COLLEGE BOTANY

Volume III

INCLUDING PLANT ANATOMY, REPRODUCTION IN FLOWERING PLANTS, BIOCHEMISTRY, PLANT PHYSIOLOGY, BIOTECHNOLOGY, ECOLOGY, ECONOMIC BOTANY, CELL BIOLOGY AND GENETICS

For Undergraduate and Postgraduate Students

Dr. B.P. PANDEY
MSc, PhD, FPSI
Former Head
Department of Botany
J.V. College, Baraut, Uttar Pradesh

S. CHAND
PUBLISHING

S Chand And Company Limited
(ISO 9001 Certified Company)

S Chand And Company Limited

(ISO 9001 Certified Company)

Head Office: D-92, Sector–2, Noida – 201301, U.P. (India), Ph. 91-120-4682700

Registered Office: A-27, 2nd Floor, Mohan Co-operative Industrial Estate, New Delhi – 110 044, Phone: 011-49731800

www.**schandpublishing.com**; e-mail: **info@schandpublishing.com**

S. CHAND PUBLISHING

Branches

Chennai	:	Ph: 23632120; chennai@schandpublishing.com
Guwahati	:	Ph: 2738811, 2735640; guwahati@schandpublishing.com
Hyderabad	:	Ph: 40186018; hyderabad@schandpublishing.com
Jalandhar	:	Ph: 4645630; jalandhar@schandpublishing.com
Kolkata	:	Ph: 23357458, 23353914; kolkata@schandpublishing.com
Lucknow	:	Ph: 4003633; lucknow@schandpublishing.com
Mumbai	:	Ph: 25000297; mumbai@schandpublishing.com
Patna	:	Ph: 4011400; patna@schandpublishing.com

First Edition 2011
Reprints 2015, 2017, 2018, 2019 (Twice), 2020, 2021 (Twice)

Low Priced Students' Paperback Edition (LPSPE), 2022*; Reprint 2024*

Reprint 2026

ISBN: 978-93-550-1062-9 **Product Code:** H6BTY68BOTN10ENAA21L

PRINTED IN INDIA

By Shri Shyamlal Printing Press Private Limited, Plot 20/4, Site-IV, Industrial Area Sahibabad, Ghaziabad – 201 010 and Published by S Chand And Company Limited, A-27, 2nd Floor, Mohan Co-operative Industrial Estate, New Delhi – 110 044.

PREFACE TO THE FIRST EDITION

This textbook, College Botany, Volume III includes **nine** units, 1. Plant Anatomy, 2. Reproduction in Flowering Plants, 3. Biochemistry, 4. Plant Physiology, 5. Biotechnology, 6. Ecology , 7. Economic Botany, 8. Cell Biology and 9. Genetics, of course, a compilation work and embodies a fairly comprehensive treatment of the fundamentals of Botany. Volume III of College Botany, has been produced on the continuous demand from degree and postgraduate students alike.

During preparation of this textbook, the syllabi of all Indian Universities have been kept in view. To cope with practical work, many chapters are provided with laboratory experiments, especially in Plant Physiology, Plant Anatomy and Genetics.

The text has been written in simple, lucid and graspable language, and illustrated with self explanatory labelled diagrams, that have been drawn either by author himself or have been quoted from authentic work of reputed authors.

My sincere thanks are due to Dr. S. Kumar, Dr. J. Mohan, Dr. (Mrs.) Rajeshwari Sharma and Dr. Ashok Kumar of J.V. College, Baraut and Dr. S.S. Sharma and Dr. (Mrs.) Shashi of H.P. University, Shimla (H.P.). Sanjeeva Pandey, I.F.S., Rahul Pandey, I.F.S and Shanti Priya, I.F.S., deserve special thanks, for their time to time, valuable suggestions. I also express my deep sense of gratitude to my friends, botanists and educationists, who have accorded their full co-operation during preparation of this textbook.

I am thankful to the Management Team and the Editorial Department of S. Chand & Company Ltd., for all help and support in the publication of this book.

The healthy suggestions and criticisms from all corners of country are invited for the improvement of subsequent editions.

'Neelkanth Kuteer'
Subhashnagar, Baraut- 250 611
January, 1, 2011

Dr. B. P. Pandey
Former Reader and Head of the
Department of Botany
J.V. College, Baraut

PREFACE TO THE FIRST EDITION

[illegible]

CONTENTS

UNIT – I : Plant Anatomy

UNIT – 2 : Reproduction in Flowering Plants

UNIT – 3 : Biochemistry

UNIT – 4 : Plant Physiology

UNIT – 5 : Biotechnology

UNIT – 6 : Ecology

UNIT – 7 : Utilization of Plants (Economic Botany)

UNIT – 8 : Cell Biology

UNIT – 9 : Genetics–Continuity of Life

UNIT - 1

PLANT ANATOMY

1

CHAPTER

Basic Body Plan of Flowering Plant

THE PLANT BODY AND ITS DEVELOPMENT

The plant body consists of a number of organs, *i.e.*, root, stem, leaf and flower. The flower consists of sepals, petals, stamens, carpels and sometimes also sterile members. Each organ, is made up of a number of tissues. Each tissue consists of many cells of one kind.

The complex multicellular body of the seed plant is a result of evolutionary specialization of long duration. This specialization has given rise to the establishment of morphological and

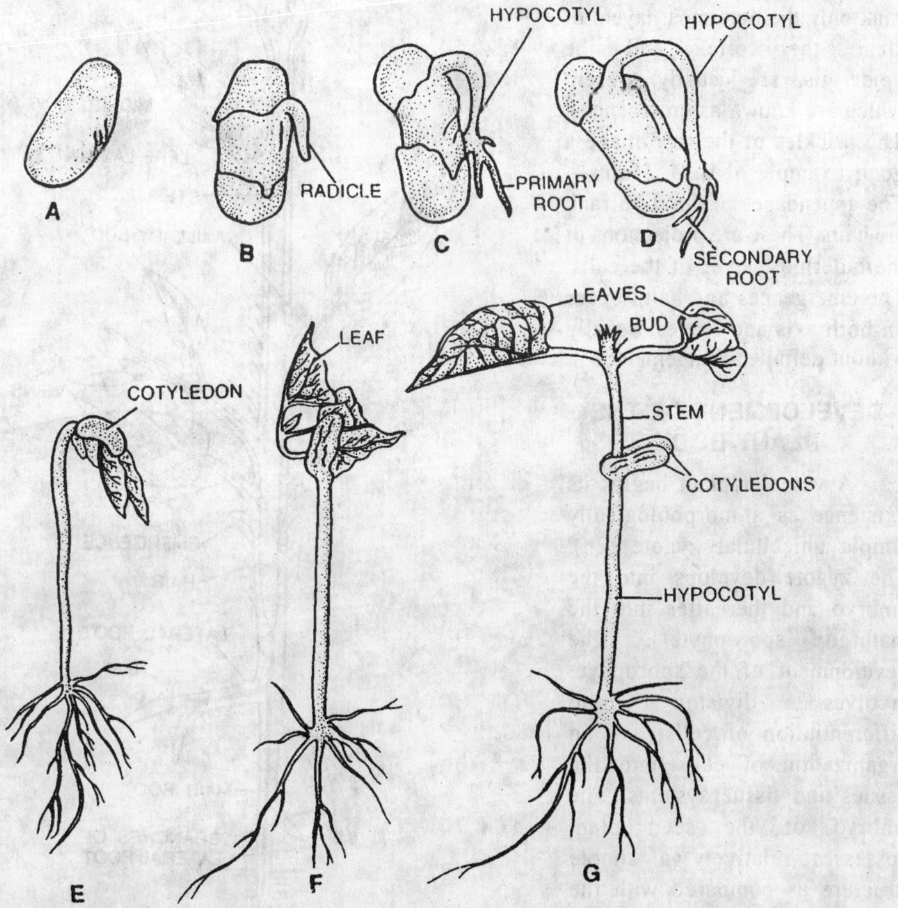

Fig. 1.1. Different stages in the germination of tne seed leading to the formation of young seedling (A–G); G, seedling with well developed roots, two young leaves, hypocotyl, cotyledons, stem and young apical bud.

physiological differences between the various parts of the plant body and also caused the development of the concept of **plant organs.**

The organization of the plant body of the oldest known land plants, the Psilophytales, suggests that the differentiation of the vegetative plant into leaf, stem and root is a result of evolutionary development from an originally simple axial structure (Arnold, 1947; Eames, 1936).

As regards the morphologic nature of the flower it is thought that the flower is homologous with a shoot and the floral parts with leaves.

Fundamental parts of the plant body: The axis, consists of two parts—that portion which is normally aerial is know as the **stem,** and the portion which is subterranean is called the **root.** There are three types of appendages arising from the axis. **1. Leaves**—The strands of vascular tissue pass through the leaves. The leaves are characteristic of the stem and do not occur on the root. The leaves are found to be arranged on the stem in a definite manner, and bear an intimate structural relation to the skeleton of the axis. The leaf is looked upon as the lateral expansion of the stem, continuous with it. All fundamental parts of the stem are concerned with the formation of the leaf. **2. Emergences**—In the appendages of the second rank only the outermost layers of stem, the cortex and the epidermis, are usually present which are known as emergences. The prickles of the rose make a good example of it. **3. Hairs**—The appendages of the third rank are hairs. These are projections of the outermost layer of the cells. The emergences and hairs occur on both axis and leaves, usually without definite arrangement.

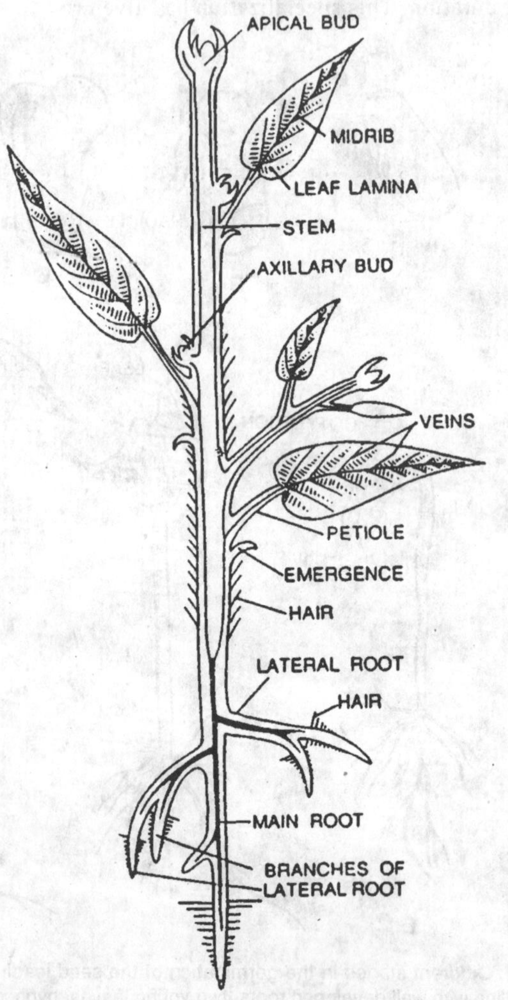

Fig. 1.2. The plant body, showing fundamental parts.

DEVELOPMENT OF THE PLANT BODY

A vascular plant begins its existence as a morphologically simple unicellular zygote (2n). The zygote develops into the embryo and thereafter into the mature sporophyte. The development of the sporophyte involves division and differentiation of cells, and an organization of cells into the tissues and tissue systems. The embryo of the seed plant possesses relatively a simple structure as compared with the mature sporophyte. The embryo bears a limited number of parts—generally only an axis bearing one or more cotyledons. The cells and tissues of this structure are less differentiated. However the embryo grows further, because of the presence of meristems, at two opposite ends of the axis, of future shoot and root. After the germination of the seed, during the development of shoot and root, the new apical meristems appear which cause a repetitive branching of these organs. After a certain period of vegetative growth, the reproductive stage of the plant is attained.

Primary and secondary growth. As mentioned above, this first-formed plant body is known as the **primary plant body**, since it is built up by means of first or **primary growth**. The tissues of this first-formed body are known as primary tissues ; for example the first-formed xylem is called **primary xylem.** In most vascular cryptogams and monocotyledons, the entire life

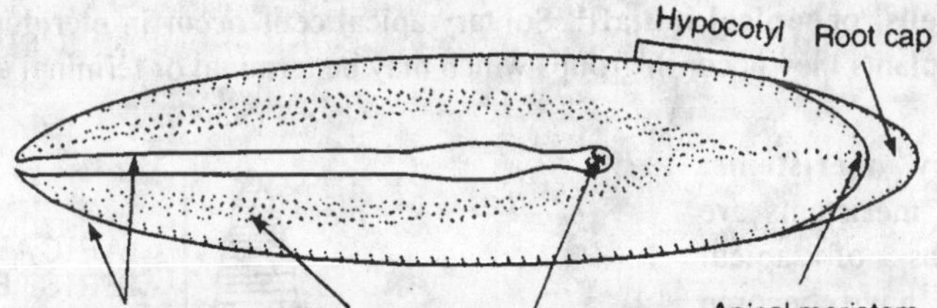

Fig. 1.3. Mature embryo of *Lactuca sativa* (After Esau).

cycle of the sporophyte is completed in a primary plant body. The gymnosperms, most dicotyledons, and some monocotyledons show an increase in thickness of stem and root by means of **secondary growth.** The tissues formed as the result of secondary growth are called **secondary tissues**. Generally the new types of cells are not formed by means of secondary growth. The bulk of the plant increases because of secondary growth. Especially the vascular tissues are developed which provide new conducting cells and additional support and protection. The secondary growth does not fundamentally change the structure of the primary body. The primary growth increases the length of the axis, forms the branches and builds up the new or young parts of the plant body. Thus, a secondary body composed of secondary tissues is added to the primary body composed of primary tissues.

A special meristem, the **cambium**, is concerned with the secondary thickening. The cambium arises between the primary xylem and the primary phloem, and lays down new xylem and phloem adjacent to these. Thus the secondary masses of xylem and phloem are found entirely within the central cylinder and between the primary xylem. The newly formed secondary xylem cloaks and ultimately surrounds the primary xylem and the pith. During this process the primary structure is not changed but engulfed intact within secondary xylem. The primary phloem and all other tissues outside the cambium are forced outward by secondary growth and ultimately crushed or destroyed.

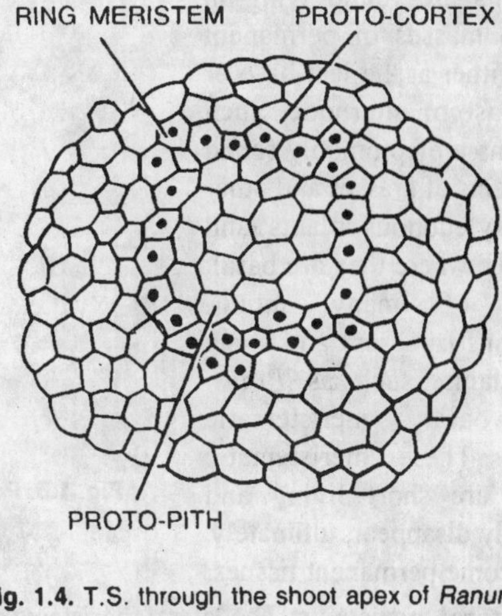

Fig. 1.4. T.S. through the shoot apex of *Ranunculus acris.*

In addition, a **cork cambium** or **phellogen** commonly develops the peripheral region of the axis and produces a periderm, a secondary tissue system assuming a protective function when the primary epidermal layer is disrupted during the secondary growth in thickness.

3. Meristems Based on Position in Plant Body

As regards their position in plant body, the meristems may be classified into three groups — **apical meristem, intercalary meristem** and **lateral meristem.**

Apical meristem: The apical meristem lies at the apex of the stem and the root of vascular plants. Very often they are also found at the apices of the leaves. Due to the activity of these meristems, the organs increase in length. The initiation of growth takes place by one or more cells situated at the tip of the organ. These cells always maintain their individuality and position and are called **'apical cells'** or **'apical initials'.** Solitary apical cells occur in pteridophytes, whereas in higher vascular plants they occur in groups which may be terminal or terminal and sub-terminal in position.

Intercalary meristems: The intercalary meristems are merely portions of apical meristems that have become separated from the apex during development by layers of more mature or permanent tissues and left behind as the apical meristem moves on in growth. The intercalary meristems are internodal in their position. In early stages, the internode is wholly or partially meristematic, but later on some of its part, becomes mature more rapidly than the rest and in the internode a definite continuous sequence of development is maintained. The intercalary meristems are found lying in between masses of permanent tissues either at the leaf base or at the base of internode. Such meristems are commonly found in the stems of grasses and other monocotyledonous plants and horsetails, where they are basal. Leaves of many monocotyledons (grasses) and some other plants, such as *Pinus*, have basal meristematic regions. These meristematic regions are short living and ultimately disappear, ultimately, they become permanent tissues.

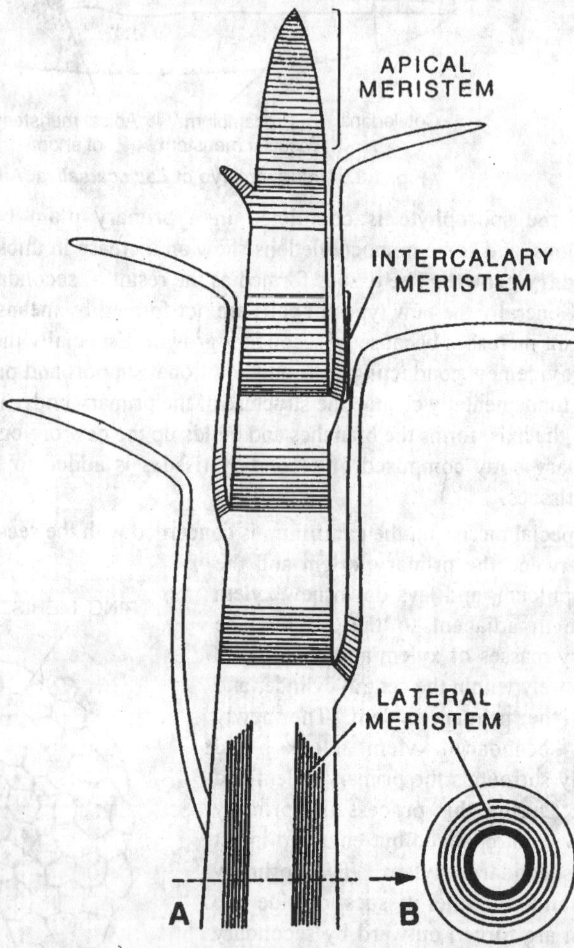

Fig. 1.5. Position of meristems. A, longitudinal view; B, cross-section.

Lateral meristems: The lateral meristems are composed of such initials which divide mainly in one plane (periclinally) and increase the diameter of an organ. They add to the bulk of existing tissues or give rise to new tissues. These tissues are responsible for growth in thickness of plant body. The cambium and the cork cambium are the examples of this type.

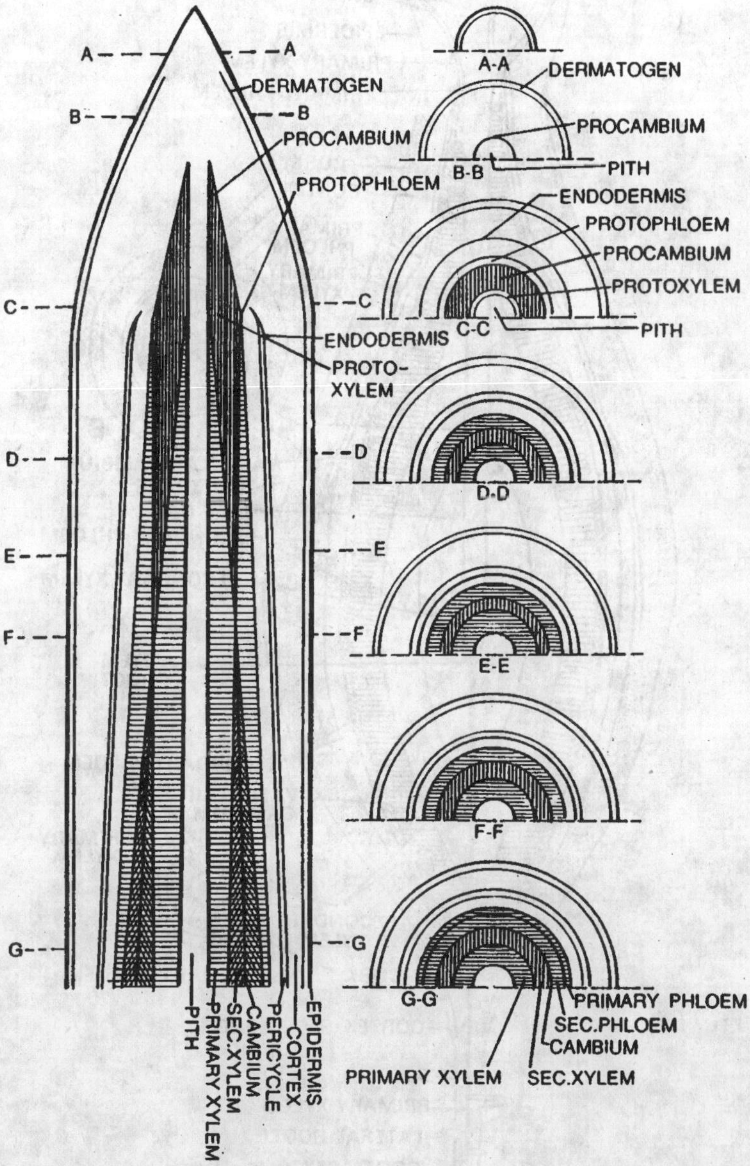

Fig. 1.6. Development of the stem. Longitudinal and cross-section of tip of elongating axis. At A – A, entire axis promeristem; B – B, dermatogen, procambium and pith in early stages of development; C – C, procambium formed a complete cylinder, outermost and innermost procambium has become protophloem and protoxylem; D – D, large portions of procambium adjacent to the protophloem and protoxylem become phloem and xylem; E – E, remaining layer of procambium becomes the cambium and forms the first secondary phloem and secondary xylem cells; F – F, secondary tissues increased in amount; G – G, further secondary growth occurred. (After Eames and MacDaniels).

The cambium does not fall definitely in either group (primary and secondary). It arises from apical meristem of which it is late and specialized stage. However, the accessory cambia are secondary. The tissues formed by the cambium are secondary, whereas the primary meristems form only primary tissues.

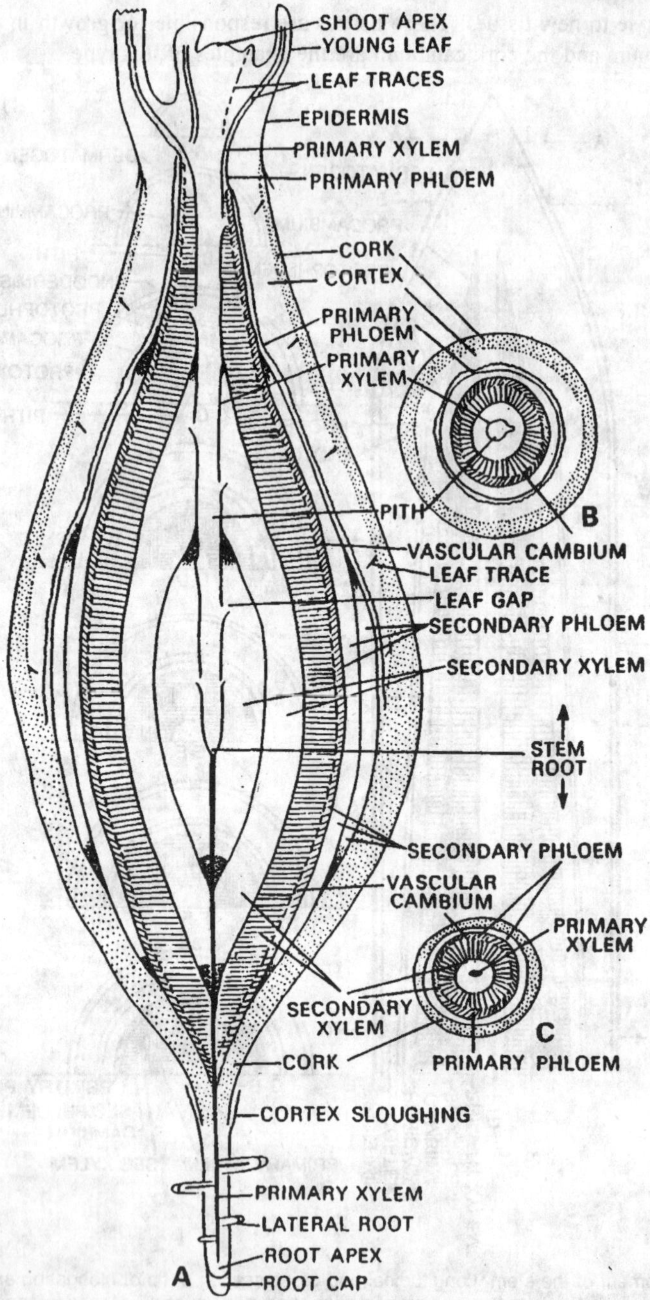

Fig. 1.7. Primary and secondary growth in a dicot plant *A*, longitudinal view of plant; *B*, transverse section of stem; *C*, transverse section of root.

The primary growth of an axis is completed in a relatively short period, whereas the secondary growth persists for a longer period and in a perennial axis the secondary growth continues indefinitely.

The stem apex like the root apex consists of a meristematic zone of cells that remain in a continuous and rapid state of division. This is called **promeristem** having cells with very thin walls. Immediately beneath the promeristem there is **zone of determination** which has no visible boundary with the promeristem. In the dicots, this zone has a group of conspicuous cells with dense cytoplasm. These cells in a transverse section are arranged in a circle (Fig. 1.4.). It is a remnant of a primordial meristem, which remains behind in a maturing segment, and it retained its activity to divide. Due to its circular appearance it is also called the **ring meristem**. The cells in the centre are **protopith** and those that are external to the ring meristem are the **protocortex**. The cells of protocortex and protopith divide and build up the mass of **ground tissue**. The cells of the ring meristem divide longitudinally and form elongated cells that later on develop in vascular bundles and are known as **procambical strands**. The first formed phloem elements and so the xylem elements differentiate from the procambial strands.

INTERNAL ORGANIZATION OF VASCULAR PLANT

The **cells** or the morphologic units of the plant body are associated in various ways with each other forming **tissues.** In the plant body the cells are of several kinds and their combinations into tissues are such that different parts of the same organ may differ from one another. The larger units of tissues may show topographic continuity or physiologic similarity, or both together. Such tissue units are called **tissue systems.** Thus the complex structure of the plant body results from variation in the form and function of cells and also from differences in the type of combination of cells into tissues and tissue systems. As pointed out by Sachs (1875), the plant body of a vascular plant is composed of three systems of tissues—(1) the **dermal,** (2) the **vascular** and (3) the **fundamental** or **ground** system.

The three vegetative organs, *i.e.*, stem, root and leaf, are distinguished by the relative distribution of the vascular and ground tissues. The vascular system of the stem is found between the epidermis and the centre of the axis. In such type of arrangement the **cortex** (ground tissue) is found between the epidermis and the vascular region and the **pith** in the centre of the stem (Fig. 1.6 B,C.). In the root, the pith may be absent (Fig. 1.6 E), and the cortex is generally shed during secondary growth (Fig. 1.6 D). The primary vascular tissues are commonly being arranged in the form of a ring of bundles as seen in transverse section of stem (Fig. 1.6 B). During secondary growth the original primary vascular system may be obscured by secondary vascular tissues between the primary xylem and the primary phloem (Fig. 1.6 C). In the leaf the vascular system consists of many interconnected strands (bundles) found in the ground tissue. In the case of leaf the ground tissue consists of photosynthetic parenchyma, and is known as **mesophyll** (Fig. 1.6 G).

The above mentioned tissue systems of the primary plant body are derived from the apical meristems (Fig. 1.6 F,H). The partly differentiated derivatives from these meristems may be classified as—**protoderm**, **procambium** and **ground meristem.** They make the meristematic precursors of the **dermal**, **vascular** and **fundamental** (ground) systems, respectively. The vascular tissue system enlarges by secondary growth which takes place in the **vascular cambium.** The periderm may be derived from a separate meristem, the **phellogen** or **cork cambium** (Fig. 1.6 D).

MODULAR GROWTH

Variation in organisational form that arises from size dependent relationship among parts is a fundamental aspect of development and evolutionary change. **Allometric analysis** is one of the earliest morphometric tools that help in revealing ontogenetic or evolutionary changes in shape as a consequence of changes in organ or body size (Gayon, 2000).

In plant population the individuals change widely in size may be due to asymmetric competition for light (Weimer, *et al*, 2001) or meagre distribution of other resources. The variability is dependent on the way plants are constructed. Plants grow through the repeated

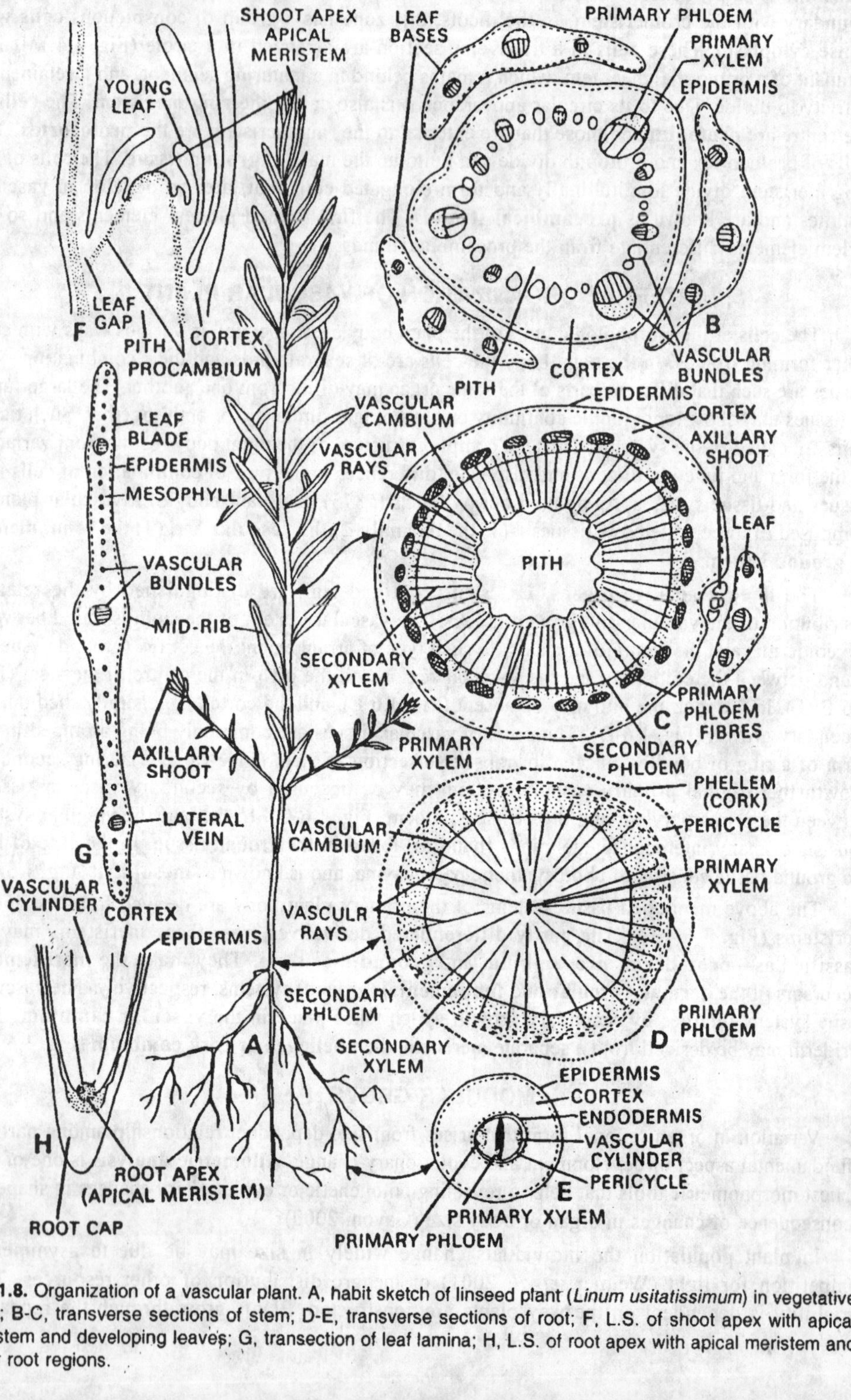

Fig. 1.8. Organization of a vascular plant. A, habit sketch of linseed plant (*Linum usitatissimum*) in vegetative state; B-C, transverse sections of stem; D-E, transverse sections of root; F, L.S. of shoot apex with apical meristem and developing leaves; G, transection of leaf lamina; H, L.S. of root apex with apical meristem and other root regions.

addition of similar morphological sub-units called **metamers** and **modules**. This mode of development contributes to size variation by creating the potential for both **indeterminate** and **exponential** growth.

Modularity presents special challenge and opportunities for allometric analysis. In biological system there are different levels of organisation, *e.g.*,

genetic families → individuals → population → communities

Modular organisms have additional levels of organisation due to their clear within individual substructure. The modular growth provides serial adjustment to the phenotype through the addition of new parts during development.

Module and **metamer** may be defined as follows :

Module is a product of an apical meristem; while **metamers** are serially homologous repeated units along an axis and are generally sub-units of modules. A vegetative metamer consists of a leaf, the segment of stem subtending it and its axillary meristem.

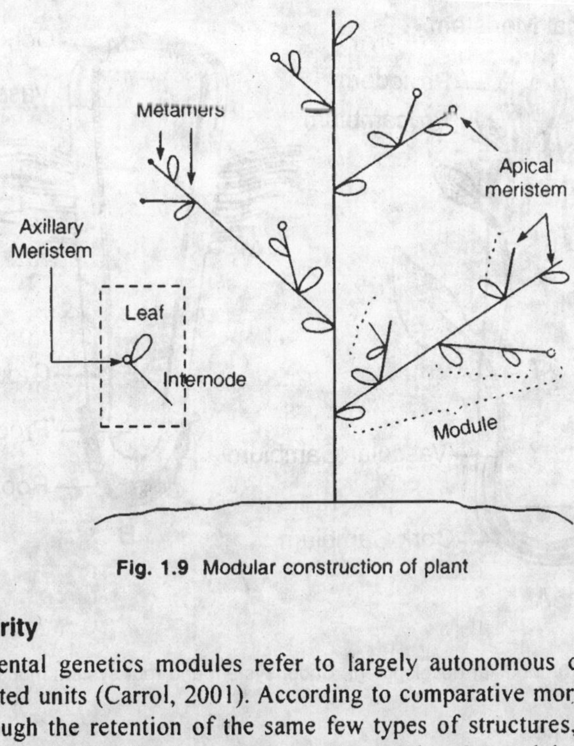

Fig. 1.9 Modular construction of plant

Types of Modularity

On developmental genetics modules refer to largely autonomous developmentally and functionally integrated units (Carrol, 2001). According to comparative morphology the modular growth occurs through the retention of the same few types of structures, *e.g.*, **branches** and **flowers** in plants. In contrast to developmental genetic modules, the modular subunits comprising an organism are similar to each other, *i.e.*, serially homologous and loosely analogous to individuals in population.

Modularity in Plants

In plants, module is the product of apical meristem, *e.g.*, branches, cones or flowers. Vegetative modules produce new meristem that may give rise to additional vegetative or reproductive modules, creating a modular hierarchy.

Usually modules themselves are composed of repeated units or **metamers**. For example, a typical vegetative metamer consists of a node and an internode, a leaf and an axillary meristem (Fig. 1.9).

Modular Development

In seed plants, *e.g.*, gymnosperms or angiosperms, the plant body is essentially **modularly** organised. The smallest elementary unit of construction in the shoot system is called a **metamer**. Metamers make branches and branches construct branching system. Each shoot apex is a potential point of further development. Development is iterative or repetitive process. The finite bit of programme is repeated to add new **metamers**. The number of iterations can be infinite in some species. In annual plants iterations certainly terminate, but their number is not strictly defined and may depend on environment (Schlichting and Smith, 2002). The number of leaves of a tree can vary with age and habitat conditions. It is due to capability of formation of organs continuously. Organs, metamers and branches are disposable without death of organism.

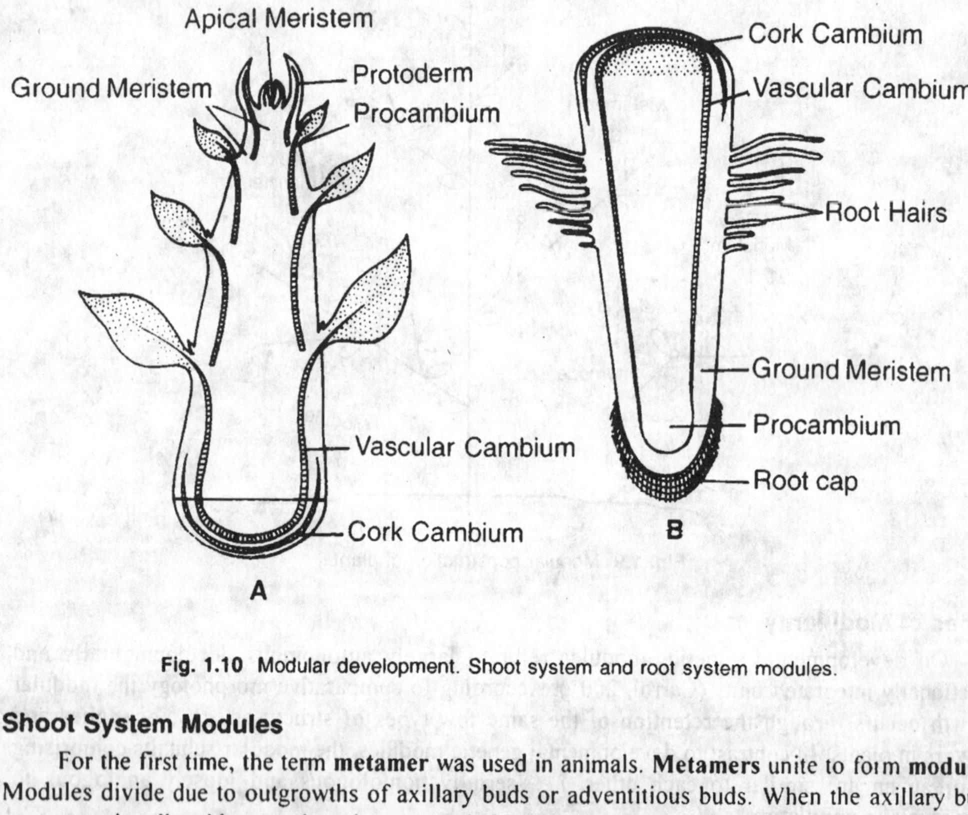

Fig. 1.10 Modular development. Shoot system and root system modules.

Shoot System Modules

For the first time, the term **metamer** was used in animals. **Metamers** unite to form **module**. Modules divide due to outgrowths of axillary buds or adventitious buds. When the axillary bud grows continually without undergoing rest period is called **sylleptic sub-module** while the axillary bud that undergoes some dormancy period is called **proleptic sub-module.**

The activity of module is directly related with that of apical meristem. After getting a stimulus, the axillary bud activates and module branches. New modules may arise some time playing an important role in **regeneration**, *e.g.*, in *Eucalyptus*, after fire new modules grow out rapidly from hidden buds produced by modification of the base of stem.

2

CHAPTER

The Tissue

Groups or masses of the cells that are alike in origin, structure, and function form tissue. The plant body consists of **vegetative tissue** and **reproductive tissue**. In the higher plants the plant body is somewhat more complex in its cellular structure. The cells differ very much in their kind, form and origin in higher plants. Morphologically, a tissue is a group or a mass of cells or vessels, alike in form, origin and function. From the study point of view, the tissues may be grouped into three principal groups — **1. Meristems or meristematic tissue; 2. Permanent tissue,** and **3. Secretory tissue.**

1. MERISTEMS OR MERISTEMATIC TISSUE

A meristematic tissue consists of a group of cells which remain in a continuous state of division or they retain their power of division. The characteristic features of meristematic tissue are as follows:

1. They are composed of immature cells which are in a state of division and growth.
2. Usually the intercellular spaces are not found among these cells.
3. The cells may be rounded, oval or polygonal in shape; they are always living and thin-walled.
4. Each cell of meristematic tissue possesses abundant cytoplasm and one or more nuclei in it.
5. The vacuoles in the cells may be quite small or altogether absent.

MERISTEMS AND GROWTH OF PLANT BODY

Beginning with the division of the oospore, the vascular plant generally produces new cells and forms new organs until it dies. In the beginning of the development of the plant embryo cell division occurs throughout the young organism. But as soon as the embryo develops and converts into an independent plant the addition of new cells is gradually restricted to certain parts of the plant body, while the other parts of the remain concerned with activities other than growth. This shows that the portions of embryonic tissue persists in the plant throughout its life, and the mature plant is a composite of adult and juvenile tissues. These juvenile tissues are known as the **meristems.** The presence of meristems remarkably differentiates the plant, from the animal. In the growth resulting from meristematic activity is possible throughout the life of the organism, whereas in animal body the multiplication of the cells mostly ceases when the organism attains adult size and the number of organs is fixed.

The term meristem (Greek *meristos*, meaning divisible) emphasizes the cell-division activity characteristic of the tissue which bears this name. It is obvious that the synthesis of new living substance is a fundamental part of the process of the formation of new cells by division. The living tissues other than the meristems may also produce new cells, but the meristems carry on such activity indefinitely, because they not only add cells to the plant body, but also perpetuate themselves, that is, some of the products of division in the meristems do not develop into adult cells but remain meristematic.

The meristems usually occur at the apices of all main and lateral shoots and roots and thus their number in a single plant becomes quite large. In addition, plants bearing secondary increase in thickness possess extensive meristems, the vascular and cork cambia, responsible for the secondary growth. The combined activities of all these meristems give rise to a complex and large plant body. The primary growth, initiated in the apical meristems expands the plant body and produces the reproductive parts. On the other hand, the cambia, aid in maintenance of the expanding body by increasing the volume of the conducting system and forming supporting and protecting cells.

CLASSIFICATION OF MERISTEMS

Various systems of classifying meristems have been proposed by many eminent workers which are based on the characteristics such as stage of development, position in plant body, origin, function and topography. No system is exclusive and rigid. A few important types have been discussed here:

1. Meristems Based on Stage of Development

Promeristem or primordial meristem. Promeristem is the region of new growth in a plant body where the foundation of new organs or parts of organs is initiated. Sometimes, it is also called **primordial meristem, urmeristem** and **embryonic meristem.** From the view point of its structure, this region consists of the initials and their immediate derivatives. The cells of this region are isodiametric, thinwalled, vacuolate, with active cytoplasm and early stages of pits. Prominent nuclei and inconspicuous intercellular spaces may be seen. As soon as the cells of this region begin to change in size, shape, and character of wall and cytoplasm, setting off thc beginning of tissue differentiation, they are no longer a part of typical meristem; they have passed beyond that earliest stage.

2. Meristems Based on Origin of Initiating Cells

Primary and secondary meristems. The meristems are classified as *primary* and *secondary*, on the basis of type of tissue in which origin occurs.

The primary meristems are those that build up the primary part of the plant and consist in part of promeristem. In primary meristems, promeristem is always the earliest stage. The possession of promeristem continuously from a early embryonic origin is characteristic of primary meristems. The main primary stems are the apices of roots, stems, leaves and similar appendages.

The secondary meristem appears later at a stage of development of an organ of a plant body. Secondary meristems always arise in permanent tissues and they are always found lying lateral along the side of the stem and root. Sometimes, some of the primary permanent tissues acquire the power of division and become meristematic. These tissues build up the secondary meristem. Secondary meristems are so called because they arise as new meristems in tissue which is not meristematic. The most striking example of secondary meristem is phellogen or cork cambium. It is formed from mature cells — cortical, epidermal or phloem cells.

The primary meristems build up the early and structurally and functionally complete plant body. The secondary meristems later add to that body forming supplementary tissues that functionally replace the early formed tissues or serve in protection and repair of wounded regions.

The cambium does not fall definitely in either group (primary and secondary). It arises from apical meristem of which it is late and specialized stage. However, the accessory cambia are secondary. The tissues formed by the cambium are secondary, whereas the primary meristems form only primary tissues.

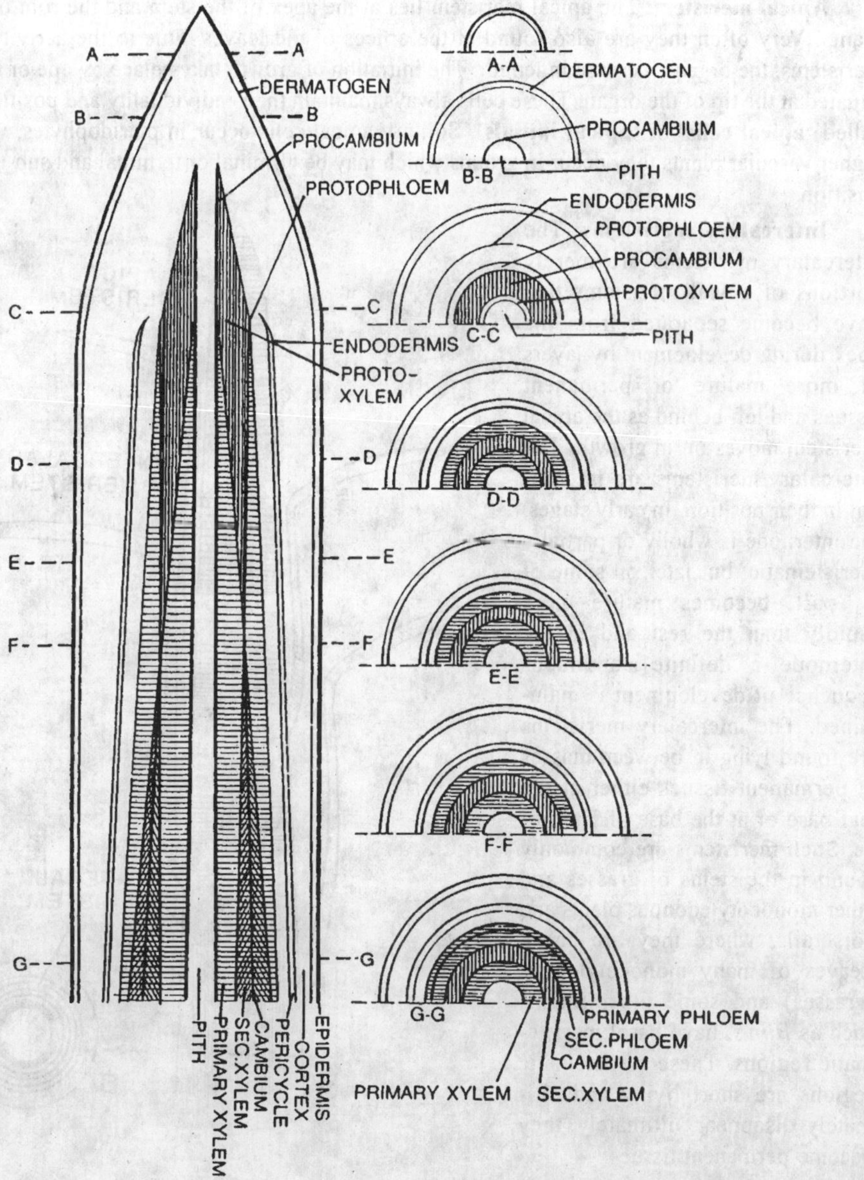

Fig. 2.1. Development of the stem. Longitudinal and cross-section of tip of elongating axis. At A – A, entire axis promeristem; B – B, dermatogen, procambium and pith in early stages of development; C – C, procambium formed a complete cylinder, outermost and innermost procambium has become protophloem and protoxylem; D – D, large portions of procambium adjacent to the protophloem and protoxylem become phloem and xylem; E – E, remaining layer of procambium becomes the cambium and forms the first secondary phloem and secondary xylem cells; F – F, secondary tissues increased in amount; G – G, further secondary growth occurred. (After Eames and MacDaniels).

3. Meristems Based on Position in Plant Body

As regards their position in plant-body, the meristems may be classified into three groups — **apical meristem, intercalary meristem and lateral meristem.**

Apical meristem. The apical meristem lies at the apex of the stem and the root of vascular plants. Very often they are also found at the apices of the leaves. Due to the activity of these meristems, the organs increase in length. The initiation of growth takes place by one or more cells situated at the tip of the organ. These cells always maintain their individuality and position and are called **'apical cells'** or **'apical initials'.** Solitary apical cells occur in pteridophytes, whereas in higher vascular plants they occur in groups which may be terminal or terminal and sub-terminal in position.

Intercalary meristems. The intercalary meristems are merely portions of apical meristems that have become separated from the apex during development by layers of more mature or permanent tissues and left behind as the apical meristem moves on in growth. The intercalary meristems are internodal in their position. In early stages, the internode is wholly or partially meristematic, but later on some of its part, becomes mature more rapidly than the rest and in the internode a definite continuous sequence of development is maintained. The intercalary meristems are found lying in between masses of permanent tissues either at the leaf base or at the base of internode. Such meristems are commonly found in the stems of grasses and other monocotyledonous plants and horsetails, where they are basal. Leaves of many monocotyledons (grasses) and some other plants, such as *Pinus*, have basal meristematic regions. These meristematic regions are short living and ultimately disappear, ultimately, they become permanent tissues.

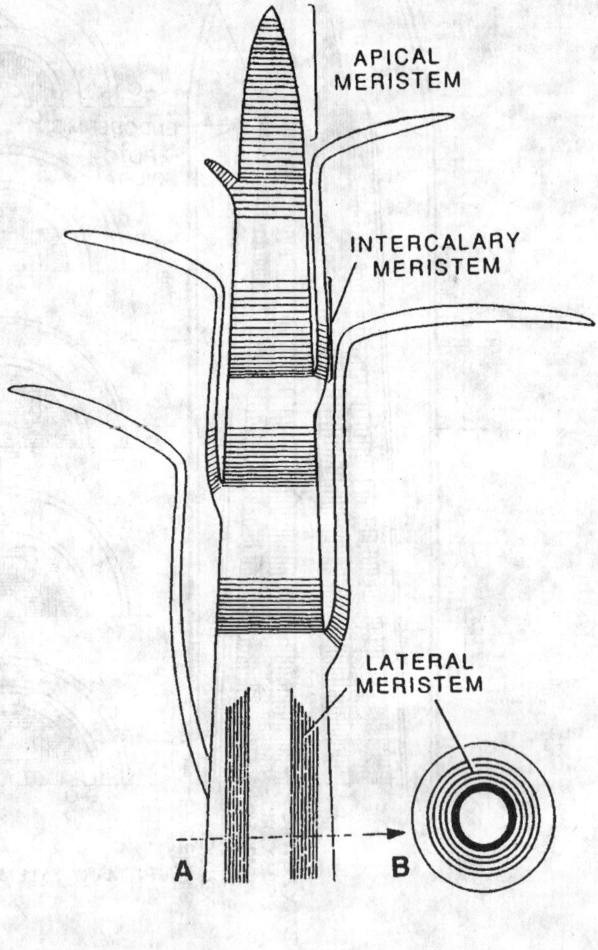

Fig. 2.2. Position of meristems. A, longitudinal view; B, cross-section.

Lateral meristems. The lateral meristems are composed of such initials which divide mainly in one plane (periclinally) and increase the diameter of an organ. They add to the bulk of existing tissues or give rise to new tissues. These tissues are responsible for growth in thickness of plant body. The cambium and the cork cambium are the examples of this type.

4. Meristems Based on Function

As regards their function a system of classification of meristems was proposed by Haberlandt in the end of nineteenth century. He suggested that the primary meristem at the apex of the stem and root is distinguished into three tissues — **protoderm, procambium and ground or**

fundamental meristem. The protoderm is the outermost tissue which develops into epidermis. The procambium develops into primary vascular tissue. It forms isolated strands of elongated cells very near to the central region; in cross-section each procambium appears as a small group of cells in the ground or fundamental meristem, but in longitudinal section the cells appear to be long and pointed. The ground or fundamental meristem develops into ground tissue and pith; the cells of this region are large, thin walled, living and isodiametric. In later stages, they become differentiated into hypodermis, cortex, endodermis, pericycle, pith rays and pith.

Meristem and meristematic. The terms meristem and meristematic, as applied to developing cells and tissues, are somewhat loose. According to Eames and MacDaniels, the term **'meristem'** is applied to regions of more or less continuous cell and tissue initiation; the adjective **'meristematic'** is used to indicate resemblance in an important way to a meristem, but not necessarily as consisting of or constituting meristem, *i.e.*, it is applied to those cells, tissues and regions that have characteristics of developing structures — especially cell division — but do not themselves strictly constitute meristems. For example, the apices of the stems and the cambium are regions of tissue initiation, developing xylem and phloem are meristematic tissues, because they form some new cells and are immature but they are not permanent or semipermanent initiating regions (meristems). On the other hand, cells in mature tissue, such as the primary cortex of stems, may divide. Such cells are meristematic, but neither they nor the tissues of which they are a part constitute a meristem.

MERISTEMS AND PERMANENT TISSUES

In active meristems there occurs a continuous separation between cells that remain meristematic — the *initiating cells* — and those that develop into the various tissue elements — the *derivatives* of the initiating cells. During this process of developing the derivatives gradually change, physiologically and morphologically, and assume more or less specialized characteristics. In other words, the derivatives differentiate into the specific elements of the various tissue-systems. As the cells of vascular plants vary in their physiologic and morphologic characteristics, they also vary in details of differentiation. Different types of cells attain different degrees of differentiation as compared with their common meristematic precursors. For example, various parenchyma cells diverge relatively little from their meristematic precursors and retain the power of division to a high degree. On the other hand, such as sieve elements, fibres, tracheary elements are more thoroughly modified and lose most, or all of their former meristematic potentialities. These variously differentiated cells are known as *mature* or *permanent* in the sense that they have reached the degree of specialization and physiological stability that normally characterizes them as components of certain tissues of an adult plant part. During the differentiation of tissues from meristems the derivatives of meristematic cells synthesize protoplasm, enlarge and divide. It is difficult to delimit the meristem proper from its recent derivatives. The development of meristematic derivatives into mature cells also is gradual. In other words, the differentiation is a continuous process.

2. PERMANENT TISSUES

The permanent tissues are those in which growth has stopped either completely or for the time being. Sometimes, they again become meristematic partially or wholly. The cells of these tissues may be living or dead and thin-walled or thick-walled. The thin-walled permanent tissues are generally living whereas the thick-walled tissues may be living or dead. The permanent tissues may be **simple** or **complex.** A simple tissue is made up of one type of cells forming a uniform of homogeneous system of cells. The common simple tissues are — **parenchyma, collenchyma** and **sclerenchyma**. A complex tissue is made up of more than one type of cells working together as a unit. The complex tissues consist of parenchymatous and sclerenchymatous cells; collenchymatous cells are not present in such tissues. The common examples are — the **xylem** and the **phloem.**

SIMPLE TISSUES

1. Parenchyma. *The parenchyma tissue is composed of living cells which are variable in their morphology and physiology, but generally having thin walls and a polyhedral shape, and concerned with vegetative activities of the plant.* The individual cells are known as **parenchyma cells.** The word parenchyma is derived from the Greek *para*, beside and *enchein*, to pour. This combination of words expresses the ancient concept of parenchyma as a semi-liquid substance *poured beside* other tissues which are formed earlier and are more solid. Phylogenetically the parenchyma is a primitive tissue since the lower plants have given rise to the higher plants through specialization and since the single type or the few types of cells found in the lower plants have become by specialization the many and elaborate types of the higher plants. The unspecialized meristematic tissue is parenchyma and is often called parenchyma thus it can be said that, ontogentically parenchyma is a primitive tissue.

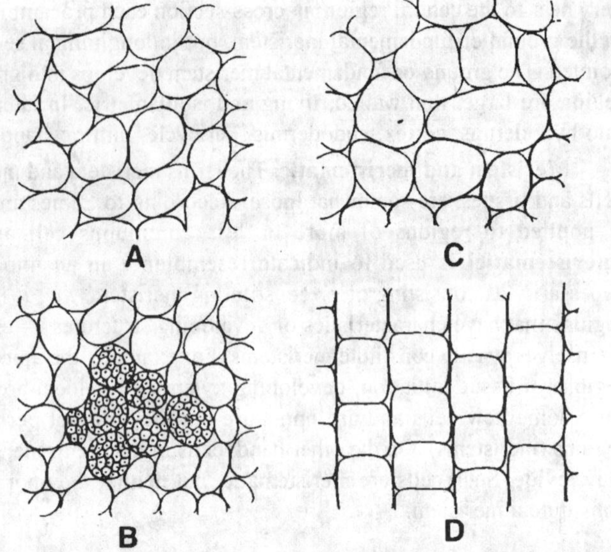

Fig. 2.3. Parenchyma. A, from pith of rhizome of *Polypodium*; B, from cortex of root of *Asclepias*, the cells containing starch grains; C and D, from pith of *Zea* in transverse and longitudinal sections.

The parenchyma consists of isodiametric, thin-walled and equally expanded cells. The parenchyma cells are oval, rounded or polygonal in shape having well developed spaces among

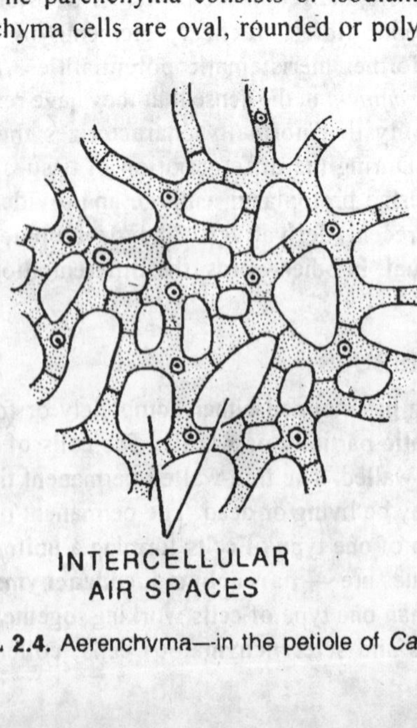

Fig. 2.4. Aerenchyma—in the petiole of *Canna*.

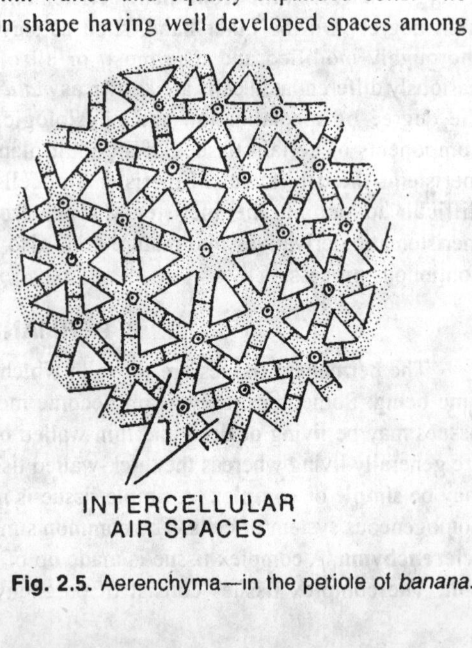

Fig. 2.5. Aerenchyma—in the petiole of *banana*.

them. The cells are not greatly elongated in any direction. The cells of this tissue are living and contain sufficient amount of cytoplasm in them. Usually each cell possesses one or more nuclei.

Parenchyma makes up large parts of various organs in many plants. Pith, mesophyll of leaves, the pulp of fruits, endosperm of seeds, cortex of stems and roots, and other organs of plants consist mainly of parenchyma. The parenchyma cells also occur in xylem and phloem.

In the aquatic plants, the parenchyma cells in the cortex possess well developed air spaces (intercellular spaces) and such tissue is known as **aerenchyma.** Parenchyma may be specialized as water storage tissue in many succulent and xerophytic plants. In *Aloe*, *Agave*, *Mesembryanthemum*, *Hakea* and many other plants chlorophyll-free, thin-walled and water-turgid cells are found which represent water storage tissue. When the parenchyma cells are exposed to light they develop chloroplasts in them, and such tissue is known as **chlorenchyma**. The chlorenchyma possesses well developed aerating system. Intercellular spaces are abundant in the photosynthetic parenchyma (chlorenchyma) of stems too.

Commonly the parenchyma cells have thin primary walls. Some such cells may have also thick primary walls. Some storage parenchyma develop remarkably thick walls and the carbohydrates deposited in these walls, the hemicellulose, are regarded by some workers as reserve materials. Thick walls occur, in the endosperm of *Phoenix dactylifera*, *Diospyros*, *Asparagus* and *Coffea arabica*. The walls of such endosperm become thinner during germination.

CHLOROPLASTS

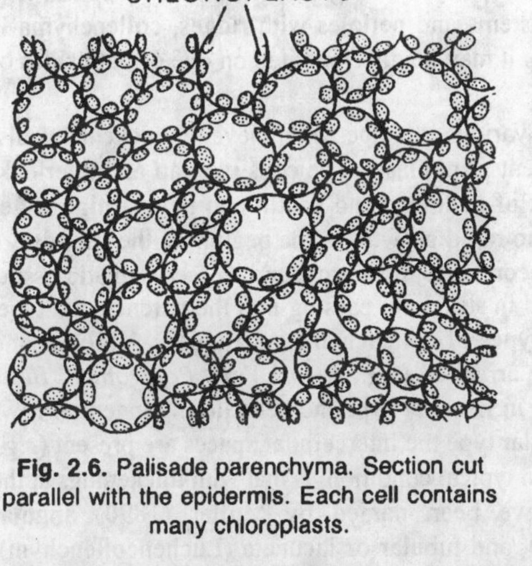

Fig. 2.6. Palisade parenchyma. Section cut parallel with the epidermis. Each cell contains many chloroplasts.

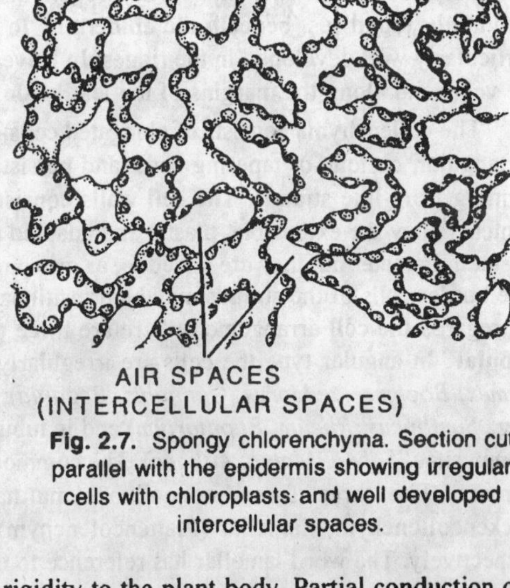

AIR SPACES (INTERCELLULAR SPACES)

Fig. 2.7. Spongy chlorenchyma. Section cut parallel with the epidermis showing irregular cells with chloroplasts and well developed intercellular spaces.

The turgid parenchyma cells help in giving rigidity to the plant body. Partial conduction of water is also maintained through parenchymatous cells. The parenchyma acts as special storage tissue to store food material in the form of starch grains, proteins, fats and oils. The parenchyma cells that contain chloroplasts in them make chlorenchyma which are responsible for photosynthesis in green plants. In water plants the aerenchyma keep up the buoyancy of the plants. Such air spaces also facilitate exchange of gases. In many succulent and xerophytic plants such tissues store water and known as water storage tissue. Vegetative propagation by cuttings takes place because of meristematic potentialities of the parenchyma cells which divide and develop into buds and adventitious roots.

Origin. As regards their origin, the parenchyma tissue of the primary plant body, that is, the parenchyma of the cortex and the pith, of the mesophyll of leaves, and of the flower parts, differentiates from the ground meristem. The parenchyma associated with the primary and secondary vascular tissues is formed by the procambium and the vascular cambium respectively.

Procambium—parenchyma associated with the primary vascular tissues.

Vascular cambium—parenchyma associated with the secondary vascular tissues.

Parenchyma may also develop from the phellogen in the form of phelloderm, and it may be increased in amount by diffuse secondary growth.

Phellogen—Phelloderm (parenchyma).

2. Collenchyma. Collenchyma is a living tissue composed of somewhat elongated cells with thick primary nonlignified walls. Important characteristics of this tissue are its early development and its adaptability to changes in the rapidly growing organ, especially those of increase in length. When the collenchyma becomes functional, no other strongly supporting tissues have appeared. It gives support to the growing organs which do not develop much woody tissue. Morphologically, collenchyma is a simple tissue, for it consists of one type of cells.

Collenchyma is a typical supporting tissue of growing organs and of those mature herbaceous organs which are only slightly modified by secondary growth or lack such growth completely. It is the first supporting tissue in stems, leaves and floral parts. It is the main supporting tissue in many dicotyledonous leaves and some green stems. Collenchyma may occur in the root cortex, particularly, if the root is exposed to light. It is not found in the leaves and stems of monocotyledons. Collenchyma chiefly occurs in the peripheral regions of stems and leaves. It is commonly found just beneath the epidermis. In stems and petioles with ridges, collenchyma is particularly well developed in the ridges. In leaves it may be differentiated on one or both sides of the veins and along the margins of the leaf blade.

The collenchyma consists of elongated cells, various in shape, with unevenly thickened walls, rectangular, oblique or tapering ends, and persistent protoplasts. The cells overlap and interlock, forming fibre-like strands. The cell walls consist of cellulose and pectin and have a high water content. They are extensible, plastic and adapted to rapid growth. In the beginning the strands are of small diameter but they are added to, as growth continues, from surrounding meristematic tissue. The border cells of the strands may be transitional in structure, passing into the parenchyma type. As regards the cell arrangement there are three types of collenchyma — **angular, lamellar** and **tubular**. In angular type the cells are irregularly arranged (*e.g.*, *Ficus*, *Vitis*, *Polygonum*, *Beta*, *Rumex*, *Boehmeria*, *Morus*, *Cannabis*, *Begonia*); in lamellar type the cells lie in tangential rows (*e.g.*, *Sambucus*, *Rheum*, *Eupatorium*) and in tubular type the intercellular spaces are present (*e.g.*, Compositae, *Salvia*, *Malva*, *Althaea*). The common typical condition, is that with thickenings at the corners. The three forms of collenchyma have been named by Muller (1890) angular (Eckencollenchym), lamellar (Plattencolenchym), and tubular or lacunate (Luchencollenchym), respectively. The word lamellar has reference to the plate like arrangement of the thickenings; the lacunate (tubular) to the presence of intercellular spaces.

The walls of collenchyma are chiefly composed of cellulose and pectic compounds and contain much water (Majumdar and Preston, 1941). In some species collenchyma walls possess an alternation of layers rich in cellulose and poor in pectic compounds with layers that are rich in pectic compounds and poor in cellulose. In many plants collenchyma is a compact tissue lacking intercellular spaces. Instead, the potential spaces are filled with intercellular material (Majumdar, 1941).

The mature collenchyma cells are living and contain protoplasts. Chloroplasts also occur in variable numbers. They are found abundantly in collenchyma which approaches parenchyma in form. Collenchyma consisting of long narrow cells contains only a few small chloroplasts or none. Tannins may be present in collenchyma cells.

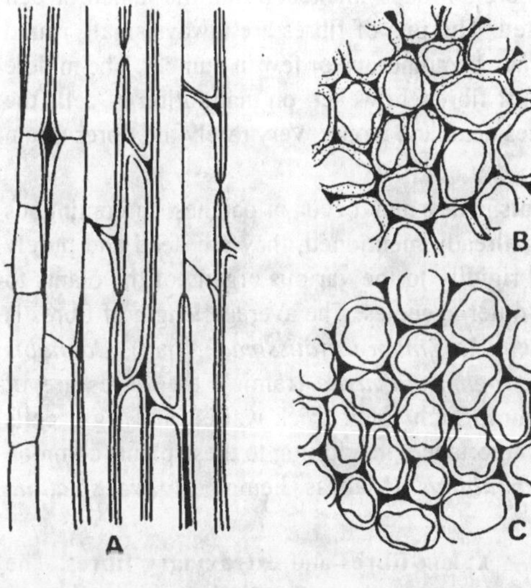

Fig. 2.8. Collenchyma. A and B, longitudinal and transverse sections from stem of *Solanum tuberosum*; C, transverse section from stem of *Abutilon*.

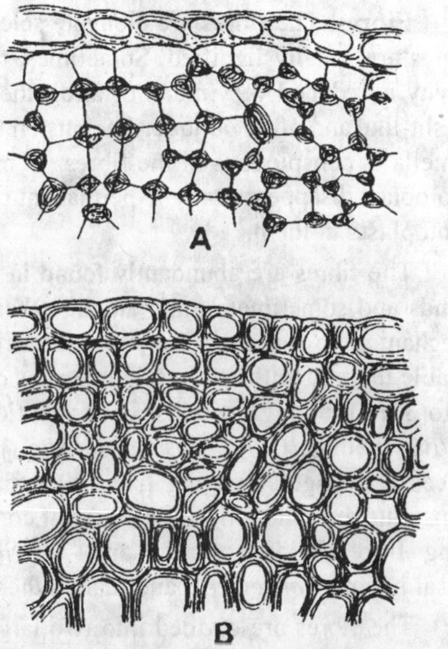

Fig. 2.9. Collenchyma. A, angular collenchyma of *Cucurbita* stem (thickenings in the angles); B, lacunar collenchyma of *Lactuca* stem where intercellular spaces are present and the thickenings are located next to these spaces.

Ontogenetically collenchyma develop from elongate, procambium like cells that appear very early in the differentiating meristem. In the beginning, small intercellular spaces are present among these cells, but they disappear in angular and lamellar types as the cells enlarge, either by the enlarging cells or filled by intercellular substance.

The chief primary function of the tissue is to give support to the plant body. Its supporting value is increased by its peripheral position in the parts of stems, petioles and leaf mid-ribs. When the chloroplasts are present in the tissue, they carry on photosynthesis.

3. Sclerenchyma. The sclerenchyma (Greek, *sclerous*, hard; *enchyma*, an infusion) consists of thick walled cells, often lignified, whose main function is mechanical. This is a supporting tissue that withstands various strains which result from stretching and bending of plant organs without any damage to the thin-walled softer cells. The individual cells of sclerenchyma are termed **sclerenchyma cells**. Collectively sclerenchyma cells make sclerenchyma tissue. Sclerenchyma cells do not possess living protoplasts at maturity. The walls of these cells are uniformly and strongly thickened. Most commonly, the sclerenchyma cells are grouped into **fibres** and **sclereids.**

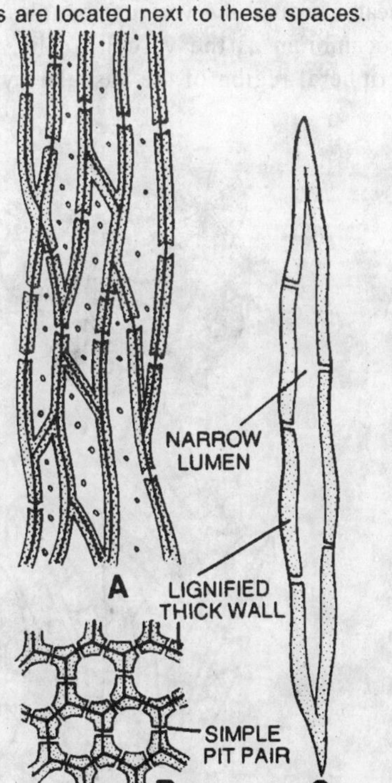

Fig. 2.10. Sclerenchyma. A, L.S. of fibres; B, T.S. of fibres; C, a single fibre as seen in longitudinal section.

Fibres. The fibres are elongate sclerenchyma cells, usually with pointed ends. The walls of fibres are usually lignified. Sometimes, their walls are so much thickened that the lumen or cell cavity is reduced very much or altogether obliterated. The pits of fibres are always small, round or slit-like and often oblique. The pits on the walls may be numerous or few in number. The middle lamella is conspicuous in the fibres. In most kinds of fibres, however, on maturation of cells the protoplast disappears and the permanent cell becomes dead and empty. Very rarely the fibres retain protoplasts in them.

The fibres are abundantly found in many plants. They may occur in patches, in continuous bands and sometimes singly among other cells. As already mentioned, they are dead and purely mechanical in function. They provide strength and rigidity to the various organs of the plants to enable them to withstand various strains caused by outer agencies. The average length of fibres is 1 to 3 mm. in angiosperms, but exceptions are there. In *Linum usitatissimum* (flax), *Cannabis sativa* (hemp), *Corchorus capsularis* (jute), and *Boehmeria nivea* (ramie), the fibres are of excessive lengths ranging from 20 mm. to 550 mm. Such long, thick-walled and rigid cells constitute exceptionally good fibres of commercial importance. In addition to these plants common long fibre yielding plants are — *Hibiscus cannabinus* (Madras hemp), *Agave sisalana* (sisal hemp), *Sansevieria* and many others.

The fibres are divided into two large groups — **xylem fibres** and **extraxylary fibres.** The xylem fibres develop from the same meristematic tissues as the other xylem cells and constitute an integral part of xylem. On the other hand, some of the extraxylary fibres are related to the phloem. The fibres that form continuous cylinders in monocotyledonous stems arise in the ground tissue under the epidermis at variable distances. They are known as **cortical fibres**. The fibres forming sheaths around the vascular bundles in the monocotyledonous stems arise partly from the same procambium as the vascular cells, partly from the ground tissue. The fibres present in the peripheral region of the vascular cylinder, often close to the phloem are known as **pericyclic**

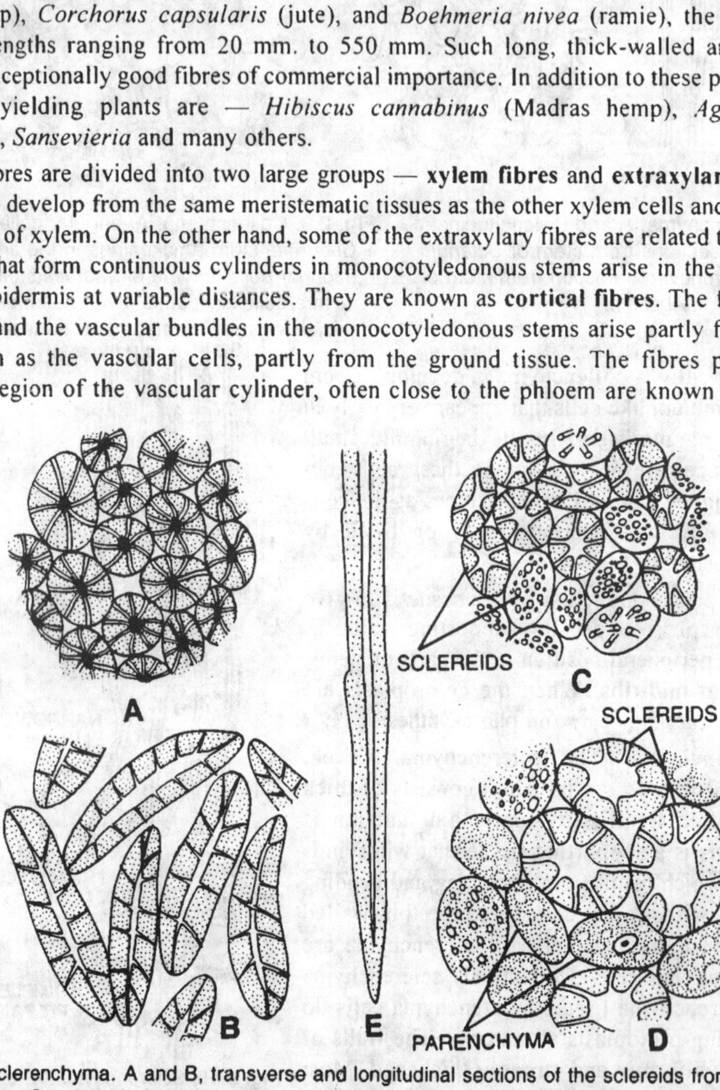

Fig. 2.11. Sclerenchyma. A and B, transverse and longitudinal sections of the sclereids from endocarp of *Cocos nucifera*; C, sclereids from the pericarp of *Pyrus communis*; D, sclereids and parenchyma cells from stem cortex of *Dracaena fragrans*; E.L.S. of fibres (After Eames and MacDaniels).

fibres. The extraxylary fibres are sometimes combined into a group termed **bast fibres**. Generally the term extraxylary fibres is used for bast fibres, which are classified as follows — **phloem fibres,** fibres originating in primary or secondary phloem; **cortical fibres,** fibres originating in the cortex; **perivascular fibres** (Van Fleet, 1948), fibres found in the peripheral region of the vascular cylinder inside the innermost cortical layer but not originating in the phloem. The extraxylary fibres may vary in length, and their ends are sometimes blunt, rather than tapering, and may be branched. The longest fibres (primary phloem fibres) measured *Boehmeria nivea* (ramie). The cell walls of extraxylary fibres are very thick. The pits are simple or slightly bordered. Some possess lignified walls, others non-lignified. The fibres of *Linum usitatissimum* are non-lignified, and their secondary walls consist of pure cellulose. On the other hand, the extraxylary fibres of the monocotyledons, are strongly lignified. Concentric lamellations are found in extraxylary fibres. In the fibres of *Linum usitatissimum* the individual lamellae vary in thickness from 0.1μ to 0.2μ.

Xylem fibres typically possess lignified secondary walls. They vary in size, shape, thickness of wall, and structure and abundance of pits.

Sclereids. The sclereids are widely distributed in the plant body. They are usually not much longer than they are broad, occurring singly or in groups. Usually these cells are isodiametric but some are elongated too. They are commonly found in the cortex and pith of gymnosperms and dicotyledons, arranged singly or in groups. In many species of plants, the sclereids occur in the leaves. The leaf sclereids may be few to abundant. In some leaves the mesophyll is completely permeated by sclereids. Sclereids are also common in fruits and seeds. In fruits they are disposed in the pulp singly or in groups (*e.g.*, *Pyrus*). The hardness and strength of the seed coat is due to the presence of abundant sclereids.

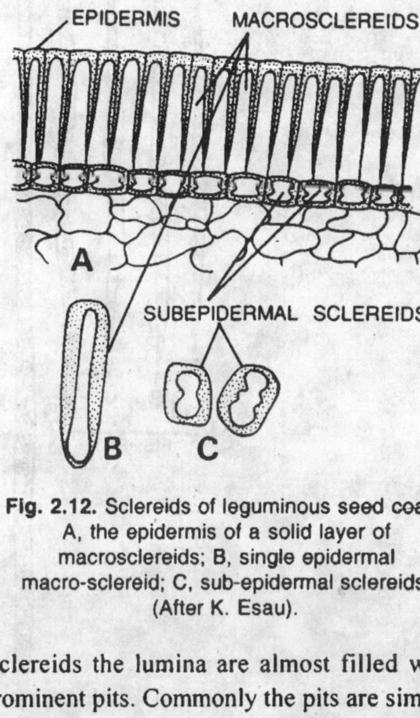

Fig. 2.12. Sclereids of leguminous seed coats. A, the epidermis of a solid layer of macrosclereids; B, single epidermal macro-sclereid; C, sub-epidermal sclereids. (After K. Esau).

The secondary walls of the sclereids are typically lignified and vary in thickness. In many sclereids the lumina are almost filled witl massive wall deposits and the secondary wall shows prominent pits. Commonly the pits are simple and rarely bordered pits may also occur.

The sclereids are grouped into four categories (Foster, 1949). They are as follows — **brachysclereids, macrosclereids, osteosclereids** and **astrosclereids.**

Brachysclereids. These stone cells or sclereids are short and more or less isodiametric. They are commonly distributed in cortex, phloem and pith of stem and in the pulp of fruits.

Macrosclereids. They are more or less rod-like cells forming palisade-like epidermal layer of many seeds (of Leguminosae) and fruits and frequently found in xerophytic leaves and stem cortices.

Osteosclereids. They are bone-shaped sclereids, *i.e.*, columnar cells are enlarged at their ends. Such sclereids are commonly found in the hypodermal layers of many seeds and fruits. They are also found in xerophytic leaves.

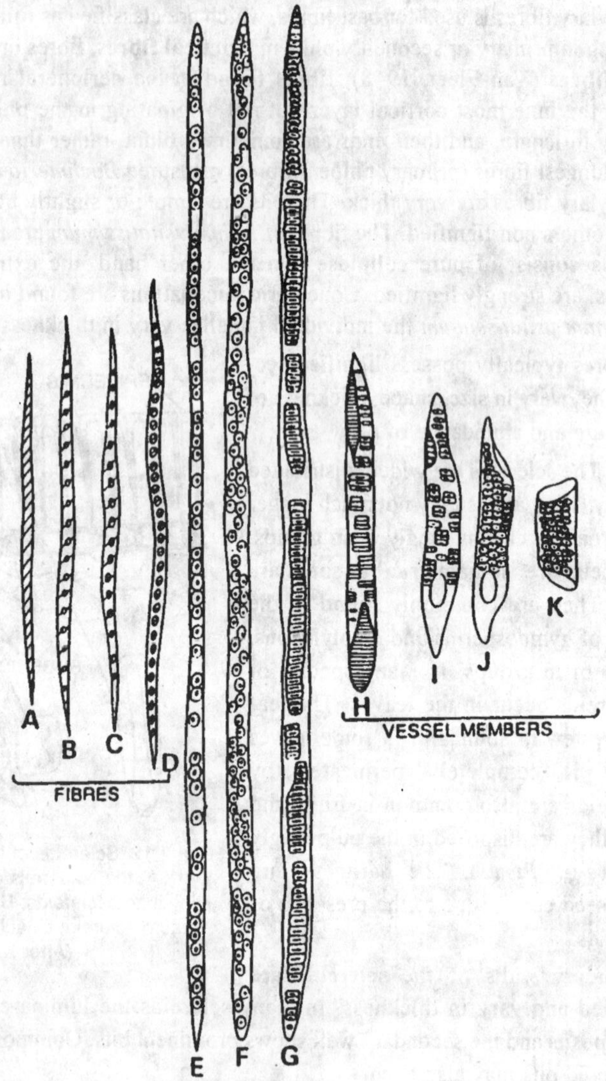

Fig. 2.13. Xylem. A – D, fibres; E – G, tracheids and H – K. vessel members. (After Bailey and Tupper).

Astrosclereids. They are star-shaped sclereids; such sclereids with lobes projecting, like hairs are commonly found in the intercellular spaces of the leaves and stems of hydrophytes.

COMPLEX TISSUES

Here the vascular tissues have been treated as **complex tissues.** The most important complex tissues are — **xylem** and **phloem.**

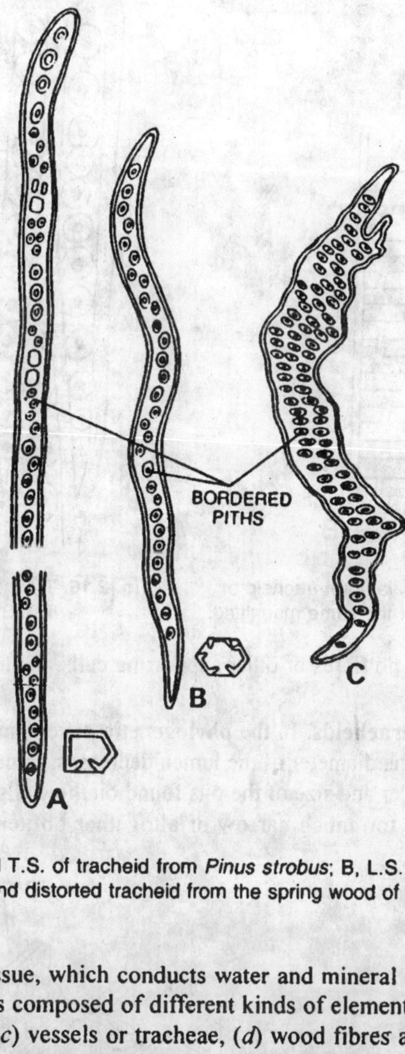

Fig. 2.14. Tracheids. A, L.S. and T.S. of tracheid from *Pinus strobus*; B, L.S. and T.S. of normal tracheid from *Quercus alba*; C, flattened and distorted tracheid from the spring wood of *Quercus alba*. (After E & M).

XYLEM

Xylem is a conducting tissue, which conducts water and mineral nutrients upward from the root to the leaves. The xylem is composed of different kinds of elements. They are: (*a*) tracheids, (*b*) fibres and fibre-tracheids, (*c*) vessels or tracheae, (*d*) wood fibres and (*e*) wood parenchyma. The xylem is also meant for mechanical support to the plant body.

(*a*) Tracheids. The tracheid is a fundamental cell type in xylem. It is an elongate tube like cell having tapering, rounded or oval ends and hard and lignified walls. The walls are not much thickened. It is without protoplast and non-living on maturity. In transverse section the tracheid is typically angular, though more or less rounded forms occur. The tracheids of secondary xylem have fewer sides and are more sharply angular than the tracheids of primary xylem. The end of a tracheid of secondary xylem is somewhat chisel-like. They are dead empty cells. Their walls are provided with abundant, bordered pits arranged in rows or in other patterns. The cell cavity or lumen of a tracheid is large and without any contents. The tracheids possess various kinds of thickenings in them and they may be distinguished as annular, spiral, scalariform, reticulate or pitted tracheids. Tracheids alone make the xylem of ferns and gymnosperms, while in the xylem of angiosperms they occur associated with the vessels and other xylary elements. The tracheids are specially adapted to function of conduction. The thick and rigid walls of tracheids also aid in

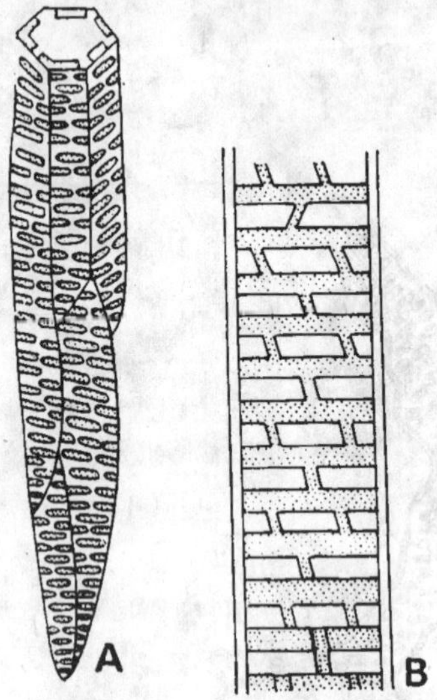

Fig. 2.15. Tracheids. A, a scalariform tracheid of fern; B, a portion of the wall of the same magnified.

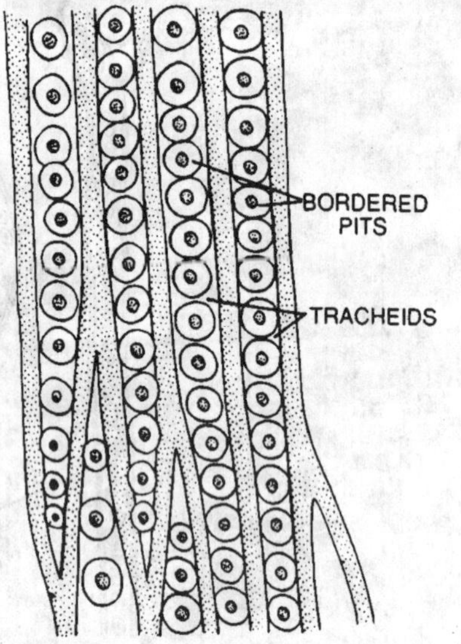

Fig. 2.16. Tracheids. Tracheids of pine stem in R.L.S. with bordered pits.

support and where there are no fibres or other supporting cells, the tracheids play a prominent part in the support of an organ.

(*b*) **Fibres and fibre-tracheids.** In the phylogenetic development of the fibre, the thickness of the wall increases while the diameter of the lumen decreases. In most types the length of the cell also decreases and the number and size of the pits found on the walls also decrease. Sometimes the lumen of the cell becomes too much narrow or altogether obliterated and simultaneously pits

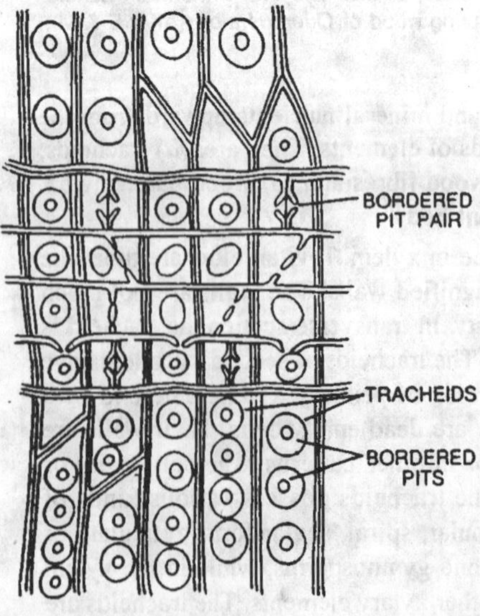

Fig. 2.17. Tracheids with bordered pits of pine stem in R.L.S.

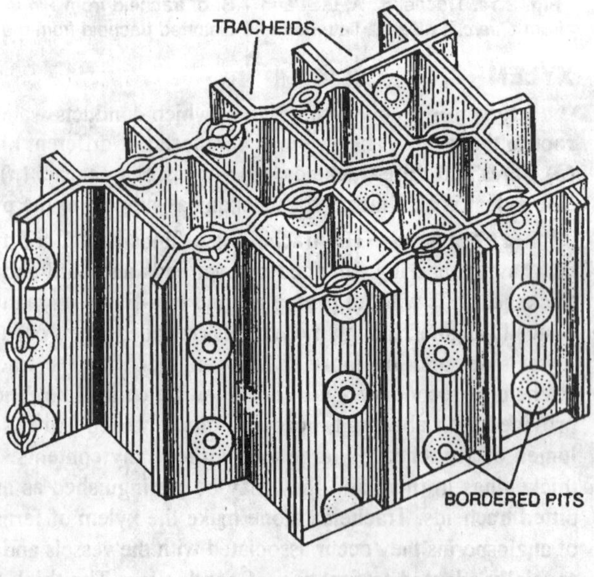

Fig. 2.18. Tracheids with bordered pits of pine stem (diagrammatic).

become quite small in size. At this stage it is assumed that either there is very little conduction of water or no conduction through such type of cells, typical **fibres** are formed. Between such cells (*i.e.*, fibres) and normal tracheids there are many transitional forms which are neither typical fibres nor typical tracheids. These transitional types are designated as **fibre-tracheids**. The pits of fibre-tracheids are smaller than those of vessels and typical tracheids. However, a line of demarcation cannot be drawn in between tracheids and fibre-tracheids and between fibre-tracheids and fibres. When the fibres possess very thick walls and reduced simple pits, they are known as libriform wood fibres because of their similarity to phloem fibres (liber = phloem fibres). The libriform wood fibres chiefly occur in woody dicotyledons (*e.g.*, in Leguminosae). The walls of fibre tracheids and fibres of many genera of different families possess gelatinous layers. The cells possessing such layers are known as **gelatinous tracheids, fibre-tracheids** and **fibres.** In certain fibre-tracheids the protoplast persists after the secondary wall is mature and may divide to produce two or more protoplasts. These protoplasts are separated by thin transverse partition walls and remain enclosed within the original wall. Such fibre tracheids are called **septate fibre-tracheids**. In fact, they are not individual cells but rows of cells. Here, the transverse partitions are true walls, and each chamber has a protoplast with nucleus.

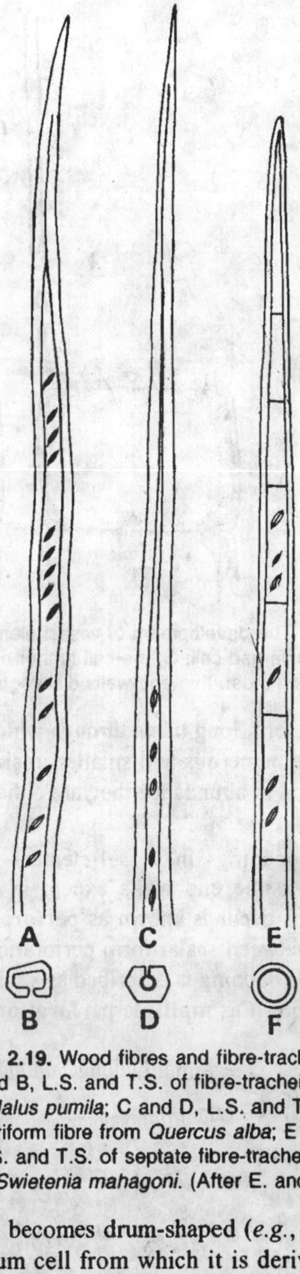

Fig. 2.19. Wood fibres and fibre-tracheids. A and B, L.S. and T.S. of fibre-tracheid from *Malus pumila*; C and D, L.S. and T.S. of libriform fibre from *Quercus alba*; E and F, L.S. and T.S. of septate fibre-tracheid from *Swietenia mahagoni*. (After E. and M.)

(c) Vessels. In the phylogenetic development of the tracheid the diameter of the cell has increased and the wall has become perforated by large openings. Due to these adaptations and specializations water can move from cell to cell without any resistance. In the more primitive types of vessels, the general form of the tracheid is retained and increase in diameter is not much. In the most advanced types, increase in diameter is much and the cell becomes drum-shaped (*e.g.*, *Quercus alba*). The tracheid is sufficiently longer than the cambium cell from which it is derived. The primitive vessel is slightly longer than the cambium cell. The most advanced type of vessel retains the length of cambium cell or is somewhat shorter, with a diameter greater than its length (drum-shaped vessel). The ends of the cells change in shape in the series from least to highest specialization. The angle formed by the tapering end wall becomes greater and greater until the end wall is at right angles to the side walls (as in drum-shaped vessel in *Quercus alba*). Some intermediate forms possess tail-like lips beyond the end wall. Usually the diameter of vessels is much greater than that of tracheids and because of the presence of perforations in the partition

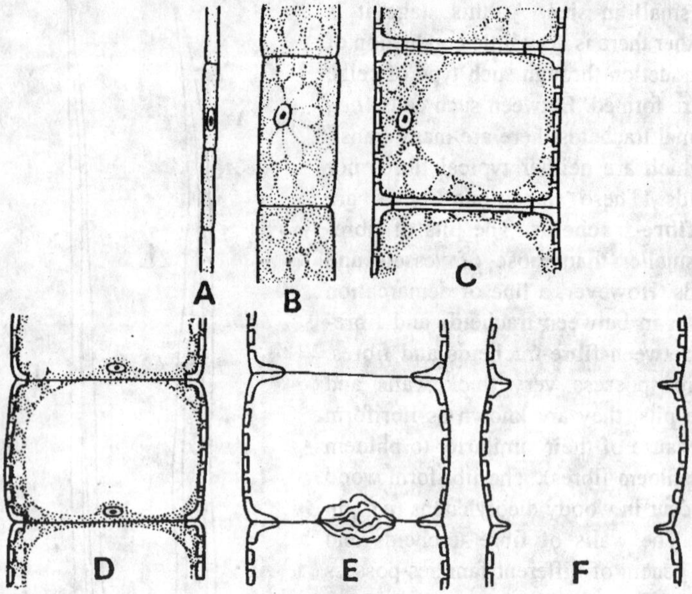

Fig. 2.20. The development of vessel element. (Ontogeny of the vessel) — A, the cambium initial; B, the much enlarged cell; C, the cell further enlarged; D, the cytoplasm restricted to the periphery; E, the cytoplasm lost, thin end walls disintegrating; F, the mature, perforated, empty cell. (After E. & M.)

walls they form long tubes through which water is being conducted from root to leaf. The pits are often more numerous and smaller in size than are those of tracheids and cover the wall closely. When found in abundance they are either scattered or arranged in definite patterns on the walls of the vessels.

The openings in vessel-element walls are known as **perforations**. These openings are restricted to the end walls except in certain slender, tapering types. The area in which the perforations occur is known as **perforation plate**. Commonly this is an end wall. The stripes of cell wall between scalariform perforations are the **perforation bars**. The perforation plate when bears single opening is described as having **simple perforation**. If there are two or more openings, they are known as **multiple perforations.**

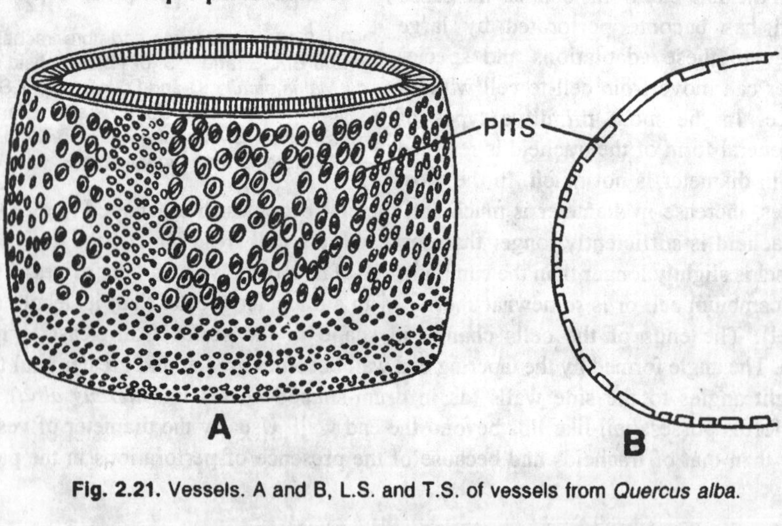

Fig. 2.21. Vessels. A and B, L.S. and T.S. of vessels from *Quercus alba*.

The secondary walls of vessel-elements develop in a wide variety of patterns. Generally, in the first-formed part of the primary xylem a more limited area of the primary wall is covered by secondary wall layers than in the later-formed primary xylem and in the secondary xylem. The secondary thickenings are deposited in the vessels as rings, continuous spirals or helices, with the individual coils of a helix here and there interconnected with each other, giving the wall a ladder-like appearance. Such secondary thickenings are called — **annular, spiral or helical** and **scalariform** respectively. In a still later ontogenetic type of vessel elements, the **reticulate** vessel elements, the secondary wall appears like a reticulum. When the meshes of the reticulum are transversely elongated, the thickening is called **scalariform-reticulate**. The **pitted** elements are characteristic of the latest primary xylem and of the secondary xylem.

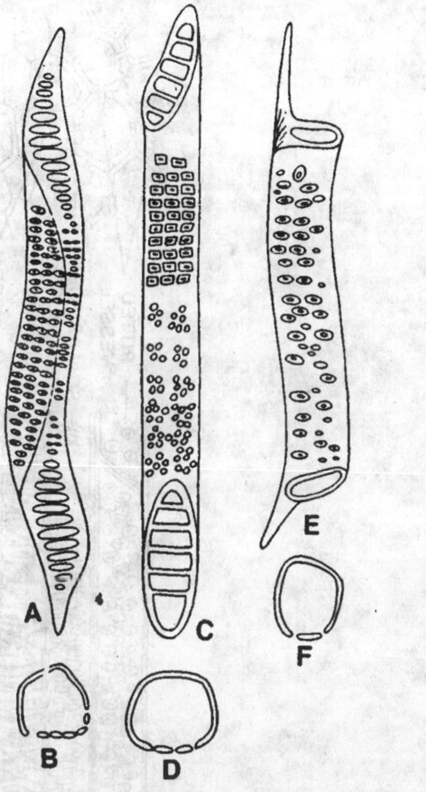

Fig. 2.22. Vessel elements. A and B, L.S. and T.S. of vessel from *Betula*; C and D, L.S. and T.S. of vessel from *Liriodendron*; E and F, L.S. and T.S. of vessel from *Malus*.

Vessels are characteristic of the angiosperms. However, certain angiospermic families lack the vessels — the Winteraceae, Trochodendraceae and Tetracentraceae. In many monocotyledons (*e.g.*, *Yucca*, *Dracaena*) they are absent from the stems and leaves. They are found in some species of *Selaginella*, in two species of *Pteridium*

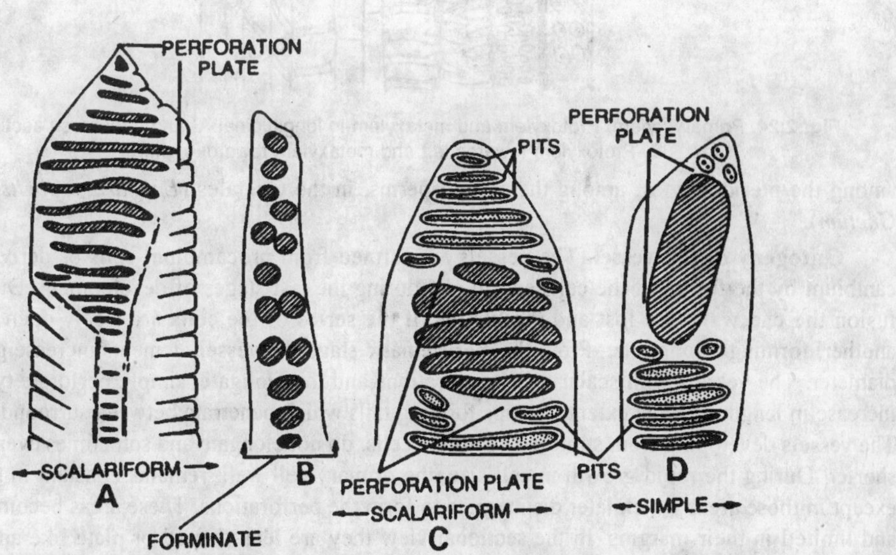

Fig. 2.23. End walls of vessels with perforation plates. A scalariform vessel of *Pteridium*; B, foraminate type of *Ephedra*; C, scalariform vessel of *Vitis* and D, simple type of *Vitis*.

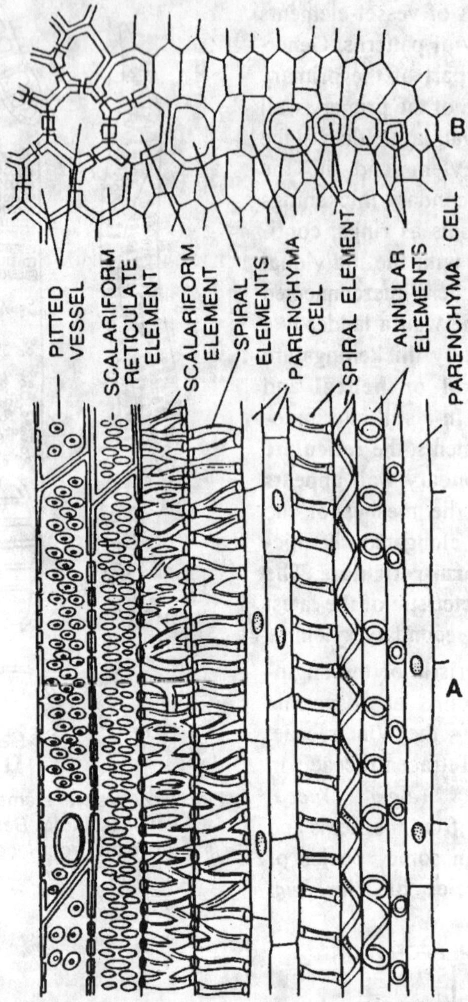

Fig. 2.24. Primary xylem. Protoxylem and metaxylem in longitudinal A, and transverse sections B, Protoxylem towards left and metaxylem towards right.

among the pteridophytes; among the gymnosperms, in the Gnetales (*Ephedra*, *Welwitschia* and *Gnetum*).

Ontogeny of the vessel. The vessels are formed from procambium cells or derivatives of cambium by the fusion of the cells end to end during the last stages of development. During this fusion the end walls are lost and the lumina of the series of the cells are freely open into one another, forming a long tube. From the meristematic stage the vessel elements increase greatly in diameter. The vessels with scalariform perforations and the elongate, simply perforate types may increase in length to some extent, the tips forming tails which penetrate between surrounding cells. The vessels developing from stratified cambium cells, do not elongate and sometimes even become shorter. During the rapid growth in cell size, the primary cell wall, remains constant in thickness except in those areas which later disintegrate to form the perforations. These areas become thicker and limited in their margins. In the sectional view they are lens-shaped or plate like and can be seen to be three layered, composing of the primary walls of the two adjacent cells and the middle lamella. When the cell reaches its maturity, the cytoplasm of the cell begins to disintegrate. In

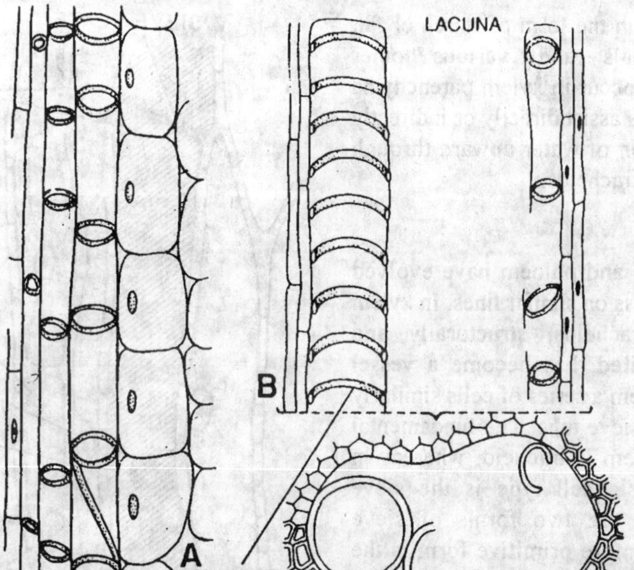

Fig. 2.25. Protoxylem. A, L.S. of protoxylem from *Arisaema* fruit, the elements are all annular; B – C, L.S. and T.S. of protoxylem from *Zea*, the surrounding parenchyma pulled away from the protoxylem elements, leaving a large lacuna.

certain woody plants the nucleus becomes quite small and flat and lies in scant cytoplasm against the wall where perforation is about to occur. As soon as the primary wall becomes mature, the perforation of the end wall and loss of the protoplast begin. The wall in the perforation area becomes thinner and thinner and ultimately disintegrates. The maturation in all members of a vessel series takes place from one end to the other and not simultaneously (see Fig. 2.22).

(*d*) **Wood parenchyma.** The parenchyma cells which frequently occur in the xylem of most plants. In secondary xylem such cells occur vertically more or less elongated and placed end to end, known as **wood or xylem parenchyma**. The radial transverse series of the cells form the wood rays and are known as **wood** or **xylem ray parenchyma.** The xylem parenchyma cells may be as long as the fusiform initials, or they may be several times shorter, if a fusiform derivative divides transversely before differentiation into parenchyma (wood parenchyma). The shorter type of xylem parenchyma cells is the more common. The ray and the xylem parenchyma cells of the secondary xylem may or may not have secondary walls. If a secondary wall is present, the pit pairs between the parenchyma cells and the tracheary elements may be simple, half-bordered or bordered. In between, parenchyma cells only simple pit pairs occur. The xylem parenchyma cells are noted for

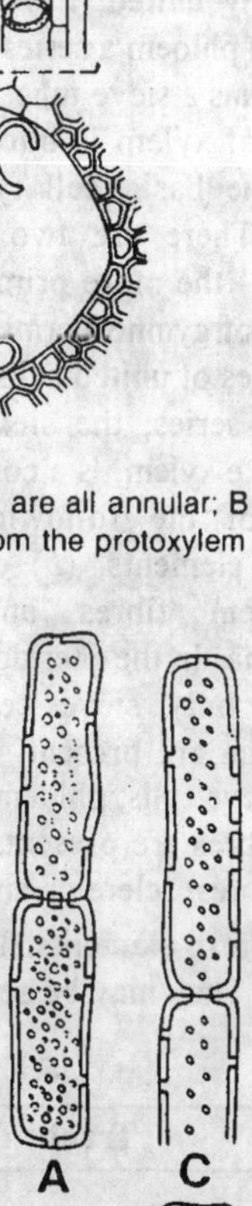

Fig. 2.26. Wood parenchyma. A and B, L.S. and T.S. of wood parenchyma from *Quercus alba*; C and D, L.S. and T.S. of wood parenchyma from *Carya ovata*.

storage of food in the form of starch or fat. Tannins, crystals and various other substances also occur in xylem parenchyma cells. These cells assist directly or indirectly in the conduction of water upward through the vessels and tracheids.

2. PHLOEM

The xylem and phloem have evolved along more or less on similar lines. In xylem a series of tracheids, structurally and functionally united, has become a vessel whereas in phloem a series of cells similarly united, forms a sieve tube. The fundamental cell type of xylem is tracheid, whereas in phloem the basic cell type is the sieve element. There are two forms of sieve element — the more primitive form is the **sieve cell** of gymnosperms and lower forms where series of united cells do not exist, the unit of a series, the sieve tube element. Phloem like xylem, is a complex tissue, and consists of the following elements — (*a*) sieve elements, (*b*) companion cells, (*c*) phloem fibres and (*d*) phloem parenchyma. In the pteridophytes and gymnosperms only sieve cells and phloem parenchyma are present. In some gymnosperms, sieve cells, phloem parenchyma and phloem fibres are present. In angiosperms, sieve tubes, companion cells, phloem parenchyma, phloem fibres, sclereids and secretory cells are present.

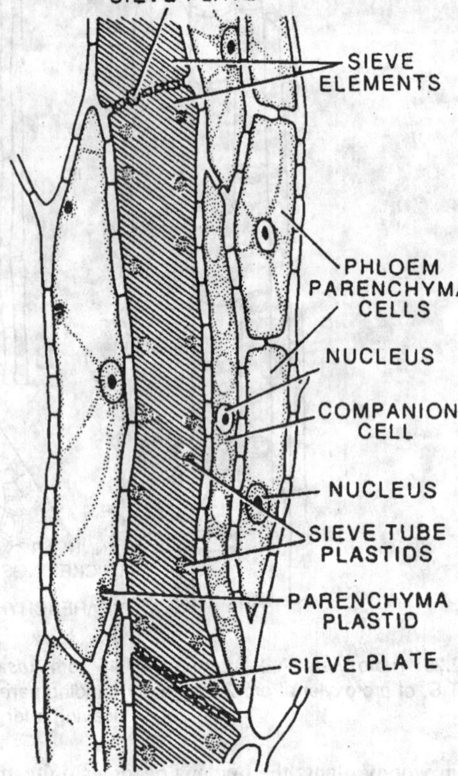

Fig. 2.27. Phloem. Phloem tissue from the stem of *Nicotiana*.

(*a*) Sieve elements. The conducting elements of the phloem are collectively known as **sieve elements**. They may be segregated into the less specialized **sieve cells** and the more specialized

Table. 2.1. Comparison of Tracheid and Vessel

Tracheid	Vessel
1. The tracheids are short and are generally upto 1 mm. in length. In rare cases their length becomes upto 1.2 cm. or so.	1. They are comparatively longer and may reach upto 10 cm. in length. In rare case they attain the length upto 2–6 metres (*e.g.*, in *Eucalytus*, *Quercus*, etc.)
2. It consists of a single elongated cell which possesses tapering end walls.	2. The vessel consists of a row of cells placed one above the other. Their intervening walls are absent.
3. The tracheids are not tubular. The tracheids found one above the other are separated by cross walls which bear bordered pits. They are not perforated.	3. The vessels are tubular and have no cross walls. They are well adapted for the conduction of water. They may be perforated by small or large pores.

sieve tubes or **sieve tube elements.** The morphologic specialization of sieve elements is expressed in the development of sieve areas on their walls and in the peculiar modifications of their protoplasts. The **sieve areas** are depressed wall areas with clusters of perforations, through which the protoplasts of the adjacent sieve elements are interconnected by **connecting strands**. In a sieve area each connecting strand remains encased in a cylinder of substance called **callose.** The wall in a sieve area is a double structure consisting of two layers of primary wall, one belonging to one cell and the other to another, cemented together by intercellular substance. Like the pits in the tracheary elements, the sieve areas occur in various numbers and are variously distributed in sieve elements of different plants. The wall parts bearing the highly specialized sieve areas are called **sieve plates** (Esau, 1950). If a sieve plate consists of a single sieve area, it is a **simple sieve plate.** Many sieve areas, arranged in scalariform, reti-culate, or any other manner, constitute a **compound sieve plate**. However,

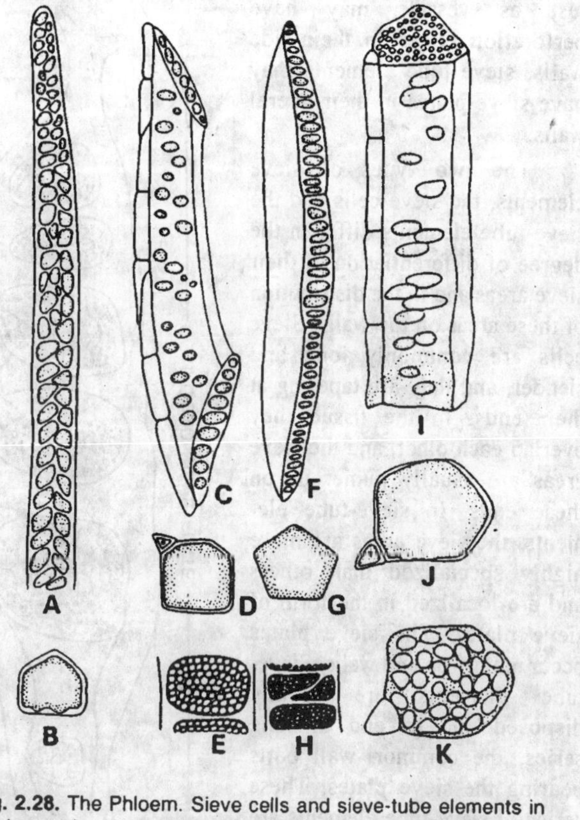

Fig. 2.28. The Phloem. Sieve cells and sieve-tube elements in side view and cross-section, with detailed structure of sieve plates. A and B, L.S. and T.S. of sieve cell of *Pteridium*; C and D, L.S. and T.S. of sieve tube with companion cells attached in *Liriodendron*; E, detail of sieve plate in the same; F and G, sieve tube from *Malus pumila* in L.S. and T.S.; H, detail of sieve plate in same; I and J sieve tube from *Robinia* in L.S. and T.S. with companion cells attached; K, detail of sieve plate in same.

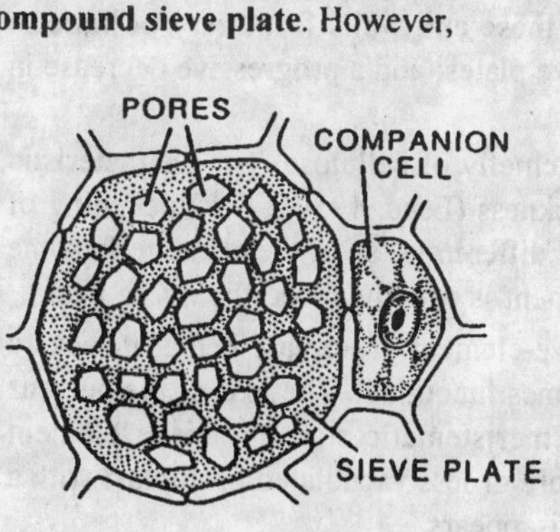

Fig. 2.29. Phloem. T.S. through a sieve plate and companion cell.

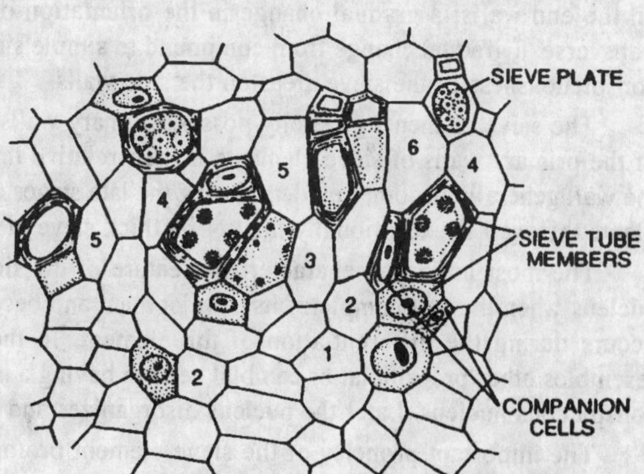

Fig. 2.30. Phloem. Differentiation of sieve tube members in *Cucurbita*.

just as vessels may have perforation plates in their side walls, sieve tube elements may have sieve plates in their lateral walls.

The two types of sieve elements, the sieve cells and the sieve-tube elements differ in the degree of differentiation of their sieve areas and in the distribution of these areas on the walls. Sieve cells are commonly long and slender, and they are tapering at their ends. In the tissue they overlap each other, and the sieve areas are usually numerous on these ends. In sieve-tube elements, the sieve areas are more highly specialized than others and are localized in the form of sieve plates. The sieve plates occur mainly on end walls. Sieve-tube elements are usually disposed end to end in long series, the common wall parts bearing the sieve plates. These series of sieve-tube elements are **sieve-tubes**.

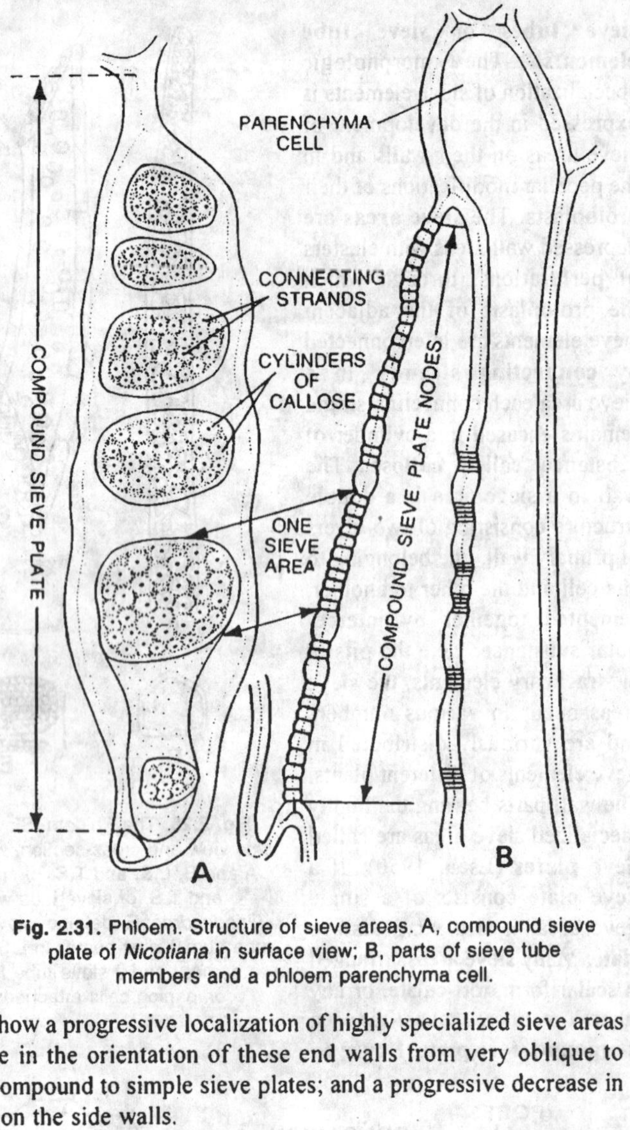

Fig. 2.31. Phloem. Structure of sieve areas. A, compound sieve plate of *Nicotiana* in surface view; B, parts of sieve tube members and a phloem parenchyma cell.

The lower vascular plants and the gymnosperms generally have sieve cells, whereas most angiosperms have sieve-tube elements. The sieve-tube elements show a progressive localization of highly specialized sieve areas on the end walls; a gradual change in the orientation of these end walls from very oblique to transverse; a gradual change from compound to simple sieve plates; and a progressive decrease in conspicuousness of the sieve areas on the side walls.

The sieve elements generally possess primary walls, chiefly of cellulose. The characteristic of the primary walls of sieve elements is their relative thickness (Esau, 1950). The thickening of the wall generally becomes evident during the late stages of differentiation of the element. In some plants this wall is exceptionally thick. The thick sieve element is usually called the *nacre wall.*

The most important characteristic feature of the sieve-element protoplast is that it lacks a nucleus when the cell completes its development and becomes functional. The loss of the nucleus occurs during the differentiation of the element. In the meristematic state the sieve element resembles other procambial or cambial cells in having a more or less vacuolated protoplast with a conspicuous nucleus. Later the nucleus disorganizes and disappears.

The important property of the sieve-element protoplast of dicotyledons is the presence of variable amounts of a relatively viscous substance, the *slime*. The slime is proteinaceous in nature. The slime appears to be located mainly in the cell-sap together with various organic and inorganic ingredients. The slime originates in the cytoplasm in the form of discrete bodies, the **slime-bodies.**

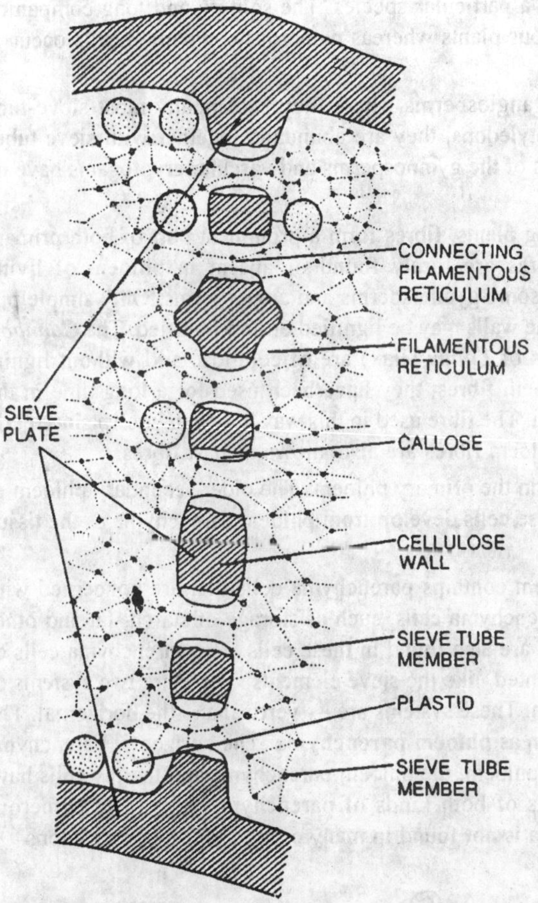

Fig. 2.32. Phloem. Diagrammatic representation of the ultra-structure of a sieve plate.

They may be spherical, or spindle shaped, or variously twisted and coiled. They occur singly or in multiples in one element.

(b) Companion cells. The *companion cell* is a specialized type of parenchyma cell which is closely associated in origin, position and function with sieve-tube elements. When seen in transverse section the companion cell is usually a small, triangular, rounded or rectangular cell beside a sieve-tube element. These cells are living having abundant granular cytoplasm and a prominent elongated nucleus which is retained throughout the life of the cell. Usually the nuclei of the companion cells serve for the nuclei of sieve tubes as they lack them. The companion cells do not contain starch. They live only so long as the sieve-tube element with which they are associated and they are crushed with those cells. The companion cells are formed by longitudinal division of the mother cell of the sieve tube element before specialization of this cell begins. One daughter cell becomes a companion cell and other a sieve tube element. The companion cell initial may divide transversely several times producing a row of companion cells so that one to several companion cells may accompany each sieve-tube element. A companion cell or a row of companion cells formed by the transverse division of a single companion-cell initial may extend the full length of the sieve-tube element. The number of companion cells accompanying

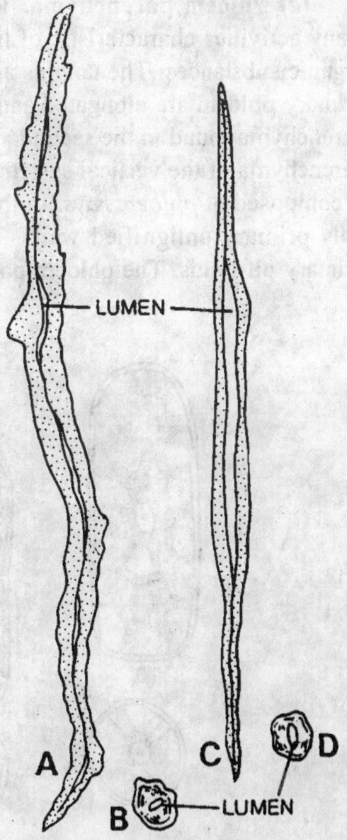

Fig. 2.33. Phloem fibres. A and B, L.S. and T.S. of phloem fibres from *Malus pumila*; C and D, L.S. and T.S. of phloem fibre from *Robinia*. (After E. & M).

a sieve-tube element is fairly constant for a particular species. The solitary and long companion cells occur in primary phloem of herbaceous plants whereas numerous companion cells occur in the secondary phloem of woody plants.

The companion cells occur only in angiosperms where they accompany most sieve-tube elements. In the phloem of many monocotyledons, they are abundant, together with sieve tubes making up the entire tissue. The sieve cells of the gymnosperms and vascular cryptogams have no companion cells.

(*c*) **Phloem fibres.** In many flowering plants, fibres form a prominent part of both primary and secondary phloem. The phloem fibres are rarely found or absent in phloem of living pteridophytes. They are also not found in some gymnosperms and angiosperms. Only simple pits are found on the walls of phloem fibres. The walls may be lignified or non-lignified. The *Cannabis* (hemp) fibres are lignifed, whereas fibres of *Linum* (flax) are of cellulose and without lignin. Because of the strength of strands of phloem fibres, they have been used for a long time in the manufacture of cords, ropes, mats and cloth. The fibre used in this way has been known since early times as **bast** or **bass,** and this way the phloem fibres are also known as bast fibres.

The sclereids are occasionally found in the primary phloem. The older secondary phloem of many trees also contains the sclereids. These cells develop from phloem parenchyma as the tissue ages and the sieve tubes cease to function.

(*d*) **Phloem parenchyma.** The phloem contains parenchyma cells that are concerned with many activities characteristic of living parenchyma cells, such as storage of starch, fat and other organic substances. The tannins and resins are also found in these cells. The parenchyma cells of primary phloem are elongated and are oriented, like the sieve elements. There are two systems of parenchyma found in the secondary phloem. These systems are — vertical and the horizontal. The parenchyma of the vertical system is known as **phloem parenchyma**. The horizontal parenchyma is composed of *phloem rays*. In the active phloem, the phloem parenchyma and the ray cells have only primary unlignified walls. The walls of both kinds of parenchyma cells have numerous primary pit fields. The phloem parenchyma is not found in many or most of monocotyledons.

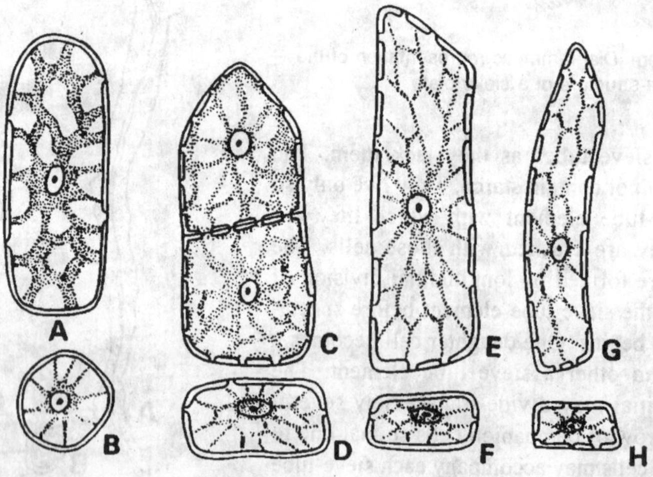

Fig. 2.34. Phloem parenchyma in L.S. and T.S. A – B, from *Salix*; C – D, from *Robinia*; E – F, from *Liriodendron*; G – H, from *Malus*.

3. SECRETORY TISSUE

The tissues that are concerned with the secretion of gums, resins, volatile oils, nectar, latex and other substances are called **secretory tissues**. These are further subdivided into two groups — (*a*) laticiferous tissue and (*b*) glandular tissue.

(*a*) **Laticiferous tissue.** Usually latex is present in the families of many flowering plants. This substance may be white, yellow or pinkish in colour. This is a viscous fluid and established to be colloidal in nature. Many substances like sugars, proteins, gums, alkaloids, enzymes, rubber, etc., remain suspended in a matrix of watery fluid. Starch grains may be abundantly present. The latex of some plants is of great importance, especially as a source of rubber (*e.g.*, *Haevea*, *Ficus*, etc.), chicle (*Achras*), and papain (*Carica*). The laticiferous ducts, in which latex is found may be of two types — **latex cells** or **non-articulate latex ducts** and **latex vessels** or **articulate latex ducts.** The functions and the contents of the two are same but they differ in their nature and morphology. They contain numerous nuclei in the thin layer of cytoplasm along the cell wall. The function of these tissues is not yet clearly understood. They may act as food storage organs or as reservoirs of waste products.

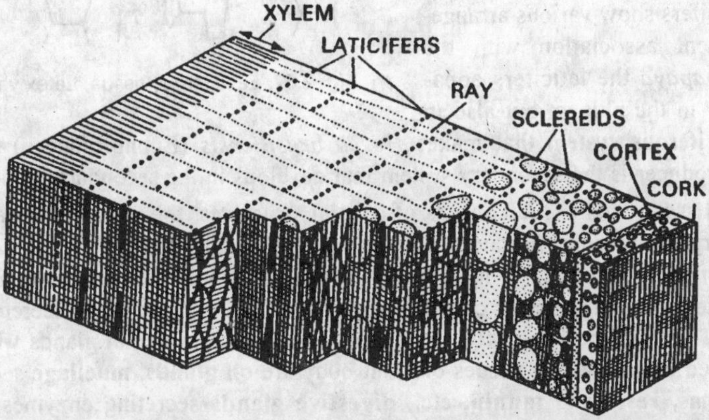

Fig. 2.35. Laticiferous tissue. Three dimensional diagram of bark of *Hevea brasiliensis* showing arrangement of articulated laticifer in secondary phloem. In tangential sections, laticifers form a reticulum.

Nonarticulate latex ducts or latex cells. These ducts are independent units which extend as branched structures for long distances in the plant body. They originate as minute structures, elongate quickly and ramify in all directions of the plant body by repeated branching, but they do not fuse together, thus no netted structures are formed as they are formed in articulate ducts. The walls of the ducts are soft and very often thick. Such ducts are commonly found in *Calotropis*, *Euphorbia*, *Nerium*, *Vinca*, etc.

Branched nonarticulated laticifers commonly occur in leaves. Here they travel through the vascular bundles, ramify in the mesophyll, and often reach the epidermis.

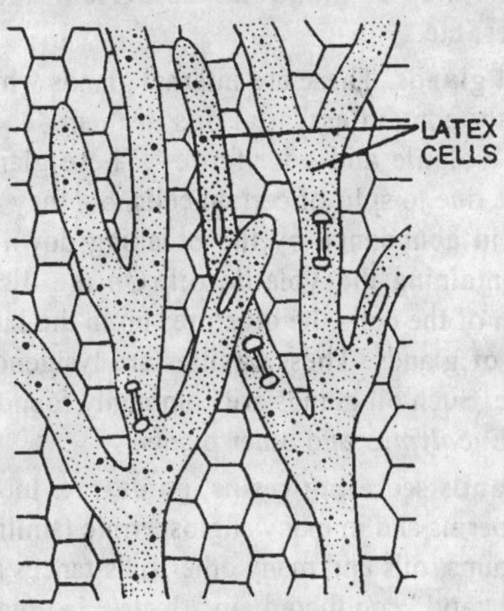

Fig. 2.36. Laticiferous tissue. Latex cells.

The unbranched nonarticulated laticifers of *Vinca* and *Cannabis* occur in the primary phloem but are apparently absent in the secondary tissues.

Articulate latex ducts or latex vessels. These ducts or vessels are the result of anastamosing of many cells together. They originate in the meristems from rows of cells by the abortion, of the separating walls early in the ontogeny of the cells. They grow more or less as parallel ducts which by means of branching and frequent anastamoses form a complex network. A duct of this type resembles with the xylem vessel only in the respect that it is made up of a series of cells united to form a tube otherwise the latex tube is living and coenocytic. Such latex vessels are commonly found in angiospermic families — Papaveraceae, Compositae, Euphor-biaceae, Moraceae, etc.

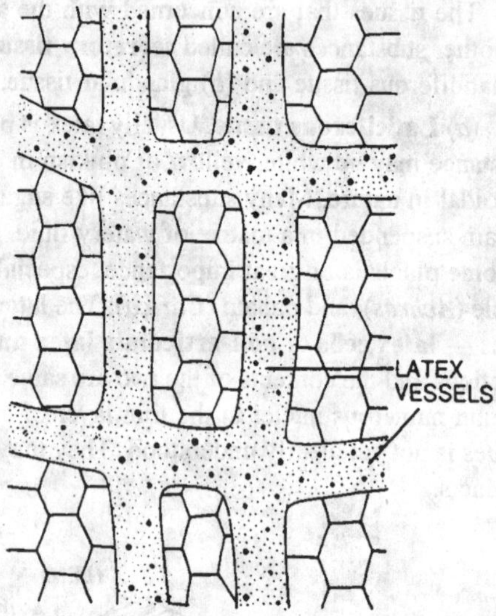

Fig. 2.37. Laticiferous tissue. Latex vessels.

Articulated laticifers show various arrangements and a frequent association with the phloem. In *Carica papaya* the laticifers apparently occur not only in the phloem but also in the xylem. The laticiferous system that makes *Hevea brasiliensis* (Euphorbiaceae) such an outstanding rubber producer is the secondary system that develops in the secondary phloem.

(*b*) Glandular tissue. This tissue consists of special structures, the *glands*. These glands contain some secretory or excretory products. The glands may consist of isolated cells or small groups of cells with or without central cavity. They are of various kinds, and more common types are those which secrete digestive enzymes, called **digestive glands** and those which secrete nectar, known as *nectaries*. They may be **internal** or **external.** The common internal glands which are usually lying embedded in the interior tissues of plant body are **oil glands, mucilage secreting, glands secreting gums, resin** and **tannin,** etc., **digestive glands** secreting enzymes, **water secreting glands** also known as **hydathodes.** The common external glands which occur on the epidermis may be **glandular epidermal hairs, nectaries,** etc.

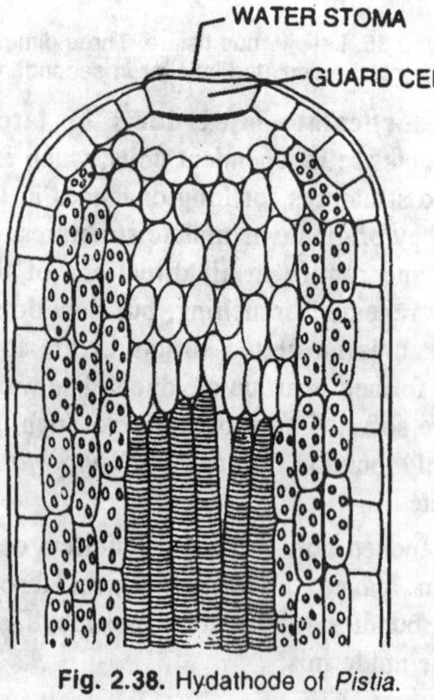

Fig. 2.38. Hydathode of *Pistia*.

Oil glands. These are internal glands which frequently contain essential oils in them. These oils are volatile and odoriferous. These glands originate due to split of certain cells, but they are formed in abundance by the breaking down of cells containing the volatile oil. On the disintegration of the cells the oil stores up in the large cavities of glands. These cavities are lysigenous in nature. Such oil glands are commonly found in *Citrus*, *Eucalyptus* and other plants.

Glands secreting resins, gums, etc. In the gymnosperms and in many angiospermic families, resins, gums, oils and many other subs-tances are secreted and conducted in ducts. In many gymnosperms (*e.g.*, in *Pinus*) these ducts or canals form extensive systems extending both vertically and horizontally. In other plants (*e.g.*, in *Umbelliferae*) the ducts are local in occurrence and limited in extent. In *Pinus* and many other gymnosperms, the resin ducts are schizogenous in nature, and when mature, have the structure of a tube with an epithelial lining. These glands are internal.

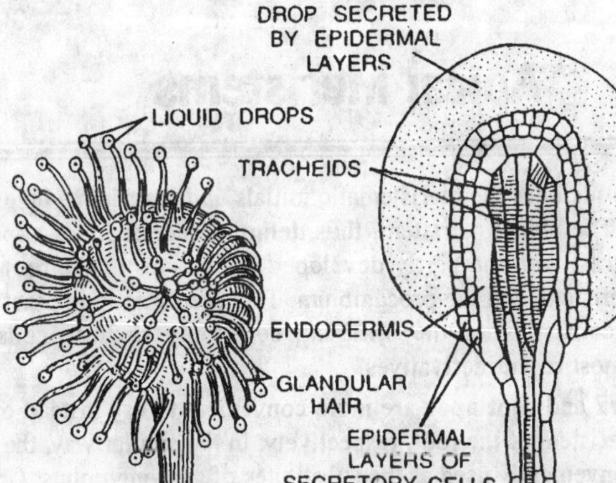

Fig. 2.39. Glands. A, leaf of Drosera plant covered with numerous glandular hairs; B, a digestive gland of sundew (*Drosera*).

Digestive glands. In certain insectivorous plants there are special glands which secrete protein-digesting enzymes. These enzymes act upon insects so that the products of digestion can be absorbed by the plant. In *Drosera*, the secretory tissue is at the tips of the leaf tentacles. Here in addition to the digestive enzymes, there are secreted viscid substances which hold the insects. These are internal glands.

Hydathodes (water secreting glands). Many plants possess special structures which exudate water under conditions of low transpiration and abundant soil moisture. These modified special structures are known as **hydathodes or water stomata.** The water stoma resembles an ordinary stoma, and morphologically it is considered to be enlarged stoma which has lost the power of movement and serves for water secretion. Commonly, the hydathodes occur at the tips of the leaves of *Pistia* and other aroids, water hyacinth, grasses, garden nasturtium and many other plants of humid climate. The hydathodes are internal glands.

Nectaries. Many insect-pollinated plants produce *nectar* which attracts insects. This substance is secreted by special cellular structures, the nectaries. Definite and elaborate nectaries occur in certain families (*e.g.*, Euphorbiaceae). In the less specialized nectaries the secreting cells are superficial upon the floral parts. Here, the epidermal cells do not possess cuticle. The nectar is exuded through the wall and exposed upon the outer surface. The **septal nectaries** are commonly found in many monocotyledonous flowers where they make pockets in the septal walls of syncarpous ovaries where the carpel walls are fused incompletely and the epidermal cells are glandular. These glands are external in nature.

3

CHAPTER

Apical Meristems

The apical meristem includes the meristematic initials and their immediate derivatives at the apex of a shoot or root. The apical meristem, thus delimited corresponds approximately to the promeristem, and to contrast with the partly developed derivatives of the promeristem, *i.e.*, the protoderm, the ground meristem, and the procambium. This seems quite impracticable, to think of the apical meristem as consisting of the initiating cells only because cells may be poorly differentiated from their most recent derivatives.

The terms **shoot apex** and **root apex** are more convenient to use instead of apical meristem of the shoot and apical meristem of the root, respectively. In the similar way, the terms shoot apex and root apex are more conveniently used as the substitutes of growing points. Growth in the sense of cell division, which is characteristic of the meristematic state, is not restricted to the so-called growing point but occurs abundantly — and may be even more intense — at some distance from the apical meristem (Wardlaw, 1945; Goodwin and Stepka, 1945). On the other hand, growth in the sense of increase in size of cells, tissues, and organs is most pronounced, not in the apical meristem, but in its derivatives.

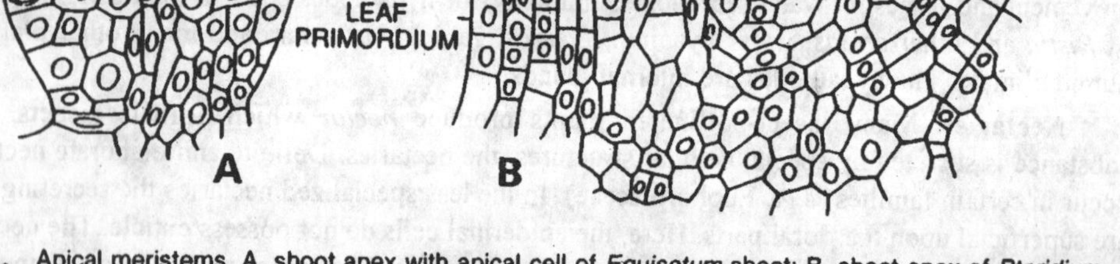

Fig. 3.1. Apical meristems. A, shoot apex with apical cell of *Equisetum* shoot; B, shoot apex of *Pteridium*.

INITIALS AND DERIVATIVES

An **initial** or initiating cell, is a cell that remains within the meristem indefinitely with the addition of cells to the plant body by combining self-perpetuation. The concept regarding meristematic initials, implies that a cell is an initial, not because of its inherent characteristics, but simply because of its particular position in the meristem, a position that cannot be treated as permanent.

The number of initials in root and shoot apices is variable. In most of pteridophytes a single initial cell occurs at the apex. In the lower vascular plants, as well as in the higher, several initials are present. The single initial in its morphology is quite distinct from its derivatives and is commonly known as the **apical cell.** If the initials are numerous, they are called apical initials.

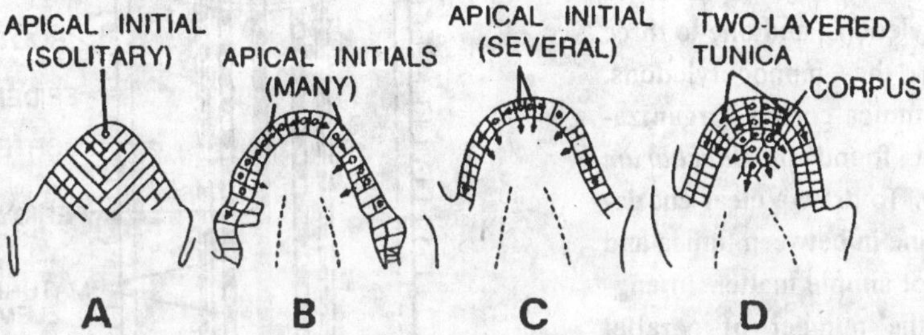

Fig. 3.2. Position and planes of division of stem-apex initials. A, initial solitary, with oblique and anticlinal divisions; B, initials many, superficial, divisions both anticlinal and periclinal; C, initials several, superficial, divisions both anticlinal and periclinal; D, initials in three tiers, the two outer, with anticlinal divisions, forming a two-layered tunica and the innermost, with divisions in all planes, forming a corpus. (After Eames and MacDaniels).

Usually the apical initials occur in one or more tiers. If there is only one tier, all cells of a plant body are ultimately derived from it. On the other hand, different parts of a plant body are derived from different groups of initials.

VEGETATIVE SHOOT APEX

The vegetative shoot apices vary in shape, size and cytohistologic structure, and in their relation to the lateral organs. The shoot apex of *Pinus* and other conifers are commonly narrow and conical in form. In *Cycas* (cycads) and *Ginkgo* they are usually broad and flat on the other hand the apical meristem of a grass and some other monocotyledons remains elevated above the youngest leaf primordium. In many dicotyledons the apical meristem rises above the primordia, and in other cases it appears to be sunken beneath them. The diameters of apices range from 90μ in some angiosperms to 3.5 mm in *Cycas revoluta* (Foster, 1949). The size and shape of the apex marked by change during the plant development.

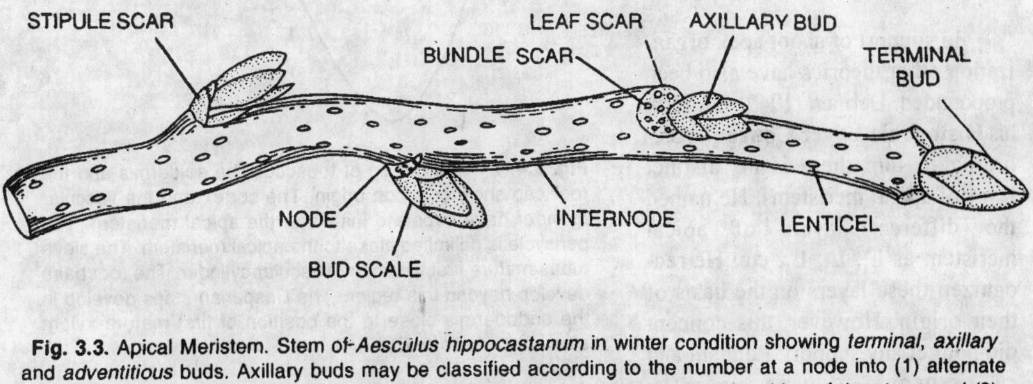

Fig. 3.3. Apical Meristem. Stem of *Aesculus hippocastanum* in winter condition showing *terminal, axillary* and *adventitious* buds. Axillary buds may be classified according to the number at a node into (1) alternate with a single bud at a node, (2) opposite, with two buds at a node on opposite sides of the stem, and (3) whorled with more than two buds at each node. Buds which arise anywhere on the plant except at the tips of stems or in the axils of leaves are called *adventitious buds.* In this figure, terminal bud is located at the tip. The leaf scars are left by the breaking away of the leaf stalks. Leaf trace scars are the broken ends of leaf traces. When the scales of terminal bud are shed a *ring* or *girdle* is left.

Angiosperms. There is **tunica-corpus organization** in the shoot apex of angiosperms. One to five layers of tunica have been observed in the dicotyledons, and one to three layered in the monocotyledons. However, tunica-corpus organization is not found in *Saccharum officinarum*. To draw a clear cut demarcation line in between tunica and corpus is not simple matter. In angiosperms, the number of parallel periclinal layers in the shoot apex may vary during the ontogeny of the plant body and under the influence of seasonal growth changes.

In the angiosperms the segregation of apical-meristem zones is more definite than in lower groups. There are two sets of initials, one above the other, which give rise to **tunica** and **corpus**. The tunica has no or only rare periclinal divisions and ranges in thickness from several layers to one with two or three layers probably most frequent. The number of layers in the tunica may vary even in an individual plant.

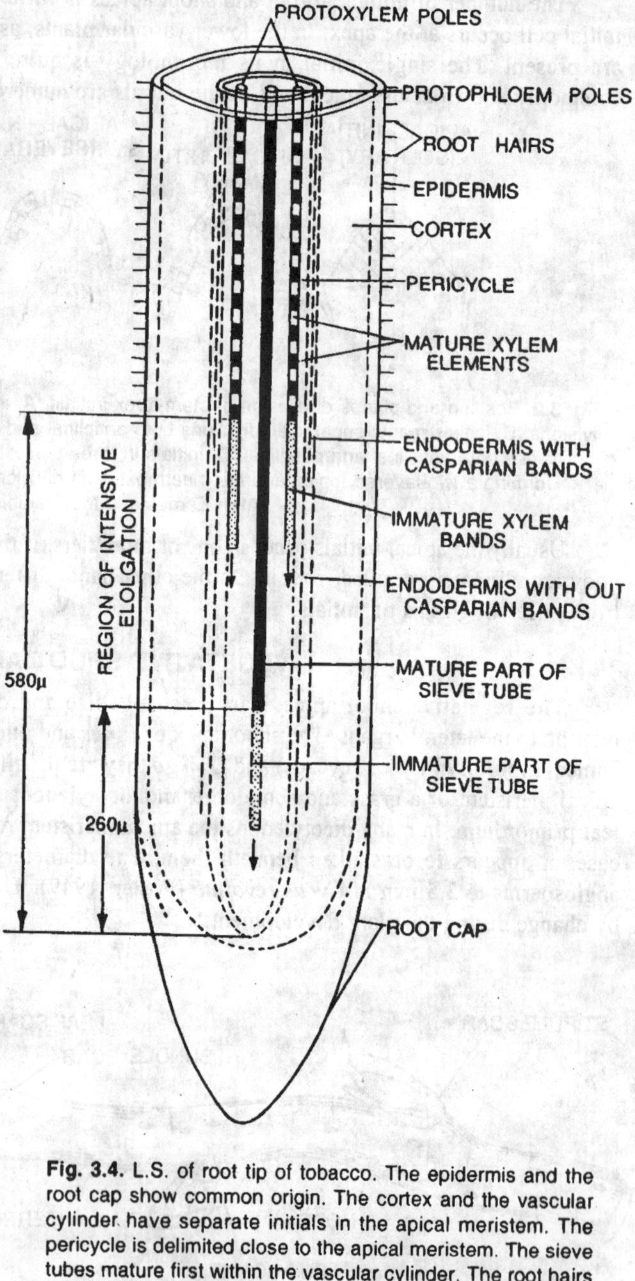

Fig. 3.4. L.S. of root tip of tobacco. The epidermis and the root cap show common origin. The cortex and the vascular cylinder have separate initials in the apical meristem. The pericycle is delimited close to the apical meristem. The sieve tubes mature first within the vascular cylinder. The root hairs develop beyond this region. The Casparian strips develop in the endodermis close to the position of first mature xylem elements. (After K. Esau).

OTHER THEORIES OF SHOOT APEX ORGANIZATION

In support of shoot apex organization other theories have also been propounded. Dermen (1947) put forth his **Histogenic Layer Concent.** According to him there is no distinct layer of apical meristems. He named the different layers of apical meristem as L_1, L_2, L_3, etc. He recognized these layers on the basis of their origin. However, this concept did not get any support. Popham and Chan (1950) put forth **Mantle Core Concept.** This concept is comparable to tunica corpus theory. They used the term mantle instead of tunica and core in place of corpus. Plantefol (1947, 1950), Buvat (1955) and Amefort (1956) propounded the **Concept of French School** and recognized three distinct regions in the apical meristem. According to these authors, peripheral active zone was known as *Anneu initial*, the zone next to it *Meristeme de attente* and the central zone was termed *Meristem medullaire*. Newman (1961) put forth his concept and recognized three kinds of shoot apices. According to him, *Monoplex* type is found in vascular cryptogams and ferns; here the shoot apex is denoted by one or more cells which divide by walls parallel to the inclined walls in the stem. The *Simplex* type is found in gymnosperms; it consists of one or more initial cells arranged in a single layer; these cells divide anticlinally and periclinally. The *Duplex* type is found in the shoot apex of angiosperms; it consists of atleast two successive layers of cells; the cells of surface layer divide anticlinally and that of inner layer divide in more than one plane.

ROOT APEX

During the later stages of development of embryo, the cells at the root pole become arranged in a pattern characteristic of the species. This group of cells comprises the **apical meristem** of the primary root. The cells of this region are all relatively undifferentiated and meristematic, densely protoplasmic and with large nuclei and they all undergo active division. The tissues of the mature root are eventually derived from a number of these cells of the apical meristem, which are termed **initials.** In contrast to the apical meristem of the shoot, that of the root produces cells not only toward the axis but also away from it, for it initiates the root cap and because of the presence of root cap the root meristem is not terminal but subterminal in its position, in the sense that it is located beneath the root cap. The root apex also differs from the shoot meristem in that it forms no lateral appendages comparable to the leaves, and no branches. The root branches are usually initiated beyond the region of most active growth, and they arise endogenously. It also produces no nodes, and internodes, and therefore, the root grows more uniformly in length than the shoot, in which the internodes elongate much more than the nodes.

APICAL CELL THEORY

This theory was put forth by Nageli. In the roots of vascular cryptogams (pteridophytes), *e.g.*, *Dryopteris*, a single tetrahedral apical cell is present, it is generally thought that by its division this gives rise to all the tissues of the root. However, the apical cell theory was superceded by the histogen theory.

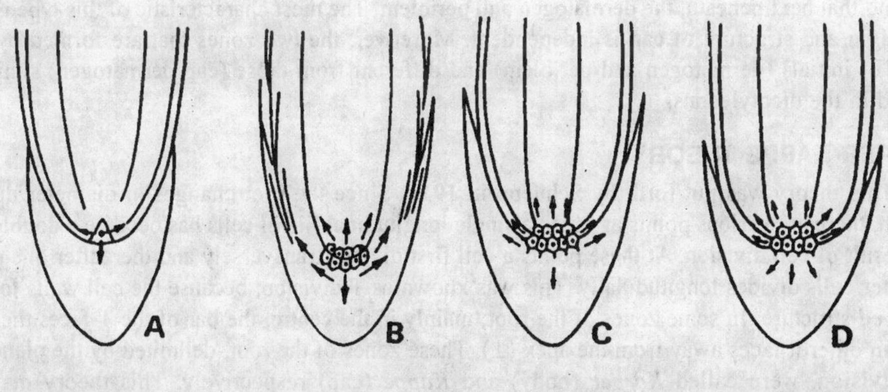

Fig. 3.5. The root apex. Diagrams showing different root apex types, A, initial solitary, cap distinct; B, initials in two groups, cap not distinct structurally; C, initials in three groups, cap not distinct; D, initials in three groups, cap distinct, and independent in origin. (After E. & M.)

In number, the initials range from one to many. Where the initials are more than one, they are arranged in one to four fairly distinct, uniseriate groups. In each group there are one to several initials. Where there is more than one group, the groups lie adjacent to one another on the longitudinal axis of the root. Each of these groups quickly develops one or more growth zones. In many plants these zones appear to represent 'the histogens'. The terms dermatogen, periblem and plerome are no longer in general use in descriptions of stem ontogeny but they have been continued to indicate general zones in studies of root development. A fourth histogen, the *calyptrogen*, is added where the cap has an independent origin. There are basic patterns for the major plant groups. The pattern is determined by the number of initials, the number of groups of these initials, the zones formed by each group, the morphological nature of the cap, and the degree of independence of the cap.

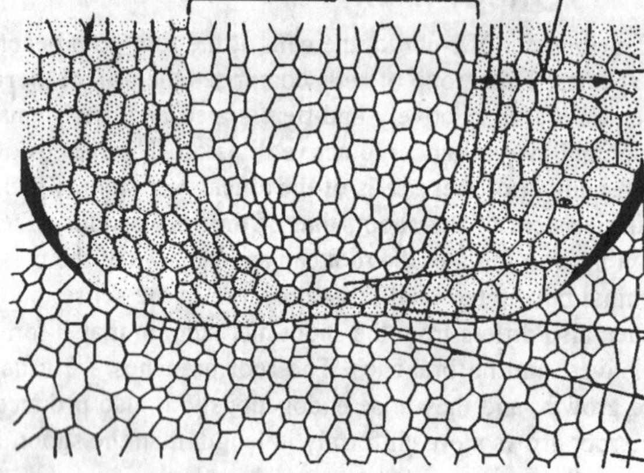

Fig. 3.6. The root apex. Root tip of *Zea mays* in L.S. The swollen wall substance originates through the gelatinization of the wall between the root cap and the protoderm.

In the angiosperms there are three, rarely four groups of initials. In the dicotyledons the distal group forms the cap and the dermatogen; the median group, the periblem; the innermost, the plerome. The most characteristic is the common origin of cap and dermatogen. In monocotyledons, there are three groups of initials which form four zones, but the outermost, independently, forms the cap, and that next beneath, the dermatogen and periblem. The most characteristic of this type is that the origin and structure of cap is independent. Moreover, the two zones that are formed by one group of initials (dermatogen and periblem) and different from those (cap dermatogen) similarly formed in the dicotyledons.

KORPER-KAPPE THEORY

This theory was put forth by Schuepp in 1917. Since the root changes in diameter during growth, there are various points at which a single longitudinal file of cells has become a double file as a result of cell division. At these points a cell first divides transversely and thereafter one of its daughter cells divides longitudinally. This was known as T division, because the cell walls form a T-shaped structure. In some zones of the root, mainly in the centre, the bar of the T faces the root apex, in other it faces away from the apex (⊥). These zones of the root, delimited by the planes of cell division, were called *Korper* (body) and *Kappe* (cap) respectively. This theory may be compared with the tunica-corpus theory in the shoot apex.

Mainly in roots with a very regular arrangement of cells in the apical meristem, such as of *Zea mays*, it is possible to conclude from the study of cell lineages that there is a central region of cells which divide rarely or not at all. The cells on the periphery of this hemispherical or cup-shaped region are meristematic. This inactive or passive region of cells is known as **'quiescent centre'**.

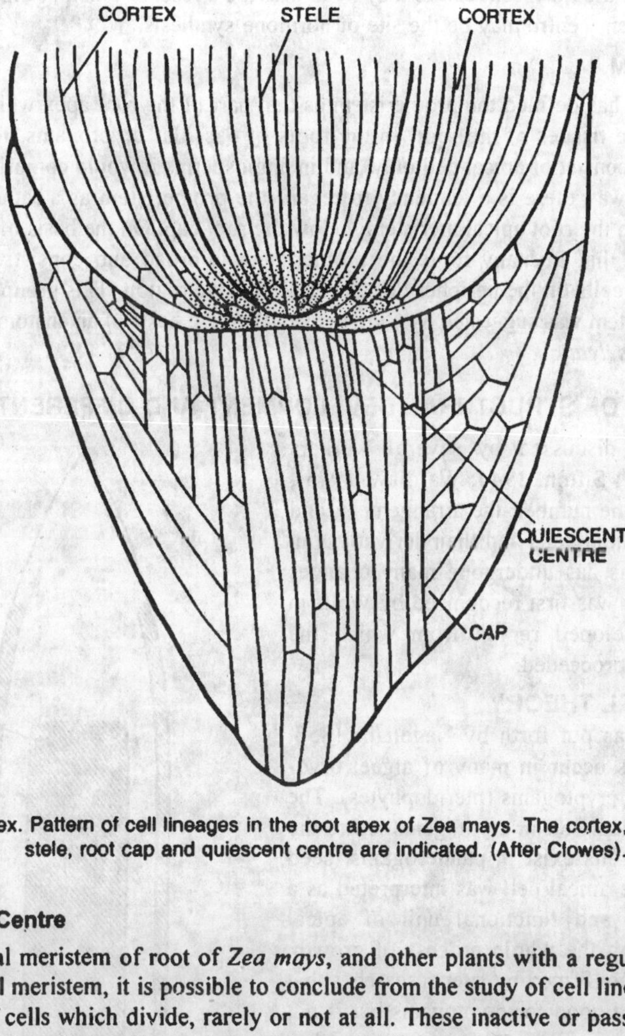

Fig. 3.7. Root apex. Pattern of cell lineages in the root apex of Zea mays. The cortex, vascular cylinder or stele, root cap and quiescent centre are indicated. (After Clowes).

The Quiescent Centre

In the apical meristem of root of *Zea mays*, and other plants with a regular arrangement of cells in the apical meristem, it is possible to conclude from the study of cell lineages that there is a central region of cells which divide, rarely or not at all. These inactive or passive cells constitute the **quiescent centre**. The cells on the periphery of this hemispherical or cupshaped region are meristematic and may be regarded as the constituents of the promeristem (Clowes, 1958). By various techniques, the existence of quiescent centre, has now been demonstrated in the root apices of a considerable number of species. The quiescent centre develops during the ontogeny of the root (Clowes, 1958). A quiescent centre is not found in the roots with a single apical cell. In 1956, Clowes was able to show that there was a central region (quiescent centre) in the roots of *Zea* where the cytoplasm had the lower content of RNA and where the cells had smaller nucleoli. He was also able to demonstrate that the cells in the quiescent centre did not actively synthesize DNA.

The physiological and cytological properties of the cells in the quiescent centre have now been studied in a number of species. The cells in the region have a lower concentration of DNA, RNA and protein than any other cells in the root apex (Clowes, 1958; Jensen, 1958). The cells of quiescent centre also have fewer mitochondria, little endoplasmic reticulum, and the smallest dictyosomes, nuclei and nucleoli (Clowes, 1964). They are less sensitive to radiation damage than other cells of the meristem (Clowes, 1959, 1964).

The function of the quiescent centre may be to provide a reserve block of diploid cells within the root. The quiescent centre may be the site of hormone synthesis.

THE PROMERISTEM

Clowes (1961) has defined the promeristem as that part of the root apex which is capable of giving rise to all the tissues of the root. In the roots of vascular cryptogams, for example, the promeristem would consist of apical cell only, and in angiosperms it would comprise the initials of the histogens. This way there is a tendency to regard the promeristem as a rather small region, situated terminally in the root apical meristem, below the root cap. On the basis of modern work it has been suggested that in many roots the promeristem is broad and consists of a somewhat cupshaped group of cells on the periphery of a central inactive region. This grouping of the initial cells of the promeristem was suggested by Clowes (1950) on the basis of an anatomical study of the root apex of *Fagus sylvatica*.

THEORIES OF STRUCTURAL DEVELOPMENT AND DIFFERENTIATION

As has been discussed by several workers (Foster, 1939, 1941; Sifton, 1944; Wardlaw, 1945), the view regarding the number, the arrangement, and the activity of the initial cells and their derivatives in the apical meristems has undergone many changes since the shoot apex was first recognized by Wolff in 1759 as an undeveloped region from which the growth of the plant proceeded.

THE APICAL CELL THEORY

This theory was put forth by Nageli in 1858. Solitary apical cells occur in many of algae, bryophytes and vascular cryptogams (pteridophytes). The discovery of the apical cell in cryptogams led to the concept that such cells exist in phanerogams (seed plants) as well. The apical cell was interpreted as a constant structural and functional unit of apical meristems governing the whole process of growth. However, this was confirmed by later researches that this theory may hold good for cryptogams but is not applicable to the phanerogams. Further researches have refuted the universal occurrence of apical cells and replaced it by a concept of independent origin of different parts of plant body. The apical cell theory was superceded by the **histogen theory.**

THE HISTOGEN THEORY

This was introduced in 1870 by Hanstein who considered that the primordial meristem was sharply separable into three distinct zones or **histogens**. According to this theory the apical meristem or growing region of the stem and root are composed of small mass of cells which are all alike and are in a state of division. These meristematic cells constitute promeristem. The cells of the promeristem soon differentiate into three regions — **dermatogen, periblem** and

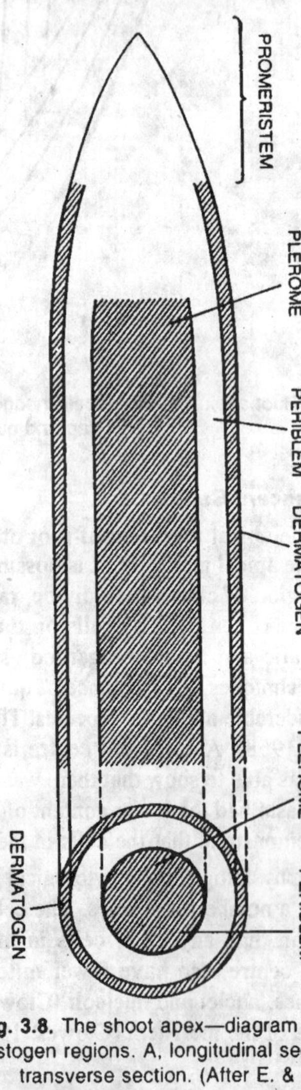

Fig. 3.8. The shoot apex—diagram showing histogen regions. A, longitudinal section; B, transverse section. (After E. & M.).

plerome. Every zone consists of a group of initials and is called a **histogen** or a **tissue builder. Dermatogen** — This is the single outermost layer of the cells which later gives rise to the epidermis of the stem. In the root it is also single layered, but at the apex it merges into the periblem and just outside the periblem the dermatogen cuts off many new cells resulting into a small celled tissue, the **calyptrogen**, which is also meristematic and gives rise to the **root cap. Periblem** — This region is found internal to the dermatogen, and is the middle region of the apical meristem. It is single layered at the apex but in central part it becomes multilayered. It develops into the cortex of the stem. In the roots it is also single layered at the apex and many layered in the central portion. In the case of root, it also develops into the cortex. **Plerome** — It is the central meristematic region of stem apex and lies internal to the periblem. It is also composed of thin walled isodiametric cells. Ultimately it develops and differentiates into the central stele consisting of primary vascular tissues and ground tissues, such as, pericycle, medullary rays, and medulla. In the roots the function of plerome is practically same as in stem. At a little distance behind the apex certain strands of cells show a tendency to

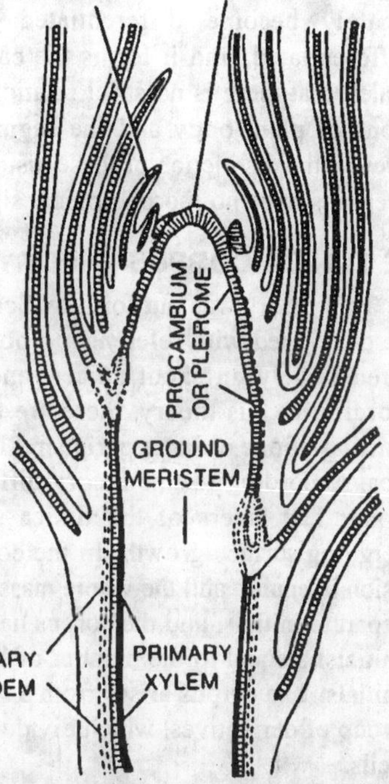

Fig. 3.9. Apical meristems. L.S. of stem tip (diagrammatic) showing the histogens.

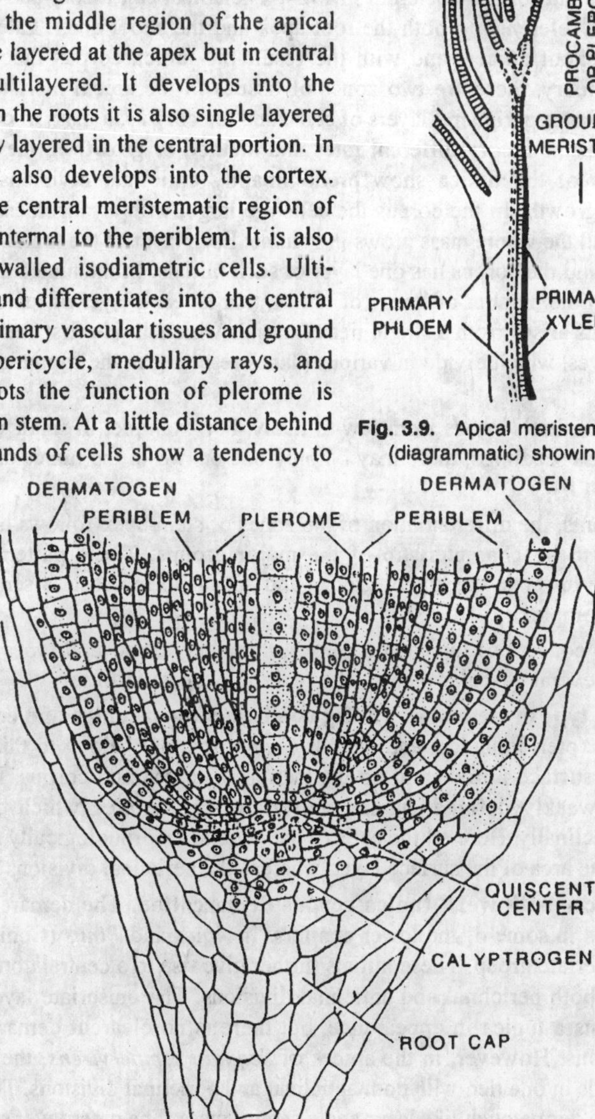

Fig. 3.10. Root apex. L.S. of a tip of onion root showing histogens and root cap.

elongate. These strands of elongated cells make the **procambium**. The procambial strands ultimately become differentiated, into vascular bundles. A portion, however, remains undifferentiated, and it forms the cambium of the vascular bundle. Recent investigations have revealed that there is no strict relationship between the development of the histogens and various regions of plant body and the segmentation and layering of the cells in the apical meristem. However, the distinction of these histogens in an apex cannot be made in some plants, and in others the regions have no morphological significance.

THE TUNICA-CORPUS THEORY

This theory was put forth by Schmidt in 1924. The apical cell theory and the histogen theory were developed with reference to both the root apex and the shoot apex. Later attention became centred largely on shoot apices, and with the result the tunica corpus theory was developed. According to this theory, there are two zones of tissues in the apical meristems — **the tunica** consisting of one or more peripheral layers of cells, and the **corpus**, a mass of cells enclosed by the tunica. According to this theory different rates and method or growth in the apex set apart two regions. The layers of the tunica show predominantly anticlinal divisions, that is, they are undergoing surface growth. In the corpus the cells are large, with arrangement and planes of cell division irregular, and the whole mass grows in volume. Each layer of the tunica arises from a group of separate initials, and the corpus has one layer of such initials. In the tunica the number of layers of initials is equal to the number of layers of tunica, that is, each layer of tunica has its own layer of initials. The corpus arises from a single tier of initials which divide first periclinally to give rise to group of derivatives, which divide in various planes resulting in the formation of the inner mass of cells.

The number of initials varies from few to many. For example, in small very slender apices, such as those of grass seedlings, there may be only one or two in the tunica and about two in the corpus.

In vascular plants, the differentiation of the zones of stem-apex follows more or less definite patterns that seem to be characteristic of the major groups. These patterns show increasing complexity from the lower to the higher groups and appear to represent a series in specialization from simplicity to complexity.

As regards the concept of tunica and corpus, there may be several types which are found in the stem apices of several vascular plants. The types may be as follows.

The primitive type of stem apex having no distinction of tunica and corpus. *Lycopodium*, *Isoetes*, *Selaginella* (pteridophytes) and **cycads** (gymnosperms) belong to this group. They have simple apices with surface initials and no distinction of tunica and corpus. In *Lycopodium*, the initiating layer is weakly defined, having uniseriate surface area which divides freely both anticlinally and periclinally. Here all the cells of the layer are morphologically alike. The anticlinal divisions increase the area of the surface layer, whereas the periclinal divisions form the inner core.

The stem apices with weak tunica-corpus demarcation. The demarcation of tunica and corpus layers begins in some of the lower conifers. In *Abies* and *Pinus* (Coniferales), the initials make an apical uniseriate group. These initials further give rise to a central core and an enveloping uniseriate layer by both periclinal and anticlinal divisions. The uniseriate layer that envelops the central core suggests a tunica in appearance, but there is no clearcut demarcation between the tissues of two regions. However, in the apices of *Sequoia sempervirens*, the initials are a small group of surface cells in one tier, with both anticlinal and periclinal divisions. These divisions result in the formation of a dermatogen like layer and a central mass. The outer layer suggests a tunica and the central mass, the corpus. The species of *Cryptomeria* and *Taxodium* (Coniferales) have a dermatogen, in which there are no periclinal divisions. There appears to be structural seggregation of tunica and corpus in the apices of many Coniferales, but there is only one tier of initials and no independent meristematic regions are recognized.

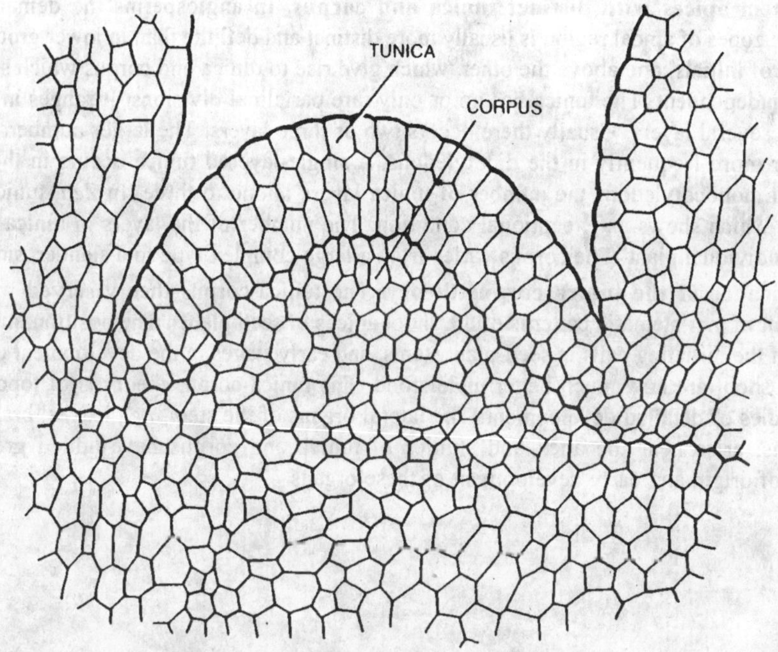

Fig. 3.11. Apical meristem. L.S. through shoot apex of *Vinca*, showing three-layered *tunica* and *corpus* beneath it.

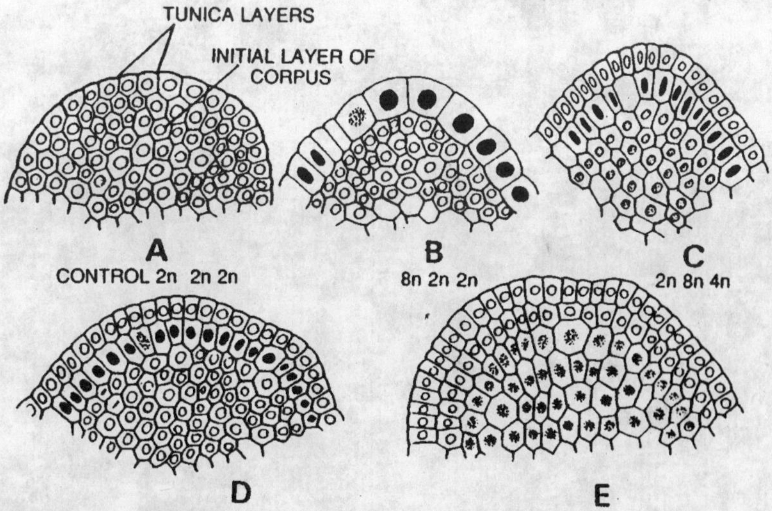

Fig. 3.12. Shoot apices of *Datura*. A, diploid plant; B – C, periclinal cytochimeras. The chromosomal combinations in the various apices are indicated by the values given below each diagrams. The first figure of each group (*i.e.*, 2n, 8n, 2n and 2n) of three refers to the first tunica layer; the second (*i.e.*, 2n, 2n, 8n, 4n and 2n) to second tunica layer; the third (*i.e.*, 2n, 2n, 4n, 2n and 4n) to the initial layer of the corpus. The 8n cells are largest the 4n cells are somewhat smaller, the 2n cells are smallest. In the tunica layer the divisions are anticlinal, in the corpus they occur in various planes. (After Satina *et. al.*, 1940).

The stem apices with distinct tunica and corpus. In angiosperms the demarcation of meristematic zones of apical region is usually more distinct and definite than in lower groups. There are two sets of initials, one above the other, which give rise to tunica and corpus which seem to be completely independent. The tunica has no or only rare periclinal divisions. It ranges in thickness from one to several layers. Usually there occurs two or three layers. The larger numbers of tunica layers occur more frequently in the dicotyledons. A single-layered tunica occurs in the grasses. However, in monocotyledons the number of tunica layers is one to three. In *Zea*, tunica divides periclinally, which shows an exceptional condition. The number of the layers in tunica may vary even in an individual plant. The corpus varies from a large complex type to a slender, simple type.

Significance of the tunica corpus theory. The tunica-corpus theory served well in the establishment of meristematic patterns of the shoot apices of seed plants. The position, number and behaviour of the initiating cells in seed-plant stems, and early stages in the development of primary body of the shoot are now much better understood. The tunica-corpus theory is of topographical value in studies of detailed development. The lateral organs of the stem, *i.e.*, leaves, branches and floral organs, arise near the apex and studies of tunica and corpus have added greatly to a knowledge of origin and early development of these organs.

4
CHAPTER

The Tissue System

"All the tissues of a plant which perform the same general function, regardless of position or continuity in the body, may be considered to form together, a tissue system."

A vascular plant comes in existence morphologically from a single unicellular zygote. By further development the zygote develops into the embryo and ultimately into the mature sporophyte or plant body. Usually in the higher plants division of labour exists, and due to this, the tissues are arranged in system called tissue system. The cells are associated in various ways with each other and form tissues. In higher plant the cells are of many different kinds and they combine into tissues in such a way that different parts of the same organ vary very much from each other. The arrangement of cells and tissue in the plant body maintain topographic continuity or physiologic similarity, or both, together. These units of the tissues are called tissue systems. Each system usually consists of only one tissue or an association of tissues which perform a common function and have the same origin. According to Sachs (1875), there are three main tissue systems —1. The dermal or epidermal tissue system. 2. The fundamental or ground tissue system and 3. The vascular tissue system.

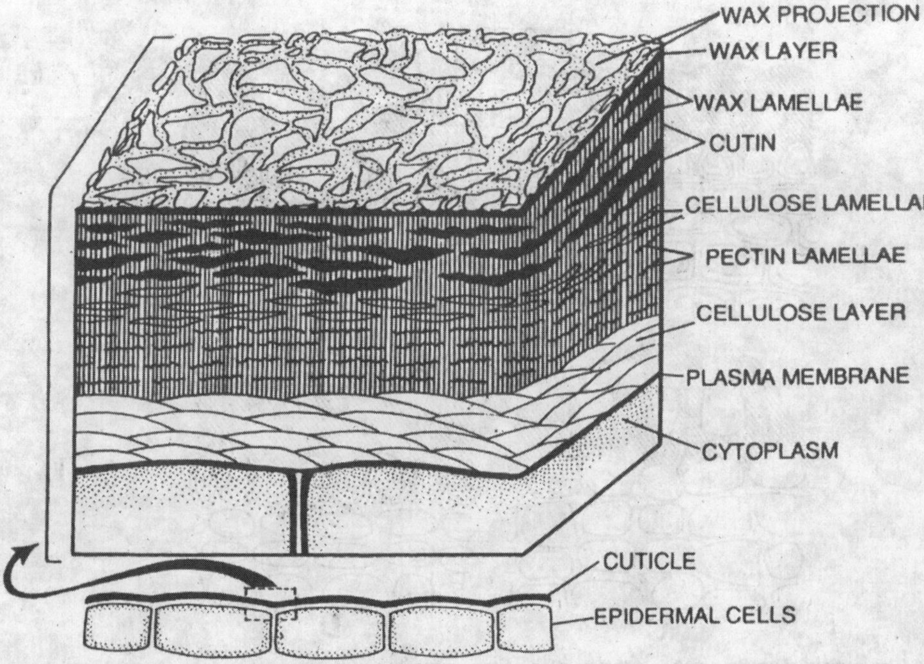

Fig. 4.1. The Epidermis. Schematic representation of the structure and composition of the cuticle and cell wall of foliar epidermal cells.

1. THE DERMAL OR EPIDERMAL TISSUE SYSTEM

The dermal system forms the outer protective covering of the plant and is represented, in the primary plant body, by the **epidermis**. During secondary growth the epidermis may be replaced by another dermal system the **periderm,** with the cork cells forming the new protective tissue.

THE EPIDERMIS

The epidermis usually consists of a single layer of cells which cover the whole outer surface of the plant body. The word is derived from two words of Greek origin, *epi*, upon, and *derma*, skin. It is a continuous lay-er except for certain small pores, called stomata and lenticels. Acc-ording to the histogen theory introduced by Hanstein in 1870, it is derived from dermatogen of apical meristem. In meristematic regions it is, ofcourse, unidiffe-rentiated, and in older stem and roots it may have been destroyed by secondary growth. Mostly the epidermis is single layered, but in many plants

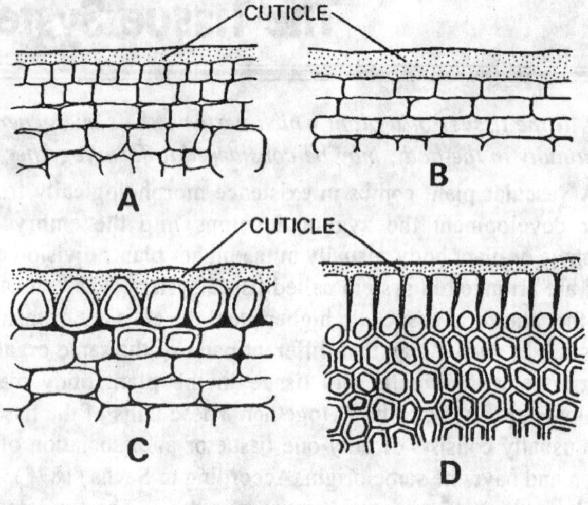

Fig. 4.2. The cuticle. A, in fruit of *Citrus sinensis*; B, in fruit of *Malus pumila*; C, in *Dracaena* stem; D, in leaf of *Dasylirion serratifolium*. (After Eames and Mac Daniels.)

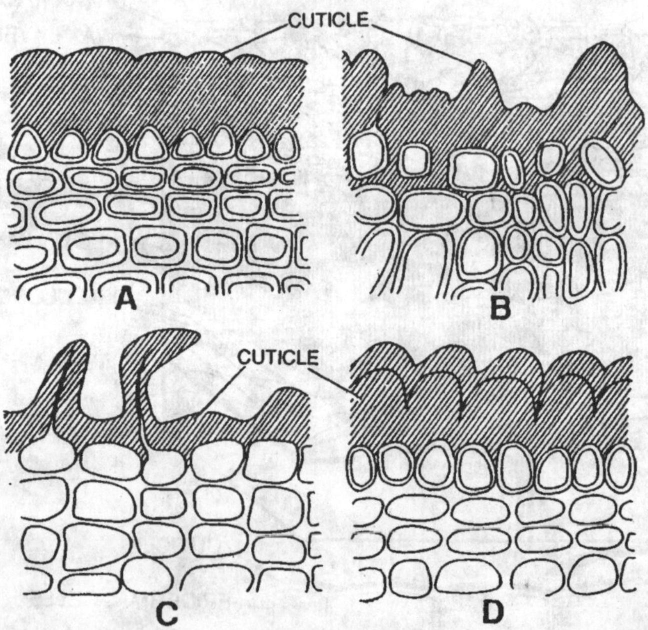

Fig. 4.3. The cuticle. The figure shows the section of the epidermis and adjacent tissues. A, thick cuticle of *Acer* stem, the older outer layer cracking and disintegrating; B, thick cuticle of *Smilax* stem; C, thick cuticle of *Vaccinum* stem; D, thick cuticle of *Cornus* stem, showing two stages, the older, outer layers are replaced by new ones developed below.

it has been described as bi-or multiseriate. In the leaves of India rubber plant (*Ficus elastica*), banyan tree (*Ficus bengalensis*), oleander (*Nerium* spp.), etc. It becomes two to multilayered. The epidermal cells may be somewhat irregular in outline, usually varying in shape and size and arranged very close to each other having no intercellular spaces among them. The cells possess a large central vacuole and thin peripheral cytoplasm. The cells may contain leucoplasts, anthocyanins and chromoplasts, but no chloroplasts except in guard cells. In the epidermal cells of certain aquatic (*e.g., Hydrilla*) and shade loving plants the chloroplasts are also found. Sometimes, the substances like muci-lage, tannin and calc- ium carbonate crystals (cystoliths) are also found in these cells. The walls of epidermal cells are unevenly thic-kened. The inner and radial walls are compa-ratively thicker. This additional thickness is due to the impregnation of suberin or cutin. The suberization and cutini-zation of the walls protect the epidermis from mechanical inju-ries and prevent from loss of water.

In the case of ro-ots the outermost layer is known as the **epibl-ema, piliferous layer or rhizodermis.** Usually its cells extend out-wards in the form of tubular unicellular root hairs, which help in the absorption of water and mineral nutrients from the soil.

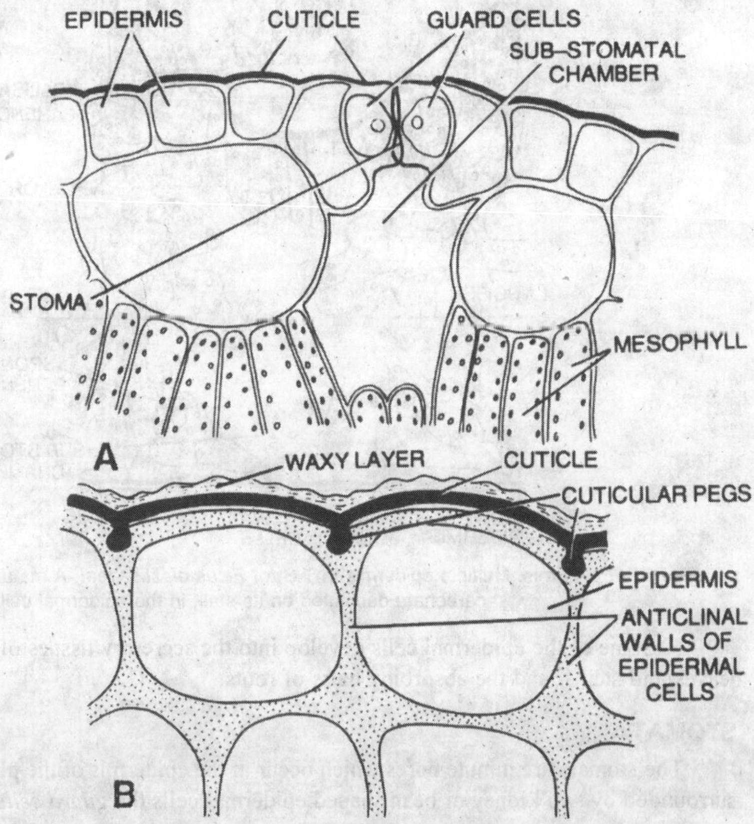

Fig. 4.4. The cuticle. A, a section of upper epidermis of *Musa* leaf through stomatal region, showing extent of cuticle over guard cells; B, section of the banana (*Musa*) leaf through pulvinar band showing *pegs* of cuticle over epidermal cells.

Functions of the Epidermis

1. The epidermis is primarily a covering layer which helps in the protection of the internal soft tissues against mechanical injury.

2. It prevents excessive evaporation of water from the internal tissues, for this, several adaptations like development of thick cuticle, wax, hairs, etc., take place.

3. It also serves in photosynthesis and secretion.

4. The epidermis acts as store house of water in many xerophytic plants.

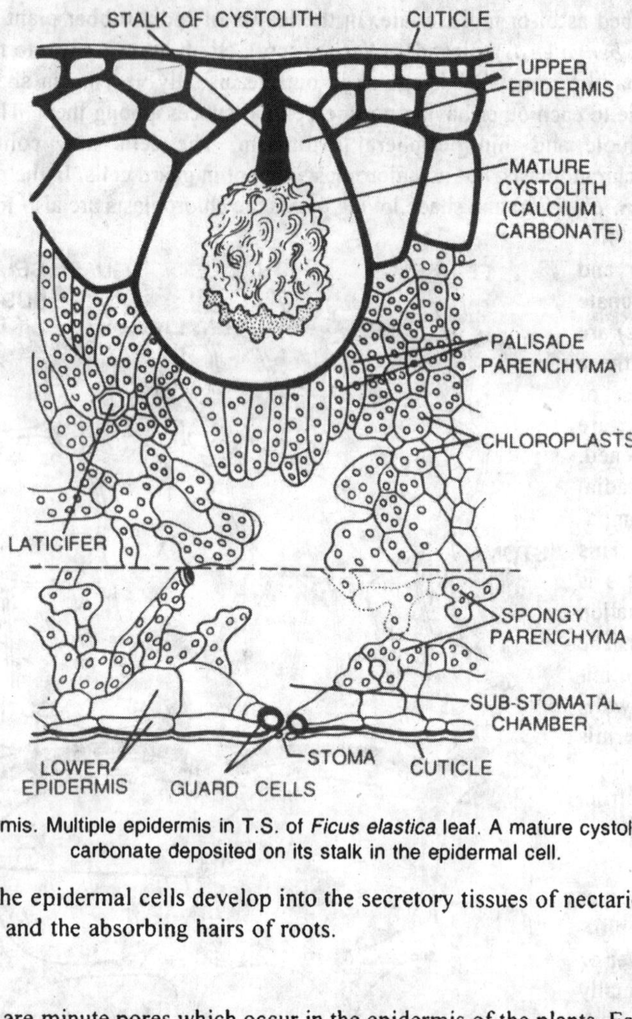

Fig. 4.5. Epidermis. Multiple epidermis in T.S. of *Ficus elastica* leaf. A mature cystolith with calcium carbonate deposited on its stalk in the epidermal cell.

5. Some of the epidermal cells develop into the secretory tissues of nectaries, the stomata of leaves and stems, and the absorbing hairs of roots.

STOMATA

The stomata are minute pores which occur in the epidermis of the plants. Each stoma remains surrounded by two kidney or bean shaped epidermal cells the *guard cells*. The stomata may occur

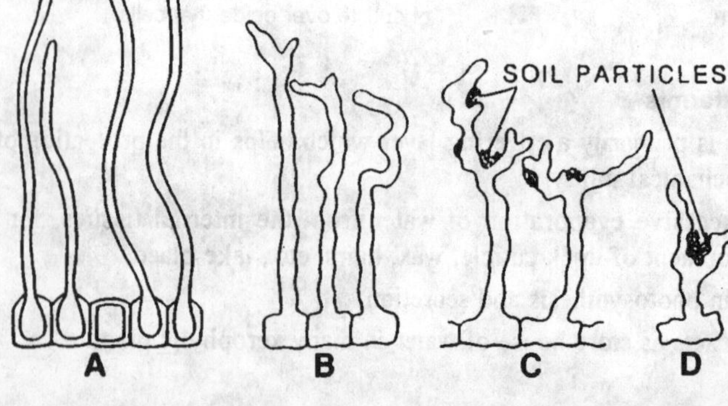

Fig. 4.6. Root hairs, A, grown in water; B, grown in moist soil; C and D, grown in dry soil. (After Schwarz).

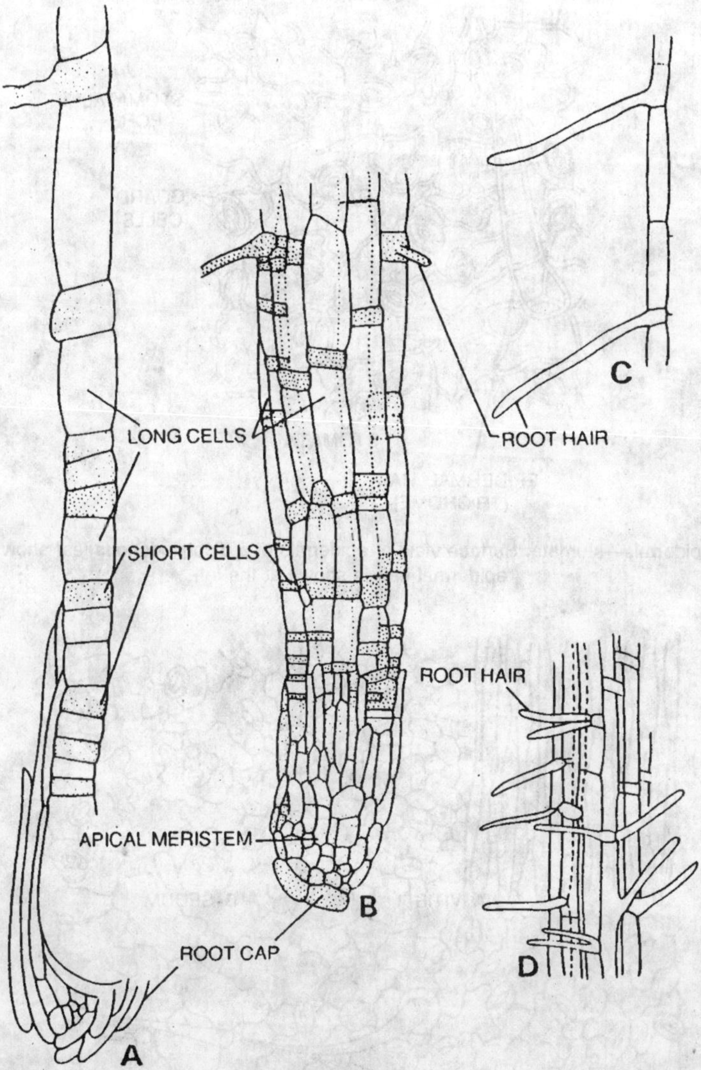

Fig. 4.7. Development of root hair from protruded cells. A,C, in *Cyperus*. B,D, in *Anigozanthos*.

on any part of a plant except the roots. The epidermal cells bordering the guard cells are called **accessory cells** or **subsidiary cells.** Generally the term stoma is applied to the stomatal opening and the guard cells. The guard cells are living and contain chloroplasts in them. They also contain a larger proportion of protoplasm than other epidermal cells. Usually in the leaves of dicotyledons the stomata remain scattered whereas in the leaves of monocotyldons they are arranged in parallel rows. The number of stomata may also range on the surface of a single leaf from a few thousand to hundreds of thousands per square centimetre. Stomata occur on both upper and lower surfaces of leaf, but especially they are confined to the lower surface. In floating leaves stomata are confined only on the upper surface of the leaf. Under normal conditions the stomata remain closed in the absence of light or in night or remain open in the presence of light or in day time. Structurally the stomata may be of different types. The four main types of stomata which occur in dicotyledons are known as 1. Ranunculaceous or anomocytic type — type A; 2. Cruci-ferous or

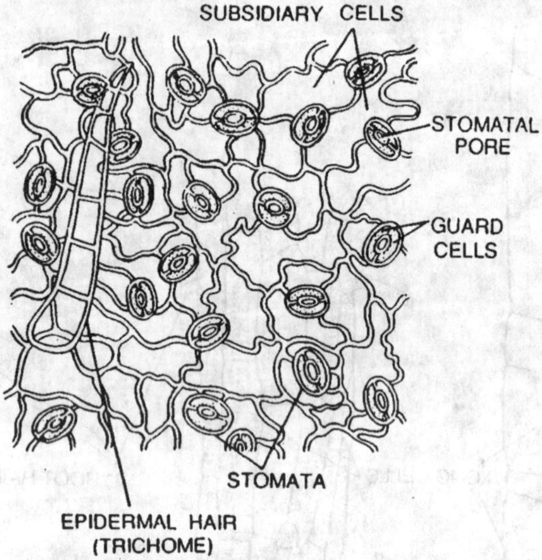

Fig. 4.8. The epidermis—stomata. Surface view of epidermis of a dicotyledonous leaf showing stomata. An epidermal hair is shown at the left.

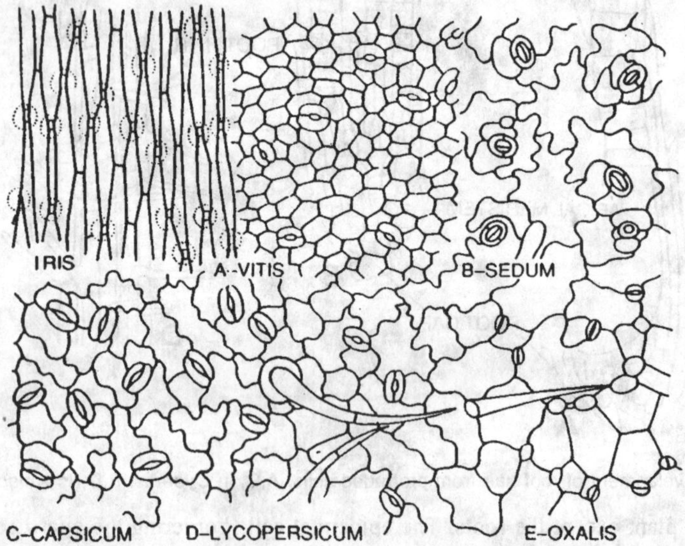

Fig. 4.9. The Epidermis. Surface views of abaxial leaf epidermis. Upper figure on left side of *Iris*, sunken stomata in longitudinal rows. A, dispersed stomata of *Vitis*; B, anisocytic stomata of *Sedum*; C, raised stomata of *Capsicum;* D, raised stomata of *Lycopersicon;* E, sunken stomata of *Oxalis*.

anisocytic—type B; 3. Caryophyllaceous or diacytic—type C; 4. Rubiaceous or paracytic—type D. the fifth type of stomata are commonly found in monocotyledons and known as—gramineous type.

1. Ranunculaceous or anomocytic. Type A — (*Anomocytic* = irregular celled). In this type the stoma remains surrounded by a limited number of subsidiary cells which are quite alike the remaining epidermal cells. The accessory or subsidiary cells are five in number.

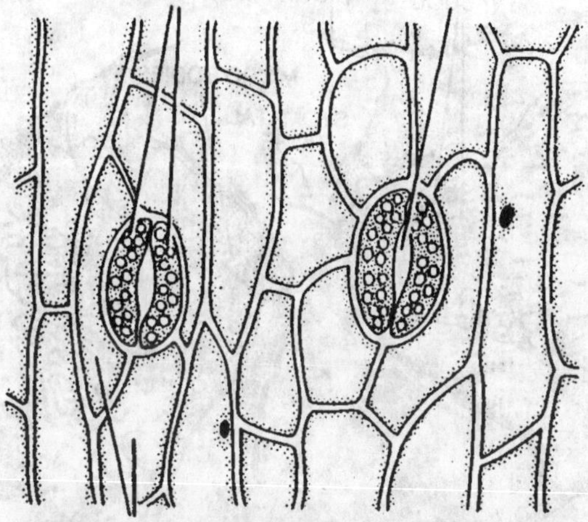

Fig. 4.10. Epidermis. Lower surface of leaf showing stomata.

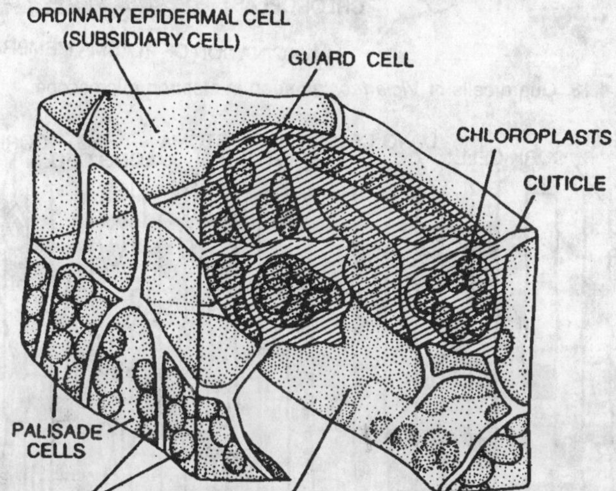

Fig. 4.11. Stomata. Diagram showing surface view and cross section of stoma.

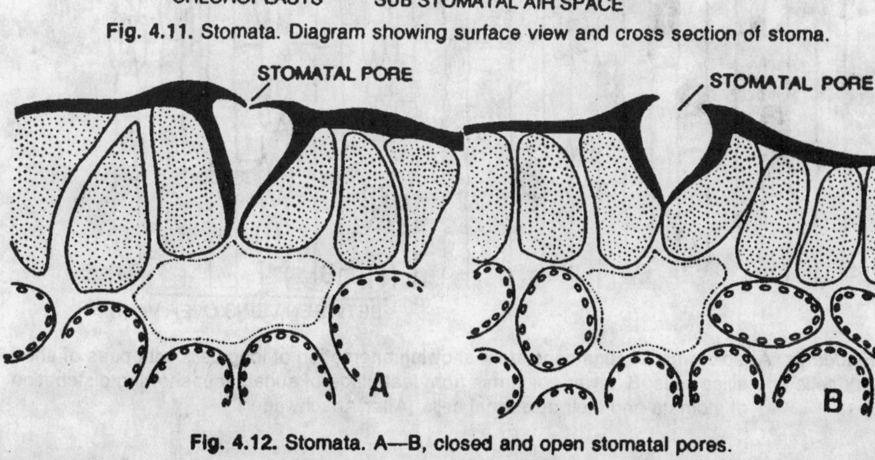

Fig. 4.12. Stomata. A—B, closed and open stomatal pores.

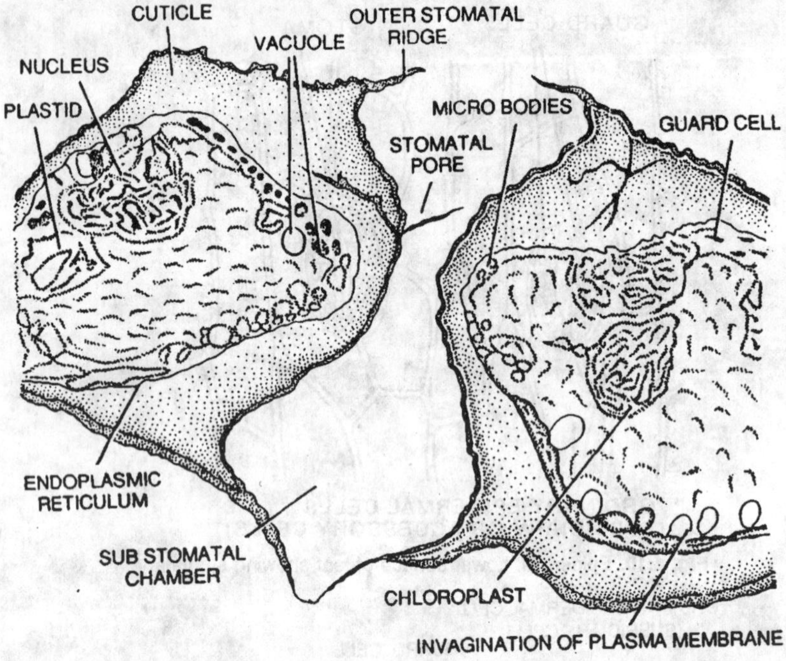

Fig. 4.13. Guard cells of *Vicia faba* as seen in electron microscope.

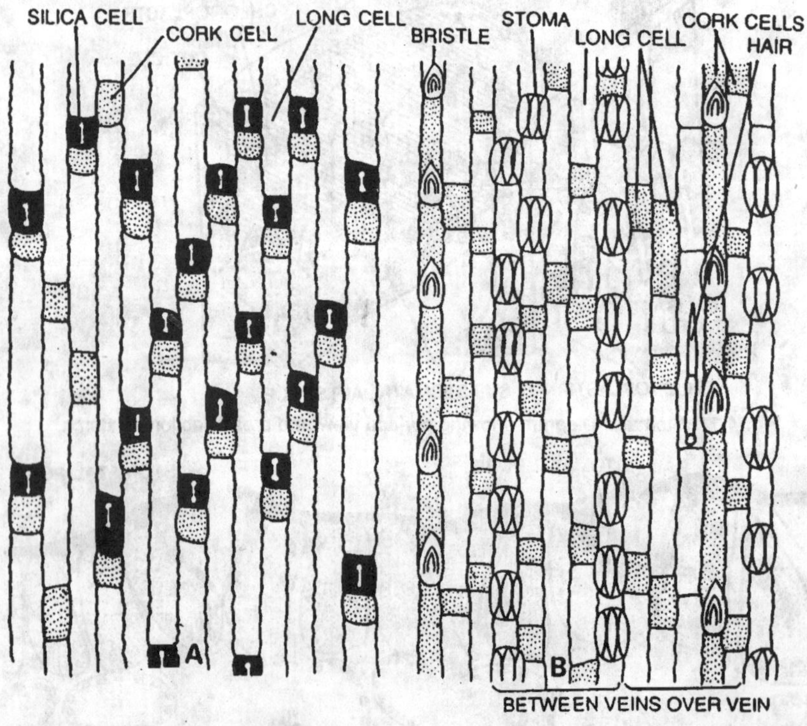

Fig. 4.14. Epidermis. A, epidermis of sugarcane stem showing alternation of long cells with pairs of short cells, the cork cells and silica cells; B, lower epidermis from leaf blade of sugarcane, showing distribution of stomata and their epidermal cells (After Artschwager).

2. Cruciferous or anisocytic. Type B – (*Anisocytic* = unequal celled). In this type stoma remains surrounded by three accessory or subsidiary cells of which one is distinctly smaller than the other two.

3. Rubiaceous or paracytic. Type C – (*Paracytic* = parallel celled). In this type, the stoma remains surrounded by two subsidiary or accessory cells which are parallel to the long axis of the pore and guard cells.

4. Caryophyllaceous or diacytic. Type D – (*Diacytic* = cross celled)–In this type the stoma remains surrounded by a pair of subsidiary or accessory cells and whose common wall is at right angles to the guard cells.

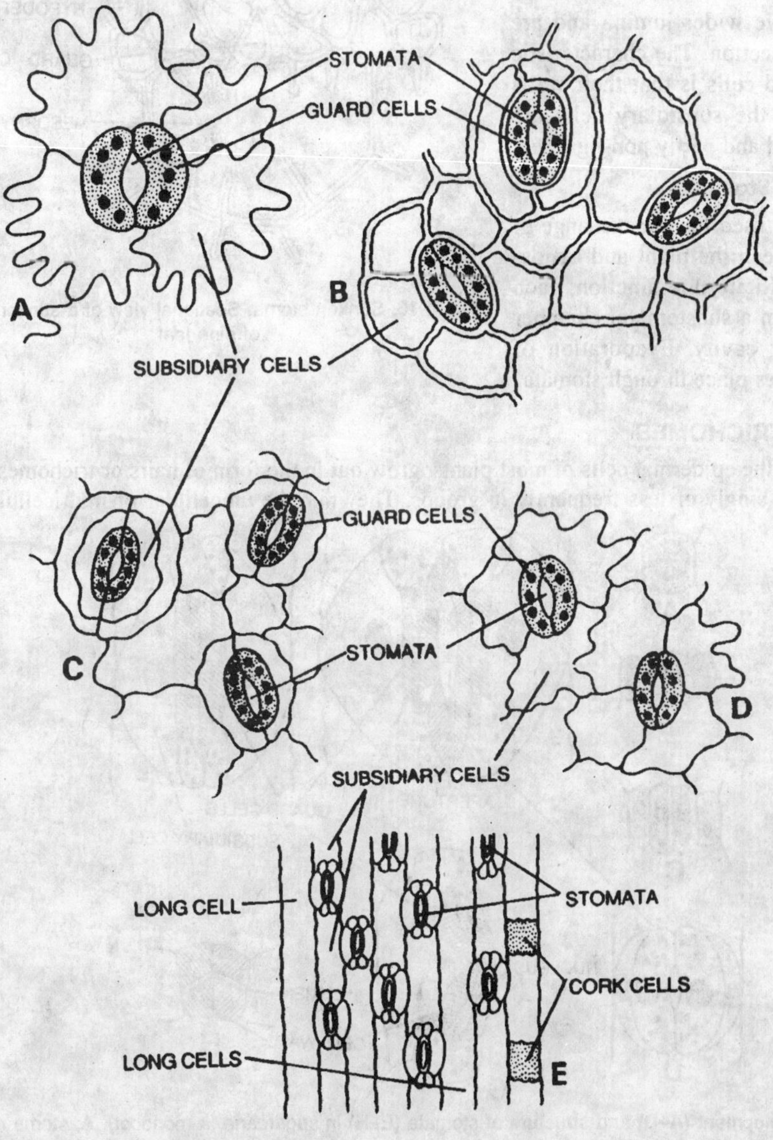

Fig. 4.15. Stomata—types of stomata. A, anomocytic or irregular celled type (ranunculaceous type); B, anisocytic or unequal celled type (cruciferous type); C, paracytic or parallel celled type (rubiaceous type); D, diacytic or cross-celled type (caryophyllaceous type); E, gramineous type.

Gramineous. The gramineous stoma possesses guard cells of which the middle portions are much narrower than the ends so that the cells appear in surface view like dump-bells. They are commonly found in Gramineae and Cyperaceae of monocotyledons.

Coniferous Stomata

They are sunken and appear as though suspended from the subsidiary cells arching over them. In their median parts the guard cells are elliptical in section and have narrow lumina. At their ends they have wider lumina and are triangular in section. The characteristic of these guard cells is that their walls and those of the subsidiary cells are partly lignified and partly non-lignified.

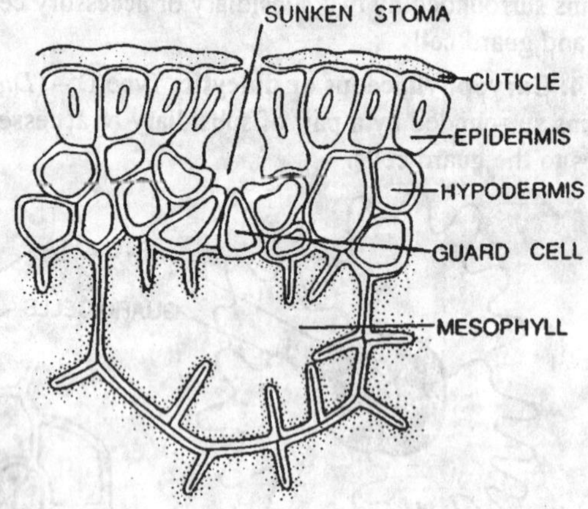

Fig. 4.16. Sunken stoma. Sectional view of a sunken stoma of pine leaf.

Functions of Stomata

They are used for the exchange of gases in between the plant and atmosphere. To facilitate this function, each stoma opens in a substomatal chamber or respiratory cavity. Evaporation of water also takes place through stomata.

HAIRS OR TRICHOMES

Some of the epidermal cells of most plants, grow out in the form of hairs or trichomes. They may be found singly or less frequently in groups. They may be unicellular or multicellular and

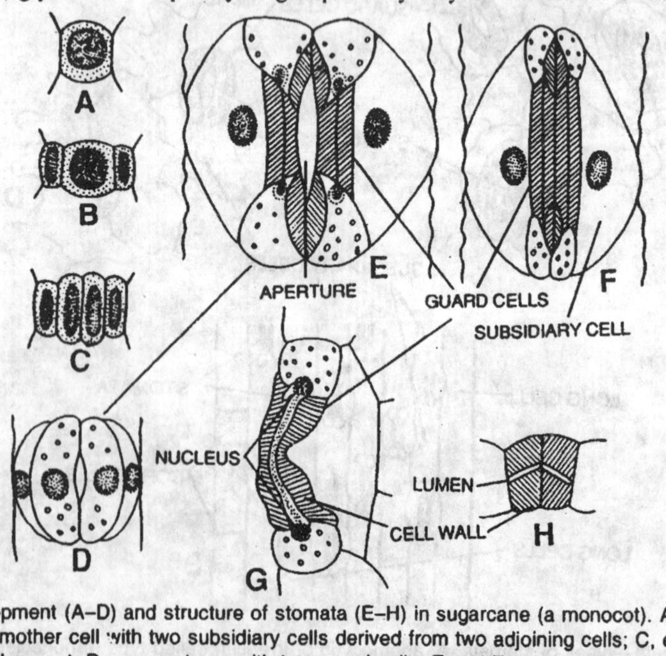

Fig. 4.17. Development (A–D) and structure of stomata (E–H) in sugarcane (a monocot). A, stoma mother cell; B, stoma mother cell with two subsidiary cells derived from two adjoining cells; C, early stage of guard-cell development; D, young stoma with two guard cells; E and F, mature stomata seen from the outer surface in open (E) and closed (F) states; G, L.S. of one guard cell; H, transection through the central portion of two guard cells from a closed stoma.

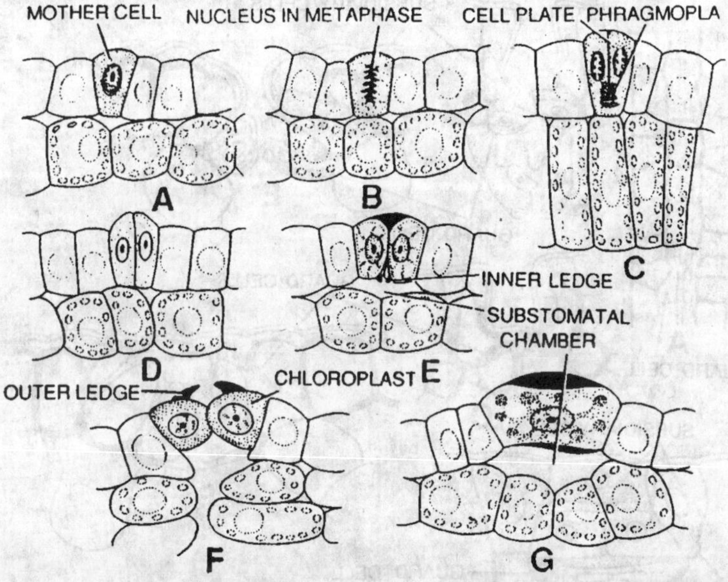

Fig. 4.18. Development of stoma in *Nicotiana* leaf as seen in sections. A–C, stoma mother cell before and during division in two guard cells; D, young guard cells with thin walls; E, thickening of the walls of guard cells begun; F, mature guard cells with unevened thickened walls; G, one mature guard cell.

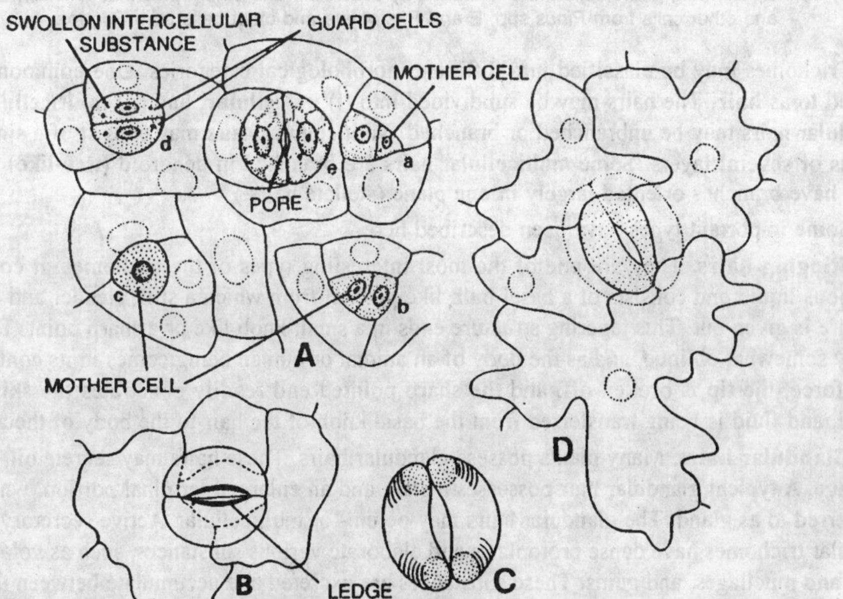

Fig. 4.19. The epidermis. Stomata of *Nicotiana* leaf in surface views. A, developmental stages. B, mature stoma; C, guard cells as they appear from the inner side of the epidermis; D, stoma seen from the inner side of the abaxial surface.

occur in various forms. They vary from small protuberances of the epidermal cells to complex branched or stellate multicellular structures. The cells of the hairs may be dead or living. Very frequently the hairs lose their protoplasm in their cells.

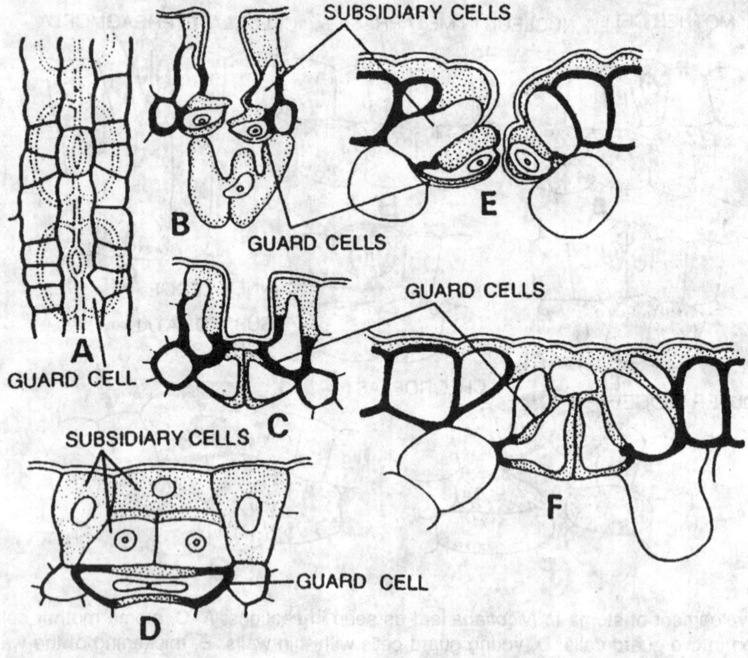

Fig. 4.20. Stomata of conifer leaves. A, surface view of the epidermis of *Pinus merkusii* showing two deepely sunken stomata, guard cells are overarched by subsidiary and other epidermal cells; B—D, stoma and other cells from *Pinus* spp; E and F, stomata and other cells from *Sequoia*.

Trichomes may be classified into different morphological categories. One common type is referred to as **hair**. The hairs may be subdivided into (i) **unicellular**; and (ii) **multicellular.** The unicellular hairs may be unbranched or branched. Multicellular hairs may consist of a single row of cells or several layers. Some multicellular hairs are branched in dendroid (tree-like) manner, others have branches oriented largely in one plane (stellate hairs.)

Some important types have been described here.

Stinging hairs. They are one of the most interesting types of the trichomes. it contains a poisonous liquid and consists of a basal bulb like portion from which a stiff, slender and tapering structure is given out. This tapering structure ends in a small knob like or a sharp point. The tip is usually somewhat oblique, and as the body of an animal or human being comes in its contact with some force, the tip is broken off, and the sharp pointed end readily penetrates the skin of the animal, and fluid is being transferred from the basal knob of the hair to the body of the animal.

Glandular hairs. Many plants possess glandular hairs. These hairs may secrete oil, resin or mucilage. A typical glandular hair possesses a stalk and an enlarged terminal portion, which may be referred to as gland. The glandular hairs may be uni- or multicellular. Active secretory cells of glandular trichomes have dense protoplasts and elaborate various substances, such as volatile oils, resins and mucilages, and gums. These substances are excreted and accumulate between the walls and cuticle. Their final removal from the hair occurs by rupture of the cuticle.

Scale or peltate hair. A common type of trichome is the **scale,** also called **peltate hair** (from the latin *peltatus*, target-shaped or shield like, and attached by its lower surface). A scale consists of a discoid plate of cells, often borne on a stalk or attached directly to the foot.

Cell Wall

The cell walls of trichomes are commonly of cellulose and are covered with a cuticle. They may be lignified. Plant hairs often produce thick secondary walls as, for instance, the cotton seed

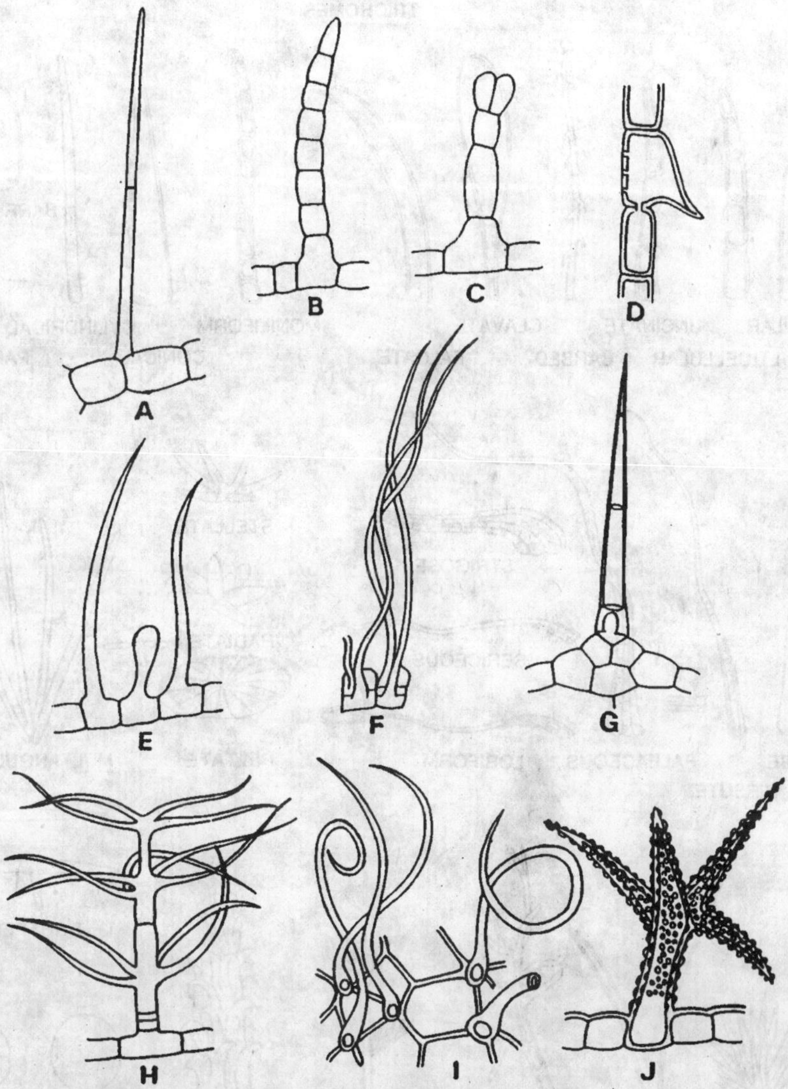

Fig. 4.21. Various types of trichomes (hairs). A, from petal of *Epigaea*; B, from leaf of *Coreopsis*; C, from petal of *Phryma*; D, from leaf of *Avena*; E, from sepal of *Heliotropium*; F, from stem of *Onopordum*; G, from *Cucumis* leaf; H, from *Platanus* leaf; I, from *Rubus* fruit; J, from *Aubrietia* stem. (After E. & M).

hairs or the climber hairs of *Humulus*. The walls or trichomes are sometimes impregnated with silica or calcium carbonate. Their contents are varied in relation to function. Cystoliths and other crystals may develop in hairs.

Developmenmt

A trichome is initiated as a protuberance from an epidermal cell. The protuberance elongates, and if it develops into a multicellular structure various divisions may follow the initial elongation.

Trichomes and Taxonomy

The trichome types have been successfully used in the classification of genera and even of species in certain families and in the recognition of interspecific hybrids (Metcalfe and Chalk, 1950; Hoff, 1950; Sporne, 1956; King and Robinson, 1969, 1970; Ramayya,

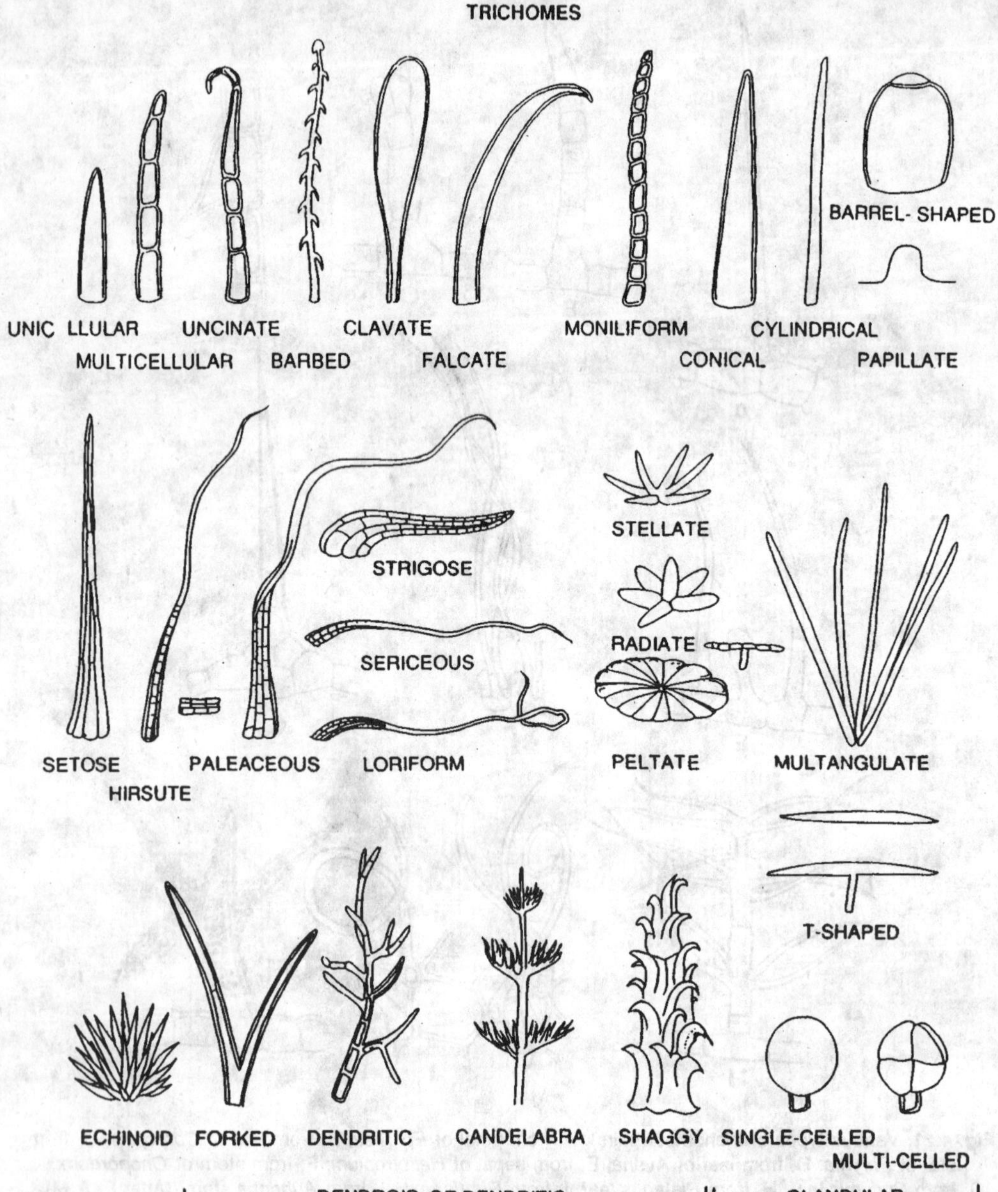

Fig. 4.22. Trichomes of different types.

1972). King and Robinson (1969, 70) used trichome types to determine genetic limits among Compositae. Ramayya (1972), used the trichome types to establish genetic limits among Magnoliales.

Functions of Trichomes

Generally a dense covering of wooly trichomes controls the rate of transpiration. They also reduce the heating effect of sunlight. They aid in the protection of plant body from outer injurious agencies.

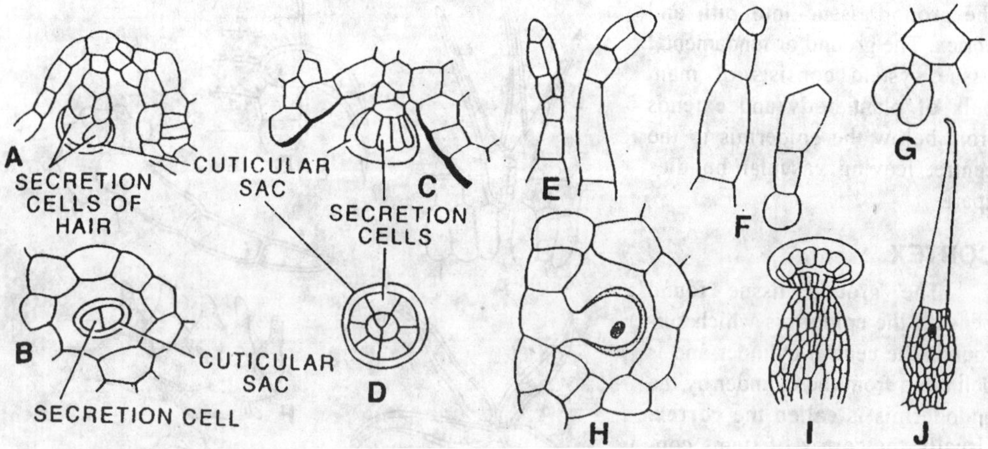

Fig. 4.23. Types of glandular hairs. A and B, section and surface view *Artemisia*; C and D, section and surface view, *Thymus*; E, *Hyascyamus*; F, *Atropa*; G, *Digitalis*; H, *Dryopteris filix-mass* (rhizomes); I, *Cannabis*; J, *Urtica dioica*.

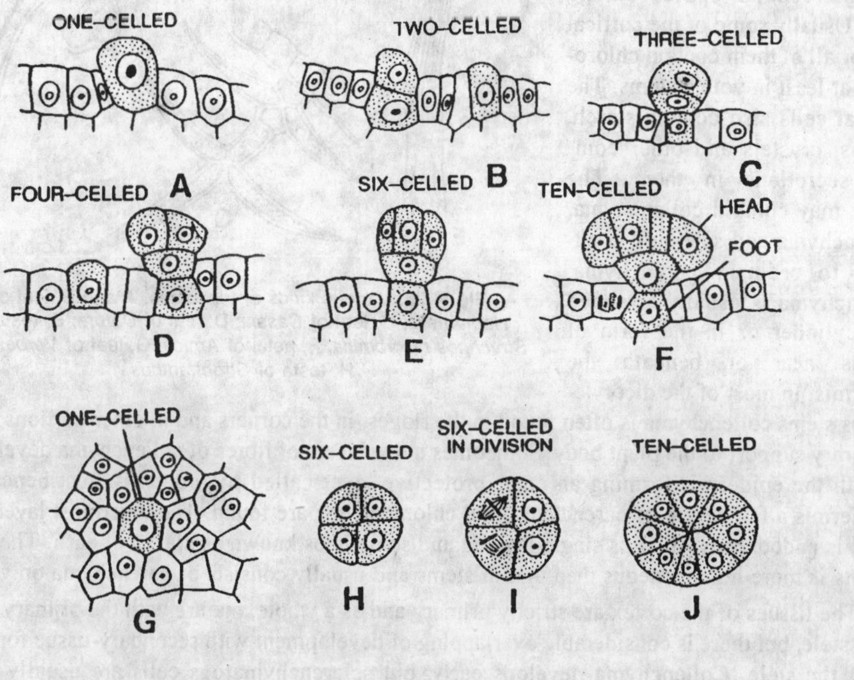

Fig. 4.24. Development of glandular trichomes in *Lingustrum* as seen in sectional (A–F) and surface (G–J) views.

2. THE FUNDAMENTAL OR GROUND TISSUE SYSTEM

Usually in stems which possess the vascular system in the form of solid cylinder, the ground tissue found in between epidermis and vascular cylinder is called **cortex.** In such vascular system the central tissue may be called medulla or pith and the rays of parenchyma cells arising from medulla or pith are termed **medullary** or **pith rays.** If the vascular bundles are found in dispersed condition throughout in the axis (as in monocotyledonous stems) then there is no delimitation of the ground tissue into pith and cortex. The ground or fundamental tissue system consists of main bulk of plant body and extends from below the epidermis to the centre, leaving vascular bundles apart.

CORTEX

The ground tissue found beneath the epidermis which surrounds the central cylinder and is delimited from the cylinder by the endodermis is called the **cortex.** Usually the cortex of stems consists of thin-walled parenchyma cells having sufficiently developed intercellular spaces among them. Usually some of the cortical cells or all of them contain chloroplasts at least in young stems. The cortical cells also contain starch, tannins, crystals and other common secretions in them. The cortex may contain collenchyma, sclerenchyma and sclereids in addition to ordinary parenchyma. Collenchyma is usually arranged as a cylinder or in the form of strands near or beneath the epidermis. In most of the dicotyledonous stems collenchyma is often found in the ridges, in the corners and in other portions to give temporary support to the plant body. Sometimes a few layers of fibres of collenchyma develop just beneath the epidermis forming an outer protective layer called **hypodermis**. Just beneath the hypodermis a few layers of parenchyma and chlorenchyma are found. The innermost layer of the cortex is endodermis which is single-layered and sometimes known as **starch sheath.** The cortex of roots is more homogeneous than that of stems and usually consists of parenchyma only.

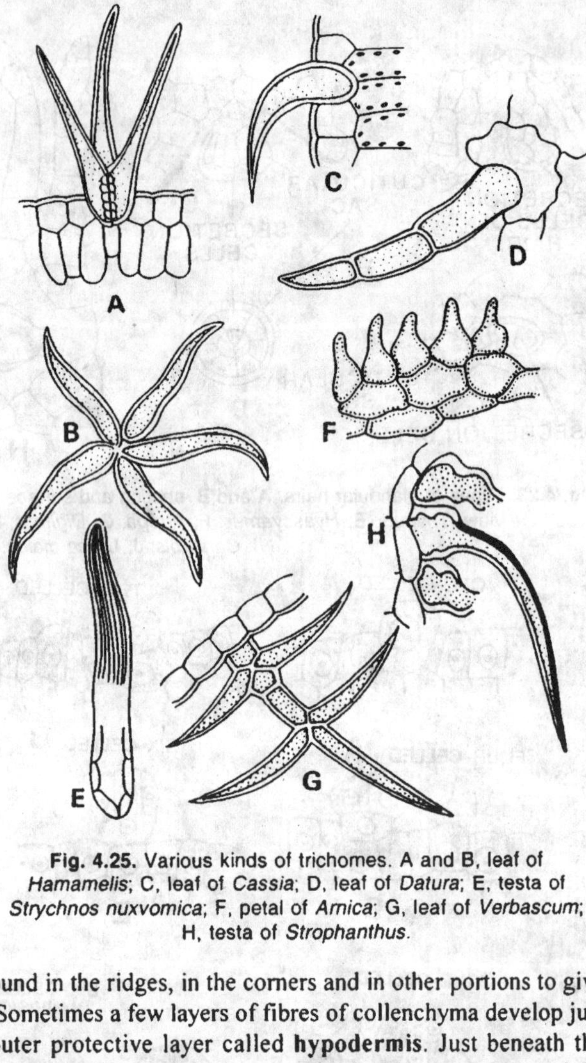

Fig. 4.25. Various kinds of trichomes. A and B, leaf of *Hamamelis*; C, leaf of *Cassia*; D, leaf of *Datura*; E, testa of *Strychnos nuxvomica*; F, petal of *Arnica*; G, leaf of *Verbascum*; H, testa of *Strophanthus*.

The tissues of the cortex are strictly primary and as a whole, mature with the primary tissues of the stele, but there is considerable overlapping of development with secondary-tissue formation within the stele. Collenchyma develops early, but sclerenchymatous cells are usually late in reaching maturity. The cortex of an axis in which marked secondary growth has occurred has tissues crowded and even more or less crushed radially.

Functions of the Cortex

In stems it acts as a protective tissue, but secondarily carbon assimilation, storage of water, storage of food and other functions are also carried on. Collenchyma of the cortical region aids in the temporary mechanical support of plant cody. In roots it is a storage tissue and helps in pumping water from hairs to the xylem.

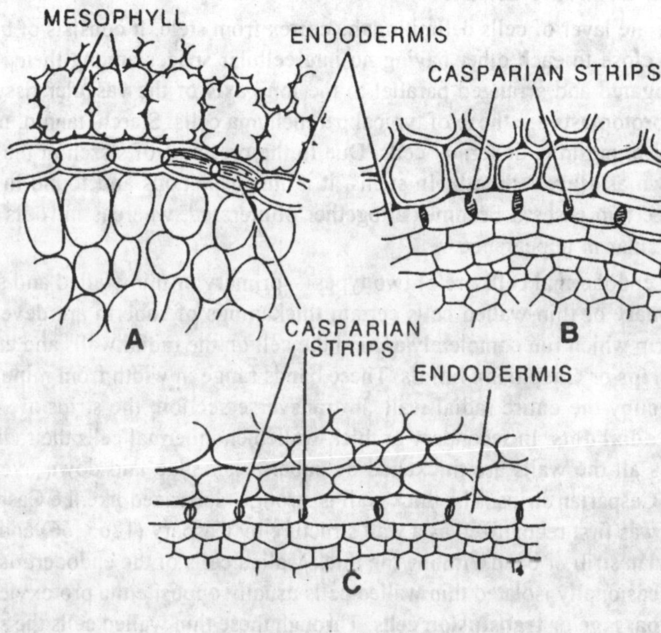

Fig. 4.26. The endodermis. A, T.S. of leaf of *Pinus*, showing the Casparian strips in the endodermal cells; B, T.S. of rhizome of *Polypodium* showing Casparian strips in endodermis; D, Casparian strips in the endodermis of stem of *Lobelia*.

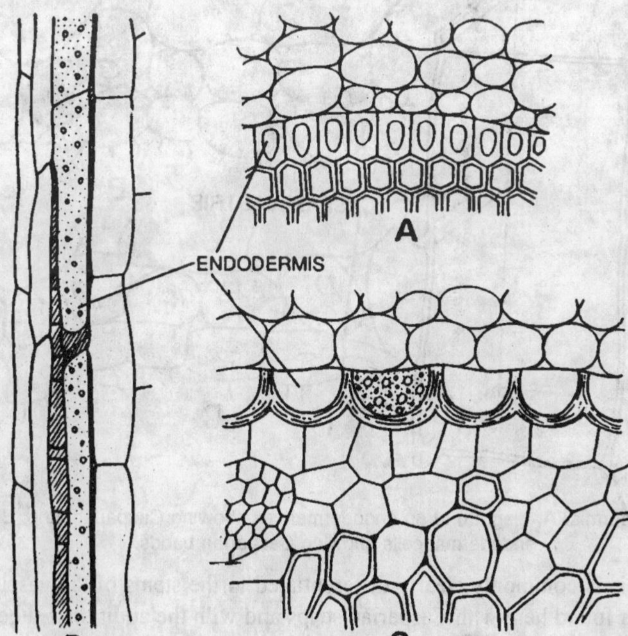

Fig. 4.27. The endodermis, thick walled types. A and B, T.S. and L.S. of *Smilax* root; C, T.S. of *Musa* root.

ENDODERMIS OR STARCH SHEATH

This is a uniseriate layer of cells delimiting the cortex from stele. It consists of barrel-shaped cells arranged quite close to each other having no intercellular spaces among them. The cells of endodermis are elongated and arranged parallel to the long axis of the vascular tissue. They are living cells and the protoplasts are those of typical parenchyma cells. Starch, tannin, mucilage and nuclei are frequently found in endodermal cells. Due to the presence of starch in the endodermal cells, it is also known as **starch sheath.** In stems, it is inconspicuous and found in the form of wavy layer, and in certain cases it becomes altogether obliterated, whereas in roots this layer is well-defined and circular in appearance.

Commonly the endodermal cells are of two types— primary or thin-walled and secondary or thick-walled. In primary or thin-walled cells certain thickenings of suberin are developed in the form of a band or strip which run completely around the cell on the radial walls and end walls, are called **Casparian strips** or **Casparian bands**. These bands range in width from minute threads to broad bands that occupy the entire radial wall. In transverse section, the strips are often called **Casparian dots** or **radial dots**. In secondary or thick-walled endodermal cells the radial and inner walls and sometimes all the walls are thickened by suberin lamellae laid down over the earlier formed wall with its Casparian strips. The thick wall is strongly suberized like the Casparian strips. The Casparian band was first recognized as a wall structure by Caspary (1865–66) and is therefore known as the Casparian strip or band. Among the thick-walled cells of the endodermis, as in many roots, there occur occasionally isolated thin walled cells usually opposite the protoxylem elements, which are known as **passage** or **transfusion cells**. Through these thin walled cells the sap absorbed by root hairs enters the xylary elements.

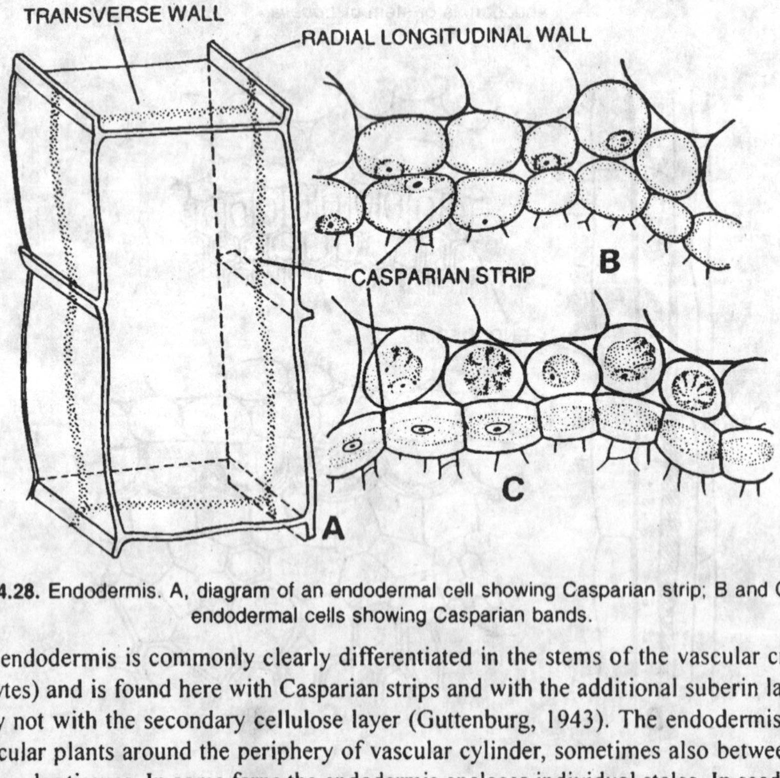

Fig. 4.28. Endodermis. A, diagram of an endodermal cell showing Casparian strip; B and C, the endodermal cells showing Casparian bands.

The endodermis is commonly clearly differentiated in the stems of the vascular cryptogams (pteridohytes) and is found here with Casparian strips and with the additional suberin lamella, but apparently not with the secondary cellulose layer (Guttenburg, 1943). The endodermis occurs in lower vascular plants around the periphery of vascular cylinder, sometimes also between the pith and the vascular tissues. In some ferns the endodermis encloses individual steles. In seed plants the endodermis is quite distinct in the roots, but in a number of herbaceous angiosperms, the stems

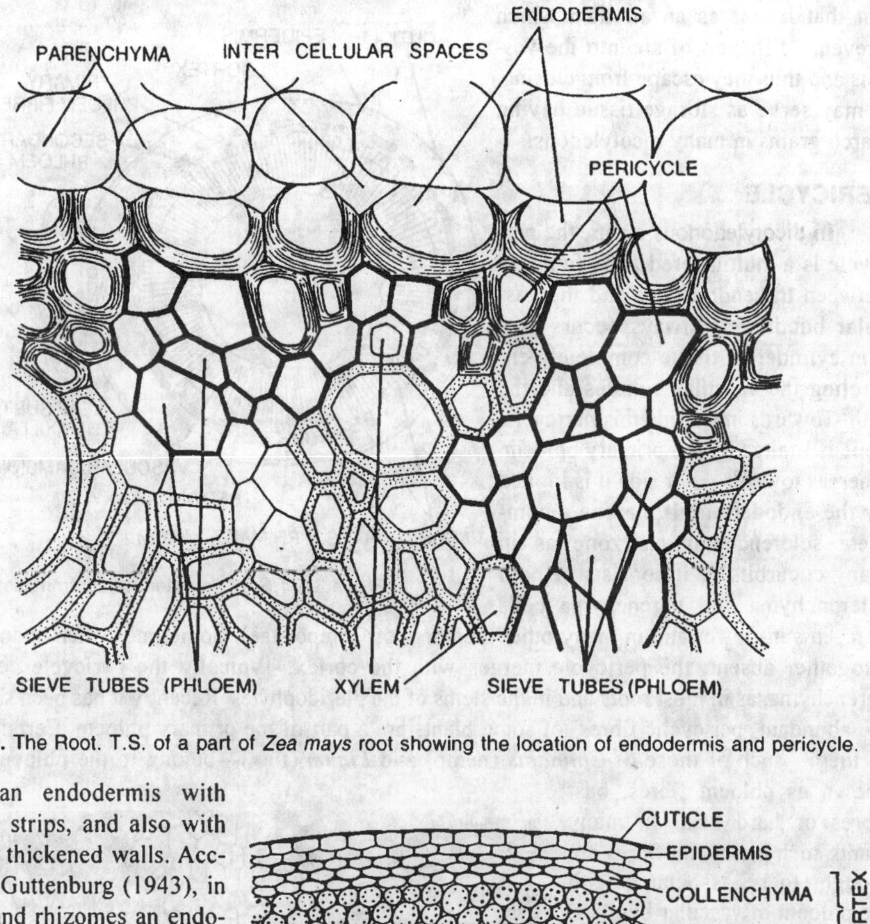

Fig. 4.29. The Root. T.S. of a part of *Zea mays* root showing the location of endodermis and pericycle.

develop an endodermis with Casparian strips, and also with somewhat thickened walls. According to Guttenburg (1943), in underground rhizomes an endodermis develops more frequently than in aerial stems. In *Senecio* and *Leonurus*, the endodermis develops in the herbaceous stem when the plant attains flowering stage (Datta, 1945; Warden, 1935). The woody gymnosperms and the dicotyledons do not possess an endodermis in the aerial stems (Plaut, 1910).

Functions of the endodermis. There is a great controversy about the functions of the endodermis. According to some workers it is a protective layer or sort of accessory inner epidermis. According to others it is connected with the maintenance of root pressure. It is also thou-

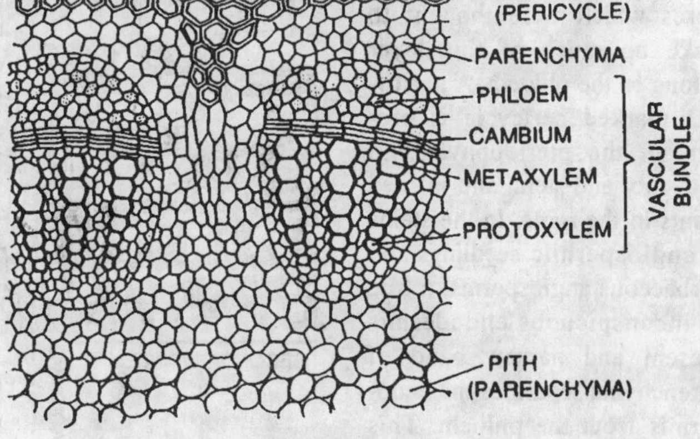

Fig. 4.30. Anatomy of dicot stem. T.S. of a part of stem of *Tinospora* showing complete band of lignified pericycle.

ght that it acts as an air dam which prevents diffusion of air into the vessels and thus they escape from closing. It may serve as storage tissue having starch grains in many dicotyledons.

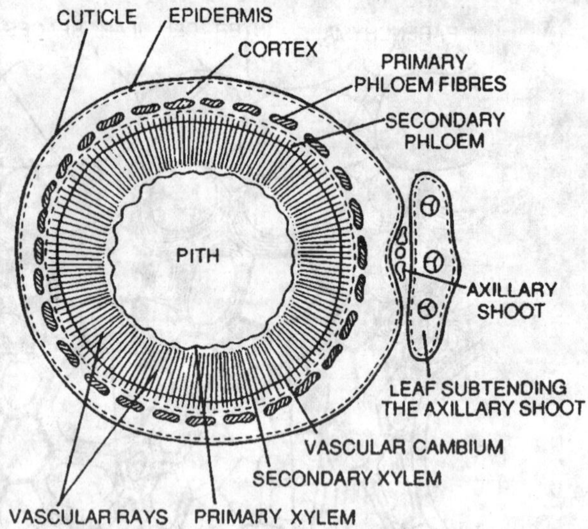

Fig. 4.31. T.S. of flax stem (diagrammatic).

PERICYCLE

In dicotyledonous stems, the pericycle is a multilayered zone found in between the endodermis and the vascular bundles. It always occurs as a thin cylinder of tissue completely encircling the vascular bundles and the pith. Towards inner side this pericyclic zone is limited by the primary phloem, whereas towards outer side it is limited by the endodermis. It may be a complete sclerenchymatous zone as in many cucurbits or it consists of both sclerenchyma and parenchyma cells (*e.g.*, in sun-flower and in many other members of Compositae). Sometimes when endodermis is altogether absent, the pericycle merges with the cortex. Typically the pericycle consists of parenchyma, as in most roots and in the stems of the pteridophytes. Recently it has been shown that the abundant 'pericyclic fibres' of some plants are a part of the primary phloem. Certainly many of them—such of those of *Cannabis* (hemp) and *Linum* (flax)—belong to the phloem and are known as phloem fibres, bast fibres or hard bast. In many plants such pericyclic fibres are thought to be associated with the phloem of vascular bundles. It is also claimed that no pericycle is present in the stems of many angiosperms because the fibres which were thought to make up much of this layer belong to the phloem. A narrow well-marked pericycle is present in the pteridophytes, in both root and stem, and in seed plants in the roots. In the stems of angiospermic seedlings and herbaceous angiosperms, a true or inconspicuous endodermis present and narrow band of parenchyma separates the endodermis from the phloem. This band represents either the outermost layer of the primary phloem or a pericycle. Usually

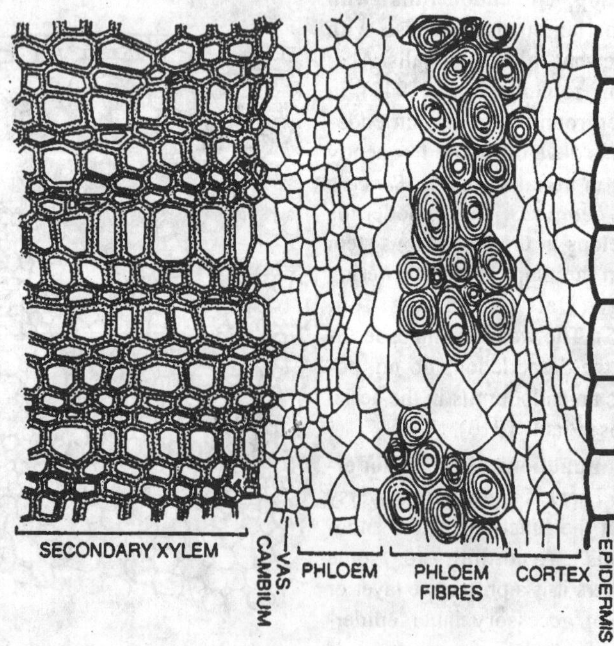

Fig. 4.32. T.S. of stem of *Linum usitatissimum* L. showing phloem fibres and their relation to other tissues of stem.

in woody herbs the protophloem fibres lie against the endodermis, and no pericycle is present.

The pericycle of roots consists of thin-walled parenchyma. The lateral roots of angiosperms arise in this tissue. Generally the pericycle is uniseriate in the roots (in *Smilax* root the pericycle is many layered and sclerenchymatous). Most of the roots possess distinct pericycle. However, the roots of certain angiospermic parasites and aquatic plants lack pericycle.

Functions of Pericycle

In the dicotyledonous roots the cells of pericycle become meristematic and form the vascular cambium and phellogen. The pericycle gives rise to lateral roots. The adventitious roots originate from pericycle in stems. Laticiferous cells, secretory cells and other specialized cells may occur in the pericycle. Some of the pericyclic cells aid in storage.

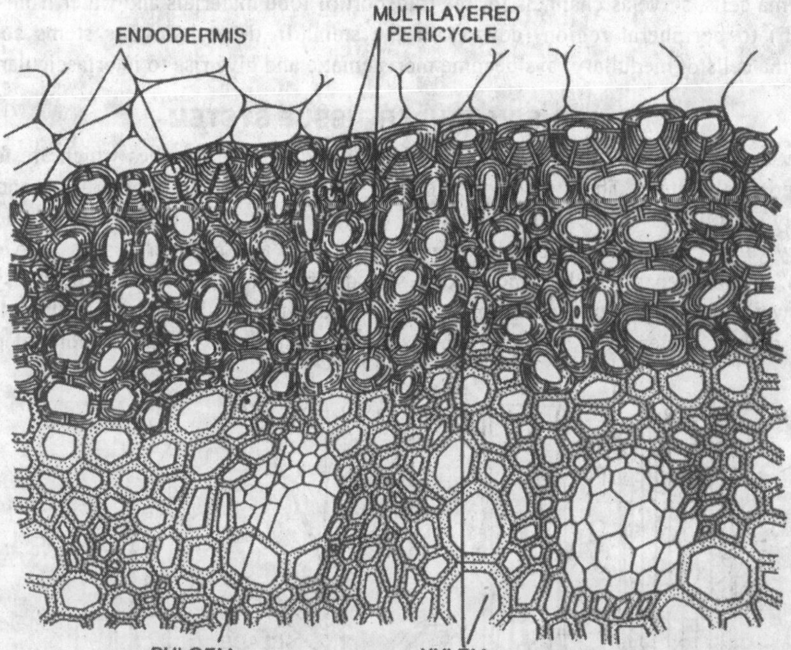

Fig. 4.33. The root. T.S. of the inner part of *Smilax* root showing endodermis (very-thick-walled cells) and multilayered sclerenchymatous pericycle.

PITH

The pith or medulla forms the central region of the stem and the root. Usually the pith of dicot stems is largely parenchymatous. It is devoid of chlorophyll in the mature state but starch forming leucoplasts are found in it. The sufficiently developed intercellular spaces are found among the pith cells. In monocotyledonous stems the vascular bundles are found scattered throughout the ground tissue and pith is not distinguishable. In the dicotyledonous roots the pith is scanty or lacking. However, in monocotyledonous roots it is well developed. In certain monocotyledonous roots (*e.g., Canna*), the pith is sclerenchymatous. The extensions of the pith in the form of narrow parenchymatous strips are called **medullary** or **pith rays.** The pith of many plants is partially obliterated during the growth of the stem and in such cases the stem becomes hollow. However, in such cases the nodes retain their pith. Certain pith cells possess tannin and crystals. Certain specialized structures like laticifers or secretory canals may also occur in the pith cells. In many cases the peripheral portion of the pith is demarcated from its central portion, due to the presence of smaller cells, their contents and sometimes even by the presence of chloroplasts in them (*e.g., Lantana, Anagalis,* etc.). In certain plants (*e.g., Equisetum*) there is an inner endodermis. In such cases the medullary rays are not connected with the central pith region. In some plants belonging to Umbelliferae and Compositae the medullary rays are composed of sclerenchymatous cells or of both sclerenchyma and parenchyma cells. As regards the ontogeny of pith it develops from the ground meristem and may be treated as the inner portion of the ground or fundamental tissue system.

Function of the Pith

The pith cells mainly serve as storage tissue. In case the pith is sclerenchymatous it acts as mechanical tissue and provides mechanical strength to the plant. The medullary ray consisting of parenchyma cells, serve as channels for the transport of food materials and water from the central part (pith) to peripheral region (cortex) of the stem. In dicotyledonous stems some of the parenchyma cells of medullary rays become meristematic and give rise to interfascicular cambium.

3. THE VASCULAR TISSUE SYSTEM

The vascular tissue system consists of a number of vascular bundles which are found to be distributed in the stele. The stele is the central cylindrical portion of the stem and the root, commonly surrounded by the endodermis, and consists of vascular bundles, pericycle, pith and medullary rays. Each vascular bundle consists of xylem and phloem tissues with or without cambium. In roots separate xylem and phloem strands are found. The function of this system is to conduct water and other nutrients from roots to leaves through the xylem and translocation of prepared carbohydrates from leaves to other storage organs and growing regions of plant body

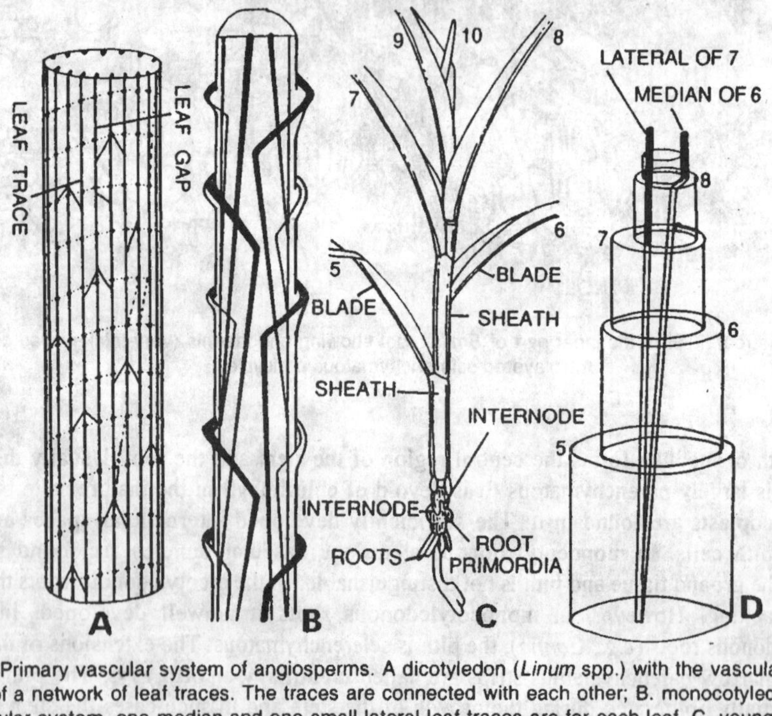

Fig. 4.34. Primary vascular system of angiosperms. A dicotyledon (*Linum* spp.) with the vascular system in the form of a network of leaf traces. The traces are connected with each other; B. monocotyledonous type of a vascular system, one median and one small lateral leaf traces are for each leaf. C, young *Zea mays* plant; D, diagram of part of plant in C showing the median trace of leaf 8 and its connection with the lateral trace of leaf. 7. (A, after Esau; B, after Linsbauer, C and D, after Sharman).

through the phloem. The vascular bundle elements are derived from the procambial strands of the primary meristem. The vascular bundles may be arranged in circular ring as in the dicotyledonous stems and the roots, on the other hand, they are found to be scattered throughout the axis in the monocotyledonous stems. In certain plants the vascular bundles remain scattered within the well defined pith, such bundles are called medullary vascular bundles (*e.g., Mirabilis, Boerhaavia, Bougainvillaea, Achyranthes, Amaranthus,* etc.). Vascular bundles may also occur in the cortical region of the stem, such bundles are known as cortical bundles (*e.g., Casuarina, Nyctanthes*).

PRIMARY VASCULAR TISSUE

The Procambium

The first cells to mature, in either leaf or stem, belong to the vascular tissue. In the promeristem, where all cells are isodiametric and alike, continuing longitudinal divisions set apart in some areas strands of elongate, slender cells with dense cytoplasm. Thus, meristematic tissue forms the primary phloem and xylem and is known as the **procambium.** Here, the term procambium is used to indicate the meristematic tissue that gives rise to the morphological vascular units. The first procambium appears as isolated strands very close to the apex in stem and root. It is continuous backward in the older tissues with older promeristem strands and mature vascular tissue. The slender procambium strands increase in diameter by longitudinal cell division within themselves and by the addition of new cells on their borders by means of promeristem cells. The increase in size of the strands is so great that a few or all of the strands fuse to form a hollow cylinder or a solid central core. Ultimately the procambium forms the vascular cylinder of the region.

As procambium develops, the diameter of the organ increases and simultaneously the promeristem cells multiply and enlarge in bulk. As the growth continues, the first phloem and first xylem cells are formed which mature on the inner and outer margins of slender strands. They are separated more and more widely from each other as the strands enlarge in size. The first maturing cells in a young strand are the phloem cells, which are followed by first xylem cells thereafter.

The first mature xylem and phloem cells are separated radially by procambium in stems and leaves and tangentially by promeristem in roots.

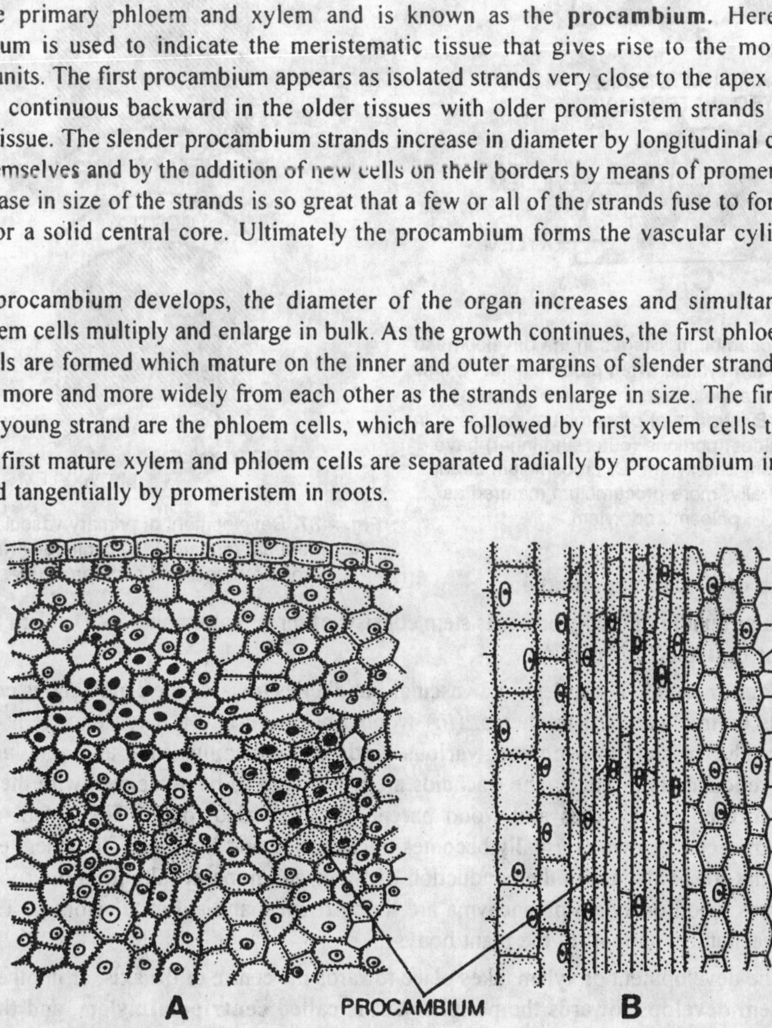

Fig. 4.35. Procambium. A and B, T.S. and L.S. of stem tip of *Linum usitatissimum* showing procambium. The procambium cells possess dense cytoplasm. (After Eames and MacDaniels).

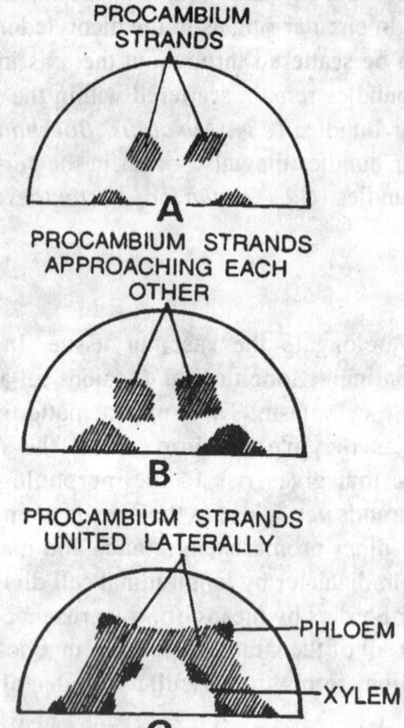

Fig. 4.36. Procambium. Stages in the development of a procambium cylinder from promeristem. A, first procambium appeared in the form of strands in promeristem; B, strands of procambium increased in diameter, oldest portions (outer and inner) have become phloem and xylem; C, procambium strands united laterally, more procambium matured as phloem and xylem.

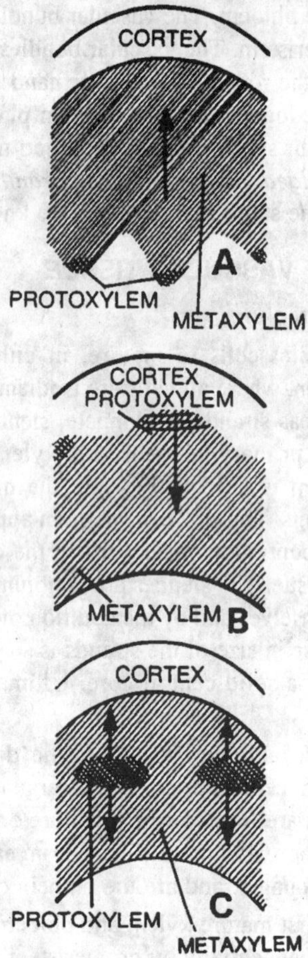

Fig. 4.37. Development of primary vascular tissue. A, centrifugal (endarch); B, centripetal (exarch); C, both centrifugal and centripetal (mesarch).

Constituents of a Vascular Bundle

A vascular bundle of dicotyledonous stem consists of three major zones—(*a*) xylem or wood, (*b*) phloem or bast and (*c*) cambium.

(*a*) Xylem or wood. The xylem of a vascular bundle lies towards the centre and is composed of (*i*) vessels or tracheae, (*ii*) tracheids, (*iii*) wood fibres and (*iv*) a patch of xylem or wood parenchyma. The vesslels may possess various kinds of thickenings such as—annular, spiral, scalariform, reticulate and pitted. The tracheids are also found to be associated with the vessels. In the similar way wood fibres and wood parenchyma are also found. The xylem or wood parenchyma of secondary wood usually becomes thick-walled and lignified. The xylem elements, *i.e.,* vessels and tracheids, aid in the conduction of water and mineral salts from the roots of the leaves, whereas wood or xylem parenchyma are living tissues, and aid in the storage. The wood fibres give mechanical support to the plant body.

When the development of xylem takes place towards the centre of the axis, or in other words, the protoxylem develops towards the periphery, it is called **centripetal xylem,** and the xylem strand is said to be **exarch.** If the development of xylem is towards periphery of the axis, or in other words, protoxylem elements develop towards the centre, it is called **centrifugal xylem,** and the xylem unit is said to be **endarch.** When development is such that both centripetal and

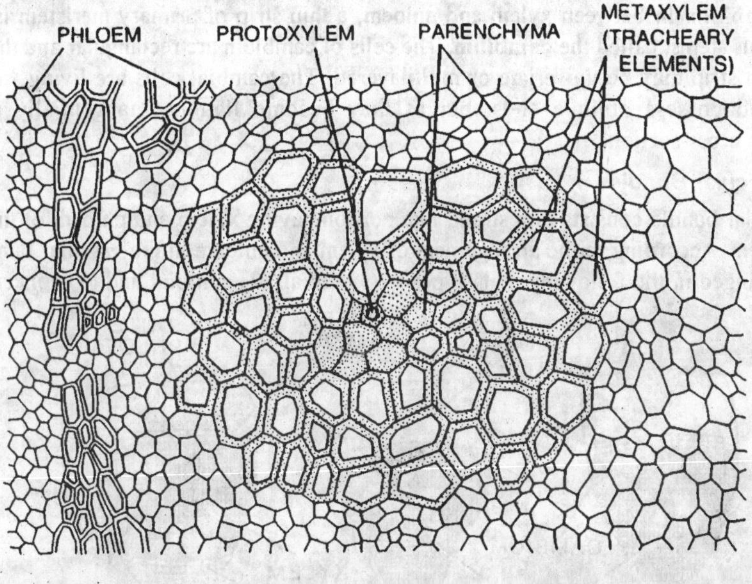

Fig. 4.38. The stem T.S. of vascular bundle of *Pteris* rhizome showing mesarch xylem.

centrifugal xylem are formed, the xylem is **mesarch**. For example, the stem of seed plants is endarch; the root is always exarch; the stem of club mosses (*Lycopodium* spp.) is exarch; mesarch xylem commonly found in the ferns and in the hypocotyl region of angiospermic seedings.

The first cells of the xylem to mature are collectively called the **protoxylem.** The protoxylem is complex tissue made up of tracheids vessels and parenchyma cells. The protoxylem consists of annular spiral and scalariform vessels which may stretch in length very easily. In the stems it lies towards the centre of the axis whereas in the root it lies towards periphery. The vessles of protoxylem have smaller cavities. The xylem which develops afterwards and possesses reticulate and pitted vessels and some tracheids is called **metaxylem.** In the roots towards the centre. The vessels of metaxylem have bigger and wider cavities.

(*b*) Phloem or bast. Usually in stems, phloem is found away from the centre of the axis towards the periphery and consists of sieve tubes or sieve cells only, or sieve tubes and companion cells only, or sieve tubes, companion cells and phloem parenchyma. In gymnosperms it is represented by sieve cells only. In most of monocotyledons it consists of sieve tubes and companion cells only, whereas in dicotyledons, sieve tubes, companion cells and phloem parenchyma possess simple pits in their walls, particularly which lie against the sieve tubes. Phloem serves for translocation of prepared carbohydrates from leaves to the storage tissue and other growing regions. Sieve tubes translocate proteins and some other carbohydrates, phloem parenchyma conducts amines, amino acids and soluble carbohydrates and companion cells also translocate many soluble food materials. All phloem elements are living and formed of cellulose. In certain cases, the primary phloem is capped by a patch of sclerenchyma called hard bast as in the *Helianthus* stem.

The first cells of the phloem to mature are known as **protophloem.** The protophloem consists of narrow sieve tubes, and is found towards periphery. The inner portion of the phloem consists of bigger sieve tubes called **metaphloem.** The metaphloem is complex tissue and consists of well developed cells of all types such as—sieve tubes, companion cells, phloem parenchyma and sometimes phloem fibres and sclereids.

(*c*) **Cambium.** In between xylem and phloem, a thin strip of primary meristem is found in dicotyledonous stems, called the **cambium.** The cells of cambium are rectangular and thin-walled. The cambium strip may be uniseriate or multilayered. The cambial cells are living, sufficiently elongated and possess oblique ends, but as they become flattened tangentially they look rectangular in cross-section.

Types of Vascular Bundles

A vascular bundle consists of a strand like portion having xylem and phloem of the primary vascular system. According to the arrangement of xylem and phloem in the vascular bundles, they are being arranged in the following main types —(1) radial, (2) conjoint and (3) concentric.

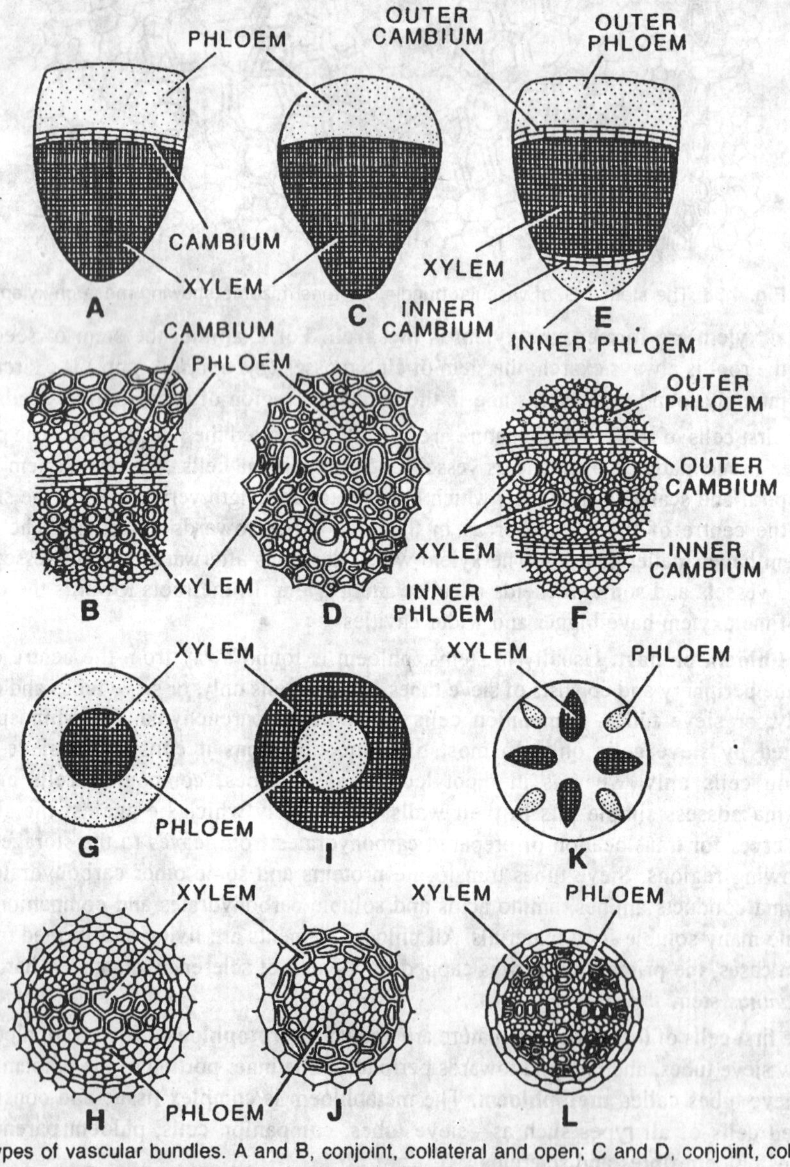

Fig. 4.39. Types of vascular bundles. A and B, conjoint, collateral and open; C and D, conjoint, collateral and closed; E and F, conjoint, bicollateral and open; G and H, concentric and amphicribral; I and J, concentric and amphivasal; K and L, radial.

(1) Radial. Those in which the xylem and the phloem lie radially side by side (*e.g.*, in roots of seed plants). This is most primitive type.

(2) Conjoint. Those in which the two types of tissues are separated from one another. Here, xylem and phloem together form a bundle. The two subtypes are— (*a*) Collateral and (*b*) Bicollateral.

(*a*) Collateral. The xylem and phloem lie together on the same radius in the position that xylem lies inwards and the phloem outwards. Here the phloem occurs on one side of the xylem strand. In dicotyledonous stem, the cambium is found to be present in between xylem and phloem, such bundles are called **open** (*e.g.*, in *Helianthus*), and when the cambium is absent it is called **closed** (*e.g.*, in monocotyledonous stems).

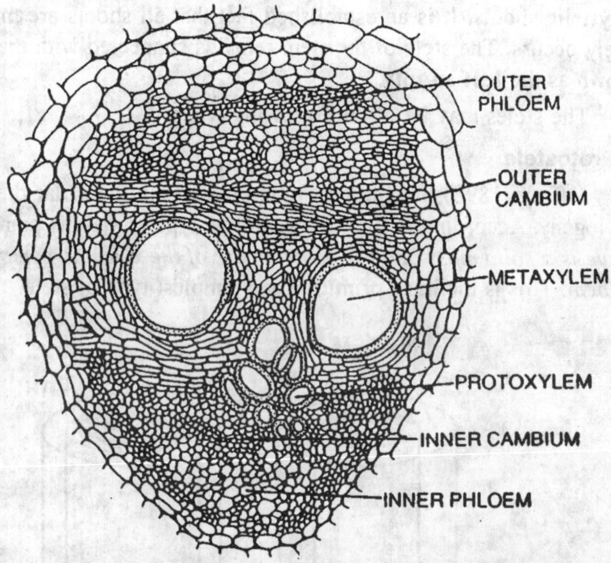

Fig. 4.40. Anatomy of dicot stem. T.S. of bicollateral bundle of *Cucurbita* stem, showing phloem on both sides of the xylem.

(*b*) Bicollateral. In such bundles the phloem is found to be present on both sides of xylem. Simultaneously two cambium strips also occur. Various elements are arranged in the following sequence—outer phloem, outer cambium, xylem, inner cambium and inner phloem. Such bundles are commonly found in the members of Cucurbitaceae. Such bundles are always open.

(3) Concentric. Those in which one type of tissue surrounds, or ensheaths, the other. The concentric bundles may be of two subtypes, **amphivasal** and **amphicribral.** If the xylem surrounds the phloem it is called amphivasal bundle as found in *Dracaena, Yucca* and other monocots and some dicots. If the phloem surrounds the xylem, it is amphicribral as found in many ferns. Such bundles are always closed.

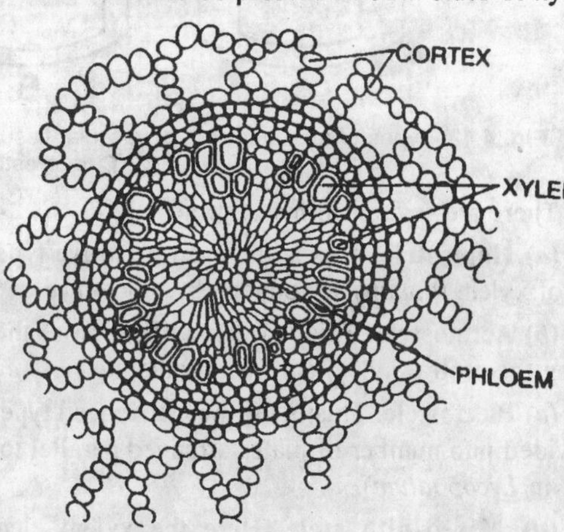

Fig. 4.41. *Iris* stem. T.S. of vascular bundle (amphivasal type)— detailed structure.

STELAR SYSTEM

According to the older botanists, the vascular bundle is the fundamental unit in the vascular system of pteridophytes and higher plants. Van Tieghem and Douliot (1886) interpreted the plant body of vascular plant in the different way. According to them, the fundamental parts of a shoot are the cortex and a central cylinder, is known as **stele.** Thus *the stele is defined as a central vascular cylinder, with or without pith and delimited the cortex by endodermis.* The term stele has been derived from a Greek word meaning pillar. Van Tieghem and Douliot (1886) recognized only three types of steles. They also thought that the monostelic shoot were rare in comparison of polystelic shoots. It is an established fact that all shoots are monostelic and polystelic condition rarely occurs. The stele of the stem remains connected with that of leaf by a vascular connection known as the **leaf supply.**

The steles may be of the following types:

1. Protostele

Jeffrey (1898), for the first time pointed out the stelar theory from the point of view of the phylogeny. According to him, the primitive type of stele is **protostele.** *In protostele, the vascular tissue is a solid mass and the central core of the xylem is completely sorrounded by the strand of phloem.* This is the most primitive and simplest type of stele.

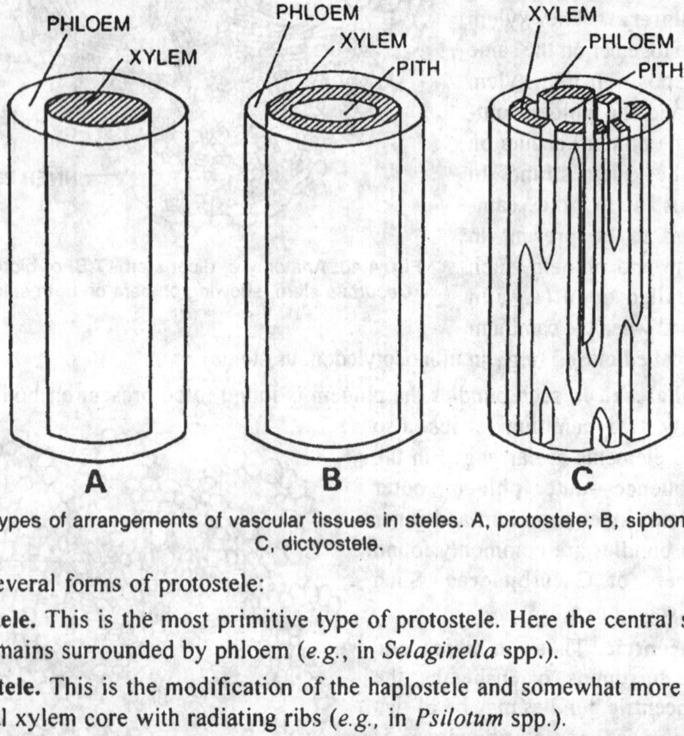

Fig. 4.42. Types of arrangements of vascular tissues in steles. A, protostele; B, siphonostele; C, dictyostele.

There are several forms of protostele:

(*a*) Haplostele. This is the most primitive type of protostele. Here the central solid smooth core of xylem remains surrounded by phloem (*e.g.*, in *Selaginella* spp.).

(*b*) Actinostele. This is the modification of the haplostele and somewhat more advanced in having the central xylem core with radiating ribs (*e.g.*, in *Psilotum* spp.).

(*c*) Plectostele. This is the most advanced type of protostele. Here the central core of xylem is divided into number of plates arranged parallel to each other. The phloem alternates the xylem (*e.g.*, in *Lycopodium*).

(*d*) Mixed-pith stele. Here the xylem elements (*i.e.*, tracheids) are mixed with the parenchymatous cells of the pith. This type is found in primitive fossils and living ferns. They are treated to be the transitional types in between true protosteles on the one hand and siphonosteles on the other (*e.g.*, in *Gleichenia* spp. and *Osmunda* spp.).

2. Siphonostele

This is the modification of protostele. A stele in which the protostele is medullated is known as **siphonostele.** Such stele contains a tubular vascular region and a parenchymatous central region. Jeffrey (1898) interpreted that the vascular portion of siphonostele possesses a parenchymatous area known as a **gap** immediately above the branch traces only or immediately above leaf and branch traces. On the basis of these branch and leaf gaps Jeffrey (1910), distinguished two types of siphonosteles. In one type, however, the leaf gaps are not found and they

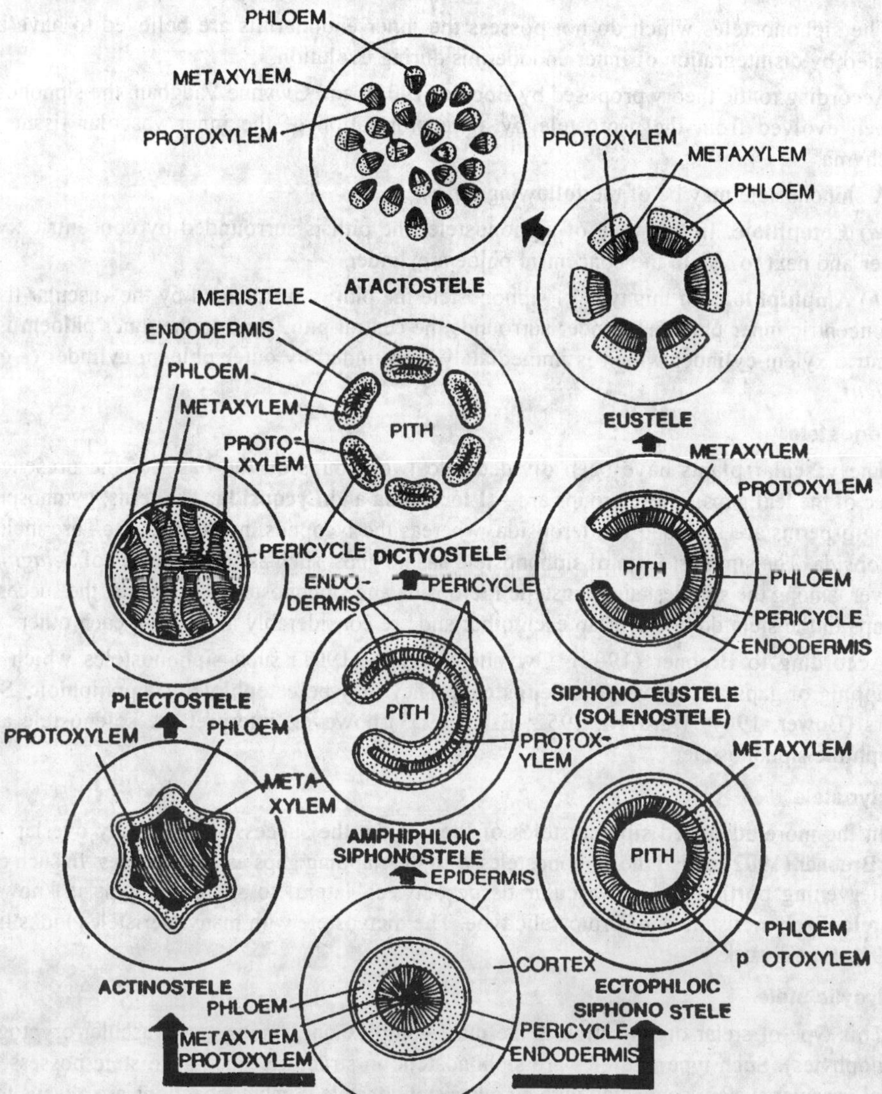

Fig. 4.43. The stelar system. Different types of steles arranged in evoluntionary sequence.

are known as **cladosiphonic siphonosteles.** In the other type both leaf and branch gaps are present and they are known as **phyllosiphonic siphonosteles.**

Jeffrey (1902, 1910, 1917) interpreted the evolution of the siphonostele from the protostele as follows. He supported that the parenchyma found internal to the phloem and xylem has been originated from the cortex. The supporters of this theory believe that the inner endodermis found to the inner face of the vascular tissue and the parenchyma encircled by this endodermis have been originated from the cortex. According to Jeffrey and other supporters of this theory the siphonosteles with internal endodermis are more primitive than those without an internal endodermis.

The siphonosteles which do not possess the inner endodermis are believed to have been originated by disintegration of inner endodermis during evolution.

According to the theory proposed by Boodle (1901), and Gwynne Vaughan, the siphonostele has been evolved from the protostele by a transformation of the inner vascular tissue into parenchyma.

A siphonostele may be of the following types:

(*a*) Ectophloic. In this type of siphonostele, the pith is surrounded by concentric xylem cylinder and next to xylem the concentric phloem cylinder.

(*b*) Amphiphloic. In this type of siphonostele the pith is surrounded by the vascular tissue. The concentric inner phloem cylinder surrounds the central pith. Next to the inner phloem is the concentric xylem cylinder which is immediately surrounded by outer phloem cylinder (*e.g.*, in *Marsilea).*

3. Solenostele

The vascular plants have been divided into two groups on the basis of the presence or absence of the leaf gaps. These groups are— **Pteropsida** and **Lycopsida.** The ferns, gymnosperms and angtosperms are included in Pteropsida, whereas the lycopods, horse-tails, etc., are included in Lycopsida. The simplest form of siphonostele has no gaps, such as some species of *Selaginella.* However, among the simplest siphonostelic Pteropsida and siphonostelic Lycopsida, the successive leaf gaps in the stele do not overlap each other and are considerably apart from each other.

According to Brebner (1902), Gwynne-Vaughan (1901) such siphonosteles which lack overlapping of gaps are known as **solenosteles.** They may be ectophloic or amphiphloic. Some authors (Bower, 1947; Wardlaw, 1952; Esau, 1953) however, interpret the solenostele as an amphiphloic siphonostele.

4. Dictyostele

In the more advanced siphonosteles of Pteropsida, the successive gaps may overlap each other. Brebner (1902) called the siphonosteles with overlapping gaps as **dictyosteles.** In such cases the intervening portion of the vascular tissue between lateral to such leaf gaps is known as **meristele.** Each meristele is of protostelic type. The dictyostele with many meristeles looks like a cylindrical meshwork.

5. Polycylic stele

This type of stelar organization is the most complex one amongst all vascular cryptogams (pteridophytes). Such type of steles are siphonostelic in structure. Each such stele possesses an internal vascular system connected with an outer siphonostele. Such connections are always found at the node. A typical polycyclic stele possesses two or more concentric rings of vascular tissue. This may be a solenostele or a dictyostele. Two concentric rings of vascular tissue are found in *Pteridium aquilinum* and three in *Matonia pectinata.*

6. Eustele

According to Brebner (1902), there is one more modification of the siphonostele known as **eustele.** Here the vascular system consists of a ring of collateral or bicollateral vascular bundles situated on the periphery of the pith. In such steles, the interfascicular areas and the leaf gaps are not distinguished from each other very clearly. The example of this type is *Equisetum.*

5

CHAPTER

Nodal Anatomy

LEAF TRACES AND LEAF GAPS

A shoot bears **nodes'** and **internodes.** At each node, portions of the vascular system are deflected into the leaf, which is attached at this node. A vascular bundle located in the stem but directly related to a leaf, to represent the lower part of the vascular supply of this leaf, is termed the **leaf trace.** The leaf trace is defined as follows—*The leaf trace is a vascular bundle that connects the vascular system of the leaf with that of the stem.* A leaf trace is extended between the base of a leaf and the point where it is completely merged with other parts of the vascular system in the stem. One or more leaf traces may be associated with each leaf.

In the shoot of a pteropsid (seed plants and ferns) where the leaf trace diverges into a leaf, it appears as though a portion of the vascular cylinder of the stem is deflected to one side. Immediately above the diverging trace, a parenchymatous tissue is being differentiated instead of vascular tissue in the vas-cular region of the stem for a limited distance. The parenchy-matous regions in the vascular system of the stem, located adaxially from the diverging leaf traces, are called **leaf gaps or lacunae.** Actually these gaps are not breaks in the continuity of the vascular system of the axis. Lateral connections occur between the tissues above and below the gap. In transverse sections of an axis at the level of a leaf gap, the gap resembles an **interfascicular area.**

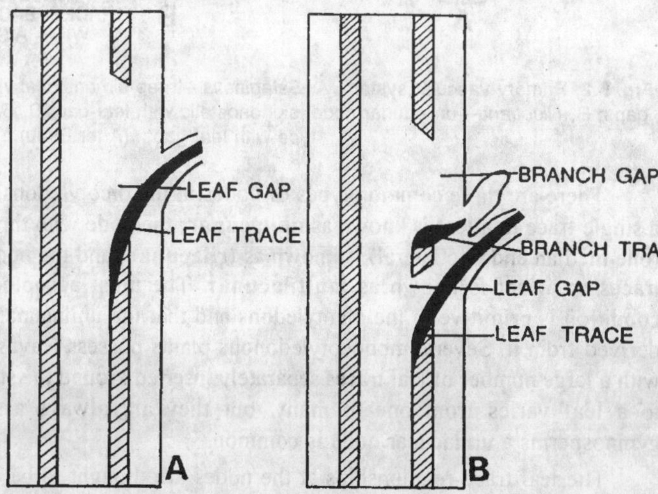

Fig. 5.1. Leaf and branch traces and gaps. A, L.S. of node through leaf trace and gap; B, L.S. of node through branch trace and gap.

The gaps are quite conspicuous in the ferns and angiosperms where the vascular system in the internodal parts of the stem forms a more or less continuous cylinder. In some ferns the leaves are so crowded that the gaps formed at the successive nodes overlap one another and the vascular cylinder appears highly dissected. The transverse sections of such stems show a circle of vascular bundles with the parenchymatous leaf gaps. In certain ferns, gymnosperms and most angiosperms the vascular system consists of anastamosing strands. In such cases, the parenchyma that occurs above the diverging leaf trace becomes confluent with the interfascicular areas, thus the recognition of the gaps become uncertain.

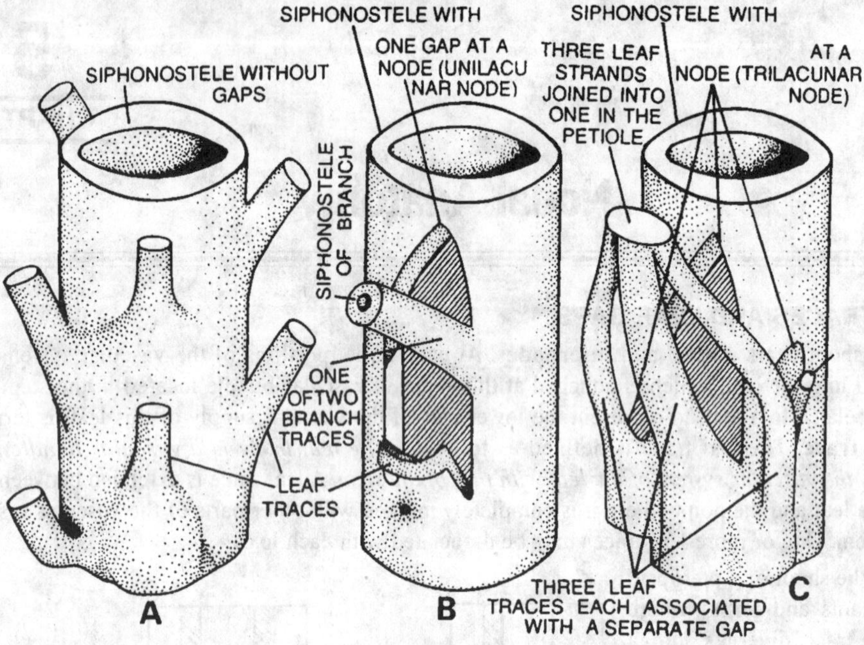

Fig. 5.2. Primary vascular system. A, *Selaginella*—three-dimensional view, siphonostelic type without leaf-gaps; B, *Nicotiana*—unilacunar node, siphonostelic with leaf gap; C, *Salix*—trilacunar node, siphonostelic type with leaf gaps. (After Esau).

There are three common types of nodes in the dicotyledons. The node with a single gap and a single trace to a leaf is known as **unilacunar;** the node with three gaps and three traces to a leaf (one median and two lateral) is known as **trilacunar;** and the node with several to many gaps and traces to a leaf is known as **multilacunar.** The most accepted concept is that the trilacunar condition is primitive in the dicotyledons and that the unilacunar and the multilacunar have been derived from it. Several monocotyledonous plants possess leaves with sheathing bases and nodes with a large number of leaf traces separately inserted around the stem. In ferns the number of traces to a leaf varies from one to many, but they are always associated with a single gap. In gymnosperms a unilacunar node is common.

The leaf trace relationships at the nodes are thought to be of phylogenetic importance, and therefore, nodal anatomy is concerned with the study of systematics and phylogeny of angiosperms.

Nodal Anatomy in Wheat (Monocot) Stem

In the wheat stem the course of the vascular bundles through the internode and the leaf sheath is almost parallel. Near the node the leaf sheath is considerably thick and attains its maximum thickness just above its union with the stem. On the other hand, the stem has the smallest diameter above the junction with the leaf sheath. The stem is hollow in the internode and solid at the node. The sheath remains open on one side at higher levels, just near the node. Massive collenchymatous bundle caps are present in the bundles of leaf sheath.

Just beneath the junction of the leaf sheath and stem the smaller of the leaf traces are prolonged in the peripheral part of the axis, and the larger leaf traces become part of the inner cylinder of strands. The internodal bundles located above the leaf insertion assume, just above the

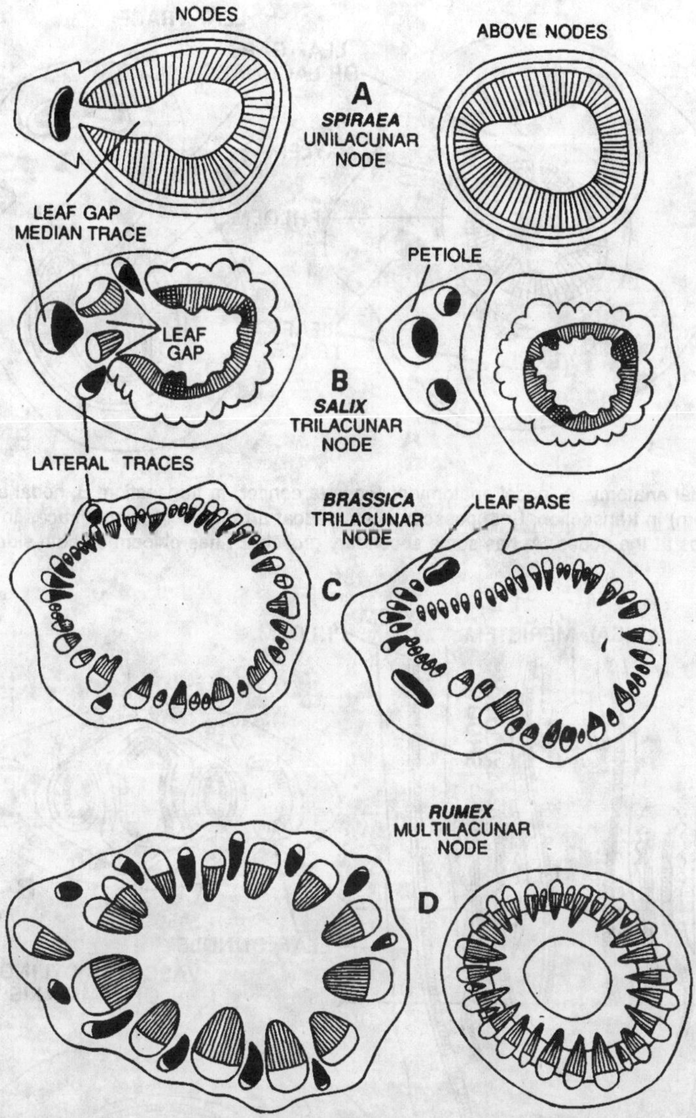

Fig. 5.3. Nodal anatomy of dicotyledons. A. *Spiraea*— each leaf has one leaf trace and one leaf gap (unilacunar node); B, *Salix*— each leaf has three leaf traces and three leaf gaps (trilacunar node); C, *Brassica*— three leaf traces and three leaf gaps per leaf (trilacunar node); D, *Rumex*— many leaf traces and many leaf gaps per leaf (multilacunar node).

node a horizontal and oblique course (Fig. 5.7 C, D), and are reoriented toward a more peripheral position in the node and below it (Fig. 5.7 D, E). These horizontal and oblique bundles variously branch and coalesce, and their number reduces. The large leaf traces and the bundles from the internode above the insertion of the leaf make the inner cylinder of the bundles of the next lower internode (Fig. 5.7 E). In this cylinder approximately half of the bundles are leaf traces from the nearest leaf above and the other half of the bundles are from the internode above the insertion of the leaf (Fig. 5.7 E). The peripheral bundles are mostly leaf traces. The most conspicuous character of grass stems is the presence of transverse bundles in the nodal regions.

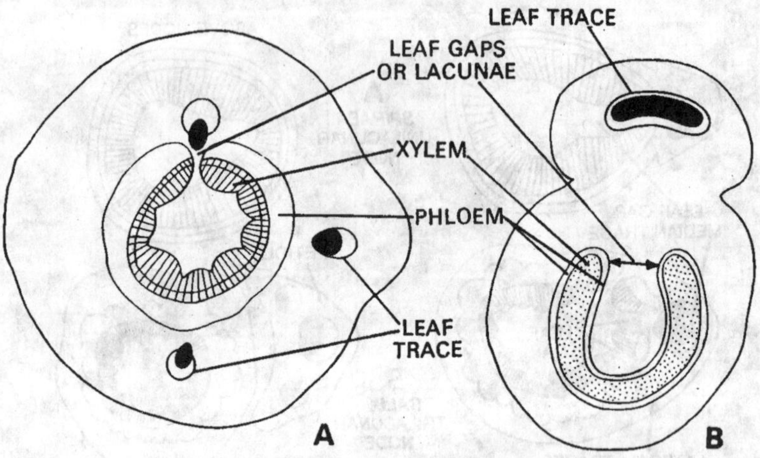

Fig. 5.4. Nodal anatomy. A, nodal anatomy of *Picea* (a conifer) in transection; B, nodal anatomy of *Adiantum* (a fern) in transection. Both possess alternate leaf arrangement, single traces to leaves, and single leaf gaps at the nodes. A, has some secondary growth; B, has phloem on both sides of xylem.

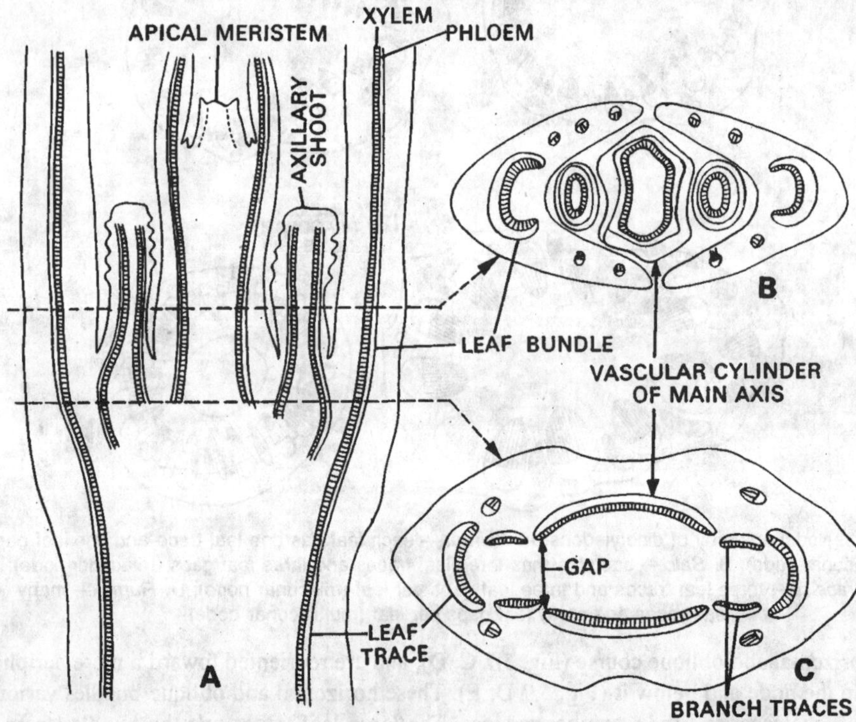

Fig. 5.5. Nodal anatomy. The diagrams depict the primary vascular system of plant with an opposite (decussate) leaf arrangement in L.S. (A) and T.S. (B and C). The branches present in the axils of the leaves are inflorescences. The leaf trace and branch traces in its axil are associated with one common gap. The two branch traces of level C are united into a tubular vascular cylinder in B.

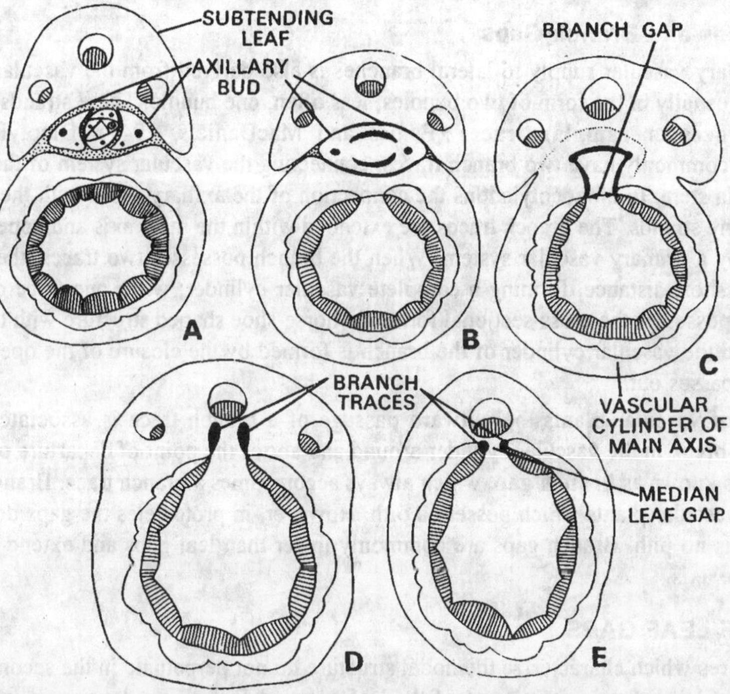

Fig. 5.6. Branch traces and gaps. Diagrams showing vascular connection between an axillary branch (bud) and the main axis in *Salix*. Vascular system of bud is shown in black in the diagram. First two leaves of bud are opposite. The branch gap and the median gap of the subtending leaf are confluent.

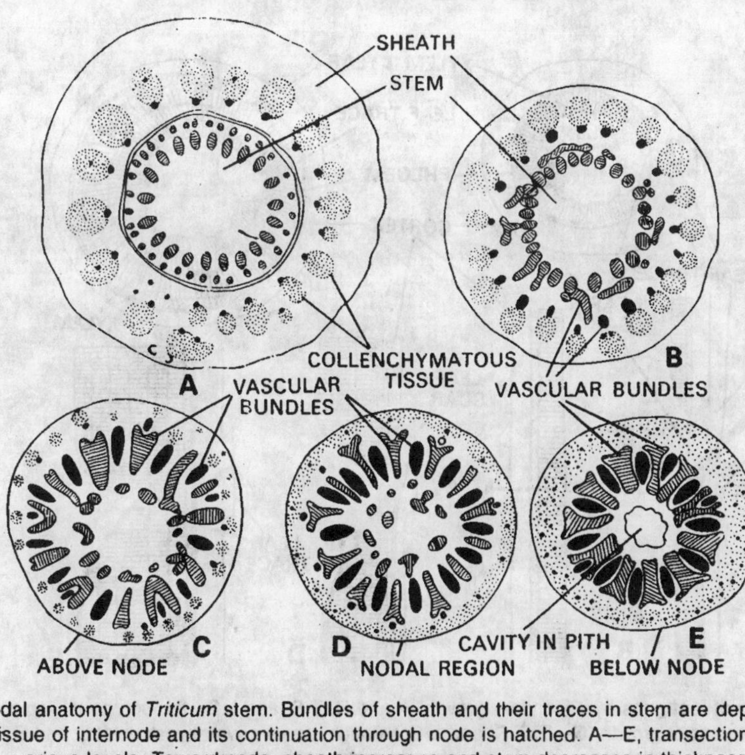

Fig. 5.7. Nodal anatomy of *Triticum* stem. Bundles of sheath and their traces in stem are depicted in black; vascular tissue of internode and its continuation through node is hatched. A—E, transections of stem at various levels. Toward node, sheath increases and stem decreases in thickness.

Branch Traces and Branch Gaps

The primary vascular supply to lateral branches is also derived from the vascular system of the main axis, usually in the form of two bundles, less often, one bundle. These strands are known as **branch traces** or **ramular traces** (Eames and MacDaniels, 1947). Dicotyledons and gymnosperms commonly have two branch traces, connecting the vascular system of the branch to that of the main stem. In monocotyledons the connection of the axillary shoot with the main stem consists of many strands. The branch traces are extended within the main axis and appendages are tied together by a primary vascular system. When the branch possesses two traces, these bundles unite within a short distance, forming a complete vascular cylinder; when one trace occurs, this strand usually possesses the cross-sectional form of a horse-shoe shaped structure with the opening downward, and the vascular cylinder of the branch is formed by the closure of the opening as the branch traces passes out.

In most of vascular plants the outward passage of a branch trace is associated with the formation of a break in the vascular cylinder around and above the point of departure of the trace. This opening is known as **branch gap,** which always accompanies a branch trace. Branch gaps are present in all vascular plants which possess a pith. However, in protosteles the gaps do not occur because there is no pith. Branch gaps are commonly lower than leaf gaps and extend for greater distances in the axis.

CLOSING OF LEAF GAPS

The features which characterize the nodal structure do not perpetuate in the secondary body. A cambium develops in the parenchyma of the leaf gap and forms vascular tissues in continuity with those bordering the gap. This phenomenon is known as closing of the gap. The parenchyma cells near the margin of the gap are the first to change into cambium and those in the inner portion

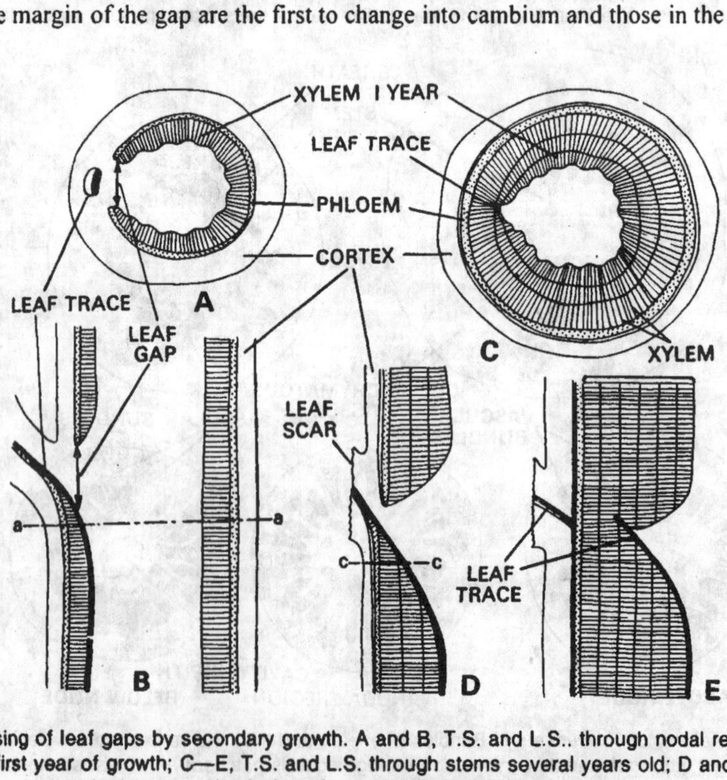

Fig. 5.8. Closing of leaf gaps by secondary growth. A and B, T.S. and L.S.. through nodal region of stems in first year of growth; C—E, T.S. and L.S. through stems several years old; D and E, depict stages in closing of gaps and rupture of leaf trace (E).

change later. This process takes place gradually, and the gap parenchyma is maintained as such within the secondary body until and cambium is differentiated throughout the entire tangential width of the gap.

In the leaf trace itself complicated changes take place during secondary growth. The primary xylem is buried by the secondary tissues while the phloem is pushed outward. The upper part of the trace diverges outwardly and crosses the plane of the cambium. The part of the cambium that differentiates above the trace in the gap region, produces vascular tissue between the trace and the vascular cylinder. This tissue which increases in amount, exerts a pressure upon the trace and ultimately causes its rupture. The break is filled with parenchyma which is changed into cambium and connects the cambium of the lower part of the trace with that formed in the gap. After this cambium has formed some secondary tissues, the end of the trace below the break becomes embedded in secondary xylem (Fig. 5.8 E). The upper severed end is carried outward, and in time it may be thrown off, together with the cortex, by the activity of the periderm. Since the cambium within the trace itself pushes the trace phloem outward, the buried part of the trace consists of xylem only.

6

CHAPTER

The Cambium

In majority of monocotyledons and pteridophytes the primary plant body is in itself structurally and functionally complete. It is evident from the fact that in these plants it alone constitutes the plant. In most dicotyledons and gymnosperms, primary growth is soon followed by secondary growth. Secondary growth is effected by definite layers of initials— in vascular tissues, by the cambium; in other tissues by similar meristem. These growing layers provide additional and constantly renewed conducting, supporting and protecting tissues. The length of the axis and appendages increases due to primary growth; secondary growth increases the girth of the axis. In certain tree ferns and few monocotyledons there a large body present which is wholly primary in nature. However, some larger monocotyledons, including some palms, *Yuccas* and *Dracaenas* possess secondary growth of special type.

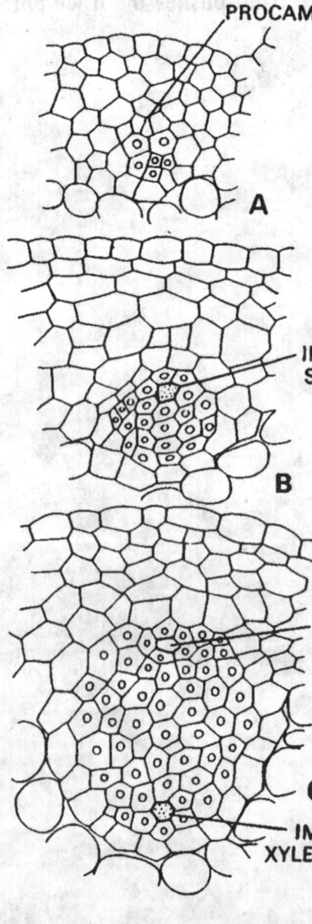

Fig. 6.1. Primary vascular differentiation, A–C, successive stages in the development of the proceambium in T.S. of *Linum* stem. The first phloem and xylem elements begin to differentiate before procambial strand completes its increase in diameter.

ORIGIN OF CAMBIUM

The primary vascular skeleton is built up by the maturing of the cells of the **procambium** strands to form xylem and phloem. The plants which do not possess secondary growth, all cells of the procambium strands mature and develop into vascular tissue. In the plant which have secondary growth later on, a part of the procambium strand remains meristematic and gives rise to the cambium proper. In roots the formation of cambium differs from that in stems because of the radial arrangement of the alternating xylem and phloem strands. Here the cambium arises as discrete strips of tissue in the procambium strands inside the groups of primary phloem. Later on, the strips of cambium by their lateral extension are joined in the pericycle opposite the rays of primary xylem. The secondary tissue formation is most rapid beneath the groups of phloem so that the cambium, as seen in the transverse section of older roots, soon forms a circle.

FASCICULAR AND INTERFASCICULAR CAMBIUM

In stems the first procambium that develops from promeristem is usually found in the form of isolated strands. In some plants these first-formed strands soon become, united laterally by additional similar strands formed between them and by the lateral extention of the first-formed strands. During further development this procambial cylinder gives rise to a cylinder of primary vascular tissue (xylem and phloem) and cambium. Later on, a cylinder of secondary vascular tissue is formed that arises in strands as does the primary cylinder. In *Ranunculus* and some other herbaceous plants, the procambium strands, and the primary vascular tissues, do not fuse laterally but remain as discrete strands. More often in herbaceous stems the cambium extends laterally across the intervening spaces until a complete cylinder is formed. Where such extension occurs, the cambium arises from interfascicular meristematic cells derived from the apical meristem. The strips of cambium that arise within collateral bundles are known as **fascicular cambium,** and the cambial strips found in between the bundles are known as **interfascicular cambium.**

DURATION OF CAMBIUM

The duration of the functional life of the cambium varies greatly in different species and also in different parts of the same plant. In a perennial woody plant the cambium of the main stem lives from the time of its formation until the death of the plant. It is only by the continued activity of the cambium in producing new xylem and phloem that such plants can maintain their existence. In leaves, inflorescenes and other deciduous parts, the functional life of the cambium is short. Here all the cambium cells mature as vascular tissue. The secondary xylem is directly found upon the secondary phloem in such bundles.

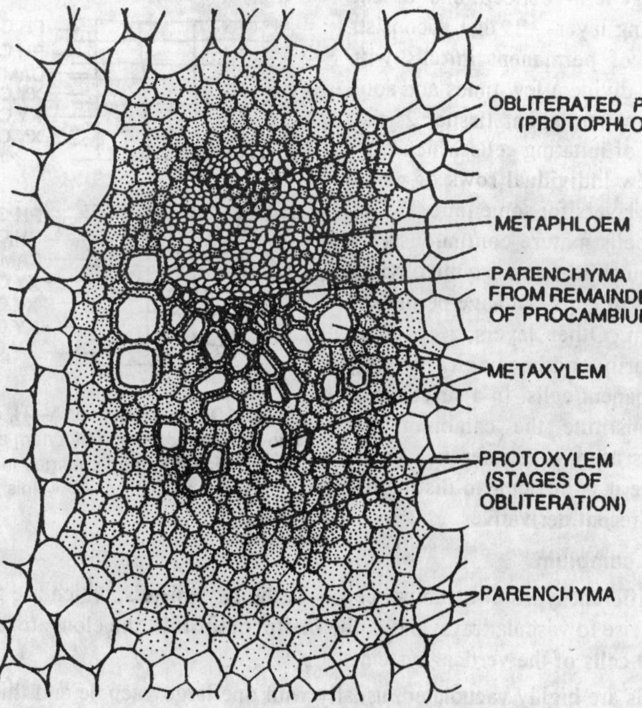

Fig. 6.2. The stem. T.S. of a vascular bundle of *Ranunculus*. This is an example of collateral bundle from a herbaceous dicotyledon lacking secondary growth. (After K. Esau.)

Function of Cambium

The meristem that forms secondary tissues consists of an uniseriate sheet of initials that form new cells usually on both sides. The cambium forms xylem internally and phloem externally. The tangential division of the cambial cell, forms two apparently identical daughter cells. One of the daughter cells remains meristematic, *i.e.* the persistent cambial cell, the other becomes a **xylem mother cell** or a **phloem mother cell** depending upon its position internal or external to the initial. The cambium cell divides continuously in a similar way; one daughter cell always remains meristematic, the cambium cell, whereas the other becomes either a xylem or a phloem mother cell. Probably there is no definite alternation and for brief periods only one kind of tissue is formed. Adjacent cambium cells divide at nearly the same time, and the daughter cells belong to the same tissue. This way, the tangential continuity of the cambium is maintained.

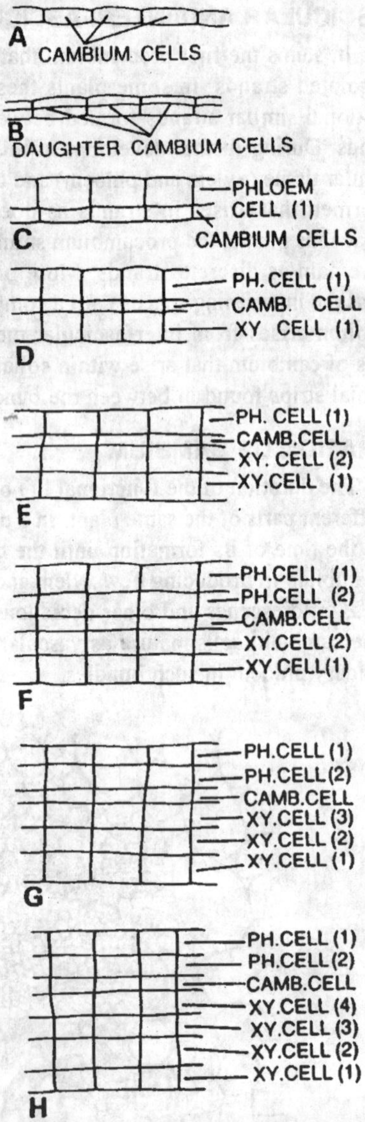

Fig. 6.3. The cambium. A—H, diagrams showing the formation of xylem and phloem by the cambium, and changes in position of phloem and cambium by this activity.

Structure of cambium

There are two general conceptions of the cambium as an initiating layer— 1. that it consists of a uniseriate layer of permanent initials with derivatives which may divide a few times and soon become converted into permanent tissue; 2. that there are several rows of initating cells which form a cambium zone, a few individual rows of which persist as cell forming layers for some time. During growing periods the cells mature continuously on both sides of the cambium it becomes quite obvious that only a single layer of cells can have permanent existence as cambium. Other layers, if present, function only temporarily and become completely transformed into permanent cells. In a strict sense, only the initials constitute the cambium, but frequently the term is used with reference to the cambial zone, because it is difficult to distinguish the initials from their recent derivatives.

Cellular structure of cambium

There are two different types of cambium cells—1. the **ray initials,** which are more or less isodiametric and give rise to vascular rays; and 2. the **fusiform initials,** the elongate tapering cells that divide to form all cells of the vertical system.

The cambial cells are highly vacuolated, usually with one large vacuole and thin peripheral cytoplasm. The nucleus is large and in the fusiform cells is much elongated. The walls of cambial cells have primary pit fields with plasmodesmata. The radial walls are thicker than tangential walls, and their primary pit fields are deeply depressed.

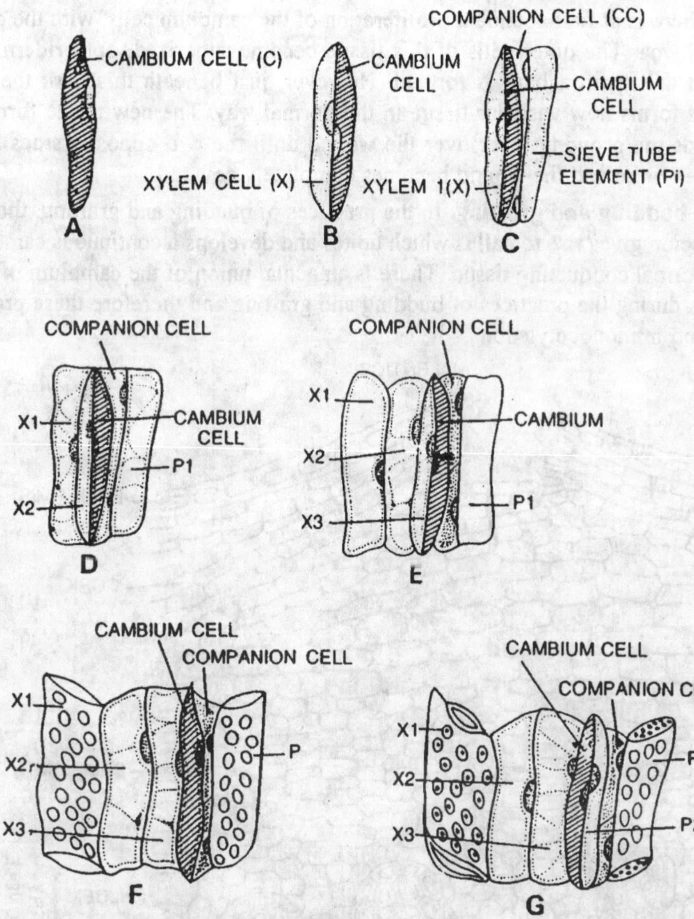

Fig. 6.4. The cambium. Differentiation of phloem and xylem from vascular cambium. A—G, diagrams as seen in radial section, showing stages in differentiation of vascular cambium cells.

Cell Division in Cambium

With the result of tangential (periclinal) divisions of cambium cells the phloem and the xylem are formed. The vascular tissues are formed in two opposite directions, the xylem cells towards the interior of the axis, the phloem cells toward its periphery. The tangential divisions of the cambium initials during the formation of vascular tissues determine the arrangement of cambial derivatives in radial rows. Since the division is tangential, the daughter cells that persist as cambium initials increase in radial diameter only. The new cambium initials formed by transverse divisions increase greatly in length; those formed by radial divisions do not increase in length.

As the xylem cylinder increases in thickness by secondary growth, the cambial cylinder also grows in circumference. The main cause of this growth is the increase in the number of cells in tangential direction, followed by a tangential expansion of these cells.

Cambium growth about wounds. One of the important functions of the cambium is the formation of **callus** or **wound tissue,** and the healing of the wounds. When wounds occur on plants, a large amount of soft parenchymatous tissue is formed on or below the injured surface; this tissue is known as callus. The callus develops from the cambium and by the division of parenchyma cells in the phloem and the cortex. During the healing process of a wound the callus is formed. In this there is at first abundant proliferation of the cambium cells, with the production of massive parenchyma. The outer cells of this tissue become suberized, or periderm develops within them, with the result a bark is formed. However, just beneath this bark the cambium remains active and forms new vascular tissue in the normal way. The new tissue formed in the normal way extends the growing layer over the wound until the two opposite sides meet. The cambium layers then unite and the wound becomes completely covered.

Cambium in budding and grafting. In the practices of budding and grafting, the cambium of both stock and scion gives rise to callus which unites and develops a continuous cambium layer that gives rise to normal conducting tissue. There is an actual union of the cambium of stock and scion of two plants during the practices of budding and grafting and therefore these practices are not commonly found in monocotyledons.

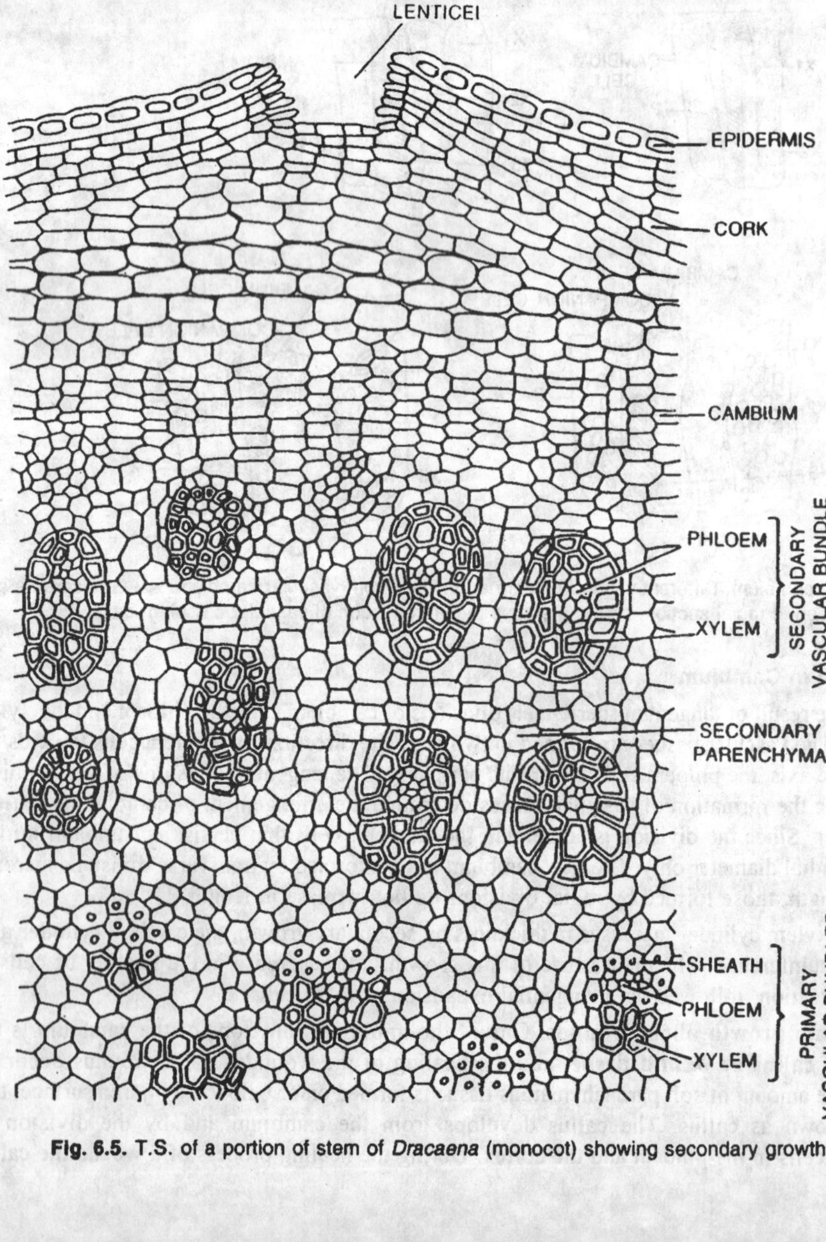

Fig. 6.5. T.S. of a portion of stem of *Dracaena* (monocot) showing secondary growth.

Cambium in monocotyledons. A special type of secondary growth occurs in few monocotyledonous forms, such as *Dracaena, Aloe, Yucca, Veratrum* and some other genera. In these plants the stem increases in diameter forming a cylinder of new bundles embedded in a tissue. Here a cambium layer develops from the meristematic parenchyma of the pericycle or the innermost cells of the cortex. In the case of roots, the cambium of this develops in the endodermis. The initials of cambium strand in tiers to form a storied cambium as found in the normal cambium of some dicotyledons.

Thickening in Palms

The palm stems do not increase in girth, because of any cambial activity but this thickening is the result of gradual increase in size of cells and of intercellular spaces and sometimes of the proliferation of fibre tissues. This is the type of long continuing primary growth. The process is as follows:

Most of the monocotyledons lack secondary growth, but with the result of intense and long continuing primary growth they may produce such large bodies as those of the palms. The

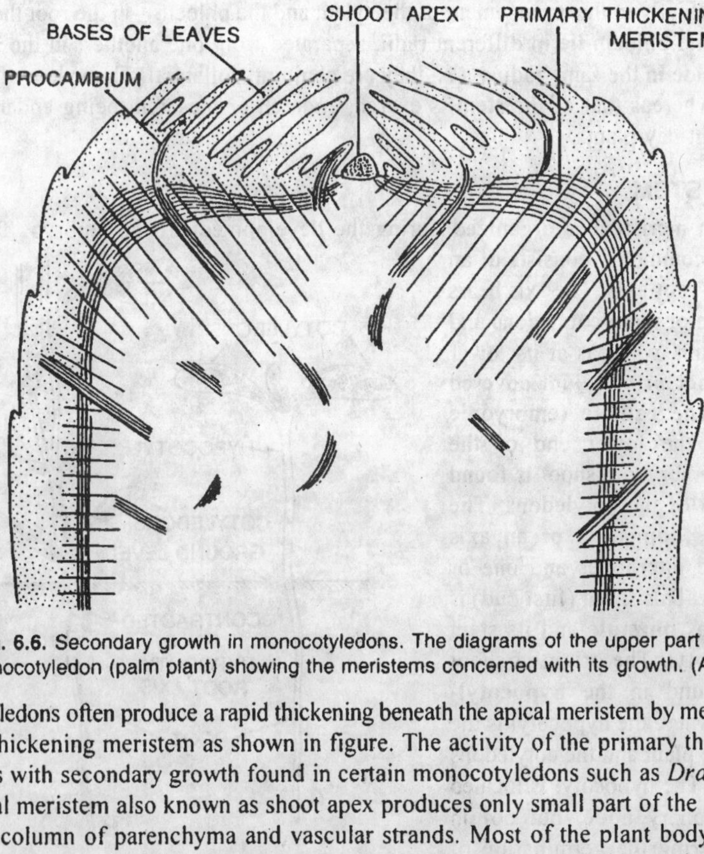

Fig. 6.6. Secondary growth in monocotyledons. The diagrams of the upper part of shoot of a monocotyledon (palm plant) showing the meristems concerned with its growth. (After Eckardt).

monocotyledons often produce a rapid thickening beneath the apical meristem by means of a peripheral primary thickening meristem as shown in figure. The activity of the primary thickening meristem resembles with secondary growth found in certain monocotyledons such as *Dracaena, Yucca,* etc. The apical meristem also known as shoot apex produces only small part of the primary body, *i.e.*, a central column of parenchyma and vascular strands. Most of the plant body is formed by the primary thickening meristem. The primary thickening meristem is found beneath the leaf-primordia, which divides periclinally producing anticlinal rows of cells. These cells differentiate into a tissue formed of ground parenchyma traversed by procambial strands. These procambial strands later on develop into vascular bundles. The ground parenchyma cells enlarge and divide repeatedly, causing increase in thickness. This way, both apical meristem and primary thickening meristem give rise to the main bulk of the stem tissues of monocotyledons. The thickening takes place in monocotyledons, such as palms, due to the activities of the two meristems mentioned above.

7

CHAPTER

The Shoot System : Primary and Secondary Structure

The part of the axis of the plant which is usually ascending and aerial in nature, and also bears the leaves and reproductive structures is called the **stem**. The stem together with the leaves which it bears constitutes the **shoot;** the relationship between leaves and stem is very close one and a separation of the shoot into its component parts is to some extent artificial. The stem bears conspicuous nodes and internodes and fundamentally differ from roots in their vascular structure. The difference lies chiefly in the arrangement of the xylem and the phloem—in the root the strands of primary xylem and phloem lie in different rádii, separated from one another; in the stem the strands lie side by side in the same radius, *i.e.*, they are conjoint, collateral. The xylem of the root is always exarch, whereas that of the stem is exarch, endarch or mesarch, being endarch most commonly in present-day plants.

ORIGIN OF THE STEM

The first stem meristem is organized during the development of the embryo. The fully developed embryo commonly consists of an axis, the **hypocotyl-root axis**. The axis bears at its upper end, one or more cotyledons and the shoot primordium, whereas at its lower end it bears the root primordium covered with a root-cap. The **radicle** (embryonic root) is found at the lower end of the hypocotyl and the embryonic shoot is found above the insertion of the cotyledons. The embryonic shoot is composed of an axis bearing unextended internodes and one or more leaf primordia. This shoot (first bud) is commonly known as **plumule** and its stem part is termed **epicotyl.** The origin of shoot organization is found in the **hypocotyl-cotyledon system** where the hypocotyl is the first stem unit of the plant and the cotyledons are the first leaves. The hypocotyl is located below the cotyledonary node, but not in between nodes. During the germination of the seed, the root meristem forms the first root, whereas the shoot meristem develops the first shoot by adding new leaves, nodes and internodes to the shoot system formed in the embryo. The lateral stems normally arise

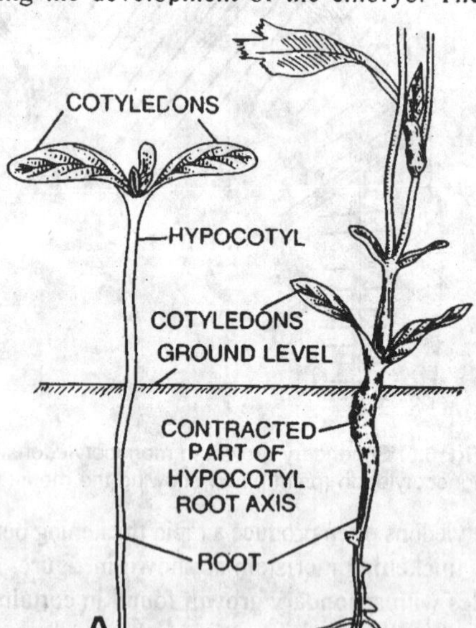

Fig. 7.1. Seedling of *Medicago sativa*. A, the younger seedling bears its cotyledons high above the ground level; B, the older seedling has pulled down the cotyledons close to the ground by contracting the hypocotyl and the upper part of the root.

by the development of new apical meristems laterally in the terminal meristem of the mother axis. The adventitious branches develop on both stem and roots, by the formation of meristems secondarily in the pericyclic, phloic or cambial regions.

ROOT-STEM TRANSITION

The root and stem make a continuous structure called the **axis** of the plant. The vascular bundles are continuous from the root to the stem. The epidermis, cortex, endodermis, pericycle and secondary vascular tissues are directly continuous in the two organs, root and stem, but the arrangement of vascular bundles is quite different in the two organs. The stems possess collateral bundles with endarch xylem, whereas the roots possess radial bundles with exarch xylem. Of course, a region exists where these changes occur and the two different types of vascular tissues

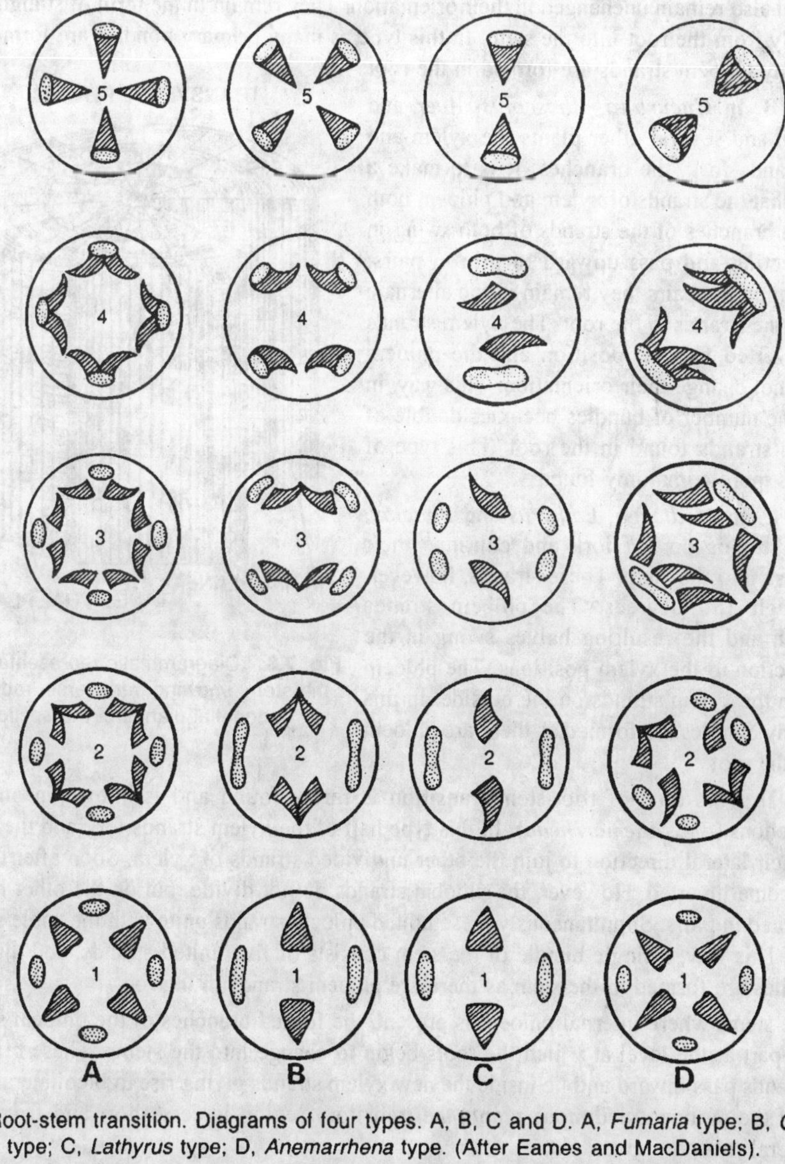

Fig. 7.2. Root-stem transition. Diagrams of four types. A, B, C and D. A, *Fumaria* type; B, *Cucurbtia* type; C, *Lathyrus* type; D, *Anemarrhena* type. (After Eames and MacDaniels).

maintain their continuity. The change of position involving inversion and twisting of xylem strands from exarch to endarch type is referred to as vascular transition, and the part of the axis where these changes occur is called **transition region.** Commonly this region is quite small and rarely of several centimetres. These changes may be found gradually or abruptly in the top of the radicle or at the base of the hypocotyl, near its middle region, or in the upper part. The phloem bundles remain practically in the same position. The transition may be of four main types which vary from species to species.

Type A. In *Mirabilis*, *Fumaria* and *Dipsacus*, and other plants each xylem strand of the root divides by radial division in the branches. As these branches pass upward, they swing in their lateral direction; one bends towards right and the other goes to the left. Simultaneously these branches join the phloem strands on the inside. The phloem strands, however, do not change their position and also remain unchanged in their orientation. They remain in the form of straight strands continuously from the root into the stem. In this type as many primary bundles are formed in the stem as many phloem strands are formed in the root.

Type B. In *Cucurbita*, *Phaseolus*, *Acer* and *Trapaeolum* and several other plants the xylem and phloem strands fork, the branches. It is to make a point here that the strands of xylem and phloem both divide. The branches of the strands of both swing in lateral direction and pass upward to join in pairs. After joining in the pairs they remain in the alternate position of the strands in the root. The xylem strands become inverted in their position and the phloem strands do not change their orientation. This way, in the stem, the number of bundles becomes double of the phloem strands found in the root. This type of transition is more commonly found.

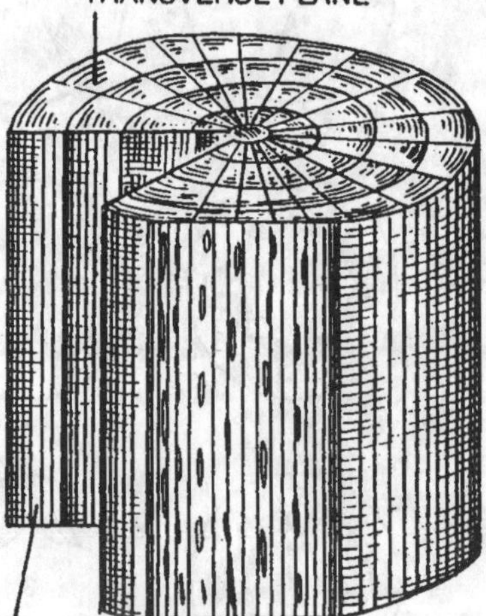

Fig. 7.3. Diagrammatic representation of the stem, showing transverse, radial and tangential planes of the section.

Type C. In *Medicago*, *Lathyrus* and *Phoenix*, the xylem strands do not fork and continue their direct course into the stem. These strands, however, twist through 180 degrees. The phloem strands divide soon and the resulting halves swing in the lateral direction to the xylem positions. The phloem strands join the xylem strands on the outside. In this type as many bundles are formed as there are phloem strands in the root.

Type D. This type of root-stem transition is rarely found and is known in only a few monocotyledons (*e.g.*, *Anemarrhena*). In this type half of the xylem strands fork and the branches swing in their lateral direction to join the other undivided strands of xylem. Soon after the xylem strands become inverted. However, the phloem strands do not divide, but on the other hand they become united in pairs. Simultaneously these united phloem strands unite with the triple strands of the xylem. This way, a single bundle of the stem consists of five united strands, and thus half as many bundles are formed in the stem as there are phloem strands in the root.

In the stems where internal phloem is present, the forked branches of the phloem strands of the root depart at the level at which the roots begin to change into the stems. These branches of phloem strands pass inward and lie inside the new xylem strands giving rise to bicollateral bundles. In some of the monocotyledonous plants the transitory region is very short and from that too several lateral roots are given out.

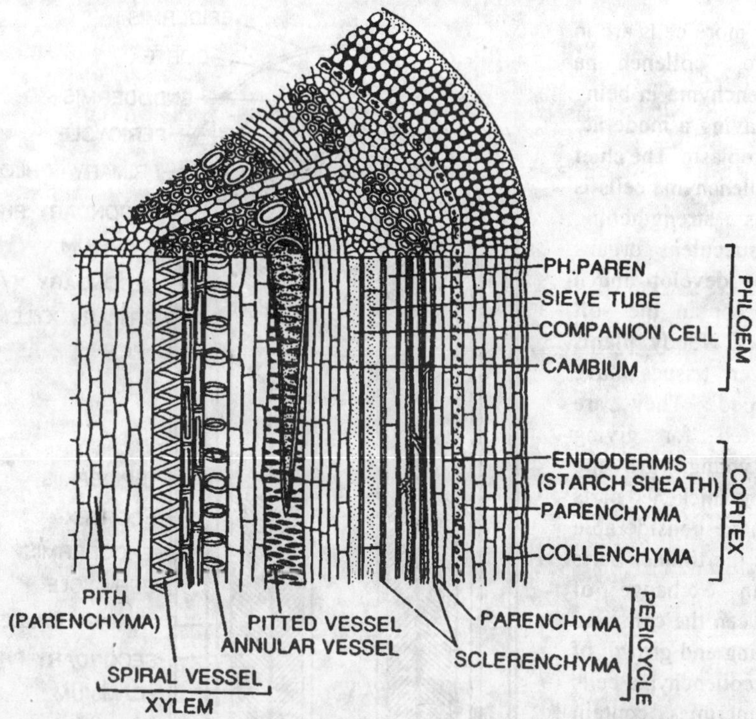

Fig. 7.4. Anatomy of dicot stem. Diagrammatic combined transverse and longitudinal sections of stem.

The seed plants are generally divided into two groups—the **angiosperms** and the **gymnosperms**. The angiosperms are further sub-divided into **dicotyledons** and **monocotyledons**. In a cross section of the stems of dicotyledons and gymnosperms the vascular bundles are found to be arranged in a ring, whereas in most of the monocotyledonous stems the vascular bundles are numerous and scattered.

ANATOMY OF DICOTYLEDONOUS STEMS

In young dicotyledonous stems there are three distinct regions—the epidermis, the cortex and the stele.

Epidermis. The epidermis consists of a single layer of cells and is the outermost layer of the stem. It contains stomata and produces various types of trichomes. The outer cell walls are greatly thickened and heavily cutinized. The cells are compactly arranged and do not possess intercellular spaces. In transverse section the cells appear almost rectangular. It serves mainly for restricting the rate of transpiration and for protecting the underlying tissues from mechanical injury and from disease-producing organisms.

Cortex. The region that lies next to the epidermis is the **cortex.** The innermost layer of the cortex is the **endodermis**, known also as the **starch-sheath.** It consists of a single layer of cells which surrounds the stele and contains numerous starch grains. Frequently it is most easily distinguishable from the surrounding tissue by the presence of these starch grains. The part of the cortex situated between the epidermis and the endodermis is generally divided into two regions, an outer zone of **collenchyma** cells and an inner zone of **parenchyma** cells.

Collenchyma. On the inside of the epidermis there is usually a band of collenchyma. The cells of the collenchyma are modified parenchyma cells with cellulose walls thickened at the angles where three or more cells are in contact. The collenchyma resembles parenchyma in being alive and in having a moderate amount of protoplasm. The chief function of collenchyma cells is to serve as strengthening material in succulent organs which do not develop much woody tissue, or in the soft young parts of woody plants before stronger tissues have been developed. They are especially fitted for giving strength to young, growing organs, since the thickened parts of the walls have considerable rigidity, while the thinner parts allow for an exchange of materials between the cells and for the stretching and growth of the cells. The collenchyma cells of stems sometimes contain chloroplasts and carry on photosynthesis.

Parenchyma. The parenchyma cells are generally regular in shape, have comparatively thin walls, and are not greatly elongated in any

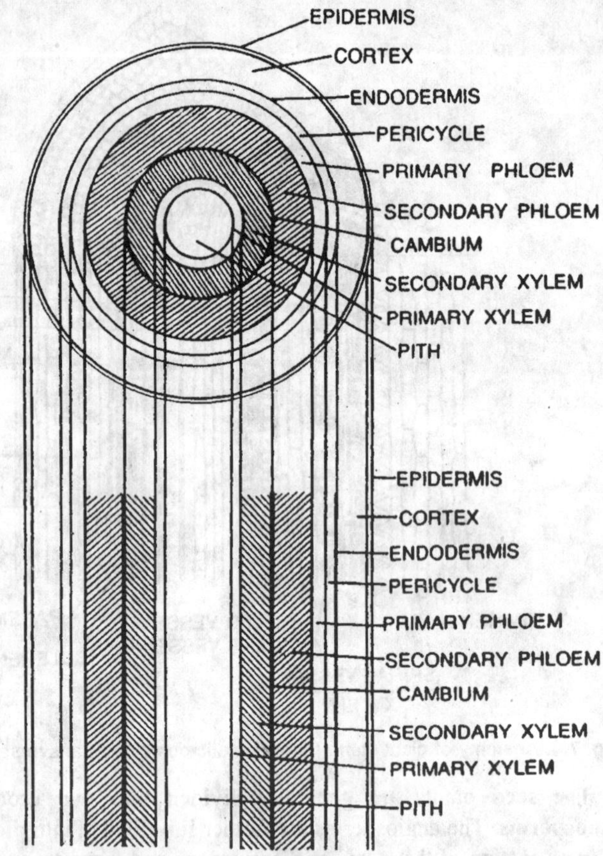

Fig. 7.5. The stem. Diagram showing structure of dicot axis. A, transverse section; B, longitudinal section. (After Eames and MacDaniels).

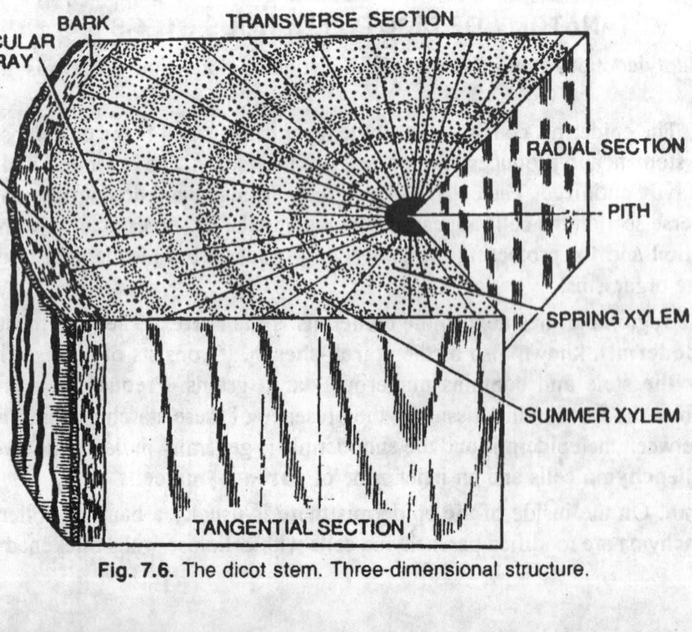

Fig. 7.6. The dicot stem. Three-dimensional structure.

direction. They are living cells and contain a moderate amount of protoplasm. When they are exposed to the light they develop chloroplasts and are known as **chlorenchyma cells.** Chlorenchyma cells are thus only a special kind of parenchyma cells. The parenchyma cells in the cortex of a stem are near enough to the light so that some or all of them develop chloroplasts and perform photosynthesis. The turgid parenchyma cells frequently help in giving rigidity to an organ. The function of parenchyma cells is important in succulent stems and in the young parts of the stems and woody plants before strong mechanical tissues have been developed. The parenchyma cells serve for the slow conduction of water and food. In the case of the cortex of stem it becomes evident that the water which is received by the collenchyma and the epidermis must be conducted through the parenchyma. The parenchyma is the special storage tissue of plants.

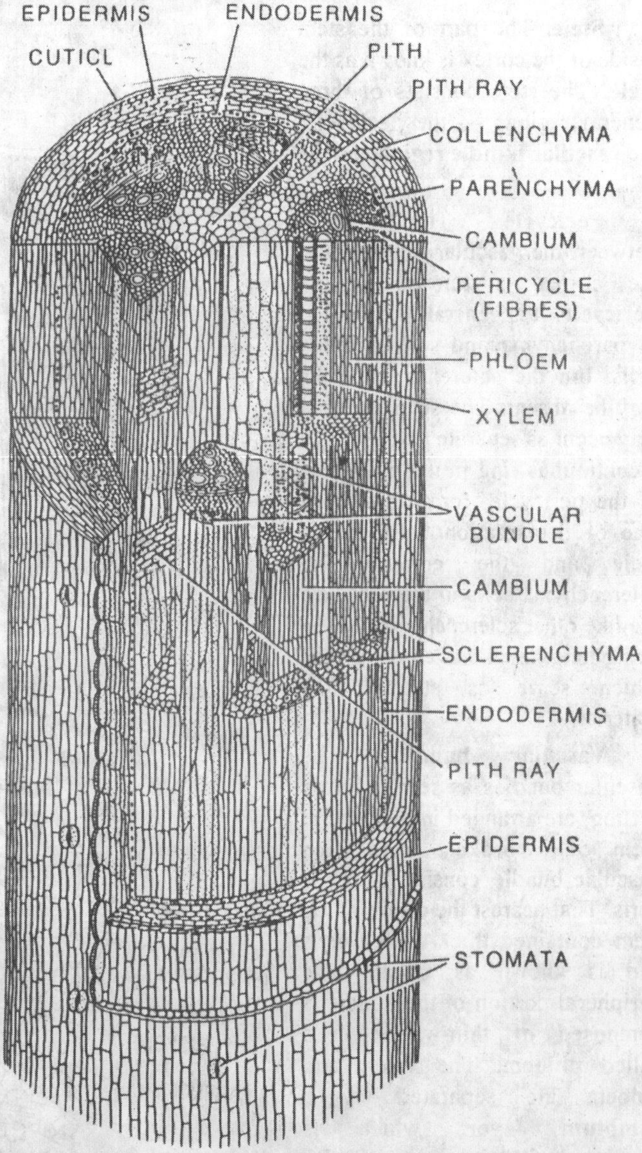

Fig. 7.7. Anatomy of dicot stem. Three dimensional diagram of a portion of an internode of a stem to show transverse, radial and tangential sections.

Sclerenchyma. The sclerenchyma cells are found in the cortex of some stems. There are two varieties of these sclerenchyma cells — short or irregularly shaped cells, known as **stone cells,** and **sclerenchyma fibres**. Sclerenchyma fibres are long, thick-walled dead cells and serve as strengthening material. Stone cells give stiffness to the cortex. The sclereids have been reported from the cortex of many water plants (*e.g.*, *Limnanthemum*, *Nymphaea,* etc.).

Endodermis. The innermost layer of the cortex is the endodermis consisting of barrel-shaped, elongated, compact cells, having no intercellular spaces among them. Usually the cells contain starch grains and thus the endodermis may be termed at starch sheath.

Stele. The part of the stem inside of the cortex is known as the **stele.** The stele consists of three general regions — the **pericycle,** the **vascular bundle region** and the **pith.**

Pericycle. The region between the vascular bundles and the cortex is known as the **pericycle.** It is generally composed of parenchyma and sclerenchyma cells, but the sclerenchyma cells may be absent. The sclerenchyma may occur as separate patches or as a continuous ring in the outer part of the pericycle, forming a sharp line of demarcation between the stele and the cortex. The sclerenchyma cells in the pericycle are like other sclerenchyma cells in being long, thick-walled dead cells which serve as strengthening material.

Vascular bundles. The vascular bundles as seen in cross section, are arranged in the general form of a broken ring. Each vascular bundle consists of three parts. That nearest the centre of the stem contained thick-walled cells and is known as **xylem.** The peripheral portion of the bundle is composed of thin-walled cells called **phloem.** The xylem and phloem are separated by a **cambium layer**, which is composed of meristematic cells. By division the cambium layer increases the size of vascular bundles by forming xylem cells on the inner side and phloem cells on the outer side. In some stems the bundles are separate and run the length of the internode. In others they are more or less united and form a hollow cylinder in which the medullary rays occur as radiating plates with slight vertical extension.

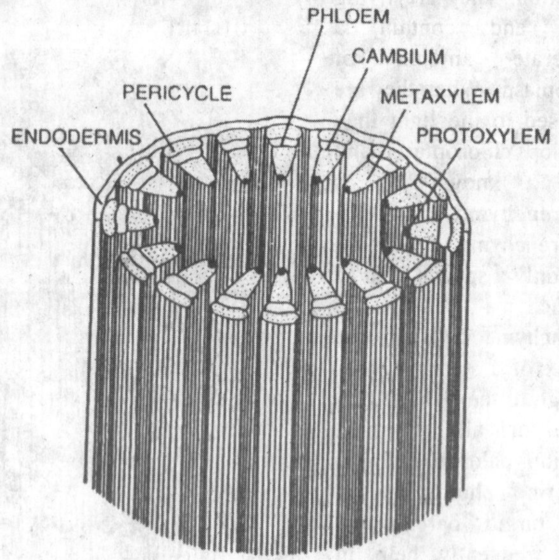

Fig. 7.8. Vascular system. Stele of a dicotyledonous stem.

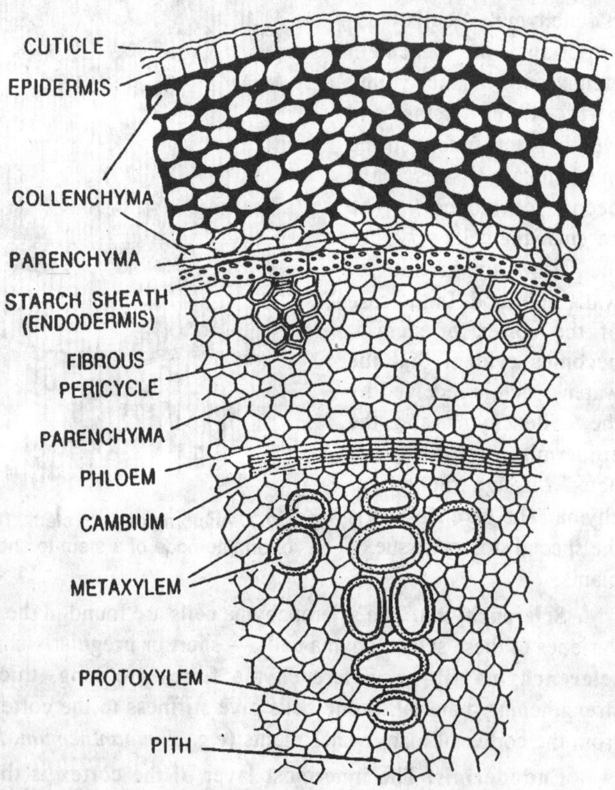

Fig. 7.9. Anatomy of dicot stem. T.S. of a sector of stem of *Ricinus communis.*

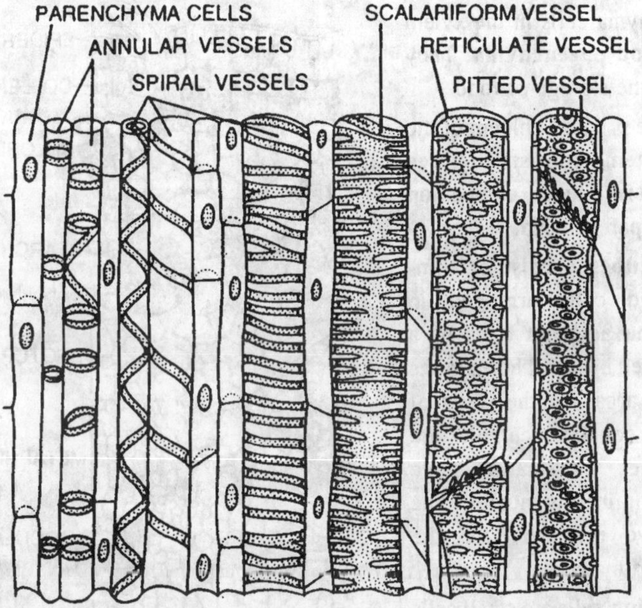

Fig. 7.10. The primary xylem. Types of vessels that occur in primary xylem in an elongating branch. Annular vessels formed first, and are therefore the oldest a more stretched. The pitted vessel formed last is the youngest. Elongation has stopped, so the pitted vessels will not be stretched.

Xylem. The xylem which is formed before the activity of the cambium has begun to produce xylem and phloem cells is called **primary xylem**. It is composed of two parts. The xylem formed first is nearest the centre of the stem and is called **protoxylem.** The more peripheral part of the primary xylem is known as **metaxylem.**

The xylem is composed of three different types of cells — tracheary cells, that include **tracheids** and **vessels; wood fibres** and **wood parenchyma.**

The **tracheids** are elongated dead cells, with walls that are thick in some places and thin in others. They serve both as water conducting and as strengthening cells. The walls of the tracheids are heavily impregnated with lignin.

The **vessels** are composed of rows of tracheary cells the cavities of which are connected by the total or partial disappearance of the cross walls. The diameter of vessels is usually much greater than that of tracheids. They form long tubes, and therefore, they constitute the principal water-conducting elements of the dicotyledonous stem.

The tracheary cells may be divided into several types according to the method by which the walls are thickened. **Annular** tracheary cells have thickenings in the form of rings, while **spiral** tracheary cells have spiral thickenings. **Pitted** tracheary cells have walls which are uniformly thickened except for thin places in the form of pits. When ladder-like thickenings are present, the vessel is said to be **scalariform.**

The protoxylem is composed largely of annular and spiral vessels and parenchyma, while the tracheary elements of the secondary xylem are pitted.

The **wood fibres** are long, slender, pointed dead cells with greatly thickened walls and only comparatively few small pits. They serve as strengthening cells. The tracheids that have a structure approaching that of wood fibres are called **fibre tracheids.**

The parenchyma cells in the xylem are known as **wood parenchyma**. They serve mainly for the storage of food.

Phloem. The primary phloem of the dicotyledonous stems consists of three types of cells — sieve tubes, companion cells and phloem parenchyma.

The **sieve tubes** consist of thin-walled, elongated cells arranged in vertical rows. The adjacent cells of a sieve tube are united by small holes in the cross walls. The areas on the walls of sieve tubes which contain such holes are called **sieve plates**. The mature sieve tubes do not contain any nuclei. The sieve tubes serve primarily for the conduction of food material.

The **companion cells** are small cells which are attached to the sieve tubes. Each companion cell is the sister cell of a sieve-tube cell, the two being formed by the division of a mother cell.

The phloem contains parenchyma cells whose structure is very similar to that of other parenchyma cells. These are known as **phloem parenchyma.**

Cambium. There lies a layer of meristematic cells between the xylem and the phloem is known as the **cambium.** The cambium consists of a single layer of cells which, by division gives rise to xylem cells toward the centre of the stem and phloem cells toward the periphery. At first the cambium is confined to the bundles, but later the parenchyma cells of the pith rays which lie between the edges of the cambium in the bundles divide and form a layer of cambium which reaches across the pith rays and connects that in the bundles, so that the cambium becomes a continuous cylinder.

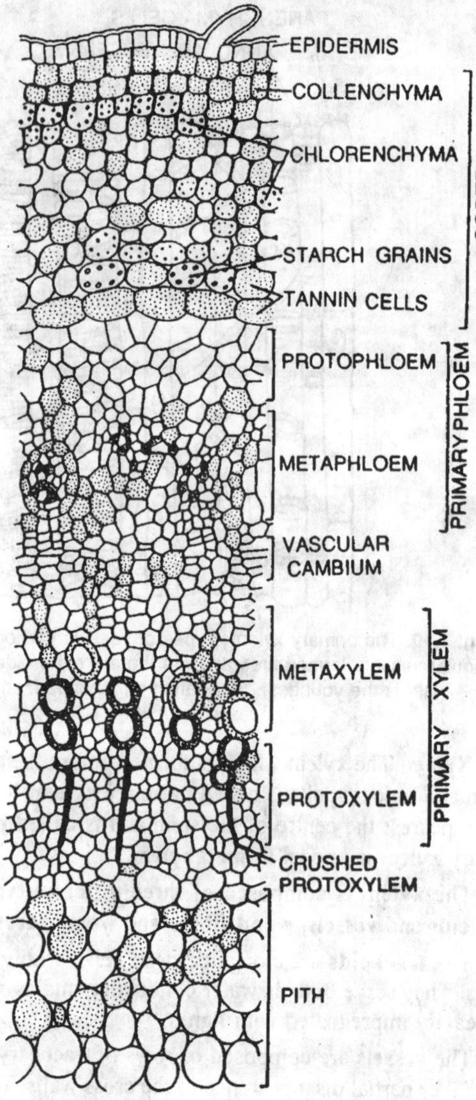

Fig. 7.11. Anatomy of dicotyledonous stem. T.S. of *Prunus* stem showing details.

Pith rays. The vascular bundles are separated from each other by radial rows of parenchyma cells known as pith rays. The pith-ray cells are usually elongated in a radial direction. They serve primarily for the conduction of food and water radially in the stem and for the storage of food.

Pith. In a dicotyledonous plant the centre of the stem is composed of thin-walled parenchyma cells and is known as the **pith.** The cells have distinct intercellular spaces.

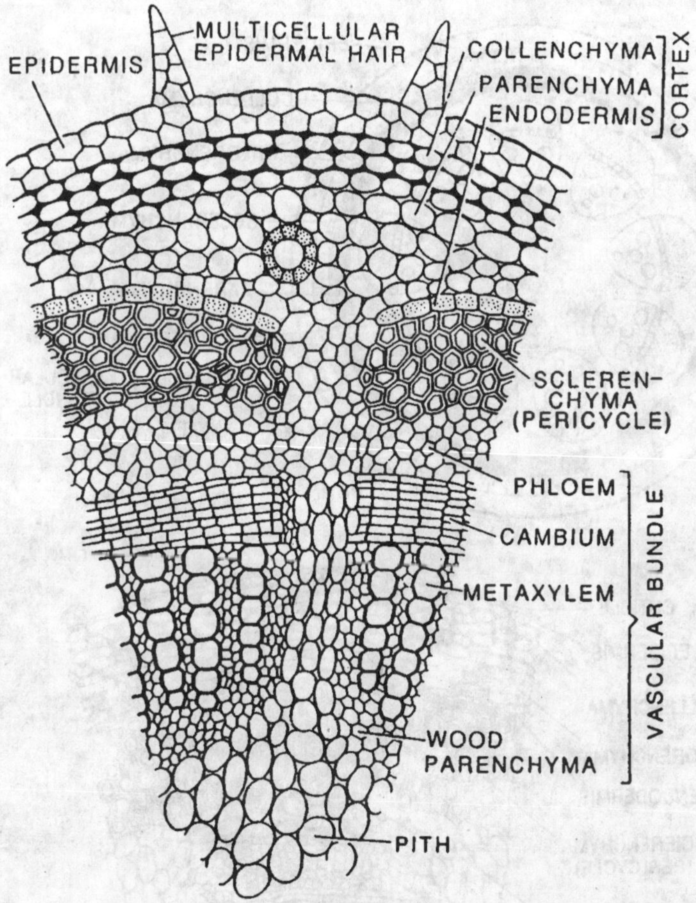

Fig. 7.12. T.S. of a dicotyledonous stem (*Helianthus annuus*).

VARIATIONS IN STEM STRUCTURE

The above mentioned description of structure of the stems is applicable to the great majority of dicotyledonous plants, but there are a few which show minor variations. The relative development of the various parts, however, varies greatly in different species. In some cases the pith is wide, while in others it is narrow. It may be wide and transitory and its early disappearance results in a hollow stem. The vascular bundles vary considerably in number and size, while the pith rays and cortex vary in width. Bundles which have the phloem only on the outside of the xylem are called **collateral** bundles. The bundles of some plants have phloem on both the outside and the inside of the xylem (*e.g.*, in the members of Cucurbitaceae) and known as **bicollateral** bundles.

ANATOMY OF *CUCURBITA* STEM

Epidermis. This single outermost layer consists of compact barrel shaped cells having no intercellular spaces. The epidermis remains covered with a thin cuticle. Some of the epidermal cells possess multicellular epidermal hairs.

Cortex. This region consists of external collenchyma, chlorenchyma (photosynthetic tissue) and endodermis.

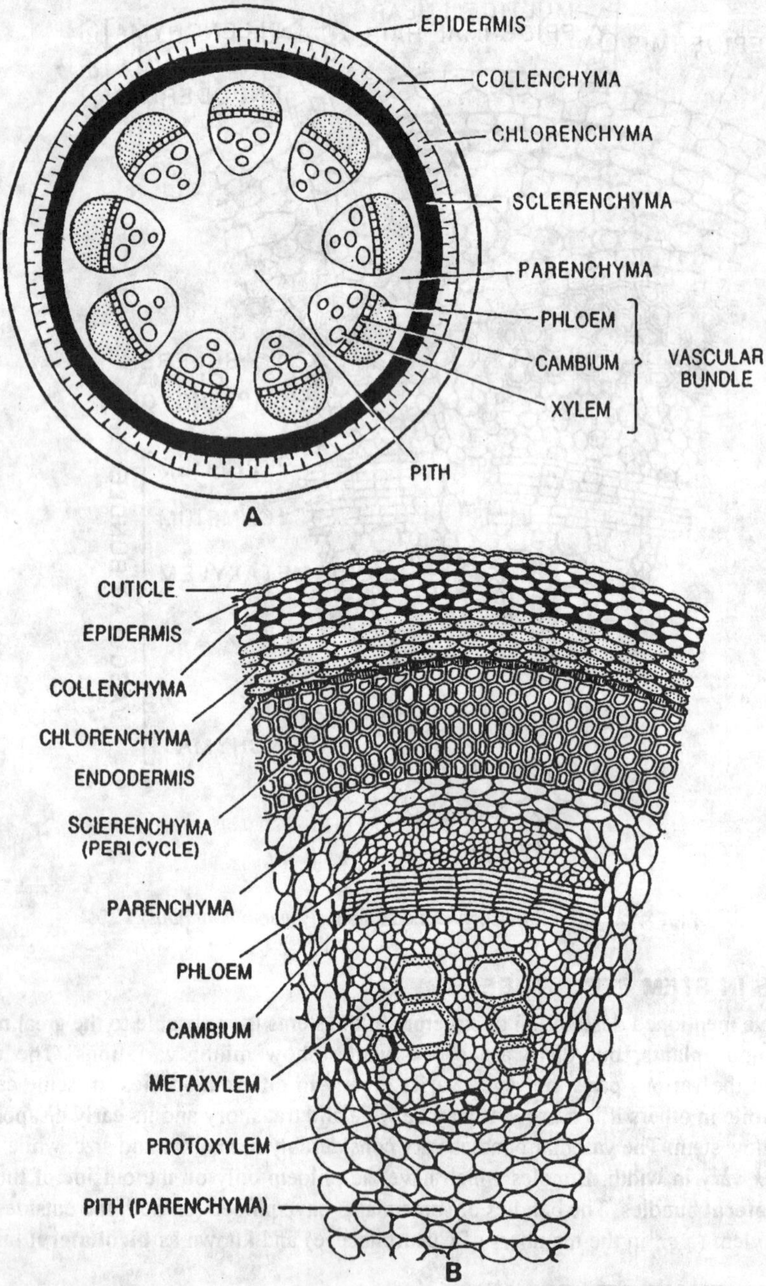

Fig. 7.13. Anatomy of dicot stem. T.S. of young stem of *Aristolochia*. A, diagrammatic; B, detail of a sector.

***(a)* Collenchyma.** This lies immediately beneath the epidermis consisting of many layers of the cells in the ridges, whereas in furrows it is only two or three layered or sometimes altogether absent.

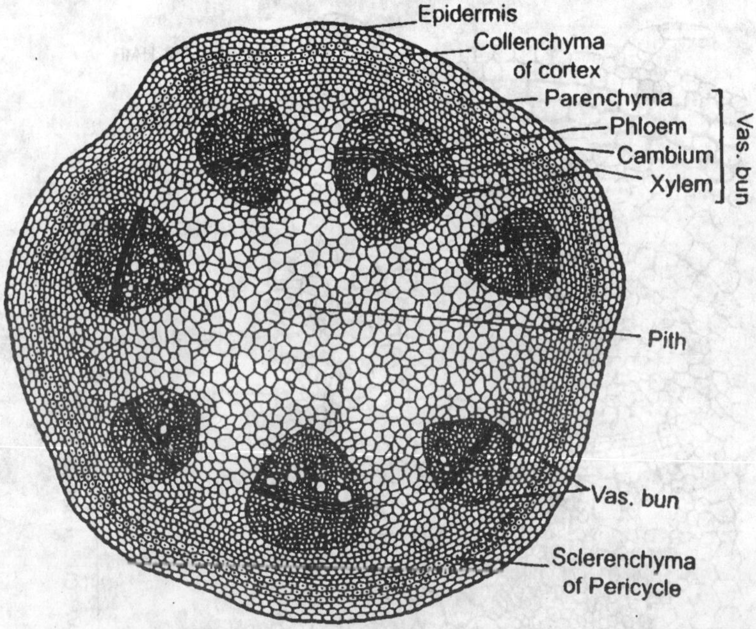

Fig. 7.14. The stem. Cross section of a young stem of *Aristolochia*. Just beneath the uniseriate layer of epidermis a few layers (2 or 3) of collenchyma are present. Chlorenchyma is also visible. The pericyclic region consists of a continuous band of sclerenchyma. Seven bundles are arranged in a ring. Each bundle shows typical dicot characteristics. Pith is large and conspicuous.

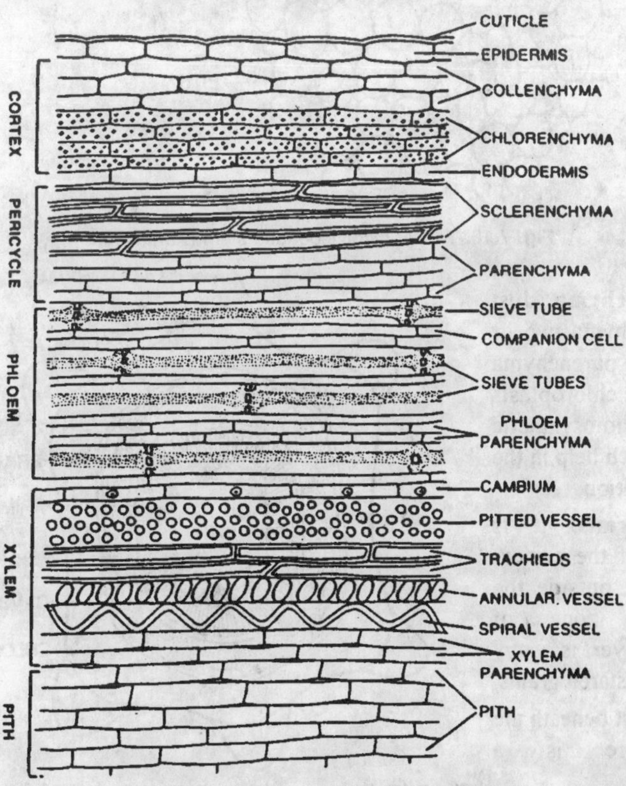

Fig. 7.15. L.S. of stem of *Aristolochia*.

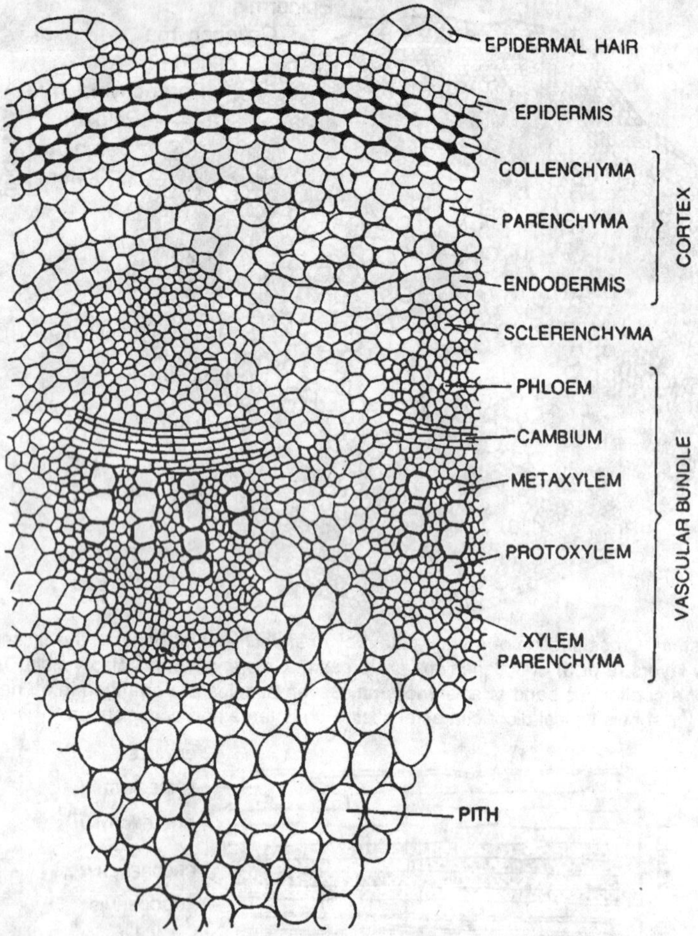

Fig. 7.16. T.S. of dicotyledonous stem (*Xanthium*).

(b) Chlorenchyma. Just below the collenchyma two or three layers of parenchyma containing chloroplasts (chlorenchyma—photosynthetic tissue) present which help in the process of assimilation.

(c) Endodermis. It is innermost layer of the cortex, lying immediately outside the sclerenchymatous zone of pericycle. This layer is wavy and contains many starch grains.

Pericycle. Just beneath the endodermis there is a

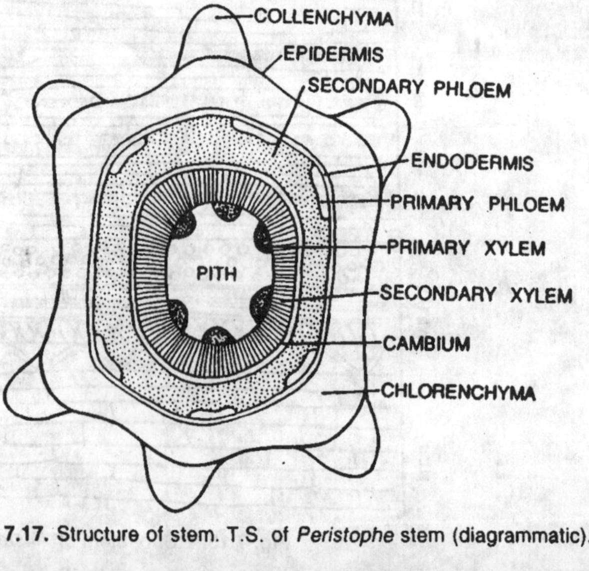

Fig. 7.17. Structure of stem. T.S. of *Peristophe* stem (diagrammatic).

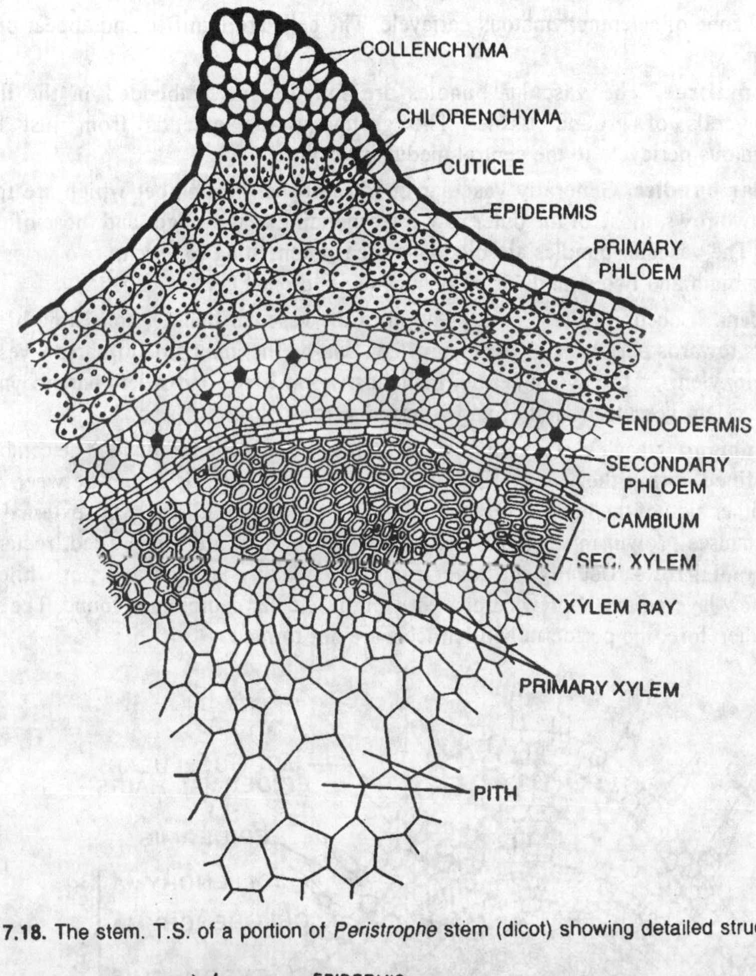

Fig. 7.18. The stem. T.S. of a portion of *Peristrophe* stem (dicot) showing detailed structure.

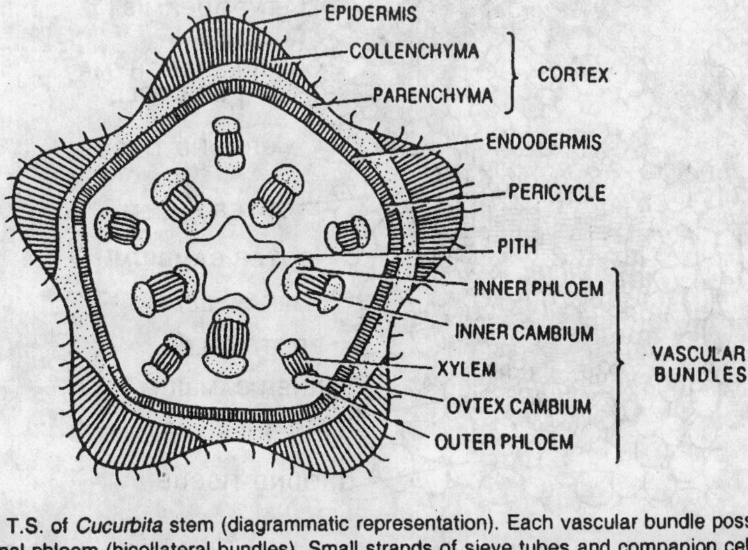

Fig. 7.19. T.S. of *Cucurbita* stem (diagrammatic representation). Each vascular bundle possesses external and internal phloem (bicollateral bundles). Small strands of sieve tubes and companion cells traverse the parenchyma of the vascular region and the tissues of the cortex. (After K. Esau).

multilayered zone of sclerenchymatous pericycle. The cells are lignified and appear polygonal in cross section.

Ground tissue. The vascular bundles are found lying embedded in the thin walled parenchyma cells of ground tissue. The ground tissue extends from just below the sclerenchymatous pericycle to the central medullary cavity.

Vascular bundles. Generally vascular bundles are ten in number which are found to be arranged in two rows, those of the outer row corresponding to the ridges and those of the inner to the furrows. The vascular bundles are bicollateral each consisting of xylem, two strips (inner and outer) of cambium and two strands of phloem (inner and outer).

(*a*) Xylem. It occupies the central position of the vascular bundle, consisting of very wide, pitted vessels towards periphery of the metaxylem, and on the inner side of narrow vessels which form the protoxylem. In the xylem certain tracheids, wood fibres and xylem parenchyma are also present. The xylem vessels are not arranged in radial rows.

(*b*) Cambium. In each vascular bundle two strips of cambium are found. The cambial activity remains confined within the vascular bundles. The cambial strip is found between xylem and phloem on either side of the bundle. Of the two strips of cambium it is only the external one which divides and causes growth in thickness. The cells of cambium are thin walled, rectangular and arranged in radial rows. Usually the outer cambium is many layered and flat while the inner cambium is few layered and somewhat curved. Only fascicular cambium is found. The stem is not woody, and therefore, the periderm and lenticels are not formed.

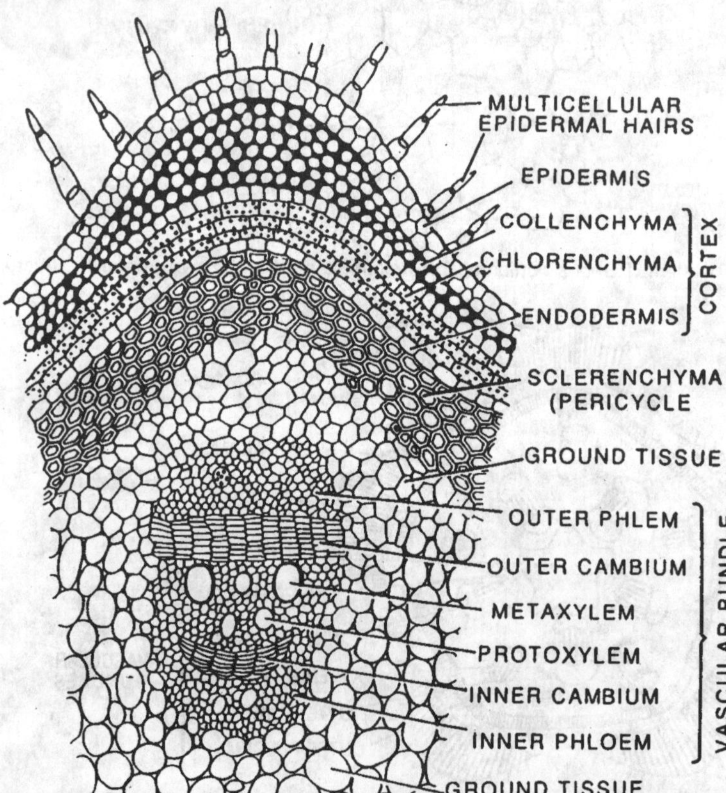

Fig. 7.20. T.S. of young *Cucurbita* stem (dicotyledonous) showing bicollateral vascular bundle.

(*c*) **Phloem.** On the extreme ends of the vascular bundle the phloem occurs in two patches, towards the periphery, the outer phloem, and towards pith, the inner phloem. Each strand of phloem consists of sieve tubes, companion cells and phloem parenchyma. Sieve tubes are very well developed. The sieve plates with perforations are also visible. Fibres and ray cells are absent.

Special Structure

The bicollateral open vascular bundles are found each consisting of xylem (central position), two strips of cambium (outer and inner) and two patches of phloem (outer and inner). (See figs. 7.19 and 7.20).

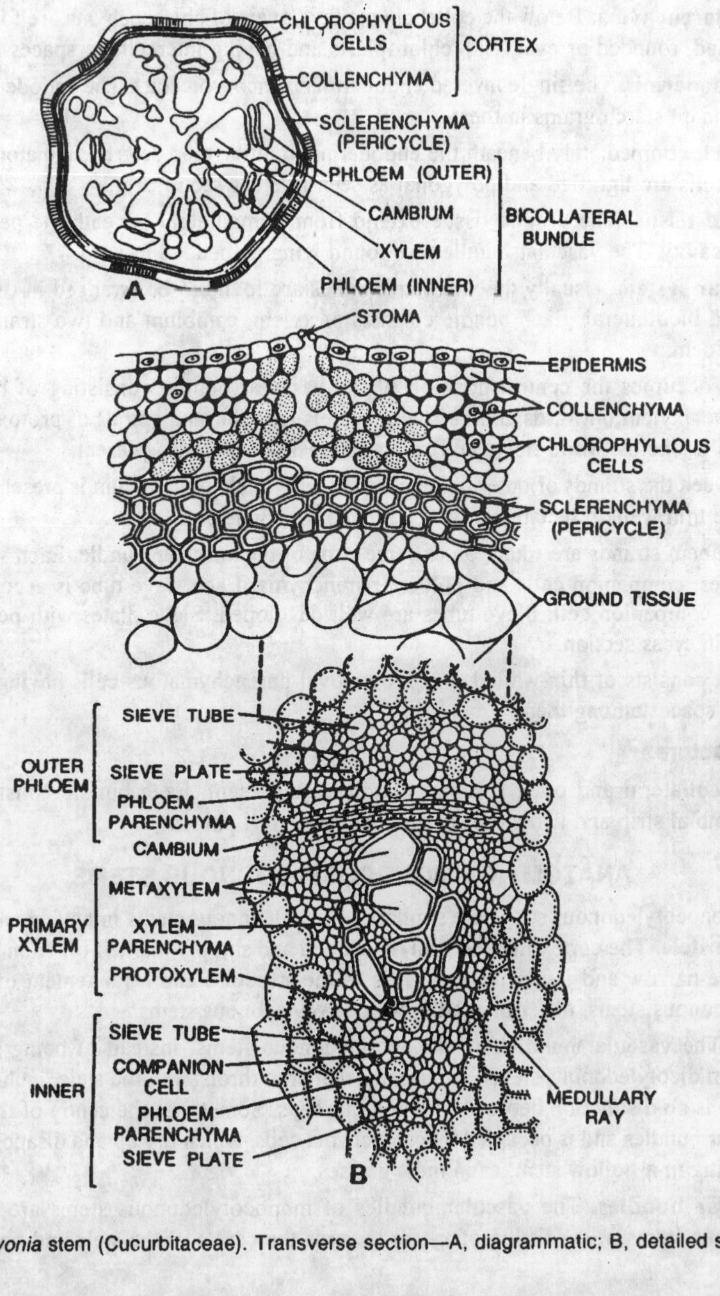

Fig. 7.21. *Bryonia* stem (Cucurbitaceae). Transverse section—A, diagrammatic; B, detailed structure.

ANATOMY OF *BRYONIA* STEM

Epidermis. The single outermost layer consists of compact barrel shaped cells having no intercellular spaces. Usually the epidermis is covered with a thin cuticle. At certain places stomata are also found.

Cortex. This consists of collenchyma, loose chlorenchyma and inconspicuous endodermis.

(*a*) Collenchyma. This lies immediately beneath the epidermis consisting of rounded or oval cells (in cross section) usually thickened laterally due to the presence of cellulose. The collenchymatous region is multilayered.

(*b*) Chlorenchyma. Below the collenchyma few layers of chlorenchyma are found. The cells are thin walled, rounded or oval, with chloroplasts and having intercellular spaces among them.

(*c*) Endodermis. The single layered endodermis is inconspicuous. The endodermal cells may contain abundant starch grains in them.

Pericycle. Immediately beneath the endodermis multilayered sclerenchymatous pericycle is found. The cells are lignified and polygonal as seen in cross section.

Ground tissue. The ground tissue extend from immediately beneath the pericycle to the central pith cavity. The vascular bundles are found lying embedded in it.

Vascular system. Usually the vascular bundles are found to be arranged in two rows. They are open and bicollateral. Each bundle consists of xylem, cambium and two strands (inner and outer) of phloem.

Xylem occupies the central position of the vascular bundle consisting of bigger vessels (pitted) of metaxylem outwards and narrower vessels (annular and spiral) of protoxylem towards pith. Certain tracheids, wood fibres and xylem parenchyma are also present.

In between the strands of outer phloem and xylem a strip of cambium is present. The cells of cambium are thin walled, rectangular and arranged in radial rows.

The phloem strands are found on extreme ends of the vascular bundle. Each strand consists of sieve tubes, companion cells and phloem parenchyma. Each sieve tube is accompanied by a conspicuous companion cell. Sieve tubes are well developed. Sieve plates with perforations are also visible in cross section.

Pith. It consists of thin-walled rounded or oval parenchymatous cells having well defined intercellular spaces among them.

Special Structure

The bicollateral and open vascular bundles are present. Each bundle consists of central xylem, a cambial strip and two strands (inner and outer) of phloem.

ANATOMY OF MONOCOTYLEDONOUS STEMS

The monocotyledonous stems are similar to dicotyledonous stems in having an **epidermis**, a **cortex** and a **stele**. The cortex may be well developed and sharply marked off from the stele, or it may be quite narrow and inconspicuous. It is in the structure and arrangement of bundles that monocotyledonous stems, differ markedly from dicotyledonous stems.

Stele. The vascular bundles of monocotyledonous stems, instead of being arranged in a cylinder as in dicotyledonous stems, are usually scattered throughout the stele, including the pith, so that there is no distinction between pith and pith rays. Sometimes the centre of the stele is free from vascular bundles and is occupied by parenchyma cells, which dry up and disappear at an early stage, resulting in a hollow stem, as in most grasses.

Vascular bundles. The vascular bundles of monocotyledonous stems are like those of dicotyledonous stems in consisting of xylem towards the centre of the stele and phloem towards

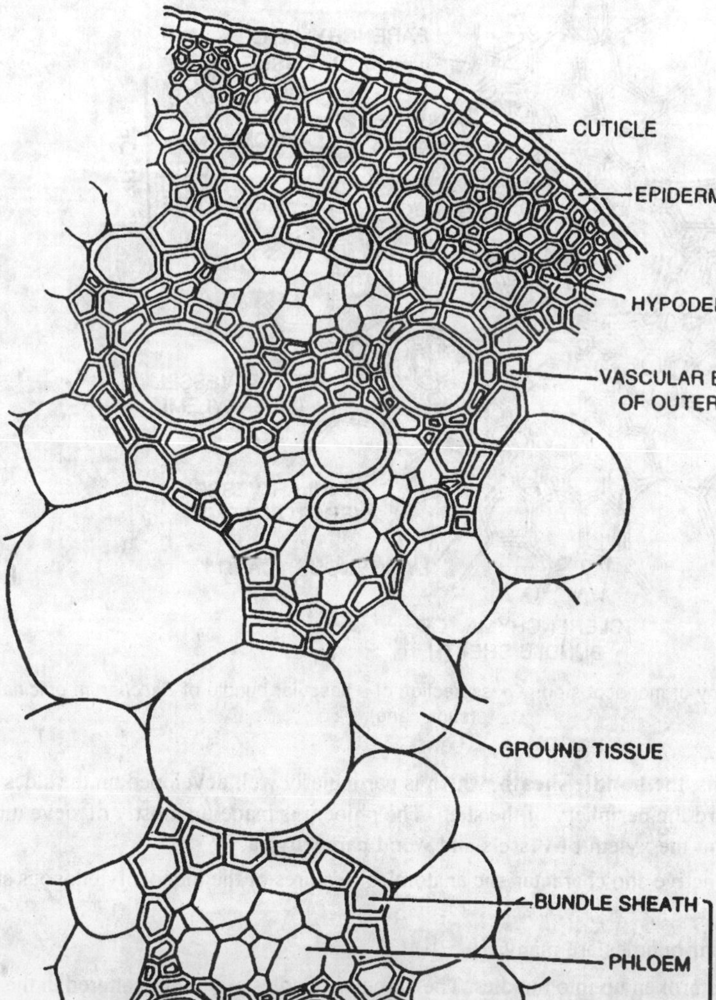

Fig. 7.22. T.S. of a portion of stem of grass (*Cynodon dactylon*) typical monocot stem, showing **detailed** internal structure.

the periphery. The vascular bundles of monocotyledonous stems do not possess a cambium layer which is found in dicotyledonous stems. This means that monocotyledonous stems usually do not have secondary thickening. Each bundle remains more or less completely surrounded by a sheath

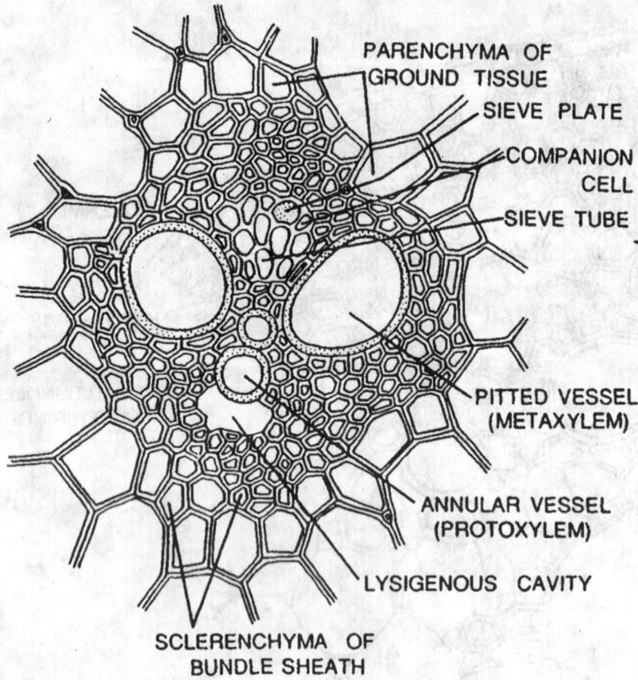

Fig. 7.23. Anatomy of monocot stem. Cross section of a vascular bundle of *Saccharum officinarum* (sugarcane).

of sclerenchyma cells, the **bundle sheath,** which is particularly well developed on the sides toward the centre and toward the periphery of the stem. The phloem is made up mostly of sieve tubes and companion cells, and the xylem of vessels and wood parenchyma.

The most distinctive and characteristic anatomical features of the monocotyledonous stem are as follows:

1. The vascular bundles are many.
2. The stele is broken up into bundles. The vascular bundles are lying scattered in the ground tissue of the axis.
3. The endodermis is not found. The cortex, pericycle and pith are not differentiated because of the presence of scattered bundles throughout the axis.
4. The vascular bundles are collateral and closed. The secondary growth of usual type is lacking, but vestiges of cambial activity in bundles may present in the plant body.
5. Leaf trace bundles are numerous. The leaf traces when enter the stem, penetrate deeply. The median traces penetrate more deeply than lateral. The bundles are common. Each common bundle somehow or other fuses with other bundle in the due course of time. The anastamoses occur at the nodes.
6. Each vascular bundle remains surrounded by a well developed sclerenchymatous sheath.
7. The vascular bundles are commonly oval shaped.
8. The phloem is represented by sieve tubes and companion cells only. The phloem parenchyma is not found.

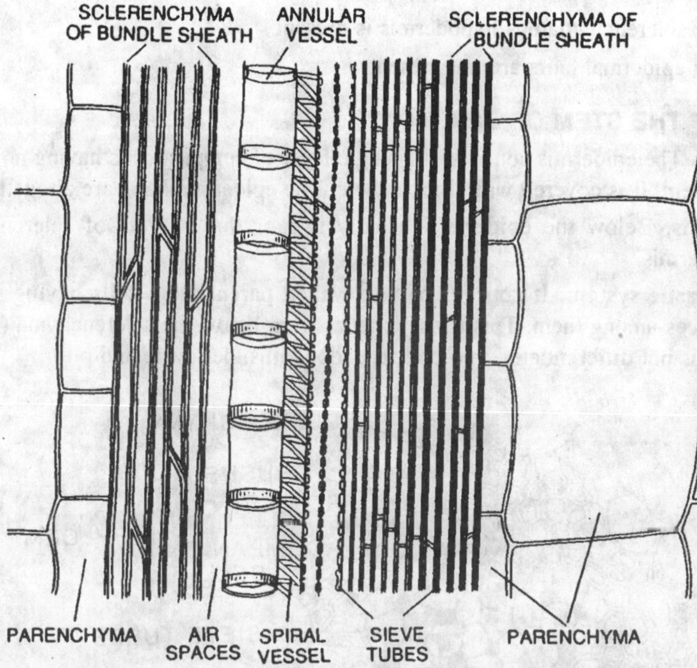

Fig. 7.24. Anatomy of monocot stem. L.S. of a vascular bundle of *Saccharum officinarum* (sugarcane).

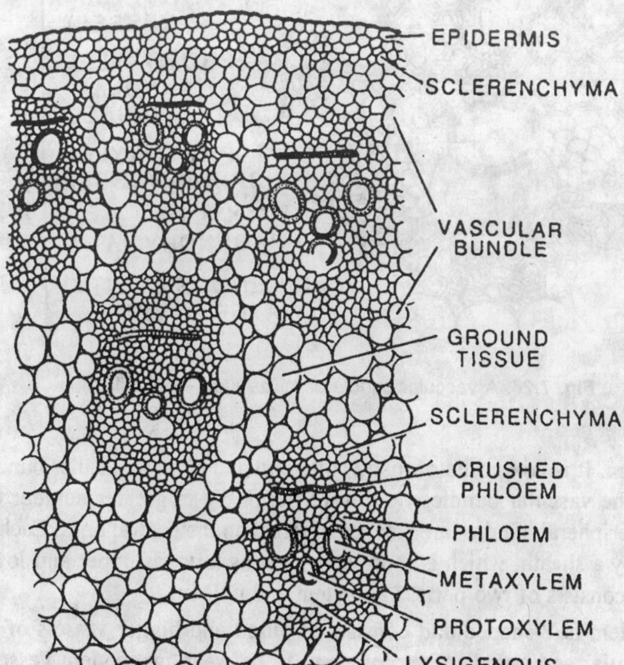

Fig. 7.25. The monocotyledonous stem. T.S. of maize stem showing sclerenchymatous hypodermis, parenchymatous ground tissue and vascular bundles.

9. The pith is not marked out.
10. Usually sclerenchymatous hypodermis is present.
11. Usually epidermal hairs are not present.

ANATOMY OF THE STEM OF *ZEA MAYS*

Epidermis. The epidermis consists of a single layer of compact cells having no intercellular spaces among them. It is covered with thick cuticle. The epidermal hairs are altogether absent.

Hypodermis. Below the epidermis, usually two or three layers of sclerenchyma cells represent hypodermis.

Ground tissue system. It consists of thin walled parenchyma cells having well-defined intercellular spaces among them. This tissue extends from below the sclerenchyma (hypodermis) to the centre. It is not differentiated into cortex, endodermis, pericycle and pith.

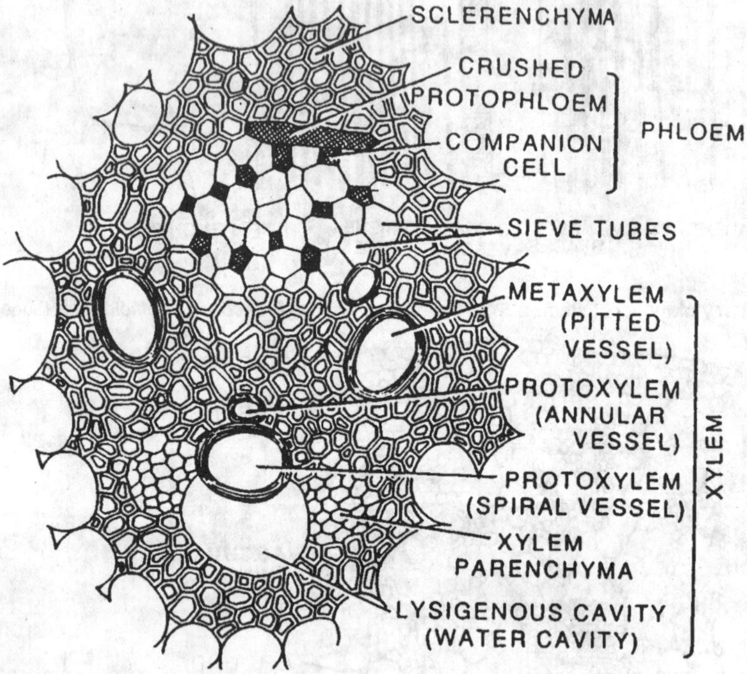

Fig. 7.26. A vascular bundle of maize stem—magnified.

Vascular system. It is composed of many collateral and closed vascular bundles scattered in the ground tissue. The vascular bundles lie toward periphery in greater number than the centre. Comparatively the peripheral bundles are smaller in size than the central ones. Each bundle is more or less surrounded by a sheath, which is more conspicuous towards upper and lower sides of the bundle. The bundle consists of two parts, *i.e.*, xylem and phloem.

Usually the xylem is Y-shaped and consists of pitted and bigger vessels of metaxylem and smaller vessels (annular and spiral) of protoxylem. In between metaxylem vessels, small pitted

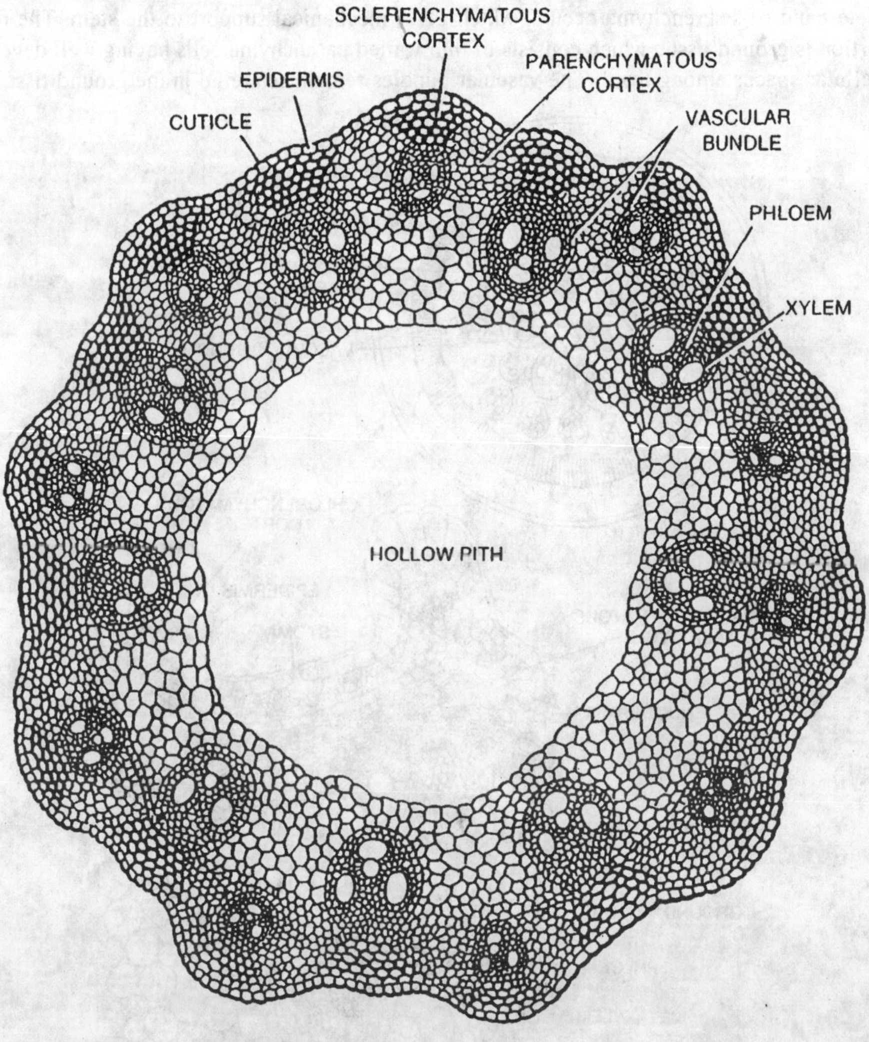

Fig. 7.27. T.S. of stem of *Avena sativa* (oat), showing hollow pith in the centre.

tracheids are also found. Around the lysigenous or water cavity wood parenchyma is present. The lysigenous cavity is formed by the breaking down of the inner protoxylem vessel.

Phloem consists of sieve tubes and companion cells. Phloem parenchyma is altogether absent in most of monocotyledonous stems. The outer phloem which is broken mass may be called as protophloem and the inner portion is metaphloem. Sieve tubes and companion cells are quite conspicuous.

ANATOMY OF THE STEM OF *ASPARAGUS*

Epidermis. It is outermost uniseriate layer composed of approximately rounded cells with cuticularized outer walls.

Ground tissue system. Just beneath the epidermis a few layers of parenchyma are found which contain chloroplasts in them. This may be called **cortex.** The innermost layer of the cortex consists of compact cells and called the **starch sheath.** Below the starch sheath a multilayered complete band of sclerenchyma occurs, which gives mechanical support to the stem. The rest of the portion is ground tissue which consists of thin walled parenchyma cells having well developed intercellular spaces among them. The vascular bundles remain scattered in the ground tissue.

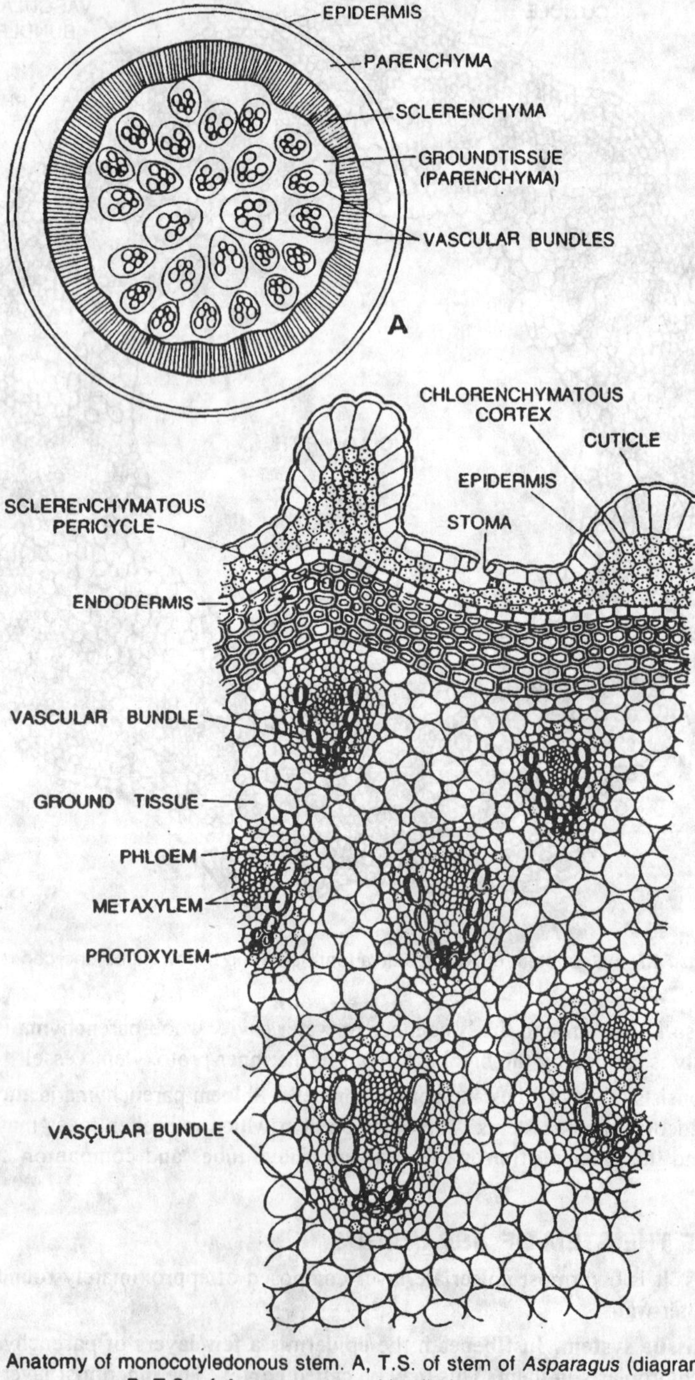

Fig. 7.28. Anatomy of monocotyledonous stem. A, T.S. of stem of *Asparagus* (diagrammatic); B, T.S. of *Asparagus* stem (detailed structure).

Vascular system. The vascular bundles remain scattered in the ground tissue. The central bundles are comparatively larger than the peripheral ones. They are always collateral and closed. Each vascular bundle consists of xylem and phloem. The xylem is Y-shaped. The metaxylem vessels form arms of Y and protoxylem, the base. Phloem consists of sieve tubes and companion cells. Bundle sheath is not found.

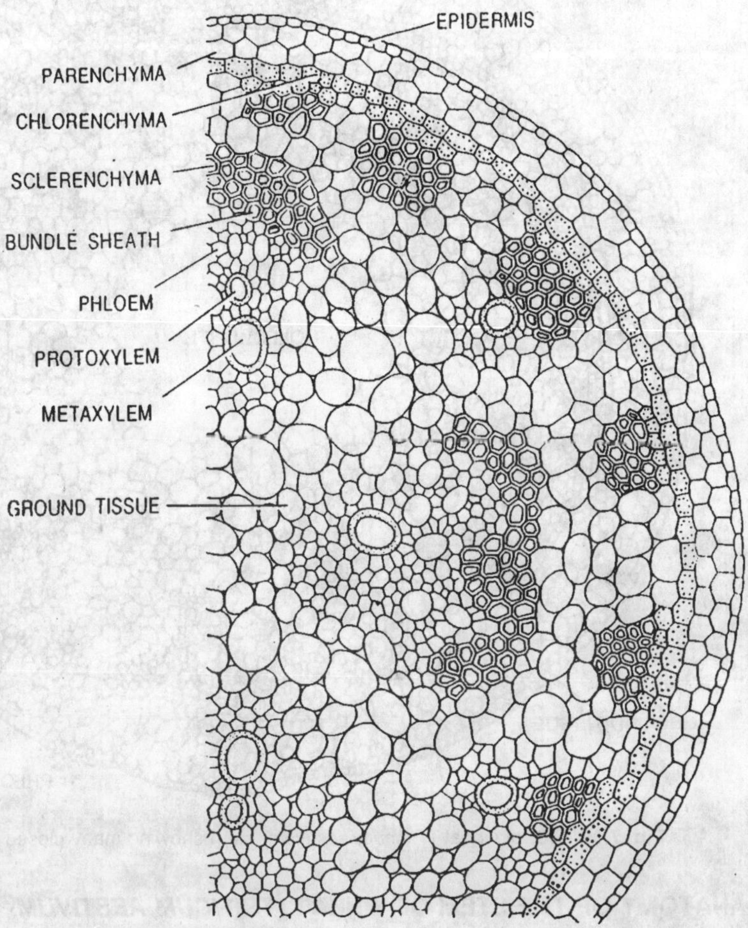

Fig. 7.29. The monocotyledonous stem. T.S. of scape of *Canna*.

ANATOMY OF THE SCAPE OF *CANNA*

Epidermis. It is the outermost uniseriate layer consisting of small, polygonal cells with cuticularized outer walls.

Ground tissue system. Just beneath the epidermis a few layers of parenchyma occur forming small cortical region. The cells of cortex are sufficiently large and polygonal. Immediately below the cortex, a single-layered chlorophyllous tissue is found consisting of chloroplast bearing cells. The sclerenchyma patches also remain attached to the chlorophyllous tissue here and there. The rest of the portion consists of a continuous mass of large, thin walled, parenchymatous cells having sufficiently developed intercellular spaces among them. It is called the ground tissue.

Vascular bundles. They are many and of various sizes, lying scattered in the ground tissue. The bundles are closed and collateral. Each bundle is incompletely surrounded by a sheath of sclerenchyma called **bundle sheath.** The outer sclerenchyma patch of the bundle is more distinct and cap like whereas inner patch is not so developed. Each bundle consists of xylem and phloem. The xylem is situated on the inner side and the phloem towards outer side. The xylem consists of a large spiral vessel with one or two smaller vessels of same nature. The phloem consists of sieve tubes and campanion cells.

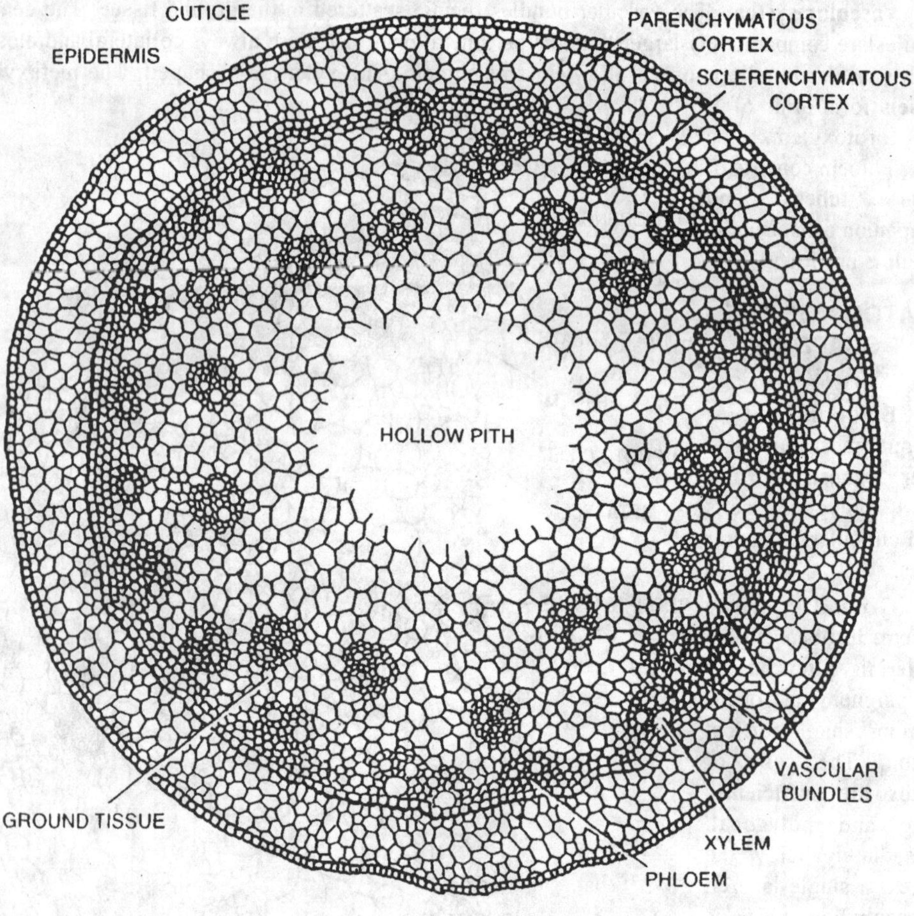

Fig. 7.30. T.S. of wheat (*Triticum aestivum*) stem showing many closed vascular bundles.

ANATOMY OF THE STEM OF WHEAT (*TRITICUM AESTIVUM*)

Epidermis. It is the outermost uniseriate layer, usually composed of compact tabular cells with cuticularized outer walls. The stomata are also seen here and there on the epidermis.

Ground tissue system. Just beneath the epidermis the sclerenchyma cells occur in small patches which are not arranged in a continuous band, but are interrupted by chlorenchyma tissue here and there. The stomata are confined on the epidermis only in chlorenchymatous regions. The rest of the ground tissue consists of thin walled rounded or oval parenchyma cells having sufficiently developed intercellular spaces among them. The central region of the stem is hollow.

Vascular bundles. The closed and collateral vascular bundles occur in two series. The peripheral series consists of smaller bundles, whereas the inner series is of bigger bundles. The vascular bundles of outer series are lying embedded in sclerenchyma band. The bundles of inner series are also surrounded by sclerenchymatous bundle sheath like that of maize stem. The bundle sheath of peripheral bundles actually touches the epidermis.

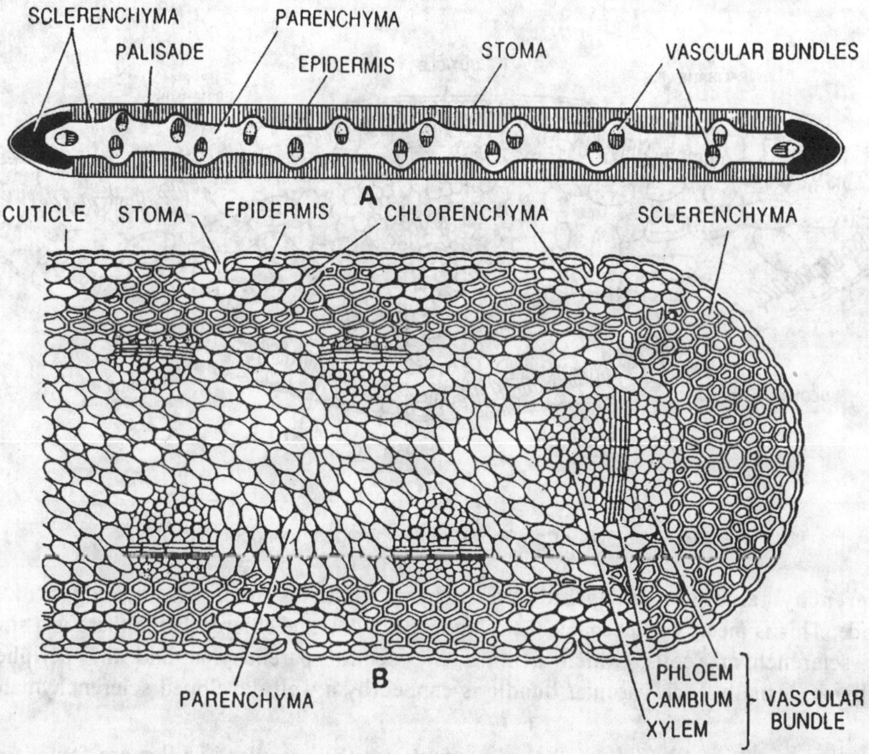

Fig. 7.31. *Homalocladium platycladum* (*Muehlenbeckia platycladus*)—phylloclade (dicot.). A. transection of phylloclade (diagrammatic); B, transaction of phylloclade showing detailed structure. The stomata, the cambium, the vascular bundles, the sclerenchyma and the chlorophyllous cells are clearly visible.

ANATOMY OF THE PHYLLOCLADE

Numerous stems are specialized for photosynthesis and take the place of leaves in the manufacture of carbohydrates. Some stems which are specialized for photosynthesis are round (*e.g., Casuarina, Euphorbia tirucalli,* etc.), others are flattened (*e.g.,* Cocoloba-*Muehlenbeckia platyclada*), and others even have the form of leaves (*e.g., Ruscus, Myrsiphyllum, Phyllocladus protractus,* etc.). Such stems as those of cacti (*e.g., Opuntia, Carnegiea,* etc.) are specialized both for photosynthesis and for water storage. In the following paragraphs, the anatomy of the phylloclade of cocoloba—(*Muehlenbeckia platyclada—Homalocladium platycladum*) and *Ruscus* has been discussed.

ANATOMY OF THE PHYLLOCLADE OF COCOLOBA (*HOMALOCLADIUM-PLATYCLADUM—MUEHLENBECKIA PLATYCLADA*). DICOT.

Epidermis. The surfaces are bounded on both the sides by upper and lower epidermal layers. A thin cuticle covers the epidermis. The epidermis is interrupted by numerous stomata on both the surfaces. Distinct guard cells of the stomata and sub-stomatal chambers are visible.

Chlorenchyma. Just beneath the epidermis there are few layers of chlorophyllous cells. The chlorophyllous cells are found only underneath the upper and lower epidermal layers. However, the chlorenchyma is not found at the edges of the phylloclade. The stomata are confined to chlorophyllous regions. There are well developed intercellular spaces among these cells. This is assimilatory tissue.

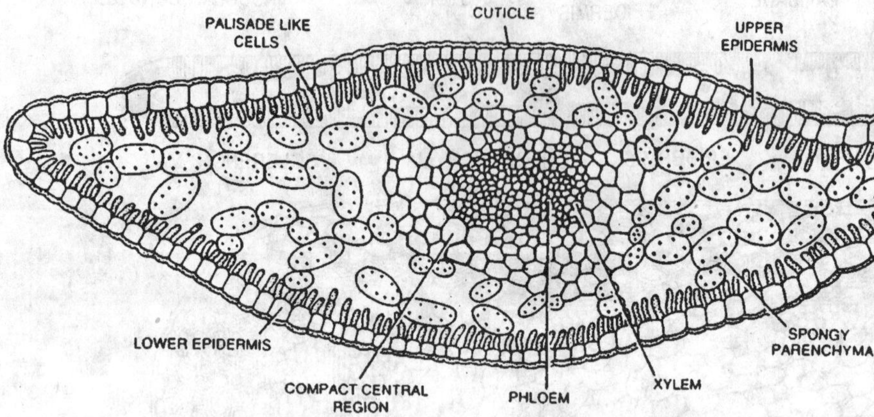

Fig. 7.32. T.S. of phylloclade of *Asparagus* (monocot).

Sclerenchyma. The multilayered sclerenchyma tissue is found at the edges of the phylloclade. This is meant for mechanical strength. Just below the chlorenchyma there is a single layer of sclerenchyma cells, which delimits the central parenchyma and the peripheral chlorenchyma. Usually each vascular bundle is capped by a well developed sclerenchymatous patch.

Vascular bundles. Around the central parenchyma the vascular bundles are found to be arranged in the peripheral region. The vascular bundles of the two corners are bigger in size than the remaining ones. Each vascular bundle is capped by a sclerenchymatous patch, and is composed of xylem, phloem and cambium. The xylem consists of metaxylem and protoxylem groups. The xylem parenchyma is also present. The phloem strand lies towards periphery. The phloem is composed of sieve tubes, companion cells and phloem parenchyma. In between xylem and phloem strands there lies the cambium. The cambium is confined to the bundle.

Parenchyma. The central region is occupied by parenchyma. It is composed of thin-walled, rounded or oval, living cells having well developed intercellular spaces. This is storage tissue.

ANATOMY OF THE PHYLLOCLADE OF *RUSCUS* (MONOCOT)

Epidermis. The phylloclade possesses two surfaces (upper and lower). Both the surfaces remain bounded by upper and lower epidermal layers. The upper epidermis consists of a single row of radially elongated epidermal cells. The epidermis is interrupted by stomata at certain places. The sub-stomatal chambers and guard cells with chloroplasts are distinctly seen. The upper surface becomes somewhat bulged in the central region. The lower surface in the central region becomes somewhat angular, otherwise the anatomy of the lower epidermis is quite similar to that of upper epidermis.

Chlorenchyma. Immediately below the upper epidermis few layers of chlorophyllous cells are present. These cells are rounded or oval shaped, containing chloroplasts and having well developed intercellular spaces among them. In between upper and lower epidermis the well developed parenchyma is present.

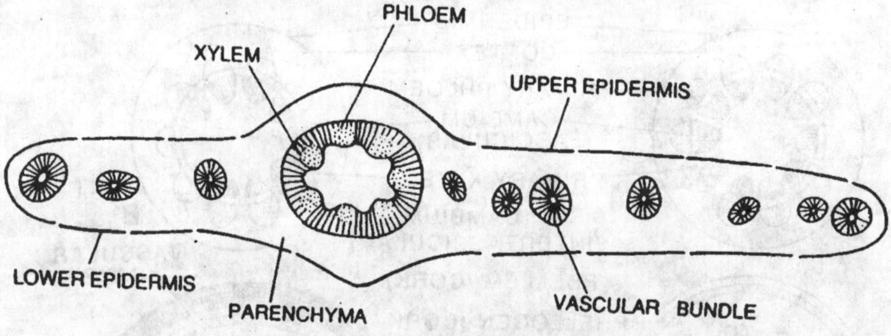

Fig. 7.33. *Ruscus* (monocot). Transection of phylloclade (diagrammatic).

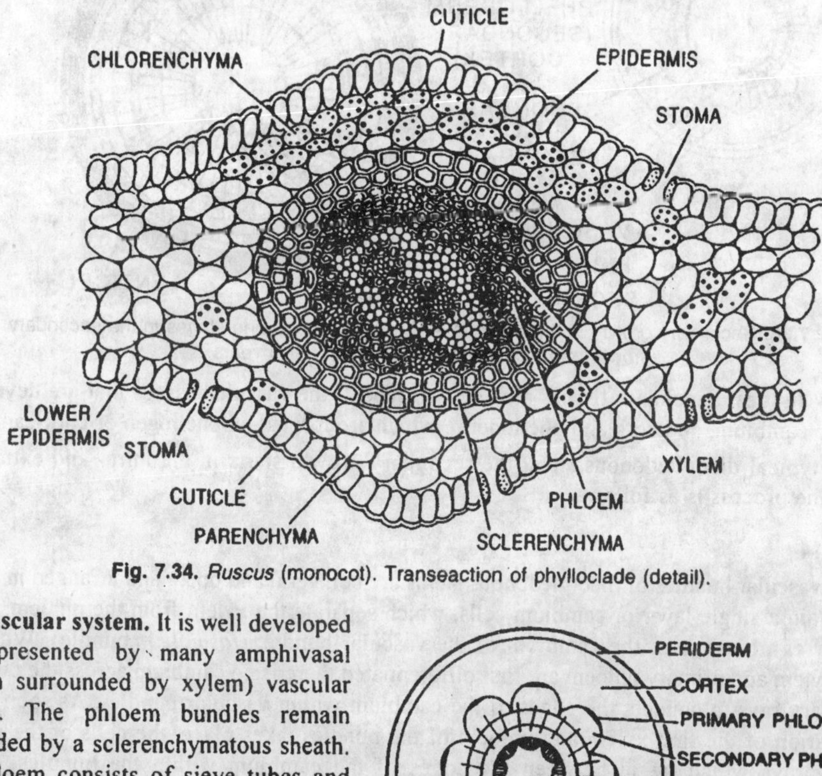

Fig. 7.34. *Ruscus* (monocot). Transeaction of phylloclade (detail).

Vascular system. It is well developed and represented by many amphivasal (phloem surrounded by xylem) vascular bundles. The phloem bundles remain surrounded by a sclerenchymatous sheath. The phloem consists of sieve tubes and companion cells.

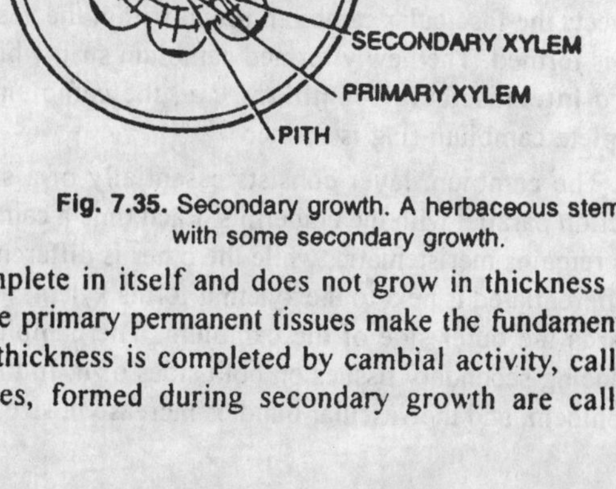

Fig. 7.35. Secondary growth. A herbaceous stem with some secondary growth.

SECONDARY GROWTH IN DICOTYLEDONOUS STEMS

The primary body of the plant is developed from the apical meristem. Sometimes as in monocotyledons and pteridophytes, the primary plant body is complete in itself and does not grow in thickness by cambial activity. However, in dicotyledons, the primary permanent tissues make the fundamental parts of the plant, and the further growth in thickness is completed by cambial activity, called **secondary growth in thickness**. The tissues, formed during secondary growth are called

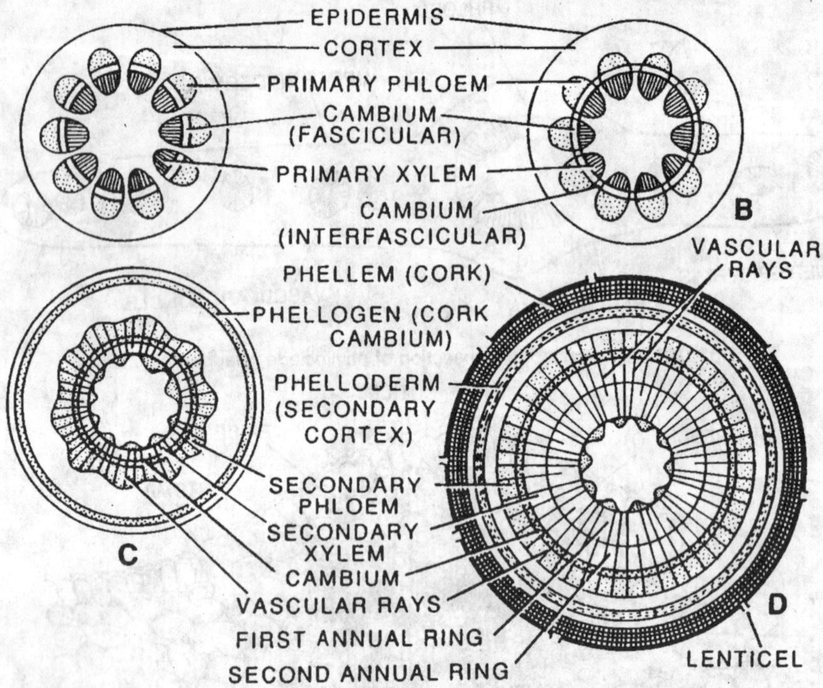

Fig. 7.36. Secondary growth in thickness. A – D, diagrams showing stages in the secondary growth of a dicotyledonous stem upto two years.

secondary tissues. Secondary tissues may be two types—the vascular tissues that are developed by the true cambium, and cork and phelloderm, which are formed by phellogen or cork-cambium.

In a typical dicotyledonous stem, the secondary growth starts in the intra- and extrastelar regions. The process is as follows.

CAMBIUM

The vascular bundles of dicotyledonous stems are collateral and open, and arranged in a ring. They contain a single layer of cambium cells, which separate the xylem from the phloem, called **fascicular cambium,** *i.e.*, the cambium of the vascular bundle, (*fascicle* = bundle). When the primary xylem and primary phloem are first differentiated there is no cambium across the pith rays or medullary rays to connect the edges of the cambium within vascular bundles. As soon as the differentiation of the first xylem and phloem of the bundles takes place, the cells of the pith or medullary rays which lie in between the edges of the cambium within the bundles, divide accordingly and form a layer of cambium across the medullary rays. The newly formed cambium connects the fascicular cambium found within the vascular bundles, and thus a complete cambium ring is formed. The newly formed cambium strip which occurs in the gaps between the bundles is called **interfascicular cambium**, *i.e*, the cambium in between two vascular bundles. Thus a complete cambium ring is formed.

The cambium layer consists essentially of a single layer of cells. These cells divide in a direction parallel with the epidermis. Each time a cambial cell divides into two, one of the daughter cells remains meristematic, while the other is differentiated into a permanent tissue. If the cell that is differentiated is next to the xylem it forms xylem, while if it is next to phloem it becomes phloem towards the outer side of the cambium. The cambium cells divide continuously in this manner producing secondary tissues on both sides of it. In this way, new cells are added to the xylem and the phloem, and the vascular bundles increase in size. While there is more or less alternation in the

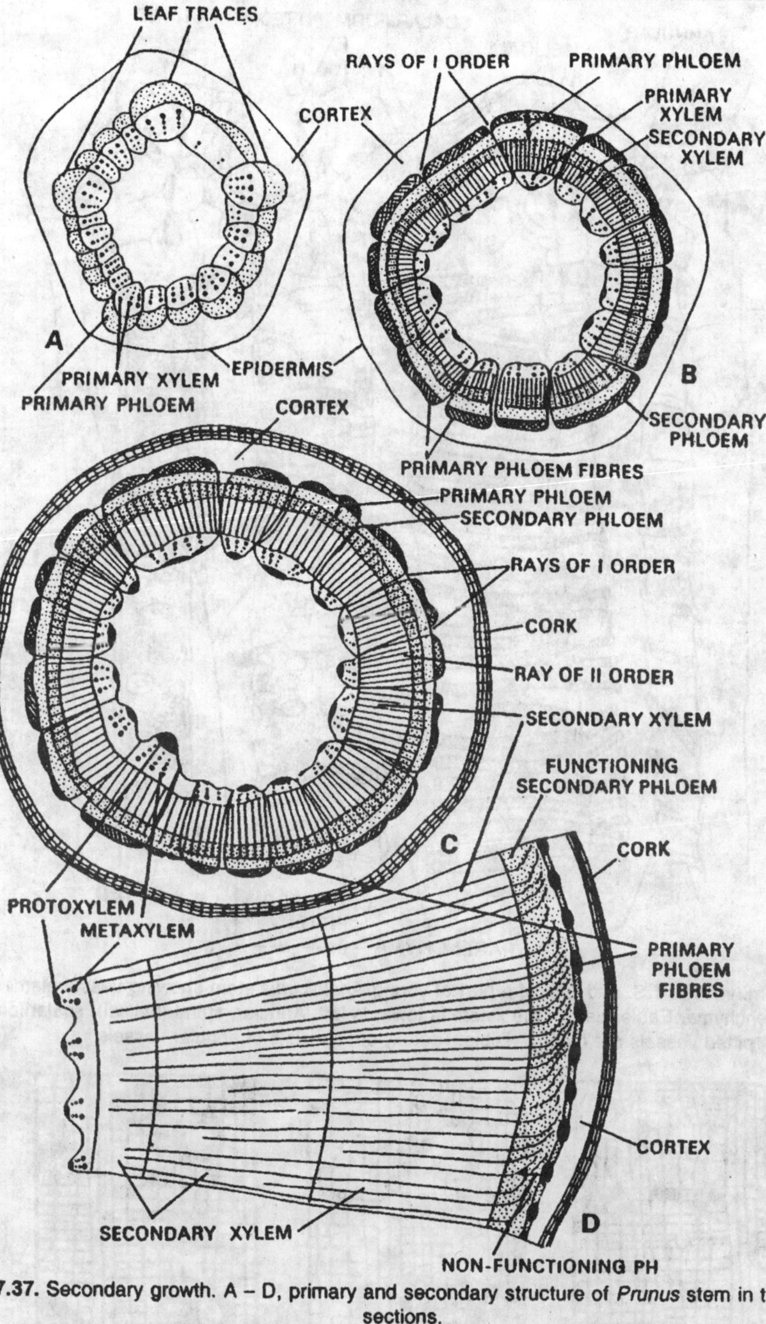

Fig. 7.37. Secondary growth. A – D, primary and secondary structure of *Prunus* stem in transverse sections.

production of xylem and phloem cells from a cambium cell, more cells are formed on the xylem side than on the phloem side. The cells formed from the cambium in the region of the pith rays become pith-ray cells. The activity of the cambium thus increases the length of the pith rays grow equally.

The formation of new cells from the cambium result in an enlargement of the stem that is known as the secondary thickening. The formation of new cells in secondary thickening continues

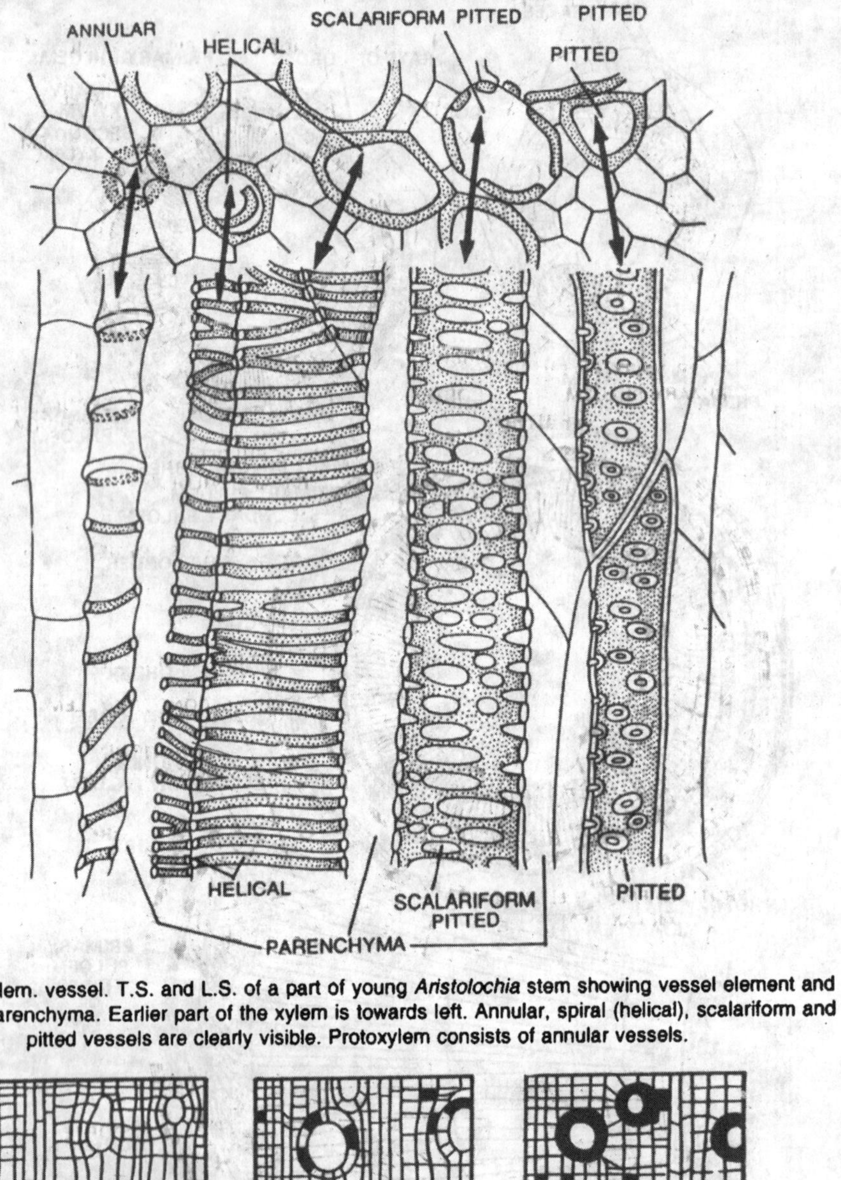

Fig. 7.38. Xylem. vessel. T.S. and L.S. of a part of young *Aristolochia* stem showing vessel element and associated parenchyma. Earlier part of the xylem is towards left. Annular, spiral (helical), scalariform and pitted vessels are clearly visible. Protoxylem consists of annular vessels.

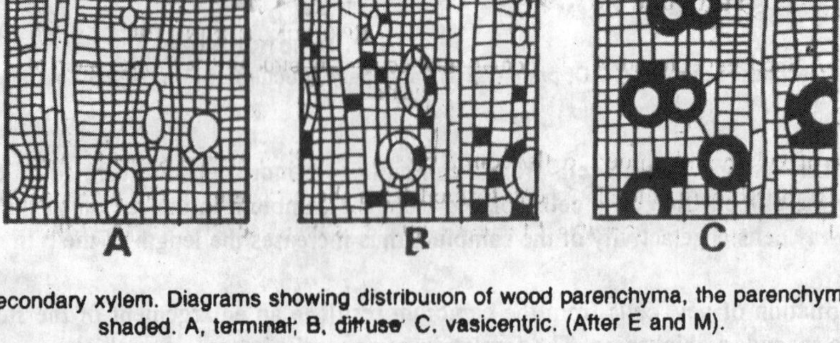

Fig. 7.39. Secondary xylem. Diagrams showing distribution of wood parenchyma, the parenchyma cells are shaded. A, terminal; B, diffuse C. vasicentric. (After E and M).

throughout the life of the plant. It is in this way that the trunks of trees continue to grow in diameter. The cambium perpetuates and remains active for a considerable long period of time.

The thin-walled cells of the vascular cambium are highly vacuolate and in this respect are unlike most other meristematic cells. The electron microscopic structure reveals their highly vacuolate nature. Many ribosomes and dictyosomes, and well developed endoplasmic reticulum, are present (Srivastava, L.M., 1966)

SECONDARY XYLEM

The cambium ring cuts off new cells on its inner side are gradually modified into xylary elements, called the **secondary xylem**. This tissue serves many important functions, such as conduction of water and nutrients, mechanical support, etc. The secondary xylem of tree trunks is of great economic value, since it constitutes the timber and wood of commerce.

The secondary xylem consists of a compact mass of thick-walled cells so arranged as to form two systems—a longitudinal (vertical) and a transverse radiating system. The longitudinal system consists of elongate, overlapping and interlocked cells—tracheids, fibres and vessel elements—and longitudinal rows of parenchyma cells. All these cells possess their long axes parallel with the long axis of the organ of which they are a part.

The secondary xylem consists of scalariform and pitted vessels, tracheids, wood fibres and wood parenchyma. These elements of secondary xylem are more or less similar to those occur in primary xylem. Vessels or tracheae are most abundant and are usually shorter than those of primary xylem. Mostly the vessels are pitted. Annular and spiral tracheids and vessels are altogether absent. Xylem parenchyma cells may be long and fusiform, but sometimes they are short. They are living cells and usually meant for storage of food material (starch and fat) in them. Tannins and crystals are frequently found in these cells. Xylem parenchyma may occur either in the association of the vessels or quite independently. The fibres of secondary xylem possess thick walls and bordered pits.

DISTRIBUTION OF WOOD (XYLEM) PARENCHYMA

Wood parenchyma is distributed in *three* ways: (*i*) Terminal wood parenchyma; (*ii*) diffuse or metatracheal wood parenchyma and (*iii*) vasicentric or paratracheal wood parenchyma.

Terminal wood parenchyma. In some gymnosperm woods, wood parenchyma is absent; in other (*e.g.*, *Larix* and *Pseudotsuga*), and in some angiosperm woods (*e.g.*, *Magnolia* and *Salix*), wood parenchyma cells occur only in the last-formed tissue of the annual ring. Such woods have **terminal wood parenchyma.**

Diffuse or metatracheal wood parenchyma. Where parenchyma occurs not only in this region, but also remains scattered throughout the annual ring, some of the cells lying among the tracheids, and fibre-tracheids the plant has **diffuse** or **metatracheal wood parenchyma** (*e.g.*, in *Malus*, *Quercus*, *Diospyros*, etc.).

Vasicentric or paratracheal wood parenchyma. Where parenchyma occurs at the edge of the annual ring and elsewhere only about vessels and does not occur isolated among tracheids and fibres, the plant possesses **vasicentric** or **paratracheal wood parenchyma** (*e.g.*, in *Acer*, *Fraxinus*, etc.).

Xylem rays. The xylem rays or wood rays, extend radially in the secondary xylem. They are strap or ribbon like. They originate from the ray initials. The xylem rays run as a continuous band to the secondary phloem through the cambium, thus forming a continuous conducting system. All vascular rays are initiated by the cambium and, once formed, are increased in length indefinitely by the cambium. Commonly these rays are known as medullary rays, or pith rays, on the basis of their similarity and parenchymatous nature with the pith rays of herbaceous dicotyledonous stems.

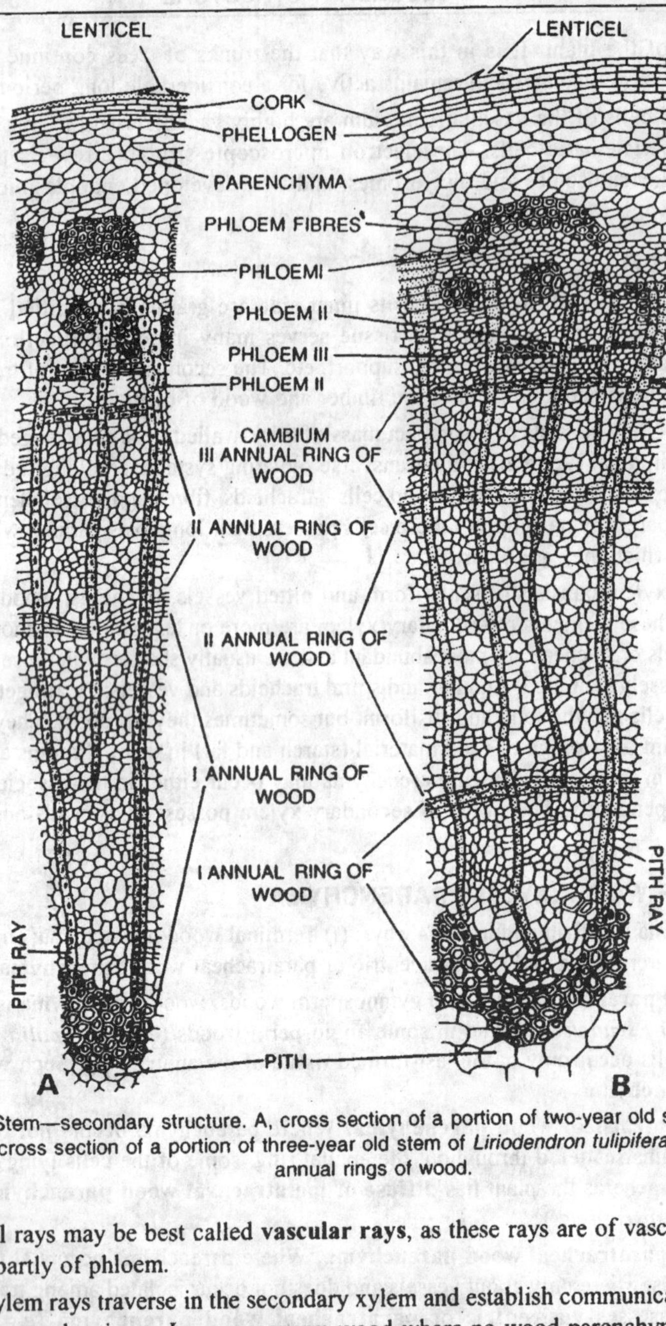

Fig. 7.40. Stem—secondary structure. A, cross section of a portion of two-year old stem of *Liriodendron tulipifera*, B, cross section of a portion of three-year old stem of *Liriodendron tulipifera* (tulip tree) with three annual rings of wood.

These radial rays may be best called **vascular rays**, as these rays are of vascular tissue partly of xylem and partly of phloem.

The xylem rays traverse in the secondary xylem and establish communication with the living cells of the vascular tissue. In gymnosperm wood where no wood parenchyma is present, every tracheid is in direct contact with at least one ray. Vessels also in their longitudinal extent, come into contact with many rays. In herbaceous stems, such as of *Ranunculus*, where vascular bundles are separated by projecting parenchymatous wedges, and in vines, such as *Clematis*, where the bundles are separated by bands of secondary parenchyma, vascular rays are not found. The xylem rays help in the exchange of gases. They also aid in the conduction of water and food from phloem to the cambium and xylem parenchyma.

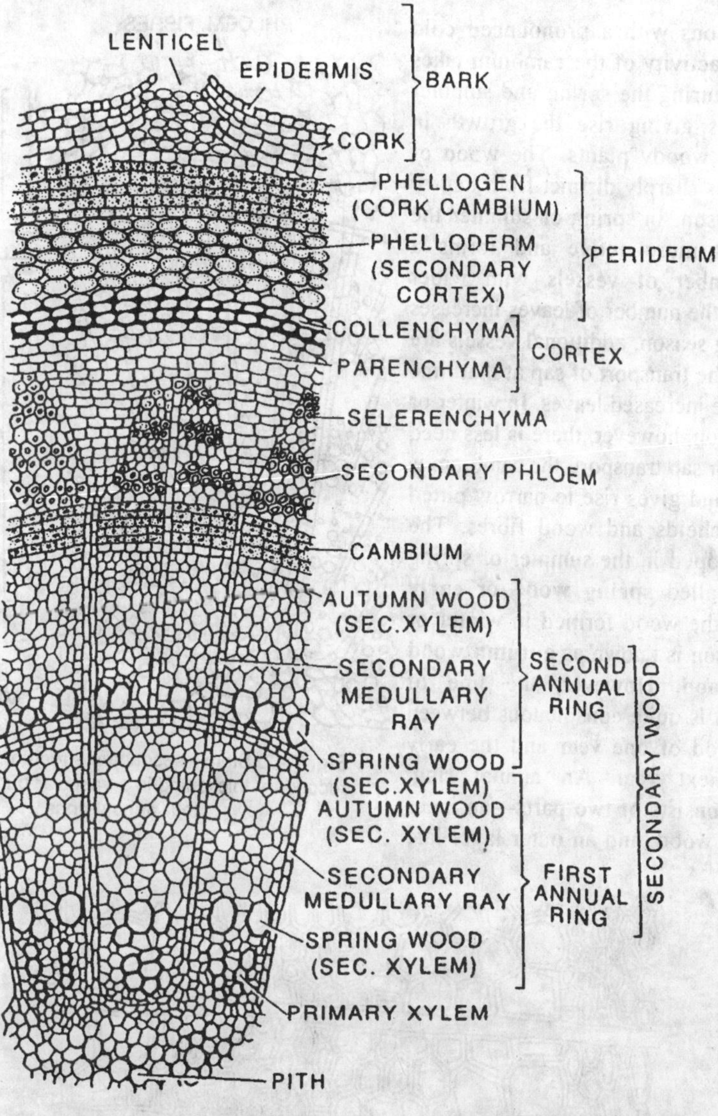

Fig. 7.41. Secondary growth in thickness. T.S. of a two-year old dicotyledonous stem.

ANNUAL RINGS OR GROWTH RINGS

The secondary xylem in the stems of perennial plants commonly consists of concentric layers, each one of which represents a seasonal increment. In transverse section of the axis, these layers appear as rings, and are called **annual rings** or **growth rings**. They are commonly termed as annual rings because in the woody plants of temperate regions and in those of tropical regions where there is an annual alternation of growing and dormant period, each layer represents the growth of one year. The width of growth rings varies greatly and depends upon the rate of the growth of tree. Unfavourable growing seasons produce narrow rings, and favourable seasons wide ones. Annual or growth rings are characteristic of woody plants of temperate climates. Such rings are weakly developed in tropical forms except where there are marked climate changes such as distinct moist and dry seasons. Annuals and herbaceous stems show, naturally, but one layer.

In regions with a pronounced cold season, the activity of the cambium takes place only during the spring and summer seasons thus giving rise the growth in diameter of woody plants. The wood of one season is sharply distinct from that of the next season. In spring or summer the cambium is more active and forms a greater number of vessels with wider cavities. As the number of leaves increases in the spring season, additional vessels are needed for the transport of sap at that time to supply the increased leaves. In winter or autumn season, however, there is less need of vessels for sap transport, the cambium is less active and gives rise to narrow pitted vessels, tracheids and wood fibres. The wood developed in the summer or spring season is called **spring wood** or **early wood,** and the wood formed in winter or autumn season is known as **autumn wood** or **late wood.** However, the line of demarcation is quite conspicuous between the late wood of one year and the early wood of next year. An annual ring, therefore, consists of two parts—an inner layer, early wood, and an outer layer late wood.

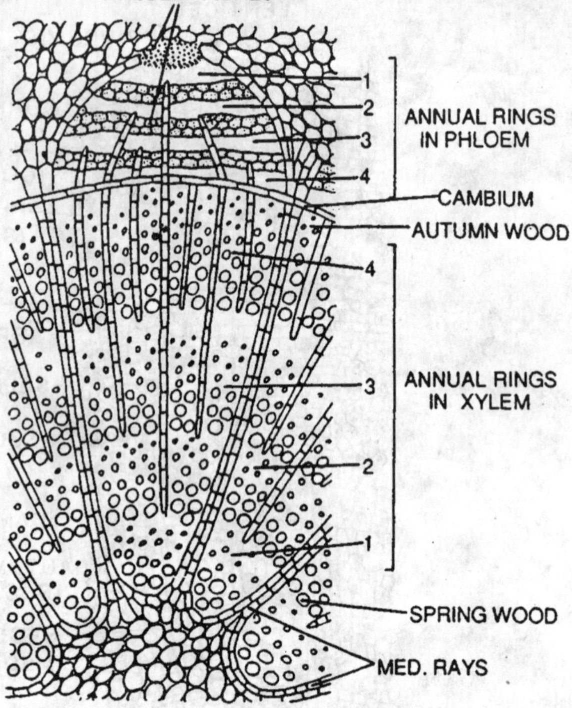

Fig. 7.42. Stem—secondary structure. Diagram of secondary thickening in a vascular bundle showing four annual rings.

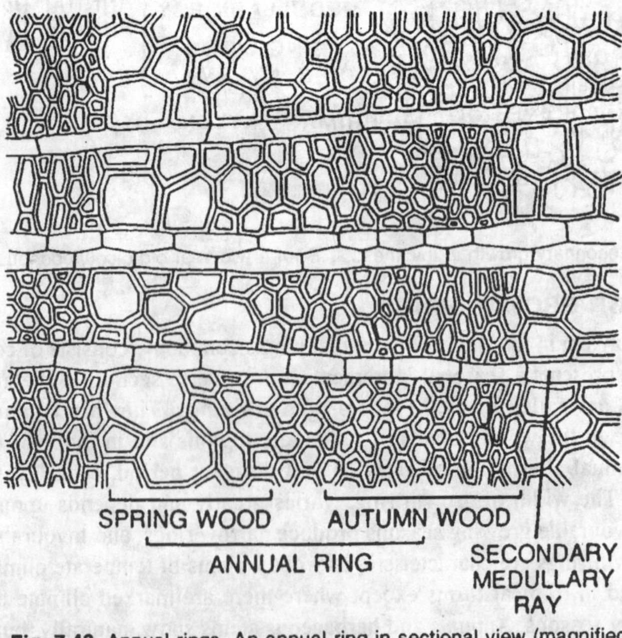

Fig. 7.43. Annual rings. An annual ring in sectional view (magnified).

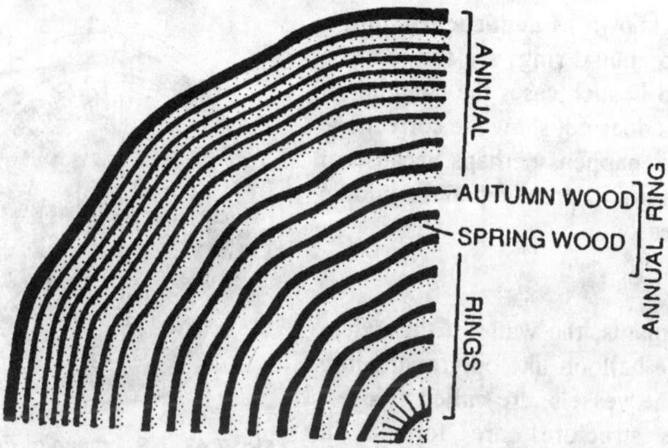

Fig. 7.44. Annual rings (growth rings)—cut surface of a stem showing annual rings.

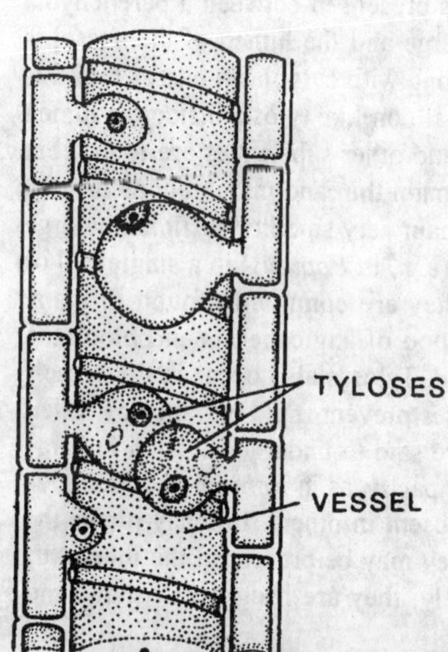

Fig. 7.45. Tyloses. A, L.S. of vessel with tyloses; B, T.S. of vessel with tyloses.

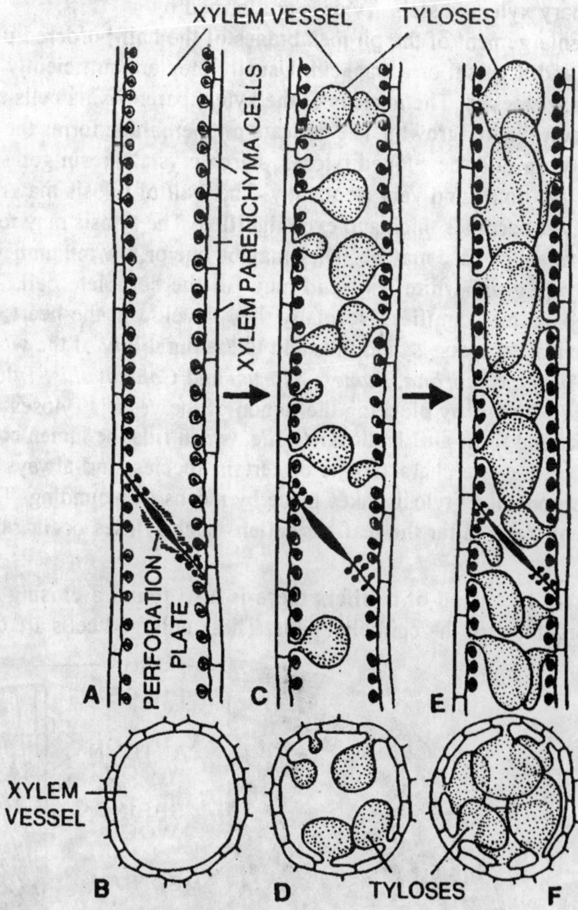

Fig. 7.46. Tyloses. A – F, development of tyloses in xylem vessels depicted in L.S. and T.S.

DENDROCHRONOLOGY

Each annual ring corresponds to one year's growth, and on the basis of these rings the age of a particular plant can easily be calculated. The determination of age of a tree by counting the annual rings is known as **dendrochronology.** Sometimes two annual rings are formed in a single year, and in such cases the counting of the annual rings does not show the correct age of the tree. This happens perhaps because of the drought conditions prevailed in the middle of a growing season.

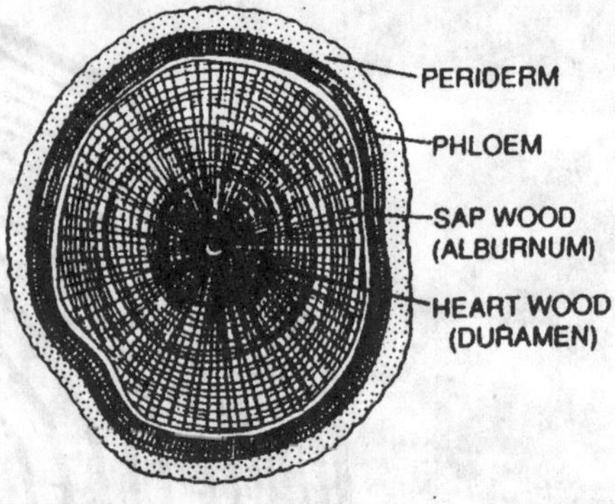

Fig. 7.47. T.S. branch of *Fraxinus*, showing heart and sapwood. (diagrammatic).

TYLOSES

In many plants, the walls of the xylem vessels produce balloon like outgrowths into the lumen of the vessels, are called **tyloses.** Usually these structures are formed in secondary xylem but they may also develop in primary xylem vessels. Tyloses are formed by the enlargement of the pit membranes of the half-bordered pits present in between a parenchyma cell and a vessel or a tracheid. Usually they are sufficiently large and the lumen of the vessel is almost blocked. The nucleus of the xylem parenchyma cells along with cytoplasm passes into this balloon like outgrowth. The delicate pit membrane forms the balloon like tylosis inside the lumen cavity. In fully developed tyloses, starch crystals, resin gums and other substances are found, but they are not found very frequently. The wall of tylosis may remain thin and membranous or very rarely it becomes thick and even lignified. The tylosis may remain very small or sufficiently large in size as the case may be. They may be one or few in number (*e.g.*, in *Populus*) in a single cell or many (*e.g.*, in white oak) and may fill the complete cell. They are commonly found in many angiospermic families. Normally they develop in the heart wood of angiosperms and block the lumen of the vessels, and thus add to the durability of the wood. Tyloses also occur in the vessels of *Coleus*, *Cucurbita*, *Rumex*, *Asarum* and *Convolvulus*. Tyloses prevent rapid entrance of water, air and fungus by blocking the lumen of the vessel. Tyloses are said to undergo division in some plants and form **multicellular tissue,** which fills the lumen compactly, as in *Robinia* and *Maclura*. The tyloses are characteristic of certain species, and always absent in others. In many plants the development of tylosis takes place by means of wounding. They may be present in the inner part of leaf traces after the leaf has fallen. Such tyloses occur rarely; they are irregular in shape and size.

In the wood of conifers there is also found a closing of the cavity of resin canals by the enlargement of the epithelial cells. These enlarged cells are commonly known as **tylosoids.**

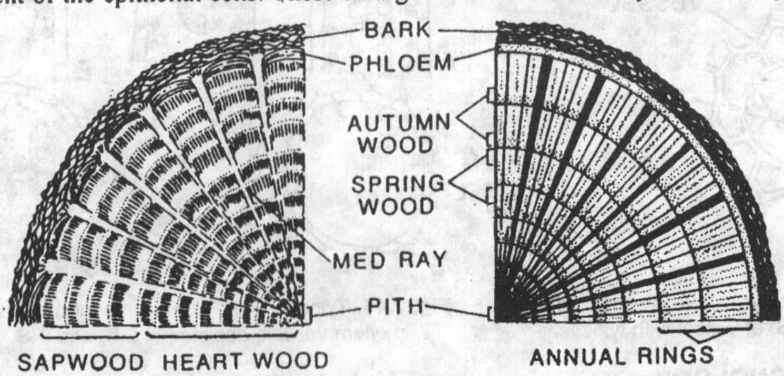

Fig. 7.48. Transections of old dicot stems—left, sector showing heartwood and sapwood; right, sector showing annual rings.

SAPWOOD AND HEARTWOOD

The outer region of the old trees consisting of recently formed xylem elements is **sapwood** or **alburnum**. This is of light colour and contains some living cells also in the association of vessels and fibres. This part of the stem performs the physiological activities, such as conduction of water and nutrients, storage of food, etc.

The central region of the old trees, which was formed earlier is filled up with tannins, resins, gums and other substances which make it hard and durable, is called **heartwood** or **duramen**. It looks black due to the presence of various substances in it. Usually the vessels remain plugged with tyloses. The function of heartwood is no longer of conduction, it gives only mechanical support to the stem.

The sapwood changes into heartwood very gradually. During the transformation a number of changes occur—all living cells lose protoplasts; water contents of cell walls are reduced; food materials are withdrawn from the living cells; tyloses are frequently formed which block the vessels; the parenchyma walls become liginified; oils, gums, tannins, resins and other substances develop in the cells. In certain plants—for example, *Ulmus* and *Malus pumila*, the heartwood remains saturated with water; in other plants, for example, in *Fraxinus* the heartwood may become very dry. The oils, resins and colouring materials infiltrate the walls, and gums and resins may fill the lumina of the cells. In *Diospyros* and *Swietenia*, the cell cavities are filled with a dark-coloured gummy substance. The colour of heartwood, in general, is the result of the presence of these substances. Generally the heartwood is darker in colour than sapwood. However, in some genera, such as *Betula*, *Populus*, *Picea*, *Agathis* the heartwood is hardly darker in colour than the sapwood.

The proportion of sapwood and heartwood is highly variable in different species. Some trees do not have clearly differentiated heartwood (*e.g.*, *Populus*, *Salix*, *Picea*, *Abies*), others possess thin sapwood (*e.g.*, *Robinia*, *Morus*, *Taxus*), the still others possess a thick sapwood (*e.g.*, *Acer*, *Fraxinus*, *Fagus*).

From economic point of view, heartwood is more useful than sapwood. Heartwood, as timber, is more durable than sapwood, because the reduction of food materials available for pathogens by

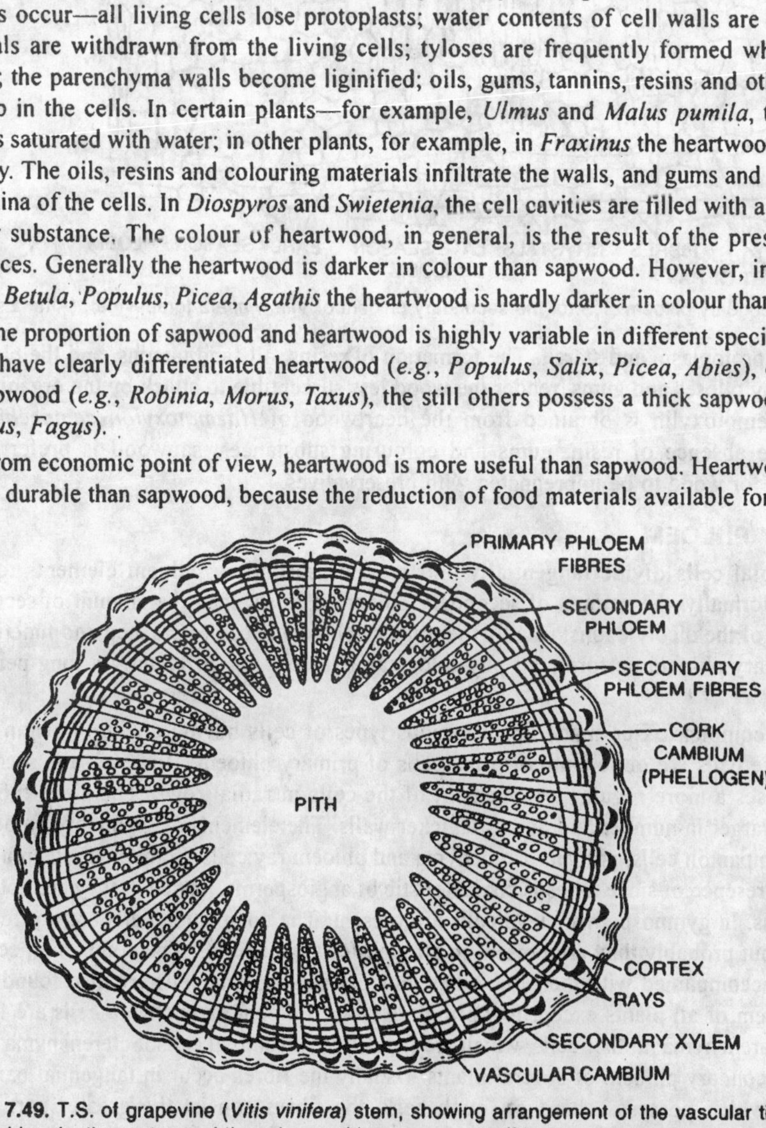

Fig. 7.49. T.S. of grapevine (*Vitis vinifera*) stem, showing arrangement of the vascular tissues. The epidermis, the cortex and the primary phloem were cut off by the activity of the cork cambium which interpolated a layer of cork between primary and secondary phloem. (After K. Esau).

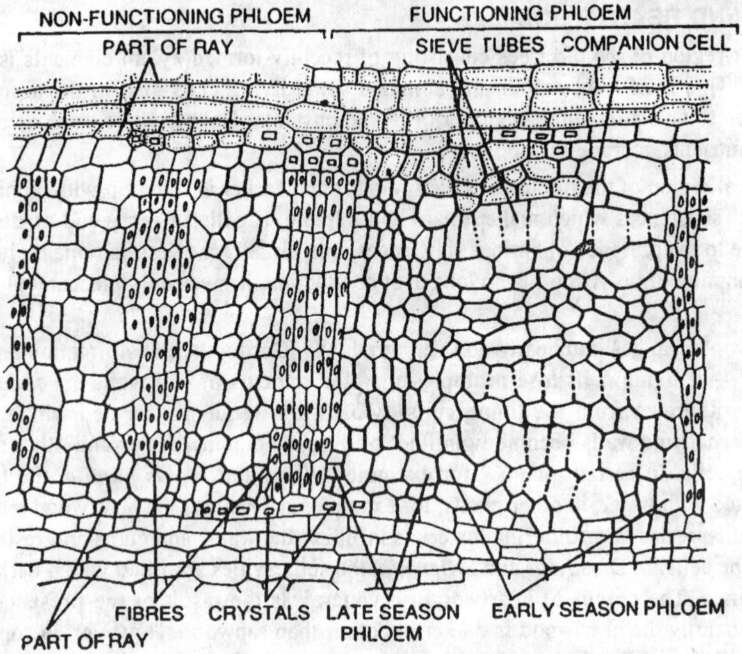

Fig. 7.50. Secondary phloem. T.S. of the secondary phloem of *Vitis vinifera* (grapevine). (After Esau).

the absence of protoplasm and starch. The formation of resins, oils and tannins, and the blocking of the vessels by tyloses and gums, render the wood less susceptible to attack by the organisms of decay. The haemotoxylin is obtained from the heartwood of *Haematoxylon campechianum*. Because of the absence of resin, gums and colouring substances, sapwood is preferred for pulpwood, and for wood to be impregnated with preservatives.

SECONDARY PHLOEM

The cambial cells divide tangentially and produce secondary phloem elements towards outside of it. Normally, the amount of secondary phloem is lesser than the amount of secondary xylem. In most of the dicotyledons; usually the primary phloem becomes crushed and functionless and the secondary phloem performs all physiological activities for sufficiently a long period of time.

This is a complex tissue made up of various types of cells having common origin in the cambium. These cells are quite similar to the cells of primary phloem. However, the secondary phloem possesses a more regular arrangement of the cells in radial rows. The sieve tubes are comparatively larger in number and possess thicker walls. The elements of secondary phloem are sieve tubes, companion cells, phloem parenchyma and phloem ray cells. Sometimes sclerenchyma is also found. Presence of sieve tubes is characteristic of angiosperms, however, they are not found in gymnosperms. In gymnosperms, sieve cells are present. The companion cells are not found in gymnosperms but probably they are present in all types of angiosperms. The companion cells are usually found accompanied with the sieve tubes. Phloem parenchyma cells are also found in the secondary phloem of all plants except few primitive types. Phloem parenchyma cells are formed directly from parenchyma mother cells, which are formed from cambial cells. Sclerenchyma is also found in the secondary phloem of several plants. Usually the fibres occur in tangential bands. In certain plants which possess a hard or tough bark, the fibres consist the greater part of the secondary phloem and surround the softer tissues.

Sieve tubes are series of sieve-tube elements attached end to end with certain sieve areas more highly specialized than others. The sieve tubes of the secondary phloem of dicotyledons are of many types as regards the shape and nature of the end and side walls. In many woody species (*e.g.*, *Carya cordiformis*), the oblique end walls of the sieve tube elements frequently extend for about half the length of the element. These oblique walls possess many areas which together make **compound sieve plates.** The other type, *i.e.*, **simple sieve plate** is found in *Robinia, Maclura* and some species of *Ulmus*. Here the terminal walls of the sievetube elements are transverse and there is a single specialized sieve area. In the majority of species, the sieve tube elements of the secondary phloem possess simple sieve plates.

Sclerenchyma of one type or another is a characteristic of the secondary phloem of several species. Fibres occur frequently in definite tangential bands (*e.g.*, in *Liriodendron* and *Populus*). In *Cephalanthus*, the fibres are found singly. However, in *Carya cordiformis*, the fibres constitute the greater part of the secondary phloem and surround the groups of softer tissues. All conditions have been reported in gymnosperms. The phloem of *Pinus strobus* lacks sclerenchyma; well developed tangential bands of fibres are found to be present in *Juniperus*, and large masses of sclereids are present in *Tsuga*. In *Thuja occidentalis*, the fibres are arranged in uniseriate tangential rows. These rows of fibres alternate with rows of sieve cells and phloem parenchyma.

In *Platanus* and *Fagus* sclereids are the only type of sclerenchyma present in the phloem. The sclereids are found abundantly in the older, living, but nonconducting phloem of the woody plants.

Phloem rays. The phloem rays are usually present in the vascular tissues developed by the cambium. The vascular rays are formed in the cambium and develop on either side of it with the secondary xylem and secondary phloem of which they are a part. The phloem rays may be one to several cells in width. Normally they are of uniform width throughout their length. They may increase in width outwardly, the increase being due to the multiplication of the cells or to the increase in size of cells toward the outer end of the ray. The phloem rays may be one cell wide (*e.g.*, in *Castanea* and *Salix*), two or three cells wide (*e.g.*, in *Malus pumila*) or many cells wide (*e.g.*, in *Robinia* and *Liriodendron*). However, in oaks there are two types of phloem rays—one very broad and the other uniseriate.

Commonly the phloem ray cells in woody plants, as seen in transverse section, are rectangular and radially elongated. In herbaceous plants, commonly the ray cells are globose. In *Cephalanthus*, *Agrimonia* and *Potentilla* the ray cells closely resemble the phloem parenchyma cells. All phloem ray cells are parenchymatous with active protoplasm, but as they become older many of them become sclereids.

A special type of ray cell known as **albuminous cell** is found in gymnosperms. These albuminous cells are found to be situated at the upper and lower margins of the phloem rays. The albuminous cells differ from the ordinary ray cells both structurally and functionally. They are joined directly with the sieve cells by sieve areas. They do not contain starch, and are of much greater vertical diameter than the normal ray cells. They retain their protoplasts as long as the sieve cells with which they are connected function. It is thought that they function like companion cells of angiosperms.

Seasonal rings in secondary phloem. The tissues of the secondary phloem are generally arranged in definite tangential bands. These layers of tissue have the appearance of annual rings. However, these ring like bands do not possess definite seasonal limits like those of secondary xylem, because there is no sharp distinction between the phloem cells formed in the early and late growing season. Seasonal formation of sclerenchyma bands may exist, but this is not constant feature. In tropical plants new layers of phloem and xylem are formed with each period of new growth.

Function. The functions of secondary phloem are normally the same as that of primary phloem. The various cells of secondary phloem are structurally adapted for the function of translocation of food. The sieve tubes, companion cells and some phloem parenchyma cells are especially adapted for lengthwise conduction, and certain phloem rays help in horizontal conduction to and from the xylem and the cambium. Some of the phloem parenchyma cells in some plants act as storage tissue of starch, crystals and other organic materials.

Economic importance. The secondary phloem of various trees and shrubs of the Malvaceae, Tiliaceae, Moraceae has provided **bast fibres** for economic purposes. The tapa cloth of Pacific islands is composed of mainly of phloem fibres. Tannin obtained from the secondary phloem of various plants is utilized for the preparation of spices and drugs. Secretory canals are abundantly found in the secondary phloem, and the secretions are of much economic value—such as rubber is obtained from the latex of *Hevea brasiliensis*, and resins from various gymnosperms.

PERIDERM

Due to continued formation of secondary tissues, in the older stem, and roots, however, the epidermis gets stretched and ultimately tends to rupture and followed by the death of epidermal cells and outer tissues, and a new protective layer is developed called **periderm**. The formation of periderm is a common phenomenon in stems and roots of dicotyledons and gymnosperms that increase in thickness by secondary growth. Structurally, the periderm consists of three parts—1. a meristem known as **phellogen** or **cork cambium**, 2. the layer of cells cut off by phellogen on the outer side, the **phellem** or **cork**, and 3. the cells cut off by phellogen towards inner side, the **phelloderm.**

The periderm appears on the surface of those plant parts that possess a continuous increase in thickness by secondary growth. Usually the periderm occurs in the roots and stems and their branches in gymnosperms and woody dicotyledons. It occurs in herbaceous dicotyledons, sometimes limited to the oldest parts of stem or root.

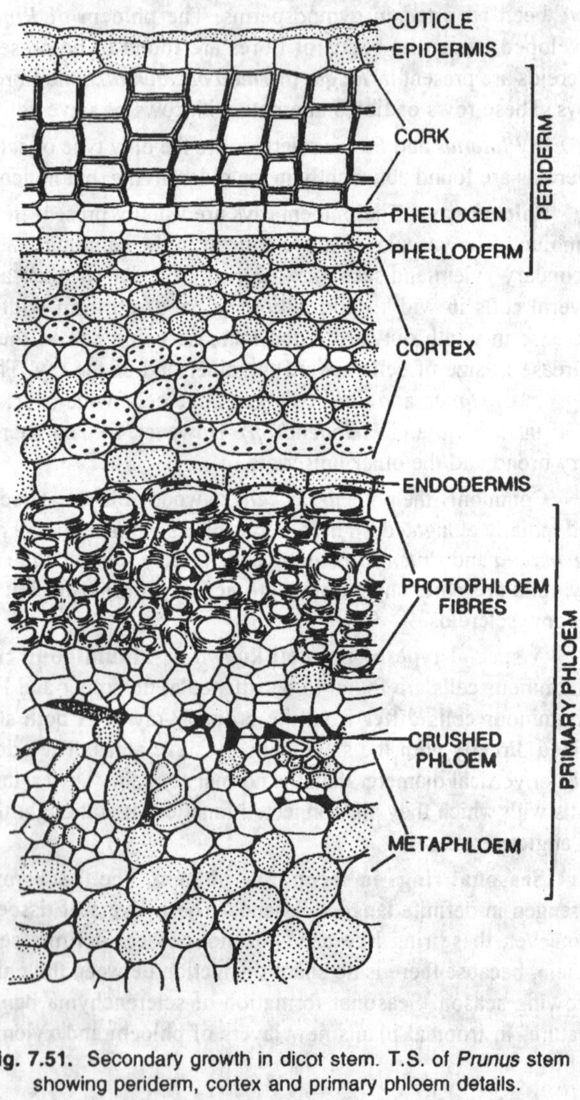

Fig. 7.51. Secondary growth in dicot stem. T.S. of *Prunus* stem showing periderm, cortex and primary phloem details.

Phellogen. In contrast to the vascular cambium, the phellogen is relatively simple in structure, and composed of one type of cells. The cells of phellogen appear rectangular in cross-section, and somewhat flattened radially. Their protoplasts are vacuolated and may contain tannins and chloroplasts, except in the lenticels, intercellular spaces lacking.

When we consider the place of origin of the meristem forming the periderm, it becomes necessary to distinguish between the first periderm, and the subsequent periderms, which arise beneath the first and replace it as the axis increases in circumference. In most stems the first phellogen arises in the subepidermal layer. In a few plants the phellogen arises in the epidermal cells (*e.g.*, *Nerium*, *Pyrus*). Sometimes only a part of the phellogen is developed from epidermis while the other part arises in subepidermal cells (*e.g.*, *Pyrus*). In some stems the second or third cortical layer initiates the development of periderm (*e.g.*, *Robinia*, *Aristolochia*, *Pinus*, *Larix*, etc.). In still other plants the phellogen arises near the vascular region or directly in the phloem (*e.g.*, in **Caryophyllaceae,** Cupressaceae, Ericaceae, *Punica*, *Vitis*, etc.). If the first periderm is followed by the formation of others, these are formed repeatedly, in successively deeper layers of the cortex or phloem.

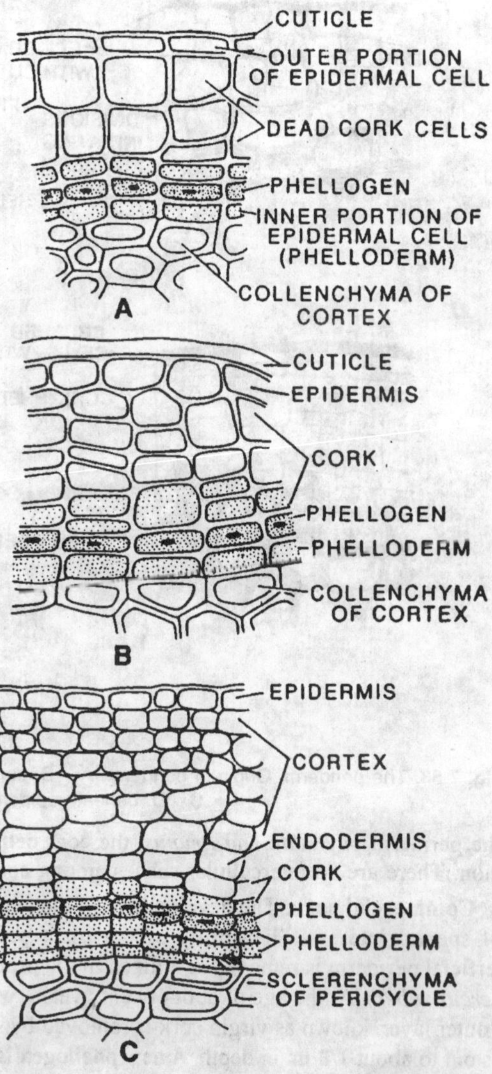

Fig. 7.52. Phellogen. Origin and its development. A, epidermal; B, hypodermal; C, deep-seated.

At the time of the beginning of the development of a phellogen in epidermal cells, the protoplasts lose their central vacuoles and the cytoplasm increases in amount and becomes more richly granular. As soon as this initial layer develops, it divides tangentially and, to a lesser extent radially, in the similar way as division takes place in true cambium. The derivative cells are normally arranged in radial rows.

Generally, several to many times as many cells are cut off toward the outside (phellem-cork cells) as toward the inside (phelloderm). Phelloderm cells are few or absent; rarely phelloderm is greater in amount than phellem.

Phellem (cork cells). The cells that constitute phellem are commonly known as **cork cells.** They are like the phellogen cells from which they are derived. As seen in tangential section, they are polygonal and uniform in shape, and often radially thin as seen in cross section of the stem. The cells of the commercial cork (*Quercus suber*) are radially elongated as seen in transverse section

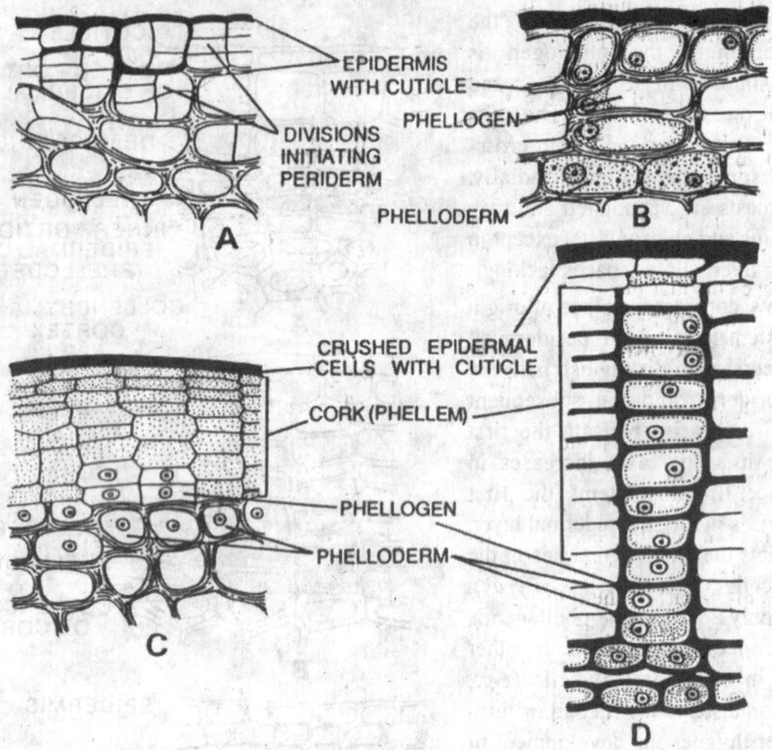

Fig. 7.53. The periderm. Origin of periderm. A – B, partly in epidermis and partly beneath it, in *Pyrus*; C – D, beneath epidermis in *Prunus*.

In the periderm of *Betula* and *Prunus*, the cork cells are elongated tangentially as seen in cross-section. There are no intercellular spaces among cork cells.

Commercial cork. The development of the periderm layers in the cork oaks (*Quercus suber*) is of special interest. The ability of the plant produce phellogen in deeper layers when the superficial periderm is removed is utilized in the production of commercial cork from the cork oak (*Quercus suber*). At the age of about twenty years, when the tree is about 40 cm in circumference, this outer layer, known as virgin cork is removed by stripping to the phellogen. The exposed tissue dries out to about 1/8 in. in depth. A new phellogen is established beneath the dry layer and rapidly produces a massive cork of a better quality than the first. After nine or ten years the new cork layer has attained sufficient thickness to be commercially valuable and is in turn removed. Of course, this cork is of better quality than the virgin cork, but of inferior quality than the cork obtained at the third and subsequent strippings. These strippings take place at intervals of about nine years until the tree is 150 or more years old. After the successive strippings the new phellogen layers develop at greater depth in the living tissue. The cortex is lost after few strippings and the subsequent cork layers are formed in the secondary phloem. The important properties of the commercial cork are its imperviousness, its lightness, toughness and elasticity.

Phelloderm. The phellogen cuts off the phelloderm cells towards inner side. The phelloderm cells are living cells with cellulose walls. In most plants, they resemble cortical cells in wall structure and contents. Their shape is similar to that of phellogen cells. They may be distinguished from cortical cells by their arrangement in radial series resulting from their origin from the tangentially dividing phellogen. In some species they act as photosynthetic tissue and aid in starch storage. They are pitted like other parenchyma cells. Occasionally, the sclereids and other such

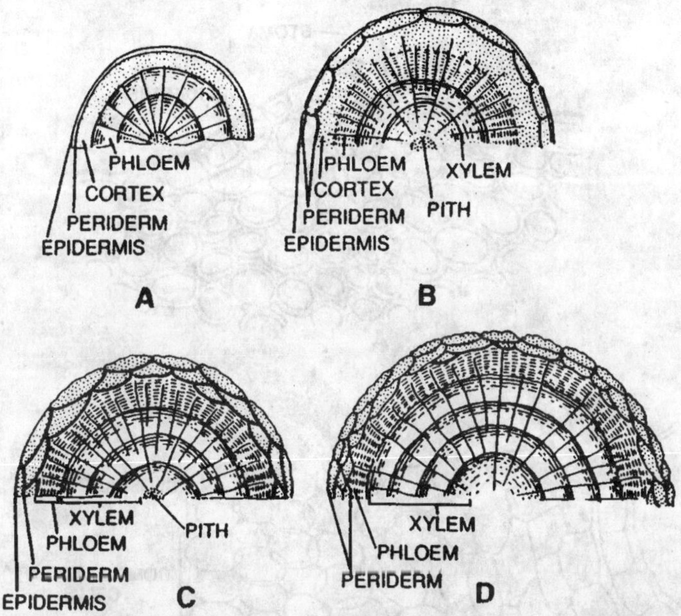

Fig. 7.54. The periderm. Diagrams showing the position and extent of successively formed periderm layers. A, a one-year-old twig, the first periderm layer, a complete cylinder formed beneath the epidermis; B, a two-year-old twig, the epidermis and first periderm ruptured; C, a three-year-old stem, the outer tissues weathered away and more periderm layer formed deeper in the stem; D, a four-year-old stem, the cortex and outer secondary phloem with their periderm layers largely weathered away.

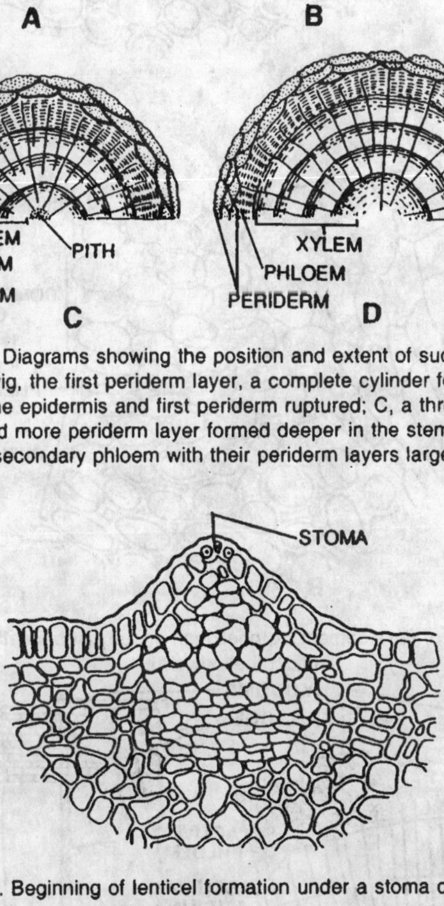

Fig. 7.55. The lenticel. Beginning of lenticel formation under a stoma of *Morus alba* (mulberry).

specialized cells occur in phelloderm. The term **secondary cortex** is sometimes applied to phelloderm, which does not seem to be appropriate.

BARK

The term **bark** is commonly applied to all tissues outside the vascular cambium of the stem, in either primary or secondary state of growth. In this way, bark includes primary phloem and cortex in stem with primary tissues only, and primary and secondary phloem, cortex and periderm in stem with secondary tissues. This term is also used to denote the tissue that is accumulated on the surface of the stem as a result of the activity of cork cambium. As the periderm develops, it becomes separated, by a non-living layer of cork cells from the living tissues. The tissue layers thus separated become dead. The term bark in restricted sense is applied to these dead tissues together

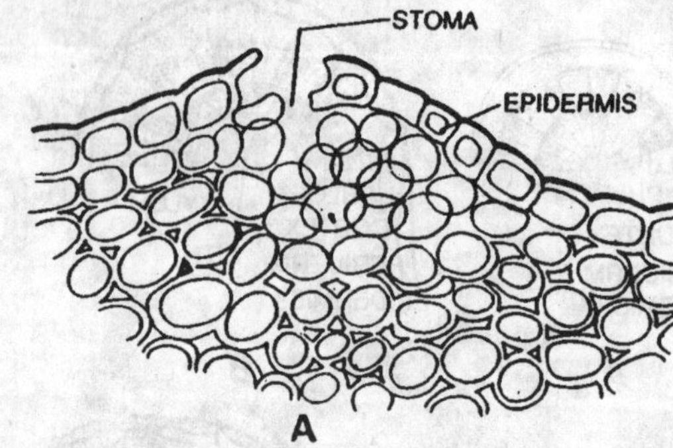

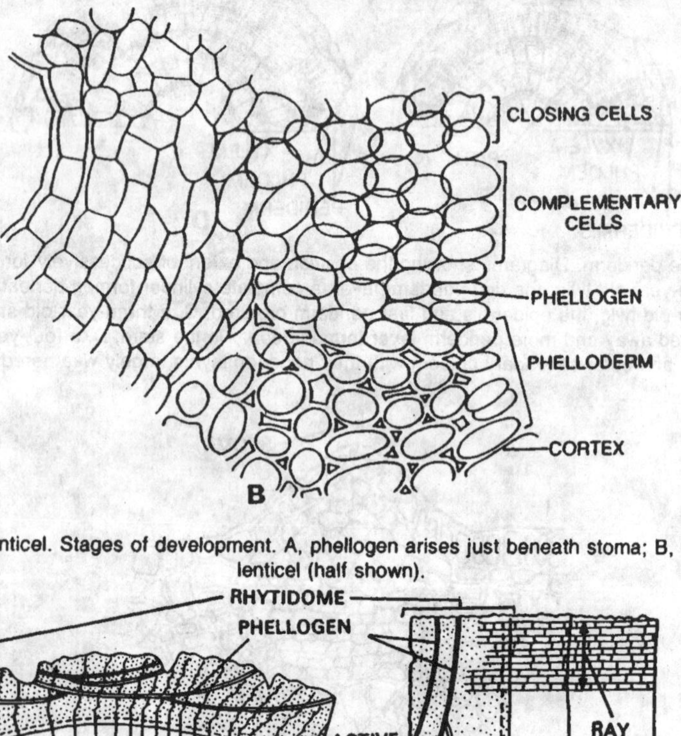

Fig. 7.56. The lenticel. Stages of development. A, phellogen arises just beneath stoma; B, well developed lenticel (half shown).

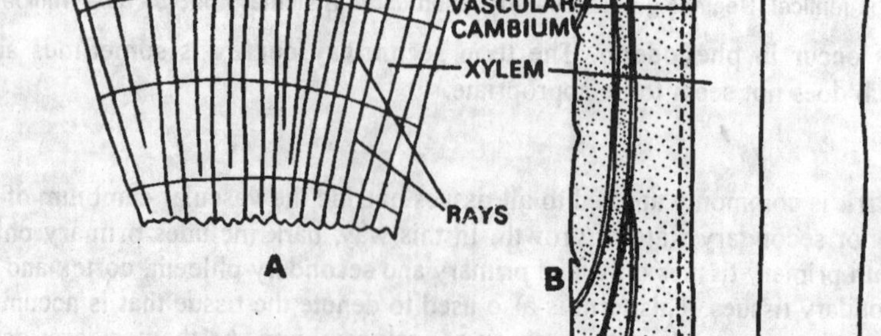

Fig. 7.57. The Periderm. A and B, Transverse and longitudinal sections of part of stem showing rhytidome and its location with reference to vascular tissues; here the rhytidome is composed of periderm and non-living secondary phloem.

with the cork layers. In wider sense the term is applied to denote the tissues outside the vascular cambium. However, the term bark is loose and non-technical.

RHYTIDOME

In most of plants, as soon as the first phellogen ceases to function, second phellogen develops in the tissue below the first one. In this way additional layers of periderm are formed in the progressively deeper regions of the stem, thus new phellogen layers arise in deeper regions of the cortex which may exceed even upto phloem. As the phellogen arises in deeper region and cuts cork cells or phellem towards outside, all the living cells outside the phellogen do not get water supply and nutrients, and become dead. These dead tissues formed outside the phellogen constitute the **rhytidome.**

In some rhytidomes parenchyma and soft cork cells predominate whereas others contain large amounts of fibres usually derived from the phloem. The manners in which the successive layers of periderm originate possesses a characteristic effect upon the appearance of the rhytidome. When the sequent periderms develop as overlapping scale-like layers, the outer tissue breaks up into units related to the layers of periderm, and thus formed outer bark is termed scale-bark. On the other hand, if the phellogen arises around the whole circumference of the stem, a ring bark is formed, which shows the separation of hollow cylinders or rings from the stem.

LENTICELS

Usually in the periderm of most plants, certain areas with loosely arranged cells have been found, which possess more or less raised and corky spots where the underneath tissues break through the epidermis. Such areas are universally found on the stems of woody plants. These broken areas are called the **lenticels.** Wutz (1955) defined a *lenticel as a small portion of the periderm where the activity of the phellogen is more than elsewhere, and the cork cells produced by it are loosely arranged and possess numerous intercellular spaces.* These areas are thicker radially than rest of the periderm because of the presence of loose complementary cells. The lenticels perform the function of exchange of gases during night or when the stomata are closed.

Lenticels are first formed immediately beneath the stomata or group of stomata and the number of lenticels, therefore, depends upon the number of stomata or groups of stomata. The lenticels may be scattered on the stems or they may be arranged in vertical or horizontal rows. The lenticels also occur on the roots.

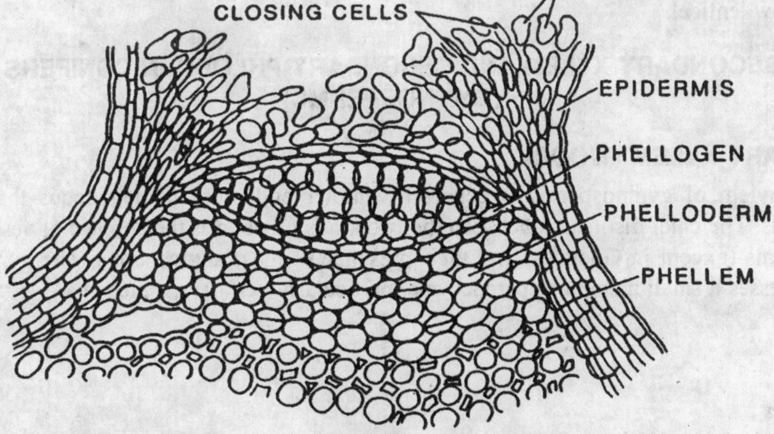

Fig. 7.58. The lenticel. A portion of T.S. of stem of *Prunus* showing lenticel. Successive layers of complementary and closing cells are visible.

The lenticels originate beneath the stomata, either just before, or simultaneously with the initiation of the first layer of the periderm. In most of plants, lenticel formation takes place in the

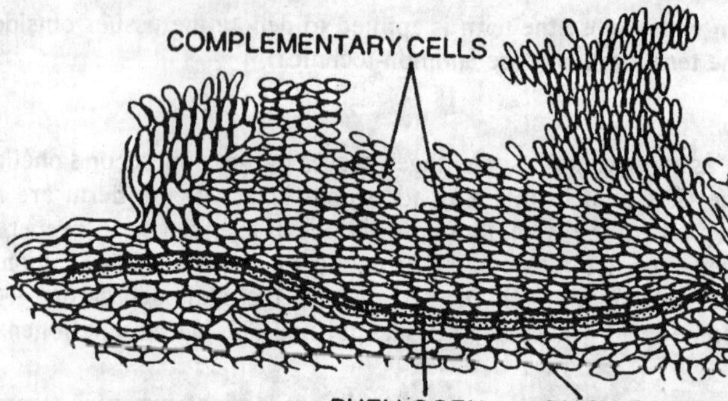

Fig. 7.59. The lenticel of *Mangifera indica* (mango).

first growing season and sometimes previous to the growth in length has stopped. As the lenticel formation begins, the parenchyma cells found nearabout the sub-stomatal cavity lose their chlorophyll and divide irregularly in different planes giving rise to a mass of colourless, rounded, thin walled, loose cells called **complementary cells.** Such cells are also produced by phellogen towards outside instead of cork cells. As the complementary cells increase in number, pressure is caused against the epidermis and it ruptures. Very often, the outer most cells die due to exposure to outer atmosphere and are replaced by the cells cut off by cork cambium or phellogen. The thin walled loose complementary cells may alternate with masses of more dense and compact cells called the **closing cells.** These cells together form a layer called **closing layer.** With the continuous formation of new loose complementary cells, the closing layers are ruptured. The lenticels are filled up with complementary cells completely in the spring season whereas in the end of the spring season the lenticel becomes closed by the formation of closing layer.

The complementary cells are thin-walled, rounded and loose with sufficiently developed intercellular spaces among them. Their cell walls are not suberized. Due to the presence of profuse intercellular spaces, the lenticels perform the function of exchange of gases between the atmosphere and internal tissues of the plant.

Sometimes, lenticels develop independent of the stomata. In such cases the phellogen cuts for sometime the cork cells and then loose complementary cells which ultimately break the cork and rise to a new lenticel.

SECONDARY XYLEM AND SECONDARY PHLOEM IN CONIFERS (GYMNOSPERMS)

SECONDARY XYLEM (WOOD)

The xylem of gymnosperms is generally simpler and more homogeneous than that of angiosperms. The chief distinction between the two kinds of wood is the absence of vessels in the gymnosperms (except in Gnetales) and their presence in most angiosperms. The gymnosperm wood possesses a small amount of parenchyma, particularly vertical parenchyma.

THE VERTICAL SYSTEM

In the secondary xylem of gymnosperms, the vertical system consists mostly of tracheids. The late wood tracheids possess relatively thick walls and pits with reduced borders, and therefore, they are known as **fibre-tracheids,** but libriform fibres do not occur. The tracheids are long cells (0.5 to 1.1 mm) with their ends overlapping those of other tracheids. The tracheids of existing gymnosperms are interconnected by circular or oval bordered pit-pairs in single, opposite or alternate arrangement. The number of pits on each tracheid may vary from 50 to 300 (Stamm, 1946). The pit-pairs are abundantly present on the ends where the tracheids overlap each other. Generally the pits are confined to the radial facets of the cells. Tori are present on the pit membranes in *Ginkgo*, Gnetales and most Coniferales. The tracheids possess thickenings of intercellular material and primary walls along the upper and lower margins of the pit-pairs. These thickenings are called **crassulae.** Another wall sculpture is represented by the **trabeculae.** They are

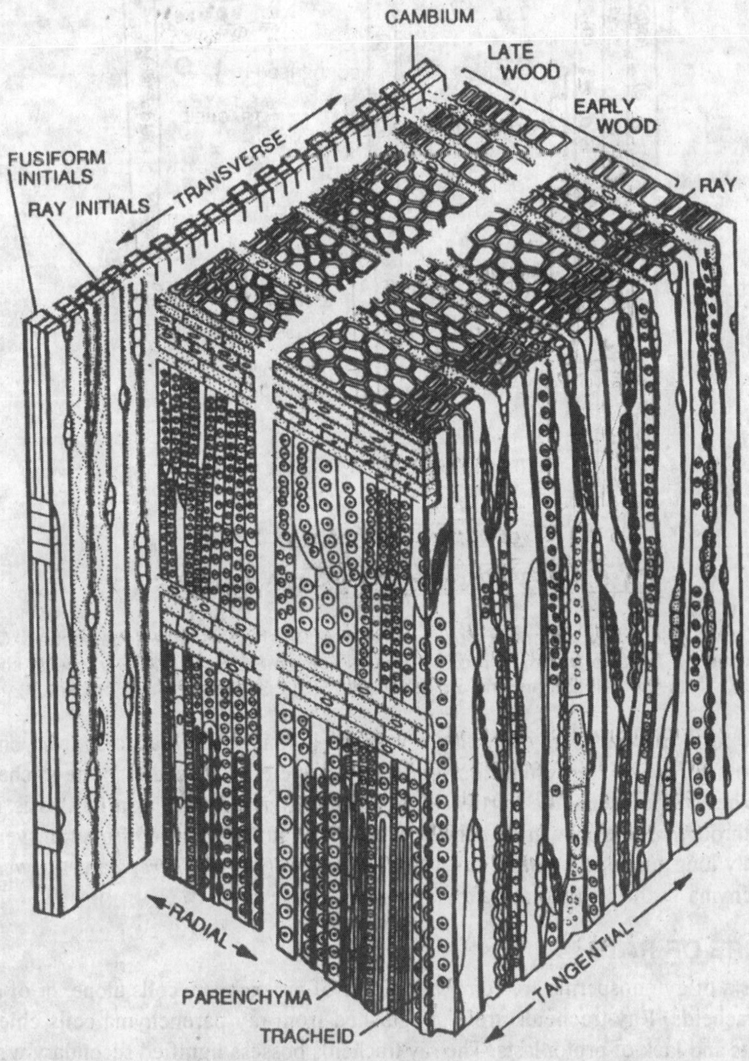

Fig. 7.60. Xylem—wood of conifers. Three-dimensional diagram of the cambium and secondary xylem of *Thuja occidentalis* Linn. (After Bailey).

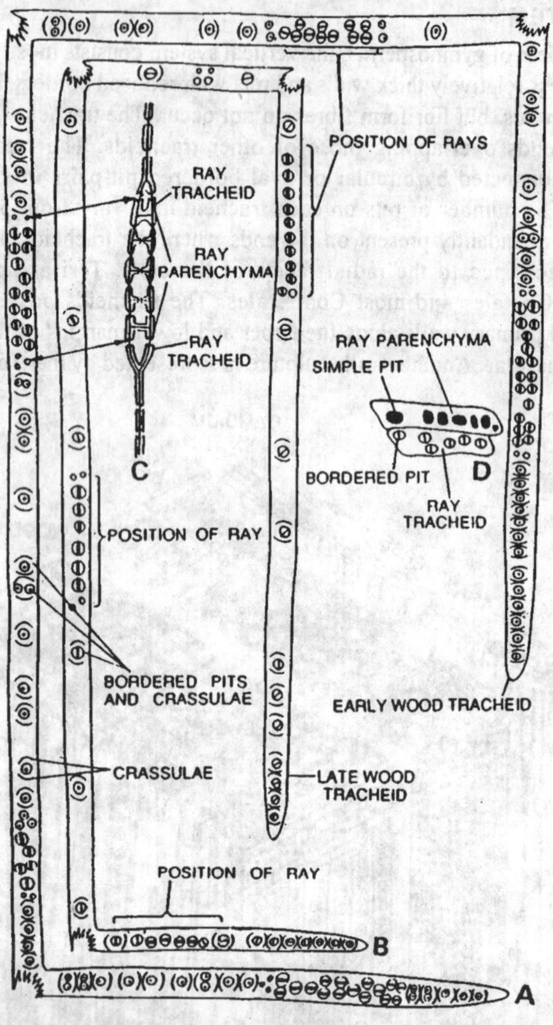

Fig. 7.61. Xylem—secondary xylem of *Pinus*. A, early-wood tracheid; B, late-wood tracheid; C, T.S. of ray as seen in T.L.S. of wood; D, two ray cells as seen in R.L.S. of wood. Tracheids show pits with full borders and are associated with crassulae., (After Forsaith).

found in the form of small bars extending across the lumina of the tracheids from one tangential wall to the other. Helical thickenings on pitted walls have been recorded in the tracheids of some conifers. Wherever present, the vertical xylem parenchyma of the Coniferales is found to be distributed throughout the growth ring and occurs in long strands derived from transverse divisions on the mostly long fusiform cambial cells. Some conifers (*Taxus*, *Torreya* and *Araucaria*) do not have parenchyma in the vertical system.

STRUCTURE OF RAYS

The rays of gymnosperms are composed either of parenchyma cells alone, or of parenchyma cells and tracheids. Ray tracheids are distinguished from ray parenchyma cells chiefly by their bordered pits and lack of protoplasts. The ray tracheids possess lignified secondary walls. In some conifers these walls are thick and sculptured, with projections in the form of bands extending across the lumen of the cell. The ray parenchyma cells possess living protoplasts in the sap wood

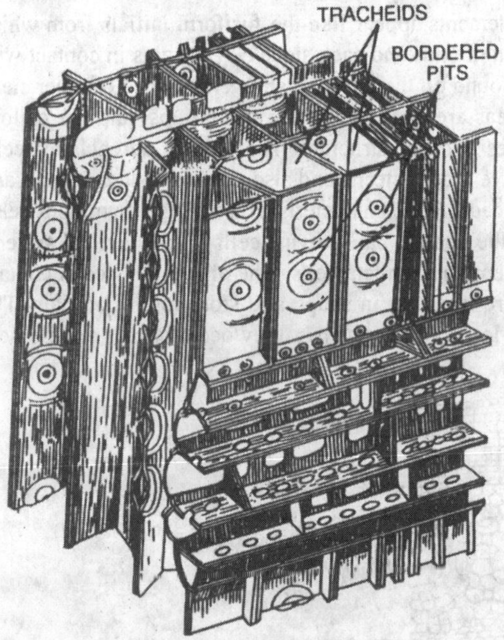

Fig. 7.62. Secondary xylem. Three-dimensional structure of wood of *Pinus strobus*. Tracheids are shown in the figure.

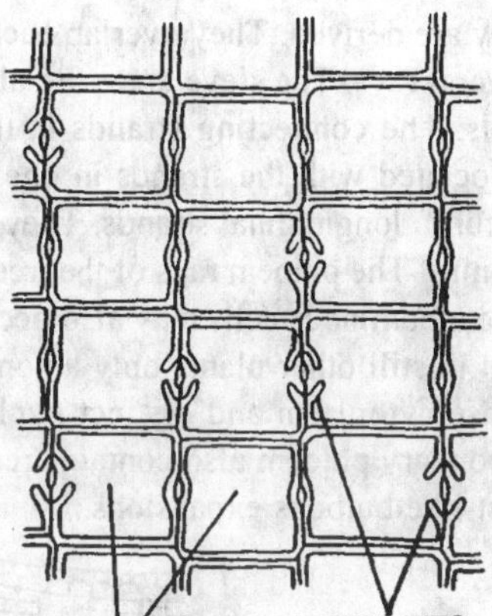

Fig. 7.63. Tracheids with bordered pits of pine stem in T.S.

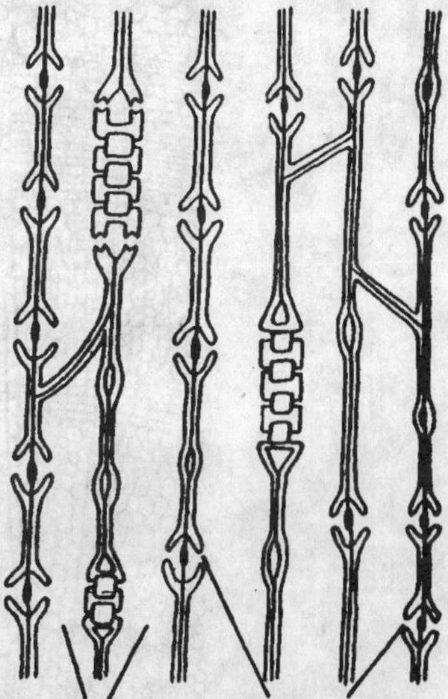

Fig. 7.64. Tracheids with bordered pits of pine stem in T.L.S.

and often dark coloured resinous deposits in the heartwood. The rays of conifers are for the most part only one cell wide and from 1 to 20 or sometimes upto 50 cells high. Ray tracheids may occur singly or in series, at the margins of a ray. The rays serve to transport the assimilation products formed in the leaves and flowing downwards in the phloem in a radial direction into the wood of the stem and roots. They conduct water away from the wood in the opposite direction. The rays penetrate equally into the xylem and the phloem and thus suited for these functions.

Resin ducts. In certain gymnosperms the resin ducts are developed in the vertical system or in both the vertical and horizontal systems. The resin ducts arise as schizogenous intercellular spaces by separation of resin producing parenchyma cells from each other. These cells make the lining, the **epithelium,** of the resin duct and excrete the resin. A resin duct may become closed by the enlarging epithelial cells. These tylosis like extensions are known as **tylosoids** (Record, 1947).

SECONDARY PHLOEM

The structure of phloem of conifers is quite simple. The vertical system contains sieve cells, parenchyma cells and frequently fibres. Companion cells are absent. The sieve plates are present on the lateral walls. The rays are mostly uniseriate and contain parenchyma only or parenchyma and albuminous cells.

The sieve cells are slender, elongated elements appear like the fusiform initials from which they are derived. They overlap each other at their ends and each sieve cell remains in contact with several rays. The sieve areas are abundantly found on the ends which overlap those of other sieve cells. The connecting strands in the sieveareas are aggregated into the groups, and the callose associated with the strands in one group fuses into one structure. The phloem parenchyma cells occur in longitudinal strands. They store reserve food material and also contain resins, crystals and tannins. The phloem rays of the trees of advanced age are characteristic in having albuminous cells. The albuminous cells may also occur among the phloem parenchyma cells (in the vertical system) and in still other plants only among the phloem parenchyma cells. The albuminous cells contain dense cytoplasm and distinct nuclei. They are irregular in shape and store food materials. The secondary phloem also contains resin canals. In *Picea canadensis*, they occur in rays and possess cyst-like bulbous expansions.

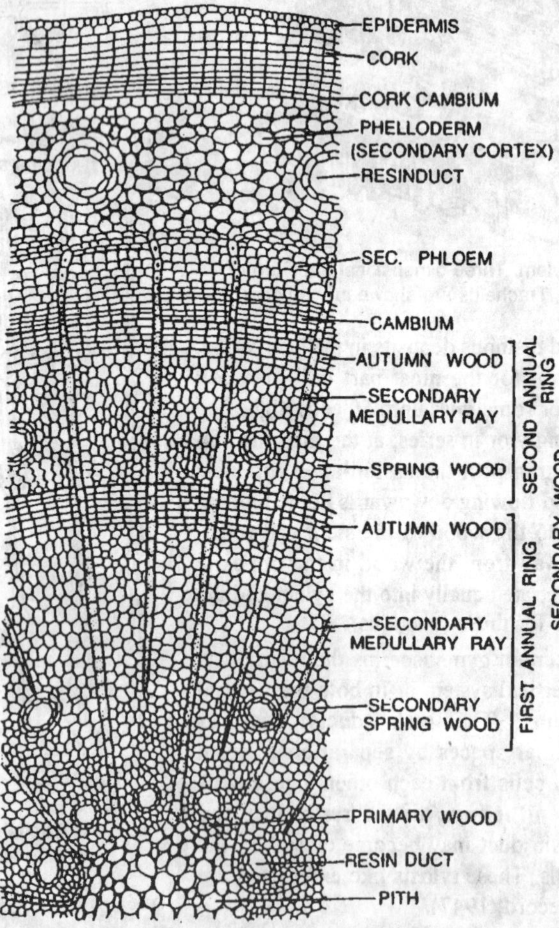

Fig. 7.65. Secondary growth in thickness of the pine stem. T.S. of a two-year-old pine stem.

SECONDARY GROWTH IN THE MONOCOTYLEDONS

Commonly, the vascular bundles of monocotyledons do not possess cambium, and therefore, there is no secondary growth. However, it occurs in some monocotyledons (*e.g.*, *Dracaena*, *Yucca*, *Veratrum*, *Aloe*, *Sansevieria*, *Xanthorrhoea*, *Kingia*, etc.). In these plants the secondary growth occurs by the formation of the cylinder of new bundles embedded in a tissue of less specialized nature. Here a cambium layer is formed from the meristematic parenchyma of the pericycle or of the innermost cortical cells. In roots of some plants, a cambium of this type forms in the endodermis. The initials of this cambium may be polygonal, rectangular or fusiform in different species. They are found in tiers forming a storied cambium.

STEM OF *PINUS*—PRIMARY AND SECONDARY STRUCTURE

ANATOMY OF YOUNG STEM

It resembles the anatomy of dicotyledonous stem in many respects. The general arrangement of the various tissues from the circumference to the centre is the same. However, it differs, from the dicot stem in having a large number of resin ducts filled with resin. These ducts are found to be distributed almost throughout the stem. The epidermis has an irregular outline. Endodermis and pericycle are like those of the dicotyledonous stem, but the pericycle contains no sclerenchyma. The vascular bundles are not wedge-shaped, as in the dicotyledons. Phloem consists of annular and spiral tracheids which are irregularly disposed towards the centre. Metaxylem consists of exclusively tracheids with bordered pits. The tracheids are arranged in radial rows as seen in the transverse section of the stem. The pits of the pine wood are large and mostly restricted to the radial walls. There are no true vessels. The details of the anatomy of young stem of pine are as follows. **Epidermis**—It consists of a single layer of cells with a very thick cuticle. **Sclerenchyma**—Sometimes a few patches of sclerenchyma occur here and there below the epidermis. **Cortex**—Many layers of more or less rounded parenchyma cells, with conspicuous resin ducts lying embedded in the cortex. **Endodermis**—A single layer lying internal to the cortex; the innermost layer of the cortex is treated as endodermis. **Pericycle**—It consists of parenchyma cells, there is no sclerenchyma in it. **Medullary rays**—They run from the pith outwards between the vascular bundles. **Pith**—There is a well defined pith, consisting of a mass of parenchyma cells. A few resin-ducts are also present in the pith. **Vascular bundles**—These are collateral and open, and arranged in a ring, as in dicot stem. Each bundle consists of phloem, cambium and xylem. **Phloem**—The phloem consists of sieve tubes and phloem parenchyma, but no companion cells. It lies on the outer side of the bundle. **Cambium**—A few layers of thin walled, rectangular cells in between xylem and phloem. **Xylem**—It consists exclusively of tracheids; there are no true vessels. Resin ducts are also present here. Protoxylem lies towards the centre and consists of a few annular and spiral tracheids which are not disposed in any regular order. Metaxylem lies towards the cambium and consists of tracheids with bordered pits which develop on the radial walls. These tracheids are four sided and are arranged in definite rows.

SECONDARY GROWTH IN THICKNESS OF STEM OF *PINUS*

The secondary growth in pine stem takes place in exactly the same way as in a dicotyledonous stem. However, the points of differentiation are as follows: The pine stem is characterized by the presence of conspicuous resin-ducts which are distributed throughout the stem. The secondary wood consists exclusively of tracheids with numerous bordered pits on their radial walls. As in the dicotyledonous stem, there are distinct annual rings, consisting of the autumn wood and spring wood. The autumn wood consists of narrow and thick-walled tracheids, and the spring wood of wider and thinner-walled tracheids. The secondary medullary rays are usually one layer of cells in thickness and a few in height. The phloem portion of the medullary ray consists of middle layers of starch—containing cells, called starch cells, and upper and lower layers of protein containing cells, called albuminous cells. The xylem portion of the medullary ray consists of similar starch cells in the middle, and empty cells with bordered pits, called tracheidal cells, in the upper and lower layers. Vessels are absent.

Table. 7.1. Anatomical differences between Dicot and Monocot Stems

	Dicotyledonous Stem	Monocotyledonous Stem
1. Hypodermis	It is collenchymatous.	It is sclerenchymatous.
2. Cortex	It consists of a few layers of parenchyma.	There is a continuous mass of parenchyma up to the centre. It is commonly known as ground tissue.
3. Endodermis	It is a wavy layer of compact cells.	
4. Pericycle	Usually it consists of parenchyma and sclerenchyma.	It is not differentiated into distinct tissues.
5. Medullary ray	There lies a strip of parenchyma in between vascular bundles.	
6. Pith	The central cylinder consists of parenchyma.	It is not marked out.
7. Vascular bundles	(*a*) They are collateral and open.	They are collateral and closed.
	(*b*) They are arranged in a ring.	They are scattered.
	(*c*) They are of uniform size.	They are larger towards the centre.
	(*d*) Phloem parenchyma present.	Phloem parenchyma absent.
	(*e*) They are wedgeshaped.	They are usually oval.
	(*f*) Bundle sheath absent.	Bundle sheath strongly developed.

8

CHAPTER

Leaf : Origin, Development and Anatomy

ORIGIN OF LEAVES

A leaf initiates by periclinal divisions in a small group of cells at the side of an apical meristem. In angiosperms, the tunica and the corpus are responsible for leaf initiation. In the dicotyledonous plants the periclinal divisions initiating the leaves occur, not in the surface layer, but in one or more layers beneath it. If the tunica is single-layered, such divisions take place within the corpus, otherwise they occur both in tunica and corpus or in the tunica only. In certain monocotyledonous plants the superficial tunica layer undergoes periclinal divisions and gives rise to some or most of the tissue. In the case of gymnosperms the leaves initiate from the peripheral tissue zone. In the vascular cryptogams (pteridophytes) the leaves are initiated either from single superficial cells or from groups of such cells.

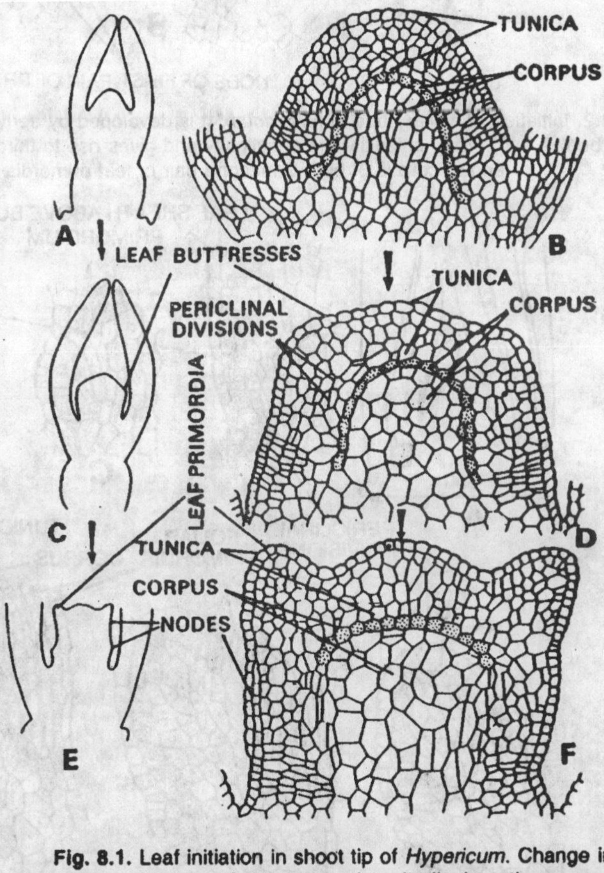

Fig. 8.1. Leaf initiation in shoot tip of *Hypericum*. Change in shape and histology of shoot apex. Longitudinal sections are seen in this figure. Leaves are in pairs at each node, in decussate arrangement. Protrusions in axis below the leaves in A, C and E are leaf bases of next lower pair of leaves; B, D and F, stippling indicates outer-boundary cells of corpus and their immediate derivatives; F, four sided figure indicates the presumptive place of origin of an axillary bud.

The periclinal divisions which initiate a leaf primordium are responsible for the formation of a lateral prominence on the side of the shoot apex. This prominence constitutes the leaf base which is also known as **leaf buttress.** Subsequently the leaf grows upwardly from the buttress. As shown in the figure, in *Hypericum* spp., the apical meristem is less prominently elevated above the youngest leaf buttress.

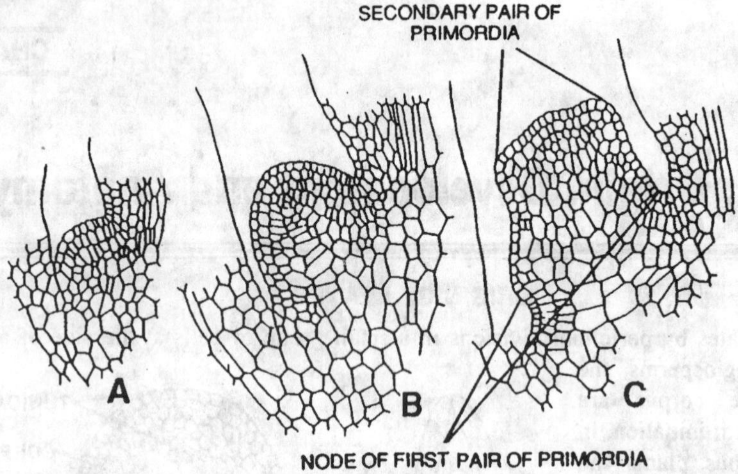

Fig. 8.2. Initiation of axillary bud in *Hypericum*. It is developed by derivatives of three layers of tunica of bud (A – C). Third layer divides periclinally and gives rise to third and fourth layers of tunica and to corpus of bud, C, second pair of leaf primordia is being initiated.

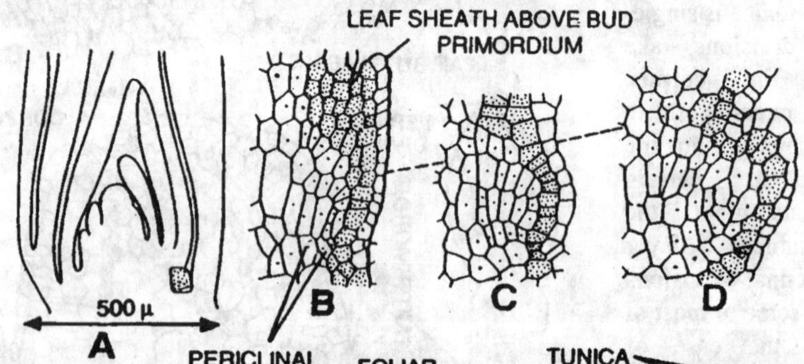

Fig. 8.3. Initiation of lateral bud in *Agropyron*. A, low-power view of shoot tip with several leaf primordia; stippled part indicates position of bud; it is developed by derivatives of the two-layered tunica and the corpus. B – G derivatives of second layer of tunica are stippled, and those of corpus indicated by a single dot in each cell. Bud is initiated by periclinal divisions in corpus derivatives (B, C). Anticlinal divisions occur in tunica derivatives; bud emerges above surface of stem (D). Tunica derivatives remain in a biseriate arrangement at apex of bud and form its two-layered tunica (E, G). Foliar primordia arise on bud (E – G).

Before the initiation of a new leaf primordium the apical meristem appears as a rounded mound. It gradually widens, and, then leaf buttresses are initiated on its sides. While the new leaf primordia grow upward from the buttresses, the apical meristem again becomes like a small mound.

ORIGIN OF BRANCHES

In angiosperms, branches commonly are initiated in close association with the leaves – They originate in the axils of the leaves, and in their nascent state they are known as **axillary buds.** The axillary buds commonly initiate somewhat later than the leaves subtending them and therefore, it is not always clear whether the meristem of the axillary bud is derived directly from the apical meristem of the main shoot or whether it originates from partly differentiated tissue of the internode. Both situations may occur because plants vary with regard to time of appearance of axillary buds. On the one hand, the axillary buds may be directly related to the apical meristem of the parent shoot; on the other hand they may intergrade, ontogenetically with the adventitious buds which arise in obviously differentiated tissue regions.

The initiation of the axillary bud in seed plants is characterized by a combination of anticlinal divisions, in one or more of the superficial layers of the young axis, and of various divisions, sometimes predominantly periclinal, in the deeper layers (see Fig. 8.2). This coordinated growth

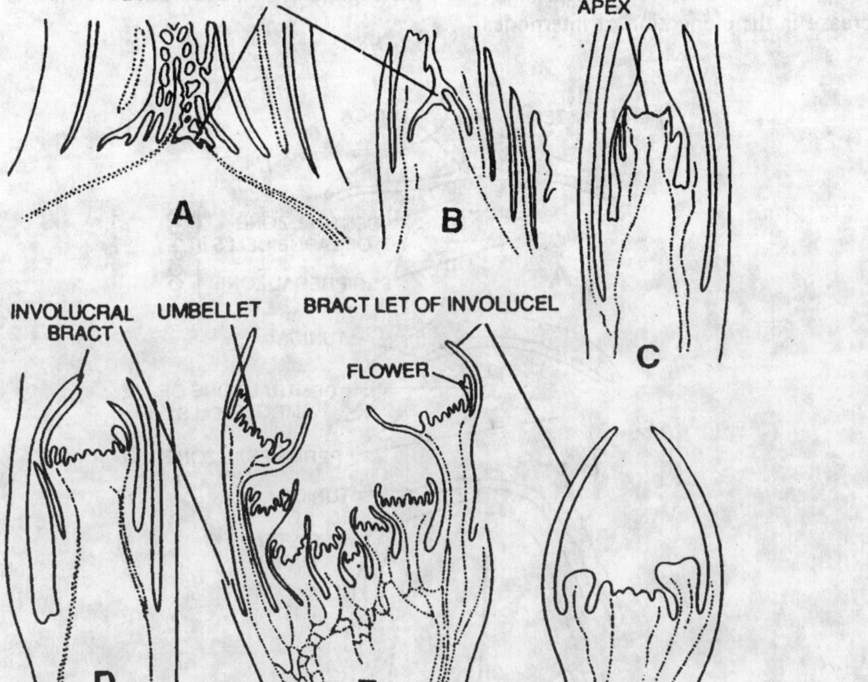

Fig. 8.4. Transformation of apical meristem during shift from vegetative growth to development of floral apices in carrot. The inflorescence is a compound umbel. A, vegetative shoot apex at base of rosette of leaves; B, shoot apex at approach of reproductive stage by internodal elongation. C, D, flattened inflorescence apices producing bracts and umbel primordia; E, compound umbel in young state; F, each flower develops a flat apex and forms floral organs.

in surface of the peripheral region and growth in volume at greater depth cause the bud to protrude above the surface of the axis. Depending on the quantitative relationships between the tunica and the corpus in the shoot apices of angiosperms. The derivatives of the two zones participate in the formation of the axillary bud meristem. If the axillary bud develops into a shoot, its apical meristem gradually organizes — commonly duplicating the pattern found in the parent shoot apex and proceeds with the formation of leaves.

ORIGIN OF REPRODUCTIVE SHOOT APEX

In the reproductive state in angiosperms, floral apices replace the vegetative apices either directly or through the development of an inflorescence. The flower, which may occur singly or as part of an inflorescence, is formed during the reproductive phase of growth. It develops from a terminal or lateral vegetative shoot apex and results in the culmination of meristematic activity of that particular meristem. Thus, the floral apex, like the leaf primordium and unlike the vegetative shoot apex, shows determinate growth.

The change to the reproductive stage may be first detected by the modified growth habit of the shoot. When the flowers develop an axillary-branch inflorescence, there appears an acceleration in production of axillary buds, which shows one of the earliest indication of approaching flowering. Simultaneously, the nature of foliar organs subtending the axillary buds also changes. They develop as bracts more or less distinct from the foliage leaves. Here during the reproductive stage the axillary buds appear earlier and grow more vigorously than the subtending bract primordia. The next feature that reveals the beginning of the reproductive state is the sudden increase in the elongation of internodes.

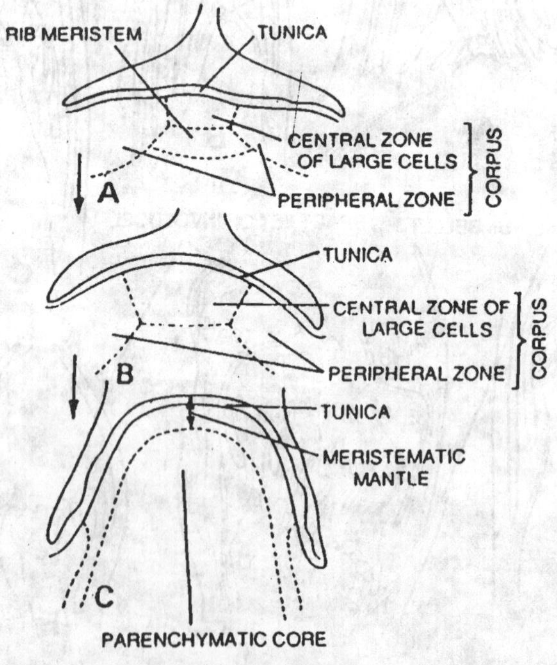

Fig. 8.5. Modification in zonation of vegetative apex during change into inflorescence in *Succisa*. A, apex when forming foliage leaves, B – C, two stages of development of inflorescence, B, initiation of inflorescence is associated with cessation of growth in length and disappearance of rib-meristem, C, central and peripheral zones are reorganized to form, together with the tunica, a meristematic mantle, overarching a parenchymatic core.

From the viewpoint of histology and cytology the reproductive meristem differs from the vegetative meristem in varying degrees. It may have the same quantitative relationship between the **tunica** and the **corpus** as was present in the vegetative apex, or the number of separate surface layers may be reduced or increased. The most conspicuous change is exhibited in the distribution of the eumeristematic and the more highly vacuolated cells. In many species the apex of the inflorescence or the flower shows a uniform, small-celled mantle-like zone of one or more layers enclosing a large celled core; this type of apex may be flatter and wider than the vegetative one. It is not necessary that the mantle may coincide with the tunica; a part of corpus may be included in it. The cells of the central tissue enlarge and become vacuolate, and the meristematic activity remains restricted to the mantle zone. This activity is concerned only with the production of floral organs.

ANATOMY OF THE LEAF

Commonly there are two types of leaves—**1. dorsiventral leaves** (dicotyledonous) and **2. isobilateral leaves** (monocotyledonous). The dorsiventral leaves usually grow in a horizontal direction with distinct upper and lower surfaces, the upper being more strongly illuminated than the

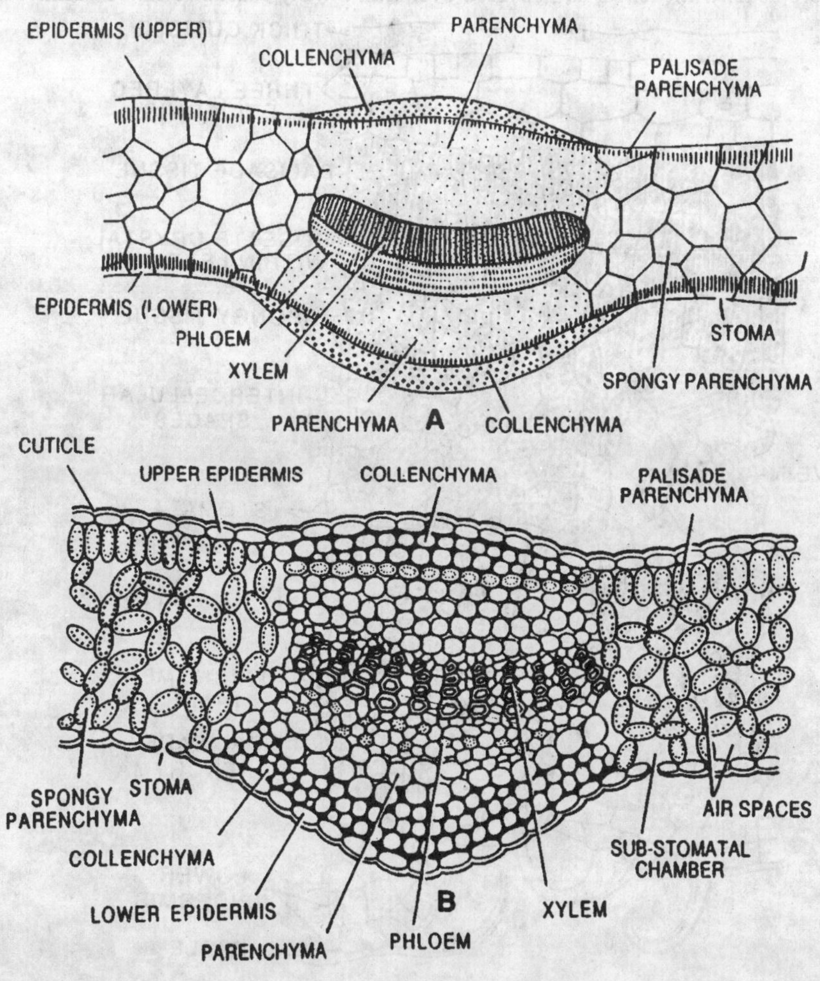

Fig. 8.6. Anatomy of bifacial dicot leaf. A, T.S. of leaf (diagrammatic); B, T.S. of leaf (detailed).

lower. There exists a difference in the internal structure between the upper and lower surfaces of the dorsiventral leaf due to its unequal illumination. Most of the dicotyledonous leaves are dorsiventral. The isobilateral leaves hang vertically so that both surfaces of the leaf receive direct and equal amount of sunlight. The isobilateral leaves possess a uniform structure on both upper and lower surfaces. A very few dicotyledons and most monocotyledons have isobilateral leaves.

Usually the leaf is composed of various tissues, which furnish various functions. In discussions of the form and anatomy of the leaf, it is customary to designate the leaf surface that is continuous with the surface of the part of the stem located above the leaf insertion as **upper, ventral**, or **adaxial** side, the opposite side as the **lower, dorsal** or **abaxial.**

ANATOMY OF DICOTYLEDONOUS LEAF

To study the anatomy of leaf, several vertical sections passing through the mid-rib are required. The internal structure of the dicotyledonous leaf is as follows:

EPIDERMIS

The leaf is covered on both surfaces by a single-layered epidermis. The outer walls of the epidermis are usually thickened, and covered over with a waxy substance called **cutin.** The outer

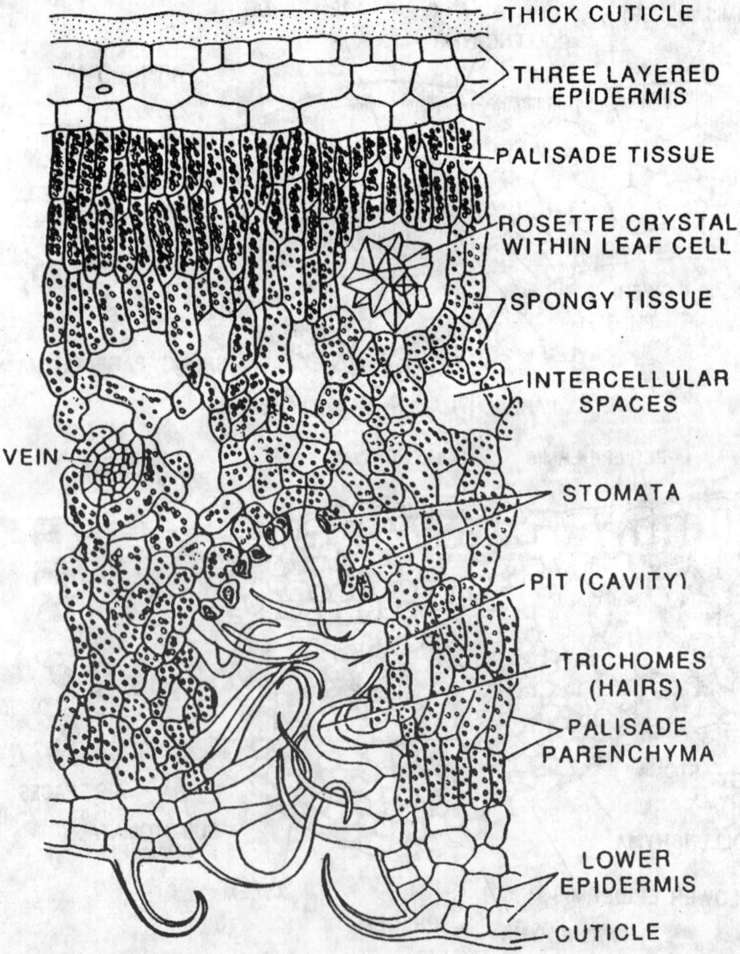

Fig. 8.7. Anatomy of a xerophytic leaf. Cross section of a leaf of *Nerium* with upper and lower palisade, three-layered upper epidermis, and stomata in a pit protected by trichomes.

surfaces of the epidermis are frequently covered with a thin or thick cuticle. This cuticular layer is formed of cutin. As the outer walls of the epidermis are thick and cutinized, water does not pass through them rapidly and the transpiration from the surface of the epidermis is greatly reduced, only small quantity of water is evaporated by transpiration. The epidermis checks the transpiration to a great extent. The epidermis also prevents the entrance of pathogens into the interior of the leaf. Another function of the epidermis is the protection of the soft internal tissue of the leaf from the mechanical injuries. Sometimes in the xerophytic leaves the epidermis cells become radially elongated and somewhat lignified. In *Nerium* leaf, the epidermis is multilayered.

Numerous small openings called stomata, are found in the epidermal layers of the leaves. Stomata are found in most abundance in the lower epidermis of the dorsiventral leaf. They are very few in the upper epidermis and sometimes altogether absent. In the floating leaves, stomata remain confined to the upper epidermis; in the submerged leaves the stomata are absent. In xerophytic leaves either stomata are sunken or situated inside the depressions.

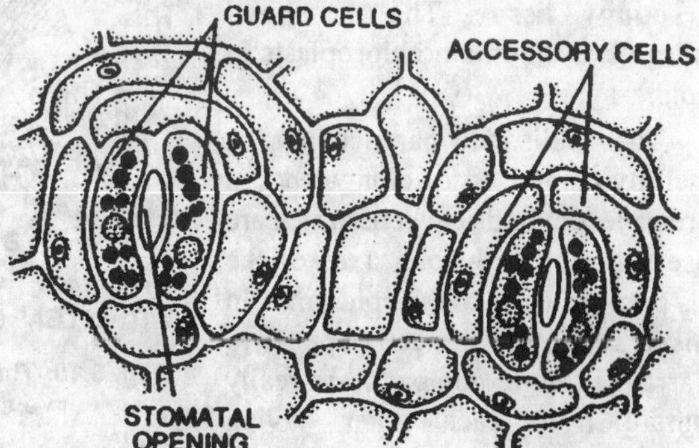

Fig. 8.8. Stomata in epidermal layer—surface view.

Each stoma remains surrounded by two semilunar guard cells. The guard cells are living and contain chloroplasts, they regulate opening and closing of stomata. The guard cells may remain surrounded by two or more **accessory cells** in addition to epidermal cells. The stomata are found in scattered condition.

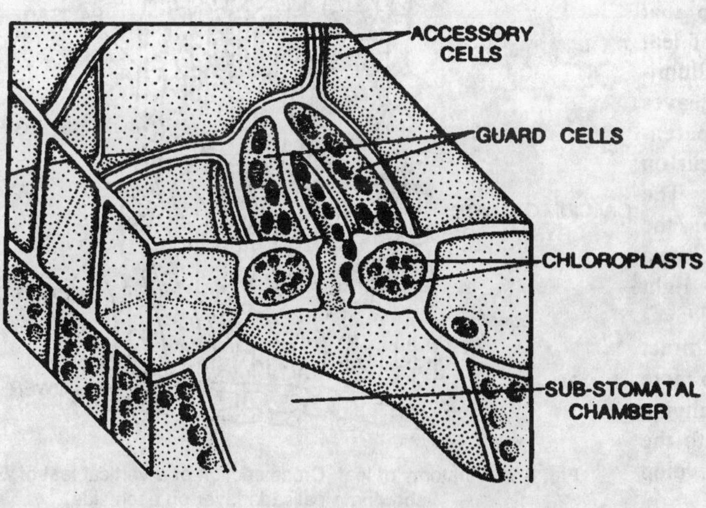

Fig. 8.9. Stomata. Diagrammatic representation of a stoma—surface and sectional views.

Usually the stomata are meant for exchange of gases in between the plant and the atmosphere. To facilitate the diffusion of gases properly, each stoma opens internally into a respiratory cavity or substomatal chamber. The transpiration takes place through the stomata, and the surplus water is being evaporated.

MESOPHYLL TISSUE

The tissue of the leaf that lies between the upper and lower epidermis and between the veins consists of typically thin walled parenchyma is known as **mesophyll.** This tissue forms the major portion of the inner of leaf. Commonly the cells of mesophyll are of two types—the **palisade parenchyma** or **palisade tissue,** and the **spongy parenchyma** or **spongy tissue**. The mesophyll tissues always contain chloroplasts in them.

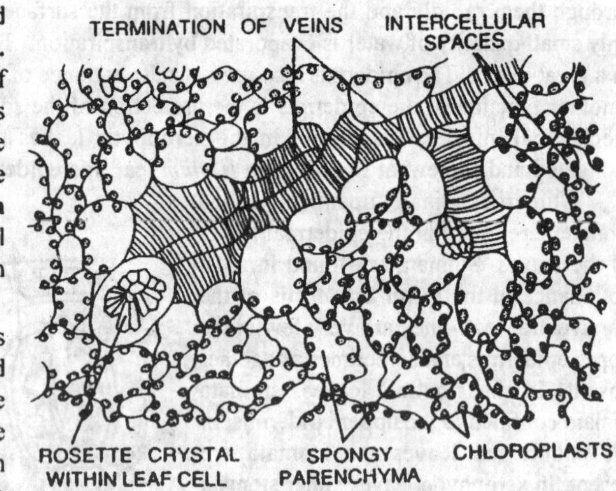

Fig. 8.10. The leaf. Termination of veins in a leaf, as seen in a section cut parallel with the epidermis.

The palisade parenchyma is generally composed of elongated and more or less cylindrical cells which are close together with long axes of the cells perpendicular to the epidermis. In transverse section the cells appear to be arranged quite compact, are really separate from each other having intercellular spaces among them. The palisade tissue may consist of a single or more layers. These cells are arranged near to the upper surface of the leaf, where they receive sunlight and facilitate to carry the function of photosynthesis. Sometimes the leaves hang vertically (*e.g., Eucalyptus*), so that both surfaces of leaf are equally illuminated. In such leaves the palisade parenchyma may occur on both sides. The compactness of the palisade parenchyma depends upon light intensity. The leaves which receive direct sunlight develop more compact parenchyma in comparison to the leaves which develop in shady places.

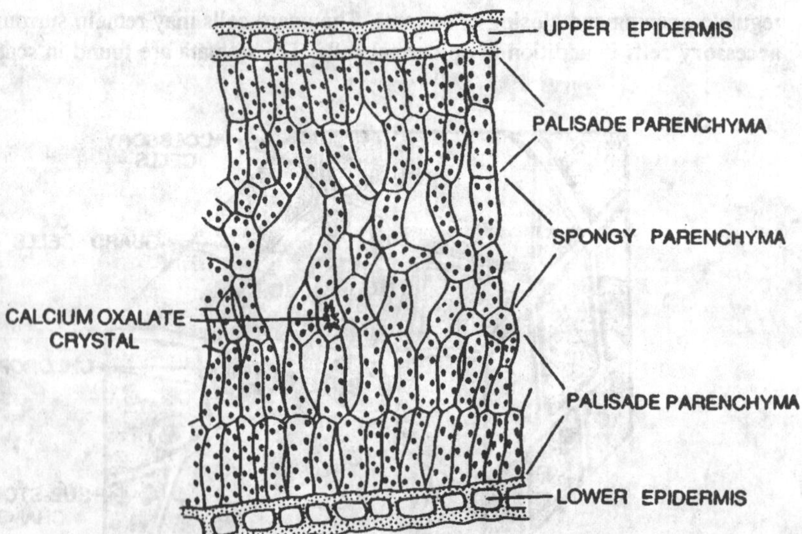

Fig. 8.11. Anatomy of leaf. Cross section of a vertical leaf of *Eucalyptus* showing a palisade layer on each side.

The lower portion of the mesophyll in the leaf is known as spongy parenchyma or spongy tissue. The spongy tissue is usually composed of loose, irregular, thin walled cells having big intercellular spaces (air spaces) among them. The cells of spongy parenchyma also contain chloroplasts and carry on photosynthesis, but in comparison of palisade parenchyma less chloroplasts are developed. Due to the presence of a large air space in the spongy tissue they are more adaptable to the exchange of gases between the cells and the atmosphere.

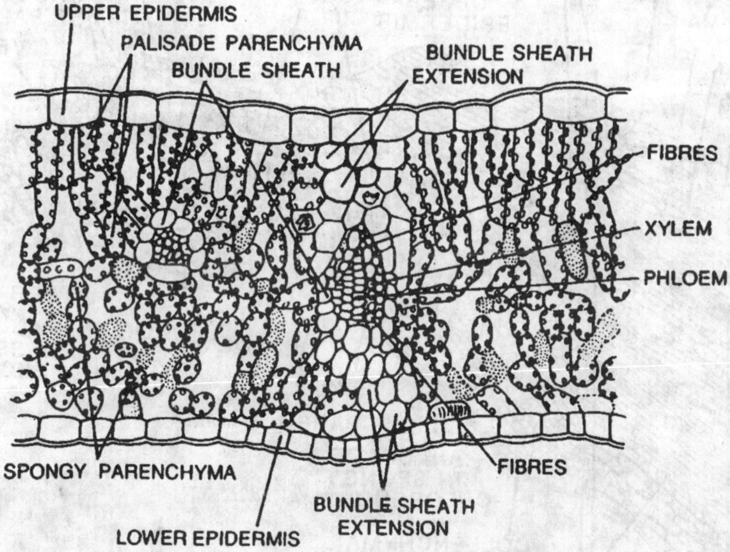

Fig. 8.12. Anatomy of leaf. T.S. of pear leaf. Palisade parenchyma towards upper side consists of 2 or 3 layers. Bundles are enclosed in bundle sheaths. The large vascular bundle has bundle sheath extensions reaching to the epidermis on both sides of the leaf.

The large air spaces that surround the spongy parenchyma cells are near the stomata and directly connected with them. There is therefore a much more free circulation of gases around these cells than around the palisade parenchyma cells, with the result that they are better suited to the exchange of gases between the cells and the surrounding atmosphere. The air spaces of the spongy chlorenchyma are not isolated chambers but a series of intercommunicating passages.

Both spongy and palisade parenchyma contain discoid chloroplasts arranged in parallel rows in the cells. As the chloroplasts are more dense in the palisade tissue than the spongy tissue the upper surface of the leaf appears to be deeper green than the lower surface.

MECHANICAL SUPPORT IN THE LEAF

The functions of the midrib and the lateral veins are to strengthen the leaf. The important tissue giving mechanical strength to leaf are—collenchyma, sclerenchyma, turgid parenchyma and woody xylem.

Collenchyma. In the centre of the upper portion of the midrib, just below the epidermis, there is usually a group of cells which give strength by having thickened walls and by being turgid. A group of the same kind of cells usually occurs also just above the lower epidermis. These cells constitute the **collenchyma**. Collenchyma is composed of living cells with walls which are thickened at the angles where three or more cells come in contact with one another. The thick places in the walls increase the strength of the cells, while the thin places allow for a more rapid transfer of materials from cell to cell than would take place if the cell walls were thickened throughout. These cells are more or less turgid, and so give strength to the leaf in the way also. The weight of the leaf causes it to tend to bend downward, with the result that there is a tendency for the upper portion to be stretched and the lower portion compressed. The collenchyma occurs, therefore, in those parts of the midrib in which there is the greatest need for strengthening material.

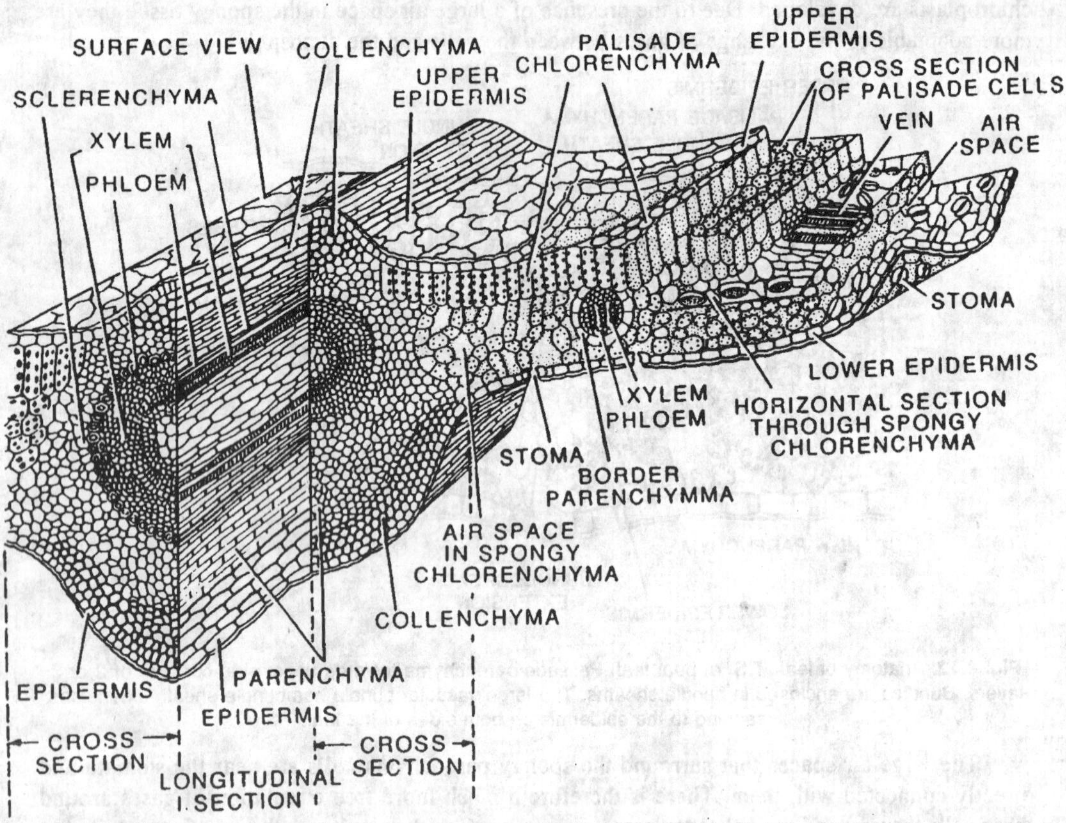

Fig. 8.13. The leaf. A three-dimensional view of a section of a midrib and a small part of the leaf blade. On the left side is a cross section of half of the midrib followed by a longitudinal section, and this by a cross section of the remainder of the midrib and a portion of the blade. The leaf on the right side is dissected in various ways to show the arrangement of the tissues. (After Brown).

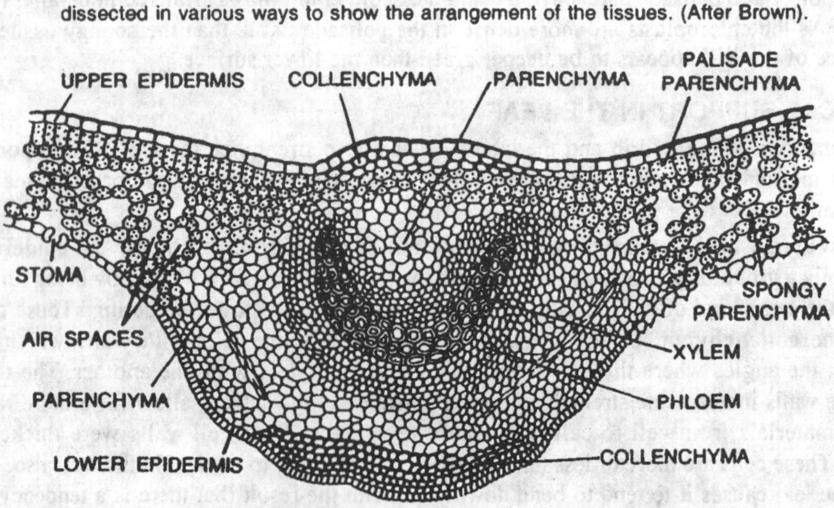

Fig. 8.14. Anatomy of dicotyledonous leaf. Cross section of midrib and leaf blade of leaf of *Erythroxylon*.

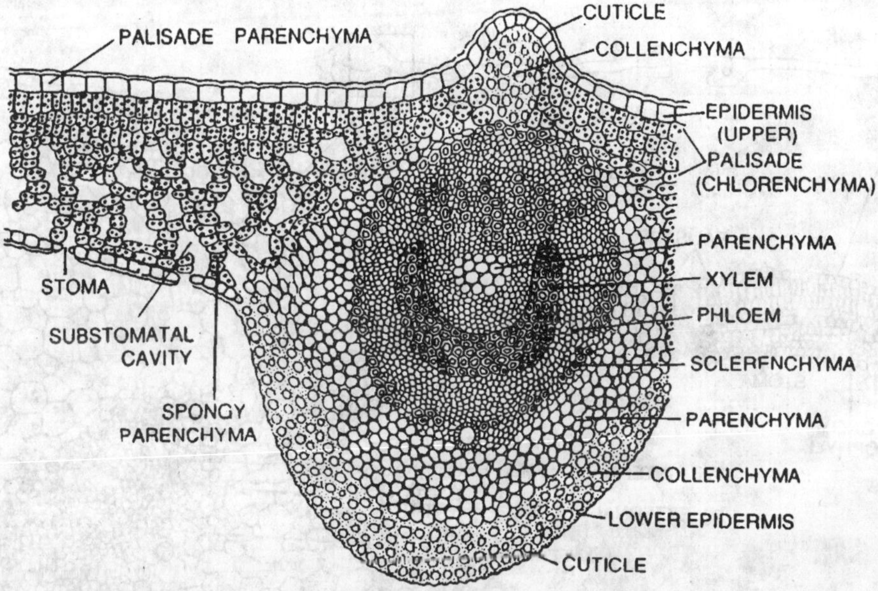

Fig. 8.15. Anatomy of dicotyledonous leaf. Cross section through a midrib and a part of leaf blade of a leaf of *Ixora*.

Sclerenchyma. Usually the sclerenchyma cells or the fibres are associated with the vascular tissues of the leaves. They occur usually as bundle caps adjacent to the phloem. Sometimes the fibres are found on both the sides of large vascular bundle of the leaves. Usually these cells are thick walled, dead and lignified. Their position just exterior to thin-walled phloem affords mechanical protection to the latter. The fibres are greatly elongated in the longitudinal direction of the midrib.

Turgid parenchyma. The regions between the collenchyma cells and the central portion of the midrib are occupied by parenchyma cells. In structure the parenchyma cells are not specially modified for any particular function, but they perform all the general functions of cells to a limited extent. Parenchyma cells have thin walls, but on account of their turgidity they strengthen the midrib.

Xylem. Usually the vessels and tracheids of xylem conduct water, but due to their thick walled nature they also give mechanical support to the leaves. The xylem elements are composed of lignified and dead cells.

ORIENTATION OF VASCULAR TISSUE

In the leaf traces of flowering plants, before they have the stele, the phloem is always found towards the outside of the stem. The leaf traces after their entrance in the petiole and lamina, also maintain the relative position of the xylem and the phloem, *i.e.*, the phloem is always found towards the lower side and the xylem towards the upper side in the leaf. Sometimes the xylem ring remains surrounded by a ring of phloem. The phloem occurs only below the xylem or rarely both above and below it.

Conducting system. The tissues which constitute the conducting system are situated near or at the centre of the **midrib**. This system may have various shapes, *e.g.*, the form of a ring, a crescent shaped ring, a crescent or scattered patches. In the ring shaped conducting system parenchyma cells are usually found in the centre of the ring. The inner part of the ring is composed of xylem (towards upper surface), and phloem (towards lower surface).

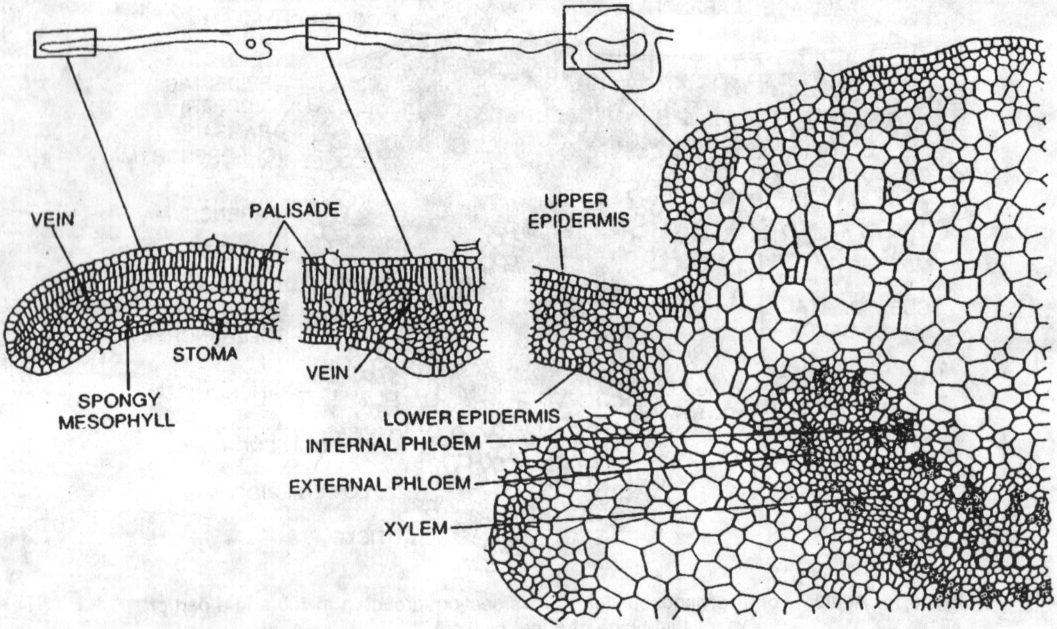

Fig. 8.16. Anatomy of dicotyledonous leaf of *Nicotiana tabacum*. T.S. through a part of leaf. Diagrammatic detail. (After Avery).

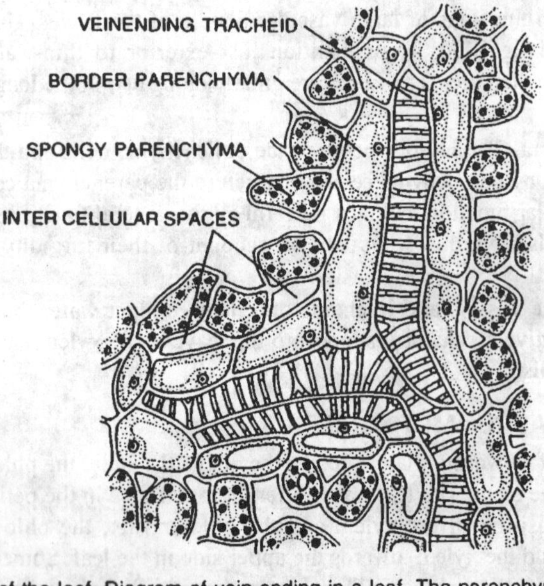

Fig. 8.17. Veins of the leaf. Diagram of vein ending in a leaf. The parenchyma tissue bordering the vein is conspicuous.

Xylem is composed of various kinds of vessels, trachieds wood fibres and wood parenchyma. Specially the vessels are annular and spiral. Xylem conducts water, raw food material and also gives mechanical support to the leaf. The phloem consists of sieve tubes, companion cells and phloem parenchyma. The phloem serves for the translocation of prepared food material from the mesophyll of the leaf.

Veins. The structure of large veins is more or less similar to that of a midrib. As they pass from the base of a leaf blade towards the apex or margin of the leaf, they get reduced in size, and simple in structure. The small veins consist of only of few conducting cells. The xylem is always found towards the upper surface and phloem towards lower even in very small veins. The cells of the mesophyll (chlorenchyma) are usually arranged so that the conduction of materials to and from the veins is facilitated.

The bundle sheath. The larger vascular bundles of dicotyledonous leaves remain surrounded by parenchyma with small number of chloroplasts, whereas the small bundles occur in the mesophyll. However, these small bundles do not remain in contact with intercellular spaces but are commonly enclosed with a layer of compactly arranged parenchyma, the **bundle sheath.** In dicotyledons the bundle-sheath parenchyma is also called **border parenchyma.** The bundle sheaths of dicotyledonous leaves usually consist of cells elongated parallel with the course of the bundle and having walls as thin as those of adjacent mesophyll. In some plants these cells have chloroplasts similar to those the mesophyll (*e.g.*, in *Humulus, Nicotiana tabacum*); in others they have few or no chloroplasts. The bundle sheath cells are in direct contact with the conducting cells of the vascular bundle of parenchyma and on the outer face with the mesophyll tissue. Individual sheath cells may contain crystals.

The parenchymatous bundle sheaths are more common, but in certain dicotyledons bundles of various sizes are enclosed in sclerenchyma, *e.g.*, Winteraceae, Melastomaceae; (Bailey and Nast, 1944; Foster, 1947).

Vertical leaves. The leaves of many species of *Eucalyptus* do not spread out horizontally but hang vertically, so that both surfaces of the leaf receive direct sunlight. In keeping with this fact, palisade chlorenchyma is developed on both sides.

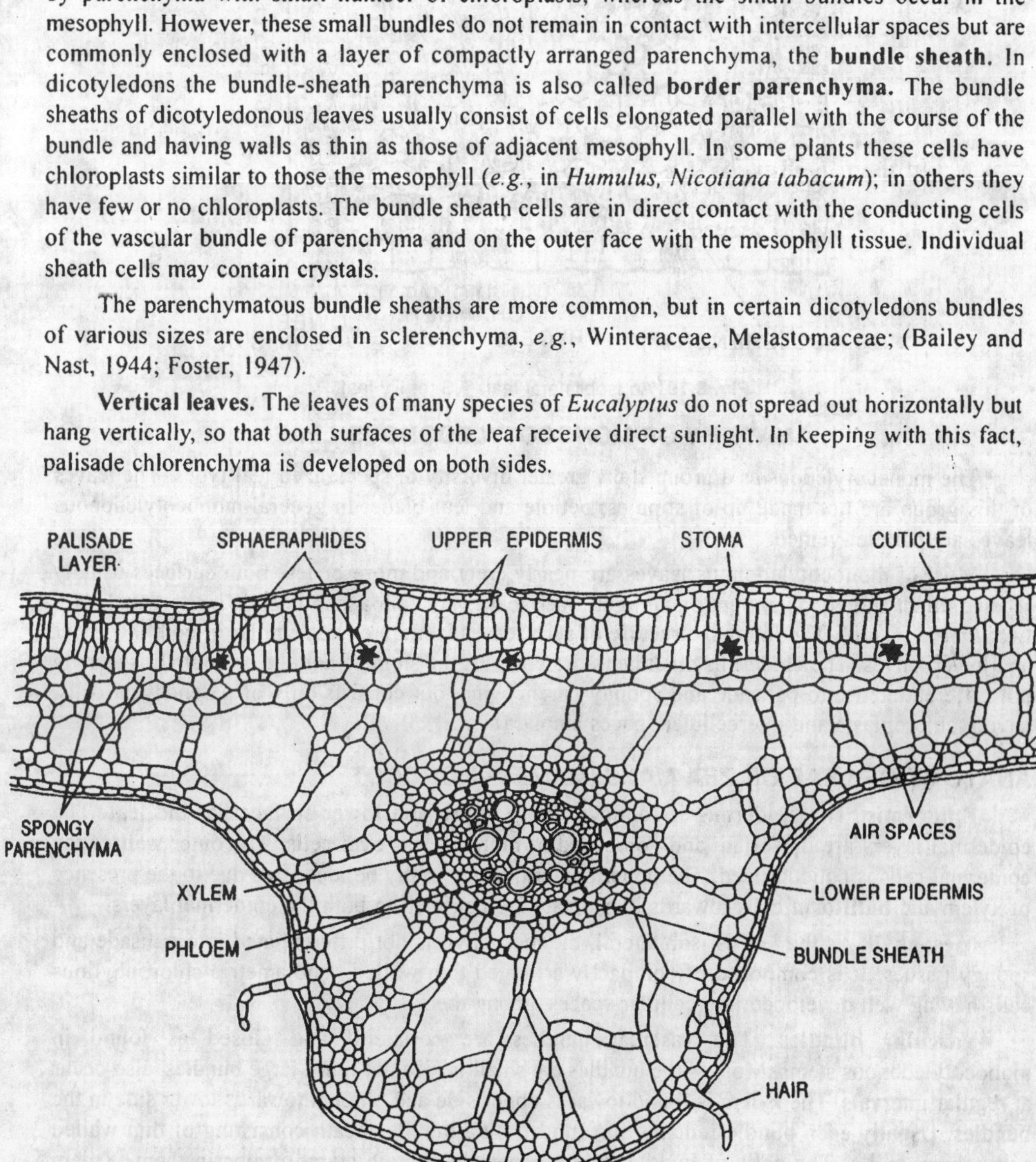

Fig. 8.18. Hydrophytic leaf. T.S. of floating leaf of *Trapa bispinosa*, showing big air spaces, the stomata confined to upper epidermis only.

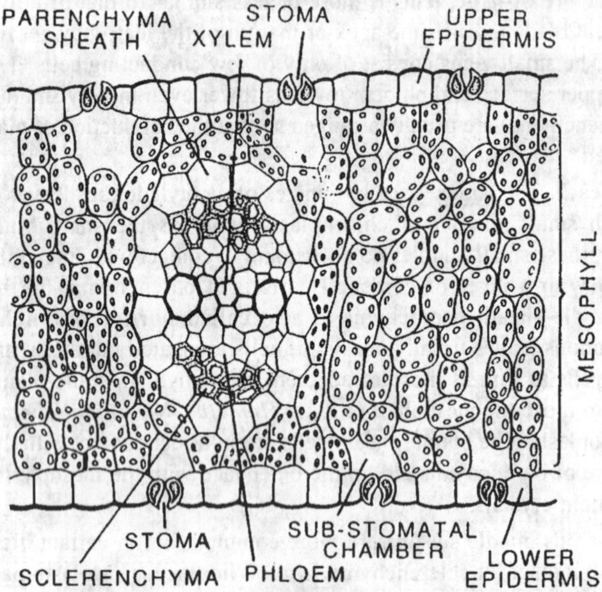

Fig. 8.19. An isobilateral leaf. T.S. of lily leaf.

ANATOMY OF MONOCOTYLEDONOUS LEAF

The monocotyledons as a group show greater diversity of specialized leaf types. The leaves of this group are not made up of stipules, petiole and leaf blade. In general monocotyledonous leaves are parallel-veined.

Most of monocotyledonous leaves are nearly erect and more or less both surfaces usually receive direct and equal amount of sunlight. Such leaves are called isobilateral (*isos* = equal; *bi* = two; *lateris* = side). The internal structure of such leaves is more or less similar in both the upper and lower halves. The epidermis on either sides contains the stomata and the mesophyll is usually not differentiated into palisade and spongy parenchyma, but consists only of parenchyma cells, having chloroplasts and intercellular spaces among them.

ANATOMY OF LEAF OF *ZEA MAYS* (MAIZE)—MONOCOT

Epidermis. The epidermis is found on both upper and lower surfaces of the leaf. The epidermal layers are uniseriate and composed of more or less oval cells. The outer wall of the epidermal cells is cuticularized. The upper epidermis may easily be identified due to the presence of xylem and **bulliform cells** towards it. Stomata are confined to both the epidermal layers.

Mesophyll. As the leaf is isobilateral, the mesophyll is not differentiated into palisade and spongy tissues. It is composed of compactly arranged thin walled, isodiametric chlorophyllous cells having well developed intercellular spaces among them.

Vascular bundles. The vascular bundles are collateral and closed as found in monocotyledonous stems. Most of the bundles are small in size but fairly large bundles, also occur at regular intervals. The xylem is found towards upper side and phloem towards lower side in the bundles. Usually each bundle remains surrounded by a bundle sheath consisting of thin walled parenchyma cells. The cells of bundle sheath generally contain starch grains in them. Xylem consists of vessels and phloem of sieve tubes and companion cells. Sclerenchyma cells occur in patches on both ends of the large vascular bundles which give mechanical support to the leaf.

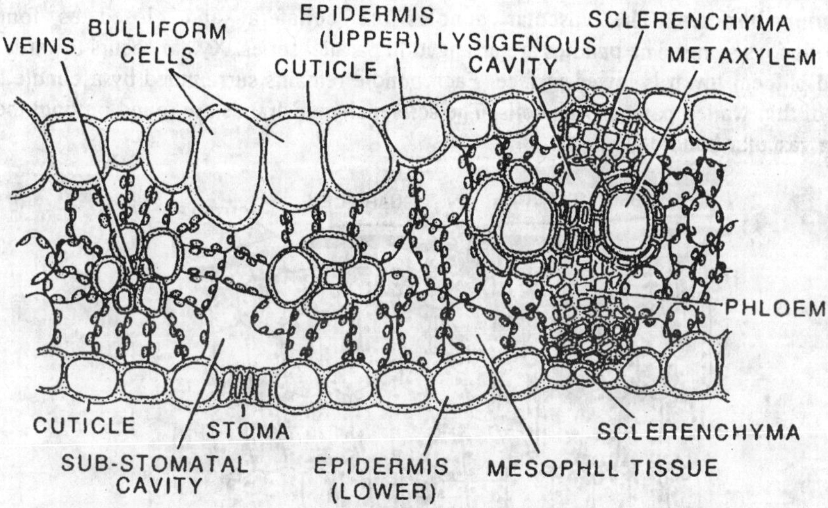

Fig. 8.20. Anatomy of monocotyledonous leaf of *Zea mays* similar structure of the two sides of vertical leaf.

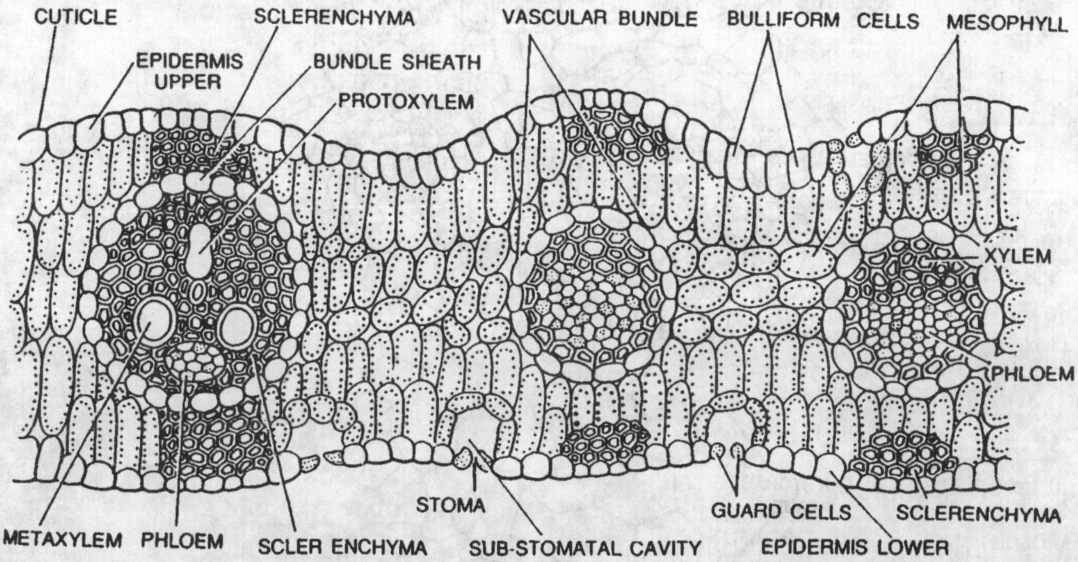

Fig. 8.21. Anatomy of isobilateral leaf. T.S. *Triticum aestivum* leaf (monocot).

ANATOMY OF THE LEAF OF *TRITICUM AESTIVUM* (WHEAT)—MONOCOT

Epidermis. As usual the epidermis layers are found on both upper and lower surfaces of the leaf. The epidermises are uniseriate and composed of more or less oval cells having no intercellular spaces among them. The outer walls of epidermal cells are cuticularized. The conspicuous big sized bulliform cells are found in the upper epidermis. The stomata are confined to both epidermis layers. The sub-stomatal chambers are also seen in vertical section.

Mesophyll. It is composed of more or less oval chlorenchyma cells having intercellular spaces among them. The mesophyll tissue is not clearly differentiated into palisade and spongy parenchyma; however, the cells towards epidermal layers are somewhat elongated and palisade-like. Substomatal chambers are seen beneath the stomata.

Vascular bundles. The vascular bundles are collateral and closed as found in monocotyledonous stems. The bundles are arranged in parallel series. Xylem occurs towards upper surface and phloem towards lower surface. Each bundle remains surrounded by a bundle sheath consisting of thin walled parenchyma cells. The sclerenchyma strands are found on both the ends of each big vascular bundle.

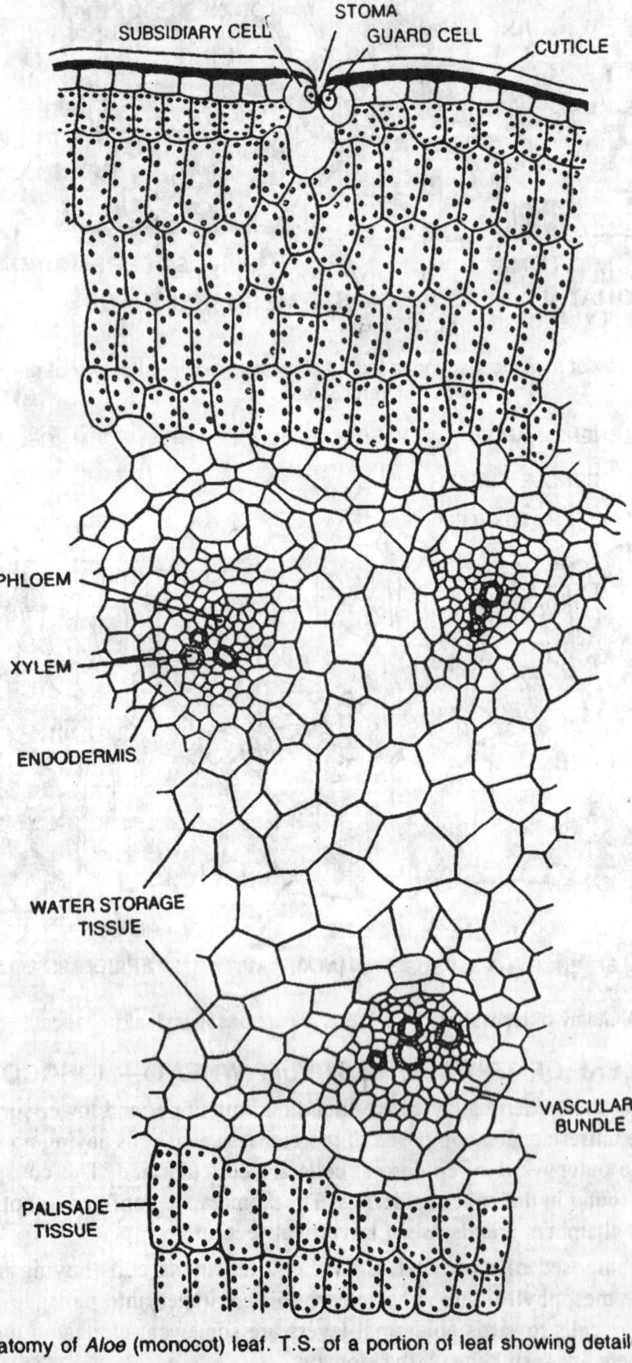

Fig. 8.22. Anatomy of *Aloe* (monocot) leaf. T.S. of a portion of leaf showing detailed internal structure.

ADAPTATIONS TO WATER STRESS: ECOLOGICAL ANATOMY

The plants which characteristically grow in certain ecological niches often show a type of structure which is believed to be adapted to that particular environment. In the course of evolution, many species have become adapted in both structural and physiological features to habitats with an excessive water supply. Plants that live wholly or partly submerged in water or in very wet places are known as **hydrophytes** (Gr. *hudor,* water; *phyton,* plant). The greatest number of plants grow under average conditions of moisture and temperature. Plants of habitats that usually show neither an excess nor a deficiency of water are known as **mesophytes** (Gr. *mesos*, middle; *phyton*, plant). Mesophytes are therefore, intermediate between hydrophytes and xerophytes. Plants that grow habitually where the evaporation stress is high and the water supply low show characteristic adaptations to a decrease in water content. They are known as **xerophytes** (Gr. *Xeros,* dry; *phyton*, plant). The plants grow in desert or in very dry places; they can withstand a prolonged period or drought uninjured. They are really drought-resistant plants. Hydrophytes, xerophytes, and mesophytes are distinguishable as groups, since each has more or less definite habitat and characteristic appearance. Between hydrophytes and mesophytes on the one hand, and extreme xerophytes and mesophytes on the other, they found all gradations of form and all degrees of structural adaptations due to intermediate habitats. Plants that grow upon other plants, but do not absorb food from them are known as **epiphytes** (Gr. *epi*, upon; *phyton*, plant), such as many orchids (*e.g., Vanda*). Plants that grow in places rich in decaying organic substances, and derive their nutrition from them, are known as **saprophytes** (Gr. *sapros*, rotten; *phyton*, plant). (*e.g., Montropa*). Plants that grow upon other living plants and absorb their food material from them, are known as **parasites.** For the purpose of the absorption of food the parasites develop haustoria, which penetrate into the tissue of the host plant, and absorb nutrition from it (*e.g., Cuscuta*). Some of the anatomical features of above mentioned groups of plants are described below:

HYDROPHYTES

Plants grow in water or very wet places. They may be **submerged** or **partly submerged, floating** or **amphibious.** Their structural adaptations are mainly due to the high water content and the deficient supply of oxygen. The various adaptations are as follows:

(*i*) The reduction of protective tissue (epidermis here is meant for absorption and not for protection).

(*ii*) The reduction of supporting or mechanical tissue (*i.e.,* lack of sclerenchyma).

(*iii*) The reduction of conducting tissue (*i.e.,* minimum development of vascular tissue).

(*iv*) The reduction of absorbing tissue (roots chiefly act as anchors, and root hairs are lacking).

(*v*) There is special development of air-chambers (aerenchyma) for aeration of internal tissues.

EPIDERMIS

In aquatic plants, the epidermis is not protective but absorbs gases and nutrients directly from the water. The epidermis in the typical hydrophyte has an extremely thin cuticle, and the thin cellulose walls permit ready absorption from the surrounding water. Commonly the chloroplasts are found in epidermal cells of leaves, especially when the leaves are very thin; these chloroplasts utilize the weak light under water for photosynthesis. In submerged plant, stomata are not present, and exchange of gases takes place directly through cell walls. The floating leaves of aquatic plants have abundant stomata on the upper surface.

Lack of sclerenchyma. Submerged plants usually have few or no sclerenchymatous tissue and cells. The water itself gives support to the plant, and protects it to some extent from injury. The

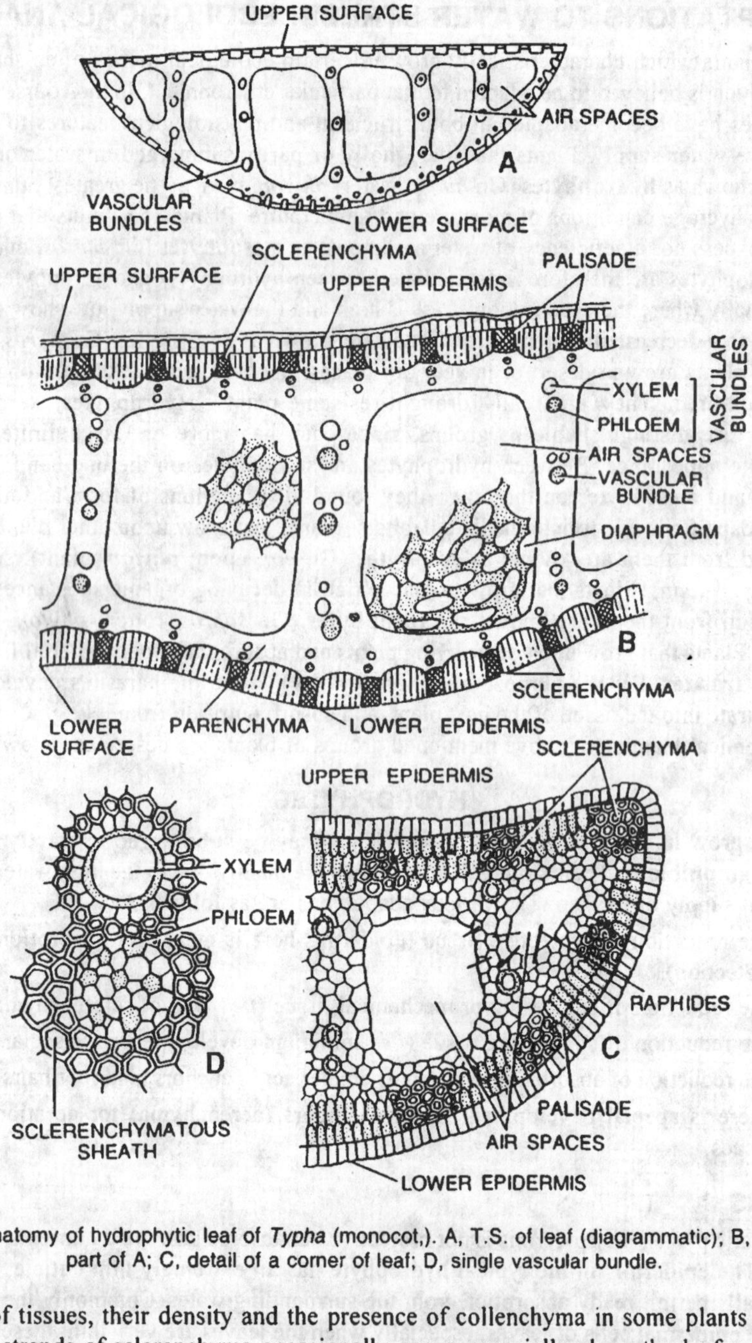

Fig. 8.23. Anatomy of hydrophytic leaf of *Typha* (monocot,). A, T.S. of leaf (diagrammatic); B, detail of a part of A; C, detail of a corner of leaf; D, single vascular bundle.

thick walls of tissues, their density and the presence of collenchyma in some plants give some rigidity. The strands of sclerenchyma occasionally occur, especially along the leaf margins, and increase tensile strength. A few star shaped idioblasts or sclereids are present, which give mechanical support to the body of aquatic plant (*e.g.*, *Limnanthemum*, *Nymphaea*).

Minimum development of vascular tissue. In the vascular tissues, the xylem shows the greatest reduction and in many aquatic plants consists of only a few elements, even in the stele and main vascular bundles (*e.g.*, *Elatine alsinastrum*). In some aquatic plants (*e.g.*, *Potamogeton*

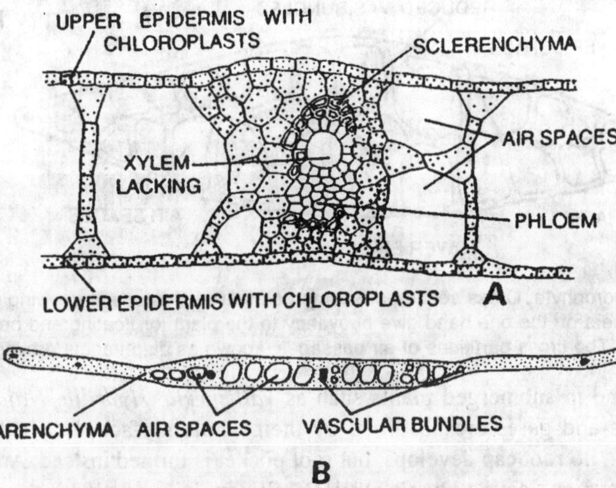

Fig. 8.24. Anatomy of hydrophytes. A, cross section of submerged leaf of *Potamogeton epihydrus* (detail); B, diagrammatic representation of the same.

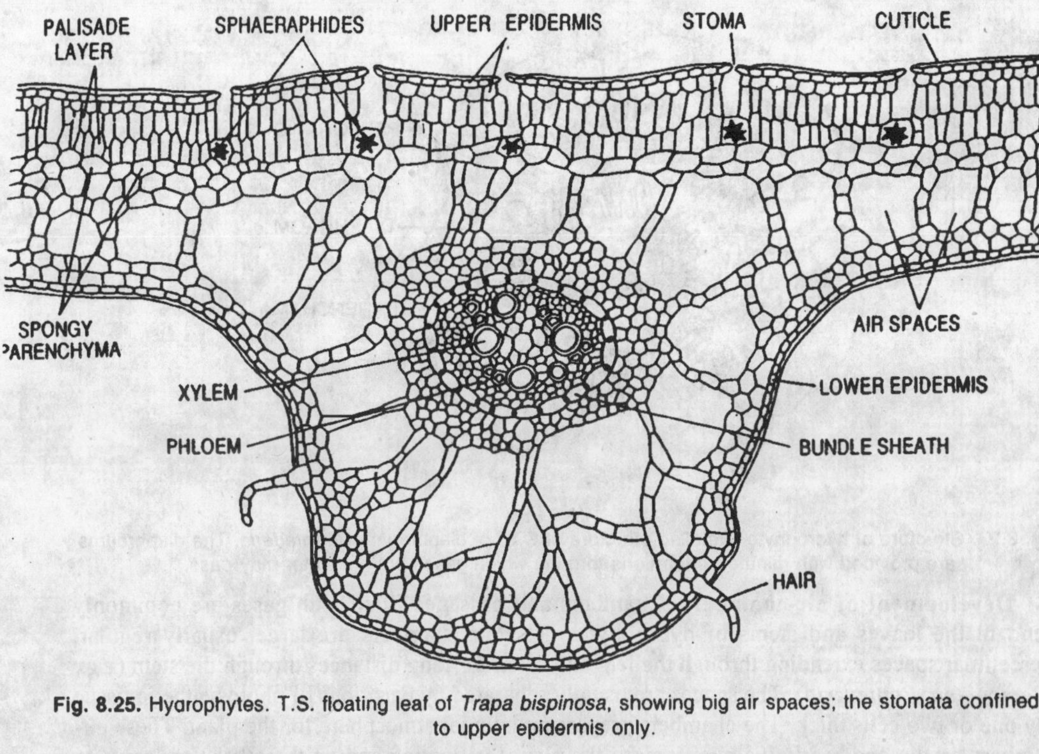

Fig. 8.25. Hyarophytes. T.S. floating leaf of *Trapa bispinosa*, showing big air spaces; the stomata confined to upper epidermis only.

pectinatus, P. epihydrus), in the stele and large bundles, and frequently in the small bundles, xylem elements are lacking. In these plants there is well developed **xylem lacuna** in the position of xylem. These lacunae resemble typical air-chambers (air spaces). In many aquatic plants, the phloem is fairly well developed as compared with the xylem. The endodermis is usually present around the stele, but it is weakly developed.

Reduction of absorbing tissue. The root-system in hydrophytes is feebly developed and root hairs and root cap are absent. In some floating plants such as *Utricularia, Ceratophyllum*, etc., no

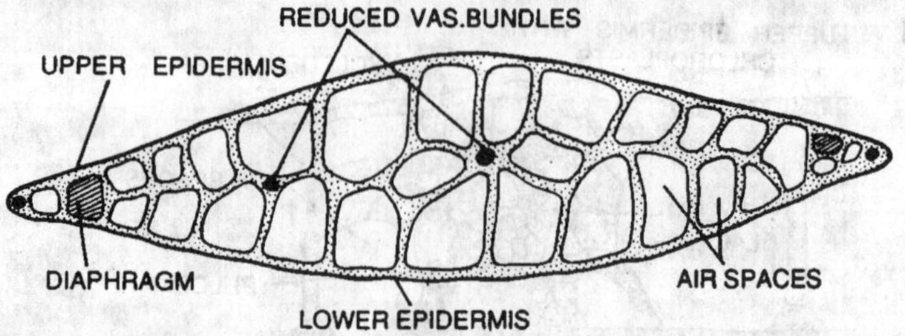

Fig. 8.26. Structure of hydrophyte. Cross section of submerged leaf of *Pontederia* showing diaphragm and air spaces. The airchambers on the one hand give buoyancy to the plant for floating and on the other they serve to store up air. The cross partitions of air passages, known as diaphragms prevent flooding.

roots are developed, and in submerged plants such as *Vallisneria, Hydrilla, Naias,* etc., water dissolved mineral salts and gases are absorbed by their whole surface. In plants like *Pistia, Eichhornia, Lemna,* etc., no root cap develops, but root pocket is formed instead. An aquatic plant is, in reality, submerged in or floating upon a nutrient solution. In hydrophytes the root system is functioning chiefly as holdfasts or anchors, and a large part of the absorption takes place through the leaves and stems.

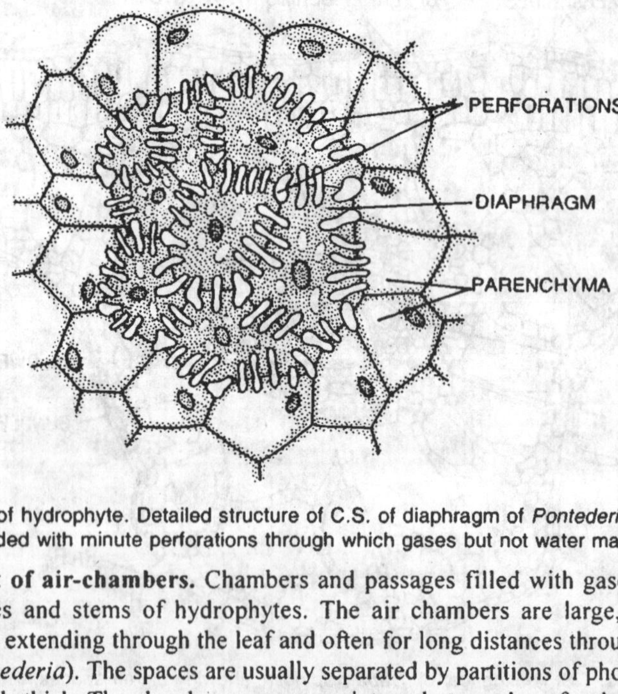

Fig. 8.27. Structure of hydrophyte. Detailed structure of C.S. of diaphragm of *Pontederia*. The diaphragms are provided with minute perforations through which gases but not water may pass.

Development of air-chambers. Chambers and passages filled with gases are commonly found in the leaves and stems of hydrophytes. The air chambers are large, usually regular, intercellular spaces extending through the leaf and often for long distances through the stem (*e.g., Potamogeton, Pontederia*). The spaces are usually separated by partitions of photosynthetic tissue only one or two cells thick. The chambers prepare an internal atmosphere for the plant. These air-chambers on the one hand give buoyancy to the plant for floating and on the other they serve to store up air (oxygen and carbon dioxide). The carbon dioxide that is given off in respiration is stored in these cavities for photosynthesis, and again the oxygen that is given off in photosynthesis during the daytime is similarly stored in them for respiration. The cross partitions of air passages, known as diaphragms, prevent flooding. The diaphragms are provided with minute perforations through which gases but not water may pass. Another specialized tissue frequently found in aquatic plants that gives buoyancy to the plant parts on which it occurs is **aerenchyma.** The presence of

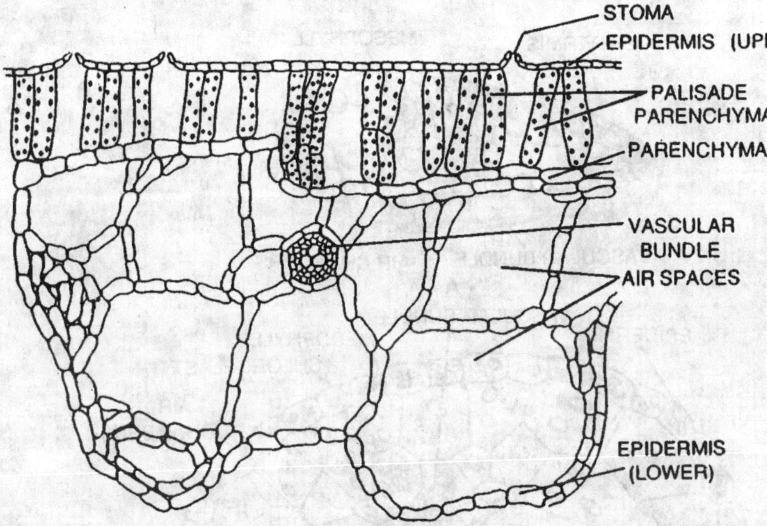

Fig. 8.28. Anatomy of hydrophytie leaf. V.S. of aquatic leaf of *Victoria regia* (dictot.) detail.

this type of aerenchyma is characteristic of species of *Decodon* and *Lythrum*. Here, very thin partitions enclose air spaces and the whole structure consists of very feeble tissue. Aerenchyma is phellem formed by a typical phellogen of epidermal or cortical origin. At regular intervals individual cells of each layer of phellem elongate greatly in the radial direction while the other cells of this layer remain small. However, the term aerenchyma is applied to any tissue with many large intercellular spaces, but such aerenchyma is quite distinct from the typical aeranchyma mentioned above (of *Decodon*) which is of secondary origin.

List of Common Aquatic Plants

Submerged— *Vallisneria, Potamogeton, Hydrilla.* **Floating**—*Ceratophyllum, Pistia, Utricularia, Eichhornia, Trapa, Neptunia.*

Plants with floating leaves—*Nymphaea, Nelumbium, Victoria regia, Euryale, Limanthemum.*

Amphibious plants—*Ranunculus aquatilis, Sagittaria, Limnophylla, Cardenthera, Typha, Alisma, Myriophyllum heterophyllum,* etc.,

MESOPHYTES

They grow in habitats that are neither extremely dry nor wet. These are plants that grow under average conditions of temperature and moisture. They are supposed to be intermediate between hydrophytes and xerophytes. In mesophytes the root system is well developed with the tap-root and its branches in dicotyledons, and a cluster of fibrous roots in monocotyledons; root hairs are abundantly produced for the absorption of water from the soil. The stem is solid, erect and normally branched. All the different kinds of tissues, particularly the mechanical and conducting tissues, have reached their full development in the mesophytes. The aerial parts of plants such as the leaves and the branches are provided with cuticle. In dorsiventral leaves the lower epidermis is provided with numerous stomata; there are few stomata or none at all on the upper surface. In erect leaves, as in most monocotyledons, stomata are more or less equally distributed on both surfaces. The stomata are relatively uniform in structure and the guard cells show a maximum capacity for movement. The anatomy of mesophytic plants is quite normal and no special adaptations are found in them. In the foregoing chapters, much emphasis has been given on the anatomical features of the plants that develop in regions of average or optimum water supply, *i.e.*, mesophytes.

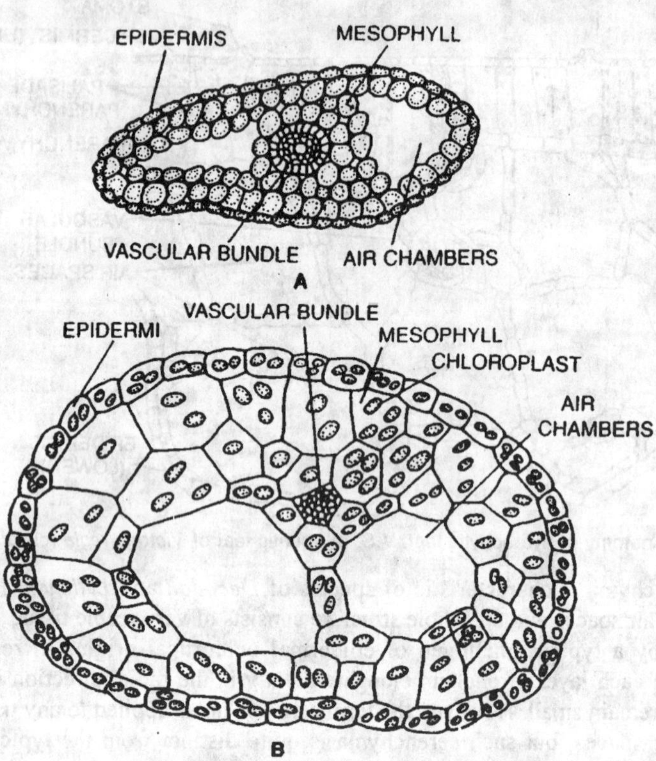

Fig. 8.29. Hydrophytes. A, T.S. through the leaf of submerged plants *Zanichellia palustris; B, T.S. through leaf of Potamogeton*

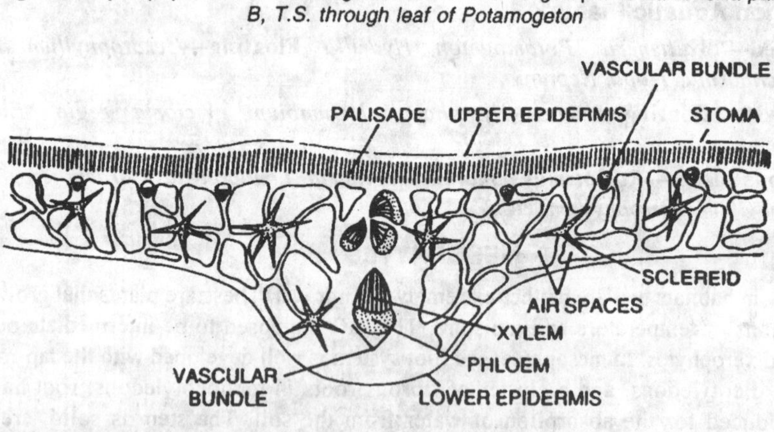

Fig. 8.30. Anatomy of hydrophyte leaf. V.S. of leaf of *Nymphaea* (dicot) showing big air spaces and sclereids (diagrammatic).

XEROPHYTES

They grow in deserts or in very dry places; they can withstand a prolonged period of drought uninjured, for this purpose they have certain peculiar adaptations. The xerophytic plants have to guard against excessive evaporation of water; this they do by reducing evaporating surfaces. Plants produce a long tap root which goes deep into the sub-soil in search of moisture. To retain the water absorbed by the roots, the leaves and stems of some plants become very thick and fleshy (*e.g.*,

Aloe, Agave). Water tissue develops in them for storing up water; this is further facilitated by the abundance of mucilage contained in them. Multiple epidermis sometimes develops in the leaf (*e.g.*, *Nerium*). Modification of the stem into phylloclade for storing water and food and at the same time performing functions of leaves is characteristic of many desert plants (*e.g.*, *Opuntia* and other cacti).

In xerophytes certain structural features are also common. Leaves are thick and leathery, with a well developed cuticle and abundant hairs. Well differentiated mesophyll is also present, and there is often more than one layer of palisade tissue (*e.g.*, *Nerium, Hakea*). The walls of epidermal and sub-epidermal cells are frequently lignified, and a distinct hypodermis, may be present. They have a well developed vascular system and often an abundance of sclerenchyma, either in the form of sclereids or fibres (*Hakea, Ammophila*). The leaf is sometimes cylindrical or rolled. This organization is to protect the stomata, which may occur in furrows. Certain fleshy leaves (*e.g.*, *Sedum*), contain abundant thin-walled cells, the water storage tissue. The characteristic anatomical features of the xerophytes are as follows:

Epidermis and Thick Cuticle

Heavy cuticularization and extreme cutinization of the epidermis and even of sub-epidermal cells are common in xerophytes. The thickness of the cuticle shows various gradations. In certain cases the thickness of cuticle is only slightly greater than normal, like that of plants of semi-xerophytic habitats. In extreme xerophytes the cuticle may be as thick as, or thicker than the diameter of the epidermal cells. In addition to the presence of thick cuticle, the walls of epidermal cells become cutinized, and sometimes also those of underlying cells. Along with well-developed cutinized layers the epidermal and sub-epidermal cells also become lignified. For example, in the leaflets of *Cycas*, the lignification may extend even to the palisade parenchyma cells. In certain cases the covering of wax is formed on the epidermis (*e.g.*, *Calotropis*). The epidermal cells are usually radially elongated. In the leaves of *Nerium* and *Ficus*, the epidermis becomes multilayered.

In many xerophytes, in addition to a cutinized epidermis, single to multilayered **hypodermis** is also present. In most plants, the hypodermis of leaves is morphologically mesophyll and may be in the form of sheet of fibrous tissue or a layer of sclereids. The hypodermis of the stems seems to be a part of the cortex. The hypodermis of stem and leaves may be cutinized to lignified. In many plants, the mucilage, gums and tannins are commonly found in the hypodermis.

Hairs. In many xerophytic plants, especially those of alpine regions exposed to strong winds, a covering of matted epidermal hairs on the underside of the leaves prevents water loss. Hairs may also be abundant over the entire aerial part of the plant. The thick matting of hairs also prevents rapid evaporation through stomata. The xerophytes that possess abundant hairs, on their leaves and stems, are commonly called **trichophyllous.**

Structure of Stomata

The stomata are very minute openings formed in the epidermal layer in green aerial parts of the plants.

The stomata are essential for intake of carbon dioxide and oxygen and for the passage inward and outward of other gases. The evaporation of the surplus water takes place through the stomata. When the stomata are open, water escapes even when water loss is harmful to the plant. This way, the reduction of transpiration is of great importance in xerophytes. The xerophytes may possess less stomata, either by reduction of leaf surface or of stomatal number per unit area. To reduce excessive transpiration, usually the stomata that remain sunken in pits are formed. Such stomata are

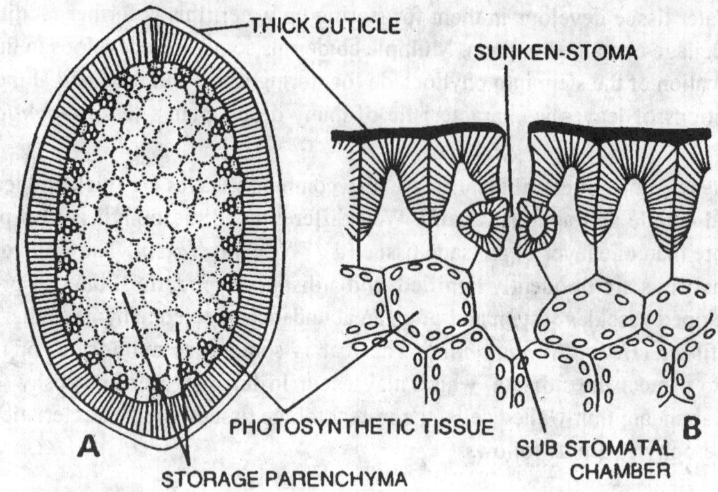

Fig 8.31. Anatomy of xerophytic leaf—*Aloe* (monocot). A, T.S. showing peripheral photosynthetic tissue and central water storage tissue (diagrammatic); B, a portion (detailed) showing thick cuticle, thickening on the radial and outer walls of the epidermal cells and sunken stomata.

commonly known as **sunken stomata** (*e.g., Pinus, Hakea, Agave,* etc,). In certain cases the stomata are found in groups and they remain confined to depressions found on leaf surface (*e.g., Nerium, Banksia,* etc.). Usually the depressions contain hairs in them which protect the stomata from direct attack of wind gusts.

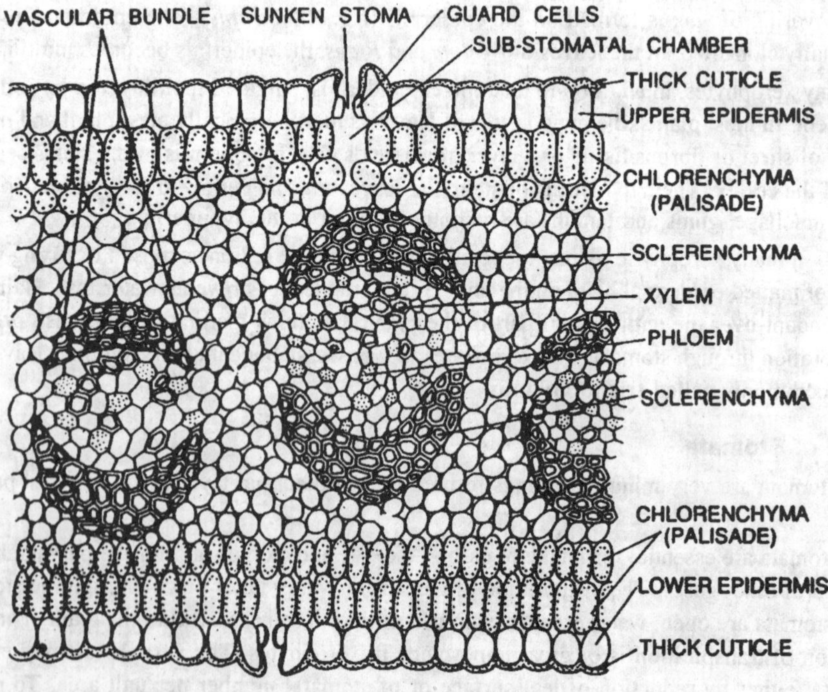

Fig. 8.32. Anatomy of xerophytic leaf. V.S. of leaf of *Agave* (monocot) showing detailed structure.

Sclerenchyma

The xerophytes commonly have a larger proportion of sclerenchyma in their leaf structure than is found normally in mesophytes. The sclerenchyma is either found in groups or in continuous sheets. For example, in *Banksia*, there is a continuous thin sheet of sclerenchyma between the hypodermis and the mesophyll. In *Dasylirion*, there is well-developed sclerenchyma below the epidermis. The sheets of sclerenchyma check excessive transpiration to some extent and also give mechanical support to the plant body. The xerophytes that possess heavy sclerification of the leaves are known as **sclerophyllous.**

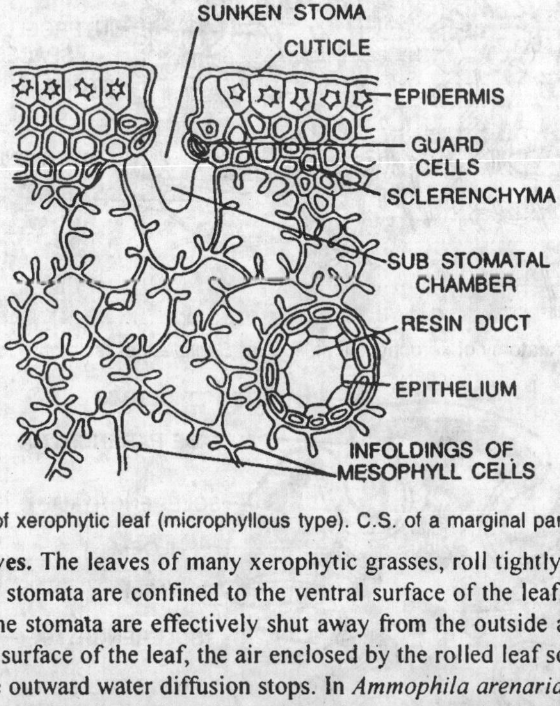

Fig. 8.33. Structure of xerophytic leaf (microphyllous type). C.S. of a marginal part of leaf of *Pinus nigra*.

Rolling of leaves. The leaves of many xerophytic grasses, roll tightly under dry conditions. In these grasses, the stomata are confined to the ventral surface of the leaf, so that when the leaf edges roll inward, the stomata are effectively shut away from the outside air. As the stomata are located on the inner surface of the leaf, the air enclosed by the rolled leaf soon becomes saturated with water under the outward water diffusion stops. In *Ammophila arenaria*, there is tight upward folding of the leaf and also the sheltered location of the stomata in furrows, greatly reduce air movement over stomatal areas. Special motor cells (hinge) on the upper surface of the leaf are responsible for the inward rolling of leaves. In the xerophytic grasses, the motor cells are well developed.

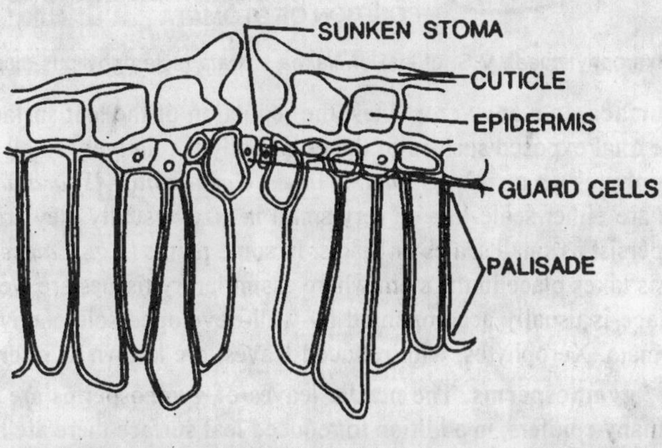

Fig. 8.34. Structure of xerophytic leaf. T.S. outer layers of cells of *Hakea* leaf.

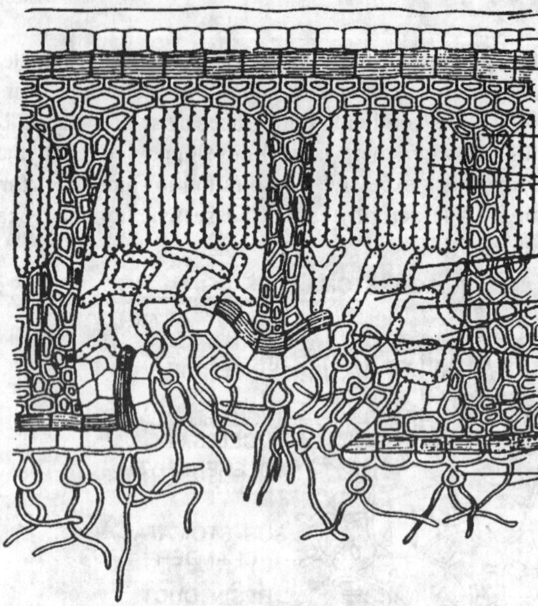

Fig. 8.35. Anatomy of xerophytic leaf. T.S. of *Banksia* leaf (sclerophyllous type).

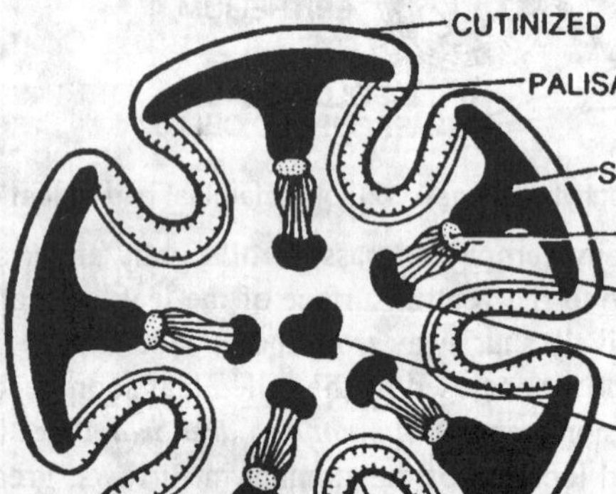

Fig. 8.36. Anatomy of xerophytic leaf. V.S. of leaf of *Hakea sulcata* (sclerophyllous-dicot)—diagrammatic.

Reduced leaf surface. In many xerophytes, the reduction of the leaf surface partly prevents water loss because the total exposed surface of the plant body is relatively small as compared with that of normal mesophytes (*e.g., Equisetum, Pinus, Casuarina, Asparagus,* etc.). In such xerophytes the leaves are either scale-like or very small in size. Usually they are not found in the mature plant, or they persist as small scales or bracts. In some plants (*e.g., Equisetum, Polygonella,* etc.) the photosynthesis takes place in the stem where assimilatory tissues are well developed. The reduction of leaf surface is usually accompanied by well-developed sclerenchyma water storage tissue and sunken stomata. Xerophytes, with reduced leaves, are known as **microphyllous.**

Needle leaves of gymnosperms. The needle leaves of gymnosperms are of microphyllous type. In the leaves of many conifers, in addition to reduced leaf surface there are heavy cutinization and sunken stomata. A characteristic illustration of this type is the needle of *Pinus*. The outer walls

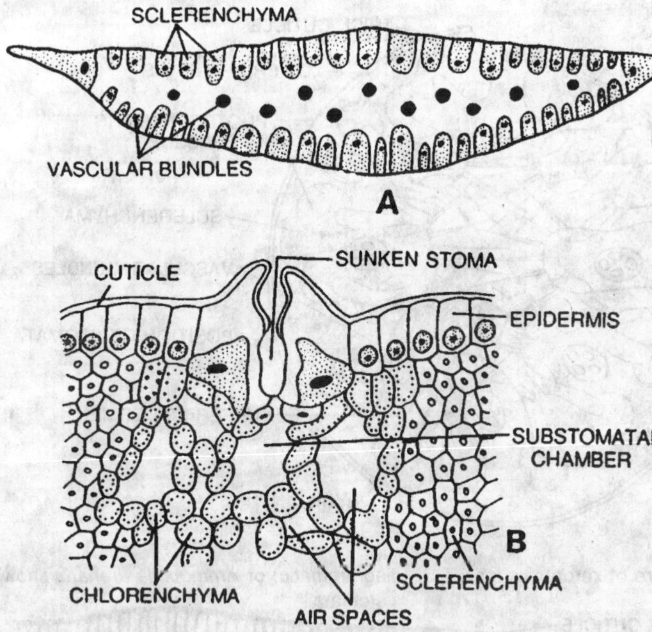

Fig. 8.37. Structure of xerophytic leaf. A, C.S. of *Dasilirion serratifolium* leaf (diagrammatic) B, detail of small portion. (After E. and M.)

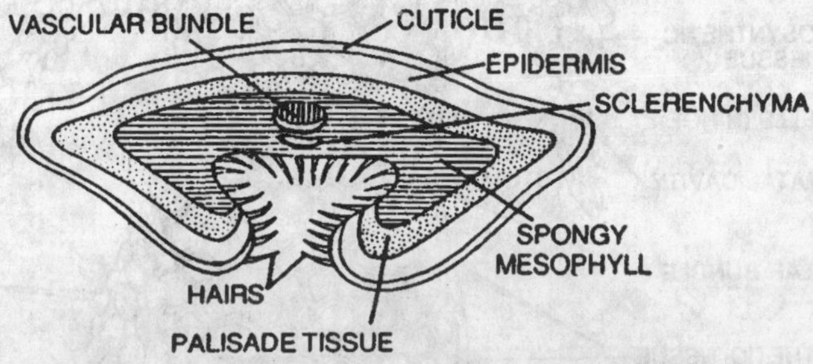

Fig. 8.38. Anatomy of xerophytic leaf. V.S.. of leaf of *Erica cinerea* (dicot). Dorsiventral rolled leaf; hairs present, cuticle more fully developed on the upper surface than on the lower surface; internal walls of epidermal hairs frequently mucilaginous; stomata confined to the grooves on the lower surface mesophyll situated at the leaf margin; vascular bundles mostly accompanied by mechanical tissue.

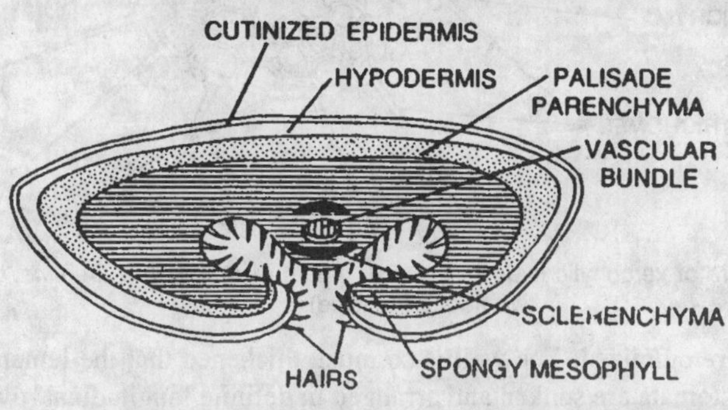

Fig. 8.39. Anatomy of xerophytic leaf. T.S. of dorsiventrally rolled leaf of *Erica tetralix*.

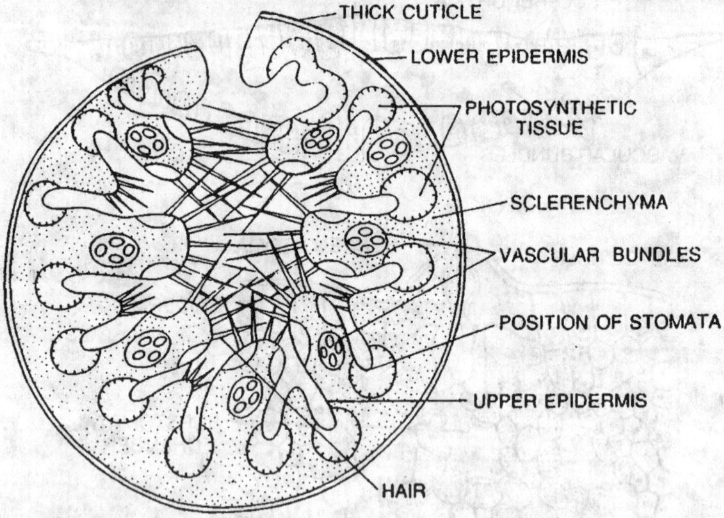

Fig. 8.40. Structure of xerophytic leaf. T.S. (diagrammatic) of *Ammophila arenaria* showing protected stomata.

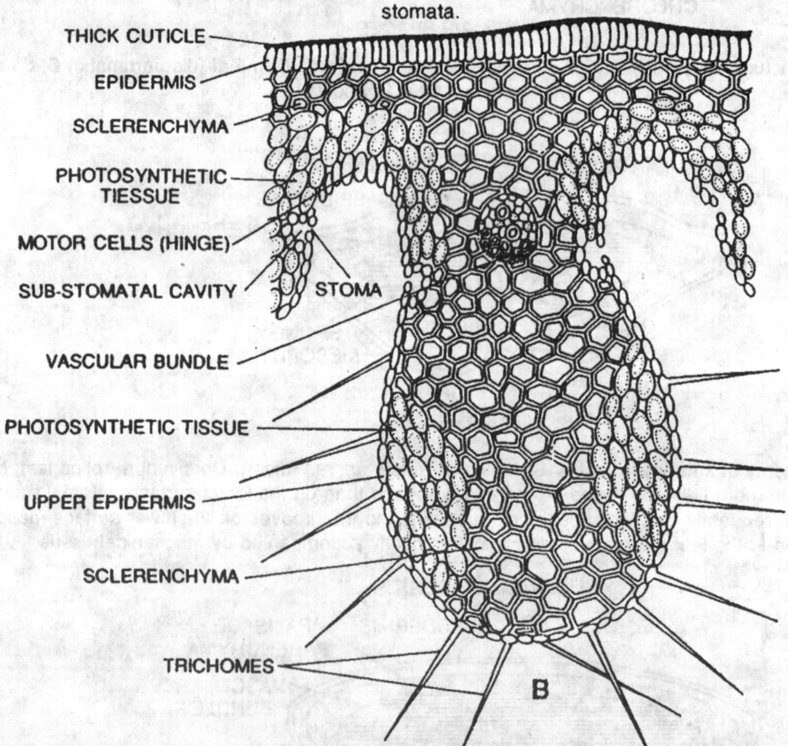

Fig. 8.41. Structure of xerophytic leaf. Part of T.S. of leaf of *Ammophila arenaria*, between two ridges (detailed).

of the epidermal cells are cutinized. The wall is so much thickened that the lumen of the cells is nearly obliterated. The stomata are sunken and arranged in definite longitudinal rows. Beneath the epidermis there is well developed hypodermis, consisting of elongate sclerenchyma cells.

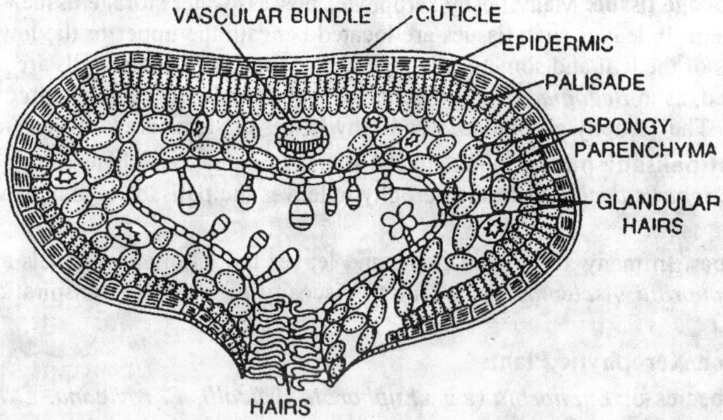

Fig. 8.42. Anatomy of xerophytic leaf. V.S. of leaf of *Empetrum nigrum* (dicot.) Leaf deeply furrowed on the lower side. The groove almost closed by hairs and thus forming a central cavity; consisting of glandular and simple unicellular hairs from a tangled mass closing the entrance to the central cavity; epidermis of the outer surface composed of cells with very thick outer and mucilaginous inner walls; epidermal cells around the central cavity are provided with their outer walls; mesophyll dorsiventral leaf consists of a palisade tissue below the upper epidermis and of spongy tissue on the inside of the lower epidermis, vascular bundles not accompanied by sclerenchymatous element; crystals—according to Solereder secreted in the form of clusters.

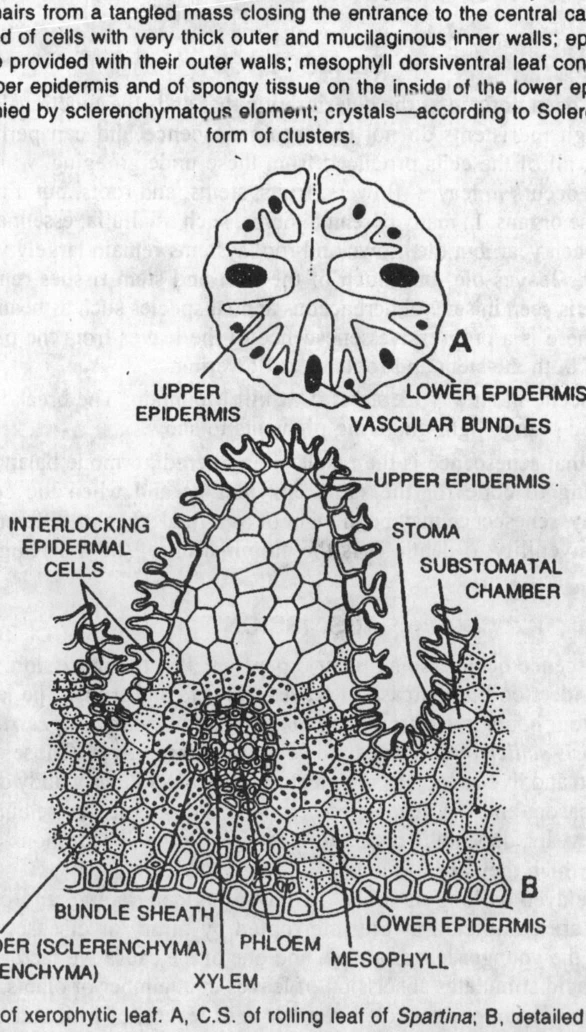

Fig. 8.43. Structure of xerophytic leaf. A, C.S. of rolling leaf of *Spartina*; B, detailed structure of same.

Water storage tissue. Many fleshy xerophytes possess water storage tissue and mucilaginous substance in them. In leaves such tissues are located beneath the upper or the lower epidermis, or upon both sides of the leaf and sometimes in the centre too. The storage cells are usually large and often thin-walled, as in *Begonia.* The storage tissue may actually serve as a source or reserve water during drought. The xerophytes, that possess fleshy leaves or stems are known as **malacophyllous.**

Abundant palisade parenchyma. In the stems of many xerophytes, the palisade tissue is present (*e.g., Capparis decidua*). In the xerophytic leaves the palisade is abundant and compactly arranged.

Latex tubes. In many xerophytic stems and leaves the laticiferous canals are present (*e.g., Calotropis, Euphorbia, Asclepias,* etc.). Due to viscosity of latex the transpiration is reduced to some extent.

List of Common Xerophytic Plants

Several species of *Euphorbia* (*e.g., Euphorbia tirucalli, E. royleana, E. neriifolia,* etc.); many cacti (*e.g., Opuntia, Cereus, Pereskia,* etc.); *Agave, Aloe; Capparis decidua; Calotropis procera; Carthamus; Portulaca; Argemone mexicana; Salsola; Alhagi, Ammophila arenaria; Dasylirion serratifolium; Nerium; Banksia; Hakea; Casuarina; Erica; Empetrum* and several others.

SENESCENCE

Senescence has been defined as the deterioration that ends the functional life of an organism or an organ. Although meristems do not undergo senescence and can perhaps be considered potentially immortal, all of the cells produced from these undergo aging, which eventually leads to death. Senescence occurs in leaves, flowers, fruits, stems, and roots, but it commonly occurs at different times in these organs. In many perennial herbs, such as alfalfa, essentially the entire above ground system dies each year, but the crown and root systems remain largely viable. In deciduous woody perennials, the leaves die, but much of the root and stem tissues remain alive. Another pattern of senescence is seen in several herbaceous annual species such as beans, tomatoes and the cereal grains. Here there is a progressive senescence of the leaves from the older to the younger, followed by death of both the stem and roots after flowering.

Senescence; A scene in New York states, Catskill Mountain; The breakdown of chlorophyll allows yellow, red and orange light-gathering pigments to show.

It is concluded that senescence is the result of an altered hormone balance that prevents the genes from continuing to code for the same enzymes as and when the cells were younger. Considered in this way, senescence may be thought of as a final stage of differentiation which itself is continuous from juvenility to death. It is the culmination of the morphogenetic information programme.

ABSCISSION

Soon after senescence occurs, some plant organs are lost by **abscission**. The physiology of this process is best understood in the case of leaves, flowers and fruits. The longevity of flowers ranges from three or four hours in *Hibiscus trionum* and *Calandrinia compressa,* upto three or four months in *Phalaenopsis scilleriana.* Leaves are generally longer lived. Those of most herbaceous annuals are never shed and live as long as the plant, those of deciduous woody dicotyledons remain intact one growing season, and the needles of certain gymnosperms are retained from about one year to seven or eight years, depending upon the species and growth conditions. Most fruits are lost during the season in which they are formed.

Abscission is delayed as long as organ is physiologically active and occur if the normal metabolic processes are completed or are interrupted by injury or disease. Leaf abscission is usually stimulated by the younger leaves above, and one of the causative factors supplied by these is an auxin. Abscisic acid stimulates abscission of leaves in a number of plants. It seems, that acid and the other abscisins play important roles in the loss of leaves, of fruit and of flowers.

Abscission benefits plants in various ways. Injury or disease often causes the abscission of the affected organ. The plant thus rids itself of a useless part or of a potential infection source.

ABSCISSION OF LEAVES

The leaves are periodically detached from the perennial plants. The phenomenon of this detachment is complex one. During this phenomenon leaves are separated from the stem without causing any injury to the living tissues in stem and the newly exposed surface is also protected from desiccation and infection. This phenomenon of the separation of leaves from the stem takes place in a particular region of the plant, known as **abscission region** or **abscission zone.** The phenomenon as a whole known as **abscission of leaves** and the separating leaf may be said to abscised. The abscission zone consists of a **separation layer** through which the actual break occurs, and the **protective layer.**

In simple dicotyledonous leaves the abscission zone occurs within the petiole or at its base. In compound leaves the abscission zones occur in the petiole of the leaf as a whole and at the base of individual leaflets.

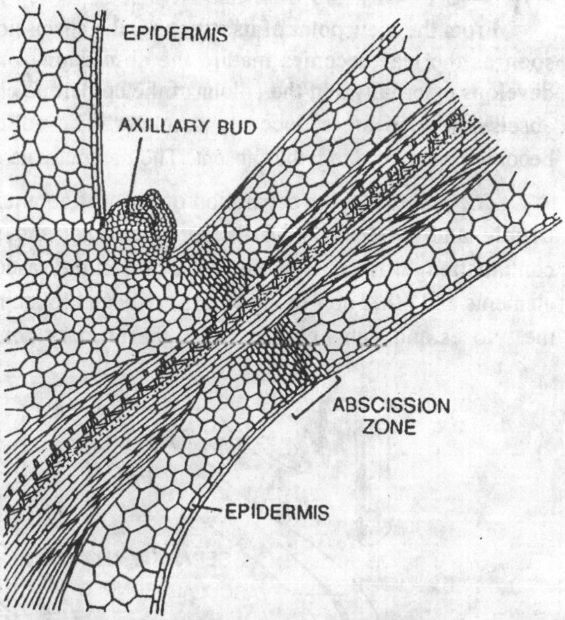

Fig. 8.44. Leaf abscission—formation of the abscission zone.

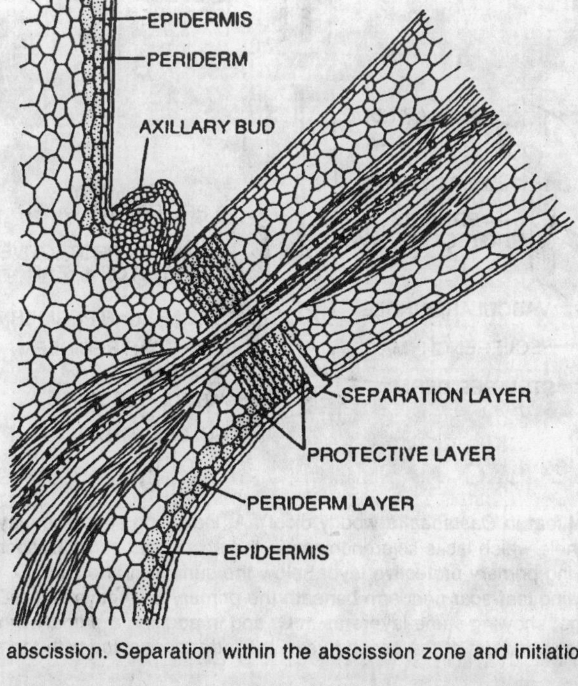

Fig. 8.45. Leaf abscission. Separation within the abscission zone and initiation of periderm.

Within the abscission zone, a few days or even weeks before actual leaf fall, a separation layer develops which aids structurally in the leaf fall. When the tissues, found beneath the separation layer are exposed after the leaf fall, they are protected from desiccation and infection by means of one or more protective layers. At least one of these protective layers lies within the abscission zone. These protective layers are of two types–a **primary protective layer** and the **secondary protective layer** or **periderm**.

From the view point of its structure, the abscission zone is the weakest part of the petiole. As soon as the leaf becomes mature the abscission zone becomes evident. A shallow depression develops externally and the colour of the epidermis changes in this zone. The vascular bundles in abscission zone are reduced in diameter. The collenchyma is lacking and the sclerenchyma becomes weak or altogether absent. The parenchyma cells of this zone possess denser cytoplasm.

The process of the separation of the leaf commonly starts from the peripheral region of the petiole and proceeds towards the middle of the petiole. The separation layer remains in continuation through the parenchyma cells in the vascular bundles, whereas the xylem and phloem elements and other non-living cells have been broken mechanically. Just before the actual leaf fall, the tyloses and gums chiefly block the primary conducting cells of the vascular bundles, but

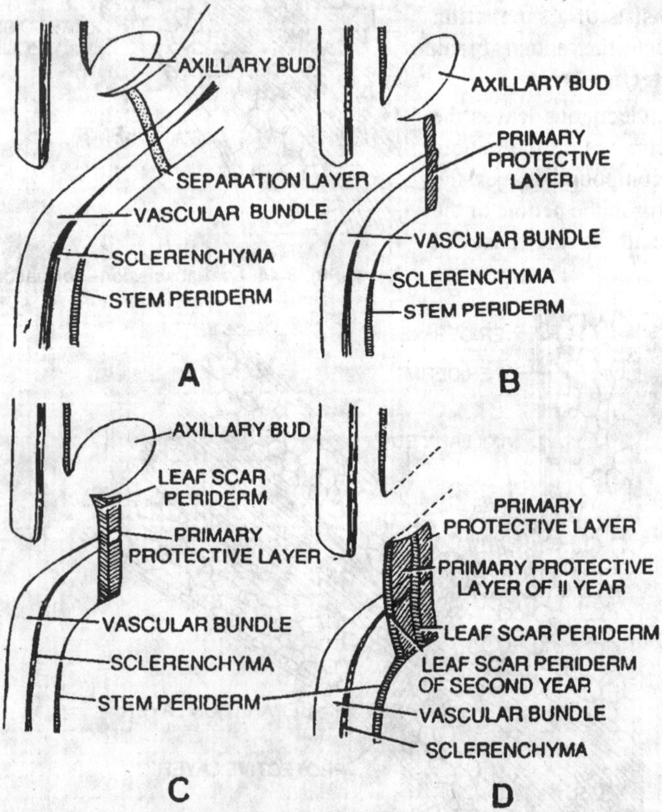

Fig. 8.46. Abscission of leaf in *Castanea* (a woody dicot). A, indicating separation layer extending through vascular bundle which lacks sclerenchyma in the abscission zone; B, soon after the leaf fall, showing primary protective layer below the surface of the scar; C, late autumn stage, showing leaf-scar periderm beneath the primary protective layer; D, second year stage, showing same layers as in C, and in addition a primary protective layer and leaf-scar periderm of the second year, the latter connected with the stem periderm.

sufficient conduction is maintained through the secondary elements which keep the leaf fresh turgid unless and until its separation is being completed. Shortly before the abscise of the leaf, the outer walls and the middle lamella of the cells become gelatinized and in the end prior to leaf fall they break down and dissolve. On the dissolution of intercellular substances and the outer cell walls, the cells become quite separate and free from each other. Ultimately the leaf is only supported by the vascular elements which break very soon by the wind and the weight of the leaf itself, thus separating the leaf from the stem. In wet weather, because of the addition of the water to the leaves, and the hydrolysis of the gelatinous cell walls, the leaf fall is accelerated to some extent.

Shortly after the leaf fall the protective layers develop on the exposed surface. The protective layers may be of the both primary and secondary origin. Sometimes they are only of secondary origin. The secondary protective layer is typical periderm. At the region of separation, a leaf scar is formed. The scar is formed because of the deposition of the substances, which protect the new surface from injuries, infection and loss of water. These substances are found beneath the separation layer in the cells and referred as suberin and lignin. In some plants the periderm develops just after leaf fall. This newly developed periderm beneath the protective layer remains in continuation with the periderm of the stem.

9

CHAPTER

The Root System : Primary and Secondary Structure

The roots are generally divided into two categories: (1) **primary**, normal roots, which originate from the embryo and usually persist throughout life, and (2) **adventitious** roots, which arise secondarily from stem, leaf or other tissues and which may be either permanent or temporary.

The functions of the primary roots are to anchor the plant in the soil, to absorb water and soluble substances and to serve as storehouses of food materials. The functions of adventitious roots are very various. Sometimes they enter the soil and act as primary roots. In other cases they may be modified into climbing organs, stilts or props, thorns, haustoria, etc.

The anatomy of roots is in many respects simpler than that of stems and it is considerably more uniform, perhaps as the result of a rather uniform environment underground, which is in marked contrast with the extreme variability of the conditions affecting aerial shoots. Root anatomy is more ancient in type than that of stems. Roots preserve, in their primary condition, the actinostely of the vascular tissues, which in the lower Pteridophyta is characteristic of both stems and roots.

GENERAL CHARACTERISTICS OF THE ROOTS

1. The roots possess a tendency to grow downwards or sideways rather than upwards.
2. There is absence of chlorophyll in the roots.
3. The roots are not susceptible to the influence of light.
4. There is absence of leaves and hence, of course, absence of buds.
5. The roots possess a root cap over the apex.
6. They possess endogenous origin and branching.
7. In roots, the phloem and xylem are situated on different radii in the primary structure.
8. There is a relatively short zone of growth at the apex.
9. They possess root hairs near the apex.

ANATOMICAL CHARACTERISTICS OF THE ROOT

ROOT CAP

The root cap consists of parenchymatous cells in various stages of differentiation. It is protective in function. Recent experiments have indicated that the root cap has another function that is physiologically of great importance. The root cap is apparently the site of the perception of gravity; thus it appears to be capable of controlling the production in the meristem of the growth-regulating substances involved in **geotropism** or their movement. However, the root cap itself is not the site of synthesis of growth substances. The experiments show that the root cap can control the movement, if not also the synthesis of endogenous auxin in the root apex.

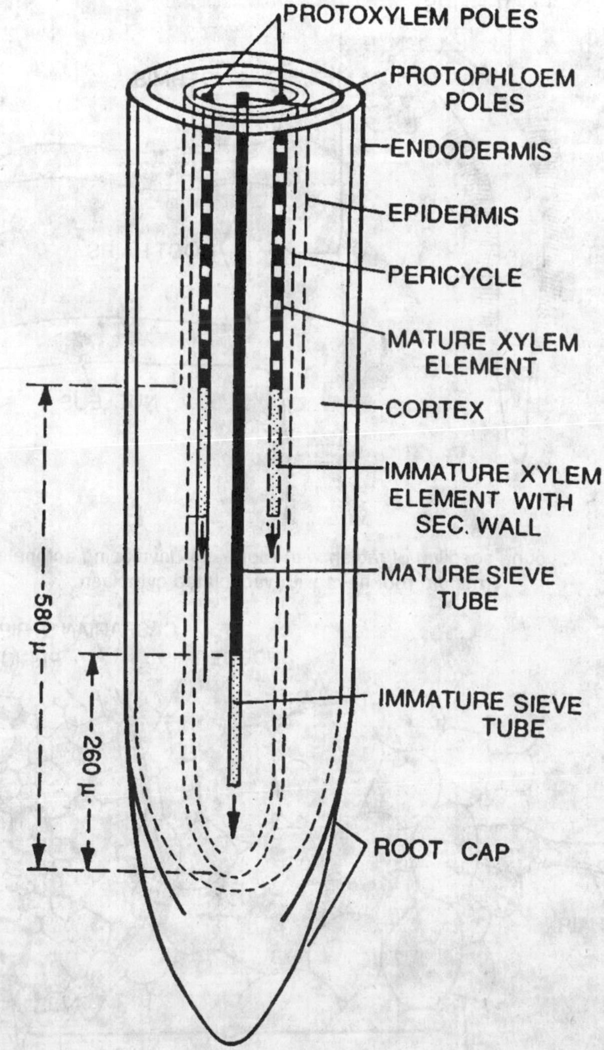

Fig. 9.1. The root. L.S. of a root tip of tobacco. (After Esau).

EPIDERMIS

The epidermis is also known as epiblema or piliferous layer. In most of roots, root hairs develop from some of the epidermal cells at a little distance from the apical meristem. The cells, giving rise to root hairs are known as **trichoblasts.** In the roots of the grass (*Phleum*), trichoblasts are formed by unequal division, of a cell of the immature epidermis, the protoderm. The trichoblast is the distally situated cell of this division. Root hairs are outgrowths of single cells, and function both in the absorption and in anchorage. Root hairs are usually eventually sloughed off, but occasionally they are persistent. Electron microscopy reveals (Leech, Mollenhauer and Whaley, 1963) that the wall of emerging root hair is a continuation of only the inner component of the wall of the epidermal cell which gives rise to it. In some species, root hairs are formed from special cells which are dintinct in size and metabolism from the neighbouring epidermal cells. These cells

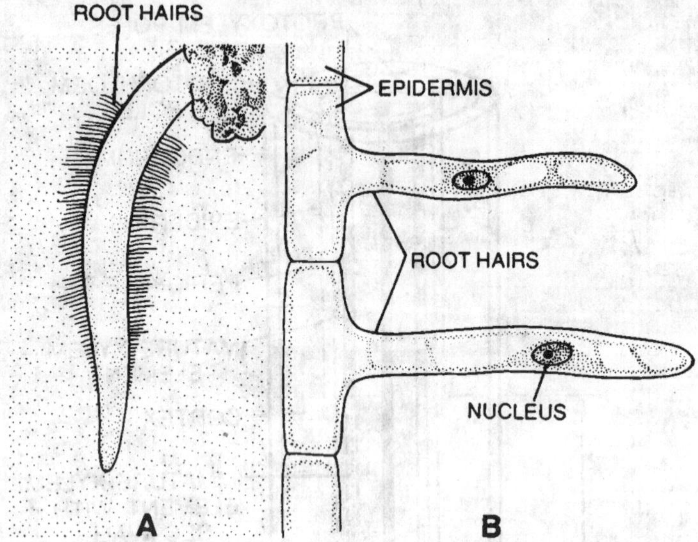

Fig. 9.2. Root hair. A, young seedling of radish with root hairs developing acropetally; B, highly magnified mature root hairs with vacuolated cytoplasm.

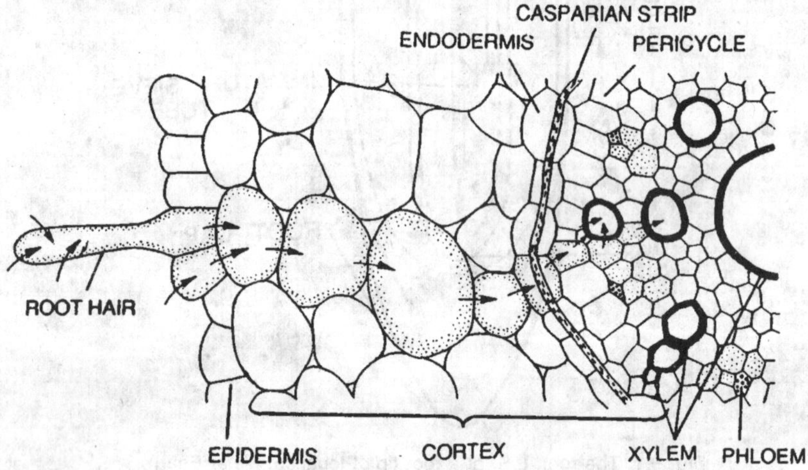

Fig. 9.3. Function of root. In this diagram the arrows indicate the movement of water and salts absorbed from the soil by root hair.

are known as **trichoblasts.** In other species, root hairs may develop from a whole row of cells, which stain more densely than their neighbours.

In the aerial roots of certain epiphytic orchids a multiple epidermis, or **velamen** is present. This tissue is derived from the epidermal initials and may be several cells thick. The cells are dead and devoid of contents, the cell walls are strengthened with bands of lignin. On the inner side of the velamen there is a specialized layer of cells which is derived from the periblem and not the dermatogen, and may therefore be considered as the outermost layer of the cortex, the **exodermis.** This layer is composed of alternating long and short cells; the long cells become thick-walled on their radial and outer tangential surface, but the small cells remain thin-walled and are called **passage cells.** The velamen is thought to function as a protective tissue, preventing undue water

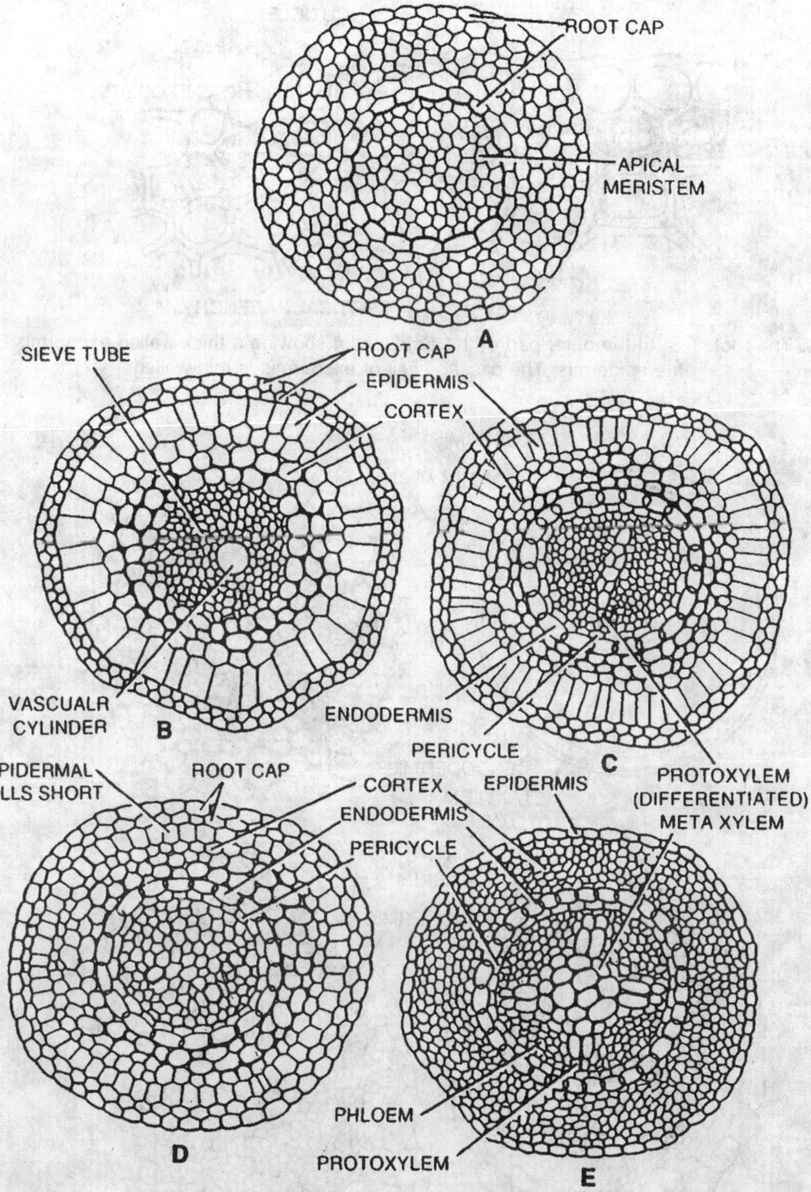

Fig. 9.4. Tissue differentiation in root. Cross sections at various levels of root showing tissue differentiation. A, T.S. root apex showing apical meristem and root tip; B, T.S. showing root cap, epidermis cortex and elements of sieve tubes; C, endodermis, pericycle, sieve elements and xylem elements are seen; D—E, show later stages of development.

loss from the delicate cortical cells of the exposed aerial root. Formally this was believed that the cells of the velamen also absorbed and conserved water drawn from the atmoshphere, but recent experiments show that the mature velamen and exodermis are nearly impermeable to water and solutes.

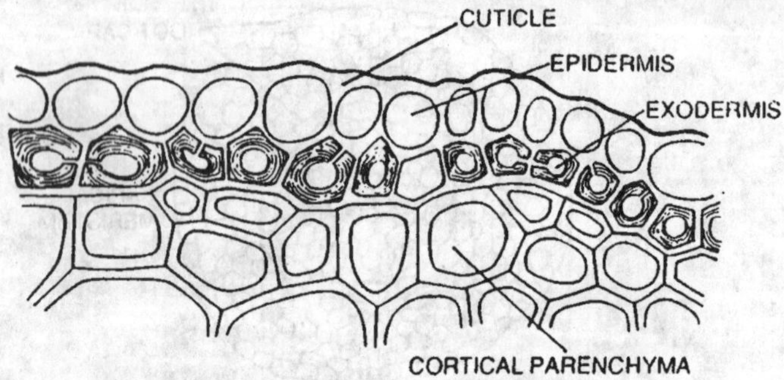

Fig. 9.5. The root. T.S. of the outer part of the *Smilax* root showing a thick-walled exodermis beneath the epidermis. The passage cell of exodermis is thin-walled.

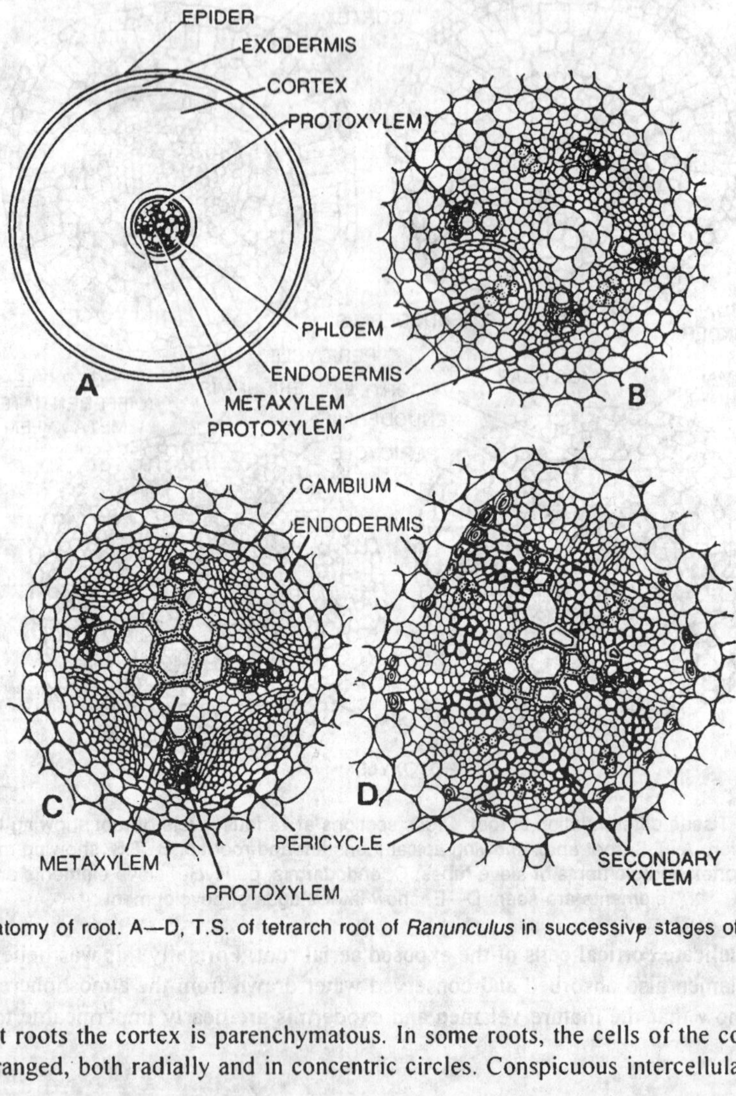

Fig. 9.6. Anatomy of root. A—D, T.S. of tetrarch root of *Ranunculus* in successive stages of development.

CORTEX

In most roots the cortex is parenchymatous. In some roots, the cells of the cortex are very regularly arranged, both radially and in concentric circles. Conspicuous intercellular spaces may

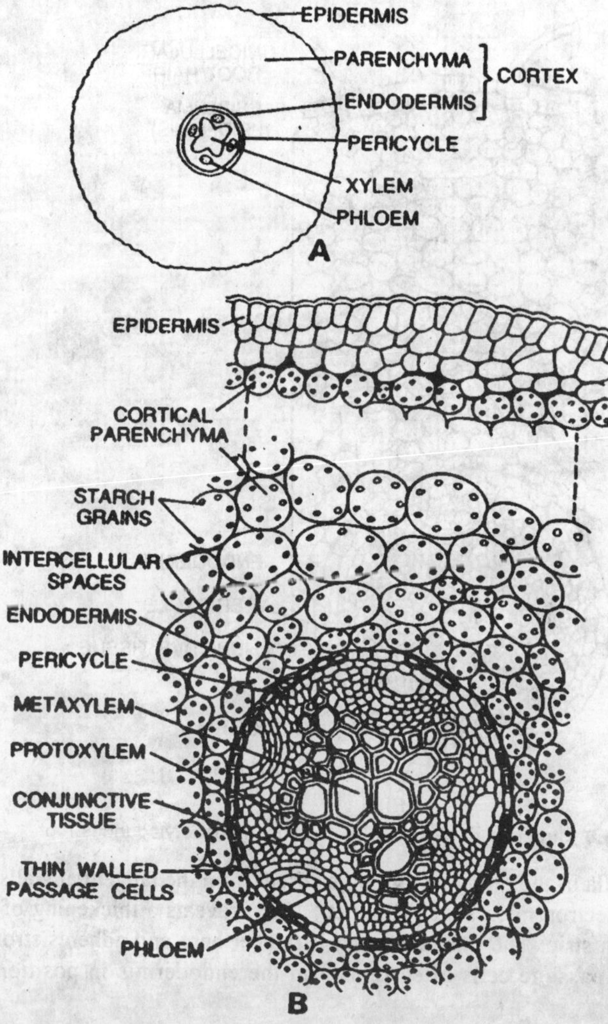

Fig. 9.7. Root of dicotyledon. T.S. of root of *Ranunculus repens*— A, diagrammatic: B, detail.

be present, and especially evident in aquatic species, where they form a type of aerenchyma. The cortical cells often contain starch, and sometimes crystals. Sclerenchyma is more common in the roots of monocotyledons than those of dicotyledons. The characteristic trichosclereids are found in the roots of *Monstera*. Collenchyma is occasionally present in roots (*e.g., Monstera*). The outermost layer or layers of the cortex, just beneath the epidermis may be differentiated as an **exodermis,** a kind of **hypodermis**, with suberized walls. The innermost layer of the cortex is usually differentiated as an **endodermis.**

ENDODERMIS

The endodermis comprises a single layer of cells differing physiologically and in structure and function from those on either side of it. In the young endodermal cells a band of suberin, **Casparian strip**, runs radially around the cell and is thus seen in the radial walls in transverse sections of roots. This suberin deposit, to which the protoplast of the cell is attached, is continuous

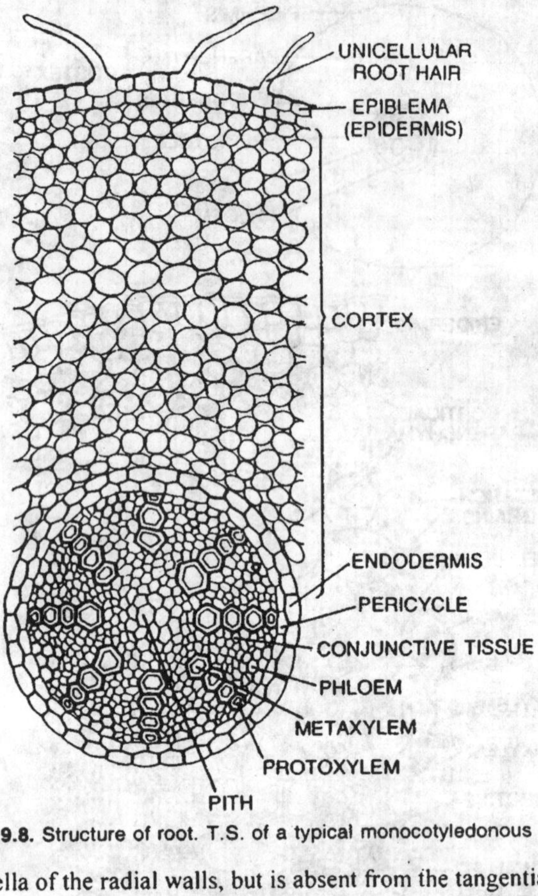

Fig. 9.8. Structure of root. T.S. of a typical monocotyledonous root.

across the middle lamella of the radial walls, but is absent from the tangential walls. A study of the endodermis with the electron microscope (Bonnett, 1968) reveals a thickening of the wall in the region of the Casparian strip. The **plasmalemma** is thicker here and adheres strongly to the cell wall. The thin-walled **passage cells** often remain in the endodermis in positions opposite the protoxylem.

PERICYCLE

The pericycle is usually a single layer of parenchymatous cells lying just within the endodermis and peripheral to the vascular tissues. The pericycle has a capacity for meristematic growth, and gives rise to lateral root primordia, parts of the vascular cambium, and usually the meristem which produces cork, the phellogen. The pericycle is sometimes called pericambium.

VASCULAR SYSTEM

The vascular system of the root as seen in transverse section consists of a variable number of triangular rays of thick-walled, lignified tracheary elements, alternating with arcs of thin-walled phloem. In the root, the xylem and phloem do not lie on the same radius. The xylem may form a solid central core, or there may be a parenchymatous or sclerenchymatous pith, as in the roots of many monocotyledons. Roots with 1, 2, 3, 4, 5 and many arcs of xylem are respectively called monarch, diarch, triarch, tetrarch, pentarch and polyarch. The xylem is exarch, *i.e.*, protoxylem lies towards periphery and metaxylem towards the centre. The xylem is always centripetal in its development. The phloem bundle consists of sieve tubes, companion cells and phloem parenchyma. The protoxylem consists of annular and spiral vessels and metaxylem of reticulate and pitted vessels.

The parenchyma found in between xylem and phloem bundles is known as **conjunctive tissue.** The pith may be large, small or altogether absent.

ANATOMY OF DICOTYLEDONOUS ROOTS

The important anatomical characteristics of the dicotyledonous roots are as follows:

1. The xylem bundles vary from two to six number, *i.e.*, they may be diarch, triarch, tetrarch, pentarch or hexarch.
2. The pericycle gives rise to lateral roots and secondary meristems (*e.g.*, cambium and phellogen).
3. The cambium appears later as a secondary meristem.
4. The pith is scanty or altogether absent.

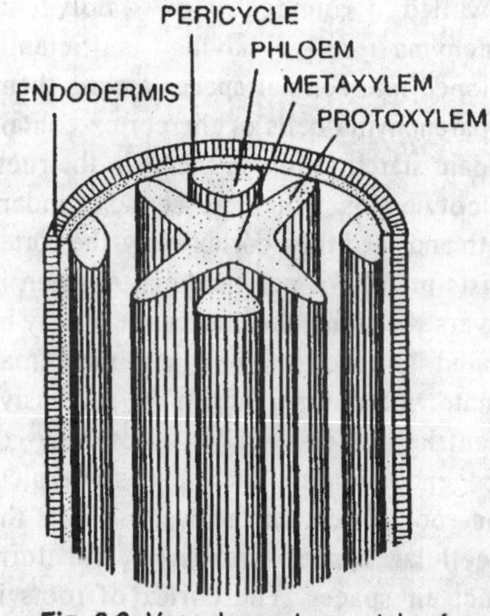

Fig. 9.9. Vascular system—stele of a dicotyledonous root.

EPIDERMIS

The epidermis consists of closely packed elongated cells with thin walls that usually lack a cuticle and stomata. In some dicotyledons thickened outer walls occur in root parts growing in air and also in roots that retain their epidermis for a long time. The root epidermis (also known as **piliferous layer, rhizodermis** or **epiblema**) is typically uniseriate. Most of the epidermal cells extend out in the form of tubular unicellular root hairs. Normally, the root hairs are confined to a region between one and several centimetres in length near the tip. They are absent in the nearest proximity of the apical meristem, and they die off in the older root parts. Some roots also develop a specialized layer—the exodermis—beneath the epidermis. The exodermis arises from one or several of the sub-epidermal layers of the cortex. The cell walls of exodermis become suberized. The exodermis is found to be present in few dicots.

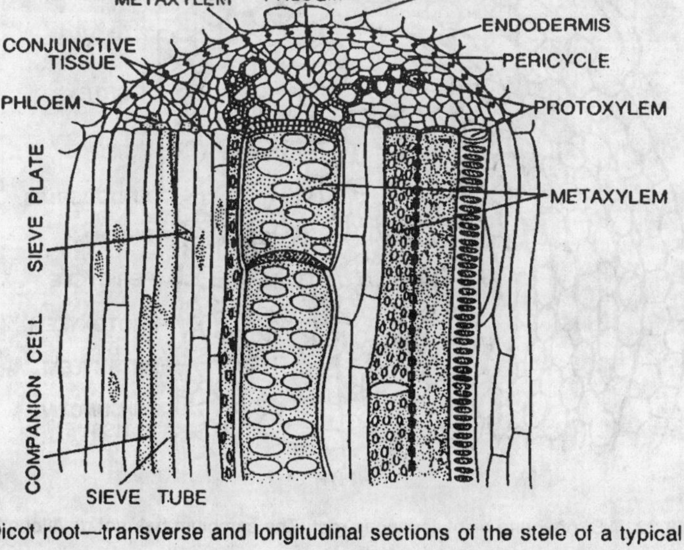

Fig. 9.10. Dicot root—transverse and longitudinal sections of the stele of a typical dicot root.

CORTEX

The cortex is massive and consists of thin-walled rounded or polygonal parenchyma cells having sufficiently developed intercellular spaces among them. The parenchyma cells of the cortex contain abundant starch grains in them. In the roots of dicotyledons which possess secondary growth and shed their cortex early, the cortex consists mainly of parenchyma. As seen in transverse sections, the cortical cells may be arranged in radial rows, or they may alternate with one another in the successive concentric layers. The presence of schizogenous intercellular spaces is typical of the root cortex. In the water plants the intercellular spaces are large and form distinct air spaces. The cortex of roots is usually devoid of chlorophyll. Exceptions are roots of some water plants and aerial roots of many epiphytes (*e.g., Tinospora* spp). Various idioblasts and secretory structures are found in the root cortex. Some dicotyledons (*e.g., Brassica, Pyrus, Prunus,*

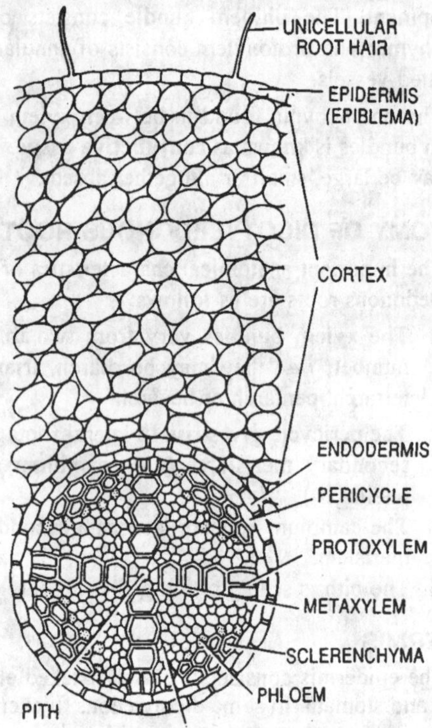

Fig. 9.11. Dicot root—T.S. of gram root.

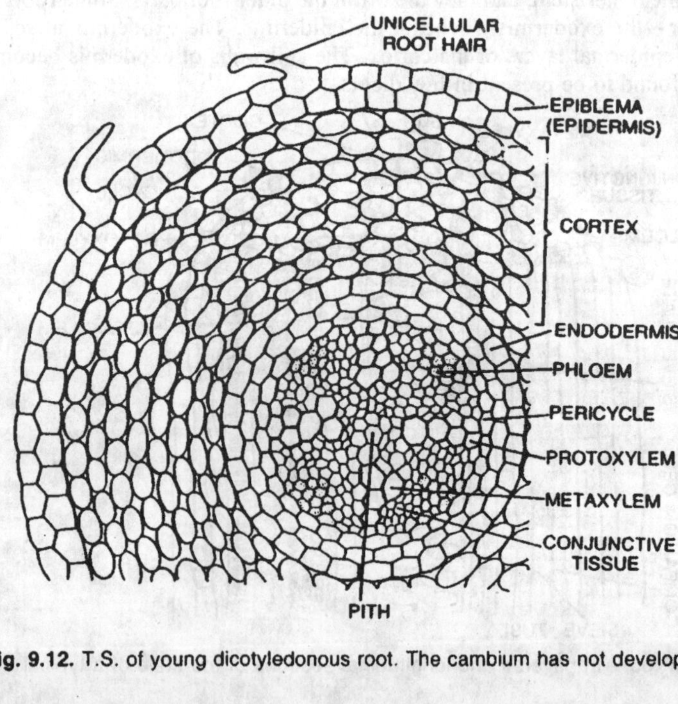

Fig. 9.12. T.S. of young dicotyledonous root. The cambium has not developed.

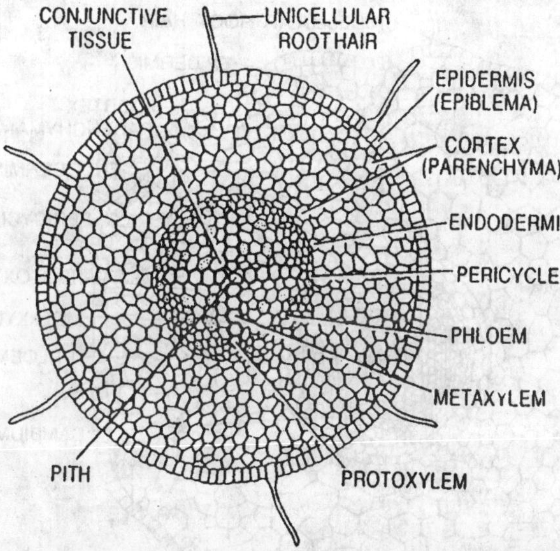

Fig. 9.13. Anatomy of dicot root. T.S. of young root of *Phaseolus radiatus* prior to cambium formation.

Spiraea, etc.) may develop prominent reticulate or band-like thickenings in cortical cells outside the endodermis.

ENDODERMIS

The innermost distinct layer of the cortex is known as **endodermis.** The endodermis is uniseriate and almost universally present in the roots. The cells of endodermis are living and characterized by the presence of **Casparian strips** or **Casparian bands** on their anticlinal walls. The strip is formed during the early ontogeny of the cell and is a part of the primary wall. The strip is typically located close to the inner tangential wall. Guttenberg (1943) says, that the suberin-like materials are found in the strips. The cytoplasm of an endodermal cell remains firmly attached to the Casparian strip. This firm attachment controls the movement of the materials in the root and their passage into xylem cells. The thin-walled **passage-cells** are also found in the endodermal layer which lie against the protoxylem poles. The passage cells either remain unmodified as long as the root lives or develop thick walls like the rest of the endodermis.

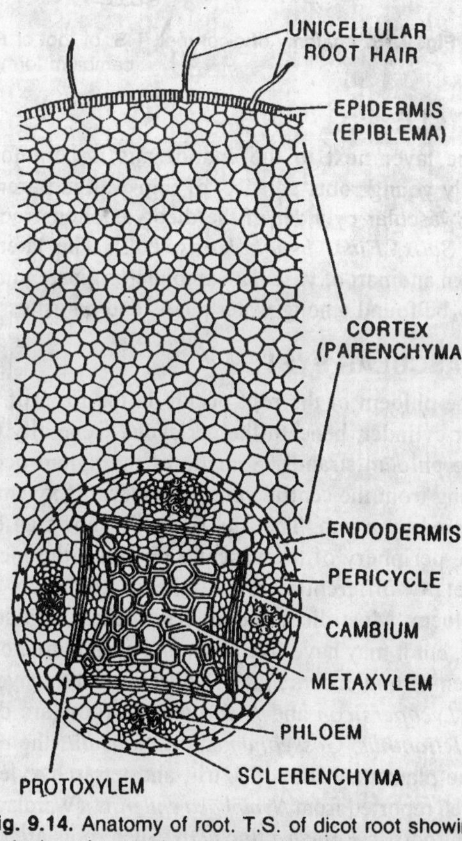

Fig. 9.14. Anatomy of root. T.S. of dicot root showing beginning of secondary growth. Details of a sector and central stele.

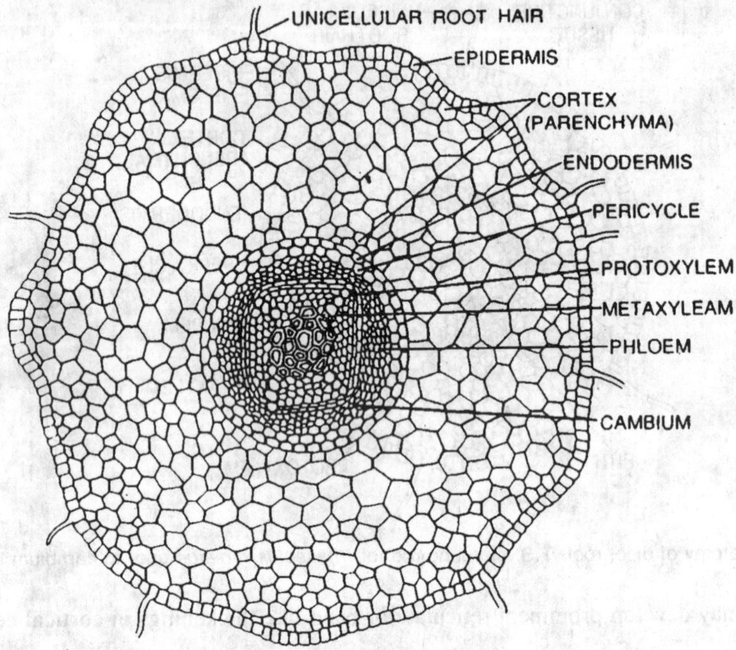

Fig. 9.15. Anatomy of dicot root. T.S. of root of *Phaseolus radiatus* showing beginning of cambium formation.

PERICYCLE

The layer next to the endodermis is commonly known as **pericycle**. The pericycle of relatively young roots consists of thin-walled parenchyma. It makes the outer boundary of the primary vascular cylinder of the dicotyledonous roots. It may be uniseriate or multiseriate (*e.g.*, *Morus, Salix, Ficus benghalensis*, etc.). The lateral roots in dicots arise in this tissue. The phellogen and part of vascular cambium originate in the pericycle. Roots without pericycle are rare but may be found among water plants and parasites.

THE VASCULAR SYSTEM

The phloem of the root occurs in the form of strands distributed near the periphery of the vascular cylinder, beneath the pericycle. Generally the xylem forms discrete strands, alternating with the phloem strands. Sometimes the xylem occupies the centre, with the strand-like parts projecting from the central core like ridges. If xylem is not differentiated in the centre, the centre is occupied by a pith. The root typically shows an exarch xylem, *i.e.*, the protoxylem is located near the periphery of the vascular cylinder, the metaxylem farther inward. The phloem is also centripetally differentiated, *i.e.*, the protophloem occurring closer to the periphery than the metaphloem. Most dicotyledons have few xylem strands. The taproot is frequently di-, tri-, or tetrarch, but it may have five to six and even more poles, (*e.g.*, many Amentiferae, *Castanea*). Only one xylem strand occurs in the slender root of the hydrophyte *Trapa natans*. In *Raphanus, Daucus, Linum, Lycopersicon* and *Nicotiana* the roots are diarch. In *Pisum* the root is triarch. In *Cicer, Vicia, Helianthus, Gossypium* and *Ranunculus* the roots are tetrarch. In certain dicots the root of the same plant may show di-, tri-, and tetrarch xylem. For example, tetrarch and polyarch roots have been reported from *Nymphaea chilensis*. (Wardlaw, 1928). Banerji (1932) reported tri-, tetra-, and pentarch roots in *Enhydra fluctuans*. Such roots are known as **heteroarchic roots.** The protoxylem consists of annular and spiral vessels whereas metaxylem of reticulate and pitted vessels. The phloem strand consists of sieve tubes, companion cells and phloem parenchyma. The parenchymatous conjunctive tissue occurs in between xylem and phloem strands. The pith is scanty or altogether absent.

ANATOMY OF MONOCOTYLEDONOUS ROOTS

The distinctive anatomical characters of the monocotyledonous roots are as follows:

1. The xylem groups are numerous (polyarch condition) and generally vary from twelve to twenty.
2. The pericycle gives rise to lateral roots only.

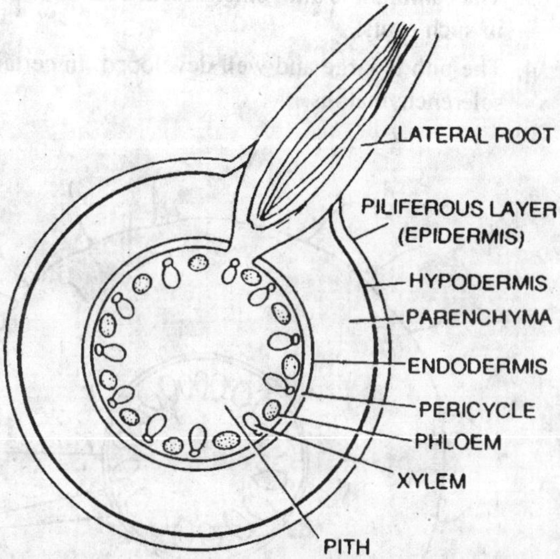

Fig. 9.16. The root. Transection through root of *Zea mays* (monocot) showing a lateral root.

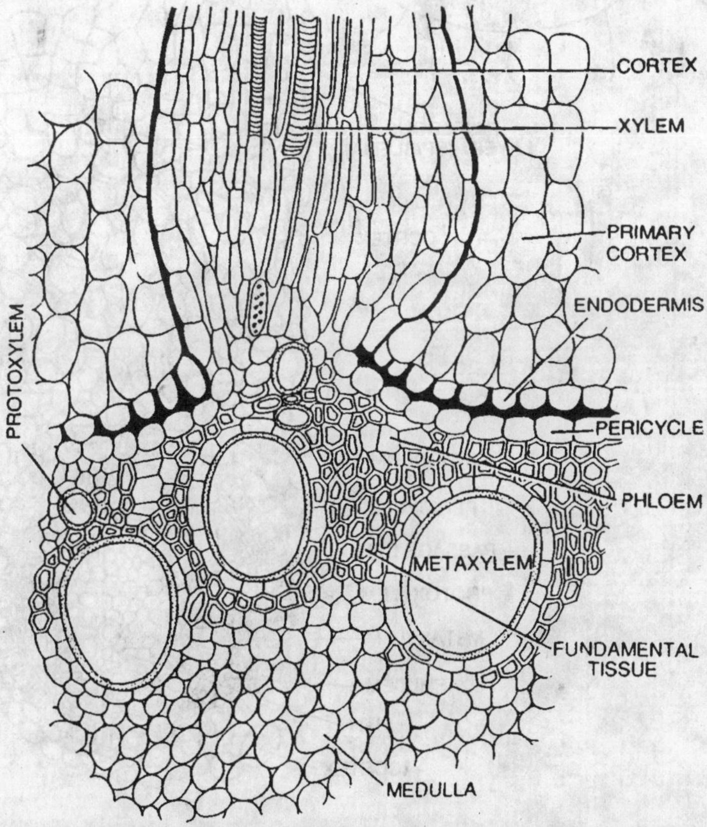

Fig. 9.17. The root. Transection through root of *Zea mays* (monocot) showing a lateral root. The cortex and xylem are clearly visible in the lateral root.

3. The cambium is altogether absent even in later stages, as there is no secondary thickening in such roots.
4. The pith is large and well developed. In certain cases (*e.g.*, in *Canna*), the pith becomes sclerenchymatous.

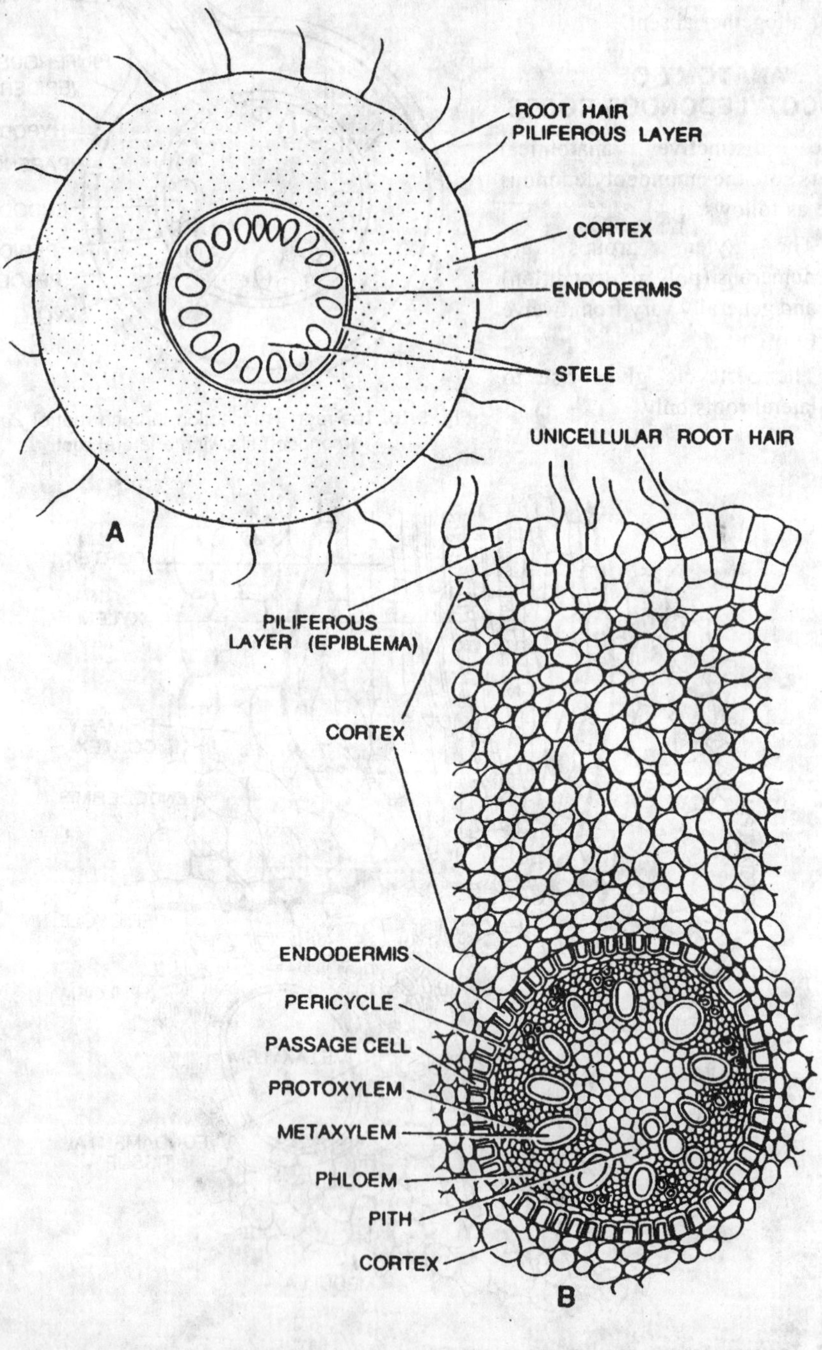

Fig. 9.18. Root. T.S. of monocotyledonous root (*Iris*). A, diagrammatic; B, detailed.

EPIDERMIS

The epidermis or outermost layer of the root is commonly known as **rhizodermis, epiblema** or **piliferous layer.** It is uniseriate and composed of compact tabular cells having no intercellular spaces and stomata. The tubular unicellular root hairs are also present on this layer. A well known example of a multiseriate epidermis is the **velamen** of aerial roots of orchids and epiphytic aroids (Guttenberg, 1940). The velamen is a parchment-like sheath consisting of compactly arranged nonliving cells with thickened walls. The cells of velamen are quite big in size and contain air and water in them. The cell walls develop fibrous thickenings. Generally, beneath the epidermis there are present one or more layers of **exodermis**. Usually the exodermis consists of a single row of cells with thickened outer and lateral walls except certain passage cells which remain thin-walled.

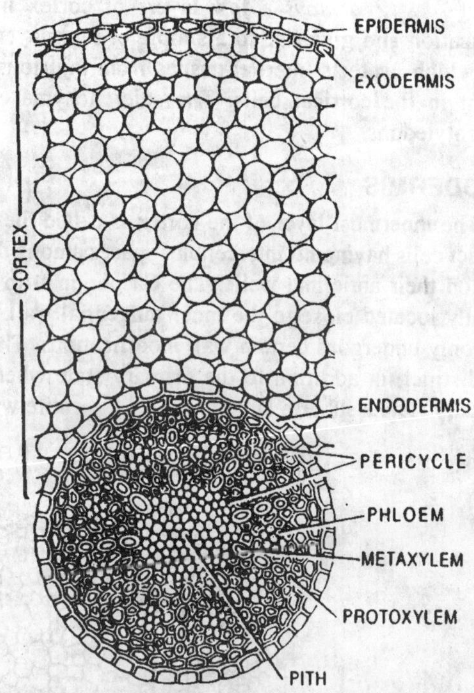

Fig. 9.19. Anatomy of root. T.S. of *Smilax* root (monocot)—detail of a sector.

CORTEX

Immediately beneath the epidermis a massive cortex lies consisting of thin-walled parenchyma cells having sufficiently developed intercellular spaces among them. Usually in an old

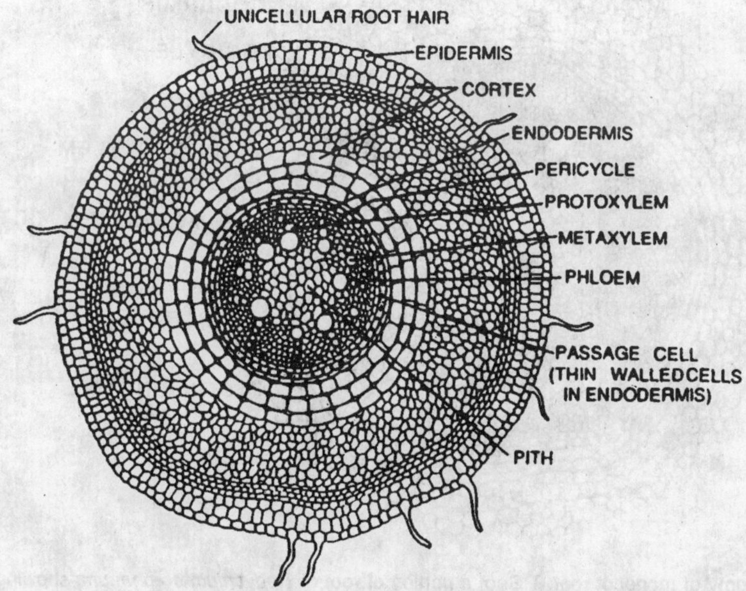

Fig. 9.20. Anatomy of monocot root. Cross section of root of *Commelina*.

root of *Zea mays* a few layers of cortex immediately beneath the epidermis undergo suberization and give rise to a simple or multilayered zone—the **exodermis.** This is protective layer which protects internal tissues from injurious agencies. The starch grains are abundantly present in the cortical cells. The sclerenchyma cells are commonly found in the cortex of monocotyledons.

ENDODERMIS

The innermost layer of the cortex is called the endodermis. It is composed of barrel-shaped compact cells having no intercellular spaces among them. The endodermal cells possess Casparian strips on their anticlinal walls. The Casparian strip is the part of primary cell wall. The strip is typically located close to the inner tangential wall. In most of monocotyledons the endodermis commonly undergoes certain wall modifications. There are two developmental states, sometimes very distinct, in addition to the primary state when only the Casparian strip is present. In the secondary state a suberin lamella covers the entire wall on the inside of the cell. At a later stage of

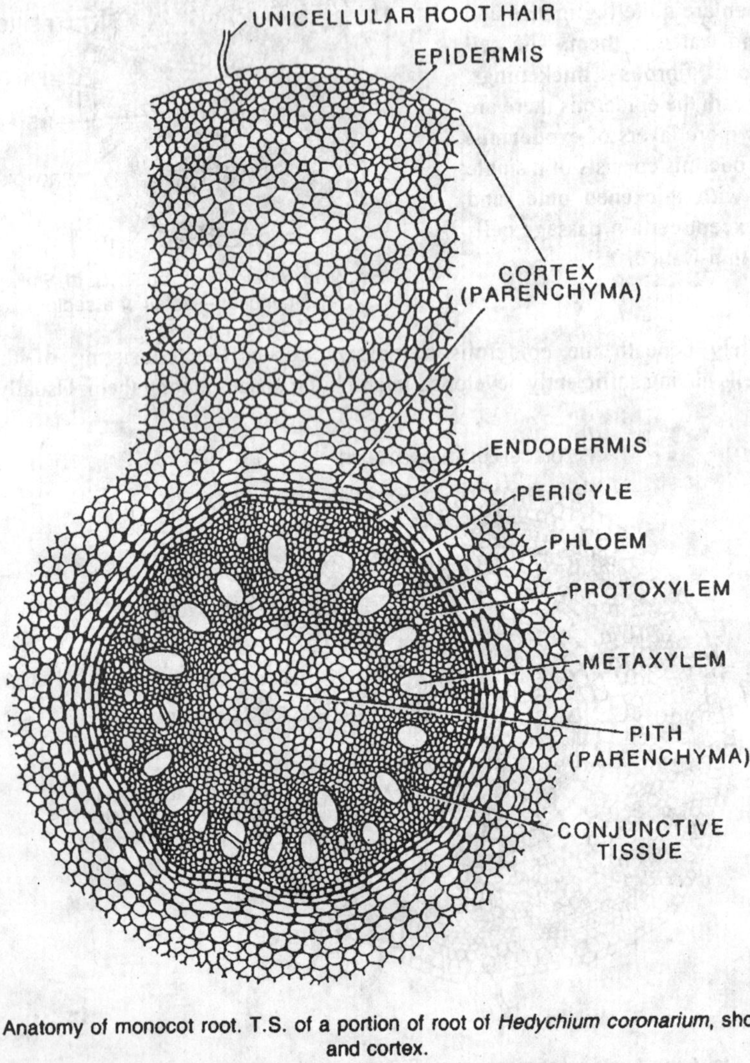

Fig. 9.21. Anatomy of monocot root. T.S. of a portion of root of *Hedychium coronarium*, showing stele and cortex.

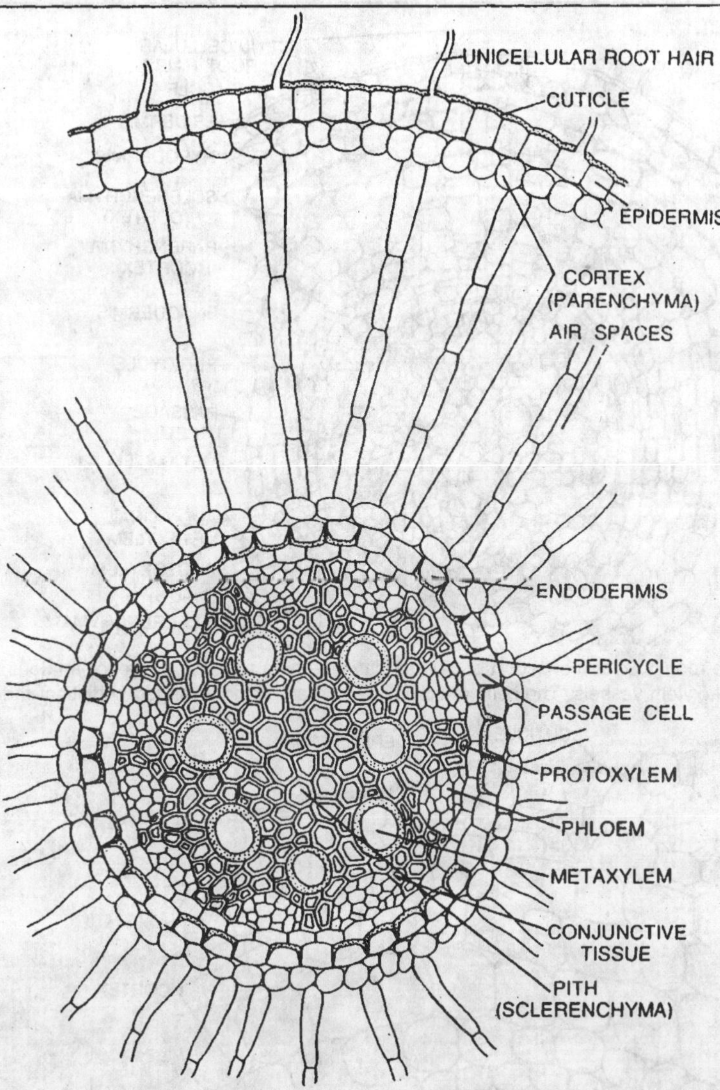

Fig. 9.22. The root. T.S. of monocot root of *Oryza sativa* (rice) showing air-spaces in cortex and sclerenchymatous pith.

development this suberin lamella is covered by a layer of cellulose which in some monocot roots attains a considerable thickness. Thus the walls of the endodermal cells become sufficiently thickened and the thick-walled **passage cells** are formed opposite the protoxylem poles. The passage cells are meant for diffusion and are also called the **transfusion cells.**

PERICYCLE

It is usually uniseriate and composed of thin-walled parenchymatous cells. In the monocotyledons, the pericycle often undergoes sclerification in older roots, partly or entirely. In many monocotyledons (*e.g.*, some Gramineae, *Smilax, Agave, Dracaena,* palms) the pericycle consists of several layers. The pericycle may be interrupted by the differentiation of xylem (many Gramineae and Cyperaceae) or phloem elements (Potamogetonaceae) next to the endodermis (Guttenberg, 1943). Here, the pericycle gives rise to lateral roots only.

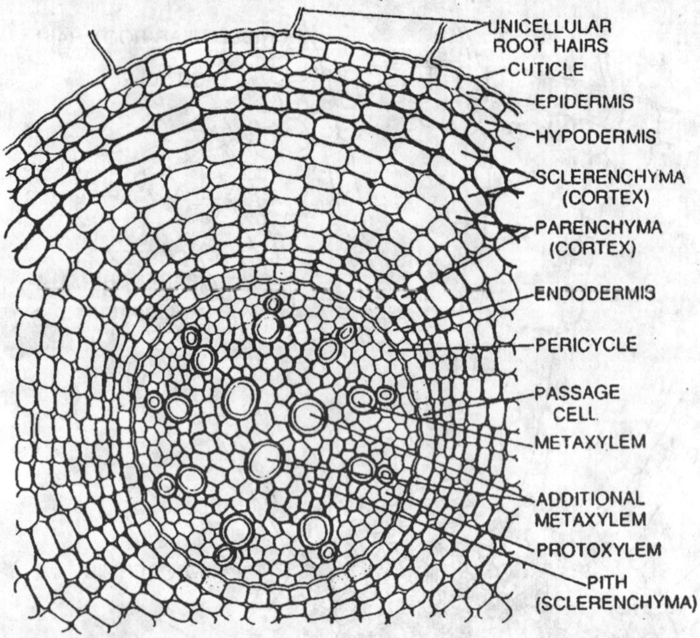

Fig. 9.23. The root. T.S. of monocot root (*Avena sativa*—Oats) showing sclerenchymatous pith and additional metaxylem vessels. The cells of cortical region are being arranged in distinct radial rows.

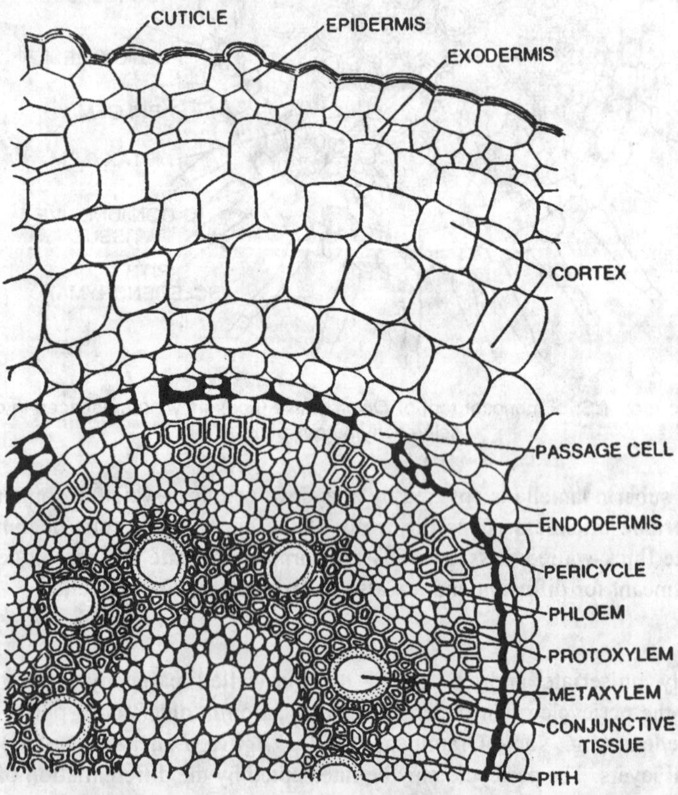

Fig. 9.24. The root. T.S. of monocotyledonous root (grass).

VASCULAR TISSUE

The vascular tissue consists of alternating strands of xylem and phloem. The phloem occurs in the form of strands near the periphery of the vascular cylinder, beneath the pericycle. The xylem forms discrete strands, alternating with the phloem strands. The centre is occupied by large pith which may be parenchymatous or sclerenchymatous. Bundles are numerous and referred as **polyarch.** The adventitious roots of Palmae and Pandanaceae have considerably higher number of vascular bundles, as many as 100 or more. In some roots (*e.g., Hydrilla, Triticum*), a single vessel occupies the centre and is separated by non-tracheary elements from the peripheral strands. In other variable numbers of large metaxylem vessels are arranged in circle around the pith (*e.g., Zea mays*). In the woody monocotyledons the inner metaxylem elements may form two to three circles (*e.g., Latana*), or they may be widely separated from each other (*e.g., Phoenix dactylifera*), or scattered throughout the centre (*e.g., Raphia hookeri*). In some monocotyledons (*e.g., Cordyline, Musa*, Pandanaceae) phloem strands are scattered among the tracheary elements in the centre of the root.

The xylem is exarch, *i.e.*, the protoxylem lies towards periphery and the metaxylem towards the centre. The vessels of protoxylem are narrow and the walls have annular and spiral thickenings whereas that of metaxylem the vessels are broad and they possess reticulate and pitted thickenings.

The phloem strands consist of sieve tubes, companion cells and phloem parenchyma. The phloem strands are also exarch having protophloem towards the periphery and metapholem towards the centre. The parenchymatous or sclerenchymatous conjunctive tissue is found in between and around the xylem and phloem strands. The central part of the stele is occupied by a well developed pith. In *Canna, Oryza sativa, Avena sativa*, the pith is sclerenchymatous.

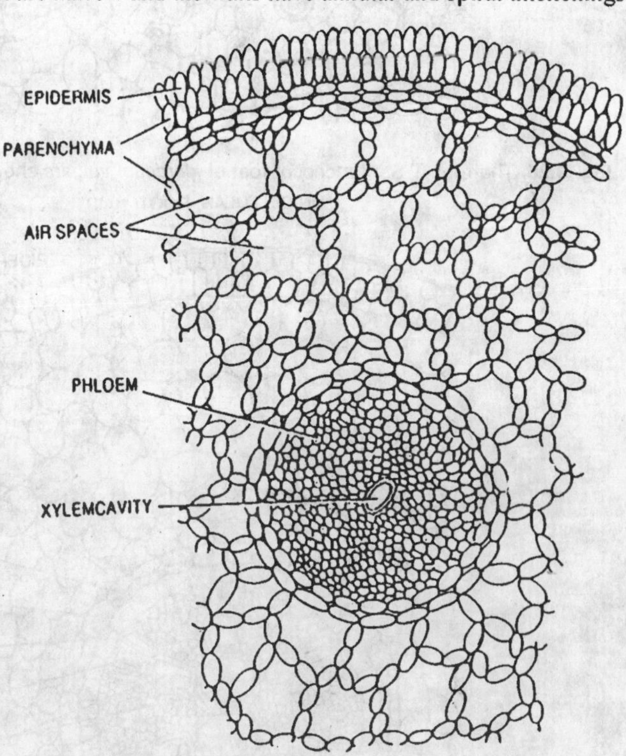

Fig. 9.25. T.S. of monocot root of *Hydrilla* showing large air spaces in cortex and single xylem cavity.

FORMATION OF LATERAL ROOTS

In flowering plants, the lateral roots are endogenous in origin, that is, they originate in the inner tissue of the mother root, and appear externally only after their growth is well begun. The root meristems arise in the pericycle found immediately beneath the endodermis. (In ferns, and other pteridophytes the lateral roots originate in the endodermis). Usually the lateral roots are restricted to the regions opposite the xylem and come out in vertical rows, the number being equal to that of xylem strands present. In the formation of a lateral root, the cells of the pericycle lying against the protoxylem become meristematic and begin to divide first tangentially and then periclinally and anticlinally,

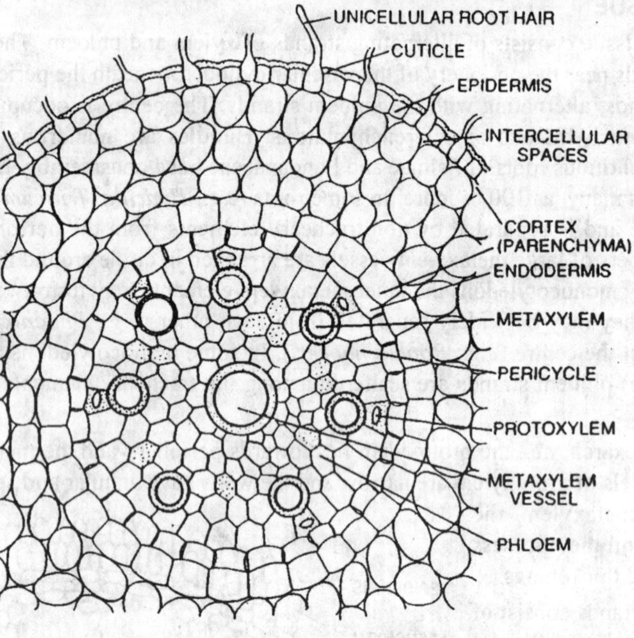

Fig. 9.26. The root. T.S. of monocot root of *Hordeum vulgare* showing the central metaxylem vessel.

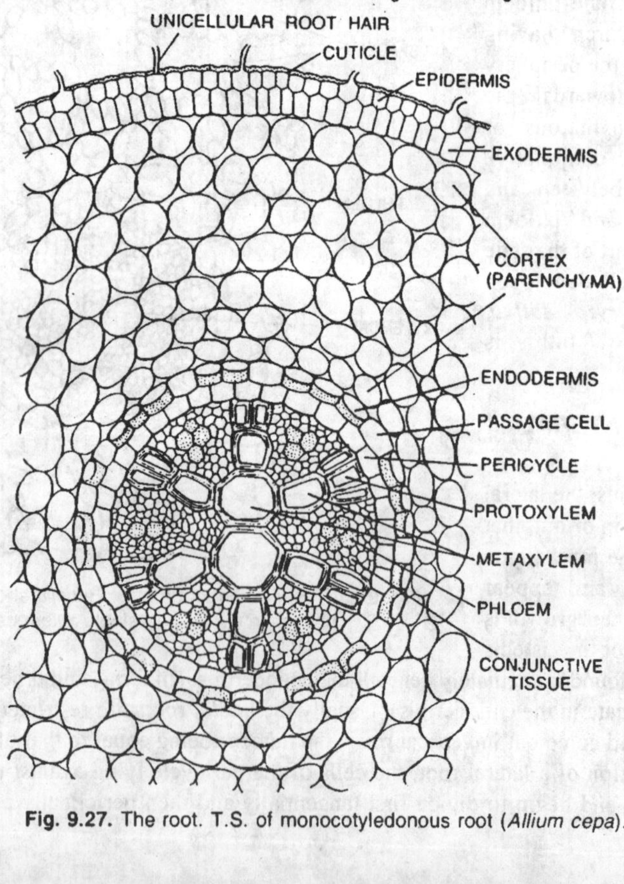

Fig. 9.27. The root. T.S. of monocotyledonous root (*Allium cepa*).

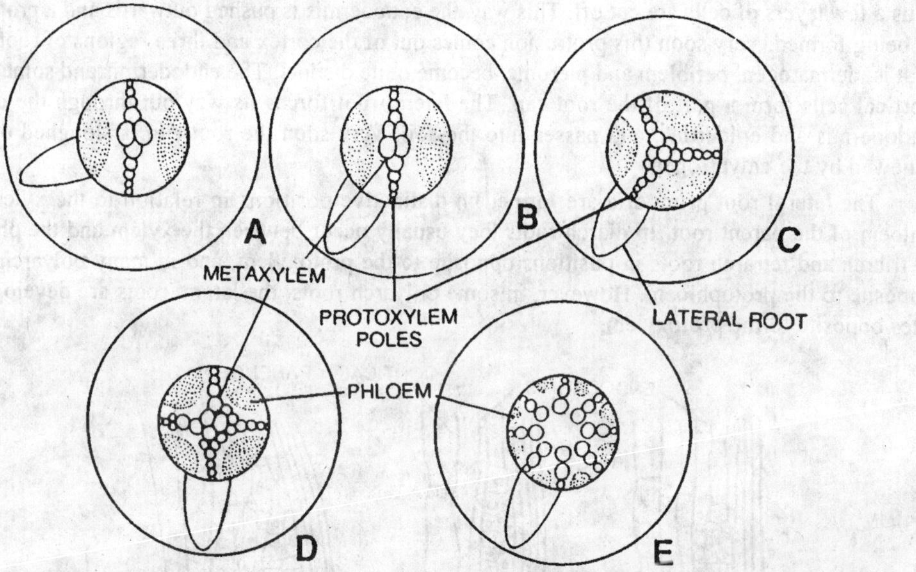

Fig. 9.28. Arrangement of primary vascular tissues and the orientation of lateral root with reference to the vascular tissues of the main root. A—D, diarch to tetrarch (in dicot); E, polyarch (in monocot). Lateral root arises opposite the phloem poles in A and E; opposite the protoxylem poles in C and D; between xylem and phloem poles in B.

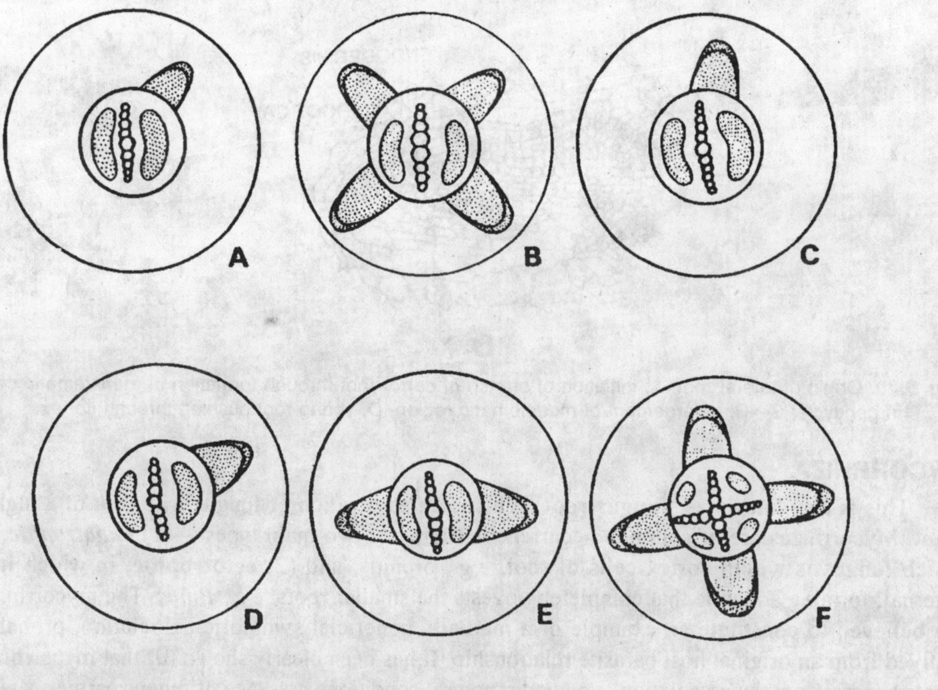

Fig. 9.29. Position of origin of lateral roots. A—E, various positions found in gymnosperms as well as in angiosperms where root has less than three xylem rays; F, position (opposite xylem rays) found in roots of all vascular plants where there are three or more xylem rays.

thus a few layers of cells are cut off. This way, the endodermis is pushed outwards and a protrusion is being formed. Very soon this protrusion comes out of the cortex and three regions of root apex, that is, dermatogen, periblem and plerome, become quite distinct. The endodermis and some of the cortical cells form a part of the root cap. The lateral root forces its way out through the cortex, endodermis and epidermis, and passes into the soil. Very soon the root cap is sloughed off and renewed by the calyptrogen.

The lateral root primodria are formed in distinctive positions in relation to the xylem and phloem of the parent root. In diarch roots they usually occur between the xylem and the phloem, in triarch and tetrarch roots in positions opposite to the protoxylem, and in many polyarch roots opposite to the protophloem. However, in some polyarch roots, the lateral roots are developed in sites opposite to the protoxylem.

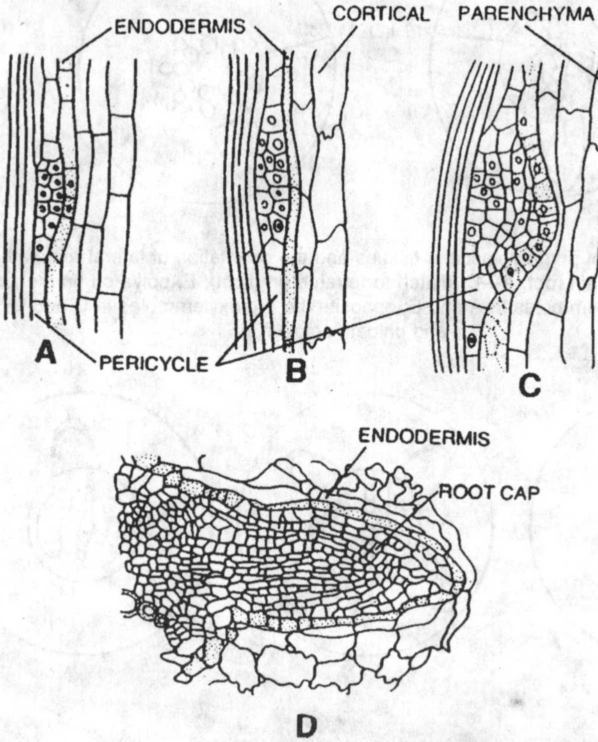

Fig. 9.30. Origin of lateral root. A, initiation of branch of carrot root through formation of meristematic cells in pericycle; B—C, enlargement of meristematic region, D, young root pushing through cortex.

MYCORRHIZA

This is also known as **'fungus root'.** This is an association of fungus with root of a higher plant. Mycorrhizas are of common occurrence. There are two main types —(1) ***endotrophic***, in which fungus is within cortex cells of root, *e.g.*, orchids, and (2) **ectotrophic,** in which it is external, forming a mantle that completely invests the smaller roots, *e.g., Pinus*. The mycorrhizas are believed to constitute an example of a mutually beneficial symbiotic association, probably evolved from an original host parasite relationship. It has been clearly shown (*a*) that mycorrhizal plants benefit from the association, *e.g.*, under natural conditions presence of fungus partner is vital for establishment and growth of seedling trees of a number of different species, *e.g.*, pines, and (*b*) that association of fungus with tree is necessary for development and reproduction by fungus.

FORMATION OF ADVENTITIOUS ROOTS

The adventitious roots may occur on the hypocotyl of a seedling, at nodes and internodes of stems, and in roots. They may be formed in young organs or in older tissues which are still meristematic. Most adventitious roots arise endogenously. Stem-borne adventitious roots make the main vascular system in vascular cryptogms (pteridophytes), in most monocotyledons, in dicotyledons propagating by means of rhizomes or runners, in water plants, in saprophytes and in parasites. The roots which are developed on cuttings, directly from the stem or from the callus tissue, are also adventitious.

Usually the adventitious roots are initiated in the vicinity of differentiating vascular tissues of the organ which gives rise to them (Datta and Majumdar, 1943). In young organ, the adventitious primordium is initiated by a group of cells near the periphery of the vascular system. In older organ, it is located deeper, near the vascular cambium. In young stems, the cells that form the root primordium are derived from the interfascicular parenchyma, while in older stems from a vascular ray. In certain cases the adventitious roots are initiated by divisions in the cambial zone (Smith, 1936). Usually the seat of the root primordium in the case of stems is known as pericycle. The origin of the adventitious roots in the vascular ray, or in the cambium places the young root close to both the xylem and the phloem of the mother axis and makes the vascular connection between the two organs (see fig. 9.30).

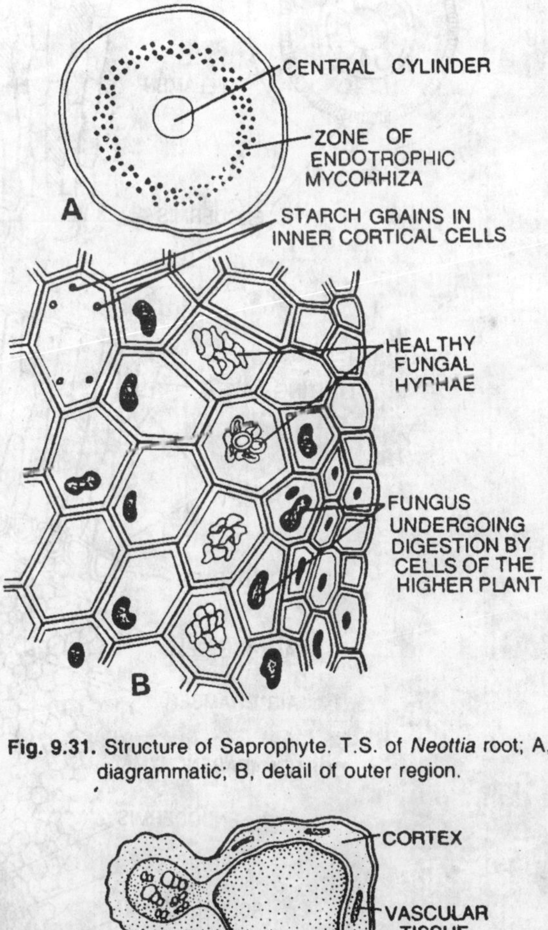

Fig. 9.31. Structure of Saprophyte. T.S. of *Neottia* root; A, diagrammatic; B, detail of outer region.

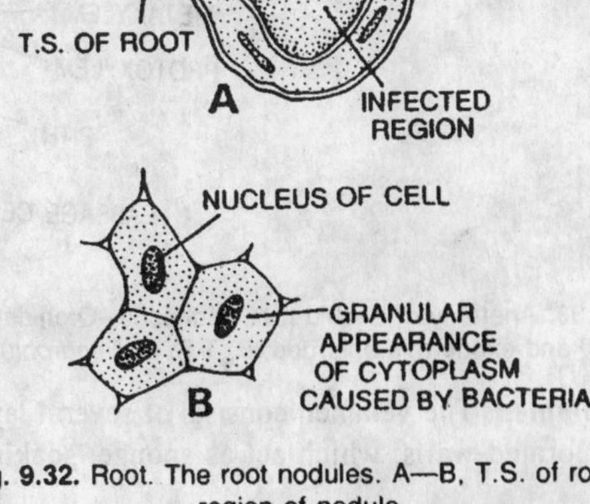

Fig. 9.32. Root. The root nodules. A—B, T.S. of root in region of nodule.

ANATOMY OF EPIPHYTIC ROOTS

ANATOMY OF ORCHID ROOT (MONOCOT)

The orchids (of family Orchidaceae-monocotyledons) are epiphytes. They possess the aerial roots hanging in the air. The anatomy of the root of *Dendrobium* (an orchid) is given here.

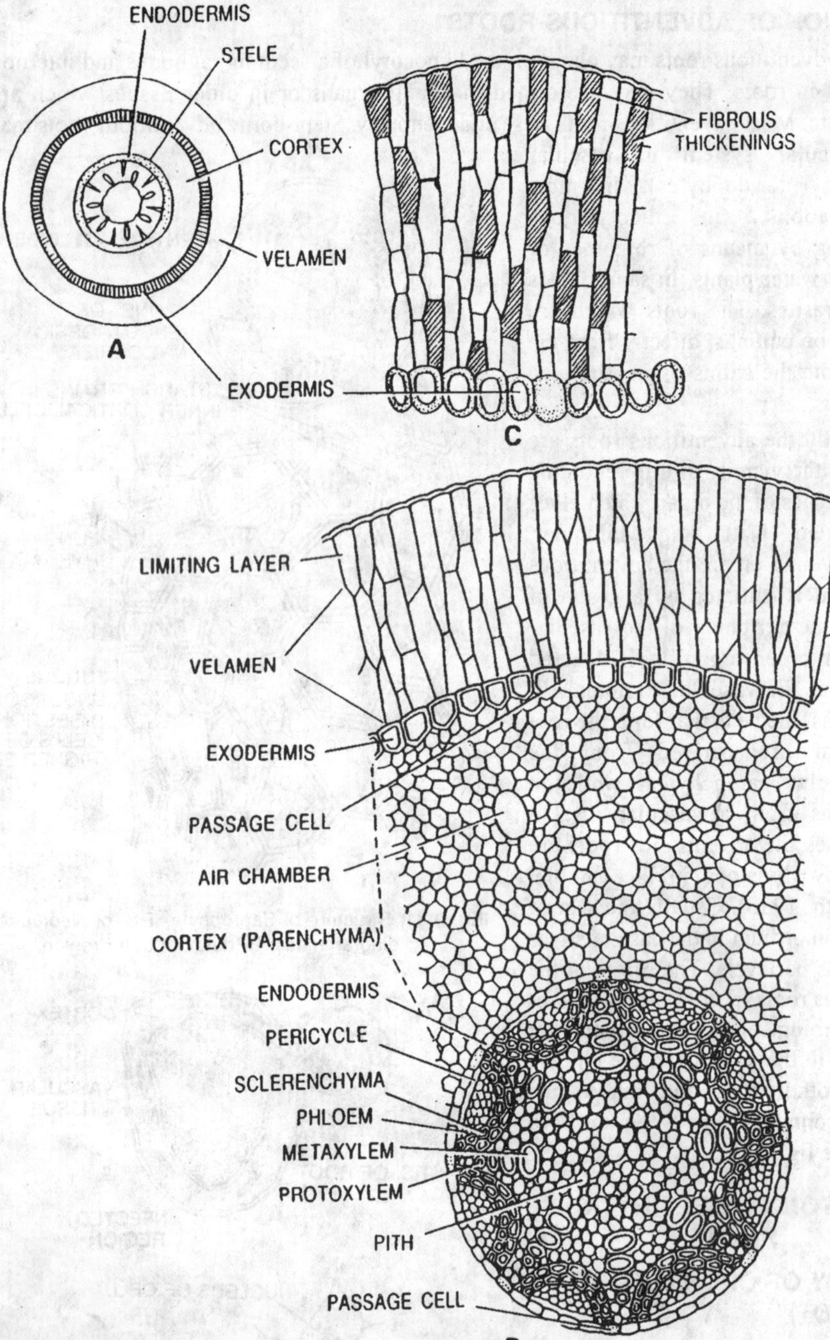

Fig. 9.33. Anatomy of Orchid root (Monocot—Orchidaceae)—A, T.S. of root (diagrammatic); C, velaman and exodermis enlarged; B, T.S. of *Dendrobium* (orchid) root showing detailed structure.

Velamen. The velamen consists of several layers of dead cells often with spirally thickened and perforated walls, which act as sponge, soaking up water that runs over it. The velamen is multiple epidermis. The velamen is thought to function as a protective tissue, preventing undue water loss from the delicate cortical cells of the exposed aerial root.

Exodermis. It is the outermost layer of the cortex. This layer is composed of alternating long and short cells; the long cells become thick-walled on their radial and outer tangential surface, but the small cells remain thin-walled and are called **passage cells.**

Cortex. The main cortex consists of thin-walled parenchyma cells having intercellular spaces among them. The innermost layer of the cortex is **endodermis** that consists of compact barrel-shaped cells having starch grains in them. The endodermis completely encircles the stele.

Pericycle. Immediately beneath the endodermis a single-layered pericycle is found. The cells are thin-walled.

Vascular system. The vascular bundles are radial, *i.e.*, the xylem and phloem strands are equal in number and arranged alternately. The bundles are more than six (*i.e.*, polyarch condition). The xylem is exarch. The protoxylem poles are found towards periphery and metaxylem towards centre. The vessels of the protoxylem are narrow and possessing annular and spiral thickenings whereas the vessels of metaxylem are broad and possessing reticulate and pitted thickenings on their walls. The phloem bundles are made up of sieve tubes, companion cells and phloem parenchyma.

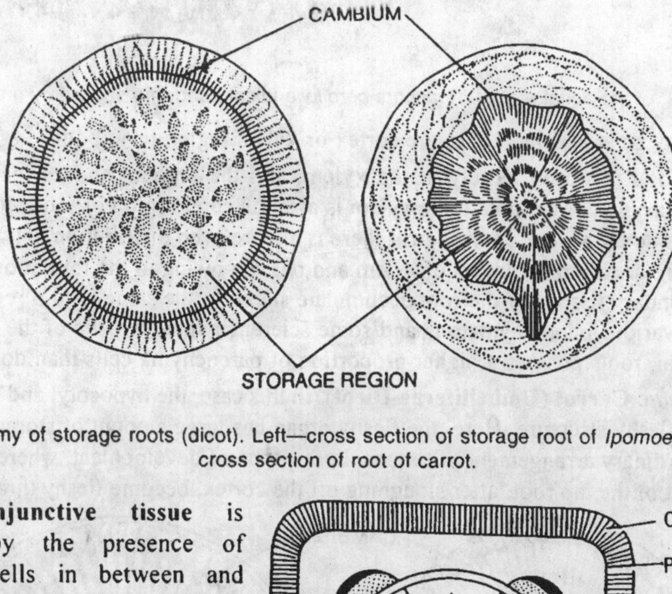

Fig. 9.34. Anatomy of storage roots (dicot). Left—cross section of storage root of *Ipomoea batatas*; right—cross section of root of carrot.

The **conjunctive tissue** is represented by the presence of parenchyma cells in between and around the vascular bundle.

ANATOMY OF STORAGE ROOTS

The underground roots may become very much thickened and serve as organs for the storage of food. Such is the case in sweet potatoes, radishes, turnips, carrots and dahlias. In such

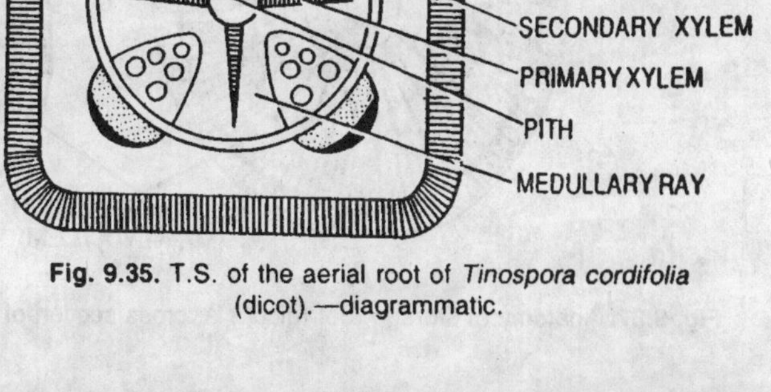

Fig. 9.35. T.S. of the aerial root of *Tinospora cordifolia* (dicot).—diagrammatic.

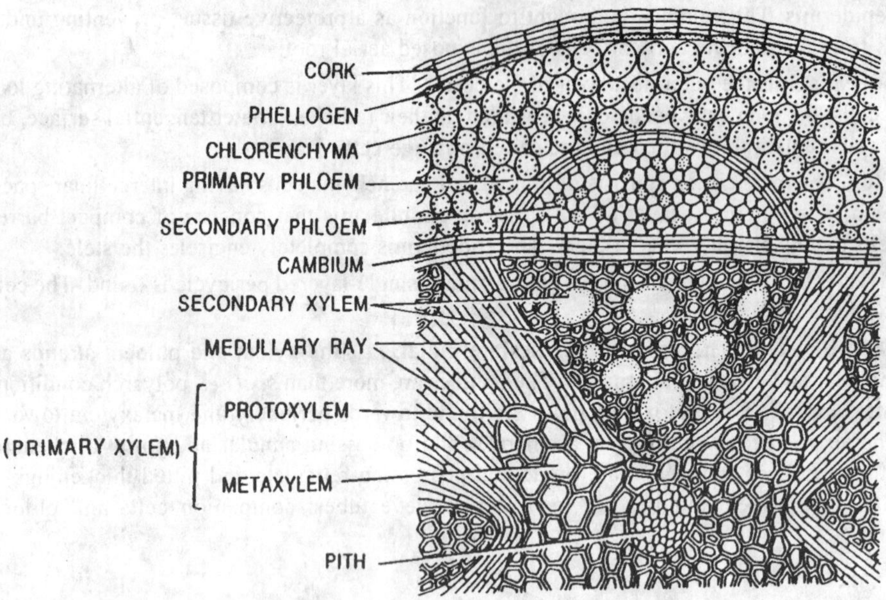

Fig. 9.36. T.S. of the aerial root of *Tinospora cordifolia* (dicot.) showing secondary growth-detail.

roots the food may be stored largely in the cortex or xylem region or in both.

In turnips food is stored largely in the xylem, and the phloem and cortex are relatively narrow. In the radish and sweet potato the xylem is also the chief region of food storage, but food is also stored outside the xylem. In the carrot there is a more even distribution between xylem and bark. In beets there are alternate layers of xylem and phloem owing to the formation of successive cambia. The secondary tissues of the root accumulate starch in the same kind of cells as those of the stem, that is various parenchymatous and some sclerenchymatous cells of the xylem and the phloem. In general, roots possess a higher proportion of parenchyma cells than do stems.

***Daucus carota.* Carrot (Umbelliferae-Dicot).** In this case, the hypocotyl and base of taproot form jointly one fleshy structure. Here, the fleshy organ has large amount of storage parenchyma associated with ordinary arrangement of tissues. In this type of development, where the hypocotyl and the upper part of the tap root, after sloughing off the cortex, become fleshy through a massive

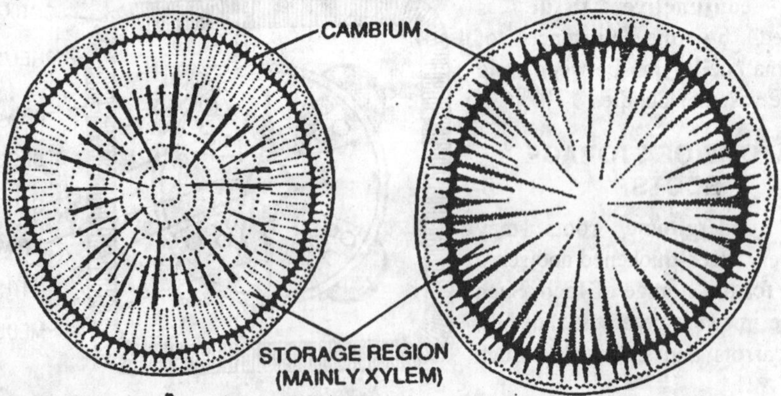

Fig. 9.37. Anatomy of storage root (dicot.). A, cross section of turnip root; B, cross section of radish root.

development of parenchyma in the phloem and the xylem. Besides the cambial activity the massive parenchyma, that makes the storage tissue, adds to the thickness of the root.

***Raphanus sativus.* Radish (Cruciferae-Dicot).** The fleshy roots of radish show a proliferation of parenchyma in the pith and in the secondary xylem, and a differentiation of concentric vascular bundles within this parenchyma. Here, the fleshy roots show a diarch primary xylem. The normal cambium cuts off secondary phloem towards periphery and secondary xylem towards the centre. Several concentric vascular bundles are seen in the transverse section of the fleshy root. The concentric bundles are composed of secondary cambial rings with a few vascular elements in the centre.

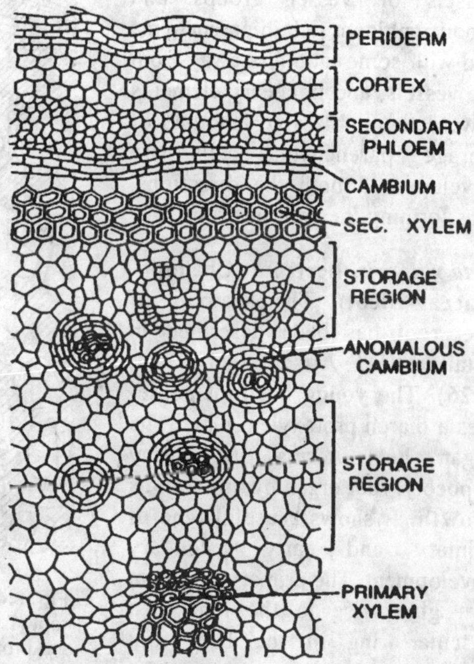

Fig. 9.38. The root. T.S. of a sector of root oi *Raphanus sativus* (dicot.)

***Ipomoea batatas.* Sweet potato (Convolvulaceae-Dicot).** It exhibits a complicated type of anomalous secondary thickening. In primary state the root is pentarch or hexarch. The cortex is delimited by a single-layered distinct endodermis from the stelar region. In the normally developed but highly parenchy-matous primary and

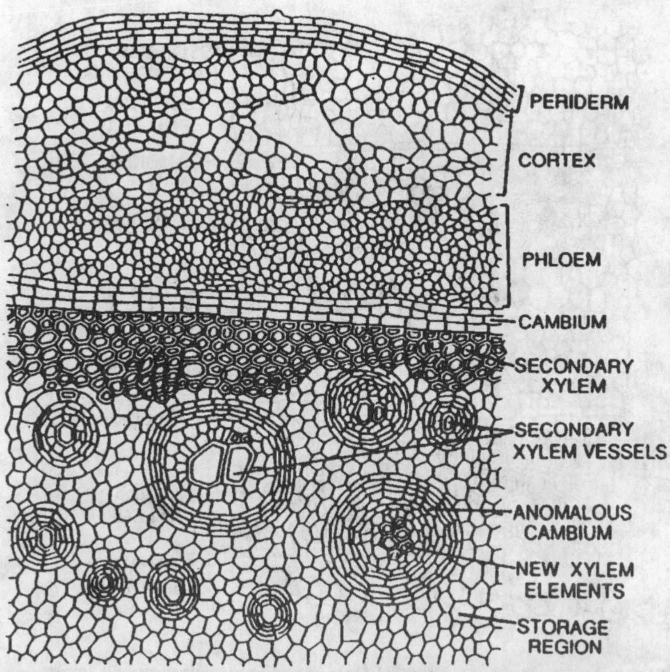

Fig. 9.39. The root. T.S. of storage root of *Ipomoea batatas* a sector.

secondary xylem, anomalous cambia arise around individual vessels or vessel groups and produce phloem rich in parenchyma and with some laticifers away from the vessels, and tracheary elements toward them. Massive amounts of storage parenchyma cells are developed in both the directions, thus forming the tuberous roots.

***Beta vulgaris*. Beetroot (Chenopodiaceae-Dicot)**. The anatomy of beet root has been described in detail by E.F. Artschwager (1924, 1926). The young beetroot possesses a diarch protoxylem plate. The sugar beet forms its fleshy hypocotyl root organ by **anomalous growth.** It shows a useful type of primary and early secondary development. The primary cambium that gives rise to the innermost vascular ring in the beet root develops in the interstitial parenchyma except opposite the two

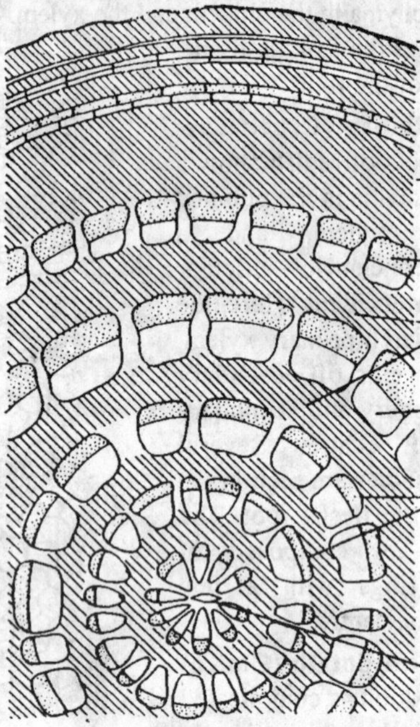

Fig. 9.40. Anomalous secondary growth in *Beta vulgaris* root (T.S.), showing alternate layers of vascular bundles and proliferated pericycle, phloem, lignified xylem cells in radial rows, xylem parenchyma and secondary interfascicular tissue. (After Eames and MacDaniels).

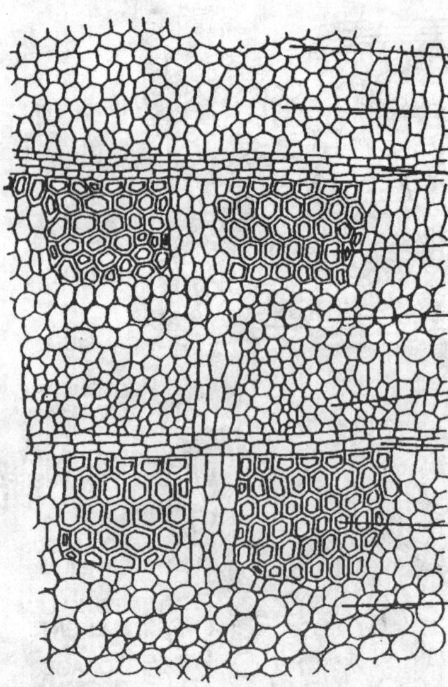

Fig. 9.41. The root. The root of *Beta vulgaris* showing growth layers.

protoxylem poles where it is derived from the pericycle. The first secondary cambium in the root and lower part of the hypocotyl arises in the phloem parenchyma, whereas in the upper part of the hypocotyl is derived from the pericycle. Later, however, a series of supernumerary cambia arise outside the normal vascular cylinder and produce several increments of vascular tissue, each consisting of a layer of parenchyma, parenchymatous xylem and parenchymatous phloem. Practically all the supernumerary cambia that give rise to the vascular rings in the mature root have already been developed when the diameter of the young root is no greater than five millimetres or so. All the cambia are active at the same time.

HETEROARCHY IN ROOTS

In certain cases, the same plant may bear roots of different types. In such plants, the roots may be tetrarch, pentarch, hexarch and even polyarch. This condition is known as **heteroarchy,** and the roots, the **heteroarchic roots.** Wardlaw (1928) reported heteroarchy in *Nymphaea chilensis*. This plant bears four types of roots. The small roots possess tetrarch condition; the slightly thicker roots possess seven xylem groups alternating with the seven phloem groups; more thicker roots possess polyarch condition (*i.e.,* 12-14 xylem groups) and still more thicker roots are also polyarch (*i.e.,* they bear 16-18 xylem groups alternating with equal number of phloem groups).

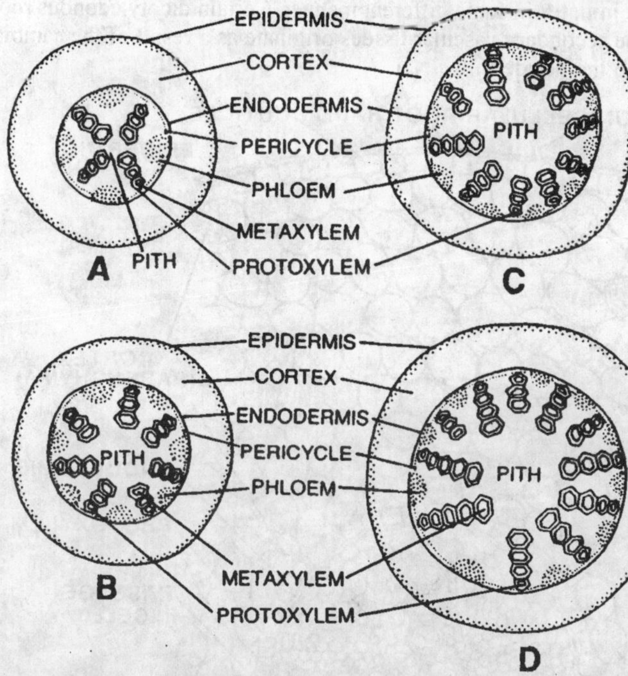

Fig. 9.42. Heteroarchy in roots of *Nymphaea chilensis*. A, root with tetrarch condition; B, root, with seven xylem strands; C, root with ten xylem strands; D, root with twelve xylem strands. (After Wardlaw, 1928).

However, these roots lack secondary growth and present on the same plant. They are of various diameters. Wardlaw (1921) reported the presence of such roots in some species of *Eryngium* (of Umbelliferae). Majumdar (1932) reported heteroarchy in the roots of *Enhydra fluctuans* (of Compositae). Here, the normal terrestrial plants bear tetrarch roots while the plants growing in marshy places bear the roots having triarch, tetrarch and pentarch conditions. (See Fig. 9.42)

Table.9.1. Differences between Dicotyledonous and Monocotyledonous Roots

		Dicotyledonous Root	Monocotyledonous Root
1.	Xylem bundles	The number varies from two to six (di- to hexarch), rarely more.	Usually they are numerous, rarely a limited number (*e.g.*, in Onion).
2.	Pith	It is small or absent.	It is large and well developed.
3.	Pericycle	It gives rise to lateral roots and secondary meristems, *i.e.*, cambium and cork-cambium.	It gives rise to lateral roots only.
4.	Cambium	It appears later as a secondary meristem.	It is altogether absent.

SECONDARY GROWTH IN DICOTYLEDONOUS ROOT

The roots of gymnosperms and most dicotyledonous undergo secondary growth. Most of the dicotyledonous roots show secondary growth in thickness, similar to that of dicotyledonous stems. However, the roots of extant vascular cryptogams and most monocotyledons do not show any secondary growth; they remain entirely primary throughout their life. The secondary tissues developed in the dicotyledonous roots are fundamentaly quite similar to that of dicotyledonous stems, but the process initiates in some different manner. Certain dicotyledonous roots do not show secondary growth. The secondary vascular tissues originate as a result of the cambial activity. The phellogen gives rise to the periderm.

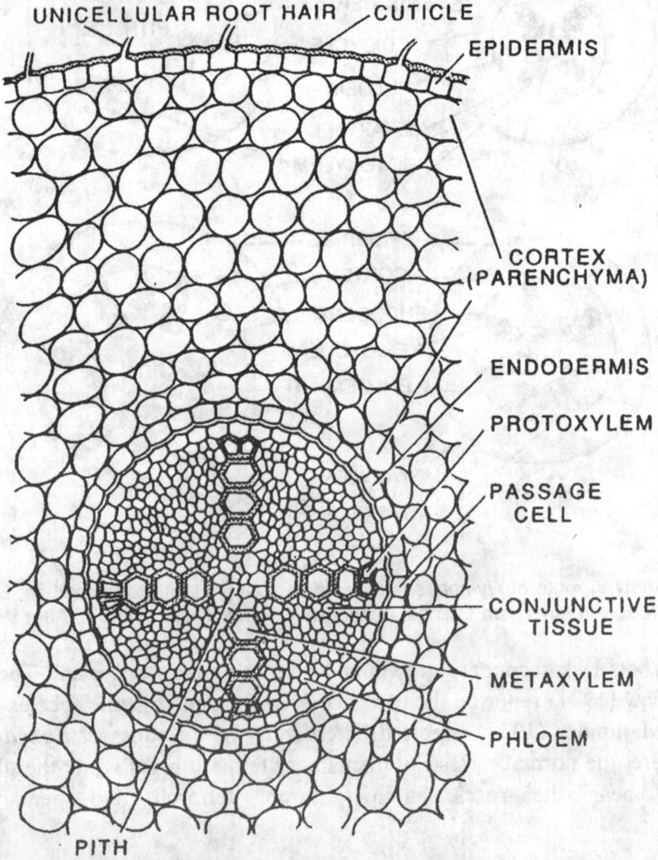

Fig. 9.43. The root. T.S. of a dicotyledonous (gram) root showing tetrarch xylem and small pith.

FORMATION OF CAMBIUM AND DEVELOPMENT OF SECONDARY TISSUES

The dicotyledonous roots posses a limited number of radial vascular bundles with exarch xylem. Normally the pith is very little or altogether absent. On the initiation of secondary growth, a few parenchyma cells beneath each group of phloem become meristematic and thus as many cambial strips are formed as the number of phloem groups. The cambial cells divide tangentially again and again and produce secondary tissues. Thereafter some of the cells of single layered pericycle become meristematic lying against the protoxylem groups, which divide and form a few layers of cells. The first formed cambium now extends towards both of its edges and reaches the inner most derivatives of the pericycle, thus giving rise to a complete ring of cambium. The cambium ring is wavy in outline, as it passes internal to phloem and external to xylem groups. The cambial cells produce more xylem elements than phloem. The first formed cambium produces

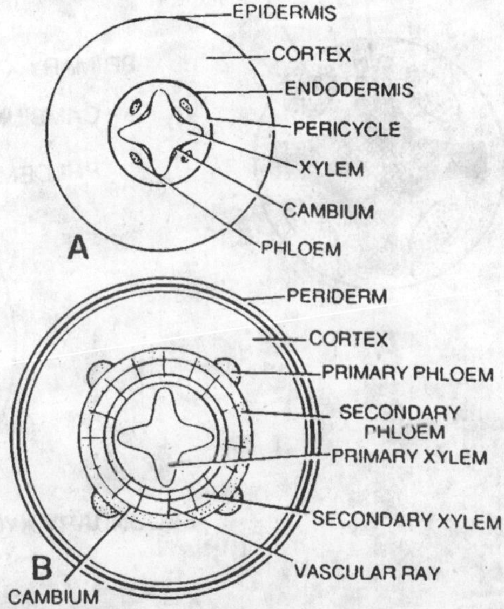

Fig. 9.44. Secondary growth in root A, cross section of a root without secondary growth; B, the same after considerable secondary growth.

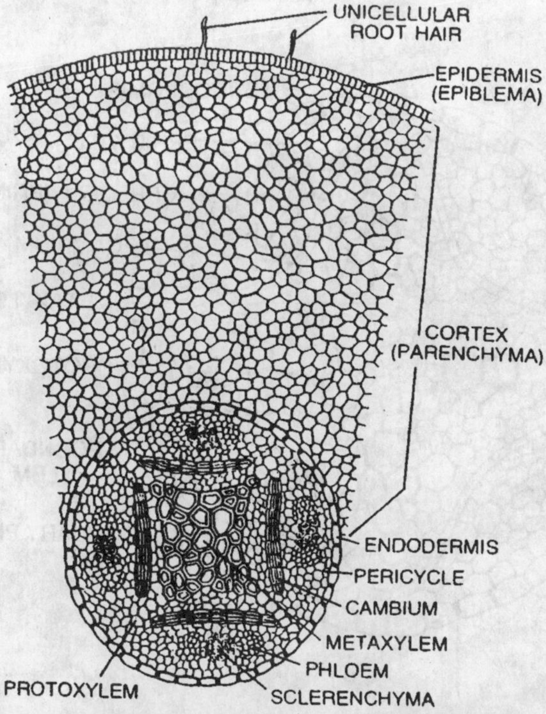

Fig. 9.45. The root. T.S. of gram root (dicot.) showing the beginning of the formation of cambium.

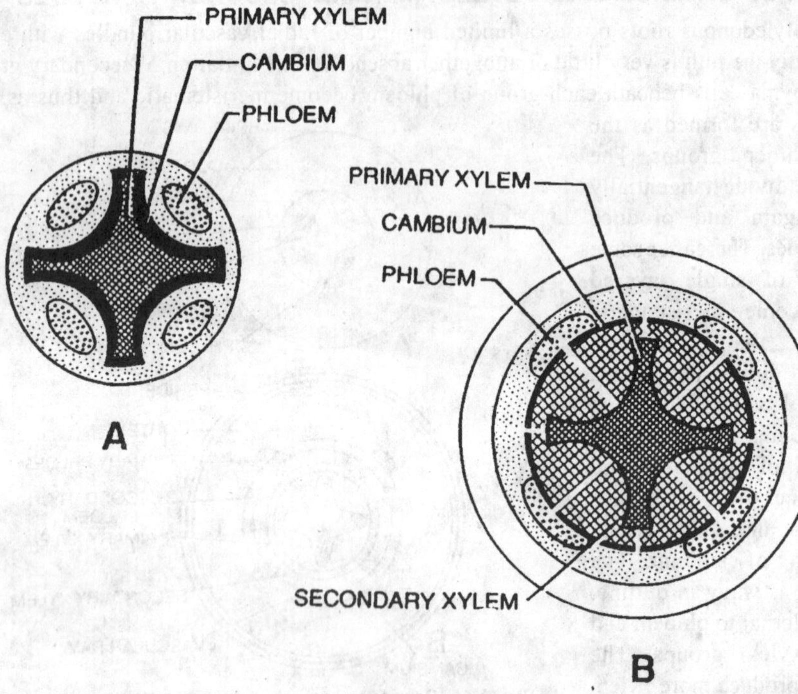

Fig. 9.46. Secondary growth of root. A, diagrammatic cross section of a dicot root showing the cambium; B, a similar section showing secondary phloem and xylem with vascular rays (medullary rays) indicated in white lines.

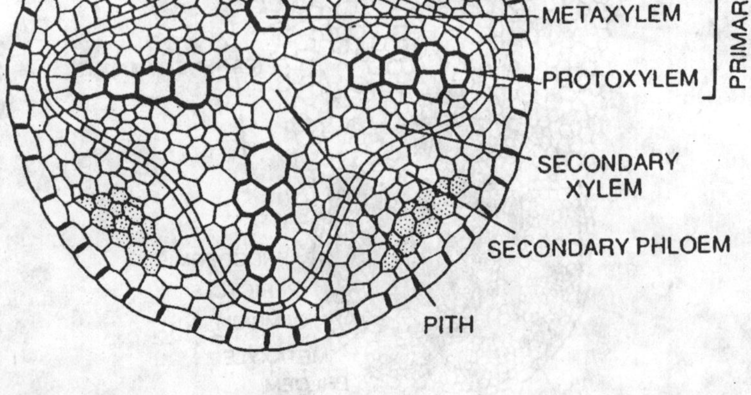

Fig. 9.47. Beginning of secondary growth in dicotyledonous root.

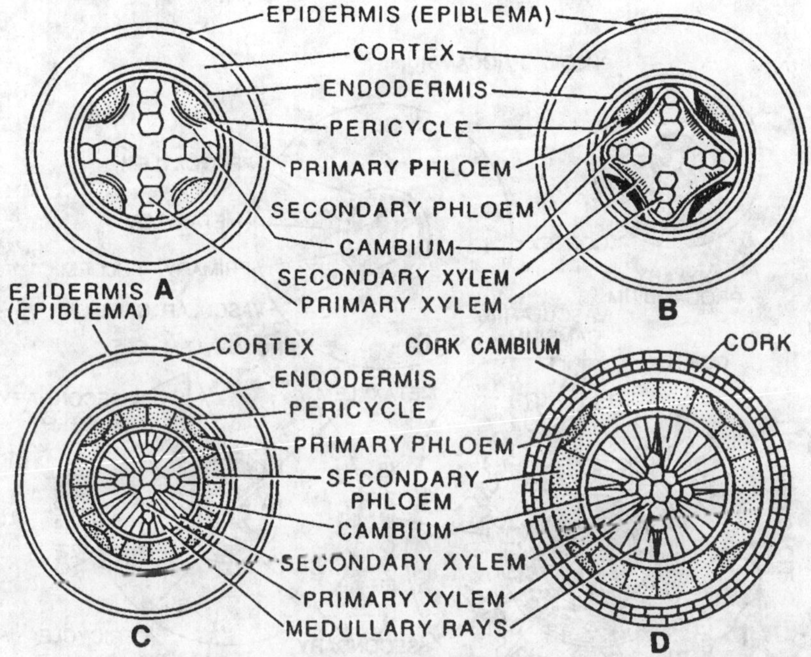

Fig. 9.48. Secondary growth in dicot root. A—D, diagrams showing stages in the secondary growth of a typical dicotyledonous root.

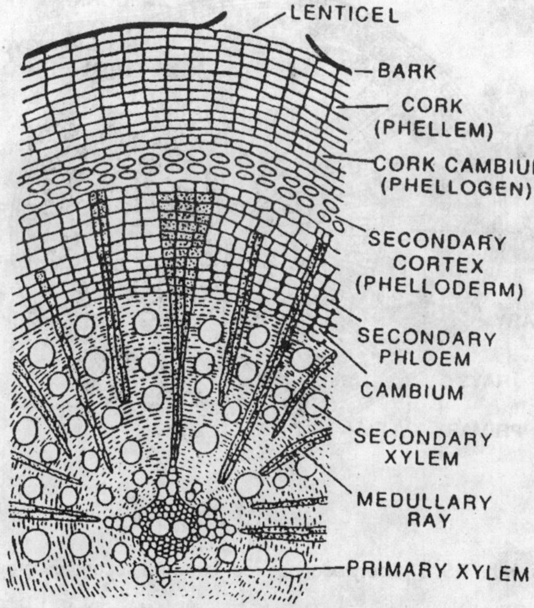

Fig. 9.49. Secondary growth, T.S. of dicotyledonous root showing secondary growth (later stage)

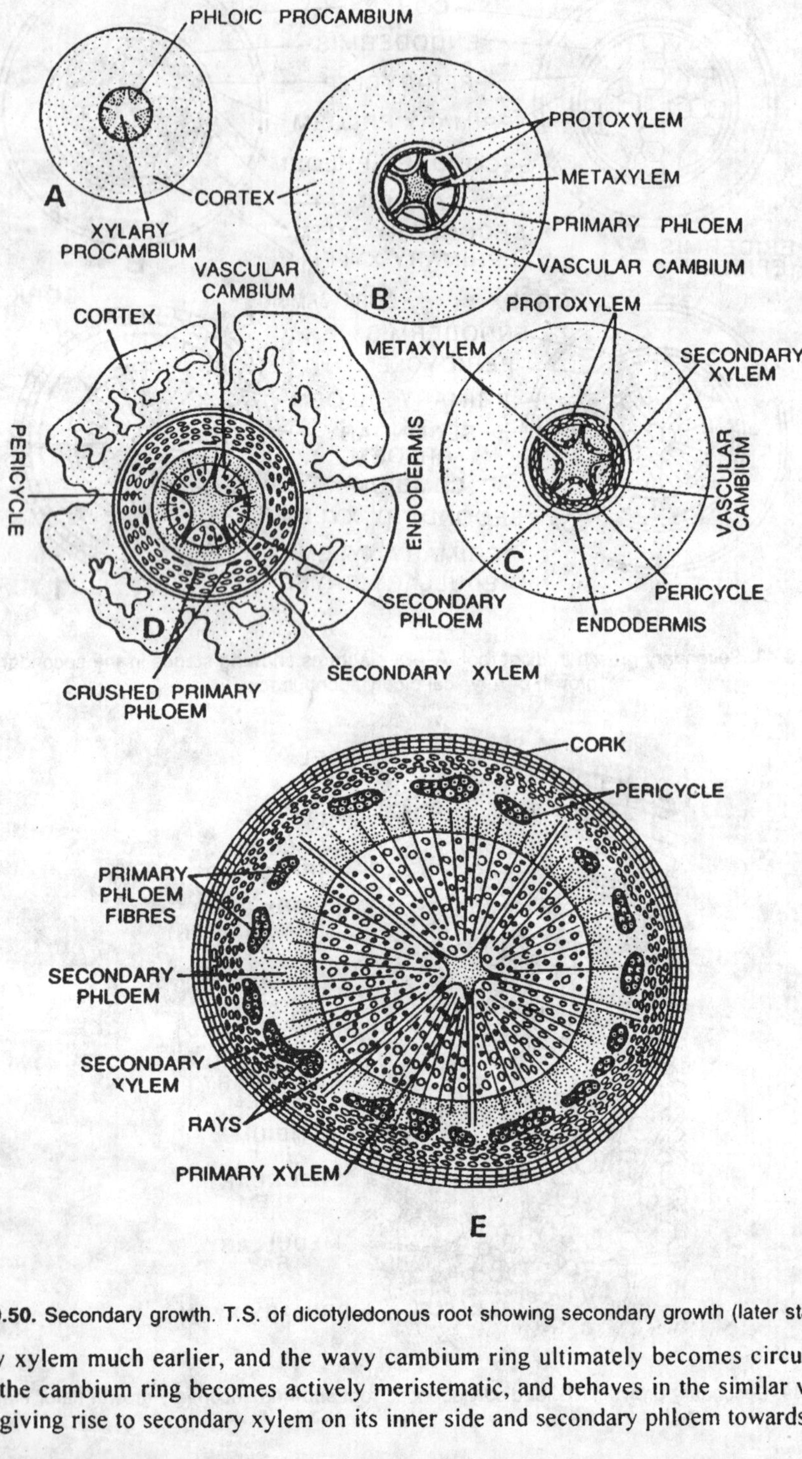

Fig. 9.50. Secondary growth. T.S. of dicotyledonous root showing secondary growth (later stage).

secondary xylem much earlier, and the wavy cambium ring ultimately becomes circular. Now whole of the cambium ring becomes actively meristematic, and behaves in the similar way as in the stem, giving rise to secondary xylem on its inner side and secondary phloem towards outside.

The secondary vascular tissues form a continuous cylinder and usually the primary xylem gets embedded in it. At this stage distinction can be made only by exarch primary xylem located in the centre. The primary phloem elements are generally seen in crushed condition. The cambial cells that originate from the pericycle lying against the groups of protoxylem function as ray initials and produce broad vascular rays. These rays are traversed in the xylem and phloem through cambium; this is characteristic feature of the roots. Normally, such rays are called **medullary rays.**

PERIDERM

Simultaneously the periderm develops in the outer region of the root. The single layered pericycle becomes meristematic and divides, giving rise to **cork cambium** or **phellogen**. It produces a few brownish layers of **cork cells** or **phellem** towards outside, and the **phelloderm** on the inside. The phelloderm does not contain chloroplasts. The pressure caused by secondary tissues ruptures the cortex with endodermis, which is ultimately sloughed off. The epiblema dies out earlier. Lenticels may also be formed.

10

CHAPTER

Anatomy of the Embryo and Young Seedling

In most embryos, the procambium is commonly found in some isolated areas and a few mature protoxylem and protophloem cells may be present. The anatomy of the embryo proper is the histology of meristems.

ANATOMY OF THE COTYLEDON

The traces of the cotyledon vary in number. Commonly only two traces are found in the lower taxa of both monocotyledons and dicotyledons. Four is a frequent number, with transition to three by the fusion of the middle pair. Three is also common with the strong central bundle sometimes double. The large number of traces are probable uncommon (*e.g.*, *Canna* and some *Araceae*). When four traces are present, the two median traces lie close together. The Iridaceae have a median trace, simple or double, with one or two pairs of laterals. The Araceae have one to many traces. The Liliaceae have all stages in the origin of an odd number of traces—two traces, four traces, a double traces, a median trace with one or more pairs of laterals. Odd numbers result from the fusion of two or more traces. Number, position and fusion of traces coincide with those of leaf traces. A single trace is characteristic of highly specialized cotyledons. In many taxa, commonly, the lateral bundles are free distally and with the median bundle, formed a three veined cotyledon. The two free laterals become major bundles in the anatomy of many specialized cotyledons.

The characteristic feature of many monocotyledons is the presence of two strong lateral traces, that supply the sides of the sheathing leaf base. The median vein that supplies the cotyledon tip, bends downward to the scutellum. The lateral veins continue upward in the sheathing wings, or rarely they also continue downward to the scutellum. The tip of the median bundle, remained unbranched in small and cylindrical forms, but becomes branched in large forms.

In most cotyledons which possess two or three free traces, all the vascular bundles continue as veins towards the tip. In the downbent cotyledons where the tip has been transformed into a scutellum, all the bundles may continue in the scutellum, but usually only the median bundle extends to it, the lateral bundles are shorter and their distal parts recurve below the point of down bending. The down bent cotyledons which show the prominent sheath as a part of the cotyledon, the lateral bundles are also prominent.

An even number of traces in the cotyledons of angiosperms denotes the primitive condition. The primitive taxa (*e.g.*, Ranales, Liliales, Helobiales) have cotyledons with two strong traces, often with pairs of lateral traces. In most gymnosperms even numbered traces are characteristic. In angiosperms the odd-numbered traces are derived from even-numbered traces.

The number of cotyledonary traces is fairly constant in families. For example, two traces are commonly found in most of the lower monocotyledonous families. The Liliaceae have two in the lower tribes; two, four and six in others. The Zingiberaceae have two traces. The Amaryllidaceae have two; the Iridaceae, one, two or three. The Araceae have one to several and the Cannaceae

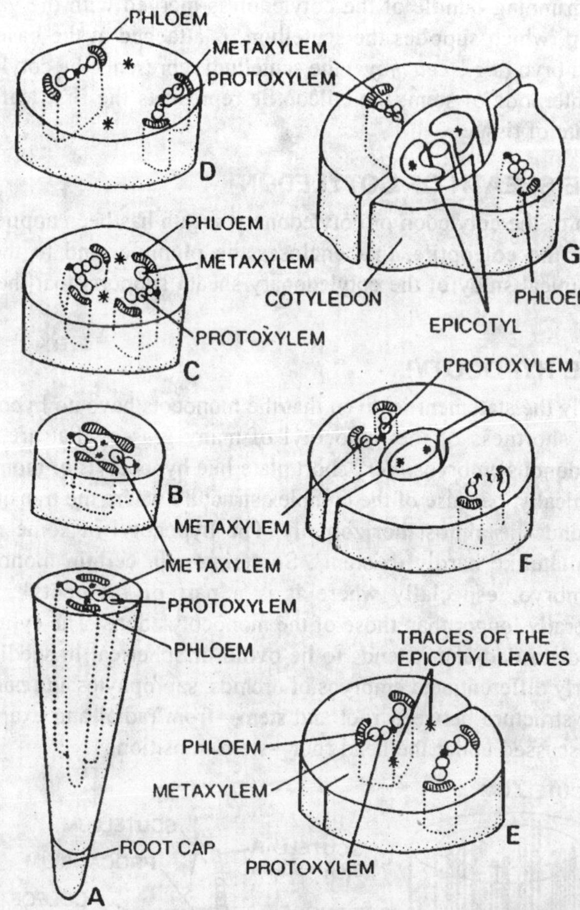

Fig. 10.1. Anatomy of seedling of dicotyledon (*Beta vulgaris*). A – E, diagram showing the connection between the root and the cotyledons in the transition region. Description in text. (After Esau).

have several. Among dicotyledons the woody Ranales have two traces. The vascular system of the cotyledon of monocots has two major bundles or two with additional vascular bundles. The cotyledons of dicot have commonly three major bundles.

ANATOMY OF MESOCOTYL

The mesocotyl is a compound structure which consists of the hypocotyl and the adnate part of the cotyledon. It contains the vascular tissues of the stele of the hypocotyl and one or more vascular bundles of the cotyledon. The external and internal effect of adnation of the cotyledon neck to the hypocotyl is frequently found. External evidence of the fusion is the presence, in some genera, of a longitudinal ridge on the axis of embryo; internal evidence is the presence of a vascular bundle running longitudinal in the cortex of hypocotyl. The superfluous bundle belongs to the down bent adnate neck of the cotyledon that makes the vascular supply of the scutellum, the median bundle of the cotyledon continued downward from the point of downbending of the cotyledon neck. The vascular supply of the scutellum thus follows a roundabout course, like an inverted V. With the result of the bending downward of the tip of the cotyledon, the adnate vascular bundles, as seen in cross sections of the mesocotyl are inverted the xylem external to the phloem.

When the downrunning bundle of the cotyledon is merged with the vascular tissue of the hypocotyl, its free tip, which supplies the scutellum, is attached at the base of hypocotyl. In a monocotyledonous embryo (*e.g.*, *Zea mays*) the scutellum represents the cotyledon; the mesocotyl represents the first internode of stem; the coleoptile represents the first leaf; and the hypocotyl represents a mere plate of tissue.

ANATOMY OF THE SHEATH OF COTYLEDON

The term sheath of the cotyledon or cotyledonary sheath has been applied to the cap-like or sheath-like structure, the coleoptile, that encloses the plumule, and to the basal part of the cotyledon. The anamotical study of the cotyledonary sheath supports that the sheath is the basal part of the cotyledon.

ANATOMY OF THE HYPOCOTYL

Very occasionally the statement is given that the monocots have no hypocotyl. The basis for this statement is the shortness of the hypocotyl of many grasses that are commonly used to illustrate monocotyledonous embryos. Very short plate like hypocotyls of monocots have received little attention anatomically, because of the complex structure where the transition occurs abruptly and the vascular strands lie almost horizontally. The hypocotyl of some monocots has been described as 'often platelike hardly existent'. Sometimes, in certain monocots it is long and prominent in the embryo, especially where it is a part of mesocotyl. The hypocotyls of dicotyledons are generally longer than those of the monocotyledons. The cylinderical or platelike hypocotyl is greatly distorded and it tends to be ovoid or spherical in seedlings of *Crocus* and *Raphanus* and in poorly differentiated embryos of orchids, saprophytes and parasites. The types of transition in vascular structure between root and stem—from radial and exarch to collateral and endarch have been discussed under the head root—stem transition.

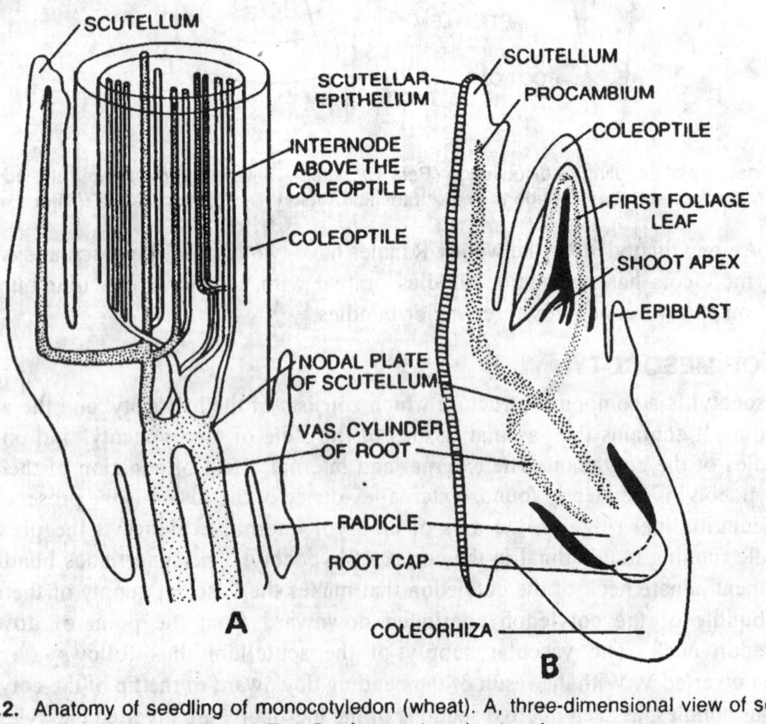

Fig. 10.2. Anatomy of seedling of monocotyledon (wheat). A, three-dimensional view of seedling of wheat; B, L.S. of an entire wheat embryo.

ANATOMY OF THE SEEDLING ROOT

The vascular cylinder of the primary root of seedlings is commonly diarch or tetrach. Monarchy is rarely found in primary roots. Polyarchy is frequently found in monocotyledons. It is believed that tetrarchy is basic type since it is associated with arborescent taxa. The diarchy is associated with herbaceous taxa. The Ranunculaceae have diarch condition, whereas the woody families have tetrarch primary roots. In the dicots there are few variations from diarchy or tetrarchy. However, in the monocots there are many variations, but polyarchy is common, the neck. the median part, differentiated as the coleoptile, and the apex, the scutellum.

In cotyledons where there is no downbending of the distal part, all the vascular bundles including those of the sides of the sheath, usually continue into the scutellum. These cotyledons, with two or four traces are simple and of primitive type. In cotyledons of advanced type, with one trace which divides to form a median and two lateral strong bundles, only the median bundle continues to the scutellum. The branches extent first upward and laterally and then downward, on the opposite of the sheath. The course of the bundles has been considered remarkable and evidence that the coleoptile is an independent organ, not a part of the cotyledon. The position and course of the veins of sheath support the interpretation that the upper part of sheath is stipular.

Where there is adnation of the cotyledon neck laterally to its lower part, the midvein is bent back upon itself. The two parts are fused and a bicollateral bundle is formed. Under continued specialization of this vascular fusion, the bundle is shortered distally and may become united with vascular stele of the hypocotyl. The shortening and adnation may extend to the point of origin of the branches of the trace of the sheath, and the branches then appear to arise directly from the hypocotyl. The origin of the trace of the sheath from the hypocotyl, shows that the sheath and the coleoptile represent the first leaf.

11

CHAPTER

Anatomy of the Floral Parts

The large majority of botanists, regard the flower as a modified shoot and its parts homologous of leaves. *Anatomically, the flower is a determinate stem with crowded appendages, with internodes much shortened or obliterated.* The appendages are of leaf rank but differ from those of the vegetative stem in function and shape. In the present text the flower is treated on the basis of the concept of homology between the flower and the shoot in their phylogeny and ontogeny.

PARTS OF THE FLOWER AND THEIR ARRANGEMENT

The flower consists of an axis, also known as receptacle and lateral appendages. The appendages are known as *floral parts* or *floral organs.* They are sterile and reproductive. The sepals and petals which constitute the *calyx* and *corolla* respectively are the sterile parts. The stamens and the carpels are the reproductive parts. The stamens compose the *androecium*, whereas the free or united carpels compose the *gynoecium.*

The vegetative shoot shows unlimited growth, whereas the flower shows the limited growth. In flower, the apical meristem ceases to be active after the formation of floral parts. In more specialized flowers there is a shorter growth period and they produce a small and more definite number of floral parts than the more primitive flowers. In still more advance flowers there are specialized characters, such as, whorled arrangement of parts instead of spiral, adnation of parts of two or more different whorls, cohesion of parts within a whorl, zygomorphic instead of actinomorphic condition, and epigynous condition instead of hypogynous condition.

Sepals. The sepals resemble leaves in their anatomy. Each sepal consists of ground parenchyma, a branched vascular system and an epidermis. The chloroplasts are found in the green sepals but usually there is no differentiation in the palisade and spongy parenchyma. They may contain crystal—containing cells, laticifers, tannin cells and other idioblasts. The epidermis of sepals may possess stomata and trichomes.

The traces are similar in origin and number. From the evidence of vascular system, sepals are clearly, in nearly every case morphologically bracts—that is, they have been derived directly from leaves and are not sterile sporophylls.

Petals. The petals also resemble leaves in their internal structure. They contain ground parenchyma, a more or less branched vascular system, and an epidermis. They may also contain crystal containing cells, tannin cells, laticifers and certain other idioblasts. They contain pigments—containing chromoplasts. Very often, the epidermal cells of the petals contain volatile oils which emit the characteristic fragrance of the flowers. In certain flowers the anticlinal epidermal walls of the petáls are wavy or internally ridged, whereas the outer walls may be convex or papillate. The epidermis may also possess stomata and trichomes.

Stamen. Commonly the stamen consists of a two-lobed four-loculed anther. The anther is found to be situated on a slender filament which bears single vascular bundle. In certain primitive dicotyledonous families the stamens are leaf-like and possess three veins, whereas in advance types they are single-veined.

The structure of filament is simple. The vascular bundle is amphicribral and remains surrounded by parenchyma. The epidermis is cutinized and bears trichomes. The stomata may also be present on the epidermis of both anther and filament. The vascular bundle is found throughout the filament and culminates blindly in the connective tissue situated in between the two anther-lobes.

The outermost wall of the anther is the epidermis. Just beneath the epidermis there is endothecium which usually possesses strips or ridges of secondary wall material mainly on those walls which do not remain in contact with the epidermis. The innermost layer is composed of multinucleate cells; this is nutritive in function and known as tapetum. The wall layers which are located in between the endothecium and tapetum are often destroyed during the development of the pollen sacs. On the maturation of the pollen the tapetum disintegrates and the outer wall of the pollen sac now consists of only the epidermis and endothecium. At the time of dehiscence of the anthers the pollen are released out through stomium.

Gynoecium. The unit of gynoecium is called the carpel. A flower may possess one carpel or more than one. If two or more carpels are present they may be united or free from one another. When the carpels are united the gynoecium is known as *syncarpous*; when they are free the gynoecium is said to be *apocarpous*. A gynoecium with single carpel is also classified as apocarpous. The apocarpous gynoecium is termed *simple pistil*, whereas the syncarpous gynoecium is termed *compound pistil*. The carpel is commonly interpreted as foliar structure. The carpel of an apocarpous or syncarpous gynoecium is being differentiated into the ovary and the style. The upper part of the style is differentiated as a stigma. The stigma is sessile.

The ovary consists of the ovary wall, the locule or locules and in a multilocular ovary, the partitions. The ovules are found to be situated on the inner or adaxial (ventral) side of the ovary wall. The ovule-bearing region forms the *placenta*. According to Puri (1952) the position of the placentae is related to the method of union of carpels. In a carpel the placenta occurs close to the margin. Since there are two margins, the placenta is double in nature. The two halves may be united or separate. The number of double placenta in compound ovaries is equal to number of carpels. When the carpels are folded, the ovary is multilocular and the placentae occur in the centre of the ovary where the margins of the carpels meet. This is *axile placentation*. When the partitions of the ovary disappear, it becomes *free-central placentation*. When the carpels are joined margin to margin and the placentae are found to be situated on the ovary placentation is *parietal*.

Most commonly the carpels has three veins, one dorsal or median and two ventral or lateral, and the vascular supply of the ovules has been derived from the ventral bundles. The vascular bundles of the ovary, possessing axile placentation appear in the center of the ovary, with the phloem turned inward and the xylem wall, the outward.

The ovary and style are composed of epidermis, ground tissue of parenchyma, and vascular bundles. The outer epidermis is cuticularized and may have stomata. The ovule consists of a nucellus which encircles the sporogenous tissue. There are two integuments of epidermal origin, and a stalk, *funiculus*. The ovule consists of parenchyma and contains a more or less dominant vascular system.

VASCULAR ANATOMY

The study of the vascular anatomy has helped in solving many intricate problems of floral morphology. It has shown that many structures are not what they appear to be or what they are commonly taken to be. The fundamental vascular plan remains more or less unaltered and can always be of some help (Puri, 1952).

Morphologically the flower is a determined shoot with appendages, and these appendages are homologous with leaves. This commonly accepted view is sustained by the anatomy of the flowers. Flowers, in their vascular skeletons, differ in no essential way from leaf stems. They are often more complex than most stems. Taxonomy and comparative morphology have in large measure determined the structural nature of the flower. Anatomy of the flower has aided in the solution of certain puzzling conditions.

Pedicel. The Pedicel and the receptacle have typical structure, with a normal vascular cylinder. The cylinder may be unbroken or it may contain a ring of vascular bundles. In the region where floral organs are borne, the pedicel expand into the *receptacle*. The vascular cylinder also expands and the vascular bundles increase somewhat in number, and finally traces begin to diverge. In the simplest cases vascular traces for different organs and whorls of organs arise quite independently (*e.g.*, in *Aquilegia*). In other cases various degrees of fusion may take place between bundles situated more or less in the same sectors.

The appendage traces are derived from the receptacular stele exactly as leaf traces are derived in typical stems. When the floral organs are numerous and closely placed, the gap of traces break the receptacular stele into a meshwork.

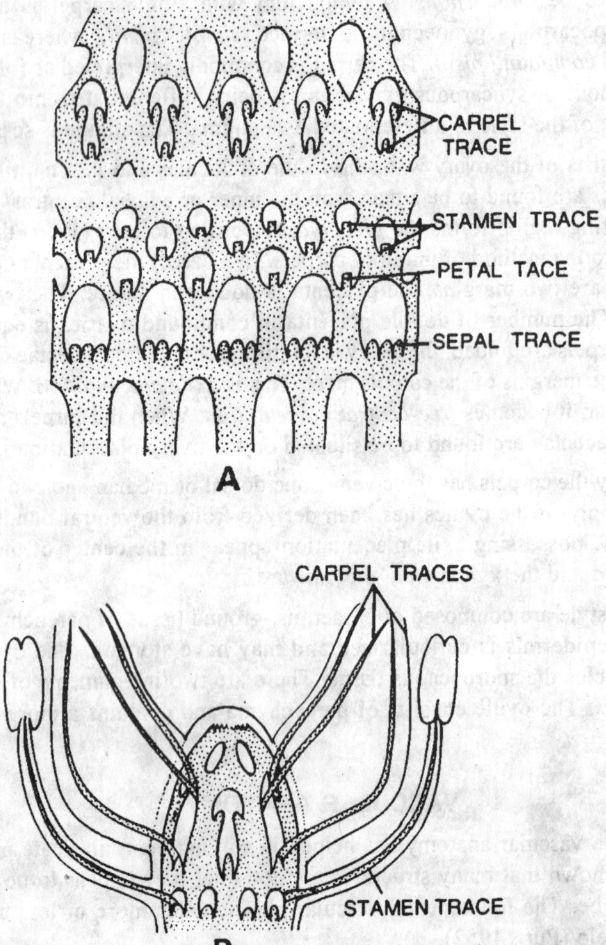

Fig. 11.1. Anatomy of the floral parts. A and B. diagram showing vascular structure of *Aquilegia*.

Sepals. The sepals are with very few exceptions, anatomically like the leaves of the plant in question. A sepal usually receives three traces derived from the same or different sources. As regards the morphological nature of the sepals, they have often been considered as equivalent to bracts and foliage leaves. Such a view is born out by a study of vascular anatomy which reveals practically the same vascular pattern as exists in foliage leaves and bracts of the same plant.

Petals. In their vascular supply the petals are sometimes leaf like, but much more often they are like stamens. The petals may have one, three or several traces. Very commonly there is but one trace. The petals appear to be sometimes modified leaves, like the sepals. but in the great majority of families they are sterile stamens. However, since stamens are the homologous of the leaves, it is not always possible to determine from anatomical evidence along whether one trace petals in certain families are modified stamens or whether they have come more directly from leaf-like structures.

Stamens. A stamen generally receives a single trace which remains almost unbranched throughout its course in the filament. In the anther region it may undergo some branching. In a few Ranalian families and rarely elsewhere as in some members of the Lauraceae and Musaceae, three traces are present in each stamen. In *Ravenala* (Musaceae) each filament is traversed by 25 to 28 small vascular bundles. Most of these disappear as the anther is approached, and the system of

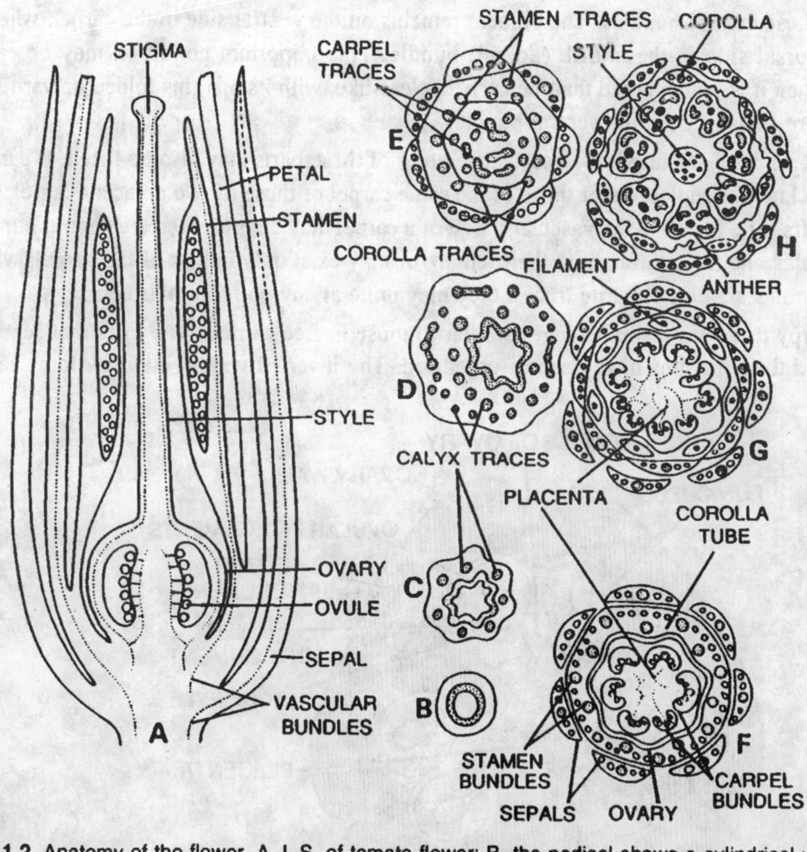

Fig. 11.2. Anatomy of the flower. A, L.S. of tomato flower; B, the pedicel shows a cylindrical vascular region encircling a pith and delimited on the outside by the cortex; C—D, in the receptacle and level of attachment of the sepals, traces diverge into these appendages; D—E, the traces diverge into the corolla, one to each petal (in most dicotyledonous flowers); E—G, traces to the stamens, typically one to each stamen; the carpellary supply of one, three, five or more traces to each carpel; H, a prolongation of the vascular supply into the style (After Esau).

central bundles consisting of three or four bundles, continues into the connective. From other evidence the above mentioned families appear to be fairly primitive, it seems highly probable that the single trace condition is one of reduction from three.

In the simple flower of *Aquilegia* the stamen traces pass off, one to each organ in several whorls. Above the supermost whorl of stamens the vascular cylinder becomes complete again.

Carpels. The carpel is commonly looked upon as a leaf-like organ folded upward, *i.e.*, ventrally with its margins more or less completely fused and bearing the ovules. This conception has been supported by the anatomy. The details of origin, number and course of the bundles forming the vascular supply are exactly like those of leaves the carpel has one, three, five or several traces. The three trace carpel is most common. The five-trace carpel is nearly as common as the three traces, and carpels with seven, nine and more traces are increasingly less and less common. The evidence that the one-trace carpel (nearly always an achene) has been derived by reduction from the three-trace type. The median trace which leaves the stele below the other carpel traces, is known as the *dorsal trace* because it becomes the dorsal (midrib) bundle of the folded organ. The outermost traces are known as *ventral* or *marginal traces* because they become the bundles that run along the ventral edge of the carpel, *i.e.*, along or near the margins of the organ if it were unfolded. The upward and inward folding of the sides of the carpel brings about the inversion of these ventral bundles. The phloem remains on the ventral side in the carpel, whereas it is on the dorsal side in the midrib (dorsal) bundle. This important condition may be easily understood when it is remembered that the carpel is leaf-like, with its margins folded upward. The ovule traces are derived from the ventral bundles.

When floral parts are fused, the vascular bundles of these parts may also be fused. If carpels are united, the lateral bundles, either those of the same carpel or those of two adjacent carpel, may be fused in pairs. The fusion in the vascular tissue of a carpel may be present in the ventral bundles from an origin as one trace throughout their length, or may exist only in part of the carpel; where the ventral bundles arise as separate traces, they may unite at any point in their course.

In syncarpy there are fusion changes similar to those in free carpels. The lines that separate the carpels and their margins have been disorganised. The inverted ventral bundles, form a ring

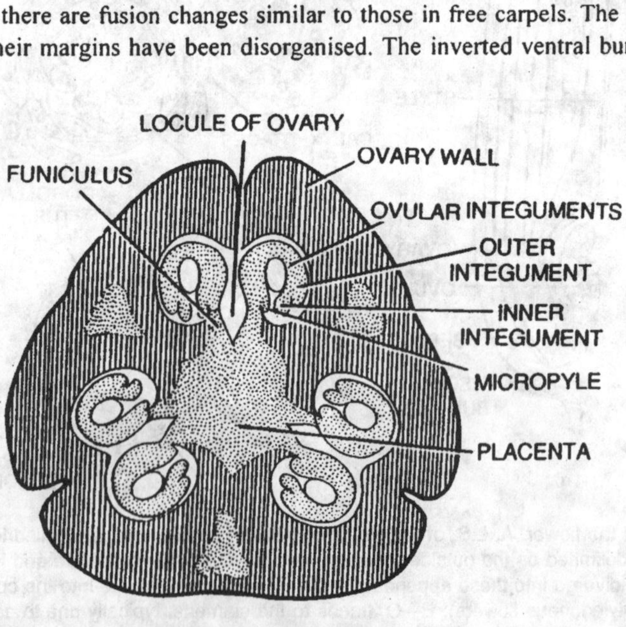

Fig. 11.3. The flower. T.S. of the ovary of *Lilium*, showing six anatropous ovules and the manner of placentation.

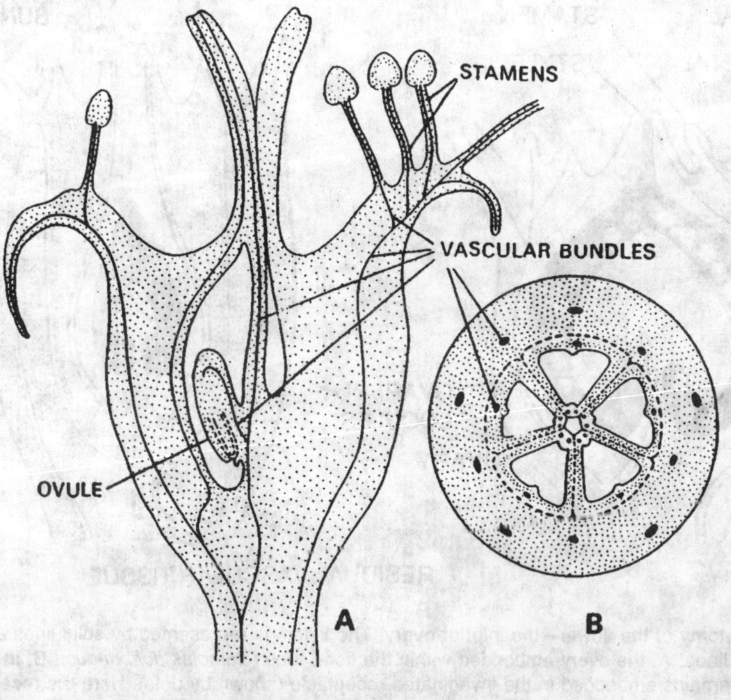

Fig. 11.4. The vascular system of the flower in *Malus pumila*. A, vertical section; B, transverse section.

of bundles in the centre. These bundles usually lie in pairs. Here each pair consists of the ventral bundles, of the same carpel, or more often of bundles from each of two adjacent carpels. In the centre of a three carpellary syncarpous ovary there may be a ring of six or three ventral bundles. If the ring consists of three bundles, each bundle is morphologically double and represents either the two ventral traces of one carpel or one from one carpel and one from the adjacent carpel.

Several workers proposed that the evolutionary changes in the structure of the gynoecium of the flower of angiosperms involve various manners of union of carpels of the same flower. In such angiospermous flower the carpel may become joined by their margins to the receptacle (Fig. 11.6 B), or they may grow together laterally in a closed folded condition (Fig. 11.6 C), or they may become laterally united in an open folded condition (Fig. 11.6. A). The junction of carpels in an open condition may result in a unilocular ovary showing parietal placentation as shown in fig. 11.6 A. Folding combined with union of carpels with each other may form an ovary with as many locules as there are carpels. In such cases the ovules are borne on the central column of tissue where the carpels come together showing, axile placentation (Fig. 11.6 B, C).

The inferior ovary. The inferior ovary is formed by the adnation of the sepals, petals and stamens to the carpels or by the sinking of the gynoecium in a hollowed receptacle with fusion of the receptacle walls about the carpels. The vascular system is thought to show this structure in that the bundles found in the appendages of different whorls are variously fused but all show the usual orientation of xylem and phloem. In certain flowers with inferior ovary (*e.g.*, Calycanthaceae, Santalaceae and Juglandaceae) there is evidence that the ovary is partially enclosed in hollowed receptacle. Here the vascular bundles are prolonged from the axis to the level below the insertion of floral parts, other than the carpels, where traces to the parts diverge. The main bundles continue

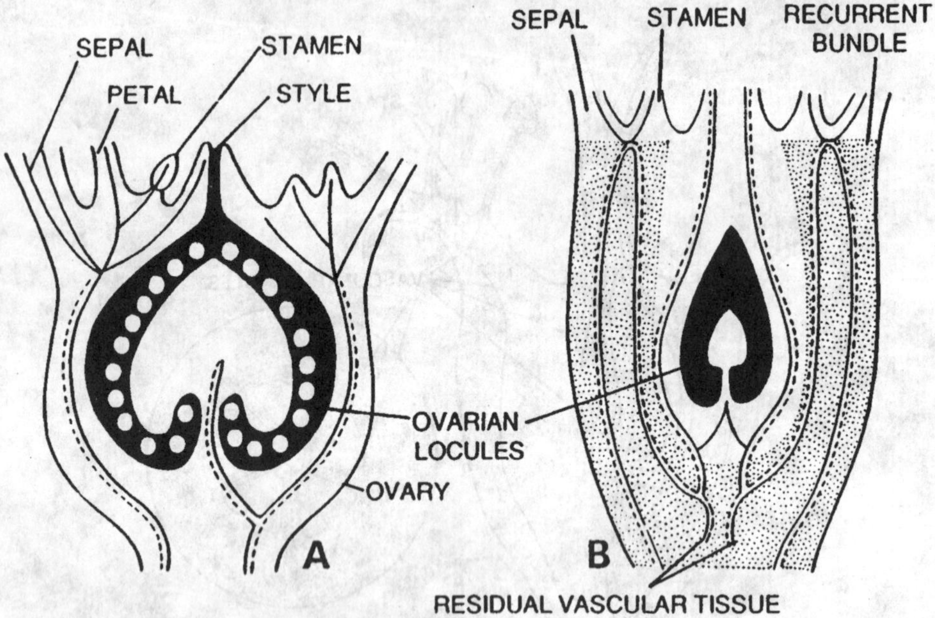

Fig. 11.5. Anatomy of the flower—the inferior ovary, The xylem is represented by solid lines and phloem by broken lines. A, the ovary embedded within the floral tube (*Samolus floribundus*); B, In *Darbya* the ovary remains embedded in the invaginated receptacle (shown by dots). Here the receptacular nature of the outer tissue is indicated by the presence of recurrent bundles with inversely oriented xylem and phloem (After Douglas, 1944).

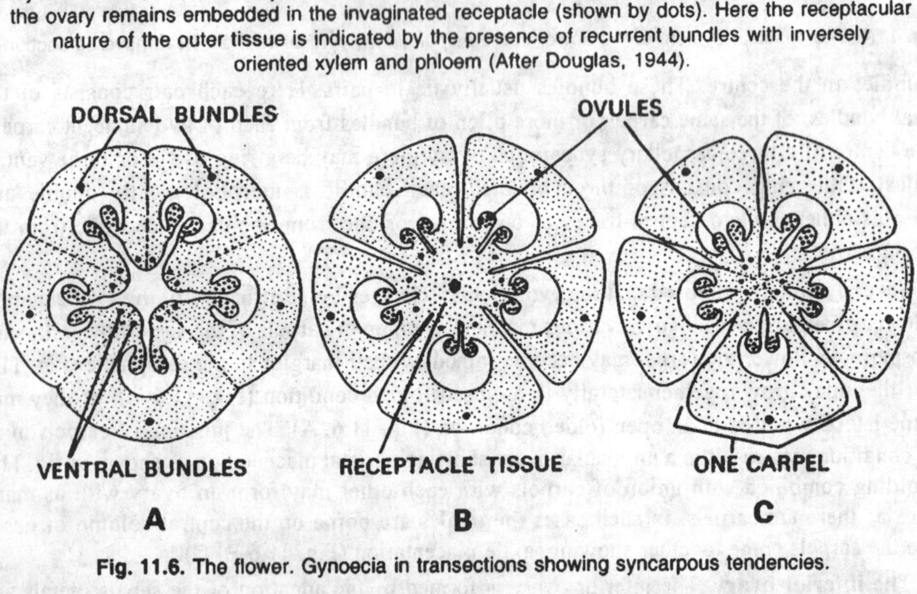

Fig. 11.6. The flower. Gynoecia in transections showing syncarpous tendencies.

farther from the periphery in a downward direction with a corresponding inversely oriented position of the xylem and the phloem. These bundles at lower levels give branches to the carpels. This type of orientation of the vascular system is thought to be the result of the invagination of the receptacular axis.

12

CHAPTER

Special Flowering Plants

SAPROPHYTES

These are plants that grow in places rich in decaying organic substances, and derive their nutrition from them. Among the angiosperms *Monotropa* (Indian pipe) and some orchids afford good examples of saprophytes. Total saprophytes are colourless; and the partial ones are green in colour. Their roots become associated with a filamentous mass of a fungus which takes the place of and acts as the root-hairs, absorbing food material from the decomposed organic substances present in the soil. The association of a fungus with the root of a higher plant is known as **mycorrhiza**. Mycorrhizal fungi commonly associated with the roots of many forest trees, orchid seedlings, pine seedlings, etc. Two types of mycorrhiza are seen— **endotrophic**, in which the fungus is internal, usually living within the cortical cells of the root, as in many orchids, and **ectotrophic**, in which the fungus is external, growing attached to the surface of the root, as in conifers and other plants.

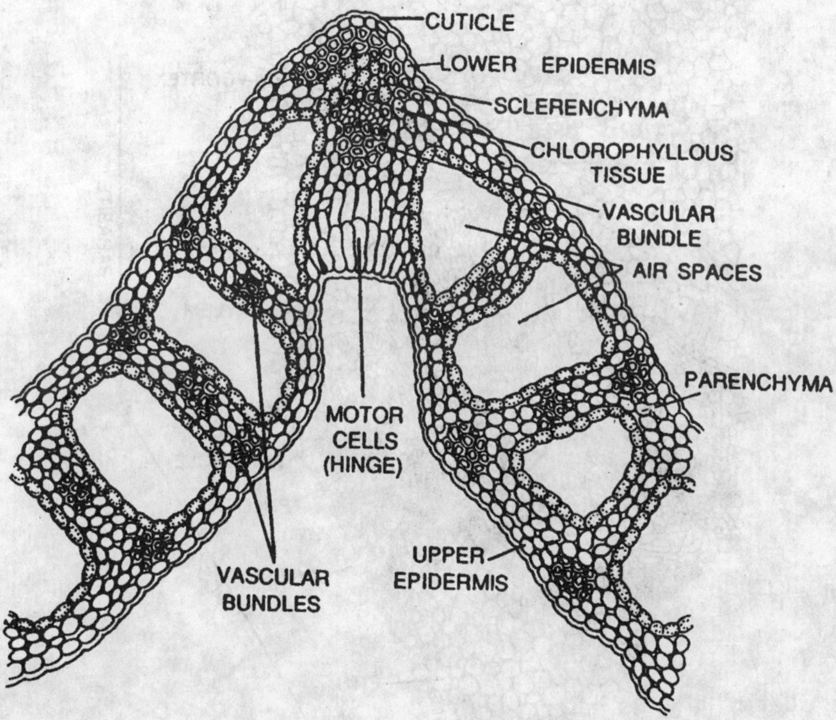

Fig. 12.1. *Molinia*—V.S. of marshy monocot leaf (detailed) showing both xerophytic and hydrophytic characters.

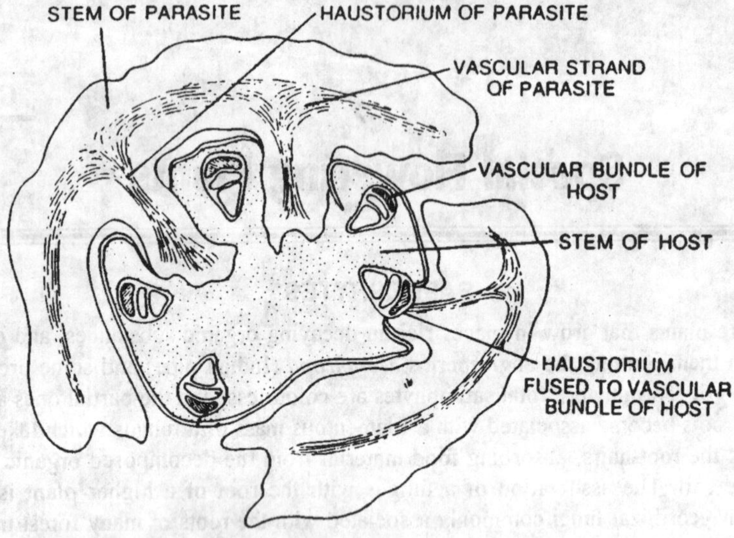

Fig. 12.2. Structure of total stem parasite. Section through haustoria and host of *Cuscuta* (diagrammatic).

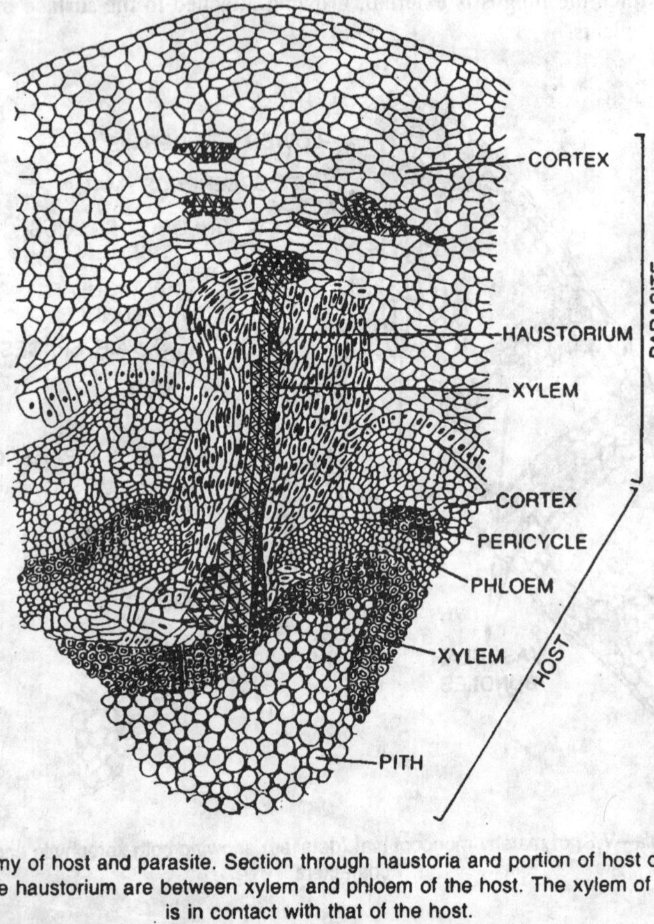

Fig. 12.3. Anatomy of host and parasite. Section through haustoria and portion of host of *Cuscuta*. The cells of the haustorium are between xylem and phloem of the host. The xylem of parasite is in contact with that of the host.

PARASITES

The plants that grow upon other living plants, absorb their food material from them. For the purpose of absorption parasites produce special roots, the **haustoria**, which penetrate into the tissue of the host plant and absorb nutrition from it. There are differential degrees of parasitism. Some are **total parasites** and other **partial parasites**. The total parasites are never green in colour as they obtain all their food from the host plant; while the partial parasites develop chlorophyll and are in a position to manufacture food to a greater or less extent. They may be parasitic on the stem and branches or on roots. Accordingly they are said to be **stem-parasites** or **root-parasites** (*e.g.*, total stem parasite—*Cuscuta*; partial stem parasite—*Viscum*; total root parasite *Orobanche*; and partial root parasite, *Striga*). (See figs. 12.2 and 12.3)

HALOPHYTES

These plants grow in saline soil or water, where there is abundance of salt in the soil; hence halophytes show some special characters. Most of halophytes have succulent leaves and some possess succulent stems. Leaves may be modified into or provided with spines. Typical examples

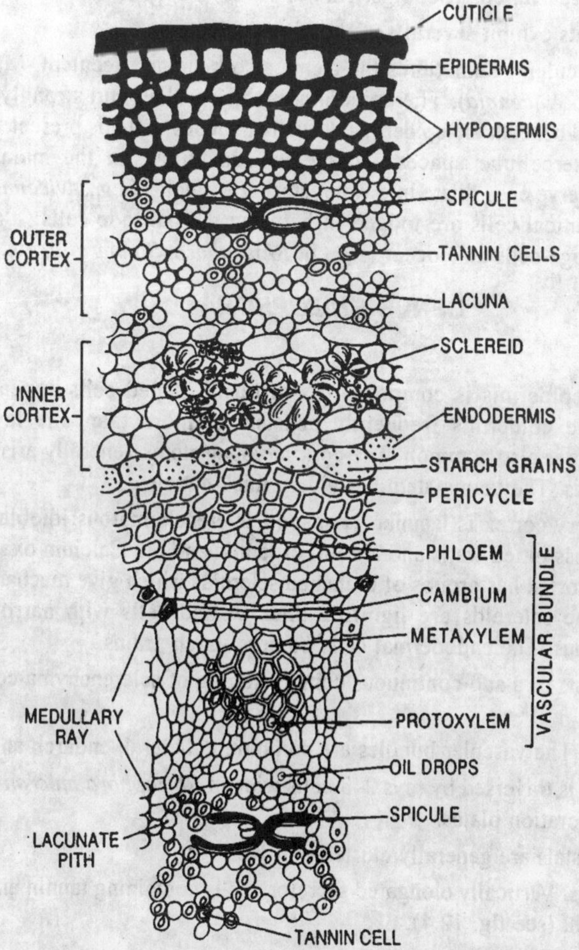

Fig. 12.4. *Rhizophora mucronata.* Transverse section of young stem (detailed structure).

of halophytes are *Suaeda maritima, Salsola, Acanthus ilicifolius, Chenopodium, Basella* and some species of Asclepiadaceae.

Halophytes growing in marshy places near the seashore, as in Sundarbans (West Bengal), form a special vegetation known as the **mangrove**.. Mangrove plants produce a large number of stilt roots from the main stem and the branches. In many cases, in addition to the stilt roots special roots, called **respiratory roots** or **pneumatophores**, are also produced in large numbers, such roots develop from underground roots, and projecting beyond the water level they look like so many conical spikes distributed all round the trunk of the tree. They are provided with numerous pores or respiratory spaces in the upper part, through which exchange of gases for respiration takes place. Mangrove species also show a peculiar type of germination. The seed germinates inside the fruit while it is still on the parent tree and is nourished by the same. Germination is almost immediate without any period of rest. The radicle elongates to a certain length and swells at the lower part. Ultimately the seedling separates from the parent tree and falls vertically down. The radicle presses into the soft mud, keeping the plumule and cotyledons clear above the saline water. This kind of germination of the seed inside the fruit while the latter still remains attached to the plant is known as **vivipary**. Typical examples of mangrove plants are—*Rhizophora, Sonneratia, Ceriops, Heritiera Excoecaria*, etc. (See figs. 12.4 to 12.10)

The mangrove plants exhibit several xeromorphic characters:

The leaves are succulent. Sometimes the stems also become succulent. Many species are covered with hairs (*e.g., Avicennia*). The epidermis is thick-walled and strongly cutinized. The sunken stomata are found beneath the epidermis. Usually aqueous tissue is present. The mesophyll is almost devoid of intercellular spaces and the palisade tissue in the main chlorenchyma (*e.g., Sonneratia*). The nerve ends dilate into water storing tracheids (*e.g., Avicennia*). Long stone cells or bast like mechanical cells are lodged in between the palisade cells (*e.g., Rhizophora, Sonneratia*, etc.). Mucilage cells also occur (*e.g.*, in *Rhizophora, Sonneratia*, etc.).

GENUS *RHIZOPHORA*

T.S. OF STEM

Epidermis. The epidermis is composed of variously shaped cells appearing conical in transverse sections. The epidermis frequently consists of more than one layer, but a true hypodermis of 3–7 layers is also common. The cork in young stems generally arises superficially, usually in the hypodermis. The young stem has a very thick cuticle.

Cortex. The primary cortex is lacunar. H-shaped sclerenchymatous idioblasts are present. The cells of cortex possess pitted walls and are full of tannin and oil. Calcium oxalate crystals are also present. The inner cortex has groups of branched sclereids which give mechanical strength to the lacunate cortex. The sclereids are lignified thick walled cells with narrow lumina. The endodermis is conspicuous. The endodermal cells possess starch grains.

Pericycle. It consists of a sub-continuous composite ring of sclerenchyma consisting of 3–4 layers of cells.

Vascular bundles. The vascular bundles are conjoint, collateral, endarch and open.

Xylem. The xylem is traversed by rays 2–3 cells wide in *Rhizophora mucronata.* The vessels possess scalariform perforation plates.

Crystals. The crystals are generally clustered.

Secretory elements. Vertically elongated secretory cells containing tannin and/or oil present in the cortex and the pith. (see fig. 12.4).

T.S. OF PETIOLE

Transverse sections of petiole exhibit a ring of bundles surrounding additional medullary strands in *Rhizophora mucronata* Lam. Mostly clustered crystals present. **Secretory elements**–cells containing tannin have been recorded in the mesophyll, cortex and pith. The inner cortex possesses H-shaped idioblasts.

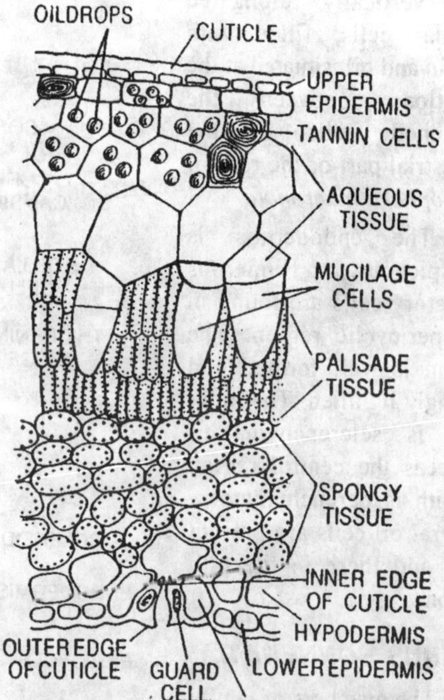

Fig. 12.5. *Rhizophora mucronata.* V.S. of leaf showing detailed structure.

Anatomy of Leaf

The leaves are usually dorsiventral. **Hairs** are mostly unicellular with thick or thin walls. The cuticle is well-developed and often quite thick on both the leaf surfaces. **Cork** warts occur as small black spots on the lower side of the leaf. The epidermis is single layered and consists of rectangular cells. The cells of upper epidermis possess some rod-shaped and cubical crystals of calcium oxalate. **The hypodermis** towards the upper surface is 2 or more layered. The **stomata** are confined to the lower surface. They are depressed and often provided with a front cavity. The mesophyll consists of palisade and spongy tissue. Palisade tissue consists of 1–4 layers. Spongy tissue usually possess large intercellular spaces. Aqueous tissue and mucilage cells are also present beneath the upper epidermis. H-shaped sclerenchymatous idioblasts occur in the palisade tissue, and variously branched ones in the spongy mesophyll.

Anatomy of Breathing Root

The well-known breathing roots (pneumatophores) of members of the Rhizophoraceae inhabiting mangrove swamps have large intercellular spaces of the spongy cortex which facilitate gaseous exchange in the special habitat in which the plants grow. The **cork** consists of suberized cells. The cork layer remains interrupted by lenticels at several places. In some cases the cork consists of alternating layers of suberized and ordinary parenchymatous cells in the aerial portion. Next to the cork there lies a thick cortex containing abundant, large, intercellular spaces, arranged radially around the stele. Intercellular spaces are larger in the subterranean than in the aerial parts of the roots. The cortex may be subdivided into two portions–the secondary cortex and the primary cortex. The **secondary cortex** consisting of few layers is found just beneath the cork. The **primary cortex** lies next to secondary cortex. The primary cortex is broad and lacunar. The primary cortex in the terrestrial part of the root is composed of cells of two kinds—(a) radially elongated cells connected with one another tangentially by short lateral arms; (b) rows of vertically elongated cells which show small, circular lumina in transverse sections. Solereder has recorded the ridges of thickening which are supposed to give mechanical support to the radially elongated cells where they are found. However, according to Bowman these are really cells filled up with mucilaginous sap. Mullan (1933) states that the cortex in the aerial part of the root system of *Rhizophora mucronata* Lam. is much reduced and the lacunae small. Sclerenchymatous **idioblasts** also occur in the cortex. H-shaped sclerenchymatous idioblasts project into the cortical intercellular spaces in the aerial part of the root, but are less numerous below ground. Mullan (1933) has also recorded the vertically elongated tubular cells, filled with tannin and oil, situated at the junctions between the branched cells in the terrestrial part or the root of *Rhizophora mucronata*.

The endodermis is conspicuous. Numerous secretory cells are found in the pericyclic region. The xylem is well formed and strongly lignified. The outer pith is sclerenchymatous whereas the central region of pith is parenchymatous. Several oil cells are present here and there in the pith region.

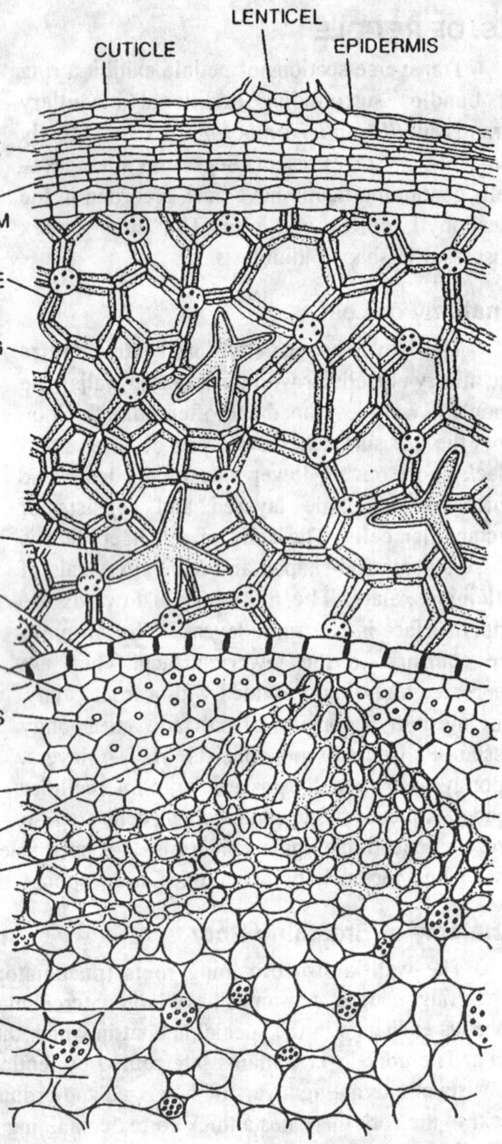

Fig. 12.6. *Rhizophora mucronata*. T.S. of a portion of subterranean stilt root.

GENUS *SONNERATIA*

The members of family Sonneratiaceae are generally trees. Some of the species of *Sonneratia* inhabiting Mangrove Swamps from Africa to Australia are provided with **vertical branches of the root** system projecting into the air or water above the mud. The occurrence of **intraxylary phloem** in *Sonneratia* is also noteworthy.

T.S. OF STEM

The young stem of *Sonneratia* is provided with collenchymatous wings. The **cork** arises in the sub-epidermis in *Sonneratia apetala* Ham. Primary **Cortex** consists of spongy parenchyma. The outer part of cortex contains branched sclerenchymatous idioblasts. **Xylem** is found in the form of a continuous cylinder traversed by narrow rays. The vessels possess simple perforations. The **phoem** includes sclerenchyma. The **endodermis** is inconspicuous. The **pericycle** is found in the form of patches over phloem. The **intraxylary** or **inner** phloem is found next to xylem around the pith. The **pith** remains supported by sclerenchymatous elements. The cells of the pith and cortex contain tannin and oil drops. The **secretory cells** occur in the phloem as well as in intraxylary phloem, of *Sonneratia apetala.* According to Mullan (1933), **crystals** in vertical

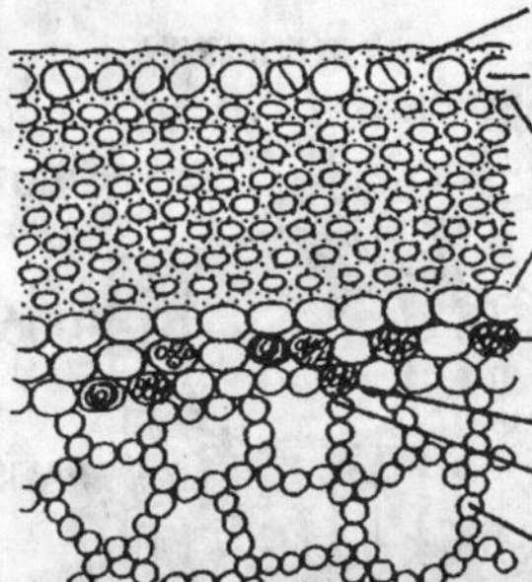

Fig. 12.7. *Sonneratia apetala*. T.S. of stem showing thick-walled hypodermal tissue with sclereids and tannin cells, well developed vascular system, and sclereids in the pith region.

rows of special cells in the secondary phloem of *Sonneratia apetala.* The **secondary cortex** is composed of tangentially elongated cells. Sclereids are also found in the secondary cortex. These cells contain oil drops and tannin.

ANATOMY OF LEAF

The leaves of *Sonneratia apetala* Ham. are isobilateral. The upper **epidermis** possesses cuticular ridges. **Cork** warts are found in some species of *Sonneratia.* The stomata are deeply sunken and present on both surfaces in *Sonneratia acida* Linn. The stomata are of rubiaceous type and they are equally numerous on both surfaces in *Sonneratia apetala* Ham. Large and rounded mucilage cells are present below the upper epidermis in the mesophyll. The central region consists of aqueous tissue and contains branched sclerenchymatous idioblasts. The oil and tannin cells are also present in the mesophyll tissue. (see fig. 12.8)

ANATOMY OF BREATHING ROOT

The vertical, negatively geotropic portions of the root system are known as **'breathing'** or **'pneumatophores'.** The **terrestrial roots** are also present.

The lenticels are present on the pneumatophores. The cork consists of a succession of lamellae each composed of three layers of cells. The cells of the outer layer of the cork are rounded externally and not suberized. The cells of the middle layer of the cork are tabular and suberized and those of inner layer are radially elongated, rounded on the inner side and suberized. Two layers

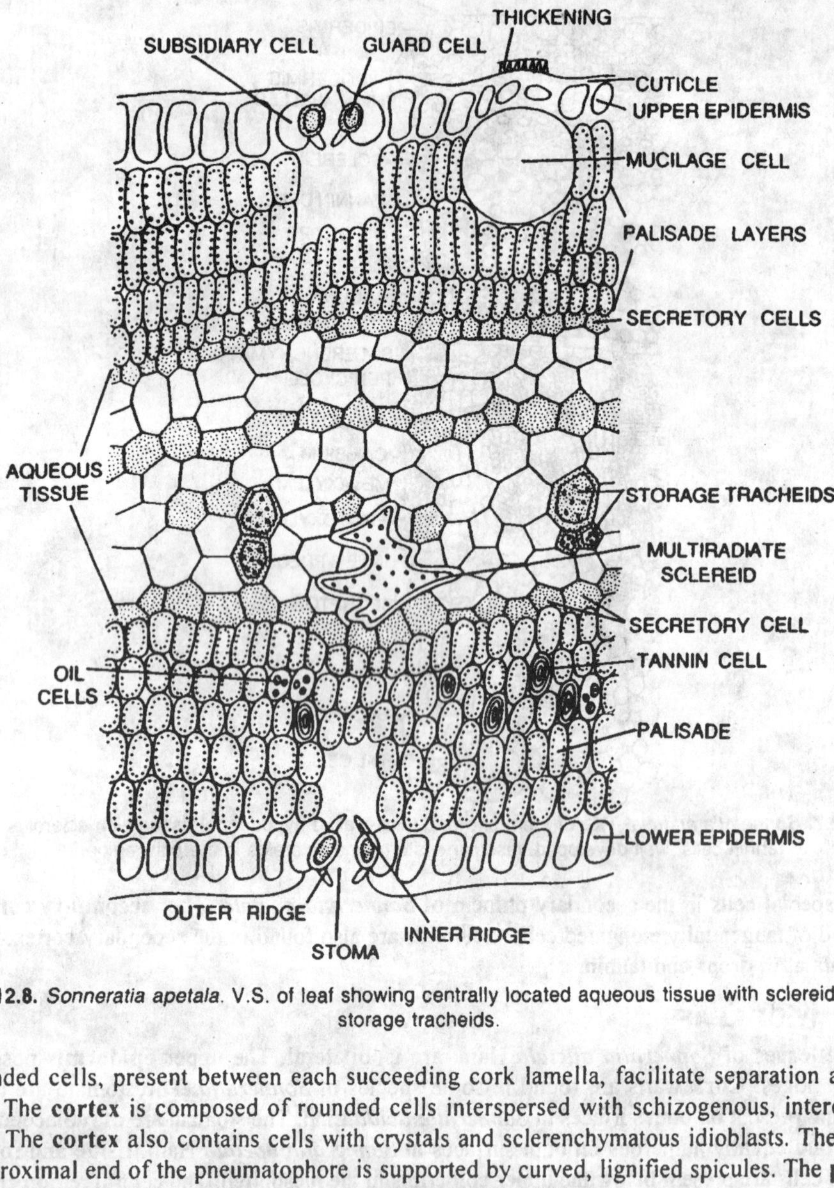

Fig. 12.8. *Sonneratia apetala*. V.S. of leaf showing centrally located aqueous tissue with sclereids and storage tracheids.

of rounded cells, present between each succeeding cork lamella, facilitate separation at these points. The **cortex** is composed of rounded cells interspersed with schizogenous, intercellular spaces. The **cortex** also contains cells with crystals and sclerenchymatous idioblasts. The cortex at the proximal end of the pneumatophore is supported by curved, lignified spicules. The **phloem** includes isolated strands of fibre and vertical rows of crystalliferous cells. The **xylem** is found in the form of a broad feebly lignified ring. The **pith** contains sclerenchymatous idioblasts at the distal end but not at the proximal end.

The terrestrial roots of *Sonneratia* show the following characteristics.

Cortex is lacunar. It is composed of cells mostly triradiate, and supported by thickening ridges and by vertically elongated cells with thick, pitted but lignified walls. Cork arises superficially.

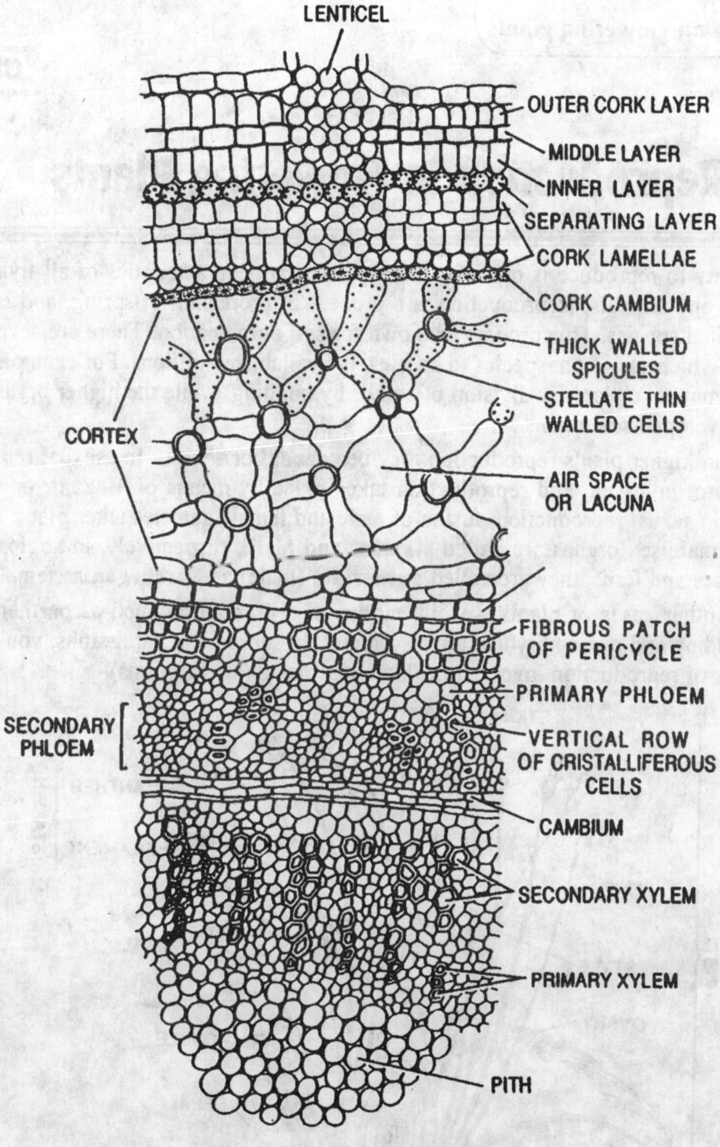

Fig. 12.9. *Sonneratia apetala*. T.S. of a portion of pneumatophore (respiratory root) showing detailed structure.

UNIT - 2

Reproduction on Flowering Plants

13

CHAPTER

Reproduction in Flowering Plants

The capacity to reproduce is one of the most important characteristics of all living beings, *i.e.*, both plants and animals. Reproduction is a process of producing offspring, and is aimed to preserve individual species. This process is known for self perpetuation. There are several modes of reproduction which vary from species to species, in available conditions. For example, in lower organisms, this may take place by division of cell or by budding, while the higher organisms may possess fully developed sex organs.

However, in higher plants reproduction may be **asexual** or **sexual**. In asexual reproduction, sex organs are not involved, and reproduction takes place by means of asexual or vegetative methods, while in sexual reproduction, fusion of male and female gametes takes place. Generally, the male and female sex organs are called **stamen** and **pistil**, respectively, in angiosperms. In liverworts, mosses and ferns, they are called **antheridia** (male) and **archegonia** (female).

In certain other cases of plants, special modes of reproduction such as parthenogenesis, sporophytic budding and polyembryony, are also found. In subsequent paragraphs, you will study various methods of reproduction involved in flowering plants (angiosperms).

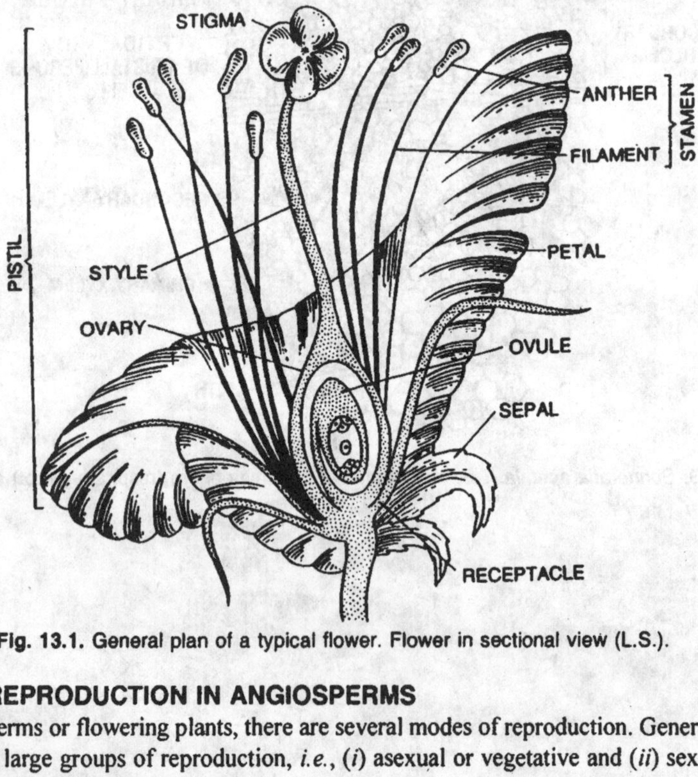

Fig. 13.1. General plan of a typical flower. Flower in sectional view (L.S.).

MODES OF REPRODUCTION IN ANGIOSPERMS

In angiosperms or flowering plants, there are several modes of reproduction. Generally, they are arranged in two large groups of reproduction, *i.e.*, (*i*) asexual or vegetative and (*ii*) sexual types.

In asexual or vegetative reproduction, the offspring are produced from the somatic cells, while in sexual reproduction there is fusion of male and female gametes.

In the case of vegetative reproduction, any part of the plant, *i.e.*, stem, root or leaf, is capable of growing into a new plant, in addition to performing its sexual functions. Sometimes, in certain plants, buds and bulbils are developed, which develop into new plants.

In sexual reproduction, the **gametes** from male and female organs of the flower are fused to produce a **zygote**. In angiosperms, these organs are generally called, **androecium** and **gynoecium**, respectively.

In some plants, certain special modes of reproduction are found, which are commonly known as parthenogenesis, sporophytic budding, polyembryony, apomixis, apospory, and micro-propagation. The production of synthetic or artificial seeds is also possible through tissue culture.

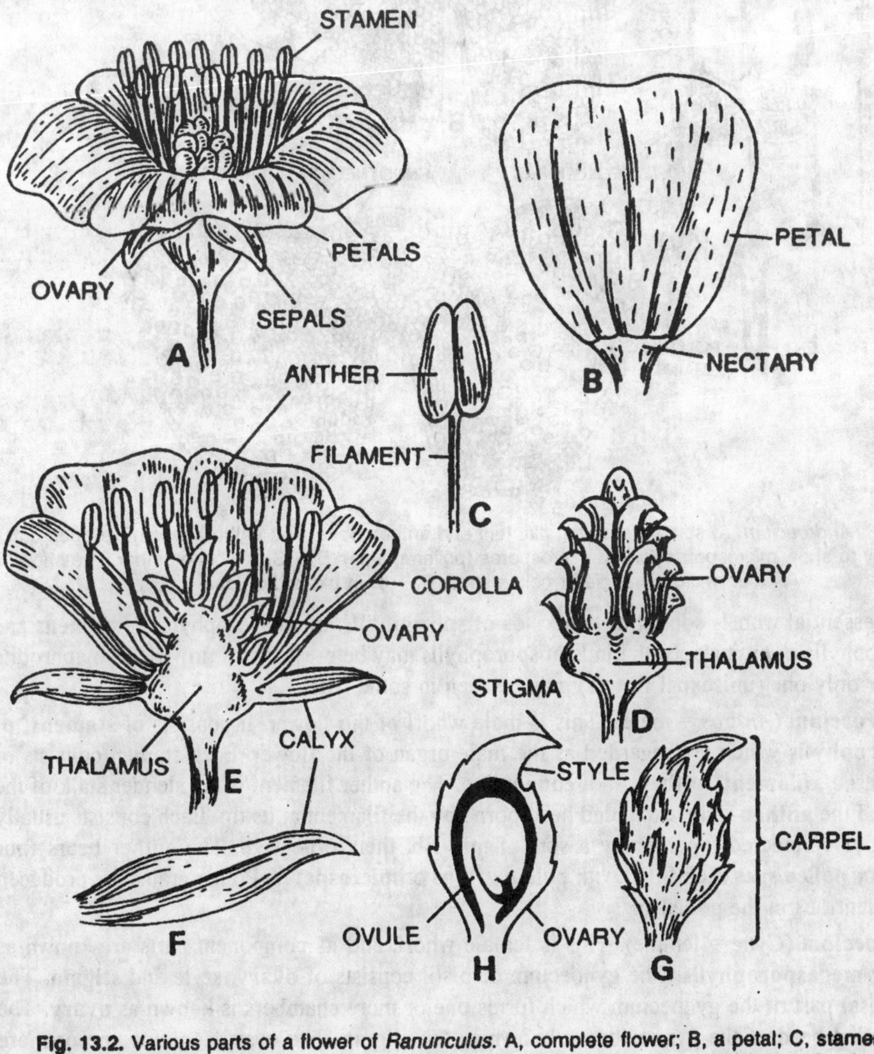

Fig. 13.2. Various parts of a flower of *Ranunculus*. A, complete flower; B, a petal; C, stamen; D, thalamus with apocarpous gynoecium; E, a sepal; F, V.S. of flower; G, a carpel; H, V.S. of carpel.

SEXUAL REPRODUCTION

The flower. The flower is a highly specialized reproductive shoot. Each typical flower consists of four distinct types of members arranged in four separate but closely set whorls, one above the other, on the top of a long or short stalk. The lower two whorls are called **accessory** whorls, and the upper two **essential** or **reproductive** whorls because only these two are directly concerned in reproduction.

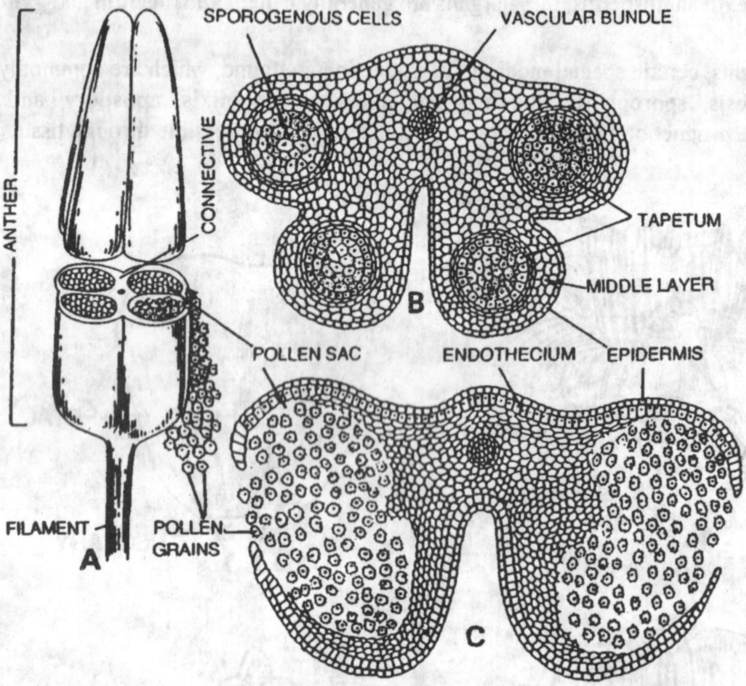

Fig. 13.3. *Androecium.* A, stamen showing filament and anther lobes. The anther lobes have been cut transversely to show microsporangia and microspores (pollen grains); B, T,S. of young anther lobe showing four microsporangia or pollen sacs; C, T.S. of old anther lobe.

The essential whorls consist of two kinds of **sporophylls**: microsporophylls or **stamens** and megasporophylls or **carpels**. Both kinds of sporophylls may be present in a flower (hermaphrodite flower), or only one (unisexual flower) may be seen in some types.

Androecium (*Andros* = male). This is male whorl of the flower. It consists of **stamens** or **microsporophylls** which are regarded as the male organ of the flower. Each stamen consists of three parts, *i.e.*, **filament, anther** and **connective**. The anther filament is the slender stalk of the stamen, and the **anther** is the expanded head borne by the filament at its tip. Each consists usually of two lobes connected together by a sort of mid-rib, the **connective**. The anther bears four chambers or **pollen sacs** each filled with **pollen grains** or **microspores**. Pollen grains are produced in large quantities in the pollen sacs.

Gynoecium (*Gyne* = female). This is female whorl, and its component parts are known as **carpels** or **megasporophylls**. The gynoecium or pistil consists of **ovary, style** and **stigma**. The swollen basal part of the gynoecium which forms one or more chambers is known as **ovary**. The small rounded head of the gynoecium is known as the **stigma**. The ovary contains one or more little, roundish or oval, egg-like bodies which are the rudiments of seeds and are known as **ovules**. Each ovule encloses a large oval cell known as the **embryo sac**. On maturation, the ovary gives **rise to the fruit** and the ovules to **seeds**.

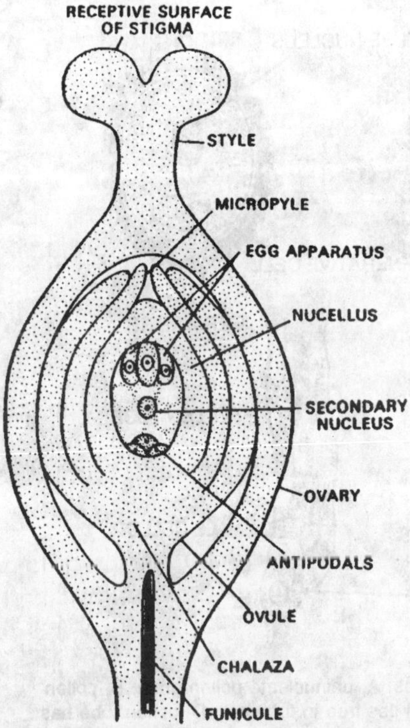

Fig. 13.4. Gynoecium in longitudinal section showing different parts of mature ovule attached to a basal placenta.

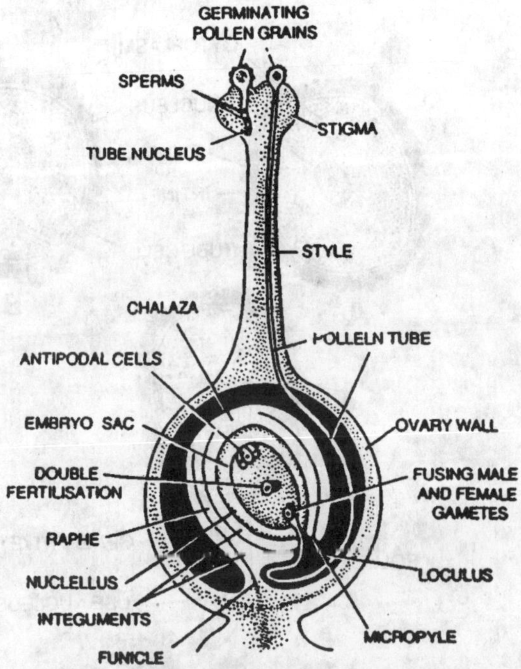

Fig. 13.5. A monocarpellary pistil cut vertically to show its external and internal parts. It also shows pollen grains on stigma.

Homologies.

Carpel = Megasporophyll

Ovule = Megasporangium

Embryo sac = Female gametophyte

Egg = Female gamete

Stamen = Microsporophyll

Anther (pollen sac) = Microsporangium

Pollen grain = Microspore

Germinating pollen grain = Male gametophyte

The reproductive process in angiosperms is as follows:

Development of the Male Gametophyte

Microsporangium (pollen sac). The **epidermis** is the outermost layer of microsporangium. The cells of epidermis are generally stretched and flattened. The layer next to the epidermis is the

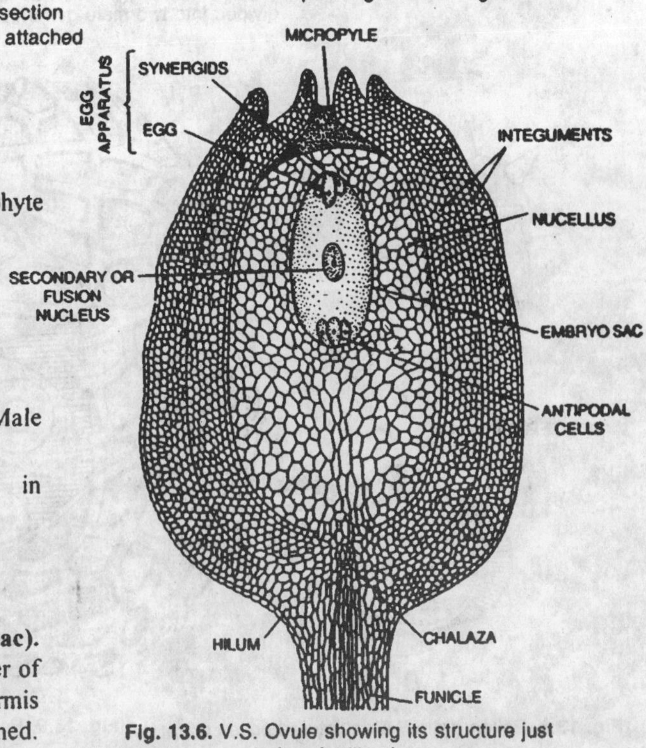

Fig. 13.6. V.S. Ovule showing its structure just before fertilization.

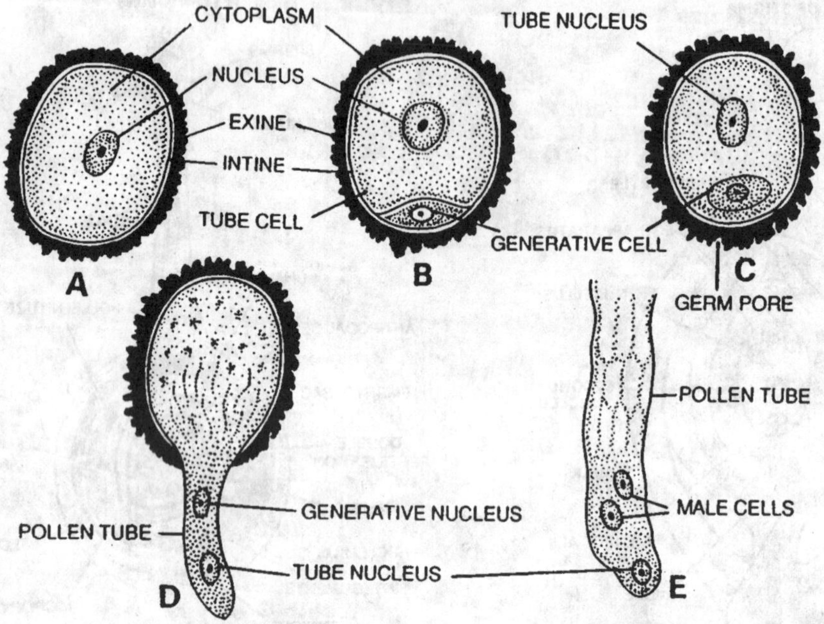

13.7. Structure and germination of pollen grain in angiosperms. A, uninucleate pollen grain; B, pollen grain with generative cell and tube nucleus; C, generative cell lies free in tube cell; D, pollen tube has developed and the generative cell and tube nucleus have migrated into it; E, generative nucleus has divided into two male gametes.

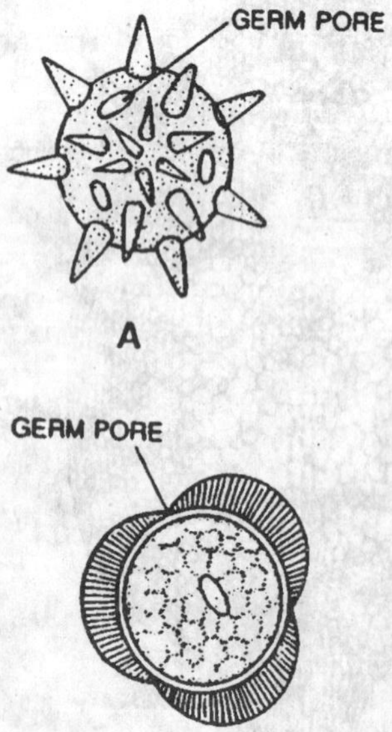

Fig. 13.8. Pollen grains. A sculptured pollen grain; B, sectional view.

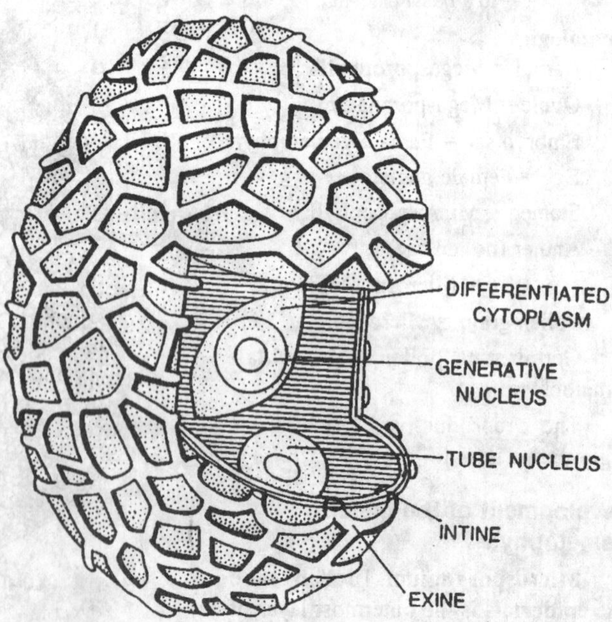

Fig. 13.9. Pollen grain of lily. Stereoscopic view.

endothecium or **fibrous layer**. As a rule, by the development of the fibrous bands of thickening the endothecium becomes hygroscopic and is, therefore, mainly responsible for the dehiscence of mature anther.

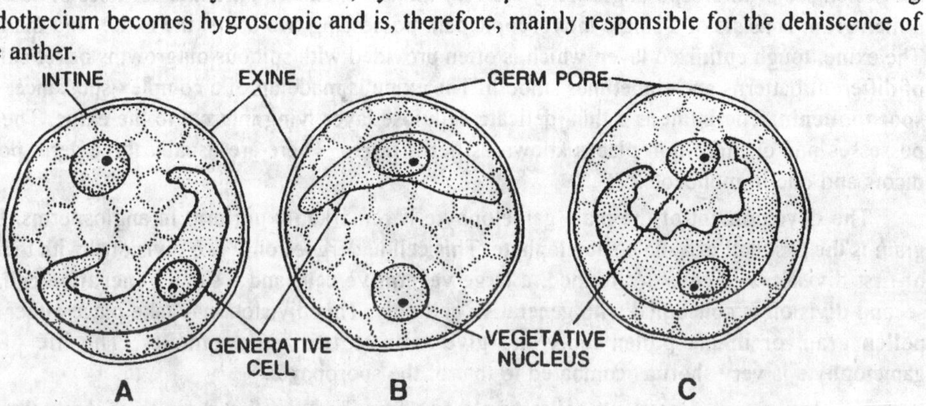

Fig. 13.10. Male gametophyte. Pollen grains showing vegetative nucleus and generative cells. In A and B, the generative cells are much elongated; where as in C the generative cell is of amoeboid nature.

The anther is generally bilobed, containing two longitudinally running chambers or pollen sacs per lobe. Each chamber contains a large number of pollen grains. The anther wall is composed of 4 to 5 layers. The innermost layer of these wall layers develops into a single layered **tapetum**. The tapetal layer is of great physiological significance as all the food material entering into the sporogenous tissue diffuses through, this layer. Ultimately the cells of tapetal layer disorganise. Thus, tapetum makes a nutritive layer for the developing microspores.

The cells of endothecium are thin walled along the line of dehiscence of each anther lobe. The opening through which the pollen grains are discharged from the pollen sac is called **stomium.** On the maturity of the anther, a strain is exerted on the stomium due to the loss of water by the cells of endothecium, with the result the stomium ruptures and the anther dehisces. Generally, the mature anther dehisces by means of slits or apical pores.

The pollen grains. The pollen grains or microspores are the male reproductive bodies of a flower, and are contained in

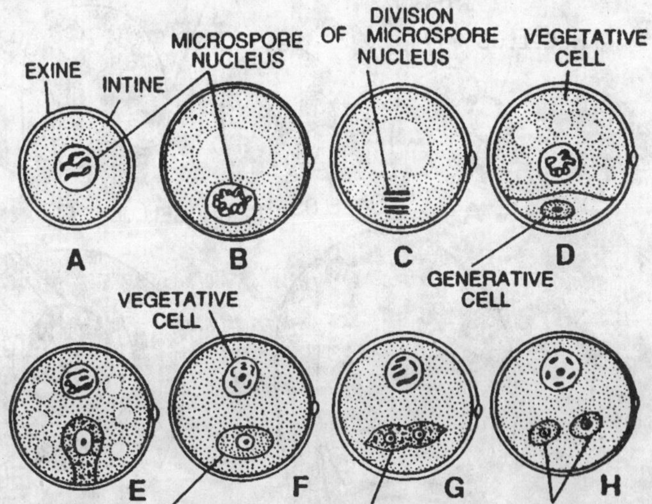

Fig. 13.11. Male gametophyte, A-J, different stages in the development of male gametophyte.

the pollen sac or microsporangia. They are very minute in size and are like particles of dust. Each pollen grain consists of a single microscopic cell, possessing two coats: the **exine** and the **intine**. The exine, tough cutinized layer, which is often provided with spinous outgrowths or reticulations of different patterns and sometimes smooth. The exine is made up of a complex substance, called **sporopollenin**. The intine is a thin, delicate cellulose layer lying internal to the exine. The exine possesses one or more thin places known as **germ pores.** There are usually three germ pores in dicots and one in monocots.

The development of the male gametophyte is remarkably uniform in angiosperms. Pollen grain is the first cell of a male gametophyte. This cell undergoes only two divisions, with the result of first division two cells are formed: a large **vegetative cell** and a small **generative cell.** The second division is concerned with generative cell only. This division may take place either in the pollen grain or in the pollen tube, and give rise to two **male gametes**. The life of male gametophyte is very short as compared to that of the sporophyte.

Vegetative and generative cells. As already described, the first division of the pollen grain gives rise to the **vegetative** and **generative** cells. The first formed walled and peripheral cell is the

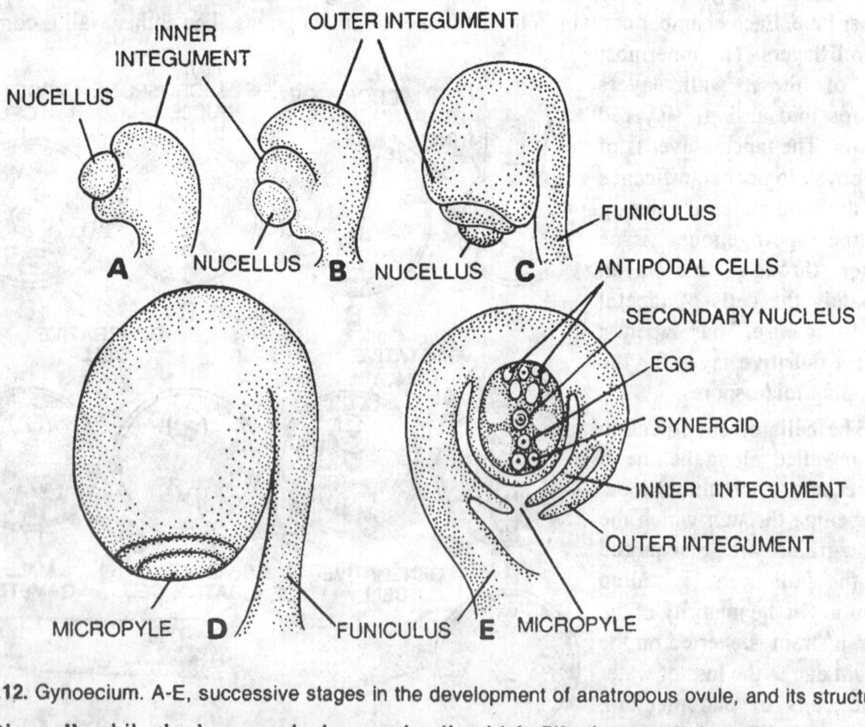

Fig. 13.12. Gynoecium. A-E, successive stages in the development of anatropous ovule, and its structure.

generative cell, while the larger, naked, central cell, which fills the remainder of the spore-wall cavity, is the **vegetative** or **tube cell**. The nuclei of generative and vegetative cells differ in size, structure and in staining qualities. The nucleus of vegetative cell possesses a prominent nucleus, while the nucleus of generative cell contains a small nucleolus. The cytoplasm of generative cell is hyaline and is almost without RNA, whereas that of vegetative cell is rich in RNA. The DNA contents of both the nuclei are same in the beginning but later on they increase in the generative nucleus. Eventually the generative cell loses contact with the microspore (pollen grain) wall, and is being shifted into the vegetative cell, where it may lie in any part of it. Thus, the pollen grain becomes two-celled. Generally, the pollen grains are being shed from the microsporangium (pollen sac) in two-celled stage for pollination.

Development of the Female Gametophyte

The megasporangium or ovule. An ovule or megasporangium develops from the base or the inner surface of the ovary. It is a small generaliy oval structure and consists chiefly of a central body of tissue, the **nucellus** and one or two **integuments.** Each ovule is attached in the placenta by a small stalk called the **funiculus.** The place of attachment of the stalk with the main body of the ovule is called the **hilum**. In an inverted ovule, the funicle fuses with the main body of the ovule, forming a sort of ridge, known as the **raphe**. The upper end of the raphe which is the junction of the integuments and the nucellus is called the **chalaza**. The nucellus makes the main body of the ovule, which is made up of parenchyma tissue. Nucellus is the megasporangium proper, and is surrounded by two coats, the **integuments**. A small opening is left at the apex of the integuments; this is called the **micropyle**. When there are two integuments then the inner integument is formed first and followed by the formation of the outer integument. A large oval cell lying embedded in the nucellus towards the micropylar end is the **embryo sac**. This makes the most important part of the mature ovule. It is the embryo sac, which bears the **embryo** later on.

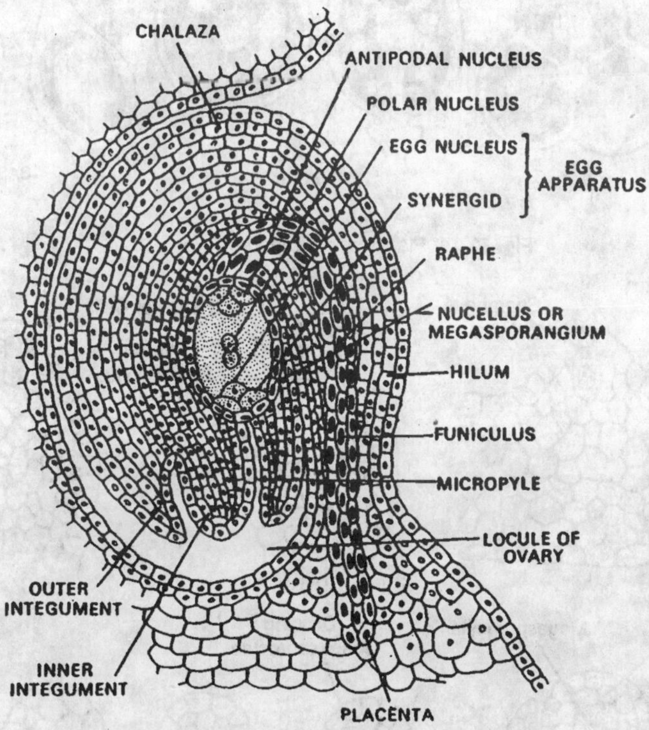

Fig. 13.13. Ovule. L.S. of a typical ovule of angiosperm.

Placentation. The **placenta** is an outgrowth of a parenchymatous tissue in the inner wall of the ovary to which the ovule or ovules (megasporangia) remain attached. The placentae usually develop on the margins of carpels, either along their whole line of union, called the **suture** or at their base or apex. The manner in which the placentae are distributed in the cavity of the ovary is known as **placentation.**

In the simple ovary (*i.e.*, of one carpel), there is one common type of placentation, known as **marginal**, and in the compound ovary (*i.e.*, of two or more carpels united together) placentation may be **axile, central** and **free-central, basal, parietal** and **superficial** as shown in fig. 13.14.

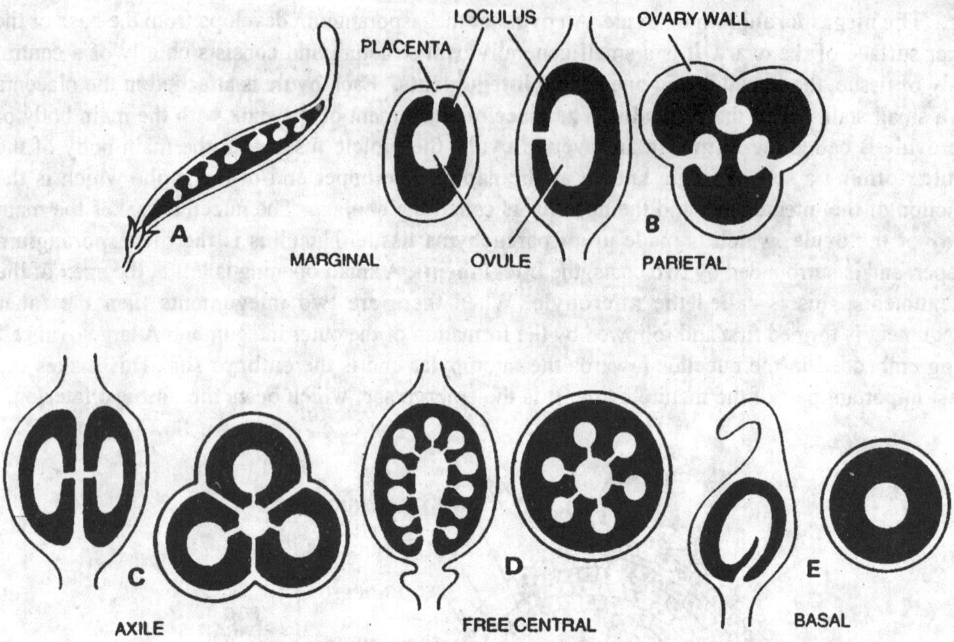

Fig. 13.14. Placentation. Different Types.

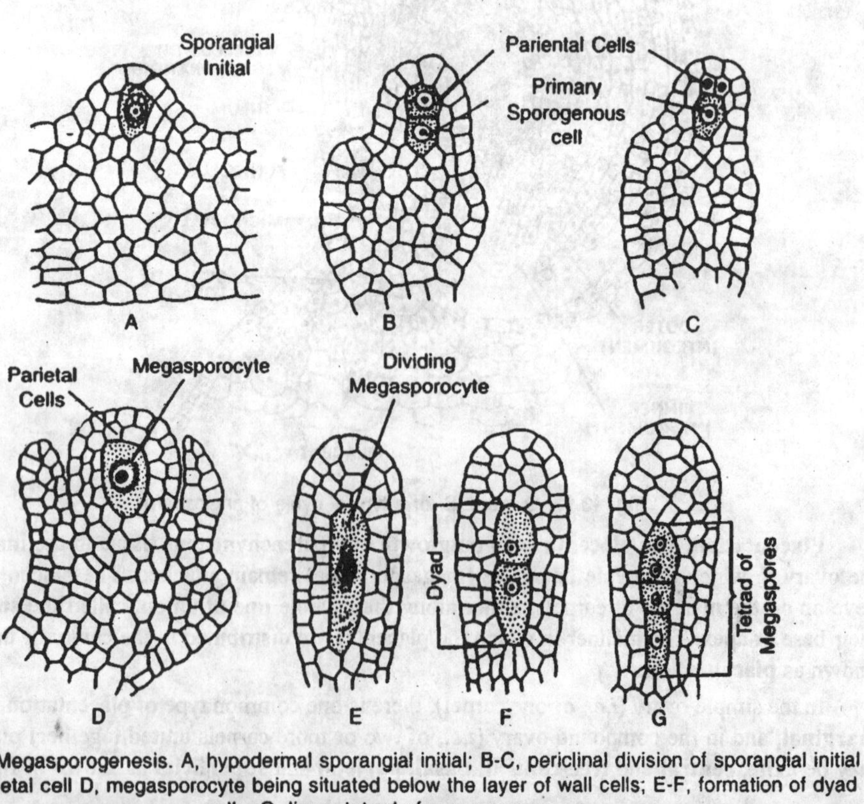

Fig. 13.15. Megasporogenesis. A, hypodermal sporangial initial; B-C, periclinal division of sporangial initial forming parietal cell D, megasporocyte being situated below the layer of wall cells; E-F, formation of dyad cells; G, linear tetrad of megaspores.

P. Maheshwari, F.R.S. (1904–1966). He worked on embryological aspects, especially the embryo sac of several plants belonging to more than 100 angiospermous families. His famous books of international fame are:

1. Introduction to the Embryology of Angiosperms
2. Recent advances in Embryology of Angiosperms (1963, edited by P. Maheswari).

He devoted his life for plant embryology, and very often referred to as 'Father of Indian Plant Embryology.' He was honoured with fellowship of Royal Society.

Megasporogenesis. The **archesporium** is hypodermal in origin. At some early stage in the development of the ovule, usually at the time of the initiation of the integumentary primordia, single hypodermal cell known as **primary archesporial cell**, becomes differentiated at the apex of the nucellus beneath the epidermis. It can be distinguished from other neighbouring cells owing to its large size, conspicuous deeply staining **nucleus**, and dense cytoplasm. Usually this primary archesporial cell divides periclinically forming an outer **primary parietal cell** and an inner **primary sporogenous cell.** The primary parietal cell may divide further several times both by anticlinal and periclinical divisions forming a variable amount of parietal tissue, or sometimes it remains undivided. The primary sporogenous cell usually does not divide further and functions directly as the **megaspore mother cell**.

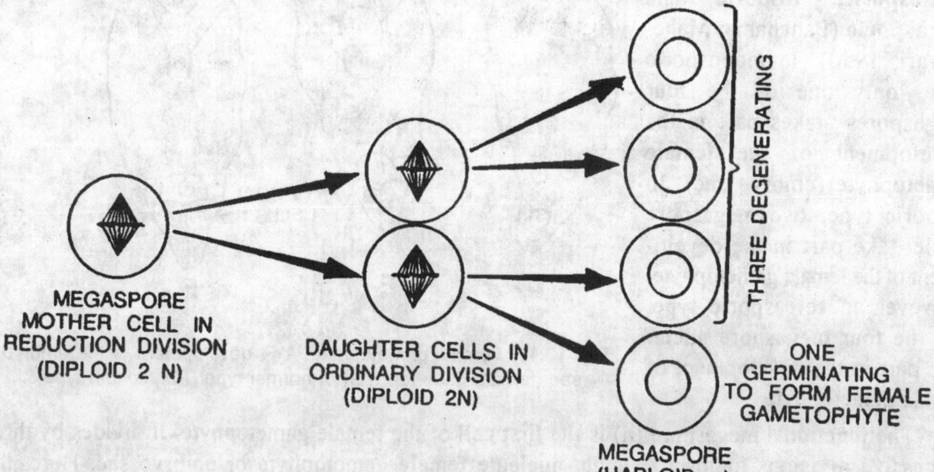

Fig. 13.16. Formation of megaspores from a megaspore mother cell. Only one megaspore is functional.

Usually the megaspore mother cell divides meiotically forming a tetrad of four megaspores. This usual process of meiotic division is termed **megasporogenesis.** Here the first division (*i.e.*, meiosis I) is always transverse and gives rise to two cells. The second is also transverse (*i.e.*, meiosis II), and thus in total four cells are being formed. The four megaspores thus formed in an axial row within the nucellus forming a **linear tetrad**.

Of the four megaspores, so formed, each with half (n) the usual number (2n) of chromosomes, the three upper ones degenerate and appear as dark caps, while the lowest one functions, and gives rise to the embryo sac. The developing megaspore encroaches upon and absorbs the other three degenerating megaspores of tetrad and the neighbouring cells of the nucellus.

Female gametophyte. The megaspore (n) makes the beginning of the female gametophyte. The nucleus of the functional megaspore divides and develops into the female gametophyte or the embryo sac. The female gametophyte of angiosperms is very much reduced and totally dependent for its nutrition upon the tissue of the sporophyte.

Depending on the number of megaspores taking part in the development, the embryo sacs (female gametophytes) of angiosperms may be classified into three main categories; **monosporic, bisporic** and **tetrasporic** (Panchanan Maheshwari, 1950). In monosporic type, only one of the four megaspores takes part in the development of the female gametophyte (embryo sac). In bisporic type, two megaspore nuclei take part in the development of the female gametophyte. However, in tetrasporic type, all the four megaspore nuclei take part in the development of female gametophyte.

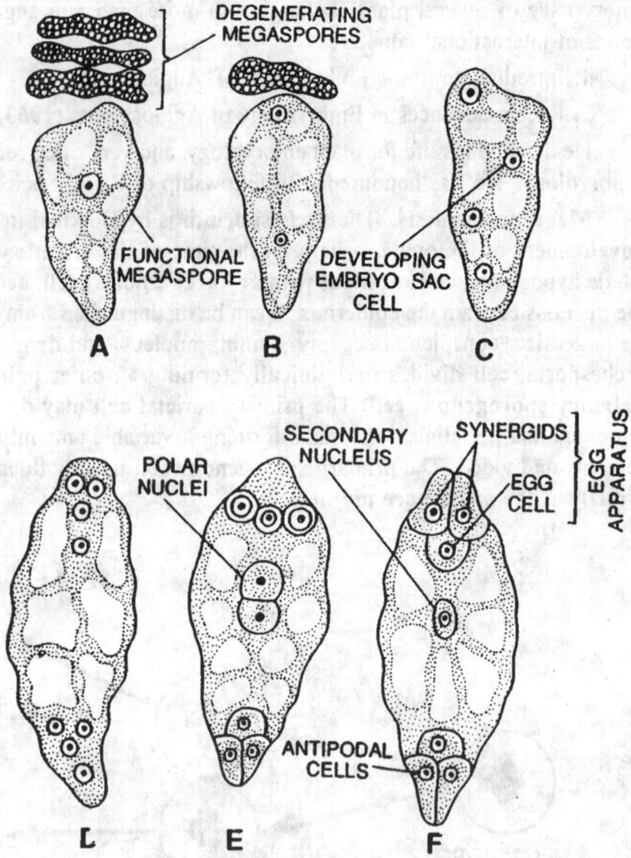

Fig. 13.17. Female gametophyte. A-F, development of the embryo sac (female gametophyte) of normal type (*Polygonum* type).

The functional megaspore (n) is the first cell of the female gametophyte. It divides by three successive divisions to form an eight-nucleate female gametophyte or embryo sac. Here, the nucleus of the functional megaspore divides to form two nuclei; the primary micropylar and the primary chalazal nuclei. These nuclei again divide, so that the number is increased to four. Each of these nuclei divides, so that altogether eight nuclei are formed in the embryo sac, four at each end. The female gametophyte increases in size. Now, one nucleus from each end or pole passes inwards, and the two polar nuclei fuse together somewhere in the middle of the embryo-sac, forming the **secondary nucleus** (2n). The remaining three nuclei at the micropylar end, each surrounded by a very thin wall, form the **egg apparatus.** The egg apparatus consists of two synergids and an egg cell. The other three nuclei at the opposite or chalazal end, lying in a group, often surrounded by very thin walls, form the **antipodal cells**. This type of embryo-sac is the most common and generally known as the **normal type**.

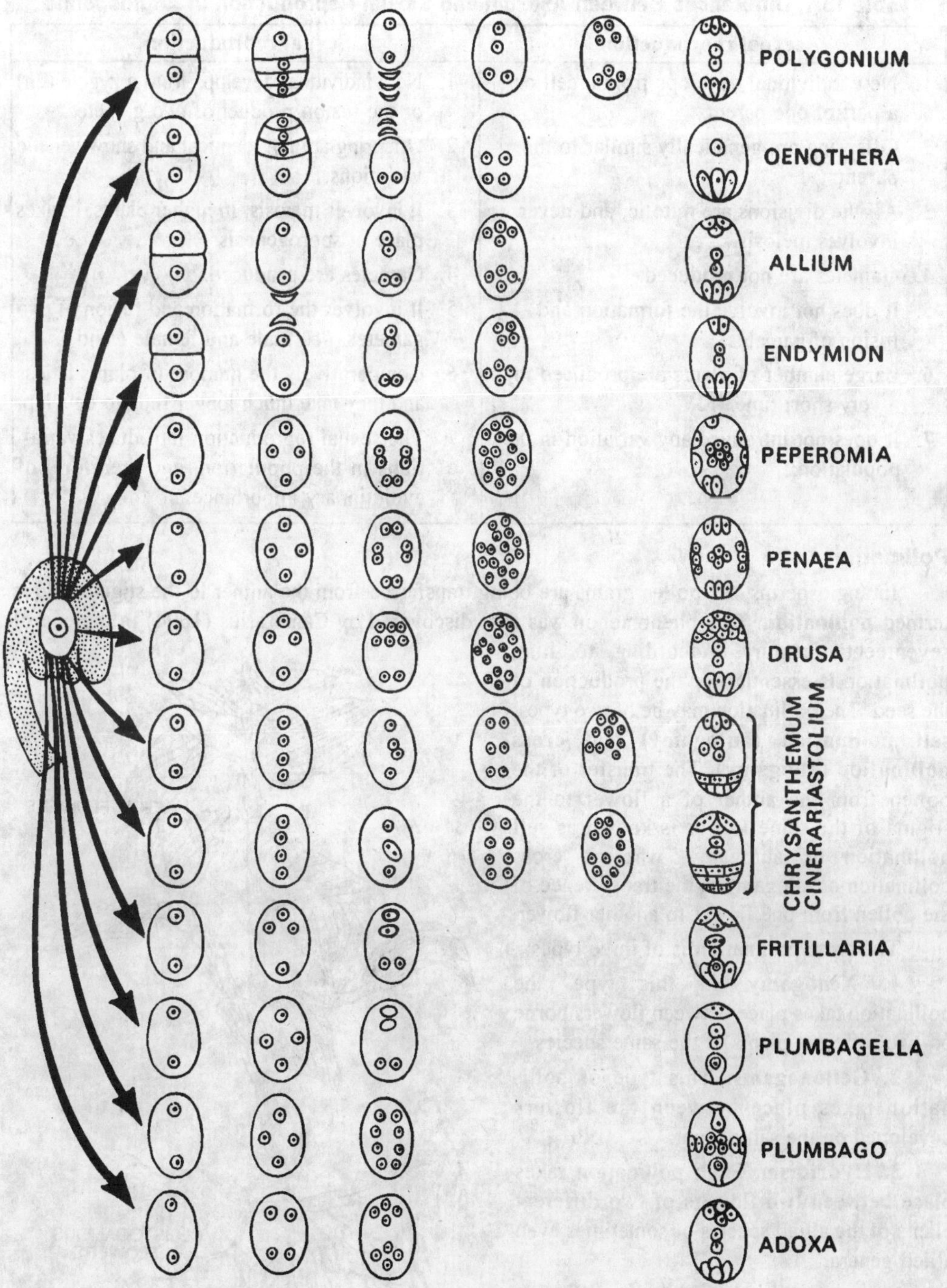

Fig. 13.18. Female gametophyte. Development of different types of embryo sacs in angiosperms.

Table 13.1. Differences Between Asexual and Sexual Reproduction in Angiosperms

Asexual reproduction	Sexual reproduction
1. New individual develops from a cell or a part of one parent.	1. New individual develops from a zygote (2n) or the fusion product of two gametes.
2. Offspring are genetically similar to the parent.	2. Offspring are not identical and show genetic variations.
3. All the divisions are mitotic, and never involves meiosis.	3. It involves meiosis. In higher plants, it takes place at sporogenesis.
4. Gametes are not produced.	4. Gametes are produced.
5. It does not involve the formation and fusion of gametes.	5. It involves the formation and fusion of two gametes, *i.e.*, male and female (and).
6. Large number of plants are produced in a very short time.	6. Comparatively the number of plants is less and they take much longer time to develop.
7. It does not introduce any variation in the population,	7. The sexual reproduction introduces variations in the population, and therefore, of evolutionary importance.

Pollination

In angiosperms, the pollen grains are being transferred from the anther to the stigma, and is termed **pollination**. This phenomenon was first discovered by Camerarius (1694) in the end of seventeenth century. According to him, pollination is essential for the production of the seed. The pollination may be of two types: **self pollination (autogamy)** and **cross pollination (allogamy)**. The transfer of the pollen from the anther of a flower to the stigma of the same flower is known as self pollination or autogamy, whereas cross pollination or allogamy is the transference of the pollen from one flower to another flower.

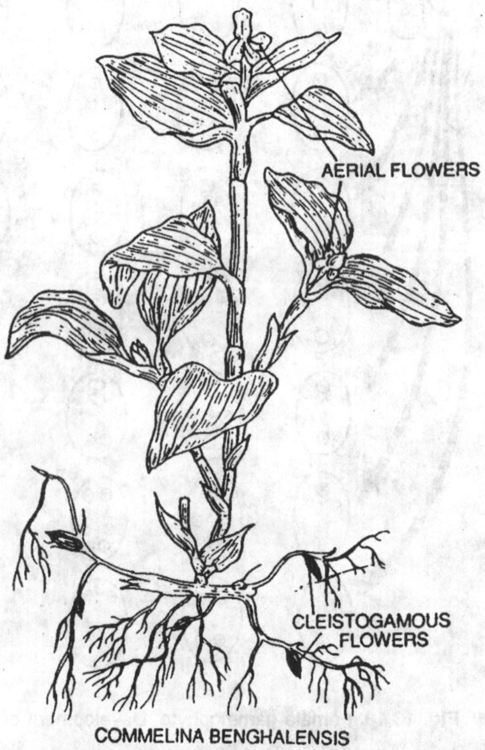

Fig. 13.19. Homogamy-cleistogamy. The cleistogamous flowers are born on underground branches of *Commelina benghalensis*.

The cross pollination is of three types:

1. Xenogamy. In this type, the pollination takes place between flowers borne on two different plants of the same species.

2. Geitonogamy. This type of pollination takes place between the flowers developed on the same plant.

3. Hydridism. Such pollination takes place between two flowers of two different plants of the allied species or sometimes even allied genera.

In the condition in which the pollen are discharged from the anther, they show considerable resistance to environmental changes. Sometimes, they remain viable for several weeks.

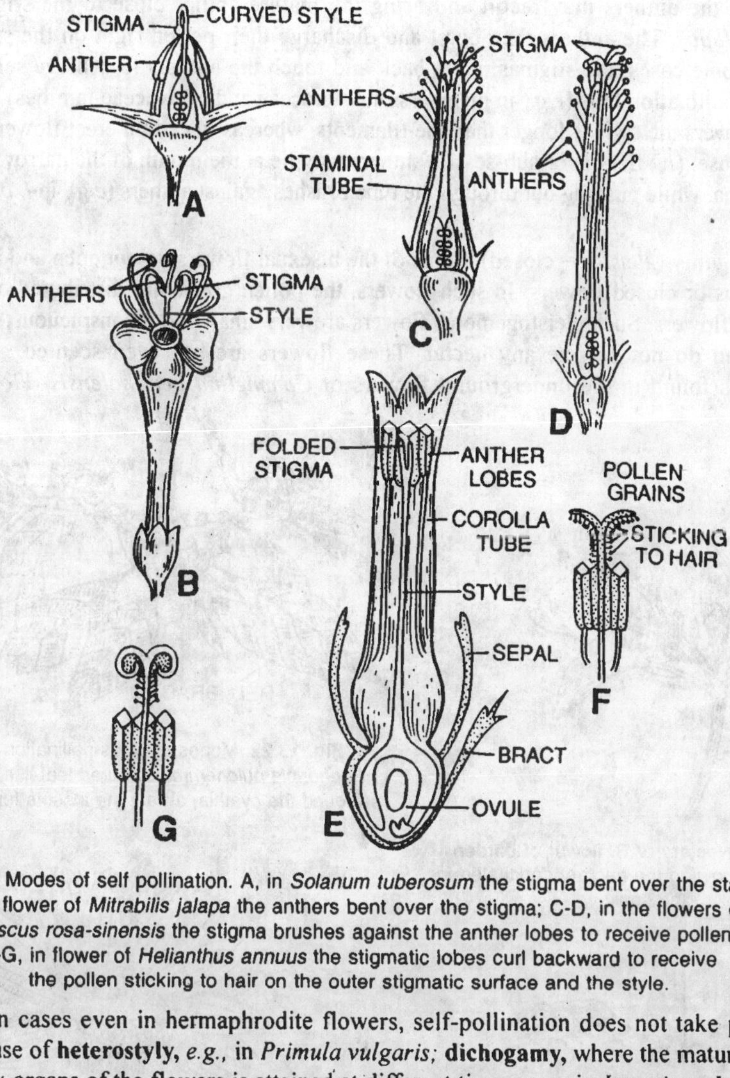

Fig. 13.20. Modes of self pollination. A, in *Solanum tuberosum* the stigma bent over the staments; B, in flower of *Mitrabilis jalapa* the anthers bent over the stigma; C-D, in the flowers of *Hibiscus rosa-sinensis* the stigma brushes against the anther lobes to receive pollen; E-G, in flower of *Helianthus annuus* the stigmatic lobes curl backward to receive the pollen sticking to hair on the outer stigmatic surface and the style.

In certain cases even in hermaphrodite flowers, self-pollination does not take place. This happens because of **heterostyly,** *e.g.,* in *Primula vulgaris;* **dichogamy,** where the maturity of male and female sex organs of the flowers is attained at different times, *e.g.*, in *Impatiens*; **herkogamy,** in which the structure of male and female sex organs in the flowers acts as barrier for self-pollination, and **self-sterility**, as found in *Petunia axillaris.*

As mentioned, pollination is of two kinds: (1) **self pollination** or **autogamy** (auto = self; *gamos* = marriage) and (2) **Cross-pollination** or **allogamy** (*allos* = different).

1. Self -pollination (autogamy). This kind of pollination is the transference of pollen grains from the anther of a flower to the stigma of the same flower or from a flower (male or bisexual) to a flower (female or bisexual), both found on the same individual plant. Here only one parent plant is concerned to give rise to the offspring. The self-pollination is, however, presented in unisexual flowers borne by two separate plants, and also in many bisexual flowers. The undermentioned adaptations are commonly found in flowers to achieve self-pollination.

Homogamy (*homos* = same). In this condition, the anthers and the stigmas of a bisexual flower mature at the same time. (*i*) Here some of the pollen grains may reach the stigma of the same flower through the agency of wind or insects, thus effecting self-pollination. (*ii*) The filaments of the anthers may recoil and bring the mature anther close to the stigma (*e.g.*, in *Mirabilis jalapa*). The anthers then burst and discharge their pollen right on the surface of the stigma. In some cases, the stigmas move back and touch the anthers to achieve self-pollination when cross-pollination fails (*e.g.*, in members of Asteraceae and Malvaceae families). (*iii*) In some drooping flowers the style is longer than the filaments, whereas in certain erect flowers the reverse may be the case. (*iv*) Sessile or sub-sessile anthers may lie at the mouth of the narrow corolla tube and the stigma, while pushing out through the tube brushes against anthers (*e.g.*, in *Ixora, Gardenia* and *Vinca*).

Cleistogamy (*kleistos* = closed). Some of the bisexual flowers do not open and are known as cleistogamous or closed flowers. In such flowers, the pollen grains are distributed on the stigma of the same flowers. Such cleistogamous flowers are very small and inconspicuous. They are not coloured, and do not secrete any nectar. These flowers are not even scented. This type of pollination is found in the underground flowers of *Commelina benghalensis, Viola, Drosera, Oxalis,* etc.

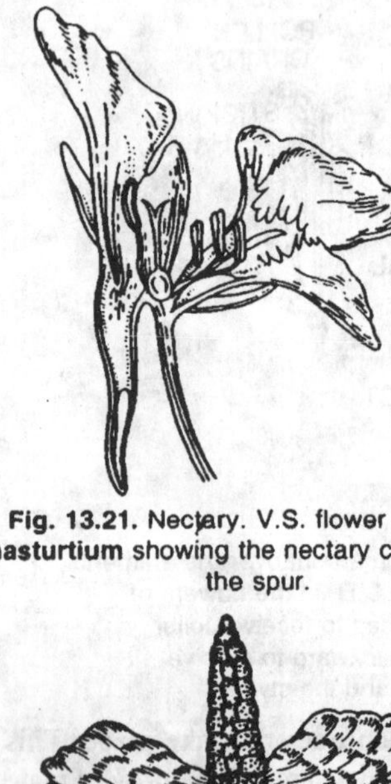

Fig. 13.21. Nectary. V.S. flower of garden **nasturtium** showing the nectary concealed in the spur.

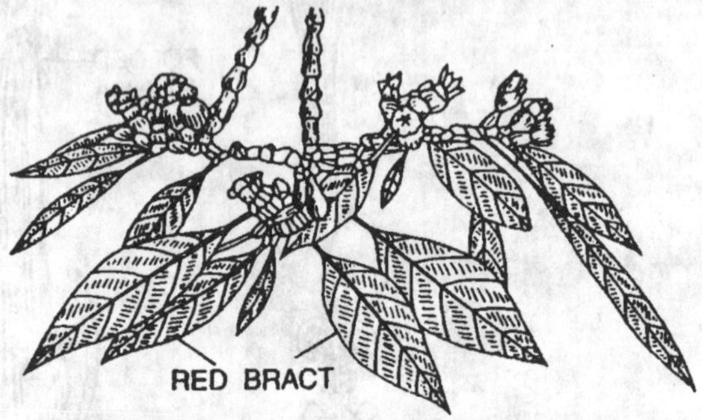

Fig. 13.22. Modes of cross-pollination-colour. In *Euphoribia pulcherrima* coloured leaf-like breacts that surround the cyathia, attract the insects for the purpose.

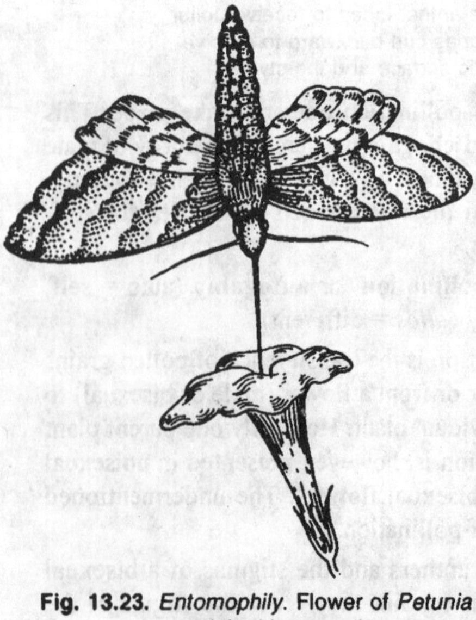

Fig. 13.23. *Entomophily*. Flower of *Petunia* being visited by a moth.

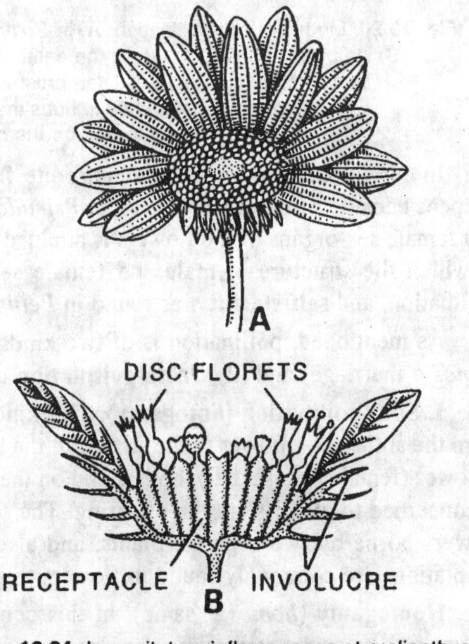

Fig. 13.24. In capitutum inflorescence of *Helianthus* (A–B), the closely arranged flowers have every chance of pollination.

2. Cross-pollination (allogamy). The cross-pollination is induced by external agents which carry the pollen grains of one flower and deposit them on the stigma of another flower, the two being borne by two separate plants of the same or closely allied species. These agencies may be **insects** (*e.g.*, bees, flies, moths, etc.), **animals** (*e.g.*, birds, snails, etc.), **wind** and **water**. The allogamy (cross-pollination) is the rule in unisexual flowers borne by two separate plants, while in bisexual flowers, it also occurs generally. Nature favours cross-pollination and there are so many adaptations in flowers to achieve this type of pollination.

Entomophily (*entomon* = insect, *phileo* = to love). This type of pollination takes place through the agency of insects. It is of general occurrence among plants. The insect-loving flower possesses various adaptations by which they attract insects and use them as carriers of pollen grains for the purpose of cross-pollination. The main such adaptations are **colour, nectar** and **scent.** The flowers of Asteraceae and Lamiaceae families are generally pollinated by the bees and butterflies.

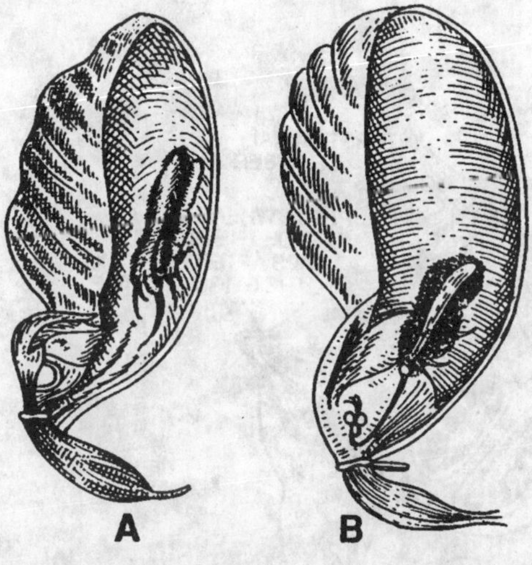

Fig. 13.25. *Entomophily* A-B, V.S. flowers of Cypripedium (can orchid) showing pollination by bee.

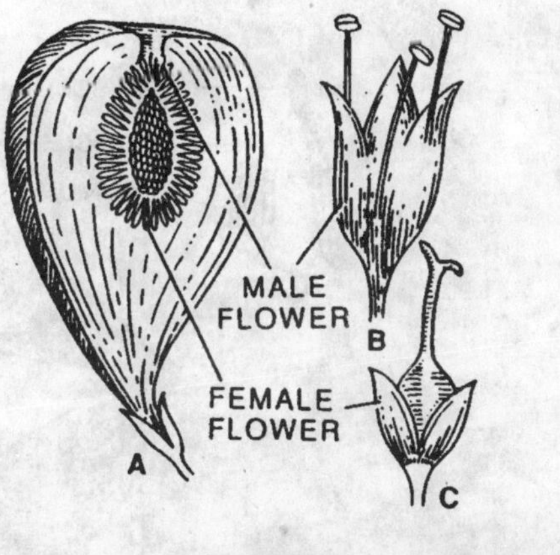

Fig. 13.26. The insects enter through the apical pore of hypanthodium in *Ficus*, to ensure pollination (A-C).

Generally, the pollen grains of entomophilous flowers are sticky. The stigma is also sticky. Pollen grains and nectar are very often used as food materials by the insects. Flowers generally attract insects by their colour, nectar or scent, or they visit the flowers in search of food, or shelter from sun and rain. Thus, as the insects visit the flowers, their body gets dusted with pollen grains, and when they fly and visit other flowers, they brush against the stigma which being sticky at once receives the pollen grains from their body. Thus, cross-pollination is achieved.

In several species of *Ficus,* the insects enter the chamber of the inflorescence (hypanthodium) through the apical pore, and as they move over the unisexual flowers inside the chamber, the pollination is achieved. Female flowers lie at the base of the cavity and open earlier, whereas male flowers lie near the apical opening and open later so that pollen grains have to be brought over from another inflorescence.

Flowers are generally adapted for pollination by some specific insects. For example, in snapdragon and other such flowers with saccate corolla, only the insects of particular size and weight can open the mouth of the corolla. On the other hand, long-tongued insects can pollinate the flowers with long corolla tubes.

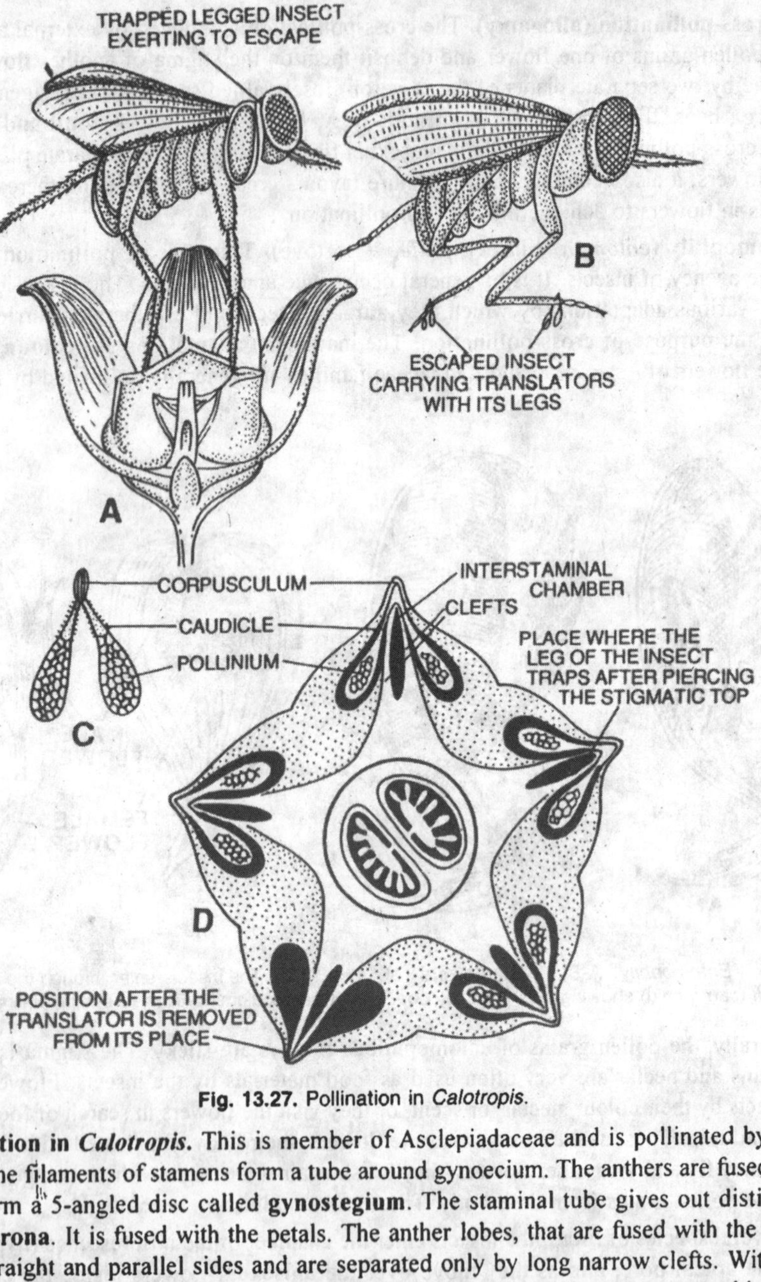

Fig. 13.27. Pollination in *Calotropis*.

Pollination in *Calotropis*. This is member of Asclepiadaceae and is pollinated by bees. In this flower, the filaments of stamens form a tube around gynoecium. The anthers are fused with the stigma to form a 5-angled disc called **gynostegium**. The staminal tube gives out distinct lobes called the **corona**. It is fused with the petals. The anther lobes, that are fused with the stigmatic disc, have straight and parallel sides and are separated only by long narrow clefts. Within these clefts there are **interstaminal chambers**. The pollen grains in the anthers are grouped in the form of mass called **pollinium**. The pollinium develops a rider mechanism or the **translator.** It consists of two arms called the **caudicles**. The caudicles carry the two pollinia on one side and are fused to form a black and sticky dot on the other side. This dot-like structure is called the **corpusculum.** There are five corpuscula at the angles of gynostegium from two adjacent anthers. An insect crawling about over the flowers is sooner or later trapped, through one of its legs becoming caught in one of the clefts between adjacent anthers. The insect can release itself only by drawing the leg upwards through the clefts and this it does, but as the leg becomes free at the top of the cleft, it catches in the notch of the corpusculum so that further movements pull this together with its attached pollinia, away from its anchorage on the gynostegium. The released insect in due course visits another flower and again becomes caught by the leg in the similar way. While drawing the leg, this time, through the anther cleft the pollinia brought from the previous flower are torn away from corpusculum and are deposited in the interstaminal chamber. The new translators are carried away and there is repetition of the whole process.

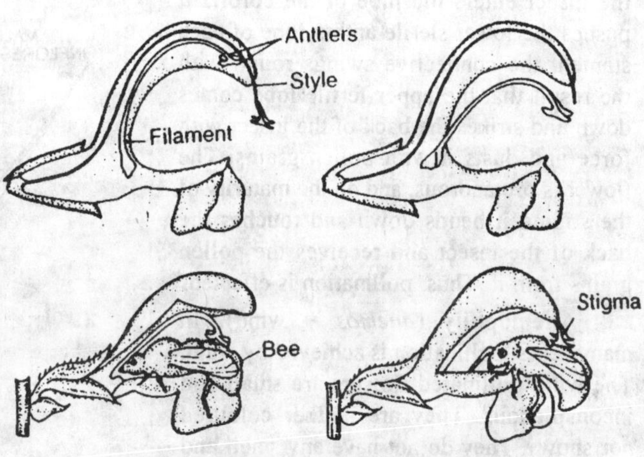

Fig. 13.28. Entomophily. An interesting type of cross-pollination in *Salvia* by insects.

Pollination in *Salvia*. An interesting type of cross-pollination takes place in *Salvia* by insects. In this flower, there are two stamens. The two anther lobes of each stamen are widely separated by the elongated curved connective which plays freely on the filament. The upper lobe is fertile and the lower one sterile. In the natural position, the connective remains upright. When

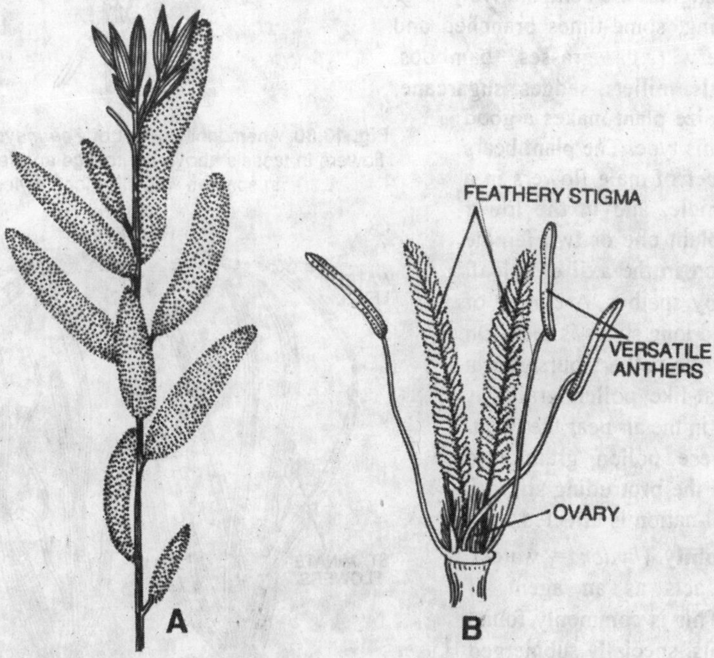

Fig. 13.29. Anemophily. A, the male catkin of *Salix;* B, the flower of *Avena sativa* with feathery stigmas.

the insect enters the tube of the corolla it pushes the lower sterile anther lobe of each stamen; the connective swings round with the result that the upper fertile lobe comes down and strikes the back of the insect with force and dusts it with pollen grains. The flower is protandrous, and on the maturity of the stigma it bends down and touches the back of the insect and receives the pollen grains from it. Thus, pollination is effected.

Anemophily (*anemos* = wind). In many cases, pollination is achieved by wind. The wind pollinated flowers are small and inconspicuous. They are neither coloured nor showy. They do not have any smell and they do not secrete any nectar. The anthers produce an immense quantity of pollen grains. A large quantity of pollen grains is being wasted during transit from one flower to another. The pollen grains are quite light and dry, and sometimes provided with wings (*e.g., in Pinus,* a gymnosperm) to facilitate distribution by wind. In the wind loving flowers, the stigmas are comparatively large and protruding, some-times branched and often feathery (*e.g.,* grasses, bamboos, palms, cereals, millets, sedges, sugarcane, etc.). The maize plant makes a good example of this type. The plant bears a large number of male flowers in a terminal panicle, and in the lower part of the plant one or two female spadices, each in the axil of a leaf, surrounded by spathes. A cluster of fine, silky and long styles is seen. On the maturity, the anthers burst and a cloud of dust-like pollen grains is seen floating in the air near the plant. Some of these pollen grains are entangled by the protruding stigmas and thus polli-nation is effected.

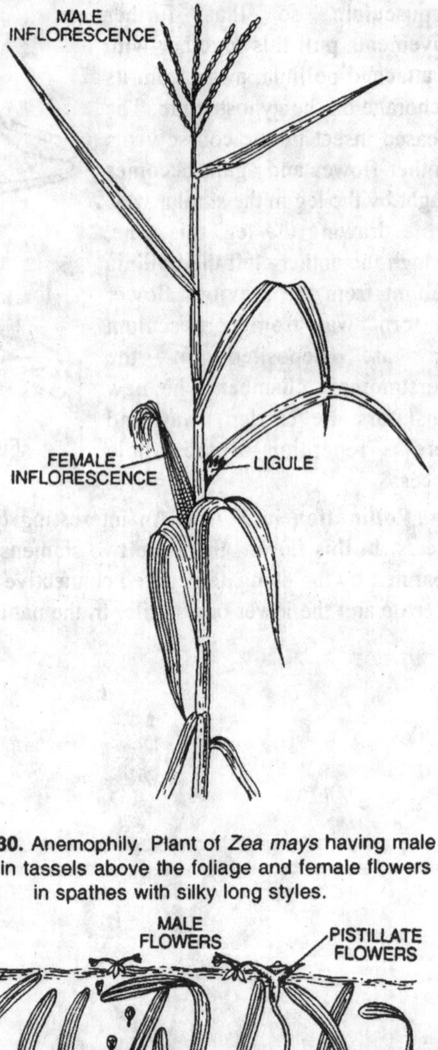

Fig. 13.30. Anemophily. Plant of *Zea mays* having male flowers in tassels above the foliage and female flowers in spathes with silky long styles.

Hydrophily (*hydor* = water). Water also acts as an agent of pollination. This is commonly found in water plants, specially submerged ones, such as *Vallisneria, Cerato-phyllum*, *Hydrilla* and *Zostera.* The mode of pollination in *Vallisneria* (submerged aquatic plant) is as

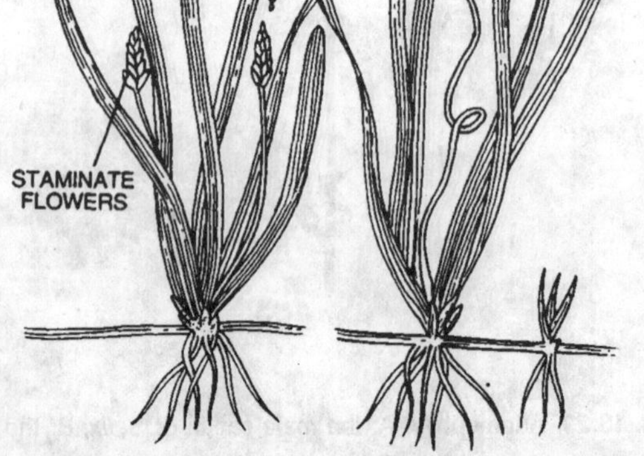

Fig. 13.31. Hydrophily. Pollination by water in *Vallisneria.*

follows: The plant is dioecious. The male plant bears a large number of minute male flowers in a small spadix surroun-ded by a spathe and borne on a short stalk, whereas the female plant bears solitary female flowers each on a long slender pedicel. This stalk of the flower elongates and takes the female flower to the surface of the water. The spathe bursts releasing the male flowers from the spadix, while still closed, and float on the surface of the water. The anthers burst and the sticky pollen grains adhere to the surface of trifid stigmas which thereafter close. As soon the pollination is over, the stalk of the female flower becomes spirally coiled and pulls the female flower down into the water. The fruit develops and matures under water a little above the bottom.

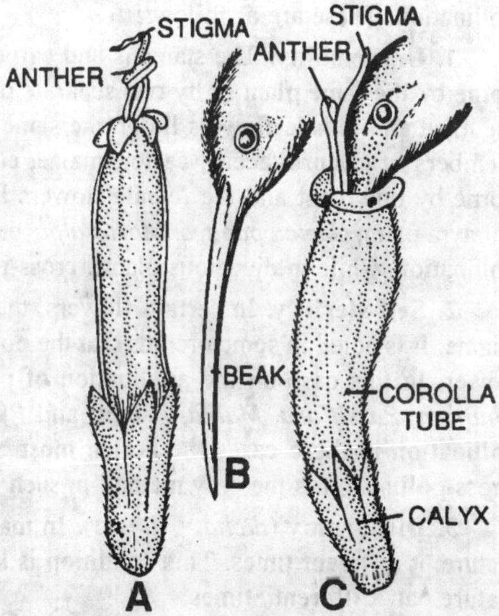

Fig. 13.32. Zoophily. Many flowers are pollinated by long-beaked birds. (ornithophily)

Zoophily (*zoo* = animals). There are so many animals, such as birds, squirrels, bats, snails, etc., which are involved in cross-pollination. The pollination by birds, generally called **ornithophily**, is common in coral tree (*Erythrina*), bottle brush *(Callistemon), Butea monosperma* and silk cotton tree (*Bombax ceiba*). The pollination in *Adansonia, Kigelia* and *Anthocephalus* are carried out by bats. This type is called **chiropterophily.** Snails are involved in pollination of several aroids (members of family Araceae). In aroids, the inflorescence is a spadix; the female flowers remain situated at the base of the spadix and the male flowers towards top. The stigmas mature first and the pollen grains are brought from another spadix.

Table 13.2. Agencies and types of Pollination

Agencies of Pollination		Types of Pollination
Abiotic	Wind	Anemophily
	Water	Hydrophily
Biotic	Insects	Entomophily
	Birds	Ornithophily
	Bats	Cheiropteriphily
	Snails	Malacophily

Significance of Pollination

1. Pollination is an important process which leads to fertilisation and production of seeds and fruits, which are responsible for continuity of plant life.

2. The seeds and fruits are also used as food both for animal and humans. They make source of vitamins and minerals.

3. The pollination, especially cross pollination is important for production of plants with a combination of characters from two plants.

4. Pollination is also important in the production of hybrid seeds.

Contrivances for cross-pollination. Certain structural devices in the flowers favour cross-pollination. These are as follows:

1. Unisexuality. The stamens and carpels lie in separate flowers—male and female, either borne by the same plant or by two separate plants. There are two kinds of unisexuality: (*i*) where the male and female flowers lie on the same plant and the plant is said to be **monoecious** (*e.g.*, members of Cucurbitaceae, castor, maize, etc.), (*ii*) where the male and the female flowers are borne by one plant and the female flowers lie on another plant, it is known as **dioecious** (*e.g.*, palmyra palm, *Carica papaya, Morus alba,* etc.). In monoecious plants, there may be self-or cross-pollination, while in dioecious plants, cross-pollination is a basic necessity.

2. Self-sterility. In certain flowers, the pollen grains are unable to germinate on its own stigma. It is noted in some orchids that the pollen has an injurious effect on the stigma of the same flower. In this case on the application of pollen to stigma, the stigma dries up and falls off, *Abutilon*, *Passiflora*, *Malva*, *Prunus* and *Pyrus* are self-sterile. To effect the successful cross-pollination in these cases the pollen must be from two such parents which differ genetically. Cross-pollination is the only method in such cases for the setting of seeds.

3. Dichogamy (*dicha* = in two). In many bisexual flowers, the anthers and stigmas often mature at different times. This condition is known as **dichogamy**. As the anther and the stigma mature at different times, dichogamy often checks the self-pollination. There are two types of dichogamy: (*i*) **protogyny** (*protos* = first; *gyne* = female) where the gynoecium matures earlier than the anthers of the same flower, and in such cases, the stigma receives the pollen grains brought from another flower and thus cross-pollination becomes indispensable (*e.g.*, *Ficus, Mirabilis, Magnolia, Annona,* etc.) and (*ii*) **protandry** (*protos* = first; *andros* = male) where the anthers mature earlier than the stigma of the same flower and hence the pollen grains, are carried over to the stigma of another flower (*e.g., Clerodendron, Hibiscus rosa-sinensis, Abelmoschus esculentus, Helianthus annuus, Coriandrum sativum,* etc.)

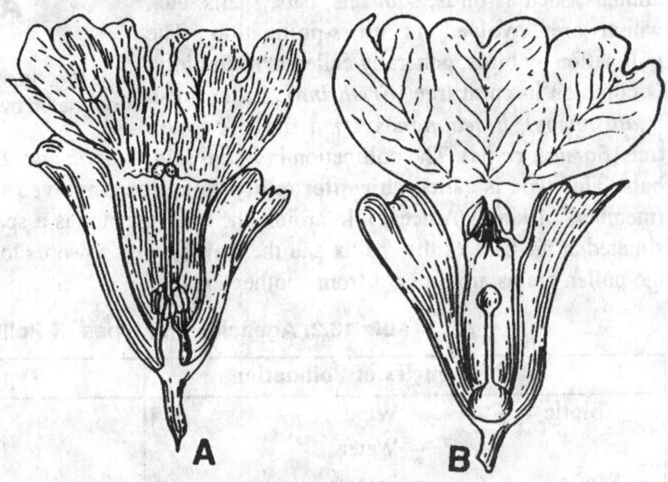

Fig. 13.33. Heterostyly in the flowers of *Primula*.

4. Heterostyly (*heteros* = different). Some plants bear flowers of two different forms. One form possesses long stamens and a short style, while the other form possesses short stamens and a long style. This kind of bearing of stamens and styles is known as **dimorphic heterostyly**. In such cases, the chances of self-pollination decrease whereas chances of cross-pollination increase. In the flowers of this type, cross-pollination readily takes place between stamens and styles of the same length borne by different flowers. Dimorphic heterostyly is seen in *Oxalis, Linum, Polygonum fagopyrum, Woodfordia,* etc.

5. Herkogamy (*hercos* = barrier). In some homogamous flowers, there are certain structural peculiarities of the floral parts which act as a barrier to self-pollination and thus favour cross-pollination by insects. Here are cited some important examples:

For example, in *Calotropis* and orchids, the pollinia are located at places where they can never come in contact with the stigma by themselves and can only be carried away by insects. The lever mechanism in *Salvia* also promotes cross-pollination and avoids self-pollination. In *Viola tricolor* the stigma is protected by a flap or a lid, that prevents contact between the stigma and anther. This flap is pushed aside by the insect and thus cross-pollination is effected.

Advantages and disadvantages of self and cross-pollination. Some of more important features are given here:

Advantages of self-pollination. This type of pollination is almost certain in a bisexual flower, if the stamens and carpels of the flower mature at the same time.

Table 13.3. Differences Between Self-pollination and Cross-pollination

Self-Pollination	Cross-Pollination
1. Pollen grains are transferred from the anther to the stigma of the same flower (autogamy) or another flower borne on the same plant (geitonogamy)	1. Pollen grains are transferred from the anther of one flower to the stigma of another flower borne on a different plant of the same species (allogamy).
2. It can occur even when the flowers are closed (cleistogamy).	2. It occurs only when the flowers are open.
3. Both the anthers and the stigmas mature at the same time.	3. The anthers and the stigmas of a flower generally mature at different times.
4. Self-pollination ultimately results in progenies which are pure lines, *i.e.*, homozygous	4. Cross-pollination produces the heterozygous offspring, and they show variations in characteristics.
5. It cannot eliminate harmful or useful characters.	5. It can eliminate harmful or useless characters.
6. External agent (insects, wind, etc.) is not required for self-pollination.	6. An external agent is required for cross-pollination.
7. Self-pollination does not help in the production of new varieties and species.	7. Cross-pollination is responsible for producing new varieties and species among plants.
8. Here the yield of the plant gradually falls with time.	8. The yield of the plant usually does not fall.
9. This type of pollination is economical for the plant.	9. This type of pollination is not economical.
10. Immunity of the race towards disease falls in the succeeding progenies.	10. Immunity of the race towards disease is generally maintained in the succeeding progenies.
11. It leads to less vigorous offspring.	11. Here the offspring are vigorous and exhibit genetic recombination.
12. Self-pollination does not introduce any variations, and therefore, the offspring are unable to adapt to the changed environment.	12. Cross-pollination introduces variations in the offspring, and therefore, the plants are better adapted in the changed environment.

Disadvantages of self-pollination. Continued self-pollination generation after generation definitely results in weaker progeny.

Advantages of cross-pollination. (*i*) It always gives rise to healthier offspring in subsequent generations which are better adapted in the struggle for existence; (*ii*) more abundant and viable seeds are produced; (*iii*) new varieties can be developed by this method; (*iv*) the adaptability of the plants to their environment is definitely better by this method.

Disadvantages of cross-pollination. (*i*) The plants have to depend upon external agencies for pollination (such as wind, water, insects, animals); (*ii*) various devices are needed to fulfil the needs of outer agencies; (*iii*) there is always a considerable waste of pollen where wind is the pollinating agent in cross-pollination.

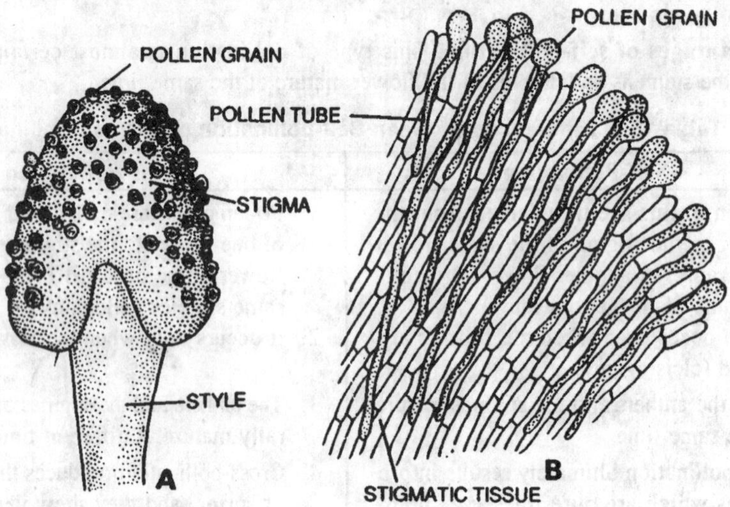

Fig. 13.34. Fertilization. A, pollen grains deposited on stigma; B, pollen grains germinating through stigmatic tissue forming pollen tubes.

Pollen Germination and Fertilisation

The fusion of two dissimilar sexual reproductive units or gametes is termed as **fertilization.** In gymnosperms, the pollen grains usually land directly on the nucellus, while in angiosperms, they fall on the stigma. In angiosperms, the fertilization is being completed as follows:

Germination of pollen grain. After being deposited on the stigma, the pollen grain absorbs liquid from the moist surface of the stigma, expands in size, and the intine protrudes out through a germ pore. The small tubular structure also known as pollen tube continues to elongate, and makes its way down the tissues of the stigma and style. Only the distal part of the pollen tube possesses living cytoplasm.

The stigma plays an important role in the germination of pollen grain. The stigma, secretes fluid containing liquids, gums, sugar and resins. The chief function of the stigmatic secretion is to protect the pollen as well as the stigma from desiccation.

After arriving to the wall of the ovary, the pollen tube enters the ovule either through the micropyle or by some other route. The entrance of the pollen tube through the micropyle is the normal condition and is known as **porogamy.** In some cases the pollen tube enters the ovule through the chalaza. This condition is known as **chalagogamy.** The chalagogamy was first reported by Treub (1891), in *Casuarina.*

The period between pollination and fertilisation varies from plant to plant. Usually this period varies from 12 to 48 hours. According to P. Maheshwari (1949), the temperature is responsible for controlling the growth of pollen tube.

Gametic fusion. In normal case, one male gamete unites with the egg to form the zygote and the second travels a little farther and unites with the secondary nucleus. This process is known as

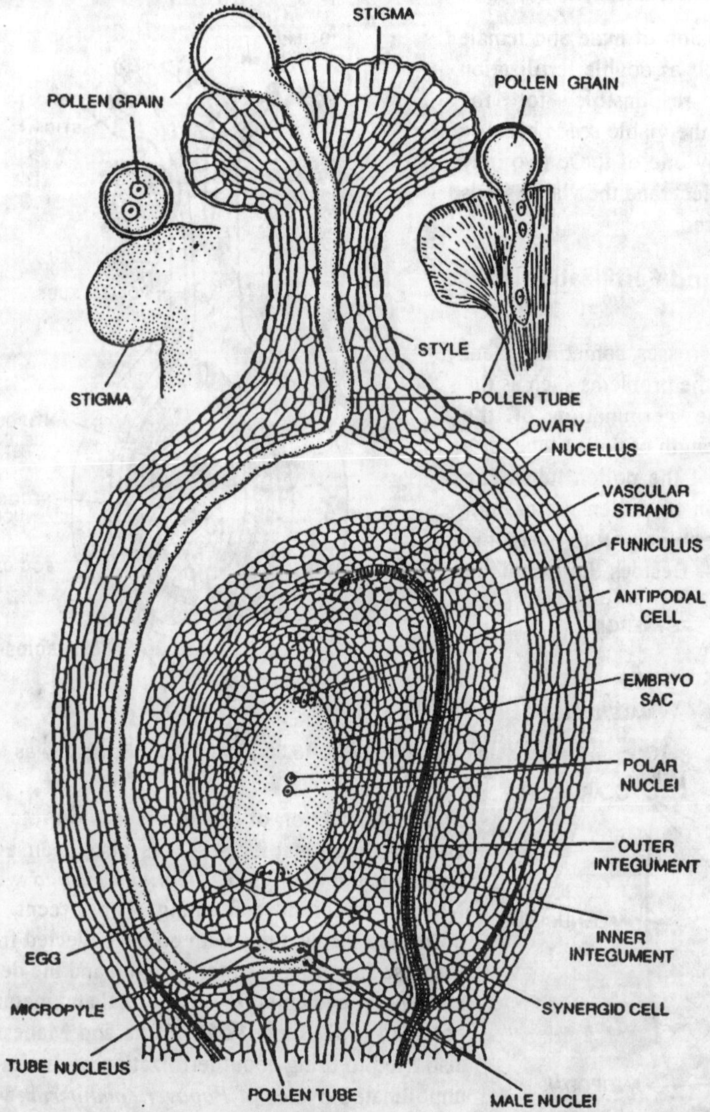

Fig. 13.35. Fertilization. C, porogamous fertilization in an anatropous ovule as seen in V.S. of carpel. A, the pollen grain is on the stigmatic surface; B, formation of pollen tube, that enters through the stigmatic tissue.

double fertilisation (Navaschin, 1898; Guignard, 1899). As the second male gamete fuses with the secondary diploid (2n) nucleus, producing a triploid (3n) primary endosperm nucleus, this is called **triple fusion.** Thus in an embryo sac there occur two sexual fusions; one in **syngamy** (*i.e.*, fusion of male gamete with egg), and the other in triple fusion, and therefore, the phenomenon is called **double fertilisation.**

Significance of double fertilization. The embryo, during its growth and development receives its nourishment from endosperm, which is a product of double fertilization. This process also gives required energy to the polar nuclei, which fail to divide further. Since the endosperm nuclei are the resultants of double feritlization, they are characterized by maternal and paternal chromosomes and thus endosperm represents the physiological aggressiveness due to hybrid vigour. The fusion of male and female gametes as well as double fertilization are equally responsible for the production of the viable seeds because absence of any one of these two may cause lethal effect, and the viable seeds are not produced.

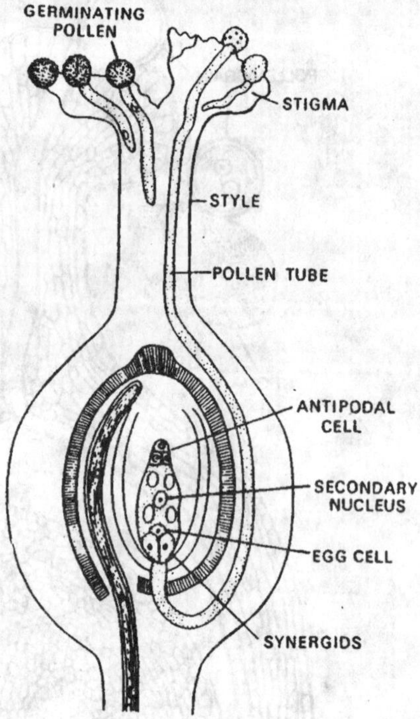

Fig. 13.36. Fertilization. Porogamy as seen in V.S. of carpel.

Pollination and Fertilization in Vitro

In many crosses, sometimes plant breeders face the problems such as the failure of the germination of the pollen, short length of pollen tube, or a slow growth of the pollen tube. The direct injection of pollen grains into the ovary may be helpful to overcome such problems. Besides the technique of direct injection of pollen suspension into the ovary, *in vitro* pollination of pistils has also been accomplished. Unpollinated ovaries of *Nicotiana rustica* were grown on Nitsch's medium containing 4 per cent sucrose and pollinated the next day with pollen collected from dehiscing anthers. The process of fertilization and the development of endosperm and embryo were normal and mature seeds were obtained (P.S. Rao, 1965). Kanta and Maheshwari (1963) also tried to bring about fertilization of ovules *in vitro*. The unpollinated ovules of *Papaver somniferum* were sown on an agar medium in a test tube. The pollen grains were dusted over the implanted ovules. The pollen grains germinated, and the pollen tubes grew rapidly and covered the ovules. Successful fertilization occurred in many ovules.

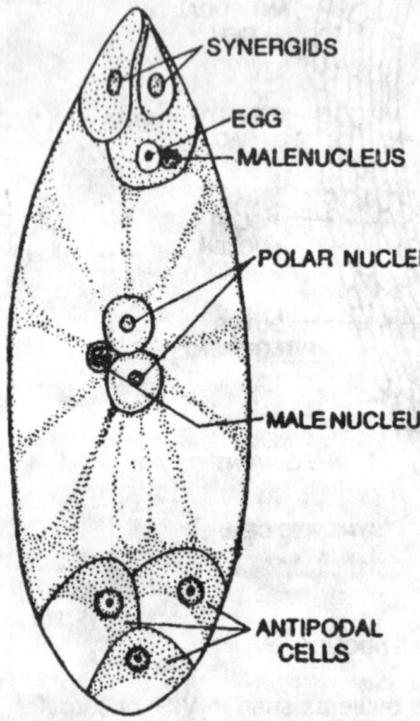

Fig. 13.37. Double fertilization in *Nicotiana*.

DEVELOPMENT OF ENDOSPERM

The Endosperm

The endosperm makes the main source of food for the embryo. In gymnosperms, the endosperm is haploid (n) and forms a continuation of the female gametophyte. On the other hand, in angiosperms it is formed mostly as the result of a fusion of the two polar nuclei and one of the male gametes. Since all the three nuclei taking part in the fusion are haploid, the endosperm becomes triploid (3n). In normal cases, the endosperm is triploid but haploid, tetraploid and polyploid endosperms are also known. Generally the endosperm nucleus divides after the division of the oospore, but in several cases the endosperm is formed to a great extent even before the first

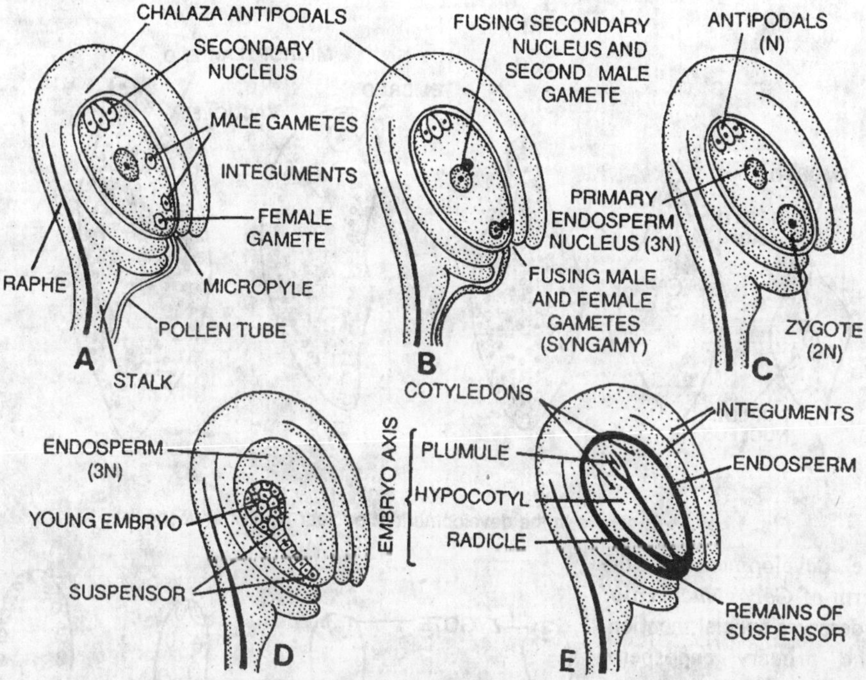

Fig. 13.38. Fertilization and post-fertilization changes. A, two male gametes discharged in the embryo sac; B, syngamy and double fertilization; C, formation of zygote (2n) and primary endospern nucleus (3n); D-E, post fertilization changes.

division of the oospore. However, endosperm formation is suppressed in two angiospermic families, the Orchidaceae and Podostemonaceae.

Types of Endosperm Formation

There are three general types of endosperm formation: (*a*) **nuclear type,** (*b*) **cellular type** and (*c*) **helobial type.**

Nuclear type. In this type, the first division and usually several of the following divisions are unaccompanied by wall formation. The nuclei may either remain free or in later stages, they may become separated by walls.

As divisions progress, the nuclei are being pushed towards the periphery, thus a large central vacuole is formed. Often the nuclei are especially aggregated at the micropylar and chalazal ends of the sac and form only a thin layer at the sides. Generally the endosperm nuclei in the chalazal part of the embryo sac have been observed to be larger than those in the micropylar end. The number of free nuclear divisions varies in different plants.

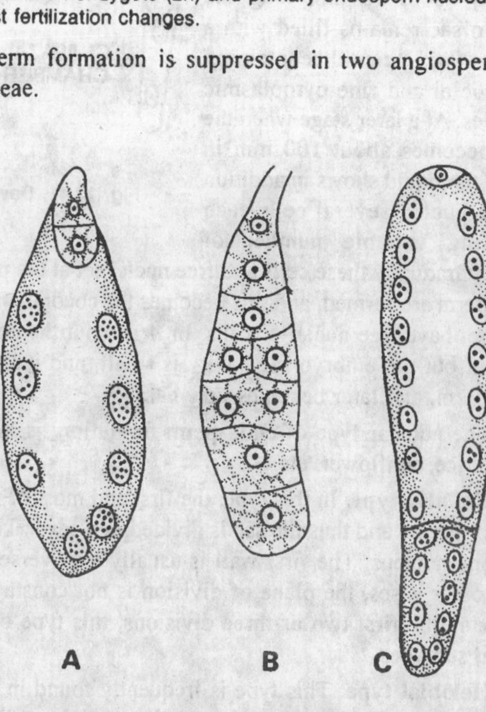

Fig. 13.39. Development of endosperm. A, nuclear type; B, cellular type and C, helobial type.

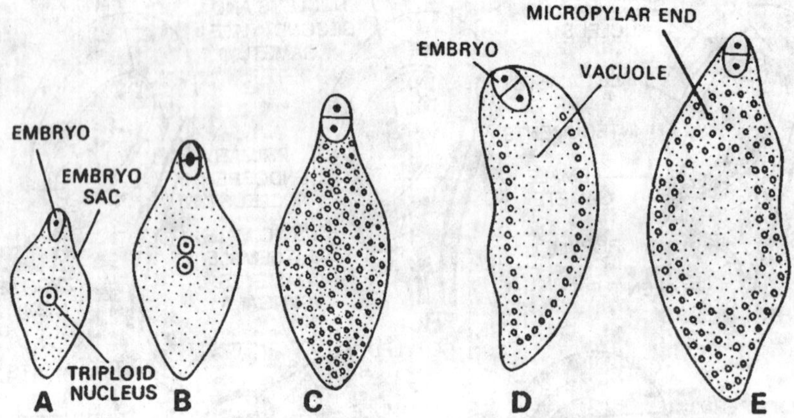

Fig. 13.40. A-E, stages in the development of nuclear type of endosperm.

The development of the endosperm of *Cocos nucifera* of Palmae deserves special mention. Here the primary endosperm nucleus undergoes a number of free nuclear divisions. When the fruit is about 50 mm long the embryo sac remains filled with a watery fluid or milk containing free nuclei and fine cytoplasmic particles. At a later stage when the fruit becomes about 100 mm in length the liquid shows in addition to free nuclei, several cells each enclosing variable number of nuclei. Gradually these cells and free nuclei set at the periphery of the cavity, and layers of cellular endosperm are formed, and this becomes the coconut meat. On maturity of coconuts the endosperm does not have free nuclei or cells. In *Areca* nut the development of the endosperm is like that of coconut but the embryo sac cavity is small, and it is completely filled up by the growth of the endosperm, and later becomes very hard.

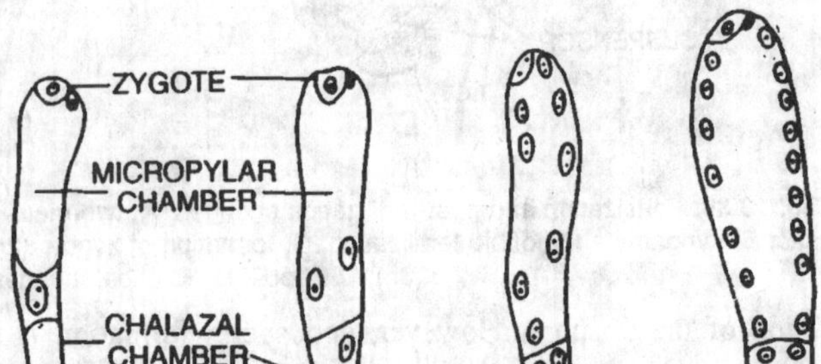

Fig. 13.41. Development of helobial type of endosperm in *Eremurus.*

The nuclear type of endosperm formation, is the most common type and found in maize, wheat, rice, sunflower, etc.

Cellular type. In this type, the first and most of the following divisions are accompanied by wall formation and thus the sac is divided into several chambers, some of which may contain more than one nucleus. The first wall is usually transverse but sometimes vertical or oblique, and in some other cases, the plane of division is not constant. On the basis of the orientation of walls following the first two or three divisions, this type of endosperm has been further divided into several subtypes.

Helobial type. This type is frequently found in the members of the order Helobiales. This type is intermediate between the **nuclear** and the **cellular** types. In this type the first division is followed by a transverse wall resulting in a micropylar and chalazal chamber. Further divisions are generally free nuclear and may be formed by the micropylar chamber only.

Eremurus is an example of a typical Helobial endosperm. Here the primary endosperm nucleus divides tranversely forming two chambers, a large micropylar and a small chalazal. Free nuclear divisions occur in both but are more rapid in micropylar chamber. Thus, when four nuclei are formed in the chalazal chamber, eight nuclei are produced in the micropylar chamber. When the chalazal chamber has eight nuclei, the micropylar chamber contains sixteen nuclei, and when there are 30 to 32 nuclei in chalazal chamber the micropylar chamber has considerably a large number of nuclei. In older ovules, the chalazal chamber begins to degenerate. Finally, when cell formation takes place in the micropylar chamber, the chalazal chamber is almost crushed and shows only a few disorganized nuclei.

DEVELOPMENT OF EMBRYO

After fertilization, the fertilized egg is called zygote or oospore which develops into an **embryo**. The oospore before it actually enters into the process undergoes a period of rest which may vary from few hours to few months. Generally the zygote (oospore) divides immediately after the first division of the primary endosperm nucleus. Unlike gymnosperms where the early stages of the development show free nuclear divisions the first division of zygote is always followed by wall-formation resulting in a two-celled proembryo. Practically there are no fundamental differences in the early stages of the development of the embryos of monocots and dicots. But in late stages, there is a marked difference between the embryos of dicotyledonous and monocotyledonous plants, hence their embryogenesis has been considered here separately.

Development of Embryo in Dicots

According to Soueges, the mode of origin of the four-celled proembryo and the contribution made by each of these cells makes the base for the classification of the embryonal type. However, Schnarf (1929), Johansen (1945) and Maheshwari (1950) have recognized *five* main types of embryos in dicotyledons. They are as follows:

I. The terminal cell of the two-celled proembryo divides by longitudinal wall.

(*i*) **Crucifer type.** Basal cell plays little or no role in the development of the embryo.

(*ii*) **Asterad type.** Basal and terminal cells play an important role in the development of the embryo.

II. The terminal cell of the two-celled proembryo divides by a transverse wall. (*a*) Basal cell plays a little or no role in the development of the embryo.

III. Solanad type. Basal cell usually forms a suspensor of two or more cells.

IV. Caryophyllod type. Basal cell does divide further.

V. Chenopodiad type. Both basal and terminal cells take part in the development of the embryo.

Here citing the example of *Capsella bursa-pastoris* (Shepherd's purse), the detailed study of **Crucifer type** of the development of the embryo has been given.

Development of dicot embryo in *Capsella bursa-pastoris* (Crucifer type). For the first time Hanstein (1870) worked out the details of the development of embryo in *Capsella bursa-pastoris*, a member of Crucifeae.

The oospore divides transversely forming two cells, a **terminal cell** and **basal cell**. The cell towards the micropylar end of the embryo sac is the **suspensor cell** (*i.e.*, basal cell) and the other one makes to the **embryo cell** (*i.e.*, terminal cell). The terminal cell by subsequent divisions gives rise to the embryo while the basal cell contributes the formation of **suspensor**. The terminal cell divides by a vertical division forming a 4-celled 1-shaped embryo. In certain plants the basal cell also forms the hypocoty1 (*i.e.*, the root end of the embryo) in addition of suspensor. The terminal

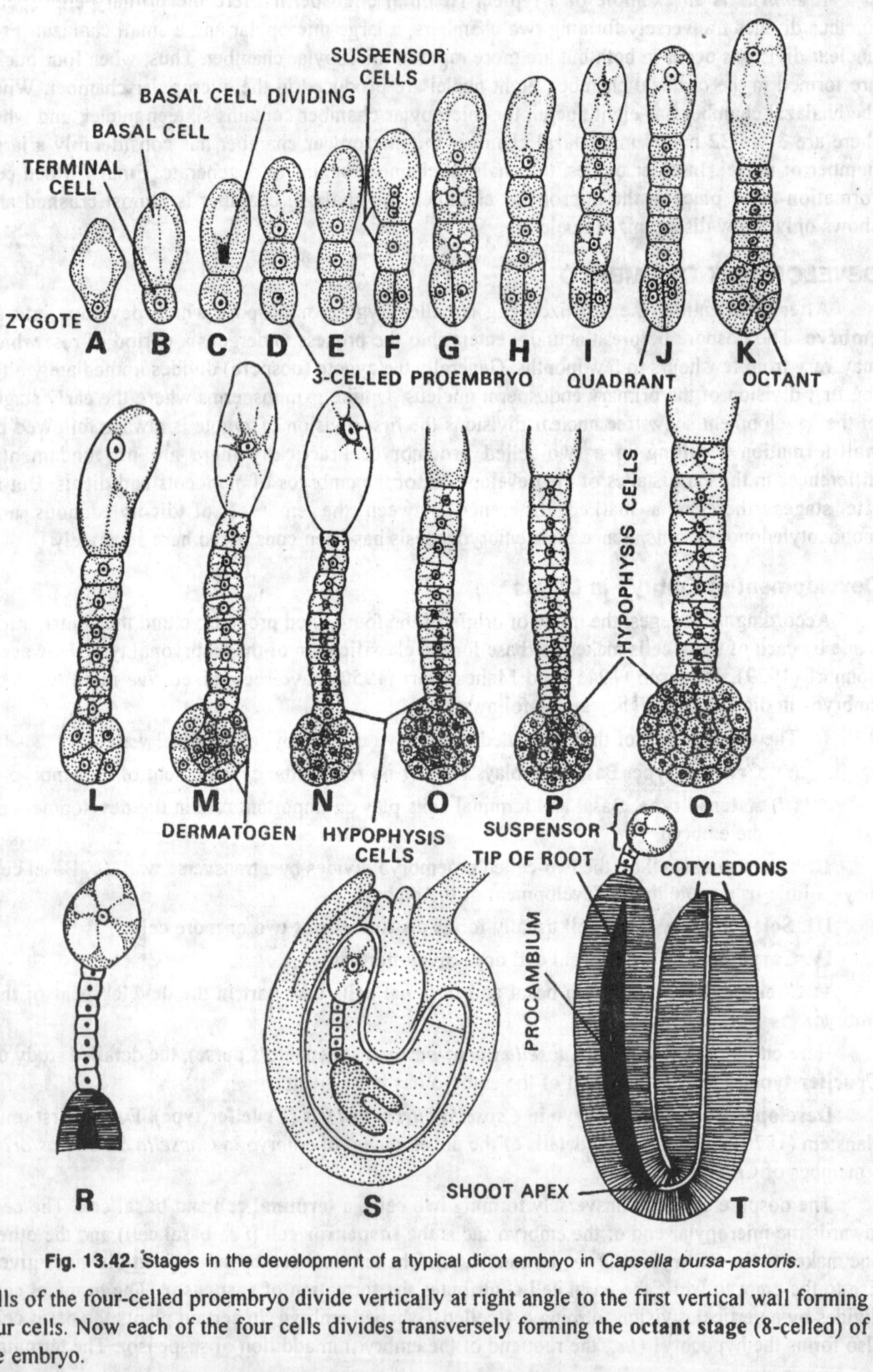

Fig. 13.42. Stages in the development of a typical dicot embryo in *Capsella bursa-pastoris*.

cells of the four-celled proembryo divide vertically at right angle to the first vertical wall forming four cells. Now each of the four cells divides transversely forming the **octant stage** (8-celled) of the embryo.

The four cells next to the suspensor are termed the **hypobasal** or **posterior octants** while the remaining four cells make the **epibasal** or **anterior octants.** The epibasal octants give rise to **plumule** and the **cotyledons,** whereas the hybobasal octants give rise to the hypocotyl with the exception of its tip. Now all the eight cells of the octant divide periclinally forming outer and inner cells. The outer cells divide further by anticlinal division forming a peripheral layer of epidermal cells, the **dermatogen.** The inner cells divide by longitudinal and transverse divisions forming **periblem** beneath the dermatogen and **plerome** in the central region. The cells of periblem give rise to the cortex while that of plerome form the stele.

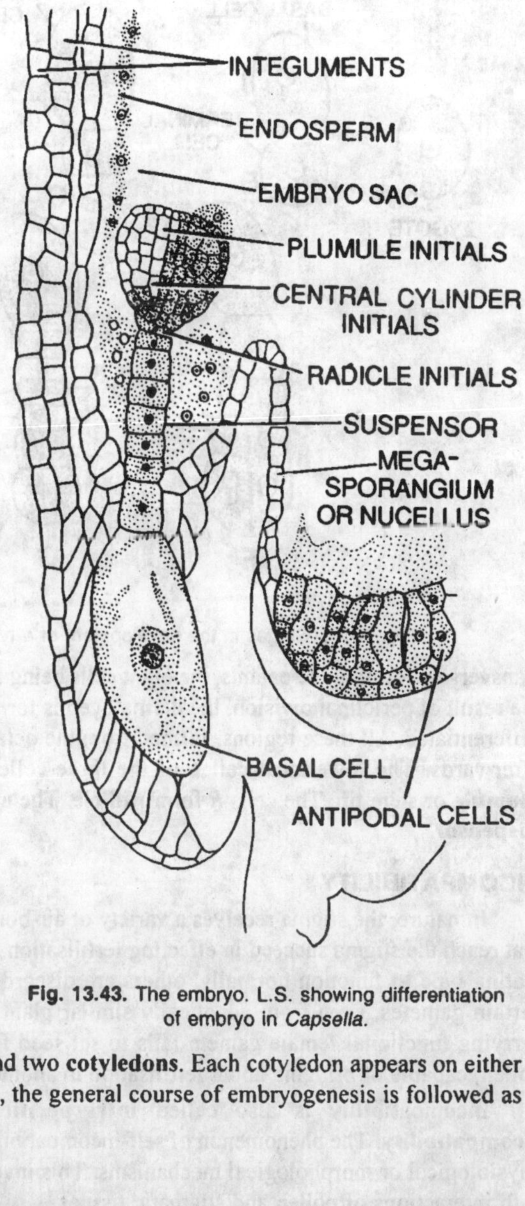

Fig. 13.43. The embryo. L.S. showing differentiation of embryo in *Capsella*.

At the time of the development of the octant stage of embryo the two basal cells divide transversely forming a 6-10 celled filament, the suspensor which attains its maximum development by the time embryo attains globular stage. The suspensor pushes the embryo cells down into the endosperm. The distal cell of the suspensor is much larger than the other cells and acts as a **haustorium.** The lowermost cell of the suspensor is known as **hypophysis.** By further divisions, the hypophysis gives rise to the embryonic root and root cap.

With the continuous growth, the embryo becomes heart-shaped which is made up of two primordia of cotyledons. The mature embryo consists of a **short axis** and two **cotyledons**. Each cotyledon appears on either side of the hypocotyl. In most of dicotyledons, the general course of embryogenesis is followed as seen in *Capsella bursa-pastoris*.

Development of Embryo in Monocots

There is no essential difference between the monocotyledons and the dicotyledons regarding the early cell divisions of the proembryo, but the mature embryos are quite different in two groups. Here the embryogeny of *Sagittaria sagittifolia* has been given as one of the examples.

The zygote divides transversely forming the terminal cell and the basal cell. The basal cell, which is the larger and lies towards the micropylar end, does not divide again but becomes transformed directly into a large vesicular cell. The terminal cell divides transversely forming the two cells. Of these, the lower cell divides vertically forming a pair of juxtaposed cells, and the middle cell divides transversely into two cells. In the next stage, the two cells once again divide vertically forming quadrants. The cell next to the quadrants also divides vertically and the cell next to the upper vesicular divides several times transversely. The quadrants now divide

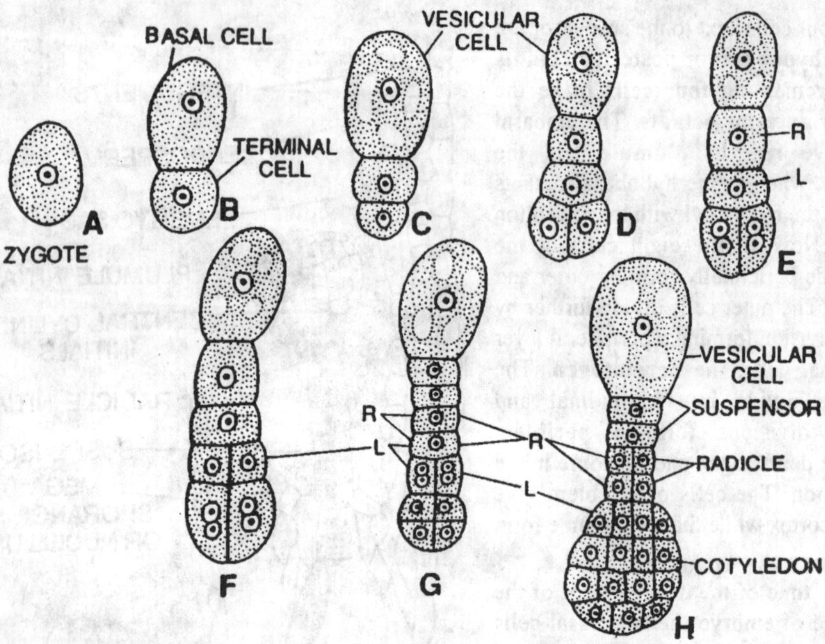

Fig. 13.44. Stages in the development of a typical monocot embryo in *Sagittaria*.

transversely forming the octants, the eight cells being arranged in two tiers of four cells each. With the result of periclinal division, the dermatogen is formed. Later the periblem and plerome are also differentiated. All these regions, formed from the octants develop into a single terminal cotyledon afterwards. The lowermost cell *L* of the three-celled suspensor divides vertically to form the **plumule** or stem tip. The cells *R* form **radicle**. The upper 3-6 cells contribute to the formation of **suspensor.**

INCOMPATIBILITY

In nature, the stigma receives a variety of air-borne or insect-carried pollen but not all pollen that reach the stigma succeed in effecting fertilisation. The pistil allows the pollen of only the right mating type to function normally, others are discarded. Thus, incompatibility is the inability of certain gametes, even from genetically similar plant species, to fuse with each other. If a pistil carrying functional female gamete fails to set seed following pollination with viable and fertile pollen, capable of bringing about fertilisation in another pistil, the two are said to be incompatible.

Incompatibility is also called **intraspecific incompatibility, self-sterility** or **self-incompatibility**. The phenomenon of self-incompatibility is geneally due to the prevention of some physiological or morphological mechanisms. This involves many complex mechanisms associated with interactions of pollen and stigmatic tissues.

Self-Incompatibility

A large number of flowering plants are successfully fertilised only by the pollen of other plants and not by their own. Such flowering plants are called **outbreeders.** In nature different floral adaptations, such as dichogamy, herkogamy and unisexuality have evolved to prevent self-pollination but the most widespread and effective natural device in such plants is seif-incompatibility, which refers to the inability of a plant producing functional male and female gametes to set seeds when self-pollinated.

Depending on the origin of factors determining the mating types on the pollen side, two categories of self-incompatibility have been recognised:

(*i*) Sporophytic incompatibility. Where the incompatibility is due to the genotype of the sporophytic stigmatic tissues, *e.g.*, in Asteraceae, Brassicaceae, etc.

(*ii*) Gametophytic incompatibility. Where the incompatibility is due to the genotype of pollen, *e.g.*, in Poaceae, Liliaceae, Solanaceae, etc. This may be due to prevention of pollen germination, retardation of growth, deorientation of pollen tube, or even failure of nuclear fusion. It is controlled by genes with multiple alleles (S-allele). Usually, it develops with the maturation of stigma.

Biological significance of incompatibility. In nature a balanced breeding of the plants is regulated by incompatibility. Extensive selfing of the plants leads to highly homozygous individuals which have a very low survival value. To overcome this, nature has imposed self-incompatibility.

Despite the natural value, incompatibility may turn out to be a serious hurdle in a plant improvement programme. For example, before the introduction of anther culture technique selfing was one of the chief methods to obtain homozygous individuals. For several plants where anther culture has failed to yield haploids, self-pollination continues to be an important approach to achieve this. In this context, self-incompatibility is a serious problem.

SPECIAL MODES OF REPRODUCTION

The vegetative and sexual modes of reproduction are generally normal and occur in nature. There are cases of special modes of reproduction where propagation takes place without the act of fertilisation. Some special modes are mentioned here:

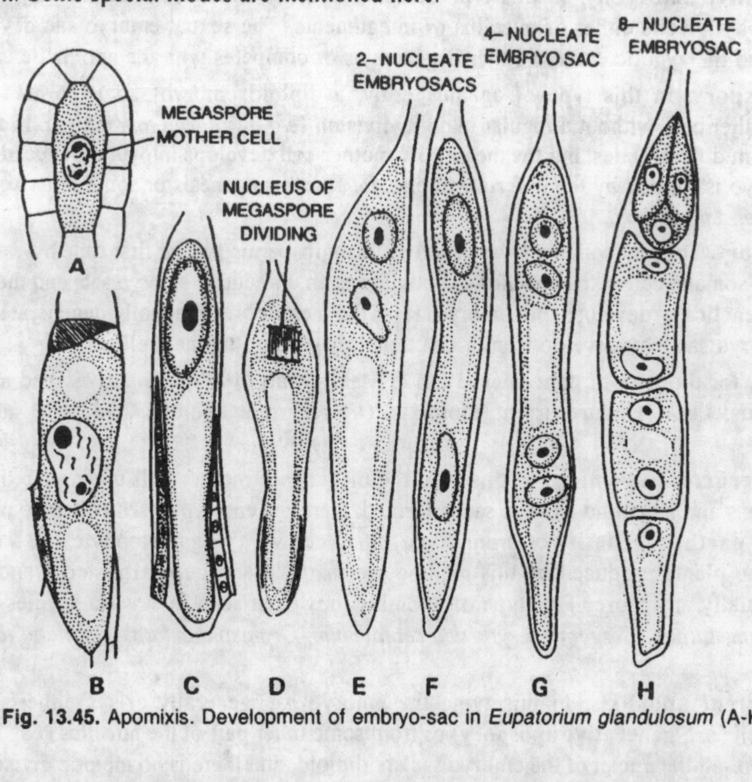

Fig. 13.45. Apomixis. Development of embryo-sac in *Eupatorium glandulosum* (A-H).

Apomixis

According to Winkler (1908, 1934), the substitution for sexual reproduction of an asexual process which does not involve any nuclear fusion. The term **apomixis** (*apo* = without; *mixis* = mingling) is a general one, and covers all types of asexual reproduction which tend to replace, or to act as substitute for the sexual method. This phenomenon covers all the non-sexual methods of reproduction in which the reproducing spores are developed without fusion, whereas the normal sexual cycle (**amphimixis**) involves two important processes : (*a*) **meiosis,** that transforms a diploid (2n) sporophytic cell into four haploid (*n*) gametophytic cells, and (*b*) **fertilization,** where two haploid gametes of opposite sex fuse and re-establish the diploid sporophytic generation. Thus, in a sexual cycle, a diploid (2*n*) or sporophytic generation alternates with the haploid (*n*) or gametophytic generation. In angiosperms, the gametophytic generations are very short and are represented by embryo sac on the female side and microspore or pollen grain on the male side. The remaining part of the life-cycle represents the sporophytic generation.

The plants where the usual sexual reproduction has been completely replaced by a type of asexual reproduction are called **apomictic**, and the phenomenon, **apomixis.**

There are two main categories of apomixis, *i.e.*, **1. Agamospermy** and **2. Vegetative reproduction.**

Agamospermy

In this category of apomixis the plants have retained seed as the agent of propagation but the embryo is formed by some process in which normal meiosis and syngamy have been eliminated. This phenomenon is known as **agamospermy**. There are three different types of agamospermy.

1. Adventive embryony. In this type of agamospermy, embryos arise directly from the diploid sporophytic cells either of nucellus or integuments. The sexual embryo sac develops in normal way and the zygotic embryo either degenerates or competes with the apomictic embryos.

2. Diplospory. In this type of agamospermy, a diploid embryo sac is formed from a megaspore mother cell, without a regular meiotic division (*e.g.*, in *Aerva tomentosa*). In this type an archesporium differentiates, but the megaspore mother cell develops into an unreduced embryo sac. The embryo is formed by the unfertilized egg, *i.e.*, parthenogenesis or some other cell of the embryo sac, *i.e.*, apogamety.

3. Apospory. This phenomenon was reported in angiosperms for the first time by Rosenberg (1907). Here a somatic cell in the nucellus directly forms an unreduced embryo sac, and the diploid egg parthenogenetically develops into embryo. Here the megaspores gradually degenerate and the aposporic embryo sac may develop from a functional megaspore mother cell.

However, for the sake of convenience Dr. P. Maheshwari (1950) has sub-divided apomixis into three types, *i.e.*, (*i*) nonrecurrent apomixis, (*ii*) recurrent apomixis, and (*iii*) adventive embryony.

1. Non-recurrent apomixis. In this type the megaspore mother cell undergoes the usual meiotic divisions and a haploid embryo sac is formed. Here the embryo arises either from the egg (*i.e.*, **haploid parthenogenesis**) or from some other cell of the gametophyte (*i.e.*, **haploid apogamy**). The plants produced by this method are, haploid and generally sterile and do not reproduce sexually any more. This type of apomixis has been seen in several species such as *Solanum nigrum, Lilium, Bergenia, Erythraea centaurium, Orchis maculata, Nicotiana tabacum,* etc.

2. Recurrent apomixis. In this type, the embryo sac generally arises either from an archesporial cell (*i.e.*, **generative apospory**) or from some other part of the nucellus (*i.e.*, **somatic apospory**). Here all the nuclei of the embryo sac are diploid, and there is no meiotic division. The embryo arises either from the egg (**diploid parthenogenesis**) or from some other cell of the gametophyte (**diploid apogamy**). Generative apospory has been observed in *Eupatorium glandulosum, Parthenium argentatum*, etc. Somatic apospory has been reported in *Hieracium excelens, H. flagellare* and *H. aurantiacum.*

3. Adventive embryony. This type of apomixis is also known as **sporophytic budding**. Here, the developed embryo sacs may be haploid or diploid, but the embryos do not arise from the cells of nucellus or the integument. There is no alternation of generations, because the diploid tissues of the present sporophyte directly give rise to the new embryo. Adventive embryony has been frequently reported in *Citrus, Euphorbia dulcis, Capparis frondosa, Mangifera indica* and *Hiptage madablota.*

Significance of apomixis. The most important apomictic crop plants are citrus, mango, mangosteen and black berries. As a reproductive system, it offers the possibility of the indefinite propagation of specially favourable biotypes, which may be highly heterozygous or sexually sterile. In obligate apomixis, this advantage is served at the expense of the long term evolutionary flexibility which is the gift of sexuality. However, in facultative apomixis, where sexual and apomictic members co-exist, the phenomenon is of special significance.

Vegetative Reproduction

In this type of apomixis, the new individual arises from a group of undifferentiated or differentiated cells, where neither embryo nor seed are produced. This type of reproduction takes place by means of bulbs, bulbils, tubers, runners, suckers, etc. Such propagules are formed by the sporophyte only. Gustafsson (1946) has distinguished three types of vegetative reproduction in angiosperms : 1. In this type, the propagules are formed outside the floral regions; though the sex organs are formed, yet no fertilization or seed setting takes place, *e.g.*, in *Agave americana* and *Elodea canadensis*. 2. In this type, the propagules are formed outside the floral regions, and the plants are sexually sterile, as found in *Fritillaria imperialis* and *Lilium bulbiferum*. 3. In this type, the propagules are formed on the floral branches either in addition to the flowers or in place of them. This phenomenon is commonly known as **vivipary**. This term is also used for those plants (*e.g.*, mangrove vegetation), in which sexually formed seeds germinate on the mother plant. Here the term vivipary will be used as **vegetative vivipary.** The vegetative vivipary is commonly found in grasses, *e.g.*, *Festuca, Poa,* and in *Allium*. The vegetative vivipary is actually an adaptation for the multiplication of a genotype under a set of environmental conditions which prevent or check to some extent the opportunity for normal pollination. However, most of the vegetative viviparous races have not lost the capacity for flowering and normal seed setting, *e.g.*, a grass, *Deschampsia caespitosa* is sexually reproducing in Sweden, while growing by vegetative vivipary in California.

Apospory

The apospory (*apo* = without) is the development of the gametophyte from a cell of the sporophyte without the intervention of a spore. In angiosperms, this phenomenon was for the first time reported by Rosenberg (1907) in *Hieracium* spp. Here the megaspore mother cell undergoes the usual meiotic divisions and forms a tetrad. In the angiosperms it is sometimes seen that an embryo may be formed from the diploid cells of the nucellus, as in *Citrus, Mangifera, Opuntia*, etc., or even from those of integument, as in *Allium cepa*. The embryo thus formed is pushed into the embryo sac during the course of its development. Since the nucellus or the integument belongs to the sporophyte, the production of the embryo from the tissue of the sporophyte without the intervention of the spore is a case of apospory.

In the aposporic members of the Asteraceae, only one nucellar cell acts as the mother cell and gives rise to a normal 8- nucleate embryo sac, while in the grasses, more than one aposporic embryo sac may develop in the same nucellus, and the organization of mature embryo sac is 4-nucleate.

Parthenogenesis

The development of the zygote from the egg-cell without the act of fertilization, or in other words, formation of embryo from an unfertilized egg is called **parthenogenesis**. In some species of angiosperms, the embryo develops parthenogenetically. In such cases the embryo may develop from haploid egg-cell or diploid egg-cell. In apomicts of Asteraceae and Rubiaceae, the development of embryo is independent of the pollination stimulus. However, in many other apomicts, the embryo develops only after pollination, and the phenomenon is known as **pseudogamy**, *e.g.*, many apomictic grasses. According to Heslop-Harrison (1972) there are three roles of pollination in pseudogamy: (*i*) to activate the growth of ovary and ovule, (*ii*) to supply the male nucleus for the development of the endosperm, and (*iii*) to stimulate the parthenogenesis.

In most of grass apomicts, the egg may divide parthenogenetically but the proembryo ceases to grow unless and until the endosperm develops. Here, the development of endosperm occurs only after the fusion of the male nucleus with the polars, and therefore, a mature apomictic embryo in these plants is formed only after pollination.

Significance of parthenogenesis. The role of parthenogenesis in nature is severely limited; the zygogenesis and other methods of reproduction are predominant. The reason is thought to be that parthenogenetic species are not adaptable enough. In ameiotic parthenogenesis, genetic variability is practically nil. In meiotic parthenogenesis, individuals tend to become homozygous, and cause the accompanying disadvantage of this condition.

The advantages of this phenomenon are several fold. In meiotic parthenogenesis which applies to homozygous genotypes, advantageous combinations of genes are maintained instead of dispersed by meiosis as in zygogenetic species. Well adapted forms thus spread rapidly, as long as the enviornmental conditions remain unchanged. As Peacock (1961) reports, the existence of hardly triploid organism becomes possible in ameiotic parthenogenesis.

Parthenocarpy

In certain cases of angiosperms the ovary normally develops into a fruit without pollination and fertilization. This type of free development of fruit is known as **parthenocarpy.** Such fruits (parthenocarpic fruits) are always seedless. Sometimes the fruit formation may be induced by artificial pollination by foreign pollen from another species, but without subsequent fertilization. The parthenocarpy may also be induced by the spraying of growth promoting substances, such as naphthalene acetic acid NAA. This is called **induced parthenocarpy.** The examples of parthenocarpy are commonly found in banana, papaya, pineapple, guava, grapes, apple, *Thalictrum, Alchemilla*, etc.

In modern days, a lot of work has been done to produce seedless fruit on seeded varieties by controlling pollination and applying certain chemical subtances to the pistil. Thimann (1934) suggested that many pollen grains possess considerable quantities of growth substances. Gustaffson (1938) used several growth substances, such as IAA, IBA, α-NAA and phenylacetic acid mixed in the lanolin paste of about 0.5 to 1 per cent strength and smeared on the stigma to produce parthenocarpic fruits. Among the species where the fruits can be set by auxins are tomato, tobacco, pepper, figs and blackberry. Here, the fruits which have been set by treating unpollinated flowers are seedless. Nitsch and other, workers used α-NAA in aqueous form to induce parthenocarpy by atomizer. Crane (1964) induced parthenocarpy in tomatoes, apples and pears by gibberellins. Cytokinins have also been used in the induction of parthenocarpy in certain fruits.

In addition to induced parthenocarpy, the natural parthenocarpy may occur in certain species. Many horticultural varieties of bananas, pineapples, cucumber, tomatoes and figs exist, where seedless fruits are normally produced without the need for any exogenous hormone. In some species, the fruits are formed without pollination while in others, pollination is necessary but fertilization does not occur, in still others fertilization occurs but the embryos abort before the fruits mature. It is not understood clearly how the growth of these parthenocarpic fruits is controlled, but it is thought that in some cases the maternal tissues, such as the placentae may produce auxin in the absence of normal embryos. It has been noticed that the ovaries of unopened flowers of parthenocarpic varieties of orange and *Vitis vinifera* (grape) possess a higher auxin content than those of normal seeded varieties.

POLYEMBRYONY

The occurrence of more than one embryo in the seed is known as **polyembryony**. Polyembryony is quite common among conifers (gymnosperms), but many species both of dicots and monocots (angiosperms) exhibit this phenomenon. Usually there are two main types of polyembryony, *i.e.*, 1. **true polyembryony** and 2. **false polyembryony.**

1. True Polyembryony

The true polyembryony may be subdivided into two types: (*i*) **cleavage polyembryony,** where the embryos arise within an embryo sac, either by a cleavage of the egg, or from the synergids, antipodals or endosperm; (*ii*) **adventive polyembryony**, where the embryos arise from the tissues living outside the embryo sac, *i.e.*, the cells of the nucellus or the integuments, but generally they come to lie within the embryo sac.

2. False Polyembryony

Sometimes the polyembryony occurs due to the presence of multiple embryo sacs within the ovule. They may arise from: (*a*) the derivatives of the same megaspore mother cell; (*b*) from two or more megaspore mother cells, or (*c*) from nucellus cells (*i.e.*, apospory).

Importance of Polyembryony

This phenomenon plays an important role in plant breeding and horticulture. Nucellar adventive polyembryony is of great value in horticulture, where the nucellar seedlings of *Citrus* have been proved to be better clones of orchard stock than cuttings. On the other hand, the nucellar embryos are supposed to be free from disease, and the nucellar seedlings rejuvenate the vigour that is generally lost after continued cutting propagation. The adventive polyembryony is much useful in the propagation of the fruit trees, such as *Citrus* and *Mango*. The application of adventive embryos is also important for providing genetically uniform seedlings in fruit trees.

The haploids can be used for the development of homozygous diploid, which are of much value. Due to the practical value of haploids in plant breeding, the methods have been recognized for the artificial production of these embryos from the eggs or synergids.

VEGETATIVE REPRODUCTION

In vegetative propagation, any part of the plant, *i.e.*, stem, root, leaf or even buds are capable to give rise to new plants. The most striking example of such reproductive capacity is seen in the leaves of *Bryophyllum*. Like other leaves they too carry on photosynthesis, their usual function, but in addition they have the capacity to produce one or more plants from the notches in their margins. If one keeps a leaf of *Bryophyllum* on damp soil, within a day or two the buds appear in the notches of the margin of leaf. These buds would later form new plants, complete with roots, leaves and stem.

More often the capacity for vegetative propagation resides in roots, *e.g.*, in sweet potato, asparagus and dahlia, or stems, *e.g.*, in ginger, turmeric, banana, potato, onion, sugarcane and canna. In all these cases the plant parts possess the power of **regeneration,** which means that a part of the plant can either replace its lost portion or bring forth a new adult plant.

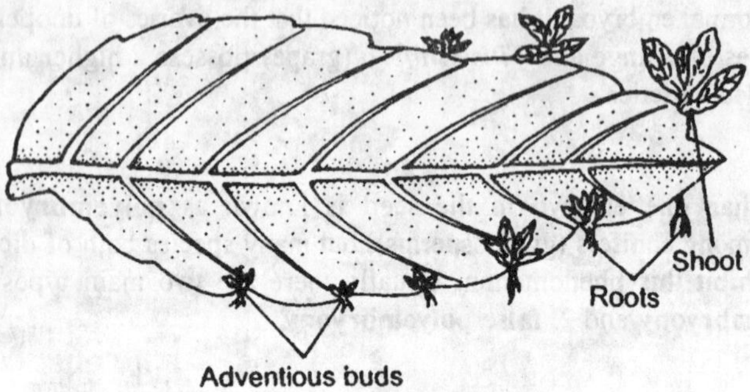

Fig. 13.46. *Bryophyllum.* Buds on margin of leaf.

Fig. 13.47. Tuberous roots of sweet potato.

The capacity for regeneration is quite common in most higher plants and has been put to great use by mankind since time immemorial. Thus, rose, coleus, pothos and glory of garden (*Bougainvillaea*) are generally propagated by placing their stem cuttings in moist soil. The cuttings soon strike roots and grow into new plants.

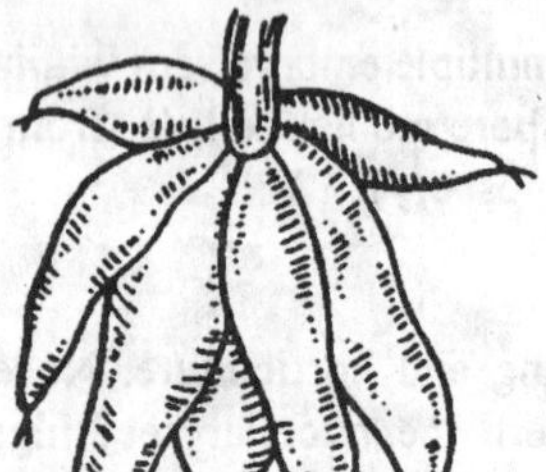

Fig. 13.48. Fasciculated tuberous roots of *Dahlia.*

Fig. 13.49. Underground modified stem rhizome of ginger with bud.

Cutting, grafting and layering are generally referred to as artificial methods of vegetative propagation. The resulting offspring are normally identical, and resemble the parent forms in almost all respects. Gardeners generally use these methods for getting plants of same types.

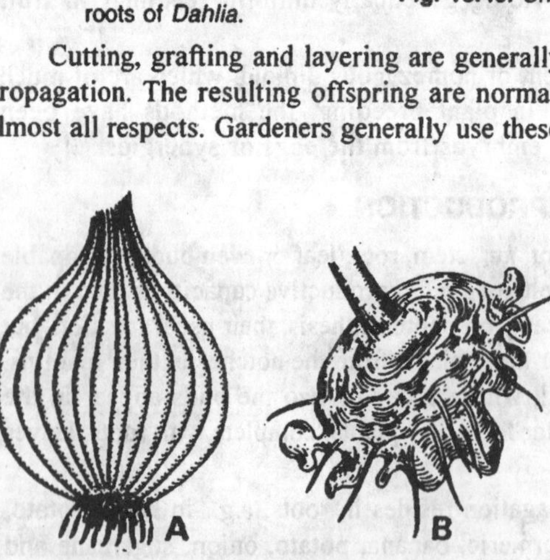

Fig. 13.50. Underground modified stems.

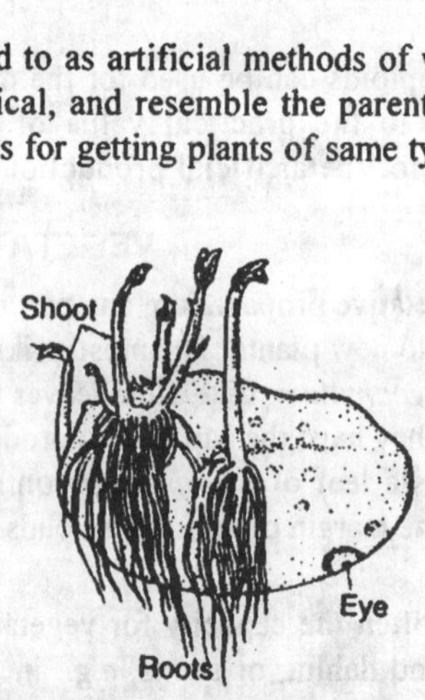

Fig. 13.51. Underground modified stem of potato.

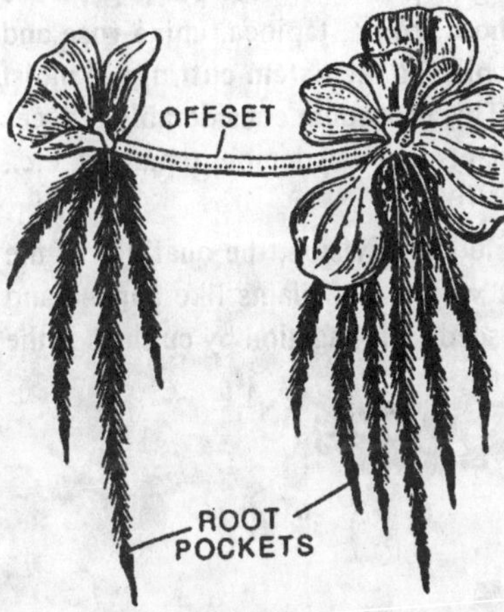

Fig. 13.52. Sub-aerial modification of stem of *Pistia*.

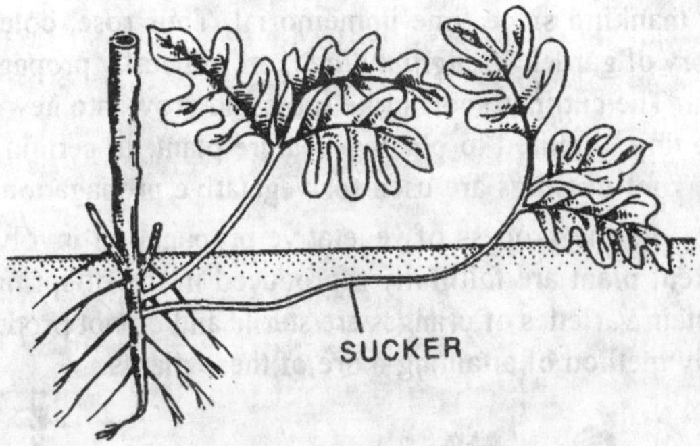

Fig. 13.53. Sub-aerial modification of stem of *Chrysanthemum*.

The methods of vegetative reproduction may be grouped into two categories, *i.e.*, (*i*) natural methods and (*ii*) artificial methods.

1. Natural methods. In such methods of vegetative propagation, a portion of the plant gets detached from the mother plant and develops into a new independent plant under suitable environmental conditions. The detached parts may be roots, stems, leaves or flowers.

The most striking example of such reproductive capacity is seen in the leaves of *Bryophyllum*. Like other leaves they too carry on photosynthesis, their usual function, but in addition they have the capacity to produce one or more plants from the notches in their margins. If one keeps a leaf of *Bryophyllum* on damp soil, within a day or two the buds appear in the notches of the margin of leaf. These buds would later form new plants, complete with roots, leaves and stem.

More often the capacity for vegetative propagation resides in roots (*e.g.*, in sweet potato, asparagus and dahlia) or stems (*e.g.*, in ginger, turmeric, banana, potato, onion, zamikand, sugarcane and canna). In all these cases the plant parts possess the power of **regeneration**, which means that a part of the plant can either replace its lost portion or bring forth a new adult plant. The stem of plants with subaerial modifications, as in *Pistia*, *Chrysanthemum*, *Eichhornia* and pine apple are also used for propagating plants.

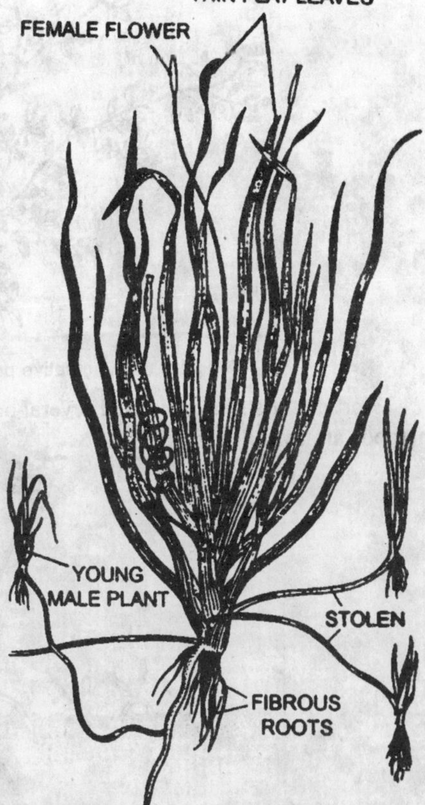

Fig. 13.54. Vegetative propagation in *Vallisneria spiralis* by means of stolons.

In plants, such as *Agave*, *Dioscorea* and *Oxalis*, small buds develop near the flower, leaf axil and tuberous root, respectively, to give rise to new plants. The capacity of regeneration is quite common in most higher plants. In *Vallisneria* (a submerged water plant), vegetative propagation takes place by means of stolons.

2. Artificial methods. The capacity for regeneration in higher plants has been put to great use by mankind since time immemorial. Thus rose, coleus, pothos, croton, tapioca, china rose and glory of garden (*Bougainvillaea*) are generally propagated by placing their **stem cuttings** in moist soil. The cuttings soon strike roots and grow into new plants. This procedure considerably reduces the time required to obtain a mature plant. In certain other plants, such as lemon, tamarind, etc., the **root cuttings** are used for vegetative propagation.

As the process of vegetative propagation involves simple cell division, the qualities of the parent plant are faithfully reproduced in the offspring. Some very useful plants like banana and certain varieties of oranges are sterile and do not produce any seeds. Propagation by cuttings is the only method of attaining more of these plants.

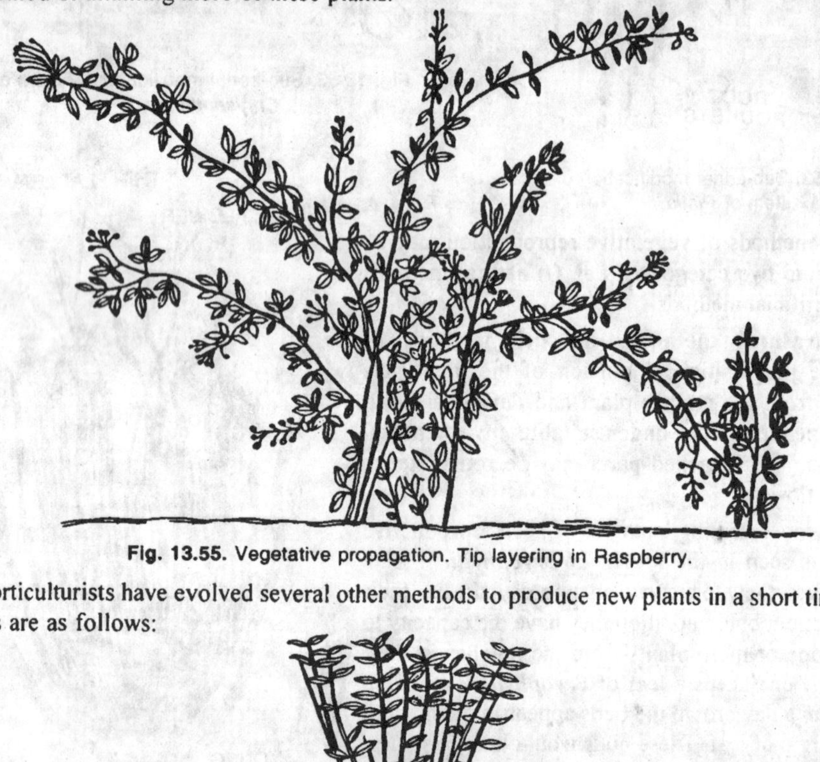

Fig. 13.55. Vegetative propagation. Tip layering in Raspberry.

Horticulturists have evolved several other methods to produce new plants in a short time. The methods are as follows:

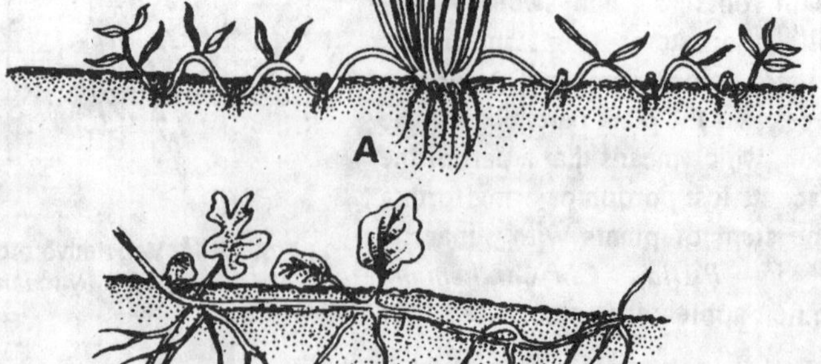

Fig. 13.56. Layering. A, serpentine layering; B, trench layering.

Layering. This is one of the most common methods used for propagating plants such as rose, jasmine, grape vine, lemon, rhododendrons and magnolias.

Layering is the development of roots on a stem while it is still attached to the parent plant. The stem or branch that develops adventitious roots while still attached to the parent plant is called a **layer**. This is a natural means of reproduction in black raspberries and trailing blackberries. Layering can be artificially induced in many plants. It can be induced by bending the branch to the ground and covering a medium portion of it below the soil. The apical portion of the branch is left exposed to the air to form the leaves. The part below the soil develops adventitious roots. Now the connection of the layered branch can be cut from the parent plant and grown independently.

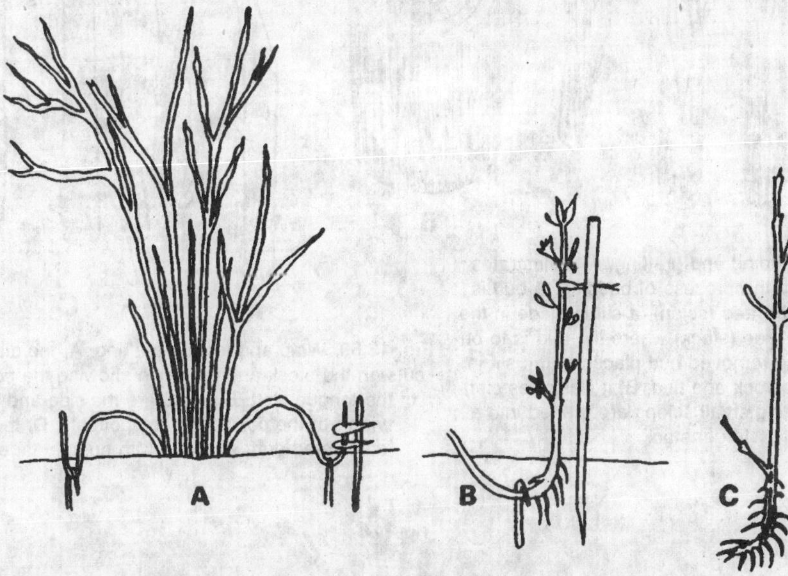

Fig. 13.57. Common method of layering. A, the branches of the plants are bent and buried under the soil; B, buried part, after it develops roots; C, the cut part is separately planted.

Grafting. This is another method in which man has remarkably exploited the regenerative capacity of higher plants. It is generally practiced in plants which do not root easily or have a weak root system. It is an art of joining parts of two plants of the same or allied species in such a way as to bring about an organic union or fusion of the tissues. This method is practiced in mango, apple, pear, citrus, guava, rose and rubber plant.

It is a common experience that from a mango tree grown a good seed will not always bear fruit of the same quality as the parent tree. Other cultivated fruit trees also show such variations. Under such conditions one may resort to grafting. In this process, a detached part of one plant is inserted into the stem or root system of another plant. The former is called **scion** (short piece of detached shoot containing several dormant buds) and the latter **stock** (longer portion of the plant which is fixed to the soil by its root system). The **scion** is generally taken from the plant having superior characters.

In successful grafting, the object is to connect or fit two pieces of living plants in such a way that they will unite and subsequently behave as one plant. This is done in such a way that the cambium tissue of both (scion and stock) comes in contact and forms a cambium layer common to both. Consequently, the two **scion** and **stock** grow together. The place where they are grafted is covered with grafting wax to avoid infection. The scion becomes a part of the plant into which it is grafted. This plant bears flowers and fruits characteristic of the **scion**. At this junction of graft,

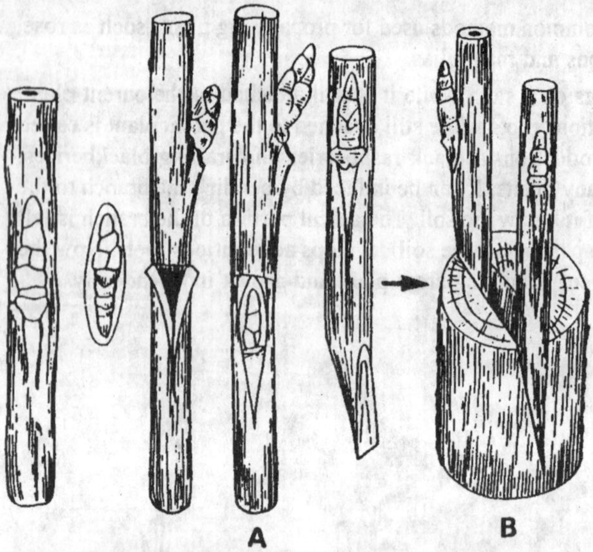

Fig. 13.58. Budding and grafting. A, it illustrates three stages in the process of budding. A bud is removed from the tree (scion), a slit is made in the bark of another tree (stock) where the bud is to be planted and the removed bud placed in the slit in the bark of the stock and tied; B, it illustrates cleft or wedge grafting small scions are grafted into a larger stock.

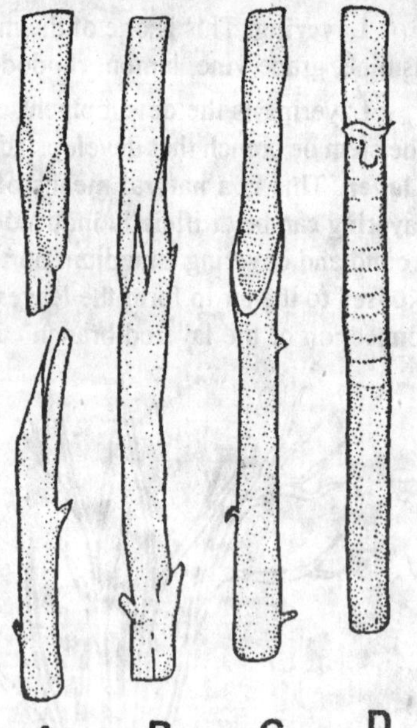

Fig. 13.59. Whip and tongue grafting. A, the diagonal cuts on the stock and the scion showing the portion of the tongue cleft. B and C are the side and face views of the positioned components; D, the completed graft wrapped with nursery tape.

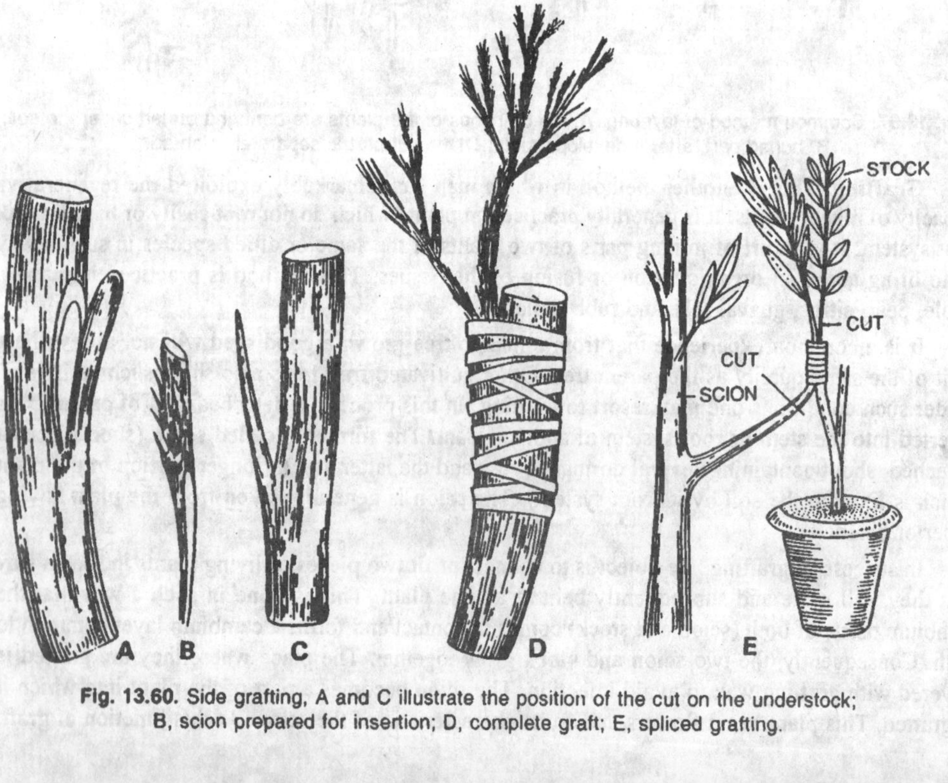

Fig. 13.60. Side grafting, A and C illustrate the position of the cut on the understock; B, scion prepared for insertion; D, complete graft; E, spliced grafting.

union a mass of parenchyma tissue develops from the living cells of both stock and the scion. This tissue heals the wound and is called **callus**. Its appearance marks successful grafting.

Gootee. This method is usually employed for vegetative propagation of lemon, orange, guava and litchi during rainy season. In this process, a healthy and woody branch is selected and the bark is sliced off in a ring form of about 3-5 cm in length. A thick plaster of grafting clay is wrapped up with rag and tied around the debarked portion. The 'grafting clay' is prepared by mixing cow-dung, finely cut hay and water. The tied up portion is kept moist by suitable supply of water. In about 2 or 3 months the roots come out and 'gootee' is ready to be cut below the tied rag for propagation.

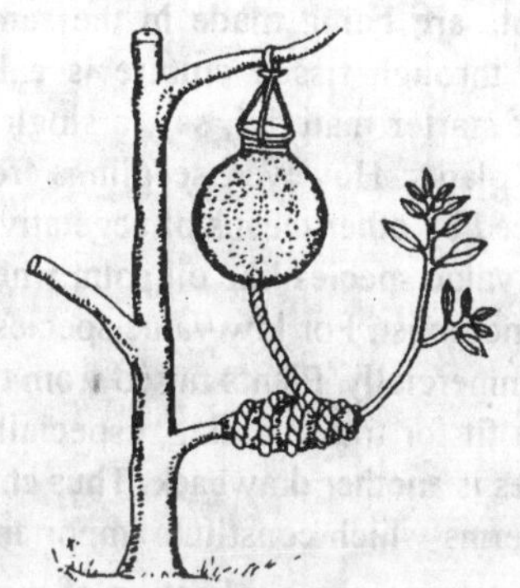

Fig. 13.61. Gootee. Method usually employed for vegetative propagation of lemon, orange, litichi, etc.

Significance of Vegetative Reproduction

1. Plants in which useful characters of parents have to be maintained, are propagated vegetatively.
2. The plants which do not produce viable seeds are propagated by this method.
3. Plants with reduced power of sexual reproduction, long dormant period of seed or poor viability are multiplied easily through this method.
4. The plants which are unable to produce seeds as a result of self-pollination cannot breed true. Such plants bear flowers that are only cross-pollinated and thus there is always mixture of characters. Such plants cannot produce seeds that will germinate to give rise to plants exactly like the parent. In such cases, vegetative propagation is the only method to get true to type plants.
5. Vegetative reproduction also helps in removing common infections from the parent plant.
6. Plants raised through vegetative propagation from a single plant constitute a genetically uniform population, the **clone**. Whereas plants developed from seeds may show variations due to genetic recombination and segregation thus by propagating plants through vegetative means a large stock of selected strains can be built up and maintained without losing the desirable characters.
7. It helps to perpetuate particular form of plants. In some individuals young stage of plants is quite different from the adult form. In order to maintain this young or juvenile form, vegetative propagation is essential.
8. Grafting helps in getting an economically important plant having useful characters of two different individuals in a short time.
9. It is a cheap and rapid method of propagation of the plants with long periods of seed dormancy.

Micropropagation

Tissue culture serves as an alternative to vegetative propagation by conventional methods, such as by rooting of cuttings. This is particularly valuable in the case of difficult-to-root species and those species like the palms which can neither be rooted by cuttings nor grafted because they lack a cambium. Recently, genetically uniform oil palms (*Elaeis guineensis*) have been produced by tissue culture.

Attempts are being made in the same direction with the coconut palm also. Vegetative propagation through tissue culture is called **micropropagation**, because it uses very small quantities of starter material, say, a single cutting or even a few grams of tissue to regenerate hundreds of plants. However, seedlings from tissue cultures are relatively more expensive than those produced by other means of vegetative propagation such as cuttings. Therefore, it is applied only to high value species like oil palm where, moreover, other alternative vegetative propagation methods do not exist. For low value species such as *Eucalyptus* rooted coppice shoot cuttings are still used commercially. Plants raised from tissue cultures require a longer hardening period before they become fit for transplanting, especially in harsh forest environments. Genetic instability of callus cultures is another drawback. Thus chromosome abnormalities are common in tissue cultures of Gymnosperms which constitute important components of temperate and arboreal forests.

In recent years, the application of micropropagation techniques as an alternative means of asexual propagation of important plants has increased the interest of workers in various fields. The micropropagation techniques are preferred over the conventional asexual propagation methods due to following reasons:

(*i*) In this method only a small amount of tissue is needed as the initial explant for regeneration of millions of clonal plants in a year.

(*ii*) This method provides a possible alternative method for developing resistance in many species.

(*iii*) It provides a mean for international exchange of plant materials, hence the problem for introduction of disease can be solved in quarantine.

(*iv*) Stock can be quickly proliferated *in vitro* as it is not season dependent.

(*v*) Valuable germplasm can be stored for a long time.

Application in horticulture and forestry. Regeneration of plantlets in cultured plant cells and tissues has been achieved in many trees of high economic value. Many of the studies are aimed at large scale micropropagation of important trees yielding fuel, pulp, timber, oil or fruits.

Hence, clonal forestry and horticulture are gaining an increasing recognition as an alternative for tree improvement. However, strategies for transferring cultured plants *in vitro* to field conditions are based on relatively higher priced horticultural species rather than agricultural and forestry species.

Regeneration of plantlets in cultured tissue has been described by Murashige (1974) into three undermentioned stages:

(*i*) Establishment of explant aseptically.

(*ii*) Multiplication of propagules by repeated subcultures on a specific nutrient medium.

(*iii*) Rooting and hardening of plantlets and planting into soil.

Later on Fossard (1987) has described the following four stages of micropropagation:

(*i*) Selection of a suitable explant and inoculation into nutrient medium.

(*ii*) Multiplication and growth of culture which takes about two months, followed by repeated subcultures.

(*iii*) Cultures are obtained by changing the medium to planting out.

(*iv*) This is 'planting out' stage where plantlets are aseptically removed from test tube environment to natural and harsh environment. At this stage, roots should be fully functional in potting mix, the soil where plantlets are transplanted.

However, at planting out stage, the plantlets fail to survive due to sudden change in the environment and invasion by soil microbes. Scientists have suggested that the 'regenerates' should be transferred first to green house and then to field. The humidity should be controlled by covering the plants with transparent polyethylene sheets. This acclimatization requires several weeks which should be followed by potting into sterile peat or soil.

In recent years, the interest has created in commercialising the *in vitro* propagation of forest trees. For betterment and improvement of tree plants of high economic value, a breakthrough in forestry research has come with production of artificial seeds in *Eucalyptus*, and genetic transformation and *in vitro* regeneration in conifers. Moreover, micropropagation has been successfully done in many trees.

Advantages of Micropropagation (Tissue Culture)

Micropropagation, an essential component of plant biotechnology, has been proved to be means of producing millions of identical plants by culturing plant tissues or organs under aseptic conditions. The advantages of micropropagation over conventional methods, of a sexual reproduction are as follows:

(*i*) Greater output
(*ii*) Economy of time and space
(*iii*) Freedom from seasonal constraints
(*iv*) Multiplication under disease-free conditions.

Hence, this technique is ideal for the species where:

(*i*) Traditional methods of propagation are inadequate to meet the demand for planting material
(*ii*) Marked variability exists in the natural population and productivity can be significantly increased by cloning of superior individuals.
(*iii*) Virus can be eliminated by culturing the shoot meristem, thus pathogen-free stock can be maintained by routine micropropagation.

In the modern days, tissue culture has been successfully employed for the multiplication of orchids and many other ornamental plants. In the developed countries, tissue culture is a routine method of multiplication while in developing countries, the techniques are largely used for producing plants for export markets.

The Department of Biotechnology (DBT), Government of India, set up two pilot-scale national facilities for large scale production of elite planting material of forest trees through tissue culture, one at the Tata Energy Research Institute (TERI), New Delhi, and the other at the National Chemical Laboratory (NCL), Pune.

QUESTION BANK

Very Short Answer Questions (1 mark each)

1. Define parthenocarpy.
2. Which are the nuclei that fuse to form endosperm?
3. What is double fertilization?
4. What is bulbil?
5. What is coleorhiza?
6. What are parthenocarpic fruits?
7. What does the term monoecious mean?
8. What is the term used for plant bearing female flowers?
9. Name a bat pollinated flower.
10. What is scutellum?
11. What type of fruit tomato is?
12. Give three examples of false fruit.
13. What is funiculus?
14. How does the mustard inflorescence differ from banana inflorescence in arrangement? Give the technical term for each.
15. Why are cucurbits referred to as monoecious?
16. What is geitonogamy?
17. What is allogamy?
18. What is ornithophily?
19. What is chiropterophily?
20. What is agamospermy?
21. Which technique is used for propagating improved varieties of mango and rose.
22. (*i*) Give the term for pollination by bat. (*ii*) Give one example of bat pollinated flowers.
23. Why are date palm plants referred to as dioecious?
24. One of the plants bearing anemophilous flowers is (*a*) *Vallisneria* (*b*) *Salvia* (*c*) Kigelia (*d*) Maize.

ANSWERS

1. The formation of fruits without fertilization; **2.** Two polar nuclei (secondary nucleus) and one male gamete; **3.** Here one male gamete fuses with egg (*i.e.*, syngamy) to form zygote, while second male gamete fuses with two polar nuclei to form primary endosperm nucleus (triple fusion), the process is double fertilization; **4.** Here floral buds become fleshy, which can give rise to new plants, *e.g.*, *Agave*; **5.** Protective cap on radicle of maize; **6.** The fruits formed without fertilization, *e.g.*, seedless fruits of papaya or banana; **7.** When both male and female flowers are borne on the same plant; **8.** Bisexual or hermaphrodite; **9.** Kadamba; **10.** Single cotyledon in caryopsis of maize is called scutellum; **11.** Berry; **12.** Apple, pine apple, jack fruit; **13.** The stalk of ovule; **14.** In mustard, the inflorescence is raceme, flowers are arranged in acropetal order on floral axis, whereas in banana, inflorescence is spadix, where fleshy axis remains covered by spathe; **15.** Because male and female flowers are borne on same plant; **16.** A type of pollination, where pollen is transferred from anther of a flower to stigma of another flower of the same plant; **17.** A type of pollination, where the pollens move from the anther of one flower to the stigma of another flower of a different plant, it is referred to as cross pollination, xenogamy or allogamy; **18.** The pollination by birds; **19.** Pollination by bats; **20.** A process of reproduction, where seeds are formed without fusion of gametes; **21.** Grafting; **22.** (*i*) Chiropterophily (*ii*) *Kigelia pinnata;* **23.** Date palms are unisexual, where male and female flowers are borne on different plants, and therefore, they are referred to as dioecious; **24.** (*d*).

Short Answer Questions (2 marks each)

1. Name the pollinating agents of flowers like maize and wheat. Give any two favourable features of such a flower.
2. Define triple fusion. What is the product of this process? What does the product develop into?
3. Name the pollinating agent of flowers like *Salvia*, Nasturtium and sunflower. Give two favourable features of such a flower for pollination.
4. Some crop plants can be grown from a seed as well as vegetatively from stem cuttings. List any four advantages of vegetative propagation in such cases.
5. Draw a labelled diagram of the L.S. of an anatropous ovule.
6. How does the coriander inflorescence differ from the mustard inflorescence in arrangement?
7. Describe the nature of three kinds of angiospermic fruits. Give an example of each.
8. Give characteristics of insect pollinated flowers.
9. Write the significance of double fertilization.
10. What is parthenogenesis? Give one example.
11. Give four characteristics of wind pollinated flowers.

Short Answer Questions (3 marks each)

1. Trace the development of megasporocyte in the ovary to a mature ovule.
2. What do you understand by ornithophily and chiropterophily.
3. Describe the structure of a typical monosporic embryo sac found in flowering plants.
4. Write a note on the need and significance of pollination in plants.
5. What do you understand by double fertilization.
6. Draw a well labelled diagram of a mature ovule, showing its internal structure.
7. Describe the structure of a pollen grain and the process of its germination.
8. What do you understand by vegetative methods of reproduction? Explain with examples.
9. Describe the importance of artificial methods of vegetative reproduction.
10. Write short notes on the following:
    (*a*) hydrophily (*b*) entomophily
    (*c*) anemophily (*d*) cross-pollination
11. Name the advantages of propagating plants without using seeds.
12. Define
    (*a*) Siphonogamy (*b*) Endosperm (*c*) Double fertilization.
13. (*i*) Give the term for pollination by bats (*ii*) Give an example of bat pollinated plant.
14. Draw labelled diagram of the longitudinal section of a pistil showing pollen germination.
15. Differentiate between geitonogamy and allogamy.
16. Trace the development of a mature ovule from a megaspore mother cell.

Long Answer Questions (5 marks each)

1. Trace the development of a megaspore mother cell of a flower into a mature ovule. Give a labelled diagram of the final stage.
2. Draw a L.S. of a pistil showing pollen germination. Explain the events in the embryo sac during the process of fertilization. Which resulting stages give rise to the embryo and endosperm respectively?
3. (*i*) Draw a neat labelled diagram of the longitudinal section of an anatropous ovule.
   (*ii*) Which cell of the ovule gets transformed into megaspore mother cell?
4. Define double fertilization. Explain the process of double fertilization in an angiospermic plant.
5. Describe the development of male gametophyte in an angiosperm.
6. Describe the development of female gametophyte in angiosperms.

7. What develops into a microspore mother cell in a flower? Trace the development of this cell into a pollen grain which is ready for germination. Draw a labelled figure of a mature pollen grain.
8. Describe in brief the various special modes of reproduction. Mention their economic significance.
9. "Incompatibility is a natural barrier in the fusion of gametes". Justify the statement.
10. Write a note on the development of endosperm. Mention the types with examples.
11. Write an essay on the development of female gametophyte. Illustrate the answer with suitable diagrams.
12. What do you understand by the development of an embryo? Support the answer with suitable diagrams.

True or False

1. Nutritive layer of cells around pollen sacs in anther is tapetum.
2. A carbohydrate layer present on the outer side of grains of maize, wheat, rice, etc. is called aleurone layer.
3. The flower with superior ovary is called hypogynous.
4. Wall of fruit having epicarp, mesocarp and endocarp is called periderm.
5. The part of the plant that is grafted on the stalk is called scion.
6. A cotyledon of bean seed is called scutellum.
7. The maintenance of purity of a given variety of plants by vegetative propagation is called cloning.
8. The transference of the pollen grains from the anther to stigma is called fertilization.
9. Double fertilization or triple fusion is characteristic of angiosperms.
10. A bean seed is albuminous, while a maize seed is exalbuminous.
11. The main causes of seed dormany are hardness of seed coat and presence of inhibitory substances.
12. Two cells present on either side of egg cell in an embryo sac are termed as antipodals.
13. Cross pollination is also known as allogamy.
14. The process of entry of pollen tube into ovule through integuments for fertilization is called porogamy.
15. Three cells present at the chalazal end in the embryo sac are known as antipodals.
16. Within each ovule, a haploid embryo sac usually containing nuclei is formed.
17. Cross-pollination requires abiotic or biotic agent.
18. Only meiotic divisions are involved in asexual reproduction.
19. Microspores are diploid.
20. In *Vallisneria*, the male flowers are released in air.

ANSWERS

1. True ;	**2.** False ;	**3.** True ;	**4.** False ;	**5.** True ;	**6.** False ;
7. True ;	**8.** False ;	**9.** True ;	**10.** Flase ;	**11.** True ;	**12.** False ;
13. True ;	**14.** False ;	**15.** True ;	**16.** True ;	**17.** True ;	**18.** False ;
19. False ;	**20.** False ;				

Fill in the Blanks

1. A technique to produce genetically identical individuals from a single cell is known as ____________.
2. A population of genetically identical plants derived from an individual is called ____________.
3. A protective sheath of radicle in monocots is called ____________.
4. The flower with superior ovary is called ____________.
5. Study of pollen grains is known as ____________.
6. Phenomenon of the formation of more than one embryo per ovule is called ____________.

7. During grafting, the part that becomes the supporting portion (usually the root) is called ________.
8. The fruit that develops from the whole of inflorescence is called ________.
9. A stamen consists of ________ and ________
10. Genetically, the megaspore mother cell is ________.
11. A small pore in the ovule through which the pollen tube enters is called ________.
12. The ovary wall develops into a fruit wall is called ________.
13. Nutritive layer of cells around pollen sacs in anther is called as ________.
14. The flowers in catkin are ________.
15. The tip of the pedicel on which different floral parts are inserted is known as ________
16. Stem cuttings are frequently used for ________.
17. *Bryophyllum* is the best example of propagation by ________.
18. Each microspore mother cell has ________ of chromosomes and therefore is ________.
19. The process of nuclear fusion to form zygote is called ________.
20. Inside ovary, ovules develop from a special tissue called ________.

ANSWERS

1. Cloning	2. Clone	3. Coleorhiza	4. Hypogynous
5. Palynology	6. Polyembryony	7. Stock	8. Sorosis
9. Filament and anther	10. Diploid	11. Micropyle	12. Pericarp
13. Tapetum	14. Unisexual	15. Thalamus	16. Propagation
17. Leaf	18. 2n, diploid	19. Syngamy	20. Placenta.

Multiple Choice Questions (Objective Type Questions)

1. Layering is used in vegetative propagation of :
   (*a*) Jasmine (*b*) Rose
   (*c*) Mango (*d*) All the above
2. Egg apparatus consists of:
   (*a*) Egg and antipodals (*b*) Polar nuclei
   (*c*) Egg and synergids (*d*) Egg
3. Sexual reproduction of flowering plants was discovered by:
   (*a*) Camerarius (*b*) Nawaschin
   (*c*) Strasburger (*d*) Maheshwari
4. In banana, edible part is:
   (*a*) Fleshy epicarp (*b*) Rudimentary mesocarp and fleshy endocarp
   (*c*) Pericarp (*d*) Rudimentary endocarp and fleshy mesocarp
5. A spike of unisexual flowers is found in:
   (*a*) *Amaranthus* (*b*) Mulberry
   (*c*) Wheat (*d*) Bottle brush
6. Cleistogamous condition present in:
   (*a*) *Brassica* (*b*) *Solanum tuberosum*
   (*c*) *Commelina* (*d*) *Allium cepa.*
7. Fusion of two dissimilar gametes is known as:
   (*a*) Fertilisation (*b*) Autogamy
   (*c*) Allogamy (*d*) Dichogamy

8. The edible part of ripe mango is morphologically:
(a) Epicarp (b) Mesocarp
(c) Pericarp (d) Endocarp

9. In monocots, grafting is almost impossible be cause they lack:
(a) Cambium (b) Ground tissue
(c) Vascular bundle (d) Parenchymatous cells

10. The outer whorl of *Bougainvillaea* flower consists of :
(a) Bracts (b) Epicalyx
(c) Sepals (d) Petals

11. *Ficus* is an example of which kind of inflorescence?
(a) Spike (b) Raceme
(c) Cyathium (d) Hypanthodium

12. Anemophilous flowers have:
(a) Sessile stigma (b) Small smooth stigma
(c) Coloured flower (d) Large feathery stigma

13. Pollination by snails and slugs is:
(a) Ornithophily (b) Cheiropterophily
(c) Entomophily (d) Malacophily

14. Pollination by ants is:
(a) Malacophily (b) Myrmecophily
(c) Entomophily (d) Ornithophily

15. In *Kigelia*, Pollination occurs by:
(a) Wind (b) Bats
(c) Birds (d) Humans

16. Feathery stigmas occur in:
(a) Pea (b) *Datura*
(c) *Caesalpinia* (d) Wheat

17. Function of tapetum is:
(a) Protective (b) Nutritive
(c) Respiratory (d) All the above

18. Formation of embryo directly from nucellus and integument is:
(a) Adventive polyembryory (b) Apospory
(c) Apogamy (d) Apomixis

19. Transfer of pollen to the stigma of another flower of the same plant is:
(a) Autogamy (b) Allogamy
(c) Xenogamy (d) Geitonogamy

20. Bicarpellary gynoecium and oblique ovary occurs in:
(a) Banana (b) Brinjal
(c) *Pisum* (d) Mustard

21. Anemophily occurs in:
(a) *Salvia* (b) *Vallisneria*
(c) Coconut (d) Bottle brush

22. The correct match for edible part of fruit is:
(a) Guava-pericarp with thalamus fused (b) Tomato-thalamus
(c) Maize-cotyledon (d) Date palm-epicarp

23. Type of placentation in which ovary is syncapous unilocular and ovules on sutures is called:
(*a*) Apical placentation (*b*) Parietal placentation
(*c*) Marginal placentation (*d*) Superficial placentation

24. Aril is the edible part of:
(*a*) Banana (*b*) Litchi
(*c*) Mango (*d*) Apple

25. The hairs present in maize corn cob is :
(*a*) Seed hairs (*b*) Modified hairs of bract
(*c*) Stigma (*d*) Style

26. A piece of potato tuber will form a new plant if it possesses:
(*a*) Roots (*b*) Eyes
(*c*) Stored food (*d*) Branches

27. Winged fruits are commonly known as:
(*a*) Cypsela (*b*) Regma
(*c*) Samara (*d*) Siliqua

28. Maturation of male and female sex organs at different times is known as:
(*a*) Herkogamy (*b*) Dichogamy
(*c*) Polygamy (*d*) Apogamy

29. Which one of the following events in a botanical garden is never directly influenced by light:
(*a*) Flowering (*b*) Photosynthesis
(*c*) Transpiration (*d*) Fertilization

30. Development of egg without fertilization:
(*a*) Parthenocarpy (*b*) Polyembryony
(*c*) Parthenogenesis (*d*) Adventive embryony

31. Food material in exalbuminous seed is mainly stored in;
(*a*) Nucellus (*b*) Testa
(*c*) Endosperm (*d*) Embryo

32. Apomixis is a type of reproduction that results in the development of a/an:
(*a*) New organism without fusion of gametes
(*b*) New organism from fusion products of gametes
(*c*) Embryo from endosperm
(*d*) Embryo from nucellus

33. The arrangement of megaspores in a tetrad in an angiosperm is:
(*a*) Decussate (*b*) Tetrahedral
(*c*) Linear (*d*) Isobilateral

34. Which among the following are pollinated by bat:
(*a*) *Salvia* (*b*) *Ophrys*
(*c*) *Kigelia* (*d*) *Brassica*

35. Fruit of *Abelmoschus esculentus* is:
(*a*) Cypsella (*b*) Capsule
(*c*) Legume (*d*) Pome

36. Father of Indian Angiosperm Embryology is:
(*a*) B.M. Johri (*b*) B.G.L. Swamy
(*c*) R.N. Kapil (*d*) P. Maheshwari

37. Censer mechanism of seed dispersal is found in:
(*a*) Papaveraceae (*b*) Liliaceae
(*c*) Leguminosae (*d*) Rosaceae

38. Allogamy is best favoured by:
(*a*) Dichogamy (*b*) Dicliny
(*c*) Cleistogamy (*d*) Homogamy

39. Cleistogamy occurs in:
(*a*) *Pisum sativum* (*b*) *Oryza sativa*
(*c*) *Allium cepa* (*d*) *Commelina bengalensis*

40. In *Bryophyllum*, vegetative propagation is by:
(*a*) Roots (*b*) Leaves
(*c*) Rhizomes (*d*) Stem

41. The development of fruit without fertilization is:
(*a*) Parthenogenesis (*b*) Parthenocarpy
(*c*) Apomixis (*d*) Apogamy

42. Translator apparatus is found in:
(*a*) Mustard (*b*) Mango
(*c*) Pea (*d*) *Calotropis*

43. Germ pore is the region where the exine is:
(*a*) Thin (*b*) Uniform
(*c*) Thick and uniform (*d*) Absent

44. Double fertilization in angiosperms was dicovered by:
(*a*) Strasburger (*b*) J.C. Bose
(*c*) Maheshwari (*d*) Nawaschin

45. In a young anther the four rows of cells, which later produce pollen, are called:
(*a*) Antheridium (*b*) Archesporium
(*c*) Tapetum (*d*) Zoosporangium

13. Double fertilization was first discovered by Nawaschin (1898) in:
(*a*) *Lilium* and *Fritillaria* (*b*) Mango and sugarcane
(*c*) Papaya and pea (*d*) *Brassica* and candytuft

47. The point where funicle joins with ovule is known as:
(*a*) Chalaza (*b*) Micropyle
(*c*) Hilum (*d*) Integument

48. Axillary buds are used to raise crop of:
(*a*) Wheat (*b*) Rice
(*c*) Groundnut (*d*) Sugarcane

49. The female gametophyte of a typical dicot at the time of fertilization is:
(*a*) 8-celled (*b*) 7-celled
(*c*) 6-celled (*d*) 4-celled

50. Embryo sac is also known as:
(*a*) Microgametophyte (*b*) Megagametophyte
(*c*) Microsporangium (*d*) Megasporangium

51. An inflorescence always forms a:
(*a*) Simple fruit (*b*) Dry dehiscent fruit
(*c*) Aggregate fruit (*d*) Multiple or composite fruit

52. Which plant propagates through leaves:

(*a*) *Agave* (*b*) *Kalonchoe*

(*c*) *Gladiolus* (*d*) Potato

53. Fertilization is depicted by the condition:

(*a*) $N \rightarrow 2N$ (*b*) $2N \rightarrow N$

(*c*) $2N \rightarrow 4N$ (*d*) $4N \rightarrow 2N$

54. Pollen grains are able to withstand extremes of temperature and desiccation because there exine is composed of :

(*a*) Cutin (*b*) Suberin

(*c*) Sporopollenin (*d*) Callose

55. The plant part which consists of two generations one within the other is:

(*a*) Germinated pollen grain (*b*) Seed

(*c*) Unfertilized ovule (*d*) Embryo

56. Synergids are:

(*a*) Haploid (*b*) Diploid

(*c*) Diploid after fertilization (*d*) Triploid after fertilization

57. Pick the odd one out:

(*a*) Chalazogamy (*b*) Porogamy

(*c*) Mesogamy (*d*) Allogamy

58. When the filament runs along the back of anther it is called:

(*a*) Adnate (*b*) Versatile

(*c*) Longitudinal (*d*) Syngenecious

59. Vegetative propagation by bulbils occur in:

(*a*) *Agave* (*b*) *Zingiber*

(*c*) *Vallisneria* (*d*) *Curcuma*

60. If any somatic cell of sporophyte produces gametophyte without reduction division. It is:

(*a*) Parthenogenesis (*b*) Apogamy

(*c*) Apospory (*d*) Amphimixis

ANSWERS

1. (*a*)	**2.** (*c*)	**3.** (*a*)	**4.** (*d*)	**5.** (*b*)	**6.** (*c*)	**7.** (*a*)	**8.** (*b*)
9. (*a*)	**10.** (*a*)	**11.** (*d*)	**12.** (*d*)	**13.** (*d*)	**14.** (*b*)	**15.** (*b*)	**16.** (*d*)
17. (*b*)	**18.** (*a*)	**19.** (*d*)	**20.** (*b*)	**21.** (*c*)	**22.** (*a*)	**23.** (*b*)	**24.** (*b*)
25. (*d*)	**26.** (*b*)	**27.** (*c*)	**28.** (*b*)	**29.** (*d*)	**30.** (*c*)	**31.** (*d*)	**32.** (*a*)
33. (*c*)	**34.** (*c*)	**35.** (*b*)	**36.** (*d*)	**37.** (*a*)	**38.** (*a*)	**39.** (*d*)	**40.** (*b*)
41. (*b*)	**42.** (*d*)	**43.** (*a*)	**44.** (*d*)	**45.** (*b*)	**13.** (*a*)	**47.** (*c*)	**48.** (*d*)
49. (*b*)	**50.** (*b*)	**51.** (*d*)	**52.** (*b*)	**53.** (*a*)	**54.** (*c*)	**55.** (*b*)	**56.** (*a*)
57. (*d*)	**58.** (*a*)	**59.** (*a*)	**60.** (*c*).				

UNIT - 3
Biochemistry : Enzymology

14
CHAPTER

Basics of Enzymology – Enzymes

An **enzyme** is a specialized protein produced within an organism or cell which is capable of catalysing a specific chemical reaction. Since the enzyme acts as a catalyst, it is sometimes referred to as **biocatalyst**. A catalyst influences the rate of a chemical reaction, usually without undergoing any change itself. Thus, an enzyme differs from a normal catalyst. The enzyme may participate in a reaction by combining with the substrate. Ultimately, however, it is set free. The DNA in each cell has the necessary message (blue print) for the production of all the enzymes required by it. The cell uses this information as and when necessary to produce the enzymes required to catalyse specific reactions at any point of time.

Enzymes are synthesised by living cells. But they retain their catalytic action even when extracted from cells. For example, Rennet tablets containing the enzyme rennin from the calf's stomach have long been used for coagulating milk protein to obtain casein (cheese from milk), for various uses, including the preparation of eatables.

Discovery of enzymes. The term enzyme was coined by **Kuhne** (1878) for catalytically active substances previously called **ferments**. Enzymes were discovered by accident. In 1897 a German chemist Edward Buchner was preparing yeast extract for medicinal purposes. The extracts he prepared invariably turned bad. He added some sugar to prevent spoilage. To his surprise the sugar fermented into alcohol. Pasteur had already demonstrated that living yeast cells promoted fermentation. Buchner discovered that living cells were not necessary but that yeast extract could bring about fermentation. The word **enzyme** was coined. It literally means **'in yeast'** but is now used as a general name for biocatalysts.

Definition. Mayrback (1952) defined 'enzymes are simple or compound proteins acting a specific catalysts'. They may also be defined as 'organic substances capable of catalysing chemical reactions in the living systems.'

However, enzymes speed up the rate of reaction without affecting the equilibrium. They exhibit a striking specificity to manifest themselves in their catalytic reactions, enhancing and controlling the course of these processes.

In 1878, **Freidrich W. Kuhne** coined the word **enzyme** (Gk. *en* + *zyme* = in yeast), and replaced the older word 'ferment' by it.

NOMENCLATURE AND CLASSIFICATION OF ENZYMES

Enzymes were variously named in the past. Enzymes, such as ptyalin (salivary amylase). pepsin and trypsin give no indication of their action. While other enzymes such as amylase, sucrase, protease and lipase were named after the substrates on which they acted — amylose (starch), sucrose, protein and lipids respectively. Still others were named according to the source from which they were obtained — papain from papaya, bromelain from pineapple (of family Bromeliaceae). Some like DNA polymerase indicate its specific action, polymerisation. To facilitate scientific communication and to maintain uniformity, enzymes are now categorised and named by an **international code of enzyme nomenclature**.

The name of each enzyme ends with an **ase** and consists of two parts. The first part indicates its **substrates** and the second the reaction catalysed. For example, glutamate pyruvate transaminase transfers an amino group from the substrate glutamate to another substrate pyruvate.

Enzymes are grouped into *six* major classes :

Class 1. Oxireductases. These catalyse oxidation or reduction of their substrates and act by removing or adding electrons from or to substrates, *e.g.*, cytochrome oxidase oxidises cytochrome.

Class 2. Transferases. These transfer specific groups from one substrate to another. The chemical group transferred in the process is not in a free state, *e.g.*, glutamate pyruvate transaminase.

Class 3. Hydrolases. These break down large molecules into smaller ones by the introduction of water (hydrolysis) and breaking of specific covalent bonds. Most digestive enzymes belong to this catagory, *e.g.*, amylase which hydrolyses starch.

Class 4. Lyases. These catalyse the cleavage of specific covalent bonds and removal of groups without hydrolysis, *e.g.*, histidine decarboxylase cleaves C–C bond in histidine to form carbon dioxide and histamine.

Class 5. Isomerases. These catalyse the rearrangement of molecular structure to form isomeres, *e.g.*, phosphohexose isomerase changes gulcose-6-phosphate to fructosc-6-phosphate (both are hexose phosphates).

Class 6. Ligases. Thse catalyse covalent bonding of two substrates to form a large molecule. The energy for reaction is derived from the hydrolysis of ATP. Pyruvate carboxylase combines pyruvate and carbon dioxide to form oxaloacetate at the expense of ATP.

ENDOENZYMES AND EXOENZYMES

The enzymes which are synthesized by the living cells usually operate inside them within the boundary of their membrane. Such enzymes are called **endoenzymes** or **intracellular enzymes.** Most of the enzymes belong to this category. But in heterotrophic microorganisms such as bacteria and fungi, some of the enzymes, *e.g.*, **protease, cellulase, amylase**, etc., produced by the cells are secreted out and are active in the outer environment of cells where they convert complex insoluble chemical compounds into simple soluble compounds, the latter are then readily absorbed by them. Such enzymes which operate externally to the cells in which they originate are called **exoenzymes** or **extracellular enzymes** exoenzymes are digestive or hydrolytic in nature and obviously their function is to make insoluble substances available as substrates to the cells for their growth. The insectivorous plants which also exhibit heterotrophic nutrition have special secretory cells to produce such enzymes especially proteolytic ones to digest their prey. During the germination of cereal grains, hydrolytic enzymes are secreted into the endosperm by **scutella** and **aleurone cells** to convert insoluble reserve food material into soluble one so that it may be made available to the growing seedling. It is believed that generally the plant cells have some limited capacity to secrete enzymes outer to them which might be located on the cell walls or they may be released into the surrounding environment. Secretion of hydrolytic enzymes into the other medium by cells of higher plants in tissue culture experiments is well known that supports this belief.

STRUCTURE OF ENZYMES

All enzymes are proteins but all proteins are not enzymes. Many enzymes contain a non-protein part called the **prosthetic group.** These are tightly bound to the enzyme. Some prosthetic groups are metal compounds. For example, iron-porphyrin complexes form the prosthetic groups of cytochromes. In addition, certain organic compounds and inorganic ions are required for enzyme activity. They are loosely bound to the enzyme and are called **co-factors.**

Nucleotides of the vitamin nicotinamide (NAD) and riboflavin (FAD) are organic **co-factors** or **coenzymes** of many oxidising enzymes of the mitochondria. In addition certain metals, especially those occurring in trace amounts, facilitate enzyme reaction. Iron (Fe^{++}) is a co-factor responsible for the catalytic action of catalase.

All enzymes have a specific three dimonsional structrue, a part of which is known as the **active site**. An enzyme may have more than one active site.

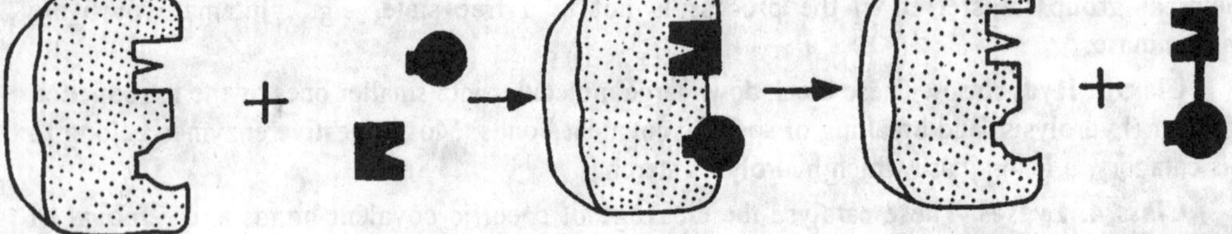

Fig. 14.1. Lock and key hypothesis of enzyme action.

The active site serves as a **'lock'** into which the reactant, commonly referred to as the substrate fits in like a **'key'** (Fig. 14.1). The points where the substrate is bound on the active site is known as the substrate-binding site. Substrate binding causes a lowering of the activation energy and allows the reaction to proceed (Fig. 14.2). Once the reaction is completed the enzyme releases the **products** and is ready to catalyse again.

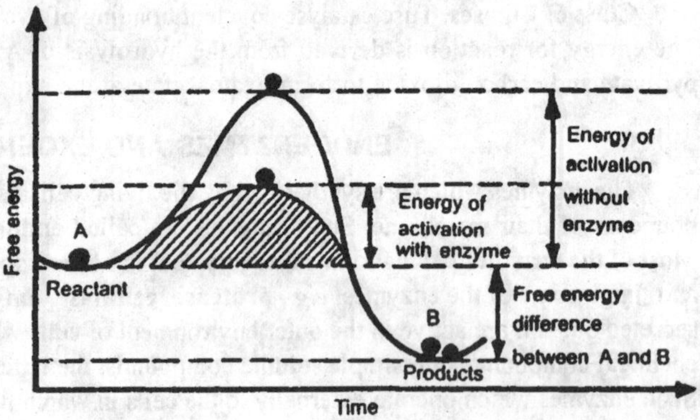

Fig. 14.2. Activation energy requirement of non-catalysed and enzyme-catalysed reactions.

A single molecule of the enzyme carbonic anhydrase, the fastest enzyme known, hyrates 36 million (36 × 10^6) molecules of carbon dioxide per minute.

$$CO_2 + H_2O \xrightarrow{\text{carbonic anhydrase}} H_2CO_3$$

The catalysed reaction is 10 million (10^7) times faster than the non-catalysed reaction.

Experiment 1.

Take 2 ml of hydrogen peroxide (H_2O_2) solution in two test tubes. Add a pinch of manganese dioxide (MnO_2) powder to one and a small piece of fresh liver or potato to the other. Keep the test tubes at room temerature in summer or in a beaker of warm water (at 38°C) in winter. Bubbles of oxygen evolve in the two test tubes. Thus both manganese dioxide and a tissue enzyme (peroxidase or catalase) can catalyse the evolution of oxygen from hydrogen peroxide. Repeat the same experiment, but use boiled and cooled manganese dioxide (MnO_2) suspension and a boiled or cooled liver/potato slice. Gas evolution still occurs in the hydrogen peroxide solution treated with boiled and cooled manganese dioxide. But the tube containing the boiled tissue slices does not evolve oxygen.

This experiment demonstrates that heat inactivates the enzyme but not the inorganic catalyst.

Table 14.1. Similarities Between Inorganic Catalysts and Enzymes

1. Inorganic catalysts and enzymes remain unchanged after reaction, chemically and quantitatively and can be used over and over again.
2. Both are required in minute quantities compared to the substrate.
3. They do not alter the equilibrium of a reversible reaction.
4. They do not initiate a reaction, but only enhance its rate by lowering the activation energy.
5. They form short-lived complexes with the reactants.

Table 14.2. Dissimilarities Between Inorganic Catalysts and Enzymes

Inorganic Catalysts	Enzymes
1. Small molecules or simple mineral ions.	1. Proteins with complex three-dimensional structure.
2. Can catalyse diverse reactions.	2. Catalyse only specific reactions of a single or only a few substrates.
3. Not regulated by any regulator molecules.	3. Can be regulated by specific molecules which can change conformation, and therefore, activity.
4. They are less sensitive to temperature and pH.	4. They are more sensitive to change in temperature and pH.

Characteristics of Enzymes

1. Specificity. Each enzyme can catalyse the change of either a specific substrate or a specific group of substrates only.

The specificity for a substrate may easily be demonstrated by an experiment as follows :

Experiment 2.

Take 3 ml of Benedict's solution containing cupric sulphate, in two test tubes. 1 ml of starch solution (1%) is addèd to one and 1 ml of sucrose solution (1%) to the other. The solutions are then boiled for a couple of minutes. No change occurs in either of the test tubes. Thus, both starch and sucrose are non-reducing carbohydrates. Neither of them can reduce Cu^{++} of the reagent to Cu^{+}. Now, saliva is collected in two fresh test tubes. Starch is added to one of them and sucrose to the other. Both test tubes are kept at room temperature in summer for about one hour and in warm water (about 38°C) in winter. Benedicti's solution is then added to both test tubes and their contents are boiled for a couple of minutes. The blue solution changes to yellow or red precipitate in the test tube containing starch.

This indicates that the enzyme salivary amylase hydrolyses starch to reducing sugars. The latter reduces Cu^{++} to Cu^{+} which forms the coloured precipitate of cuprous oxide (Cu_2O). But the test tube containing sucrose shows no change. Thus, salivary amylase cannot hydrolyse sucrose. No reducing sugar is produced and the colour of benedict's soloution remains unchanged.

2. Optimum temperature. Enzymes generally work over a narrow range of temperatures. Usually it corresponds to the body temperature of the organism. For instance, human enzymes work at the normal body temperature. Each enzyme shows its highest activity at a particular temperature. This is called the **optimum temperature**. Activity declines both above and below the optimum temperatrure. Cold preserves the enzyme in a temporarily inactive state. Food may be preserved for long in a frozen state because neither microbial enzyme nor enzymes in the food can act at low temperatures to cause its spoilage. As demonstrated earlier (experiment 1), very high temperatures destroy enzyme activity. This is because proteins are denatured by heat. For this reason, few cells can tolerate temperatures above 45°C. Some heat resistant species like microoganisms living in hot springs at temperatures close to 100°C, possess heat-resistant enzymes.

3. Optimum pH. Each enzyme shows its highest activity at a specific pH. This is called the **optimum pH**. Activity declines both above and below the optimum pH. Most intracellular enzymes function best around neutral pH. Some digestive enzymes have their optimum in the acidic or alkaline range. For example, the protein digesting enzyme pepsin found in the stomach, has an optimum pH of 2.0. Another protein-digesting enzyme, trypsin, found in the duodenum, functions best in an alkaline pH of 8.5.

Experiment 3.

Take 2 ml starch solution (1%) in two test tubes. Some saliva is collected mixed with the contents of each tube. A few drops of dilute hydrochloric acid are added to one of the tubes. Both test tubes are then kept for one hour at room temperature in summer or in beaker containing warm water (about 38^{0}C) in winter. Subsequently a drop of dilute iodine solution is added to each tube. In the test tube whose contents were acidified, a blue colour develops due to the reactions of unchanged starch with iodine. But the content of the other test tube is not coloured blue with iodine, indicating that starch has been hydrolysed by salivary amylase.

This shows that amylase hydrolyses starch at salivery pH, but fails to act at a more acid pH. In the stomach, salivary amylase swallowed with food is inactivated by the hydrochloric acid present in the gastric juice.

4. Enzyme-substrate complex. Each enzyme (E) possesses a substrate-binding site on the active site in its molecule. A highly reactive enzyme-substrate complex is consequently produced. The latter almost immediately dissociates into the product or products (P) and the unchanged enzyme.

$$E + S \rightleftharpoons \underset{\text{short-lived}}{ES} \longrightarrow EP \longrightarrow E + P$$

Formation of the enzyme-substrate complex is essential for catalysis. The higher the affinity of the enzyme for its substrate, the greater is its catalytic activity.

5. Effect of substrate concentration. With the increase in substrate concentration (S), the velocity (V) of the enzymatic reaction rises at first. But the rise in V decreases progressively with the rise in (S). The reaction ultimately reaches a maximum velocity, which is not exceeded by any further rise in substrate concentration (Fig. 14.3). This happens because enzyme molecules are fewer than the substrate molecules. Any more increase in substrate concentration will saturate all the enzyme molecules. No enzyme is left free to bind with additional molecules of the substrate.

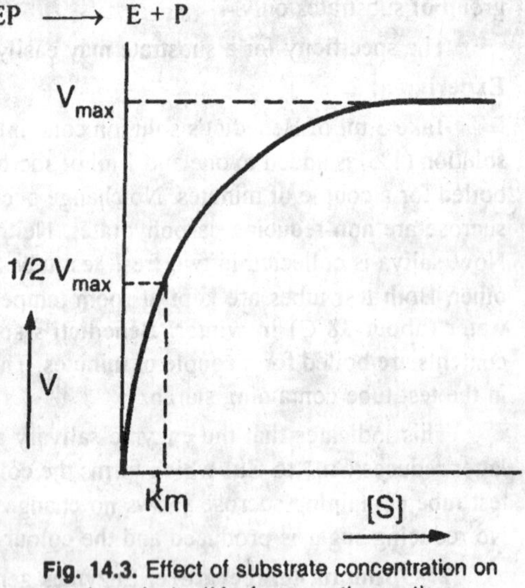

Fig. 14.3. Effect of substrate concentration on the velocity (*V*) of enzymatic reactiony V_{max} = maximum velocity.

Michaelis constant (K_m). Michaelis constant (K_m) of an enzyme is the substrate concentration at which the reaction attains half its maximum velocity (Fig. 14.3). It is a measure of the affinity of the enzyme for its substrate. The lower the K_m, the higher is the substrate affinity of the enzyme. An enzyme possesses different affinities for different substrates. Thus, its K_m value differs from substrate to substrate. Proteases can act on a variety of proteins. The K_m value of the protease will vary with the type of protein.

Inhibition or Regulation of Enzyme Activity

Enzyme action can be inhibited in **four** different ways. Inhibition of enzyme action by denaturation of proteins has already been discussed. The other **three** ways in which enzymes can be inhibited are as follows :

1. Competitive Inhibition. The action of an enzyme may be reduced or inhibited in the presence of a substance that closely resembles the substrate in molecular structure. Such an inhibition is called a **competitive inhibition** of that enzyme. Due to its closed structural similarity with the substrate, the inhibitor competes with the latter for the substrate-binding site of the enzyme (Fig. 14.4). Consequently, the enzyme cannot participate in catalysing the change of the substrate. As a result, the enzyme action declines, *e.g.*, the inhibition of succinate dehydrogenase by malonate, which closely resembles succinate in structure.

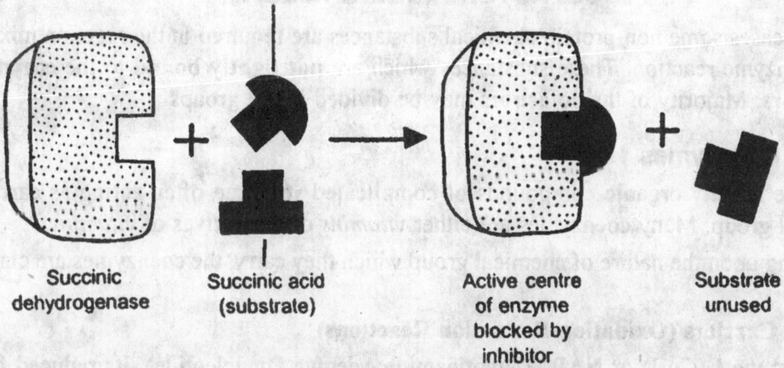

Fig. 14.4. Competitive inhibition of enzyme action

This may be compared to a lock jammed by a key similar to the original key. Such competitive inhibitors are often used in the control of bacterial pathogens. For instance, sulpha drugs are competitive inhibitors of folic acid synthesis in bacteria as they substitute for p-amino benzoic acid, thus preventing the next step in the synthesis.

2. Non-competitive inhibition. Cyanide kills an animal by inhibiting cytochrome oxidase, a mitochondrial enzyme essential for cellular respiration. This is an example of non-competitive inhibition of an enzyme. Here the inhibitor (cyanide) has no structural similarity wtih the substrate (cytrochrome c) and does not bind with the substrate-binding site but at some other site of the enzyme. Thus, in non-competitive inhibition substrate binding takes place but no products are formed.

3. Allosteric Modulation or Feedback Inhibition. The activites of some enzymes, particularly those which form a part of a chain of reactions (metabolic pathway), are regulated internally. Some specific low molecular weight substance, such as the product/products of another enzyme further on in the chain, acts as the inhibitor. Such a modulator substance binds with a specific site of the enzyme different from its substrate-binding site. This binding increases or decreases the enzyme action. Such enzymes are called **allosteric enzymes** (Fig. 14.5).

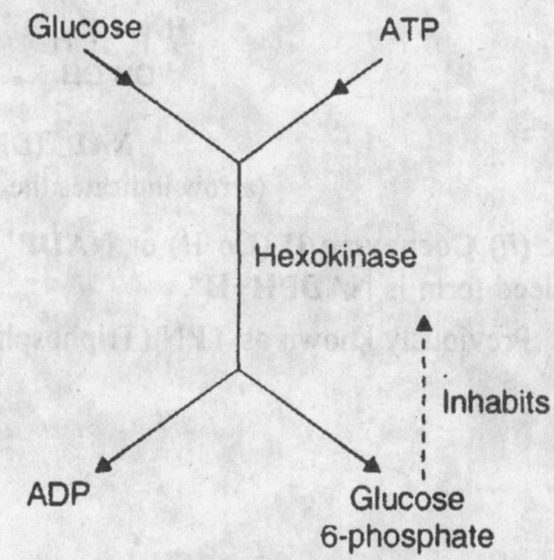

Fig. 14.5. Feedback allosteric inhibition

Coenzymes or Cofactors

For some chemical reactions a substance other than an enzyme and substrates are necessary. These substances are called **coenzymes** or **cofactors.** For example, the formation of **acetyl-CoA** can occur only in the presence of **coenzyme-A.** The **coenzymes** are therefore, necessary if a particular enzyme is to be active. Like enzymes, coenzymes also remain unchanged at the end of a reaction.

Coenzymes, however, differ from enzymes in that they are not proteins. They are of low molecular weight (500 or so) and are heat stable. Enzymes, which are proteins have a comparatively higher molecular weight and undergo denaturation at temperatures, 50° to 60°C. However, an enzyme may function independently of a coenzyme but a coenzyme cannot function without an enzyme.

COFACTORS (COENZYMES)

In many cases some non-protein chemical substances are required in the reaction mixture to catalyse the enzyme reaction. These substances which are **not tightly bound** to the enzyme are called **cofactors**. Majority of the cofactrors may be divided into 2 groups :

(A) Specific Coenzymes

These are usually organic compounds of complicated structrue often acting as carriers of some chemical group. Many coenzymes are either *vitamins* or derivatives of *vitamins.*

Depending upon the nature of chemical group which they carry, the coenzymes are classified as follows :

(1) Hydrogen Carriers (Oxidation-Reduction Reactions)

(i) **Coenzyme I** (Co I) or **NAD⁺** (Nicotinamide Adenine Dinucleotide). Its reduced form is **NADH + H⁺**.

Previously known as DPN (Diphospho Pyridine Dinucleotide) contains vitamin *Nicotinic acid* (*Niacin*) in amide form.

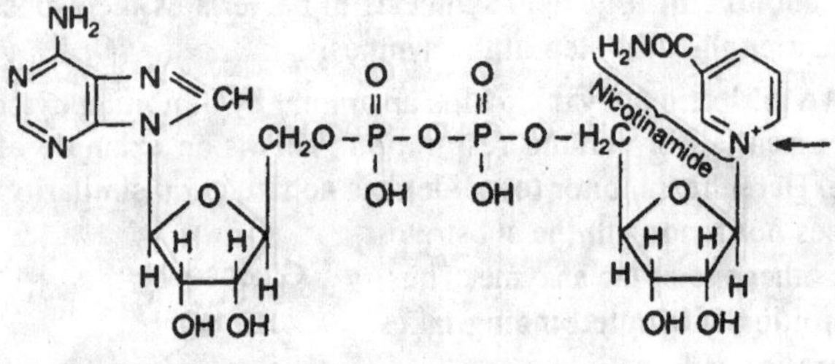

NAD⁺ (DPN⁺) – oxidised form.*
(arrow indicates the position where reduction occurs)

(ii) **Coenzyme II** (Co II) or **NADP⁺** (Nicotinamide Adenine Dinucleotide Phosphate). Its reduced form is **NADPH+H⁺.**

Previously known as **TPN** (Triphospho Pyridine Dinucleotide).

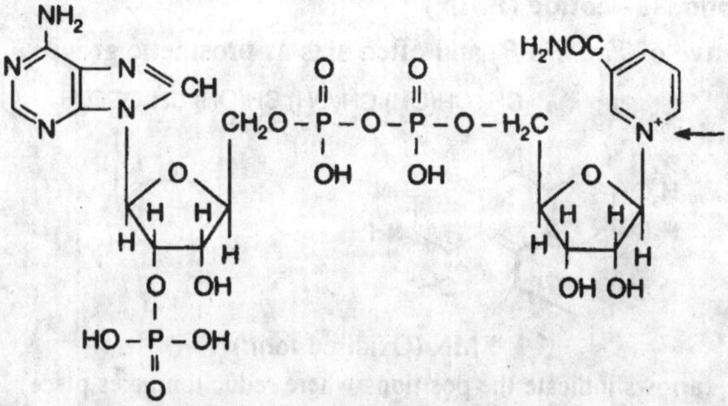

NADP⁺ (TPN⁺)-oxidised form. *

(arrow indicates the position where reduction occurs)

***(iii)* Lipoic Acid** (also helps in oxidative decarboxylation of α-keto acids)

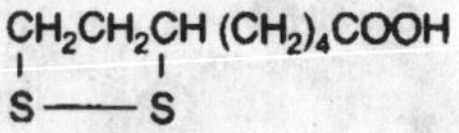

Oxidised

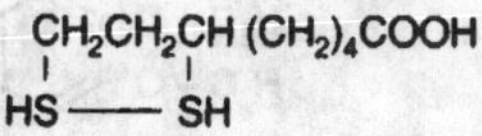

Reduced

***(iv)* Ascorbic Acid** (*Vitamin C*)

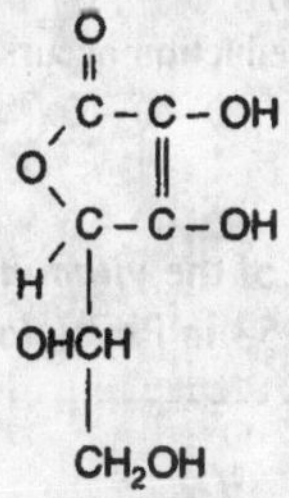

Reduced

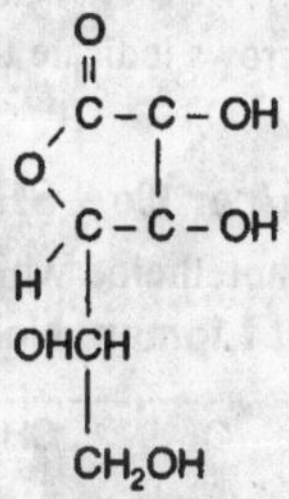

Oxidised

***(v)* Glutathione** (GSH reduced form)/GSSG (oxidised form). It is a tripeptide (γ-glutamyl cyseinly glycine) that acts as coenzyme in some oxidation-reduction reactions in cells.

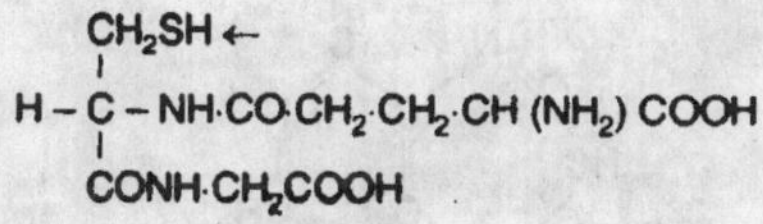

Reduced form

(arrow indicates the reaction group)

***(vi)* Flavin Adenine Dinucleotide (FAD)**

It is derivative of *Vitamin B_2 i.e., Riboflavin.* Often it acts as prosthetic group.

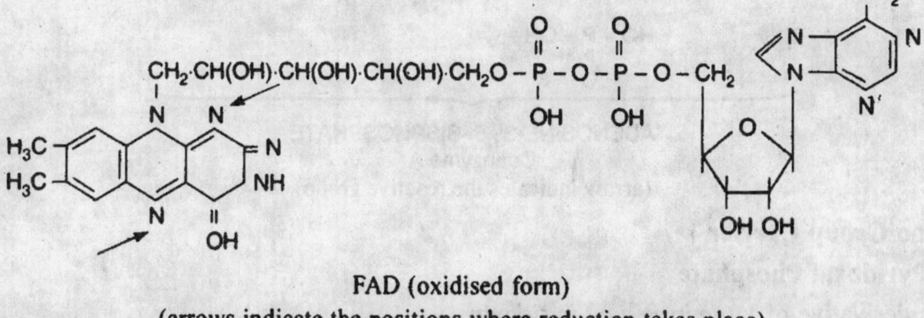

FAD (oxidised form)

(arrows indicate the positions where reduction takes place)

(*vii*) Flavin Mono Nucleotide (FMN)

It is also derivative of *Vitamin B_2* and often acts as prosthetic group.

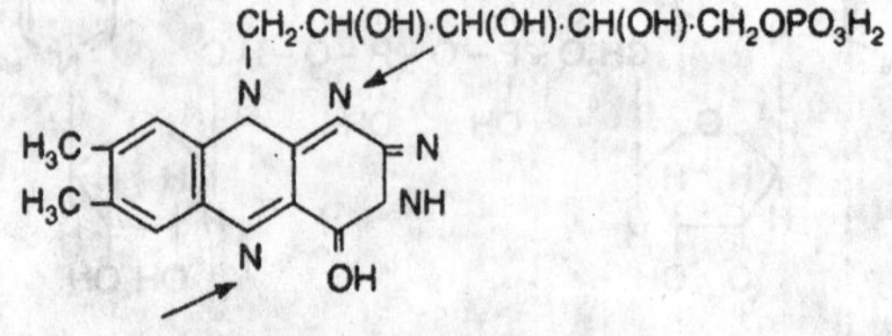

FMN (Oxidised form)
(arrows indicate the positions where reduciton takes place)

(*viii*) Coenzyme Q (CO-Q) or Ubiquinone

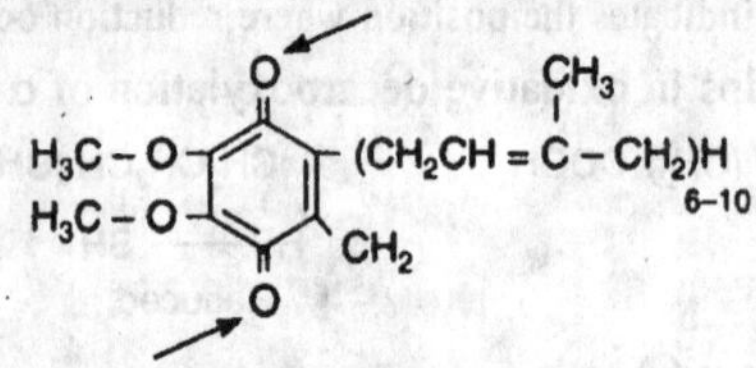

CO-Q (Oxidised form)
(arrows indicate the position where reduction occurs)

(2) Acyl Group Carrier

(*i*) Coenzyme-A (CoA or CoA-SH)

It contains phosphopantetheine which is a derivative of the *vitamin pantothenic acid.* It was discovered by **Fritz Albert Lipman.** Nobel Laureate of 1953 in Physiology or Medicine category.

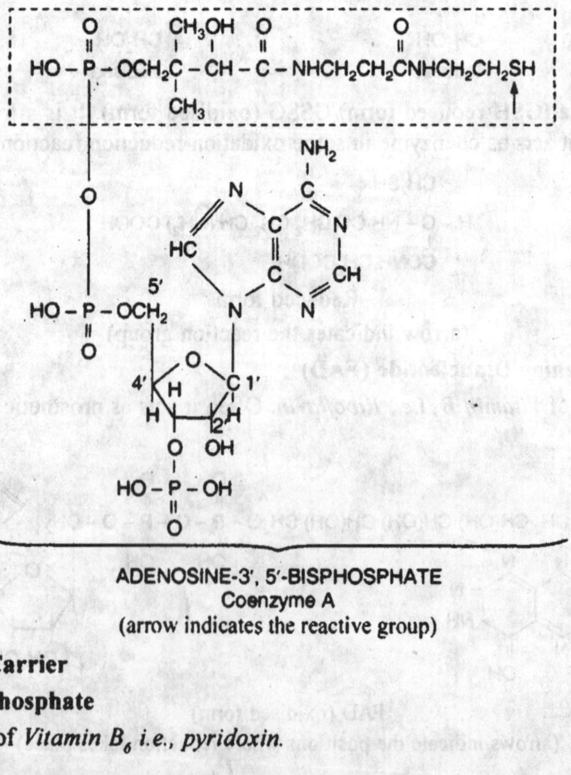

ADENOSINE-3′, 5′-BISPHOSPHATE
Coenzyme A
(arrow indicates the reactive group)

(3) Amino Group Carrier

(*i*) Pyridoxal Phosphate

It is derivative of *Vitamin B_6 i.e., pyridoxin.*

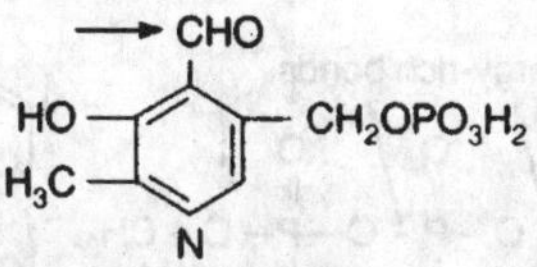

Pyridoxal phosphate
(arrow indicates the reactive group)

(4) CO_2 Carrier

(*i*) Biotin (Coenzyme R)

This is a *vitamin* and often acts as prosthetic group.

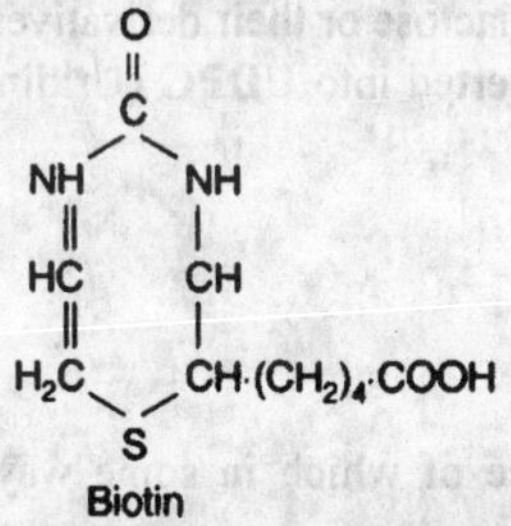

Biotin

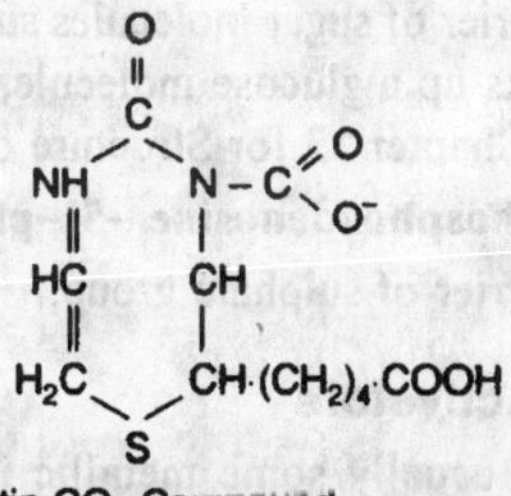

Biotin CO_2-Compound

(5) Thiamine Pyrophosphate (TPP) or Cocarboxylase

This is a derivative of *Vitamin B_1 i.e., thiamine* and plays an important role as coenzyme in the oxidative decarboxylation of α-keto acids (*e.g.*, pyruvic acid α-ketoglutaric acid).

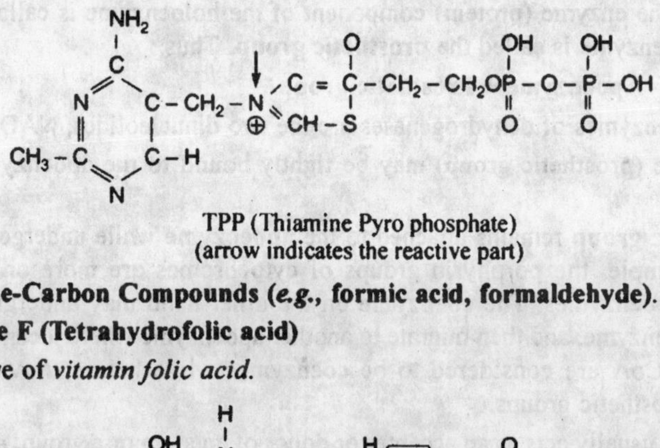

TPP (Thiamine Pyro phosphate)
(arrow indicates the reactive part)

(6) Carrier of One-Carbon Compounds (*e.g.*, formic acid, formaldehyde).

(*i*) Coenzyme F (Tetrahydrofolic acid)

It is derivative of *vitamin folic acid*.

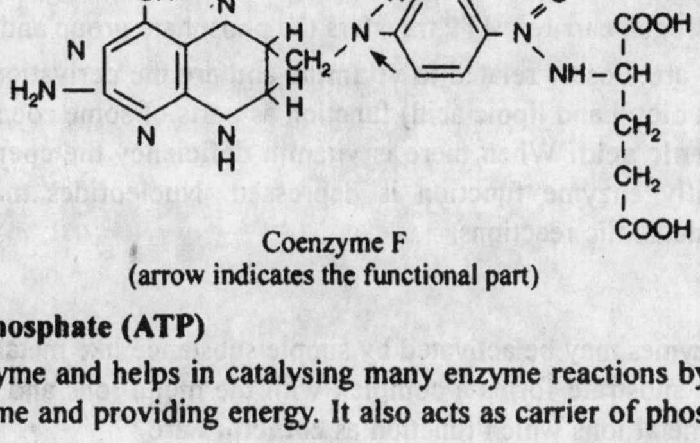

Coenzyme F
(arrow indicates the functional part)

(7) Adenosine Tri Phosphate (ATP)

It acts as coenzyme and helps in catalysing many enzyme reactions by activating either the substrate or the enzyme and providing energy. It also acts as carrier of phosphate group.

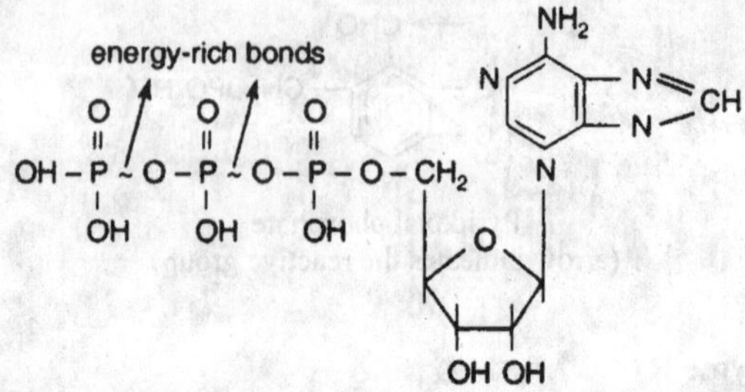

(8) UDP (Uridine Diphosphate)

This is carrier of sugar molecules such as glucose, galactose or their derivatives. For instance, when UDP picks up a glucose molecule, it becomes converted into **UDPG** (Uridine Diphosphate Glucose). See Chapter 13 for Structure of UDPG.

(9) PAPS (3' phosphoadenosine –5'–phosphosulphate)

This is carrier of sulphate group.

(B) General Activators

These are usually some metallic ions, the presence of which in some way activates the enzyme reaction.

HOLOENZYMES AND APOENZYMES

An enzyme and a coenzyme together form an enzymatically active conjugated protein called the **holoenzyme.** The enzyme (protein) component of the holoenzyme is called an **apoenzyme.** The non-protein coenzyme is called the **prosthetic group.** Thus :

Holoenzyme = Apoenzyme + Prosthetic group.

The major coenzymes of dehydrogenases are the two dinucleotides, NAD and NADP.

The coenzyme (prosthetic group) may be tightly bound to the apoenzyme or may easily dissociate from it.

The **prosthetic group** remains attached to the **apoenzyme** while undergoing oxidation and reduction. For example, the porphyrin groups of cytochromes are more or less permanently attached to their apoenzymes. The **coenzyme** on the other hand may undergo reduction while attached to one apoenzyme, and then migrate to another apoenzyme where it can be oxidised. Thus NAD, NADP and CoA are considered to be coenzymes while hemes, flavins and biotin are considered to be prosthetic groups.

The coenzyme usually acts as an accepter or donor of an atom or a group, *e.g.*, NAD, NADP, FMN and CoQ are hydrogen carrires, ATP transfers the phosphate group and CoA the acyl group.

Many coenzymes are closely related to **vitamins** and are the derivation of vitamins. The B group vitamins (except biotin and lipoic acid) function as parts of some coenzyme, *e.g.*, CoA is a derivative of **pantothenic acid.** When there is vitamin deficiency the coenzyme concentration decreases. Consequently enzyme function is depressed. Nucleotides may also function as coenzymes in certain metabolic reactions.

Activators

In same cases enzymes may be activated by simple substance like metal ions which are then called **activators.** The substrate forms a complex with the metal ions and then reacts with the enzyme. Examples of metal ions which function as **cofactors** are :

Na^+, K^+, Ca^{++}, Co^{++}, Mg^{++}, Mn^{++}, Cd^{++}, Fe^{++}, Cr^{+++} and Al^{+++}

MECHANISM OF THE ENZYME ACTION

Swante August Arrhenius, the Nobel Prize winner of 1903 in Chemistry, first pointed out that all the molecules in a given population do not have the same kinetic energy. Some molecules due to collisions have more energy and are **energy-rich molecules** while the others are **energy-poor molecules.**

In an ordinary chemical reaction only energy rich molecules can take part at normal temperature due to an **energy barrier** to reaction, hence the rate of reaction is lower. The higher is the energy barrier for a molecule, the greater is its stability or inactiveness to take part in reaction. The energy required to hurdle molecules over this energy barrier is called the **energy of activation.**

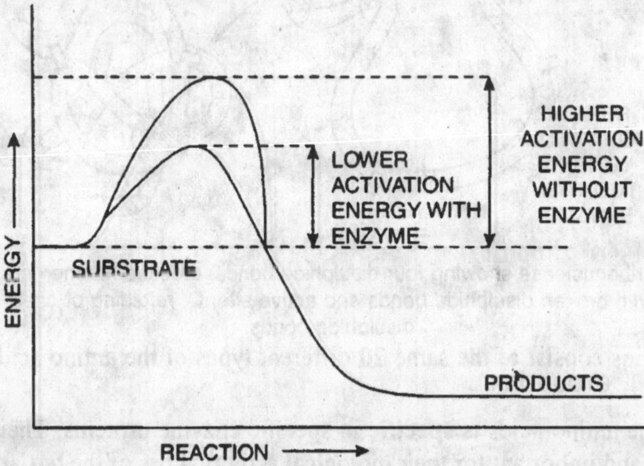

Fig. 14.6. Activation energy of an enzyme catalysed reaction is lower than that of an uncatalysed reaction.

At higher temperature the rate of chemical reaction becomes faster because increased temprature brings about an increase in the number of **activated molecules** by increasing their movement and number of collisions due to thermal agitation.

However, in case of **enzyme catalysed reactions** the rate of reaction is **optimum** at normal body temeratures. It is because all the molecules (energy-rich and energy-poor) can combine with the active sites of enzyme to form **enzyme substrate complex** which later on breaks into enzyme and the product. Thus, the enzymes act by lowering the energy of activation of the reactions (Fig. 14.6).

STRUCTURE OF ENZYMES

1. Protein part the enzyme (apoenzyme)

Major part of the enzyme consists of protein whose molecular weight may vary from few thousands to over a million. For example :

Enzyme	Molecular weight
Ribonuclease	approx 12700
Papain	" 20700
Glutamic dehydrogenase	" over a million

Usually the enzymic proteins consist of only one polypeptide chain, but sometimes there may be more than one polypeptide chains.

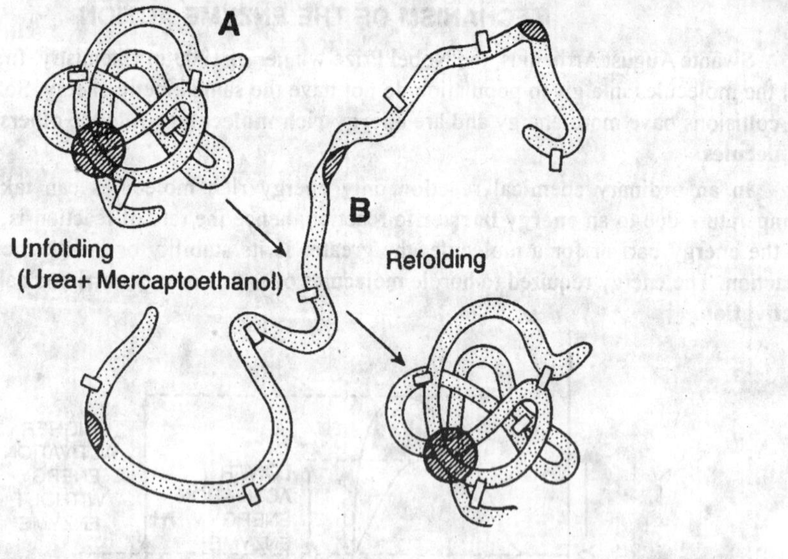

Fig. 14.7. A, Native ribonuclease showing four disulphide bonds, crossed hatched area is the active site; B, unfolded chain with broken disulphide bonds and active site; C, refolding of chain and restoration of disulphide bonds.

Enzymic proteins consist of the same 20 different types of the amino acids which constitute other proteins.

Sequence of the amino acids is **specific** in specific enzyme proteins. Their tertiary structure is also very specific and important for their biological activity. Loss of the tertiary structure renders the enzyme inactive. For example, in enzyme **ribonuclease** different folds of the polypeptide chain are held together by **four disulphide linkages** (S-S) to give it a compact shape (Fig. 14.7 A). If these linkages are reduced with mercaptoethanol, the disulphide groups are converted to **sulphydryl groups** (– SH) resulting in unfolding of the polypetide chain and loss of enzymic activity (Fig. 14.7 B). Reoxidation of the protein in air results in information of the disulphide bonds and return of its enzymic activity (1.7 C).

2. Active Centre or Active Site

Active centre or the active site is that part of the enzyme which takes part in the reaction. Specific substrate combines with it and this combination brings about the biochemical reaction.

Active centre is very **specific.** There may be one or more active centre on a single enzyme molecule.

It is believed that the active centre consists of amino acids residues which are very close to each other in native structure of the enzyme because of the folding of the polypeptide chain, but in fact may be far apart in the primary sequence (Fig. 14.8). This also explains why unfolding of the polypeptide chain by denaturing agents results in loss of its activity.

Fig. 14.8. Description in the text.

If the active centre is present only on one fold of the polypeptide chain and does not extend over the different folds as shown in Fig. 14.9, the unfolding of the polypeptide chain may not necessarily result in loss of enzme activity.

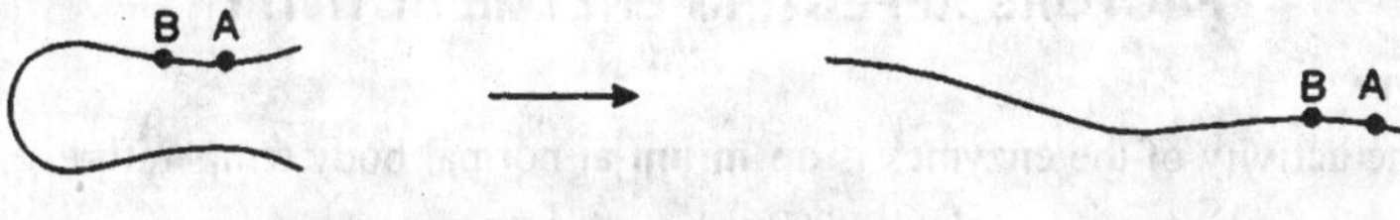

Fig. 14.9. Description in text.

In enzymes consisting of more than one polypeptide chains, the active centre may extend an individual chain or over different polypeptide chains.

The neighbouring groups of amino acids although not constituting the active centre, may also have profound influence on its specificity.

3. Prosthetic Group (non-protein part of the enzyme)

Sometimes a non-protein substance is required at the active centre for enzyme activity which is **bound tightly** to the enzyme protein by covalent linkages and is known as **prosthetic group.**

The prosthetic group may consist of (*a*) an organic compound or (*b*) simple metal ions, such as Cu, Zu, Mn, Mo, etc. The organic compounds acting as prosthetic groups are usually (*i*) a flavin compound, such as **FMN** (Flavin Mono-nucleotide), **FAD** (Flavin Adenine Dinucleotide) (*ii*) heme iron, *i.e.*, iron-porphyrin or (*iii*) biotin, etc.

PROPERTIES OF ENZYMES

(1) Catalytic Property

Like inorganic catalysts the enzymes are active in very small or catalytic amounts and remain unchanged after the reaction. Only a small amount of enzyme is enough to convert large quantity of the substrate into products. Their **turnover number (*k* cat)** *i.e.*, the number of substrate molecules converted to product by one molecule of enzyme per second per active site may range from 0.5 to 4×10^7. The turnover number for ***catalase*** has been calculated as 4×10^7 and is among the highest known. ***Lysozyme*** on the other extreme, has lowest value of turnover number *i.e.*, 0.5.

(2) Specificity

Enzymes are very specific in their action. A particular enzyme usually acts on a particular substrate to catalyse a particular type of reaction. In some cases the specificity of the enzymes may not be so strong but rather general and a particular enzyme may act on a group of substrates.

(3) Reversibility

In most of the cases the reactions catalysed by the enzymes are reversible depending upon the requirements of the cell. But, in some cases there are separate enzymes for forward and backward reactions. Or, a reaction catalysed by a particular enzyme may not be reversible at all.

(4) Sensitiveness to Heat and Inhibitors

(*i*) The enzymes are very sensitive to heat, *i.e.*, they are **themolabile.** They are inactivated at very low temperatures. At very high temperatures 60°-70°C usually they are destroyed (denatured). Low molecular weight enzymes are comparatively more heat stable.

(*ii*) Enzymes are also sensitive to inhibitors. While some inhibitors may partially inhibit their activity, other inhibitors like poisons destroy them permanently and inhibit their activity.

(5) Colloidal Nature

The enzymes are of colloidal dimensions and present large surfaces for reactants in water to facilitate the enzyme reaction.

FACTORS AFFECTING ENZYME ACTIVITY

(1) Temperature

Usually the activity of the enzymes is **optimum** at normal body temperature.

At very low temperature (*i.e.*, about 0°C) the activity of the enzymes is **minimum.**

An increase in temperature up to a certain limit increases the enzyme activity, **maximum** being at about 45°C after whcih the enzyme activity is retarded (Fig.14.10) Beyond 60°–70°C usually their activity is permanently stopped due to the **denaturation** of enzymes.

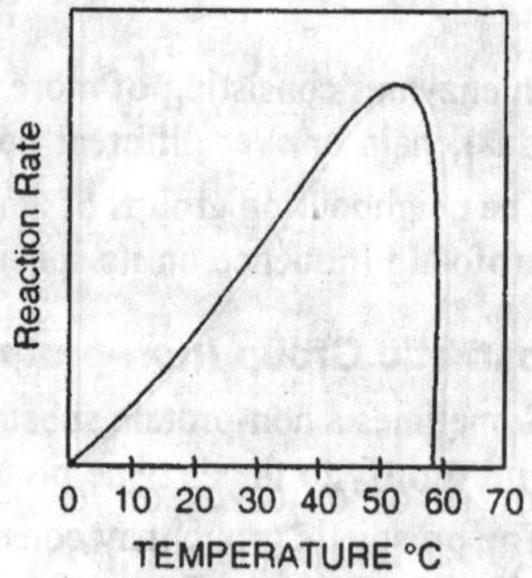

Fig. 14.10. Effect of temperature on enzymic reaction.

(2) Hydrogen Ion Concentration (pH)

Enzymes are active only over a limited range of pH. Some enzymes, *e.g.*, *trypsin* are active in alkaline medium (high pH.), *diastase* in neutral medium, while *pepsin* shows optimum activity in acidic medium (low pH).

(3) Water

In absence of water the enzyme activity is suppressed so much so that in dry seeds the enzymes are almost inactive.

Proper hydration of the cells is neccessary for enzyme activity because (*i*) water provides medium for enzyme reaction to take place, and (*ii*) in many cases it is one of the reactants.

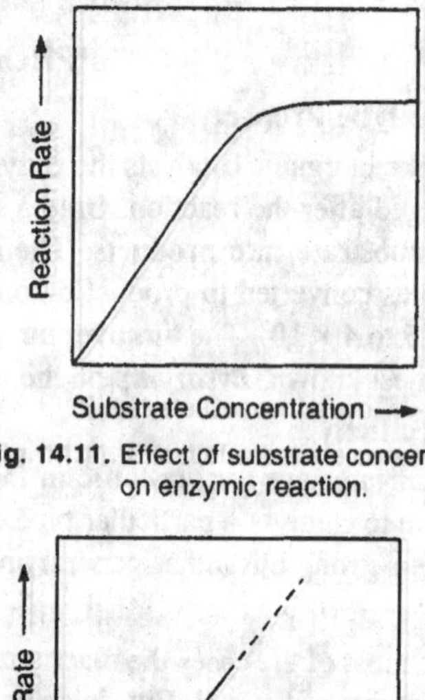

Fig. 14.11. Effect of substrate concentration on enzymic reaction.

(4) Concentration of the Substrate

Increase in the concentration. of the substrate brings about an increase in the activity of the enzyme till all the **active sites** of the enzyme molecules are saturated with substrate. After this the rate of enzyme reaction becomes steady and addition of the substrate will not have positive effect (Fig. 14.11).

(5) Enzyme Concentration

Usually a very small amount of the enzyme can consume large amount of the substrate. Increase in the concentration of the enzyme will increase the rate of reaction catalysed by it provided there is enough concentration of substrate (Fig. 14.12). It is because (*i*) increased number of enzyme molecules will have more active sites, and (*ii*) at higher concentration of the enzyme the inhibitors will fall short.

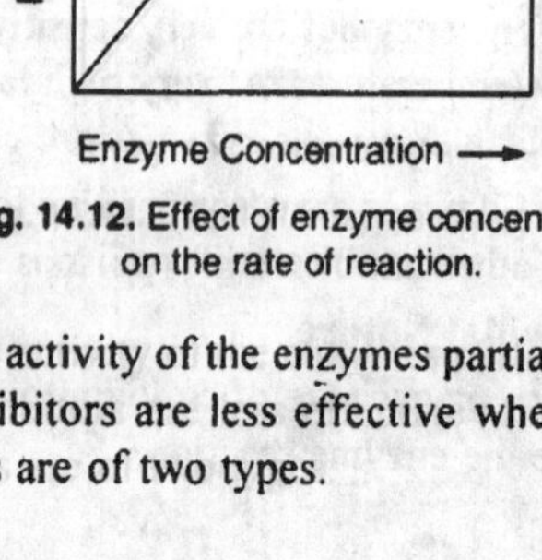

Fig. 14.12. Effect of enzyme concentration on the rate of reaction.

(6) Inhibitors

Presence of inhibitors in the reaction mixture inhibits the activity of the enzymes partially or completely depending upon the nature of the inhibitors. Inhibitors are less effective when the concentration of the enzyme and substrate is higher. Inhibitors are of two types.

(*i*) Competitive Inhibitors

Such inhibitors have structural similarity with the substrate both of which **compete** for the **same** active site of enzyme. If competitive inhibitor pre-occupies the active site, the substrate molecule will be unable to combine with the enzyme and hence, the enzyme activity will be inhibited. But, this inhibition is of **reversible type** because removal of the competitive inhibitor restores the activity of the enzyme.

(*ii*) Non-Competitive Inhibitors

These are usually **poisons** which do not compete for the active sites but destroy the structure of the enzyme and cause permanent or **irreversible inhibition** of the acitvity of the enzyme.

(7) Accumulation of End-Products

Accumulation of the end-products retards the enzymic activity mainly because the active sites of the enzymes are crowded by them and substrate molecules will have comparatively lesser chance of combining with the active sites.

SUMMARY

1. The living world can sustain its busy pace entirely because of the presence of **enzymes.**
2. Enzymes, the **bio-catalysts** synthesised in living cells, are **proteins.**
3. Some have a non-protein part called the **prosthetic group** or **coenzyme.**
4. Many require the presence of **co-factors** like mineral ions to function.
5. According to the nature of reactions catalysed, enzymes are classified into **oxireductases, transferases, hydrolases, lyases, isomerases** and **ligases**.
6. Enzymes are required in minute amounts and are not used up or changed at the end of a reaction.
7. They accelerate the rate of a reaction by reducing the energy required for it.
8. Reactions catalysed by enzymes are often a million times faster than the non-catalysed ones.
9. The three-dimensional form of enzymes makes the enzyme more versatile than inorganic catalysts.
10. Generally an enzyme acts on some specific **substrates.**
11. Every enzyme acts best at optimum pH and at optimim temperature.
12. High temperature may permanently destroy enzyme action.
13. Cold preserves the enzyme in a temporarily inactive state.
14. Enzyme activity is also controlled by substrate concentration.
15. The substrate binds with a **specific site** of the enzyme.
16. The highly reactive **enzyme-substrate complex** almost immediately dissociates to give the product and the unchanged enzymes.
17. Sometimes a substance which structurally resembles the substrate, inhibits the enzymes by occupying its substrate-binding site. This is called **competitive inhibition.**
18. **Non-competitive inhibition** results from the interaction with a substance which is not structurally similar to the substrate.
19. **Allosteric modulation** or **feedback inhibition** is due to inhibition of enzyme action by the product/products of the reaction.

TERMS TO REMEMBER

Activation energy. An initial input of energy to start the reaction.

Active site. All enzymes have specific three-dimensional structrue, a part of which is known as **active site** which serves as a **'lock'** into which the reactant (substrate) fits in like a **'key'**.

Allosteric enzymes. Where a modulator substance binds with a specific site of the enzyme different from its substrate binding site. This binding increases or decreases the enzyme action. Such enzymes are called allosteric enzymes.

Catalyst. A small amount of a substance that influences significantly the rate of a chemical reaction. The substance itself is not used up or changed at the end of reaction.

Catalysis. The phenomenon is called catalysis.

Coenzymes or Co-factors. Certain organic compounds and inorganic ions are required for enzyme activity ; they are loosely bound to the enzyme, such as NAD and FAD (*i.e.*, nucleotides of the vitamin nicotinamide and riboflavin).

Enzymes. Molecules synthesized by the cells; they are biological catalysts.

Feedback inhibition. Decline in enzyme activity by the allosteric effect of the product, *e.g.*, allosteric inhibition of hexokinase by glucose-6-phosphate.

Michaelis constant (K_m). Substrate concentration at which the reaction attains half its maximum velocity.

QUESTION BANK

N.B. Undermentioned questions are repeatedly asked in various Indian Universities and competitive examinations.

Short and Long Answer Questions

1. What are enzymes ? Give a brief account of the enzyme you have studied.
2. What are enzymes ? State their characteristics and discuss the role in digestion.
3. What are enzymes ? Give an account of the general properties and nomenclature of enzymes.
4. Wrtie short note on prosthetic group.
5. Write note on coenzymes.
6. Write an esssay on enzymes.
7. What are enzymes ? Discuss their mechanism of action.
8. What are enzymes ? Discuss their properties and mode of action.
9. Discuss the chemical natrue, mechanism of action and properties of enzymes.
10. Discuss the structure and the mechanism of the enzyme action.
11. Enzymes are 'biological middle men'. Justify the statement.
12. Write short note on enzymes.
13. Boiled yeast cannot ferment sugar. Comment.
14. Give an example and importance of coenzyme.
15. Where are the following enzymes located in the plant cell? In what process do they participate ?
    (*a*) hydrolases (*b*) dehydrogenases
    (*c*) lyases (*d*) transferases.
16. What kind of reaction does each of the following group of enzymes catalyse ?
17. List threee important properties of enzymes.
18. How does competitive inhibition differ from allosteric inhibition ?
19. How does competitive inhibition of an enzyme occur ? How is such inhibiton useful ?
20. What role does temperature play in food preservation ? Explain.
21. How are enzymes named ? How have enzymes been classified ?
22. What does an enzyme do in terms of energy requirement of a reaction ? What would happen if the enzyme did not play this role ?
23. What is the name given to that part of the enzyme where catalytic work is carried out ?
24. Explain differences in the following :
    (*a*) coenzyme (*b*) prosthetic group (*c*) co-factor
25. Explain the following :
    Frozen and boiled leaf extract hardly exhibit any enzyme activity but when brought to room temperature, the former shows enzyme activity and the later fails to do so.
26. What are enzymes ? Write about their :
    (*a*) Mode of action (*b*) Role in plant metabolism (*c*) Classification

27. Give a short account of the mechanism of action of enzymes.
28. Differentiate between :
    (*a*) Competitive and non-competitive inhibitors
    (*b*) Coenzymes and co-factors
    (*c*) NAD^+ and $NADP^+$
29. Describe chemical nature and characteristics of enzymes.
30. What is Michaelis-Meten Constant ? What is its significance.
31. What are coenzymes ? Illustrate your answer with two examples.
32. What are enzymes? Describe the various factors affecting the enzymes activity.
33. Give an account of classification and mechanism of action of enzymes.
34. What kind of reaction does each of the following group of enzymes catalyse
    (*a*) hydrolases (*b*) dehydrogenases
    (*c*) lyases (*d*) transferases
35. What is the name given to that part of the enzyme where catalytic work is carried out ?
36. How does competitive inhibition differ from allosteric inhibition ?
37. How does competitive inhibition of an enzyme occur ? How is such inhibition useful ?
38. List three important properties of enzymes.
39. How are enzymes named ? How have enzymes been classified recently ?
40. What role does temperature play in food preservation ? Explain.

Multiple Choice Questions

1. Which of the following statements is not correct ?
   (*a*) Enzymes are simple or combined proteins acting as specific catalysts.
   (*b*) Enzymes are organic catalysts.
   (*c*) Enzymes are biological catalysts.
   (*d*) None of the above.
2. Protein part of the enzyme is called
   (*a*) holoenzyme (*b*) prosthetic group (*c*) apoenzyme (*d*) none of the above
3. The specific region of the enzymic protien which is involved in biochemical reaction is called :
   (*a*) active region (*b*) active site (*c*) both (*a*) and (*b*) (*d*) none of the above
4. The enzymes differ from inorganic catalysts in being :
   (*a*) products of living cells
   (*b*) proteinaceous in nature
   (*c*) remarkably specific toward their substrates
   (*d*) all of above
5. The enzymes which operate externally to the cells in which they originate are called :
   (*a*) exoenzymes (*b*) extracellular enzymes
   (*c*) exocellular enzymes (*d*) all of above
6. One of the first enzymes discovered in isozyme form is :
   (*a*) aspartate kinase (*b*) lactate dehydrogenase
   (*c*) malate dehydrogenase (*d*) none of the above
7. If an enzyme substrate system has lower value of Km, then binding of substrate to its enzyme will be :
   (*a*) more strong (*b*) less strong (*c*) inhibited (*d*) none of the above
8. Concentration of substrate to half saturate the enzyme or to cause half the maximal recaction rate is called :
   (*a*) Michaelis constant (*b*) Michaelis-Menten constant
   (*c*) Km (*d*) all of above

9. Allosteric enzymes have
   (*a*) Active sites (*b*) allosteric sites (*c*) both (*a*) and (*b*) (*d*) none of the above
10. Competitive inhibitor of the activity of the enzyme succinic dehydrogenase is :
   (*a*) malonic acid (*b*) succinic acid (*c*) fumaric acid (*d*) none of the above
11. Which of the following statements is not correct ?
   (*a*) Enzymes act in very small amounts
   (*b*) Enzymes are sensitive to heat, pH and inhibitors
   (*c*) Enzymes are specific in their action
   (*d*) Enzymes catalyse only reversible reactions
12. The enzymes act by :
   (*a*) loweirng the energy of activation of reactions
   (*b*) increasing the energy of activation of reactions
   (*c*) conserving the energy of activation of reactions
   (*d*) none of the above
13. Which of the following coenzymes is a carrier of acyl group ?
   (*a*) Coenzyme A (*b*) Coenzyme Q (*c*) Coenzyme II (*d*) Coenzyme F
14. Which of following organic compounds act as prosthetic groups in some enzymic reactions and as cofactor in some others ?
   (*a*) FMN (*b*) FAD (*c*) Biotin (*d*) All of above
15. Non-protien chemical substances which are required for enzymic reatcion but are not tightly bound to the enzyme (by covalent linkages) are called :
   (*a*) prosthetic groups (*b*) cofactors
   (*c*) general activators (*d*) coenzymes
16. Which of the following hydrolysing enzymes do not hydrolyse ester bonds
   (*a*) Phosphatases (*b*) Phosphatidases (*c*) Lipases (*d*) Peptidases
17. According to new system of classification the enzymes are grouped into :
   (*a*) four major groups (*b*) five major groups
   (*c*) six major groups (*d*) seven major groups
18. First enzyme to be isolated in pure crystalline form was :
   (*a*) zymase (*b*) urease (*c*) invertase (*d*) diastase
19. The word enzyme was coined by :
   (*a*) F.W. Kuhne (*b*) Louis Pastur (*c*) Alexopoulos (*d*) C.E. Bessey
20. Except for small group of catalytic RNA molecules, all enzymes are :
   (*a*) proteins (*b*) lipids (*c*) protiens and lipids (*d*) none of the above
21. Different enzymes show optimum activity in :
   (*a*) acidic medium (*b*) alkaline medium (*c*) neutral medium (*d*) either of the above
22. Coenzyme is
   (*a*) always. a protein (*b*) often a metal
   (*c*) always an inorganic compound (*d*) often a vitamin
23. Enzymes generally have :
   (*a*) same pH and temperature optima
   (*b*) same pH but different temperature optima
   (*c*) different pH but same temperature optima
   (*d*) different pH and different temperature optima
24. The term feed-back refers to :
   (*a*) the effect of substrate on the rate of enzymatic reaction

(*b*) the effect of end product on the rate of enzymatic reaction
(*c*) the effect of enzyme concentration on its rate of reaction
(*d*) the effect of an external compound on the rate of enzymatic reaction.

25. Which of the following is the best evidence for the lock and key theory of enzyme action ?
(*a*) All isolated enzymes have been identified as proteins
(*b*) Compounds similar in structure to the substrate inhibit the reaction.
(*c*) Enzymes are found in living organisms and speed up certain reactions.
(*d*) Enzymes determine the direction of a reaction.

ANSWERS

1. (*d*)	2. (*c*)	3. (*b*)	4. (*d*)	5. (*d*)	6. (*b*)	7. (*a*)	8. (*d*)	9. (*c*)	10. (*a*)
11. (*d*)	12. (*a*)	13. (*a*)	14. (*d*)	15. (*b*)	16. (*d*)	17. (*c*)	18. (*b*)	19. (*a*)	20. (*a*)
21. (*d*)	22. (*b*)	23. (*d*)	24. (*b*)	25. (*c*)					

UNIT - 4
Plant Physiology

15
CHAPTER

Plant Water Relations

The plants absorb water and soluble mineral salts from the soil by their root system. This function of absorption is facilitated by the unicellular root hairs present on the roots. These unicellular root hairs enter in the interspaces of the soil particles, irregularly. These root hairs absorb the water found in the form of thin films around these soil particles.

Cell as a physiological unit. Cells are the building blocks from which living things are made. A single cell may make up an entire organism, or groups of cells may be loosely organised and live together.

Scientists have known about cells for a long time. About two hundred years back biologists realised that 'the cell is the basic unit of all living organisms, hence **cell theory** was proposed by two German scientists, 'Schleiden and Schwann'.

The major ideas of cell theory are:

1. Living things are made up of cells and cell products.
2. Cells are very much alike in their structure and composition.
3. Cells have a set of functions that they carry out in order to stay alive.
4. New cells arise from old cells by cell reproduction.

However, plant cells are composed of cell wall and protoplast.

The term **protoplast** is generally used to refer collectively to the **plasma membrane** and **protoplasm**.

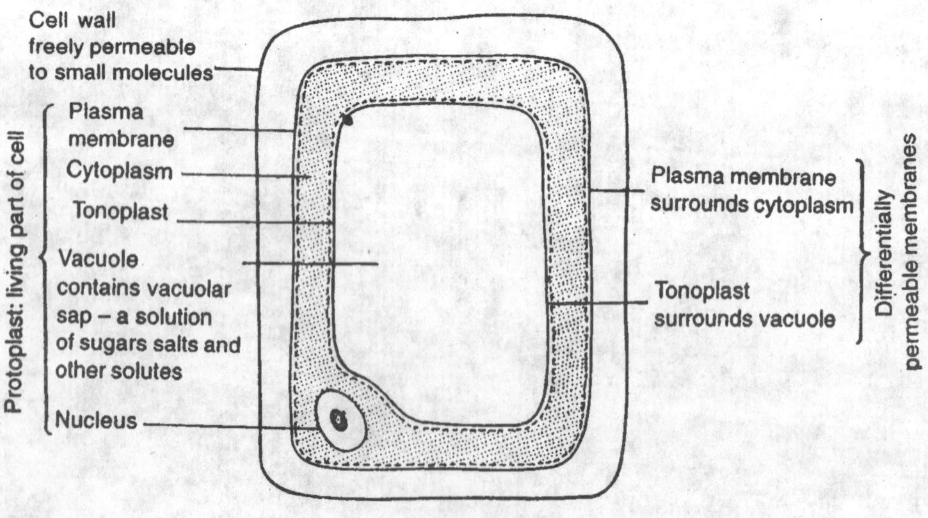

Fig. 15.1. Structure of a plant cell.

The protoplasm refers to the living contents of the cells and consists of **cytoplasm** and **nucleus**.

Generally, the plant cell possesses three compartments:

(*i*) Vacuole, (*ii*) protoplasm and (*iii*) cell wall. These compartments are separated from each other by **plasma membranes,** *i.e.*, the tonoplast is found in between the vacuole and the protoplasm, while plasmalemma between the protoplasm and the cell wall. Plasmodesmata, connect the protoplasm of one cell to that of other cell.

The plasma membrane is **selectively permeable**. This means, it allows some materials to pass through and not others.

The plasma membrane is made up almost of protein and lipid molecules.

Protoplasm. According to modern view, the protoplasm is a colourless, semi-transparent and viscous substance. It is considered as complex colloidal system of many phases.

Table 15.1. Differences Between Plant Cells and Animal Cells

Plant Cells	Animal Cells
1. Plant cells have a rigid cell wall made of **cellulose**.	1. Cellulose cell wall absent.
2. **Plastids** present. Photosynthesis takes place in **chloroplasts**.	2. Plastids absent. No photosynthesis, no chloroplasts.
3. Each plant cell has a large vacuole containing water and salt.	3. Vacuoles absent.
4. Centrioles absent.	4. They have **centrioles**, which are active during reproduction of cell. Centrioles contain microtubules which help to separate and to sort chromosome material during cell division.

However, it is well established that water is chief component of all physiologically active protoplasm and in such cases may constitute upto 90% of the protoplasm and in cases of hydrophytes even more. In dry seeds where the protoplasm is rather inactive, water may be less than 10% of the total protoplasm.

The Water

Importance of water. The water is the most important factor for the vital functions of the plants. The plants cannot survive in its absence. Water is a very important solvent, and usually consists most of the part of the protoplasm. Many biochemical reactions going on in the plants are catalysed by many enzymes, formed in the protoplasm. Usually 75% quantity of water is found in the cytoplasm. Usually in the leaves, the quantity of water is 75% , whereas in the stems it is 60%. In several hydrophytes, *e.g.*, algae, etc., this quantity exceeds up to 98%. In the same way, the quantity of water in the xerophytes is usually 60% or lesser than this. In the dormant seeds, this

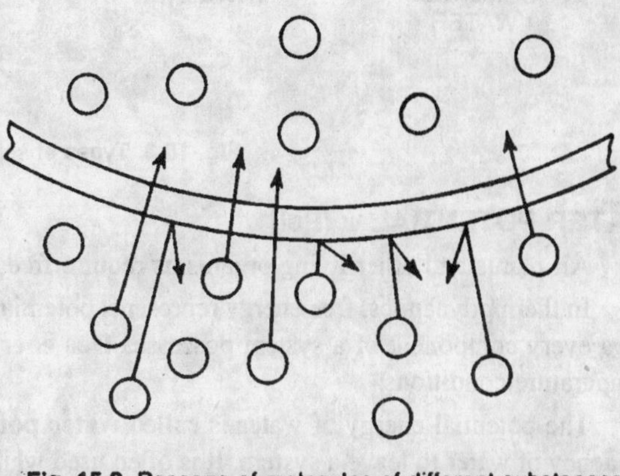

Fig. 15.2. Passage of molecules of different substances through a selectively permeable membrane.

quantity of water is only about 10%. This is, of course very much less for any vital function, and therefore, the germination of these seeds is only then possible, when they get sufficient moisture. The cytoplasm can remain viable only in the presence of sufficient amount of water. In the scarcity of water, it dies. The water also plays an important role in the function of photosynthesis. The water is a good solvent, the minerals cannot be absorbed unless they are not soluble in water. The cell of the plants remain turgid by water; and give temporary mechanical support to the young plants.

The water found in the plants, is a very small part of the water absorbed by the plants, rest of the larger part of the water goes out from the surface of the plants, by a vital process, called **transpiration**.

Availability of the water in the soil. About three forms of water are found in the soil. Just after the rains, because of gravitation some amount of water along with some mineral salts goes in the lower strata of the earth. This is called **gravitational** or **free water** and cannot be used by the plants. Besides this, every particle of soil holds some imbibed water in it. This water is hold up in the soil particle with such a great imbibition force, that it cannot be separated from it for the use of the plant. This is called **hygroscopic water**, which also cannot be absorbed from the soil by the plants. Besides these each soil particle is surrounded by a loose film of water; this film is attracted by the capillary force to the soil particle, and such water film is called **capillary water**. Now it is to be noticed, that only this capillary water may be absorbed by the root hairs of the plants. The mineral salts are also found in this water in soluble state, and are absorbed by the plants along with water. If soil lacks this capillary water, the plants very soon begin to wither and ultimately die.

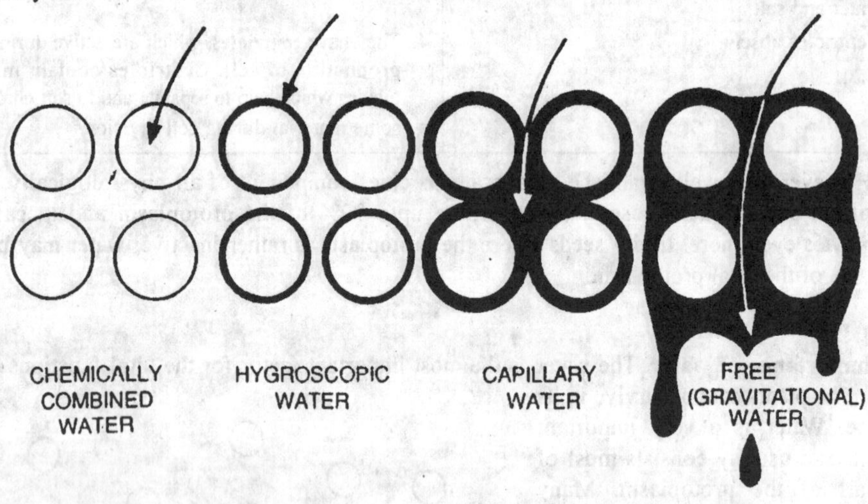

Fig. 15.3. Types of soil water.

WATER POTENTIAL ψ (Psi)

All plants and other living organisms require free energy to grow and reproduce.

In thermodynamics, free energy represents potential to do work. According to thermodynamic laws every component of a system possesses **free energy** capable of doing work under constant temperature conditions.

The potential energy of water is called **water potential**. Water potential is regarded as the tendency of water to leave a system. It is often used while explaining the direction in which water will flow from one cell to another, or from one part of the plant to another such as from soil to root, from root to leaves, from leaves to air, or from soil to air.

Water always moves from a region of higher water potential to that of lower water potential. It can also be said that the difference in water potential between two points is a measure of the amount of work, *i.e.*, energy, needed to move water from one point to the other.

Osmotic movement of water involves certain work done and in fact the main driving force behind this movement is the difference between free energies of water on two sides of the selectively permeable membrane. For water free energy molecule is known as water potential (ψ_w).

Water potential is measured in terms of pressure. Common measurement unit of water potential is **Pascal**, *Pa* ; *1* Megapascal represents 10 bars, *i.e.*, 1 **Megapascal** = 10 **bars**. One bar is close to one atmosphere of pressure, *i.e.*, 1 bar = 0.987 atmosphere of pressure.

At atmospheric pressure water potential of pure water is zero, and therefore, all solutions at atmospheric pressure have lower water potentials than water, *i.e.*, they have a negative value.

Water potential ψ_w is measured in relative quantity, and expressed as the difference between the potential of a solution in a given state and the potential of the same solution in a standard state.

Water potential is lowered by the addition of solutes and as water potential value is zero for pure water, all other water potential values will be negative. Thus, the movement of water will take place in osmotic or other systems from a region of **higher water potential** (*i.e.*, less negative) to a region of **lower water potential** (*i.e.*, more negative).

Water potential of any solution (ψ_w) is influenced by three factors. (*i*) concentration, (*ii*) pressure and (*iii*) gravity. This can be represented by following equation:

$$\psi_w = \psi_s + \psi_p + \psi_g$$

i.e., ψ_s effect of solutes (*i.e.*, **solute potential** or **osmotic potential)**

ψ_p effect of pressure (*i.e.*, **pressure potential** or **hydrostatic pressure)**

ψ_g effect of gravity (*i.e.*, **gravity potential)**

This means, pure water has a higher potential than the water inside a cell. In other words ψ_w of pure water is zero, and therefore, water potential ψ_w inside plant cells is negative.

Solute potential (ψ_s). Solutes present in a cell reduce the free energy of water, or the water potential.

Pressure potential (ψ_p) or hydrostatic pressure. The positive hydrostatic pressure is called **turgor pressure**. The pressure potential for pure water in an open beaker is zero.

Gravity potential (ψ_g). This term represents the effect of gravity on water potential. It depends on the height of water. If vertical height is less than five meters, the ψ_g is negligible. In a plant cell only ψ_s and ψ_p are important, and considered, *i.e.*, $\psi_w = \psi_s + \psi_p$.

According to this equation when water moves into the cell from outside, the hydrostatic pressure, *i.e.*, pressure potential (ψ_p) increases, which results in an increased water potential (ψ_w) of the cell, and the difference between the inside and outside ψ_w ($\Delta\ \psi_w$) is reduced.

On the other hand, when concentration of solute is increased in the cell, the solute potential (ψ_s) is lowered, and therefore, water potential (ψ_w) is decreased.

Table 15.2. Differences Between DPD and Water Potential

Diffusion Pressure Deficit (DPD)	Water Potential ψ (Psi)
1. It is measure of actual pressure.	1. It is measure of free energy.
2. It is measure of decrease in diffusion pressure of water (pure solvent) due to addition of solute molecules.	2. It is measure of difference of energy of pure water and an aqueous solution.
3. It is equal in magnitude and opposite in direction to water potential (ψ Psi).	3. It is equal in magnitude and opposite in direction to diffusion.

Thus, water moves into the cell from outside due to a water potential gradient. If a pressure is created on the cell, water moves out of it. Here, external pressure raises the water potential (ψ_w) of the cell, and thus the difference in water potential (ψ_w) inside and outside ($\Delta\ \psi_w$) will be such that water will flow out of cell.

There are two basic factors that affect the water potential : (*i*) amount of solute and (*ii*) external pressure.

(*i*) **Amount of solute.** Pure water at atmospheric pressure has a zero water potential. An addition of solutes lowers the water potential (ψ_w), *i.e.*, it becomes negative in value.

(*ii*) **External pressure.** Effect of pressure on water potential is just opposite to the effect of solutes, *i.e.*, the increase in pressure increases the water potential (ψ_w).

ABSORPTION AND MOVEMENT OF WATER

The absorption of water and solutes from the soil seems to have been the first physiological processes to receive the attention of early writers on botanical subjects. According to Aristotle plant foods are complex substances which have been so prepared in the soil that they can be absorbed and used by the plant without any changes, hence without the necessity of excreting any

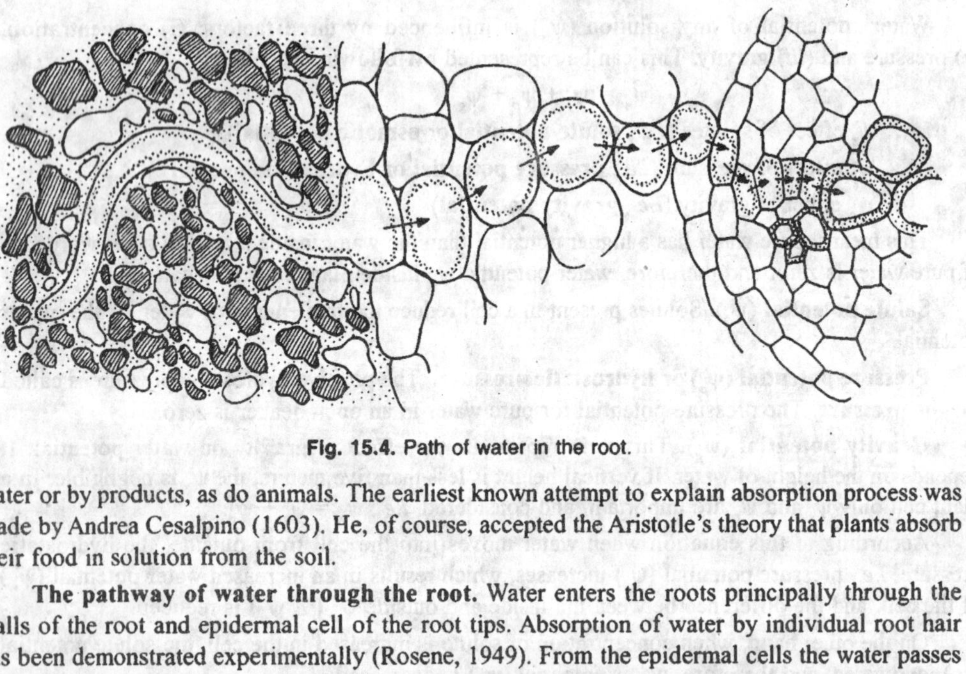

Fig. 15.4. Path of water in the root.

water or by products, as do animals. The earliest known attempt to explain absorption process was made by Andrea Cesalpino (1603). He, of course, accepted the Aristotle's theory that plants absorb their food in solution from the soil.

The pathway of water through the root. Water enters the roots principally through the walls of the root and epidermal cell of the root tips. Absorption of water by individual root hair has been demonstrated experimentally (Rosene, 1949). From the epidermal cells the water passes through successive rows of thin walled cortical cells and then through the cells of endodermis.

After passing through the endodermis water moves into xylem tissue ducts. Once in the xylem ducts its general direction of movement is upward. The xylem tissue is continuous from just back of the tips of roots, through the roots, into and through the stems, the petioles of leaves and ultimately terminates in the mesophyll of the leaf. The xylem tissue through which the water moves thus a continuous system with the body of the plant.

Water in the root moves through two pathways:

(*i*) **Apoplast pathway** and

(*ii*) **Symplast pathway.**

E. Munch of Germany introduced **apoplast-symplast** concept in 1932. He suggested that the interconnecting cell walls and intercellular spaces including the water-filled (or air-filled) xylem elements should be considered as a single system and called the **apoplast.**

The remaining part of the plant consists of the protoplasts of the cells. Evidence based upon electron micrograph now indicates that the cytoplasm connected from cell to cell via the

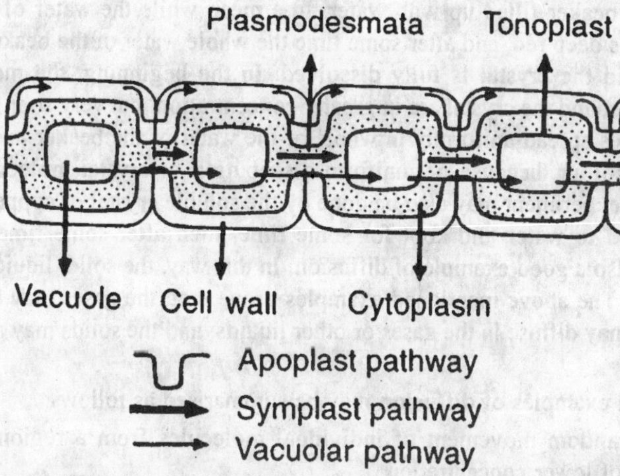

Fig. 15.5. Pathways of water movement.

plasmodesmata also constitutes an interconnected system. This system of interconnected protoplasm (excluding vacuoles) was termed by Munch the **symplast**.

Major proportion of water flow in the root cortex occurs via the **apoplast**, as cells of cortex are loosely packed, and therefore, cortex does not show any resistance.

However, apoplastic water movement beyond cortical region is blocked by casparian strip, present in endodermis. The casparian strip consists of a wax-like substance called suberin, which blocks water and solute movement through the cell wall of endodermis.

Thus, beyond endodermis, water is forced to move through cell membranes. Such movement of water through cell membrane is called **transmembrane pathway**. In this pathway water may also cross through the **tonoplast** surrounding the vacuole.

Once the water reaches root xylem, transpiration pull drives the water to move the leaves through the stem.

Diffusion

If we keep hydrogen sulphide gas (H_2S) exposed in any corner of the room, after a very short time the whole room is filled up with bad odour of the gas. In fact, this happens because the molecules of hydrogen sulphide gas gradually spread in the whole room. In other words, it can be said that the molecules of the gas gradually mix with the molecules of the air present in the room, uniformly. This process is called **diffusion**. During respiration the oxygen is used in the leaf, and the carbon dioxide is accumulated in the intercellular spaces of the leaf. Now this carbon dioxide comes outside in the atmosphere, by diffusion and the oxygen is taken in the cells by diffusion. This process of diffusion may take place in all kinds of matters such as solid, liquid and gas. In other words, it can be said that the molecules of these matters may spread uniformly in the solvent.

If the volatile substances, such as petroleum, alcohol, ether and perfumes, etc., are kept exposed in a room, then in a meanwhile, the whole room fills up with the odour of the volatile substance. It means, the molecules of these substances spread in the whole room, and gradually mix with the molecules of the air present in the room. Besides these, if the solid substances such as naphthalene balls and camphor are kept exposed in the room, very soon their molecules spread, and mix with air molecules, and the whole room fills up with their odour. The solid substances are also diffused in the liquid substance, but with a slow speed. For example, a crystal of potassium permanganate ($KMnO_4$) is dropped in a beaker filled up with water. In a mean while the water of the beaker around this crystal becomes deep red, and after some time the whole water of the beaker becomes of uniform red colour, and the crystal is fully dissolved. In the beginning, the molecules of potassium permanganate, around the crystal are in greater concentration, but very soon, the crystal dissolves, and the molecules spread uniformly in whole of the water of the beaker and the water becomes of uniform red colour, because of uniform distribution of crystal molecules, in the solvent, by diffusion. This experiment may also be done by the soluble crystal of copper sulphate. If sugar crystals are added to water and kept for some time, then after some time the water becomes sweet — this is also a good example of diffusion. In this way, the solid, liquid and gases diffuse in different media. The above mentioned examples prove that, the gases may be diffused in other gases; the liquids may diffuse in the gases or other liquids; and the solids may also diffuse either in gas or in liquid.

The above mentioned examples of **diffusion** may be summarised as follows:

That diffusion is a random movement of individual molecules from a region of higher concentration to a region of lower concentration.

Larger the difference in concentration more rapid is the flow of molecules.

Diffusion is more rapid in gases than in liquids.

When there is no further movement of molecules, a state of equilibrium is acquired, which means that the diffusing substance is evenly distributed.

In diffusion, the movement of molecules is random and independent of each other.

Suitable examples of diffusion in plants are: supply of carbon dioxide from atmosphere to the leaves for photosynthesis, and loss of water vapour from leaves to the atmosphere.

Permeability

The concept of permeability is inseparable from the idea of a membrane. Permeability is a property of the membrane, not of substance which diffuses through it.

Some membranes are impermeable to all substances, others allow all or most substances to diffuse through them with little resistance. Many biologically important membranes are of the type known as **differentially permeable**. Such membranes allow some substances to pass through them much more readily than others. The extent to which a membrane permits or restricts the movement of a substance is called **membrane permeability**. It depends on the membrane composition, as well as chemical nature of solute. Permeability can be measured readily by determining the rate at which solute passes through a membrane under a specific set of conditions.

Osmosis

It is usually seen, that when two liquids of different densities are separated from each other by placing a membrane between them, by which the water of the liquid of lower density flows towards the liquid of higher density, then such separating membrane is called the **semipermeable membrane**. In other words, only the solvent or water may pass through such membrane, the solute or the dissolved substance in the water cannot pass through it. The parchment paper, egg membrane, goat bladder, etc., are the good examples of semipermeable membranes. In the plant cell, the cell wall is permeable whereas the protoplasmic membrane is semipermeable. When concentrated and dilute solutions or the solutions of lower density and higher density are separated from each other by such membrane, then the solvent moves from a concentrated solution to dilute solution. This process is called the **'osmosis'**.

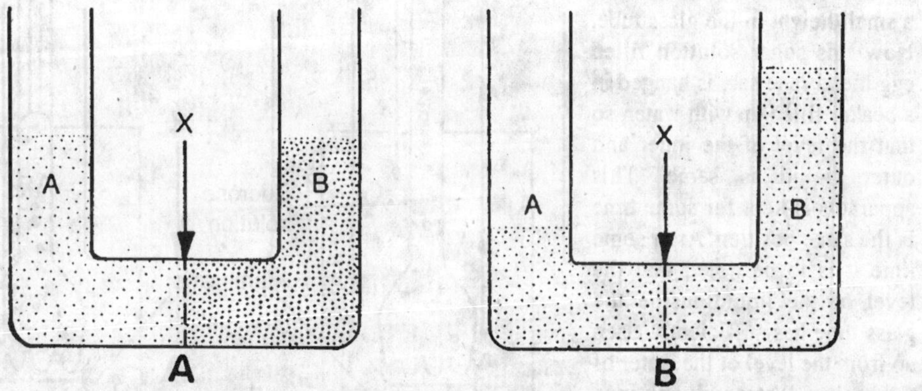

Fig. 15.6. Diagrammatic representation of osmosis, *x* indicates the semipermeable membrane.

Table 15.3. Differences Between Diffusion and Osmosis

Diffusion	Osmosis
1. Diffusion can occur in any medium.	1. It occurs only in liquid medium.
2. The diffusing molecules may be solids, liquids or gases.	2. It involves movement of solvent molecules only.
3. Semipermeable membrane is not required.	3. Semipermeable membrane is required.
4. It is dependent upon the free energy of the molecules of diffusing substance only; presence of other substances in the system is of no importance.	4. Though it is the diffusion of solvent molecules only, yet influenced by the presence of other substances (solutes) in the system.
5. It is not influenced by the pressures other than diffusion pressure.	5. It is influenced by turgor or hydrosttic pressure of the system.
6. An equilibrium in the free energy of diffusion molecules is achieved in the system.	6. Equilibrium in the free energy of solvent molecules is never achieved.
7. Factors like water potential, solute potential and pressure potential do not affect diffusion.	7. Water potential, solute potential and pressure potential do not affect osmosis in a living system.

In other words, diffusion of water through a semipermeable membrane is called **osmosis.**

The diffusion of water molecules continues to occur across the membrane till an equilibrium is acquired. At equilibrium **water potential** (ψ_w) on both sides of membrane is equal.

To demonstrate osmosis experimentally following experiments may be done:

1. Egg membrane experiment. To demonstrate osmosis by this experiment an egg is taken. On the pointed side of the egg a small hole is formed and all the white and yellow matter of the egg is taken out through this hole. Now the empty egg is placed in the dilute solution of hydrochloric acid (HCl), so that the hard shell of the egg constituted of calcium carbonate is dissolved in it. The membrane of the egg, found just beneath the cell remains intact. Now this egg membrane is thoroughly washed with tap water, and a glass tube is inserted in it through its hole and tied tightly with a piece of thread, so that the end of the glass tube remains inside the egg membrane. Now, the concentrated solution of sugar is poured in it through glass tube with the help of a thistle funnel. The sugar solution is filled up in such a quantity, so that after completely filling the egg membrane sac, it also reaches to a small height in the glass tube. Now this sugar solution filled egg membrane sac, is hanged in a beaker filled up with water, so that the level of the inner and outer liquid is same. This apparatus is kept for some time in the same position. After some time it is to be noted that the level of the liquid inside the glass tube has sufficiently risen up from the level of the water of the beaker. Water will continue to move across the membrane, resulting in the rise of solution in the funnel until an equilibrium is reached.

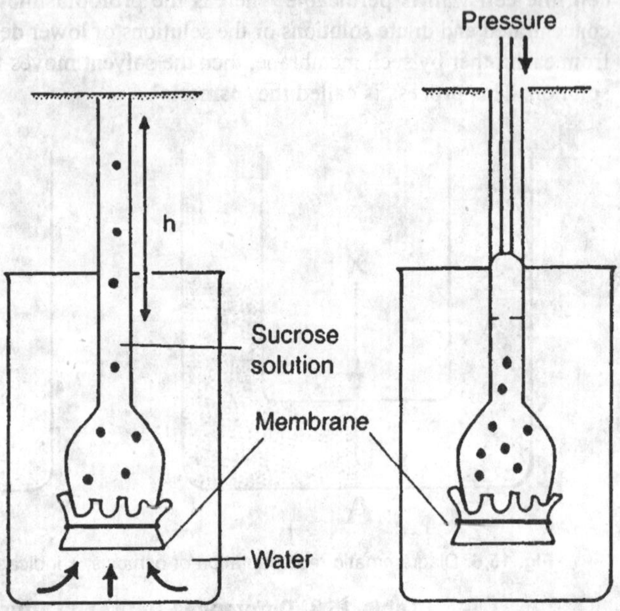

Fig. 15.7. Demonstration of osmosis by egg membrane experiment.

Pressure can be applied to the solution from upper part of funnel to prevent movement of water into it through egg membrane.

The pressure required to stop the movement of water completely is called **osmotic pressure.** This may be also referred as **osmotic potential** or **solute potential** (ψ_s).

Osmotic pressure and osmotic potential are numerically equal, but osmotic potential has a negative (–) sign.

An isolated solution without solute, and not bounded by any membrane, has no osmotic pressure. It has only the potential to result into a pressure when placed in an osmometer.

Thus, a solution has an osmotic potential (ψ_s), which is negative (–) of osmotic pressure (π, pi). The equation is

$$\psi_s = -\pi$$

If one reverses the experiment by filling up the water in the egg membrane sac and the sugar solution in the beaker then the water moves from inner side to outer side. This process is called **reverse osmosis**. The process of reverse osmosis is used for removing salts from saline water.

Process of osmosis is controlled by two important factors :

(*i*) Concentration of dissolved solutes in a solution, and

(*ii*) Pressure difference.

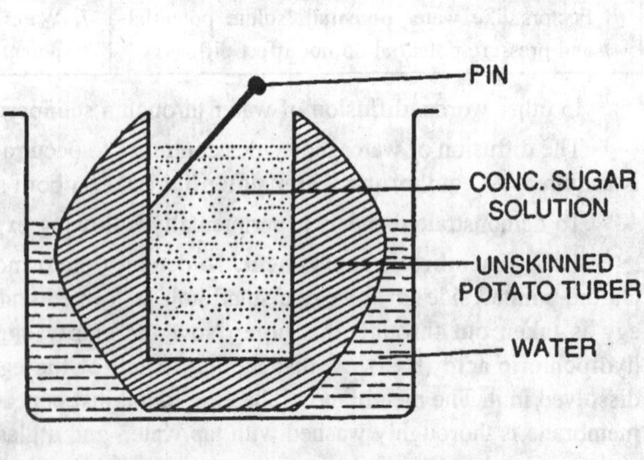

Fig. 15.8. Osmosis. Demonstration with potato osmoscope.

These two factors determine the **chemical potential** of water, which acts as driving force for water movement in plants.

Water moves from a region of high chemical potential of water to a region of low chemical potential of water.

Chemical potential of water is also called water potential, and denotes free energy associated with water.

2. Potato osmoscope experiment. One peeled potato tuber is taken. Now make it flat at its one end. Also make a deep and broad cavity on the other end of it, so that the bed of the cavity may reach up to flat surface, and the outer walls of the cavity become somewhat thin. Now fill up this cavity with concentrated sugar solution and place this potato osmoscope in a beaker containing water, so that the level of the outer and inner liquids may remain the same. After a short time, it is to be noted that the level of the liquid filled in the cavity of the potato osmoscope goes higher, because of endosmosis. The density of the sugar solution, filled up inside the potato cavity is higher than the water of the beaker. Here, the tissues of the tuber act as a semipermeable membrane, and thus the water moves from outside to inner side.

Plasmolysis

To demonstrate this process experimentally, one will have to take the red coloured epidermal peel of the lower surface of *Tradescantia* leaf. Now, this peel is mounted in a drop of water on a microscopic slide and then examined under the microscope. At this moment the cells are fully turgid, and are filled up with red coloured cell sap. Now, this epidermal peel is kept in a drop of salt or sugar solution and again examined under the microscope. The exosmosis occurs and the cell shrinks in its size. The cell soon reaches to its minimum volume. If the exosmosis continues further, there is no further shrinkage in the cell wall, but the protoplasmic membrane begins to recede or contract from the corners first. This stage is called the **incipient plasmolysis**. If exosmosis continues further, there is further contraction of the protoplasmic membrane, thus reaching the **complete plasmolysis** stage. In the case of complete plasmolysis the cell sap, protoplasm and nucleus, etc., are completely contracted in the centre of the cell leaving away the cell wall. The in-between part of the cell is filled up with the sugar or salt solution. Here, around the vacuole, the protoplasmic membrane acts as a semipermeable membrane, which allows water to come out through it and leaving other contents inside the cell. If the plasmolysed cells are again placed in water, there is recovery to the original condition due to endosmosis of water, and this process is called **deplasmolysis**.

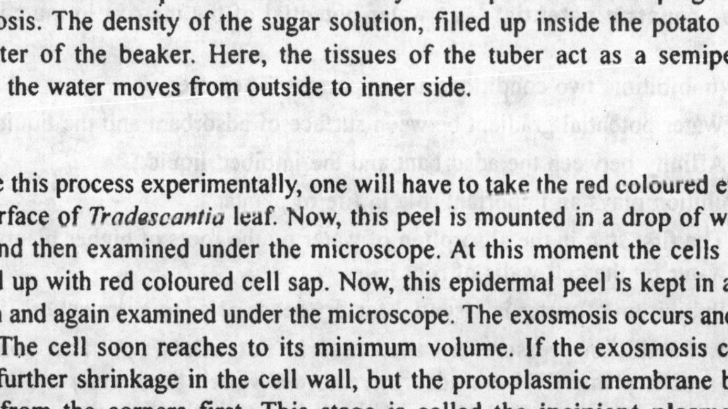

Fig. 15.9. Plasmolysis. Stages in plasmolysis of a plant cell.

Continuous loss of water from plant cells results in wilting and drooping of leaves and stems.

Imbibition

This process is a type of diffusion by which movement of water takes place along a diffusion gradient. Due to this process certain dried and half-dried matters absorb water. Such substances (*e.g.*, fibres, wood pieces, proteins and sponges) are called **adsorbants**. An adsorbant is required for the **imbibition** to occur. The cell wall and the protoplasm also absorb water by the process of imbibition. The absorption by imbibition is possible only in those conditions, where there is a great affinity between adsorbant and water, otherwise this is not possible. For example, cotton fibres absorb water by this process, whereas rubber sheet does not, as there is no affinity between rubber and water. Dry plant material or seeds act as adsorbant to imbibe water and swell. The swollen seeds produce a large pressure developed by imbibition. This pressure forces the seedlings to emerge above the ground through the soil surface. Here, with the result of imbibition pressure, the seed coat bursts and seedling comes out of ground. This pressure is called **imbibition pressure** or **matric potential** (*i.e.*, water potential of the matrix) in the context of plant water relations.

For imbibition, two conditions are important. They are:

(*i*) Water potential gradient between surface of adsorbant and the liquid imbibed.

(*ii*) Affinity between the adsorbant and the imbibed liquid.

Imbibition plays an important role in life of plants.

(*i*) The first step in the absorption of water by the roots of higher plants is the imbibition of water by the cell walls of root hairs.

(*ii*) Imbibition of water is essential for dry seeds prior to germination.

Now, imbibition pressure is called **matric potential** (ψ_m). The matric potential in an imbibant results primarily from adsorptive forces which bind water molecules to micelles or molecules of the adsorbant (imbibant) and is analogous to the osmotic potential of a solution. In a solution, the greater the amount of water present in proportion to a given amount of solute, the less negative (or higher) is the osmotic potential. Similarly, in an imbibant the greater the amount of water present in proportion to a given amount of imbibant, the less negative is the matric potential. With reference to pure water, the values of matric potentials are always negative.

The water potential of an imbibant is equal to its matric potential (always negative) plus any turgor or other pressure (pressure potential) which may be imposed upon the imbibant.

$$\psi_w = \psi_m + \psi_s$$

If the imbibant is unconfined no turgor or such pressure is involved and hence the above equation is simplified as:

$$\psi_w = \psi_m$$

THEORIES OF WATER TRANSLOCATION

A suction pump can lift water only to the barometric height, (*i.e.*, about 10.3 m or 34 feet at 1 atm pressure). Yet some trees are 130 meters (*i.e.*, 400 feet) tall from their water collecting roots in the soil to the upper tips of their branches. If the water is lifted to that height by pushing from below, some 13 atm or bars of pressure would be required in addition to that required to overcome the resistance and to maintain the flow. Different theories have been put forth to explain this phenomenon. The three important theories are:

(*i*) Capillarity

(*ii*) Root pressure

(*iii*) Cohesion theory.

Capillarity

Question arises, can the water be raised to the top of such trees by **capillarity**?

Such a rise of water in small tubes comes about because of the **adhesion** between water molecules and the wall of the tube in which the process is taking place. This adhesion forms a **meniscus** in which the water tends to climb up the side of the container. The smaller the diameter of the tube, the greater is the lifting force of the meniscus compared to the amount of water to be lifted. Hence the smaller the tube, the higher the column of capillary water will rise. Force of gravity also affects water uptake by capillarity.

According to this theory, water is first driven in due to force of adhesion between water and the walls of thin xylem vessels, *i.e.*, tracheids. As the water flows upward along the wall, strong cohesive forces between water molecules begin to function and pull the water upward. This upward pull of water continues until the forces of adhesion and cohesion are balanced by downward force of gravity.

However, capillarity alone in the usual sense does not operate in plants. This seems to be an insufficient force to lift water in tall trees. Water is lifted less than one meter in glass or cellulose tubes the size of xylem elements.

Root Pressure

Such pressures from below, produced by the roots have been observed in several species. Grapevines, for example, are capable of showing fairly high root pressure (about 5 or 6 bars), yet no one considers root pressure as a mechanism for the translocation of water in tall trees.

If a stem of plant is cut transversely above the soil surface, xylem sap will exude in the form of a drop from the cut surface. This exhibits the presence of a positive pressure in the xylem. This pressure is called **root pressure**.

Although, root pressure which is developed in the xylem of the roots can raise water to a certain height but it does not seem to be an effective force in ascent of sap due to following reasons:

(*i*) Magnitude of root pressure is quite low (about 2 bars).

(*ii*) Even in the absence of root pressure, ascent of sap continues.

(*iii*) Root pressures are not observed in conifers.

(*iv*) Mineral ions from the soil are taken up by roots and get deposited in the xylem vessels. Accumulation of ions in vessels leads to the lowering of osmotic potential.

(*v*) Root pressures are usually negligible, in temperate regions, where during summer transpiration is rapid.

Cohesion Theory

This theory was given by Henry Dixon in 1914. This theory is quite convincing and has been widely accepted. As the name suggests, the cohesion theory is based on the force of cohesion between water molecules. This forms a continuous water column throughout the xylem vessels of the plant, from the top to the root.

Water molecules remain joined to each other due to presence of **H-bonds** between them. Although H-bond is very weak, but when they are present in enormous numbers as in case of water, a very strong mutual force of attraction or cohesive force develops between water molecules and hence they remain in the form of a **continuous water column** in the xylem. The magnitude of this force is very high (about 350 atm or bars), therefore, continuous water column in the xylem cannot be broken easily due to force of gravity or any other means of resistance.

According to this theory, evaporation of water from the leaf to the atmosphere results in a decrease in the water potential of the epidermal cells, which are in direct contact with the atmosphere.

The water lost from epidermal cells is replaced by the water moving from the adjacent cells along a water potential gradient. The water lost from leaf cells is replaced by the water moving from the xylem elements in leaf veins (*i.e.*, xylem elements). Due to this pattern of water movement, a **tention** is created in water in the xylem elements of the leaves. This tention is transmitted downward to water in xylem elements of the roots through the xylem of petiole and stem and the water is pulled upward in the form of continuous unbroken **water column** to reach the transpiring surface upto the top of plants.

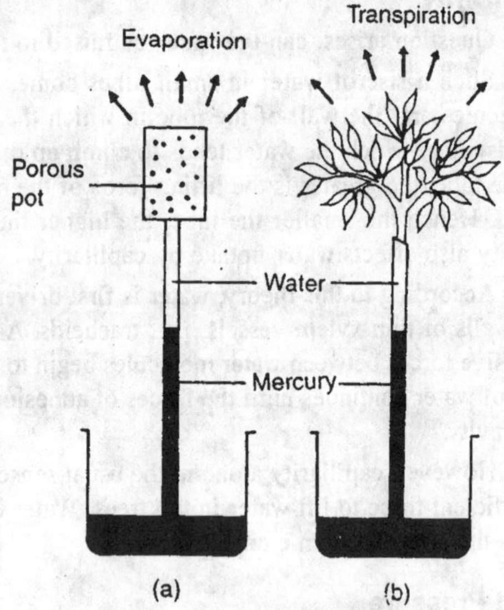

Fig. 15.10. Demonstration of cohesion theory: (*a*) evaporation and (*b*) transpiration.

Also the walls of xylem vessels are constituted of ligno-cellulose have strong affinity for water molecules. The water potential of root cells is lower than the water potential of soil, and therefore, movement of water occurs from soil to the roots. Uplift of water, is also referred to as **transpiration pull**.

TRANSPIRATION

The plants absorb sufficient quantity of water from the soil by means of their root hairs. Some part of this water is used up in the metabolic activities going on within the plant body and the rest of it evaporates from the stem and leaves. The evaporation of the water from the aerial parts of the plant is known as **transpiration**. Many authors described this phenomenon of transpiration from time to time in the following words:

'Transpiration is the loss of water in the form of water vapour from stem and leaves'. (Miller, 1930)

'The loss of water vapour from aerial parts of living plants is known as transpiration'. (Meyer, 1953)

'Transpiration is giving off of water vapour from the surface of a plant.' (Thomas, 1956)

The transpiration differs from ordinary evaporation this way, that the former is controlled by the protoplasm whereas latter does not. The transpiration is a metabolic activity, which is controlled by protoplasm and may be reduced or increased where needed by the nature.

Kinds of transpiration. In general, there are three kinds of transpiration *viz.* (1) cuticular, (2) lenticular and (3) stomatal. The cuticular transpiration takes place through the cuticle found on the surface of the stem and leaves. The lenticular transpiration takes place through the lenticels found upon the stem. During night the stomata remain closed and the plants transpire through lenticels and cuticle.The stomatal transpiration is the most important. This takes place through the stomata situated on the leaves and sometimes on the green stems. The number of stomata is usually always greater on the lower surface of the leaf. About 90 to 97% of the transpiration takes place through the stomata.

Mechanism of transpiration. About 90 to 97% of the transpiration takes place through stomata, and 3 to 10% through the cuticle. The lenticular transpiration is negligible. Here the mechanism of stomatal transpiration has been given in detail. As we know well the water rises up in the stem of the plant through xylem vessels. From the xylem vessels of the veins of the leaves, the water diffuses to the mesophyll tissue making gradually the assimilatory cells, fully turgid. The moist cellular walls release the water in the form of vapour which reaches the intercellular spaces. This way, the intercellular spaces become more saturated than the outer atmosphere. As the intercellular spaces are interconnected with the sub-stomatal chambers, they also become saturated with water vapour. The outer atmosphere is comparatively drier than the inner tissues and therefore, the water vapour diffuses from the sub-stomatal chambers to the outside through the stomata. The outer air remains in close contact of the leaves, evaporating the water from their surfaces. This process goes on continuously. The stomatal transpiration is controlled by the guard cells of the stomata.

Significance of transpiration. Transpiration helps in the movement of xylem sap, which also increases the absorption of mineral nutrients by the roots from the soil.

Transpiration causes cooling of leaves. Some solar radiations cause heating of the leaves. However, transpiration reduces heating of leaves. The additional water is transpired to the atmosphere from the aerial parts of the plants.

Factors Affecting Transpiration

The transpiration is affected by several external and internal factors. They are as follows:

External Factors

1. Light. The light affects indirectly the transpiration. The rate of transpiration is always higher in light than in darkness. The main reason is that the stomata remain open in the presence of light or in the day time, and the transpiration takes place through them. In the absence of light or in the night, the stomata remain closed, and the transpiration is checked. During night only lenticular and cuticular transpiration takes place. The leaves receive heat from the sun, which accelerates the rate to some extent.

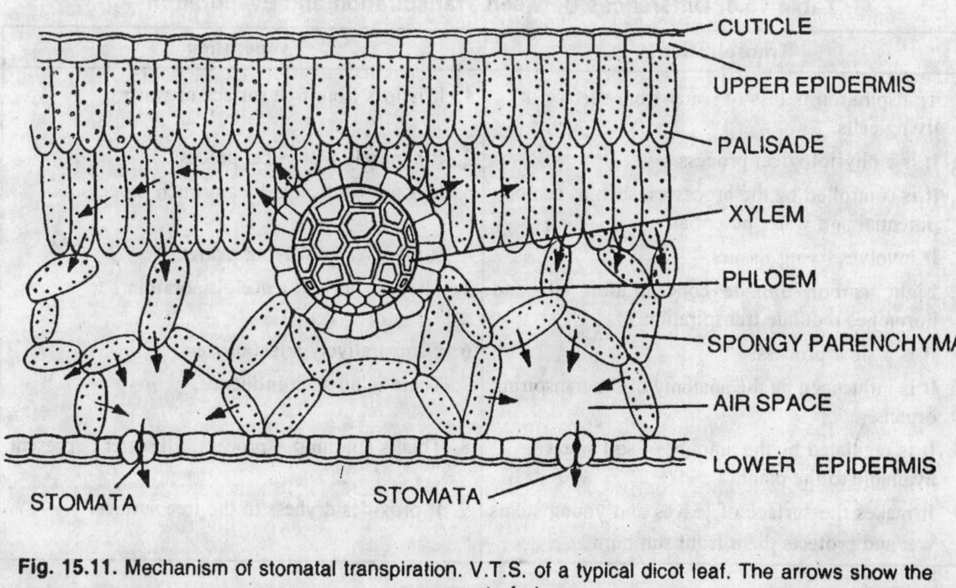

Fig. 15.11. Mechanism of stomatal transpiration. V.T.S. of a typical dicot leaf. The arrows show the movement of air.

2. Atmospheric moisture. Both the dryness and the humidity of the atmosphere affect the transpiration. When the atmosphere is very dry, then the water evaporates very rapidly from the surface of the leaves. On the other hand, in saturated atmosphere the rate of transpiration is quite slow.

3. Wind velocity. When wind blows very fast, the rate of transpiration also becomes very high, and on becoming the atmosphere calm and quiet, the transpiration lessens sufficiently due to moist air in close contact of the transpiring plants.

4. Air temperature. As the atmospheric temperature rises, the rate of transpiration also rises. In high temperatures the water evaporates from the leaf surface quite rapidly. In dry and hot air the rate of transpiration rises further.

5. Solar radiation. This factor is deeply related to the transpiration. The temperature of the leaves rises due to solar radiation, thus increasing the rate of transpiration. This way, solar radiation affects the transpiration indirectly.

6. Soil environment. This factor also affects the transpiration indirectly. The soil environment is much related to the water absorption. We know well, that the transpiring mesophyll cells of the leaves receive water from the soil. This way, the factor affecting the absorption of water from the soil, such as (1) soil water content, (2) concentration of soil solution, (3) soil temperature and (4) oxygen of soil air, etc., affect the transpiration indirectly. If there is enough of absorption of water, the transpiration takes place to a greater extent, on the other hand if the absorption of water is less the transpiration is also less.

Internal Factors

1. The root system. If the roots reach deep in the soil up to the moist layers, the root hairs absorb sufficient quantity of water and at the same time the transpiration increases from the aerial parts of the plants. On the other hand, if the root system of the plant remains confined in the upper layers of the soil, there is less absorption of water and less transpiration.

2. The stem. As we know that the water rises from the roots to the stem and leaves through the xylem vessels, and therefore, the rate of transpiration much depends upon the narrowness and broadness of the xylem vessels present in the stem. If the xylem vessels are sufficiently broad, the rate of transpiration increases, and if they are narrow there is comparatively less transpiration.

Table 15.4. Differences Between Transpiration and Evaporation

Transpiration	Evaporation
1. Transpiration is loss of water from surface of living cells.	1. It is loss from free surface of water.
2. It is a physiological process.	2. It is purely a physical process.
3. It is controlled by the processes, such as osmotic potential and water potential.	3. It is not controlled by any such process.
4. It involves living tissues.	4. It involves non-living matter.
5. Light, carbon dioxide concentration, pH and hormones regulate transpiration.	5. They do not influence evaporation.
6. It is a slow process.	6. Comparatively a fast process.
7. It is influenced by the anatomy of the transpiring organs.	7. There is no such influence.
8. It is regulated by the amount of soil water available to the plant.	8. This is continuous process, till water is present.
9. It makes the surface of leaves and young stems wet and protects them from sun burn.	9. It provides dryness to the free surface.

3. Leaf structure. The leaves of many xerophytes are too much divided and this way the total leaf area becomes very much decreased. Sometimes, some plants completely lack the leaves, and the stems of such plants become flat, leaf like, angular or rounded and green. They are called phylloclades, *e.g.*, phylloclades of *Ruscus*, *Opuntia*, etc. Less amount of water is transpired from the surface of the phylloclades. The leaves of *Asparagus* are scale-like and the cladodes are developed for photosynthesis. Very less amount of water transpires from the surface of these cladodes.

Several leaves bear the special adaptations to check the excessive transpiration. These leaves also differ anatomically from the ordinary typical leaves. Sometimes in certain leaves a waxy substance accumulates on the epidermis and the cuticle becomes quite thick, which checks the excessive transpiration. The leaves of other plants bear special cavities or depressions. The stomata are situated in these depressions which are usually surrounded by hairs. These special adaptations check transpiration to a large extent, *e.g.*, *Nerium*, *Banksia*, etc. In addition to these, the epidermis becomes multilayered, *e.g.*, *Nerium*, *Ficus*, etc., which lessens the transpiration. In several xerophytic plants, the cells of epidermis are radially elongated, which retard excessive transpiration. The sunken stomata are found in xerophytic leaves which help in retarding the transpiration. The leaves of certain xerophytes become infolded, and the stomata are protected from the direct gusts of wind, thus decreasing the rate of transpiration, *e.g.*, *Ammo-phila arenaria*. This way, the leaves bear several special adaptations which check thc excessive transpirations.

STOMATAL MECHANISM

The stomata are very minute apertures, usually found on the epidermis of the leaves, Each stoma is surrounded by two kidney-shaped special epidermal cells, known as **guard cells**. The stomata may be found in all the aerial parts of the plant. They are never found on its roots. The epidermal cells surrounding the guard cells of the stoma are known as **accessory** or **subsidiary cells**. Usually the term stoma stands for the stomatal opening and the guard cells. The guard cells are always living and contain chloroplasts. These cells, however, contain much amount of protoplasm than the other ordinary cells. Usually the stomata are found scattered on the dicotyledonous leaves whereas they are arranged in parallel rows in the case of monocotyledonous leaves. The number of stomata may range from thousands to lacs per square centimeter on the surface of the leaf. The stomata may be found on both the surfaces of the leaf, but their number is always greater on the lower surface. However, the upper surface of the leaves of banyan and rubber trees lack stomata. The upper surface of the leaves of several xerophytes also lack the stomata. The free floating leaves of the water plants bear stomata only on their upper surface. In normal condition the stomata remain closed in the absence of light. They are always open in the day time or in the presence of light.

Table 15.5. Number of Stomata on Upper and Lower Surfaces of Leaves

Plants	Number of Stomata/mm^2	
	Upper surface	Lower surface
Monocot		
Wheat	50	40
Barley	70	85
Onion	175	175
Dicot		
Sunflower	120	175
Alfalfa	169	188
Geranium	29	179

Stomatal Opening and Closing

Each stoma is surrounded by two guard cells. The kidney-shaped guard cells contain chloroplasts. A respiratory cavity or chamber is found under each stoma. The mechanism of the closing and opening of the stomata depends upon the presence of sugar and starch in the guard cells. During day time or in the presence of light, the guard cells of the stomata contain sugar synthesized by their chloroplasts. The sugar is soluble and increases the concentration of the sap of guard cells. Due to higher concentration of the cytoplasm of guard cells, the water comes to them from the neighbouring cells by osmosis and they become turgid. With the result the stomata remain open. In the night or in the absence of light the sugar present in guard cells converts into the starch. The starch is insoluble, and this way the cell sap of the guard cells remains of much lower concentration than those of neighbouring cells, and the neighbouring cells take out the water from the guard cells by osmosis making them flaccid and the stomata closed. The conversion of sugar into starch during night and vice-versa in day time depends upon the acidity (pH) and alkalinity of the cell sap of guard cells. During night there is no photosynthesis and the carbon dioxide accumulates in the guard cells., converting the cell sap into weak acidic starch. During day time the carbon dioxide is used in the process of photosynthesis, the cell sap becomes alkaline and the starch converts into sugar.

Concentration of CO_2 hypothesis by Bonner and Galston. Bonner and Galston have proposed the following mechanism of opening and closing of stomata. This depends upon the concentration of the carbon dioxide (CO_2) found in the stomatal chamber and not upon the presence or absence of light.

Normally .03% of carbon dioxide is found in the atmosphere, and when the density of the CO_2 in the sub-stomatal chamber also remains .03%, then the guard cells become flaccid and the stomata closed. As the density of CO_2 retards gradually, the stoma begins to open and it opens gradually lengthwise until the density of CO_2 becomes .01%. Now the stomata are perfectly open and they are not open further beyond this density. The photosynthesis takes place in day time and much of the carbon dioxide is being used in the process, the density becomes lesser than .03% and the stomata remain open during day time. During night or in the darkness, there is no

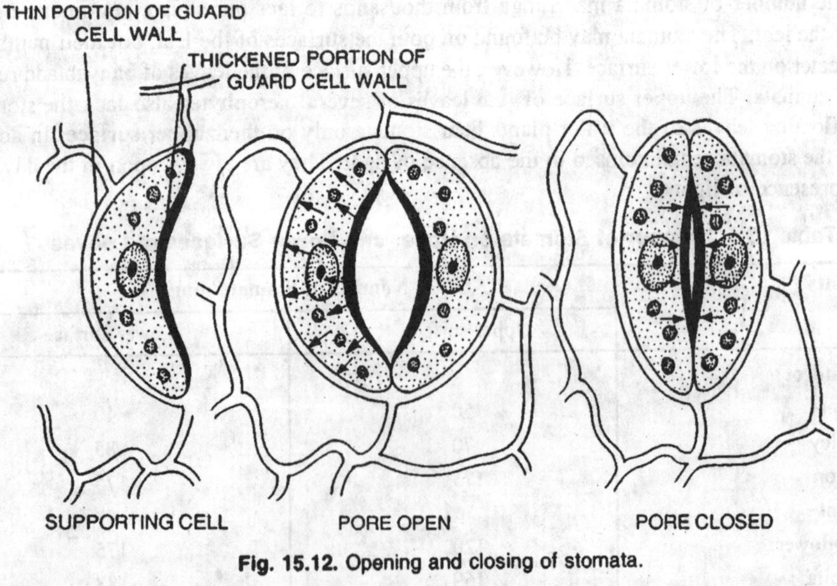

Fig. 15.12. Opening and closing of stomata.

photosynthesis, the density of carbon dioxide remains .03%, the guard cells remain flaccid and the stomata closed.

Active potassium (K^+) theory (Levitt, 1974). Role of potassium K^+ in stomatal opening is now universally accepted. This was observed for the first time by Fujino (1967) that opening of stomata occurs due to the influx of K^+ ions into the guard cells. The source of K^+ ions are nearby subsidiary and epidermal cells, thereby increasing the concentration from 50 mM to 300 mM in guard cells. The increase in K^+ ions concentration increases the osmotic concentration of guard cells thus leading to stomatal opening. The uptake of potassium K^+ controls the gradient in the water potential. This in turn triggers osmotic flow of water into the guard cells raising the turgor pressure. ATP helps in entry of K^+ ions into the guard cells. Levitt (1974) observed that proton (H^+) uptake by guard cell's chloroplasts takes place with the help of ATP. This leads to increase in value of pH in guard cells. Rise in pH converts starch into organic acid, such as malic acid.

$$\text{Starch} \rightarrow \text{phosphoglyceric acid} \xrightarrow{\text{carboxylase}} \text{Phosphophenol pyruvic acid} + CO_2$$

$$\downarrow$$

$$\text{Oxaloacetic acid}$$

$$\downarrow$$

$$\text{Malic acid}$$

Malic acid further dissociates to form H^+ and malate anion. The uptake of potassium K^+ ions is balanced by one of the following:

(*i*) uptake of Cl^-

(*ii*) transport of H^+ ions from organic acids, such as malic acid

(*iii*) by negative charges of organic acids when they lose H^+ ions.

The accumulation of large amounts of K^+ ions in guard cells is electrically balanced by the uptake of negatively charged ions, *i.e.*, chloride and malate. The high amount of malate in guard cells of open stomata accumulates by hydrolysis of starch.

The stomatal closure is considered to be brought about by a passive or highly catalysed excretion of K^+ and Cl^- from the guard cells to the epidermal tissue in general and subsidiary cells in particular. It is thought that subsidiary cells have an active reabsorption mechanism of K^+.

Factors Affecting Stomatal Movement

Most prominent factors that affect stomatal movement (opening and closing of stomata) include (*i*) light, (*ii*) temperature, (*iii*) water availability to plants and (*iv*) carbon dioxide (CO_2) concentration.

1. Light. Light has strong controlling influence on stomatal movements. Stomata generally open in light and close in darkness. The amount of light required to achieve optimum stomatal opening varies from species to species. For example, some plants, such as tobacco require low light intensities, while others may require full sunlight. However, light intensity required to open the stomata is very low, as compared to the intensity required for photosyn-thesis. The stomata of plants showing CAM (Crassulacean Acid Meta-bolism) are exceptional, as they open at night and close during the day. Even moonlight is sufficient to keep the stomata open in some CAM plant species. This unique behaviour of stomata is a kind of adaptation to conserve moisture in CAM plants, such as pineapple, agave, aloe, etc. The period during which stomata remain open in daylight and close at night varies from species to species of plants. The effect of different wavelengths of light on stomatal move-ment also varies.

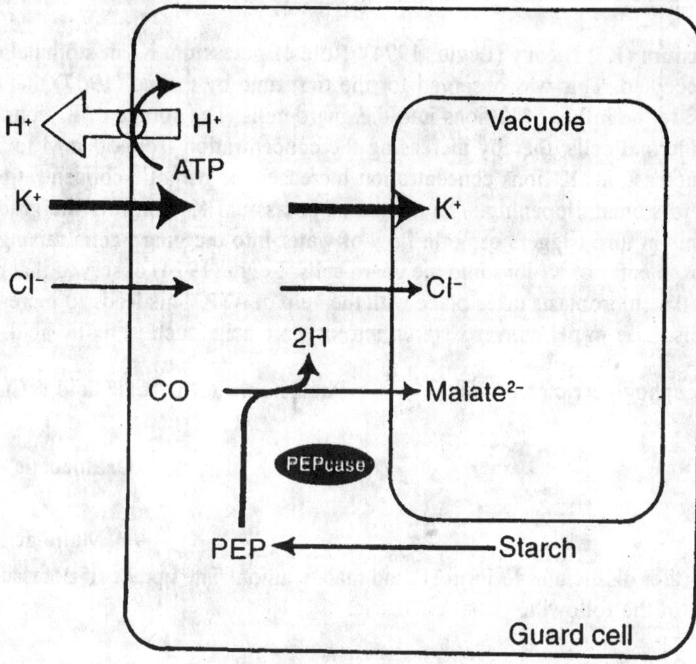

Fig. 15.13. Role of potassium K^+ ions in stomatal opening.

2. Temperature. Usually an increase in temperature leads to increase stomatal opening provided water does not become a limiting factor. In some plant species, stomata remain closed even under continuous light at 0°C. For example, in *Camellia* (tea plant), stomata do not open at very low temperature (below 0°C) even in strong light. However, if the temperature is increased, stomatal opening in such species increases. At temperatures higher than 30°C, there is decline in stomatal opening in some species.

3. Water availability. When availability of water is less, and rate of transpiration is high, plants undergo **water stress.** Water stress is also called **water deficit or moisture deficit.** Such plants begin to show signs of wilting and are known as **water-stressed plants.** Most of the mesophytes under such conditions close their stomata quite tightly and completely in order to protect them from the damage which may result due to extreme water shortage. The stomata reopen only when water potential of these plants is restored. This type of control of stomatal movement by water is called **hydropassive control.**

Accumulation of phytohormone **abscisic acid (ABA)** in the guard cells of several water stressed plants is now well established. The ABA causes stomata of such plants to close. When water potential of water-stressed plant is restored, the stomata reopen and ABA gradually disappears from the guard cells. The type of control of stomata by water, mediated through ABA, is called **hydroactive control.** Externally applied ABA to leaves of normal plants also induces closure of stomata.

4. Carbon dioxide (CO_2) concentration. CO_2 concentration has pronounced effect on stomatal movement. Reduced CO_2 concentration favours opening of stomata while an increase in CO_2 concentration causes stomatal closing. This happens even under the light. In certain species of plants, stomata also close merely by breathing near leaves.

The stomata which are forced to close by increased CO_2 concentration, do not reopen rapidly simply by flushing the leaf with CO_2 free air, and in dark. However, during subsequent light exposure, such stomata open soon. This happens because CO_2 trapped inside the leaf is consumed in photosynthesis during light exposure. This shows, it is the internal leaf CO_2 concentration rather than the atmospheric carbon dioxide that is responsible for stomatal opening.

However, the cuticle present over the guard cells, and epidermal cells is quite impermeable to CO_2 and ensures response of stomata to CO_2 present in the leaf rather than that of outer atmosphere.

Table 15.6. Differences Between Stomata and Hydathodes

Stomata	Hydathodes
1. They are found in epidermis of leaves, stems and fruits.	1. They are found on the tips and margins of young leaves at their vein endings.
2. They are surrounded by pairs of chlorophyllous guard cells.	2. They are surrounded by a ring of cuticularised achlorophyllous cells.
3. They are subtended by a substomatal cavity.	3. They are subtended by a mass of loosely arranged cells.
4. The stomata are surrounded by subsidiary epidermal cells.	4. Subsidiary cells are absent.
5. The stomata have no connection with main ends.	5. They are situated on the vein ends.
6. Their opening and closing is regulated by guard cells.	6. They are always open.
7. They are concerned with the process of 'transpiration'.	7. They are concerned with the process of 'guttation'.

Some endogenous factors, such as K^+, Cl^+ and H^- ions and organic acids, also influence stomatal movement.

EXPERIMENTAL WORK : Practicals

Plasmolysis

Experiment 1.

Object : To demonstrate plasmolysis.

Requirements : Red coloured *Tradescantia* leaves. Water, sugar solution, slide and microscope.

Experiment : To demonstrate plasmolysis, red coloured *Tradescantia* leaves are taken. With a sudden jerk a small segment can be peeled off from the lower surface of leaf. Cut this piece of peel into two parts. First part is put in a drop of water on a slide, second part is put in a drop of sugar solution on another slide. Now both slides are observed under the microscope respectively.

Observation : In first slide the cell structure is seen clearly. Almost most of the cells are turgid. Another slide shows that the cell contents have been separated from their cell walls and so a space is being formed nearer the cell wall.

If the sugar solutions are used with higher concentrations, then the cell contents of the cells will shrink continuously.

Explanation : First slide represents the normal condition. Only a slightly inflated condition may be observed after a considerable time.

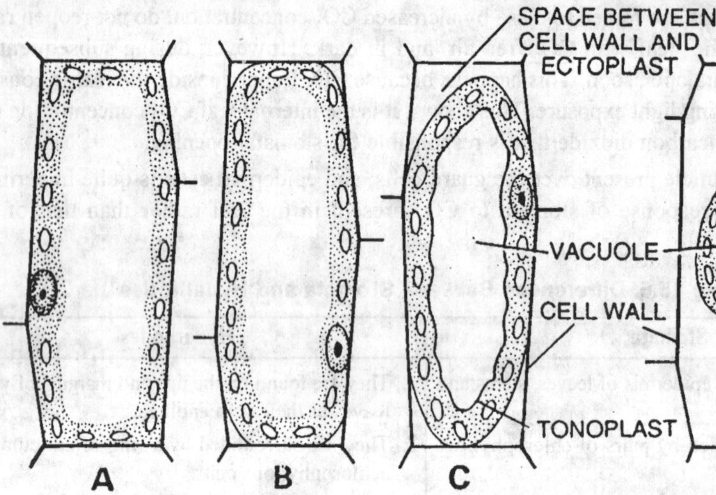

Fig. 15.14. Plasmolysis. A, turgid cell; B-D, successive stages in the shrinkage of protoplasm from the cell wall.

The second slide shows the separation of cell contents from the cell wall. It is due to loss of water from the cell. Here so-called space shows the beginning of the plasmolysis and so it is called as **incipient type of plasmolysis.**

When the concentration of outer medium is increased, the space becomes more widened due to complete loss of water from the cell. This condition is of **complete plasmolysis.**

Note : Here in the fully plasmolysed cell the hypertonic solution, *i.e.*, the sugar solution fills the space formed between cell wall and cell contents.

If the first slide in which incipient plasmolysis has been completed, is provided by pure water or hypotonic solution, the cell will attain its normal position of turgidity. This process is known as **deplasmolysis.**

Osmosis

Experiment 2.

Object : Demonstration of osmosis by Egg Membrane Osmoscope.

Requirements : An egg, thistle funnel, dilute HCl, water beaker, sugar (sucrose) solution, stand, etc.

Experiment : To set this experiment, an egg is taken. One small hole is made at one end of the egg. The yolk and albumen are taken out of the egg shell through this hole. Now the egg shell is kept in dilute HCl for some time, with the result the hard egg shell of calcium carbonate dissolves in the dilute HCl and the

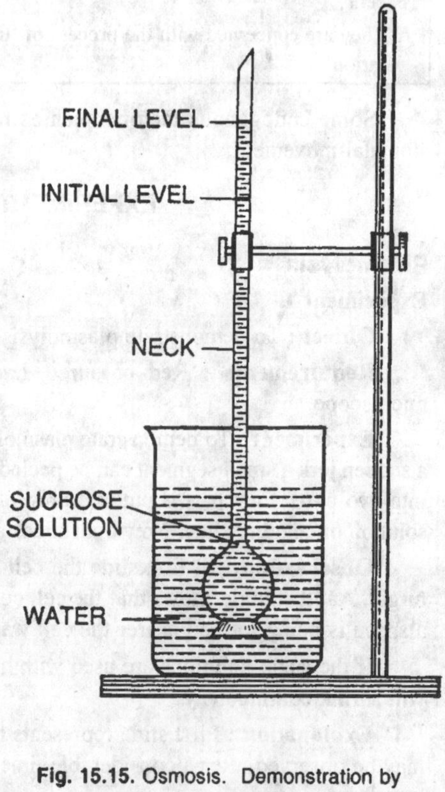

Fig. 15.15. Osmosis. Demonstration by egg membrane osmoscope.

semipermeable egg membrane adhering to the shell remains unaffected. Now this semipermeable membrane is washed with water.

Thus the prepared membrane is put on the mouth of a thistle funnel with the help of a thread. Now a sugar solution of suitable concentration is poured in this funnel that the level of it rises to some extent in the glass tube. This whole apparatus is put in a beaker full of water. This apparatus is kept as such for some time.

Observation : After some time the level in the glass tube of thistle funnel is seen higher from that of the previous one.

Explanation : It is inferred, that the water enters through the egg membrane, and the level of the liquid inside the tube rises sufficiently. The density of the inner liquid is greater than that of outer, and in between two, there is semipermeable membrane, and therefore, the outer fluid enters inside through this membrane. This process is called **endosmosis**. In the same way, if the fluids are reversed, the fluid of lower density seeps out, and the process is called **exosmosis**.

Experiment 3.

Object : Demonstration of osmosis by Potato Osmoscope.

Requirements : Potato, sugar solution, water and beaker.

Experiment : A peeled potato is made flat on its one end, and towards other end a cavity is made. This cavity must be sufficiently deep and broad, so that this may reach to the bottom, and the walls may not remain thick. Now, fill up this cavity with concentrated sugar solution and place this potato in a beaker filled up with water. The level of the outer and inner solutions must be same. After some time it is observed, that the level of the fluid inside the potato cavity rises sufficiently.

Explanation : This happens because of **endosmosis**. The density of the sugar solution is greater than that of water, and the potato tissues collectively act as semipermeable membrane, and thus the water moves in from outside.

Note : If sugar solution is placed in the beaker and water is placed in the cavity of potato, the result will be reversed. It happens because of **exosmosis**, *i.e.*, water moves out from the inside.

Imbibition

Experiment 4.

Object : Demonstration of phenomenon of imbibition.

Requirements : Gram seeds, water and watch glasses.

Experiment : Take some gram seeds in the water in the watch glasses. Keep them for some time.

Observation : After some time the seeds got swollen.

Explanation : Here no cell membrane is involved in this process. The pectic or proteinaceous surface attracts the water molecules by intermolecular forces. These pectic substances are hydrophilic in nature.

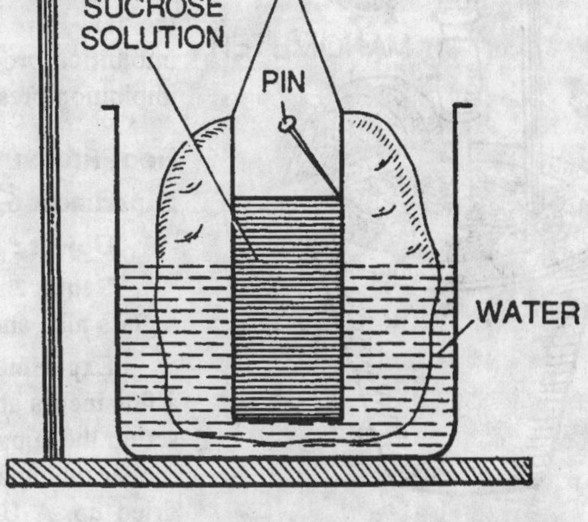

Fig. 15.16. Osmosis. Demonstration by potato osmoscope.

As the diffusion pressure of dry seeds is zero, therefore the water is absorbed in the seeds. This process remains continued till the diffusion pressure of the seeds and water becomes equal. Thus, the seeds get swollen here.

Experiment 5.

Object : Demonstration of developing pressure during imbibition.

Requirements : A corked jar, a disc fitting in it, a round scale and a pointer attached with the disc, stand, experimental gram seeds and water.

Fig. 15.17. Imbibition. Demonstration of the phenomenon.

Experiment : Take seeds and water in the jar as directed in the figure 2.18. Fit the disc over these seeds. To this disc attach the pointer indicating initial reading at zero on the round scale.

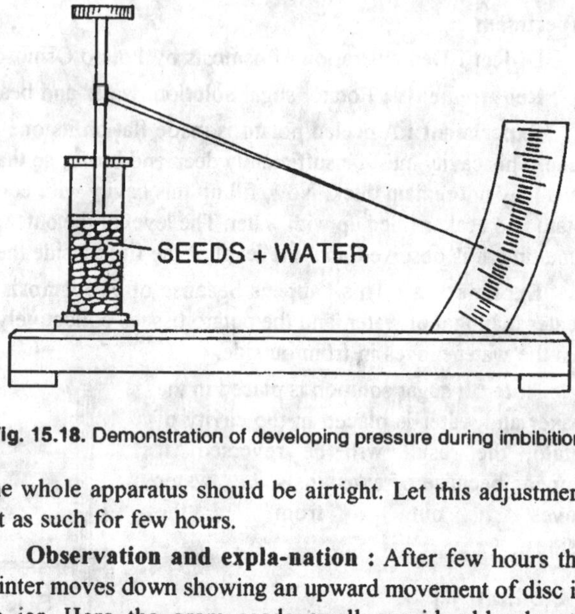

Fig. 15.18. Demonstration of developing pressure during imbibition.

The whole apparatus should be airtight. Let this adjustment put as such for few hours.

Observation and expla-nation : After few hours the pointer moves down showing an upward movement of disc in the jar. Here the gram seeds swell considerably due to imbibition process. These seeds cause a pressure known as imbibition pressure.

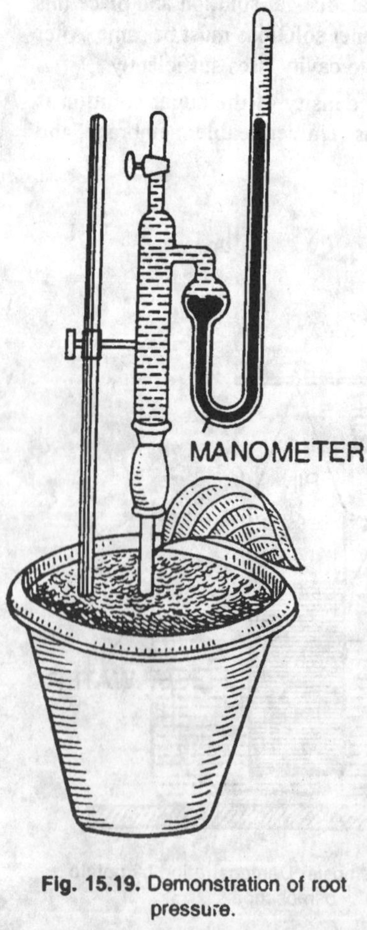

Fig. 15.19. Demonstration of root pressure.

Root Pressure

Experiment 6.

Object : Demonstration of root pressure.

Requirements : A potted balsam plant, a rubber tubing, a glass tube and a U-shaped manometer.

Experiment : The stem of a healthy balsam plant is cut a few inches above the ground level in the morning time and set up the apparatus as shown in the figure. With the help of rubber tubing a glass tube is fitted just above the stem is not dried up. A U-shaped manometer, partially filled up with mercury is connected to the glass tube. The whole apparatus must be air-tight.

Observation : When again observed the apparatus after few hours, the mercury is found on the higher level in the open tube of the manometer, and simultaneously the quantity of water is also increased in the glass tube.

Explanation : Due to accumulation of water in the glass tube, the pressure is exerted on the mercury, and it is pushed upwards in the open glass tube of manometer. This water exudates, because of root pressure from the cut end of the stem and accumulates in the glass tube fitted just above the cut end of the stem. This is also proved by this experiment that root pressure helps the ascent of sap.

Guttation

Experiment 7.

Object : Demonstration of phenomenon of Guttation.

Requirements : Well developed potted plant of Garden nasturtium, bell jar, cork, a glass tube.

Experiment : Put the watered plant under the bell jar for some time (as shown in the figure).

Observation : After some time water droplets are observed at the tip of veins near the margin of leaf.

Explanation : It is due to the fact that the rate of water absorption by roots is higher than that of transpiration. As a result of which the excess amount of water collected in the veins of leaf which is forced to come out at their tip in the form of water droplets. The oozing out of the water in the form of water droplets from uninjured part of leaf is known as **guttation**. These so-called uninjured parts are called **hydathodes** or water stomata.

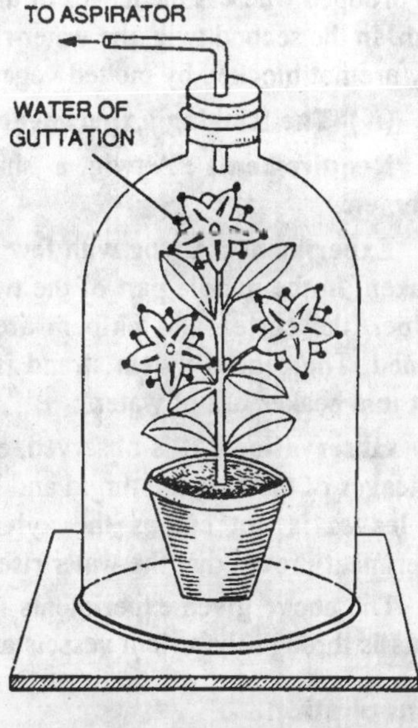

Fig. 15.20. Guttation. Demonstration of the phenomenon.

Ascent of Sap

Experiment 8.

Object : Demonstration of movement of water through xylem.

This may be shown in various ways. Some important ones are given here.

(*i*) **Requirements :** Balsam plant, water, safranin, microscope.

Experiment : The stem of the balsam plant is cut under the water. Now, to make the water red coloured, a few drops of safranin or euosine are added in the beaker full of water. Thereafter, the balsam stem, cut under the water is kept in this coloured water. After some time the stem is cut into transverse sections at various levels, and the sections are studied under the lens of the microscope.

Observation : Here, we find that only the vessels and tracheids are red stained. This way, this experiment proves, that water rises in the stem through the vessels and tracheids only.

(*ii*) **Requirements :** Plant of *Arundo donax*, vegetable ghee, coloured water in a beaker.

Experiment : Two white and linear leaves of *Arundo donax* are taken. The vessels of one of the leaves have been blocked by applying the melted vegetable ghee at its base; the other leaf is kept without blocking its vessels. Now, both the leaves are kept in the beaker full of coloured water.

Observation : After a few hours, it is observed that the leaf with blocked base is as before and the veins of the leaf with unblocked base have become coloured. This indicates the rising of water through the veins (xylem vessels).

(*iii*) **Requirements :** Two twigs of a plant, vegetable ghee, two beakers of water, etc.

Experiments : We take the two twigs of plant cut under water. The base of one of the twigs is blocked with melted vegetable ghee whereas of the other twig is not blocked. These twigs are kept in two separate beakers full of water.

Observation : After a sufficiently long time, it is observed that the leaves of the twig with blocked end have been wilted and drooped whereas the leaves of the other twig are turgid and fresh. In the second twig, the water rises through the vessels, as they are not blocked by melted vegetable ghee.

(*iv*) **The Ringing Experiment :**

Requirements : A twig, a sharp scalpel, beaker full of water, etc.

Experiment : A twig with few leaves cut under the water is taken. In the middle part of the twig, with the help of sharp scalpel, the cortex and phloem are removed, and a ring is formed. The central xylem strand is kept intact. This twig is kept in a beaker full of water.

Observation : It is observed, even after a long time that the leaves of the twig are turgid and fresh. The water supply of the leaves is not cut as the xylem strand is intact. This experiment proves that the water rises in the plant through xylem vessels.

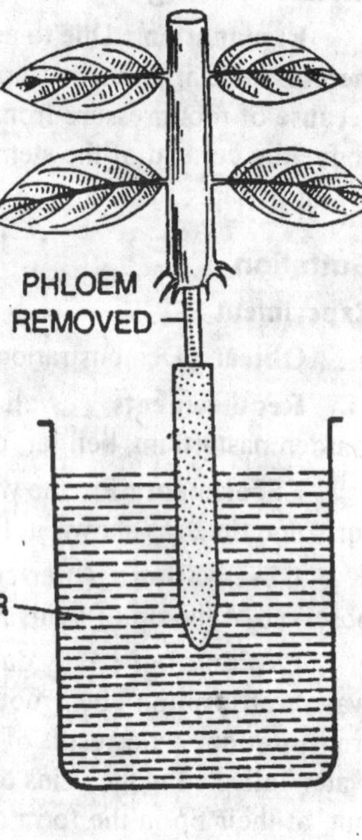

Fig. 15.21. Movement of water through xylem.

The above given experiments indicate clearly that the pathway of the ascent of sap in the plants is through the xylem vessels and the tracheids.

Transpiration

Experiment 9.

Object : Demonstration of transpiration by keeping a plant under a bell jar.

Requirements : A potted plant, rubber sheet, water, bell jar, glass plate, vaseline.

Experiment : A healthy potted plant is taken for this purpose. Now, the soil surface of the pot is being covered by the rubber sheet so that there is no evaporation of water from the moist surface of the soil. Thereafter the potted plant is kept on a glass plate is being covered over by a bell-jar. The margins of the bell-jar are vaselined, so that the atmospheric air may not enter the bell-jar. Now the covered potted plant is kept at room temperature.

Observation : After some time, the droplets of water appear on the inner surface of bell-jar.

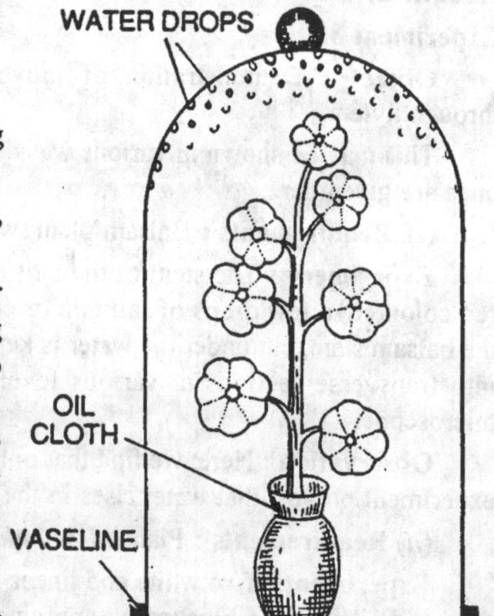

Fig. 15.22. Transpiration. Demonstration of the phenomenon.

Explanation : As all the precautions have been taken for checking the entrance of any moisture from outside, and the release of moisture from the soil surface, these droplets of water adhered to the inner surface of the bell jar are definitely given off from the aerial parts of the plant by means of transpiration.

Experiment 10.

Object : Demonstration of transpiration by cobalt-chloride screen.

Requirements : Filter paper, cobalt-chloride solution, a potted plant, clip.

Experiment : Some pieces of the filter paper are dipped in cobalt chloride solution and then dried off. They are blue coloured. Now, two such pieces of filter paper are taken and pressed on both the surfaces of the leaf of a potted plant with the help of a clip. This apparatus is kept for some time as such.

Observation : After a few hours, when it is observed, the cobalt chloride paper of the lower surface of the leaf becomes pink coloured.

Explanation : The dried blue coloured cobalt chloride paper turns red as it becomes moist. The stomata are confined mostly on the lower surface of the leaf, and therefore, the cobalt chloride paper of that surface becomes moist and turns red. The paper of the upper side of the leaf may also become pink to some extent, as few stomata are found on this side.

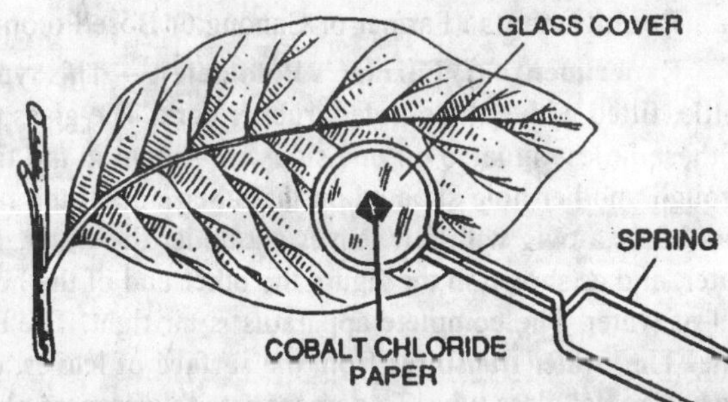

Fig. 15.23. Transpiration. Demonstration of phenomenon. (Cobaltchloride method).

Experiment 11.

Object : Demonstration of transpiration by four–leaf experiment.

Requirements : Four leaves, vaseline and a string.

Experiment : To demonstrate the transpiration from the leaf surface, four banyan leaves are taken. Both the surfaces of the A leaf, lower surface (with stomata) of B leaf, upper surface (without stomata) of C leaf are vaselined. The vaseline is not applied on the D leaf. Now, as shown in the figure the leaves are hanged so that they may transpire freely.

Observation and explanation : When the observations are taken after a day or two, they are as follows — the A leaf, which is vaselined on its both the surfaces, looks fresh and green, as no surface transpires. The B leaf is vaselined on its lower surface (with stomata), and transpiration takes place only from the upper surface which is negligible. This leaf also remains turgid and green like the A leaf. If few stomata are present on the upper surface of the leaf, then it shrivels to some extent. The C leaf is vaselined on its upper surface, which contains

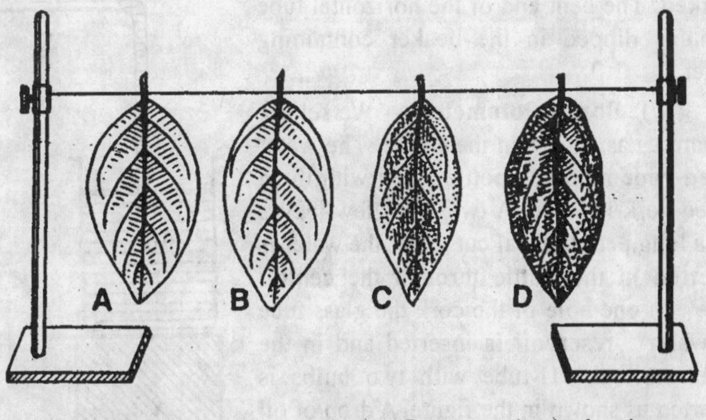

Fig. 15.24. Comparison of transpiration. Demonstration by four leaves.

less number of stomata or no stomata. The transpiration takes place from the lower stomatal surface, and the leaf shrivels to a large extent. The D leaf is not vaselined and both the surfaces transpire freely releasing much water. The leaf wilts completely in this case. This experiment proves that the rate of stomatal transpiration is fairly higher than the cuticular transpiration.

Rate of transpiration : The rate of transpiration is measured by potometer. There are many types of potometers which are designed by various scientists from time to time. These potometers are after the names of Farmer, Ganong, Garreau and Bose.

Experiment 12.

Object : Demonstration of rate of transpiration by potometers.

Requirements : Farmer or Ganong or Bose Potomer, water, plants, vaseline, stop watch, etc.

Experiment : (*i*) Farmer's Potometer — This type of potometer consists of a wide mouthed bottle, fitted with a three-holed rubber cork. The glass tube of water reservoir passes through one of these holes situated on one side. As shown in the figure another bent glass tube finds its way through another hole situated on the other side of the rubber cork. The central hole of the rubber cork bears a twig with few leaves cut under the water. The apparatus is completely filled up with water, and as shown in the figure the other end of the horizontal glass tube is dipped in the beaker full of water. The complete apparatus is air tight. The apparatus is kept in this position for some time. The water transpires from the surface of leaves, and to fulfil the vacuum the water rises in the horizontal glass tube. To demonstrate this process clearly, an air bubble is entered with the help of a dropper from the other end of the horizontal tube.

(*ii*) **Ganong's Potometer** — The mode of action of this potometer resembles to that of Farmer's potometer. The apparatus is completely filled up with water. A twig with few leaves cut under the water is entered in the wide mouthed bent tube on one side through the hole of the rubber cork, like that of Farmer's potometer. There is a water reservoir, from which the water may be taken inside the apparatus when needed. The horizontal tube of the potometer is well marked. The bent end of the horizontal tube remains dipped in the beaker containing water.

(*iii*) **Bose's Potometer** — We set the apparatus as shown in the figure. The water filled wide mouthed bottle fitted with three holed cork is taken. A twig with few leaves or a long petioled leaf cut under the water is inserted in the bottle through the central hole. In one hole of the cork the glass tube of water reservoir is inserted and in the other hole the U-tube with two bulbs is inserted as shown in the figure. A drop of oil is put in the U-tube. Now, the apparatus is kept in such condition so that the aerial parts of the twig transpire freely.

Observation : (*i*) As water transpires, the air-bubble moves towards the bottle

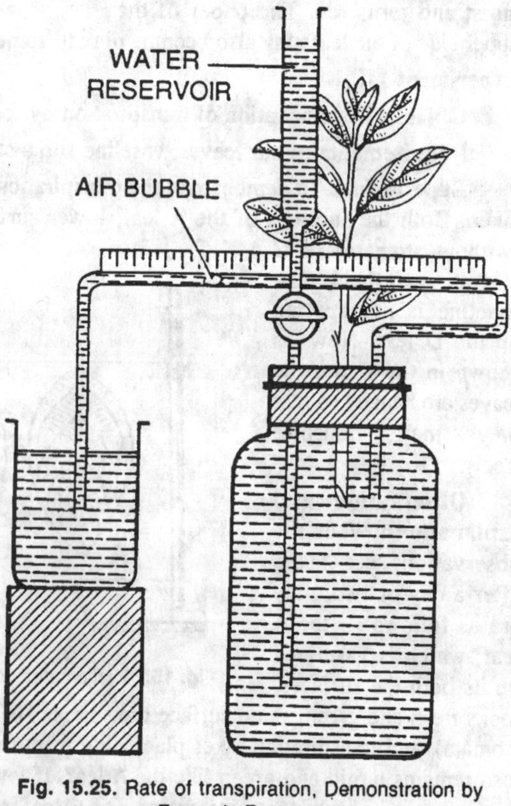

Fig. 15.25. Rate of transpiration, Demonstration by Farmer's Potometer.

along with water. This air-bubble may be brought back by adding the water in the bottle from the reservoir which is controlled by a stop cock. There is a scale behind the horizontal tube. With the help of a stop watch, the time may be noted, which is consumed in the travelling of the air-bubble from one particular mark to another particular mark on the scale. Several readings may be taken in different conditions. The rate of transpiration may easily be calculated, if one knows the actual volume of water in between two particular points on the horizontal tube.

(*ii*) As the leaves transpire, the water flows towards the twig in the horizontal tube. At the end of the bent horizontal tube there is a subterminal hole. With the help of a dropper or otherwise an air bubble is entered through this hole in the tube. As the leaves transpire the water from the beaker rushes towards the twig in the horizontal tube along with air bubble. The time spent in the travel of the air bubble from one particular mark to another on the horizontal tube may be noted. The air bubble may be brought back on the first mark in the tube by releasing water from the reservoir. Several observations may be taken in different transpiring conditions and the rate of the transpiration may be calculated. The apparatus must be completely air-tight.

(*iii*) The vacuum develops within the bottle because of the transpiration, and the oil drop gradually rises up in the U-tube towards the twig. As the oil drop reaches the inner bulb, it bursts and goes back again in its original position. The time taken in rising and bursting of the oil drop is being noted. Serveral such readings may be taken in different conditions. The apparatus must be completely air-tight.

Various modifications for transpiring plants : (1) Potometer kept in atmosphere of high humidity. (2) Potometer kept under the fan. (3) Potometer kept in higher temperature. (4) Potometer kept in dark.

(1) Potometer kept in atmosphere of high humidity : Here the air bubble moves with a slow speed. Stomatal transpiration is caused by the diffusion of water vapours from the intercellular spaces of the mesophyll cells into the outer atmosphere through the stomata. This condition is only possible when outer atmosphere possesses less humidity or less vapour contents. Here in the given condition the outer atmosphere is of higher humidity, so the loss of water from the leaves is negligible and consequently the transpiration is lowered. Therefore higher the humidity of air, lower is the transpiration.

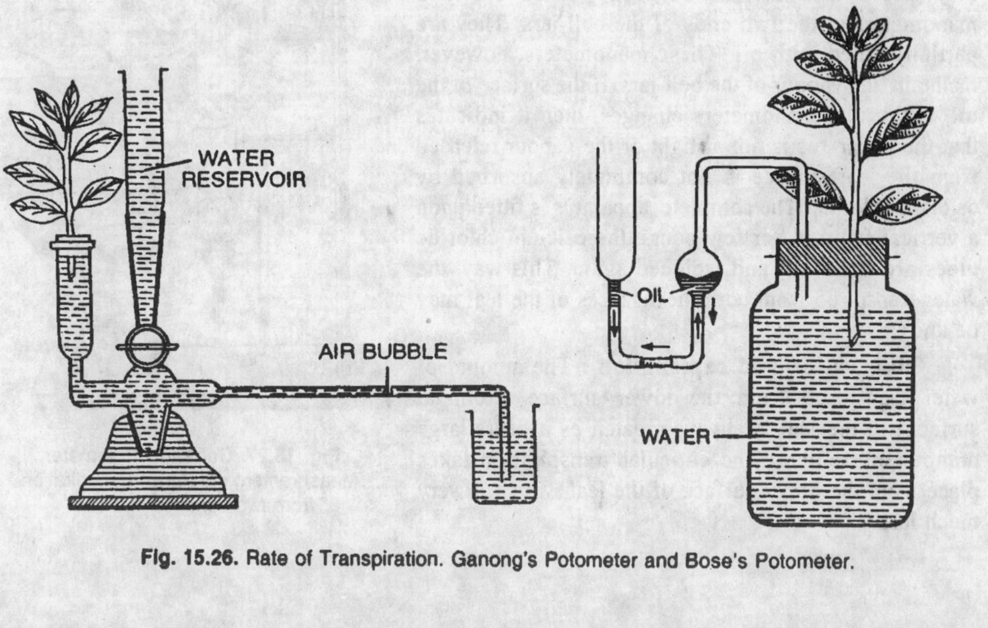

Fig. 15.26. Rate of Transpiration. Ganong's Potometer and Bose's Potometer.

(2) Potometer kept under the fan : Here the air bubble will move with a greater speed. The running fan causes to increase the rate of transpiration by sweeping away the water vapours that are present in the vicinity of transpiring plant. Therefore in this area the humidity of air becomes lower and the râte of transpiration is promoted.

(3) Potometer kept in higher temperature : Here the air bubble moves with a faster speed.

Temperature has an indirect influence on the rate of transpiration. Increase in temperature causes the following effects.

(*A*) Stomata get widened with the increase in temperature. So the loss of water is more, increasing the rate of transpiration.

(*B*) A rise in temperature decreases the relative humidity of surrounding air. The drier the air, the more rapid is transpiration.

(4) Potometer kept in dark : The air bubble does not move at all. It is due to fact that the stomata get closed when it is dark. Lowering of pH value (pH - 5) favours in closing of stomata. In dark the reducing osmotically active sugars change into the osmotically inactive starch. So the pH value lowers to 5 and the stomata are closed. On closing the stomata, no transpiration takes place, hence, the air bubble remains stable.

Experiment 13.

Object : Comparison of rate of transpiration from both the surfaces of leaf by Garreau's Potometer.

Apparatus : Garreau's potometer, stand, leaf, etc.

Experiment : ***Garreau's Potometer*** — With the help of this apparatus, the comparative study of the transpiration from both the surfaces of the leaf is being done. This apparatus consists of two small bell-jars, which are kept together in close contact as shown in the figure. A leaf of a potted plant is kept in between these two bell-jars. In each of these bell-jars a small test tube is kept. Each small test tube contains equal amount of anhydrous calcium chloride ($CaCl_2$). The apparatus is made air-tight, applying vaseline where they press the leaf in between. There are two manometers at the two ends of the bell-jars. They are partially filled with oil. These manometers, however, maintain the vapour of the bell-jars. If the surface of the oil, within the manometers changes, then it indicates that the apparatus is not airtight or the vapour released from the leaf surface is not completely absorbed by calcium chloride. The complete apparatus is fitted upon a vertical stand. After few hours, the calcium chloride tubes are taken out and weighed again. This way, the water transpired from both the surfaces of the leaf may be known.

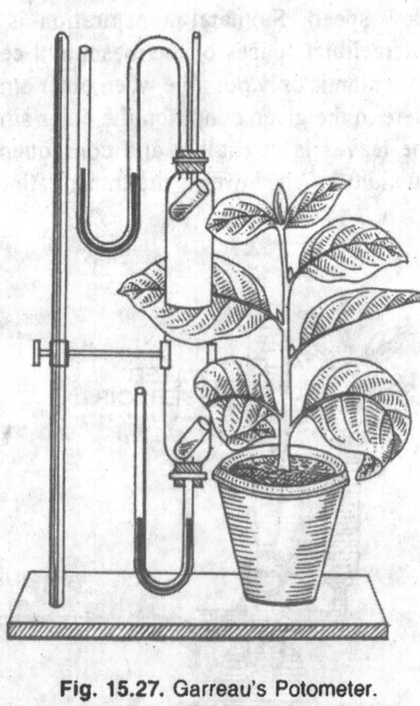

Fig. 15.27. Garreau's Potometer. Measurement of relative transpiration from two surfaces of a leaf.

Observation and explanation : The amount of water transpired from the lower surface (stomatal surface) of the leaf is always greater, as it bears large number of stomata. The cuticular transpiration takes place from the upper surface of the leaf, which is very much less.

Stomata

Experiment 14.

Object : Demonstration of the stomatal opening by Drawin's porometer.

Requirements : Darwin's porometer, water or mercury, a potted plant, stop watch, etc.

Experiment : This apparatus functions on the principle that the stomatal apertures govern the rate of flow of water. Cement the glass cup to the surface of the leaf by an adhesive (durofix, etc.) and immerse the vertical arm of tube in water or mercury. Open the clip and suck the water to a predetermined height in the vertical arm, close the clip.

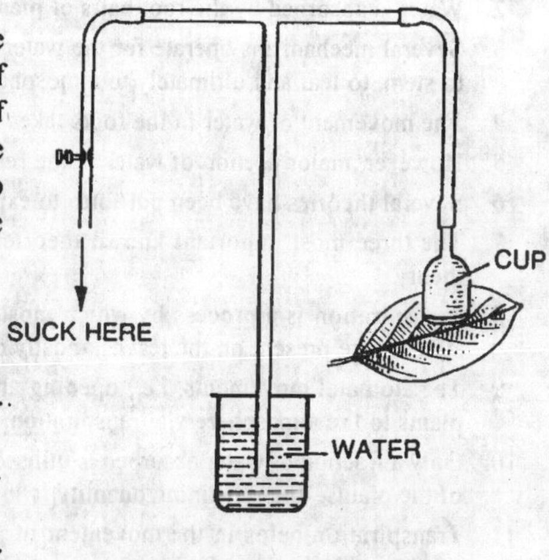

Fig. 15.28. Darwin's porometer.

Observation : Two possibilities occur here;

(*A*) The water level in arm remains unchanged.

(*B*) The water column begins to fall.

Explanation : On the closing of the clip, the air inside the porometer undergoes a reduced pressure.

(*A*) If the stomata under the cup are closed, the water level in the arm will not change.

(*B*) If the stomata under the cup are open, the air will find its way through them and water column in the arm will begin to fall.

Absorption of Water

Experiment 15.

Object : Demonstration of relation between Transpiration and Absorption.

Requirements : A bottle with a side, tube, cork, a plant, oil, balance, etc.

Experiment : Here, the apparatus must be completely filled up with water and air-tight. In the side marked tube of the apparatus some oil drops are being added so that the water may not evaporate. The cork is fitted in the wide mouth of the bottle in the way that the aerial part of a complete plant remains outside of it and the root system or the plant remains within the bottle. Now the apparatus is weighed on a pan balance to note its weight and thereafter it is kept for few hours in such a place where sufficient transpiration from the aerial parts of the plant takes place. In the end the apparatus is weighed once again and the difference from that of the original weight may be calculated.

Observation : This way the quantity of transpired water is known in grams. The oil drops present on the surface of water in the marked side tube travel somewhat downward and we know the actual quantity of absorbed water in ml by the roots. By comparison, it is noted that the quantity of absorbed water is always

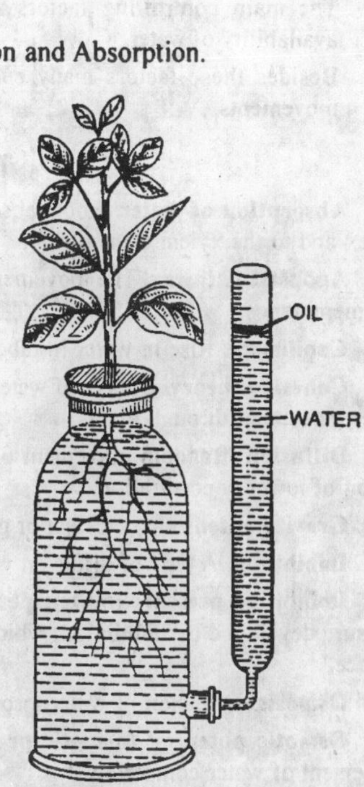

Fig. 15.29. Relation between transpiration and absorption. Demonstration of the phenomenon.

greater than the transpired water because some of the water is used in other metabolic activities.

SUMMARY

1. Water is most essential for plant growth and development.
2. Water is absorbed by the root hairs of plants from soil, and translocated to the leaves.
3. Several mechanisms operate for the water to move from one cell to another, and it passes from root to stem, to leaf and ultimately to atmosphere.
4. The movement of water in the roots takes place through apoplast pathway and symplast pathway.
5. However, major portion of water in the root flows through apoplast pathway.
6. Several theories have been put forth to explain water translocation within a plant.
7. The three most important known theories are (*i*) root pressure, (*ii*) capillarity and (*iii*) Cohesion theory.
8. Transpiration is a process by which most of the water taken up by plants is lost to the number of stomata are present on the leaves, mostly on the lower leaf surfaçe.
9. The stomatal movements, *i.e.*, opening and closing of stomata, control the flow of water from the plants to the atmosphere via transpiration.
10. Only a fraction of water absorbed is utilised for the purpose of growth, maintenance, and reproduction of the plants. The remaining quantity is lost in atmosphere by transpiration.
11. Transpiration helps in the movement of xylem sap, also called ascent of sap, and simultaneously increases absorption of mineral nutrients by the roots from the soil.
12. Transpiration also assists in cooling by evaporation of water, thus reducing heat load on the leaves.
13. There are several environmental factors which contribute to the occurrence of transpiration and control of stomatal movements.
14. The main controlling factors include — light, temperature, humidity, CO_2 concentration and availability of water.
15. Besides these factors many endogenous factors also influence both transpiration and stomatal movements.

TERMS TO REMEMBER

Absorption of water. Roots absorb water in plants. From root hair, water moves through the root cortex and to the xylem elements.

Apoplast pathway. The movement of water occurs exclusively through the cell wall without crossing any membranes.

Capillarity. Rise in water in tubes of small diameter (capillaries) kept in a vessel containing water.

Cohesion theory. Uptake of water takes place by transpirational pull. This is most accepted theory of water movement through plants.

Diffusion. Random movement of individual molecules from a region of higher concentration to a region of lower concentration.

Gravity potential ψ_g. Effect of gravity on water potential.

Imbibition. A type of diffusion where movement of water takes place along a diffusion gradient.

Imbibition pressure (matric potential). When seeds imbibe water and swell, they produce a large pressure developed by imbibition, which makes the seedlings to emerge above the ground through the soil surface.

Osmosis. Diffusion of water through a semipermeable membrane.

Osmotic potential (osmotic pressure or solute potential) ψ_s. The pressure required to stop the movement of water completely.

Pascal. The common measurement unit of water potential.

Permeability of membrane. The extent to which a membrane permits or restricts the movement of a substance.

Plasmolysis. Cell when placed in a concentrated sucrose solution loses water, and plasma membrane starts contracting.

Pressure potential (hydrostatic pressure) ψ_p. Positive hydrostatic pressure (also known as turgor pressure) is zero for pure water in an open beaker.

Root pressure. Water from soil is absorbed by root hairs and conducted through xylem vessels, which indicates the presence of a positive pressure in the xylem.

Stomata. Tiny pores, located on the surface of the epidermal layer of leaves. Each stoma has two guard cells, which contain chloroplasts.

Suberin. A wax-like substance.

Symplast pathway. Movement of water occurs from cell to cell through the plasmodesmata.

Transmembrane pathway. Movement of water through the cell membrane.

Transpiration. Loss of water in the form of water vapour from the plant to the atmosphere.

Water potential ψ_w. The potential energy of water.

QUESTION BANK

Very Short Answer Questions

1. What is protoplast ?
2. What is water potential ?
3. Give common measurement unit of water potential.
4. Where does apoplastic movement of water occur ?
5. Where does symplastic movement of water occur ?
6. Define the term 'diffusion'.
7. How would you define 'membrane permeability' ?
8. Define the term 'osmosis'.
9. What is imbibition ?
10. What is capillarity ?
11. Which theory of water translocation was given by Henry Dixon in 1914 ?
12. What is transpiration ?
13. What the term, ψ_s, is called ?
14. What the term, ψ_p is called ?
15. What the term, ψ_g is called ?
16. What is the other name of 'imbibition pressure' ?
17. Which fraction of soil water is available to plants for absorption by roots ?
18. What is 'guttation' ?
19. What will happen if a plant cell is kept in hypotonic solution for some time ?
20. When a plant cell kept in a solution is plasmolysed; what is nature of solution ?
21. Name the pore through which guttation takes place.
22. What is an isotonic solution ?
23. Name the plant process carried by hydathodes.
24. Name the pores through which guttation occurs.
25. Define plasmolysis.
26. What are antitranspirants ?
27. Who proposed K^+ exchange hypothesis for the opening and closing of stomata ?
28. Some plants close their stomata to conserve water under severe drought conditions. Name the phytohormone that helps them to do so.

ANSWERS

1. Plasma membrane + protoplasm ; 2. The potential energy of water is referred to as water potential ; 3. This is pascal, Pa (1 megapascal, Mpa = 10 bars) and is represented by Greek letter, Psi (ψ) ; 4. The apoplastic movement of water occurs exclusively through the cell wall without crossing any membranes ; 5. The symplastic movement of water occurs from cell to cell through the plasmodesmata ; 6. Diffusion is a random movement of individual molecules from a region of higher concentration to a region of lower concentration ; 7. The extent to which a membrane permits or restricts the movement of a substance is called membrane permeability; 8. Diffusion of water through a semipermeable membrane is known as osmosis ; 9. A type of diffusion by which movement of water takes place along a diffusion gradient ; 10. Capillarity refers to a rise in water in tubes of small diameter kept in a vessel containing water ; 11. Cohesion theory ; 12. Loss of water in the form of water vapour from the plant to the atmosphere is called transpiration ; 13. Solute potential or osmotic potential ; 14. Pressure potential or hydrostatic pressure ; 15. Gravity potential ; 16. Matric potential (*i.e.*, water potential of the matrix) ; 17. Capillary water; 18. The excretion of water in the form of liquid droplets from the leaves and other parts of an uninjured or intact plant is called guttation ; 19. Endosmosis ; 20. Hypertonic solution ; 21. Hydathode ; 22. When a solution has a concentration, where no gain and loss of water by osmosis separated by a semipermeable membrave from a specified solution ; 23. Guttation ; 24. Hydathodes ; 25. Shrinkage of protoplasm of a cell when placed in a hypertonic solution as a result of osmosis, is called plasmolysis ; 26. A substance applied to the plant for reducing transpiration is called anti-transpirant ; 27. Levitt (1974) ; 28. Abscisic acid.

Short Answer Questions

1. A well watered potted herbaceous plant shows wilting in the afternoon of a dry sunny day. Why ?
2. Write short notes on : (*a*) Plasmolysis (*b*) Imbibition (*c*) Osmosis (*d*) Root pressure.
3. Write brief explanatory notes on (*a*) Root pressure (*b*) Water potential (*c*) Guttation (*d*) Significance of transpiration.
4. Distinguish between the following :
   (*a*) Osmotic pressure and osmotic potential (*b*) Osmotic potential and matric potential
   (*c*) Diffusion and osmosis (*d*) Osmosis and imbibition
5. How is transpiration different from guttation ?
6. Mention any two uses of transpiration.
7. Describe in brief opening and closing of stomata.
8. List any four mechanisms that contribute to the ascent of sap in tall trees.
9. Does transpiration serve any useful function in the plant ?
10. Define guttation. How would you differentiate from transpiration ?
11. Who proposed K^+ hypothesis for opening and closing of stomata ?
12. How do potassium ions regulate the opening and closing of stomata ?
13. A farmer observed drops of water along the margins of leaves of tomato plants growing in his well irrigated field on a winter morning. Give reasons of this occurrence. Why had the water drops appeared only along the leaf margins ?
14. Write the role of osmosis in the life of plants.
15. Why do some herbaceous plants have hydathodes ? Under what conditions do they help the plants ?
16. Describe the role of osmotic potential in regulating water potential of plant cells.
17. Describe the theories related to translocation of water.
18. Define osmosis and explain how it influences other components of cell-water relations in plants.
19. Of what importance is potassium in the opening and closing of stomata ?
20. Discuss Dixon's theory of ascent of sap.
21. How do guard cells control opening and closing of stomata.
22. How do potassium ions regulate the opening and closing of stomata ?

23. How does cohesion tension theory explain the ascent of sap ?
24. Define hygroscopic and capillary waters. Which is not available to plants and why ?
25. Give the different factors that influence stomata.
26. How does transpiration differ from guttation ? What is significance of transpiration ?
27. Is there a general mechanism to explain the opening and closing of stomata ? Justify your answer.
28. Why is transpiration in higher plants called a 'necessary evil' ?
29. What is root pressure ? How can you demonstrate experimentally ?
30. How do rise in temperature and increased wind velocity affect transpiration ? Write any two adaptations shown by certain plants to reduce transpiration.
31. List the three prominent theories to explain water translocation in trees. Describe the most accepted theory out of these.

Long Answer Questions

1. Mention some of the factors that influence stomatal opening and closing. How are these factors involved in regulating stomatal behaviour ?
2. Describe the theories related to translocation of water.
3. Explain why transpiration in higher plants is considered a necessary evil ?
4. Of what importance is potassium in the opening and closing of stomata ?
5. How do potassium ions regulate the opening and closing of stomata ?
6. What is ascent of sap ? Give Dixon's cohesive theory for it.
7. What is transpiration ? Explain various factors affecting it.

MULTIPLE CHOICE QUESTIONS (Objective Type Questions)

1. When a cell is fully turgid, which one of the following is zero ?
   (*a*) Turgor pressure (*b*) Wall pressure
   (*c*) Diffusion pressure deficit (*d*) Osmotic pressure
2. If a piece of potato tuber is placed is concentrated sugar solution
   (*a*) It would become limp due to the loss of water from its cells
   (*b*) It would become turgid by abrsorbing water from sugar solution
   (*c*) The cells will show endosmosis
   (*d*) It swells up due to imbibition
3. Bacteria cannot survive in a highly salted pickle because
   (*a*) Salt inhibits reproduction
   (*b*) Bacteria do not get enough light for photosynthesis
   (*c*) They become plasmolysed and consequently killer
   (*d*) The pickle do not contain nutrients necessary for bacteria to live
4. When beet root cylinders are washed and then placed in cold water none of the anthocyanins come out. This indicates most likely that plasma membrane is
   (*a*) Permeable to anthocyanins (*b*) Impermeable to anthocyanins
   (*c*) Differentially permeable to anthocyanins (*d*) Dead
5. Selective permeability identifies the process of
   (*a*) diffusion (*b*) osmosis (*c*) imbibition (*d*) plasmolysis
6. Seeds swell when placed in water because of
   (*a*) Osmosis (*b*) Imbibition (*c*) Hydrolysis (*d*) None
7. A cell when placed in solution gets plasmolysed. What is largely present in between the cell wall and the plasmolysed contents ?
   (*a*) Water (*b*) Cell sap
   (*c*) Hypotonic solution (*d*) Hypertonic solution

8. In the process of osmosis
   (*a*) both protoplasm and cell wall act as a single layer
   (*b*) only protoplast acts as a single layer
   (*c*) only cell membrane acts as a single layer
   (*d*) none of the above
9. The movement of water from one cell of the cortex to the adjacent one in roots is due to
   (*a*) accumulation of inorganic salts in the cells
   (*b*) accumulation of organic compounds in the cells
   (*c*) chemical potential gradient
   (*d*) water potential gradient
10. The path of water and solutes from the soil to the conducting tissue of the root is
   (*a*) soil ⟶ root hair ⟶ cortex ⟶ endodermis ⟶ pericycle ⟶ protoxylem ⟶ phloem
   (*b*) soil ⟶ root hair ⟶ cortex ⟶ pericycle ⟶ endodermis ⟶ protoxylem ⟶ metaxylem
   (*c*) soil ⟶ epidermal cell of the root ⟶ cortex ⟶ endodermis ⟶ pericycle ⟶ protoxylem ⟶ metaxylem ⟶ secondary xylem
   (*d*) soil ⟶ root hair ⟶ cortex ⟶ endodermis pericycle ⟶ protoxylem ⟶ metaxylem
11. Root cap has no role in absorption because it has
   (*a*) no direct connection with vascular system
   (*b*) loosely arranged cells
   (*c*) no cells containing chloroplasts
   (*d*) no root hairs
12. Water available to the plant is
   (*a*) run off water (*b*) gravitational water
   (*c*) hygroscopic water (*d*) capillary water
13. According to one vital force theory, ascent of sap is due to active pulsations of innermost layer of cortex just outside the endodermis. This theory was given by
   (*a*) J.C. Bose (*b*) Dixon (*c*) Strasburger (*d*) Sachs
14. Xylem transport of water in tall trees appears mainly due to
   (*a*) metabolic activity in xylem cells
   (*b*) root pressure
   (*c*) capillarity rise in xylem open pipes
   (*d*) transpiration pull and cohesion of water molecules.
15. Which one of the following is the most widely accepted explanation for ascent of sap ?
   (*a*) Capillarity (*b*) Atmospheric pressure
   (*c*) Pulsation activity (*d*) Transpiration pull
16. The metal ion involved in stomatal regulation is
   (*a*) iron (*b*) magnesium (*c*) zinc (*d*) potassium
17. Increase in CO_2 concentration around leaf causes
   (*a*) rapid opening of stomata
   (*b*) partial closure of stomata
   (*c*) complete closure of stomata
   (*d*) there will be no effect on stomatal opening

18. Which one by following is used for measuring the rate of traspiration.
(*a*) potometer (*b*) porometer (*c*) osmometer (*d*) Moll's experiment
19. Which one of the following factors is the most important in the regulation of transpiration ?
(*a*) Humidity (*b*) Light (*c*) Temperature (*d*) Wind
20. Process of water exudation through hydathodes is called
(*a*) guttation (*b*) transpiration (*c*) excretion (*d*) hydrolysis
21. Increase in the CO_2 concentration of microenvironment of leaf would cause
(*a*) closure of stomata (*b*) opening of stomata
(*c*) no effect of stomata (*d*) wider opening of stomata
22. Conversion of starch to organic acid is essential for stomata
(*a*) closure (*b*) opening (*c*) initiation (*d*) growth
23. Generally the number of stomata per square cm leaf area is
(*a*) in millions (*b*) less than one hundred
(*c*) in thousands (*d*) none of the above
24. In many thin leaved mesophytes, stomata open during day and close at night, this comes under
(*a*) Barley type (*b*) Potato type (*c*) Alfalfa type (*d*) Bean type
25. Of the processes which occur in leaves, the one which may lower their temperature is
(*a*) respiration (*b*) photosynthesis (*c*) transpiration (*d*) hydrolysis
26. The following percentage of water absorbed by herbaceous plants is lost during transpiration
(*a*) 80 (*b*) 60 (*c*) 90 (*d*) 40
27. Stomata open during the day time because the guard cells
(*a*) photosynthesise and produce osmotically active sugars
(*b*) are thin walled
(*c*) are bean shaped
(*d*) have to help in gaseous exchange
28. Active K^+ exchange mechanism for opening and closing of stomata was given by
(*a*) Darwin (*b*) Levitt (*c*) Scarth (*d*) Khorana
29. In which of the following plants would metabolism be hindered if the leaves are coated with wax on their upper surface ?
(*a*) Hydrilla (*b*) Lotus (*c*) Pistia (*d*) Vallisneria
30. Root pressure is maximum when
(*a*) transpiration is high and absorption is very low
(*b*) transpiration is very low and absorption is high
(*c*) transpiration is very high and absorption is also high
(*d*) transpiration and absorption both are low
31. Water potential is equal to
(*a*) ψ (*b*) p + WP (*c*) p + TP (*d*) $y_s + y_p$
32. In rainy season, wooden door swells up due to
(*a*) imbibition (*b*) capillarity (*c*) endosmosis (*d*) exosmosis
33. Cohesion theory of ascent of sap was given by
(*a*) Dixon and Jolly (*b*) Bose (*c*) Munch (*d*) Stephen Hales
34. Instrument used in determination of transpiration is
(*a*) Tensiometer (*b*) Auxanometer (*c*) Porometer (*d*) Potometer
35. Exudation of xylem sap on cutting the shoot is due to
(*a*) transpiration (*b*) guttation (*c*) root pressure (*d*) none of the above

36. Plasmolysis occurs due to
(*a*) Absorption (*b*) Osmosis (*c*) Endosmosis (*d*) Exosmosis
37. Water exudation through hydathodes is
(*a*) Guttation (*b*) Hydrolysis (*c*) Transpiration (*d*) Excretion
38. High carbon dioxide concentration in leaf interior will result in
(*a*) Stomatal opening (*b*) Stomatal closure
(*c*) No effect on stoma (*d*) Destruction of stomata
39. Plant cooling is due to
(*a*) Assimilation (*b*) Guttation (*c*) Photorespiration (*d*) Transpiration
40. Movement of water in the cortex of root from outside to inside is due to
(*a*) Gradient of water potential (*b*) Gradient of chemical potential
(*c*) Accumulation of organic solutes (*d*) Accumulation of inorganic salts
41. Osmotic pressure is highest in
(*a*) Hydrophytes (*b*) Mesophytes (*c*) Xerophytes (*d*) Halophytes
42. A cell placed in solution gets plasmolysed. This solution is
(*a*) Hypotonic (*b*) Hypertonic (*c*) Isotonic (*d*) Ditonic
43. Hydathodes are found in
(*a*) Stem (*b*) Leaves (*c*) Roots (*d*) All the above
44. The water potential and osmotic potential of pure water are
(*a*) 100 and zero (*b*) zero and zero (*c*) 100 and 100 (*d*) zero and 100
45. A cell will become fully turgid if it is placed in
(*a*) Hypotonic solution (*b*) Isotonic solution
(*c*) Hypertonic solution (*d*) All the above
46. Cohesion-tension theory is related to
(*a*) Respiratiom (*b*) Ascent of sap (*c*) Transpiration (*d*) Photosynthesis
47. Dry wooden stakes driven in cracks of a rock and soaked will develop pressure that will split the rock. The phenomenon is
(*a*) Osmotic pressure (*b*) Imbibition
(*c*) Turgor pressure (*d*) Deplasmolysis
48. A cell placed in hypotonic solution will
(*a*) Shrink (*b*) Show exosmosis
(*c*) Show endosmosis (*d*) Not change in shape or size
49. Which one will reduce rate of transpiration ?
(*a*) Rise in temperature (*b*) Increase in water uptake
(*c*) Increase in wind velocity (*d*) Decrease in light intensity
50. Root hair absorbs water from soil through
(*a*) Turgor pressure (*b*) Ion exchange (*c*) Osmosis (*d*) DPD
51. Wooden doors swell up and get stuck up during rainy season due to
(*a*) Endosmosis (*b*) Imbibition (*c*) Capillarity (*d*) Exosmosis
52. Rate of transpiration is measured by
(*a*) Ganong's potometer (*b*) Porometer
(*c*) Auxanometer (*d*) Respirometer
53. When water enters the plant cell one of the pressures is exerted on the cell wall :
(*a*) Turgor pressure (*b*) Suction pressure
(*c*) Root pressure (*d*) Osmotic pressure

54. Presence of glycolate in the cells will help to open stomata when there is :
(*a*) High concentration of CO_2 (*b*) Low concentration of O_2
(*c*) High concentration of CO_2 and low O_2 (*d*) High concentration of O_2 and low CO_2

55. In soil water available for plants is :
(*a*) Gravitational water (*b*) Hygroscopic water
(*c*) Capillary water (*d*) Chemically bound water

56. The water potential and osmotic potential of pure water are :
(*a*) Zero and 100 (*b*) Zero and zero (*c*) 100 and zero (*d*) 100 and 100

57. If a cell A with, DPD, 4 bars is connected to cells B, C, D whose OP and TP are respectively 4 and 4, 10 and 5 and 7 and 3 bar, the flow of water will be :
(*a*) C to A, B and D (*b*) A and D to B and C
(*c*) A to B, C and D (*d*) B to A, C and D

58. Water potential in the leaf tissue is positive (+ ve) during :
(*a*) Excessive transpiration (*b*) Low absorption
(*c*) Low transpiration (*d*) Guttation

59. With increase in turgity of a cell surrounded by water the wall pressure will :
(*a*) Increase (*b*) Decrease
(*c*) Fluctuate (*d*) Remain unchanged

60. Endosmosis of water occurs when in comparison with the outer solution, the water potential of cell sap is :
(*a*) Higher (*b*) Lower (*c*) Equal (*d*) None of these

61. The rate of absorption of water is slow at temperature near freezing point :
(*a*) It is mainly a metabolic process (*b*) Cell membrane becomes more viscous
(*c*) Growth of cells stop (*d*) Transpiration is retarded

62. What will be the nature of sugar solution, if the cell of an epidermal peel of *Rhoeodiscolor* shows plasmolysis ?
(*a*) Hydrophoric (*b*) Hypertonic (*c*) Isotonic (*d*) Hypotonic

63. It is desirable to add a pinch of salt to water to prolong the life of cut flower, which of the following is correct explanation ?
(*a*) Salt causes exosmosis
(*b*) Salt checks transpiration of flowering twig
(*c*) Salt inhibits the growth of microorganisms
(*d*) Salt gives the uptake of water by flower

64. If alcohol treated cell is kept in hypertonic solution it :
(*a*) Bursts (*b*) Plasmolysed (*c*) Remains same (*d*) None

65. Stomata usually open during the day time because the guard cells :
(*a*) are thin walled
(*b*) help in gas exchange
(*c*) are bean shaped
(*d*) photosynthesise and produce osmotically active sugars.

66. Plants will undergo wilting under one of these conditions :
(*a*) High temperature (*b*) High humidity
(*c*) Heavy rainfall (*d*) Absorption of water

67. If CO_2 concentration suddenly increases around the leaf, one of the following events occurs :
(*a*) Stomata open gradually
(*b*) Stomata open suddenly

(*c*) Transpiration will not be affected

(*d*) Decrease in transpiration due to sudden closure of stomata

68. Wilting in plants occurs due to increase in :
(*a*) Photosynthesis (*b*) Photoperiodism (*c*) Transpiration (*d*) Osmosis

69. Rate of transpiration can be measured by :
(*a*) Ganong's potometer (*b*) Porometer (*c*) Auxanometer (*d*) Respirometer

70. The osmotic potential of a solution is denoted by the symbol :
(*a*) y_x (*b*) DY (*c*) y_P (*d*) y_s

71. If cohesion-tention transpiration theory is correct then a break in water column in xylem vessels :
(*a*) should cause the mesophyll cells to become flaccid and result in wilting of leaves
(*b*) should increase the water content of leaves
(*c*) should have no effect at all
(*d*) should increase the rate of photosynthesis

72. Dumb-bell shaped guard cells are found in :
(*a*) Wheat (*b*) Bean (*c*) Groundnut (*c*) Sunflower

73. Who had said that 'transpiration is a necessary evil' ?
(*a*) Curtis (*b*) Steward (*c*) Anderson (*d*) J.C. Bose

74. Osmosis is defined as the process in which :
(*a*) Water diffuses from lower concentration to higher concentration
(*b*) Solutes diffuse from lower concentration to higher concentration
(*c*) Active transport of ions take place
(*d*) Passive transport of ions take place

75. Plant cells submerged in distilled water will become :
(*a*) Turgid (*b*) Flaccid (*c*) Plasmolysed (*d*) Impermeable

76. To initiate cell plasmolysis, the salt solution should be :
(*a*) Isotonic (*b*) Hypertonic (*c*) Hypotonic (*d*) None of these

77. Plant cooling occurs due to :
(*a*) Assimilation (*b*) Guttation (*c*) Photorespiration (*d*) Transpiration

78. Rate of transpiration increases :
(*a*) When there is no light (*b*) In water
(*c*) When temperature is high (*d*) In rainy season

79. Which of the following factors is most important in regulation of temperature ?
(*a*) Light (*b*) Wind (*c*) Temperature (*d*) Humidity

80. The phytohormone which is supposed to be one of the factor responsible for regulating the opening and closeing of stomata :
(*a*) ABA (*b*) GA (*c*) IBA (*d*) Kinetin

81. Transpiration pull will be maximum under which of the following conditions ?
(*a*) Open stomata, high humid atmosphere and well irrigated soil
(*b*) Open stomata, dry atmosphere and moist soil
(*c*) Open stomata, high humid atmosphere and dry soil
(*d*) Closed stomata, low light intensity and humid atmosphere

82. Osmosis is defined as :
(*a*) The flow of solvent molecules from a region of higher concentration to a region of lower concentration through a semipermeable membrane.
(*b*) The flow of low concentration liquid
(*c*) The flow of solvent molecules from a higher concentration to a lower concentration region
(*d*) The flow of solvent molecules from a lower concentration to a higher concentration region.

83. A plasmolysed cell can be deplasmolysed by placing it in :
(*a*) Pure water or hypotonic solution (*b*) Hypertonic solution
(*c*) Isotonic solution (*d*) Saturated solution

84. A cell becomes turgid when placed in :
(*a*) Isotonic solution (*b*) Hypertonic solution
(*c*) Hypotonic solution (*d*) All of these

85. Process of water exudation through hydathodes is called :
(*a*) Guttation (*b*) Transpiration (*c*) Excretion (*d*) Hydrolysis

86. Maximum transpiration occurs from :
(*a*) Protoderm and procombium (*b*) Dermal tissue
(*c*) Periderm and lenticels (*d*) Ground tissue and scale leaves

87. The degree of opening of stomata is determined by :
(*a*) Porometer (*b*) Calorimeter (*c*) Potometer (*d*) All of these

88. During absorption of water by roots the water potential of cell sap is lower than that of :
(*a*) Pure water and soil solution
(*b*) Neither pure water nor soil solution
(*c*) Pure water but higher than that of soil solution
(*d*) Soil solution but higher than that of pure water

89. A twig kept in water remain fresh for a longer time if some salt is added to it is due to :
(*a*) Absorption of more water (*b*) Exosmosis
(*c*) Decrease in transpiration rate (*d*) Decrease in bacterial degradation activity

90. The bulliform cells of leaves lose their turgidity during excessive :
(*a*) Assimilation (*b*) Transpiration (*c*) Photosynthesis (*d*) Respiration

91. Root hairs are found :
(*a*) In the zone of elongation (*b*) Adventitious roots
(*c*) On the root cap (*d*) In the zone of maturation

92. Osmotic pressure of a solution is :
(*a*) Greater than the pure solvent (*b*) Lesser than the pure solvent
(*c*) Equal to the pure solvent (*d*) More or less the pure solvent

93. Plasmodesmata connections help in :
(*a*) Cytoplasmic streaming (*b*) Synchronous mitotic divisions
(*c*) Locomotion of unicellular organisms (*d*) Movement of substances between cells

94. The cohesive force existing between molecules of water is contributing to :
(*a*) Plasmolysis (*b*) Translocation (*c*) Ascent of sap (*d*) Osmosis

95. Opening and closing of stomata is due to the :
(*a*) Hormonal change in guard cells. (*b*) Change in turgor pressure of guard cells
(*c*) Gaseous exchange (*d*) Respiration

96. Stomata of a plant open due to :
(*a*) Influx of hydrogen ions (*b*) Efflux of potassium ions
(*c*) Influx of calcium ions (*d*) Influx of potassium ions

97. Water is released as droplets — this is known as :
(*a*) Root pressure (*b*) Transpiration (*c*) Guttation (*d*) None

98. If the concentration of external solution is more than the cytoplasm, the solution is known as :
(*a*) Hypertonic (*b*) Isotonic (*c*) Hypotonic (*d*) None

99. The cause of guttation is mainly :
(*a*) Root pressure (*b*) Osmosis (*c*) Transpiration pull (*d*) Cohesive force

100. The water potential and osmotic potential of pure water are :
(*a*) 100 and zero (*b*) Zero and zero (*c*) 100 and 200 (*d*) Zero and hundred
101. Which one of the following is a rapid type of absorption?
(*a*) passive absorption (*b*) active absorption
(*c*) root absorption (*d*) salt absorption
102. Active absorption of water from the soil by the root is mainly effected by
(*a*) respiratory activity of root (*b*) tension in cell sap to transpiration
(*c*) tissue organisation (*d*) none of the above
103. In soil, water available for roots is
(*a*) capillary water (*b*) gravitational water
(*c*) hygroscopic water (*d*) none of the above
104. Water will be absorbed by root hairs when the external medium is
(*a*) isotonic (*b*) hypertonic (*c*) viscous (*d*) hypotonic
105. Water absorption through roots can be increased by
(*a*) decreased transpiration (*b*) increased transpiration
(*c*) increased rate of photosynthesis (*d*) decreased absorption of ions
106. The ultimate cause for the movement of water against gravity in a tree is
(*a*) osmosis (*b*) transpiration (*c*) imbibition (*d*) photosynthesis
107. The path of water from soil upto secondary xylem is
(*a*) soil → root hair cell wall → cortex → endodermis → pericycle → protoxylem → metaxylem
(*b*) cortex → root hair → endodermis → pericycle → protoxylem → metaxylem
(*c*) pericycle → soil → root hair → cortex → endodermis → protoxylem → metaxylem
(*d*) soil → root hair cell wall → cortex → pericycle → endodermis → protoxylem → metaxylem
108. The water held tightly by the soil particles around them is known as
(*a*) capillary water (*b*) hygroscopic water (*c*) runaway water (*d*) gravitational water
109. The initial stage of water absorption by root cells is by
(*a*) absorption (*b*) imbibition (*c*) osmosis (*d*) respiration
110. Which one of the following is connected with transport of water in plants?
(*a*) phloem (*b*) xylem (*c*) epidermis (*d*) cambium
111. Osmosis is the movement of
(*a*) solute particles from higher concentration to lower concentration
(*b*) solvent particles from higher water potential to lower water potential
(*c*) solute particles from higher concentration to lower concentration through a semipermeable membrane
(*d*) solvent particle from lower water potential to higher water potential
112. Freshly cut potato chip is put into a strong solution of sugar, later it is found to be
(*a*) flaccid (*b*) turgid
(*c*) filled up with more starch (*d*) filled up with more sugar
113. The movement of water from one cell of the cortex to the adjacent one in roots is due to
(*a*) accumulation of inorganic salts in the cells
(*b*) accumulation of organic salts in the cells
(*c*) chemical potential gradient
(*d*) water potential gradient
114. A cell is plasmolysed after being kept in a hypertonic solution. What will be present between cell wall and plasmalemma ?
(*a*) Hypertonic solution (*b*) Air
(*c*) Hypotonic solution (*d*) Isotonic solution

115. Dry seeds when placed in water swell due to
(*a*) diffusion (*b*) absorption (*c*) imbibition (*d*) inhibition

116. An innovative professor, who wanted to give a live demonstration of a physiological process, filled a glass bottle with previously moistened mustard seeds and water. He screw capped the bottle and kept it away in a corner and resumed his lecture. Towards the end of his lecture, there was a sudden explosion with glass pieces of the bottle thrown around. Which of the following phenomenon did the professor want to demonstrate ?
(*a*) Imbibition (*b*) Osmosis
(*c*) Anaerobic respiration (*d*) Diffusion

117. The form and structure of growing cells are maintained because of the
(*a*) osmosis (*b*) plasmolysis (*c*) turgidity (*d*) wall pressure

118. Turgidity of cells is maintained by
(*a*) wall pressure (*b*) turgor pressure
(*c*) diffusion pressure (*d*) osmotic pressure

119. Of the process which occurs in leaves, the one which may lower their temperature is
(*a*) photosynthesis (*b*) transpiration (*c*) hydrolysis (*d*) respiration

120. Which of the following has the lowest water potential ?
(*a*) soil (*b*) root xylem (*c*) leaf cell walls (*d*) leaf air spaces

121. In hypertonic solution a cell's water potential
(*a*) increases (*b*) decreases
(*c*) first increases, then decreases (*d*) no change

122. The stomata in angiosporms open and close due to
(*a*) pressure of gases inside the leaves (*b*) their genetic constitution
(*c*) turgor pressure of the guard cells (*d*) turgor pressure of the subsidiary cells

123. When the contents of a cell are in the shrinkage state, the process is called
(*a*) hypotonic (*b*) osmosis (*c*) endosmosis (*d*) plasmolysis

124. The stage when plasmolysis just begins and the plasmalemma starts receding the cell walls, it is called
(*a*) deplasmolysis (*b*) plasmolysis
(*c*) incipient plasmolysis (*d*) none of the above

125. Due to low atmospheric pressure the rate of transpiration will
(*a*) increase (*b*) decrease slowly (*c*) decrease rapidly (*d*) remain unaffected

126. The vacuolar membrane is called
(*a*) plasmalemma (*b*) middle lamella (*c*) tonoplast (*d*) chromoplast

127. In a terrestrial habitat which of the following factors affect temperature and rainfall conditions ?
(*a*) translocation (*b*) transformation (*c*) transpiration (*d*) transduction

128. The transpiration in the plants will be lowest
(*a*) when there is high humidity in the atmosphere
(*b*) high wind velocity
(*c*) environmental conditions are very dry
(*d*) there is excess of water in the cell

129. Which of the following is used for determining the rate of transpiration in plants ?
(*a*) Auxanometer (*b*) Potentiometer (*c*) Porometer (*d*) Potometer

130. Which of the following is the most common type of transpiration ?
(*a*) Cuticular (*b*) Stomatal (*c*) Foliar (*d*) Lenticular

131. To compare the rate of transpiration from two surfaces of a leaf, a piece of dry paper, previously soaked in the solution of a chemical which changes colour when becomes moist, is taken one such chemical is
(*a*) Cobalt chloride (*b*) Calcium chloride (*c*) Sodium chloride (*d*) Cobalt nitrate

132. Root pressure is maximum when
(*a*) transpiration is very low and absorption is high
(*b*) transpiration is very high and absorption is also high
(*c*) transpiration and absorption both are low
(*d*) transpiration is high and absorption is low

133. Wilting in plant occurs when
(*a*) phloem is blocked (*b*) xylem is blocked
(*c*) epidermis is peeled off (*d*) pith is blocked

134. Loss of turgor from the cells causes drooping of leaves during day, but they recover from it at night. This is called
(*a*) temporary wilting (*b*) guttation (*c*) permanent wilting (*d*) exudation

135. In both evaporation and transpiration water is lost in the form of vapour, yet they differ because
(*a*) frequency of water loss is different in both of them
(*b*) transpiration is a physical process and evaporation is physiological process
(*c*) transpiration is a physiological process and evaporation is a physical process
(*d*) both evaporation and transpiration are similar but the rate of water loss differs

136. Increase in CO_2 concentration around leaf results in
(*a*) partial closure of stomata (*b*) complete closure of stomata
(*c*) opening of stomata (*d*) no effect on stomatal opening and closing

137. Which one of the following is produced during water stress and causes closure of stomata ?
(*a*) Abscisic acid (*b*) Auxin (*c*) Gibberellin (*d*) Ethylene

138. Which of the following plant keeps its stomata open during the night and closed during the day ?
(*a*) Water lily (*b*) Maize plant (*c*) Cactus (*d*) Cucurbit

139. Conversion of starch to organic acid is essential for
(*a*) stomatal closure (*b*) stomatal growth (*c*) stomatal opening (*d*) stomatal initiation

140. Guard cells differ from epidermal cells in having
(*a*) chloroplasts (*b*) mitochondria (*c*) cell wall (*d*) vacuole

141. Active K^+ exchange mechanism for opening and closing of stomata was given by
(*a*) Khorana (*b*) Sachs (*c*) Levitt (*d*) Strasburger

142. In succulent plants the stomata open in night and close in day. Which among the following would be best hypothesis to explain the mechanism of stomatal opening in night only ?
(*a*) CO_2 accumulates, reduces pH, stimulates enzymes, resulting in accumulation of sugars.
(*b*) decrease in CO_2 concentration in dark, starch is broken down into organic acids particularly malic acid resulting in K^+ transport and osmotic concentration of guard cells increases.
(*c*) CO_2 used up, increase pH results in accumulation of sugars.
(*d*) low CO_2 concentration accumulates organic acid resulting in the increased concentration of cell sap.

143. Stomata will open, if there is accumulation of the following element in the guard cells
(*a*) Magnesium (*b*) Potassium (*c*) Iron (*d*) Zinc

144. In many thin leaved mesophytes the stomata open during the day time and close at night. This comes under
(*a*) Alfalfa type (*b*) Potato type (*c*) Barley type (*d*) Bean type

145. The process of the escape of liquid from the tip of uninjured leaf or through hydathodes is called
(*a*) guttation (*b*) transpiration (*c*) evaporation (*d*) none of above

146. Which of the following is responsible for guttation ?
(*a*) Transpiration (*b*) Root pressure (*c*) Photosynthesis (*d*) Osmosis

147. Transpiration - cohesion - tention theory operates in
 (*a*) Active absorption (*b*) Passive absorption
 (*c*) Both (*a*) and (*b*) (*d*) None of the above

148. Many transplanted seedlings do not survive because
 (*a*) they do not like the new soil
 (*b*) they do not get required minerals
 (*c*) most of root hairs are lost during transplantation
 (*d*) root apex is damaged during this process

149. The most widely accepted theory for ascent of sap in trees is
 (*a*) Role of atmospheric pressure
 (*b*) Pulsating action of living cells
 (*c*) Transpiration pull and cohesion theory of Dixon and Jolly
 (*d*) Cytoplasmic theory of Hugo de Vries.

150. Which of the following contributes most to transport of water from the ground to the leaves of a tall tree ?
 (*a*) Capillary rise of water through xylem vessels
 (*b*) Root pressure
 (*c*) Cohesion of water and transpiration pull
 (*d*) Break down of ATP

ANSWERS

1. (*c*)	2. (*a*)	3. (*c*)	4. (*b*)	5. (*b*)	6. (*b*)	7. (*d*)	8. (*b*)	9. (*d*)	10. (*d*)
11. (*d*)	12. (*d*)	13. (*a*)	14. (*d*)	15. (*d*)	16. (*d*)	17. (*c*)	18. (*a*)	19. (*a*)	20. (*a*)
21. (*a*)	22. (*b*)	23. (*c*)	24. (*c*)	25. (*c*)	26. (*c*)	27. (*a*)	28. (*b*)	29. (*b*)	30. (*b*)
31. (*d*)	32. (*a*)	33. (*a*)	34. (*c*)	35. (*d*)	36. (*d*)	37. (*b*)	38. (*c*)	39. (*d*)	40. (*a*)
41. (*d*)	42. (*b*)	43. (*b*)	44. (*b*)	45. (*a*)	46. (*b*)	47. (*b*)	48. (*c*)	49. (*d*)	50. (*c*)
51. (*b*)	52. (*a*)	53. (*a*)	54. (*d*)	55. (*c*)	56. (*b*)	57. (*d*)	58. (*a*)	59. (*a*)	60. (*b*)
61. (*d*)	62. (*b*)	63. (*b*)	64. (*c*)	65. (*d*)	66. (*a*)	67. (*d*)	68. (*c*)	69. (*a*)	70. (*d*)
71. (*a*)	72. (*a*)	73. (*a*)	74. (*a*)	75. (*a*)	76. (*b*)	77. (*d*)	78. (*c*)	79. (*a*)	80. (*a*)
81. (*b*)	82. (*a*)	83. (*a*)	84. (*a*)	85. (*a*)	86. (*b*)	87. (*a*)	88. (*b*)	89. (*c*)	90. (*b*)
91. (*a*)	92. (*a*)	93. (*d*)	94. (*c*)	95. (*b*)	96. (*d*)	97. (*c*)	98. (*a*)	99. (*a*)	100. (*b*)
101. (*a*)	102. (*a*)	103. (*a*)	104. (*d*)	105. (*b*)	106. (*b*)	107. (*a*)	108. (*b*)	109. (*b*)	110. (*b*)
111. (*b*)	112. (*a*)	113. (*d*)	114. (*a*)	115. (*c*)	116. (*a*)	117. (*c*)	118. (*b*)	119. (*b*)	120. (*d*)
121. (*b*)	122. (*c*)	123. (*d*)	124. (*c*)	125. (*a*)	126. (*c*)	127. (*c*)	128. (*a*)	129. (*d*)	130. (*b*)
131. (*a*)	132. (*a*)	133. (*b*)	134. (*a*)	135. (*c*)	136. (*a*)	137. (*a*)	138. (*c*)	139. (*c*)	140. (*a*)
141. (*c*)	142. (*b*)	143. (*b*)	144. (*a*)	145. (*a*)	146. (*b*)	147. (*b*)	148. (*c*)	149. (*c*)	150. (*c*)

16

CHAPTER

Mineral Nutrition and Nitrogen Metabolism

The basic needs of all living organisms are similar and they require macromolecules, such as carbohydrates, proteins and fats for their growth and development. They also require minerals for their development.

However, green plants prepare their food from simple substances, such as water and carbon dioxide, through process of photosynthesis. This type of green organisms, which prepare their food through photosynthesis are called **autotrophs**.

While other organisms, and non-green plants cannot prepare their own food, as autotrophs do. They obtain their nutrition from autotrophs, and are called **heterotrophs**.

In the formation of carbohydrates, proteins and fats, carbon (C), hydrogen (H) and oxygen (O) are required. In addition to these elements (*i.e.*, C, H and O), plants need several other important elements, called **mineral elements**.

The mineral elements that are essential in the life of a plant, with the exception of carbon and oxygen, are obtained through the root system from the soil. Carbon and oxygen are obtained from the atmosphere. The utilization for various absorbed ions by a plant for growth and development is called the **mineral nutrition** of the plant. It has been demonstrated by water and sand culture experiments that carbon, hydrogen, oxygen, nitrogen, sulphur, phosphorus, calcium, magnesium and iron are essential for the healthy growth and development of plants. These elements are referred to as the **macronutrients** or **major elements** because of the relatively large quantities in which they are needed for plant life. Plants also require some elements in minute or trace quantities which are called the **micronutrients** or **trace** or **minor elements**. Some important micronutrients are manganese, zinc, boron, copper and molybdenum.

ESSENTIAL MINERAL ELEMENTS

An **essential element** is known, without which the plant cannot complete its life cycle. It has clear physiological role to play. The important criteria for an essential element are as follows:

(*i*) This element is absolutely necessary for supporting normal growth and reproduction of plant.

(*ii*) This element is always specific, and cannot be replaced by any other element.

(*iii*) This element is directly involved in the metabolism of the plant.

However, among the mineral elements absorbed by the plants, not all are essential.

Out of 105 or more elements discovered so far, only 20 elements have been found to be essential for growth and development of the plant.

These essential elements are classified into two broad categories called (*i*) **macronutrients** and (*ii*) **micronutrients**.

The **macronutrients** are: carbon, hydrogen, oxygen, nitrogen, phosphorus, sulphur, potassium, calcium, magnesium and silicon.

The macronutrients are generally present in plant tissues in concentrations of 1 to 10 mg per gram of dry matter.

The **micronutrients** or **trace elements** are: iron, manganese, copper, molybdenum, zinc, boron and chlorine. Recently some other such elements have also been discovered, *e.g.*, cobalt, vanadium and nickel.

The microelements are required in very low amounts, *i.e.*, about 0.1 mg per gram of dry matter.

SOURCES OF ESSENTIAL ELEMENTS FOR PLANTS

All-elements incorporated into plants are ultimately derived from the atmosphere, water and soil.

Carbon (C). It is derived from atmosphere as CO_2.

Hydrogen (H). It is mainly obtained from water.

Oxygen (O). It is either derived from the air or from the water in the form of inorganic ions.

Nitrogen (N). The plants are unable to use atmospheric nitrogen. It is inert and plants cannot make use of it directly. However, by means of atmospheric activities nitrogen combines with oxygen and is brought down by rain to the soil. Besides, there are certain highly specialised organisms called **nitrogen fixers**, such as bacteria, and cyanobacteria. They fix atmospheric nitrogen into the soil in the form of nitrites (NO_2), and nitrates (NO_3). These heterotrophic organisms, occurring in the soil convert nitrogen gas (N_2) to anionic forms such as nitrates (NO_3) or nitrite (NO_2^-), or a reduced cationic form such as NH_4^+ (ammonium). These nitrogenous compounds enter plants as nutrients through the roots and are assimilated as organic nitrogen. The plants, in turn, provide organic nitrogen to heterotrophic organisms.

The other elements are absorbed from the soil, such as phosphorus (P) as phosphate (PO_4), and sulphur (S) mainly as sulphate (SO_4).

ROLE OF ESSENTIAL ELEMENTS

The essential elements perform several important roles. They may be as follows:

The most important role of the elements is to participate in various metabolic activities, such as regulation of permeability of cell membranes; some elements are required for maintenance of osmotic pressure of cell sap, while others take part in an electron transport system. Some elements are responsible for buffer action, and some for electrical neutrality.

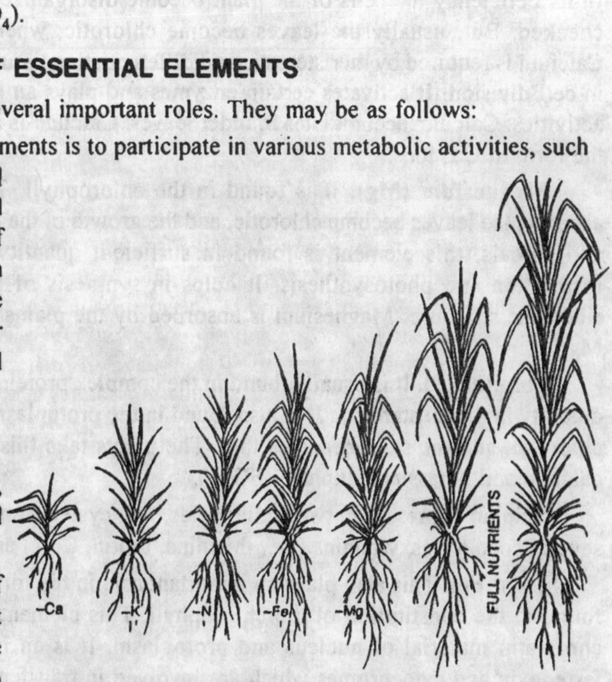

Fig. 16.1. Barley plants grown in water culture showing deficiency of certain nutrients.

Macronutrients

Mineral elements include N, P, K, Ca, Mg, S and Fe. They are absorbed from soil.

Nitrogen (N). About 78% of nitrogen is found in atmospheric air, but this is of no use to plants, in its free state. This enters in the plants through stomata along with other gases, and comes out in the same state, unused. The plants can take nitrogen, found in the soil in the form of NO_2^-, NO_3^- or NH_4^+. This is required by all parts of a plant, particularly the meristematic tissues. Nitrogen is found in the constituents of proteins, chlorophyll, protoplasm, nucleic acids, vitamins and hormones. For proper and normal growth of leaves of plants, it is one of the most essential elements.

Phosphorus (P). It is usually found in nucleoproteins and protoplasm. It also helps in the division of nucleus and the cell. It also helps in the decomposition of carbohydrates during respiration. Phosphorus is a constituent of cell membranes, nucleic acids and nucleotides. This is needed for all phosphorylation reactions. It plays a very important role in the ripening of the grains and fruits. This also helps a lot in the development of root system. For the development of underground parts of radish, beet root, and potato, etc., this element is required. Phosphorus is absorbed from the soil in the form of phosphate $H_2PO_4^-$ ions.

Potassium (K). This element is usually found in the growing regions of the plant. It is one of the constituents of the protoplasm. It is related to metabolic activities. This helps in the synthesis of carbohydrates and proteins. The plant grows normally in its presence, and the fruits and seeds remain quite healthy. On the scarcity of potassium, the normal growth of the leaves become yellowish, and the stem becomes somewhat thin. The plants take potassium from the soil in the form of potassium nitrate and potassium chloride, etc.

Potassium helps to determine anion-cation balance in cells, and is involved in protein synthesis, opening and closing of stomata, activation of enzymes, and maintenance of turgidity of cells. It is absorbed as K^+ ion by plants from the soil.

Calcium (Ca). This element is always found in green plants. The middle lamella of the cell wall consists of calcuim pectate. Only because of this element, the permeability of the protoplasm is maintained. Usually for the growth and development of the fruits, the calcuim is very essential. In its deficiency the cells of the plant become disorganized, and the growth of the plant is also checked. But, usually the leaves become chlorotic, when its overdose is present in the soil. Calcium is required by meristematic and differentiating tissues. It is also used in the mitotic spindle in cell division. It activates certain enzymes and plays an important role in regulating metabolic activities. Calcium accumulates in older leaves. Calcium is absorbed by the plants from the soil in the form of Ca^+ ions.

Magnesium (Mg). It is found in the chlorophyll. The chlorophyll does not form in its absence, the leaves become chlorotic, and the growth of the plant is retarded. In the seeds of pulses and cereals, this element is found in sufficient quantity. Magnesium activates enzymes in respiration and photosynthesis. It helps in synthesis of DNA and RNA. This also maintains ribosome structure. Magnesium is absorbed by the plants from the soil in the form of divalent Mg^{2+}.

Sulphur (S). It is usually found in the complex proteins of the plants. It is found in sufficient quantity in the mustard oil. It is also found in the protoplasm. In its deficiency, the leaves become chlorotic, and the stem becomes thin. The plants take this element from the soil in the form of calcium and potassium sulphate (SO_4^{2-}).

Sulphur is present in two amino acids, *i.e.*, cysteine and methionine. It is main constituent of several coenzymes, vitamins (*i.e.*, thiamine, biotin, CoA) and ferredoxin.

Iron (Fe). This also plays an important role in the formation of chlorophyll, though it is not found in the constitution of the chlorophyll. This element is always found to be present in the chromatin material of nucleus and protoplasm. It is an important constituent of proteins like ferredoxin and cytochromes which are involved in transfer of electrons. It is reversibly oxidised from Fe^{2+} to Fe^{3+} during electron transfer. It activates catalase. Iron is absorbed by the plants from the soil in the form of ferric (Fe^{3+}) ions.

Non-mineral elements include C, H and O

Carbon (C). Carbon is the main constituent of the plant material. The main part of the plant consists of it. It is usually half of plant's dry weight. Carbon is found in all organic compounds present in the plant. The plants get, carbon from the atmosphere in the form of carbon dioxide. Usually, .03% carbon dioxide is found in the atmosphere, but this percentage goes down even to .01% in day time, because of its use in the photosynthesis.

Hydrogen (H). Free hydrogen does not play any role in the plant life. When it combines with oxygen, water is formed, which is absorbed by the plants. The hydrogen is found in so many organic and inorganic compounds of the plant.

Oxygen (O). Free oxygen is taken from the atmosphere by the plants, which helps in the respiration of the living cells. Besides this, the oxygen is found in many organic compounds of the plant.

Micronutrients

Boron (B). This is also an essential element for the growth of nearly all the plants. The plants of tomato, tobacco, lemon, root, mustard, cotton and others are sufficiently benefitted by these elements. Boron also helps in the formation of the nodules of the leguminous plants. It also adds to the quantity of the sugar of beet root. The beet root becomes susceptible to various diseases, because of its deficiency. In its deficiency, the normal growth of the plant is obstructed and various leaf spots are developed. In its absence, the apices of roots and stems become brittle, and gradually they die.

Boron is also required for uptake and utilisation of Ca^{2+}, membrane function, pollen germination, cell elongation, cell differentiation and carbohydrate translocation.

Manganese (Mn). Manganese activates many enzymes which are involved in photosynthesis, respiration and nitrogen metabolism. Manganese helps in splitting of water to liberate oxygen during photosynthesis. Various vitamins are formed in the fruits, only because of its presence. The cabbage plants, pine trees and the leguminous plants require its optimum doses. Manganese is absorbed by plants in the form of manganous cation (Mn^{2+}).

Zinc (Zn). Zinc helps in the formation of chloroplasts. It activates various enzymes, especially carboxylases. Zinc is required in synthesis of auxin. It is absorbed by plants from soil in the form of (Zn^{2+}) ions.

Copper (Cu). Copper helps in formation of starch. It is required for the overall metabolism in plants. It is associated with certain enzymes involved in redox reactions and is reversibly oxidised from Cu^{+} to Cu^{2+}. Copper is absorbed by plants as cupric ion (Cu^{2+}).

Molybdenum (Mo). This helps in formation of proteins. It also helps in fixation of nitrogen in soil by *Azotobacter* and *Rhizobium*. This is a constituent of several enzymes, including nitrogenase and nitrate reductase which take part in nitrogen metabolism. This is absorbed by plants from soil in the form of molybdate ion (MoO_2^{2+}).

Chlorine (Cl). With Na^{+} and K^{+}, chlorine helps in determining solute concentration and anion-cation balance in cells. It is required for cell division in roots and leaves. It is needed to perform water-splitting reaction in photosynthesis, which evolves oxygen.

DEFICIENCY SYMPTOMS

Deficiency Symptoms (Macronutrients)

Nitrogen (N). Nitrogen deficiency causes yellowing of older leaves (chlorosis). The plant growth is stunted as protein content, cell division and cell enlargement are decreased. It also causes dormancy of lateral buds, late flowering, purple colouration and shoot axis surface and wrinkling of cereal grains.

Phosphorus (P). Phosphorus deficiency causes premature leaf fall. Dead necrotic areas develop on leaves or fruits, and leaves turn dark to blue-green in colour. It also causes delay in seed germination.

Potassium (K). Mottled chlorosis of leaves occurs. Necrotic areas are developed at the tips and margins of leaves, and they curve downward. Internodes become short, and plants adopt bushy habit. It also causes loss of cambial activity, disintegration of plastids and increase in rate of respiration.

Calcium (Ca). Calcium deficiency causes disintegration of growing meristematic regions of the root, stem and leaves. Chlorosis occurs along the margins of the younger leaves, and malformation occurs. This also leads to stunted growth of the plant.

Magnesium (Mg). Magnesium deficiency causes interveinal chlorosis of the leaves. The older leaves are affected first, and dead necrotic patches appear on the leaves. This also causes premature leaf abscission.

Sulphur (S). Sulphur deficiency causes yellowing (*i.e.*, chlorosis) of leaves, younger leaves are affected first, tips and margins of leaves roll inward, and stem becomes hard due to development of sclerenchyma. These symptoms are similar to those of nitrogen deficiency symptoms, as sulphur and nitrogen are constituents of proteins.

Iron (Fe). Iron deficiency causes rapid chlorosis of the leaves which is generally interveinal.

Deficiency Symptoms (Micronutrients)

Manganese (Mn). Manganese deficiency causes chlorotic and necrotic spots in the interveinal areas of leaves.

Zinc (Zn). Zinc deficiency causes chlorosis of older leaves which starts from tips and margins. Malformation of leaves takes place, and stunted growth of plant occurs. Its deficiency causes **mottle leaf** disease in apple, citrus, walnut, etc., and **khaira** disease in rice.

Copper (Cu). Copper deficiency causes necrosis of the tips of young leaves. It causes **die-back** of citrus and other fruit trees where leaves wither and fall, bark becomes rough and splits exuding gummy substances. **Reclamation disease** of cereals and leguminous plants is also caused due to its deficiency.

Boron (B). Boron deficiency causes death of the shoot tip. Flower formation is suppressed, root growth is stunted and shoot apices die. Fruits become of small size and root nodules in leguminous plants are not formed, and leaves become coppery in texture.

Molybdenum (Mo). Molybdenum deficiency causes chlorotic interveinal mottling of the older leaves. This may cause nitrogen deficiency, as it is component of enzymes involved in nitrogen metabolism. Flower formation is inhibited, and also causes **whip tail** disease in cauliflower plants.

Chlorine (Cl). The deficiency of chlorine in plants causes wilting of leaves, stunted root growth and reduced fruiting.

MECHANISM OF ABSORPTION OF ELEMENTS

Here the term mineral salt is used for those substances which contain nitrogen, sulphur and phosphorus in inorganic and organic combinations. The upward translocation of nitrogen, sulphur and phosphorus occurs in both organic and inorganic combinations.

Earlier this was universally agreed that upward translocation of mineral salts takes place through the xylem. But most studies of the sap present in the xylem indicated that it contains more inorganic solutes than organic ones. During the seasons, appreciable concentrations of mineral salts are commonly present in the sap vessels when upward flow of water occurs at its most rapid rate.

Table 16.1. Roles of Mineral Elements in Plants.

Element	Obtained as	Regions of plant in which required	Functions	Deficiency symptoms
Nitrogen N	NO_2^-, NO_3^- or NH_4^+	In all tissues, particularly in meristematic tissues.	Constitutent of proteins, nucleic acids, vitamins, hormones, coenzymes, ATP, chlorophyll.	Stunted growth, chlorosis.
Phosphorus P	$H_2PO_4^-$	Young tissues, withdrawn from the older metabolically less active cells.	Constituent of cell membrane. Required for the synthesis of nucleic acids, nucleotides, ATP, NAD and NADP.	Poor growth of plant, leaves dull green.
Potassium K	K^+	Meristematic tissues, buds, leaves, root tips.	Involved in protein synthesis; involved in formation of cell membrane and in opening and closing of stomata; increases hardness; helps in determination of anion cation balance in cells; activates enzymes and helps in maintenance of turgidity of cells.	Stunted growth; yellow edges to leaves; premature death and mottled appearance of leaves.
Calcium Ca	Ca^{++}	Meristematic and differentiating tissues, accumulates in older leaves.	Involved in selective permeability of cell membranes; activates certain enzymes; required for development of stem and root apices, and as calcium pectate in the middle lamella of the cell wall.	Stunted growth; chlorosis of young leaves; die back of shoots.
Magnesium Mg	Mg^{++}	All the leaves of plants; withdrawn from ageing leaves and directed to developing seeds.	Activates enzymes in phosphate metabolism; constituent of chlorophyll; maintains ribosome structure.	Chlorosis
Sulphur S	SO_4^{++}	Young leaves; stem and root tips; remobilized during senescence.	Constituent of amino acids, cysteine, methionine and proteins, coenzyme A, and ferredoxin.	Chlorosis

Element	Obtained as	Regions of plant in which required	Functions	Deficiency symptoms
Iron Fe	Fe^{+++}	Everywhere in leaves, along leaf veins.	Constituent of ferredoxin and cytochromes; required for synthesis of chlorophyll.	Chlorosis
Manganese (trace) Mn	Mn^{++}	Leaves and seeds	Activates certain enzymes (carboxylases).	Chlorosis; grey spots on leaves
Molybdenum (trace) Mo	Mo^{+++}	All parts; particularly in roots.	Activates certain enzymes in nitrogen metabolism.	Retardation of growth to some extent.
Boron (trace) B	B^{---}	Leaves and seeds	Increases the uptake of water and Ca; essential for meristematic activity and growth of pollen tube; involved in translocation of carbohydrates.	Death of stem and root apices; leaves become curled and brittle; reduces flowering; causes brown heart disease.
Copper (trace) Cu	Cu^{++}	All parts of plant	Activates certain enzymes	
Zinc (trace) Zn	Zn^{++}	All parts of plant	Activates various enzymes especially carboxylases, carbonic anhydrate and various dehydrogenases; required for auxin synthesis.	Malformation of leaves Dieback of shoots.
Chlorine Cl	Cl^-	All parts of plant	With Na^+ and K^+ helps in determining solute concentration and anion-cation balance in cells; essential for oxygen evolution in photosynthesis.	

The experiments of Clements and Engard (1938), Phillis and Mason (1940) and others have shown that ringing stems of various species do not prevent upward transport of mineral salts through the plant. This shows that upward translocation of mineral salts can take place in the xylem. Experiments on ringing often show that mineral salts can be conducted in the xylem and experiments on intercepting wood often show that they can be conducted in the phloem.

Stout and Hoagland (1939), employed the radioactive tracer technique in experiments designed to ascertain the path of upward movement of mineral salts in plants. The results of experiments conducted by these workers showed that upward movement of mineral salts occurs in the xylem, but the possibility of some such movement in the ploem also is not excluded even though it is clear that lateral movement from xylem to phloem takes place readily. The similar experiments of Gustafson (1939) also indicate that a limited amount of upward translocation of radioctive phosphate may occur through the phloem.

(*i*) The **outer space** includes the intercellular space and the cell wall. The **inner space** refers to most of cytoplasm and vacuole.

(*ii*) Entry of ions into outer space is considered as **passive**.

(*iii*) Entry into, or exit from the inner space is **active**.

(*iv*) passive entry does not require expenditure of metabolic energy.

(*v*) Active process requires metabolic energy.

(*vi*) Movement of ions is termed **flux**. The movement into the cell is **influx**, whereas outward movement is **efflux**.

Conclusively it can be said that upward translocation of mineral salts occurs in the xylem, and it appears quite certain that this is the main pathway along which their general upward translocation of mineral salts from roots to leaves occurs. Some upward translocation of mineral salts also occurs in the phloem under certain circumstances.

Absorption of Solute (Mineral Salts)

Besides water, the plant absorbs from the environment considerable quantities of mineral salts, gases and various other salts. All these are absorbed in the form of aqueous solutions. The mineral salts are absorbed from the external solutions by the roots. It is believed that they are not absorbed as whole molecules but as ions. This is evident from the unequal accumulation of the anions and cations of the same salt in the cell sap.

For many years it was supposed that various solutes entered the roots along with soil water in the process of osmosis; in other words the salts swept in with the water current. This view is erroneous because the diffusion of solute is quite different from the diffusion of water. Bonner (1953) has shown that salts can be absorbed by a cell even if there is higher concentration of a particular salt. Hoagland (1944) also found that solutes can be absorbed from a culture solution either more less rapidly than water is absorbed depending on the kind of solutes.

Passive Absorption

Passive absorption. In most cases, the movement of mineral ions into the root occurs by diffusion. Molecules or ions diffused from a region of their higher concentration to a region of their lower concentration. As these substances diffuse they exert a pressure called **diffusion pressure**. The movement of mineral ions into root cells as a result of diffusion is called **passive absorption**.

Ion exchange theory. According to the theory of **ion exchange** ions from the external solution (in which tissue is immersed) are exchanged with the ions of similar charge absorbed on the surface of the cell wall or membrane of the tissue. The colloidal fraction of the soil has an important role in ion exchange. These colloidal particles are known as **micelles**, possess negative charge and attract cations such as calcium, magnesium, potassium, ammonium, sodium, as well as hydrogen ions arising from biological activity. In the similar way, the root surface, which has a negative charge, carries many cations on its surface. These cations can be exchanged with other cations present in the soil. Thus a new cation can be absorbed on the root surface. Further transport of cations inside the root cell takes place by diffusion. Like cations, anions can also be exchanged with free 'OH^-' ions.

Donnan equilibrium. This theory explains the passive accumulation of ions, that are non-diffusible, which may be present on one side of the membrane (Donnan, 1927). Unlike diffusible ions, the membrane is not permeable to non-diffusible ions. Such ions are called **fixed ions**. They may be anions or cations. In a system, in which there are no fixed ions, there are equal number of anions and cations on both sides of the membrane at equilibrium. But in Donnan equilibrium, in order to balance, the charge of the fixed ions (anions), more ions of the other charge (cations) would be required.

For example, there is a membrane that separates a cell from the external medium and allows exchange of some ions and not others. To the inner side of this membrane there are anions, which are fixed and non-diffusible, and therefore, the membrane becomes inpermeable to these anions. In such a situation, for equilibrium to be reached, additional cations are needed to balance the negative charges of the anions that are structurally formed to the inner side of the above membrane.

According to the theory, Donnan equilibrium is attained if the product of anions⁻ and cations⁺ in the internal solution becomes equal to the product of anions⁻ and cations⁺ in the external solution, depicted by the equation as follows:

$$\frac{\text{Cations inside, } Ci^+}{\text{Cations outside } Co^+} = \frac{\text{Anions outside, } Ao^-}{\text{Anions inside, } A\,i^-}$$

For example, a membrane which is permeable to Mg^+ and Cl^- ions and to X^- ions (*i.e.*, fixed ions) present inside the cell. Here, membrane has $6X^-$ fixed ions on the inner side. Cl^- ions make across the membrane by diffusion along the concentration gradient. The concentration of anions⁻ on the inner side is now more than that of cations⁺. In order to balance electrochemical equilibrium within the cell sap, Mg^{++} ions move across the membrane against the concentration gradient. Similarly, if there are fixed cations the anions shall move against the concentration gradient to bring about equilibrium.

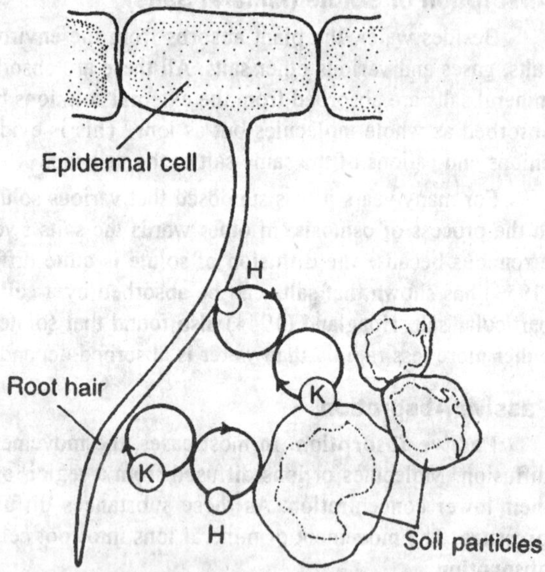

Fig. 16.2. Contact exchange theory.

Mass flow hypothesis. According to this hypothesis, roots also absorb a large quantity of ions along with absorption of water, due to transpiration. The ion absorption increases with increase in transpiration. The ions have been considered to move in a mass flow with water from the soil solution through the root and eventually to the shoot. This occurs due to passive absorption of ions by free diffusion into the free space of a tissue. Thus, mass flow of ions through root tissue occurs as a result of transpirational pull in the absence of metabolic energy. This theory was supported by Kramer (1956), Russel and Barber (1960).

Active Absorption

Generally, the lipid-protein membrane of a cell is largely permeable to free ions. The energy is considered to be involved in the transport of such free ions across the membrane. Thus *the absorption of ions, involving use of metabolic energy is called active absorption.*

The absorption of solutes takes place only in some cases by simple diffusion. Only limited quantities of minerals can pass into the cells by this method. Hoagland and Davies (1923) and many scientists have found that there is also a movement of salts against the concentration gradient, *i.e.*, from lower concentration to higher concentration for each ion. This cannot be explained on the basis of osmosis and most scientists now accept the theory of **"active absorption of solutes"** put forward by Hoagland (1923).

Active absorption of solutes or theory of salt accumulation. According to this theory Hoagland (1923) suggested that absorption of solutes takes place against higher concentration of salts. The cells near the tips of roots also have the capacity of accumulating ions (Hoagland and Broyer, 1936). If the initial salt content of the root cells is low and if other conditions are favourable, the concentration of ions in the absorbing cells may greatly be increased than that present in soil solution.This involves an expenditure of energy. This energy is supplied by the respiratory activity of the absorbing cells. The rate of accumulation is often influenced, therefore, by the previous metabolic status of the absorbing cells.

The phenomenon of salt accumulation seems confined largely to cells which have the capacity for cell division and growth. Meristematic cells and cells in the early stages of enlargement are particularly active in absorbing ions. As cells lose their capacity for growth, they also lose their capacity of mineral salt accumulation. As already referred earlier, that accumulation of salt requires expenditure of energy which is supplied by respiratory activity of cells.

Hoagland and Broyer (1936) found that if excised roots (young roots) are immersed in dilute solutions of mineral salts through which N_2 is bubbled, little or no accumulation of salts occurs in the root cells. If on the other hand, O_2 is bubbled through the solution, a rapid accumulation of salts within root cells takes place. Lack of O_2 checks aerobic respiration and prevents absorption of ions. The accumulation of ions of root cells and their retention within these cells in a free condition requires an expenditure of energy which is supplied by the process of respiration.

Salt accumulation is also affected by the rate of photosynthesis because on this process depends the supply of carbohydrates which are the respiratory substrates for efficient respiration. So any factor, which reduces photosynthesis, also reduces salt accumulation.

The fact that salt accumulation by root cells is dependent on respiration, suggests that temperature may have also marked effect on salt accumulation process.

Carrier concept. Ions, which are accumulated in cells, may move into the inner space against concentration and for this movement additional energy is required. This

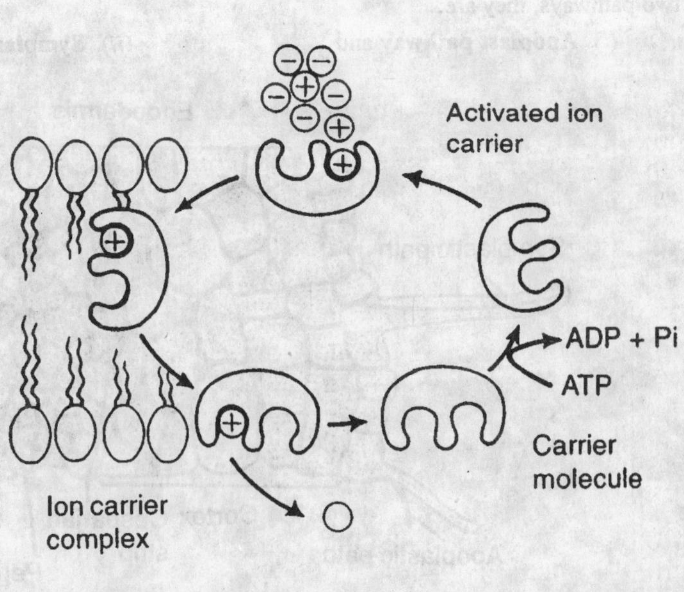

Fig. 16.3. Carrier concept.

additional energy is derived directly or indirectly through metabolism. This theory of active absorption has been supported by various evidences which show that active ion uptake is carried out by **carrier mechanism** for both influx and efflux of ions.

Unlike ion channels, the carrier proteins do not have pores. The membrane does not allow the ions to pass through as it is. The activated ions combine with carrier proteins and form **ion-carrier complex**, which is capable of moving across the membrane. This complex moves across the membrane and reaches the inner surface. Here, the complex breaks and releases ions into the cytoplasm of the cell. Carriers are specific, and combine with a particular type of ion.

Table 16.2. Differences Between Passive Absorption and Active Absorption

Passive Absorption	Active Absorption
1. This processes physical driving force, which is non-metallic.	1. Here, the driving force is energy derived from metabollic processes.
2. This type of absorption of ions and molecules is spontaneous and proceeds towards equilibrium.	2. This type of absorption is not spontaneous and does not proceed towards equilibrium.
3. Such absorption of a substance occurs across a protoplasmic membrane from its higher to lower chemical potential	3. The active absorption of a substance occurs across a protoplasmic membrane from its lower to higher chemical potential, *i.e.*, against concentration gradient.
4. In passive absorption, the energy yielding metabolic processes are not involved.	4. When energy yielding metabolic processes are weakened, active transport system is also checked.
5. The passive transport takes place through the protoplasmic layer in between the cell wall and the vacuole.	5. The active transport takes place across the protoplasmic membrane (*i.e.*, plasme membrane, tonoplast, etc.)

Ion Movement into the Root

Mineral nutrients absorbed by the root are carried to the xylem. This absorption takes place by two pathways, they are:

(*i*) **Apoplast pathway** and (*ii*) **Symplast pathway**

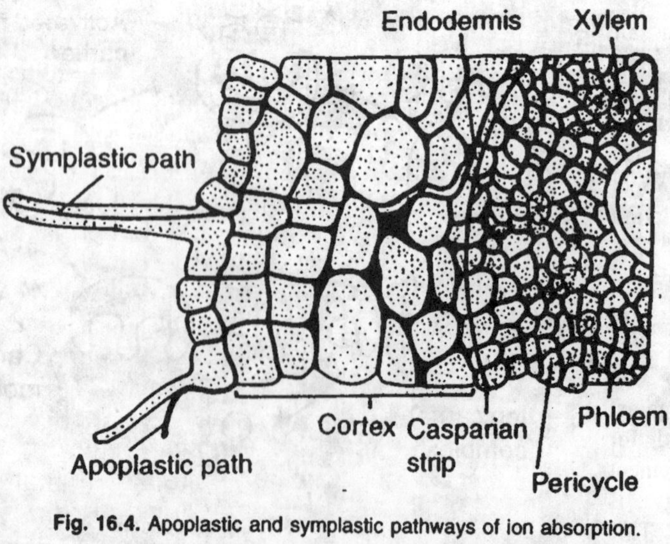

Fig. 16.4. Apoplastic and symplastic pathways of ion absorption.

(*i*) **Apoplastic pathway.** This pathway, essentially involves diffusion, and mass flow of water from cell to cell through spaces between cell wall polysaccharides.

The ions that enter the cell wall of epidermis move across cell wall of cortex, cytoplasm of endodermis, cell wall of pericycle, and finally accumulate in xylem vessels.

(*ii*) **Symplastic pathway.** In this pathway, ions that enter the cytoplasm of epidermis move across the cytoplasm, cortex, endodermis and pericycle through plasmodesmata, and finally reach to xylem vessels.

TRANSLOCATION OF SOLUTES

Upward Translocation of Mineral Salts

Here the term mineral salt is used for those substances which contain nitrogen, sulphur and phosphorus in inorganic and organic combinations. The upward translocation of nitrogen, sulphur and phosphorus occurs in both organic and inorganic combination.

Earlier this was universally agreed that upward translocation of mineral salts takes place through the xylem. But most studies of the sap present in the xylem indicated that it contains more inorganic solutes than organic ones. During the seasons appreciable concentrations of mineral salts are commonly present in the sap of vessels when upward flow of water occurs at its most rapid rate. The experiments of Clements and Engard (1938), Phillis and Mason (1940) and others have shown that ringing stems of various species do not prevent upward transport of mineral salts through the plant. This shows that upward translocation of mineral salts can take place in the xylem. Experiments on ringing often show that mineral salts can be conducted in the xylem and experiments on intercepting wood often show that they can be conducted in the phloem.

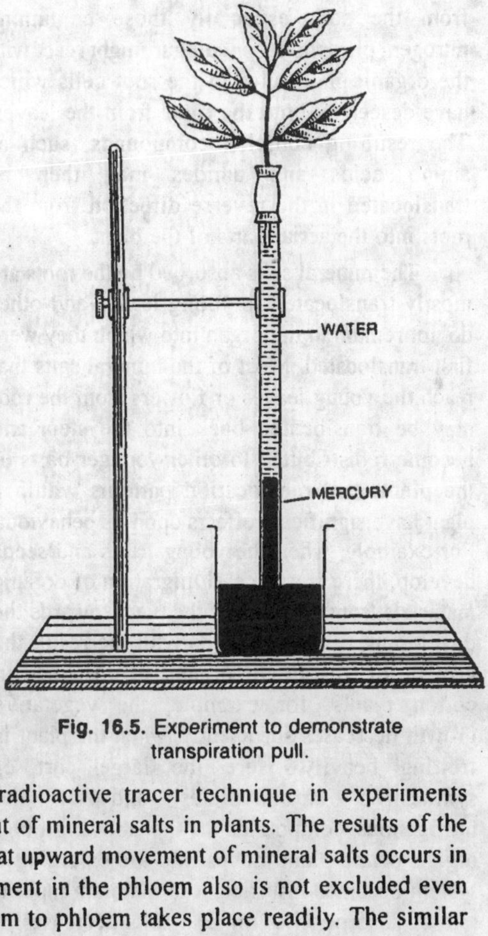

Fig. 16.5. Experiment to demonstrate transpiration pull.

Stout and Hoagland (1939) employed the radioactive tracer technique in experiments designed to ascertain the path of upward movement of mineral salts in plants. The results of the experiments conducted by these workers showed that upward movement of mineral salts occurs in the xylem, but the possibility of some such movement in the phloem also is not excluded even though it is clear that lateral movement from xylem to phloem takes place readily. The similar experiments of Gustafson (1939) also indicate that limited amount of upward translocation of radioactive phosphate may occur through the phloem.

Conclusively it can be said that upward translocation of mineral salts occurs in the xylem, and it appears quite certain that this is the main pathway along which their general upward translocation of mineral salts from roots to leaves occurs. Some upward translocation of mineral salts also occurs in the pholem under certain circumstances.

However, analysis of xylem sap shows the presence of inorganic salts, and by feeding plants with isotopes, it has exhibited that inorganic substances move up the plant through xylem.

General Aspects of the Translocation of Solutes in Plants

From the time when a young plant starts to grow until its death, there is continuous movement of solutes through the conducting elements of every organ of the plants. In the early stages of the development of the seedling, the food is generally translocated upward in the growing stems and downward in the developing roots from the storage tissues of that seed. Once the leaves are formed and plant begins to photosynthesize, the food starts flowing in downward direction, from the leaves towards the stem and the root. Likewise, as soon as the developing roots make effective contact with the soil particles, absorption of mineral salts begins, and the mineral solutes absorbed by the roots move in an upward direction, towards the shoot. Some of the solutes absorbed from the soil, especially those containing nitrogen, phosphorus or sulphur might react with the organic molecules in the root cells which have descended into the roots from the leaves. The resulting complex compounds, such as amino acids and amides may then be translocated in the reverse direction from the roots into the aerial parts of the plant.

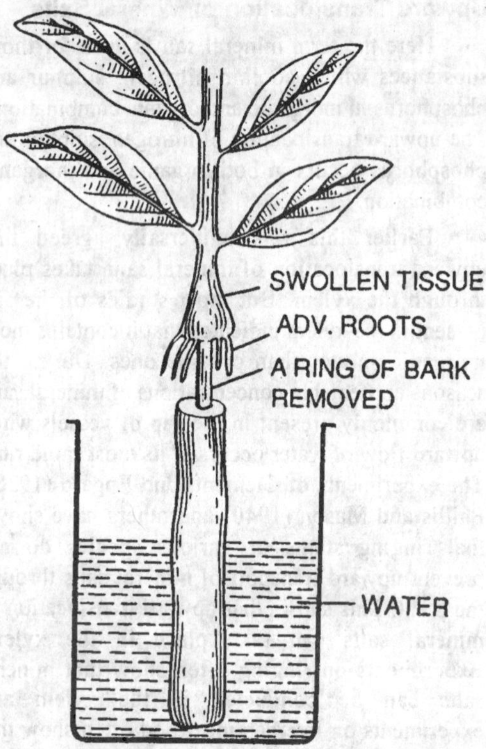

Fig. 16.6. Ringing experiment.

The mineral salts absorbed by the roots are mostly translocated to young leaves and other do not remain in the organ into which they were first translocated. Most of the mineral salts that reach the young leaves or flowers from the root may be translocated back into the stem and become redistributed to other younger parts of the plant, the translocation patterns within a plant have significant effects upon its behaviour. For example, when the young fruits and seeds develop, there is a general migration of organic materials from all parts of the plant towards the developing fruits and seeds with the result the growth of vegetative organs is checked. In cotton plants, for example, the vegetative growth decreases sufficiently, when the plant is fruiting heavily. Here the large part of synthesized carbohydrates and of the nitrogenous compounds in the above ground organs of the plant moves into the enlarging fruits. The carbohydrate supply reaching the root system becomes insufficient to maintain rapid respiration and root elongation. With the result the rate of absorption of mineral salts decreases, which in turn checks or even stops the vegetative growth of the plant (Eaton and Johan. 1944).

Evidence from ringing experiments. Much of the evidence indicating that organic solutes move towards the basal portions of the plant in the phloem has been obtained by ringing experiments. 'Ringing' means the removal of a narrow continuous band of tissues external to the xylem. Since ringing entirely encircles the stem, all tissues external to the xylem are completely intercepted. This operation is also called 'girdling'. This operation which is performed beneath the foliage region of the stem, produces two effects. They are as follows:

1. The organic food accumulates in the region above the ring which swells up as a result of this accumulation whereas the food content of the tissue below the ring is greatly diminished on

account of their being used up locally. 2. Secondly vigorous growth takes place in the region above the ring and sometimes the adventitious roots are developed. This happens, because of the accumulation of food materials in this region. The tissues below the ring are soon dried up because of starvation. Here the growth of tissues is inhibited, root development is checked and the tissues ultimately die. If the ringing is done in such a way that the phloem is not interrupted, translocation of food is not affected and the normal development of the roots beneath the ring continues.

The ringing is of much practical value in the case of fruit trees. At the time of the development of fruits the rings are being formed at different places on the trunks of the fruit tree. The ringing of the stem in such a manner prevents the downward flow of the food across the ring. With the result the food synthesized in the leaves above the ring is diverted to the fruits which become much larger in size. Normally the narrow rings are being made, so that the cambium may be affected and after some time the wound heals up.

METABOLISM OF NITROGEN

Nitrogen Cycle

As already mentioned although nitrogen occurs to the extent of about seventy eight percent of air by volume, it is not as a rule utilized by plants in its free state. However, nitrogen occurs in the dry substances of the plant to the extent of 1-3 percent only. Nevertheless, it is indispensable to the life of the plant, as it is an essential constituent of proteins, chlorophyll and protoplasm. Moreover it is essential for growth, particularly of the leaves. An excess of nitrogen causes vigorous growth of vegetative parts, specially the leaves, but delays reproduction activity.

One of the fundamental biological requirements for life to persist is that the nitrogen cycle should continue to function. During this process, the atomospheric nitrogen is fixed into organic combinations, such as amino-acids, proteins, nucleic acids, etc., in living organisms via inorganic forms as NH_4^+ (ammonia).

As living organisms die and decay, inorganic nitrogen is liberated.

Ammonification. The dead remains of animals and plants are decomposed through microbial activities to produce ammonia (NH_3).

Nitrification. Here, ammonia is rapidly converted first to nitrites (NO_2), and then to nitrates (NO_3). The conversion of ammonia to nitrite is carried out by bacteria *Nitrosomonas*, and of nitrite to Nitrate by *Nitrobacter*. Now, nitrate is available to the plant.

$$2NH_3 + 3O_2 \xrightarrow{\text{Nitrosomonas}} 2NO_2^- + 2H^+ + \text{-}2H_2O$$

$$2NO_2^- + O_2 \xrightarrow{\text{Nitrobacter}} 2NO_3^-$$

Denitrification. Where nitrate (NO_3) may convert into N_2 gas by bacteria *Pseudomonas*. This nitrogen gas may be again fixed in the form of NH_4^+ through the process of biological **nitrogen fixation.**

Nitrogen of the soil. The amount of nitrogen in the soil varies from 0.096 to 0.21 per cent. However, the soil makes the main source of nitrogen for the plant. In the plant the nitrogen exists as inorganic and organic compounds. The chief forms of inorganic compounds are the nitrates and nitrites of potassium and calcium, and also ammonia and its compounds; while the organic compounds are chiefly the proteins. Normally the ammonium compounds found in the soil are made available for the use of the green plants after conversion into nitrate by the action of certain nitrifying bacteria living in the soil. This process is known as **nitrification**. During this process the ammonium compounds are oxidized into nitrate in two stages—(*i*) these are acted upon by the nitrite-bacteria (*Nitrosomonas*) and oxidized into ($-NO_2$) and (*ii*) the nitrite thus formed is again acted upon by the nitrate-bacteria (*Nitrobacter*) and further oxidized into nitrate ($-NO_3$). The nitrate, thus produced is readily absorbed by the green plants.

Biological Nitrogen Fixation

Biological nitrogen fixation is carried out by both free-living and symbiotic bacteria.

The free-living nitrogen fixing bacteria are : Cyanobacteria, *Azotobacter* and *Clostridium*.

Symbiotic N_2 fixation. Sometimes the ammonium compounds (NH_4) are made available to the plants by the nitrogen fixers. The best known nitrogen-fixing symbiotic bacterium is *Rhizobium* (*R. leguminosarum*). This bacterium lives in soil to form root nodules in plants of the family Leguminosae such as gram, pea, groundnut, beans, etc. Root nodules are little outgrowths on roots. When a section of the fresh root nodule is examined, it looks pinkish in colour due to the presence of a pigment called **leghaemoglobin**. This pigment is closely related to **haemoglobin**, the red pigment of human blood. Like haemoglobin, legha emoglobin is an oxygen scavenger. The enzyme-nitrogenase which catalyses the fixation of nitrogen function under anaerobic conditions. Leghaemoglobin combines with oxygen and protects nitrogenase.

Nodule acts as a site for N_2 fixation. It contains all the necessary biochemical compounds, such as **nitrogenase** and **leghaemoglobin**. The enzyme nitrogenase is a Mo-Fe protein and catalyses the conversion of atmospheric N_2 to NH_3. This enzyme is extremely sensitive to oxygen to protect it from oxygen, nodules contain an **oxygen scavenger**, called **leghaemoglobin**.

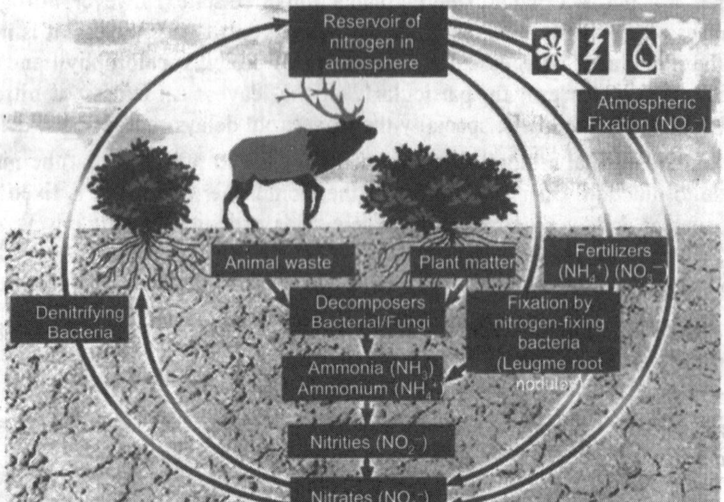

Fig. 16.7. Nitrogen cycle.

Formation of root nodules in leguminous plant. When a root hair of a leguminous plant comes in contact with *Rhizobium* (a bacterium) it is curled or deformed. Certain specific chemical substances secreted by bacteria (*Rhizobium*) are responsible for curling.

At the site of curling of root hair, rhizobia (bacteria) invade the root tissue and proliferate within the root hair.

Some of the bacteria enlarge to become membrane bound structures called **bacteroids**. The bacteroids cannot divide, and therefore, some bacteria remain untransformed, and they allow infection to spread.

An infection thread made up of plasma membrane is formed, which grows inward from the infected cell of the plant, that separates the infected tissue from rest of the plant.

Cell division is stimulated in the infected tissue and more bacteria invade the newly formed tissues.

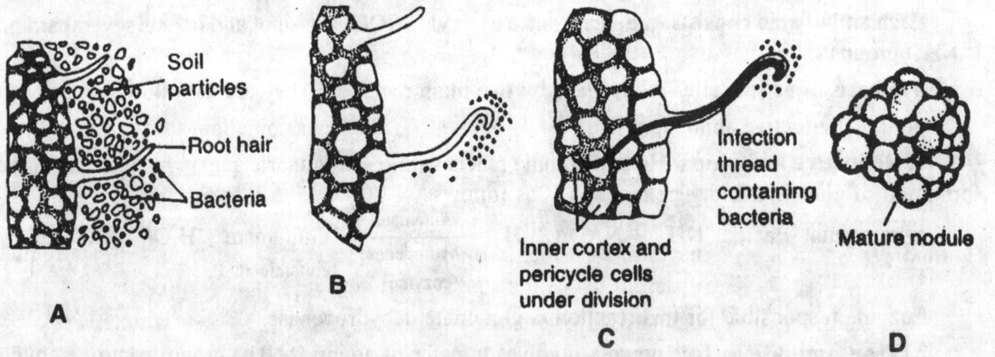

Fig. 16.8. Formation of root nodule in leguminous plant.

It is believed that a combination of **cytokinin** produced by the invading bacteria and **auxin** produced by plant cells, promotes cell division and extention, which leads to molecule formation.

The nodule thus formed, is responsible for direct vascular connection with the host for exchange of nutrients.

However, N_2 fixation, occurs under the control of plant *nod* genes and bacterial *nod, nif* and *fix* gene cluster.

Reduction of atmospheric N_2. Here, atmospheric nitrogen is reduced by the addition of hydrogen atoms.

The three bonds betwen two nitrogen atoms (N°N) are broken and ammonia is formed.

Three main components are required for nitrogen fixation, they are:

(*i*) A strong reducing agent.

(*ii*) ATP to transfer hydrogen atoms to dinitrogen, and

(*iii*) The enzyme systems.

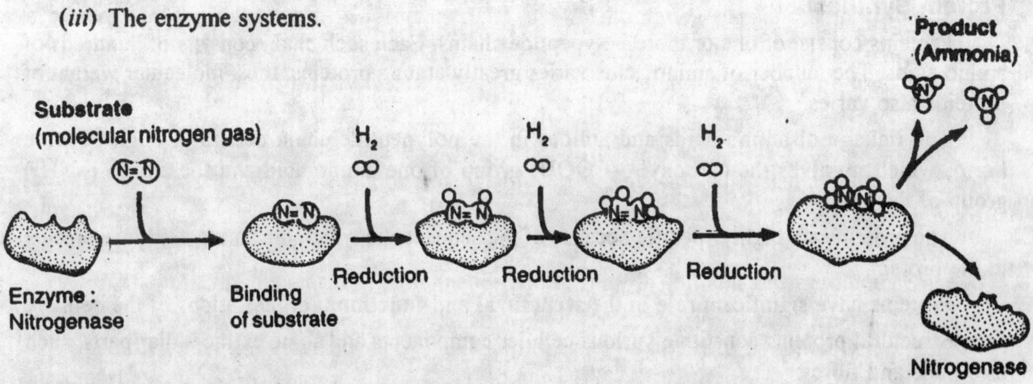

Fig. 16.9. Reduction of one molecule of N_2 in a series of reactions catalysed by nitrogenase enzyme.

The reducing agent FAD and ATP are provided by photosynthesis and respiration respectively.

Thus formed ammonia is utilised for the synthesis of amino-acids.

These amino-acids are translocated to other parts of the plant, which act as building blocks for the synthesis of various proteins.

Synthesis of Amino Acids

Amino-acids are supposed to be initial products of nitrogen assimilation.

Each amino-acid consists of at least one carboxyl (–COOH) group, and one or several amino ($-NH_2$) groups.

Synthesis of amino-acids takes place by two main methods. They are as follows:

(*i*) Reductive amination, and (*ii*) Transamination.

1. Reductive amination. Here, ammonia reacts with α-ketoglutaric acid, which results in the formation of glutamic acid. The reaction is as follows:

$$\alpha\text{-ketoglutaric acid} + NH_4^+ + NAD\,(P)\,H \xrightarrow[\text{dehydrogenase (enzyme)}]{\text{Glutamate}} \underset{\text{(glutamic acid)}}{\text{Glutamate}} + H_2O + NAD\,(P)$$

Enzyme responsible for this reaction is glutamate dehydrogenase.

2. Transamination. This process involves transfer of amino ($-NH_2$) group from one amino acid to the keto group of keto acid.

Glutamic acid is main from which other seventeen amino acids are formed through transamination.

The enzyme responsible for this reaction is called **transaminase.**

Amides. There are two most important amides found in plants. They are (*i*) asparagine, and (*ii*) glutamine.

They are formed from two amino acids, called

(*i*) glutamic acid, and (*ii*) aspartic acid.

During this process hydroxyl (–OH) part of the acid is replaced by another ($-NH_2$) radicle.

The enzymes responsible for such reaction may be glutamine synthetase or asparagine synthetase.

Amides have more nitrogen than amino acids, and make structural part of most proteins.

Protein Synthesis

Proteins consist of one or more polypeptide chains. Each such chain consists of hundreds of amino acids. The number of amino acids varies greatly among proteins, thus, molecular weight of proteins also varies.

The linkage of amino acids and amides in the polypeptide chain occurs through **peptide bond**, which involves the carboxyl (–COOH) group of one amino acid and the amino ($-NH_2$) group of the next.

The proteins are highly specific because of the sequence in which the amino acids are present in the protein.

Proteins have significant role in the **structural** and **functional** organisations of the cell.

Structural proteins constitute various cellular components and some extracellular parts, such as cuticle and fibres.

Functional (enzymatic and hormonal) proteins control almost all metabolic, biosynthetic, bioenergetic, growth regulating, sensory and reproductive activities of the cell.

All the proteins that are required by the cell for its different purposes are synthesized by the cell itself intracellularly.

Water Culture or Soil Less Culture (Hydroponics)

In general, soil supplies the mineral nutrients for plant growth. Since the minerals required by plants for their growth are easily absorbed in solution and therefore, it is possible to grow plants in water containing the required amount of mineral salts taking care that aerial parts of the plants are exposed to air and light. Thus, cultivation of plants by placing the roots in the nutrient solution is called **hydroponics**. It is necessary to aerate the solution to provide roots with adequate oxygen supply.

The earliest experiment using a culture solution was done by Sachs (1860) and he showed the essentiality of nitrogen for plant growth. Later Knop (1865) gave the formula of nutrient solution. His prescription for preparing a nutrient solution was used for a long time. About seventy years later Arnon and Hoagland developed a formulation to study the micronutrients as well. Iron was supplied as ferrous sulphate and often it precipitated out. This problem has now been solved by dissolving the ferrous sulphate along with a chelating agent Na-EDTA (*i.e.*, disodium salt of ethylene - diaminetetra acetic acid.)

In water culture experiments, the seedlings are grown in water containing the known nutrients in a particular proportion. The culture solutions may contain all essential elements except that whose importance has to be studied. By excluding a particular element in a culture solution, characteristic deficiency symptoms can be observed. Deficiency symptoms may vary from species to species. The result obtained from soil-less culture may then be used to determine deficiencies under field conditions.

Table 16.3. Formula of Two Nutrient Media.

Knop (1865)	g/l	Arnon and Hoagland (1940)	g/l
KNO_3	0.2	KNO_3	1.02
$Ca(NO_3)_2$	0.8	$Ca(NO_3)_2$	0.492
KH_2PO_4	0.2	$NH_4H_2PO_4$	0.23
$MgSO_4$, $7H_2O$	0.1	$MgSO_4$, $7H_2O$	0.49 mg/l
$FePO_4$	0.1	H_3BO_3	2.86
		$MnCl_2$, $4H_2O$	1.81
		$ZnSO_4$, $5H_2O$	0.08
		$CuSO_4$, $7H_2O$	0.22
		H_2MoO_4, H_2O	0.09
		$FeSO_4$, $7H_2O$ 0.5%	0.6 ml/l
		Tartaric Acid 0.4%	3x weekly

Application of Fertilizers

Soil fertility is defined as the ability of the soil to provide all essential plant nutrients in appropriate form and in a suitable balance. A soil can be highly fertile, *i.e.*, it has a ready supply of nutrients in suitable form. A fertile soil may be highly saline or alkaline which may not be good for agriculture. The soil poor in fertility may be made fertile by adding fertilizers in suitable dosages. Soils generally contain sufficient quantities of essential minerals. However, three important elements (*i.e.*, NPK–nitrogen, phosphorus and potassium) need to be replenished in crop fields as they are depleted by repeated cultivation. The common sources of N, P and K in this country are - sodium nitrate, ammonium sulphate, ammonium nitrate, ammonium chloride, urea, calcium ammonium nitrate, superphosphate, bonemeal, rock phosphate and calcium magnesium phosphate. The bags of NPK fertilizers are labelled 15-15-15 or 17-18-9 which refer to the percentage by weight of nitrogen, phosphorus and water soluble potassium. These fertilizers are used in different dosages according to the climatic conditions, soil and crop.

SUMMARY

1. There are three main sources which supply inorganic nutrients to plants. They are (*i*) soil, (*ii*) air and (*iii*) water.

2. Plants absorb a wide range of mineral elements.
3. So far, more than 105 elements have been discovered.
4. However, only about 20 elements are essential for the normal growth and metabolism of plants.
5. Some elements are required in large quantities by the plants, and are known as macro-elements.
6. Some elements are required in less amount, and are called micro-nutrients.
7. The elements required by the plants become the essential constituents of protein, carbohydrate, fat, nucleic acid, etc., and take part in various metabolic processes.
8. Some of these elements serve as activators or co-factors for several enzymes.
9. Deficiency of any element in plants may lead to symptoms of deficiency, such as chlorosis, necrosis, stunted growth, etc.
10. Plants absorb mineral elements through root by passive or active absorption.
11. The absorbed elements are transported from the root to the xylem by apoplastic and symplastic pathways.
12. The most essential element for sustenance of life, is nitrogen.
13. However, plants cannot use atmospheric nitrogen directly.
14. For this purpose, prior to absorption, atmospheric nitrogen is fixed into organic combination.
15. Nitrogen fixation requires — (*i*) a strong reducing agent, (*ii*) energy in the form of ATP and (*iii*) the enzyme systems.
16. This task is completed by certain nitrogen fixing bacteria and cyanobacteria. Rhizobium is associated symbiotically with the roots of leguminous plants and form nodules in the roots.
17. The atmospheric nitrogen is fixed in the form NH_4^+ (ammonia) through the process of nitrogen fixation. Ammonia converts to nitrates.
18. Plants absorb nitrates, which again convert to ammonia by enzymatic reactions.
19. Ammonium ions are then used for the synthesis of amino acids, proteins and other nitrogenous compounds in the plant.

TERMS TO REMEMBER

Active absorption. Ions accumulated in cells may move against concentration or ecp gradients.

Ammonification. The dead remains of animals and plants are decomposed through microbial activities to produce ammonia.

Autotrophs. The organisms, which can prepare their own food through photosynthesis.

Bacteroids. Some of the bacteria that enlarge to become membrane bound structures.

Denitrification. Where nitrates convert to nitrogen gas.

Donnan equilibrium. Theory, explains the passive accumulation of ions that are fixed or non-diffusible, against an ecp gradient.

Essential element. An element without which the plant cannot complete its life cycle.

Flux. Movement of ions. The movement into the cell is **influx** and the outward movement is **efflux**.

Heterotrophs. Organisms, including non-green plants, which cannot make their own food and obtain their nutrition from autotrophs.

Hydroponics. Soil-less culture of plants, where roots are immersed in nutrient solution without soil.

Ion exchange. The process of exchange between adsorbed ions and ions in solution.

Leghaemoglobin. Pink coloured substance, similar to haemoglobin of vertebrates.

Macronutrients. Generally present in plant tissues in concentration of 1 to 10 mg per gm of dry matter.

Mass flow hypothesis. Mass flow of ions through root tissue occurs as a result of transpirational pull in the absence of metabolic energy.

Micronutrients. Also known as trace elements, generally present in plant tissues in very small amounts, *i.e.*, equal to or less than 0.1 mg per gm of dry matter.

Mineral nutrition. The study of how plants obtain mineral elements, either through water, air or soil and utilise them for their growth and development.

Nitrification. Ammonia, first converts to nitrites and then to nitrates.

Passive absorption. Absorption of minerals by physical processes not involving direct expenditure of metabolic energy.

Reductive amination. In this process ammonia reacts with α-ketoglutaric acid and forms glutamic acid.

Transamination. Transfer of amino group from one amino acid to the keto group of keto acid. The enzyme responsible for such reaction is transaminase.

QUESTION BANK

Very Short Answer Questions

1. What are autotrophs ?
2. What are heterotrophs ?
3. Define mineral nutrition.
4. What is an essential element ?
5. Name the macronutrients.
6. Give names of micronutrients.
7. Define the term 'flux'.
8. What is ammonification ?
9. What is nitrification ?
10. What is denitrification ?
11. What is leghaemoglobin ?
12. What are symbionts ?
13. Name the best known symbiotic nitrogen fixing bacterium.
14. Name the enzyme involved in biological nitrogen fixation.
15. What are bacteroids ?
16. What is transamination ?
17. Name the enzyme involved in transamination.
18. Who discovered 'translocation of solutes' ?
19. Give symptom of iron deficiency in plants.
20. Give symptoms of zinc deficiency in plants.
21. What type of condition is created by leghaemoglobin in root nodules of a legume ?
22. Name the red pigment present in the root nodules of leguminous plants.
23. Name the best known symbiotic nitrogen fixing bacterium.
24. Pick out from the following list the two minerals which are not needed by the majority of plants but very much needed by almost all animals:

    Calcium, Sodium, Potassium, Iron, Iodine
25. Name one most mobile element and one most immobile element.
26. What protects nitrogenase ?
27. What is common to *Nepenthes, Utricularia* and *Drosera* as regard to a special mode of nutrition?

ANSWERS

1. Organisms, which can prepare their own food through photosynthesis; 2. Organisms, including non-green plants, which cannot prepare their own food and obtain their nutrition from autotrophs; 3. The study of how plants obtain mineral elements, either through water, air or soil, and utilise them for their

growth and development; 4. An element without which the plant cannot complete its life cycle; 5. They include carbon, hydrogen, oxygen, nitrogen, phosphorus, sulphur, potassium, calcium, magnesium and silicon; 6. They include iron, manganese, copper, molybdenum, zinc, boron and chlorine; 7. The movement of ions is termed flux; the movement into the cell is influx, while the outward movement is efflux; 8. When the dead remains of animals and plants are decomposed through microbial activities to produce ammonia; 9. When ammonia is rapidly converted first to nitrites, and then to nitrates; 10. When nitrate converts to nitrogen gas by other microorganisms, *e.g.*, *Pseudomonas*; 11. Root nodules of leguminous plant contain an oxygen scavanger of pink colour and similar to haemoglobin of vertebrates; 12. Two organisms that live in close physical association, and are of mutual benefit to each other, *e.g.*, lichen, mycorrhiza, etc; 13. *Rhizobium*; 14. Nitrogenase; 15. Some of the bacteria enlarge to become membrane-bound structures, called bacteroids; 16. This process involves the transfer of amino group from one amino acid to the keto group of keto acid; 17. Transaminase; 18. P.R. Stout and D.R. Hoagland (1939); 19. Chlorosis of leaves ; 20. Malformed leaves, inter-veinal chlorosis in leaves, and stunted growth; 21. Anaerobic; 22. Leghaemoglobin; 23. *Rhizobium*; 24. Sodium and iodine; 25. Potassium and iron; 26. The pigment leghaemoglobin; 27. All are insectivorous plants.

Short Answer Questions

1. List the macronutrients and mention their major functions.
2. Why do farmers use leguminous crops to provide nitrogen to the soil ? Explain.
3. Name the organism that fixes nitrogen in symbiotic association with a water fern. Where does it live in such plants ?
4. Prior to sowing rice, a legume crop was cultivated and ploughed back in the field, why ? Explain.
5. How are ions absorbed by the roots ? Explain.
6. What do you understand by Donnan's equilibrium ? Explain.
7. Write down deficiency symptoms produced by following elements: (*i*) Nitrogen (*ii*) Phosphorus and (*iii*) Potassium.
8. Define the following : (*i*) Micronutrients (*ii*) Macronutrients.
9. Write short notes on : (*i*) Symplastic pathway (*ii*) Apoplastic pathway.
10. Give three criteria of essentiality of an element.
11. Why do plants of the legume family usually contain more protein than other plants ?
12. Name any two autotrophic plants which also show heterotrophic mode of nutrition.
13. Prior to sowing rice, a legume crop was cultivated and ploughed back in the field, why ? Explain.
14. Explain the terms plant macroelements and plant microelements. Give one example of each.
15. Name the nitrifying bacteria of the soil. Why are they called chemoautotrophs ?
16. Mention the symptoms of any four mineral deficiencies in plants.
17. What is nitrification ?
18. A farmer adds Azotobacter culture to the soil before sowing maize. How does it increase the yield of maize.
19. Name the respective mineral nutrient element that :
    (*i*) forms the constituent of the ring structure of chlorophyll
    (*ii*) activates carboxylases
    (*iii*) forms the component of nitrogenase
    (*iv*) synthesises middle lamella in plants cells.
20. Write an explanatory note on biological nitrogen fixation.
21. Define the following : (*i*) Nutrients (*ii*) Active absorption (*iii*) Symplastic pathway.
22. Differentiate between macronutrients and micronutrients.
23. What are various steps involved in the biological nitrogen fixation in plants ?
24. Name the nitrifying bacteria of the soil. Why are they called chemoautotrophs ?
25. Why do farmers use leguminous crops to provide nitrogen to the soil ? Explain.

26. Differentiate between essential and non essential mineral elements.
27. Write short notes on:
    (*i*) Reductive amination (*ii*) Transamination.
28. Make a list of macronutrients and mention their major functions.
29. Write short notes on:
    (*i*) Donnan equilibrium (*ii*) Mass flow hypothesis.
30. State deficiency symptoms of Manganese, Boron, Iron and Zinc.
31. Why do plants need potassium and magnesium ?
32. Why do farmers use leguminous crops to provide nitrogen to the soil ? Explain.
33. Differentiate between the two manners of absorption of minerals in plants from the soil through roots.
34. What are the various steps involved in the biological nitrogen fixation in plants ?

Long Answer Questions

1. Differentiate between two types of absorption of minerals from soil through roots.
2. Describe two important functions each of K, Fe and Zn in green plants and also write deficiency symptoms of any two of them.
3. Discuss the process of biological nitrogen fixation in plants.
4. Write an essay on mineral nutrition in plants.
5. List the macronutrients and mention their major functions.
6. Differentiate between micronutrients and macronutrients. How they are helpful in plant growth ?
7. Evaluate the importance of potassium, sulphur, iron, zinc, copper and molybdenum in plants.
8. What are trace elements ? What symptoms are caused by their deficiency ?
9. Describe the role and deficiency symptoms of the following elements in plants : (*a*) Nitrogen, (*b*) Molybdenum, (*c*) Zinc, (*d*) Phosphorus, and (*e*) Copper.
10. What are macronutrients ? Discuss the role of potassium, phosphorus, sulphur and iron in plant metabolism.
11. Describe the process of symbiotic biological nitrogen fixation.
12. Describe two important functions each of the element P, B and S in green plants and also write the deficiency symptoms of any two of them.
13. Make a table showing macroelements, regions of plants in which required, functions and their deficiency symptoms.
14. Make a list of macronutrients and mention their major functions.

MULTIPLE CHOICE QUESTIONS (Objective Type Questions)

1. Nitrogen is an important constituent of
   (*a*) proteins (*b*) lipids (*c*) carbohydrates (*d*) phopholipids
2. Zinc is essential for
   (*a*) biosynthesis of chlorophyll (*b*) biosynthesis of 3- IAA
   (*c*) stomatal opening (*d*) oxidation of carbohydrates
3. The micronutrient among these is
   (*a*) Zn (*b*) N (*c*) P (*d*) Ca
4. Presence of phosphorus
   (*a*) brings about healthy root growth (*b*) promotes fruit ripening
   (*c*) retards protein formation (*d*) none of the above
5. In plants a common symptom caused by deficiencies of P, K, Ca and Mg is
   (*a*) bending of leaf tip (*b*) formation of anthocyanin
   (*c*) poor development of vasculature (*d*) appearance of dead necrotic areas

6. Chlorosis occurs when plants are grown in
   (*a*) dark (*b*) shade (*c*) strong light (*d*) Fe-free medium
7. Which of the following elements is a component of Ferredoxin ?
   (*a*) Copper (*b*) Manganese (*c*) Zinc (*d*) Iron
8. A trace element is an element which
   (*a*) is a radioactive element and can be traced by Geiger counter
   (*b*) is required in very minute amounts
   (*c*) draws other elements out of protoplasm
   (*d*) was one of the first to be discovered
9. Mineral salts absorbed by the roots from the soil are in the form of
   (*a*) very dilute solution (*b*) dilute solution
   (*c*) concentrated solution (*d*) very concentrated solution
10. The presence of an element in plant ash
    (*a*) does not guarantee that it is essential
    (*b*) proves that it is essential
    (*c*) proves that it takes part in the physiology of plants
    (*d*) indicates that it occurs in abundance in soil
11. 'Khaira' disease of rice is developed due to the deficiency of
    (*a*) copper (*b*) sodium (*c*) zinc (*d*) molybdenum
12. Ash is of what significance in the study of mineral nutrition of plants?
    (*a*) It tells what minerals are present in the soil
    (*b*) It informs which element is essential and in which amount it is necessary for a particular plant
    (*c*) It is of no practical significance
    (*d*) It indicates how much irrigation is needed by the plant.
13. Active transport occurs
    (*a*) Against concentration gradient and requires ATP
    (*b*) Against concentration gradient but does not requires ATP
    (*c*) Along concentration gradient but requires ATP
    (*d*) Along concentration gradient but does not require ATP
14. Magnesium is an important component of
    (*a*) Haemoglobin (*b*) Florigen (*c*) Enzymes (*d*) Chlorophyll
15. Plants use zinc as
    (*a*) Zn (*b*) Zn^{2+} (*c*) $ZnSO_4$ (*d*) $Zn(NO_3)_2$
16. Loading of phloem means
    (*a*) elongation of phloem cells (*b*) separation of phloem parenchyma
    (*c*) strengthening of phloem fibres (*d*) pouring of sugar into phloem
17. Radioactive tracer studies with ^{14}C have shown that
    (*a*) phloem transports organic nutrients (*b*) phloem transports inorganic nutrients
    (*c*) xylem transports inorganic nutrients (*d*) xylem transports organic nutrients
18. Direction of conduction of food through phloem is
    (*a*) from below upward (*b*) from tip to bottom
    (*c*) from leaves to roots (*d*) phloem never conducts food
19. Most widely accepted theory of carbohydrates translocation is
    (*a*) Mass flow theory (*b*) Root pressure theory
    (*c*) Imbibition theory (*d*) Transpiration theory

20. Brown heart disease is due to deficiency
(*a*) Molybdenum (*b*) Potassium (*c*) Iron (*d*) Boron
21. Which is required for nitrogen fixation ?
(*a*) Mn (*b*) *n* (*c*) Cu (*d*) Mo
22. Premature leaf fall is due to deficiency of
(*a*) Sodium (*b*) Potassium (*c*) Zinc (*d*) Phosphorus
23. Nitrogen is an important constituent of
(*a*) Polyphosphates (*b*) Carbohydrates (*c*) Proteins (*d*) Lipids
24. Element present in middle lamella
(*a*) Zn (*b*) Ca (*c*) Cu (*d*) K
25. Plants require sulphur for
(*a*) ATP synthesis (*b*) Protein synthesis (*c*) Glucose synthesis (*d*) DNA replication
26. Nitrogen absorbed by plants is
(*a*) Converted to nitrate (*b*) Reduced to ammonia
(*c*) Changed to nitrite (*d*) Combined with oxygen
27. Which important greenhouse gas other than methane is being produced from the agricultural field ?
(*a*) Arsine (*b*) Sulphur dioxide (*c*) Ammonia (*d*) Nitrous oxide
28. Supply end in solute transport is
(*a*) root (*b*) stem
(*c*) green leaves and storage organs (*d*) xylem and phloem
29. Which is not a micronutrient
(*a*) P / Mg (*b*) Cu / B (*c*) Mo / Zn (*d*) Mn / Cu
30. Hydroponics is
(*a*) growing of aquatic plants (*b*) growing of submerged aquatic plants
(*c*) growing of floating aquatic plants (*d*) soil-less cultivation of plants
31. Increase in fertility of soil without adding any nutrients is due to :
(*a*) Floods (*b*) Crop residue
(*c*) Favourable temperature (*d*) Microbial activity
32. The presence of large amount of nitrogen in the atmosphere is due to :
(*a*) Decomposers (*b*) Nitrites (*c*) Nitrogen cycle (*d*) Ammonia
33. 80 per cent of cells has :
(*a*) Minerals (*b*) Water (*c*) Proteins (*d*) Carbohydrates
34. Plants require one of the following for formation of ATP :
(*a*) N, Ca (*b*) N, P (*c*) N, Cu (*d*) K
35. The core-element of chlorophyll is :
(*a*) Mn (*b*) Mg (*c*) Zn (*d*) Fe
36. One of the following elements of not of much importance to plants :
(*a*) Calcium (*b*) Zinc (*c*) Copper (*d*) Sodium
37. The largest and sessile pitchers are produced by :
(*a*) Nepenthes (*b*) Dischidia (*c*) Darlington (*d*) Sarracenia
38. The theory which suggests that CO_2 produced in respiration plays an important role in mineral absorption is :
(*a*) Contact exchange theory (*b*) Carbonic acid exchange theory
(*c*) Active absorption theory (*d*) None of these.
39. Cyanobacteria help farmers by :
(*a*) Reducing the alkalinity of soil (*b*) Increasing soil fertility of soil
(*c*) Neutralising alkalinity of soil (*d*) Water logging

40. Plants can be cultivated in soil less medium where all nutrients are supplied from outside in water solution and this method comes under :
(*a*) Water culture (*b*) Hydroponics
(*c*) Hybrid culture (*d*) Critical culture media

41. In fruit trees a disease exanthema is caused by the deficiency of :
(*a*) Na (*b*) Ca (*c*) Cu (*d*) P

42. The essential nutrient element required by plants in the least quantity is :
(*a*) Chlorine (*b*) Zinc (*c*) Molybdenum (*d*) Manganese

43. Enzyme catalyzed reactions can be inhibited by :
(*a*) Mg^{2++} (*b*) Zn^{2++} (*c*) Cu^{2++} (*d*) Hg^{2++}

44. Permeability of protoplasm is accelerated by :
(*a*) Na (*b*) K (*c*) Ca (*d*) P

45. The brown colour of leaves of cabbage is due to the deficiency of :
(*a*) Boron (*b*) Nitrogen (*c*) Sulphur (*d*) Calcium

46. Soil salinity is measured by :
(*a*) Porometer (*b*) Potometer (*c*) Conductivity meter (*d*) Calorimeter

47. Biofertilizer present in root nodules of non-leguminous plants is :
(*a*) *Azotobacter* (*b*) *Clostridium* (*c*) *Frankia* (*d*) *Aerohizobium*

48. The major portion of the dry weight of plants comprises of :
(*a*) Calcium, magnesium and sulphur (*b*) Carbon, nitrogen and hydrogen
(*c*) Carbon, hydrogen and oxygen (*d*) Nitrogen, phosphorus and potassium

49. Boron in green plants assists in :
(*a*) Acting as enzyme cofactor (*b*) Photosynthesis
(*c*) Sugar transport (*d*) Activation of enzymes

50. Which organism is used in rice fields for nitrogen fixation :
(*a*) Nostoc (*b*) Azolla (*c*) Trifolium (*d*) All of these

51. Zn is used up by plants in the form of :
(*a*) Zn (*b*) Zn^{++} (*c*) $ZnSO_4$ (*d*) $Zn(NO_3)_2$

52. Which of the following is not major element ?
(*a*) Zn (*b*) Ca (*c*) Mg (*d*) P

53. Function of Mg and Fe is :
(*a*) Synthesis of chlorophyll (*b*) Synthesis of proteins
(*c*) Synthesis of fat (*d*) Synthesis of organic acids

54. Which of the following is macronutrient ?
(*a*) Ca (*b*) Mn (*c*) Zn (*d*) Cu

55. Which of the following is macronutrient ?
(*a*) Zn (*b*) Ca (*c*) P (*d*) Mg

56. A facultative parasite is one which :
(*a*) Always requires a living host
(*b*) is normally a saprophytic but can also become a parasite
(*c*) Never requires a living host
(*d*) None of these

57. The movement of mineral ions into plant root cells as a result of diffusion is called :
(*a*) Endocytosis (*b*) Osmosis
(*c*) Passive absorption (*d*) Active absorption

58. The role of inorganic nutrients in plant growth was at first indicated by :
(*a*) Wood Ward (*b*) Knop (*c*) Stewart (*d*) De Saussure
59. Zinc is essential for :
(*a*) Biosynthesis of chlorophylls (*b*) Biosynthesis of 3-IAA
(*c*) Stomatal closing (*d*) Oxidation of carbohydrates
60. Cultivation by sand culture is also called :
(*a*) Soilless cultivation (*b*) Green house effect
(*c*) Photorespiration (*d*) None of these
61. Inorganic nutrients are present in the soil in the form of :
(*a*) Molecules (*b*) Atoms
(*c*) Electrically charged ions (*d*) Parasites
62. Function of Zinc is :
(*a*) Metabolism of carbohydrates (*b*) Production of IAA
(*c*) Both above (*d*) None of these
63. Which of the following is the importance of molybdenum in plant metabolism ?
(*a*) Carbon assimilation (*b*) Nitrogen reduction
(*c*) Plant breeding (*d*) Chromosome contraction
64. Phosphorus is a structural element in :
(*a*) Fat (*b*) Starch (*c*) Nucleotide (*d*) Carbohydrate
65. The leaves become yellow due to deficiency of :
(*a*) Zinc and Boron (*b*) Potassium and Calcium
(*c*) Iron and Magnesium (*d*) None of these
66. Premature leaf fall occurs due to deficiency of :
(*a*) Calcium (*b*) Iron (*c*) Phosphorus (*d*) Sulphur
67. Carnivorous plants are found on :
(*a*) nitrogen deficient soil (*b*) O_2 deficient soil
(*c*) CO_2 deficient soil (*d*) none of these
68. Hydroponics is :
(*a*) water (*b*) solution containing all the nutrients
(*c*) green house (*d*) liquid
69. The major portion of the dry weight of plants comprises of :
(*a*) Nitrogen, phosphorus and potassium (*b*) Calcium, magnesium and sulphur
(*c*) Carbon, nitrogen and hydrogen (*d*) Carbon, hydrogen and oxygen
70. Gray spots of oat are caused by deficiency of :
(*a*) Cu (*b*) Zn (*c*) Mn (*d*) Fe
71. Active transport of ions by the cell requires :
(*a*) High temperature (*b*) ATP (*c*) Alkaline pH (*d*) Salts
72. Tracer elements are :
(*a*) Microelements (*b*) Macroelements (*c*) Radio isotopes (*d*) Vitamins
73. Trace element in plants is :
(*a*) K (*b*) P (*c*) Zn (*d*) None of these
74. Plants deficients of element zinc, show its effect on the biosynthesis of plant growth hormonce :
(*a*) Auxin (*b*) Cytokinin (*c*) Ethylene (*d*) Abscisic acid
75. Which one of the following mineral elements plays an important role in biological nitrogen fixation ?
(*a*) Copper (*b*) Manganase (*c*) Zinc (*d*) Molybdenum

76. An essential element is one which
(*a*) is present in plant ash (*b*) is available in soil
(*c*) is indispensable for growth (*d*) improves plant growth
77. Mineral salts, which are absorbed by the roots from the soil, are present in
(*a*) very dilute solution (*b*) concentrated solution
(*c*) very concentrated solution (*d*) dilute solution
78. Conduction of inorganic materials in plants occurs mainly through
(*a*) xylem (*b*) phloem (*c*) sieve tube (*d*) cambium
79. In plant nutrition, elements are classified as major or minor depending on
(*a*) their relative production in the ash obtained after burning the plant
(*b*) the relative amounts required by the plants
(*c*) their relative importance in plant growth
(*d*) their availability in the soil
80. The framework elements are
(*a*) magnesium, copper and iron (*b*) copper, carbon and oxygen
(*c*) manganese, calcium and nitrogen (*d*) carbon, hydrogen and oxygen
81. Which one of the following plays an independent role in energy metabolism ?
(*a*) calcium (*b*) sodium (*c*) sulphur (*d*) phosphorus
82. Stem and root tips die due to deficiency of
(*a*) nitrogen (*b*) phosphorus (*c*) calcium (*d*) sulphur
83. The plant ash is an indication of
(*a*) mineral salts absorbed by the plant (*b*) organic matter of the plant
(*c*) both the mineral salts and organic matter (*d*) none of the above
84. Which one of the following essential elements can land plants normally take directly from the air ?
(*a*) Carbon (*b*) Nitrogen (*c*) Phosphorus (*d*) Hydrogen
85. Micronutrients
(*a*) are called 'micro' becuase they play only a minor role in plant nutrition
(*b*) may be omitted from culture media without any detrimental effect on the plants
(*c*) are as important in nutrition as the macronutrients
(*d*) are more important in nutrition than macronutrients
86. A trace element
(*a*) is a radioactive and can be traced by Geiger - count
(*b*) is required in very minute amounts
(*c*) draws other elements out of protoplasm
(*d*) was one of the first to be discovered in protoplasm
87. Which of the following is a micronutrient
(*a*) Mg (*b*) Zn (*c*) P (*d*) K
88. Which of the following is a macronutrient ?
(*a*) Ca (*b*) Mo (*c*) Zn (*d*) Mn
89. Which of the following elements has not been proved to be essential for plants ?
(*a*) Carbon (*b*) Sodium (*c*) Zinc (*d*) Potassium
90. Active mineral absorption depends on
(*a*) expenditure of energy (*b*) ions move freely
(*c*) ions move passively (*d*) ions are active

91. Carbon becomes available to crop plants in the form of
(*a*) carbonates (*b*) carbon dioxide (*c*) element carbon (*d*) amino acids
92. Most of the plants obtain nitrogen from the soil in the form of
(*a*) nitric acid (*b*) nitrites (*c*) nitrates (*d*) free nitrogen gas
93. The bulk of nitrogen in nature is fixed by
(*a*) chemical industries (*b*) symbiotic bacteria
(*c*) lightning (*d*) denitrifying bacteria
94. All the following contributes to the availability of nitrogen compounds in the soil except
(*a*) *Azotobacter* (*b*) thunders from clouds
(*c*) bacterial decay of animal refuge (*d*) addition of lime
95. Which of the following does NPK denote ?
(*a*) Nitrogen, Protein, Kinetin (*b*) Nitrogen, Protein, Potassium
(*c*) Nitrogen, Phosphorus, Potassium (*d*) Nitrogen, Phosphorus, Kinetin
96. In plants, a common symptom caused by deficiency of P, K, Ca and Mg is
(*a*) formation of anthocyanin (*b*) shredding of leaf
(*c*) bending of leaf tip (*d*) development of necrotic areas on leaves
97. Which of the following is a component of middle lamella in plant cells ?
(*a*) Mg (*b*) K (*c*) Ca (*d*) Fe
98. Death of stem and root tips occurs due to deficiency of
(*a*) Calcium (*b*) Nitrogen (*c*) Carbon (*d*) Phosphorus
99. Absence of magnesium from plant tissue results in
(*a*) etiolation (*b*) hydrolysis (*c*) chlorosis (*d*) necrosis
100. Which element forms part of structure of chlorophyll molecule ?
(*a*) Mg (*b*) Mn (*c*) K (*d*) Fe
101. Deficiency of iron causes
(*a*) decrease in protein synthesis (*b*) interveinal chlorosis first on young leaves
(*c*) bending of stem tip (*d*) reduced leaves and stunted growth
102. Which of the following element is a component of ferredoxin ?
(*a*) Manganese (*b*) Zinc (*c*) Iron (*d*) Copper
103. Iron is mainly absorbed in
(*a*) ferrous form (*b*) ferric form (*c*) both (*a*) and (*b*) (*d*) None of above
104. Plants requiring the two metallic compounds for chlorophyll synthesis, they are
(*a*) Fe and Mg (*b*) Cu and Ca (*c*) Ca and K (*d*) Mg and Ca
105. Phosphorus is a structural element in
(*a*) proteins (*b*) carbohydrates (*c*) DNA (*d*) cytochrome
106. Which of the following essential element is not a constituent of any enzyme but stimulate the activity of many enzymes ?
(*a*) Zn (*b*) K (*c*) Mg (*d*) Mn
107. The most important use of potassium is that
(*a*) regulates many plant processes
(*b*) it provides red colour to the fruit
(*c*) it helps in photosynthesis
(*d*) it influences enzyme activity, which regulates many plant processes

108. Deficiency of molybdenum causes
(*a*) bending of leaf tip (*b*) chlorosis of leaves
(*c*) mottling and necrosis of leaves (*d*) poor development of vasculature

109. Which of the following element is necessary for translocation of sugars in plants ?
(*a*) Boron (*b*) Molybdenum (*c*) Manganese (*d*) Iron

110. Which one of the following micronutrient can be absorbed by foliage ?
(*a*) Zinc (*b*) Iron (*c*) Phosphorus (*d*) None of the above

111. Which of the following is not an essential micronutrient ?
(*a*) Nickel (*b*) Manganese (*c*) Cobalt (*d*) Boron

112. Which of these is not a nutrient for plants
(*a*) water (*b*) mineral ions (*c*) carbon dioxide (*d*) nitrogen gas

113. Symbiotic nitrogen fixation by *Rhizobium* was discovered by
(*a*) Louis Pasteur (*b*) Lister (*c*) Beijerinck (*d*) Pfeffer

114. Which pigment is essential for nitrogen fixation by leguminous plants ?
(*a*) phycocyanin (*b*) phycoerythrin (*c*) leghemoglobin (*d*) myoglobin

115. Which root tissue primarily contributes to the formation of nodules particularly in legume family ?
(*a*) epidermis (*b*) xylem (*c*) cortex (*d*) endodermis

116. The symbiotic fixation of atmospheric nitrogen in root nodules of leguminous crops is brought about by
(*a*) *Rhizobium* (*b*) *Rhizopus* (*c*) *Rhizoclonium* (*d*) *Rhizoctonia*

117. In nitrogen cycle nitrite is converted to nitrate by
(*a*) *Azotobacter* (*b*) *Rhizobium* (*c*) *Nitrobacter* (*d*) *Nitrosomonas*

118. The enzyme responsible for the reduction of molecular nitrogen to the level of ammonia in leguminous root nodules is
(*a*) nitrogenase (*b*) nitrate reductase (*c*) nitrite reductase (*d*) hexokinase

119. A bulk of nitrogen in nature is fixed by
(*a*) Lightnfng (*b*) Denitrifying bacteria
(*c*) Symbiotic bacteria (*d*) None of above

120. A crop plant that can grow well in nitrogen deficient soils without addition of manure is
(*a*) *Allium sativum* (*b*) *Triticum aestivum*
(*c*) *Solanum melongena* (*d*) *Cajanus cajan*

121. Conversion of organic nitrogenous compound into ammonium compound is called
(*a*) nitrification (*b*) denitrification (*c*) amononification (*d*) none of above

122. Root hairs do not play a role in
(*a*) mineral uptake (*b*) oxygen uptake (*c*) water uptake (*d*) CO_2 uptake

123. Organisms that fix nitrogen in aquatic habitats are
(*a*) diatoms (*b*) protozoans (*c*) desmids (*d*) cyanobacteria

124. Which one of the following statements is correct ?
(*a*) Legumes fix nitrogen only through specialised bacteria that live in their leaves
(*b*) Legumes fix nitrogen independently of the specialised bacteria that live in their roots
(*c*) Legumes fix nitrogen only through the specialised bacteria that live in their roots
(*d*) Legumes are incapable of fixing nitrogen

125. Exanthema, a disease of citrus plant is caused by the deficiency of
(*a*) zinc (*b*) magnesium (*c*) manganese (*d*) copper

ANSWERS

1. (*a*)	2. (*b*)	3. (*a*)	4. (*c*)	5. (*d*)	6. (*d*)	7. (*d*)	8. (*b*)	9. (*a*)	10. (*c*)
11. (*c*)	12. (*b*)	13. (*a*)	14. (*d*)	15. (*b*)	16. (*d*)	17. (*a*)	18. (*c*)	19. (*a*)	20. (*d*)
21. (*d*)	22. (*d*)	23. (*c*)	24. (*c*)	25. (*b*)	26. (*b*)	27. (*d*)	28. (*c*)	29. (*a*)	30. (*d*)
31. (*b*)	32. (*c*)	33. (*b*)	34. (*b*)	35. (*b*)	36. (*d*)	37. (*d*)	38. (*b*)	39. (*b*)	40. (*b*)
41. (*c*)	42. (*c*)	43. (*d*)	44. (*b*)	45. (*a*)	46. (*c*)	47. (*c*)	48. (*c*)	49. (*c*)	50. (*d*)
51. (*b*)	52. (*a*)	53. (*a*)	54. (*a*)	55. (*a*)	56. (*b*)	57. (*c*)	58. (*b*)	59. (*b*)	60. (*d*)
61. (*c*)	62. (*d*)	63. (*b*)	64. (*c*)	65. (*c*)	66. (*c*)	67. (*a*)	68. (*b*)	69. (*d*)	70. (*c*)
71. (*b*)	72. (*c*)	73. (*c*)	74. (*a*)	75. (*d*)	76. (*c*)	77. (*a*)	78. (*a*)	79. (*b*)	80. (*d*)
81. (*d*)	82. (*c*)	83. (*a*)	84. (*a*)	85. (*c*)	86. (*b*)	87. (*b*)	88. (*a*)	89. (*b*)	90. (*a*)
91. (*b*)	92. (*c*)	93. (*b*)	94. (*d*)	95. (*c*)	96. (*d*)	97. (*c*).	98. (*a*)	99. (*c*)	100. (*a*)
101. (*b*)	102. (*c*)	103. (*b*)	104. (*a*)	105. (*c*)	106. (*b*)	107. (*d*)	108. (*c*)	109. (*a*)	110. (*a*)
111. (*a*)	112. (*d*)	113. (*c*)	114. (*c*)	115. (*c*)	116. (*a*)	117. (*c*)	118. (*a*)	119. (*c*)	120. (*d*)
121. (*c*)	122. (*d*)	123. (*d*)	124. (*c*)	125. (*d*)					

17

CHAPTER

Respiration

We know that during photosynthesis, light energy is converted into chemical energy, and is stored in carbohydrate molecules, such as glucose and starch. Organisms make use of such energy for their activities by oxidising these high energy food molecules into simple low energy molecules, *i.e.*, carbon dioxide and water. The reactions involved in process of oxidation are known as **respiration**. The compounds that are oxidised during process of respiration are called **respiratory substrates**.

Technically, respiration is defined as follows :

This is a process by which living cells break down complex high energy food molecules into simple low energy molecules, *i.e.*, CO_2 and H_2O, releasing the energy trapped within the chemical bonds.

The energy released during oxidation of energy rich compounds is made available for activities of cells through an intermediate compound called **adenosine triphosphate** (ATP).

During process of respiration, the whole of energy contained in respiratory substrates is not released all at a time. It is released slowly in several steps of reactions controlled by different enzymes.

Respiration takes place in all types of living cells, and generally called **cellular respiration**. During the process of respiration oxygen is utilised, and CO_2 water and energy are released as products. The released energy is utilised in various energy-requiring activities of the organisms, and the carbon dioxide released during respiration is used for biosynthesis of other molecules in the cell.

As we know, important life processes, such as synthesis of proteins, fats and carbohydrates, require a certain expenditure of energy. Where does this energy come from, how is it stored, and how is it made available to the living cell, are some of the questions, which are to be answered by process of respiration.

The reaction that occurs in common respiration of glucose may be summed up as follows:

$$C_6H_{12}O_6 + 6O_2 \xrightarrow{\text{enzymes}} 6CO_2 + 6H_2O + \underset{\text{(2870 kJ or 686 kcal)}}{\text{Energy}}$$

Here, 686 kcal or 2870 kJ of energy is liberated per molecule of glucose. Formerly, this calculated value was 673 kcal. One kcal is equal to 1000 calories. This means that one molecule of glucose on complete oxidation yields 686 kcal (kilocalories) of energy, (*i.e.*, 686, 000 calories).

The main facts associated with respiration are :

1. Consumption of atmospheric oxygen.
2. Oxidation and decomposition of a portion of the stored food resulting in a loss of dry weight as seen in the seeds germinating in dark.

3. Liberation of carbon dioxide and a small quantity of water (the volume of CO_2 liberated is equal to volume of O_2 consumed).
4. Release of energy by breakdown of organic food, (such as carbohydrates).

Adenosine Triphosphate (ATP)

This is an **energy intermediate**. As we know, both energy-yielding and energy-consuming reactions occur within the living cell.

The potential or stored energy of one compound, such as glucose, is released and utilised, in a most efficient manner, to drive the synthesis of other compounds, such as proteins.

This energy, now stored in the newly synthesised compound (*e.g.*, protein), can in turn made be available for other synthetic reactions.

However, energy-yielding reactions of the cell occur in many instances in the absence of energy-consuming reactions. The energy released in such situation is in the form of heat and lost to the organism.

However, nature has provided the living cell with a means of temporary energy storage in the form of adenosine triphosphate (ATP).

Thus, energy released in oxidation of compounds, such as carbohydrates, lipids, proteins, etc., is immediately utilised in the synthesis of ATP from adenosine diphosphate (ADP) and inorganic phosphate (i.P.).

The chemical energy transferred to ATP can be used to drive synthetic reactions, while ADP and iP are released during the process. ATP is called **energy currency** of the cell.

ATP is capable of receiving energy from one reaction and transferring this to drive another reaction. This is of obvious advantage to the living system, as ATP can be formed in the oxidation of a variety of compounds and can be used for synthesis of a variety of compounds.

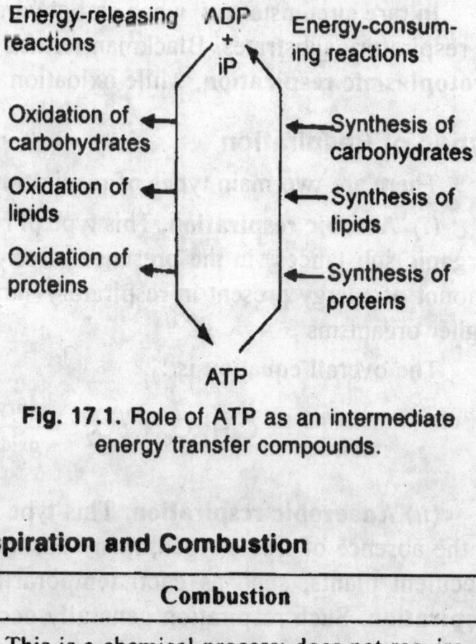

Fig. 17.1. Role of ATP as an intermediate energy transfer compounds.

Table 17.1. Differences Between Respiration and Combustion

Respiration	Combustion
1. This is a vital process; occurs inside living cells.	1. This is a chemical process; does not require living cells.
2. This is biochemical process.	2. This is physico-chemical process.
3. Energy is released step by step.	3. All the energy is released suddenly.
4. Less than 50 per cent energy is liberated as heat.	4. Most of energy is liberated as heat.
5. There is very small rise in temperature.	5. There is large increase in temperature.
6. Most of the energy is stored in ATP molecules.	6. ATP is not formed.
7. Respiratory reactions are regulated by enzymes.	7. This is a non-enzymatic process.
8. Several intermediates are formed.	8. In the process of combustion, no such intermediates are produced.
9. Oxidation takes place at the end of reaction between reduced coenzymes and oxygen.	9. Substrate directly oxidises.

In other words, oxidation of a compound, such as glucose, can provide the energy, through ATP, for synthesis of several cellular materials.

On the other hand, fuel burned in engines, where a large amount of released energy is lost in the form of heat, the oxidation of substances in the cell occurs with relatively little loss of energy. This is due to reason of the cell's very efficient energy transfer system mediated by ATP.

Here it is notable that the energy locked in a biological compound may be transferred repeatedly. Thus, in the living cell, the stored energy of glucose may be found at one time in ATP and at another time locked in the bonds of a protein molecule.

Respiratory Substrates

Respiratory substrates are those organic substances which are oxidised during respiration. They are high energy compounds and are called **respiratory substrates**. They may be carbohydrates, fats and proteins. Carbohydrates, such as glucose, fructose (hexoses), sucrose (disaccharide) or starch, inulin, hemicellulose (polysaccharide), etc., are main respiratory substrates.

Besides, fats are used as respiratory substrates by a variety of organisms as they contain more energy than carbohydrates.

In rare circumstances, when carbohydrate reserves are exhausted, fats and proteins also serve as respiratory substrates. Blackman termed the respiratory oxidation of protoplasmic protein as **protoplasmic respiration**, while oxidation of carbohydrates as **floating respiration.**

Types of Respiration

There are two main types of respiration, (*i*) **aerobic** and (*ii*) **anaerobic**.

(*i*) **Aerobic respiration.** This type of respiration leads to a complete oxidation of stored food (organic substances) in the presence of oxygen, and releases carbon dioxide, water and a large amount of energy present in respiratory substrate. Such type of respiration is generally found in higher organisms.

The overall equation is :

$$C_6H_{12}O_6 + 6O_2 \xrightarrow[\text{oxidation}]{\text{enzymes}} 6CO_2 + 6H_2O + \text{energy}$$

(2870 kJ) or (686 k cal)

(*ii*) **Anaerobic respiration.** This type of respiration occurs in complete absence of oxygen. In the absence of free oxygen, many tissues of higher plants, seeds in storage, fleshy fruits, and succulent plants, such as cacti temporarily take to a kind of respiration, called **anaerobic respiration**. Such respiration generally occurs in lower organisms like bacteria and fungi. This results in incomplete oxidation of stored food and formation of carbon dioxide and ethyl alcohol, and sometimes also various organic acids, such as malic, citric, oxalic, tartaric, etc. Very little energy is released by this process to maintain activity of protoplasm.

The equation is as follows :

$$C_6H_{12}O_6 \longrightarrow 2C_2H_5OH + 2CO_2 + \text{Energy}$$

(247 kJ) or (28 k cal)

This process of oxidation in microbes is known as **fermentation**. This is quite similar to that of anaerobic respiration in case of higher plants.

Table 17.2. Differences between Aerobic and Anaerobic Respiration

Aerobic Respiration	Anaerobic Respiration
1. Occurs in all living cells.	1. Occurs in microbes (*e.g.*, bacteria and fungi), and in germinating seeds, fleshy fruits and succulent plants.
2. This requires oxygen.	2. This does not require oxygen.
3. The end products are carbon dioxide and water.	3. The end products are carbon dioxide and alcohol.
4. Complete oxidation of one molecule of glucose produces a net of 38 ATP molecules.	4. Only two ATP molecules are produced.
5. Reactions of glycolysis occur in cytoplasm, whereas of Krebs cycle in mitochondria.	5. All reactions occur in cytoplasm. There is no need of mitochondria for this process.

Respiratory Quotient (RQ) or Respiratory Ratio

As we know, during aerobic respiration, oxygen is consumed and carbon dioxide is released. The ratio of the volume of carbon dioxide given out to the volume of oxygen absorbed in respiration, *i.e.*, $\frac{CO_2}{O_2}$ is called **respiratory quotient (RQ) or respiratory ratio.**

$$RQ = \frac{\text{volume of } CO_2 \text{ evolved}}{\text{volume of } O_2 \text{ consumed}}$$

The value of respiratory quotient depends upon the nature of respiratory substance used during respiration. This varies for different types of substrates.

Carbohydrates (RQ equal to unity). The value of respiratory quotient is unity (one) when hexose sugars are consumed in respiration. Here equal volumes of CO_2 and O_2 are evolved and consumed, respectively. This is obvious from overall equation of respiration.

$$C_6H_{12}O_6 + 6O_2 \longrightarrow 6CO_2 + 6H_2O$$

$$RQ = \frac{6CO_2}{6O_2} = 1.0$$

Fats (RQ less than unity). When substances poorer in oxygen than carbohydrates, *e.g.*, fats are oxidised in respiration, the value of respiratory quotient is less than one. It is explained in tripalmitin and triolein as follows :

$$\underset{\text{Tripalmitin}}{2C_{51}H_{98}O_6} + 145O_2 \longrightarrow 102CO_2 + 98H_2O$$

$$RQ = \frac{CO_2}{O_2} = \frac{102}{145} = 0.7 \text{ (less than unity)}$$

$$\underset{\text{Triolein}}{C_{57}H_{104}O_6} + 80O_2 \longrightarrow 57CO_2 + 52H_2O$$

$$RQ = \frac{CO_2}{O_2} = \frac{57}{80} = 0.7 \text{ (less than unity)}$$

RQ in above-mentioned examples is less than unity, *i.e.*, 0.7, because fats contain less oxygen than the carbohydrates, and therefore, they require relatively greater amount of oxygen for oxidation.

In case of proteins RQ is 0.5 (approximately).

Succulents (RQ is zero). Where incomplete oxidation of carbohydrates takes place RQ is zero. In such cases oxygen absorbed does not oxidise the carbohydrates completely to CO_2 and water but produces intermediate products of partial oxidation. This occurs especially in respiration of succulent plants, such as cacti (*Opuntia*). In such plants respiration of carbohydrates occurs at night when stomata are open which results in production of organic acids that utilise O_2 but do not evolve CO_2. The equation is as follows :

$$2C_6H_{12}O_6 + 3O_2 \longrightarrow \underset{\text{Malic acid}}{3C_4H_6O_5} + 3H_2O$$

$$RQ = \frac{CO_2}{O_2} = \frac{0}{3} = 0$$

Organic acids (RQ more than unity). When substances rich in oxygen are respired, the value of RQ is more than unity. This occurs in respiration of organic acids. Organic acids contain more oxygen than carbohydrates, and therefore, relatively less amount of oxygen is required for their oxidation. The examples are shown by following equations :

(*i*)
$$\underset{\text{Oxalic acid}}{2(COOH)_2} + O_2 \longrightarrow 4CO_2 + 2H_2O$$

$$RQ = \frac{CO_2}{O_2} = \frac{4}{1} = 4$$

Here RQ is 4 in case of oxalic acid.

(*ii*)
$$\underset{\text{Tartaric acid}}{2C_4H_6O_6} + 5O_2 \longrightarrow 8CO_2 + 6H_2O$$

$$RQ = \frac{CO_2}{O_2} = \frac{8}{5} = 1.6$$

This means, RQ is 1.6 in case of tartaric acid.

(*iii*)
$$\underset{\text{Malic acid}}{C_4H_6O_5} + 3O_2 \longrightarrow 4CO_2 + 3H_2O$$

$$RQ = \frac{CO_2}{O_2} = \frac{4}{3} = 1.3$$

In case of malic acid, RQ is 1.3.

Anaerobic respiration (RQ infinity). As we know, in anaerobic respiration CO_2 is evolved but O_2 is not consumed, and therefore RQ is infinite (∞). Equation is as follows :

$$C_6H_{12}O_6 \xrightarrow[\text{enzyme}]{\text{zymase}} 2C_2H_5OH + 2CO_2 + \text{energy}$$

$$RQ = \frac{CO_2}{O_2} = \frac{2}{0} = \text{Infinity } (\infty)$$

Significance of RQ. The RQ value of a respiring tissue may provide valuable information to an investigation. From an RQ value, one can obtain a rough indication of the nature of substrate being oxidised.

It also helps in knowing the type of respiration being performed. It may also provide some information about major transformation of food materials.

If RQ is less than one, then substrate is of low oxygen content, *e.g.*, fats.

In starvation the cell material itself becomes substrate. According to Blackman, in starving conditions, if cellular proteins are the respiratory substrates then it is called **protoplasmic respiration**.

MECHANISM OF RESPIRATION

There are two major phases of respiration :

(*i*) **Glycolysis** and

(*ii*) **Krebs cycle**

During process of respiration, carbohydrates are converted into pyruvic acid through a series of enzymatic reactions. This series of reactions is known as **glycolysis** which takes place in cytosol.

Now, pyruvic acid enters mitochondria, where several enzymes catalyse the reactions, and pyruvic acid finally converts into CO_2 and water. This series of enzymatic reactions is known as **Krebs cycle** (after name of its discoverer Sir Hans Adolf Krebs (1900-1981), awarded Nobel Prize in 1953), or **tricarboxylic acid** (TCA) or **citric acid cycle**.

Glycolysis

Glycolysis is a term used to describe the sequential series of reactions present in a wide variety of tissues that starts with a hexose sugar (usually glucose) and ends with pyruvic acid. This term has originated from Greek words, *glycos* = sugar and *lysis* = splitting.

The scheme of glycolysis was discovered by three German Scientists, Gustav Embden, Otto Meyerhof and J. Parnas, and therefore, referred as **EMP pathway**, after the abbreviation of their last names.

Glycolysis is the first stage in the breakdown of glucose and is common to all organisms. This means, glycolysis is common to both aerobic and anaerobic modes of respiration. In anaerobic organisms, this is only process in respiration. Glycolysis occurs in cytoplasm of cells. During this process, glucose undergoes partial oxidation to form two molecules of pyruvic acid.

In plants, glucose is derived from sucrose, which is the end product of photosynthetic carbon reactions (also known as dark reactions) or from storage carbohydrates.

Sucrose is converted into glucose and fructose by the enzyme **invertase**. Now, these two monosaccharides (*i.e.*, glucose and fructose) enter glycolysis or EMP pathway. The main steps of glycolytic pathway are as follows:

Glycolysis is carried out in following different steps.

1. Phosphorylation of sugar (*i.e.*, first phosphorylation). Glucose and fructose are phosphorylated to give rise to glucose-6-phosphate and fructose-6-phosphate, respectively, by the activity of enzyme **hexokinase**, in presence of ATP. The phosphorylated form of glucose then isomerises to produce fructose-6-phosphate. Isomerisation takes place with the help of enzyme **phosphohexose isomerase**.

Further steps of metabolism of glucose and fructose are quite similar.

Equations are as follows :

$$\text{Glucose (6C)} + \text{ATP} \xrightarrow[\text{Mg}^{2+}]{\text{hexokinase}} \text{Glucose-6-phosphate} + \text{ADP}$$

Now isomerisation occurs :

$$\text{Glucose-6-phosphate} \underset{\text{isomerase Mg}^{2+}}{\overset{\text{phosphohexose}}{\rightleftharpoons}} \text{Fructose-6-phosphate}$$

2. Phosphorylation of fructose-6-phosphate (i.e., second phosphorylation). Now, fructose-6-phosphate is phosphorylated and fructose-1, 6-bisphosphate produced by the action of enzyme **phosphofructokinase** in presence of ATP.

$$\text{Fructose-6-phosphate} + \text{ATP} \xrightarrow[\text{Mg}^{2+}]{\text{phosphofructokinase}} \text{Fructose-1, 6-bisphosphate} + \text{ADP}$$

3. Splitting. Now, fructose-1, 6-bisphosphate splits into two molecules of triose phosphate, *i.e.*, 3-phosphoglyceraldehyde (PGAL) and dihydroxyacetone phosphate (Di HAP), which are interconvertible.

$$\text{Fructose-1, 6-bisphosphate} \xrightleftharpoons{\text{aldolase}} \text{3-phosphoglyceraldehyde (PGAL)} + \text{dihydroxyacetone phosphate (Di HAP)}.$$

4. Oxidative dehydrogenation. After formation of 3-phosphoglyceraldehyde (PGAL), the glycolytic pathway enters the energy conserving phase. Here, it is oxidised to a carboxylic acid, *i.e.*, 1, 3-bisphosphoglycerate, and NAD is reduced to NADH.

$$\text{3-phosphoglyceraldehyde} + \text{NAD} \xrightleftharpoons[\text{dehydrogenase}]{\text{glyceraldehyde phosphate}} \text{1, 3-bisphosphoglycerate} + \text{NADH} + \text{H}_+$$

5. Formation of ATP. In next step of glycolysis, 3-phosphoglycerate is formed from 1, 3-bisphosphoglycerate by enzymatic activity of **phosphoglycerate kinase**, and ATP is generated during this process. Direct synthesis of ATP from intermediate metabolites is called **substrate level phosphorylation**.

$$\text{1, 3-bisphosphoglycerate} + \text{ADP} \xrightleftharpoons[\text{kinase} + \text{Mg}^{2+}]{\text{phosphoglycerate}} \text{3-phosphoglycerate} + \text{ATP}$$

This type of formation of ATP, where a phosphate group is directly transferred from a substrate to ADP to form ATP, is different from the ATP produced by ATP synthase during oxidative phosphorylation in mitochondria or in chloroplasts (during photophosphorylation in photosynthesis).

6. Isomerisation. In next step 3-phosphoglycerate converts into its isomer 2-phosphoglycerate by catalytic activity of enzyme phosphoglyceromutase.

$$\text{3-phosphoglycerate} \xrightleftharpoons[\text{glyceromutase} + \text{Mg}^{2+}]{\text{phospho-}} \text{2-phosphoglycerate}$$

7. Dehydration. In subsequent step 2-phosphoglycerate converts into phosphoenol pyruvate (PEP) in the presence of enzyme pyruvate kinase and liberates ATP.

$$\text{2-phosphoglycerate} \xrightleftharpoons{\text{pyruvate kinase}} \text{phosphoenol pyruvate} + \text{ATP}$$

$$\text{2-phosphoenol pyruvate} + 2\,\text{ADP} \rightleftharpoons \text{pyruvic acid} + 2\,\text{ATP}$$

8. Generation and utilisation of ATP during glycolysis. During glycolytic pathway, the molecules of ATP are produced as follows :

(*i*) Direct transfer of phosphate to ATP.

(*ii*) Oxidation of NADH produced during glycolytic pathway to NAD^+.

9. In the end of glycolysis net gain of ATP.

(*i*) During glycolysis two triose phosphate molecules are formed from one glucose molecule, and 4 ATP molecules are produced.

(*ii*) Out of 4 ATP molecules, 2 ATP molecules are utilised in first few steps in converting glucose to fructose-1, 6-bisphosphate.

(*iii*) Moreover, three ATP molecules are produced from oxidation of each of two molecules of NADH produced during catabolism of glucose.

(*iv*) In all, a net gain of 8 molecules occurs during process of glycolysis.

(*v*) However, in anaerobic respiration, NADH + H^+ is not converted to ATP, and therefore, only 2 ATP molecules are produced.

Oxidative Decarboxylation of Pyruvic Acid

(Acrobic Oxidation of Pyruvic Acid)

Now, pyruvic acid generated in cytoplasm through glycolysis is transferred to mitochondria. This is initiation of second phase of respiration. As soon as, pyruvic acid enters the mitochondria, one of the three carbon atoms of pyruvic acid is oxidised to carbon dioxide in a reaction called **oxidative decarboxylation**. Here, pyruvate is first decarboxylated, and thereafter oxidised by enzyme **pyruvate dehydrogenase**. This enzyme is made up of a decarboxylase, lipoic acid, TPP, transacetylase and Mg^{2+}.

Acetyl Co-A acts as substrate entrant for Krebs cycle. The equation is as follows :

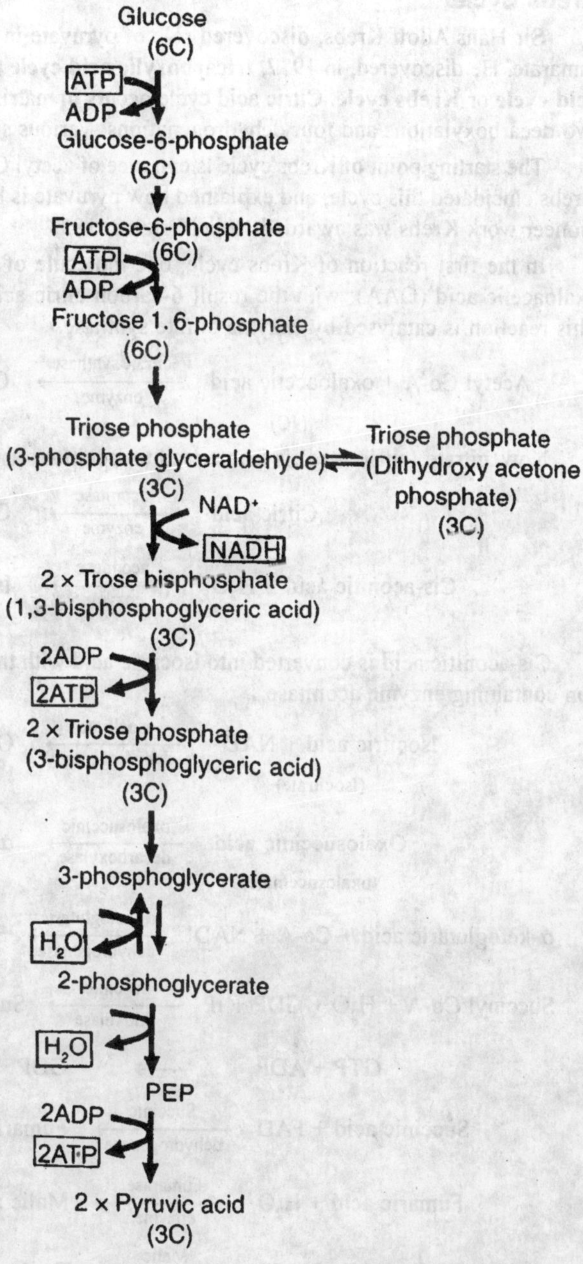

Fig. 17.2. Main steps of glycolysis or EMP pathway.

$$\text{Pyruvate} + \text{NAD+} + \text{Co-A} \xrightarrow[\text{dehydrogenase}]{\text{pyruvate}} \text{Acetyl Co-A} + \text{NADH} + H^+ + CO_2^-$$

Acetyl Co-A can enter into mitochondria while pyruvic acid cannot.

Krebs Cycle

Sir Hans Adolf Krebs, discovered role of pyruvate in conversion of glucose hydrogens into fumarate. He discovered, in 1937, **tricarboxylic acid cycle** (*i.e.*, TCA cycle), also known as **Citric acid cycle** or **Krebs cycle**. Citric acid cycle occurs in matrix of mitochondria. This cycle involves two decarboxylations and four dehydrogenations. Various steps of these reactions are as follows :

The starting point of Krebs cycle is entrance of acetyl Co-A into a reaction to form citric acid. Krebs elucidated this cycle, and explained how pyruvate is broken down to CO_2 and H_2O. For this pioneer work Krebs was awarded Nobel Prize in 1953.

In the first reaction of Krebs cycle, one molecule of acetyl Co-A combines with 4-carbon oxaloacetic acid (OAA); with the result 6-carbon citric acid is produced, and Co-A is released. This reaction is catalysed by enzyme citrate synthase.

$$\underset{(4C)}{\text{Acetyl Co-A + oxaloacetic acid}} \xrightarrow[\text{enzyme}]{\text{citrate synthase}} \underset{(6C)}{\text{Citric acid + Co-A}}$$

Now, citrate (citric acid) is isomerised to isocitrate (isocitric acid).

$$\text{Citric acid} \xrightarrow[\text{enzyme}]{\text{aconitase}} \text{Cis-aconitic acid} + H_2O$$

$$\text{Cis-aconitic acid} + H_2O \xrightarrow[\text{enzyme}]{\text{aconitase}} \underset{\text{(Isocitrate)}}{\text{Isocitric acid}}$$

Cis-aconitic acid is converted into isocitric acid with the addition of water in the presence of iron containing enzyme aconitase.

$$\underset{\text{(Isocitrate)}}{\text{Isocitric acid}} + NAD^+ \xrightarrow[\text{dehydrogenase}]{\text{isocitrate}} \underset{\text{(oxalosuccinate)}}{\text{Oxalosuccinic acid}} + NADH + H^+$$

$$\underset{\text{(oxalosuccinate)}}{\text{Oxalosuccinic acid}} \xrightarrow[\text{decarboxylase}]{\text{oxalosuccinic}} \alpha\text{-Ketoglutaric acid} + CO_2$$

$$\alpha\text{-ketoglutaric acid + Co-A} + NAD^+ \xrightarrow[\text{dehydrogenase}]{\alpha\text{-ketoglutaric}} \text{Succinyl Co-A} + NADH + H^+ + CO_2$$

$$\text{Succinyl Co-A} + H_2O + GDP + iP \xrightarrow[\text{thiokinase}]{\text{succinic}} \text{Succinic acid + Co-A} + GTP$$

$$GTP + ADP \longrightarrow GDP + ATP \text{ (substrate phosphorylation)}$$

$$\text{Succinic acid} + FAD \xrightarrow[\text{dehydrogenase}]{\text{Succinic}} \text{Fumaric acid} + FADH_2$$

$$\text{Fumaric acid} + H_2O \xrightarrow[\text{enzyme}]{\text{Fumarase}} \text{Malic acid}$$

$$\text{Malic acid} + NAD^+ \xrightarrow[\text{dehydrogenase}]{\text{Malic}} \text{Oxaloacetic acid (OAA)} + NADH + H^+$$

During citric acid cycle (Krebs cycle) 3 molecules of NAD^+ and one molecule of FAD (Flavin Adenine Dinucleotide) are reduced to produce NADH and $FADH_2$, respectively.

During citric acid cycle NADH and $FADH_2$ are produced. Now, they are linked with electron transport system (ETS) and produce ATP by oxidative phosphorylation. This may be summarised in following equation :

$$\text{Pyruvic acid} + 4NAD^+ + FAD + 2H_2O + ADP + iP$$
$$\downarrow \text{mitochondrial matrix}$$
$$3CO_2 + 4NADH + 4H^+ + FADH_2 + ATP$$

In the end of Krebs cycle, glucose molecule is completely oxidised. From one glucose molecule, two pyruvic acid molecules are formed. After oxidation of one pyruvic acid molecule, three CO_2 molecules are released. Thus, in all 6 molecules of CO_2 are released.

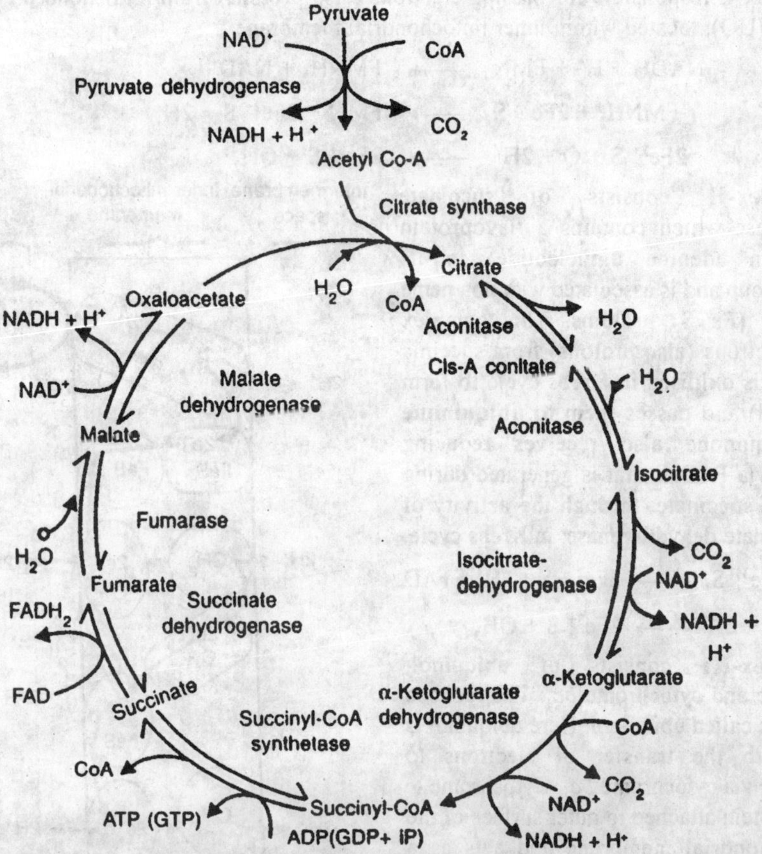

Fig. 17.3. Krebs cycle or citric acid cycle.

Electron Transport System (ETS)

By the end of Krebs cycle, glucose molecule oxidises completely, but the energy does not release till NADH and $FADH_2$ oxidise through electron transport system (ETS). The metabolic pathway through which electron passes from one carrier to another, is called **electron transport system** (ETS). The electron transport system is also known as **electron transport chain** or **mitochondrial respiratory chain**. The electron transport system consists of a series of coenzymes and cytochromes that take part in passage of electrons from a chemical to its ultimate acceptor. The passage of electrons from one-enzyme or cytochrome to the next takes place with a loss of energy at each step. Electron transport system is operative in the inner mitochondrial membrane.

The electron carriers include flavins, iron sulphur complexes, quinones and cytochromes. Most of them are prosthetic groups of proteins.

Electron transport system in mitochondria consists of **four complexes** which are found in bases of stalked particles in the **inner mitochondrial membrane**, and also **ubiquinone** (UQ) or coenzyme Q and **cytochrome** *c* which are not bound to stalked particles but act as mobile electron carriers between the complexes.

Complex-I consists of NADH-dehydrogenase or NADH-Q reductase which contains a flavoprotein FMN (flavin mononucleotide) and is associated with iron-sulphur (Fe-S) proteins. This complex is responsible for passing electrons (also protons) from mitochondrial NADH to ubiquinone (UQ), located within inner mitochondrial membrane.

$$NADH + H^+ + FMN \longrightarrow FMNH_2 + NAD^+$$

$$FMNH_2 + 2Fe^{3+} S \longrightarrow FMN + 2Fe^{2+} S + 2H^+$$

$$2Fe^{2+} S + Q + 2H^+ \longrightarrow 2Fe^{3+} S + QH_2$$

Complex-II consists of succinate dehydrogenase which contains a flavoprotein FAD (flavin adenine dinucleotide) in its prosthetic group and is associated with non heme iron-sulphur (Fe S) proteins. This complex receives electrons (also protons) from succinic acid (which is oxidised in Krebs cycle to form fumaric acid) and passes them to **ubiquinone** (UQ). Ubiquinone also receives reducing equivalents via $FADH_2$ that is generated during oxidation of succinate, through the activity of energy succinate dehydrogenase, in Krebs cycle.

$$FADH_2 + 2Fe^{3+} S \longrightarrow 2Fe^{2} + S + 2H^+ + FAD$$

$$2Fe^{2+} S + Q + 2H^+ \longrightarrow 2Fe^{3+} S + QH_2$$

Complex-III consists of ubiquinol, cytochrome c and cytochrome bc_1. The reduced ubiquinone is called ubiquinol. Here ubiquinol is oxidised with the transfer of electrons to cytochrome *c* via cytochrome bc_1. Cytochrome *c* is a small protein attached to outer surface of the inner mitochondrial membrane and acts as a mobile carrier for transfer of electrons between complex III and complex IV.

This complex is called QH_2-cytochrome *c* reductase complex. This bears three components, *i.e.*, cytochrome *b*, non-heme iron sulphur (Fe - S), and cytochrome c_1. Coenzyme Q is also involved between Fe-S and cytochrome c_1. The equations are as follows :

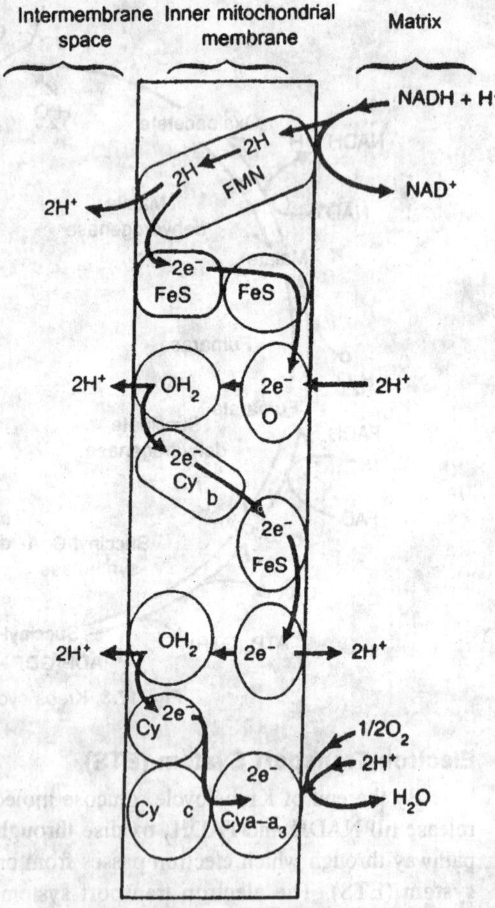

Fig. 17.4. Electron transport system (ETS)

$$QH_2 + 2Fe^{3+}\text{-}cy\ b \longrightarrow Q + 2H^+ + 2Fe^{2+} cy\ b$$

$$2Fe^{2+} cy\ b + 2Fe^{3+} S \longrightarrow 2Fe^{3+} cy\ b + 2Fe^{2+} S$$

$$2Fe^{2+} S + Q + 2H^+ \longrightarrow 2Fe^{3+} S + QH_2$$

$$QH_2 + 2Fe^{3+} cy\ c_1 \longrightarrow Q + 2H^+ + 2Fe^{2+} cy\ c_1$$

Now, cytochrome c_1 transfers electrons to cy *c*. Like coenzyme Q, cy *c* is also mobile carrier of electrons.

Complex-IV is known as cytochrome *c* oxidase complex. This contains cytochromes *a* and a_3, along with two copper centres. This complex receives electrons from cytochrome *c* and passes them to 1/2 O_2. Two protons are needed and H_2O molecule is formed (terminal oxidation). Here, O_2 is ultimate acceptor of electrons. It combines with protons to form metabolic water or respiratory water.

$$\underset{(Fe^{++})}{\text{2 Ferrocytochrome}} + 2H^+ + 1/2\ O_2 \rightleftharpoons \underset{(Fe^{+++})}{\text{2 ferricytochrome } c} + H_2O$$

Complex-V. When electrons are transferred from one carrier to next carrier via complexes I to IV in electron transport system (ETS), they are coupled to ATP synthase enzyme complex for production of ATP from ADP and inorganic phosphate (iP).

Here, number of ATP molecules synthesised during ETS, depends on nature of electron donor. Oxidation of one molecule of NADH gives rise to 3 molecules of ATP, and one molecule of $FADH_2$ gives rise to 2 molecules of ATP. ATP synthase complex is called **complex V**.

During transportation of electrons, hydrogen atoms split into protons and electrons. The electrons are carried by cytochromes. Before last stage, where hydrogen atom is accepted by oxygen to form water, the electrons again recombine with their protons. Oxygen acts as final hydrogen acceptor.

Oxidative phosphorylation. The whole process, where oxygen effectively allows the production of ATP by phosphorylation of ADP, is called **oxidative phosphorylation**. In other words, synthesis of ATP is called phosphorylation, and as it takes place in presence of oxygen, it is called oxidative phosphorylation.

$$2H \rightleftharpoons 2H^+ + 2e^-$$

$$NAD^+ + H^+ + H^+ + e^- + e^- \longrightarrow NADH + H^+$$

The enzyme required for synthesis of ATP, is called ATP synthase. This is located in F_1 or head piece of $F_0 - F_1$ or elementary particles. ATP synthase enzyme becomes active in ATP formation, where there is a proton gradient saving higher concentration of H_2.

ATP synthase, also known as **complex V** consists of two major components, *i.e.*, F_1 and F_0. The F_1 headpiece is a peripheral membrane protein complex and contains the site for ATP from ADP and inorganic phosphate (iP).

Whereas, F_0 is an integral membrane protein complex which forms the channel through which protons cross the inner membrane. The passage of protons through the channel is coupled to the catalytic site of the F_1 component for the production of ATP.

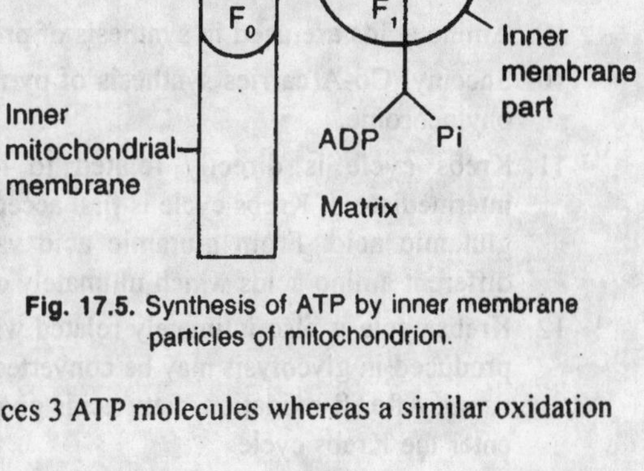

Fig. 17.5. Synthesis of ATP by inner membrane particles of mitochondrion.

Oxidation of one molecule of $NADH_2$ produces 3 ATP molecules whereas a similar oxidation of $FADH_2$ produces 2 ATP molecules.

Net gain of ATP. Complete oxidation of glucose to CO_2 and water shows that there is a net gain of 38 ATP. Each NADH + H^+ produces 3 ATP molecules, while $FADH_2$ forms only 2 ATP molecules at the end of reaction.

$$NADH + H^+ + 1/2\ O_2 + 3\ ADP + 3\ iP \longrightarrow NAD + 3\ ATP + H_2O$$

$$FADH_2 + 1/2\ O_2 + 2\ ADP + 2\ iP \longrightarrow FAD + 2\ ATP + H_2O$$

Thus, total gain of ATP in aerobic respiration is as follows :

Glycolysis ⟶ 8 ATP

Pyruvic acid ⟶ Acetyl Co-A ⟶ 6 ATP

Krebs cycle ⟶ 24 ATP

Total ⟶ 38 ATP

$$C_6H_{12}O_6 + 6O_2 + 8H_2O + 38\ (ADP + H_3PO_4) \longrightarrow 6CO_2 + 14H_2O + 38\ (ATP + H_2O).$$

However, in most eukaryotic cells, 2 molecules of ATP are required for transport of NADH produced in glycolysis into mitochondrion for further oxidation, and therefore, net gain of ATP is 36 molecules.

Significance of Krebs Cycle

1. During Krebs cycle, carbon skeletons are obtained for use in growth and maintenance of the cell.
2. Many intermediate compounds are formed which are used in synthesis of other biomolecules, such as amino acids, nucleotides, chlorophyll, cytochromes and fats.
3. During this pathway amino acids are synthesised from α-ketoglutaric acid, pyruvic acid and oxaloacetic acid.
4. Here succinyl Co-A acts as starting molecule for synthesis of chlorophyll.
5. Krebs cycle is major pathway for generation of ATP molecules, which make **energy currency** of the cell.
6. Energy is released from glucose, and is used in various biochemical reactions.
7. Phenol, anthocyanin, etc., are produced from acetyl Co-A, whereas fatty acids are formed from glycerol.
8. Glutamic acid is formed from α-ketoglutaric acid; aspartic acid from oxaloacetic acid, and alanine from aspartic acid.
9. Amino acids are used in synthesis of proteins, nucleic acids, purines and pyrimidines.
10. Succinyl Co-A carries synthesis of pyrrole compounds of chlorophyll, cytochrome and phytochrome.
11. Krebs cycle is directly related to nitrogen metabolism. α-ketoglutaric acid, an intermediate of Krebs cycle is first acceptor molecule of NH_3 forming an amino acid, the glutamic acid. From glutamic acid various transamination reactions begin to form different amino acids which ultimately condense to form proteins.
12. Krebs cycle is also intimately related with fat metabolism. Dihydroxyacetone phosphate produced in glycolysis may be converted into glycerol via glycerol-3-phosphate and *vice versa*. After β-oxidation, fatty acids give rise to active 2-C units, the acetyl Co-A which enter the Krebs cycle.

PENTOSE PHOSPHATE PATHWAY (PPP)

(Hexose Monophosphate Shunt)

As we know, major pathway for aerobic respiration of glucose is through **glycolysis** and **Krebs cycle**, however, an alternate pathway exists in many organisms. This pathway, which requires the presence of oxygen, is called **pentose phosphate pathway (PPP)** or **hexose monophosphate shunt (HMS).** As shown in figure that reduced NADP is formed in the reactions forming 6-phosphogluconic acid and ribulose-5-P. If the equivalent of a molecule of glucose is oxidised to CO_2 and H_2O via this cyclic pathway (six turns of cycle), then 12 molecules of reduced NADP would be formed. In the presence of enzyme transhydrogenase the hydrogens of NADPH can be transferred to NAD to form NADH. Hence the formation of 12 molecules of reduced NADP via hexose monophosphate shunt ultimately can lead to synthesis of 36 molecules of ATP. Thus, capture of energy released in oxidation of glucose via this pathway (hexose monophosphate shunt) is as effective as that of glycolytic-Krebs cycle pathway.

This pathway (PPP) is also known as **Warburg-Limpam-Dickens cycle** and **phosphogluconate shunt**. This was first studied by Warburg (1935) and Dickens (1938). This pathway occurs within the cytosol, where all enzymes of pentose phosphate pathway (PPP) are present.

Starting from 6 molecules of glucose 6-phosphate, the various reactions of PPP are as follows

1. 6 molecules of glucose-6-phosphate in the presence of coenzyme NADP are oxidised into 6 molecules of 6-phosphogluconolactone by the enzyme **glucose-6-phosphate dehydrogenase**. 6 molecules of NADP are reduced in the reaction which is reversible.

$$\text{Glucose-6-phosphate} + \text{NADP} \xrightleftharpoons[\text{dehydrogenase}]{\text{glucose-6-phosphate}} \text{6-Phosphogluconolactone} + \text{NADPH}_2$$

2. 6-phosphogluconolactone is hydrolysed by the enzyme **lactonase** to produce 6 molecules of 6-phosphogluconic acid.

$$\text{6-phosphogluconolactone} + H_2O \xrightarrow[Mg^{2+}]{\text{lactonase}} \text{6-phosphogluconic acid}$$

3. Phosphogluconic acid is oxidatively decarboxylated by the enzyme **6-phosphogluconic acid dehydrogenase.** 6 molecules of NADP are reduced, 6 molecules of CO_2 are released, and 6 molecules of ribulose-5-phosphate are produced.

$$\text{6-phosphogluconic acid} + \text{NADP} \xrightarrow[\text{dehydrogenase}]{\text{phosphogluconic acid}} \text{Ribulose-5-phosphate} + \text{NADPH}_2 + CO_2$$

4. 6 molecules of ribulose-5-phosphate isomerise into 4 molecules of xylulose-5-phosphate and 2 molecules of ribose-5-phosphate in the presence of enzymes **ribulose phosphate-3-epimerase and pentose phosphate isomerase**, respectively.

$$\text{Ribulose-5-phosphate} \xrightleftharpoons{\text{epimerase}} \text{xylulose-5-phosphate}$$

$$\text{Ribulose-5-phosphate} \xrightleftharpoons{\text{isomerase}} \text{ribose-5-phosphate}$$

That is,

$$\text{Ribulose-5-phosphate} \xrightleftharpoons[\text{isomerase}]{\text{epimerase and}} \text{xylulose-5-phosphate} + \text{ribose-5-phosphate}$$

5. 2 molecules of xylulose-5-phosphate and 2 molecules of ribose-5-phosphate combine in the presence of the enzyme **transketolase** to form 2 molecules of sedoheptulose-7-phosphate and 2 molecules of phosphoglyceraldehyde.

$$\text{Ribose-5-phosphate} + \text{xylulose-5-phosphate} \xrightleftharpoons[\text{TPP } Mg^{2+}]{\text{transketolase}} \text{sedoheptulose-7-phosphate} + \text{glyceraldehyde-3-phosphate}$$

6. 2 molecules of sedoheptulose-7-phosphate and 2 molecules of 3-phosphoglyceraldehyde combine in the presence of enzyme **transaldolase** to form 2 molecules of fructose-6-phosphate and 2 molecules of erythrose-4-phosphate.

$$\text{Sedoheptulose-7-phosphate} + \text{glyceraldehyde-3-phosphate} \xrightleftharpoons{\text{transaldolase}} \text{Fructose-6-phosphate} + \text{erythrose-4-phosphate}$$

7. 2 molecules of erythrose-4-phosphate react with remaining 2 molecules of xylulose-5-phosphate (reactions 4 and 5) in the presence of **transketolase** to form 2 molecules of fructose-6-phosphate and 2 molecules of 3-phosphoglyceraldehyde.

i.e., $$\text{xylulose-5-phosphate} + \text{erythrose-4-phosphate} \xrightleftharpoons{\text{transketolase}} \text{Fructose-6-phosphate} + \text{glyceraldehyde-3-phosphate}$$

8. One molecule of phosphoglyceraldehyde isomerises into dihydroxyacetone phosphate, in the presence of enzyme **phosphotriose isomerase**.

$$\text{Glyceraldehyde-3-phosphate} \xrightleftharpoons[\text{isomerase}]{\text{phosphotriose}} \text{dihydroxyacetone-3-phosphate}$$

9. Remaining one molecule of 3-phosphoglyceraldehyde unites with dihydroxyacetone phosphate in presence of enzyme **aldolase** to form one molecule of fructose 1, 6-diphosphate, which in the presence of **phosphatase** forms one molecule of fructose-6-phosphate.

$$\text{3-phosphoglyceraldehyde} + \text{dihydroxyacetone phosphate} \xrightleftharpoons{\text{aldolase}} \text{Fructose 1, 6-diphosphate}$$

10. 5 molecules of fructose-6-phosphate produced in reactions 6, 7 and 9, isomerise into 5 molecules of glucose-6-phosphate in presence of enzyme **phosphohexose isomerase**.

$$\text{Fructose-6-phosphate} \xrightleftharpoons[\text{isomerase}]{\text{phosphohexose}} \text{glucose-6-phosphate}$$

To summarise, 6 molecules of glucose-6-phosphate which enter into this pathway, produce 6 molecules of CO_2, after oxidation, and 12 molecules of reduced coenzyme $NADPH_2$, while 5 molecules of glucose-6-phosphate are regenerated.

$$\text{6 glucose-6-phosphate} + 12\ NADP^+ \longrightarrow \text{5-glucose-6-phosphate} + 12\ NADPH_2 + 6\ CO_2$$

Complete oxidation of a molecule of glucose produces 12 molecules of $NADPH_2$, which is equal to 36 ATP molecules. This capture of energy released in oxidation of glucose via this pathway (PPP) is as effective as that of glycolytic-Krebs cycle pathway, where 38 ATP molecules per glucose molecule are produced.

Significance of Pentose Phosphate Pathway (PPP)

1. This pathway provides alternative route for carbohydrate degradation.
2. This pathway (PPP) generates NADPH molecules which are used as reductants in biosynthetic processes under conditions when NADPH molecules are not generated by photosynthesis. It is, therefore, important in non-photosynthetic tissues, such as differentiating tissues, germinating seeds and during period of darkness. Production of NADPH is not linked to ATP generation in pentose phosphate pathway (PPP).

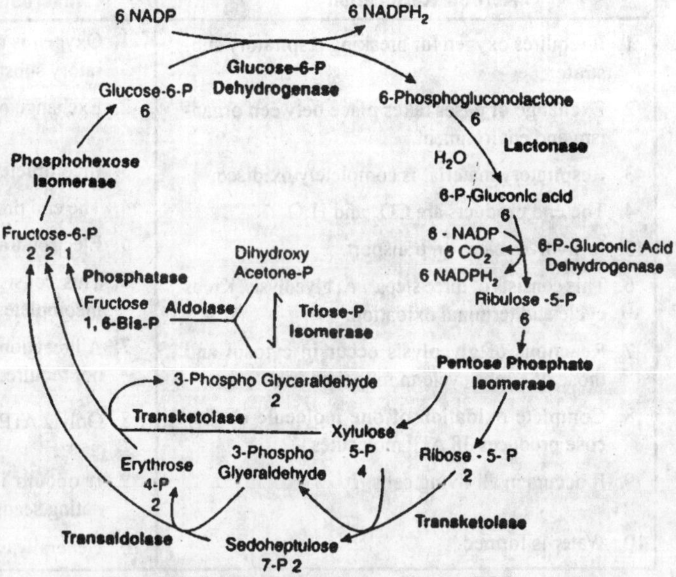

Fig. 17.6. Pentose phosphate pathway (PPP).

3. It produces ribose sugars for synthesis of nucleic acids.
4. It plays an important role in fixation of CO_2 in photosynthesis through ribulose-5-phosphate; ribulose 1, 5-phosphate derived from ribulose-5-phosphate is the primary acceptor of CO_2 in photosynthesis.
5. It provides erythrose-4-phosphate, which is required for synthesis of shikimic acid. The latter is precursor of aromatic ring compounds.
6. It produces a number of tetroses and pentoses for synthesis of nucleosides, nucleotides, nucleic acids, anthocyanins and other compounds.

ANAEROBIC RESPIRATION

When oxygen is not available for oxidation of carbohydrates then CO_2 and ethanol (C_2H_5OH) or lactic acid ($CH_3.CHOH.COOH$) are formed. This is called **anaerobic respiration**. This results in incomplete oxidation of substrate, hence energy released is much less in comparison of aerobic respiration. It generally occurs in lower organisms, such as bacteria and fungi. It also occurs in higher plants and animals under specific conditions, particularly when oxygen is limiting. Anaerobic respiration can be represented by following equation.

$$C_6H_{12}O_6 \longrightarrow 2\ C_2H_5OH + 2\ CO_2 + \text{Energy } 247 \text{ kJ or } 28 \text{ k cal}$$

Fermentation

In microorganisms, such as bacteria and yeasts, the term fermentation is more commonly used where anaerobic respiration takes place, after the name of product like alcoholic fermentation, lactic acid fermentation, etc. The enzyme complex, present in the process was named as **zymase**. However, fermentation is defined as anaerobic breakdown of carbohydrates and other organic compounds into alcohol, organic acids, gases, etc., with the help of microorganisms or their enzymes.

Table 17.3. Differences Between Aerobic and Anaerobic Respiration

Aerobic Respiration	Anaerobic Respiration
1. It requires oxygen for breaking respiratory substrate.	1. Oxygen is not required for breakdown of respiratory substrate.
2. Exchange of gases takes place between organism and environment.	2. Exchange of gases is absent.
3. Respiratory material is completely oxidised.	3. Incomplete breakdown of respiratory material.
4. The end products are CO_2 and H_2O	4. The end products are CO_2 and alcohol.
5. It involves electron transport.	5. Electron transport is absent.
6. This consists of three steps, *i.e.*, glycolysis, Krebs cycle and terminal oxidation.	6. This consists of two steps, *i.e.*, glycolysis and incomplete breakdown of pyruvic acid.
7. Reactions of glycolysis occur in cytosol and those of Krebs cycle in mitochondria.	7. All reactions occur in cytosol. Mitochondria are not required.
8. Complete oxidation of one molecule of glucose produces 38 ATP molecules.	8. Only 2 ATP molecules are produced.
9. It occurs in all living cells.	9. It occurs in certain bacteria, fungi, germinating seeds, fleshy fruits, etc.
10. Water is formed.	10. Generally, water is not formed.

The mechanism of anaerobic respiration or fermentation is similar to common pathway of aerobic respiration upto glycolysis. However, oxidation of pyruvic acid and NADH by mitochondria requires oxygen. When oxygen is limiting, NADH and pyruvic acid begin to accumulate. Under such condition, plants carry out **fermentation** (anaerobic respiration) which leads to the formation of CO_2 and either ethanol (ethyl alcohol) or lactic acid. In most of cases ethanol is produced. Two types of fermentation are common :

1. Alcoholic fermentation. In this type, the pyruvic acid is first decarboxylated to acetaldehyde in the presence of enzyme **carboxylase**. Thiamine pyrophosphate (TPP) is required as co-factor.

$$\underset{\text{Pyruvic acid}}{2\ CH_3COCOOH} \xrightarrow[\text{TPP}]{\text{carboxylase}} \underset{\text{Acetaldehyde}}{2\ CH_3CHO} + 2\ CO_2$$

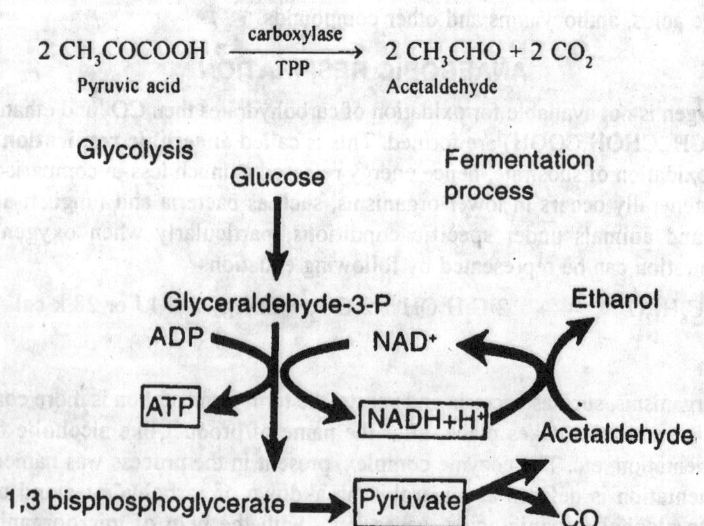

Fig. 17.7. Pathway of fermentation (anaerobic respiration) in yeast.

Acetaldehyde is then reduced to ethanol (ethyl alcohol) by the enzyme **alcohol dehydrogenase**. Coenzyme $NADH_2$ (produced in glycolysis) is oxidised.

$$\underset{\text{Acetaldehyde}}{2\ CH_3CHO} + \underset{\text{Reduced}}{NADH_2} \xrightarrow[\text{dehydrogenase}]{\text{alcoholic}} \underset{\text{Ethanol}}{CH_3CH_2OH} + \underset{\text{Oxidised}}{NAD}$$

The overall equation for anaerobic respiration involving alcoholic fermentation is as follows :

$$C_6H_{12}O_6 \longrightarrow 2\ CH_3CH_2OH + 2\ CO_2$$

2. Lactic acid fermentation. This type of fermentation occurs in lactic acid bacteria, certain fungi and muscles. Here, pyruvic acid is converted into lactic acid by the enzyme **lactic dehydrogenase**. Coenzyme $NADH_2$, produced in glycolysis, is oxidised.

$$\underset{\text{pyruvic acid}}{CH_3CO.COOH} + NADH_2 \xrightarrow[\text{dehydrogenase}]{\text{lactic}} \underset{\text{lactic acid}}{CH_3CHOH.COOH} + NAD$$

The overall equation for anaerobic respiration (lactic acid fermentation) is as follows :

$$\underset{\text{glucose}}{C_6H_{12}O_6} \longrightarrow \underset{\text{lactic acid}}{2\ CH_3CHOH.COOH}$$

There is net gain of only 2 ATP molecules (in glycolysis stage) during anaerobic respiration (or fermentation) and most of energy contained in glucose molecule is released as heat.

Importance. Many of the fermentive processes are of great importance in the household and industry. An example of the household is souring of milk or formation of curd. In the latter category are the alcoholic and acid fermentations. The **ripening** of cheese, the **retting** of flax, sannhemp, ramie, and jute, the **curing** of tobacco and tea leaves, and the **tanning** of leather are some very important examples of commercial processes dependent upon fermentations brought about by different species of bacteria. Alcoholic fermentation is used in brewing industry, where various types of beers, whisky and wines are produced, whereas CO_2 of alcoholic fermentation is used in baking industry for making bread and biscuits. Vinegar is produced by fermentation activity of acetic acid bacteria. Cleaning of raw hides is done by fermentive activity of bacteria.

Efficiency of the System

The total energy production from 38 ATP molecules is 1292 kJ. This means, one ATP molecule produces 34 kJ of energy, *i.e.*, $38 \times 34 = 1292$ kJ energy.

However, energy released by complete oxidation of one molecule of glucose is 2870 kJ. This shows, the efficiency is 45 per cent, *i.e.*, $\frac{1292 \times 100}{2870} = 45.01$.

Thus, it becomes clear that only a part of this energy is used to make ATP, and more than half of energy generated during respiration is released in the form of heat.

COMPENSATION POINT

When the need of oxygen (O_2) and carbon dioxide (CO_2) is fulfilled in the plant itself without any gaseous exchange, this is called **compensation point**.

This is a point in light intensity and atmospheric CO_2 concentration, when the rate of photosynthesis is just equivalent to the rate of respiration in the photosynthetic organs, and therefore, there is no gaseous exchange.

This means, the atmospheric concentration of carbon dioxide (CO_2) at which photosynthesis just compensates for respiration, is called **CO_2 compensation point**.

This shows, at given low concentration of CO_2 and non-limiting light intensity, the photosynthetic rate of a given plant will be equal to the total amount of respiration, *i.e.*, true respiration plus photorespiration.

The CO_2 compensation point is achieved when the amount of CO_2 uptake is equal to that generated through respiration at a non-limiting light intensity, where net photosynthesis is zero.

The value of CO_2 compensation point in C_3 plants is usually much higher (50-100 ppm) than in C_4 plants (5-10 ppm).

EXPERIMENTAL WORK : PRACTICALS

Respiration

Experiment 1

Object : Measurement of R.Q. by Ganong's Respirometer.

Requirements : Ganong's Respirometer, respiratory substrate, etc.

Experiment : The respiratory quotient may easily be measured by Ganong's respirometer. In Ganong's respirometer the amount of oxygen absorbed and carbon dioxide released out during respiration are determined simultaneously. The respirometer consists of a bulb with a graduated side tube. The volume of the apparatus is about 102 c.c. The stopper and neck of the bulb are each provided with hole. The stopper may be turned to bring the two holes opposite each other so that the air inside the bulb may communicate with the outer air and is at the atmospheric pressure. The side graduated tube is connected with a levelling tube by a rubber tubing.

For the determination of respiratory quotient the manometer is filled with mercury or a saturated solution of common salt. The water cannot be used since carbon dioxide dissolves in it. Carbon dioxide is slightly soluble in salt solution and therefore, best results can be obtained when mercury is used.

Two c.c. of plant material, the R.Q. of which is to be measured is being placed inside the bulb. In the beginning the air of the graduated tube is kept in direct communication with the atmospheric air at the atmospheric pressure. The mercury in both the tubes is brought to the same level by raising or lowering the levelling tube. Now the stopper in the neck of the bulb is turned so that the two holes get apart and the air in the apparatus is cut off from the outside air and respiration proceeds in closed chamber.

Observation and explanation : The initial level of mercury in the graduated tube is noted. The level is again noted after about an hour. If the respiratory substrate kept in the bulb is carbohydrate, the amount of carbon dioxide released during respiration will be equal to the amount of oxygen absorbed and therefore, there will be neither a rise and nor a fall in the mercury level. If caustic potash (KOH) is now added to the apparatus, the accumulated carbon dioxide, will be absorbed, and hence a rise in the mercury level, and thus the amount of carbon dioxide can be measured. The volume of oxygen absorbed will be equal to the volume of carbon dioxide measured. Hence the R.Q. is unity.

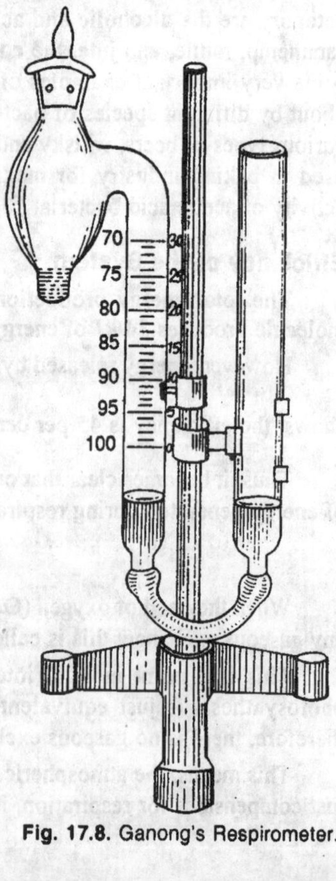

Fig. 17.8. Ganong's Respirometer.

When the respiratory substrate is a fat, the respiratory quotient is less than one. Here the amount of carbon dioxide released is less than the amount of oxygen absorbed and therefore, a vacuum is created in the closed chamber. This results in the rise of mercury level. This rise of mercury level is denoted by V_1 c.c. that is equivalent to the excess oxygen. Now the caustic potash (KOH) is added and there is a further rise of mercury level. The second rise in the mercury level is denoted by V_2 c.c. This represents the volume of carbon dioxide liberated. This way, the total amount of oxygen absorbed is equal to $V_1 + V_2$ c.c. the respiratory quotient will therefore, be less than one.

$$R.Q. = \frac{CO_2}{O_2} = \frac{V_2}{V_1 + V_2}$$

When the respiratory substrate is such that the carbon dioxide released is more than the volume of oxygen absorbed during respiration, the mercury level falls. The fall in the mercury level is denoted by V_1 c.c. that is equivalent to the excess carbon dioxide. Now the caustic potash is added to the tube. It absorbs the total amount of carbon dioxide and therefore, the mercury level rises. The rise is denoted by V_2 c.c. that is equivalent to the total volume of oxygen absorbed is then $V_2 - V_1$ c.c. The respiratory quotient will, therefore, be more than one.

$$R.Q. = \frac{CO_2}{O_2} = \frac{V_2}{V_1 - V_2}$$

R.Q. values for different respiratory substrates

R.Q.	Respiratory substrate
> 1.0	Carbohydrate with some anaerobic respiration. Carbohydrate synthesized from Organic acids.
1.0	Carbohydrates
0.99	Proteins with NH_3 formation
0.8	Proteins with amide formation
0.7	Fats, *e.g.*, tripalmitin
0.5	Fats with associated carbohydrate synthesis
0.3	Carbohydrates with associated organic acid synthesis

Experiment 2

Object : Demonstration of release of CO_2 during respiration.

(*i*) **Requirements :** Germinating seeds, a bottle, a bent tube, two holed cork, water neservoir, beaker, etc.

Experiment : Inside the bottle some germinating seeds are placed. The bottle is closed with the help of a two-holed cork. Here one of the holes is provided by glass tube bent twice at right angles. Another hole possesses a water reservoir which remains closed by a stopcock. The free end of bent glass tube is dipped in a beaker of water which also acts as a seal. Now this apparatus is left undisturbed for some time.

After some time the water of beaker is replaced by lime water and the stop cock of reservior is opened. The water runs in the bottle and so it drives out the air of bottle in the beaker through the bent glass tube.

Observation : The lime water turns milky.

Explanation : The germinating seeds undergo the respiration releasing CO_2 in this process. The CO_2 passes through the bent glass tube making the lime water milky.

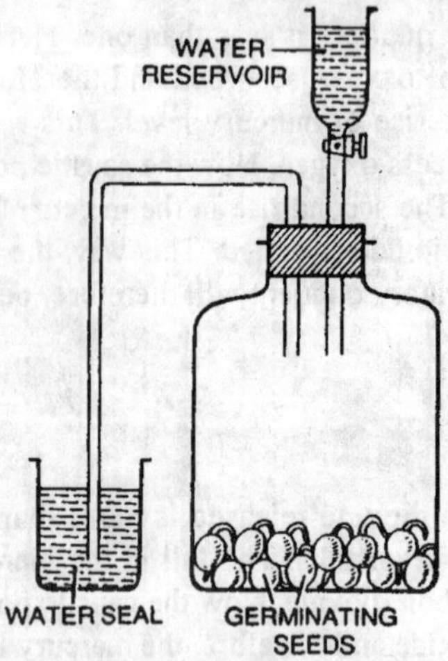

Fig. 17.9. Release of CO_2 during respiration. Demonstration of the phenomenon.

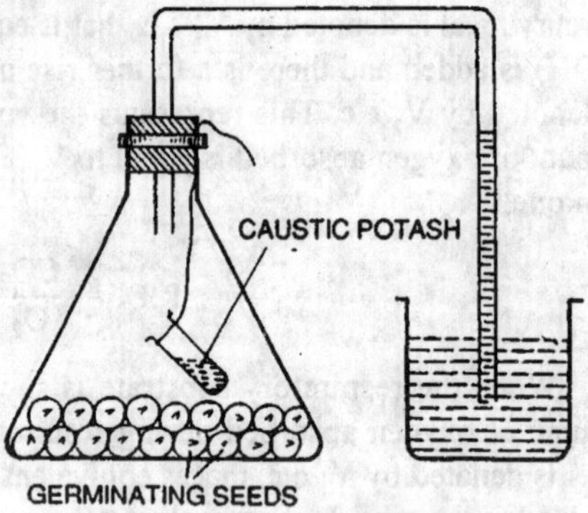

Fig. 17.10. Release of CO_2 during respiration. Demonstration for the phenomenon

(*ii*) **Requirements :** Germinating seeds, a conical flask, a single holed cork, caustic potash in a test tube, a bent glass tube, water beaker, etc.

Experiment : Inside the conical flask some germinating seeds are placed. The bottle is closed with a single-holed cork through which a glass tube bent twice at right angles is inserted. Another free end of this tube is put in a beaker of water. A test tube of caustic potash is hung inside the conical flask. Now this apparatus is put as such for some time.

Observation : Water rises in the far end of glass tube from the beaker.

Explanation : Germinating seeds undergo the anaerobic respiration, releasing CO_2 gas which is absorbed by the caustic potash. Thus a vacuum is created inside the conical flask and consequently water rises in the tube to fulfil it.

Note : The experiment should be performed in dark in case the green leaves are used as the respiratory substrate.

Experiment 3

Object : Demonstration of utility of oxygen in Respiration.

Requirements : A conical flask, a bent tube, germinating seeds, caustic potash in a small container, a mercury dish.

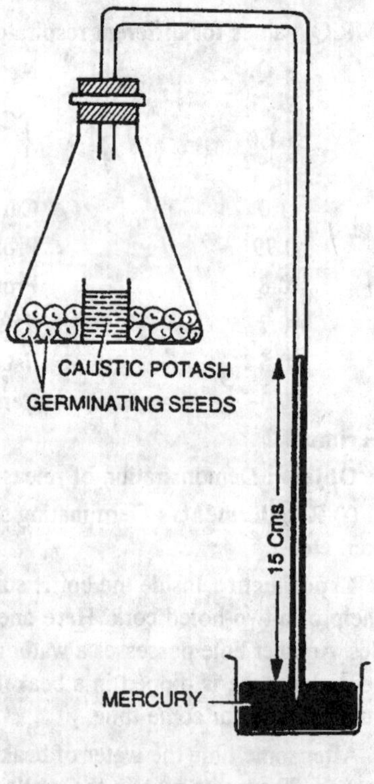

Fig. 17.11. Utility of O_2 in Respiration. Demonstration of the phenomenon.

Experiment : Germinating seeds are taken in a conical flask in which a container of caustic potash is also put. The mouth of this conical flask is closed by a single-holed cork through which a glass tube bent twice at right angles in inserted. The far end of this tube is put in the mercury dish. Now this apparatus is left undisturbed for some time.

Observation : The mercury in far end of bent glass tube rises to a height of 15 cm.

Explanation : The germinating seeds undergo aerobic respiration as they use the oxygen available inside the conical flask. As whole of the oxygen is used up by the germinating seeds, the pressure inside the flask is decreased. Hence, consequently the mercury level rises in the far end of the bent glass tube. This level reaches only a height of 15 cm in the glass tube. As this level is about one-fifth the air. As oxygen constitutes one fifth of total composition, it is reasonable to infer that the seeds have used this gas of the air in respiration.

Experiment 4

Object : Demonstration of production of heat in respiration.

Requirements : Two thermos bottles, germinating seeds, dry seeds, corks with a single hole, two thermometers.

Experiment : Half fill both the thermos bottles with germinating and dry seeds respectively. Now close their mouths with the help of single-holed corks through which a thermometer passes respectively. Put this experiment for about 24 hours.

Observation : There is a rise in temperature in the thermometer which is placed in the thermos bottle of germinating seeds. Another thermos bottle shows no change in previous temperature.

Explanation : The dry seeds or physiologically died seeds do not undergo respiration so there is no change in temperature. But the germinating seeds are going to make respiration where **(Table : 16.3)** energy also releases along with CO_2 gas. Thus, this energy causes a higher temperature in another thermos bottle. This release in energy is due to many biological activities going on stepwise with a gradual release of energy.

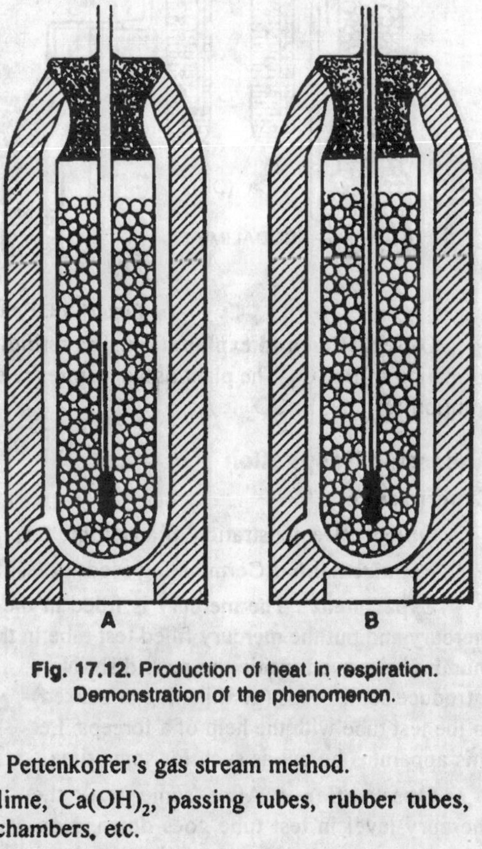

Fig. 17.12. Production of heat in respiration. Demonstration of the phenomenon.

Experiment 5

Object : Demonstration of release of CO_2 by Pettenkoffer's gas stream method.

Requirements : Pettenkoffer's tube, soda lime, $Ca(OH)_2$, passing tubes, rubber tubes, respiratory tissue, aspirator water, $Ba(OH)_2$, plant chambers, etc.

Experiment : The experiment is set as follows :

Firstly, there is a soda lime tower which is open to air by a tube. This tower is connected by passing tubes to the bottles of $Ca(OH_2)$ solution. Usually two bottles are used in the experiment. The second bottle is connected to the plant chamber by another passing tube. Pettenkoffer's tube is put between the plant chamber and aspirator by some rubber tubing connections. A two-way tap is also connected to the Pettenkoffer's tube. This tube is filled with $Ba(OH)_2$ solution.

With the help of two-way tap and aspirator the air is sucked out. Due to a lower pressure, a current of air gets in the soda lime tower. The soda lime and $Ca(OH)_2$ solution remove the whole CO_2 of air. Now the CO_2 free air reaches to plant-chamber from which it gets in the Pettenkoffer's tube. Here the $Ba(OH)_2$ solution is turned turbid. The aspirator is set in the way to regulate the slow movement of air in the form of bubbles.

After some time the turbid solution of Pettenkoffer's tube is titrated by using N/10 HCl and phenolphthalein-indicator.

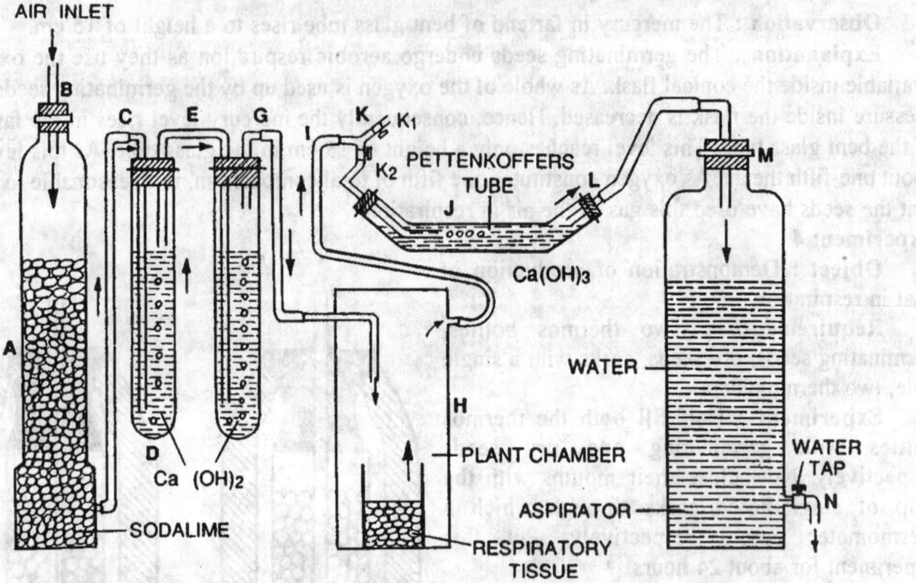

Fig. 17.13. Pettenkoffer's Tube.

Observation and explanation. The turbidity of the solution of Pettenkoffer's Tube is due to formation of $BaCO_3$. The plant tissue respires releasing CO_2 gas. The CO_2 gas reacts with $Ba(OH)_2$ solution forming $BaCO_3$.

Anaerobic Respiration

Experiment 6

Object : Demonstration of anaerobic respiration.

Requirements : Germinating seeds, a test tube, mercury, KOH crystals, petri dish, etc.

Experiment : The mercury is filled in the test tube up to the rim. Take a petri dish full of mercury and put the mercury filled test tube in the inverted condition with the help of thumb. The thumb is removed inside the petri dish. Now introduce some seeds (germinating or soaked) in the test tube with the help of a forceps. Let this apparatus be put as such for some time.

Observation : After some time the mercury level in test tube goes down. Now introduce some KOH crystals in the above test tube. After a little while the mercury level will go up to the former position.

Explanation : The lowering of mercury level in test tube indicates that some gas has been released by germinating seeds. Only CO_2 gas may be absorbed by KOH crystals. We see that with the introduction of KOH crystals the level of mercury goes high, hence the seeds have released CO_2 under the anaerobic conditions.

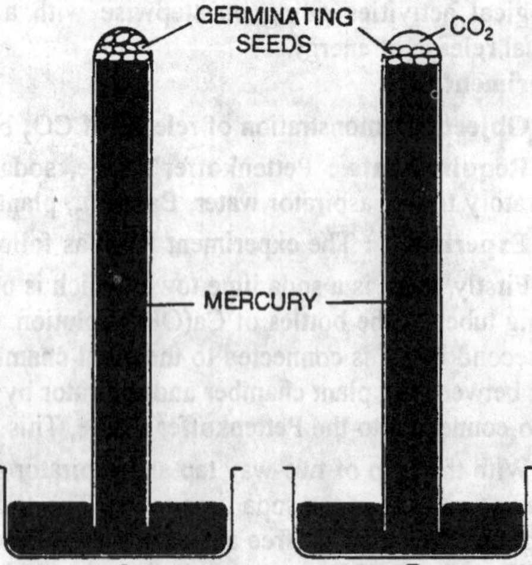

Fig. 17.14. Anaerobic Respiration. Demonstration of the phenomenon.

Alcoholic Fermentation

Experiment 7

Object : Demonstration of "Alcoholic-Fermentation" by yeast cells.

Requirements : Kuhne's fermentation tube, glucose or sucrose solution (10% aqueous solution), yeast powder (Baker's yeast), beaker, etc.

Experiment : Take some glucose solution in beaker and add 1 gm yeast powder to it. Now fill the Kuhne's fermentation tube with this solution. The half of the bulb and complete vertical tube is filled with the solution. The open end of the bulb is plugged with some cotton.

Observation : There is a consequent fall in the level of solution in vertical tube.

Explanation : The gas produced in vertical tube is proved to be CO_2 with the help of caustic potash. At the same time ethyl alcohol is also liberated :

$$\underset{}{C_{12}H_{22}O_{12}} \xrightarrow{\text{yeast Invertase}} \underset{\text{Glucose}}{C_6H_{12}O_6} + \underset{\text{Fructose}}{C_6H_{12}O_6}$$

$$C_6H_{12}O_6 \xrightarrow{\text{Fermentation}} 2C_2H_5OH + 2CO_2$$

Alcohol may also be tested 'by Iodoform test'.

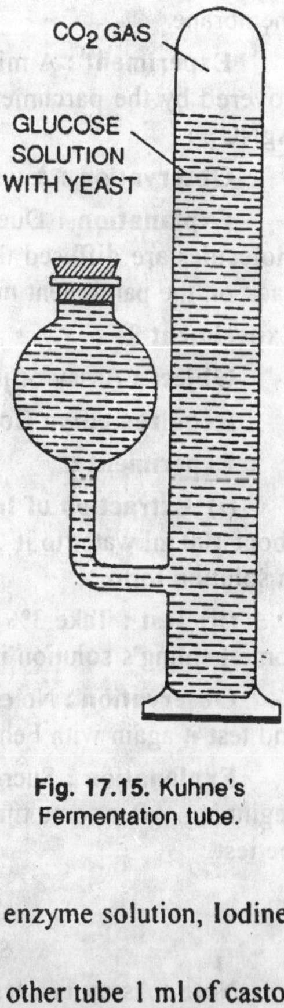

Fig. 17.15. Kuhne's Fermentation tube.

Enzymes

Experiment 8

Object : Demonstration of properties of enzyme : (*i*) specificity; (*ii*) thermolability and (*iii*) colloidal nature.

(*i*) **Specific Nature (Specificity) :**

Requirements : Test tubes, 1% starch solution, castor oil, diastase enzyme solution, Iodine, Sudan III, etc.

Experiment : Take 1 ml of 1% starch solution in a test tube and in other tube 1 ml of castor oil. Add 2 ml of diastase enzyme solution to each test tube. After about 5 minutes add few drops of iodine solution to the starch solution and few drops of Sudan III to castor oil.

Observation : The former tube shows no test of starch while in the latter castor oil is turned red.

Explanation : In the test tube of starchy solution the diastase enzyme has hydrolysed this solution indicating that the diastase enzyme is specific for starch in action.

(*ii*) **Sensitivity to heat (Thermolability) :**

Requirements : Four test tubes, diastase enzyme solution, beaker, water, starch solution, Iodine, etc.

Experiment : Take four test tubes and pour diastase enzyme solution in each of it. The temperature for these four test tubes is quite different, *i.e.*, 0°, 20°, 40° and 50°C respectively. Four beakers with water of 0°, 20°, 40° and 50°C temperature are used here to obtain the required condition. Add 10 c.c. of starch solution after some time. Now take few drops from each test tube and treat it with iodine solution.

Observation : Solution gives no colour at about 40°C.

Explanation : It shows that the rate of enzymatic reaction is optimum at this temperature. In other cases the positive iodine test is obtained.

(*iii*) **Colloidal Nature :**

Requirements : NaCl solution, enzyme solution, thistle funnel, beaker, $AgNO_3$, parchment membrane.

Experiment : A mixture of NaCl solution and enzyme solution is taken in a thistle funnel covered by the parchment membrane. Immerse it in a solution of starch. Test the filtrate with $AgNO_3$.

Observation : A white ppt. of AgCl is obtained here.

Explanation : Due to colloidal nature the enzyme molecules are large. Here only NaCl molecules are diffused through the parchment membrane, while the colloidal particles are held back on the parchment membrane.

Experiment 9

Object : Assay of invertase.

Requirements : Commercial yeast, distilled water, 3% sugar solution, Fehling's solution.

Experiment :

(*i*) **Extraction of Invertase :** Take 5 gm. of commercial yeast in a dish. Powder it and add about 100 ml water to it. After sometime filter the yeast in a beaker. The filtrate contains invertase in solution form.

(ii) **Test :** Take 3% sugar solution. Add 10 c.c. of each of the solutions in a test tube. Pour some Fehling's solution in this test tube.

Observation : No colour develops here. Put the enzyme sugar (sucrose) solution for an hour and test it again with Fehling's solution. Here red colour appears.

Explanation : Sucrose (sugar solution) is not a reducing agent so no change appears in the beginning. After some time (about an hour) it has broken down into reducing hexoses which give the test.

$$\underset{\text{Sugar solution}}{C_{12}H_{22}O_{12}} \xrightarrow[\text{Enzyme}]{H_2O} \underbrace{C_6H_{12}O_6 + C_6H_{12}O_6}_{\text{Hexoses}}$$

Note : Assay is a test of biologically active substance which is done by a living material.

Experiment 10

Object : To prepare the enzymes from wheat or rice seeds.

Requirements : Rice or wheat seeds, water, mortar and pestle, centrifuge, phosphate buffer at pH 6.9, ice bucket, etc.

Method : Take rice or wheat seeds soaked and germinated for 0, 24 and 48 hours. Place 50 seeds in a mortar and pestle with a little bit of 10 ml phosphate buffer at pH 6.9. Now grind seeds adding more fluid to extract thoroughly until 35 ml has been added. Now this process may be repeated with each set of seeds (for 0, 24 and 48 hours). Allow the homogenate to stand approximately for 10 minutes in the ice bucket. After doing so, centrifuge the debris, starch grains and other major organelles at 15,000 rpm for 10 minutes. Use the supernatant as enzyme sources.

SUMMARY

1. Respiration is a metabolic process in which carbon compounds synthesised by photosynthesis are oxidised, in the presence of various enzymes, into carbon dioxide and water with the release of energy.

2. The ratio of carbon dioxide evolved to the volume of O_2 consumed during oxidation of carbon compounds is called respiratory quotient (RQ).
3. Respiratory quotient depends upon the respiratory substrate being used in respiration.
4. Respiration is basically of two types : (*i*) aerobic respiration which occurs in the presence of oxygen, and (*ii*) anaerobic respiration that does not require oxygen.
5. Anaerobic respiration occurs in the absence of oxygen. It takes place in the cytoplasm of the cell. The end products of anaerobic respiration are ethanol or lactic acid, and very little energy is released.
6. The initial stages in respiration, which constitute the process of glycolysis, are common to both anaerobic and aerobic respiration.
7. During glycolysis, glucose converts into pyruvic acid. There is a net gain of 8 ATP molecules during glycolysis.
8. Aerobic respiration occurs in mitochondria.
9. In the mitochondria, the pyruvic acid is oxidised to acetyl-CoA, which then enters the TCA (tricarboxylic acid cycle or Krebs cycle) or citric acid cycle where it oxidises further.
10. During this process, CO_2 and NADH and $FADH_2$ are produced and take part in electron transport system (ETS) which carries the electrons in a chain to molecular oxygen, ultimately producing water.
11. The energy released during electron transport system (ETS) is utilised to synthesise ATP. This process is called oxidative phosphorylation.
12. The energy trapped in ATP is utilised in various metabolic processes by the living organisms.
13. Most organisms have an alternate route also for glucose metabolism, called oxidative pentose phosphate pathway. This pathway also operates in cytosol of the cell and produces pentose sugars and NADPH.
14. The atmospheric concentration of CO_2 at which photosynthesis just compensates for respiration, is called CO_2 compensation point.

TERMS TO REMEMBER

Aerobic respiration. This process of respiration leads to a complete oxidation of organic substances in the presence of O_2 and release CO_2, water and a large amount of energy present in the substrate.

Anaerobic respiration. This type of respiration takes place in the complete absence of oxygen.

Compensation point. The atmospheric concentration of CO_2 at which photosynthesis just compensates for respiration.

Citric acid cycle (Krebs cycle or tricarboxylic acid cycle TCA). Begins when acetyl-Co-A enters into a reaction to form citric acid.

Electron transport system (ETS). The metabolic pathway through which the electron passes from one carrier to another.

Fermentation. Process of oxidation in microbes.

Glycolysis (EMP pathway). In the process of respiration, the carbohydrates are converted into pyruvic acid through a series of enzymatic reactions, which take place in the cytosol.

Hans Adolf Krebs (1900-1981). He discovered citric acid cycle (Krebs cycle or tricarboxylic acid cycle) for production of energy in the cell in 1937. He was awarded Nobel Prize in 1953.

Hexokinase. An enzyme, which catalyses reaction where glucose and fructose are phosphorylated to give rise to glucose-6-phosphate and fructose-6-phosphate, respectively.

Invertase. An enzyme, by which sucrose is converted into glucose and fructose.

Oxidative decarboxylation. Here, pyruvate is first decarboxylated and then oxidised by the enzyme pyruvate dehydrogenase.

Oxidative phosphorylation. Production of ATP by phosphorylation of ADP.

Pentose phosphate pathway (PPP). Here, glucose-6-phosphate produced during early stages of glycolysis. This reaction takes place in the presence of the enzyme glucose-6-phosphate dehydrogenase.

Phosphofructokinase. An enzyme, which catalyses the reaction where fructose-6-phosphate is phosphorylated and fructose 1, 6-bisphosphate is produced.

Respiration. Phenomenon of release of energy by oxidation of various organic molecules, for cellular use.

Respiratory quotient (RQ) or respiratory ratio. The ratio of the volume of CO_2 evolved to the volume of O_2 consumed in respiration, *i.e.*, $RQ = \frac{CO_2}{O_2}$.

Respiratory substrate. The compounds that are oxidised during respiration.

QUESTION BANK

Very short answer questions

1. Give equation of cellular respiration.
2. What are respiratory substrates?
3. What is respiratory quotient?
4. Give equation of an aerobic respiration.
5. What is glycolysis?
6. Where does glycolysis take place?
7. Who discovered citric acid cycle?
8. Expand TCA.
9. Who discovered glycolysis?
10. Which enzyme is responsible for conversion of sucrose into glucose and fructose?
11. Expand FAD.
12. What is net ATP production in glycolysis?
13. Expand PPP.
14. Define compensation point.
15. What is net gain of ATP during aerobic respiration of one molecule of glucose?

ANSWERS

1. $C_6H_{12}O_6 + 6O_2 \longrightarrow 6CO_2 + 6H_2O$ + Energy (2870 kJ) ; 2. The compounds that are oxidised during respiration ; 3. The ratio of volume of CO_2 evolved to the volume of O_2 consumed during respiration, *i.e.*, CO_2/O_2 ; 4. $C_6H_{12}O_6 \xrightarrow[\text{enzyme}]{\text{zymase}} 2C_2H_5OH + 2CO_2$ + Energy (247 KJ) ; 5. During respiration, the carbohydrates convert into pyruvic acid through a series of enzymatic reactions, they are together known as glycolysis ; 6. In cytosol ; 7. Hans Adolf Krebs ; 8. Tricarboxylic acid ; 9. Embden, Meyerhof and Parnas ; 10. Invertase ; 11. Flavin adenine dinucleotide ; 12. 2 ATP ; 13. Pentose phosphate pathway ; 14. The atmospheric concentration of CO_2 at which photosynthesis just compensates for respiration, is called CO_2 compensation point ; 15. 38 ATP molecules.

Short Answer Questions

1. Define respiration. What are respiratory substrates?
2. Why respiration is called cellular respiration?
3. Give equation of cellular respiration.
4. Define the following :
   (*a*) Respiratory quotient (*b*) Anaerobic respiration
5. How would you differentiate between aerobic respiration and anaerobic respiration ?
6. What is fermentation? Give its economic importance.

7. Distinguish between respiration and combustion.
8. Give types of respiration and their overall equations.
9. Give R.Q. value of carbohydrates and fats.
10. What is significance of R.Q ?
11. What is meant by respiration quotient (RQ)? When will the value of RQ be 1 and when will if be less than 1?
12. Distinguish between glycolysis and citric acid cycle.
13. Differentiate between glycolysis and fermentation.
14. What is oxidative phosphorylation?
15. Write short notes on :
(*a*) Glycolysis (*b*) Electron transport chain.
16. What is respiratory substrate? Enumerate the steps involved in the breakdown of carbohydrates upto pyruvic acid.
17. Differentiate between glycolysis and Krebs cycle.
18. Distinguish between respiration and photorespiration.
19. Why does anaerobic respiration produce less energy than aerobic respiration?
20. Write the significance of citric acid cycle.

Long Answer Questions

1. Illustrate the mechanism of electron transport system.
2. Describe the pentose phosphate pathway.
3. Describe the process and role of citric acid cycle in living organism.
4. Discuss various steps of Krebs cycle. Also give the estimates of water, CO_2 and formation of ATP.
5. Define respiration. Explain the complete process of respiration in plants.
6. Where does glycolysis occur in a cell? Explain its different steps.
7. Explain non-cyclic photophosphorylation in plants. Why is this process called so?

MULTIPLE CHOICE QUESTIONS (Objective Type Questions)

1. During Krebs cycle, dehydrogenase enzyme removes hydrogen from the substance. The hydrogen atom becomes ionised into proton and electron. The electrons are passed to oxygen through a series of substances, the penultimate electron acceptor that supplies the electrons directly to oxygen is
(*a*) DNA (*b*) ubiquinone (*c*) cytochrome a_3 (*d*) cytochrome *a*
2. The importance of Krebs cycle is
(*a*) production of amino acids
(*b*) production of vitamins
(*c*) production of ATP molecules through oxidative phosphorylation.
(*d*) to encourage gluconeogenesis
3. Which of the following is required, both in the processes of respiration as well as photosynthesis?
(*a*) organic fuel (*b*) green cells
(*c*) cytochrome (*d*) energy from carbon bonds
4. Glycolysis takes place in
(*a*) cytoplasm (*b*) chloroplast (*c*) ribosome (*d*) mitochondria
5. Pentose phosphate pathway an alternative pathway of respiration, was elucidated by
(*a*) Warburg (*b*) Dickens (*c*) Forecker (*d*) Blackman
6. Cytochromes in plant cells function mainly as
(*a*) oxygen acceptor (*b*) CO_2 acceptor (*c*) electron acceptor (*d*) H_2O acceptor

7. The respiration of young maturing seeds is quite high but as water content decreases during further maturation respiration
(*a*) remains high (*b*) stops completely (*c*) increases steadily (*d*) decreases steadily
8. Total ATP production during EMP pathway is
(*a*) 24 ATP molecules (*b*) 8 ATP molecules (*c*) 38 ATP molecules (*d*) 6 ATP molecules
9. Respiration in cells takes place in
(*a*) ribosomes (*b*) nucleus (*c*) golgi body (*d*) mitochondria
10. Under glycolysis, the pyruvic acid is reduced to lactic acid anaerobically in
(*a*) liver (*b*) muscles (*c*) skin (*d*) brain
11. Conversion of sugar into alcohol during fermentation is due to the direct action of
(*a*) temperature (*b*) microorganisms
(*c*) concentration of sugar solution (*d*) zymase
12. The end product of glycolysis is
(*a*) pyruvic acid (*b*) ethyl alcohol (*c*) glucose (*d*) carbon dioxide
13. One of the products of anaerobic respiration is
(*a*) malic acid (*b*) lactic acid (*c*) pyruvic acid (*d*) ethyl alcohol
14. Biological oxidation in Krebs cycle involves
(*a*) N_2 (*b*) CO_2 (*c*) O_2 (*d*) SO_2
15. Adenosine diphosphate contains
(*a*) one high energy bond (*b*) two high energy bonds
(*c*) no high energy bonds (*d*) three high energy bonds
16. The formation of Acetyl coenzyme A from pyruvic acid is the result of its
(*a*) reduction (*b*) dehydration
(*c*) dephosphorylation (*d*) oxidative decarboxylation
17. The end products of aerobic respiration in plants are
(*a*) CO_2, H_2O and energy (*b*) H_2O and energy
(*c*) CO_2 and energy (*d*) CO_2 and H_2O
18. Respiratory quotient refers to
(*a*) The ratio between the amount of CO_2 produced to the amount of O_2 absorbed
(*b*) Amount of ATP produced to the amount lost during respiration
(*c*) Amount of CO_2 produced
(*d*) The number of glucose molecules breaking up to produce energy in one hour
19. Glycolysis operates in
(*a*) endoplasmic reticulum (*b*) cytoplasm
(*c*) golgi apparatus (*d*) perinuclear space
20. Common source of energy for cellular activity is
(*a*) ATP (*b*) NAD (*c*) Fat (*d*) Protein
21. Oxidation of pyruvate occurs in
(*a*) Krebs cycle (*b*) Tricarboxylic acid (*c*) Citric acid cycle (*d*) All the above
22. End product of Krebs cycle is
(*a*) Citric acid (*b*) Pyruvic acid (*c*) $CO_2 + H_2O$ (*d*) Lactic acid
23. End product of glycolysis is
(*a*) Glucose-1-phosphate (*b*) Acetyl Co-A
(*c*) Fructose-1-phosphate (*d*) Pyruvic acid
24. In aerobic respiration one gram mole of glucose yields
(*a*) 4 ATP (*b*) 24 ATP (*c*) 38 ATP (*d*) 40 ATP

25. Which is product of aerobic respiration
(*a*) pyruvic acid (*b*) malic acid (*c*) lactic acid (*d*) ethyl alcohol
26. The end product of oxidative phosphorylation is
(*a*) NADH (*b*) Oxygen (*c*) ATP (*d*) ATP + H_2O
27. Enzyme which changes glucose to glucose 6-phosphatase is
(*a*) Glucose synthetase (*b*) Hexokinase
(*c*) Glucose 6-phosphatase (*d*) Phosphorylase
28. Protein is substance in
(*a*) Anaerobic respiration (*b*) Protoplasmic respiration
(*c*) Seedling stage (*d*) Floating respiration
29. Krebs cycle occurs in
(*a*) E.R. (*b*) Chloroplasts (*c*) Mitochondria (*d*) Dictyosomes
30. Fructose 6-phosphate is changed to fructose 1, 6 diphosphate by
(*a*) Phosphoglycerate (*b*) Phosphofructokinase
(*c*) Phosphatase (*d*) Enolase
31. Metabolism of one palmitic acid molecule yields
(*a*) 36 ATP (*b*) 56 ATP (*c*) 48 ATP (*d*) 136 ATP
32. Anaerobic respiration of yeast produces
(*a*) N_2 (*b*) O_2 (*c*) CO_2 (*d*) H_2O
33. Site for glycolysis or EMP is
(*a*) cytoplasm (*b*) mitochondrion (*c*) chloroplast (*d*) nucleus
34. Anaerobic respiration is also called
(*a*) Glycolysis (*b*) Fermentation (*c*) Krebs cycle (*d*) Fragmentation
35. Production of alcohol by yeast in
(*a*) Aerobic (*b*) Light dependent (*c*) Anaerobic (*d*) both (*b*) and (*c*)
36. R.Q. is more than one in case the substrate is
(*a*) Fat (*b*) Glucose (*c*) Protein (*d*) Organic acid
37. Currency of cell is
(*a*) Granum (*b*) Mitochondria (*c*) ATP (*d*) Fat
38. ADP contains
(*a*) 1 high energy bond (*b*) 2 high energy bonds
(*c*) 3 high energy bonds (*d*) 4 high energy bonds
39. What is released at the time of seed germination ?
(*a*) Starch (*b*) Fat (*c*) Heat (*d*) Light
40. Respiratory substrate (s) in respiration is
(*a*) Glucose and sucrose (*b*) Glucose and carbon
(*c*) Glucose and oxygen (*d*) Glucose and carbon dioxide
41. Respiration occurs in
(*a*) In all living cells in light (*b*) In all living cells in dark
(*c*) Both (*a*) and (*b*) (*d*) In non green cells in dark only
42. Respiration may occur in absence of O_2 in
(*a*) Potato (*b*) *Spirogyra* (*c*) Yeast (*d*) Humans
43. Krebs cycle is also called as
(*a*) Glycolate cycle (*b*) EMP pathway (*c*) Glyoxylate cycle (*d*) Citric acid cycle
44. The nét gain of energy from one gram mole of glucose during aerobic respiration is
(*a*) 38 ATP (*b*) 40 ATP (*c*) 36 ATP (*d*) 2 ATP

45. Both respiration and photosynthesis require
(*a*) Sunlight (*b*) Green pigment (*c*) Cytochromes (*d*) Phytochrome

46. Where do we observe both photosynthesis and respiration
(*a*) virus (*b*) fungi (*c*) bacteria (*d*) green plants

47. Respiratory enzymes are located in
(*a*) Matrix of mitochondria (*b*) Perimitochondrial space
(*c*) Cristae (*d*) Outer membrane

48. ATP synthesis occurs in which part of mitochondria
(*a*) Mitochondria as a whole (*b*) Inner membrane of mitochondria
(*c*) Outer membrane of mitochondria (*d*) Mitochondrial matrix

49. The amount of energy given by one molecule of ATP is
(*a*) 7.3 kcal (*b*) 7.61 kcal (*c*) 6.86 kcal (*d*) 7.06 kcal

50. EMP can produce a total of :
(*a*) 2 ATP (*b*) 6 ATP (*c*) 8 ATP (*d*) 10 ATP

51. Hexose monophosphate shunt is called :
(*a*) Pentose phosphate pathway (*b*) Total of metabolic reactions
(*c*) Conversion of glucose into pyruvate (*d*) EMP pathway

52. Pentose phosphate pathway was discovered by
(*a*) Horecker (*b*) Warburg and Dickens
(*c*) Lipmann *et al* (*d*) Kostytchen

53. Glycolysis is part of
(*a*) Aerobic respiration (*b*) Anaerobic respiration
(*c*) Both (*a*) and (*b*) (*d*) Krebs cycle

54. Reaction of glycolysis occurs in
(*a*) cytoplasm (*b*) mitochondria
(*c*) chloroplast (*d*) perimitochondrial space

55. Oxidation of $NADH_2$ yields
(*a*) 1 ATP (*b*) 2 ATP (*c*) 3 ATP (*d*) 4 ATP

56. The first substance that enters the mitochondria after cytoplasmic part of respiratory reactions is
(*a*) Oxaloacetic acid (*b*) Pyruvic acid (*c*) Citric acid (*d*) Acetyl Co-A

57. Respiratory quotient is always less than one in succulent plants because of
(*a*) Complete oxidation (*b*) Complete reduction
(*c*) Incomplete oxidation (*d*) Incomplete reduction

58. Which of the following does not involve EMP cycle
(*a*) Conversion of glucose in ethyl alcohol
(*b*) Conversion of glucose in PGAL
(*c*) Reduction of glucose into pyruvic acid
(*d*) Conversion of pyruvic acid into CO_2 and H_2O

59. How many $NADH_2$ are formed during glycolysis
(*a*) 1 (*b*) 2 (*c*) 3 (*d*) 4

60. Cheese and yogurt are products of
(*a*) Pasteurisation (*b*) Distillation (*c*) Fermentation (*d*) Dehydrogenation

61. Complete oxidation of one molecule of acetyl Co-A results in the formation of
(*a*) 12 ATP (*b*) 15 ATP (*c*) 19 ATP (*d*) 38 ATP

62. In which of the following process 2 electrons and 2 protons are used
(*a*) Dehydrogenation (*b*) Deamination (*c*) Decarboxylation (*d*) Hydrogenation

63. The process of Acetyl Co-A synthesis from pyruvic acid is called
(*a*) Reduction (*b*) Dehydrogenation
(*c*) Dephosphorylation (*d*) Oxidative decarboxylation

64. End products of aerobic respiration are
(*a*) $CO_2 + H_2O$ (*b*) $O_2 + H_2O$ + Energy
(*c*) Energy (*d*) $CO_2 + H_2O$ + Energy

65. The number of carbons in pyruvic acid is
(*a*) 3 (*b*) 4 (*c*) 6 (*d*) 2

66. Terminal cytochrome of respiratory chain which donates electrons to oxygen is
(*a*) Cyt . *b* (*b*) Cyt . *c* (*c*) Cyt . a_3 (*d*) Cyt . a_1

67. Metabolic water is
(*a*) Produced during fermentation
(*b*) Produced during transpiration
(*c*) Produced during aerobic utilisation of glucose
(*d*) Produced during condensation of glucose molecules in photosynthesis

68. Which one is a product of glycolysis ?
(*a*) FAD (*b*) NAD (*c*) NADP (*d*) NADH

69. Hydrogen atoms released at succinate level in Krebs cycle are accepted by
(*a*) FAD (*b*) NAD (*c*) NADP (*d*) AMP

70. Anaerobic respiration of organisms produces
(*a*) $CO_2 + H_2O$ (*b*) Alcohol + CO_2
(*c*) Lactic acid + H_2O (*d*) $CO_2 + H_2O$ + Energy

71. Correct sequence of electron acceptor in ATP synthesis is
(*a*) Cyt. a_1, a_3, *b*, *c* (*b*) Cyt. *b*, *c*, *a*, a_3 (*c*) Cyt. *c*, *b*, *a*, a_3 (*d*) Cyt. *b*, *c*, a_3, *a*

72. Which one transfers electrons to ETS ?
(*a*) Cytochrome (*b*) FeS
(*c*) Phytochromes (*d*) FeS and Cytochrome

73. End product of citric acid cycle or Krebs cycle is
(*a*) Citric acid (*b*) Lactic acid (*c*) $CO_2 + H_2O$ (*d*) H_2O

74. R.Q. is
(*a*) CO_2 / O_2 (*b*) O_2 / CO_2 (*c*) $1 + \frac{O_2}{CO_2}$ (*d*) $1 + \frac{CO_2}{O_2}$

75. The reactions of Krebs cycle take place
(*a*) In cytoplasm (*b*) In mitochondria
(*c*) On surface of mitochondria (*d*) In E.R. and cytoplasm

76. Glycolysis occurs in
(*a*) Muscle cells (*b*) Nerve cells (*c*) Virtually all cells (*d*) Eukaryotes

77. Respiratory Quotient is
(*a*) $\frac{CO_2}{O_2}$ (*b*) $\frac{O_2}{CO_2}$ (*c*) $\frac{N_2}{CO_2}$ (*d*) $\frac{CO_2}{N_2}$

78. Centre of phosphorylation is
(*a*) Oxysome (*b*) Peroxisome (*c*) Ribosomes (*d*) Mitochondria

79. Which of the following are essential for ATP synthesis?
(*a*) Fe and Mo (*b*) N and P (*c*) Fe and P (*d*) Mg and Mn

80. Organism used in the industrial preparation of ethanol is
(*a*) *Lactobacillus* (*b*) *Azotobacter* (*c*) *Penicillium* (*d*) *Saccharomyces*

81. Metabolism of one lipid molecule produces
(a) 36 ATP (b) 38 ATP (c) 147 ATP (d) 56 ATP
82. Anaerobic respiration of yeast produces
(a) N_2 (b) O_2 (c) CO_2 (d) H_2O
83. Who receives electron at the end of electron transport chain ?
(a) H_2O (b) H_2 (c) CO_2 (d) cytochrome a_3
84. What is the total production of ATP by breakdown of one glucose molecule during aerobic respiration ?
(a) 34 (b) 38 (c) 40 (d) 32
85. RQ of sprouting potato tubers will be
(a) > 1 (b) 0 (c) 1 (d) < 1
86. Anaerobic respiration after glycolysis is called
(a) Krebs cycle (b) Fermentation
(c) Zymoses (d) Oxidative phosphorylation
87. Production of ATP by oxidative phosphorylation is driven by energy from
(a) Coenzyme A
(b) $NADH_2$
(c) Pyruvic acid
(d) Movement of protons from inner mitochondrial membrane to cytoplasm
88. Krebs cycle is a part of .... respiration.
(a) Aerobic (b) Anaerobic (c) Fermentation (d) Facultative
89. How many ATP molecules are formed in ETS from the reduced nicotinamide adenine dinucleotide generated in one turn cycle of Krebs cycle ?
(a) 3 (b) 6 (c) 9 (d) 12
90. RQ fat is
(a) More than one (b) Zero (c) One (d) Less than one
91. Respiration is a process in which
(a) energy is used up
(b) energy is released
(c) energy is released and stored in the form of ATP
(d) energy is stored in the form of ADP
92. Chief site of respiration in plants is
(a) lysosomes (b) mitochondria (c) ribosomes (d) chloroplasts
93. In the process of respiration the potential energy stored in the organic compounds is released in the form of
(a) physical energy (b) kinetic energy (c) chemical energy (d) radiant energy
94. Why do fishes in an aquarium thrive better if green plants are growing there ? Because they
(a) inhale oxygen released by green plants (b) inhale CO_2 released by green plants
(c) can feed on green plants (d) none of the above
95. Which of the following statements regarding respiration and breathing is correct
(a) plants respire, while animals breathe
(b) higher animals breathe, as well as respire
(c) higher plants respire during day, and breathe at night
(d) none of the above
96. Complete oxidation of 1 -gm molecule yields
(a) 6,860,000 calories (b) 686,000 calories (c) 68600 calories (d) 6860 calories

97. The energy yield as a result of total oxidation of 1 glucose molecule during cellular respiration is to convert
(*a*) 32 molecules of ADP into 32 molecules of ADP
(*b*) 38 molecules of ADP into 38 molecules of ATP
(*c*) 30 molecules of ADP into 30 molecules of ATP
(*d*) 34 molecules of ADP into 34 molecules of ATP

98. The end products of respiration in plants are
(*a*) starch and O_2 (*b*) H_2O and energy
(*c*) CO_2, H_2O and energy (*d*) sugar and O_2

99. Anaerobic respiration is also known as
(*a*) intramolecular respiration (*b*) intermolecular respiration
(*c*) extramolecular respiration (*d*) molecular respiration

100. In which of the following, anaerobic respiration taken place ?
(*a*) yeast (*b*) *Spirogyra* (*c*) potato (*d*) *Spirulina*

101. How many molecules of ATP are gained during anaerobic respiration of one molecule of glucose ?
(*a*) 36 (*b*) 38 (*c*) 2 (*d*) 4

102. When a molecule of pyruvic acid is subjected to anaerobic oxidation and forms lactic acid, there is
(*a*) gain of 2 ATP molecules (*b*) loss of 3 ATP molecules
(*c*) loss of 6 ATP molecules (*d*) gain of 3 ATP molecules

103. Which one of the following process releases a CO_2 molecule ?
(*a*) Alcoholic fermentation (*b*) Glycolysis
(*c*) Lactic acid fermentation (*d*) Hydrolysis of glycogen

104. Which of the following molecules is a product of fermentation of glucose by yeast ?
(*a*) $C_6H_{12}O_6$ (*b*) $(C_6H_{10}O_5)_n$ (*c*) C_2H_5OH (*d*) CH_3OH

105. When yeast ferments glucose, the products are
(*a*) ethanol and water (*b*) water and CO_2 (*c*) methanol and CO_2 (*d*) ethanol and CO_2

106. Glycolysis is found in
(*a*) most body cells (*b*) anaerobic bacteria (*c*) eukaryotic cells (*d*) virtually all cells

107. The common phase in aerobic and anaerobic respiration is
(*a*) glycolysis (*b*) tricarboxylic acid cycle
(*c*) oxidative phosphorylation (*d*) Krebs cycle

108. The other term for glycolysis is
(*a*) TCA pathway (*b*) Carbon pathway (*c*) EMP pathway (*d*) HMS pathway

109. Enzymes taking part in glycolysis are present in
(*a*) mitochondria (*b*) cytosol (*c*) cell sap (*d*) none of above

110. What is end product of glycolysis
(*a*) C_2H_5OH (*b*) pyruvic acid (*c*) CO_2 (*d*) Glucose

111. The enzyme, which converts glucose to glucose-6-phosphate is
(*a*) glucose synthase (*b*) hexokinase (*c*) phosphorylase (*d*) arginase

112. In glycolysis net gain is two ATP molecules and two molecules of
(*a*) $NADH_2$ (*b*) $FADH_2$ (*c*) $FMNH_2$ (*d*) $NADPH_2$

113. Krebs cycle takes place in
(*a*) dictyosomes (*b*) mitochondrial matrix
(*c*) lysosomes (*d*) endoplasmic reticulum

114. Which is the connecting link between glycolysis and Krebs cycle ?
(*a*) Pyruvic acid (*b*) Oxaloacetic acid (*c*) Acetyl-CoA (*d*) Cytochrome

115. Krebs cycle starts with the formation of a 6-carbon compound by chemical reaction between
(*a*) succinic acid and acetyl-CoA (*b*) fumaric acid and pyruvic acid
(*c*) oxaloacetic acid and acetyl-CoA (*d*) malic acid and acetyl-CoA
116. What is the other name for Krebs cycle?
(*a*) Citric acid cycle (*b*) Glycolate cycle (*c*) EMP pathway (*d*) Glyoxylate cycle
117. The Krebs cycle begins with
(*a*) pyruvic acid (*b*) fumaric acid
(*c*) phosphoglyceraldehyde (*d*) lysine
118. Pyruvate dehydrogenase enzyme is used in conversion of
(*a*) glucose to pyruvate (*b*) pyruvic acid to lactic acid
(*c*) pyruvate to acetyl-CoA (*d*) pyruvate to glucose
119. Fumarase enzyme converts
(*a*) fumaric acid to malic acid (*b*) fumaric acid to isocitric acid
(*c*) malic acid to succinic acid (*d*) succinic acid to fumaric acid
120. Organelles which are regarded as 'power house' of the cell and in which the oxidative reactions of the respiratory process take place are
(*a*) lysosomes (*b*) dictyosomes (*c*) chloroplasts (*d*) mitochondria
121. Synthesis of ATP in mitochondria takes place
(*a*) in the matrix (*b*) in cristae (*c*) in outer membrane (*d*) in intracristae space
122. ATP is
(*a*) an enzyme, which brings about oxidation
(*b*) a molecule, which contains high-energy phosphate bonds
(*c*) a hormone
(*d*) a protein
123. What is 'energy currency' of living organisms ?
(*a*) chlorophyll (*b*) ATP (*c*) NADP (*d*) FAD
124. During ATP synthesis electrons pass through which one of the following ?
(*a*) CO_2 (*b*) H_2O (*c*) O_2 (*d*) cytochromes
125. An indispensable role in energy metabolism is played by
(*a*) sodium (*b*) calcium (*c*) phosphorus (*d*) boron
126. Which is also formed along with ATP in glycolysis ?
(*a*) $NADPH_2$ (*b*) $NADH_2$ (*c*) $FADH_2$ (*d*) FAD
127. Synthesis of ATP in mitochondria requires
(*a*) NADP (*b*) FMN (*c*) Oxygen (*d*) pyruvic acid
128. The atom within each cytochrome molecule that actually accepts and releases electrons is
(*a*) iron (*b*) oxygen (*c*) zinc (*d*) carbon
129. Within the mitochondrion, the proton gradient develops across the
(*a*) outer membrane (*b*) inner membrane
(*c*) intermembrane space (*d*) matrix
130. R.Q. of respiratory substrate rich in oxygen is
(*a*) equal to one (*b*) more than one (*c*) less than one (*d*) none of above
131. R.Q. of fatty substances is generally
(*a*) zero (*b*) unity (*c*) more than one (*d*) less than one
132. R.Q. is maximum, when respiratory substrate is
(*a*) fat (*b*) glucose (*c*) malic acid (*d*) protein

133. In succulent plants respiratory quotient is always less than one because of
(*a*) complete oxidation (*b*) complete reduction
(*c*) incomplete oxidation (*d*) incomplete reduction

134. If the volume of CO_2 liberated during respiration is more than the volume of O_2 used, the respiratory substrate will be
(*a*) fats (*b*) organic acids (*c*) proteins (*d*) carbohydrates

135. Hexose monophosphate shunt is
(*a*) pentose phosphate pathway
(*b*) conversion of glucose into pyruvic acid
(*c*) a process by which new products are synthesized
(*d*) glycolytic pathway

136. Photorespiration takes place in
(*a*) mitochondria (*b*) glyoxysomes (*c*) peroxisomes (*d*) Golgi bodies

137. In hospitals plants are removed from patient's room at night because
(*a*) they compete with patient for available oxygen in the room
(*b*) they produce CO_2 at night
(*c*) they produce CO_2 all the 24 hours, but give out oxygen during day
(*d*) this practice has no practical significance

138. When the bread is baked, it becomes light and spongy, becuase
(*a*) the evaporation of alcohol from fermented flour
(*b*) the evolution of CO_2 from the kneaded flour
(*c*) the presence of yeast
(*d*) none of above

139. Food products are kept under refrigeration or in cold storage because
(*a*) they remain very cool
(*b*) respiration is negligible under very low temperature and the food products maintain their flavour and freshness better and longer
(*c*) foodstuff becomes tasty
(*d*) they can be used in off-season

140. Respiration and photosynthesis, both require
(*a*) organic fuel (*b*) cytochrome
(*c*) sunlight (*d*) energy from carbon bonds

141. Which of the following statements about NAD^+ is false ?
(*a*) NAD^+ is reduced to NADH during both glycolysis and the Krebs cycle
(*b*) NAD^+ is reduced by the action of dehydrogenases
(*c*) NAD^+ can receive electrons for use in oxidative phosphorylation
(*d*) NAD^+ has more chemical energy than NADH

142. The colour of cytochrome is
(*a*) Blue (*b*) Black (*c*) Pink (*d*) Colourless

143. One stearic acid molecule releases
(*a*) 140 ATP (*b*) 147 ATP (*c*) 145 ATP (*d*) 180 ATP

144. Krebs cycle is a
(*a*) catabolic cycle (*b*) anabolic cycle (*c*) amphoteric cycle (*d*) amphibolic cycle

145. Electron acceptor in cyt a_3
(*a*) Fe (*b*) Cu (*c*) As (*d*) Both (*a*) and (*b*)

ANSWERS

1. (*c*)	2. (*c*)	3. (*c*)	4. (*a*)	5. (*c*)	6. (*c*)	7. (*c*)	8. (*b*)	9. (*d*)	10. (*b*)
11. (*b*)	12. (*a*)	13. (*d*)	14. (*c*)	15. (*b*)	16. (*d*)	17. (*a*)	18. (*a*)	19. (*b*)	20. (*a*)
21. (*d*)	22. (*c*)	23. (*d*)	24. (*c*)	25. (*b*)	26. (*d*)	27. (*b*)	28. (*b*)	29. (*c*)	30. (*b*)
31. (*d*)	32. (*c*)	33. (*a*)	34. (*b*)	35. (*c*)	36. (*d*)	37. (*c*)	38. (*a*)	39. (*c*)	40. (*c*)
41. (*c*)	42. (*c*)	43. (*d*)	44. (*a*)	45. (*c*)	46. (*d*)	47. (*a*)	48. (*b*)	49. (*a*)	50. (*c*)
51. (*a*)	52. (*b*)	53. (*c*)	54. (*a*)	55. (*c*)	56. (*d*)	57. (*c*)	58. (*d*)	59. (*b*)	60. (*c*)
61. (*a*)	62. (*a*)	63. (*d*)	64. (*d*)	65. (*a*)	66. (*c*)	67. (*c*)	68. (*d*)	69. (*a*)	70. (*c*)
71. (*b*)	72. (*d*)	73. (*c*)	74. (*a*)	75. (*b*)	76. (*c*)	77. (*a*)	78. (*a*)	79. (*c*)	80. (*d*)
81. (*c*)	82. (*c*)	83. (*d*)	84. (*b*)	85. (*c*)	86. (*b*)	87. (*b*)	88. (*a*)	89. (*c*)	90. (*d*)
91. (*c*)	92. (*b*)	93. (*c*)	94. (*a*)	95. (*b*)	96. (*b*)	97. (*b*)	98. (*c*)	99. (*a*)	100. (*a*)
101. (*c*)	102. (*c*)	103. (*a*)	104. (*c*)	105. (*d*)	106. (*d*)	107. (*a*)	108. (*c*)	109. (*b*)	110. (*b*)
111. (*b*)	112. (*a*)	113. (*b*)	114. (*c*)	115. (*c*)	116. (*a*)	117. (*a*)	118. (*c*)	119. (*a*)	120. (*d*)
121. (*b*)	122. (*b*)	123. (*b*)	124. (*d*)	125. (*c*)	126. (*b*)	127. (*c*)	128. (*a*)	129. (*b*)	130. (*a*)
131. (*d*)	132. (*c*)	133. (*c*)	134. (*b*)	135. (*a*)	136. (*c*)	137. (*c*)	138. (*b*)	139. (*b*)	140. (*b*)
141. (*d*)	142. (*c*)	143. (*b*)	144. (*d*)	145. (*a*)					

18

CHAPTER

Photosynthesis and Transport of Organic Substances

The process in which certain carbohydrates are synthesized from carbon dioxide and water by chlorophyllous cells in the presence of light, oxygen being a by-product, is generally called **photosynthesis**. The summary equation of photosynthesis is as follows :

$$6CO_2 + 6H_2O \xrightarrow[\text{chlorophyllous cells}]{\text{radiant 673 kg. cal of radiant energy}} C_6H_{12}O_6 + 6O_2$$

This equation, although properly balanced, gives an erroneous impression of the mechanism by which the reaction is accomplished. By the use of H_2O and CO_2 labelled with isotopic oxygen (O^{18}), biochemists have been able to demonstrate that the oxygen released in photosynthesis comes not from CO_2 but from water.

Definition. "Photosynthesis (*Photos* = light; *synthesis* = putting together) is an anabolic process in which green plants or green parts of the plants synthesize or manufacture complex carbonaceous organic food substances (carbohydrates) with carbon dioxide and water (respectively taken from air and water) in the presence of sunlight and evolve oxygen as a by-product. Thus, in this process radiant energy is converted into chemical energy."

However, green plants apart from taking nutrients from soil, make their own food by utilising carbon dioxide, water and sunlight. This is basis of photosynthesis. During this process, oxygen is evolved and released to the atmosphere.

A simple equation given by C. B. van Niel of Stanford University, U.S.A. is as follows :

$$CO_2 + 2H_2O \xrightarrow[\text{green plants}]{\text{light energy}} (CH_2O)_n + H_2O + O_2$$

During photosynthesis, carbon dioxide CO_2 is chemically reduced to carbohydrate $(CH_2O)_n$. Here, n is an integer.

In glucose, n is 6, *i.e.*, formula of glucose is $C_6H_{12}O_6$.

Water molecule splits in presence of light. This process is called *photolysis* and O_2 is released.

Thus, released O_2 comes from water and not from CO_2.

Importance of photosynthesis. Food is the source of energy needed by animal and plant life. And this food is manufactured by green plants from inorganic substances with the aid of sunlight energy during photosynthesis. Food represents the stored energy of sunrays. Fuel in the form of wood is also the indirect result of photosynthesis activity of plants and it is also thought that coal, petroleum, etc., are also the remote consequences of photosynthesis. A number of other substances are also produced as the by-products, for example, the oxygen needed by animals and human being continues to be supplied by photosynthesis.

Historical Perspective

Study on photosynthesis originated only about 300 years ago.

For the first time Belgian physician, Jan Baptista van Helomont, on the basis of his simple experiment concluded that all the substance of the plant was produced from the water and none from the soil.

By the end of the eighteenth century, Joseph Priestley (1733-1804), in 1771-72, performed first experiment on photosynthesis, and showed that plants have ability to take up CO_2 from the atmosphere and release O_2.

Later, Dutch physician Jan Ingenhousz (1730-1799), in 1780 confirmed Prietley's work, and made following important conclusions:

(*i*) The evolution of O_2 took place only within a few hours and not weeks.

(*ii*) The evolution of O_2 took place only during day time, *i.e.*, in presence of sunlight.

(*iii*) Only green parts of plants could restore used air.

Ingenhousz was first to give an equation for photosynthesis :

$$CO_2 + H_2O \xrightarrow[\text{green plants}]{\text{light}} O_2 + \text{Organic matter}$$

In 1804, a Swiss scholar Nicholas Theodore de Saussure observed that water is essential for photosynthesis. He also correlated the importance of light during intake of CO_2 and evolution of O_2.

In 1837, Dutrochet experimentally demonstrated that chlorophyll is necessary for photosynthesis.

In 1845, Liebig told that CO_2 is the main source of all organic compounds synthesised by green plants.

In 1864, Sachs told for first time that organic matters produced by plants were carbohydrates.

SITE FOR PHOTOSYNTHESIS

Photosynthesis takes place only in the green parts of the plants, such as leaves, stems, etc.

Within a leaf photosynthesis occurs particularly in **mesophyll cells** which have **chloroplasts**.

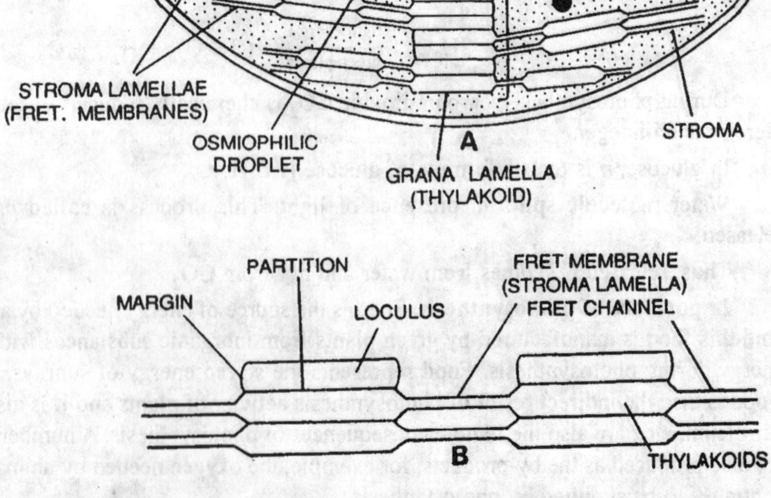

Fig. 18.1. Chloroplast. A, internal structure; B, few enlarged thylakoids from two grana.

Table 18.1. Advancement of Photosynthesis in Twentieth Century.

Year	Scientists	Work
1905	Blackman	Explained and formulated the law of limiting factors; discovered the existence of dark reaction in photosynthesis.
1920	Warburg	Introduced the unicellular green algae *Chlorella* as a suitable material to study photosynthesis.
1931	Van Neil	Reported that O_2 is released by the photolysis of water and not from CO_2.
1932	Emerson and Arnold	Reformed the 'flashing light experiment' to show the existence of light and dark reactions.
1937	Hill	Demonstrated 'photolysis of water by isolated chloroplasts' in the presence of suitable electron acceptor.
1941	Ruben and Kamen	Demonstrated that the oxygen given out during photosynthesis is from water by using O^{18} isotope.
1954	Arnon, Allen and Whatley	Used radioactive CO_2 (*i.e.*, $^{14}CO_2$) to show fixation of C by isolated chloroplasts.
1954	Calvin (Nobel Prize, 1960)	Traced the path of carbon in photosynthesis and established C_3 cycle (Calvin cycle).
1957	Emerson *et. al.*	Reported two photosystems PS I and PS II.
1963	Park and Sane	Reported that light reactions take place on the thylakoid membranes in grana and dark reactions occur in the stroma of the chloroplasts.
1965	Hatch and Slack	Reported C_4 pathway for CO_2 fixation in certain tropical grasses.
1970	Kok *et. al*	Reported that an unknown water oxidising enzyme complex is associated with photooxidation of water.
1985	Huber, Michael and Dissenhofer (Nobel prize in Chemistry in 1988)	Crystallized the photosynthetic reaction centre of bacterium *Rhodobacter* and analysed its structure by X-ray diffraction.

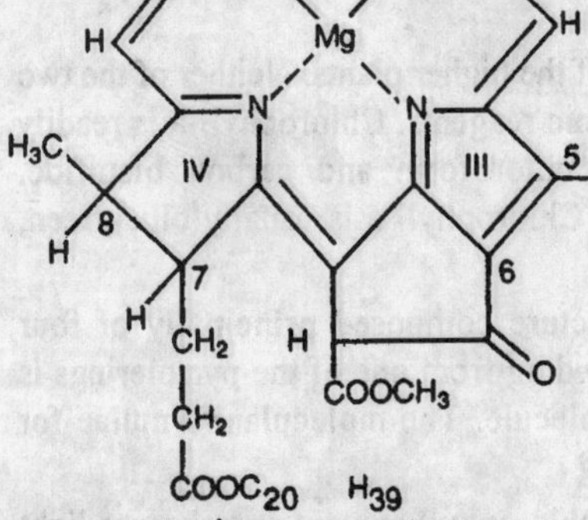

Fig. 18.2. Structural formula of Chlorophyll a.

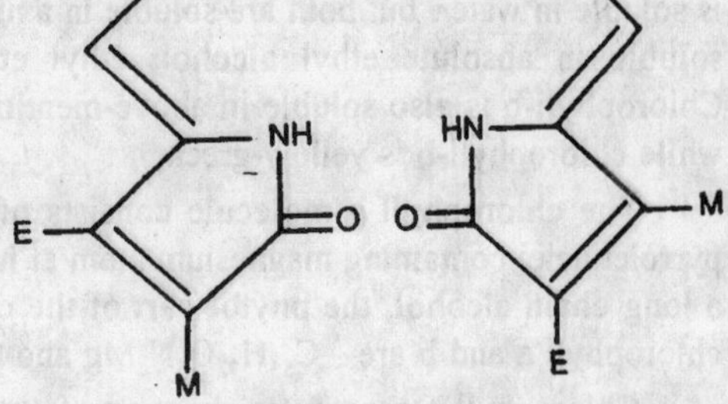

Fig. 18.3. Structure of Phycoerythrobilin.

Chloroplasts make actual sites for photosynthesis in green plants. Chloroplasts are located at the outer margins with their broad surfaces parallel to the cell wall of the mesophyll cells.

This type of arrangement helps in easy diffusion of CO_2 required for photosynthesis from atmosphere to the inside of chloroplasts.

Chloroplast

The complex process of photosynthesis takes place from beginning to end in the chloroplast. The absorption of light energy and carbon dioxide and the conversion of the carbon dioxide to starch and evolution of oxygen all take place within the illuminated chloroplast.

Structure of the chloroplast. The contents of the fully developed chloroplast are enclosed in an envelope consisting of two membranes with an enclosed space. Each membrane being 40 to 60 Å thick and the space between them vary from 25 to 75 Å. Inside is filled with proteinaceous matrix called stroma contains starch grains and osmophilic droplets. Eye spots and pyrenoid bodies, often found in algal cells, are also found in the matrix (stroma).

Several membranes stacked on top of each other are exhibited in the cross section of the chloroplast. These membranes are paired, forming stacks of discs. On or within the lamellae the chlorophyll and other pigments are found. In the lower forms of plant life, the pigments are evenly distributed over the entire surface of the lamellae, while in the higher forms of plant life, they are restricted to certain areas of lamellae. If these concentrated areas are layered one on the top of the other, the complete stack is known as a **granum**. According to Wolken (1961) and Calvin (1959) the chloroplast is a lamellar structure composed of lipid and aqueous protein layers.

The thylakoids in the chloroplasts contain most of the machinery for photochemical reactions of photosynthesis they contain pigments required for capturing solar energy. The most important pigments are chlorophylls.

Chlorophyll Pigments

The chlorophylls, the green pigments of plants, are the most important pigments active in the process of photosynthesis. There are at least eight types of chlorophyll pigments. They are chlorophyll a, b, c, d, and e; bacteriochlorophyll-a; bacteriochlorophyll-b and chlorobium chlorophyll (bacterioviridin); of these chlorophyll a is most nearly of universal occurrence being present, in all photosynthetic organisms except the green and purple bacteria. Chlorophyll b is found in all higher plants and in the green algae, but is not found in algae of most other classes (*e.g.*, blue-green, brown and red algae). The other chlorophylls (*i.e.*, c, d and e) are found only in algae and in combination with chlorophyll a, bacteriochlorophyll (a and b) are present in the purple bacteria, whereas the green bacteria contain the pigment called bacteriovir-idin (chlorobium chlorophyll). All of the chlorophylls are very similar in chemical composition and all of them are compounds which contain magnesium.

Chlorophyll a and b are the characteristic chlorophylls of the higher plants. Neither of the two is soluble in water, but both are soluble in a number of organic reagents. Chlorophyll-a is readily soluble in absolute ethyl alcohol, ethyl ether, acetone, chloroform and carbon bisulfide. Chlorophyll-b is also soluble in above-mentioned reagents. Chlorophyll a is usually blue-green, while chlorophyll-b is yellow-green.

The chlorophyll a molecule consists of a cyclic structure composed principally of four pyrrolenuclei containing magnesium atom at its centre. Extending from one of the pyrrolerings is a long chain alcohol, the phytol part of the chlorophyll molecule. The molecular formulae for chlorophyll a and b are—$C_{55}H_{72}O_5N_4Mg$ and $C_{55}A_{70}O_6N_4Mg$

Chlorophyll b constitutes about one-fourth of the total chlorophyll content and absorbs light of different wavelength than the chlorophyll a. On absorbing light, the chlorophyll b molecule is excited and transfers its energy to the chlorophyll a molecule. Finally, the chlorophyll a molecule converts the light energy into electrical energy by bringing about charge separation. Here, chlorophyll a molecules act as **reaction centres**.

The Carotenoids (Carotenoid Pigments)

The carotenoids are lipid compounds. They are found to be distributed widely in both animals and plants. They are red, orange, yellow and brownish pigments. They are present in variable concentrations in nearly all higher plants and many microorganisms such as — red and green algae, photosynthetic bacteria and fungi.

β-carotene, the major carotenoid is orange-yellow pigment and found in plant tissues. This is generally accompanied by a-carotene.

The carotenoids which consist of carbon and hydrogen are known as **carotenes**, while the carotenoids containing oxygen are called **xanthophylls** which are found more frequently in nature than the carotenes. The major xanthophylls are generally found in green leaves.

The carotenoids are located in the chloroplasts and chromatophores. They occur there as water-insoluble protein complexes.

Like chlorophyll carotenoids are also embedded in the thylakoid membranes of chloroplasts. These accessory pigments act as antenna complexes and procure light from different regions of the spectrum than the chlorophyll. The light captured by these pigments is transferred to the reaction centres of chlorophyll-a for conversion into electrical energy. The accessory pigments (carotenoids) and the reaction centre (chlorophyll-a), together form **photosystem**.

Phycobilins

The phycobilins are found only in algae. The red and blue phycobilins are called **phycoerythrins** and **phycocyanins**, respectively. They are active in the transfer of light energy to chlorophyll for utilization in the process of photosynthesis. The role of phycobilins and carotenoids is indirect in the sense that the energy they absorb is transferred to chlorophyll before it becomes active in photosynthesis.

PHOTOCHEMICAL AND BIOSYNTHETIC PHASES

Radiant Energy

The pigment system of the chloroplast first absorbs light energy and then passes it on via intermediates to the products of photosynthesis.

When a chlorophyll molecule absorbs a light quantum (*i.e.*, photon) the molecule is excited; it means that it has been brought from its normal ground state to an excited state (*i.e.*, higher energy level). All quanta are not able to lift chlorophyll to a higher state of energy. Firstly the light is being absorbed and, therefore, the quantum absorbed possesses a sufficient amount of energy to facilitate this job. The quantum energy may be determined from the wavelength of radiation; the shorter the wavelength greater the energy.

White light, as it comes from the sun is composed of different wavelengths, ranging from the relatively long waves of red light, through successively shorter waves to violet light. **Wave length** (l) denotes the linear length by which a wave travels forward in one complete vibration. This is generally shown by units such as millimicron (mμ) or Angstrom (Å)—(1 cm = 10^{-8} Å). When white light is passed through a glass prism, it is resolved into these colours. The band of colours, is the visible spectrum. The complete visible spectrum is composed of red, orange, yellow, green, blue, indigo and violet colours. Our eyes can perceive only the **visible rays** whose wave lengths are between 390 nm to 780 nm. The wavelengths exist that we are unable to perceive with our eyes. Beyond the red are still longer, invisible rays, the **infrared**; and beyond the violet are

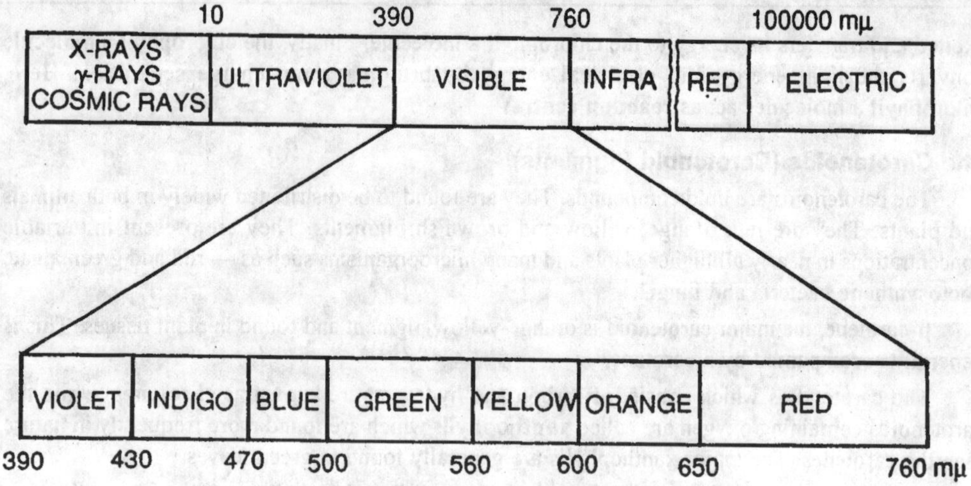

Fig. 18.4. Spectrum of radiant energy.

shorter, invisible rays, the **ultraviolet**. This way, the visible rays represent only a part of the radiant energy that comes to the earth from the sun. Here only a part of the visible spectrum is effective in photosynthesis.

Chlorophyll, however, is a pigment that gives green colour to the leaves. It absorbs light in the violet and blue wavelengths, and also in the red region of the visible spectrum of the light. This portion of the spectrum between 400 nm and 700 nm is called **photosynthetically active radiation (PAR)**. As chlorophylls reflect the green light, thus they impart green colour to the leaves.

Transfer of Energy

Not all of the pigment molecules absorb light or are activated at once. Light energy absorbed by one pigment molecule is thought to be transferred through many other pigment molecules before reaching its site of action. All the pigments except chlorophyll a are known as accessory pigments. Here the transfer of light energy may be from one chlorophyll a molecule to another, from chlorophyll b to chlorophyll a, from carotenoids to chlorophyll a, or from phycobilins to chlorophyll a.

The energy can be transferred from molecule to molecule as follows—the normal state of molecules is known as **ground state** or

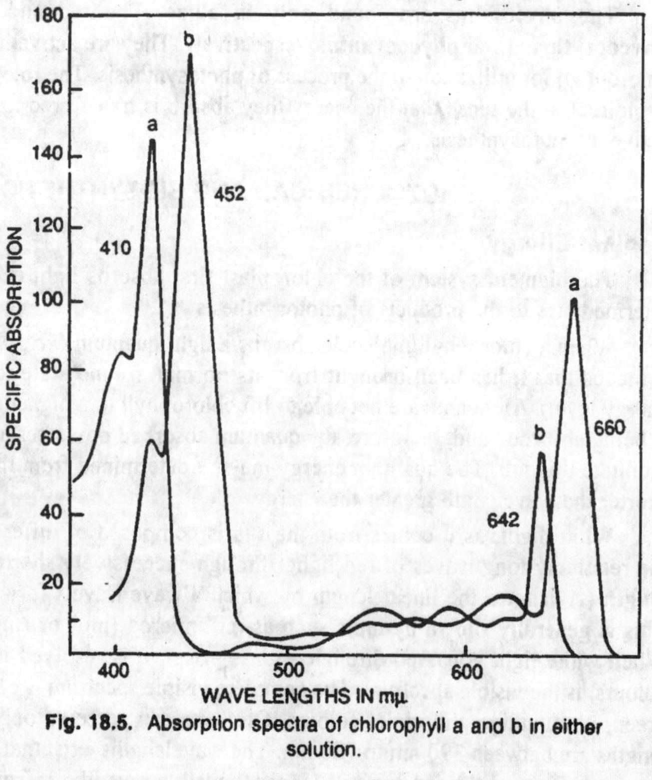

Fig. 18.5. Absorption spectra of chlorophyll a and b in either solution.

singlet state. When an electron of a molecule or atom absorbs a quantum of light, (light rays consist of tiny particles known as **photons**. The energy carried by a photon is known as **quantum** which is represented by **hv**.) It is raised to a higher energy level which is called **excited second singlet** state. This is unstable and has a half-life to 10^{-12} seconds.

The electron comes to the next higher energy level by the loss of some of its extra energy in the form of **heat**. This is called as excited first singlet state and is also unstable with a half life of 10^{-9} seconds.

From the first singlet state the excited electron may return to the ground state in two ways: (*i*) either losing its remaining extra energy in the form of heat, or (*ii*) by losing extra energy in the form of **radiant energy**. The latter process is known as **fluorescence**. The substances which show this property of fluorescence emit fluorescent light **only during the period they are exposed to incident light**. Secondly, the **fluorescent light is of higher wavelength than the incident light**. It is because some energy lost during the change of excited second singlet state to excited first singlet state.

The excited molecule or the atom may also lose its electronic excitation energy by **'internal conversion'** and comes to another exicited state known as triplet state which is **metastable** with a half life of 10^{-3} seconds. In this excited state the electron carrying extra energy can take part in further reaction.

From the triplet state the excited molecule or the atom may return to the ground state in three ways: (*i*) by losing its remaining extra energy in the form of heat: (*ii*) by losing the extra energy in the form of radiant energy. The latter process is termed **phosphorescence**. The substances which show this property of phosphorescence emit phosphorescent light **even after the incident radiant light is cut off**. Secondly, the **phosphorescent light is of higher wave length than the incident light and also fluorescent light**; (*iii*) the electron carrying the extra energy may be expelled from the molecule and is consumed in some further chemical reaction and a fresh normal electron returns to the molecule and is consumed in some further chemical reactions and a fresh normal electron which has now become unexcited returns to the molecule. **This is what exactly happens with excited triplet state of chlorophyll-a molecule which takes part in primary photochemical reaction in photosynthesis.**

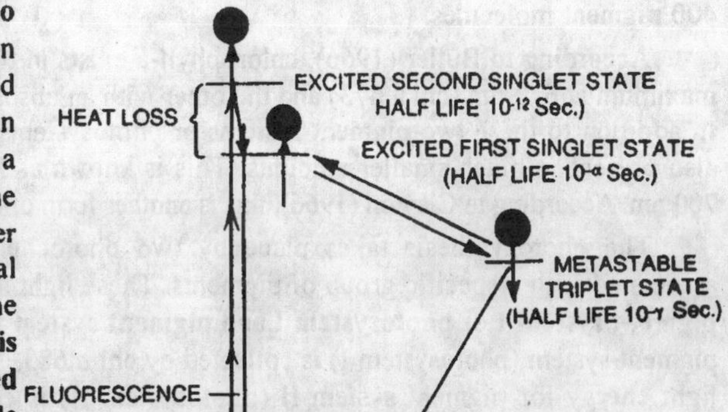

Fig. 18.6. Diagram to show excitation of molecules to fluorescence or phosphorescence.

Two Pigment Systems (Photosystems I and II)

Chlorophyll a is present in different forms, which have maximum absorption at different wavelengths of visible sight. Here, one of the forms shows an absorption peak at a wavelength of 673 nanometers (nm) and is called **chl a 673**.

Table 18.2. Differences between Photosystem I and Photosystem II

Photosystem I (PS I)	Photosystem II (PS II)
1. It is involved both in the cyclic and non-cyclic photophosphorylation.	1. It is involved only in non-cyclic photophosphorylation.
2. It receives the electrons from the photosystem II. This system produces a strong reductant which reduces $NADP^+$ to $NADPH_2$	2. PS II donates electron to PS I where $NADP^+$ is reduced.
3. Molecular oxygen is not evolved in this system.	3. This system is responsible for the photolysis of water and involves the evolution of molecular oxygen.
4. PS I is located on the outer surface of the thylakoid, *i.e.*, appressed regions of grana.	4. It is located on the inner surface of the thylakoid, *i.e.*, in the stroma and non-appressed region of grana.
5. The reaction centre of PS I is P_{700}.	5. The reaction centre of PS II is P_{680}.
6. Chlorophyll, carotenoid pigments are in the ratio 20-30 : 1.	6. Chlorophyll, carotenoid pigments are in the ratio of 3-7 : 1.
7. Chlorophyll *a* with maximum absorption at 700 nm (P_{700}).	7. Chlorophyll *a* with peak absorption at 680 nm (P_{680}).

In the similar way two other forms of chlorophyll a are **chl a 683 (P_{680})** and **chl a 703 (P_{700})**, with peak absorption at 683 and 703 nm, respectively. These pigment are anchored in thylakoids in separate units of organisation called **photosystems**. A single photosystem consists of about 250 to 400 pigment molecules.

According to Butler (1966), chlorophyll-a exists in two forms, one form with an absorption maximum at 673 nm (chl a 673) and the other with an absorption maximum at 683 nm (chl a 683). In addition to these two pigment systems or photosystems a long wave absorbing chlorophyll is also present in much smaller amounts. This is known as P 700 with an absorption maximum at 700 nm. According to Clayton (1966), this is another form of chlorophyll. Here, P stands for pigments.

The photosynthesis takes place by two photochemical processes, each process being associated with a specific group of pigments. These light absorbing group of pigments are called **pigment system I** or **photosystem I** and **pigment system II** or **photosystem II.** Light energy for pigment system (photosystem I) is collected by chl *a* 683, P 700 and the carotenoids, whereas the light energy for pigment system II (photosystem II) is collected by chl *a* 673, chlorophyll b, phycobilins (Jones and Myers, 1964). The primary function of the two photosystems (PS I and II), which interact with each other is to trap light energy and convert it to the chemical energy (ATP). This chemical energy (ATP) is utilised by living cells.

Photosynthetic Unit

Now this has been proved that the chloroplasts are composed of numerous minute photosynthetic units. A photosynthetic unit is the smallest group of collaborating pigment molecules necessary to effect a photochemical act. Park and Biggins (1946) isolated the photosynthetic unit from chloroplast lamellae. They called the photosynthetic units as **quantasomes**.

Hydrogen acceptor. There are two principal forms of hydrogen acceptor which can receive hydrogen from a substrate under the action of the appropriate dehydrogenase.

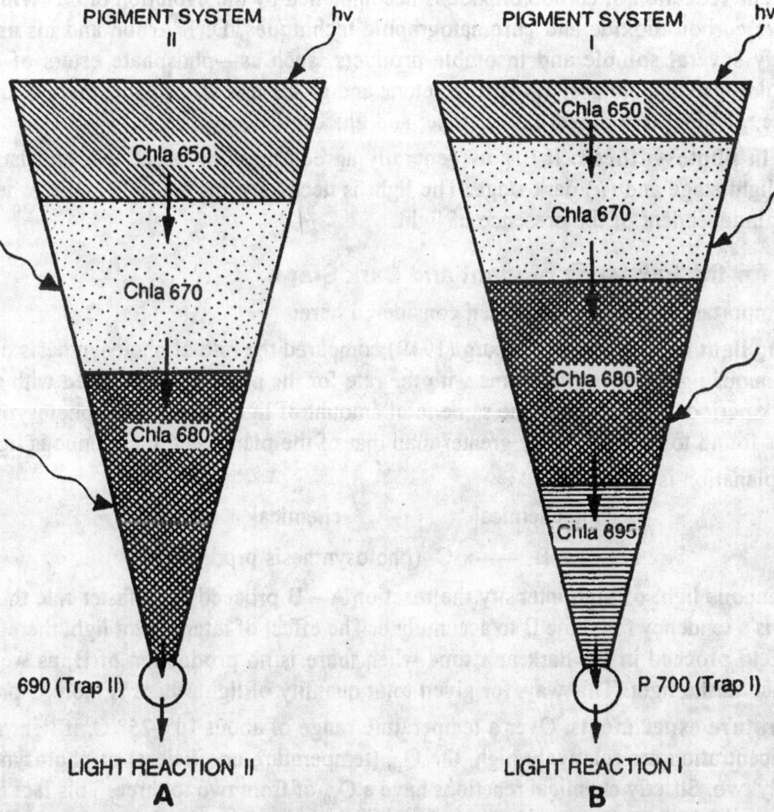

Fig. 18.7. A hypothetical scheme for the distribution of the chlorophyll in two pigment systems in green algae and higher plants.

According to the latest nomenclature, recommended by the international commission they are:

Coenzyme I–nicotinamide adenine dinucleotide (NAD)

Coenzyme II–nicotinamide adenine dinucleotide phosphate (NADP).

Adenosine triphosphate (ATP). This compound occurs in all living cells and consists of the nucleotide adenosine (A) and three phosphate radicals (—P).

A—P—P—P

For the most part it is only ATP which is able to carry out the actual transference of the high energy phosphate. (~ P) so that the ~ P formed from low energy sources is used to regenerate ATP from adenosine diphosphate (ADP) rather than be used directly.

"ATP is the main fuel of life produced in photosynthesis and oxidative phosphorylation. In both cases it is produced by an electric current, that is, energy released by a 'dropping' electron".

MECHANISM OF PHOTOSYNTHESIS

Carbon dioxide assimilation. Arnon is 1954 found that isolated chloroplasts under suitable experimental conditions, could assimilate CO_2. The enzymes involved in the reduction (assimilation) of carbon dioxide, therefore, must be present and perhaps produced within the chloroplast. The reduction of carbon dioxide is accompanied by the evolution of O_2. With the use of radioactive carbon dioxide and chromatographic techniques, D. I. Arnon and his associates could identify several soluble and insoluble products, such as—phosphate esters of glucose; fructose; ribulose; sedoheptulose; dihydroxyacetone and glyceric acid; glycolic, malic and aspartic acids; alanine, glycine; free dihydroxy-acetone; and glucose.

Stages in photosynthesis. It is now generally agreed that photosynthesis consists of two stages— (*i*) light stage and (*ii*) dark stage. The light is necessary for the light stage, whereas the dark stage is independent of the presence of light.

Evidences for the Existence of Light and Dark Stage

Three important evidences have been considered here.

Flashing light experiments. Warburg (1919) compared the rate of photosynthesis of a plant kept in continuous light for a certain time with the rate for the plant when supplied with alternate light and dark periods but receiving the same total amount of light. The rate of photosynthesis of the latter was found to be sufficiently greater than that of the plant kept in continuous light.

The explanation is as follows :

$$A \xrightarrow{\text{Photochemical}} B \xrightarrow{\text{chemical}} C \text{ (photosynthesis product).}$$

In continuous light of high intensity the reaction A—B proceeds at a faster rate than B—C so that there is a tendency for some B to accumulate. The effect of intermittent light therefore is to enable B—C to proceed in the dark at a time when there is no production of B, as well as for B—C continue in the light. This way, for given total quantity of light, there is more C produced.

Temperature experiments. Over a temperature range of about 10°–25° C, if light intensity and CO_2 concentration are relatively high, the Q_{10} (temperature coefficient) of photosynthesis is approximately two. Strictly chemical reactions have a Q_{10} of from two to three. This fact indicates that at least one of the reactions involved in photosynthesis is of purely chemical type. Since this fact was first pointed out by Blackman, this reaction is known as **Blackman reaction**. This is also called the **dark reaction**, since it does not require light and therefore, may take place in either the light or the dark.

A chemical reaction which proceeds only at the expense of absorbed light is called a photochemical reaction. The Q_{10} of a photochemical reaction is approximately one.

Temperature coefficient Q_{10}. The temperature coefficient of a physiological, chemical or physical process is the ratio of the process at any stated temperature of the rate at a lower temperature usually 10° C lower, and designed as the Q_{10} of the process. Thus, if a process is 2.3 times as fast at 25° as at 15° C, the temperature coefficient, Q_{10} is 2.3.

Temperature does not accelerate photochemical reactions. Under conditions of high light intensity, increased temperature accelerates the reaction B—C at the expense of the excess B (Q_{10} = 2).

When there is a low light intensity, A—B is slower than B—C will not affect the overall production of C. The limiting reaction A—B is photochemical (Q_{10} = 1):

Dark pick-up of CO_2. Under conditions of intense illumination but lacking CO_2, 'B' would accumulate and this would react with CO_2 in the dark.

ELECTRON TRANSPORT CHAIN

Photosystem II (PS II)

The light-driven reaction of photosynthesis also called **light reaction (Hill reaction)**, referred to as **electron transport chain**, were first propounded by Robert Hill in 1939.

The electron transport chain of photosynthesis is initiated by absorption of light by **photosystem II (P_{680})**.

When P680 absorbs light, it is excited and its electrons are transferred to an **electron acceptor molecule**.

Therefore, P_{680} becomes a strong oxidising agent, and splits a molecule of water to release oxygen. This light-dependent splitting of water molecule is called **photolysis**.

However, manganese, calcium and chloride ions play important roles in photolysis of water.

After photolysis of water, electrons are generated, which are then passed to the **oxidised** P_{680}.

Now, the electron deficient P_{680} (as it had already transferred its electrons to an acceptor molecule) is able to restore its electrons from the water molecule.

After accepting electron from the excited P_{680}, the primary electron acceptor is reduced. The primary electron acceptor in plants is **pheophytin**.

The reduced acceptor which is a strong reducing agent, now donates its electrons to the downstream components of the electron transport chain.

Photosystem I (PS I)

Similar to photosystem II (P_{680}), photosystem I (P_{700}) is excited on absorption of light and gets oxidised, and transfers its electrons to the primary electron acceptor (pheophytin), which, in turn gets reduced.

While the oxidised P_{700} draws electrons from photosystem II, the reduced electron acceptor of photosystem I, transfers electrons to ferredoxin and ferredoxin–NADP reductase to reduce NADP to $NADPH_2$.

$NADPH_2$ is a powerful reducing agent, and is utilised in the reduction of CO_2 to carbohydrates in the carbon reaction of photosynthesis.

The reduction of CO_2 to carbohydrates requires energy in the form of ATP, produced through electron transport chain.

Process of ATP formation from ADP in the presence of light in chloroplasts is called **photophosphorylation**.

The Light Reaction (Hill Reaction)

The light reaction is thought to be responsible for the production of a 'reducing power' and oxygen from water as a result of light energy. This is as follows :

The light energy, after absorption by chlorophyll, splits H_2O.

$$H_2O + \text{Light} \longrightarrow (H) + (OH)$$

(*i*) The (H) combines with an unidentified compound (probably ferredoxin) and is passed from this to NADP.

(*ii*) The $NADPH_2$ can cause the reduction of phosphoglyceric acid .... Phosphoglyceraldehyde, together with some ATP production.

(*iii*) The (OH) forms H_2O and oxygen :

$$4\,(OH) \longrightarrow 2H_2O + O_2$$

The light reaction gives rise to two very important production .... (*i*) a reducing agent $NADPH_2$ and (*ii*) an energy rich compound ATP. These two products of the light reaction are utilized in the dark phase of photosynthesis.

The energy transformations in photosynthesis are as follows :

(1) The radiant energy of an absorbed quantum is transformed into the energy of an activated pigment molecule

$$P + \text{Light energy} \longrightarrow P$$

(pigment molecule or activated pigment)

(2) Now the activated pigment removes an electron from the hydroxyl ion derived from the water molecule. The (OH) represents the 'free radical'. These are uncharged, but highly reactive forms.

$$H_2O \rightleftharpoons H_+ + OH^- + P$$

$$(OH)\ Pe^-$$

(3) The free radicals react in many ways; the release of oxygen and formation of free radicals of hydrogen takes place.

$$2\,(OH) \longrightarrow O_2 + 2\,(H)$$

(4) The H^+ ions from water, together with the electron attached to the pigment are transferred to certain molecules, which then carry the reducing power to other reactions.

$$NADP + H^+ + e^- \longrightarrow NADP.H$$

(reducing power)

(5) Another reaction is the recombination of the split products of water into the water molecules itself.

$$(H) + (OH) \longrightarrow H_2O$$

This reaction is strongly energy-releasing. The chloroplast puts this reaction to work by causing it to synthesize energy-rich ATP from a precursor molecule ADP and inorganic phosphate (P_i):

$$(H) + (OH) \longrightarrow H_2O \qquad ADP + P_i \longrightarrow ATP$$

(6) The energy of the ATP can now be used, in the reduction of CO_2 to sugar by the reducing power (NADP.H) generated in the light reaction.

$$CO_2 + NADP.H \xrightarrow{ATP \;\to\; ADP + P_i} (CH_2O) + H_2O + NADP$$

This way, the radiant energy has been converted to the chemical energy of the sugar molecule by passing through a photoactivated pigment, photolyzed water fragments, and ATP. The main function of light energy in photosynthesis is to produce ATP through a complex of reactions called **photophosphorylation.**

The subsequent reactions leading to the formation of sugar from CO_2 can proceed entirely in darkness.

Photophosphorylation

Photosynthetic phosphorylation. With the discovery that CO_2 can be assimilated in isolated chloroplasts, this came into existence that the chloroplast must contain the enzymes necessary for this assimilation and must be able to produce the ATP (adenosine tri-phosphate) essential for the formation of the main photosynthesis products. Arnon and his co-workers (1954) demonstrated that the isolated chloroplasts can produce ATP in the presence of light. They gave the name to this process **photosynthetic phosphorylation**. This was revealed for the first time that mitochondria are not the only cytoplasmic particles that produce ATP. ATP formation in chloroplasts differs from that in mitochondria in that it is free from respiratory oxidations. During this process the light energy is being converted to ATP. In other words, there is a conversion to light energy of chemical energy.

ATP is only one of the necessary requirements for the reduction of carbon dioxide to the carbohydrate level. A reductant must be formed in photosynthesis that will provide the hydrogens or electrons for this reduction. Arnon (1951) demonstrated that isolated chloroplasts are capable of reducing pyridine nucleotides in light. The photochemical reaction and an enzyme system are capable of utilizing the reduced pyridine nucleotide as soon as this was formed, Arnon *et al.*, (1957) found that NADP. H_2 is the reduced pyridine nucleotide in photosynthesis. In the presence of H_2O, ADP (adenosine di-phosphate) and orthophosphate (P), substrate amounts of NADP (nicotinamide adenine dinucleotide phosphate) were reduced, accompanied by the evolution of oxygen. The equation is as follows :

$$2ADP + 2P + 2NADP + 4H_2O \longrightarrow 2ATP + O_2 + 2NADPH_2 + 2H_2O$$

As shown by the equation the evolution of one molecule of oxygen is accompanied by the reduction of two molecules of NADP and esterification of two molecules of orthophosphate. Together, ATP and $NADPH_2$ provide the energy requirements for CO_2 assimilation. Arnon gave name to this power **assimilatory power** (*i.e.*, ATP + $NADPH_2$).

According to Arnon (1967), in bacterial photosynthesis $NADH_2$ is utilized of $NADPH_2$.

Ferredoxin. In the late 1950's the reduction of $NADP^+$ was thought to be associated with a soluble protein factor found in chloroplasts. Arnon *et al.* (1957) observed that this protein reduced $NADP^+$ accompanied by the evolution of oxygen. They termed it the 'NADP reducing factor.' Thereafter the NADP reducing factor was purified and called photosynthetic pyridine nucleotide reductase (PPNR), since its catalytic activity was only apparent when chloroplasts were kept in light (San Pietro and Lang, 1958). Tagawa and Arnon (1962) recognized that PPNR is one of a family of nonhemenonflavin, iron-containing proteins that is universally present in chloroplasts. These proteins were given a generic name **ferredoxin**.

When ferredoxin was not discovered, NADP was thought to be the terminal electron acceptor of the photosynthetic light reaction. Arnon (1967) revealed that illuminated chlorophyll reacts directly with ferredoxin and not with $NADP^+$. The exposition of chlorophyll to light causes a flow of electrons to ferredoxin. Now the reduced ferredoxin causes the reduction of $NADP^+$ in an enzyme catalyzed reaction that is independent of light (Arnon, 1967). In other words, ferredoxin is termed as terminal **electron acceptor** of the photosynthetic light reaction.

The reduction of NADP takes place by ferredoxin. Under normal condition, in photosynthesis ferredoxin reduced by the acceptance of an electron is immediately reoxidized by $NADP^+$. The reduction of NADP by ferredoxin is catalyzed by ferredoxin-NADP reductase. This shows that the mechanism of $NADP^+$ reduction in photosynthesis completes in three steps (Shin and Arnon, 1965). These steps are–(*i*) photochemical reduction of ferredoxin; (*ii*) reoxidation of ferredoxin by ferredoxin $NADP^+$ reductase and (*iii*) reoxidation of ferredoxin-$NADP^+$ reductase by $NADP^+$. According to Arnon there are two types of photophosphorylation: (*i*) non-cyclic photophosphorylation and (*ii*) cyclic photophosphorylation.

Non-cyclic photophosphorylation. This is a result of an interaction of photosystem I (PSI) and photosystem II (PSII). In non-cyclic photophosphorylation, the electron is not returned to the chlorophyll molecule, but is taken up by NADP ± which thereafter reduces to NADPH. Here the electron that returns to the chlorophyll molecule is derived from an outside source which is water.

In this process oxygen is released and both $NADPH_2^-$ and ATP are formed. In green plants and many photosynthetic bacteria, however, illumination is known to produce also $NADPH_2^-$ which provides hydrogen for the reduction of carbon dioxide in the day. The electron lost by the excited chlorophyll is accepted by NADP along with a proton resulting in the formation of $NADPH_2$. The light energy is now stored in the $NADPH_2$ molecule. The proton required for the reduction of NADP is released from the dissociation of water molecule by photolysis into hydrogen $H^{\pm}$ and hydroxyl ions OH.

$$2H_2O \longrightarrow 2H^+ + 2\,(OH)$$

The hydroxyl ions react to produce water and molecular oxygen. The reaction is as follows:

$$4\,(OH) \longrightarrow 2H_2O + O_2 + 4e^-$$

Here the hydroxyl ion also releases an electron that is accepted by the cytochromes of the chloroplast. In turn, the cytochrome donates this electron to the chlorophyll molecule, which already lost an electron earlier. The energy released during this transfer of electron from the cytochrome is utilized in the formation of ATP by the photophosphorylation of ADP.

In water molecule hydrogen is strongly bound to oxygen and this can be cleaved only by the use of energy. This energy is supplied by light. This way, in non-cyclic photophosphorylation light energy takes part in two processes, *i.e.*, the activation of chlorophyll molecule and photolysis (cleavage) of water.

In non-cyclic photophosphorylation one molecule of $NADPH_2$ and one molecule of ATP are produced by the activation of chlorophyll molecule by a photon, while in cyclic photophosphorylation two molecules of ATP are produced for each photon absorbed by chlorophyll. The overall reaction of photophosphorylation is as follows:

$$2ADP + 2iP + 4H_2O + 2NADP \xrightarrow{\text{Light}} O_2 + 2ATP + 2NADPH_2 + 2H_2O$$

Cyclic photophosphorylation. When non-cyclic photophosphorylation is stopped under certain conditions, cyclic photophosphorylation takes place. The non-cyclic photophosphorylation can be stopped by illuminating isolated chloroplasts with light of wavelength greater than 680 nm.

By this way, only photosystem I (PS I) is activated, as it has a maximum absorption at 700 nm, and photosystem II (PS II), which absorbs at 680 nm, remains inactivated.

Due to inactivation of PS II, the electron flow from water to NADP is stopped, and also CO_2 fixation is retarded.

When CO_2 fixation stops, electrons are not removed from reduced NADPH. Thus, NADPH will not be oxidised and NADP will not be available as an electron acceptor.

Under above-mentioned conditions, cyclic-photophosphorylation occurs.

During cyclic-photophosphorylation, electrons from photosystem I (PS I) are not passed to NADP from the electron acceptor, as NADP is not available in oxidised state to receive electrons.

Hence, the electrons are transferred back to P_{700}.

This type of movement of electrons from an electron acceptor to P_{700} result in the formation of ATP from ADP, and the process is called cyclic photophosphorylation.

During cyclic photophosphorylation oxygen is not released, as there is no photolysis of water and $NADPH_2$ is also not produced.

In cyclic photophosphorylation the excited electron lost by the chlorophyll is returned to it through vitamin K or FMN (flavin mononucleotide) and cytochromes. The chlorophyll molecule on losing an electron assumes a positive charge and subsequently the electron is transferred to a second acceptor. This second acceptor is a group of substances collectively known as **cytochrome**

system. All the members of cytochrome system are variants of cytochrome. Ultimately these cytochromes transfer the electron to the chlorophyll molecule from where it was lost initially.

The electromagnetic energy of the light is utilized in the formation of ATP. This means that light energy is being converted into chemical energy. Here the electron after leaving a chlorophyll travels in a cyclic way and ultimately returns to the same molecule from which it initiated, and therefore, this process has been termed by Arnon as cyclic photophosphorylation. The final electron acceptor and the initial electron donor is the same substance—the chlorophyll. No outside material takes part in the process. During cyclic photophosphorylation, one electron and two ATP molecules are formed. One ATP molecule is being formed when the electron travels from the cofactor (*i.e.*, vitamin K or FMN) to the cytochromes while the other when it travels from the cytochromes back to the chlorophyll molecule.

Here the light energy is being converted into chemical energy.

In nature both processes of photophosphorylation proceed simultaneously. In green plants the non-cyclic electron transfer is essential for the production of $NADPH_2$ and ATP. The oxygen is evolved during the process. The cyclic electron transfer fulfills the requirement of the low yield of ATP during non-cyclic process. This way, the complete light phase of photophosphorylation produces ATP and $NADPH_2$ and oxygen is evolved.

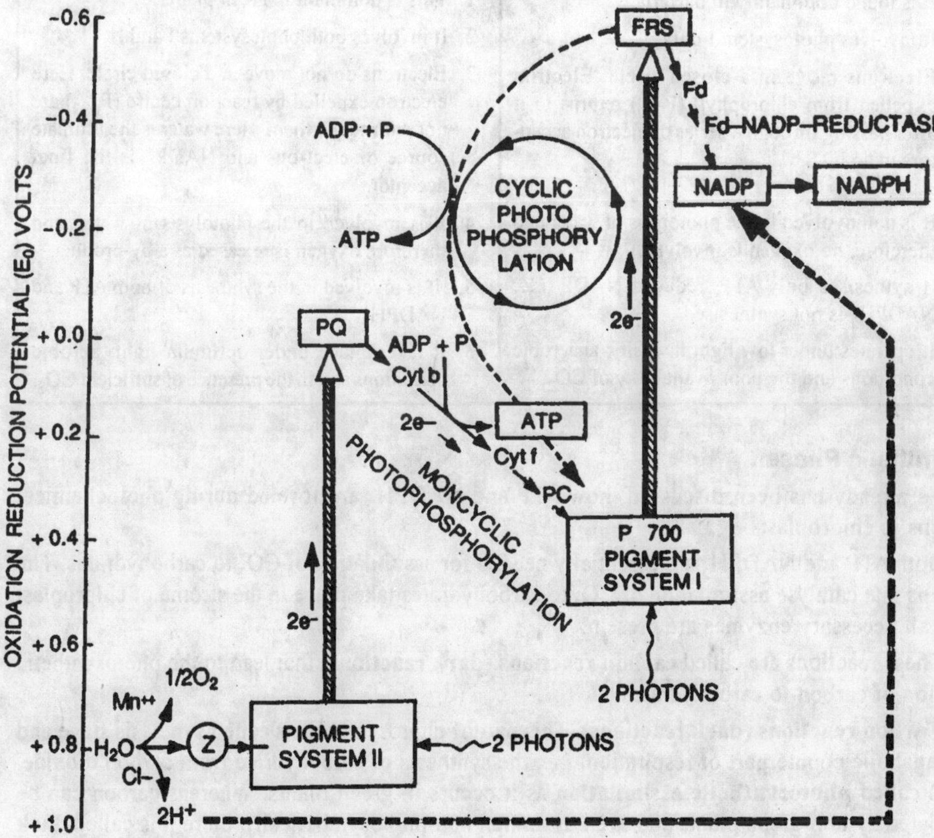

Fig. 18.8. Schematic representation of the electron transport and photophosphorylation in photosynthesis.

$NADPH_2$ is a biological reductant that brings about the reduction of carbon dioxide to carbohydrates in the dark phase of photosynthesis. Here both $NADPH_2$ and ATP provide energy for reduction. The assimilatory power of the cell is constituted by these two components. The energy of these components is derived from visible part of sunlight. In the dark phase of photosynthesis the energy, that is stored in $NADPH_2$ and ATP, is being transferred to the molecules of organic substances and stored there in the form of chemical energy.

During photosynthesis the electromagnetic energy of visible light is being converted into chemical energy. Now this energy is utilized by living cells as the driving force for various vital activities. This act of the conversion of energy is brought about by the photosynthetic cells of green plants or photosynthetic bacteria. Here the solar energy is trapped by the chlorophyll apparatus. As soon as the light energy is being transformed into chemical energy, it may be used in the formation of carbohydrates, protein synthesis and other important vital activities. The living are so designed that they can use only chemical energy for various metabolic activities. The light energy cannot be directly used for these vital activities. The light reaction of the higher plants takes place in the grana of the chloroplasts.

Table 18.3. Differences Between Cyclic and non-cyclic Photophosphorylation.

Cyclic photophosphorylation	Non-cyclic photophosphorylation
1. It is found dominantly in bacteria.	1. This is dominant in green plants.
2. It involves photosystem I only.	2. It involves both photosystems I and II.
3. Electrons move in a closed circle. Electron expelled from chlorophyll (P_{700}) returns to it after passing through a series of electron acceptors in an ETS.	3. Electrons do not move in a closed circle. Here electron expelled by reaction centre (P_{680}) are not returned to them. Here water is the ultimate source of electrons and $NADP^+$ is the final acceptor.
4. It is not involved in the photolysis of water and therefore, no oxygen is involved.	4. It is involved in the photolysis of water, and therefore oxygen is released as a by-product.
5. It sythesises only ATP, reduced NADP, *i.e.*, $NADPH_2$ is not synthesised.	5. It is involved in the synthesis of both ATP and $NADPH_2$.
6. It operates under low light intensity, anaerobic conditions and the poor availability of CO_2.	6. It takes place under optimum light, aerobic conditions and in the presence of sufficient CO_2.

Biosynthetic Phase

As already has been discussed, how ATP and $NADPH_2$ are formed during photochemical reactions in chloroplasts.

Both ATP and $NADPH_2$ are essentially needed for assimilation of CO_2 to carbohydrates. The reactions that catalyse assimilation of CO_2 to carbohydrates take place in the stroma of chloroplast where all necessary enzymes are present.

These reactions are called **carbon reactions (dark reactions)** that lead to the photosynthetic reduction of carbon to carbohydrates.

Carbon reactions (dark reactions). This part of photosynthesis is called synthesis stage and is the anabolic counterpart of respiration, *i.e.*, the synthesis of carbohydrate from carbon dioxide. This is called **photosynthetic assimilation** as it occurs in green plants. Whereas carbon can be assimilated by non-green plants and even by animal non-photosynthetically, there it is called **dark carbon** assimilation. Both these processes (dark C-assimilation and photosynthesis C-assimilation) differ in nature of end product. Carbohydrates are formed as a result of photosynthesis C-assimilation but organic acids are formed as end products in dark C-assimilation. During this process carbon dioxide and water build up carbohydrate, oxygen being released. Energy is absorbed in form of light energy and converted into chemical energy of carbohydrate molecule.

$$CO_2 + H_2O \xrightarrow[\text{Chlorophyll}]{\text{Light}} (CH_2O) + O_2$$

In first phase of carbon reactions (dark reactions), CO_2 is accepted by a 5-carbon molecule, ribulose-1, 5-bisphosphate (RuBP) and two molecules of 3-carbon compound, *i.e.*, 3-phosphoglycerate (PGA) are formed.

The 3-carbon molecule, *i.e.*, 3-phosphoglycerate, is first stable product, and therefore, this is called **C_3 pathway**.

Formation of 3-phosphoglycerate (PGA) is known as **carboxylation**. This reaction is catalysed by an enzyme called **ribulose bisphosphate carboxylase** (*i.e.*, **Rubisco**).

In addition to carboxylase activity this enzyme (Rubisco) also possesses oxygenase activity, and therefore abbreviated as **Rubisco** (*i.e.*, **ribulose bisphosphate carboxylase oxygenase**).

The oxygenase activity of the enzyme allows O_2 to complete with CO_2 for combining with RuBP (*i.e.*, **ribulose bisphosphate**) in photorespiration.

After carboxylation reaction, reduction of PGA takes place, where ATP and NADPH, formed during photochemical reactions are utilised.

With the reduction of PGA (*i.e.*, **3-phosphoglycerate**), **a carbohydrate, glyceraldehyde-**3-phosphate, is formed.

These 3-carbon molecules (carbohydrates) are also called **triose phosphates**. They are diverted from Calvin cycle and act as precursors for synthesis of sucrose and starch.

For the completion of Calvin cycle, and for its process of continuation, on its own, **regeneration** of the initial 5-carbon acceptor molecule, *i.e.*, ribulose-1, 5-bisphosphate (RuBP), takes place.

The regeneration of RuBP from glyceraldehyde-3-phosphate requires another ATP molecule formed with the result of photophosphorylation during light reactions.

Path of carbon in photosynthesis. Our knowledge of the path of carbon in photosynthesis comes mainly from a series of brilliant researches initiated by Melvin Calvin (1946) and his co-workers. They made use of the radioactive isotope of carbon, C^{14}, from which they prepared radioactive carbon dioxide (C^{14} O_2) and then fed this to unicellular algae—*Chlorella* and *Scenedesmus*—for periods of time ranging from five seconds to several minutes. After these short periods of photosynthesis in $C^{14}O_2$ the cells were plunged into boiling ethyl alcohol in order to kill them. The cells were instantaneously killed and their enzymes denatured. The compounds into which C^{14} had been incorporated by photosynthesis were then separated from the alcoholic extract. Among the many compounds found are:

Phosphoglyceric acid (a 3-C compound) after only five seconds exposure.

Phosphoglyceraldehyde
Dihydroxyacetone phosphate } after 30 seconds exposure.

Tetroses, pentoses, hexoses and heptoses after 90 seconds exposure.

After an exposure of only 5 seconds to $C^{14}O_2$ most of the radioactive carbon is found in 3-phosphoglyceric acid (3-PGA), a three carbon compound normally considered a constituent of glycolysis. Increase in the time of exposure to $C^{14}O_2$ to 30-90 seconds found most of the isotopic carbon in phosphoglyceraldehyde dihydroxyaçetone phosphate and hexose phosphates as well as 3-PGA.

The C_3 type of carbon reactions occur in the stroma of chloroplast. This **C_3 pathway** is also called **Calvin cycle** after its discoverer, Melvin Calvin, who was awarded Nobel Prize for the discovery of this pathway.

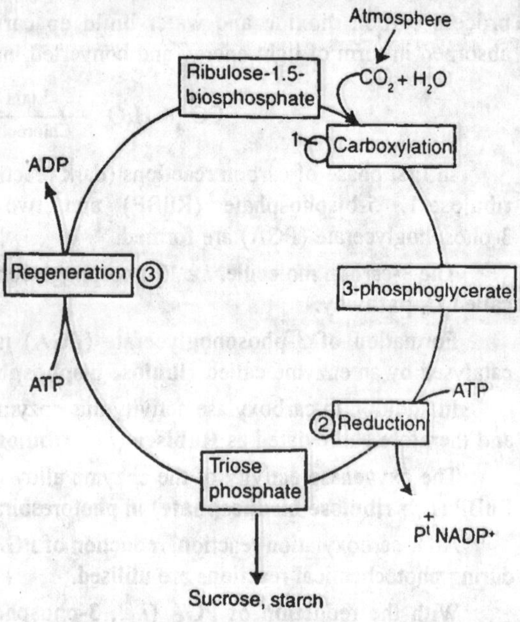

Fig. 18.9. Calvin Cycle.

Initial acceptor of carbon dioxide. The question arises as to what compound or compounds give rise to 3-PGA. In other words, what compound is the initial acceptor of the carbon dioxide molecule? It might be anticipated that the fed $C^{14}O_2$ would couple with some 2-carbon compound to produce the 3-carbon compound (3-PGA), but this seems not to be true. Calvin obtained evidence that a 5-carbon compound ribulose-1, 5, bisphosphate (RuBP), is formed from ribulose-5- phosphate. The $C^{14}O_2$ appears to attach to a 5-carbon compound ribulose-1, 5 bisphosphate (RuBP) to form an unstable 6-carbon compound, which then spontaneously decomposes to two PGA molecules. RuBP is now accepted to be the compound with which carbon dioxide first combines in photosynthesis under the influence of the enzyme, carboxydismutase. This has been confirmed that the 6-carbon compound formed by combination of CO_2 with RuBP is quite unstable and immediately splits to give rise to two molecules of PGA.

The study of the radioactive carbon labelling of the 7-carbon (C_7) and 5-carbon (C_5) sugar phosphates has shown that PGA was starting material for their synthesis and therefore, the precursor, not only of hexoses, but of RuBP.

$$\begin{array}{l} CH_2OPO_3H_2 \\ | \\ C=O \\ | \\ HCOH \\ | \\ HCOH \\ | \\ CH_2OPO_3H_2 \end{array} + C^{14}O_2 + H_2O \longrightarrow \begin{array}{l} CH_2OPO_3H \\ | \\ HCOH \\ | \\ C^{14}OOH \end{array} + \begin{array}{l} COOH \\ | \\ HCOH \\ | \\ CH_2OPO_3H \end{array}$$

Ribulose 1, 5 bisphosphate + CO_2 + H_2O $\longrightarrow$ 2, 3-phosphoglyceric acid.

The carboxylation enzyme occurs in chloroplasts together with phosphoribulokinase which catalyzes the following reaction.

$$\text{Ribulose 1, 5 -phosphate + ATP} \xrightarrow{\text{Phosphoribulokinase}} \text{ribulose 1, 5-diphosphate + ADP.}$$

PHOTORESPIRATION

Respiration that is initiated in chloroplasts and occurs in light only, is called **photorespiration**.

Photorespiration or glycolate pathway. It is interesting to know that in the plants possessing Calvin cycle, the enzyme RuBP carboxylase can initiate the reversal of photosynthetic reactions. This process occurs when there is low CO_2 concentration but high O_2 concentration. At mid-day, when temperature and CO_2 content are high, the affinity of RuBP carboxylase increases for O_2 but decreases for CO_2. Thus, it converts RuBP to 3-carbon compound (PGA) and a 2-carbon compound (phosphoglycolate). The phosphoglycolate is converted rapidly to glycolate in the peroxisomes. Glycolate is further converted to glycine, serine, CO_2 and NH_3 without the generation of ATP or NADPH. Thus net result is oxidation of organic food synthesized during photosynthesis. This process is called **photorespiration** or glycolate pathway as it occurs at high rate in the presence of light. As already mentioned that photorespiration is a loss to the net productivity of green plants having Calvin cycle. The green plants having Calvin cycle are **C_3 plants**. Overcoming photo-respiratory loss poses a challenge to plants growing in the tropics.

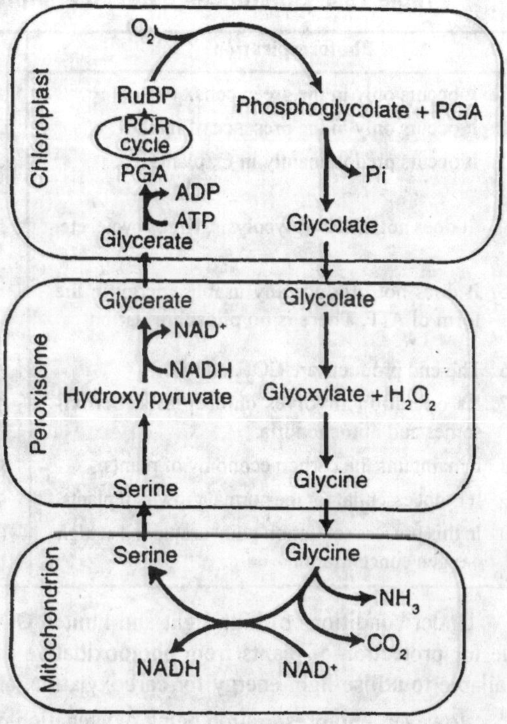

Fig. 18.10. Photorespiration.

Photorespiration occurs due to fact that the active site of enzyme Rubisco (ribulose bisphosphate carboxylase oxygenase) is same for both carboxylation and oxygenation.

The oxygenation of RuBP (ribulose bisphosphate) in the presence of O_2 is first reaction of photorespiration that leads to the formation of one molecule of phosphoglycolate, a two-carbon compound and one molecule of PGA.

Where PGA is used in Calvin cycle, and phosphoglycolate is dephosphorylated to form glycolate in the chloroplast.

From chloroplast, glycolate is diffused to **peroxisome** where it is oxidised to in glyoxylate. Here, glyoxylate is used to form amino acid, glycine. Now, glycine enters mitochondria where two glycine molecules (4 carbons) give rise to one molecule of serine (3 carbons) and one molecule of CO_2 (one carbon).

Now, serene is taken up by peroxisome, and through a series of reactions is being converted into glycerate.

This glycerate leaves the peroxisome and enters the chloroplast, where it is phosphorylated to form PGA.

Now PGA molecule enters the Calvin cycle to make carbohydrates, but one CO_2 molecule released in mitochondria during photorespiration has to be re-fixed. This means, 75 per cent of the carbon lost by the oxygenation of RuBP is recovered and 25 per cent is lost as release of one molecule of CO_2.

Photorespiration is also known as **photosynthetic carbon oxidation cycle**.

As already discussed in foregoing paragraph, this process involves an interaction of three organelles, *i.e.*, (*i*) chloroplast (*ii*) peroxisome and (*iii*) mitochondria.

Table 18.4. Differences between Photorespiration and Aerobic Respiration.

Photorespiration	Aerobic respiration
1. It occurs only in the green cells.	1. It occurs both in green and non-green cells.
2. It occurs only in the presence of light.	2. It occurs all the time irrespective of light.
3. It occurs predominantly in C_3 plants.	3. It takes place in all the plants, except anaerobic microbes.
4. It does not involve glycolysis, Krebs cycle, etc.	4. It involves glycolysis, Krebs cycle or terminal oxidation.
5. It does not produce any usable energy in the form of ATP. There is no phosphorylation.	5. It produces usable energy in the form of ATP. Substrate and oxidative phosphorylations take place.
6. The end products are CO_2 and PGA.	6. The end products are CO_2 and H_2O.
7. Its operation involves chloroplasts, peroxisomes and mitochondria.	7. Its operation involves cytoplasm, matrix and mitochondria only.
8. It maintains the carbon economy of plants.	8. There is no such role.
9. It is not essential for the normal growth of plants.	9. It is essential for the normal growth of plants.
10. In this process saturation point is attained at high oxygen concentration.	10. Here saturation point is attained at comparatively lower oxygen concentration.

Under conditions of high light and limited CO_2 supply, photorespiration plays an important role for protection of plants from photooxidative damage. This shows that if enough CO_2 is not available to utilise light energy for carboxylation, and excess energy inflicts damage to plants.

However, photorespiration being oxygenation of RuBP, utilises part of light energy and saves the plant from photooxidative damage.

The relative levels of O_2 and CO_2 are responsible for determination of the occurrence of photorespiration as both of these gases (O_2 and CO_2) compete for the same active site of enzyme Rubisco.

Increased O_2 level increases photorespiration; while increased CO_2 level decreases photorespiration, and increases C_3 photosynthesis.

Photorespiration and aerobic respiration. Photorespiration is not related to aerobic respiration. Aerobic respiration occurs throughout day and night in all types of cells, whereas photorespiration occurs in illuminated cells only. The main differences between photorespiration and aerobic respiration are as follows :

C_4 PATHWAY (HATCH-SLACK PATHWAY)

The discovery of C_4 cycle in monocots such as sugarcane, maize and sorghum has indicated that these plants have solved the problem of photorespiration. The carbon dioxide is fixed in the mesophyll cells. The initial product being a-4 carbon compound, the process is called C_4 pathway of carbon dioxide fixation.

Hatch-Slack pathway. Two Australian botanists Hatch and Slack (1966) discovered that there are two types of chloroplasts in sugarcane. One type restricted to bundle sheath cells have the normal grana. These chloroplasts carry on Hatch-Slack or C_4 cycle. Hence, Hatch-Slack cycle or C_4 cycle has been found in most monocots and some dicots. The plants having C_4 cycle are known as C_4 plants, and the plants C_3 (Calvin cycle) are C_3 plants.

Photorespiration occurs in C_3 plants (Calvin cycle), which leads to a 25 percent loss of the fixed CO_2. Photorespiration occurs in C_3 plants only, as the enzyme Rubisco catalysis both carboxylation and oxygenation reactions of the initial acceptor molecule that is RuBP.

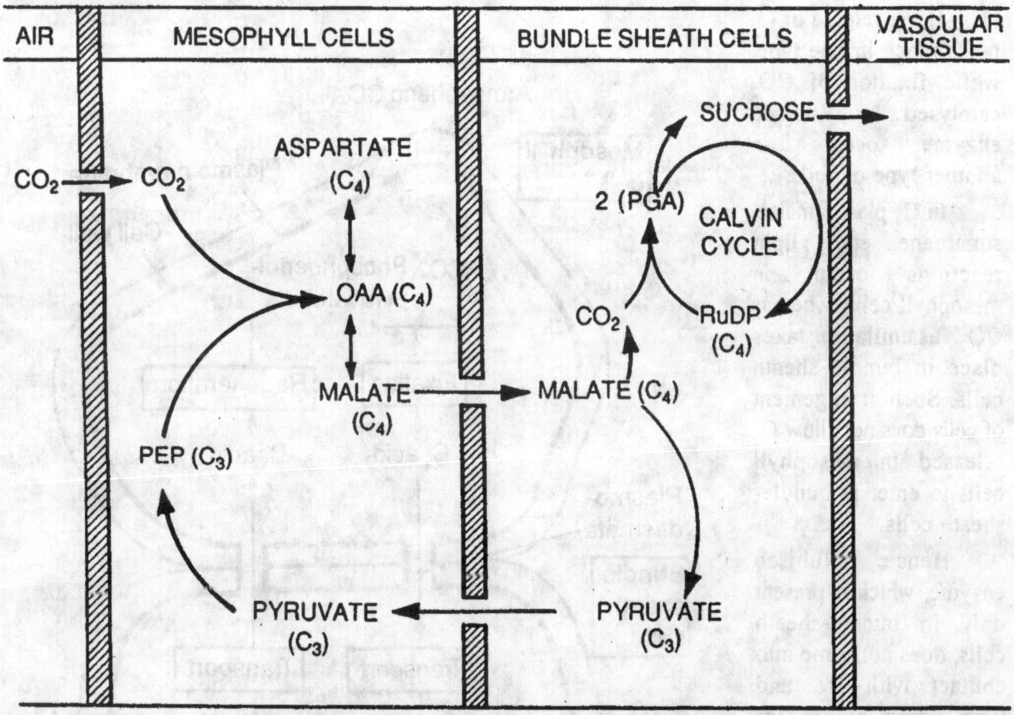

Fig. 18.11. Hatch Slack Pathway of CO_2 fixation.

In C_3 plants, photosynthesis occurs only in mesophyll cells. Photosynthesis has two types of reactions, *i.e.*, light reactions and carbon or dark reactions.

In light reactions, ATP and $NADPH_2$ are produced, and as a result of photolysis of water O_2 is released.

During carbon or dark reactions, CO_2 is assimilated and carbohydrates are produced.

As both light reactions and carbon (dark) reactions occur in mesophyll cells in C_3 plants, it becomes essential for enzyme Rubisco to catalyse both oxygenation and carboxylation reactions of RuBP, simultaneously.

However, in category of C_4 plants, nature has evolved a mechanism to avoid occurrence of photorespiration, which is thought to be a harmful process.

C_4 pathway requires the presence of two types of photosynthetic cells, *i.e.*, mesophyll cells and bundle sheath cells. The bundle sheath cells are arranged in a wreath like manner. This kind of arrangement of cells is called **Kranz anatomy** (Kranz : wreath). In Kranz anatomy, the mesophyll and bundle sheath cells are connected by plasmodesmata or cytoplasmic bridges.

The C_4 plants contain dimorphic chloroplasts. The chloroplasts in mesophyll cells are granal, whereas in bundle sheath cells they are agranal.

The granal chloroplasts contain thylakoids which are stacked to form grana, as formed in C_3 plants. However, in agranal chloroplasts of bundle sheath cells, grana are absent and thylakoids are present only as stroma lamellae.

The presence of two types of cells (granal and agranal) allows occurrence of **light** and **carbon (dark)** reactions separately in each type.

Here, release of O_2 takes place in one type, while fixation of CO_2 catalysed by Rubisco enzyme occurs in another type of cells.

In C_4 plants (maize, sugarcane, etc.), light reactions occur in mesophyll cells, whereas CO_2 assimilation takes place in bundle sheath cells. Such arrangement of cells does not allow O_2 released in mesophyll cells to enter in bundle-sheath cells.

Hence, Rubisco enzyme, which is present only in bundle-sheath cells, does not come into contact with O_2, and thus, oxygenation of RuBP is completely avoided.

In C_4 plants, a CO_2 concentrating mechanism is present which helps in reducing the occurrence of photorespiration (*i.e.*, oxygenation of initial acceptor RuBP). This type of CO_2 concentrating mechanism is called **C_4 pathway.**

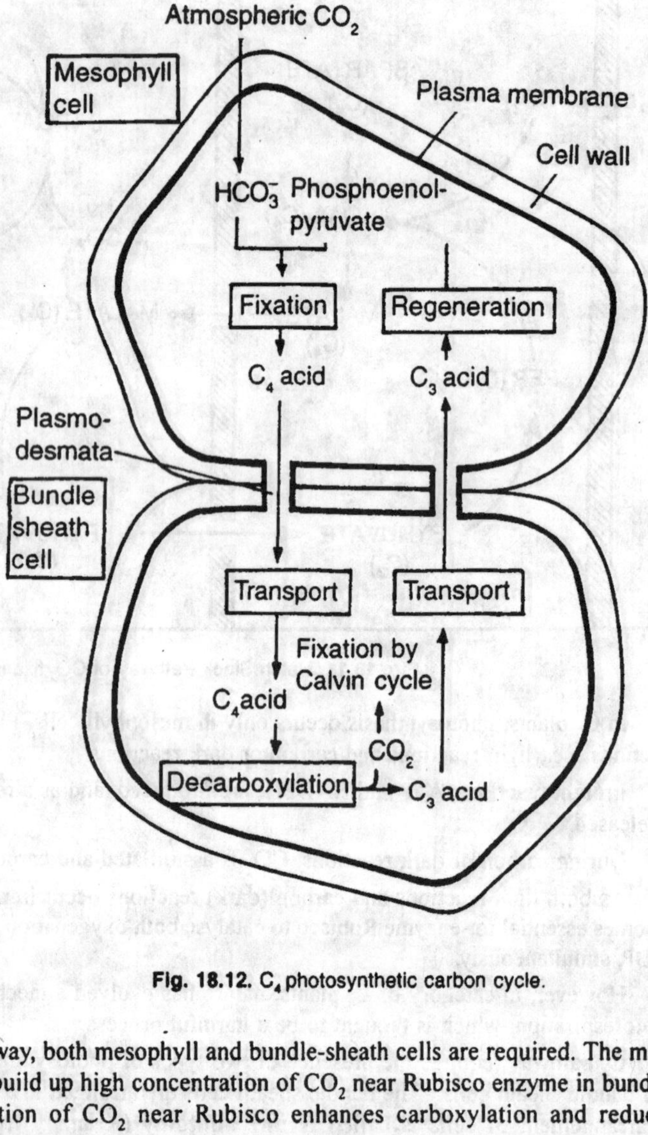

Fig. 18.12. C_4 photosynthetic carbon cycle.

For operation of C_4 pathway, both mesophyll and bundle-sheath cells are required. The main objective of C_4 pathway is to build up high concentration of CO_2 near Rubisco enzyme in bundle-sheath cells. High concentration of CO_2 near Rubisco enhances carboxylation and reduces photorespiration.

C_4 photosynthetic carbon cycle. In C_4 pathway, CO_2 from the atmosphere enters through stomata into the mesophyll cells and combines with phosphoenol pyruvate (3-carbon compound). This reaction is catalysed by an enzyme known as phosphoenol pyruvate carboxylase, *i.e.*, **PEPCase**. With the result, a C_4 acid, oxaloacetic acid (OAA) is formed.

$$CO_2 + PEP + H_2O \xrightarrow[\text{enzyme}]{\text{PEPCase}} \text{Oxaloacetic acid (OAA)} + H_3PO_4$$

The above-mentioned reaction occurs in cytosol of the mesophyll cells and is called **fixation of CO_2 or carboxylation.**

Table 18.5. Differences between Calvin Cycle and Hatch-Slack C_4 Cycle.

Calvin cycle (C_3 cycle)	Hatch-Slack cycle (C_4 cycle)
1. It operates in all plants.	1. It operates in C_4 plants only.
2. It has a slower rate of CO_2 fixation.	2. It has a faster rate of CO_2 fixation.
3. CO_2 once fixed is not released back.	3. Fixed CO_2 is released back in bundle sheath cells where it is finally fixed and reduced by Calvin cycle.
4. The primary acceptor of CO_2 is RuBP, a 5-carbon compound.	4. The primary acceptor of CO_2 is PEP, a 3-carbon compound.
5. The first stable product is 3-PGA, 3-carbon compound.	5. The first stable product is OAA, a 4-carbon compound.
6. It cannot operate under very low CO_2 concentration.	6. It can operate under very low CO_2 concentration.
7. Fixation of one molecule of CO_2 requires 3 ATP and 2 $NADPH_2$ molecules.	7. Fixation of one molecule of CO_2 requires 2 ATP molecules in addition to that required in C_3 cycle.
8. Optimum temperature for the operation of C_3 cycle is 10-25°C.	8. Optimum temperature for the operation of C_4 cycle is 30 to 45°C.
9. There is a net gain of one hexose sugar of 6 CO_2 molecules fixed and reduced.	9. It has no such gain.

Since this gives rise to the first stable product C_4 acid, and therefore, known as C_4 pathway.

The next step of reaction is **transport** of oxalo acetic acid (OAA - 4 C compound) from cytosol of mesophyll cells to chloroplasts of bundle- sheath cells, where it is decarboxylated to release fixed CO_2 and high concentration of CO_2 is generated near Rubisco.

The other product of decarboxylation reaction is a 3-carbon compound callèd pyruvic acid. Now, this is transported back to mesophyll cells, where if regenerates phosphoenol pyruvate to its own for continuation of C_4 pathway.

However, the C_4 pathway is more efficient than C_3 pathway due to absence of photorespiration in C_4 plants.

Table 18.6. Comparison of C_3 and C_4 Plants.

C_3 plants	C_4 plants
1. CO_2 acceptor is RuBP (Ribulose bisphosphate).	1. CO_2—acceptor is PEP (Phosphoenol pyruvate).
2. Only one type of chloroplasts occur in the cells. Grana present in chloroplasts.	2. Two types of chloroplasts, bundle sheath chloroplasts possess C_3 cycle (Calvin cycle) and do not have grana; and mesophyll chloroplasts possess C_4 cycle (Hatch Slack cycle), and have grana.
3. First stable compound after CO_2 fixation is PGA.	3. First stable compound after CO_2 fixation is oxaloacetate.
4. Plants photosynthesize well, if CO_2 concentration is high.	4. Plants synthesize well, even if CO_2 concentration is low.
5. They possess photorespiration that results in a low overall efficiency in synthesis of carbohydrates.	5. They lack photorespiration and conserve more organic food and thus an overall higher photosynthetic efficiency.
6. Excess of atmospheric oxygen inhibits photosynthetic activity.	6. Excess of atmospheric oxygen has no effect on photosynthesis.

FACTORS AFFECTING PHOTOSYNTHESIS

Limiting Factors

Sachs in 1860 for the first time propounded the concept of the three **cardinal points**. According to this concept, there is a **minimum**, **optimum** and **maximum** for each factor in relation to photosynthesis. This way, with any given species there may be a minimum temperature below which no photosynthesis takes place, an optimum temperature at which the highest rate takes place and a maximum temperature beyond which no photosynthesis will take place.

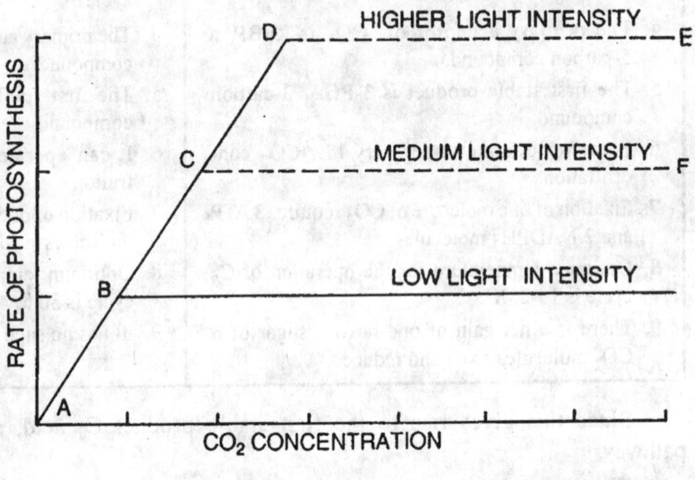

Fig. 18.13. Diagram to illustrate Blackman's law of limiting factors.

In the twentieth century Blackman (1905) proposed his **principle of limiting factors.*** According to this principle the rate of photosynthesis controlled by several factors is only as rapid as the slowest factor permits. He claimed that, if all other factors are kept constant the factor under consideration will affect the rate of photosynthesis, starting at a minimum below which no photosynthesis takes place and ending with an optimum at which a horizontal would be established, that is, the rate would remain constant despite further increases in that factor. At this point some other factor becomes limiting.

The explanation of Blackman's principle can best be presented in terms of the illustration given by Blackman himself. It is to be assumed that light intensity supplied to a leaf is just sufficient to utilize 5 mg of carbon dioxide per hour in photosynthesis. As the carbon dioxide supply is increased the rate of photosynthesis is also increased until 5 mg of carbon dioxide enters the leaf per hour. Any further increase in the supply of carbon dioxide will have no influence upon the rate of photosynthesis. Light has now become the limiting factor and further increase in the rate of photosynthesis can be brought about only by an increase in the intensity of light.

These results are indicated graphically. Here the effects of three different light intensities have been shown on the rate of photosynthesis under increasing concentrations of carbon dioxide. Under low light intensity, the rate of photosynthesis increasing concentrations of carbon dioxide. Concentration is raised until B is reached where further increase in carbon dioxide concentration is not accompanied by any increase in the rate of photosynthesis. The rate of photosynthesis becomes constant along the line BC. Any further increase in the supply of carbon dioxide will have no effect single upon the rate of photosynthesis, because light intensity has now become the limiting factor. If light intensity is now further increased, the rate of photosynthesis also increases until light again becomes a limiting factor. Here light becomes the limiting factor at the point C and there is another sharp break in the rate of photosynthesis along the line CF. Further increase in light intensity causes an increase in the rate of photosynthesis along the line CD with a

* When a process is conditioned as to its rapidity by a number of separate factors, the rate of the process limited by the pace of the slowest factors. Blackman, 1905

proportional increase in carbon dioxide concentration. The rate of photosynthesis becomes constant along the line DE where light again becomes limiting factor. At the points B, C and D the increase in the rate of photosynthesis stops abruptly because one or the other factors becomes limiting.

Light and carbon dioxide are not the only factors which can be limiting in the process of photosynthesis; other factors of photosynthesis can also become limiting under certain conditions.

It becomes clear from the above discussion that when photosynthesis is under the influence of several factors simultaneously, an increase in that factor and the limiting factor will bring about an increase in the rate of photosynthesis.

EXTERNAL FACTORS

Light

A study of the effect of light on the rate and quantity of photosynthesis would have to include light reflected, absorbed and transmitted; intensity, quality and duration of available light, and destructive effects of light.

The plant is capable of using only a very small portion of the incident electromagnetic radiation that falls on a leaf. This radiation is absorbed by the pigment complex of the leaf. Each pigment has its own absorption spectrum. The chlorophylls absorb heavily in the blue and red region of the spectrum and β-carotene mostly in the blue region. Most of the light is being reflected in the green region, giving a leaf the green colour. The greater absorption of light is found in thicker leaves with, a lower percentage of transmitted light as compared to thinner leaves.

Light intensity. There may be a direct relationship between the rate of photosynthesis and the intensity of light, provided that no other factor is limiting. For example, on bright sunny days the carbon dioxide concentration of the atmosphere is usually the limiting factor, not light intensity. However, on cloudy days light may be the limiting factor. Heinicke and Childers (1937) have found that the rate of photosynthesis steadily increased with light intensity up to about full sunlight even through saturation intensity for a single exposed leaf would be sufficiently lower. The need for higher light intensities for maximum photosynthesis of an entire tree is due to partial illumination of the inner leaves.

Both quality and intensity of light influence photosynthesis. Light between wavelength of 400 nm and 700 nm is most effective, for photosynthesis. This light is called **photosynthetically active radiation (PAR)**.

Photo-oxidation. When the light intensity is increased beyond a certain point, the cells of the leaf or other photosynthesizing organ become vulnerable to chlorophyll-catalyzed photooxidations. With the result, many more chlorophyll molecules become excited than can be utilized causing the bleaching of chlorophyll and inactivation of important enzymes. The presence or absence of carotenoids and the concentration of carbon dioxide also influence the amount of photooxidation. The carotenoids have a protective role in photo-oxidation. With high concentrations of carbon dioxide, the consumption of oxygen of photo-oxidation takes place at much higher light intensities.

Light quality. White light, that comes from the sun, is composed of different wave lengths, ranging from the relatively long wave or red light (700 nm) through successively shorter waves to violet light (440 nm). When passed through a glass prism, white light is resolved into seven colours. The band of colours is the **visible spectrum**. The complete visible spectrum is composed of red, orange, yellow, green, blue, indigo and violet colours. The wave length of light that we are unable to perceive with our eyes, beyond the red and still longer, invisible rays, the **infrared**; and beyond the violet are shorter invisible rays, the **ultraviolet**. As we know, the absorption spectrum of chlorophyll shows a sharp peak at the red end and a wider but less definite peak at the blue end.

Green light is mostly transmitted or reflected and therefore, is not utilized in photosynthesis. Red and blue lights are effective in photosynthesis. Hoover (1937) while working on wheat plants found that the wavelength (655 μm) in the red is most effective and a wave length (440 μm) in the blue to be the second most effective in photosynthesis.

Duration of light period. It is assumed that a greater quantity of photosynthesis will take place in a plant exposed to longer periods of light. In general plant carries on much photosynthesis if it is provided with light for 10 to 12 hours per day. Bohning (1949) found that the leaves on young apple trees exposed to a continuous illumination and the usual atmospheric concentration of CO_2 photosynthesize at an undiminished rate of periods of at least 18 days without any noticeable damaging effect on the plant.

Carbon Dioxide

The carbon dioxide, which constitutes on the average only about 0.03 per cent by volume of the atmosphere, plays a role of the greatest significance in the biological world. As a result of the photosynthetic activity of green plants, the carbon dioxide from the atmosphere becomes chemically bound for indefinite period of the organic molecules which are the basis of all life.

Carbon dioxide supply. The green plants utilize the atmospheric carbon dioxide, while the other sources supply the gas to the atmosphere. Carbon dioxide is continually being returned to the atmosphere as a product of the respiration of plants and animals. The organic residues of plants are decomposed as a result of activities of bacteria and fungi. During decay the carbon of these residues is released in the carbon dioxide as a result of the metabolic activities of these organisms, and escapes into the atmosphere. The respiration of the soil bacteria alone results in a greater return of carbon dioxide to the atmosphere than the respiration of all animals. Carbon dioxide is

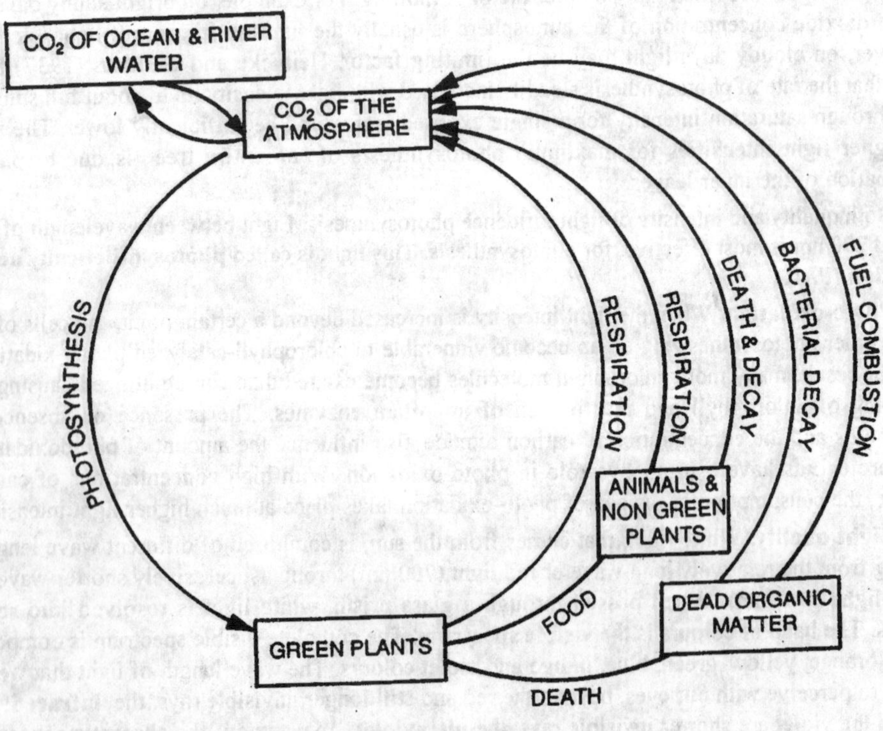

Fig. 18.14. Carbon cycle in nature.

also released into the atmosphere from volcanoes, mineral springs, and in the combustion of coal, oil, gasoline, wood and other fuel materials.

Oceans are much more important reservoirs of carbon than the atmosphere. The marine plants consume carbon dioxide in photosynthesis and release carbon dioxide in the process of respiration.

There is a constant exchange of carbon dioxide between the ocean and the atmosphere. On theoretical grounds it is assumed that the carbon dioxide concentration of the atmosphere is more or less maintained in dynamic equilibrium with that of the oceans. Carbon dioxide that escapes from the oceans whenever its atmospheric concentration falls below the usual value, and dissolves in the oceans whenever a contrary shift in atmospheric carbon dioxide concentration occurs. The maintenance of such a dynamic equilibrium between the oceans and the atmosphere is the principal factor for the constant value of carbon dioxide concentration of the atmosphere.

Absorption of carbon dioxide. Carbon dioxide in the air surrounding the leaves ultimately reaches the chloroplasts. Its inward diffusion path is through the stomata to the intercellular spaces, through walls of palisade and spongy parenchyma cells to the cytoplasm and thereafter into the chloroplasts. The walls of palisade and spongy parenchyma possess water. Carbon dioxide dissolves in water and ultimately passes through the walls in aqueous solution.

Carbon dioxide concentration. If light intensity and temperature are favourable, the carbon dioxide of the atmosphere limits the rate of photosynthesis.

The workers like Kreuslar (1887), Brown and Escombe (1902) and Pantanelli (1903) investigated that there is an increase in the rate of photosynthesis with an increase in the concentration of carbon dioxide at the lower levels of carbon dioxide concentrations. A decline in rate was observed in higher concentrations. Blackman and his co-workers claimed that after an optimum concentration is reached, the rate of photosynthesis remains constant over a wide range of carbon dioxide concentrations.

It has been demonstrated experimentally that at usual temperature and light intensities, artificial increase of carbon dioxide up to a concentration of 0.5 per cent may give an increased rate of photosynthesis, but only for a limited period. It appears that the high level of carbon dioxide is injurious to plants.

Water

Water is one of the raw material utilized in the process of photosynthesis. In land plants, the soil is the source of water. Only about one per cent or less of the water absorbed by the roots is actually used in photosynthesis.

Investigators noted reduction in the rate of photosynthesis in water deficient soils. These inhibitory effects are primarily because of decreased hydration of the protoplasm and closing of stomata. Removal of water from protoplasm affects its colloidal structure and therefore, affects metabolic processes such as photosynthesis, respiration. According to Rabinowitch (1945), photosynthesis is more sensitive to dehydration than other metabolic processes, such as respiration.

Many workers think that the primary factor in the retardation of photosynthesis by dehydration is closing of stomata. When a water deficit occurs in a plant it causes the closing of the stomata, and therefore, there is a decrease in the absorption of carbon dioxide. Since carbon dioxide concentration of the atmosphere is usually low enough to be the limiting factor in the photosynthesis under natural conditions, a decrease in its absorption, therefore, slows down the rate of photosynthesis.

Nutrient Supply

Among various nutrients, nitrogen has direct relationship with photosynthesis. As we know, nitrogen is a basic constituent of chlorophyll and all enzymes involved in carbon reactions, any reduction in nitrogen supply has an adverse effect on photosynthesis.

The major enzyme of carbon metabolism in plants is Rubisco, which alone accounts for more than half of the total leaf nitrogen.

In general, all essential elements affect the rate of photosynthesis.

Temperature

Photosynthesis can take place over a wide range of temperature. Plants of cold climates photosynthesise at much lower temperatures than do those of warm climates. The photosynthesis takes place in certain evergreen species of cold regions, even at temperatures below than 0°C. It has been reported to occur in some species of conifers at temperatures as low as –35°, and in some kinds of lichens at –20°C. Tropical plants normally do not photosynthesize below about 5°C. On the other hand algae in the water of hot springs may carry on photosynthesis at a temperature as high as 75°C. Many semi-desert and tropical species can withstand air temperatures of 55°C. Most ordinary temperate climate plants, however, photosynthesize best between temperature of 10° and 35°C.

If there is adequate light intensity and a normal supply of carbon dioxide (*i.e.*, no factor is limiting), the rate of photosynthesis of most ordinary land plants increases with rise in temperature up to a point (usually 25°C) which varies somewhat from one kind of a plant to another; above this range there is rapid decline in the rate of photosynthesis primarily form injurious effects of higher temperatures on the protoplasm. At these higher temperatures the time of exposure is of importance. The higher the temperature the sooner the decline in photosynthetic rate. The decline in the rate of photosynthesis with time particularly marked at higher temperatures, is evidence of the increasingly limiting effect of some internal factor generally called the "time-factor". As regards the nature of this time factor, it is possible that it may represent the composite influence of several internal conditions. They are as follows:

(*i*) An inactivation of enzymes at higher temperatures.

(*ii*) The accumulation of the end products of the reaction which may exert a retarding effect on the rate of photosynthesis.

(*iii*) Failure of the diffusion of carbon dioxide toward the chloroplasts to keep pace with its use in photosynthesis.

(*iv*) Similar time factor effects are present in the temperature relations of other plant processes such as respiration and growth.

Oxygen Concentration

In most plants, increase in the oxygen concentration results in a decrease in the rate of photosynthesis. The normal atmospheric concentration of oxygen is high enough to induce a lower rate of photosynthesis than obtains at lower concentration of oxygen. This is demonstrated by the work of McAlister and Myers (1940) showing the effect of high and low concentrations of oxygen on the rate of photosynthesis of wheat plants. The explanation of this seems to be that oxygen actually exerts as direct inhibitory effect on photosynthesis, and the greater the concentration of oxygen the greater this effect.

Contrary to above statement the energy product in oxygen respiration is necessary for photosynthesis. Even small amount of this energy, may supplement light energy.

Chemical Compounds

Many different kinds of chemical compounds have direct or indirect effect upon the rate of photosynthesis. Especially the effects of certain substances are noticeable which markedly influence the rates of photosynthesis when present only in minute quantities. Among these chemical compounds are hydrocyanic acid, hydroxylamine, hydrogen sulphide and certain compounds containing the iodoacetyl radical.

Narcotics such as chloroform, ether and urethans, exert retarding or inhibitory effects on photosynthesis when present in very low concentrations.

INTERNAL FACTORS

Chlorophyll Content

Chlorophyll is indispensable for photosynthesis. Scientists, devised the **photosynthetic number (assimilation number)**. This assimilation number is the number of grams of carbon dioxide per hour per gram of chlorophyll. Other investigations show that there is not proportional relationship between chlorophyll content and photosynthesis in the leaves of vascular plants.

Leaf Anatomy

The rate of photosynthesis is also influenced by the anatomy of the leaf. Here the structural features of the leaf influence the amount of carbon dioxide that reaches the chloroplasts. The size, position and structure of the stomata, the size and distribution of the intercellular spaces, the relative proportions and distribution of palisade and spongy layers, thickness of the cuticle and epidermis, the amount and position of sclerenchyma, the presence of epidermal hairs, the arrangement of mesophyll cells, distribution and efficiency of vascular system, position of chloroplasts in the cells, all influence the rate of photosynthesis. The effect of the leaf anatomy upon the rate of photosynthesis is because of influences upon the rate of carbon dioxide entry, upon the light intensity penetrating to chlorenchyma cells, upon the turgidity of leaf cells and upon the rate of translocation of solutes from green cells.

Protoplasmic Factors

The rate of photosynthesis is also affected by protoplasmic factors. The most important protoplasmic factor is the enzyme complement of the protoplasmic system. A number of enzymes play an important role in the process of photosynthesis. The hydration of protoplasm is essential. If the cells lack water and protoplasm is dehydrated, the rate of photosynthesis slows down.

TRANSPORT OF ORGANIC SUBSTANCES

Food materials are manufactured mainly in the leaves and are translocated to the other regions of the plant through the phloem. Some of this is utilized for the growth of the plant, while the excess is stored. Whenever needed, the stored food material is drawn to the regions of necessity again through the phloem. The organs of the plants that store the food materials are called the storage organs. The storage of food materials occurs in fruits and seeds. In some plants root and stems are modified to perform this function, for example, rhizomes, bulbs, corms and tubers are the modifications of the stem which store the food in the form of carbohydrates, fats and proteins. The conversion of sucrose into starch at the storage region maintains the sucrose concentration low at the storage region and, thus, the concentration gradient is maintained until a sufficient quantity is accumulated. In the storage cells, starch is usually stored in the form of grains. Starch grains are formed in plastid, known as amyloplasts (leucoplasts). Starch is the common storage material in seeds and cereal grains. The growth of a starch grain takes place by apposition of successive shells around a growth centre of hilum. Some of the other polysaccharides of storage are hemicellulose and inulin.

Photosynthates are energy rich carbon compounds formed during process of photosynthesis, are transported from the leaf to non-photosynthetic organs and tissues such as roots, stem tissues and developing seeds. This type of long distance transport of photosynthates occurring through phloem is called **translocation**.

Sucrose is the principal form of carbohydrates that is translocated from leaf to the non-photosynthetic organs. Sucrose is a non-reducing sugar, and therefore, it is chemically stable. Due to this property, this does not react with other substances during translocation.

Photosynthates provide energy to non-photosynthetic tissues through respiration.

Mechanism of translocation of solutes in phloem. Several theories have been advanced to explain the mechanism of the translcoation of solutes in phloem tissues, none theory has ever received general acceptance. In order to consider the principal theories that have been proposed, a general review of various facts regarding the problem of translocation of solutes in the phloem will be useful.

1. The translocation in the conducting elements of the phloem ceases when the cells are killed. This shows that living cells are absolutely essential for the purpose.

2. The movement of solutes may be bidirectional. There is no doubt that movement of solutes in the phloem can sometimes occur in one direction and sometimes in the other. Experiments conducted by various workers have shown that both carbohydrates and phosphates move both up and down into the phloem of a stem from the point at which they enter it from the petiole of a leaf. But this phenomenon does not involve a bidirectional movement through the same phloem at the same time.

3. Relatively the large amounts of solutes are transported. The amount of carbohydrate translocated through the phloem is sufficiently large in the case of fleshy roots, tubers or fruits. Crafts and Lorenz (1944) calculated that in 33 day growing period the pumpkin fruit gained the weight to be about 5500 gms. A large amount of the increase is water but they showed that every hour the fruit gained 0.61 gram of dry weight. All this food material entered the developing fruit through one slender stalk that connects the fruit to the vine.

4. The velocity of translocation of organic solutes through the sieve tubes is quite rapid.

5. The movements of organic and inorganic solutes exhibit a periodicity. The movements of these solutes do not occur at a constant rate both day and night. There is more rapid translocation of radioactive phosphate from leaves of bean plants during the day than during the night. Mason and Mashell (1928) have reported that most of the carbohydrates that enter the developing bolls of cotton appears to move into add them during day time rather than at night. These diurnal variations occur in plants but do not follow the same pattern in all species.

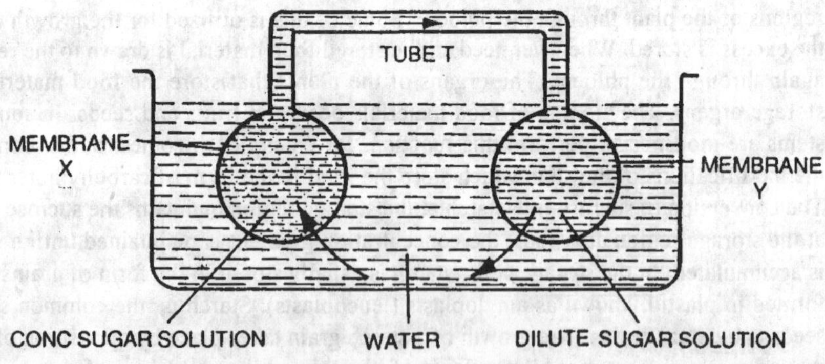

Fig. 18.15. Diagram to illustrate the principle of Munch mass flow hypothesis.

The mass flow hypothesis. This theory of translocation of solutes through phloem was advanced by Munch (1927, 1930). This theory has also put forth in modified forms by Crafts (1933, 1938) and others. The principles involved in this hypothesis can be clarified by a simple physical system. This is as follows:

As shown in the figure, two bulbs with membranes permeable only to water, are dipped in a trough containing water and are connected by a tube to form a closed system. Membrane X encloses a stronger solution of sucrose than membrane Y. Firstly, the water will enter both membranes, but greater turgor pressure develops in X which is soon to be transmitted throughout the system. With the result greater pressure in the water in Y membrane than in the pure water of the trough in which the membranes are immersed. As a result the water passes out of the membrane Y, and there is a flow of solution along the horizontal tube from X to Y. This mass flow of solution from X to Y continues unless and until the concentrations of the sugar solutions in both membranes become equal. At this point the flow of solution in the tube stops and a dynamic equilibrium establishes between the solution in the closed system and the surrounding water. If such an apparatus could be set up that we are able to arrange removal of sugar from the weaker solution (Y) as soon as it reaches it and replace the sugar lost by the stronger solution (X), flow of solution from X to Y would continue indefinitely.

According to Munch hypothesis an analogous system exists in plants. This hypothesis assumes that the translocation of solutes in plants through phloem is similar to the situations found in the experiment described in the preceding paragraph. The adjacent figure shows how it is supposed to operate as applied to the downward translocation of solutes. The photosynthetic cells of the leaf correspond to membrane X; the root cells correspond to Y and the continuous system of phloem connecting leaf and cells correspond the horizontal connecting tube. Besides xylem and cambium are also there. The osmotic pressure of the leaf cells is high as a result of photosynthesis. In the root cells the osmotic pressure is usually lower because most of the sugars translocated into them are used in metabolic activities or are converted into insoluble storage forms. Water supply to the leaf cells remains continuous through the xylem.

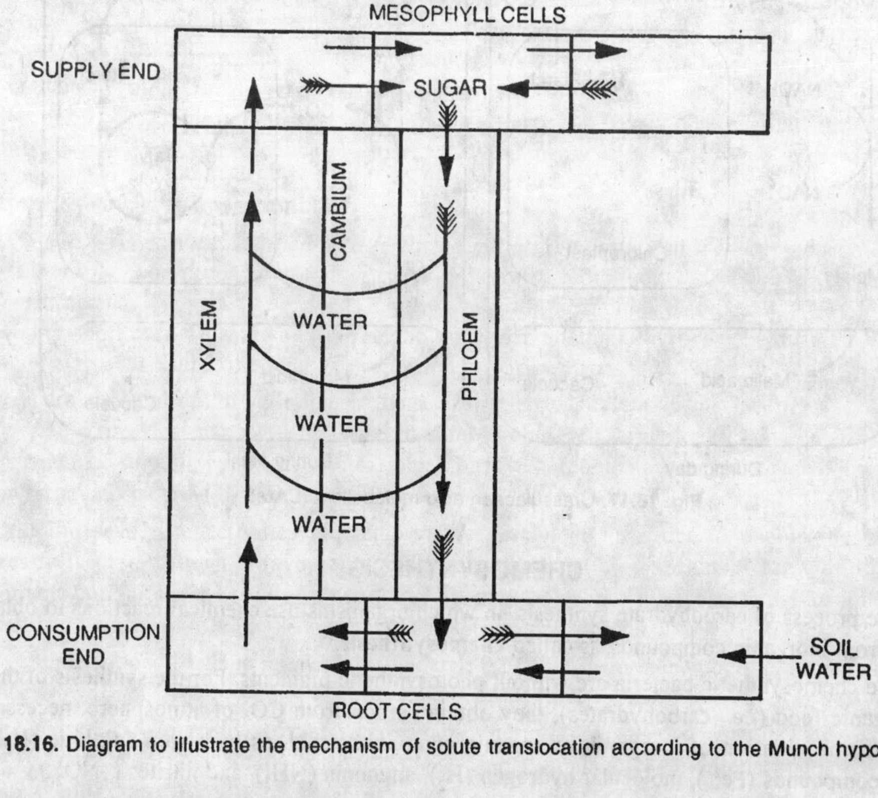

Fig. 18.16. Diagram to illustrate the mechanism of solute translocation according to the Munch hypothesis.

CRASSULACEAN ACID METABOLISM (CAM)

This type of metabolism, refers to a mechanism of photosynthesis, that is, different from C_3 and C_4 pathways. Crassulacean acid metabolism (CAM) is found only in succulents and other xerophytes or plants that grow in dry conditions.

In this type of metabolism, CO_2 is taken up by the leaves on green stems through stomata which remain open during night. However, during day time, stomata in such plants remain closed to conserve moisture.

The CO_2 taken up by succulent plants in night is fixed in the similar way as it takes place in C_4 plants to form malic acid, which is being stored in vacuole.

Hence, malic acid formed during night is used during day time as a source of CO_2 for photosynthesis to proceed through C_3 pathway.

Crassulacean metabolism is a kind of adaptation found in certain succulent plants such as pineapple to proceed photosynthesis without much loss of water, which generally occurs in plants with C_3 and C_4 pathways.

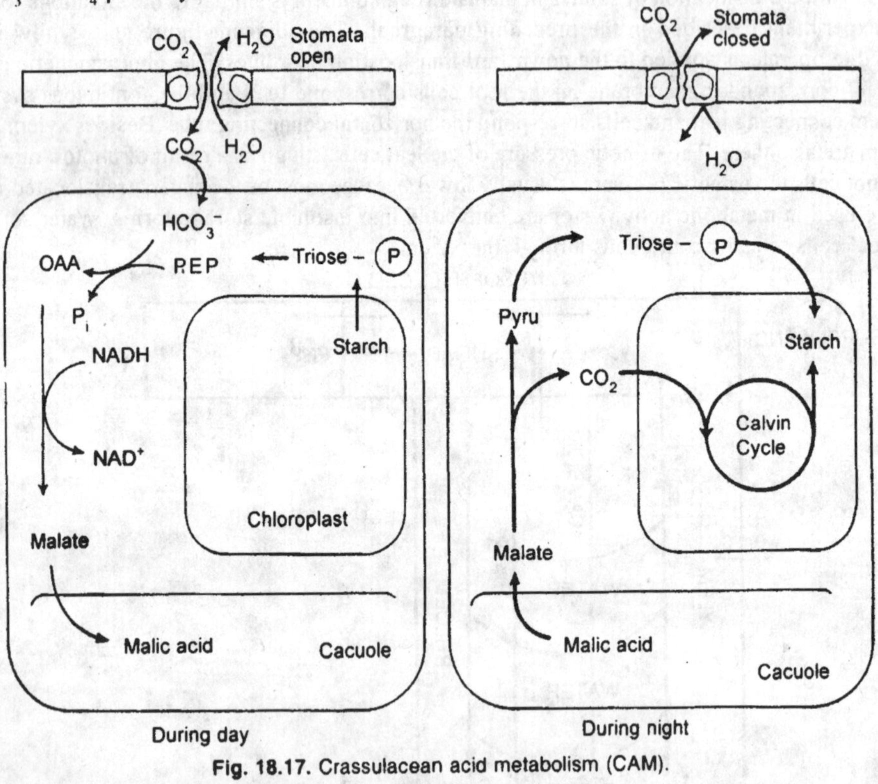

Fig. 18.17. Crassulacean acid metabolism (CAM).

CHEMOSYNTHESIS

The process of carbohydrate synthesis, in which organisms use chemical reactions to obtain energy from inorganic compounds, is called **chemosynthesis**.

The chemosynthetic bacteria are without photosynthetic pigments. For the synthesis of their own organic food (*i.e.*, carbohydrates), they obtain carbon from CO_2 of atmosphere, necessary energy from oxidation of inorganic or organic compounds such as hydrogen sulphide (H_2S), ferrous compounds (Fe^{2+}), molecular hydrogen (H_2), ammonia (NH_3), and nitrites ($-NO_2^-$).

For example bacteria of genus *Nitrosomonas* oxidise ammonia to nitrite. The energy released during oxidation is used by bacteria in the similar way as plants use energy from sunlight during photosynthesis, for converting CO_2 to carbohydrates. Such bacteria are known as **chemosynthetic autotrophs**.

The nitrifying bacteria (*Nitrosomonas*) are found in soil. Through their metabolic activates, they convert (NH_3) or ammonium ion (NH_4^+), which is formed by breakdown of animal and plant proteins during decay, to nitrates (NO_3^-). The formation of from NH_3 or NH_4^+ is termed **nitrification**. This process occurs in two steps:

(*i*) *Nitrosomonas* is most common organism found in soil that oxidises ammonia into nitrite ion ($-NO_2^-$) and (*ii*) *Nitrobacter* oxidises nitrite ion into nitrate ($-NO_3^-$) ion. These microbes obtain energy by oxidising ammonia or nitrite

$$(i)\ \underset{\text{Ammonia}}{2NH_3} + 3O_2 \xrightarrow{\textit{Nitrosomonas}} \underset{\text{Nitrite ion}}{2NO_2^-} + 2H^+ + 2H_2O + \text{energy}$$

$$(ii)\ \underset{\text{Nitrite ion}}{2NO_2^-} + O_2 \xrightarrow{\textit{Nitrobacter}} \underset{\text{Nitrate ion}}{2NO_3^-} + \text{energy}$$

HETEROTROPHIC NUTRITION

Green plants are autotrophic (*auto* = self; *trophe* = food) and manufacture carbohydrates by means of photosynthesis and nourish themselves. Non-green plants on the other hand are heterotrophic (*heteros* = different). Such plants cannot prepare carbohydrates, and they get nourishment from different sources. The heterotrophic plants may be classified as— (*i*) **parasites**; (*ii*) **saprophytes**, (*iii*) **symbionts** (*iv*) **insectivorous plants**.

1. Parasites. The total parasites, like dodder (*Cuscuta*) and broomrape (*Orobanche*) are never green and cannot synthesize their own food. In such cases, they develop haustoria or sucking roots which go into the vascular bundles of the host plant and absorb from them the prepared food and water.

2. Saprophytes. For example, *Monotropa*, bacteria and fungi grow on decaying vegetable or animal matter and absorb organic food material from their substrata.

3. Symbionts. Two organisms that live in close physical association and are of mutual benefit to each other are called **symbionts** and the condition is known as **symbiosis**. Lichens and mycorrhiza are examples of symbionts.

Lichens. A lichen is a plant consisting of two separate plants a fungus and an alga, so closely associated with each other as to appear a single plant.

Mycorrhiza. Some fungi live in close association of other higher plants where they are mutually beneficial to each other. Here fungi develop in the roots of higher plants.

Fig. 18.18. Parasite. *Cuscuta (dodder).*

4. Insectivorous plants. On the other hand the insectivorous plants are capable of manufacturing carbohydrates due to the presence of chlorophyll, but since they grow in swampy soil which are deficient in nitrogen they cannot synthesize enough proteins. They overcome this deficiency by catching small insects and digesting them. For this purpose, their leaves are specially modified in various ways. The best known examples of insectivorous plants are–the pitcher plants (*Nepenthes*), the sundew (*Drosera*), venus fly trap (*Dionaea*), butterwort (*Pinguicula*) and the bladderwort (*Utricularia*).

Fig. 18.19. Saprophyte. *Agaricus.*

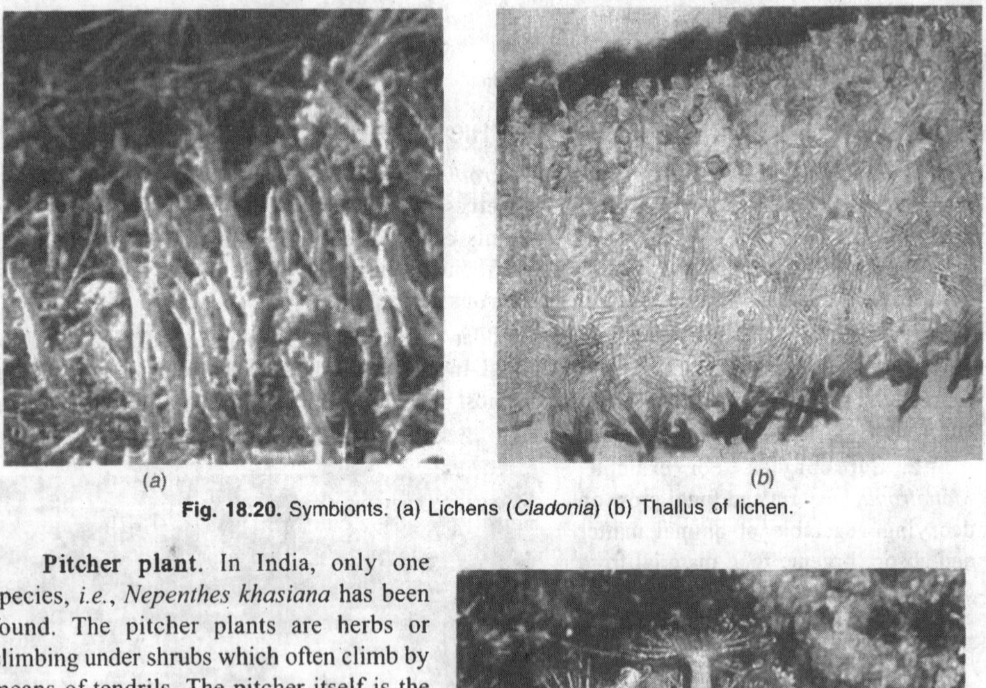

(*a*) (*b*)

Fig. 18.20. Symbionts. (a) Lichens (*Cladonia*) (b) Thallus of lichen.

Pitcher plant. In India, only one species, *i.e.*, *Nepenthes khasiana* has been found. The pitcher plants are herbs or climbing under shrubs which often climb by means of tendrils. The pitcher itself is the modification of the leaf-blade. The insects are attracted to these pitchers either by their bright colours or by their nectar. Below the mouth the inside of the pitcher is covered with numerous smooth and sharp hairs, all pointing downwards. The insects that slip into water are prevented from coming out by the hairs present in the pitcher. The trapped insects eventually die and are decomposed by microorganisms. The proteins are converted into amines and are absorbed by the inner surface of the pitcher.

Fig. 18.21. Insectivorous plant : *Drosera.*

The sundew plant. Three species of *Drosera* are found in India. The sundew plant is a small herb. Each leaf of *Drosera* remains covered on the upper surface with numerous glandular hairs known as **tentacles**. Each gland secretes a viscous fluid which glitters in the sun like dew-drops and hence the name sundew. An insect landing on the leaf gets stuck and the glandular hairs bend down and prevent the insect from escaping. The enzymes secreted by the hairs digest the insect and the products are absorbed by the leaf surface. The enzyme called pepsin hydrochloric acid, acts on the insect and changes the proteins of its body into soluble and simple forms.

SIGNIFICANCE OF PHOTOSYNTHESIS

Photosynthesis is a vital process for life on this planet. This process links the physical and biological world. This process helps conversion of solar energy into organic matter that makes bulk of dry matter of any organism.

The plants biomass (dry matter), derived through photosynthesis supports humans and all other heterotrophic organisms living in biosphere.

Survival of all organisms is dependent upon food (carbohydrates, etc.), a photosynthetic product. All organisms need energy for different life activities which they derive from food (carbohydrates, fats and proteins).

Green plants are unique in the character that they are able to synthesise food for whole biokingdom.

During photosynthesis, O_2 is released, which is helpful to living organisms mainly in two ways. Firstly, in efficient utilisation of the energy rich molecules, *i.e.*, carbohydrates, in respiration.

Secondly, in making ozone (O_3) in outer layer of atmosphere, which is required to stop harmful ultraviolet (UV) rays from reaching the earth.

During photosynthesis green plants take CO_2 from atmosphere and release O_2, thus purifying air. Without O_2, life of all aerobic organisms including humans is not possible.

Crops are totally dependent on photosynthesis. This process feeds whole biokingdom directly or indirectly.

EXPERIMENTAL WORK : PRACTICALS

Photosynthesis

Experiment 1.

Object : Demonstration of starch test.

Requirements : Green leaves of a plant, burner, water, 70% alcohol, dilute iodine solution.

Experiment and observation : The green leaves of any healthy plant may be boiled in the day time thereafter, by keeping the leaves in 70% alcohol, the chlorophyll is extracted from them. Now these chlorophyll-less leaves are kept for sometime in dilute iodine solution. The leaves become deep blue or blue black in colour. This is known as 'starch test'. If the plant is kept for a long time, viz., 24 or 48 hours, in darkness, and thereafter the leaves are tested for starch test, it is always negative. The leaves do not become blue black in colour.

Explanation : As the plant was kept in darkness continuously for a long period, there was no photosynthesis, and the starch already prepared was shifted to the lower part of the plant during this period.

Experiment 2.

Object : Demonstration of release of oxygen during photosynthesis.

Requirements : Few branches of an aquatic plant, i.e., Hydrilla, etc., beaker, glass funnel, test tube, sodium bicarbonate, etc.

Experiment : The release of oxygen during photosynthetic process may be proved experimentally. A few branches of an aquatic plant, Hydrilla are kept in a big beaker full of the same pond water. Thereafter, the branches are covered with a glass funnel, and a test tube full of water is inverted at the end of the funnel as shown in the figure. If required, a small quantity of sodium bicarbonate may be added in the water, so that the supply of carbon dioxide may become adequate for the photosynthesis. Now, the apparatus is kept in the sunlight.

Observation : The gas bubbles may be observed from the ends of the *Hydrilla* branches kept under the glass funnel in the beaker. These gas bubbles are accumulated in the end of the test tube inverted over the end of the funnel, and the water within the tube goes downward. On test the gas is to be proved oxygen.

Note : To test the gas, the pyrogallol solution is taken in a beaker, and with the help of the thumb the tube partially filled with gas is kept inverted in the pyragallol solution. The solution enters the test tube and the tube again fills up completely because the pyragallol solution is soluble in oxygen.

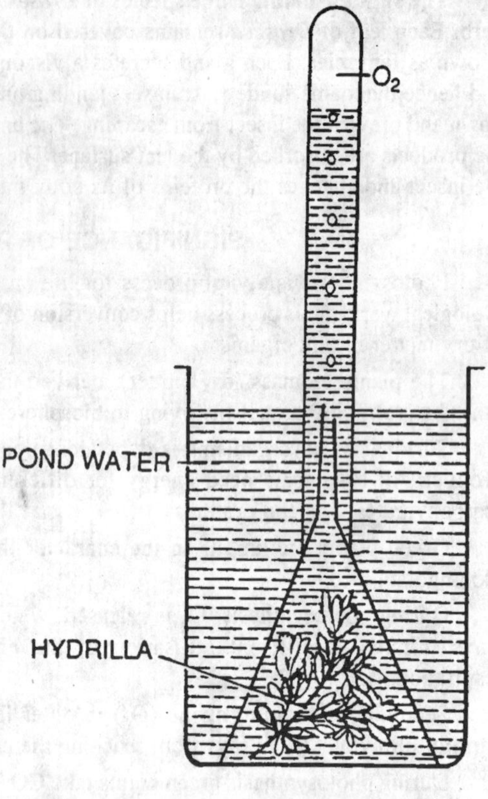

Fig. 18.22. Liberation of oxygen in photosynthesis. Demonstration of the phenomenon.

Various modifications for this experiment :

(1) When the pond water of beaker is replaced by boiled or distilled water.

(2) When the above experiment is covered by a black cloth.

(3) When the *Hydrilla* twigs are replaced by terrestrial plants.

(1) When pond water of beaker is replaced by boiled or distilled water : If the pond water in the beaker is replaced by boiled or distilled water, the gas bubbles are not released from the ends of the *Hydrilla* branches kept under the glass funnel in the beaker. Why? The reason is quite clear, that during distillation or boiling of the water, the dissolved carbon dioxide goes out, which is necessary factor for photosynthesis. The photosynthesis does not take place. With the help of this modification of the experiment, the necessity of the carbon dioxide for the photosynthesis of water plants may be proved.

(2) When the above experiment is covered by a black cloth : If this apparatus is covered with black cloth, or kept in darkness, the gas bubbles are not released showing that the light is one of the essential factors for the photosynthesis in the case of water plants.

(3) When the *Hydrilla* twigs are replaced by terrestrial plants : Here the photosynthesis is completely checked. Only hydrophytes may absorb CO_2 from the water, the terrestrial plants, being of different habitat, fail to absorb CO_2 from water, and therefore, the photosynthesis is stopped here.

Experiment 3.

Object : Demonstration of comparison of rate of photosynthesis under different conditions.

(A) Different concentrations of CO_2 (by sodium bicarbonate)

(B) Reaction of sunlight and shade.

(C) Reaction in red, green and blue coloured-light.

(D) Reaction of different temperatures.

Requirements : Willmott's bubbler, *Hydrilla* plant, sodium bicarbonate, different coloured papers, burner, thermometer, pond water, stop watch, etc.

Experiment : Willmott's bubbler : It can easily be prepared in the laboratory. Take a wide mouthed bottle and fix a cork in it. Pass wide glass tube through this cork. Another narrow glass tube having a jet at its one end is introduced in the former one. Fill this apparatus with pond water and tie the twigs of *Hydrilla* at the lower end of narrow glass tube as shown in the figure.

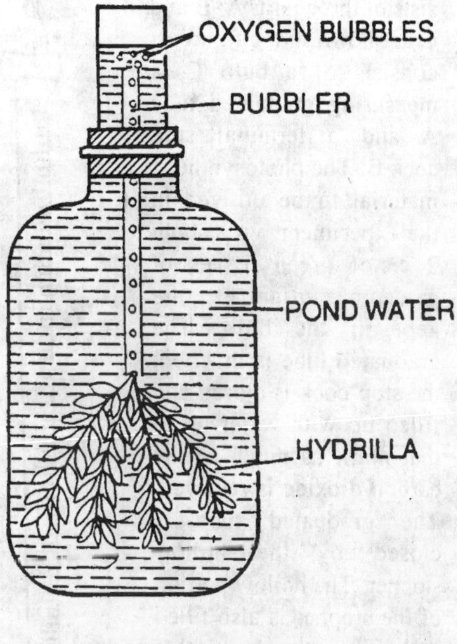

Fig. 18.23. Willmott's bubbler.

For different conditions the following factors are provided here.

(A) Add sodium bicarbonate to the water of the bottle and count the bubbles coming out in each case in definite time.

(B) Put the apparatus as such in sun and shade respectively for definite intervals and count the bubbles coming out in each case.

(C) Put the apparatus in double walled bell jar providing different coloured papers. Count the bubbles coming out in each case for definite time intervals.

(D) Take another beaker of hot water and put the apparatus in it at definite temperatures. Count the bubbles coming out in each case for definite time intervals.

Explanation :

(A) With the increasing concentration of $NaHCO_3$, the rate of photosynthesis increases. This rate of photosynthesis goes on increasing till light or some other factor acts as a limiting factor

(B) The readings show that the rate of photosynthesis is more in sun.

(C) The readings show that the rate of photosynthesis is the highest in red light and lowest in green.

(D) This experiment shows that photosynthesis occurs at a rapid rate from 10 to 35°C, provided other factors are not limiting.

Experiment 4.

Object : Demonstration of measurement of photosynthesis by Ganong's photosynthetometer.

Requirements : Ganong's photosynthetometer, green leaf, water, KOH, Kipp's apparatus, etc.

Experiment and observation : With the help of this apparatus, the quantity of released oxygen, and the quantity of utilized carbon dioxide during photosynthesis in a green leaf may easily be detected. This way, the photosynthetic quotient O_2/CO_2 may be known.

This apparatus consists of three parts A, B and C as shown in the figure. It consists of a bulb C, a measuring graduated tube A and a terminal stop cock B. The photosynthetic material to be utilized in the experiment, viz., about 2 c.c.of green leaves of garden nasturtium, etc., are kept in the bulb. The graduated tube is inverted, the stop-cock is closed and filled up with water up to that mark as much as the carbon dioxide is required. The graduated tube is closed by the hollow stopper. The hollow portion of the stopper is also filled up with water. Now, this end of the tube is to be closed with the help of the hand, and inverted in the trough full of water. Thereafter it is clamped this way that the level of water remains at par to the level of the hole of the stop-cock. Now, the stop-cock of the lower end is opened and the upper end of the graduated tube is connected with the Kipp's apparatus to receive the carbon-dioxide. The upper stop-cock is opened carefully, the carbon dioxide enters the tube, this is closed again, when the water of the tube is replaced by carbon dioxide, and its level becomes at par of the level of the outer water. Now, both the stop-cocks are being closed, and the complete tube is attached to the bulb with photosynthetic material. Now, the lower stop-cock is opened, and the carbon dioxide diffuses in the bulb containing photosynthetic material. This apparatus is kept for 3 to 4 hours in sunlight and after noting the time the lower stop-cock is closed and the tube is pulled out from the bulb. Now, this is placed in the trough filled with water, and by keeping it in the water, the hollow stopper is removed. Now, the zero mark of this measuring graduated tube is kept at par of the water

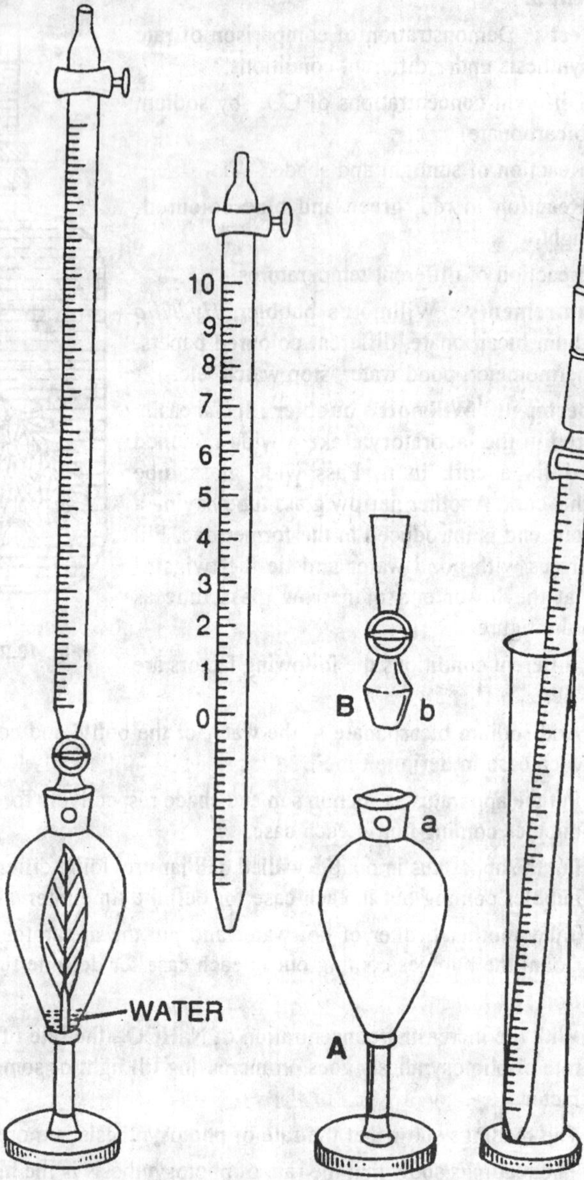

Fig. 18.24. Ganong's photosynthetometer.

level, and gradually the stop-cock of the upper end is opened and make the water rise up to the zero mark of the tube.

Now a test tube is filled up with 30% caustic potash (KOH) solution and this tube is connected with the graduated tube with the help of rubber tubing. Thereafter, this apparatus is taken out from the water and removed the clamp and let the caustic potash solution enter the graduated tube. The graduated tube is shaken thoroughly and the caustic potash solution is again transferred to the test tube and the rubber tube is clasped. The end of the graduated tube is kept in water by keeping the zero mark at the water level, and the test tube is removed. Now, in the graduated tube that much amount of water rises, as much carbon-dioxide is absorbed by caustic potash solution. This way, the volume of carbon dioxide is known which has been used by the leaf in the process of photosynthesis. If this experiment is furnished by filling the test tube with alkaline pyragalol solution the released oxygen is absorbed.

Explanation : The reduction in the volume of carbon dioxide and addition in the volume of oxygen indicate the volume of utilized carbon dioxide and released oxygen during photosynthesis. Their values are usually identical and this way, the photosynthetic quotient is usually one.

$$P.Q. = \frac{6O_2}{6CO_2} = \frac{6}{6} = 1$$

Experiment 5.

Object : Demonstration of necessity of light for photosynthesis.

This may be shown in various ways, some important ones are given here.

(*i*) **Requirements :** A potted plant, 70% alcohol, iodine solution, water, etc.

Experiment and observation : A potted plant is kept for 48 hours in dark so that it becomes starch free. Now, on testing the leaves for the starch, they give negative test. This shows that in the absence of light there is no photosynthesis.

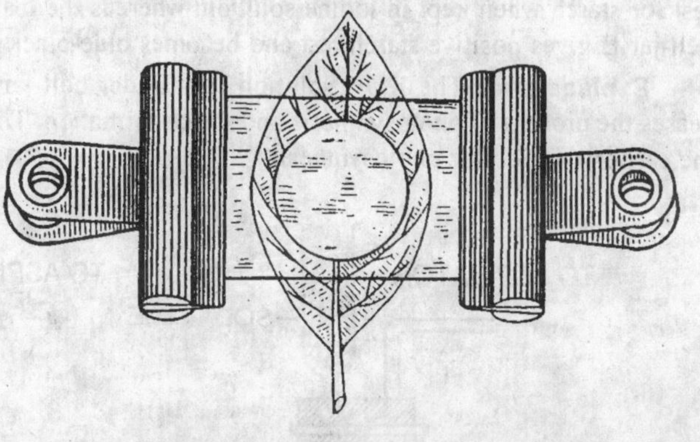

Fig. 18.25. Ganong's light screen.

(*ii*) **Requirements :** A potted plant, a piece of paper, iodine, 70% alcohol, water, etc.

Experiment : A potted plant is kept in dark continuously for 48 hours, to make it free from light. Now, again the plant is kept in the light and one of its leaves covered as in the figure. The photosynthesis begins after keeping the plant in light. After some time the partially covered leaf is detached from the plant and tested for starch.

Observation : The exposed portions of the leaf give positive test and the covered portion of the leaf gives negative test. This experiment shows that the photosynthesis takes place only in those portions of the leaf which were exposed to the light and not in covered portions.

(*ii*) **Ganong's Light Screen Test.**

Requirements : A potted plant, a Ganong's Screen, 70% alcohol, burner, iodine, water, etc.

Experiment : A potted plant is kept in darkness for about 48 hours, so that its leaves become starch free. A small Ganong's light screen is attached to a leaf of the plant as shown in the figure.

The Ganong's light screen partially covers the leaf. There is proper arrangement in the screen for the aeration of the leaf. Now, the plant along with light screen is kept in the light for photosynthesis. After 3 or 4 hours, the leaf is detached from the plant and tested for starch.

Observation : The portion of the leaf exposed to light gives positive starch test, *i.e.*, it becomes deep blue in iodine solution, whereas, the covered portion of the leaf gives negative starch test and does not become blue-black in iodine solution. This experiment proves the necessity of light for photosynthesis.

Experiment 6.

Object : Demonstration of necessity of CO_2 for photosynthesis:

Requirements : Two small sized potted plants, two bell jars, KOH solution in a petri dish, water, 70% alcohol, iodine, water, etc.

Experiment : Two small sized potted plants are taken. They are kept in the darkness at least for 48 hours, so that their leaves become starch free. Now, these potted plants are kept under two separate bell-jars. A petri dish partially filled up with KOH solution is kept under bell-jar 'A' and another petri dish parially filled with water is kept under bell-jar B. Now the apparatus is kept in sunlight for photosynthesis. After some time (3 to 4 hours), the leaves from both the potted plants are tested for starch by extracting their chlorophyll and keeping them in iodine solution.

Observation : The leaf detached from the plant kept under bell-jar, does not give positive test for starch when kept in iodine solution, whereas the leaf detached from the plant kept under bell-jar B gives positive starch test and becomes blue-black in colour, in iodine solutions.

Explanation : The KOH solution kept under bell-jar 'A' absorbs all the carbon dioxide, ceases the process of photosynthesis and starch formation. This experiment proves the necessity of the carbon dioxide for photosynthesis.

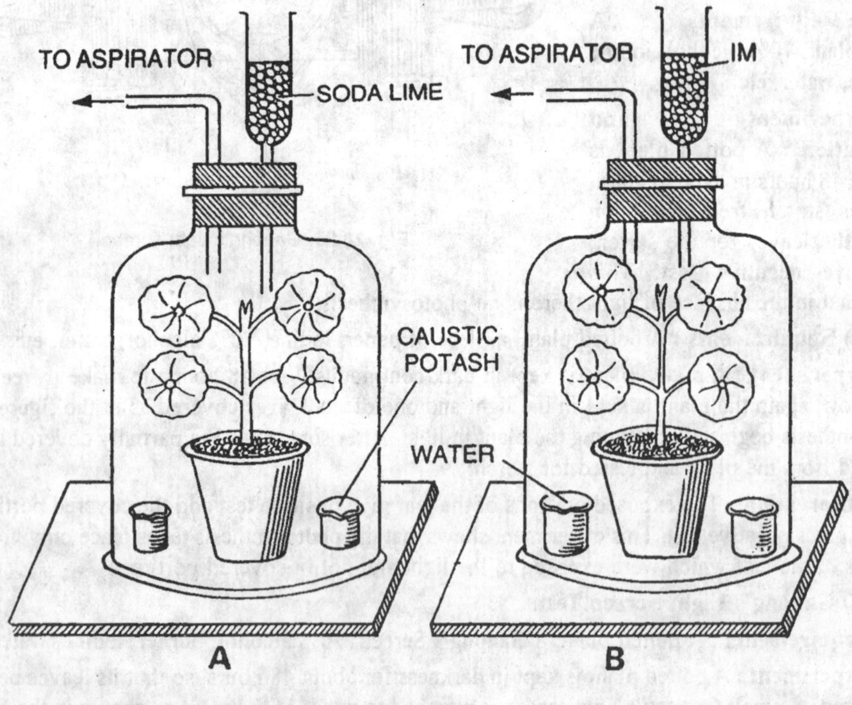

Fig. 18.26. Necessity of CO_2 for photosynthesis. Demonstration of phenomenon.

Experiment 7.

Object : Demonstration of Moll's experiment :

Requirements : A wide mouthed bottle, a split cork, conc. KOH solution, a leaf, water, beaker, wax, etc.

Experiment : A wide mouthed bottle with a split cork in two equal halves is taken. The bottle is partially filled up with concentrated caustic potash (KOH) solution. A leaf detached from the plant previously kept in darkness at least for 48 hours is pressed in between the two halves of the cork of the bottle so that half the leaf remains within the bottle and the other half outside the bottle. The petiole of the leaf remains outside which is kept in water filled beaker, so that the leaf may not become dry soon. The apparatus is made air-tight by applying melted wax so that the atmospheric air may not enter the bottle. Thereafter the apparatus is kept in the sunlight for photosynthesis.

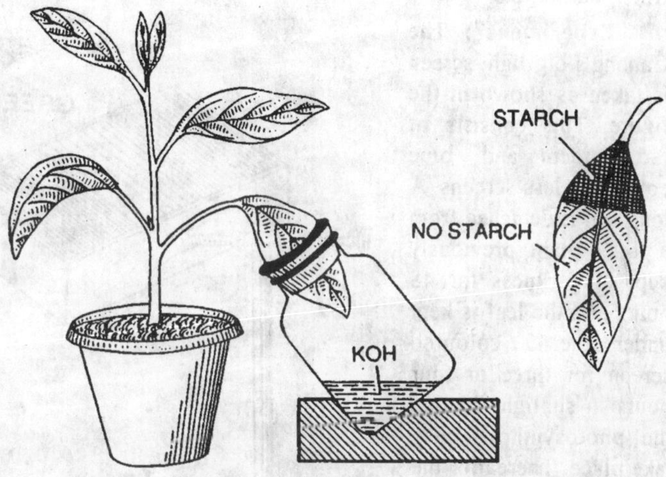

Fig. 18.27. Moll's experiment.

Observation : After few hours the leaf is tested for starch by extracting its chlorophyll and keeping it in iodine solution. The portion of the leaf which remained inside the bottle gives negative test, *i.e.*, this does not become blue-black.

Explanation : The carbon dioxide within the bottle is absorbed by caustic potash (KOH) solution and in the absence of carbon dioxide, the photosynthesis does not take place and the starch is not formed. The portion of the leaf which remained outside the bottle could receive all the necessary factors for photosynthesis and the photosynthesis took place in this portion forming starch. This portion of the leaf gives positive starch test and becomes blue when comes in contact of iodine solution after extracting the chlorophyll.

In addition to it some portion of the leaf remains pressed in between the two halves of the cork. This portion does not get light. With the result there is no photosynthesis and starch formation in this portion of the leaf. This portion also does not give positive starch test. This way, this experiment proves the necessity of carbon dioxide and light for photosynthesis at one time.

Experiment 8.

Object : Demonstration of necessity of chlorophyll for photosynthesis.

Requirements : Some variegated leaves, 70% alcohol, iodine, water, burner, etc.

Experiment : To prove the necessity of chlorophyll for photosynthesis some variegated leaves are taken and tested for starch as usual.

Observation and explanation : The portions of the leaves containing white or yellow spots do not give positive starch test. They do not become blue when brought in contact of iodine solution. This experiment proves that the photosynthesis takes place only in the green coloured portion of the leaves.

Experiment 9.

Object : Demonstration of importance of light's colour for photosynthesis in land plants by Ganong's big light screen.

Requirements : Ganong's big light screen, a potted plant, 70% alcohol, iodine solution, water, burner, etc.

Experiment : The Ganong's big light screen is taken as shown in the figure. This consists of red, green and blue coloured glass screens. A long leaf is detached from a potted plant, previously kept in darkness for 48 hours and the leaf is kept under the 3 coloured screen for three or four hours in sunlight so that the photosynthesis may take place. Thereafter the leaf is tested for starch.

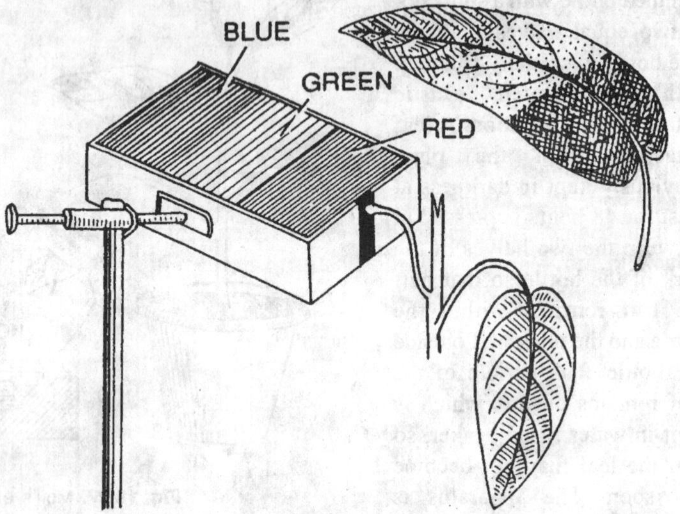

Fig. 18.28. Importance of light's colour for photosynthesis (Ganong's big light screen).

Observation : The portion of the leaf remained under red-coloured screen gives the positive starch test with deep blue colour. The portion of the leaf remained under the blue coloured screen also give positive starch test, but with fade blue colour. The part of the leaf remained under green-coloured screen either gives negative starch test or very less formation of the starch.

Explanation : This way, this experiment proves that the red and blue coloured rays are absorbed to the utmost by the chlorophyll. The absorption of the green rays by the chlorophyll is the lowest. The rate of photosynthesis is the highest under red screen and lowest under green screen.

Experiment 10.

Object : Demonstration of an increase in the mass of leaves due to formation of photosynthetic products by Ganong's leaf-area cutter.

Requirements : Ganong's leaf-area cutter, green leaves, an oven, balance, etc.

Experiment : Take two green plants. Put one in the light and another in dark. Now pick some leaves from each of the plants after putting them in their

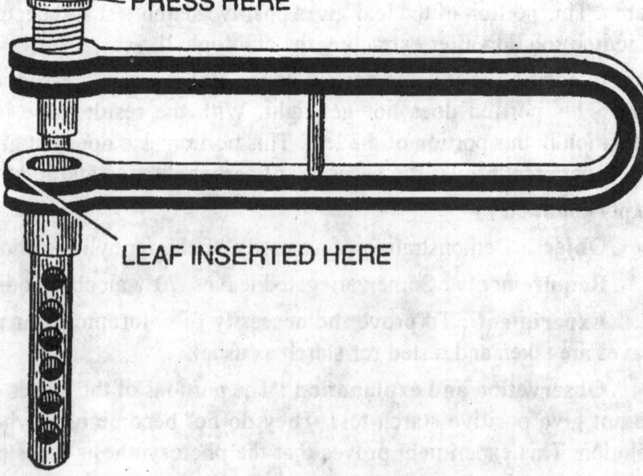

Fig. 18.29. Ganong's leaf punch.

respective conditions for few hours. Using the Ganong's leaf-area cutter, cut few circular discs from respective sets of leaves. Now put these sets in an oven and heat. After heating they are weighed properly by a balance.

Observation : The weight of the set (leaves form the plant kept in light) is found much enough than that of another set (leaves from the plants kept in dark).

Explanation : This simple experiment shows that there is a rise in dry weight of leaves which is due to accumulation of photosynthetic products.

Chlorophyll

Experiment 11.

Object : Demonstration of separation of chlorophyll by paper chromatography.

Requirements : Tecoma leaves, mortar and pestle, acetone, petroleum ether, beaker, tube, etc.

Experiment : Take about 10 gm of Tecoma leaves in a mortar and crush them by a pestle. Add about 12 to 15 ml of acetone to it and filter in a beaker. This so obtained filtrate is being concentrated by heating. Take a paper strip and sketch a pencil line 2 cm. above the base of it. Point out the centre of it and pour the acetone filtrate on it drop by drop. The size of spot on the paper strip should be small. Now, add a few drops of petroleum ether in a separate tube and place the above paper strip in a vertical position in this tube. Close the tube tightly.

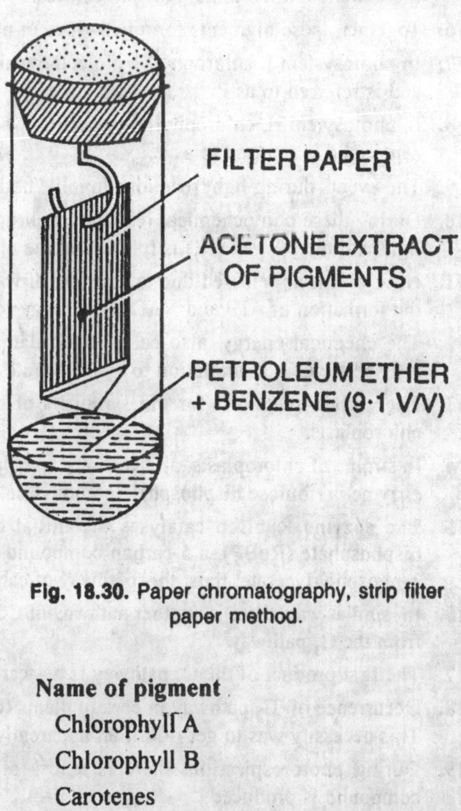

Fig. 18.30. Paper chromatography, strip filter paper method.

Observation : Observe the paper strip after some time. The level of solvent, *i.e.*, petroleum ether and different colours should be pointed out by a pencil. Here the pigment may be identified by their different colours.

Colour	Name of pigment
Blue green	Chlorophyll A
Yellow green	Chlorophyll B
Orange	Carotenes
Yellow	Xanthophyll

Experiment 12.

Object : Demonstration of extraction of chlorophyll by chemical method.

Requirements : Green leaves of spinach, 95% ethyl alcohol, distilled water, benzene, beaker, etc.

Experiment : Boil about 50 gm green leaves of spinach for some time. Dry these leaves and chop them into small pieces. Now put these pieces in a test tube containing 95% alcohol. Place this tube overnight in a dark place and filter it the following day. Dilute the filtrate with some distilled water and add a few amount of benzene to it. Shake the mixture and stand it for some time.

Observation : Observe the colour of the pigments. The upper layer is of green pigments, these are two, chlorophyll A and chlorophyll B. The lower layer is of yellow pigments, these are also two, xanthophyll and carotene.

SUMMARY

1. Photosynthesis is one of the most important phenomena of bio-kingdom that occurs in plants, algae and certain pigmented bacteria.
2. During process of photosynthesis, carbon dioxide from the atmosphere is taken in by leaves through stomata, and is used for making carbohydrates, primarily sucrose and starch.
3. This process occurs inside chloroplasts, where green pigments called chlorophyll, and other accessory pigments called carotenoids, are located on thylakoids often stacked to form grana.
4. Chlorophyll, mainly chlorophyll *a* which acts as reaction centre, takes part in the photochemical reactions.
5. Initially, light energy is absorbed by various chlorophyll molecules and accessory pigments, and thereafter supplied to the reaction centres.
6. Together, these pigments form two types of photosystems, *i.e.*, photosystem I and photosystem II.
7. In photosystem I, chlorophyll *a* molecule which absorbs light at a 700 nm acts as the reaction centre and is referred to as P_{700}.
8. In photosytem II, chlorophyll *a* molecule, which has maximum absorption at 680 nm, is the reaction centre and is referred to as P_{680}
9. The events during light reactions involve both photosystem I and photosystem II.
10. During these photochemical reactions, splitting of water molecule initially occurs in the presence of light and the oxygen (O_2) is released at the photosystem II site.
11. Now, electrons released due to splitting of water initiate the electron transport chain, which leads to the formation of ATP and $NADPH_2$, energy required for conversion of CO_2 to carbohydrates.
12. The chemical energy, also called assimilatory power stored in the form of ATP and $NADPH_2$ is utilised for CO_2 assimilation to carbohydrates.
13. The carbon reactions for the synthesis of carbohydrates from CO_2 take place in the stroma of chloroplasts.
14. In stroma of chloroplasts, all necessary enzymes required for reactions, are present. The most notable enzyme is ribulose bisphosphate carboxylase oxygenase (Rubisco).
15. The enzyme Rubisco catalyses the initial carbon reaction, where CO_2 combines with ribulose bisphosphate (RuBP), a 5-carbon compound. The product of this reaction is a 3-carbon compound, 3-phosphoglycerate, thus, this pathway of carbon reactions is called C_3 pathway or the Calvin cycle.
16. In similar way, there is another pathway of CO_2 fixation called as C_4 pathway, which is quite different from the C_3 pathway.
17. The first product of the C_4 pathway is a 4-carbon compound, *i.e.*, oxaloacetic acid.
18. Occurrence of C_4 pathway in certain plants (called C_4 plants) in nature is an outcome of a necessity. This necessity was to get rid off an apparently wasteful process of photorespiration.
19. During photorespiration, there is a loss of fixed carbon (*i.e.*, 25 percent) and no energy rich compound is produced.
20. Certain environmental factors affect the rate of photosynthesis in plants. Such factors include (*i*) quality of light (*ii*) intensity of light, (*iii*) carbon dioxide, (*iv*) water and (*v*) temperature.
21. Certain other factors, such as (*i*) age of leaf, (*ii*) chlorophyll content, (*iii*) nutritional states of leaves also affect the rate of photosynthesis.
22. The end product of photosynthesis is sucrose, which is synthesised in the cytosol of a mesophyll cell. However, starch is synthesised inside chloroplasts only under certain conditions.
23. The sucrose moves from leaves to other organs of the plants (translocation), where it is used either for growth, or for storage in storage organs.

TERMS TO REMEMBER

Calvin cycle. Also called C_3 pathway. C_3 type of carbon reactions occur in the stroma of chloroplast.

C_3 Pathway. Where first stable product, 3-carbon molecule, 3-phosphoglycerate (PGA) is formed; reaction is catalysed by an enzyme Rubisco.

C_4 Pathway. C_4 plants possess a CO_2 concentrating mechanism.

Carbon reactions (dark reactions). Take place in the stroma of chloroplast, leading to the photosynthetic reaction of carbon to carbohydrates.

Carboxylation. Fixation of carbon dioxide. For example, formation of 3-Carbon compound, 3-phosphoglycerate (PGA).

Carotenoids. Red, orange and yellow coloured pigments.

Chemosynthesis. The process of carbohydrate synthesis, where organisms use chemical reactions to obtain energy from inorganic compounds.

Chemosynthetic autotrophs. When *Nitrosomonas* (bacteria) oxidise ammonia to nitrite, the released energy is used by the bacteria for converting CO_2 to carbohydrate. Such bacteria are chemosynthetic autotrophs.

Crassulacean acid metabolism (CAM). A different mechanism of photosynthesis that occurs in succulent plants.

Electron transport chain. The light driven reactions of photosynthesis.

Jan Ingenhousz (1730-1799). A physician, discovered that release of oxygen by plants was possible only in sunlight and only by the green parts of the plants.

Joseph Priestley (1733-1804). Discovered that plants have the ability to take up CO_2 from the atmosphere and release O_2.

Kranz anatomy. The C_4 plants contain dimorphic chloroplasts, *i.e.*, granal and agranal; granal in mesophyll cells and agranal in bundle-sheath cells.

Photolysis. Light dependent splitting of water molecule.

PEPC. Phosphoenol pyruvate carboxylase, an enzyme, which catalyses formation of a C_4 acid, oxaloacetic acid (OAA).

Photophosphorylation. The process of ATP formation from ADP in the presence of light in chloroplasts.

Photorespiration. Respiration that is initiated in chloroplasts and occurs in light only, also called **photosynthetic carbon oxidation cycle.**

Photosystem. The accessory pigments and the reaction centre together *i.e.*, PS I and PS II. Here, pigments are anchored in thylakoids in discrete units of organisation.

Photosynthesis. A process by which plants synthesise their own food in the presence of light. It takes place only in the green parts of the plant.

Photosynthetically active radiation (PAR). Portion of the spectrum between 400 nm and 700 nm.

Phytol chain. Side chain of chlorophyll molecule which extends from one of the pyrrole rings.

Pyrrole rings. Chlorophyll molecule composed of four 5-membered rings.

Reaction centre. Chlorophyll *a* molecules which convert light energy into electrical energy by bringing about electrical charge separation.

Rubisco. Ribulose bisphosphate carboxylase oxygenase, an enzyme which catalyses **carboxylation** (*i.e.*, formation of PGA).

Theodore de Saussure. He found that water is an essential requirement for photosynthesis to occur.

Translocation. Long distance transport of photosynthates which occurs through phloem.

QUESTION BANK

Very Short Answer Questions

1. Where does photosynthesis take place ?
2. What are actual sites for photosynthesis ?
3. Expand PAR.
4. Which molecules act as reaction centres in photosynthesis ?
5. What are accessory pigments ?
6. Define photophosphorylation.

7. Who formulated electron transport chain ?
8. What is photolysis ?
9. Where does photophosphorylation occur ?
10. What are essential requirements for the assimilation of CO_2 to carbohydrates ?
11. Expand Rubisco.
12. Expand RuBP.
13. Where C_3 type of carbon reactions occur ?
14. Give another appropriate name for C_3 pathway.
15. What is photorespiration ?
16. What is main function of enzyme Rubisco?
17. What is Kranz anatomy ?
18. Expand PEPC.
19. Who postulated law of limiting factors ?
20. Define chemosynthesis.
21. What are chemosynthetic autotrophs ?
22. What is end product of photosynthesis, and where it is synthesised ?
23. Which chlorophyll is known as universal photosynthetic pigment ?
24. Give name of central element found in chlorophyll molecule.
25. Mention the site of formation of glycoxylate from glycolate.
26. Name two photosynthetic pigments belonging to caretenoids.
27. Name any two C_4 plants.
28. Give single chemical equation of photosynthesis.
29. Expand the term RuBP.
30. Write one anatomical feature of C_4 plants.
31. Which of the following is not a useful function of the light reaction in photosynthesis ?
(*a*) splitting water. (*b*) synthesis of NADPH
(*c*) converting light energy into chemical energy (*d*) releasing oxygen for photorespiration.
32. What is the first stable product of C_4 cycle ?

ANSWERS

1. Photosynthesis takes place only in the green parts of the plant; **2.** The chloroplasts are actual sites for photosynthesis in green plants; **3.** Photosynthetically active radiation; **4.** Chlorophyll *a* molecules; **5.** These pigments, called carotenoids, are of red, orange and yellow colours; **6.** Process of ATP formation from ADP in the presence of light in chloroplasts is called photophosphorylation; **7.** Robert Hill (1939); **8.** Light-dependent splitting of water molecule is called photolysis; **9.** Photophosphorylation occurs in chloroplasts; **10.** ATP and $NADPH_2$; **11.** Ribulose bisphosphate carboxylase oxygenase; **12.** Ribulose bisphosphate; **13.** They occur in stroma of chloroplast; **14.** C_3 pathway is also called Calvin cycle after its discoverer Nobel Laureate Melvin Calvin; **15.** Respiration that is initiated in chloroplasts and occurs in light only; **16.** Photorespiration involves oxygenation of ribulose bisphosphate (RuBP) catalysed by the enzyme Rubisco; **17.** In C_4 plants where chloroplasts in mesophyll cells are granal, while in bundle-sheath cells are agranal; **18.** Phosphoenol pyruvate carboxylase; **19.** F.F. Blackman (1905); **20.** Process of carbohydrate synthesis, in which the organisms use chemical reactions to obtain energy from inorganic compound; **21.** They are certain bacteria (*e.g.*, *Nitrosomonas*), where energy released during oxidation is used for converting carbon dioxide to carbohydrates; **22.** The end product of photosynthesis is sucrose which is synthesised in the cytosol of a mesophyll cell; **23.** Chlorophyll *a*; **24.** Magnesium; **25.** Peroxisomes of mesophyll cell; **26.** Carotene, xanthophyll; **27.** Sugarcane and maize; **28.** $6CO_2 + 12H_2O \xrightarrow[\text{chlorophyll}]{\text{Light}} C_6H_{12}O_6 + 6O_2 + 6H_2O$; **29.** Ribulose bisphosphate; **30.** Leaves show 'Kranz' anatomy; **31.** (*d*) **32.** Oxaloacetic acid.

Short Answer Questions

1. What is significance of photosystem ?
2. What is Hill reaction ? Explain.
3. Describe photosynthetic unit.
4. Give a graphic outline of Calvin cycle.
5. Give a graphic outline of Hatch and Slack cycle.
6. Differentiate between C_3 and C_4 plants.
7. What are the steps that are common to C_3 and C_4 photosynthesis?
8. Differentiate between PS I and PS II.
9. Differentiate between photorespiration and aerobic respiration.
10. What is mass flow hypothesis? Explain.
11. Describe very briefly the contribution of the following scientists :
    (*i*) Jan Ingenhousz (*ii*) C. B. van Niel (*iii*) Joseph Priestley
12. Give comparison between the following:
    (*i*) C_3 and C_4 pathways
    (*ii*) Cyclic and non-cyclic photophosphorylation
    (*iii*) Carboxylation and oxygenation
    (*iv*) Anatomy of leaf in C_3 and C_4 plants.
13. Specify how a pentose phosphate is a CO_2 acceptor in the dark reaction of photosynthesis.
14. What is Rubisco? Explain its role in C_3 and C_4 photosynthesis.
15. Give the importance of C_4 plants.
16. Explain why photosynthesis is considered the most important process in the biosphere.
17. All life on earth is bottled 'sun's energy'. Justify.
18. Name the hormones which increase and decrease the rate of photosynthesis.
19. What is Blackman's law of limiting factors ?
20. Describe the importance of C_4 plants.

Short Answer Questions

21. Give the path and magnitude of translocation of organic materials.
22. Name the three phases of Calvin cycle. Explain the significance of each of them.
23. Describe Blackman's law of limiting factors.
24. How would you know that the source of oxygen in photosynthesis is water and not carbon dioxide?
25. Draw a labelled diagram of the cross-section of chloroplast as seen under microscope.
26. Give the precise location where the dark and light reactions of photosynthesis take place. What are the final products of each of these reactions ?
27. Give the salient features of Kranz anatomy.
28. Distinguish between cyclic and non-cyclic photophosphorylation.
29. How would you prove experimentally that light is essential for photosynthesis ?
30. Why photosynthesis is considered the most important process in the biosphere ? Explain.
31. Write short note on Crassulacean acid metabolism.
32. What is the advantage of having more than one pigment molecule in a photocentre ?
33. What is kranz anatomy? Write a note on photosynthesis of those plants in which this anatomy is found.
34. Write a brief account on the chloroplast pigment.
35. Describe the mechanism of Hatch and Slack pathway in C_4 plants.
36. Write short notes on *Nepenthes* and *Drosera*.
37. Write a short note on chloroplast pigments.

38. List the three phases of Calvin cycle of photosynthesis. Describe in short the chemical steps in these phases.
39. List the various external and internal factors affecting photosynthesis.
40. Name any two C_4 plants. Describe how CO_2 is fixed in such plants.
41. Expand PEP. Where is it produced in C_4 plants? What is its role in the biosynthetic process ?
42. Expand RuBP. Where is it found in a C_3 plant? What is its role in the biosynthetic process ?
43. Name any two C_4 plants. Give anatomical characters of these plants.
44. Where does carboxylation take place in C_3 plants? Explain the process.
45. How did Hill prove experimentally that oxygen evolved during photosynthesis comes from water ?
46. Why does the rate of photosynthesis decrease at higher light intensities? What plays a protective role in such situations ?

Long Answer Questions

1. Describe cyclic photophosphorylation. What is the purpose of proton gradient created during the process in the thylakoids ?
2. What is Hill reaction? Write a brief note.
3. Describe photosystem I and photosystem II in green plants. How these photosystems cooperate in producing NADPH and ATP in light reactions of photosynthesis ?
4. Define carbon fixation in plants. What was the contribution of M. Calvin in regard to photosynthesis? Describe the three phases of Calvin cycle.
5. What is photorespiration? Explain how plants like sugarcane and sorghum have adapted themselves to overcome photorespiration?
6. What is the term used for long distance movement of carbohydrates in plants? How and in what form are the carbohydrates synthesised in leaves, reach long distance parts in plants? Explain the most accepted view.
7. Explain the photochemical phase of photosynthesis. Where does it take place?
8. How are ATP, NADPH and oxygen produced in non-cyclic photophosphorylation?
9. What is photophosphorylation? Distinguish between cyclic and non-cyclic photophosphorylation. Give schematic sketches of both the pathways.
10. Describe the light reaction of photosynthesis with special reference to non-cyclic and cyclic photophosphorylation.
11. Compare C_4 and C_3 pathways of CO_2 fixation during photosynthesis. Give well labelled and schematic sketch of C_4 pathways.
12. Describe the light dependent steps of photosynthesis. How are they linked to the dark reaction ?
13. Calvin cycle consists three phases. What are they ? Explain the significance of each of them.
14. Name any two C_4 plants. Describe how carbon dioxide is fixed in such plants.
15. Explain photochemical phase of photosynthesis. Where does it take place ?
16. Give an account of external factors affecting photosynthesis.
17. Explain the process of oxidation reduction occurring in photosynthesis to generate ATP and NADPH.
18. Describe cyclic photophosphorylation. What is the purpose of proton gradient created during the process in the thylakoids ?
19. Where does Calvin cycle take place ? Explain the process in detail.
20. Describe the light dependent steps of photosynthesis. How are they linked to the dark reactions ?
21. Describe the C_4 pathway in a sugarcane plant. How is this pathway an adaptive advantage to the plant ?
22. Name the pentose phosphate that fixes CO_2 in a C_3 plant. Explain Calvin cycle in such plants.
23. Mention the steps where the products of light reaction are utilised in the dark reaction.
24. Define photophosphorylation. Describe cyclic and non-cyclic photophosphorylation.
25. What is Blackman's law of limiting factors ? Explain it with reference to photosynthesis.

MULTIPLE CHOICE QUESTIONS (Objective Type Questions)

1. Who among the following proved for the first time that O_2 in photosynthesis comes out by photolysis of water ?
   (*a*) Arnon (*b*) Hill
   (*c*) Ruben, Hassid and Kamen (*d*) Blackman
2. The energy wastage occurs during
   (*a*) Dark reaction (*b*) Photorespiration (*c*) Photosynthesis (*d*) None of the above
3. Which of the following equations most adequately sums up the photosynthetic reaction ?
   (*a*) $CO_2 + H_2O = CH_2O + O_2$ (*b*) $C_6H_{12}O_6 + 6O_2 = 6CO_2 + 6H_2O$
   (*c*) $6CO_2 + 6H_2O = C_6H_{12}O_6 + 6O_2$ (*d*) $6CO_2 + 6H_2O = C_6H_{12}O_6 + 6O_2 + 6H_2O$
4. Which one of the following would not be limiting factor for photosynthesis?
   (*a*) Oxygen (*b*) Carbon dioxide (*c*) Chlorophyll (*d*) Light
5. During photosynthesis oxygen in glucose comes from
   (*a*) Water (*b*) CO_2
   (*c*) Both water and CO_2 (*d*) From air
6. Dark reaction in photosynthesis is called so because
   (*a*) It can also occur in dark (*b*) It does not require light energy
   (*c*) Of neither of these (*d*) Of both of these
7. During photosynthesis when PGA is changed into phosphoglyceraldehyde which of the following reaction occur
   (*a*) Oxidation (*b*) Reduction (*c*) Electrolysis (*d*) Hydrolysis
8. Bacteriochlorophyll differs from chlorophyll in having
   (*a*) One hydrogenated pyrrole ring (*b*) Two hydrogenated pyrrole rings
   (*c*) Three hydrogenated pyrrole rings (*d*) Four hydrogenated pyrrole rings
9. Blackman demonstrated that increasing illumination increased the photosynthetic rate upto a point when CO_2 became limiting. If light was not limiting, temperature became limiting. Emerson found that maximum CO_2 fixation would be achieved with brief flashes of light. Mark the correct statement in the following.
   (*a*) Only one factor can be limiting in photosynthesis
   (*b*) Photosynthesis consists of a light and a dark reaction
   (*c*) The trapping of light by chloroplasts is temperature dependent
   (*d*) The trapping of light by chloroplasts can occur only if CO_2 is present
10. Which of the following radioactive isotope was employed by Calvin for tracing the path of carbon in photosynthesis?
    (*a*) C^{11} (*b*) C^{14} (*c*) O^{18} (*d*) P^{35}
11. The first step in photosynthesis is
    (*a*) Joining of 3 carbon atoms to form glucose
    (*b*) Formation of ATP
    (*c*) Ionization of water
    (*d*) Excitement of an electron of chlorophyll *a* by a photon of light
12. The C_4 plants differ from C_3 plants with reference to the
    (*a*) Substance that accepts CO_2 in carbon assimilation
    (*b*) Type of end products of photosynthesis
    (*c*) Number of ATPs that are consumed in synthesising sugar
    (*d*) Type of pigments involved in photosynthesis

13. Which one of the following is a C_4 plant ?
(*a*) Papaya (*b*) Potato (*c*) Maize (*d*) Pea

14. Discovery of Emerson effect has already shown the
(*a*) Two distinct photochemical reactions (*b*) Light and dark reactions of photosynthesis
(*c*) Photophosphorylation (*d*) Photorespiration

15. The percentage of light energy utilised by higher plants for photosynthesis is
(*a*) 10 per cent (*b*) 50 per cent (*c*) 20 per cent (*d*) 1-2 per cent

16. Which of the following have high CO_2 compensation point?
(*a*) C_2 plants (*b*) C_3 plants (*c*) C_4 plants (*d*) Alpine herbs

17. Which of the following statements regarding 'compensation point' is incorrect?
(*a*) The rate of photosynthesis exactly balances that of respiration
(*b*) Neither oxygen nor carbon dioxide is given off from the leaves
(*c*) No growth occurs
(*d*) It occurs when the light intensity falls to about 20 per cent of that found on bright sunny day.

18. The percentage of light energy fixed in photosynthesis is generally around
(*a*) 35 per cent (*b*) 10 per cent (*c*) 50 per cent (*d*) 1 per cent

19. The inner envelope of chloroplast is permeable to
(*a*) Triose phosphate (*b*) Orthophosphate (*c*) Sucrose (*d*) Glutamine

20. First stable product of dark reaction in C-3 plants is
(*a*) PGA (*b*) RuBP (*c*) PEP (*d*) OAA

21. Calvin cycle is
(*a*) Dependent on light (*b*) Not dependent on light
(*c*) Inhibited by light (*d*) Partly dependent on light

22. Photosynthesis is a process in which
(*a*) CO_2 is reduced to carbohydrate (*b*) NADH is reduced to NAD
(*c*) ATP is generated (*d*) Oxidative phosphorylation occurs

23. The presumed size of chlorophyll molecule is
(*a*) Head 15 × 15Å Tail 20 Å (*b*) Head 10 × 12 Å Tail 15 Å
(*c*) Head 20 × 20 Å Tail 25 Å (*d*) Head 15 × 15Å Tail 25 Å

24. Photolysis of water is associated with
(*a*) PS I (*b*) PS II (*c*) Cyt. b (*d*) quinone

25. Photorespiration occurs in
(*a*) C_3 plants (*b*) C_4 plants (*c*) All plants (*d*) Algae

26. CO_2 fixation during C_4 pathway occurs in the chloroplast of
(*a*) guard cells (*b*) mesophyll cells (*c*) spongy parenchyma (*d*) bundle sheath cells

27. 'Kranz' type of anatomy is found in
(*a*) C_4 plants (*b*) C_3 plants (*c*) Succulents (*d*) None of the above

28. Structural component of chlorophyll among the following is
(*a*) Mg (*b*) Mn (*c*) Zn (*d*) Fe

29. In experiments on photosynthesis the isotope used by Calvin was
(*a*) O^{18} (*b*) C^{14} (*c*) C^{11} (*d*) N^{14}

30. Quantasomes occur on the surface of
(*a*) Plasmalemma (*b*) Cristae (*c*) Thylakoids (*d*) Nuclear envelope

31. At carbon-3, Chlorophyll *a* has
(*a*) – CHO group (*b*) – CH_3 group (*c*) – COOH group (*d*) No functional group

32. Photorespiration is favoured by
(*a*) High temperature and low oxygen (*b*) High humidity and temperature
(*c*) High carbon dioxide and low oxygen (*d*) High oxygen and low carbon dioxide

33. C_4 plants differ form C_3 plants with respect to
(*a*) Number of ATP molecules consumed (*b*) First product
(*c*) Substrate which accepts carbon dioxide (*d*) All the above

34. Which one of the following statements about Cytochrome P_{450} is wrong?
(*a*) It has an important role in metabolism (*b*) It contains iron
(*c*) It is an enzyme involved in oxidation (*d*) It is coloured cell

35. Pigments of PS I occur in
(*a*) Appressed part of granal thylakoids
(*b*) Stromal thylakoids and non-appressed parts of granal thylakoids
(*c*) Both appressed and non-appressed parts of granal thylakoids
(*d*) Stroma

36. Enzyme required in early CO_2 fixation in C_4 cycle is
(*a*) RuBP carboxylase (*b*) RuBP oxygenase
(*c*) PEP Carboxylase (*d*) PGA dehydrogenase

37. For fixing one molecule of CO_2 in Calvin cycle, are required
(*a*) 3 ATP + 1 $NADPH_2$ (*b*) 3 ATP + 2 $NADPH_2$
(*c*) 2ATP + 3 $NADPH_2$ (*d*) 3 ATP + $NADPH_2$

38. Carbon dioxide is fixed in
(*a*) Light reaction (*b*) Dark reaction
(*c*) Aerobic respiration (*d*) Anaerobic respiration

39. The pigment present universally in all green oxygenic plants is
(*a*) Chlorophyll *a* (*b*) Chlorophyll *b* (*c*) Chlorophyll *c* (*d*) Chlorophyll *m*

40. In photosynthesis, photolysis of water is used in
(*a*) Reduction of NADP (*b*) Oxidation of NADP
(*c*) Oxidation of FAD (*d*) None of the above

41. Scientist awarded Nobel Prize in 1960 for tracing the path of carbon is
(*a*) Hatch (*b*) Huber (*c*) Calvin (*d*) Ruben

42. Pigment system connected with oxidation of water is
(*a*) PS I (*b*) PS II (*c*) Phycobilisome (*d*) Carotenoids

43. Carotenes protect plants from
(*a*) Photo-oxidation (*b*) Desiccation (*c*) Photorespiration (*d*) Photosynthesis

44. Chemical which absorbs light energy and changes it to chemical energy is
(*a*) Xanthophyll (*b*) Chlorophyll *a* (*c*) Chlorophyll *b* (*d*) Chlorophyll *c*

45. Which of the following occurs in dark reaction of photosynthesis?
(*a*) Formation of ATP (*b*) Release of O_2 (*c*) Release of H_2 (*d*) Synthesis of PGAL

46. *Orobanche* plant is
(*a*) Partial parasite (*b*) Total root parasite (*c*) Symbiont (*d*) Total stem parasite

47. Insectivorous plants kill insects because
(*a*) insects eat their leaves (*b*) insects eat their fruits
(*c*) they are heterotrophs (*d*) they obtain nitrogen from killed insects

48. Insectivorous plants grow in soil which is deficient in
(*a*) calcium (*b*) magnesium (*c*) nitrogen (*d*) water

49. A pair of insectivorous plants is
(*a*) *Drosera* and *Rafflesia* (*b*) *Nepenthes* and Bladderwort
(*c*) *Dionaca* and *Viscum* (*d*) Venus fly trap and *Rafflesia*

50. Insectivorous plant is
(*a*) *Opuntia* (*b*) *Crotolaria* (*c*) *Eichhornia* (*d*) *Utricularia*

51. The mass flow hypothesis was first described by
(*a*) Swanson (*b*) Buchanan (*c*) Kurosawa (*d*) Munch

52. Which would do maximum harm to a tree ?
(*a*) The loss of half of its leaves (*b*) The loss of all its leaves
(*c*) The loss of half its branches (*d*) The loss of its bark

53. Organic substances such as sugars are translocated in the phloem can be demonstrated by
(*a*) Grafting (*b*) Root pressure (*c*) Defoliation (*d*) Ringing the stem

54. Photosynthates are transported to other part of higher plants through
(*a*) Cambial cells (*b*) Pith cells (*c*) Xylem cells (*d*) Phloem cells

55. Translocation of sugar in flowering plants occurs in the form of
(*a*) glucose (*b*) sucrose (*c*) starch (*d*) maltose

56. Rubisco (RuBP-carboxylase oxygenase), a protein which comprises
(*a*) 5% of total chloroplast portion (*b*) 11% of total chloroplast portion
(*c*) 16% of total chloroplast portion (*d*) 20% of total chloroplast portion

57. Photo-oxidation refers to
(*a*) Photolysis of water
(*b*) Photorespiration
(*c*) Light induced breakdown of substance in the presence of oxygen
(*d*) All of the above

58. Action spectrum of photosynthesis in 1883 was described by
(*a*) Calvin (*b*) Hill (*c*) Arnon (*d*) Englemann

59. The electron energy transfer between accessory pigments and chlorophyll molecules takes place by
(*a*) Transduction (*b*) Radiation (*c*) Resonance (*d*) Flourescence

60. The two enzymes responsible for primary carboxylation in C_3 and C_4 plants, respectively are
(*a*) RuBP carboxylase and pyruvate carboxylase
(*b*) PEP carboxylase and RuBP carboxylase
(*c*) RuBP carboxylase and PEP carboxylase
(*d*) PEP carboxylase and pyruvate carboxylase

61. Photorespiration is affected by
(*a*) Light intensity (*b*) Temperature (*c*) CO_2 and O_2 (*d*) All of these

62. Chlorophyll *a* is present in
(*a*) All photosynthetic eukaryotes as well as prokaryotes
(*b*) All plants except fungi
(*c*) All higher plants carrying photosynthesis
(*d*) All O_2 evolving photosynthetic organisms

63. Calvin cycle expands the following for fixation of 3-molecules of CO_2
(*a*) 9 ATP and 6 $NADPH_2$ (*b*) 8 ATP and 6 $NADPH_2$
(*c*) 9 ATP and 3 $NADPH_2$ (*d*) 6 ATP and 9 $NADPH_2$

64. Which of the following is the first product of photorespiration
(*a*) Glycolic acid (*b*) Serine (*c*) Phosphoglycolate (*d*) Glycine

65. Which element is essential for photolysis of water
(*a*) Nitrogen (*b*) Chlorine (*c*) Ingenhousz (*d*) Oxygen

66. In C_4 plants initial CO_2 fixation takes place in the chloroplasts of
(*a*) Guard cells (*b*) Spongy mesophyll (*c*) Palisade tissue (*d*) Bundle sheath

67. Photorespiration takes place only in
(*a*) Green parts of the plant (*b*) All the living cells of the plant
(*c*) Mitochondria (*d*) Root

68. The organelle associated with photorespiration is called as
(*a*) Lysosome (*b*) Peroxisome (*c*) Glyoxisome (*d*) Mesosome

69. The wavelength of light most absorbed during photosynthesis is
(*a*) 400 nm (*b*) 500 nm (*c*) 550 nm (*d*) 660 nm

70. Non-cyclic photophosphorylation involves
(*a*) Pigment system II only (*b*) Pigment system I only
(*c*) Both pigment systems I and II (*d*) None of these

71. Photophosphorylation means
(*a*) Formation of ATP from ADP (*b*) Formation of NADP
(*c*) Formation of ADP from ATP (*d*) Formation of PGA

72. Which one of the following is needed in both photosynthesis and respiration ?
(*a*) Sunlight (*b*) Chlorophyll (*c*) Glucose (*d*) Cytochrome

73. The first CO_2 acceptor in C_4 plants is
(*a*) PEP (*b*) RuBP (*c*) PGA (*d*) OAA

74. NADPH is generated through
(*a*) Photosystem I (*b*) Photosystem II
(*c*) Anaerobic respiration (*d*) Glycolysis

75. The core metal of chlorophyll is
(*a*) Fe (*b*) Mg (*c*) Ni (*d*) Cu

76. Most plants are green in colour because
(*a*) The atmosphere filters out all the colours of the visible light spectrum except green
(*b*) Green light allows maximum photosynthesis
(*c*) Green light is the most effective wavelength region of the visible spectrum in sunlight for photosynthesis
(*d*) Chlorophyll is least effective in absorbing green light

77. Protochlorophyll differs from chlorophyll in lacking
(*a*) 4 hydrogen atoms in one of its pyrrole rings
(*b*) 4 hydrogen atoms in two of its pyrrole rings
(*c*) 2 hydrogen atoms in one of its pyrrrole rings
(*d*) 2 hydrogen atoms in two of its pyrrole rings

78. Which one of the following statements about cytochrome P 450 is wrong ?
(*a*) It has an important role in metabolism (*b*) It contains iron
(*c*) It is an enzyme involved in oxidation (*d*) It is a coloured cell

79. Warburg effect is decreased rate of photosynthesis at
(*a*) Low concentration of CO_2 (*b*) High concentration of CO_2
(*c*) Higher concentration of O_2 (*d*) None of these

80. Which one of the following prokaryotic algae possesses chlorophyll *b*
(*a*) *Anacystis* (*b*) *Oscillatoria* (*c*) *Prochloron* (*d*) *Segtonema*

81. Which of the following statements is correct about C_4 type of photosynthesis ?
(*a*) C_4 cycle is independent cycle
(*b*) C_4 cycle is adjunct of Calvin cycle
(*c*) RuBP carboxylase has higher affinity for CO_2
(*d*) Carboxylase is present in the bundle sheath cells

82. Assimilatory powers during photosynthesis are
(*a*) H_2O and O_2 (*b*) RuDP and RuMP
(*c*) $C_6H_{12}O_6$ and PGAL (*d*) ATP and $NADPH_2$

83. Who for the first time experimentally demonstrated that oxygen is evolved from water during photosynthesis?
(*a*) Calvin (*b*) Robert Hill (*c*) Govindji (*d*) Ruben and Kamen

84. The source of oxygen liberated in photosynthesis is
(*a*) Carbohydrate already present in the leaf (*b*) Water
(*c*) A photosynthetic enzym (*d*) Carbon dioxide

85. The isotopes that have proved useful in researches on photosynthesis are
(*a*) O^{18} and O^{14} (*b*) C^{11} and P^{32} (*c*) P^{32} and O^{18} (*d*) C^{14} and O^{18}

86. Acid concentration in CAM plants is more at :
(*a*) Right (*b*) Daytime (*c*) Down (*d*) Dusk

87. In PS-II, first known electron acceptor is :
(*a*) Cytochrome (*b*) PQ (*c*) FRS (*d*) Ferredoxin

88. In C_4 plants :
(*a*) Grana present in mesophyll cells and absent in bundle sheath cells
(*b*) Grana absent in mesophyll cells and present in bundle sheath cells
(*c*) Grana present in both mesophyll and bundle sheath cells
(*d*) Grana absent in both mesophyll and bundle and bundle sheath cells

89. Hill reaction occurs in :
(*a*) High altitude plants (*b*) Total darkness
(*c*) Absence of water (*d*) Presence of ferredoxin

90. Photorespiration in C_3 Plants starts from :
(*a*) Phosphoglycerate (*b*) Phosphoglycolate (*c*) Glycerate (*d*) Glycine

91. Which of the following helps in translocation of food in plants :
(*a*) Xylem (*b*) Phloem (*c*) Sclerenchyma (*d*) Collenchyma

92. Number of carboxylation in C_4 cycle are :
(*a*) Four (*b*) Three (*c*) Two (*d*) One

93. O_2 evolution is directly associated with :
(*a*) PS I (*b*) PS II (*c*) Phytochrome (*d*) Phycocyanin

94. Chlorophyll molecules are green in colour because they :
(*a*) Transmit green light (*b*) Transform green light
(*c*) Reflect green light (*d*) Absorb green light

95. This is not an electron transferring molecule:
(*a*) Coenzyme Q (*b*) Fe ~ S protin (*c*) ATP (*d*) NAD

96. Which one of the following is the aim of Moll's half leaf experiment? To show that :
(*a*) CO_2 is produced during anaerobic respiration (*b*) CO_2 is produced during aerobic respiration
(*c*) CO_2 is essential for photosynthesis (*d*) Chlorophyll is essential for photosynthesis

97. Orange and red colour of flower and fruit is due to :
(*a*) Leucoplast (*b*) Chloroplast (*c*) Protoplast (*d*) Chromoplast

98. Maximum photosynthesis occurs in :
(*a*) Continuous light (*b*) Green light (*c*) Red light (*d*) Blue light

99. In photosynthesis, energy from light reaction to dark reaction is transferred in the form of :
(*a*) ADP (*b*) ATP (*c*) RuBP (*d*) Chlorophyll

100. Stomata of CAM plants :
(*a*) are always open
(*b*) open during the day and close at night
(*c*) open during the night and close during the day
(*d*) never open

101. Which fraction of the visible spectrum of solar radiation are primarily absorbsed by carotenoids of the higher plants?
(*a*) Blue and green (*b*) Green and red (*c*) Red and violet (*d*) Violet and blue

102. Which one of the following in wrong in relation to photorespiration?
(*a*) It occurs in chloroplast (*b*) It occurs in daytime only
(*c*) It is characteristic of C_4 plants (*d*) It is characteristic of C_3 plants

103. Which one of the following concerns photophosphorylation?
(*a*) $ADP + AMP \xrightarrow{\text{Light energy}} ATP$ (*b*) $ADP + \text{Inorganic } PO_4 \xrightarrow{\text{Light energy}} ATP$
(*c*) $ADP + \text{Inorganic } PO_4 \longrightarrow ATP$ (*d*) $AMP + \text{Inorganic } PO_4 \xrightarrow{\text{Light energy}} ATP$

104. In sugarcane plant 14 CO_2 is fixed in malic acid in which the enzyme that fixes CO_2 is:
(*a*) Photophosnal pyruvic carboxylase (*b*) Ribulose bisphosphate carboxylase
(*c*) Ribulose phosphate Kinase (*d*) Fructose phosphatase

105. Enerson effects explain the phenomenon of :
(*a*) Transpiration (*b*) Absorption of water by roots
(*c*) Photosynthesis (*d*) Respiration

106. Photosynthesis is
(*a*) catabolic process (*b*) anabolic process (*c*) exothermic process (*d*) exergonic process

107. For photosynthesis, the plant requires
(*a*) chlorophyll (*b*) CO_2 and H_2O (*c*) light (*d*) all the above

108. CO_2 and O_2 balance in atmosphere is maintained due to
(*a*) respiration (*b*) photorespiration (*c*) photosynthesis (*d*) nitrogen metabolism

109. Which of the following equations is most adequate in summing up the photosynthesis ?
(*a*) $6CO_2 + 12H_2O + \text{light} \longrightarrow C_6H_{12}O_6 + 6O_2 + 6H_2O$
(*b*) $6CO_2 + 6H_2O \longrightarrow C_6H_{12}O_6 + 6O_2$
(*c*) $C_6H_{12}O_6 + 6O_2 \longrightarrow 6CO_2 + 6H_2O$
(*d*) $CO_2 + H_2O + \text{light} \longrightarrow CH_2O + O_2$

110. Which of the following crop plants is very efficient converter of solar energy ana whose net productive value ranges from 2 kg to 4 kg / m^2 or even higher ?
(*a*) rice (*b*) wheat (*c*) bajra (*d*) sugarcane

111. The bulk fixation of carbon through photosynthesis takes place in
(*a*) terrestrial vegetation (*b*) tropical rain forests (*c*) crop plants (*d*) oceans

112. Nine-tenth of all photosynthesis of the world is carried by
(*a*) herbs (*b*) shrubs (*c*) algae of oceans (*d*) forests

113. The maximum evolution of oxygen is by
(*a*) crops (*b*) forests

(c) siberian vegetation (d) phytoplanktons of sea

114. During photosynthesis the oxygen in glucose comes from
(a) carbon dioxide (b) water and carbondioxide
(c) oxygen in air (d) water

115. The main constituents of Hill reaction are
(a) ATP and $NADPH_2$ in chloroplast (b) ATP and $NADPH_2$ in mitochondria
(c) A reduced substance and O_2 in chloroplast (d) only oxygen

116. Where do the energy-capturing reactions of photosynthesis occur ?
(a) thylakoids (b) stroma (c) plasma membrane (d) cytoplasm

117. The process in which water is split, and essential for photosynthesis
(a) hydrolysis (b) photolysis (c) plasmolysis (d) hemolysis

118. The source of O_2 liberated in photosynthesis is
(a) photosynthetic enzyme (b) carbohydrates
(c) water (d) carbon dioxide

119. Which enzymes most abundantly found on earth?
(a) nitrogenase (b) invertase (c) rubisco (d) catalase

120. Chlorophyll is present
(a) in grana of chloroplasts (b) on surface of chloroplasts
(c) in stroma of chloroplasts (d) dispersed throughout chloroplasts

121. Grana refers to
(a) glycolysis of glucose (b) byproduct of photosynthesis
(c) stacks of quantasome (d) stacks of thylakoids

122. Quantasomes are found in
(a) chloroplast (b) nucleus (c) lysosome (d) mitochondria

123. Where does the primary photochemical reaction occur in the chloroplast ?
(a) stroma (b) quantasome
(c) inner membrane of chloroplast (d) outer membrane of chloroplast

124. Chemical formula for chlorophyll *a* is
(a) $C_{55}H_{72}O_5N_4Mg$ (b) $C_{55}H_{70}O_5N_4Mg$ (c) $C_{55}H_{77}O_6N_4Mg$ (d) None of above

125. The basic structure of all chlorophyll comprises of
(a) porphyrin system (b) cytochrome system (c) plastocyanin system (d) flavoprotein only

126. Which of the following wavelength of light is absorbed maximum for photosynthesis ?
(a) green light (b) red light (c) blue light (d) yellow light

127. Which wavelength of light carries out photosynthesis in bacteria ?
(a) blue (b) red (c) far red (d) ultraviolet

128. The assimilatory power in photosynthesis is
(a) ATP (b) ATP and $NADPH_2$
(c) NADPH (d) ATP, NADPH and CO_2

129. The oxygen produced during photosynthesis comes from photolysis of water proved by
(a) M.Calvin (b) Robert Major (c) Blackman (d) Ruben and Kamin

130. The process of photophosphorylation was discovered by
(a) Calvin (b) Arnon (c) Warburg (d) Weismann

131. Photosynthesis can be increased if light, instead of being administered continuously is given as brief flashes. This phenomenon was first observed by
(a) Emerson and Arnold (b) Benson and Calvin
(c) Hatch and Slack (d) Calvin and Hill

132. The two-pigment theory of photosynthesis was proposed by
(*a*) Blackman (*b*) Emerson (*c*) Arnon (*d*) Hill

133. The source of hydrogen atoms for the synthesis of glucose is
(*a*) $NADPH_2$ (*b*) $FADH_2$ (*c*) H_2O (*d*) ATP

134. The primary electron acceptor in cyclic photophosphorylation is
(*a*) carbon dioxide (*b*) a protein that contains iron and sulphur
(*c*) NADP (*d*) FAD

135. Through which of the following substances the photosystem I passes an electron to *NADP* during light reactions ?
(*a*) Plastocyanin (*b*) Cytochrome (*c*) Ferredoxin (*d*) Plastoquinone

136. ATP formation during photosynthesis is called
(*a*) substrate level phosphorylation (*b*) oxidative phosphorylation
(*c*) photophosphorylation (*d*) phosphorylation

137. Photosystem II occurs in
(*a*) stroma (*b*) grana (*c*) mitochondria (*d*) ribosomes

138. In the electron transport system in terminal oxidation the cytochrome, which donates electron to O_2 is
(*a*) cytochrome *b* (*b*) cytochrome *a* (*c*) cytochrome a_3 (*d*) cytochrome *c*

139. NADP is converted into $NADPH_2$ in
(*a*) photosystem I (*b*) photosystem II
(*c*) non-cyclic photophosphorylation (*d*) cyclic photophosphorylation

140. During cyclic photophosphorylation energy molecules are obtained in the form of
(*a*) ADP (*b*) ATP (*c*) GTP (*d*) ATP and $NADPH_2$

141. Dark reaction in photosynthesis is called, because
(*a*) it does not require light energy (*b*) cannot occur during day time
(*c*) occurs more rapidly at night (*d*) it can also occur in darkness

142. Calvin cycle occurs in
(*a*) chloroplast (*b*) mitochondria (*c*) glyoxysomes (*d*) cytoplasm

143. C_4 cycle was discovered by
(*a*) Hatch and Slack (*b*) Hill (*c*) Arnon (*d*) Calvin

144. During photochemical reactions of photosynthesis
(*a*) liberation of O_2 and formation of ATP and $NADPH_2$ takes place
(*b*) assimilation of CO_2 takes place
(*c*) liberation of O_2 and formation of $NADPH_2$
(*d*) formation of ATP and $NADPH_2$ takes place

145. CO_2 joins the photosynthetic pathway during
(*a*) dark reaction (*b*) photosystem I (*c*) photosystem II (*d*) photolysis

146. The primary acceptor during CO_2 fixation in C_3 plants is
(*a*) Ribulose bisphosphate (*b*) Glycolate
(*c*) Phosphoenolpyruvate (*d*) Triosephosphate

147. First stable compound in C_3 cycle is
(*a*) phosphoglyceraldehyde (*b*) phosphoglyceric acid
(*b*) fructose – 1, 6 diphosphate (*d*) glucose – 6 phosphate

148. Who enunciated law of limiting factor for photosynthesis ?
(*a*) Hill (*b*) Calvin (*c*) Arnold (*d*) Blackman

149. Which of the following have high CO_2 compensation point ?
(*a*) C_2 plants (*b*) C_3 plants (*c*) C_4 plants (*d*) Aquatic plants

150. Compensation point is
(*a*) where there is neither photosynthesis nor respiration
(*b*) where rate of photosynthesis is equal to rate of respiration
(*c*) when there is enough water to meet the requirements of plant
(*d*) when the entire food synthesised in photosynthesis remains unutilised

151. Photosynthesis is maximum during
(*a*) continuous weak light (*b*) continuous strong light
(*c*) intermittent light (*d*) darkness

152. What will happen to the rate of photosynthesis if sodium bicarbonate is added in the water having *Hydrilla* plant in a beaker ?
(*a*) it will be retarded (*b*) it will be remain ormal
(*c*) it will be accelerated (*d*) none of above

153. Rate of photosynthesis is independent of
(*a*) intensity of light (*b*) duration of light (*c*) temperature (*d*) quality of light

154. Kranz type of anatomy is found in
(*a*) C_2 plants (*b*) C_3 plants (*c*) C_4 plants (*d*) CAM plants

155. In C_4 plants Calvin cycle
(*a*) occurs in stroma of bundle sheath chloroplasts
(*b*) occurs in chloroplasts of mesophyll
(*c*) occurs in grana of bundle sheath chloroplasts
(*d*) does not occur

156. In C_4 cycle, CO_2 is fixed by
(*a*) phosphoglyceric acid (*b*) phosphophenol pyruvate
(*c*) oxaloacetic acid (*d*) RuBP

157. The enzyme, which catalyses the photosynthetic C_4 cycle is
(*a*) RuBP carboxylase (*b*) PEP carboxylase (*c*) carbonic anhydrase (*d*) hexokinase

158. C_4 photosynthetic pathway is found in
(*a*) corn (*b*) mustard (*c*) potato (*d*) brinjal

159. Tropical plant like sugarcane shows high efficiency of CO_2 fixation, becuase of
(*a*) Hatch-Slack cycle (*b*) EMP pathway (*c*) TCA cycle (*d*) Calvin cycle

160. Which of the following plants fixes carbon dioxide by way of crassulacean acid metabolism ?
(*a*) cactus (*b*) grass (*c*) Red alga (*d*) *Hibiscus*

161. Energy waste occurs during
(*a*) photosynthesis (*b*) glycolysis
(*c*) photorespiration (*d*) pentose - phosphate pathway

162. What is substrate for photorespiration ?
(*a*) Glycolic acid (*b*) Serine (*c*) Malic acid (*d*) Indole acetic acid

163. All life on earth derives energy, directly or indirectly from sun, except
(*a*) chemosynthetic bacteria (*b*) moulds
(*c*) pathogenic bacteria (*d*) symbiotic bacteria

164. Which of the following photosynthetic bacteria have both PS I and PS II ?
(*a*) green-sulphur bacteria (*b*) purple non-sulphur bacteria
(*c*) purple-sulphur bacteria (*d*) cyanobacteria

165. The bacterial photosynthesis is different from that of other green plants as
(*a*) light is not required (*b*) oxygen is not released
(*b*) a host organism is required (*d*) energy is not fixed

166. Translocation of solutes primarily taken place through
(*a*) phloem (*b*) xylem (*c*) cortex (*d*) pith

167. The carbohydrates synthesised in the leaves are transported through sieve tubes most commonly in the form of
(*a*) glucose (*b*) sucrose (c) triose sugar (*d*) soluble starch

168. If the rate of translocation of food is slow, the the rate of photosynthesis will
(*a*) remain the same (*b*) decrease (*c*) become double (*d*) increase

169. Munch mass flow hypothesis explains
(*a*) Transcription (*b*) Translocation (*c*) Transduction (*d*) Transpiration

170. The *Orobanche* plant is
(*a*) partial stem parasite (*b*) partial root parasite (*c*) total stem parasite (*d*) total root parasite

171. *Cuscuta* is a
(*a*) partial stem parasite (*b*) partial root parasite (*c*) total stem parasite (*d*) total root parasite

172. Which of the following is an example of insectivorous plants
(*a*) *Nepenthes* (*b*) *Cuscuta* (*c*) *Rafflesia* (*d*) *Viscum*

173. Which of the following is an insectivorous plant
(*a*) *Cuscuta* (*b*) *Drosera* (*c*) *Monotropa* (*d*) *Orobanche*

174. Common name of *Utricularia* is
(*a*) Venus fly trap (*b*) bladderwort (*c*) butterwort (*d*) sundew plant

175. The example of saprophyte is
(*a*) *Nepenthes* (*b*) *Drosera* (*c*) *Cuscuta* (*d*) *Monotropa*

ANSWERS

1. (*c*)	**2.** (*b*)	**3.** (*d*)	**4.** (*a*)	**5.** (*b*)	**6.** (*b*)	**7.** (*b*)	**8.** (*b*)	**9.** (*b*)	**10.** (*b*)
11. (*d*)	**12.** (*a*)	**13.** (*c*)	**14.** (*a*)	**15.** (*d*)	**16.** (*b*)	**17.** (*c*)	**18.** (*d*)	**19.** (*b*)	**20.** (*a*)
21. (*b*)	**22.** (*a*)	**23.** (*d*)	**24.** (*b*)	**25.** (*b*)	**26.** (*d*)	**27.** (*a*)	**28.** (*a*)	**29.** (*b*)	**30.** (*c*)
31. (*b*)	**32.** (*d*)	**33.** (*d*)	**34.** (*d*)	**35.** (*b*)	**36.** (*c*)	**37.** (*b*)	**38.** (*b*)	**39.** (*a*)	**40.** (*a*)
41. (*c*)	**42.** (*b*)	**43.** (*a*)	**44.** (*b*)	**45.** (*d*)	**46.** (*b*)	**47.** (*d*)	**48.** (*c*)	**49.** (*b*)	**50.** (*d*)
51. (*d*)	**52.** (*d*)	**53.** (*d*)	**54.** (*d*)	**55.** (*b*)	**56.** (*c*)	**57.** (*d*)	**58.** (*d*)	**59.** (*a*)	**60.** (*c*)
61. (*d*)	**62.** (*d*)	**63.** (*d*)	**64.** (*c*)	**65.** (*b*)	**66.** (*a*)	**67.** (*a*)	**68.** (*b*)	**69.** (*d*)	**70.** (*c*)
71. (*a*)	**72.** (*d*)	**73.** (*a*)	**74.** (*b*)	**75.** (*b*)	**76.** (*d*)	**77.** (*c*)	**78.** (*d*)	**79.** (*c*)	**80.** (*c*)
81. (*b*)	**82.** (*d*)	**83.** (*b*)	**84.** (*b*)	**85.** (*d*)	**86.** (*a*)	**87.** (*b*)	**88.** (*a*)	**89.** (*d*)	**90.** (*b*)
91. (*b*)	**92.** (*c*)	**93.** (*b*)	**94.** (*a*)	**95.** (*c*)	**96.** (*c*)	**97.** (*d*)	**98.** (*c*)	**99.** (*b*)	**100.** (*c*)
101. (*d*)	**102.** (*c*)	**103.** (*b*)	**104.** (*a*)	**105.** (*c*)	**106.** (*b*)	**107.** (*d*)	**108.** (*c*)	**109.** (*a*)	**110.** (*d*)
111. (*d*)	**112.** (*c*)	**113.** (*d*)	**114.** (*a*)	**115.** (*c*)	**116.** (*a*)	**117.** (*b*)	**118.** (*c*)	**119.** (*c*)	**120.** (*a*)
121. (*d*)	**122.** (*a*)	**123.** (*b*)	**124.** (*a*)	**125.** (*a*)	**126.** (*c*)	**127.** (*c*)	**128.** (*b*)	**129.** (*d*)	**130.** (*b*)
131. (*a*)	**132.** (*b*)	**133.** (*a*)	**134.** (*b*)	**135.** (*c*)	**136.** (*c*)	**137.** (*b*)	**138.** (*c*)	**139.** (*c*)	**140.** (*b*)
141. (*a*)	**142.** (*a*)	**143.** (*a*)	**144.** (*a*)	**145.** (*a*)	**146.** (*a*)	**147.** (*b*)	**148.** (*d*)	**149.** (*b*)	**150.** (*b*)
151. (*c*)	**152.** (*c*)	**153.** (*b*)	**154.** (*c*)	**155.** (*a*)	**156.** (*b*)	**157.** (*b*)	**158.** (*a*)	**159.** (*a*)	**160.** (*a*)
161. (*c*)	**162.** (*a*)	**163.** (*a*)	**164.** (*d*)	**165.** (*b*)	**166.** (*a*)	**167.** (*b*)	**168.** (*b*)	**169.** (*b*)	**170.** (*d*)
171. (*c*)	**172.** (*a*)	**173.** (*b*)	**174.** (*b*)	**175.** (*d*)					

19
CHAPTER

Plant Growth and Development

When a seed is sown in soil, it germinates and forms a small seedling which grows over a period of time, and converts into a large and mature plant. This process is termed as **growth**.

Growth is regarded as one of the most fundamental and conspicuous characteristic of a living being. Growth can be defined as an irreversible permanent increase in size of an organ or its parts or even of an individual cell. Generally growth is accompanied by metabolic process (both anabolic and catabolic), that occur at the expense of energy. Therefore, expansion of a leaf is growth but the swelling of wood submerged in water is not.

The most complex of all the physiological processes is **growth**. The process of growth results from an increase in protoplasm, leading to an irreversible increase in size and weight. The growth involves three stages: **stage of cell division**, **stage of cell elongation** and **stage of cell differentiation**. **Growth** is associated with differentiation of cell which is a change in form and physiological activity. **Development** refers to the sequence of processes in the overall life history of a cell or an organism including growth, differentiation, maturation and senescence.

In unicellular organisms, growth involves increase in their volume and numbers. Cell division serves as a means of reproduction in these organisms, and leads to increase in population. In the multicellular organisms, however, growth is much more complex.

The life of flowering plant begins with the fertilized egg. Through a series of divisions, an embryo is formed which is enclosed in a seed. Germination then takes place leading to the formation of a seedling. After passing through the juvenile phases, a mature plant is finally formed. After a period of vegetative growth, the plant enters the reproductive stage. With the initiation and development of flowers, fruits and seeds are formed. A new generation of plants starts again. Annual plants like wheat undergo senescence and die after bearing grain. Development associated with each of three steps is controlled by several factors, both internal and external.

In plants, growth is associated with both anabolic and catabolic activities. This is a quantitative phenomenon and can be measured in relation to time. In living organisms, growth is intrinsic, while in non-living objects, it is extrinsic.

In plants, growth is confined only to **meristems**. The extreme apices of root and shoot are occupied by primary meristems, while in their older parts, secondary meristems, *i.e.*, cambia, give rise to additional vascular tissues and to protective layers of cork cells.

The activity of each meristem influences the other meristems which are close to it, giving rise to **growth correlations**. For example, while the main apical shoot meristem is active it retards the activity of more recently initiated lateral bud meristems, a phenomenon called **apical dominance**.

Besides growth, plants also show movements, both at organ-level, as well as whole-plant level. In this chapter, various aspects of growth, such as dormancy and seed germination, characteristics and conditions for growth, its measurement, growth regulators and types of movements have been discussed in detail.

Plant Growth Generally is Indeterminate

Plants are unique in that they retain the capacity for unlimited growth throughout their life. This ability is due to the presence of meristems at certain locations in their body. The cell(s) of such meristems have the capacity to divide and self-perpetuate. The form of growth wherein new cells are always being added to the plant body by the activity of the meristem is called open form of growth.

The root apical meristem (RAM) and the shoot apical meristem (SAM) are responsible for the primary growth of the plant and principally contribute to the elongation of the plant parallel to its axis. In dicotyledonous plants and gymnosperms, the lateral meristems, vascular cambium and cork cambium appear later in life. These meristems that cause increase in girth of the organ in which they are active, contributing to what is generally known as **secondary growth** of the plant.

The intercalary meristem, located just above the nodes of grasses and related plants contribute to the elongation growth. Thus, root apical meristem (RAM), shoot apical meristem (SAM), vascular cambium, cork-cambium and intercalary meristem are all called **indeterminate meristem**. However the meristem such as those involved in leaf and flower formation are active only for a short period and are primarily responsible for the formation of an organ. These are called **determinate** meristems. (Also see the chapter : Anatomy of Flowering Plants).

Growth is Measurable

Growth is measured by a variety of parameters. Some of such parameters are : (*i*) increase in fresh weight; (*ii*) increase in dry weight; (*iii*) increase in length; (*iv*) increase in area; (*v*) increase in volume; and (*vi*) increase in cell number, etc. For example, one single maize root apical meristem can give rise to more than 17,500 new cells per hour, whereas cells in a watermelon fruit may increase in size by upto 3,50,000 times. In the former, growth is expressed as increase in cell number; the latter expresses growth as increase in size of the cell. Though every cell, tissue organ and organism exhibit growth, yet all the above parameters are not applicable to all forms of growth at all times. For example, an increase in length is a good parameter for a pollen tube growth, while the growth in a dorsiventral leaf can be more easily be measured as an increase in area.

Dormancy and seed Germination

Seed. *A true seed is defined as a fertilized mature ovule that possesses embryonic plant, stored material, and a protective coat or coats.* Seed is the reproductive structure characteristic of all phanerogams. The structure of seeds may be studied in such common types of pea, gram, bean, almond or sunflower. They are all built on the same plan although there may be differences in the shape or size of the seed, the relative proportion of various parts.

There are hundreds of variations in the seed size, shape, colour and surface. The seeds range in size from tiny dust particles, as found in some orchids, to large double-coconuts. The seed surface may be smooth, wrinkled, striate, ribbed, furrowed, reticulate, tuberculate, alveolate, hairy, pulpy or having patterns like finger prints.

In the seed, life activities are temporarily suspended in order to enable the plant to successfully pass through unfavourable and injurious climatic conditions. On the approach of favourable conditions, the seed resumes active life and grows into full plant. In the form of seeds, a plant can be carried to long distances without special precautions.

The developed seeds in many plants undergo a period of dormancy before germination and further growth.

Quiescence. Generally, all plants experience a period of suspended growth. This suspension may be due to exogenous control, such as a change in environmental conditions, and is referred to as **quiescence**.

Seed dormancy. Many kinds of seeds, apparently ripe, fail to germinate even if placed under such conditions that all environmental factors are favourable. In such seeds, resumption of growth by the embryo is arrested by the conditions within the seeds themselves. The state of inhibited growth of seeds or other plant organs as a result of internal causes is usually called **dormancy** but is sometimes referred to as the rest period. Seed dormancy is of considerable advantage to the plant. It enables the embryo to safely pass the unfavourable part of the year and germinate when the conditions are suitable for the establishment of the seedlings. In nature, dormancy period coincides with the unfavourable period for the seedling of the species. Dormancy of seeds results from one or a combination of several undermentioned factors.

Impermeability of seed-coats to water. The seed coats of many species are completely impermeable to water at the time of their maturity. This condition is very common in the seeds of many legumes, (*e.g.*, clovers, alfalfa, etc.) of the water lotus, and of the morning glory. Germination fails to occur until water penetrates through the seed coats.

Mechanically resistant seed coats. In some seeds as those of mustard (*Brassica*), pigweed (*Amaranthus*), shepherd's purse (*Capsella*), etc., the seed-coats are so strong that they do not yield to the pressure of the expanding embryo. The embryos of these seeds have no dormant period and will grow readily if the seed coats are removed.

Seed-coats impermeable to oxygen. The two seeds in a fruit of cocklebur (*Xanthium*) are not equally dormant. Under natural conditions, the lower seed usually germinates in the spring following maturity while the upper seed remains dormant until the next year. The dormancy of these seeds has been demonstrated to result from the impermeability of the seed coats to oxygen.

Rudimentary embryos. In plants like ginkgo (*Ginkgo biloba*), European ash (*Fraxinus*), holly (*Ilex*) and many orchids, the embryo is unorganized when the seed is shed and attains full development before it germinates.

Dormant embryos. In many species, although the embryos are completely developed when the seed is ripe, the seed fails to germinate even when environmental conditions are favourable. Dormancy of such seed is a result of the physiological condition of the embryo. The embryos of such seeds will not grow when the seeds first ripen even if the seed coats are removed. During the period of dormancy, some physiological changes called after-ripening occur in the embryo before the seed is capable of germination. The seeds of apple, peach, iris and pine belong to this group. In nature, after-ripening occurs in winter and the seeds formed in autumn germinate the coming spring.

Germination inhibitors. Germination of seeds is sometimes checked or prevented by the presence of compounds known as **inhibitors**. These are often substances produced in one or more plant organs. For example, the juice of tomato fruits inhibits the germination of tomato seeds and many other seeds as well. Inhibitors may be present in the embryo (*e.g.*, in *Xanthium*), endosperm, (*e.g.*, in *Iris*) or in the seed coat (*e.g.*, in *Cucurbita*). Abscissic acid (ABA) is one of the most commonly detected inhibitors of germination.

Methods of Breaking the Dormancy of Seeds

The dormancy of seeds presents a practical problem of considerable economic importance. Plant growers are often interested in securing seed that will germinate soon after it is harvested. Several methods have been devised for breaking the dormancy of seeds and for shortening the period of dormancy so that they may germinate promptly.

Whenever dormancy results of any of the causes inherent in the seed coats it can be interrupted by **scarification**. For example, machine thrashed legumes seeds usually show a higher percentage of germination than those that have been harvested by hand. Strong mineral acids have been used successfully to interrupt seed dormancy caused by resistant or impermeable seed coats.

Soaking the seeds in certain chemicals like potassium nitrate, ethylene, chlorohydrine, thiourea or in certain plant hormones is known to break dormancy. After ripening of many seeds occurs more rapidly when they are kept at low temperatures than when stored at higher temperatures. Temperature from 5° to 10°C for two or three months are effective with seeds of conifers. Under natural conditions, seed dormancy is gradually overcome by processes such as weakening of the seed coat by the digestive juices in the alimentary canal of fruit-eating birds and other animals, or in still due to the action of microbes or due to mechanical abrasions. Dormancy of seeds is also broken by subjecting the seeds alternately to relatively low and high temperatures. Light is also considered as means of breaking dormancy of seeds. Seeds of sweet clover (*Melilotus alba*) and alfalfa (*Medicago sativa*) showed greatly improved germination after being subjected to hydraulic pressures of 2000 atm. at 18°C.

Germination of Seed

This is the first step towards plant growth. In favourable conditions of environment, seeds germinate. After the dormancy period is over or dormancy is broken, and other necessary conditions for growth are present, the dormant embryo resumes metabolic activities and growth.

The embryo lies dormant in the seed, but when the latter is supplied with moisture, the embryo becomes active and tends to grow and develop into a small seedling. *The resumption of metabolic activity and growth by the seed tissue, involving rehydration, utilization of reserves and gradual development of synthetic systems which enable the plant to assume an autophytic or autotrophic existence, is called germination.* In other words, *the process by which the dormant embryo wakes up and begins to grow is known as germination.* The embryo grows by absorbing the food material stored up in the cotyledons, or the endosperm when it is present. At first the seed absorbs moisture and swells up considerably, then the radicle elongates and comes out often through the micropyle and gives rise to the root. In whatever position the seed be placed in the soil, the radicle always grows downwards and gives rise to the root system. Its rate of growth is much faster than that of the plumule. As a result of swelling, the seed-coat bursts and the cotyledons partially or completely separate from each other to give way to the plumule which lies within. Prior to germination, several intricate physiological processes occur within the seed. A rapid increase in respiration occurs. This is accompanied by the appearance of some hydrolytic enzymes that break down food materials stored in the seed to simpler molecules that can be utilized by the seedling until the latter can become photosynthetically efficient.

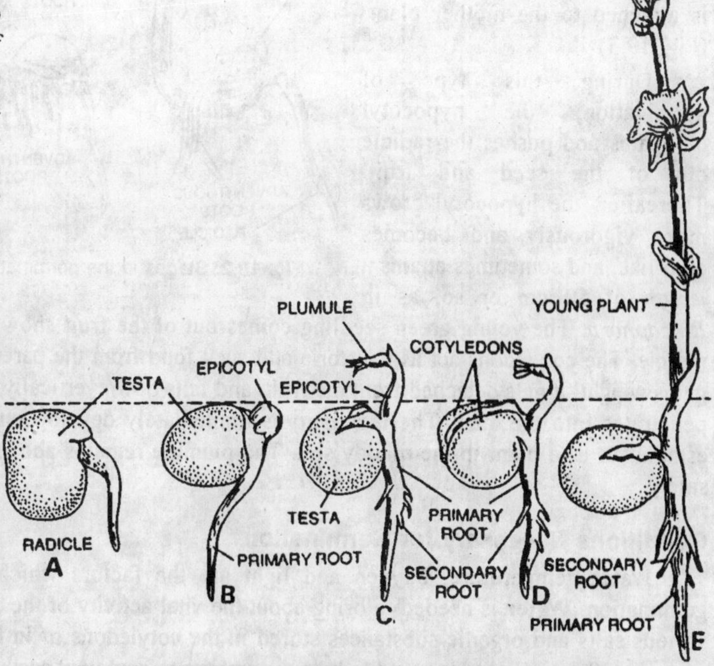

Fig. 19.1. Stages in the germination of pea seed (hypogeal germination in dicot).

Based on the behaviour of the cotyledons, germination is of two types: **epigeal** and **hypogeal**. In some seeds such as tamarind, cucumber, cotton, gourd, castor, etc., the cotyledons are seen to be pushed upwards above the soil, the germination is said to be **epigeal**. In other seeds such as gram, pea, broad bean, groundnut, mango, etc., the cotyledons remain below the soil and the germination is known as **hypogeal**. In the seeds of all monocotyledonous plants, the germination is of hypogeal type.

Vivipary

This is a special type of germination of seed. This is the phenomenon of germination of seeds within the fruit, while the fruit is still attached to the mother plant. This type of seed germination occurs in several species of the plants to mangrove vegetation, such as *Rhizophora*, *Sonneratia*, *Ceriops*, *Kandelia*, etc. The seeds in such plants do not germinate in the soil due to high salt contents and deficiency of oxygen in the marshy habitats. In such plants, the seed dormancy is absent. Instead, embryo grows continuously without any hinderance inside the fruit while it is attached to the mother plant. (Fig. 19.3)

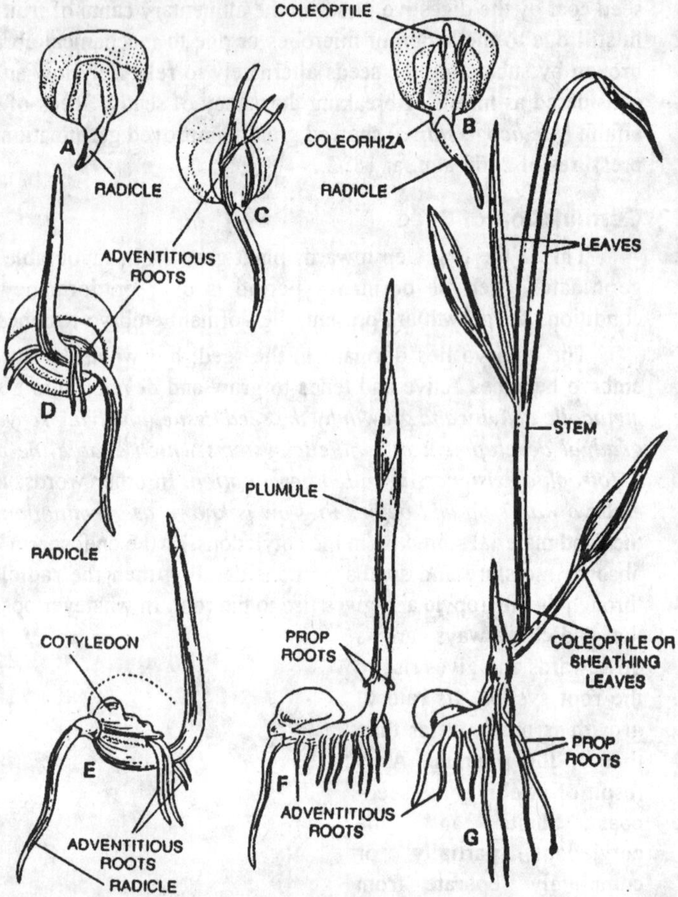

Fig. 19.2. Stages in the germination of maize grain (A-G).

During this type of germination, the hypocotyl elongates and pushes the radicle out of the seed and fruit. Thereafter, the hypocotyl grows more vigorously and becomes club-like, and sometimes attains a length of 50 cm or so, as in *Rhizophora*. The young green seedling comes out of the fruit showing the long hypocotyl and radicle. The cotyledons act as haustoria and suck food from the parent plant. When the seedling gains weight, it gets detached from the fruit, and falls down vertically like a dart. Now the radicle penetrates into the mud. The lateral roots immediately develop on this seedling, and it soon establishes as a plant in the muddy soil. The plumule remains above the water level and grows safely.

Conditions Necessary for Germination

Water, temperature, oxygen and light are the factors which are responsible for seed germination. **Water** is needed to bring about the vital activity of the dormant embryo to dissolve various salts and organic substances stored in the cotyledons or in the endosperm; to facilitate necessary chemical changes; and to help the embryo to come out easily by softening the seed-coat. **Temperature** requirement of seeds varies depending on the species. Seeds of many species germinate only if the temperature is within a certain range. Very low and very high temperatures retard or prevent germination. Wheat grains may germinate at a temperature a little above 0° C while the lowest limit for maize is 5-10°C. **Oxygen** is essential for the germination of germinating seeds. Seeds buried in the deeper layers of the soil remain dormant for want of oxygen. They readily germinate when the soil is ploughed. Seeds of aquatic plants can obtain their oxygen requirements from the air dissolved in water. *Light* is an essential factor for the germination of seeds of mistletoe and many epiphytes. They will not germinate in the dark. In some plants seed germination is favoured by light. This is the case with seeds of lettuce (*Lactuca sativa*) and many grasses. Many secds are however, indifferent to light. In others, light has a retarding effect and may even completely prevent germination (*e.g.*, *Nigella*, *Phlox*, onion, and lilies).

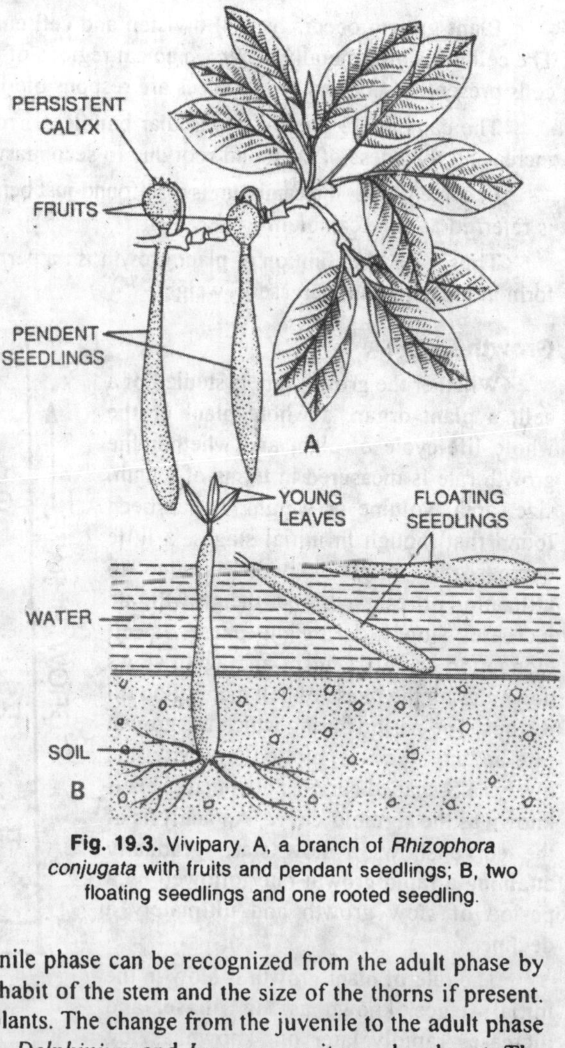

Fig. 19.3. Vivipary. A, a branch of *Rhizophora conjugata* with fruits and pendant seedlings; B, two floating seedlings and one rooted seedling.

Juvenility

After germination, a young plant develops vegetatively for some time and lacks the capacity to form flowers. This early phase of the vegetative growth of the plant is known as **juvenile phase**. The juvenile phase can be recognized from the adult phase by certain striking features such as leaf shape, habit of the stem and the size of the thorns if present. Such differences also occur in some lower plants. The change from the juvenile to the adult phase is gradual, as shown in the leaves of cotton, *Delphinium* and *Ipomoea*, or it may be abrupt. The latter condition represents heteroblastic development. For example, in some plants the first few leaves are normal, whereas the subsequent leaves may be phyllodes, (*e.g.*, *Acacia* spp).

It has been advocated that the juvenile and adult parts of the plants are also physiologically different. In the juvenile phase, the plant does not respond to stimuli that can induce flower formation. In woody plants, branches cut from the juvenile stage root more readily than those derived from the adult stage. This is a point of significance in vegetative propagation.

CHARACTERISTICS OF GROWTH

Plant growth is a complex phenomenon associated with numerous physiological processes, both of constructive and destructive types.

Constructive process leads to the formation of various nutritive substances and the protoplasm, while destructive process is responsible for their breakdown.

The protoplasm assimilates the protein food and increases in bulk, while the carbohydrates are utilised in respiration and in the formation of cell-wall substance, cellulose.

Plant growth occurs by cell division and cell enlargement followed by cell differentiation. The cell division generally occurs in apical regions of shoot and root, and therefore, meristematic cells present at root and shoot apices are responsible for growth in plants.

The cambia are present in vascular bundles of root and shoot of dicot plants. They help in increasing thickness of stem and root due to secondary growth.

In some plants, the cambium is also found just beneath the epidermis and above cortex, which is referred as cork cambium.

Thus, overall definition of plant growth is : a permanent and irreversible increase in size and form attended by an increase in weight.

Growth Curve

Whether the growth rate is studied of a cell, a plant organ, a whole plant or the whole life-cycle of plant and whether the growth rate is measured in terms of length, size, area, volume or weight. It has been found that though in initial stages, a little decrease in weight may occur due to utilization of reserved food, the growth rate increases slowly during the phase of cell elongation or enlargement and again slows down during the phase of cell maturation till it stops. The period during which the growth rate in any term is plotted against time always a S-shaped curve is obtained. This is known as the **sigmoid curve**. An analysis of the curve shows a slow start, gradually attaining a rapid growth rate followed by a period of slow growth and ultimately a decline.

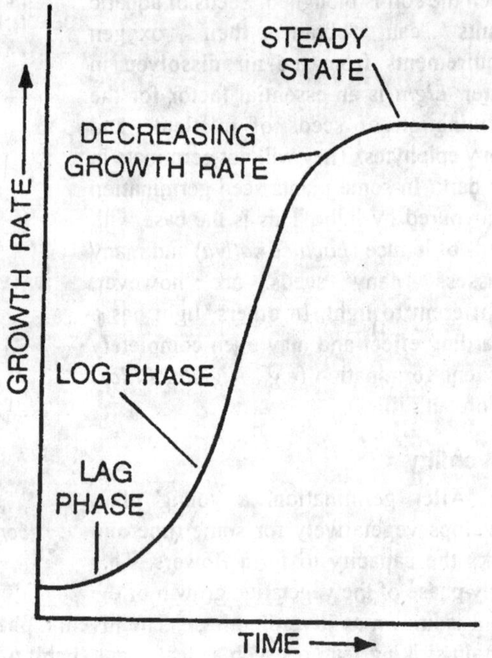

Fig. 19.4. Sigmoid curve.

The rate of plant growth is slow in the initial stages, known as **lag phase**, and increases rapidly later on, known as **log phase** (exponential phase). The growth again slows down due to the limitation of nutrients, and called **steady phase**.

The rate of growth can be measured by an increase in size or area of an organ of the plant, such as leaf, flower or fruit in a unit time. The rate of growth is called **efficiency index**.

CONDITIONS NECESSARY FOR GROWTH

As growth is brought about by the protoplasm, the conditions for growth are the same as those that maintain the activity of the protoplasm. They are as follows :

1. Supply of nutritive materials. Growth can only take place when the protoplasm of the growing region is supplied with nutritive materials. The protoplasm assimilates these materials and builds up the body of the plant. Carbohydrates make a source of energy.

2. Supply of water. An adequate supply of water is absolutely necessary to maintain the turgidity of the growing cells. Turgidity is the first step towards growth. The protoplasm can only function when it is saturated with water. However, abundant supply of water is lost due to transpiration, and only small amount is required for actual growth.

3. Supply of oxygen. Supply of free oxygen is indispensable for the respiration of all living cells. This is an oxidation process by which the **potential** energy stored in the food is released in the form of **kinetic** energy, and used by the protoplasm for hundreds of activities.

4. Suitable temperature. The protoplasm requires a suitable temperature for its activities. At a low temperature, it ceases to perform its functions or does so very slowly, whereas a temperature of 45° to 50°C coagulates and kills the protoplasm. However, the protoplasm maintains its activities within a certain range of temperature. This is called the **thermotonic** effect of temperature. The optimum temperature is generally from 28° to 30°C, while the minimum temperature is about 4°C.

5. Light. However, this condition for growth is not absolutely necessary in initial stages. In fact, plants grow more rapidly in the dark than in the light. However, stomata remain open and chloroplasts function normally preparing food substances (carbohydrates) only in the presence of light. All this happens due to **phototonic** or stimulating effect of light. Continued absence of light is quite harmful to plants.

Plants grown in the dark or in very weak light have delicate, soft and slender stems and branches with elongated internodes, are pale-green or pale-yellow in colour and sickly in appearance. On such plants generally the flowers and fruits are not produced. The leaves of such plants are small, pale-yellow in colour and often remain under-developed, and the roots are poorly developed. Plants showing such characteristics are called **etiolated**, and the phenomenon, **etiolation**.

The relative length of day and night has a profound influence on the production of flowers and fruits (see topic photoperiodism in this chapter).

6. Gravity. This factor determines the direction of growth of particular organs of the plant body. The roots grow towards force of gravity, and the stem against it. This process is called **geotropism**. The roots are **positively geotropic**, while the stems are **negatively geotropic**.

Besides all-above-mentioned factors, salt, mineral deficiencies and stress factors also influence the rate of growth.

PHASES OF GROWTH

Generally in plants growth is restricted to meristematic regions only. These **meristems** may be **apical, lateral** or **intercalary**. The growth in length is due to gradual enlargement and elongation of the cells of the apical meristems, *i.e.*, root-apex and shoot-apex. However, in dicotyledonous angiosperms and gymnosperms the growth in thickness is due to the activity of the lateral meristems, *i.e.*, interfascicular cambium, intrafascicular cambium and cork cambium. Growth is not a very simple process. Before completion of this process a meristematic cell has to pass to three important phases : 1. The formative or meristematic phase; 2. The phase of elongation and 3. The phase of maturation; 4. Grand period of growth.

1. The formative or meristematic phase. This is restricted to the apical meristem of root and stem. The cells of this region constantly divide and multiply in number. They have abundant protoplasm, a large nucleus and a thin cellulose wall.

The meristematic phase has constantly dividing cells both at the root apex and the shoot apex. The cells in this region are rich in protoplasm, possess large conspicuous nuclei and their cell walls are primary, thin and cellulosic with abundant plasmodesmata.

2. The phase of elongation. This lies immediately behind the formative phase. The cells do not divide in this phase, but they increase in size. The cells enlarge in size and elongate until they reach their maximum dimension. In the root, this phase occupies a length of a few millimeters, and in the stem a few centimeters.

The cells just next to meristematic zone represent the phase of elongation. Increased vacuolation cell enlargement and new cell wall deposition are the characteristics of cells in this phase.

3. The phase of maturation. This is further behind, and here, the cells start maturing to obtain a permanent size. The thickening of the cell-wall takes place in this phase.

Further, away from the apex, *i.e.*, more proximal to the phase of elongation lies the portion of the axis which is undergoing the phase of maturation. The cells occupying this zone, attain their final size, wall thickening and protoplasmic modifications. Most of the tissue/cell types represent this phase. Hence, at this phase, all the diverse tissue types observed in epidermis, cortex, vascular tissue, etc., both in root and apical end of a stem.

4. Grand period of growth. The time interval from the formative phase to maturation phase is called the grand period of growth. Every cell of the organ of plant body, shows a variation in the rate of its growth. The growth is at first slow, then it accelerates till a maximum is attained, then it falls off quickly, and gradually slows down till it comes to a standstill. This growth of organ or cell of a plant as a whole extending over the whole period is actual **grand period of growth**.

Within the grand period, variations in growth occur due to external and other causes. There is thus the **diurnal variation of growth**. Light inhibits growth, and too intense light even checks growth altogether. Thus plants grow quicker in night than in comparison of day.

There is also **seasonal variation of growth**. During winter, the growth of many plants is checked or becomes very slow, while during spring, growth proceeds rapidly.

MEASUREMENT OF GROWTH

As already mentioned, growth is a complex natural phenomenon, and generally takes place at the apical regions of the plant. Thus, the growth in length can easily be measured with the help of **auxanometer**. This phenomenon, you can understand by following simple experiments :

An auxanometer is used to measure the rate of growth in terms of shoot length.

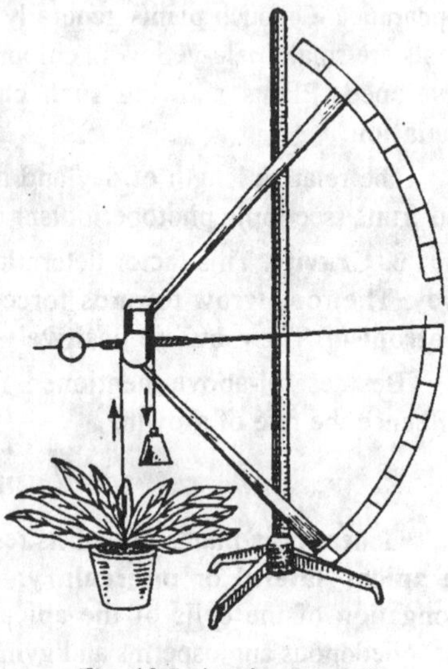

Fig. 19.5. Arc Auxanometer.

PRACTICALS

Experiment

Object : Measurement of growth in plants.

Requirements : Auxanometers : (*i*) Arc auxanometer (*ii*) Pfeffer's automatic auxanometer.

(*i*) **Arc auxanometer :** It consists of a vertical stand with a pulley to which is attached a long thread and a needle or pointer movable over a graduated arc. One end of the thread is tied with the growing point of the plant and another is stretched with a suitable weight.

(*ii*) **Pfeffer's automatic auxanometer :** It consists of a vertical stand with two pulleys. One of these two pulleys possesses a thread carrying two weights at either ends to keep it stretched. This thread on one side is also attached with a fine scratching pointer which touches a smoked drum. Another pulley is also provided with a thread of which one end is tied with the growing point of plant and another is stretched with a suitable weight.

Observation and Explanation : (*i*) With the growth of plant, the weight moves the thread down and the movement of needle can be read easily on the scale.

There exists a notable ratio between the size of pulley and the needle. If pulley is 4 inches with the needle 20 inches from the centre of the disc of pulley, growth will be magnified ten times on the scale. It can easily be illustrated by an example :

If indicator moves 4 cm in 8 hours and the magnification is 10 times, then the actual growth is:

$\because$ Growth in 8 hours = 4/10 cm

= 0.4 cm or 4 mm

$\therefore$ Growth in one hour = 4/8

= 0.5 mm/hour

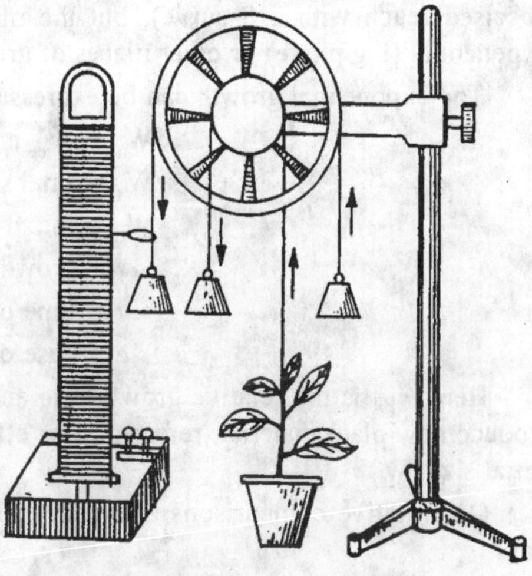

Fig. 19.6. Pfeffer's Auxanometer.

(*ii*) With the growth of plant first pulley makes moving the another which in turn moves the pointer. This pointer moves downwards and traces a spiral on the rotating smoked drum. Thus the growth for a certain period is recorded.

Growth can also be measured by an increase in weight both fresh and dry, and volume of the plant. The increase in the number of cells, especially in algae, cyanobacteria, yeast, etc. The measurement of area or volume of an organ of the plant also gives information about the rate of growth.

Growth Rates

The expression of increased growth per unit time is termed **growth rate**. Thus, rate of growth can be expressed mathematically. An organism, or a part of the organism can produce more cells in a variety of ways.

The growth rate can be **arithmetic** or **geometrical** increase :

In **arithmetic growth**, following mitotic cell division only one daughter cell continues to divide while the other differentiates and matures. The simplest expression is arithmetic growth, *e.g.*, a root elongating at a constant rate. Mathematically, it is expressed as :

$$L_t = L_o + r_t$$

L_t = length at time 't'

L_o = length at time 'zero'

r = growth rate/elongation per unit time.

Geometrical growth. However, in most systems, the initial growth is slow (lag phase), and it increases rapidly thereafter at an on exponential rate (log or exponential phase). Here, both the progeny cells following a mitotic cell division retain the ability to divide and continue to do so. However, with limited nutrient supply, the growth slows down leading to a stationary phase. If we plot the parameter of growth against time, we get a typical **sigmoid** or **S-curve**. S-curve is characteristic of every living organism growing in a natural environment. It is typical for all cells, tissues and organs of a plant. However, S-curve of the individual cells/tissues/organs/organisms may not be synchronous, *i.e.*, not at the same phase of the curve. For example, one cell may enter stationary phase while other is just entering the lag phase. Individual leaves are initiated, and abscised (each with a S-curve), but the plant/branch on which they occur could be still in exponential (log phase) or other places of growth.

The exponential growth can be expressed as :

$$W_1 = W_{oe}\, r_t$$

W_1 = final stage (weight, height, number, etc.)

W_0 = initial size at the beginning of the period

r = growth rate

t = time of growth

e = base of natural logarithms

Here, r = is the relative growth rate and is also the measure of the ability of the plant to produce new plant material, referred to as **efficiency index**. Hence, final size of W_1 depends on initial size, W_0.

Quantitative comparisons between the growth of living system can be also made in two ways :

(*i*) Measurement and the comparison of total growth per unit is called absolute **growth rate**.

(*ii*) The growth of the given system per unit time expressed on a common basis, *e.g.*, per unit initial parameter is called **relative growth rate**. For example, two leaves A and B of different area sizes show exact absolute increase in area in the given time to give leaves A′ and B′. However, one of them has much higher relative growth rate.

Apical Dominance

In many herbaceous plants which produce aerial stems, growth in length takes place at the apex of the main axis of the plant. Although a lateral bud is present in the axil of every leaf, side branches do not often develop from these buds as long as the terminal bud retains its vigour and continues to grow. If the terminal bud is destroyed or is artificially removed, development of the lateral buds usually starts at once. This inhibiting effect of a terminal bud upon lateral bud development is called **apical dominance** and is much more pronounced in some species than in others.

The phenomenon of apical dominance is usually also in evidence in all woody plants on which true terminal buds form. The lateral buds on current shoots usually do not develop unless the terminal bud is destroyed or injured. Development of the lateral buds on older shoot segments is of more frequent occurrence, indicating that the inhibitory effect of the apical bud diminishes with greater distance of the lateral buds from the apex of the stem.

The controlling effect of the apical bud in apical dominance results from its auxin content. Several other growth regulating compounds have similar effects upon the growth of lateral buds, if applied to the cut surface of a detipped stem. For example, when potato tubers begin to sprout the apical buds grow rapidly but the lateral buds usually fail to elongate. If, however, the apical and lateral buds are cut out of the parent tuber both grow at similar rates. Treatment of the tubers with ethylene chlorohydrin which causes the destruction of auxin, results in the rapid growth of both lateral and apical buds. This supports that the growth of lateral buds is checked by auxins formed in the apical buds.

Conditions for Growth

Water, oxygen and nutrients are very essential for growth. The plant cells grow in size by cell enlargement which in turn requires water. Thus, plant growth and further development is intimately linked to water status/availability water also provides medium for enzymatic activity.

Oxygen helps in releasing metabolic energy, so essential for growth activities.

Nutrients (macro and micro essential elements) are required by plants for synthesis of protoplasm and act as source of energy.

Temperature. In addition, every plant organism has an optimum temperature range best suited for its growth. Any deviation from this range could be detrimental to its survival.

Environmental signals such as light and gravity also affect certain phases/stages of growth.

GROWTH REGULATORS

Plants produce some specific chemical substances, which are capable of moving from one organ to the other, and provide physiological control on growth. These substances, which are active in very small amounts are called **plant hormones** or **growth regulators**.

The genetic make up and **growth regulations** constitute important internal factors that regulate plant growth and development. The main naturally occurring plant growth regulators are **auxins, gibberellins, cytokinins, ethylene** and **abscisic acid**. The first four are called plant hormones. Abscisic acid (ABA) is naturally occurring growth inhibitor. A plant hormone is an organic compound synthesized in one tissue of plant and migrates to another tissue wherein very minute quantity affects the growth.

1. Auxins (*Gk. auxein = to grow*). Auxin is a group of hormone produced by the apical apices of stem and roots which migrate from the apex to the zone of elongation. The role of auxin is essential for the elongation process. Most of the knowledge about auxins comes from the work

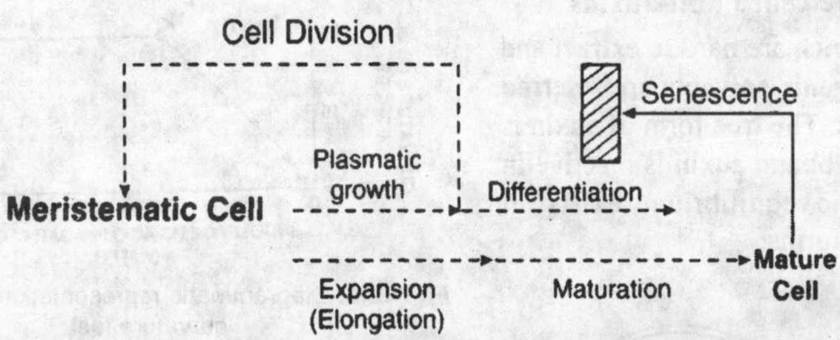

Fig. 19.7. Structures of some common synthetic auxins.

on oat (*Avena sativa*). If the growing tip of oat coleoptile is removed, the remaining portion of coleoptile will show a marked decrease in growth which will ultimately stop. This means growth is restricted to or dependent on upper region. If the removed tip is placed on agar block for a period of several hours and then removed and the agar block now transferred to the cut stem, it is observed that block partially substitutes for the tip and the growth is resumed. This may be concluded that substance synthesized in the tip migrates downwards (in agar block) and is responsible for elongation of tip. This substance was denoted as auxin. Went (1928) performed ***Avena*-curvature test.** He placed several freshly cut coleoptile tips on agar block, after few hours which is cut into several pieces. He placed the agar block eccentrically on the coleoptile cut portion for two hours in dark. The growth curvature occurred and the coleoptile bends on one side opposite to the agar block. It occurred due to auxin diffusion from block to coleoptile resulting in elongation and growth on that side, as a result coleoptile bends. The experiments performed by Went shared that auxin is synthesized in the coleoptile tip and is translocated downward.

Auxins are synthesized in the shoot tips, young leaf primordia, developing seeds and from there they migrate to the regions of elongation. The movement of auxin is polar and in stems, it takes place in a basipetal direction whereas in the roots, it is in an acropetal direction. Auxins cause elongation of the stems and roots.

Extensive work has been done on auxin and several related compounds have been isolated in pure forms. Among them the most common one is Indole 3-acetic acid (IAA) which is derivative of amino acid tryptophan.

The primary physiological effect of auxin is to promote the elongation of the cells which may be due to increasing osmotic pressure and permeability of cytoplasm to water and decreasing wall pressure. Some work done by Coartney *et al* (1967), Masuda *et al* (1967) and Nooden (1968) indicates that auxin is associated with nucleic acid metabolism. It affects the site of DNA responsible for increasing plasticity of walls and its extension.

The compounds which can be converted into auxins are called **auxin precursors**.

The compounds which inhibit the actions of auxins are called **anti-auxins**.

The auxins which are hard to extract and need the use of organic solvents are referred to as **bound auxins**. The free form of auxin is active, whereas the bound auxin is inactive in growth. A dynamic equilibrium exists in between these two forms.

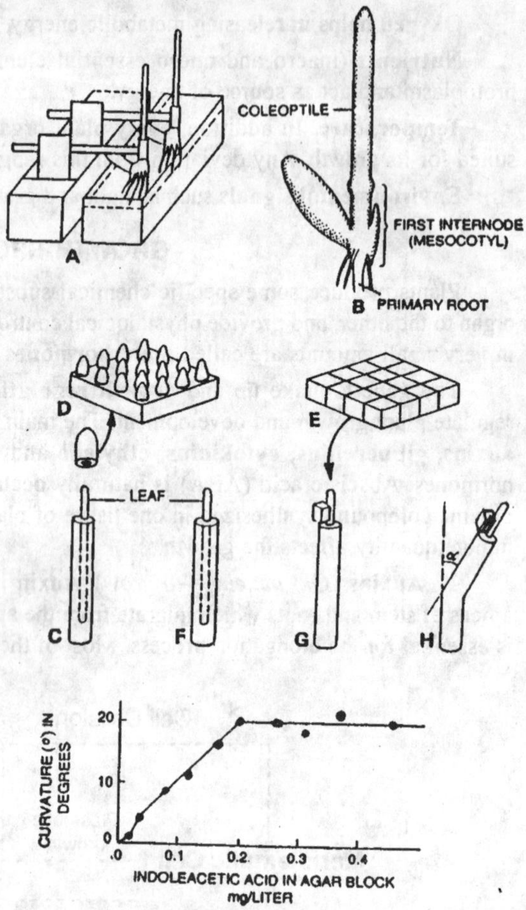

Fig. 19.8. Diagrammatic representation of the *Avena* curvature test.

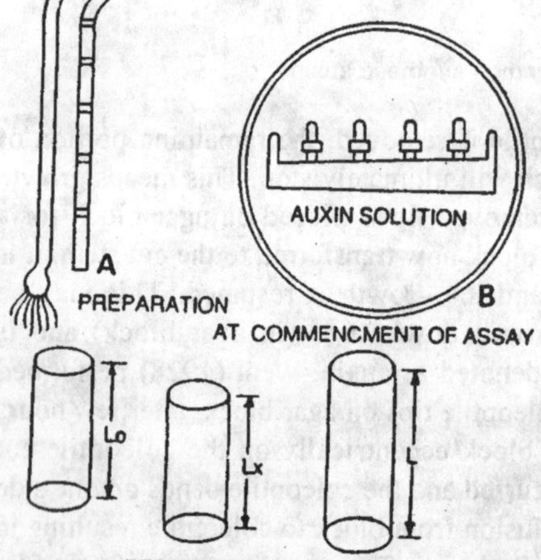

Fig. 19.9. Avena Section Test. LO = length of freshly cut segment. LX = Length of untreated segment after floating in water for length of test period ; L = length of treated segment after floating in test solution for length of test period.

The functions of auxins are generally tested with the help of bioassays. **Bioassay** means the testing of substance for its activity in causing a growth response in a living plant or its organ. This test is quantitative in nature, which measures the concentration required to produce the effect.

For example, *Avena* curvature test, and root growth inhibition test, are bioassays for examining auxin activity.

Uses of auxins. There are several horticultural and agricultural uses of auxins. They are as follows :

The applications of auxins have a wide range, such as (*i*) enhancing the formation of roots, (*ii*) development of parthenocarpic fruits (*iii*) thinning of flowers and fruits for healthy growth of remaining ones, (*iv*) control of preharvest fruit drop, (*v*) enhancement of flowering, (*vi*) improving quality during storage, (*vii*) weed control by herbicidal action, (*viii*) control of apical dominance.

Some specific uses of auxins are as follows :

(*i*) **As weedicides.** 2, 4–D (*i.e.*, 2, 4-Dichlorophenoxyacetic acid) is a selective weedicide. It destroys broad-leaved dicot weeds. It is used in cereal crops and in lawns to kill the weeds. It does not affect the growth of monocots.

(*ii*) **For fruiting and root initiation.** Naphthalene acetic acid (NAA) and indole butyric acid (IBA) induce fruiting. The foliar spray on litchi and pineapple induces flowering and when applied to cuttings they induce root initiation. They also retard abscission, and therefore prevent premature fruit fall.

(*iii*) **For potato storage.** Methyl ester of naphthalene acetic acid (NAA) inhibits the sprouting of potatoes, and therefore used for storage.

(*iv*) **To inhibit or stimulate the growth of lateral buds.** The pruning of plants is done to stimulate growth in the desired area. If apex is removed lateral buds develop, giving a branching appearance. In roses and many fruit trees, the pruning is done to improve the quality of flowers and fruits.

Characteristics of Plant Growth Regulators

The plant growth regulators (PGR) are small, simple molecules of diverse chemical composition. They could be **indole compounds** (indole-3-acetic acid IAA); **adenine derivatives** (N^6 – furfurylamino purine, Kinetin); **derivatives of carotenoids** and **fatty acids** (abscisic acid, ABA); **terpenes** (gibberellic acid, GA_3) or **gases** (ethylene, C_2H_4).

Plant growth regulators are variously described as **plant growth substances, plant hormones** or **phytohormones.**

The plant growth regulators (PGR) can be broadly divided into two groups based on their functions in a living plant body.

One group of PGRs are involved in growth promoting activities, such as cell division, cell enlargement, pattern formation, tropic growth, flowering, fruiting and seed formation. These are also called **plant growth promoters**, *e.g.*, Auxins, gibberellins and cytokinins.

The PGRs of other group play an important role in plant responses to wounding and stress of biotic and abiotic origin. They also are involved in various growth inhibiting activities such as promotion of dormancy and abscission. The PGR abscisic acid (ABA) belongs to this group.

The gaseous PGR, ethylene (C_2H_4), could fit either of the groups, but it is largely inhibits growth activities.

Functions of PGRs. Each of these PGRs belonging to any group bring about a variety of growth and developmental responses, and not all responses are similar and simultaneous at any given time, *e.g.*, a given concentration of auxin which promotes shoot growth may inhibit root growth.

Secondly, similar responses are affected by different PGRs, *e.g.*, both auxins and gibberellins can result in cell enlargement, while cell division could be promoted by auxins, gibberellins and cytokinins.

The PGRs are active at very low concentrations usually in 10^{-6} M range. However, site of production and sites of action (target cells) of PGRs could be same or different. Also they are synthesised at several sites and in different tissues within a plant body and not in any specialised gland or tissue, as in animals.

Moreover, each of the major classes of PGR bring about a variety of growth and differentiation responses.

The Discovery of Plant Growth Regulators

The discovery of each of the five major groups of PGRs have been accidental.

1. All this started with the observation of Charles Darwin and his son Francis Darwin when they observed that the coleoptiles of canary grass (*Phalaris canarensis*) responded to unilateral illumination by growing towards the light source (phototropism). After a series of experiments, it was concluded that the tip of coleoptile was the site of transmittable influence that caused the bending of the entire coleoptile.

   Thereafter, several experiments in different laboratories, culminated in the discovery of first PGR, the **auxin**, by F.W. Went (1928) in coleoptile tips of *Avena sativa* seedlings.
2. The *bakane* (foolish seedling) disease of rice seedlings which resulted in weak, elongated stems that produced little or no grains. Japanese plant pathologist indentified the causal organism, *Gibberella fujikoroi*, a fungus. In 1926 Kurosawa reported the appearance of symptoms of disease in uninfected rice seedlings. When they were treated with sterile filtrates of the fungus, the active substance was later identified as **gibberelic acid**.
3. F. Skoog (USA) and his co-workers were studying the nutritional requirements of tissue cultures derived from the internodal segments of tobacco stems. They observed that the callus proliferated only, it in addition to auxins nutrient medium was supplemented with one of the following extracts of vascular tissues or yeast extract or coconut milk or DNA. Skoog and Miller, soon identified and crystallized the cytokinesis-promoting active substance that they termed **kinetin**.
4. As the research in plant growth regulators was progressing, it became apparent that certain substances of plant origin interfered with auxin responses. Advent of paper chromatography technique as an analytical tool helped to identify the PGR, **abscisic acid** in 1967.
5. Businessmen involved in shipping and storing fruits have been aware that ripe and rotten fruits could accelerate the ripening of other fruits stored nearby. Cousins (1910) confirmed the release of a volatile substance from ripened oranges that hastened the ripening of unripened bananas stored nearby. R. Gane (1934) provided undisputable evidence that this volatile substance was **ethylene** (C_2H_4), a gaseous PGR using gas chromatography technique.

PHYSIOLOGICAL EFFECTS OF PLANT GROWTH REGULATORS

Auxins

Auxins (GK *Auxein* = to grow), isolated initially from human urine were the first plant PGR to be discovered.

However, IAA also occurs in human urine, especially in persons suffering from pellagra (niacin or nicotinic acid deficiency)

The term **auxin** is applied to the indole-3-acetic acid (IAA), and to other natural and synthetic compounds having certain growth regulating properties. They are generally produced by the growing apices of the stems and roots, from where they migrate to the regions of their action.

Auxins, like IAA and indole butyric acid, IBA, have been isolated from plants.

2, 4–D (2, 4 dichlorophenoxyacetic), NAA (naphthalene acetic acid) are the synthetic auxins.

All above mentioned auxins have been used extensively, particularly in agricultural practices.

Applications of auxins have a wide range. They have been used for more than 50 years in horticulture and agriculture. They help to initiate rooting in stem cuttings, an application widely used for plant propagation. Auxins promote flowering, *e.g.*, in pineapples. They help to prevent fruit and leaf drops at early stages but promote the abscission older/mature leaves and fruits.

In most higher plants, the growing apical bad inhibits the growth of lateral (axillary) buds, a phenomenon called **apical dominance**.

Removeal of shoot tips (decapitation) usually results in the growth of lateral buds. It is widely applied in tea plucking, hedge-making.

Auxins also induce parthenocarpy, *e.g.*, in tomatoes. They are widely used as herbicides. Auxin 2, 4–D, is widely does not affect mature monocotyledonous plants. It is also spread to kill dandelions/daisies in lawns by gardeners. Auxin also control xylem differentiation and help cell-division.

Gibberellins

This is another kind of promotery PGR. There are more than 100 gibberellins reported from different organism such as fungi and higher plants, and the number is still increasing.

They are denoted as GA_1, GA_2, GA_3 and so on. However, GA_3 was one of the first gibberellins to be discovered and remains the most intensively studied form.

All GA_5 are acidic. They produce a wide range of physiological responses in the plants. They specifically make genetic dwarfs, *e.g.*, in peas, grow tall. Their ability to cause increase in length of axis is used to make the stalks of graphs lengthy, thereby allowing the grapes to grow larger.

Gibberellins GA_4 and GA_7 cause apple fruits to elongate and improve shape. They also delay senescence, thus the fruits can be left on the tree longer to extend market period.

GA_3 is used to speed up malting process in brewing industry.

Spraying sugarcane crop with gibberellins increases the length of the stem. It helps increase yield an much as by 20 tons per acre.

Spraying juvenile conifers with GA_4 and GA_7 hastens the maturity period. Thus leading to early seed production. Gibberellins also promote bolting (*i.e.*, internode elongation prior to flowering) in beet, cabbages and many plants with rosette habit.

Cytokinins

These PGRs have specific effects on cytokinesis, and were discovered as **kinetin** (a modified form of adenine, a purine) from the herring sperm DNA. Kinetin does not occur naturally in plants. The searches for natural substances with cytokinin like activities led to the isolation of **Zeatin** from corn-kernels and coconnt milk, etc. Since the discovery of zeatin, several naturally occurring cytokinins, and some synthetic compounds, with cell division promoting activity, have been identified from plants.

Natural cytokinins are synthesised in regions where rapid cell division is occurring, *e.g.*, root apices, developing shoot buds, young fruits, etc.

They help in production of new leaves, chloroplasts in leaves, lateral shoot growth as well as adventitious shoot formation. Cytokinins overcome apical dominance. They promote nutrient mobilization that helps in delay of leaf senescence.

Ethylene

This is a simple gaseous PGR. It is aynthesised in large amounts by tissues undergoing senescence and ripening of fruits. Ethylent influences of plants include horizontal growth of seedlings, swelling of the axis, tighter apical look formation in dicot seedlings.

Ethylene promotes senescence and abscission of plant organs (especially leaves, flowers etc.)

Ethylene is highly effective in fruit ripening. It enhances the respiration rate during ripening of fruit. This rise in rate of respirsation is called **respiratory climacteric**.

Exposure of plants to ethylen causes drooping of leaves and flowers, a phenomenon known as **epinasty**.

Ethylene is a natural PGR and product of metabolism in plants.

Ethylene break seed and bud dormancy, initiate germination in peanut seeds, sprouting of potato tubers.

Ethylene promotes rapid internode/petiole elongation in deep water rice plants. It also helps leaves/upper parts of shoot to remain above water.

This also promotes root growth and root hair formation. Thus helping plant to have more absorption surface.

Ethylene promotes in pineapple family (Bromeliaceae), and is used for synchronizing fruit set.

Ethylene also induces flowering in mango. Ethylene regulates so many physiological processes.

It is one of the most widely used PGR in agriculture. The most widely used compound is **ethepon, 2-chloroethyl phosphonic acid (Ether).** Ethepon in aqueous solution is readily absorbed and transported within the plant and release ethylene slowly. Ethepon hastens fruit ripening in tomatoes and apples. It accelerates abscission in flowers and fruits (thinning of cotton, cherry, walnut, etc.). It promotes female flowers in cucumbers, and therefore, increases the yield.

Abscissic Acid

Abscissic acid regulates abscission and dormancy. However, like other PGRs it also has wide range of effects on plant growth and development. It acts as general plant growth inhibitor and also inhibits plant metabolism. Abscissic acid (ABA) inhibits closure of stomata in epidermis, and increases tolerance of plant to various kinds of stresses, and therefore, it is also called **stress hormone**.

ABA plays an important role in seed development, maturation and dormancy. By inducing dormancy, ABA helps seeds to withstand desiccation and other factors unfavourable for growth. In most situations ABA acts as an antagonist to gibberellins.

However, for any and every phase of growth, differentiation and development of plants, one or the other PGR has to play some role. Such roles may be complimentary or antagonistic. They could be individualistic or synergistic.

Abscission. The shedding of leaves, flowers and fruits from the living plant is known as abscission. These parts abscise in a region called the **abscission zone**, which is located near the base of petioles of leaves. In most plants leaf abscission is preceded by the differentiation of a distinct layer of cells, the **abscission layer**. During abscission the walls of the cells in the abscission layers are digested, which causes them to become soft and weak.

Auxins delay the onset of early stages of leaf abscission but promote the later stages.

Auxin level within leaves is very high in young leaves and progressively decreases in maturing leaves and in very low in senescent old leaves.

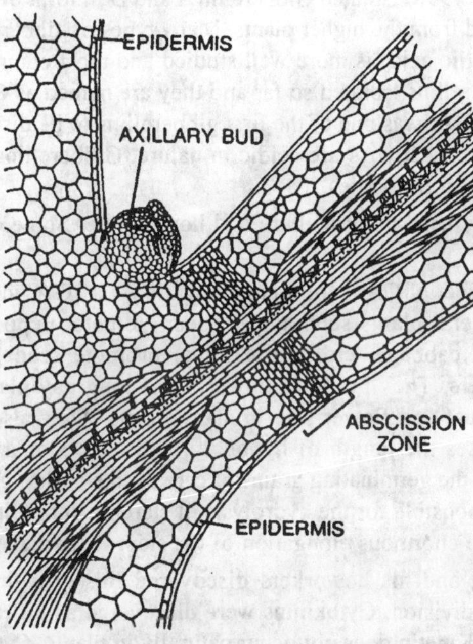

Fig. 19.10. Leaf abscission. Formation of abscission zone.

When applied externally to young leaves, IAA (indole acetic acid) inhibits leaf drop. However in later stages of leaf growth, if applied externally, it hastens the process.

It is also known that high levels of auxin trigger biosynthesis of ethylene within cells. Ethylene strongly hastens the formation of abscission zone.

There is an interaction between auxin and ethylene for an event, *i.e.*, the abscission zone formation.

In the similar way, there are so many events in the life of a plant where more than one PGRs interact to affect that event, *e.g.*, dormancy in seeds/buds, senescence, apical dominance, etc.

PRACTICALS

Experiment

Object : Demonstration of effect of auxin by *Avena* section test.

Requirements : Coleoptiles, distilled water, auxin solution, petri dishes.

Experiment : Take some germinating *Avena* seedlings. Cut the coleoptiles, 25-30 mm in length. Remove the tip of coleoptile and sections 3-5 mm in length of each coleoptile. Put all the sections for an hour in distilled water and then transfer them into other petri dishes containing auxin solution. Keep the experiment as such for a day or two.

Observation : The length of each section, measured after some time is found more than the previous one.

Explanation : This experiment explains the growth response of the solution which is found to be directly proportional to the logarithm of the concentration of auxin used.

2. Gibberellins. Gibberellin was first extracted from the fungus *Gibberella fujikuroi*, the causal organism of **'foolish seeding'** disease of rice. The infected plants were distinctly taller, seedless and pale in colour. These symptoms were produced due to a substance secreted by a fungus. Yabuta and Sumuki (1938) isolated Gibberellin A and B in form of crystals from the fungus but soon after it was isolated from the higher plants. Many types of gibberellins have been isolated among which GA_3 (gibberellic acid) is more well studied and most common in plants. There are 100 different types of gibberellins isolated so far and they are named as GA_1, GA_2, GA_3, to up to GA_{100} and so on. However, GA_3 was one of the first gibberellins to be discovered and remains the most intensively studied form. All GAs are acidic in nature. Gibberellins contain a gibbane ring system with specific biological properties.

Gibberellins are widely used in agriculture and horticulture. Some of important uses are as follows :

The most important effect of GA is the stem elongation, *i.e.*, GA, induces cell elongation. It has been confirmed on several plants such as pea, bean, tomato, pepper, sweet corn, summer squash, cucumber, lettuce, cabbage, etc. Gibberellins promote seed germination and break dormancy of buds and tubers. They promote flowering of long day plant under non-inductive conditions. They increase leaf and flower size in many plants. They also induce parthenocarpy (seedless fruit). GA increases the length of hypocotyl and cotyledonary leaf area. GA affects positively on fruit setting. In the germinating grains of cereals like barley, gibberellins stimulate the formation of *a*-amylase, responsible for the hydrolysis of starch. Bolting in cabbage is induced by gibberellin application. Here enormous elongation of the stem takes place, and flowering occurs.

3. Cytokinins. Skoog and his coworkers discovered this growth regulator. Its specific property is to promote cell division. Cytokinins were discovered as kinetin (a modified form of adenine) from sperm DNA. Kinetin does not occur naturally in plants. Cytokinins are synthesised in areas where cell division occurs, *e.g.*, in root apices, developing shoot buds, young fruits, etc.

Patan, Das and Skoog reported that kinetin promotes cell division in tobacco pith by activating DNA synthesis. (Cytokinin promotes cell division by activating DNA synthesis). It has antagonistic property with auxin. Kinetin promotes the growth of lateral buds by neutralizing the effect of natural auxin. Thimann (1960) reported that kinetin activates protein synthesis in buds by incorporation of labelled amino acids. Owing to its ability to bring about cytokinesis in cells, the

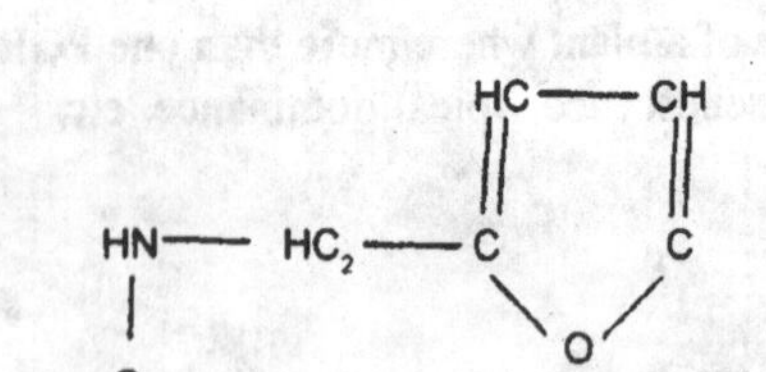

Fig. 19.11. Structure of Kinetin.

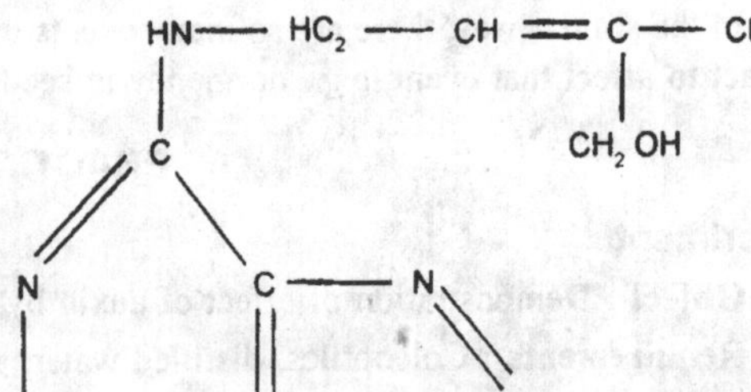

Fig. 19.12. Structure of Zeatin.

name kinetin was given. The presence of kinetin is reported in the extracts from coconut milk, maize endosperm and tender apple fruits.

Letham (1963) isolated another type of cytokinin from fractionation of sweet corn extract and termed it as **Zeatin**. The high activity of Zeatin is due to side chain of a very reactive allylic hydroxyl group.

Cytokinins reduce apical dominance, and cause delay in senescence. The common bioassays for cytokinins include promotion of cell division in tobaçco pith culture, expansion of excised radish cotyledons, delay in senescence, etc.

Practicals

Two experiments on gibberellins and cytokinins are given here :

Experiment

Object : Demonstration of effect of gibberellic acid GA_3 on elongation.

Requirements : Prepared aqueous (1000.0) solutions of GA_3 having 0.01, 0.1, 1.0, 10.0 and 1000.0 mg/ml, young plants of dwarf and tall varieties of peas, distilled water.

Experiment : Take ten dwarf variety plants and ten tall variety plants. Apply 1 ml. of a GA_3 solution to a young leaf of each of the plants. Do this application again after one week. Distilled water is applied as a control in separate plants. Measure the height of each daily for fifteen days.

Observation and Explanation **:** Each time there is a clear elongation in the plant height. The growth response in dwarf variety increases with the increase of concentration of GA_3.

Experiment

Object : Demonstration of effect of kinetin of senescence.

Requirements : Solutions of kinetin containing 0, 0.001, 0.01 and 100.0 mg./litre of hormone, mature fresh leaves of radish, sterile distilled water, petri dish, filter paper, etc.

Experiment : Take mature fresh leaves of radish plant and wash them with sterile distilled water. Keep them in petri dishes on moist filter paper. Apply 0.5 ml of one of the kinetin solutions per leaf. Examine the leaves daily for a week.

Observation and Explanation : The leaves turn yellow after a week. This is due to disappearance of chlorophyll and degradation of proteins.

4. Abscisic acid (ABA). In contrast to the above discussed growth hormones, abscisic acid (ABA) retards or suppresses growth (growth inhibitor). Abscisic acid has been isolated from several parts of higher plants including dormant buds and seeds.

Abscisic acid promotes leaf fall and dormancy of buds. In some seeds, it is present in the seed coats and causes dormancy. ABA decreases the synthesis of RNA and protein in the leaves. It inhibits the formation of amylase in germinating cereal grains. Most of the activities of abscisic acid are reverse to those induced by gibberellic acid and cytokinins.

Eagles and Wareing (1962) isolated an inhibitor from the birch leaves held under short day conditions. When this substance was reapplied to the leaves of the birch seedlings, apical growth was completely arrested. As this substance induced dormancy, they named it as **dormin**. Later in 1965, Ohkuma and others isolated an inhibitor from cotton fruits and named it **abscission II,** when abscisic acid is applied exogenously (from outside) bud dormancy, seed dormancy, tuber formation and boll abscission in cotton is caused. Many physiological effects by abscisic acid such as dormancy, etc., are reversed by either the application of gibberellins or cytokinins. So it is proposed that dormancy is effected by the ratio of abscisic acid to gibberellins and cytokinins.

Besides its role in abscission and bud dormancy, ABA inhibits seed germination and growth of excised embryos. It also inhibits growth in duckweeds and stimulates stomatal closure in epidermal strips. It increases tolerance of plants against various kinds of stresses. ABA plays a major role in seed development and its maturation.

5. Ethylene. Ethylene is the only hormone which is found in the form of gas. It was previously used for early ripening of fruits. Now it is proved that plant cells produce ethylene when there is a stress on them. When ethylene is applied to a plant, loss of sensitivity of gravity (ageotropism) in roots and shoot **abscission** of leaves, ripening of fruits, adventitious root formation and hook formation in germinating seedlings takes place. When microorganisms invade a plant or cut is made in it, large quantity of ethylene is produced. This ethylene promotes the formation and secretion of peroxidase enzymes, *e.g.*, sweet potato tuber. This wound repair is done by ethylene. Ethylene is evolved by plants, specially during the ripening of fruits. This effect of ethylene has been utilized in citrus industry where oranges, lemons and grape fruits are sometimes picked while green and ripened in gas chambers containing ethylene (similar is the case now with many fruits, including bananas and mangoes.)

Ethylene is a natural product of metabolism in plants.

Exposure of plants to ethylene causes drooping of leaves and flowers. This phenomenon is called **epinasty**.

6. Vitamins. Vitamins (*vita*, life) are a heterogeneous group of organic products of plants, which are invaluable for normal growth and development of the body, maintenance of health, vigour, nervous stability, and proper function of the digestive system.

Vitamins are also essential in preventing or curing certain deficiency diseases such as scurvy, beriberi, rickets, malnutrition, loss of appetite, poor physical growth, eye infection, nervous breakdown, etc., caused by the absence of vitamins in the food or their faulty absorption due to intestinal troubles.

Up till now several vitamins have been discovered and their value established. It is known that vitamins do not take any direct part in body-building nor they make a source of energy. However, they play a very important role in the metabolism of proteins, fats and carbohydrates, and their proper assimilation into the body. They also help proper utilisation of certain minerals in the body.

Some of the vitamins act as prosthetic groups or coenzymes and help in synthesis of certain enzymes, and control many important biochemical reactions in both plants and animals.

Vitamins are required in minute quantities for a particular effect, and are used up in the metabolic processes.

Vitamins are mostly synthesized by plants and stored up in their different organs. Certain vitamins are also formed by bacteria and fungi.

However, animals including human beings, cannot synthesize them in their body, and therefore, plants are the sources of vitamins for them.

Vitamins are of many types, such as vitamins A, B (B complex – B_1, B_2, B_6, B_{12}, etc.), C, D, E and K. Some common and important vitamins are as follows :

Vitamin A is growth-promoting and anti-infective vitamin, soluble in fats and oils, less soluble in water and fairly resistant to heat.

Deficiency of vitamin A results in eye-diseases, loss of weight, skin diseases, nervous weakness and respiratory diseases.

Main sources of this vitamin are carrot, green leafy vegetables, cereals, sprouting pulses, many fruits, such as tomato, mango, orange, banana, apple, papaya, etc., milk, butter, meat, liver of mammals, egg yolk, fish, cod liver oil, etc.

Carotene of plants is the source of this vitamin, and animals can synthesize vitamin A in their body by taking food containing carotene. Excess of vitamin A is stored in the liver and utilized when deficiency occurs.

Vitamin B consists of a group of closely allied vitamins, commonly called **vitamin B complex**. This is required for proper maintenance of health throughout life.

Deficiency of this results in digestive troubles, loss of appetite, diarrhoea, constipation, beriberi and neuritis. Some of the vitamins of this group are—thiamine, riboflavin, pyridoxine, niacin, etc.

Vitamin B complex is widely distributed in plants in almost all their parts. Rich sources are—dried yeast, whole grains, pulses, green vegetables, many fruits, *e.g.*, tomato, papaya, mango, banana, apple etc., nuts, milk, cheese, egg-yolk, meat, liver, fish, etc.

Vitamin C also known as ascorbic acid, soluble in water, sensitive to heat, and therefore, lost by cooking, destroyed when exposed to sunlight. Vitamin C is a general activator of metabolic processes. It cannot be stored in the body, and therefore, a daily supply of this vitamin is a necessity.

Vitamin C prevents scurvy, mental depression, swelling and bleeding of gums, degeneration of teeth, cold and sore mouth.

It is found in high concentrations in the fruits, such as orange, lemon, guava, tomato, pineapple, emblic myrobalan, papaya, etc. This is also found in green vegetables, sprouting pulses, cereals and milk.

Vitamin D also known as calciferol. This is an anti-ricket vitamin, soluble in fats and oils.

Its deficiency causes rickets and dental carries in children, and osteomalacia in adults.

It is essential for normal development of bones and teeth, and for general growth.

Vitamin D is commonly found in dried yeast, milk, butter, cheese, egg-yolk, fish and cod-liver oil. Vitamin D can also be produced in the human body by sunrays.

Vitamin E or anti-sterility vitamin. This is soluble in fats and oils, resistant to heat and light but destroyed by ultra-violet rays.

Its deficiency causes sterility in animals, degeneration of muscles and falling-out of hairs.

It is found in green vegetables, germinating grains, wheat embryo, milk, egg-yolk, meat, etc.

Vitamin K is fat-soluble.

Its deficiency causes lowering of pro-thrombin value of the blood. This means, this does not help proper blood clotting in wounds and cuts. This vitamin is found in green vegetables, fresh fruits, and in yeast.

Differentiation

The cells derived from root apical meristem (RAM) and shoot apical meristem (SAM) and cambium differentiate, mature to perform specific functions. This act leading to maturation is termed **differentiation**. They, undergo a few or major structural changes both in their cell walls and protoplasm. For example, to form, a trachery element the cells lose its protoplasm but develops a very strong, elastic, lignocellulosic secondary cell wall is best suited to carry water to long distances even under extreme tension. Similarly, cells designated to be mesophyll come to possess many chloroplasts so as to, perform photosynthesis. On one hand, a parenchyma in hydrophytes develop large schizogenous interspaces for mechanical support, buoyancy and aeration, but on the other hand, in a potato tuber (or perennating organs) develops more amyloplasts.

Dedifferentiation

In plants, the living differentiated cells can regain the capacity to divide mitotically under certain conditions. The sum of events, that bestow this capacity to divide once again, are termed

dedifferentiation. A dedifferentiated tissue can act as meristem (*e.g.*, interfascicular vascular cambium, wound meristem, cork cambium).

Redifferentiation

The product of dedifferentiated cells/tissue which lose the ability to divide are called redifferentiate cells/tissues and the event, **redifferentiation**.

However, the growth in plants is open, and even differentiation in plants is open, because, *e.g.*, the same apical meristem cells give rise to xylem phloem, fibres, etc., cells/tissues arising out of same meristem have different structures at maturity. The final structure at maturity of a cell/tissue arising out of same meristem is determined by the location of the cell within. For example, cells positioned distal to root apical meristem (RAM) differentiate as root cap cells, while those pushed to periphery mature as epidermis. However we do not know for as well as determined is called **commitment**. Terms **determination** and **commitment** are used as synonyms.

DEVELOPMENT

Development is a term that includes all changes that an organism goes through during its life cycle from germination of the seed through growth, maturation, flowering, seed formation and senescence. The term is also applied to formation of cells/tissues/organs. It can also applied for change in phases of life, *e.g.*, from vegetative to flowering, and from leaf initiation to leaf expansion. It is also used at sub-cellular level, *e.g.*, appearance of chloroplasts in cells exposed to light. The last phase of the development process in plants is **senescence** during which, events leading to ageing and death take place.

Diagrammatic representation of the sequence of processes of development of a cell are summarised as follows :

The plants follow different pathways in response to environment or phases of life to form different kinds of structures. This ability is called **plasticity**, *e.g.*, heterophylly in cotton, coriander and larkspur. In such plants the leaves of the juvenile plant are different in shape than those in mature plants. On other hand, difference in shapes of leaves produced in air and while in water in buttercup (*Ranunculus*) also represent heterophyllous development due to environment. This phenomenon of heterophylly is an example of plasticity.

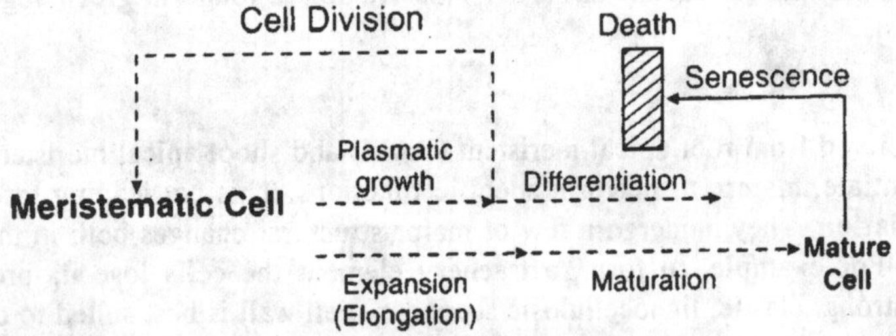

Fig. 19.13. Sequence of development process in a plant cell

Thus, growth differentiation and development are very closely related events in the life of a plant. However, development in considered as sum of growth and differentiation. The development in plants (*i.e.*, both growth and differentiation) is under control of **intrinsic** and **extrinsic** factors. The former includes both intracellular (genetic) or intercellular factors (chemicals such as plant growth regulators) while extrinsic factors include light, temperature, water, oxygen, nutrition, etc.

Table 19.1. Comparison of influences of PGRs on plant development
Plant growth regulators (PGRs)

	Auxin	Gibberellins	Cytokinins	ABA	Ethylene
Root development	×	×	×		×
Extension growth	×	×	×	×	×
Juvenility	×	×			
Flowering	×	×	×	×	×
Fruit development	×	×	×	×	×
Senescence	×	×	×		×
Dormancy		×	×	×	×

× = Involvement of PGR in the plant development

However, the role(s) of PGRs are only one kind of intrinsic control. Along with genomic control and extrinsic factors, they play an important role in plant growth and development. The extrinsic factors, such as temperature and light control plant growth and development via PGR. Such events are : vernalisation, flowering, dormancy, seed germination, plant movements, etc.

PHOTOPERIODISM

During the last few decades, it has been observed that plants respond to day length in their flowering. This has come to be known as the phenomenon of **photoperiodism**. The plants have been classified as **short day**, **long day**, **day neutral**, **short-long day** or **long-short day types**. Interestingly SD, LD or ND types have now been observed not only within the same genus but also among the ecotypes or variants within the same species.

The observation of Garner and Allard (1920) that a variety of tobacco, maryland mammoth flowered when the relative length of the day was shorter than the length of dark period led to the discovery of photoperiodism. They used the term photoperiodism to designate the response of organism to the relative length of day and light and photoperiod to designate the favourable length of day for each plant.

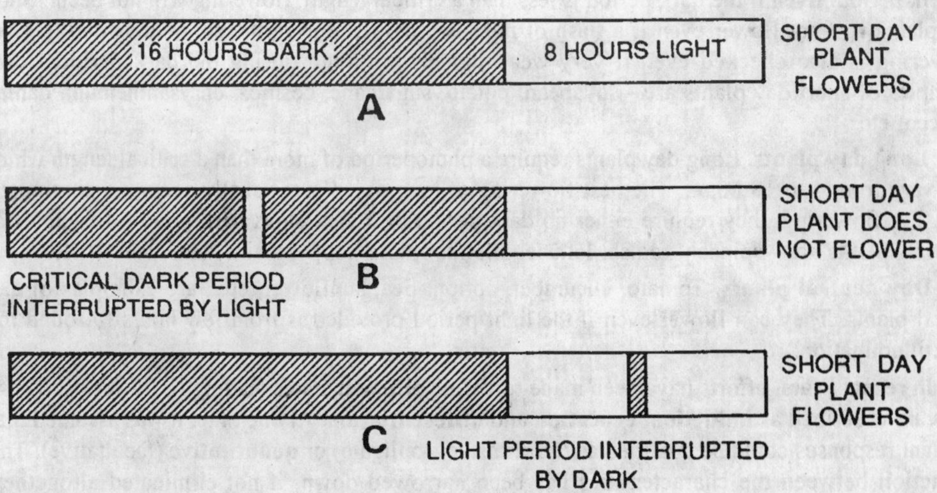

Fig. 19.14. Photoperiodism. Effect of a brief exposure of red light during dark and light periods on flowering in short day plant.

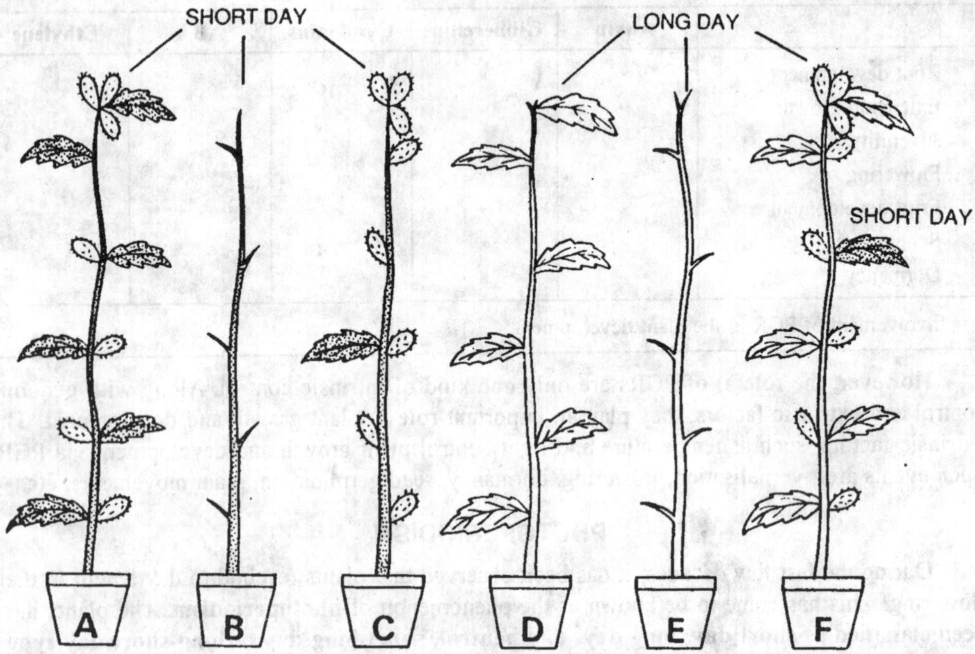

Fig. 19.15. Photoperiodism. Experiment on cocklebur plants to show that photoperiodic stimulus is perceived by the leaves. Flowering occurs even if a single leaf is exposed to appropriate photoperiod.

Short day plants. For flowering of short day plants, the day length must not exceed a certain critical value, the day length required is less than a certain critical length. Short day plants be more correctly called as long night plants, as a certain minimum of uninterrupted dark period in 24 hours is necessary for their flowering. In the case of the short day plants, the critical thing is the length of dark period. Even if the dark period is less than a critical length, flowering will not occur. Short day plants will not flower even if a flash of light is provided during the continuous dark period. Flowering is also checked even if very weak light is provided during the dark period. Some examples of short day plants are—soyabean, potato, sugarcane, cosmos, chrysanthemum, dahlia, tobacco, etc.

Long day plants. Long day plants require a photoperiod of more than a critical length which may vary from 4 to 18 hours. The best flowering of long day plants usually occurs in continuous light. For flowering, they require either no dark period or a very short dark period. Examples of long day plants are—spinach, radish, lettuce, alfalfa, opium poppy, maize, oats, wheat, etc.

Day neutral plants. Tomato, cucumber, cotton, pea, sunflower, etc., are examples of day neutral plants. They can flower even if the light period provided is from few hours to round the clock illumination.

In recent years, efforts have been made to define different states leading to flowering. These states are described as **induction, evocation** and **differentiation.** At one time, it was assumed that the plant responses could be qualified as **'qualitative'** (obligate) or **quantitative** (facultative). The distinction between the characteristics has been narrowed down, if not eliminated altogether. Furthermore, it has become clear that the intensity of flowering is a quantitative expression even in qualitative plants.

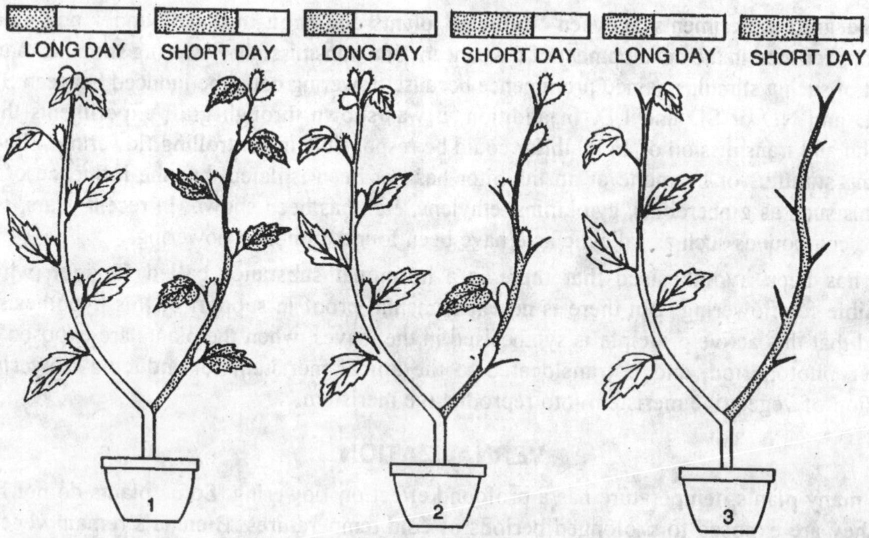

Fig. 19.16. Photoperiodism. Experiments on cocklebur plants to show that the photoperiod stimulus can be transmitted from one branch of the plant to another.

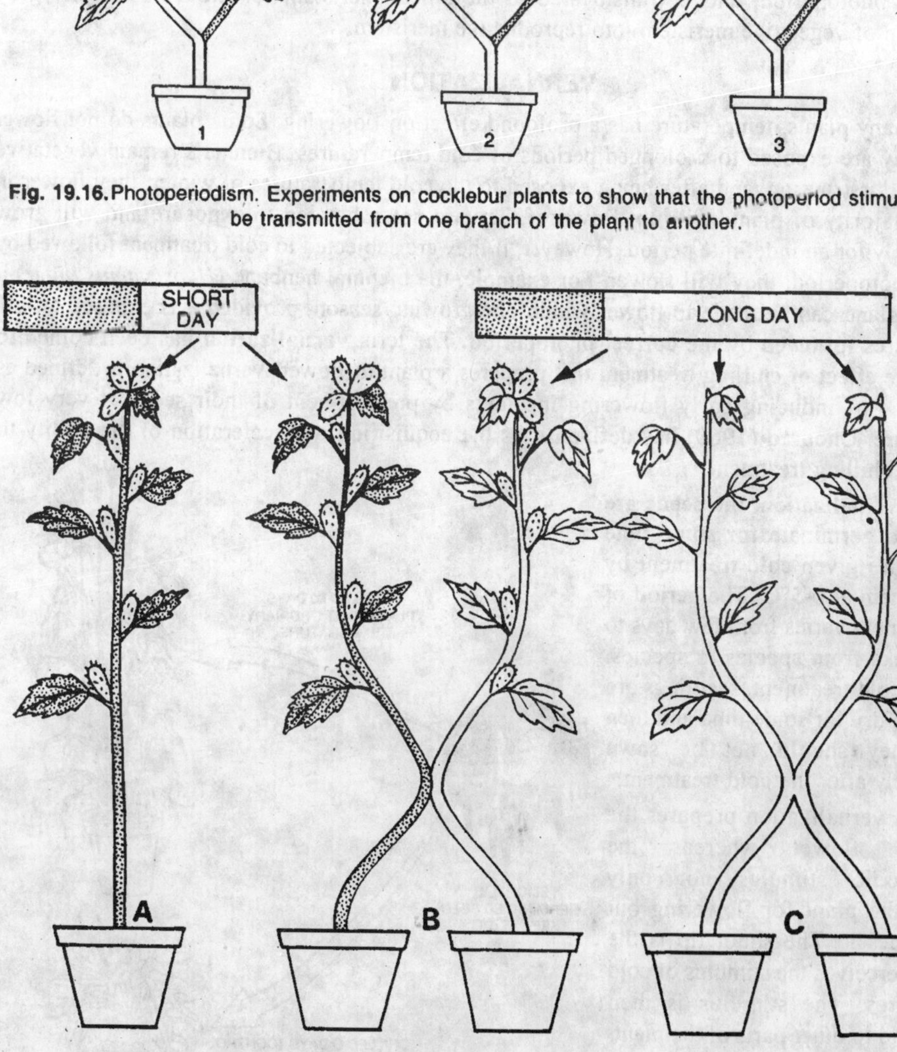

Fig. 19.17. Photoperiodism. Grafting experiments in cocklebur plants to show the translocation of floral hormone from one plant to another through graft union.

The graft experiments between **'induced'** plants and **'non-induced'** under non-inductive conditions resulted in the development of the concept of a transmissible flowering stimulus. A unified concept of such a stimulus gained prominence because flowering could be induced between SD and ND, LD and ND or SD and LD. In addition, it was shown through graft experiments that the formation and transmission of an inhibitor could be responsible in controlling flowering. Either any flowering stimulus or hormone or an inhibitor has not been isolated, but the influence of many chemicals such as gibberellins, cytokinins, ethylene, etc., has been shown. In recent years, several phenolic compounds such as salicylic acid have been found to induce flowering.

It has been hypothesised that there is a hormonal substance called **florigen** which is responsible for flowering. But there is no experimental proof in support of this hypothesis. It is believed that this active principle is synthesised in the leaves, when the plants are exposed to the inductive photoperiod, and is translocated to the apical meristem for inducing flowering by conversion of vegetative meristem into reproductive meristem.

VERNALIZATION

In many plants, temperature has a profound effect on flowering. Some plants do not flower unless they are exposed to prolonged periods of cold temperatures. Biennials remain vegetative during the first season, and after being exposed to the cold temperatures of winter, they flower in spring. Majority of plants will not flower if they are not subjected to exposure and will grow vegetatively for an indefinite period. However, if they are subjected to cold treatment followed by correct photoperiod, they will flower. For example, the biennial henbane (*Hyoscyamus niger*) a long day plant, can be made to flower within one growing season, provided it is exposed to low temperatures followed by the correct photoperiod. The term **vernalization** has been coined to explain the effect of chilling treatment that prepares a plant to flower. Vernalization is defined as the method of inducing early flowering in plants by pretreatment of their seeds at very low temperature. Chourad (1960) has defined it as the acquisition of acceleration of the ability to flower by chilling treatment.

For vernalization, the seeds are allowed to germinate for some time and then are given cold treatment by keeping them at 0-5°C. The period of cold treatment varies from few days to many weeks from species to species. After the cold treatment, seedlings are allowed to dry for some time and then sown. They should not be sown immediately after the cold treatment.

Thus vernalization prepares the plant to flower whereas the photoperiodic stimulus not only prepares the plant for flowering but also induces it. The shoot tip is the part that perceives the stimulus of cold temperatures. The stimulus is then translocated to other parts of the plant. In some plants, application of gibberellin may replace the cold treatment.

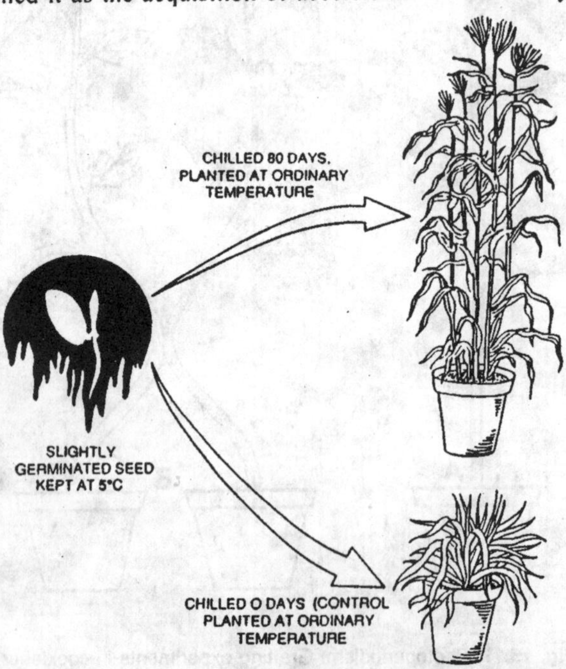

Fig. 19.18. Vernalization. Diagram to illustrate effects of vernalization.

Vernalization is defined as the method of inducing early flowering in plants by pretreatment of their seeds at very low temperatures. Chourad (1960) has defined it as the acquisition or acceleration of the ability to flower by chilling treatment. *Hyoscyamus niger* has two types, one is annual and the other is biennial. Both of them are long day plants and when exposed to short day will grow vegetatively. Even the biennial type can be made to flower if its ten days old seedlings are subjected to cold treatments. For vernalization the seeds are allowed to germinate for some time and then are given cold treatment by keeping them at 0-5°C. The period of cold treatment varies from few days to many weeks from species to species.

Temperature as a vernalization effect as well as during photoperiodic treatments has been found to be an important factor regulating flowering. There is evidence to suggest that vernalization effect could involve such substances as gibberellins. The interaction between photoperiod and temperature is considered important in the flowering of many crop plants.

SENESCENCE

Senescence has been defined as the deterioration that ends the functional life of an organism or an organ. Although meristems do not undergo senescence and can perhaps be considered potentially immortal, all of the cells produced from these undergo aging, which eventually leads to death. Senescence occurs in leaves, flowers, fruits, stems, and roots, but it commonly occurs at different times in these organs. In many perennial herbs, such as alfalfa, essentially the entire above ground system dies each year, but the crown and root systems remain largely viable. In deciduous woody perennials, the leaves die, but much of the root and stem tissues remain alive. Another pattern of senescence is seen in several herbaceous annual species such as beans, tomatoes and the cereal grains. Here there is a progressive senescence of the leaves from the older to the younger, followed by death of both the stem and roots after flowering.

Senescence; A scene in New York states, Catskill Mountain; The breakdown of chlorophyll allows yellow, red and orange light-gathering pigments to show.

It is concluded that senescence is the result of an altered hormone balance that prevents the genes from continuing to code for the same enzymes as when the cells were younger. Considered in this way, senescence may be thought of as a final stage of differentiation which itself is continuous from juvenility to death. It is the culmination of the morphogenetic information programme.

ABSCISSION

Soon after senescence occurs, some plant organs are lost by **abscission**. The physiology of this process is best understood in the case of leaves, flowers and fruits. The longevity of flowers ranges from three or four hours in *Hibiscus trionum* and *Calandrinia compressa* upto three or four months in *Phalaenopsis scilleriana*. Leaves are generally longer lived. Those of most herbaceous annuals are never shed and live as long as the plant, those of deciduous woody dicotyledons remain intact one growing season, and the needles of certain gymnosperms are retained from about one year to seven or eight years, depending upon the species and growth conditions. Most fruits are lost during the season in which they are formed.

Abscission is delayed as long as organ is physiologically active and occurs only if the normal metabolic processes are completed or are interrupted by injury or disease. Leaf abscission is usually stimulated by the younger leaves above, and one of the causative factors supplied by these is an auxin. Abscisic acid stimulates abscission of leaves in a number of plants. It seems, that abscisic acid and the other abscisins play important roles in the loss of leaves, of fruit and of flowers.

Abscission benefits plants in various ways. Injury or disease often causes the abscission of the affected organ. The plant thus rids itself of a useless part or of a potential infection source.

PHOTOMORPHOGENESIS

Growth and development of plants are influenced by several environmental factors including light. However, light causes several responses other than photosynthesis. These responses greatly influence the course of plant development and the final plant appearance. They are **photomorphogenetic responses**. For example, the seeds of many plants do not germinate unless they are exposed to light. Germination of seeds in light shows that the seedlings require light to grow. Phototropic responses of seedlings and of leaves of mature plants are also beneficial photomorphogenetic processes. Photomorphogenetic responses are also important to older plants. Many such responses respond to the relative lengths of day and night by forming reproductive structures or by forming dormant buds that can resist a cold winter (*i.e.*, phenomenon of photoperiodism and vernalization.)

Photoperiodism. The discovery of photoperiodism, *i.e.*, the growth response to the length of light and dark periods by Garner and Allard, completely changed the concept of flower initiation. It was demonstrated by experiments that the length of the dark period rather than the light period is the critical factor in the photoperiod response. As per the result of investigations, it became apparent that a majority of plants fell into one of three categories : (*i*) short day, (*ii*) long day and (*iii*) day-neutral plants. Short-day plants require a dark period exceeding some critical length to flower, and cannot flower under continuous illumination (light). Long-day plants are inhibited from flowering when the dark period exceeds some critical length, and they can flower under continuous illumination. Day-neutral plants can flower under any night length. In some plants, the leaves need only to be exposed to one light-dark cycle of the proper day length to cause flower initiation, whereas most plants require several or many such cycles.

It has been shown that photoperiodic responses may be altered by brief exposure to low light intensity. For example, interruption of the dark period in short-day plants has shown that it is red light (wave length 660 mμ) which is effective. Similarly it has been proved experimentally that, far-red light (wave length 730 mμ) reverses the red light effect, *i.e.*, if exposure to red light is followed by exposure to far-red, the result is as if there had been no exposure at all. If repeated alternating exposure to red and far-red are given, the final exposure determines the response.

Phytochrome

The above given observations led to the discovery of the pigment system isolated from the leaf called **phytochrome**. This pigment system specifically receives the external photoperiodic message. The phytochrome was discovered by H.A Borthwick and Sterling B. Hendricks for the first time in 1959. Phytochrome is a pigment present in small amounts in all plants. Under short-day conditions, an interruption of the dark period with light (specifically red light) causes an intramolecular shift in phytochrome that brings about flowering in long-day plants and prevents flowering in short-day plants.

Characteristics of phytochrome. The cytoplasmic pigment system phytochrome now identified as a protein and partially purified, which is sensitive to red light.

This pigment can exist in two forms, one that absorbs red light (Pr) and one that absorbs far-red light (Pfr). Red light converts Pr to Pfr, but this form is unstable and is gradually converted back to the Pr form.

$$\text{Pr 660} \xrightarrow{\text{red}} \text{Pfr 730}$$

$$\text{Pr 660} \xleftarrow[\text{or dark (slow)}]{\text{Far-red (rapid)}} \text{Pfr 730}$$

Phytochrome is active in the Pfr form and thus the responses are produced by red light. In relation to flowering, reactions promoted by Pfr interfere with the dark reaction that promotes flowering in short-day plants and inhibits the flowering of long-day plants. Since it is the length of the dark period that is critical, and therefore, it is supposed that the reversion of Pfr to Pr determines the critical length of the dark period. The reversion takes place only about four hours in the dark.

Apart from photoperiodic phenomena, many other light effects upon plants are exerted through the phytochrome system. The germination of lettuce seeds for example, required a light stimulus, and this is effected by red light and reversed by far-red light. Stem elongation and leaf expansion could be influenced by red light, and the effect of etiolation could be checked by exposure to red light.

Phytochrome is a protein with chromophoric (pigment) groups. The molecular weight of phytochrome is about 60,000 with three chromophores per molecule. The chromophore pigment is closely similar but not identical to the chromophore of c-phycocyanin, an algal (blue alga) chromoprotein.

It is believed that phytochrome is also involved in other photoperiodically controlled processes such as tuber and bulk formation, and dormancy.

About the functioning of the phytochrome, it has been suggested that it may operate by influencing membrane permeability in the cells, not only of the plasma membrane but also of those of the nucleus and the mitochondria, thus influencing the metabolism of cells.

Though the discovery of phytochrome has made a very significant contribution towards explaining the first step in the mechanism of flowering, yet much experimentation is required, so that the substances specifically causing the transition of the apical meristems from the vegetative to the flowering conditions could be isolated and their mode of action determined.

PLANT MOVEMENTS

Though ordinarily we do not associate plants with movements, they do exhibit shift in the positions of their several organs. These adjustments are necessary so that the plant organs may fulfil their function adequately. Though largely, the movements that we come across in plants are not locomotory; movement of locomotion involving the shift of the entire body are not wanting. The swimming movements of Volvocales and the male gametes of several plants are examples of locomotory movements.

A movement is made in response to a stimulus. This ability to respond is reflection of irritability, a property inherent in all organisms. Certain plant movements are rapid and thereafter clearly visible and certain other movements take place over a long period of time and therefore are imperceptible. The rapid folding up of leaves exhibited by 'touch-me-not' is an instance of the former kind.

A stimulus is essentially a change in environment. This change may be of the nature of a shock or chemical or atmospheric. All parts of plants are sensitive to stimuli. Specialized parts called perceptive regions receive the stimulus and transmit it to regions where responsive movements are effected and these latter areas are "responsive regions".

A stimulus does not produce a response immediately. It has to act for some time before the plant organ may respond. This period necessary for a stimulus to induce a response is called **presentation time**. A weak stimulus requires a long presentation time and a strong one a short presentation time. A stimulation repeated a number of times before the effect of the previous stimulation wears out, brings about the response. In other words, the effect of each stimulation adds up to the total effect of the previous stimulations. The behaviour is embodied in a law called the **law of summation of stimuli**. The time taken by a plant organ to manifest its response to a stimulus is called the "reaction time". This is equal to presentation time plus the time taken for the stimulus to be conducted from the region of perception of the region of response (transmission time) plus the time necessary for the internal changes in the cells of the responsive region.

The movements exhibited by the organs of plants are classified into three groups: (1) **growth movements** caused by changes in the position of the organs due to enlargement of cells, or increase in the number of cells, or both; (2) **turgor movements** caused by reversible changes in cell volume, and (3) **hydration movements** concerned usually with non-living plant tissues or organs and resulting from hydration or dehydration of the cell walls. Here we deal with some of the growth and turgor movements that occur most commonly in plants.

Growth Movements

Growth movements are divided into three sub-groups: (1) **Tropic movements** occur in response to always related to the direction of the stimulus. (2) **Nastic movements** in which the response has no relation to the direction of the stimulus. It is diffused. (3) **Nutation** is a movement which is usually independent of the environmental factors. It is characterized by spiral type of growth of the shoot apex.

Tropic Movements

Most commonly found in the radially symmetrical organs of the plant such as roots and stems; tropic movements are curvature movements caused due to stimulus coming from one side. These movements controlled by the direction of the stimulus occur in one direction due to differences in the rates of growth on the two sides of the moving organs which results in curvature. A tropic movement may be phototropism (in response to light), geotropism (in response to gravity), chemotropism (in response to chemicals), hydrotropism (in response to water) and haptotropism or thigmotropism (in response to touch).

(*i*) **Phototropism.** Phototropic or curvature movements that take place when plant is provided with artificial or natural light only from one direction. If curvature movement is towards the source of light it is known as **positive phototropism** and if away from the source of light is known as **negative phototropism**. Leaves of some plants can keep themselves perpendicular to the source of light and diaphototropic. One example of phototropic movement is the leaves of *Neptunia oleracea* which keeping their faces towards sun keep on moving throughout the day turning from east to west. The flowers of *Helianthus annuus* (sun flower) also move the same way always keeping their faces towards sun. Ovary stalk of *Arachis hypogea* shows different type of phototropic movements

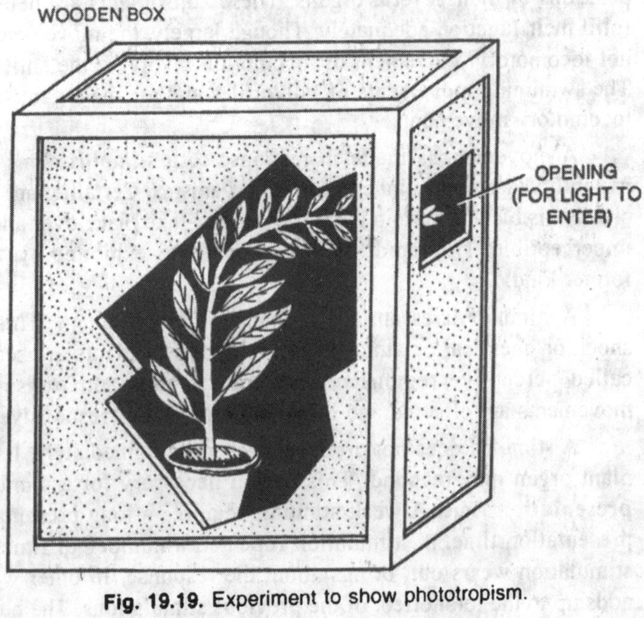

Fig. 19.19. Experiment to show phototropism.

during different phases of its life. It is positively phototropic when the ovary is unfertilized but after the ovary is fertilized, it becomes negatively phototropic with the result that it bends towards soil and moves the ovary inside the soil. The dispersal of spores in *Pilobolus* (a fungus) occurs when the sporangiophores have moved towards light.

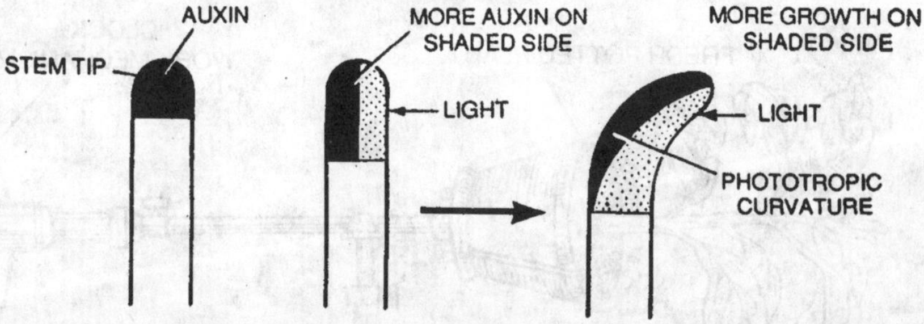

Fig. 19.20. Interaction of light and auxin in causing phototropic curvature in stem

The phototropic movements are thought to be controlled by growth regulatory substances which collect on the side away from the light to increase its growth and result in curvature.

In the laboratory, phototropism can be demonstrated by keeping a potted plant inside a box with a small opening only on one side to provide light. After sometime it will be found that stem has bent towards the opening through which the light is coming.

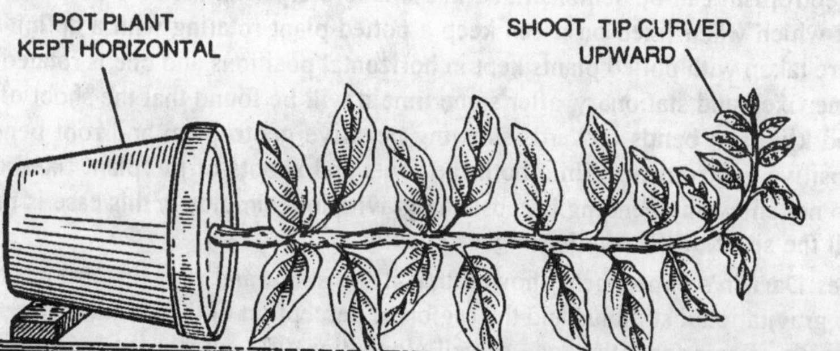

Fig. 19.21. Experiment to show geotropic curvature.

(*ii*) **Geotropism.** Geotropism is the movement caused in response to gravitational stimulus. Positive geotropism is observed in the primary roots of many plants and negative geotropism in their shoots. The secondary branches of roots and stems are diageotropic or plagiogeotropic or apogeotropic as they grow laterally at an angle to the gravitational force, called ageotropic are tertiary and further branches of roots which are not sensitive to gravitational stimulus. The flower stalk of poppy flower shows different response to gravitational stimulus during different phases of its life.

It is positively geotropic and keeps the unopened bud hanging down but as the bud opens and changes into flower, it becomes negatively geotropic with the result that the direction of the stalk changes and flower grows upwards. The change in the direction occurs due to unequal growth on the two sides of the stalk.

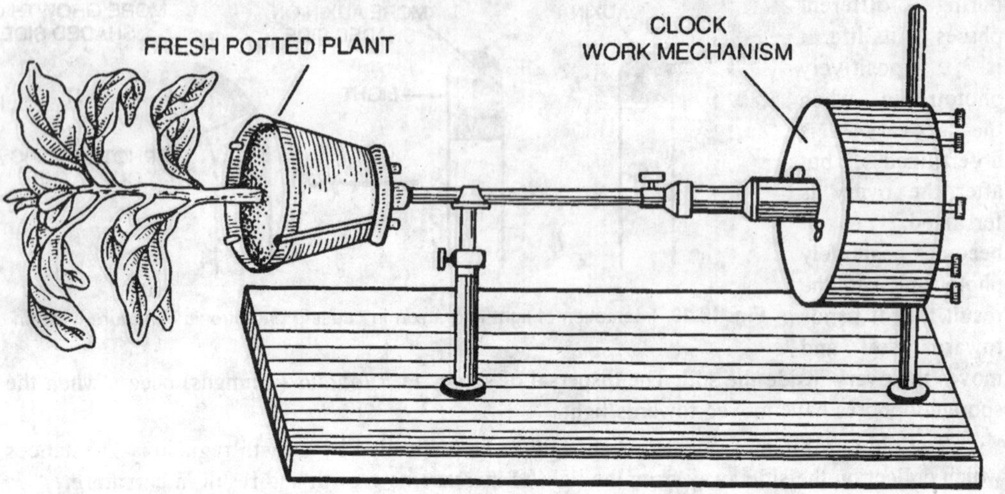

Fig. 19.22. Klinostat.

Depending on the contour, the rhizome of many plants also grows horizontally in the soil due to some reason.

The geotropism can be demonstrated in the laboratory with the help of an instrument known as klinostat which when fixed on it can keep a potted plant rotating with a definite speed. If two klinostats are taken with potted plants kept in horizontal positions and one is rotated while keeping the other one fixed and stationary, after some time it will be found that the shoot of the plant kept on the fixed klinostat bends upwards showing negative geotropism and root bends downwards showing positive geotropism. While both the roots and shoots of the plant fixed on the rotating klinostat do not show any bending because the gravitation stimulus in this case is not unilateral as it affects all the sides of the rotating organs equally.

Charles Darwin's experiment showed that if the shoot and root tips are cut off, there is no response to gravitational stimulus and the region of perception of the stimulus (the tip) is different from the region of response (the zone of cell elongation). To explain the reason of the curvature and bending of the roots and shoots, various theories have been put forward by Vernon, Nemec, Haberlandt, etc., in the part but the most convincing evidences are for the hormone theory proposed by Cholodny, Dolk, Bennet, Clark, Ball, etc. According to this theory, the hormones synthesized in the apical meristem uniformly distributed flow towards mature regions due to gravitational force when the plant is upright, but when it is kept in horizontal position, the concentration of flowing hormone becomes more on low side due to gravitational force and less on the other side. This unequal concentration of hormones on the two sides of the organ concerned results in an unequal growth rate of two sides affecting the tendency of the organ

(*iii*) **Hydrotropism.** This is the movement of the plant organs to unilateral stimulus of water. This also results in curvature of the organ concerned due to unequal growth on its sides. Roots are positively hydrotropic. The demonstration of the hydrotropism is possible in the laboratory with the help of a shallow sieve in which moist saw dust is kept and some seeds are germinated. After some time, it will be observed that the radicles come out of holes due to positive geotropism but immediately after coming out start bending up and reenter the moist saw dust through other neighbouring holes of the sieve due to hydrotropism towards water.

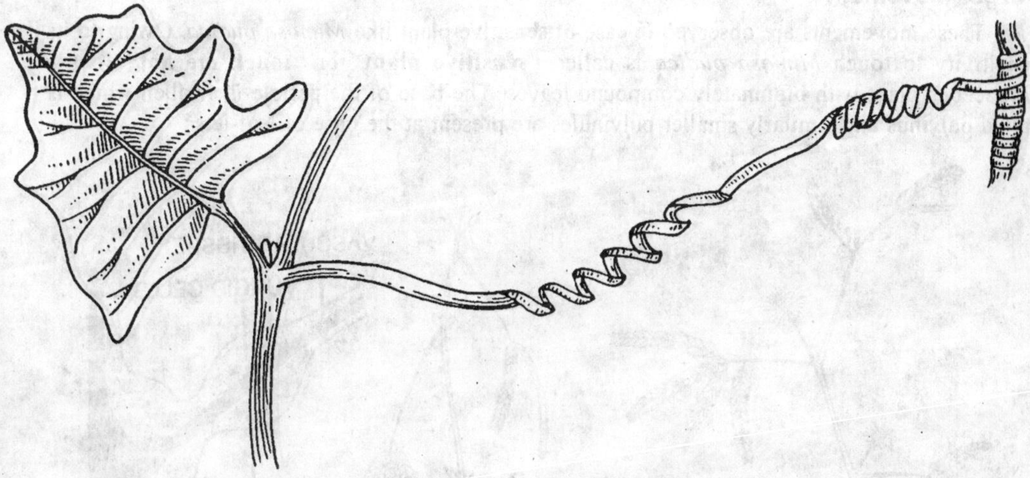

Fig. 19.23. Experiment to show hydrotropism.

(*iv*) **Chemotropism.** Chemotropism is the movement caused due to unilateral stimulus of some chemical. The pollen tube in many cases which moves through the style towards ovary due to chemical stimulus is a good example. Another example can be that of fungus mycelium which when grown in culture medium moves and grows towards the region of the medium where more nutrients are concentrated.

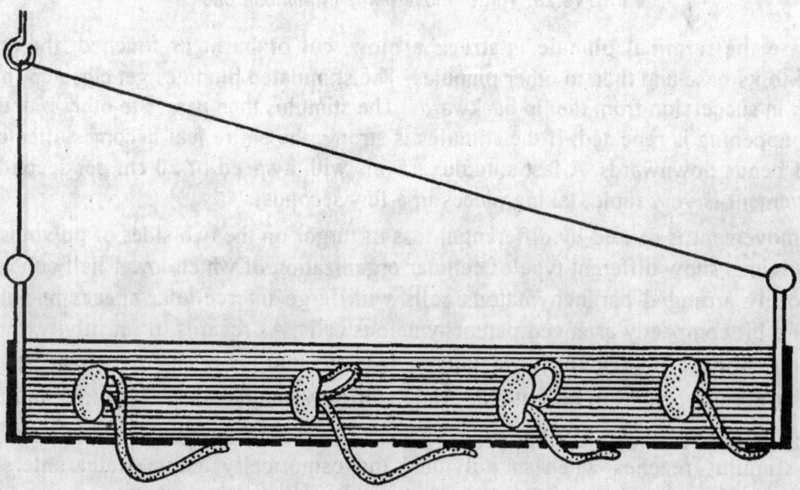

Fig. 19.24. Thigmotropic curvature of the tendril.

(*v*) **Thigmotropism.** Thigmotropism is the curvature movement of plant response to unilateral stimulus of touch and can be observed in so many twiners and climbers. Whenever the supporting organ touches a support, it makes a curvature movement to catch hold the object and tightens its hold. In tendril climbers, the tendrils first show nutation and as soon as its apex touches a support it makes thigmotropic movements to turn round it.

Turgor Movements

These movements are observed in case of sensitive plant like *Mimosa pudica.* Owing to its sensitivity to touch *Mimosa pudica* is called **"sensitive plant"** or **"touch me not"** It is a herbaceous plant with bipinnately compound leaves. The base of the petiole is swollen which is called pulvinus and similarly smaller pulvinules are present at the base of leaf-lets.

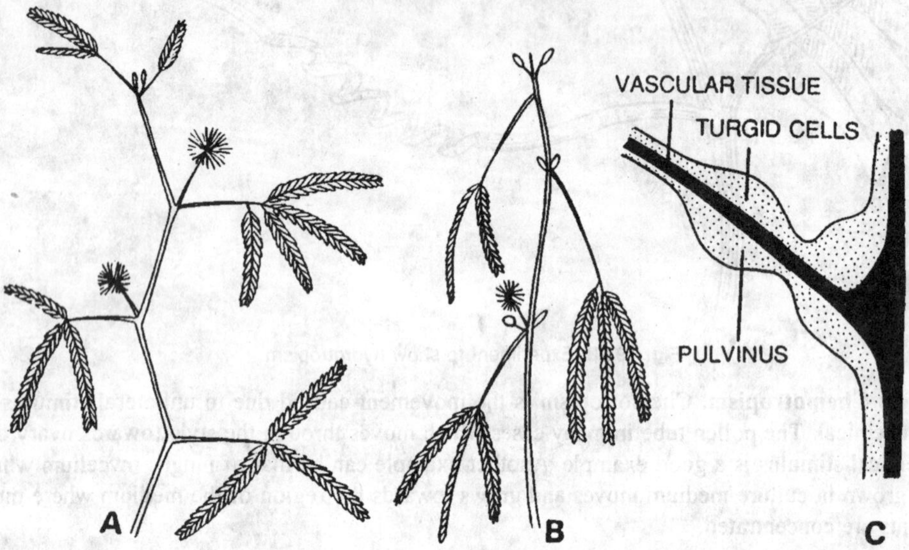

Fig. 19.25. Turgor movements in *Mimosa pudica.*

In case the terminal pinnule is struck a blow, cut or burnt or touched, the stimulus is conducted to its base and then to other pinnules. The stimulated pinnules get close up in pairs and drop down in succession from the tip backwards. The stimulus then passes to other pinnules where the same happening is repeated. If the stimulus is strong, the entire leaf becomes affected and the whole leaf bends downwards. A fast stimulus travels with a speed of 20 cm per second, thus the entire movement is very rapid, taking places in a few seconds.

The movement is caused by differential loss of turgor on the two sides of pulvinus. The two sides of pulvinus show different type of cellular organization of which lower half consists of thin walled loosely arranged parenchymatous cells with large intercellular spaces and upper half consists of a bit compactly arranged parenchymatous cells. As regards to sensitivity, the vascular trace passing through this region shows upper side stable and lower side sensitive.

During normal condition on both sides cells of pulvinus remain fully turgid and the leaf is held erect.

The stimulus reaches when in pulvinus, the osmotically active water enters into the cyptoplasm of cells present on the lower half of pulvinus lowering the osmotic pressure of these cells effectively and forcing out water into the intercellular spaces. These flaccid cells now fail to hold pinnules erect and cause the dropping down of pulvinules and ultimately pulvinus. The whole leaf bends downwards and pulvinus and pulvinules act as hinges. The stimulus may pass from one leaf to another one. It is believed that the whole mechanism is operated under the influence of some hormone which produced in the stimulated part and travels to the pulvinus through the xylem. The reverse is the case true for restoring normal position.

SUMMARY

1. The irreversible increase in shape, size and weight of an organism or its part is called growth.
2. In plants, growth is generally confined to apical regions and in meristematic tissues.
3. Almost all the plants have a period of suspended growth and even a period of rest, is called dormancy.
4. The dormancy in seeds may be due to impermeable and mechanically resistant seed coat, physiologically immature and rudimentary embryo, or even due to presence of inhibitors.
5. Dormancy can be broken or its period can be reduced by mechanical or chemical scarification of seed coat, stratification of seeds, and by changing the environmental conditions.
6. In some cases, light plays an important role in seed germination.
7. Cell division and cell enlargement, followed by cell differentiation, result in growth.
8. The rate of growth is slow in beginning, rapid thereafter, and then becomes stationary.
9. The rate of growth of a plant or its organs can be measured with the help of an instrument, called auxanometer.
10. The period of growth is generally divided into formative, elongation and maturation phases.
11. Plants synthesise some organic compounds, called hormones. Even in very small quantities, hormones may influence the physiology of plants and are responsible for growth. Hormones are also called, growth regulatory substances.
12. There are five main categories of these substances. They are (*i*) auxins, (*ii*) gibberellins, (*iii*) cytokinins, (*iv*) ethylene and (*v*) abscisic acid.
13. Jasmonic acid, salicylic acid, brassinosteroids and some vitamins also help in regulating the process of growth.
14. Auxins are involved in regulating apical dominance, cell elongation, cell division in cambium, and root induction, etc.
15. Gibberellins are required for enhancing seed germination, cell elongation and flowering, overcoming dwarfism, and certain other general functions.
16. Cytokinins play main role in cell division, and help in delaying senescence and reducing apical dominance.
17. Ethylene and abscisic acid generally have a negative role and are responsible for immature falling of leaves, rapid fading of flowers, inhibiting germination, etc.
18. Sometimes these negative roles become beneficial for us, as inducing fruit ripening, breaking dormancy in potato, inhibiting the growth of duckweeds and stimulating the closure of stomata.
19. Vitamins are responsible for normal growth and development of plants.
20. Flowering of plants has a close relationship with the period of exposure to light. Some plants flower in longer periods of exposure to light, whereas others in shorter photoperiods. This phenomenon is called photoperiodism. Some flowering plants are neutral towards duration of light.
21. Low temperature, in particular, has profound effect on growth and flowering of plants. This phenomenon is known as vernalisation.
22. The period between complete maturity and final death of an organ or organism is called senescence.
23. Abscission is shedding of leaves, flowers or fruits by a plant.
24. The movement in plants is very slow process and can be observed at the interval of several days.
25. The streaming movement of protoplasm is spontaneous, whereas the movement in plastids is due to effect of light.
26. Induced movements are called taxis and they may be due to effect of chemical, light and heat.
27. In certain plants, the curvature is produced by diffused stimuli and affects the whole plant uniformity. This is called nastic movement or nastism.
28. In other plants, the stimuli do not affect the whole plant, and the curvature developed is called tropic movement or tropism. The stimuli that trigger movement in plants are light, heat, water, touch, chemical, gravity, etc.

29. Growth is open in higher plants. It is also called indeterminate.
30. Following cell division in root apical meristem and shoot apical meristem cells, the growth could be arithmetic or geometrical.
31. Growth rates could be absolute or relative
32. Growth is generally not sustained at higher rate throughout the life of cell/tissue/organ/organism.
33. There are three principal phases of growth, *i.e.*, lag, log and senescent phase.
34. When a cell loses the capactiy to divide it leads to differentiation.
35. Differentiation provides structures or is commensurate with the function the product has to perform.
36. General principles for differentiation for cell, tissues and organs are similar.
37. A differentiated cell may be differentiate and then redifferentiate.
38. Development is the sum of growth and differentiation.
39. Plant exhibits plasticity in development along with open differentiation.
40. Plants growth and development are under control of both intrinsic and extrinsic factors.
41. Intercellular intrinsic factors are the chemical substances, called plant growth regulators.
42. There are diverse groups of PGRs in plants, principally belonging to 5 groups : (*i*) auxins, (*ii*) gibberellins, (*iii*) cytokinins, (*iv*) abscisic acid, (*v*) ethylene.
43. The PGRs are produced in various parts of the plant; they control different differentiation and developmental events.
44. Any PGR has direct physiological effects on plant; similar affects are manifested by diverse PGRs.
45. PGRs may act synergistically or antagonistically.
46. Plant growth and development are also affected by light, temperature, nutrition, oxygen, gravity and such external factors.

TERMS TO REMEMBER

Abscission. The phenomenon of breaking of leaves and fruits from the plant.

Apical dominance. When the growth of apical bud at the apex of shoot inhibits the growth of lateral buds into branches, it is called apical dominance.

Aleurone layer. The outer layer of endosperm in cereal grains, (*e.g.*, maize, wheat, etc.) which produces hydrolysing enzymes, such as amylase and protease.

Autonomic movement. The self controlled growth movements of the plants.

Catabolism. The breaking down phase of metabolism. Such as digestion and respiration.

Cytokinin. A growth regulator concerned with stimulation of cell division and nucleic acid metabolism.

Day-neutral plants. The plants that flower after a period of vegetative growth indifferent to day length or the photoperiod.

Emergence. The appearance of root and shoot from seed.

Epigeal germination. During germination, the cotyledons are pushed above the ground level due to rapid elongation of hypocotyl.

Germination. The awakening of dormant embryo in the seed.

Growth. The phenomenon of growth represents an increase in mass or volume of an organism accompanied by an irreversible change in form and structure.

Hypogeal germination. In this type of germination, the cotyledons and endosperm remain below the soil and epicotyl elongates.

Imbibition. Initial intake of water by the seed.

Indole acetic acid (IAA). A type of auxin (a growth promoter).

Long-day plants. Such plants flower when the day length exceeds critical length.

Nastic movement. Non-directional growth movements.

NAA. Naphthalene acetic acid.

Paratonic movements. The growth movements induced by external stimuli.

Photoperiodism. Response of a plant to the changing relative lengths of the day and night.

Phototropism. Growth movements of plants induced by stimulus of light.

Phytochrome. A light sensitive protein pigment involved in several plant activities.

Response. The reaction of a plant to a stimulus.

Senescence. Gradual decline in the smooth functioning of the organisms ultimately leading to death.

Short-day plant. When the flowering of a plant is induced by uninterrupted dark period, longer than the critical length.

Vernalization. Low temperature treatment required by plants for flowering.

QUESTION BANK

Very short answer questions

1. Gibberellins promote the production of :
   (*a*) male flowers (*b*) female flowers (*c*) neutral flowers (*d*) abscission layer
2. Give any one function of phytochrome.
3. A student cultures a callus from the tobacco pith in a sterilised minimal nutritive medium but adds more cytokinins than auxins. What would develop first from the callus-the shoot buds or the roots
4. Name the stress hormone in plants that functions during drought.
5. What is the full form of IBA ?
6. What is the full form of NAA ?
7. Name the two synthetic auxins used for inducing the rooting in woody plants.
8. What is vernalisation ?
9. Certain plants will flower only when they are exposed to low temperature for a few weeks. What do you call for this requirement ?
10. Name any two synthetic auxins in agriculture.
11. What induces parthenocarpy in grapes ?
12. Which is the only one gaseous natural plant growth regulator ?
13. What does an overripe apple release which affects other apples in the basket ?
14. Name the substances which cause seed dormancy.
15. Placing a ripe apple in a bag of green bananas will cause them to ripen quickly. This occurs because the apple:
    (*a*) absorbs cytokinin (*b*) forms digestive enzymes
    (*c*) lacks auxin (*d*) produces ethylene

ANSWERS

1. (*a*) ; **2.** It is required for breaking dormancy and initiation of germination in some light sensitive seeds, such as lettuce ; **3.** The shoot buds ; **4.** Abscisic acid (ABA) ; **5.** Indole butyric acid (IBA) ; **6.** Naphthalene acetic acid (NAA) ; **7.** Indole butyric acid (IBA) and Naphthalene acetic acid (NAA) ; **8.** This is low temperature treatment to plants for flowering ; **9.** Vernalisation; **10.** IBA and NAA ; **11.** Auxins ; **12.** Ethylene ; **13.** Ethylene ; **14.** They are germination inhibitors, which include organic acids, phenolics, alkaloids, etc. ; **15.** (*d*).

Short Answer Questions

1. Explain inhibitory effect of auxins with the help of one example.
2. Taking the examples of auxins and cytokinins together explain :
   (*i*) synergetic action in plants (*ii*) an antagonistic action in plants
3. What is bolting ? What conditions can induce bolting naturally and how can it be induced artificially ?

4. What is the effect of each of the following on germination of seeds :
   (*i*) Abscisic acid (*ii*) Far-red region of light
5. Write the full forms of two synthetic auxins NAA and IBA. What for are they used ?
6. What are nastic movements ? Give one example.
7. List any four uses of auxins.
8. What will you do to prevent leaf fall and fruit drop in plant ? Support your answer with reason.
9. Which among the following is a long day plant? Why is it so called ? Sugarbeet, sugarcane, tomato.
10. How does abscisic acid act antagonistically to auxins and gibberellins ?
11. What is the role of phytochrome in seed germination ?
12. Name two synthetic auxins. How are they used in agriculture ?
13. What is senescence ? What are its causes ?
14. In most plants the terminal bud suppresses the development of lateral buds. What is this phenomenon called ? Name the phytochrome that can promote the phenomenon.
15. Give at least four roles of gibberellins on plant growth.
16. Differentiate between quiescence and dormancy with reference to seed germination.
17. What is seed dormancy ? What causes it ? How is it broken naturally and how can it be broken artificially ?
18. Name the only gaseous natural plant hormone. Describe its three different actions in plants.
19. Write briefly about abscisic acid.
20. Describe the various steps involved in the process of seed germination.
21. "Growth is an important phenomenon of living". Justify the statement with reasons.
22. Explain different phases of growth with the help of a diagram.
23. What do you understand by photoperiodism and vernalisation ? Describe their significance.
24. Write an essay on growth regulators in plants.
25. How will you measure the rate of growth ? Describe an instrument used to measure the increase in height of an angiospermic plant.
26. What are the important characteristics of growth ? Describe in brief.
27. Describe an experiment that would demonstrate that growth stimulating hormone is produced at the tip of coleoptile.
28. Mention any two causes of seed dormancy. Add a note on the significance of this phenomenon.
29. Describe the phenomenon of photoperiodism.
30. Explain briefly the role of auxins on plant growth.
31. Describe the experiment conducted by F. Went regarding discovery of auxins.

Long Answer Questions

1. What do you understand by the spontaneous and induced movements in plants ? Illustrate your answer with suitable diagrams.
2. Write an essay on growth regulators in plants.
3. Write short notes on the following :
   (*a*) Senescence (*b*) Abscission (*c*) Quiescence (*d*) Vivipary
4. What do you understand by photoperiodism and vernalization ? Describe their significance.
5. Discuss the practical applications of growth regulators.
6. Describe the important factors that affect growth and development of plants.
7. Write a note on short day, long day and day neutral plants.
8. Write a note on seed germination and seed dormancy. What are the methods of breaking dormancy of seeds ?
9. Write an essay on vernalization.
10. Write the physiological effects of gibberellins and cytokinins.

MULTIPLE CHOICE QUESTIONS (Objective Type Questions)

1. The substance related phototropism in the shoot is :
(*a*) Ethanol (*b*) Cytokinin (*c*) Auxin (*d*) Gibberellin
2. In leaves of grasses bulliform cells show :
(*a*) Tropic movements (*b*) Growth movements
(*c*) Nastic movements (*d*) Turgor movements
3. Some flowers open during the day time and close at night. This is known as :
(*a*) Phototaxy (*b*) Phototropism (*c*) Photoperiodism (*d*) Photonasty
4. Gibberellins cause :
(*a*) Shortening of genetically tall plants (*b*) Elongation of genetically dwarf plants
(*c*) Promotion of rooting (*d*) Yellowing of young leaves
5. The hormone which has negative effect on apical dominance is :
(*a*) Cytokinin (*b*) Auxin (*c*) Gibberellin (*d*) Ethylene
6. A genetically dwarf plant can be converted into a tall plant by the use of :
(*a*) Kinetin (*b*) AA/X-rays (*c*) 2, 4–D (*d*) GA_3
7. Which one of the following hormones is not found in plants :
(*a*) 2, 4–D (*b*) GA_3 (*c*) Gibberellin (*d*) IAA
8. The chemical nature of Kinetin is :
(*a*) Butyric acid (*b*) Indole butyric acid
(*c*) 6-furfuryl amino purine (*d*) Indole acetic acid
9. Which of the following hormones owes its discovery to tissue culture technique ?
(*a*) Auxin (*b*) Abscisic acid (*c*) Gibberellin (*d*) Cytokinin
10. Germination of the seed is promoted by :
(*a*) Green light (*b*) Red light (*c*) Blue light (*d*) Infrared light
11. Which of the following induces cell division in a cell :
(*a*) Cytokinins (*b*) Gibberellins (*c*) Auxins (*d*) ABA
12. Movement of *Drosera* is :
(*a*) Thigmotropism (*b*) Thigmonastic (*c*) Thermonastic (*d*) Photonastic
13. Which one of the following induces flowering in long day plants?
(*a*) Gibberellins (*b*) Cytokinin (*c*) Auxins (*d*) Ethylene
14. Thigmotropism is best exemplified by :
(*a*) Root apex (*b*) Thorns (*c*) Tendrils (*d*) Lamina
15. The rate of growth of a plant stem can be measured by means of :
(*a*) Potometer (*b*) Auxanometer (*c*) Osmometer (*d*) Hydrometer
16. Touch induced closure of leaflets in *Mimosa pudica* is the case of :
(*a*) Thigmotropism (*b*) Phototropism (*c*) Thermotropism (*d*) Siesmonasty
17. Which hormones promote flowering in long day plants and also control sex expression ?
(*a*) Cytokinins (*b*) Gibberellins (*c*) Ethylene (*d*) Auxin
18. *Avena* coleoptile test was conducted by :
(*a*) Darwin (*b*) N. Smit (*c*) Paal (*d*) F.W. Went
19. The growth hormones responsible for bolting are :
(*a*) Auxins (*b*) Kinetin (*c*) Coumarins (*d*) Gibberellins
20. In short day plants, flowering is interrupted by :
(*a*) Dark condition is interrupted by white or red light
(*b*) Dark condition is interrupted by far-red light

(*c*) Dark condition is interrupted by red followed by far-red light
(*d*) In short day plants, flowering cannot be interrupted.

21. Growth regulator ethylene is used for :
(*a*) Retarding ripening of bananas (*b*) Speeding up ripening of fruits
(*c*) Slowing down ripening of apples (*d*) Both (*b*) and (*c*)

22. Coconut milk factor is :
(*a*) an auxin (*b*) a gibberellin (*c*) abscisic acid (*d*) cytokinin

23. Differentiation of shoot is controlled by :
(*a*) High auxin : cytokinin ratio (*b*) High cytokinin : auxin ratio
(*c*) High gibberellin : auxin ratio (*d*) High gibberellin : cytokinin ratio

24. Seed dormancy is due to the :
(*a*) Ethylene (*b*) Abscisic acid (*c*) IAA (*d*) Starch

25. By which of the following means the testa is made permeable to water :
(*a*) Scarification (*b*) Stratification (*c*) Vernalization (*d*) Denudation

26. One of these prevents elongation in plants :
(*a*) Auxin (*b*) Gibberellin (*c*) ABA (*d*) Cytokinin

27. Long day plant amongst the following is :
(*a*) *Glycine max* (*b*) Spinach (*c*) *Mirabilis jalapa* (*d*) Soya bean

28. Hormone responsible for preventing seeds during drought is :
(*a*) IAA (*b*) NAA (*c*) IBA (*d*) ABA

29. What will happen if terminal buds are removed from a plant ?
(*a*) The plant will die (*b*) The lateral buds will grow profusely
(*c*) The roots will die (*d*) The shoot will die

30. The closing and opening of leaves of *Mimosa pudica* is due to :
(*a*) Thermonastic movement (*b*) Hydrotropic movement
(*c*) Seismonastic movement (*d*) Chemonastic movement

31. ABA is involved in :
(*a*) Dormancy of seeds (*b*) Root elongation
(*c*) Shoot elongation (*d*) Increased cell division

32. A plant hormone used for inducing morphogenesis in tissue culture is :
(*a*) ABA (*b*) Ethylene (*c*) Gibberellin (*d*) Cytokinin

33. Gibberellins can be extracted from :
(*a*) Rice only (*b*) Fungus only
(*c*) Germinating seeds only (*d*) Many healthy plants

34. Thigmotropism is the response of the plant to :
(*a*) Gravity (*b*) Water (*c*) Light (*d*) Contact

35. Auxanometer is an instrument with which we can measure the :
(*a*) Rate of respiration (*b*) Rate of photosynthesis
(*c*) Geotropism (*d*) Rate of growth

36. During germination, stem grows upward and root grows downward because :
(*a*) it depends upon light (*b*) of auxin
(*c*) it does not depend on light (*d*) of epinasty and hyponasty

37. 2, 4–D is a :
(*a*) Flowering hormone (*b*) Rooting hormone
(*c*) Herbicide (*d*) Pesticide

38. To promote the growth of lateral branches of a plant :
(*a*) Axillary buds are removed (*b*) Apical bud is removed
(*c*) Auxin is applied to the apical bud (*d*) Auxin is applied to the decapitated shoot tip

39. The plants respond to photoperiods due to the presence of :
(*a*) Phytochromes (*b*) Stomata (*c*) Enzymes (*d*) Phytohormones

40. The hormone present in the liquid endosperm of coconut is :
(*a*) Ethylene (*b*) Gibberellin (*c*) Auxin (*d*) Cytokinin

41. Stress hormone is :
(*a*) Auxin (*b*) Gibberellin (*c*) ABA (*d*) Cytokinin

42. To remove seed dormancy by mechanical removing of seed-coat is called :
(*a*) Stratification (*b*) Vernalization (*c*) Scarification (*d*) Photoperiodism

43. Vernalization is done at :
(*a*) Low temperature (*b*) Low light intensity
(*c*) High temperature (*d*) High light intensity

44. Which one of the following statements is true for the phytochrome :
(*a*) Phytochrome is a phytohormone
(*b*) Phytochrome is a photosynthetic pigment
(*c*) Phytochrome is a pigment that controls growth, photomorphogenesis and development of many plants
(*d*) Phytochrome is a regulatory protein that controls several dark dependent development processes.

45. All the cytokinins are :
(*a*) Acidic (*b*) Aminopurines (*c*) Phenol (*d*) Glucosides

46. Certain chemical substances having profound effect on growth, are called :
(*a*) Compost (*b*) Catalytic agent (*c*) Enzymes (*d*) Phytohormones

47. The presence of auxins in a solution could be tested by :
(*a*) *Avena sativa* stem tip test (*b*) Carbon tetrachloride test
(*c*) Iodine test (*d*) Defoliation test

48. The photoperiodic stimulus is perceived by :
(*a*) Leaves (*b*) Flowers (*c*) Buds (*d*) Meristem

49. The activity of α–amylase in the endosperm of barley germinating seed is induced by :
(*a*) Ethylene (*b*) Cytokinin (*c*) IAA (*d*) Gibberellin

50. Leaf fall starts when the amount of :
(*a*) Auxin increases (*b*) Auxin decreases
(*c*) Abscisic acid decreases (*d*) Gibberellic acid decreases

51. The rate of growth of any organism follows :
(*a*) Hyperbolic curve (*b*) J-shaped curve (*c*) Sigmoid curve (*d*) Parabolic curve

52. Which of the following fungus is associated with the discovery of gibberellins :
(*a*) *Fusarium* (*b*) *Rhizopus* (*c*) *Aspergillus* (*d*) *Penicillium*

53. Induction of formation of interfascicular cambium is by :
(*a*) Kinetin (*b*) Gibberellin
(*c*) Auxin (*d*) Ethylene

54. The following is a naturally occurring growth inhibitor :
(*a*) IAA (*b*) ABA (*c*) NAA (*d*) GA_3

55. In plants, the induction of flowering, by low temperature treatment, is called :
(*a*) Pruning (*b*) Cryobiology (*c*) Vernalisation (*d*) Photoperiodism

ANSWERS

1. (*c*)	**2.** (*d*)	**3.** (*d*)	**4.** (*b*)	**5.** (*a*)	**6.** (*d*)	**7.** (*a*)	**8.** (*c*)	**9.** (*d*)	**10.** (*b*)
11. (*a*)	**12.** (*b*)	**13.** (*a*)	**14.** (*c*)	**15.** (*b*)	**16.** (*d*)	**17.** (*b*)	**18.** (*d*)	**19.** (*d*)	**20.** (*a*)
21. (*b*)	**22.** (*d*)	**23.** (*b*)	**24.** (*b*)	**25.** (*a*)	**26.** (*c*)	**27.** (*b*)	**28.** (*d*)	**29.** (*b*)	**30.** (*c*)
31. (*a*)	**32.** (*d*)	**33.** (*d*)	**34.** (*d*)	**35.** (*d*)	**36.** (*b*)	**37.** (*c*)	**38.** (*b*)	**39.** (*a*)	**40.** (*d*)
41. (*c*)	**42.** (*c*)	**43.** (*a*)	**44.** (*c*)	**45.** (*b*)	**46.** (*d*)	**47.** (*a*)	**48.** (*a*)	**49.** (*d*)	**50.** (*b*)
51. (*c*)	**52.** (*a*)	**53.** (*a*)	**54.** (*b*)	**55.** (*c*)					

20

CHAPTER

Lipid (Fat) Metabolism

What are lipids ? The term lipid is derived from the Greek word *lipos*, meaning fat. It is an operational term for a variety of substances that are not soluble in polar solvent, such as water but dissolve in non-polar solvents, such as benzene, ether and chloroform. This occurs because lipids contain relatively long or complex hydrocarbon chains that are non-polar and thus hydrophobic.

The main groups of compounds classified as lipids are : **(*i*) triglycerides, (*ii*) phospholipids, (*iii*) steroids and (*iv*) waxes.**

Triglycerides

One important group of stored lipids is **triglycerides,** a category that includes **fats and oils.** Triglycerides are composed of a single molecule of glycerol bound to threc fatty acids (Fig. 20.1).

Glycerol is a 3 carbon alcohol with 3 OH groups that serve as binding sites.

Fatty acids are long chain hydrocarbon molecules with a carboxyl group (COOH) at one end which is free to bind to one of the OH groups of the glycerol, thus forming a bond called ester bond.

The hydrocarbon portion of a fatty acid can vary in length from 4 – 24 carbons.

The fats may be saturated or unsaturated. If the carbons in the chain are single bonded, the fat is saturated; if there is at least one C = C double bond in the chain, it is unsaturated. The structure of fatty acids is responsible for the physical nature of fats and oils (liquid fats) which are greasy and insoluble.

In general, solid fats are saturated, and oils are unsaturated.

In most cells for long term, triglycerides are stored in concentrated form as droplets or globules.

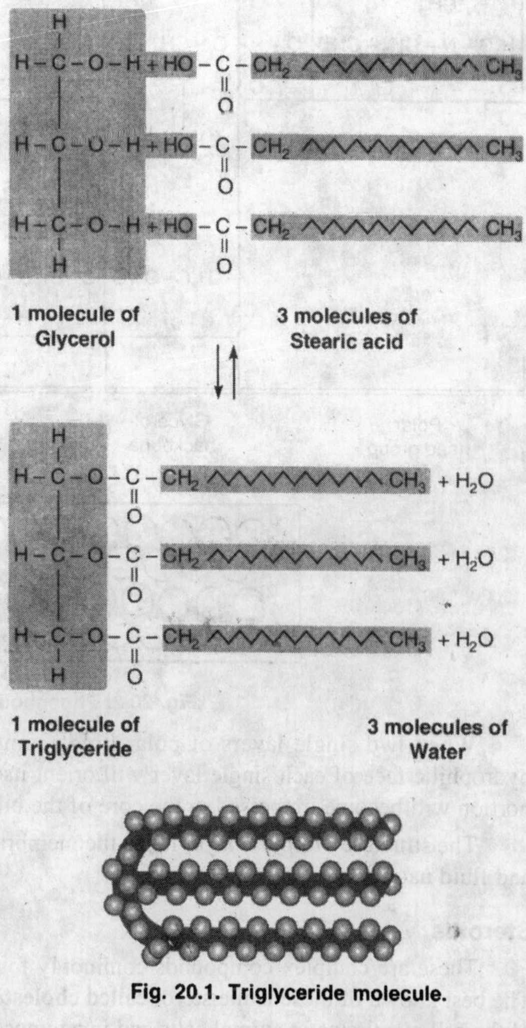

Fig. 20.1. Triglyceride molecule.

Phospholipids (Membrane Lipids)

A class of lipids that serve as major structural component of cell membranes is **phospholipids.** Although phospholipids are similar to triglycerides in containing glycerol and fatty acids, there are some significant differences. Phospholipids contain only two fatty acids attached to the glycerol, while the third glycerol binding site holds a phosphate group (Fig. 20.2). This phosphate is in turn bonded to an alcohol. These lipids have both **hydrophilic** and **hydrophobic** regions due to a change on the phosphoric acid/alcohol 'head' of the molecule and lack of a charge on the long 'tail' of the molecule (formed by the fatty acids).

When exposed to an aqueous solution, the charged heads are attracted to the water phase and the non-polar tails are repelled from the water phase.

The way lipids naturally assume single and double layered (bilayer) configuration makes them a valuable component of the primary framework of cell membranes.

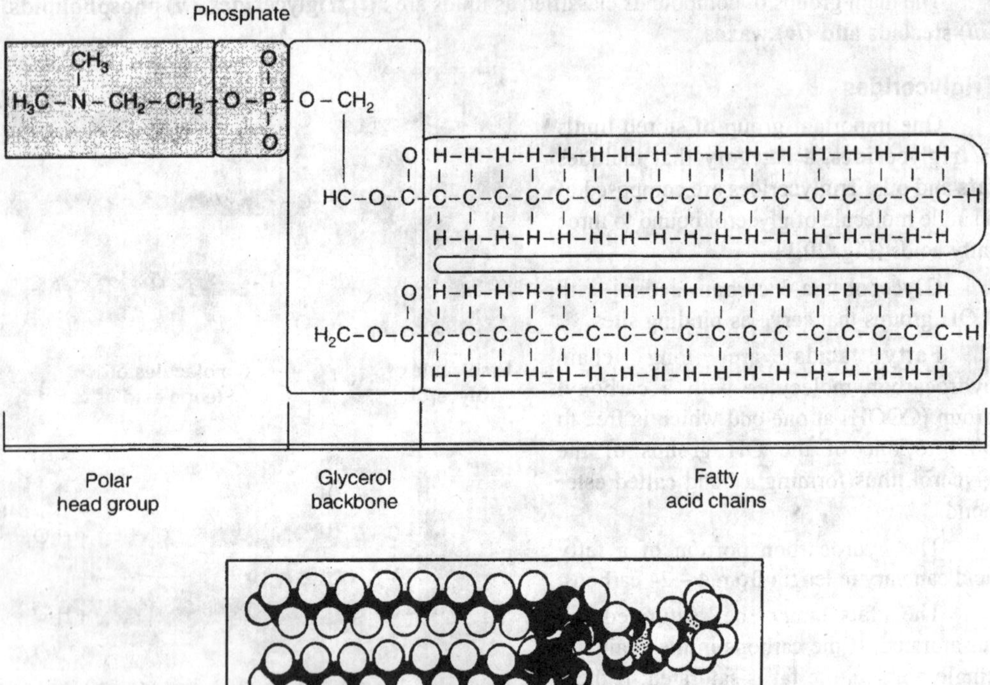

Fig. 20.2. Phospholipid molecule.

When two single layers of polar lipids come together to form a double layer, the outer hydrophilic face of each single layer will orient itself towards, the solution and the hydrophobic portion will become immersed in the core of the bilayer.

The structure of lipid bilayer helps the membrane in functions such as selective permeability and fluid nature.

Steroids

These are complex compounds commonly found in cell membranes and animal hormones. The best known of these is the sterol called **cholesterol** (Fig. 20.3) which reinforces the structure of the cell membrane in animal cells and in an unusual group of cell-wall deficient bacteria called **mycoplasmas.** The cell membrane of fungi also contains a sterol called **ergosterol.**

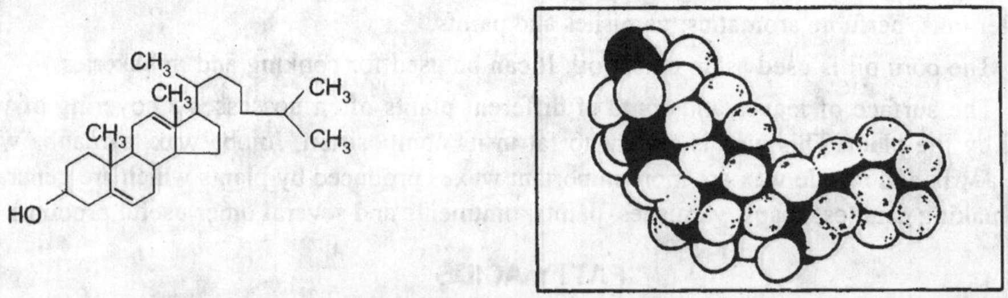

Fig. 20.3. Cholesterol molecule.

Wax

Waxes are esters formed between a long chain alcohol and saturated fatty acids (Fig. 20.4). This material is typically pliable and soft when warm but hard and water resistant when cold (*e.g.*, paraffin).

Fur, feathers, fruits, leaves, human skin and insect exoskeleton are naturally waterproofed with a coating of wax. Bacteria that cause tuberculosis and leprosy produce a wax (wax-D) that contributes to their pathogenicity. The formula of beewax is as follows (Fig. 20.3a).

$$\underset{\text{Palmitic acid}}{CH_3(CH_2)_{14}-\overset{O}{\overset{\|}{C}}-OH} + \underset{\text{Hexacosonal}}{H\ O-CH_2(CH_2)_{24}CH_3}$$

$$\downarrow \rightarrow H_2O$$

$$\underset{\text{Hexacosyl palmitate}}{CH_3(CH_2)_{14}-\overset{O}{\overset{\|}{C}}-O-CH_2(CH_2)_{24}CH_3}$$

Fig. 20.3(a). Beewax.

Fats in Plants

Fats are commonly found in higher plants. They are especially formed in reproductive tissues (*e.g.*, seeds and fruits) of higher plants where they form reserve food material, such as in cotyledons of sunflower (*Helianthus annuus)*, rape (*Brassica napus*), peanuts (*Arachis hypogaea*), almonds (*Prunus amygdalus*), endosperm of castor beans, coconuts, etc., and mesocarp of avocado fruit. Some cereals, such as wheat and barley possess rich fat content in cells of aleurone layer. Generally the fats are stored in cell-organelles called **spherosomes**, which are distributed in cytoplasm of cells.

Importance of Lipids

1. Fats serve as reserve food in seeds. They are deposited during the development of seed and are mobilized and reutilized as a source of energy during the germination and growth of the seedling.

2. Oils are used by people for various purposes. The edible oils are obtained from the seeds of mustard, cotton, groundnut, soybean, sunflower, sesame and fruits of coconut.

3. Lipids provide the structural frame-work to the living tissues of plants and animals. Plasma membrane and other cell organelles, such as chloroplasts, mitochondria, endoplasmic reticulum, lysosomes and golgi complex contain the lipids in the form of layers. In the plants they are found in the form of small droplets dispersed in the cytoplasm.

4. Lipids serve as the main fuel reserve for metobolism and provide more energy than carbohydrate and proteins.

5. Linseed oil is primarily used in the manufacture of paints and varnishes. It is also used in the manufacture of linoleum and oil-cloth, printing and lithographic inks and soft soap.

6. Castor oil is used as a purgative. It is also used for making transparent soap, textile soap, typewriter inks, perfume aromatics, varnishes and paints.

7. The corn oil is used as an edible oil. It can be used for cooking and in bakeries.

8. The surface of leaves and fruits of different plants often possesses a covering of wax secreted by the plant. This wax is similar to fat in its composition. Jojoba wax, carnauba wax, candelilla wax and myrtle wax are more important waxes produced by plants which are generally used in making candles, soaps, varnishes, paints, ointments and several other useful products.

FATTY ACIDS

The acids which are combined with glycerol in the naturally occurring fats are called **fatty acids.** These acids contain even number of carbon atoms linked together in long chains which are in general unbranched. The chain contains from six to about twenty carbon atoms in plant triglycerides and the most frequent number being 16 or 18. The long chain molecule possesses the carboxyl group at one end, while the remainder part consists of carbon and hydrogen atoms only.

Classification of Fatty Acids

The fatty acids can be classified into four groups as follows :

1. **Saturated fatty acids**
2. **Unsaturated fatty acids**
3. **Branched chain fatty acids**
4. **Cyclic fatty acids.**

N.B. Only (1) saturated fatty acids and (2) unsaturated fatty acids are described.

1. Saturated fatty acids. Saturated fatty acids are those which contain only single bonds in their hydrocarbon chain. The general formula is :

$$R - COOH$$

where R is $CH_3(CH_2)n$; *n* varies from zero in acetic acid to 24 in cerotic acid and to 86 in mycolic acid.

The most commonly occurring saturated fatty acids of the higher plants are palmitic acid (C_{16}) and stearic acid (C_{18}). Other major saturated fatty acids found in plant lipids are shown in table.

Table 20.1. Major Saturated fatty acids and their sources

S. No.	Name of fatty acids	Structure	Source
1.	Butyric acid	$CH_3(CH_2)_2COOH$	Butter
2.	Caproic acid	$CH_3(CH_2)_4COOH$	Butter, palm oil, coconut oil
3.	Caprylic acid	$CH_3(CH_2)_6COOH$	Palm oil, coconut oil
4.	Capric acid	$CH_3(CH_2)_8COOH$	Palm oil, coconut oil
5.	Lauric acid	$CH_3(CH_2)_{10}COOH$	Plants of lauraceae, coconut oil, palm oil.
6.	Myristic acid	$CH_3(CH_2)_{12}COOH$	Seed fats of mace, butter, coconut oil
7.	Palmitic acid	$CH_3(CH_2)_{14}COOH$	Plant fats, palm oil, peanut oil.
8.	Stearic acid	$CH_3(CH_2)_{16}COOH$	Plant and animal fats

S. No.	Name of fatty acids	Structure	Source
9.	Arachidic acid	$CH_3(CH_2)_{18}COOH$	Peanut oil
10.	Behenic acid	$CH_3(CH_2)_{20}COOH$	Plant lipids
11.	Lignoceric acid	$CH_3(CH_2)_{22}COOH$	Plant lipids
12.	Cerotic acid	$CH_3(CH_2)_{24}COOH$	Beewax, wool

2. Unsaturated fatty acids. Unsaturated fatty acids are those which contain one or more double bonds in their hydrocarbon chain. The general formula is :

$$R - CH = CH\ (CH_2)_n - COOH$$

These fatty acids are also characterized by the presence of cis-trans isomerism at their double bonds. The most common examples of unsaturated fatty acids are mentioned in table. Oleic and linoleic unsaturated fatty acids are widely distributed in plants.

Table 20.2. Major Unsaturated fatty acids and their sources

S. No.	Name of fatty acids	Structure	Source
1.	Palmitoleic acid	$CH_3(CH_2)_5CH = CH(CH_2)_7COOH$	Sardine oil
2.	Oleic acid	$CH_3(CH_2)_7CH = CH(CH_2)_7COOH$	Olive oil, peanut oil, linseed oil
3.	Linoleic acid	$CH_3(CH_2)_4CH = CHCH_2CH = CH(CH_2)_7COOH$	Olive oil, peanut oil, linseed oil, soyben oil
4.	γ-linolenic acid	$CH_3(CH_2)_4CH = CHCH_2\ CH = CHCH_2CH = CH(CH_2)_4COOH$	linseed oil
5.	Parinaric acid	$CH_3CH_2CH = CHCH = CHCH = CH(CH_2)_7COOH$	Plant lipids
6.	Erucic acid	$CH_3(CH_2)_7CH = CH(CH_2)_{11}COOH$	Rapeseed oil
7.	Arachidonic acid	$CH_3(CH_2)_4CH = CHCH_2CH = CHCH_2CH = CHCH_2CH = CH(CH_2)_3COOH$	Peanut oil

Properties of Fatty Acids and Fats

Physical Properties

1. Fats and fatty acids are soluble in organic solvents, such as petroleum ether, benzene and chloroform. They are insoluble in water.
2. Saturated fatty acids are solid at room temperature, while unsaturated fatty acids are liquid.
3. Unsaturated fatty acids show cis-trans isomerism due to presence of double bonds.
4. They are bad conductors of heat.
5. Saturated glycerides containing fats require high temperature for melting, whereas unsaturated glycerides containing fats require relatively lower temperature for its melting.

Chemical Properties

1. Hydrolysis. Fats undergo hydrolysis when treated with mineral acids, the alkalies or fat splitting enzyme *lipase* or hydrolases to yield glycerol and the constituent fatty acids.

$$\begin{array}{l} CH_2O\ \boxed{OC{\cdot}C_{15}H_{31}\ HO}\ H \\ CHO\ \boxed{OC{\cdot}C_{15}H_{31}\ HO}\ H \\ CH_2O\ \boxed{OC{\cdot}C_{15}H_{31}\ HO}\ H \end{array} \xrightarrow[\textit{Lipase}]{\text{Enzyme}} \begin{array}{l} CH_2OH \\ CHOH \\ CH_2OH \end{array} + 3C_{15}H_{31}COOH$$

Fat (tripalmitin) Water Glycerol Palmitic acid

Hydrolysis by alkalies, such as NaOH or KOH leads to the formation of sodium or potassium salts of fatty acids. The salts are known as **soaps** and process of its formation is **saponification.**

2. Hydrogenation. Oils containing unsaturated fatty acids can be hydrogenated in presence of high temperature, pressure and finely divided nickel. By this process the oils are converted into solid fats (glycerides of saturated fatty acids). This reaction forms the basis of the industrial production of hydrogenated oil (vegetable ghee).

$$\begin{array}{l} CH_2OOC\,C_{17}H_{33} \\ | \\ CHOOC\,C_{17}H_{33} \\ | \\ CH_2OOC\,C_{17}H_{33} \end{array} \xrightarrow[\text{Ni } 180^\circ - 200^\circ C]{3H_2} \begin{array}{l} CH_2OOC\,C_{17}H_{35} \\ | \\ CHOOC\,C_{17}H_{35} \\ | \\ CH_2OOC\,C_{17}H_{35} \end{array}$$

Triolein (m.p.17°C) (oil) — Tristearin (m.p.60°C) (solid fat)

3. Hydrogenolysis. Oils and fats are converted into glycerol and a long chain aliphatic alcohol when excess of hydrogen is passed through them under pressure and in presence of copper-chromium catalyst. This splitting of fat by hydrogen is called **hydrogenolysis.**

4. Halogenation. When unsaturated fatty acids are treated with halogens, such as iodine and chlorine, they take up iodine or other halogens at their double bond site. This process of taking of iodine is called **halogenation** which is an indication of unsaturation. **Iodine number** is the percentage of iodine absorbed by a fat.

5. Rancidity. Oils and fats on long storage in contact with heat, light, air and moisture, develop an unpleasant odour. Such oils and fats are known as **rancid oils** and **fats.**

The rancidity develops due to certain chemical changes taking place in the fat. These changes include (*i*) enzymatic hydrolysis, (*ii*) air oxidation of unsaturated fatty acids, and (*iii*) β-oxidation of saturated fatty acids.

In all above mentioned changes, hydrolysis of fats is caused by enzyme *lipase* which is produced by microorganisms present in them. To check the rancidity, it becomes essential to protect oils and fats from air, light and moisture during storage.

6. Emulsification. The process of breaking of large-sized fat molecules into smaller ones is called **emulsification.** In animals, this process is brought about by bile juice liberated from liver. Other emulsifying agents are water, soaps, proteins and gums.

Breakdown (Degradation) of Fats

Fats are found in dynamic state in plants, *i.e.*, at one time they are synthesized; while at other time they break down to meet specific requirement of the cells.

Active breakdown of fats (insoluble) takes place as follows :

(*i*) During germination of fatty seeds so that the decomposition products may enter into glycolysis and Kreb's cycle to release energy and also to synthesise soluble **sucrose** through **glyoxylic acid cycle** which is then translocated to the growing regions of the young germinating seedling till it develops green leaves to manufacture its own food.

(*ii*) In plants, when carbohydrates reserve declines, the fats (and also proteins), may form the **respiratory substrates** which are broken down and oxidised to release energy.

The fats are first hydrolysed in the presence of the enzymes *lipases* to yield fatty acids and glycerol.

$$\begin{array}{l} CH_2OOC{\cdot}R \\ | \\ CHOOC{\cdot}R \\ | \\ CH_2OOC{\cdot}R \\ \text{Fat} \\ \text{(Triglyceride)} \end{array} + 3H_2O \xrightarrow{\text{Lipase}} \begin{array}{l} CH_2OH \\ | \\ CHOH \\ | \\ CH_2OH \\ \text{Glycerol} \end{array} + \begin{array}{c} 3R{\cdot}COOH \\ \text{Long chain} \\ \text{fatty acids} \end{array}$$

OXIDATION OF GLYCEROL

The glycerol may react with ATP under the catalytic influence of *glycerol kinase* to form **glycerol-3-phosphate** which is then oxidised in the presence of *glycerol-3-phasphate dehydrogenase* and NAD^+ to produce **dihydroxyacetone phosphate** and enters into glycolysis.

$$\begin{array}{l} CH_2OH \\ | \\ CHOH \\ | \\ CH_2OH \\ \text{glycerol} \end{array} + ATP \longrightarrow \begin{array}{l} CH_2OH \\ | \\ CHOH \\ | \\ CH_2OPO_3H_2 \\ \text{glycerol-3-phosphate} \end{array} + ADP$$

$$\begin{array}{l} CH_2OH \\ | \\ CHOH \\ | \\ CH_2OPO_3H_2 \\ \text{glycerol-3-phosphate} \end{array} + NAD^+ \longrightarrow \begin{array}{l} CH_2OH \\ | \\ C=O \\ | \\ CH_2OPO_3H_2 \\ \text{dihydroxyacetone phosphate} \end{array} + NADH + H^+$$

$$\text{Dihydroxyacetone phosphate} \xrightleftharpoons{\text{Glycolytic pathway}} \text{Pyruvic acid} + 2ATP_S + NADH + H^+$$

The conversion of glycerol into pyruvic acid that takes place in cytoplasm yields 2ATPs by substrate level phosphorylation and 2NADH which on reoxidation by terminal electron transport chain *via* the external NADH dehydrogenase (located on the outer surface of the inner mitochondrial membrane in plants) further generate 4 ATP molecules (2 mol./NADH oxidised). If the pyruvic acid also undergoes complete oxidation into CO_2 and H_2O in Kreb's cycle (or TCA cycle), it will produce another 15ATP moleccules. Thus a total of 2 + 4 + 15 = 21ATPs are produced per glycerol moleule oxidised. However, 1ATP molecule is consumed in the *glycerol kinase* catalysed reaction. Hence, the net gain is 21 – 1 = 20 ATPs per glycerol molecule oxidised. Thus :

$$\text{Glycerol} + ATP \longrightarrow \text{Glycerol-3-phosphate} + ADP$$

$$\text{Glycerol-3-phosphate} + NAD^+ \longrightarrow \text{Dihydroxyacetone phosphate} + NADH + H^+$$

$$\text{Dihydroxyacetone phosphate} \underset{\text{isomerase}}{\overset{\text{Phosphotriose}}{\rightleftharpoons}} \text{3-phosphoglyceraldehyde}$$

$$\left.\begin{array}{c} \text{Dihydroxyacetone} \\ \text{phosphate} \\ + \\ \text{3-phosphoglyceraldehyde} \end{array}\right\rangle \xrightarrow{\text{aldolase}} \text{Fructose 1,6 bisphosphate}$$

$$\text{Fructose 1, 6 bisphosphate} \xrightarrow[\text{bis-phosphatase}]{\text{Fructolse 1, 6}} \text{Fructose-6-phosphate}$$

$$\text{Fructose-6-phosphate} \underset{\text{isome rase}}{\overset{\text{Phoasphohexose}}{\rightleftharpoons}} \text{Glucose-6-phosphate}$$

$$\text{Glucose-6-phosphate} \xrightleftharpoons{\text{Glucose-6-phosphatase}} \textbf{Glucose}$$

$$\text{Glucose-6-phosphate} \xrightleftharpoons{\text{Phosphoglucomutase}} \text{Glucose-1-phosphate}$$

$$\text{Glucose-1-phosphate} \longrightarrow \textbf{Oligo and polysaccharides}$$

OXIDATION (BREAKDOWN) OF FATTY ACIDS

Now, long chain fatty acids are broken down by **α-oxidation** and **β-oxidation.** The β-oxidation ultimately produces the **active 2-C units,** the **acetyl-CoA** ($CH_3CO{\cdot}CoA$).

α-Oxidation

Here, the long chain of fatty acid is gradually broken down until it is reduced to **12C-atoms.** Fatty acids with less than 13-C atoms are not affected by this process. One complete α-oxidation results in the elimination of one carbon atom in the form of CO_2 from the — COOH group of the fatty acid, whereas **α–C–atom**, *i.e.*, C-atom no., 2, adjacent to COOH is oxidised (α-oxidation).

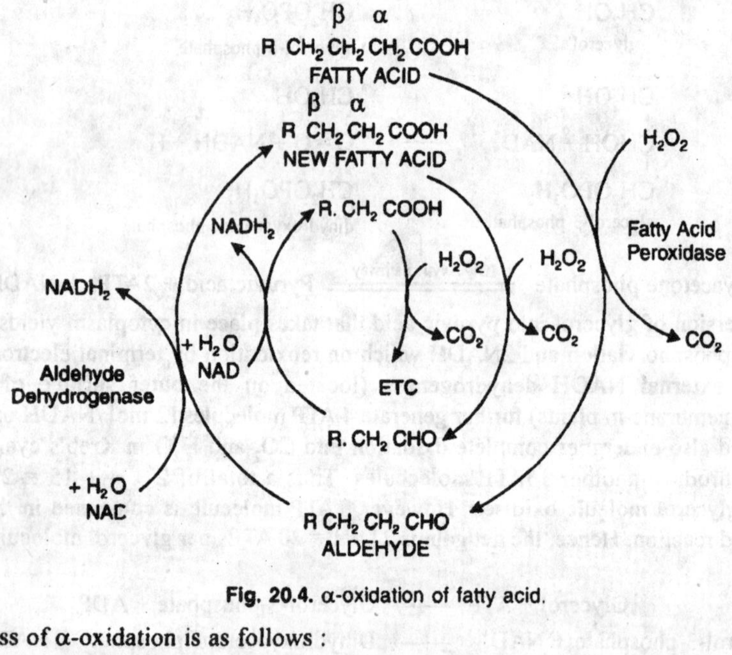

Fig. 20.4. α-oxidation of fatty acid.

Process of α-oxidation is as follows :

(*i*) The fatty acid is **oxidatively decarboxylated** in presence of enzyme *fatty acid peroxidase* and H_2O_2 to form an **aldehyde.** Here, CO_2 comes out from the carboxylic group and oxidation takes place at **α–C–atom** that converts into aldehyde group.

$$\underset{\text{Fatty acid}}{R{\cdot}CH_2\overset{\beta}{C}H_2\overset{\alpha}{C}H_2COOH} \xrightarrow[2(H_2O_2)]{\text{fatty acid peroxidase}} \underset{\text{Aldehyde}}{R{\cdot}CH_2CH_2CHO} + CO_2 + H_2O$$

(*ii*) Now, the aldehyde is further oxidised in the presence of enzyme *aldehyde dehydrogenase* to form the new fatty acid containing one carbon atom less than in the original fatty acid. NAD+ is reduced in the reaction.

$$\underset{\text{Aldehyde}}{R \cdot CH_2CH_2CHO} \xrightarrow[H_2O]{\text{Aldehyde dehydrogenase}} \underset{\text{New fatty acid}}{R \cdot CH_2CH_2COOH} + NADH + H^+$$

The new fatty acid will oxidise repeatedly, till it consists of 12 – C atoms by the same process of α-oxidation.

β-Oxidation

β-oxidation is the main process of fatty acid degradation in plants. This mechanism is well established for saturated fatty acids, while obscure for unsaturated fatty acids.

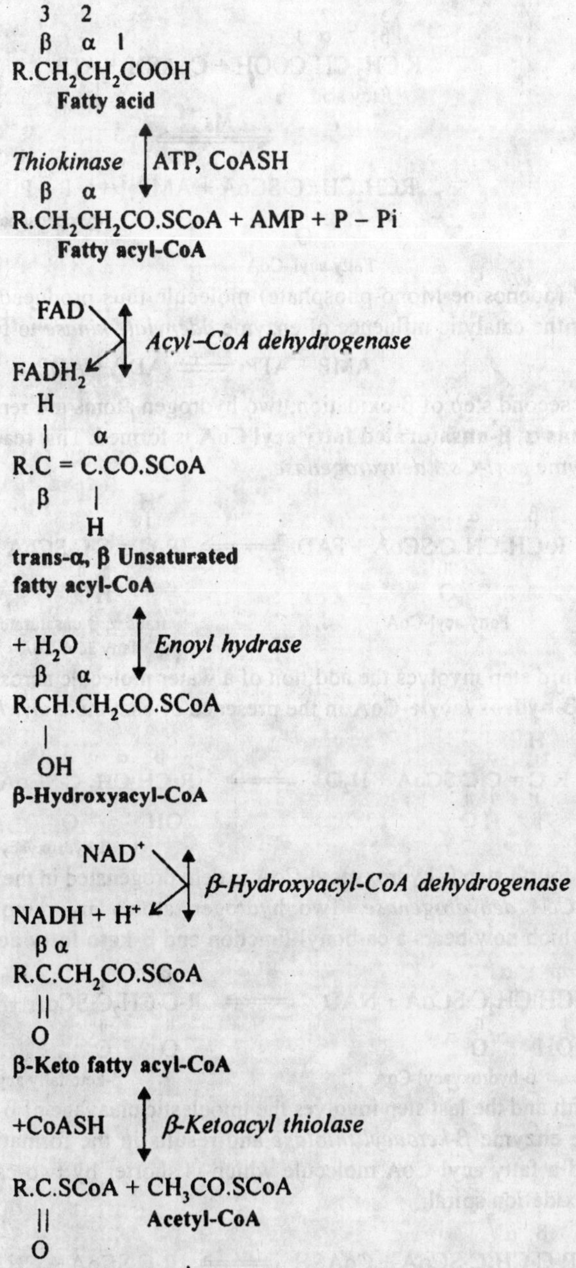

Fig. 20.5. β-oxidation of fatty acid.

β-oxidation takes place in mitochondria and also in glyoxysomes. It involves sequential removal of 2–C in the form of acetyl-CoA ($CH_3CO \cdot SCoA$) molecules from the carboxyl end of the fatty acid. This is called β-oxidation because β-C (*i.e.*, C atom No. 3) of the fatty acid is oxidised during this process. Various steps of this process are as follows :

(*i*) The first step involves the activation of fatty acid in the presence of ATP and enzyme *thiokinase*. CoASH is consumed and CoA derivative of fatty acid is produced.

$$\underset{\text{Fatty acid}}{R{\cdot}\overset{\overset{3}{\beta}}{C}H_2{\cdot}\overset{\overset{2}{\alpha}}{C}H_2\overset{1}{C}OOH} + CoASH + ATP \xrightleftharpoons{Mg^{++}} \underset{\text{Fatty acyl–CoA}}{RCH_2CH_2,\underset{\underset{O}{\|}}{C}{\cdot}SCoA} + AMP + \underset{\text{Pyrophosphate}}{P-Pi}$$

The AMP (adenosine Mono-phosphate) molecule thus produced reacts with another ATP molecule under the catalytic influence of enzyme *adenylate kinase* to form 2 ADP molecules.

$$AMP + ATP \rightleftharpoons ADP + ADP$$

(*ii*) In the second step of β-oxidation, two hydrogen atoms are removed between α and β-C atoms and a **trans α, β-unsaturated fatty acyl CoA** is formed. This reaction is catalysed by FAD-containing enzyme *acyl-CoA dehydrogenase.*

$$\underset{\text{Fatty acyl-CoA}}{R{\cdot}\overset{\beta}{C}H_2\overset{\alpha}{C}H_2\underset{\underset{O}{\|}}{C}{\cdot}SCoA} + FAD \rightleftharpoons \underset{\text{trans α, β-unsaturated fatty acyl-CoA}}{R{\cdot}\overset{H}{\overset{|}{C}} = \underset{\underset{H}{|}}{C}{\cdot}\underset{\underset{O}{\|}}{C}{\cdot}SCoA} + FADH_2$$

(*iii*) The third step involves the addition of a water molecule across the double bond to form corresponding **β-hydroxyacyle-CoA** in the presence of enzyme *enoyl hydrase.*

$$R{\cdot}\underset{\underset{\beta}{|}}{\overset{H}{\overset{|}{C}}} = \underset{\underset{H}{|}}{\overset{\alpha}{C}}{\cdot}\underset{\underset{O}{\|}}{C}{\cdot}SCoA + H_2O \rightleftharpoons \underset{\text{β-hydroxyacyl-CoA}}{R{\cdot}\underset{\underset{OH}{\|}}{\overset{\beta}{C}H}{\cdot}\overset{\alpha}{C}H_2{\cdot}\underset{\underset{O}{\|}}{C}{\cdot}SCoA} + NADH + H^+$$

(*iv*) In the fourth step β-hydroxyacyl-CoA is dehydrogenated in the presence of NAD-specific *β-hydroxyacyl-CoA dehydrogenase.* Two hydrogen atoms are removed from the β-C atom (β-oxidation) which now bears a carbonyl function and **β-keto fatty acyl CoA** is formed.

$$\underset{\text{β-hydroxyacyl-CoA}}{R{\cdot}\underset{\underset{OH}{|}}{\overset{\beta}{C}H}{\cdot}\overset{\alpha}{C}H_2\underset{\underset{O}{\|}}{C}{\cdot}SCoA} + NAD^+ \rightleftharpoons \underset{\text{β-keto fatty acyl-CoA}}{R{\cdot}\underset{\underset{O}{\|}}{\overset{\beta}{C}}{\cdot}\overset{\alpha}{C}H_2\underset{\underset{O}{\|}}{C}{\cdot}SCoA} + NADH + H^+$$

(*v*) The fifth and the last step involves the thioclastic cleavage of β-ketofatty acyl-CoA in the presence of the enzyme *β-ketoacyl thiolase* and results in the formation of an active 2-C unit acetyl-CoA and a fatty acyl-CoA molecule which is shorter by two-carbon atoms than when it entered the β-oxidation spiral.

$$R{\cdot}\underset{\underset{O}{\|}}{\overset{\beta}{C}}{\cdot}\overset{\alpha}{C}H_2\underset{\underset{O}{\|}}{C}{\cdot}SCoA + CoASH \rightleftharpoons \underset{\text{Fatty acyl-CoA}}{R{\cdot}\underset{\underset{O}{\|}}{C}{\cdot}SCoA} + \underset{\text{Acetyl CoA}}{CH_3CO{\cdot}SCoA}$$

The fatty acyl-CoA so produced again re-enters the β-oxidation spiral at step 2, by passing the first step as it is already activated, and losing a further 2-C unit. This sequence continues till whole molecule is degraded.

Each turn of the β-oxidation generates one $FADH_2$ (step 2), one $NADH + H^+$ (step 4) and one acetyl-CoA molecule (step 5). However, in the last turn of the spiral two acetyl-CoA molecules will be produced. Reoxidation of $FADH_2$ and $NADH + H^+$ by the electron transport chain will yield 2 and 3 ATP molecules respectively. Thus each turn of β-oxidation generates 5 ATP molecules. However, in the first turn 2 ATPs are consumed in the first step, thus in this turn there will be a net gain of only 3 ATP molecules.

Complete oxidation of one acetyl-CoA molecule in TCA cycle to CO_2 and H_2O will result in the production of 12 ATP molecules.

Thus huge amount of energy is generated in the form of ATP molecules by the mitochondrial oxidation of fatty acids through the β-oxidation spiral and TCA cycle. For instance, one molecule of palmitic acid (with 16 C atoms) on complete oxidation will produce 129 ATP molecules.

While complete oxidation of stearic acid (with 18 C atoms) through β-oxidation spiral and TCA cycle will result in production of 146 ATP molecules.

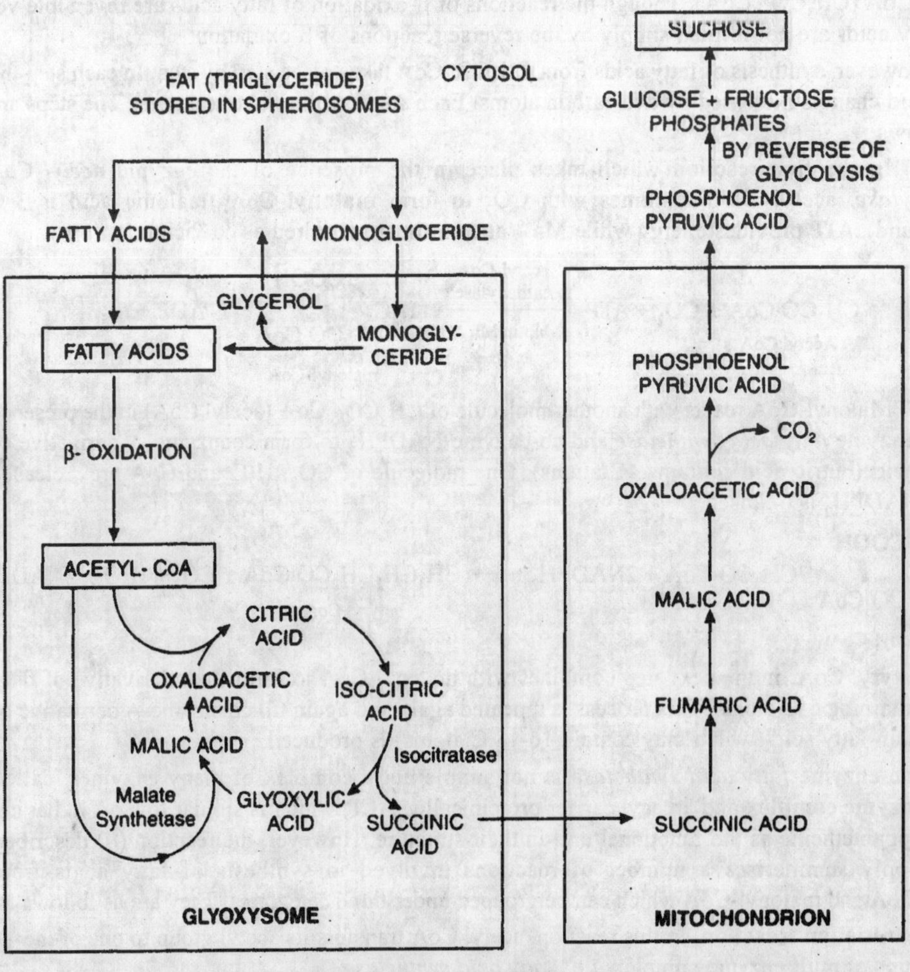

Fig. 20.6. Glyoxylate cycle.

Fate of acetyl–CoA ($CH_3CO{\cdot}CoA$). Acetyl-CoA units are end products of β-oxidation of fatty acids, which may enter (*i*) into Kreb's cycle (TCA cycle) and are oxidised to release energy as mentioned in preceding paragraphs, or (*ii*) in case of germination of fatty acids, they are converted into soluble sucrose through the **glyoxylic acid cycle.**

GLYOXYLATE CYCLE

(Glyoxylic Acid Cycle)

Korenberg and **Krebs** (1957) framed a cycle which is known as **Glyoxylic acid cycle** or **Glyoxylate cycle** through which the fats could be converted into sucrose (carbohydrates) during the germination of fatty seeds in plants.

The glyoxylate cycle is completed in **glyoxysomes, mitochondria** and **cytosol.** Various steps of this cycle occurring in higher plants especially during the germination of fatty seeds are shown in Fig. 20.6. (Glyoxylate cycle) that occur in **glyoxysome and mitochondrion.**

BIOSYNTHESIS OF FATTY ACIDS

Long chain saturated fatty acids are synthesized in plants from active two carbon units, the acetyl-CoA ($CH_3CO \cdot CoA$). Though the reactions of β-oxidation of fatty acids are reversible yet the fatty acids are not formed simply by the reverse reactions of β-oxidation.

However, synthesis of fatty acids from $CH_3CO{\cdot}$ CoA takes place step by step. In each step the fatty acid chain is increased by two carbon atoms. Each step involves two reactions. The steps are as follows :

(*i*) In the first reaction which takes place in the presence of the enzyme *acetyl-CoA carboxylase,* acetyl–CoA combines with CO_2 to form **malonyl-CoA** (malonic acid is 3-C compound). ATP provides energy while Mn^{++} and biotin are required as co-factors.

$$\underset{\text{Acetyl CoA}}{CH_3CO{\cdot}CoA} + CO_2 + ATP \xrightarrow[\text{biotin } Mn^{++}]{\text{acetyl-CoA carboxylase}} \underset{\text{malonyl-CoA}}{H_2C\begin{matrix} \diagup COOH \\ \diagdown CO{\cdot}CoA \end{matrix}} + ADP + iP$$

(*ii*) Malonyl-CoA reacts with another molecule of $CH_3CO \cdot CoA$ (acetyl CoA) in the presence of the enzyme *fatty acid synthetase* and co-enzyme $NADPH_2$ to form coenzyme-A derivative of butric acid (butric acid contains 4C-atoms). One molecule of CO_2, H_2O and CoA are released while $NADPH_2$ is oxidised.

$$\underset{\text{malonyl-CoA}}{H_2C\begin{matrix} \diagup COOH \\ \diagdown CO{\cdot}CoA \end{matrix}} + CH_3CO{\cdot}CoA + 2NADPH_2 \longrightarrow \underset{\text{butyryl CoA}}{CH_3CH_2CH_2CO{\cdot}CoA} + CO_2 + H_2O + 2NADP$$

Butyryl CoA, in the next step combines with malonyl CoA to form CoA derivative of fatty acid containing 6-C atoms. This process is repeated again and again till coenzyme-A derivative of long chain fatty acid (which may contain 16-18 C atoms) is produced.

The enzyme *fatty acid synthetase* is not simple but a complex of many enzymes, called **multienzyme complex** and an acyl carrier protein called ACP, which is similar to CoA in having phosphopantetheine as the functional unit in their structure. However, the reaction (*ii*) described above only summarises a number of reactions involved in synthesis of fatty acids from acetyl-CoA and malonyl-CoA which can be grouped under three categories. They are as follows :

1. Initiation Reaction. In this reaction, acetyl CoA transfers its acetyl group to one of the —SH groups of multienzyme complex, *i.e., fatty acid synthetase.*

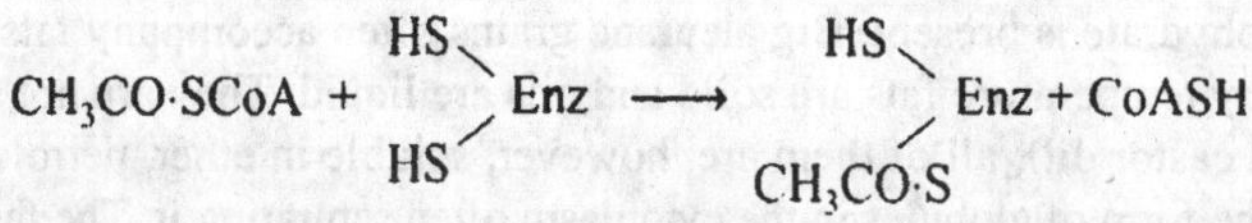

2. Chain Elongation Reactions. Six different reactions involved are — (*i*) malonyl transfer, (*ii*) condensation, (*iii*) reduction, (*iv*) dehydration, (*v*) reduction and (*vi*) acyl transfer.

Chain elongation starts with the transfer of malonyl group from malonyl-CoA to second – SH group of the multienzyme complex. Thereafter, there is condensation of the latter so that a 4-C unit is produced. This unit by next three reactions, *i.e.*, reduction, dehydration and reduction converts into a saturated 4-C unit (*i.e.*, butyryl-CoA). In acyl transfer reaction the fatty acid residue is transferred back to the —SH group to which the acetyl group was transferred in initiation reaction. The cycle is repeated again and again with malonyl transfer, condensation, etc., till the fatty acid residue consists of up to 16 to 18 C atoms. Each such turn elongates fatty acid chain by 2-C atoms. Chain elongation reactions are as follows :

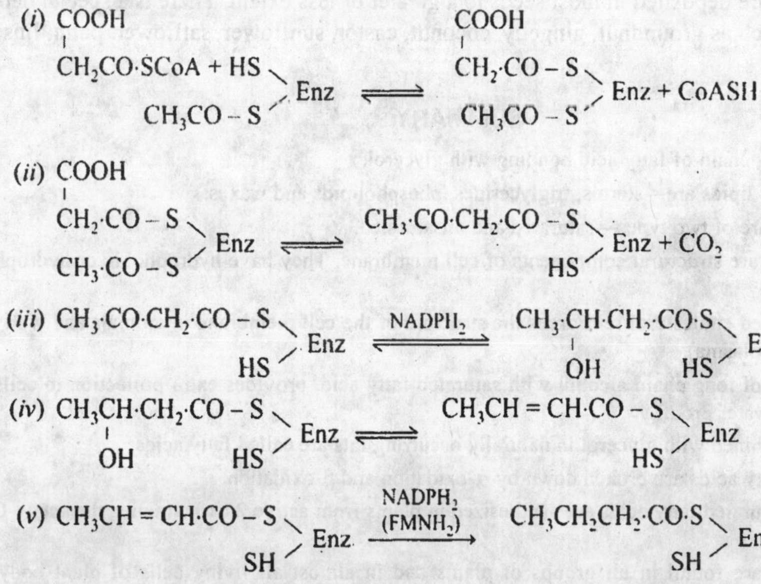

3. Termination Reaction. When the fatty acid residue attains a desired length, the chain elongation stops at reaction (*v*) and the cycle is not repeated. The acyl group instead of being transferred to the —SH of the enzyme, is transferred to—SH group of Co-enzyme A (CoA SH) molecule. Thus, CoA derivate of the fatty acid is produced which can then be utilised in fat synthesis. The enzyme becomes free.

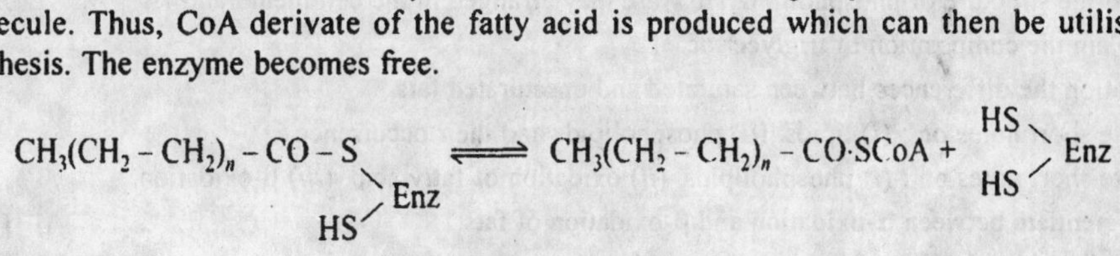

STORAGE AND MOBILIZATION

Fats and oils are found in all groups of plants and in almost all living cells of the plant body. In angiosperms they are specially common in seeds and fruits. When oil is in abundance usually very little carbohydrate is present. Big aleurane grains often accompany fats and oils, as in castor seed. At ordinary temperature fats are solid and oils are liquid. They are not soluble in water or in alcohol (except castor oil); all of them are, however, soluble in ether, petroleum, chloroform, etc. They occur in the form of globules in the cytoplasm often saturating it. The fats and oils are formed from fatty acids and glycerine.

It is a well known fact that these substances enter into the composition of protoplasm; but they undergo many chemical changes before they are utilised by the protoplasm. They are decomposed by the enzyme *lipase* into fatty acids and glycerol. By this decomposition a large amount of heat is liberated.

When oily or fatty seeds germinate a considerable quantity of fatty acids may be detected in them, while glycerol disappears almost immediately.

Fatty acids and glycerol may also be translocated to the growing regions where they are utilised by the protoplasm. Both of them may readily pass through cell walls.

Oils and fats are deposited in most seeds to a greater or less extent. There is a special deposit of them in seeds such as groundnut, gingelly, coconut, castor, sunflower, safflower, palm, linseed, etc.

SUMMARY

1. Lipids are long chain of fatty acid bonding with glycerol.
2. Major types of lipids are—sterols, triglycerides, phospholipids and waxes.
3. Triglycerides are of two types—saturated and unsaturated.
4. Phospholipids are structural components of cell membrane. They have hydrophobic or hydrophilic ends.
5. The sterol called cholesterol reinforces the structure of the cell membrane in animals and wall less bacteria (mycoplasma).
6. Wax, an ester of long chain alcohol with saturated fatty acid, provides extra protection to cells by making them water proof.
7. The acids combined with glycerol in naturally occurring fats are called fatty acids.
8. Long chain fatty acids are broken down by α-oxidation and β-oxidation.
9. Long chain saturated fatty acids are synthesized in plants from active 2 carbon units, the acetyl-CoA ($CH_3CO \cdot CoA$).
10. Fats and oils are found in all groups of plants and in almost all living cells of plant body. In angiosperms, they are commonly found in seeds and fruits.

QUESTION BANK

Short and Long Answer Questions

1. Write short notes on : (*i*) steroids (*ii*) wax.
2. Describe structure of phospholipid. How are they arranged in the cell membrane ?
3. Explain the composition of triglyceride.
4. Mention the differences between saturated and unsaturated fats.
5. Write short notes on : (*i*) lipids, (*ii*) phospholipids and their occurrence.
6. Write short notes on : (*i*) phospholipids, (*ii*) oxidation of fatty acid, (*iii*) β-oxidation.
7. Differentiate between α-oxidation and β-oxidation of fats.
8. Describe classification of lipids.
9. Differentiate between saturated and unsaturated fatty acids.
10. Explain the chain elongation reactions in fat synthesis.
11. Describe the β-oxidation path way of fatty acids.

12. Give the structure and mechanism of fat synthesis in plants.
13. What are lipids ? Explain the distribution and degradation of lipids in plants.
14. Draw β-oxidation path way. No description is required.
15. What are plant lipids ? How are they biosynthesised ? Discuss mechanism of their biosynthesis.
16. Describe degradation of fats. What is the fate of end product of their oxidation ?
17. Enumerate the steps leading to the synthesis of fatty acids.
28. Give an account of fat synthesis in plants.

Multiple Choice Questions

1. Fats are found in abundance in plants especially in
   (*a*) reproductive tissues (*b*) vegetative tissus
   (*c*) meristematic tissues (*d*) all the above.
2. Which of the following is not a component of triglycerides ?
   (*a*) glycerol (*b*) long chain saturated fatty acid
   (*c*) long chain unsaturated fatty acid (*d*) long chain monohydric alcohol.
3. In cells, fats are stored in
   (*a*) spherosomes (*b*) lysosomes (*c*) cytosol (*d*) all the above.
4. β-oxidation of fatty acids takes place in
   (*a*) mitochondria (*b*) glyoxysomes (*c*) both (*a*) and (*b*) (*d*) cytosol.
5. The reactions of β-oxidation of fatty acids in plants are
   (*a*) reversible (*b*) irreversible (*c*) both (*a*) and (*b*) (*d*) non-enzymatic.
6. Which of the following is not a phospholipid ?
   (*a*) lecithin (*b*) cephalin (*c*) cardiolipin (*d*) none of the above.
7. Phospholipids make important structural component of
   (*a*) plasmamembrane (*b*) tonoplast (*c*) all cell membranes (*d*) none of the above.
8. Conversion of succinate into fumarate in glyoxylate cycle takes place in
   (*a*) glyoxysome (*b*) mitochondrion (*c*) cytosol (*d*) all the above.
9. Conversion of fats into carbohydrates through glyoxylate cycle is an example of
   (*a*) gluconeogenesis (*b*) glucogenesis (*c*) synthesis of sucrose (*d*) none of the above.
10. Glyoxylate cycle was discovered by
    (*a*) Hans A. Krebs (*b*) Korenberg and Krebs
    (*c*) Harden and Youngs (*d*) none of the above.
11. Glyoxylate cycle is completed in
    (*a*) glyoxysome (*b*) glyoxysome and mitochondrion
    (*c*) glyoxysome, mitochondrion and cytosol (*d*) none of the above.
12. The acetyl-CoA molecules produced at the end of β-oxidation spiral may be converted into sucrose through
    (*a*) glyoxylate cycle (*b*) glycolate cycle (*c*) TCA cycle (*d*) none of the above.
13. How many carbon atoms are removed in complete turn of α-oxidation spiral in plants ?
    (*a*) one (*b*) two (*c*) three (*d*) none of the above.
14. α-oxidation of fatty acids in plants is
    (*a*) one step process (*b*) two step process (*c*) three step process (*d*) none of the above.
15. In eukaryotic plants, complete aerobic oxidation of one molecule of glycerol results in net gain of
    (*a*) 5 ATP_S (*b*) 20 ATP_S (*c*) 15 ATP_S (*d*) none of the above.
16. Common 18–C unsaturated fatty acid, oleic acid contains.
    (*a*) one double bond (*b*) two double bonds (*c*) one triple bond (*d*) none of the above.

17. The phospholipids are broken down (hydrolysed) to their residues by the action of enzymes called
(*a*) phosphatases (*b*) phosphatidases (*c*) phosphorylases (*d*) none of the above.

18. Which of the following is not a saturated fatty acid ?
(*a*) lauric acid (*b*) myristic acid (*c*) palmitic acid (*d*) none of the above.

19. Palmitic acid contains
(*a*) 14-C atoms (*b*) 16-C atoms (*c*) 18-C atoms (*d*) 20-C atoms.

20. Complete oxidation of one palmitic acid molecule (16-C) through β-oxidation spiral and TCA cycle results in net gain of
(*a*) 127 ATP mols (*b*) 128 ATP mols (*c*) 129 ATP mols (*d*) 130 ATP mols.

21. In each turn of β-oxidation spiral, there is sequential removal of 2-C atoms in the form of
(*a*) two CO_2 mols (*b*) one CO_2 and one acetyl-CoA mol
(*c*) one acetyl-CoA mol (*d*) none of the above.

22. The enzyme fatty acid synthase is a complex of many enzymes (multienzymes complex) plus
(*a*) CoASH (*b*) ACP (*c*) FMN (*d*) none of the above.

23. Each turn of β-oxidation spiral generates two reduced coenzymes in the form of
(*a*) two NADH mols (*b*) two $FADH_2$ mols
(*c*) one NADH and one $FADH_2$ mols (*d*) none of the above.

24. Which of the following are called neutral lipids ?
(*a*) triglycerides and waxes (*b*) phospholipids and glycolipids
(*c*) sterols (*d*) none of the above.

25. The two key enzymes of glyoxylate cycle are
(*a*) malate synthetase and citrate synthase (*b*) malate synthetase and isocitratase
(*c*) citrate synthease and isocitratase (*d*) none of the above.

ANSWERS

1. (*a*) **2.** (*d*) **3.** (*a*) **4.** (*c*) **5.** (*a*) **6.** (*d*) **7.** (*c*) **8.** (*b*) **9.** (*a*) **10.** (*b*)
11. (*c*) **12.** (*a*) **13.** (*a*) **14.** (*b*) **15.** (*b*) **16.** (*a*) **17.** (*b*) **18.** (*d*) **19.** (*b*) **20.** (*c*)
21. (*c*) **22.** (*b*) **23.** (*c*) **24.** (*a*) **25.** (*b*)

UNIT - 5
Biotechnology

21
CHAPTER

Genetic Engineering, Cloning and Genomics

As we know, genes regulate growth and differentiation, and all fundamental life processes are also regulated by them. Ageing and cancer result from differential gene expression. Several other pathological disorders are also caused by some defective gene. Thus, it becomes quite important to understand the structure of genes and their organization and how their expression is regulated. However, in microorganisms, it is easy to study the organization and expression of genes. This is because several mutants, with altered characteristics can be isolated. In bacteria, conjugation and transduction experiments can also be carried out, where the functional characters could easily be related to specific genes and their arrangement.

In this chapter, we will learn about the tools and techniques of molecular biology for cleaving and rejoining DNA sequences from two or more different organisms.

Such genetically modified DNA fragments are known as recombinant DNA molecules. This process involves manipulation or engineering of the DNA (genes) involved in the process and thus the term **'genetic engineering'** has been coined.

The recombinant DNA molecules can be cloned and amplified virtually to an unlimited extent.

Application of DNA manipulation or genetic engineering ranges from cloning genes to cloning organisms including transgenic microbes, agriculturally important crops and farm animals.

Thus by the process of genetic engineering we can get genetically modified food products, human gene products, pharmacologically and therapeutically useful products.

Gene therapy or gene replacement can be used in the treatment of hereditary diseases which are otherwise incurable.

In modern days, DNA fingerprinting has been successfully used in forensic investigations.

Now human genome has been worked out, which reveals the blue print of our life itself.

The latest of this series is claim of first human clone, which was announced by Brigitte Boisselier, head of a company known Clonaid on December 26, 2002, a baby girl called Eve by scientists.

GENETIC ENGINEERING

Genetic engineering is considered as a kind of biotechnology.

This is a process in which the alteration of the genetic make up of cells is done by deliberate and artificial means.

This process involves transfer or replacement of genes to create recombinant DNA.

This can be done by cutting DNA molecules at specific sites to get fragments containing desirable and useful genes from one type of cell.

Thereafter, these genes can be inserted into a suitable carrier or vector.

Now, these recombinant DNA can be put into completely different cell of a bacterium or plant or animal cell.

By this technique they acquire useful characteristics, such as disease resistance or to make useful enzymes, hormones, vaccines, etc.

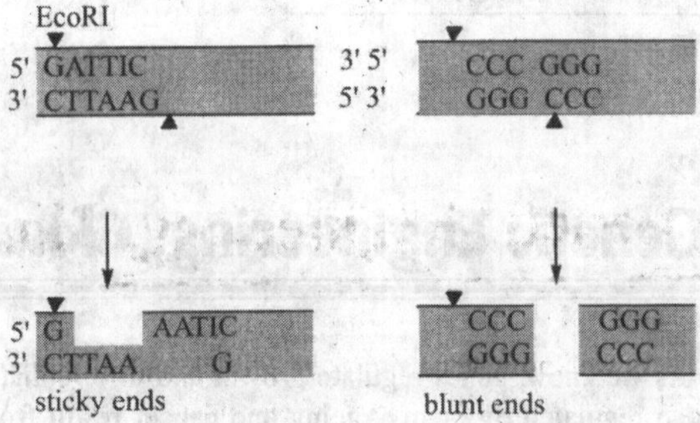

Fig. 21.1. Restriction enzymes.

Tools and Techniques of Genetic Engineering

Genetic engineering involves cutting and pasting fragments of DNA may be cut and pasted in the vector, a plasmid or a virus whose DNA then becomes the recombinant DNA.

Tools of genetic engineering. The three tools for recombinant DNA technology are as follows :

1. Cell culture containing cells with the desired DNA segment (gene).

2. DNA modifying enzymes such as : (*a*) Restriction endonuclease from various bacteria. It cleaves double stranded DNA but only at a limited number of sites (*b*) DNA ligase from *Escherichia coli* which joins DNA molecules. (*c*) DNA polymerase from *E. coli* which synthesises a new strand of DNA complementary to an existing DNA or RNA template.

DNA segment can be excised by **"molecular scissors"** or **'chemical scalpels'** which are known as **restriction enzymes** in biotechnological language.

Restriction enzymes, synthesized by microbes as a defense mechanism, are specific endonucleases, which can cleave double-stranded DNA.

However, they can do this only at limited number of sites depending on the number of recognition sequences in DNA.

With the use of **restriction enzymes** it is possible to cut a DNA sequence. For example, a restriction enzyme EcoR1 will cut DNA only if sequence $\begin{matrix}\text{GAATC}\\\text{CTTAG}\end{matrix}$ is present in the double stranded DNA. Hundreds of such restriction enzymes with different sequence specificities have been isolated from several bacteria and are commercially available. These enzymes are known as **restriction enzymes** because they restrict infection by bacteria by certain bacteriophages, by degrading the viral DNA without affecting the bacterial DNA. Thus, such enzymes are helpful in breaking DNA molecule at a specific point. In recombinant DNA technology, they are used to cut DNA into specific fragments that contain specific genes.

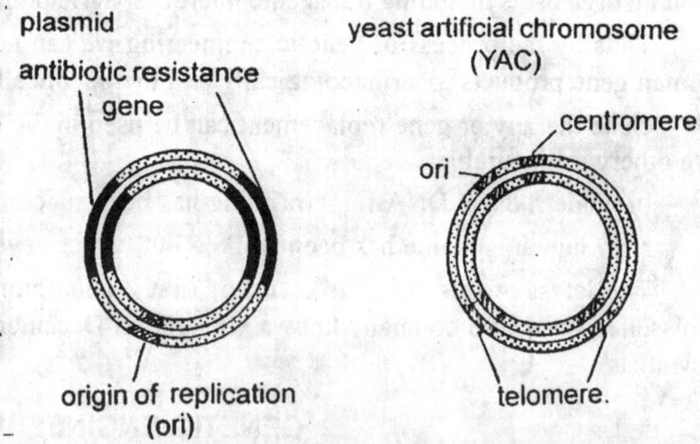

Fig. 21.2. Plasmid and yeast artificial chromosome

DNA synthesising enzymes. DNA synthesising enzymes, such as **DNA polymerase** or **reverse transcriptase** to make DNA complementary to an existing DNA or RNA template respectively called c DNA (complementary or copy DNA) are also required.

Because of the presence of an universal genetic code, the DNA polymerases (synthesising enzymes) can accurately transcribe a DNA sequence from one organism to another organism, and finally molecular sutures, the **DNA ligase** enzymes to join DNA fragments.

This happens so by the formation of phosphodiester bond, again.

Any pair of fragments produced by the same restriction enzyme, from any DNA source (*e.g.*, fruit fly, any other animal or human), can be joined together.

3. **Cloning vectors.** The desired gene is inserted in the vectors or gene carrier to form DNA. Vectors carrying recombinant DNA (r-DNA) divide and thus help in producing several copies of the r-DNA.

There are five cloning vectors which are used in experiments with *E. coli* animals/humans are:

(*a*) plasmids (*b*) bacteriophages (viruses that infect bacteria) (*c*) plant/animal viruses (*d*) transposons (jumping genes) and (*e*) artificial chromosomes of bacteria, yeast and mammals.

The most commonly used vectors are plasmids and viruses.

Recombinant DNA (r-DNA) technique. The sequence of steps in r-DNA technology are as follows :

(*i*) Cell culture of cells with the required DNA sequences is obtained through tissue culture technique. (*ii*) Specific restriction endonuclease is selected from the specific bacterium. (*iii*) Restriction endonuclease cuts the specific DNA (desired gene) at the two ends which becomes the **restriction fragment**. (*iv*) Same restriction endonuclease cuts a matching DNA sequence from a plasmid. (*v*) Ligase enzyme which acts as a molecular glue joins the restriction fragment in the place vacated by the cut DNA segment of the plasmid. The plasmid DNA now contains foreign DNA and its DNA is called **recombinant DNA** (r-DNA). (*vi*) Recombinant plasmids containing recombinant DNA are now inserted into a host cell, *e.g.*, *E. coli*. This is commonly done by a process called **electroporation** in which transient temporary pores are created in the cell membrane of the host for the uptake of foreign DNA molecules. (*vi*) Host bacterium divides to give multiple copies of the recombinant DNA which may be preserved in a DNA library which is also called genomic DNA library.

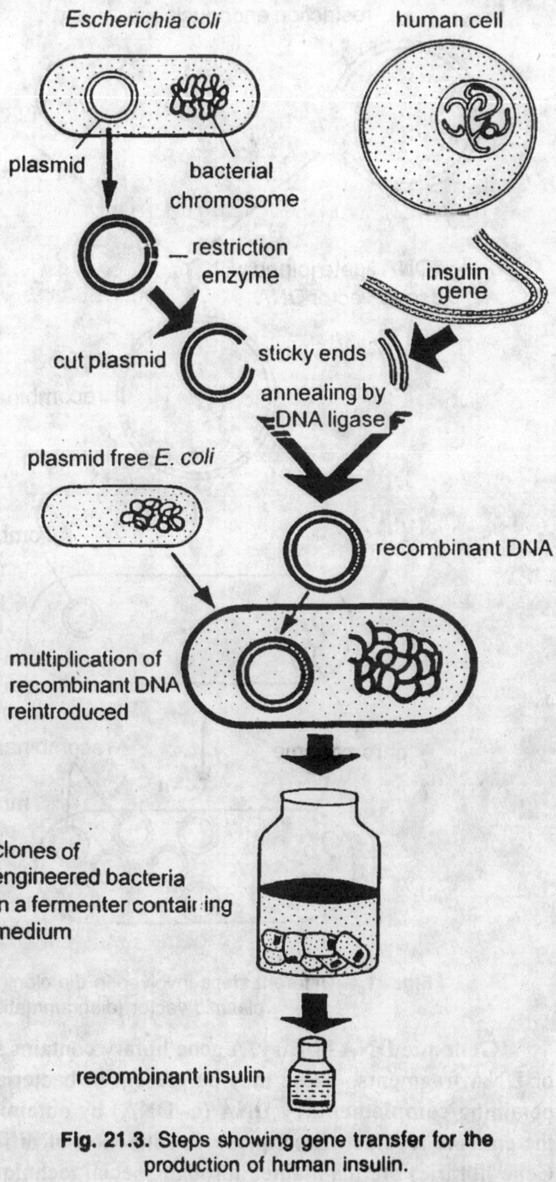

Fig. 21.3. Steps showing gene transfer for the production of human insulin.

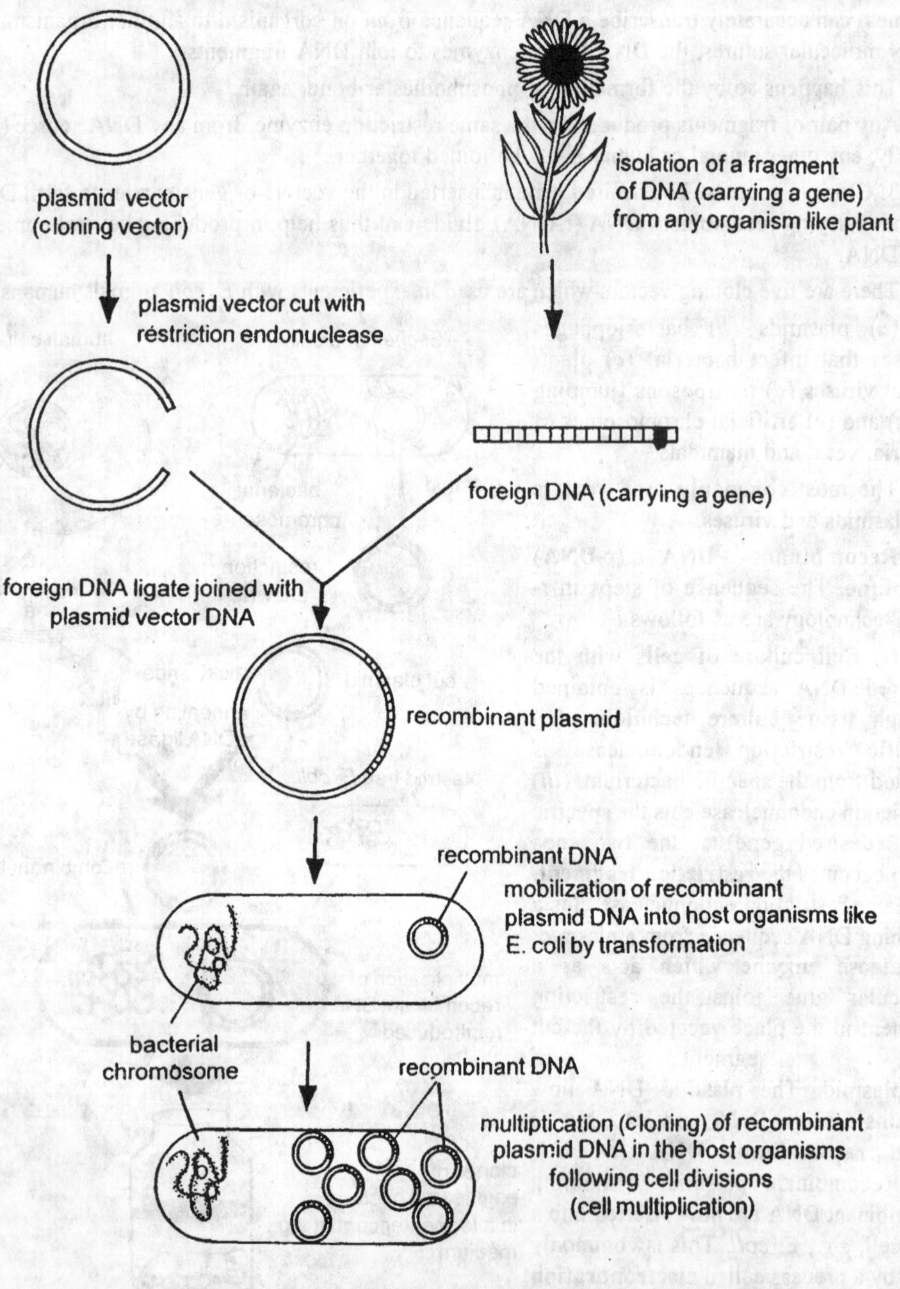

Fig. 21.4. Different steps involved in the cloning of a foreign DNA fragment into a plasmid vector (diagrammatic representation).

Genomic DNA library. A gene library contains several copies of many of the desired genes or DNA fragments. These may be present in bacterial clones with **recombination DNA** or by obtaining **complementary DNA** (c- DNA) by obtaining a DNA from an RNA template by using the enzyme reverse transcriptase. A collection of different c-DNA fragments is a c-DNA library. Gene libraries are maintained through special techniques.

Gene Transfer

Gene transfer can be done by two methods :

(*i*) indirect method through vectors or carriers and

(*ii*) direct or vectorless transfer method.

The first method includes (*a*) plasmids and viruses and (*b*) natural genetic engineer.

(*a*) **plasmids and viruses.** Recombinant DNA technology involves the transfer of desired genes into vectors such as plasmids or viruses. Cloning of the recombinant DNA (r-DNA) then provides multiple copies.

Natural genetic engineer tumor inducing (ti) plasmid. For example, *Agrobacterium tumefaciens* is a plant pathogenic bacterium which can transfer part of its plasmid DNA as it infects host plants. Species of *Agrobacterium* produce crown galls or plant tumors in several dicot plants such as tobacco, tomato, potato, etc.

These bacteria contain large Ti-plasmids (*i.e.*, tumor-inducing plasmids in *Agrobacterium tumefaciens*) which pass on their tumour causing gene into the genome of the host plant. Thus, galls are formed on the host plant and therefore, these bacteria are known as *natural genetic engineers of plants*. Ti-plasmids can be used as gene vectors for delivering useful foreign genes into target plant cells and tissues. Ti-plasmid vectors can be used for genetic transformation of many important dicot (*e.g.*, potato, tomato, cotton, sunflower, etc.) and monocot (*e.g.*, wheat, rice, etc.) plants.

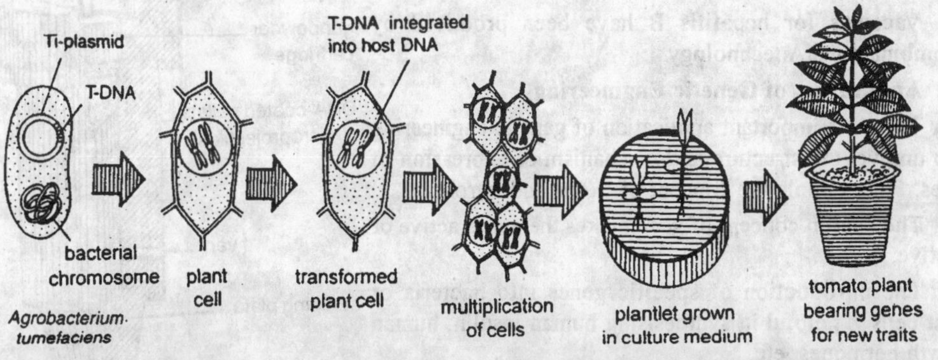

Fig. 21.5. *Agrobacterium*. Tumor inducing (Ti) plasmid-mediated genetic transformation in plants.

Fig. 21.6. Tumor inducing (Ti) plasmid. Crown caused on turnip by bacteria (*Agrobacterium tume-faciens*) carrying Ti plasmid.

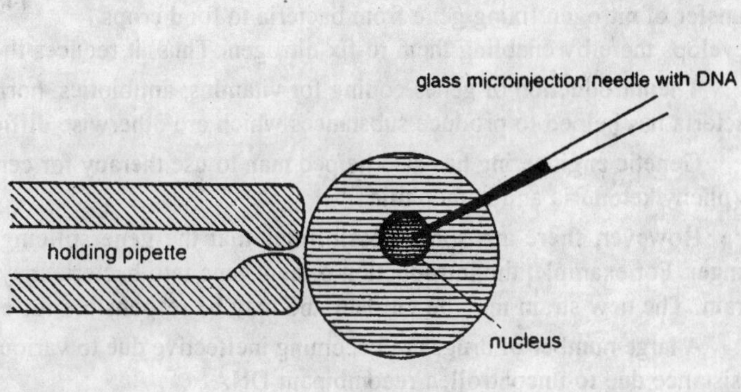

Fig. 21.7. Microinjection. Micropipette is used for injecting DNA into the nucleus of a cell.

The **vectorless gene transfer** includes the following four important methods :

(*a*) Electroporation. In which temporary holes produced in plasma membrane of the cell mediate entry of foreign DNA.

(*b*) Chemical mediated gene transfer. In which certain chemicals (*e.g.*, polyethylene glycol) help in the uptake of foreign DNA into host cell.

(*c*) Microinjection. Introduction of foreign genes into plant or animal cells using micropipettes.

(*d*) Particle gun. In which Tungsten particles coated with foreign DNA are bombarded into target cells.

APPLICATIONS OF RECOMBINANT DNA TECHNOLOGY

The technique of recombinant DNA can be used as follows :

It can be used to elucidate molecular events in the biological process of cellular differentiation and ageing.

This can also be utilised in making gene maps with precision.

This can be used to spell out the complete nucleotide sequence of genome of various organisms including humans.

By this technique, useful chemical compounds can be produced cheaply and efficiently.

Vaccines for hepatitis B have been produced by recombinant DNA technology.

Application of Genetic Engineering

The most important application of genetic engineering is to unravel the structure and mechanism of expression of genes. For example the concept of exons and introns.

The operon concept of gene makes the genes active or inactive.

The introduction of specific genes into bacteria or yeast cells is helpful in synthesising human insulin, human growth hormones, etc.

It makes possible to introduce useful procaryotic genes into eucaryotes. For example, the possibility of the transfer of nitrogen fixing gene from bacteria to food crops develops there by enabling them to fix nitrogen. Thus, it reduces the need of nitrate fertilizers.

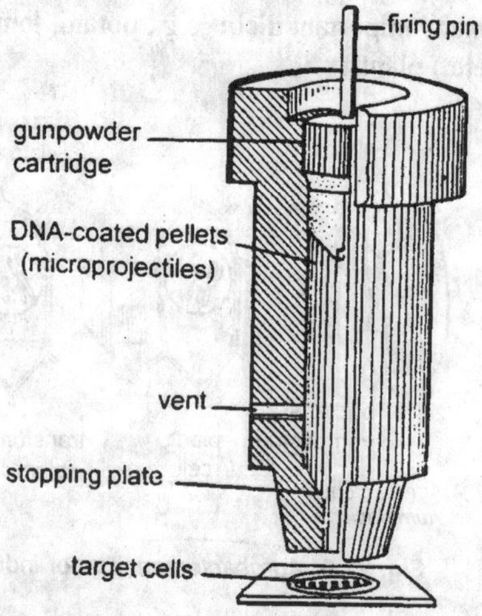

Fig. 21.8. Particle gene gun.

The introduction of genes coding for vitamins, antibiotics, hormones from higher animals to bacteria has helped to produce substances which are otherwise difficult to synthesise.

Genetic engineering has also helped man to use therapy for certain hereditary diseases, such as phenylketonuria and hemophilia.

However, there are some possibilities that the gene splicing are tempered with possible danger. For example, the introduction of new gene into bacteria may lead to the formation of new strain. The new strain may be virulent and may be responsible for epidemics.

A large number of drugs are becoming ineffective due to various microorganisms developing resistance due to uncontrolled recombinant DNA.

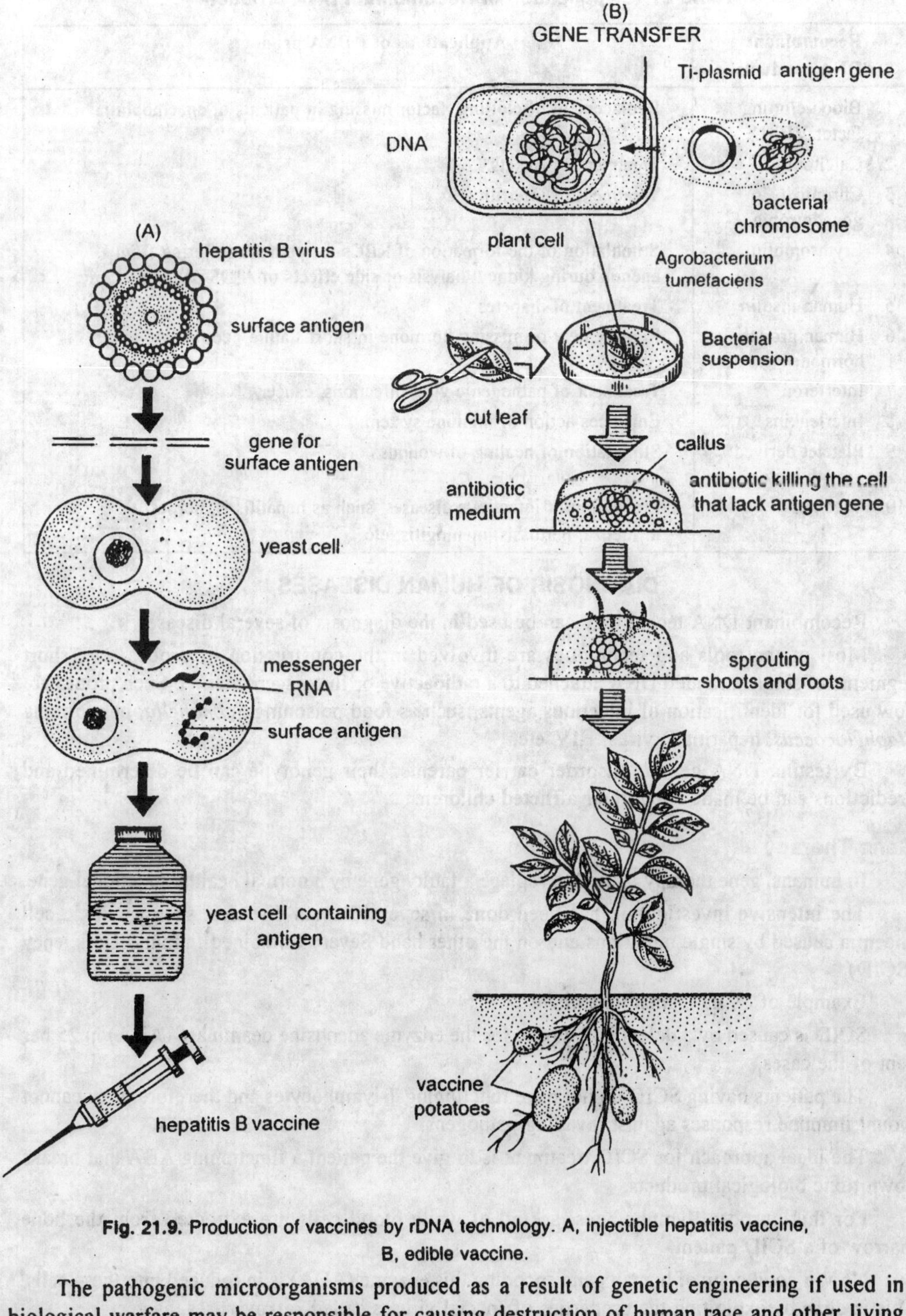

Fig. 21.9. Production of vaccines by rDNA technology. A, injectible hepatitis vaccine, B, edible vaccine.

The pathogenic microorganisms produced as a result of genetic engineering if used in biological warfare may be responsible for causing destruction of human race and other living beings.

Table 21.1. Application of Recombinant DNA products

Recombinant DNA products	Applications of r DNA products
1. Blood clotting factor VIII/IX	Replacement of clotting factor missing in patients of anaemophilia A / B.
2. Calcitonin	Treatment of rickets.
3. Chronic gonadotropin	Treatment of infertility.
4. Erythropiotin	Stimulation of the formation of RBCs for patients suffering from anemia during kidney dialysis or side effects of AIDS patients
5. Human insulin	Treatment of diabetes.
6. Human growth hormone	Replacement of missing hormone in short stature people.
7. Interferon	Treatment of pathogenic viral infections, cancer.
8. Interleukins	Enhances action of immune system.
9. Platelet derived growth factor	Stimulation of healing of wounds.
10. Vaccines	Prevention of infectious diseases, such as hepatitis B, herpes, influenza, pertussis, meningitis, etc.

DIAGNOSIS OF HUMAN DISEASES

Recombinant DNA technology can be used in the diagnosis of several diseases.

Most of the tools and techniques are involved in the construction of probes, *i.e.*, short segments of single stranded DNA attached to a radioactive or fluorescent marker. Such probes are now used for identification of infectious agents, such as food poisoning *Salmonella*, pus forming *Staphylococcus*, hepatitis B virus, HIV, etc.

By testing DNA genetic disorder carrier parents, their genotype can be determined and predictions can be made about their afflicted children.

Gene Therapy

In humans, gene therapy is used to replace a faulty gene by a normal healthy functional gene.

The intensive investigation has been done in several human diseases, such as sickle cell anaemia caused by single mutations and on the other hand Severe Combined Immuno-Deficiency (SCID)

Example of SCID is mentioned here :

SCID is caused by a defect in the gene for the enzyme adenosine deaminase (ADA) in 25 per cent of the cases.

The patients having SCID do not have functioning T-lymphocytes and therefore, they cannot mount immune responses against invading pathogens.

The ideal approach for SCID treatment is to give the patient a functioning ADA that breaks down toxic biological products.

For this purpose, lymphocytes, a kind of white blood cells are extracted from the bone marrow of a SCID patient.

Now, a good copy of human gene encoding this enzyme (ADA) is introduced into these cells. This is done by exploiting the properties of special viruses called **retroviruses**, as vector.

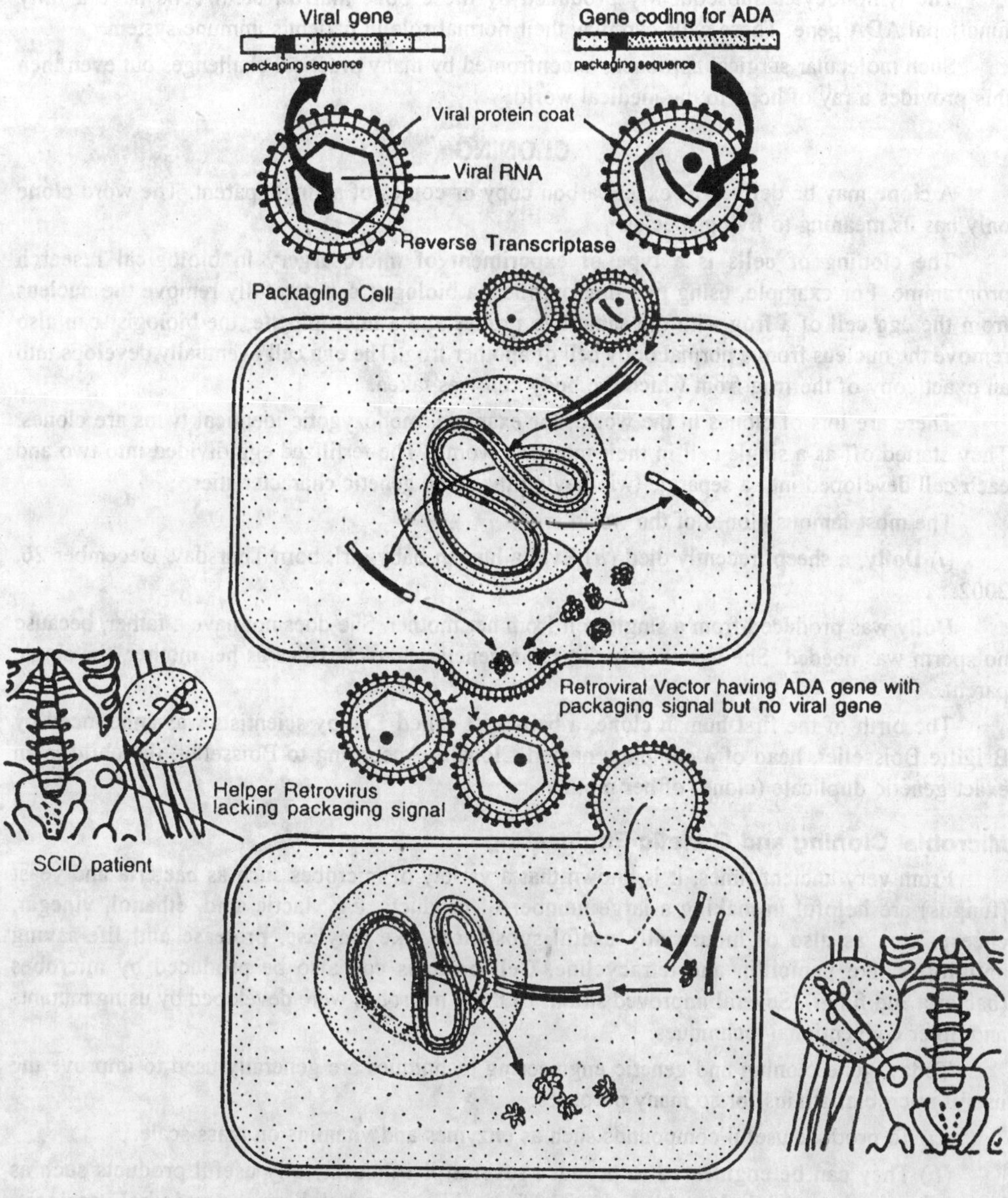

Fig. 21.10. Gene Therapy to treat Severe Combined Immuno-Deficiency (SCID).

This vector (retrovirus) is engineered to incorporate the ADA gene which has the packing sequence but no viral genes.

Now, co-infection of the bone marrow stem cells, removed from a SCID patient, with this vector and helper virus produces new virus particles with ADA gene inserted inside, but lacks the packing sequence.

This equips these cells with a good copy of the gene, in addition to the existing faulty copy of the gene.

Now, the treated cells are reinjected to the patient's bone marrow.

The lymphocytes subsequently produced by these bone marrow stem cells have a fully functional ADA gene. These cells can play their normal role in patient's immune system.

Such molecular surgical approach, is confronted by many practical challenges but even then this provides a ray of hope to the medical world.

CLONING

A **clone** may be defined as exact carbon copy or copies of a single parent. The word **clone** only has its meaning to living species.

The cloning of cells is a type of experiment of microsurgery in biological research programme. For example, using two microprobes, a biologist can carefully remove the nucleus from the egg cell of a frog with the same two probes and a micropipette, the biologist can also remove the nucleus from a normal body cell of another frog. The egg cell eventually develops into an exact copy of the frog from which the body cell was taken.

There are lots of clones in the world, for example, monozygotic identical twins are clones. They started off as a single cell in their mother's womb. The fertilized egg divided into two and each cell developed into a separate twin having the same genetic characteristics.

The most famous clones of the world are :

(*i*) **Dolly**, a sheep, recently died (*ii*) **Eve**, a human baby girl, born Thursday, December 26, 2002.

Dolly was produced from a single cell from her mother. She does not have a father, because no sperm was needed. She has exactly the same genetic characteristics as her mother, the single parent.

The birth of the first human clone, a baby girl called **Eve** by scientists was announced by Brigitte Boisselier, head of a company named Clonaid. According to Boisselier, the child is an exact genetic duplicate (clone) of her mother.

Microbial Cloning and Genetic Engineering

From very ancient times, it is known that a variety of microbes such as bacteria and yeast (fungus) are helpful in making a large number of products, *e.g.*, lactic acid, ethanol, vinegar, cheese, etc., as also of industrially useful substances like amylase, protease and life-saving antibiotics like penicillin and tetracycline. Cell proteins can also be produced by microbes (bacteria and fungi). Several improved strains of these microbes were developed by using mutants and other conventional techniques.

Today, gene cloning and genetic engineering techniques are generally used to improve the useful microbial strains for so many purposes.

(*a*) To produce useful compounds such as enzymes and vitamins on mass scale.

(*b*) They can be engineered to produce several pharmaceutically useful products such as human insulin (*e.g.*, in *Escherichia coli*), interferon, human growth hormone and viral vaccines.

(*c*) Several microbial strains are used in the various industries for performing many important functions such as the removal of undesired lignin (*e.g.*, *Trametes*).

(*d*) Microbes (*e.g.*, heavy-metal accumulating bacteria like *Pseudomonas*) can be used to purify polluted environment (called bioremediation).

(*e*) Certain microbes such as *Trichoderma* (fungus) and *Rhizobium* (bacterium) are used for bio-control (against plant diseases and pests) and as biofertilisers respectively.

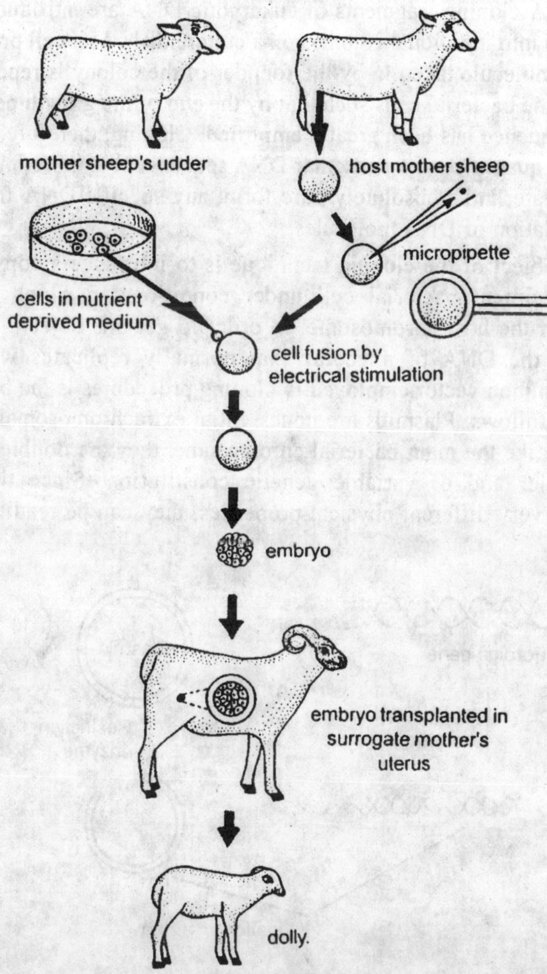

Fig. 21.11. Dolly. Steps in cloning of sheep.

Table. 21.2 Application of Genetically Engineered Microbes

Microbes	*Applications*
1. *Bacillus thuringiensis* (a soil bacterium)	Production of endotoxin (Bt toxin), a biodegradable insecticide for plant protection.
2. *Escherichia coli.* (a gut bacterium)	Production of human insulin, human growth factor interferons and interleukin.
3. *Pseudomonas fluorescence* (a bacterium)	Prevention of frost damage to the plants.
4. *Pseudomonas putida* (a bacterium)	Scavanging of oil spills. Digests hydrocarbons of crude oil.
5. *Rhizobium meliloti* (bacterium)	Nitrogen fixation by incorporating "nif" gene in cereal crops.
6. *Trichoderma* (a fungus)	Produces enzyme chitinase for biocontrol of fungal diseases in plants.

In the process of DNA cloning fragments of eukaryotic DNA are introduced into bacterial cells, which are then grown into individual colonies on a culture dish. As a cell proliferates to form a colony, the single DNA molecule taken in by the founder of the colony is repeatedly replicated by the enzymes present in the bacterial cells such that by the end of the growth period, the number of copies of the foreign sequence has been greatly amplified. Cloning, therefore, can be used as a technique to produce large quantities of a particular DNA sequence, but more important, it can be used as a technique to isolate, in an absolutely pure form, any specific DNA fragment among a large, heterogeneous population of DNA molecules.

Gene cloning. The object of the cloning technique is to introduce a copy of a eukaryotic DNA fragment into a recipient bacterial cell under conditions in which it will replicate autonomously from that of the host chromosome. In order to get this objective, the eukaryotic DNA must be linked to the DNA of a **vector** that normally replicates within a bacterial environment. The most common vector employed in cloning procedures is the bacterial **plasmid**. The use of plasmids is as follows: Plasmids are nonessential extrachromosomal DNA molecules present in many bacteria. Like the main bacterial chromosome, they are double-stranded circles, but they are much smaller and of variable genetic constitution. Since the plasmids and chromosomal DNAs have very different physical properties, they can be readily separated from one another.

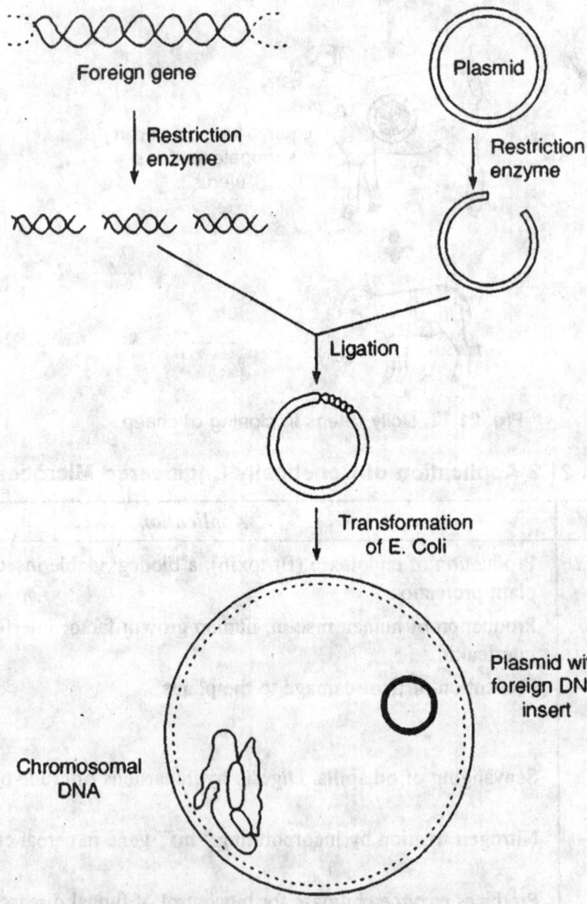

Fig. 21.12. Plasmid. Vectors and transformation.

The foreign DNA to be cloned is inserted into the plasmid to form the recombinant DNA molecule. This modified plasmid is then added to a bacterial culture as naked DNA, and in the presence of $CaCl_2$, a small percentage of the bacteria will pick up one of these molecules from the medium. Once a plasmid is taken up, it will replicate autonomously within the recipient and will be passed on to its progeny during cell division. A wide variety of plasmids have been isolated, many of which carry genes for resistance to antibiotics. If these plasmids are added to a bacterial culture and the cells are then treated with specific antibiotics, only these bacteria which have taken up the plasmid will be able to survive.

How is the DNA of the vector combined with that form the eukaryotic genome? Recombinant DNA molecules can be formed in several ways.

Recombinant DNAs can be constructed between DNA fragments having blunt ends. This can be done by enzymatically adding a string of A- or C- bearing nucleotides to one strand of the fragment and a complementary string of T- or G- bearing nucleotides to the opposite strand of the vector, mixing the two populations, and sealing the molecules with the ligase.

Cloning genomic fragments. When working with genomic DNA, one has to isolate a particular gene or genes, such as those which code for the histones, from among the thousands of unrelated sequences. The first step in this type of experiment is to fragment the DNA with restriction endonucleases. These enzymes recognize sequences from 4 to 6 nucleotides in length. Once the DNA is fragmented, the fragments are combined with the DNA of the vector, and the diverse population of recombinant DNA molecules is subjected to the DNA cloning procedure. Since a given bacterial cell takes up only one plasmid, all the cells of a given colony will contain copies of the same recombinant DNA molecule.

Cell cloning. The bacterial cell is at one and the same time is the somatic and the germ cell. Having selected a single bacterium, one can grow large populations of cells, all identical in morphology and biochemistry. In modern times by means of refined culture techniques the cell cloning has become possible, and the pure populations of cells have been grown from a single isolated cell.

The smallest viable unit of plant one can at present envisage as reproducing, growing and developing in culture is a single cell. Several workers established method which would allow the growth of isolated plant organs and tissues *in vitro*, in culture.

Cell cloning is based on the property of **totipotency** in plants or **pluriopotency** in animals. Totipotency is the potential ability of a plant cell to grow into a complete plant, whereas pluriopotency is the potential ability of a cell into develop any type of the cell in the animal body, *e.g.*, nerve cells, kidney cells or heart cells.

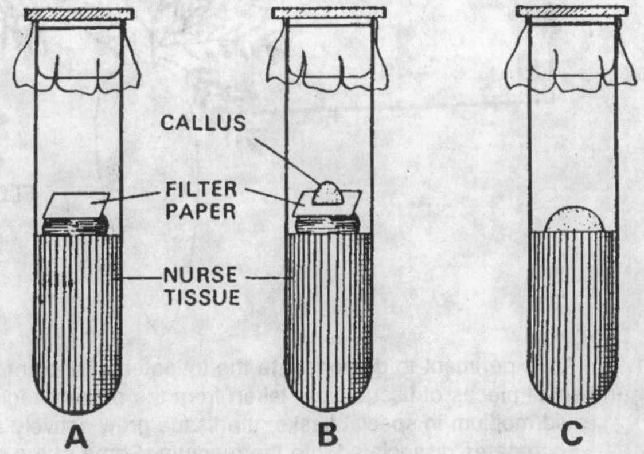

Fig. 21.13. Nurse-tissue technique to raise single-cell clones. A, a single cell from the callus is placed on filter paper lying on the top of a large callus (nurse tissue); B, the cell divides and forms a small tissue; C, this tissue is transferred from the filter paper to the medium directly where it is able to grow further.

Virtually all plants are totipotent but in animals only fertilized egg and stem cells in the embryonic blastocyst are totipotent.

Plant cloning. Cellular totipotency is the capacity of mature cells showing that when freed from the plant body, they have the ability to reorganize themselves into the new individuals. Steward and his co-workers, showed this phenomenon in the carrot cultures. Here the small pieces of mature carrot root, were grown in a liquid medium supplemented with coconut milk in special containers. These cultures were shaken generally which freed all the cell clusters into the medium. Some of them developed into rooting clumps. When these were transferred to the tubes containing a semi-solid medium, they gave rise to whole plant that flowered and set seeds.

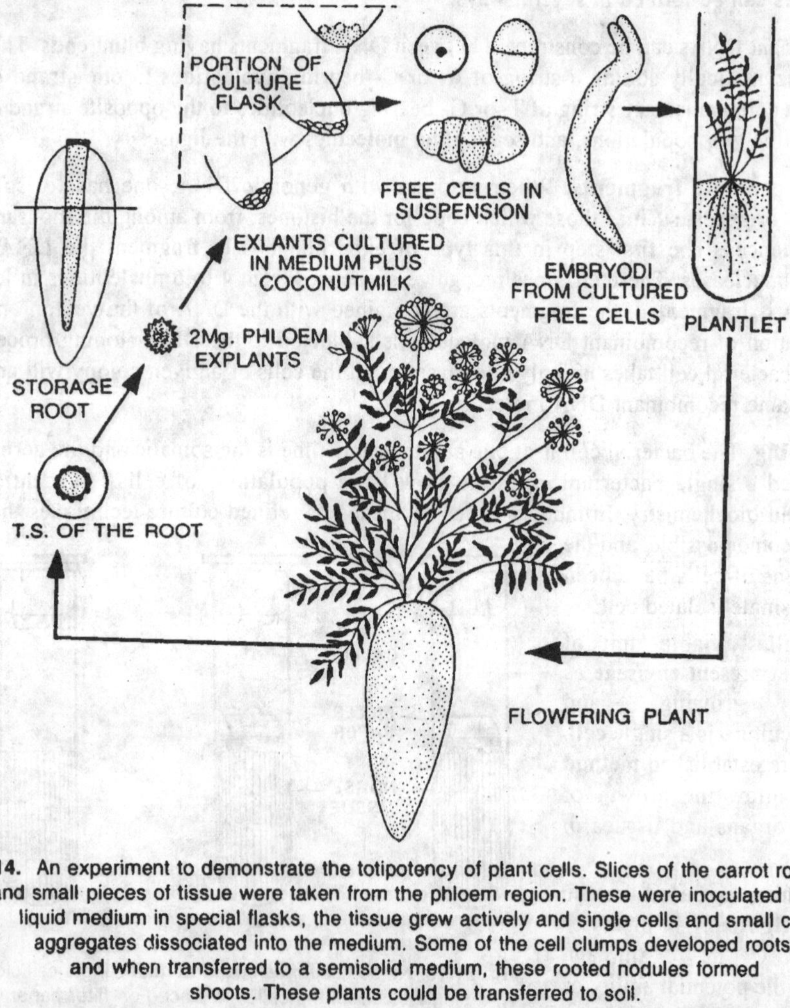

Fig. 21.14. An experiment to demonstrate the totipotency of plant cells. Slices of the carrot root were cut and small pieces of tissue were taken from the phloem region. These were inoculated into a liquid medium in special flasks, the tissue grew actively and single cells and small cell aggregates dissociated into the medium. Some of the cell clumps developed roots, and when transferred to a semisolid medium, these rooted nodules formed shoots. These plants could be transferred to soil.

Organismal cloning. It is characteristic of vegetative reproduction that a vegetative part, when removed from the plant and placed under suitable conditions, will replace the missing parts and produce a complete individual. It has been possible to grow several types of plant organs in sterile culture including roots, shoot apices, leaves, floral parts and fruits. The nutrient requirements for such organ culture vary considerably from species to species and according to the type of organ in question but certain general requirements can be recognised.

Intact higher plants are autotrophic, that is, they are able to synthesize all the organic substances required for their own life from water, carbon dioxide, oxygen and mineral nutrients. But since most sterile cultures are unable to carry on photosynthesis, it is clear that they will require atleast a carbon source, usually supplied in the form of a sugar as sucrose or glucose. In addition, sterile cultures require the same mineral nutrients as the intact plant, including both macronutrients (*e.g.*, nitrogen, phosphorus, potassium and calcium) and micronutrients or trace elements (*e.g.*, Mg, Fe, Mn, Zn, etc.). In addition to the requirements for a carbon source and mineral nutrients, it is found that most isolated organs have also a requirement for certain special organic substances, such as vitamins, nicotinic acid, etc.

This type of reproduction is applied extensively to horticulturally important plants. Horticulturists usually refer to it as vegetative propagation. Its practical advantage is that a single individual can give rise to a large number of plants that will be uniform because all of them have the same genetic constitution, or genotype. Such a group of plants derived from a single one by vegetative propagation is called a **clone**. Now a days the organismal cloning is a common practice for the development of the clones of horticultural as well as forest plants.

Many orchids producing beautiful flowers on cloned plants. Scientists have genetically engineered agronomically important crop plants. Rapid production of such plants can be achieved using actively dividing meristematic cells, which occur at the apices of root and shoot of the plant.

For the agriculture, disease, drought, insect pest-resistant as well as herbicide-tolerant crops have been successfully produced by gene manipulation.

Genetically Modified Food (GMF), such as vitamin A-rich rice and lysine-rich pulse seeds are now becoming popular components of human staple food.

PLANT CLONING AND GENETIC ENGINEERING

In plants, agronomically important traits are governed by the genetic information stored in the nuclear and organellar (*i.e.*, chloroplasts and mitochondria) genome and gene transfer can be done in all these genomes. However, gene transfer in organelles specially in mitochondria is relatively difficult as compared to nuclear genetic transformation. The uptake of genes by cells in microbes and plants is termed as transformation.

Steps in plant genetic engineering. The important steps involved in plant genetic engineering are as follows:

1. The first step is the identification and isolation of agronomically important gene. 2. The second step is cloning the isolated gene in a plant transformation vector. 3. The third important step is introduction of the gene into plant protoplasts, cells or tissues using gene transfer methods.

4. Now comes culture and regeneration of complete plants from gentically transformed cells on suitable selection medium. 5. The last important step is demonstration of the integration and expression of foreign gene in the transgenic plants by using molecular techniques.

Applications of plant genetic engineering. Till now, the plant genetic engineering has been successful in producing disease and pest resistant as well as herbicide tolerant transgenic plants. For example, in tomato the slow ripening process of the fruits is developed; in soybean, corn and cotton herbicide tolerance is developed; in potato, tomato, tobacco and rice viral resistance is developed.

ANIMAL CLONING AND GENETIC ENGINEERING

Animal cloning. Animal cloning is more difficult than plant cloning because animal cells lose their totipotency on reaching the gastrula stage of animal development. However, animal tissue cultures from tumours and embryonic tissue cells have been successful. Standard techniques are available for isolating animal cells and tissues from different systems. Some more important

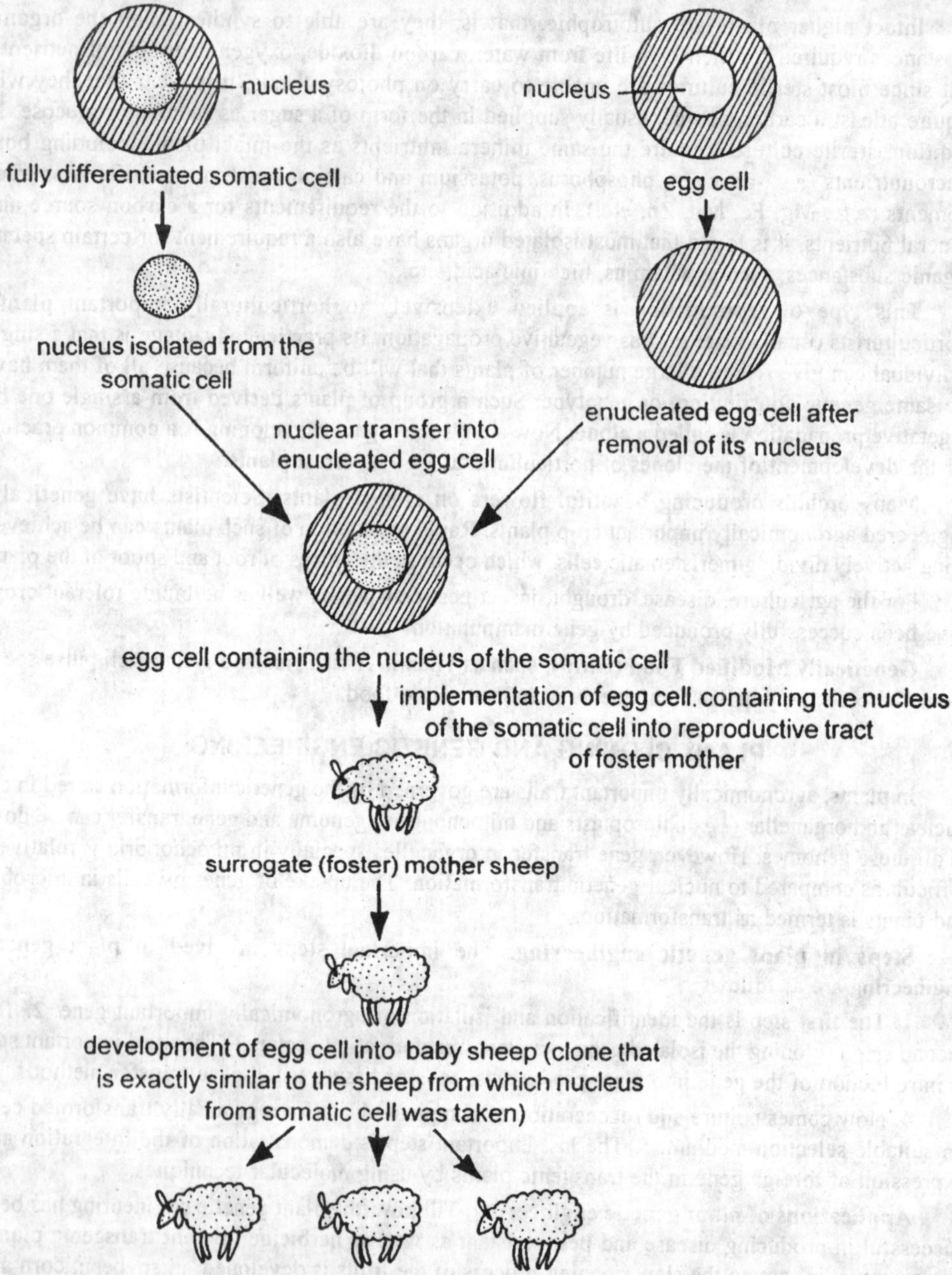

Fig. 21.15. Steps involved in the cloning of the sheep **Dolly.**

examples of animal cloning are tissue culture, somatic cell fusion, cell cloning and creating transgenics.

Gene transfer in animals. Gene transfer in animals is mostly through direct methods such as electroporation or microinjection or using particle gun. In creating 'Dolly' the cloned sheep, fertilised egg of its mother was removed by microneedle and nucleus from an udder cell of a donor sheep was microinjected in the egg after removing egg nucleus. The egg developed into 'Dolly' with genes identical to its mother.

Applications of animal cloning and genetic engineering. Examples of animal products (medicines) produced through genetic engineering are : (*i*) chick embryo fluid which produces vaccines for influenza, measles and mumps. (*ii*) duck embryo fluid which produces vaccines for rabies and rubella.

How sheep 'Dolly' cloned ? Ian Wilmut and his associates at the Roslin Research Institute, Scotland, took cells from ewe (mother sheep's udder). An udder cell is different from a skin cell or a muscle cell or a nerve cell.

They managed to store these udder cells in nutrient deprived culture. This checked the starved cells from dividing, and switched off their active genes.

Now, one udder cell complete with its nucleus was selected, as this nucleus carries the mother's genetic information.

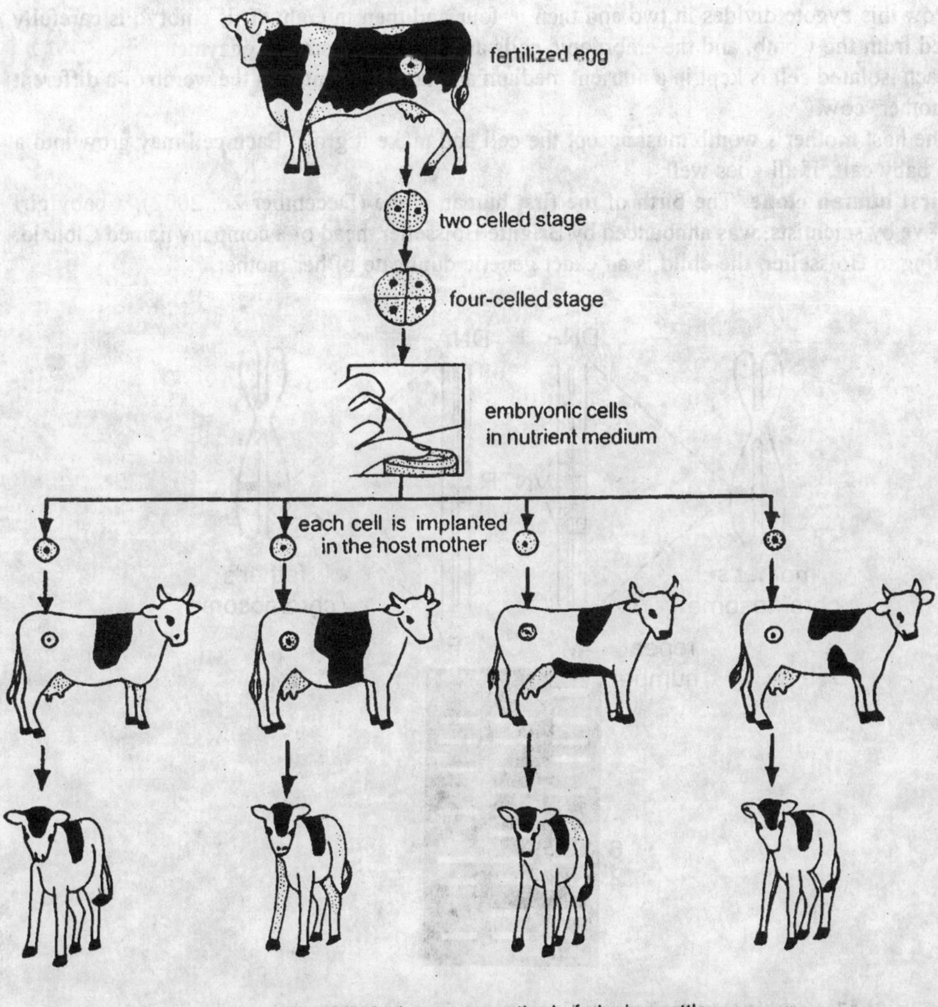

Fig. 21.16. Japanese method of cloning cattle.

Meanwhile, unfertilized egg cell was taken from a different ewe (host mother sheep). Its nucleus was sucked out leaving an empty cell containing all the necessary components to produce an embryo. This cell was now ready to receive udder cell nucleus.

They now fused udder cell nucleus with the empty egg cell by electrical stimulation. Then this egg cell had the mother's nucleus.

When a normal or altered egg is implanted in a different female is termed **'surrogate mother'**. This means, substitute mother.

Then the altered egg was cultured for six days. Out of many resulting embryos, one was implanted in the uterus of the surrogate mother, where it grew into a lamb.

Thus, **Dolly** was born genetically identical to mother sheep as her first cell nucleus came from mother's cell.

How calves are cloned in Japan ? Scientists from Japan have cloned cattle in a different way.

They have got success in growing as many as eight identical calves from one fertilized cell of their mother. The process is as follows :

When the mother cow has mated with the bull, she has a fertilized egg in her womb.

Now this zygote divides in two and then in four and then in eight. This embryo is carefully removed from the womb, and the embryonic cells are separated using as enzyme.

Each isolated cell is kept in a nutrient medium and later implanted in the womb of a different 'host mother' cow.

The host mother's womb must accept the cell and make it grow. Each cell may grow into a normal baby calf, if all goes well.

First human clone. The birth of the first human clone (December 26, 2002), a baby girl called **Eve** by scientists, was announced by Brigitte Boisselier, head of a company named Clonaid. According to Boisselier, the child is an exact genetic duplicate of her mother.

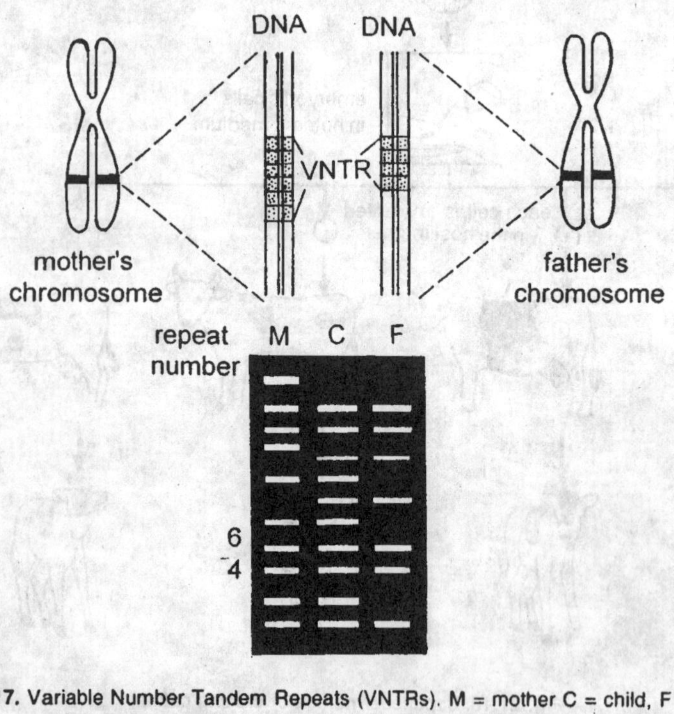

Fig. 21.17. Variable Number Tandem Repeats (VNTRs). M = mother C = child, F = father.

To clone, scientists slip the nucleus of an adult cell, like a skin cell, into an unfertilized egg from which its own genetic material has been removed.

Then, if stimulated to act like a fertilised egg, the newly altered genetic material can then direct the egg to divide and grow into an embryo, then a foetus, then a newborn, if all goes well. Yet, as scientists have discovered, only rarely does all go well.

In animal work so far only about 1 to 5 per cent of cloning attempts succeed, said Randall Prather, a cloning expert. That is, for every 100 eggs, one to five clones are born.

DNA FINGERPRINTING

Every individual organism is unique.

Each person has a unique DNA fingerprint.

A DNA fingerprint of a person is the same for every cell, tissue and organ.

DNA fingerprint cannot be altered by any known treatment.

The ideal way to distinguish an individual from other people on Earth would be to describe entire genomic DNA sequence of the person.

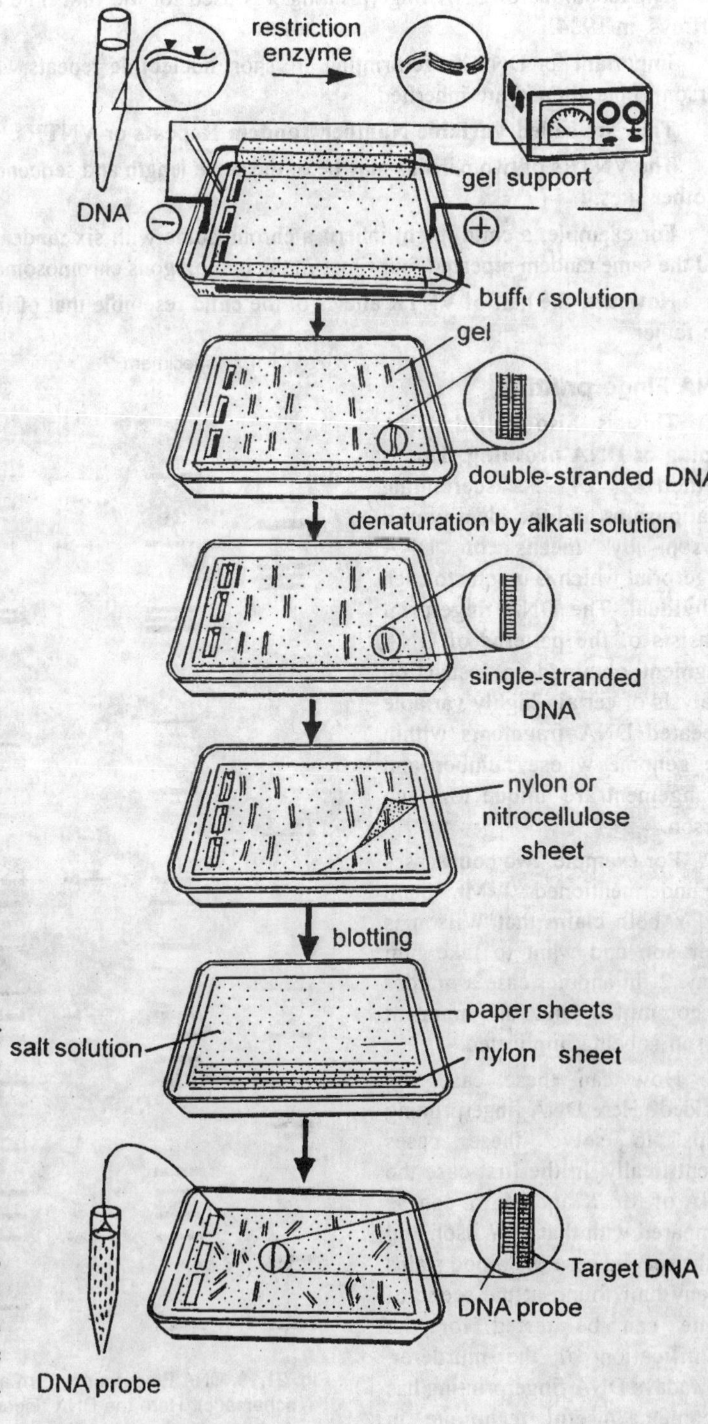

Fig. 21.18. Steps in technique of DNA fingerprinting.

The technique of DNA fingerprinting was used for the first time by English geneticist Alec Jeffreys, in 1984.

Important for DNA fingerprinting are short nucleotide repeats which vary in number from person to person and are inherited.

They are called **Variable Number Tandem Repeats** or **VNTRs.**

The VNTRs of two persons may be of the same length and sequence at certain sites, but vary at other sites.

For example, a child might inherit a chromosome with six tandem repeats from the mother and the same tandem repeated four times in the homologous chromosome inherited from the father.

However, the half of VNTR alleles of the child resemble that of the mother and half that of the father.

DNA Fingerprinting

This is also called **DNA typing** or **DNA profiling.** This is method of ascertaining relationships and the identity of a person by means of DNA fingerprint which is unique to each individual. The DNA fingerprint consists of the patterns of DNA fragment obtained in restriction analysis of certain highly variable repeated DNA fragments within the genome whose number and arrangement are unique for each person.

For example, two court cases are undermentioned : 1. Mr. X and Mr. Y both claim that Wilson is their son and want to take him away. 2. In another case a murder is committed and an innocent person is being implicated.

How can these cases be decided? Here DNA fingerprinting helps to solve these cases scientifically. In the first case the DNA of Mr. X and Mr. Y can be compared with that of Wilson and in the second case the blood stains or any hair found at the scene of crime can be tested for the identification of the murderer. Nowadays DNA fingerprinting has become a useful technique in forensic science to reach at correct decisions.

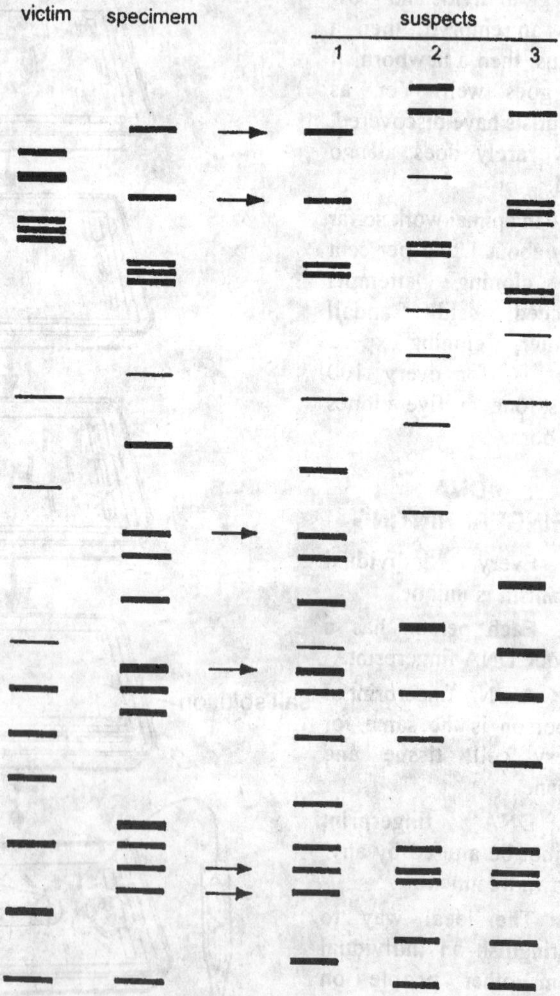

Fig. 21.19. DNA Fingerprints from a Murder Case (somewhat schematic). Here the DNA fingerprint of the specimen (evidence such as blood stain which does not belong to the victim but to the suspected murderer) obtained from the crime-scene, appears to match with that of suspect No. 1.

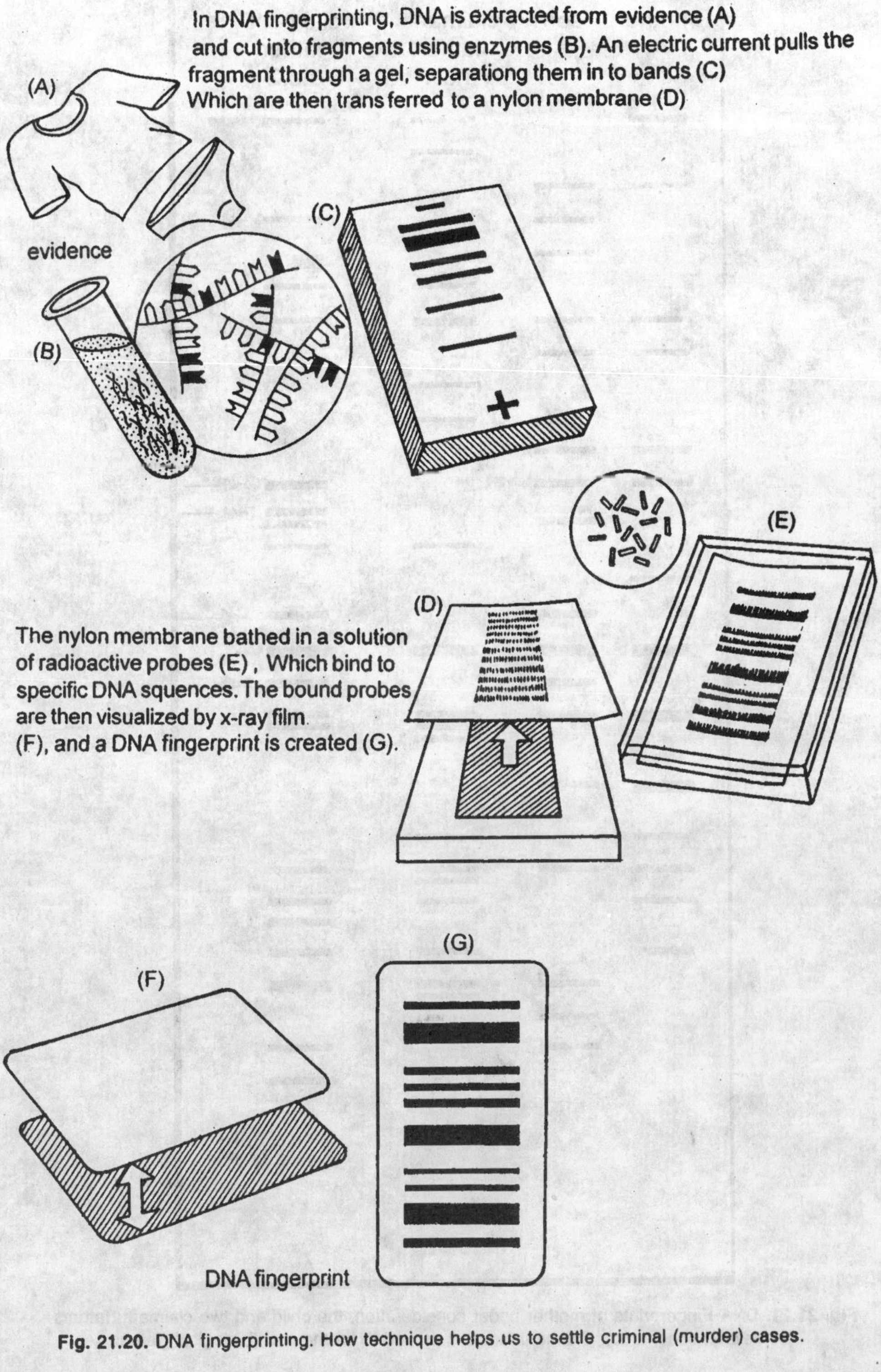

Fig. 21.20. DNA fingerprinting. How technique helps us to settle criminal (murder) cases.

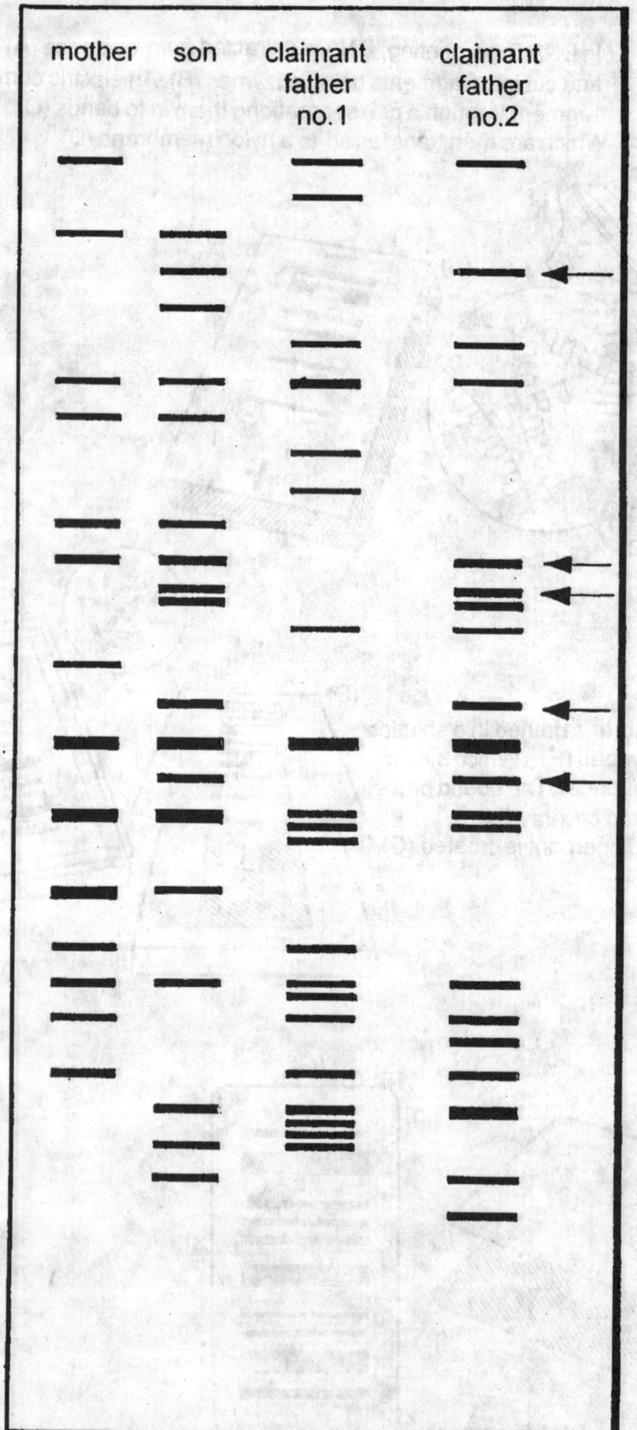

Fig. 21.21. DNA Fingerprints of mother under consideration, the child and two claimant "fathers (somewhat schematic). Claimant No. 2 is proved to be the real (biological) father.

Principle involved in DNA fingerprinting. The DNA of every individual has distinctive characteristics which is not the same for two humans except monozygotic (identical) twins. There are twenty three pairs of human chromosomes. Each set of 23 pairs of chromosomes has 1.5 million pairs of genes. The genes are segments of DNA which differ in the sequence of their nucleotides. Not all segments of DNA code for proteins. Some DNA segments have a regulatory function, while others are intervening sequences (introns) and still others are repeated DNA sequences. The non-repetitive or unique DNA sequences form almost half of the haploid genome (DNA in one set of 23 chromosomes) and except identical twins, no two humans have genomes with same DNA nucleotide sequences.

In DNA finger printing short repetitive nucleotide sequences are quite important as they vary from person to person. They are called the **Variable Number Tandem Repeats (VNTRs).** The VNTRs of two persons may be of the same length and sequences at certain sites and vary at other sites. When chromosomal DNA samples are digested with restricted enzymes, DNA from different individuals yield specific patterns when subjected to gel electrophoresis.

Mechanism of DNA fingerprinting. DNA fingerprints can be prepared from extremely minute amounts of blood, semen, hair bulk or any other cells of the body. The main steps are as follows.

The first step is called **extraction.** In this step DNA is extracted from any of the above mentioned cells. Thereafter many copies of this DNA are made by a technique called Polymerase Chain Reaction. Making of many copies of DNA is called **amplification.** Then DNA is cut with restriction enzymes into precise reproducible sequences, this is called **restriction digestion.**

In the next step DNA restricted sequences are then separated by gel electrophoresis, *i.e.*, separation of DNA sequences. Now separated DNA sequences are transferred from gel onto a trinitrocellulose or nylon membrane, *i.e.*, known as **Southern blotting** after the name of the inventor E. M. Southern.

Then an already available complementary DNA is made to hybridise with the isolated DNA, *i.e.*, **hybridisation.** Many such DNA strands with specific nucleotide sequences complementary to VNTR sequences are available, which are called **probes.**

Lastly, the membrane is exposed to X-ray film on which specific bonds can be seen as depicted in the figure.

Applications of DNA fingerprinting. 1. The tests for paternity can be done for identifying the true (biological) father. The bands of child's DNA should match the DNA prints of the biological parents. 2. Identification of the criminal is made possible by DNA fingerprinting. Here DNA finger prints of suspects and from blood or hair or semen picked up from the scene of crime are prepared and compared. The DNA fingerprint of the person matching the one obtained from sample obtained from site of crime can give clue to the actual criminal. 3. To verify whether a hopeful immigrant is, as he or she claims, really a close relative of already an established resident. 4. To identify social groups to rewrite biological evolution.

GENOMICS

All the DNA in the cells of an organism, such as cells from skin, muscle or brain and every thing including genes, is called its **genome.**

Human body contains 100 million cells of over 260 different kinds.

In all, there are 23 different chromosomes containing packed DNA in a haploid set of human genome.

Additional DNA is in cell's mitochondria which is inherited from one's mother.

In human genome, according to estimates there are about three billion of biochemical letters, *i.e.*, nucleotide base pairs (in human genome), and 30,000 genes per cell.

Human Genome Project

This project began in 1990. The main aims of the project are as follows :

1. To develop the ways of mapping the human genome.

2. To store this information in databases and to develop tools for data analysis.

3. To address the ethical, legal and social issues that may arise from this ambitious human genome project.

Fig. 21.22. Human genome.

Genomic Revelations

The human gene count is approximately 30,000 to 40,000. This count is nearabout the same in mice.

Nine-tenths of human genes are identical to that of the mouse which is generally used for experimental purposes.

The fruit fly (*Drosophila melanogaster*) has about 13,000 genes per cell.

Escherichia coli has about 4,000 genes.

Humans are incredibly 99.9 per cent identical with *E. coli* at the DNA level. In other words, genomically humans and bacteria are similar.

However, most of human differences are shared among all ethnicities and races spread into the geographic regions around the planet.

Different human genes vary widely in the length often over thousands of base pairs.

White β -globin and insulin gene are less than 10 kilo base pairs.

The gene responsible for Duchenne Muscular Dystrophy on X chromosome is made up of 2400 kilo base pairs, most probably the longest gene known.

However, a lily has 18 times more DNA than a human, *i.e.,* 106 billion base pairs per cell.

Such large amounts of genes are split by long non-coding introns. Only less than 2 per cent of the genome is known to include the exons, the protein coding sequences. In fact, a lily produces fewer proteins than a human.

As already studied, clusters of VNTRs of variable lengths, arranged in tandem.

Approximately one million copies of short 5 to 8 base pair repeated sequence clustered around the centromeres and near the ends of the chromosomes represent, the **junk DNA**.

Prospects and Implications of Human Genome

It is expected and seems possible that we will soon get snapshots of more than 1200 genes that are responsible for common cardiovascular ailments, endocrine diseases like diabetes, neurological disorders like Alzheimer's disease, deadly cancers and many other such diseases.

Even single gene defects may account for several inherited diseases.

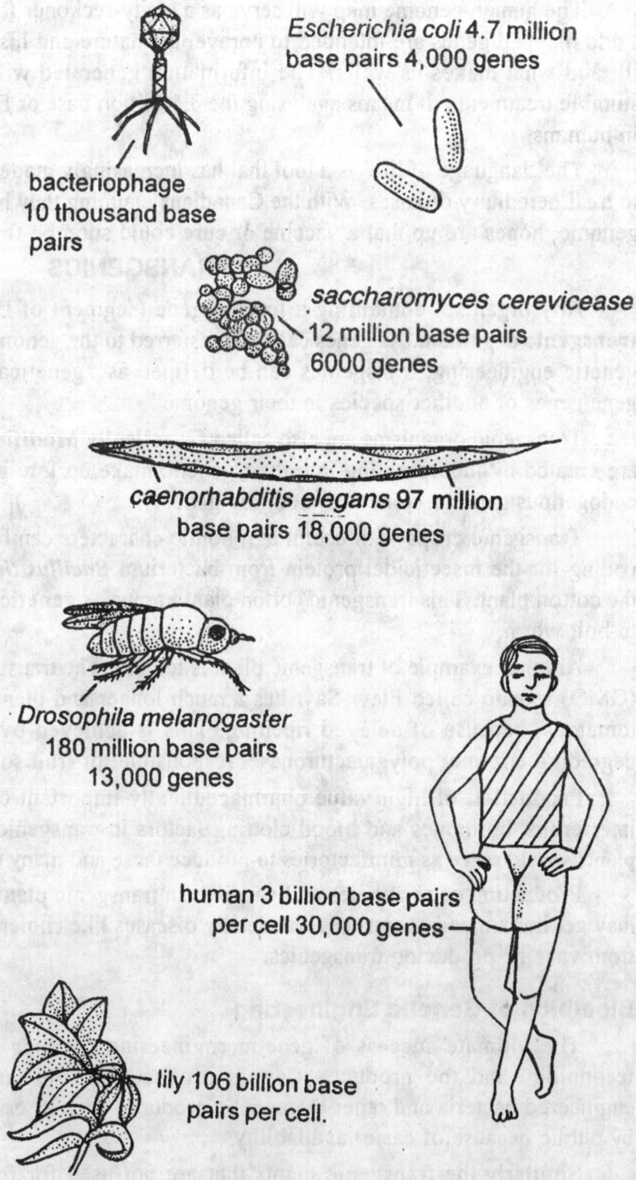

Fig. 21.23. Comparative genomes.

Efforts are in progress to determine genes that will revert cancerous cells to normal.

The human genome will definitely make a halthier living.

The human genome also holds the prospects of vast database of knowledge about designer drugs, genetically modified diets and genetic identity.

Human Genome Revelations

The year 2003 marks fifty years of the discovery of the double-helix of DNA, twenty five years of the world's first test-tube baby and now the complete mapping of the human genome.

The Human Genome Project that commenced in 1990 under a US-UK led public consortium of academic centres headed by Francis Collins, has now announced that the map, valued at nearly $800 million, is complete two years ahead of schedule.

Three draft maps of human genome have already made public, and this is the final one, as the scientists say. This however, does not mean the end of genome mapping as the work will shift to other species.

Also, variations in the human genome will have to be studied and then there is the whole task of analysing the tomes of data generated by the map. For, it is in data-crunching that applications can be formulated.

It all began with the discovery of the structure of DNA by James D. Watson and Francis Crick. They made their stunning discovery public in an article that first appeared in **Nature** magazine on April 25, 1953.

Since then, biology, has got transformed into a dynamic field of study, generating whole new subjects : **genetics, biotechnology, proteomics, pharmacogenomics, bio-informatics and chem-informatics**, among others.

The human genome map will serve as a ready-reckoner for human body functions. Its 35,000 - odd mapped genes are intended to unravel the nature and history of disease, *i.e.*, what makes us ill, and what makes us well ? The information generated will enable gene therapists formulate suitable treatments. It means analysing the 3.1 billion base or DNA letters responsible for heredity in humans.

The 'language of life' is a tool that has increasingly made designer drugs possible, especially to treat hereditary diseases. With the Canadians claiming they have now sequenced the SARS virus genome, hopes are up that a vaccine or cure could soon be found for the killer-pneumonia.

TRANSGENICS

Any organism containing a foreign gene (segment of DNA) from a different species is a **transgenic organism**. As genes can be transferred to the genome of another organism only through genetic engineering, transgenics can be defined as "genetically engineered organisms carrying gene/genes of another species in their genome".

Transgenic organisms are also called **Genetically Modified Organisms** (GMOs). The GMOs are created by incorporating into their genetic make up foreign gene/genes or extra copies of an endogenous gene or cloned or modified gene.

Transgenic crops with useful agronomic characters can be produced. For example, the gene coding for the insecticidal protein from bacterium *Bacillus thuringiensis* has been transferred to the cotton plant. This transgenic cotton plant known as **genetically modified cotton** Bt is resistant to boll worm.

Another example of transgenic plant is tomato. The transgenic genetically modified organism (GMO) tomato called Flavr Savr has a much longer and blended with flavour than conventional tomatoes, because of delayed ripening. This is achieved by reducing the amount of cell wall degrading enzyme 'polygalacturonase' responsible for fruit softening.

Production of high value pharmaceutically important compounds such as human insulin, interferons, hormones and blood clotting factors in transgenic plants or seeds. In fact transgenic plants would serve as minifactories to produce these and many other compounds in huge quantities.

Production of antibodies and vaccines in transgenic plants like banana and tomato. Children may get immunized against several deadly diseases like cholera by eating banana or raw tomatoes from vaccine producing transgenics.

Bioethics of Genetic Engineering

The ultimate success of genetic engineering depends upon consumer acceptance of the technology and the products. Certain products like human insulin produced in genetically engineered bacteria and other therapeutic products, such as oral vaccines may be readily accepted by public because of easier availability.

Similarly the transgenic plants that are not used for food are less likely to cause public concern.

On the other hand transgenic crop plants that are used for human consumption have led to lot of controversies about their safety because of the presence of certain unwanted properties.

Transgenic cattle that have received additional gene, for instance, to increase growth rate, can be marketed more quickly.

Transgenic animals have been genetically engineered with human genes in order to make products that can be used in human medicine.

For example, transgenic cattle (cow, sheep and goat) have been produced with the intention of increased milk yield, as well as, therapeutic human proteins. The cattle secrete there useful proteins in their milk from where it can be obtained easily.

Transgenic pigs have been given human genes so that their organs carry human antigens. These pig organs like heart, kidney, pancreas can be safely transplanted into humans.

However, the thorough assessment of the risks associated with transgenics for both plants and animals is important before they are released. Many scientists believe that genetic engineering is the technology which can solve various human problems especially hunger and disease.

GENE LIBRARIES AND GENE BANKS

Gene libraries

Each chromosome is like a volume of a book in a library.

Even the genome of a bacterium *Escherichia coli* contains 4,000 genes.

Gene cloning or DNA cloning is done to construct several copies of the desired genes in large amounts. This precise technique allows specific DNA sequences to be separated from other sequences permitting detailed analysis or manipulation.

Gene libraries can also be created using RNA.

The enzyme Reverse Transcriptase, a RNA-directed DNA polymerase, is used to convert the RNA into complementary DNA (*i.e.*, cDNA), which can then be converted in the same way as DNA cloning.

Such gene libraries are maintained through special techniques.

Gene Banks

A gene bank is a repository of clones of known DNA fragments, genes, gene maps, seeds, spores, frozen sperms or eggs or embryos.

These stored genes may be used in genetic engineering and breeding experiments where species have become extinct.

These gene banks will be used increasingly as the rate of extinction increases, depleting the Earth's biodiversity and genetic variety.

Now the genomic information is available for a dozen of species. The most remarkable is the prospects and contribution of Human Genome Project.

The Human Genome Project that commenced in 1990, has now announced that the map, is complete two years ahead of schedule in year 2003.

SUMMARY

1. Genetic engineering involves the isolation of specific genes, making of copies of genes and their transfer to target genomes.
2. The key to genetic engineering technology is a special class of enzymes known as restriction endonucleases, which recognise specific sites and cleave DNA molecules into sticky or blunt fragments.
3. The cleaved two strands of DNA can be joined back together with the aid of a sealing enzyme, ligase.
4. Plasmids and artificial chromosomes from bacteria and yeast are important tools for indirect gene transfer.
5. Bacteria, yeast and cultured plant and animal cells are commonly used as hosts for recombinant DNA experiments.
6. Agriculture is a major focus of genetic engineering activity. Successes have included incorporation of genes for herbicide resistance into crop plants, conferring natural resistance to insect pests.

7. Genetic technologies have made many advancements in the production of drugs, such as insulin and interferon.
8. Several recombinant vaccines directed against human diseases such as hepatitis and herpes, are now available as a therapeutic tool in the prevention of disease.
9. In gene therapy, a faulty gene is replaced with a normal healthy gene, to treat diseases where other medical treatments are not effective.
10. With cloning of 'Dolly' sheep the cloning of any mammalian species is now virtually possible.
11. The first human clone, a baby girl called Eve by scientists, was announced on December 26, 2002.
12. Many useful transgenic microbes, crop plants and farm animals have been cloned successfully.
13. Because the DNA of an individual or species is unique, the genetic analysis methods can be used to identify an organism from a small sample of its cells, that is, to create a DNA fingerprint. DNA fingerprinting is effectively applied in forensic science.
14. Genomic libraries can be created as sources of genes for cloning and their use.
15. The map of entire DNA sequence of a human besides many other comparative genomes, is the most significant achievement of Human Genome Project.
16. Besides many benefits, the ethical, social and legal implications of these potent gene technologies have led to considerable concern about the possibility of accidentally producing new pathogens responsible, for fatal diseases or developing 'genetic monsters'.

TERMS TO REMEMBER

Bacteriophage. A virus capable of infecting a bacterium and replicating in it.

Bioethics. Considering of what is good or bad from morality point of view in the application of biological innovations specially on humans.

Biotechnology. The use of living cells or microorganisms (*e.g.*, bacteria) in industry and technology to manufacture drugs and chemicals or to break down wastes, etc. In recent years, it specially refers to the use of genetically modified cells and microorganisms.

Callus. Mass of undifferentiated cells that initially arises from plant cell or tissue in artificial culture.

Cellular totipotency. Ability of a plant or animal cell to repeatedly divide and differentiate into a complete organism on a defined nutrient medium under suitable laboratory conditions.

Cloning. Producing a population of identical DNA molecules, cells or individuals derived from a single such unit.

DNA fingerprinting. Also called DNA typing or DNA profiling. A method of ascertaining relationships and the identity of a person by means of DNA fingerprint which is unique to each individual.

DNA library. A collection of cloned DNA fragments, usually representing an entire genome present in an organism. Also called genomic DNA library.

DNA ligase. An enzyme that can seal one DNA fragment with another DNA segment both having sticky ends. Ligase is the 'molecular glue'.

Electroporation. Creation of transient (temporary) pores in the cell membrane of a host allow the entry of foreign DNA.

Enucleation. Removal of the nucleus from the cell used, in cloning.

Gene cloning. Also called DNA cloning. Technique for obtaining clones or identical copies of a particular DNA molecule.

Gene therapy. Replacement and alteration of a faulty gene. Technique used for hereditary disease.

Genetic engineering. A technique for artificially and deliberately modifying DNA (genes) to suit human needs.

Genome. Total number of genes contained in one haploid set of chromosomes of a diploid organism.

Genome library. DNA library consisting of fragments of chromosomal DNA.

Microinjection. Introduction of foreign genes into animal or plant cell by injecting DNA directly.

Molecular scissors. Restriction endonuclease enzyme.

Particle gun. A technique for bombarding microprojectiles (gold or tungsten particles) coated with foreign DNA with great velocity into the target cells.

Plasmid. Extrachromosomal small circular double stranded DNA molecules in a bacterial cell which have sequences matching those of the required gene and can be similarly cut by the same restriction enzyme. Plasmids are autonomous and replicate separately from the host chromosome.

Probes. DNA strands with specific nucleotide sequences complementary to VNTR (Variable Number Tandem Repeats) sequences.

Recombinant DNA or r DNA. DNA produced by joining together genes from different sources.

Restriction endonuclease. Any such enzyme which very specifically recognises a particular DNA sequence, and cuts it. These enzymes are the 'molecular scissors'.

Southern blotting. A technique named after the inventor, Southern, involving hybridisation of DNA with probes.

Surrogate mother. A female who grows someone else's zygote/embryo in her own uterus for full gestation period and delivers the baby.

Syndrome. A group of symptoms appearing together for a particular condition.

Transgenic. Genetically modified organism (GMO) carrying foreign genes. The introduced foreign gene is called **transgene**.

Vector. An intermediate carrier (in genetic engineering), a phage, plasmid or virus DNA into which another DNA is inserted for introduction into bacterial or other cells for amplification (DNA cloning).

QUESTION BANK

N.B. Undermentioned questions are asked repeatedly in various Indian Universities and competitive examinations.

Very Short Answer Questions

1. What is 'genetic engineering' ?
2. Define cell cloning and gene cloning.
3. What is gene therapy ?
4. Give exact meaning of cloning.
5. What are cloning vectors ?
6. What is restriction fragment ?
7. What is electroporation ?
8. Define 'genomic DNA library'.
9. Give an example of 'natural genetic engineer'.
10. Give the name of engineered microbe which produces human insulin:
11. Give one famous example of cloned sheep.
12. Give two examples of transgenic plants with their useful characters.
13. What is 'transgenics' ?
14. What is 'DNA' 'fingerprinting' ?
15. Expand VNTR and GMO.

ANSWERS

1. Genetic engineering is a technique for artificially and deliberately modifying DNA (genes) to suit human needs, **2.** Cell cloning is a technique by which genetically identical cells may be produced from a single cell; gene cloning is the technique to obtain clones or identical copies of a particular DNA molecule; **3.** To cut genes responsible for hereditary diseases and replace them with normal genes; **4.** Cloning means producing exact copy/copies of a single parent; **5.** The desired gene is inserted in the vectors or gene carrier to form DNA, *e.g.*, plasmids and viruses; **6.** Restriction endonuclease cuts the specific DNA (desired gene) at the two ends which becomes the restriction fragment; **7.** This is a process in which transient (temporary) pores are created in the cell membrane of the host for uptake of foreign DNA molecules; **8.** A gene library contains several copies of many of the desired genes or DNA fragments; **9.** *Agrobacterium tumefaciens*, a plant pathogenic bacterium which can transfer part of its plasmid DNA as it infects host plants; **10.** *Escherichia coli* ; **11.** Dolly; **12.** Tomato : increased shelf life of fruits (slow ripening); Rice : Vitamin A rich; **13.** 'Genetically engineered organisms carrying gene/genes of another species in their genome'; **14.** DNA typing or DNA profiling, DNA fingerprint is unique to each individual; **15.** Variable Number Tandem Repeats and Genetically Modified Organism.

Short Answer Questions

1. Name two of the common pharmaceutically important products obtained through genetic engineering.
2. What is meant by 'genetic engineering' ? List the various steps involved in this technology.
3. What are the proposed benefits of genetic engineering in crop improvement?
4. Explain the principles involved in DNA fingerprinting.
5. List two applications of DNA fingerprinting.
6. Gene therapy can cure the important genetic disorders in human. Comment.
7. Give one example each of transgenic plant and transgenic animal.
8. What are Variable Number Tandem Repeats or VNTRs ?
9. Name at least three diseases against which genetically engineered vaccines are now available.
10. What is a cloned animal ? Give one example.
11. What is Human Genome Project ?
12. Give an outline of the steps involved in DNA fingerprinting.
13. Name the various cloning vectors and explain how a plasmid can be used for genetic engineering.
14. Describe different methods to introduce foreign genes into animal cells.
15. List three applications of DNA fingerprinting.
16. Why is "Agrobacterium-mediated genetic transformation" in plants described as natural genetic engineering of plants ?
17. What is Southern blotting ? Give an example where it is applied.

Long Answer Questions

1. What is the Human Genome Project ? What has been revealed about our genome so far ?
2. What is genetic engineering ? Explain briefly the distinct steps common to all genetic engineering technology.
3. Differentiate between
   (*i*) Cell cloning and organismal cloning.
   (*ii*) Direct gene transfer and indirect gene transfer.
4. Write short notes on :
   (*i*) Recombinant DNA; (*ii*) Transgenics (*iii*) Genomics.
5. Write a comprehensive account of " Tools and Techniques of Genetic Engineering".
6. Write notes on :
   (*i*) Applications of Recombinant DNA Technology.
   (*ii*) Diagnosis of human diseases by recombinant DNA technology.
7. Write a comprehensive account of gene therapy, citing example of Severe Combined Immuno Deficiency (SCID).
8. Write an account of cloning, citing atleast three important examples.
9. How sheep 'Dolly' was cloned ? Give the process of cloning step wise.
10. Write short notes on :
    (*i*) How calves are cloned in Japan ? (*ii*) First human clone.

Multiple Choice Questions (Objective Type Questions)

Select the most appropriate alternative:

1. The technique in which a foreign DNA precipitated on the surface of tungsten or gold particles and shot into the target cells is known as
   (*a*) Microinjection (*b*) Chemical-mediated gene transfer
   (*c*) Particle gun (*d*) Electroporation.
2. The enzyme that cuts specifically recognition sites in the DNA is known as:
   (*a*) DNA ligase (*b*) DNA polymerase
   (*c*) Reverse transcriptase (*d*) Restriction endonuclease.

3. Restriction endonucleases
   (*a*) cleave DNA at highly specific recognition sequences,
   (*b*) are inserted into bacteria by bacteriophages
   (*c*) are made only by eukaryotic cells.
   (*d*) add methyl groups to specific DNA sequences.
4. Plasmids
   (*a*) are circular protein molecules. (*b*) are required by bacteria.
   (*c*) are tiny bacteria (*d*) confer resistance to antibiotics.
5. Genetic diagnosis by DNA testing
   (*a*) detects only mutants and normal alleles (*b*) can be done only on eggs or sperms
   (*c*) involves hybridization to ribosomal RNA.
   (*d*) utilizes restriction enzymes and a polymorphic site.
6. DNA can be introduced into any cell by
   (*a*) injection. (*b*) being complexed with calcium salts.
   (*c*) gel electrophoresis. (*d*) being placed along with the cells into a gene gun.
7. In DNA fingerprinting
   (*a*) The variability of repeated sequences between two restriction sites is evaluated.
   (*b*) a positive identification can be made.
   (*c*) The polymerase chain reaction amplifies fewer DNA.
   (*d*) multiple restriction enzyme digests/generate unique fragments.
8. Ability of a plant or animal cell to repeatedly divide and differentiate into a complete organism is :
   (*a*) Cloning (*b*) DNA fingerprinting
   (*c*) Cellular totipotency (*d*) Mitosis.
9. Restriction endonuclease is also known as :
   (*a*) Molecular glue (*b*) DNA ligase
   (*c*) DNA polymerase (*d*) Molecular scissors.
10. Extrachromosomal small circular double stranded DNA molecule in a bacterial cell is :
   (*a*) Plastid (*b*) Plasmid
   (*c*) Mitochondrion (*d*) Chloroplast.
11. Introduction of foreign genes into plant or animal cells using micropipettes is
   (*a*) Electroporation (*b*) Chemical-mediated gene transfer
   (*c*) Microinjection (*d*) Particle gun.
12. Natural genetic engineer is
   (*a*) *Agrobacterium* spp. (*b*) *Rhizobium* spp.
   (*c*) *Bacillus* spp. (*d*) Bacteriophage.
13. The vectorless gene transfer includes
   (*a*) Particle gun (*b*) Microinjection
   (*c*) Electroporation (*d*) All the above.
14. Three billion base pairs are found in
   (*a*) Lily (*b*) Human
   (*c*) Fruit fly (*d*) Yeast

ANSWERS

1. (*c*) **2.** (*d*) **3.** (*a*) **4.** (*a*) **5.** (*d*) **6.** (*d*) **7.** (*c*) **8.** (*c*) **9.** (*d*) **10.** (*b*)
11. (*c*) **12.** (*a*) **13.** (*d*) **14.** (*b*)

22
CHAPTER

Plant Tissue Culture and Biotechnology

The technique of **plant cell culture** occupies a key role in the second green revolution in which gene modifications and biotechnology are being used to improve crop yield and quality. In recent years, plant protoplast, cell and tissue cultures have become an important tool for crop improvement, commercial production of natural compounds and many more in the development of forestry.

M.S. Swaminathan (1987), emphasized the significance of biotechnological application of *in vitro* cultured plant protoplasts/cells/tissues as mentioned here :

(*i*) Tissue culture applications in order to capitalise upon the totipotency of cells.

(*ii*) Cell and protoplast cultures coupled with DNA vectors to overcome problems caused by barriers to gene transfer through sexual means.

(*iii*) Culture of plant cells for the production of useful compounds.

(*iv*) Transfer of genes for nitrogen fixing (*nif*) ability to non-fixing species.

This technology has been employed to a wide range of crop plants and tree species to solve the problems. Now, with the better understanding of the technique of plant tissue culture and nutritional requirements of plant cell, it has become possible to develop newer technologies by culturing plant organs, such as an anther, ovary, ovule, petal, leaf and meristem, which leads to establishment of new research lines, *viz.*, haploids, virus-free plants, *in-vitro* fertilisation, embryo rescue and direct regeneration from leaf disc for genetic engineering.

Biotechnology is defined by different organisations in different ways. It has been broadly defined as "the development and utilisation of biological processes, forms and systems for obtaining maximum benefits to man and other forms of life". Thus, "biotechnology is the application of scientific and engineering principles to the processing of materials by biological agents to provide goods and service".

In recent years revolution in biology has occurred due to the potential of biotechnology. Techniques have been developed to produce rare and medicinally valuable molecules, to change hereditary traits of plants and animals, to diagnose diseases to produce useful chemicals, and to clean up and restore the environment. Thus, biotechnology has great impact in the field of health, agriculture and environmental protection.

In most of the developing countries, the recombinant DNA technology has become one of the major thrusts. In 1982, Government of India has set up an official agency, The National Biotechnology Board (NBTB) which started functioning under The Department of Science and Technology (CDST) in the Ministry of Science and Technology for planning, promotion and coordination of various biotechnological programmes.

PLANT TISSUE CULTURE

Plant tissue culture is the maintenance and growth of plant cells, tissues and organs on a suitable culture medium *in vitro*, *e.g.*, in a test tube or any other suitable vessel.

Plant tissue cultures are often classified according to the type of *in vitro* growth, such as callus and suspension cultures, or the explant used for culture initiation, *e.g.* embryo culture, anther culture, etc.

An **explant** is the part of a plant that is excised from its original location and used for initiating a culture.

Surface sterilisation and sterilisation. It is essential that the explants, glassware, culture containers or vessels, media and the instruments used for plant tissue culture must be free from microbes.

Hence the explants are treated with specific anti-microbial chemicals, and the process is called **surface sterilisation.** Suitable sized plant material (explant) is sterilised as follows :

(*i*) Bring the explant to be sterilised in well sterilised laboratory and prepare pieces for sterilisation.

(*ii*) Clean the working area and hands with alcohol, put on mask and cap, and light the spirit lamp.

(*iii*) Keep 3 or 4 petridishes in a line, add disinfectant (*e.g.*, mecuric chloride 0.01 to 0.1% aqueous solution, or 20% sodium hydrochloride) in first plate and autoclaved distilled water in subsequent plates.

(*iv*) Place plant pieces in first plate and immerse the material with the help of sterilised forceps for 5–10 minutes depending upon the disinfectant used.

(*v*) Transfer material from first to second petriplate, rinse gently and pass to third and fourth plates, one by one with thorough rinsing.

(*vi*) Finally drain the distilled water, and prepare suitable sized explants.

A quick dip in 70% ethanol (15–30 seconds), is always advantageous, before surface sterilisation with disinfectant.

The vessels, media and instruments are also suitably treated with steam, dry heat, alcohol or subjected to filtration to make them free from microbes.

Generally, autoclave is used to sterilise medium, glassware and tools for the purpose of plant tissue culture. Sterilisation of material is carried out by increasing moist heat (121°C) due to increased pressure inside the vessel (15–22 *psi, i.e.*, pounds per square inch) for 15 minutes for routine sterilisation. Moist heat kills the microorganisms and makes the material free from microbes.

Surface strerilisation of explants and their transfer to culture media must be done under aseptic conditions.

Nutrient media could be prepared in a separate room where sufficient space is available for keeping and weighing chemicals, and putting glassware.

Vitamins and growth hormones are carefully weighed.

Stock solutions of chemicals are kept in refrigerator to avoid contamination.

Culture Technique

As already mentioned, the technique of plant tissue culture enables us to study the cells, tissue or organs by isolating them from the plant body and growing aseptically, in suitable containers, on an artificial nutrient medium, under controlled environmental conditions. Thus (*i*) **nutrient medium,** (*ii*) **aseptic conditions** and (*iii*) **aeration of the tissue** are important aspects of the technique of *in vitro* culture.

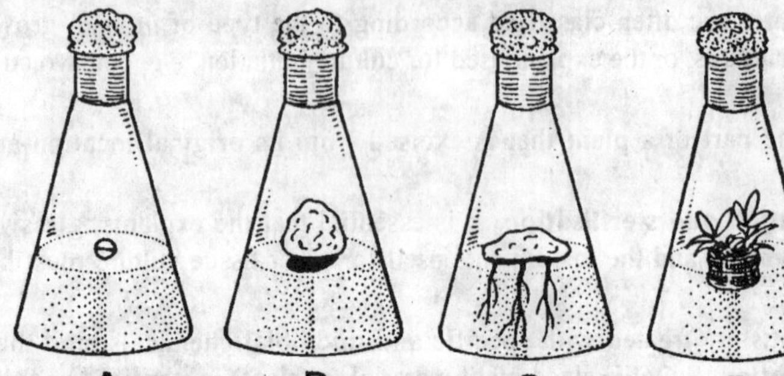

Fig. 22.1. An experiment to demonstrate the effect of growth regulators (auxins and cytokinins) on growth and differentiation in plant tissue culture. A, on the nutrient medium lacking a growth regulator the tobacco pith tissue showed very poor growth; B, in the presence of a cytokinin a vigorously growing callus was formed; C, when transferred to a medium containing 3 mg/l of indole acetic acid and 0.2 mg/l of kinetin this callus differentiated only roots; D, if a portion of the same callus was planted on a medium with higher concentration of kinetin (1 mg/1) and lower concentration of indole acetic acid (0.03 mg/1), it differentiated only shoots.

Table 22.1. Composition of Nutrient Medium (Murashige and Shoog, 1962)

	Chemical constituents		*Mg/l*
1.	**Macronutrients**		
	NH_4 No_3	...	1650
	KNO_3	...	1900
	$CaCl_2 . 2H_2O$	...	440
	$MgSO_4 . 6H_2O$	...	370
	KH_2PO_4	...	170
2.	**Iron**		
	Na_2 EDTA	...	37.3
	$FeSO_4 . 7 H_2O$	...	27.8
3.	**Micronutrients**		
	$MnSO_4 . 4H_2O$	...	22.3
	$ZnSO_4 . 4H_2O$	...	8.6
	$Na_2MO_4 . 2H_2O$	...	0.25
	$CuSO_4 . 5H_2O$	...	0.025
	$COCl_2 . 6H_2O$	...	0.025
	KI	...	0.83
	H_3BO_3	...	6.2
4.	**Vitamins**		
	Glycine	...	2.0
	Nicototinic acid	...	0.5
	Pyrodoxime-HCL	...	0.5
	Thiamine- HCL	...	0.1
5.	**Cytokinins**		
	Kinetin	...	0.04–10.0
	Myo-inositol	...	100.0
	Indole acetic acid (IAA)	...	1.0–30.0
	Sucrose (g)	...	30.0
	pH	...	5.7

Nutrient Medium

Every tissue and organ has its special requirements for optimal growth and these need to be worked out when starting work with a new system (Table 9.1). However, most of the media contain inorganic salts of major and minor elements, vitamins and sucrose. A medium with these ingredients will be referred to as basal medium. sometimes, growth regulators, such as auxins, gibberellins and cytokinins, may also be added to the basal medium. Growth regulators are required for cell division and organ regeneration from the cultures. The cultures are usually kept in a culture room at about 24°C with some illumination. These all constituents are dissolved in distilled water. If necessary, the medium is solidified with about 0.8% agar. The *pH* of the medium is adjusted around 5.8 (slightly acidic). Now equal quantities of the medium are dispersed in culture vials, which are usually glass tubes or flasks. The culture vials, containing medium, are plugged with non-absorbent cotton wrapped in cheese cloth. Such a closure allows the exchange of gases but does not permit the entry of micro-organisms into culture vials.

Aseptic Conditions

The sugar content of the nutrient media may support a luxuriant growth of many micro-organisms, like bacteria and fungi. It is, therefore, extremely important to maintain a completely aseptic environment inside the culture vials. Micro-organisms can contaminate the medium in at least three ways :

(*a*) The micro-organisms present in the medium right from the beginning many be destroyed by sterilizing the properly plugged culture vials. It can be done by maintaining the temperature at 120°C for about 15 minutes.

(*b*) The micro-organisms may also be carried along with tissue that is being cultured. To prevent this, the plant material from which the tissue is to be excised is surface sterilized. The material may be surface sterilized with saturated chlorine water and then thoroughly washed with sterilized distilled water and to remove all traces of chlorine. If the material is fairly hard, as are some fruits and seeds, it may be surface sterilized by rinsing in alcohol.

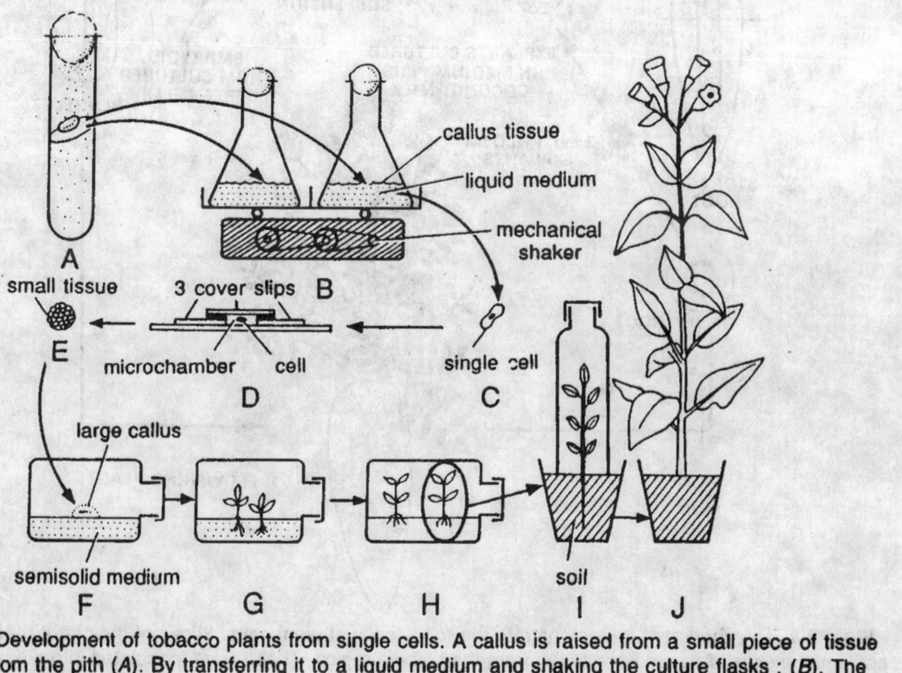

Fig. 22.2. Development of tobacco plants from single cells. A callus is raised from a small piece of tissue excised from the pith (*A*). By transferring it to a liquid medium and shaking the culture flasks ; (*B*), The callus is dissociated into a single cell; (*C*), is mechanically removed from the flask, and is placed on a slide in a drop of culture medium; (*D*), a microchamber is formed around the culture drop using the three-cover slips; (*D*), a small tissue ; (*E*) derived from the cell through repeated division is then transferred to a semi-solid medium where it grows into large callus (*E*) and eventually differentiated plants (*F, G*), when transferred to soil; (*H*), these plants grow to maturity, flower and set seeds (*I*).

(*c*) Finally, precautions must also be taken to prevent the entry of micro-organisms while/the plug of a culture vial is removed to transfer the tissue to the nutrient medium (inoculation). For this, all operations from surface sterilization of the tissue up to inoculation are done in an aseptic environment.

Aeration

Proper aeration of the cultured tissue is also an important aspect of culture technique. If the tissue is grown on the surface of a semi-solid medium it acquires enough aeration without special device for liquid medium, special device "filter paper bridge" is used. Here, two legs remain dipping in the medium and the horizontal part carrying the tissue is raised above the level of the medium.

Cellular Totipotency

This is the capacity of mature cells showing that when freed from the plant body, they had the ability to reorganize themselves into the new individuals. Steward and his co-workers, showed this phenomenon in the carrot cultures. Here the small pieces of mature carrot root, were grown in a liquid medium supplemented with coconut milk, in special containers. These cultures were

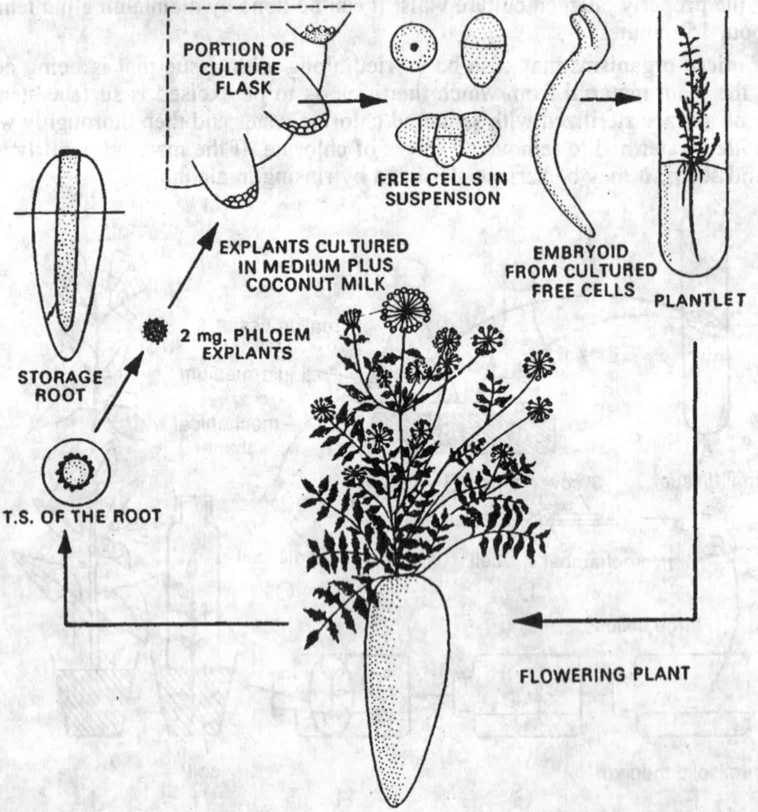

Fig. 22.3. An experiment to demonstrate the totipotency of plant cells. Slices of the carrot root were cut and small pieces of tissue were taken from the phloem region. These were inoculated into a liquid medium in special flasks, the tissue grew actively and single cells and small cell aggregates dissociated into the medium. Some of the cell clumps developed roots, and when transferred to a semisolid medium, these rooted nodules formed shoots. These plants could be transferred to soil.

shaken generally which freed all the cell clusters into the medium. Some of them developed into rooting clumps. When these were transferred to the tubes containing a semi-solid medium, they gave rise to whole plant that flowered and set seeds. On the basis of these experiments, it can be inferred that, at least theoretically, every living plant cell, irrespective of its age and location, is totipotent. However, this phenomenon cannot be compared with the mode of the development of the zygote, wherein the divisions give predictable manner. But in case of cultured cells, the isolated single cells of tobacco divide, quite irregularly to form a mass from which roots and shoot buds differentiate eventually.

However, Guha and Maheswari, while culturing mature anthers of *Datura innoxia* with an aim of understanding the physiology of meiosis, accidentally noticed that on basal nutrient medium containing kinetin, coconut milk, or grape juice numerous embryo-like structures appeared from the inside of anthers, which eventually, developed into plants. Later on, these workers confirmed the origin of the embryoids from pollen grain. As expected, the plantlets of pollen-origin were haploid.

Applications of Tissue Culture

(*a*) The technique provides a way for rapid multiplication of desirable and rare plants.

(*b*) As the experiments reveal, we may obtain healthy stocks from virus infected plants through shoot-tip culture.

(*c*) The development of haploids through the techniques of anther culture is having its potential significance in basic and applied genetics and plant breeding. During the past 30 years, the technique has been succesfully extended to about 20 species including some economic plants, *e.g. Atropa, Brassica, Hordeum, Lycopersicon, Nicotiana, Oryza* and *Triticum*.

(*d*) The embryo culture has been useful in overcoming seed dormancy. It is also utilized for producing viable plants from crosses which normally fail due to the death of immature embryos, *e.g.*. jute, rice.

(*e*) The embryo tissue culture is also applied for the propagation of rare plants, *e.g.*, "makapuno". Here, some coconuts develop soft, solid, fatty tissue in place of the liquid endosperm. These are rare and very expensive, served only at special banquets in the Philippines. Under normal conditions the coconut seeds fail to germinate. Using the technique of *in vitro* culture of excised embryos, the scientists have succeeded in plantlets from makapuno nuts.

(*f*) Another important use of embryo culture is in obtaining some rare hybrids. It is possible to raise complete hybrid plants through embryo culture. This method has been profitably used for many interspecific crosses.

Culture of Plant Materials

Explant culture. There are a variety of forms of seed plants, such as trees, herbs, grass, which exhibit the basic morphological units, *i.e.*, root, stem and leaves. Parenchyma is the most versatile of all types of tissues. They are capable of division and growth. Development of a tissue is characterised by (*i*) cell division, (*ii*) cell elongation and (*iii*) cell differentiation. For this reason, the explant from healthy and young part of the plant is used. Presence of parenchyma is first consideration in a particular species. parenchyma from stems, rhizomes, tubers, root is easily accessible and will generally respond quickly to culture conditions *in vitro*.

Callus formation and its culture. In nature, callus develops by infection of microorganisms from wounds due to stimulation by endogenous growth hormones, the auxins and cytokinins. However, it has been artificially developed by adopting tissue culture techniques. A callus is an amorphous mass of loosely arranged thin walled parenchyma cells developing from proliferating cells of the parent tissue. The unique feature of callus is that the abnormal growth has biological potential to develop normal root, shoots and embryoids ultimately forming a plant.

In callus culture, cell division in the explant forms a callus, an unorganised mass of cells. It is maintained on a medium gelled usually with agar. The medium ordinarily contains the auxin 2, 4 – D (2, 4 – dichlorophenoxyacetic acid), and often a cytokinin BAP (benzylaminopurine). When an explant is placed on such a medium, many of the cells become meristematic and begin to divide. In about 2 to 3 weeks, a callus mass is obtained.

Cell (suspension) culture. A suspension culture consists of single cells and small groups of cells suspended in liquid medium. Cell suspension is prepared by transferring a fragment of callus (about 500 mg.) to the liquid medium (500 ml.) and agitating them aseptically to make the cells free in medium. The medium ordinarily contains the auxin 2, 4 – D. Suspension cultures must be constantly agitated at 100 – 250 rpm (revolutions per minute).

Agitation serves three important purposes. They are as follows :

(*i*) aeration of culture; (*ii*) constant mixing of the medium and (*iii*) breakage of cell aggregates into smaller cell groups. Suspension cultures grow much faster than callus cultures.

It is difficult to have suspenstion of single cell. However, the suspension includes single cell, cell aggregates (varied number of cells), residual inoculum and dead cells. King (1980) has described that a good suspension consists of a high proportion of single cells than small cluster of cells.

Cell suspension cultures have many advantages over the callus cultures. They are as follows.

(*i*) The suspension can be pipetted.

(*ii*) They are less heterogeneous and cell differentiation is less pronounced.

(*iii*) They can be cultured in volumes upto 1500 litres.

(*iv*) They can be subjected to more stringent environmental controls.

(*v*) They can be manipulated for production of natural products by feeding precursors.

Subculturing. After some time, the undermentioned three things happen in all types of plant tissue cultures :

(*i*) Cell/tissue dry matter known as biomass increases, (*ii*) the level of nutrients in the medium decreases, and (*iii*) the medium volume declines due to evaporation.

Hence, if tissue cultures were kept in the same culture vessel, they will die in due course of time. Due to this reason, cells/tissues are regularly transferred into new culture vessels containing fresh media. This process is called **subculturing.**

Precaution is taken that during subculture, only a part of the culture from a vessel is transferred into the new culture vessel.

Table 22.2. Difference Between Callus and Suspension cultures.

Callus culture	Suspension culture
1. Her cell division in the explant forms a callus, which is an unorganised mass of cells.	1. Suspension culture consists of single cells and small groups of cells.
2. It is maintained on a medium gelled usually with agar.	2. Here, cells are suspended in liquid medium.
3. The medium ordinarily contains the auxin 2, 4-D, and often a cytokinin like BAP.	3. Usually the medium contains the auxin 2, 4-D.
4. There is no need of agitation.	4. They must be constantly agitated at 100-250 rpm (revolutions per minute).
5. In about 2-3 weeks, a callus mass is obtained	5. Suspension culture grow much faster than callus cultures.

Uses of callus and suspension cultures. The callus and suspension cultures can be used to achieve cell biomass production which may be used for biochemical isolation.

Also used for regeneration of plantlets, *i.e.*, newly regenerated plants through tissue culture.

Production of transgenic plants and isolation of protoplasts.

Regeneration of Plantlets

Plants cells cultured *in vitro* can ultimately give rise to complete plants. Potentiality of a plant cell to regenerate the entire organism or plant is called **totipotency.** This potentiality has been exploited through the culture of protoplasts, cells, tissues and organs *in vitro*. Gottlieb Haberlandt in 1902, for the first time started the technique of plant tissue culture, when he attempted to culture isolated single cells from leaf mesophyll to determine their totipotency.

Regeneration describes the development of an organised structure, such as root, shoot or somatic embryo from cultured cells. However, plantlets can be obtained from cultured cells by two different ways:

(*i*) Where shoot regeneration is followed by rooting of the shoots and

(*ii*) Where regeneration of somatic embryos followed by their germination.

In cultured materials it has been possible to study such process as differentiation of a parenchyma cell into tracheid (*i.e.*, cytodifferentiation), organ formation (*i.e.*, organogenesis) and somatic embryo formation (*i.e.*, somatic embryogenesis). Besides the study of fundamental process of differentiation, the capacity of cell to form organs and embryos can be exploited to regenerate plantlets for clonal propagation.

Organogenesis. The process by which cells and tissues are forced to undergo changes which lead to the production of a structure, known as shoot or root primordium. This system is commonly produced in callus cultures. The earliest reports on controlled organogenesis *in vitro* were by White (1939) who obtained shoots on callus of a tobacco hybrid and by Nobecourt (1939), who observed root formation in carrot callus.

The earliest report on controlled **somatic embryogenesis** *in vitro* was with carrot reported simultaneously in 1958 by Reinert and Steward (see Fig 9.3). The process occurs naturally in a wide range of species from both reproductive and somatic tissues. Somatic embryos can be formed on callus, in cell suspensions and protoplasts cultures, or directly from cells of organised structures, such as stem segments or zygotic embryo.

Advantages of plantlet regeneration. There are several advantages of plantlet regeneration through plant biotechnological methods using organogenesis or embryogenesis, in comparison to conventional methods of propagation. The advantages include the efficiency of process, *i.e.*, formation of plantlet in fewer steps, with reduction in labour, time and cost, and the potential for the production of much higher number of plantlets, and their morphological and cytological uniformity. Till now about 150 species from angiosperms and gymnosperms have been reported to produce somatic embryos in culture.

Shoot and root regeneration. Shoot regeneration is promoted by a cytokinin, such as BAP (benzylaminopurine). While root regeneration is promoted by an auxin, such as NAA (naphthalene acetic acid). Thus, shoot and root regenerations are generally controlled by auxin-cytokinin balance. Usually, an excess of auxin promotes root generation, and that of cytokinin promotes shoot generation.

Callus cultures are first kept on a BAP (cytokinin) containing medium. After sometime shoots regenerate from callus cells. When the shoots become 2-3 cm long, they are excised and transferred to an auxin-containing medium. After sometime, roots regenerate from the lower ends of these shoots to give rise to complete plantlets.

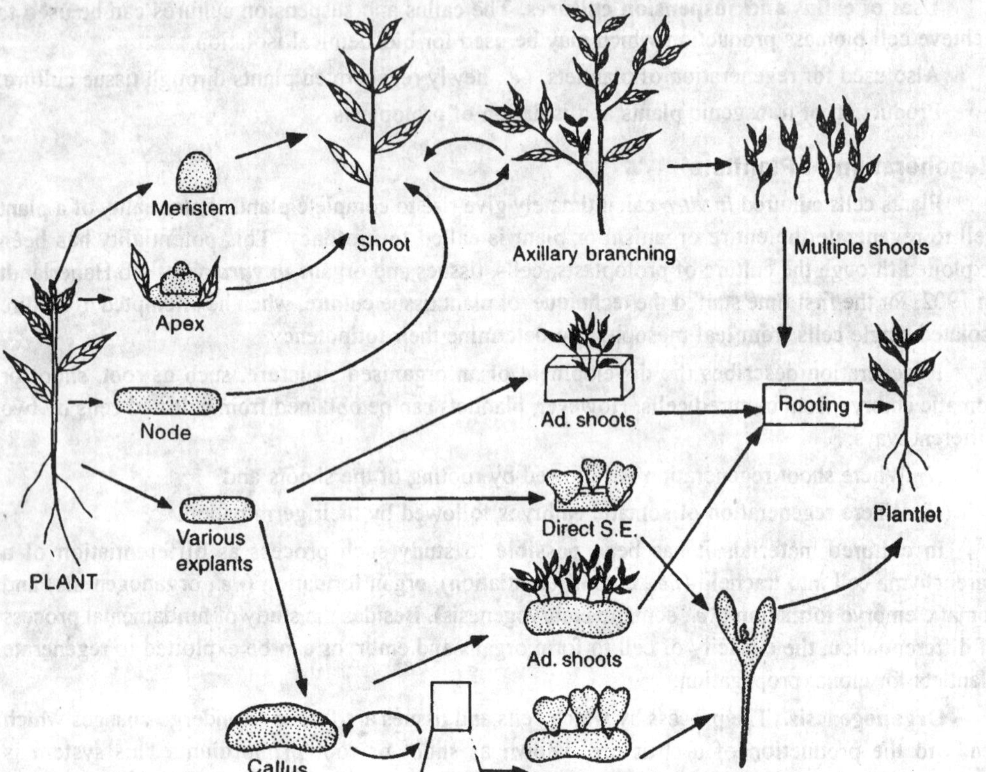

Fig. 22.4. Different methods of regeneration from explant and callus/cell cultures.

Somatic embryo regeneration. Plant cells are totipotent and can produce complete new plants under favourable conditions of nutrients and plant growth regulators. Steward and Reneirt, almost simultaneously reported for the first time, somatic embryo formation in carrot cell suspension cultures in 1958. These somatic embryos were similar to zygotic embryos in development and structure.

A somatic embryo develops from a somatic cell. The pattern of development of a somatic embryo is similar to that of a zygotic embryo.

Somatic embryo regeneration is induced usually by a relatively high concentration of an auxin like 2, 4-D (2, 4-dichorophenoxyacetic acid). The young embryos develop into mature embryos either in the same medium or on another medium. Mature somatic embryos germinate to yield complete plantlets.

During somatic embryo generation in cell suspension cultures, embryos of different sizes are produced. For any experimental or micropropagation method, embryos of uniform size are required. This can be achieved by sieving or fractionation of suspension with appropriate sieve size.

Somatic embryo regeneration is a versatile technique for micropropagation of plant species. A large number of herbaceous dicots and monocots have been regenerated through somatic embryogenesis.

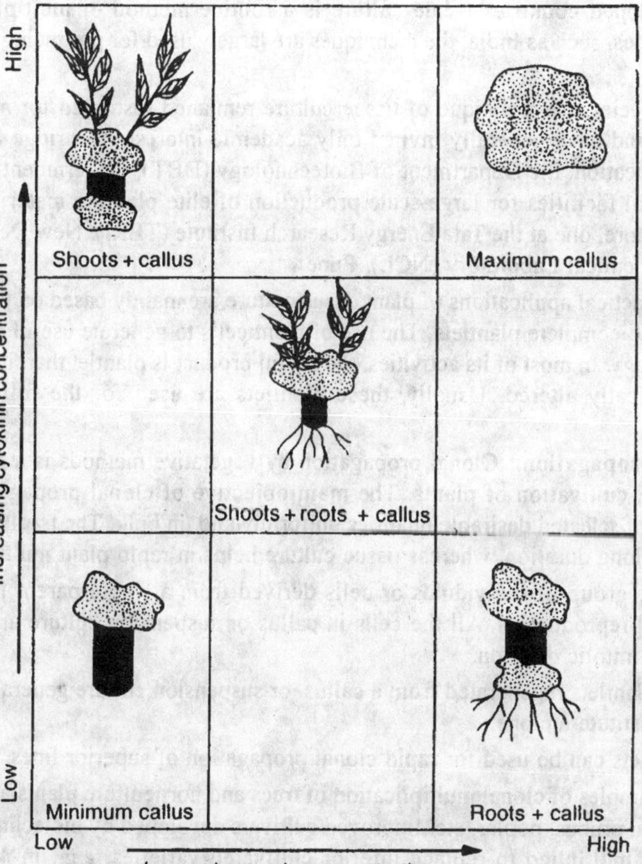

Fig. 22.5. Effect of a combination of auxin and cytokinin ratio.

Establishment of plantlets in the field. Plantlets are produced through rooting of isolated shoots or germination of somatic embryos. Now, the plantlets can be removed from culture vessels and established in the field. This stage is concerned with transfer of plantlets in pots, their **hardening** and establishment in soil. Hardening of plants imparts some tolerance to moisture stress and plants become autotrophic from heterotrophic condition. During hardening, plantlets are kept under a reduced light and high humidity for a suitable period of time. Hardening procedures make the plantlets capable of tolerating the relatively harsher environments outside the culture vessels.

Hardened plants are then transferred to glass or poly-houses with normal environmental conditions. Generally the poly-houses are erected by mounting polythene or polycarbonate sheets on metal frame support. Now, plants are irrigated frequently and their growth and variation monitored regularly. Plants are generally transferred to fields, *e.g.*, plantation crops, after 4-6 weeks of acclimatization.

In India, there are now many commercial companies which produce millions of plantlets through micropropagation.

Large glass houses and green houses are essential components of micropropagation industry. Hardening and acclimatization of delicate *in vitro* raised plantlets is carried out in these glass houses. Now a days chambers made of polycarbonate and polypropylene sheets are used for creating large working place. These houses are fitted with mist and fog generating units with cyclic auto-regulation. Light is provided through proper light sources.

Application of plant tissue culture. Tissue culture has been successfully employed for the multiplication of orchids and many other ornamental plants.

In the developed countries tissue culture is a routine method of multiplication while in developing countries, such as India, the techniques are largely used for producing plants for export markets.

With tree species, the technique of tissue culture remianed restricted for many years to the laboratory stage and have generally invited only academic interest. To bridge this gap between research and application, the Department of Biotechnology (DBT), Government of India, set two pilot-scale national facilities for large-scale production of elite planting material of forest trees through tissue culture, one at the Tata Energy Research Institute (TERI), New Delhi, and the other at the National Chemical Laboratory (NCL), Pune.

However, practical applications of plant tissue culture are mainly based on the ability of plant cells to give rise to complete plantlets. The use of plant cells to generate useful products is called **plant biotechnology.** In most of its activities, the useful product is plantlet that, in many cases may have been genetically altered. Usually, these plantlets are used for the following important purposes:

(*i*) Clonal propagation. Clonal propagation by vegetative methods is a practice followed since man started cultivation of plants. The main objective of clonal propagation has been to reproduce plants of selected desirable qualities uniformly and in bulk. The traditional propagation methods, require long duration, whereas tissue culture helps in rapid plant multiplication.

A **clone** is a group of individuals or cells derived from a single parent individual or cell through a asexual reproduction. All the cells in callus or suspension culture are derived from a single explant by mitotic division.

Hence, all plantlets regenerated from a callus or suspension culture generally have the same genotype and constitute a clone.

These plantlets can be used for rapid clonal propagation of superior lines.

Selected examples of clonal multiplication of trees and horticulture plants are as follows : oil palm, citrus peach, prunus, poplar, etc. Improved cultivars developed by biotechnological methods are then clonally multiplied to replace inferior cultivated varieties, *e.g.*, in *Mentha* and other aromatic plants.

(*ii*) Somaclonal variation. Genetic variation present among plant cells of a culture is called **somaclonal variation.**

In vitro cell and tissue cultures of plant give rise to genetic variation spontaneously. While spontaneous variation is not desired during propagule multiplication, it has been useful in providing some genetic variants among crop species. The observed frequencies of such somaclonal variants vary widely and are probably related to both time and culture. Several point mutations have been observed, the majority of analysed spontaneous genetic variants from somatic cultures appear to have resulted from induction of aneuploidy, loss of interchanges or intra-chromosomal segment duplication, deletions or structural arrangements.

Spontaneous or mutagen induced genetic variation in somatic cell culture coupled with *in vitro* selection techniques have been effective in isolating desired novel genetic variants with cellular level expression while in heterozygous condition. The somaclonal variation has been used to develop several useful varieties of crop plants.

(*iii*) Transgenic plants. A gene that is transferred into an organism by genetic engineering is called **transgene**. An organism that contains and expresses a transgene is called **transgenic organism.**

The plants, in which a functional foreign gene has been incorporated by any biotechnological methods that generally not present in plant, are called **transgenic plants.** However, a number of transgenic plants carrying genes for traits of economic importance have either been released for commercial cultivation or are under field trials.

However, transgenes can be introducd into individual plant cells. The cells containing and expressing transgenes can be easily selected *in vitro.* Ultimately, plantlets can be regenerated from these cells. These plantlets yield highly valuable transgenic plants.

Some of the commercially grown transgenic crop plants in developed countries are : 'Flavr Savri' and 'Endless Summer' tomatoes, 'Freedom II' squash, 'High lauric' rapeseed and 'Roundup Ready' soybean. So far more than 60 transgenic dicot plants including herbs, shrubs and trees, and several monocots, such as maize, oat, rice, wheat, etc., have been produced. In future the number of these crops certainly will go up. These transgenic plants contain certain selected traits such as herbicide resistance, insect resistance, virus resistance, seed storage protein, modified ripening, modified seed oil, agglutinin, etc.

Meristem Culture

The meristem is a dome of actively dividing cells about 0·1 mm in diameter and 0·25 mm in length. Shoots of all flowering plants grow by virtue of their apical meristems. The totipotency of the plant cells forms the basis of meristem culture.

Here, one can use an explant containing pre-existing shoot meristems, and produce shoots from them. Such cultures are known as **meristem culture.** The explants generally used in meristem culture are shoot tips or nodal segments.

These explants may be cultured on a medium containing a cytokinin, usually BAP (benzylaminopurine). Cytokinins promote axillary branching by overcoming apical dominance. Hence, they support multiple shoot development from each explant.

When axillary branching takes place, individual shoots are cultured, whereas when axillary branching does not take place, the single shoot is cut into nodal segments, which are then cultured. Shoots of 2-3 cm are excised and rooted on a suitable medium.

The *in vitro* culture of meristem and shoot tip involves several phases such as initiation of culture and establishment of explant, growth and differentiation, proliferation of shoots and finally plantlet fomation by rooting of shoots.

The plantlets thus obtained are subjected to hardening and ultimately established in the field.

Uses of meristem cultures. Meristem cultures are used for rapid clonal multiplication. Development of virus free plants is one of the most significant application of meristem culture. Generally this technique has applications in diverse areas such as clonal multiplication of vegetatively propagated crop plants, virus elimination and germplasm preservation.

Embryo Culture

Interspecific crosses may fail due to several reasons, but when the development of embryo is arrested owing to the degeneration of the endosperm, or when the embryo aborts at an early stage of development, embryo culture is the only technique to recover hybrid plants. It is being used extensively in the extraction of haploid barley (*Hordeum vulgare*) from the crosses *H. vulgare* × *H. bulbosum.* Embryo culture is also a routine technique employed in orchid propagation and inbreeding of those species that show dormancy. Das and Burman (1992) developed the method of regeneration of tea shoots from embryo callus.

Excision of young embryos from developing seeds and their cultivation on a nutrient medium is called **embryo culture.** *In vitro* older embryos are more easily cultured than young embryos.

The objective of embryo culture is to allow the young embryos to complete development and ultimately, give rise to seedlings.

More recently, a number of hybrids have been successfully raised through embryo culture : *Hordeum vulgare* × *Secale cereale*, *H. vulgare* × *Agropyron repens*, *H. vulgare* × *Triticum aestivum*, interspecific hybrids in *Abelmoschus* and *Secale*.

In some interspecific crosses, the endosperm of developing hybrid seeds degenerates at an early stage. Here, young embryos also die on the degeneration of endosperm. Hence such interspecific crosses cannot be normally made. In such cases, young hybrid embryos are excised and cultured *in vitro* to obtain hybrid seedlings.

The orchid industry owes a great deal to the technique of embryo culture. The culture of orchid embryos was initiated at the Singapore Botanic Garden in 1928. Orchids lack stored food. Here, embryo culture allows development of seedlings from most of the embryos. In such cases, embryo culture is also used for rapid clonal propagation.

Embryo culture has helped in overcoming self-sterility of seeds, especially of crop plants propagated vegetatively, when the seeds do not germinate in nature. In a wild relative of commercial banana, *Musa balbisiana*, for example, the seeds do not germinate under natural conditions. However, if the embryos are excised and grown on a simple culture medium of mineral salts, seedlings are readily obtained.

Indian work. Sometimes some interspecific hybrids of *Oryza* show quite a low percentage of seed germination under normal conditons because the hybrid embryos succumb at an early stage of their development. The scientists raised seedllings of certain interspecific crosses in *Oryza* by culturing the excised embryos on Nitsch's medium . The embryo culture technique has also been successfully employed in *Colocasia esculenta* where the seeds fail to germinate in nature. They grew the excised embroys on synthetic media and obtained seedlings which on transplanting in soil gave rise to normal healthy plants.

Rangaswamy and Rangan (1963) have cultured the embroys of a stem parasite, *Cassytha filiformis*, in the absence of the host, on a modified White's medium supplemented with IAA. The embryos of *Cuscuta reflexa*, a total stem parasite, were also cultured. Somewhat similar results have been obtained with the embryos of *Dendrophthoe falcata*, a partial stem parasite. Like the embryos of stem parasites, those of some root parasites have also shown considerable capacity for proliferation. In cultures of seeds of *Orobanche aegyptiaca*, a total root parasite, the ovoid unorganized embryos produced a massive callus capable of continuous growth followed by differentiation into shoot tips.

Anther Culture and Haploid Production

Anther, a male reproductive organ, is diploid (2n) in chromosome numbers. As a result of microsporogenesis, tetrads of microspores or pollen grains are formed from a single spore mother cell (2n), which are haploid (n).

In nature, haploid plants originate from unfertilised egg cells. However, in laboratory, they can be produced from both male and female gametes. In many plant species, haploids are produced when their anthers are cultured on a suitable medium. This process is called **anther culture.**

The first successful pollen cultures were established by Tulecke in the 1950's using mature pollen grains of certain gymnosperms. In 1964, Guha and Maheshwari discovered that when excised anthers of *Datura innoxia* were cultured intact in a mineral salt medium in conjunction with coconut milk and other complex organic substances and growth hormones, embryo-like outgrowths appeared from the sides of the anther in about 6-7 weeks. In subsequent studies, they confirmed the haploid nature of the embryoids and their origin from microspores.

Investigations have shown that for some reason, anthers from flowers of the Solanaceae respond best to excision and culture by production of embryoids. Convincing demonstration of the direct transformation of microspores into embryoids has been provided by several workers in different species of the genera of Solanaceae, *i.e., Datura, Nicotiana, Atropa, Lycium, Petunia, Solanum, Capsicum* and *Hyoscyamus.* It has been observed that embryoids go through the globular, heart-shaped and torpedo stages typical of the ontogeny of normal diploid zygotic embryos before they finally elongate and form shoot and root meristems. Embryoids have also been obtained form cultured anthers of certain cereals like rice. All in all therefore, the capacity of microspores in cultured anthers to form haploid embryoids and plants can now scarcely be questioned.

In some other plants, haploids do not arise directly from the microspores, but do through tne intervention of a callus. The microspores first develop into multicellular bodies which later give rise to an exceedingly dense callus. Subculture of the callus in an embryogenesis-inducing medium containing specific concentration of auxins and a cytokinin led to the initiation of haploid seedlings. There, thus seem to exist the following alternative pathways for haploidy in anther cultures :

1. Microspore → callus → embryogenesis → plantlet *e.g.,* Solanaceae
2. Microspore → callus → embryogenesis → plantlet *e.g., Oryza, Brassica, Hordeum, Coffea, Populus.*
3. Microspore → callus → plantlet, *e.g., Datura metelloides.*

In several species, the pollen grains can be isolated and cultured to obtain haploids. In many species of plants, haploids can also be produced by culturing unfertilised ovaries or ovules.

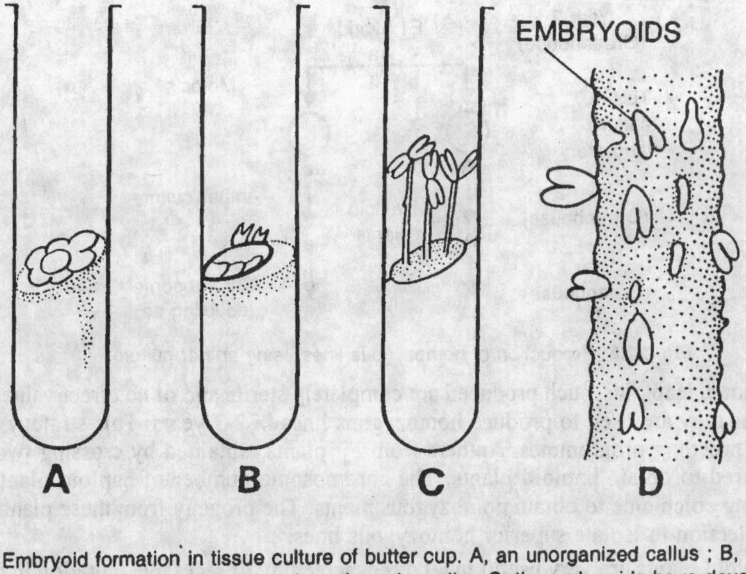

Fig. 22.6. Embryoid formation in tissue culture of butter cup. A, an unorganized callus ; B, six-week old culture showing numerous embryoids arising from the cells ; C, the embryoids have developed into plantlets and a fresh crop of embryoids is seen arising from the surface of the hypocotyledonary region of these plants; D, the embryoid-bearing portion enlarged from C.

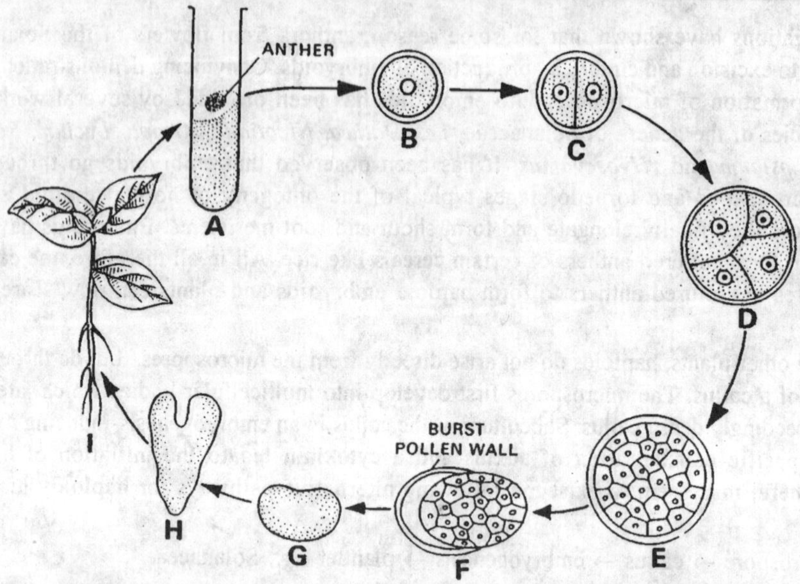

Fig. 9·7. Diagram showing the development of haploid plants from the pollen grains of tobacco. The anther of the right stage is excised from the flower bud and cultured on a suitable medium (A). Some of the pollen inside the anther undergoes repeated division (B-D), forming a multicellular tissue within the parent wall (E). Eventually, the pollen wall bursts, releasing the tissue mass directly develops into an embryoid and germinates to form a haploid plant.

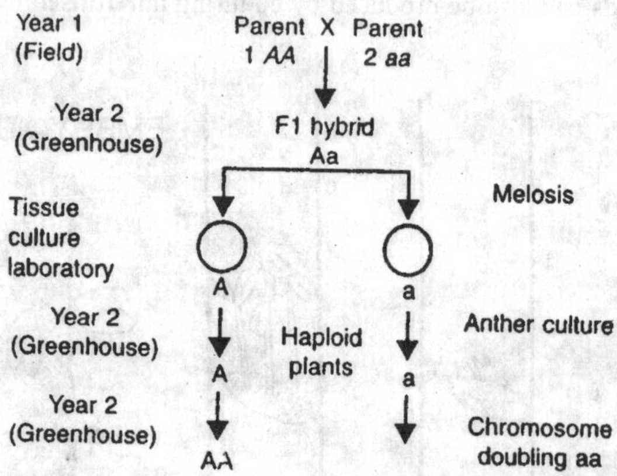

Fig. 22.8. Production of homozygous lines using anther culture.

Applications. Haploids, such produced are completely sterile and of no direct value. But they are important as they are used to produce homozygous lines in 2-3 years. This strategy can be of much value in breeding programmes. Anthers from F_1, plants, obtained by crossing two or more lines, are cultured to obtain haploid plants. The chromosome number of haploid plants may be doubled by using colchicine to obtain homozygous plants. The progeny from these plants are then subjected to selection to isolate superior homozygous lines.

Thus, haploid plants are very useful in (*i*) direct screening of recessive mutation in diploid or polyploid, screening of recessive mutation is not possible, and (*ii*) development of homozygous diploid plants following chromosome doubling of haploid plant cells.

In China, the most widely grown wheat is a doubled haploid produced through homozygous diploid lines. Anther culture of rice is also successfully grown. Haploid plants have been produced in tobacco, wheat and rice through pollen culture which are used for the development of disease resistant and superior diploid lines.

At present, more than 247 plant species and hybrids belonging to 38 genera and 34 families of dicots and monocots have been regenerated using anther culture technique. They include economically important crops and trees, such as rice, wheat, maize, coconut, rubber plantation, etc.

Protoplast Culture and Somatic Hybridisation

An even more advanced technique of free cell culture is that involving the culture of isolated protoplasts. Essentially, the method consists of , first, breaking down the cell wall mechanically or chemically using enzymes and thus freeing the protoplasts which are then cultured like whole cells using appropriate culture media. The cells are, in other words, rendered naked and then cultured.

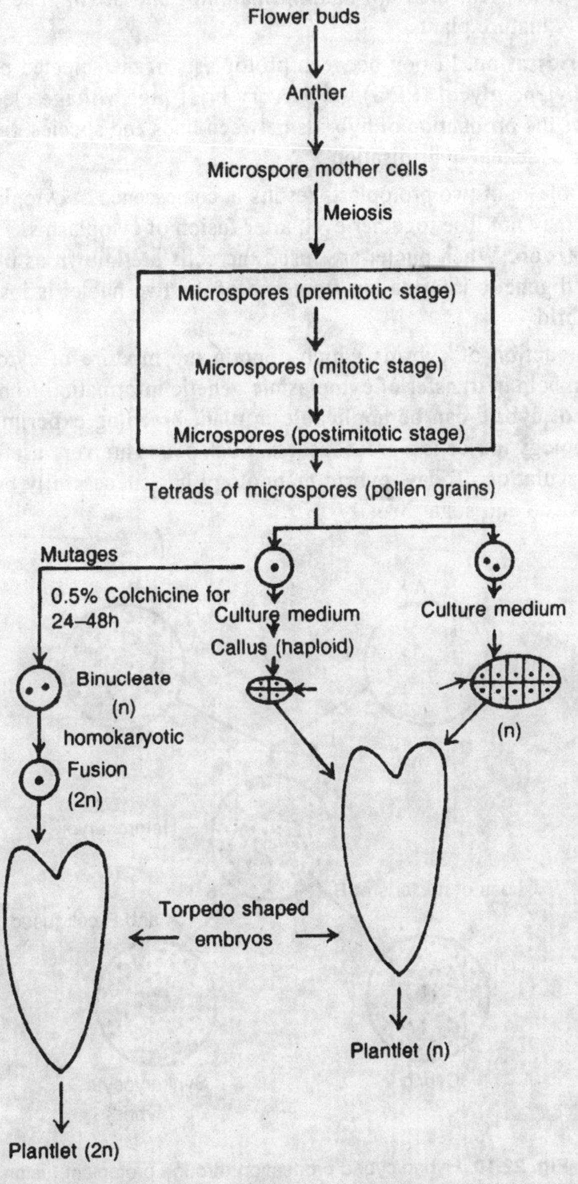

Fig. 22.9. Methods of anther culture, and production of haploid and diploid plants *in vitro*.

When cell wall is mechanically or enzymatically removed, the isolated protoplast is known as 'naked plant cell' on which most of recent researches are based.

Plant cell wall acts as physical barrier and protects cytoplasm from microbial invasion and environmental stress. Cooking (1960), for the first time isolated the protoplasts of plant tissues by using cell wall degrading enzymes, *viz.*, cellulose, hemicellulose, pectinase and protease extracted from a saprophytic fungus *Trichoderma viride.* Later on protoplasts were cultured *in vitro.*

Protoplast culture and regeneration. The protoplasts regenerate a cell wall, undergo cell division and form callus. The callus can also be subcultured. Embryogenesis begins from callus when it is placed on nutrient medium lacking mannitol and auxin. The embryo develops into seedlings and finally mature plants.

Somatic hybridisation. Fusion between protoplasts of the selected parents is induced by a solution of polyethylene glycol (PEG), or by very brief high voltage electric current. Somatic bybridisation allows the production of hybrids between lines and species, that cannot be produced normally by means of sexual hybridisation.

Fusion of cytoplasm of two protoplasts results in coalescence of cytoplasm. The nuclei of two protoplasts may or may not fuse together even after fusion of cytoplasms. The binueleate cells are known as **heterokaryon.** When nuclei are fused the cells are known as **hybrid,** and when only cytoplasms fuse and genetic information from one of the two nuclei is lost is known as **cybrid,** *i.e.,*cytoplasmic hybrid.

However, production of cybrids which contain the mixture of cytoplasms but only one nuclear genome can help in transfer of cytoplasmic genetic information from one plant to another. Thus, information of cybrid can be applicable in plant breeding experiments. For example, in China, cybrid technology in rice is a great success. Such plants are very useful in producing hybrid seeds without emasculation. Today, cybrid technology has successfully been applied to carrot, mustard, citrus, tobacco and sugar beet.

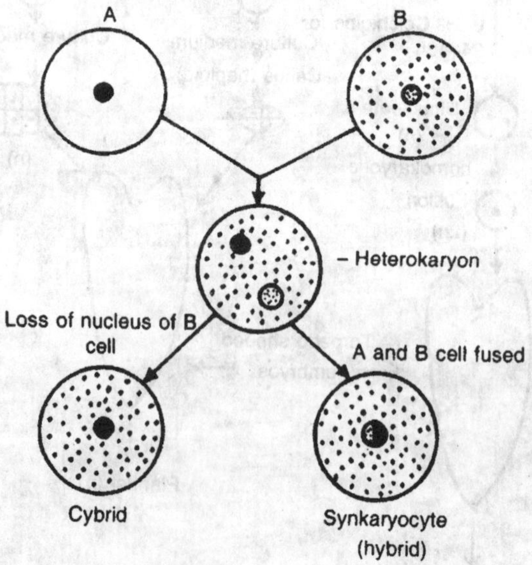

Fig. 22.10. Hybrid/cybrid production through protoplast fusion.

Somatic hybrids may also be used for gene transfer, transfer of cytoplasm and production of useful allopolypoloids.

Tissue and protoplast cultures have been used in genetic engineering for the transfer of DNA and extrachromosomal bodies — plasmids, mitochondria, chloroplasts, *nif* (nitrogen fixing) genes from the nitrogen fixing bacterium *Klebsiella pneumoniae* to a strain of the colon bacterium *Escherichia coli*. Isolated protoplasts have great advantage in all the afore mentioned uses. For transformation purposes cultured apical meristems are also usable because these can easily be regenerated into whole plants and also because intact DNA taken up by plants appears to be rapidly transported to meristematic regions, where growth and differentiation are centred.

Root culture. Excised roots were the first plant organs of higher plants to be successfully brought into sterile culture. In addition to the usual requirements for a carbon source and mineral nutrients most isolated roots grown in sterile culture required to be supplied with certain vitamins. This is because, in the intact plant, certain vitamins, are synthesized in the leaves and the roots are dependent upon shoots for the supply of these substances which they are unable to synthesize themselves. For example, tomato roots require only sucrose, mineral nutrients and thiamin, and given all these, will grow successfully in culture for many years. But excised roots of some monocotyledonous plants fail to grow even when supplied with a full complement of β-vitamins and other vitamins. In some of these (*e.g.*, rye), an exogenous auxin supplement to the nutrient medium allows growth to proceed. In order to maintain the culture, the excised roots must be regularly subcultured on to a fresh medium, by excising a piece of root bearing a lateral which then proceeds to grow rapidly and maintain the culture.

As a rule, excised root of most species produce only root tissues in culture. There are exceptions, however, where they regenerate shoot buds as well as further roots, *e.g.*, *Convolvulus*, *Taraxacum* and *Rumex*.

Generally excised root is cultured in liquid medium. The techniques of root culture give certain important informations such as, (*i*) nutritional requirements, (*ii*) infection by *Rhizobium* and nodulation and (*iii*) physiological activities.

Culture of Shoot Apices and Leaves

Like roots, isolated shoot apical meristems and leaf primordia can also be grown in sterile culture. These are often preferred in fact, because these frequently produce roots and can hence eventually develop into complete plants. The shoot apices and leaves of vascular cryptogams, such as ferns, are relatively more autotrophic than those of angiosperms. Thus, even a small fern apex can be grown on a medium containing only carbohydrate source and mineral nutrients. Small angiosperm apices (less than 0.5 mm in diameter) require a general source of organic nitrogen and certain specific amino acids and vitamins in addition to the basic medium, but larger apices will grow on a simple medium. The simpler requirements of larger apices may be due to the fact that they carry larger leaf primordia, which apparently can supply some of the requirements of the apex for vitamins and other organic nutrients.

Isolated young leaves of the fern *Osmunda cinnamomea* and of the sunflower (*Helianthus annuus*) and tobacco (*Nicotiana tabacum*) have been successfully grown on a simple medium containing only sucrose and inorganic salts. Such isolated leaf primordia continue to grow and develop into normally differentiated leaves, although the latter are usually very much smaller than normal leaves developed *in vivo, i.e.*, on the plant.

Culture of Ovaries

Rau (1956) attempted to culture pollinated ovaries of *Phlox drummondii* and studied the influence of extraneous chemicals on the pattern of development of the endosperm and embryo.

The addition of colchicine to the medium caused aberrant divisions, fusion and aggregation of endosperm nuclei and finally a degeneration of the endosperm. In 12 to 14-days old cultures the embryo also aborted and the seeds were malformed.

Nirmala Maheshwari and Lal (1961) excised the flowers of *Iberis amara* one day after pollination and planted them on agar nutrient media. Fruits of normal size were obtained in two weeks on a medium containing Knop's mineral salts + Nitsch's trace elements + sucrose + B vitamins. The seeds formed *in vitro* contained viable embryos. Removal of the sepals slowed down the growth of the ovaries showing that the calyx is by no means an unessential structure but has an important role in the physiology of the fruit.

Pollinated ovaries of a few other plants have also been reared into fruits, but when unpollinated ovaries are taken, the fruits are either not formed or are seedless.

Johri and Sehgal (1963) cultured the ovaries of *Anethum graveolens* at the zygote stage on White's basal medium containing yeast extract and /or casein hydrolysate thirteen to twenty weeks later, a polyembryonate mass developed by the proliferation of the zygotic proembryo and ruptured the pericarp. Further growth resulted in the production of multiple shoots some of which flowered in the test tube after about seven months. Thus this was possible to obtain several seedlings from a single fertilized ovule.

However, it is easier to maintain ovules in sterile culture when they are left *in situ* within the ovary. The physiological requirements of fertilized ovules do not appear to be species specific, since young ovules of widely different species have grown to mature seeds following transplantation on to the placenta of *Capsicum* fruits.

Culture of Ovules and Parts of Ovules

White (1932) was the pioneer to culture the ovules. White and La Rue cultured ovules of *Erythronium* and *Antirrhinum* on White basic medium containing indole acetic acid IAA.

Nirmala Maheshwari and Lal (1961) cultured the ovules of *Papaver somniferum* excised six days after pollination when they contained only a 2-celled proembryo and a free nuclear endosperm. These grew to maturity in twenty days and even germinated and produced seedlings in the culture tubes.

Several genera, such as *Citrus, Eugenia* and *Mangifera* show the occurrence of nucellar embryos. Since they have the same genetical composition as the maternal parent, they are of much importance for the clonal propagation of desirable varieties. Rangaswamy (1961) reported that if the nucellar tissue of *Citrus microcarpa* is grown on a suitable nutrient medium containing casein hydrolysate, it proliferates profusely and on subculturing produces embryo-like regenerants termed **"pseudobulbils"**, which can develop into seedlings so that an indefinite number of new plants can be obtained from a single nucellus.

A. N. Rao (1963) successfully germinated seeds of an interspecific hybrid of *Vanda* on a simple agar nutrient medium. Some of the fertilized ovules directly produced seedlings; others gave rise to a callus from which new plants arose subsequently.

Culture of Endosperms

It is somewhat more difficult to raise tissue cultures from the endosperm. However, Rangaswamy and Rao (1963) established a continuously growing tissue from the mature endosperm of *Santalum album* when they cultured it along with the embryo on White's medium containing yeast extract, kinetin and 2, 4-D. On the other hand, the endosperm failed to callus when it was grown without the embryo. Johri and Bhojwani (1965), also cultured the endosperm of *Exocarpus cupressiformis* on White's medium containing indole actic acid IAA, kinetin and casein hydrolysate. If merely the endosperm devoid of the embryo was grown, it did not proliferate. In their experiments, the shoots were differentiated and not the roots.

BIOTECHNOLOGY

Biotechnology is that portion of microbiological science which deals with the possible utilisation of micro-organisms in industrial processes, or in processes in which their activities may become of indusrial or technical significance. Thus, biotechnology may be defined as the use of microorganisms, animal or plant cells, or their components to generate products and services useful to human beings. However, the use of complete animals and plants is not generally included in biotechnology.

For several decades it has been known that numerous kinds of yeasts, moulds and other lower fungi, and several types of groups of bacteria have direct relation, to certain types of economic processes carried out in connection with industrial or factory operations, such as brewing, wine making, cheese making, etc. However, people did not know that microorganisms were involved in these processes. Microorganisms were used for the first time to produce some organic compounds like citric acid in the beginning of twentieth century. Thereafter, micro-organisms were employed to generate a variety of products, including antibiotics. In all such processes, only the natural capabilities of the organisms and cells are exploited. All such activities carried over by micro-organisms were grouped under **old biotechnology.**

In recent years revolution in biology has occurred due to the potential of biotechnology. Techniques have been developed to produce rare and medicinally valuable molecules, to change hereditary traits of plants and animals, to diagnose diseases, to produce useful chemicals, and to clean up and restore the environment. Thus, biotechnology has great impact in the fields of health, food, agriculture and environment protection.

During 1970, the technique of recombinant DNA technology was developed. Recombinant DNA technology is popularly known as genetic engineering. Recombinant DNA technology is responsible for the isolation of desired gene from any organism, and its transfer and expression into the organism of choice. In most of the developed countries, the recombinant DNA technology has become one of the major thrusts. The United Nations Industrial Development Organisation (UNIDO) has recognised the potential of genetic engineering and biotehnology for promoting the economic progress of the developing countries.

Transgenic micro-organisms are produced to obtain novel pharmaceutical proteins, such as human insulin is commercially produced from a transgenic *Escherichia coli* (bacterium) strain, that contains and expresses the human insulin gene. Proteins poduced by transgenes are called **recombinant proteins.**

Many valuable recombinant proteins, also have been produced by use of transgenic animal cell lines and transgenic plants. However, the recombinant proteins cannot be naturally produced by the concerned cells or organisms. The production technologies based on genetic engineering are grouped under **modern biotechnology.**

In India, in 1988, a full fledged Department of Biotechnology (DBT) has been set up, in the Ministry of Science and Technology for planning, promotion and coordination of various biotechnological programmes.

Recombinant DNA technology has made it easier to detect the genetic diseases and cure before the birth of a child. In genetic engineering programmes, it has become possible to map the whole genome of an organism. Gene bank and DNA clone bank have been constructed to make available different types of genes of its known function.

Table 22.3. Area of Biotechnology

Area of interest	Products
1. Recombinant DNA technology (genetic engineering)	Fine chemicals, enzymems, vaccines, growth hormones, antibiotics, interferon.
2. Treatment and utilisation of biomaterials (biomass)	Single cell protein, mycoprotein, alcohol and biofuels.
3. Plant and animal cell culture.	Fine chemicals (alkaloids, essential oils, dyes, steriods), somatic embryos, encapsulated seeds, interferon, monoclonal antibodies.
4. Nitrogen fixation	Microbial inoculants (biofertilizers).
5. Biofuels (bioenergy)	Hydrogen (via photolysis), alcoholos (from biomass), methane (biogas produced from wastes and aquatic weeds).
6. Enzymes (biocatylysts)	Fine chemicals, food processing, biosenser, chemotherapy.
7. Fermentation	Acids, enzymes alcohols, antibiotics, fine chemicals, vitamins, toxins (biopesticides).
8. Process engineering	Effluent, water recycling, product extraction, novel reactor, harvesting.

Genetically Modified Crops

The plants, in which a functional foreign gene has been incorporated by any biotechnological methods that generally not present in plant, are called **transgenic plants**. A transgenic crop that contains and expresses a **transgene** (*i.e.*, functional foreign gene). Generally, transgenic crops are called **genetically modified crops** or **GM crops**.

The techniques used for production of transgenic crops have two great advantages. They are as follows :

(*i*) Any gene (from any organism or chemically synthesised) can be used as a transgene.

(*ii*) The change in genotype can be controlled to some extent as only the transgene is added into the crop genome.

In contrast, breeding activities can use only those genes which are present in such species that can be hybridised with them. Moreover, changes occur in all those traits for which the parents used in hybridisation differ from each other.

However, when a transgene is introduced into the genome of an organism, it can achieve one of the following characteristics :

(*i*) Produces the desired protein.

(*ii*) Produces a protein which itself produces the desired phenotype.

(*iii*) Modifies an existing biosynthetic pathway, and therefore, a new end product is obtained.

Some examples are mentioned here :

For example, **hirudin** is a protein that prevents blood clotting. The gene encoding hirudin was chemically synthesised. Thereafter, this gene was transferred into *Brassica napus,* where hirudin accumulates in seeds. Now, the hirudin is purified and used medicinally. Here, the transgene product itself is the desired product.

The other example is of a soil bacterium *Bacillus thuringiensis* which produces a crystal (Cry) protein. The Cry protein is toxic to larvae of certain insects. There are several different types of Cry proteins, and each of them is toxic to a different group of insects. The gene encoding Cry protein is *cry* gene, which has been isolated and transferred into several crops. A crop, that

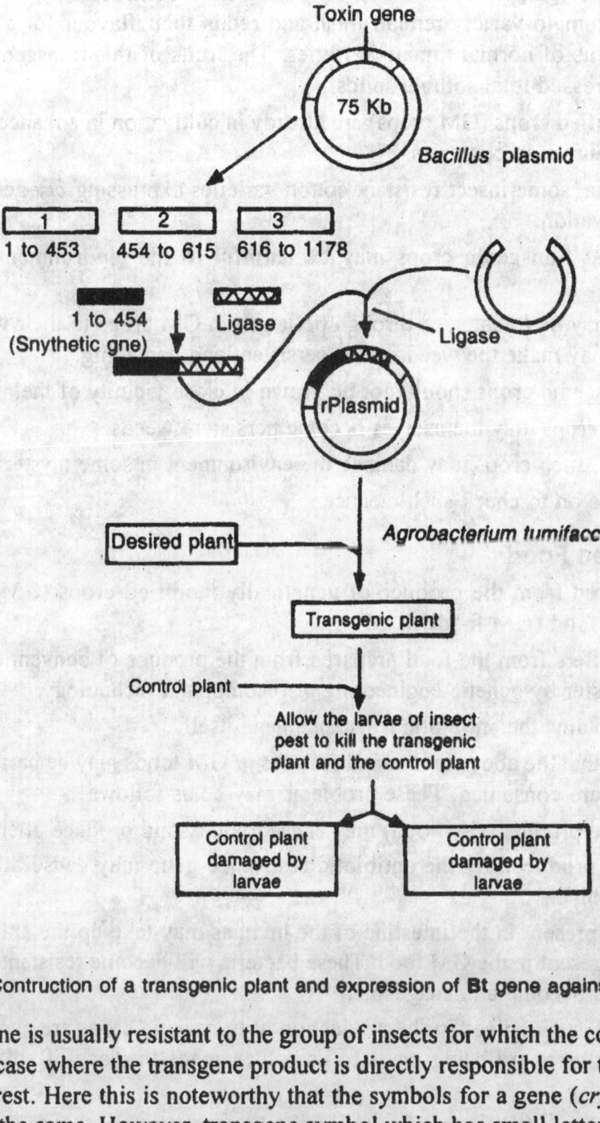

Fig. 22.11. Contruction of a transgenic plant and expression of **Bt** gene against insect larvae.

expresses a *cry* gene is usually resistant to the group of insects for which the concerned Cry protein is toxic. This is a case where the transgene product is directly responsible for the production of the phenotype of interest. Here this is noteworthy that the symbols for a gene (*cry*) and for its protein (Cry) product are the same. However, transgene symbol which has small letters is written in italics (*cry*), whereas the first letter of protein symbol is capital and written in Roman (Cry).

Insect-resistant transgenic plants. The *Bt* gene of a bacterium, *Bacillus thruingiensis* has been found to encode the toxins called endotoxins which have cidal effect of certain insect pests. These toxins are of different types, such as beta-endotoxin and delta-endotoxin. Preparations of *Bt* gene in powder form have been made available in market for commercial use.

The other approach has been isolation of the toxin gene *Bt 2* from *Bacillus thruingiensis* and its introduction into Ti-DNA plasmid of *Agrobacterium tumefaciens.* Thus, Ti-plasmid mediated transformation of several plants has been done, *e.g.*, tobacco, cotton, tomato, corn, etc.

Tomato variety 'Flavr Savr' is an example where expression of a native tomato gene has been blocked. Expression of native gene can be blocked by several methods. For example, fruit softening is promoted by the enzyme **polygalacturonase**, which is responsible for degrading pectin. Production of polygalacturonase was blocked in the transgenic tomato variety 'Flavr Savr'. Hence, fruits of this tomato variety remian fresh and retain their flavour for a longer period in comparison of the fruits of normal tomato varieties. The fruits of this transgenic variety have a superior taste and increased total soluble solids.

Genetically modified crops (GM crops) are already in cultivation in advanced countries, such as U.S.A. and many European countries.

However, in India, some insect resistant cotton varieties expressing *cry* genes have reached onto farmers for cultivation.

It is thought that transgenic crops may be harmful to the environment because of the following reasons :

(*i*) The transgene may be transferred through pollen from GM crops to their wild relatives and such a gene transfer may make the weeds more persistent and damaging.

In such cases, transgenic crops should not be grown in close vicinity of their wild relatives.

(*ii*) The transgenic crops may themselves become persistent weeds.

(*iii*) In view of this, such crops may damage the environment in some mysterious manner.

Investigations are on to check such menace.

Genetically Modified Food

The food prepared from the produce of genetically modified crops (GM crops) is called **genetically modified food** (GM food).

The GM food differs from the food prepared from the produce of conventionally developed used during gene transfer by genetic engineering or recombinant technology.

(*iii*) GM food contains the antibiotic resistance gene itself.

It has been argued that the above mentioned features of GM foods may be harmful and problem making if such foods are consumed. These problems may be as follows :

(*i*) The transgene product (GM food) may cause toxicity and produce allergies.

(*ii*) The enzyme produced by the antibiotic resistance gene may cause allergies, as it is a foreign protein.

(*iii*) The bacteria present in the intestine of the humans may take up the antibiotic resistance gene that is present in the GM food. These bacteria will become resistant to the concerned antibiotic and become unmanageable.

The biotechnologists involved in the production of transgenic crops are aware of above men tioned aspects, and effortrs are being made to use other genes in place of antibiotic resistance genes.

Ban on genetic food. It is a growing concern all over the world that the genetic food may pose risks to human health, ecology and the environment. However, it has forced the governments of many countries to rethink on introduction of such crop. For the first time the European Commission's Scientific Advisors have recommended that a genetically engineered potato be withheld from the market because they cannot guarantee its safety. The United States, the world's biggest producers of genetically modified foods, has also threatened New Zealand to ban his genetically engineered foods.

Sustainable Agriculture

In modern days, in agricultural practices non-renewable resources are utilised which cause pollution. However, such practices cannot be continued indefinitely. This means, they are not sustainable.

Sustainable development may be defined in several ways. **Sustainable agriculture** primarily have renewable resources, which cause minimum pollution and maintain the optimum yield level.

Any such development which reduces the use of non-renewable resources, and level of pollution, will definitely enhance the sustainability of agriculture.

Biotechnology contributes in several ways for enhancement of the sustainability of agriculture. They are as follows :

Biofertilizers. The term 'biofertilizers' denotes all the 'nutrient inputs of biological origin for plant growth' (Subba Rao, 1982). However, micro-organisms employed to enhance the availability of nutrients like nitrogen, and phosphorus to crops are called biofertilizers.

As we know, nitrogen is available in atmosphere in high amount in the form of gas. It is converted into combined form of organic compounds by some prokaryotic micro-organisms through biological reactions. The phenomenon of fixation of atmospheric nitrogen by biological means is known as '**diazotrophy**' or 'biological nitrogen fixation' and these prokaryotes as 'diazotrophs' or 'nitrogen fixers' (nif). They may be in free living or in symbiotic forms.

Examples of nitrogen-fixing micro-organisms are bacteria and cyanobacteria (blue-green algae). Some of these micro-organisms are free-living, while others form symbiotic association with plant roots. **Rhizobia** form root nodules in leguminous crops, while cyanobacteria form symbiotic association with the pteridophyte *Azolla*.

On the other hand, insoluble forms of soil phosphorus are converted into soluble forms by certain micro-organisms. This makes the phosphorus available to the plants.

Phosphate is made soluble by some bacteria and by some fungi that form association with roots of higher plants. The fungus and plant root association is called *mycorrhiza*. Here the fungi absorb their food from the roots and in response are beneficial to the plants. The mycorrhiza may be external or internal. The external mycorrhiza also called 'ectophytic mycorrhiza' are confined to the outer region of the roots, whereas the internal mycorrhiza are found deeply in the root cells. These fungi solubilise phosphorus, produce plant growth promoting substances and protect host plants from soil pathogens.

Advantages. Biofertilizers make a low cost and easy technique and can be used by small farmers.

It is free from pollution hazards and increases soil fertility. Cyanobacteria secrete growth promoting substances, amino acids, proteins, vitamins, etc. They add sufficient amount of organic matter in soil.

Rhizobial biofertilizer can fix 50-150 kg N/ha/annum.

Azolla supplies N, increases organic matter and fertility in soil and shows tolerance against heavy metals.

The biofertilizers increase physico-chemical properties of soil, such as soil structure, texture, water holding capacity, etc.

The mycorrhizal biofertilizers make the host plants available with certain elements, increase longevity and surface area of roots, reduce plant response to soil stresses, and increase resistance in plants. In general, plant growth, survival and yield are increased.

However, extensive efforts are made to enhance the effectiveness and the contribution of biofertilizers to agricultural production.

Biopesticides. Biopesticides are those biological agents which are used to control weeds insects and pathogens. There is a vast majority of micro-organisms, such as viruses, bacteria, fungi, protozoa and mycoplasma known to kill the insect pests. The suitable preparations of such micro-organisms for control of insects are called 'microbial insecticides'. The microbial insecticides are non-hazardous, non-phytotoxic and selective in their action. Pathogenic micro-organisms which kill insects are viruses (DNA containing viruses), bacteria (*e.g., Bacillus thuringiensis*), and fungi (*e.g., Aspergillus, Fusarium,* etc.). Now a days, some of the biopesticides are being used even at commercial scale.

For example, *Bacillus thuringiensis* is a widely distributed soil bacterium, and can be isolated from soil, litters and dead insects. It is a spore forming bacterium and produces several toxins. Spores of this bacterium produce the insecticidal Cry protein. Therefore, spores of this bacterium kill larvae of certain insects. After ingestation of spores, larvae are damaged, as the rod-shaped bacterial cell secretes at the opposite end, a single large crystal (Cry) in the cell. This crystal is toxic and proteinaceous in nature. The commercial preparations of *B. thuringiensis* contain a mixture of spores, Cry protein (toxin) and an inert carrier.

Bacillus thuringiensis, was the first biopesticide to be used on a commercial scale. Certain other bacteria and fungi are also used for control of some weeds and diseases of various crop plants.

Microbial pesticides are produced by many multi-national companies by using viruses, bacteria and fungi. *B. thuringiensis* preparations have been produced in U.S.A., France, Russia and U.K. in the form of wettable powder and water suspensions.

A number of **viruses** have been discovered which belong to groups Baculoviruses and cytoplasmic polyhedrosis viruses (CPV). Preparations of viruses or their products have been developed as effective biopesticides and being successfully used for the control of insect pests in agriculture and horticulture.

Recent studies on the use of **mycopesticides** for the control of insect pests are of much value. Mode of action of these fungi is different from viruses and bacteria. The infective conidia, spores, etc., of the antagonistic fungi reach the haemocoel of the insect either through integument or mouth. They multiply in haemocoel followed by secretion of mycotoxins which result in death of insect hosts.

The use of biopesticides may reduce the application of synthetic chemicals for control of diseases, insect pests and weeds. The synthetic insecticides, generally affect non-target organisms, and many beneficial organisms for agriculture, are killed. In turn, they cast hazardous effects on human health, and therefore, use of biopesticides has been suggested.

Disease-resistant Varieties

Genetic engineering has been also used in the development of such crop varieties which are resistant to certain diseases. Usually, plant diseases are caused by fungi, bacteria, viruses and nematodes.

The most successful approach for the production of virus resistant plants is the transfer of the virus coat protein gene into the plants. The genetic material of viruses is found enclosed in a protein coat.

The gene that encodes coat protein is isolated from the genome of the virus that causes concerned disease. Now this gene is transferred and expressed in the host of the concerned virus.

Expression of the coat protein produces resistance in the host to this virus. This approach has been used in producing a virus-resistant variety of squash. Such disease-resistant varieties are used to minimise the use of chemicals which are generally used for control of crop diseases. This approach also reduces pollution. Such varieties are successful in reducing yield losses due to various crop diseases, thus they enhance agricultural production.

Single Cell Protein (SCP)

The dried cells of micro-organisms, such as algae, bacteria, actinomycetes and fungi, used as food or feed are collectively known as **microbial protein.** Since the time immemorial a number of micro-organisms have been used as part of human diet. Micro-organisms are widely used for preparation of a variety of fermented foods, such as cheese, butter, leavened bread, *idlis* and several other bakery products. Some other micro-organisms have long been used as human food, *e.g.*, the blue green alga (cyanobacteria), *Spirulina*, and the fungi commonly called edible mushrooms.

The term 'microbial protein' was replaced by a new term 'single cell protein' (SCP) during first International Conference on 'microbial protein' held in 1967, at Masachusetts, U.S.A. In recent years, NBRI, Lucknow and CFTRI, Mysore, have established centres for mass production of SCP from *Spirulina* (cyanobacteria).

Substrates used for production of SCP. A variety of substrates are used for SCP production. Algae which contain chlorophylls, do not require organic wastes. They use free energy from sunlight and carbondioxide from air, while bacteria and fungi require organic wastes, as they do not contain chlorophylls, the major components of substrates are the raw materials which contain sugars, starch, lignocellulose from woody plants and herbs having residue with nitrogen and phosphorus contents and other raw materials.

Nutritional value of SCP. SCP is rich in high quality protien and poor in fats. They are ideal for human food. SCP provides a valuable protein-rich supplement in human diet.

Now a days, many pilot plants for the production of *Spirulina* powder have been established in Japan, U.S.A. and European countries. In India, food grade *Spirulina* at two main centres, one at MCRC, Chennai and the other at Central Food Technology and Research Institute (CFTRI), Mysore. The products are marketed in India and abroad.

The use of *spirutina* (SCP) should help bridge the gap between the requirement and the supply of proteins in the human diet. *Spirulina* (SCP) is a rich source of protein, amino acids, vitamins, minerals, crude fibres, etc., it is used as supplemented food in diets of under-nourished children, adults and old aged people in developing countries. *Spirulina* is also popular as health food.

SCP as therapeutic and natural medicine. *Spirulina* posseses many medicinal properties. It has been recommended by medicinal experts for reducing body weight, cholesterol and for better health. It lowers sugar level in blood of diabetics. It is a good source of β-carotenes, and helps in monitoring healthy eyes and skin.

Biopatent

Dictionary meaning of **patent** is, 'an official right to be the only person to make, use or sell a product or an invention'. Thus, a patent is the right granted by a government to prevent others from commercial use of his invention.

A patent is granted for :

(*i*) an invention, including a product,

(*ii*) an improvement in an earlier invention,

(*iii*) the process of generating a product, and

(*iv*) a concept or design.

Initially, patents were granted for industrial inventions by a particular company, such as patent medicines, etc.

But, now a days, patents are also being granted for biological entities and for products derived from them, such patents are called **biopatents**, *e.g.*, *neem* and its products; *haldi* and its products.

However, industrialised countries, such as U.S.A. , Japan and European Union Countries, are awarding Biopatents.

Biopatents are awarded for the following :

(*i*) strains of micro-organisms,

(*ii*) cell lines,

(*iii*) genetically modified strains of plants and animals,

(*iv*) DNA sequences,

(*v*) the proteins enclosed by DNA sequences

(*vi*) various biotechnological products

(*vii*) production processes

(*viii*) products, and

(*ix*) product applications.

On the basis of ethical and political reasons, such biopatents have been opposed from time to time by different societies of the world. However, arguments in favour of biopatents are given primarily of increased economic growth.

Many biotechnological patents are quite broad in their coverage. For example, one patent covers 'all transgenic plants of family Brassicaceae/mustard family. Such broad patents are unacceptable and not fair, as they would enable financially powerful corporations to have their monopoly control over biotechnological processes. Such powerful corporations try to control the direction of whole agricultural research, including plant breeding. Such a position seems to be a threat to the food security of the world.

Biopiracy

When big organisations and multinational companies exploit patent biological resources or bioresources of other nations without proper authorisation from the countries concerned; such exploitation is called **biopiracy.**

The advanced or industrialised nations are generally rich in technology and financial resources. However, they are poor in biodiversity and traditional knowledge related to bioresources. While developing nations are poor in technology and financial resources, but quite rich in biodiversity and traditional knowledge related to bioresources.

Biological resources or **bioresources** are those organisms which can be used to derive commercial benefits from them.

Traditional knowledge related to bioresources is the knowledge developed by various communities from time immemorial, regarding the utilisation of the bioresources, *e.g.*, use of plants and other organisms in healing art. Such traditional knowledge of a particular nation can be exploited to develop modern commercial processes. Here, the traditional knowledge is primarily used in the direction to be followed which saves a lot of time, and bioresources are easily commercialised.

Institutions and multinational companies of industrialised advanced nations are collecting and exploiting the bioresources, as follows :

(*i*) They collect and patent the genetic resources themselves. For example, a patent granted in U.S.A. covers entire 'basmati' rice germplasm indigenous to our country.

(*ii*) The bioresources are analysed for identification of valuable biomolecules. A **biomolecule** is a compound produced by a living organism.

(*iii*) Useful genes are isolated from the bioresources and patented, and thereafter, used to generate useful commercial products.

(*iv*) Sometimes, even traditional knowledge itself of other countries may be patented.

For example, a plant, *Pentadiplandra brazzeana* of West Africa, produces a protein called **brazzein.** This protein is approximately two thousand times as sweet as sugar. Moreover, this is a low calorie sweetner.

Local people of West Africa have known and used the super-sweet berries of this plant for centuries. However, the protein brazzein was patented in U.S.A. , where the gene encoding this protein was also isolated, sequenced and patented.

It is proposed to transfer the brazzein gene into maize and express it in maize grains. These grains (kernels) will be used for the extraction of brazzein, which can give a serious jolt to the countries exporting large quantities of sugar.

Bioresources of third world countries have always been commercially exploited by the industrialised nations without an adequate compensation. This exploitation has increased a lot with the development of biotechnological techniques. Some developing nations coming forward and raising voice to make laws to prevent unauthorised exploitation of bioresources and traditional knowledge.

Biowar

This word denotes, the use of harmful bacteria as weapons of war. The biological weapons are generally used against humans, and their crops and animals. A **bioweapon** is a device that carries and delivers to the target organisms, a pathogen or a toxin derived from it.

The **bioweapon agent**, is kept in a suitable container so that it remains acitive and virulent during delivery. The container with bioweapons could be delivered to the target by several ways, including missiles and aircrafts.

For example, anthrax is an acute infectious disease caused by the spore-forming bacterium *Bacillus anthracis*. Spores of *B. anthracis* can be produced and stored in a dry form keeping them viable for several decades in storage or after release. A cloud of anthrax spores, if released at a strategic location to be inhaled by the individuals under attack may act as an agent of effective weapon of **biowar**. For example, the anthrax bacteria were sent through letters after September 2001, in U.S.A.

An attack with bioweapons using antibiotic-resistant strains would initiate the incidence and spread of communicable diseases, such as anthrax and plague, on either an endemic or epidemic scale.

Bioweapons are low cost weapons, and cause far more casualities than chemical or conventional weapons. Bioweapon agents are microscopic and invisible with naked eyes, and therefore, difficult to detect.

Such type of biowar and use of bioweapons against civilised human society is a major threat for all inhabitants of this planet, the earth.

The possible defences against bioweapons include use of gas mask, vaccination, administration of specific antibiotics, and decontamination. However, biologists should play an important role in creating awareness about the impact of misuse of biology on the human society and the whole Biokingdom.

Bioethics

Ethics includes 'moral principles' that control or influence a person's behaviour. This is connected with beliefs and principles about what is right or wrong, morally correct or acceptable. This includes a set of standards by which a community regulates its behaviour and decides as to which activity is legitimate and which is not.

Thus, **bioethics** makes a set of standards which is used to regulate our activities in relation to the whole biokingdom.

Now a days, biotechnology, particularly recombinant DNA technology, is used for exploitation of the biological world by various ways. Biotechnology has been used in various ways, from 'unnatural' to 'detrimental' to 'biodiversity'. The major bioethical ways concerning to biotechnology, are as follows :

1. Use of animals in biotechnology is cruelty towards animals which causes great suffering to them.

2. When animals are used for production of certain pharmaceutical proteins, they are treated as a 'factory' or 'machine'.

3. Introduction of a transgene from one species into another species threats integrity of species.

4. Transfer of human genes into animals or *vice-versa* is great ethic threat for humanness.

5. Biotechnology is only used for fulfilment of the motive of selfishness by humans. This is used only for the benefit of human beings.

6. However, biotechnology poses unforeseen risks to the environment and biodiversity.

Besides ethical arguments, techniques of biotechnology are used in the production of things on a much larger scale and at a much faster rate. Each society has to evaluate bioethical issues and take right decision about their application.

SUMMARY

1. Plant cells and plant organs can be cultured *in vitro* (*e.g.*, in test tube or any other container) on a suitable medium (*e.g.*, agar medium), is called plant tissue culture.
2. A plant part excised from its original location and used for initiating a culture is known as explant.
3. The explants, media, vessels and instruments used in tissue culture must be sterilised to make them free from any microbes.
4. Culture medium should be provided with nutrition that is required for growth and development of explants.
5. Culture of explants on an agar medium provided with 2, 4-D yields callus cultures.
6. Plant cells can also be grown in a liquid medium as a suspension of single cells as well as groups.
7. A constant agitation of suspension cultures is essential.
8. Complete plantlets can be obtained from agar and suspension cultures.
9. Explants that contain pre-existing shoot meristems and produce shoots from them are called meristem culture.
10. Excision of young embryos from developing seeds and their cultivation on a nutrient medium is called embryo culture.
11. Haploids may be produced in many plant species when anthers are cultured on a suitable medium, this is called anther culture.
12. Chromosome numbers of haploid plants can be doubled (diploid, 2n) to produce homozygous lines within 2 to 3 years.
13. A hybrid produced by fusion of somatic cells of two species is called somatic hybrid, and process is known as somatic hybridisation.
14. Cell walls can be digested with a combination of pectinase and cellulase.
15. The plant cells lacking cell walls are called protoplasts.
16. The fusion of protoplasts can produce somatic hybrids.
17. Biotechnology may be defined as the use of microorganisms, animal or plant cells, or their components to generate products and services useful to humans.

18. Recombinant DNA technology or genetic engineering permits the isolation of desired gene from any organism, and its transfer and expression into the organism of choice. Generally this is used to produce transgenic organisms that possess novel specialties.
19. The most important application of plant tissue culture is production of transgenic crops.
20. A transgenic crop contains one or more genes transferred by recombinant DNA technology (genetic engineering).
21. Transgenic crops resistant to insects and pests, with changed quality, capable of producing a medicinal protein, are already cultivated.
22. Food obtained from transgenic crops is called genetically modified food (GMF).
23. However, such foods may be toxic, may cause allergies and may affect useful microbial populations of alimentary canal. Efforts are in progress to check this obnoxity.
24. Modern agricultural practices utilise non-renewable resources and cause pollution. These practices are not sustainable. However, sustainable agriculture would use renewable resources, would cause minimum pollution and maintain optimum yield level.
25. Biotechnology contributes to sustainable agriculture by developing biofertilisers, biopesticides, disease and insect resistant varieties and single-cell proteins.
26. The microorganisms that are employed to enhance the availability of nutrients, such as nitrogen (N) and phosphorus (P) to crops are called biofertilisers.
27. Biopesticides consist of viruses, bacteria, protozoans, fungi and mites that help in controlling diseases, insects and weeds.
28. The use of biofertilisers, biopesticides and resistant varieties helps to save non-renewable resources and checks pollution.
29. Single-cell protein is microbial biomass rich in high quality protein. They serve as valuable food and feed supplements.
30. Patents that are granted for biological entities and for products derived from them are called biopatents. Developments in biotechnology have accelerated biopatenting.
31. Biopiracy is unauthorised use of bioresources and traditional knowledge related to bioresources foı commercial benefits.
32. Such developments of biotechnology favour rich industrialised nations, at the cost of developing nations.
33. Now, some nations are developing comprehensive laws to prevent unauthorised exploitation of their bioresources and traditional knowledge.
34. Biowar or biological war is the use of biological weapons, or disease causing agents, such as viruses, bacteria and fungi to destroy crops, domesticated animals and human beings.
35. Bioethics is a set of standards by which a community regulates its behaviour and decides as to which activity is legitimate and which is not. Each society has to evaluate such issues and take right decision regarding them. However, biotechnology may pose unforeseen risks to biodiversity.

TERMS TO REMEMBER

Anther culture. Haploids are produced, when anthers are cultured on a suitable medium.

Bioethics. A set of standards which may be used to regulate own activities in relation to the biological world.

Biofertilizers. Micro-organisms employed to enhance the availability of nutrients.

Biomolecule. A compound produced by a living organism.

Biopatents. The patents granted for biological entities and products derived from them.

Biopesticides. Biological agents used for control of weeds, insects and pathogens.

Biopiracy. Exploitation of bioresources of other nations without proper authorisation from the countries concerned.

Bioresources. All these organisms that can be used to derive commercial benefits.

Biotechnology. Use of organisms, and their cells or components to generate products and services useful to human beings.

Biowar. Use of biological weapons against humans, or their crops and animals.

Bioweapon. A device that carries and delivers to the target organisms a pathological agent or a toxin derived from it.

Bioweapon agent. A biological agent or toxin.

Brazzein. A plant, *Pentadiplandra brazzeana* produces a protein called brazzein, which is about 2000 times as sweet as sugar. A low-calorie sweetener.

Callus culture. Cell division in the explant forms a callus, an unorganised mass of cells is called callus culture.

Clone. A group of individuals or cells derived from a single parent individual or cell through asexual reproduction.

Embryo culture. Excision of young embryos from developing seeds and their cultivation on a nutrient medium.

Explant. A plant part, excised from its original location and used for initiating a culture.

G.M. crop. Genetically modified crop or transgenic crop that contains and expresses a transgene.

G.M. food. The food prepared from genetically modified (transgenic) crops.

Hardening. The procedure done, when plantlets are transferred from culture vessels and established in the field.

Hirudin. A protein that prevents blood clotting.

Meristem culture. Use of an explant that contains pre-existing shoot meristems and produce shoots from them.

Mycorrhiza. The fungus and plant root association.

Plant tissue culture. Maintenance and growth of plant cells, tissues and organs on a suitable culture medium *in vitro*.

Protoplasts. The plant cell lacking cell wall.

Recombinant proteins. Proteins produced by transgenes.

Regeneration. Development of an organised structure (*e.g.*, root, shoot, embryo) from cultured cells.

Rhizobia. The bacteria which form root nodules in legume crops.

Somatic hybrid. A hybrid produced by fusion of somatic cells of two varieties or species.

Subculturing. When tissues/cells are regularly transferred into new culture vessels containing fresh media, the process is called subculturing.

Suspension culture. It consists of single cells and small groups of cells suspended in a liquid medium.

Sustainable agriculture. Primarily use renewable resources, cause minimum pollution and obtain optimum yield level.

Totipotency. The ability of plant cells to regenerate into complete plants is called totipotency.

Transgenic crop. A crop that contains and expresses a transgene.

QUESTION BANK

Very Short Answer Questions

1. Surface sterilisation
2. Subculture
3. Somatic embryo
4. Protoplast
5. Somatic hybrid
6. Biotechnology
7. Transgene
8. Transgenic organism

9. Sustainable agriculture
10. Sterilisation
11. What is plant tissue culture ?
12. What is an explant ?
13. What is callus culture ?
14. What is a suspension culture ?
15. What is totipotency ?
16. What is regeneration ?
17. What is plant biotechnology ?
18. What are protoplasts ?
19. What is modern biotechnology ?
20. What is a transgenic crop or/GM crop ?
21. What is GM food ?
22. What are biopesticides ?

ANSWERS

1. When the explants are treated with specific anti-microbial chemicals, the procedure is called surface sterilisation; **2.** The regular transference of tissues, into new culture vessels containing fresh media, is called subculturing ; **3.** A somatic embryo develops from a somatic cell, which is comparable to a zygotic embryo; **4.** Plant cells lacking cell wall are called protoplasts ; **5.** A hybrid produced by fusion of somatic cells of two species is called somatic hybrid ; **6.** Biotechnology may be defined as the use of microorganisms, animals or plant cells, or their components to generate products and services useful to human beings ; **7.** A gene that is transferred into an organism by genetic engineering is called transgene ; **8.** An organism that contains and expresses a transgene is called transgenic organism ; **9.** Sustainable agriculture primarily uses renewable resources, which cause minimum pollution and obtain optimum yield level ; **10.** When media and instruments are treated with steam, dry heat or alcohol, or subjected to filtration to make them free from microbes is called sterilisation ; **11.** It is maintenance and growth of plant cells, tissues and organs on a suitable culture medium *in vitro* ; **12.** It is a plant part that is excised from its original location and used for initiating a culture ; **13.** In callus culture, cell division in the explant forms a callus which is an unorganised mass of cells ; **14.** It consists of single cells and small groups of cells suspended in a liquid medium ; **15.** The ability of plant cells to regenerate into complete plants is called totipotency ; **16.** The development of an organised structure, like root, shoot or somatic embryo from cultured cells, **17.** It is the use of plant cells to generate useful products and/or services ; **18.** Plant cells lacking cell wall are called protoplasts ; **19.** The production technologies based on genetic engineering are often referred to as modern biotechnology; **20.** A crop that contains and expresses a transgene ; **21.** The food prepared from the produce of transgenic crops (genetically modified GM) ; **22.** Biopesticides are those biological agents that are used for control of weeds, insects and pathogens.

Short Answer Questions

1. Write a note on single-cell protein (SCP).
2. Explain the term 'biopatent'.
3. Explain the term 'biowar'.
4. What is 'biopiracy' ?
5. What are 'biowar agents' ?
6. Explain the term 'bioethics'.
7. What is 'genetically modified food' ? Explain.
8. What is 'sustainable agriculture' ? Explain.
9. What are 'bioweapons' ? Explain.
10. Write a note an 'suspension cultures'.
11. What is 'subculturing' ? Explain the process.

12. What are uses of somatic hybrids ?
13. What is Hirudin ? How is it obtained ?
14. What is anther culture ? Explain.
15. What is old biotechnology ? Write a note.
16. Explain the terms 'callus and 'suspension cultures'.
17. What is 'meristem culture' ? Explain.
18. What is 'biopiracy' ? Write a note.
19. Write a note on 'embryo culture'.
20. What are biofertilizers ? Explain.
21. Describe the importance of mycorrhiza, cyanobacteria and bacteria in biofertilizers.
22. Why are biofertilizers preferred over chemical fertilizers ?
23. What are green manures ? What are their uses ?
24. What are biofertilizers ? How do mycorrhiza act as an entity ?
25. Explain the meaning of the following and their relevance to human welfare in not more than 100 words.
26. Why are biofertilizers or biopesticides preferred to chemical fertilizers or pesticides ?
27. What are advantages and disadvantages of biofertilizers ?

Long Answer Questions

1. Discuss the role of plant tissue culture in increasing food production.
2. Elaborate as to how biotechnology can be helpful in achieving sustainable agriculture.
3. 'Biotechnology can greatly promote human welfare, but it can also be misused to increase human sufferings', comment on the statement with the help of suitable examples.
4. Bring out the salient features through which biotechnology can lead to higher food production.
5. Give a schematic representation of initiation of callus and suspension cultures ?
6. How would you differentiate between callus and suspension cultures ?
7. Give a schematic representation of micropropagation.
8. What are biopatents ? Give their advantages and disadvantages.
9. How does GM food differ from conventional food ? What harm is expected from it ?
10. What can a transgene do on entering the genome of another organisation ?
11. Define biofertilizers. Describe any four sources of biofertilizers.
12. Dicuss the biological methods for the control of insect pests.

MULTIPLE CHOICE QUESTIONS (Objective Type Questions)

1. The tool of genetic engineering which makes it successful is

   (*a*) DNA polymerase (*b*) Permease
   (*c*) Restriction endonuclease (*d*) Topoisomerase

2. Restriction endonucleases are :

   (*a*) Synthesised by bacteria
   (*b*) Present in mammalian cells for degradation of DNA
   (*c*) Used for *in vitro* DNA synthesis
   (*d*) Used in genetic engineering

3. Restriction endonucleases are used in genetic engineering, because :

   (*a*) They can degrade harmful proteins
   (*b*) They can join DNA fragments
   (*c*) They can cut DNA at specific base sequences

(*d*) They can cut DNA at variable sites.

4. Structure involved in genetic engineering is :

(*a*) Plasmid (*b*) Codon (*c*) Plastid (*d*) Scissors

5. One of the following is used to join the segments of DNA during genetic engineering :

(*a*) Lipase (*b*) Ligase (*c*) Gyrase (*d*) Helicase

6. Genetic engineering is possible because :

(*a*) Phenomenon of transduction in bacteria is well understood

(*b*) We can see DNA by electron microscope

(*c*) We can cut DNA at specific sites by endonucleases like DNAase I

(*d*) Restriction endonucleases purified from bacteria can be used *in vitro*.

7. The transgenic animals are those which have :

(*a*) Foreign DNA in some of their cells (*b*) Foreign DNA in all of their cells

(*c*) Foreign RNA in all of their cells (*d*) Both (*a*) and (*c*)

8. Wine and beer are produced directly by fermentation. Brandy and whisky require both fermentation and distillation because :

(*a*) Fermentation is inhibited at an alcoholic level of 10-18%

(*b*) Distillation prolongs storage

(*c*) Distillation improves quality

(*d*) Distillation purifies the beverage

9. Which of the following organelles is related with genetic engineering :

(*a*) Mitochondria (*b*) Golgi apparatus (*c*) Plasmids (*d*) Lysosomes

10. Genetically engineered bacteria have been used in commercial production of :

(*a*) Thyroxine (*b*) Testosterone (*c*) Human insulin (*d*) Melatonin

11. The main technique involved in agricultural biotechnology is called :

(*a*) Tissue culture (*b*) Transformation (*c*) Plant breeding (*d*) NA replication

12. When the genotype of an organism is improved by the addition of foreign genes, the process is called :

(*a*) Biotechnology (*b*) Tissue culture (*c*) Genetic engineering (*d*) Genetic diversity

13. Genetic engineering would not have been possible if which of the following were not known :

(*a*) DNA polymerase (*b*) RNA synthetase

(*c*) DNA ligase (*d*) Reverse transcriptase

14. Which of the following is a genetic vector :

(*a*) Plasmid (*b*) Phage (*c*) Cosmid (*d*) All of these

15. Genetic engineering is :

(*a*) Plastic surgery (*b*) Addition or removal of genes

(*c*) Study of extranuclear genes (*d*) All the above

16. Plasmids occur in :

(*a*) Viruses (*b*) Chromosomes (*c*) Bacteria (*d*) Chloroplasts

17. 'Molecular scissors' used in genetic engineering is :

(*a*) DNA polymerase (*b*) DNA ligase

(*c*) Restriction endonuclease (*d*) Helicase

18. Which of the following correctly defines a transgenic animal ?

(*a*) An animal which has foreign DNA in all its cells because of an injection of DNA into the nuclei of the zygote from which it is developed

(*b*) An animal which has foreign DNA in all its cells because of an injection of DNA into the nuclei of some of the cells in adulthood.

(*c*) An animal which has foreign DNA and RNA in some of its cells because of an injection of DNA and RNA into the nucleus of the zyyote from which it is developed.

(*d*) An animal which has foreign DNA in some of its cells because of an injection of DNA, into the nuclei of some of the cells of the blastocyst.

19. A chemical substance derived from a living source that has the capacity to inhibit growth or destroy microbes is called :

(*a*) Vaccine (*b*) Toxoid (*c*) Toxin (*d*) Antibiotic

20. Biopiracy is related to which of the following :

(*a*) Traditional knowledge

(*b*) Biomolecules and regarding bioresources, genes isolated from bioresources

(*c*) Bioresources

(*d*) All of the above

21. Which of the following is used in biowar ?

(*a*) A pathogen

(*b*) Toxin from a pathogen

(*c*) A delivery system for the bioweapon agent

(*d*) All of the above

22. Which of the following can be controlled by using biopesticides ?

(*a*) Insects (*b*) Diseases (*c*) Weeds (*d*) All of them

23. Which of the following is included in biopesticides ?

(*a*) Viruses and bacteria

(*b*) Viruses, bacteria and fungi

(*c*) Viruses, bacteria, fungi, protozoa and mites

(*d*) Viruses, bacteria, fungi and protozoa

24. Biofertilizers include :

(*a*) Blue-green algae, rhizobia, other nitrogen-fixing bacteria and mycorrhiza fungi

(*b*) Blue-green algae, rhizobia and other nitrogen-fixing bacteria

(*c*) Rhizobia, other nitrogen-fixing bacteria and mycorrhiza fungi

(*d*) Blue-green algae, rhizobia and mycorrhiza fungi.

25. Embryo culture is used for :

(*a*) establishing suspension culture (*b*) recovery of interspecific hybrids

(*c*) somatic hybridization (*d*) haploid production

ANSWERS

1. (*c*) **2.** (*d*) **3.** (*c*) **4.** (*a*) **5.** (*b*) **6.** (*d*) **7.** (*b*) **8.** (*a*) **9.** (*c*) **10.** (*c*)
11. (*a*) **12.** (*a*) **13.** (*c*) **14.** (*a*) **15.** (*c*) **16.** (*c*) **17.** (*c*) **18.** (*a*) **19.** (*d*) **20.** (*d*)
21. (*d*) **22.** (*d*) **23.** (*c*) **24.** (*a*) **25.** (*b*)

UNIT - 6
ECOLOGY

23
CHAPTER

Organisms and the Environment

The world 'environment' commonly means 'a surrounding'. The life containing and life supporting environment is restricted to a very irregular layer, five to twenty ten thick, around the globe. Life could orignate and flourish on earth only because the environment of this planet provides the necessary conditions for it.

Every organism lives amongst living (biotic) and non-living (abiotic) objects, events, and influences, the aggregate of which constitutes the environment for their sustenance. Close interaction between the organism and the environment of which it is a part, is essential to satisfy the basic necessities of life.

Thus, the environment can be defined as the sum total of all the physical and biotic conditions which influence the response of organisms.

Ecology is the branch of biology that deals with the study of interaction between organism and their environment. For the first time, the term ecology was coined by a German biologist, Ernst Haeckel in 1869. The origin of this word, was from the Greek word Oikos meaning 'home' and logos meaning 'to study'.

Like other fields of learning, the developments in the field of ecology have been gradual. This science has progressed from natural history and biography to ecosystem ecology. In modern days, global ecology with an emphasis on climate change, biodiversity conservation and ecological sustainability has been emphasised.

What do we study in ecology ? In ecology, we study the distribution and abundance of organism, their interactions among themselves and with the physical environment. The physical environment consists of (*i*) lithosphere (*ii*) hydrosphere and the (*iii*) atmosphere.

In this chapter, the effects of environment factors on organisms, the significance of the range of tolerance, and adaptation of organisms to varying physical environmental conditons have been discussed.

LEVELS OF ORGANISATON

Biology is a field of enquiry from genes to the ecosystems, which form a spectrum of several levels of organisation.

These levels, in the ascending order of complexity are arranged into a graded series, they are : genes → cells → organs → individual organism → population → biological community → ecosystem → land scape → biome → biosphere.

Here, one level of organisation integrates with the other level. However, there are no sharp lines in the functional sense among various levels. The ecological levels of organisation are as follows :

Organisms. They make the basic unit of study in ecology. At each level, the biological unit has a specific structure and function. At this level, the form, physiology, behaviour, distribution and adptations in relation to the environmental conditions are studied.

The organisms of the smilar type have the potential for interbreeding, and produce fertile offspring, which are called **species**.

The organism performs all the life processes independently. However, parts of organism cannot exist independently of one another.

An organism is fully adapted to its environment. It has a definite life span including definite series of stages like birth, hatching, growth, maturity, senescence, aging and death.

Competition, mutualism and predation are various types of interaction between organisms.

Population. In ecology, a population is a group of individuals of the same species, inhabiting the same area, and functioning as a unit of biotic community.

For example, all individuals of the common grass, *Cynodon*, in a given area constitute its population. Similarly, the individuals of elephants or tigers in an area constitute their population.

The interaction between populations are generally studied. These interactions may be a predator and its prey, or a parasite with its host. Competition, mutualism, commensalism, parasitism, and predation are various types of interactions.

Biological community. Biotic community organisation results from intedependence and interactions amongst population of different species in a habitat. This is an assemblage of populations of plants, animals, bacteria and fungi that live in an area and interact with each other.

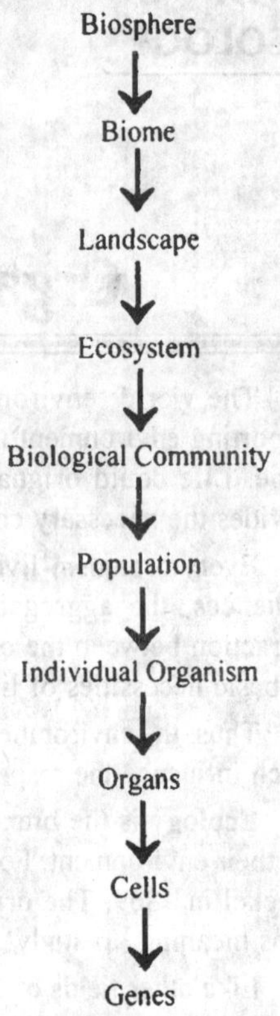

Fig. 23.1. Levels of organisation in ascending series.

A biotic community is a higher ecological category next to population. These are three types of biotic community, they are : animals, plants and decomposers (*i.e.*, bacteria and fungi). A biotic community has a distinet species composition and structure.

Ecosystem. The ecosystems are parts of nature where living organisms interact amongst themselves and with their physical environment. An ecosystem in composed of a biotic community, integrated with its physical environment through the exchange of energy and recycling of the nutrients. The term ecosystem was coined by Sir Arthur Tansley in 1935.

Ecosystems can be recognised as self-regulating and self-sustaining units of landscape, *e.g.*, a pond or a forest. An ecosystem has two basic components : (*i*) abiotic (non-living) and (*ii*) biotic (living organisms). Abiotic components comprise inorganic materials, such as carbon, nitrogen, oxygen, CO_2, water etc., while biotic components include producers, consumers and decomposers.

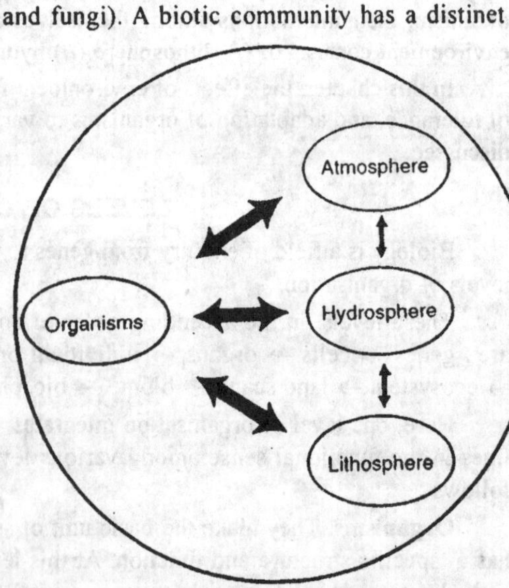

Fig. 23.2. The interaction of organisms with atmosphere.

Landscape. A landscape is a unit of land with a natural boundary having a mosaic of patches, which generally represent different ecosystems.

Biome. This is a large regional unit characterised by a major vegetation type and associated fauna found in a specific climate zone. The biome includes all associated developing and modified communities occurring within the same climatic region, *e.g.*, forest biomes, grassland and savanna biomes, desert biome, etc.

On a global scale, all the earth's terrestrial biomes and aquatic systems constitute the biosphere.

Biosphere. The entire inhabited part of the earth and its atmosphere including the living components is called the biosphere. The global environment consists of three main sub-divisions : (*i*) the hydrosphere which includes all the water components, (*ii*) the lithosphere comprises the solid components of the earth's crust, and (*iii*) the atmosphere formed of the gaseous envelope of the earth. The biosphere consists of the lower atmosphere, the land and the oceans, rivers and lakes, where living beings are found.

ENVIRONMENT, HABITAT AND NICHE

Environment

The word 'environment' commonly means 'a surrounding', but in the context of life it means much more. Life could originate and flourish on earth only because this environment of this planet provides the necessary conditions for it. All organisms, *i.e.* microbes, plants and animals including man, depend upon the environment for their sustenance.

Thus, environment is the sum total of all biotic (living) and abiotic (non-living) factors that surround and potentially influence an organism. Every organism lives in the midst of various living and non-living objects, events and influences. Some components of the environment act as resource, which others act as regulatory factor.

The environment and the organisms are both products of a continuing process of universal change. Each plant or animal species of today is the outcome of millions of years of biological evolution, and any form of life once lost cannot be recreated. Thus, all existing living forms including man are related somehow to one another through common ancestry.

The different components, of the environments are interlinked and interdependent.

Spatial and Time Scales of Environment

Interaction of organisms with their environment takes place at several spatial and time scale.

For example, a single bacterium in soil, interacts with air and water within a fraction of a cubic centimeter space.

On the other land, a tree interacts with a large volume of air, water and soil at a large spatial scale.

The environment varies from place to place due to variations in climate, soil type and topography.

The activities of the organisms influence the hydrosphere, the lower atmosphere and the near surface part of the lithosphere. These activities happen due to exchanges of matter and energy.

On the other land, organisms have to cope with the external environment over a range of time scales. The time scales may be of few minutes, days, seasons or even much longer periods of geological time scale.

For example, phytoplankton populations may change within a few days with the change in light conditions in aquatic systems.

However, the variations in lithosphere occur very slowly over a long period of time.

The ecological factors that influence theorganisms have been classified into two major groups. They are :

(*i*) **Direct factors.** For example : light, temperature, humidity, soil moisture, soil nutrients, soil air, etc.

(*ii*) **Indirect factors.** For example : soil structure, precipitation, wind, soil organisms, altitude, slope, etc.

Climate

Climate is the referred to as the average weather of an area, including general patterns of atmospheric conditions seasonal variations and weather extremes averaged over a long period.

While, the short-term properties of the atmosphere, such as temperature, pressure, humidity, rainfall, sunshine, cloud cover and wind, at a given place and time, as a whole called weather.

The weather reflects the hourly, daily or weekly changes in the above mentioned properties, while the climate exhibits the longer periods, such as season or years together.

Temperature and the rainfall are two most important factors which determine the climate of an area. Thus the climate includes the undermentioned main factors : (*a*) Light, (*b*) Temperature (*c*) Rainfall and atmospheric humidity and (*d*) Air and atmosphere.

Global variations of temperature and rainfall result from : (*i*) differential input of solar radiation in different regions, and (*ii*) from the redistribution of heat energy by winds and ocean currents.

Variations in temperature, rainfall and humidity in different regions of the world form global climate patterns, which govern all life that prevails on earth.

Climatic zones. On the basis of variation in mean temperature along latitude, the main climatic regions are follows :

They are distributed in four categories.

(*i*) Tropical region (0°– 20° latitude)

(*ii*) Sub-tropical region (20°– 40° latitude)

(*iii*) Temperate region (40°– 60° latitude)

(*iv*) Arctic and Antarctic regions (60°– 80° latitude)

The special characteristic of climatic zones are as follows :

(*i*) The mean temperature declines from tropical to arctic region.

(*ii*) In the similar way, as we move from the lower altitude to the higher altitude, in the mountains the mean temperature decreases. Thus, a mountain located in a tropical region will sucessively have tropical → subtropical → temperate and → alpine zones, with increasing alitutude.

(*iii*) Similarly, in temperate zone, the high altitudes will have alpine climatic conditions.

(*iv*) Within each temperature-based climatic zone, the annual rainfall or snowfall varies considerably, and these two factors, *i.e.* temperature and rainfall, determine the vegetation and soil types.

Generally, climate in of two types : (*i*) Microclimate and (*ii*) Macroclimate.

(*i*) **Microclimate.** The microclimate represents the climatic conditions that prevail at local scale or in areas of limited size, *e.g.* the immediate surroundings of plants and animals. This is owing to the uneven topography, plants cover, etc. The microclimates are recognisable only in a very small area and they are sufficient to induce marked local variations in type of composition of vegetation. Thus, microclimate is of much ecological value in the study of plant and animal behaviour.

Microclimate generally differs from the prevailing regional climatic conditions. For example, in a forest, dense foliage reduces the amount of light reaching the ground.

Microclimate also results in changed air temperature profile. In day-time, the air temperature inside the forest is lower than the outside. The interior of a forest in generally more humid than a non-forested area in close vicinity.

(*ii*) **Macroclimate.** In one macroclimatic region there may exist a number of microclimates differing in several respects from the general climate. Forest is an example of macroclimate, where dense forest tall trees are exposed to high intensity of light and temperature, but shrubs growing in the shade of trees do not get the same climatic conditions. Thus, shrubs grow in the environment of dim light, high moisture and low temperature, and again at ground level the conditions are changed where only some peculiar shade loving herbs can thrive.

Habitat and Niche

Habitat. This is a specific place or locality where an organism lives. It is a physical entity that comprises of the sum total of the abiotic factors to which a species or a group of species is exposed. Habitat usually refers to a relatively large area, such as a pond, a forest, an estuary or an ocean.

Habitats are characterised by conspicuous physical features, which include the dominant forms of plant and animal life. The habitat may be referred to the place occupied by an entire biological community. For example, a large number of species of plants and animals are formed in a forest habitat.

The habitats can be further subdivided into parts, which exhibit distinct properties and give shelter to different types of organisms, such habitats are called **microhabitats**. For example, the muddy bottom and a surface water of a pond tree canopy and forest floor are microhabitats.

Some animals are very specific to their habitat, while others have wider choices. For example, *Fubifex*, an annelid lives in flowing fresh water which is rich both in organic content and oxygen on the other hand, the *Chironomous* larvae (insect larvae) can survive in water with very low oxygen content. Certain fishes can live only in fresh water, while others e.g. Hilsa can live in both fresh water and saline water.

Ecological niche. The ecological niche of an organism represents the range of conditions that if can tolerate, the resources it utilises, and its functional role in ecological system. Each species of a community lives in a very specific part of a habitat and performs certain functions. The habitat together with the functions forms the niche of the species.

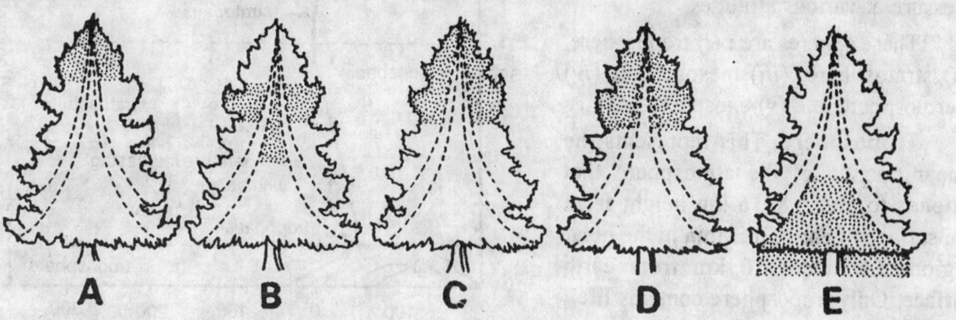

Fig. 23.3. Several species of birds often use the same tree for feeding and nesting, but each species uses a specific zone.

In other words, the concept of ecological niche includes factors, such as food relations, predators, tolerance levels and other habits as well as abiotic factors. Each species within a community has a separate ecological niche. No two species within a given community can have exactly the same niche and live permanently together. In such case, there would be a direct competition with each other till one eliminates the other.

ENVIRONMENTAL FACTORS

As we know, the global environment consists of three main sub-divisions :

1. The Hydrosphere. It includes all the water (liquid) component of the oceans, seas, rivers and other inland water bodies.

2. The Lithosphere. This comprises of solid components of the earth's crust, i.e., rocks, soil and minerals.

3. The Atmosphere. This is formed of the gaseous cover which envelops the hydrosphere and the lithosphere.

The entire inhabited part of the earth and its atmosphere including the living and the non-living components forms the **biosphere**. Thus, biosphere is the combination of all the ecosystem or indefinite units of the earth environment's.

The physical environment consists of factors, such as air, light, heat, water, soil and wind. These abiotic factors determine the success of an organism through their effect on structure, life-history, physiology and behaviour.

Growth and reproduction of an organism are also affected by biotic factors, which include all other organisms in the habitat.

Role of various factors in biotic and abiotic process have been discussed here.

The Atmosphere

The atmosphere is divided into a series of **atmospheric layers** or **spheres,** due to variations in temperature and pressure at various attitudes.

These spheres are : (*i*) troposphere, (*ii*) stratosphere, (*iii*) mesosphere, (*iv*) thermosphere and (*v*) exosphere.

Troposphere. This represents the linear portion of the atmosphere that extends to about 8–16 km height from the surface of earth. It is thin in the polar regions *i.e.* about 10 km from earth surface. Only troposphere contains life.

It contains more than 90 per cent of gases in the atmosphere. Nitrogen and

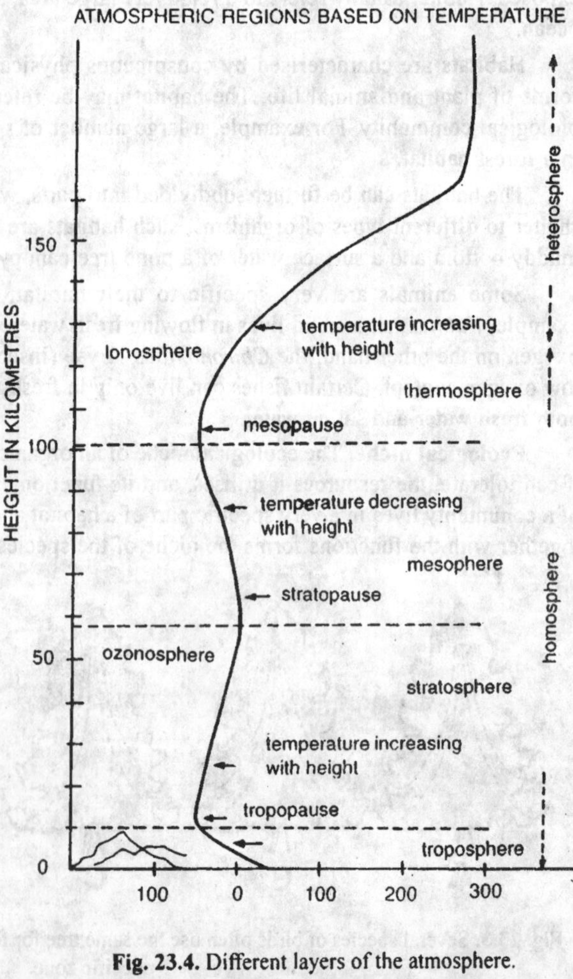

Fig. 23.4. Different layers of the atmosphere.

oxygen are the most aboundant gases in the troposphere, constituting 78.0 per cent and 20.9 per cent of the volume of total gases, respectively.

Generally temperature decreases with increasing height upto **tropopause**, *i.e.*, top of troposphere. The average temperature near the soil surface in about 15°C. The temperature lowers down to –57°C at the tropopause, which denote the transition to the stratosphere.

Stratosphere. The second layer of air mass above tropopause is called stratosphere. It extends upto 30 – 50 km. There is little mixing of gases between the troposphere and stratosphere. However, a thin layer of ozone is present in the stratosphere at the height of 15 to 30 km. The uppermost layer of stratosphere is **stratosphere**, which is the transition layer between the stratosphere and the mesosphere. In this zone, the temperature shows an increase in temperature from a minimum of about – 60°C to maximum of 5°C. The increase in temperature is due to ozone formation under the influence of UV (ultraviolet) rays of solar radiation.

Mesosphere. The third layer of atmosphere next to stratopause in called mesosphere. It extends upto an altitude of 80 km and shows a decrease of temperature with height. The mesosphere is characterised by low atmospheric pressure and low temperature. The temperature begins to drop down from stratopause, goes on decreasing with the increase in height, and seconds a minimum of about 95°C at a level of 80 km or above. The upper limit of the mesosphere is called mesopause.

Thermosphere. Next to mesosphere is thermosphere, which extends upto 500 km above the earth surface. Thermosphere is characterised by steady temperature increase with the height from mesopause. The thermosphere includes the regions in which ultraviolet radiations and cosmic rays cause ionisation of molecules like oxygen and nitric oxide. This region is called **ionosphere**. In ionosphere, molecules of gases are so widely spaced that high frequency audible sound is not carried by the atmosphere.

Exosphere. The rest of the region of the atmosphere above the thermosphere is called **exosphere** or outer space, which lacks atoms, except those of hydrogen and helium. This extends upto 32190 km above the earth surface. Exosphere has a very high temperature due to solar radiation. The earth's magnetic field becomes more important than gravity in distribution in of atomic particles in the exosphere.

Homosphere extends upto 100 km from earth's surface. It is homogeneous due to air circulation in it.

Hetrosphere is the outer region of thermosphere, which bears gases mixed with radioactive substances.

Air

Air Compositon. Nitrogen and oxygen are major gases in the troposphere, where nitrogen is 78 per cent while oxygen 20.9 per cent. The remaining 1 per cent consists of Argon, water vapour, carbon dioxide, ozone and other gases.

Table 23.1. Air composition

Constituent	*Percentage of volume*
Nitrogen	78 per cent
Oxygen	20.9 per cent
Carbon dioxide	0.03 per cent
Argon	0.23 per cent

Though water vapour, carbon dioxide and ozone (O_3) occur in minute quantities in the atmosphere, yet they are essential for maintaining life on earth.

Ozone occurs only in minute traces in the atmosphere and has a peak concentration around 25 km above the surface of the earth. At no level is its concentration more than a millionth of the main atmosphere. If the entire ozone content is compressed at normal temperature and pressure, it will constitute a layer only 3 mm thick. But it has played a vital role in the evolution of life. The life sustaining role comes from the fact that radiations below 300 mm are biologically harmful, the UV radiation. Any large scale depletion of the ozone content can have devastatory effect on all biological systems, including plants.

Water vapour regulates the hydrological cycle, which sustain life in both terrestrial and aquatic systems. This also absorbs infrared radiation from the earth.

Carbon dioxide, water vapour and ozone play an important role in maintaining the heat balance of the earth. The composition of the atmosphere is a product of the activities of living organisms.

Gases in water. In the aquatic systems, oxygen (O_2), carbon dioxide (CO_2), and other gases are paritally dissolved in water.

In water bodies, oxygen may be a limiting factor for the growth of phytoplankton, and other aquatic organisms, generally in deep lakes, which receive heavy loads of organic materials.

The oxygen supply in water in regulated through diffussion from the air and from photosynthetic activity.

Carbondioxide is highly soluble in water and may be found in variable amounts. CO_2 combines with water and results in carbonic acid (H_2CO_3). The carbonic acid reacts with available limestone and form carbonates (CO_3^{-2}) and bicarbonates (HCO_3^{-1}).

Light

Light is the most essential abiotic factor without which no life can sustain on earth. It is non-lethal limiting factor both at the maximum and minimum levels. The main natural sources of light are-sunlight, moonlight, star light and light producing or luminescent organisms.

Light affects many physiological activities of the plants, *e.g.* photosynthesis, respiration, opening and closing of stomata, growth and flowering of plants, etc. Similarly, light as a complex physical factor, affects the colour vision, eye-size, skin pigmentation, reproduction and biological periodicity of the animals.

Electromagnetic spectrum. Sun is the ultimate source of energy for most organisms on earth, directly or indirectly. The radiant energy coming from the sun in the form of visible spectrum is called light or luminous energy. When the visible sublight in passed through a prism, it is disposed into a series of wavelengths exihibiting seven different colours, *i.e.* violet, indigo, blue, green, yellow, orange and red (VIBGYOR).

Solar radiation, before entering the atmosphere, at 83 km above the earth surface carries energy at a constant rate of 2 cal cm^{-2} min^{-1} in known as solar constant.

Solar spectrum comprises short wave radiation, light and long wave radiation. The short wave radiations include cosmic rays, X-rays and ultraviolet (UV)rays, which have wavelengths shorter than 0.4 to 0.7 mm. This is also known as photosynthetically active radiation (PAR). However, the infrared wavelengths are longer than 0.740 mm.

The ultraviolet (UV) radiation wavelengths are 0.1 mm to 0.4 mm. They are strongly absorbed by ozone (O3) layer present in the stratosphere, and only a small fraction of UV radiation reaches the surface of the earth.

As regards to their wavelength, these are three types of ultraviolet radiation. These are : (*i*) **UV–C** (0.100 to 0.280 mm), (*ii*) **UV–B** (0.280 to 0.320 mm) and (*iii*) **UV–A** (0.320 to 0.400 mm). Out of these three radiation types, **UV–C** radiation type is lethal, and UV–B is harmful to the organisms.

Earth is a very small object in solar system and if receives only 1–50 millionth part of the total solar radiation reaching the universe. The journey of solar energy from sun to earth surface is very much moderated while if passes through stratosphere and the atmospheric envelope surrounding the earth. In the strasphere lies the ozone layer which absorbs the harmful solar radiations of short wavelengths. At any place on the earth surface the energy flux varies with season, time of day and atmospheric humidity and drought.

From the ecological point of view, the energy and its utilisation is most important in sustenance of life. Many of the environmental phenonmena, such as movement of wind currents, rainfall, chemical actions and organic behaviour are controlled by energy.

Effects of light on plants. Light affects many physiological activities of the plants the quality, the intensity and duration of light are important to organisms. Here quality of light means, its wavelength, the intensity means, energy measured in calories and the duration means, the length of day.

The intensity of light varies with latitude and time of the day.

Light affects the processes of (*i*) photosynthesis, (*ii*) respiration, (*iii*) opening and closing of stomata, (*iv*) growth and flowering of plants, (*v*) movements, (*vi*) germination of seeds and (*vii*) reproduction. Light is also an important factor in distribution of plants. Some plants grow and flourish in full sunlight, while others prefer shade and called shade loving plants.

The quality of light plays an important role in flower induction, seed germination and plant movements.

The duration of light regulates the phenological processes, such as flowering and fruiting in plants. The timing of seasonal activites of plants in relation to change in environmental comditions is called **phenology**.

For more details you can consult chapters 3, 4 and 13, *i.e.*, Photosynthesis, Respiration, Plant Growth and Movements, respectively.

On the other hand, in many animals, migration, hibernation and reproduction are controlled by the relative lengths of day and night. The photoperiod is known to affect breeding behaviour of

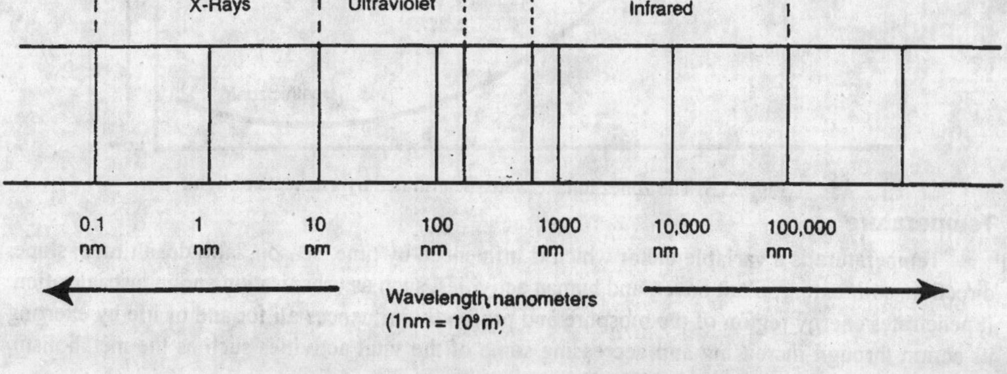

Fig. 23.5. The electromagnetic spectrum of solar radiation.

insects, certain birds and mammals. The animals are divided into three categories : (*i*) short-day animals, *e.g.* sheep, deer, etc. (*ii*) long-day animals, *e.g.*, turkeys, starlings, etc, and (*iii*) day-neutral animals, rabbit, ground squirrel, etc.

Effects of light on aquatic systems. Life activity under water is often controlled by the availability of light.

Light makes a limiting factor for plants in deep waters, *e.g.*, in oceans and deep lakes.

In aquatic systems, the pressure of light determines where producers and consumers are to live in water. For example, ther phytoplanktons (phyto=plants, plankton = small) live in illuminated surface layer of water, whereas benthic organisms are found in the sediments of a lake.

According to penetration of light, a deep lake can be divided into three zones :

1. The littoral zone. This is shallow water around the edge of the lake that supports rooted vegetation. The light penetrates through shallow water.

2. The limnetic zone. The open water zone found beyond the littoral zone in called limnetic zone. In this zone, phytoplankton grows in abundance,. Here light can penetrate, 20 to 40 m depth depending upon clarity of water.

3. The profundal zone. The dark zone, where light does not reach, is called **profundal zone**. The sediments at the bottom of lakes and ponds form the **benthic** region which makes a habitat for benthic organisms, such as snails, slugs and microorganisms.

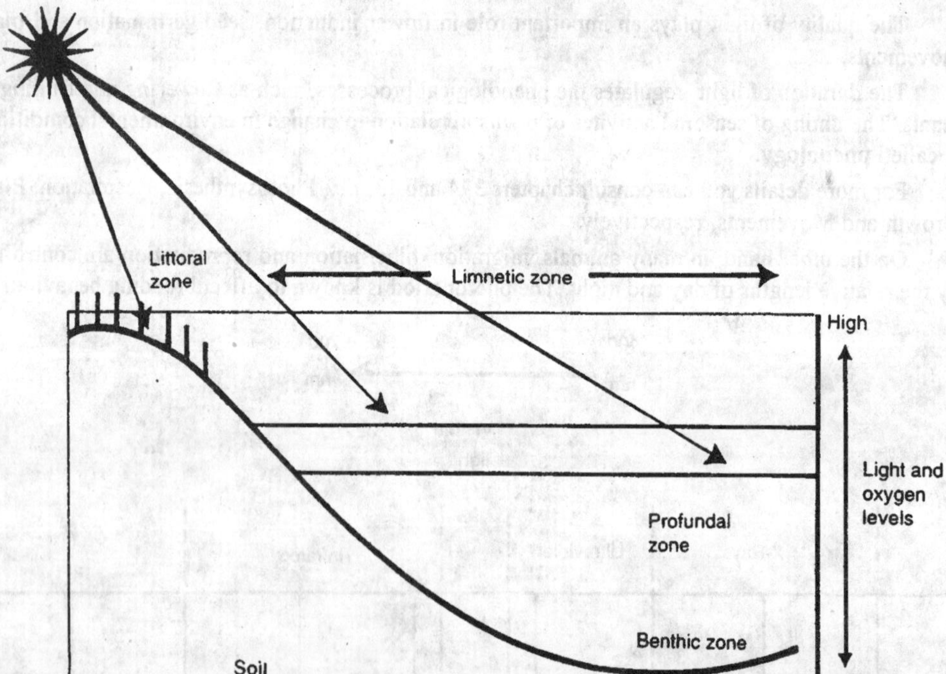

Fig. 23.6. The zones in lake water determined by gradients of light.

Temperature

Temperature is a variable factor which is influenced by time, season, latitude, altitude, slope, direction, soil texture, plant cover, and human activities, such as urbanisation and industrialisation. It penetrates energy region of the biosphre and profundly influences all for and of life by exerting its action through increasing and decreasing some of the vital activities such as the metabolism, reproductive behaviour, enbryonic development and growth.

Temperature is a measure of intensity of heat. In terms of standard unit its is commonly expressed as degrees either in Fahrehenit or Celcius scale. Heat is a form of energy, called thermal energy. Thermal energy is exchanged between animal and environment by radiation, conduction, convection and evaporation. These four basic needs of transfer of heat energy occur within the organisms and in the interface between the organisms and their environment.

Temperature is the degree of hotness or coldness of a substance. The vertical temperature gradient over earth's surface is called **lapse rate**, the value of which is 6.5°C per 1000 m elevation.

Temperature has an emphatic effect on the climatic conditions, growth responses of plants and activities of organisms.

Temperature also acts as a stimulus for plants, determining the timing of their development. for example, thermoperodism (*i.e.*, a day-night temperature differential) is essential for optimum growth of some plants.

Exposure to cold, (*i.e.*, vermalisation) enhances seed germination, as well as induces flouering in some plants.

Thermoregulation and homeostasis. Temperature also controls the rate of processes inside an organism, and other activities.

In cold-blooded animals, also known as **ectotherm**, the body temperaure tends to match with the temperature of the environment, in which they live.

Many active ectotherms, *e.g.*, frogs and snakes, control their body temperature by moving around or by seeking shade. While some ectotherms are nocturnal in habit and they feed during the night.

On the other hand, the **endotherms**, *i.e.*, warm-blooded animals, such as birds and mammals, regulate their body temperature by physiological processes and maintain a more or less constant temperature within their bodies even when the temperature of the environment fluctuates.

The warm-blooded animals (endotherms) have certain physiological mechanisms to keep their body temperature constant or within tolerance limits.

The maintenance of relatively constant internal environment is called **homeostasis**. To maintain a constant body temperature in the case of endotherm or warm-blooded animals provides them a metabolic advantage over other organisms.

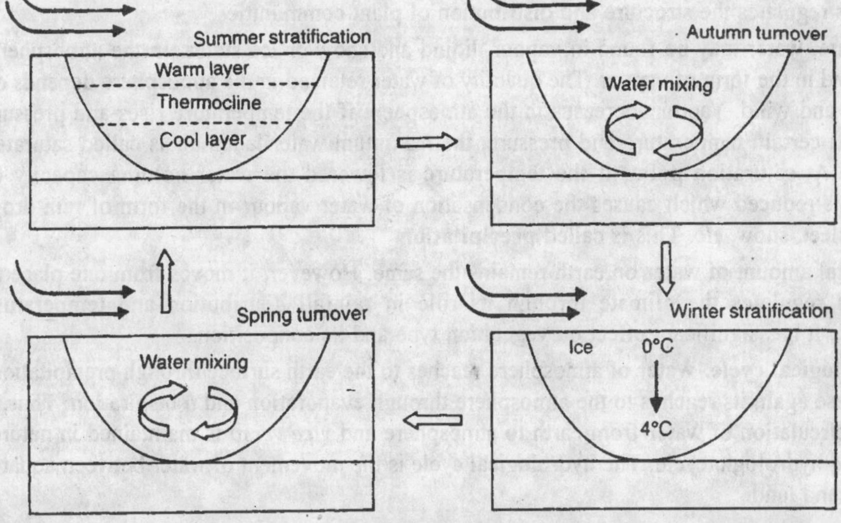

Fig. 23.7. Thermal stratification in temperate lakes.

This is an established fact that biochemical pathways and enzymes often function at their maximum at a temperature about 37°C in endotherms, and threfore, these animals may remain active even under cold conditions by exhibiting different types of adaptations to minimise the loss & heat.

Thermal stratification in lakes. Differences in temperature of at different depths in deep lakes, result in thermal stratification.

During summer, temperature is higher in the surface water, which is separated from the deeper water mass by a **thermocline,** *i.e.*, a zone of gradual change in temperature. During summer, surface water bears a higher temperature, which is separated by deep cold water by thermocline zone. A thermocline often creates two different layers : (*i*) epilimnion, and (*ii*) hypolimnion.

1. Epilimnion. The epilimnion represents the upper layers of water. During winter, in a temperate lake water is at a freezing temperature on the surface. The surface water is cool during autumn and warm in spring. This results in a free mixing of autumn and **spring turnover**. This turnover redistributes oxygen and nutrients, resulting in a bloom of shytoplankton growth.

2. Hypolimnion. The hypolimnion represents the lower layer of water. During winter, the temperature of lower layer remains about 4°C in temperate lakes.

Due to stratified conditions, both in winter and summer, growth of phytoplankton in low due to low nutrients and oxygen supply.

In terrestrial environment temperature fluctuations are varied and marked. Lowest temperature recorded for any land mass is –70°C (in Siberia). Higher temperature, may often reach upto 85°C in deserts at noon. In Rajasthan, the highest temperature exceeds 50°C. Water in hotsprings and geysers may be as high as 100°C.

The temperature varies from place to place and likewise the vegetations of different areas also differ considerably. Desert plants grow in extreme heat; aquatic plants grow in low temperature range, and grasses prefer to grow in the area of moderate temperature.

Water

Water is one of the most important climatic factors. It affects the vital piocesses of all the living beings. This is the sole agent that sets in motion the nutrients of the soil and makes them available to plants. It affects the morphology and physiology of the plants. It in combination with other factors regulates the structure and distribution of plant communities.

In nature, water may be found in vapour, liqiud and snow or ice states. In the atmosphere, water is found in the form of vapour. The quantity of water retained in the atmosphere depends on temperature and wind. Vapour increases in the atmosphere if the temperature rises and pressure decreases. At certain temperature and pressure, the maximum water-laden air is called saturated atmosphere. At saturation point, if the temperature is lowered the water holding capacity of atmosphere is reduced which causes the condensation of water vapour in the form of rain drop, dew, front, sleet, snow, etc. This is called **precipitation**.

The total amount of water on earth remains the same. However, it moves from one place to another and regulates the climate through its role in rainfall distribution and temperature modification. It has significant effect on vegetation type and its conposition.

Hydrological cycle. Water of atmosphere reaches to the earth surface through precipitation, and from these again its reaches to the atmosphere through evaporation and transpiration. Thus, a continuous circulation of water from earth to atmosphere and *vice versa* is maintained in nature. This is called hydrologic cycle. The hydrological cycle is the movement of water between aquatic systems, air and land.

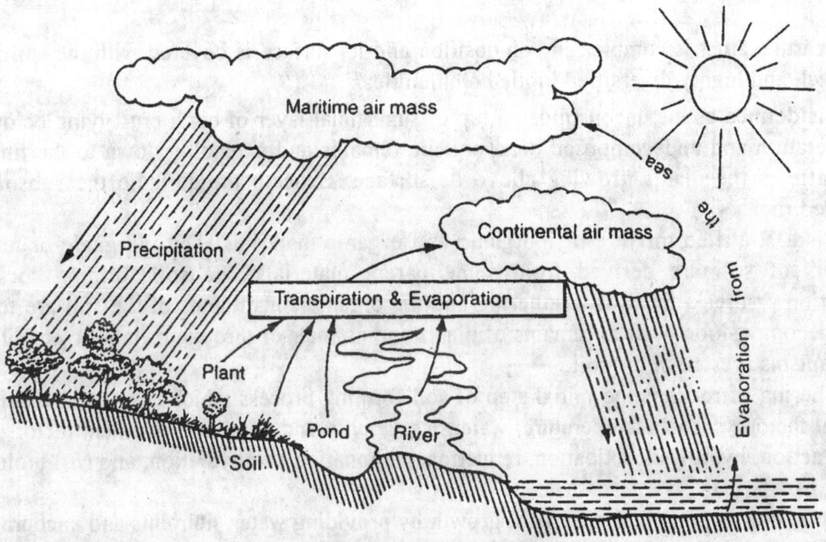

Fig. 23.8. Hydrological cycle in nature.

Water vapour, an important constituent of the atmosphere, can condense to form clouds, and eventually rainfall. Plants play an important role in the hydrological cycle through the process of transpiration. In tropical forests as much as 75 per cent of annual rainfall is returned to the atmosphere by plants, which recharges the atmospheric water vapour.

Rainfall is uneven on earth's surface. For example, deserts recieve very low rainfall, (*i.e.*, less than 100 mm $year^{-1}$) each year, while same areas receive high rainfall, *e.g.*, in Cherrapunji, average rainfall is more than 11,000 mm per year.

Atmospheric humidity. The water vapour present in unit volume of air is called **absolute humidity**. This is expressed in terms of percentage of water vapour present in unit volume of air at certain temperature. The amount of water vapour required to saturate the same unit volume of air under constant physical conditions is called **relative humidity**. This is affected by light intensity, temperature, wind velocity, vegetation and soil water. Relative humidity (RH) is measured by an instrument called hygrometer. It plays an important role both in life of plants and animals.

Plant-water relations. For land plants, the main source of water to soil is rainfall and melting of snow.

The potential energy of water is referred to as water potential. This is the source with which soils hold water and it is quantified in terms of pressure.

At sea level pressure exerted by the atmosphere is one bar which equals about 0.1 megapascals (MPa).

The upper limit of water availability of a soil is called **field capacity**. The water potential of a soil at field capacity is about – 0.01 MPa.

The lower limit of water availability of a soil is called wiliting point. The water potential of a soil at wilting point is about – 1.5 MPa.

While the **osmotic potential** in the roots of plants is responsible for the entrance of water in the roots from the soil.

Plants have adapted to variations in water availability by habitat selection (*e.g.* xerophytes, mesophytes, hydrophytes, etc.) phenological adjustments, or by having higher water use efficiency.

Soil

The earth's crust is complex in composition and its surface is covered with the soil which supports rich and highly diversified biotic communities.

Soil is defined as the unconsolidated top or superficial layer of earth crust lying below any aerial vegetation and undecomposed dead organic remains and extending down to the limits to which if affects the plants growing above its surface. Beneath the soil, lie the subsoil and unweathered rocks.

Soil is a stratified mixture of inorganic and organic materials. The inorganic or mineral constituents of soil are derived from some parent materials, the soil forming rocks by fragmentation or break-down of weathering and the organic constituents of the soil are formed either by decomposition of dead remains of plants and animals or through metabolic activities of living organisms present in the soil.

Weathering of rocks is the initial step of soil forming process which is brought about by : (*i*) physical factors, such as temperature, water, ice, gravity and wind, (*ii*) chemical factors, such as solvent action, hydrolysis, oxidation, reduction, carbonation and hydration, and (*iii*) biological factors.

Soil plays an important role in plant growth by providing water, nutrients and anchorage.

Soils support the growth of crops, grassland and forests on which we depend for food, fibre, wood and building materials.

Edaphic factors are those which are dependent on the soil, such as soil constitution, soil water, soil air, soil organisms, etc.

Soil at different places vary considerably in their structure, components and properties. These differences in the soils are often largely responsible for differences in vegetation within the same climatic region, and consequently of great significance in the distribution of plant communities.

The mineral composition of soils depends on the minerals in the parent material and the extent of weathering.

Soil profile. The vertical layered structure of soil is called the **soil profile**. It develops due to weathering process, accumulation of organic matter and the leaching of mineral matter.

These are four main horizons in a soil profile : the O-horizon is the organic layer composed of lead organic residues, found above the A-horizon.

The A-horizon, also called the **top soil**, is the uppermost mineral layer, which also contains roots and partially decomposed organic matter. The A-horizon designates the top stratum which is subjected to marked leaching.

The B-horizon is the subsoil, lying under A-horizon has little organic matter, very few plant roots and a sparse microflora and fauna. In it, iron and aluminium compounds are often accumulated. A and B-horizons collectively represent the true soil.

The C-horizon represent, the less weathered parent maeatrial. In this layer the organic matters are present in small amounts and little or no life is present.

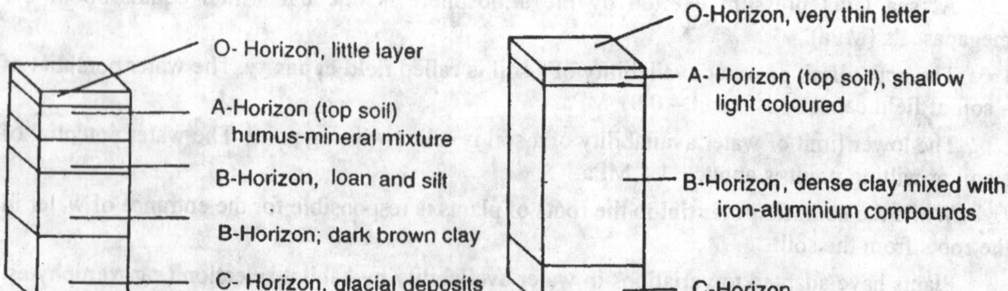

Fig. 23.9. Soil profile. A, temperate deciduous forests; B, tropical rain forests.

The development of soil profile is mainly governed by the climate and the kind of vegetation. Here, in the following figures, the soil profiles of a temperate deciduous forest and tropical rain forest are given :

Characteristics of soil profile. Soils in forest, grasslands and deserts differ markedly in colour, clay, organic matter content and depth.

In desert soils, the top soil (A-horizon) has little or no humus, while subsoils (B-horizon) make a mixture of sand, clay, minerals and salts.

However, in the grasslands the roots of native plants penetrate deep in the ground, forming a dense sod that holds moisture and prevents erosion. This adds large amount of organic material to soil each year.

While in temperate forest soils, the top soil (A-horizon) is a rich mixture of humus and inorganic soil components as exhibited in Fig. 16.9 A.

In tropical rain forest, dense clay subsoil (B-horizon), heavy rainfall, and high temperatures result in nutrient-poor and shallow soils, as exhibited in Fig. 16.9 B.

Properties of soils. Soils are made up of four components : The two solid substances are : (*i*) small mineral particles and (*ii*) organic matter. The other components are : (*iii*) air (gaseous), and (*iv*) water (liquid).

(*i*) The small mineral particles come from weathering of rocks. They include about 25 elements and of which 16 elements are essential. These are divided into two categories, *i.e.*, macronutrients, such as C, H, O, N, P, S, Ca^{++}, K^{+}, Mg^{++} and micronutirents, such as Fe, Mn, B, Mo, Cu, Zn, and Cl.

(*ii*) The organic matter is of plant and animal origin, both from dead and living organisms.

In an average soil, about 45 percent of the volume is filled with mineral particles and about 5 percent ley organic matter.

The remaining 50 percent of the volume is filled with soil (*iii*) air and (*iv*) water. The amount of air or water varies greatly, depending on how wet soil is at the time.

The proportion of mineral particles of different sizes in soil represents its texture. According to varying soil particles they are divided into following categories. The particles vary in sizes, such as **gravel** (more than 2 mm); **coarse sand** (between 0.2 to 2 mm); **fine sand** (0.02 to 0.2 mm); **silt** (0.002 to 0.02); **clay** (less than 0.002 mm).

Fine texture soils have a predominance of clay and silt particles; while the coarse textured soils have a predominance of sand particles.

Sandy soils. It is formed of 85 percent sand and 15 percent clay and silt, also known as **light soil**. This soil is not rich in nutrients and is less fertile. It is characterised by xerophytic vegetation.

Clayey soil. It is formed of 50 per cent clay and 50 per cent silt or sand or both also known as **cold** or heavy soil. It has high water holding capacity and less water logging.

Silt soil. It has 90 percent silt and 10 percent sand. It has good soil porosity and water holding capacity. This is poor in nutrient supply.

Loamy soil. It is composed of 70 per cent sand and 30 per cent clay or silt or both. This is considered best soil for plant growth. It has good water holding capacity, water infiltration and adequate aeration. Roots penetrate deep in loamy soils.

Soil moisture. Plants absorb a small quantity of rain water and dew directly, but they take a large quantity of water from the soil. Water held in the soil is of following types :

(*i*) **Gravitational water.** This is free water which percolates downwardly through the pore spaces between soil particles and is accumulated in the pore spaces in the form of **ground water**.

(*ii*) **Capillary water.** The amount of water present around the soil particles and held by surface tension and attraction force of water moelcules. Capillary water remains readily available to the roots upto a certain soil moisture tension.

(*iii*) **Hygroscopic water.** Water, which is adsorbed on the soil particles and held on the surface of particles by forces of attraction and cohesion of its molecules. This is the moisture, remaining in air-dry soil, and cannot be used by the plants.

Soil organic matter. The organic matter stored in soil may be divided into two categories:

(*i*) **Detritus or litter.** This is freshly dead and partially decomposed plant and animal material.

(*ii*) **Humus.** This is colloidal, amorphous and dark coloured substance that constitutes the organic component of soil. It is formed by the decomposition of plant and animal remains and has a complex and variable chemical composition. Being a colloid, it can hold water and therefore improves the water retaining properties of soil; it also enhances soil fertilily. **Acidic humus (mor)** is found in region of coniferous forest, where the decay is brought about mainly by fungi. **Alkaline humus (mull)** is typically found in grassland and deciduous forest : it supports an abundance of micro-organisms and small annelids, *e.g.*, earthworms.

A part from the dead organic matter, soil harbours very large number of organisms which include detritus feeders, such as termites, earthworms, carpenter ants and crabs; bacteria and fungi.

The soil organisms act as decomposers and play an important role in decomposition of plant and animal residues.

Fire

Fire is a biological factor rather than a physical factor as it is mostly caused by man's activity. Lightning initiated fires have destroyed plants and animals since their early appearance on earth. A large body of information has been developed on the effects of fire on grassland and forests as well as on the use of fire in land management. Native people in various lands have used fire to enhance hunting, improve visibility and provide forage, etc.

The branch of ecology which deals with the effects of the fire an ecosystem is called **'fire ecology'** or **'ecopyrology'** plants having ability to withstand fire with little or no damage are referred to as **pyrophytes**. Many pyrophytes are known to occur in Siwalik hills of India. The examples of pyrophytes are *Cochlospermum religiosa*, *Combretum nanum*, *Grewia sapida*, etc. These small plants are supposed to have become permanently dwarf by annual forest fires. Pyrophytes are generally woody plants with thick bark.

Fires caused by man's activity are responsible for complete destruction of vegetation at certain places resulting in temporary or permanent alterations in the characters of vegetations. Fire has marked effects on the physical environment through removal of the plant cover, burning of litter mass present on the soil surface, and loss of nutrients due to volatilisation.

There is mortality among a variety of animal groups due to occasional or recurrent fires.

Generally in fires the aerial parts of plants are destroyed completely but their roots, rhizomes or other underground parts may sometimes remain unaffected which under favourable conditions may grow and produce new plants.

Fire generally makes the area suitable for the growth of grasses and thus imporves the quality of forage. Post-burn plants are preferred by herbivores. Animals grazing on burnt grasslands are found to gain in weight more rapidly than these grazing on unburnt grasslands. Fire removes harmful plant parasites and pests.

Fire is an important factor in temperate forest and grassland regions, as well as in tropical areas having dry seasons.

Biotic Factors

The biotic factors include the influence of living organisms,both plants and animals upon the vegetation. The living species may be the producers, (*e.g.*, the green plants) of food or consumers such as herbivores predators, parasites or omnivores.

Any activity of the living organism, which may cause marked effects on vegetation in any way is referred to as **biotic effect**. The biotic effect may be both direct and indirect. It may be beneficial to the plants in some respects but detrimental in other respects. The species may have positive, negative or neutral effect on population growth and well-being of other species.

The plants live together in a community and influence one another. In the forest there are many plant communities, such as trees, shrubs, herbs, mosses and lichens. These communities interact with one another and adjust according to environmental conditions. Trees cast their shadow on many shade-loving plants, which grow around or beneath them. The micro-organisms, such as bacteria, algae and fungi affect the life of plants of a given area in many ways.

Many animals use plants as their food and for shelter as well. Besides animals, the man is most significant agent for modifying the vegetation.

Range of tolerance

The environmental factors vary in their effects, and biological species have a range of tolerance for these factors. Any of these factors which is present in least amount may become limiting. The examples of such limiting factors are as follows :

(*i*) Low temperature limits plant growth at higher elevations.

(*ii*) Water availability limits plant growth in deserts.

(*iii*) Whereas low phosphorus availability limits the growth of phytoplankton in deep lakes.

However, this is noticeable that not only too little amount of something is a limiting factor, but also too much may be a limiting factor for the growth and distribution of an organism.

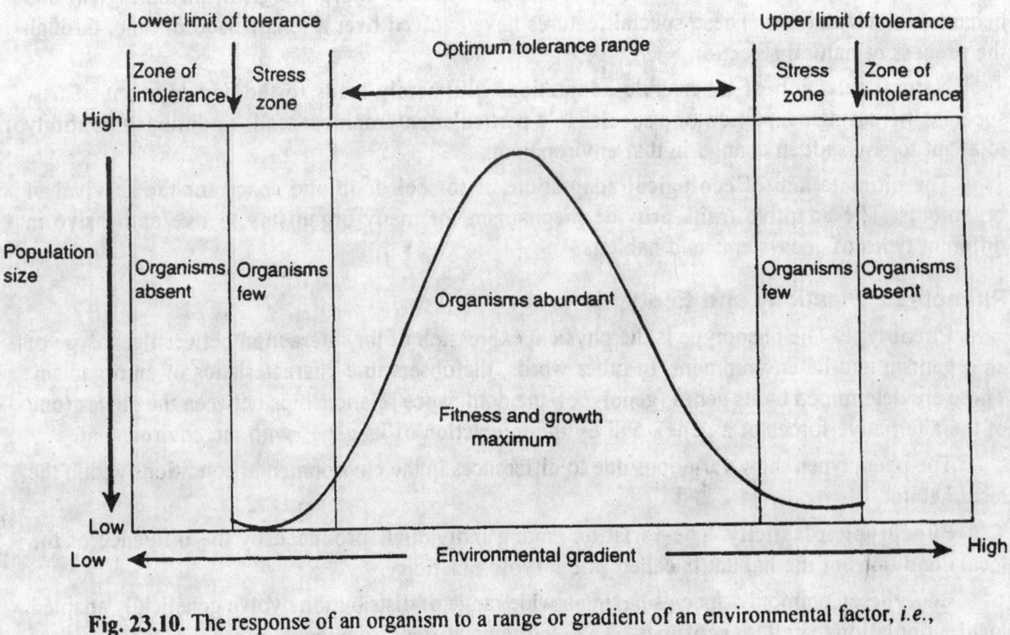

Fig. 23.10. The response of an organism to a range or gradient of an environmental factor, *i.e.*, temperature, light, nutrient.

The organisms show a bell shaped curve (Fig. 23.8) to a range or gradient of a single environmental factor, such as temperature, sunlight or nutrient concentration.

In this curve, the organisms are abundant in the central **optimum** range showing greatest fitness, growth and survival.

On the other hand, in the zone of **stress**, only a few organisms survive and are not able to reproduce. While in the zone of **intolerance** the organisms are absent.

Thus, the range between 'too little' and 'too much' shows the range of tolerance that determines the existence and abundance of an organism.

If the range of tolerance is wide then the organisms are widely distributed, on the other hand when this range is narrow, the distribution of organisms is restricted.

Acclimatisation

The gradual physiological adjustment to slowly changing new environmental conditions is known as **acclimatisation.**

The limits of tolerance and optimal range of distibution may vary in different seasons, in some species of animals. If some environmental factor shifts beyond the limit of tolerance of an organism; in such conditions, the organisms can come to the resting stage or migrate or they can acclimatise them in new environmental conditions.

ECOLOGICAL ADAPTATIONS

The term **adaptation** may be defined : Any change in the structure or functioning of an organism that makes it better suited to its environment. However, the special charcteristics of plants and animals that enable them to be successful under prevailing set of environmental conditions are called **adaptations.**

The organisms in natural world have various types of morphological, physiological and behavioural adaptations. These special features have evolved over a long period of time, through the process of natural selection.

Natural selection of inheritable adaptations ulitimately leads to the development of new species. Increasing adaptation of a species to a particular environment tends to diminish its ability to adapt to any sudden change in that environment.

The ultimate aim of ecological adaptations is to seek food and space for the survival of organioms. The adaptive traits provide mechanism for many organisms to live and thrive in different types of ecosystems and habitats.

Phenotypic Plasticity and Ecotypes

Phenotype. The phenotype is the physical expression of the interaction between genotype of an organism and its environment. In other words, the observable characteristics of an organism. These are determined by its genes (genotype), the dominance relationships between the alleles (one of the alternative forces of a gene), and by the interaction of its genes with the environment.

The phenotypes show variations due to differences in the environmental conditions within the local habitat.

Phenotypic plasticity. The variation among individuals produced by the influence of the local conditions of the habitat is called **phenotypic plasticity**.

Ecotypes. Commonly, species having a wide range of distribution evolve genetically adapted local populations, called **ecotypes**. The ecotypes differ from each other on the basis of morphological and physiological characters. Though ecotypes of a species differ genetically yet they are interfertile. Such ecotypes are commonly found in plants and sessile animals.

Strategies of Adaptations in Plants

The living organisms react with their environments and they bear full impression of the environments in which they grow. In order to withstand adverse conditions of the environment and utilise to their maximum benefit the nutrients and other conditions prevailing therein, the organisms develop certain morphological, anatomical, physiological and reproductive features. Any feature of an organism or its part which enables it to exist under condition of its habitat is called **adaptation**. Every organism develops certain adaptations and so does the population or a community.

Plants have special traits that help them to enlarge their tolerance lmits to : (*i*) light regimes, (*ii*) dry conditions, (*iii*) high temperature, (*iv*) water saturated condition and (*v*) saline environments.

In plants, flowers evolve special structures to ensure pollination by insects or other animals.

Plants also deveop various mechanisms to deal with stress conditions of the environment.

Adaptation to light. Plant communities, as well as individual plants, adapt to different light intensites. These are two categories of such plants :

(*i*) **Sciophytes.** They are also known as shade loving plants. The shade loving or shade adapted plants generally have low photosynthetic, respiratory and metabolic activities. For example, several ferns and other herbaceous plants growing on the ground under dense canopy of trees in forests, are shade tolerant plants.

(*ii*) **Heliophytes.** Such plants are adapted to high intensity of light. They are higher temperature optima for photosynthesis, as well as have high rates of respiration. For example, many tropical plants, particularly grasses which grow in not and arid climates possissing C_4 pathway of photosynthesis.

Adaptations to Water Scarcity and Heat

Plants of hot deserts are adapted to survive in dry conditions of soil and high temperature. Places where available water is not present in adequate quantity are termed **xeric** habitats.The plants growing in xeric conditions are xerophytes. Xeric habitats may be of following types :

(*i*) Habitats physically dry; where water retaining capacity of the soil is very low and the climate is dry, *e.g.*, desert, rock surface, waste land, etc.

(*ii*) Habitats physiologically dry; places water is present in excess amount but it is not such as can be absorbed by the plants easily. Such habitats may be either too salty or too acidic, too hot or too cold.

(*iii*) Habitats dry physically, as well as physiologically, *e.g.*, slopes of mountains.

Drought evading plants. The plants which evade dry conditions are known as **ephemerals.** They are short lived plants. During critical dry periods, they survive in the form of seeds and fruits which have hard and resistant seedcoats and pericarps respectively. For example, in desert areas of Rajasthan, many annual plants germinate from seeds, complete their life cycle quickly during the rainy season and survive in the form of seeds in the following dry season. Thus, plants remain unaffected by extreme dry conditions. Such plants (ephemerals) are quite common in the semiarid zones where rainy season is of short duration. The common examples are : *Astragalus*, *Artemesia*, members Zygophyllaceae, Boraginaceae, grasses, etc.

Deep rooted plants. Some plants have deep tap roots, which can reach even upto water table, in arid climates, hence they are capable of absorbing water from deep soil. Some examples of deep rooted plants are : *Prosopis* (mosquito), palms and some species of *Acacia.*

Plants having deciduous leaves. Many shrubs and trees of dry climate, such as *Acacia nilotica* and *Capparis decidua* have deciduous leaves. But in the majority of the plants the leaves are generally reduced to seeds, as in *Casuarina*, *Ruscus*, *Asparagus*, etc.

Leaves with sunken stomata. For example, stomata are found is sunken pits in the common *Nerium* plant, reducing the rate of transpiration.

In many xerophytes, the leathery leaf surface and waxy cuticle also check the transpiration.

Sometimes the leaves may be reduced to spines, *e.g.* in *Ulex*, *Opuntia*, *Enphorbia*, *Capparis*, *Acacia*, etc.

Succulence. Succulents are those plants in which some organs become smaller and fleshy due to active accumulation of water, or the bulk of the plant body is composed of water storing tissues. Water stored in these tissues is consumed up during the period of extreme arid conditons when the soil becomes depleted of available water. In cacti leaves are reduced to spines, while stems are modified into fleshy and spongy structures.

In leaf succulents, the leaves swell remarkably and become very fleshy owing to storage of excess amount of water and latex in them. Plants with succulent leaves generally develop very reduced stems. The examples of leaf succulents are : *Sedum*, *Aloe*, *Mesembryanthenum*, *Kleinia* and several members of family Chenopodiaceae.

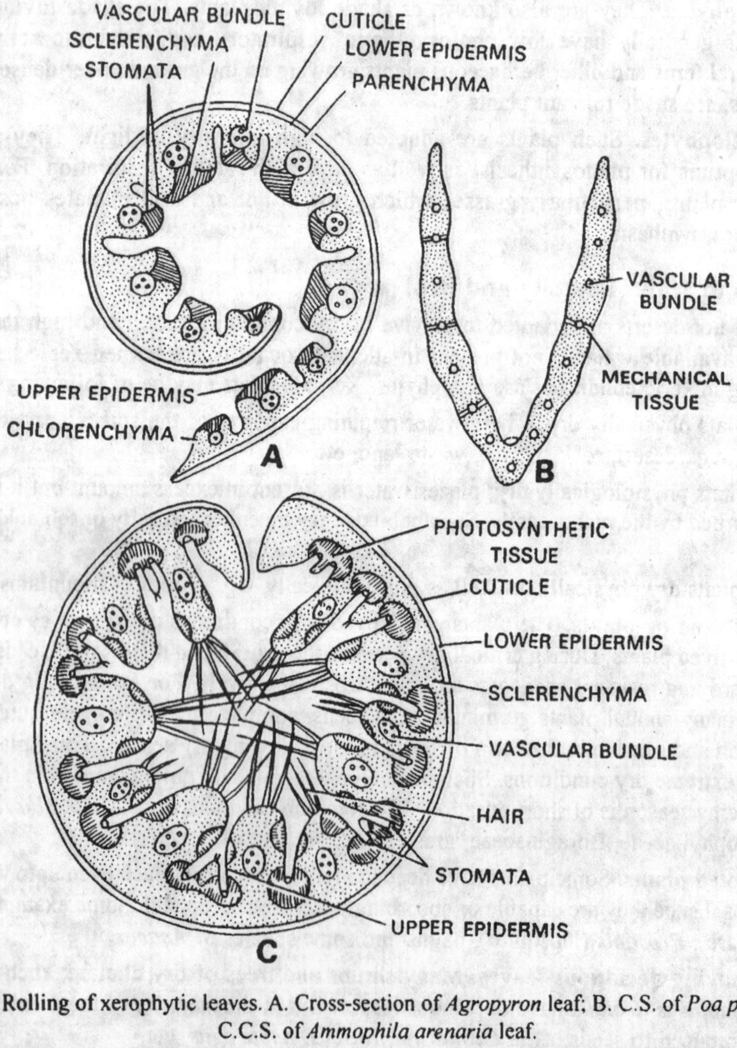

Fig. 23.11. Rolling of xerophytic leaves. A. Cross-section of *Agropyron* leaf; B. C.S. of *Poa pratensis* leaf; C.C.S. of *Ammophila arenaria* leaf.

Trichophylly. In some xerophytes, especially these growing well exposed to strong wind, the undersurfaces of the leaves are covered with thick mats of hairs which protect the stomatal guard cells and check the transpiration. These xerophytes which have hairy covering on the leaves and stems are known as trichophyllous plants, *e.g.*, *Zizyphus*, *Calotropis*, *Banksia*, *Nerium*, etc.

Rolling of leaves. The leaves of many xerophytic grasses, roll tightly under dry conditions. In these grasses, the stomata are combined to the ventral surface of the leaf, so that when the leaf edges roll inward, the stomata are effectively shut away from to outside air. As the stomata are located on the inner surface of the leaf, the air enclosed by the rolled leaf soon becomes saturated with water and the outward diffusion steps, *e.g.*, *Ammophila*, *Erica*, *Spartina*, etc.

Other significant adaptations. Many tropical plants, especially grasses which grow in hot and arid climates, have C_4 pathway of photosynthesis. The plants having C_4 pathway of photosynthesis perform better in low soil water environments. Thus, such plants use less water to achieve higher rates of photosynthesis, at higher temperatures.

Many other xerophytes, such as cacti and succulents close their stomata during the day and open them in the night, hence reducing transpiration. Crassulacean acid metabolism (CAM) occurs in succulents and other plants that normally grow in dry conditions.

Many xerophytes accumulate proline (an amino acid) in the cells which maintain osmotic and water potential in their leaves.

On the other hand, the heat shock proteins (chaperonins) provide physiological adaptations to plants to high temperatures. Such protein help other protein to maintain their structure and avoid denaturisation at high temperature.

Characteristics of xerophytes. The peculiar characteristics of xerophytes are as follows :

1. They grow in deserts or in very dry places; they can withstand a prolonged period of drought uninjured, for this purpose they have certain peculiar adaptations.

2. The xerophytic plants have to guard against excessive evaporation of water; this they do by reducing evaporating surfaces.

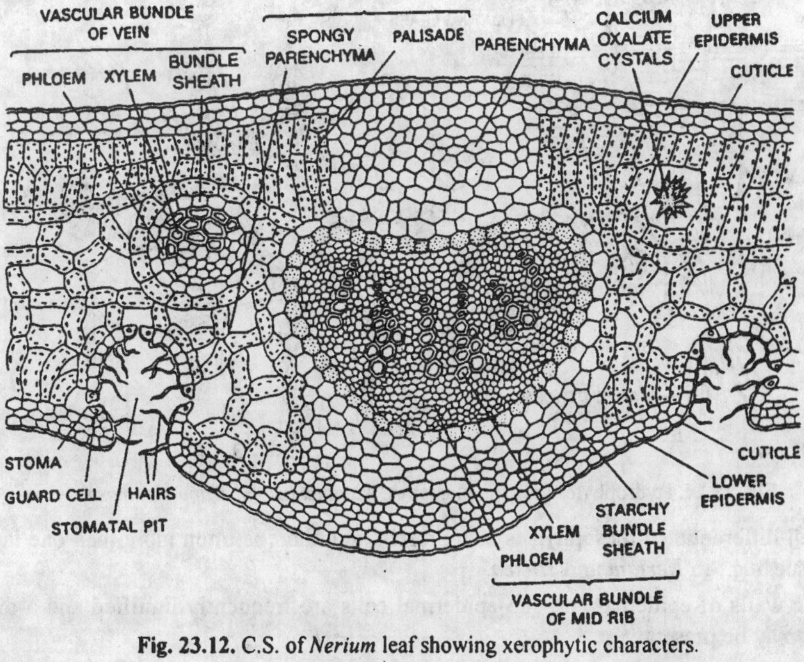

Fig. 23.12. C.S. of *Nerium* leaf showing xerophytic characters.

3. Plants produce a long top root which goes deep into the sub-soil in search of moisture.

4. To retain the water absorbed by the roots, the leaves and stems of some plants become very thick and fleshy, *e.g.*, *Aloe*, *Agave*, etc. Water tissue develops in them for storing upwater; this is further facilitated by the abundance of mucilage contained in them.

5. Multiple epidermis sometimes develops in the leaf, *e.g.*, in *Nerium*.

6. Modification of the stem into phylloclade for storing water and food at the same time performing functions of leaves is characteristic of many desert plants, *e.g.*, *Opuntia* and other cacti.

7. In xerophytes, certain structural features are also common. Leaves are thick and leathery, with a well developed cuticle and abundant hairs.

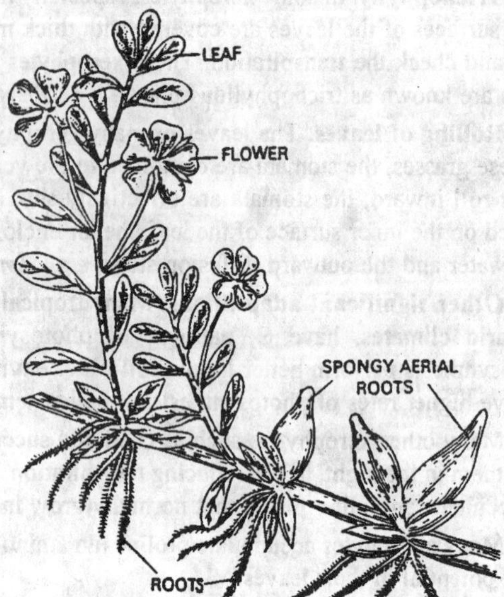

Fig. 23.13. *Jussiaea,* a typical hydrophyte.

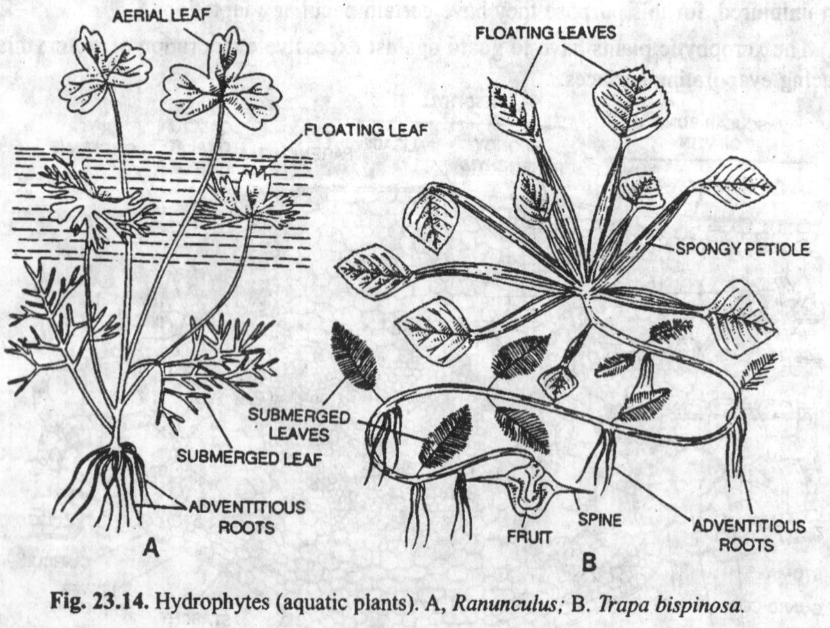

Fig. 23.14. Hydrophytes (aquatic plants). A, *Ranunculus;* B. *Trapa bispinosa.*

8. Well differentiated mesophyll is also present, and there is often more than one layer of palisade tissue, *e.g.*, in *Nerium* and *Hakea*.

9. The walls of epidemal and sub-epidermal cells are frequently lignified and a distinct hypodermis may be present.

10. They have well developed vascular system and often an abundance of sclernchyma, either in the form of sclereids or fibres, *e.g.*, in *Hakea* and *Ammophila.*

11. The leaf is sometimes cylindrical or related. This organisation is to protect the stomata, which may occur in furrows.

Adaptations in aquatic environments. Plants which remain permanently immersed in water are called **hydrophytes**. Such plants grow in water or very wet places. They may be submerged or partially submerged, floating or amphibious. Their structural adaptations are mainly due to the high water content and the deficient supply of oxygen. The various adaptations are as follows:

Epidermis. In aquatic plants, the epidermis is not protective but absorbs gases and nutrients directly from the water. The epidermis in the typical hydrophyte has an extremely thin cuticle, and the thin cellulose walls permit ready absorption from the surrounding water. Commonly chloroplasts are found in epidermal cells of leaves, especially when the leaves are very thin; these chloroplasts utilise the weak light under water for photosynthesis.

In submerged plants, stomata are not present, and exchange of gases takes place directly through cell walls. The floating leaves of aquatic plants have abundant stomata on the upper surface.

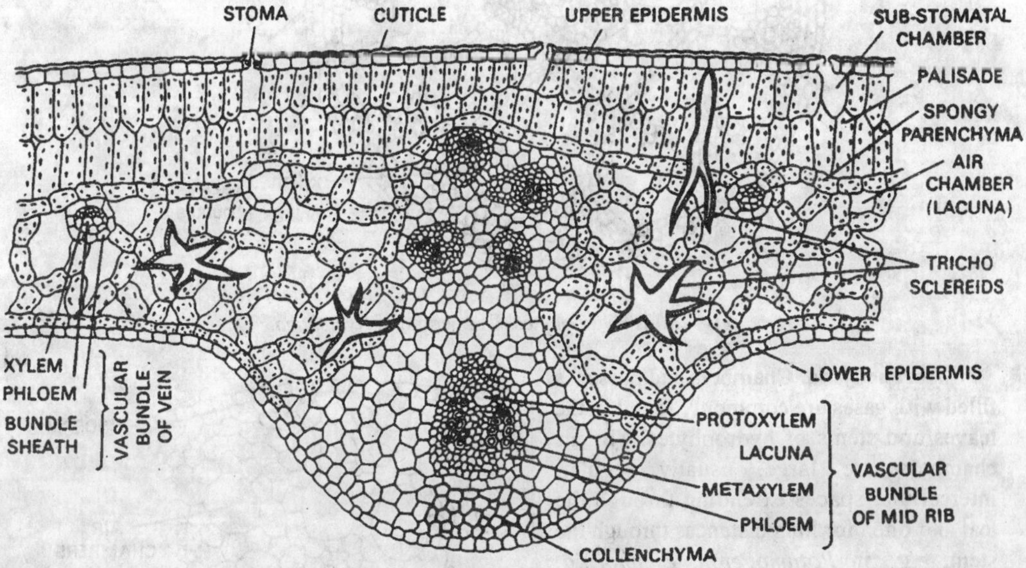

Fig. 23.15. Cross-section of Nymphaea leaf (a floating hydrophyte).

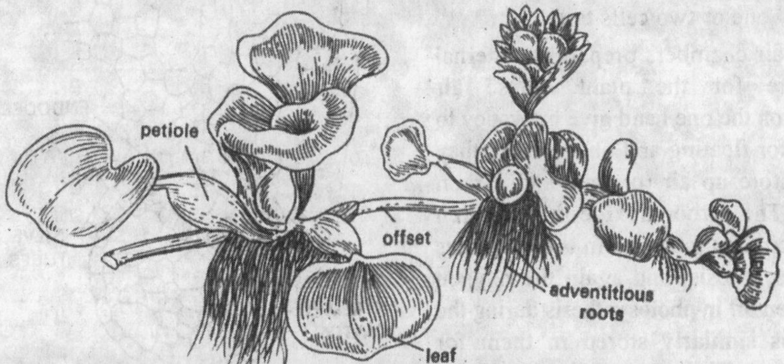

Fig. 23.16. Hydrophytes. *Eichhornia* (a floating hydrophyte).

Reduction of absorbing tissue. The root-system in hydrophytes is feebly developed and root hairs and root caps are absent. In some floating plants, such as *Utrieularia*, *Ceratophyllum*, etc., no roots are developed, and in submerged plants, such as *Vallisneria*, *Hydrilla*, etc., water dissolved mineral salts and gases are absorbed by their whole surface. An aquatic plant is in reality, submerged in or floating upon a nutrient solution. In hydrophytes the root-system is functioning chiefly as holdfasts or anchors and a large part of the absorption takes place through leaves and stems.

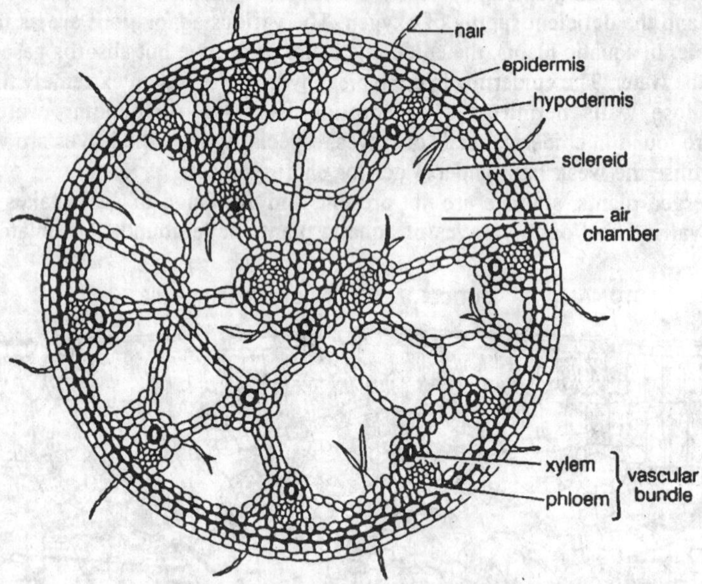

Fig. 23.17. Hydrophytes. T.S. petiole of *Nymphaea*.

Aerenchyma. Chambers and passeges filled with gases are commonly found in the leaves and stems of hydrophytes. The air chambers are large, usually regular, intercellular spaces extending through the leaf and often for long distances through the stem, *e.g.*, in *Potamogeton*, *Eichhornia*, *Pontederia*, etc. The spaces are usually separated by partitions of photosynthetic tissue only one or two cells thick.

The air chambers prepare an internal atmosphere for the plant. These air chambers on the one hand give buoyancy to the plant for floating and on the other they serve to store up air (oxygen and carbon dioxide). The carbondioxide that is given off in respiration is stored in these cavities for photosynthesis, and again the oxygen that is given off in photosynthesis during the daytime is similarly stored in them for respiration. The specialised tissue frequently found in aquatic plants that gives

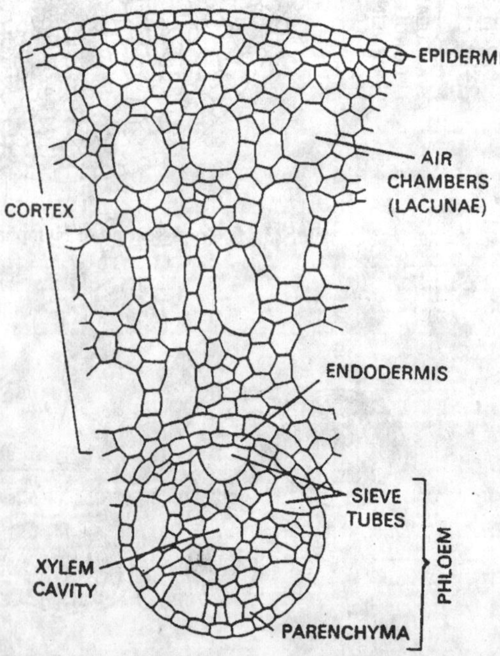

Fig. 23.18. Hydrophytes. T.S. root of *Potamogeton*.

buoyancy to the plant parts on which it occurs is **aernechyma**. This tissue helps to transport oxygen produced during photosynthesis and permits its free diffusion to other parts, including roots located in anaerobic soil.

Presewa of inflated peteioles in Eichhornia (water hyacinth) Keeps the plants floating on the surface of water.

Roots are poorly developed or absent in free floating hydrophytes, such as *Wolffia*, *Solvinia* and *Ceratophyllum*, or poorly developed, as in *Hydrilla. Nymphora* and *Nelumbo* are examples of rooted hydrophytes which grow in fresh water pond.

Examples of aquatic plants are :

Submerged – *Vallisneria, Potamogeton, Hydrilla*, etc.

Floating – *Ceratophyllum, Pistia, Utricularia, Trapa, Eichhornia, Neptunia*, etc.

Plants with floating leaves – *Nymphaea, Nelumbo, Victoria, Euryale, Limnanthemum*, etc.

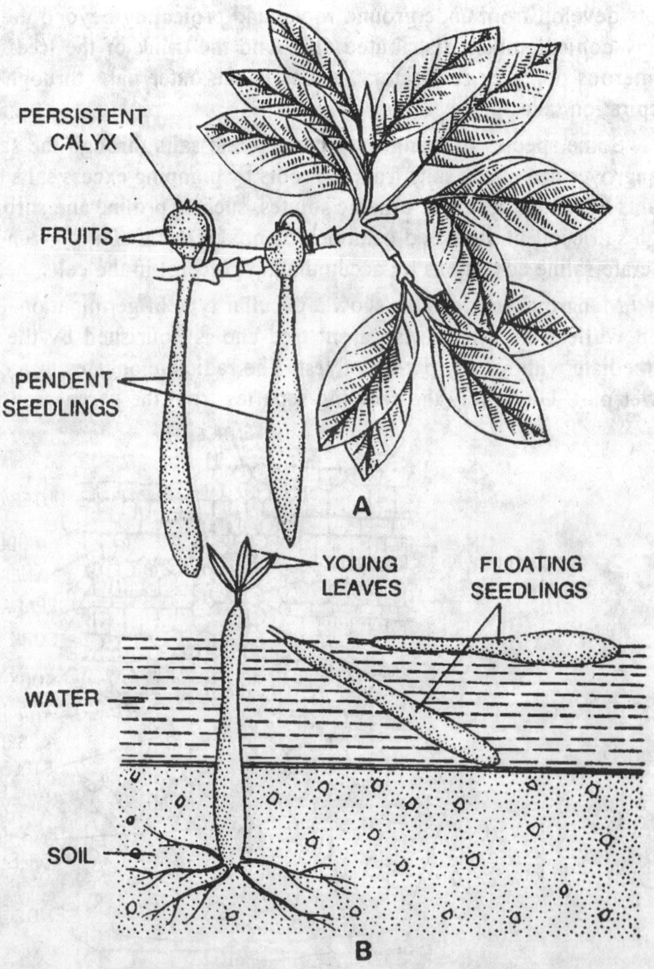

Fig. 23.19. Vivipary. Germination of the seed inside the fruit while the latter still remains attached to the plant.

Amphibious plants – *Ranunculus aquatilis, Sagittaria, Typha, Alisma, Cardenthera, Myriophyllum* etc.

Adaptations in saline environments. Some plants grow and complete their life cycle in the habitats with a high salt content. They are called salt plants or **halophytes**. Halophytes occur in tidal marshes and coastal dunes, mangroves and saline soils. They show some special characters. The halophytic plants, under hot and dry conditions, may become succulent and dilute the ion cocnentration of salts with, water they store in cells by stems and leaves. Leaves may be modified into or provided with spines. Typical examples of such plants are : *Suaeda maritima, Salsola, Acanthus ilicifolius. Chenopodium* and some species of family Asclepiadaceae.

Halophytes growing in marshy places near the seashore, as in Sundarbans (West Bengal), from a special vegetation known as the **mangrove**. Mangrove plant produce a large number of stilt roots from the main stem and the branches. In many cases, in addition to the still roots, special roots called **respiratory roots or pneumatophores**, are also produced in large numbers. Such roots develop from underground roots, and projecting beyond the water level, they look like so many conical spikes distributed all round the trunk of the tree. Such roots are provided with numerous pores or respiratory spaces in the outer part, thruogh which exchange of gases for respiration takes place.

Some species of mangroves can excrete salts through the salt glands on the leaves. Some mangroves can exude salts from the roots by pumping excess salts back into soil. Many mangrove plants have high levels of organic solutes, such as proline and sorbitol, to cope with conditions of high salt concentration and osmotic potential. *Dumaliella*, a green alga found in saline lakes, can tolerate saline conditions by accumulating glycerol in the cells, helping in osmoregulation.

Mangrove species also show a peculiar type of germination. The seed germinates inside the fruit while it is still on its parent tree and is nourished by the same. Germination is almost immediate without any period of rest. The radicle elongates to a certain length and swells at the lower part. Ultimately the seedling separtes from the parent tree and falls vertically down. The

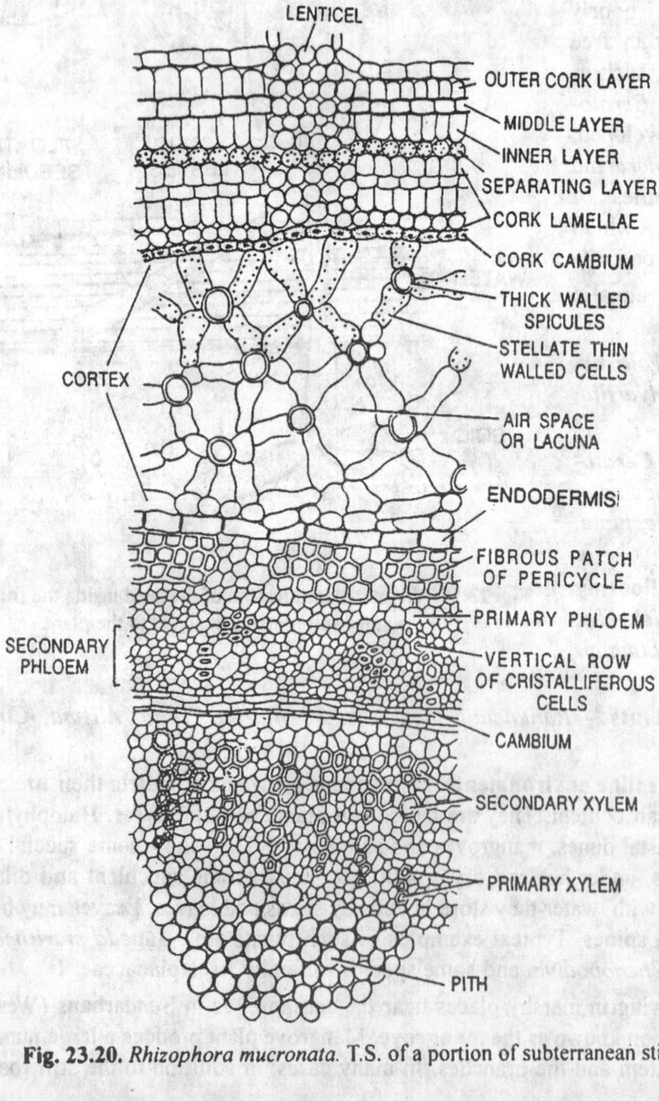

Fig. 23.20. *Rhizophora mucronata.* T.S. of a portion of subterranean stilt root.

radicle presses into the soft mud, keeping the plumule and cotyledons clear above the saline water. This kind of germination of the seed inside the plant is known as **vivipary**. Typical examples of mangrove plants are : *Rhizophora, Avicennia, Sonneratia, Ceriops, Heritiera*, etc.

Avicennia and *Rhizophora* are the domiant species in mangrove forests. The pneumatophores are capable to take up oxygen from the atmosphere and transport it to the main roots. The stilt roots give support to the mangrove plants in wet and muddy substratum, while vivipary permits plants to escape the effect of salinity on seed germination.

Adaptations to oligotrophic soils. The oligotrophic soils are those which contain lone amounts of nutrients. Such soils are generally found in geologically stable areas, such as soils of tropical rain forest region. Due to intense weathering and high rates of leaching, such soils have a poor nutrient retention capacity.

However, in nutrient poor soils, nutrient accumulation in vegetation is high.

Mycorrhizae. Many plants that grow in nutrient-poor soils have mycorrhizae or fungus root which have mutualistic association of roots with fungi. These are two types of mycorrhizae

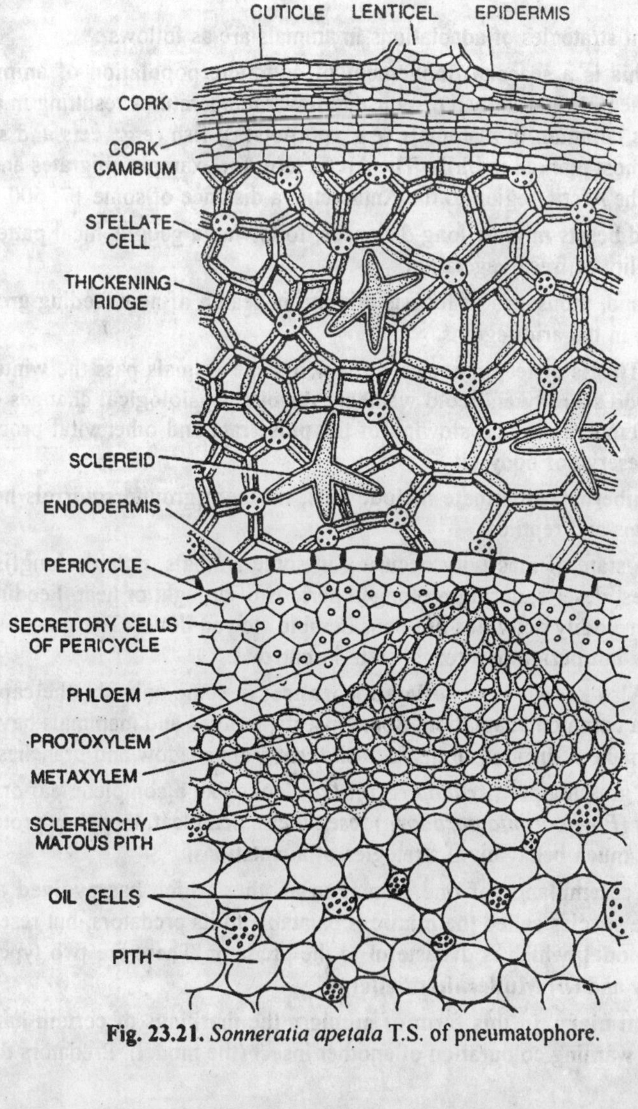

Fig. 23.21. *Sonneratia apetala* T.S. of pneumatophore.

(*i*) **endomycorrhizae** and (*ii*) **ecotomycorrhizae**. In endophytic mycorrhizae, the fungal hyphae are found within the tissues of roots in several vascular plants. While in ectomycorrhizae, the fungal mycelium forms a mantle of mat outside the root of vascular plant. Ectomycorrhizae generally occur in roots of shrubs and trees of temperate regions :

Mycorrhizae help in efficient absorption of nutrients, such as phosphorus and other nutrients, thus fulfil the scarcity of nutrient-poor soils.

Strategies of Adaptations in Animals

Several strategies of adaptations are found in animals. Many animals adjust themselves in different environmental conditions to survive and flourish.

For example, carnivores and herbivores have adaptations to eat a specific kind of food. On the other hand, some animals have adaptation to avoid being eaten by the predators.

Some animals have behavioural adaptations to attract a mate. The moles of some animals have bright colouration., particularly the plumage of the birds, which are helpful to attract their mates.

Some important strategies of adaptations in animals are as follows :

Migration. This is a seasonal movement of complete population of animals to a more favourable environment. It is usually a response to lower temperatures resulting in a reduced food supply. Migration is common in mammals (*e.g.*, porpoises), fish (*e.g.*, eels and salmon) and in some insects but is most marked in birds. The Arctic tern, for example, migrates annually from its freeding ground in the Arctic region to the Antaractic, a distance of some 17, 600 km.

In Africa, wild beasts migrate long distances, following a geographical pattern of seasonal rainfall and availability of fresh vegetation.

On the other land, thousands of locusts migrate in search of new feeding grounds from the food depleted areas, in the arid regions.

Hibernation. This is a sleeplike state in which some animals pass the winter months as a way of surviving/food scarcity and cold weather. Various physiological changes occur, such as lowering the body temperature and slowing of the pulse rate and other vital processes, and the animal lives on its reserve of body fat.

Animals that hibernate libermate include bats, northern ground squirrels hedgehogs, and many fish, amphibians and reptiles.

Aestivation. A state of inactivity occuring in some animals, notably lungfish and ground squirrels in south-west deserts, during prolonged periods of drought or heat. Feeding, respiration, movement, and other bodily activities are considerable slowed down. The gound squirels, avoid heat by spending dry-hot period in a torpid state in burrows.

Camouflage. Also known as **cryptic appearance**; in some animals, the capacity to blend with surrounding is a common adaptation. Some insects, reptiles and mammals have markings on their bodies, which make it difficult to distinguish them from shadow and branches.

For example, a grasshopper (*Arantia rectifolia*), looks like a complete leaf or a part of leaf, while praying mantis (*Phyllocrania paradoxa*) resembles a dead leaf, thus they protect themselves from the enemies by much behavioural strategies of adaptations.

Mimicry. The resemblance of one animal to another which has evolved as a means of protection. Here, one species called the **mimic** is palatable to its predators, but resembles another species, called the **model**, which is distasteful to the predator. There are two types of minicry : (*i*) **Batesian minicry** and (*ii*) **Mullerain mimicry**.

(*i*) **Batesian mimicry.** In this form of mimicry the markings of certain harmless insects closely resemble the warning colouration of another insect (the model). Predators that have learnt to avoid the model will also avoid good minics of it. This phenomenon is often found among butterflies. For examples, monarch butterfly and the mimics vicerory butterfly. Here, monarch butterfly contains toxins in its body and mimicked by vicreroy butterfly which has no toxins.

(*ii*) **Mullerian mimicry.** This form of mimicry involves the mutual resemblance of a group of animals, all harmful, such as the wasp, bee and hornet, so that predator, having experienced one will subsquently avoid all of them. The other examples are-monoarch butterfly and the mimic queen butterfly. Here the mimic shares the same defensive mechanisms as the model.

Echolocation. A method used by some animals (such as bats, dolphins and certain birds) to detect objects in the dark. The animal emits a series of high-pitched sounds that echo back from the object and are detected by the ear or some other sensory receptor. From the direction of the echo and from the time between emission and reception of the sounds the object is located, often very accurately.

For example, horseshoe bat produces high frequency sound, and detects the pressure of echoes produced from the objects.

Warning colouration (aposematic colouration). The conspicous markings of an animal that make it easily recognisable and warm would-be predators that it is a poisonous, foul-tasting, or dangerous species. For example, the brightly colored and highly poisonous dart frogs (*Phylobates bicolour*), of the tropical rain forests of South America are easily recognised and avoided by the predators. The other example is the yellow and black striped abdomen of the wasp warns of its sting.

Adaptations to water scarcity. Two main types of adaptations are found in animals of arid regions, *i.e.*, (*i*) lowering of water loss as much as possible and (*ii*) adapting to arid conditions. The examples are as follows :

The kangaroo rat conserves water by excreting solid urine, and can live throughout life without drinking water.

On the other hand, the camels show unique adjustments to desert conditions. They are very economical in water use they can tolerate the wide fluctuations in body temperature and can maintain blood stream moisture even during extreme heat stress.

Adaptations to cold. Some sessile animals, such as barnacles and molluses which live in very cold inter-tidal zones of northern shores, and several insects and spiders resist the effect of cold spells by a process known as **cold hardening**.

The organisms that tolerate freezing conditions passes ice nucleating proteins which induce ice formation in the extracellular spaces at low rule zero temperatures.

While some free-avoiding animals can tolerate environmental temperature below 0°C by accumulating glycerol or antifreeze proteins that lower freezing point of their body fluids. Presence of such antifreeze substances allows the fish in Antarctica region to remain active in sea water.

SUMMARY

1. Ecology is the study of reciprocal relationships between organisms and their environment.
2. The levels of biological organisation of interest in ecology are : Organism-Population-Community-Ecosystem-Biosphere.
3. A community contains many organisms of different species.
4. An ecosystem includes biological community, integrated with its physical environmet.
5. Biosphere includes all ecosystems on the earth.
6. The prevaling regional environment has large-scale effets on climate, biota and vegetation.
7. Microclimate represents the climatic conditions closer to living organisms.
8. Habitat is the place where an organisms lives.

9. Ecological niche is the functional role of an organisms.
10. Light and temperature affect climate, activities of plants and animals, and metabolic process of organisms.
11. Hydrological cycle is regulated by water vapour in atmosphere, evaporation and precipitation.
12. Soil plays an important role in plant growth by providing water, nutrients and anchorage, and a habitat for diverse population of soil organisms.
13. Moisture and temperature are generally responsible for limiting the activities of terrestrial organisms.
14. However, aquatic organisms are mainly affected by oxygen and light.
15. Organisms with broad range of tolerance have wide distribution.
16. Organisms with narrow range of tolerance have restricted distribution.
17. Desert plants adapt to water scarcity by mining water with deep tap root system, storing water in succulent leaves and stems, and having low transpiration.
18. Plants adapt to high concentration of salt in soil or water by salt excretion, or by accumulating organic solutes in stems and roots.
19. The oligotrophic soils are nutrient-poor soils. In such soils, nutrient retention is high in vege tation and mycorrhizae help in mineral nutrition of plants.
20. A large number of animal adaptations, are physiological and behavioral that include migration, regulation of body temperature, and mimicry to avoid predators.
21. In *Batesian* mimicry, the mimic is defenseless.
22. In *Mullerian* mimicry, the mimic shares the same defensive mechanisms as the model.
23. Some organisms avoid predation by cryptic appearance or warning colouration.
24. In cold environments, organisms adapt by super cooling their body fluids, or by lowering the freezing point of their body fluids by anitfreeze compounds.

TERMS TO REMEMBER

Acclimatisation. The gradual physiological adjustment to slowly changing new environmental conditions.

Adaptations. The special characteristics of organisms that enable them to be successful under prevailing set of environmental conditions.

Aestivation. Bounding the dry-hot period in an inactive state.

Biological community. This is an assemblage of populations of plants, animals, bacteria and fungi that live in an area and interact with each other.

Biomes. A large regional unit characterised by a major vegetation type and associated fauna found in a specific climatic zone.

Benthic region. The sediments at the bottome of lakes and ponds.

Batesian mimicry. Here, the mimic is defenseless, but has anti-predatory marks, like the model which has a defense against predators.

Climate. The average weather of an area.

Comouflage. The capacity to blend with surroudings.

Detrius. Freshly dead and partially decomposed plant and animal material.

Ecology. The branch of biology that deals with the study of interactions between organisms and their environment.

Ernst Haeckel. German biologist, coined word 'ecology' in 1869, (*oikos* = home; *logos* = to study).

Ecosystem. This is composed of a biological community integrated with its physical environment through the exchange of energy and recycling of the nutrients.

Environment. The sum total of all biotic and abiotic factors that surround and influence organisms.

Ecotypes. The species having a wide range of distribution evolve genetically adapted local population.

Ecological niche. The ecological niche of an organisms represents the range of conditions that if can tolerate the resources, its utilities and its functional role in the ecological system.

Ectotherms. Cold-blood animals, the body temperature tends to match with the environmental temperature is which they live.

Endotherms. Warm-blooded animals, regulate their body temperature by physiological means.

Ephemerals. The plants which evade dry conditions.

Endomycorrhizae. The fungal hyphae live inside roots.

Ectomycorrhizae. The fungal mycelium forms a mat outside the root.

Epilimmion. Upper layer of water in a simple body of water.

Field capacity. The upper limit of water availability.

Habitat. The place where an organism lives.

Homostasis. The maintenance of relatively constant internal environment under varying external environment.

Hypolimnion. Linear layer of water in a single body of water.

Hydrological cycle. This is the movement of water between aquatic systems, air and land.

Humus. Colloidal, amorphous and dark coloured substance.

Heliophytes. The plants adapted to high intensity of light.

Hydrophytes. Plants which remain permanently immersed in water.

Halophytes. Plants of saline environments which are adapted to grow in high concentrations of salt in soil or water.

Hibernation. Spending winter in dormant conditon.

Landscape. A unit of land with a natural boundary having a mosaic of patches.

Littoral zone. The shallow water zone around the edge of the lake which supports vegetation.

Limnetic zone. The open water zone beyond the littoral zone, where phytoplankton grows in abundance.

Lapse rate. The vertical temperature gradient over earth's surface, the value being 6.5°C per 1000 m elevation.

Litter. See detritus.

Mullerian mimicry. The process when the mimic shares the same defensive mechanism as the model.

Migration. Long-distance or short-distance movement of animals from one region to another.

Mimicry. Two species resemble each other closely, one species called the mimic which resembles another species called the model. The former is palatable, while the latter distasteful to the predator.

Mycorrhizae. Mutualistic association of roots with fungi (fungus root).

Mesosphere. Beyond stratosphere is extends up to an altitude of 80 km and shows a decrease of temperature with height.

Microclimate. The climatic conditions that prevail at a local scale, or in areas of limited size.

Oligotrophic soils. The soils, which contain low amounts of nutrients.

Phenotype. The physical expression of the interaction between genotype of an organism and its environment.

Profundal zone. The dark zone in water, where light does not reach.

Phenology. The timing of seasonal activities of plants in relation to change in environmental conditions.

Photosynthetically active radiaton (PAR). Light or visible spectrum having wavelengths of 0.4 to 0.7 mm.

Population. A group of individuals of a plant or an animal species, inhabiting a given area.

Species. Similar organisms having the potential for interbreeding and producing fertile offspring.

Stratopause. The transition layer between stratosphere and the mesosphere.

Solar constant. Solar radiation, befoer entering the atmosphere, carries energy at a constant rate of 2 cal cm^{-2} min^{-1}.

Soil. The uppermost weathers layer of earth's crust and is composed of minerals and partly decomposed organic matter.

Soil profile. The vertical layered structure of soil.

Sciophytes. Shade tolerant plants

Succulents. The plants having fleshy leaves and stems to store water.

Troposphere. The lower portion of the atmosphere, extending to about 8 to 16 km height from the earth surface.

Tropopause. Top of troposphere, where temperature remains –57°C.

Warning colouration. Concealing form and colouration enables a species to avoid its naturale predator.

Wilting point. The lower limit of water availability in soil.

Weather. The short term properties of the atmosphere, at a given place and time.

QUESTION BANK

Very Short Answer Questions

1. Define 'ecology'.
2. What is 'biological community'?
3. Which are the main climatic zones ?
4. What is PAR ?
5. What does 'phenology' refer to ?
6. What is 'biome'?
7. What is environment ?
8. What do you understand by the term 'microclimate'?
9. What is 'troposphere' ?
10. Give the ecological levels of organisation in ascending or desending order.
11. What is 'littoral zone' of a lake ?
12. Define 'hydrological cycle'?
13. What are lithophytes ?
14. What are eutrophic soils ?
15. Define hibernation.
16. What are microothermal organious ?
17. Where the mangrove vegetation in found ?
18. What is warning colouration ?
19. What are 'ecotypes'?
20. What is profundal zone of water ?

ANSWERS

1. Ecology is the branch of biology that deals with the study of interactions between organisms and their environment; **2.** The biological community is an assemblage of population of plants, animals, bacteria and fungi that live in an area and interact with each other; **3.** Depending on variation of mean temperature, the main zones are : tropical, subtropical, temperate, Arctic and Antarctic; **4.** Light or visible spectrum, which has wavelength 0.4 to 0.7 mm is called 'photosynthetically active radiation, *i.e.*, PAR; **5.** Phenology refers to the time of seasonal activities of plants with respect to the change in environmental conditions; **6.** A biome is a large regional unit characterised by a major vegetation type and associated fauna found in a specific climate zone; **7.** Environment is the sum total of all biotic and abiotic factors that surround and potentially influence an organism; **8.** The microclimate repersents the climatic conditions that prevail at a local scale; **9.** The lower portion of the atmosphere, extending to about 8-16 km hight from the earth surface; **10.** Biome-ecosystem-community-population-species-organisms; **11.** The littoral zone is the shallow water zone around the edge of the lake which supports rooted vegetation; **12.** The hydrological cycle is the movement of water between aquatic system, air and land; **13.** Plants found on rocky surface; **14.** The soils which have almost optimum concentration of minerals in soil solution; **15.** Hibernation is the period of dormancy during winter; **16.** Organisms living at moderate summer temperature and low winter temperature; **17.** Mangroves are found in marshy condition of tropical deltas and along ocean edges; **18.** Concealing form and colouration enables a species to avoid its natural predator; **19.** The species having a wide range of distribution evolve genetically adapted local population, called ecotypes; **20.** The dark zone where light does not reach is called profoundal zone.

Short Answer Questions

1. What is the difference between climate and weather ?
2. Distinguish between comouflage and mimicry.
3. How do plants adapt to oligotrophic soils.
4. What do you understand by ecological niche ?
5. What is solar constant ?
6. Some freeze avoiding animals can tolerate temperatures below 0°C. How ?
7. What type of plants are called ephemerals ? Cite an appropriate example.
8. What are the types of ultraviolet radiation, on what basis their division is being done ?
9. How does Dunaliella tolerate saline conditions?
10. Classify the vegetation of world into major groups.
11. Give a brief account of wilting coefficient.
12. What is the effect of temperature on metabolism of plants ?
13. Describe environmental factors and their importance to plants and animals.
14. How do plants adapt to water scarcity and saline environments ?
15. Define the following terms :
    (*a*) Migration (*b*) Stratosphere (*c*) Community (*d*) Biosphere
16. How do kangaroo rats and camels adapt to arid conditions ?
17. How do plants adapt in saline environment and oligotrophic soils ?
18. Distinguish between :
    (*a*) Batesian mimicry and Mullerian mimicry
    (*b*) Endomycorrhizae and Ectomycorrhizae
19. Differentiate between ectotherms and endotherms.
20. What do you understand by ecological factors?
21. Give a comprehensive account of soil moisutre.
22. What is the importance of soil in determining the vegetation of a place ?
23. Explain the importance of climatic factors in determining the nature of plant community.
24. How do sessile animals like barnacles and molluscs combat very cold spells in the intertidal zones of northern shores.

Long Answer Questions

1. Explain the following terms :
    (*a*) Mimicry (*b*) Acclimatisation (*c*) Ectotherms (*d*) Endotherms
2. Explain how tolerance to environmental factors determines distribution of species.
3. What are the different of the different types of adaptation in animals ? Explain with suitable examples.
4. Give a brief account of the different layers of atmosphere.
5. Give a comprehensive account of the effect of light on aquatic systems.
6. Define soil profile. How does it develop ? What are the main horizons in a soil profile ?
7. What are biotic factors ? Explain the effect of humans on vegetation.

8. Describe the effect of soil composition and soil texture on the growth and distribution of plants.
9. What is soil ? What is the role of microorganisms in soil formation ?
10. Descirbe in brief the main edaphic factors that affect the vegetation of a given area.
11. Give the importance of soil reaction, soil organisms and soil cover.
12. Explain the effect of light on the growth and distribution of plants.

MULTIPLE CHOICE QUESTIONS (OBJECTIVE TYPE QUESTIONS)

1. A zone of gradual change in temperature is :
(*a*) Thermostat (*b*) Thermal (*c*) Thermocline (*d*) Thermal tolerance
2. The branch of biology that deals with the study of interaction between organisms and environ ment is called :
(*a*) Physiology (*b*) Morphology (*c*) Ecology (*d*) Methology
3. Who coined the word 'ecology':
(*a*) Strasburger (*b*) P. Odum (*c*) Ernst Haeckel (*d*) Roxburgh
4. Whose organisms occur with other individuals of the same species form a part of :
(*a*) Biome (*b*) Biosphere (*c*) Population (*d*) Environment
5. Organisms interact with physical environment that comprises of :
(*a*) Atmosphere (*b*) Hydrosphere (*c*) Lithosphere (*d*) All of these
6. Warm-blooded animals are called :
(*a*) Ectotherms (*b*) Endotherms (*c*) Homeostasis (*d*) None of these
7. An association of different interelated poplation belonging to different species in common environment which can survive in nature in called :
(*a*) Family (*b*) Hard (*c*) Population (*d*) Biotic community
8. A direct food relation between two species of animals in which one animal kills and feeds on another is referred to as :
(*a*) Scavanging (*b*) Predation (*c*) Parasitism (*d*) Symbiosis
9. Which are of the following is protective device :
(*a*) Commensalism (*b*) Mutualism (*c*) Camouflage (*d*) Competition
10. Synecology is the study of :
(*a*) Biosphere (*b*) Individuals
(*c*) Environment (*d*) Community in relation to envirionment
11. Plants growing on burnt soil are called :
(*a*) Heliophilous (*b*) Hetrophyllous (*c*) Hydrophylous (*d*) Pyrophilous
12. When one population is harmed and the other remains unaffected the relationship is called :
(*a*) Amensalism (*b*) Commensalism (*c*) Parasitism (*d*) Mutualism
13. The relationship between a climber and the host correspond to :
(*a*) Mutualism (*b*) Parasitism (*c*) Commensalism (*d*) Neutralism
14. The mangrove plants are generally characterised by :
(*a*) Microphylly (*b*) Pneumatophores and vivipary
(*c*) Absence of aernchyma (*d*) Poor water storage
15. Plant groups growing in zones where high temperatuer alternates with low temperature are called :
(*a*) Megatherms (*b*) Mesotherms (*c*) Microtherms (*d*) Hekistotherms
16. Plants growing on sand and gravel are called :
(*a*) Eremophytes (*b*) Prammophytes (*c*) Prilophytes (*d*) Oxylophytes
17. The mesophytes are characterised by :
(*a*) Uniform mesophyll (*b*) Absence of cuticle
(*c*) Well developed root-shoot systems (*d*) All of these
18. Plants growing on cold soil are called :
(*a*) Psychrophytes (*b*) Premmophytes (*c*) Sciophytes (*d*) Oxylophytes
19. The biome is :
(*a*) That part of earth and its atmosphere, which inhabits living organisms.

(*b*) A complex of community interacting with one another
(*c*, The flora in an ocean
(*d*) The flora on land

20. Ecosystem has two components :
(*a*) Plants and animals' (*b*) Needs and trees (*c*) Biotic and abiotic (*d*) Frogs and lizards

21. Which one of the following animals can live from birth to death without even drinking water ?
(*a*) Kangaroo rat (*b*) Kangaroo (*c*) Camel (*d*) Desert cat

22. The study of periodic biological events such as flowering, breeding, migration etc., in relation to climatic and other environmental factors :
(*a*) Polynology (*b*) Pomology (*c*) Anthology (*d*) Phenology

23. Hydrilla is a :
(*a*) Free floating hydrophyte (*b*) Floating and anchored hydrophyte
(*c*) Submerged hydrophyte (*d*) Suspended hydrophyte

24. Among the following which plant is completely devoid of roots :
(*a*) Azolla (*b*) hydrilla (*c*) Ceratophyllum (*d*) Vallisneria

25. Among the following characters which one does not characterise a hydrophyte ?
(*a*) Poor development of roots
(*b*) Leaves having stomata only on the upper surface or none
(*c*) Plentiful xylem and sclerenchyma
(*d*) Abundant air spaces and air chambers

26. Aerenchyma is very extensive in almost all the vegetative organs of :
(*a*) Epiphytes (*b*) Mesophytes (*c*) Xerophytes (*d*) Hydrophytes

27. Xerophytes have deep roots in soil :
(*a*) Due to light (*b*) To draw water from deep water beds
(*c*) To give mechanical support (*d*) None of these

28. Mechanical tissues are very poorly developed in :
(*a*) Mesophytes (*b*) Hydrophytes (*c*) Halophytes (*d*) Lithophytes

29. Which of the following is the most characteristic feature of a xeric environment ?
(*a*) Low atmospheric humidity (*b*) High rate of vaporisation
(*c*) Extremes of temperature (*d*) The precipitation

30. Humus is an example of :
(*a*) Crystalloids (*b*) Organic colloids (*c*) Soil structure (*d*) None of these

31. The substance having organic and inorganic constituent is :
(*a*) Water (*b*) Soil (*c*) Air (*d*) All of these

32. Who proposed the term 'ecosystem'?
(*a*) Gardner (*b*) Tansley (*c*) Tansley (*d*) Clements

33. Who coined the term 'biocoemosis'
(*a*) Huxley (*b*) Tensley (*c*) Haeckel (*d*) Carl Mobius

34. The role of an organism in the ecological system is known as :
(*a*) Habitat (*b*) Herbivary (*c*) Niche (*d*) Interaction

35. Adaptation to low temperature and freezing in animals occurs due to the production of :
(*a*) Antifreeze proteins (*b*) Chaperonins (*c*) Proling (*d*) Analine

ANSWERS

1. (*a*)	**2.** (*c*)	**3.** (*c*)	**4.** (*c*)	**5.** (*d*)	**6.** (*b*)	**7.** (*d*)	**8.** (*b*)	**9.** (*c*)	**10.** (*d*)
11. (*d*)	**12.** (*a*)	**13.** (*c*)	**14.** (*b*)	**15.** (*b*)	**16.** (*a*)	**17.** (*c*)	**18.** (*a*)	**19.** (*b*)	**20.** (*c*)
21. (*a*)	**22.** (*d*)	**23.** (*c*)	**24.** (*c*)	**25.** (*c*)	**26.** (*d*)	**27.** (*b*)	**28.** (*b*)	**29.** (*c*)	**30.** (*b*)
31. (*b*)	**32.** (*c*)	**33.** (*d*)	**34.** (*c*)	**35.** (*a*)					

24

CHAPTER

Population, Biotic Community and Succession

The organization of an ecosystem starts with the **organism**. This organism may be simple and one-celled or complex and multicellular. A group of organisms of the same species living in a particular place at the same time makes a **population**. For instance, a population may be a single flock of animals or all the members of a plant species growing on a mountain range, or a mass of slime mold. It is not possible to study all the members of a species, and therefore, the ecologist must decide on the size of the sample group to be studied. It may be the antelope of a sanctuary or the rats of a particular area.

Social interaction in a marine population of guppies exhibiting sexual dimorphism : The male (left) is normally much brighter in color than the female.

All population of organisms that live together in a specific area and depend upon one another for food and shelter make up a **biological (biotic) community**. Different types of environments, support different populations. A desert community consists of populations of plants and animals different from those in a tropical rain forest.

However, the organisms in a habitat are not there simply by chance; their presence and suitability to a particular environment shows a long-drawn struggle for existence.

In this chapter population and community levels of organisation, population characteristics and growth, species interaction in the community and change in community, are dealt with.

POPULATION

The term **population** has been interpreted in several ways, they are as follows :

1. In human demography, a population is a set of humans in a given area, such as village, town, city, state or country or even the whole world.

2. In genetics, a population is a group of interbreeding individuals of the same species, which is isolated from other groups.

3. In ecology, a population is a group of individuals of the same species, inhabiting the same area, and functioning as a unit of biotic community.

For example, all individuals of the common grass snails or pine trees, of particular habitats, constitute their population.

Organisms in a population undergo the same life cycle. They experience similar ecological process at a particular stage of the life cycle.

Populations can be defined at various spatial scales. For example, local population can occupy very small habitat patches, like a temporary pond of water. A set of local populations connected by dispersing individuals is called a **metapopulation**.

Populations can also be considered at the scale of regions, islands, continents or oceans. Even the entire species can be treated as a population.

Characteristics of Population

A population has group characterstics, such as density, natality (birth rate), mortality (death rate), dispersal, age distribution (*i.e.*, ratio of one age group to the other), biotic potential and growth forms.

Populations are groups of individuals of the same species living in a particular place at the same time. They may differ in their number, patterns of living together, behaviour and organization. All of these factors are important when considering the interactions of a population with its environment and other populations. The description of a population involves several parameters such as (*i*) the number and kind of individuals of a species, (*ii*) a given space or an area, and (*iii*) time.

Density. The number of individuals of a species living in a particular area is the **density** of that population. Density is dependent upon many factors, such as danger of predators and the availability of food, water, light, heat and nesting places. The density of a population increases when conditions are favourable to the populations and decreases when they are not favourable. Population density is determined by counting all the individuals and dividing it by the number of units of space. For terrestrial organisms usually two dimensional units m^2 (a quadrate of 1m × 1m) or soil surface are taken. For aquatic organisms and organisms suspended in a medium, space is expressed in three dimensions (m^3). If the total number of individuals is taken as N and the number of units of space as S, the population density D can be calculated as

$$D = \frac{N}{S}$$

For example, 50 individuals of a tree species may occur per hectare, or 70 individuals of the grass *Cynodon* per square metre. Density of plants is determined by counting individuals in sample units of predetermined sizes. Species density varies from time to time and from one area to another. For human population, counting is being done every ten years.

Distribution. The arrangement of the individuals of a population within a particular space is called the distribution. While population density gives us knowledge that how many individuals exist in an area, whereas the distribution tells us how those individuals are arranged in that area. The patterns of distribution are **random, uniform** and **clumped**. In random distribution organisms occur in no particular order. The organisms that are distributed in an uniform manner are spread evenly over an area, whereas the clumped organisms are concentrated at points throughout an area. Clusters may offer the population protection from enemies, wind and cold.

Factors Affecting Population

Populations can change in many ways. They can get larger or smaller. The areas they occupy can increase or decrease. The ratio of males to females can vary. Changes in a population occur in response to some change in the factors that influence the population. A population tends to increase as individuals are added by **natality,** *i.e.*, birth, hatching or germination, and **immigration**, *i.e.*, moving in from outside. On the other hand, a population tends to decrease by **mortality** or death, and **emigration** or moving out. However, in the case of land plants incapable of locomotion, active immigration or emigration do not occur. An occasional addition to a plant population may occur through arrival of seeds from a long distance dispersed by air, water or animals.

Natality. The increase in number of individuals in a population under given environmental conditions is called **natality**. For example, birth, hatching, germination and vegetative propagation are main causes which are responsible for increase of number of individuals.

When the increase in individuals is expressed per unit time, it is called, **natality rate.**

Natality is calculated as follows :

$$\text{Birth rate or natality (B)} = \frac{\text{number of births per unit time}}{\text{average population}}$$

The maximum number of births produced per individual under ideal conditions of environment is called **potential natality**.

Natality varies from organism to organism. It depends upon the population density and environmental factors. It is a general rule that if the population density is low, the birth rate is also low, because the chances of mating between males and females are low. On the other hand, if population density is unusually high, the birth rate may also be low due to poor nutrition, or physiological or other probelms related to crowding.

The maximum or absolute natality is observed when the species exists under ideal ecological and genetic conditions. The actual number of births occurring under the existing environmental conditions is mush less as compared to absolute natality. It is referred to as **ecological natality** or **realised natality**. It is not constant for population and may vary with the size of population as well as with the time.

Mortality. The loss of individuals due to death in a population under given environmental conditons is called **mortality**.

Mortality refers to the number of deaths per unit time.

Mortality rate = $\frac{D}{t}$ where D is the number of deaths in the time t.

Mortality can be expressed as follows :

(*i*) **Minimum or specific or potential mortality.** It represents the minimum or theoretical loss of individuals under ideal or non-limiting conditions. Thus even under the best conditions individuals of a population would die of old age determined by their physiological longevity. So it is constant for a population.

(*ii*) **Ecological or realised mortality.** It refers to the death of individuals of a population under existing environmental conditions. Since it varies with environmental conditions, it is never constant. The maximum mortality occurs at the egg, larval, seedling and old age.

Mortality is affected by a number of factors, such as density, competition, disease, predation and environment. Death rates vary among the species and are correlated with birth rates. When the rate of natality is equal to the rate of mortality, the population is stationary.

A birth-death ratio $\left(\frac{\text{Births}}{\text{Deaths}} \times 100\right)$ is called **vital index**.

For a population, the survival of individuals is more important than the death. The number of births in relation to the carrying capacity of the habitat is a fundamental factor influencing the moratality rate. When more youngs are born than the habitat can support, the surplus must either die or leave the area. As the number of survivors is more important than the number of dying individuals, mortality is better expressed as survival or as **life expectancy**. The life expectancy refers to the average number of years the members of population have left to live.

Dispersal. The majority of organisms disperse at one time or the other during their life cycles. The individuals move into (immigration) and move out of the population (emigration), and such movements affect the size of population.

Movement of individiuals into and out of the population is called **population dispersal**. It plays important role in the geographical distribution of organisms even to the areas previously occupied by the members of population. Dispersal of oraganisms occurs for various reasons such as food, protection, prevention from overcrowding, action of wind and water, environmental factors such as light, temperature, breeding behaviour, physiological reasons or for interchange of genetic materials between the populations.

Population dispersal occurs in nature as follows :

(*i*) **Emigration.** It is one way movement of individuals out of a population. This movement is permanent and causes spread of a species to new areas. Emigration under natural conditions occurs when there is overcrowding in the population and is generally regarded as an adaptive behaviour that regulates the population on a particular site and prevents over-exploitation of the habitat. This type of dispersal offers new opportunity to the indiviudals of a population to interbreed with those of the other population leading to more genetic heterozygosity and adaptability.

(*ii*) **Immigration.** This is one way movement of individuals into a population. It leads to rise in density of population. It may result in decreased mortality among the immigrants or decreased reproductive capacity of the individuals.

(*iii*) **Migration.** Migration is two way mass movement of the entire population. It involves a periodic departure and return of the individuals of a population and occurs only in mobile organisms during unfavourable periods. It is shown by many birds, fishes and certain animals. In most cases, migration of population occurs for food, shelter or reproduction.

Age distribution. Age distribution is an important characteristic of population which influences natality and mortality. Mortality, usually varies with age, as chances of death are more in early and later periods of life span. Similarly, natality is restricted to certain age groups, *e.g.*, in middle age-groups in higher animals.

The individuals of a population can be divided in three ecological stages. They are : (*i*) **pre-reproductive**, (*ii*) **reproductive** and (*iii*) **post-reproductive**. The individuals of pre-reproductive group are young, those of reproductive group are mature and those in post-reproductive group are old.

The distribution of ages may be constant or variable. It is directly related to the growth rate of the population. Depending upon the proportion of the three age groups, populations can be said to be **growing, mature** or **stable**, and **diminishing**. Rapidly increasing population contains a large proportion of young individuals, a stable population shows even distribution of individuals in reproductive age group, and declining or diminishing population contains a large propotions of old individuals.

Age pyramids. Age pyramid a model in which the numbers or proportions of individuals in various age groups at any given time are geometrically presented. In an age pyramid, the number of pre-reproductive individuals is shown at the base, that of reproductive age group in the middle and the number of post-reproductive individuals at the top. The age pyramid indicates whether a population is expanding or stable or diminishing. The hypothetical age pyramids are as follows :

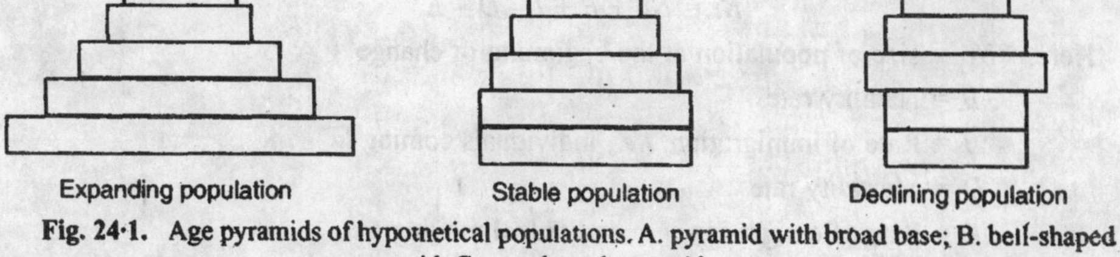

Fig. 24·1. Age pyramids of hypothetical populations. A. pyramid with broad base; B. bell-shaped pyramid; C. urn-shaped pyramid.

(*i*) **Pyramid with broad base.** This pyramid shows a high percentage of young individuals and an exponential growth of population due to high birth rate, *e.g.*, yeast, housefly, etc.

(*ii*) **Bell-shaped pyramid.** This type of age pyramid shows a stable population having, more or less equal number of young and middle-aged individuals and post-reproductive individuals being smallest in number.

(*iii*) **Pyramid with narrow base.** This is an urn-shaped pyramid which shows increased numbers of middle-aged and old organisms as compared to young ones in the population. This shows diminishing of population.

Biotic potential and environmental resistance. Every kind of organism produces more offspring than are necessary for that species to survive. The maximum reproduction rate of a population, under ideal conditions, is called **biotic potential**. This factor assumes that all of the young will live long enough to reproduce. To reach its biotic potential a population must have all of the food or raw materials, water and space it needs to survive. It also needs an ideal climate and the absence of competitors and disease. For instance, some bacteria divide about every 20 minutes. In 24 hours, the number of individuals produced would be enough to cover the entire surface of the earth to a depth of over 20 cm. However, populations do not reach their biotic potential. Many factors influence the growth rate of population. **Environmental resistance** means the collection of factors that reduce the growth rate of a population.

Biotic and abiotic factors influencing population growth. Biotic factors that influence population growth are living organisms or their characteristics. For example, the biotic factors that influence a population are the presence of predators or hunters, the food supply, the density of the population itself, the biotic potential of the species and disease. Abiotic factors are nonliving physical elements in the environment, such as temperature, water, humidity, light, soil, slope, air and wind.

Density dependent and density independent factors. Density dependent factors influence a population differently if the population is crowded than if it is not crowded. The effects of predators, disease and competition vary with the cocentration of the population. For example, a disease spreads more rapidly through a crowded population severely. The biotic factors influence all population than through a sparse one. The loss of a food source affects a crowded population, regardless of their density, and are called **density-independent**. For example, a forest fire affects the food supply and shelter of all organisms in the areas whether they are crowded or not crowded.

Population Growth Forms

The growth is one of the dynamic features of species population. Population size increases in a characteristic way. The growth of a population can be measured as increase in its size over a period of time. The change in population size may be expressed as follows :

Population having initial size, No

Population increases to size, Nt, and

Time interval, t

$$Nt = No + B + I - D - E$$

Here, No = size of population at the beginning of change

B = Natality rate

I = Rate of immigration, *i.e.*, individuals coming in

D = Mortality rate

E = Rate of emigration, *i.e.*, individual moving out.

When the number of individuals of population is plotted on the y-axis, and the time on the x-axis, a curve is obtained that indicates the trend in the growth of population size in a given time. This curve is called **population growth curve**. There are two types of growth curves :

(*i*) **J-shaped curve.** In the case of J-shaped growth form, the population grows exponentially, and after attaining the peak value, the population may abruptly crash. This increase in population is continued till large amount of food materials exist in the habitat. After some time, due to increase in population size, food supply in the habitat becomes limited which ultimately results in decrease in population size. For example, many insect populations show explosive increase in numbers during the rainy season, followd by their disappearance at the end of the season.

The following equation exhibits J-shaped growth :

$$\frac{dN}{dt} = rN$$

Here dN/dt represents rate of change in population size, r is biotic potential and N stands for population size.

2. **S-shaped or sigmoid curve.** When a few organisms are introduced in an area, the population increase is very slow in the beginning, *i.e.*, **positive acceleration phase** or **lag phase**, in the middle phase, the population increase becomes very rapid, *i.e.*, logarithmic phase, and finally in the last phase the population increase is slowed down, *i.e.*, **negative acceleration phase**, until an equilibrium is attained around which the population size fluctuates according to variability of environment. The level beyond which no major increase can occur is referred to as **saturation level or carrying capacity** (K). In the last phase the new organisms are almost equal to the number of dying individuals and thus there is no more increase in population size.

The S-shaped sigmoid growth form is represented by the following equation :

$$\frac{dN}{dt} = rN\left(\frac{K-N}{K}\right) = rN\left(1-\frac{N}{K}\right)$$

where, dN/dt is the rate of change in population size,
r is biotic potential
N is population size,
$K - N/K$ or $1 - (N/K)$ is for environmental resistance.

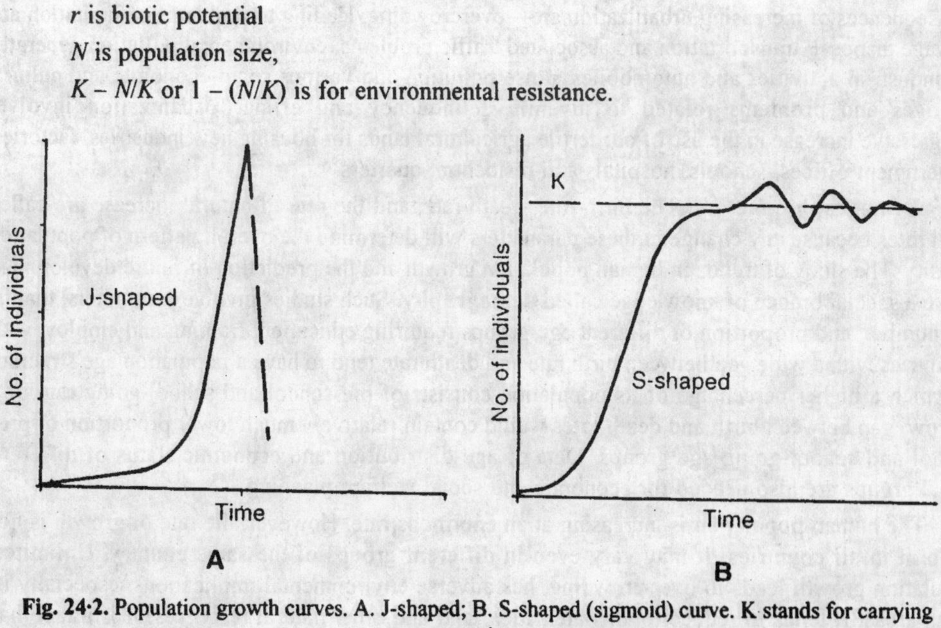

Fig. 24·2. Population growth curves. A. J-shaped; B. S-shaped (sigmoid) curve. K stands for carrying capacity.

Human Population

The distribution of human population in various regions of the world has been and is quite uneven in terms of its density mainly because of geographical, socio-economic and demographic factors. Only about thirty per cent of the world's land area is inhabited by man.

The pattern of human population and population growth depend upon several complex factors, such as—(1) geographical factors like climate, location of water, soil, energy, mineral resources, transportation etc., (2) socio-economic factors, and (3) demographic factors.

Geographical factors. The north and south poles are free of human habitation mainly because they are extremely cold and also agriculturally unproductive. Human settlements occur in places where adequate sources of water are available. The fertility of the soil for farming is another important determinant of population distribution. For instance, the main basis of the highly dense populations in the Indus valley and Indo-Gangetic plains is the alluvial nature of the soils in these regions.

In certain places both iron ore and coal and other fossil energy sources are located close together. Industrial cities based around steel plants have come up in Jamshedpur, Bokaro, Durgapur, Bhilai and Rourkela.

Means of transportation have played an important role in the redistribution of population. This made it possible for the first time for persons to live far away from the source of produce or of goods required for living. Transportation by water is cheaper than by land or air and this is probably the main basis for the coastal location of most big cities such as Kolkata, Mumbai, London, New York and Tokyo.

Socio-economic factors. The size of population, and birth and death rates have great significance on the standard of living of the people, their aspirations, and their economic and social development. The birth rate of human population is regulated more by socio-economic factors than biological factors. These factors may be social status of women, age of women at marriage, family structure, education, acceptability of family planning practices, and religious beliefs.

Prosperity in the cities is the basic cause of continued urban growth. Some important consequences of increasing urbanization are—overcrowding, leading to problems of sanitation and sewage disposal; transportation and associated traffic problems; environmental pollution generated by industrial activities and automobiles; noise pollution and various socio-economic and cultural changes and problems related to juvenile delinquency and crime. Urbanization involves progressive increase in the use of our fertile agricultural lands for housing new industries, factories, government offices, schools, hospitals and residential quarters.

Demographic factors. The birth-rate, death-rate, and the rate of natural increase are called vital rates because any change in these parameters will determine the overall pattern of population density. The study of trends in human population growth and the prediction of future development make a special branch of knowledge called **demography**. Such studies involve parameters, that is, the number, and proportion of different age-groups requiring education, training and employment. Countries with a wide gap between birth rate and death rate tend to have a population age structure in which a higher percentage of its population consists of pre-school and school-going rate of a narrow gap between birth and death rates would contain relatively much lower proportion of pre-school and school-going age groups. Data of age distribution and economic status of different social groups are also needed for economic and social welfare planning.

The human population is increasing at an enormous rate. However, the rate of growth is not uniform in all countries. It may vary even in different groups of the same country. Unlimited population growth leads to over-crowding, has adverse environmental implications, especially in urban areas. It tends to reduce food, water, fuel, land and other natural resources. It is a fact that the growth of human population is more stable in the developed countries, *i.e.*, both the birth rates and death rates are low. When the birth rate of a population is hign, the population increases, and on the other hand when the death rate is high the population decreases. In the United States of America, France and Germany, the population growth is more stable than in the developing countries like Pakistan, Bangladesh, India and China. Usually, the relationship between population growth rate and the level of industrial development and education is inversely proportional. Such relationship is also found among different groups of the people in the same country.

SPECIES, ECOLOGICAL INTERDEPENDENCE AND INTERACTIONS

The Individual Organism

The individual organism is a distinct package carrying out life processes within its body as a entity separate from those being preformed in the bodies of others. The organisms may be unicellular or multicellular. The example of individual organisms are potato plants, bean plants, cats, rats, tigers and others. Such organisms can be counted, measured and studied. However, in may cases they remain organically connected with one another such as in grasses or in colonies of corals and sponges. The individual organisms always develop from pre-existing ones by means of reproduction which may be vegetative, asexual or sexual.

Species

A large variety and numerous individual organisms are found in nature. The organisms do not occur in isolation. Such organisms may be of a kind, as cats, rats, tiger, bean plants, humans, etc. The individual organisms aggregate and form population. A geographically localised group of individuals of the same kind form a **species**. The individual organisms of a species may differ in structure and function depending upon their sex, stage of development or specialisation for specific functions. For example, in many insects the adult, larval and pupal stages are considerably different. In frogs, toads and salamanders the adults and larval stages are quite different in structure and function. On the other hand, the sporophyte and gametophyte of a fern or moss are quite different in their structure and function.

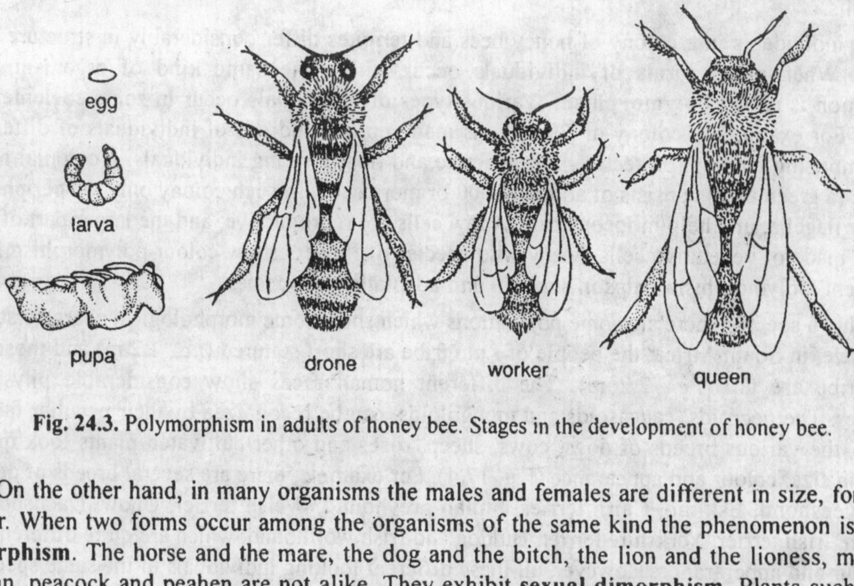

Fig. 24.3. Polymorphism in adults of honey bee. Stages in the development of honey bee.

On the other hand, in many organisms the males and females are different in size, form and colour. When two forms occur among the organisms of the same kind the phenomenon is called **dimorphism**. The horse and the mare, the dog and the bitch, the lion and the lioness, man and woman, peacock and peahen are not alike. They exhibit **sexual dimorphism**. Plants such as the

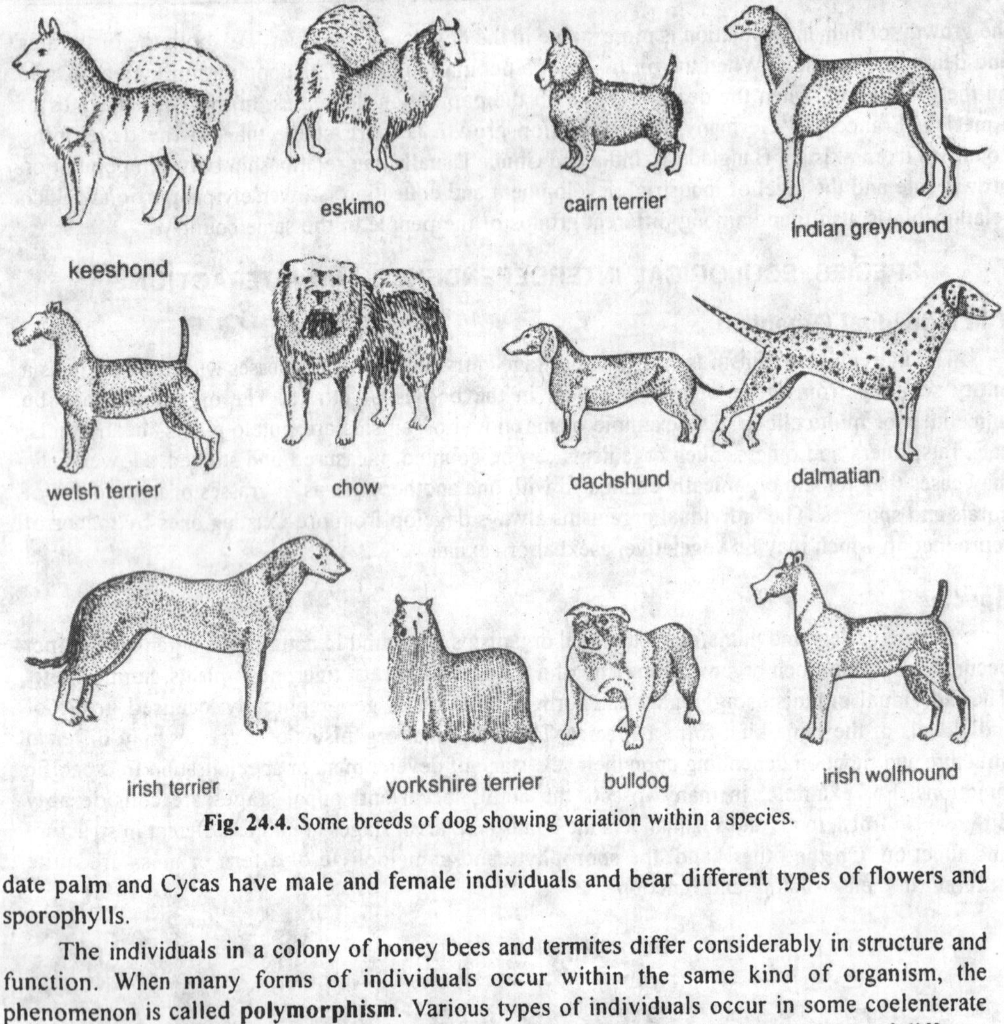

Fig. 24.4. Some breeds of dog showing variation within a species.

date palm and Cycas have male and female individuals and bear different types of flowers and sporophylls.

The individuals in a colony of honey bees and termites differ considerably in structure and function. When many forms of individuals occur within the same kind of organism, the phenomenon is called **polymorphism**. Various types of individuals occur in some coelenterate colonies. For example, a colony of *Physalia* is made up of hundreds of individuals of different kinds comprising feeding, protective, reproductive and float forming individuals. A colonial form of *Volvox* (a green alga) consists of about 60,000 or more cells. In such colony only the peripheral cells bear flagella, and help in locomotion. A few cells are reproductive, and the larger part of the colony is made of vegetative cells. Many wild species of flowers show colour polymorphism. To some extent, polymorphism helps in survival and adaptation of species.

Within a species, there are some populations which show some morphological characterstics. For instance, in South Africa, the people of Zulu tribe are short statured (*i.e.*, 1.2 m) and those of Watusi tribe are tall (*i.e.*, 2.2 m). The different human races show considerable physical differences. The negroids, caucasoids and mongoloids, can be recognized by their peculiar faces. Similarly, the various breeds of dogs, cows, sheep, roses and other cultivated plants look quite different in size, colour and appearance (Fig. 17.4). For example, there are several breeds of dogs, such as Keeshond, Eskimo, Cairn terrier, Indian greyhound, Welsh terrier, Chow, Dachshund, Dalmatian, Irish terrier, Yorkshire terrier, Buldog and Irish wolfhound, which are quite different in size, colour and apperarance. However, all these different looking individuals of the same species may interbreed among themselves. While the populations or individuals belonging to different species may appear quite similar but do not breed in natural conditions.

Thus, a species can be defined as a *group of closely related, structurally and functionally similar organisms which interbreed with one another in nature, but not with organisms of other groups.*

The inability to interbreed or reproductive isolation makes the most important distinction between different species. Thus, reproductive isolation is the main factor that maintains the distinctness of different species. But there are several examples where members of two species are alike and still do not interbreed. However, members of two different species may breed under captivity or under artificial conditions. As we know, the horses and donkeys are of distinct species but they interbreed and produce sterile offspring, the **mule** (*i.e.*, progeny of male donkey and mare) or **hinny** (*i.e.*, progeny of stallion and female donkey). The artificially produced hybrids between bull frogs leopard frogs die before attaining the reproductive age. There are some examples of species that interbreed under captivity to produce fertile offspring, they are—the mallard and pintail duck, the tiger and the lion, the polar bear and the Alaskan brown bear, the platy and swordtail fishes. The interbreeding between members of two different species can occur only when the isolating condition is removed artificially. There is great diversity in the living world. To study the diversity, the scientists have developed several hierarchical terms–many similar species make a **genus** ; many related genera constitute a **family**, and several related families form the **order**.

Origin of Species

It has already been mentioned in the preceding paragraphs that prevention of interbreeding between members of different species is essential for the maintenance of identity of the species. It is an established fact that life arises only from pre-existing life. It is also thought, that new species is derived from the par-existing ancestral species. Now the question arises, how does a new species originate. Here, we will consider the origin of a terrestrial species which has a wide range of distribution. For example, due to development of a physical barrier, such as a high mountain range or a large body of water, it becomes impossible to maintain interbreeding between the members of the groups thus separated. Sometimes the long distance between populations may act as a reproductive barrier between them. In the initial stages, interbreeding between the individuals of these two populations will be possible if the isolation factor is artificially removed. However, the absence of a reproductive contact for a long time will lead to a loss of capacity for interbreeding. In the due course of time, the individuals of these populations undergo physical and physiological changes depending upon their environment, so that, they become morphologically different from each other. They would gradually go away from each other in structure and function and ways of living, and become so different as to give rise to a new species.

Interactions Between Members of a Species

The individuals of a species interact with each other in several ways, such as cooperation, communication and competition.

Cooperative interaction. This type of interaction is essential for reproduction and prepetuation of the species. Organized social interactions offer the advantages of cooperation in reproduction, caring for the young, obtaining food and in defence. A herd of musk oxen form a circle for protection. Social organization may be very simple or very complex. The simplest social behaviour is herding, schooling or flocking. The individuals are less likely to be captured by a predator while in a school than if alone. Social organization also aids in reproduction and rearing. For the seal, meeting at the breeding area makes contact between male and female easier. The baboons and monkeys live together for such advantages as grooming each other and caring for the young. Herding, rank establishment and territory and other interactions are restricted to certain animals only.

Group formation. Family life or group formation in different animals varies. It is found only in few types of animals. Foxes, wolves and swans are **monogamous**, *i.e.*, once a male and female come together the partnership lasts throughout life. However, in sparrow the partnership breaks down at the end of a breeding season, and the male and female birds find new partners in the subsequent years. Seals, walruses and deers are **polygamous**. A male keeps a harem of many females. Rats, mice and some other animals do not have any fixed partners.

Many animals, such as geese, ducks, parrots, antelopes, deer, zebras, elephants and monkeys live in groups or herds. Members of each herd cooperate for mutual protection and for finding food and water for the herd. For example, it has been observed in the Bandipur Santuary of Karnataka that when a group of cheetals is attacked by a predator, such as the wild dog, panther or tiger, the stag with the best antlers is closely surrounded by other individuals so that it is saved from destruction. This is a unique example of the self-sacrifice of a few individual deer allowing themselves to be killed in the interest of the species.

Usually a community has a few populations that are more important in determining the nature of community than the others. These **dominant species** strongly influence the food supply and the envrionment of the other species. In a forest, the large trees are usually dominant species. Large trees dominate forests because their canopy of leaves over the other populations determines how much light is available to other plants.

On the other hand, within the herd there is a social organisation and ranking of individuals. Usually the females are subordinate to males and the young are subordinate to the adult. In the red deer the female is the leader of the herd. **Dominance** or ranking of individuals is generally settled by battles. Dominance is also established by an aggressive posture or display of feathers by birds. In most species, the individuals of the highest rank has the first choice of mate and food followed by individuals of subsequent ranks.

The honey bees, ants and termites form well organised societies having division of labour among its members showing **polymorphism**. In these social insects (honey bees) the individuals of different kinds (*i.e.*, polymorphic) live together in a colony and work together for the benefit of the group. Here the insect societies are formed of different castes such as workers, males (drones) and queen. All of them are specialized for different kinds of work. The workers collect and store food. They also build houses of complicated design, and also do other special tasks. The males and the queen are mainly involved in reproduction and act as the progenitors of future colony.

In the termites incomplete metamorphosis is found, which shows that the insects hatched from eggs are very similar to adults and develop into adults through growth and moulting. Most of these function as worker termites, and have perpetual adolescent phase and do not develop into adults. Only the **king** and the **queen** reach the adulthood and produce future colony through sexual reproduction.

The insect societies are quite different from the human society. They differ both in origin and organisation. Human societies show more psychosocial evolution than biological evolution. The members are made of numerous family units composed of males and females, adults and juveniles. However, the insect societies are the products of biological evolution based on learnt behaviour. All the members of the colony are derived from common parents.

Home range and territory. Individuals, pairs or groups of vertebrates and higher invertebrates, commonly restrict their activities to a definite area. This area over which the animals wander in search of food and mates, is called their **home range**. Variations in home range are associated with the species, sex, age, season and with such ecological condition as availability of food, shelter and intraspecific struggle. Home range provides an animal with its necessities of life, such as food, cover, shelter and to rear young ones.

A number of breeding groups, that is pairs and herds inhabit a home range. Each breeding group, or an individual occupies a particular **territory**. The home range of different groups can overlap but not the territory. Each territory centres round the individuals or group's home, nests, holes, burrow or other types of shelter. The special odours of the urine or faeces delineate the territory of animals like dogs and tigers. The territory is defended by its members. The territorial concept is most developed in birds where the male first establishes a territory. It drives off all other males of the same species from this territory and sometimes also females other than its mate.

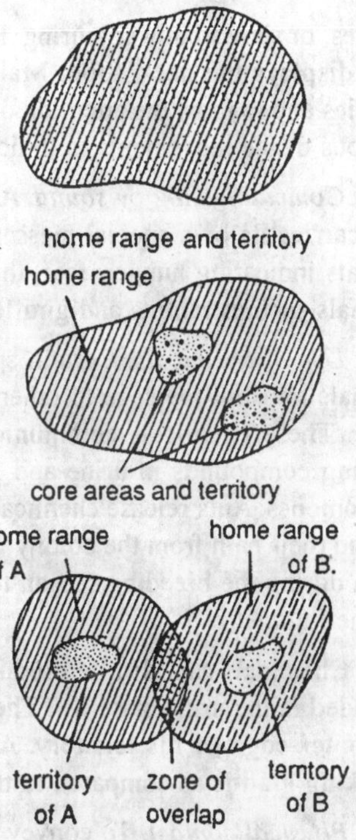

Fig. 24.5. Home ranges and territories of two species.

Communication. The survival and well-being of an animal population is largely dependent upon the communication among the members of the population. Even simple organisms have developed methods of communication, such as sight, sound, chemicals or contact. Through these methods of communication, members of a population indicate dominance, submission, the source of food, the presence of danger, hunger, the urge to mate, and the limits of territory.

Visual displays. Animals may use visual displays to communicate. This is the way where the animal stands,

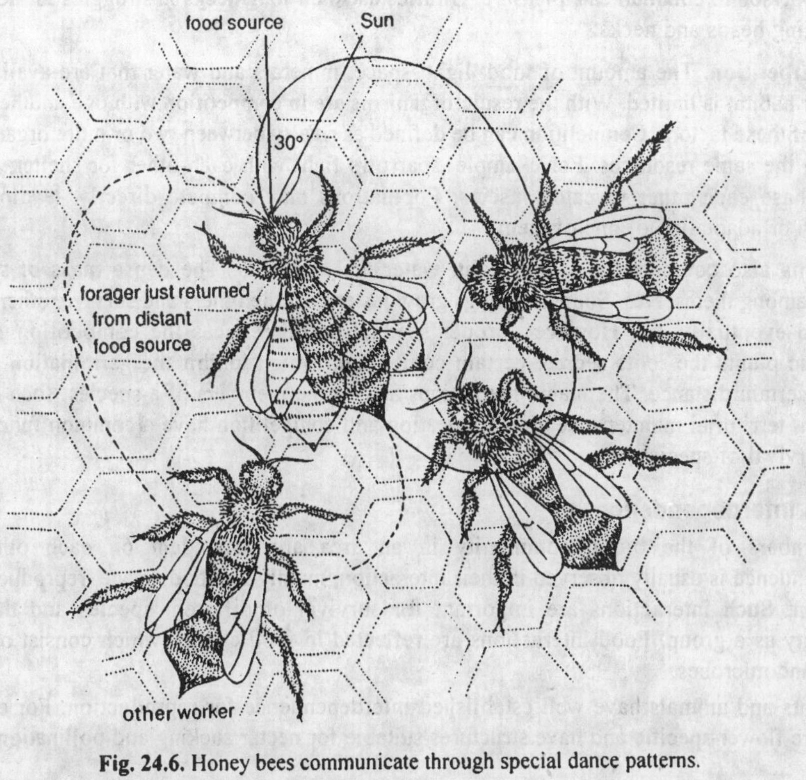

Fig. 24.6. Honey bees communicate through special dance patterns.

moves, or shows body colouring. For example, an aggressive cobra arches its back, bares its fangs, and displays the neck hood. Male birds are often brightly coloured to attract females of their species and to draw the attention of enemies away from the female and young. Honey bees perform various dance movements to indicate the distance and direction of the food source.

Communicating by sound. Animals may also communicate by making sounds. Each call or cry carries its own special message. Some animals have as many as two dozen different sound signals indicating hunger, fear, threat, annoyance, desire for mating and parental concern. Even animals such as rabbits and giraffes, utter sounds when they are intensely afraid.

Use of chemicals. Certain special chemical compounds such as **pheromones**, secreted by animals transmit message to other members of the species. Pheromones are detected by smell or taste. These chemicals communicate territorial rights, fear, or a desire to mate. The territory making compounds in urine and faeces as already mentioned in preceding paragraphs are also pheromones. Ants release chemicals containing pheromones, which enable the members of colony to find their path from the colony to the source of food and back. The sex pheromones are used by bitch during the breeding season to attract the male dog. A dog can smell a bitch from a distance of one kilometre.

Chemicals can also be produced and secreted by **specialized glands** or **tissues** and may be included in the urine or saliva. The male lion marks his territory by spraying urine at points along the outer edge of his territory. Among social animals, the dominant males have large **scent-marking glands** as compared to the others on the group and use them more often.

Physical contact. To convey concern, hunger, play or aggression, animals may use physical contact. A young bird pecks at the parent's bill to communicate hunger. A pet cat will rub up against a person to communicate pleasure. Giraffes use their long necks in struggles for dominance by knocking heads and necks.

Competition. The amount of food, light, space, minerals and water that are available in a particular habitat is limited. With the result, organisms are in competition with one another for one or more of these factors. Competition can be defined as rivalry between two or more organisms for obtaining the same resources. For example, sparrows fight with each other for shelter, and wall lizards chase each other to catch insects. Populations may compete directly, leading to the extinction or adaptation of one of them.

Plants also compete for space, light, water and minerals. The dense mass of seedlings compete among themselves. Some seedlings grow faster than the others and survive, others remain weak and eventually die. However, proper seed dispersal reduces the competition. In some xerophytic plants the roots secrete certain compounds which inhibit the germination of seeds within a certain distance. The many interactions among the members of a species, such as group formation, territorial maintenance, communication and competition have a common function and that is survival of species.

Species Interdependence

Members of the biotic community in an area are dependent on each other. The interdependence is usually observed in their interaction, mainly for food, space, reproduction and protection. Such interactions are important for survival of different species and the biotic community as a group. Food interactions are reflected in food chains, which consist of plants, animals and microbes.

Plants and animals have well established interdependence for reproduction. For example, insects are flower-specific and have structures suitable for nectar sucking and pollination.

Contrary to it, some flowers are insect-specific. For example, snapdragon flower possesses lip-like petals, which facilitate insect entry and landing. Here, both flowers and insects have developed and evolved in a way leading to their interdependence. The nectar of flowers is main attraction for insects. Insects visit the flowers in search of nectar and pollination is effected. The fluctuations in insect pollination would affect pollination that leads to plant reproduction.

Birds and mammals help in the dispersal of seeds and fruits. Interdependence may also be shown by certain other specific examples. For example, cuckoo lays eggs in the nest of other birds, and gall wasps bury their eggs deep into the tissues of plants that ensure hatching and protection.

Camouflage. Some members of biotic community, particularly animals, sometimes camouflage to avoid detection. For example, butterflies and moths have colours which match the colours of flowers, and therefore, their detection becomes difficult. The camouflage can be observed in praying mantis and leaf insect, which mimic the shapes of leaves and branches.

Mimicry. For example, orchids mimick the butterfly, as their colours are concerned. Generally, weaker members of animals, mimic the strong, fast moving species and which have a fewer natural enemies. For example, non-poisonous snakes mimic the poisonous snakes to avoid their enemies. Usually, birds mimic voice of other animals.

Interaction Between Different Species

In the great web of life, which exists in nature, living organisms not only live in an environment, but are also themselves a part of the dynamic environment for other organisms. The relationship between one species and another within a community has evolved through their interactions, based on the requirement and the mode of nutrition and shelter and also on the habits of species. The relationships between members of different populations are termed **interspecific relations**.

The interactions between populations of species in a community are broadly divided into two categories : (*i*) **positive** (beneficial) and (*ii*) **negative** (inhibition) **interactions**. This depends upon the nature of effect on the interacting organisms of different species.

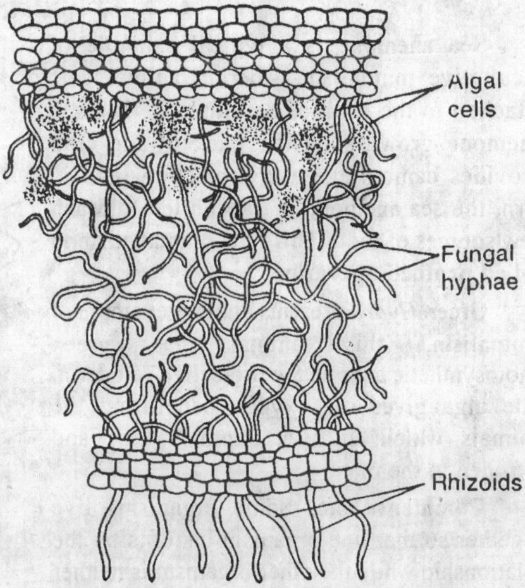

Fig. 24.7. V.S. of Lichen thallus showing association of alga and fungus.

Positive interactions

Symbiosis or mutualism. When two species live together in a close association that is helpful to both species, the relationship is known as **symbiosis**. The oxpecker bird and the rhinoceros exhibit this relationship. The oxpecker receives protection and obtains food from the ticks and other pests infesting the rhino's skin. The rhino receives cleaning and warning of approaching dangers. Algae and fungi live together in symbiotic relationship in **lichens**, whereas the fungi live on the roots of higher plants, and the association is known as **mycorrhiza**. In lichens, the algae are able to produce food by photosynthesis, and the fungi obtain water and minerals and provide attachment for the lichen. The bacterium *Rhizobium leguminosarum* found in the root nodules of leguminous plants fixes atmospheric nitrogen in the soil in the form of nitrates which is used by the plant, and in return plant supplies water, minerals and organic food to the bacterium. The cyanobaterium *Anabaena* also lives in symbiotic association with water fern *Azolla*. Bacteria in the gut of some domestic animals help in cellulose digestion.

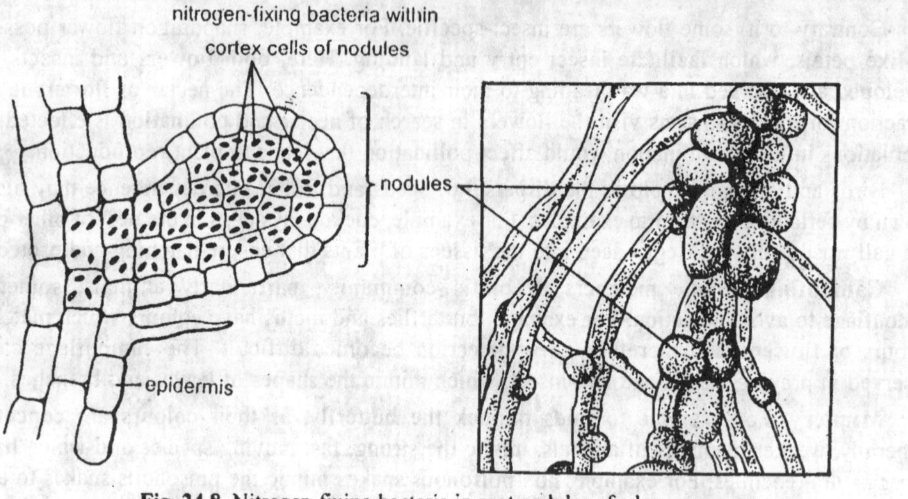

Fig. 24.8. Nitrogen-fixing bacteria in root nodules of a legume.

Sea anemone is a typical example of facultative mutualism, wherein animal gets attached to the shell of hermit crab. The sea anemone growing on the back of the crab provides camouflage and protection, and in turn, the sea anemone is transported to reach new sources of food. This type of mutualism in called **protoco-operation**.

Fig. 24.9. Crab and sea anemone mutualism.

Green *Hydra* presents another example of mutualism, this animal has green photosynthetic alga in the protective ectoderm. The alga gives off oxygen benefitting the animals which, in turn supplies CO_2 and nitrogen to the plant.

Commensalism. Some organisms live together so that one organism benefits by the relationship while the other organism is neither helped nor harmed. This type of relationship is known as **commensalism**. An example of this association is the relationship between the shark and the small remora fish. The remoras may attach themselves to the shark as it swims through the water. When the shark finds food, the remoras eat some of the food not consumed by the shark. The shark is not harmed by the remora, while the remora is

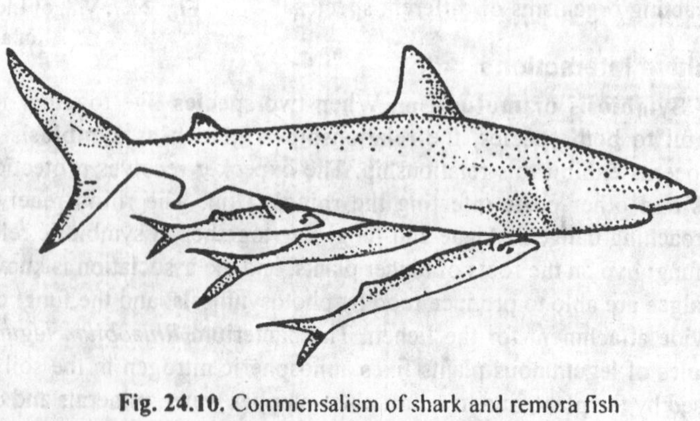

Fig. 24.10. Commensalism of shark and remora fish

helped. The attachment of the sedentary sea anemone to the body of a hermit crab and barnacles to a whale are other examples of commensalism.

Some epiphytes, such as orchids, mosses, ferns, etc., are the best examples. Epiphytes depend upon the other trees for support and nutrients. They manufacture their own food but do not help the supporting plant any way.

Several woody climbers (lianas) take the support of the trees for exposing their canopy above ground without doing any harm to the supporting trees.

Negative Interactions

Certain interactions between different species give rise to negative effect on either or both species. Parasitism and predation are interaction where one species gains and the other suffers. While in the interaction called competition both species are harmed.

Parasitism. This is a relationship in which one organism, the **parasite** spends much or all of its life living in or another organism, the **host**. The parasite is dependent upon the host for food. The parasite benefits from the relationship and the host is always harmed. Parasites may bring about the death of their host, but most often only weaken their host. Human parasites may be external **(ectoparasites)** such as body lice, ticks, mites and leeches, or internal **(endoparasites)** such as tapeworms, some types of roundworms, malarial parasite, microfilaria and guineaworm. The dodder (*Cuscuta*), broomrape (*Orobanche*), mistletoe (*Viscum*), *Dendrophthoe*, *Striga* and *Rafflesia* are parasitic plants. Certain bacteria are parasitic on human beings and animals and cause fatal diseases such as *Vibrio coma* (cholera), *Mycobacterium tuberculosis* (tuberculosis), *Salmonella typhosa* (typhoid fever), *Mycobacterium leprae* (leprosy), etc. A large number of fungi are parasitic on several crop plants causing diseases like rusts, smuts, blights, mildews and wilts.

A parasite usually parasitises a host which is larger in body size than it, and ordinarily it does not kill the host, at least not until it has completed its reproductive cycle.

Predation. This is commonly associated with the idea of strong attacking the weak such as the tiger pouncing upon the deer, the hawk upon the sparrow, the frog upon the insects and so on. A species such as the frog may be both a prey and a predator. The relationship between a snake and a rat is more than that between a prey and a predator as the snake also seeks shelter in the rat holes. Thus "predation represents a direct and often complex interaction of two or more species, of the eaters and being eaten." This is a negative interaction which results in negative effects on the growth and survival of one of the two populations.

In this type of association and interaction one species (**predator**) kills and feeds on second species (**prey**). Predation is important process in the community dynamism. Predator is always stronger than pery. From population ecology point of view predation is the action and reaction in the transfer of energy from one trophic level to the other. It represents a direct and complex interaction between two or more species of eaters and eaten.

Parasites and predators have some points of difference, they are as follows :

Parasites, like the predators, limit the population of the host species, but they are generally host-specific, and do not have choice or alternatives like predators.

Parasites are smaller in size and have higher biotic or reproductive potential composed to the predators.

Parasites have poor means of dispersal and require specialised structures to reach or invade the host. While the predators are quite mobile and swift, and capable of capturing the prey.

However, newly acquired predators and parasites are more damaging than the older ones, as the latter are familiar and the species getting affected have adjusted by then.

Competition. The amount of food, light, space, minerals and water that are available in a particular habitat is limited. As a result, organisms are in competition with one another for one or more of these factors. Competiton occurs not only among individuals of a given species but also between members of two or more species. For instance, carnivorous animals such as tigers and leopards, compete for the prey. The members of kingdom Plantae, such as trees, shrubs and herbs in a forest are to compete for sunlight, nutrients and water and biological agents for pollination and dispersal.

Populations may compete directly, leading to the extinction or adaptation of one of them. Many animals establish territories within which they live and which they will defend against other of their species who try to intrude. By staying in their own territories, competition and combat are lessened.

This is of two types :

(*i*) **Interspecific competition** occurs between the individuals of the same species and their requirements are common and,

(*ii*) **Interspecific competition** occurs between individuals of two different species occurring in a habitat.

Generally the intraspecific competition is more intense than interspecific competition. Requirements of individuals of same species are similar, and therefore, competition is more intense.

Scavanging. This is a type of direct food relationship where animals such as a vulture or hyena, or a jackal feed on other animals which have died naturally or have been killed by another animal. For instance, the omnivorous animals such as the common crow consume many types of foods including dead animals.

Other relationships. Many insects, reptiles, birds and mammals get shelter and protection on trees and shrubs. Many animals protect them by a highly interesting device, called **mimicry**. This phenomenon is seen in many insects where they develop a superficial resemblance in shape and colour to specific plant parts on which they live. The examples are—the stick insect (*Carausius morosus*) mimics thin dry branches; the dead leaf butterfly (*Kalima parolecta*) resembles a dry leaf, whereas the praying mantis (*Mantis religiosa*) and *Rhyllium frondosum* resemble with the green leaves. By their mimicry, they conceal themselves from predators and other foes.

For the survival of a community, the availability of the other nonliving components is also important, and sometimes one of the components plays a dominant role in determining the character of the community. For example, a community having fruit bearing trees may consist mainly of fruit eating animals, such as bats and insects. On the other hand, in a grassland there will be only seed eating birds, mice, voles and predatory birds living on others lower down the food chain. In a marshy land, frogs, toads, fish, aquatic insects and water birds which feed on aquatic insects are maximum. Aquatic plants adapted to different intensities of light may be found either at the surface or at different depths in water. Thus the environmental factors act as the determinants of the types of individuals in a community.

BIOTIC COMMUNITY ORGANISATION

All the living things make the biotic system of the earth. Neither organisms nor species populations exist by themselves in nature, but are always part of an assemblage of different species populations living together in the same area. *Any assemblage of populations of living organisms in the prescribed area or habitat is termed biotic community.* For example, the different species of organisms occurring in a pond constitute the **pond community**. Some other communities such as swamps, deserts, large lakes, grass lands and many others of different dimensions. Similarly, the interdependent species in any environment, such as a forest, a lawn or a desert track, constitute biotic communities. A community may be composed primarily of animals, or primarily of plants, but most communities consist of both animals and plants. The factors that influence the living orgnisms are known as **biotic factors**. In the natural world there is interdependence of one form of life on another. A population of single species is not a viable entity by itself. It will not be able to survive for long. For example, the sparrows require worms, insects or seeds or some other kind of food. Thus the most appropriate definition of biotic community— "a biotic community is a naturally occurring assemblage of plants and animals that live in the same environment, are mutually sustaining and interdependent, and are constantly fixing and dissipating energy."

However, the different species in a biotic community share a common environment and their relationships are based on direct or indirect functional interactions. The nature of relationship is determined by the requirements of the members of the community.

Biotic community organisation results from interdependence and interaction among populations of different species in a habitat. Large number of biotic communities found in nature due to two specific reasons. They are as follows :

(*i*) Existence of diverse habitats with characterstic environmental conditions and

(*ii*) Co-occurrence of different species whose tolerance ranges overlap with the environmental condition obtained in that habitat. When similar habitat conditions are repeated at another location, the same biotic community gets established there.

Characteristics of Community

Each biotic community consists of very diverse organisms belonging to different kingdoms of living things. The number of species and abundance of population in communities also vary greatly. As mentioned earlier, the organisms in a community depend upon each other as well as upon the non-living environment for food, shelter and reproduction.

Species composition. The kinds of plants and other organisms present in a community indicate its **species composition**, which differs from one community to another. Sometimes, in the same community, there may be seasonal variation in plant species.

Each species of community has got definite range of tolerance towards the physical and biological enviromental conditions of the habitat. The range of environment a species can tolerate is called its **ecological amplitude**. The nature of community of a particular habitat is determined by the species, and physical and biotic influences prevailing in the locale of community.

Dominance. A biotic community may have major categories of growth forms, such as trees, shrubs, herbs and mosses. Out of hundreds of species present in the community, relatively only a few exert a major controlling influence due to their large size, numbers of activities. The phenomenon is called **dominance**. "Dominant species are those which are highly successful ecologically and which determine to a considerable extent the conditions under which the associated species must grow."

The dominance in the community may be the result of co-action between two or more species. Different communities are generally recognised and named on the basis of dominant species occurring in them. For example, a forest community in which pine trees are dominant is called pine forest. Grassland represents a community which has grass species dominating over the other herbs. Sometimes, communities are named after environmental factors, such as desert community, marine community, mangrove vegetation, etc.

Physiognomy. General appearance of vegetation is referred to as **physiognomy**. It constitutes general stature, shape and life-forms of the species comprising the vegetation and actually the classification of vegetation types has been done on the basis of physiognomy. The species of a community can be grouped into several life-forms on the basis of general appearance and growth. The physiognomy is the total effect created by the combination of vertical structure and architecture of dominant species of vegetation. For example, the high physiognomy of a forest differs distinctly from a low physiognomy of a grassland. However, several communities though possess similar physiognomy, yet differ markedly on the basis of species composition and dominants, *e.g.*, different types of forests.

Stratification. Every biotic community has a vertical layering or **stratification** of organisms or environmental conditions. A number of examples can be cited to support the concept of community stratification from different habitats. In **grassland community** three strata, namely (1) **subterranean**, (2) **floor** and (3) **herbaceous** may be recognized. The subterranean stratum contains the roots of the principal vegetation and provides permanent shelter to bacteria, fungi, protozoans, nematodes, earthworms, ringworms and several other invertebrates. The floor stratum consists of basal parts of the vegetation, including the rhizomes of grass plants. In this stratum, generally the insects, spiders, reptiles and rodents are peresent. The herbaceous stratum of grassland community is represented by upper parts of grasses and herbs. Several types of insects, birds and grazing mammals are included in this stratum.

In a **forest community**, five vertical strata are present. They are (1) **overstorey stratum**, (2) **understorey stratum**, (3) **transgressive stratum**, (4) **seedling stratum** and (5) **subterranean stratum**. A typical forest may have an overstorey stratum comprised of trees that are more than forty feet in height. These trees make a canopy. Just beneath this canopy there is an understorey stratum that extends from twenty feet in height to a short distance below the overstorey. A transgressive stratum extends from four feet to twenty feet or more and comprises of shorter shade loving species. The seedling stratum begins at the soil level and extends to the lower limit of the transgressive strautm. The subterranean stratum in the forest community is moist and contains a large amount of humus. It is very prominent upto a depth of two to three meters. Each strautm has its own group of animals. However, most animals can move from one stratum to another in search of food or in response to many biotic factors, such as insects, snails, birds and squirrels. The animals found above the soil include turtles, snakes, some birds, insects and a variety of mammals, such as rabbits, deer, wolves and foxes. The animals living in humus soil are beetles, fly larvae, spiders, annelids, antipedes, mites, protozoans, nematodes and some springtails.

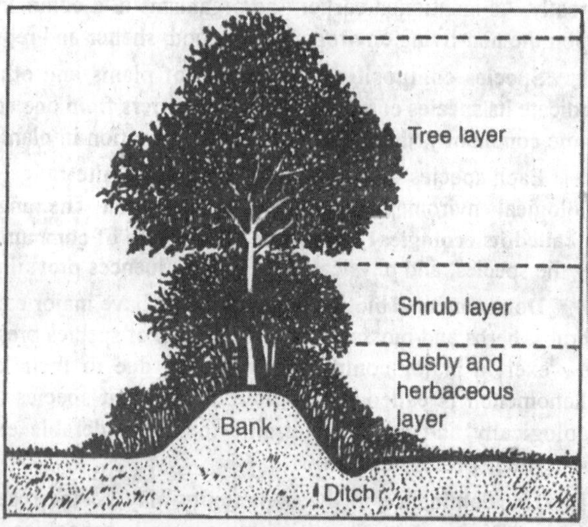

Fig. 24.11. Stratification.

In **pond community**, vertical stratification is very little. However, in deep ponds and lakes three strata—(1) **littoral zone**, (2) **limnetic zone** and (3) **profundal zone** can be recognized. The littoral zone comprises shallow water region and is occupied by rooted plants. The limnetic zone occupies the depth upto which the light penetrates and inhabited by planktons, nektons and neustons. In profundal zone, there is no penetration of light, and therefore, it has no photosynthetic organisms.

Species diversity. The biotic community is a natural assemblage of a large number of plant and animal species in an area. However, in any particular habitat there is no considerable variation in environmental condition, the plants growing together in a community show unique uniformity in their behaviour. Vegetation, therefore, is reflection of a climate and, in general, widely separated areas having similar climate have similar aspects of landscape.

Some communities, for example, tropical rain forest and coral reef community, show high species diversity with many different kinds of species living at each trophic level.

Some community areas have limits but more often the community boundaries are hard to define. A clearly distinguished area or a type of area with uniform habitat conditions and supporting characteristic type of vegetation is termed **biotype**.

Ecotone and edge effect. The zone where two or more different communities meet and integrate, is called **transition zone or ecotone**. This zone of integration may be narrow or wide, local (*e.g.*, a zone between field and a forest) or regional (*e.g.*, the transition between forest and grass land). Ecotone contains few species from both communities. The total number of species is often greater in the ecotone than in the adjoining communities. The ecotone or transition zone exhibits a shift in dominance of the conspicuous species of both sides. It may also include a number of highly adaptable species that tend to colonize such transitional areas. Beacause of this, the variety (*i.e.*, species diversity) and density of life is often greatest in such areas. This potential for the ecotone to act as a habitat for species found in neither major community is called **edge effect**. Thus the tendency of increased variety and density of some organisms at the community border is known as **edge effect**. The organisms that occur primarily, or most abundantly, or spend the greatest amount of their time in junctions between communities are called **edge species**. A common example of the edge effect in action can be seen in those species of owl that live in or near ecotones between forests and grasslands. They depend on forest trees for nesting and do their hunting in the grassland, where they depend on field rodents for food.

In man-made communities such as agricultural fields, the ecotone between the field and the forest act as refuge for species formerly found in the ploughed area, as well as for other plants such as weeds. Ecotones of this type are also the prime habitat of may species of insects, game birds, and mammals.

Keystone species. The species, which have much greater influence on community characteristics, relative to their low abundance or biomass, are known as **keystone species**. Such species play a vital role in controlling the relative abundance of other species.

When keystone species is removed, it causes serious disruption in the functioning of the community. For example, in the tropical rain forests, the different species of figs are the keystone species as they produce large quantity of fruits. During the time of food scarcity, these fruits are consumed by monkeys, bats, birds, etc. Thus, by protecting the fig trees, the animals dependent on them are also conserved.

Link species. However, only a few species act as keystone species, while others act as **link species**. For example, mycorrhizal fungi in soil are critical link species as they establish essential links in the absorption of nutrients from the soil and other organic substances.

Some critical link species are responsible for providing food to the network species, while others act as pollinators of flowers, and some act as agents for dispersal of seeds and fruits. Tropical rain forests are rich in critical link species due to high degree of animal dependent pollination and dispersal.

Analysis of Plant Communities

Generally, analysis of community characters is being done for two specific purposes :

(*i*) to record variation within and between communities and

(*ii*) for naming and calssifying communities.

Analytical characteristics are those features of community which can be observed or measured directly in each aspect. It involves measurements of various charactrs in sample plots, commonly known as **quadrats**. Measurements made in sample plots (quadrats) are scientifically processed to reflect the characteristics of the entire community.

Two sets of characters, *viz.*, (*i*) **analytical** and (*ii*) **synthetic** are studied in a community at the same time.

1. Analytic characters. They are directly observed or measured in sample plots. They include kinds and number of species, distribution of individuals, number of individuals, height of plants, etc.

2. Synthetic characters. They are derived from the measurements of analytic characters and utilise data obtained in the analysis of a number of stands.

Analytical characters are of two types :

(*i*) **Qualitative.** They are based on non-quantitative observations, *e.g.*, species composition and stratification of vegetation. They are expressed only in qualitative way.

(*ii*) **Quantitative.** They are expressed in quantitative terms. They are measured. The major quantitative characters include frequency, diversity, cover, biomass, leaf size, abundance, dominace, etc. They are as follows :

Frequency. This is based on precentage of sample plots in which a species is present, indicating its dispersion in space. This frequency of each species is calculated as follows :

$$\text{Frequency percentage} = \frac{\text{number of sampling units in which that species occurred}}{\text{total number of sampling units studied}} \times 100$$

Diversity. This is denoted by number of individuals per unit area, indicating the relative abundance of a species.

Cover and basal area. This is percentage land area occupied by a species, indicating the influence zone of a species. Although sometimes used in general sense for the area occupied by a plant, (which may be the herbage cover or the cover of basal area), it is generally used for above ground parts. Thus, cover or herbage cover signifies primarily the area of the ground occupied by the above ground parts of plants, such as leaves, stems and inflorescences as viewed from above.

However, basal area refers to the gound actually penetrated by the stems and is readily seen when the leaves and stems are clipped at the ground surface. It is one of the chief characterstics to determine dominance. It is measured either at 2.5 cm above ground or actually on the ground level.

Biomass. This expresses quantity of living materials per unit area, indicating the growth of a species. Thus, **biomass** is the standing crop expressed in terms of weight (*i.e.*, organism mass) of the living matter present. The amount of living material, present in a component population at any time, is known as the **standing crop**, which may be expressed in terms of weight per unit area.

Leaf area. The precentages of species having different leaf sizes, indicating the adaptation of the vegetation to the prevailing environment. As the leaves are essential part and are very much affected by climate condition, their shapes and sizes have been taken as important criteria in determination of quantitative characters.

Density. Density represents the numerical strength of a species in the community. The number of individuals of that species in any unit area is its **density**. This gives an idea of degree of competition. It is calculated as follows :

$$\text{Density} = \frac{\text{Total number of individuals of the species in all the sampling units}}{\text{Total number of sampling units studied}}$$

The value thus obtained is then expressed as number of individuals per unit area.

Abundance. This is the number of individuals of any species per sampling unit of occurrence. It is calculated as follows :

$$\text{Abundance} = \frac{\text{Total number of individuals of the species in all the sampling units}}{\text{Number of sampling units studied}}$$

Synthetic characters. These are determined after computing the data on the quantitative and qualititative characters of the community. For comparing the vegetation of different areas, community comparison needs the calculation of their synthetic characters. These are determined in terms of presence and constance, fidelity, etc.

Presence and constance. It expresses the extent of occurrence of the individuals of a particular species in the community.

Fidelity. This is the degree with which a species is restricted in distribution to one kind of community. Such species are sometimes known as **indicators.**

Dominance. Here, the dominance is expressed in synthetic form. On the basis of density, frequency and dominance (cover) values, there has been proposed idea of **Importance Value Index** (IVI). IVI of a species in the community give the idea of its relative importance. For IVI, values of **Relative density, Relative frequency** and **Relative dominance** (cover basis) are obtained as follows :

$$\text{Relative density} = \frac{\text{Density of the species} \times 100}{\text{Total density of all the species}}$$

$$\text{Relative frequency} = \frac{\text{Frequency of the species} \times 100}{\text{Total frequency of all the species}}$$

$$\text{Relative dominance (cover)} = \frac{\text{Dominance (cover) of the species} \times 100}{\text{Total dominance (cover) of all the species}}$$

Now for IVI, three values are added. IVI values of different species are then arranged in decreasing order.

Other synthetic characters. In addition to above mentioned characters, there are some other synthetic characters. They are quite useful in comparative studies on communities. Such characters include, **interspecific association** and **association index, index of similarity, dominance index, species diversity** and **diversity index**, etc.

BIOTIC SUCCESSION

Abiotic factors such as water, solar energy and minerals determine which populations, especially plant populations, can survive in an area. In general, climate and soil are the main factors that control where plants can survive on land. It is noticeable that plants serve as food for animals and other consumers. The result is that plant distribution will determine which animal populations will be present . On the other hand, it is true that the nonliving environment influences populations, and it is also true that populations influence the nonliving environment.

Abiotic factor and biotic factors interact to produce changes in the ecosystem. As conditions change with time, some populations gradually become less capable of surviving while others become more capable. The ecologists have studied that there is a successive replacement of one community by another. This sequence of replacement of one community of organisms with another is called **ecological** or **biotic succession**. Succession is a process with certain types of organisms always present in a particular stage of development in a given area.

The plants that invade the base land initially, are called **pioneer species**. The accumulation of pioneer species becomes the **pioneer community**. Generally, the pioneer species show high rate of growth but of short life span.

In time, a pioneer community is replaced by another community with combination of different species. This second community is replaced by third community, and process goes on. Different communities, are represented by combinations of lichens, mosses, herbs, shrubs and trees replacing one another during succession, they are called **seral stages** or **seral communities**.

The plant species which are established later are called late succcessional species.

For any particular kind of climate and soil, succession leads to a certain community structrure that is relatively stable and undergoes little further change. The stable commuinity structure of an ecosystem is called the **climax community**. A specific sequence of development of a community is related to a particualr set of physical and chemical conditions. This is known as a **sere** and is composed of a number of biotic successions replacing each other in course of time.

The biotic succession may be of two types—(1) **primary succession** and (2) **secondary succession**. When the succession proceeds from a bare and sterile area or from an area which has not been changed physically by organism, is known as **primary succession**. For example, succession on a bare rock **(xerarch)**, succession in a pond **(hydrarch)** succession in a newly exposed sea floor, lava sediments or sand dunes.

The succession occurring in terrestrial areas with low moisture, such as bare rock, is known as **xerarch**. The succession, that occurs in water bodies, such as ponds and lakes is called **hydrarch** succession.

These two types of succession are described here :

Succession on a Bare Rock (Xerarch)

For example, in the succession from bare rock, there must first be the long process of rebuilding the soil. Organisms such as lichens can survive on bare rock. Gradually, the effects of the lichens together with wind, rain, ice and temperature changes begin to break rocks into soil. The lichens also trap soil that is transported by wind and water. As soil formation takes place, other plants such as mosses, grasses and flowering herbs are able to survive and reproduce. After hundreds of years such succession from bare rocks may result in a climax forest in the area.

The pioneer colonisers on the bare rock are crustose lichens which occur on the rock surface in the form of membranous crusts. Their spongy nature enables them absorb excess amount of water and minerals. The lichens secrete carbonic

Fig. 24.12. Ecological succession on a bare rock (xerarch).

acid (H_2CO_3) in excess, which reacts with the rocky materials and loosens the rock particles. The corroded rock particles together with decaying lichens make the first thin layer of the soil on the rock surface. After accumulation of little soil and humus the rock surface previously occupied by crustose lichens, now gets covered with foliose and fruticose lichens. Now because of enough moisture mosses also invade, and a lichen-moss carpet is formed which provides suitable substratum for the germination of seeds of herbaceous plants which are dispersed in it.

The seeds of higher plants germinate and grow successfully in pockets of newly formed soil on the rock. When the soil increases in thickness, the herbaceous vegetation, which consists mainly of annual and perennial herbs, develops very quickly. The roots of these plants penetrate deep in the crevices of the rock, where they secrete acids and accelerate the process of rock disintegration. Decaying roots, stems, leaves and other parts of the plants become deposited on the soil surface in the form of humus. This further increases the water holding capacity of the soil. These reactions make the habitat more suited for woody plants than to the existing herbs. Now herbaceous species make way for the invasion of shrubs followed by the trees. Decaying roots, leaves, twigs, etc., of these shrubs also enrich the soil with humus. These important reactions bring about such conditions in the habitat, that are most suited to the trees rather than to shrubs or herbs. Now the trees invade the area which has been occupied previously by shrubs. The first trees growing in such areas are dwarf and widely spaced. With the increase in the water holding capacity of the soil these trees gradually disappear and subsequently the mesophytic large trees are developed. Passing through seral stages in course of time, **climax community** gets established, which is generally dominated by trees.

Dominance of species. This refers to the fact that not all the species in the community are equally importnat in determining the nature of the community out of hndreds of species present in the community, relatively only a few exert a major controlling influence due to their large size.

The stability of a community depends upon the large number of species of a community, the larger the number of speices that interact, the more stable that community will be. For example, if a biotic community is represented by a single species of eucalyptus or casuarina (*i.e.*, monoculture), it may be completely wiped out if it is infested by fungal, viral or bacterial disease. However, when a mixture of many species of trees is raised up, only one species would be destroyed by a particular disease, and the rest species will survive.

Various studies and records have revealed that development of a climax forest from bare rocks or sand dunes in primary succession takes about 1000 years or more, whereas a secondary succession requires a shorter period of time. A destroyed grassland recovers in 50 to 100 years, while a destroyed forest in more than 200 years. When a man destroys a forest by felling the trees, or denudes a grassland by overgrazing his cattle, the process of community succession reverses.

Succession in Aquatic Environment (Hydrarch)

Hydrarch succession occurs in the aquatic environment. Such succession is recognisable only if the colonisation of plant communities takes place in small shallow ponds, lakes, etc., where wave action speeds up the process by allowing the erosion of soil towards edge regions. Water bodies are prove to sitting as a result of soil erosion from surrounding areas. On the other hand, blockage of rivers by landslides and construction of dams lead to formation of new lakes, where hydrarch succession proceeds in due to invasion of aquatic species. Thus, the filling process speeds up quickly and consequently the body of water disappears within few years time.

In a new and virgin pond hydrarch starts with the colonisation of phytoplankton and zooplankton which constitute the pioneer community. The simple forms of life, such as bacteria, algae and many other aquatic forms of plants (phytoplankton) and minute animals (zooplankton) floating in water are the pioneer colonisers. All these organisms add large amount of organic matter and nutrients due to their various life activities and after their death, they settle in the bottom of pond to form a layer of silt.

The phytoplankton stage is flollowed by submerged plant stage. The submerged plants, with their roots anchored in the mud are next to colonise the pond. When these plants die their remains are deposited at the bottom of the ponds or lakes. This process gradually raises the bottom of the ponds and lakes up. As this process progresses, the body of water becomes more and more shallow, consequently the habitat becomes less suited for the submerged plants but more favourable for other plants.

Now the **floating plant species** invade the pond. In the beginning the submerged and floating plants grow intermingled but in the course of time the submerged plants are replaced completely. The most tolerant species in the area are able to reproduce and perpetuate. Due to continuous interaction between plant communities and aquatic environment, the habitat becomes changed chemically as well as physically. More water and air borne soil and dead remains of plants are deposited at the bottom. Thus, the substratum rises up in vertical direction. Important floating plants that replace the submerged vegetation are : *Nelumbo*, *Trapa*, *Nymphaea*, *Pistia*, *Limnanthemum*, etc.

With the continued siltation, the pond bottom is gradually raised and water layer becomes shallow and rich in nutrients. The habitat is changed so much that it becomes less suiting to the floating plants, some other plants, such as reeds, are able to colonise the pond. This is accompanied by the invasion of dragon flies, crustaceans and more rooted species, such as *Typha*, *Phragmites*, etc. The foliage leaves of such plants are exposed much above the surface of water and roots are generally found either in mud or submerged in water. The foliage leaves form a cover over a submerged and floating plants and thus they cut off light from the plants underneath them. Under such condition neither submerged nor floating plants can survive. Further deposition of soil and plant debris at the bottom reduces the depth of water and makes the habitat less suitable for the pre-existing plants. When the bottom reaches very close to the water surface many secondary species of plants, such as *Polygonum*, *Sagittaria*, etc., make their appearance. Thus, the species composition of the pond keeps changing with time.

The filling process finally results in a marshy soil which may be too dry for the plants of pre-existing community. Now the plants well adapted to this new habitat begin to appear in the pre-existing community in mixed state. As most of the plant species are sedges and rushes, and therefore, this is called **sedge marsh stage**. With increased setting of silt and deposition of dead organic matter derived from pre-existing community of plants, the pond becomes shallower until it gets transformed into a terrestrial habitat.

Gradually grasses, bushes and other mesophytes start appearing and after sometime the sedge and marshy vegetation is totally replaced by them.

In the beginning some shrubs and later medium sized trees form open vegetaion or **woodland stage**. These plants produce more shade and absorb and transpire very large quantity of water. Ultimately these terrestrial species colonise the pond area and a **climax community** is established. In the climax forest, all types of plants are met with. Trees are dominant and they have control over the entire vegetation. During hydrarch succession, the colonisation by land plants usually progresses from margins toward the centre of the pond area. At the climax stage, a complete harmony is established among plant community and habitat.

Characteristics of Community that change during Succession

The characteristics of the community and their species that appear during primary or secondary succession, vary with their habitats and its conditions.

The seral stages differ from climax stages with regard to their structure and function. The average size of individual plants or animals increases and the organisation of community becomes more complex in comparison to seral community.

Now the food webs become more complex during various successional stages. At the same time, the efficiency of energy use and nutrient conservation increase as the community progresses towards the climax stage.

The composition of species at the climax stage is determined by the climate of particular region, as well as local edaphic factors or soil conditions.

Topography of the region and water availabilty are also responsible for species composition. Where heavy rains are available the forests appear.

The climax stage shows the highest level of vegetaion and the associated fauna that can be supported under the surroundings of environment.

SUMMARY

1. Population is defined as a group of individuals of the same species that inhabit the same area.
2. The members of the population are capable of interbreeding among themselves.
3. The characteristic parameters of population are : density, natality, mortality, age distribution, growth form, biotic potential, etc.
4. Under favourable conditions, the magnitude of population increases.
5. Two patterns of growth form occur, which are known as J-shaped and S-shaped.
6. The size of population is determined by the balance between number of individuals added usually by natality and immigration.
7. The highest magnitude of the population that can be supported in a given habitat is called its carrying capacity.
8. Population of different species that occur in a particular habitat make the biotic community.
9. The characteristic features of biotic community are : dominance, stratification and species interactions.
10. Community analysis may be done on the basis of qualitative, quantitative and synthetic characters.
11. The characters of quantitative analysis include frequency, density, cover, biomass and leaf size of species present in the community.
12. The transition zone between two communities is known as ecotone.
13. The members of the community are interdependent for food, reproduction and protection.
14. The insects and moths play an important role in pollination of plants.
15. The interaction in between members of the biotic community may have positive or negative effects
16. Organisms living together when benefit each other, the process is called mutualism.
17. When one organism may benefit the other without affecting it, the process is commensalism.
18. In certain cases one organism may adversely affect the other, they are called predator and prey respectively.
19. The relationship in whih the smaller organism, called parasite adversely affects the larger host, is called parasitism.
20. The biotic community is always dynamic, and undergoes changes with the passage of time; such changes are sequentially ordered and constitute succession.
21. The process of succession involves replacement of one community by the other.
22. Succession begins with invasion of the barren area by the pioneer species and thereafter other suitable species develop.
23. Ultimately succession leads to a climax community. The climax community is stable till the environment does not change.

TERMS TO REMEMBER

Analytic characters. The characters, which are directly observed or measured in sample plots.

Biomass. Quantity of living materials per unit area, indicating the growth of a species.

Biotic community. Poupulations of a variety of plants, animals and micro-organisms living together within a habitat.

Biotic potential. The inherent maximum capacity of an organism to reproduce or increase in number.

Carrying capacity. The maximum number of individuals of a population that can be sustained indefinitely in a given habitat in carrying capacity (K).

Commensalism. A relationship between two species where one species in benefitted, while the other neither gets any benefit nor adversely affected.

Climax community. The terminal stage of succession.

Competition. Interaction between two species, where both suffer adverse effects.

Cover. Percentage of land area occupied by a species, indicating the influence zone of a species.

Density. It is expressed as the total number of individuals present per unit area or volume at a given time.

Dominance. Where one or few species in a community are in abundance to dominate and influence other species in terms of numbers and biomass production.

Diversity. Number of individuals per unit area, indicating the relative abundance of a species.

Ecological succession. The succession replacement of communitites in an area over a period of time.

Ecotone. The transition zone between two communities.

Ectoparasites. The parasites which remian outside the host.

Edge species. The organisms which spend greatest amount of their time in junctions between communities.

Edge effect. The tendency of increased variety and density of some organisms at the community border.

Environmental resistance. The environmental check on population size, or its biotic potential.

Frequency. It is based on precentage of plots in which a species is present, indicating its dispersion in space.

Hydrarch. Succession in aquatic environment.

Keystone species. The species having much greater influence on community characteristics, relative to their low abundance or biomass.

Leaf size. Percentages of species having different leaf sizes, which indicate adaptation of vegetation to the prevailing environment.

Mortality. The loss of individuals due to death in a population under given environmental condition.

Metapopulation. A set of local populations connected by dispersing individuals.

Mutualism. An association of two species where both species are benefitted.

Natality. The increase in number of individuals in a population under given environmental conditions.

Parasitism. In the interaction, the parasite lives on the host, i.e., host parasite relationship.

Pioneer species. The plants that invade the base land initially during succession.

Physiognomy. External look or appearance of the community.

Pioneer community. The assemblage of pioneer species.

Population. A group of individuals of the same species, inhabiting the same area, and functioning as a unit of biotic community.

Population growth forms. Population characteristic patterns of growth with time.

Symbiosis. The condition in which there is a close physical association between the individuals (symbionts) of a pair of species, benefitting each other.

Xerarch. Succession on a bare rock.

QUESTION BANK

Very Short Answer Questions

1. Select the statement which best explains commensalism :
   (*a*) One organism is benefitted
   (*b*) Both the organisms are benefitted
   (*c*) One organism is benefitted; other is not affected
   (*d*) One organism is benefitted; other is affected
2. Community is defined as aggregation of :
   (*a*) individuals of the same kind (*b*) individuals of different kinds
   (*c*) individuals of a population (*d*) population of different species.
3. Parasite can be explained as an organism which depends on others :
   (*a*) for food (*b*) for shelter
   (*c*) for both food and shelter (*d*) for reproduction
4. Define symbiosis, and name the organisms that form lichens.
5. Define the term succession.
6. What is 'hydrarch succession' ?
7. What is 'xerarch succession' ?
8. Define the term 'climax community'.
9. What are 'link species' ? Give one example.
10. What is 'mutualism' ?
11. What is 'biotic potential' ?
12. What is 'ecotone' ? Give one example.

ANSWERS

1. (*c*) ; **2.** (*d*) ; **3.** (*c*) ; **4.** The condition in which there is a close physical association between the individuals of a pair of species; algae and fungi ; **5.** The successive replacement of communites in an area over a period of time ; **6.** The succession occurring in water bodies like ponds and lakes ; **7.** The succession that occurs in terrestrial areas with low moisture ; **8.** The terminal stage of succession, which is stable and does not show changes in species composition ; **9.** Link species are those which establish esential links in the absorption of nutrients from the soil and organic residues, *e.g.*, mycorrhizae ; **10.** An association of two species, in which both species are benefitted ; **11.** The inherent maximum capacity of an organism to reproduce or increase in number ; **12.** The transition zone between two communities; *e.g.*, the ecotone between the grassland and the forest.

Short Answer Questions

1. Write a short note on 'natality'.
2. What is 'environmental resistance' ? Support your answer with suitable example.
3. Write a note on 'population growth forms'.
4. What is 'parasitism' ? Give suitable examples.
5. What do you understand 'edge effect' and 'edge species' ? Write a note.
6. Write a note on 'camouflage' and 'mimicry'. Give suitable examples.
7. Write a note on 'commensalism' with one suitable example.
8. What do you understand by 'predation' ? Write a note.
9. Distinguish between population and community.
10. Explain J-shaped pattern of population growth.
11. Give any example of mimicry in organisms.
12. How is a biotic community named ? Give examples.

13. Compare J-shaped pattern with S-shaped pattern of population growth.
14. What are the important analytic characteristics in community analysis ?
15. Write some special characteristics of a parasite.
16. Explain how predation is beneficial in the long run.
17. Define biotic community. How is it different from the term community used in human population ?
18. What do you understand by the term 'physiognomy' ? Support your answer with suitable examples.
19. What is 'stratification' ? Support your answer with suitable examples.

Long Answer Questions

1. Describe the process of succession on a bare rock.
2. How does succession differ in terrestrial and aquatic systems ?
3. Explain the differences between the seral stage and the climax community during succession.
4. Explain species interaction under :
   (*a*) Positive interaction (*b*) Negative interaction
5. Describe the different community characteristics.
6. How do you distinguish the following ?
   (*a*) Ecotones and edge effect
   (*b*) Kestone species and Critical link species
   (*c*) Ectoparasite and endoparasite
   (*d*) Primary succession and secondary succession
   (*e*) Pioneer community and Climax community
7. Describe the process of succession in lakes.

MULTIPLE CHOICE QUESTIONS (OBJECTIVE TYPE QUESTIONS)

1. A mutually beneficial association which is neceassary for the survival of both the partners is called :
   (*a*) Symbiosis (*b*) Commensalism (*c*) Parasitism (*d*) Mutualism
2. A parasite living in the tissues of a host is :
   (*a*) Ectophyte (*b*) Endophyte (*c*) Epiphyte (*d*) None of these
3. A saprophyte which can act as parasite is :
   (*a*) Facultative saprophyte (*b*) Obligate saprophyte
   (*c*) Facultatative parasite (*d*) Obligate parasite
4. In which of the following association, one of the species gets benefit and the other is unaffected ?
   (*a*) Commensalism (*b*) Mutualism (*c*) Symbiosis (*d*) Parasitism
5. Food derived by killing organism is known as :
   (*a*) Commensalism (*b*) Symbiosis (*c*) Parasitism (*d*) Predation
6. Obligate parasites are the organisms that :
   (*a*) Live on dead, decaying organic matter
   (*b*) Live on living organism only
   (*c*) are essentially saprophytes but can also become parasites
   (*d*) are essentially parasites but can also become saprophytes
7. Relationship between Remora and Shark is :
   (*a*) Symbiosis (*b*) Commensalism (*c*) Parasitism (*d*) Protocooperation
8. Mycorrhiza show :
   (*a*) Amensalism (*b*) Parasitism (*c*) Commensalism (*d*) Mutualism
9. Lichen is the asociation of :
   (*a*) Alga and alga (*b*) Alga and fungus
   (*c*) Alga and roots of higher plant (*d*) Fungus and fungus

10. The tiny free-floating animals in surface water constitute :
(*a*) Phytoplankton (*b*) Symbiosis (*c*) Benthos (*d*) Zooplankton

11. A bird introduced from another country becomes a serious pest due to :
(*a*) Better adaptation to new area (*b*) Increased sexual reproduction
(*c*) Better nesting habitats (*d*) Absence of natural competition

12. Relationship between sea anemone and hermit crab is called :
(*a*) Symbiosis (*b*) Mutualism (*c*) Commensalism (*d*) None of them

13. Interaction in which one partner is benefitted and other is unaffected is called :
(*a*) Amensalism (*b*) Scavanging (*c*) Commensalism (*d*) Symbiosis

14. Association of animals in which both the partners are benefitted :
(*a*) Colony (*b*) Commensalism (*c*) Mutualism (*d*) Amensalism

15. Individuals of one kind (species) occupying a particular geographic area at a given time form :
(*a*) Community (*b*) Population (*c*) Species (*d*) Biome

16. Which of the following utilises inorganic materials :
(*a*) Autotrophs (*b*) Decomposers (*c*) Saprophytes (*d*) Heterotrophs

17. The independent evolution of flowering plants and pollinating insects together is known as :
(*a*) Mutualism (*b*) Coevolution (*c*) Commensalism (*d*) Cooperation

18. Climax community is :
(*a*) Unstable community (*b*) First stable community
(*c*) Intermediate community (*d*) Last stable community

19. The effect of individuals of the same species upon each other is called as :
(*a*) Reaction (*b*) Competition (*c*) Coaction (*d*) Ecesis

20. The invasion of a new community in a bare area is initiated by :
(*a*) Aggregation (*b*) Ecesis (*c*) Migration (*d*) All the above

21. Primary succession on rocks starts with :
(*a*) Herbs (*b*) Shrubs (*c*) Trees (*d*) Lichens

22. The ultimate seral community appears in an area as a result of :
(*a*) Reaction (*b*) Invasion (*c*) Nudation (*d*) Ecesis

23. In a 'hydrarch', the submerged stage in followed by :
(*a*) Reed-swamps (*b*) Sedges (*c*) Floating plants (*d*) Phytoplanktons

24. Plant succession occurring in sand dune is :
(*a*) Psammosere (*b*) Halosere (*c*) Xerosere (*d*) Hydrosere

25. Primary succession is development of biotic communities on :
(*a*) Newly exposed habitat (*b*) Cleared forest area
(*c*) Freshly harvested crop field (*d*) Pond filled after a dry season

ANSWERS

1. (*d*) **2.** (*b*) **3.** (*a*) **4.** (*a*) **5.** (*d*) **6.** (*b*) **7.** (*b*) **8.** (*d*) **9.** (*b*) **10.** (*d*)
11. (*d*) **12.** (*b*) **13.** (*c*) **14.** (*c*) **15.** (*b*) **16.** (*a*) **17.** (*b*) **18.** (*d*) **19.** (*a*) **20.** (*b*)
21. (*d*) **22.** (*a*) **23.** (*c*) **24.** (*a*) **25.** (*a*)

25
CHAPTER

Ecosystem: Structure and Function

The populations of organisms interact with each other in biological communities, and no biotic community can live in isolation. It lives in an environment which supplies its material and energy requirements and provides other living conditions. A biological community interacting with the non-living environment is called an **ecosystem**. An ecosystem can be natural or artificial, temporary or permanent. A pond, a lake, a tract of forest, a coral reef, a large grassland, a village, an aquarium, a field of sugarcane, a manned spaceship, or a laboratory culture can all be regarded as ecosystems. Thus, an ecosystem may be defined as *a dynamic system which includes both organisms (biotic component) and abiotic environment influencing the properties of each other and both necessary for the maintenance of life.*

The concept of ecosystem was first put forth by Sir Arthur Tansley in 1935. Ecosystems can be recognised as self-regulating and self-sustaining units of landscape. Ecosystem is the major ecological unit. In nature, two major categories of ecosystems may be distinguished: (*i*) **terrestrial** and (*ii*) **aquatic**. Forests, grasslands and deserts are main examples of terrestrial ecosystems, while ponds, lakes, streams or salt water (marine estuaries) represent aquatic ecosystems.

Ecosystem has both **structure** and **function**. The structure is related to species diversity. The more complex is the structure the greater is the diversity of the species in the ecosystem. The function of ecosystem is related to flow of energy and cycling of materials through structural components of the ecosystem.

According to E.P. Odum, the ecosystem is the basic fundamental unit of organisms and their environmental interacting with each other and with their own components. All the ecosystems of the earth are connected to one another, *e.g.*, river ecosystem is connected with the ecosystem of oceans, and a small ecosystem of dead logs is a part of large ecosystem of a forest.

However, human activities may modify natural ecosystems into man -made or anthropogenic ecosystems. For example, natural forests have been cut and the land converted to tree plantations or agricultural systems. Sometimes dam construction involves submergence of forests and conversion to water reservoirs.

COMPONENTS OF ECOSYSTEM

Organisation of the Ecosystem

The living parts **(biotic component)** and the non-living parts **(abiotic component)** of ecosystems are very closely interconnected. As we have studied that the energy flows in the form of food from one organism to another organism within a community. This is being done through feeding relationships such as grazing, predation and parasitism. The biotic community is only one part of ecosystem. Another important part of ecosystem is the **abiotic** portion. The abiotic part of the ecosystem includes chemical elements such as oxygen, carbon and nitrogen. It also includes physical elements such as oxygen, carbon and nitrogen. It also includes physical elements such as wind, fire and climate. Together, the biotic and abiotic parts determine the characteristics of the ecosystem.

The study of the functional aspect of an ecosystem consists of the volume and the rate at which various materials circulate and the rate at which energy flows through it. Energy moves through the food chain in one direction only. The movement of matter, is **cyclic** or circular. Energy flows through the ecosystem and is finally lost to space in the form of heat. Matter may be changed from one form to another, but it always remains in the ecosystem. The study of the functional aspect of an ecosystem also includes the processes by which living organisms change the non-living or abiotic environment. The processes by which abiotic environment affects living organisms and the events by which population levels of organisms are regulated.

Biotic Components

All organisms require energy for their life processes, and this energy enters the world of living things through the process of photosynthesis carried on by green plants. Green plants produce carbohydrates by photosynthesis and also synthesise proteins and fats. The green plants are called **primary producers**. Producers are autotrophic, *i.e.*, self-nourishing. A variety of photosynthetic bacteria, chemosynthetic bacteria and photosynthetic protozoans also produce organic substances in terrestrial and aquatic habitats, in very small amounts. In terrestrial ecosystems, the autotrophs are usually rooted plants, such as herbs, shrubs and trees, while in deep aquatic ecosystems, floating plants called **phytoplankton** are the major autotrophs. The dominant producers of shallow water are called **macrophytes**, which are generally rooted plants.

All other populations in a community are dependent upon green plants and are referred to as **consumers**. Under this category are included all different kinds of animals that are found in an ecosystem. Consumers are also known as **phagotrophs** (*phago* = to eat). They are **hetrotrophic** organisms, mostly animals which generally ingest or swallow their food. There are different categories of consumers, such as primary, secondary, tertiary, and scavangers, etc.

Primary consumers are purely herbivorous animals that are dependent for their food on producers or green plants, *e.g.*, insects, rodents, rabbit, deer, cow, buffalo, goat, etc. The herbivores serve as the chief food source for carnivores.

Secondary consumers are carnivores. Generally, they are flesh eating animals that are adapted to consume herbivores, *e.g.*, fox, wolves, cats, snakes, etc.

Tertiary consumers are the top carnivores which prey upon other carnivores and herbivores, *e.g.*, lion, tiger, hawk, vulture, etc.

Besides different categories of consumers, the parasites, scavangers and saprobes are also included among consumers. The parasitic plants and animals utilize the living tissues of different plants and animals. The scavangers and saprobes utilize dead remains of animals and plants as their food.

The non-green organisms like the fungi and some bacteria, which are incapable of producing their food, live on dead and decaying plants or animal parts, and are consumers of a special kind, called the **decomposers**. These simplify step by step the organic constituents of each dead body. Their activities make chemical substances available for other living beings, the producers. Decomposers are also known as **saprotrophs** (*sapro* = to decompose). Generally, they are hetrotrophic organisms, consisting mostly of bacteria and fungi which live on dead organic matter. However, decomposers or saprotrophs release different enzymes from their bodies into the dead and decaying plant and animal remains. The extracellular digestion of the dead remains leads to the release of simpler inorganic substances which are then used by the decomposers. The decomposers play an important role in maintaining the dynamic nature of ecosystems.

Food-getting interactions are made up of several **feeding**, or trophic levels. The first trophic level is made up of populations of green plants and other autotrophs which use energy from sunlight to make food through the process of photosynthesis. These organisms which are mostly green plants, are called **primary producers**. The organisms depending for their food on primary producers are **consumers**. The herbivores such as cattle, deer and goat are **primary consumers** or the **first order consumers**. Animal populations that feed upon other consumers are **secondary consumers** or **second order consumers**, such as lion, tiger, leopard, etc. Secondary consumers that only eat other animals are **carnivores**. Within a food chain, primary and secondary carnivores can be found. **Primary carnivores** eat animals and are in turn eaten by other animals, **secondary carnivores**. **Omnivores** are consumers that eat both plants and animals. For example, humans are omnivores.

Abiotic Components

The living parts and the non-living parts of ecosystems are very closely interconnected. The biotic community is only one part of the ecosystem. Another important part of the ecosystem is the **abiotic** portion. The abiotic part of the ecosystem includes chemical elements such as oxygen, carbon and nitrogen. Among the abiotic factors the most important are **climatic** and **edaphic** factors. The climatic factors consist of temperature, humidity, rain and snowfall. The edaphic factors comprise the soil and substratum

Temperature. A certain temperature is essential for all the vital functions of the plant and for its growth. All living organisms can survive only in a narrow range of temperatue which allows their metabolism. For instance, plants normally prefer a temperature varying from 20°C to 40°C. Most flowering plants are killed at a temperature below 0°C and above 45°C, while seeds remain injured at a temperature far beyond these limits. However, many living organisms develop physiological and behavioural adaptations to withstand extremes of temperature, such as the polar bear can live in very cold regions and hibernates during winter. Some birds and mammals migrate to warmer places in winter to avoid extreme cold. Some desert animals live inside burrows to avoid the intense heat of the desert.

Water. Without water the life cannot exist. The unique chemical properties of water make it the supporter and carrier of life, and all biological activities depend on it. A given molecule of water does not necessarily stay in the same place forever. It may evaporate from a lake into the atmosphere or it may precipitate from the atmosphere as rain or snow. It may be taken up by plant roots and become part of plant tissue. It may be frozen into a glacier or run off the land to meet the ocean. This movement of water throughout the biosphere is called the **hydrologic cycle**.

Plants, in relation to the factor of water are divided into three groups, *i.e.*, **hydrophytes**, **mesophytes** and **xerophytes**. Hydrophytes are adapted to extremely wet situations. The leaves of such plants are fine and thin and possess little cutin. Mesophytes are plants adapted to inhabit regions with a moderate water supply. Examples are cultivated crops, garden vegetables, trees, ferns and mosses. Xerophytes are plants adapted to inhabit in arid or semiarid regions, such as cactus, yucca, etc.

Whether an animal lives in the water, or on land, the water balance in its body must be maintained. The amphibians and earthworms always live in a moist environment. Most animals obtain water by drinking. Many animals get most of the water they need from their food. Some carnivorous animals obtain their water from the blood of their prey. The termites live without the intake of water. They satisfy their water requirements from the water of metabolism. The camel can live for long periods without drinking water partly because it has a flexible water temperature.

The animals that cannot actively swim live under stones or in burrows and crevices, to avoid the strong water currents. The plants found in fast flowing water possess finely divided or thin ribbon-shaped leaves. Sea anemones and limpets, living in the intertidal zone of sea have sessile habit, whereas *Neries* and some tube worms live in the burrows in soil. The sea weeds such as *Fucus*, *Laminaria*, *Macrocystis* and *Nereocystis* are found in attached condition to face the waves and water currents.

Humidity. The humidity of the atmosphere directly regulates the rate of transpiration and perspiration from the plants and animals respectively. Various plants and animals develop several adaptations to face dry conditions.

Light. Light is an important ecological factor which is essential for photosynthetic organisms for the preparation of food, on which the whole living world depends. The reproductive cycle of many species of plants is affected by duration of light or length of day. The response of plants to day length is called **photoperiodism**. Light has been involved in the evolution of **photoreceptors** in the various animal groups. These photoreceptors, such as the pigment spots of many invertebrates, play a prominent role in the procurement of food, the avoidance of enemies, and the recognition of mates during the breeding season. Animals such as true frogs and chameleons have the ability to change their colour. They do so by photic stimulation through the eyes. Relative lengths of day and night make an important factor in periodical animal migration. Some animals, such as the deer, mate in autumn when the days are short. Poultrymen have been able to increase egg production by exposing hens to longer light periods through the use of artificial light.

Light plays an important role in determining the periods of activity of animals. Some animals are active only at dawn, others are active through the morning hours, and still others are active only during brightest hours of the day. At night diurnal forms withdraw from the scene and nocturnal animals become active. Many nocturnal animals have eyes specialized for nocturnal vision. The leaves of many leguminous plants fold up or droop at night.

Wind. Air gusts or wind affect the plants in several ways. It enhances transpiration. In the forests it has been noticed that some plants can resist the action of wind far better than others. On seashore the coconut-palms can withstand them well because their leaves are cut into narrow segments with stout mid-rib. Where the wind gusts are quite strong, only the plants with tough roots and stems can survive. Wind is useful in disseminating seeds and fruits, particularly those provided with some kind of appendages.

Soil pH. The living organisms require an optimal pH range for their survival. Certain plants and animals thrive best in acidic conditions, other prefer neutral or alkaline conditions. pH of the soil and water is responsible to a great extent for the distribution of organisms.

Mineral elements. Soil is defined 'as mineral material that may exist in solid or unbroken form, such as boulders and gravels or as finely divided particles of mineral matter referred to as sands, silts or clays, depending upon the texture'. Often these finely divided soils will contain considerable amounts of organic matter that form a very rich productive humus. A soil is described as 'a complex physical and biological system providing support, water, nutrient and oxygen for the plant'. The major elements present in the soil are aluminium, silicon, calcium, magnesium, sodium, potassium and iron. The minor elements are -cobalt, boron, iodine, zinc, arsenic, etc. The concentration and availability of essential mineral elements control the distribution of all living organisms. Plants found in nitrogen deficient soil develop special adaptations to obtain it, such as harbouring nitrogen-fixing bacteria, and the insectivorous habit of plants.

The salinity of soil or water has great influence on the distribution of organisms. Special salt secreting glands develop in plants and animals to eliminate excessive salt. The fresh water species cannot survive in a marine habitat. Animals living in the estuaries near the seashore have special physiological adaptations for facing fluctuations in salinity accompanying tidal rhythms. The pneumatophores and vivipary are special adaptations in the mangrove vegetation.

Topography. The topography of an area is represented by physical features, such as hills, plains or slopes. It influences distribution of organisms in the direct way. Sometimes, it indirectly affects the factors, such as wind, water current, light or wave action. The centre and edge of a pond, top-side and under-side of a rock or boulder, north and south faces of a ridge are generally occupied by different species of organisms.

Background. The background of the habitat is responsible for the distribution of animals by enabling them to paint against the colour, pattern and general texture, such as desert animals like lion and the camel are sand-coloured. The jelly fishes and sea cucumbers are glassy in appearance. The chameleon changes its colour according to its background.

STRUCTURE AND FUNCTION OF ECOSYSTEM

Structure

As described earlier, biotic and abiotic components are physically organised to provide a characteristic structure of the ecosystem. Important structural features are:

(*i*) **Species composition** and (*ii*) **Stratification**

For example, some ecosystems, such as tropical rain forests, show a canopy of tall plants and a large number of biological species. On the other hand, a desert ecosytem shows a low discontinuous layer of herbs or small shrubs which consist of less number of species and extensive bare patches of soil.

In the forest, tallest trees, influence the under storey plants and ground vegetation. The plants form more or less, distinct strata or storeys on vertical as well as in horizontal planes, which is characteristically known as **stratification**. The individuals of different layers represent different species of plants.

Trophic levels. There is another way to depict the structure of ecosystem through food relationships of producers and consumers. Trophic or food structure of ecosystem is based on the existence of several trophic levels.

The energy in a community is passed from one organism to another in feeding patterns. These patterns of energy transference together form a **food chain**. Each step in the food chain represents a **trophic level**. The plants represent the **first trophic level**, the herbivores make the **second trophic level**, the primary carnivores constitute the **third trophic level**, and the secondary carnivores, such as large fish, man, etc., constitute the **fourth trophic level** of an ecosystem. Thus energy from the sun enters the living world through photosynthetic organisms and passes open from one organism to another in the form of food.

Trophic structure may be described in terms of living material, called **standing crop**, found in different trophic levels at a given time. The standing crop is commonly expressed as the **biomass** of organisms per unit area. The biomass is defined as the total weight of dry matter (dry weight) present in the ecosystem at any one time.

Nutrients are required for the proper growth and development of living organisms. They flow from abiotic to biotic components and back to the non-living component again in a more or less cyclic manner. This is known as biogeochemical cycle or inorganic-organic cycle. The amounts of nutrients, such as nitrogen, phosphorus and calcium present in the soil at any given time, is called the **standing state**. The standing states of nutrients differ from one ecosystem to another, or with seasons even in the same ecosystem.

Function of Ecosystem

An ecosystem is a discrete structural, functional and life sustaining environmental system. The environmental system consists of biotic and abiotic components in a habitat. The synthesis and perpetuation processes involve energy exchange and this energy comes from the sun in the form of light or solar energy. Thus, in any ecosystem, there are three functional components:

(*i*) Inorganic constituents (*i.e.*, air, water and minerals)

(*ii*) Organisms (*i.e.*, plants, animals and microbes), and

(*iii*) Energy input which enters from outside (*i.e.*, sun).

These three interact and form an environmental system. Inorganic constituents are synthesized into organic structures by the green plants (primary producers) through photosynthesis and solar energy is utilized in the process. Green plants become the source of energy of renewals (herbivores) which, in turn become source of energy for the flesh eating animals (carnivores). Animals, of all types grow and add organic matter to their body weight and their source of energy is complex organic compound taken as food. They are known as secondary producers. All the living organisms, whether plants or animals in an ecosystem have a definite life span after which they die.

The dead organic remains of plants and animals provide food for saprophytic microbes, such as bacteria, fungi, and many other animals. The saprobes ultimately decompose the organic structure and break the complex molecules and liberate the inorganic compounds into their environment. These organisms are known as decomposers.

During the process of decomposition of organic molecules the energy which kept the inorganic components bound together in the form of organic molecules gets liberated into the environment as heat energy. Thus, in an ecosystem energy from the sun, the input is fixed by the plants and transferred to animal components.

The ecosystems operating in different habitats, such as deserts, forests, grasslands and seas are interdependent on one another. The energy and nutrients of one way find their way into another, so that, ultimately all parts of the earth are interrelated, each comprising a part of the total system that keeps the biosphere functioning.

Thus, principal functions of ecosystems are as follows:

(*i*) Reception of radiant energy of sun.

(*ii*) Manufacture of organic materials from inorganic ones by producers.

(*iii*) Consumption of producers by consumers and further elaboration of consumed materials

(*iv*) After the death of producers and consumers, complex organic compounds are degraded and finally converted by decomposers and converters into such forms as are suitable for reutilisation by producers.

PRODUCTIVITY

The relationship between the amount of energy accumulated and the amount of energy utilised within one trophic level of food chain has an important bearing on how much energy one trophic level passes on to the next trophic level in the food chain. The ratio of output of energy to input of energy is referred to as **ecological efficiency**.

Productivity

The rate of biomass production is called **productivity**. The portion of fixed energy, a trophic level passes on to the next trophic level is called **production**. Productivity in ecosystems is of two kinds, i.e., primary and secondary. Green plants fix solar energy and accumulate it in organic forms as chemical energy. As this is the first and basic form of energy storage, the rate at which the energy accumulates in the green plants or producers is known as **primary productivity**. Productivity is a rate function, and is expressed in terms of dry matter produced or energy captured per unit area of land, per unit time. It is more often expressed as energy in calories /cm^2/yr or dry organic matter in g/m^2/ yr ($g/m^2 \times 8.92$ = lb/acre). Hence, the productivity of different ecosystems can be easily compared.

Primary productivity has two aspects (*i*) gross and (*ii*) net. The total solar energy trapped in the food material by photosynthesis is referred to as **gross primary productivity** (GPP).

However, a good fraction of gross primary productivity is utilised in respiration of green plants. The amount of energy-bound organic matter created per unit area and time that is left after respiration is **net primary productivity** (NPP).

Net productivity of energy = Gross productivity — Energy lost in respiration.

The rates at which the heterotrophic organisms resynthesise the energy-yielding substances is called **secondary productivity**. Here, the net primary productivity (NPP) results in the accumulation of plant biomass, which serves the food of herbivores and decomposers. It is notable that the food of consumers has been produced by the primary producers, and secondary productivity depicts only the utilisation of this food for the production of consumer biomass Secondary productivity is the productivity of animals and saprobes in ecosystem.

There are three fundamental concepts of productivity:

1. Standing crop
2. Materials removed and
3. Production rate.

1. Standing crop. This is abundance of organisms existing in the area at any one time. It may be expressed in terms of number of individuals, as biomass of organisms, as energy content or in some other suitable terms. Measurement of standing crop reveals the concentration of individuals in various populations of the ecosystem.

2. Materials removed. The second concept of productivity is the materials removed from the area per unit time. It includes the yield to man, organisms removed from the ecosystem by migration, and the material withdrawn as organic deposit.

3. Production rate. The third concept of productivity is the production rate, at which the growth processes are going forward within the area. The amount of material formed by each link in the food chain per unit of time per unit area or volume is the production rate.

Environmental factors affecting the production processes in an ecosystem are as follows:

1. Solar radiation and temperature

2. Moisture, *i.e.*, leaf water potential, soil moisture, fluctuation of precipitation, and transpiration

3. Mineral nutrition, *i.e.*, uptake of minerals from the soil, rhizosphere effects, fire effects, salinity, heavy metals and nitrogen metabolism.

4. Biotic activities, *i.e.*, grazing, above ground herbivores, below ground herbivores, predators and parasites and diseases of primary producers.

5. Impact of human populations, *i.e.*, populations of different sorts, ionising radiations, such as atomic explosions, etc.

6. In aquatic systems, productivity is generally limited by **light**, which decreases with increasing water depth. In deep oceans **nutrients** often become limiting for productivity. **Nitrogen** is most important nutrient limiting productivity in marine ecosystems.

The largeness of primary productivity depends on the photosynthetic capacity of producers and the existing environmental conditions, such as solar radiation, temperature and soil moisture.

In tropical conditions, primary productivity may remain continuous throughout the year, provided adequate soil moisture remain available.

While in temperate regions, primary productivity is limited by cold climate and a short snow-free growing period during the year.

Primary productivity of the major ecosystems of the world is as follows:

Table 25.1. Geographical area, mean plant biomass and net productivity in major world ecosystems

Major world ecosystems	*Geographical area 10^6 km²*	*Mean plant biomass ($t\ ha^{-1}$)*	*Mean net primary productivity ($t\ ha^{-1}\ year^{-1}$)*
1. Tropical rain forest	17	440	20
2. Tropical deciduous forest	8	360	15
3. Temperate deciduous forest	7	300	12
4. Temperate coniferous forest	12	200	8
5. Savanna	15	40	9
6. Temperate grassland	9	20	5
7. Desert shrub	18	10	0.7
t = ton = 1000 kg ; ha = 10,000 m²			

Decomposition

Decomposers and **transformers** are the living components of the ecosystem and they are **fungi** and **bacteria**. Decomposers attack the dead remains of producers and consumers and degrade the complex organic substances into simpler compounds. The simple organic matters are then attacked by another kind of bacteria, and transformers which change these organic compounds into the inorganic forms that are suitable for reuse by producers or green plants.The decomposers and transformers play very important role in maintaining the dynamic nature of ecosystems.

Decomposition concerns breakdown of complex organic matter by decomposers to inorganic raw materials like carbon dioxide, water and various nutrients. The upper layer of soil is the main site for decomposition processes in the ecosystem.

Dead plant parts and animal remains are called **detritus**.

Dried plant parts, such as leaves, stems, bark, flowers, etc., and dead remains of animals, including faecal matter, drop over the soil which constitute the **aboveground detritus**, which is also known as **litter fall**.

Contrary to it, the **belowground detritus** is composed of dead roots and also known as root **detritus**.

As the time passes, decomposing detritus loses weight, until it disappears completely.

Sometimes, when decomposition is retarded or stopped, large amount of partially decomposed organic matter is accumulated in the ecosystem.

Processes of Decomposition

Generally, there are three main processes of decomposition. They are: (*i*) fragmentation of detritus, (*ii*) leaching and (*iii*) catabolism.

1. Fragmentation of detritus. This process takes place, mainly due to the action of detritus feeding invertebrates, also known as **detrivores,** where detritus is broken into smaller particles. Here, the detritus is pulverised, when passes through the digestive tracts (alimentary canals) of animals. Due to this process, the surface area of detritus particles is greatly increased.

2. Leaching. During this process, water percolating through soil removes soluble substances, such as sugars and several other nutrients, from the fragmented detritus due to leaching action.

3. Catabolism. During process of catabolism, the extracellular enzymes released by bacteria and fungi carry out enzymatic conversion of the decomposing detritus to simpler compounds and inorganic substances.

It is notable that all the above mentioned processes of decomposition operate simultaneously on the detritus.

Besides above mentioned decomposition processes, **humification** and **mineralisation** occur during decomposition in the soil.

Humification. During this process of decomposition a dark coloured amorphous substance is formed and accumulated, which is called **humus**. This is highly resistant to microbial action and undergoes quite slow decomposition. Humus serves as a reservoir of nutrients.

Mineralisation. A process, which results in the release of inorganic substances, such as CO_2, H_2O and other nutrients like NH_4^+, Ca^{++}, Mg^{++}, K^+, etc., in the soil.

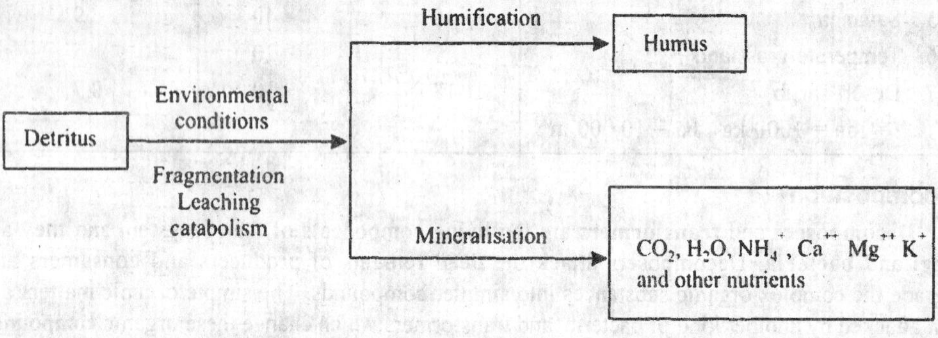

Nutrient immobilisation. During process of decomposition, under certain specific conditions, soil nutrients get tied up with the biomass of microbes and become temporarily unavailable to other organisms. This type of incorporation of nutrients in living microbes is called **nutrient immobilisation.**

Such nutrients remain immobilised for variable periods and get mineralised later, after the death of microbes.

The immobilisation of nutrients prevent them from being washed out from the ecosystem.

Factors Affecting Decomposition

The rate of decomposition of detritus is primarily regulated by factors categorised under two important heads, (*i*) climatic conditions and (*ii*) chemical quality of detritus.

1. Climatic conditions. Here, key role is played by temperature and soil moisture, which have their effect on the activities of soil microbes.

Detritus decomposes very rapidly, within a few weeks or months, in a climate where higher temperature prevails, *i.e.*, more than 25°C, and moist conditions remain constant for long time, *e.g.*, in humid tropical regions.

However, low temperature, *i.e.*, less than 10°C, sharply reduces decomposition rate even if moisture is in abundance. For example, in regions of high altitude, complete decomposition of detritus takes place in several years or decades.

Decomposition rate is lowered in prolonged dryness of soil, even if the temperature remains high, as found in tropical deserts.

2. Chemical quality of detritus. The accumulation of certain substances is responsible for promotion or retardation of rate of decomposition. The chemical quality of detritus is determined by the relative proportions of water soluble substances, which include sugars, polyphenols, lignin and nitrogen.

Even, within same climatic conditions decomposition rate becomes slower, if the detritus is rich in lignin and chitin.

The nitrogen-rich detritus, on the other hand, having low amounts of lignin, decomposes relatively rapidly.

However, the overall rate of decomposition of detritus in natural conditions depends upon the combined effect of environmental conditions and quality of detritus.

BIOSPHERE

The entire global environment is basically made of **abiotic** (non-living) and **biotic** (living) components. These components together constitute the **biosphere** or **ecosphere**. *Biosphere is, therefore, defined as that part of the globe where life exists.* The abiotic global environment is composed of the **atmosphere** (air), the **lithosphere** (earth) and the **hydrosphere** (water), and the biotic component is made of various forms of life inhabiting in the abiotic environment. However, so far it is known, life exists only on the planet we live, *i.e.*, the earth. Life exists only on earth because it possesses all the physical conditions essential for sustaining life; earth too, possesses only certain areas having optimal conditions for the sustenance of life, and also all types of environmental conditions are not favourable to all kinds of organisms, *e.g.*, terrestrial animals like lion or tiger, etc., cannot live in water and aquatic fishes do not survive on land. In fact, living organisms cannot survive without non-living environment around them and the maintenance of non-living environment also depends on its living counter-parts.

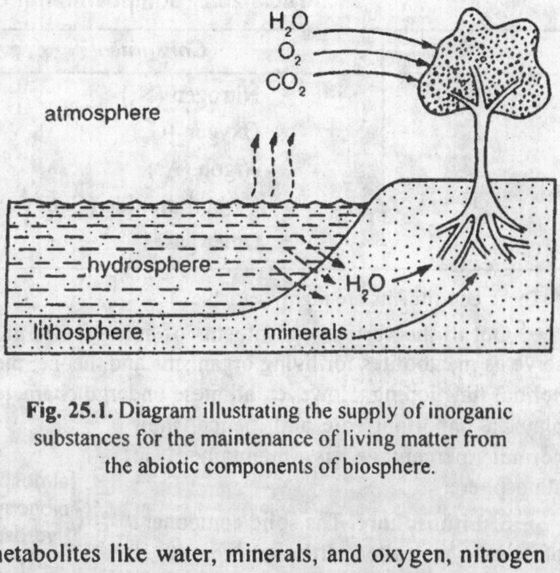

Fig. 25.1. Diagram illustrating the supply of inorganic substances for the maintenance of living matter from the abiotic components of biosphere.

Biosphere is made of different types of ecosystem. It is, therefore, a biochemical system capable of capturing, converting, storing and utilising the energy of sun.

Living organisms require inorganic metabolites like water, minerals, and oxygen, nitrogen and carbon dioxide, etc., for building and maintenance of lives. Living organisms obtain all such inorganic substances from the abiotic counter-parts of the biosphere (Fig. 25.1). Thus, these components are described in detail in the following pages.

1. Hydrosphere. It includes water in the oceans, lakes, ponds, etc., and covers about 73% area of the earth's surface. Water is the major inogranic nutrient needed by all living organisms, hence, water is essential to all life. First life originated in water. The means of obtaining and conserving water have shaped the nature of terrestrial life; means of living within the water have the overwhelming influence on aquatic life. Water is one of the main agents in pedogenesis and is also the medium for several different ecosystems.

Water continuously circulates between atmosphere and the earth's surface; this cycle is referred to as the **water cycle**. The energy for driving the cycle and, thus, ensuring a constant supply of fresh water on land comes from the sun. Solar heat evaporates water from the ocean which is the great reservoir of water. A lesser amount of water is also evaporated from the surface of the land from plants, a process known as **evapotranspiration**. All this vaporized water forms clouds which moved by winds, may pass over land where they are cooled enough to precipitate the water as rain or snow. Some of the precipitated water soaks into ground, some runs off the surface into stream and goes directly back to the seas. The ground water is returned to the surface by springs, by pumps and the transpiration—the movement of water in plants from roots to leaves. Water inevitably ends up back in the sea, but it may become incorporated into the bodies of several different organisms, one after another, *en route*.

2. Atmosphere. It is a thick gaseous mantle which envelopes the hydrosphere and earth's surface, called the **air**. It supplies oxygen, nitrogen, carbon dioxide and other gases and is subjected to physical cycles by the sun and spin of earth. Cooled polar air sinks, while warm equatorial air rises and the axial rotation of the earth causes to shift air masses laterally resulting into the formation of global air currents. The composition of atmosphere is somewhat uniform upto a height of about 80 kms (Table 12.1). Higher levels have lighter gases. The atmosphere is denser near the earth and rarer away from the earth. The atmospheric pressure is more near the earth than away from it. The atmosphere has a layer of ozone at a height of about 32–48 km; this layer acts as a barrier that checks ultraviolet rays of sun from reaching the earth which could be lethal for living organisms.

Table 25.2. Composition of dry atmosphere.

S.No.	*Constituent*	*Percentage*
1.	Nitrogen (N_2)	78.084
2.	Oxygen (O_2)	20.947
3.	Argon (Ar)	0.934
4.	Carbon dioxide (CO_2)	0.0314*
5.	Other gases	0.003

* These constituents are highly variable.

Out of the various constituents of atmospheric gases, oxygen, nitrogen and carbon dioxide serve as metabolites for living organisms and, hence, they are essentially needed by them for their normal functioning. However, all these undergo characteristic cycles in nature in which organisms play an important role and, hence, their normal percentage is maintained in atmosphere.

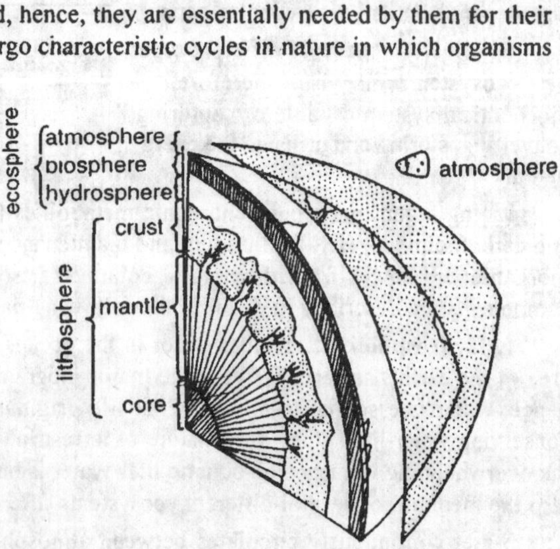

Fig. 25.2. Cross section of earth showing different layers.

3. Lithosphere. The solid component of earth is called **lithosphere**. It is multilayered and includes following three main layers: **crust**, **mantle** and **core** (outer and inner). The core is the central fluid or vapourized sphere having diameter of about 2500 km from the **centre** and is possibly composed of nickel-iron. The **mantle** extends about 2900 km above the core. This is in a molten state. The **crust** is the outermost solid zone of the earth and it is about 8 to 40 km above mantle. The crust is very complex and its surface is covered with the **soil** supporting rich and varied biotic communities. The soil provides food, shelter, anchorage and concealment from predators to living organisms.

The soil is the most characteristic feature of terrestrial environment. It is the top layer of earth's crust and is the mixture of weathered rock materials (*i.e.*, minerals) and organic detritus, both of which are formed through the physical, chemical and biological processes occurring slowly and slowly for a long period at the earth's surface. Besides being the source for the entry of nutrients and water in plants, the soil is the medium for the detritus food chain : nutrients released in detritus are decomposed by various soil microbes like bacteria, algae, fungi, protozoa, etc., bound in or on soil particles and taken back into plants through their roots. Soil (mud) is also the main source of nutrients for all aquatic plants; rooted, submerged or free-floating. In addition, soil is the means to support for all terrestrial organisms: plants are anchored to the soil by their root systems; animals walk upon it and are supported by it, as many animals like nematodes, polychaetes, arachnids, insects, rodents, etc., live under the soil. However, the chemical composition of earth's crust has been shown in Table 12.2. In addition, soil also contains organic matters like **humus**, etc.

Table 25.3. Chemical composition of earth's crust.

S.No.	*Constituent*	*Percentage*
1.	Oxygen (O)	46.6
2.	Silicon (Si)	27.7
3.	Aluminium (Al)	8.1
4.	Iron (Fe)	5.0
5.	Calcium (Ca)	3.6
6.	Sodium (Na)	2.8
7.	Potassium (K)	2.6
8.	Magnesium (Mg)	2.1
9.	Compounds of elements like B, Mn, Cu, Zn, Mo, Co, I, F, etc.	1.4

Thus, these three ecological components and the biotic component of the world constitute the **biosphere**. All these four components, thus, represent the four major global components of the world ecosystem. These four spheres continuously exchange matter with one another in a cyclical manner. Thus, biosphere is that part of the earth in which life exists. More specifically, the sum of those portions of the hydrosphere, lithosphere and atmosphere into which life penetrates, is the biosphere. However, together with the geological, chemical features of the totality of our habitats, these (air, water, earth and organisms) are sometimes grouped under the term **ecosphere**. Biosphere or ecosphere may be thought as a biochemical system capable of capturing, converting, storing and utilizing the energy of the sun. Approximately three hundred thousand species of green plants and microorganisms are recognized as **primary producers** which utilize inorganic elements and compounds to synthesize the organic minerals of life. Their productivity is consumed by more than a million other species of organisms which convert this organic store-house into animal form, adding to the beauty, and value of the biosphere as well as its complexity. Still other species, primarily bacteria and fungi, accomplish the recycling process by returning plant and animal wastes and residues to inorganic form so the process may be renewed. In this cyclic process of life, many elements are shared form a common global pool and are converted from inorganic to organic form and back again. Examples of such elements which commonly shuttle among the air, water, earth and organism are carbon, oxygen, hydrogen, nitrogen, phosphorus, sulphur, sodium, potassium, calcium, magnesium, iron, manganese, cobalt, copper, and zinc.

In physical terms, the biosphere is a relatively thin and incomplete envelope covering most of the world. It represents a mosaic of different biotic communities from simple to complex, aquatic to terrestrial, and tropical to polar. It does not exist in the extremities of the polar regions, the highest mountains, the deepest ocean troughs, the most extreme deserts, or the most highly polluted areas of land and water. Its total thickness, including all portions of the earth where living organisms can exist, is less than 26 kilometres. Its zone of active biological production, in terms of photosynthesis, is much narrower, and varies from a few centimetres to over 100 metres. This zone would, for instance, be only a few centimetres in muddy or turbid water, whereas in very clear ocean water, it could be more than 100 metres in thickness. On land, the zone of biological production might be only a few millimetres in a desert or rock environment, whereas it might again be more than 100 metres in a sequoia or tropical rain forest. Living organisms can exist,of course, beyond the range of active biological production; some insects or birds may be airborne to altitudes above 20,000 feet, and viable spores, seeds of plants, and microorganisms may be found in the atmosphere and mountain tops above 25,000 feet. In the ocean depths, many animals can exist well below a thousand feet—one hydra-like animal has been photographed at a depth of 15,900 feet in the south Atlantic. However, in both extreme altitude and extreme depth, the organisms depend upon the much thinner zone of active biological production, that portion of the system which converts the energy of sunlight into the chemical and physical energy of living organisms.

Spaceship Earth

The earth is the third planet of our solar system which revolves round the sun. In the initial stages of earth's formation, it probably lost some materials in form of light gases. But, as the conditions became suitable for the origin of life on it, the material loss had been reduced and at the same time there is a little inflow of material, from outside the earth. Therefore, the earth together with its atmosphere can be considered a **closed system**. The amount of materials like oxygen, carbon, nitrogen, water and minerals, essential for sustaining life, is finite. The supply of these materials in forms that can be utilised by the living organisms is exhaustible.

On the other hand, earth is an **open system** as far as energy is concerned. The sole source of its energy is the sun. Earth receives solar energy in form of heat, light, X-rays, ultraviolet rays, electric waves and in other forms; some forms of energy which are harmful to life are filtered by the atmosphere. In fact, a very small amount of energy received from the sun is utilised by the living organisms for their energy need and an enormous amount of it is radiated by the earth in its outer space.

Concepts of Matter and Energy

In fact, matter and energy determine the environment, *e.g.*, all objects are formed of matter and any phenomenon or process or activity involves **energy**. Thus, matter and energy are essential for the existence of all living and non-living objects, processes of life and the physical, chemical and biological events taking place in the environment. Therefore, what we see, feel, hear, taste, touch or use are all manifestations of matter and energy.

Matter has mass and volume. It exists in solid, liquid or gaseous states. These states of matter are inter-convertible, *e.g.*, liquid water can be changed into solid ice and gaseous vapours but cannot be destroyed. Matter, in normal conditions, neither can be created nor destroyed. But, it can be broken down into its constituent components, *e.g.*, water can be broken down into its elements of hydrogen and oxygen by electrolysis. Destruction of matter, as it occurs during nuclear fission, generates a large amount of energy.

It is a well known fact that an individual organism is a well organised orderly system. Every organised system tends towards disorganisation due to entropy. So, to reduce entropy energy is required. Therefore, we need energy to be living, so even if we sleep energy is needed, pumping of heart, ventilation of lungs, digestion of food, etc., all need energy. In the same way all non-living affairs, *e.g.*, falling of rain, the blowing of breeze, the running of a car or scooter, etc., involve energy. Objects emit energy as light, heat and sound in the non-living environment and our senses perceive these forms of energy to make us aware of the changes happening in our surroundings. Energy may be in form of kinetic or potential; either directly involved in doing an activity, or may be stored in form of energy-rich chemical bonds, *e.g.*, ATP in living beings. One form of energy can by changed into other form, *e.g.*, electrical energy can be changed into mechanical energy. Thus, energy cannot be created or destroyed but can be changed from one form to other. However, under specific conditions, energy can be changed into matter and vice-versa. Therefore, both these are so closely associated to each other that it is difficult to isolate them. Hence, it is true that matter and energy determine the environment.

TRAPPING OF SOLAR ENERGY BY LIVING ORGANISMS

Amongst the living organisms green plants are only equipped to trap solar energy, the process is called **photosynthesis**. This process is complex one and essentially involves two stages. First of all, **chlorophyll** present in green plants absorbs energy from sunlight. This solar energy is finally converted and captured in the form of chemical energy as a substance called ATP. This acts as transporter and temporary store of energy in the cell. For long-term storage of energy compounds more stable than ATP are needed. Hence, in the second stage which goes without light, carbon dioxide is taken into the plant cell and reduced to organic compounds. The energy needed for this reaction is supplied by ATP. The organic compounds, thus, formed, are various types of sugars. These are used for building new tissues, for food storage, or for respiration to generate energy essential to keep the plant cells alive and functioning. The most important by-product of the process of photosynthesis is oxygen, which is liberated in the atmosphere. However, plants constitute the source of energy for animals.

ENERGY FLOW IN ECOSYSTEM

Energy has been defined as the capacity to do work. Energy exists in two forms: (*i*) **potential** and (*ii*) **kinetic**. Potentical energy is the energy at rest, *i.e.*, stored energy, capable of performing work. Kinetic energy is the energy of motion, *i.e.*, free energy. It results in work performance at the expense of potential energy. Conversion of potential energy into kinetic energy involves the imparting of motion.

The source of energy required by all living organisms is the chemical energy of their food. The chemical energy is obtained by the conversion of the radiant energy of sun. The radiant energy is in the form of electromagnetic waves which are released from the sun during the transmutation of hydrogen to helium. The chemical energy stored in the food of living organisms is converted into potential energy by the arrangement of the constituent atoms of food in a particular manner.

In any ecosystem there should be unidirectional flow of energy. This energy flow is based on two important laws of thermodynamics, which are as follows:

1. **First law of thermodynamics.** It states that the amount of energy in the universe is constant. It may change from one form to another, but it can neither be created nor destroyed. Light energy can be neither created nor destroyed as it passes through the atmosphere. It may, however, be transformed into another type of energy, such as chemical energy or heat energy. There forms of energy can be transformed into electro magnetic radiation.

2. **Second law of thermodynamics.** It states that non-random energy, *i.e.*, mechanical, chemical and radiant energy, cannot be changed, without some degradation into heat energy. The change of energy from one form to another takes place in such a way that a part of energy assumes

waste form, *i.e.*, heat energy. Thus, after transformation the capacity of energy to perform work is decreased, and energy flows from higher to lower level.

Thus, in ecosystem, the transfer of food energy from one organism to another leads to degradation and loss of a major fraction of food energy as heat due to metabolic activities, with only a small fraction being stored in living tissues or biomass. Energy in food is in concentrated form, while heat energy is highly dispersed. All changes in energy forms can be accounted for in any system.

Main source of energy is sun. Approximately 57 percent of sun energy is absorbed in the atmosphere and scattered in the space. Some 35 per cent is expanded to heat, water and land areas and to evaporate water of the approximately 88 per cent of light energy striking plant surface, 10 percent to 15 per cent is reflected, 5 per cent is transmitted and 80 per cent to 85 per cent is absorbed, and an average of only 2 per cent (0.5 to 3.5 per cent) of the total light energy striking on a leaf is used in photosynthesis and rest is transformed into heat energy.

However, only the visible light, *i.e.*, the **photosynthetically active radiation** (PAR), which carries about 50 per cent of the energy of total incident solar radiation, is available to primary producers for absorption.

By multiplying the estimated productivity with the **calorific value**, *i.e.*, energy content per unit weight, of biomass, the energy captured can be determined. The calorific value is determined by burning known weight of dry biomass in a bomb calorimeter in the presence of oxygen, and measuring the heat evolved.

Energy flow in ecosystems. Living organisms can use energy in several forms: **radiant** and **fixed energy**. Radiant energy is in the form of electromagnetic waves such as light. Fixed energy

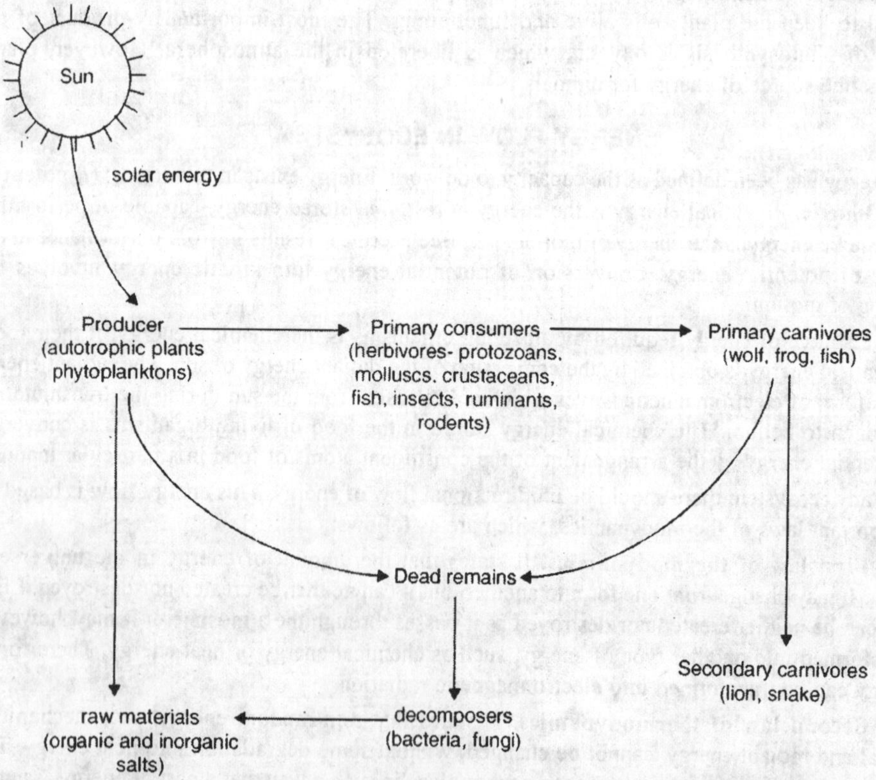

Fig. 25.3. Flow of energy at different levels of ecosystem.

is potential chemical energy bound in various organic substances which can be broken down in order to release their energy content.

Organisms that can fix energy from inorganic sources into organic molecules are called **autotrophs**. Organisms that cannot obtain energy from abiotic source but depend on energy-rich organic molecules synthesised by autotrophy are called **heterotrophs**. Those which obtain energy from living organisms are called consumers and those which obtain energy from dead organisms are called **decomposers**.

When the light energy falls on the green surfaces of plants, a part of it is transformed into chemical energy which is stored in various organic products in the plants. When the **herbivores** consume plants as food and convert chemical energy accumulated in plant products into kinetic energy, degradation of energy will occur through its conversion into heat. When herbivores arc consumed by **carnivores** of the first order, *i.e.*, **secondary consumers**, further degradation will occur. Similarly, when primary carnivores are consumed by **top carnivores**, again energy will be degraded.

However, under favourable environmental conditions, only about 1-5 per cent energy of incident radiation, or 2–10 per cent of photosynthetically active radiation, as actually captured by the photosynthetic process, *i.e.*, gross primary productivity, and the remaining portion is dispersed.

As the simultaneously occurring respiratory processes are energy consuming and use up the part of photosynthetic gain, the net capture of energy, i.e., net primary productivity is reduced to only 0.8 – 4 per cent of the incident total radiation, or 1.6 to 8 per cent of photosynthetically active process (PAR). Only the energy captured in net productivity is used by other trophic levels.

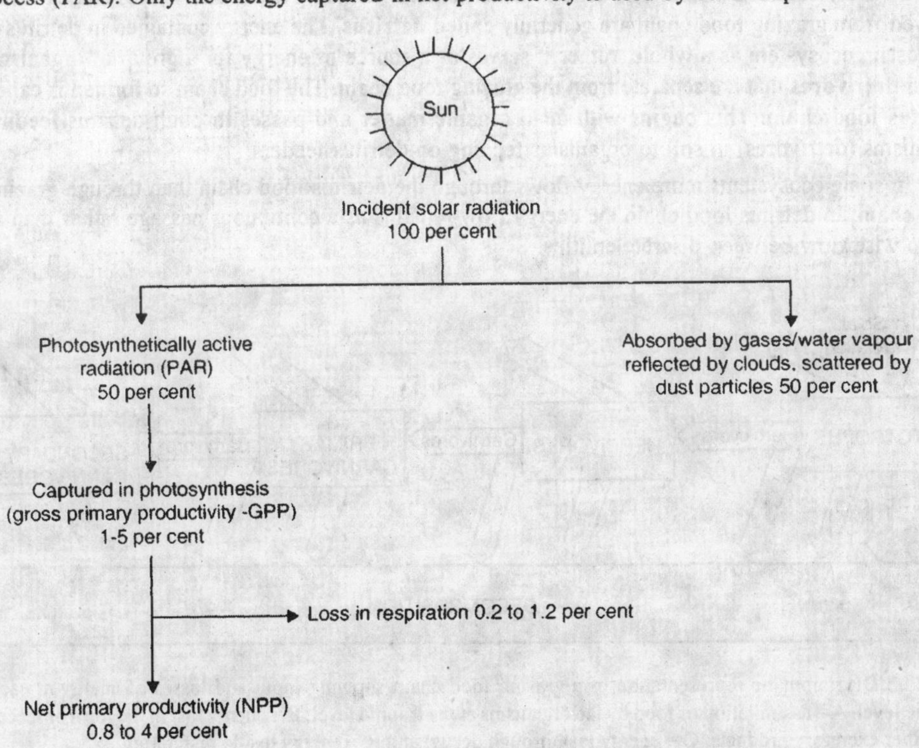

Fig. 25.4. Fate of solar radiation.

Trophic level. The producers and consumers in ecosystem can be arranged into several feeding groups each known as **trophic level** or **feeding level**. In any ecosystem, **producers** represent the first trophic level, **herbivores** represent the second trophic level, **primary carnivores** represent the third trophic level and **top carnivores** represent the last trophic level.

Food Chain and Food Web

In the ecosystem, green plants alone are able to trap in solar energy and convert it into chemical energy. The chemical energy is locked up in the various organic compounds, such as carbohydrates, fats and proteins present in the green plants. All trophic levels in 'an ecosystem are connected by transfer of food or energy. The transfer of energy from one trophic level, *e.g.*, producers, to the next trophic level, *e.g.*, consumers; is called **food chain**. Thus, a food chain may be defined as the transfer of energy and nutrients through a succession of organisms through repeated process of eating and being eaten. Mainly, food chains are of two types: (*i*) **grazing food chain** and (*ii*) **detritus food chain.**

1. Grazing food chain. The grazing food chain starts from green plants and goes from herbivores (primary consumers) to primary carnivores (secondary consumers) and then to secondary carnivores (tertiary consumers) and so on. Cattle grazing in grasslands, deer grazing in forest, and insects feeding on crops and trees, are most common biotic constituents of the grazing food chain.

Autotroph ⟶ Herbivore ⟶ Primary carnivore ⟶ Secondary crnivore, etc.

2. Detritus food chain. The dead organic remains including metabolic wastes and exudates derived from grazing food chain are generally called **detritus**. The energy contained in detritus is not lost in ecosystem as a whole, rather it serves as a source of energy for a group of organisms called **detrivores** that are separate from the grazing food chain. The food chain so formed is called detritus food chain. This begins with dead organic matter and passes through detritus feeding organisms (detrivores) in soil to organisms feeding on detritus-feeders.

In some ecosystems more energy flows through the detritus food chain than through grazing food chain. In detritus food chain the energy flow remains as a continuous passage rather than as a step wise flow between discrete entities.

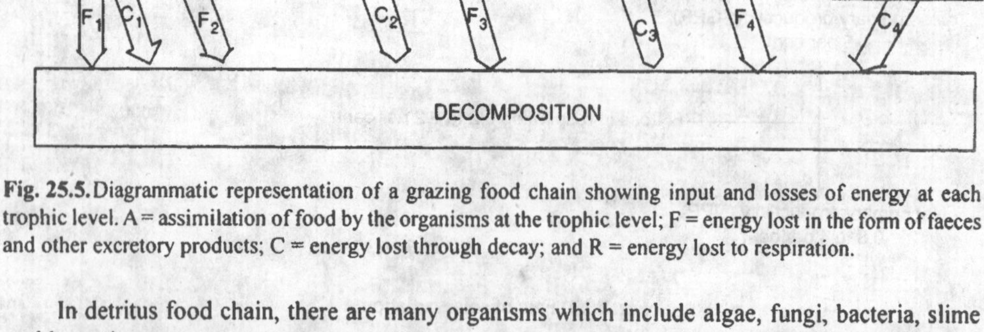

Fig. 25.5. Diagrammatic representation of a grazing food chain showing input and losses of energy at each trophic level. A = assimilation of food by the organisms at the trophic level; F = energy lost in the form of faeces and other excretory products; C = energy lost through decay; and R = energy lost to respiration.

In detritus food chain, there are many organisms which include algae, fungi, bacteria, slime molds, actinomycetes, protozoa, etc. Detritus organisms ingest pieces of partially decomposed organic matter, digest them partially and after extracting some of the chemical energy in the food to run their metabolism excrete the remainder in the form of slightly simpler organic molecules. The waste from one organism can be immediately utilised by a second which repeats the process. Gradually the complex organic molecules present in the organic wastes or dead tissues are broken down to much simpler compounds, sometimes to carbon dioxide and water, and whatever is left that is humus. In a normal environment the humus is quite stable and forms an essential part of the soil.

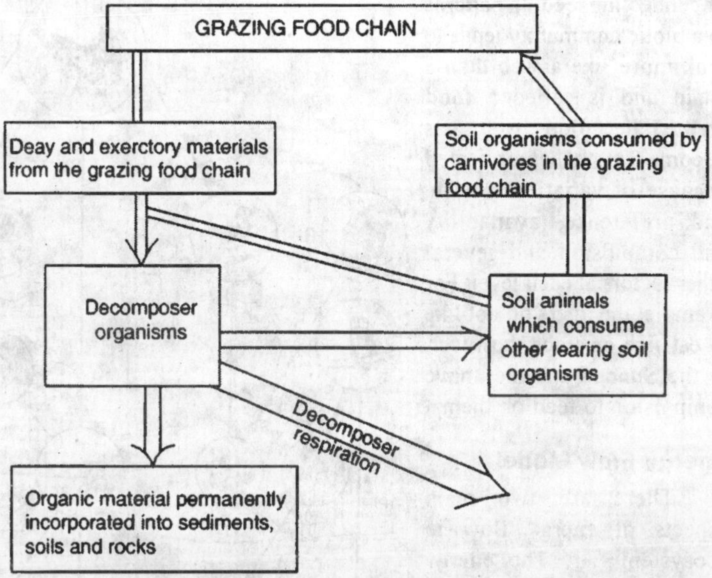

Fig. 25.6. Diagrammatic representation of detritus food chain showing energy transfers between it and the grazing food chain.

3. Links Between Grazing and Detritus Food Chains

Just as energy enters the detritus food chain from the grazing food chain as leaf litter, or dead organisms, energy can re-enter the grazing food chain from the detritus food chain if organism from the latter are consumed by grazers. Considering the diversity of the detritus community, it is not surprising that many of these serve as prey for carnivores in the grazing food chain. A common example is robin eating earthworms. In addition, many insects, among them beetles and flies, spend their larval period in the detritus food chain and their adulthood in the grazing food chain. But through such links through which energy passes from detritus food chain basic into grazing food chain, very little amount of energy is passed in comparison to the amount of energy which flows from grazing food chain to detritus food chain.

Food web. In nature simple food chains occur rarely. The same organism may operate in the ecosystem at more than one trophic level, *i.e.*, it may derive its food from more than one source. Even the same organism may be eaten by several organisms of a higher trophic level or an organism may feed upon several different organisms of a lower trophic level. Usually the kind of food changes with the age of the organism and the food availability. Thus, in a given ecosystem various food chains are linked together and intersect each other to form a complex network called food web.

Communities are not made up of unrelated chains. A consumer often has several major sources of food. A predator such as a lion or a tiger may feed on several different species of herbivores. Ticks and mites, leeches and blood sucking mosquitoes and other insects are dependent on herbivores and even on carnivores. On the other hand, a population of rabbits may be the prey of several different predators. Thus different organisms at each level have food relationship with more than one organism at the lower levels, such as a rat feeds on several kinds of grains and fruits; a snake eats the rat, and a falcon eats the snake. The snakes eat both frogs and rats. The collection of connecting feeding patterns in a biotic community tends to look more like a web than a chain and is called a **food web**. The food web has become more complicated because of variation in taste and preference, availability and compulsion and several other factors at each level. For example, the tigers do not like to eat fish or crabs, however, in the Sunderbans they have compulsion to feed on them.

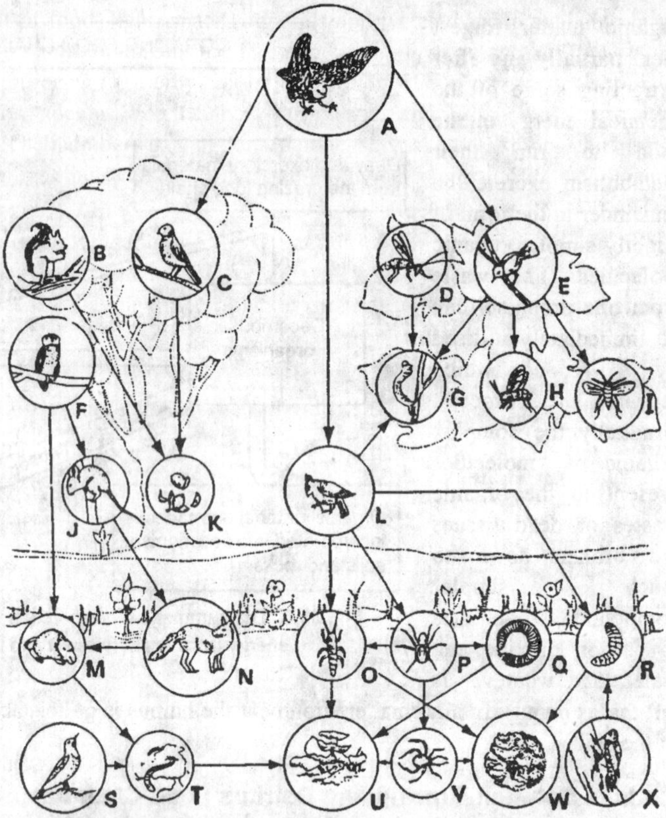

Fig. 25.7. A food web. A, hawk, B, squirrel; C, fruit eating bird ; D, insect ; E, L and S, birds feeding on insects, worms etc.; F, owl ; G, caterpillar; H and I, insects ; J, rodent ; K, fruits and nuts ; M, shrew ; N, fox ; O, insect ; P, spider; Q, millipede ; R, grule ; T, earthworm; U, mushroom; V, mite ; W, bracket fungus ; X, woodpecker.

Energy Flow Model

There are two main aspects of energy flow in ecosystem : 1. The energy flows one way, *i.e.*, from producers through herbivores to carnivores. This cannot be transferred in reverse direction. 2. The amount of energy flow decreases with successive trophic levels.

Producers capture only a small fraction of solar energy, *i.e.*, only 1-5 per cent of total solar radiation, and the bulk of unutilised energy is dispersed mostly as heat.

However, part of energy captured in gross production of producers is used for maintenance of their standing crop (respiration) and for providing food to **herbivores**, *i.e.*, **herbivory**.

The unutilised net primary production is ultimately converted to detritus, which serves as source of energy to decomposers.

Thus, energy actually used by the herbivore trophic level is only a small fraction of the energy captured at the producer level.

On an average, in different ecosystems, the herbivore assimilation or productivity approximately comes to 10 per cent of gross productivity of producers.

The energy assimilated by herbivores is used in respiration and a fraction of unassimilated energy is transferred to decomposers, *e.g.*, faecal matter.

The remaining herbivore level energy is either utilised by the carnivores, or gets transferred to decomposers after the death of herbivores.

The energy available at carnivore trophic level is again partitioned, leaving a very small fraction to support the next trophic level.

The species which occupy each trophic level in the food chain form a link, called the **food - link**. The links of one food chain are a flower, a butterfly, a dragonfly, a frog, a snake and a hawk. Here the flower nectar is eaten by butterfly, the butterfly is eaten by dragon fly, and so on through each successive link of the food chain. The chain ends with the hawk. When a hawk dies, its cells and tissues are digested and used as food by bacteria and other organisms of decay. In this way, the organic materials of the food chain are returned to the soil and recycled through another chain. However, the organisms that trap solar energy and act as producers also use up some energy for their own life processes. Animals being more active than plants use much of the energy acquired before they are consumed by the next trophic level. The studies have shown that only about ten per cent of the food energy in green plants is utilized by themselves at the primary consumer level. Much of the other 90 per cent of the energy goes to heat and movement. The actual percentages of energy from food at one level converted to energy from food at the next level be more than 10 per cent or less than 10 per cent. This general pattern forms an **energy pyramid** as each successive trophic level has less energy available to it. So, at each stage of energy transfer, a considerable energy is lost from the food chain. The decomposition of dead organisms also releases chemical energy. The chemical energy is transferred to living world through food. Food means "materials containing energy that organisms can use". Since food is the means of transfer of both matter and energy in the living world hence the study of food relation becomes necessary to understand the community and environment.

Ecological Pyramids

Studies of various food chains and food webs show that starting from the producers there is a regular decrease in the characteristics (number, energy and biomass) of the organisms occupying a trophic level, whether in a food chain or a level as a whole. If shown graphically these relationships will show a figure of a pyramid, known as **ecological pyramid**. Generally the pyramids are of three types — 1. pyramid of numbers; 2. pyramid of energy and 3. pyramid of biomass.

Pyramid of numbers. In a food chain the members at the successive higher levels are smaller in number. For example in a pond the lowest trophic level is represented by algae and diatoms, which are largest in number. The second trophic level is represented by herbivorous zooplankton, such as copepods, *Ranatra* etc., which are less abundant in number. While the third and fourth trophic levels are occupied by smaller and larger fish, respectively. There is a considerable reduction in the number of individuals from the base to the top of the pyramid. Another example may be quoted of a forest.

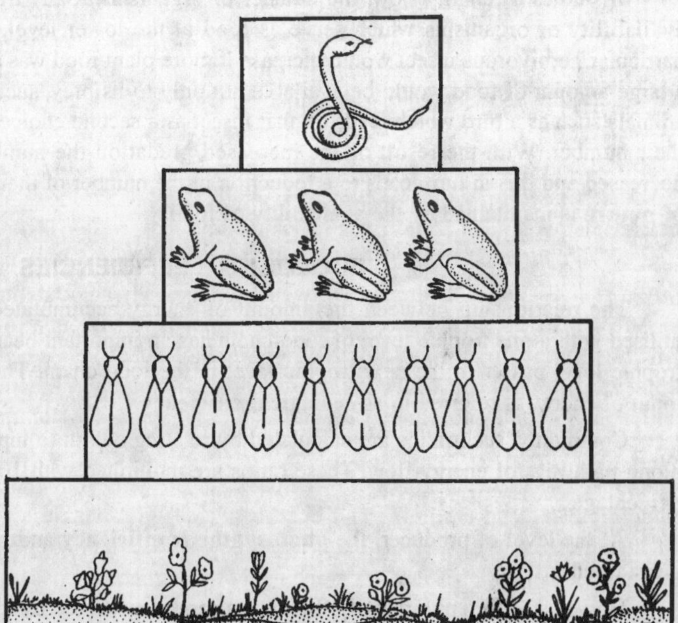

Fig. 25.8. Pyramid of number in food chain.

In a forest the small herbivorous insects are more abundant than the insectivorous birds. Similarly the preying birds, such as hawks are fewer than insectivorous birds.

Pyramid of energy. The amount of energy and matter transferred through food to successive higher levels become less and less. Greater amount of energy is available at the producer level than at the primary consumer level (herbivores). The energy production of the primary consumer is greater than that of the secondary consumers (*i.e.*, primary carnivores) which form next link in the energy chain. The energy at the tertiary consumer level (secondary carnivores) is produced in minimum amount. The actual fractions or percentages of energy from food at one level converted to energy from food at the next level may be more than 10 per cent or less than 10 per cent. This general pattern forms an **energy pyramid**, because each successive trophic level has less energy available to it.

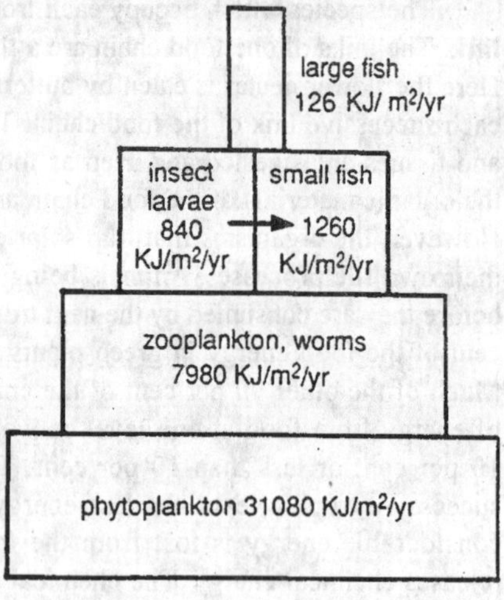

Fig. 25.9. Pyramid of energy.

Pyramid of biomass. The biomass is defined as the total weight of dry matter (dry weight) present in the ecosystem at any one time. The biomass can be measured graphically. This graph represents the shape of a pyramid which is known as **pyramid of biomass**. This pyramid shows the total mass of organisms and gives a rough picture of the overall effect of food chain relationships for the ecological group as a whole.

In studies of energy flow, the number of organisms at any trophic level depends upon the availability of organisms which serve as food at the lower level. For example the number of particular herbivorous insect would increase if more plant food was available to them. In this way, a large amount of food would be available not only to its prey, such as the frog but also to other animals such as a bird which feeds on that insect as a second choice which leads to an increase in their number. With the result of the increased predation the number of herbivorous insects is decreased and this in turn leads to a reduction in the number of their predators. Thus the **balance of nature** is maintained by the availability of food.

ECOLOGICAL EFFICIENCIES

The relationship between the amount of energy accumulated, and the amount of energy utilised within one trophic level of food chain has an important bearing on how much energy one trophic level passes to the next trophic level in the food chain. The ratio of output of energy to input of energy is referred to as **ecological efficiency**.

Commonly, such ratios are calculated by relating output to input of energy at various points along pathways of energy flow. These ratios are multiplied with 100 to express the efficiency as percentage.

At the level of producer, the **photosynthetic efficiency** and **net production efficiency** are considered.

However, different kinds of efficiencies can be measured by different parameters, which are as follows:

(*i*) **Ingestion.** This indicates quantity of food or energy taken by trophic level. This is referred as **exploitation efficiency**. The ability of herbivores and carnivores to use the food energy ingested, varies from one species to another.

(*ii*) **Assimilation.** This indicates the amount of food absorbed and fixed.

(*iii*) **Respiration.** This indicates the energy lost in metabolism.

The photosynthetic efficiency measures the ability to utilise incident solar radiation. This efficiency is expressed in relation to photosynthetically active radiation (PAR).

However **net production efficiency** varies widely in different species. For example, tree species having larger nonphotosynthetic biomass, *i.e.*, huge trunks and thick branches, depict lesser net production efficieny.

The major ecological efficiencies may be summarised as follows:

Percentage of photosynthetic efficiency

$$= \frac{\text{Gross primary productivity} \times 100}{\text{Incident total solar radiation}}$$

Percentage of net production efficiency

$$= \frac{\text{Net primary productivity} \times 100}{\text{Gross primary productivity}}$$

Percentage of assimilation efficiency

$$= \frac{\text{Food energy assimilated} \times 100}{\text{Food energy ingested}}$$

Percentage of ecological efficiency

$$= \frac{\text{Energy of biomass production at a trophic level} \times 100}{\text{Energy in biomass production at previous trophic level}}$$

NUTRIENT CYCLING-BIOGEOCHEMICAL CYCLES

Out of over 105 elements discovered so far, only about 20 of them have been found to be essential for plant growth and metabolism. These essential elements are divided into two broad categories, (*i*) macronutrients and (*ii*) micronutrients. The macronutrients include C, H, O, N, P, S, K, Ca, Mg, and Si, while micronutrients include Mn, Cu, Mo, Zn, B and Cl. These materials flow from abiotic to biotic compounds and back to the non-living component in a more or less cyclic manner, and referred to as **nutrient cycling**.

Plants can photosynthesise simple compounds, such as carbohydrates, using C, H, and O obtained from carbon dioxide and water. On the other hand, for the synthesis of more complex substances, such as proteins, they require supply of additional essential elements or nutrients. Some nutrients, such as nitrogen and phosphorus are required in large amounts (macronutrients), while others are needed in trace amounts, *e.g.*, zinc, molybdenum, copper, etc. Nutrient cycles involve storage and transfer of nutrients through various components of the ecosystem, and therefore, they are repeatedly used.

The nutrient cycle is also known as the **biogeochemical cycle** or **inorganic-organic cycle.** The flow of the elements through the ecosystem must be cyclic with matter being consistently reused. As the flow involves not only living organisms, but also a series of chemical reactions in the abiotic environments, such cycles are called biogeochemical cycles. Nutrient cycles, are of two types: (*i*) **gaseous** and (*ii*) **sedimentary**.

1. Gaseous. The reservoir of gaseous type of nutrient cycle is generally located in the atmosphere or hydrosphere, *e.g.*, nitrogen (reservoir in atmosphere).

2. Sedimentary. However, in the sedimentary type, the reservoir exists in the earth's crust, *e.g.*, phosphorus (reservoir in lithosphere).

Nutrient cycles are generally considered under three aspects, which are as follows:

Input of Nutrients

Ecosystem receives nutrients from external sources and stores them for further use through biological processes, *e.g.*, nutrients in dissoloved state are received from rainfall, *i.e.*, **wet deposition**. When nutrients are gained from dust fall, it is called **dry deposition**.

Symbiotic biological fixation of nitrogen in soil is also an input of nutrients.

Another example of input is weathering of soil parent materials, which releases available nutrients from their fixed state.

Output of Nutrients

Here, nutrients are moved out of an ecosystem and many become input to another ecosystem. For example, lot of loss of nutrients like calcium and magnesium occurs through run off water or through soil erosion.

The other example is considerable loss of nitrogen in gaseous form by the process of denitrification in soil.

Harvesting of agricultural crops, and transportation of logs from forests, represent loss of nutrients from these ecosystems.

Internal Nutrient Cycling

Nutrients in varying amounts are absorbed by the plants from the soil.

Nutrients are continuously regenerated and stored in soil due to process of decomposition of dead organic matter.

Both processes, *i.e.*, regeneration and absorption of nutrients occur simultaneously.

The transfer of nutrients from the soil to the plants by absorption is called **uptake** process.

The absorbed nutrients are used metabolically for the use of plant growth. At the time of death, when plant debris again goes to soil, nutrients are recycled and brought back to soil through **litter fall** of organisms.

Both aboveground and root detritus are decomposed, with the result, nutrients are regenerated.

However, when the uptake of nutrients exceeds the amount recycled, a fraction of the uptake is retained in the **standing crop**. This type of **retention** of balance nutrients in the standing crop increases the nutrient content of the ecosystem. This means:

Retention = uptake–recycle.

Rates of nutrient uptake, retention and recycle vary in different ecosystems, and may be calculated by various chemical methods.

ECOSYSTEM NITROGEN CYCLE

Of all the elements that plants absorb from the soil, nitrogen is most important for plant growth. This is required in greatest quantity. Nitrogen is required for the synthesis of amino acids, proteins, enzymes, chlorophylls, nucleic acids, etc. Green plants obtain nitrogen from the soil solution in the form of ammonium, nitrate and nitrite ions, but the main source of all these nitrogen compounds is the atmospheric nitrogen. The ultimate source of nitrogen to the ecosystems is molecular nitrogen in the atmosphere, which cannot be directly metabolised by plants or animals. Thus, all the nitrogen accumulated in biomass, detritus and humus in various ecosystems, is derived from the atmosphere by biological activities. Nitrogen cycle consists of the following steps:

(*i*) Nitrogen fixation. (*ii*) nitrogen assimilation, (*iii*) ammonification, (*iv*) nitrification, (*v*) denitrification and (*vi*) sedimentation. The details are as follows:

1. Nitrogen fixation. Conversion of free nitrogen of atmosphere into the biologically acceptable form or nitrogenous compounds is referred to as **nitrogen fixation**. This process is of two types: (*i*) physicochemical or non-biological nitrogen fixation. and (*ii*) biological nitrogen fixation.

In **physico-chemical process**, the atmospheric nitrogen combines with oxygen (as ozone) during lightning or electrical discharges in the clouds and produces different nitrogen oxides. The equations are as follows:

$$N_2 + 2(O) \xrightarrow[\text{discharge}]{\text{electric}} 2NO$$

$$2NO + 2(O) \longrightarrow 2NO_2$$

$$2NO_2 + (O) \longrightarrow N_2O_5$$

These nitrogen oxides get dissolved in rain water, and on reaching earth surface they react with mineral compounds to form nitrates and other nitrogenous compounds:

$$N_2O_5 + H_2O \longrightarrow 2HNO_2$$

$$2HNO_2 + CaCO_2 \longrightarrow Ca(NO_3)_2 + CO_2 + H_2O$$

During combustion of various types, some nitrogenous compounds are formed, which are washed down along with rain water.

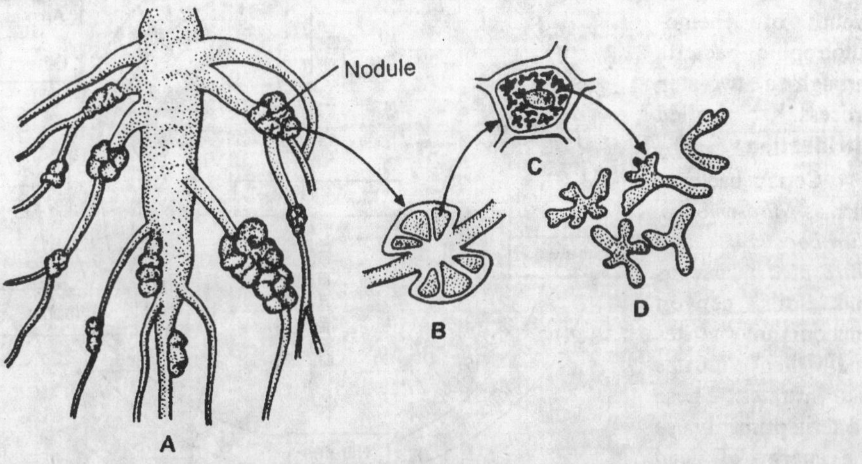

Fig. 25.10. Root nodules of a legume plant. A, legume root with nodules; B, T.S. of root nodule; C, single cell of nodule; D, nitrogen fixing bacterium, *Rhizobium*.

Biological nitrogen fixation is carried out by certain prokaryotes. The cyanobacteria (blue-green algae) fix significant amounts of nitrogen in the oceans, lakes and soils. Symbiotic bacteria (*Rhizobium*) inhabiting the root rodules of legumes and symbiotic cyanobacteria, such as *Nostoc*, *Anabaena*, etc., found in free state, or in thalli of *Anthoceros* (*bryophyte*), *Azolla* (water fern), coralloid roots of *Cycas* (gymnosperm) fix atmospheric nitrogen.

Certain **free living** nitrogen fixing bacteria, such as *Azotobacter*, *Clostridium*, *Beijerinckia*, etc., also fix free nitrogen of atmosphere in the soil. Frankia, an actinomycetous fungus found in the roots of higher plants, such as *Alnus* and *Casuarina*, also fix nitrogen.

Nitrogen fixing organisms combine the gaseous nitrogen of atmosphere with hydrogen obtained from respiratory pathway to form ammonia, which then reacts with organic acids to form amino acids.

Biological nitrogen fixation is the major source of fixed nitrogen upto 140 – 700 mg/m^2/year as against 35 mg/m^2/year by electrical discharge and photochemical fixation.

2. Nitrogen assimilation. Inorganic nitrogen in the form of nitrates, nitrites and ammonia is absorbed by the green plants and converted into nitrogenous organic compounds. Nitrates are first converted into ammonia which combines to organic acids to form amino acids. Aminoacids are used in the synthesis of proteins, enzymes, chlorophylls, nucleic acids, etc.

Animals derive their nitrogen requirement from the plant proteins. Plant proteins are not directly utilised by the animals. They are first broken down into aminoacids during digestion and then the aminoacids are absorbed and manipulated into animal proteins, nucleic acids, etc.

3. Ammonification. The dead organic remains of plants and animals and excreta of animals are acted upon by a number of microorganisms, especially actinomycetes and bacilli, such as Bacillus ramosus, B. vulgaris, etc. These organisms utilise organic compounds in their metabolism and release ammonia. This process is called **ammonification**. After meeting their own metabolic requirement, these microbes release the excess ammonia in the soil.

4. Nitrification. In next step of ammonia formation, ammonia is converted into nitrate by a group of chemo-autotrophic bacteria through a two-step process called **nitrification**.

Certain bacteria, such as *Nitrosomonas*, *Nitrococcus* and *Nitrospira* in oceans and soils convert ammonia into nitrites and then nitrites into nitrates. These bacteria primarily use the energy of dead organic matter in their metabolism. The equation is as follows:

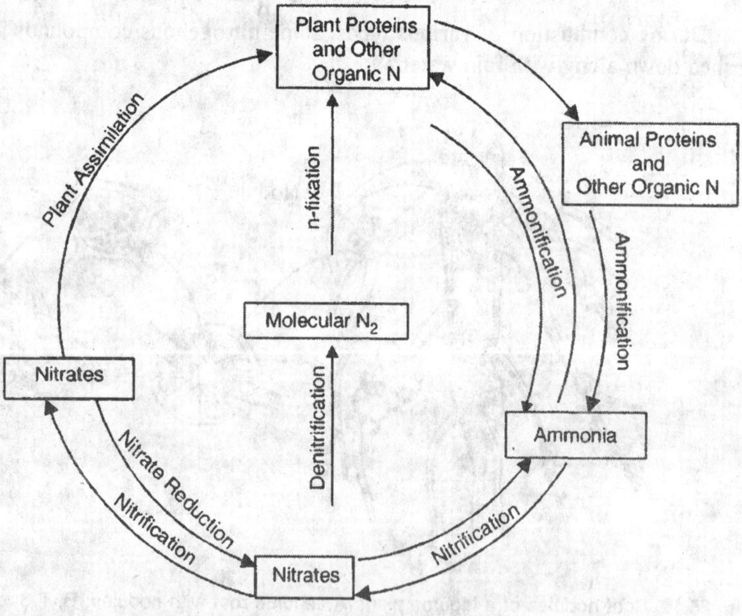

Fig. 25.11. Nitrogen cycle in ecosystem.

$$2NH_4 + 2O_2 \longrightarrow NO_2^- + 2H_2O + \text{energy}$$

Conversion of nitrites to nitrates is brought about by several microbes, such as *Penicillium* (a fungus), *Nitrobacter*, etc.

$$2NO_2^- + O_2 \xrightarrow{\textit{Nitrobacter}} 2NO_3^- + \text{energy}$$

Some nitrates are also made available through weathering of nitrate containing rocks.

5. Denitrification. Ammonia and nitrates are converted into free nitrogen by certain microbes. This process is referred to as **denitrification**. *Pseudomonas*, the most common denitrifying bacterium, thrives best under poorly aerated and detritus-rich conditions. Denitrifying bacteria transform nitrate nitrogen to nitrous and nitric oxides, and ultimately to gaseous nitrogen, which goes to atmosphere.

Denitrification by denitrifying bacteria.

$$2NO_3^- \longrightarrow 2NO_2^- \longrightarrow 2NO \longrightarrow N_2$$

6. Sedimentation. Nitrates of the soil are washed away to the sea or leached deep into the earth along with percolating water. Nitrates thus lost from the soil surface are locked up in the rocks. This process is called **sedimentation** of nitrogen. Nitrogen of rock is released only when the rocks are exposed and weathered.

Thus a large part of nitrogen is fixed up and stored up in plants, animals and microbes. Most higher plants absorb nitrate from the soil; the absorbed nitrate is ultimately converted to organic nitrogen. A fraction of nitrogen incorporated in plant tissues is used by consumers, and ultimately all dead remains convert into detritus and used by decomposers. Thus, complex nitrogen cycle completes.

Carbon Cycle

The carbon is the basic constituent of all organic compounds found in the protoplasm, such as carbohydrates, proteins, fats and nucleic acids. In the non-living world, there are three main sources of carbon; 1. the carbon dioxide in air and found dissolved in water, 2. carbonates of earth's crust derived from rocks give rise to carbon dioxide on chemical changes, and 3. the fossil fuels like coal and petroleum give rise to carbon dioxide on burning.

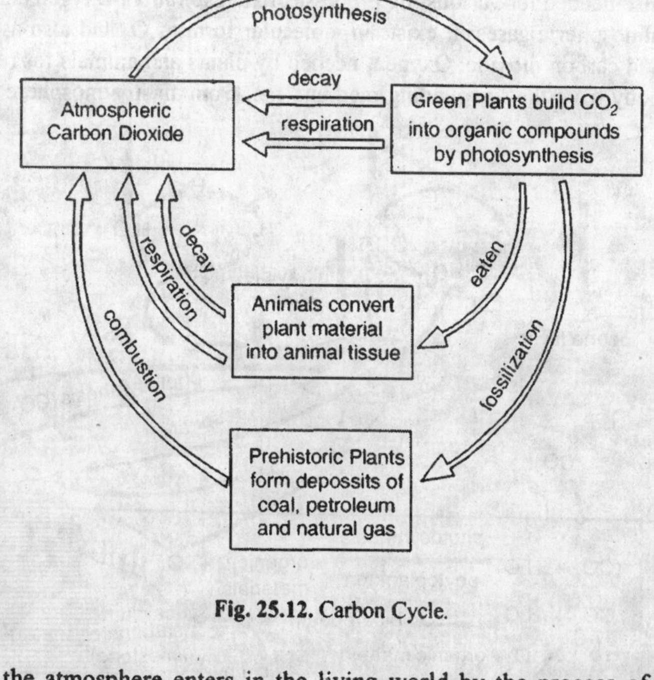

Fig. 25.12. Carbon Cycle.

The basic source of carbon for the living organisms is carbon dioxide. Atmosphere, having a concentration of 0.031 per cent of carbon dioxide, acts as its reservoir. Carbon dioxide from the atmosphere enters in the living world by the process of photosynthesis in green plants (producers). The amount of carbon fixed by photosynthesizers is nearly 7×10^{13} kg per year. As we know, during photosynthesis simple sugar like glucose ($C_6H_{12}O_6$) is synthesized which is subsequently converted into other organic compounds like polysaccharides (sucrose, starch, glucose, etc.), proteins and lipids. These are passed from plants (producers) to the herbivorous and carnivorous animals (consumers).

Available data suggest that one hectare of a healthy forest can produce about 10 tonnes of oxygen and absorb 30 tonnes of carbon dioxide in a year.

The respiratory activity of plants and animals return back fixed carbon as carbon dioxide into the atmosphere. The excretory wastes of living organisms having accumulated carbon compounds and they after their death are decomposed by microorganisms (decomposers) in the soil to release carbon dioxide back into the environment. Burning of wood and fossil fuels, dissolution of carbonate rocks and volcanic activities, all release carbon dioxide into the environment for its recycling (Fig. 25.12).

Under certain conditions, large number of organisms got buried deep into the layers of the earth and they gradually transformed into coal, petroleum and natural gas under high pressure, and temperature. Or, if the process of decay is extremely slow then a sufficient amount of carbon goes out of the cycle. Such events take millions of years. But, when such fuels are burnt, carbon dioxide goes back to the cycle. Similarly, carbon is also locked up in hard calcareous shells of animals and also in their skeletal structures which the decomposers cannot act upon. Therefore, the chief pathway of carbon cycle is from the atmosphere or hydrosphere into the living organisms and back. The carbon cycle is essentially a self-regulating feedback system but may be disturbed by man by the over-use of fossil fuels.

Oxygen Cycle

Oxygen, like carbon, is another essential element for the construction of living body and it is also needed for various life processes like respiration. Oxygen constitutes nearly 21 per cent of the atmospheric gases. It exists in molecular form as O_2 and also as a part of compounds like water and carbon dioxide. Oxygen, needed by plants and animals for respiration, enters directly in their body from the surrounding medium, *i.e.*, from air in atmosphere or from water.

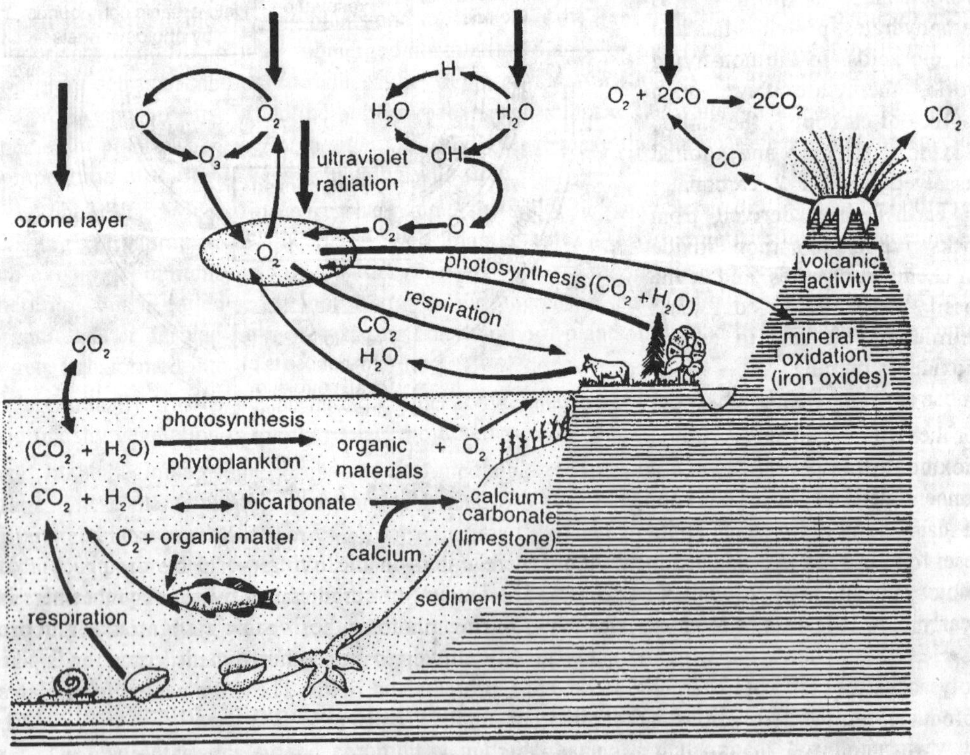

Fig. 25.13. Oxygen cycle.

However, cycling of oxygen is very complex (Fig. 25.13). As a constituent of CO_2, it circulates freely throughout the biosphere. Some carbon dioxide combines with calcium to form carbonates. Oxygen combines with nitrogen compounds to form nitrates, with iron to ferric oxides, and with many other materials to form various other oxides. In these states oxygen is temporarily withdrawn from circulation. In photosynthesis the oxygen freed is split from the water molecule. This oxygen is then reconstituted into water during plant and animal respiration. Some part of atmospheric oxygen that reaches the higher levels is reduced to ozone (O_3) by high energy ultraviolet radiations. Thus, in this way oxygen level in the atmosphere is maintained at a constant level.

The earth's atmosphere, after its formation, has undergone a slow but steady change due to various human activities. Human activity, however, has not had much effect on the oxygen content of the atmosphere because it is always replenished by photosynthesizers. But the condition is altogether different for other atmospheric gases, collectively these are called **greenhouse gases** and the effect they produce is called the **greenhouse effect**.

The greenhouse gases allow the penetration of incoming solar radiations having short wave lengths (0.15 to 4 m m) but they prevent the escaping of long wave length radiations into the outer space and reflect back on the earth causing rise in temperature of the earth. This is referred to as greenhouse effect. For example, carbon dioxide (a greenhouse gas) tends to prevent the long wave radiations (*i.e.*, infra-red heat radiation) from earth from escaping into outer space and reflect it back to the earth. This has caused an increase in earth's temperature. Since, carbon dioxide content of the atmosphere is increasing with an alarming rate due to excessive use of fossil fuels liberating carbon dioxide into the earth's atmosphere, it has a greenhouse effect (Fig. 25.14).

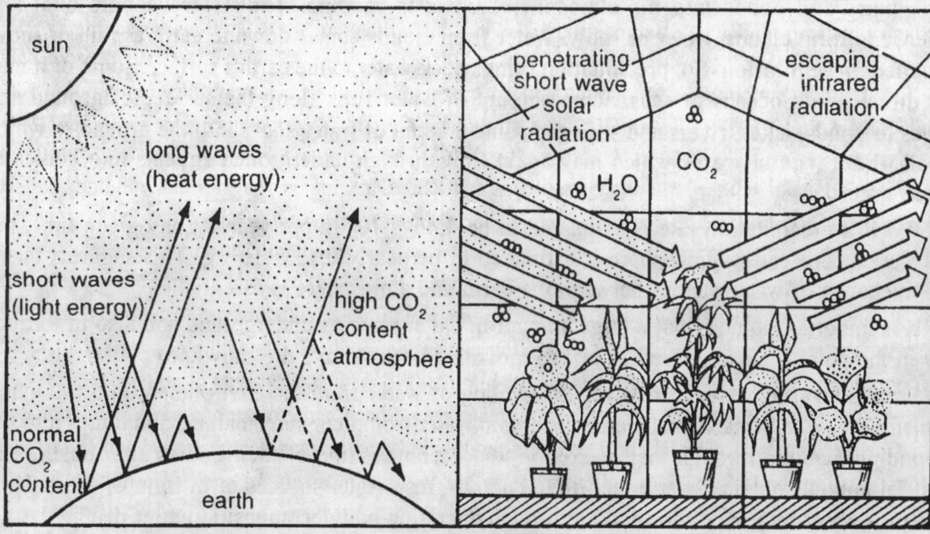

Fig. 25.14. Greenhouse effect caused due to high concentration of carbon dioxide.

Water Cycle

Water cycle basically forms a link between gaseous and sedimentary biogeochemical cycles. Hence, it needs a discussion at this stage before discussing the sedimentary cycles.

Water is indispensable for life constituting more than 80 per cent of living cells. The water cycle is represented by two overlapping cycles in nature. (*i*) **Global water cycle**, being controlled by physical processes involving no life, and (*ii*) **Smaller water cycle**, being controlled by biological processes involving life.

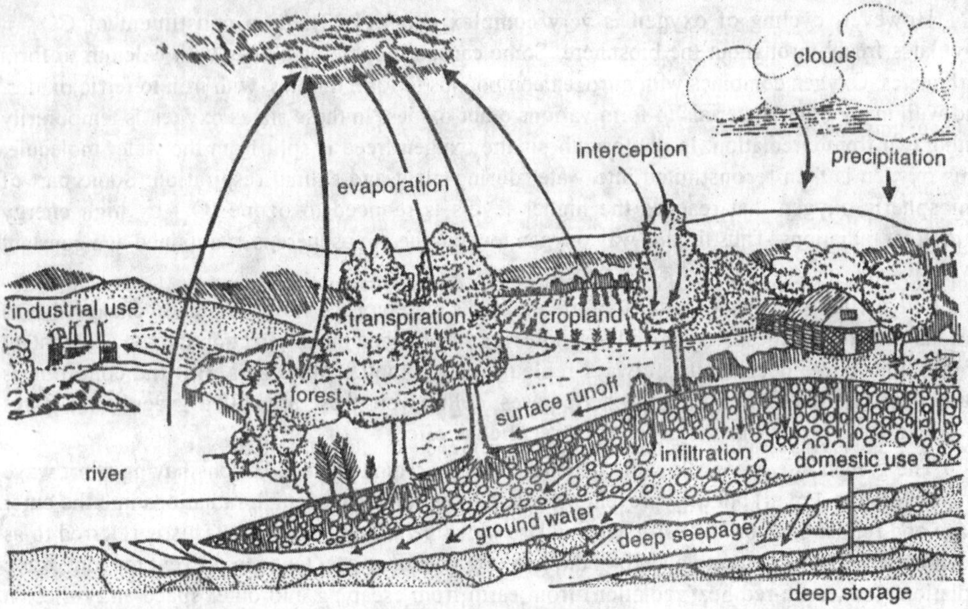

Fig. 25.15. Water cycle.

Global water cycle. It involves evaporation of water from hydrosphere such as oceans, seas, rivers, lakes and ponds into the atmosphere as water vapours. The water vapours cool and condense to form clouds, water or snow. Water from clouds comes down to earth as rain or snow, it is called **precipitation**. So, precipitation brings back water to the earth's surface, some of it may drop directly into oceans or seas, some amount of water runs along the surface of ground and reaches to ponds, lakes, rivers and seas and some amount of water soaks into the ground to which we call **underground water** which may again flow through underground streams into bodies of surface water.

World's precipitation rate is estimated to be 4.46×10^{20} g per year. At any given time, the water vapour present in atmosphere is estimated to be nearly 0.13×10^{20} g. This suggests that a rapid exchange of water vapour between the earth and atmosphere is essential.

It is important to note that a large amount of water remains underground and also in form of snow in the polar regions as well as on the mountain peaks above the snowline.

Smaller water cycle. It involves the cycling of water from the environment into the living organisms and vice-versa. Aquatic animals obtain water from their surroundings and return it to the surrounding medium through their excretion and decomposition of their bodies after death. The terrestrial animals obtain water either directly from fresh water sources or in form of food. They also return water into their surrounding through excretion and decomposition after death.

The plants absorb water from the soil by their roots. These retain some amount of water in their bodies and the rest is given out in the environment as water vapours during the process of transpiration and amount of water left in their bodies returns back to the environment after the death and decomposition of their bodies. Evaporation of water from terrestrial plants cools the surrounding air and, thus, it helps in maintaining a microclimate around them.

The smaller water cycle is complicated one and differs considerably from the global water cycle but both of these operate simultaneously in nature to keep a water balance between the living and non-living world.

ECOSYSTEM PHOSPHORUS CYCLE

Plants and animals obtain phosphorus from the environment. Phosphorus is a component of nucleic acids, ADP, ATP, NADP, phospholipids, etc. It occurs in the soil as rock phosphate, apatite or calcium phosphate, fluorapatite Ca_{10} Fe_2 $(PO_4)_6$ ironphosphate or aluminium phosphate. Soils derived from the rock beds rich in phosphates are rich in phosphorus.

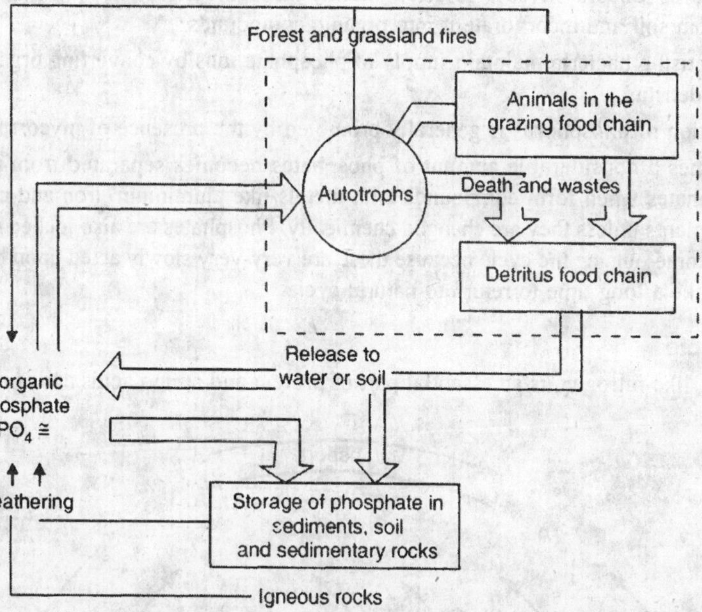

Fig. 25.16. Phosphorus cycle in ecosystem.

Phosphorus occurs in the soil in five forms:

P_1 (stable organic), P_2 (labile organic), P_3 (labile inorganic), P_4 (soluble) and P_5 (mineral form) and of these forms P_3 and P_4 are in equilibrium and entry of phosphorus in the green plants is considered to occur via labile inorganic pool.

The dissolved phosphorus is absorbed by plants and converted to organic form. From plants it travels to various trophic levels in the form of organic phosphates. When the plants and animals die, the decomposers attack them and liberate phosphorus to the environment. Thus this process proceeds in cyclic way.

Phosphorus along with many other mineral elements reaches the oceans and settles down as

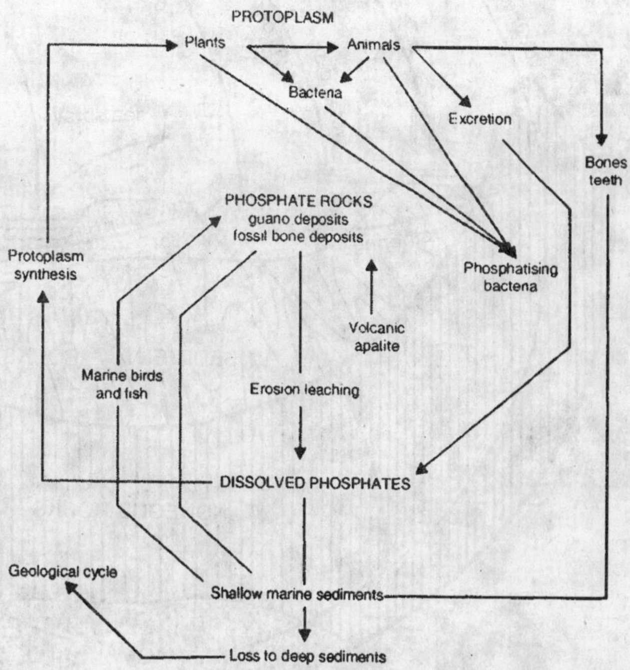

Fig. 25.17. The phosphorus cycle.

sediment. A good proportion of phosphorus leaches down to deep layers of soil. In this way, major proportion of phosphate becomes lost to this cycle by physical processes, such as sedimentation and leaching. Biological processes such as formation of teeth and bones also keep phosphorus locked up for some time.

Phosphorus occurs in soil solution mainly as orthophosphate (PO_4^{3-}). Plants absorb phosphate from soil and incorporate it into organic compounds.

Phosphatising bacteria maintain supply of phosphate ions by converting organic phosphorus contained in detritus.

Absorption of phosphorus is generally promoted by the presence of mycorrhizae.

Sometimes a considerable amount of phosphates becomes separated from the phosphorus cycle ; phosphates when form compounds with metals like aluminium, iron and calcium become unusable for plants unless they are changed chemically. Phosphates are also locked up in bones and teeth, and become outside the cycle because these are very-very slowly acted upon by decomposers and, hence, take a long time to return to natural cycle.

Sulphur Cycle

Sulphur, like nitrogen, is an essential part of protein and amino acids and is characteristic of

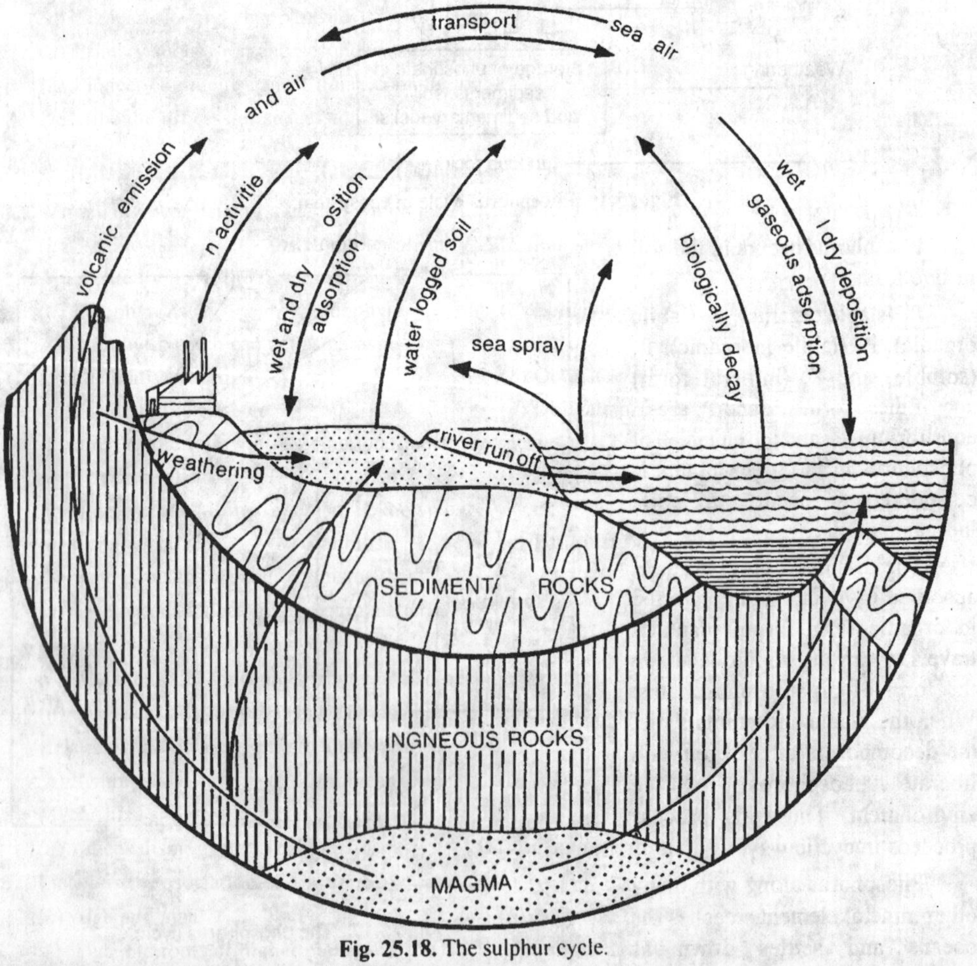

Fig. 25.18. The sulphur cycle.

organic compounds. The main source of sulphur for living organisms is the inorganic sulphur in form of sulphates.

The photosynthesizers (producers) obtain sulphur in form of sulphates from the soil or from water in case of aquatic plants and make use in their protein synthesis. This organic sulphur reaches to animals through food. After death, the animals and plants are decomposed in the soil by microorganisms like *Aspergillus*, *Neurospora* and *Escherichia* under aerobic conditions as sulphates ; these sulphates are mineralised in the soil. But under anaerobic conditions such as in marshes, it is reduced to sulphides. Sulphides, thus, produced are converted into soluble sulphates by sulphur bacteria, *viz.*, *Thiobacillus* into sulphates.

Sulphur is added in the atmospheric air as sulphur dioxide from various industries The fossil fuels also add sulphur dioxide to the environment when they are burnt During rains, sulphur dioxide of the atmosphere forms H_2SO_4 (sulphuric acid) which later on decomposed to give rise to SO_4 ions and then incorporated into living body.

Sulphur is removed from the organic phase in form of elemental sulphur which is insoluble and accumulates into reservoir pool in deep sediments.

Other Minerals and their Cycling

Calcium, magnesium, iron and other minerals (micronutrients), are also cycled in nature like other cycles, as they are also required by living organisms.These are slowly released from the rocks either by water or wind actions and finally reach to the soil and water. Plants obtain these through their roots and animals get them in form of food. Animals like molluscs and corals, deposit a good amount of calcium in their shells and skeletons which is locked for a considerable period and, hence, not available for cycling. The sedimentary elements in the sea return very slowly to the cycle through marine food chains and through coastal sea water sprays. The process may take hundred to millions of years.

Flow of Energy

As referred to, sun is the only source of energy to our planet earth. The solar energy is released in form of invisible ultra-violet light and infra-red light, and visible light. Most of the ultra-violet light is absorbed by **ozone layer** in the upper atmosphere and most of the infra-red light having longer wavelengths are absorbed by atmospheric gases and some are reflected back in the environment. Visible light constitutes nearly 50 per cent of solar energy; a part of it is reflected by clouds and dust particles, and a part is absorbed by the atmosphere (Fig. 25.19). In fact, sun radiates energy of nearly 10^{26} Joules/second but the earth gets only a fraction of it. On the top of the atmosphere, the earth receives energy equal to 173×10^{15} Joules/second , of this about one-third is reflected back into the space by the atmosphere.

However, whatever amount of energy from the sun reaches the earth in form of light and heat regulates the climatic phenomena on this planet. The green plants trap only a very small fraction (nearly one per cent) of available solar energy during the process of photosynthesis. It has already been mentioned that green plants trap light energy with the help of the pigment chlorophyll and convert it in chemical energy. Thus, the energy trapped by green plants, *i.e.*, **autotrophs** is utilised then in synthesizing organic compounds during the process of photosynthesis. The green plants, thus, are the only organisms which can trap and fix solar energy and can manufacture food used by them as well as by other organisms ; hence, these are called **producers**.

The rate at which organic compounds are synthesized in a green plant or a population of green plants is called **gross primary productivity** (GPP). GPP gives us an idea of the proportion of assimilation of light energy into living matter of the plant. The organic compounds synthesized

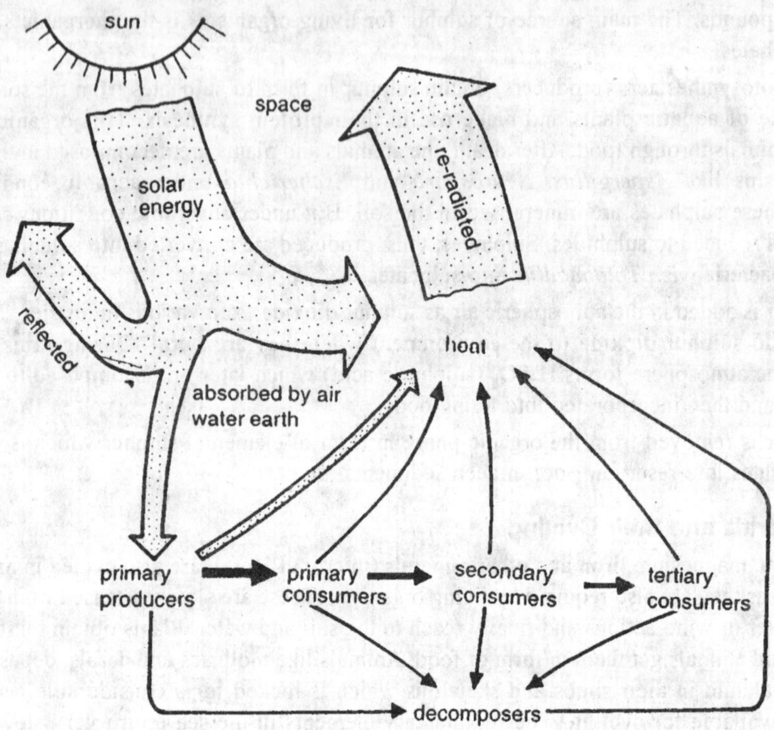

Fig. 25.19. Flow of energy and cycling of materials.

by plants are used as a source of energy for their body building, storage and various catabolic activities. The total stored energy in form of organic matter (which is not used by the producer itself) is called **net primary productivity** (NPP). Exactly in the manner as a single plant contributes to the gross primary productivity and net primary productivity, all autotrophs in a community contribute to **community productivity**.

It has been mentioned earlier that all heterotrophs depend upon autotrophs (producers) directly or indirectly for food. So, by consuming autotrophs, heterotrophs consume organic matter from them. Energy, thus, enters the ecosystem through photosynthesis and passes through the different trophic levels. In other words, flow of energy takes place from the sun to autotrophs to heterotrophs. The food consumed by heterotrophs is utilized in their maintenance and for storage too. If there is more storage than consumption, the biomass of the population would be higher at the end of a time period than at the beginning. So, this rate of increase in the biomass of heterotrophs is referred to as **secondary productivity**.

There occurs a continuous loss of energy all along the path when it is transferred from producer to a consumer and from consumer to the next consumer at the higher trophic level. For this, Lindemann (1942) formulated a concept called **10 per cent law**. To explain, when plants (producers) are eaten by a herbivore (primary consumer), about 10 per cent of energy in the food is fixed in herbivore's body and when a carnivore (secondary consumer) eats up the herbivore, only about 10 per cent of energy in food is fixed in carnivore's body. Therefore, the second level consumer gain in ènergy is only 0.01 per cent of the net productivity of a plant (producer). This clearly shows that there is a loss of energy at each trophic level. So, the longer the food chain, the minimum is the energy available to the last member of the chain. It is, therefore, there are usually four or five steps in natural food chains.

The flow of energy is, however, unidirectional.

Ecological Imbalance

Ecological studies suggest that there exists an **ecological** balance between various constituents of abiotic and biotic components in the **biosphere**. For example, the various biogeochemical cycles operate in nature without any interruption and the abiotic as well as biotic components including producers, consumers and decomposers are significant. If producers be destroyed, carbon from atmospheric carbon dioxide cannot move to organic compounds in living organism and if consumers and decomposers be destroyed the organic compounds will accumulate resulting into locking up of carbon and further not available for cycling. However, when all organisms of an area are studied, it becomes evident that in spite of different types of competitions and struggles between them, they cooperate each other on many ways or they seem to be interdependent. This dependence is called ecological balance. It is very necessary for the continuity of ecosystems and, hence, the biosphere.

However, man being a dominant organism of most ecosystems controls and modifies environment more extensively than any other organism. In fact, there have been significant changes in the natural environments due to man's intervention and his rapid progress in colonization, urbanization, industrialization, agriculture, transportation and technology. Thus, deforestation has provided land for agriculture and rural inhabitation, rural land has been converted into urban settlements and open spaces are fast vanishing. All these have resulted into a mass-scale destruction of flora and fauna which has become detrimental to ecological balance. If, this balance is disturbed for long, it is bound to create a number of crisis to the biological world including our lives. Hence, considering this importance, a number of ways are being adopted by government and private agencies so that ecological balance could be maintained.

MAJOR BIOMES OF THE WORLD

Natural ecosystems of plants and animals extend over large areas of the world. Each of such major terrestrial ecosystem or distinct terrestrial areas with their natural groupings of climax plants and associated animals make **biomes**. Thus a biome is a group of ecosystems similar in types of dominant vegetation. A biome is the largest terrestrial biotic community. The abiotic factors such as temperature, sunlight, soil barriers, latitude, altitude and availability of water are important in determining the nature and extent of biomes. Across the surface of the earth, examples of the same biome a desert, for example can be found wherever the climate and soil conditions are similar. Similarly there are distinct major ecosystems or life supporting zones in marine and fresh water environments. However, the characteristic of the aquatic systems are different from the terrestrial biomes. Ecosystems of the same biome from anywhere on earth are similar in many ways.

The major biomes of the world are (*i*) Tundra, (*ii*) Northern conifer forest or Taiga, (*iii*) Temperate deciduous forest, (*iv*) Tropical rain forest, (*v*) Chapparal, (*vi*) Tropical Savannah, (*vii*) Grassland, (*viii*) Desert.

Tundra. The literal meaning of word **Tundra** is north of the timberline. The tundra extends above 60°N latitude. It is almost treeless plain in the far northern parts of Asia, Europe and North America. A tundra consists of plains characterised by snow, ice and frozen soil most of the year. The permanent frozen soil of tundra is called **permafrost**. Winters are very long on the tundra with little daylight. In contrast summers are short but there are many daylight hours. Precipitation is low, mounting to only 25 cm or less per year, because cold air can hold relatively little moisture. The ground is soggy in the summer because moisture cannot soak into the permanently frozen ground. Ponds, small lakes and marshes are abundant due to the nearly flat terrain.

There are no upright trees on the tundra. Only trees such as dwarf willows and birches, which grow low to the ground, can escape the drying effect of the wind which upright trees would

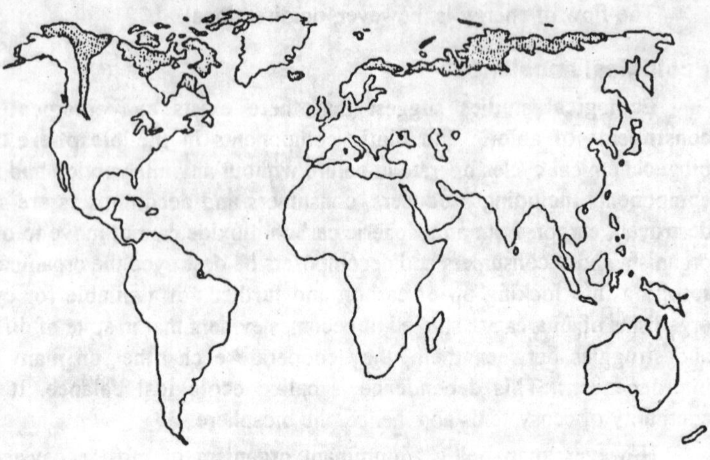

Fig. 25.20. Tundra biome.

experience. This biome consists mainly of mosses, grasses, sedges, lichens and some shrubs. Seasonal thawing of the frozen soil occurs only upto a few centimetres depth, which permits the growth of shallow rooted plants.

Caribon, arctic hare and musk ox are important herbivores of tundra biome. Some important carnivores that prey on the herbivores are the arctic fox, arctic wolf, bobcat and snowy owl. Polar bears live along coastal areas, and prey on seals. Because of the severe winters, many of the animals are migratory and move from one region to another with the change in seasons. Many shorebirds and water fowls, such as ducks and geese, nest on the tundra during the summer but migrate south for the winter. The tundra make a very delicate ecosystem, and may be recovered from any disturbance very slowly.

Northern conifer forest or taiga. The northern coniferous forest or **taiga** is a 1300-1450 km wide band south of the tundra. This extends as an east-west band across North America, Europe and Asia. This area also has long, cold winters, but summer temperatures may reach 10-12°C, and the summer and the growing season are longer than in the tundra. Precipitation is higher than in the tundra, ranging from 10 to 35 cm annually. The moisture is the combined result of summer rains and winter snows. Lakes, ponds and bogs are abundant. The duration of growing period of plants is only about 150 days. Since five physical conditions are variable, the organisms are resistant to fluctuations of temperature.

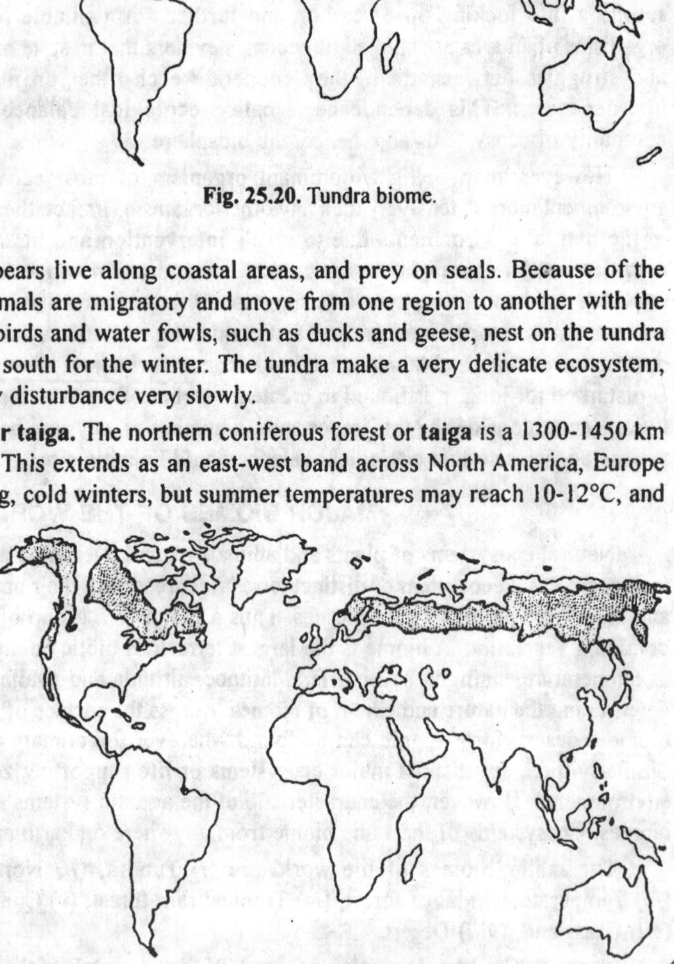

Fig. 25.21. Taiga biome.

The taiga makes really a northern forest of coniferous trees such as spruce, fir, pine, cedàr and hemlock. In disturbed areas, deciduous trees such as birch, willow and poplar are abundant. In certain areas the trees are so dense that little light may reach the floor of the forest. Vines, maple and spring wild flowers are common. Mosses and ferns also grow in moist areas.

The common smaller mammals are herbivores, such as squirrels, snowshoe hare, and predatory martens. Important migratory herbivores include moose, elk, deer and caribon. Moose and caribon migrate to the taiga for winters and to the tundra for summers. Important predators are the timber wolf, grizzly bear, black bear, bobcat and wolverine. Many insects are found during the warmer months. Migratory shore birds and waterfowls are abundant during summer months.

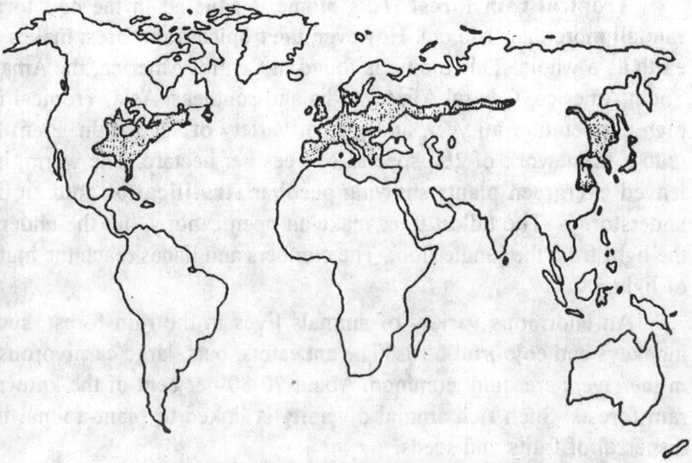

Fig. 18.22. Temperate deciduous forest biome.

Temperate deciduous forests. The deciduous forests are found in the temperate regions of north central Europe, east Asia and the eastern United States, that is, south of the taiga in the Northern Hemisphere. Such forests occur in regions having hot summers, cold winter, rich soil and abundant rain. Annual rainfall is typically around 100 cm per year.

Common deciduous trees are the hardwoods such as beech, maple, oak, hickory and walnut. They are broad-leaved trees. The trees shed their leaves in the late fall so the biome has an entirely different appearance in the winter than in the summer. The fallen leaves provide food for a large variety of consumer and decomposer populations, such as millipedes, snails and fungi living in or on the soil. The temperate deciduous forest produces flowers, fruits and seeds of many types which provide a variety of food for animals.

The common herbivores of this biome are deer, chipmunks, squirrels, rabbits and beavers. Tree-dwelling birds are abundant in number and diversity. Important predators are—black bears, bobcats, and foxes. Predatory birds are also found, such as hawks, owls and eagles. The cold-blooded or ectothermic animals, such as snakes, lizards, frogs, and salamanders are also common.

The temperate deciduous forest makes a very complex biome. Many changes take place during the year, and a large variety of species inhabit the soil, trees and air.

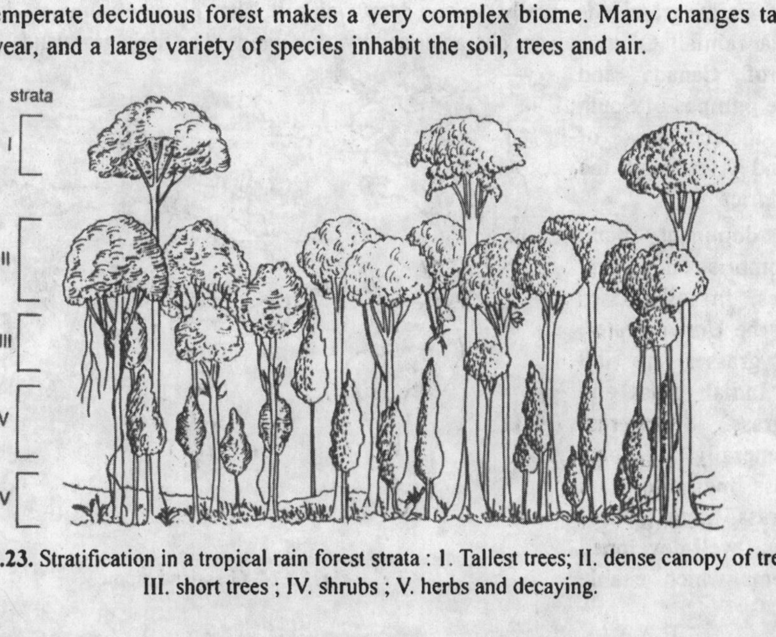

Fig. 25.23. Stratification in a tropical rain forest strata : I. Tallest trees; II. dense canopy of trees ; III. short trees ; IV. shrubs ; V. herbs and decaying.

Tropical rain forest. This biome is situated in the equatorial regions having the annual rainfall more than 140 cm. However, the tropical rain forest makes an important biome across the earth as a whole. This biome is found in Central America, the Amazon Basin, Orinocon Basin of South America, Central Africa, India and southeast Asia. Tropical rain forests have high rainfall, high temperature all year, and a great variety of vegetation. Plant life is highly diverse reaching upto a framework of 200 species of trees per hectare. The warm, humid climate supports broad-leaved evergreen plants showing peculiar **stratification** into an upper storey and two or three understoreys. The tallest trees make an open canopy, but the understoreyed plants block most of the light from the jungle floor. The climbers and lianas reach the highest level of the trees in search of light.

An enormous variety of animals lives in the rain forest, such as insects, lizards, snakes, monkeys and colourful birds. The ant eaters, bats, large carnivorous animals, and a variety of fish in the rivers are quite common. About 70-80 per cent of the known insects are found in tropical rain forests. Such rich animal diversity is linked to plant-animal interaction for pollination and dispersal of fruits and seeds.

Chapparal. This biome is also known as mediterranian scrub forest. This is marked by limited winter rain followed by drought in the rest of the year. The temperature is moderate under the influence of cool, moist air of the oceans. The biome extends along the mediterranian, Pacific coast of North America, Chile, South Africa and South Australia. This biome has broad-leaved evergreen vegetation. The vegetation is generally made up of fire resistant resinous plants and drought-adapted animals. Bush fires are very common in this biome.

Tropical savannah. The savannahs are warm climate plants characterised by coarse grass and scattered trees on the margins of tropics having seasonal rainfall. Primarily they are situated in South America, Africa and Australia. However, there is no savannah **vegetation** in India. The average total rainfall in such regions is 100 to 150 cm. There is alternation of wet and dry seasons. Plants and animals are drought tolerant and do not have much diversity. The animal life of tropical savannah biome consists of hoofed herbivorous species, such as giraffe, zebra, elephant, rhinoceros and several kinds of antelope. Kangaroos are found in the savannahs of Australia.

Grassland. Some grasslands occur in temperate areas of the earth and some occur in tropical regions. Temperate grasslands usually possess deep, rich soil. They have hot summers cold winters and irregular rainfall. Often they are characterised by high winds. The main grasslands include the **prairies** of Canada and U.S.A., the **pampas** of South America, the **steppes** of Europe and Asia, and the **veldts** of Africa.

The dominant plant species comprise short and tall grasses. In tall-grasses prairies in the United States, important grasses are tall bluestem, Indian grass and slough grass. Short-grass prairies generally have blue grama grass, mesquite grass and bluegrass. Many grasses have long, well-developed root systems which enable

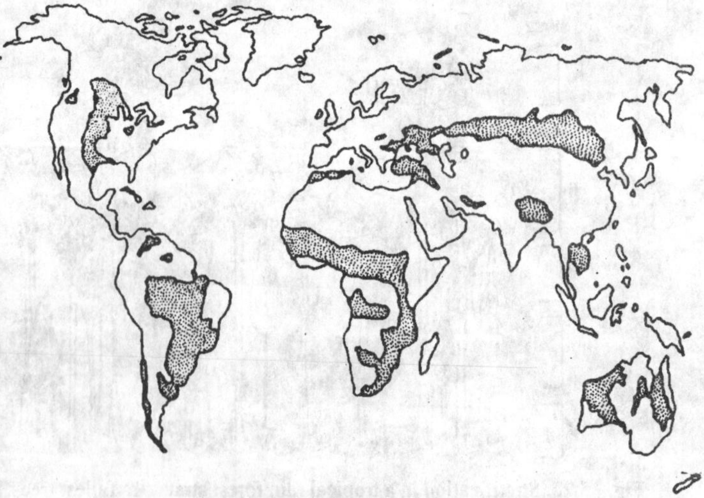

Fig. 25.24. Grassland biome.

them to survive limited rainfall and the effects of fire. The main animals of this biome are—the prong-horned antelopes, bison, wild horse, jack rabbit, ground squirrel and prairie dogs. Larks, the burrowing owl and badgers are also found. Important grassland predators include coyotes, foxes, hawks and snakes.

Desert. The desert biome is characterised by its very low rainfall, which is usually 25 cm per year or less. Most of this limited moisture comes as short, hard showers. Primarily the deserts of the world are located in the south-west U.S.A., Mexico, Chile, Peru, North Africa (Sahara desert), Asia (Tibet, Gobi, Thar) and central western Australia. Deserts generally have hot days and cold nights, and they often have high winds. The reason for the difference of temperature between day and night is due to the lack of water vapour in the air. Deserts are characterised by scanty flora and fauna. Desert organisms must meet some initial requirements if they are to survive. The plants must be able to obtain and conserve water. In order to meet these requirements, many adaptations have been made by desert plants. Such adaptations are—reduced leaf surface area, which reduces evaporation from the plants, loss of leaves during long dry spell; small hairs on the leaf surfaces, and the ability to store large amount of water. The example of important desert plants are—yuccas, acacias, euphorbias, cacti, many other succulents and hardy grasses. Many of the small plants are annuals.

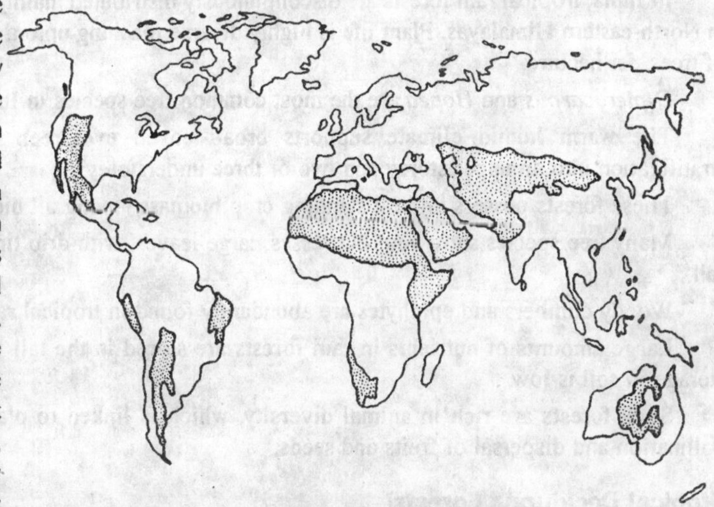

Fig. 25.25. Desert biome.

Animals also must meet the requirements of heat, cold and limited water. Many desert animals are nocturnal in habit, and are active mainly at night. Many reptiles and small mammals burrow to get away from the intense heat of midday. The other common desert animals are the herbivorous kangaroo, rat, ground squirrel, and jack rabbit. The important predators are—coyotes, badgers, kit fox, eagles, hawks, falcons and owls. Ants, locusts, wasps, scorpions, spiders, insect-eating birds, such as swifts and swallows, seed-eating quails, doves and various cats are other common desert animals.

Altitudinal Biomes

The biomes can also be noted along the slopes of high mountain ranges, such as Himalayas (Asia), Andes (South America) and the Rockies. In such mountain ranges the gradual change in the biome types follows the altitude rather than latitude. The biomes extending thousand of kilometres in horizontal or latitudinal sequence may be seen only in few thousand metres in altitudinal sequence. Temperature and precipitation, *i.e.*, rain fall and snowfall have much effect on these biomes. In the tropical mountains the sequence of biomes from base to snowline is as follows—tropical forest (known as Terai forest in India), deciduous forest, coniferous forest and tundra. In the higher latitude, where the mountain is situated, its community and other conditions will be more of the northern type. Thus the number of habitats that cover its slopes is much reduced.

Major biomes of India may be divided in categories mentioned below:

FOREST BIOMES OF INDIA

Major forest biomes in India are commonly divided in four categories; they are as follows :

(*i*) Tropical rain forest biome,

(*ii*) Tropical deciduous forest biome,

(*iii*) Temperate broad-leaf forest biome and

(*iv*) Temperate needle-leaf or coniferous forest biome.

Tropical Rain Forests

The tropical rain forest makes an important biome across the earth as a whole. Tropical rain forests have high rainfall, high temperature all the year, and a great variety of vegetation.

In India, tropical rain forests are discontinuously distributed mainly along Western Ghats and in North-eastern Himalayas. Plant life is highly diverse reaching upto a framework of 200 species of trees per hectare.

Dipterocarpus and *Hopea* are the most common tree species in Indian rain forests.

The warm humid climate supports broad-leaved evergreen plants showing peculiar stratification into an upper storey and two or three understoreys.

These forests possess highest standing crop biomass among all biomes.

Many tree species show root buttresses, large leaves, with drip tips and round the year leaf fall.

Woody climbers and epiphytes are abundantly found in tropical rain forests.

Large amounts of nutrients in rain forests are stored in the tall vegetation, while nutrient storage in soil is low.

Such forests are rich in animal diversity, which is linked to plant-animal interaction for pollination and dispersal of fruits and seeds.

Tropical Deciduous Forests

In India, the tropical deciduous forests occur widely in the northern and southern parts both in hilly areas and plains. Towards the north-west zone, they make scrub thorn forests. Sal (*Shorea robusta*) and teak (*Tectona grandis*) trees are the dominant tree species in tropical deciduous forest of India.

Other common species in deciduous forests are tendu (*Diospyros melanoxylon*), chiraunji (*Buchanania lanzan*) and khair (*Acacia catechu*), which are of great economic importance.

The trees of deciduous forests are generally short statured, only 10 to 20 metres high.

During rainy season, such forests are lush green, while the leaves of most trees fall before advent of summer, and the whole forest becomes leafless along with dried herbs. The forests are rich in nutrients due to scarce leaching.

Temperate Broad-leaf Forests

In India, temperate broad-leaf forests mainly occur between 1500 and 2400 m altitude in the western Himalayas, *i.e.*, Himachal Pradesh and Jammu and Kashmir.

Several species of oak (*Quercus*) are dominating in the temperate broad-leaf forests. The main species of oak found in western Himalayas are: banj oak (*Q. leucotrichophora*), khrsn oak (*Q. semecarpifolia*), tilonaj oak (*Q. floribunda*) and rianj oak (*Q. lanuginose*). Though species of oak in western Himalayas are evergreen, yet their leaves drop during summer, but the trees never become naked.

The trees of oak of different species are 25 to 30 m in height. The trees are thickly populated, and tree canopy is dense. The epiphytes are common on oak trees.

Temperate Coniferous Forests

They are also known as needle-leaf forests. In the Himalayas, the temperate coniferous or needle-leaf forests are generally distributed over 1700 to 3000 m altitude, a.s.l. Such forests mainly consist of gymnosperms, *e.g.*, blue pine (Pinus wallichiana), deodar (*Cedrus deodera*), spruce (*Picea smithiana*) and silver fir (*Abies pindrow*). The wood of these trees is of great economic value, and they yield resins, etc. The trees are quite tall (30 – 35 m) and possess evergreen needle-like leaves. The canopy is generally cone-shaped.

AQUATIC ECOSYSTEMS

Aquatic Ecosystems

Many kinds of aquatic ecosystems are found. They differ widely with regard to abiotic factors. The biotic communities living in such ecosystems also vary. The aquatic ecosystems range from open ocean to temporary puddles, ponds and lakes. These possess the conditions of salinity, depth and fluctuations of temperature. The depth of the water is important for vegetation, since more light penetrates near the surface of the water than farther down in deep water. The fresh water and marine environments have many ecosystems with overlapping boundaries which cannot be clearly demarcated.

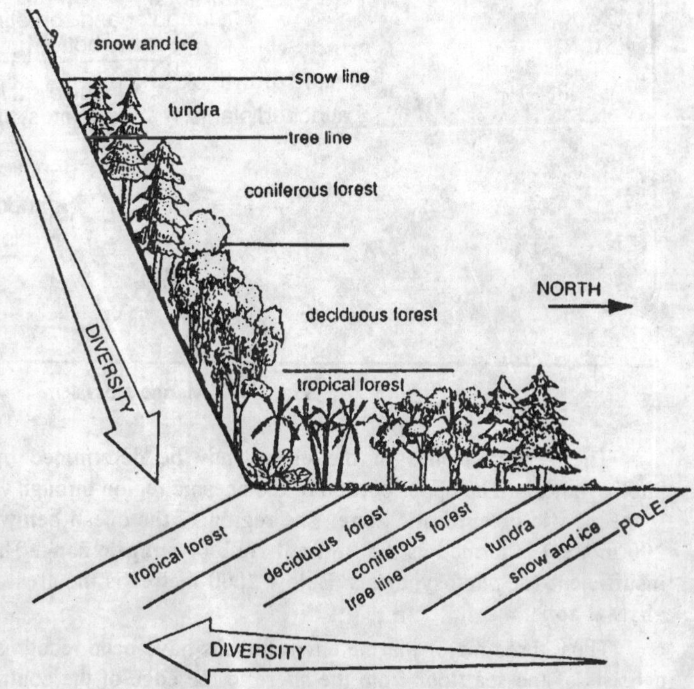

Fig. 25.26. Altitudinal and latitudinal biomes showing correlation.

The adaptations of aquatic organisms have great diversity. For instance, fishes live exclusively in water. On the other hand, the frogs, crocodiles, hippopotamus and aquatic birds are amphibious in nature. The animals like coelenterates and echinoderms live only in saline water, while hilsa fish can live in fresh water as well as in sea.

Marine Environment

Marine biomes are the biomes of the oceans. The marine environment is characterised by its high concentration of salt and mineral ions. The salt concentration in the open sea is about 3.5 per cent. The most dominant ions are sodium and chloride followed by sulphur, magnesium and calcium. The sea is not a single environment. It is subdivided into distinct ecosystems both in abiotic and biotic composition. More important determinants of marine ecosystems are—depth of the water, currents, tide, light penetration and temperature. Ocean coasts are fascinating areas in

which the communities are made up of populations which at high tide are under water but at low tide actually on land.

The sea is divided into regions or zones and each region or zone is characterised by different physical conditions and by different plant and animal inhabitants. From the coastline of the sea a gradually sloping region extends to an average of 160 km in the sea. This zone of depth of 8-200 metres is known as the **continental shelf**. Beyond this zone there is **continental slope**, extending from the outer edge of the shelf into deeper water. The continental slopes do possess the ridges, basins and trenches formed of mud and sand, deposited by slow-flowing rivers. The sea is divided into two major regions or zones, *i.e.*, **neritic** and **oceanic**. The neritic zone, adjacent to the shore, is a shallow-water zone which lies above the continental shelf. The oceanic region is the deep water region beyond the neritic zone and beyond the continental shelf.

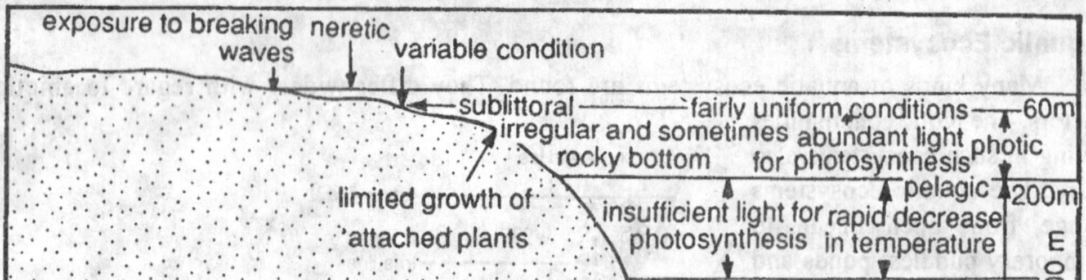

Fig. 25.27. Marine ecosystems.

The vertical zones of the ocean may be determined by the availability of light for photosynthesis. The upper portion of the oceanic region through which light effectively penetrates is the **photic** or **euphotic zone**. The region of the ocean below the euphotic zone (*i.e.*, below 200 metres) is termed as the **bathyal zone** or **aphotic zone**. This zone gets less light which is insufficient for photosynthesis. Below 2000 metres is the area of constant darkness, called the **abyssal zone**.

Thus, three major marine environments have been recognised (*i*) **the littoral zone**, which consists of the sea floor from the shore to the edge of the continental shelf; (*ii*) **the benthonic zone**, comprising of the sea floor along with the continental slope and the aphotic and abyssal zones and (*iii*) **the pelagic zone**, which constitutes the water of the ocean basin.

Life in the sea is abundant and diverse and extends to all its depths. The total mass of marine organisms is greater than the combined masses of terrestrial fresh water organisms.

Marine organisms can be classified as **plankton, nekton, benthos** and **neuston**.

1. Plankton. The plankton consists of floating organisms. Most of these minute organisms are confined to the euphotic zone. The plankton includes photosynthesizing organisms including diatoms are termed **phytoplankton**, and heterotrophic organisms are **zooplankton**. Zooplankton includes many of the protozoans, especially the dinoflagellates, radiolarians, foraminifera and a large number of small crustaceans.

2. Nekton. They comprise of actively moving organisms with well-developed locomotory organs. They include actively swimming organisms found in the surface or deep waters. They feed on planktons or smaller nektons.

3. Benthos. The benthonic organisms are found along the floor of sea-bed. They include creeping, crawling and sessile organisms. Most of these organisms are scavangers.

The open sea. The open sea has **photic, aphotic** and **abyssal** regions. The photic region contains largest number of organisms including phytoplanktons and zooplanktons. The nekton comprises of large and small fishes, squids and whales. The nektons are met within the both photic and aphotic zones.

The producers are not found in abyssal zones, and they are inhabited by predators. Some of these predators have stout jaws and sharp teeth (shark fish). Some animals are luminescent and attract other organisms. The examples of such animals are devil fish and hatchet fish.

The benthonic fauna consists of less producers, and more consumers, decomposers and scavangers. Among the benthic animals are star fish, snails, clams, crabs, worms, brancles, sponges, sea anemones, corals, oysters, tunicates and others.

Coastal region. The continental shelf adjacent to coastal region can be divided into **littoral** (substratum), **neretic** (water) and **intertidal zones**. Since there is no wave action in neretic zone, and therefore, it harbours a large variety of planktons and other organisms. The organisms found in the littoral zones face the strong wave action, and therefore they adhere strongly to the substratum, such as many large and small sea weeds. The organisms found in the intertidal zones face rhythmic alteration between aquatic and sub-terrestrial conditions. In the estuaries the physical conditions are different as the fresh water from the rivers mixes with the sea water. The estuaries make the most fertile ecosystems of the world.

Fresh Water Environment

Such biomes occur in ponds, lakes, streams and rivers.

Lakes and ponds. The lakes and ponds have stagnant fresh water. They occur practically in every biome. They vary in size from less than a hectare to hundreds of hectares. The life span of ponds ranges from a few weeks or months in the case of small seasonal ponds to several hundred years for large lakes. Lakes also differ in their origin, and may be of direct or indirect result of **glaciation**. Certain ponds or lakes are natural or man-made. The depth of ponds and lakes varies from a few centimetres to over a hundred metres. The shallow lakes, also known as **eutrophic lakes** have a rich accumulation of organic products. The deep lakes, having steep and rocky side are called **oligotrophic lakes**. Such lakes are poor in circulating nutrients, such as phosphates. Some lakes contain saline or brackish water, such as Sambar lake of Rajasthan.

The **autotrophic** and **heterotrophic** components are found in perfect harmony in a pond or lake. The fresh water pond autotrophs include microscopic phytoplankton such as *Chlamydomonas*, *Volvox*, *Euglena* and other such organisms. Other free floating plants are found on the surface of water such as *Azolla*, *Lemna*, *Wolffia* and *Pistia*. Macrophytes like *Ceratophyllum*, and *Utricularia* are free-floating plants found beneath the surface of water. *Vallisneria*, *Nelumbo*, and *Typha* are the common rooted plants.

The heterotrophs or first order consumers include ciliates, flagellates, rotifers and small crustaceans, such as *Daphnia*, *Cypris*, *Cyclops* and eggs and larvae of various aquatic animals. Other common consumers are leeches, molluscs, fishes, frogs and larger carnivorous fishes.

Streams and rivers. The flowing fresh water makes the streams, rivers and brooks. Such bodies of flowing fresh water differ widely in their volume of water, speed of flow, oxygen content, temperature and other chemical and physical conditions. The flora and fauna depend on the source of river and the environment of land through which the stream or river passes.

The rivers which originate from melting glaciers or springs are penennial and have cool water with swift currents. Floating populations of plankton are generally not found in such waters. When the water reaches in the plains, the current becomes slower and the river-body wider. Sediments deposit in the river-bed. The total volume of water is also increased. Since the water surface remains exposed to sun light the temperature of water rises up. The rate of photosynthesis and other biological activities also become higher. In the lower reaches, the water current diminishes further. The water becomes muddy, and the light becomes poor at the river bed. Both phytoplankton and zooplankton develop in abundance. The nature and composition of fauna becomes like that of lakes. Many mammals, birds and reptiles obtain their food from the water of river or stream.

MAN-MADE ECOSYSTEMS — AGROECOSYSTEM

The man-made ecosystems are artifical and also known as **agroecosystem**. Such ecosystems are variable in their duration and stability. The terrestrial ecosystems developed by man may be villages, cities, parks, plantations, orchards, gardens and crop fields. The man-made aquatic ecosystems are dams, reservoirs, lakes, ponds, canals, fishery tanks and aquaria.

The important man-made modifications in the biotic community are brought by cultivation of plants, domestication of animals and use of fire. The human civilisation has been established and supported by agriculture. Most of the human population depends upon agriculture for their food. The agriculture is the process of cultivating soil for raising the economically important plants. In broad sense, the term agriculture is used for both animal husbandry and crop production. Man has converted very large areas of forests and grasslands by cutting them into croplands for growing cereals, pulses, oilseeds and fodder crops. Thus, the cropland and pastoral land are essentially grasslands with economic plants of choice.

The **agroecology** is the science of the study of the relation between agricultural crops and environment. The biotic communities and the physical conditions of the different croplands vary widely. These croplands possess some common features and are called **agroecosystems**. The physical condition of the cropland depends upon latitude, climatic conditions and edaphic factors. The physical deficiencies of cropland are removed by proper irrigation and use of fertilisers, biofertilisers and manures. The climate, season and choice of farmer, are the main determinants of the type of crop.

Generally one crop **(monoculture)** is grown in a field and there is a strong selective pressure to reduce diversity. However, some weeds grow in the crop field, but their number is quite less as compared to a natural grassland. The animal population of cultivable land consists of earthworms, nematodes, insects, domestic animals, pests, pollinators, birds and rodents.

The man-made ecosystems are simple and efficient because of less diversity of organisms. They do not have the diversity of natural ecosystems. A diversified ecosystem (natural ecosystem) is more stable because some species of organisms would survive even if they are affected by certain pests and pathogens. A monoculture would be destroyed completely by drought, floods, pests or pathogens, whereas a natural diversified ecosystem has capacity for many adjustments.

BOUNDARIES OF ECOSYSTEMS

An ecosystem is considered as an area where the inputs and outputs can be studied across its boundaries, and it is treated as a separate entity. The ecosystems are not strictly separate and isolated. Their boundaries are indistinct and overlapping. For example, a pond may be a separate entity from forest or grassland, but birds of their regions can feed on fishes and crabs of the pond. The movement of energy and materials can be achieved by biological, climatic, and geological processes. The top soil from Himalayas is brought in the deltas of the rivers such as Ganga, Jamuna and Brahmputra. Siberian cranes migrate to Ghana bird sanctuary for overwintering. Thousands of the ecosystems are interrelated with each other, and a single global ecosystem is formed, which is known as **biosphere**.

SUMMARY

1. Ecosystems are self-regulating and self-sustaining units of landscape.
2. The term ecosystem was coined by Sir Arthur Tansley in 1935.
3. Ecosystem is comprised of two basic components: (*i*) abiotic (inorganic materials, air, soil, water, etc.) and (*ii*) biotic (producer, consumer and decomposer organisms).
4. Biotic and abiotic components are physically organised to provide a characteristic structure, such as species composition, stratification, etc., of the ecosystem.
5. Ecosystem structure can also be depicted through food relationship of producers and consumers, which is called trophic structure.
6. Productivity and decomposition are two important functions in ecosystem.
7. Productivity is involved in production of food.
8. While decomposition leads to the breakdown of organic matter.
9. Primary productivity is the rate of capture of solar energy or production of biomass by producers.
10. The rate of total production of organic material or capture of energy is known as gross primary productivity.
11. Net primary productivity represents the balance after meeting the cost of respiration.
12. Secondary productivity is the rate at which food energy is assimilated at the trophic levels of consumers.
13. Decomposition is the process of breakdown of complex organic compounds in detritus to carbon dioxide, water and inorganic nutrients by decomposers.
14. There are three main processes of decomposition, that is, (*i*) fragmentation of detritus, (*ii*) leaching and (*iii*) catabolism, which operate simultaneously on the detritus.
15. Energy flow and nutrient cycling are important functions in the ecosystem.
16. Energy flow is unidirectional, which involves (*i*) the conversion of light energy into food and (*ii*) transfer of energy from one organism to another.
17. The trophic levels are connected by the transfer of food or energy along the food chain.
18. Ecological efficiencies show the efficiency with which the organisms exploit their food and convert the food into biomass make available to the next higher trophic level.
19. Nutrient cycles involve strorage and transfer of nutrients through various components of the ecosystem, and the nutrients are repeatedly used.
20. Nutrient cycles are of two kinds : (*i*) gaseous and (*ii*) sedimentary.
21. The reservoir of gaseous type of nutrient cycle is generally located in the atmosphere or the hydrosphere; while the reservoir of sedimentary type exists in the earth's crust.
22. Ecosystem nutrient cycles possess three aspects: (*i*) input, (*ii*) output and (*iii*) internal cycling of nutrients.
23. Nitrogen, oxygen, carbon dioxide are good examples of gaseous nutrient cycle, while Phosphorus, sulphur are examples of sedimentary types.
24. The biomes are the life forms of the climax vegetation.
25. Forest, grassland, savanna, and desert biomes occupy most of the land area under natural vegetation.
26. Forest biomes are generally dominated by trees having a closed canopy.

27. Grasslands are dominated by herbaceous species.

28. Savanna is characterised by herbs interspersed with trees.

29. Deserts show scarce vegetation. They have low herb or shrub cover with mostly base ground.

TERMS TO REMEMBER

Abiotic components. They include inorganic materials and dead organic matter.

Aboveground detritus or litter fall. Dried plant parts, and dead remains of animals, including faecal matter.

Ammonification. Formation of ammonia from organic nitrogenous compounds.

Associative symbiosis. A type of combination of bacterium and root of higher plant, where nitrogen-fixing microbe does not penetrate deep into host tissues.

Biotic components. They include producers, consumers and decomposers.

Biogeochemical cycle. Nutrient cycle, generally considered in a regional or global context.

Belowground detritus. Dead organic material primarily composed of dead roots.

Biomes. The regional biotic units, recognised by the life form of climax vegetation.

Carnivore. The secondary consumer, an animal that eats flesh of other animals.

Consumers or phagotrophs. The heterotrophic organisms, mostly animals which generally ingest their food.

Decomposers or saprotrophs. The heterotrophic organisms, consisting mostly of bacteria and fungi which live on dead organic matter or detritus.

Detritus. Dead plant parts and animals remains.

Ecosystems. Parts of nature where living organisms interact amongst themselves and with their physical environment.

Food chain. The transfer of energy from one trophic level to the next trophic level.

Food web. Interconnected matrix of food chains is called food web.

Grassland. Such ecosystems have treeless herbaceous plant cover, dominated by a wide variety of grass species (family Poaceae).

Gross primary productivity. The rate of total capture of energy or the rate of total production of organic material (biomass).

Macrophytes. Rooted plants, in shallow waters.

Nitrification. Ammonia is converted into nitrate by a group of chemo-autotrophic bacteria through a two-step process.

Nutrient cycle. They involve storage and transfer of nutrients through various components of the ecosystem so that the nutrients are repeatedly used.

Net primary productivity. The balance energy or biomass remaining after meeting the cost of respiration of producers.

Phytoplankton. In deep aquatic ecosystems, floating plants called phytoplankton are the major autotrophs.

Productivity. The rate of biomass production.

Producers. They are autotrophic, generally chlorophyll-bearing organisms which produce their own food by photosynthesis.

Primary productivity. This refers to the rate at which sunlight is captured by producers for the synthesis of energy-rich organic compounds through photosynthesis.

Savanna. A well developed grass cover, interspersed with scattered shrubs or small trees.

Secondary productivity. At the trophic level of consumers, the rate at which food energy is assimilated.

Standing crop. Trophic structure may be described in terms of the amount of living material, called standing crop, present in different trophic levels at a given time.

QUESTION BANK

Very Short Answer Questions

1. What man made ecosystems are called?
2. Who coined the term 'ecosystem'?
3. Expand PAR.
4. What are biomes?
5. Which are the types of food chains in all ecosystems?
6. Cite three examples of N_2- fixing cyanobacteria.
7. What is detritus ?
8. Several higher plant species other than legumes also produce nodules. Name them.
9. Name two most common trees found in Indian tropical rain forest.
10. Name any two dominant deciduous tree species.
11. What are coral reefs?
12. Define leaching.
13. Give the name for a network formed by interlinking of a number of food chains.
14. Name two components of ecosystem.
15. Give the term for the formation of soil.
16. Give the terms for the plants found on saline soils and sandy soils
17. Name the term used to indicate the soil factors affecting the organisms.
18. Give the term for the grasslands with scattered trees.
19. Name the most productive agro-ecosystem.
20. Name two kinds of cycles of materials.
21. Name the process by which CO_2 enters into living world.
22. Name a denitrifying bacterium.
23. Name greenhouse gas.
24. Give the alternative term for 'biosphere'.
25. Give the term for the amount of living matter in a component population of a specific trophic level at a given time.

ANSWERS

1. Anthropogenic ecosystem; **2.** Sir Arthur Tanslay, 1935; **3.** Photosynthetically active radiation; **4.** Biomes are major ecosystem delimited by particular climates or geographical areas; **5.** Grazing food chain and detritus food chain; **6.** Anabaena, Aulosira and Nostoc; **7.** The dead parts of plants and animal remains; **8.** Casuarina and Alnus, which produce nodules harbouring Frankia, a nitrogen-fixing actinomycete; **9.** Dipterocarpus and Hopea; **10.** Sal and Teak; **11.** Rocks formed in the coastal seas by calcareous secretions of Cnidarian polyps; **12.** Loss of soluble substances from A-horizon of soil as these are carried by downward moving gravitational water; **13.** Food web; **14.** Abiotic component and biotic component; **15.** Pedogenesis; **16.** Halophytes and psammophytes; **17.** Edaphic; **18.** Savannah; **19.** Sugarcane crop; **20.** Gaseous and sedimentary cycles; **21.** Photosynthesis; **22.** Pseudomonas; **23.** Carbon dioxide; **24.** Ecosphere; **25.** Standing crop.

Short Answer Questions

1. What are the processes involved in decomposition of detritus?
2. What are the two basic components of ecosystem? Define them.
3. Define food chain and food web.
4. What do you understand by ecological efficiency?
5. Enlist basic requirements of an ecosystem.

6. Define ecological pyramids. Give their different types.
7. Define biogeochemical cycles. Name two types of them.
8. Differentiated between grazing food chain and detritus food chain.
9. Give the main characteristics of Tundra biome.
10. Differentiate between gaseous and sedimentary types of nutrient cycling.
11. What is ecological efficiency? Give its significance.
12. What is a grassland? How does it differ from savannah?
13. Differentiate between abiotic and biotic components.
14. Briefly describe the processes and products of decomposition.
15. What are greenhouse gases? Name two gases exerting greenhouse effect?
16. Differentiate between food chain and food web.
17. Distinguish between Net primary productivity and Gross primary productivity.
18. What is xerosere? Name its two types.
19. What is greenhouse effect?
20. List the processes involved in nitrogen cycle.
21. Distinguish between wet deposition and dry deposition.
22. With the help of labelled diagram only, give nitrogen cycle.
23. Explain phosphorus cycle by line diagram.
24. Give an account of biotic components of ecosystem.
25. Give an account of factors affecting the rate of decomposition.
26. Give an account of energy flow in ecosystem.
27. What is biosphere? What are the main sub-divisions of biosphere?
28. Explain ten per cent law of flow of energy.
29. Give the major characteristics of the desert biome.
30. Explain the concept of food chain.
31. What is biome? Enumerate the factors that determine the characteristics of a biome.
32. What is primary productivity? Give the range of primary productivity in different ecosystems of the world.
33. Explain three biotic components of any natural ecosystem.
34. Explain the term 'stratification' in relation to a tropical rain forest.
35. Describe the various kinds of food chains in a food web.
36. Give an account of keystone species.
37. Define an ecosystem. Mention some important instances of an ecosystem.
38. Name the two fundamental trophic levels and describe their general characteristics.
39. Describe in brief the biotic components found in an ecosystem.
40. Give a schematic representation of nitrogen cycle of a terrestrial ecosystem. Name any two microorganisms involved in it.

Long Answer Questions

1. Briefly describe the tropical forest biomes.
2. Outline the salient features of the ecosystem nitrogen cycling.
3. What are ecological pyramids? Mention their various types.
4. Give an account of major forest biomes found in India.
5. Explain the pond ecosystem as a classical example of ecosystem.
6. What is meant by nutrient cycling? Explain nitrogen cycle.
7. What are sedimentary cycles? Depict phosphorus cycle diagrammatically.

8. Describe the marine ecosystems.
9. Give the major characteristics of the desert.
10. Define the term 'biome' and list the factors that determine characteristics of a biome.
11. Discuss briefly the abiotic components of an ecosystem.

MULTIPLE CHOICE QUESTIONS (OBJECTIVE TYPE QUESTIONS)

1. Succulent plants grow in :
(*a*) Tundra (*b*) Deserts
(*c*) Tropical rain forests (*d*) Temperate deciduous forests
2. Total amount of living material at the various trophic levels of a food chain is dipicted by pyramids of :
(*a*) Number (*b*) Energy (*c*) Biomass (*d*) All of these
3. In an upright pyramid of biomass the herbivores occupy the position :
(*a*) 1st (*b*) 2nd (*c*) 3rd (*d*) 4th
4. In submerged plants, the stomata lie on :
(*a*) Upper surface (*b*) Lower surface
(*c*) None on any surface (*d*) Equally on both surfaces
5. Pyramid of energy in a pond ecosystem is always :
(*a*) Upright (*b*) Inverted (*c*) Both (*a*) and (*b*) (*d*) None of these
6. Acacia arabica is a :
(*a*) Halophyte (*b*) Mesophyte (*c*) Xerophyte (*d*) Hydrophyte
7. N_2 content is kept constant in the biosphere due to :
(*a*) N_2 fixation (*b*) Industrial pollution (*c*) N_2 cycle (*d*) Absorption of N_2
8. Zone of atmosphere that lies near the ground is :
(*a*) Troposphere (*b*) Stratosphere (*c*) Homosphere (*d*) All of these
9. Greenhouse effect is due to :
(*a*) CFCs
(*b*) O_3
(*c*) Gases that check reflected infra-red radiations to pass through
(*d*) All of these
10. Mangrove of marshy Sunderbans is characterised by :
(*a*) Pneumatophores (*b*) Prop roots (*c*) Vivipary (*d*) All of these
11. The food chain in which micro-organisms breakdown the energy rich compounds, is called :
(*a*) Ecosystem (*b*) Detritus food chain (*c*) Parastic food chain (*d*) Predator food chain
12. The relationship in an ecosystem can be depicted by :
(*a*) Pyramid of energy (*b*) Pyramid of biomass (*c*) Pyramid of numbers (*d*) All of these
13. The biome which is characterised by broad-leaved vegetation, fire resistant resinous plants and drought evading plants, is known as :
(*a*) Savannah (*b*) Chapparal (*c*) Steppes (*d*) Deciduous forests
14. The niche of the population is the :
(*a*) Place where it lives (*b*) Geographical area that it covers
(*c*) Set of conditions that interacts (*d*) Geographical and resources it uses
15. In a lake, the upper warmer oxygen rich water zone is called :
(*a*) Epilimnion (*b*) Hypolimnion (*c*) Limenetic zone (*d*) Profundal zone
16. Which part of the world has a high density of organisms :
(*a*) Grasslands (*b*) Savannahs (*c*) Deciduous forests (*d*) Tropical rain forests

17. An ecological pyramid of biomass represents :
(*a*) Population in each food web (*b*) Tissue organisation at each trophic level
(*c*) Energy flow through each trophic level (*d*) All of these
18. Which of the following is correctly matched :
(*a*) Butterfly .... camouflage (*b*) Garden lizard .... mimicry
(*c*) House lizard .... autotomy (*d*) None of these
19. Organisms found at the bottom of the sea are :
(*a*) Planktons (*b*) Nekton (*c*) Benthos (*d*) Phytons
20. In the submerged hydrophytes exchange of gases occurs through :
(*a*) Hydathodes (*b*) Lenticels (*c*) Stomata (*d*) General surface
21. The plants growing in deserts, to tolerate water stress have :
(*a*) No stomata (*b*) Long roots reaching water table
(*c*) Stem modified into leaf-like form (*d*) Stipular spines
22. Food chain refers to :
(*a*) Number of humans forming a chain for food
(*b*) Animals gathered near a source of food
(*c*) Transfer of energy from producers to consumers
(*d*) None of these.
23. Deciduous forests have :
(*a*) Variety of grasses (*b*) Broad-leaved trees (*c*) Narrow-leaved trees (*d*) Variety of crocodiles
24. Transition zone between vegetational types is :
(*a*) Ecotone (*b*) Ecotype (*c*) Ecocline (*d*) Ecosystem
25. Which of the following can be recognised as a major environment in oceanic basin :
(*a*) Littoral zone (*b*) Benthonic zone (*c*) Pellagic zone (*d*) All of these
26. When the number of organisms at successive trophic levels are plotted, they assume the shape of a pyramid. This is called the pyramid of :
(*a*) Number (*b*) Energy (*c*) Biomass (*d*) None of these
27. How much energy is consumed from one trophic level to another trophic level ?
(*a*) 5% (*b*) 10% (*c*) 15% (*d*) 20%
28. Desert can be converted into green land by planting :
(*a*) Oxylophytes (*b*) Psammophytes (*c*) Halophytes (*d*) Tropical trees
29. Two similar halophytes are called :
(*a*) Isotype (*b*) Neotype (*c*) Synotype (*d*) Mesotype
30. Halophytes are peculiar in having :
(*a*) Pneumatophoric stems (*b*) Velamen tissue
(*c*) Vivipary (*d*) Saline soil
31. Deer in a forest ecosystem acts as a :
(*a*) Primary consumer (*b*) Secondary consumer
(*c*) Decomposer (*d*) None of these
32. Pyramid of energy is always :
(*a*) Inverted (*b*) Upright (*c*) Spindle-shaped (*d*) Cup-shaped
33. In India, tropical rain forests are found in :
(*a*) Darjeeling (*b*) Karnataka (*c*) Andaman (*d*) J&K
34. Halophytes grow on physiologically dry soil due to presaence of :
(*a*) Excess salts in water (*b*) Excess salts in plants
(*c*) Excess humidity outside (*d*) Dry soil

35. The free floating organisms of an open sea and sea shore are collectively called :
(*a*) Planktons (*b*) Nektons (*c*) Benthonic (*d*) Sea anemones
36. In an ecosystem, bacteria are considered as :
(*a*) Microconsumers (*b*) Macroconsumers
(*c*) Primary consumers (*d*) Secondary consumers
37. Field capacity is :
(*a*) Higher for sandy soils than clay soils (*b*) Amount of water in soil available to plants
(*c*) Same as permanent wilting point (*d*) Amount of water left in soil after drainage
38. Soil salinity is measured by :
(*a*) Porometer (*b*) Potometer (*c*) Conductivity meter (*d*) Calorimeter
39. The factors governing the structure of soil are called :
(*a*) Topographic (*b*) Edaphic (*c*) Biotic (*d*) Temperature
40. Concept of ecological pyramids was developed by :
(*a*) Reiter (*b*) Odum (*c*) Darwin (*d*) Elton
41. In an ecosystem, which one of the following is natural controlling force :
(*a*) Soil moisture (*b*) Temperature (*c*) Food (*d*) Predators
42. The maximum energy amongst escosystems is contributed by :
(*a*) Crops (*b*) Forests (*c*) Coal (*d*) Fuel gas
43. The most recently discovered ecosystem is :
(*a*) Vent (*b*) Crater (*c*) Tundra (*d*) Floating iceberg
44. Inverted pyramid of biomass can be traced in one of the following ecosysteme :
(*a*) Rain forest (*b*) Desert (*c*) Ocean (*d*) Tundra
45. The study of energy transfer in different trophic levels of an ecosystem is called :
(*a*) Bioenergetics (*b*) Biogeocoenosis (*c*) Holocoenosis (*d*) Biosystem
46. The 10% law for energy transfer in food chains was given by :
(*a*) Stanley (*b*) Tranley (*c*) Lindemann (*d*) Weismann
47. Frog that feeds on insects is :
(*a*) Primary consumer (*b*) Secondary consumer (*c*) Tertiary consumer (*d*) Decomposer
48. Atmospheric humidity is measured by :
(*a*) Auxanometer (*b*) Hygrometer (*c*) Photometer (*d*) Potometer
49. In a comparative study of grassland ecosystem and pond ecosystem, it may be observed that :
(*a*) Primary and secondary consumers are similar
(*b*) Both biotic and abiotic components are different
(*c*) Biotic components are almost similar
(*d*) Abiotic components are almost similar
50. Phytoplanktons of a pond ecosystem act as :
(*a*) Producers (*b*) Primary consumers
(*b*) Secondary consumers (*d*) Decomposers
51. The lentic ecosystem includes :
(*a*) Gravitational water (*b*) Standing water (*c*) Rain water (*d*) Running water
52. A rat feeding on potato tuber is a :
(*a*) Producer (*b*) Primary consumer (*c*) Carnivore (*d*) Decomposer
53. Which of the following habitats show highest density of living species ?
(*a*) Grassland (*b*) Deserts
(*c*) Tropical rain forests (*d*) Temperate forests

54. This is an inverted pyramid :
(*a*) Pyramid of number in a grassland (*b*) Pyramid of energy in pond system
(*c*) Pyramid of biomass in a grassland (*d*) Pyramid of biomass in pond ecosystem

55. Food chains are met only in the :
(*a*) Sea (*b*) Forests (*c*) Deserts (*d*) All of these

56. The zooplankton forms are :
(*a*) Primary consumers (*b*) Secondary consumers
(*c*) Carnivores (*d*) Primary producers

57. The driving force of the ecosystem is :
(*a*) Carbohydrates in plants (*b*) Biomass
(*c*) Producers (*d*) Solar energy

58. The snakes are included under :
(*a*) Saprophytes (*b*) Primary consumers
(*c*) Secondary consumers (*d*) None of these

59. Transfer of energy from organisms to organisms in a natural community establishes :
(*a*) Food chains (*b*) Biological control (*c*) Natural barriers (*d*) All of these

60. Green plants constitute :
(*a*) 1st trophic level (*b*) 2nd trophic level (*c*) 3rd trophic level (*d*) 4th trophic level

61. In an ecosystem, one of the following occurs as abiotic compounds :
(*a*) Flow of energy (*b*) Cycling of materials (*c*) Consumers (*d*) Both (*a*) and (*b*)

62. Which of the following habitat is most unsuitable for primary productivity ?
(*a*) Meadow (*b*) Forested river bank (*c*) Cave (*d*) Pond

63. Ecosystem has two components :
(*a*) Plants and animals (*b*) Weeds and trees (*c*) Biotic and abiotic (*d*) Frogs and men

64. The pyramid of number in a grassland ecosystem is :
(*a*) Linear (*b*) Upright (*c*) Inverted (*d*) Irregular

65. Biological equilibrium is found between :
(*a*) Producers and consumers (*b*) Producers and decomposers
(*c*) Producers and light (*d*) Producers, consumers and decomposers

66. The number of individuals of a species in a particular ecosystem at a given time remains constant due to :
(*a*) Human beings (*b*) Parasites (*c*) Predators (*d*) Food availability

67. Ecological pyramids are of :
(*a*) Two types (*b*) Three types (*c*) Four types (*d*) Five types

68. A lake ecosystem is :
(*a*) Artificial (*b*) Abiotic (*c*) Natural (*d*) Hydrological

69. Food level in an ecosystem is called :
(*a*) Trophic level (*b*) Consumer level (*c*) Producer level (*d*) Herbivore level

70. Savannahs are :
(*a*) Tropical rain forests (*b*) Dense forests with close canopy
(*c*) Grasslands with scattered trees (*c*) Desert scrub

71. The maximum biomass occurs in :
(*a*) Tropical forests (*b*) Temperate forests (*c*) Taiga (*d*) Alpine vegetation

72. Which is correct :
(*a*) Least productive ecosystem is desert and deep lake
(*b*) Sugarcane is the most productive agroecosystem

(*c*) Most productive ecosystem is coral reef
(*a*) All of the above

73. Stratification is more common in :
(*a*) Deciduous forest (*b*) Tropical rain forest (*c*) Temperate forest (*d*) Tropical savannan

74. Hygrometer is used to measure the :
(*a*) Temperature (*b*) Wind velocity (*c*) Relative humidity (*d*) Turbidity

75. Which of the following is an abiotic component of the ecosystem ?
(*a*) Bacteria (*b*) Humus (*c*) Plants (*d*) Fungi

76. What fraction of assimilated energy is used in respiration by the herbivore ?
(*a*) 20 per cent (*b*) 30 per cent (*c*) 40 per cent (*d*) 60 per cent

77. Which of the following is a free living nitrogen-fixing bacteria present in soil ?
(*a*) Azotobacter (*b*) Nitrosomonas (*c*) Rhizobium (*d*) Pseudomonas

78. Which of the following represents the sedimentary type of nutrient cycle ?
(*a*) Nitrogen (*b*) Carbon (*c*) Phosphorus (*d*) Oxygen

79. Which of the following processes helps in nutrient conservation ?
(*a*) Mineralisation (*b*) Immobilisation (*c*) Leaching (*d*) Nitrification

80. Decomposers are :
(*a*) Animalia and Monera (*b*) Protista and Monera
(*c*) Fungi and Plantae (*d*) Bacteria and Fungi

81. Transition zone between vegetational types is :
(*a*) Ecotone (*b*) Ecotype (*c*) Ecoline (*d*) Ecosystem

82. Bacterial role in carbon cycle is :
(*a*) Chemosynthesis (*b*) Photosynthesis
(*c*) Breakdown of organic matter (*d*) Assimilation

83. The rate at which light energy is changed into chemical energy of organic molecules is :
(*a*) Net primary productivity (*b*) Gross primary productivity
(*c*) Net secondary productivity (*d*) Gross secondary productivity

84. If there was no CO_2 in the earth's atmosphere, the temperature of earth's surface would be :
(*a*) Same as present (*b*) Less than present
(*c*) Higher than present (*d*) Depends upon amount of O_2

85. If we completely remove the decomposers from an ecosystem, its functioning will be adversely affected because :
(*a*) Energy flow will be blocked (*b*) Herbivores will not receive solar energy
(*c*) Mineral movement will be blocked (*d*) The rate of decomposition will be high

86. In a biotic community (ecosystem), the primary consumers are :
(*a*) Carnivores (*b*) Omnivores (*c*) Detritivores (*d*) Herbivores

87. What is true about photolithotrops ?
(*a*) Obtain energy from radiations and hydrogen from organic compounds
(*b*) Obtain energy from radiations and hydrogen from inorganic compounds
(*c*) Obtain energy from organic compounds
(*d*) Obtain energy from inorganic compounds

88. The frog that feeds on an insect is a :
(*a*) Tertiary consumer (*b*) Decomposer (*c*) Primary consumer (*d*) Secondary consumer

89. Relative Biological Effectiveness (RBE) is caused due to :
(*a*) Soil (*b*) Water (*c*) Radiation (*d*) Pollution

90. Pneumatophores are characteristics of :
(*a*) Halophytes (*b*) Oxylophytes (*c*) Fresh water plants (*d*) Psammophytes

91. Forest cover of India according to 'State of Forest Report 1997' is :
(*a*) 11.5% (*b*) 17.55% (*c*) 18.27% (*d*) 19.27%

92. Which of the following communities is more vulnerable to invasion by outside animals and plants ?
(*a*) Mangrove (*b*) Tropical evergreen
(*c*) Temperate forests (*d*) Oceanic island communities

93. In a terrestrial ecosystem (*e.g.*, forest) maximum energy is in which trophic level :
(*a*) T_1 (*b*) T_2 (*c*) T_3 (*d*) T_4

94. Plants such as Prosopis, Acacia and Capparis are found in tropical :
(*a*) Grasslands (*b*) Thorny forests (*c*) Deciduous forests (*d*) Evergreen forests

95. Which of the following ecosystems has the highest gross primary productivity ?
(*a*) Grassland (*b*) Coral reef (*c*) Mangroves (*d*) Tropical rain forest

96. The 'niche' of a species is meant for :
(*a*) Specific space where an organism lives
(*b*) Habitat and specific functions of a species
(*c*) Specific species function and its competitive power
(*d*) None of these

97. Benthonic animals are those, which are :
(*a*) Deep dwellers in sea (*b*) Free floating
(*c*) Submerged in sea (*d*) Float on sea surface

98. In any food chain, the largest population is that of :
(*a*) Primary consumers (*b*) Tertiary consumers (*c*) Producers (*d*) Decomposers

99. Which of the following is the most stable ecosystem ?
(*a*) Forest (*b*) Desert (*c*) Mountain (*d*) Ocean

100. In desert grasslands, which type of animals are relatively more abundant ?
(*a*) Diurnal (*b*) Arboreal (*c*) Aquatic (*d*) Fossorial

ANSWERS

1. (*b*)	**2.** (*c*)	**3.** (*b*)	**4.** (*c*)	**5.** (*a*)	**6.** (*c*)	**7.** (*c*)	**8.** (*a*)	**9.** (*d*)	**10.** (*d*)
11. (*b*)	**12.** (*c*)	**13.** (*b*)	**14.** (*d*)	**15.** (*a*)	**16.** (*d*)	**17.** (*c*)	**18.** (*c*)	**19.** (*c*)	**20.** (*d*)
21. (*c*)	**22.** (*c*)	**23.** (*b*)	**24.** (*a*)	**25.** (*c*)	**26.** (*a*)	**27.** (*b*)	**28.** (*b*)	**29.** (*a*)	**30.** (*c*)
31. (*a*)	**32.** (*b*)	**33.** (*c*)	**34.** (*a*)	**35.** (*a*)	**36.** (*a*)	**37.** (*d*)	**38.** (*c*)	**39.** (*b*)	**40.** (*d*)
41. (*d*)	**42.** (*b*)	**43.** (*b*)	**44.** (*c*)	**45.** (*a*)	**46.** (*c*)	**47.** (*b*)	**48.** (*b*)	**49.** (*d*)	**50.** (*a*)
51. (*b*)	**52.** (*b*)	**53.** (*c*)	**54.** (*d*)	**55.** (*d*)	**56.** (*a*)	**57.** (*d*)	**58.** (*c*)	**59.** (*a*)	**60.** (*a*)
61. (*d*)	**62.** (*c*)	**63.** (*c*)	**64.** (*b*)	**65.** (*d*)	**66.** (*c*)	**67.** (*b*)	**68.** (*c*)	**69.** (*a*)	**70.** (*c*)
71. (*a*)	**72.** (*d*)	**73.** (*b*)	**74.** (*c*)	**75.** (*b*)	**76.** (*b*)	**77.** (*a*)	**78.** (*c*)	**79.** (*a*)	**80.** (*d*)
81. (*a*)	**82.** (*c*)	**83.** (*b*)	**84.** (*b*)	**85.** (*c*)	**86.** (*d*)	**87.** (*b*)	**88.** (*d*)	**89.** (*a*)	**90.** (*a*)
91. (*a*)	**92.** (*a*)	**93.** (*a*)	**94.** (*b*)	**95.** (*d*)	**96.** (*c*)	**97.** (*a*)	**98.** (*d*)	**99.** (*d*)	**100.** (*d*)

26
CHAPTER

Natural Resources and Vegetation Types of India

Man lives in nature and depends on the resources of nature. The progress of human beings depends upon the exploitation of different natural resources. The utilisation of soil, water, coal, electricity, oil, gas and nuclear energy is important for the development of a nation. Any component of the natural environment that can be utilised by man to promote his welfare is considered as a **natural resource**.

Food, shelter and clothing are the primary requirements of the man. Today, man's dependence on the environment is greater than that of other organisms because he is more than a mere biological creature. Modern man has developed an obsession for greater comfort and security. To meet his requirements, he consumes larger amounts of material and energy than any other organism. He has developed a new kind of environment–the **socio-cultural environment**–within the natural environment. Such environment consists of things developed by man through his tools, skills, efforts and social institutions. It depends on and draws sustenance from the natural environment.

Human civilisation has evolved gradually and passed through several distinct stages. The hunting, fishing and food-gathering stages of the primitive man were followed by the agricultural and the industrial stages. With these events the biosphere became transformed into a human-dominated environment or **noosphere** (*noo* = mind; *sphere* = domain).

Due to increase in human population, India is facing an ecological crisis and is depleting her natural resources day by day. Now the shortage of natural resources is a matter of international concern. There is increasing deficiency of energy, metals, coal, non-fuel and non-metallic materials. In the subsequent paragraphs, the natural resources, causes of their degradation and conservation will be discussed.

CLASSIFICATION OF NATURAL RESOURCES

Natural Resources

The word 'resource' means a source of supply or support generally held in reserve.

In other words, natural resources are the components of the atmosphere, hydrosphere and lithosphere, which can be drawn upon for supporting life.

The 'natural resources' include energy, air, water, land, minerals, plants and animals.

For human-beings resources are those materials and sources of energy which are needed for their survival and prosperity.

The nature of resources varies from society to society depending on a number of factors, such as culture, the level of development and the nature of work of that particular society. For example, uranium, gold or silver are of no use for the Onge tribals of Andamans.

Natural resources vary greatly in their location, quantity and quality. For example, a particular type of forest may occur only in certain countries.

Classification

Natural resources can be classified in different ways. A most convenient classification of resources is based upon their exhaustibility and renewability. They are most commonly classified as (*i*) **inexhaustible**, and (*ii*) **exhaustible** on the basis of their abundance and availability.

Inexhaustible Resources

Inexhaustible resources are available in unlimited quantities on the earth.

Some inexhaustible resources remain unaffected by human activities, while others may show changes in their quality, but their quantity is not affected.

Inexhaustible resources like solar energy, wind power, tide power, rainfall and even atomic energy cannot be exhausted significantly at global level due to human activities.

However, they may sometimes be affected at local level by human activities, *e.g.*, pollution may change the quality of air.

Exhaustible Resources

A large number of natural resources are exhaustible, *i.e.*, they have limited supply on the earth and can be exhausted if used indiscriminately. For example, the availability of water in lakes and rivers and water stream energy can be diminished or degraded if used improperly.

Exhaustible resources are classified as (*i*) **renewable**, and (*ii*) **non-renewable**.

Renewable resources. Resources that have the inherent capacity to reappear or replenish themselves by quick recycling, reproduction and replacement within a reasonable time and maintain themselves. The growth and reproduction of such resources can be successfully managed so that these resources are continuously regenerated. Soil, water and living organisms are the main renewable resources. The rate at which their renewal occurs varies.

However, if the consumption of renewable resources continues to exceed their rate of renewal, not only their quality becomes affected, they may even get totally exhausted.

Natural Resources

- **Inexhaustible**
  - Solar energy
  - Wind power
  - Rainfall
  - Power of tides
  - Hydro-power
- **Exhaustible**
  - **Renewable**
    - Water
    - Soil fertility
    - Natural vegetation
    - Wildlife
    - Aquatic animals
    - Humans
  - **Non-renewable**
    - Biological species
    - Minerals

Fig. 26.1. Basic types of natural resources

Some important ecosystems and their renewable resources are :

(*i*) **Forests.** They yield timber and other plant products.

(*ii*) **Rangelands.** They sustain grazing animals for milk, meat and wool production.

(*iii*) **Wild life.** They maintain food chain.

(*iv*) **Agricultural systems.** They yield food, fibre, spices, etc.

(*v*) **Marine and fresh water systems.** They provide various products from plants and animals.

(*vi*) **Soil and water.** They are other renewable resources of great importance.

Non-renewable resources. Resources that lack the ability for recycling and replacement are called non-renewable resources. Substances with a very long recycling time are also regarded as non-renewable resources. For example, fossil fuels, like coal and petroleum, and minerals are non-renewable resources. Biological species, which have evolved in nature during the course of millions of years, are considered non-renewable. Once a biological species becomes extinct, it cannot be recreated again by man.

Resources such as underground water, forests and wildlife are renewable resources but can become non-renewable if used too rapidly by improper management.

Principal Natural Resources, that contribute significantly to human welfare are :

(*i*) Soil, (*ii*) Water, (*iii*) Land, (*iv*) Energy, (*v*) Marine, and (*vi*) Mineral.

SOIL RESOURCES

Land is a major constituent of the lithosphere and the source of many minerals essential to man and other organisms. It forms about one-fifth of the earth's surface, covering about 13, 393 million hectares. About 36.6 per cent of the land area is occupied by human dwellings and factories, roads and railways, deserts and dunes, glaciers, polar ice marshes, rocks and mountains. About 30 per cent of the total land mass is under forests, approximately 22 per cent is occupied by meadows and pastures and only 11 per cent is arable land (*i.e.*, suitable for growing crops).

The surface layer of the land is called soil. About four-fifths of the land area is covered by soil. Soil is composed of inorganic particles, organic matter, air, water and a variety of organisms. It takes hundreds of years for the development of soil horizons having different physico-chemical properties.

The physical properties of soil depend on its texture, structure, bulk, density, porosity and water retentivity. The salt content, pH, and organic and inorganic nutrients like nitrogen, phosphorus and potassium determine its chemical properties. The topography, climate and biotic factors control the conditions of the soil.

Human activities often create worldwide problems. Soil erosion, salinisation, water-logging, and acidification and alkalisation of soil by erroneous human activities are the great dangers to the land resources.

Construction of dams, roads, and railways, urban encroachment and industrialisation and mining activities are responsible for causing depletion of productive land.

Soil Erosion

The word 'erosion' literally means 'to wearing away'. In soil erosion, fertile soil surfaces are detached and removed from their original places and are deposited at some other places. According to Fox (1950), the soil erosion covers a wide range of physical and chemical actions, such as removal of soluble matters, chemical changes, disintegration by frost or by rapid changes of temperature, attrition by dust charged wind, scouring by silt laden currents, alternate impact and succession by storm waves, land slides and so on. Thus, soil erosion is the removal of top soil by movement of water and air.

Human activities accelerate soil erosion by removing natural plant cover. From croplands in India, millions of tons of top soil are eroded into sea each year. Deforestation, undesirable forest biota, and mechanical practices by man are important factors which cause soil erosion. Erosion causes a significant loss of soil fertility by transporting organic matter and nutrients that are essential part of the soil.

The eroded soil, which gets into streams, rivers and lakes in the form of sediments, affects water quality and the habitats of aquatic organisms. There are several serious effects of soil erosion, which are as follows :

1. Due to uprooting of trees, scarcity of timber and fuelwood.
2. Loss of soil stability and fertility.
3. Shortage of fodder.
4. Destruction of cropable land in plains.
5. Formation of sand dunes.
6. Greater frequency of floods and threat to communication channels.
7. Silting of river beds, lakes and dams.
8. Higher temperature and lower rainfall.

However, abundant plant cover significantly reduces soil erosion.

Depletion of Soil Fertility

If the rate of removal or loss of components is greater than the rate of addition, the soil will naturally less fertile. Leaching is an important factor which makes the soil poor in its resources. In this process minerals and organic substances are removed from the top layer of soil by rain water. Biological agencies are also active in causing loss of resources from the soil. Cultivation of crops regularly year after year makes the soil less productive. In cultivation there are little chances for the compensation of lost nutrients of the soil by way of death and decay of the vegetation which grows on it.

On the other hand, when natural vegetation is removed to develop agricultural systems, as in many parts of India, not only the nutrients stored in vegetation are removed, the organic matter and nutrients accumulated in the soil are also lost. From agricultural systems, nutrients are exported through crop harvest, thus depleting soil fertility.

Leguminous plants, however, compensate the loss of nitrogenous compounds because bacteria (rhizobia, etc.) inhabiting in their root nodules fix considerable amount of free atmospheric nitrogen into its compounds, such as ammonia, nitrites, nitrates, etc.

Soil Conservation

The main aims of soil conservation are : (*i*) to protect the soil from erosion, and (*ii*) to maintain the productive capacity of the soil.

Both engineering and biological methods have been used to check the soil erosion but it is still without a plausible check. In India, we are aware of advancing deserts of Rajasthan, and erosional losses, floods, etc., in other parts of the country. The problem has received the attention of forest ecologists, soil scientists and engineers these days. With the result several soil and crop management practices have been evolved which can minimise erosion and reduce nutrient depletion of agricultural soils. Such practices include (*i*) conservation tillage, (*ii*) organic farming, (*iii*) crop rotation (especially cereals with legumes), (*iv*) contour ploughing, and (*v*) strip-cropping terraces, etc.

(*i*) **Tillage conservation.** Many researches support the view that in dry areas, shallow ploughing gives comparatively good crop yields. Shallow ploughing removes the weeds and enables the soil to absorb water. Deep ploughing often leads to soil erosion but in the areas where rainfall is sufficiently high, deep ploughing (upto 15 to 30 cm deep) is effective in removing weeds and increasing crop yields.

In contrast to conventional tillage, conservational tillage incorporates residues from previous crops into the soil, thus increasing the organic matter which in turn improves soil moisture and nutrients. There are two kinds of conservation tillage : (i) reduced tillage, and (ii) no-tillage.

The efforts to improve erosion-affected soils are summarised in two steps. They are :

(*i*) stabilising the soil to prevent further erosion, and

(*ii*) restoration of soil fertility.

For soil stabilization, seeding of base ground with plants that can survive adverse conditions is required. For this purpose usually drought resistant grasses are grown. Such plants eventually establish vegetation cover on the soil, preventing further erosion.

(*ii*) **Organic farming.** With increasing addition of detritus, the soil organic matter, nutrient and moisture levels improve. Application of biofertilizers is also useful for enhancement of soil fertility. Various organic farming measures that provide increased organic input to soil have long-term beneficial effects on soil fertility.

Humus is formed by the accumulation of partially decayed and partially synthesized organic materials. Humus helps in making the soil granular. It causes air spaces to be formed in the clay soil and increases the water holding capacity of sandy soils. Humus is rich in nutrients and therefore, enhances plant growth. Being black humus absorbs heat and warms up the soil.

WATER RESOURCES

Water is the major constituent of the hydrosphere and covers four-fifths of the earth's surface. In fact, water is all around us. Every cubic millimetre of air, even over dry deserts, has water vapour. Water is present in the soil and also hidden in underground pools.

The total volume of water in the hydrosphere is 1.4 billion cubic kilometres (km^3), about 97.5 per cent of the earth's water is found in oceans, which is strongly saline. The rest 2.5 per cent is fresh water, and all of this is not available for direct human use. Most of the fresh water is frozen as polar or glacial ice (*i.e.*, 1.97 per cent). Remaining fresh water occurs as ground water (*i.e.*, 0.5 per cent), and water in lakes and rivers (0.02 per cent), soil (0.01 per cent) and atmosphere (0.001 per cent). Thus, only a small fraction of fresh water is available for human consumption.

About 84 per cent of the total global evaporation occurs from ocean surface and 16 per cent from land surface.

At any given time the amount of moisture in the air is only enough to meet a total rainfall requirement of ten days. Thus, there is a fast movement of water from ocean and land into the atmosphere, and an average stay time of water in the air is only about ten days.

About 77 per cent of the total rainfall on earth is received on the sea surface (as against 84 per cent evaporation from ocean surface) and 23 per cent on land (as against 16 per cent from land surface). Thus, there is net gain of 7 per cent rainfall water on land, and this excess is returned to the oceans by surface run off through rivers and sub-surface water flows.

However, on global basis, the hydrological cycle is perfectly balanced as the total annual evaporation matches with annual rainfall.

Global water is unequally distributed. Precipitation is seasonal and, therefore, the amount of water in inland bodies is variable. Irregularity in the duration and intensity of rainfall often causes floods or droughts. Scarcity of fresh water results in serious regional disparities. Arid regions suffer perennially from water shortage.

Table 26.1. Global Distribution of Fresh Water

	Water : Cubic km (km^3)
1. Water in snow caps, ice sheets, glaciers, etc.	24, 000, 000
2. Surface ponds, lakes and reservoirs	280, 000
3. Water in streams and rivers	1, 200
4. Water present as soil moisture	85, 000
5. Ground water	60, 000, 000
Total amount of fresh water on our planet	84, 366, 200

The global distribution of fresh water on our planet is only about 84.4 million cubic km. The global distribution of fresh water on earth's crust including ground water and water present as vapours in the atmosphere is given in table 13.1.

Table 26.2. Annual Water Budget of our Planet

	Water in cubic km (km^3)
1. Evaporation from sea surface	452, 600
2. Evaporation from land surface	72, 500
3. Precipitation on ocean surface	411, 600
4. Precipitation on land surface	113, 500
5. Surface and ground water run-off	41, 000
Total evaporation from land and sea surface	525, 100
Total precipitation on land and sea surface	525, 100

The excess water received by land surface, about 41, 000 cubic km has to flow back to sea, it cannot be retained on earth's surface ordinarily.

Water Use

On global basis, the water use has increased 4 to 8 per cent per year since 1950, and the consumption rate varies among different countries.

Agriculture sector is the biggest consumer of freshwater. Worldwide, about 70 per cent of total water use is accounted by agriculture.

Following agriculture, power generation (6.2 per cent), and industries (5.7 per cent) are the biggest consumers of fresh water.

Domestic requirement and livestock management taken together consume only 4.3 per cent of the total water drawn.

However, only about 1.1 per cent of fresh water is used for domestic and municipal supplies. The rest of water is consumed by various industries, such as cement, mining, pharmaceutical, detergent and leather industry, etc.

Fisheries, hydro-electric power generation, recreational activities, etc., also require a huge quantity of water, much of which flows down to the sea.

Problems Related with Water Resources

Today in almost all spheres of human activity more water is drawn than what is actually needed. Due to carelessness much of it is wasted and allowed to flow out in an impure state. At many places enough clean water is no longer available. The rapid rise in demand for fresh water is naturally a result of an equally rapid growth in the number of consumers. But there are many other causes as well which have contributed significantly to the wastage and degeneration of fresh water.

For example, about 40 per cent of the world's population lives in arid or semi-arid regions. These people spend lot of energy, time and effort in obtaining water for their domestic and agricultural uses.

To meet the needs of huge population, surface waters, *i.e.*, ponds, lakes, rivers, streams, etc., are overdrawn. Due to over use of surface water, the nearby wetlands may dry up.

When more ground water is removed for human use than can be recycled by rainfall or snow-melt, the ground water may also dry out.

However, everywhere we tend to use more water than is actually needed. A little care can result in substantial savings and longer life for our resource base or else, the water thus saved can be diverted to regions where there is shortage.

Excessive irrigation in arid and semi-arid regions can cause salt accumulation in the soil, due to which crop productivity will decline.

On the other hand, the continuous depletion of ground water along the coastal regions often leads to the movement of saline sea water into fresh water wells, spoiling the quality of water. Estuaries become more saline and consequently less productive when surface waters are over drawn.

Addition of wastes and sewage causes the water body to become exceedingly rich in plant nutrients. Blooms of algae and other organisms appear and make the water useless for human purposes. The entire biomass may suddenly die and start decomposing causing several other problems. Organically rich waters also support a population of many pathogenic organisms and vectors which transfer diseases from one individual to another.

Heavy rainfall results in rapid run-off from areas having exposed soil, particularly on mountain slopes. This causes soil erosion which results in heavy floods. Uncontrolled soil erosion is the main cause of sedimentation of water ways which causes harm to fisheries.

Now a days, pressure of demand on underground water resourses has gone up considerably. Every year more and more water is drawn up from sub-surface layers whereas recharging of underground waters has been slowed down. Massive deforestation has caused disappearance of plant cover over a large area of land surface. In absence of plant cover most of the rain water flows down quickly in streams and rivers. Little of it percolates down to sub-surface layers to recharge the ground water stock. With rapidly flowing waters considerable amount of top soil is lost with torrential flow of water. In a number of localities where underground water is regularly drawn, the water table is receding deeper, thus output exceeds the input.

Conservation and Management of Water

As we know, water is the basic need of living organisms. An acute crisis of water is expected to follow in some regions of the world, particularly in our country. The shortage of water shall make many localities barren, dry and devoid of life. Fertile land will convert into deserts. Conservation of fresh water is therefore, an absolute necessity of today. A number of steps are being undertaken to minimise wastage of fresh water resources and to make more efficient use of the available water. Main approaches for conservation of water are as follows :

(*i*) Reducing agricultural water wastage by increasing efficiency of irrigation.

(*ii*) Reducing water wastage in industry by recycling the used water.

(*iii*) Reducing domestic water wastage by constructing waste water treatment plants and recycling the treated water.

(*iv*) Rainwater harvesting by using practices to store rainwater and recharge groundwater.

(*v*) Afforestation and protection of water sheds to improve water economy.

(*vi*) Reducing pollution and recycling of water.

(*vii*) By development of an efficient distribution system of water.

(*viii*) By enhancement of surface water storage capacity.

(*ix*) By improvement of underground water storage capacity.

(*x*) By adopting water economy.

Main approaches for management of water are as follows :

(*i*) Construction of dams and reservoirs to regulate year-round supply of water. They are also helpful in controlling flood and generating electricity.

(*ii*) Desalinisation of sea water and saline groundwater, making it fit for drinking and agricultural purposes. Desalinisation plants are already under operation in Middle East countries.

(*iii*) Diversion of water and bodies (*e.g.*, through canals) to increase the natural supply of water to a particular area.

(*iv*) Regular dredging and desiltation of water bodies.

Swajaldhara. Reforms in the Rural Drinking Water Sector were adopted in 1999 and also a few projects were launched as pilots. They were intended to be implemented during the Ninth Five Year Plan and with the experience gained there on, the reform initiatives were to be firmed up and scaled up during the Tenth Plan period for adopting the demand responsive strategy and also for institutionalising community participation for the sustainability of drinking water supply system and sources in rural areas. On 15.12.2002, the reform initiative in the Rural Drinking Water Sector were scaled up throughout the country by launching the **Swajaldhara** by the Hon'ble Prime Minister of India.

LAND RESOURCES

Land is a major constituent of the lithosphere and is the source of many materials essential to man and other organisms. Earth's one fourth area is formed by land which is largely covered with natural forests, grasslands, wetlands and man made urban and rural settlements along with agriculture. About 36.6 per cent of the land area is occupied by human dwellings and factories, roads and railways, deserts and dunes, glaciers, polar ice marshes, rocks and mountains. About 30 per cent of the total land mass is under forests, approximately 22 per cent is occupied by meadows and pastures and only 11 per cent for agriculture. Low-lying areas covered with shallow water are called wetlands. The wetlands make the transitional zones between terrestrial and aquatic areas.

FORESTS

The forest is 'a plant community predominantly of trees and other woody vegetation, usually with a closed canopy'. The word **forest** has been derived from the Latin '*foris*' meaning outside, the reference being to a village boundary or fence, and it must have included all uncultivated and uninhabited land. Today a forest is any land managed for the diverse purpose of forestry, whether covered with trees, shrubs, climbers, lianes, etc., or not. The Indian word 'jungle' has been adopted in the English language to describe a collection of trees, shrubs, etc., that are not grown in a regular manner. Forests are a very striking feature of the land surface. They vary greatly in composition and density, and stand in marked contrast with meadows and pastures. Certain forests are evergreen, like the Deodar forests of Kashmir and Himachal Pradesh, while others are deciduous, becoming leafless either before the advent of winter when vegetative activity almost ceases, such as the oak forests of the Himalayas, or else just before the onset of intense dry summer, to reduce transpiration to the minimum, like the teak forests of Madhya Pradesh.

Importance of Forests

The forests of a country make a natural asset of immense value. Unlike its mineral resources, including fossil fuels, which in course of time will either get exhausted or their utilisation will become uneconomic due to increased costs for obtaining and processing them, the forests, if of adequate extent ideally dispersed, scientifically managed, and judiciously utilised can be kept perpetually productive and useful, conferring many benefits, direct and indirect, on the people. Directly, forests meet the needs of timber wood, fuel, bamboos and a variety of other products, including fodder which are indispensable requirements of the people living in close proximity of the forests. The forests provide facility for the grazing of livestock, a yield and variety of products, of commercial and industrial value such as structural timber, charcoal, raw materials for making paper, newsprint, panel products, **bidi** leaves, gums, resin, tanstuff and a number of other economic products including medicinal drugs. Indirectly, forests preserve the physical features, check soil runoff, mitigate floods and make the stream flow perennially and thus help agriculture. Forests make the climate equable and have a considerable hygienic and strategic value. They also provide shelter to the wildlife.

In developing countries the heaviest demand on forests is for fuel wood. More than 1500 million people depend on wood for cooking and other purposes. The world consumption of wood for fuel is estimated to be more than 1,000 million m^3. This is well over 80 per cent of the total use. About 58 per cent of the total energy used in Africa and 42 per cent in South East Asia is obtained from fuel wood.

Bamboos are tall, perennial, arborescent grasses. More than 100 species of them are found in the Indian forests. Bamboos are characterised by woody stems, called culms. The strength of culms, their straightness, hardness, and the facility with which they can be split make them suitable for a variety of purposes. Indeed bamboos are the poor man's timber, used as rafters, scaffolding, roofing, walling, flooring, matting, basketry, carthoods, cordage, etc. Tender shoots are eaten and pickled. Bamboos are the only indigenous plant of wide occurrence in the Indian forests which has a comparatively long fibre suitable for making paper and rayon. Canes, that come from family Palmaceae, and occur in the forests of Andamans, Assam, Kerala, Tamil Nadu, Maharashtra, Bihar, Orissa and Uttar Pradesh, are used as plaiting material, as ropes and cables of suspension bridges in the forests, for furniture, walking sticks, umbrella handles, and sports goods.

Essential oils are obtained from a variety of forest plants. These are used in the manufacture of soaps, cosmetics, pharmaceuticals, confectionery, tobacco flavouring and incense. Important from the commercial point of view are the oils of *Eucalyptus*, used in medicine, rusa grass, khus and sandalwood. Tannins, dyes, gums, resins and oleoresins are other important forest products. Babul bark (*Acacia nilotica*) is an important tanning material used in northern India, the main centre being Kanpur. Gums and resins are exuded by plants. The gum is used in the textile trade, cosmetics, dentrifices, cigar and food industry. The chief producing centres of gum are Madhya Pradesh, Uttar Pradesh, Rajasthan and Gujarat. The most important resin is that obtained by tapping the chir pine (*Pinus roxburghii*). It is a flourishing forest industry. Natural camphor is also a forest product. Drugs, spices, poisons and insecticides are other important forest products. They are derived from trees, shrubs, climbers, herbs, ferns, mosses, lichens and consist of fruits, flowers, leaves, bark, stem or root. **Sarpagandha**, a famous drug is obtained from the roots of *Rauwolfia serpentina*, whereas quinine, a drug used against malaria fever, is obtained from the *bark of Cinchona*. **Kala zira** is the seed of *Carum carvi*, a much valued spice. Several forest fruits, flowers and even leaves and tuberous roots are eatern, such as **bel**, **ber**, **phalsa**, **jamun**, **khirni** and **tendu**. The parts of many plants are used as pickles or vegetables. Such important trees and shrubs are— **amla**, **anar**, **imli**, **karaunda**, **kokam**, **kachnar** and **kaith**. Mushrooms and morels are found in wild state in Kashmir and Himachal Pradesh. They are edible and used as delicacy. Palmyra palm yields a fermented drink **nira**. **Mahua** corollas are fermented to get a liquor. **Phulwara** butter is obtained from the seeds of Indian butter tree (*Diploknema butyracea*). **Shahtoot** fruit is eaten or made into a sherbet. **Bhilama** fruits are salted and pickled.

The leaves of **tendu** (*Diospyros melanoxylon*) are used as wrappers of tobacco to make **bidis**. Leaves of the woody climber *Bauhinia vahlii* found in deciduous forests are collected in large quantities and made into plates and leaf cups used for feasts and other festive occasions.

Miscellaneous forest products include leaves of certain species used for various purposes, soap substitutes, such as **ritha** (seeds of *Sapindus emarginatus*), pods of *Acacia concinna* called **shikakai**, sola pith, ornamental seeds, such as **gumchi** and **rudraksha** (the drupes of *Elaeocarpus ganitrus*).

Lac is the most important animal product obtained from forests. It is a resinous secretion, formed as a protective covering on the bodies of larvae of a minute insect *Laccifer lacca*. The lac insects live on the hosts, such as **palas** (*Butea monosperma*) and **ber**. India produces about 85 per cent of the world production. Lac has been mentioned in Vedas, and known from ancient times in India. Other animal products from forests are honey and wax. **Tussar** or **kosa** silk moths, horns and hides of dead animals are also the products of forests. Antlers of deer and ivory are also animal forest products.

The forests play an important role in the life of tribal people living in forests. The forests provide them food, fruits, meat, medicines, hides, skins and other products of commercial use.

Forests make large biotic communities, and they give shelter to diverse species of plants, animals and micro-organisms.

Forests protect the environment. A forest and its environment are always interacting. The most important environmental factors are micro-climate soil characteristics, moisture availability and action of animals and insects. Micro-climate is governed by solar radiation, rainfall, wind, humidity and temperature of the air and the soil. In a dense forest temperature range is narrow, and although the air temperature in and outside a forest is more or less the same, the humidity is greater inside. Soil temperature is also influenced by the forests, which in turn affects the biological activity in the top layer of the soil. Heavy winds may cause a serious erosion if the soil is dry and not covered with vegetation. Extensive forests condense low clouds and thus to some extent increase precipitation. When the tree canopy is open there is little humus on the forest floor and, therefore, rain strikes the bare soil with full fury and brings about soil erosion, which leads to denudation. In rocky tracts, roots of trees penetrate deep into the soil and thus bind it together.

The need for adopting soil conservation measures is the practice of forestry. A well managed and properly stocked forest reduces soil runoff. Rain water is absorbed by the humus and then it seeps into the sub-soil and finally moves underground, thus keeping the streams flowing perennially. Forests thus mitigate floods which can otherwise do immense damage to agricultural land in the lower region. The forest soil absorbs water during rains, and does not allow it to evaporate or run off swiftly. This ensures a perennial supply of water in springs and wells. The hill slopes with forest cover conserve water and gradually release it into streams, rivers and sub-soil springs. Forests help to increase the humidity of the atmosphere by drawing subsoil water and sending it out in the air by means of transpiration. The increased humidity of the forest helps plants and animals for their survival in a warm season by making it cool and pleasant. Forests reduce atmospheric pollution by collecting the suspended particulate matter and by absorbing carbon dioxide from atmosphere.

Forests have a great aesthetic value. All people appreciate the beauty and tranquillity of forests. In ancient times, to arrest devastation of forests, which was adversely affecting the life of people, some wise ancestors and **rishis** declared cutting of trees a sin and planting and protecting them an act of piety. Several useful species were thus saved from extinction, such as the banyan, the **pipal** and **bel**. Forests are of great educative value. The forests are supposed to be nature's laboratories which have contributed to the study and research in various branches of natural sciences. Indian culture was born in **ashramas** situated in deep forests, where the **rishis** sang— "May the gods, the water, the plants and the forest trees, accept our prayers. and may their blessings protect us for ever, and ever".

The forests are storehouse of biodiversity and provide important environmental services to mankind. These services originate from the undermentioned key functions of forests :

(*i*) **Productive functions.** They include production of wood, fruits and a wide variety of compounds, such as resins, alkaloids, essential oils, latex, pharmaceuticals, etc.

(*ii*) **Protective functions.** They include conservation of soil and water; prevention of drought, shelter against wind cold, radiation, noise, sights and smells, etc.

(*iii*) **Regulative functions.** They include absorption, storage and release of gases (CO_2, O_2), water, mineral elements and radiant energy.

Forests effectively regulate floods and drought and the global biogeochemical cycles, particularly carbon cycle.

The regulative functions also improve atmospheric and temperature conditions. They enhance the economic and environmental value of the landscape.

Forest Area in India

At the beginning of the twentieth century, about 30 per cent of land in India was covered with forests.

However, by the end of the twentieth century, the forest cover was reduced to 19.4 per cent.

This is less than the optimum 33 per cent area recommended by the National Forest Policy (1988) for the plains, and 67 per cent for the hills.

Of the existing forests, less than two-third are dense forests, and the rest are open degraded forests.

Today, per capita forest area avaiable in India is 0.06 ha, comparatively, which is much below the average for the world, *i.e.*, 0.64 ha per capita.

Table 26.3. Forest Cover in India, 1999

Class	*Area (km^2)*	*Percentage-Geographic area*
Dense forest	3,77,358	11.5
Open degraded forest	2,55,064	7.8
Mangrove	4,871	0.1
Scrub forest	5,896	1.6
Non-forest (other land use)	25,98,074	79.0
Total	32,87,263	100.0

Forests in India

Palaeobotanical studies have shown that there were dense forests in India in the Permian period, 250 million years ago. Man was evolved in the beginning of the Pleistocene Age, only a million years ago. At this time India had thick forests except in Rajasthan and parts of Punjab which lay buried under a swamp. Archaeological evidence shows that the Rajasthan swamps existed till as late as 4000 B.C., when Mohenjodaro culture flourished. During **Ramayana era** there were dense forests in Naimisharanya, Chitrakoot, Dandakaranya and Panchwati which abounded in wild life. The chronicles of Chinese pilgrims mention dense Indian forests in the birth place of Lord Krishna. Records relating to the invasion of Alexander in 327 B.C. mention the existence of almost dark and deep forests along the Indus. Later in Kautilya's time, protection of forests, planting of new species of trees and preservation of wild life were considered desirable. By the time of Samrat Ashoka, the inroads were into the forests. Ashoka also encouraged the cultivation of exotic, medicinal plants. Emperor Jahangir introduced the famous **chinar** tree in Kashmir valley. Over-population and unplanned felling of trees have drastically reduced the forest area and the quality of forests in India today.

The area under forests in India is about 75 million ha and consists of about 23 per cent of the total land area. The National Forest Policy lays down that India should maintain one-third of its land under forests. The forests of India may be classified into three classes : (*i*) reserved forests, (*ii*) protected forests, and (*iii*) unclassed forests, forming 47.1, 30.3 and 22.6 per cent respectively of the total forest area. The forests in India are largely owned (about 96 per cent) or managed by the states.

Forest types. The distribution of natural forests in India is governed principally by rainfall which may vary from 12 cm to 125 cm annually in different parts of the country resulting in a wide variety of vegetation, from xerophytic scrub forests in the arid zones in Rajasthan to evergreen rain forests in the tropics as in the Western Ghats, Assam, North Bengal, Andamans and conifers in the temperate region. In between the extremes, there are many intermediate types and sub-types. The major forest types are : (*i*) moist tropical forests, (*ii*) dry tropical forests, (*iii*) montane sub-tropical forests, (*iv*) montane temperate forests, (*v*) sub-alpine forests, and (*vi*) alpine scrub forests.

Moist tropical forests occur in Western Ghats, Andamans and Assam. They consist of many evergreen species, such as dipterocarps, hopea, irul, toon, terminalias and several others.

Dry tropical forests occur in areas with rainfall 75 cm to 125 cm containing thorn forests. Tropical thorn forests are found in the desert and arid zones of Rajasthan, Punjab, Haryana, Gujarat, Western U.P. and Madhya Pradesh. They consist mainly of acacias.

Montane sub-tropical forests occur at elevations of 750 to 1800 m in the Himalayas and also at the similar elevations in the Nilgiris in South India. The forest flora is represented by pines.

Montane temperate forests occur at elevation of 1800 to 2700 m and with a rainfall of about 125 cm to 200 cm. Deodar, blue pine, spruce and fir and the important conifers in the Western Himalayas mixed with oaks, maples, walnut and *Ulmus*.

Sub-alpine forests occur between 2900 to 3500 m a.s.l. The vegetation consists of a dense growth of small crooked trees or large shrubs with patches of conifers like *Abies* and blue pine. Birch and *Rhododendron* are the common broadleaved trees.

Alpine scrub forests occur above 3500 m along the entire length of the Himalayas. The vegetation consists of low evergreen forests mostly of *Rhododendron* with birch and other deciduous trees forming a dense growth with short branchy stems.

Deforestation. Deforestation is a serious threat to the economy, quality of life and future of the environment of this country. The forests in India have declined from about 7,000 million hectares in 1900 to 2890 million hectares in 1975. It is estimated that by the year 2000 only 2370 million hectares will be left. Tropical rain forests have been reduced from 1,600 million hectares to 938 million hectares.

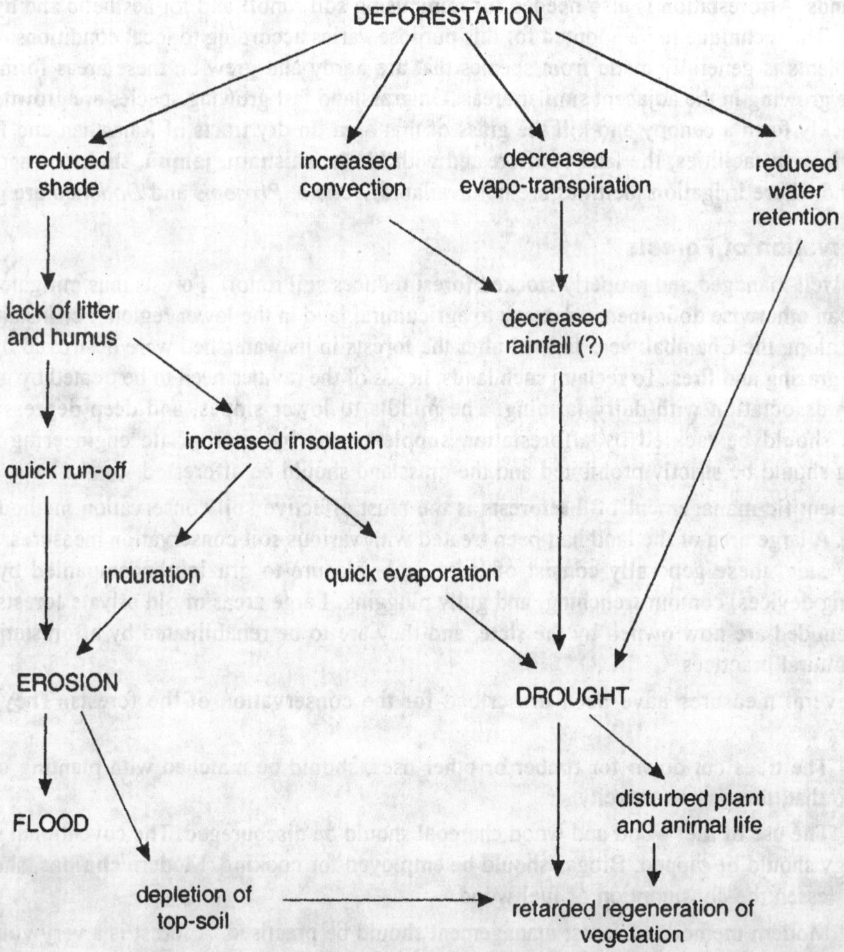

Fig. 26.2. Deforestation.

In India, the main causes of deforestation are : explosion of human and livestock population, increased requirement of timber and fuel wood, expansion of croplands for farming and enhanced grazing by cattle. Construction of roads in the hilly terrain is another important factor for deforestation. The total length of such roads is about 30,000 km in ecologically fragile areas. Development of industries, extension work for mining, quarrying, irrigation and agriculture are other causes of deforestation. Increased demand for fuel wood, timber, wooden crates, paper, newsprint and paper board led to felling of trees on large scale.

Deforestation is the main cause of soil erosion. The floods, drought and loss of precious wild life are also due to deforestation. Thus the economy of the country and quality of life of weaker sections have been much deteriorated. In this country, particularly in the Himalayan region, shortage of fire wood and water has been causing great misery to the womenfolk. They have to spend the whole day in the collection of fuel wood for cooking the meals of the day. It is thought that time is not far when the cost of food would be lesser than the cost of fuel to cook it.

Afforestation. As there is a general shortage of forests and as wood is a bulky commodity which cannot be transported to a long distance, it would be desirable to develop forests on all the wastelands. Afforestation is also needed for minimising soil runoff and for aesthetic and hygienic reasons. The technique to be adopted for this purpose varies according to local conditions. Choice of the plants is generally made from species that are hardy and grew on these areas formerly or they are growing in the adjacent similar areas. On grassland fast growing species are grown, which can quickly form a canopy and kill the grass of that area. In dry tracts of Rajasthan and Punjab, with irrigation facilities, the land is afforested with **khair**, **shisham**, **jamun**, **shahtoot** and **safed siris**, and where irrigation facilities are not available, *Acacia*, *Prosopis* and *Dodonea* are grown.

Conservation of Forests

A well-managed and properly stocked forest reduces soil runoff. Forests thus mitigate floods which can otherwise do immense damage to agricultural land in the lower region. For instance, the ravines along the Chambal were formed after the forests in its watershed were destroyed by over-felling, grazing and fires. To reclaim such lands, heads of the ravines need to be treated by growing grass in association with dairy farming. The middle to lower slopes, and deep depressions of ravines should be tackled by afforestation supplemented by appropriate engineering works. Grazing should be strictly prohibited and the grassland should be afforested.

Scientific management of the forests is the most effective soil conservation method in the country. A large area of the land had been treated with various soil conservation measures. On the forestry side, these generally consist of large-scale closure to grazing accompanied by water disposing devices, contour trenching, and gully plugging. Large areas of old private forests which were denuded are now owned by the state, and they are to be rehabilitated by afforestation and other cultural practices.

Several measures have been prescribed for the conservation of the forests. They are as follows :

1. The trees cut down for timber or other uses, should be matched with planting of more trees, so that, there is no scarcity.

2. The use of fuel wood and wood charcoal should be discouraged. The coventional sources of energy should be tapped. Biogas should be employed for cooking. Modern **chulhas**, should be used to lessen the consumption of fuel wood.

3. Modern methods of forest management should be practised. A forest is a very vulnerable asset. The slight neglect or unscientific working can rapidly deplete and may even annihilate it after which reforesting of the area may not be economically feasible.

4. The silvicultural practices should be adopted. Cultivation of forest crops consists of regeneration, that is, renewal of forest crop, and tending, that is carrying on operations from time to time for the benefit of the growing forest crop during its lifetime. The silvicultural practices include use of irrigation, fertilisers, bacterial and mycorrhizal inoculations, disease and pest management, control of weeds, cleaning, thinning, breeding of elite trees and use of tissue culture techniques.

5. The Social Forestry Programme (1976) should be encouraged. Under this programme, the so called waste lands should be utilised to produce fire wood, fodder and small timber for the use of agricultural implements. This programme includes raising, planting and protecting trees for various purposes. This programme is a boon for rural community.

6. The annual deforestation must be followed by annual reforestation of the deforested areas. Thus the forest is conserved. There should be intensification of afforestation or reforestation rates to nearly three times of the existing rate.

7. The agroforestry programme should be encouraged. Under this programme the attempt should be made to use the same land for farming, forestry and animal husbandry.

8. The urban forestry programme should also be encouraged. Under this programme, the small gardens and house compounds should be well maintained by planting flower and fruit trees. The trees of aesthetic value should also be planted along the road side. The ornamental trees should be grown in the parks and other wasteland. Such forestry programme will give nice look to the town, and mitigate the foul environment.

According to the opinion of experts in this field, it is believed that economy of this country would be sound if at least one-third of country's land comes under forest. To achieve this, there should be prompt action at the levels of individuals, community and the government. In India, several such movements have been taken by the people. For instance, *Chipko* movement of Tehri-Garwal region, and the public agitation against the construction of the hydroelectric project in silent valley, are current examples. India became independent in 1947, and thereafter, attention of the government was drawn to the need for remodelling the management of Indian forests so that they could play an increasingly useful role in promoting national welfare. As a first step towards making the people forest-conscious, a nation-wide celebration of an annual tree-planting festival, called **Van-Mahotsava** was conceived. All the waste-lands, road sides, railway track sides, parks and barren lands should be planted to regenerate forests.

Forest conservation and management programmes may be summarised as follows :

(*i*) They should ensure sustainable supply of tree products and services to people and industry.

(*ii*) They should ensure the maintenance of long-term ecological balance through protection, restoration and conservation of forest cover.

Extensive programmes of **afforestation** are needed to save the diminishing forest cover. The goals can be achieved by undermentioned practices :

(*i*) **Conservation forestry.** Also known as **protection forestry.** This involves protection of degraded forests to allow recoupment of their flora and fauna.

In such forestry practices, forest areas designated as national parks and sanctuaries are protected from human interference.

On the other hand, well-stocked forests are managed scientifically for producing timber and other forest products without causing any negative environmental impact on the forest.

(*ii*) **Production forestry.** Also known as **commercial forestry**. This aims to fulfil the commercial demand, without causing denudation of natural forests, through intensive plantation in available land. Social forestry and agro-forestry programmes are also included in this category.

Social forestry. This programme aims to plant trees and shrubs on all unused and fallow land to provide fuel wood, fodder, etc., thus, reducing pressure on existing forests. For example, unused farmland, usar land, community land, road and rail sides, etc., are planted with suitable tree species.

Agro-forestry. This includes a variety of land uses, where woody species are grown in combination with herbaceous crops, either at the same time or in time sequence.

Taungya system involves growing agricultural crops between rows of planted trees, such as sal, teak, poplars, etc.

Jhum system is well known shifting cultivation. This is a traditional agro-forestry system usually practiced in the north-eastern region of our country. This system involves felling and burning of forests, followed by cultivation of crops for few years and then gain abondoning cultivation to allow forest regrowth.

FORESTS AND WILDLIFE LAWS

National Forest Policy (1988). The National Forest Policy, 1988, emphasizes on scientific forestry research toward attainment of policy objectives which aim at restoring ecological balance and conservation of country's natural heritage by evolving socially acceptable, technically viable and ecologically sustainable management practices. Some priority areas of research broadly indicated in the policy are :

(*i*) Increasing forest productivity per unit area and per unit time.

(*ii*) Conservation eco-restoration and management of existing forest resources.

(*iii*) Social forestry in rural/tribal development.

(*iv*) Efficient utilisation of forest produce and substitutes for wood

(*v*) Formulate a meaningful curriculum and training model for forestry education to ensure professional competence.

(*vi*) Creating awakening amongst masses for increasing tree cover and adopting agroforestry models using suitable extension methodologies.

To enhance the effectiveness of management, conservation, sustainable development and utilisation of forest resources it becomes expedient to build up technical skills and improve the quality of human resources, research capability and support, forestry extension, information dissemination system and public education.

The principal aim of Forest Policy is to ensure environmental stability and maintenance of ecological balance, including atmospheric equilibrium, which are vital for all life forms, human, animal and plant.

Wildlife (Protection) Act 1972 (Amended 1991). This Act aims to protect wild animals, birds and plants. The main objectives of this Act are :

(*i*) Restriction and prohibition on hunting of animals.

(*ii*) Protection of specified plants ;

(*iii*) Setting up and managing sanctuaries and national parks;

(*iv*) Empowering zoo authority with control of zoos and captive breeding; and

(*v*) Control of trade and commerce in wildlife, wildlife products and trophies.

Forest Act 1927. This Act aims to consolidate the law relating to forests. The basic objectives of this act are :

(*i*) Setting up and managing reserved forests, protected forests and village forests ;

(*ii*) Protection of non-government forests and forest land;

(*iii*) Control of movement of forest produce ; and

(*iv*) Control of cattle grazing.

WWF – INDIA

The Word Wide Fund for Nature-India (WWF – India) has been working to promote harmony between humankind and nature for almost three decades. Today it is recognised as a premier NGO (non-government organisation) in the country dealing with conservation and development issues.

At a time when the Web of Life has come under increasing threats, WWF – India's attempts have been to find and implement solutions so that human beings can live in harmony with nature, and leave for future generations a world rich in natural resources and natural wonders.

Formerly known as the World Wildlife Fund, WWF – India was established as a Charitable Trust in 1969. With its network of State/Divisional and Field offices spread across the country to implement its programmes. WWF – India is the largest and one of the most experienced conservation organisations in the country. The Secretariat functions from New Delhi. The organisation is part of the WWF – India family with 27 independent National Organisations. The coordinating body, the WWF – International, is located at Gland in Switzerland.

WWF – India Mission

'The promotion of nature conservation and environmental protection as the basis for sustainable and equitable development'

To achieve this Mission WWF – India undertakes the following activities :

(*i*) **Tiger and Wildlife conservation**
(*ii*) **Freshwater and Wetland Conservation Programme**
(*iii*) **Educational Awareness**
(*iv*) **Centre for Environmental Law**
(*v*) **Oceans and Coasts Programme**
(*vi*) **Library and Documentation Services**
(*vii*) **Communication and Fund Raising**
(*viii*) **Indira Gandhi Conservation Monitoring Centre (IGCMC)**

WWF – India, through its biodiversity conservation, ecorestoration and environment education programmes has been extending its support to the conservation efforts and trying to maintain the ecological balance.

Table 26.4. Environmental Calendar

Month	*Date*	*Event*
January	14 – 30	Animal Welfare Fortnight
February	2	World Wetlands Day
February	28	National Science Day
March	21	World Forestry Day
March	22	World Water Day
April	22	World Earth Day
April	28	World Heritage Day
June	5	World Environment Day
June	17	World Day to Combat Desertification
July	1	Vanmahotsava Day
July	11	World Population Day
September	16	World Ozone Day
October	1 – 7	Worldlife Week
October	2	International National Disaster Prevention Day
October	5	World Habitat Day
November	1	World Ecology Day
November	10	Forest Martyr's Day
November	19	
	to	National Environment Month
December	18	
December	29	International Day for Biological Diversity

GRASSLANDS

The **grasslands**, also known as **rangeland**, provide forage and habitat to domestic animals and wildlife. Natural grasslands occur where rainfall is intermediate between that of desert lands and forest lands. In the temperate zone this generally means an annual precipitation between 10 and 30 inches, depending on temperature, seasonal distribution of the rainfall, and the water-holding capacity of the soil. Tropical grasslands may receive up to 60 inches concentrated in a wet season that alternates with a prolonged dry season. Grasslands are one of the most important of terrestrial ecosystem types.

A well-developed grassland community contains species with different temperature adaptations, one group growing in the cool part of the season (*i.e.*, spring and winter) and another in the hot part (summer). Forbs (*i.e.*, nongrassy herbs) are often important components, and woody plants (trees and shrubs) also occur in grasslands either as scattered individuals (savanna) or in belts or groups along streams and rivers.

In India, the area under various kinds of grass cover, including fallow and waste lands is about 18 per cent of the total land area. While forest cover is about 19 per cent of total land. This means, about 37 per cent of land can be said to be available for grazing.

Uses. In rural areas of our country, dried hay obtained from grasslands, particularly from tall grasses, is used as fuel or thatching material.

Grass cover is extremely effective in binding soil particles with the help of highly branched fibrous root system, thus significantly reducing soil erosion.

The annual average production of dry grass or hay in India is about 250 million tons.

Large herbivores are a characteristic feature of grasslands.

When man uses grasslands as natural pastures he usually replaces the native grazers with its domestic animals, *i.e.*, cattle, sheep and goats.

Since grasslands are adapted to heavy energy flow along the grazing food chain, such a switch is ecologically sound.

Degradation of Grassland

However, man has had a persistent history of misuse of grassland resources by virtue of allowing overgrazing and overplowing. The result is that many grasslands are now man-made deserts. The conversion of grassland (or forest) to desert is called **desertification**.

Degradation of destruction of grassland is mainly related to overpopulation. To enhance food production, grasslands possessing fertile soils are ploughed and converted to agricultural lands.

In India, grassland areas are frequently overgrazed. For example, the number of animals grazing in the arid and semi-arid regions has been found to be 2 – 10 times greater than the capacity of the grassland to feed the animals.

The lack of plant cover due to overgrazing causes soil erosion. When overgrazing occurs in combination with drought, the deserts are resulted.

Grassland Management

The important measures of grassland management are :

(*i*) **Protection from grazing.** This allows recovery of severely damaged vegetation.

(*ii*) **Use of rotational grazing.** While some areas are closed to grazing, allowing the plant cover to recover, grazing is permitted in other selected areas.

(*iii*) **Removal of unwanted plants.** This includes removal of woody bushes or shrubs and weeds, which usually adversely affect the productivity of grasses.

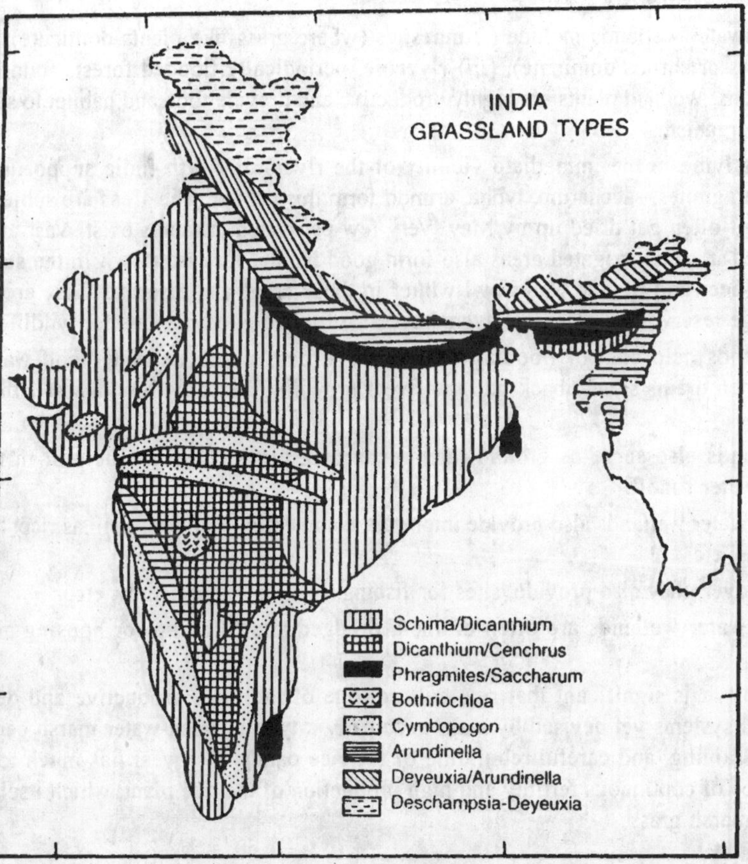

Fig. 26.3. Major grassland types of India.

(*iv*) **Conservation of soil and water.** This may be done by reducing loss of soil and water from the grassland.

(*v*) **Use of controlled burning.** This promotes recycling of nutrients stored in dried mulch and to reduce woody species invasion.

Grassland Types of India

The tropical grasslands of India may be classified as follows :

(*i*) **Xerophilous grasslands.** They are found in dry regions of North West India under semiarid conditions. The common examples are : *Andropogon contortus*, *Cenchrus ciliaris*, *C. barbatus*, etc.

(*ii*) **Mesophilous grasslands.** Also known as 'savannahs' they are extensive grassy plains typically occurring in moist deciduous forests of Uttaranchal. The dominant species are : *Saccharum munja*, *Saccharum narenga*, etc.

(*iii*) **Hygrophilous grasslands.** These are called wet 'savannahs' adapted to wet soil.

WETLANDS

Wetlands are low-lying areas, usually covered by shallow water and have characteristic soil and water tolerant vegetation. Wetlands may be either freshwater or salt water.

Wetlands occupy almost 6 per cent of the world's land surface and provide crucial environmental services. Now a days the wetlands are increasingly threatened by agriculture, pollution and construction of dams, etc.

Freshwater Wetlands

Freshwater wetlands include (*i*) **marshes** (where grass-like plants dominate), (*ii*) **swamps** (where trees or shrubs dominate), (*iii*) **riverine**, periodically flooded forests found in lowlands along streams. Wetland plants are highly productive and provide food and habitat to support a wide variety of organisms.

Areas lying in the immediate vicinity of the rivers of North India supporting tamarisks, acacias, phragmites, saccharum, typha, arundo form this habitat. The areas are subject to summer flooding but often get dried up by May. Very few permanent swamps exist. Vast areas rendered waterlogged in canal irrigated areas also form good habitat for waterfowl. In the stabilised areas occur hog deer and nilgai. Waterfowl winter in these areas and also use these areas as staging points; large reservoirs created on rivers have also formed good habitats for wildlife.

Wetlands help control flooding by holding excess water, and the flood water stored in wetlands then drains slowly back into the rivers providing a steady flow of water throughout the year.

Wetlands also serve as groundwater recharging areas. They are helpful in cleaning and purifying water runoff.

Freshwater wetlands also provide important commercial products, such as rice, black berries, blue berries, etc.

Moreover, they also provide, sites for fishing, boating, nature study, etc.

Freshwater wetlands are often drained, dredged and filled up for housing and industrial purposes.

Finally, it is significant that rice culture, one of the most productive and dependable of agricultural systems yet devised by man, is actually a type of fresh-water marsh ecosystem. The flooding, draining, and careful rebuilding of the rice paddy each year has much to do with the maintenance of continuous fertility and high production of the rice plant, which itself is a kind of cultivated marsh grass.

Saltwater Wetlands

Coastal wetlands are also known as saltwater wetlands. They include highly productive estuaries which provide food and habitat for a large number of marine organisms. Between the seas and the continents lie a belt of diverse ecosystems that are not just transition zones but have ecological characteristics of their own. Whereas physical factors such as salinity and temperature are much more variable near shore than in the sea itself, food conditions are so much better that the region is packed with life.

Along the shore live thousands of adapted species that are not to be found in the open sea, on land, or in freshwater. The word 'estuary' (Latin, *aestus* = tide) refers to a river mouth or coastal bay where the salinity is intermediate between the sea and freshwater and where tidal action is an important physical regulator. Estuaries and inshore marine waters are amongst the most naturally fertile in the world.

Tidal action promotes a rapid circulation of nutrients and food, and aids in the rapid removal of the waste products of metabolism. A diversity of plant species and life forms provides a continuous photosynthetic carpet despite variable physical conditions.

Mangrove swamps are coastal wetlands in tropical regions which contain certain trees and shrubs growing best in the intertidal zone. As mangroves expand into the ocean, other plants colonise the soil left behind. Mangrove roots provide habitat for oysters, crabs and other marine organisms. However, the coastal wetlands are also being destroyed for coastal development and agricultural lands.

Organisms have evolved many adaptations to cope. with tidal cycles, thereby enabling them to exploit the many advantages of living in an estuary. Some animals such as fiddler crabs, have internal 'biological crops' that help to time their feeding activities to the most favourable part of the tidal cycle.

Wetland Conservation

Conservationists and trained marine environmental engineers have become alarmed by the needless destruction of coastal resources. Ultimately it may be necessary to set up some kind of conservation plan so that the use of such areas by man can be placed on a sound ecological basis. Some wetland conservation programmes are as follows :

(*i*) Preparation of wetland inventories

(*ii*) Identification of wetlands of critical importance for their protection.

(*iii*) Checking waste disposal in wetlands

(*iv*) Reduction of excessive inflow of nutrients and silt into wetlands from surrounding uplands by keeping them under plant cover.

ENERGY RESOURCES

The energy crisis is a global problem today. The survival of the man will be difficult if the energy problem is not solved on the priority basis. Future energy needs of rapidly expanding human population will demand the exploitation of most energy resources. The energy consumption is maximum in developed countries as compared to developing nations.

The nineteenth century industrial societies used fossil fuels, and the daily per capita energy utilisation jumped to 70,000 kcal. Today we require energy for agriculture, industry, transport, communication, comfort and defence. The per capita energy consumption per day in the USA has reached about 2,50,000 kcal. People in other countries use far less energy. It is as low as 10,000 kcal in several developing countries. However, it is increasing fast with rapid industrialisation.

Today the world's energy resources have reached a critical stage. The reasons are many. First, the world's almost total dependence on the fossil fuels-coal, petroleum and natural gas has caused such depletion that these fuels may last only another few centuries.

Today, 30 per cent of the world's population, living in industrialised countries, consumes about 80 per cent of the global energy. On the other hand the poorer nations rely more on firewood for cooking and heating and animal power for transport.

(*i*) **Non-renewable energy resources.** Such resources include various fossil fuels and nuclear energy. Fossil fuels include petroleum products, natural gas and coal. While nuclear energy is mainly obtained from the nuclear fission of the uranium.

The world reserves of fossil fuels and uranium are limited and will eventually be depleted. It is estimated that the stock of the mineral oil will be depleted in twenty first century, if it continues to be used at present rate.

However burning fossil fuels for energy has negative environmental consequences, such as global warming, air pollution, acid rain and oil spills. Now, this has become necessary to minimise use of non-renewable energy resources, and to replace them with renewable resources.

(*ii*) **Renewable energy resources.** Such energy resources are regenerated by natural processes so that they could be used indefinitely.

Renewable energy generally causes much less negative environmental impact than fossil fuels or nuclear energy. However, the generation of renewable energy is often more expensive than energy produced by fossil fuels or nuclear energy. With the advancement of technology, the costs of renewable energy is expected to decrease.

The most important renewable energy is solar energy, while other resources of renewable energy are hydropower, wind geothermal energy, ocean waves and tidal energy.

Solar Energy

There are two types of solar energy :

(*i*) Direct solar energy, and

(*ii*) Indirect solar energy.

Direct solar energy is the radiant energy, while **indirect solar energy** is obtained from materials that have previously incorporated the sun's radiant energy.

Solar energy can be used for direct heating and alternatively the heat converted into electricity, *i.e.*, thermal electric generation. Solar thermal pumps have been developed and are being tested under actual field conditions. Photovoltaic cells convert direct solar energy into electricity. However, a back-up system is required to store and generate electricity when solar power is not operative at night or during cloudy days. Solar photovoltaic panels, cookers, heaters and solar battery driven cars are being made and are in use.

Biomass energy. Among various energy resources, where solar energy is utilised indirectly, biomass energy is most important one. This is detained from those materials whose origin can be traced to photosynthesis, *e.g.*, live plant material and dried residues, freshwater and marine algae, agricultural and forest residues, such as straw, husks, corn cobs, bark, sawdust, roots, animal wastes, etc. Biomass also includes biodegradable organic wastes from industries, such as sugar mills, breweries, etc. About half of the world's population depends upon biomass as their main source of energy for domestic use.

In India, fuel wood is still a major source of energy for domestic purposes, at least in rural areas. Biomass fuel, may be solid, liquid or gas. This is burned to release its energy. Solid biomass includes wood, charcoal, animal dung and peat.

Biomass can be converted to liquid fuels, such as methanol (methyl alcohol) and ethanol (ethyl alcohol), which can be used in internal combustion engines of automobiles. Gasoline mixed with 10–20 per cent ethanol can be used in conventional gasoline engines.

Biogas. Biomass in the form of animal waste and hydrophytes, such as *Eichhornia* can be converted into biogas in biogas digesters by using the process of anaerobic microbial decomposition. This is a clean anaerobic fuel whose combustion produces less pollutants than other combustible energy resources. The biogas is composed of 60 per cent methane and 40 per cent carbon dioxide.

Energy Plantations

Production of biomass for energy requires sufficient area of land and water. Fuel wood has been the primary energy source for mankind from the beginning of civilisation and still continues to be the main source of energy in the developing countries, particularly in rural areas. Plant based energy is obtained through energy plantations which can produce biomass from slected species of trees in the shortest possible time at a low cost. These plants yield solid, liquid or gaseous fuel through burning, gasification, digestion, etc. Such plantations can be raised in both hills and plains particularly on marginal land. It has been calculated that about four tons of dry matter can be obtained in 0.25 ha land, which is sufficient for an average family.

Some important plants for energy plantation, which are extensively grown in India are *Leucaena leucocephala*, *Casuarina*, poplar tree and *Eucalyptus*.

Petroplants. Also called **hydrocarbon plants** are known to yield liquid hydrocarbons the substitute for liquid fuels. The hydrocarbons present in such plants can be converted into petroleum hydrocarbons of high molecular weight. *Jatropha curcas* tree yields 2 kg of seed oil per plant/year. The oil obtained from this plant is expected to replace the conventional diesel fuel. These plants can easily be grown in arid regions and other waste lands.

Other Renewable Resources of Energy

Among other renewable resources of energy some are important which are mentioned here

(*i*) **Hydropower.** Hydroelectric power is the most important and widely used resource of renewable energy. This is generated from water. Water falling from a height turns turbines at the bottom of dams to generate electricity. Hydropower produces approximately one-fourth of the worlds electricity, and is usually cheaper than electricity produced by thermal power plants. India has big potential for hydroelectric power generation. The energy obtained from hydropower is widely used in agriculture, industry, transport, domestic sectors, etc.

However, building a dam to hold the water results in several environmental problems, such as submergence of plant and animal habitats and displacement of people.

(*ii*) **Wind energy.** The wind can also be exploited as a source of energy in different ways. When fans are rotated by the action of wind, its energy can be used for generation of electricity. National Aeronautics Limitd, Bangalore is engaged in research and development of power generation through wind mills. In many states wind mills have been set up for irrgation purposes. However, harvesting wind energy is possible only in the areas that receive fairly continual winds, such as islands, coastal areas and mountain passes. Wind energy may be converted into mechanical and electrical energy. Now a days, wind energy is being used for pumping water is rural areas. According to an estimate, about 20,000 mw electricity can be generated in India from wind alone.

(*iii*) **Tidal energy.** The difference in the level of water between high tide and low tide can be used to generate electricity.

(*iv*) **Geothermal energy.** Heated groundwater flowing upward as hot water or steam, or as hot springs, can be used to turn turbines and generate electricity is geothermal power plants.

(*v*) **Ocean waves energy.** Ocean waves, produced by winds, possess the potential to turn a turbine and generate electricity.

The present critical energy position demands an organised effort at all levels from individual practices to international action. Considerable amount of energy can be saved by reducing wastage and using energy efficient devices. Some of such measures are :

(*i*) Reduction in man's dependence on fossil fuels and development of newer alternative sources of energy.

(*ii*) Preparation of smokeless and efficient chulhas (wood stoves).

(*iii*) Improvement and expansion of sources of solar energy. Solar photovoltaic panels, cookers, heaters, and solar-battery driven cars need to be improved technically and made cost-effective.

(*iv*) The use of biogas plants must be encouraged so that agricultural and animal wastes can be used to produce both energy and fertiliser.

(*v*) Improvement in design, manufacture and maintenance of biogas plants, engines and pumps.

(*vi*) Generation of hydroelectric, wind and tidal power has to be explored more extensively.

(*vii*) Programmes for growing fuel wood trees and shrubs under the control and maintenance of local communities have to be implemented in the rural areas of the developing countries.

MARINE RESOURCES

The oceans cover nearly three-fourth of earth's surface. Ocean has been the source of many needs of man from the time immemorial. The rapid growth of human population and the advancement of industrialisation have exerted great pressure on the resources and the environment of oceans. Land resources are depleting at tremendous rate and in view of this man has started thinking to exploit the oceanic resources.

Marine resources can be broadly divided into two major categories : (*i*) **Living resources**, such as algae and the animals of the sea, (*ii*) **Non-living resources**, *e.g.*, various kinds of minerals.

Alga Resources

Marine algae vary greatly in form and range from one-called microscopic phytoplanktons to giant helps, which attain a length of 100 to 150 metres, *e.g.*, *Nereocystis*, *Macrocystis*, etc.

Green, blue, red and brown algae are commonly found in oceans. From time immemorial, algae have been widely used as human food. The algae are used as direct source of food by several sea animals and fishes. Marine planktonic diatoms are of fundamental biological importance since all life of sea is dependent upon them. Since the prehistoric times several sea weeds have been used as direct source of food to human beings. The sea weeds form the most important part of the diet of Japan and China. **Suimono** is a Japanese preparation of dried fish and several sea weeds. **Mitsu** is another Japanese preparation which contains sea weeds, fruits, sugars and dried kidney beans.

In many countries, animals are still regularly fed on fresh or processed sea weed (*e.g.*, *Laminaria* and *Fucus*).

Marine algae have been used as a manure in many countries because of their high nutrient content. Balanced fertiliser can be made by mixing sheep manure, fish and shells with seaweeds. Seaweeds are a store-house of the important potash, ionic sulphate, microelements and growth substances, besides having every other element and radical required by plants. Seaweed manure seems to increase disease resistanc to plants.

Agar extraction. Mainly red algae, *e.g.*, Gracilaria, Gelidium, etc., are used for the extraction of commercially important agar. Japan produces the largest quantity of agar, and exports to most of the countries of the world. The agar is used in several ways. It is employed in the preparation of ice creams, jellies, desserts, pharmaceuticals, photography, metal plating, lithography, metallurgy, and also in the manufacture of explosives, detergents, pesticides, in sizing the textiles and clearing many liquids. It is also used in preparing shaving creams, cosmetics and shoe polishes. The agar has constantly been used in biological laboratories for media preparation for fungal and bacteriological cultures.

Animal Resources

Fish, molluscs, crustaceans and many mammals found in sea waters are used as human food. Oceans provide an excellent habitat for above mentioned organisms.

Fish. The bulk of fish and other aquatic animals come from marine habitats. Marine fish provide considerable amount of food throughout the world. Fish are also used for the manufacture of several edible products, such as_fish glue, fish meal, fish oil, fish proteins and vitamins.

Economically important fish are generally divided into two categories : (*i*) **demersal fish** and (*ii*) **pelagic fish**. The demersal fish are found at the sea-bottom, while pelagic fish floating free in the water column.

Fishing activity near the shore-line is carried on by small boats and vessels. This is called **coastal fishing**. On the other hand a large part of the total annual catch of fish comes from deep waters, and called **deep sea fishing**. This type of fishing is done by large boats or ships. In developed countries, where fishing is an organised industry, large boats and vessels are used for the purpose.

Molluscs. They are soft-bodied and shelled animals, (Latin, molluscus = soft bodied). Important molluscs from commercial point of view are the mussel, oyster, clam, etc. Many types of molluscs are used as food. However, pearl oyster is commercially important. The pearl worn as jewellery is secreted by certain oysters (bivalves). The inner calcareous surface of several bivalve shells is iridescent and pearl-like (nacreous) in appearance.

Crustaceans. They include crabs and prawns. They are the dominant arthropods of the sea. Prawns, lobsters and crabs are important economically. They make valuable items of food. India ranks first among the prawn producing countries of the world.

Phytoplankton-feeding, tiny crustaceans form an important link in the food chain of oceans.

Mammals. Whales, dolphins and porpoises are the economically important mammals found in the sea. The blue whales are the largest animals, some 30 m in length. Whales may be filter-feeders, living on planktons, or may feed on fish. Whales provide many valuable primary products, such as meat, ivory, skin, and frozen glands. They also produce many secondary products, such as oils, liver oil, etc. Fresh meet of all cetaceans, *i.e.*, whales, dolphins, porpoises, etc., has been used for human consumption.

Minerals in Sea

The sea is a store house of many valuable minerals. Most abundant elements in sea water are sodium, chlorine, magnesium, and bromine, that are commercially extracted from sea water. Phosphorite nodules are also found in sea, which can meet the shortage of phosphate fertilizers.

The sea weeds make an unique supplement for a well balanced diet. Potassium, sodium and chloride are found in the ionic form in sea weeds. The significance of iodine, as a constituent of food, is that besides being present in organic combination it is also available in part in the readily available form of the precursor of thyroxine and hence this source of iodine surpasses mineral iodine in drinking water and iodised table salt. The another micronutrients besides iodine which are important in human metabolism are iron, copper, manganese and zinc and all of them present as the trace elements of sea weeds. The highest copper content is found is *Sarconema* and *Acanthophora*. Today, iodine is produced from brown algae (seaweeds) in Japan, France, Norway and Jawa.

MINERAL RESOURCES

Some mineral elements are essential for the formation and functioning of the living body of all organisms, including man. Most of the essential elements enter animals through food chains and food webs. However, minerals are essential to our industrialised society and daily life. Mineral resources are non-renewable. The geographical distribution of essential minerals is unequal. Industry, transport, agriculture and defence preparation are making ever-increasing demands on the limited mineral deposits of the world. Depletion of almost all known and easily accessible deposits are anticipated within a few decades. Moreover, there may be shortage of some crucial elements, such as mercury, silver, gold, platinum, copper, tungsten within next 20 to 100 years. The limited resources of phosphorus which is an essential component of fertilisers may also cause retardation of agricultural growth.

Minerals can be divided into two groups : (*i*) metallic, *e.g.*, iron, copper, gold, silver, platinum, etc., and (*ii*) non-metallic, *e.g.*, sand, stone, salt, phosphates, asbestos, sulphur, corundum, etc.

Mining. This includes extraction, processing and disposal of minerals. However, mining has adverse effects on environment. This not only disturbs and damages the land, but also pollutes the soil, water and air.

The land that has been destroyed due to mining is known as **mine spoil**. Such destroyed lands can be reclaimed to a semi-natural condition by revegetation to prevent further degradation.

Conservation of Minerals

Efforts are being made to check the wasteful and injudicious use of minerals by recycling and adopting more efficient technologies, exploiting untapped deposits and by deep sea-mining. In process of recycling, used and discarded items are collected, remelted and reprocessed into new products, such as iron scraps, aluminium cans, etc.

The problem of high mineral consumption can be minimised by scientific and technological developments. Search for new production processes, designing smaller equipment, use of new raw materials and restrained use of materials have to be intensified. Finding new uses for glass, plastics, ceramics and synthetic fibres and using them as substitutes for exhaustible minerals is in progress.

Some minerals present in products can be recycled, e.g., gold, silver, lead, copper, nickel, steel, zinc, aluminium, etc. However, minerals in several other products are lost through normal use, such as paints containing lead, zinc, chromium, etc.

Table 26.5. Some Important Minerals and Their Uses

Minerals	*Uses*
1. Metallic	
Uranium	Nuclear bombs, electricity, tinting glass
Iron	Steel
Manganese	Alloy steel, disinfectants
Chromium	Metallurgy, refractory, chemicals
Nickel	Over 3000 alloys, coins, metal plating
Copper	Electrical products, alloys, gold jewellery, silver, etc.
Lead	Batteries, gasoline, paints, pipes, etc.
Tin	Tin plate, solder, chemicals, cans, containers, alloys.
Zinc	Galvanising, solder, die-casting, chemicals, brass, electrodes
Aluminum	Air crafts, rockets, building materials, electrical wiring, utensils
Gold	Monetary purposes, jewellery, dentistry, alloys
Silver	Jewellery, photography, utensils, alloys
Potassium	Fertiliser, glass, photography
Platinum	Jewellery, equipments, industrial catalyst
Radium	Medical and industrial uses, radiography
2. Non-metallic	
Phosphorus	Fertilisers, chemicals, medicine, detergents
Sulphur	Fertilisers, acid, iron and steel industries, insecticides, medicines
Corundum	Abrasives
3. Metallic liquid	
Mercury	Thermometers, dentistry, electric switches, etc.

Recycling and reusing not only renew the mineral resources, but also help in : (*i*) saving land from disruption of mining, (*ii*) reducing the amount of solid waste that is disposeable, and (*iii*) reducing pollution and consumption of energy.

However, to maintain the extended supply of minerals for a longer time, consumers must decrease their mineral consumption.

Durable and repairable products should be encouraged to be used again. Manufacturing industries should use the waste products of one manufacturing process as the raw materials for mother industry.

ENVIRONMENTAL ETHICS AND RESOURCE USE

Every morning the sun rises, and enlightens the whole land. The darkness disappears, and all becomes lighted. Besides light, we get energy from sun. All greens absorb light and food is produced for us. This great phenomenon of nature is **photosynthesis**. Only the plants are capable of this phenomenon. The plants give us food; they give us life. The plants are producers while rest consumers. The plants are biggest creation of god for us ; they are ideal donors. They only give, and from the time immemorial we worship them. The tree is eternal in its origin, and provides us the eternal peace. Beyond the kingdom of plants there is absolute darkness. Hundreds of plants are being considered sacred by the great people of this country, dealing with cultural heritage, festivals and religious ceremonies, starting from birth till death.

Lord Krishna says (Gita X, 26), "of all trees (I am) *Asvattha* (peepal tree)".

"They speak of the imperishable *asvattham* (peepal tree) as having its root above and branches below. Its leaves are the *Vedas* and he who knows this is the knower of the *Vedas*". (Gita XV, 1).

"Its branches extend below and above, nourished by the modes, with sense objects for its twigs and below in the world of men stretch forth the roots resulting in action". (Gita XV, 2).

"Its real form is not thus perceived here, nor its end nor beginning nor its foundation. Having cut off this firm-rooted *asvattham* (peepal tree) with the strong sword of non-attachment". (Gita XV, 3).

It is said in *Taittiriya Upnishad*, I, 10

"I am the originator of the world tree"

The cosmic tree is supreme–to know the cosmic tree is true knowledge, and the knower is complete in wisdom.

Plato says, "As regards the most lordly part of our soul, we must conceive of it in this wise ; we declare that God has given to each of us, as his demon, that kind of soul which is housed in the top of our body and which raises us-seeing that we are not an earthly but a heavenly plant-up from earth towards our kindred in heaven". (*Timaeus*, 90–A).

Dr. Sarvapallai Radhakrishnan says in his famous work '*The Bhagavadgita*' : 'As the tree originates in god, it is said to have its roots 'above' ; as it extends into the world, its branches are said to go downwards'.

He further says; "According to ancient belief, the vedic sacrificial cult is said to sustain the world and so the hymns are said to be the leaves which keep the tree with its trunk and branches alive".

"India is a unique country with a great cultural diversity associated with all kinds of climates and rich flora and fauna. The human societies in our country have evolved within magnificent environments and reverence to nature is inherent in our cultural ethos". I quote the lines: "The vast sky; and so the vast land; The vast ocean and the great Mountains; The great people and the majestic animals; The beautiful birds and the colourful butterflies; All the insects and all the moths; The creator has created them. Why ? Because they are need of creation; They are components of creation". One can enjoy nature by giving up greed.

Here I quote 'the philosophy I ever dreamt': "Where I find, no concrete walls, and no cement pillars; No chimneys and no factories; Neither transport nor poisonous gases, nothing like pollution, Only nature, the vast nature; Nature from horizon to horizon; great Nature in full grandeur ; Only huts and hamlets and their inhabitants; the innocense and serenity; the philosophy I ever dreamt; This is life; This is God; The 'beauty' and 'love' at the same time; great elements *khsiti* (soil), *Jal* (water), *Pavak* (fire) *gagan* (ether) and *Samira* (air), are components of great Nature; Where air develops from ether and water from air; where fire bakes our bread and earth makes base to stand; Then survival of all creatures and survival of whole 'global family'; The philosophy I ever dreamt".

Through history, the Indian people have not been exploiters but utilisers of nature. We belive in 'Live and let live'. We must recognise our responsibility to conserve earth resources for future generations. We must grow trees to maximum to protect the environment from poisonous gases. "In this hour of peril; Every hand is on trigger, and waits for order to fire; where does this race end, they do not know; Humanity is on brink of disaster; War mongers are roaming to convert the world in flames and ashes; Whole bio-kingdom is under threat; Count down has begun; By order or by mistake; All have to face doom's day; Oh contractors of humanity; Thou trust in God; Then why thou do not know; what His sons and daughters need; I tell thee, they need 'plain drinking water' ; Neither *agni* nor fire.

To conclude, I may say that the plant is the biggest creation of God; the gift of nature for us; static *Brahmarishi*, the ideal of donors, what he takes, takes from the mother, mother the land, mother the sole donor; sucks the nectar from the mother and gives to us. Grow more plants; protect the earth; protect the environment.

I worship the plants; I bow my head to plant kingdom.

SUMMARY

1. Any component of the natural environment that can be utilised by man to promote his welfare is known as a natural resource.
2. The natural resource can be a substance, an energy unit or a natural process, or phenomenon.
3. Natural resources can be divided into two categories: inexhaustible and exhaustible.
4. Inexhaustible resources, such as solar energy, wind power, are available in unlimited quantities on the earth.
5. Exhaustible resources have finite supply and can be either renewable or non-renewable.
6. The growth and reproduction of renewable resources, such as products from forests, grasslands, etc., can be managed so that these resources are continuously regenerated.
7. Non-renewable resources, such as biological species cannot be regenerated or reconstructed once they are used up.
8. Amongst the natural resources of earth, soil, water, land, energy and mineral resources contribute a lot to human welfare.
9. Soil resource regulates the yield of biotic products in terrestrial ecosystems.
10. Erosion by water and air makes a significant loss of soil.
11. World's fresh water reserves consist of 2.5 per cent of the total water, while the rest of water is saline.
12. The water reserves play significant role in global hydrological cycle.
13. The world's use of water has been increasing, and agriculture and industries account for most of the water consumption.
14. Thus, water conservation practices are significantly important to ensure water availability.

15. Amongst land resources the most important are; forests, grasslands and wetlands.
16. World's forest cover is shrinking rapidly, especially in the developing countries.
17. Deforestation is the main cause for the extinction of plant, animal and microbial species, and may induce regional and global climatic changes.
18. Massive afforestation programmes are required to save forest cover.
19. On the other hand, grasslands provide forage and habitat to domestic animals and wildlife. The grass cover also effectively binds the soil with its highly branched fibrous root system.
20. Wetlands of freshwater or salt water provide important environmental services, such as high productivity, control of floods, and serve as groundwater recharging areas.
21. Energy resources are non-renewable, such as fossil fuel, nuclear energy or renewable, such as hydropower, wind, geothermal energy, ocean waves, tidal energy, etc.
22. Renewable energy generally causes much less negative environmental impact than fossil fuels or nuclear energy.
23. Amongst various solar energy resources, biomass energy is most important.
24. Various algae and animals form important marine resources.
25. However, minerals are non-renewable resources.
26. India is a unique country with a great cultural diversity, associated with all kinds of climates and rich flora and fauna.
27. The human societies in this great country have evolved within magnificent environments, and reverence to nature is inherent in our culture.
28. *Isha-Upanishad* states : 'The whole universe together with its creatures belongs to the Lord. Let no one species encroach over the rights and privileges of other species. One can enjoy nature by giving up greed'.

TERMS TO REMEMBER

Afforestation. Extensive planting of trees.

Agro-forestry. Growing of woody species in combination with herbaceous crops.

Biogas. Biomass, particularly animal waste can be converted into biogas in biogas digesters, by the process of anaerobic microbial decomposition.

Biomass energy. This may be obtained from those materials whose origin can be traced to photosynthesis.

Conservation forestry. Involved protection of degraded forests to allow recoupment of their flora and fauna.

Commercial forestry. To fulfil the commercial demand, without causing denudation of natural forests, through intensive plantation in available land.

Deforestation. Destruction of forests by cutting or felling of trees.

Desertification. The conversion of grassland or forest to desert.

Direct solar energy. The radiant energy from sun.

Energy plantations. Plant species, showing high calorific value and growth rate.

Exhaustible resources. They have finite supply on the earth and can be exhausted.

Forest Act. This act aims to consolidate the law relating to forests.

Geothermal energy. Where hot springs, can be used to turn turbines to generate electricity.

Grasslands. Also called rangeland, which provides forage and habitat to domestic animals and wildlife.

Hydropower. Water falling from a height turns turbines at the bottom of dams to generate electricity.

Indirect solar energy. Energy obtained from materials that have previously incorporated the sun's radiant energy.

Inexhaustible resources. Resources available in unlimited quantities on the earth, e.g., solar energy, wind power, etc.

Jhum. The shifting cultivation, a traditional agro-forestry system.

Mineral conservation. Recycling and reuse of minerals.

Mine spoil. The land that has been destroyed due to mining.

Mangrove swamps. Coastal wetlands in tropics having certain trees and shrubs growing best in the intertidal zone.

Marshes. Where grass-like plants dominate in wetlands.

Natural resource. Any component of the natural environment utilised by man for his welfare.

Non-renewable resources. Such resources cannot be regained or reconstructed once they are used up.

Non-renewable energy. Resources include various fossil fuels and nuclear energy.

National Forest Policy. To ensure environmental stability and maintenance of ecological balance.

Ocean waves energy. Ocean waves produced by winds are capable to turn a turbine and generate electricity.

Production forestry. See commercial forestry.

Protection forestry. See conservation forestry.

Renewable energy. Resources are regenerated by natural processes so that they can be used indefinitely.

Riverine forests. Forests found in lowlands along streams.

Renewable resources. Such resources can be successfully managed so that they are continuously regenerated.

Soil conservation. Soil and crop management practices which can minimise erosion and deplete nutrient depletion of agricultural soils.

Social forestry. Planting of trees and shrubs on all unused and fallow land to provide fuel wood, fodder, etc.

Swamps. Where trees or shrubs dominate in wetlands.

Tidal energy. The difference in the level of water between high tide and low tide can be used to generate electricity.

Taungya system. This involves growing agricultural crops between rows of planted trees.

Wetlands. Low-lying areas covered with shallow water.

Wind energy. When fans are rotated by the action of wind, its energy can be used to generate electricity.

Wildlife Laws. Legal provisions to safeguard the national interests related to wildlife.

QUESTION BANK

Very Short Answer Questions

1. What do you understand by natural resources ?
2. Why marine algae are used as manure ?
3. What is India's share in total global fish catch ?
4. In which part of atmosphere ozone layer is found ?
5. What is the percentage of forest of our country, and what should it be ?
6. What is total land area under forests in the world ?
7. How will you classify land vegetation ?
8. What are wetlands ?
9. What is weathering ?
10. Give few examples of inexhaustible natural resources.
11. Give some examples of renewable exhaustible natural resources.
12. Give two examples of non-renewable exhaustible natural resources.
13. What is per capita forest area available in India ?

14. What is social forestry ?
15. What is desertification ?
16. Give a single main cause of soil erosion and flood.
17. Name the sea weeds that are processed and fed to animals.
18. Which algae are used for extraction of agar.

ANSWERS

1. Any component of the natural environment that can be utilised by man to promote his welfare; **2.** Due to their high nutrient content; **3.** 2.5 million tons; **4.** Stratosphere; **5.** 19.4 per cent and 33.0 per cent; **6.** 30.0 per cent; **7.** Forests, grasslands, shrubs and crops; **8.** Low lying areas covered with shallow water; **9.** This is destructive process of transformation of solid rocks into soil; **10.** Solar energy, wind power, rainfall, power of tides and hydro-power; **11.** Water, soil fertility, natural vegetation, wildlife, aquatic animals and humans; **12.** Biological species and minerals; **13.** 0.06 ha per person; **14.** Planting of trees and shrubs on all unused and fallow land to provide fuel wood, fodder, etc; **15.** The conversion of grassland or forest to desert; **16.** Deforestation; **17.** Laminaria and Fucus; **18.** Gracilaria and Gelidium of a group called the red algae.

Short Answer Questions

1. What is desertification ? How is it caused ?
2. What is soil erosion ? How is it accelerated ?
3. What are the advantages of recycling and reusing ?
4. What are the kinds of solar energy ?
5. What are the forms of forests ?
6. Give a short account of fresh water wetlands.
7. What are the advantages of energy plantation ?
8. What is humus ? Give its two main functions.
9. How is land vegetation classified ?
10. Write a short note on agroforestry.
11. How is soil fertility depleted ?
12. How can you say that global hydrological cycle is perfectly balanced ?
13. What are the steps involved to improve erosion affected soil ?
14. List some legal provisions for safeguard of wildlife.
15. Explain why soil resource is important for human welfare.
16. What are the methods of conserving water resources ?
17. What is the importance of forest resources ?
18. How do we manage our grassland ?
19. Why are wetlands considered ecologically important ?
20. Explain the significance of biomass energy.
21. Describe major marine resources.
22. What do you mean by field capacity ?
23. What is agar ? From which organisms is it obtained ?
24. What is the importance of humus in the soil ?
25. Explain the value of minerals as natural resources.
26. What are the main sources of energy in the world ?
27. What role do the animals play in the soil ?
28. Give important marine resources.
29. Name the various regions of the atmosphere, and give the position of each of them.
30. What are alternative sources of energy ?

31. How can mineral resources be conserved ?
32. Give an account of soil profile.
33. Give a comprehensive account of commercial and social forestry.
34. How is water present in the earth ?

Long Answer Questions

1. Distinguish between the following :
   (*a*) Inexhaustible and exhaustible resources (*b*) Renewable and non-renewable resources
   (*c*) Afforestation and agro-forestry
2. Distinguish between the following :
   (*a*) Freshwater wetlands and marine wetlands (*b*) Grasslands and wetlands
   (*c*) Deforestation and desertification
3. What are the main approaches for conservation of water ?
4. What are the frequently employed measures of grassland management ?
5. Discuss the methods of soil conservation.
6. Give the list of different categories of natural resources. Illustrate your answer with suitable examples.
7. Explain the role of plants as essential resources.
8. Describe the major marine resources.

MULTIPLE CHOICE QUESTIONS (OBJECTIVE QUESTIONS)

1. Tick the correct answer. Soil erosion can be prevented by :
   (*a*) Overgrazing (*b*) Removal of vegetation
   (*c*) Afforestation (*d*) Deforestation
2. Mild grazing in grassland by herbivores :
   (*a*) Retards growth of grasses (*b*) Arrests growth of grasses
   (*c*) Stimulates growth of grasses (*d*) Destroys vegetation
3. Deforestation generally decreases :
   (*a*) Rainfall (*b*) Soil erosion (*c*) Drought (*d*) Global warming
4. Forest area in India is about :
   (*a*) 9 per cent of geographical area (*b*) 19 per cent of geographical area
   (*c*) 29 per cent of geographical area (*d*) 37 per cent of geographical area
5. Which one of the following represents a renewable source of energy :
   (*a*) Petroleum (*b*) Coal (*c*) Nuclear fuel (*d*) Trees
6. Which of the following represents the regulative function of forest :
   (*a*) Storage and release of gases (*b*) Production of wood
   (*c*) Production of essential oils (*d*) Conservation of soil and water
7. In India per capita forest area is :
   (*a*) 0.06 ha (*b*) 0.60 ha (*c*) 1.0 ha (*d*) 1.6 ha
8. Extensive planting of trees to increase forest cover is called :
   (*a*) Afforestation (*b*) Agro-forestry (*c*) Deforestation (*d*) Social forestry
9. Wetlands occupy :
   (*a*) 6 per cent of world's land (*b*) 10 per cent of world's land
   (*c*) 12 per cent of world's land (*d*) 14 per cent of world's land
10. Which of the following functions performed by a forest help most in controlling drought :
    (*a*) Forests prevent soil erosion (*b*) Forests bring rainfall
    (*c*) Forests have lot of water plants (*d*) Forests act as water sheds

11. The value of a resource depends upon :
(*a*) Quantity of resource (*b*) Quality of resource
(*c*) Type of society and its needs (*d*) All the above

12. All the following are proper plans for increasing agriculture production except :
(*a*) Expansion of irrigation facilities
(*b*) Increase in application of fertilisers
(*c*) Mechanisation of various aspects of farming
(*d*) Cutting of forests to add land for cultivation

13. Amount of water a soil can hold against the pull of gravity is known as :
(*a*) Hygroscopic water (*b*) Storage capacity (*c*) Gravitational water (*d*) Field capacity

14. Edaphic factors are related to :
(*a*) Man (*b*) Soil (*c*) Animals (*d*) Temperature

15. Quantity of water the soil can hold against the force of gravity is known :
(*a*) Storage water (*b*) Gravitational water (*c*) Hygroscopic water (*d*) Field capacity

16. American water plant which has become a troublesome water weed in India is :
(*a*) Cyperus rotundus (*b*) Trapa latifolia (*c*) Eichhornia crassipes (*d*) Trapa bispinosa

17. The least porous soil among the following is :
(*a*) Sandy soil (*b*) Clayey soil (*c*) Loamy soil (*d*) Gravel soil

18. Waterlogging occurs in :
(*a*) Sandy soil (*b*) Gravel soil (*c*) Loamy soil (*d*) Clay soil

19. Humus is an example of :
(*a*) Soil structure (*b*) Crystalloids (*c*) Organic colloids (*d*) None of these

20. Alluvial soil is mostly found in which region :
(*a*) Southern India (*b*) Northern India
(*c*) Gangetic Jamuna Plains (*d*) Eastern India

21. Water remaining in the soil after a plant has permanently wilted is :
(*a*) Hygroscopic water (*b*) Ground water (*c*) Gravitational water (*d*) Capillary water

22. Desertification is due to :
(*a*) Deforestation (*b*) Soil-erosion due to water
(*c*) Soil-erosion due to wind (*d*) Very high temperature and low rainfall.

23. Geothermal energy is :
(*a*) Non-renewable, conventional source of energy
(*b*) Non-renewable, non-conventional source of energy
(*c*) Renewable, non-conventional source of energy
(*d*) Renewable conventional source of energy

24. Deforestation has an alarming effect on :
(*a*) Soil erosion (*b*) Weed control
(*c*) Sunlight (*d*) Increase in grazing area

25. The best soil for healthy and vigrous growth of most plants is :
(*a*) Sandy soil (*b*) Loam soil (*c*) Clay soil (*d*) None of these

26. Who will maintain the organic matter of the soil :
(*a*) Fungi and semiparasites (*b*) Cyanobacteria and parasitic animals
(*c*) Protozoans and slime molds (*d*) Bacteria and Fungi

27. Terai forest is :
(*a*) Tropical forest (*b*) Coniferous forest
(*c*) Deciduous forest (*d*) Temperate deciduous forest

28. Soil erosion can be prevented by :
(*a*) Deforestation (*b*) Afforestation (*c*) Overgrazing (*d*) All of these

29. Soil water available to plants is :
(*a*) Surface water (*b*) Hygroscopic water (*c*) Capillary water (*d*) Gravitational water

30. Water holding capacity is maximum in :
(*a*) Silt soil (*b*) Sandy soil (*c*) Clayey soil (*d*) Loamy soil

31. Source of energy which does not produce CO_2 is :
(*a*) Oil (*b*) Coal (*c*) Nuclear energy (*d*) Organic compounds

32. A non-renewable resource is :
(*a*) Coal and minerals (*b*) Plants and coal
(*c*) Water and natural gas (*d*) Energy and water

33. Non-conventional source of energy is :
(*a*) Coal (*b*) Wood (*c*) Petroleum (*d*) Biogas/solar energy

34. Bulk of carbon fixation by photosynthesis occurs in :
(*a*) Oceans (*b*) Croplands (*c*) Tropical rain forests (*d*) (*b*) and (*c*)

35. Plants die in water-logged soil because of :
(*a*) Nutrient leaching (*b*) Dilution of soil nutrients
(*c*) Stoppage of root respiration (*d*) Dilution of cell sap

36. Main reason of animal extinction is :
(*a*) Felling of trees (*b*) Habitat destruction (*c*) Predation (*d*) Pollution

37. Soil best suited for plant growth is :
(*a*) Loamy (*b*) Clayey (*c*) Sandy (*d*) Gravelly

38. Soil fertility is reduced by :
(*a*) Nitrogen-fixing bacteria (*b*) Decaying organic matter
(*c*) Crop rotation (*d*) Intensive agriculture

39. Black soil is due to the presence in it of :
(*a*) Organic matter (*b*) More moisture (*c*) Minerals (*d*) Air

40. The renewable source of energy is :
(*a*) Coal (*b*) Petroleum (*c*) Biomass (*d*) Kerosene

41. Black soil is productive because of abundant :
(*a*) Gravel and calcium (*b*) Clay and humus (*c*) Silt and earthworms (*d*) Sand and zinc

42. A non-renewable resource is :
(*a*) Water (*b*) Forest (*c*) Wild life (*d*) Coal/Petroleum

43. Fertility of soil is determined by its ability to :
(*a*) Hold organic matter (*b*) Retain water (*c*) Retain nutrients (*d*) Support life

44. Of the total amount of water, the water found in the seas and oceans forms about :
(*a*) 60 per cent (*b*) 70 per cent (*c*) 80 per cent (*d*) 95 per cent

45. Soil is composed of :
(*a*) Minerals, water and air (*b*) Minerals, organic matter and water
(*c*) Minerals, organic matter, air and water (*d*) Organic matter and water.

ANSWERS

1. (*c*)	**2.** (*c*)	**3.** (*a*)	**4.** (*b*)	**5.** (*d*)	**6.** (*a*)	**7.** (*a*)	**8.** (*a*)	**9.** (*a*)	**10.** (*b*)
11. (*c*)	**12.** (*d*)	**13.** (*d*)	**14.** (*b*)	**15.** (*d*)	**16.** (*c*)	**17.** (*b*)	**18.** (*d*)	**19.** (*c*)	**20.** (*c*)
21. (*a*)	**22.** (*a*)	**23.** (*b*)	**24.** (*a*)	**25.** (*b*)	**26.** (*d*)	**27.** (*a*)	**28.** (*b*)	**29.** (*c*)	**30.** (*c*)
31. (*c*)	**32.** (*a*)	**33.** (*d*)	**34.** (*a*)	**35.** (*c*)	**36.** (*b*)	**37.** (*a*)	**38.** (*d*)	**39.** (*a*)	**40.** (*c*)
41. (*b*)	**42.** (*d*)	**43.** (*d*)	**44.** (*d*)	**45.** (*c*)					

27

CHAPTER

Biodiversity and Biogeographical Regions of India

'Biological diversity' encompasses all species of plants, animals, and microorganisms and the ecosystems and ecological processes of which they are parts. It is an umbrella term for the degree of nature's variety including both the number and frequency of ecosystems, species, or genes in a given assemblage. Thus, the term '**biodiversity**' refers to the totality of 'genes, species and ecosystems' of a region.

It is usually considered at three different levels: (*i*) genetic diversity, (*ii*) species diversity and (*iii*) ecosystem diversity.

Genetic diversity is the sum total of genetic information, contained in the genes of individuals of plants, animals and microorganisms that inhabit the earth.

Species diversity refers to the variety of living organisms on earth and has been variously estimated to be between 5 and 50 million or more, though only about 1.4 million have actually been described.

Ecosystem diversity relates to the variety of habitats, biotic communities, and ecological processes in the biosphere, as well as the tremendous diversity within ecosystems in terms of habitat differences and the variety of ecological processes.

Biodiversity is defined as "the variability among living organisms from all sources, including terrestrial, marine and other aquatic ecosystems and the ecological complexes of which they are a part; this includes diversity within species, between species and of ecosystems."

Conservation and sustainable use of biodiversity is fundamental to ecologically sustainable development. Biodiversity is part of our daily lives and livelihood, and constitutes resources upon which families, communities, nations and future generations depend.

Every country has the responsibility to conserve, restore and sustainably use the biological diversity within its jurisdiction. Biological diversity is fundamental to the fulfilment of human needs. An environment rich in biological diversity offers the broadest array of options for sustainable economic ability, for sustaining human welfare and for adapting to change. Loss of biodiversity has serious economic and social costs for any country.

The experience of the past few decades has shown that as industrialisation and economic development in the classical sense takes place, patterns of consumption, production and needs, change, straining, altering and even destroying ecosystems.

India, a megabiodiversity country, while following the path of development, has been sensitive to needs of conservation and hence is still rich in biological resources. Ethos of conservation and harmonious living with nature is very much ingrained in the lifestyles of India's people.

MAGNITUDE OF BIODIVERSITY

The foundation for assessing the importance of biodiversity is an inventory of how many species exist and which species exist where. At the global level the plants and vertebrates are relatively well known. Erwin (1982), for example, suggests as many as 30 million species in total, with most undescribed species living in tropical forests. The known and described number of species of all organisms on the earth is between 1.7 and 1.8 million which is fewer than 15 per cent of the actual number'. About 61 per cent of the known species are insects. Only 4650 species of mammals are known to biological science. A large number of plant species (2,70,000) and vertebrates are known. But the fact remains that basic knowledge of the organisms that make up most ecosystems, especially in the tropics is inadequate. Information about bacteria,viruses, protists and Archaea is only fragmentary.

For convenience, many assume that about 10 million species exist, though the final figure is likely to be 30-50 million.

Given these limitations, the following table 14.1, represents a summary of the current state of knowledge (from Wilson, 1988):

Table 27.1. How many species exist

Group	*Number of described species*
Bacteria and blue-green algae: (*i.e.*, cyanobacteria)	4760
Fungi:	46,983
Algae:	26,900
Bryophytes (mosses and liverworms):	17,000 (WCMC, 1988)
Gymnosperms (conifers):	750 (Raven *et al.*, 1986)
Angiosperms (flowering plants):	250,000 (Raven *et al.*, 1986)
Protozoans:	30,800
Sponges:	5,000
Corals and Jellyfish:	9,000
Roundworms and earthworms:	24,000
Crustaceans:	38,000
Insects:	751,000
Other arthropods and minor invertebrates:	132,461
Molluscs:	50,000
Starfish:	6,100
Fishes (Teleosts):	19,056
Amphibians:	4,184
Reptiles:	6,300
Birds:	9,198 (Clements, 1981)
Mammals:	4,170 (Honacki *et al.*, 1982)
Total	**1,435,662**

However, new species are being discovered faster than ever before due to the efforts of Global Biodiversity Information Facility and the Species, 2000. The approximate number of species is being mentioned in the table 27.2.

Table 27.2. Approximate Numbers of Species.

Group	*Number of described species*
Higher plants	2,70,000
Algae	40,000
Fungi	72,000
Bacteria and cyanobacteria	4,000
Viruses	1,550
Mammals	4,650
Birds	9,700
Reptiles	7,150
Fish	26,959
Amphibians	4,780
Insects	10,25,000
Crustaceans	43,000
Molluscs	70,000
Nematodes and worms	25,000
Protozoa	40,000
Others	1,10,000

The number of plant and animal species in different groups recorded in India are given in table 14.3.

Table 27.3. Number of Species of Different Taxonomic Groups

Plants		*Animals*	
Group	*No. of species*	*Group*	*No. of species*
Angiosperms:	17,500	Mammalia:	390
Gymnosperms:	64	Aves:	1232
Pteridophytes:	1100	Reptilia:	456
Bryophytes:	2850	Amphibia:	209
Lichens:	200	Pisces:	2546
Fungi:	14,500	Protochordata:	119
Algae:	6,500	Other invertebrates:	8329
Bacteria:	850	Arthropoda:	68389
		Mollusca:	5070
		Protozoa:	2577

India has 47,000 species of flowering and non-flowering plants representing about 12 per cent of the recorded world's flora. Out of 47,000 species of plants, 5,150 are endemic and 2532 species are found in the Himalayas and adjoining regions and 1,782 in the peninsular India. India is also rich in the number of endemic faunal species it possesses.

Table 27.4. Comparative statement of recorded number of animal species in India and the world

Taxa	*INDIA*			*World*	*Percentage of India to the world*
	Species	*Endemic species*	*Threatened species*		
Protista	2577			31,259	8.24
Mollusca	5070	967		66,535	7.62
Arthropoda	68389	16214 (insects)		987,949	6.90
Other Invertebrates	8329		22	87,121	9.56
Protochordata	119			2106	5.65
Pisces	2546		4	21,723	11.72
Amphibia	209	110	3	5150	4.06
Reptilia	456	214	16	5817	7.84
Aves	1232	69	73	9026	13.66
Mammalia	390	38	75	4629	8.42

Source: MoEF 1999; Baillie 1996.

LEVELS OF BIODIVERSITY

Biodiversity is usually considered at three different hierarchical levels:

(*i*) Genetic diversity,

(*ii*) Species diversity, and

(*iii*) Community and ecosystem diversity.

Though these levels of biodiversity are interrelated yet distinct and can be studied separately to understand the interrelationships that sustain life on earth.

Genetic Diversity

Genetic diversity is the sum total of genetic information, contained in the genes of individuals of plants, animals, and microorganisms that inhabit the earth. Each species, stores an immense amount of genetic information.

For example, the number of genes is about 450-700 in Mycoplasma; 4000 in *Escherichia coli*; 13,000 in *Drosophila melanogaster*; 32,000-50,000 in *Oryza sativa* and 35,000 to 45,000 in *Homo sapiens*.

The characteristics of genetic diversity are as follows:

Genetic diversity refers to the variation of genes within species. The differences could be in alleles, *i.e.*, different variants of same genes; in entire genes, *i.e.*, the traits that determine particular characteristics or in chromosomal structures.

The genetic diversity enables a population to adapt to its environment and to respond to natural selection. On the other hand, if a species has more genetic diversity, it can adapt better to the changed environmental conditions.

Lower diversity in a species leads to uniformity, for example, in large monocultures of genetically similar crop plants. This may be an advantage when increased crop production is considered, whereas this may be a problem when a pest or pathogen attacks the crop field, and the whole crop is threatened.

The amount of genetic variation is the basis of **speciation**, *i.e.*, evolution of new species. It has a key role to play in the maintenance of diversity at species and community levels.

The total genetic diversity of a community will be greater if there are many species, as compared to an area with few species. Genetic diversity within a species often increases with environmental variability.

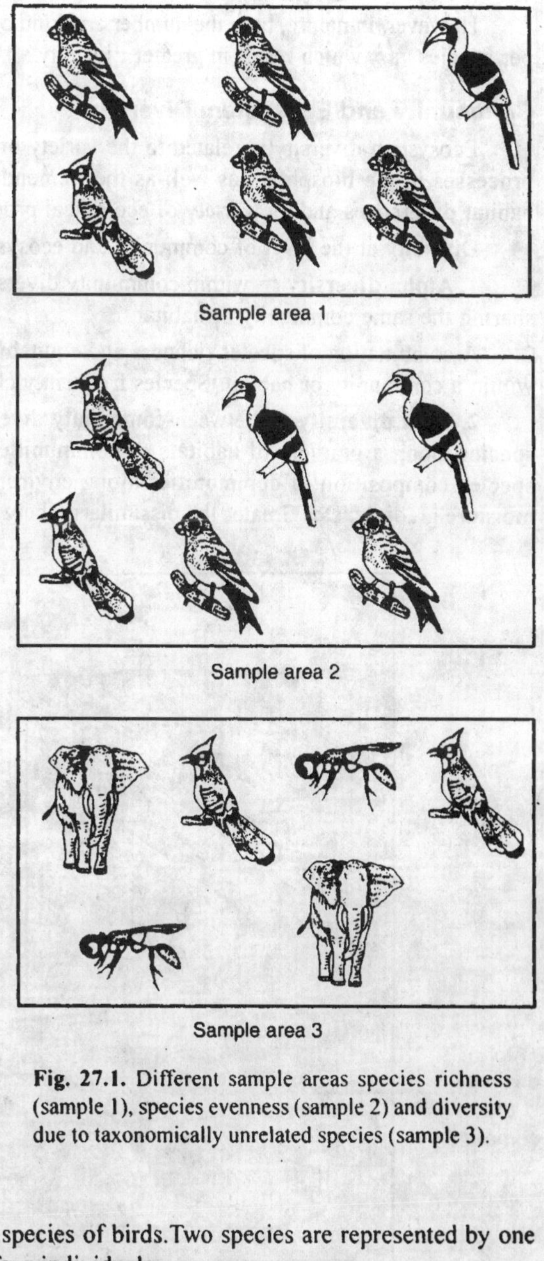

Fig. 27.1. Different sample areas species richness (sample 1), species evenness (sample 2) and diversity due to taxonomically unrelated species (sample 3).

Species Diversity

Species diversity refers to the variety of living organisms on earth and has been variously estimated to be between 5 and 50 million or more, though only about 1.4 million have actually been described.

Species are distinct units of diversity, and each unit plays a specific role in an ecosystem. Thus, loss of species has consequences for the whole ecosystem.

Species diversity refers to the variety of species within a region.

Species richness or the number of species per unit area, denotes the measure of species diversity. The number of species increases with the area of the site, that is greater the species richness, greater is the species diversity. On the other hand, number of individuals among the species may also vary, resulting into differences in **evenness**, or **equitability** and consequently in diversity.

Here the example of three sample areas may be quoted:

1. The sample area 1, consists of three species of birds. Two species are represented by one individual each, while the third species has four individuals.

2. The sample area 2, also consists of three species, here, each species is represented by two individuals. This sample area exhibits greater evenness, and there are equal chances for a species being represented in a sample. The sample area 2 is more diverse than sample area 1.

3. The sample area 3, depicts the presence of an insect, a mammal and a bird. This sample area is considered most diverse, as it comprises of taxonomically unrelated species.

This example shows, there are equal number of species in each sample area, *i.e.*, samples 1, 2 and 3, but having varying number of individuals per species.

However, in nature, both the number and kind of species, as well as the number of individuals per species vary,which result in greater diversity.

Community and Ecosystem Diversity

Ecosystem diversity is related to the variety of habitats, biotic communities, and ecological processes in the biosphere, as well as the tremendous diversity within ecosystems in terms of habitat differences and the variety of ecological processes.

Diversity at the level of community and ecosystem has been divided into three categories:

1. Alpha diversity (= within community diversity). This refers to the diversity of organisms sharing the same community or habitat.

A combination of species richness and equitability or evenness is used to represent diversity within a community or habitat. Species frequently change when habitat or community changes.

2. Beta diversity (= between-community diversity). This refers the rate of replacement of species along a gradient of habitats or communities. In beta diversity, there are differences in species composition of communities along environmental gradients, *e.g.*, altitudinal gradient, moisture gradient, etc. Greater the dissimilarity between communities, higher is the beta diversity.

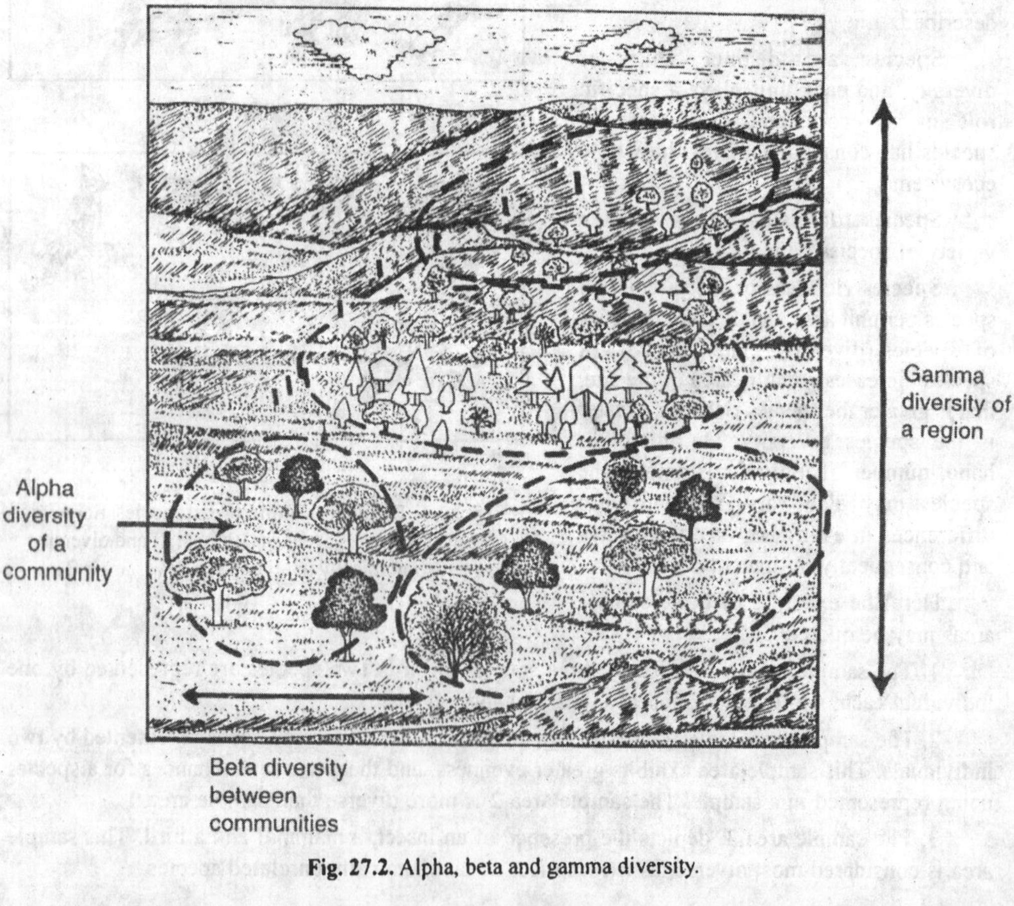

Fig. 27.2. Alpha, beta and gamma diversity.

3. Gamma diversity. This refers to the diversity of the habitats over the total landscape or geographical area.

Characteristics of ecosystem diversity. In ecosystem diversity there are a number of ecological niches, trophic levels and various ecological processes that sustain energy flow, food needs and the recycling of nutrients.

Ecosystem diversity has a focus on various biotic interactions and the role and function of keystone species.

However, the diverse communities are functionally more productive and stable, even under environmental stresses, such as dry or drought conditions.

STATUS OF BIODIVERSITY IN INDIA

India occupies only 2.4 per cent of the world's land area but its contribution to the world's biodiversity is approximately 8 per cent of the total number of species, which is estimated to be 1.75 million. Of these, 126,188 have been described in India. The species recorded includes flowering plants (angiosperms), mammals, fish, birds, reptiles and amphibians, constitute 17.3 per cent of the total wheareas nearly 60 per cent of India's bio-wealth is contributed by fungi and insects.

Based on the available data, India ranks tenth in the world and fourth in Asia in plant diversity, and ranks tenth in the number of endemic species of higher vertebrates in the world. There are ten biogeographical zones in India. They can be classified as follows:

1. Trans-Himalayas. An extension of the Tibetan Plateau, harbouring high-altitude cold desert in Laddakh (J and K) and Lahaul Spiti (H.P.) comprising 5.7 per cent of the country's landmass.

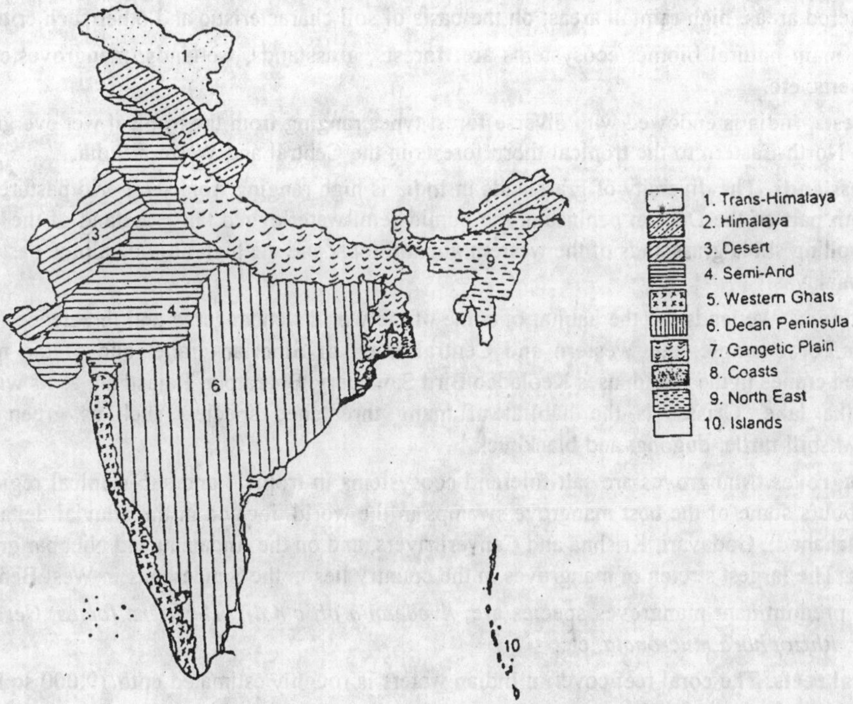

Fig. 27.2(*a*). Biogeographical regions of India (source WII Dehradun).

2. Himalayas. The entire mountain chain running from north-western to north-eastern India, comprising a diverse range of biotic provinces and biomes, 7.2 per cent of the country's landmass.

3. Desert. The extremely arid area west of the Aravalli hill range, comprising both the salty desert of Gujarat and the sand desert of Rajasthan. 6.9 per cent of the country's landmass.

4. Semi-arid. The zone between the desert and the Deccan plateau, including the Aravalli hill range. 15.6 per cent of the country's landmass.

5. Western ghats. The hill ranges and plains running along the western coast line, south of the Tapti river, covering an extremely diverse range of biotic provinces and biomes. 5.8 per cent of the country's landmass.

6. Deccan peninsula. The largest of the zones, covering much of the southern and south-central plateau with a predominantly deciduous vegetation. 4.3 per cent of the country's landmass.

7. Gangetic plain. Defined by the Gangas river system, these plains are relatively homogenous. 11 per cent of the country's landmass.

8. North-east India. The plains and non-Himalayan hill ranges of north eastern India, with a wide variation of vegetation. 5.2 per cent of the country's landmass.

9. Islands. The Andaman and Nicobar Islands in the Bay of Bengal, with a highly diverse set of biomes. 0.03 per cent of the country's landmass.

10. Coasts. A large coastline distributed both to the west and east, with distinct differences between the two; Lakshadeep Islands are included in this with the percent area being negligible.

Apart from the above mentioned biogeographic classification, ecosystems can also be demarcated on the basis of purely geographical or geological features, such as mountains, islands, valleys, plateau, oceans, etc., on the basis of vegetative cover like forests, grasslands, mangroves and deserts; on the basis of climatic conditions, such as arid and semi-arid areas, permanently snow-covered areas, high rainfall areas; on the basis of soil characteristic and other such criteria.

The main natural biomes/ecosystems are: forests, grasslands, wetlands, mangroves,coral reefs, deserts, etc.

Forests. India is endowed with diverse forest types ranging from the tropical wet evergreen forests in North-Eastern to the tropical thorn forests in the Central and Western India.

Grasslands. The diversity of grasslands in India is high ranging from semi-arid pastures of the western part of the Deccan peninsula, the humid semi-waterlogged tall grassland of theTerai belt, the rolling shola grasslands of the western ghat hilltops, and the high-altitude alpine pastures of the Himalayas.

Wetlands. Wetlands are the habitat of some of the world's endangered and threatened flora and fauna.For example, the Western and Central flock of Siberian crane, one of the most endangered cranes in the world, uses Keoladeo Bird Sanctuary, Bharatpur, Rajasthan, as its winter site. Chilka lake, Orissa, is the habitat of many threatened species, such as green sea turtle,Hawksbill turtle, dugong, and blackbuck.

Mangroves. Mangroves are salt-tolerand ecosystems in tropical and sub-tropical regions. India harbours some of the best mangrove swamps in the world, located in the alluvial deltas of Ganga, Mahanadi, Godavari, Krishna and Cauveri rivers, and on the Andaman and Nicobar group of Islands. The largest stretch of mangroves in the country lies in the Sunderbans in West Bengal.

The predominant mangroves species are; *Avecennia officinalis*, *Heritiera fomes*, *Ceriops decandra*, *Rhizophora mucronata*, etc.

Coral reefs. The coral reef cover in Indian waters is roughly estimated upto 19,000 sq.Km. Indian coral reefs are as follows:

Palk Bay and Gulf of Mannar; Gulf of Kachchh; Andaman and Nicobar Islands; Lakshadeep Islands and Central West Coast.

Deserts. Three kinds of deserts are noticeable in India:

1. The sand desert of western Rajasthan and neighbouring areas.
2. The vast salt desert of Gujarat
3. The high-altitude cold desert of Jammu and Kashmir and Himachal Pradesh.

Desert fox, desert cat, houbara bustard and some sandgrouse species are restricted to Thar Desert, Rajasthan.

In the Rann of Kachchh, lies the nesting ground of Flamingoes and the only known population of Asiatic wild ass.

The distinctive animals of cold desert are:

Kiang (relative of wild ass of Kachchh), snow leopard, Yak, Tibetan antelope, Ibex, Blue sheep, Tibetan gazelle, Woolly hare, etc.

GRADIENTS OF BIODIVERSITY

Biodiversity varies with change in latitude or altitude.When one moves from high to low latitudes (*i.e.*, from the poles to the equator), the biodiversiy increases.

In the temperate region, the climate is severe having short growing period for plants. On the other hand, in tropical rain forest the conditions are favourable for growth of plants throughout the year. Favourable conditions are helpful for speciation, and large number of species develop and grow.

The mean number of species of vascular plants per 0.1 ha sample area in tropical rain forests varies from 118-236, while in temperate zones, this range is 21-48 species.

Such a correlation between diversity and latitude is also found for a variety of several other taxa, such as ants, birds, butterflies, moths, etc.

In the similar way, there is a decrease in species diversity from lower to higher altitudes on a mountain. Increase of 1000 metres in altitude results in a temperature drop of about 6.5° C. Such

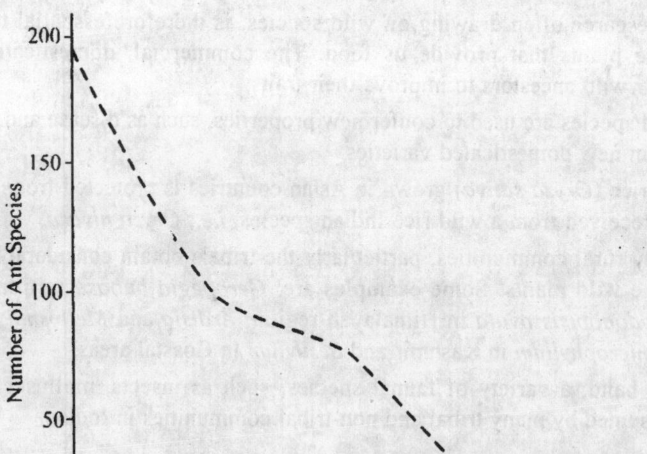

Fig. 27.3. Latitudinal gradient of biodiversity.

temperature drop and seasonal variability at higher altitudes are responsible for lowering the diversity.

The **latitudinal** and **altitudinal** gradients of species diversity are two master gradients. To some extent regional and taxa-related gradients also affect biodiversity. It is expected that prevalence of more complex and heterogeneous environment makes the flora and fauna more diverse and complex.

USES OF BIODIVERSITY

Humans derive many direct and indirect benifits from biological diversity. All our food comes from wild species brought into domestication. Most of our medicines, pharmaceutical, fibres, rubber and timber come from biological resources. The biodiversity also provides many ecological services free of charge that are responsible for maintaining ecosystems. Our water is supplied by one of nature's most important processes, called the 'hydrological cycle'. Forested watersheds provide clear,high-quality water for domestic or agricultural use,while healthy rivers provide water, transport and fish.

Source of Food and Improved Varieties

Biodiversity has direct consumptive value in agriculture. In modern agriculture, biodiversity is used as follows:

(*i*) As a source of new crops

(*ii*) As a source material for breeding improved varieties, and

(*iii*) As a source new biodegradable pesticides.

Approximately 80,000 edible plants have been used at one time or another in human history, of which only about 150 have even been cultivated on a large scale. Today a mere 10 to 20 species provide 80 to 90 per cent requirements of the world. Over half of human nutrition is provided by the three major carbohydrate crops, *i.e.*, rice, wheat and maize. Fats, oils, fibres, etc., are other uses for which many new species are to be investigated.

Continuous research,often drawing on wild species, is therefore essential to maintain the productivity of the plants that provide us food. The commercial, domesticated species are crossbred with their wild ancestors to improve their traits.

Genes of wild species are used to confer new properties, such as disease and pest resistance or increased yield in new domesticated varieties.

For example rice (*Oryza sativa*) grown in Asian countries is protected from the four major diseases by genes received from a wild rice Indian species, *i.e.*, *Oryza nivara*.

In India, many rural communities, particularly the tribals obtain considerable part of their daily food from the wild plants. Some examples are: *Ceropegia bubosa* in Central India and Western Ghats; *Codonopisis ovata* in Himalayan region; *Ardisia* and *Meliosma pinnata* in the North-east; *Cicer microphyllum* in Kashmir and *Sesuvium* in Coastal areas.

On the other hand, a variety of faunal species, such as insects, molluscs, spiders, wild herbivores are consumed by many tribal and non-tribal communities in India.

Drugs and Medicines

At one time, nearly all medicines were derived from biological resources. Even today they remain vital and as much as 67 to 70 per cent of modern medicine are derived from natural products.

In India, almost 95 per cent of the prescriptions are plant-based in the traditional systems of Ayurveda, Unani and Sidha. Many indigenous medicines also utilise medicines and their parts or extracts as remedies for various diseases.

Examples of plant-derived substances developed into valuable drugs are: Morphine obtained from *Papaver somniferum* and used as an analgesic; Quinine obtained from *Cinchona ledgeriana*, used for treatment of Malaria, and Taxol, an anticancer drug obtained from the bark of yew tree (*Taxas baccata, T.brevifolia*).

Botanochemicals. Many plants are also used for the manufacture of hundreds of synthetic products, which are called 'botanochemicals'.

Aesthetic and Cultural Benefits

Biodiversity has also great aesthetic value. Diverse habitats and species have non-consumptive use-value. Examples of aesthetic benefits include ecotourism, bird watching, wildlife, pet keeping, gardening, recreation and scientific research.

Many plants, animals and their parts are used in rituals all over the country. In a majority of Indian villages and towns, plants like *Ocimum sanctum* (Tulsi), *Ficus religiosa* (Pipal), *F. bengalensis* (Bargad), etc., are considered sacred and worshipped by the people. Flowers of *Hibiscus*, *Datura* and *Euphorbia*, leaves of *Aegle marmelos* (Bel), *Eragrostis cynasuroides* (Kusa grass), rice, til, chenopods sacred, odorous roots of *Dolomiaea macrocephala* (Dhup) are used in rituals. Besides, sacred values are attached to entire ecosystems, for example, patches of forests were believed to be the abode of demigods and are used only for prayers and rituals. Many 'sacred groves' exist in different parts of our country.

Several birds, snakes and other animals are treated sacred and worshipped.

Ecosystem Services

The indirect use-value of biodiversity includes ecosystem process of biological diversity, which provides valuable ecological services to the biosphere.

For example, the ecosystem's ability to absorb pollution, maintain soil fertility and microclimates, recharge groundwater and other invaluable services. These services include maintenance of gaseous composition of the atmosphere, climate control by forests and oceanic systems, natural pest control, pollination of plants by insects and birds, formation and protection of soil, conservation and purification of water, and nutrient cycling, etc.

The above mentioned ecosystem services have been valued in the range of 16 to 54 trillion US dollars per year.

THREATS TO BIODIVERSITY

Major biodiversity threats are as follows:

(*i*) Habitat destruction and fragmentation

(*ii*) Extention of agriçulture

(*iii*) Filling up of wetlands

(*iv*) Conversion of rich biodiversity site for luman settlement and industrial development

(*v*) Destruction of coastal areas,

(*vi*) Uncontrolled commercial exploitation

(*vii*) Disturbance and pollution, and

(*viii*) Introduction of non-native (exotic) species

Habitat Loss and Fragmentation

The destruction of habitats is the primary reason for the loss of biodiversity. This erosion of biodiversity is largely due to habitat loss caused by the expansion of various development projects, such as mines, dams, roads and canal construction. When people cut down trees, fill a wetland, plough a grassland or burn a forest the natural habitat of a species is changed or destroyed. Such changes can kill or force out many plants, animals and microorganisms. These changes also disrupt complex interactions among the species.

Habitat loss leads to the fragmentation of continuous stretches of land and consequently fragments wildlife populations inhabiting them. These small populations are increasingly vulnerable to inbreeding depression, high infant mortality, susceptibility to environmental stochasticity and in the long run possibly to extinction.

Apart from the primary loss of habitats, there are many other problems contributing to the loss and endangered status of several plant and animal species. Habitat degradation can lead to declines in primary food species for wildlife.

Poaching is another threat as one of the primary reasons for extinction of species such as the tiger.

Population pressures, such as collection of fuelwood and fodder, and grazing in forests by local communities also take their toll on the forests and consequently its biodiversity.

Other minor factors include fire, and natural calamities like droughts, diseases, cyclones and land slides.

It is estimated that, after independence, the country has lost 4,696 million ha of forest land to non-forestry purposes.

Disturbance and Pollution

Communities are affected by natural disturbances, such as fire, tree fall, landslides and defoliation by insects.

Anthropogenic disturbances differ from natural disturbances in intensity, rate and spatial extent. For example, man by using fire more frequently may change species richness of a community.

The new anthropogenic impacts may be large number of synthetic compounds, massive releases of radiations by nuclear projects, and spill over of oil in sea. These impacts may lead to a change in the habitat quality.

Over exploitation of natural resourses, such as fishing by boats, mechanical catching of other animal species, etc., are serious threats to wildlife. Disturbance in migratory routes of several fishes, due to construction of dams, etc., hence they are not able to reach their spawning grounds and face extinction.

Pollution is also responsible for reduction and elimination of populations of sensitive species. For example, pesticide linked decline of fish-eating birds and falcons.

Lead poisoning of water is also a cause of mortality of many species, such as ducks, swans and cranes, as they take in the spent shotgun pellets that fell into lakes and marshes. Eutrophication, *i.e.*, nutrient enrichment of water bodies is also responsible for reduction of species diversity.

Introduction of Exotic Species

New species that enter a geographical region are called **exotic** or alien species. The invasion of such species may cause disappearance of native species through changed biotic interactions. The invasion of exotic species is considered second one to habitat destruction as a major threat to extinction of species.

Exotic species have more effective impact in island ecosystems, which give shelter to the world's threatened biological diversity. Examples are as follows:

(*i*) An exotic species *Lantana camara* has invaded many forest lands in different parts of our country, and strongly competes with the native species.

(*ii*) On the other hand water hyacinth (*Eichhornia crassipes*), an exotic aquatic species, clogs rivers, lakes and village ponds in different parts of India and several other tropical countries, which threaten, the survival of several native aquatic species.

(*iii*) Nile perch, an exotic predatory fish has been introduced into Lake Victoria of South Africa, where this has threatened the entire ecosystem of the lake, and eliminated several native species of small fish, *e.g.*, Cichild fish species.

(*iv*) *Periplaneta americana* (American cockroach) has threatened the existence of native cockroach, *i.e.*, *Blatta orientalis*.

(*v*) *Parthenium hysterophorus* has threatened several native herbs and shrubs of this country.

(*vi*) Goats and rabbits introduced in the islands of Indian and Pacific oceans are destroying the habitats of several plants, birds and reptiles.

Extinction of Species

Extinction has been a fact of life since life first emerged. The present few million species are the modern-day survivers of the estimated several billion species that have ever existed. All past extinctions have occurred by natural processes, but today humans are the main cause of extinction.

The rapid destruction of the world's most diverse ecosystems, especially in the tropics,has led most experts to conclude that perhaps a quarter of the earth's total biological diversity is at serious risk of extinction during the next 20-30 years. By many indications, the world is already experiencing extinction rates of greater scale and impact than at any previous time in the earth's history.

More species than even before are threatened with extinction, with thousands, mostly insects, disappearing each year. There are three main types of extinction processes:

1. Natural extinction. With the change in environmental conditions, some species become extinct, while others, which are more adapted to changed conditions,take their place.This type of extinction of species which took place in the geological past at a very slow rate, is called **natural extinction**.

2. Mass extinction. As we know, there have been several periods in the geological history of earth when large number of species disappeared because of catastrophes. This kind of extinction is called '**mass extinction**'. Such mass extinctions occurred in millions of years.

3. Anthropogenic extinction. All past extinctions occurred either by natural or mass extinctions, but today humans are the main cause of extinctions. Today an alarming number of species are disappearing from the surface of earth due to irresponsible human activities. This man-made extinction of species represents a very severe depletion of biodiversity, particularly because this occurs within a short period of time.

It has been estimated at World Conservation Monitoring Centre (WCMC), that 533 species of animals (mostly vertebrates) and 384 species of plants (mostly angiosperms) have become extinct since 1600 AD. More species have gone extinct from the islands than from the mainland or oceans. The current rate of extinction of species is 1000 to 10,000 times higher than the background rate of extinction. Some interesting observations about the current rate extinction of species are as follows:

1. From ten high-diversity localities in tropical forests which cover about 300,000 sq. km, some17,000 endemic plant species and 350,000 endemic animal species are threatened and could be lost in near future.

2. The tropical forests alone are losing about 14,000 to 40,000 species per year,which comes about 2-5 species per hour.

3. It is estimated that by the end of twenty first century, if the current rate continues, the earth will lose up to fifty per cent of the species.

Susceptibility to Extinction

The characteristics of species that make them susceptible for extinction are as follows:

1. Large body size. Many animals are large-sized, *e.g.*, Bengal tiger, lion and elephant.

2. Small population size and low reproductive rate. This characteristic of species is responsible for susceptibility to extinction, *e.g.*, Blue whale and Giant panda.

3. Feeding at high trophic levels in the food chain. This characteristic also makes the animals susceptible to extinction. The examples are: Bengal tiger and Bald eagle.

4. Fixed migratory routes and habitat. Such routes cannot be changed, if any interruption occurs that leads towards extinction. The examples are; Blue whale and Whooping crane.

5. Localised and narrow range of distribution. This characteristic also makes the species susceptible to extinction, *e.g.*, woodland caribon and many island species.

THE IUCN RED LIST CATEGORIES

The World Conservation Union (WCU), formerly known as International Union for the Conservation of Nature and Natural Resources (IUCN), has recognised eight Red List Categories of species. They are as follows:

1. Extinct. A taxon is **Extinct** when there is no reasonable doubt that the last individual has died.

2. Extinct in the Wild. A taxon is **Extinct in the Wild** when exhaustive surveys, in known and/or expected habitats, have failed to record an individual.

3. Critically Endangered. A taxon is **Critically Endangered** when it is facing an extremely high risk of extinction in the wild in the immediate future.

4. Endangered. A taxon is **Endangered** when it is not Critically Endangered, but is facing a very high risk of extinction in the wild in the near future.

5. Vulnerable. A taxon is **Vulnerable** when it is not Critically Endangered or Endangered, but is facing a high risk of extinction in the wild in the medium-term future.

6. Lower Risk. A taxon is **Lower Risk** when it has been evaluated and does not satisfy the criteria for Critically Endangered, Endangered or Vulnerable.

7. Data Deficient. A taxon is **Data Deficient** when there is inadequate information to make a direct, or indirect, assessment of its risk of extinction.

8. Not Evaluated. A taxon is **Not Evaluated** when it has not yet been assessed against the above criteria.

The IUCN Red List is a catalogue of those taxa which are facing the risk of extinction.

The uses of the Red List are:

(*i*) To develop awareness about the importance of threatened biological diversity.

(*ii*) Identification and documentation of endangered species.

(*iii*) Providing a global index of the decline of biodiversity.

(*iv*) Defining conservation priorities at the local level and guiding conservation action.

The species which are threatened with extinction are included in **Vulnerable, Endangered** or **Critically Endangered** categories.

Rare species. Taxa with small world populations that are not at present 'Endangered' or 'Vulnerable' but are at risk.

In practice, 'Endangered' and 'Vulnerable' categories may include, temporarily, taxa whose populations are beginning to recover as a result of remedial action, but whose recovery is insufficient to justify that transfer to another category. These taxa are usually localised within restricted geographical areas or habitats or are thinly scattered over a more extensive range.

Indeterminate. Taxa known to be 'Endangered', 'Vulnerable', or 'Rare', but where there is not enough information to say which of the three categories is appropriate.

The IUCN Red List System was initiated in 1963, and since then evaluation of the conservation status of species and subspecies is continuing on a global scale.

The 2000 IUCN Red List is the most comprehensive inventory of the global conservation status both of plant and animal species.

The 2000 IUCN Red List contains assessments of more than 18,000 species, of which 11,000 are threatened.

Status of Threatened Species. According to 2000 IUCN Red List, there are 11,046 species listed as threatened, *i.e.*, Critically Endangered, Endangered, or Vulnerable. Of these 5,485 are animals and 5,611 are plants. 1939 species are listed as Critically Endangered, of which 925 are animals and 1,014 are plants.

The percentage of threatened species of Angiosperms and four verteberate groups of animals are as follows:

Table 27.5. Percentage of Threatened Species

Categories	*Angiosperms*	*Amphibians*	*Reptiles*	*Birds*	*Mammals*
1. Critically Endangered	16%	14%	15%	9.0%	10%
2. Endangered	19%	22%	21%	17%	19%
3. Vulnerable	51%	48%	43%	48%	34%
4. Lower Risk	14%	16%	21%	16%	37%

According to 2000 IUCN Red List, in India 44 species of plants are critically endangered; 113 endangered and 87 vulnerable. While amongst animals 18 species are critically endangered, 54 endangered and 143 species, vulnerable.

Table 27.6. The Number of Plant and Animal Species of Various Threat Categories in India

Categories	*Plants*	*Animals*
1. Critically Endangered	44	18
2. Endangered	113	54
3. Vulnerable	87	143
4. Lower Risk	73	109
5. Data Deficient	14	31

Table 27.7. Examples of Threatened Species in India

Categories	*Plants*	*Animals*
1. **Critically Endangered**	*Berberis nilghiriensis*	**Sus salvanius** (Pigmy hog)
2. **Endangered**	*Bentinckia nicobarica*	**Ailurus fulgens** (Red Panda)
3. **Vulnerable**	*Cupressus cashmeriana*	**Antilope cerbicapra** (Black buck)

CONSERVATION OF BIODIVERSITY

The complex threats to biological diversity call for a wide range of responses across a large number of private and public sectors. All are necessary, with the mix of responses adjusted to the local conditions. As government policies are often responsible for depleting biological resources, it stands to reason that policy changes are often a necessary first step toward conservation.

National policies dealing directly with wildlands management or forestry, or influencing biodiversity indirectly through land tenure, rural development, family planning, and subsidies for food, pesticides, or energy can have significant impacts on the conservation of biodiversity.

Protecting species can best be done through protecting habitats. Most national governments have established legal means for protecting habitats that are important for conserving biological resources. These can include: national parks and other categories of reserves; local laws protecting particular forests, reefs or wetlands; planning restrictions on certain types of land; and customary laws protecting sacred groves or other special sites. The responsibility for such management is often spread widely among public and private institutions.

The Ministry of Environment and Forests (MOEF) is the main agency in the Government of India for planning, promotion, coordination and overseeing the implementation of the environmental and forestry programmes. The Mandates of the MOEF included survey of flora, fauna, forests and wildlife, and conservation of natural resources. A number of institutions affiliated with the Ministry are involved in the work related to various aspects of biological diversity.

Today, the ecosystems are undergoing change due to pollution, invasive species, anthropogenic over exploitation and climate change. Biodiversity at all the three levels (*i.e.*, genetic, species and ecosystem or community biodiversity) is important and needs to be conserved. The most effective and efficient mechanism for conserving biodiversity is to prevent further destruction or degradation of habitats by us.

People form the foundation for the sustainable use of biological resources. Local communities need to be more or involved in the management of biological resources, and to benefit from their sustainable use.

There are two basic strategies of biodiversity conservation, (*i*) *in situ* (on site) and (*ii*) *ex situ* (off site).

In situ Conservation (Within natural habitat) Strategies

Protected areas. The areas of land and/or sea especially for protection and maintenance of biodiversity, and of natural and associated cultural resources. These areas are managed through legal or other effective means, *e.g.*, National Parks and Wildlife Sanctuaries. The earliest national parks are: The Yellowstone National Park in USA and the Royal National Park near Sydney, Australia. These parks were chosen because of their scenic beauty and recreational values.

Today, many such protected areas throughout the world protect rare species. World Conservation Monitoring Centre (WCMC) has recognised 37,000 protected areas around the world.

In India, some important measures are taken. They are as follows:

Approximately 4.7 per cent of the total geographical area of the country has been earmarked for extensive *in situ* conservation of habitats and ecosystems. A protected area network of 89 National Parks and 492 Wildlife Sanctuaries have been created (MOEF, 2002). The results of this network have been significant in restoring viable population of large mammals, such as tiger, lion, rhinoceros, crocodiles, elephants, etc.

The Jim Corbett National Park, Nainital, Uttaranchal, was the first National Park, in India.

The Indian Council of Forestry Research (ICFRE) has identified 309 forest preservation plots of representative forest types for conservation of viable and representative areas of biodiversity. 187 of these plots are in natural forests and 112 in plantations covering a total area of 8,500 hectares.

Eco-development. A programme entitled 'eco-development' for *in situ* conservation of biological diversity involving local communities has been initiated in recent years. The concept of 'eco-development' includes the ecological and economic parameters for sustained conservation of ecosystems by involving the local communities with the maintenance of earmarked regions surrounding protected areas. The economic needs of the local communities are taken care of under this programme through provision of alternative sources of income and a steady availability of forest and related produce.

The main benefits of protected areas are:

1. To maintain viable populations of all native species and subspecies.
2. To maintain the number and distribution of communities and habitats. Conservation of the genetic diversity of all the existing species.
3. To prevent human caused introductions of alien species.
4. To make it possible for species and habitats and shift in response to environmental changes.

Biosphere reserve programme. Biosphere reserves are a special category of protected areas of land and/or coastal environments, wherein people are an integral component of the system.

The biosphere reserves are representative examples of natural biomes and contain unique biological communities.

The concept of Biosphere Reserves was launched in 1975 as a, part of UNESCO's 'Man and Biosphere Programme, dealing with the conservation of ecosystems and the genetic resources contained therein.

Till May 2002, there were 408 biosphere reserves dispersed in 94 countries.

In India, thirteen biodiversity rich areas have been designated as Biosphere Reserves applying the diversity and genetic integrity of plants, animals and microorganisms. (See map and table 14.8).

In India, Biosphere Reserves are also notified as National Parks.

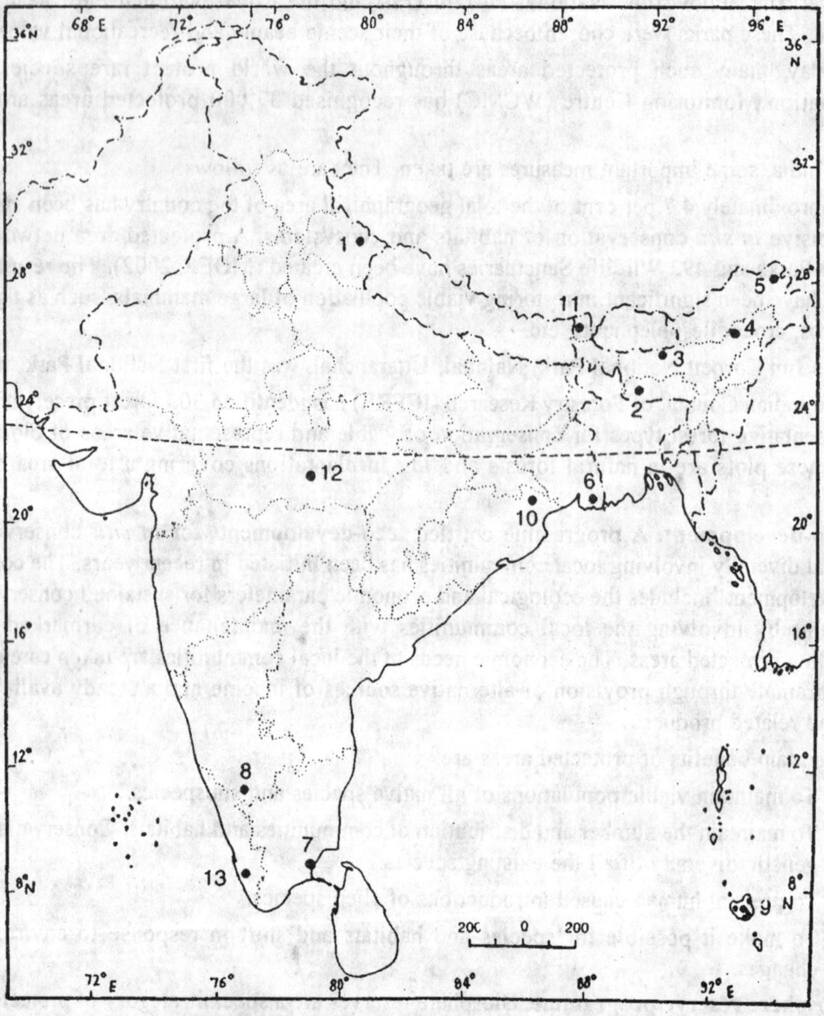

Fig. 27.4. The Biosphere Reserves in India.

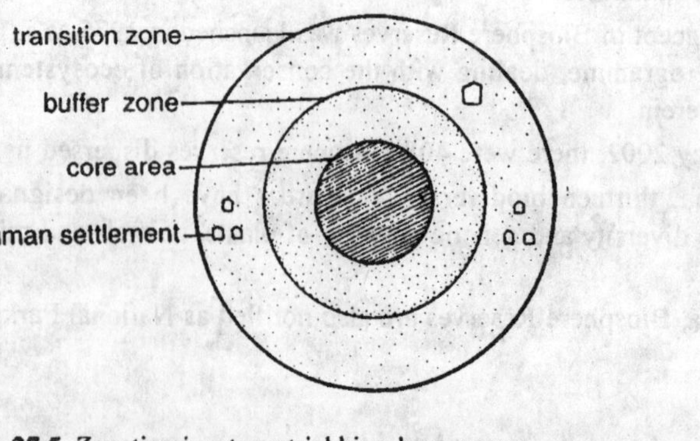

Fig. 27.5. Zonation in a terrestrial biosphere reserve.

Table 27.8. Biosphere Reserves

Name of the site	*Location (State)*
1. Nanda Devi	Part of Chamoli, Pithoragarh, Almora Districts (Uttaranchal)
2. Nokrek	Part of Gora Hills (Meghalaya)
3. Manas	Part of Kokrajhar, Bongaigaon, Barpeta, Nalbari Kamprup and Darang District (Assam)
4. Dibru-Saikhowa	Part of Dibrugarh and Tinsukia District (Assam)
5. Dehang Debang	Part of Siang and Debang Valley in Arunachal Pradesh
6. Sunderbans	Part of delta of Ganga and Brahamputra river system (West Bengal)
7. Gulf of Mannar	Indian part of Gulf of Mannar between India and Sri Lanka (Tamil Nadu)
8. Nilgiri	Part of Wynad, Nagarhole, Bandipur and Madhumalai, Nilambur, Silent Valley and Siruvani Hills (Tamil Nadu)
9. Great Nicobar	Southern most islands of Andaman and Nicobar (A and N islands)
10. Similipal	Part of Mayurbhanj District, (Orissa)
11. Khanghendzonga	Part of Kanchanjanga Hills and Sikkim (Kanchanjanga)
12. Pachmarhi	Parts of Betul, Hoshangabad and Chindwara Districts of Madhya Pradesh
13. Agasthyamalai	Part of Kerala State

Zonatism of a terrestrial biosphere reserve. A terrestrial biosphere reserve consists of **core, buffer** and **transition** zones.

(*i*) The **natural** or **core zone** comprises an undisturbed and legally protected ecosystem.

(*ii*) The **buffer zone** surrounds the core area, and is managed to accommodate a greater variety of resource use strategies, and research and educational activities.

(*iii*) The **transition zone**, the outermost part of the Biosphere Reserve. This is an area of active cooperation between reserve management and the local people, wherein activities like settlements, cropping, forestry, recreation and other economic uses continue in harmony with people and conservation goals.

The main functions of biosphere reserves are:

(*i*) **Conservation.** To conserve the ecosystems, a biosphere reserve programme is being implemented, for example, conservation of landscapes, species and genetic resources. It also encourages traditional resource use.

(*ii*) **Eco-development.** The concept of eco-development integrates the ecological and economic parameters for sustained conservation of ecosystems by involving the local people with the maintenance of earmarked regions. Biosphere reserves are also used to promote economic development which is culturally, socially and ecologically sustainable.

(*iii*) **Scientific research programme.** Programmes have also been launched for scientific management and wise use of fragile ecosystem. Specific programmes for management and conservation of wetlands, mangroves and coral reef systems are also being implemented. Under this programme, 21 wetlands,15 mangrove areas and 4 coral reef areas have been identified for management. National and sub-national level committees oversee and guide these programmes to ensure strong policy and strategic support.

Sacred forests and sacred lakes. In India and some other Asian countries, a traditional strategy for the protection of biodiversity has been in practice in the form of **sacred forests** or **groves**. These forest patches of varying dimensions are protected by local people due to their religious sanctity. Generally, they are most undisturbed forests without any human impact. In India, sacred forests are located in several parts, such as Karnataka, Maharashtra, Kerala, Meghalaya, Uttaranchal, Uttar Pradesh, etc., and serve as refuge for a number of rare and endangered taxa.

Similarly several water bodies are declared sacred by the people, *e.g.*, Khecheopalri lake in Sikkim. Such water bodies protect aquatic flora and fauna.

Ramsar sites. Six internationally significant wetlands of India have been declared as **Ramsar Sites** under the Ramsar Convention. To focus attention on urban wetlands threatened by pollution and other *anthropogenic* activities, state Governments were requested to identify lakes that could be include the National Lake Conservation Plan (NLCP).

World heritage sites. Under the World Heritage Convention, five natural sites have been declared as 'World Heritage Sites'.

Table 27.9. World Heritage Sites

Site	*Location*
1. Kaziranga National Park	Assam
2. Keoladeo Ghana National Park	Rajasthan
3. Manas Wildlife Sanctuary	Assam
4. Nanda Devi National Park	Uttaranchal
5. Sunderban National Park	West Bengal

Five natural World Heritage Sites are as follows:

1. The Tura Range in Gora Hills of Meghalaya is a gene sanctuary for preserving the rich native diversity of wild *Citrus* and *Musa* species.

2. Sanctuaries for rhodendrous and orchids have been established in Sikkim.

3. **Project tiger.** A potential example of an highly endangered species in the Indian Tiger (*Panthera tigris*). It is estimated that India had about 40,000 tigers in 1900, and the number declined to a mere about 1,800 in 1972. Hence project tiger was launched in 1973.

At present these are 25 Tiger Reserves spreading over in 14 states and covering an area of about 33875 sq. km and the tiger population has more than doubled now due to total ban on hunting and trading tiger products at national and international levels.

4. **Project elephant.** This project was launched in 1991-92 to assist states having free ranging population of wild elephants to ensure long term survival of elephants in their natural habitats.

5. **Rhinos.** Rhinos have been given special atention in selected sanctuaries and national parks in the North East and North West India.

All these programmes, though focussed on a single species, have a wider impact as they conserve habitats and a variety of other species in those habitats.

Ex-situ Conservation (outside natural habitats) Strategies

The *ex situ* conservation strategies include: botanical gardens, zoological gardens, conservation stands and gene, pollen, seed, seedling, tissue culture and DNA banks.

Seed gene banks make the easiest way to store germplasm of wild and cultivated plants at low temperature.

While in **field gene banks**, preservation of genetic resources is being done under normal growing conditions.

Table 27.10. In Situ and Ex-situ Biodiversity Conservation

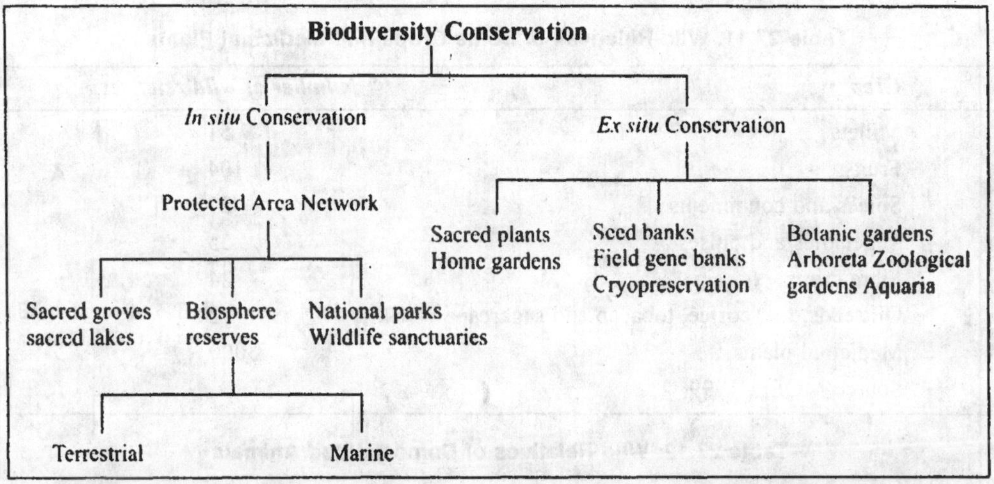

Cryopreservation. This type of *in vitro* conservation is done in liquid nitrogen at a temperature of –196ºC. This is particularly useful for conserving vegetatively propagated crops, *e.g.*, potato.

Cryopreservation is the storage of material at ultra-low temperature (*i.e.*, –196° C) either by very rapid cooling, as used for storing seeds, or by gradual cooling and simultaneous dehydration, as being done in tissue culture.

In cryopreservation, the material can be stored for a considerable long period of time in compact low maintenance refrigeration units.

Botanical gardens. According to currently available survey, Central Government and State Governments together run and manage 33 Botanical Gardens, while Universities have their own botanic gardens.

An scheme entitled Assistance to Botanic Gardens provides one-time assistance to botainc gardens to strengthen and institute measure for *ex situ* conservation of threatened and endangered species in their respective regions.

There are more than 1500 botanic gardens and arboreta in the world containing more than 80,000 species. Many of these botanic gardens now have seed banks, tissue culture facilities and other *ex situ* technologies.

Zoological gardens (zoos). In India, there are 275 zoos, deer parks, safari parks, aquaria, etc. A Central Zoo Authority was set up to secure better management of zoos.

There are more than 800 professionally managed zoos around the world with about 3000 species of mammals, birds, reptiles and amphibians.

Many of these zoos have well developed captive breeding programmes.

Conservation of wild species. The conservation of wild relatives of crop plants, animals or cultures of microorganisms provides breeders and genetic engineers with a ready source of genetic material.

India has 47,000 species of flowering and non-flowering plants representing about 12 per cent of the recorded world's flora. Out of 47,000 species of plants, 5150 are endemic and 2532 species are found in the Himalayas and adjoining regions, and 1782 in peninsular India.

India is also rich in the number of endemic faunal species it possesses, while its record in agro-biodiversity is very impressive as well.

There are 166 crop species and 320 wild relatives along with numerous wild relatives of domesticated animals. Overall India ranks seventh in terms of contribution to world agriculture.

Table 27.11. Wild Relatives of Some Crops and Medicinal Plants

Crop	*Number of wild relatives*
Millets	51
Fruits	104
Spices and condiments	27
Vegetables and pulses	55
Fibre crops	24
Oil seeds, tea, coffee, tobacco and sugarcane	12
Medicinal plants	3000
Source MOEE, 1999	

Table 27.12. Wild Relatives of Domesticated Animals

Group	*Numbers*
Cattle	27
Sheep	40
Goats	22
Camels	8
Horses	6
Donkeys	2
Poultry	18
Buffalo	8
Source MOEF, 1999	

HOT SPOTS OF BIODIVERSITY

Norman Myers developed the **hot spots** concept in 1988 to designate priority areas for in situ conservation.

Biodiversity hot spots are areas that are unusually rich in species, most of which are endemic, and are under a constant threat of being overexploited.

The main criteria for determining a hot spot are:

(*i*) Number of endemic species (*i.e.*, the species confined to that area, and not found elsewhere).

(*ii*) Degree of threat, which is measured in terms of habitat loss.

Among the 25 hot spots in the world, two are found in India.

These are two distinct areas:

(*i*) The Eastern Himalayas, and

(*ii*) The Western Ghats.

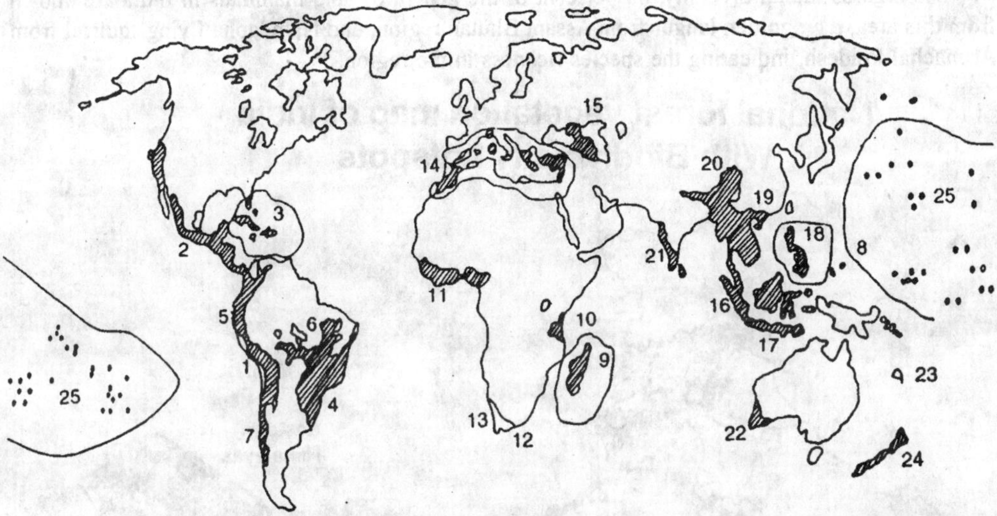

1. Tropical Andes, 2. Mesoamerica, 3. Caribbean, 4. Brazil's Atlantic Forests, 5. Choco/Darien/Western Ecuador, 6.Brazil's Cerrado, 7. Central Chile, 8. California Floristic Province, 9. Madagascar, 10. Eastern Arc & Coastal Forests of Tanzania/Kenya, 11. West African Forests, 12. Cape Floristic Province, 13. Succulent Karoo, 14. Mediterranean Basin, 15. Causcasus, 16. Sundland, 17. Wallacea, 18. Philippines, 19. Indo-burna, 20, South-Central China, 21. Western Ghats Sri Lanka, 22. Southwest Australia, 23. New Caledonia, 24. New Zealand, 25. Polynesia/Micronesia.

Fig. 27.6. The terrestrial biodiversity worldwide hot spots.

These hot spots extend into the neighbouring countries also. These areas are rich in angiosperms (flowering plants), also in reptiles, amphibians, swallow-tailed butterflies and some mammals. Most of the species are endemic.

Together these 25 sites of the world contain approximately 49,955 endemic plant species or 20 per cent of the world's recorded plant species, in only 746,400 sq km or 0.5 per cent of the earth's land surface.

1. **Eastern Himalayas.** Phytogeographically, the Eastern Himalayas forms a distinct floral region and comprises Nepal, Bhutan, neighbouring states of east and north-east India, and a part of southwestern China.

The temperate forests are found at altitudes of 1780 to 3500 metres a.s.l. In the whole of Eastern Himalayas, there are an estimated 9000 plant species, with 3500, *i.e.*, 39 per cent of them are endemic.

In India's sector of the area, there occur 5800 plant species, approximately 2000, *i.e.*, 36 per cent of them are endemic.

At least 55 flowering plants endemic to this area are recognised as rare, *e.g.*, the pitcher plant (*Nepenthes khasiana*). The species of numerous primitive angiosperm families such as Magnoliaceae and Winteraceae, and primitive genera of plants, like *Magnolia* and *Betula* are found in Eastern Himalayas.

The area is also rich in wild relatives of plants of economic significance, such as rice, banana, citrus, ginger, chilli, jute and sugarcane. The rigion is regarded as the centre of origin and diversification of commercially important palms, like coconut, arecanut, palmyra palm, sugar palm and wild date-palm.

As regards faunal diversity, 63 per cent of the genera of land mammals in India are known from this area, *e.g.*, golden langur from Assam Bhutan region, and Namdapha flying squirrel from Arunachal Pradesh, indicating the species richness in the region.

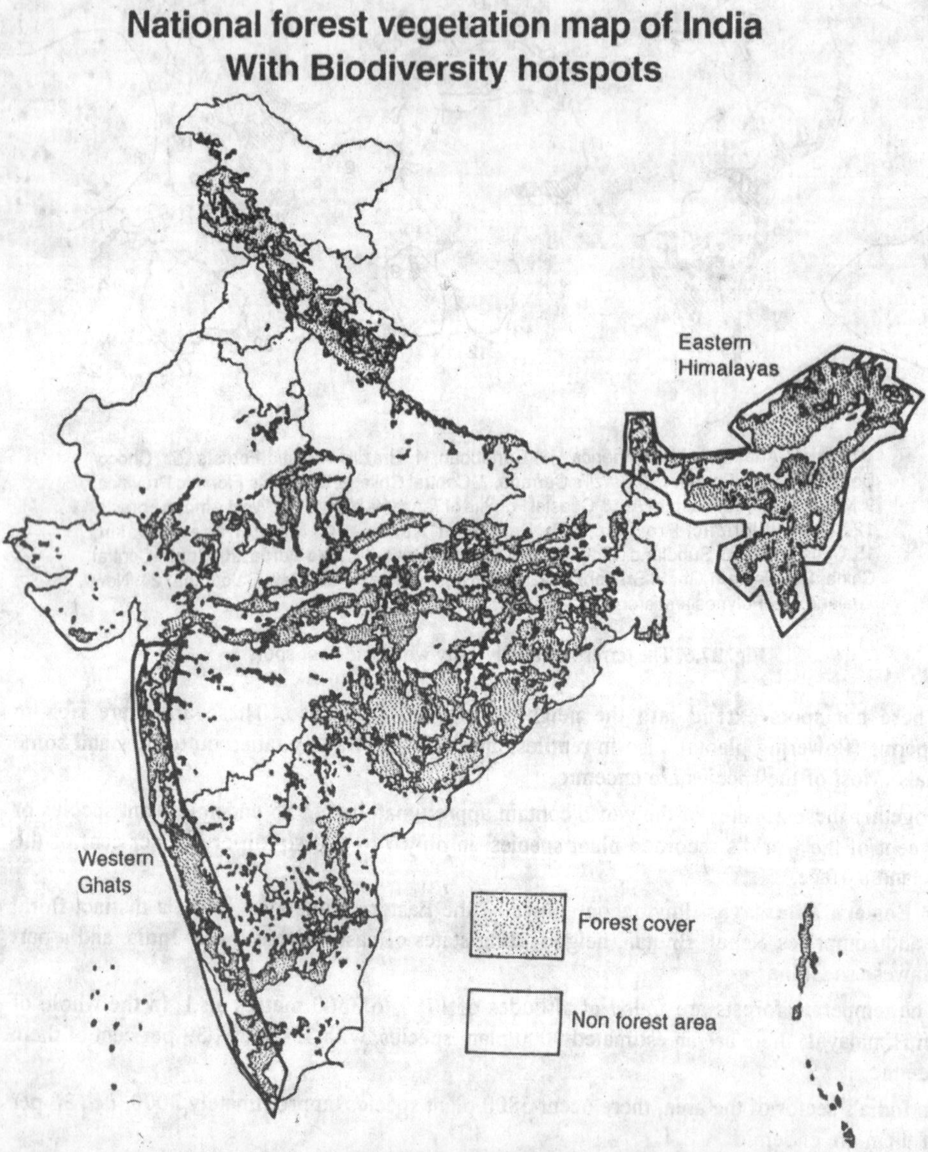

Fig. 27.7. National forest vegetation map of India with biodiversity hotspots.

2. **The Western Ghats.** The Western Ghats region is considered as one of the most important biogeographic zones of India, as it is one of the richest centres of endemic species. This region lies parallel to the western coast of Indian peninsula for almost 1600 km in Maharashtra, Karnataka, Tamil Nadu and Kerala. The forest at low elevation (500 m a.s.l.) are mostly evergreen, while those found at 500 to 1500 metres a.s.l. are generally semi-evergreen forests.

Due to varied topography and micro-climate, some areas within the region are considered to be active zones of speciation.

The region has 490 arborescent taxa, of which 308 species are endemic. About 1500 endemic species of dicotyledonous plants are reported from the Western Ghats. 245 species of orchids (monocotyledons) belonging to 75 genera are found in this region, of which 112 species in ten genera are endemic to this region.

As regards the fauna, as many as 315 species of vertebrates belonging to 22 genera are endemic, which include 12 species of mammals, 13 species of birds, 89 species of reptiles, 87 species of amphibians and 104 species of fish.

Nearly 235 species of endemic flowering plants are considered endangered.

Rare fauna of the region includes: Lion Tailed Macaque, Nilgiri Langur, Nilgiri Tahr, Flying Squirrel, and Malabar Gray Hornbill.

In the Wester Ghats, the Agasthyamalai hills, the Silent Valley, and the new Amambalam Reserve, are the main centres of diversity.

BIODIVERSITY CONSERVATION IN INDIA

India is one of 12 megadiversity countries of the world. The innumerable life forms harboured by the forests, deserts, mountains, other land, air and oceans provide food, fodder, fuel, medicine, textiles, etc. There are innumerable species, the potential of which is not as yet known. It would therefore be prudent to not only conserve the species we already have information about, but also species we have not get identified and described from economic point of view.

Taxus baccata, a tree found in the sub-Himalayan regions, once believed to be of no value is now considered to be effective in the treatment of certain types of cancer. The diversity of genes, species and ecosystem is a valuable resource that can be tapped as human needs and demands change, the still more basic reasons for conservation are the moral, cultural and religious values.

Major problems with biodiversity conservation in India are:

(*i*) Low priority for conservation of living natural resources.

(*ii*) Exploitation of living natural resources for monetary gain.

(*iii*) Values and knowledge about the species and ecosystem inadequately known.

(*iv*) Unplanned urbanisation and uncontrolled industrialisation.

Biodiversity conservation in India is also impeded by a lack of knowledge of the magnitude, patterns, causes and rates of deforestation and biodiversity loss at the ecosystem and landscape level. Poaching and trade in wildlife species are among the most important concerns in the management of protected areas today but information on poaching, trade and trade routes is sketchy and current wildlife protection and law enforcement measures are inadequate and inefficient.

Existing Policy of Biodiversity Conservation

1. A protected area network of National Parks and Wildlife Sanctuaries have been created.

2. The Indian Council of Forestry Research and Education (ICFRE) has identified forest preservation plots of representative forest types for conservation of viable and representative areas of biodiversity.

3. A programme entitled **'ecodevelopment'** for *in situ* conservation of biological diversity involving local communities has been initiated.

4. To conserve the respective ecosystems, a **Biosphere Reserve Programme** is being implemented.

5. Programmes have also been launched for scientific management and wise use of fragile ecosystem.

6. Specific programmes for management and conservation of wetlands, mangroves and coral reef systems are also being implemented.

7. Six internationally significant wetlands of India have been declared as '**Ramsar Sites**' under the Ramsar Convention.

8. Wildlife Protection Act is in the final stage of revision and provisions have been made for conservation reserves and community reserves to allow restrictive use to make it more people oriented. There will also be State Biodiversity Boards to control access to domestic consumers.

9. Under the World Heritage Convention, five natural sites in India, have been declared as **World Heritage Sites**.

10. Project Tiger and Project Elephant have been launched to protect the wildlife. Rhinos have been given special attention in selected sanctuaries and national parks.

11. The Ministry of Environment and Forests (MOEF) constituted the National Afforestation and Ecodevelopment Board (NAEB) in August 1992, which has evolved specific schemes for promoting afforestation and management strategies and ecodevelopment packages for promoting biomass production through a participatory planning process of Joint Forest Management (JFM) and microplanning.

Certain *Ex situ* conservation strategies are as follows:

Central Government and State Government together run and manage Botanical Gardens, zoos, deer parks, safari parks, aquaria, etc. A Central Zoo Authority has been set up to secure better management of zoos. A scheme entitled Assistance to Botanic Gardens provides asstistance to botanic gardens.

State Governments have already received the funds for the preparation of management action plans for Pongdam in Himachal Pradesh, Wullar lake in Kashmir, Loktak in Manipur, Rudrasagar in Tripura and Kolleru in Andhra Pradesh.

The National Bureau of Plant, Animal and Fish Genetic Resources has a number of programmes to collect and conserve the germplasm of plants and animals in seed gene banks, and field gene banks *in vitro* conservation.

The diverse food and medicinal plants are also being conserved successfully by the tribal people. The women particularly have an important role in the conservation of agrobiodiversity. The contribution of natural and agricultural biodiversity in terms of crops, live stock, fisheries, etc., is very substantial in terms of commercial value.

Biodiversity Contribution To Indian Economy

Biodiversity products have obtained a commercial value and have been increasingly exchanged in the markets having a monetary value, from which their share in the national economy can be judged.

The contribution of natural and agricultural biodiversity has a major contribution to the Indian GDP (gross domestic product).

The large economic implication of biodiversity in its wild and domesticated forms is the rice improvement programme. Rice accounts for 22 per cent of the total cropped area and 39 per cent of the total area under cereals, which reflects its importance in the country's struggle to attain self sufficiency in food.

When the rice crop was doomed in the 1970s, one single gene from the wild strain of rice, namely *Oryza nivara* from Uttar Pradesh, showed resistance to this virus and proved vital in the fight against the virus.

With respect to the commercial value of the plant species of medicinal value, the world trade is of several billion dollars and this is growing. The export market for medicinal plants has also increased. India's foreign exchange reserves from horticultural products are from high yielding varieties. Increased production of oilseeds also helped in saving large amounts of foreign exchange spent on edible oil import.

International Efforts For Conserving Biodiversity

It is apparent that action plans and strategies, when designed appropriately and implemented, can make important contributions to conservation. A collaborate effort of the World Resources Institute, IUCN (International Union for Conservation of Nature and Natural Resources), and UNEP (United Nations Environment Programme), working with other institutions, is leading to the preparation of a Global Strategy for the Conservation of Biodiversity, as a companion to the new version of the **World Conservation Strategy** now being prepared. The aim of the Strategy is to provide a comprehensive framework to stimulate urgent, positive, innovative and coordinated action to stem the loss and degradation of the world's biological resources and enhance the contribution of these resources to human well-being. The strategy will be developed by and for national governments, NGOs (Non-government organisations), resource managers, scientists, international institutions, multilateral banks, and bilateral aid agencies. The development of the Global Strategy will be centred around a series of regional workshops in Asia, Africa, Europe, Latin America and North America. The Global strategy will include considerations of a variety of factors influencing biological resource conservation, such as international financing, international cooperation, research, education, training, public awareness, and ecological restoration.

The Earth Summit held in 1992 at Rio de Janeiro, Brazil resulted into a Convention on Biodiversity, which came into force on December, 29, 1993. The Convention has three main objectives:

(*i*) Conservation of biological diversity

(*ii*) Sustainable use of biodiversity, and

(*iii*) Fair and equitable sharing of benefits that arise by the utilisation of genetic resources.

The World Conservation Strategy (WTS) and the World Wide Fund for Nature (WWF) support projects worldwide to promote conservation of biological diversity.

WILDLIFE CONSERVATION

When we hear the term "wildlife", it generally refers to large ferocious animals living in jungles and forests such as tigers, lions, elephants, wolves, etc. But in fact, "wildlife" implies to any living organism in its natural habitat which includes all plants, animals and microorganisms except cultivated plants and domesticated animals. From ecological view point, wildlife is a renewable resource.

Necessity for Wildlife Conservation

The conservation of wildlife is required for the following benefits:

1. The wildlife helps us in maintaining the '**balance of nature**'. Once this equilibrium is disturbed it leads to many problems. The destruction of carnivores or insectivores often leads to the increase of herbivores which in turn affects the forest vegetation or crops.

2. The wildlife can be used **commercially** to earn money. It can increase our earning of foreign exchange, if linked with tourism.

3. The preservation of wildlife helps many naturalists and behaviour biologists to study morphology, anatomy, physiology, ecology, behaviour biology of the wild animals under their natural surroundings.

4. The wildlife provides best means of **sports** and **recreation**.

5. The wildlife of India is our **cultural asset** and has deep-rooted effect on Indian art, sculpture, literature and religion.

Reasons for Depletion of Wildlife

Many wild animals have become extinct due to various human and natural activities:

1. Absence of cover or shelter to wild animals.

2. Due to deforestation for cultivation or for urbanisation, reduction in area for free movement of wild animals which retard reproductive capacity of certain wild animals like deer, bison, rhino, tiger, etc.

3. Destruction of wild plants of forests for timber, charcoal and fire wood often deprives wild animals their most palatable food and affects their survival.

4. Noise pollution by different transporting media (trucks, buses, rails, aeroplanes, etc.) and polluting river water have adversely affected wild animals.

5. Various natural calamities such as floods, droughts, fires, epidemics,etc., have also caused great destruction of wild animals.

6. Hunting methods of all kinds and for any purpose (*i.e.*, for food, recreation, hide, fur, plumage, musk, tusk, horn, etc.) have caused destruction of wildlife.

SOME IMPORTANT WILDLIFE OF INDIA

Indian subcontinent is unique in having immense natural beauty in its different regions (like Himalayas, Gangetic Plain and Plateau of Deccan, etc.) and also in possessing a rich and diverse wildlife fauna. However, some of the mammalian wildlife representatives of our country are:

1. **The Majestic Elephants** (*Elephas maximus*). It is the largest terrestrial mammal and is confined to the Terai and foot-hills because of its dependence on succulent grass, bamboo and plenty of water. It is gregarious and its herds move constantly in search of new feeding grounds; it cannot tolerate high temperature. It is an intelligent animal and can be domesticated easily. Its lifespan is about 70 years. Its population is hunted out for tusk and, therefore, its number is decreasing slowly.

2. **The great one-horned Rhinoceros** (*Rhinoceros unicornis*). It is found in the grasslands and jungle areas of the foot hills of the Himalayas and also in the plains of West Bengal and Assam. It prefers swamps and open savannah, covered with tall elephant grass. It has a single horn near the tip of its snout; the horn is made of keratinized skin and matted hair and it is said to have aphrodisiac and other medicinal values. It is, therefore, hunted for this purpose and is at the verge of extinction.

3. **The Sloth Bear** (*Melursus ursinus*). It is a stout carnivore which is found in the hilly forests like Mount Abu and Erinpura ranges. It lives mostly on fruits, honey and insects, it sucks up white ants from their hills which are broken by its claws with great speed. It is rapidly vanishing due to ruthless hunting and it needs conservation. **Brown Bears** (*Ursus arctus*) are found on mountains upto 3,000 metres height and **Black Bears** (*Selenarctos tibetanus*) at 1500–3000 metres height.

4. **The lion** (*Panthera leo*). It is a rare mammal and was found in Thar desert, in arid plains of Sind, Rajasthan and Punjab but now it is restricted to Gir forest of Gujarat. It is somewhat nocturnal and referred to as the **King of Animals**. Male possesses mane which is not found in **female**. This animal is said to possess enormous strength. The lion is the emblem of the **Government** of India. Its extermination is well known.

5. **Indian Panther** (*Panthera paradus fusca*). It is smaller than tiger and is spotted. It can live in all types of forests. Once it was found all over India but now its number has been drastically reduced. Now, it is under protection in Mount Abu sanctuary. It is commonly called the **Leopard**. The **snow leopard** (*Panthera unica*) is found in the high Himalayas from Kashmir to Sikkim near snow line. It has a creamy grey coat with large black rings. The leopards, especially the snow leopards are greatly hunted for their fur. It is an endangered species.

6. **The Indian Tiger** (*Panthera tigris*). It is gracious carnivore and distributed in Uttar Pradesh from the Himalayas to the Vindhya forests in the South. It lives in a variety of habitats, from thorn forests to the dense terai forests. It is carnivorous and nocturnal. Its number, once estimated to be nearly 25,000 in 1948, has gone considerably down nearly 1540 in 1970. Realizing this fact, Government of India has launched a project commonly called **Project Tiger** to save the tigers from extinction. This project was launched in 1972; due to this effort the population of tiger has improved considerably.

The **White Tiger** is a mutant variety of Tiger which was first noticed in the forests of Gidhaur in Monghyr District of Bihar State.

7. **The Cheetah** (*Acinonyx jubatus*). It was found in Central India,Deccan region and in Thar desert upto Jaipur in Rajasthan. Now the Cheetah, one of the most beautiful, agile and fastest animals, is regarded to be extinct from India.

8. **The Clouded Leopard** (*Neofelis nebulosa*). It is found in the evergreen forests of Assam. It is black in colour and lives on trees, *i.e.*, arboreal in habit. It feeds on birds and small animals.

9. **Striped Hyaena** (*Hyaena striata*). It is found generally roaming near jungles throughout our country. It is terrestrial and carnivorous; it feeds on goat, sheep, etc.

10. **Wolf** (*Canis lupus*). It is found in the plains throughout our country. It preys on goat, sheep and deer.

11. **Wild Ass** (*Equus hemionus khur*). It had a fairly wide distribution in the dry regions of North-West India (Jaisalmer and Bikaner), but its distribution has become restricted to the southern part of the Thar desert. Its number is estimated to be nearly 870. Its population is severely reduced due to hunting, catching for breeding mules and surra disease, etc. Since, it is the only true **wild ass** of the world, hence, it needs protection and conservation.

12. **Wild Boar** (*Sus cristatus*). The wild boar or pig has a long mobile snout with terminal nostrils. The canines of both jaws grow continuously and form long triangular and up curved tusks for defence and digging roots; the tusks are better developed in males. It is omnivorous, it feeds on carrion, snakes, insects, roots, tubers and cultivated crops. It is gregarious living in families in grass or bush of marshy places. It is now rare animal and is mostly found in small numbers along the Aravalli ranges in the eastern part of Thar desert where it inhabits rocky slopes.

13. **Wild goat and sheep.** These are restricted only to the Northern part of our country. The **Nilgiri Tahr** (*Hemitragus hylocrius*) is a variety of wild sheep; the only variety found in south (in Nilgiris, Tamil Nadu). It lives in groups and grazes on grasses. This species is greatly endangered due to habitat disturbance, predation by black panther, wild dogs and hunting by poachers. The **Himalayan Ibex** is a variety of wild goat, *Capara siberica*.

14. **Nilgai or Blue Bull** (*Boselaphus tragocamelus*). It lives in plains and Rajasthan deserts in groups of 4 to 10 in number. It prefers to live near cultivated lands and is also found in desert grasslands.Males have small cone-shaped curved horns. Both sexes have a short dark mane on the neck. It is hunted under Crop-Protection Act, because herds of Nilgai inflict severe damage to crops. In Thar desert it is regarded sacred like 'cow', so is spared from hunting.

15. **Wild-Buffalo** (*Bas bubalis*). It is large-sized, robust animal having streamlined body. It prefers tall grassy forests close to marshy areas in the vicinity of rivers and lakes. It was once distributed over the grass jungles and rivers in forests of Gangetic plain and in the foot-hills of Assam, Madhya Pradesh and Nepal. Its number has also decreased rapidly due to great hunting.

16. **Indian Bison** (*Bos gaurus*). It is related to bull and is found in Andhra Pradesh, Orissa, Madhya Pradesh and Bihar. Due to various reasons, it is now confined only to Bandipur of Karnataka. Its number has also reduced down to a considerable extent.

17. **Indian Gazelle** (*Gazella bennetii*). It is also called **Chinkara** and is mostly found through out desert region of Southern part of Uttar Pradesh and Rajasthan. It lives in herds and adapted to live in extremely arid conditions. It prefers to live in open grass-lands with thick bushes.

18. **Four-horned Antelope** (*Tetracerus quadricornis*). It is also called **Chausingha** and has two pairs of horns. It is found in the foot-hills of Himalayas and in Bundelkhand region. It generally leads solitary life.

19. **The Black Buck** (*Antelope cervicapra*). It has four subspecies in India. It is a graceful and fast running animal, found in the grassy plains of India and avoids forests. Males have spirally ringed, unbranched long and permanent horns. It has been hunted out from the most parts of India and now it is confined only in certain localities in Rajasthan.

20. **The Musk Deer** (*Moschus moschiferus*). It is found in Himachal Pradesh, Northern Uttar Pradesh, Nepal and Sikkim. It is a shy animal and lives a solitary life. Male possesses a musk gland for which it is hunted. The secretion of this gland is a valuable product used as perfume fixative, and as an important ingredient of several Aurvedic and Homeopathic drugs.

21. **The Barking Deer** (*Cervulus muntjac*). It is found in the foot-hills and plain. It has suborbital glands below eyes, antlers and non-protruding canines. It is diurnal and lives in pairs.

22. **The Dancing Deer** (*Cervus unicolor*). It is also called **Sambhar**. It is a rare beautiful deer, lives in herds and found in the forests all over the country. It has very long antlers. It comes out on plains only at mid-night. It is mostly hunted for its skin and its flesh is used as food by many people.

23. **The Spotted Deer** (*Axis axis*). It is also called **Cheetal**. It is beautiful deer with white spots on its brown coat. It has long slender antlers, each having three branches which shed annually. It is mostly found in the forests of Indian plains and is also reported from Assam, Punjab and Rajasthan. It is also hunted greatly for skin and meat.

24. **The Hog Deer** (*Axis porcinus*). It is smaller and stout in build and has hog-like appearance. It lives either solitary or in pair and prefers to live in grass patches at the borders of the forests. It is diurnal and comes out to feed only during morning and evening.

25. **The Nilgiri Langur** (*Cercopithecus johni*).

26. **The Lion-tailed Monkey** (*Macaca silensus*).

27. **The Hanuman Monkey** (*Semnopithecus entellus*).

28. **The Rhesus Monkey** (*Macaca mulatta*).

29. **The Indian Giant Squirrel** (*Rotufa indica*).

30. **The Porcupine** (*Hystrix lencura*).

31. **The Pangolin** (*Manis crassicaudata*).

The above mentioned list is related to mammals only. Likewise, a large number of birds, reptiles, etc., are also among wildlife of India.

PROTECTED SPECIES OF INDIAN WILDLIFE

The Government of India has declared followings species as protected:

1. Tiger,
2. White tiger,
3. Lion,
4. Panther,
5. Snow Leopard,
6. Clouded Leopard,
7. Leopard cat,
8. Kashmir stag,
9. Brown Antlered Deer,
10. Black Buck,
11. Chital,
12. Indian swamp deer,
13. Four-horned Antelope,
14. Golden Cat,
15. Indian Bison,
16. Indian Rhinoceros,
17. Wild Ass,
18. Barking Deer,
19. Slender Loris,
20. Pigmy hog,
21. Musk deer,
22. Indian Gazelle,
23. Gibbons,
24. Nilgiri Langur,
25. Slow Loris,
26. Golden Langur,
27. Lion-tailed Monkey,
28. Great Indian Bustard,
29. Mountain Quail
30. Grey Jungle Fowl,
31. White Winged Wood Duck,
32. Pea Fowl,
33. Horned Owl,
34. Indian Gharials,
35. Crocodiles.

Measures for Wildlife Conservation in India

In India, following measures have been undertaken for wildlife conservation:

(*i*) **Protection of natural habitats.** Jungles and forests are the natural habitats of many wild animals. Hence, these natural habitats should not be destroyed and for this law should be framed to protect such areas from any damage and hunting should be prohibited. However, realizing the importance of natural resources, several national and international organisations have been established to look after such problems.

An international organisation **IUCN** was established in Switzerland in 1948. This organisation has framed many projects to overcome such problems for which this organisation arranges a meeting once a year in any country. Its 10th general meeting was held in New Delhi in 1969. For the normal and effective functioning of this organisation, an additional organisation referred to as **WWF** (World Wildlife Fund) has been established. The **WWF** is related to the collection of funds from its member countries, of course, India is also a member, which are 24 in number. This fund is utilized to run several projects dealing with the conservation of natural resources. The **Tiger Project** in India has been financed by **WWF** and working efficiently since 1972.

(*ii*) **Protection by Law.** India was probably the first country to enact a Wildlife Protection Act. The **Wild birds and Animals Protection Act** was passed in 1887 and repealed in 1912. For game protection in the states the **Forest Act XVI** was enacted in 1927. Then **Indian Board of Wildlife** was established in 1952 which is followed by setting up of Wildlife Boards in different states. In 1972, new **Wildlife Protection Act** was passed. Under this Act, possession, trapping, shooting of wild animals alive or dead; serving their meat for eating, their transport and export and all controlled and watched by special staff (Chief Wildlife Warden and anthorized officers). This Act prohibits hunting of females and young ones under this Act, threatened species are absolutely protected and the rest and provided graded protection according to the condition of their population size. However, in India every year we observe a **Wildlife Week** from 1st October to 8th October.

(*iii*) **Establishment of sanctuaries and national parks.** In India, nearly 200 sanctuaries and national parks have been established for wildlife management. These are meant for providing natural habitat to wild animals.

A **sanctuary** is a place or area with natural environment having optimum living conditions and protection for wild animals; in fact, in a sanctuary wild indigenous animals are kept for protection. Shooting and hunting is prohibited in a sanctuary. A sanctuary is established by **State Forest Department** by Notification and it can be abolished by similar procedures. Contrary to a sanctuary, **a national park** is a permanent place or area established by **Central Legislation** for preserving flora, fauna, landscapes and historic objects of a particular area. However, shooting and hunting is prohibited in such areas also.

Conservation Strategies

For the judicious use of resources, the scientists from nearly 100 countries of the world have formulated some conservation strategies. Few of the steps proposed to save the existing species of the wildlife are given below:

1. Every effort should be made to preserve the endangered species; these species should be given priority over a vulnerable one, a vulnerable species over a rare one and a rare species over other categories.

2. Proper management and planning should be made to preserve wildlife in their natural habitat (*in situ*) and in zoos and national parks (*ex situ*).

3. A wide range of varieties of livestock, animals for aquaculture and their wild varieties should be preserved, and priority should be given to those that are most threatened and needed for national and international breeding programme.

4. Each country should locate the habitats of wild relatives of the economically valuable and useful animals and ensure their preservation in protected areas.

5. The feeding, breeding, nursery and resting areas of species should be safeguarded.

6. In case of migratory animals, a network of protected areas should be established to preserve their habitats. For those species which migrate from one national jurisdiction to another, bilateral or multilateral agreements should be made to meet out the required network.

7. Unique ecosystems should be protected as a matter of priority.

8. The national protection programmes should be coordinated with the international programmes like UNESCO's Man and Biosphere Project 8 and national parks and protected areas of International Union for Conservation of Nature and Natural Resources. This would safeguard the genetic diversity and their continuing evolution.

9. The productive capacities of species should be determined, so that, their utilisation should not exceed those capacities.

10. Proper legislative and administrative measures should be taken to regulate the International trade of wild animals.

Protected Areas in India

As referred to, Indian subcontinent is very rich in possessing natural beauty. Its biogeographical range consists of the coldest Ladakh and Spiti, the hot deserts of Thar, the temperate forest in Himalayas to the lush green tropical rain forests of the low lands; Indian subcontinent also possesses large fresh water bodies such as Wular and the Manasbal lakes in Kashmir, the Chilka in Orissa and Kolleru lake in Andhra Pradesh and the ruggest and rich coastline and coral reefs of the Deccan.

Government of India passed the Wildlife Protection Act in 1972, under which national parks and sanctuaries could be created.

However, out of 434 national parks and sanctuaries in India, 17 have been selected as "Project Tiger" areas.

During the past twenty years UNESCO has evolved **Biosphere Reserves** under its Man and Biosphere (MAB) Programme. Accordingly, India has located 13 areas as Biosphere Reserves; from these Nilgiri Biosphere Reserve, including parts of Karnataka, Kerala and Tamil Nadu was declared in 1986 and the Nanda Devi Biosphere Reserve in 1988. Probably two more Biosphere Reserves, one at Uttaranchal (including the Valley of Flowers in North-Western Himalayas) and another at Nokrek (North-Eastern Himalaya), has also been included in the list of Biosphere Reserve.

In a Biosphere Reserve, the land is designated into different zones; these are the **core zone** (where no human activity is allowed), the **buffer zone** (where limited human activity is allowed) and the **manipulation zone** (where a large number of human activity may go on). In Biosphere Reserves, wild population as well as traditional life styles are protected.

Some Important Wildlife Sanctuaries

1. **Annamalai Sanctuary.** This sanctuary is situated in the southern part of Coimbatore District in Tamil Nadu and extends in a vast area of 958 sq km. This sanctuary has rich fauna of animals like elephant, gaur, sambhar, spotted deer, barking deer, Nilgiri tahr, lion-tailed monkeys, tiger, panther, sloth bear, langur, porcupine and pangolin.

2. **Kaziranga Wildlife Sanctuary.** This sanctuary is situated on the south bank of the river Brahmaputra in Sibsagar district of Jorhat subdivision of Assam. It consists of 430 sq km of forest grasslands and swamps and supports a fauna of nearly 700 rhinoeros. Besides, it also has elephant, wild buffalo, bison, tiger, leopard, sloth bear, sambhar, swamp deer, hog deer, barking deer, wild boar, gibbon, and birds like pelicon, stork and ring-tailed fishing eagles. This is, in fact, a **Rhino Sanctuary**.

3. **Jaldapara Wildlife Sanctuary.** This sanctuary is situated in Jalpaiguri district of West Bengal and is extended in a 65 sq km stretch of grassland. It is known for rhinoceros and, hence, referred to as a **Rhino Sanctuary**. Besides, it also has gaur, elephant, tiger, leopard, deer, and a variety of birds and reptilian fauna.

4. **Manas Wildlife Sanctuary and Tiger Reserve.** This sanctuary is situated in Kamrup district in Assam and is extended in an area of 540 sq km. River Manas passes through it. It contains the following wild animals: tiger, panther, wild dog, wild boar, rhinoceros, gaur, wild buffalo, sambhar, swamp deer and golden langur.

5. **Periyar Wildlife Sanctuary.** This sanctuary is situated in Kerala and has an area of 777 sq km. It has the fauna of wild elephants, gaur, leopards, sloth bear, sambhar, barking deer, wild dogs, wild boars, black Nilgiri Langur and some birds.

6. **Mudumalai Wildlife Sanctuary.** This sanctuary is situated in north-western part of Nilgiris in Tamil Nadu and extends in an area of 22 sq km. It has diverse fauna of wild elephant, gaur, sambhar, chital, barking deer, mouse deer, four-horned antelope, tiger, panther, bonnet monkey, langur, giant squirrel, flying squirrel, wild dog, jackal, wild cat, sloth bear, porcupine, pangolin, flying lizard, monitor lizard, rat snake, python and various birds.

7. **Bandipur Wildlife Sanctuary.** This sanctuary is situated in south of Mysore city of Karnataka state and extends in an area of 874 sq km. Its fauna includes elephant, leopard, sloth bear, wild dog, chital, panther, barking deer, porcupine and langur.

8. **Sesan Gir Sanctuary.** This sanctuary is situated near Ahmedabad in Gujarat state and extends in a vast area of 1295 sq km. It is the largest sanctuary of our country. It is known for Asiatic lions and other fauna includes spotted dear, blue bull, four-horned antelope, chinkara, striped hyaena, wild boar, porcupine, langur, python, crocodiles and some birds.

9. **Dachigam Wildlife Sanctuary.** This sanctuary is situated in Kashmir and extends in an area of 89 sq km. Its fauna includes Kashmir stag or hungal, musk deer, leopard, black bear, brown bear and baboon.

10. **Bharatpur Bird Sanctuary.** It is also named as Koeldeo Ghana Sanctuary. This sanctuary is situated at Bharatpur of Rajasthan state and extends in an area of 29 sq. km. It is a'sanctuary meant for various bird fauna.

In addition to these, the mention of the following sanctuaries may also be made:

(*i*) **Point Calimera Wildlife Sanctuary** in Tamil Nadu and includes the fauna of Chital, wild boar and black buck.

(*ii*) **Sariska Sanctuary** near Alwar in Rajasthan and includes tiger, leopard, spotted deer, four-horned antelope, etc.

(*iii*) **Chilka Lake Sanctuary** in Orissa and has variety of water birds.

(*iv*) **Shivpuri Sanctuary** in Madhya Pradesh and is known for its tiger fauna.

(*v*) **Gautam Buddha Sanctuary** in Gaya of Bihar state and has tiger, leopard, chital, sambhar, etc.

(*vi*) **Bhimbadh Sanctuary** of Monghyr district in Bihar state and has wolf, tiger, leopard, etc.

(*vii*) **Valmikinagar Sanctuary** in Champaran of Bihar state and has tiger, leopard, sambhar, chital, etc.

Some Important National Parks

1. **Simlipal National Park.** This national park is situated in Mayurbhanj district in Orissa state and is extended in an area of 2750 sq km. It is covered over by dense sal forests and is chosen for **project tiger**. Its fauna includes tiger, elephant, deer, pea fowl, talking mynas, chital, sambhar, panther, gaur, hyaena and sloth bear. It is the largest national park of our country.

2. **Corbett National Park.** This national park is situated between Nainital and Garhwal districts of Uttar Pradesh and extends in an area of 525 sq km. It supports rich and diverse fauna of tiger, panther, sloth bear, elephant, blue bull, swamp deer, barking deer, Indian antelope, porcupine, and many birds and reptiles. This national park is one of the most prestigious wildlife parks of our country.

3. **Hailey National Park.** This national park is situated in Ramnagar in the valley of Nainital in Uttar Pradesh and covers an area of 200 sq km. It supports the fauna of elephant, sambhar, chital, langur, wild fowls, pea fowls, etc.

4. **Palamu or Betla National Park.** This national park is situated in Daltonganj district of Bihar state and covers an area of 345 sq km. It supports the fauna of tiger, panther, sloth bear, elephant, chital, gaur, nilgai, chinkara, mouse deer, etc.

5. **Hazaribagh National Park.** This national park is situated in Hazaribagh district of Bihar state and covers an area of 184 sq km. It supports the fauna of wild boar, sambhar, nilgai, tiger, leopard, sloth bear, hyaena and gaur.

6. **Kanha National Park.** This national park is situated in Mandala district of Madhya Pradesh and extends in an area of 160 sq km. It supports the fauna of tiger, chital, deer, black buck, sambhar, blue bull, bison, panther, wild dogs, hyaena, etc.

7. **Tandoba National Park.** This national park is situated in Chandrapur district of Maharashtra state and covers an area of 116 sq km. It supports the fauna of tiger, sambhar, sloth bear, bison, chital, chinkara, barking deer, blue bull, four-horned deer, langur, pea fowl, and few crocodiles.

Zoological Gardens

The **zoological gardens** are somewhat different from sanctuaries and wildlife national parks as the animals are kept in cages in zoological gardens for show. The animals, thus, do not get natural habitat in zoological gardens. There are various zoological gardens in our country but the zoological garden (Zoo) of Delhi is worth mentioning

SUMMARY

1. The totality of genes, species and ecosystems of a region, as a whole are known as biodiversity.
2. Biodiversity has many medicinal and economic use to its credit.
3. Genes of wild species are used to confer new properties, such as disease resistance or improved yield in domesticated species of animals and plants.
4. Biodiversity provides valuable indirect services through natural ecosystems.
5. The total number of species found on earth is estimated to range from 5 to 50 million.
6. However, only about 1.8 million species have so far been described.
7. Biodiversity has three levels to its credit: (*i*) genetic, (*ii*) species, and (*iii*) community and ecosystem.
8. Species are distinct units of diversity and each species is responsible for a specific role in an ecosystem.
9. However, the diversity within a species often increases with the variability of environment.
10. Species diversity refers to the variety of species within a region.
11. Within community,diversity is known as alpha diversity.
12. Between communities, diversity is called beta diversity.
13. Overall diversity of a region is called gamma diversity.
14. Biodiversity increases from poles towards equator, and from high elevations to low elevations.
15. Loss of habitat, fragmentation, disturbance and introduction of alien species seem to be greatest threats to biodiversity.
16. Invasive species are second only to habitat destruction as a major cause of extinction of species.
17. Exotic species especially are having large impacts in island ecosystems, which harbour much of the worlds threatened biodiversity.
18. In the name of modernity, humans have caused the extinction of many species and the rate of species loss is increasing day by day.
19. According to approximate estimation about 14,000—40,000 species are being lost every year from the tropical forests alone.
20. There are three main categories for species threatened with extinction, they are: (*i*) Vulnerable (*ii*) Endangered, and (*iii*) Critically Endangered.
21. The 2000 IUCN (International Union for the Conservation of Nature and Natural Resources) Red List is the world's most comprehensive inventory of the global conservation status of threatened plant and animal species.
22. The IUCN is important to ensure the conservation of landscapes, ecosystems, species and genetic resources.
23. Conservation strategies include *in situ* (on site) and *ex situ* (off site) approaches.
24. Protected Area Network, includes: national parks, wildlife sanctuaries, and biosphere reserves, etc.
25. Sacred groves are traditionally protected areas, which serve as refuge for a number of rare and endangered species.
26. The hot spots are the richest and most threatened reservoirs of plant and animal life on earth.

27. Twenty-five terrestrial hot spots for conservation of biodiversity have been identified worldwide.

28. Amongst the 25 hot spots of the world, two are found in India, *i.e.*, (*i*) Western Ghats, and (*ii*) Eastern Himalayas.

29. The World Conservation Union and World Wildlife Fund (WWF) support projects worldwide to promote conservation and development of Biosphere Reserves.

TERMS TO REMEMBER

Alpha diversity. Means within community diversity, refers to the diversity of organisms sharing the same community/habitat.

Anthropogenic extinction. Many species are disappearing from the face of the earth due to human activities.

Biodiversity. The totality of genes, species and ecosystems of a region.

Beta diversity. Means between community diversity.

Botanochemicals. Plants are used for the manufacture of many synthetic products.

Biosphere reserves. They are a special category of protected areas of land and coastal environments, wherein people are an integral component of the system.

Buffer zone. Surrounds the core area, and is managed to accommodate a great variety of resource use strategies, and research and educational activities.

Core zone. An undisturbed and legally protected ecosystem.

Earth Summit. Held in 1992 at Rio de Janeiro resulted into a convention on biodiversity.

Genetic diversity. Each species, stores an immense amount of genetic information.

Gamma diversity. Diversity of the habitats over the total landscape or geographical area.

Hot spots. Norman Myers, in 1988 developed this concept to designate priority areas for *in situ* conservation.

Mass extinction. When large number of species become extinct.

Natural zone. See core zone.

Natural extinction. When some species disappear and others, which are more adapted to changed conditions, take their place.

Protected areas. Areas of land and/or sea, especially dedicated to the protection and maintenance of biological diversity, and of natural and associated cultural resources.

Speciation. Evolution of new species.

Species diversity. The variety of species within a region.

Species richness. The number of species per unit area.

Sacred forest. Forest patches protected by people due to religious sanctity.

Transition zone. The outermost part of the Biosphere Reserve, is an area of active cooperation between reserve management and the local people.

QUESTION BANK

Very Short Answer Questions (1 mark each)

1. What is biodiversity?

2. How many species of mammals are known to science?

3. Give hierarchical levels of biodiversity.

4. Name three zones of a biosphere reserve.

5. Expand BNHS and WPSI.

6. The number of genes in *Escherichia coli* is_________.

7. What is genetic diversity?

8. What do you understand by 'species diversity'?

9. What is alpha diversity?
10. Define gamma diversity.
11. What are sacred forests?
12. Who developed hot spots concept?
13. How many terrestrial hot spots for conservation of biodiversity are identified worldwide?
14. Which day is celebrated as 'World environment day'?
15. Which State of India has richest flora and fauna?
16. Name the national parks famous for rhinoceros, and lion respectively.
17. What are the threats to biodiversity?
18. Where the Wildlife Institute of India is situated?

ANSWERS

1. The totality of genes, species, and ecosystems of a region are referred to as biodiversity; **2.** 4650 species of mammals; **3.** There are three hierarchical levels of biodiversity, they are: (*i*) general diversity, (*ii*) species diversity and (*iii*) community and ecosystem diversity; **4.** They are: core, buffer and manipulative zones; **5.** Bombay Natural History Society and Wildlife Preservation Society of India; **6.** 4000; **7.** Genetic diversity refers to the variation of genes within species; **8.** Species diversity refers to the variety of species within a region; **9.** Diversity within-community; **10.** Diversity of the habitats over the total landscape is called gamma diversity; **11.** They are forest patches protected by tribals due to religious sanctity accorded to them; **12.** Norman Myers developed the hot spots concept in1988; **13.** Twenty five hot spots; **14.** 5th, June; **15.** Madhya Pradesh; **16.** Kaziranga National Park, Assam and Gir National Park, Gujarat; **17.** Increased human population, resources consumption, pollution; **18.** Dehradun, Uttaranchal

Short Answer Questions

1. Define genetic diversity, species diversity and community or ecosystem diversity.
2. How do forests help in maintenance of climate?
3. How biodiversity is used in agriculture?
4. How does latitude or altitude effect biodiversity?
5. Describe the role of the wildlife in modern agriculture.
6. Give the list of threats to biodiversity.
7. Define wildlife. Which animal is used as symbol for WWF?
8. Define extinction. List the causes of extinction.
9. What are threatened species? Give three categories of threatened species.
10. Name the international organisations involved in the conservation of wildlife.
11. How conservation of wildlife is defined? What are three objectives of conservation of wildlife.
12. Give an account of biogeographical regions of India.
13. What efforts have been taken in India to conserve wildlife?
14. What are the key criteria for determining a hot spot?
15. Name three endangered animal species of India.
16. Why would it be unethical to destroy wild species?
17. What are the patterns of biodiversity.
18. Explain what is meant by species diversity.
19. What is biodiversity? Why has it become important recently?
20. What kinds of threats to the biodiversity may lead to its loss?
21. How is diversity at all levels generally conserved?
22. Broadly classify the extinction processes.
23. Why should killing wild animals be regarded unethical?

24. Distinguish between endangered, critically endangered and vulnerable species.
25. What do you understand by management of wild life?
26. Which organisations are working for the safety of wildlife in India?
27. What is the social forestry?
28. What are the specific objectives of conservation of wildlife?

Long Answer Questions

1. What are the three major threat categories of species? Describe with examples.
2. Write an explanatory note on the efforts for conservation of biodiversity in India.
3. How is biodiversity distributed along major environmental gradients?
4. Write short notes on the following:
   (*a*) Ex-situ conservation (*b*) Hot spots of biodiversity
   (*c*) Biosphere reserves (*d*) IUCN Red List
   (*e*) Protected areas
5. What is the economic importance of a forest?
6. What is deforestation? Give its causes, and explain them.
7. What are exotic species? How do they threaten biodiversity?
8. Define conservation of wildlife. What are the various steps taken to conserve wildlife?
9. How is extinction process distinguished? Explain its types.
10. What are the effects of deforestation?
11. What is wildlife? How does it help in the maintenance of environment?
12. Give three main causes of extinction of a species by human intervention.
13. Give the *in situ* and ex situ approaches of conserving biodiversity in India.
14. Write a note on forest and grassland management.

MULTIPLE CHOICE QUESTIONS (OBJECTIVE TYPE QUESTIONS)

1. The Earth Summit held at Rio de Janeiro in 1992 resulted into:
   (*a*) Compilation of Red List (*b*) Establishment of Biosphere reserves
   (*c*) Convention of Biodiversity (*d*) IUCN
2. Approximate percentage of endemic flowering plants in India is:
   (*a*) 23 (*b*) 33 (*c*) 53 (*d*) 63
3. The species become extinct most easily by:
   (*a*) Urbanisation (*b*) Heavy rains (*c*) Deforestation (*d*) Sliding of hills
4. Bandipur in Karnataka is the site of project:
   (*a*) Elephant (*b*) Hangul (*c*) Tiger (*d*) Peacock
5. Red Data Book deals with:
   (*a*) Endemic plant (*b*) Plants that are extinct
   (*c*) Animals on verge of extinction (*d*) Plants showing photoperiodism
6. Lions in India are now found in:
   (*a*) Jim Corbett N.P. (*b*) Forests of M.P.
   (*c*) Forests of Western Ghats (*d*) Gir forests
7. Saffron is obtained from:
   (*a*) Styles and stigmas of *Crocus* (*b*) Stamens of *Hibiscus*
   (*c*) Petals of *Hibiscus* (*d*) Stamens of *Crocus*
8. Wildlife of Nature is renamed as:
   (*a*) World Wildlife Conservation of Nature (*b*) World Wildlife of Nature
   (*c*) World Wild Fauna (*d*) World Wild Flora

9. Commercial latex is obtained from:
(*a*) Euphorbiaclae (*b*) Acacia arabica (*c*) Tectona grandis (*d*) Manihot esculenta
10. Which animal is the symbol of the World Wildlife Fund?
(*a*) Tiger (*b*) Red Panda (*c*) Horn bill (*d*) White bear
11. In a national park, protection is provided to:
(*a*) Flora only (*b*) Fauna only (*c*) Both flora and fauna (*d*) Entire ecosystem
12. Which one of the following is First National Park in India?
(*a*) Kanha NP (*b*) Periyar NP (*c*) Corbett NP (*d*) Bandipur NP
13. Forest Research Institute is situated at:
(*a*) Nainital (*b*) Madras (*c*) Calcutta (*d*) Dehradun
14. Animals and plants are best protected in:
(*a*) Zoos (*b*) Botanical gardens (*c*) Sanctuaries (*d*) National Parks
15. The species of animals protected in Kaziranga sanctuary is :
(*a*) Macaca mullata (*b*) Panthera tigris (*c*) P. leo (*d*) Rhinoceros unicornis
16. Red Data Books are produced by:
(*a*) IUCN (*b*) WWF (*c*) IBWL (*d*) None of these
17. The national bird of India is:
(*a*) Horn bill (*b*) Black swan (*c*) House sparrow (*d*) Peacock
18. Nandan Kanan Zoo is known for the:
(*a*) Nilgiri Tahr (*b*) Hippopotamus (*c*) White tiger (*d*) Whale
19. Dudhwa National Park is located in:
(*a*) Himachal Pradesh (*b*) Uttar Pradesh (*c*) Madhya Pradesh (*d*) Arunachal Pradesh
20. The biological name of the domestic cat is:
(*a*) Panthera domestica (*b*) Panthera indica (*c*) Felis leo (*d*) Felis domestica
21. Kanha National Park is famous for:
(*a*) Birds (*b*) Rhinocers (*c*) Tigers (*d*) Crocodiles
22. 'Project tiger' in India was started in the year:
(*a*) 1973 (*b*) 1981 (*c*) 1985 (*d*) 1986
23. The lion-tailed monkeys Macaca silenus are found only in:
(*a*) Kaziranga
(*b*) Eastern Ghats and Chennai
(*c*) Western Ghats including Travancore and Mysore
(*d*) Himalayas
24. Now a days, biological reserves are commonly destroyed by:
(*a*) Pollution (*b*) Population (*c*) Rains (*d*) None of these
25. *Idri Idri* is found in:
(*a*) Australia (*b*) Madagascar (*c*) Mauritius (*d*) Tasmania
26. What is major cause of diminishing wildlife numbers?
(*a*) Cannabalism (*b*) Felling trees
(*c*) Paucity of drinking water (*d*) Habitat destruction
27. The animal extinct from India is:
(*a*) Panthera leo (*b*) Antelope (*c*) Rhinoceros (*d*) Acinomyx
28. At present the most significant cause of dwindling biodiversity is:
(*a*) Biological magnification of DDT (*b*) Global warming
(*c*) Destruction of habitat (*d*) Destruction of ozone layer

29. A high density of a protected animal in a National Park can result into:
(*a*) Emigration (*b*) Predation
(*c*) Mutualism (*d*) Intraspecific competition

30. Best method to conserve genetic material of wildlife is:
(*a*) Cold storage (*b*) Tissue culture
(*c*) Seed storage (*d*) Growing in natural habitats

31. The Ranthambore National Park is located in:
(*a*) Rajasthan (*b*) Gujarat (*c*) U.P. (*d*) Maharashtra

32. MAB stands for:
(*a*) Man and Biology Programme (*b*) Mammals and Biology Programme
(*c*) Mammals and Biosphere (*d*) Man and Biosphere Programme

33. Which one of the following fish is introduced in India by foreigners:
(*a*) Labeo rohita (*b*) Pomphret (*c*) Mystus singhala (*d*) Clarius betrachus

34. The breeding place of Flamingo (Hansawar) in India is most likely in:
(*a*) Sambhar lake (*b*) Chilka lake (*c*) Rann of Kachchh (*d*) Ghana vihar

35. Which monkey has prehensile tail?
(*a*) Spider monkey (*b*) Semnopithecus (*c*) Rhesus monkey (*d*) Bounet monkey

ANSWERS

1. (*c*)	**2.** (*b*)	**3.** (*c*)	**4.** (*c*)	**5.** (*c*)	**6.** (*d*)	**7.** (*a*)	**8.** (*d*)	**9.** (*a*)	**10.** (*b*)
11. (*d*)	**12.** (*c*)	**13.** (*d*)	**14.** (*d*)	**15.** (*d*)	**16.** (*a*)	**17.** (*d*)	**18.** (*c*)	**19.** (*b*)	**20.** (*d*)
21. (*c*)	**22.** (*a*)	**23.** (*c*)	**24.** (*a*)	**25.** (*b*)	**26.** (*d*)	**27.** (*d*)	**28.** (*c*)	**29.** (*d*)	**30.** (*d*)
31. (*a*)	**32.** (*d*)	**33.** (*c*)	**34.** (*b*)	**35.** (*a*)					

28
CHAPTER

Environmental Changes

POLLUTION

Pollution of the environment is one of the most horrible **ecological crisis** to which we are subjected today. The air, land (soil) and water are the three basic amenities for living organisms. Sometimes in the past, these amenities were pure, virgin, undisturbed, uncontaminated and basically most hospitable for living organisms. But, the situation is just reverse today because our environment has become foul, contaminated, undesirable and, therefore, harmful for the health of living organisms including man. The various factors responsible for it are numerous but the apparent ones are the explosive population, rapid industrialization, urbanization leading to maximum destruction of natural resources, etc., are of utmost importance. Thus, pollution is an undesirable change in the physico-chemical and biological characteristics of our basic amenities causing harmful effect on our life or that of other desirable species and cultural assets. However, **Southwick** (1976) has defined pollution as **the unfavourable alteration of our environment, largely as a result of human activities.**

Pollution adversely affects biological species, including humans. It damages our industrial processes, living conditions and cultural assets. Other significant changes brought about through human activities are seen in the lower atmosphere. Such changes occur due to the increase in concentration of carbon dioxide and other greenhouse gases, and the depletion of ozone layer of stratosphere. These environmental changes, occur on a global scale, which influence the air, water, land resources, biological diversity and human health.

The loss of forests, fertility of soil, productivity and energy crisis have created many problems. The pollution created by industry, technology and over-consumption by the affluent society lead to the rapid depletion of basic natural resources. Many human problems are also due to mismanagement which is created by humans themselves.

Environmental implications due to pollution are in various aspects. These produce serious problem for human beings to maintain its existence, protection, survival and for the improvement of general standard. The basic needs of human beings have disturbed natural resources and finally led to a situation which has threatened to be disastrous. In the recent years every one has started thinking over the problem of over-population and its consequences, which is primarily concerned with the environmental pollution and every effort should be made to focus public attention to save mankind from self destruction, and steps should be taken at national and international levels so that the consequences may not become worse.

The ecological state of biosphere is becoming more and more disbalanced day by day due to technical and industrial advancements as well as population explosion. Vast changes are taking place in the environment due to interaction between human society and environment itself. Man is exploiting the natural resources for its own interest and many such instances are there as clearly indicate that man has disturbed the natural balance for the sake of small benefits and has changed the environment of many places to such an extent that they are not fit for inhabitation by living beings.

Environmental pollution is the unfavourable alteration of our surroundings, wholly or largely as byproducts of man's action through direct or indirect effects of changes in energy patterns, radiation levels, chemical and physical constitutions and abundance of organisms. These changes may affect man directly or through his supplies of water and of agricultural and other biological products, his physical objects or possessions, or his opportunities for recreation and appreciation in nature.

"The environment is very important in the aspects of peace because when we destroy our resources, they become scarce and we fight over that."

Wangart Maathai, 2004 *Nobel Peace Prize Winner*

POLLUTANTS

The materials which cause pollution of environment are called **pollutants**. The pollutants are, all man made because these are the residues of various materials we make, use and throw away. Certain common pollutants of well-developed and developing countries are as under : **1. Deposited matter** such as soot, smoke, tar, dust and grit. **2. Gases** like sulphur dioxide, carbon monoxide, carbon dioxide, nitrogen oxide, hydrogen sulphide, ammonia, fluorine, chlorine, etc. **3. Chemical compounds** such as aldehydes, arsines, hydrogen fluorides, phosgenes, detergents, etc. **4. Metals** like lead, iron, zinc, mercury, etc. **5. Economic poisons** like herbicides, fungicides, pesticides, nematocides, insecticides, rodenticides and other biocides. **6. Fertilizers, 7. Sewage, 8. Radioactive substances, 9. Noise** and **heat**, etc.

On the other hand, from the viewpoint of ecosystem, pollutants can be divided into two main categories, *i.e.* (*i*) **non-biodegradable** and (*ii*) **biodegradable** pollutants.

1. Non-biodegradable pollutants. Such pollutants are not acted upon by microbes but can be oxidised and dissociated automatically :

For example, chlorinated hydrocarbon pesticides (*i.e.*, dichloro diphenyl trichloroethane (DDT), benzene hexachloride (BHC), waste plastic bottles and bags, polyethylene bags, used soft drink cans, and other plastic materials. They are either not degraded or degraded very slowly in the nature.

However, non-biodegradable pollutants are difficult to manage, and in most cases there is no process of treatment to handle this man-made menace in the ecosystem.

2. Biodegradable pollutants. These include market garbage, livestock wastes, municipal sewage, etc. Such pollutants can be decomposed efficiently by the decomposers.

The biodegradable pollutants are easily manageable by natural processes, or in engineered systems, such as the waste treatment plants.

Pollutants are also classified into the following two categories on the basis of their forms they exist in the environment after their release :

A. Primary pollutants. These are the pollutants which exist as such after being added or released into the environment, *e.g.*, oxides of sulphur, nitrogen, etc.

B. Secondary pollutants. These are the pollutants formed by the reactions of primary pollutants, particularly in the environment in presence of sunlight, *e.g.*, hydrocarbons and nitrogen oxides react in atmosphere in presence of sunlight to form a group of nitrous compounds like **peroxyacetyl nitrate (PAN)**.

An air pollutant may be a **gas or particulate matter**, *i.e.*, suspended aecrosols composed of solids and liquids.

Concentrations of atmospheric pollutants depend mainly on the total mass emitted into the atmosphere, and the atmospheric conditions that affect their fate and transport.

Most of the air we breathe constitutes of O_2 and N_2. About 1 per cent is composed of other constituents, such as CO_2 (.03 per cent) and water vapour.

A small part of this 1 per cent may be air pollutants including gases and particulate matter. This small concentration is sufficient to harm life and property.

Natural sources of air pollution consist of pollen, dust, smoke from forest fires, volcanic ash, which are emitted into the atmosphere.

On the other hand, anthropogenic air pollutants enter the atmosphere from (*i*) **fixed** and (*ii*) **mobile** sources.

Fixed sources are those which include large factories electrical power plants, mineral smelters and different small-scale industries.

Mobile sources include all sorts of transport vehicles moving by road, rail or air.

However, air pollutants can be divided into two broad categories : (*i*) **primary** and (*ii*) **secondary** air pollutants.

Primary air pollutants enter the atmosphere directly from various sources.

While **secondary air pollutants** are formed during chemical reactions between primary air pollutants and other atmospheric constituents, such as water vapour. Generally these reactions take place in the presence of sunlight.

Primary Air Pollutants and their Effects

The most important primary air pollutants are particulate matter, carbon monoxide (CO), hydrocarbons, sulphur dioxide (SO_2) and nitrogen oxides (NO_x).

Particulate matter. Solid and liquid aerosols suspended in the atmosphere are referred to as particulate matters. They arise from grinding, erosion, spraying, etc. Aerosols are the chemicals which are released in the air with force in the form of a mist on vapour. The examples are soot, smoke, dust, asbestos, fibres, pesticides, some metals, including mercury, lead, copper and iron, and also biological agents like tiny dust mites, and flower pollen.

Atmospheric particles having diameter approximately about 10 μm, generally settle out in a day or so, while particles with diameter 1 μm or less can remain suspended in air for weeks.

Suspended particulate matter in the lower atmosphere (troposphere) causes human respiratory ailments, like asthma and chronic bronchitis, etc.

Particulate matter, when accumulated in the upper atmosphere (stratosphere) alters the radiation and thermal budgets of the atmosphere, lowering the temperature at the surface of the earth.

The aerosols containing fluorocarbons deplete the ozone layer in the stratosphere and thus permit more harmful ultraviolet radiations to reach the earth surface. Ozone acts as a preventive covering against ultraviolet rays.

From the emission of supersonic aeroplanes nitrogen and sulphur oxides are released which also cause thinning of ozone layer.

The effects of particulate matter include corrosion of metals, erosion and soiling of buildings, sculptures, painted surfaces, and soiling of clothings, damage of electrical equipments, etc.

Many toxic particles including metal dusts, asbestos, aromatic hydrocarbons have been discovered in a polluted urban atmosphere. Lead from vehicle exhausts, resulting from the use of tetraethyl lead as an anti-knock additive to petrol may build up to dangerous levels in urban areas. In small dose, it shortens life span and causes deterioration of nervous system.

Carbon monoxide (CO). It is one of the important gaseous air pollutants. It originates from incomplete combustion of fossil fuels. Nearly 50 per cent of all CO emission originates from automobiles. Carbon monoxide is also present in cigarette smoke. It is short-lived in the atmosphere and oxidises to CO_2. Carbon monoxide is highly poisonous to humans and other animals. The toxic effects of CO on human beings or animals arise from its reversible combination with haemoglobin in the blood. Haemoglobin has much greater affinity with CO, and it lessens the oxygen carrying capacity of blood. However, when inhaled it reduces the oxygen carrying capacity of blood and also reduces the dissociation of oxyhaemoglobin.

Hydrocarbons. They are also known as **volatile organic carbons**. These compounds are composed of hydrogen (H) and carbon (C). Natural sources of hydrocarbons are largely biological. Hydrocarbons are produced naturally during decomposition of organic matter and by certain types of plants, such as pine trees. Worldwide methane production mainly from anaerobic decay of organic matter probably amounts to one billion metric tons annually. Methane (CH_4), the most abundant hydrocarbon in the atmosphere, is evolved from soil in flooded rice fields and swamps. Hydrocarbons are also generated during the burning of fossil fuels, *i.e.*, coal and petroleum.

Benzene and its derivatives, such as formaldehyde, carcinogenic or cancer causing substances.

In urban areas, ethylene is known to inhibit the plant growth. Many aromatic compounds cause irritation and injury in the mucous membrane.

Hydrocarbons are of particular concern because of their involvement in the production of photochemical oxidants which cause irritation and other effects.

Formaldehyde emitted from indoor sources, such as newly manufactured carpeting, causes indoor pollution.

Sulphur dioxide (SO_2). The most important air pollutant is SO_2. About one-third of SO_2 present in the atmosphere is believed to be produced by activities of human beings. SO_2 is the major constituent in the emission when sulphur containing coal is burnt. SO_2 present in atmosphere comes largely from coal and petroleum combustion. Biologically produced H_2S when oxidised produces SO_2. Ore smelters and oil refineries also emit large amounts of SO_2.

SO_2 can damage building materials and buildings, mainly through its conversion into the highly reactive H_2SO_4.

It accelerates corrosion of metals, especially iron, steel and zinc.

A high concentration of SO_2 causes severe respiratory problems in human beings.

Exposure to high SO_2 concentration is harmful to plants. High concentration of SO_2 over short period of time can produce leaf necrosis and browning of pine leaves.

Nitrogen oxides (NO_x). Nitrogen oxides are formed mainly from N_2 and O_2 during combustion of fossil fuels in automobile engines. The biological production of NO and NO_2 amounts to about one billion metric tons annually, while man's combustion processes produce 48 million metric tons NO_2 annually.

Nitrogen oxides produce fading of textile dyes; deterioration of cotton and nylon and corrosion of metals due to production of particulate nitrates.

Nitrogen oxides cause the reddish-brown haze, known as **brown air**, in traffic congested city air, which contributes to heart and lung problems and may be carcinogenic for human beings.

NO_2 causes leaf injury and reduction of growth in several NO_2 sensitive plants.

Nitrogen oxides also contribute to acid rain because they combine with water droplets to produce nitric acid and other acids.

Besides, it is considered to be a major factor in causing eye irritation.

Secondary Air Pollutants and their Effects

Photochemical smog. This is a secondary air pollutant, and generally formed in traffic congested metropolitan cities where warm conditions and intense solar radiation are present.

Photochemical smog mainly consist of ozone (O_3), peroxyacetyl nitrate (PAN) and Nitrogen oxides (NO_x).

It is often called **brown air** where solar radiation is intense. When lesser solar radiation prevails, smog formation is incomplete and the air is referred to as **grey air**.

Automobile exhaust contains hydrocarbons and nitrogen oxides, which play an important role in ozone (O_3) and peroxyacetyl nitrate (PAN) formation in environment of metropolitan cities.

Photochemical reactions involved in smog formation are as follows :

Reaction that occurs inside engine of automobile :

$$N_2 + O_2 \longrightarrow 2NO$$

Reactions that occur in atmosphere :

$$2NO + O_2 \longrightarrow 2NO_2$$

$$NO_2 \xrightarrow{\text{ultraviolet radiation}} NO + O$$

$$O + O_2 \longrightarrow O_3$$

$$NO + O_3 \longrightarrow NO_2 + O_2$$

$$HC + NO + O_2 \longrightarrow NO_2 + \text{peroxyacetylnitrate (PAN)}$$

The effects of photochemical smog are as follows :

(*i*) Smog ozone causes damage to plants as well as animal life. In plants, generally the leaves are affected.

(*ii*) Ozone (O_3) is responsible for causing lung diseases in humans.

(*iii*) Ozone (O_3) is also an effective oxidant, corrodes the building surfaces of historical importance and damages marble surfaces and statues.

(*iv*) Several species of plants are susceptible to PAN in smog. With the result, chloroplasts are damaged and photosynthetic efficiency is reduced.

(*v*) Smog also inhibits electron transport system in plants and interferes with enzyme systems that play important role in cellular metabolism.

(*vi*) PAN causes acute irritation of eyes.

Acid rain. Acid rain refers to several ways in which acids from the atmosphere are deposited on the earth. The term acid rain was first used by Robert Angus in 1872. Literally it means presence of excessive acids in rain water. In fact, acid rain is a mixture of acids, such as H_2SO_4, HNO_3 and HCl. These acids may travel long distances in the atmosphere and undergo several physical and chemical transformations to produce more hazardous substances, which may fall on earth with rain.

Acid deposition includes wet and dry deposition :

Wet deposition refers to acidic water received through rain, fog, snow, dew, mist, etc.

Dry deposition refers to the wind blown acidic gases and particles in the atmosphere, which settle down on the earth.

About half of the acidity is transferred to earth through dry deposition. Dry deposited gases and particles can also be washed from trees and other surfaces by rain fall.

In the atmosphere the following reactions take place in case of sulphur :

$$S + O_2 \longrightarrow SO_2$$

$$2SO_2 + O_2 \longrightarrow 2SO_3$$

SO_3 in humid atmosphere forms droplets of H_2SO_4

$$SO_3 + H_2O \longrightarrow H_2SO_4$$

In case of nitrogen following reactions take place :

$$NO + O_3 \longrightarrow NO_2 + O_2$$

$$NO_2 + O_3 \longrightarrow NO_3 + O_2$$

$$NO_3 + NO_2 \longrightarrow N_2O_5$$

N_2O_5 in humid atmosphere gives rise to nitric acid

$$N_2O_5 + H_2O \longrightarrow 2HNO_3 \text{ (nitric acid)}$$

HNO_3 and H_2SO_4 combine with HCl to generate precipitation, which is referred to as acid rain

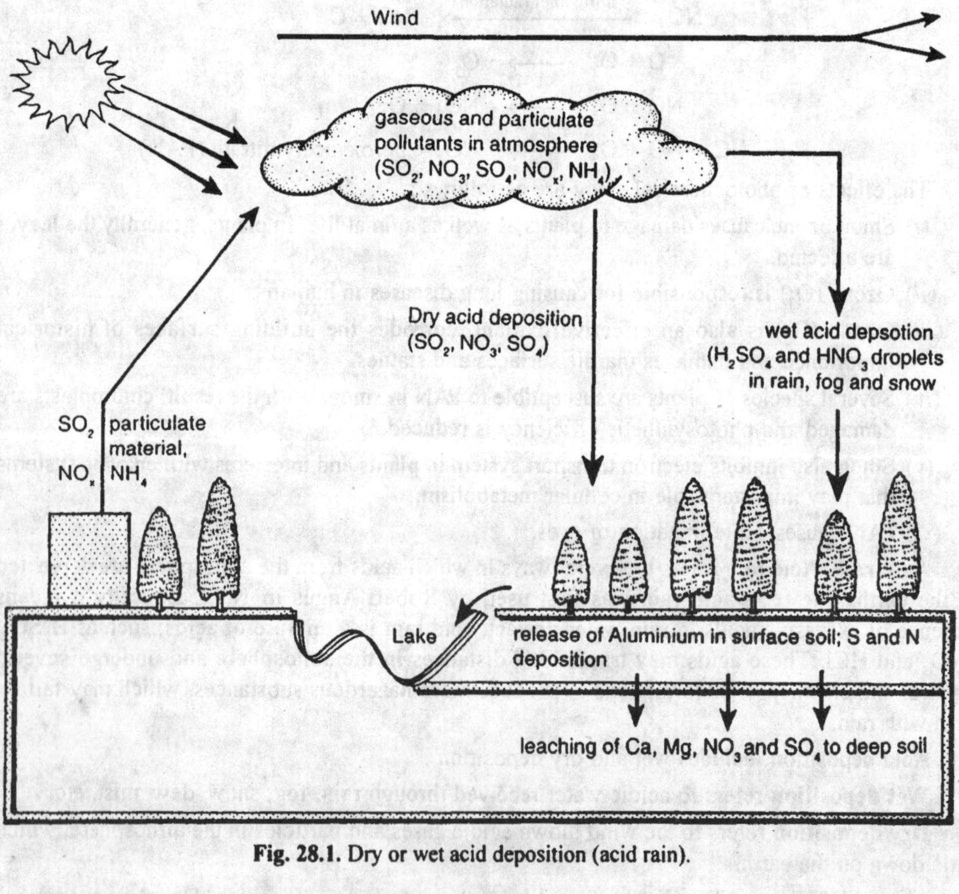

Fig. 28.1. Dry or wet acid deposition (acid rain).

Nitrogen oxides (NO_x), volatile organic carbons (VOCs) and sulphur dioxide (SO_2) are produced during the combustion of coal and petroleum in industries and automobiles respectively.

Lightning in sky also produces NO_x naturally.

The above mentioned gases are highly reactive in air. They rapidly oxidise to acids, sulphuric acid (H_2SO_4) or nitric acid (HNO_3), which dissolve in water and are washed out to the ground as **acid rain**.

In normal cases, the rain water is slightly acidic (pH 5.6 to 6.5) as water and carbon dioxide combine in air to form a weak acid.

While pH of acid rain in less than 5.6 and sometimes as low as 4 or lesser.

Adverse effects of acid rain are as follows :

(*i*) Acid rain causes extensive damage to buildings and structural materials such as marble, lime, stone, mortar and slate. Our heritage monuments, such as Taj Mahal at Agra, are threatened by the corrosive action of acid deposition.

(*ii*) Acid rain adversely affects terrestrial and aquatic vegetation.

(*iii*) The fish and molluscs of rivers and lakes cannot tolerate water having pH below 5.0.

(*iv*) Low pH conditions also damage the soil microbial community.

Control of Particulate Matter

Generally, two important devices are used to remove particulate air pollutants. These devices are:

(*i*) **Arresters.** Such devices are used to separate particulate matters from contaminated air.

(*ii*) **Scrubbers.** These devices are used to clean air for both dusts and gases by passing the contaminated air through a dry or wet packing material.

Particulate matter arresters are of different kinds. The most common are **cyclonic separators** and **trajectory separators**. They are generally used to separate out particulate matters from industrial emissions with minimum moisture content. These separators work on the principle of dust separation by centrifugal force and efficiently work for coarser dust particles.

Filters are usually used for the collection of extremely fine particulate matters. Different types of filters are used for different size and quality of the particulate matters.

Electrostatic precipitator (ESP) is considered the most effective device to remove particulate matters. This type of precipitator works on the principle of electrical charging of the dust particles and collecting it on a differently charged platform.

Scrubbers are also used for dust separation. They are either dry or wet types. However, scrubber is the least used device for separation of particulate matters from the emissions. This device is suitable for the removal of gaseous pollutants.

Control of Gaseous Pollutants

There are some well known techniques that are used to control gaseous pollutants. These techniques are as follows :

(*i*) **Combustion.** In this process, oxidisable gaseous pollutants are completely burnt at a high temperature.

Petro-chemical, fertiliser, paints and varnish industries use this type of combustion device to control gaseous pollutants.

(*ii*) **Absorption.** In this process, gaseous pollutants are absorbed in suitable absorbent materials.

(*iii*) **Adsorption.** This technique is applied to control toxic gases, vapours and inflammable compounds. Such air pollutants are adsorbed on large solid surfaces.

Control of Automobile Exhaust

An efficient type of automobile engine can reduce the unburnt hydrocarbons (HC_x) in auto-emissions.

Catalytic converter filters in the vehicle can convert nitrogen oxides (NO_x) to nitrogen, reducing the hazards of nitrogen oxides.

The automobile fuels of good quality can also reduce the toxic contaminants in exhaust. Lead-free petrol to some extent reduces the load of lead in the exhaust.

Automobile engines operated with **compressed natural gas** (CNG) reduce significantly toxic contaminants in exhaust. The buses with CNG fuel are now running on roads of metropolitan cities like Delhi and Mumbai, which have reduced toxic contamination in exhaust.

Kinds of Pollution

Pollution can be classified as follows :

Generally pollution is classified on the basis of part of environment where it occurs, such as atmosphere, hydrosphere and lithosphere, where it can be classified as (*i*) **air pollution**, (*ii*) **water pollution** and (*iii*) **soil pollution**.

In terms of origin, pollution may be classified into two important categories :

1. Natural. This originates from natural processes, such as volcanic eruptions, forest fires, natural organic and inorganic decays; tons of toxic gases released from volcanic eruptions and forest fires and particulate matter, dust and pollen, etc., naturally present in atmosphere.

2. Anthropogenic. This is called man-made pollution, *e.g.*, industrial pollution, agricultural pollution, etc.

According to the physical nature of the pollutants, the pollution may be categorised as follows :

(*i*) **Gaseous pollution**, where pollution is produced by toxic gases.

(*ii*) **Dust pollution**, is produced by particulate matter in atmosphere.

(*iii*) **Thermal pollution** is produced by higher temperature.

(*iv*) **Noise pollution**, where furious sound is produced by man-made instruments.

(*v*) **Radioactive pollution**, generally produced by nuclear weapons, etc.

AIR POLLUTION

Degradation of air quality and natural atmospheric conditions constitute **air pollution**. When, due to some natural processes or human activities, the amount of solid wastes or concentration of gases other than oxygen increase in the air which are harmful to man and his environment, then the air is said to be polluted and this process is referred to as **air** or **atmospheric pollution**. Air pollution is one of the most dangerous and common kind of environmental pollution that is reported in most industrial towns and metropolitan cities of our country and abroad such as Delhi, Mumbai, Kolkata, Kanpur, Chennai, Hyderabad, Bhopal, Jaipur, Ahmedabad, Nagpur, Firozabad, Agra and also in London, New York, Tokyo, Pittsburg, etc. The importance of air pollution can be estimated by a calculated fact that air constitutes nearly 80 per cent of man's daily intake by weight. A man breathes about 22,000 times a day inhaling about 16 kg of air.

Sources of Air Pollution

Pollution of air started from the very moment when the primitive man knew to make fire, since then it has increased and still increasing every moment. However, the major causes of air pollution are **increase in population, deforestation, burning of fossil fuels and fires, emissions from vehicles, industrialization, agricultural activities, wars** and **natural causes**.

Increase in population. We are worried about our fast increasing population. It is believed that the present world population is likely to be doubled by the year 2000 reaching about six billion. If this rate remains the same then the population would be doubled after every 35 years. The increase in population has resulted several serious problems including the worsening of the condition of environment. An estimate suggests that man alone has dumped 36,00,00,00,000 tons of carbon dioxide in the atmosphere. If its concentration goes on increasing in the atmosphere, in addition to increase in atmospheric temperature it also pollutes the environment making it unsuitable for animal life.

Deforestation. Since, plants purify the air by taking in carbon dioxide for their use and liberating oxygen which is used up by animals during respiratory activity liberating carbon dioxide used by the plants, hence, plants maintain a balance of these gases in nature. Deforestation, i.e., cutting of plants, trees and cleaning of the jungles and forests indiscriminately by man for his own need has disturbed the balance referred to. This has caused in an increase in carbon dioxide and decrease in oxygen concentration in the atmosphere.

Burning of fossil fuels and fibres. Wood, charcoal and fossil fuels are the conventional sources of energy. Burning of these sources causes air pollution. We see smoke coming out from every house every morning and evening. In fact, the by-products of burning are poisonous gases like carbon dioxide, carbon monoxide, sulphur dioxide, etc. The kind, quality and concentration of these gases depend on the type of fuel being used. In the surroundings of factories, the concentration of sulphur dioxide in air is much higher. Sometimes, sulphur dioxide (SO_2) mixes in the air with small particles of metals near the factories and gets oxidised into sulphur trioxide (SO_3). These gases are harmful and they react with water to form sulphuric acid (H_2SO_4) or sulphurous acid (H_2SO_3) and come down to the earth with rain water; it is called **acid rain** or **acid precipitation**. Thus, various poisonous gases coming out from the burning of fossil fuels and fibres, pollute the air making it foul or unfit for breathing.

Emissions from vehicles. Nearly 80 per cent of total air pollution is caused by automobile, locomotives, aircrafts, exhausts, *i.e.*. emissions from vehicles in cities. These vehicles release poisonous fumes by incomplete combustion of petrol and diesel which react with oxides of nitrogen in presence of sunlight in atmosphere to form photochemical smog; it is very toxic. The important pollutants released from vehicles are carbon monoxide—77.2 per cent, nitrogen oxide—7.7 per cent and hydrocarbons—13.7 per cent; in addition it also contains leaded gas and particulate lead.

In a survey conducted at Kolkata, it was estimated that carbon monoxide concentration of 35 ppm (parts per million) due to auto exhaust during the peak hours at selected points was the highest incidence of air pollution in India. Particulates measured about 530 microgram per cubic metre. In a similar survey conducted in New York city suggests that a man who remains outdoors for 24 hours, inhales fumes and smoke equivalent to the smoke of 38 cigarettes.

Industrialization. Industries such as metallurgical plants and smelters, chemical plants, petroleum refineries, pulp and paper mills, sugar mills, cotton mills, and synthetic rubber manufacturing plants are responsible for about one-fifth of air pollution. They release various types of inorganic and organic gases in smoke they produce. The most common pollutants in this case are carbon dioxide, carbon monoxide, sulphur dioxide, hydrogen sulphide, nitrogen oxide, etc. in addition to small particles of dust, carbon, metals, other solids, liquids and radioactive materials which get mixed into the smoke, and pollute the air. All such gases and suspended particles in them are injurious to human health.

Accidental release of poisonous gases, due to carelessness of authorities and other faults, from the industries also pollute the air badly and sometimes fatal instantaneously. An example is **Bhopal gas tragedy** in which methyl isocynate **(MIC)** gas was released accidentally killing thousands of persons while they were asleep.

Cotton dusts, released from the industries located at Ahmedabad and Surat, are one of the most important air pollutants in these cities. The pesticide industries are also concern of threat to the environment. Food processing factories and tanneries produce repulsive odours.

Smog. Smog is yet another problem to which industrial areas are subjected. It envelops the entire areas like a thick blanket. In addition to reducing visibility, it harms animals and even plants and trees. The harmful particles suspended in air block the stomatal openings of plant and tree leaves rendering then to wilt. These suspended particles come down to the earth with rain and enter the root. Sometimes they are harmful to the extent that they kill the entire vegetation of the area.

Tokyo is the most polluted city of the world; it is estimated that nearly 34 tonnes of carbon particles mixed with other waste particles fall per square km every day in this city. The air in Tokyo is polluted to the extent that the traffic policemen have to breathe pure oxygen from oxygen booths. New York is, however, next polluted city of the world where nearly 17 tonnes of carbon and other waste particles fall per square km/day.

Agricultural activities. Different types of biocides used in agricultural practices like pesticides, insecticides, larvicides, herbicides, etc., also cause air pollution because some amount of these poisonous substances is carried away by wind, during their spray over crops, to distant places making the air foul for human health as well as for other animals.

Wars. Various types of explosives used during wars also pollute the air. Radioactive rays coming out of nuclear explosions pollute the air extensively and bring sufferings to mankind to a very large extent. The effects of nuclear explosions on Hiroshima and Nagasaki during the World War II are well known to us.

Natural causes. The natural sources of air pollution are volcanic eruptions releasing poisonous gases, forest fires, natural organic and inorganic decays, marsh gases, pollen grains of flowers and fungal spores. All these are produced naturally and released in the air, making it foul and injurious for human health.

Air Pollution in India

Nearly 80 per cent of industries, the major source of air pollution in India, are located in few big cities; these cities are often referred to as the industrial centres. The major pollutants in the atmosphere of these cities are smoke dust, carbon dioxide, sulphur dioxide, carbon monoxide, hydrogen fluorides, hydrocarbons, nitrogen oxides, fly ash, soot and rarely radioactive substances. A survey conducted regarding sulphur dioxide, nitrous oxide and suspended particulate matter (SPM) in the air of certain important industrial cities of India suggests the data given in the following table :

Table 28.1. Air quality over some Indian cities (annual average of 24 hours). All values are in microgram/cubic meter.

Cities	*SPM*	SO_2	NO_2
Agra	308.0	15.50	–
Ahmedabad	249.47	41.57	25.67
Baroda	316.9	14.2	37.9
Chennai	143.34	13.32	12.6
Cochin	114.5	33.35	7.7
Delhi	400.88	31.14	31.06
Hyderabad	248.66	21.8	9.54
Jaipur	301.74	7.98	11.94

Cities	*SPM*	SO_2	NO_2
Kanpur	326.34	15.4	14.28
Kolkata	430.58	53.26	26.76
Mumbai	190.6	38.34	19.88
Nagpur	209.78	10.62	14.96
Vishakhapatnum	129.08	24.35	8.5

From the above table, it is evident that Kolkata is the most polluted city of our country.

Common Air Pollutants

The most common air pollutants are : **Oxides of carbon** such as carbon dioxide and carbon monoxide primarily produced by cigarette smoking, automobiles, burning of fuels in houses, industrial plants, power houses and carbon dioxide is also produced by respiratory activity of animals and plants. **Oxides of sulphur** such as sulphur dioxide and sulphur trioxide produced while melting metallic ores having sulphur impurities, by burning coal and fossil fuels. **Oxides of nitrogen** such as nitrogen monoxide and nitrous oxide released by motor vehicles and particularly fertilizer industries. **Photochemical oxidants**, formed by photochemical reactions between primary pollutants like oxides of nitrogen and hydrocarbons; the oxides of nitrogen react with unburnt hydrocarbons derived from incomplete combustion of automobile fuel in presence of sunlight, *e.g.*, peroxyacetyl nitrate (PAN), ozone, aldehydes and other organic compounds in the air. These are called secondary pollutants. **Aerosols** such as fluorocarbons (carbon compounds having fluorine) released by jet aeroplane emission causing thinning of ozone layer which forms a protective shield against harmful ultraviolet radiations reaching the earth. **Hydrocarbons**, these are unburnt discharges from incomplete combustion of automobile fuels. These form very toxic PAN after reacting with oxides of nitrogen in atmosphere. **Smog**, formed by condensation of smoke and exhausts from industries and automobiles, contains several gaseous and non-gaseous air pollutants. **Radioactive substances** released during nuclear explosions used in wars and experimentations.

Effects of Air Pollution

Air pollution effects our health, our vegetation, our livestock and our belongings in different ways. However, few important of them are discussed below.

1. Effects on human health. Severe air pollution affects our health causing many fatal disceases and disorders. Some of the effects caused by inhaling polluted air are listed below.

(*i*) Flower's pollen grains, fungal spores and suspended fine dust particles responsible for causing various allergic reactions.

(*ii*) Sulphur dioxide enters the soft tissues causing drying of the mouth, scratchy throat and smarting eyes.

(*iii*) Oxides of carbon, sulphur and nitrogen diffuse into the blood stream to combine with haemoglobin causing reduction in its oxygen carrying capacity. Carbon monoxide severely damages cardiovascular system and disturbs psychomotor functions.

(*iv*) Hydrocarbons and many other air pollutants are responsible for causing cancer.

(*v*) Air pollutants cause a number of respiratory diseases like emphysema, chronic bronchitis and lung cancer.

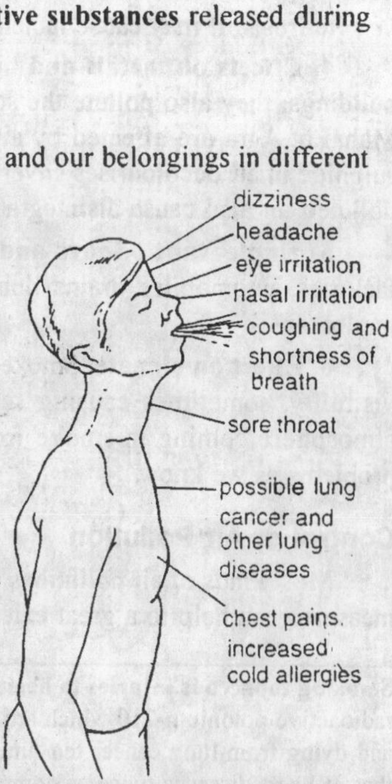

Fig. 28.2. Diseases in man caused due to air pollution.

(*vi*) Fine dust particles and cotton dusts cause bronchitis and asthma.

(*vii*) Cough, sore throat, wheezes, eye irritations, nasal irritations, headache, dizziness, etc., are commonly caused if a person inhales polluted air.

(*viii*) Black lung disease is caused among coal miners who inhale mine dust for many years.

(*ix*) Asbestosis is caused among pipe fitters and insulation workers exposed to airborne asbestos fibres.

2. Effects on vegetation. Air pollution has serious harmful effects on vegetation causing severe economic loss to us. Some of such effects are listed below.

(*i*) Sulphur dioxide causes chlorosis, *i.e.*, loss of chlorophyll and, therefore, it has deleterious effects on trees, plants and vegetation. Its effect completely kills the vegetation.

(*ii*) Oxides of nitrogen and fluorides reduce crop yields.

(*iii*) Fluorides destroy the leaf tissues causing chlorosis and necrosis of leaf apex and margins.

(*iv*) Photochemical smog bleaches and blazes foliage of economically important plants and crops.

(*v*) Hydrocarbons like ethylene cause immature leaf fall, shedding of floral buds, curling and discolouration of petals.

(*vi*) Suspended particles in air and smoke when cover the leaf surface, hamper the photosynthetic activity of the plant causing heavy reduction in yield.

(*vii*) Ozone damages cereals, fruits, cotton, crop, etc. It also causes immature yellowing and shedding of leaves.

3. Effects on livestock. Pollutants present in air also cause widespread damage to our livestock. The general effects of such pollutants on livestock are the same as in the case of human beings. In addition, various fluorine compounds which fall on foliage of plants are eaten by livestock causing abnormal calcification of bones and teeth in them. It is called fluoride toxicity, *i.e.*, fluorosis. It may cause lameness, loss of weight and frequent diarrhoea in animals.

4. Effects on metals and buildings. Acid rains and photochemical smog affect metals and buildings; they also pollute the soil and water. A large number of historical monuments, like Taj Mahal at Agra are affected by air pollution particularly created by Mathura refinery. Hydrogen sulphide in air decolourises silver and lead paints, ozone oxides, rubber goods. Acidic products in polluted air also cause disintegration of textiles, papers and marbles.

5. Unpleasant odours and asthetic insult. Smoke and foul smelling odours emitted by factories, automobiles, drains, dumped garbages, etc., make the urban life most discomfortable and unpleasant.

6. Effect on climate. Smoke, smog and dust make the atmosphere less transparent and reduce visibility, sometimes causing severe accidents on roads and rails. The various gases in the atmosphere coming in smoke from factories imbalance the composition of air causing severe problems as we know.

Control of Air Pollution

Most kinds of air pollutions can be controlled by modern technology. However, the following measures can help to a great extent in keeping the environment free from air pollution :

Smoking tobacco is injuries to health because its smoke contains nearly seven polycyclic hydrocarbons and radioactive polonium-210 which are said to be carcinogenic. An average smoker has the risk of developing and dying from lung cancer ten times more than a non-smoker. The risk of lung diseases is six times and that of heart diseases twice as compared to a non-smoker. A number of other diseases are also said to be linked to smoking.

1. The use of crude fuels should be avoided and the use of high quality fuels should be recommended. This will considerably reduce sulphur contents and hydrocarbons in the atmosphere.

2. Use of automobiles should be minimised which will reduce the nitrogen contents in the atmosphere.

3. The industrial smokes must be filtered before releasing into the atmosphere.

4. The population growth which is supposed to be a major cause of pollution should be brought under control.

5. The gaseous pollutants from industries and power plants can be removed by chemical means.

6. Nuclear explosions should be avoided.

7. Tree plantation should be increased which will reduce carbon dioxide contents of the environment and make it pure by releasing oxygen.

8. Legal control of air pollution is also helpful in making the environment free from air pollutants to some extent. We have **Air Pollution Boards** at central and state level. Their power is to issue and cancel licences to polluting industries, enforce emission standards and frame rules and regulations for the control of air pollution.

In fact, some pollutant gases which are more soluble in a particular liquid than in air can be separated by dissolving them before being released in the atmosphere. It is done by the technique of electrostatic precipitation device. For this, cyclone collectors consisting of a spirally made

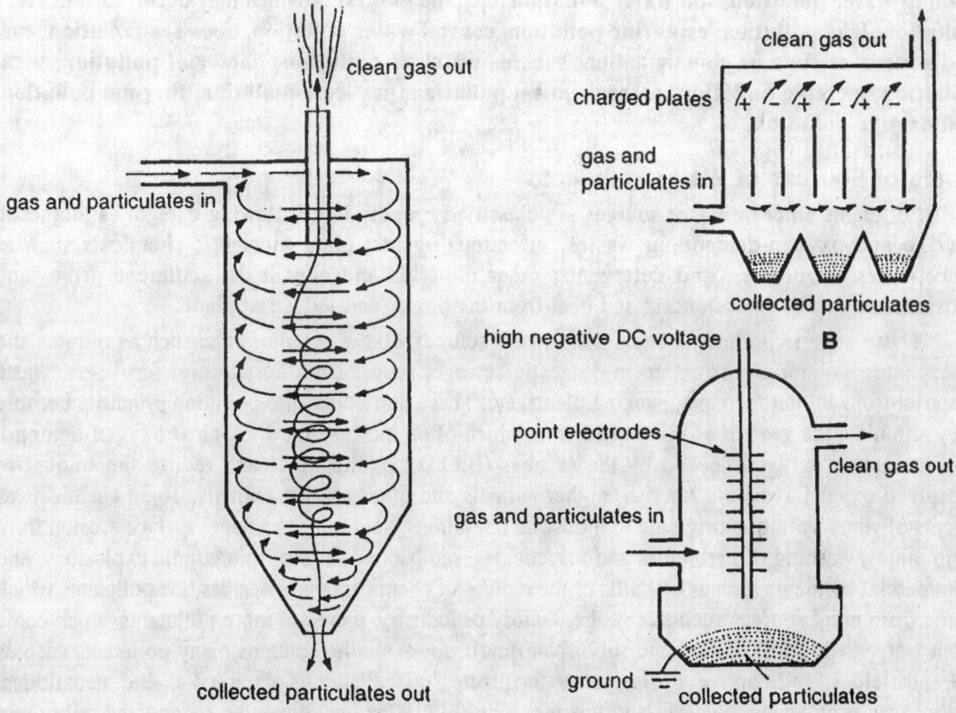

Fig. 28.3. Common types of electrostatic precipitators. A-Cyclone collector; B, Plate-type precipitator; C, Tube type precipitator.

Air pollution inhibits the growth of lichens on trees, hence, lichens can serve as pollution indicators; clean air is indicated by heavy growth of lichens on trees.

chamber or any type of precipitator is taken. In this, the gas to be cleaned, is passed and whirled round through a tight circular spiral. The pollutant particles are centrifuged outward and collected which is removed periodically. For this purpose different types of collectors used are shown in Fig. 28.3.

WATER POLLUTION

'Water is life' is a common saying because all organisms including man need water for various purposes; it is needed for various metabolic activities and some organisms use it as habitat as well; man needs water for several purposes like bathing, washing, cooking, irrigation, flushing away wastes, generating electricity, manufacturing different products in industries, navigation, etc. However, during all these processes the wastes and undesirable substances are continuously added to the water sources. A general survey has revealed that nearly 70% streams and rivers in our country contain polluted water. Rivers of our country like Ganga, Jamuna, Hooghly, Godawari, Cauvery, etc., which were once very pure in their waters, are polluted to the extent of 70%. Realizing the importance, the Government has now started several projects to clean the waters of these rivers in phases to make them free from pollutants. The term **water pollution**, therefore, refers to any type of aquatic contamination which affects the living organisms.

Types of Water pollution

It may be classified by the **medium** in which they occur, such as **surface water pollution, ground water pollution, soil water pollution**, etc.; the **habitat** in which they occur, such as **river pollution, lake pollution, estuarine pollution, coastal water pollution, open sea pollution**, etc.; and **source** or **type** of contamination, such as **nutrient pollution, bacterial pollution, viral pollution, metallic pollution, petrochemical pollution, pesticide pollution, thermal pollution, radioactive pollution**, etc.

Kinds of Sources of Water Pollutants

Pollutants entering water sources are classified broadly into following categories: domestic sewage and oxygen-demanding wastes; infectious agents; plant nutrients; chemicals such as insecticides, herbicides, and detergents; other minerals and chemicals; sediments from land erosions; radioactive substances; and heat from the power and industrial plants.

These aquatic pollutants come from many sources. Excessive nutrients, such as nitrates and phosphates, commonly originate in domestic sewage, runoff from agricultural fertilizers, waste material from animal feed lots, packing plants, etc. These nutrients cause pollution primarily because they stimulate the growth of microorganisms which often increase the **biological oxygen demand**, *i.e.*, amount of oxygen needed by the aerobes (B.O.D.) of the water and reduce the amount of dissolved oxygen available for fish, higher animals and other aquatic animals. Toxic chemicals as agents of water pollution originate in industrial operations, acid mine drainage, surface erosion from strip mines, washing of herbicides and insecticides, radioactive fallout from atomic explosions, and commercial accidents such as oil spills or the rupture of chemical tanks. Besides, the pollutants which come from point sources such as sewage, factory or industry, there are more pollutants which come from watershed runoff. Urban and sub-urban runoff, for example, contains many pollutants such as oil, pesticides, radioactive dusts, salts, fertilizers, miscellaneous chemicals, and nematodes, pathogenic protozoans, bacteria and viruses. **Kimbal** (1975) has, however, recognized only three major sources of pollution of water : **domestic, industrial** and **agricultural**.

Effects of Water Pollution

Each type of water pollution affects the abiotic and biotic factors of different aquatic systems in different degrees and its ultimate effect on man remains quite in medical, asthetic, and economical sense. Some of the well known effects of water pollution are following :

1. Sewage pollution. Contamination of fresh-waters and shallow offshore seas by sewage is a common occurrence. Sewage generally includes biodegradable pollutants such as human faecal matter, animal wastes and certain dissolved organic compounds (*e.g.*, carbohydrates, proteins, urea, etc.) and inorganic salts such as nitrates and phosphates of detergents and sodium, potassium, calcium and chloride ions. Under natural processes most of the biodegradable pollutants of sewage are rapidly decomposed, but when they accumulate in large quantities, they create problem, *i.e.*, when their input in the environment exceeds the decomposition capacity of the latter. Most cities of developed countries like USA, Britain, etc., and some cities of developing countries like India have evolved certain engineering systems, such as, **septic tanks, oxidation ponds, filter beds, waste-water treatment plants and municipal sewage treatment plants** for the removal of many harmful bacteria and other microbes, organic wastes and other pollutants from the sewage, before it is tipped into river or sea.

The sewage treatment is usually performed in following three stages : **(1) primary treatment**, which removes large objects and suspended undissolved solids of raw sewage and converts them into a biologically inactive and aesthetically inoffensive state, called the **sludge**, a valuable fertilizer. **(2) secondary treatment**, which supplies aeration and bacteriological action to decompose organic compounds into harmless substances such as carbon dioxide, sulphate and water. During later stages of secondary treatment, whole waste water is chlorinated (*i.e.*, treated with chlorine) to reduce its contents of bacteria. **(3) tertiary treatment**, which removes nitrates and phosphates and releases pure water. These three stages of sewage treatment have become increasingly expensive and only in most advanced countries all the three treatments of sewage are done. However, most Indian cities either lack any sewage or waste-water treatment plant or have inadequate sewage treatment facilities. Consequently, normally and especially during heavy downpour and floods raw sewage or incompletely treated sewage is dumped into rivers which causes severe water pollution problems.

2. Industrial pollution. Most of the Indian rivers and fresh-water streams are seriously polluted by industrial wastes or effluents (Table 15.2 and 15.3) which come along waste waters of different industries such as petro-chemical complexes, fertilizer factories, oil refineries, pulp, paper, textile, sugar, steel mills, tanneries, distilleries, drugs, fibres, rubber, plastic, etc. All these

Table 28.2. Some important Indian rivers and their major sources of pollution

Name of the river	*Sources of pollution*
1. Yamuna near Delhi	1. D.D.T. factory, sewage, Indraprastha Power Station, Delhi.
2. Ganga at Kanpur (U.P.)	2. June, chemical, metal and surgical industries, tanneries, textile mills and a great bulk of domestic sewage of highly organic nature.
3. Gomati near Lucknow (U.P.)	3. Paper and pulp mills; sewage.
4. Damodar between Bokaro and Panchet (Bihar)	4. Fertilizers, flyash from steel mills, suspended coal particles from washeries, and thermal power station.
5. Hoogly at Kolkata	5. Power stations, paper and pulp, jute, textile, chemical mills, metal steel, varnishes, rayon and soap and a huge bulk of sewage.
6. Sone at Dalminagar (Bihar)	6. Cement, pulp and paper mills.
7. Godavari	7. Paper mills.
8. Cauvery (Tamil Nadu)	8. Sewage, tanneries, distillaries, paper and rayon mills.

chemicals of industrial wastes are toxic to animals and may cause death or damage to different body systems of the aquatic fauna and flora.

3. Thermal pollution. Various industrial processes may utilize water for cooling and resultant warmed water has often been discharged into streams or lakes. Coal or oil-fired generators and atomic energy plants generate large amounts of waste heat which iscarried away as hot water and cause **thermal pollution**. The thermal pollution produces distinct changes in aquatic biota. However, the thermal pollution can exert a disruptive effect on aquatic ecosystem.

4. Effects on aquatic ecosystem. Organic and inorganic wastes decrease the **dissolved oxygen** (DO) ¢ontent of water bodies.

Water having DO content less than 8.0 mg L^{-1} is considered containinated. Heavily polluted waters have DO content less than 4.0 mg L^{-1}.

DO content water is important for the survival of aquatic organisms.

The turbidity, photosynthetic activity, oxygen consumption by organisms and decomposition of organic matter are the factors that determine the amount of DO present in water.

Higher amounts of organic waste increase the rate of oxygen consumption, thus causes drop in DO content of water.

The demand of oxygen is directly related to increasing input of organic wastes and is referred to as **biochemical oxygen demand** (BOD) of water.

BOD is a measure of oxygen required by aerobic decomposers for the biochemical degradation of organic materials (biodegradable materials) in water.

Higher the BOD, lower would be dissolved oxygen (DO).

Chemical oxygen demand (COD) is also a measure of pollution load in water. This is measure of oxygen equivalent of the requirement for oxidation of total organic matter, (i.e., biodegradable and non-biodegradable) present in water.

Thus, contamination of water bodies by pollutants reduces DO content, and therefore, sensitive organisms, such as plankton, mollusc and fish are eliminated.

In such state, only a few tolerant species, like annelid *Tubifex* and some insect larvae, survive in highly polluted, low DO water, and they are referred to as **indicator species** for polluted waters. Biocide residues, PCBs and heavy metals like Hg, Cd, Pb, Cu, As, etc., can eliminate different species of organisms.

Higher the temperature of water, lower is the rate of dissolution of oxygen in water.

However, hot wastewaters discharged from industries, when added to water bodies, cause lowering of DO content of water.

5. Biological magnification. The phenomenon through which certain pollutants are accumulated in tissues in increasing concentration along the food chain, is refered to as **biological magnification**. Such pollutants are non-biodegradable, such as DDT. Once they are absorbed by an organism, they cannot be metabolised and broken down or excreted out.

Such pollutants (non-biodegradable), generally get accumulated in fat containing tissues of the organism.

For example, DDT an insecticide, is sprayed on water bodies to check the growth of mosquitoes.

BOD is measured by keeping a sample of water containing known amount of oxygen for five days at 20°C in the dark. At the end of this period, the oxygen content is again measured. A high BOD indicates intense level of microbial pollution.

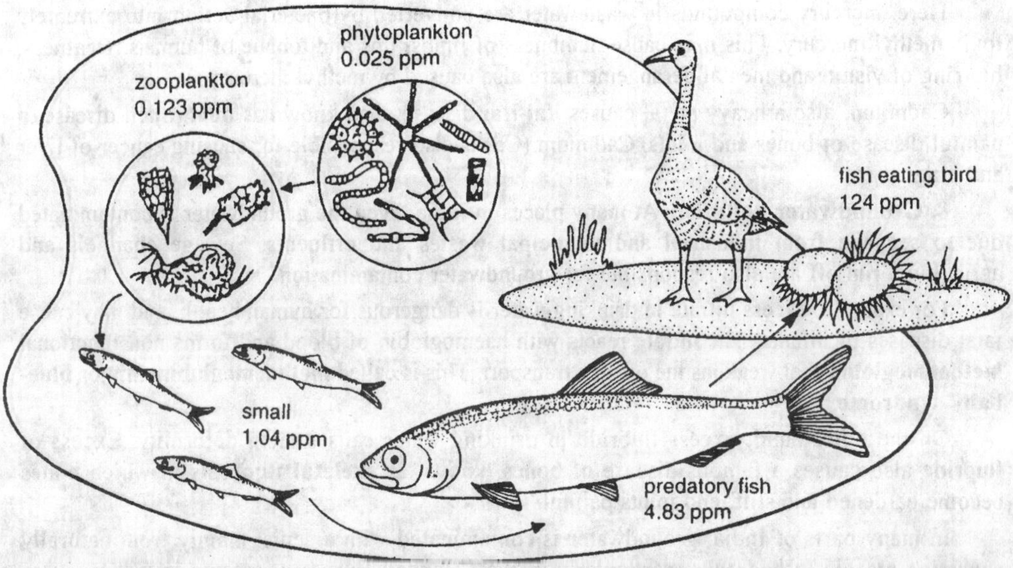

Fig. 28.4. Process of biological magnification. DDT concentrations increase in organisms along food chain.

In an island of USA, after regular DDT spraying for few years, the population of fish-eating birds decreased. Later, this was found that the concentration of DDT had increased about 800 times in the phytoplankton relative to the concentration in water.

However, zooplankton contained about five times greater DDT than phytoplankton.

In different fish, the DDT concentration increased 9 to 40 times, relative to the concentrations in zooplankton.

Birds showed about 25 times greater DDT concentration relative to that in fish.

Many other persistent pesticides and radionuclides also show biological magnification.

6. Eutrophication. Here, instead of inorganic nutrient input with the inflow of waste water, decomposition of organic wastes, increases the nutrient content of the water bodies.

The excess of nutrients causes profuse growth of algae, especially the blue-green algae (cyanobacteria). Such profuse growth of algae is called **algal bloom**.

Such algal blooms completely cover the water surface.

The blue-green algae release toxins in water, and sometimes cause deficiency of oxygen in water. Therefore, in bloom-infected water body the growth of other fresh water is checked due to toxins, and aquatic animals may die because of toxic effect or lack of oxygen.

The process of enrichment of nutrients of water, and then loss of species diversity is known as **eutrophication**.

7. Effects on human health. Domestic sewage contains pathogens, such as virus, bacteria, parasitic protozoans, and several types of worms.

Contaminated water with above mentioned pathogens causes several water borne diseases, like jaundice, cholera, typhoid, amoebiasis, etc. The contamination makes the water unfit for drinking purpose. Such water cannot be used even for bathing, swimming and irrigation purposes.

On the other hand, the heavy metal contamination of water causes serious ailments of human beings. Mercury poisoning, also known as **Minamata disease** is caused by consumption of fish captured from Hg-contaminated Minamata Bay in Japan. This disease was detected for first time in 1952.

Here, mercury compounds in wastewater are converted by bacterial action into extremely toxic methyl mercury. This may cause numbness of limbs, lips and tongue of humans. Deafness, blurring of vision and mental derangement are also caused by methyl mercury.

Cadmium, also a heavy metal causes **itai-itai** disease, also known as **ouch-ouch** disease, a painful disease of bones and joints. Cadmium (Cd) is also responsible for causing cancer of liver and lungs.

8. Groundwater pollution. At many places in India, even the groundwater is contaminated due to seepage from industrial and municipal wastes and effluents. Sewage channels and agricultural run off are also responsible for groundwater contamination.

For example, excess nitrate in drinking water is dangerous for human health, and may cause fatal diseases of infants. The nitrate reacts with haemoglobin of blood and forms non functional **methaemoglobin** that weakens the oxygen transport. This is called **methaemoglobinemia** or **blue-baby syndrome**.

On the other hand, excess fluoride in drinking water causes teeth deformity. Excess of fluoride also causes a famous disease of bones, known as **skeletal fluorosis** in which bones become hardened and stiff, and joints painful.

In many parts of India, groundwater is contaminated with arsenic, mainly from naturally occurring arsenic in bedrocks, particularly in West Bengal. Excess of arsenic in water causes **black-food disease**. Arsenic also causes diarrhoea, peripheral neutritis, hyperkeratosis, and also skin and lung cancers.

Improving Water Quality

The industrial and municipal waste waters are treated in **Effluent Treatment Plant (ETP)** prior to disposal in water bodies.

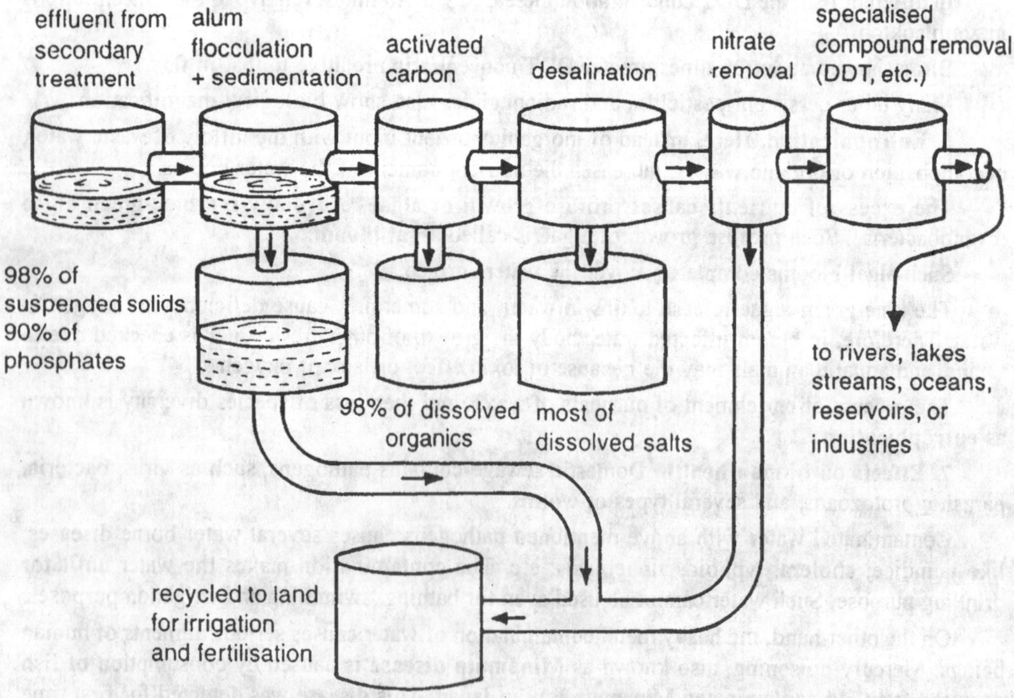

Fig. 28.5. Treatment of wastewaters in Effluent Treatment Plant (ETP).

Generally the undermentioned treatments are given in ETP :

(*i*) **Primary treatment.** This is a physical process, when the separation of large debris is done, which is followed by sedimentation in tanks or clarifiers of improved type.

(*ii*) **Secondary treatment.** This is a biological process and carried out by the activity of microorganisms. In this treatment, the waste water is pumped in shallow **stabilisation or oxidation** ponds, where the microorganisms (microbes) oxidise its organic matter.

This process results in release of carbon dioxide and formation of **sludge** also known as **biosolid**. The sludge is continuously aerated to accelerate its oxidation.

Algae grown in the upper lighted zone of the wastewater provide aeration by generating oxygen.

(*iii*) **Tertiary treatment.** This is physicochemical process, which removes turbidity in wastewater caused by nutrients, such as nitrogen, phosphorus, etc., dissolved organic matter, heavy metals or pathogens.

Table 28.3. Various organic and inorganic pollutants of water and their sources

Type of Industry	*Organic pollutants*	*Organic pollutants*
Mining	**Mine wastes:** Chlorides, various metals, ferrous sulphate, sulphuric acid hydrogen sulphide, ferric hydroxide, surface wash offs, suspended solids, chlorides and heavy metals.	—
Iron and steel	Suspended, solids, iron cyanide thiocyanate, sulphides, oxides, of copper, chromium, cadmium, and mercury.	Oil, phenol and naptha
Chemical plants	Various acids and alkalies, sulphates, nitrates of metals, phosphorus, fluorine, silica, and suspended particles.	Aromatic compound solvents, organic acids, nitro compound dyes, etc.
Pharmaceuticals	—	Proteins, carbohydrates, organic solvents, intermediate products, drugs and antibiotics.
Soap and detergent	Tertiary ammonia compounds, alkalies.	Fats and fatty acids, glycerol, polyphosphates, sulphonated hydrocarbons.
Food processing	—	Highly putrescible organic matter and pathogens
Paper and pulp	Sulphides, bleaching liquors	Cellulose fibres, bark, wood, sugars and organic acids.

This step involves chemical oxidation of wastewater by strong oxidising agents like chlorine gas, perchlorate salts, ozone gas and ultra-violet (UV) radiation.

After tertiary treatment, the wastewater is discharged into natural waters and may be used for irrigation.

Control of water pollution. It is very difficult to check the pollution of water but the intensity of pollution can be minimised to a great extent by the following methods :

1. Adequate sewage treatment. Raw sewage should not be dumped into rivers or oceans. Before its release into them, sewage should be properly treated in sewage treatment plants.

2. Treatment of industrial effluents. The industrial effluents should be cleaned before they are discharged into rivers.

3. Recycling. The best method of prevention and control of water pollution is the recycling of various kinds of wastes. Dung of cows and buffaloes can be used for the production of **gobar gas**, a cheap source of fuel and also of manure.

Ganga Action Plan

As referred to, it is one of the largest projects adopted recently by the Government of India, with a cost of nearly 292 crores of rupees, to clean Ganga water.

Ganga, the sacred river of India, is one of first ten mighty rivers of the world. It travels nearly 2,525 km through U.P., Bihar and West Bengal supporting about 45 million people. Once, the purest water of Ganga is now polluted at a number of places by the pollutants of domestic and industrial wastes (see Table 15.2). An estimate suggests that nearly 1,200 million litres of waste water are released everyday in it from nearly 27 major cities situated at its banks. At Varanasi, a city in U.P., it receives the largest amount of biological and chemical filths from millions of people taking bath every year. Besides this, nearly 60 million litres of untreated sewage are dumped into it every day. It also receives ashes of about 40,000 human bodies, about 10,000 incompletely burnt dead human bodies and those of the dead bodies of animals are dumped annually into it at Varanasi. A survey conducted by CBPCWP (Central Board for the Prevention and Control of Water Pollution) suggests that B.O.D. in the river reaches upto 9.7 mg/litre as against the acceptable limit of 3 mg/litre.

However, realising the consequences of the pollution of Ganga water, Government of India has recently prepared a project to clean its water; this project is called **Ganga Action Plan**. This project is to be implemented in phases. This Action Plan covers nearly 27 cities (6 in U.P., 4 in Bihar and 17 in West Bengal). Government has established "**Ganga Project Directorate**" in 1985 as a wing of the **Department of Environment** to coordinate the activities taken by the Action Plan and another government agency called **Central Ganga Authority** was also established in the same year to look into the implementation of the Action Plan. Now, its first phase is on with the following tasks :

1. Renovation of existing trunk sewers to prevent the outflow of sewage into the Ganga.
2. Construction of interceptors, drains and sewers to divert the flow of sewage and other liquid wastes.
3. Renovation and installation of sewage treatment plants with special emphasis on recovery of resources like methane gas for the generation of power and treated water for irrigation and agriculture.
4. Low cost sanitation schemes in the areas adjoining the river.
5. Biological conservation measures.
6. River front developments including afforestation on the banks.
7. Prevention of industrial pollution particularly from main pollutors, in cooperation with regulatory agencies and other schemes.
8. Regular monitoring of water quality.

SOIL POLLUTION

Land and soil are very essential like air and water, either directly or indirectly for the survival and maintenance of living organisms including man. Soil supports vegetation on which every living animal depends. However, like air and water soil may also get polluted. There are many natural and synthetic materials that can adversely affect the physical, chemical and biological properties of soil and seriously affect its productivity. Therefore, any substance that reduces the productivity of soil is called soil pollutant and such soil is referred to as polluted.

Soil gets polluted either directly by dumping and disposal of solid wastes or indirectly by air pollution. The major soil pollutants are different types of biocides used in agricultural practices, fertilizers, industrial wastes such as chemicals, flyash and cinders which are residues of combustion of solid fuels, garbage, discarded food, paper, plastics, rubbers, cloth, leather, asphalt, tin, iron, lead, copper, building materials, dead animals like cattle, dogs, cats, birds, and discarded goods like refrigerators and autos, etc. Huge quantity of unwanted materials causes serious disposal problems. From these, the organic wastes decompose and befoul the air; others do not decompose, hence, cause a problem for their disposal.

Biocides such as pesticides, insecticides, larvaecides, herbicides reduce the population of undesired species as also of the desired microorganisms in the soil. Therefore, their uncontrolled use affects the structure and fertility of the soil. Several pesticides or their residues are absorbed by the plants, that affect the entire food chains and food webs.

The excretory products of humans and livestock, and digested sewage sludge used as manure pollute the soil. In underdeveloped and developing countries the poor sanitary condition aggravates soil pollution. Several disease germs contained in such wastes contaminate the soil and vegetables causing severe health hazards for human beings and domestic animals.

Salination of soil also affects its productivity and degrades the quality of land. Intensive farming with poor drainage also results in salination of the soil. An estimate suggests that there are nearly six million hectares of saline land in our country. In Punjab alone nearly 6000—8000 hectares of farm land are becoming saline and unfit for agriculture. About one-sixth of the arid and semi-arid lands of the world has high salinity.

Control of Soil Pollution

Several modes adopted to control soil pollution are given below :

1. Transfer stations should be established at various places in a city for bulk transfer of refuge to ultimate discharge sites.
2. Pneumatic pipes should be used for collecting and disposing wastes.
3. Materials such as paper, plastics and glass should be recycled.
4. Animal refuge should be used for production of biogas for various domestic as well as industrial use.

Fluorosis. Fluoride containing minerals are most widely distributed in our country. Most underground and surface waters are contaminated with fluoride ions. High amounts of fluoride ions are reported in drinking water nearly in 13 states of our country. A human body can tolerate fluoride to the extent of 1.5 ppm (mg/litre of water). When its concentration reaches beyond the tolerance level, it causes fluorisis resulting into various neuro-muscular disorders, gastro-intestinal problems, allergies, dental disorders and skeletal disorders leading to crippling of people. So, it is very essential to check and minimise fluorine content in drinking and cooking waters within the range of tolerance. Industrial fluorisis has also been reported to affect agriculture and horticulture. Hence, defluoridation technology must be adopted in India, unfortunately this technology has not yet been introduced in our country.

5. Use of chemical fertilizers should be minimised by applying biofertilizers and manures.
6. Use of biocides should be minimised by adopting biological control methods.
7. Soil erosion can be checked by planting more trees and the process of deforestation should be checked.

Degradation of Land

In addition to pollution, soil and land face several other problems. These include erosion, deforestation and overgrazing, flooding and water logging, salination, desertification and ill-planned urbanization. It is estimated that if the present rate of soil depletion and land degradation continues, about one-third of arable land will be destroyed by the end of the present century.

Erosion. Removal of top, fertile layer of soil is called soil erosion. The agencies responsible for it are water, wind, ocean waves, glaciers, rains, over-grazing, over-cropping, and improper tilling. In fact, erosion occurs both in dry and wet regions and results in floods. In India, soil erosion is a serious problem in northern and north-eastern regions. Soil erosion is a global problem especially in countries like Nepal, India, China, Spain, Australia, U.S.A., USSR and Central Asia.

Deforestation and over-grazing. In India, these are the main causes of soil erosion. An estimate suggests that nearly 40,000 hectares of land are affected by wind and water erosion. The quality of top soil loss in India is about 18.5% of the total global loss. India has highest number of livestock in the world, the pressure of grazing, therefore, is intensively higher.

Roots of grasses, plants and trees are excellent binding material and keep the soil intact. Disruption of grass cover by plough, intensive grazing, deforestation, etc., loosen the soil making it suitable for being washed away by wind or rain.

Shifting cultivation. It is also one of the causes of land degradation. Many tribal communities, particularly in the north-eastern India, follow the practice of cutting trees, burning them and raising crops on resulting ashes called **jhuming**. This practice is most prevalent in Jhum forests covering an area of about 30,000,000 km^2. It degrades forests and disturbs soil stability.

Desertification. It results from erosion of top soils, shifting of sand dunes by wind and over-grazing in lands sparsely covered by grass. Many deserts are believed to be man-made.

In addition to above causes, various developmental activities like rapid urbanisation and human settlements, construction of dams, canals, mining, roads, railways, airports and establishment of industries have considerably reduced the areas of fertile and productive crop lands, woodlands and grasslands. All these have, thus, aggravated the problem of land degradation.

Control of land degradation. Degradation of land can be controlled by adopting following measures :

1. By restoring forests and grass cover, soil erosion and flood can be checked.
2. Shifting cultivation can be replaced by crop rotation practices. Mixed cropping or developing plantation crops would improve soil fertility and support a larger population.
3. Adequate drainage should be made to prevent salinity of soil.
4. Salt affected lands can be recovered by bleaching them with more water.
5. Sufficient plantation of appropriate plant species can prevent shifting sand; mulching or covering the area with artificial protective covering also prevents shifting sand.

India is basically an agricultural country. Out of India's total land mass of 305 million hectares nearly half is waste land, hence, nearly 143 million hectares are used for agricultural purposes. From remaining, nearly 18 million hectares are under urban productive use, 21 million hectares are rocky or snowcapped, 17 million hectares are culturable waste lands, 23 million hectares are fallows, 83 million hectares are forests and pasture lands.

Due to rapid increase in population the demand of land for agriculture, settlement and industry is increasing rapidly but, on the other hand good land is shrinking considerably because of soil degradation problems. Obviously, the only solution of the problem appears to develop the waste lands so that they may be used by man for their various needs.

The waste lands are grouped into two categories, *viz.*, **culturable** and **unculturable waste lands**. The culturable waste lands are those which can be brought to use by their development and reclamation. Examples of such lands are ravinous and gullied lands, surface water-logged land and marsh, saline lands, forest lands, strip lands, industrial waste lands, shifting cultivation areas, etc. The unculturable waste lands are those which cannot be used. Examples of such lands are barren rocky areas, steep slopes, snow-capped mountains, glaciers, etc. So, the development and reclamation of culturable waste lands can increase the availability of productive land.

No doubt, reclamation of waste lands involves high expenditure, expertise hands and manpower. Even then, proper steps within the financial means must be undertaken by the Government agencies immediately which will definitely solve the crisis of productive land to some extent.

Water Management in India

Implementation of environmentally unsound developmental programmes, practices and defective land use in mountains have created severe problems in the plains of countries like ours, Pakistan and Bangladesh. Nearly 400 million people are ravaged by recurring floods and their consequences. Even today, the canal irrigated land's productivity in our country is very poor in comparison to other countries due to salinity and water logging. So, proper drainage development and desalination methods should be taken to overcome such problems.

In our country, however, we have not yet thoroughly tapped underground water. It should be tapped because of the following advantages :

1. It involves very low cost, *i.e.*, installation of tube-wells.
2. It takes very short time.
3. A large amount of underground water is available even in desert areas.
4. The underground water is especially suitable in canal command areas because it helps in lowering the water tables.
5. Irrigation by underground water is economical because it does not involve storage and transportation.
6. It is easier to rouse the interest of the farmers.
7. The underground water is not vulnerable to evaporation and seepage losses.

RADIOACTIVE POLLUTION

It is a phenomenon of physical pollution to all life-supporting system like air, water and land. **Radioactivity is spontaneous disintegration of a radioactive substance which results in the emission of radioactive rays.** In fact, in this phenomenon, the nuclei of radioactive substances spontaneously disintegrate to emit protons (α-particles), electrons (β-particles) and gamma rays (short wave electromagnetic waves). The emitted radiations of radioactive elements affect the biotic community in various ways. Though the biotic community including human beings has been exposed to low levels of radiations from natural sources for several millenniam, but the danger of radiations exposure has increased in the recents years.

Sources of environmental radiations are both **natural**, comprising cosmic rays that reach the surface of the earth from space and terrestrial radiations from radioactive element's nuclei present in the earth's crust (*e.g.*, radium-224, Uranium-235 and 238, thorium-232, radon-222, potassium-40 and carbon-14), and **man-made** (*e.g.*, mining and refining of plutonium and thorium, production and explosion of nuclear weapons, nuclear power plants and fuels and preparation of radioactive isotopes).

Nuclear Weapons

Amongst the nuclear weapons, atomic bombs were first used in World War II on the twin cities of Japan, Nagasaki and Hiroshima in 1945. Since then the craze for possessing nuclear weapons has caused the nuclear race by the big powers of the world.

Tests of nuclear arms comprise the use of uranium-235 and plutonium-239 for fission and hydrogen or lithium as fusion material. Nuclear explosions are uncontrolled chain reactions, they give rise to very large neutron flux conditions that make other materials radioactive in the surroundings. Such materials include iodine-131, strontium-90, cesium-137. These materials are transformed into gases and fine particles which are thrown high up into the air like a mushroom cloud. The radioactive particles are blown away by winds and, thus, get distributed in wide areas. When rain drops containing these particles fall on the ground, the radioactivity is transferred to the soil. Thus, soil and water get polluted by radioactive substances. These substances, from the soil, enter into the food chain affecting different forms of life including man.

Radioactive isotopes like C^{14}, I^{125}, P^{32} and their compounds are widely used in scientific research. Waste waters containing these radioactive substances reach the rivers and lakes through sewer. These radioactive isotopes enter the food chain and finally reach to man (final victim of radioactive pollution) through fish. Man also receives radiations voluntarily from diagnostic X-rays and radiation therapy for cancer. People living in nearby areas and also those who work in nuclear reactors, fuel processors and power plants are vulnerable to radiation exposure.

The radiation exposure sources may be summarised as under :

1. Natural

A. Cosmic rays

B. Environmental

(*i*) Terrestrial

(*ii*) Atmospheric

(*iii*) Internal

2. Man-made

A. Diagnostic exposures, *i.e.*, medical and dental
(X-rays and radiation therapy)

B. Nuclear explosions, leakages and exposures
(Radioactive fallout, nuclear reactor wastes, etc.)

C. Occupational exposures

D. Miscellaneous exposures
(TV. luminous dials, luminous markers, isotope tagged products, etc.)

The nuclei of radioactive elements possess a constant rate of disintegration. Half-life is the time taken for half of the atoms to disintegrate. This varies from a fraction of second to thousands of years. The nuclei of elements having long half-life are usually the main sources of environmental concern.

Effects of Radioactive Pollution

Atomspheric and climatic conditions such as wind, temperature, rainfall and also half-life, energy releasing capacity and rate of diffusion of the radioactive pollutants determine their effects. However, some generalized effects are listed below :

1. In lower doses, it can affect seriously and impair their functions.
2. In higher doses it can cause instantaneous death.
3. Long and repeated exposures can cause cancer and leukemia, and induce mutations.
4. The mutant genes having deleterious effects can persist and passed on to the progeny where they show their effects.

Control of Radioactive Pollution

In fact, there is no cure of radiation damage, hence, every precaution should be taken to prevent radioactive pollution, such as :

1. Leakages of radioactive substances from nuclear reactors, careless handling, transport and use of radioactive fuels, fission products and radioisotopes have to be totally stopped.
2. Safety measures against accidents in the power plants, fuel processors, nuclear reactors should be strictly enforced to avoid any chance of leakage.
3. The disposal of waste must be very safe.
4. Regular monitoring through frequent sampling and quantitative analysis has to be ensured in the risk areas.
5. Use of nuclear weapons should be completely banned.

NOISE POLLUTION

Noise is defined as sound without value or any sound that is undesirable by the recipient. In other words, noise can be defined as **wrong sound, in the wrong place, at the wrong time.** Noise pollution, thus, refers to the unwanted sound dumped into the atmosphere leading to health hazards. Noise is a physical form of pollution and has no persistent effects on the life-supporting systems but it has direct effects on the recipients.

Sources of Noise Pollution

Noise is either **natural** such as thunder or **man-made**. The main sources of man-made noise in developed urban areas are automobiles such as motors, trucks, buses, scootors, fire engines, police cars, ambulances, etc., factories, industries, trains, air-planes, and accessory noise producers such as horns, sirens, musical instruments, TV, radio, transistors, barking of dogs, shouting, loud-speakers, etc. There has been a considerable increase in noise from man-made sources during the last 100 years which is now doubling after every 10 years.

Effects of Noise Pollution

The various effects of noise pollution on human beings are summarised as under :

1. Auditory effects. The most acute and immediate effect of noise pollution is impairing of hearing leading to auditory fatigue and may finally lead to deafness.

The unit of noise is deciBels (dB). Modern conversation has a noise value of 60 deciBels, any value greater than 80 dB causes noise pollution. Noise becomes unbearable at 140 dB. A man subjected for long periods continuously with 85 dB sound noise, his hearing ability is affected. A jet plane when takes off produces 120 dB and big cities where cars and trucks are continuously running produce a noise of 90 dB.

2. Non-auditory effects. These effects are very alarming as they may cause severe diseases. These effects can be briefed as under :

(*i*) Interference with speech communication.

(*ii*) Annoyance leading to ill-temper, bickering, mental disorientation and violent behaviour.

(*iii*) Loss of working efficiency due to physiological disorders. These may lead to cause neurosis, anxiety, insomnia, hypertension, cardio-vascular diseases, hepatic stress, giddiness, nausea, fatigue, visual disturbance, change in skin temperature and blood circulation, quickening of human foetus's heart rate and malformation of its nervous system.

Control of Noise Pollution

The different methods to control noise pollution are as under :

1. Control of noise at source may be achieved by designing and fabricating silencing devices and their use in air-craft engines, trucks, cars, auto-scooters and industrial machines.
2. Noise at source can be minimised by proper lubrication and better maintenance of machines.
3. Noise producing parts of machines may be insulated in sound proof materials.
4. Noise producing industries should be installed away from dwelling areas.
5. Use of loudspeakers and aimplifiers should be restricted at a fixed intensity and hours of the day.
6. Stuffing of cotton balls in the ears, covering our ears with hands under noise conditions, being away from the sources of noise and using ear plugs to reduce noise pollution to the intensity of about 40–50 dB are personal protection measures.

The Central Pollution Control Board has recommended zone wise ambient noise levels. They are as follows :

Table 28.4. Zone-wise permissible Ambient Noise Levels

Zones	*Day : 6.00 to 21.00 hr*	*Night : 21.00 to 6.00 hr*
1. Industry	75 dB	70 dB
2. Commercial	65 dB	55 dB
3. Residential	55 dB	45 dB
4. Silent	50 dB	40 dB

ENVIRONMENTAL LAWS FOR CONTROLLING POLLUTION

The Insecticide Act, 1968

This act deals with the regulation of import, manufacture, sale, transport, distribution and use of insecticides with a view to prevent risk to human health and other organisms.

The Water (Prevention and Control of Pollution) Act, 1974

An Act to provide for the prevention and control of water pollution and the maintaining or restoring of wholesomeness of water, for the establishment, with a view to carrying out the purposes aforesaid, of Boards for the prevention and control of water pollution, for conferring on and assigning to such boards powers and functions relating thereto and for matters connected therewith.

In brief, this Act deals with the preservation of water quality and the control of water pollution with a concern for the detrimental effects of water pollutants on human health and also on the biological world.

The Air (Prevention and Control of Pollution) Act, 1981

An Act to provide for the prevention, control and abatement of air pollution, for the establishment, with a view to carrying out the aforesaid purposes, of Boards, for conferring on and assigning to such Boards powers and functions relating thereto and for matters connected therewith.

In brief, this Act deals with the preservation of air quality and the control of air pollution with a concern for the detrimental effects of air pollutants on human health and also on the biological world.

In 1987, important amendments to the Air Act 1981 were made and noise was recognised as an air pollutant.

The Environment (protection) Act, 1986

(*a*) In this Act, unless the context otherwise requires; 'environment' includes water, air and land and the inter-relationship which exists among and between water, air and land, and human beings, other living creatures, plants, microorganisms and property;

(*b*) 'environmental pollutant' means any solid, liquid or gaseous substance present in such concentration as may be, or tend to be, injurious to environment;

(*c*) 'environmental pollutant' means the presence in the environment of any environmental pollutant;

(*d*) 'handling', in relation to any substance, means the manufacture, processing, treatment, package, storage, transportation, use, collection, destruction, conversion, offering for sale, transfer or like of such substance;

(*e*) 'hazardous substance' means any substance or preparation which, by reason of its chemical or physicochemical properties or handling, is liable to cause harm to human beings, other living creatures, plant, micro-organism, property or the environment;

(*f*) 'occupier', in relation to any factory or premises, means a person who has, control over the affairs of the factory or the premises and includes in relation to any substance, the person in possession of the substance;

(*g*) 'prescribed' means prescribed by rules made under this Act.

In brief, this Act deals with the protection of air, water and soil quality, and the control of environmental pollutants, including noise under its purview.

GLOBAL ENVIRONMENTAL CHANGE

An outcome of the atmospheric pollution is warming of the earth's environment. This is a serious problem and in twenty-first century this may be a major global problem. The temperature of the earth has increased to some extent during the past fifty years has been exhibited in the following Fig. 28.6. This increase in temperature of atmosphere is dangerous for living organisms. The human activities are mainly responsible for global warming. Though there are several causes for global warming, however, some important ones are mentioned here: They include deforestation, industrialisation, energy production from fossil fuels, such as diesel, petroleum, coal, etc., and urbanisation. The conversion of a forest to a grazing land or a cropland through deforestation causes loss of carbon stored in soil and vegetation to the atmosphere, and affects the global carbon cycle.

Biomass burning associated with agricultural practices releases a large amount of CO_2 into the atmosphere. Besides, due to domestic and industrial coal burning, huge amount of carbon dioxide is also released in the atmosphere.

Besides carbondioxide, some other gases like methane (CH_4), nitrous oxide (N_2O) and chlorofluorocarbons (CFCs) are also responsible for increasing the temperature of the earth and its environment.

These gases CO_2, CH_4, N_2O and CFCs are **radiatively active gases**, also called **greenhouse gases** as they can absorb long wave infrared radiation.

The increased amounts of greenhouse gases in the atmosphere affect the global climate, and this phenomenon is called **global change**.

Greenhouse Gases (Greenhouse Effect)

The gaseous mantle around the globe allows a considerable portion of solar radiations to enter right upto the surface of earth which absorbs it and radiates back infra-red and heat waves. This heat is transferred to layers above, as warm layer rises and in turn passes on to higher and higher layers. The outgoing longwave infrared radiation is absorbed by the greenhouse gases normally present in the atmosphere. The atmosphere radiates part of this energy back to the earth. This downward flux of radiation, known as **greenhouse flux**, keeps the earth warm. Thus, the greenhouse gases of the atmosphere form a blanket over the earth that controls the escape of heat from the surface of earth to outer space so as to keep it warm and cosy. This phenomenon is called **greenhouse effect**.

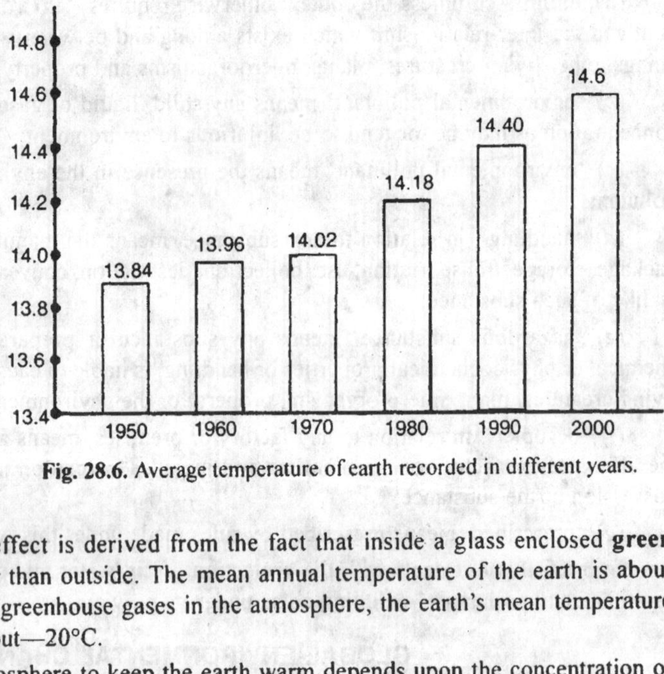

Fig. 28.6. Average temperature of earth recorded in different years.

The name, greenhouse effect is derived from the fact that inside a glass enclosed **green house**, temperature is warmer than outside. The mean annual temperature of the earth is about 15°C. If there would have no greenhouse gases in the atmosphere, the earth's mean temperature would go sharply down to about—20°C.

This capacity of the atmosphere to keep the earth warm depends upon the concentration of the greenhouse gases. The excessive increase in concentrations of greenhouse gases in the atmosphere would retain more and more of the infrared radiation, resulting in enhanced **green house effect**. The consequent increase in the global mean temperature is referred to as **global warming**.

The rise in temperature of earth's atmosphere caused due to greenhouse effect depends on the amount of CO_2 present in the atmosphere. At normal CO_2 concentration (0.03 per cent) in the atmosphere the surface temperature of the earth remains constant due to energy balance of the sun rays which strike on the earth, heat it and then radiate back into the space. This is called **energy budget**. But when there is increase in CO_2 concentration in the atmosphere, the thick layer of CO_2 prevents the heat from being radiated out into space. This layer of CO_2 thus functions as a glass pane of green house which allows the sunlight to filter through it but prevents heat from being radiated back into the outer space.

However, an international panel on climate change periodically makes an assessment of the atmospheric abundance of greenhouse gases and its possible impact on climate and other such issues.

The trends in the increase in concentrations of greenhouse gases since pre-industrial times, are as follows :

Carbon dioxide. CO_2 is the most abundant greenhouse gas in the atmosphere. This is about sixty per cent of the greenhouse gases. The level of the concentration of carbon dioxide in the

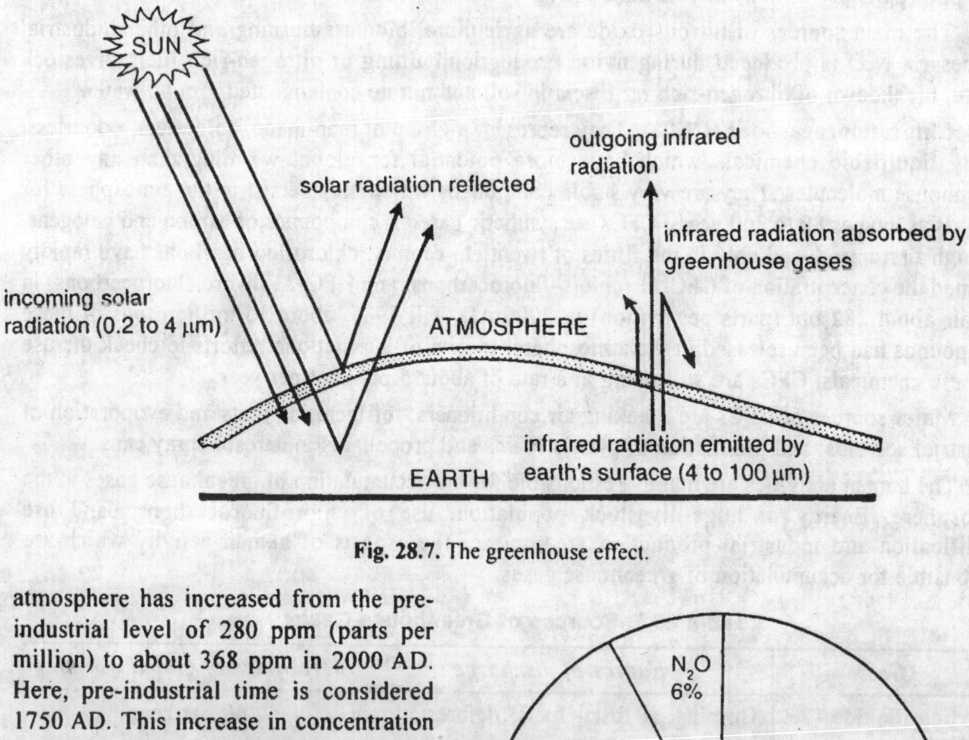

Fig. 28.7. The greenhouse effect.

atmosphere has increased from the pre-industrial level of 280 ppm (parts per million) to about 368 ppm in 2000 AD. Here, pre-industrial time is considered 1750 AD. This increase in concentration is mainly due to fossil fuel burning, deforestation and change in land use.

Methane. CH_4 is another greenhouse gas which is produced when organic matter decays under anaerobic conditions. Methane concentration in atmosphere was about 750 ppb (parts per billion) in pre-industrial level, *i.e.*, 1750 AD., which had become 1750 ppb in 2000 AD. Methane is generally produced as a result of incomplete decomposition by a group of bacteria called **methanogens**, under anaerobic conditions. The concentration of this gas is rising at a rate

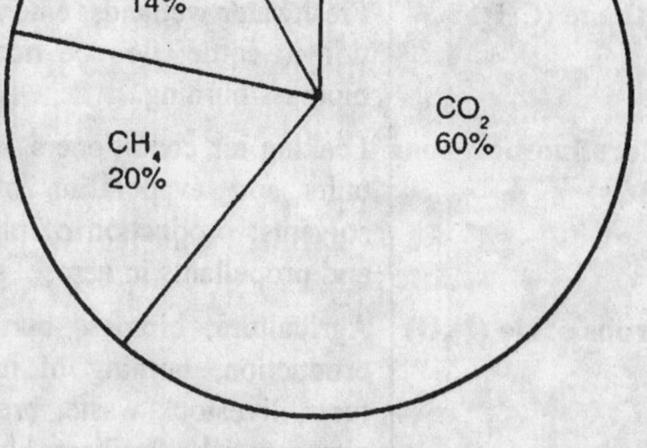

Fig. 28.8. Contribution of percentage of greenhouse gases to global warming.

of about one per cent per year. Between the years 1980-90 about 15 per cent of the total warming has been attributed to this gas alone.

The major sources of methane are : freshwater wetlands, enteric fermentation in cattle, and flooded rice fields. Biomass burning is also a source of methane. In the atmosphere, methane undergoes oxidation to carbon dioxide and water, both of which tend to emphasize the greenhouse effect.

Nitrous oxide. N_2O is another troublesome greenhouse gas. Other oxides of nitrogen are reacted upon or cleared rapidly, while nitrous oxide undergoes decomposition very slowly, and therefore, it tends to accumulate in the atmosphere. The concentration of nitrous oxide in the atmosphere has increased from about 270 ppb in pre-industrial time (*i.e.*, 1750 AD.) to about 316 ppb (parts per billion) in year 2000 AD.

The main sources of nitrous oxide are agriculture, biomass burning and other industrial processes. N_2O is produced during nylon production,burning of nitrogen-rich fuels, livestock waste, breakdown of nitrogen-rich fertilisers in soil and nitrate contaminated ground water.

Chlorofluorocarbons (CFCs). They represent a group of man-made, colourless, odourless, easily liquifiable chemicals which have more potential for global warming than any other greenhouse molecules. They are very stable compounds which may persist in the atmosphere for periods as long as 80 to 260 years. CFCs are synthetic gaseous compounds of carbon and halogens. Though first introduced only in the fifties of twentieth century, chlorofluorocarbons have rapidly attained the concentration of CFC-11 (chloro-fluorocarbons) and HFC-23 (hydro-fluorocarbons) in the air about 282 ppt (parts per trillion) in 2000 AD. Till 1985, about 15 million tons of these compounds had been released in the atmosphere. Inspite of international efforts to check the use of these chemicals, CFCs are still rising at a rate of about 5 per cent per year.

Major sources of CFCs are : leaking air conditioners, refrigeration units and evoporation of industrial solvents; and production of plastic foams and propellants in aerosol spray cans.

The human activities are mainly responsible for the accumulation of greenhouse gases in the atmosphere. Energy of huge livestock population, use of chlorofluorocarbons, land use modification and industrial production are some of the aspects of human activity which are responsible for accumulation of greenhouse gases.

Table 28.5. Sources of Greenhouse Gases

Gas	*Source of discharge*	*Percentage of global warming*
Carbon dioxide (CO_2)	Burning of fossil fuels; deforestation; change in land use.	60 per cent
Methane (CH_4)	Freshwater wetlands; enteric fermentation in cattle; flooded rice fields and biomass burning.	20 per cent
Chlorofluorocarbons (CFCs)	Leaking air conditioners, refrigeration units and evaporation of industrial solvents; production of plastic foams and propellants in aerosol spray cans.	14 per cent
Nitrous oxide (N_2O)	Agriculture, biomass burning; nylon production, burning of nitrogen-rich fuels, livestock waste, breakdown of nitrogen-rich fertilisers in soil and nitrate contaminated ground water.	6 per cent

Percentage of greenhouse gases. It is estimated that carbon dioxide contributes about 60 per cent of the total global warming. The share of methane is 20 per cent, while that of chlorofluorocarbons is 14 per cent. However, a smaller contribution to global warming is made by nitrous oxide, *i.e.*, 6 per cent.

EFFECTS OF GREENHOUSE GASES

The increasing abundance of greenhouse gases in the atmosphere has the following three main effects :

(*i*) CO_2 fertilisation effect on plants

(*ii*) Global warming and

(*iii*) Depletion of ozone (O_3) layer in the stratosphere.

Carbondioxide (CO_2) Fertilisation Effect on Plants

The data produced in USA have shown that atmospheric carbondioxide concentration has been rapidly rising since 1959 as shown in the graph. If such rising trend continues, by the end of twenty first century the atmospheric concentration of CO_2 shall increase to a level between 540 and 970 ppm.

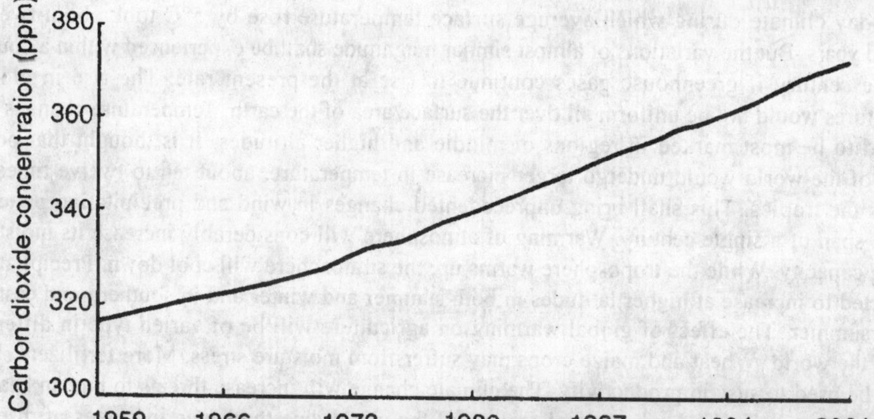

Fig. 28.9. Increase in CO_2 concentration in atmosphere from 1959 to 2001.

When the CO_2 concentration of the atmosphere is more or less doubled, the growth of many plants, *i.e.*, C_3 plants in particular, under favourable conditions of water, nutrients, light and temperature, could increase by about thirty per cent on average, in the short term of few years or so.

The response of plants to elevated concentrations of CO_2 is called **carbon dioxide fertilisation effect.**

Due to increased carbondioxide concentration, the rate of photosynthesis also increases, and the stomatal conductance decreases due to partial closure of stomata. Hence, the transpiration rate reduces, and water-use efficiency increases.

Such effect allows many species to grow successfully in regions of water scarcity.

Under higher atmospheric carbon dioxide concentrations, plants allocate, a greater proportion of photosynthate to roots. However, greater root production increases development of mycorrhiza and fixation of nitrogen in root nodules, thus, makes possible the plants to grow in soils which are poor in nutrition.

However, in natural conditions the beneficial effects of increased carbon dioxide may not be there because of negative effects of global warming.

Possible Effects of Global Warming

Global records of earth's surface temperatures indicate that a warming of about 0.6° (*i.e.*, 0.3° – 0.7°C) has occurred during the last century alone. Results from recent climatic models suggest that mean global temperatures would rise by 2° – 6°C during the twenty first century, if we assume that carbon dioxide concentration increases to 600 ppm (parts per million). The predicted global warming in near future has the potential to affect the (*i*) weather and climate, (*ii*) sea level change, (*iii*) distribution and phenology of species and (*iv*) food production and the fishery resources in the oceans.

(*i*) **Effects on weather and climate.** As already mentioned in the preceding paragraph, the global mean temperature has increased about 0.6°C in the twentieth century. It is thought, that mean global temperature may increase by 1.4 to 5.8°C by the end of twenty first century, (*i.e.*, 2100 AD).

The projected change in mean surface temperatures may appear insignificant because variatious of this magnitude are experienced in course of seasonal or even daily weather. The world climate was very much different from what it is today. The transition from the great Ice Age to present-day climate during which average surface temperature rose by 5°C took about twelve thousand years. But the variations of almost similar magnitude shall be experienced within a course of single century if greenhouse gases continue to rise at the present rate. The rise in global temperatures would not be uniform all over the surface area of the earth. Temperature changes are expected to be most marked in regions of middle and higher altitudes. It is thought that polar regions of the world would undergo larger increase in temperature, about ten to twelve times as much as the tropics. This shall bring unprecedented changes in wind and precipitation patterns within a span of a single century. Warming of atmosphere will considerably increase its moisture carrying capacity. While the troposphere warms up, the stratosphere will cool down. Precipitation is expected to increase at higher latitudes in both summer and winter and in southern and eastern Asia in summer. The effect of global warming on agriculture will be of varied type in different parts of the world. Wheat and maize crops may suffer from moisture stress. More fertilizers shall have to be used to sustain productivity. The climate change will increase threats to human health, particularly in tropical and sub-tropical regions of the world, due to change in ranges of disease vectors, water-born pathogens, etc. Global warming shall bring with it an entirely new environment in which life though not impossible yet its existence shall be tougher to maintain.

(*ii*) **Sea level change.** Though there are so many uncertainties regarding the consequences of global warming, one of the obvious results of the general heating up of earth's surface shall be a rather rapid rise in mean sea level. Evidences suggest that in Ice Age, about 12,000 years back it was nearly 100 m lower than the present-day level. It is expected that global rise in temperature shall further enhance the rate of already rising sea level in two ways : (*i*) Large deposits of ice present on earth's surface shall melt, which will add more water to the oceans. (*ii*) Rise in temperature shall also cause thermal expansion of the upper layers of the water.

Sea level has been raised by 1 to 2 mm per year during the twentieth century. It is expected that by the end of twenty first century (*i.e.*, 2100 AD.), the global mean sea level can increase upto 0.88 m over the 1990 level. A rise of even half a meter in sea level would largely effect human population, one-third of which lives within 60 km of a coastline.

Thus, many of the world's important cities and coastal areas will come under the threat of flood, and several low-lying islands will be submerged.

The flooding of coastal salt marshes and estuaries will deprive many important birds and fish their breeding grounds and their extinction will be imminent.

Thus, sea-level rise is predicted to have negative impacts on human settlements, such as tourism, fresh-water supplies, fisheries, wetlands, etc.

(*iii*) **Effects on distribution and phenology of species.** As the climatic belts shift away from equator towards poles, vegetation will also shift in the same direction to stay in favourable climatic conditions. Those species, which will not do so shall die. There will be losses of genetic resources on large scale. Only hardy and resistant forms shall come up and survive. For example, with a global temperature rise by 2 to 5°C during the twenty first century, the temperate region vegetation may shift 250-600 km poleward.

As trees are more sensitive to temperature stress, a rapid rise in temperature may cause large scale death of trees and there replacement by scrub vegetation.

As temperature changes will affect wind and precipitation patterns also water could play an important role in altering the biotic communities. It has been suggested that some rise in precipitation, however, shall be balanced by an enhanced evaporation and this could lead to water deficit and moisture stress in many regions of the world. Insects and pests may increase as warmer conditions could be more favourable to their growth and coupled with higher humidity pathogens shall multiply.

(*iv*) **Food production.** Increased temperature will cause eruption of plant diseases and pests. Besides, there will be explosive growth of weeds and increased basal rate of respiration of plants. Thus, all these factors will be responsible for decrease of crop production.

However, small temperature increase may slightly enhance crop productivity in temperate regions, but larger temperature changes will reduce crop productivity there also.

Even a small rise in temperature will have detrimental effect on crop-productivity, both in tropical and sub-tropical regions.

It is expected that rice yield alone, in southeast Asia will go down by 5 per cent for each 1°C rise in temperature. However, in spite of beneficial carbon dioxide fertilisation effect, the overall world crop productivity will decline considerably due to projected global warming, and the food supply of the whole world shall be affected.

As the climatic belts will shift away from equator towards poles, vegetation will shift in the same direction to stay in favourable climatic conditions. Those species which shall be unable to do so, they will die.

There will be losses of genetic resources on large scale. Only hardy and resistant species shall come up and survive. An altogether changed biotic spectrum shall replace the earlier ones and almost all important biomes shall be affected.

Alterations in cropping pattern shall occur and pest resistant varieties more suitably to warmer conditions shall have to be developed. In brief greenhouse warming (global warming) shall bring with if an entirely new environment in which life though not impossible yet its existence shall be tougher to meet with.

Approaches to Deal with Global Warming

Some strategies which could reduce the global warming are as follows :

(*i*) Reduction of the greenhouse gas emissions by the use of limited fossil fuels, by developing alternative renewable sources of energy, such as solar energy, wind energy, etc.

(*ii*) By increasing the vegetation cover, particularly the forests, for photosynthetic utilisation of corbon dioxide.

(*iii*) By using minimum nitrogen fertilisers in agriculture, so that, the N_2O emissions may be reduced.

(*iv*) By developing substitutes for chlorofluorocarbons (CFCs).

Besides, above mentioned strategies, adaptations to address localised impacts of climate change shall be important.

Stratospheric Ozone Depletion

Sun emits radiations at all wavelengths. Of these, radiations important to our planet are : ultraviolet (UV) radiations, light rays, and infrared rays or heat waves. Radiations of visible spectrum and infrared rays carry little energy which does not harm living beings. However, the energy content of ultraviolet radiations is larger than the limits of tolerance of a living cell, and therefore, is harmful or even lethal to a living system.

Stratospheric O_3 layer. High up in the stratosphere, that is, about 20 to 26 km above the sea level, short wavelength ultraviolet radiations are absorbed by molecular oxygen which splits up into its constituent atoms. These atoms combine with molecular oxygen to produce ozone.

$$O_2 \xrightarrow{\text{UV rays}} O + O$$

$$O_2 + O \xrightarrow{\text{UV rays}} O_3$$

Thus, ozone is a result of photochemical reactions in which the starting molecule is oxygen. Along with this reaction another photochemical reaction which causes breakdown of ozone molecules due to absorption of radiations also occur :

$$O_3 \longrightarrow O_2 + O$$

$$O_3 + O \longrightarrow 2O_2$$

The two reactions, *i.e.*, the formation and destruction of ozone molecule normally balances each other and ultimately result in effective absorption of short wavelength ultraviolet radiations in the stratospheric region. Life underneath is thus protected from the biocidal solar radiations.

Most of the ozone present in the atmosphere, almost 90 per cent is concentrated in the stratosphere at an altitude of about 20 to 26 km above the surface of earth. The thickness of the vertical column of stratospheric ozone layer, condensed to standard temperature and pressure, averages 0.29 cm above the equator and may exceed 0.40 cm above the poles at the end of the winter season. Though maximum amount of ozone production occurs over equator, yet its concentration is lowest here, as most of the ozone formed is displaced towards the poles with massive movement of atmospheric air.

Ozone shield. The stratospheric ozone layer acts as the ozone shield, which protects the earth biota from harmful effects of strong UV radiation. Absorption of UV radiation by ozone layer increases more rapidly with its thickness. Thus, maximum amount of UV radiation passing through the atmosphere reaches the earth surface in the tropics, *i.e.*, near the equator, and this amount decreases towards the poles.

The concentration of ozone in the stratosphere changes with seasons. In spring season (February to April), this is highest, while during fall season (July to October), this is lowest.

Ozone hole. During the period 1956-1970, the spring season O_3 layer thickness above Antarctica varied from 280 to 325 Dobson Unit (DU), *i.e.*, 1 DU = 1 ppb (part per billion). The thickness was sharply reduced to 225 DU in 1979 and to 136 DU in 1985. Later the O_3 layer thickness continued to decline to about 94 DU in 1994.

The decline in spring time ozone layer thickness is termed **ozone hole**. The ozone hole was first discovered in 1985 over Antarctica. The presence of ozone hole was also discovered above

Arctic in 1990. The global average total column ozone amount for the period 1997-2001 was about 3 per cent below the pre-1980 average values.

Ozone hole is formed by intense UV activity on CFCs. It starts appearing at the end of winter, shows maximum display in spring and disappears in summer. This is because in winter the air is heavy and industrial gases like CFCs get concentrated over an area in Antarctica where the maximum damage of ozone layer has been noticed. In Antarctica CFCs bearing winds in winter become frozen to form ice crystals. During spring time when ice melts the trapped CFCs and ClO are freed at once which in turn release nascent chlorine to attack ozone. Thus, ozone hole becomes large in the spring season.

CFCs, CH_4 and N_2O escape into the stratosphere and cause destruction of O_3 there. Most damaging effect is of CFCs (chlorofluorocarbons) which produce active chlorine (*i.e.*, Cl and ClO radicals) in the presence of UV radiation. These radicals catalytically destroy ozone and convert it into oxygen. CH_4 and N_2O also cause ozone destruction through a series of reactions.

For making above mentioned discoveries related to O_3 destruction, Sherwood Rowland and Mario Molina, along with Paul Crutzen, were awarded Nobal Prize for chemistry in 1995.

Effect of ozone depletion. Ozone layer shields us from biocidal UV radiations. Depletion of stratospheric ozone concentration shall result in an increased penetration of UV–B radiations. A higher loss of stratospheric ozone could cause entry of not only UV–B radiations but also UV–C radiations. This could turn the geological clock back to the era when the ozone umbrella was very thin. Terrestrial life shall be drastically affected so also will be aquatic life which occurs in shallow waters.

The thinning of the O_3 layer results in an increase in the UV–B radiation reaching the earth surface. A 5 per cent loss of ozone results in a 10 per cent increase in UV–B radiation.

In humans the increased UV–B radiation increases the chances of cataract and skin cancer. This also diminishes the functioning of immune system.

Increased levels of UV–B radiation affect photosynthesis, and damage nucleic acids in living organisms. UV–B radiation inhibits photosynthesis in most phytoplankton as it penetrates through the clear open sea waters. Thus, the whole food chain of the organisms would be affected that depend on phytoplankton for thier food.

INTERNATIONAL CONCERN FOR MITIGATING GLOBAL CHANGE

Global warming is the global concern. The long term challenge of stabilising the atmospheric concentrations of greenhouse gases requires that global emissions be significantly lowered than what they are today. In this context, the representatives of many countries assembled from time to time to pass some resolutions, which can be implemented.

Montreal Protocol. In 1987, seventy seven industrially developed countries signed the Montreal Protocol. This conference was held at Montreal. This was a landmark international agreement to protect the stratospheric ozone by agreeing to limit the production and use of ozone-depleting substances. It was decided in the conference to limit the use of CFCs and cut level of CFCs production to 50 per cent by 1999. To-date, more than 175 countries have signed the Montreal Protocol. However, India and China did not sign the Protocol. Developed countries have also agreed to establish a multilateral fund under Montreal Protocol to provide financial support to developing countries for that purpose.

London Protocol. In 1990, London Protocol was signed. In London Protocol, India, China and several other countries demanded more time to reduce CFCs consumption. However, the developed countries agreed to stop CFCs consumption completely by 2000 AD, and for developing nations the time limit was extended to 2010 AD.

Toronto Conference. In 1988, the world conference on the changing atmosphere was held in Toronto (Canada). There it was decided to reduce 20 per cent carbon dioxide emissions by the year 2005.

Earth Summit. In 1992, The First Earth Summit was held in Rio de Janeiro, Brazil. The Earth Summit, was held under the banner of UNCED (*i.e.*, The United Nations Conference on Environment and Development). This summit, established the principles for reducing greenhouse gas emission.

Kyoto Protocol. The Kyoto Protocol, approved by a follow-up conference held in Kyoto, Japan, during December 1997, has specified the commuitments of different countries to mitigate climate change. This protocol has established the rules to reduce overall greenhouse gas emissions to a level at least 5 per cent below the 1990 level by 2008-2012.

At present, on the basis of Montreal Protocol, India has established **ozone cell** under the Ministry of Forests and Environment with the help of UNDP (United Nations Development Programme). By now, India has developed R-22, and R-134 as CFCs substitutes which are presently at trial stage.

SUMMARY

1. Pollution may be defined as an undesirable change in physical, chemical or biological characteristics of air, water and land, resulting in air pollution, water pollution and soil pollution.
2. There are five types of primary air pollutants : (*i*) particulate matter, (*ii*) carbon monoxide (CO), (*iii*) hydrocarbons (HCs), (*iv*) sulphur dioxide (SO_2) and (*v*) nitrogen oxides (NO_2).
3. Secondary air pollutants are formed during chemical reactions between primary air pollutants and other atmospheric constituents, such as water vapour.
4. Different types of control measures are adopted to combat pollution from gaseous and particulate matters in industrial emissions and automobile exhausts.
5. Types of water pollutants may be (*i*) biological, such as pathogens like viruses, bacteria, protozoa, blue-green algae and helminths, (*ii*) chemical, *e.g.*, organic chemicals like biocides, polychlorinated biphenyls (PCBs) and (*iii*) inorganic chemicals, such as phosphates, nitrates, fluoride, etc., and also heavy metals, such as arsenic, lead, cadmium, mercury, etc., and (*iv*) physical, such as hot water from industries, oil spills from oil carriers, etc.
6. Water pollutants adversely affect the physical, chemical and biological health of the aquatic ecosystems, quality of ground water and human health.
7. Most of the industrial and municipal waste waters are treated in Effluent Treatment Plants (ETPs) for safe disposal.
8. Soil pollution and land degradation usually result from different human activities, such as waste dumping, agricultural practices, deforestation, mining operations and urbanisation.
9. Control measures for soil pollution are : safe disposal and management of soil wastes from industries and human habitations.
10. Noise pollution : man-made noise that originates from industry, transport, sound amplifiers pollute our environment.
11. Several laws have been enacted in India for controlling air water, soil and noise pollution.
12. Major issues of global environmental change are global warming and ozone depletion in stratosphere.
13. Naturally occurring greenhouse gases, such as carbon dioxide, methane and nitrous oxide, in the atmosphere absorb long-wave radiations and help in maintaining the average temperature of earth around 15°C.
14. The increase in concentrations of greenhouse gases is casusing enhanced green house effect, increased global temperature, sea level rise, and change in rainfall pattern.
15. The ozone layer of stratosphere plays an important role by protecting the living organisms from the harmful effects of ultraviolet radiations.

16. Ozone hole is referred to as thinning of stratospheric ozone layer during spring. For the first time, ozone hole was discovered over Antarctica, but it also occurs over the Arctic region.

17. The man-made chemicals such as chlorofluorocarbons (CFCs) are mainly responsible for ozone depletion.

TERMS TO REMEMBER

Acid rain. The ways, in which acids from the atmosphere are deposited on the earth.

Air pollution. Degradation of air quality and natural atmospheric condition.

Algal bloom. Profuse growth of algae.

Anthropogenic pollution. Man-made pollution, *e.g.*, industrial pollution, agricultural pollution.

Biodegradable pollutants. The pollutants, which can be decomposed efficiently by the decomposers, *e.g.*, market garbage, livestock wastes, etc.

Brown air. Nitrogen oxides cause reddish brown haze in traffic congested city air, called brown air.

Biochemical oxygen demand (BOD). A measure of oxygen required by aerobic decomposers for the biochemical degradation of organic materials (*i.e.*, biodegradable materials) in water.

Biological magnification. The phenomenon through which certain pollutants get accumulated in tissues in increasing concentrations along the food chain.

Carbon dioxide fertilisation effect. The response of plants to elevated concentrations of CO_2.

Chlorofluorocarbons (CFCs). They are non-toxic and non-flammable, highly stable and synthetic gaseous compounds of carbon and halogens.

Chemical oxygen demand (COD). The measure of oxygen equivalent of the requirement for oxidation of total organic matter present in water.

Decibel (dB). The unit of sound level.

Earth Summit. Held at Rio de Janeiro, Brazil in 1992.

Eutrophication. The process of nutrient enrichment of water, and consequent loss of species diversity, is called eutrophication.

ETP. Effluent Treatement Plant. The industrial and municipal waste waters are treated in this plant prior to disposal in water bodies.

Grey air. In areas of lesser solar radiation, smog formation is incomplete and the air is referred to as 'grey air'.

Greenhouse gases. These gases (CO_2, CH_4, N_2O and CFCs) are radiatively active gases, because they can absorb, long wave infrared radiation.

Global change. The increased amounts of greenhouse gases in the atmosphere that affect the global climate, the phenomenon is global change.

Greenhouse flux. Downward flux of radiation.

Greenhouse effect. The atmospheric greenhouse gases forming a blanket over the earth, control the escape of heat from the earth's surface to outer space so as to keep it warm and hospitable, the phenomenon is greenhouse effect.

Global warming. The increase in the global mean temperature.

Hydrocarbons (HCs) or volatile organic carbons. They are compounds composed of hydrogen and carbon.

Incineration. Burning the solid wastes in presence of oxygen.

Indicator species. Tolerant or resistant species that survive in highly polluted water.

Kyoto Protocol. Conference held in Kyoto, Japan, in 1997.

Montreal Protocol. A landmark international agreement to protect the stratospheric ozone, in Montreal, in 1987.

Noise pollution. The loud disturbing sound dumped into the ambient atmosphere without regard to the adverse effects it may have.

Non-biodegradable. The pollutants, which are not decomposed by decomposers.

Oil spills. The accidental discharge of petroleum in oceans or estuaries.

Ozone hole. The decline in spring-time ozone layer thickness is termed ozone hole.

Photochemical smog. Mainly formed in traffic congested metropolitan cities where warm conditions and intense solar radiation are present. This is composed mainly of ozone (O_3), peroxyacetyl nitrate (PAN) and NO_2.

Physical pollution. Pollution caused by changes in physical properties of water, *e.g.*, change in temperature.

Smog. Combination of smoke ang fog.

Synergism. Increase in toxicity from primary pollutants to secondary pollutants.

QUESTION BANK

Very Short Answer Questions

1. Define pollution.
2. Classify pollution, on the basis of part of environment.
3. Name types of pollution in terms of origin.
4. Give at least four types of pollution in terms of physical nature of pollutants.
5. Give the important categories of the pollutants from the ecosystem viewpoint.
6. Give four examples of biodegradable pollutants.
7. Expand PAN.
8. Expand BOD.
9. What is COD ?
10. Expand DDT.
11. Expand BHC.
12. Give four examples of non-biodegradable materials.
13. What are hydrocarbons ?
14. Give five examples of primary air pollutants.
15. Give two examples of secondary air pollutants.
16. What is grey air ?
17. What is acid rain ?
18. What is combustion ?
19. Classify water pollutants.
20. What is algal bloom ?
21. What is Minamata Disease, where this was discovered ?
22. Name greenhouse gases.
23. When and where, ozone hole was discovered ?
24. When Montreal Protocol was signed ?
25. When and where Earth Summit was held ?
26. What are aerosols ?
27. Define greenhouse effect.
28. Which aerosol pollutant is present in jet aeroplane emission ?
29. Name main components of photochemical smog.
30. What is jhuming ?
31. Expand ODS.
32. Which one of the following is not a greenhouse gas ?

    CO_2, CH_4, O_3, CFCs

ANSWERS

1. Pollution is an undesirable change in physical, chemical or biological characteristics of air, land or water, caused by excssive accumulation of pollutants; **2.** Air pollution, water pollution and soil pollution; **3.** Natural or anthropogenic; **4.** Gaseous pollution, dust pollution, thermal pollution and noise pollution; **5.** Biodegradable and non-biodegradable pollutants; **6.** Market garbage, livestock wastes, municipal sewage, faecal matter; **7.** Peroxyacetyl nitrate; **8.** Biochemical oxygen demand; **9.** Chemical oxygen demand; **10.** Dichloro diphenyl trichloro ethane; **11.** Benzene hexachloride; **12.** DDT, BHC, waste plastic bottles, polyethylene bags; **13.** Compounds composed of hydrogen and carbon, also called volatile organic carbon; **14.** Particulate matter, carbon monoxide (CO), hydrocarbons (HCs), sulphur dioxide (SO_2) and nitrogen oxides (NO_x); 15. Photochemical smog and acid rain; **16.** Where smog formation is incomplete, the air is referred to as grey air; **17.** Acid rain refers to several ways in which acids from the atmosphere are deposited on the earth; **18.** A process, in which oxidisable gaseous pollutants are completely burnt at a high temperature; **19.** (*i*) Biological, (*ii*) chemical and (*iii*) physical; **20.** Profuse growth of algae; **21.** Mercury poisoning due to consumption of fish captured from Hg-contaminated Minamata Bay in Japan, detected in 1952; **22.** CO_2, CH_4, N_2O and CFCs; **23.** The ozone hole was first discovered in 1985 over Antarctica; **24.** In 1987; **25.** Earth Summit was held at Rio de Janeiro, Brazil in 1992; **26.** Chlorofluorocarbons compressed in the form of droplets released by jet aeroplanes; **27.** Increase in environmental temperature due to increased concentration of green house gases (CO_2, CH_4, N_2O and CFCs); **28.** Chlorofluorocarbons (CFCs); **29.** PAN and O_3; **30.** Raising crops on the resulting ash due to burning of trees; **31.** Ozone Depleting substances; **32.** O_3.

Short Answer Questions

1. What is photochemical smog composed of ? How does this affect the plants ?
2. Define pollution. Compare the biodegradable and non-biodegradable pollutants.
3. What do you understand by fixed and mobile sources of air pollution ?
4. Distinguish between the primary and secondary air pollutants.
5. What is particulate matter ? How do particulate matters harm human health ?
6. What is photochemical smog ? How does smog affect the biological world ?
7. What is acid rain ? What are its effects on plants ?
8. Distinguish between point and non-point sources of water pollution.
9. State the consequences of stratospheric ozone depletion.
10. What do you mean by 'biochemical oxygen demand' (BOD) ?
11. What is Minimata disease ? Where and when this was detected ?
12. Name three types of particulate pollutants of air.
13. What is thermal pollution ?
14. Give two harmful effects of ozone.
15. What causes enhanced greenhouse effect ?
16. Mention the effects of excess fluoride in drinking water.
17. What is global change ?
18. What is greenhouse effect ?
19. What are the effects of increased greenhouse gases in the atmosphere ?
20. What are the harmful effects of PAN ?
21. Explain the phenomenon of biological magnification.
22. What measures do you suggest to control pollution from automobile exhausts ?
23. Why are industrial effluents more difficult to manage than municipal sewage ? Name a disease that is caused by heavy metal contamination.
24. How can pollution by domestic sewage be controlled ?
25. Describe the ways by which soil gets polluted.
26. What is noise ? Describe briefly the effects of noise on human health.

27. Discuss the causes and effects of global warming.
28. What are the effects of ultraviolet radiations on humans ?
29. What is the environmental significance of the increasing Antarctica ozone hole ?
30. How are gaseous pollutants controlled ?
31. How can automobile exhaust be controlled ?
32. Give the steps involved in management of solid wastes.
33. What are pollutants ? How are they classified?
34. How is soil salinity caused ?
35. What do you understand by ocean water pollution ?

Long Answer Questions

1. What is meant by the ozone shield ? How do the CFCs and ozone depleting substances affect ozone shield ?
2. Explain the following :
   (*i*) Greenhouse effect
   (*ii*) CO_2 fertilisation effect
   (*iii*) Ozone hole.
3. What are the control measures used for controlling soil pollution.
4. Give an account of the possible effects of global warming.
5. What is 'ozone shield' ? How does O_3 depleting substances affect it ?
6. Give the details of various sources of air pollution.
7. Write a comprehensive note on control measures used for controlling soil pollution.
8. What is environmental pollution ? How this is being affected by human activities ?
9. Mention the steps which can reduce noise pollution.
10. How can water pollution be controlled ?
11. What is radioactivity ? Discuss the man-made radioactive pollution.

MULTIPLE CHOICE QUESTIONS (OBJECTIVE TYPE QUESTIONS)

1. Ozone layer of upper atmosphere is being destroyed by :
   (*a*) Sulphur dioxide (*b*) Photochemical oxidants
   (*c*) Chloroflurocarbons (*d*) Smog
2. Acid rain is caused by increase in the atmospheric concentration of :
   (*a*) Ozone and dust (*b*) SO_2 and NO_2 (*c*) SO_3 and CO (*d*) CO_2 and CO
3. Ozone depletion in the stratosphere will cause:
   (*a*) Increased incidence of skin cancer (*b*) Forest fires
   (*c*) Global warming (*d*) None of these.
4. Attack of asthma in certain persons may be due to :
   (*a*) Eating of some seasonal vegetables
   (*b*) Inhalation of certain air-borne pollens
   (*c*) Exposure to cold temperature
   (*d*) Absence of CO_2 in the air due to increased rate of photosynthesis.
5. Eutrophication causes decrease in :
   (*a*) Dissolved hydrogen (*b*) Dissolved salts (*c*) Dissolved oxygen (*d*) All of these
6. Positive pollution of soil is due to :
   (*a*) Reduction in soil productivity (*b*) Addition of wastes on soil
   (*c*) Excess use of fertilisers (*d*) All of these

7. If the fertilisers are added to fresh water :
(*a*) Plants will die (*b*) Eutrophication will occur
(*c*) Fish population will decrease (*d*) Overall animal population will increase
8. Photochemical smog formed in congested metropolitan cities mainly consists of :
(*a*) Oxides of nitrogen (*b*) Suspended particulate matter
(*c*) Carbon dioxide and carbon monoxide (*d*) Oxides of sulphur
9. Biological Oxygen Demand (BOD) is a measure of :
(*a*) Amount of oxygen needed by green plants during night
(*b*) Amount of carbon monoxide inseparately combined with haemoglobin
(*c*) Industrial wastes poured into water bodies
(*d*) Extent to which water is polluted with organic compounds
10. A person is suffering from impaired nervous system and madness after prolonged consumption of polluted water. Which metal is responsible :
(*a*) Hg (*b*) Ca (*c*) Mn (*d*) Pb
11. The major source of methane in India is :
(*a*) Rice fields (*b*) Wheat fields
(*c*) Sugarcane plantation (*d*) Fruit orchard
12. Natural sink of stratospheric ozone layer is :
(*a*) SO_2 (*b*) HFCs
(*c*) Ferons (*d*) Sulphur flux of oceans
13. Which of the following has been declared a killer disease under Factory Act ?
(*a*) Asbestosis (*b*) Tuberculosis (*c*) Silicosis (*d*) Shigellosis
14. Green house effect is caused by :
(*a*) Green plants (*b*) Infra red rays (*c*) UV-rays (*d*) X-rays
15. Peeling of ozone hole is due to :
(*a*) CFCs (*b*) PAN (*c*) CO_2 (*d*) Coal mining
16. Acid rains are caused due to :
(*a*) Production of SO_2 and NO_2 (*b*) Phosphates
(*c*) SO_2 and CO (*d*) All of these
17. Ozone hole refers to :
(*a*) Reduction in thickness of ozone layer in trophosphere
(*b*) Reduction of thickness of ozone layer in stratosphere
(*c*) Hole in ozone layer in stratosphere
(*d*) Increased concentration of ozone
18. Ozone umbrella is affected by :
(*a*) CFM (*b*) CO_2 (*c*) Methane (*d*) PHN
19. Greenhouse effect is because of :
(*a*) CFC
(*b*) O_3
(c) Those gases which fail to allow reflected infra-red radiations through them
(*d*) All of these
20. DDT is considered harmful because :
(*a*) It is organochloride compound (*b*) It is pesticide
(*c*) It is non-biodegradable (*d*) It is easily degradable
21. The pollutants released by jet planes are :
(*a*) Fogs (*b*) Smogs (*c*) Colloids (*d*) Aerosols

22. Greenhouse effect refers to :
(*a*) Ozone hole moon light (*b*) Global warming caused by increasing CO_2
(*c*) Increased chlorofluorocarbons (*d*) Plants grown in green houses
23. The compound associated with Bhopal gas tragedy is :
(*a*) DDT (*b*) Atomic radiations (*c*) methyl isocyanate (*d*) Malathion
24. Sudden mass scale death of fishes from O_2 depletion is more likely in case of :
(*a*) Oligotrophic lake (*b*) Mesotrophic lake (*c*) Eutrophic lake (*d*) Oxbow lake
25. The World Environment Day is on :
(*a*) 7th, August (*b*) 5th, June (*c*) 10th, April (*d*) 28th, February
26. Greenhouse effect is due to :
(*a*) Higher CO_2 concentration
(*b*) Absorption of infra-red gases and dust particles
(*c*) Both (*a*) and (*b*)
(*d*) Rarification of atmosphere
27. Gas leaked in Bhopal tragedy was :
(*a*) Potassium isocyanide (*b*) Sodium isocyanate
(*c*) Ethyl isothiocyanide (*d*) Methyl isocyanate
28. Which of the following is not a pollutant ?
(*a*) SO_2 (*b*) CO_2 (*c*) CO (*d*) NO_2
29. Which of the following on inhalation dissolves in the haemoglobin more rapidly than oxygen ?
(*a*) SO_2 (*b*) O_3 (*c*) CO (*d*) N_2O
30. The most harmful environmental pollutants are :
(*a*) Human organic wastes (*b*) Wastes from fields
(*c*) Non-biodegradable (*d*) Natural nutrients in excess
31. Acid rain is caused by :
(*a*) SO_2 (*b*) NO_2
(*c*) Both (*a*) and (*b*) (*d*) None of these
32. Smog is a combination of :
(*a*) Fire and water (*b*) Smoke and fog (*c*) Water and smoke (*d*) Air and water
33. As it travels along the food chain, the concentration of DDT :
(*a*) Increases (*b*) Stays constant (*c*) Decreases (*d*) Fluctuates randomly
34. Result of ozone hole is :
(*a*) Greenhouse effect (*b*) Global warming
(*c*) Acid rain (*d*) Increased UV radiations
35. The term biomagnification refers to :
(*a*) Increase in concentration of non-degradable pollutant through a food chain
(*b*) Increase in population size
(*c*) Growth of organisms due to food consumption
(*d*) Blowing up of environment issues by man
36. Acid rain is due to :
(*a*) Excess CO_2 (*b*) Excess O_2
(*c*) A natural phenomenon (*d*) Excess of SO_2
37. DDT-spraying on the crop results in the pollution of :
(*a*) Soil and water (*b*) Air and soil (*c*) Crops and air (*d*) Air and water
38. Which one is not dangerous for life ?
(*a*) Biopollutants (*b*) Ionosphere (*c*) Nuclear blast (*d*) Deforestation

39. Acid rain is due to :
(*a*) Sulphur dioxide pollution (*b*) Carbon monoxide pollution
(*c*) Pesticide pollution (*d*) Dust particles

40. Plants are known as purifiers of air due to process of :
(*a*) Respiration (*b*) Transpiration (*c*) Photosynthesis (*d*) Desiccation

41. Carbon monoxide is a major pollutant of :
(*a*) Water (*b*) Air (*c*) Noise (*d*) Soil

42. Air pollution effects are usually found on :
(*a*) Roots (*b*) Stems (*c*) Flowers (*d*) Leaves

43. One of the important effect of SO_2 and transformation products on plants is :
(*a*) Plasmolysis (*b*) Destruction of chlorophyll
(*c*) Destruction of Golgi bodies (*d*) Destruction of cell wall

44. Major pollutant in the jet plane emission is :
(*a*) Carbon tetrachloride (*b*) SO_2 (*c*) CO (*d*) Fluorocarbons

45. Pollutants having most lasting effects are :
(*a*) Pesticides (*b*) Smoke from chimneys
(*c*) SO_2 (*d*) CO

46. Thermal pollution is more common near :
(*a*) Hot water springs (*b*) Coal based power plants
(*c*) Tropical regions (*d*) Temperate regions

47. Pollution indicator plants :
(*a*) Purify atmosphere (*b*) Resist pollution
(*c*) Are sensitive to pollutants (*d*) Can indicate onset of rain

48. Sound becomes a hazardous noise pollution if its level is above :
(*a*) 30 dB (*b*) 80 dB (*c*) 120 dB (*d*) 150 dB

49. Pollution of water is caused by :
(*a*) Industrial effluents (*b*) Sewage (*c*) Form run off (*d*) All of these

50. Photochemical smog always contains :
(*a*) PAN and O_3 (*b*) CH_4 and O_3 (*c*) CO and O_3 (*d*) PAN and CH_4

51. Greenhouse effect is due to the presence of :
(*a*) NO_2, CO_2, SO_2, CFC (*b*) CO, CO_2 H_2
(*c*) CO, O_2, H_2, CH_4 (*d*) CO_2 and CH_4 only

52. Acid rains are caused due to :
(*a*) SO_3 only (*b*) CO_2 only (*c*) NO_2 and SO_2 (*d*) SO_3 and CO_2

53. The depletion of ozone layer is due to :
(*a*) Chlorofluorocarbons (*b*) Oxides of nitrogen (*c*) Hydrocarbons (*d*) All of these

54. The indiscriminate use of fertilizers causes :
(*a*) Air pollution (*b*) Water pollution (*c*) Soil pollution (*d*) None of these.

55. In big cities, air pollution is mainly due to :
(*a*) Burning of fossil fuels (*b*) Thermal power plants
(*c*) Sewage (*d*) Suspended particles

56. As compared to tap water, BOD of a water polluted with sewage waste would be :
(*a*) High (*b*) Low (*c*) Normal (*d*) Nil

57. Which of the following does not occur when the sewage is discharged into the rivers ?
(*a*) Eutrophication (*b*) Depletion of O_2 occurs
(*c*) Increasing O_2 (*d*) Cyanophycean bloom occurs

58. Increase in the concentration of pollutants in higher trophic levels is known as :
(*a*) Biomagnification (*b*) Biodegradation (*c*) Eutrofication (*d*) Recycling

59. Greenhouse effect is increasing due to :
(*a*) Increasing CO_2 concentration (*b*) Increasing SO_2 concentration
(*c*) Ozone hole (*d*) Increasing CFCs concentration

60. Major cause of air pollution in big cities is due to :
(*a*) Domestic exhaust (*b*) Burning of fossil fuels
(*c*) Thermal power plants (*d*) Automobile exhaust

61. Effect of pollution is on :
(*a*) Cell division (*b*) Crop rotation (*c*) Mutations (*d*) Ecological balance

62. The UV-rays in atmosphere are checked by :
(*a*) O_3 (*b*) O_2 (*c*) H_2 (*d*) Cl_2

63. Which of the following is indiçatar of SO_2 pollution ?
(*a*) Moss (*b*) Lichens (*c*) Algae (*d*) Pteridophytes

64. One of these contributes maximum air pollution :
(*a*) India (*b*) USA (*c*) Russia (*d*) Britain

65. Which of the following wili not be found in polluted water ?
(*a*) Blue-green algae (*b*) Larvae of stone fly (*c*) Water hyacinth (*d*) Sewage fungi

66. Greenhouse effect is related to :
(*a*) Global warming (*b*) Terrace gardening
(*c*) Kitchen gardens (*d*) Increased growth of algae

67. The lake, in which fishes will die in bulk, is :
(*a*) Oligotrophic lake (*b*) Eutrophic lake
(*c*) Organotrophic lake (*d*) None of these

68. Taj Mahal is threatened due to effect of :
(*a*) Chlorine (*b*) SO_2 (*c*) O_2 (*d*) Hydrogen.

69. The major contribution of greenhouse gases to the atmosphere is :
(*a*) Russia (*b*) Germany (*c*) Brazil (*d*) USA

70. In the coming time, skin-related disorders might be more common due to :
(*a*) Use of detergents (*b*) Water pollution
(*c*) Depletion of ozone layer (*d*) Air pollution

71. The CO_2 content in the atmospheric air is approximately :
(*a*) 0.034 % (*b*) 0.34 % (*c*) 3.34 % (*d*) 6.5 %

72. Phosphate pollution is mainly caused by :
(*a*) Sewage and phosphate rocks (*b*) Phosphate rocks only
(*c*) Sewage and agricultural fertilisers (*d*) Agricultural fertilisers only.

73. Formation of ozone hole is maximum over :
(*a*) Antarctica (*b*) Africa (*c*) Europe (*d*) India

74. A sewage treatment process, in which a portion of the decomposer bacteria present in the waste is recycled into the beginning of process, is called :
(*a*) Cyclic treatment (*b*) Primary treatment
(*c*) Activated sludge treatment (*d*) Tertiary treatment

75. Which important greenhouse gas other than methane is being produced from the agricultural fields ?
(*a*) Arsine (*b*) SO_2 (*c*) Ammonia (*d*) Nitrous oxide

76. If there was no CO_2 in the earth's atmosphere, the temperature of earth's surface would be :

(*a*) Dependent on amount of O_2 in the atmosphere

(*b*) Higher than the present

(*c*) Less than the present

(*d*) The same

77. Greenhouse effect with respect to global climate refers to :

(*a*) Cooling of earth (*b*) Warming of earth

(*c*) Increased rainfall and greenery (*d*) Desertification

78. Which of the following is secondary air pollutant ?

(*a*) SO_2 (*b*) CO_2 (*c*) PAN (*d*) Aerosol

79. In the year 1984, the Bhopal gas tragedy was caused by the leakage of :

(*a*) CO (*b*) SO_2 (*c*) NO_2 (*d*) Methyl isocyanate

80. What is the intensity of sound in normal conversation ?

(*a*) 10–20 decibel (*b*) 30–60 decibel (*c*) 70–90 decibel (*d*) 120–150 decibel

81. What is BOD ?

(*a*) Amount of O_2 utilised by organisms in water

(*b*) Total amount of O_2 present in water

(*c*) Amount of O_2 utilised by microorganisms for decomposition

(*d*) All of these

82. Effective Biological Resistance (EBR) is associated with :

(*a*) High temperture (*b*) Low temperature (*c*) Radiation (*d*) Pollution

83. Which of the following is a pollution-related occupational health hazard ?

(*a*) Fluorosis (*b*) Silicosis (*c*) Pneumoconiosis (*d*) Asthma

84. At present the most significant cause of dwindling biodiveristy is :

(*a*) Biological magnification of DDT (*b*) Global warming

(*c*) Deterioration of ozone layer (*d*) Destruction of habitat

85. Fluoride pollution mainly affects :

(*a*) Brain (*b*) Teeth (*c*) Heart (*b*) Kidney

86. *Escherichia coli* is used as an indicator organism to determine pollution of water with :

(*a*) Industrial effluents (*b*) Heavy metals

(*c*) Pollen of aquatic plants (*d*) Faecal matter

ANSWERS

1. (*c*)	**2.** (*b*)	**3.** (*a*)	**4.** (*b*)	**5.** (*c*)	**6.** (*d*)	**7.** (*b*)	**8.** (*c*)	**9.** (*d*)	**10.** (*d*)
11. (*a*)	**12.** (*c*)	**13.** (*a*)	**14.** (*b*)	**15.** (*a*)	**16.** (*a*)	**17.** (*b*)	**18.** (*b*)	**19.** (*c*)	**20.** (*c*)
21. (*d*)	**22.** (*b*)	**23.** (*c*)	**24.** (*c*)	**25.** (*b*)	**26.** (*c*)	**27.** (*d*)	**28.** (*c*)	**29.** (*c*)	**30.** (*c*)
31. (*c*)	**32.** (*b*)	**33.** (*a*)	**34.** (*d*)	**35.** (*a*)	**36.** (*d*)	**37.** (*a*)	**38.** (*b*)	**39.** (*a*)	**40.** (*c*)
41. (*b*)	**42.** (*d*)	**43.** (*b*)	**44.** (*d*)	**45.** (*a*)	**46.** (*b*)	**47.** (*b*)	**48.** (*b*)	**49.** (*d*)	**50.** (*a*)
51. (*a*)	**52.** (*c*)	**53.** (*a*)	**54.** (*b*)	**55.** (*a*)	**56.** (*a*)	**57.** (*c*)	**58.** (*a*)	**59.** (*a*)	**60.** (*d*)
61. (*d*)	**62.** (*a*)	**63.** (*b*)	**64.** (*b*)	**65.** (*b*)	**66.** (*a*)	**67.** (*b*)	**68.** (*d*)	**69.** (*d*)	**70.** (*c*)
71. (*a*)	**72.** (*c*)	**73.** (*a*)	**74.** (*c*)	**75.** (*d*)	**76.** (*c*)	**77.** (*b*)	**78.** (*c*)	**79.** (*d*)	**80.** (*b*)
81. (*c*)	**82.** (*b*)	**83.** (*c*)	**84.** (*d*)	**85.** (*b*)	**86.** (*d*)				

UNIT - 7
Utilization of Plants Economic Botany

29
CHAPTER

Introduction

The economic botany deals with application of botanical knowledge to the well-being of mankind. The primary necessities of man are threefold—*food, clothing and shelter*. The most essential need of man is food. The food primarily comes from plants in the forms of cereals (*e.g.*, rice, wheat, maize, oat, barley and rye), millets (*e.g.*, sorghum, pearl millet, finger millet, etc.), pulses, vegetables and fruits. For clothing again plants are indispensable. The plants that yield fibres are second only to food plants. From the times immemorial the man needed some form of clothing, and this need was fulfilled only by fibre-yielding plants. In this respect cotton occupies an all important position, supplemented by jute and some other fibres for coarse clothing. To meet an everincreasing demand for food and clothing an application of the knowledge of botany has been considered to be of great importance for better utilization of plant products. From the time immemorial shelter from the weather inclemencies and as a protection against natural enemy has been felt too much. In this respect the forest products have been of service to mankind from the very beginning of his history. The most familiar and most important, of these products is wood, which is used in all types of construction work. Other products like bamboo, reed, cane, thatch grass, etc., are of equal value for house making. With the advancement of civilization the need of man is also ever on the increase. To meet his requirements he has tried to tap plants as sources for his comforts and varied use by exploiting his scientific knowledge and has been successful in this direction to a great extent. Other useful plant products include—wood (for furniture, boat building, bridge building, railway sleepers, fuel, etc.), fibres (for gunny bags, rope, cordage, matting, canvas, carpet, etc.), drugs, tannins, dyes, paper, sugar, starch, gum, resin, rubber, vegetable fats, fatty oils, essential oils, tea, coffee, cocoa, tobacco, spices, condiments, cork, etc. Utility of bacteria, yeasts, other edible and antibiotics producing fungi, algae and lichens cannot be denied. It becomes quite evident that a knowledge of botany and its proper application led to the well-being of humanity in several ways. The more important plants and their products have been grouped in several important categories. In the present text the plants and their products have been grouped as follows:

FOOD PLANTS

Cereals and millets. *Cereals*: The cereals are the most important sources of plant food for man. They constitute the most important group in the food plants of India. The cereals are the members of family Gramineae. There are six true cereals rice, wheat, maize, barley, oat and rye. They contain a high percentage of carbohydrates, together with a considerable amount of proteins and some fats. Even vitamins are present.

Millets: They are also known as small grains. They are considered to have been cultivated in India from prehistoric times. Some of the commonly grown millets in India are sorghum, pearl millet and finger millet.

Legumes and nuts. *Legumes*: The legumes or pulses are next in importance to cereals as sources of food. They belong to the family Leguminosae. They contain more protein material than any other vegetable products. Carbohydrates and fats are also present in the legumes. The pulses form an important item in India where the majority of the population consists of vegetarians. The important Indian pulses are gram, black gram, green gram, pea, pigeon pea, lentil, etc.

Nuts: A nut is a one-celled, one-seeded dry fruit with a hard pericarp. Only a few nuts of commerce fulfil this description, *e.g.*, chestnut. The others included among nuts may be peanuts, almonds, coconuts, cashewnuts, walnuts, pistachio nuts, etc. These "so called" nuts make a valuable food material. The food value is due to a high protein and fat content.

Vegetables. The term vegetable is usually applied to edible plants which store up reserve food in roots, stems, leaves and fruits and which are eaten cooked, or raw as salad. The vegetables rank next to cereals as sources of carbohydrate food. The nutritive value of vegetables is tremendous, because of the presence of indispensable mineral salts and vitamins.

Fruits. Morphologically a fruit is the seed-bearing portion of the plant, and consists of the ripened ovary and its contents. Simple fruits are derived from a single ovary, and compound fruits from more than one. The aggregate fruits are formed from numerous carpels of the same flower,

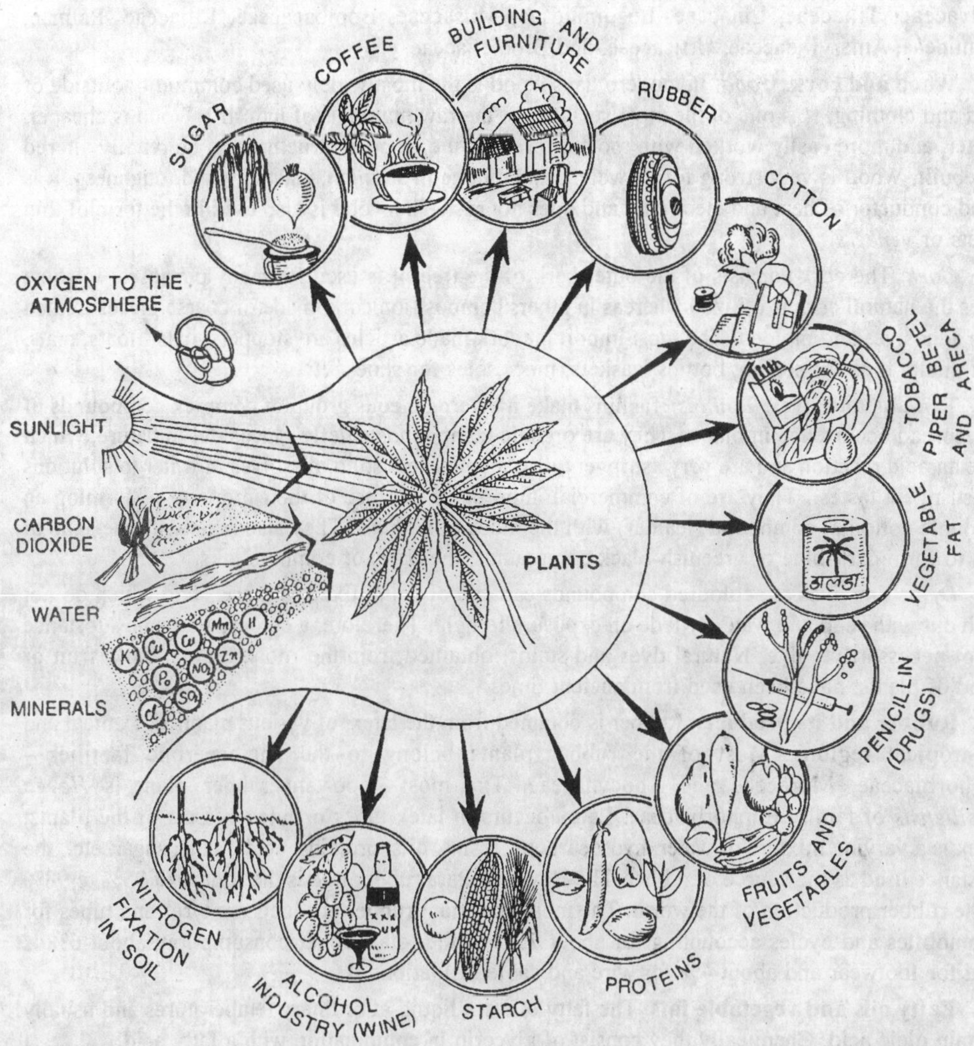

Fig. 29.1. Plants and human welfare

while composite fruits develop from ovaries of different flowers. In economic botany only those fruits are considered which are usually eaten without cooking. For convenience the fruits have been divided into two groups *tropical fruits* (*e.g.*, mango, citrus fruits, litchi, banana, guava, sugar apple, fig, papaya, pine-apple, etc.) and *temperate fruits* (*e.g.*, apple, pear, plum, peach, strawberries, grape, etc.).

PLANTS AND PLANT PRODUCTS OF INDUSTRIAL VALUE

Fibres and fibre-yielding plants. The fibre-yielding plants rank second only to food plants in their usefulness to human kind. The utilization of fibres is directly related to the advancement of civilization. As civilization advanced, the use of vegetable fibres increased greatly. They are of enormous value in our daily life. About two thousand species of the plants yield various fibres all over the world. The chief fibres of commercial importance have been classified in six groups— textile fibres (*e.g.*, cotton, flax, etc.), brush fibres, filling fibres, rough weaving fibres, natural fabrics and paper-making fibres. The most important fibre-yielding plants belong to the families— Malvaceae, Tiliaceae, Linaceae, Leguminosae, Musaceae, Bombacaceae, Liliaceae, Palmae, Gramineae, Amaryllidaceae, Urticaceae, and Bromeliaceae.

Wood and cork. *Wood*: In modern days wood is the most widely used commodity outside of food and clothing. It is one of the most versatile of the raw materials of industry. Wood is cheaper, lighter, and more easily worked with tools. Moreover the wooden structure can be readily altered or rebuilt. Wood is very strong for its weight and unique in strength, elasticity and toughness. It is a bad conductor of heat and electricity and does not rust. The wood is also used in the form of thin sheets or *veneers*.

Cork: The cork consists of the outer bark of the tree. It is used for many purposes. In some cases the natural cork is utilized whereas in others composition cork, made of coarse pieces treated with adhesives and molded. The most important cork made articles are stoppers, hats, floats, mats, tiles, metal tops for sealing bottles, gaskets, inner soles for shoes, etc.

Tannins and dyes. *Tannins*: Tannins make a heterogeneous group of complex compounds of widespread occurrence in plants. They are organic compounds chiefly glucosidal in nature, which have an acid reaction and are very astringent. It is a colourless solid, dissolves in water to solutions of astringent tastes. They are of commercial importance because of their property of forming an insoluble colloidal compound (leather) with the hides of animals. They also react with the salts of iron to form dark-blue or greenish-black compounds, the basis of common inks.

Dyes: The dyes are coloured compounds capable of being fixed to fabrics and which do not wash out with soap and water or fade on exposure to light. Therefore, a coloured organic substance is not necessarily a dye. Natural dyes and stains, obtained from the roots, leaves, bark, fruit or wood of plants, have been used from ancient times.

Rubber and its products. Rubber is obtained from the latex, of various plants of tropical and sub-tropical regions. Most of the rubber plants belong to the angiospermic families— Euphorbiaceae, Moraceae and Apocynaceae. The most important rubber plant is *Hevea brasiliensis* of family Euphorbiaceae. Latex occurs in latex tubes or latex vessels of the plants. Latex is a varying mixture of water, hydrocarbons, resins, oils, proteins, acids, salts, sugar, etc., the substance used as the source of rubber. The Hevea or Para rubber tree is the source of 95% to 98% of the rubber production of the world. The most important rubber products are tyres and tubes for automobiles and cycles accounting for about 75% of the total rubber consumption, about 6% is used for footwear and about 4% for wire and cable insulations.

Fatty oils and vegetable fats. The fatty oils are liquid at ordinary temperatures and usually contain oleic acid. Chemically they consist of glycerin in combination with a fatty acid.

The fats are solid at ordinary temperatures and contain stearic or palmitic acid. When a fat is boiled with an alkali, it decomposes and the fatty acid unites with alkali to form soap.

Usually the fatty oils are stored up in seeds of the plants belonging to many angiospermic families. Sometimes, to a less extent they are also stored in fruits, stems and other plant organs. Several fatty oils are edible and used as cooking media. These edible oils contain both solid and liquid fats.

Sugars and starches. *Sugars*: The glucose manufactured by the green plant in photosynthesis, is almost universally present in plant cells. This basic material of metabolism, the glucose, has the formula $C_6H_{12}O_6$. Fruit sugar or fructose is another product of photosynthesis which has the same formula. The more complex sugars are built up from these simple sugars. The most important complex sugar is sucrose or cane sugar, which has the formula $C_{12}H_{22}O_{11}$. This sugar is accumulated in abundance in sugarcane and sugar beets. Today, the sugar industry is the second largest in India, next only to textiles.

Starch: Starch occurs in all green plants. It is a complex carbohydrate with the formula $(C_6H_{10}O_5)\ n$. Like the sugars, they are derived also from glucose and constitute the first visible product of photosynthesis. This is the commonest type of reserve food in green plants and plays the most important role in their metabolism. Commercial sources of starch are wheat, barley, maize, potatoes and arrowroot. In these plants starch occurs in the form of starch grains which vary in shape and size.

Pulp and paper. The paper is a cellulose product. Cellulose is the most complex carbohydrate and is universally present in the cell walls of plants. One of the important uses of cellulose is in the manufacture of paper. Paper can be made from any natural fibrous material.

Gums and resins. *Gums*: The true gums are formed as the result of disintegration of internal tissues, for the most part from the decomposition of cellulose. The gums are insoluble in alcohol but soluble in water, readily swell up in it, and form a viscous mass. They are colloidal in nature. They contain a large amount of sugar and are closely allied to the pectins. The gums are formed in various kinds of plants. *Acacia senegal* yields the best gum-arabic of commerce. The gums exude naturally from the stems, or in response to wounding. The commercial gums are the dried exudations of the plants.

Resins: They represent oxidation products of various essential oils and are very complex and varied in their chemical composition. They are mostly found in the stems of the trees, and occur in abundance in special canals or ducts. They are yellowish solids, insoluble in water but soluble in alcohol, turpentine and spirit. It normally oozes out through the bark and hardens on exposure to the air.

MEDICINAL PLANTS AND DRUGS

Medicinal plants. The branch of medical science, which deals with the drug plants, is known as *pharmacognosy*. This branch of medical science is concerned with the history, commerce, collection, selection, identification and preservation of crude drugs and raw materials. Most of the drugs are obtained from wild plants growing in all parts of the world, and especially in tropical regions. The medicinal value of drug plants is due to the presence in the plant tissues of some chemical substances that produce a definite physiological action on the human body. The most important of these substances are alkaloids. Some of these chemicals are powerful poisons and therefore the drugs should be prepared and prescribed only by expert physicians.

Fumitories and masticatories. From the time immemorial the human beings have smoked or chewed various substances for pleasure. For example, the bulk of tobacco is used for smoking in the form of cigarette, *bidi*, cigar, cheroot and *chuttas* and in pipe and *hookah*. Large quantities of tobacco are also consumed for chewing.

On the other hand betel leaves and arecanuts are widely used as a masticatory. The basic preparation for chewing purposes consists of betel leaf smeared with hydrated lime, and catechu to which scrapings of arecanut are added; flavourings such as coconut shavings, clove, cardamom, fennel, powdered liquorice, nutmeg, and also tobacco are used according to one's taste. Chewing of betel leaves with various adjuncts is an ancient practice in India and other countries of East Asia.

FOOD ADJUNCTS

Spices and condiments. The spices cannot be grouped as foods, for they contain less nutritive value. They stimulate the appetite and increase the secretion and flow of gastric juices. They give a good flavour and aroma to food, and add greatly to the pleasure of eating. For this reason they are commonly known as "*food adjuncts*". The aromatic value of the spices is due to the presence of the essential oils. Sometimes the term "spice" is restricted to hard parts of plants, which are generally used in a pulverized state. Condiments are spices or other flavouring substances which possess a sharp taste, and are commonly added to food after it has been cooked.

Vitamins. The vitamins are absolutely essential for well-being of both plants and animals. They are formed by plants. They are necessary for normal metabolism, growth, development and reproduction. Vitamins are also essential for the prevention of several human diseases. Fruits, vegetables and seeds of various plants are good sources of vitamins. Seaweeds contain nearly all the known vitamins. The yeasts also contain several important vitamins.

Non-alcoholic beverages. The beverages containing caffeine are used all over the world for their stimulating and refreshing qualities. Caffeine is an alkaloid, which has definite medicinal values and acts as a diuretic and nerve stimulant. The most important non-alcoholic beverages are—tea, coffee and cocoa. Caffeine is harmful in large quantities, it is present in these beverages in very small amounts, not exceeding two per cent. The other beverages which do not contain alcohol are commonly known as *soft drinks*. They contain high sugar content and make a good source of energy. The fruit juices are the simplest soft drinks.

LOWER PLANTS IN ECONOMIC BOTANY

Fungi. Some fungi have been esteemed as articles of food from early times. Edible fungi have delicate flavours and are often valued delicacies. The important edible fungi are—*Agaricus* spp., *Cantharellus* spp., *Volvaria* spp., *Lycoperdon* spp., *Morchella* spp., *Tuber* spp. and many others.

The fungi, like yeasts are responsible for fermentation. The baking industry depends solely on the enormous budding of the yeast cells.

Penicillium is best known to the non-botanist because it is the source from which the antibiotic penicillin is extracted. The famous drug, ergotine is obtained from *Claviceps purpurea*, the causal organism of plant disease, ergot of rye.

Lichens. As food lichens have been used from the earliest times as animal feed and also as food for human consumption in times of scarcity. Lichens were once employed for dyeing wool and silk and colouring materials derived from them were highly valued before the advent of synthetic dyes. Lichens were formerly used as sources of fermentable sugars for the production of ethyl alcohol. Several lichens possess medicinal properties.

Algae. From the earliest times several sea weeds have been used as direct source of food to human beings. High mineral content up to 5% of the wet material, in which all the mineral elements important in human and animal physiology are found, makes sea weeds a unique supplement for a well balanced diet. The sea weeds (marine algae) are the richest source of vitamins. The vitamins A, B and E are found in abundance in sea weeds. Several important foodstuffs prepared by algae are—suimono, mitsu, dulse, seatron, laver, kompu, carrageen, etc.

30
CHAPTER

Food Plants

CEREALS

The cereals are the most important source of plant food for man. They constitute the most important group in the food plants of India. The cereals are the members of family Gramineae, and possess the characteristic fruit, the caryopsis. In this fruit the wall of the seed becomes fused with the ovary wall to form the husk. The term 'grain' is applied to this type of fruit. There are six true cereals—rice, wheat, maize, barley, oats and rye. Of which rice, wheat and maize, are most important, and they have played an important part in the development of civilization. Sometimes the millets and sorghums are erroneously referred to as cereals. Cereals contain a high percentage of carbohydrates, together with a considerable amount of proteins and some fats. Even vitamins are present.

RICE

Oryza sativa Linn; family—Gramineae (Poaceae); Eng.—rice; Hindi—*chaval*, *dhan*, Sanskrit—*dhanya*, *vrihi*, *nivara*, *syali*; Bengali—*chal*; Marathi—*tandula*, *dhan*, *bhat*; Gujarati—*choka*, *dangar*; Telugu—*vadlu*, *varidhanyamu*, *biyyamu*; Tamil—*nellu*, *arisi*; Kannada—*akki*, *bhatta*, *nelu*; Malayalam—*nellu ari*.

History. The earliest mention of rice cultivation is connected with China. According to Stanislas Julien, a ceremony was established in that country about 2800 B.C., by the Emperor Chin-nung, in which the sowing of five kinds of grain is the chief observance. The reigning Emperor himself has to sow the rice, but he may delegate the sowing of the other four kinds to the princes of his family. However De Candolle, affirms that rice cultivation in India, though subsequent to that of China, in point of date of first record, has been a valued crop since classic periods. One of its Sanskrit names *Dhanya* means the supporter or nourisher of mankind. By the Hindus it is regarded as the emblem of wealth or fortune.

According to Dutt's *Materia Medica of the Hindus*, there are three principal classes of rice—*Sali*, or that reaped in the cold season, *Vrihi*, or that ripens in the rainy season, and *Shashtika*, or that grown in the hot weather in low lands. It may be said that rice enters extensively into the ordinances of Hinduism. Several kinds of rice are used as votive offerings at many religious ceremonies. The Sanskrit word *syala* denotes the custom of the bride's brother scattering fried grains at the marriage ceremony. In the *Ordinances of Manu* the word *food* is given as synonymous with *rice*. Wild rice in Sanskrit works is spoken of as *nivara*, and various Sanskrit names are given to the cultivated rices, such as *dhanya*, *vrihi*, *syali*, *jiva-sadhana*, *tanonu* and *shashtika*. Most of these names are traceable to roots which denote life, existence and subsistence. As a possible historic fact, which would have a bearing on the cultivation of rice in Upper India, it may be said the word *vrihi*, is met with in the *Atharva Veda*.

The most general vernacular name for wild rice is, however, *uri* and the plant occurs mainly in Tamil Nadu, Orissa, Bengal and Kerala. The area of wild rice, corresponding to that in which *uri* and other such names are used leads to the concept that in India rice cultivation may have spread from there all over the rest of the peninsula and ultimately across the Himalayas.

The chief wild habitat of the plant is from south India. The cultivation of rice appears to have spread from there eastward to China, perhaps 3,000 years before the Christian era, and at perhaps a slightly more recent date, westward and northward, throughout India to Persia and Arabia, and ultimately to Egypt and Europe.

The Chinese were the first to cultivate rice (approximately 4,000 B.C.). In classical Chinese the words for agriculture and rice culture are synonymous. It is believed that the cultivation of rice in India dates back to ancient periods even earlier than 3,000 B.C. (Parthasarathy, 1954). The cultivation of rice was introduced into India before the time of Greeks, and then reached Syria and Northern Africa. The rice was first cultivated in Europe in 1468 in Italy. In America this was first grown in 1694 in South Carolina.

Rice is predominantly a crop of Asia, 95% of the world's area being concentrated in south-eastern Asia extending from West Pakistan to Japan. India has the largest area, 79 million acres in the world under rice cultivation, and production is about 28 million tons per year. India and Indo-China are supposed to be the centres of origin of rice (Ramiah, Ghose and Vachhani, 1952).

The traditional use of rice in the religious ceremonies of the Hindus, associated with birth, marriage and death is a testimony to its great antiquity as also to the intimate place it has in the life of the people. The crop is cultivated in almost all the states of India, extending from the delta region of the south to the higher altitudes of 3,000 to 5,000 feet above sea level in the Kashmir valley in the north. It is mostly cultivated in the valley of the Ganga and its delta and the low-lying coastal areas in southern and north-eastern India.

Of all the principal crops grown in the country rice has the largest area under it. Andhra Pradesh, Assam, Bihar, Maharashtra, Madhya Pradesh, Tamil Nadu, Orissa, Uttar Pradesh and West Bengal are the main producing states; together they account for more than 90% of the total area under the crop.

Cultivation. The rice grows best on damp soils underlaid with a semi-impervious subsoil in places where it can be flooded. A considerable interest has been aroused in India during last two decades in the Japanese method of rice cultivation. This combines improved cultural practices with proper manuring and plant protection measures. The increased acre yields obtained by this method have naturally led to its popularity. The results of breeding for high yield have also been very satisfactory, and many improved varieties have been evolved which give an enhanced yield. It has also been realized that the newer intensive methods of cultivation and manuring demand varieties which are capable of giving higher yields. With this aim in view, there has been started an intensive hybridization programme between the *japonica* and *indica* varieties of rice. The *japonica* varieties are high yielding, while the *indica* varieties have a better tillering capacity and are resistant to disease and adverse climatic conditions.

The fields are ploughed and the rice is transplanted from seed beds when 9 or 10 in. high. The young plants are covered with water, and the water is kept in circulation. As soon as ripening starts, the water is drawn off and the field is allowed to dry out. Rice is harvested and the stalks are stacked up to dry.

Investigations have been carried out to determine the role of blue-green algae in rice nutrition and their effect on the fertility of soil. The results indicate that the fixation of nitrogen is increased by the activity of blue-green algae.

It has been established that incorporation of green matter in paddy soil improves yield. It provides the cheapest way of manuring rice fields wherever facilities for raising green-manure crops are available. *Sesbanea aculeata* (*dhaincha*) has been found to be the most suitable crop for

Fig. 30.1. Rice *(Oryza sativa)* variety 'IET 4106' takes about 102 days for maturity with a yield potential of 40–45 q/ha.

rice areas as it can stand the soil and water conditions prevailing in these areas. In Kashmir valley, green manuring of rice crop with *Lens esculentus* has been found to be very effective. In U.P. *Crotalaria juncea* is becoming popular.

Milling. The grains of rice are removed by threshing. The grains are to be husked when they are to be used, and are then pounded in a mortar (*okhli*) with a wooden mallet (*musal*) and winnowed. The resulting grain is very nutritious for it contains protein and fat as well as starch.

In the commercial preparation the impurities are removed and the paddy is passed between millstones to break up the husk. This chaff is moved by blowers. Now the grain is pounded in huge mortars and a portion of the bran layer and embryo is removed. The waste is called rice bran. The white rice is then scoured by friction and polished. In polishing the embryo which contains proteins, vitamins and oils is knocked out due to lack of strong link between the embryo and the endosperm. During this process the outer, more nutritive parts of the grain are removed.

Uses. The chief use of rice is as food, and more people use it than any other cereal. The rice is generally eaten with pulses (legumes) or some other food rich in proteins. A diet of rice and soyabeans makes the food of millions. The rice straw is used for making straw boards, paper and mats. Rice bran oil is used for making soaps and cosmetics. Rice starch is much used in European countries. In several tropical countries intoxicating beverages are prepared from rice. Important beverage of Japan, *Sake* is prepared by fermenting rice. In India also in some parts of Orissa and Andhra Pradesh intoxicating beverages are prepared from rice.

This starch-rich food is eaten after boiling. It may also be converted into parched rice, beaten rice or rice flakes, and puffed rice; mixed with black gram (*urd*) powder, used for fermented preparations like *idli* and *dosa*. Broken grains obtained during milling, used as human and cattle food, for making alcoholic beverages, and as a source of starch and rice flour. Paddy husk is used as fuel; the bran is also used as cattle feed. The fatty oil obtained from bran is used for edible purposes.

WHEAT

Triticum aestivum Linn.; family—Gramineae (Poaceae); Hindi—*Gehu*; Sanskrit—*Godhuma*; Bengali—*Giun, gom, gam*; Marathi—*Gahum, gahung*; Gujarati—*Ghavum, gawn, govum*; Telgu—*Goodhumalu*; Tamil—*Godumai, godumbayarisi*; Kannada—*Godhi*; Malayalam—*Gendum, kotanpam, godamba.*

History. According to M.A. de Candolle, the cultivation of wheat is prehistoric in Old World. Very ancient Egyptian monuments show the establishment of this cultivation. However, when Egyptians or Greeks speak of its origin, they attribute it to mythical personages—Isis, Ceres, Triptolemus, etc. A small-grained wheat has been found at the earliest lake dwellings of Western Switzerland, the inhabitants of which were at least contemporary with the Trojan war, and perhaps earlier. The same form of wheat, *i.e.*, *Triticum vulgare antiquorum* Heer, was found by Unger in a brick of the pyramid of Dashur in Egypt, to which he assigns a date of 3359 B.C. Another small-grained wheat, *T. vulgare compactum muticum* Heer, was less common in Switzerland in the earliest stone age, while a third intermediate form was cultivated in Hungary at the same period. However, De Candolle believes that the wheat cultivation in the temperate parts of Europe, Asia and Africa is probably older than the most ancient known languages. The Chinese certainly grew it in 2700 B.C., and considered it a gift direct from heaven. In the annual ceremony of sowing five kinds of seeds, instituted by the Emperor Shen-nung or Chin-nung, wheat was one of the species employed.

De Candolle has written in his famous work the *Origin of Cultivated Plants* that the original home of wheat in very early prehistoric times was in Mesopotamia. According to Berosus, the earliest of all Western Historians, and a Chaldean priest who wrote some twenty-three centuries ago, it occurred wild there. According to Strabo, who was born 50 B.C., a grain very similar to wheat grew wild upon the banks of the Indus.

According to De Candolle there is strong evidence in favour of India being the home of some of the forms of wheat as can be shown for any other part of the globe. India possesses perhaps as comprehensive a series of time honoured forms of wheat as can be shown for any other country. India has its hard wheats and soft wheats ; its starch wheats and speltwheats ; its bearded and beardless wheats. It has been established that most of these have been grown for countless ages on the same fields as they are to be found at the present day. It has also been proved that wheat cultivation in India is as ancient as in Europe or any other part of the world. The wheat grains discovered as a result of Indus valley excavations at Mohenjo-Daro indicate that north-western India was one of the ancestral lands of this cereal (Pal, B.P., 1954). The carbonised grains resemble those of *Triticum sphaerococcum* Percival, an endemic species which is still found in a few places in India.

According to Vavilov, the wheats have had a multiple origin, the soft wheats have come from the mountains of Afghanistan and the southwestern Himalayas ; the durum wheats from Abyssinia, Algeria and Greece; and einkorn from Asia Minor. The archaeological evidences establish that the wheat has been cultivated for at least 6000 years.

However, it must be kept in mind, while discussing the question of the origin of this ancient, cultivated cereal, that it is very nearly impossible, whatever the original home of wheat may have been, to determine with accuracy the character of the first parent from which it was derived.

India accounts for about 3.5 per cent of the global wheat production. The area under wheat constitutes roughly 14.0 per cent of the total area under cereals, and 10.0 per cent of the total area under food grains in the country. The crop is grown mainly in the northern and central parts. It is not much significance in the south.

It is cultivated as a food crop mainly in Uttar Pradesh, Punjab, Madhya Pradesh, Maharashtra, Bihar and Rajasthan.

Wheat is the second staple food crop of India and occupies about 29 million acres of land. It is consumed mainly by the people in the north. The wheat grains discovered as a result of Indus Valley excavations at Mohenjo-Daro indicate that north-western India was one of the ancestral lands of this cereal (Pal, B.P., 1954). The carbonised grains resemble those of *Triticum sphaerococcum* Percival an endemic species which is still found in a few places in India. The wheat growing area in India can be divided into three zones—the Gangetic alluvium, the Indus valley, and the black soil tract of Peninsular India. Wheat is also cultivated in Gujarat. A special feature of Indian wheat is the relatively short season in which it completes its life cycle. While the crop stands in the field for 9 to 10 months in some western countries, in India it is ready for harvest in four to six months after sowing. However, in the hilly tracts of Northern India the growing season for wheat is about nine months but the area under the crop in this region is very small.

Of the 18 recognized species under the genus *Triticum*, five are cultivated in India (Mirchandani and Khan, 1953). Of these *Triticum aestivum* Linn., commonly known as bread wheat, occupies the largest area and is mainly grown in the northern regions. Next in importance is the macaroni wheat, *T. durum* Desf., which is the predominant species in Central and Western

Fig. 30.2. *Triticum aestivum* : Wheat **(Gehu)** 'Moti'. A trigenic variety of wheat

India. The area under *T. dicoccum* Schrank is grown in South India. *T. turgidum* Linn., the rivet wheat, and *T. sphaerococcum* Percival, the dwarf wheat are even less important.

Wheat was the first crop to attract the attention of Indian breeders. The main object was to evolve high-yielding varieties with good grain quality. A notable achievement of the last few years has been the evolution of a new series of improved wheats. Their special characters include adaptability to certain regions, high yield, good grain quality, tolerance to rusts, and resistance to loose smut.

Cultivation, harvesting and threshing. In northern India sowing of wheat is done in October-November. Wheat may be sown broadcast, either by hand or by sowing machines.

Germination begins immediately and the first leaves appear within a fortnight. Wheat is properly manured and irrigated. The crop is harvested by cutting the plants with a sickle close to the ground, in March–April. Threshing is the next process, and this involves the separation of the grain from the spike. Threshing is generally done under the feet of bullocks or by threshing machines. After threshing the wheat is winnowed and sifted. In the Punjab, recently the *combines* are introduced for the purpose. The combines reap, clean, thresh, winnow and sift the grains ; wheat must be stored in firmly built structures, and it must be well ventilated.

Milling. In India in most of the motor driven flour mills there remains a fixed lower stone upon which a movable upper one revolves. The grains are dropped in the openings in the upper stone and gradually worked out between the stones which possess grinding surfaces cut in radiating lines. In this process whole grain is used.

The roller process of milling is an advanced and perfect process. The first step in this process comprises cleaning and scouring. After making the grains clean they are thoroughly washed and scoured. The next step is tempering. In this process a little water is added, which toughens the bran and prevents its breaking up, so that it will flake out all in one piece. In the last the conditioned and tempered wheat is submitted to breaking, grinding and rolling. The grain is first cracked or crushed gradually through a series of four to six pairs of chilled iron break rolls. The surface of the break rolls is made rough by sharp lengthwise foldings. The break flour is separated out by sieves, while the main portion goes to the second break. This process is repeated until five sets of rollers have been utilised. All bran is removed during this process and the purified material is passed to smooth rollers for final granulation. The final product is the flour.

Uses. There are three main kinds of flour—*suji*, *maida*, and *ata* which are used for various purposes. The flour is used chiefly for making 'bread' and 'chapatis'. The flour is also used for making biscuits, cakes, pastry and similar articles. Wheat flakes are used as breakfast food.

Wheat is also used in the manufacture of beer and other alcoholic beverages. Wheat straw is used for seating chairs, stuffing mattresses, etc. It makes a good food for livestock. Wheat straw is also used as fodder.

This makes a staple food in most parts of the world. Properties of gluten in the grains are such that it produces bread-stuffs generally superior to those from any other cereal grains. By products of wheat milling, such as bran, germ and middlings constitute valuable feed for stock, readily eaten; supplementary feeds are provided to supply protein and minerals in which the straw is deficient. The straw is used as bedding for cattle; it is also used for padding, as in mattresses, for packing fragile goods, for thatching and many other purposes. It may be used also for production of furfuryl alcohol. Straw-pulp is utilized for the manufacture of paper, straw-board, and building-board.

Non-feed industrial uses of wheat include the manufacture of starch, industrial alcohol, malted wheat, and core-binder flour; only small quantities of wheat are used for starch and gluten manufacture. Grain is regarded as a stand-by for alcohol production. Low-grade flours are utilized in the preparation of pastes for wall papering and ply-wood adhesives, and in iron foundries as a core binder.

Wheat products include peeled wheat ; *Bulgur*, a parboiled wheat product; *Wurld wheat*, similar to *Bulgur*, but of lighter colour ; *Instant* or *agglomerated* flour; Farina or *semolina*; *Wheat flakes*; *Shredded wheat* ; *Puffed wheat* ; *Grape-nuts*, prepared from toasted slices of malted bread; *Gluten*, used in special breads; and *wheat germ*, rich in vitamin E.

MAIZE

Zea mays Linn., family—Gramineae (Poaceae) ; Eng.—Maize, corn, Indian corn; Hindi—*Makai, Makka, Bhutta* ; Bengali—*Janar, bhutta, jonar*; Marathi—*Maka, makai, buta*; Gujarati—

Makkari, makkai; Telugu—*Mokka-janna, makka jonnalu*; Tamil—*Makka-cholam*; Kannada—*Mekkejola, musukojola, goinjol*; Malayalam—*Cholam*; Oriya—*Maka, buta*; Assam—*Gomdhan, makoi*; Manipur—*Chujak, nahom.*

History. It is now universally admitted that Maize or Indian corn is a native of America. This species probably originated in a wild state in the tropical South America. In Andes its cultivation goes back to prehistoric time. It has been established by evidence that the plant must have been grown for many centuries prior to the period of the Inca civilization. The maize was grown by the Indians in new Mexico as early as 2000 B.C. De Candolle on this subject writes—"No one denies that maize was unknown in Europe at the time of Roman Empire but it has been said that it was brought from the east in the Middle ages". The various names which it bears in Europe, Egypt and

Fig. 30.3. 'Protina Opaque 2 Composite', a protein-rich variety of maize *(Zea mays)* (developed by Govind Ballabh Pant University of Agriculture and Technology Pantnagar).

Asia only show that in each country it was supposed to come from some not very distant region. Thus it is Turkish-wheat, Indian Corn, Roman Corn, Sicilian Corn, Barbary and Guinea Corn, etc. The Turks call it Egyptian Corn and the Egyptians speak of it as Syrian grain. Its most general name in India may be rendered Mecca Corn (*Makkai*). However, there is no authentic Sanskrit name for the plant, nor is the grain in any way associated with the Hindus. Crawfurd also writes, — "Maize is, beyond all question, a native of America, and before the discovery of the New World was wholly unknown to the old." Royle says that the Portuguese very probably introduced the richest products of America into India, such as maize, capsicum, guava, custard-apple and pine-apple. Abul Fazl writes in *Ain-i-Akbari* about *kewarah*, where he says that its leaves are like those of "maize". Rox-burgh wrote about the beginning of last (nineteenth) century, that Indian-Corn was "cultivated in various parts of India in gardens, and only as a delicacy; but not any where on the continent of India, so far as I can learn, as an extensive crop." Buchanan-Hamilton (1819) wrote about Kangra—"The poor people live much on Maize." Graham (1839) wrote about Western India that maize was commonly cultivated. Dalzell and Gibson (1861) wrote that maize was extensively grown in the early part of the rains, especially near large towns. It is thus very probably that in the Upper India maize was much more extensively grown at the beginning of the last (nineteenth) century. It is a field crop upon which at least the bulk of the aboriginal tribes of the hilly tracts of India are very largely dependent for subsistence.

According to De Candolle, the Maize was brought to China after the discovery of America (1492). The Portuguese came to Java in 1496, that is to say four years after the discovery of America and to China in 1516, Magellan's voyage from South America to Philippines took place in 1520. It is thought, that the seeds of maize may have been taken to China by navigators from America or from Europe. Maize had reached Europe a short time before the dates mentioned for India and China. Dodoens (1583), Camerarius (1588) and Matthiole, adopted the name Mays, which they knew to be American.

Conclusively this can be said that Maize was first introduced into Europe by Columbus, and into Asia by the earlier Portuguese explorers. Maize had acclimatized wherever the climate permitted, and has now spread all over the world.

Maize also known as 'Indian corn' or simply as 'corn', is a food crop of considerable importance in many parts of the world, especially in the U.S.A., which produces nearly 57 per cent or the total maize grown in the world as compared to about 1.4 per cent produced in India. The other important maize producing countries are—China (4.4 per cent), the Russia (3.3 per cent), Manchuria (2.9 per cent), Yugoslavia (2.4 per cent) and Mexico (2.3 per cent).

A tall annual cultivated grass ; it has been introduced in this country from tropical America about the beginning of the seventeenth century. The area under this crop measures 9.6 million acres with an annual total production of three million tons. Maize is mainly grown as 'kharif crop'. Although it is grown throughout India, the chief concentration is in the north-eastern parts. The crop is of special importance in the hilly and submontane regions where it makes the staple food of people. It is grown as a food crop mainly in Uttar Pradesh, Punjab, Madhya Pradesh, Bihar, Andhra Pradesh, Jammu and Kashmir.

Cultivation and harvesting. Maize is a summer annual. It thrives best in fertile, well irrigated, medium, heavy loamy soil. It is also commonly grown in the coarse gravel soils of hilly tracts. In India the crop is generally sown in June–July and harvested in September–October. The maize stems are cut close to the ground with the help of corn knife or sickle. The stalks are stacked to allow the grain to ripe further. After a month of this curing process, the ears (cobs) are husked by hand or by machine. Maize must be stored in well ventilated bins so that the excess of moisture is evaporated.

The table shows that maize contains all the essential nutrients of food when compared to Wheat and other foodgrains.

Uses. The chief use is as a food for man and livestock. The grain is very nutritious, with a high percentage of carbohydrates, fats and proteins. Not only is the grain valuable as a stock feed, but the plant as a whole is an important fodder crop. The immature cobs are largely eaten after roasting. The grains are also used in making corn starch and industrial alcohol. The glucose is also manufactured from the grain. The corn oil is prepared which is used for soap making, lubrication and as salad oil. Corn flakes make a good breakfast food. The fibres in the stalks are utilized for making paper and yarn. Zein, the protein which occurs in maize grain, is utilized for making artificial fibres with good tensile strength and wool-like qualities.

Table 30.1

Cereals	*Proteins (Gms)*	*Fat (Gms)*	*Calories*	*Calcium Mgs*	*Iron Mgs*	*Vit 'A' I.U.*	*Vit 'B' Rib-oflavin Mgs*	*Vit 'C' Mgs*
Maize (Tender)	4.7	0.9	125	9	1.1	54	0.17	6
Maize (Dry)	11.1	3.6	342	10	2.0	1502	0.10	-
Ragi	7.3	1.3	328	344	17.4	70	0.10	-
Rice (milled)	6.8	0.5	345	10	3.1	-	0.03	-
Jowar	10.4	1.9	349	25	5.8	79	0.28	-
Wheat (whole)	11.8	1.5	46	41	4.9	108	0.12	-

It is of special importance in the hilly and sub-montane regions of the country where it forms the staple diet of the people, particularly in the winter months. In the northern parts, it is also extensively grown as a fodder.

Maize Products	**Uses**
1. **Maize grits**	Can be used directly for maufacture of breakfast foods like corn flakes. This can also be used in the manufacture of starch.
2. **Maize rice**	Can be used in replacement of rice or in conjunction with rice. This can also be used in the manufacture of starch.
3. **Poultry grits**	Can be used in replacement of rice and other cereals in breweries and distilleries.
4. **Brewer's grits**	Can be used in replacement of rice and other cereals in breweries and distilleries.
5. **Maize flakes**	Can be used to prepare various types of dishes in place of beaten rice. This can also be used in the preparation of soup and in breweries and distilleries in replacement of rice and other cereals.
6. **Maize soji** } 7. **Pre-cooked Maize soji** }	Can be used in the preparation of sweet and savoury dishes like Kesaribhath, Kharabhath, Idli, Dosa, Vermicelli, etc. Pre-cooked Maize Soji can be used in the manufacture of Balahar and snack foods.
8. **Maize maida**	Can be used in the preparation of Bread, Biscuit, Vermicelli, Nippottu, Obbattu, Bajji, Pakoda, Kodubale, etc. This can also be

	used by mixing with Wheat, Maida and Bengal gram flour for preparing the above said dishes. Also used in gum manufacturing industry.
9. Maize flour **10. Pre-cooked Maize flour**	Can be used in the preparation of Ragi balls by mixing with ragi flour. Can also be used in the preparation of sweet and savoury dishes like Pakoda, Bajji, Kodubale, Chapaties, etc. As raw materials in the manufacture of binders (Gum) for being used in the foundry and paper industry. Pre-cooked flour can be used in the preparation of Soup, Curry, Sambar, Majjigehuli (khadi) and in the manufacture of cereal and other foods for babies.
11. Maize oil	Used as edible oil. This oil has got certain advantages like easy blood circulation, reducing body fat, etc. This can also be used in soap manufacturing industry.
12. Maize cake **13. Animal meal** **14. Bran**	Can be used in Cattle and Poultry Feed industry.

Other uses. However, due to low gluten content, it does not form dough with elastic properties, but dough with good elastic properties can be made from flour made from dehulled grain. Maize starch is extensively used as a sizing material in the textiles and paper industries. In the food industry it is used in the preparation of pies, puddings, salad dressings and confections. Maize starch is used for the production of dextrose and corn syrup; also employed as a diluent for pharmaceutical preparations, dusting material to prevent articles like surgeons gloves, from sticking together, ingredient of oil-well drilling muds, and as a depressant in ore-floatation process. In cosmetics, maize starch form an ingredient of various forms of toilet powders. Dried germs yield a semi-drying oil, known as maize oil or corn oil used as salad or cooking oil; it may also be used with linseed oil for paints. Zein, recovered from maize gluten used as a binder for cork particles in forming composition cork. A textile fibre has been produced from zein under the trade name *Vicara*; it combines the virtues of cotton and wool. Cobs are rich in pentosans and used for furfural production. They may also be used for making building-boards which are water and fire-resistant. Maize silk (styles) is astringent, diuretic and chloretic. Some of the maize products include dextrose, maize starch, syrup, corn flakes and popcorns.

VEGETABLES

The term vegetable is usually applied to edible plants which store up reserve food in roots, stems, leaves and fruits and which are eaten cooked, or raw as salad. The vegetables rank next to cereals as sources of carbohydrate food. The nutritive value of vegetables is tremendous, because of the presence of indispensable mineral salts and vitamins. India grows a large variety of vegetables belonging to the tropical, sub-tropical and temperate groups. However their present availability is only 1.3 ounces per adult per day. On the other hand a balanced diet requires ten ounces of vegetables per adult per day. A good number of the vegetables in India are introductions from foreign countries. For convenience the vegetables may be classified in three categories (*i*) underground vegetables, (*ii*) herbage vegetables, and (*iii*) fruit vegetables.

UNDERGROUND VEGETABLES

In these vegetables the food is stored in underground parts. The storage organs may be true roots or modified stems, such as rootstock, tubers, corms and bulbs. From earliest time roots and tubers have furnished food for man. The underground vegetables may be classified in two groups—(*i*) roots and (*ii*) underground stems. Underground stem vegetable **potato** is described.

UNDERGROUND STEM VEGETABLE

POTATO

Solanum tuberosum Linn.; Eng. Potato; Hindi—*Alu*; Family—Solanaceae.

Bengali and Hindi—*Alu*; Marathi and Gujarati—*Batata*; Telugu—*Bangaladumpa, uralagadda*; Tamil—*Uralakilangu, wallaraikilangu*; Kannada—*Batate, alu-gidde*; Malayalam—*Urulan kizhangu*; Punjab, Kumaon, Bihar, Orissa and Assam—*Alu*.

History. It has been firmly established that at the time of the discovery of America, the cultivation of the potato (*S. tuberosum* Linn.) was practised in the temperate regions extending from Chile to New Grenada. In Europe the potato was first introduced, at some period between 1535 and 1585, into Spain when its cultivation spread into Portugal, Italy, France, Belgium, and then into Germany. The introduction into Ireland in 1585 or 1586, was independent but after the era of its first cultivation in Spain.

The date of the introduction of the potato into India is uncertain. According to Roxburgh, it has been cultivated in India before the beginning of the eighteenth century (*i.e.*, middle or end of seventeenth century). The probability is that the cultivation of potato was introduced into India from Spain, sometimes in the seventeenth century.

This is one of the most important food plants of the world. It is native of South America now grown, chiefly in Uttar Pradesh, Assam, Punjab, West Bengal and Bihar.

Potato is also a cash crop of great importance. With proper care, it can be stored for several months and transported without much damage from the producing centres to the consuming area. The crop is mainly suited to colder latitudes and temperate zones. India accounts for only 0.7 per cent of the world production. The important potato producing countries are the Russia (32.0 percent), Poland (14.6 per cent), West Germany (10.5 per cent), France (5.7 per cent), the U.S.A. (4.6 per cent), United Kingdom (3.9 per cent), Czechoslovakia (3.0 per cent) and China (0.8 per cent).

Fig. 30.4. Potato, germinating tubers.
Healthy sprouts emerge from healthy tubers.

The potato was introduced into India in the seventeenth century. The tubers are consumed in India as a vegetable rather than as a staple food. The per capita annual consumption of potatoes is estimated at nine lbs., while in some of the Western countries the figure is as high as 440 lbs. (Pushkernath, 1955). With an area of 702,000 acres the annual production is estimated at 1,674,000 tons (Maheshwari, 1959). About 90% of the crop is grown in the north Indian plains in winter and the rest in hills in the summer. In the Nilgiris, the crop is cultivated all the year round. In the plains, two successive crops are sometimes raised on the same land. The commonly grown varieties are 'Phulwa', 'Darjeeling Red Round', 'Up-to-date', and 'Gola'. Several newly evolved high-yielding hybrids, such as 208, 209, 2236 and No. 45, have been found to be very suitable for cultivation in north Indian plains.

The plant is a spreading annual. It has pinnately compound leaves, fibrous roots, and numerous rhizomes which are swollen at the tip to form the tubers.

They can be cultivated in many soils and many climates. The best environment is a cool moist climate, and a rich light soil. They are usually propagated vegetatively by means of tubers, or parts of tubers, the so-called 'seed potatoes'. The essential parts of the seed potatoes used for propagation are the eyes. The eyes are really groups of buds situated in the axils of aborted leaves. There is usually a central bud in each eye, surrounded by smaller lateral ones. The eyes are more numerous toward the apex of the tuber. Pieces of the tubers are cut at right angles to the main axis. The larger the piece, the more vigorous is the vegetative growth, and there is greater yield. In any case, at least one eye must be present. The tubers require a rest period of several weeks for maturation. Potatoes contain about 78% water, 18% carbohydrates, 2% proteins, 9.1% fat and 1% potash.

Uses. The tubers are used as vegetable. In European countries they make a universal table food. Small tubers are utilized for the production of starch and industrial alcohol. The potatoes are also fed to livestock.

Potato chips made from fresh potatoes are famous in the South while "*katri* and *patri*" are quite common in Maharashtra and Gujarat.

Katri and patri. The fresh potatoes are made into potato chips and shavings after boiling the potatoes. These are dried in the sun. These dried chips are deep fried as and when required.

Surplus and cull potatoes are used as feed for livestock and also as raw material for manufacture of starch, ethyl alcohol, and some other industrial products. Potato is among richest foods in potassium. Biological value of potato protein is 68 and protein efficiency ratio 1.9 and it decreases on storage, more so at room temperature than at 4°C. Cooking improves digestibility of potato protein. Tuberin has a high nutritive value, being superior to wheat protein. Potatoes contain phosphorylase, amylase and several other enzymes including proteolytic enzymes. Potato flesh, even at its natural high moisture content, is superior to 72 per cent extraction of wheat flour as a source of vitamin B1, riboflavin and nicotinic acid. Concentration of thiamine is lower and that of riboflavin and folic acid is higher at the periphery than in the interior of tuber. Potato leaf haulms are useful source of a-cellulose. Potatoes are used as antiscorbutic, aperient, diuretic, and galactagogue. Extract of leaves is used as antispasmodic in cough. Tuber is ground and made into a paste for application to burns with much benefit.

Potato products include potato chips, frozen French fries, potato granules, potato flakes, potato flour, spaghetti-like potato, canned potatoes, potato starch and fermentation products.

Potatoes are used for the preparation of nutrient media, *e.g.*, potato dextrose agar media (PDA), for culture of microorganism and for potato broth, used in microbiological work.

Variety: *Kufri Alankar*—Flourishes well in the plains of Northern India. Plants are tall, erect and vigorous. Flowers white in colour. Tubers are oval, white with medium deep to fleet eyes. Flesh is white with floury texture on cooking. It takes 80–90 days to mature. In the plains, the average yield is about 250–300 quintals per hectare. Early variety.

Variety : *Kufri Jyoti*—It is most suitable for hills and plains of Northern India. The plants are tall, erect, vigorous and medium compact and the flowers are white and abundant. The tubers are oval, white with fleet eyes. Flesh is dull white. It takes about 100 days in the plains and 120 days in hills to mature. Average yield 150 quintals per hectare. Early variety.

Variety : *Kufri Sheetman*—It is best suited for the plains of Punjab, western Rajasthan, Haryana and Tarai region of Uttar Pradesh. The plants are tall, vigorous, erect, open and the flowers have blue purple colour with white tips. The tubers are round oval slightly flattened with fleet eyes. The flesh is dull white and texture floury on cooking. It takes about 100–110 days to mature in the plains and 140–150 days in hills. It yields 230 quintals per hectare on an average. Medium variety.

SUGAR

SUGARCANE

Saccharum officinarum Linn.; Eng. Sugarcane; Hindi—*Ganna, Ikh*; Sanskrit—*Ikshu, khanda, sarkara* ; Bengali—*Paunda, Pundia* ; Telugu—*Cheruku* ; Tamil—*Poovan karumbu* ; Kannada—*Patta patti kabbu* ; Malayalam—*Karimbu*; Family—Gramineae/Poaceae.

History. Charaka wrote the oldest treatise extant on Hindu medicine, at about the beginning of the Christian era. The glossary of Sanskrit names in this work denotes an intimate knowledge with the various forms and preparations of sugar which is considerately more than 2000 years old. The term *Sarkara* appears to have given origin not only to the Arabic, Persian, Greek and Latin classic names, but to the extensive assortment of words in the modern languages of India and Europe which are every nearly the direct equivalents of the English word sugar. However, there are several sources of information that carry the Hindu knowledge in cane-sugar considerably further back than can perhaps be shown for any other country. The sugar-cane plant and the cane-sugar are frequently mentioned in the *Institutes of Manu*. The more generally accepted view is that these *Institutes* were begun two or three centuries before the advent of Christ. It may thus be safely accepted that the reference to a field of sugar-cane, in *Manusmriti*, is more than 2000 years old. It may thus be accepted that sugar-cane was very generally cultivated in India, during the time the *Institutes of Manu* were written. It is thus probable that sugar-cane has been cultivated in India for at least 3,000 years.

The culms of the wild species such as *Saccharum arundinaceum* (of Deccan) and *S. spontaneum* (of Kar-Nicobar) yield a certain amount of saccharine fluid, and it may be possible that one of these wild forms might have given origin to the sugar-cane, the cultivation of 3,000 years having destroyed its original specific characteristics.

In the *Ain-i-Akbari* (Abul Fazl, 1590 A.D.) a description of the methods of cultivation, manufacture of all forms of sugar, and the distillation of spirits from it, is being given in detail.

The Spaniards carried the cultivation and manufacture of sugar-cane to the Canary Islands in the fifteenth century, but prior to that in 1420 the Portuguese had conveyed it from Sicily to Madeira and to St. Thomas Island. In 1506 it was taken from the Canary Islands to San Domingo. The Dutch first established sugar works in Brazil in 1580, and then they carried the art of sugar manufacture to the West Indies in 1655. Sugar was manufactured by the English in Barbadoes in 1643 and in Jamaica in 1664. Sugar-cane was first introduced into the United States of America in Louisiana in 1741.

It is grown chiefly in Uttar Pradesh, Bihar, South India (especially Coimbatore) and the Punjab. The Indo-Gangetic belt previously grew mostly thin canes (*Saccharum barberi* Jeswiet). These are popularly known as Indian canes, have been extensively cultivated in the country for a long time. They are characterized by high fibre and an intermediate sucrose content. In the peninsular belt the thick canes (*Saccharum officinarum* Linn.) are the chief types. They have all the desirable agronomic and milling qualities. They are characterized by a thin rind and are low in fibre and high in sucrose content. The greatest landmark in the sugar industry is the evolution of improved canes in India. Ever since its inception in 1912 the Sugarcane Breeding Institute at Coimbatore has been engaged in the evolution of improved varieties for the sub-tropical regions of India and since 1926 for the tropical regions also. Its programme of hybridization has included various species of *Saccharum* and related genera. The improved Coimbatore canes now occupy 93% of the sugarcane area in India. They have increased the yields by at least 50%. Some of the improved types are: Co. 213, Co. 290, Co. 312, Co. 313, Co. 419, Co. 421, Co. 453, Co. 527, Co. 658, Co. 997, and Co. 1148. Of these, Co. 419 yields from 40 to 90 tons of cane per acre and contains 13 to 16% sugar.

The sugar industry in India is the second largest industry in the country, next only in importance to cotton textiles. The chief source of sugar is the sugarcane. This plant is a rapid growing perennial grass, which reaches a height in cultivation of 8 to 12 feet or more and a diameter of about 2 inches. It grows in clumps. The stem is solid with a tough rind and numerous fibrous strands and contains about 10% of juice, the sugar content of which varies greatly.

The commercial sugarcane is not known in a wild state. By 327 B.C. the sugarcane had become an important crop in India. The name "sugar" comes from the Sanskrit "sarkara", meaning gravel, and refers to the crude sugar.

Breeding for effective utilization of sunlight throughout the year. Sugarcane being a C. 4 plant has a very efficient photosynthetic system. Many of the tropical sugarcane varieties take 14 to 18 months from planting to harvest. This long duration also leads to sugar factories remaining idle for considerable periods. Hence, a breeding programme was initiated at the Sugarcane Breeding Institute, Coimbatore for selection of early ripening canes. Some of the cultures give good sugar recovery and yield in about 8 months. The production system with early ripening canes can be made even more efficient with the help of chemical ripeners. Such strains can enable either taking 3 crops (one main and two ratoon) of sugar cane in 2 years or promoting rice-sugarcane (with sugarcane planting in early autumn) and wheat-sugarcane (with sugarcane planting in late spring) rotations. By properly distributing the areas under spring and autumn planting the sugarcane crushing period can be considerably extended. In trials carried out at the Sugarcane Breeding Station, Coimbatore one variety recorded in 1977 about 19% sucrose with 88% purity in 240 days. During 1978 also, trials with short duration varieties gave over 18% sucrose in juice at 7 months, whereas the mid season variety (Co. 6304) used as control recorded only 12.5% sucrose at that time. (M.S. Swaminathan, 1978).

Fig. 30.5. *Sugarcane.* Sugarcane is cultivated practically in every state in India, but Uttar Pradesh has the largest area under the crop and accounts for about 50 per cent of the total area under sugarcane in the country. Andhra Pradesh, Bihar, Haryana, Punjab, Tamil Nadu and Karnataka are other major cane growing states which account for about 40 per cent of the total cane area in the country. Crop harvest is seen in the picture in Meerut district.

Cultivation. The sugarcane is propagated by cuttings of various sizes made from upper joints of old canes. These cuttings known as *seed*, are placed in trenches and nearly covered with soil. They begin to sprout in two weeks. The crop is harvested from 10 to 20 months after sprouting. The stems are cut close to the ground for the lower end of the cane is richest in sugar. The rhizomes will normally give rise to two or three more crops, known as *ratoons* before another planting is necessary. The canes are brought to the sugar mills by rail road or any available means of transportation.

Table 30.2. Sugarcane Varieties in Cultivation

Variety	*Parentage*	*Characteristics*	*Areas where cultivated*
Co. 312	Co. 213 x Co. 244	Grown well in all types of soil but lodges in rich loose soil; good ratooner; drought and frost resistant; suitable for Sugar and *Gur*.	Uttar Pradesh, Haryana, Madhya Pradesh and Rajasthan.
Co. 313	Co. 213 x Co. 244	Suited to light loamy soils; requires irrigation or well distributed rainfall; gives *gur* of good quality.	Uttar Pradesh and Assam.
Co. 419	POJ 2878 x Co. 290	Suited to all kinds of soils, but at its best in soils of medium depth and in soils with fairly high pH; good ratooner; good variety from factory point of view; *gur* hard, crystalline.	Andhra Pradesh, Maharashtra, Karnataka, Tamil Nadu, Madhya Pradesh, Orissa, Gujarat and Assam.
Co. 453	Black Cheribon x Co. 285	More suited to heavy soils; moderate tillerer and good ratooner; *gur* not of good quality.	Punjab and Haryana.
Co. 527	Co. 349 x Co. 312	Suited to well-drained rich loam; good tillerer, good for *rab* and sugar: *gur* golden yellow; highly crystalline and hard.	West Bengal, Eastern Uttar Pradesh and Andhra Pradesh.
Co. 785	Co. 443 x Co. 453	Satisfactory under flooded condition; tillering very good.	Kerala.
Co. 1148	Co. 301 x P. 4383	A good ratooner; *gur* outturn high.	Uttar Pradesh, Punjab and Haryana.
Co. 1158	Co. 421 x Co. 419	Mid season maturing cane with good yield of canes and sugar. Canes uniform and erect making harvest easy.	In large-scale cultivation in U.P.
Co. S. 510	Co. 453 x Co. 557	Adapted to sandy and loamy soils; tolerant to drought; tillering heavy, good ratooner; heavy yielder with high sucrose content.	Uttar Pradesh.

Variety	*Parentage*	*Characteristics*	*Areas where cultivated*
B.O. 17	Co. 331 x Co. 326	Suited for loamy soils, tolerant to water logged conditions and *usar* and saline soils; moderate tillering and good ratooning; yields *gur* of good keeping quality.	Uttar Pradesh and Bihar.
Co. L. 9	Co. 312 x Co. 285	Fairly frost resistant; good ratooner; produces *gur* of good quality.	Punjab and Haryana.
Co. L. 29	Co. 312 x Co. 285	Good tillerer and good ratooner; frost resistant; gives *gur* of very good quality.	Punjab and Haryana.

Sucrose or cane sugar. Cane sugar has been known from early days and its crude form was separated from cane juice. India has been the chief producer of cane-sugar from time immemorial. Later on, other countries like Java, Cuba, Philippines, etc., also started producing sugar and they contributed towards the development of better techniques for the production of refined sugar. The main sources of sugar are sugarcane and beet. In cold countries like Russia where beet is in abundance, it is extracted from beet. In tropical countries like India it is mostly obtained from sugarcane. Indian cane contains about 12–13% of sugar.

MANUFACTURE OF CANE-SUGAR

The process of manufacture of cane-sugar as followed in India involves the following steps:

Extraction of the juice. The canes are thoroughly cleaned and cut into small pieces. These cane pieces are dropped over a continuous belt of steel plates called the cane-carrier, moving over roller chains. From the cane-carrier, these are conveyed to a crusher fitted with a set of revolving knives, and cut into very small pieces. These small pieces in the form of a compact blanket are made to pass through two roller crushers and four sets of mills. After major quantity of the juice has been extracted by the crushers and the first two mills, cold or hot water is sprinkled over the *bagasse* whereby residual juice gets diluted and can be easily extracted by further milling. About 90-95% of the juice is usually extracted. The juice extracted is weighed or measured as desired and sent for clarification.

In case sugar is to be extracted from sugar-beet, it is sliced and put in hot water when the sugar present in the beet diffuses out. A number of tanks are used and worked on the principle of counter currents—concentrated solution comes in contact with fresh slices and the exhausted slices come in contact with fresh water and lose last traces of sugar in them. The solution obtained is treated like cane-juice.

Clarification of juice. The raw juice is dark opaque liquid containing about 15% sucrose and small quantities of glucose, fructose, vegetable proteins, mineral salts, organic acids, colouring matter, gums and fine particles of bagasse suspended in it. Allowed to remain untreated for some time, it begins to ferment and the sucrose present changes to mixture of glucose and fructose. In order to avoid this, the juice is not allowed to stand untreated for a long time.

There are two main processes for clarification of juice:

(*i*) *Sulphitation.* Adding milk of lime and treating with sulphur dioxide.

(*ii*) *Carbonation.* Adding milk of lime and treating with carbon dioxide.

Both processes have advantages of their own. In fact combination of both is made use of to get better results.

(*a*) *Defecation.* The juice is strained to remove suspended matter and treated with 2-3% lime till pH value reaches 7.2 in tanks heated with steam coils.

Heating of the juice helps the coagulation of albuminoids by lime. The vegetable proteins are thus coagulated and the organic acids neutralized. These form a scum on the surface of the juice when the hot juice is transferred to settling tanks called subsiders. The scum at the surface and the mud settling at the bottom are mechanically removed by passing the whole through a filter press and the clear solution sent on to the conical tanks for carbonation or sulphitation.

(*b*) *Carbonation or Sulphitation.* A current of carbon dioxide is passed through the defecated juice, which contains unreacted lime and calcium sucrosate (*carbonation*). This removes the excess of lime as calcium carbonate and decomposes calcium sucrosate.

Very often defecated juice is treated with sulphur dioxide (*sulphitation*) instead of carbon dioxide which serves the same purpose and bleaches the juice in addition, and produces a juice with much lighter colour. It prevents formation of brown mass by oxidation, and brings about coagulation of gums and albuminoids more effectively. During the process of sulphitation the solution is maintained neutral. In some cases 'sulphitation' follows 'carbonation'. The juice is filtered again to remove the precipitates.

At present all big sugar factories in India are following double carbonation and double sulphitation process for the manufacture of cane-sugar.

Concentration and crystallisation. The clear juice is concentrated in a multiple effect evaporator. Juice in the first pan is heated by exhaust steam from the engines of the factory. The concentrated juice from the first pan is taken to the second pan and heated there at a lower pressure, by steam from the first evaporator. The concentrated solution from the second pan is taken to the third pan and heated there at a still lower pressure by exhaust steam from the second evaporator.

To this concentrated juice sulphur dioxide is again applied. All through this process a strict control is maintained over the acidity of the solution otherwise there will be losses due to inversion, destruction or even discolouration may be there.

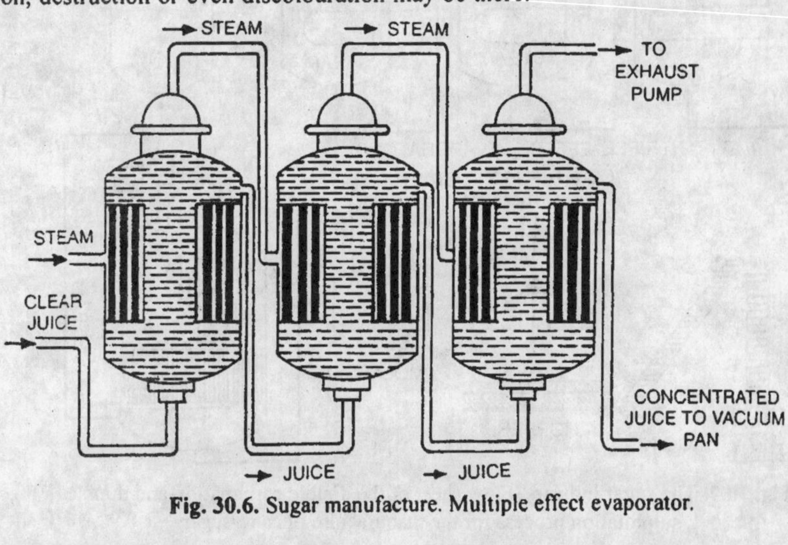

Fig. 30.6. Sugar manufacture. Multiple effect evaporator.

The clear syrupy juice is just boiled in a vacuum pan till formation of sugar crystals begins. The contents of the vacuum pan (*massecuite*) are taken into the crystallizing tank and allowed to cool slowly when the tiny crystals of sugar grow in size.

Separation of crystals. The crystals alongwith the mother liquor (molasses) are whirled in centrifugal machines wherein the molasses is removed. A little molasses adhering to the crystals is removed by spraying cold water and whirling in the centrifuge again. The crystals are given a little

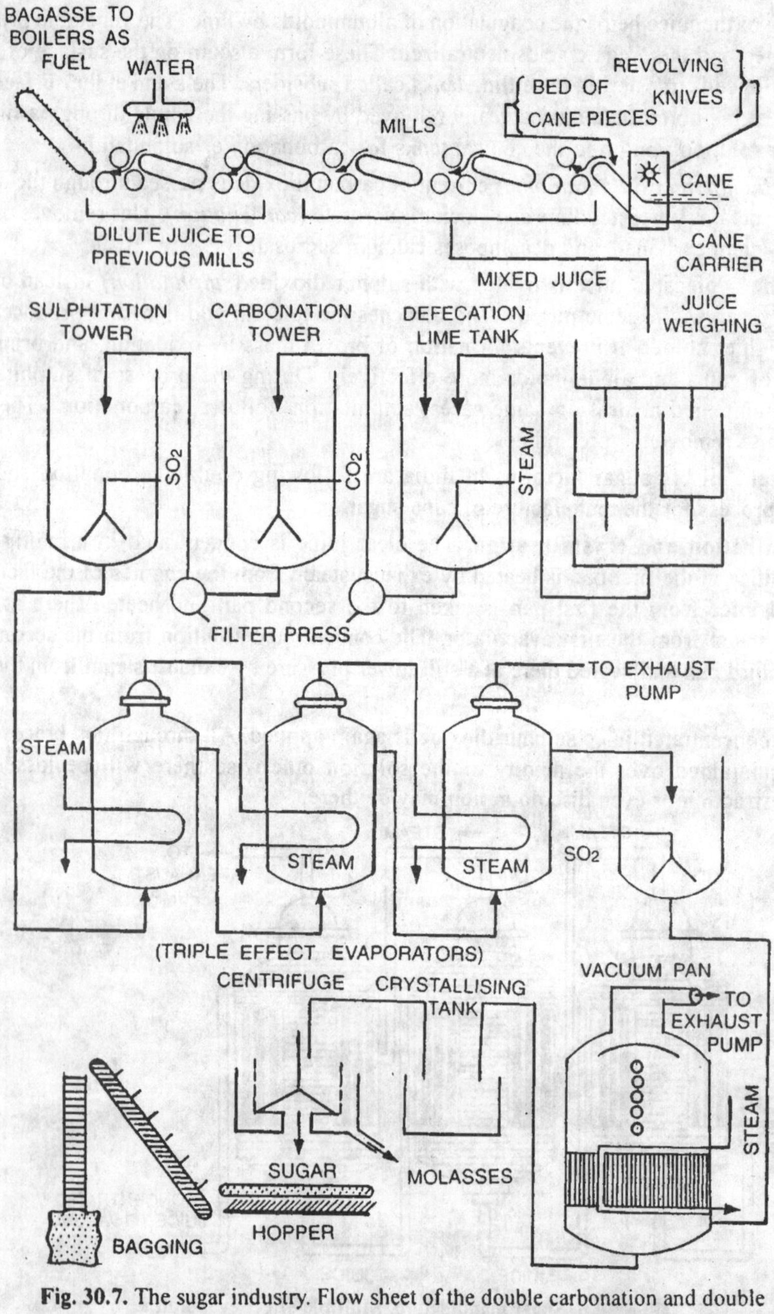

Fig. 30.7. The sugar industry. Flow sheet of the double carbonation and double sulphitation process for the manufacture of cane-sugar.

blue colour and dried by dropping through a long pipe through which hot air is passing up and bagged.

Refining of sugar. Sugar in India is generally put in the market as obtained in the above process. In U.S.A. and other foreign countries it is further refined by dissolving the crystals in hot water and decolourising the solution with animal charcoal or coconut charcoal. It is followed by filtration, concentration under reduced pressure and crystallization as usual.

Recovery of sugar molasses. The molasses still contains sufficient amount of sugar. It is boiled over again to get a fresh crop of crystals. To recover sugar from the final molasses, the latter is treated chemically. It is diluted and treated with hot concentrated solution of strontium hydroxide. Sucrose present forms a precipitate of strontium sucrosate. This is separated, suspended in water and treated with carbon dioxide when strontium carbonate separates as a white precipitate and sucrose present in the solution is decolourised, concentrated and crystallized as above.

In India sugar is not extracted chemically from molasses although still about 30 to 35% sugar is there. It is now being sent to distilleries where it is fermented and used in the manufacture of alcohol.

Sugar Industry in India. India is the accredited birth place of sugar cane and sugar. However, the Industry progressed considerably after 1931 when it was granted protection. Today, the industry is the second largest in India, next only to textiles. The industry employs about 3 lakh workers, both skilled and unskilled. The industry is highly concentrated in Uttar Pradesh and Bihar.

ESTIMATED CAPACITY AND PRODUCTION OF SUGAR IN INDIA

The present output has outstripped annual home consumption considerably, thus presenting a serious problem of surplus stocks. The industry is experiencing difficulty in promoting exports as well, because of the high cost of domestic sugar. This is due to several weaknesses of the industry *viz.* (*i*) low yield per acre of cane in India which is just 15 tonnes as against 62 and 56 tonnes in Hawaii and Java, (*ii*) high price of cane which constitutes 60% of the cost of production of sugar ahd low sucrose content, (*iii*) uneconomic size of many factories and (*iv*) short crushing season which lasts only for 145 days in a year in India.

By-Products. There are three by-products of sugar industry, *viz.*, bagasse, molasses and press-mud. Bagasse was being used mainly as fuel for steam raising. Now it is used also for the manufacture of paper pulp, cardboard and insulation board. Molasses has demand in the preparation of acetic acid, aconitic acid, power alcohol, chemicals, chloroform, plastics, etc. Pressmud finds use in the manufacture of carbon paper and polish.

Uses of sugar. The sugar is used as an article of food and as sweetening agent in sweets and drinks. It is used in food preservation and in the preparation of oxalic acids in the laboratory. It is used also for the manufacture of octa-acetate.

Sugarcane juice is used mainly for three products used in foods and beverages, for sweetening purposes, *viz.*, *Gur* and jaggery, vacuum pan sugar, and open pan sugar or *khandsari*. A good quantity of sugar is also used for chewing. Byproducts obtained during the manufacture of *gur* and sugar are molasses. *Gur* is used for direct consumption by human beings and livestock. Sugar is used for sweetening milk, tea and coffee, and for making sweets.

31

CHAPTER

Fibres and Fibre Yielding Plants

It goes without saying that the fibre yielding plants rank second only to food plants in their usefulness to humankind. The utilization of fibres is directly related to the advancement of civilization. From the earliest times the man required three things for his living—food, clothing and shelter. Though other things were at hand to fulfil these demands yet they were insufficient and incomplete too without the genuine aid of the plants. As far as the clothing was concerned the skins and hides were not sufficient. He needed somewhat more and that gap was fulfilled by the plant fibre. As there was advancement of civilization the needs of man multiplied several fold and the use of the plant fibres increased greatly. Till now more than two thousand species of plants have been worked out which yield fibres. However, the commercial fibre yielding plants are few in number. The fibres from other plants are used by primitive tribal people of the world.

Economically the fibres may be grouped as follows:

Textile fibres. Fibres utilized for the manufacture of fabrics, netting and cordage, etc.

Brush fibres. Fibres utilized in the manufacture of brushes and brooms.

Rough weaving fibres. Fibres utilized in making baskets, chairs, mats, etc.

Filling fibres. Fibres used for stuffing mattresses, cushions, pillows, etc.

Natural fibres. Natural fibres used as cloth without weaving.

Paper-making fibres. Wood fibres, etc., utilized for paper-making.

As regards their structure, the sclerenchyma cells are grouped into fibres. Fibres are described as long cells with thick walls, correspondingly small cavities, and usually pointed ends. The walls of fibres usually consist of lining as well as cellulose. The fibres may occur singly or in small groups. The fibres may be found in any part of the plant—stems, leaves, roots, fruits and even seeds.

The plants belonging to several families of angiosperms yield fibres. They are chiefly tropical plants. The important families of the fibre yielding plants are—Malvaceae, Linaceae, Tiliaceae, Gramineae, Musaceae, Bombacaceae, Leguminosae, Palmae, Liliaceae, Urticaceae, Amaryllidaceae, Moraceae, Asclepiadaceae, and Bromeliaceae.

TEXTILE FIBRES

These fibres are supposed to be most important because they are connected with the textile industry. This industry is concerned with the manufacture of fabrics, netting and cordage. For making fabrics and netting, the flexible fibres are twisted together into yarn and thereafter woven, spun and knitted. For making cordage the individual fibres are twisted together rather than woven. The textile fibres are always long and possess high tensile strength, together with cohesiveness and pliability. They possess a fine, uniform, lustrous staple. The chief textiles are included in three categories—(*i*) surface fibres, (*ii*) soft fibres and (*iii*) hard fibres.

Surface fibres, *e.g.*, Cottons.

Soft fibres, *e.g.*, Flax, hemp, jute and ramie.

Hard fibres, *e.g.*, Sisal, coconut, pineapple, abaca, etc.

SURFACE FIBRES

COTTON

Gossypium Linn.; Eng.—Cotton; Hindi—*Kapas*; Bengali, Hindi, Gujarati, Punjabi and Marathi—*Kapas, rui, tula*; Kannada—*Hathi*; Telugu—*Patti, karpasamu*; Tamil and Malayalam—*Paruthi, panji*; Oriya—*Karpaso, kopa*; Family—Malvaceae.

History. The history of cotton (*Gossypium* sp.) is most interesting, and perhaps no more remarkable example of a sudden development exists in the whole history of Economic Products, than in the case of cotton. Only a few hundred years ago cotton and its products were practically unknown to the civilized nations of the West. However, evidences exist amongst certain of the aboriginal tribes of India which indicate a much more ancient knowledge of the plant. For example. the Khonds grow a cotton-bush in the place selected for a new settlement, and in after years the village plant is tended as sacred and carefully watered. This custom is probably of very ancient origin, and may denote a superstitious regard for the plant, probably derived from the knowledge and appreciation of its valuable properties.

The Sanskrit word translated 'cotton' is perhaps first mentioned in the *Institutes of Manu*, where it is stated that, "the sacrificial thread of a Brahman must be made of cotton, so as to be put on over his head in three strings." The word used in that passage and translated cotton is *Karpusi* from which has been derived, the *Kapas*.

However, it is certain that at the time of *Institutes of Manu* spinning and weaving were not only known, but the art of starching or weighing a textile was also practised, and the admissible amount prescribed. A still earlier notice of the process of starching probably occurs in the *Rigveda*. The picture thus raised of the character of the textile industries of India, some two thousand years ago. *Institutes of Manu* also deal with the regulations concerning washerman. We are thus led to believe that the arts of spinning, weaving and washing were perfectly understood in the East, at a time when the textile industries of the West, through ignorance of cotton, were in a much more backward condition.

Katan is an old Arabic word for flax, but may also have been used for cotton, since it apparently gave origin to the European words such as Cotton (*Eng.*) Cotone (*Ital.*), Cotn (*Fr.*), etc. In Greek the word *Karpason* is generally translated cotton. It is significant to mention that, with writers at the beginning of the Christian era, it was customary to speak of cotton and cotton goods by names not in use prior to that date. Herodotus is perhaps the first who seems to refer to the fibre. But perhaps the first unmistakable reference to cotton is by Theophrastus, subsequent to the expedition of Alexander into India. He mentions, that the plant was cultivated, at least in North-Western India, at that early date.

The muslins of Dacca seem also to have been known. They are described as superior to all others, and are said to have been called *gangitiki* by the Greeks, a name indicative of their manufacture on the banks of the Ganges.

The knowledge of the manufacture of cotton appears to have extended into Arabia and Persia about the beginning of the Christian era. From India, there is no doubt, the cultivation of cotton spread into Persia, Arabia and Egypt, from where it probably extended into Central and Western Africa. From Persia the culture migrated into Syria and Asia Minor, also into Turkey in Europe and thereafter into other parts of southern Europe. The earliest account of its cultivation on the

European shores, is to be found in the works of Eben el Awan of Seville who lived in the twelfth century.

In the new world, we find that cotton has probably been used from the earliest times. It is connected with some of the most ancient beliefs of the aboriginal peoples of South America. Columbus found cotton in use among the natives of Hispaniola, but only in the most primitive way. Cortez found the manufacture in a much more advanced condition in Mexico.

With the rise of Muhammadanism the knowledge of spinning and weaving cotton probably spread to Europe, consequently the delicate cotton fabrics of the East were first imitated in Italy and Spain during the twelfth or thirteenth century. From these localities the art of cotton manufacture became diffused and extensively established all along the southern shores of the Mediterranean, but it was confined to that area till sixteenth century. From the low countries the industry passed over to England in the seventeenth century. Towards the end of the seventeenth century cotton printing was established in England. Up to the commencement of the nineteenth century America contributed but a very insignificant portion of the cotton was consumed. At the close of the war in 1815, the production of cotton in America received a fresh impetus, and the subsequent progress was rapid and continuous. This great increase in the importance of America, as a cotton-growing country early led the East India Company to commence operation for the purpose of improving the quality and increasing the quantity of Indian cotton for export to England. The imports into Great Britain from India during the years 1800 to 1809 averaged 12,700 bales per annum.

This is the world's greatest industrial crop, the chief fibre plant. It was known to the ancient world long before written records were made. References to it are to be found in the works of the Greek and Roman writers. Cotton has been in the use in India since 1800 B.C., and from 1500 B.C. to A.D. 1500 India was the centre of the industry. The Hindus were the first people to weave cloth. Cotton was introduced into Europe by the Mohammedans. This was first grown in the United States soon after the first settlements were made. The first cotton mill was established in 1787.

All the cultivated cottons fall under four species, two belonging to the Old World and two to the New World. These are *Gossypium arboreum*, *G. herbaceum*; *G. hirsutum*, and *G. barbadense*.

G. arboreum. This is most widespread of all the species of Old World cottons, being distributed throughout the rain-fed savannah areas from Africa, through Arabia and India, to China, Japan and E. Indies. Its origin is obscure, but it is obviously Asian, since the area of its greatest variability is found around the Bay of Bengal. This species comprises a large number of varieties and races including many of the cultivated cottons in and around India.

The staple is coarse and very short, only 3/8 to 3/4 inch in length, but it is strong.

G. herbaceum. This is also an Old World species. It occurs in Africa, Middle East countries, Central Asia and Western India. It has been grown in India from time immemorial. Commercially the cottons belonging to this species constitute a fairly large percentage of medium staple cotton grown in India. The major part of the cotton crop in Maharashtra state comprises this species. This species comprises a large number of cultivated races.

Fig. 31.1. Staple cotton. **'Kanchana'** variety.

It is utilized for low-quality fabrics, carpets, and blankets and is especially suitable for blending with wool.

G. hirsutum. This is a New world species. The centre of variability for this species is Central America. It comprises a large number of varieties or races. Only three races—*punctatum*, *marie galante* and *latifoliam*—extend beyond Central America. The last one is of great importance agriculturally, as it comprises the Upland cotton, which has spread over vast areas in America, Asia and Africa. The types of cotton belonging to this race constitute the bulk of long staple cottons grown at present in India. The fibres are white with a considerable range in staple length, from 5/8 to $1^3/_8$ inch.

G. barbadense. This is a New World species. It includes perennial shrubs or small trees, 3–15 feet high, or annual shrub moderately high.

The centre of origin of this group is tropical South America particularly its north-western parts.

Two distinct types of cotton belongs to:

Sea-island Cotton. This is one of the most important selections which yields lint of perhaps the highest quality which the genus *Gossypium* has so far proved capable of yielding. Its fine, strong, light cream-coloured fibres are more regular in the number and uniformity of the twists and have silkier appearance than those of other cottons. Sea-island cotton was brought to the United States from the West Indies in 1785. The finest types yielded staples 2 in. or more in length, surpassing all the others in strength and firmness. Another form of sea-island cotton is grown along the coast in Georgia and Florida and in the West Indies and South America. This has a staple form 1½ to 1¾ in. in length.

Egyptian Cotton. The second important line of annual types derived from the perennial stock is the Egyptian cotton. Egyptian cotton is derived from a hybrid stock between a perennial G. barbadense and the annual sea island cotton. It is ecologically quite distinct from sea island cotton and is well adapted for irrigated conditions in the subtropics. Its practical value lies in its greater earliness. Some of the important commercial types at present in cultivation are Karnak, Menoui, Ashmuni, and Giza. The lint length of these cotton ranges from $1^1/_8$ in. (Ashmuni) to 1½ in (Karnak). Considerable quantities of these Egyptian types are imported every year into India for supplementing indigenous long staple cotton supplies. Besides Egypt, significant quantities of this cotton are produced in Sudan, U.S.A., Peru, French North Africa and Russia.

Because of its staple's length, strength and firmness this cotton is used for thread, underwear, hosiery, tire fabrics and fine dress goods.

Cultivation. Cotton is essentially a tropical crop, but its cultivation is carried on successfully over many parts of the world, far removed from the tropics. The limits of cultivation may be said to be the 40th latitude on both sides of the Equator. It is grown either at sea level or at moderate elevations not exceeding 3,000 feet. Cultivation is confined largely to flat open country and rough hilly tracts, where the minimum temperature does not fall below 70°F. Higher temperatures are very favourable, and the upper limit may go up even to 105°F in the picking season. The crop thrives well in moderate rainfall. Rainfall exceeding 35 inches is supposed to be harmful to the crop. The lower limit for a purely rain-fed crop is 20 inches. On black cotton soils, hardly any rainfall is needed over most of the growing period provided good showers have been received before the crop was sown and a satisfactory start has been made. Cotton is grown both as a dry crop and as an irrigated crop. If the rainfall is distributed over both the monsoons, the extra-ordinary fertility of the black cotton soil allows a wide variety of crops to be grown, and also taking of two crops in the year—one in the north-east monsoon period, and the other in the south-west monsoon period. On the other hand, if the rainfall is low and is confined to the north-east monsoon period, the only one crop is grown in the year. There is considerable mixed cropping practice with cotton. Pulses such as *arhar*, blackgram and green-gram and other crops such as groundnut and the castor, into the mixture. The 'New World' cottons are, however, grown pure—whether as dry crops or as irrigated crops.

THE COTTON INDUSTRY

Several operations are necessary in order to prepare the raw cotton fibre, as it comes from the field, for use in the textile industry. In brief these operations are as follows—ginning; baling; transporting to the mills; picking, a process in which a machine removes any foreign matter and delivers the cotton in a uniform layer; lapping, an operation whereby three layers are combined into one; carding, combing, and drawing during which the short fibres are extracted and the others are straightened and evenly distributed; and finally twisting the fibres into thread.

Harvest and yield. The cotton crop is usually harvested in three or four pickings, taken at suitable intervals. Picking is carried out by hand, mostly by women, the amount of cotton collected ranging from 20 to 50 lb. per day per person. Cotton should be picked only when the bolls are fully mature, fully open and the floss has puffed up consequent on exposure to sun.

The yield per acre is low in India as compared to yield in other countries.

Cotton marketing. The bulk of cotton produced in India is sold as *Kapas* or unginned cotton. *Kapas* is transported to the local markets or ginneries mainly in carts or, sometimes, on pack animals. The cultivator sells his cotton in the village market. The purchasers are village merchants, or agents of ginneries, spinning mills or exporting firms. In some states, co-operative societies organized by cultivators have taken up the purchase and sale of the cotton.

Ginning. Kapas or seed cotton collected from the field contains both lint and seed. For use in industry, cotton should be cleaned and the lint separated from the seed. A small amount of seed cotton is ginned in villages by the use of *charkha* gin. The bulk of it, however, is ginned in factories by power-driven machinery. The yield and quality of lint depend on the type of cotton and the machinery used for ginning.

Baling. Cotton is packed for trade purposes both in loose and compressed bales. Loose packing is adopted for inland transit of ginned cotton to a pressing factory, while compressed packing is adopted for transporting ginned cotton to the market and for storing in the godowns. Each loose bale contains 200 to 300 lb. of cotton. The usual weight of compressed bale is 392 lb. net with density of 40 lb. per cubic foot.

DEVELOPMENT OF FIBRE IN COTTON

A cotton fibre is a delicate tubular prolongation of the peripheral wall of the seed. The fibres are formed by the outer epidermis of the outer integuments. These hairs are single celled and thick walled and attain a length of up to 45 mm These fibres also show characteristic twists and are called *lint fibres*. Intermingled with the lint hairs are some *fuzz hairs*. The maximum length attained by the latter is 10 mm They are thick walled with the narrow lumen and lack the twists.

USES OF COTTON

The bulk of cotton production is consumed in the manufacture of woven goods, alone or in combination with other fibres. The principal types of woven fabrics are—print cloth, yarn fabrics, sheetings, fine cotton goods, napped fabrics, duck, tyre fabrics and towels. Products in the form of yarn and cord include unwoven tyre cord, thread, cordage and twine and crochet yarns. Unspun cotton finds use in mattresses, pads and upholsteries. Cotton constitutes one of the basic raw materials for cellulose industries including plastics, rayon and explosives. Sterilized absorbent cotton finds use in medical and surgical practice.

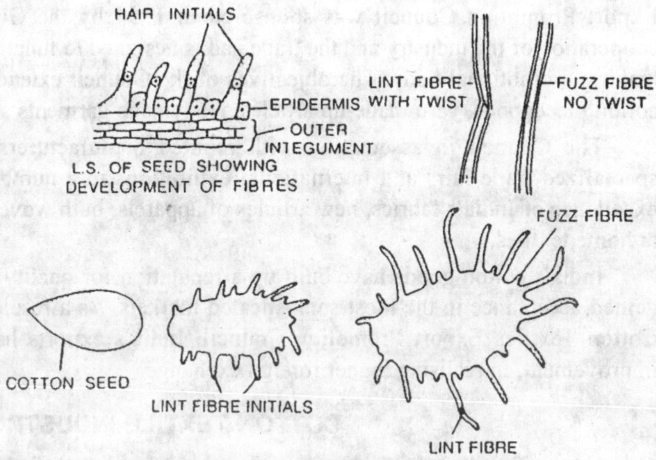

Fig. 31.2. Development of fibre in cotton.

Yarns of varying size and fineness are needed in the production of fabrics. Coarse yarns are spun from short staple cottons and fine one from medium and long staple types. Long and uniform staples are utilized for yarns of high counts required for fine fabrics.

Cotton waste is a by-product of the spinning and weaving mills and consists principally of short fibres rejected by combing and carding machines, floor sweepings, odds and ends from weaving and various scraps. The amount of waste given by cotton is an important factor in its quality evaluation. Cotton waste of good grade is employed in making cotton blankets, sheets, towels and flannelettes. Cylindrical strips from carding machine, which are constituted of fibres of good strength, are used for warps, twines, ropes and nets; they are also useful for wadding, padding for upholstery, bed quilts, etc. Strips from Egyptian cottons are mixed with wool for making mixed woollen goods. Floor sweeping and fibres unfit for spinning are bleached and used for gun-cotton, cellulose and artificial silk. Short remnants and thread waste that can not be respun are used as wiping and polishing material.

The *stalks* of plant contain a fibre that can be used in paper making or for fuel, and the *roots* possess a crude drug. The seeds are of the greatest importance and every portion is utilized. The *hulls* are used for stock feed; as fertilizer; for lining oil wells; as a source of xylose, a sugar that can be converted into alcohol and for many other purposes. The *kernels* yield one of the most important fatty oils, cottonseed oil and an oil cake and meal which are used for fertilizer, stock feed, flour, and as a dyestuff.

THE COTTON TEXTILES EXPORT PROMOTION COUNCIL OF INDIA—REPORT

As an exporter of quality textiles India's reputation dates back to the pre-Christian era. India's textile goods were shipped to distant corners of the world and they drew appreciation of high and mighty. To this day, these fabrics are known for the novelty and creativeness. The textile industry of India in those days was a cottage industry and the cloth was woven on handlooms. The skill and craftsmanship were handed over from generation to generation and this imparted a rare aesthetic quality to product. The glory of the beautiful handwoven cloth suffered a sort of eclipse in the wake of industrial revolution in the middle of the nineteenth century which created a vogue for mass produced textile products manufactured by mechanised mills. The beginning was made in India when a modern cotton mill was set up in 1854 in Bombay. The industry passed through many vicissitudes and pressure of competition from abroad in the process of its development until 1947 when India gained independence. The conditions created by the Second World War and the demand from many countries for their supplies of cotton textiles from India created an outlook for exports among the coteries of cotton mill industrialists. Cotton textiles are India's major source of foreign exchange. In 1974 cotton textiles brought in foreign exchange worth more than rupees 3,000 million.

A great need was felt to systematise the efforts to boost exports of textiles and the Government of India decided to sponsor an organisation towards the end. The Cotton Textile

Export Promotion Council was sponsored in 1954 by the Government of India with active cooperation of the industry and the trade and is designed to function as an autonomous non-profit-making promotional body. The objectives of the Council extend to the promotion of exports of cotton piecegoods, yarn made-up articles, readymade garments and hosiery articles.

The Council in association with reputed manufacturers and exporters participates in specialized trade fairs and international exhibitions in a number of countries to highlight the excellence of India's fabrics, new articles of apparels, both woven and knitted and the new range at home textiles.

India's cotton goods have built up a reputation for quality in all markets of the world and gained acceptance in the most sophisticated markets. As a result of the functions carried out by Cotton Textiles Export Promotion Council, India's exports have been helped by qualitative improvement, in realising higher foreign exchange.

COTTON TEXTILE INDUSTRY

Cotton Textile industry is one of the oldest and largest industries of India, which has made rapid strides during the current century. The industry is well organised in our country either in terms of value of annual output or number of labour employed. India has the world's highest acreage under cotton, but in terms of production among fifty-five major countries, it ranks only fourth after the U.S.A., Russia and China. Cotton is grown in our country over an area of about eight million hectares and average production during the last few seasons had been around eighty seven lakh bales. At present the industry provides direct employment to nearly twelve lakh workers. It also provides indirect employment to many millions like the cotton growers, processors, handloom and powerloom weavers who alone are estimated over three million and innumerable cloth dealers and shopkeepers. The industry contributes in ever increasing measures to the Central and State Governments by way of taxes and duties. A large domestic market and plentiful supply of domestic cotton were the two basic factors responsible for the growth and development of cotton textiles into a major key industry. The first factor still holds good. With an annual growth of 2.5 per cent in population the domestic demand for textiles is rising. But the second factor has been weakening and has tended to undermine the strength and stability of the industry. It may be said that the future of this premier industry primarily depends on our ability to increase the cotton production efficiently and economically. In this industry, concentration of management and ownership is mostly in the hands of the private sector.

Location

Though cotton textile industry being the largest industry in India has spread practically over all parts of the country, it is mostly localised in the states of Maharashtra and Gujarat. This is obvious from that these two states claim more than half of the spindlage and about 2/3 of the loomage. At the end of 1983 there were 805 mills in India. Out of this, 525 were spinning units and 280 were composite mills. Tamil Nadu, with 303, had the largest number of textile mills. But out of these only 24 weré composite mills and the remaining made yarn. In Maharashtra, there were 108, out of these, 80 were composite mills. There were 89 composite units in Gujarat, out of a total of 114 mills. These three States account for the block of the production of yarn and growth in the organised sector. Gujarat and Maharashtra put together account for two-third of the mill loomage.

Reasons for this location are (*i*) availability of raw material both in good qualities and quantities; (*ii*) cheap and developed transport facilities including ports like Bombay and Kandla; (*iii*) availability of commercial and financial facilities like export and import houses and banking institutions; (*iv*) suitable climate and (*v*) enterprising capital. In recent years, the cotton textile industry has also spread to a number of other states like Madhya Pradesh, Bihar, Kerala, Andhra Pradesh, Tamil Nadu and Uttar Pradesh.

Size

On the whole, Indian market favour the organisation of the small or moderate sized mills. Cotton mills in Tamil Nadu, Kerala, Karnataka, West Bengal, Orissa, Assam and Bihar are small in size. Size of the cotton mill industry in these states ranges from ten to fifteen thousand spindles and 200 to 400 looms. In Andhra Pradesh, Uttar Pradesh, Madhya Pradesh and in Maharashtra the units are considered as medium sized. The size of model units in these regions ranges from fifteen to thirty thousand spindles and 400 to 600 looms. Big sized units with a range from 30 to 60 thousand spindles and 750 to 1500 looms are localised at Mumbai.

The Textile Policy

The textile policy announced by the Government in August 1978 emphasises the need for encouragement of handloom sector. The policy stated that the government would freeze the loomage of mills and powerlooms and the responsibility of meeting the additional requirements arising from the increase in population and also any improvement in the per capita consumption will be entrusted to the handloom sector. This policy is aimed at in view of the fact that this would create additional jobs in the rural areas. A number of handloom development centres have been proposed to be started. As far as the policy on controlled cloth is concerned, it has been stated that mill made controlled cloth would be limited to 400 million sq. metres and would be produced by both the National Textile Corporation and the private sector mills. The policy further laid that, "it is intended that the handloom sector should to the maximum extent possible and in the shortest period of time, meet the requirements of cloth for the weaker sections of the population. The manufacture of controlled cloth in the organised sector would be phased out over a period of time consistent with the growth of production of the required variety of cloth in the handloom sector.

Again, the Government of India announced its textile policy on the sixth June 1985, indicating significant changes in the Government's approach to the growth and development of the textile industry. It aims at free and unrestricted growth of the industry by removing sector-specific and fibre specific rigidities in production and capacity creation, prevention of unregulated growth of power looms, treating mill and powerloom sectors at par, providing protection to handloom sector, restructuring of the industry in terms of stages of manufacturing process and rationalisation of excise duty structure. It also emphasises rehabilitation of viable sick units, modernisation and upgradation of technology, as well as improvement in product quality and reduction in cost of production.

SOFT OR BAST FIBRES

JUTE

Corchorus Linn.; Eng. Jute; Hindi—*Patsan*; Sanskrit—*Kalasaka*; Hindi—*Narcha*; Bengali—*Chinalitapat, narcha, nalita, titapat*; Assam—*Titamara*; Family—Tiliaceae.

History. J. F. Duthie found *C. capsularis* on the banks of the Gumpti near Judalpur in a wild state. However, Roxburgh reported the non-jute yielding species of *Corchorus* as natives of India. A special enquiry was, in 1873-74 in Madras of wild or cultivated jute found in that Presidency, and *C. olitorius* was reported to have been discovered both wild and cultivated. However, De Candolle was not convinced that the species existed in a truly wild state in the north of Calcutta. It might be found possible to produce forms of Corchorus from some of the truly wild species which would closely approximate to *C. capsularis* and *C. olitorius*. There are no Sanskrit names for these plants. There are neither Arabic nor Persian names for the species of *Corchorus*, known to the people of India. Mr. Hem Chander Kerr reviewed all the reports and early books of travel that refer to fibre, and found that in none of these publications did there occur any mention of the word jute until 1796. In several works *pat* was mentioned as a fibre in India as a form of hemp. By the beginning of the nineteenth century the word pat was completely superseded by jute in all commercial correspondence. With the facts of this kind it is believed that jute plant is a comparatively modern development from some wild stock which was unknown to the Sanskrit writers. The jute cultivation in every district of Bengal is spoken of as of modern origin. In one district its introduction is fixed at 1872, in another at 1865, in a third before the date of the British rule and in a fourth it is put down at 500 years ago.

Fig. 31.3. A Jute plant.

The commercial fibre jute is obtained from either one or both of the following species of *Corchorus*, *viz.*, *C. capsularis* Linn., grown in West Bengal and Bangladesh, and *C. olitorius* Linn., raised in the vicinity of Calcutta. Little or no jute is produced in the other states of India.

Cultivation. In India, the crop is sown between March and May, and harvested between July and September, It is grown mainly in West Bengal, Assam and Bihar, which together account for 90 per cent of the total area sown. Orissa, Uttar Pradesh and Tripura are the other states, which contribute the remaining 10 per cent area.

Jute is a bast fibre obtained from the secondary phloem. The bast fibre is obtained from *C. capsularis*, a species with round pods which is grown in lowland areas subject to inundation. Fibre from *C. olitorius*, an upland species with long pods, is but little inferior.

In India, the time for harvesting the crop depends entirely upon the date of sowing; the season commences with the earliest crops about the end of June, and extends to the beginning of October. The crop is harvested within three or four months after planting, while the flowers are still in bloom.

Separation of fibre by retting. The fibre is separated from the stems by a process of retting in pools of stagnant water. The crop is stacked in bundles for two or three days, to give time for the decay of the leaves, which are said to discolour the fibre in the retting process. The period of retting depends upon the nature of the water, the kind of fibre, and condition of the atmosphere. It varies from two to twenty–five days. The operator has therefore to visit the tank daily, and ascertain, by means of his nail, if the fibre has begun to separate from the stem. This period must not be exceeded, otherwise the fibre becomes rotten and almost useless for commercial purposes. The bundles are made to sink in the water by placing on the top of them sods and mud. When the proper stage has been reached, the retting is rapidly completed. The cultivator, standing up to the waist in the foetid water proceeds to remove small portion of the bark from the ends next the roots. Grasping them together, he strips off the whole with a little management from end to end without breaking either stem or fibre. Thereafter the washing is done to remove the impurities. It is now wrung out so as to remove as much water as possible, and then hung up on lines prepared on the spot, to dry in the sun.

The very long pale-yellow fibres from six to ten feet in length, are quite stiff, as they are considerably lignified; they possess a silky lustre. They are very abundant, but are not particularly strong, and they tend to deteriorate rapidly when exposed to moisture, to which they are quite susceptible. Besides these disadvantages the jute is cheap and easily spun makes it valuable.

Utilization. Jute is used chiefly for rough weaving. The thick cloth made from jute fibre is used for making gunny-bags. Another type of fine cloth prepared from jute fibre is chiefly used as a cloth to sleep on. Another type of coarse cloth is largely used for making the sails of country boats, and also for bags to hold large seeds or fruits.

Jute is extensively used in the manufacture of carpets, curtains, shirtings, and is also mixed with silk or used for imitating silk fabrics. The fibre is also used for making twine and ropes. Short fibres and pieces from the lower ends of the stalks constitute jute butts, which are used to some extent in paper making.

India not only grows most of the jute, but it is the largest manufacturer and exporter of jute products.

JUTE INDUSTRY

In the industrial economy of India, Jute industry occupies an important place both in terms of value of annual foreign exchange and the number of people employed. This industry accounts for Rs. 300 crores by way of capital employed, provides employment to nearly four lakh workers and exports more than 75 per cent of the production. The 75 per cent of the production accounts for nearly 5 per cent of total foreign earnings of all commodities. This industry has an installed capacity of 13.0 lakh tonnes spreading over 44,516 looms and 5.92 lakh spindles. Besides, India is the largest producer of jute goods in the world. Apart from all these, about three million families of farmers derive a substantial part of their income from jute cultivation. In 1885, India's first jute factory was set up at Serampore in Bengal, followed by several others. However, after country's partition, nearly 75 per cent of India's jute growing areas went to East Bengal (Bangladesh) whereas most of the jute mills remained on the Indian territory, which gave a severe blow to the industry. In spite of this the industry made serious effort to increase jute production through both extensive and intensive cultivation. As days passed on Bangladesh became most powerful competitor which has built considerable jute manufacturing capacity over the years by putting up more productive modern machines as against India's old factories.

Fig. 31.4. The jute industry. A gunny bag, a jute product.

Location

Jute industry has been located in five states in India, *i.e.*, West Bengal, Andhra Pradesh, Bihar, Uttar Pradesh and Madhya Pradesh. Though the units engaged in the industry are located in all these five states, the main concentration of the industry is only in the State of West Bengal particularly about sixty miles long and two miles broad along both the banks of Hoogly, above and below Calcutta. The reasons for nearly ninety per cent of concentration of this industry around Calcutta are (*i*) raw jute is cheap and cannot afford much transport cost, as such the mills were forced to establish around Calcutta because of the availability of raw material in abundance in that area; (*ii*) availability of cheap power especially coal in West Bengal; (*iii*) transports, port, financial and commercial development of export market in Calcutta. The Central Government as well as some State Governments are encouraging the farming of jute with a view to feed our jute industry and to establish new units in various locations throughout the country. For example, Tamil Nadu proposes to launch a scheme for cultivation of jute with the ultimate aim of starting a jute mill.

Size

Market and managerial integration determine, to a large extent, the optimum size of units in the jute industry. The loomage capacity of a vast number of Indian mills ranges from 1,400 to 5,000 though mills outside West Bengal have less than 500 looms each. The reason for such large size in West Bengal is mainly influenced by location advantage. It is because of availability of adequate supplies of raw jute. Marketing and managerial integration has accelerated the situation and created an atmosphere which made the units big. It is not possible to say that a unit working with a particular loomage capacity is at optimum level because the problem of optimum size for the Indian jute industry becomes more complicated. It is complicated because of scarcity of raw material, the growing adoption of substitutes in other countries and increasing rate of development of technology and modernisation in the competing countries. If we say today that a particular unit is at optimum level it may not hold good tomorrow due to the dynamic conditions arising in day-to-day life of jute industry.

Competition from substitutes. The Indian jute goods are becoming dearer day by day because of increase in the cost of production due to increase in the price of raw material. Many foreign countries have developed the cheap substitutes of the jute goods. In recent years, the synthetic materials and other alternatives such as paper have emerged as major competitors of jute goods in the field of packing. Unless and until we don't reduce our cost of production and offer the jute goods at cheap rate, there will be no bright future for our jute industry.

Cost of production. In the last few decades the cost of production has gone up by about 75 per cent. Among the various components of cost, there has been a steep rise in wages while the increase in the cost of raw material is of lesser magnitude. The cost of other components such as dyes, chemicals and power charges have also increased.

Competition. The main competitor of India in this industry is Bangladesh. Bangladesh produces raw jute of fine quality and manufactures a variety of jute goods. Bangladesh has been underquoting Indian jute goods in foreign markets. In most of cases the foreign buyers have been placing orders first with Bangladesh; and India gets only residual orders. It is being stated that the jute goods of Bangladesh are cheaper than Indian jute products.

Modernisation. The survival of Industry is mostly dependent on its ability to accelerate the pace of modernisation. The Indian jute industry lags behind Bangladesh both in capital equipment and techniques. The Planning Commission has pointed out that the existing machinery has become to a large extent worn out and obsolete.

32
CHAPTER

Vegetable and Fatty Oils

The fatty oils are liquid at ordinary temperatures and usually contain oleic acid. They are sometimes called 'fixed oils' because, unlike the essential oils they do not evaporate. Chemically, the fatty oils consist of glycerine in combination with a fatty acid.

However, the fats are solid at ordinary temperatures and contain stearic or palmitic acid. When a fat is boiled with an alkali, it decomposes and the fatty acid unites with alkali to form soap.

Usually the fatty oils are stored up in seeds of the plants belonging to many families. Sometimes, to a less extent they are also stored in fruits, stems and other plant organs. Several fatty oils are edible and used as cooking media. The edible oils contain both solid and liquid fats.

Extraction of fatty oils. The seed coats are removed and the material is being converted into a fine meal. The oils may be removed by solvents or by hydraulic pressure. The hydraulic pressure method is commonly used for extracting the edible oils. The residue or oil cake is rich in protein and makes a good cattle feed. The pressure causes the cell walls to break and the fatty oils escape. These oils are filtered and purified. The refined oil is used for food purpose, and the lower grades of oil are used in industries.

Classification of fatty oils. There are three categories of fatty oils–(1) drying and semi-drying oils, (2) nondrying oils, and (3) vegetable fats. The refined grades of drying and semi-drying oils are used as edible oils, whereas the inferior grades are used in making soaps, varnishes, paints, candles and other such articles. The nondrying oils are edible and can be used for soap and lubricants. The fats are solid or semisolid at ordinary temperatures. They are edible and are also used in the soap and candle industries.

DRYING AND SEMI-DRYING OILS

SARSON OIL

Brassica campestris Linn.; var. ***sarson*** Prain; Eng. Yellow sarson, Indian colza; Hindi—*Sarson*; Family—Cruciferae (Brassicaceae).

A herb. It is grown as an oil-seed crop mainly in Uttar Pradesh, the Punjab, Bihar and Assam. The oil content is 30 to 45 percent, and the oil is extracted by expression or solvents.

Uses. The oil is used for cooking and burning purposes. The oil-cake is used as cattle feed.

NUTS WITH HIGH FAT CONTENT

COCONUT

Cocos nucifera Linn.; Family—Palmae/Palmacea/Arecaceae; Eng.—Coconut; Hindi—*Nariyal*; Sanskrit—*Narikela*; Bengali—*Dab, narikel*; Marathi—*Narel, naral*; Telugu—*Kobbarichettu, narikelamu, tenkaya*; Tamil—*Tennaimaram, tenaki*; Kannada—*Tengu*; Malayalam—*Thenna, thenga, marikelam*.

Fig. 32.1. *Cocos nucifera*; Coconut **(Nariyal).** A coconut grove.

History. De Candolle argues in favour of an American as well as those of an Asiatic origin for coconut tree (*Cocos nucifera* Linn.) and concludes that it most probably belongs to the Indian Archipelago. According to him its introduction into India, Sri Lanka and China does not date further back than three thousand years, but the transport by sea to the coasts of America and Africa took place perhaps in a more remote epoch.

A tall palm; cultivated chiefly in Kerala, Tamil Nadu and Karnataka. The coconut has been called a *Kalpavriksha* because it provides a large range of useful products, among which ripe coconut, copra, coconut oil and coir are important. The value of this tree has been recognized from very ancient times. Indeed, the region from South Kanara to Cape Comorin is known as '*Kerala*', meaning the land of the coconut. In Malayalam or Sanskrit "*Keralam*" means land of coconut. The Kerala state in

Fig. 32.2. Germinating coconut.
I, II and III stages

Malayalam is known as "*Keralam*". In these parts, the coconut plays a vital part in the life and economy of the people. The coconut is mainly grown for nuts which it yields almost at monthly interval all through its life of about eighty years.

Varieties and cultivation. Of the varieties of coconuts grown in India, the West Coast variety, is the one that is extensively cultivated. It is a long-lived, hardy, multipurpose palm, yielding a large number of medium-sized nuts in almost every leaf axil. This variety has been cultivated from very ancient times and may be considered as indigenous to the county. Among other varieties are the Dwarf, New Guinea, Cochin-China, Java, Siam, Laccadive ordinary and Laccadive small. The New Guinea variety yields about 65 nuts a year, the Cochin-China about 90, the Java about 95, the Laccadive ordinary about 127 and the Laccadive small 160.

The primary requirements for the successful cultivation of coconut are a tropical climate, abundant rainfall and a well-drained soil. Seashores, river banks and hill-slopes afford ideal situations. In India, the principal areas of cultivation are Kerala, Karnataka, Tamil Nadu, Andhra Pradesh, Maharashtra, West Bengal and Orissa; 85 per cent of the total output comes from Kerala State.

Uses. The tender nuts are in demand for their liquid which provides a very refreshing and delicious drink. It is said to have laxative and diuretic properties. The soft kernel inside the tender nut is also scraped and eaten. The mature nuts are used mainly to make copra (dried meat or kernel) and for edible purposes as fresh kernel in food preparations.

The copra is crushed to obtain coconut oil which is in great demand for edible purposes. It is used as an adjunct for milk-fat, as a filler and thickener for milk and as an ingredient of artificial milk for infants. The cake left after the extraction of oil is largely used to feed cattle and poultry. It is occasionally used as food by poor people. The coconut cake helps to increase the milk content when fed to cows and the butter made from such milk has a firmer texture and better flavour than when other cakes are used.

Fig. 32.3. *Cocos nucifera.* VHC-1 coconut hybrid.

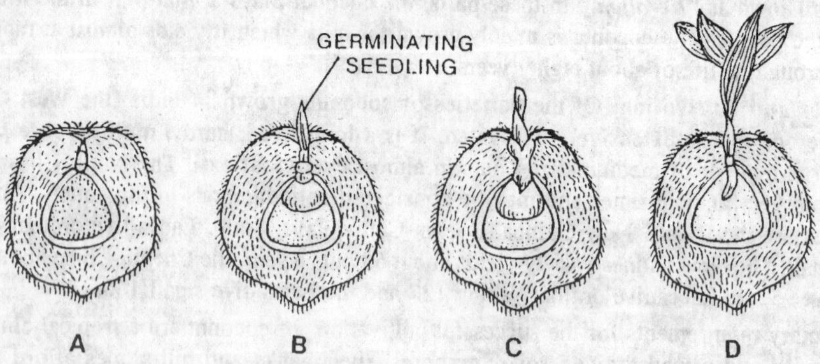

Fig. 32.4. *Cocos nucifera* (coconut). A–D, successive stages (line diagram) showing germination of coconut (seedling stage).

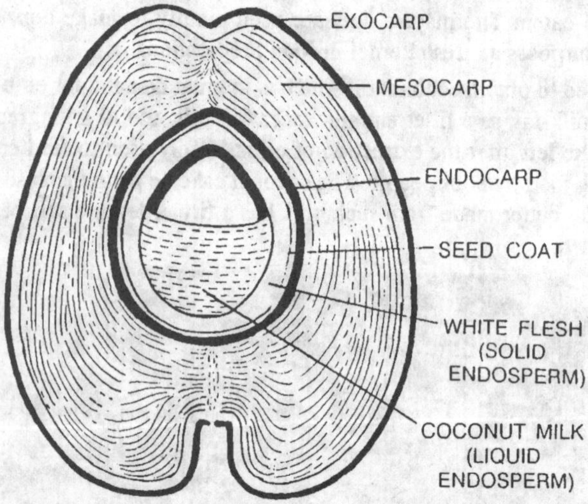

Fig. 32.5. *Cocos nucifera* (coconut). L.S. of fruit with seed.

The coconut inflorescences (spadices) are tapped to extract the juice which is converted into sweet or fermented toddy. Vinegar, jaggery, sugar or arrack (alcohol) are also made from the juice.

Shell of coconut is used for handicrafts; mesocarp (fibre) is used for coir manufacturing. The Kerala State is second to Philippines in the production of coir materials. The dry woven leaves are used for thatching the house and for temporary sheds and pandals in Southern States especially in Kerala.

GROUNDNUT

Arachis hypogaea Linn,: Eng. Peanut, groundnut, Hindi—*Mungphali*; Family—Leguminosae (Papilionaceae).

Bengali—*Chini* *badam*; Marathi—*Bhui mug*; Telugu—*Verusenagalu*; Tamil—*Verkadalai*; Kannada—*Nela-gadale*; Malayalam—

Nelakadala.

History. The peanut (*Arachis hypogea* Linn.) is a native of South America, now generally cultivated throughout India. This was not known in the Old World before the discovery of America. According to Dymock this plant reached India through China. It does not appear to have been cultivated for more than 150 years. This was brought to western India from Africa.

It is native of Brazil. It is widely grown in South India, Maharashtra and Uttar Pradesh. North Gujarat is famous for peanut cultivation. The plant is a bushy or creeping annual with the peculiar habit of ripening its fruit underground. A sandy soil is best for its cultivation. The soil must be friable so that the ripening fruit can be buried, and it must be well fertilized.

Uses. The peanuts (seeds) are used for roasting or salting and for the preparation of peanut butter. Peanuts are a very nutritious food. One lb. of peanuts yields 2700 cal. The filtered refined oil is used for cooking and in making margarine. Peanut oil is an important food oil. The oilcake is used as fodder. The protein in peanuts is used in the manufacture of ardil, a synthetic fibre. The vegetable *ghee* is made from the peanut oil after hydrogenation.

Fig. 32.6. Groundnut. High yielding variety.

The kernels are also used in various foods and confectionery. They are ground and made into peanut butter. Peanut flour is prepared by grinding the finest grades of peanut cake; it is used for supplementing the white flour. Cake is used as feed for cattle and other farm animals; also used as manure. Cake has high nutritive value. Seedcoats are mixed with groundnut husk and the product is called groundnut bran. Some commercial products are groundnut milk, peanut ice-cream and peanut massage oil for infantile paralysis. Hulls are used as filler for fertilizers, or ground into meal for insulation blocks, floor sweeping compounds, bedding the stables, etc. Peanut oil also finds some use as a lubricant, and blends with mineral oil have been developed.

33

CHAPTER

Wood and Cork

From the time immemorial foo7d, clothing and shelter have been the three great necessities of mankind. The wood is the most familiar and most important forest products. The wood has contributed a lot to the advancement of civilization. Today the wood is the most widely used commodity other than food and clothing. It is one of the most important and versatile of the raw materials of the industry. It has so many advantages over the metals.

It is cheap, light and may easily be worked with tools. It is very strong for its weight and it is embodiment of strength, toughness and elasticity. It is a bad conductor of heat and electricity. Wood is also used in the form of thin sheets or veneers. The wood is definitely superior to metals in several respects.

DIAGNOSTIC FEATURES OF WOODS

On the basis of several important diagnostic features the commercial woods may be identified to some extent. The more important diagnostic features are mentioned here:

Porous and nonporous woods. The presence or absence, and the nature and arrangement of pores, serve as a ready means of classifying woods. The coniferous woods do not possess pores, and are known as *nonporous* woods, whereas the angiospermic woods possess numerous pores and are termed as *porous* woods. On the basis of the distribution of pores, the woods may be of two types—*ring porous* and *diffuse porous* woods. In ring porous woods (*e.g.*, ash, elm, oak, etc.) the pores are found to be arranged in concentric circles, the outer and inner portions of which differ with regard to the number and size of the pores. In diffuse porous woods (*e.g.*, beech maple, walnut, etc.) the pores are small and nearly of the same size and are found to be scattered uniformly throughout the wood.

Early wood and late wood. In temperate regions, every year new wood is formed in a limited growing season, with the result definite growth layers develop, which show two distinct areas within each layer. The wood thus formed in the spring is called the *spring wood* or early wood, and that formed in winter is called the *autumn wood* or late wood. There is a sharp contrast between the late autumn wood and the early spring wood, and this makes the successive rings distinct. The growth ring of a single year is called an annual ring and the number of these annual rings gives an indication of the age of tree. Annual rings of successive years may vary greatly in width. Wide rings are formed under favourable conditions of growth of the tree, and narrow ones are formed when conditions are unfavourable.

Sapwood and heartwood. The outer region of the wood which is of lighter colour is known as the *sapwood*, and this alone is used for conduction of water and salt solutions. The cells of this region are alive and physiologically active. In old trees the central region of the secondary wood is filled up with tannin and other substances which make it hard and durable. This region is known as the *heartwood*. It looks black owing to the presence of tannins, oils, gums, resins, etc., in it. The vessels often become plugged with tyloses. The function of the heartwood is no longer conduction of water, but it simply gives mechanical support to the stem. The heartwood usually takes good polish and is used for cabinet work, furniture and other high grade wood-working industries.

Texture, grain and figure. *Texture* refers to the relative size and quality of the various woods, while *grain* refers to their structural arrangement. *Figure* is applied to the design or pattern which appears on the surface of wood.

Rays. The rays are made of parenchyma cells that are oriented at right angles to the main axis of the stem. They vary greatly in width, height and arrangement.

MECHANICAL PROPERTIES OF WOOD

Wood possesses some important mechanical properties which either alone or in combination, determine its usefulness and suitability for various purposes. These properties may differ in different species. The mechanical properties enable the wood to resist various external forces which tend to change its shape and size and produce deformations. The important mechanical properties of wood are mentioned here.

Strength

The strength is restricted to the ability to resist certain definite forces which may be termed—crushing strength, tensile strength, shearing strength and cross-breaking strength. They are as follows:

Crushing strength. It is the resistance offered to forces that tend to crush wood.

Tensile strength. It is the resistance to forces that tend to pull wood apart.

Shearing strength. It is resistance to those forces which tend to make the fibres slide past one another.

Cross-breaking strength. This is the resistance to forces which cause the beams to break, and all the above-mentioned forces are involved.

Stiffness. It is the measure of the ability of wood to resist forces that tend to change its shape.

Toughness. It is referred to the ability of wood to absorb a large amount of energy, and so resist repeated, sudden sharp blows or shock.

Hardness. It is the measure of the power of wood to resist indentations, abrasion and wear.

Cleavability. It is an expression of the ease with which wood can be split.

STRENGTH AND OTHER PROPERTIES OF WOOD

The strength of wood is the most important property in determining the value of any species for structural purposes. It is a very variable property, and is influenced by the density of the wood, the moisture content, the presence of defects and many other factors. Suitability figures for eight different properties have been calculated by taking into consideration the various strength functions of both green and seasoned timber as shown in the table.

Suitability	*Strength and other properties of wood*
1. **Weight**	Specific gravity based on weight oven dry and the volume of seasoned timber (approximately 12%) moisture content.
2. **Strength as a beam**	Modulus of rupture and fibre stress as the elastic limit in static bending. Fibre stress at the elastic limit in impact bending.
3. **Stiffiness as a beam**	Modulus of elasticity in static bending. Modulus of elasticity in impact bending.

Suitability	*Strength and other properties of wood*
4. **Suitability as a post**	Maximum crushing strength and strength at the elastic limit in compression parallel to grain. Modulus of elasticity in static bending.
5. **Shock-resisting ability**	Work to maximum load and total work in static bending.
6. **Retention of shape**	Shrinkage green to oven dry in volume and in the radial and tangential directions.
7. **Shear**	Shearing strength in the radial and tangential directions.
8. **Hardness**	Fibre stress at the elastic limit in compression perpendicular to the grain. Radial, tangential and end hardness.

SEASONING OF WOOD

Wood always contains moisture, the amount of which varies from 40 per cent to 100 per cent or more of the dry weight. The water found within the wood is known as *hygroscopic water*. The amount of hygroscopic water constitutes from 20 to 35 per cent of dry weight. This property of wood is known as *hygroscopicity*. The moisture content of wood has an important bearing on its weight, density, and often on its strength. It is only the loss of hygroscopic water which is responsible for the increase in strength, that accompanies seasoning, as the drying out of wood is called. The loss of hygroscopic water causes the shrinkage of wood. This tendency of wood to shrink as it dries is one of the great drawbacks to its use. As the result of uneven shrinkage, warping and other defects may develop, which tend to counteract any increase in strength. However, dried or seasoned wood is for the most part stronger, harder, stiffer and more durable than unseasoned wood. Artificial methods, of wood seasoning are employed. There are two chief types of artificial wood seasoning—1. *air seasoning* and 2. *kiln drying*.

Air seasoning. Here, the moisture is removed by exposure to air without resorting to artificial heat. It is carried out in open until the wood ceases to lose weight. The ultimate water content varies from 12 to 30 per cent. The main objects of air-seasoning are to reduce weight, the amount of shrinkage and other defects. This is a long-time process.

Kiln drying. Here, heat is applied to wood in an enclosed space. In this process, the moisture is removed more rapidly and more completely. The final moisture content varies from 4 to 12 percent. If green wood is kiln-dried, warping and other defects may be prevented. This process is completed in short duration.

PRINCIPAL WOODS OF INDIA

Babul

Acacia nilotica (Linn.) Del.; Syn. *A. arabica* Willd.; Trade name—Babul; Hindi—*Babul, kikar*; Bengali—*Babul*; Hindi—Punjab and Uttar Pradesh—*Kikar*; Gujarati—*Baval*; Telugu—*Nallatumma*; Tamil—*Karuvelei*; Kannada—*Jaali, gobbli*; Malayalam—*Karivelan*; Family—Mimosaceae.

The sapwood is yellowish-white and usually wide. The heart-wood when freshly cut, is a pinkish or old rose colour, but it darkens on exposure to a dull red or reddish brown. It is often mottled with darker streaks. The wood is dull and without taste or smell, hard, fairly close-textured and with straight or slightly twisted grain.

There are several varieties of *babul*. The two best known are the *telia* and *kauria* varieties, the wood of the former having a better reputation than the latter.

Seasoning. Babul is a wood which can be air-seasoned with fairly good results if care is taken. One year is sufficient to air-season babul boards up to 2 in. in thickness. It can be kiln-seasoned without difficulty.

Strength. Babul is an extremely strong, hard and tough wood. It is nearly twice as hard as teak and has a very good shock resisting ability.

Durability. The sapwood is not durable. The heartwood is durable in most situations but not to the same degree as teak and sal.

Working qualities. An easy wood to convert and to saw when green, but it becomes harder and tougher when seasoned. It works well by hand, and machines and finishes to a good surface. It takes a fair polish but requires careful filling.

Uses. It is popular for parts of carts (body work, spokes, naves, axles, felloes, yokes and shafts), and for agricultural implements such as ploughs, harrows and clod-crushers. It is a useful tool handle wood but not for all types of handle, and it can be used for tent pegs. It can be

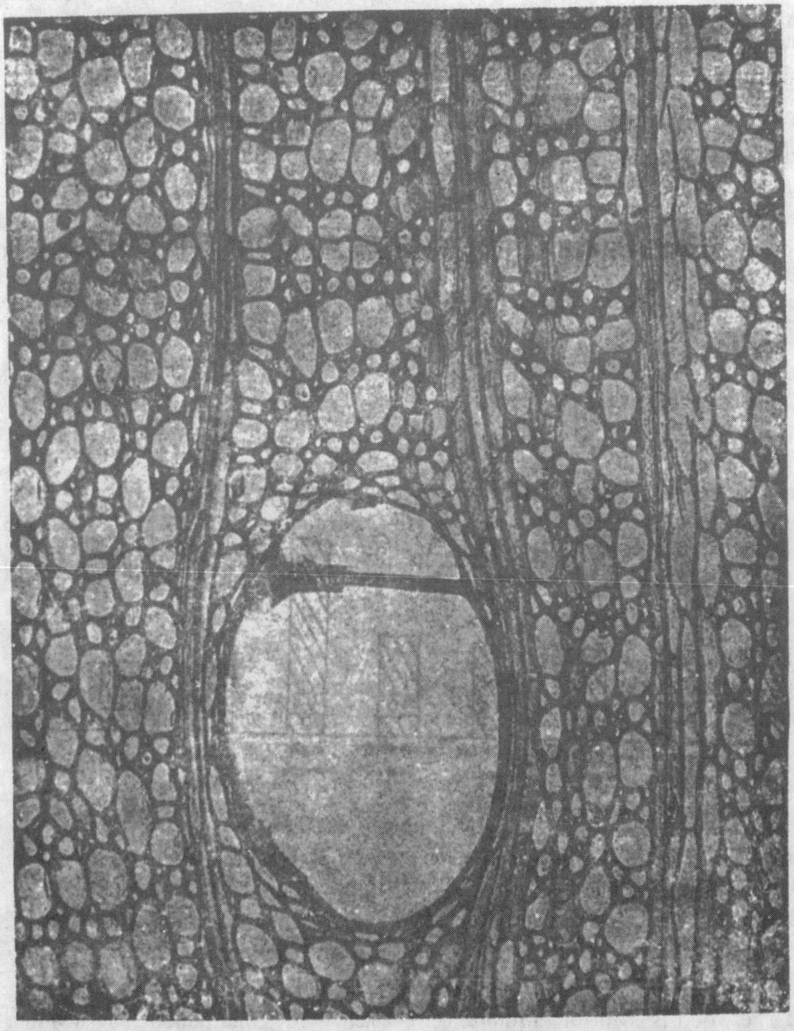

Fig. 33.1. *Bombax ceiba* **(Semul)**. Micrograph X110, of wood.

described as one of the best Indian utility woods where hardness and toughness are required. It is a good turnery wood.

Sources of supply. Babul is usually available in small logs only, but in some districts larger logs are available. It is found throughout the drier regions of North, Central and South India.

Simul

Bombax ceiba L.; Syn. *Salmalia insiginis* (Wall.) Schott & Endl.; Hindi—*Semul*; Sanskrit—*Salmali, rakta-pushpa*; Bengali—*Simul, roktosimul*; Marathi—*Saur, simlo*; Gujarati—*Sawar, simalo*; Telugu—*Booruga, konda-buruga*; Tamil—*Mullialava*; Kannada—*Booruga*; Malayalam—*Pula-maram*; Oriya—*Bour*; Garo—*Panchu*; Mundari—*Edelsong*; Family—Bombacaceae.

A large tree found in the Western Ghats, Assam and the Andaman Islands. The wood is very soft creamy white or pale pink timber, very light in weight and with large open pores.

Seasoning. Quick drying can be achieved by exposing freshly converted timber directly to the drying action of the sun and wind or by kiln-seasoning. If air-seasoning is to be done, the best method is to stack the freshly sawn stock in a vertical position against a building or railing with the planks facing the sun. The boards should be turned from time to time so that both surfaces are exposed, kiln-seasoning is the surest and best method of drying *simul*.

Uses. The wood is used for matches, packing cases, penholders, veneers and ply-wood.

Wood is most widely used in match industry, especially for match boxes. Suitable for shingles, canoes, toys, scabbards, cooperage, bush handles, tea-chest plywood and picture frames. Also used for cushioning mine-props and for inside portions of opium chests. Floss used for stuffing life belts, mattresses, cushions and pillows, upholstry and quilts. Tree yields a gum called *mocharus*.

Albizia

There are several common commercial *Albizia* woods. The best known is perhaps ***Albizia lebbeck*** (Linn.) Benth.; the others *A. odoratissima, A. procera*, and *A. stipulata*.

Red Cedar

Toona ciliata Roem.; Eng. Cedrela tree, Red cedar; Hindi—*Toon*; Sanskrit—*Nandivriksha, tunna*; Hindi and Bengali—*Tun, mahanim*; Marathi—*Kuruk*; Tamil—*Santhanavembu, tunumaram*; Telugu—*Nandichettu*; Kannada—*Mandurike*; Malayalam—*Malarveppu*; Assam—*Poma*; Family—Meliaceae.

A tree cultivated in the Punjab, Assam, Bihar, the Western Ghats, Maharashtra, Madhya Pradesh and the Nilgiris.

Description of wood. The wood is a pinkish brick red, when freshly cut, toning to a light brownish red on exposure. The wood is a light weight, and usually straight grained timber. The wood has a distinct cedar like smell.

Seasoning. *Toon* is a fairly easy wood to air-season if care is taken with the stacking. Kiln-seasoning can also be done.

Strength. *Toon* is a timber of only moderate strength qualities. Hill *toon* is strongest and has about 80% the strength of teak.

Working qualities. *Toon* is one of the easiest of Indian woods to saw and work. If properly finished and filled, it takes a very good polish. It makes up into a good type of plywood. It makes high quality congealated wood.

Uses. The wood is used for furniture, tea-chests, shuttles and picking sticks which are used in the textile industry, and cigar boxes.

Walnut

Juglans regia Linn.; Eng. English walnut, Persian walnut; Hindi—*Akhrot*; Family—Juglandaceae. Found in Kashmir, Himachal Pradesh, the Khasia hills and in the hills of Uttar Pradesh.

Indian walnut varies considerably in colour, sometimes being a dull grey, while other wood may be a dark brown with even darker markings. It is relatively light wood for its strength and it works very easily and finishes to a fine surface. Its most important quality, however, is that, when once dried it does not shrink, swell or split. This, combined with its lightness, strength and good working qualities gives it pre-eminence as a wood for rifle parts, gun stocks, high class cabinet making, and delicate carvings.

Seasoning. Walnut wood seasons slowly and springs considerably while drying out, but apart from this, it is a model wood in so far as seasoning is concerned, both in air-drying and kiln-drying. Green conversion, followed by stacking under cover with a good air circulation is the method of seasoning recommended.

Strength. For its weight, walnut is a relatively strong wood. It is about 85% the weight of teak and in shock resistance is about equal to teak.

Working qualities. An extremely easy and pleasant wood to saw and work to a fine finish. It takes an excellent polish and needs very little filling.

Uses. The wood is used for musical instruments and cabinet work. Used extensively in Kashmir and North India for carving. Well known as an excellent veneer and plywood timber. It is also used for gun stocks.

White Willow

Salix alba Linn.; Eng. White willow; Hindi—*Bis*; Kashmir—*Vivir*; Punjab—*Bis, madnu, bhushan*; Family—Salicaceae.

A small tree, found in the North-Western Himalayas and in the valley of Kashmir. The twigs are used for making baskets. Cricket bats are made of the wood.

Used also for house building, match-boxes and splints, shoes, tool-handles, agricultural implements, boats, boxes, combs and toothpicks; suitable for paper pulp and charcoal making.

Mulberry

Morus alba, Linn; Eng. White mulberry; Hindi—*Tut*; Family—Moraceae. A tree, native of China. In India, it is grown in Punjab, Uttar Pradesh, Kashmir and the North-Western Himalayas. It is also cultivated in Karnataka state for silk worm cultivation.

Description of the wood. The sapwood is white and sharply delimited from the heartwood, which is a bright yellowish brown when freshly cut. No odour or taste. Straight-grained and of rather open medium coarse texture.

Seasoning. The best results have been obtained by storing the logs for some months before final conversion. The wood can be kiln-seasoned without difficulty. In practice, the most of the mulberry used in Punjab is used in a green state by the sports goods manufacturers. The timber is converted green, steam bent, and the dried out in a bent form tightly held in a clamp.

Strength. It is approximately the same in weight as teak, and in shock resistance, shear and hardness it is considerably higher than teak.

Uses. The primary use is for sports goods, for which purpose it is eminently suitable. It is used mainly for the manufacture of hockey sticks. It is also used for tennis rackets, badminton and squash rackets, presses, cricket stumps, etc.

Fig. 33.2. *Cedrus deodara* (**Deodar**). A tree at Forest Division, Chakrata, Uttarákhand

Also suitable for house-building, agricultural implements, furniture, spokes, poles, shafts, bent parts of carriages and carts and for turnery. Bark is used for paper making; also yields a textile fibre.

Deodar

Cedrus deodara Loud.; Eng. Deodar; Hindi—*Deodar*, *Diar*; Family—Pinaceae.

A tall evergreen tree found in the North-Western Himalayas from Kashmir to Garhwal.

Description of the wood. It is of light yellow-brown colour and possesses distinctive odour. It is a medium weight wood which is very sturdy in use and durable. It is usually even-grained and of medium to fine texture, but the presence of large knots is a common feature

Seasoning. It is an easy wood to air-season. It can also be kiln-seasoned.

Strength. Deodar is the strongest of the Indian conifers. Its weight is 20% less than teak and its strength is also about 20% less.

Working qualities. It is an easy timber to saw and work to a smooth finish.

Uses. The timber is used for construction work and for railway sleepers. It is also suitable for beams, floor boards, ports, window frames, light furniture and shingles.

This is strongest of Indian coniferous woods, also used for doors, furniture, packing cases, masts, spars and also for wooden bridges. Wood yields an oleoresin and a dark coloured oil used for ulcers and skin diseases.

Himalayan Spruce

Picea smithiana (Wall.) Boiss. ; Eng. Himalayan spruce; Hindi—*Bajur*; North West Himalayan region—*Rai, rau, re, kachal, salla, tos*; Jaunsar, Garhwal and Kumaon—*Roi, rhai, ragha, morinda*; Trade—Spruce; Family—Pinaceae.

A tree commonly found in the Western Himalayas. The wood is used for construction work, railway sleepers, cabinet making, packing cases and wood pulp.

One of the most useful timber trees of the Western Himalayas. Wood is used for planking, general fittings and joinery, rough furniture, tea-boxes and packing cases. This is one of the best light boxwood of India. Wood is suitable also for match boxes, battery separators, for fence posts, transmission poles, piles and newsprint manufacture.

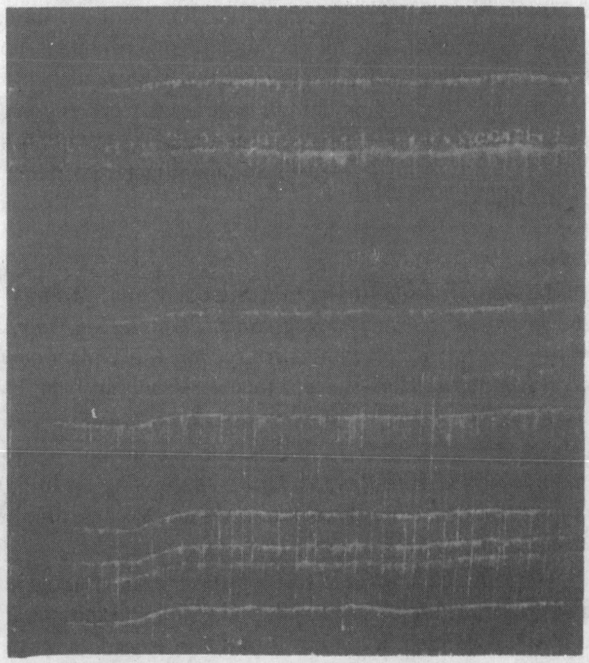

Fig. 33.3. Deodar wood (non-porous), sectional view of micrograph X 10.

Pine Wood

Pinus roxburghii Sar.; Eng. Long-leaved pine; Hindi—*Chir, Salla*; Family—Pinaceae.

An evergreen coniferous tree. It is found in the Western and Eastern Himalayas. The wood is used for construction work, railway sleepers, packing cases, furniture and in match industry.

Pinus merkusii Jungh & de Vries. A tree. The wood is very resinous with reddish-brown heartwood and yellow sapwood. It is used for building purposes and general carpentry.

Pinus wallichiana A. B. Jackson; Eng. Indian blue-pine; Hindi—*Kail, Chil*. A coniferous tree. The wood is used for pencils, penholders, splints, match boxes, construction work, railway sleepers, and furniture. Also used for shingles, packing cases, constructional work and house fitments. It is a good wood for pattern making, cores for laminboards, drawing boards, and planetables.

Indian Rosewood

Dalbergia latifolia Roxb.; Eng. Indian rosewood; Verna. *Kali Shisham*; Sanskrit—*Shishapa*; Bengali—*Sitsal, swetasal*; Marathi—*Shisham, siswa*; Gujarati—*Shissam, kalaruk*; Telugu—*Cittegi, irgudu*; Tamil—*Itti, karundorviral*; Kannada—*Bite, todagatti*; Malayalam—*Itti, colavitti*; Oriya—*Sisua*; Trade—Indian Rosewood; Family—Papilionaceae.

A large deciduous or nearly evergreen tree with cylindrical, fairly straight bole and full rounded crown, found in the sub-Himalayan tract of Eastern Uttar Pradesh, Bihar, Orissa and central, western and southern India. It attains its maximum development in the southern region of western ghats, where trees 130 ft. high up to 20 ft. in girth and 70 ft. clear bole are sometimes found. The minimum exploitable size is 6 ft. girth.

The sapwood is narrow and pale yellowish white in colour, often with a purple tinge. The heartwood ranges in colour from golden brown through shades of light rose, purple with darker streaks, to deep purple with rather distant, nearly black lines, darkening with age. It is fragrant, heavy, narrowly interlocked grained and medium coarse-textured. The timber is stronger and much harder than teak.

Indian rosewood ranks among the first wood for furniture and cabinet work. It is a valuable decorative wood suitable for carving and ornamental ply-boards and veneers. It is specially useful for pattern-making, calico printing blocks, mathematical instruments and screws. It is also used for gun carriage wheels, ammunition boxes and army wagons, pulleys, handles, shelves, decorative carriage parts, temple chariots, boat knees, agricultural implements, combs, razor handles and brush backs. Carefully selected and manufactured Indian rosewood ply-boards satisfy aircraft specifications.

Sissoo

Dalbergia sissoo Roxb.; Eng. Sissoo; Verna. *Shisham*; Sanskrit—*Shinshapa, aguru*; Hindi—*Shisham, sissu, sissai*; Bengali—*Shisu*; Gujarati—*Sisam, tanach*; Telugu—*Errasissu, sinsupa*; Tamil—*Sisu itti*; Kannada—*Agaru, biridi*; Malayalam—*Iruvil*; Oriya—*Sisu, simsapa*; Punjab—*Tali, shisham*; Marathi—*Sissu*; Trade—Sissoo, Shisham; Family—Papilionaceae.

A deciduous tree, often with crooked trunk and light crown. Normally the tree attains a height of about 100 ft., a girth up to 8 ft. and a clear bole up to 35 ft. It occurs throughout the sub-Himalayan tract from Ravi to Assam, ascending up to 5,000 ft. It is extensively cultivated in Punjab. Uttar Pradesh, Bengal and Assam. No other timber tree, except teak is cultivated to a greater extent.

The sapwood is white to pale brownish white in colour and the heartwood, golden brown to dark brown with deep brown streaks becoming dull on exposure. It is heavy, narrowly interlocked grained and medium textured. It can be air or kiln-seasoned. However, kiln-seasoning enhances the value of timber as the colour darkness and the difference between lighter and darker bands gets intensified. The wood can be converted into ornamental veneers or commercial plywood of good quality.

Sissoo (*Shisham*), is a high class furniture and cabinet wood widely used throughout north India. On account of its great strength, elasticity and durability, it is highly valued as constructional and general utility timber and is used for all the purposes for which Indian rosewood is employed in the south. It is esteemed also for railway sleepers, musical instruments, *Charpai* legs, hammer handles, shoe heels, *hookah* tubes and tobacco pipes. Carefully selected and manufactured plywood logs satisfy the specifications prescribed for aircraft, and for this purpose, the wood from trees, growing on canal banks and in plantations is considered to be the best. Sissoo wood is suitable for making laminated skiis. It can be worked into decorative ornamental carvings.

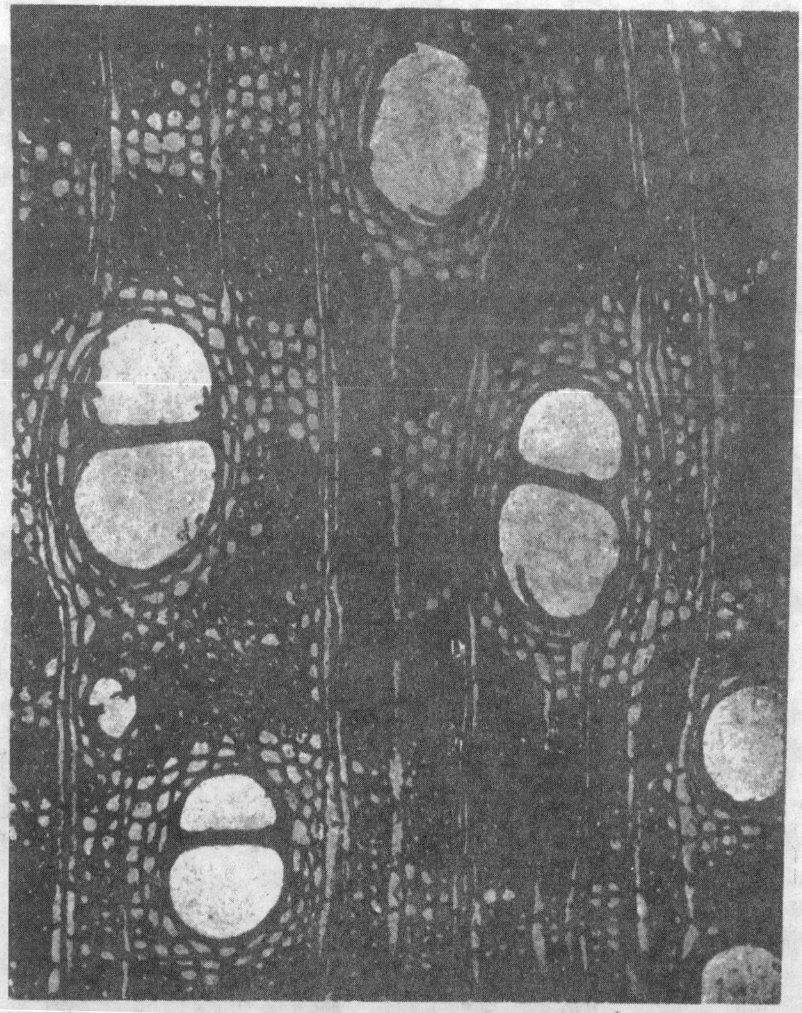

Fig. 33.4. *Dalbergia sissoo* (porous wood) micrograph of wood x 110.

Andaman Redwood

Pterocarpus indicus Willd; Eng. Andaman redwood; Verna. *Padauk*. It is a large and lofty tree found in the Andaman islands. Sapwood is small. Heartwood is dark-red, close-grained, moderately hard with a slight aromatic scent. It is durable and not attacked by white ants. When thoroughly seasoned it is unaffected by alternate dryness and moisture of the atmosphere. It seasons well, works well and takes a very fine polish. It is used for furniture, carts, guncarriages, and other purposes, and is said to be the most useful wood in the Andamans, and where it grows to an enormous size.

Indian Kino Tree

Pterocarpus marsupium Roxb. Sanskrit—*Pitasara*; Hindi—*Bijasal*; Bengali—*Pitshal*; Marathi—*Asan, bibla*; Gujarati—*Biyo*; Telugu—*Yegi, peddagi*; Tamil—*Vengai*; Kannada—*Honne, Bange*; Malayalam—*Venga*; Oriya—*Byasa*; Trade—Bijasal; Family—*Leguminosae*.

Fig. 33.5. *Pterocarpus marsupium.* Indian Kino Tree. The trees in Karnataka State.

The wood is used chiefly for building purposes, such as doors, window frames, rafters, beams and posts. It is also used in railway carriages, wagons, carts, boats, ships, electric poles, pit-props in mines, agricultural implements, drums, tool handles, camp furniture, mathematical instruments, picture frames, combs, and parts of textile looms. It is a very important timber in peninsular India.

Red Sandalwood

Pterocarpus santalinus Linn.; Eng. Red sandalwood; Verna. *Rukhto-chandan*; Sanskrit—*Raktachandana*; Hindi and Bengali—*Raktachandan, lalchandan*; Marathi—*Tambada chandana*; Gujarati—*Ratanjali*; Telugu—*Agarugandhamu, raktagandhamu*; Tamil—*Atti, sivappu chandanam*; Kannada—*Agaru, honne, kempugandha*; Malayalam—*Patrangam*; Oriya—*Raktachandan*; Trade—Red Sanders.

A small tree of South India, chiefly found in Cuddapah, North Arcot, and the southern portion of the Karnul district. It favours a dry, rather rocky soil, and a hot fairly dry climate. Sapwood is white. Heartwood is purplish-black dark orange-red when fresh cut, extremely hard, the shavings giving a blood red-orange colour. It is used for building and for turning, and is said to be much prized because it is not subject to the attacks of white ants. It is much used for carvings in Andhra Pradesh especially at Tirupati.

Wood is highly prized for house posts; also used for agricultural implements, poles, shafts and bent rims of carts, picture frames, boxes and other joinery work. In Japan, it is used for a musical instrument called **Shamisen**. Wood is ground and used for dyeing wool, cotton and leather, and staining other woods; *santalin* is the colouring principle.

Ebony

Diospyros ebenum Koenig.; Eng. Ebony; Verna. *Abnus*; Hindi—*Ebans, abnus*; Telugu—*Vallavalludu*; Tamil—*Tumbi, karunkali*; Kannada—*Karemara*; Malayalam—*Karu, vauari*; Oriya—*Kendhu*; Trade—Ebony.

It is a moderate to large sized evergreen tree with a dense crown, sometimes attaining a height up to 80 ft. and a girth of 7 ft. The girth of heartwood is not more than 4 ft. It is found in the dry evergreen forests of Deccan, Karnataka, Coimbatore, Malabar, Cochin and Travancore. It prefers well-drained rocky soil and grows well on sandy loam. It is found sparsely scattered in the forests in mixture with other trees.

This is perhaps the best ebony yielding tree and the only one which yields jet black heartwood without streaks or markings, the true ebony of commerce, *D. ebenum* is not very commonly found in India, nor do the trees, where they occur, attain any large size. Only limited supply of ebony is available in the area of its occurrence.

The sapwood is light yellowish grey, often streaked with black. The heartwood is jet black, rarely with a few dark or light brown or golden streaks. It has a metallic lustre when smoothed. It is heavy, straight-grained or somewhat irregular or wavy-grained, fine and even-textured.

Ebony is difficult to season. It is best to convert the green logs to the smallest size permissible and to store them under cover, well protected from hot winds.

The heartwood is resistant to attack by insects and fungi. It is very durable. The value of this wood depends on its intense blackness, working quality and the high finish it takes. It is difficult to work, especially when dry, but finishes to a glossy surface. It requires little hand finishing and takes a high lasting polish. It is one of the most valuable woods in the fancy wood market. It is used for ornamental carving and turnery, and for special purposes in decoration. It is used for veneers, inlaying, musical instruments, sports goods, mathematical instruments, piano keys and caskets.

Diospyros virginianum Linn. is widely used for weaving shuttles and is the standard wood for the heads of golf clubs.

Saffron Teak

Adina cordifolia Hook. f.; Eng. Saffron teak; Verna, *Haldu*, Hindi—*Haldu*; Bengali—*Petpuria, dakom*; Marathi—*Heddi*; Telugu—*Pasupukadamba*; Tamil and Malayalam—*Manjakadamba*; Kannada—*Arsintega, yettega*; Trade—Haldu; Family—Rubiaceae;

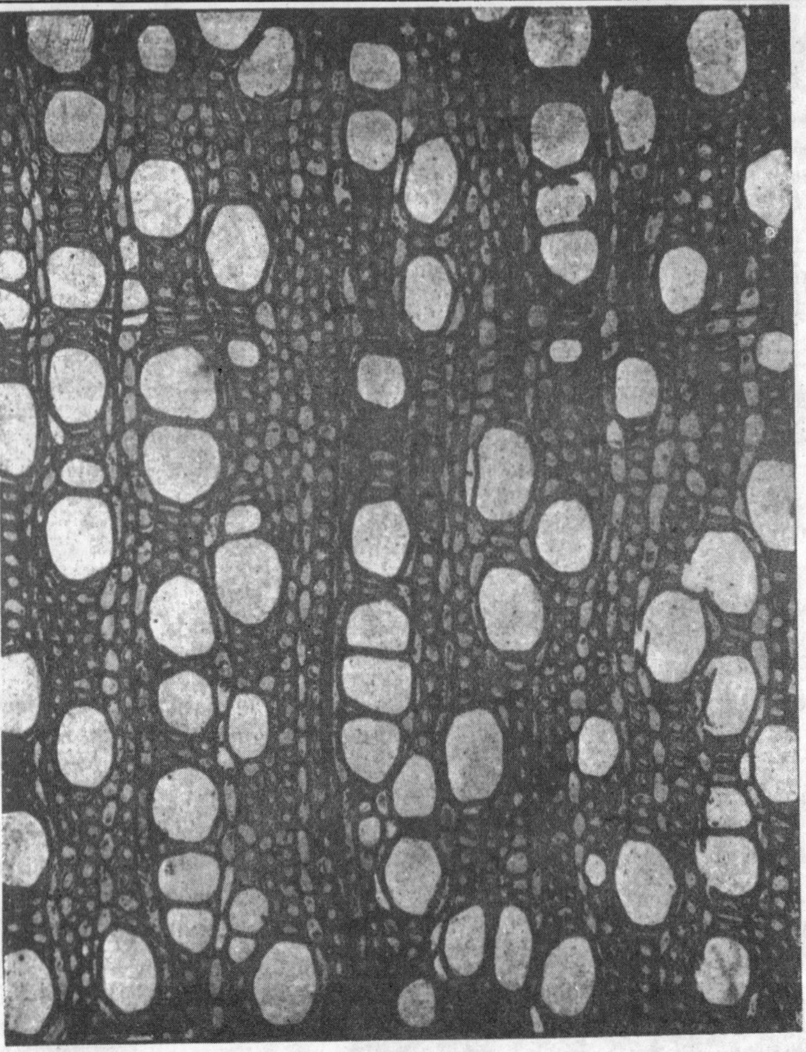

Fig. 33.6. *Adina cordifolia* **(Haldu)**. Micrograph x 110, of porous wood.

This makes an important Indian timber, used for a great variety of purposes; Pearson and Brown (1932) state that it is one of the best turnery wood in India and that selected pieces are attractively figured. The wood is commonly used for carvings, construction work, flooring and for railway carriages.

Timber is easy to saw, seasons well and takes good polish; durable under cover, resistant against subterranean termites, but highly susceptible to drywood termites. Haldu is accepted as grade I commercial and moisture-proof plywood timber.

Wrapping, writing and printing paper is manufactured from the wood pulp.

Teak

Tectona grandis Linn.; Eng. Teak; Hindi—*Sagaun*; Sanskrit—*Saka*; Bengali—*Segun*; Marathi—*Sag, sagwan*; Gujarati—*Saga*; Telugu—*Adaviteeku, teeku*; Tamil—*Tekkumaram, tekku*; Kannada—*Jadi, sagwani*; Malayalam—*Thekku, tekha*; Oriya—*Singuru*; Assam—*Chingjagu*; **Lepcha—*Ripnyok*; Family—Verbenaceae.**

A large, deciduous tree, indigenous to both peninsulas of India. In Western India it does not extend far beyond the Mhye. In Central India it attains its northern most point in the Jhansi district, and from that point the line of its northern limit continues in a south-east direction to the Mahanadi river in Orissa. It is found wild in Assam. It is, however, cultivated throughout Bengal, Assam and Sikkim, and in North-West India without difficulty as far as Saharanpur. The forests richest in large timber on the west side of the Peninsula are the Travancore, Anamally, Wynad, South-west Karnataka and North Kanara forests. In the centre of the Peninsula the Godavary forests are most compact and valuable.

Structure and utility of wood. Sapwood white and small; the heartwood when cut green, has a pleasant and strong aromatic fragrance and a beautiful dark golden yellow colour, which on seasoning soon darkens into brown, mottled with darker streaks. The timber retains its fragrance to a great age, the characteristic odour being apparent whenever a fresh cut is made. It is moderately hard, exceedingly durable and strong, does not split, crack, warp, shrink or alter its shape when once seasoned; it works easily, takes a good polish. Teak owes its chief value to its great durability, which is ascribed, probably with justice, to the circumstance that it contains a large quantity of fluid resinous matter which fills up the pores and resists the action of water. (At the Karli caves near Poona the teak-wood-work, two thousand years old, seems perfectly good at the present day).

The many uses of teak are well known. In India it is highly prized for construction, ship building, and for making sleepers and furniture.

Wood is very durable and resistant to fungi. It is used for poles, beams, trusses, columns, roofs, doors, window frames, flooring, planking, panelling, stair cases, and other constructional work. It is one of the best timbers for furniture and cabinet making, wagons and railway carriages. Due to its better shape-retention ability, teak is popular in marine constructions and is a class by itself for boat and ship–building, particularly for decking. On account of its resistance to chemicals, teak articles are used in chemical industries and for making laboratory bench-tops; suitable for casks and vats for shipping corrosive liquids and for storing vegetable oils, fruit syrups, chutneys, etc. Teak is employed for sound-boards of musical instruments, keys, etc., and for different grades of plywood. Wood waste in the form of wood-shavings and sawdust is used for chip-boards, fibre-boards and plastic-boards.

Sal

Shorea robusta; Eng. Sal tree; Hindi—*Sal*; Bengali and Hindi—*Sal, sakhu*; Marathi and Gujarati—*Ral*; Telugu—*Gugal*; Tamil—*Kungiliyam*; Kannada—*Kabba*; Malayalam—*Maramaram*; Oriya—*Sal, sagua*; Punjab and Haryana—*Sal*; Lepcha—*Taksal-Kung*; Assam—*Sal, bolsal*; Trade—Sal; Family—Dipterocarpaceae.

A large gregarious tree, often covering certain interrupted tracts without the existence of connecting patches. It occurs along the base of Tropical Himalayas from the Sutlej to Assam, in the eastern districts of Central India, and on the Western Bengal Hills.

Structure and utility of wood. The *sal*, one of the most valuable timber trees in India, has a distinct sapwood which is small in amount, whitish and not durable. The heartwood is brown in colour, finely streaked with darker lines, coarse grained, hard, strong and tough, with a remarkably fibrous and cross-grained, structure. The fibres of successive concentric strata do not run parallel, but at oblique angles, to each other, so that when the wood is dressed the fibres appear interlaced. It does not season well, but warps and splits in drying, and even when thoroughly seasoned, absorbs moisture with avidity in wet weather. During the process of seasoning, it dries when first cut, and evaporation goes on afterwards with extreme slowness. *Sal*, when once thoroughly seasoned, stands almost without a rival, as a timber, for strength, elasticity, and durability, which

Fig. 33.7. Scientifically managed Sal Forest, at Dehradun.

qualities it retains without being sensibly affected, for an immense length of time. Average weight of the seasoned *sal* about 35 lb. per cubic foot (Brandis; Gamble).

The timber is the one most extensively used in Northern India. It is in constant request for piles, beams, planking and railing of bridges, doors, and window posts of houses, for the bodies of carts, and above all, for railway sleepers. In Assam it is favourite wood for boat-building, and in the hills of Northern Bengal where it is found, perhaps, of the largest size available, the trunks are hollowed out into canoes. Owing to the fact that when unseasoned it is not floatable, difficulty is experienced in most sal forests in getting the timber out of the forests in log. This is, however, overcome by floating the logs either with the assistance of the boats or with floats of light wood or bamboos (Gamble).

Sal wood ranks with teak and deodar as one of the best sleeper woods in India; also used in form of bellies and poles. After treatment, the poles are suitable for overhead electric, telegraph and telephone lines. As domestic timber it is used for beams, scantlings, rafters and floors; also used for piles, mine work and pit props, bridges, dug-out boats, carriages and wagon building, spokes, fellows and hubs of wheels, agricultural implements, tool-handles, tent pegs, liquid storage vats, and beer and oil casks.

WOODS FOR VARIOUS USES

Agricultural implements. Agricultural implements is a term of rather wide application but it refers in the main to such appliances as ploughs, harrows, rollers and clod crushers. A strong, hard tough timber is required for this type of work. *Acacia nilotica* (*Babul*), *Anogeissus latifolia* (*axle wood*), *Syzygium cumini* (*Jaman*), *Grewia tiliifolia* (*Dhaman*), *Shorea robusta* (*Sal*), *Xylia xylocarpa* (*Irul*), etc., are used for agricultural implements of different kinds.

Axe helves and tool handles. Woods for helves and tool handles must be strong and tough and must also possess great shock resisting abilities. *Dalbergia* spp. (*Shisham*), *Grewia* spp. (*Dhaman*), *Diospyros* spp. (ebony), etc., are recommended for this purpose.

Boat and ship-building. Timber used in all small boats and large ships is subjected to very great strains, and is often employed under circumstances which tax its durability to the utmost. For this reason any timber used for ship and boat-building should be strong, elastic, durable and free from defects. *Tectona grandis* (Teak—*Sagaun*) is the best ship-building timber in the world, due to its relatively small co-efficient of expansion and contraction and to its durability. The other recommended timbers for this purpose are—*Acacia nilotica* (*Babul*), *Dalbergia* spp., *Dipterocarpus* spp., *Shorea* spp., *Xylia* spp., *Grewia* spp., *Morus* spp., *Terminalia* spp., *Bombax* spp., etc.

Boot lasts and shoe heels. There is a considerable demand in India for boot and shoe lasts, and recently demand for shoe heels, and especially ladies shoe heels, has grown enormously. For boot lasts and shoe heels, a tough wood which is not too hard is required. In addition, the wood must be able to stand repeated nailing. The important woods used for the purpose are—*Dalbergia sissoo* (*Shisham*), *Gardenia* spp., *Mitragyna parviflora* (*Kaim*), *Mangifera indica* (*Am*), etc.

Cart and carriage building. The various parts of a cart or carriage are subjected to different kinds of stresses and strains, and require different qualities of wood for real efficiency. The important woods recommended for various parts of the carts are—*Dalbergia* spp., *Shorea* spp., *Dipterocarpus* spp., *Syzygium* spp., *Acacia* spp., *Grewia* spp., *Anogeissus* spp., *Terminalia* spp., and several others.

Construction and general joinery work. Constructional woods are those timbers used for superstructures, which include all parts of houses and buildings, bridges and similar structures not actually in contact with water or the earth. For this purpose a timber should be strong and durable. Lightness of wood is sometimes an asset if strength and durability are not sacrificed. Floor and wall planking should be non-warping and non–shrinking and the wood for interior work and panels should be ornamental. There are three very important woods which stand out above all others as building timbers. These are—*Tectona grandis* (Teak—*Sagaun*), *Shorea robusta* (*Sal*) and *Cedrus deodara* (*Deodar*). The other important timbers used for this purpose are—*Acacia* spp., *Toona ciliata* (*toon*), *Dalbergia* spp., *Mangifera indica* (*Am*), *Pinus* spp., *Terminalia* spp., *Xylia* spp.

Cooperage. Cooperage or barrel-making consists of two types, "*tight cooperage*", *i.e.*, barrels used for liquids, and "loose or slack cooperage" used for dry goods like cement. The oaks, dhaman are used for tight cooperage for beer and liquor casks. *Bombax ceiba* (*Simul*), mango spruce, etc., are used for slack cooperage.

Electric poles. The qualities necessary to make a good pole are that it should be straight, *i.e.*, without crooks and bends, that it should not split or crack excessively, and that it should have the required strength for the work it has to do. The woods used in India for use as electrical transmission poles are—*Pinus roxburghii* (*Chir*), *Shorea robusta* (*Sal*), *Tectona grandis* (*Teak*), *Cedrus deodara* (*Deodar*), *Terminalia tomentosa* (Laurel), etc.

Engraving and printing blocks. *Dalbergia sissoo* (*Shisham*) in North India, and *Dalbergia latifolia* (Rosewood) in South India, are the most popular woods for calico-printing blocks. Sissoo (*Shisham*) is considered to be excellent for the purpose. *Toona ciliata* (toon) and *Tectona grandis* (teak) are also sometimes used. *Tamarindus* (*Imli*) is also said to be good for printing by the Indian method.

Furniture, cabinet making and panelling. For high class furniture, cabinet-making and decorative panel work, there are several very ornamental and excellent woods in India. The chief characteristics required for these uses are non-liability to crack and split, retention of shape, ease of working and good colour figure and grain. The most commonly used and recommended timbers for the purpose are *Albizia* spp., *Toona ciliata* (toona), *Dalbergia* spp., *Juglans regia* (walnut), *Tectona grandis* (teak), *Terminalia tomentosa* (Laurel), etc.

Artocarpus spp., is wildly grown and commonly used for making furniture in South India especially in Kerala it is a valuable wood. It is also preferred in temple works in Kerala.

Match splints and boxes. A good match wood for splint manufacture must be soft, straight-grained, white and cheap. India possesses many woods which are suitable for box making and splints. The woods are—*Bombax ceiba* (*simul*), *Anthocephalus indicus* (kadam), *Salix* spp., etc.

Mathematical instruments. The better class of mathematical instruments such as set squares, rulers, etc., are usually made of *Buxus wallichiana* (box wood), *Juglans regia* (walnut) and *Aesculus indica* (horse chestnut), but cheaper instruments intended for school use are often made of *Adina cordifolia* (*Haldu*), *Toona ciliata* (Toon), *Gardenia* spp., etc. For set square and ruler edgings, good quality hardwoods such as rosewood sissoo and ebony are most frequently used.

Musical instruments. In India, many woods are used for making musical instruments as tanpura, sitars, violins, etc., *teak, toon, sissoo, mulberry, haldu* being among the commonest. For *sitars*, teak is used for the long neck and *deodar* or *shisham* for keys. Toon is almost universally used for the bodies. For banjos, teak is most commonly used. For drums, *mulberry, sissoo, siris* etc, are used. *Canarium euphyllum* (*Dhup*) is used for guitars.

Packing cases and boxes. Wood for these purposes must be light, easily worked and cheap. They must have good nail-holding power and should preferably be of whitish colour. Tea is now generally packed in plywood chests, which are strong, light and cheap. *Hollock* (*Terminalia myriocarpa*) and *hollong* are used for making good plywood tea chests. The commonest Indian woods for packing cases and boxes are—*Dalbergia* spp., toon, teak, mango, siris, kadam, *Terminalia chebula, Pinus* spp., etc., Cigar boxes are used made in South India of *Toona ciliata, Melia azedarach*, etc. *Terminalia chebula* is a popular wood in South India for coffee boxes, while poplar (*Populus* spp.) is much used in Kashmir for fruit crates.

Pencils and pen-holders. Amongst the timbers used in India for pencil making may be mentioned Cypress, blue pine or *kail, simul, toon, Salix tetrasperma, Melia* spp., etc. Pen-holders may be made of *Haldu, Gardenia* spp., *Kaim*, etc., Spruce and fir are used in North India for cheap pen-holders.

Picture framing. No very special qualities are required for picture framing, so long as the wood used is well seasoned and not liable to warp. There are two distinct types of picture framing, one in which the wood is used in its natural state, either polished or waxed, and the other in which the framing is painted or covered with a plaster composition which is moulded to the form required and covered with gilt or other colouring media. For the former type of framing and steady ornamental wood is suitable, the most commonly used being teak, sissoo, rosewood, ebony and *haldu*. For cheaper frames, in plain moulded form or painted, light conifer woods such as fir and spruce are the best. School slate frames can be made from a variety of woods, *e.g. Trewia nudiflora* (*gutel*), *Terameles nudiflora* (maina), *Terminalia chebula, Mangifera indica* (*Am*), spruce and fir, etc.

Railway carriage and wagon building. The qualities required of a wood to be in railway carriage and wagon work are that it should be sufficiently strong and durable. It should be free from bad seasoning defects, and it should be available in sufficient quantities. Teak complies with this specification better than any other timber, and for this reason teak is the main timber used by all the railway wagon and carriage works in India. The other important timbers used for this purpose are—*Shorea robusta, Pterocarpus* spp., *Adina cordifolia, Cedrus deodara, Dalbergia latifolia, Toona ciliata, Acacia nilotica, Dipterocarpus* spp., *Pinus* spp., and several others.

Railway sleepers. The woods most commonly used are—sal, deodar, teak, *pyinkado*, and *bijasal*.

Rifle parts. Walnut (*Juglans regia*) is the chief timber used for the manufacture of rifle work all over the world, as it stands up exceptionally well when worked to a fine finish on high speed cutting and drilling machines. The wood is also very steady and is not prone to excessive shrinking, swelling, warping or splitting, once it is properly seasoned.

Shuttles. The subject of shuttles is a very important one in India. All cotton, jute, wool and other textile mills use wooden shuttles in large quantities. The important wood which may be used for making shuttles are—*Diospyros melanoxylon* (ebony), *Gardenia latifola*, *Acacia nilotica*, *Mitragyna parvifiora*, *Dalbergia latifolia*, *Dalbergia sissoo*, etc.

Sporting requisites. Billiard cue shafts in India are made of *Diospyros melanoxylon* (*tendu*), *Grewia tilaefolia* (*dhaman*), *Polyalthia fragrans*. For the butts of cues ebony, *Hardwickia pinnata* and *Dysoxylum glandulosum* are used.

More than 200 manufacturers in India are involved in the production and export of world-class sports goods. These goods are of such superior quality that over 70 countries import from India. Professional players use them in national, international and even Olympic tournaments. There are several good reasons for the tremendous popularity of Indian sports goods abroad: excellent quality, superb finish, carefully selected raw material, enhanced durability. And to top it all master craftsmanship from India, the land of traditional skills.

Cricket bats are made of *Salix* spp. (williow). *Populus* spp. has also been used for cheap types of bat.

Indian cricket bats have scored many a century for the world champions. Made from strong Kashmir willows (*Salix* spp.), the bats are designed for force and flexibility.

Golf clubs are made of *Terminalia* spp., *Grewia* spp., *Anogeissus* spp., and *Pyinma*.

Hockey sticks are made of *Morus alba* (mulberry). Hockey sticks from India are known the world over for their balance and strong drive.

The timbers employed for the skis are *Dalbergia sissoo* (*shisham*) and *Anogeissus latifolia* (axle wood).

Stumps and bales are made of *Morus* spp. (mulberry) and *Grewia tiliaefolia* (dhaman).

In India, tennis and badminton rackets are made of mahogany and maple wood. The racket frames are made of *Prunus padus*, *Dalbergia sissoo*, *Toona ciliata*, *Melia azedarach*, etc.

Turnery, carving, combs, toys, etc. Very close-grained woods are acquired for high class turnery and carving. Walnut is much in demand in North India and Kashmir for this purpose. The sandalwood carvings of Mysore are equally well known. Sissoo and ebony are also used high class carving and inlay work in North India.

Dalbergia latifolia is commonly used in Kerala for carvings of idols, animals, birds, etc.

Wood carving is an ancient craft in which the West Bengal excels. The items include are dolls and toys, owl, horse, etc. Recently many piece goods including stands for table lamps are being manufactured. Shisham wood is used in abundance.

Erythrina spp., *Gyrocarpus* spp., *Bauhinia malabarica* are used for making toys in Karnataka. *Hymenodictyon excelsum* (*Kuthan*) is the best toy wood in U.P.

Indian combs such as those used by Sikhs in the hair are made of *Buxus* spp. (boxwood), *Adina cordifolia* (*Haldu*), ebony and sandal-wood.

VENEERS

The veneers are thin slices or sheets of wood of uniform thickness. The common thickness is about 1/20 in. to 3/8 in. In making veneers or logs pieces of woods are peeled and boiled and then cut with sharp knife. Usually the veneers are cut by **rotary process** which involves turning a log on a lathe against a stationary knife, with the formation of a continuous sheet of veneer. The other process is known as **slicing process**. Here the logs are quartersawed and therefore show a more attractive figure. The logs are first quartered and thereafter sliced with a stationary knife, resulting in the formation of separate sheets. Freshly cut veneers are usually wet and must be thoroughly dried.

Uses. The veneers are used in the manufacture of boxes, baskets, door panels, cooperage, trunks, mirrors, musical instruments and several other articles.

PLYWOOD

To overcome some of the natural defects in wood is the manufacture of so-called "*built up*" stock or plywood. The plywood is made by gluing together from three to nine thin veneers. The grain of each successive layer is at an angle to the next, so that the strength is redistributed. With the result the finished product becomes very strong and stable and does not warp or twist like ordinary wood. The plywood does not split when the nails and screws are driven close to its edge.

The manufacture of a five-ply plywood panel consists of preparing the face, back, cross band, and core sheets; applying the adhesive; pressing the glued stock into a panel; and drying and finishing the product. The soft woods are generally used for the purpose, as they can be glued more easily. Several resins and gums are used in the manufacture of plywood.

Uses. The plywood is extensively used in the home for doors, walls, flooring, cabinets, shelves, partitions, furniture and interior trim. A large quantity of plywood is utilized in making concrete forms, boats, prefabricated houses, airplanes, railroad cars and the body making of station wagons.

LAMINBOARDS

Laminboards are usually made up with cheap inferior woods for the cores, and better quality decorative good for the faces. Such timber as pine, spruce, fir, *Bombax ceiba*, *Ailanthus grandis*, *Tetrameles nudiflora* and *Kydia calycina* are very suitable for core work, while better class timbers such as teak, rosewood, sissoo and toon make excellent face veneers. Face veneers are usually sliced.

Uses. The laminboards are commonly used for making doors and cabinets.

CORK

Most commercial cork is obtained from the cork oak (*Quercus suber*). Cork or "corkwood" consists of the outer bark of the tree. This can be removed without injury to the tree. At the age of about 20 years, when the tree is about 40 cm in circumference, this outer layer, known as virgin cork, is removed by stripping. The operation consists of making vertical and horizontal cuts with knives or saws, and then prying off large pieces of the bark. The underlying exposed phelloderm and cortical cells die, and a new cork cambium layer is formed several millimetres deeper in the cortex. By this cork cambium (*phellogen*) new cork is formed more rapidly than by the first layer, and after 9 to 10 years the new cork layer has attained sufficient thickness to be commercially valuable and is in turn removed. This cork is of better quality than the nearly useless virgin cork, but is not so good as that obtained at the third and subsequent stripings which take place at intervals of about 9 or 10 years until the tree is 150 years old. Usually the trees live for 100 to 500 years, and have an average yield of 40 to 500 lb. per tree. After stripping the pieces of cork are dried for several days. They are first boiled in large copper vats. This process removes the sap and tannic acid, increases the volume and elasticity and flattens pieces. The rough edges are then trimmed off and the flat pieces are sorted and baled.

Cork is exceedingly buoyant due to its composition of dead watertight cells. It is highly compressible. It is durable, a bad conductor of heat and electricity, and is resistant to passage of moisture and liquids. It absorbs sound and vibrations and also possesses some frictional characteristics.

Uses of Cork

It is used for many purposes and for the manufacture of several products. In some cases the natural cork is used whereas in other cases composition cork, made of finely ground pieces treated with adhesives and molded.

The natural cork is used to make stoppers, hats, helmets, cigarette tips, handles of golf clubs, penholders, fishing rods, floats, life preservers, life jackets, base balls, mats, tiles and several other such products. Cork board is used as an insulating material for cold storage plants, houses and refrigerators.

Composition cork is utilized for the lining of crown caps, the metal tops for sealing bottles; gaskets; toes, counters and innersoles for shoes.

LINOLEUM

A type of floor covering is made from cork or wood flour, linseed oil, resins, such as rosin or kauri gum, pigments and burlap. The oil is boiled and allowed to solidify by dripping on pieces of cloth. The solidified oil is ground up and melted with the resins. This mixture is cooled and hardened, and after 'curing' for several days it is mixed with the cork, which has been ground as fine dust, and with the dry colour pigments. It is then pressed into burlap cloth with hydraulic presses. It is then seasoned in ovens and finished by giving it a protective surface of nitrocellulose lacquer. The tiles, known as linotiles are made from ground cork and linseed oil, but thicker than linoleum.

FUELWOOD

Fuel is one of the great necessities of modern life and it is indispensable, both in the home and in industry, as a source of heat and power. Any material that burns readily in air can be utilised, and a great variety of plant products are so used. The most important of these are wood and coal.

Though much less wood is used for fuel at the present time than formerly, the total consumption is probably greater than for any other purpose. However, the extensive use of wood for fuel does not represent a proportional drain on the forest resources, for much waste material is used as well as wood unfit for other purposes.

Wood is 99 per cent combustible when perfectly dry, and thus makes an excellent fuel. It is also a flaming fuel and well adapted for heating large surfaces. Hard woods have the greatest fuel value. The woods of *Fagus*, *Betula*, *Pinus*, *Acacia*, *Mangifera*, *Quercus*, etc., are of much value for fuel purposes.

Coal comprises the fossilized remains of plants that lived in former geological periods. The original plant tissue has been more fully decomposed and converted into carbon. Coal possesses a great heating power. Anthracite or hard coals are the oldest and contain about 95 per cent carbon.

It is generally supposed that petroleum had an organic origin and was formed under pressure from the plant and animal life of former shallow seas.

Fuelwood in India

According to an ADE publication of 1984, 'A Perspective on Demand for Energy in India up to 2004–05', the population of India in 2004–05 would be 1046 million. The estimated energy requirement for this population would be 312 million tonnes of firewood, 17 million tonnes of kerosene, 94 million tonnes of agro-waste, 207 million tonnes of cattle dung, 176 million cu. metres of biogas and 100 twh of electricity. The Working Group on Energy Policy (1979) estimated the consumption of fuelwood, agriculture waste and animal dung to be 133.1, 41.0 and 73.0 million tonnes respectively, whereas the total production of fuelwood was estimated at 49 million tonnes by the Fuelwood Committee, Planning Commission (1982). Therefore, research in increasing the production of fuelwood assumes great significance. A number of steps towards the objectives, *e.g.*, high density planting, introduction of fast growing species, genetic improvement for higher biomas, production and afforestation of stress sites, etc., have been advanced by the Council.

34
CHAPTER

Bamboos in India

INTRODUCTION

Bamboos are integral not only to the culture of India but that of the entire Southeast Asia. The wide range of their uses qualifies this group of species to be the one foremost associated with the mainstay of rural life and culture in our country. Its versatility has led to the coinage of such terms as "bamboo culture", "green gold", "poor man's timber", "friend of the people" and "cradle to coffin timber". In fact, bamboo can be used as a substitute of timber in many respects.

Bamboos belong to the grass family *Poaceae* (Gramineae). In India, there are 125 indigenous as well as exotic species of bamboos belonging to 23 genera. Bamboo forests occupy an area of 10.03 million ha, roughly 12.8% of the total forest area in the country. They are found in almost all the states of the country, from the tropical to the temperate regions and the alluvial plains to the high mountains, the only exception where they do not occur naturally is Kashmir. The principal bamboo genera occurring in India are *Arundinaria*, *Bambusa*, *Chimonobambusa*, *Dendrocalamus*, *Dinochloa*, *Gigantochloa*, *Indocalamus*, *Ochlandra*, *Drepanostachyum*, *Phyllostachys*, *Pleioblastus*, *Pseudoxytenanthera*, *Schizostachyum*, and *Thamnocalamus*. More than 50 per cent of the bamboo species occur in Eastern India – Arunachal Pradesh, Assam, Manipur, Meghalaya, Mizoram, Nagaland, Sikkim, Tripura and West Bengal. Other areas rich in bamboos are the Andamans, Bastar region of Madhya Pradesh and the Western Ghats.

Bamboos in India.

HABITAT AND DISTRIBUTION

Bamboos grow from sea level, in the tropics, to 4000 metres above sea level, in the temperate region. Although, bamboos are more common to the tropics, they also occur naturally in subtropical and temperate zones of the world, except in Europe.

The geographical distribution of bamboos is governed largely by the conditions of rainfall, temperature, altitude and soil. Most of the bamboos require a temperature from 8 degree celcius to 36 degree celcius, a minimum annual rainfall of 1000 mm and high atmospheric humidity for good growth.

They form an important constituent of many deciduous and evergreen forests. In nature bamboos seldom occur as pure crops, but are generally found as an understorey in tropical evergreen, tropical moist deciduous, tropical dry deciduous, montane sub-tropical, montane wet temperate and Himalayan wet temperate forests. Generally, the genera *Bambusa* and *Dendrocalamus* are found under tropical conditions, whereas *Arundinaria* and its allies occur in the temperate region and are by far, most common on high elevations in the western and eastern Himalayas. *Dendrocalamus strictus* is predominant in dry deciduous forests, while *Bambusa bambos* flourishes best in moist deciduous forests. The most important bamboo of the semi-evergreen forests of the Andamans in *Gigantochloa rostrata*. In the eastern region, *i.e.*, West Bengal, Assam and north-eastern Himalayas, the commercially important bamboos are *Bambusa tulda*, *Dendrocalamus hamiltonii* and *Melocanna baccifera*.

Bamboos are usually found in moist valleys, sheltered depressions, along steams and the lower hill slopes, but occasionally also occur on higher slopes and hill tops. They usually occur mixed with or under tree species, except in case when they form secondary brakes, and then, they are more or less pure. Though many species form brakes, those of *Arundinaria*, *Ochlandra*, *Melocanna* and *Bambusa bambos* are typically more extensive. Where shifting cultivation is practised, the bamboo brakes are more common.

The distribution and site factors of some commercially important bamboos occurring in India are:

Table 34.1

Sl. No.	*Species*	*Nature of soil*	*Topography status*	*Moisture*	*Distribution*
1	*2*	*3*	*4*	*5*	*6*
1.	***Drepanostachyum falcata***	Rich sandy loam to clayey loam often mixed with stones.	Hill slopes and high terraces.	Moist situation.	Western Himalayas, at an elevation of 1300–2200 m.
2.	***Arundinaria racemosa***	–do–	–do–	–do–	Eastern Himalayas, at an elevation of 2200–3050 m.
3.	***Indocalamus wightianus***	Fertile loam	High hills	–do–	Evergreen Sholas of southern India, especially Nilgiris.
4.	***Bambusa bambos***	Flat alluvial and rich moist soil; prefers moderately fine clayey soils, and tolerates slight water-logging; avoids coarse-grained soils and open ridges.	Fluorishes best along river banks, in valleys, and ravines.	Moist localities.	All over the country except in the dry regions and desert areas; mostly in the Indian peninsula; cultivated in sub-himalayan tract and Indo-gangetic plains; scarce in Assam and Bengal.
5.	***Bambusa tulda***	Alluvial soils along water courses.	Flat land.	Prefers moist areas.	Hill tracts of Assam, West Bengal, central India and the Deccan

Sl. No.	Species	Nature of soil	Topography status	Moisture	Distribution
1	2	3	4	5	6
					plateau; in moist mixed deciduous forests.
6.	***Schizostachyum pergracile***	Well-drained fresh loam.	Low hill country.	Between dry and moist sites.	Assam, central India and the Deccan plateau; in dry and moist deciduous forests.
7.	***Dendrocalamus brandisii***	Black loam and loam with lateritic nodules and other good soils.	Along the rivers.	Moist localities.	Keral, Karnataka and Tamil Nadu; in moist west coast climate.
8.	***Dendrocalamus hamiltonii***	Rich loamy soil	Valley and along streams	Moist places	Central and Eastern Himalayas; upto an elevation of 1000 m; in moist deciduous and semi-evergreen forests.
9.	***Dendrocalamus longispathus***	Fertile loam	Most along streams	Moist	West Bengal, Assam, Kerala and Tamil Nadu; as an associate of moist mixed forests.
10.	***Dendrocalamus strictus***	Poor, coarse grained, well-drained dry soils and stony soils on hill slopes; avoids poorly drained and moist heavy clay soils.	Hill slopes, alluvial plains and ravines.	Dry areas	Most widely distributed all over the country except northern parts of Bengal, Assam and other very moist areas; occurs in dry, open type deciduous forests; common associate of dry sal and dry teak forests. Also occurs on hills, and ascends to 1000 m.
11.	***Melocanna baccifera***	Fertile loam	Hill slopes and abandoned clearings by shifting cultivation.	Moist areas.	Moist and wet hill tracts of Bengal, Assam and other parts of the country.
12.	***Ochlandra travancorica***	Rich loam soil	Banks of perennial or semi-perennial steams, lower slopes and flat lands.	Moist areas; prefers running water	Western ghats; as under-growth in evergreen and semi-evergreen forests; ascending upto 1600 m.

Sl. No.	Species	Nature of soil	Topography status	Moisture	Distribution
1	2	3	4	5	6
13.	***Psudoxytenanthera ritcheyi***	Shallow rocky soils.	Hill tops and ridges.	Dry areas	Western ghats and hills of Indian peninsula; as undergrowth in mixed deciduous forests.
14.	***Gigantochloa rostrata***	Fertile loam	Along streams and lower slips.	Moist areas	Orissa, Assam, central India and Deccan plateau; gregarious in semi-deciduous forests of Andaman and Nicobar islands.

UTILIZATION

Properties. Bamboo is considered to be the most efficient natural resource as far as strength vis-a-vis cost. Strength of the bamboo depends upon the species, climatic factors and its moisture content. Bamboo is strong, though not stronger than timbers like Sal and Teak. Seasoning is a essential pre-requisite for maintaining the appearance and strength of bamboo products and structures. Unseasoned bamboo is highly susceptible to insects and fungal attack, decay and mechanical degradation.

Seasoning of bamboos has to be done properly and carefully as rapid drying results in splitting. To prevent cracks during seasoning green bamboos may be split into halves. The bamboos are best dried by air seasoning under overhead cover for 2–3 months. Kiln drying under controlled conditions can be done successfully in about 2–3 weeks.

Bamboo can be cut and split easily with hand saw. Strips of any measurement can be made with knife. Immature bamboos are soft and pliable and can be moulded to desired shape. Bamboo takes polish and paint well.

Uses. The strength of the culms, their straightness and lightness, combined with hardness, range in size, hollowness, long fibre and easy working qualities, make the bamboos suitable for a variety of purposes. Whether it is the tender shoots, used for pickles and curries, the slivers, used for tooth picks and meat barbecues, ribs for fans or slats for sun screens, or the dried culm as the sturdy lathi and for construction of the so called bamboo houses, the versatility of bamboo is legendary. The thousand and one uses for bamboos have long been known and established. Some of the traditional uses are: Agricultural implements, anchors, arrows, back scratchers, baskets, beds, blinds, boats, bottles, bows, bridges, brooms, brushes, buildings, caps, cart-yokes, caulking material, chairs, chicks, chopsticks, coffins, combs, containers, cooking utensils, cordages, dust-pans, fans, fences, fish-traps, fishing-nets, fishing rods, flag-poles, floats

Weaving combs of bamboo.

for timber, flutes, flower-pots, food, food-baskets, fuel, furniture, hats, handicrafts, haystack stabilisers, hedges, hookah-pipes, joss-sticks, kites, ladders, ladles, lamps, lance staves, lanterns, lining of hats and sandals, masts, match-sticks, mats, musical instruments, nails, net floats, ornaments, props, paper, pens, polo mallets, rafts, rayon pulp, roofing, sails, scaffoldings, scoops, seed-drills, shoes, shuttles, slats, sports goods, sprayers, stools, sticks, tables, thatching, tobacco pipes, toys, tool handles, traps, trays, tubes, umbrella-handles, walking-sticks, walls, vessels and wrappers.

Weaving Fish trap and containers of bamboo

Structural utilisation of bamboos

Bamboo has been traditionally in use in building construction from times immemorial. It is used in foundation, frames, floors, walls, partitions, ceilings, door and windows, roofs and for reinforcement in cement concrete. Although, there are more than 125 species of bamboo reported to be occurring in India, 20 important species have been tested so far for their physical and mechanical properties. The mean values and ranges of specific gravity, ultimate bending and compressive strength (MOR and MCS) of bamboo in green condition are given below.

	Mean	*Ranges*
Specific gravity	0.639	0.515–0.817
Ultimate bending strength (MOR) (kg/sq cm)	559	172–986
Compressive strength (MCS) (kg/sq cm)	401	262–539

The classification of timber species for structural use in building is done on the basis of modulus of rupture (MOR) and modulus of elasticity (MOE) while for other structural uses like piles and mine use, timbers have been classified on the basis of modulus of rupture (MOR), modulus of elasticity (MOE) and maximum crushing stress (MCS). Similarly, bamboos have been classified on the basis of MOR, MOE and MCS in green condition in three groups as given below. The limits of these properties for the three groups have been fixed keeping in view the corresponding limits for wood and spread of ultimate bending and compressive strength of bamboos.

	MOR (kg/sq cm)	*MOE (1000 kg/sq cm)*	*MCS (kg/sq cm)*
Group I	> 700	> 90	> 350
Group II	500–700	> 60	> 300
Group III	300–500	> 30	> 250

Suitable species for constructional use are given below alongwith some traditional timber species falling in these groups.

Table 34.2

Group I	Group II	Group III
Bambusa multiplex (Syn. *B. nana*)	*Bambusa balcooa*	*Bambusa ventricosa*
Dendrocalamus strictus	*Bambusa pallida*	*Bambusa vulgaris*
Oxytenanthera abyssinica	*Bambusa nutans*	*Dendrocalamus longispathus*
	Bambusa tulda	*Bambusa bambos* (Syn. *B. arundinacea*)
	Bambusa auriculata	
	Bambusa burmanica	
	Schizostachyum pergracile	
	Melocanna baccifera	
	Thrysostachys oliveri	
	Timber species	
Shorea robusta	*Tectona grandis*	*Pinus roxburghii*
Albizia odoratissima	*Lagerstroemia lanceolata*	*Pinus wallichiana*
Mesua ferrea	*Terminelia paniculata*	
Hopea sp.		

For facilitating proper designing in bamboo safe working stresses of these species have also been worked out.

Uses deserving specific mention:

1. **Bamboo parquet:** (Block flooring). The term parquet is applied to flooring in which strips, 3.81 cm × 6.71 cm, are cut and laid out in geometric patterns.

2. **Laminated bamboo:** The bamboo culms are cracked, spread out and flattened into sheets, with suitable binding and filling material. Then the sheets are combined, lapped, arranged, glued, treated and pressed to the desired form. They are then cut and trimmed to the desired size and shape and finally given finishing touches, according to one's fancy.

3. **Bamboo-reinforced concrete:** Bamboo reinforcement was first used in China in 1919 in concrete piles in railways. It is also used for construction purposes.

4. **Artificially-shaped bamboo:** Bamboo can be made to grow into square, rectangular and triangular shapes for low cost housing, handicrafts, decoration items and cottage industries. Japan has successfully grown artificially-shaped bamboos. Production is simple, like moulding hollow blocks, but needs practice.

5. **Medicine:** Banslochan or Tabashir is a siliceous secretion found in the internodes of the culms of various species of bamboos. It occurs in fragments or masses, up to 2 cm thick. It is used as a cooling tonic and aphrodisiac; also in the treatment of asthma, cough and other debilitating diseases.

6. **Charcoal:** It is superior to many other charcoals for use in electric batteries; in India, used for pharmaceutical purposes. Jewellers prefer bamboo charcoal.

7. **Deodorizer:** The dried, mature bamboo leaves are used for deodorizing fish-oil in Asian countries.

8. **Soil conservation:** Many bamboos are quite useful for soil conservation due to their intricate rhizome system and roots.

SOME BAMBOOS AND THEIR USES

1. ***Bambusa polymorpha*** (Assam—*Betua*; Beng—*Jamabetua*)

This handsome species is distributed in Northeastern India. The clean culms attain a height of 20 to 27 m and a diameter of 15 cm. It is one of the best for construction, thatching and roofing; also used for paper, agarbati sticks, fibre boards, etc. tender shoots are of best quality for edible purposes.

2. ***Bambusa striata*** = *B. vulgaris* var. *striata* (Bengali—*Basini Bans*; Marathi—*Kalaka*; Tamil—*Ponmungil*)

This is a moderate sized bamboo 6 m to 10 m in height and 5–8 cms in diameter, with yellow or green striped culms. Commonly cultivated all over India upto an altitude of 1000 m. It forms loose clumps. It is widely used for furniture, toys, cages, etc., also used for construction. Commonly used as an ornamental.

3. ***Bambusa tulda*** (Bengali—*Tulda*; Hindi—*Peka*; Santal—Mak)

This bamboo is a native of eastern India and grows gregariously between 400 and 600 m above m.s.l. It is also cultivated in the plains and foothills of north India. It is one of the most useful bamboos. Due to its strong culms; it is used for building purposes, scaffolding and roofing; also used for general purposes, specially for mats and baskets, often for paper pulp.

4. ***Dendrocalamus giganteus***

This is the largest of the bamboos, cultivated often in northeastern parts and occasionally in other parts of our country. Indigenous to Myanmar (Burma). It is 24–35 m high and 20–30 cm in diameter. It is used for building purposes, water buckets, boxes, masts of boats, flower vases, etc. Tender shoot is of good quality for edible purposes. It is better than *D. strictus* for paper making.

5. ***Dendrocalamus hamiltonii*** (Assam—*Kokua*; Bengali—*Pecha*; Hindi—*Kaghzi bans*)

This species is found mainly in northwest and northeastern Himalayas mostly between an altitude of 600–1200 m. It is a large bamboo; with culms often over hanging, and up to 25 m long and 10–18 cm diameter, thin-walled. The most important use is for paper manufacture; also used for construction, baskets, mats, water and milk vessels, rafts, etc.

6. ***Dendrocalamus strictus*** (Hindi—*Narbans*; Marathi—*Nanvel*; Oriya—*Salia bhanso*; Tamil and Malayalam—*Kalmungil*; Telugu—*Sadanapa veduru*)

Distributed in deciduous forests almost all over India especially in drier zones usually upto an altitude 1000 m; it is commonly cultivated throughout India in the plains and foothills. The culms are 8–16 m high and 2.5–8 cm in diameter, almost solid or internodes are thick-walled. It is the most universally used Indian bamboo for house construction, baskets, mats, furniture, agriculture implements, tool handles, chicks, etc. The important raw material for paper and rayon in India.

7. ***Drepanostachyum falcatum*** = *Arundinaria falcata* (Hindi—*Ringal*)

This is a low level bamboo of the western Himalaya, ranging from Jammu to Nepal, at elevations between 1200–2200 m. It grows gregariously, forming an undergrowth in the forests of deodar, oak, etc., usually in moist shady locations. Its rhizome spreads widely and give out loosely a large number of culms, sometimes more than a hundred. The culms are 1.8 to 2.0 m high. It is used for basket work, hookah pipes, etc. It is especially prized for fishing rods.

8. ***Gigantochloa rostrata*** = *Oxytenanthera nigrociliata* (Bengali—*Kalia*; Oriya—*Bolangi*; Garo—Washut; Bastar—Pani bans)

This is a tufted bamboo, with culms 5–8 m high and 2.5–5 cm in diameter. It is distributed mainly in eastern India and to a limited extent in Madhya Pradesh, Maharashtra and Karnatak. It is usually gregarious. It is used for building huts, basket work and paper manufacture.

9. ***Indocalamus wightianus*** = *Arundinaria wightiana* (Tamil—*Chevani*)

This bamboo occurs in the Nilgiris, Palghat and Tinnevelly, in South India, at an elevation of 1800–2600 m. It forms a gregarious undergrowth in the evergreen sholas. Culms are 2 to 3 m high and about 1.2 cm diameter. It flowers annually. The split culms are used for making mats, baskets and fences.

10. ***Melocanna baccifera*** (Bengali—*Muli*; Assam—*Tarai*)

This species is the most common bamboo of northeastern India in the plains and lower hills. The culms do not form clumps, are straight thin-walled and attain a height of 10–20 m and a diameter of 4–7 cm. It is strong and extensively used for construction, baskets, mats, chicks, food grain containers, umbrella sticks, hats, toys, etc., an important material for superior paper pulp.

11. ***Ochlandra scriptoria*** (Malayalam—*Ammei*, *Ottal*)

A shrubby bamboo, with culms upto 5 m in height and 2.5 m in diameter. It occurs gregariously mostly along river banks and wetter parts of Western Ghats at low elevations. It is cultivated along the margins of ponds and paddy fields as a soil binder; also used for making mats, baskets and paper.

12. ***Ochlandra travancorica*** (Malayalam—*Eetta*; Tamil—*Eeral*, *Odai*)

This shrubby bamboo occurs mostly in Kerala, and in Tamil Nadu in hills of Kannyakumari and Tinnevelly districts upto an altitude of 1500 m. The culms grow up to 6 m in length and 5 cm in diameter, with rough thin-walled internodes upto 1.5 m in length. This is one of the main raw materials for paper pulp; also commonly used for mats, baskets and for making temporary huts. One of the best soil binders along water courses and other moist slopy areas.

13. ***Pseudoxytenanthera ritcheyi*** = *Oxytenanthera ritcheyi* (Kannada—*Chiwa*, *Choua*; Marathi—*Huda*, *Manga*)

This is an erect, thick-walled bamboo, occurring from the Konkan to the Anamalai hills on the western ghats. It is often cultivated. The culms are upto 6 m in height and 2.5 cm in diameter. They are strong and are used for tent poles, walking stricks, baskets and umbrella handles.

14. ***Schizostachyum polymorphum*** = *Pseudostachyum polymorphum* (Assam—*Bajal*, *Tolli*)

This is a thin-walled, shrubby bamboo, found along river banks and valleys in Northeastern states. It is in considerable demand among tea planters for baskets; also used for mats.

15. ***Thamnocalamus spathiflorus*** = *Arundinaria spathiflora* (Hindi—*Nigal*, *Ringal*)

This is a small bamboo, 3.5–6.0 m high, growing gregariously as an undergrowth in the fir, spruce and deodar forests of the western Himalayas from 2100–2700 m. The culms are used for hookah pipes, mats, baskets, fishing rod, etc.

35
CHAPTER

Spices and Condiments

The spices and condiments have played a prominent part in all the civilizations of antiquity, in ancient India and China. The majority of spices originated in the Asiatic tropics and were among the first objects of commerce between the East and the West. The quest for condiments and spices was once a powerful force in world history. The search for a sea route to the spice Islands of the East led to the voyages of Columbus, Magellan and many others.

Arabs brought the products of southern India and the spice Islands by caravan to Arabia, and then to Europe. Later other countries took over the spice trade. In the sixteenth century the Portuguese monopolized the trade for two hundred years. Later the British Empire owned most of the spice trade of the world.

The spices cannot be grouped as foods, for they contain less nutritive value. However, they give a good flavour and aroma to food, and add greatly to the pleasure of eating. They stimulate the appetite and increase the secretion and flow of gastric juices. For this reason they are commonly known as "*food adjuncts*". The aromatic value of the spices is due to the presence of the essential oils.

In general, all aromatic vegetable products that are used for flavouring foods and drinks are known as spices. Sometimes the term "*spice*" is restricted to hard or hardened parts of plants, which are generally used in a pulverized state. *Condiments* are spices or other flavouring substances which possess a sharp taste, and are commonly added to food after it has been cooked.

The majority of spices are obtained from the tropics, chiefly from Asia. In India, the major spices are pepper, chillies, cardamom, ginger and turmeric. Besides several others are also quite common, such as: coriander, cinnamon, clove, nutmeg, etc. The pepper plant (*Piper nigrum* L.) is indigenous to the forests of Kerala and has been cultivated in India from time immemorial. Large-scale cultivation of the crop is confined to the Western Ghat of Peninsular India. Chillies (*Capsicum* spp.) are an important condiment crop in India. They are indigenous to South America, and are said to have been introduced into India by the Portuguese. The principal cardamom (*Elettaria cardamomum*) producing countries are India, Ceylon and Indo-China. The big cardamom (*Amomum* spp.) are grown in Sikkim, Nepal, Cambodia, Java and some other tropical countries. Ginger of commerce is a dry product prepared from the rhizomes of the plant *Zinjiber officinale*. The most important producers of commercial dry ginger are India, Jamaica and Sierra Leone. Turmeric (*Curcuma longa* Linn.), is used as an important condiment almost in every Indian house, and has been cultivated in India from very ancient times. Coriander (*Coriandrum sativum* Linn.) is an important condiment used widely in all parts of India, Russia, Central Europe, Asia Minor and Morocco. The cinnamon of commerce is the bark of tree *Cinnamomum zeylanicum* Breyn., which is indigenous to Sri Lanka, Southern India, Myanmar and the Malayan Peninsula. The clove of commerce is the dried unopened flower bud of the clove tree, *Syzyzium aromaticum*. A native of Moluccas, it has spread to a number of countries, *viz.*, Zanzibar, the Spice Islands, the West Indies, the Mascarene Islands, Sumatra, Java, Sri Lanka etc. The cultivation of clove in India is limited to South India. The nutmeg of commerce is the de-arilled dried seed of *Myristica fragrans* Houtt. A native of eastern island of the Moluccas, it is also indigenous to Banda island, Amboyna, Gilolo and Western New Guinea. It was introduced in India towards the end of the eighteenth century. Its cultivation is confined to the south, in the Nilgiris, the Tenkasi Hills and the coastal areas of Kerala. The important minor spices grown in India are ajowan, aniseed, caraway, celery, coriander, cumin, dill seed, fennel, fenugreek, garlic, onion, saffron and vanilla, etc. Several other spice yielding plants of India and abroad have been discussed in the present text.

India is one of the largest suppliers of spices and condiments. India alone contributes 25-30 per cent of the total world trade.

Most of the important spices are grown in India. The classification of *spices* and *condiments* in the present text is based on the morphology of the plant organ which is used for the purpose. The general categories of the plants yielding *spices* and *condiments* are as follows:

SPICES AND CONDIMENTS OBTAINED FROM ROOTS

Asafetida

Ferula Linn.; English—Asafetida; Hindi—*Hing*; Kashmiri—*Anjudan*; Gujarati—*Hing*; Mumbai—*Hing*; Tamil—*Kyam*, *perungayam*; Sanskrit—*Hingu*; Family—Umbelliferae (Apiaceae).

This is a genus of perennial herbs commonly distributed from the Mediterranean region to central Asia. Some of the species are important as sources of oleogum - resins, used as condiment and in medicine. Three species are found in India. The Main bulk of asafetida and other ferula gum - resins are being imported in India from Afghanistan.

Asafetida is the dried latex obtained mainly from living rootstocks or taproots of several species of *Ferula*, such as : *F. foetida* Regel, *F. alliacea* Boiss., *F. rubricaulis* Boiss., *F. assafoetida* Linn. and *F. narthex* Boiss., found in Central Asia. *F. narthex* and *F. assafoetida* are found in Himachal Pradesh and Kashmir.

The plants from which the asafetida of commerce is obtained bear massive carrot-shaped roots (5-6 inches in diameter at the crown when they are 4-5 year old). In March-April when the plants are about to flower, the upper part of the root is laid bare and the stem cut off close to the crown. The exposed surface is covered by a dome-shaped structure made of twigs and earth. A milky juice (latex) exudes from the cut surface. After some days the exudate is scraped off and a fresh slice of the root cut when more latex exudes. The collection of the resin and the slicing of the root are repeated until exudation stops (about three months after the first cut). Sometimes the resin is being collected from successive incisions made at the junction of the stem and the tap root. With three incisions, some plants yield 1 kg. or more of gum-resin.

Asafetida (asafoetida) occurs in commerce in three forms—(*i*) *tears*, (*ii*) *mass* and (*iii*) *paste*. The *tears* make the purest form of the resin. They are rounded or flattened, 5-30 mm. in diameter and greyish or dull yellow in colour. *Mass asafetida* is the common commercial form. It consists of tears united into a more or less uniform mass usually mixed with fragments of root, earth, etc. The paste also contains foreign matter.

Asafetida is adulterated with gum arabic, other gum-resins, gypsum, chalk, wheat or barley flour, etc.

Asafetida contains 40-64% resin, 25% gum, 10-17% volatile oil and 1.5 to 10% ash. The resin portion chiefly contains asaresinotannol, free or combined with ferulic acid.

Uses. Asafetida is bitter and acrid in taste and emits a strong and peculiar odour. In India, it is used for flavouring curries, sauces and pickles. It is also used in Ayurvedic medicines. It stimulates the intestinal and respiratory tracts and the nervous system. It is useful in asthma, whooping cough and chronic bronchitis. It is used as an enema for intestinal flatulence. It is also used in epileptic and hysterical affections and in cholera. It is also used in veterinary medicine.

Lovage

Levisticum officinale Koth., English—Lovage; Family—Umbelliferae (Apiaceae).

This is a perennial plant, introduced from Europe. It is grown as a garden plant. It thrives best in well-drained soil. It is propagated either by seeds or roots. The roots are dug out in October of second or third year after setting the plants. The freshly dug roots are washed, cut into slices and dried.

Uses. Generally the roots are used for flavouring foods. Sometimes the seeds are used for flavouring confectionery. The leaves and stems are also eaten as salad. The dried roots; on steam distillation yield volatile oil known as 'lovage oil'. The oil is used for flavouring foods.

SPICES AND CONDIMENTS OBTAINED FROM UNDERGROUND STEMS

Onion

Allium cepa Linn.; English—Onion; Hindi—*Piyaz*; Tamil—*Vella-vengayam, irulli*; Telugu—*Vulli-gaddalu*; Kannada—*Vengayam, nirulli*; Malayalam—*Bawang*. They are cultivated all over India. Onion seed will not keep for certain more than one year. The selected bulbs be planted, and

Fig. 35.1. Onion. A hybrid VL Piaz 3. It is less-prone to bolting during storage.

seed obtained from these. If planted in the cold season, they will produce seed in the beginning of the hot season, and if carefully preserved, after being well ripened and dry, the seed obtained in this way will be found to yield a good crop in the following cold season, from October to February.

Uses. The bulbs are used as food and condiment.

Garlic

Allium sativum Linn.; English—Garlic; Hindi—*Lasan, lahsun*; Bengali—*Lashan*; Sanskrit—*Maha-ushadha*; Tamil—*Vallaipundu*; Telugu—*Vellulli fella-gadda*; Kannada—*Belluli*; Family—Liliaceae. Cultivated all over the country. It is propagated by planting out the cloves

Fig. 35.2. Garlic bulbs.

singly, in October, in drills about 6-7 inches apart and 2-3 inches deep. The crop is taken up in the hot weather, and after being dried in the sun the bulbs are stored for further use.

Numerous bulbs remain enclosed in a common membranous covering. Stem simple, about 2 feet high; scape is smooth and shining, solid terminated by a membranous pointed spathe enclosing a mass of flowers and solid bulbils prolonged into leafy points; leaves long, flat, acute, sheathing the lower half of the stem; flowers small, white.

Uses. The bulbs (rhizomes) are used as a condiment and flavouring substance. Garlic powder is used as a condiment. It is a carminative, diuretic, stomachic, alterative, emmenagogue, and tonic.

Turmeric

Curcuma domestica Valet; Syn. *C. longa* Auct. non Linn.; English—Turmeric; Hindi—*Haldi*; Bengali—*Halud*; Punjabi—*Haldar*, *halja*; Tamil—*Manjal*; Telugu—*Pasupu*; Malayalam—*Mannal*, *marinalu*; Kannada—*Arishina*; Marathi—*Halede*; Gujarati—*Halada*; Sanskrit—*Haridra*, *nisa*; Persian—*Zard-chobah*, *dar-zard*; Family—Zingiberaceae.

Turmeric has been cultivated in India from very ancient times. It prefers sandy and clayey loams for its cultivation. The crop cannot stand water-logging or alkalinity in the soils. The largest supplies of turmeric are obtained from Guntur district of Andhra Pradesh. Orissa is the next important growing area for turmeric where production is concentrated in the districts of Ganjam, Phulbani and Koraput. In Maharashtra, the main centres of turmeric production are in Gujarat, Thane and Khandesh districts. Tiruchirapally, Salem and Coimbatore districts of Tamil Nadu are also important turmeric growing areas. Other important states for this crop are - Uttar Pradesh, Madhya Pradesh, Karnataka, West Bengal, Rajasthan and the Punjab. The total average under turmeric in India has been estimated variously from 60,000 to 100,000 acres, and the production is nearly 100,000 tonnes of rhizomes per annum. A large part is consumed within the country, but a portion is exported to the U.K., Pakistan, Sri Lanka and U.S.A.

Cultivation. The crop is propagated vegetatively by means of corms (swollen under ground stems). The preparatory cultivation requires deep ploughing several times (six time or so). It needs a fine tilth and heavy application of manure. The field is prepared into narrow beds with facilities for irrigation and drainage. The corms are planted from April to July in these beds, 6-9 inches apart in the furrows and 16 inches apart between the furrows. After planting the beds are levelled and covered with a mulch of leaves. The corms develop aerial shoots above the ground in a month or so. One or two weedings are given, and the beds are earthed up. By November, the leafy growth is complete and the corms beneath the soil begin to thicken and to develop uniformly deep colour. In the month of February the leaves turn yellow and dry up, which is an indication of maturity of the underground corms. Harvesting is done in March which continues till the end of April.

A great care has to be taken in harvesting operations. The whole clump consisting of both primary and secondary branches known as "*fingers*", and the main thickened portion, the "*bulb*", are to be lifted up without injuring the corms. The leaves and roots are then cut off, and the bulb and fingers separated from each other. Very small quantities are sold in this raw form. In India, the bulb of the crop is marketed as dry cured turmeric (*haldi*).

Curing. The raw produce of turmeric has to be cured properly before the commercial dry turmeric can be obtained. Curing consists mainly of three phases - 1. boiling, 2. drying and 3. polishing. After harvesting, the raw green turmeric is heaped up covered with turmeric leaves, and kept in this condition for some time. The entire produce is then transferred to an earthen pot or larger iron pan which is filled up with water, the water level is kept 2-3 inches above the level of the turmeric. After covering the bulk with dry turmeric leaves, it is boiled over fire. As soon as the rhizomes become soft to touch, they are removed from the vessel, thinly spread out and dried in the sun. After 5-7 days of drying, the produce becomes fit for sale and storage. When it is quite dry, it is cleaned to remove roots and other parts, and then rubbed well between hands. The dry turmeric is also polished by special appliances. Now the produce is sorted out into *bulbs*, *fingers* and *splits*, and graded into large and small sizes according to need.

The plant of turmeric is a robust perennial with a short stem and tufted leaves. The pale-yellow flowers are found in dense spikes, topped by a tuft of pinkish bracts. The rhizomes, which yield the colourful condiment, are short and thick with blunt tubers. They are cleaned, washed and dried in the sun, it is very aromatic, with a musky odour and yellow colour. It has a pungent bitter taste.

Uses. It is used as a condiment. It is used to flavour and colour pickles, and foodstuffs. It is one of the principal ingredients of curry.

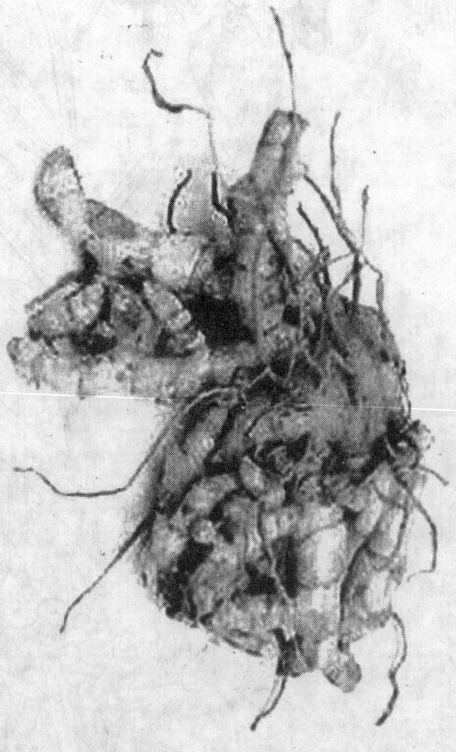

Fig. 35.3. Turmeric. Roots and rhizomes.

Ginger

Zingiber officinale Rosc.; English—Ginger; Hindi—Plant = *adrak*, Dried rhizome = *sonth*, fresh rhizome = *adrak*; Bengali—Plant = *ada*, dried rhizome = *sont*, fresh root = *adrak*, *ada*; Assamese—Plant = *ada*; Nepalese—Dried rhizome = *sunt*; Oriya—Plant = *ada*; Punjabi—Plant = *ada*, *adrak*, dried rhizome = *zangzabil*, *sunt*, fresh rhizome = *zunjbel*, *adrak*; Marathi—Plant = *ale*, Gujarati—Dried rhizome = *sunt*, fresh rhizomes *adu*, *adhu*; Tamil—Dried rhizome = *shukku*, fresh rhizome = *inji*; Telugu—Plant = *allam*, dried rhizome = *sonti*, *sonthi*, *allam*, fresh rhizomes = *allam*; Kannanda—Dried rhizomes = *vana sunthi*, fresh rhizome = *hasisunthi*; Malayalam—Dried rhizome = *Chukka*, fresh rhizome = *inchi*; Sanskrit—Plant = *adraka*, *sringavera*, dried rhizome = *vishva-bhishagam*, *nagara*, *sunti*, *mahaushadha*, fresh rhizome = *ardrakam*; Persian—Dried rhizome = *zanjabile-khushk*, fresh rhizome = *zanjabile-tar*; Family—Zingiberaceae.

Ginger of commerce is a dry product prepared from the green underground stems or rhizomes. The most important producers of commercial dry ginger are India, Jamaica and Sierra

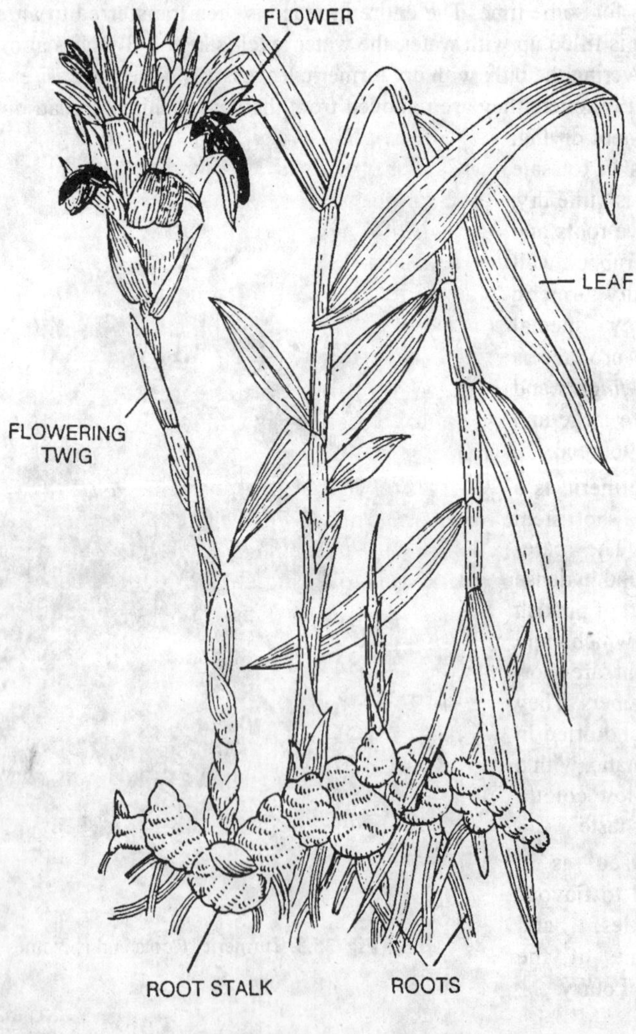

Fig. 35.4. *Zingiber officinale*. Ginger (*Adrak*). Rhizomes are used as spice and condiment.

Leone. The most important ginger growing area in India is Kerala State. The preparation of the dry ginger (sonth) of commerce is also exclusively confined to this area. In Kerala, the main producing centres lie in the Kottayam division. The other main producing areas in the West Coast are in the Malabar district.

Ginger is grown generally in areas of heavy rainfall. It requires a rich and well drained soil for its cultivation. The most suited soils are sandy or clayey loams and laterites of the Malabar Coast. Ginger is cultivated usually in small home gardens.

Cultivation. Though a perennial plant, yet it is cultivated as an annual crop. It takes 9-10 months to mature, and every year a fresh crop is taken. The plant is propagated vegetatively by means of rhizomes. The field is well ploughed, and long and narrow beds are prepared. The beds are heavily manured with cattle-manure. Seed ginger, consisting of small portions of the rhizomes, collected from the previous crop, is then planted in these beds in small pits at a distance of about 6-10 inches each way. Planting is done in May-June, and the beds are covered with mulch leaves to protect the seed from following rains. In about 2-3 weeks, the beds shoot up. The plant grows to a height of about two feet, and develop several lateral shoots in each clump. The rhizomes develop and become ready for harvest by December-January. As the crop matures, the aerial shoots begin to dry up and lodge on the ground. The leaves also become yellow. Harvesting is done by digging the whole crop or only portions of it.

After digging out, the rhizomes are thoroughly washed with water to remove the soil and dirt sticking to them. These underground stems are kept in the sun for a day or so, and then taken to the market for sale as green ginger (*adrak*). The preparation of dry ginger (*sonth*) is a local craft of Kerala State. For purpose of export only dry ginger is used.

In India, about 48,000 acres are under the crop, and the estimated production of cured ginger is 24,000 tonnes of which about 18,000 tonnes are produced on the west coast alone. About 25 per cent of the produce on the west coast is sold as the green ginger (*adrak*) and (*sonth*) and exported to other countries. The chief countries which import ginger from India are the U.K., U.S.A., France, Germany and Arabia.

Chemical composition. Moisture 10.5%; volatile oil 1.8%; oleoresin 6.5%; water extract 19.6%; cold alcohol extract 6.0%; starch 53.0%; crude fibre 7.17%; crude protein 12.4%; total ash 6.64%.

Uses. Ginger is used more as a condiment than as a spice. The aroma of ginger is due to essential oil, whereas the pungent taste is due to the presence of carminative and digestive stimulant. The essential oil, obtained from the rhizomes, is used for flavouring food stuffs. Ginger is exceedingly popular for flavouring beverages, such as ginger bear and ginger malt.

Zerumbet Ginger

Zingiber zerumbet (Linn.) Rosc. ex Smith; English—Zerumbet ginger; Hindi—*Mahabari bach, nar kachur*; Punjabi—*Kachur, nar kachur*; Malayalam—*Kathu-inshi-kua*; Sanskrit—*Sthula granthi*; Family—Zingiberaceae.

A perennial herb. Found throughout India.

Uses. The rhizomes are used as spice and condiment. The rhizomes has a slightly aromatic odour and possesses similar properties to those of *Zingiber officinale*, but in a minor degree.

SPICES AND CONDIMENTS OBTAINED FROM BARK

Cassia China

Cinnamomum aromaticum Nees.; English—Cassia China; Family—Lauraceae.

Cassia China is obtained from *C. aromaticum* Nees cultivated in China. The bark is the regular cassia China of commerce. Because of its brittle nature, much of the bark is broken, thus yielding the '*broken grade*'. The main grades are: 1. Whole Quills or China Rolls, 2. Selected Brokens or Canton Rolls, and 3. Extra selected brokens. Trees growing at higher altitude (180-300 metres) yield better quality bark with higher volatile oil content. The bark has been known from the earliest times. The dried immature fruits constitute the well known '*Cassia buds*', known in India as *Kala Nagkesar*. This species of Cassia is not grown in India but considerable quantities of it are imported into the country.

When the trees are about six years old, the first cut of bark is obtained. The season for barking commences in March and continues till the end of May, after which the bark loses its aroma. The bark, after its removal and while it is still moist with sap, is then laid with the convex side downwards. The bark is left to dry for about 24 hours, and tied up in bundles of about 45 cm. diameter and sent for marketing.

Uses. It is used as a spice or condiment in curries and similar preparations. The important constituent of commercial importance is the volatile oil which finds numerous uses in the various culinary preparations, perfumery and cosmetics as well as pharmaceutical preparations.

Indian Cassia

Cinnamomum tamala Nees. & Eberm.; English—Indian Cassia; Hindi, Bengali and Punjabi—*Tejpat, tejput*; Gujarati—*Tamalapatra*; Marathi—*Darchini*; Sanskrit—*Tamalaka, tejpatra*; Tamil—*Talishapattiri*; Telugu—*Talishapatri*; Family—Lauraceae.

A moderate-sized evergreen tree. Distributed in tropical and subtropical Himalayas (915 to 2440 metres altitude), Khasi and Jaintia hills (915-1220 metres altitude).

The bark of the tree, known in trade as Indian Cassia or Indian Cassia Lignea, is collected from trees growing at the foot of the Sikkim Himalayas. Regular plantations of *C. tamala* are grown in Khasi and Jaintia Hills, Gara Hills, Mikir Hills, Manipur and Arunachal.

Uses. The bark is aromatic. It is coarser than the bark of true cinnamon and is one of the common adulterants of true cinnamon. The essential oil from the bark is pale yellow and contains 70–85 per cent cinnamic aldehyde.

Cinnamon

Cinnamomum zeylanicum Bl.; English—Cinnamon; Hindi—*Dalchini, qalmi-dar-chini*; Bengali—*Dalchini*; Punjabi—*Dar-chini, kirfa*; Mumbai—*Taj, dalchini, tikhi*; Marathi—*Darachini, dalchini*; Tamil—*Karruwa, lavangap-pattai*; Telugu—*Sanalinga, lavanga-patta*; Malayalam—*Lavanga-patta*; Kannada—*Lavanga-patta, dalachini*; Sanskrit—*Gudatvak*; Persian—*Tali khahe, dar-chini*; Family—Lauraceae.

Cinnamon is one of the oldest known spices. The true cinnamon, also called as Ceylon Cinnamon is the dried bark of *Cinnamomum zeylanicum* Bl.

It is native of Sri Lanka. In India, it is grown in the Nilgiris, South Kanara, Malabar, Assam and Kumaon. It is an evergreen tree. The tree attains a height of 8 to 12 metres, but in cultivation it is coppiced or cut back to a height of about 2 metres. Its highly aromatic leaves are 12 to 17 cm. long, dark glossy green above and lighter beneath. The flowers are small, yellow and inconspicuous developing into dark purple ovoid and one seeded berries, about 1.5 to 2.5 cm. long.

Soil and climate. It is a hardy plant which can very well grow in almost all types of soils under a wide variety of tropical conditions. The quality of the bark is highly influenced by the soil and ecological factors. In Sri Lanka which is the major cinnamon growing country in the world the plants are cultivated on white sandy soil. Sandy or siliceous soils with an admixture of humus are considered to be ideal for cinnamon cultivation. Sheltered situations upto an altitude of 800 to 1000 metres receiving an annual rainfall of 200 to 250 cm. are considered to be good for the crop.

Propagation. The easiest and most widely adopted method of cinnamon propagation is by seed. It can also be propagated by planting, cutting and layers.

Cinnamon fruits ripen in July-August. The fruits fall down when fully ripe. The fleshy berries are left in heaps in shade to soften and rot. The mass is then trempled. The pulp free seeds are washed and dried in shade. They are sown without much delay as they have a short period of viability. The nursery is raised in a suitable spot in soil, rich in organic matter. The place is dug well twice or thrice. The soil is broken to powder and made loose, making it altogether free from stones, root bits, etc. The seed beds are made 1 metre wide and of suitable length with adequate provision for drainage. The seeds are sown in lines 12 cm. apart and are covered with a layer of soil to a thickness of about 2.5 cm. Germination of seed occurs in about 20 days. The beds have to be provided with artificial shade and watered regularly. The shade should continue untill the plants are about 12 cm. in height and then removed gradually. Transplanting is best done when the plants are about 10 to 12 month old.

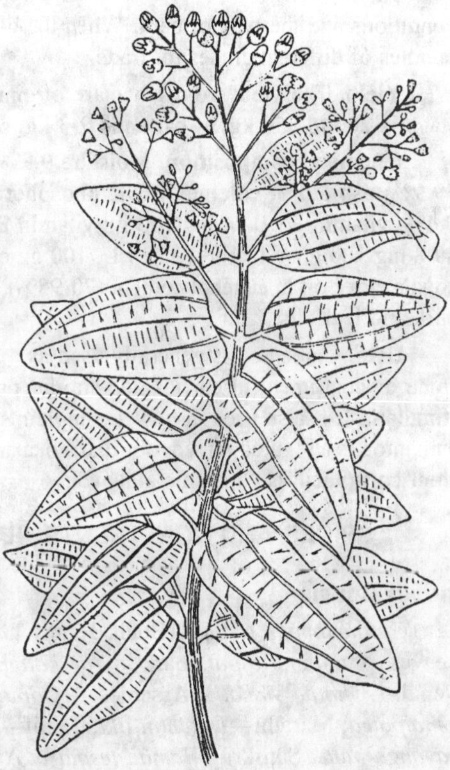

Fig. 35.5. Spices and condiments. *Cinnamomum zeylanicum* Blume; Eng. Cinnamon (Lauraceae). A flowering twig.

Planting. Seedlings are transplanted when they are about 12 months old at a distance of about 2 metres between plants and rows. The planting is done in ideal weather conditions, preferably in June-July.

Harvesting and Curing. There are two regular cutting seasons in South India, which more or less synchronize with two monsoons. The appropriate time for cutting the shoots for peeling is determined with reference to the circulation of sap between the wood and the corky layer. The sap flow and the time for peeling are judged by the peelers by making a test cut on the stem with a sharp knife. If the bark separates readily, the cutting is commenced immediately. The shoots should be of at least two years growth with the bark having a uniform brown colour and should have attained a length of 1 to 1.25 m. and a thickness of not less than 1.25 cm. Shoots satisfying these requirements are cut and bundled after the leaves and the terminal shoots have been removed.

Cutting is followed by scraping and peeling operations. The peeling is a specialized operation peculiar to this industry which requires some skill and considerable experience. It is done by using a specially made knife which has a small and round pointed end with a projection on one side to facilitate ripping of the bark. The peeler takes the cut shoots one by one and after scraping outer skin, first makes a longitudinal slit from one end to the other. Then working the knife between the bark is ripped quickly. The twigs cut in the morning are peeled on the same day. The peeled slips are gathered and kept overnight under shade for what is called '*fermentation*'. However, while no real fermentation process develops during the course of a night, a little softening of the bark does occur with the result that peels become more easy and pliable for ensuring piping operation. The bark as it dries contracts and assumes the shape of a pipe otherwise known as quill. The smaller quills or pipes are inserted into larger ones to form compound quills. They are then arranged systematically end to end in length of about 90 cm. The quills are rolled by hand when they are soft and fresh and after rolling they are dried on mats in shade. The drying lasts for 2-5 days, depending upon the weather conditions and the type of bark. When the drying is complete the bark is collected and packed in bundles of different grades for trade.

Yield. The yield from 1 hectare of cinnamon plantation after attaining the proper yielding stage is 200 to 350 kg. of bark and 2-3 kg. of leaf oil per year on an average.

Chemical composition. Moisture 9.9%; protein 4.6% fat 2.2%; fibre 20.3%; carbohydrates 59.9%; ash 3.5%; calcium 1.6%; phosphorus 0.05%; iron 0.004%; sodium 0.01%; potassium 0.4%; vitamin B1 0.14 mg/100 g.; vitamin B2 0.21 mg/100 g.; niacin 1.9 mg/100 g.; vitamin C 39.8 mg/100 g.; Vitamin A 175 I.U./100 g.; calorific value 355 calories/100 g.; cinnamon leaf oil equals clove oil in eugenol content (70-95%), root bark yields 3% oil which differs from both stem bark and leaf oils.

Uses. Cinnamon is generally used as a spice or ingredients of curry powder. It is used as a spice or condiment in curries and similar preparations. It is also used in medicine as a cordial stimulant. It is also used in bowel complaints such as dyspepsia, diarrhoea and vomiting. Powder cinnamon is a reputed remedy for diarrhoea and dysentery. The bark also yields an oil of which the chief constituent is Cinnamic aldehyde.

SPICES AND CONDIMENTS OBTAINED FROM LEAVES AND TWIGS

Indian Cassia

Cinnamomum tamala (Buch.-Ham.) T. Nees & Eberm.; English—Indian Cassia; Hindi—Leaves = *tejpat*, *tajpat*, bark = *taj kalami*, *dalchini*, *talispatri*, *silkanti*; Bengali—*Tejpat*; Nepali—*Chota sinkoli*; Assamese—*Dopatti*; Mumbai—*Darchini*, *tamala*; Gujarati—*Taj*, *tamalpatra*; Marathi—*Dalchini tiki*; Tamil—*Talisha-pattiri*; Telugu—*Tallisha-patri*; Kannada—*Lavanga patte*; Sanskrit—*Tamal*, *tespatra*; Arabic—*Zarnab*; Family—Lauraceae.

Fig. 35.6. *Cinnamomum tamala* (Tejpat). A plant with inflorescence and leaves.

A moderate-sized evergreen tree, found on the Himalayas, between 3,000 and 7,000 feet, in Bengal, the Khasia hills and Assam.

A cinnamon known as Indian Cassia is obtained from this plant. It is a coarser and sold in larger pieces than the true cinnamon or bark of *C. zeylanicum* Bl., for which it is often used as an adulterant. The bark of the root is quite as good as the true cinnamon bark. In Manipur, the natives collect the root-bark instead of the stem-bark.

Cassia buds. These are the immature fruits of tree yielding Indian Cassia. They are something like cloves, and consist of the unexpanded flower-heads. They possess properties similar to those of the bark. Cassia buds were once employed in preparing the speed wine called *Hippocras*.

Cassia bark. The bark has a general resemblance to cinnamon, but is in simple quills, not inserted one within the other. The quills, are less straight, even and regular, and of dark-brown colour. It breaks with a short fracture.

Uses. The leaves are known as *tejpat*, and bark as *taj*. The bark and dried leaves are used to flavour dishes. The leaves are commonly used as a condiment. They are famous for their pungency and added in cooked rice (*pulao*) and curries.

Leaves are also used medicinally. They are stimulant, carminative, used in rheumatism, colic, diarrhoea, and in scorpion sting. Bark is aromatic and used in gonorrhoea.

Leaves yield an essential oil, which contains d–phellandrene and 78% eugenol.

Sweet Marjoram

Majorana hortensis Moench; English—Sweet marjoram; Hindi—*Murwa*; Bengali—*Murru*; Kannada—*Maruga*; Malayalam—*Maruvamu*; Tamil—*Marru*; in Kumaon it is called Bantulsi and in Dakshin Bharat Murwa; Family—Labiatae (Lamiaceae).

This is an aromatic, branched perennial, 1-2 feet high. It is native of mediterranean region, North Africa and Asia Minor. The herb is commonly grown in Indian gardens. It is well suited for hilly places in India. Leaves oblong-ovate; flowers small, whitish or purplish, in terminal clusters; seeds minute, oval, dark brown.

It is treated as an annual under cultivation. It thrives well in well-drained fertile garden loam. It is propagated by seeds and cuttings. Seeds are sown in pots and seedlings, when large enough, are transplanted in the field 8-10" apart in rows. The crop becomes ready for harvesting in three and half months. The tops are cut when the plants are coming into flower and dried in the shade. The volatile oil content of leaves is maximum when the plant is harvested before seed formation.

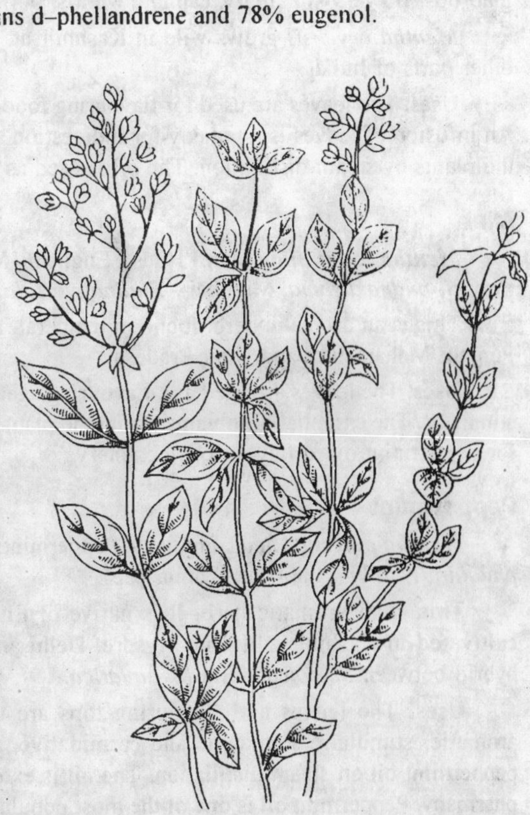

Fig. 35.7. Spices and condiments. *Majorana hortensis* Moench., Eng. Marjoram (Labiatae, Lamiaceae). The dried leaves of the herb are used as spice and flavouring agent.

Sweet marjoram possesses a strong, spicy and pleasant odour and flavour. The dry herb contains - water, 7.61%; protein 14.31%; fixed oil 5.6%; volatile oil 1.72%; pentosans 7.68%; fibre 22.06%; and ash 9.69%. Tannin and ursolic acid are also present.

Steam distillation of the leaves and flowering heads yields a volatile oil, known in the trade as *Oil of Sweet Marjoram*. The oil is colourless or pale-yellow to yellow-green with a peculiar odour.

Uses. The leaves of the plant are used fresh or dried and highly esteemed as a condiment for seasoning food. Fresh leaves are employed as garnish and incorporated in salad. They are used also for flavouring vinegar. The aromatic seeds are used in confectionery. It is a carminative, expectorant and tonic. Leaves and seeds are astringent. An infusion of the plant is used as stimulant, emmenagogue and gulactagogue. The oil is used in high grade flavour preparations and perfumes, and in soap and liqueur industries. It is used as an external application for sprains, bruises, paralytic limbs and toothache.

Field mint or Corn mint

Mentha arvensis Linn.; English—Field mint or corn mint; Hindi—*Podina*, *Pudina*; Bengali—*Mar.*; Gujarati and Telugu—*Podina, Pudina*; Kannada—*Chetni maragu*; Family—Labiatae (Lamiaceae).

An erect herb, 10-60 cm. in height found throughout temperate North Asia. Leaves 2.5-5 cm. long, shortly petioled or sessile, oblong ovate or lanceolate, serrate, cuneate at the base, hairy or glabrous; flowers in axillary, capitate whorls, borne on axils of leaves on upper stem.

Mentha arvensis grows wild in Kashmir at 1,500-3,000 m. It has also been reported from other parts of India.

Uses. The leaves are used for flavouring food stuffs. It is used as a stimulant and carminative. An infusion of leaves is a remedy for indigestion and rheumatism. A volatile oil is obtained from the plants by steam-distillation. The oil is used as a flavouring ingredient.

Mint

Mentha longifolia (Linn.) Huds.; English—Mint; Hindi—*Pudina, jungli pudina*; Punjabi—*Baburi, pudnakúshma*; Mumbai—*Pudina, vartalau*; Family—Labiatae (Lamiaceae).

This is an aromatic herb, found in temperate Himalayas and in Kashmir, Garhwal, Kumaon, Punjab, Maharashtra and Uttar Pradesh.

Uses. The leaves are used as a flavouring agent. The dried leaves are used as carminative and stimulant. The essential oil obtained from the plant on steam distillation can be used as a substitute for peppermint oil to flavour confectionery.

Peppetrmint

Mentha piperita Linn.; English—Peppermint; Hindi—*Vilaiti pudina, paparaminta, gamathi phudina*; Family—Labiatae (Lamiaceae).

This is an aromatic herb. It is native of Europe. It is grown in Indian gardens and also cultivated in Kashmir, Nilgiris, Mysore, Delhi and Dehradun. *M. piperita* is considered to be hybrid between *M. spicata* and *M. aquatica*.

Uses. The leaves and flavouring tops are used for flavouring food stuffs. The herb is aromatic. stimulant, stomachic and carminative, and used medicinally. The herb yields a true peppermint oil on steam distillation. The oil is extensively used for flavouring food stuffs and in pharmacy. Peppermint oil is one of the most popular and widely used essential oils. It is employed for flavouring chewing gums, candies, ice creams, confectionery, mouth washes, pharmaceuticals, dental preparations and alcoholic liqueurs. It is widely employed for nausea, flatulence and vomiting. It has a refreshing odour and a persistent cooling taste. It may be taken with sugar or in the form of tablets or lozenges.

Spearmint

Mentha spicata Linn.; English—Spearmint; Hindi—*Pahari pudina*, *pudina*; Family—Labiatae (Lamiaceae).

A perennial aromatic herb, 1 to 3 feet high, with creeping rhizomes. It is native of temperate Europe and Asia. In India, it is cultivated in the Punjab, Uttar Pradesh and Maharashtra.

Uses. Both fresh and dried leaves are used for mint sauce and jelly and to flavour soups, stews, sauces and beverages. The leaves are the source of spearmint oil, which is used for flavouring food products. Spearmint oil is used in U.S.A. for flavouring chewing gums, confectionery and pharmaceuticals. In India, green leaves are used for making chutney and for flavouring culinary preparations, vinegars, jellies and iced drinks. The herb is considered stimulant and carminative. A soothing tea is brewed from the leaves.

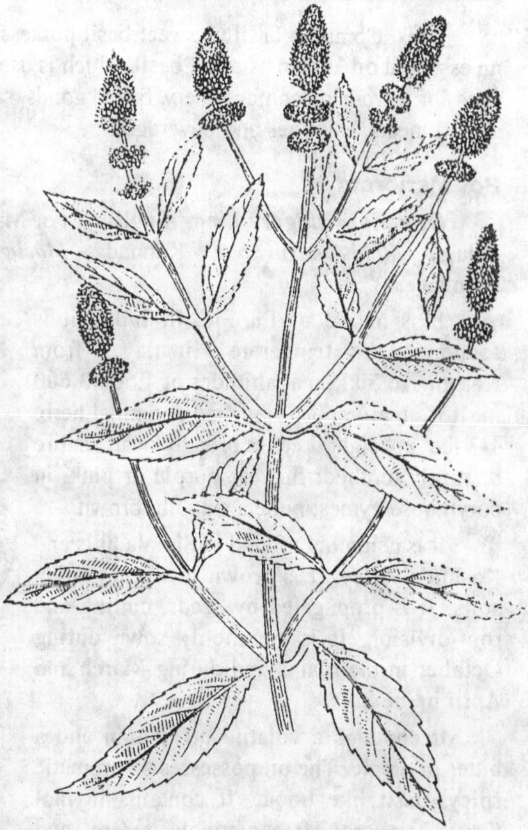

Fig. 35.8. Spices and condiments. *Mentha piperita* Linn.; Eng. Peppermint (Labiatae, Lamiaceae). A flowering twig. The leaves and flowering tops are used for flavouring purposes.

Curry Leaf Tree

Murraya koenigii (Linn.) Spreng.; English—Curry leaf tree; Hindi—*Kathnim*, *mitha nim*; Bengali—*Barsanga*; Marathi—*Karhinimb*; Gujarati—*Goranimb*; Telugu—*Karepaku*; Tamil—*Kattuveppilei*; Oriya—*Barsan*; Family—Rutaceae.

A large aromatic shrub or a small tree, upto 6 m. in height and 15-40 cm. in diameter, found throughout India and the Andaman Islands uptoan altitude of 1,500 m. Bark dark-brown or almost black; leaves imparipinnate; leaflets 9-25, ovate, lanceolate, crenate-dentate, obtuse or acute, glabrous above, pubescent beneath, gland dotted, strongly aromatic; flowers in terminal corymbose cymes, white, fragrant, berries sub-globose or ellipsoid, purplish black when ripe, 2-seeded. The plant is much cultivated for its aromatic leaves. Propagation is by seeds.

Uses. The leaves of the plant are extensively employed as flavouring agent in curries and chutneys. The leaves, root and bark are used also as tonic, stomachic and carminative.

Common Basil

Ocimum basilicum Linn.; English—Common basil, sweet basil; Hindi—*Babui-tulsi*, *Kali-tulsi*, *sabzah*, *marua*; Bengali—*Babui tulsi*, *khub kalam*, *debunsha*; Oriya—*Dhala tulasi*; Punjabi—*Baburi tulsi*, *rehan*; Marathi—*Sabza*; Tamil—*Tirmutpatchie*; Telugu—*Bhu-tulasi*, *rudra jada*, *vibudi-patri*; Kannada—*Kam-kasturi*; Malayalam—*Tiru-nitru*; Sanskrit—*Munjariki*, *Varvara*; Persian—*Firanj-Mushk*; Family—Labiatae (Lamiaceae).

An erect, herbaceous, glabrous or pubescent annual, 1-3 feet high, native of Central Asia and North-West Asia, growing throughout India. Leaves ovate - lanceolate, gland dotted; flowers white or pale purple. It is cultivated throughout tropical India from the Punjab to West Bengal.

Uses. Common basil or sweet basil possesses a clove like scent and a saline taste. It yields an essential oil known as oil of basil, which is used as a flavouring agent. Oil of basil is commonly used for flavouring confectionery, baked goods, sauces, ketchups, tomato pastes, pickles, vinegars, spiced meats, sausages and beverages.

Pot Marjoram

Origanum vulgare Linn.; English—Pot Marjoram or Common Marjoram; Hindi—*Sathra*; Telugu—*Mridu-maruvamu*; Kannada—*Maruga*; Punjabi—*Mirzanjosh*; Family—Labiatae (Lamiaceae).

It is native of Europe. In India, it is found in the temperate Himalayas from Kashmir to Sikkim at altitudes of 1,500-3,600 m. It is an aromatic, branched perennial herb, 1-3 feet in height. Leaves broadly ovate, entire or rarely toothed; flowers purple or pink, in corymbose cymes; nutlets smooth, brown.

It is commonly found in Shimla hills and Kashmir valley. It is grown in warm garden soils. It is propagated by seeds, cutting and root-division. It is commonly sown during October in the plains and during March and April in the hills.

It contains a volatile oil, tannin and a bitter principle. The oil possesses an aromatic spicy, basil like odour. It contains thymol (7%), carvacrol, free alcohols, esters, and bicyclic sesquiterpene.

Chemical composition of the leaves. Moisture 8.0%; protein 11.7%; fat 6.4%; crude fibre 11.0%; carbohydrates 53.9%; total ash 9.0%; calcium 1.7%; phosphorus 0.20%; iron 0.05%; sodium 0.02%; potassium 1.7%; vitamin A 1010 international units (I.U.)/100 g.; vitamin B_1 0.34 mg/100 g.; vitamin B_2 0.41 mg/100 g.; niacin 6.2 mg/100 g. and vitamin C 12 mg/100 g; calorific value 360 calories/100 g.

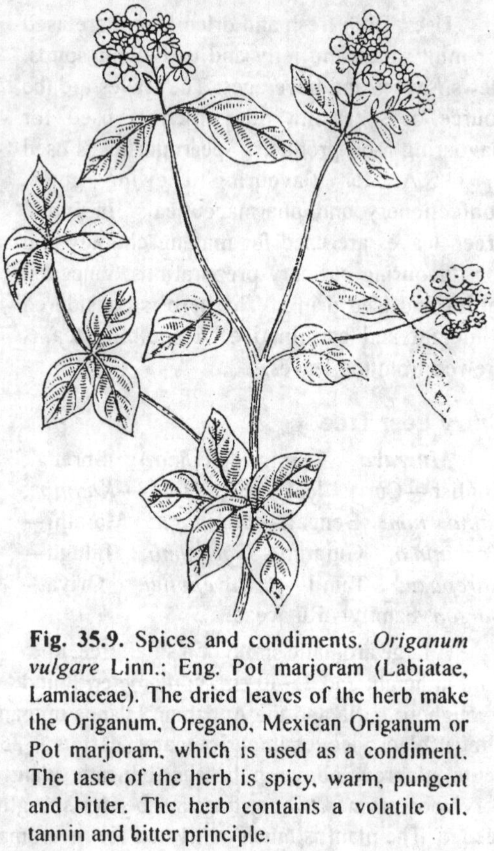

Fig. 35.9. Spices and condiments. *Origanum vulgare* Linn.; Eng. Pot marjoram (Labiatae, Lamiaceae). The dried leaves of the herb make the Origanum, Oregano, Mexican Origanum or Pot marjoram, which is used as a condiment. The taste of the herb is spicy, warm, pungent and bitter. The herb contains a volatile oil, tannin and bitter principle.

Uses. The leaves and tops of the herb cut prior to blooming are used to flavour food stuffs especially meats, egg preparations and salads. The volatile oil from herb is aromatic, carminative, stimulant, tonic, stomachic, diaphoretic, emmenagógue, rubifacient, given in colic, diarrhoea and hysteria, also applied in toothache.

Rosemary

Rosmarinus officinulis Linn.; English—***Rosemary***; Hindi—*Rusmary*; Family—***Labiatae* (*Lamiaceae*)**.

A small shrub, native of Mediterranean region. It is found wild on dry rocky hill in the Mediterranean region. In India, it is cultivated to some extent in the temperate Himalayas and Nilgiris hills in dry to moderately moist climate.

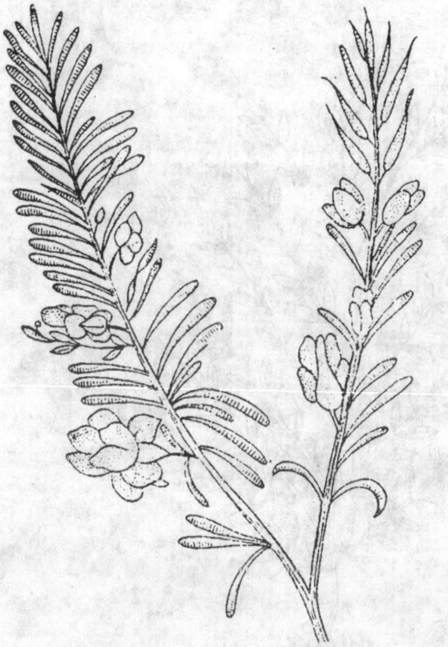

Fig. 35.10. Spices and condiments. *Rosmarinus officinalis* Linn: Eng. Rosemary (Labiatae, Lamiaceae). A flowering twig. The dried leaves of *R. officinalis* Linn., make the rosemary of commerce.

A small shrub. It is native of Mediterranean region, cultivated as a spice and for medicinal purposes. Stems shrubby, white woolly; flavouring branches tomentose-pubescent, leaves aromatic, petiolate, entire, oblong, base narrowed; flowers, purple, blue or white, in racemes. The greyish-green hairy leaves are very aromatic.

Uses. The leaves and tender twigs are used for flavouring food products. Sage has been extensively employed in the food industry as a standard spice in making stuffing for fowl, meats and sausage. Dried and powdered aromatic leaves are mixed with cooked vegetables and sprinkled on cheese dishes, cooked meats and other curries. Fresh sage leaves are used in salads, vegetable sandwiches.

Chemical composition of dried leaves. Moisture 5.7%; Protein 10.2%; fat 14.1%; crude fibre 16.0%; carbohydrates 46.3%; total ash 7.7%; Calcium 1.8%;

Leaves of rosemary possess an agreeable aromatic odour and a pungent, bitter and camphoraceous taste. It yields a volatile oil known as oil of rosemary. The volatile oil is obtained by steam distillation of leaves, flavouring tops and twigs. The finest produce is being obtained from the dried leaves freed of stalks. The oil is pale-yellow or colourless liquid with the characteristic odour of the leaves and a warm camphor, borneol and bornyl acetate.

Uses. The leaves are employed as a condiment dried and powdered. They are added to cooked meats, fish, eggs, soups, stews, sauces, dressings, preserves and jams. They are mixed with sage in pork and veal stuffings and added to biscuits. Carminative, diaphoretic, astringent, diuretic, emmenagogue, stimulant and stomachic oil or rosemary is used for flavouring of meats, sausages, soups, table sauces and other food products. The oil is mainly used in perfumery. It is also used in medicinal preparations.

Garden Sage

Salvia officinalis Linn.; English—Sage, Garden sage; Hindi—Salvia sefakuss; Family—Labiatae (Lamiaceae).

Fig. 35.11. Spices and condiments. *Salvia officinalis* Linn.; Eng. Sage, Garden sage (Labiatae, Lamiaceae). A flowering twig. The dried leaves of *S. officinalis* Linn., make the "sage" of commerce.

Phosphorus 0.09%; Iron 0.03%, Sodium 0.01%; Potassium 1.0%; vitamin B_1 0.75 mg/100 g.; vitamin B_2 0.34 mg/100 g.; vitamin C 39.8 mg/100 g.; niacin 5.7 mg/100 g.; vitamin A 2395 International Units (I.U.)/100 g.; calorific value 415 calories/100 g.

Thyme

Thymus vulgaris Linn.; English—Thyme; Family—Labiatae (Lamiaceae).

A flowering plant. It is a perennial garden plant. It is native of Mediterranean region. In India it is found in Himalayas from Kashmir to Kumaon.

The dried leaves and tender tops make "thyme" of commerce. A volatile oil of pleasant odour is obtained on steam distillation of herb.

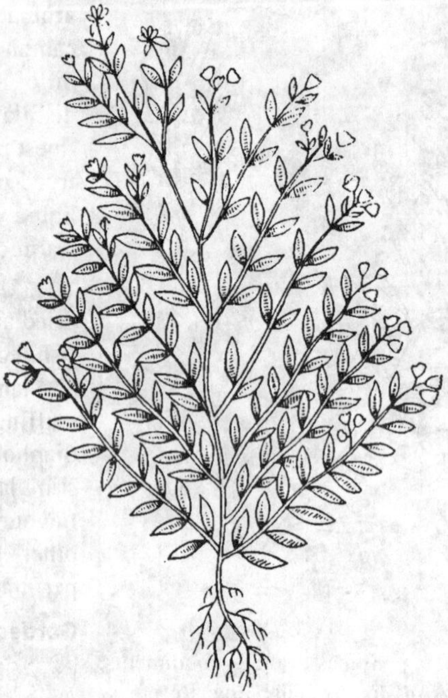

Fig. 35.12. Spices and condiments. *Thymus vulgaris* Linn.; Eng. Thyme (Labiatae, Lamiaceae). A flowering plant. The dried leaves and tender tops of *T. vulgaris* Linn., make "thyme" of commercial value. It is a perennial garden plant.

Chemical composition of dried leaves. Moisture 7.1%; Protein 6.8%; fat 4.6%; crude fibre 24.3%; carbohydrates 44.0%; mineral matter 13.2%; Calcium 2.1%; Phosphorus 0.20%; Iron 0.14%, Sodium 0.08%; Potassium 0.9%; vitamin B_1 51 mg/100 g.; vitamin B_2 0.4 mg/100 g.; vitamin C 12.0 mg/100 g.; niacin 4.9 mg/100 g.; vitamin A 175 International Units (I.U.)/100 g.; calorific value 340 calories/100 g.

Uses. The dried leaves are used for dressing and seasoning meat preparations, egg curries, pork sausage, etc.

SPICES AND CONDIMENTS OBTAINED FROM FLOWER BUDS, FLOWERS AND INFLORESCENCE

Saffron

Crocus sativus Linn.; English—Saffron; Hindi—*Kesar, zafran*; Bengali—*Jafran*; Mumbai—*Safran, kessar, kecara*; Marathi—*Kecara*; Gujarati—*Keshar*; Tamil—*Kungumapu*; Telugu—*Kumkum apave*; Kashmiri—*Kong*; Sanskrit—*Kunkuma, kashmirajanma, kumkuma*; Arabic & Persian—*Zaafaran*; Family—Iridaceae.

A rhizomatous herb. It is cultivated in Kashmir at Pampur near Srinagar. To a small extent it is cultivated also at Bhersar and Chaubattia in Uttar Pradesh. The dried stigmas and tops of the styles make the saffron of commerce. The product is obtained from the stigmas of the flowers, 4,000 of which are required to produce 25 gms. of saffron.

Uses. The saffron is used as a spice and dyestuff. It possesses a pleasant aroma. Saffron is an ingredient of many Indian dishes, particularly cooked rice and sweet rice (Kesaria chaval) and pulao.

Clove

Syzygium aromaticum (Linn.) Merr. & Perry; Syn. *Eugenia aromatica* O. Kuntze; *E. caryophyllata* Thunb.; English—Clove; Hindi—*Laung*; Bengali—*Lavange, langa*; Punjabi—*Laung, karanfal*; Kashmiri—*Raung*; Marathi & Gujarati—*Lawanga, lavinga*; Tamil—*Kiramber, ilavang ap-pu*; Telugu—*Lavangalu*; Malayalam—*Chanki*; Sanskrit—*Lavanga*; Persian—*Mekhak*; Family—Myrtaceae.

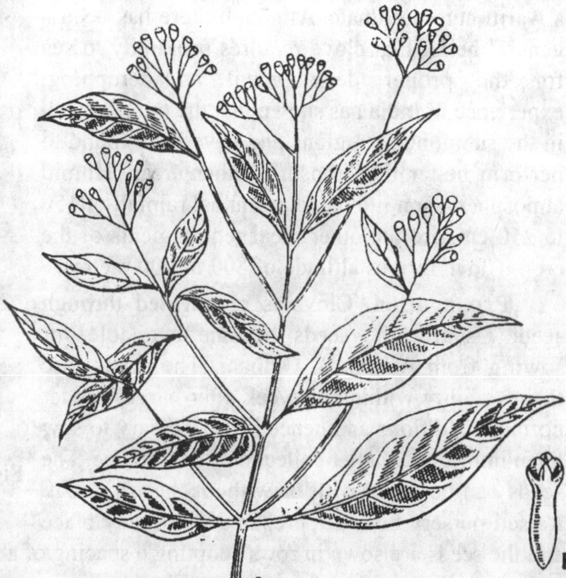

Fig. 35.13. Spices and condiments. *Syzygium aromaticum* (Linn.) Merr. & Perry, syn. *Eugenia aromatica* O. Kuntze, *E. caryophyllata* Thunb; Eng. Clove (Myrtaceae). A, a flowering twig; B, dried unopened flower bud.

Clove is one of the most ancient and valuable spices of the orient and holds a unique position in the international spice trade. Native to Moluccas, the so called 'Spice Islands' in the East Indian Archipelago, this spice was first introduced in India around 1800 A.D. by the East India company. The company's spice garden in Courtallam in Tamil Nadu was then established to cultivate clove and nutmeg as the principal spice crops. Induced by the success of the cultivation in Courtallam, cultivation of clove was extended during the period after 1850 A.D. to Nilgiris (Burliar) in Tamil Nadu, Southern regions of Travancore and also to Cochin State on the slope of Western Ghats. The Important clove growing regions in India now are Nilgiris, Tenkasi hills, and Kanyakumari districts of Tamil Nadu and Kottayam and Quilon districts of Kerala.

Although clove has been under cultivation in India for over about 170 years, its development has been very slow owing probably to its long pre-bearing period and lack of knowledge regarding the method and economics of its cultivation.

Clove is the dried unopened flower bud of *Syzygium aromaticum*, a medium statured, cone-shaped ever-green tree belonging to the Family—Myrtaceae. Clove tree attains a height of 10 to 12 metres. The stem is usually forked near its base with two or three main branches. Smaller branches are slender, rather brittle and covered with grey bark. The leaves appearing in pairs, are lanceolate, acute at both ends and are of dark shining green colour. The aromatic nature of the leaves is due to numerous oil glands found on their under-surfaces. The flower buds are greenish when fresh and are borne on ends, which are picked green and dried in the sun till they become dark brown, form the 'clove' of commerce. The buds have slightly cylindrical base and are surmounted by the plump ball like unopened corolla which is surmounted by the four toothed calyx. If the bud is left unpicked, the flower develops after fertilization into a fleshy, purple and one-seeded oval fruit as 'Mother of clove'. The fruit is about 2.5 cm. long and 1.25 cm. in width. The seed is oblong, rather soft in texture and grooved on one side. The leaves, unripe fruit and broken clove, including the stalk are all aromatic and yield an essential oil.

Soil and climate. Deep and rich loams with high humus content are best suited for clove cultivation. In India, clove has developed well in the open sandy loams and the laterite soils of South Kerala region. But the best growth is seen in black loams of the semi forest regions. Clove abhors water logging and, therefore, perfect drainage is essential.

Clove is strictly a tropical plant and it requires a warm humid climate. Although there has been a general belief that clove requires proximity to sea for the proper development and cropping, experience in India has shown that the trees do well in the submontane regions and have been found to perform better than those in other areas. Humid atmospheric condition and an annual rainfall of 150 to 250 cm. are the other ideal requirements of the crop. Clove thrives altitude of 800 to 900 metres.

Fig. 35.14. *Syzygium aromaticum*-clove (**laung**). The dried flower buds are used as spice.

Propagation. Clove is propagated through seed. Usually the seeds become available for sowing from August to October. The seeds lose their viability within one week after harvest under normal conditions and hence it is necessary to sow them immediately after collection from the tree. The seeds can be sown with or without the fruit coat. Raised nursery beds are prepared in a shady place and the seeds are sown in rows adopting a spacing of about 12 cms. The seeds begin to germinate in four to five weeks after sowing. The seedlings are very slender and delicate and grow very slowly. Watering is necessary throughout the nursery period. The seedlings after about six months of nursery life are transferred to baskets made of bamboo or mud pots and nurtured properly under the shade till they attain an age of 12 to 18 months. Clove can also be propagated vegetatively by grafting on its own stock.

Clove can conveniently be grown mixed with other commercial crops like arecanut, coconut, nutmeg, etc. The shade cast by these crops will provide enough protection to clove from the sun.

Harvesting and curing. Clove tree begins to yield from the seventh or eighth years after planting. The full bearing stage is attained after about 15 to 20 years. The flowering season is September-October in the plains and December-January in high altitudes. The buds are ready for harvest in about four months.

Just before flowering there is fresh flush of young leaves and soon after this, the flower buds begin to appear. The optimum stage for picking clove buds is indicated by the change in the colour from green to slightly pinkish tinge. The unopened clove buds are carefully picked with hand when they turn pink in colour. It is necessary to pick the buds before they open, otherwise, the value of spice will be lost to a considerable extent.

The harvested buds are spread evenly to dry in the sun either on grass-mats or on cement drying floor. During nights the buds should be stored under cover, lest they re-absorb moisture. Normally it is possible to dry the cloves in four to five days under direct sun and in about four hours when they are heated in zinc trays over a regulated fire. Fully dried buds develop the characteristic dark brown colour and crisp. If the produce is uniformly good, approximately 8,000 to 10,000 cloves would weigh one kilogram. Clove is graded according to its appearance and impurity content. Good quality clove should be brownish black in colour, with full and plump crown, somewhat rough to the touch and without wrinkles and it should not contain more than 16% moisture and 5% foreign matter. Also it should have fine aroma and flavour and should readily exude oil when the stem is pressed with the finger nail.

Yield. There is considerable variation in the yield of clove. Under favourable conditions well grown trees may yield as much 4 to 8 kg. of cloves. It is, however, common to meet with low yielding tree in clove plantations, sometimes in large numbers, resulting in low and uneconomic production, particularly in certain years. The average yield from a bearing tree in a well maintained plantation, in India is reported to be about 2.5 kg. considering that the percentage of bearing tree will be around 60, one hectare of plantation containing about 250 trees will yield about 375 kg. of cloves.

Uses. Clove is very aromatic and fine flavoured and imparts warming qualities. In all Indian homes, it is used as a culinary spice as the flavour blends well with both sweet and savoury dishes. Clove is used for flavouring pickle, curries, ketchup and sauces. It is highly valued in medicine as a carminative, aromatic and stimulant. Clove has stimulating properties and is one of the ingredients of betel chewing. In Jawa, clove is used in preparation of a special brand of cigarette for smoking. The essential oil which is obtained by distilling clove with water or steam, has even more uses. It is used medicinally in several ways. The chief constituent of the oil eugenol, is extracted and used as an imitation carnation in perfumes.

Clove requirement in India. The requirement of clove in India is being met through imports. We have been importing large quantities of clove in the past. The average annual imports of cloves was about 2,940 tonnes valuable at about Rs. 183 lakhs in the 1950's. However, owing to the restrictions imposed from time to time, it has been possible to cut down the imports considerably and in the 1960's the annual import was of the order of 500 tonnes valued at about Rs. 47 lakhs.

The chief clove producing countries are Zanzibar, which grow 90% of the total output, Indonesia, Mauritius, and the West Indies.

Chemical composition. Moisture 5.4%; protein 6.3%; volatile oil 13.2%; fat (non volatile ether extract) 15.5%; crude fibre 11.1%; carbohydrates 57.7%; mineral matter 5.0%; ash 0.24%; calcium 0.7%; phosphorus 0.11%; iron 0.01%; sodium 0.25%; potassium 1.2%; vitamin B_1 0.11 mg/100 g.; vitamin B_2 0.04 mg/100 g.; niacin 1.5 mg/100 g.; vitamin C 80.9 mg/100 g. and vitamin A 175 International Units (I.U.), calorific value 430 calories per 100 g.

SPICES AND CONDIMENTS OBTAINED FROM FRUITS

Celery

Apium graveolens Linn. var. *dulce* DC.; English—Celery, celery seed, garden celery; Hindi—*Ajmud, bari-ajmud, karafs*; Bengali—*Chanu, randhuni*; Mumbai—*Bori ajamoda, ajmud*; Punjabi—*Bhut jhata*; Arabic—*Karafs*; Persian—*Karasb*; Family—Umbelliferae (Apiaceae).

It is native of England and other parts of Europe. In India, it is cultivated in the North-Western Himalayas and in the hills of Uttar Pradesh, the Punjab and South India. In Indian plains, it is cultivated during the cold weather, chiefly as a garden crop in the vicinity of towns. The fruits are small and dark brown with peculiar flavour.

Uses. The herb is eaten as salad, or made into soup. The seed (fruit) is eaten as spice. The seed tied into a piece of cloth are used to flavour soup. The soil extracted from the seeds is stimulant and used chiefly for flavouring soups and curries. The seeds are also cordial, tonic, carminative, diuretic, emmenagogue and antiseptic.

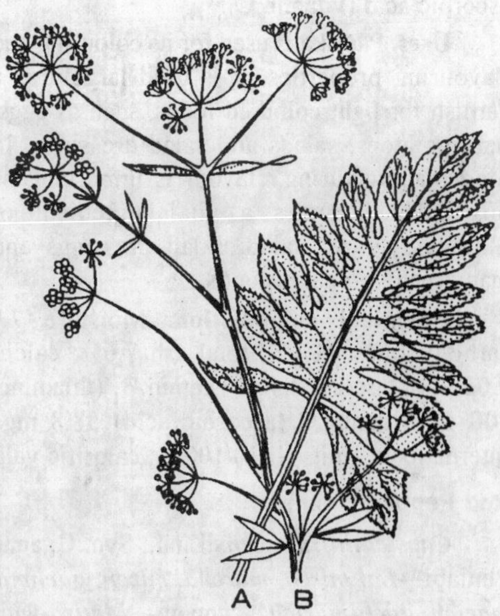

Fig. 35.15. Spices and condiments. *Apium graveolens* Linn. var. *dulce* DC.; Eng. Celery, Celery seed, Garden celery (Umbelliferae, Apiaceae). A, leaf; B, floral axis with typical umbels.

Chemical composition. Moisture 5.1%; protein 18.1%; fat (ether extract) 22.8%; crude fibre 2.9%; carbohydrates 40.9%; total ash 10.2%; calcium 1.8%; phosphorus 0.55%; iron 0.45%; sodium 0.17%; potassium 1.4%; iron 0.53%; vitamin B_1 (thiamine) 0.41 mg/100 g.; vitamin B_2 (riboflavin) 0.49 mg/100 g.; vitamin C (ascorbic acid) 17.2 mg/100 g.; niacin 4.4 mg/100 g.; vitamin A 650 international unit (I.U.); calorific value 450 calories/100 g.

Sweet Pepper

Capsicum annuum Linn.; English—Sweet pepper, paprika, Hungarian paprika, Spanish pimento; Family—Solanaceae.

This is a non-pungent variety of chilli. The red paprikas are famous for their brilliant red colour and mild flavour. Several varieties of paprika have been successfully grown at the IARI, New Delhi and Central Food Technology Research Institute (CFTRI), Mysore. Since several varieties of *Capsicum annuum* Linn. are used to produce paprika, pods in one growing area may differ in shape and appearance of those from another. Some pods are round in shape with pointed end whereas, the others are elongated. They are medium to small and quite fleshy. They are produced on small, bushy plants. When ripe, the pods are picked and dried in the sun. It is processed into powder where it is grown. The paprika pods are supposed to be one of the richest sources of ascorbic acid (vitamin C).

Uses. Paprika is used for its colouring and flavouring properties. It is used largely as a garnish for light coloured foods, such as eggs, fish, potatoes, salads and salad dressings. In food manufacturing, flavour is important, as this spice becomes a vital ingredient of sausages, soups, salad, salad dressings and many ready prepared foods.

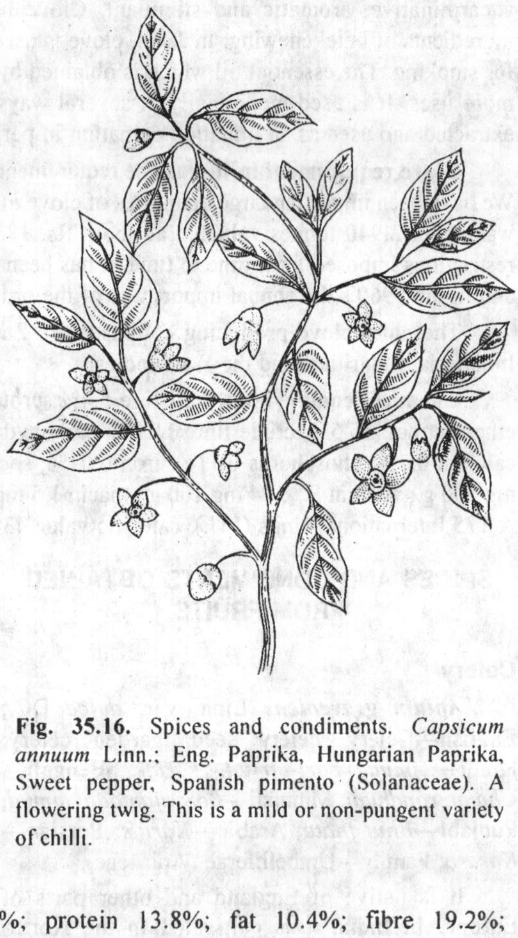

Fig. 35.16. Spices and condiments. *Capsicum annuum* Linn.; Eng. Paprika, Hungarian Paprika, Sweet pepper, Spanish pimento (Solanaceae). A flowering twig. This is a mild or non-pungent variety of chilli.

Chemical composition. Moisture 7.9%; protein 13.8%; fat 10.4%; fibre 19.2%; carbohydrates 41.1%; total ash 7.6%; calcium 0.2%; phosphorus 0.3%; iron 0.23%; sodium 0.02%; potassium 2.4%; vitamin B_1 (thiamine) 0.60 mg/100 g.; vitamin B_2 (riboflavin) 1.36 mg/100 g.; vitamin C (ascorbic acid) 58.8 mg/100 g.; niacin 15.3 mg/100 g.; vitamin A 4915 International Units (I.U.)/100 g.; calorific value 390 calories/100 g.

Red Pepper, Chillies

Capsicum frutescens Linn.; Syn. C. annuum Linn.; English—Red pepper; chillies; Hindi & Punjabi—*Lal mirch, marcha, mirch, gachmirch, mattisa, wangru*; Bengali—*Lal-mirch, lanka-marich, gach-marich*; Kumaon—*Matisa-wangru*; Kashmiri—*Mirtz-a-vangun, mirch-wangum*; Gujarati—*Lal-mirch, marchu*; Marathi—*Mirsinga*; Tamil—*Milagay, mollagu*; Telugu—*Mirapakaya*; Malayalam—*Kappal-melaka*; Kannada—*Mena-sina-kayi*; Sanskrit—*Marichi-phalam*; Persian—*Filfile-surkh, pilpile-surkh*; Family—Solanaceae.

It is native of the West Indies and tropical America, most probably of Brazil. Commonly cultivated for its fruit throughout the plains of India, and on the lower hills such as Kashmir, and in the Chenab valley upto altitude 6,500 feet. When grown on the hills it is said to be very pungent. There are several varieties, differing chiefly in the length, shape, and colour of the fruit, some being round, others oblong, obtuse, pointed or bifid, smooth or rugose, and red, white, yellow or varigated. The very pungent principles are present in the flesh and rind as well as seeds. The ripe fruits are dried in the sun and used whole or powdered.

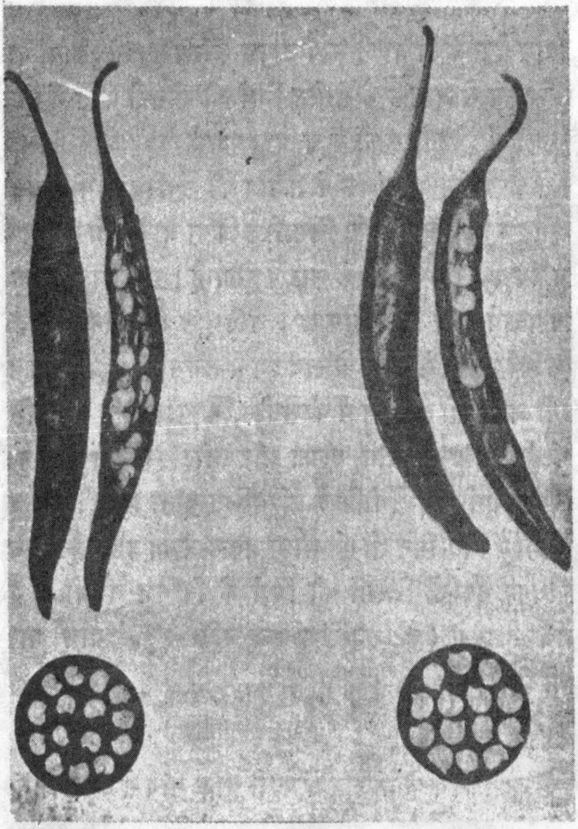

Fig. 35.17. *Capsicum frutescens* (red pepper - **Lal mirch**). Fruits and seeds.

It is a herb, 2 or 3 feet in height, with entire ovate leaves, white flowers with a rotate corolla, and many-seeded fruits, which are technically berries.

Cultivation. Chillies can be cultivated as a field crop over a wide range of tropical and sub-tropical conditions. It grows well up to an altitude of 5,000 feet a.s. l., in tracts receiving an annual rainfall of about 25 to 50 inches. Heavy rains during the growing period lead to rotting of leaves and fruits. The crop can be grown both in the rainy season commencing from about June and in the hot weather about February. In areas of heavy rainfall the crop is taken after the monsoon period. In tracts of low rainfall, the crop is grown under irrigation.

The soils best suited for the cultivation are of the heavy loam type, from grit, gravel, and stones and well drained.

The seed is sown in the end of June or in the beginning of July in well prepared nursery beds. When the seedlings are about 40-45 days old, they are transplanted. At the nursery stage frequent irrigation is required. The flowering of the plants begin after about a month of transplanting. In another one month, the first crop of green chillies is ready for picking. From about the month of November the fruits begin to ripen and change in colour, first to a deep orange and then to red. The fruits are gathered as they become red. About the middle of December the picking is in full swing. The plants continue to bear the fruit to the end of February. After being gathered, the fruits are dried in the sun. If the colour is not fully developed, they are heaped up until the colour develops fully, and then dried in the sun. They are usually trampled lightly when they are drying, so that they may be flattened and their packing in bags for storage and transport may become easy. Process of drying usually takes about a fortnight. Well irrigated crops yield 1,500 lb. to 2,500 lb. per acre.

Uses. The fruit when green is used for pickling and when ripe is mixed with tomatoes to make sauces. It is also dried and ground for use. The consumption of chillies is very great, and both rich and poor daily use them. The chillies form the principal ingredient in all chutneys and curries. They are ground into a paste, between two stones (Silbatta), with a little mustard oil, ginger and salt, they form the only seasoning which the millions of poor can obtain to eat with rice.

Caraway

Carum carvi **Linn.**; English—Caraway; Hindi—*Shiajira, zira*; Bengali—*Jira*; Punjabi—*Zira siyah*; Kashmiri—*Gunyun*; Ladakh—*Unbu*; Tamil—*Shimai-shombu*; Telugu—*Shimai-sapu*; Sanskrit—*Sushavi*; Persian—*Karoya*; Family—Umbelliferae (Apiaceae).

A herb; native of Europe and West Asia, now cultivated in Bihar, Orissa, the Punjab, Bengal and Andhra Pradesh, as a cold season crop. It is frequently cultivated on the hills, as a summer crop in Kashmir and Garhwal at an altitude of between 9,000 and 12,000 feet. It is a perennial with thick roots, compound leaves with linear segments and small white flowers. The fruits are brown in colour, slightly curved and tapering. The spice seems to have come into use in Europe about the thirteenth century, and it was known in England at the close of the fourteenth century.

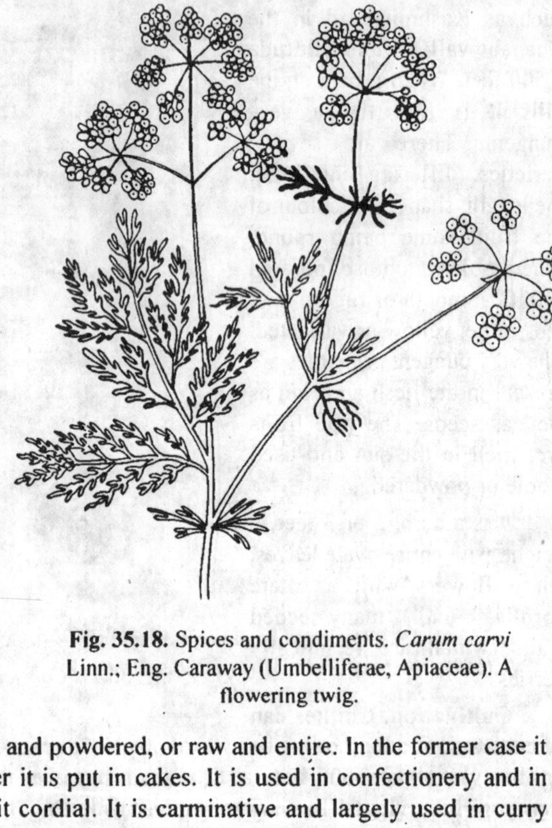

Fig. 35.18. Spices and condiments. *Carum carvi* Linn.; Eng. Caraway (Umbelliferae, Apiaceae). A flowering twig.

Uses. The fruit (seed) is used parched and powdered, or raw and entire. In the former case it is employed to flavour curries; in the latter it is put in cakes. It is used in confectionery and in flavouring drinks. It also produces a spirit cordial. It is carminative and largely used in curry powder.

A valuable essential oil is obtained from the "seeds" called caraway oil. The oil is a mixture of a hydrocarbon $C_{10}H_{16}$ (*carvene*) and an oxygenated oil, $C_{10}H_{14}O$ (*carvol*). The oil possesses a strong odour and flavour of the fruit. It is used medicinally and to flavour curries.

Chemical composition of fruit of *Carum carvi* Linn. Moisture 4.5%; protein 7.6%; fat 8.8%; fibre 25.2%; carbohydrates 50.2%; total ash 3.7%; calcium 1.0%; phosphorus 0.11%; sodium 0.02%; potassium 1.9%; iron 0.09%; vitamin B_1 (thiamine) 0.38 mg/100 g.; vitamin B_2 (riboflavin) 0.38 mg/100 g.; vitamin C (ascorbic acid) 12.0 mg/100 g.; niacin 8.1 mg/100 g.; vitamin A 580 International Units (I.U.); calorific value 465 calories/100 g. of spice.

Coriander

Coriandrum sativum Linn.; English—Coriander; Hindi—*Dhaniya*; Bengali—*Dhane*; Sanskrit—*Dhanyaka*; Tamil—*Kotamalli*; Telugu—*Danyalu, kotimiri*; Kannada—*Kotambari*, Nepali—*Danya*; Persian—*Kushniz*; Family—Umbelliferae (Apiaceae).

It is a native of the Mediterranean region. It is grown extensively in India, Russia, Central Europe, Asia Minor and Morocco. In India, it is cultivated in all the States. The more important

States for its cultivation are - Andhra Pradesh, Assam, Maharashtra, Tamil Nadu, Uttar Pradesh, Karnataka, Himachal Pradesh and Madhya Pradesh.

The plant is generally 2-3 feet in height, with white or pinkish flowers. The lower leaves have broad segments, while the upper are very narrow. The fruits are small, oval and aromatic. Technically the fruit is known as "cremocarp". Each fruit consists of two one-seeded carpels, or mericarps with numerous oil ducts (vittae).

Cultivation. It is cultivated mostly as rain-fed crop, either pure or mixed with other crops. It is also grown as an irrigated crop in some areas. The sowing time differs in different parts of India. In Northern India, the seeds are sown during winter; in Maharashtra during rainy season; in Tamil Nadu during autumn and in Karnataka and some parts of Tamil Nadu from May to August and from October to January.

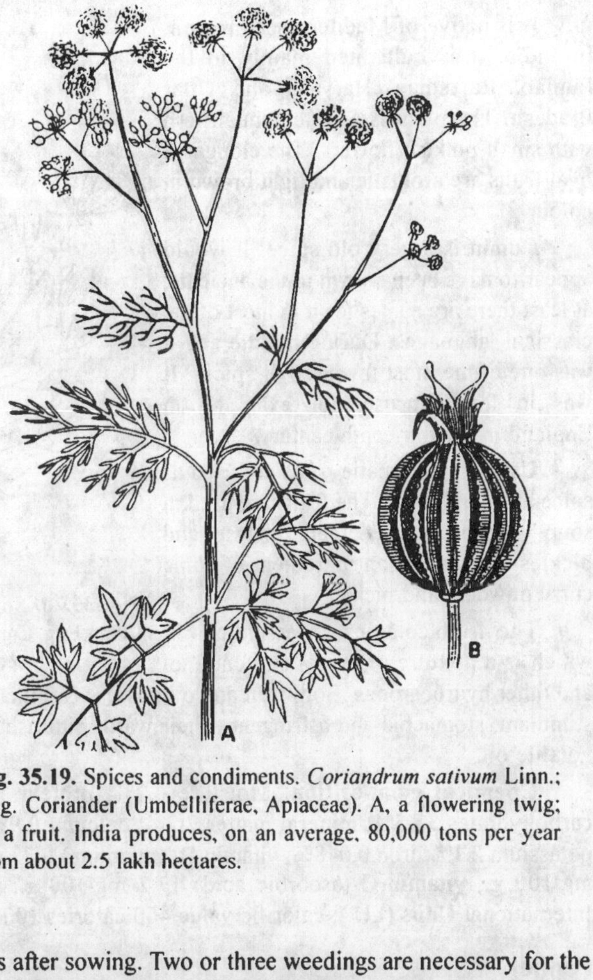

Fig. 35.19. Spices and condiments. *Coriandrum sativum* Linn.; Eng. Coriander (Umbelliferae, Apiaceae). A, a flowering twig; B, a fruit. India produces, on an average, 80,000 tons per year from about 2.5 lakh hectares.

The seed germinates in 10-25 days after sowing. Two or three weedings are necessary for the crop. Irrigation is done when it is needed. Proper manuring increases the yield. The crop is ready in three to three and half months after sowing. The plants are pulled out along with the roots and dried. Therefore, the fruits are threshed out, further dried in the sun, winnowed and stored. The yields vary from place to place. It ranges from 300 kg. to 900 kg. per acre.

Uses. The fruits and leaves are aromatic and used as flavouring materials. The fruits are used extensively in the preparation of curry powder, pickles, sauces, soups, sausages and seasonings. They are also employed for flavouring pastries, cookies, buns and cakes and tobacco products. It is also used for flavouring liqueurs, particularly gin. The fruits are used both as spice and condiment. It is an important condiment used widely in all parts of India. A major part of the produce is used within the country. The fruits are also used as stimulant, carminative, stomachic, diuretic, antibilous, refrigerant, aphrodisiac and tonic. Oil of Coriander is used in medicine and for flavouring beverages. The Coriander leaves make one of the richest sources of vitamin C (*i.e.*, 250 mg/100 g.) and vitamin A (*i.e.*, 5200 I.U./100 g.).

Cumin

Cuminum cyminum Linn.; English—*Cumin*; Hindi—*Zira*; Bengali—*Jira*; Gujarati—*Jiru*, *jira-utmi*; Marathi—*Jire*; Tamil—*Shirangam*; Telugu—*Jiraka*, *Jilakarra*; Kannada—*Jiringe*, *jirage*; Malayalam—*Jirakam*; Sanskrit—*Jiraka*, *jirana*; Persian--*Zira*; Arabic—*Kamun*; Family—Umbelliferae (Apiaceae).

It is native of Mediterranean region. In India, it is cultivated mainly in the Punjab, Rajasthan, Haryana and Uttar Pradesh. The plant is a little annual herb with small pinkish flowers. The elongated oval fruits are aromatic and light brown in colour.

Cumin is a very old spice. It would appear to have been known to the ancients; at least there are names for it in most of the classical languages. During middle age it was one of the most favoured of spices. It was in frequent use, for example, in England in the thirteenth century.

Uses. The aromatic fruits are used as spice and condiment. The fruits are used in soup, curries, cake, bread, cheese and pickles. They form an ingredient of some curry powders and pickles.

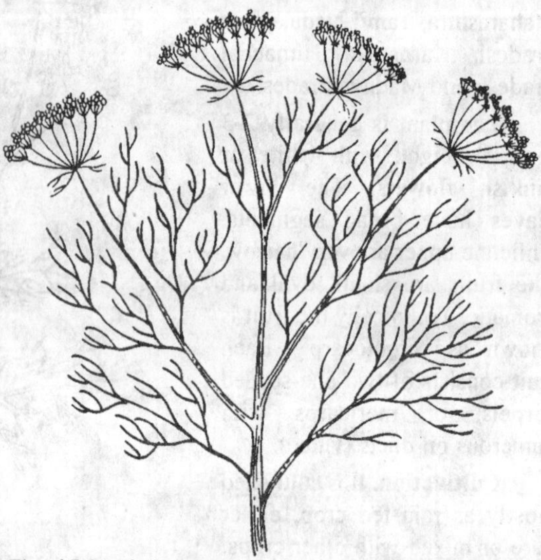

Fig. 35.20. Spices and condiments. *Cuminum cyminum* Linn.; Eng. Cumin (Umbelliferae, Apiaceae). A flowering

The fruit contains an essential oil, which is a mixture of cymol and cuminol and other hydrocarbons. Both fruit and oil possess carminative properties. They are also aromatic, stimulant, stomachic and astringent. Their warm bitterish taste and aromatic odour reside in the volatile oil.

Chemical composition. Moisture 6.2%; protein 17.7%; fat 23.8%; crude fibre 9.1%; carbohydrates 35.5%; mineral matter 7.7%; calcium 0.9%; phosphorus 0.45%; sodium 0.16%; potassium 2.1%; iron 0.048%; vitamin B_1 (thiamine) 0.73 mg/100 g.; vitamin B_2 (riboflavin) 0.38 mg/100 g.; vitamin C (ascorbic acid) 17.2 mg/100 g.; niacin 2.5 mg/100 g.; vitamin A 175 International Units (I.U.); calorific value 460 calories/100 g.

Fennel

Foeniculum vulgare Mill.; English—Fennel; Hindi—*Saunf*; Bengali—*Mauri, pan-muhori*; Mumbai—*Bari-shopha, panmohuri*; Gujarati—*variari, Variyali*; Marathi—*Badishep*; Kannada—*Badisopu*; Tamil—*Sohikira*; Telugu—*Pedda-jila-kurra*; Sanskrit—*Madhurika*; Family—Umbelliferae (Apiaceae).

It is a stout, glabrous, aromatic herb, 5-6 feet high; leaves pinnately decompound; flowers small, yellow, in compound terminal umbels; fruit oblong, ellipsoid or cylindrical, 6-7 mm. in length, straight or slightly curved, greenish or yellowish brown; mericarp 5-ridged with prominent vittae.

Fennel is a very old flavouring substance. It was known to the ancient Hindus, Chinese and Egyptians as a culinary spice. It is native of Mediterranean region. In India, it is cultivated mainly in the Punjab, Uttar Pradesh, Assam, Maharashtra and Baroda. It is cultivated mostly as a garden or homeyard crop throughout India at all altitudes upto 6,000 feet. It requires a fairly mild climate and is cultivated as a cold weather crop in parts of Northern India.

Cultivation. It grows well in any good soil, but thrives best in rich, well-drained loam or black sandy soil containing sufficient lime. It is propagated mainly by seeds. Seeds are sown broadcast by hand or by shallow drills. The time of sowing is October-November in the plains of India and March-April on the hills. When 3-4 inches high, the plants are thinned out to about 1 feet apart. Occasional weeding and irrigation once a week during dry weather is being done.

Harvesting. The crop is harvested before the fruits are fully ripe. The stems are cut with a sickle and spread out to dry in the sun. When dry (4-5 days after cutting) the fruits are threshed out and cleaned by winnowing. The yield ranges from 2800 to 1120 lb. per acre.

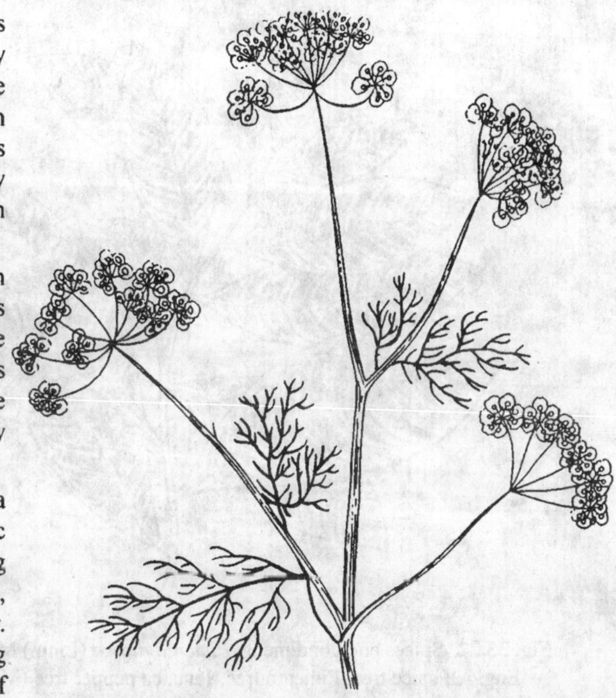

Fig. 35.21. Spices and condiments. *Foeniculum vulgare* Mill.; Eng. Fennel (Umbelliferae, Apiaceae). A flowering twig.

Uses. The leaves are used in fish sauce and for garnishing. Leaf stalks are used in salad. The leaf stalks are also used as vegetable. The leaves also possess diuretic properties. The roots are used as purgative and they possess an aromatic odour and taste.

Dried fruits of fennel have a fragrant odour and a pleasant aromatic taste. They are used for flavouring curries, soups, meat dishes, sauces, bread rolls, pastries and confectionery. They are also used for flavouring liqueurs and in the manufacturing of pickles.

The fruits are aromatic, stimulant and carminative. They are useful in the diseases of chest, spleen and kidney. It is used as one of the condiments in liquorice powder. A hot infusion of the fruits is used to increase lacteal secretion and to stimulate sweating. Fennel fruits from Lucknow are considered to be the best and are priced higher than those from other areas.

Fennel oil. The fruit of fennel also contains a volatile oil. The oil is obtained by steam distillation of crushed fruits. It is a colourless or pale yellow liquid with a characteristic taste and odour. The main constituent of the fennel oil is anethole. Oil of good quality contains 50-60% anethole. Fennel oil is largely used as a flavouring agent in culinary preparations, confectionery, cordials and liqueurs. It is a good aromatic and widely carminative. It is used in colic and flatulence of infants. It makes a good vermicide against hookworm. It is used in the preparation of fennel water. It is used in perfumery and in scenting soaps.

Chemical composition. Moisture 6.3%; protein 9.5%; fat 1.0%; crude fibre 18.5%; carbohydrates 42.3%; mineral matter 13.4%; calcium 1.3%; phosphorus 0.48%; sodium 0.09%; potassium 1.7%; iron 0.01%; vitamin B_1 (thiamine) 0.41 mg/100 g.; vitamin B_2 (riboflavin) 0.36 mg/100 g.; vitamin C (ascorbic acid) 12.0 mg/100 g.; niacin 6.0 mg/100 g.; vitamin A 1040 International Units (I.U.); calorific value 370 calories/100 g.

Allspice

Pimenta dioica (Linn) Merrill syn. *P. officinalis* Lindl.; English—Allspice tree, Jamaica Pepper tree; Family—Myrtaceae.

It is a bushy evergreen tree, 6-9 m. high. It is native of West Indies and tropical America. It is grown in gardens in India. Leaves oblong-lanceolate, coriaceous; flowers white, in terminal and

Fig. 35.22. Spices and condiments *Pimenta dioica* (Linn.) Merrill, syn. *P. officinalis* Lindl.; Eng. All spice tree, Pimento tree, Jamaica pepper tree (Myrtaceae). A flowering twig.

axillary trichotomous paniculate cymes; fruit a globose berry, about the size of a pea seed, black or purple, two seeded; seeds deep brown, reniform.

The unripe berries, when rapidly dried, form the Allspice, Jamaica Pepper or Pimento of commerce. In India, the plant is cultivated in gardens, especially in Bengal, Bihar, Orissa and Mysore. It grows well in Mysore and fruits heavily. The plants are propagated by seeds. Seeds are sown under shade in freshly prepared beds or in pots. The beds should be well watered before sowing, and the seeds should be thinly broadcast and lightly covered with coir waste. Seedlings are potted in large containers at the 2- and 4- leaf stage and are ready for planting in the field when they are 25-35 cm. in height. The tree begins fruiting when about seven years old and continues so upto twenty years. The berries are picked when mature, but still green. The berries are quickly dried in the sun for 4-10 days; They become wrinkled like black pepper and turn reddish brown in colour and the aroma becomes more pronounced. Average yield of a tree is about 35-45 kg. of berries. Dried berries are nearly globular, 4-7 mm. in diameter, reddish brown and with a wrinkled surface. The berries possess an aromatic taste and flavour resembling a mixture of cinnamon, cloves and nutmeg, and hence the name Allspice. Allspice owes its characteristic odour to the presence of an essential oil (3.3-4.5%), found mainly in the pericarp. Allspice is available whole or ground.

Uses. The berries are used as a condiment, as a flavouring agent in sauces, soups, pickles, canned meats, sausages, etc., It is an important ingredient of whole mixed pickling spice, and spice mixtures, *viz.*, curry powders, mincemeat spice, poultry dressing, pastry spice, etc., They are used for flavouring liqueurs. Pimenta berry oil is used for flavouring condiments and food products. The oil is used also as a carminative and stimulant.

Chemical composition of ground berries. Moisture 8.8%; protein 6.0%; fat 6.6%; fibre 21.6%; carbohydrates 52.8%; total ash 4.2%; calcium 0.8%; potassium 1.1%; iron 7.5%; vitamin B_1 (thiamine) 0.1 mg/100 g.; vitamin B_2 (riboflavin) 0.06 mg/100 g.; vitamin C (ascorbic acid) 39.2 mg/100 g.; niacin 2.9 mg/100 g.; vitamin A 1445 International Units (I.U.); calorific value 380 calories/100 g.

Anise

Pimpinella anisum Linn.; English—Aniseed, Hindi—*Saunf, badian*; Bengali—*Muhuri, mitha-jira*; Marathi—*Somp*; Gujarati—*Anisa*; Telugu—*Kuppi*; Tamil—*Shombu*; Kannada—*Shombu*; Oriya—*Sop*; Family—Umbelliferae (Apiaceae).

It is native of the Eastern Mediterranean region. It is widely cultivated in Europe, Russia, North Africa, Mexico and South America. In India, it is grown to a small extent. It is grown in Uttar Pradesh, the Punjab and Orissa. It is stated that a commodity commonly available in Indian market under the name *Lucknow saunf* is called Indian Aniseed.

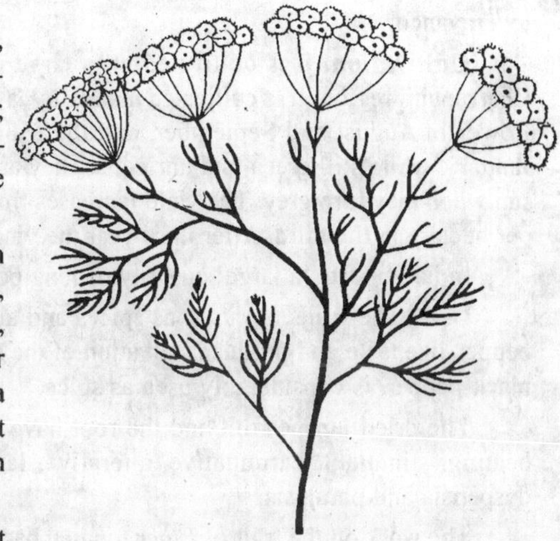

Fig. 35.23. Spices and condiments. *Pimpinella anisum* Linn.; Eng. Anise, Aniseed (Umbelliferae, Apiaceae). A flowering twig.

The plant is an annual about 2 feet in height with simple based leaves and pinnately dissected steam leaves. The small fruits are greyish brown and covered with short hairs.

The plant is well grown in light, fertile or moderately rich, well drained sandy loam. It is propagated by seeds. Seeds are sown broadcast or in drills, 20-40 cm apart. It is commonly sown from the middle of October to the end of November in the plains, and from the beginning of April to the end of May on hills. When the seedlings are 5-8 cm. in height, they are thinned to stand 10-15 cm. apart in a row. The plants require, occasional weeding and watering once a week. The crop is ready to harvest in three and half months after planting when the fruits turn greyish green. The plants are tied in bundles and then stacked with the fruiting heads towards the centre. Fruits ripen in 4-5 days and are then threshed out, cleaned and bagged for the market. A yield of 445-665 kg. of fruit per hectare is expected.

Aniseed on steam distillation yields an essential oil, known as oil of anise, anise oil is a colourless or pale yellow liquid having the characteristic odour and taste of the fruit.

Uses. The fruits are used as condiment. Now, oil of anise replaces the fruits for medicinal and flavouring purposes. Aniseed possesses a sweet aromatic taste and emits when crushed, a characteristic agreeable odour and is used for flavouring food, confectionery, bakery products, beverages and other liqueurs. The fruits are expectorant, stimulating, carminative, diuretic and diaphoretic.

Fresh leaves of the plant are used as a garnish and for flavouring salads.

Chemical composition of fruits. Moisture 9-13%; protein 18%; fatty oil 8-23%; essential oil 2-7%; sugars 3-5%; starch 5%; nitrogen free extract 22-28%; fibre 12-25%; ash 6-10%; choline is also present.

Indian Long Pepper

Piper Longum Linn.; English—India long pepper; Hindi—*Pipal, pipulmul, pipli, gaz pipal*; Bengali—*Pipul, pipli*; Nepali—*Popal pipal*; Punjabi—*Pipal, pipla mul*; Mumbai—*Pipli, pipla mul*; Marathi—*Pimpli*; Gujarati- -*Pipli, piper*; Tamil—*Tippili, pipili, pippallu*; Telugu—*Pipili, pippali katte*; Kannada—*Yippali*; Malayalam—*Lada, mulagu*; Sanskrit—*Pippali, upukulya, videhi, ushuna*; Persian—*Pilpil, filfil-i-daraz*; Family—Piperaceae.

It is a native of India, Sri Lanka and Philippines Islands. It is a slender aromatic climber with perennial woody roots occurring in the hotter parts of India, from central Himalayas to Assam,

Khasi and Mikir hills, lower hills of Bengal and evergreen forests of Western Ghats from Konkan to Travancore.

Cultivation. It is cultivated on a large scale in limestone soil, 450 to 600 m. below the Cherrapunji region. It is cultivated mainly by layering of mature branches or by suckers. The plants flower in August and September, and the fruits mature in January. The spikes are harvested in January, while still green and unripe, as they are most pungent at this stage. They are dried in the sun when they turn grey. The yield increases from 560 kg. per hectare in the first year to 1,680 kg. per hectare in the third. After third year the vines become less productive and should be replaced.

India imports 'a large' quantity of long pepper from Malaysia and Singapore.

Uses. The fruits are used as spices and also in pickles and preserves. They have a pungent pepper-like taste and produce salivation of the mouth. Long pepper, though considered inferior to black pepper, is considerably used as spice.

The dried unripe fruit and the root have long been used in medicine. They are considered heating, stimulant, carminative, alterative, laxative, and useful in cough, hoarseness, asthma, dyspepsia and paralysis.

The work on the fruit of *Piper longum* has shown the presence of the alkaloids—*piperine* and *piplartine*.

Black Pepper

Piper nigrum Linn.; English—Black pepper; Hindi—*Kalimirch, golmirch, choca mirch*; Bengali—*Kalamorich, golmorich*; Marathi—*Kalimirch, mire*; Gujarati—*Kalamari, kalomirich*; Tamil—*Milagu*; Telugu—*Miriyala tige*; Kannada—*Kare menasu*; Malayalam—*Kurumulaku, nallamulaku*; Punjabi—*Golmirich*; Kashmiri—*Martz*; Sanskrit—*Maricha, ushana, hapusha*; Family—Piperaceae.

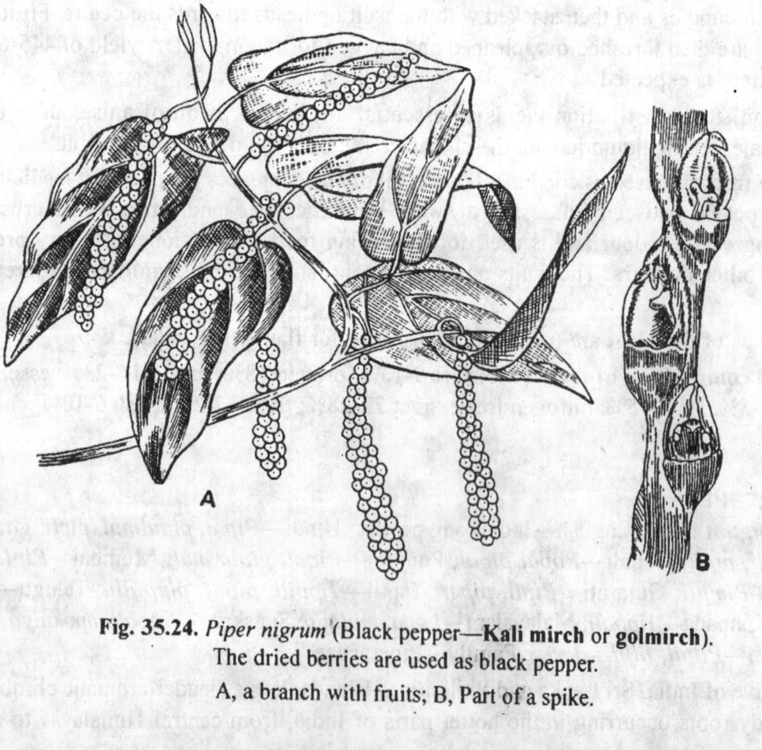

Fig. 35.24. *Piper nigrum* (Black pepper—**Kali mirch** or **golmirch**).
The dried berries are used as black pepper.
A, a branch with fruits; B, Part of a spike.

A branching, climbing perennial shrub, mostly found cultivated in the hot and moist parts of India, Ceylon and other tropical countries. Branches stout, trailing and rooting at the nodes; leaves entire, 12.5-17.5 by 5.0-12.5 cm., very variable in breadth, sometimes glaucous beneath, base acute rounded or cordate, equal or unequal; flowers minute in spikes, usually dioecious; fruiting spikes very variable in length and robustness, rachis glabrous; fruits ovoid or globose, bright red when ripe; seeds usually globose, testa thin, albumin hard.

Pepper is one of the most ancient crops cultivated in India and has probably originated in the hills of south-western India, where it is met with in a wild state in the rain forests from North Kanara to Kanyakumari. The pepper vine in its wild state is mostly dioecious and consequently rarely sets fruit. Under cultivated condition, however, the fruiting is very much better, since most of the cultivated types are bisexual. Almost all the types cultivated at present are selections from wild plants. Some crosses have already been evolved at the Pepper Research Station, Panniyur (Kerala). Of these, the hybrid, *Panniyur I*, a progeny from a cross between *Taliparamba No. 1*, noted for its high yield. *Panniyur I* is a good hardy climber and has long spikes with close set, large fruits.

Cultivation. In India, pepper is cultivated mostly as a mixed crop in homestead gardens. Under this system, the vines are trained on to existing trees like jack, mango, coconut or arecanut. The vines receive intensive care and continue to be productive upto 60 or even 100 years. The vines are also grown as in inter - or subsidiary crop along with other plantation crops like coffee, cardamom, arecanut, coconut and orange. This practice is more common in North Kanara, Coorg and parts of Kerala. As a pure crop, pepper is grown on a plantation scale only in small areas in the sub-montane tracts and lower altitudes in South Kanara, Malabar, Wynad and Travancore. India has been a leading producer and exporter of pepper. India, Indonesia, Ceylon, Cambodia and Sarawak, Brazil and Malagasy are main producers of pepper. In India Kerala on the west coast produces nearly 95% of the total output. In India, pepper is grown mainly in Kerala, Tamil Nadu and Mysore and to a less extent in Assam.

Climate and soil. The pepper vine is found growing upto an altitude of 1,500 m., but thrives best at about 500 m. Pepper requires a warm and humid climate. It thrives in places where the annual rainfall is well over 200 cm. Pepper plants are pollinated by rain-water and consequently satisfactory yields are obtained when frequent showers of rain occur during blossoming period.

Pepper thrives best on virgin soil rich in humus and other plant nutrients. Naturally well drained, red laterite soils or alluvial soils rich in humus seem to be highly suitable for this crop. In Kerala, major part of the pepper cultivation is on laterite or sandy loam along the alluvial banks of the rivers.

Propagation. The pepper vine can be propagated either vegetatively or by seeds. Vegetative propagation is universally adopted. However, it is believed that the plants raised from seeds live longer, and give heavier crops in later years than plants raised vegetatively.

There are two types of vegetative shoots preferred for planting, *viz.*, the runners which are usually confined to the bottom portion of the vines, and the terminal shoots towards the top region. The runners form the most common material for propagation. In some areas, particularly in North Kanara, the terminal shoots of the top fruiting branches are preferred. Plants raised from such cuttings are said to yield even in the second year of planting and produce a satisfactory crop from the fourth year onwards while vines raised from runner shoots give satisfactory yields only from the sixth or seventh year.

Planting. The planting of the pepper vine is done either in July or August. The pits for planting are made preferably on the north and north-eastern sides of the standard so that the severe western sun is avoided.

Manuring. Pepper is an exhausting crop and the soil needs high level of nitrogenous manuring.

Harvesting and yield. An adult vine yields annually 0.5 kg. dried fruits under Indian conditions. The yield goes on increasing as the vines get older upto about the tenth year. Usually there are two crops in a year. One in August-September and the other in March-April. When the fruits are ready for harvest, the whole spikes are removed from the vines with the aid of a ladder. They are dried in the sun for 3-4 days, and the fruits separated from the stalks by beating the dried spikes with a stick or by trampling under foot. When completely dry, the outer skin of the fruits become black and wrinkled. It is estimated that 100 kg. of green pepper roughly yield 33 kg. of dried pepper.

In India, the average yield of commercial black pepper has been found to vary from 110 to 335 kg. per hectare.

Black Pepper. Black pepper consists of the dried, fully developed unripe fruits. It is nearly globular in shape, about 4-5 mm in diameter with the characteristic coat with deep set wrinkles. The freshly harvested spikes are spread on cement floors or mats and dried in the sun for about a week. During drying the green or red fruits gradually change in colour to dark brown or almost black and their skin becomes tough and wrinkled. The fruits are detached from the stalks by beating the heaped up material with sticks or treading upon it barefooted. The outturn of dried black pepper obtained from green fruits varies from 26-29% depending upon the type.

White Pepper. It consists of dried ripe fruits, freed of their pericarp. In preparing white pepper the separation is done through the zone of fibro-vascular bundles, *i.e.*, only a part of the mesocarp is removed. In India, the production is limited to very small quantities, by some households in Kerala, for medicinal and domestic usage. For this purpose, the fully ripe fruits are rubbed with hand to remove the soft rind, and dried. The white fruits obtained are then washed and finally dried.

Uses. Pepper fruits are used as spice or condiment. In Kerala, fresh green pepper is sometimes used for preparing pickles. Black and white pepper make the major condiments employed for seasoning freshly cooked and prepared foods. In U.S.A. and other European countries they are used mainly for preserving meat. The whole fruits are added to pickles, certain types of sausages, etc., but the bulk of the product is generally ground before use. Black pepper is mostly used for its characteristic aroma and pungent taste. White pepper is less pungent. The aromatic odour of pepper is due to a volatile oil, while the pungent taste is caused by an *oleoresin*. An alkaloid is also present. Pepper stimulates the flow of saliva and the gastric juices and has a cooling effect. In modern Indian medicine, it is much employed as an aromatic stimulant in cholera, weakness following fevers, coma, etc., as a stomachic in dyspepsia, as an antiperiodic in malarial fever.

Chemical composition of different type of black pepper (*Piper nigrum* Linn.) varies. Moisture 8.7-14.1%; total nitrogen 1.55-2.60%; nitrogen in non-volatile ether extract 2.70-4.22%; volatile ether extract 0.3-4.2%; non-volatile ether extract 3.9-11.5%; alcohol extract 4.4-12.0%; starch 28.0-49.0%; ash 3.6-5.7%; crude fibre 8.7-18.0%; crude piperine 2.8-9.0%; piperine 1.7-7.4%; Alkaloid piperine makes the biting taste.

Ammi

Trachyspermum ammi (Linn.) Sprague; English—Ammi, Lovage; Hindi—*Ajwain, ajowan*; Bengali—*Jowan, juvani*; Gujarati—*Ajamo*; Marathi—*Owa*; Kashmiri—*Jawind*; Tamil—*Aman, oman*; Telugu—*Omami, omamu*; Kannada—*Omu, oma*; Mumbai—*Ajwan owa*; Sanskrit—*Yamani*; Persian—*Zinian*; Family—Umbelliferae (Apiaceae).

This is an aromatic herb. Cultivated extensively in India for its fruits (seeds); from the Punjab and Bengal to the South Deccan. It is first mentioned in Europe as brought from Egypt about 1549 A.D.

Uses. The fruits are used as spice. They yield an oil of distillation with water, which is used medicinally. The fruits (seeds) are much valued for their antispasmodic, stimulant, tonic and carminative properties. They are considered to combine the stimulant quality of capsicum or mustard with the bitter property of chiretta, and the antispasmodic virtues of asafoetida.

Vanilla

Vanilla planifolia Andr.; Syn. *V. fragrans* (Salibs) Ames; English—Vanilla; Family—Orchidaceae.

It is climbing vine with fleshy adventitious roots, large succulent leaves, and greenish-yellow flowers. The fruits are long, thin, pod like capsules, known as vanilla beans. It is a tropical species and thrives in hot climate with frequent rains. It is propagated by means of cuttings. It is native of tropical America. In India, it is cultivated in the Nilgiris, Wynad, Coorg and Mysore.

The flavour and aroma are not present in the pods until they have been cured. The unripe fruits are subjected to a sweating process. They are exposed to the sun in the morning and are then protected by blankets in the afternoon, while at night they are placed in airtight boxes. During curing process a glucoside is changed by enzyme action into a crystalline substance, vanillin, which possesses the characteristic odour.

Chemical composition. Moisture 25.85-30.93%; protein 2.56-4.87%; fatty oil 1.68-6.74%; volatile oil 0.0-0.64%; nitrogen free extract 30.35-32.90%; fibre 15.27-19.6%; carbohydrates 7.1-9.1%; ash 4.5-4.7%; vanilline 1.48-2.90%; resins 1.5-2.6%; calcium 19.7%; phosphorus 9.5%; sodium 6.7%; potassium 16.2%; iron 0.3%.

Fig. 35.25. Spices and condiments. *Vanilla planifolia* Andr.; Eng. Vanilla (Orchidaceae). A, a flowering twig; B, a seed. The vanilla pods or sticks of commerce are the cured fruits, or beans of *V. planifolia* Andr. (an orchid).

Uses. The pods are used for flavouring confectionery and in perfumery. Vanilla is used in flavouring chocolate, ice creams, candy, beverages, cakes and other food products.

SPICES AND CONDIMENTS OBTAINED FROM SEEDS

Bengal Cardamom

Amomum aromaticum Roxb; English—Bengal cardamom, Nepal cardamom; Hindi—*Bari elaichi*; Marathi—*Veldode*; Family—Zingiberaceae.

It is a perennial herb, grown in North Bengal and Khasia hills. The fruit ripens in September; the capsules are then carefully gathered by the natives and sold to the druggists.

Uses. The fruits and seeds are used as a condiment. It is one of the chief ingredients of 'garam masala'.

Fig. 35.26. *Amomum aromaticum* (**Bari elaichi**). The fruits and the seeds are used as spice.

White Mustard

Brassica hirta Moench; Syn. *B. alba* (Linn.) Boiss.; English—White mustard; Hindi—*Safed rai, safed rayan*; Bengali—*Dhop-rai*; Marathi—*Pandhora-mohare*; Gujarati—*Ujlo-rai*; Tamil—*Vellai-Kadugu*; Telugu—*Tella-avalu*; Malayalam—*Vella-Katuka*; Kannada—*Bili-sasave*; Sanskrit—*Siddhartha*; Persian—*Sipandane-supid*; Family—Cruciferae (Brassicaceae).

This is considered native of Europe and Western Asia. It is a herb, 2-6 feet high, with yellow flowers, hairy lobed leaves and a long-beaked pod with bristles. The small round seeds are yellow on the outside and white within. The seeds contain a glucoside, *sinalbin*. When ground seeds, are treated with water, the glucoside breaks down through enzyme action, and yields a sulphur compound with a characteristic sharp and pungent taste.

Uses. It is used as a condiment in food stuffs and pickles. The powdered seeds made into a paste with cold water act as a stimulant. It is used also in medicine. The seeds yield fatty oil.

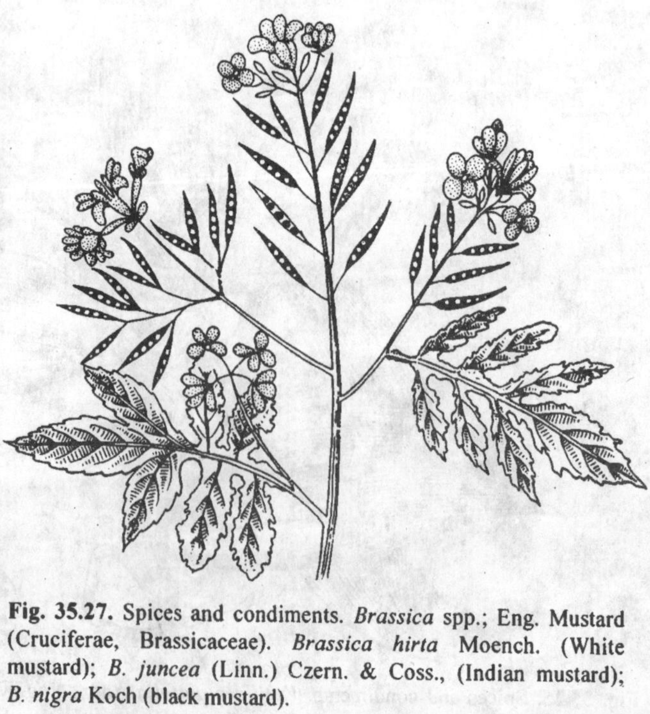

Fig. 35.27. Spices and condiments. *Brassica* spp.; Eng. Mustard (Cruciferae, Brassicaceae). *Brassica hirta* Moench. (White mustard); *B. juncea* (Linn.) Czern. & Coss., (Indian mustard); *B. nigra* Koch (black mustard).

Indian Mustard

Brassica juncea (Linn.) Czern. & Coss; English—Indian Mustard; Hindi—*Rai, sarson, sarson-lahi, gohna-sarson, barirai, barlai, badshahi-rai, shahzada-rai, khas-rai*; Bengali—*Rai sarisha*; Kashmiri—*Asur*; Gujarati—*Rai*; Mumbai—*Rai, sarson, rajika*; Marathi—*Mohari, rayan*; Sanskrit—*Rajika*; Family—Cruciferae (Brassicaceae).

A tall, erect annual herb, 3-5 feet high, with bright green foliage; racemes terminal, with a rough reticulate testa. It is cultivated chiefly in the Punjab, West Bengal and Uttar Pradesh. It is sown in October-November and cut in March-April.

Uses. The seeds are used as a condiment in pickles. The seed oil is used for pickles and cooking purposes.

Black Mustard

Brassica nigra Koch; English—Black mustard; Hindi—*Kali rai, rai, tira, tara mira, lahi, jag rai, makra rai*; Bengali—*Rai sarisha*; Gujarati—*Rai, kalirai*; Mumbai—*Rai, sarson*; Tamil—*Kadagho*; Telugu—*Avalo*; Kannada—*Bile sasive*; Sanskrit—*Rajika*; Persian—*Jarshaf*; Family—Cruciferae (Brassicaceae).

It is a native of Eurasia. In India, it is cultivated mainly in the Punjab, Uttar Pradesh and Tamil Nadu. The plant is smaller than the white mustard. It has smooth pods with dark brown seeds, which are yellow inside. The seeds contain a glucoside, sinigrin. This glucoside yields on decomposition a volatile oil containing sulphur, which is responsible for the aromatic odour and pungency.

Uses. Ground black mustard seeds are used as a condiment in pickles. The seed oil is used for cooking purposes.

Chemical composition of Brassica seeds. Moisture 7.6%; nitrogen substances 29.1%; nitrogen free extract 19.2%; ether extract 28.2%; crude fibre 11%; ash 5%; seed oil 27-33%.

Lesser Cardamom

Elettaria cardamomum Maton; English—Lesser cardamom, cardamom; Hindi—*Chhoti elaichi*; Bengali—*Ilachi*; Gujarati—*elachi*; Punjabi—*Illachi*; Mumbai—*Malabari elachi*; Marathi—*Velloda*; Tamil—*Ellakay, aila-cheddi, elakaya*; Telugu—*Ellakay, elaki chettu, ela-kaya*; Kannada—*Yalakki, yelaki, yerakki*; Sanskrit—*Prith weeka, chundruvala, ela, bahoola*; Family—Zingiberaceae.

This is a tall herbaceous perennial, with branching subterranean rootstock, from which arise a number of upright leafy shoots, 5-18 feet high, bearing alternate, elliptical or lanceolate sheathing leaves, 1-3 feet long. Flowers borne in panicles 2-4 feet long, arising from the base of vegetative shoots; panicles upright throughout their length

Fig. 35.28. Spices and condiments. ***Elettaria cardamomum.*** Maton.; Eng. Lesser cardamom, Cardamom. (Zingiberaceae). A plant with inflorescence and fruits.

or upright at first and ultimately pendent or prostrate; flowers about 1.5 inches long, white or pale green in colour with a central lip streaked with violet, borne in a close series on the rachis; bisexual. Fruits trilocular capsules, fusiform to ovoid, pale green to yellow in colour, containing 15-20 hard, brownish black, angled and rugose seeds, covered by a thin mucilaginous membrane.

It is native of the moist evergreen forests of South India, growing wild in the Western Ghats, between 2,500 and 5,000 feet. It is found wherever the overhead canopy has been thinned. It is also found along stream banks, where the overhead shade is less dense.

There are two varieties: 1. *E. cardamomum* var. *major* Thw. comprising all the wild races and 2. *E. cardamomum* var. *minor* Watt. (syn. *E. cardamomum* var. *minuscula* Burkill) comprising all the cultivated races, particularly those included under the names Malabar and Mysore cardamoms. Variety major is the more primitive variety from which the cultivated variety minor is derived. The minor variety is commonly grown in India.

Malabar cardamom is characterised by a short leafy shoot, rarely exceeding 9 feet in height, leaves 1-1.5 feet long, hairy on the under-surface; panicles 2-3 feet long and prostrate; fruits globose, rounded or ovoid and lightly ribbed. It is chiefly cultivated in Mysore and Coorg, and to some extent in Travancore.

Mysore cardamom is characterised by robust growth, leafy stem, upto 17 feet high, and large leaves with smooth underside; panicles erect; fruit fusiform, three-angled and ribbed. It is cultivated mainly in Travancore, Annamalai and Nelliampathy hills.

Distribution. It is usually cultivated in those regions which form the natural habitat of the species. They are chiefly cultivated in Kerala, Mysore, Maharashtra, Assam, Sikkim and Tamil Nadu.

Cultivation. The mode of cultivation varies considerably in different regions. The Mysore system of cultivation is the most important for commercial production and accounts for about 90% of the total cardamom crop in India. This type consists in clearing selected areas of jungle land of all undergrowth, thinning out the overhead shade, planting cardamom seedlings at regular distances and cultivating according to a regular schedule. In Mysore, cardamom is planted mostly on the margins of ravines.

The cultivation of cardamoms is confined to regions with an annual rainfall of 60-130 in., a temperature range of 50-95°F. and an altitude of 2,000 to 5,000 feet. It grows on a variety of soils. Under ravine cultivation in Mysore, cardamom attains good growth in pockets of soil among boulders, even though the soil is not deep. The soil should be moist and well drained.

It thrives best under moderate natural shade. When inter-planted in coffee and arecanut plantations, shade is indirectly provided by coffee plants and areca palms.

Where cardamom is cultivated on a plantation scale in virgin forest areas, the initial work consists in clearing all undergrowth and thinning out the overhead canopy in order to obtain an even density of shade. Pits are dug in cleared land for planting cardamom seedlings. The usual size of the pit is 2' × 2' × 1-1/2' deep. The spacing between pits varies from 5 feet to 10 feet in different areas. The spacing depends on the type of cardamom grown and also on the natural fertility of the soil. In richer soils, the spacing is about 12 feet each way however, it is much less in poor soil. The spacing for Mysore cardamom ranges from 8 to 10 feet each way, while for Malabar cardamom it is 6 ft. × 6 ft.

Propagation. Cardamom is propagated either vegetatively by division of rhizomes or by seedling transplantation. Rhizomes from large clumps of growing plants are taken out, separated into small clumps, each consisting of atleast one old and one young shoot and planted in prepared pits. The method, however, is unsatisfactory for planting large areas as the number of rhizomes obtainable is limited.

Propagation by seedlings is common adopted in North Kanara, Mysore, Coorg, Tamil Nadu and Travancore-Cochin. Seedlings which come up spontaneously in jungle clearings and those which occur in old cardamom plantings are collected and planted in prepared nursery beds until they are required for planting in permanent positions. The seeds may be sown broadcast in favourable positions on cleared land and transplanted into permanent positions when they are sufficiently developed. The sowing time is usually August-October in Coorg, Mysore and North Kanara, and February-March in Tamil Nadu.

Seeds germinate in 6-7 weeks after sowing. Seed beds are prepared on raised ground and seeds are sown broadcast and covered with soft earth. Nurseries are generally opened near stream with abundant water. The beds are not shaded from the sun until after the seedlings appear. Low pandals are put up, 4-5 feet above the beds to provide shade for seedlings. Seedlings when 3-4 months old are transplanted 6-18 in. apart in nursery beds. Seedlings are usually kept in the nursery for about two years. The time of planting out seedlings is June-July, before the onset of monsoon rains. Generally two seedlings are planted in each pit, one of which is later used for filling up gaps in the plantation. Frequent weedings are necessary in the first two years to prevent young cardamom plants from being choked up.

Harvesting. Cardamom comes into bearing in three years after planting, which may be the fourth or fifth year after sowing. Flowering commences in April-May and continues till July-August; flowers may be seen almost throughout the year. The peak flowering period is May-June and as flowers appear for long, fruits ripen irregularly at intervals necessitating several pickings. Fruits are gathered at intervals of 30-40 days. Only those fruits which are just to ripe are picked. This is necessary to prevent capsules from splitting on the drying floors. If picked in the under-ripe stage, the fruits shrink on drying and have a shrivelled appearance. Individual fruits are picked with the peduncle and each clump has to be periodically visited to gather the fruits. The first crop obtained in the third or fourth year is usually small, higher and sustained yields are obtained in subsequent years upto the tenth or fifteenth year, depending upon the type cultivated, after which the plants become exhausted.

Drying and curing. The fruits are dried after harvesting either in the sun on barbecues of beaten earth or by artificial heat in drying houses. Artificial drying takes about 48 hours and cardamoms so dried retain their green colour, which is much liked in European and American markets. Sun drying, on the other hand, takes 3-5 days, but the mucilaginous coats on the seeds remain intact in sun-dried capsules and the seeds possess a characteristic sweetish aroma. A certain amount of bleaching also takes place during sun-drying and the capsules attain a straw colour. Dried capsules are hand-rubbed and winnowed to remove stalks, calyces and foreign matter, and then bagged.

The average yield of dry capsules from a well maintained cardamom estate is 100-150 lb. per acre.

Uses. Cardamom is used as a spice and masticatory, and in medicine. The seeds possess a pleasant aroma and a characteristic, warm, slightly pungent taste. It is used for flavouring curries, cakes, bread and for other culinary purposes. It is also used for flavouring liqueurs. In the Arab countries, cardamom is used for flavouring coffee and tea. In medicine, it is used as an aromatic, stimulant, carminative and flavouring agent.

The cardamom capsules contain—Moisture 20%; protein 10.2%; ether extract 2.2% mineral matter 5.4% crude fibre 20.1% carbohydrate 42.1% calcium 0.13% phosphorous 0.16% iron 5.0 mg/100 g. The seeds of cardamom contain 2-8% volatile oil. Seeds of green cardamom yield appreciably more oil than those of bleached cardamom.

Chemical composition of seeds. Moisture 8.3%; volatile oil 8.3%; total ash 3.7%; non-volatile ether extract 2.9%; crude fibre 9.2%; crude protein 10.3%; calcium 0.3%; phosphorus

0.21%; sodium 0.01%; potassium 1.2%; iron 0.012%; vitamin B_1 (thiamine) 0.18 mg/100 g.; vitamin B_2 (riboflavin) 0.23 mg/100 g.; vitamin C (ascorbic acid) 12.0 mg/100 g.; niacin 2.3 mg/100 g.; vitamin A 175 International Units (I.U.) per 100 g. of seeds.

Cardamom oil of commerce is obtained by the distillation of the whole fruits of *E. cardamomum*. The cardamom oil is a colourless or pale yellow liquid with a penetrating, camphoraceous odour and a strong pungent taste. The main constituents of the oil are - cineol, terpineol, terpinene, limonene, sabinene and terpineol in the form of formic and acetic esters. Cardamom oil is used in flavouring beverages.

The chief importing countries of Indian cardamom are - Arabia, Sweden, U.K., U.S.A., Germany and Middle East countries.

Nutmeg and Mace

Myristica fragrans Houtt.; English—Nutmeg tree; Hindi—Jaiphal (fruit kernel), Japatri (aril); Bengali—Jaiphal (nut), jotri (aril); Punjabi—Japhal (nut), jauntari (aril); Marathi—Jaiphala (fruit), jayapatri (aril); Gujarati—Jayephal (nut), javantari, japatri (aril); Tamil—Jadikkay (nut), jadi-pattiri (aril); Telugu—Zevangam, jajikaya (nut), japatri (aril); Malayalam—Jatikka (nut), jati-pattiri (aril); Sanskrit—Jajiphalam (nut), jajipatri (aril); Family—Myristicaceae.

It is native of the Moluccas Islands. In India, it is grown in the Nilgiris, Kerala, Mysore, Andhra Pradesh, Assam and West Bengal.

This is a dioecious or rarely monoecious evergreen aromatic tree, usually 30-40 feet high. The bark is greyish black and longitudinally fissured in old trees. The leaves are elliptic or oblong-lanceolate, coriaceous. The flowers are arranged in umbellate cymes. The flowers are creamy-yellow and fragrant. The fruits are yellow, broadly pyriform or globose, 6-9 cm. long, glabrous often drooping. The pericarp is fleshy, 1.25 cm. thick, splitting into two halves at maturity. The seeds are broadly ovoid, arillate, albuminous, with a shell like purplish brown testa. The aril is red and fleshy.

Fig. 35.29. Spices and condiments. *Myristica fragrans* Houtt.; Eng. Nutmeg (kernel) and mace (aril) (Myristicaceae). A flowering twig.

Cultivation and propagation. It requires a hot and moist climate with a rainfall of 150-300 cm. per annum. It grows best at low elevations in alluvium formed of deep friable loam with good drainage, well sheltered from high winds.

The plant is propagated from seeds. Fresh seeds with shells, collected from mature fruits and dried for a day, are sown either directly at the site or in nursery beds, sheltered from wind and strong sun. Seeds are sown 30 cm. apart, 2.5 cm. below the soil in nursery beds and take 2-3 months to germinate. The seedlings are transplanted when 60-90 cm. high to their permanent in the field during wet weather. The spacing between trees varies from 6-7.5 m., depending upon the gradient and fertility of the soil; wider spacing is adopted in rich level lands. Young plants require shade. This is provided by growing bananas in advance of planting. It may also be cultivated as a mixed crop in orchard, and in coffee, coconut, arecanut and rubber plantations.

In plantations raised from seeds there are usually more male than female trees and the sex is not determined until the plants are 6-7 years old and begin to bear flowers. In order to ensure a sufficient number of female trees in the plantation, two seedlings are planted close together and the one which has proved to be female is retained.

Harvesting and yield. Under favourable conditions, the tree starts to bear fruit from the seventh year or earlier and the yield increases upto the fifteenth year or beyond. Trees continue to bear for many years and 70-80 years old trees give good and sustained yields. Fruits are borne more or less throughout the year but the main harvesting season is June-October. The fruits are picked up every morning from the ground or are gathered from the trees by the use of a long stick to which a hook is attached. Seeds that drop out of split fruits are also gathered. The average annual yield at Burliar is 1,250-4,000 fruits per tree.

Preparation of nutmeg and mace. The harvested ripe fruit with the valves split, discloses the seed with a shell-like testa covered by a scarlet fibrous aril. After collection, the pericarp is removed and the seed separated from the aril and dried. Drying is complete when the kernel rattles in the shell. The shells are cracked off with wooden hammers and the kernels removed and sorted. Dried kernels make the nutmeg of commerce.

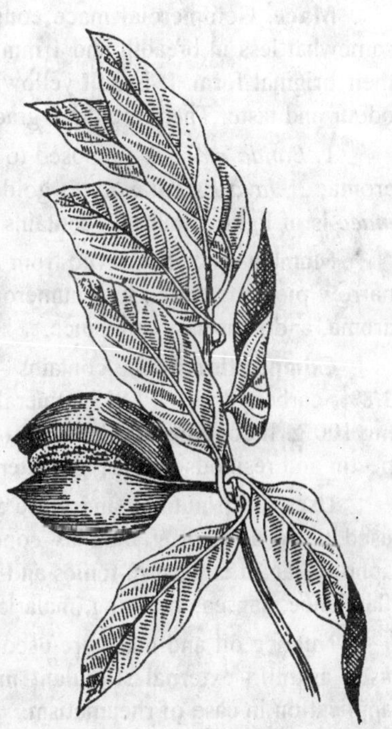

Fig. 35.30. Spices and condiments. *Myristica fragrans* Houtt; Eng. Nutmeg (kernel) and mace (aril) (Myristicaceae). A twig with an opened fruit.

Mace is the dried fibrous aril covering the testa. It is obtained by separating the arils and drying in the sun. Mace of superior quality is produced by drying in specially constructed ovens. During drying the arils at first become dark red and brittle, and in about six weeks they become bright amber coloured.

Nutmeg. The commercial nutmeg is ovoid, 2.0-3.5 cm. long × 1.5-2.8 cm. diameter, greyish brown in colour with minute reddish brown spots and lines and reticulately furrowed. East Indian nutmeg is of three grades - 1. Banda nutmeg is supposed to be the best which contains upto 8% essential oil; 2. Siauw nutmeg is of second grade containing 6.5% essential oil and 3. Penag nutmeg, which is suitable only for distillation purposes.

Composition. The nutmeg contains - Moisture 14.3%; protein 7.5%; ether extract 36.4%; fibre 11.6%; carbohydrates 28.5%; mineral matter 1.7%; calcium 0.12%; phosphorus 0.24%; iron 4.6 mg/100 g.; Nutmeg contains a volatile oil (6-16%), starch (14.6-24.2%); pentosans (2.25%); furfural (1.5%), and pectin (0.5-0.6%). The flavour and therapeutic action are due to the volatile oil.

Nutmeg oil. The percentage of volatile oil varies from 6-16% according to the origin and quality of the spice. Commercial oil is derived from broken and wormy nutmegs. The material is comminuted, pressed to remove fixed oil, and immediately subjected to steam distillation.

The nutmeg oil is a mobile, colourless or pale yellow liquid with a characteristic odour. The major constituents of the oil are *d*-pinene and *d*-camphene.

Nutmeg butter. Commercial nutmeg butter, a highly aromatic fat, is obtained from undersized, damaged or worm-eaten kernels which are unfit for sale as spice. The material is ground and cooked or steamed before pressing.

The nutmeg butter is a soft solid, yellow or yellowish red in colour, with the odour and taste of nutmeg.

Mace. Commercial mace consists of flattened lobed pieces, 2.5 cm. or more in length, somewhat less in breadth and 1 mm. thick. When soaked in water the lobes swell up and regain their original form. It is dull yellowish red in colour, translucent and brittle. It is nutmeg-like in odour and taste. There are three grades of mace.

1. *Banda mace* is supposed to be finest — it is bright orange in colour and possesses fine aroma; 2. *Java Estate mace* is golden yellow in colour with brilliant crimson streaks; 3. *Siauw mace* is of light colour and contains less volatile oil.

Mumbai mace is derived from *Myristica malabarica*, it is dark red in colour and consists of narrow pieces, divided into numerous lobes twisted together at the apex. It is almost devoid of aroma, and is useless as a spice.

Composition. Mace contains — Moisture 15.9%; protein 6.5%; ether extract 24.4%; fibre 3.8%; carbohydrates 47.8%; mineral matter 1.6%; calcium 0.18%; phosphorus 0.10%; iron 12.6 mg/100 g. It contains a volatile oil (4-15%; average 10%), amylodextrin (25%), reducing sugars, pectin and resinous colouring matter. The chief constituents are volatile oils and amylodextrin.

Uses. Both nutmeg and mace are used as condiment and in medicine. They are commonly used more as a drug than as condiment. Nutmeg is stimulant, carminative, astringent and aphrodisiac. It is used in tonics and forms a constituent of preparations prescribed for dysentery, flatulence, nausea, vomiting, malaria, rheumatism, sciatica and leprosy.

Nutmeg oil and mace are used for flavouring food products and liqueurs. Nutmeg butter is used as mild external stimulant in ointments, hair lotions and plasters, and forms a useful application in case of rheumatism.

Black Cumin

Nigella sativa Linn; English—Black cumin, small fennel; Hindi—*Kalonji, kalajira*; Bengali—*Mugrela, kala-jira*; Kashmiri—*Tukm-i-gandna*; Mumbai—*Kalonji, kalenjire*; Tamil—*Karunshirogam*; Telugu—*Nalla-jilakra*; Kannada—*Karijirigi, kare-jirage*; Malayalam—*Karun-chirakam*; Sanskrit—*Krishna-jirata*; Persian—*Siyah-danah*; Myanmar—*Samon-ne*; Family—Ranunculaceae.

A herb. It is a native of Southern Europe. In India, it is cultivated in the Punjab, Bengal, Assam and Bihar for its seeds. Its Sanskrit names indicate, its introduction at a very early period.

Uses. The seeds, possess a strong, pungent, aromatic taste, and therefore, are much used in curries, pickles and other dishes. They are also frequently sprinkled over the surface of bread along with sesamum seed. French cooks employ the seeds of this plant under the name of *Quatre epices* or *toute epices*, and they were formerly used as a substitute for pepper.

Poppy Seeds

Papaver somniferum Linn. var. album; English—Poppy seeds; Hindi—*Post*; Bengali—*Pasto*; Marathi—*Posta*; Gujarati—*Posta*; Family—Papaveraceae.

It is native of West Asia. In India, it is cultivated in the East Punjab, Uttar Pradesh, Rajasthan and Madhya Pradesh. The plant is an erect, rarely branched, usually glaucous annual herb, 60-120 cm. in height. Leaves ovate-oblong or linear-oblong, amplexicaul, lobed, dentate or serrate; flowers large, usually bluish white with a purplish base or white, purple or variegated; capsules large, 2.5 cm. diameter, globose, stalked; seeds white or black, very minute, reniform.

As we know poppy is cultivated also for its seeds. In India, var. *album*, with white seeds has been cultivated for many years for the production of seeds (*post*) under licence in Dehradun and Tehri Garhwal districts of Uttar Pradesh, and in Jalandhar, Kapurthala, Hoshiarpur and Patiala districts of the Punjab. In India, best seeds are obtained when the capsules have not been incised for extraction of opium. The crop yields 220-275 kg. of seeds per hectare.

Uses. Poppy seeds are considered nutritive and are used in breads, curries, sweets and confectionery. Poppy seeds contain upto 50% of an edible oil. The oil is odourless and possesses a pleasant almond - like taste. In India the oil is extracted by cold-pressing the seed in small presses. The oil is widely used for culinary purposes. It is free from narcotic properties and used as a salad oil. The cake or the meal left after extraction of the oil from the seeds is sweet and nutritious and is eaten by poor people.

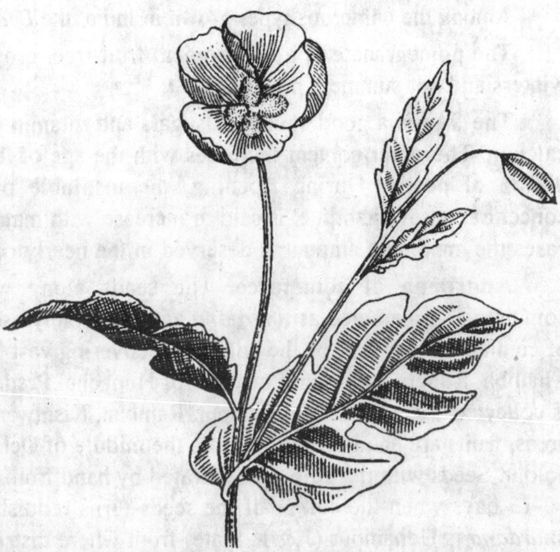

Fig. 35.31. Spices and condiments. *Papaver somniferum* Linn. var. *album*; Eng. Poppy seeds (Papaveraceae). A flowering twig. The poppy seeds are white and very small.

Chemical composition of seeds. Moisture 4.3-5.2%; protein 22.3-24.4%; ether extract 46.5-49.1%; nitrogen free extract 11.7-14.3%; crude fibre 4.8-5.8%; ash 5.6-6.0%; calcium 1.03-1.45%; phosphorus 0.79-0.89%; iron 8.5-11.1 mg/100 g.; thiamine 740-1181 ug/100 g.; riboflavin 756-1203 ug/100 g.; nicotinic acid 800-1280 ug/100 g; iodine 6 ug/kg.; manganese 29 mg/kg.; copper 22.9 mg/kg.; magnesium 15.6 g/kg.; zinc 130 mg/kg.; lecithin 2.80%; Oxalic acid 1.62%; pentosans 3.0-3.6%; traces of narcotin, an amorphous alkaloid and enzymes—diastase, emulsin.

Pomegranate

Punica granatum Linn.; English—Pomegranate; Hindi—*Anardana*; Assamese—*Dalim*; Bengali—*Dalimb*; Gujarati—*Dalamb*; Kannada—*Dalimbari*; Kashmiri—*Daan*; Malayalam—*Mathalam pazham*; Marathi—*Dalimb*; Tamil—*Mathalam pazham*; Telugu—*Dannima pandu*; Punjabi—*Anardana*; Sanskrit—*Dadima*; Family—Punicaceae.

A shrub or small tree, 5-10 m. high, native of Iran, Afghanistan and Baluchistan, found growing wild in the warm valleys and outer hills of the Himalayas between 900 and 1,800 m. and cultivated throughout India. Leaves 2.0-8.0 cm. long, oblong or obvate, shining above; flowers usually scarlet red; fruits globose, crowned by persistent calyx, with a coriaceous woody rind and an interior septate with membranous walls, containing numerous seeds; seeds angular with a fleshy testa which is red, pink or whitish.

Though mostly found cultivated in many parts of India, the tree is also very common and gregarious in the gravel and boulder deposits of dry ravines in the outer Himalayas, upto about 1,800 m. In Jammu, it is found gregariously on dry limestone soils in the upper extremities of sub-tropical forests; it is also found in Chamba, Kangra and Mandi districts of Himachal Pradesh and valleys below 1,800 m. in Jaunsar and Tehri - Garhwal districts of Uttar Pradesh. As a cultivated crop, maximum area is said to be devoted to it in Maharashtra, particularly in Pune, Sholapur and Satara districts. In Gujarat, its cultivation is concentrated in Dholka taluka. It is cultivated in the districts of Almora, Aligarh, Tehri - Garhwal, Meerut and Farrukhabad in Uttar Pradesh; Uthukuli, Michaelpatti, Vellodu and Dindigul in Tamil Nadu state; Penukonda and Madakasira in Andhra Pradesh; Tumkur, Kolar, Bangalore and Mysore districts in Karnataka state.

Among the numerous types grown in India, the *Bedana* and *Kandhari* are considered the best.

The pomegranate is a sub-tropical fruit tree, growing best in semiarid climate where cool winters and hot summers prevail.

The fruit is a good source of sugars and vitamin C, and a fair source of iron but is poor in calcium. The sugar content increases with the age of the fruit and of the tree. The fruit contains 0.27% of pectin. During ripening, the insoluble pectin changes into soluble pectin. The concentration of vitamin C is said to increase with maturity and ripening of the fruit, and in most cases the maximum amount is deserved in the nearly ripe fruit.

Anardana of commerce. The seeds along with the fleshy portions are dried and commercially marketed as *anardana* and are widely used as condiment. The source of *anardana* of commerce is said to be the wild trees, covering vast tracts of hill slopes in Jammu, and parts of Chamba, Kangra and Mandi districts of Himachal Pradesh. The main areas from where *anardana* is collected are the Riasu, Udhampur, Ramban, Kishtwar and Bhadarwah Forest Divisions. In these areas, fruits are hand-picked towards the middle of October, when they are ripe and brown red in colour. Seeds with the pulp are separated by hand from the rind and are dried in the sun for about 10-15 days when the colour of the seeds turns reddish brown. The main assembling centre for *anardana* is Udhampur (J & K State) from where distribution is done all over the country.

Fenugreek

Trigonella foenum-graecum Linn.; English—Fenugreek; Hindi—*Methi*, *muthi*; Bengali—*Methi*, *methika*; Punjabi—*Methi*, *methri*; Gujarati—*Methi*, *methini*; Tamil—*Vendayam*; Telugu—*Menti kura*; Kannada—*Menthya*; Malayalam—*Ventayam*; Sanskrit—*Methi*, *methika*; Persian—*Shanbalid*; Family—Papilionaceae.

It is a native of Southern Europe and Asia. It is grown mainly in Northern India. It is an annual legume with white flowers and long slender pods with a pronounced beak. The crop is sown in October-November. It is ready to harvest in April.

Uses. The seeds are chiefly used as a condiment to flavour curries made of rice, pulse, flour and meat, or as a relish with unleavened bread. The aromatic leaves are used as vegetable. The seeds are carminative, tonic and aphrodisiac.

SPICES AND CONDIMENTS OBTAINED FROM LICHENS

Parmelia

Parmelia abessinica Kremp.; Telugu—*Rathipoovvu*; Family—Parmeliaceae.

This is a crustaceous lichen found in rocky areas of Bellary, Anantpur and Guddapah districts of Andhra Pradesh. The lichen is available in large quantities in the market and used as food material and condiment. It contains atranorin (1.1%), lecanoric acid (3.3%), salazinic acid (0.1-0.5%) and isolichenin (3.4%).

Parmelia tinctorum Despr. is a foliose lichen commonly found in the plains of India and in the Himalayas on tree bark and rocks. It is commonly used in certain parts of South India as a component of various food preparations. It contains—crude protein, 13.8; ether extract, 6.0; isolichenin, 25.0; crude fibre, 13.4; and ash, 12.6%; calcium 1,728 mg.; ascorbic acid, 5.0 mg.; and riboflavin 100 mg./100 g.

Uses. The above mentioned lichens are used as spice and condiment.

36

CHAPTER

The Medicinal Plants–Pharmacognosy

The branch of medical science which deals with the drug plants is known as *pharmacognosy*. This science is concerned with the history, commerce, collection, selection, identification and preservation of crude drugs and raw materials. The study of the action of the drugs is known as *pharmacology*. There are several thousand drug yielding plants all over the world. Most of the plants are known and utilized by herb doctors and *ayurevdic vaids*. Only a few drug plants are cultivated. Most of the supply of drugs is obtained from wild plants growing in all parts of the world and especially in tropical regions These drug-yielding wild plants are popularly known as *jari-butis* in India. The drug plants are collected and prepared in crude indigenous way. The medicinal value of drug plants is due to the presence of some chemical substances in the plant tissues which produce a definite physiological action on the human body. The most important chemical substances are alkaloids, carbon compounds, hydrogen, oxygen, nitrogen, glucosides, essential oils, fatty oils, resins, mucilages, tannins, gum, etc. Some of these substances are powerful poisons, and, therefore, the preparation and administering of drugs should be done by competent physicians.

CLASSIFICATION OF DRUGS

The classification of drugs in the present text is based on the morphology of the plant organ from which the drug is obtained. Here the drug plants have been considered and arranged on a morphological basis. The general categories of the drug plants are as follows:

1. **Drugs obtained from roots.**
2. **Drugs obtained from underground stems.**
3. **Drugs obtained from bark.**
4. **Drugs obtained from stem and wood.**
5. **Drugs obtained from leaves.**
6. **Drugs obtained from flowers.**
7. **Drugs obtained from fruits.**
8. **Drugs obtained from seeds.**
9. **Drugs obtained from all parts of plant.**

DRUGS OBTAINED FROM ROOTS

Aconite

Aconitum heterophyllum Wall., of family Ranuncualceae; Eng. Aconite; Hindi—*Atis*; Sanskrit—*Ativisha*.

This herb is commonly found in the subalpine and alpine zones of the Himalayas from the Indus to Kumaon, from 6,000 to 15,000 feet.

Uses. The drug commonly known as aconite is obtained from the roots. The roots are used as astringent, tonic, antiperiodic in diarrhoea, dyspepsia and cough. It contains the alkaloids, atisine, dihydroatisine, heteratisine and hetisine. It is used externally for rheumatism and internally to relieve pain and fever.

Total alkaloidal content is 0.79 per cent. Plant is considered a valuable febrifuge and bitter tonic. Roots are used for hysteria, throat infections, dyspepsia and vomiting, abdominal pain and diabetes.

Indian Belladona

Atropa acuminata Royle ex Lindley, of family Solanaceae; Eng. Indian belladonna; Hindi—*Sag-angur*.

This is tall erect herb, 3-5 feet high. It is found in Kashmir and Himachal Pradesh.

Uses. The roots are used in the manufacture of tinctures and plasters. It is used as an anodyne of rheumatism, neuralgia and local inflammations.

Belladona

Atropa belladonna Linn., of family Solanaceae; Eng. Belladona; Hindi—*Sag angur*.

This is also a tall erect herb. It is native of Europe, now cultivated in Kashmir.

Uses. The roots are used as sedative, stimulant and antispasmodic. It is used externally to relieve pain and internally to check excessive sweat, cough, etc.

Dried roots and leaves are used as sedative, antispasmodic, and anodyne; also used in ophthalmology to dilate pupils. Leaves are stimulant and narcotic, contains atropine and hyoscyamine, extremely toxic alkaloids.

Liquorice

Glycyrrhiza glabra Linn., of family Papilionaceae, Eng. Liquorice, sweetwood; Hindi—*Mulhatti*; Sanskrjt—*Madhuka*; Bengali—*Jashtimadhu*; Marathi—*Jestha madha*; Gujarati—*Jethi madha*; Telugu—*Atimadhuramu*; Tamil—*Atimadhuram*; Kannda—*Atimadhura*; Malayalam—*Iratimadhuram*.

This is a perennial herb; native of the Mediterranean region but grown in Himachal Pradesh, Jammu and Kashmir.

Uses. The root contains glycyrrhizic acid. It is sweet demulcent, emollient, pectoral, alterative; laxative and expectorant; it is given in cough, bronchitis and other chest complaints, catarrhal condition of bowels, urinary passages, asthma, hoarseness of voice, etc. Its infusion is given in sore throat. It is also used in preparation of nauseous drugs.

Liquorice is also chewed with betel leaves. Principal constituents of liquorice to which it owes its characteristic sweet taste is *glycyrrhizin*, 2 to 14 per cent.

Chitraka

Plumbago zeylanica; Hindi—*Chitraka*; Family Plumbaginaceae. The plants grow as perennial herbs in the plains of West Bengal and South India. The root has been reported to be a powerful poison. It yields *plumbagin* (chitraka) a crystalline substance. It is when given internally or applied to the *osuteri* causes abortion. Plumbagin has been reported to be a powerful irritant to the smooth muscles and uterus.

Serpentine

Rauvolfia serpentina Benth., of family Apocynaceae; Eng. Serpentine; Hindi—*Sarpagandha*; Sanskrit—*Sarpagandha*; Bengali—*Chandra*; Marathi—*Harkaya*; Telugu—*Paataalagani*; Tamil—

Chivan amelpodi; Kannda—*Sarpagandhi*; Malayalam—*Chuvannavilpori*; Oriya—*Patalgarur*; Mundari—*Simjenga*; Assam—*Arachontita*; Khasi Hills—*Todong-pait-parao*; Trade—*Rauvolfia.*

Habitat. A large climbing or twining shrub, found in the tropical Himalayas and plains near the foot of the hills from Sirhind and Moradabad to Sikkim. It occurs also in Assam (up to 4000') and in South India Peninsula along the Ghats to Travancore and Kerala. The genus is distributed in the tropics, *i.e.*, Central and South America, Africa, India, Sri Lanka, Burma, China and Japan. The largest number of species are found in Africa and South America. It is also distributed to Malaysia and Java.

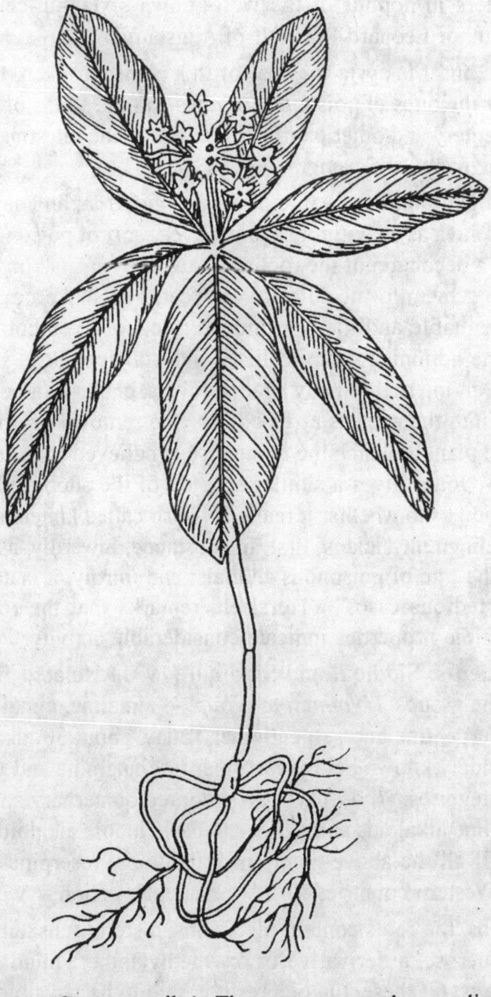

Fig. 36.1. *Rauvolfia serpentina* (*Sarpa-gandha*). The roots are used as medicine. It has been used in indigenous medicine for hundreds of years, has acquired great importance in modern therapeutics following recent scientific research. It is being extensively used in reducing blood pressure in hyperplesis and as a sedative in the treatment of insomnia, hypochondria, mental disorders and certain forms of insanity. It has been recently used to advantage in numerous other diseases like intractable skin disorders such as psoriasis, excessive sweating and itching, gynaecological ailments such as menopausal syndrome; in old-age afflictions such as toxic goitre; and in conditions such as angina pectoris and rapid or irregular heart action. As high blood pressure now is one of the commonest constitutional diseases, the drug is considered a great boon and is assured of an ever increasing demand.

History. The story of *Rauvolfia serpentina* is a most fascinating one. The plant is mentioned in ancient literature including the works of Charaka (1000-800 B.C.) where it is described under its Sanskrit name of Sarpagandha as a useful antidote against snake-bite and insect stings. There are many folk-lores about rauvolfia. One such is that a mongoose would first chew upon its leaves to gain strength before engaging a cobra in combat. According to another, its leaves when freshly ground and applied to the toes, could serve as an antidote for snake poison. A third one has it that the mentally deranged person is relieved of his madness if he eats the pieces of the root. Because of this supposed curative effect in case of insanity the plant has also been known in India as '*Pagal-ki-dava*'. Its generic name was coined towards the end of the seventeenth century by the French Botanist, Plumiers in honour of the well-known sixteenth-century German physician, botanist, traveller and author Leonard Rauwolf of Augsburg.

Medicine. In India and Malaysia the root of this plant has been, from ancient times, much valued as an antidote for the bites of poisonous reptiles and the stings of insects, also as febrifuge, and as a remedy for dysentery and other painful affections of the intestinal canal. In Sanskrit works it is mentioned under the name of *Sarpagandha.*

Rumphius speaks of it under the name of *Radix musteloe*, and says that in his time it was widely used in India and Java as an antidote against every sort of poison. It was administered both internally in the form of a decoction of the root and externally by making a plaster of the roots and fresh leaves and applying them to the soles of the feet. For snake poison, he continues, it was esteemed as specially valuable and the poisonous effects of even cobra's bite were viewed as rendered harmless by the administration of this wonderful root. It is said by him to have been universally employed as an internal remedy against fevers, cholera and dysentery, and the juice of the leaves was instilled into the eyes as a remedy for the removal of opacities of the cornea. He states also that this is the plant to which the mongoose is believed to have recourse when bitten by poisonous snakes. Sir W. Jones gives a similar account of the supposed medicinal virtues of the plant, but expresses a doubt as to whether it really is the so called khneumon plant. Roxburgh states that it is used by the "Telinga physicians, first, in substance, inwardly, as a febrifuge; secondly, in the same manner, after the bite of poisonous animals; and thirdly, it is administered, in substance to promote delivery in tedious cases". Horsfield remarks that the root yields a strong bitter infusion and that its sensible properties indicate considerable activity.

Chemical constituents. Siddiqui and Siddiqui (1931) isolated five crystalline alkaloids. These are divided into the groups: (*i*) *ajmaline group*; —ajmaline, ajmalinine and ajmalicine; and (*ii*) *serpentine group*—serpentine and serpentinine. Today, about 30 alkaloids are known to exist in this plant, the more widely known being reserpine, rescinnamine and yohimbine. Now they can be grouped into three categories: (*i*) deep-yellow coloured quaternary anhydronium bases, (*ii*) the intermediate strong indoline alkaloids and (*iii*) weak basic indole alkaloids; the last mentioned two groups are colourless. Of all the above-mentioned alkaloids, reserpine (serpasil) has gained the greatest prominence in Western countries for its therapeutic action.

Besides the alkaloids, the roots contain oleoresins, a sterol, unsaturated alcohols, oleic acid, fumaric acid, glucose, sucrose, a derivative or oxymethylantheraquinone, a strongly fluorescent substance and mineral salts. Of these, the oleoresin is said to be physiologically active and shows typical hypnotic and sedative action of the drug.

Uses as a drug. Vast developments have been made in the chemistry of its different alkaloids and their role in hypertension, neuropsychiatric and other pharmacodynamics. The two main pharmacological actions of reserpine, *viz.*, lowering the blood pressure and sedative influence, have led to successful trials of the drug in hypertension, neuropsychiatric, gynaecological and geriatrics. With a moderate hypotensive action it controls mainly subjective symptom of high blood pressure when given alone. The drug is also reported to be useful in certain gynaecological conditions, such as menstrual, moliminia, frigidity and women complaining of menopausal syndrome. In the clinical use of reserpine in geriatrics it is reported to be of value in hypertension, nervousness, insomnia, etc.

Some important preparations are as follows:

Rauvolfia serpentina (tablets)—Gluconate Limited Calcutta.

Ralfen (alcoholic preparation) (tablets)—Bengal Chemical and Pharmaceutical Works, Calcutta.

Serpina or S 117—Himalaya Drug Company, Dehradun.

Raudixin (tablets)—Sarabhai Chemicals, Ahmedabad.

Adelphene-CIBA India Limited, Mumbai.

Serpasil—CIBA Pharma Limited, Basle, Switzerland.

Ashwagandha

Withania somnifera Dunal.; Hindi—*Ashwagandha* of family Solanaceae; Sanskrit—*Ashwagandha*; Bengali—*Ashvagandha*; Marathi—*Askandha*; Gujarati—*Ghodakun*; Telugu—*Pulivendram*, *panneru*; Tamil—*Amukkura*; *aswagandhi*; Kannada—*Panneru*, *aswagandhi*; Punjab—*Asgand*; Rajasthan—*Chirpotan*; Trade—Aswagandha.

The wild plants are generally erect branching shrubs up to one metre in height. The cultivated plants are morphologically distinct from wild plants. The cultivated plants are "different from the wild ones not only in their therapeutic properties but in all morphological characters like roots, stems, leaves, flowers, pollen grains, mature seeds and the enlarged calyx." (Kaul, K.N., 1957).

Except for a limited collection of roots from *W. somnifera* plants growing wild, the supplies of Ashwagandha roots are obtained exclusively from cultivated sources.

The entire plants are uprooted for the collection of roots. The roots are separated from the overground parts as soon as possible after collection by cutting the stems 1-2 cm. above the crown. The entire root system along with the remains of aerial stems is either cut transversely into smaller pieces or dried in the whole in the sun. The roots undergo further cleaning, trimming and grading before they are despatched to the various drug markets of India.

Uses. This is used as a tonic in geriatrics, being efficacious in relieving hand and limb tremors of elderly people. It is prescribed for all kinds of weaknesses and is supposed to promote strength and vigour, being regarded as an aphrodisiac and rejuvenator. It is used for the treatment of rheumatic pain, inflammation of joints and certain paralytic conditions. Several preparations of this drug are used for all types of nervous disorders and as sedatives in the treatment of insanity and in hypertension. The leaves of the plant are used as a local application for all types of skin lesions, ulcers, boils, and swelling to reduce pus formation, inflammation to promote healing processes.

Roots have long been in use for hiccup, cough, dropsy, rheumatism, and female disorders. The pharmacological activity is ascribed to the presence of several alkaloids. The leaves are used as a febrifuge and applied to lesions, painful swellings and sore eyes. Withaferin A is the most important withanolide to which the curative properties of leaves are attributed.

Asafetida

Ferula asafoetida Linn., of family Umbelliferae (Apiaceae); Eng. Asafetida; Hindi—*Hing*; Sanskrit—*Balhika*, *hingu*; Hindi, Bengali, Marathi, Gujarati and Kannada—*Hing*; Telugu—*Inguva*; Tamil and Malayalam—*Perungayam*; Oriya—*Hengu*; Kashmir—*Yang*; Mumbai—*Hing*.

This is an unpleasant smelling perennial herb, commonly grown in the Punjab and Kashmir.

Uses. The oleo-resin gum that exudes from the root-stock is carminative, antispasmodic, nervine, stimulant, digestive, sedative, expectorant, diuretic, anthelmintic and emmenagogue. It is prescribed in flatulent colic, dyspepsia, asthma, hysteria, convulsions, cholera, chronic constipation, chronic bronchitis, whooping cough, cough, spasmodic disorders of the bowels and angina pectoris. The fried gum is given either as a solution or emulsion or pills, preferably as pills.

DRUGS OBTAINED FROM UNDERGROUND STEM

Turmeric

Curcuma longa Linn., of family Zingiberaceae; Eng. Turmeric; Hindi—*Haldi*; Sanskrit—*Haridra*; Hindi, Bengali, Marathi and Gujarati—*Haldi*, *Halada*; Tamil—*Manjal*; Telugu—*Pasupa*; Kannada—*Arishina*.

A herb, cultivated commonly in Maharashtra, Bengal, Tamil Nadu, Andhra Pradesh and Orissa for its rhizomes.

Uses. The rhizome is aromatic, stimulant, antiperiodic, tonic, alterative and carminative. It is given in diarrhoea, intermittent fevers, dropsy, jaundice, liver disorders and urinary troubles. The fresh juice of rhizome is used as an anthelmintic. It is commonly used for cleaning foul ulcers. Along with lime or alum it makes a good dressing for sprains, bruises, wounds, etc. Its decotion is an effective eye wash in ophthalmia. The fresh juice is also used as antiparasitic for many skin affections.

Fig. 36.2. The rhizomes/corms of turmeric – a medicinal plant.

Curcuma paper is used as an indicator of chemicals. Rhizomes yield an oil used as a carminative, stomachic and tonic.

Mango Ginger

Curcuma amada Roxb., of family Zingiberaceae; Eng. Mango ginger; Hindi—*Amahaldi*; Sanskrit—*Karpura-haridra*; Bengali—*Amada*; Marathi—*Amba haladi*, Telugu—*Mamidiallam*; Tamil—*Mangai inji*.

This herb is grown in Bengal, Andhra Pradesh and Tamil Nadu. Also found wild in parts of Bengal, Konkan and Tamil Nadu.

Uses. The rhizome is carminative, stomachic and cooling. It is applied over contusions and sprains.

Garlic

Allium sativum Linn., of family Liliaceae; Eng. Garlic; Verna. *Lahsuna*; Sanskrit—*Arishta*, *lashuna*; Hindi, Gujarati, Bengali and Marathi—*Lasun*, *lasan*; Telugu and Malayalam—*Velluli*, *tellagadda*; Tamil—*Vellaipundu*; Kannada—*Bellulli*; Punjab—*Thom*.

This is a strong smelling, glabrous, bulbous-rooted, perennial about a foot in height. The bulbs are short, compressed, breaking up into 10-12 bulbils or cloves, surrounded by a few, dry membranous scales. It is cultivated throughout the country.

Uses. Garlic is of great medicinal value. It is given in fevers, coughs, flatulence, disorders of the nervous system, pulmonary phthisis, whooping cough and dilated bronchitis. It has diuretic properties. A decoction of garlic made with milk and water is given in small doses in hysteria, flatulence, sciatica, etc. In the form of syrup, it is a valuable remedy for asthma, and disorders of the chest and lungs. It is used as an anthelmintic. Externally it is used as rubefacient, vesicant and disinfectant. Its juice is introduced in the ear for relief of earache. The oil in which garlic has been fried is a useful liniment for rheumatic pains, nervous diseases like scabies and maggot infested wounds.

Fig. 36.3. Garlic bulbs.

Ginger

Zingiber officinale Rosc., of family Zingiberaceae; Eng. Ginger; Hindi—*Adrak*; Sanskrit—*Ardraka*; Bengali—*Ada*; Marathi—*Ale*; Telugu—*Allamu*, *sonthi* (dry); Tamil—*Allam*; Kannada—*Hasisunti*; Malayalam—*Andrakam*, *inchi*.

This is a perennial herb; the root stock is horizontal, tuberous and aromatic; native of South-East Asia but now cultivated mainly in Kerala, Uttar Pradesh, West Bengal, Maharashtra, Himachal Pradesh and Andhra Pradesh for the rhizomes.

Uses. The rhizome is used as a stimulant, carminative and flavouring agent. It is given in dyspepsia and flatulent colic. It is administered as an adjunct to many tonic and stimulating remedies. It makes a valuable drug for disorders of the digestive system, rheumatism, piles, pulmonary and catarrhal diseases, dropsy, febrile diseases, neuralgia, etc. The juice of fresh rhizome, with honey is a remedy for coughs and asthma. A paste of ginger is a local stimulant and rubefacient in headache and toothache.

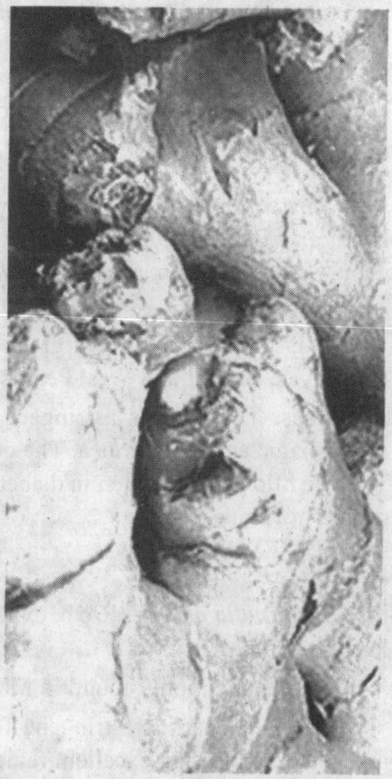

Fig. 36.4. Ginger rhizomes

DRUGS OBTAINED FROM BARKS

Cinnamon

Cinnamomum zeylanicum Bl., of family Lauraceae; Eng. Cinnamon; Hindi—*Dalchini*.

This is native of Sri Lanka but grown in the Nilgiris, South Kanara, Malabar, Assam and Kumaon.

Uses. The bark is aromatic, cordial, astringent, carminative and stimulant; it is given in diarrhoea, nausea, gastric irritation, flatulence, vomiting, spasmodic affections of the bowels, toothache, paralysis of the tongue and labour caused by defective uterine contractions. It is administered in the form of a powder, infusion or decoction. A paste made of the bark is applied to the temples to get relief from neuralgic pains and severe headaches. The oil obtained from the stem bark is used as a carminative, antiseptic and astringent.

Fig. 36.5. Cinnamon. The bark quills.

Quinine

Cinchona calisaya Wedd., *C. ledgerina* Moens. ex Trimen; *C. officinalis* Linn; *C. robusta* How., *C. succirubra* Pavon ex Klotzsch. of family Rubiaceae; Eng. Quinine; Hindi—*Kunain.*

The quinine tree is native to the Andes of South America. In India it is found in West Bengal, the Khasia hills, Nilgiris, South India, Sikkim and Madhya Pradesh.

Uses. Quinine is one of the most important drugs known and it is the only adequate cure for malaria. Quinine is obtained from the hard thick bark of above mentioned species of *Cinchona.* The most important constituent of Cinchona bark is quinine, a very bitter, white, granular substance. In addition to its use in the treatment of Malaria, it is a valuable tonic and antiseptic. It is also used in the treatment of other fevers. Some 29 other alkaloids have been isolated from the bark, including cinchonidine, cinchonine, and quinidine, all of which are useful in medicine.

Asoka Tree

Saraca indica Linn., of family Caesalpiniaceae; Eng. Asoka tree; Hindi—*Ashok*; Sanskrit, Hindi and Bengali—*Asok*, *ashoka*; Marathi—*Ashoka*; Gujarati—*Ashopalava*; Telugu—*Asoka*; Tamil—*Asogam*; Kannada—*Asokadamara*; Malayalam—*Asokam*; Oriya—*Oshoko*; Khasi Hills—*Dieng-sohkyrkha*.

This is a spreading evergreen tree; native of India; commonly found in Central and East Himalayas, Bengal and West Peninsula.

Uses. The bark is astringent. Its decoction is given in uterine disorders, especially in menorrhagia and leucorrhoea. The decoction is also an efficacious remedy for piles and dysentery. The dried flowers are given in diabetes. The dried flowers of it are fried and used even by common people in Kerala.

Arjun Tree

Terminalia arjuna (Roxb. ex DC.) Wight and Arn., of family Combretaceae; Eng. Arjun tree; Hindi—*Arjuna.*

A tree, commonly found in Madhya Pradesh, Bihar and the Western Peninsula.

Uses. The bark is astringent, febrifuge, cooling, cardiac stimulant, cholagogal, lithontriptic and vulnerary. It is an excellent remedy for heart diseases. The decoction with milk is given every morning on an empty stomach. The decoction is also used for cleaning sores and ulcers.

DRUGS OBTAINED FROM STEMS AND WOODS

Ephedrine

Ephedra gerardiana Wall., of family Gnetaceae or Ephedraceae; Eng. Ephedrine; Hindi—*Khanda.*

A small shrub, found in the drier regions of the temperate and Alpine Himalayas from Kashmir to Sikkim at 7,000 to 16,000 feet elevation.

Uses. The stems are the source of famous drug ephedrine. The liquid extract of stem is used for controlling asthma. The tincture of the plant is cardiac and circulatory stimulant. The decoction of stems and roots is used as a remedy for rheumatism and syphilis in Russia. Juice of berries is used in affections of the respiratory passages. The stems contain the alkaloids—ephedrine and pseudo-ephedrine.

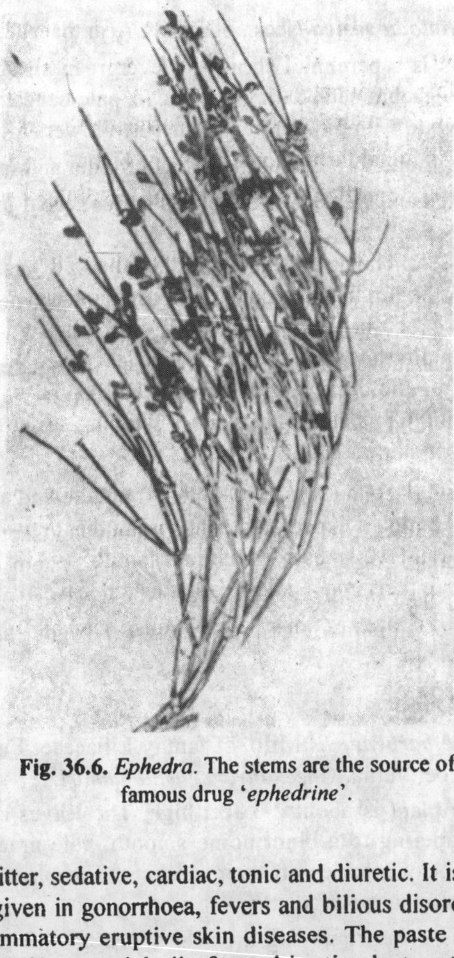

Fig. 36.6. *Ephedra*. The stems are the source of famous drug '*ephedrine*'.

White Sandal Wood

Santalum album Linn., of family Santalaceae; Eng. White sandalwood; Hindi—*Safed chandan.*

A tree, found in the Western Peninsula, Karnataka, Tamil Nadu, and forests of Kerala.

Uses. The wood is cooling, astringent, bitter, sedative, cardiac, tonic and diuretic. It is given in fevers and thirst. The powder of wood is given in gonorrhoea, fevers and bilious disorders. A paste of wood is a cooling dressing in inflammatory eruptive skin diseases. The paste is also applied to the temple in headache and fever. The essential oil of wood is stimulant, antiseptic demulcent and diuretic. It is used in gonorrhoea, chronic catarrh of the bladder, urethral haemorrhage, chronic bronchitis and intermittent fevers. The oil is applied over scabies and other skin diseases.

Catechu

Acacia catechu Willd., of family Mimosaceae; Eng.. Catechu tree; Verna. *Kattha, Khair.*

Uses. It is a valuable astringent. It is generally used for disorders in which a mild, non-irritating and powerful astringent is required, such as chronic diarrhoea, dysentery, bleeding piles, uterine haemorrhage, leucorrhoea, etc. It is very efficacious for mercurial salivation bleeding or ulcerated or spongy gums, hypertrophy of the tonsils, enlarged uvula, aphthous ulceration of the mouth, etc. It may be used as lozenge made with the addition of gum arabic and sugar. A powder of catechu is used for plugging the cavity of an aching tooth to relieve pain. A tincture of catechu is useful for bed sores and painful mammary glands. A mixture of catechu and myrh, known as *Kathbol*, is used as a tonic, as a galactagogue for nursing mothers. Khersal or catechuic acid, found in small fragments in cavities of the wood, is a useful drug for chest diseases. The juice of the fresh bark is given with asafoetida in haemoptysis.

DRUGS OBTAINED FROM LEAVES

Vasaka

Adhatoda vasica Nees., of family Acanthaceae; Eng. Malabo nut; Verna—*Arusi, rusa.*

This is a perennial shrub. An evergreen shrub about 4-8 feet in height. Leaves elliptic, lanceolate, acuminate, dark green above, pale beneath. Flowers in short dense–axillary peduncled spikes, white with pink or purple stripes. Flowers after rainy season.

It is found throughout the plains of India and in the sub–Himalayan tract up to 4,000 feet.

Twigs and flowers of the plants are collected in March-April. The dried drug is sold in the market.

Uses. The leaves contain the alkaloid vascine; they are a powerful expectorant and antispasmodic; they are commonly used in chest diseases, especially phthisis. A decoction of the leaves or their powder is also given, especially for chronic bronchitis and asthma. The leaf juice is given in diarrhoea and dysentery. The leaves are given as a febrifuge in malarial fevers. For relief of asthma the dried leaves are smoked. A poultice of the leaves is applied over fresh wounds, rheumatic joints and inflammatory swellings. A warm decoction of the leaves is used for scabies and other skin diseases.

The flowers and fruits are bitter, aromatic and antispasmodic.

The root is expectorant, antispasmodic, antiseptic, antiperiodic and anthelmintic. It is given in malarial fevers, diseases of the respiratory system, diphtheria and gonorrhoea. The root and the bark have the same medicinal uses as the leaves.

The preparations are—Vansa Khand and Chyavanprash.

Indian Aloe

Aloe barbedensis Mill., of family Liliaceae; Eng. Indian Aloe; Verna. *Gheekunvar, ghrita kumari.*

The plant is about 2-3 feet high. The leaves are fleshly tapering to a blunt point, smooth, pale green, having horny prickles on their margins. The plant is found throughout our country.

Uses. After removing the skin of leaves they are given in fevers, enlargement of the liver, spleen and other glands, skin diseases, gonorrhoea, constipation, menstrual suppression, piles, jaundice and rheumatic affections. In the diseases of liver and spleen the pulp of one leaf is administered with black salt and ginger. The juice of roasted leaf is being given with honey for cough and cold. The pulp of one leaf is being given daily in abdominal tumors, dropsy, carbuncles, piles, sciatica, rheumatism and retention of urine in fevers. A salad of leaves is eaten in indigestion, constipation and flatulence. The leaf juice is given as a remedy for intestinal worms in children. A poultice of the leaves is applied to tumours, cysts, inflamed parts and scalds.

Fig. 36.7. *Aloe barbedensis*. A common medicinal plant with succulent leaves. The pulp of leaves is given in fever and liver enlargement.

Life Plant

Bryophyllum pinnatum Kurz., of family Crassulaceae; Eng. Life plant; Hindi—*Ghamari.*

This is a succulent perennial plant. Distributed throughout India.

Uses. The leaf juice is given in diarrhoea, dysentery, calculous affections and cholera. The leaves are styptic, astringent and antiseptic; they are slightly toasted before they are applied to wounds, bruises, boils, cuts, ulcers, bites of venomous insects; by its application swelling is prevented, incised wounds heal rapidly and irritation is allayed.

Fig. 36.8. *Bryophyllum*. A common medicinal plant. The leaves possess antiseptic properties.

Indian Pennywort

Centella asiatica (L.) Urban., of family Umbelliferae (Apiaceae); Eng. Indian pennywort; Hindi—*Brahmi*.

Fig. 36.9. A flowering twig of *Tulsi*. The leaves on steam distillation yield a bright yellow volatile oil possessing a pleasant odour. The oil is reported to possess antibacterial and insecticidal properties. It has marked insecticidal activity against mosquitoes. Besides the volatile oil the plant is reported to contain alkaloids, glycosides, saponins and tannins.

This is a common trailing herb, rooting at the nodes. Commonly found throughout India.

Uses. The weed is alterative, tonic, diuretic, antiphlogistic, blood purifier and local stimulant. It is a remedy for skin diseases, like chronic eczema, chronic ulcers etc., enlargement of glands, chronic rheumatism, chronic nervous diseases, madness, cholera, amenorrhoea and piles. The leaves are a household remedy in early stages of dysentery of children. The powder of leaves is given with milk in small doses in mental weakness and to improve memory. The fresh juice of leaves mixed with milk is given as an alterative in gonorrhoea, jaundice and fevers; this is also useful for children in skin diseases and for improving the blood and nervous system. An ointment made of leaf juice and lanoline is of great value in elephantiasis.

Holy Basil

Ocimum sanctum Linn., of family Labiatae; Eng. Holy basil; Hindi—*Tulsi*.

This is an erect softy hairy aromatic herb or undershrub. Found throughout India.

Uses. The leaves are expectorant, stomachic, anticatarrhal, diaphoretic and aromatic; their decoction or infusion is given in malaria, gastric diseases of children and liver disorders; as a prophylactic against malaria fresh leaves are taken with black pepper in the morning. The leaf juice is given in chronic fever, haemorrhage dysentery and dyspepsia; it is also used to check vomiting and as an anthelmintic.

Betel Pepper

Piper betle Linn., of family Piperaceae; Eng. Betel pepper; Hindi—*Pan*.

This is a climbing shrub cultivated for its leaves.

Uses. The leaves are astringent, aromatic, antiseptic, carminative, aphrodisiac, stimulant, expectorant and sialogogue. The leaf juice with honey is given to children in colic, indigestion, diarrhoea and laryngitis. The leaves are chewed to remove foul odour from the mouth. The leaf juice is used as eye drops in ophthalmia, and other painful eye diseases and night blindness. Oil coated leaves are a useful dressing for blistered surfaces and ulcers. The essential oil extracted from the leaves, is given in catarrhal and pulmonary diseases.

Fig. 36.10. *Piper betle*. The leaves are of medicinal value.

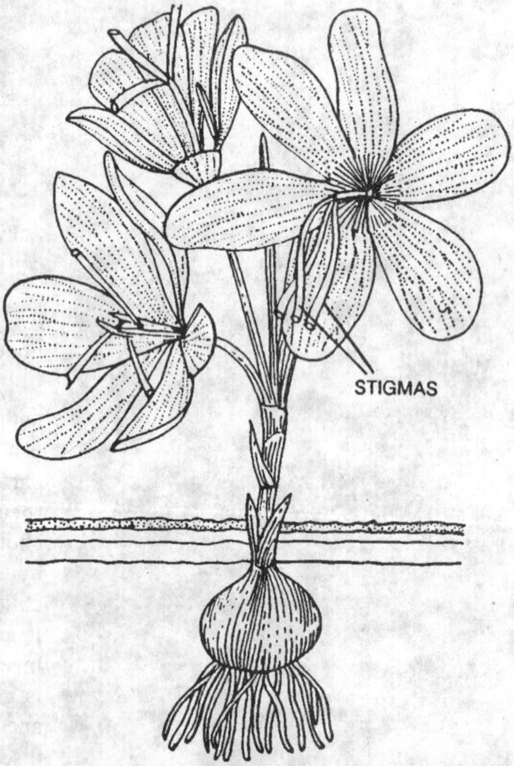

Fig. 36.11. *Crocus sativus* (Saffron). The stigmas and tops of the styles make the saffron of commerce.

Tylophora

Tylophora asthmatica; Syn. *Tylo-phora indica*; Hindi—*Jangli Pikavan* or *Antamul*; Family—Asclepiadaceae.

It is a trailing creeper, growing abundantly in Northern India, Bengal, Assam; the Western Ghats, Burma and Sri Lanka. The leaves are thick and deep green, 5 to 12 cm long and 2 to 6 cm wide. In dry state, they are rather, thick and of a pale-yellow colour.

Uses. The chewing and swallowing of leaves by the patient of asthma have shown wonderful results. The leaf was also tried at Vallabhbhai Patel Chest Institute, Delhi on the patients suffering from bronchial asthma, the results were quite satisfactory.

DRUGS OBTAINED FROM FLOWERS

Saffron

Crocus sativus Linn., of family Iridaceae; Eng. Saffron; Hindi—*Kesar*.

This is a herb, cultivated in Kashmir (Pampur), Bhersar and Chaubattia in Uttar Pradesh

Uses. The dried stigmas and tops of the styles make the saffron of commerce. It is of medicinal value. It contains the bitter principle picrocrocin. Saffron is mild stimulant, stomachic, carminative, antispasmodic, nerve sedative, mild narcotic, diuretic and emmenagogue. It is a remedy for promoting menstruation. It is also used in fevers, hysteria, flatulent colic, asthma, leucorrhoea, piles and catarrhal diseases of children.

Iron Wood

Mesua ferrea Linn., of family Guttiferae; Eng. Ironwood; Hindi—*Nagkesar*.

A tree, found in the Eastern Himalayas, Assam, West Bengal, the Western Ghats, Travancore and the Andaman Islands.

Uses. The flowers are astringent and stomachic. The dried flowers are given in vomiting, dysentery, coughs, thirst, irritability of the stomach, excessive perspiration and bleeding pile.

Violet

Viola odorata Linn., of family Violaceae; Eng. Violet; Hindi—*Banafsha*.

A herb; native of Europe but now cultivated in Kashmir.

Uses. The flowers are demulcent astringent, diuretic, emollient, diaphoretic and laxative. They are given in biliousness and lung troubles. The flowers are used for the treatment of coughs, sore throat, kidney diseases, liver disorders and infantile affections.

DRUGS OBTAINED FROM FRUITS

Bael

Aegle marmelos Corr., of family Rutaceae; Eng. Bael tree; Verna. Bael, *Siriphal*.

This is a tree.

Uses. The fruit is of great medicinal value. The ripe fruit is aromatic, astringent, cooling and laxative. The unripe or half-ripe fruit is astringent, stomachic, antiscorbutic and digestive. It is best given in sub-acute or chronic cases of diarrhoea and dysentery and in irritation of the elementary canal; it is a useful adjunct in after treatment of bacillary dysentery. The ripe fruit is prescribed in intestinal disorders and certain forms of dyspepsia characterized by alternate constipation and diarrhoea. A sherbet of the ripe fruit is given for chronic constipation and dyspepsia.

Coriander

Coriandrum sativum Linn., of family Umbelliferae (Apiaceae); Eng. Coriander: Hindi—*Dhaniya*.

This is an aromatic herb; native of the Mediterranean region now cultivated in Madhya Pradesh, Maharashtra, Karnataka, Bihar and throughout India.

Uses. The fruit is aromatic, stimulant, carminative antispasmodis, correctivem diuretic, aphrodisiac, and refrigerant. A decoction of the dried fruits is given in flatulent colic, rehumatism and neuralgia. The volatile oil distilled from the fruits is given in flatulent colic, rheumatism and neuralgia. The watery paste of seeds is used for the cure of ulcers of the mouth and throat.

Cumin

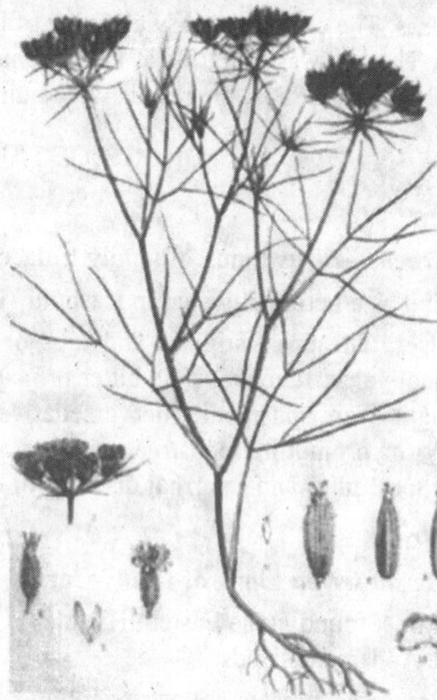

Fig. 36.12. *Cumin*. An aromatic herb.

Cuminum cyminum Linn., of family Umbelliferae (Apiaceae); Eng. Cumin; Hindi—*Zira*.

This is an annula aromatic 1-3 feet high herb. It is native of Mediterranean region but now commonly grown in the Punjab and Uttar Pradesh fro aromatic fruits.

North Gujarat especially Unja is well known for its cultivation and market.

Uses. The fruit is a good source of thymol; it is a stomachic, diuretic, carminative, stimulant, astringent and emmenagouge. It is prescribed in dyspepsia, diarrhoea, and hoarseness of voice. The fruit is given with lime juice to pregnant women for checking nausea; for promoting secretion of milk, cumin seeds are given after childbirth.

Emblic

Emblica officinalis Gaertn., of family Euphorbiaceae; Eng. Emblic; Hindi—*Amla*.

A tree found throughout India.

Uses. The fruit is of great medicinal value. It is one of the richest sources of vitamin C. The fresh fruit is refrigerant, tonic, antiscorbutic, diuretic and laxative. It is used in fevers, vomiting, indigestion, habitual constipation and other digestion troubles. The dried fruit is a good astringent, refrigerant, stomachic, antiscorbutic and blood purifier. It is given in diarrhoea, dysentery and haemorrhage. The infusion of seeds is a useful eye-wash in ophthalmic diseases.

Fig. 36.13. *Emblica officinalis* (*Amla*). The fruit is one of the richest sources of vitamin C.

Fennel

Foeniculum vulgare Mill., of family Umbelliferae (Apiaceae, Fennel; Hindi—*Saunf*.

This is an aromatic herb. It is native of Mediterranean region, now cultivated mainly in the Punjab, Assam, Maharashtra and Baroda.

Uses. The fruit is sweet, laxative, aphrodisiac, stomachic, stimulant, aromatic, corrective of flatulence, appetizer, anthelmintic, carminative, lactagogue, diuretic, stimulant and antidotal. It is administered in eye diseases, burning sensation, fever, thirst, wounds, dysentery, diseases of the chest, spleen and kidney, headache, amenorrhoea and bellyache of children; it also promotes female monthly regularity. In dysentery a decoction of fruit is given; in fever a decoction of fruit is given with sugar. The oil extracted from the seed is an anthelmintic against hookworms. The leaves are diuretic, digestive, stimulant and aromatic; they are useful in cough, flatulence, colic and thirst. They are also eaten to improve the eyesight.

Opium

Papaver somniferum Linn., of family Papaveraceae; Eng. Opium; Hindi—*Afim*.

A herb; native of W. Asia, now grown in Uttar Pradesh, in the East Punjab, Rajasthan and Madhya Pradesh.

An inspissated juice obtained by scratching the unripe capsules of *Papaver somniferum* Linn.; and allowing the milky sap, which exudes thereby, to dry spontaneously. The bulk of the medicinal article is obtained from Asia Minor, at the present day, as it has been for nearly the past 2,000 years. Indian Opium is, however, the most important form commercially, being that which is smoked, eaten or drunk, in various preparations by the inhabitants of Asiatic countries, chiefly the Chinese.

In India the opium-poppy is grown here and there throughout the country, but its cultivation is mainly confined to three centres, which afford the following opiums—'Patna Opium' in Bihar, 'Benares Opium' in Uttar Pradesh, and 'Malwa Opium' in Madhya Pradesh and certain parts of Rajasthan.

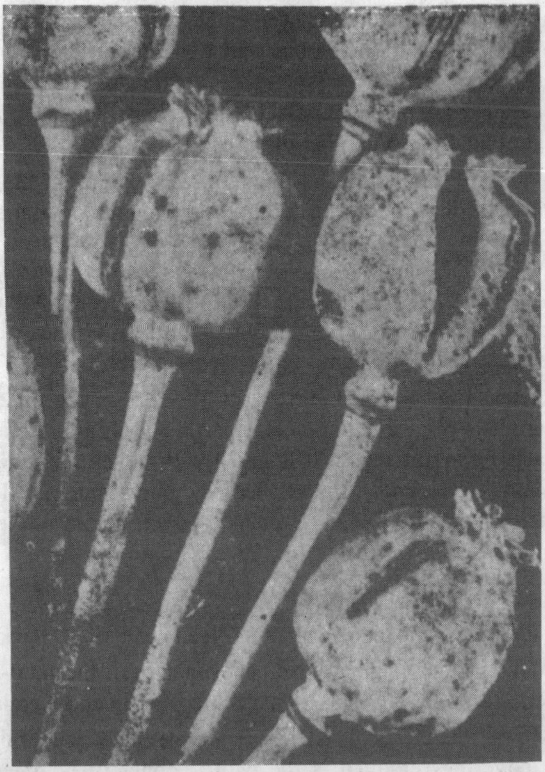

Fig. 36.14. *Papaver somniferum* (*Afim*)—The latex is obtained by scrapping the capsules. The latex, obtained from the immature fruits; is the source of opium, which is used to induce sleep, relieve pain, and relax spasms.

Medicinal properties of opium. Opium is well known to the medical profession. The medicinal drug of Europe is mainly derived from Asia Minor and is the produce of *P. somniferum* var. *glabrum*.

In the words of Pharmacopaeia of India it may be said that opium in its primary effects medicinally is stimulant, and its secondary action narcotic, anodyne, and antispasmodic. "It operates chiefly on the cerebrospinal system, and, through the nerves arising therefrom, it affects more or less every organ of the body. It tends to diminish every secretion excepting that of the skin, which increases under its use. In overdoses it is a powerful poison." In inflammation, especially of serious membranes, it has been employed extensively either alone, or in combination with calomel, antimony, and other remedies. As a general rule it is less applicable to inflammatory and other diseases, in which the tendency to death is by coma or by apnoea, then to those which produce death by asthenia. In the latter, as in peritonitis, it holds the first place as a remedial agent. In fevers, especially in the advanced stages, it is of the highest value, either alone or in combination with antimony, camphor, allaying vascular and nervous excitement, and procuring sleep; but as a general rule, it is inadmissible when contraction of the pupil is strongly marked. In painful spasmodic affections, opium in large and repeated doses often affords immediate relief. In various morbid states of the abdominal viscera, *e.g.*, simple or cancerous ulceration of the stomach, chronic gastritis, gastrodynia, nervous and sympathetic vomiting, diarrhoea, dysentery, colica pictonum, strangulated hernia, visceral destructions, it is often given with the best results. In diseases of the genito-urinary system, *e.g.*, cystitis, cistirrhoea, spasmodic stricture of the urethra, also in menorrhagia, dysmenorrohea, irritable states of the uterus, metritis, it is a remedy of the highest value. Tetanus, acute rheumatism, and delirium tremens are amongst the other diseases in which opium has been employed as a sheet anchor. In cholera it has been used but with doubtful results. In cancerous and gangrenous ulceration, opium, by allaying constitutional disturbances, often exercises a favourable influence on the local symptoms. As an external application, opium proves valuable in various rheumatic, neuralgic, and other painful affections; also in ophthalmia and other diseases of the eye".

"*Dose.* From a quarter of a grain to two grains or more according to circumstances, in many painful affections the sole criterion for the regulation of the dose is the amount of relief afforded".

Long Pepper

Piper longum Linn., of family Piperaceae, Eng. Long pepper; Hindi—*Pipar*, *Piplamul*.

This is a slender creeping undershrub. It is native of India and cultivated in the Western Ghats, Karnataka and Tamil Nadu for the fruits.

Uses. The sun-dried unripe fruit (berries) or the spike of the small flowers is known as long pepper. It is a cardiac, stimulant carminative, alterative tonic, laxative, digestive, emollient, stomachic and antiseptic. It is given with honey for indigestion, dyspepsia, cough, bronchitis, asthma, hysteria, cholera, fever, leprosy, piles, gout, etc. To prevent fever after childbirth it is an efficacious remedy. The dried root (*Piplamul*) possesses the same medicinal qualities as the berries but in an inferior degree.

Black and White Pepper

Piper nigrum Linn., of family Piperaceae; Eng. Black pepper; Hindi—*Kali mirch*; *gol mirch*.

This is a stout glabrous creeper; native of the Indo-Malayan region, also cultivated in the Western Ghats, Karnataka, Maharashtra, Assam and Kerala.

Uses. The unripe dried berries are the black pepper of commerce; and the ripe fruit with the outer covering removed is the white pepper of commerce. The berries contain the alkaloid piperine, The fruits are aromatic, stimulant, carminative, digestive, stomachic, nervine tonic, diuretic emmenagogue and antiperiodic. It is given in dyspepsia, flatulence, diarrhoea, cholera, piles, disorders of the urinary system, cough, coma, gonorrhoea and malarial fever. It is given either as an infusion or powder. White pepper is more aromatic and less pungent than black pepper. It is given in dyspepsia and constipation.

Belleric Myrobalan

Terminalia bellirica Roxb., of family Combretaceae; Eng. Belleric myrobalan; Hindi—*Bahera*.

A common tree grown as an avenue.

Uses. The ripe dry fruit known as belleric myrobalan (bahera) is astringent, bitter, tonic and laxative. It is given in piles, dropsy, diarrhoea, leprosy, biliousness, dyspepsia and headache. Half ripe fruit is given as purgative and fully ripe as an astringent.

Chebulic Myrobalan

Terminalia chebula Retz., of family Combretaceae; Eng. Chebulic myrobalan; Hindi—*Harara*, *Haritaki*.

A tree. Commonly found in Northern India. Also found in South India in the Deccan tablelands at 1,000–3,000 feet and up to 6,000 feet in Travancore; higher forests of the Mumbai Ghats, Satpuras, Belgaum and Kanara.

Uses. The fruit is the chebulic myrobalan of commerce. It is an efficacious laxative, astringent, stomachic, tonic and alterative. The fruit pulp is given in chronic diarrhoea, dysentery, flatulence, asthma, urinary disorders, vomiting, enlarged spleen and liver, etc. It is used externally as a local application to chronic ulcers and wounds and as a gargle in stomatitis. Fine powder of fruit is used as a dentrifice and considered useful in various teeth, bleeding and ulcerations of the gums.

Ammi

Trachyspermum ammi (L.) Sprague of family Umbelliferae. Eng. Ammi; Hindi *Ajwain*.

A herb, cultivated throughout India.

Uses. The fruits are carminative, stimulant, antispasmodic and tonic. They are given in colic, flatulence, dyspepsia, indigestion, diarrhoea, cholera, tympanites, hysteria, etc. The fruit yields an essential oil containing thymol.

Solanum

Solanum viarum Dunal; Syn. *Solanum khasianum* var. *Chatterjeeanum*, Sengupta; family Solanaceae.

Solanum viarum, is a wild perennial herb. It grows well in the hilly areas particularly of Khasia and Jaintia hills (Assam) in North East and Nilgiri hills of South India.

Morphology. It is a stout herb, with a woody stem, of about 2 feet in height. Nearly whole body of the plant is covered with yellow hairs (hirsute). The stem bears two types of prickles, hooked and straight. Stem is cymosely branched.

Leaf is 7" to 5" long and is deeply lobed, hirsute and bears only straight prickles.

Flowers are white in colour, and are produced in large number. The berry is about 2.5 cms. in diameter which contains about 350 seeds.

Alkaloid and medicinal uses. The berries of *S. viarum* contain the alkaloid *Solasodine*. It is a glycon which is used by pharmaceutical companies for the preparation of many important drugs. It is a nitrogen analogue of diosyenin and is a good source of *sapogenin*. Sapogenin is used as a base for the preparation of *Cortisone* and allied products. The synthetic substitutes are not known for these drugs, hence the importance of this source.

The gluco-alkaloid percentage of the berries is about 6 per cent which in turn produces one-third or 2 per cent of *Solasodine*. It can be extracted from dry as well as fresh berries.

Cortisone, a steroidal hormone prepared from solasodine, is found to be effective in the treatment of acute stages of rheumatoid arthritis, chronic cases of asthma, leukemia, obesity and many skin diseases.

Induced mutations have yielded favourable results regarding the increases in alkaloid content of the berries. (Dhyansagar and Pingle). *Material received from P.N. Purekar.*

DRUGS OBTAINED FROM SEEDS

Carrot

Daucus carota Linn. var ***sativa*** D.C. of family Umbelliferae (Apiaceae); Eng. Carrot; Hindi—*Gajar*.

An annual or biennial herb, grown chiefly in the Punjab, Uttar Pradesh and Madhya Pradesh.

Uses. The seeds are aromatic, stimulant, carminative, useful in the diseases of the kidney and in dropsy, nervine tonic, aphrodisiac, given in uterine pain.

Lesser Cardamom

Elettaria cardamomum Maton., of family Zingiberaceae; Eng. Lesser cardamom; Hindi—*Chotti ilaichi.*

This is a herb; native of India, cultivated in Kerala, Karnataka, Maharashtra, Assam and Tamil Nadu.

Uses. The seeds are aromatic, stimulant, stomachic, carminative, diuretic, cooling, abortifacient, emmenagogue and antidotal; they are useful in asthma, bronchitis, piles, diseases of the bladder, kidney, liver, uterus, rectum and throat. They are also remedy of scabies, headache, earache and toothache.

Blonde Psyllium

Plantago ovata Forsk., of family Plantaginaceae. Blonde psyllium; Hindi—*Isafgol.*

This is an annual herb. It is cultivated in parts of Rajasthan and Maharashtra.

Uses. The seeds are mildly laxative, demulcent, mucilaginous cooling, emollient, astringent and diuretic. They are used in the treatment of dysentery, constipation and disorders of the digestive system. The mucilaginous matter is found in the seed coat, and therefore, the seed coat or husk is used.

Castor Oil Plant

Ricinus communis Linn. of family Euphorbiaceae; Eng. Castor oil plant; Hindi—*Arand.*

This is a small tree, cultivated chiefly in Andhra Pradesh, Maharashtra, Karnataka and Orissa.

Uses. The seeds contain the alkaloid ricinine; the cold drawn oil from the seed is medicinally the most useful part of the plant; it is an effective purgative generally given in acute diarrhoea. As an enema the oil is given in constipation. The oil is locally applied in conjunctivitis. The leaves are applied to the head to relieve headache and as poultice for boils.

Nux-Vomica

Strychnos nux-vomica Linn., of family Loganiaceae; Eng. Nuxvomica; Hindi—*Kuchla.*

A tree, found in Orissa, Bihar, Andhra Pradesh and Tamil Nadu.

Uses. The dried ripe seeds are the source of a drug nux vomica which is used as a tonic stimulant and in the treatment of paralysis and nervous disorders. The powdered seeds are also given in general debility, chronic rheumatism, dyspepsia, intermittent fevers, diarrhoea, hysteria, general constipation, hydrophobia, impotence, cholera and epilepsy.

Fenugreek

Tirgonella foenumgraecum Linn., of family Papilionaceae; Eng. Fenugreek; Hindi—*Methi.*

A herb; native of South Europe, grown mainly in Northern India.

Uses. The seeds are aromatic, diuretic, nutritive, tonic, lactagogue, astringent, emollient, carminative and aphrodisiac. The seeds are given, boiled or roasted in dyspepsia, diarrhoea, dysentery, colic, flatulence, dropsy, rheumatism, chronic cough, liver and spleen enlargement. The seeds contain the alkaloid trigonelline.

DRUGS OBTAINED FROM ALL PARTS OF PLANTS

Absinthe

Artemisia absinthum Linn. of family Compositae (Asteraceae); Eng. Absinthe; Verna; *Vilayati Afsanthin.*

This is an aromatic, bitter, herbaceous hairy perennial herb. It is found in Kashmir from 5,000 to 7,000 feet elevation.

Uses. The whole herb is used medicinally but the leaves are preferred. The fresh plant is more efficacious than the dry plant. It is a tonic, stomachic and anthelmintic. Small doses of its infusion are given for dispersing the yellow bile of jaundice from the skin. It is also given in the disease of the digestive system, nocturnal pollution, anaemia, wasting diseases, etc. The poultice of its leaves is applied for fomentation to gouty or rheumatic joints. It is a useful antiseptic and detergent in skin diseases. An infusion of the leaves is given as an enema for killing worms in the rectum.

Neem Tree

Azadirachta indica A. Juss., (Syn. *Melia azadirachta* Linn)., of family Meliaceae; Eng. Margosa tree, Neem tree; Hindi—*Nim*.

It is native of Myanmar but grown all over India.

Uses. The leaves are carminative, expectorant, anthelmintic, antidotal, diuretic and insecticidal. The fresh juice of the leaves is given for intestinal worms; with honey the juice is prescribed for jaundice and skin diseases. An infusion of the fresh leaves is a bitter vegetable tonic and alterative, especially in chronic malarial fevers, because of its action on the liver. Externally the leaves are applied over skin diseases as a discutient, stimulant and antiseptic; they are specially used for boils, chronic ulcers, eruptions of small pox, syphilitic sores, glandular swellings, wounds, etc. The bark is also a bitter tonic, astringent, alterative, anthelmintic, antispasmodic and stimulant. It is used in the same way as the leaves. The root bark has the same properties as the bark of the stem. The nim gum is a stimulant and demulcent tonic. The fermented sap that exudes from the trunk is a refrigerant, nutrient, stomachic and alterative tonic.

The fruit is recommended for urinary diseases, piles, leprosy, intestinal worms, etc. The seeds are emetic, laxative and anthelmintic. Seed oil is applied as an antiseptic dressing in leprosy and chronic skin diseases.

Spiny Bamboo

Bambusa bambos Voss., of family Gramineae (Poaceae); Eng. Spiny bamboo; Hindi—*Bans*.

This is a tall woody grass, found throughout India, particularly along river valleys and in moist situations.

Uses. The leaf buds are administered for thread-worms. The leaf juice is given with aromatics in vomiting of blood. A decoction of the leaves is used to induce lochia after childbirth.

The young shoots contain hydrocyanic and benzoic acids; they are stomachic and stimulant; they are used in lung diseases. A decoction of the joints of bamboo stem is a useful emmenagogue; it is also used as an abortifacient.

Banșlochan, a silicious crystalline secretion found in the culms of the female plants, is a febrifuge, expectorant, tonic, aphrodisiac, demulcent and pectoral. It is given in hectic fever, phthisis, asthma, paralytic complaints, etc.

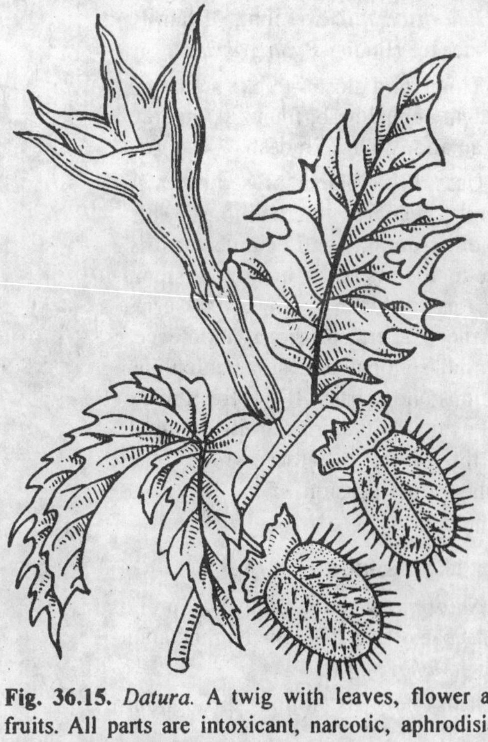

Fig. 36.15. *Datura.* A twig with leaves, flower and fruits. All parts are intoxicant, narcotic, aphrodisiac, toxic, antispasmodic and anodyne.

Apple of Peru

Datura metel Linn., of family Solanaceae, Eng. Apple of Peru; Hindi—*Dhatura.*

This is a herbaceous plant covered with fine, minute hairs. Commonly found throughout India.

Uses. All parts of the plant are strongly intoxicant, narcotic, aphrodisiac, toxic, antispasmodic and anodynous. The young leaves and seeds contain the drugs hyoscine, hyoscyamine and atropine. The dried leaves and twigs of the plants are smoked as an antispasmodic in asthma, whooping cough, bronchitis, etc. The juice of the fruits is a useful dressing for the scalp to check dandruff and falling of the hair. The seeds are astringent, antispasmodic, narcotic, anodynous, intoxicating, aphrodisiac, bitter, carminative and stomachic. The paste of seeds is used for decaying teeth, piles, fistula, tumors and parasitic skin diseases.

Achyranthes

Achyranthes aspera Linn., Hindi—*Chirchita, Latzira, Apamarg*; family Amarantaceae.

This is a common roadside weed with spike inflorescence. Flowering throughout year. It is of common occurrence throughout India.

Uses. The plants are used medicinally for several diseases such as piles, colic, boils, etc. It is pungent, purgative, diuretic and astringent. Roots are used for pyrrhoea. Also used in cough and fevers.

Pedalium

Pedalium murex Linn., of family Pedaliaceae; Hindi—*Bada gokru.*

This is a low, thick stemmed succulent annual herb; found in Gujarat, Konkan and Andhra Pradesh.

Uses. Fresh plants infused in water or milk become mucilaginous. This infusion is diuretic and demulcent; it is given in disorders of urinary system, such as ardour urine, dysuria, gonorrhoea, spermatorrhoea, impotence, nocturnal seminal emission, calculous affections and dropsy. If the fresh plant is not available the dried fruits are used for the diseases for which the mucilaginous infusion of the leaves is recommended.

Black Nightshade

Solanum nigrum Linn., of family Solanaceae; Eng. Black Nightshade; Hindi—*Makoy.*

This herb is found throughout India.

Uses. The herb is a cardiac tonic, alterative, diuretic, sedative, diaphoretic,

Fig. 36.16. *Solanum nigrum.* (Black Nightshade). A common medicinal plant. It makes the medicine for liver enlargement and jaundice.

cathartic, anodyne, expectorant and hydragogue. It is used as a decoction in dropsy; enlargement of the liver and jaundice. The syrup of herb is given as an expectorant. In fevers it is given as a cooling drink. The leaf juice is given in inflammation of the kidneys and bladder and in gonorrhoea, dropsy, heart diseases, piles and enlargement of spleen. Hot leaves are applied over the swollen and painful testicles. The berries are alterative, and tonic. They are given in fevers, diarrhoea and heart diseases.

Indian Solanum

Solanum xanthocarpum Schrad & Wendl., of family Solanaceae; Eng. Indian Solanum; Hindi—*Kateli.*

A common prickly herb found throughout India.

Uses. The herb is expectorant, bitter, stomachic, astringent, diuretic, alterative and anthelmintic. Its decoction is given in fevers, coughs, asthma, dropsy, flatulence, gonorrhoea, pain in the chest and heart disease.

Chiretta

Swertia chirata Buch-Ham., of family Gentianaceae; Eng. Chiretta; Hindi—*Charayatah.*

This is a shrub commonly found in temperate Himalayas from Kashmir to Bhutan and the Khasia hills.

Uses. The shrub contains two bitter principles ophelic acid and chiratin. It is a bitter tonic, stomachic, febrifuge, appetizer, anthelmintic, alterative, laxative, antidiarrhoeic, and antiperiodic. It makes a good drug for skin diseases, intermittent fevers, intestinal worms, bronchial asthma and regulating the bowels. It is given as an infusion or tincture.

Heart-leaved Moonseed

Tinospora cordifolia (Willd.) Miers of family Menispermaceae; Eng. Heart-leaved moonseed; Hindi—*Gulancha.*

A common climbing shrub (liane). Found throughout tropical India and the Andamans.

Uses. The fresh plant is antiperiodic, alterative, tonic, hepatic, stimulant and diuretic; its watery extract is very effective in fevers. The plant is commonly used in rheumatism, urinary diseases, dyspepsia, general debility, syphilis, skin diseases, piles, bronchitis, impotence, gonorrhoea and jaundice. The fecula prepared from the roots and stem, known as *sat giloe* is a valued drug for intermittent fevers, chronic diarrhoea, chronic dysentery, jaundice and rheumatism.

Lochnera

Lochnera rosea (Linn.) Reichb.,—*Catharanthus roseus* G. Don. Syn. *Vinca rosea* Hindi—*Sadabahar*; family Apocynaceae.

An erect annual or perennial herb; native of Madagascar but now commonly grown in India as an ornamental plant. Leaves opposite, oval, obovate or oblong, glossy; flowers usually 2-3, in cymose axillary clusters; fruit a cylindrical follicle, manyseeded. Flowers white or pink.

Fig. 36.17. *Catharanthus roseus* (**Sadabahar**). Commonly grown in gardens. It is propagated by seeds or cuttings. It blooms almost throughout the year. The alkaloids possess hypotensive, sedative and tranquillizing properties.

Alkaloids. All parts of the plant, particularly the root bark contain alkaloids; these include three alkaloids of the Rauvolfia group; *viz.*, ajmalicine, serpentine and reserpine. The alkaloids of this plant possess hypotensive, sedative and tranquillizing properties. They also cause relaxation of plain muscles and depression of the central nervous system.

Uses. The plant has been used as a folk remedy for diabetes in various parts of South Africa and also in India and Sri Lanka. It is reported to be toxic to cattle. The juice of the leaves is used as an application for wasp stings. An infusion of the leaves is given in the treatment of menorrhagia. The root is considered tonic and stomachic. The alkaloids possess hypotensive, sedative and tranquillizing properties. The alkaloids inhibit the growth of Vibrio cholerae and Micrococcus pyogenes var. aureus. Vindoline and the other alkaloids from leaves are active against M. pyogenes var. aureus and var. albus, Streptococcus haemolyticus, Corynebacterium diphtheriae and a few other bacteria; leaf extracts form a useful anti-bacterial agent for the treatment of staphylococcal and streptococcal infections.

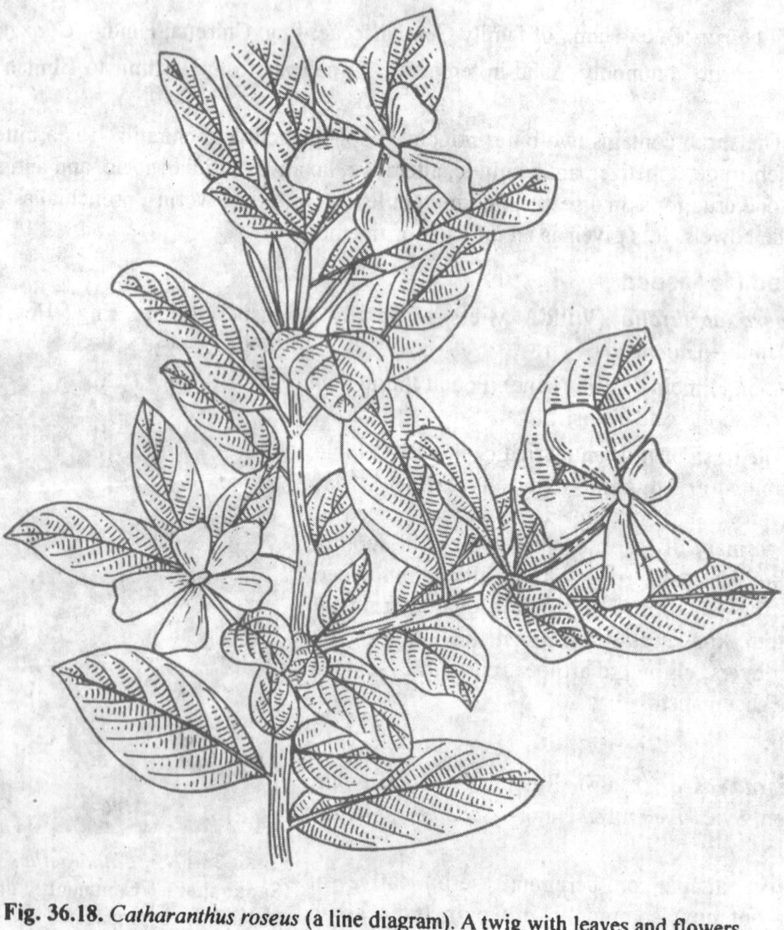

Fig. 36.18. *Catharanthus roseus* (a line diagram). A twig with leaves and flowers. The plant is useful as a medicine in cancer and diabetes.

37 CHAPTER

Non-Alcoholic Beverages and Beverage Plants

The beverages containing caffeine are used all over the world for their stimulating and refreshing qualities. Caffeine is an alkaloid, which has definite medicinal values and acts as a diuretic and nerve stimulant. The most important non-alcoholic beverages are—*tea*, *coffee* and *cocoa*. Caffeine is harmful in large quantities, it is present in these beverages in very small amounts, not exceeding two per cent. The other beverages which do not contain alcohol are commonly known as *soft drinks*. They contain high sugar content and make a good source of energy. The fruit juices are the simplest soft drinks.

INDIAN TEA

Tea

Camellia sinensis (Linn.) O. Kuntze; Eng.—Tea; Hindi—*Chq*; Family—Theaceae.

History. "According to Japanese folklore, the discovery of tea is attributed to an Indian Buddhist monk *Daruma* who lived hundreds of years ago. He left India to preach the message of the Enlightened One—The Lord Buddha—in China. Arriving at Peking, he vowed not to sleep for nine years till he finished his prayers. But, during his meditation he felt tired and his eyes closed. Waking up in disgust, he tore off his eyelids and threw them away. Where the latter fell there sprang up an evergreen bush. Surprised, *Daruma* plucked the leaves, boiled them and drank the liquid. Soon, he felt refreshed and was able to continue his prayers. *Daruma* eventually left China and went to Japan where he died."

In China the people have been drinking tea probably since the 4th century A.D. and the people of Upper Burma, along the Indo-Burmese border and Upper Assam have been used to tea for just as long a period.

Tea was brought to the notice of Europe in 1559 by Ramusio, the noted Venetian writer on voyages and travels, long after it was accepted beverage of the people of Asia. Half a century after Ramusio's notice of tea, the enterprising Dutch began to import it into Europe. England was strangely casual to the beverage during the first half of the 17th century. Tea then was far beyond the reach of the average person. The 2 lbs, 2 oz. tea, brought by the Governors of the East India Company in 1664, as a gift to King Charles II, cost them 85 shillings. Two years later the Company gave him a more ample present of *thea*, consisting of 22¾ lbs., costing 50 shillings per lb. Half a century later the retail price of tea in London was between 20-30 shillings per lb. for *Bohea* (black tea) and 12-30 shillings for the finest *Hyson* (green tea). It took another hundred years before consumption began to spread to the rural areas. According to Prof. Northcote Parkinson, it was presumably between 1784 and 1789 that tea "may literally be said to have descended from the palace to the cottage". About that time it became the breakfast beverage of practically the whole population. It was also drunk at other times which led Raynal (the French historian. 1713-96) to exclaim that tea had done more for English sobriety than any laws, sermons or moral treatises could have achieved.

Tea was sold publicly in London in 1657 and two years later, on 14th November 1659, Mercurius Politicus carried the news that tea was sold "almost in every street" of London. The first order by the East India Company for 100 lb. of the best tea was sent to its agent at Bantam in Java in 1667. In 1669 import of tea into England from Continental Europe was prohibited, thus making absolute the East Indian Company's monopoly in tea.

The British imported China tea from Bantam (Java) when they were dispossessed in 1684. From this period Madras and Surat became centres for the import of "secondhand" Chinese tea. Though, direct British trade with China did not weaken till the 1780 when the merchants of Canton decided to organise the conduct of their country's foreign tea trade.

Meanwhile, the Company's officials in India had realised the possibilities of raising this valuable commodity of trade in India. In 1780, Warren Hastings, the Governor-General, passed on some seeds of *Hyson* for propagation in Bhutan. A tea enthusiast Col. Robert Kyd, who later became Superintendent of the Botanical Gardens in Calcutta, similarly experimented with tea cultivation. In 1788, Sir Joseph Banks tried to interest the East India Company in the possibilities of growing tea in India; but the Company was not agreed to the suggestion as such a venture was against the monopoly of its tea trade with China. However, after five years, Lord Macartney's Embassy was making arrangements to send seeds of the tea locally cultivated to Calcutta. Although imported tea seeds gave the idea and the sustenance for the commercial cultivation of tea in India, the rise of the Tea Industry, as it is today, owes origin to the momentous discovery of the indigenous tea plant in Assam in India.

Many have claimed the discovery of the indigenous Indian tea plant which eventually became the foundation of the world's Tea Trade and Industry during the next century. There were some who believed that Moneram Dewan was the discoverer who led Major Robert Bruce to it; but it was Charles Bruce, his brother, who played a significant role in the development of tea culture in India during the ensuing twenty years.

As we have realised, the East India Company at first was averse to the idea of starting any tea plantation in India; but its officials in the country were eager and the discovery of the indigenous growth of tea in Assam acted as a catalyst in the great movement to develop the industry in the country. If there was difficulty in the early stages, it came largely from the application of Chinese tea labour since the general belief persisted that only such imported methods of tea manufacture were the safe ones to follow. This belief, however, lasted for a while till experience with Assam tea and the response to the indigenous tea in London overcame existing influences and the foundation of a truly Indian Tea Industry was laid.

An index of the steady rise in Britain's consumption of Indian tea can be seen from the figures of her tea imports. In 1836, the import of tea into Britain reached 49 million lbs. and all of it was China tea. Two years later, India sent her first consignment of Assam tea to London to be sold there, on January 10, 1839. In 1859, the last year of the East India Company before the crown took over, Britain imported 69 million lbs. of which only 2 million or 3 per cent came from India. By the close of the century Britain was importing about 250 million lbs. of tea of which 55 per cent came from India, 37 per cent from Ceylon and only 5 per cent from China.

In 1900, Indian production reached 170.5 million lbs., with exports at 164.6 million lbs. and out of which 154 million lbs. went to Great Britain. Within another five years Indian exports reached 214 million lbs., and India became the leading tea supplier to the world and she has retained that position.

Today the total output of this industry is over 779 million lbs.—176 million lbs. in South India and the rest in North-East India. It accounts for about 20% of the country's total exports in value.

Tea is the queen of beverages, and no other beverage except water is consumed by so many. Tea, a treasure of the world, is the most important non-alcoholic beverage; it is a pure, safe and helpful stimulant and one of the chief joys of life. A billion cups of tea all over the world add daily to the zest of life. They bring good cheer with health, stimulation without intoxication, and are refreshing and energising without any exacting demand on the family budget.

The tea plant is considered to be a native of Assam and the adjoining areas of Upper Burma, some regard it to be a native of southern Yunnan and Upper Indo-China. The major areas of production are situated in the northeast region comprising the Brahmaputra and Surma valleys of Assam, and Darjeeling and Jalpaiguri districts of West Bengal. These areas are the Terai, the Dooars and the Brahmaputra valley where tea is grown on the north and south banks of the river Brahmaputra. In addition, considerable quantities of tea are sown in the Cachar district in Assam and in Tripura. In North-West India a fair amount of tea is grown in Kangra, Mandi and a smaller quantity in Dehradun. Down South tea is grown on the Nilgiris, on the Kanan Devan or the High Range, Anamallais and on the slopes of the mountain stretching down to the plains of Kerala.

Brahmaputra valley. Tea is grown mostly on flat land, between 160 to 400 feet above sea level, on both banks of the river Brahmaputra. Soils are alluvial and the mostly sandy loam with some red clay. The average annual rainfall is 80–120 inches and it is well distributed. The cropping season is from April to December, May/June and October/November.

Teas of orthodox manufacture are black, clean, flinty well-twisted leaf with a good show of golden tip in the best grades, throwing creamy, strong, pungent, full-bodied top quality liquors. Teas of C.T.C. manufacture from this region are brown, rich, grainy, small leaf grades throwing exceptionally strong, coloury, pungent liquors. These teas are in great demand almost all over the world and are particularly suited for blending with flavoury teas to improve strength and colour.

The Terai and Dooars. Tea is grown on flat land and hill slopes bordering the Himalayan foot-hills, from 100–1000 feet above sea level. The average rainfall is 120–200 inches but it is not very evenly distributed. The cropping season is from March to November, with the vintage periods in spring and autumn.

The Terai and Dooars produce colour, full creamy liquoring teas. The orthodox teas are black, stylish and well-twisted, while the C.T.C. tea are hard, grainy and even. A number of gardens produce very small brown leaf Leg-cut teas which throw bright coloury liquors. These teas are in great demand by blenders for mixing with flavoury teas to contribute to colour and body.

Cachar and Tripura. Tea is mostly grown on hillocks peculiar to the region and to some extent on the flat lands surrounding them. Soils are red sand and clay with some areas of peat. The annual rainfall varies from 120–200 inches but distribution is uneven and severe winter droughts are common. The cropping season is from March to November.

Fig. 37.1. *Camellia sinensis* : Tea. The garden looks best, brightest and of course, busiest during the plucking season.

The districts of Cachar and Tripura produce black, well-made teas throwing colouty, sweet liquors very popular with blenders.

Darjeeling Tea

The town of Darjeeling in India is situated in the extreme north of the State of West Bengal, at a height of 7,000 feet, surrounded by the lower hills and valleys of the Himalayas and overlooks the State of Sikkim.

The town is clustered in a bowl among the hills, looking north toward Kanchenjungha, a mere 35 miles away and a very magnificent sight when it is to be seen. Most of Darjeeling's livelihood is derived from the tea gardens which surrounded the town on all sides, at lower levels.

Early in the nineteenth century tea seed was imported from China and planted both on the plains of N.E. India and also in these hills. But it was soon discovered than an indigenous tea plant was to be found in Assam. This proved to be more vigorous, in 'plains' conditions; it gave a large crop and the leaf was more easily harvested, and so the old 'China' bushes were gradually uprooted and replaced. The original bushed plantes in Darjeeling have still remained, they are up to 100 years old and still yielding good crops.

We have continued to use these bushes because they, and they alone, can produce the flavour for which Darjeeling tea is renowned. The crop yield per acre is small and the leaf is small in size and expensive to harvest. And yet, it is this climate and high altitude, the slow growth of leaf, which help to give to Darjeeling teas the flavour for which they are known throughout the world.

In South India, Sri Lanka, Indonesia and Africa the tea bush produces leaf throughout the whole year, but in N.E. India it hibernates in winter. Growth starts again in the spring when the tea bushes of Darjeeling are covered with a mass of small soft bushes. This is the first 'flush' when the tea made is of good quality. When this 'flush' is finished there is a lull in growth until the second 'flush' appears; this is usually small in appearance, the quantity of leaf on the bushes is not great, but this is the vintage period of the whole year.

The monsoon reaches Darjeeling about mid June and from July onwards the quality of tea is of standard character until the rains end in October. Then for a short period until the end of the season in November a small crop of 'autumnal' leaf is harvested which has a flavoury but 'thin' liquor.

The quantity of fine Darjeeling tea produced each year is comparatively small. Of the total crop of 16,000,000 lbs. from this district, the first and second flushes and the autumnal teas are highly prized. Most of these good, flavoury teas are used for blending with teas from other places; the latter add strength and colour; while the lighter liquor of the Darjeeling tea supplies the flavour to the blended mixture.

Public demand in many countries requires a 'strong colour' tea which the 'Assam' variety of bush contains; but for those who appreciate flavour they will find this in full measure in a pure Darjeeling tea.

In countries where tea is drunk without milk or sugar—as for example, in Russia—tea is appreciated for its flavour, and indeed it is true that the delicate flavour of a Darjeeling tea can best be appreciated by drinking the liquor 'straight'.

Good Darjeeling teas are indeed the champagne of teas. There is no other area in the world which can produce the 'muscatel' flavour of these fine teas produced on the mountain sides of this small district.

Darjeeling tea is grown on the mountain slopes of the Himalayas at elevations ranging from 1000 to 6000 feet above sea level. Soils are red loams and sandy loams. Annual rainfall varies between 100 and 200 inches; the winter season being fairly cold and dry. The cropping season is from April to November and vintage teas are produced in April/May and October.

Teas with exquisite aroma come from the Darjeeling district. Stylish, large leaf teas are the main feature with golden tips in the top grades. The liquors are famous for their flavour derived from the high elevation at which the teas are grown.

Kangra and Mandi. The tea plantations are on the mountain slopes of the Kangra Valley in the Himalayas, at elevations from 2000-5000 feet above sea level. The average annual rainfall but it is not evenly distributed; the winter and early summer being dry and droughty. The cropping season is from April to November.

Kangra and Mandi mostly produce green teas which are in demand in many parts of the world.

South India. Tea is grown on hill slopes in the States of Tamil Nadu, Kerala and Karnataka, the main tea districats being the Nilgiris, Nilgiri—Wynaad, High Range and Central Kerala. The plantations are at elevations ranging from 1,000 to 7,000 feet above sea level. Soils are red and yellow loams and are lateritic in origin. Most tea plantations in South India get two monsoons and the annual rainfall ranges from 50–275 inches and it is fairly well distributed throughout the year. The cropping season lasts throughout the year, and vintage teas are produced in December/January.

Fine flavoury teas are produced in the Nilgiris—stylish leaf throwing very bright, brisk, quality liquors with pungency and pronounced flavour; cup character is the dominating feature of these teas. Flavour is derived from the high elevation and prevails throughout the year in varying degrees.

Anamallai produces good, black, heavy, flinty well-made teas with a sprinkling of tips in the top grades during the tipping season and are the pride of this district. Liquors are coloury heavy, full-bodied, brisk, malty with quite useful strength and character, with cup quality during December/January.

Kerala teas are black or blackish, clean, heavy well-made grades, throwing exceptionally coloury, strong liquors with briskness and character and occasional quality. These are very useful for blending with flavoury teas of comparatively lighter liquors, and with others of different liquoring properties.

Karnataka produces black, well-made teas with malty medium liquors.

Nilgiri Tea

The Nilgiris, which literally means the "Blue Mountains" are situated in the state of Tamil Nadu in South India. The place derives its name from the blue haze that covers its wooded slopes. This range, with its half English air and rolling down is undoubtedly one of the most beautiful hill resorts in the world.

Apart from its scenic charms the region constitutes one of the most important tea-growing districts in India. It is the home of famed 'Nilgiri tea'. The Nilgiri district has about 23,000 hectares of land under tea cultivation producing nearly 34 to 35 million kg. of tea every year. The other main districts in the South are Coimbatore and the Anamallai hills in Tamil Nadu producing about 18.50 million kg. of tea and the Idukki high ranges in Kerala producing about 32 million kg. Nilgiri teas are, however, a class by themselves. They have a flavour unique to the high grown teas of South India.

The plantations are spread out over every slope, valley and plateau at elevations ranging from 30 to 2,000 metres above sea level on a soil that is predominantly red and yellow loam and lateritic in origin.

Unlike the gardens in Northern India, where tea growth slides off during a period of "winter dormancy", the gardens of the South enjoy a steady growth throughout the year. The two monsoons are a determining factor in facilitating throughout the year plucking. There are, however, two big flushing periods the first from April to May when about 25% of the annual crop is gathered, and the second from September to December fetching about 32 to 40 per cent of the annual crop. Most of the manufacturing is done in the 'Orthodox' process.

No other tea has the unique Nilgiri flavour. The characteristic is a gift of nature—a result of various natural stimuli on the plant. It almost appears as if the leaves take their special qualities from the breath-taking beauty that surrounds them. This assumption is not far from the truth. The flavour prevails throughout the year in varying degrees. Nilgiri teas are famous for their stylish leaves that produce very bright, brisk and quality liquors having body and strength. Cup character is the dominant feature of these teas.

The importance of South India as a tea-producing region is tremendous, Cochin serving as its nearest auction centre and port. The largest tea-packing factory in India belonging to the Tata-Finlay group is situated in Bangalore. Besides, both the instant tea manufacturing units are in Munar and Cholari in the South. The United Planters Association of South India (UPASI) Tea Research Station in the Anamallai hills in Coimbatore, is yet another factor contributing towards the phenomenal growth in the tea industry in this region.

Nilgiri teas a blender's dream, and a large portion of these teas find their way into overseas markets in Russia, U.K., the Middle East, U.S.A., Canada and Australia to meet the ever growing demand for the Nilgiri flavour. With the emergence of India as a packet tea exporter, packets of fresh high grown Nilgiri teas are available for consumers all over the world.

The Story of Indian Tea

The fascinating story of tea from the seed to your cup is one filled with colourful legend and romance of modern organisation and commerce in India. It is end product of the patient toil of tens of thousands of tea-growers, the ingenuity of scientists, the expert skill of the blenders, business acumen of traders, care and promptness of shippers and the service and courtesy of retailers. It has passed through many phases, thousands of hands, and across the oceans of the world to reach you and to give you satisfaction.

The tea plant is an evergreen of the *Camellia* genus and is known as *Camellia sinensis* and flourishes in warm tropical and subtropical rainy regions. The highest yield will be obtained from

Fig. 37.2. *Camellia sinensis*. Indian tea. The cured leaves are used as a beverage.

tea which is grown in tropical climate. Paradoxically, the finest quality teas are produced from leaves grown in the cooler altitudes of 1,000 to 2,000 metres. The great 'Darjeeling teas' are grown against the background of *Mount Kanchenjungha* of the Himalayas; nowhere else in the world has the 'Darjeeling flavour' been duplicated. From here come the most delicate, the most fragrant teas ever produced.

Our story starts with the tea seeds, round and hard like brown marbles. The seed itself is taken from the tea trees. Many estates have a plot of selected trees which are allowed to grow to their full size of 5 metres to 10 metres. During July to October the trees blossom and tea flowers appear. But only after a year will the seed be ripe. When the shells crack the seeds are removed and planted in the nursery beds. Within a month they germinate into seedlings and green shoots start to grow. In 9 to 12 months the young plants are ready for removal to the tea garden—their permanent home. For another four years the plants must be expertly pruned before they are ready for the first plucking. By this time they have become wide and flat-topped like a waist-high table to make the plucking easier. If tea plants were left unpruned, they would grow as high as 30 feet.

Plucking. Plucking takes place over 7 to 14 days and the deft fingers of the expert plucker (mostly women) can gather as much as 60 lb. of leaf in one day, or enough to make 15 lb. of black tea. Only two small leaves and a bud are gathered from each shoot.

In North India, during March or April the spring or 'First Flush' materialises; the 'Second Flush' comes a month later in May. After the 'Second Flush', the other flushes are not so well marked and the bush gives more or less a continuous supply of green leaf until November.

In India, plucking is carried on throughout the year. Even then, there are two big flushing periods, from April to May when about 25 per cent of the annual crop is gathered, and a second flush in September to December when about 35 to 40 per cent of the annual crop is harvested.

Commercially, tea may be divided into three basic classes:

(1) Black or fermented (2) Green or unfermented and (3) Oblong or semi-fermented.

Black tea is most important commercially and the production of major world supplies—viz., India, Ceylon, Indonesia and recently East Africa—is mostly of this type.

There are four principal operations in the preparation of black tea: (1) withering, (2) rolling; (3) fermenting, and (4) firing.

Withering. About 75% of the weight of a fresh leaf consists of water even on a dry day and nearly half of this has to be removed before the fibre of the leaf and stalk will stand the strain of rolling, without breaking up. The leaf is spread thinly over withering racks arranged one above the other horizontally, and allowed to remain there for 12 to 18 hours to lose its excessive moisture. Sometimes, heated air is forced over these racks if the atmosphere around is humid. The leaf slowly and evenly becomes soft and flaccid like soft leather and is ready for rolling.

Rolling. It imparts the characteristic twist to the leaf, breaks the leaf cells, exposes the juices to the air for fermentation to set in. After half-an-hour's rolling the leaf is removed in aluminium trolleys to a sifter and ball breaker. This machine consists of a long and flat metal sheet with perforations fixed on a frame which makes reciprocating motion. The movement causes the broken leaf and fine particles to fall below and the rest is taken out after sieving. The latter is again rolled for the second time with increased pressure. After the second roll, all the leaf still more or less green and quite flaccid removed to the fermenting room.

Fermentation. During fermentation, the tannin in tea is partly oxidised and the leaf changes colour and turns bright coppery-red. The rolled leaf is spread on tiles or aluminium or even glass sheets and the oxidation which has commenced during rolling continues, the leaf coming into contact with air. The period of fermentation generally extends from 3 to 3 1/2 hours, but this includes rolling time as well. As a general rule, the *shorter* the fermentation the more pungent the liquor: and the *longer* the fermentation the softer the liquor and deeper the colour.

Drying or firing. After the leaf has changed its colour, comes the final operation; namely *drying* or *firing*. The essential function of this process is to arrest further oxidation of the leaf and to remove all moisture excepting a small amount of roughly 3 to 5 per cent.

The driving machine is the largest machine required in a tea estate factory. The automatic tea drier is a large steel oven inside which the leaves, spread on tray, travel slowly from top to bottom while hot dry air is continuously forced into the oven. Careful regulation of temperature is essential as excessive heat will scorch the leaves while lack of it will result in improper drying.

Generally the process is known as first firing, removes only three-fourths of the total moisture of the fermented leaves. After a period of cooling, they are fed into another drier. The latter known as second firing removes the remaining moisture. The tea from this second drier is the finished product. There now remains only sorting or grading and packing before the tea is ready to be sent from the factory.

As the leaves come out of the driers, large and small broken and unbroken leaves are mixed together. Now they are sent through sieves, with graduated mesh, and the different sizes of tea are removed carefully so that final packages are of uniform-sized leaves or particles.

After sorting, the tea is graded and given various names such as *Orange Pekoe*, *Pekoe*, *Fannings* and *Dust*; but these are only indicative of size and not of quality.

The manufacturing process being now complete, the different grades of tea that come from the sorters are bulked, packed in plywood tea chests with linings of aluminium-foil and paper, and are ready for their adventurous journey to all corners of the world.

The process of making tea already described is generally known as the 'orthodox' method and is in vogue in most gardens in India. Recently, however, some import variations have been introduced in the process of manufacturing especially in North India. The variations consist of the use of a machine named C.T.C. or, to give its full name a *Crushing*, *Tearing* and *Curling machine*, all in one. Here, the rollers are either wholly or partly eliminated. The leaf after withering is lightly rolled without any pressure. Then the fine leaf is separated and the coarse leaf is fed into this machine two, three or even four times.

Leg-cut teas. Manufacture is vogue in the Dooars, Terai and in some Cachar gardens of North East India. This process eliminates withering, which is often difficult in these highly humid areas, and also produces a type of tea which is quick brewing and gives an instant liquor of good strength and colour.

Green tea. Most of the teas made in China and Japan are of this type. A small quantity is made in North India also but mainly for sale in Afghanistan, Iran and some for the American market. The essential difference between *green* and *black* varieties of tea is in the fermentation—green tea being completely unfermented. The leaf meant for the manufacture of green tea is generally plucked without stalk.

Oolong tea. It can be described as a cross between *black* and *green*. The fresh leaf is slightly withered before panning; during the process a light ferment is allowed to develop, the leaf is then rolled and fired. Its colour is slightly changed and the resultant teas are of greenish-brown colour. The Oolongs which have long enjoyed a special market in America, are now almost exclusively manufactured in Formosa.

Leaf Grades

These are made up of larger leaves after the broken grades have been sifted out. In brewing, flavour and colour come out of these grades more slowly but, given the necessary brewing time, they produce flavoury liquor. 'Orange Pekoe', 'Pekoe', and 'Pekoe Souchong' are the three generally used grades in this category.

Orange Pekoe (O.P.): This consists of long, thin, wiry leaves containing tip or bud leaf. These teas generally come from the finer portions of the shoot that is the bud, first leaf and softer parts of the stalk. The liquors are generally light or pale in colour and, it produced from high grown teas, usually flavoury.

Pekoe (P): The leaves are slightly shorter and so not wiry as those of O.P., the buds also are present. The liquors, however, have more colour and this grade is generally quicker brewing than the O.P.

Pekoe Souchong (P.S.): A bold and round leaf with pale liquors.

Broken Grades

These are of smaller and broken leaves and are roughly 80% of the crop including the dust varieties, which are also strictly to be classified under broken grades. There are 4 main grades in this category.

Broken Orange Pekoe (B.O.P.): They are much smaller than any of the leaf grades and usually contain tips, hence the word orange is added. The liquors have good colour and strength and this is one of the chief attractions.

Broken Pekoe (B.P): They are slightly larger than B.O.P. but tips or buds will be absent. The liquors are paler and are less coloury in the cup. These are mainly used as 'fillers'.

Broken Pekoe Souchong (B.P.S.): They are a little large or bolder than B.P. and in consequence lighter in the cup, but useful as 'fillers'.

Fannings or Pekoe Fannings: These are much smaller than B.P.S. and are quick brewing and give good coloured liquors.

Dusts

Finally, the smallest particles excluding 'fluff' and 'stalk' are graded as Dusts. These teas are useful in quick brewing, the liquors produced have both strength and colour. They are in a good demand for catering purposes.

Tea Board of India

The Tea Board's major functions at present are: promotion of the tea habit; helping the development of the Industry, more especially of its marginal units; mediation to secure essential goods and services; provision of educational facilities for the dependants of garden workers. For the buyers from abroad it is enabled by the Act to render effective assistance in ensuring the standard of tea shipments from India. But, the Tea Board is more important than its functions would signify. For it embodies the organised knowledge and experience of all tea interests, reflects the attitudes of the industry as a whole and is the only statutorily recognised link between the Industry and the Government.

India continues to be world's largest exporter of tea, and more cups of tea are drunk throughout the world than any other beverage—except water—because it is a good tranquilliser and at the same time acts as a mild stimulant. To relax over a cup of tea is a virtue worth cultivating before the human system, through stress and tension, is allowed to reach a stage when life seems distorted and the mind refuses to adjust itself. Tea's contribution to reduce tension and instil a sense of general comfort has been recognised today by eminent medical experts, though it is by no means a new claim for this little plant whose written origin dates back to some 5000 years. From the distant past an ancient philosopher has left this image of tea to posterity:

"*When I drink tea, I am conscious of peace,*
The cool breath of heaven rises in my sleeves
And blows my cares away."

Five Golden Steps to a Good Cup of Tea

1. Take fresh water from the cold tap and boil.
2. Warm teapot by rinsing out with hot water.
3. Put into teapot one teaspoonful of tea leaf for each cup.
4. Pour boiling water into the teapot. Cover and wait for three minutes. Give more time for bigger leaf teas.
5. Pour liquid tea from teapot into cup. Add milk or a slice of lemon and sugar to taste. Enjoy the taste and flavour of Indian tea.

INDIAN COFFEE

History. It has been stated that the coffee plant of commerce is native of Abyssinia, where it is called *bun* or *boun*, and coffee must have been used in that country from very early times. There is very fair evidence in Arabic literature that the use of coffee was introduced into Aden by a certain Sheikh Shihabuddin Dhabhani, sometime about the middle of the fifteenth century. From Yemen it spread to Mecca in 1511, then to Cairo to Damascus and Aleppo, and to Constantinople, where the first coffee house was established in 1554. The first European mention of coffee of Aleppo is in 1573. The first mention of a coffee shop in Great Britain occurs in 1652. Coffee is spoken of as being in use in France in 1640, and the first public cafe was opened in Paris in 1669. Shortly after it became general throughout Europe.

Fig. 37.3. *Coffee berries.* There was a record production of coffee in India, one lakh and twenty thousand tonnes valued at Rs. 89 crores were exported in 1977-78.

It was introduced into Ceylon by the Arabs, prior to the invasion of this island by the Portuguese. Its systematic cultivation about 1690 was undertaken by the Dutch but on the cession of their territory its cultivation was continued by the natives of Ceylon (Sri Lanka).

As regards the history of its introduction into India, most writers agree that it was brought to Mysore (now Karnataka) some three centuries ago by a Muslim pilgrim named Baba Budan, who on his return from Mecca, brought seven seeds with him. George Watt writes in his 'Dictionary of the Economic Products of India': "Coffee planting in India at the present day is concentrated in the Madras Presidency, and as a European Industry it may be said to date from Mr. Cannon's plantation at Chikmuglur in Mysore. This was established in 1830, but as a curiosity Major Bevan grew coffee in the Wynaad in 1882. It was cultivated by Mr. Cockburn on the Shevaroys in 1830; Mr. Glasson formed a plantation at Manantoddy in 1840; the plant was taken to the Nilgiris in 1846 and to Darjeeling in 1856."

Location and area. Coffee is grown in India on the sunny slopes of the Western Ghats and it spurs extending eastwards where the ecological conditions are ideal for the growth of firstclass coffee. The F.A.O. has listed India as one of the eight countries in the world possessing optimum conditions for the growing of coffee.

The total area under coffee in India is 3,20,570 acres (or 1,29,730 hectares). About 58% of this coffee area is in the Karnataka State, 20% is in the Tamil Nadu State and 21% in the Kerala State. The remaining 1% is scattered, in small pockets in Andhra Pradesh, Maharashtra, Orissa, Assam and West Bengal States, besides the Andamans.

India produces about 100,000 metric tonnes of coffee every year. About 60,000 metric tonnes are exported to different destinations like U.S.A., Russia, West Germany, France, Italy, Netherlands, Sweden, U.K., Belgium and Canada. Indian Coffee in all grades—is among the best in the world and is used to blend with coffees of other origin to improve the quality.

Two varieties. Two main varieties of coffee are grown in India. They are *Coffea arabica* Linn.; and *Coffea robusta* Linden.

Indian Coffee is processed in two ways, i.e., by wet process (washed coffee) and by dry process (unwashed coffee). The washed coffee is known as Plantation or Parchment coffee. The unwashed coffee is called cherry coffee. Thus according to the process, coffee under arabica and robusta is described as under:

	ARABICA	**ROBUSTA**
Wet Process (*i.e.*, washed coffee)	Plantation	Parchment
Dry Process (*i.e.*, unwashed coffee)	Cherry	Cherry

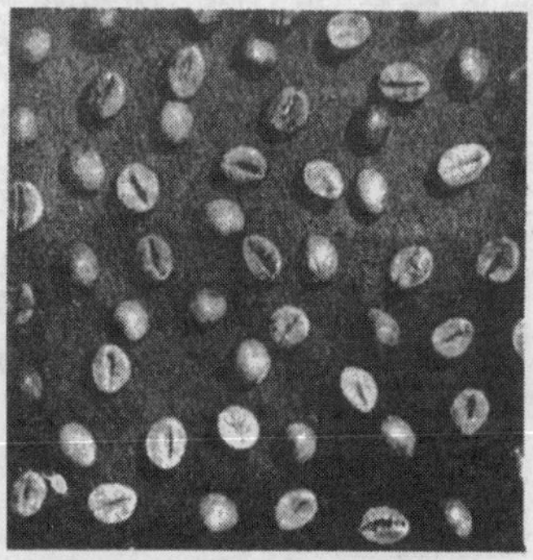

Fig. 37.4. Indian coffee. Coffee beans of *Coffea arabica.*

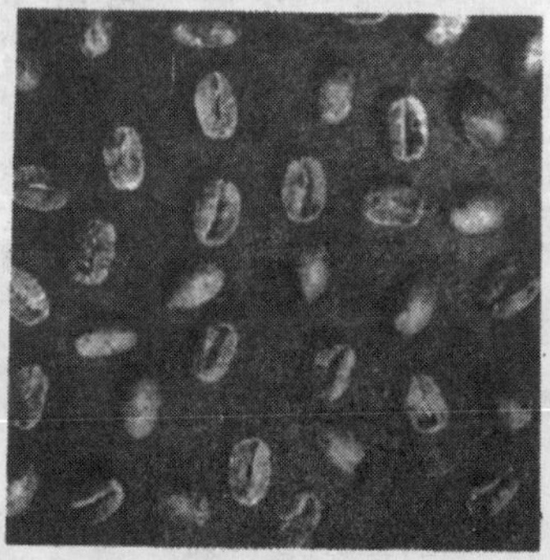

Fig. 37.5. Indian coffee. Coffee beans of *Coffea robusta.*

Plantation coffee. Arabica coffee processed by the wet or washed method is called Plantation coffee. This is an elaborate and time-consuming process in which the outer skin of the fruit and the mucilaginous matter beneath it are removed, by pulping and subsequent washing with fresh water, channelled from the springs in coffee-growing areas. The pulping and washing release the coffee beans from the coffee berries. But each bean is still encased in a soft parchment covering. The parchment-covered coffee is then dried in the sun on barbecues in the estates. Coffee in this form is known as Parchment coffee.

Curing. Parchment coffee is sent to curing works where it is further dried in the sun, if necessary, to a moisture content of not more than 10 percent. The well-dried parchment coffee is fed through the peeling machine to remove the thin brittle parchment cover.

The beans obtained are then graded according to shape and size, and carefully garbled by hand, or using electronic sorters and pneumatic separators to remove blemished and defective beans. The final product of these processes gives the Plantation coffee of commerce.

Cherry coffee. The other method of preparing Arabica coffee for the market is simpler. The berries are harvested, dried in the sun till their outer skin, the parchment cover and pulpy matter in between, dry up to form a thick husk leaving the beans loose inside. The dried cherry is then decorticated by passing through a huller, graded and garbled according to prescribed standards. The final produce of this process is known as Arabica cherry coffee or simply cherry coffee.

Robusta coffee. Robusta coffee is also processed by both wet and dry methods, and the resultant beans are known in trade parlance as Robusta Parchment or washed Robusta and Robusta cherry respectively.

Characteristics. The two types of coffee have certain characteristics:

Variety	*Type*	*Characteristics*
Arabica	Plantation	Long and wide beans, greyish or bluish in colour.
	Cherry	Same as above, but colour golden brown to brown.
Robusta	Plantation (Parchment)	Broad oval beans, smaller in size than Arabica, greyish in colour.
	Cherry	Same as above, but colour golden brown to brown.

Grading. Both Arabica and Robusta can have round beans, called PEABERRY (PB) or flat seeds called FLATS. Classification into A or B or AB is done according to the size of seeds.

The main grades of coffee released for export are Plantation A, B and Triage; Arabica Cherry AB and Triage; Robusta Cherry AB and Triage; Robusta Parchment AB. The main grades are tabulated below:

Arabica Plantation		*Arabica Cherry*		*Robusta Parchment*		*Robusta Cherry*	
Grade	*Sieve Size (mm)*	*Grade*	*Sieve Size (mm)*	*Grade*	*Sieve Size (mm)*	*Grade*	*Sieve Size (mm)*
PB	—	PB	—	PB	—	PB	—
A	6.65 and above	AB	6.00	AB	6.00	AB	6.00
B	6.00						
T	5.50	T	5.50	T	5.50	T	5.50

Coffee board. The production, internal marketing, export marketing, quality control, research, etc., are controlled by the Coffee Board which is a Statutory Body under the Ministry of Commerce of the Government of India. All coffee produced in India is delivered to the Coffee Board, Bangalore, a statutory organization, comprising representatives of coffee growers, curers, traders, workers, consumers and others connected with the industry.

Marketing. One of the major functions of the Coffee Board is the marketing of Indian coffee, through a common pool (as prescribed by the Indian Coffee Act). At the beginning of each season the coffee crop is estimated and after making provision for the internal market, the export allotment is made, so that the coffee trade may operate on the assurance of known quantities of coffee available for export. This quantity is subsequently increased, if warranted by actual crop realisations.

Exports. Coffee for export is sold in open auctions in which exporters who have registered with the Board, bid for the lots. Foreign firms can participate in these export sales by registering their names with the Coffee Board, through their Agents or Branch offices in India.

Export auctions are held once in two to three weeks. The dates of the sales are widely notified in advance. Facilities are provided for drawing the samples of coffee offered for sale and the despatch of the coffee to prospective buyers abroad.

Coffee is normally exported from the West Coast ports of Mangalore and Cochin. The normal packing is in new gunnies of 60 kg. net. Prices are normally quoted in rupees per 50 kg., f.o.b. New Mangalore/Cochin.

There was a record production of coffee, one lakh and twenty thousand tonnes in 1977-78. Thirty-six thousand tonnes of coffee worth Rs. 89 crores were exported in 1977-78.

Quality. Many steps are taken by the Coffee Board to ensure the export of only the best quality of Indian coffee. The measures are aimed at maintaining and improving the quality of coffee right from the stage when the coffee is a tender plant in plantations to the time it is fully cured and exported. Use of improved strains of coffee, scientific control of pests, application of balanced nutrition and extension of coffee research results to the field ensure growth of quality coffees.

Curing of the coffee is done so as to conform to rigid standards set for curing. The cured coffee is again examined by a screening panel before being made available for exports. Production of quality coffee on estates is encouraged by awarding premium points for good quality coffee. A cup testing unit has been established by the Coffee Board to select the best coffee for exports, on the basis of cup test.

Instant Coffee. India can also offer instant coffee of the highest standards in 50 gms., 100 gms. and 25 kg. bulk packings. This instant coffee is manufactured from Green Coffees of other origin to raise the quality of the latter.

Monsooned coffee. A speciality of Indian coffee is the Monsooned coffee, which is in good demand in several countries of Europe, particularly the Scandinavian countries.

Monsooning of coffee is done by coffee curers on the West Coast of India. Monsooned coffee had its origin in the days of sailing ships, when it took about six months for unwashed coffee to be sent to Europe. During this period of voyage, the coffee in the damp holds of the ship lost its original colour and acquired a special flavour which has been liked by consumers in Norway, France and Switzerland. With the opening of the Suez and speedy transport of steamships, consumers in Europe complained that they missed the special flavour of the unwashed Indian coffee ! The curers on the West Coast rose to the occasion and perfected the process known as 'monsooning', by which coffee acquired the special flavour. Indian monsooned coffee is coffee with a golden colour.

With the outbreak of the South-West Monsoon, late in May or early in June, unwashed coffee (Arabica Cherry or Robusta Cherry coffees) is evenly spread, about 4 to 6 inches thick, in airy godowns, open on all sides. It is racked, from time to time, for about four or five days. It is packed loose in gunny bags and stacked in piles with sufficient space between rows, to enable the monsoon air to circulate freely around each bag.

The coffee beans are bulked and repacked, once a week, or they are poured from one leaf to another, prevent their getting mouldy and ensure even monsooning. In about a month and a half, the coffee assumes golden colour, when it is considered to be fully monsooned. At this stage, the coffee beans are carefully hand-garbled to remove those beans that are not up to the required standard. After mild fumigation treatment to prevent attacks by weevils, the monsooned coffee is ready for shipment.

Monsooned coffee is generally sold for export during October to December, every year. The grades offered for sale are *Monsooned Malabar* AA, *Monsooned Basanally* and *Monsooned Robusta* AB.

Why Indian Coffee is one of the Finest? Lovers of good coffee often wonder how Indian coffee is distinctive, delicious and distinguishable. To comprehend fully the principal reasons for Indian coffee being one of the world's finest coffees is to understand pretty well a whole range of coffee facts and operations in the country.

Nature with its generous Indian climate and rich soil, pampers coffee's growth. Careful scientific cultivation of the coffee on hill slopes, programmed picking of the coffee fruits by deft human hands and the gentle painstaking manner in which they are processed, unlock the full flavour latent in every bean. Rigid assessment of quality leads to the export of only the finest beans accounting for the superiority and fine aroma of India's high grown mild coffees.

Many of the different growths of Indian coffee, like Biligiris, Bababudans, other Mysores, Coorgs, Nilgiris, Naidubattams, Shevaroys, Anamallais, Pulneys, Nelliampathis, and Nilagiris Wynaad are familiar to importers of coffee in different countries of the world, as being synonymous, with supreme quality coffee. This is because the Indian Coffee Industry has to its credit three hundred years of continuous service in growing and making available high grown, good quality, mild coffee.

Indian coffee has a high reputation in the world market. This is because of the high quality of Indian coffee and the infinite care taken by the Coffee Board to maintain high standard at each stage of processing Indian coffee from the seed to the cup and special attention given to the screening and selection of only the best coffee for export, so that coffee connoisseurs around the world can always enjoy the superior and fine aroma of India's high-grown mild coffees.

38
CHAPTER

Rubber and its Products

Rubber is obtained from the *latex*, of various plants of tropical or sub-tropical regions. Most of the rubber plants belong to the Moraceae, Euphorbiaceae and Apocynaceae families. Though several species are available as sources of rubber, yet *Hevea brasiliensis* supersedes all. The cultivated *Hevea* trees, the so-called plantation rubber furnish about 98% of the supply. Rubber is the most recent of the major crops of the world. The industry is little more than a century old, and cultivation has been carried on about 80 years or so.

The latex occurs in latex tubes or latex vessels found in the various parts of the plants. Generally the commercial rubber is obtained from the lower part of the stem of tree. Latex is a gummy white liquid full of minute globules. It is mixture of water, hydrocarbons, resins, oils, proteins, acids, salts, sugars and caoutchouc. The physical and chemical properties of rubber have been considered separately in the following paragraph:

PROPERTIES OF RUBBER

Physical properties. The physical properties of rubber vary with temperature. Natural rubber is soft and translucent at 20°C ; when chilled to 0–10°C, it becomes hard and opaque ; at the temperature of liquid air, it is brittle and transparent like glass. At temperatures exceeding 25°, rubber loses elasticity and becomes sticky. Rubber melts to a viscous fluid at about 200°C. Rubber is insoluble in water and is unaffected by alkalies or moderately strong acids. It is soluble in benzene, naphtha, carbon disulphide, ether, chloroform and chlorinated hydrocarbons. When rubber is dissolved in a solvent, it first swells to gel-like consistency and then forms a solution. The elastic property of rubber is closely related to its molecular structure. Rubber is amorphous in the unstretched state, but shows crystalline behaviour when kept at 0° for a long time or when stretched. Rubber is one of the best insulating and dielectric materials available.

Chemical properties. First grade latex plantation rubber contains : rubber hydrocarbon 92–94%, resin 3%, protein 2% and ash 0.2% in Hevea rubber. Rubber hydrocarbon, also known as caoutchouc, is colourless, odourless, transparent and elastic. It consists of long chains of isoprene units connected end to end through 1 : 4 linkages. Rubber forms compounds with halogens, halogen acids and metallic halides, ozone and oxides of nitrogen. Hydrogenation at elevated temperatures and pressures in the presence of a catalyst gives fully saturated hydrorubber. Rubber is oxidised by nitric acid, potassium permanganate and hydrogen peroxide.

Hevea Aubl. (Euphorbiaceae).

A small genus of trees distributed chiefly in the Amazon region of South America. One species *Hevea brasiliensis* ; the source of Para Rubber, has been introduced in India and cultivated as a plantation crop.

Hevea brasiliensis (H.B.K.) Muell. Arg. (Eng. Para rubber ; Verna. *Rabar*). It is a large tree attaining a height of 60–100 ft. or more and a girth of 8–12 ft. The stem is smooth, straight, generally unbranched up to a considerable height, with a much branched leafy canopy. It is considered indigenous to the Amazon valley of Brazil, Venezuela, Peru, Ecuador and Colombia.

The rubber plantation industry in South-East Asia dates back to 1876 ; when 1,900 seedlings raised at Kew, were despatched to Ceylon. Plantations were raised and by 1930 a number of strains had been developed by breeding and selection, some of them superior to the stock originally obtained from Kew.

In India, rubber plantations were first started in Kerala state in 1905. Since then many other areas have been brought under rubber cultivation. At present, Kerala is the most important rubber producing state in India with plantations concentrated particularly in Kottayam and Quilon districts. Kanyakumari district in Tamil Nadu state is also an important rubber-growing area; there are small areas in Coimbatore and Nilgiris in Tamil Nadu state, Coorg in Karnataka state and in Andaman Islands. Rubber is produced in India, in plantations ranging from less than one acre to about 3,000 acres in area. Areas above 50 acres are classified as large estates and those of 50 acres and below, as Holdings.

Fig. 38.1. The rubber plantations in India registered phenomenal growth since independence. Production increased ten-fold in a span of 30 years and area enhanced four-fold while average yield shot up 2½ times. As a result from an importer of 35,000 tonnes of natural rubber in 1963, India gradually attained self-sufficiency and emerged a net exporter since 1973. Natural rubber, has spread now to over 230,000 hectares producing annually over 150,000 tonnes valued at Rs. 1200 million. Over a million people depend on this industry for their livelihood.

Hevea brasiliensis thrives in the tropical belt of the equator, in which the climate is warm, humid and equable and the temperature ranges from 74°F to 95°F. It requires a well distributed rainfall of 70 to 100 inches per annum. In South India, the plantations are located mostly in areas with a prolonged dry season and severe South West monsoon. The temperature ranges from 60°F to 95°F and there is a large variation between winter and summer temperatures.

Hevea brasiliensis thrives best in deep, well drained loamy soils. The soils in the rubber plantations of South India are red lateritic or clayey loams. The soils are generally deep and well drained. They are fairly rich in nitrogen, but poor in mineral constituents.

Rubber is a long duration tree crop which stays on the ground for several years. The economic life of rubber tree is 30–35 years. Newly opened jungle is considered to be the most suitable for rubber cultivation. The area to be planted is cleared of the jungle by cutting down the undergrowth and felling the trees. The cleared area is then lined and marked and terraces prepared. Provision is made for roads and drainage.

Tapping. Para rubber (*Hevea brasiliensis*) is valued for the latex obtained by tapping, *i.e.*, opening up the latex vessels situated in the bark with a sharp incision on the main trunk. When the vessels are cut, the latex flows out, quickly at first, then slowly, and finally coagulating on the cut surface. The tree is rested after each cut for varying periods according to age, climate and condition of the tree. When the tree is tapped again, the coagulated latex of 'plug' from the old cut surface is removed and a thin strip of bark is cut off. During the first tapping, only a small amount of viscous latex exudes. The flow increases with each successive tapping, the cuts being opened always at an angle to the horizontal. Usually, the cut extends half way around the trunk, but quite often, may completely encircle it.

Yield. The average yield of latex per acre in India from unselected ordinary seedling trees is 300 lb. The yield from budgrafted trees of approved clones and from clonal seedlings of approved parentage is twice, or more. An average yield of 700–800 lb. per acre has been obtained with improved planting materials in India.

Latex. Fresh latex is usually milky white in colour. The latex drawn from a tree which has been rested for sometime is yellow. The latex obtained by tapping is essentially a colloidal suspension of rubber particles in an aqueous serum.

Fresh latex is readily susceptible to enzymic and bacterial action leading to acid formation, and preservatives and bactericides are usually added to latex at the time of collection to inhibit acid development and consequent coagulation.

Raw rubber. Rubber of commerce is obtained from latex of *Hevea brasiliensis* by coagulation; rolling and drying. Two forms of raw rubber are known in trade, namely, *Smoked Sheet Rubber* and *Crepe Rubber*.

Grading. The system adopted in our country for grading raw rubber is based on the type description of the Rubber Manufacturers' Association and endorsed by the Rubber Trade Association of New York. These types are recognised as universal standards by producing and consuming countries alike.

Packing. The raw rubber is packed in bales in accordance with R.M.A. packing specifications.

Marketing. The raw rubber is marketed in the form of dry rubber. About two-thirds of total production is marketed by managing agents after grading. Petty merchants and dealers sell the collection to the nearest depot of a purchasing firm or take them to dealers in Kottayam, Trivandrum, Trichur or other market centres.

Uses. The raw rubber as such has few important applications. Its chief uses are in making insulation tapes, shoe soles, adhesives and erasers.

Rubber is used for the production of a wide variety of products utilized in industries and services, and for domestic purposes. It has been estimated that about 50,000 different products are fabricated from rubber directly or indirectly. Tyres and tubes for automobiles and cycles account for about 75% of the total rubber consumption. About 6% is used for footwear ; about 4% for wire and cable insulations. Among miscellaneous manufactured articles mention may be made of rubberised fabrics, motor mountings for absorbing vibrations and shocks, washers and gaskets, transmission and conveyor belting, garden hose, fire hose and hose for gasoline, pneumatic tools, paints, sports goods, household and hospital supplies, such as sheets, hot water bags, ice bags, surgeon's gloves, bathing caps and prophylactics, toys, such as balls, dolls and balloons, erasers and rubber bands and adhesives. Metals are coated with rubber to protect them from wear and corrosion. Sponge rubber from foamed latex finds uses in cushioning, seating and bedding. Elastic fabrics are made from latex threads. It is also employed in the fabrication of battery boxes, fountain pen barrels, tobacco pipe stems, telephones and combs.

Natural rubber latex, in preserved and concentrated forms, finds many commercial applications. Compounded latex is largely replacing rubber solutions for the manufacture of such articles as balloons, gloves, contraceptive appliances, finger stalls and teats. Over 65% of the latex is used in the manufacture of foam rubber and the rest for dipped goods, fabric coatings, impregnation and moulded goods. Uncured latex is used as an adhesive in footwear manufacture. The bulk of latex goods is made from vulcanised latex.

Reclaimed rubber prepared from discarded rubber products and rubber scrap, is used alone or in admixture with raw rubber in the manufacture of heels, soles, mechanical rubber goods, tyres and adhesives for use in fabric dipping, carpet backing, flooring, etc., and hard rubber used for battery containers, tubes and rods.

OTHER RUBBERS

Besides *Hevea*, several plants have been tried from time to time as sources of rubber as shown in the table :

Table 38.1.

Rubber plants percentage	*Rubber hydro-carbon*	*Resin*	*Protein*	*Ash*
Hevea brasiliensis	94	3	2	0.2
Castilla elastica	93	6	0.5	0.1
Landolphia thollonii	93	5	1	0.5
L. owariensis	93	6	0.1	1.0
L. kirkii	91	8	0.1	1.0
Taraxacum kok-saghyz	90		2	3.0
Funtumia elastica	88	8	3	0.5
Manihot glaziovii	88	4	6	1.5
Cryptostegia grandiflora	88	9	2	0.3
Ficus elastica	78	20	1	0.5
Parthenium argentatum	72	22	3	2.5

Of these the Russian Dandelion (*Taraxacum kok-saghyz* Rodin) and the Mexican Guayule *Parthenium argentatum*. A. Gray) may specially be mentioned. The Russian Dandelion is grown on C. 2,000,000 acres of land in Russia and rubber of good quality is reported to be obtained from the roots of the plant. The Mexican Guayule is extracted from the whole plant; it is of inferior quality. Other rubber producing plants of local importance are — *Manihot glaziovii* Muell. Arg. (Ceara rubber), *Castilla elastica* Cerv. (Castilla or Panama rubber), *Hancornia speciosa* Gomez (Mangabeira rubber), *Ficus elastica* Roxb. (India or Assam rubber) and *Funtumia elastica* Stapf. (Lagos silk rubber).

Question Bank

N.B. Questions from UGC Question Bank

LONG ANSWER QUESTIONS

1. Give an account of drugs obtained from plants (15 minutes; 15 marks).
2. Assume that you and a small group of your friends are transported to an uninhabited island in the Indian Ocean to live and that you are permitted to take the seeds or propagative organs of 12 species of plants with you. List them in order of preference (mention the botanical name and family) and give reasons for your selection (10 mts.; 10 mks.).
3. By means of outline sketches only, show the morphology of the economically important of any five of the following plants: saffron, opium, poppy, cocoa, black pepper, citrus, coffee, and clove; give the botanical name of each source and comment on the uses (15 mts.; 15 mks.).
4. State the botanical names, families and morphology of the parts from which the following are obtained: (*a*) cotton, (*b*) jute, (*c*) coir, (*d*) hemp. How would you differentiate one from the other? (15 mts.; 15 mks.).
5. Name five important drug plants of India and write detailed account of any two of them. (15 mts.; 15 mks.).
6. List the chief fatty oil-yielding crops in India. Classify the oils on the basis of their drying properties and mention their uses. What do you mean by the term hydrogenation. (15 mts.; 15 mks.).
7. By simple sketches only, show the morphology of the economically important parts of the following: clove, cashew, coriander and black pepper. Mention their latin names and uses. (15 mts.; 15 mks.).
8. What are essential oils? Give a brief account of the botany, cultivation, extraction and uses of important essential oils produced in India. (15 mts.; 15 mks.).
9. Give the method of extraction, properties and economic uses of the following: (*a*) groundnut oil, (*b*) linseed oil and (*c*) castor oil. (10 mts.; 10 mks.).
10. Name any *four* fibre yielding plants, giving their families. Describe the methods of fibre extraction from them and their commercial uses. (15 mts.; 15 mks.).
11. Give the methods of cultivation of any *one* of the following: (*a*) cotton; (*b*) rubber. (10 mts.; 10 mks.).
12. Explain how the latex is processed to get rubber? (10 mts.; 10 mks.).
13. The whole coconut tree is economically useful. Justify the above statement. (20 mts.; 10 mks.).

SHORT ANSWER QUESTIONS

1. Write what do you know of the source and economic importance of the cork. (3 minutes; 3 marks).
2. Write what do you know of the source and economic importance of coconut. (5 mts.; 5 mks.).
3. List the botanical names of six plants from Cruciferae (Brassicaceae) used as vegetables and mention the morphology of the useful part in each. (5 mts.; 5 mks.).
4. Name the species of cottons exploited for commercial purposes. How would you distinguish between the Old World and New World cottons? (5 mts.; 5 mks.).
5. How is opium obtained and how is it used? (5 mts.; 5 mks.).
6. Write note on any *one* of the following:

   (*a*) *Oryza*. (5 mts.; 5 mks.).

   (*b*) *Rauwolfia*. (5 mts.; 5 mks.).

   (*c*) *Cannabis*. (6 mts.; 6 mks.).

7. Give botanical names of *three* important timber-yielding plants of India. (3 mts.; 3 mks.).
8. Name the sources of any *one* of the following products; mention the plant part from which they are obtained and indicate the main areas of cultivation of these plants in India.
   (*a*) Ephedrine. (3 mts.; 3 mks.).
   (*b*) Tobacco. (3 mts.; 3 mks.).
   (*c*) Clove. (3 mts.; 3 mks.).
   (*d*) Saffron. (3 mts.; 3 mks.).
9. Describe the medicinal importance of *Adhatoda*, *Zingiber* and *Penicillium*. (6 mts.; 6 mks.).
10. What is the morphology of the edible part in (*i*) orange, (*ii*) potato, (*iii*) papaya? (3 mts.; 3 mks.).
11. Distinguish between any *one* pair of the following:
    (*a*) Ring porous and diffuse porous. (3 mts.; 3 mks.).
    (*b*) Sap wood and heart wood. (3 mts.; 8 mks.).
    (*c*) Beedi and cigarette. (3 mts.; 3 mks.).
    (*d*) Green tea and black tea. (3 mts.; 3 mks.).
    (*e*) Lint and fuzz. (3 mts.; 3 mks.).
12. Name a plant each yielding a worldwide commodity which owes its origin to (*i*) epidermis, (*ii*) tuberous stem, (*iii*) periderm, and (*iv*) whole leaf.
13. what plant materials (mention Latin names) are used in manufacture of essential oils. (3 mts.; 3 mks.).
14. Write short note on any *one* of the following:
    (*a*) Indigenous raw materials of paper production. (5 mts.; 5 mks.).
    (*b*) Wood seasoning. (5 mts.; 5 mks.).
    (*c*) Molasses. (5 mts.; 5 mks.).
    (*d*) Papain. (5 mts.; 5 mks.).
15. How would you distinguish any *one* of the following pairs:
    (*a*) *Curcuma* from *Zingiber*. (3 mts.; 3 mks.).
    (*b*) Starch of wheat from that of rice and maize (3 mts.; 3 mks.).
    (*c*) Essential oil from fatty oil. (3 mts.; 3 mks.).
    (*d*) Fibres of cotton from those of jute. (3 mts.; 3 mks.).
16. Give the botanical names, morphological nature of plant parts yielding economic products, and uses of any *one* of the following:
    (*a*) Sugarcane. (3 mts.; 3 mks.).
    (*b*) Jute. (3 mts.; 3 mks.).
    (*c*) Potato. (3 mts.; 3 mks.).
    (*d*) Wheat. (3 mts.; 3 mks.).
17. Write botanical names of any *six* plants in which either the stem or the leaf is of economic importance.
18. Explain giving suitable reasons for the following:
    Farmers generally use leguminous plants, with nodulated roots, for rotation of crops. (5 mts.; 5 mks.).
19. Write briefly: Extraction of essential oils from rose and Sandal wood. (3 mts.; 3 mks.).
20. In India cotton textile industry is largely confined to Bombay and other parts of Western India, whereas jute industry is mostly restricted to Calcutta and other parts of West Bengal. Comment. (5 mts.; 5 mks.).
21. Write short note on any one of the following:
    (*a*) Bye-products of sugar industry. (5 mts.; 5 mks.).
    (*b*) Extraction of essential oils. (5 mts.; 5 mks.).
    (*c*) Important Indian spices. (5 mts.; 5 mks.).

22. *Cannabis sativa* hits the front lines in many of the leading magazines of the world. Comment. (5 mts.; 5 mks.).
23. Write a short note on Soybean (5 mts.; 5 mks.).
24. Distinguish between any *one* of the following pairs:
    (*a*) Pine wood and teak wood. (3 mts.; 3 mks.).
    (*b*) Fennel and Coriander. (3 mts.; 3 mks.).
    (*c*) Essential oil and fatty oil. (3 mts.; 3 mks.).
    (*d*) Flue curing and sun curing. (3 mts.; 3 mks.).
25. Name the principal states in India in which the following are cultivated:
    (*i*) Jute, (*ii*) coconut, (*iii*) tea, (*iv*) mango. and (*v*) black pepper. (3 mts.; 3 mks.).
26. How does milling affect the quality of rice, (3 mts.; 3 mks.).
27. Name drugs of plant origin which could be used in the following:
    Malaria, hypertension, rheumatism, heart disorders and dysentery. (3 mts.; 3 mks.).
28. Write what you know of the source and economic importance of Ginger. (3 mts.; 3 mks.).
29. Write briefly: Tobacco and health hazards. (5 mts.; 5 mks.).
30. Write briefly: Harvesting, grading and processing of tea. (5 mts.; 5 mks.).
31. Write briefly: Origin of wheat (5 mts.; 5 mks.).
32. Write briefly: Principal uses of wood. (5 mts.; 5 mks.).
33. Write briefly: Extraction of sugar and by-products of sugar industry. (5 mts.; 5 mks.).
34. What are the principal sources of vegetable oils in India. List the four major uses of oils.
35. Give the botanical name of the plant yielding any *one* of the following product and explain its morphology and economic importance:
    (*a*) Reserpine. (5 mts.; 5 mks.).
    (*b*) Coffee. (5 mts.; 5 mks.).
    (*c*) Rose-wood. (5 mts.; 5 mks.).
36. Name a useful plant product that is derived from (*i*) epidermis, (*ii*) whole leaf, (*iii*) mesocarp, (*iv*) periderm, (*v*) tuberous root and (*vi*) heart wood.
37. Mention some algae as source of food to human beings. (3 mts.; 3 mks.).
38. Mention the importance of Gramineae (Poaceae) as a source of food. (3 mts.; 3 mks.).
39. Write notes on: Economic uses of tannins. (6 mts.; 6 mks.).
40. Write any *three* economic uses of Euphorbiaceae members. (3 mts.; 3 mks.).
41. Outline the processing of coffee by wet method. (3 mts.; 3 mks.).
42. What kind of soil will be preferred for growing rubber. (2 mts.; 2 mks.).
43. How will you start to process the Paddy grains soon after harvesting them (Mention only the first two steps.). (2 mts.; 3 mks.).
44. Mention 5 rubber yielding plants and their families, cultivated in India. (2 mts.; 5 mks.).
45. The natural habit of tea is tree but under cultivation it is a shrub. How is it so? (2 mts.; 2 mks.).
46. Mention the other uses of Paddy, other than the grains being used as a staple food. (2 mts.; 2 mks.).
47. Give the technical name of the fruit and mention the morphology of the useful parts and their actual use in the fruits of the following:
    (*a*) Mango, (*b*) Cashew and (*c*) Jack fruit. (8 mts.; 12 mks.).
48. State what you know about the morphological nature of the following: (i) Apple, (ii) Cauliflower, (iii) Radish.
49. Give the technical name of the fruit and mention the morphology of the edible portion of the following:
    (*i*) Tomato, (*ii*) Rice, (*iii*) Coco, (*iv*) Apple and (*v*) Groundnut. (5 mts.; 10 mks.).

50. Which is the active principle in coffee? (2 mts.; 2 mks.).
51. How is the mesocarp of coconut fruit used in industry? (3 mts.; 2 mks.).
52. Name any two economic uses of cotton other than using it in textile industry. (2 mts.; 3 mks.).

SIMPLE QUESTIONS

1. Arrange the following in the order of their food value: tapioca, groundnut, soybean, potato, rice and Citrus. (2 mts.; 2 mks.).
2. Name five plant products which earn foreign exchange for our country (2 mts.; 2 mks.).
3. Mention the titles and names of authors of four books on economic botany. (2 mts.; 2 mks.).
4. What is the nature of the chief food reserve in (*i*) tapioca, (*ii*) mango, (*iii*) soybean, (*iv*) maize. (2 mts.; 2 mks.).
5. Which of the Indian states are the leading producers for Cane sugar, Sandal wood, Potato, Jute and Teak. (2 mts.; 2 mks.).
6. What are the 'active' chemical principles in the following: Coffee, Ergot, Opium, Rauwolfia and Tobacco? (3 mts.; 3 mks.).
7. What plant materials (mention Latin names) are used in the manufacture of any one of the following:
   (*a*) Sugar. (2 mts.; 2 mks.).
   (*b*) Spice powder for flavouring foods. (2 mts.; 2 mks.).
   (*c*) Paper. (2 mts.; 2 mks.).
   (*d*) Soap. (2 mts.; 2 mks.).
8. Name the Research Institute along with its location where improvement work in any one of the following crop plants is being carried out in India:
   (*a*) Jute. (1 mt.; 1 mk.).
   (*b*) Wheat. (1 mt.; 1 mk.).
   (*c*) Sugarcane. (1 mt.; 1 mk.).
   (*d*) Rice. (1 mt.; 1 mk.).
   (*e*) Potato. (1 mt.; 1 mk.).
9. Give the botanical name from which the following is obtained:
   (*a*) Caffeine. (1 mt.; 1 mk.).
   (*b*) Papain. (1 mt.; 1 mk.).
   (*c*) Morphine. (1 mt.; 1 mk.).
   (*d*) Hashish. (1 mt.; 1 mk.).
10. Which of the Indian states are leading producers of the following:
   (*a*) Tea. (1 mt.; 1 mk.).
   (*b*) Tobacco. (1 mt.; 1 mk.).
   (*c*) Rubber. (1 mt.; 1 mk.).
   (*d*) Banana. (1 mt.; 1 mk.).
   (*e*) Belladonna. (1 mt.; 1 mk.).
   (*f*) Deodar. (1 mt.; 1 mk.).
11. What is the centre of the origin of the following:
   (*a*) Coffee. (1 mt.; 1 mk.).
   (*b*) Cocoa. (1 mt.; 1 mk.).
   (*c*) Clove. (1 mt.; 1 mk.).
   (*d*) Cinchona. (1 mt.; 1 mk.).
   (*e*) Groundnut. (1 mt.; 1 mk.).
   (*f*) Black pepper (1 mt.; 1 mk.).

(*g*) Eucalyptus. (1 mt.; 1 mk.).
(*h*) Mango. (1 mt.; 1 mk.).
(*i*) Red pepper. (1 mt.; 1 mk.).
(*j*) Soybean. (1 mt.; 1 mk.).

12. Mention one important source (botanical name) for the following:
(*a*) Atropine. (1 mt.; 1 mk.).
(*b*) Cigar. (1 mt.; 1 mk.).
(*c*) Match sticks. (1 mt.; 1 mk.).
(*d*) Tapioca. (1 mt.; 1 mk.).
13. How is hydrogenation of oil done? (2 mts.; 2 mks.).
14. In what ways does paddy differ from rice? (2 mts.; 2 mks.).
15. Where did maize originate? (2 mts.; 2 mks.).
16. What makes a wood heavy? (2 mts.; 2 mks.).
17. Give the botanical name and the morphology of the product used in
(*a*) Cinchona. (1 mt.; 1 mk.).
(*b*) Groundnut. (1 mt.; 1 mk.).
(*c*) Rubber. (1 mt.; 1 mk.).
(*d*) Coir. (1 mt.; 1 mk.).
(*e*) Sorghum. (1 mt.; 1 mk.).
(*f*) Cardamum. (1 mt.; 1 mk.).
(*g*) Castor. (1 mt.; 1 mk.).
18. Describe how Cichorium intybus is used as an economically important product. (2 mts.; 2 mks.).
19. Name any two fibre-yielding plants. (2 mts.; 2 mks.).
20. Give the botanical name which yields the following: (*a*) Rose wood, (*b*) Satin wood, (*c*) Sandal wood, (*d*) Laurel wood. (3 mts.; 4+ mks.).
21. Name two essential oil-yielding plants. (2 mts.; 2 mks.).
22. Describe the morphology of the useful part in: (*a*) Ganja. (2 mts.; 2 mks.), (*b*) Taro. (2 mts.; 2 mks.), (*c*) Cardamom (2 mts.; 2 mks.), (*d*) Groundnut (2 mts.; 2 mks.), (*e*) Pepper (2 mts.; 1 mk.), (*f*) Coriander (2 mts.; 1 mk.), (g) Cloves. (2 mts.; 1 mk.).
23. Name the plant which yields Quinine. How is it extracted? (5 mts.; 5 mks.).
24. Give the botanical name for the following:
(*a*) Bengal gram, (*b*) Green gram, (*c*) Black gram, (*d*) Red gram. (1 mt.; 4+ mks.).
25. Give the botanical name of the following:
(*a*) The plant produces Aconitum, (*b*) The plant produces cabbage, (*c*) The plant produces Melia oil, (*d*) The plant produces Bengal gram. (2 mts.; 2 mks.).
26. Name a plant for which desuckering is done. (1 mt.; 1 mk.).
27. Mention one cultivated species and one wild species of sugarcane. (1 mt.; 1 mk.).
28. Give the use of bagasse. (1 mt.; 2 mks.).
29. What is meant by retting? (2 mts.; 1 mk.).
30. Which plant produces chicory? (1 mt.; 1 mk.).
31. Give the name of the plant which produces coffee. (1 mt.; 1 mk.).
32. Describe the morphology of the useful parts of cotton. (2 mts.; 2 mks.).
33. Give the names of any two major rice research stations, their location in India. (2 mts.; 2 mks.).
34. Describe the morphology of the useful part in groundnut and cotton. (2 mts.; 2 mks.).
35. Arrange in order of highest protein value: (*a*) Soybean, (*b*) Potato, (*c*) Rice, (*d*) Wheat, (*e*) Sugarcane.
36. Give one example each of plant/plant-products used in the manufacture of following: (*a*) Macroni, (*b*) rum, (*c*) morphine, (*d*) haematoxylin. (2 mts.; 2 mks.).

MULTIPLE CHOICE QUESTIONS

1. Botanical name of jute is:
(*a*) *Cannabis sativa* (*b*) *Linum usitatissimum*
(*c*) *Corchorus capsularis* (*d*) None of the above (1 minute; 1 mark)
2. Teak wood which is obtained from Tectona grandis belongs to the family of:
(*a*) Labiatae (lamiaceae) (*b*) Verbenaceae (*c*) Rubiaceae (*d*) Apocynaceae
(1 mt.; 1 mk.).
3. Digitalis purpurea belongs to the family of:
(*a*) Papilionanceae (*b*) Acanthaceae (*c*) Scrophulariaceae (*d*) Solanaceae
(1 mt.; 1 mk.).
4. Sunhemp is obtained from:
(*a*) *Crotolaria juncea* (*b*) *Cannabis sativa* (*c*) *Musa textiles* (*d*) *Cocos nucifera*
(1 mt.; 1 mk.).
5. Cloves are obtained from Eugenia aromatica and the morphology of the product being:
(*a*) product petioles (*b*) dried pedicels (*c*) dried flower buds (*d*) dried seeds
(1 mts.; 1 mk.).
6. Botanical name of the plant that yields pararubber:
(*a*) *Ficus elastica* (*b*) *Hevea brasiliensis* (*c*) *Manihot glaziovii* (*d*) *Castilla elastica*
(1 mt.; 1 mk.).
7. Reserpine, a drug is extracted from:
(*a*) *Rauwolfia serpentina* (*b*) *Ferula asafoetida*
(*c*) *Atropa belladona* (*d*) *Digitalis purpurea* (1 mt.; 1 mk.).
8. Plant parts useful for extraction of opium from Papaver somniferum are:
(*a*) young seedlings (*b*) old leaves (*c*) unripe fruits (*d*) ripened seeds
(1 mt.; 1 mk.).
9. Botanical name of cauliflower is:
(*a*) *Brassica oleracea* var. *botrytis* (*b*) Brassica oleracea var. *gongylodes*
(*c*) *Brassica oleracea* var. *capitata* (*d*) Brassica oleracea var. *gemmifera*
(1 mt.; 1 mk.).
10. The common name of *Eleusine coracana is:*
(*a*) Ragi (*b*) Barley (*c*) Wheat (*d*) Oats
11. The cotton fibre from cotton is obtained from:
(*a*) roots (*b*) stems (*c*) seeds (*d*) leaves
12. The commercial jute fibres are:
(*a*) Phloem fibre (*b*) Xylem fibres (*c*) Interxylary fibres (1 mt.; 1 mk.).
13. Cotton fibre is derived from:
(*a*) Phloem fibres (*b*) Epidermal hairs on seed
(*c*) Outgrowth on the stem (*d*) Sclerenchymatous cells (1 mt.; 1 mk.).
14. Paddy is suitable for cultivation in:
(*a*) Red soils (*b*) Dry soils (*c*) Black soils (*d*) Irrigated soils
(1 mt.; 1 mk.).
15. The economic product of tobacco plant is:
(*a*) Flowers (*b*) Leaves (*c*) Roots (*d*) Stems
(1 mt.; 1 mk.).
16. Fibre yielding plant is:
(*a*) *Triticum* (*b*) *Pennisetum* (*c*) *Gossypium* (*d*) *Rauwolfia*
(1 mt.; 1 mk.).

17. The quality of tobacco depends mainly on:
(*a*) Curing process (*b*) Variety and curing process
(*c*) Climatic conditions in which plant grows. (*d*) Nutrition of the plant in the field (1 mt.; 1 mk.).

18. Opium is obtained from:
(*a*) dried leaves (*b*) roots
(*c*) latex from unripe capsules (*d*) seeds that are fried (1 mt.; 1 mk.).

19. Coir is obtained from
(*a*) roots of date palm tree (*b*) leaf bases of areca nut palm
(*c*) mesocarp of coconut (*d*) leaves of Cocos nucifera (1 mt.; 1 mk.).

20. The centre of origin of rice plant is:
(*a*) India (*b*) Indo-Malayan region
(*c*) India and Africa (*d*) Africa (1 mt.; 1 mk.).

21. Rubber is collected from:
(*a*) Crushing the stem of *Euphorbias.*
(*b*) Tapping the stem of *Carica papaya*
(*c*) Tapping the stem of *Hevea brasiliensis*
(*d*) Crushing the fruits and collecting the latex of *Achras sapota* (1 mt.; 1 mk.).

22. Essential oils are those:
(*a*) oils which are essential for human beings.
(*b*) oils which are essential to the plants which produce them
(*c*) oils which are used as lubricants
(*d*) oils which yield perfumes (1 mt.; 1 mk.).

23. Asafoetida is obtained by:
(*a*) exudation from the stem (*b*) extraction from the fruits
(*c*) extraction from the root (*d*) extracted from the leaves. (1 mt.; 1 mk.).

24. Short fibres are known as:
(*a*) lint (*b*) fluff (*c*) fuzz (*d*) flint (1 mt.; 1 mk.).

25. Long fibres are known as:
(*a*) flint (*b*) lint (*c*) fluff (*d*) fuzz (1 mt.; 1 mk.).

26. The bark of *Cinnamomum zeylanicum* is used as spice because of:
(*a*) A sweet flavour (*b*) Aromatic oils secreted
(*c*) Ethereal oils secreted (1 mt.; 1 mk.).

27. Corms and root tubers of Araceae have a pungent acrid taste because they contain:
(*a*) Aromatic oil (*b*) Oxalate crystals (*c*) Alkaloid (*d*) Latex (1 mt.; 1 mk.).

28. The composition of the cotton fibre is:
(*a*) cellulose (*b*) callose (*c*) chitin (*d*) pectin (1 mt.; 1 mk.).

29. Tea can be grown:
(*a*) at sea level (*b*) sea shore (*c*) in elevated areas (*d*) in dry places (1 mt.; 1 mk.).

30. If tea leaves are kept in hot water for longer period, the liquid becomes bitter because:
(*a*) of the defect in the tea leaves (*b*) the volatile oil in the leaves dissolves out
(*c*) the thein dissolves out (*d*) the tannin dissolves out (1 mt.; 1 mk.).

31. Tea and coffee can be classified as:
(*a*) distilled beverages (*b*) non-alcoholic beverages
(*c*) fermented beverages (*d*) alcoholic beverages (1 mt.; 1 mk.).

32. The products of commercial importance, yielded by coconut palm are:
(*a*) latex and oil (*b*) rubber and wood (*c*) oil and fibre (*d*) fibre and rubber
(*e*) medicines (1 mt.; 1 mk.).

33. Potatoes are usually propagated by vegetative means because:
(*a*) they do not produce seeds
(*b*) by this method it is possible to maintain genetic quality
(*c*) by this method incidence of diseases may be reduced
(*d*) potato seeds have long dormancy period (1 mt.; 1 mk.).

34. The banana plant is:
(*a*) tree (*b*) shrub (*c*) herb (1 mt.; 1 mk.).

35. The true stem of banana is:
(*a*) Bulb (*b*) Rhizome (*c*) Corm (1 mt.; 1 mk.).

36. The major composition of banana fruit is:
(*a*) starch (*b*) protein (*c*) glucose (*d*) fat (1 mt.; 1 mk.).

37. Commercial tea is prepared from:
(*a*) stem (*b*) leaves (*c*) flowers (*d*) root
(*e*) bark (1 mt.; 1 mk.).

38. Rubber is obtained from:
(*a*) cell sap (*b*) gum (*c*) resin (*d*) latex (1 mt.; 1 mk.).

39. The commercial coffee is prepared from:
(*a*) leaves (*b*) flowers (*c*) fruits (*d*) root
(*e*) seed (1 mt.; 1 mk.).

40. Most of the rubber plants belong to the family
(*a*) Euphorbiaceae (*b*) Cannaceae (*c*) Rubiaceae (*d*) Rutaceae
(1 mt.; 1 mk.).

41. Latex cells occur in:
(*a*) xylem (*b*) cambium (*c*) bark (*d*) cortex
(1 mt.; 1 mk.).

42. The artificial ripening of banana is done by:
(*a*) Keeping them in a room having temperature below 0°C.
(*b*) Keeping them at room temperature.
(*c*) Keeping them in a room where the temperature is high. (1 mt.; 1 mk.).

43. Coconut oil derived from the copra can be classified as:
(*a*) essential oil (*b*) drying oil (*c*) semi-drying oil (*d*) vegetable fat.
(1 mt.; 1 mk.).

44. What is the source of chewing gum:
(*a*) Sugar from sugar-cane (*b*) Gum arabic from *Acacia* spp.
(*c*) Latex from *Achras sapota* (*d*) Fluid from *Musa* spp. (1 mt.; 1 mk.).

ANSWERS

1. (*c*)	2. (*b*)	3. (*c*)	4. (*a*)	5. (*c*)	6. (*b*)	7. (*a*)	8. (*c*)	9. (*a*)	10. (*a*)
11. (*c*)	12. (*a*)	13. (*b*)	14. (*d*)	15. (*b*)	16. (*c*)	17. (*a*)	18. (*c*)	19. (*c*)	20. (*b*)
21. (*c*)	22. (*d*)	23. (*c*)	24. (*c*)	25. (*b*)	26. (*a*)	27. (*b*)	28. (*a*)	29. (*c*)	30. (*d*)
31. (*b*)	32. (*c*)	33. (*b*)	34. (*c*)	35. (*b*)	36. (*a*)	37. (*b*)	38. (*d*)	39. (*d*)	40. (*a*)
41. (*c*)	42. (*c*)	43. (*d*)	44. (*c*)						

39
CHAPTER

The Cell: Structure and its Components

The plant body consists of a number of small, microscopic, box-like compartments called **cells.** In other words, **the cells are the universal elementary units of organic structure.** A plant cell may be defined as microcosm having a definite boundary or the cell-wall within which complicated chemical reactions are going on. A cell devoid of this chemical reaction is inert and is considered to be a dead cell.

THE CELL THEORY

Schleiden (1838) a German botanist and Schwann (1839) a German zoologist sponsored a theory that all animal and plant organisms are composed of cells.

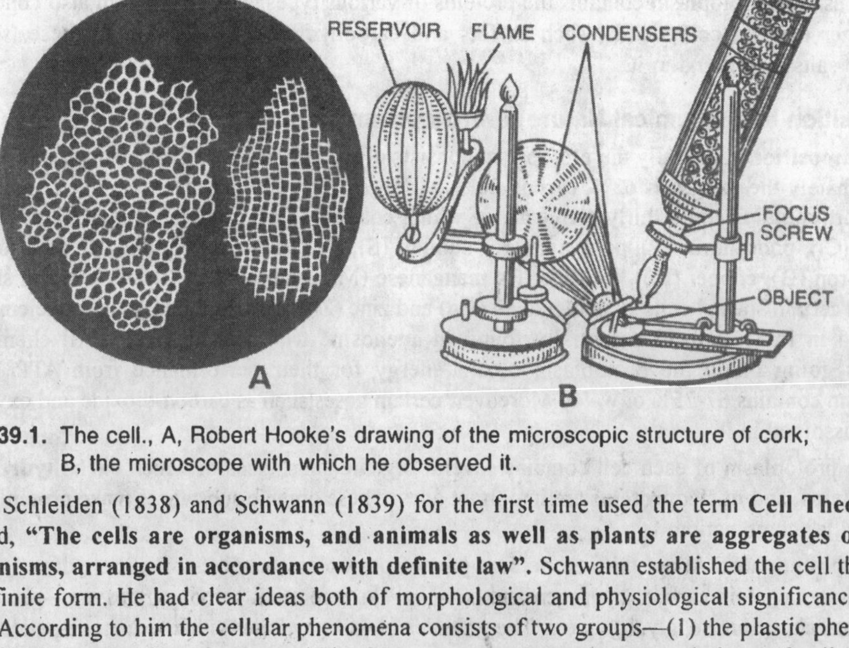

Fig. 39.1. The cell., A, Robert Hooke's drawing of the microscopic structure of cork; B, the microscope with which he observed it.

Schleiden (1838) and Schwann (1839) for the first time used the term **Cell Theory** and stated, **"The cells are organisms, and animals as well as plants are aggregates of these organisms, arranged in accordance with definite law".** Schwann established the cell theory in a definite form. He had clear ideas both of morphological and physiological significance of the cell. According to him the cellular phenomena consists of two groups—(1) the plastic phenomena and (2) the **metabolic phenomena.** The former one corresponds to morphology of cell and also includes in it "the combination of molecules which form the cell". On the other hand the metabolic phenomena (physiologic phenomena) includes **"the chemical changes, whether in the particles constituting the cell itself, or in the surrounding "cytoblastema".** Thus, about a century back Schwann expressed the present view point of cytology and, therefore, he is generally considered as 'father of modern cytology'.

The cell theory postulates, in brief that the cells from the structural units of living organisms and the latter show a characteristic cellular construction. In addition, they are also functional units in that all the vital funcitons of the living organism are traceable ultimately to the living substance, the protoplasm contained in them.

THE PROTOPLASM

According to Huxley **the protoplasm is the physical basis of life.** Inside the cell wall of living cell the living substance is known as *protoplasm*. The protoplasm is a thick fluid or jelly-like substance. These two forms are not much differentiable from each other and may easily be transformed from one form to another. When found fluid state it seems to be more active. Generally it is greyish or somewhat yellowish in colour. It is always transparent. Many small granules found in it are food granules. It is a very complex substance and found to be dispersed in the medium of water. It consists of ninety percent of water. The protoplasm found in the cells of the seeds contains less percentage of water, and therefore, it is of thick consistency. In such cases the protoplasm is somewhat inactive and becomes active only when sufficient amount of water is absorbed. In addition to water other substances are also found in the protoplasm. Among these substances the most important ones are proteins which are found in large quantity. The proteins remain dispersed in the water. The proteins are highly complex chemical compounds. The protein molecules are very large and of very high molecular weight. These complex compounds always contain carbon, hydrogen, oxygen and nitrogen. In addition to these elements sulphur and phosphorus are generally found. The proteins of protoplasm always contain sulphur and phosphorus. The protoplasm contains the proteins of various types. The protoplasm also contains some other organic compounds, such as fats and carbohydrates. In addition to these, some inorganic salts also found in it.

Composition and Chemical Nature of Protoplasm

Composition. Generally the protoplasm consists of oxygen, carbon, hydrogen and nitrogen. Approximately the oxygen is 62%, carbon 20%, hydrogen 10% and nitrogen 3%. The remainder of 5% part contains about thirty elements, of which calcium (Ca), iron (Fe), magnesium (Mg), chlorine (Cl), phosphorus (P), potassium (K), sulphur (S), etc., are important ones. In addition to these, boron (B), copper (Cu), fluorine (F), manganese (Mn) and silicon (Si) are found in small traces. In certain special cells alcohol, cobalt (Co) and zinc (Zn) are also found. All these elements are found in ionic state or essentially found in adenosine triphosphate (ATP). All chemical reactions going on in the protoplasm obtain energy for their performance from ATP. The protoplasm contains 67-75% of water. Moreover, certain gases such as carbon-dioxide and oxygen remain dissolved in it.

The protoplasm of each cell contains several organic substances of which **carbohydrates, fats, proteins,** and **nucleoproteins** are important ones. These organic substances make protoplasm by molecular combination.

Carbohydrates. About thirteen percent part of protoplasm consists of carbohydrates. The carbohydrates contain carbon, hydrogen and oxygen. The important carbohydrates are—glucose, sucrose, starch, cellulose, glycogen, etc. The granules of carbohydrates either remain suspended or dissolved in the cytoplasm. They are mainly responsible for the production of energy.

Fats. The fats or lipids consist of carbon, hydrogen and oxygen elements. They are formed by the combination of glycerol and fatty acids. They contain lesser amount of oxygen than carbohydrates. When they are chemically decomposed the energy is being liberated. They contain much more energy in comparison to carbohydrates. The cell membrane consists of fat.

Proteins. About fifteen per cent of the protoplasm consists of proteins. In addition to carbon, hydrogen and oxygen elements, the proteins essentially contain nitrogen. Usually they contain sulphur and sometimes phosphorus too. The proteins are formed by the combination of the molecules of amino-acids. About twenty amino-acids are found in the nature, that give rise to different kinds of proteins by their molecular combination. A protein molecule is made of hundreds or thousands of amino-acid molecules joined together by peptide links into one or more chains, which are variously folded. There are 20 different kinds of amino-acids commonly found in proteins, and most of these usually occur in any one protein molecule; they are arranged in the chain in a sequence which is exactly the same in all molecules of a given kind of protein. The possible different arrangement of the amino-acids are evidently practically infinite, and the diversity is fully exploited by living things, every species having kinds of protein molecule peculiar to itself. A protein molecule is very large (molecular weight from about 20,000 up to several millions), and dissolved proteins form therefore colloidal solutions. Proteins are not soluble in fat solvents. Many are soluble in water or dilute salt solutions (*e.g.*, globulins); others, with elongated (fibrous) molecules, are insoluble in these solvents (*e.g.*, scleroproteins, myosin). Proteins are synthesized from amino-acids by all living things; the precise sequence of the amino-acids being determined by the sequence of nucleotides in nucleic acids. The proteins are destroyed by proteolytic enzymes. They are frequently combined with other substances, especially nucleic acids (nucleo-proteins), carbohydrates (glycoproteins), fats (lipoproteins).

Nucleoproteins. They are most complex substances ever found. They are compounds of nucleic acid and protein. The protoplasm contains two types of nucleic acids—ribonucleic acid (RNA) and deoxyribonucleic acid (DNA). The RNA is found in the complete cell, whereas DNA remains confirmed in the nucleus. Ribonucleic acid (RNA), a molecule consisting of a large number of nucleotides attached together to form a long strand one nucleotide thick. Deoxyribonucleic acid (DNA) is mainly found in the genes of chromosomes. The DNA, a compound consisting of large number of nucleotides attached together in a single file to form a long strand. Usually two such strands are linked together parallel to each other by base pairing, and coiled into a helix. In each cell the DNA and RNA are mainly concerned with the metabolic activities. Numerous RNA and DNA are formed within the living cells. The nucleic acids of two different living beings are never identical. The RNA and DNA control all the metabolic activities going on within the living cells. They play an important role in the origin of life. DNA is the material of inheritance of almost all living beings.

Other chemical substances. Besides abovementioned organic substances several other inorganic substances are also found in the living cells in small quantities. These substances are specially concerned with the cell metabolism. Some of these substances are found in all cells whereas some are confined to certain special cells. Various pigments, latex, alkaloids, vitamins, hormones, antibiotics and some other substances are found within the plant cells.

Thus, the carbohydrates, fats, proteins, nucleoproteins and several other chemical substances make the protoplasm by their molecular combination. The molecules of all these substances are well organized and form protoplasm. In addition to these the molecules of living cells possess special characteristics by which various chemical reactions take place and with the result the energy liberates. This energy is utilized in the performance of the metabolic activities of the cells. Thus, this becomes an established fact that all constituents of the cell form a very powerful organization by their combination, which is living and quite active.

Physical Nature of Protoplasm

Colloidal state. The proteins of protoplasm are found in water in colloidal state. The proteins are formed in the form of very minute granules. Each granule consists of several molecules. Generally the protoplasm is an amulsoid, in which the proteins remain dispersed in the water. Many colloidal particles possess the power of holding and absorption of water. This is called

hydration and the colloids which absorbed the water are said to be **hydrated.** The colloids of protoplasm remain hydrated, and the amount of hydration depends upon various conditions.

Distribution. Generally the protoplasm remains divided into two parts—**the nucleus** and the **cytoplasm.** Usually the young cells remain filled up with the protoplasm. In mature cells, the cytoplasm forms the inner layer of the cell wall and a layer around the nucleus. The nucleus remains embedded in this layer of cytoplasm. All the protoplasm of a cell excluding the nucleus is known as **cytoplasm.** The cytoplasm is usually a transparent slightly viscous fluid with inclusions of various sizes.

Permeability. Permeability of membrane, exhibits to which molecules of a given kind can pass through it. Substances differ greatly in the case with which they pass through a given membrane, *e.g.*, water or fatty substances pass easily, many ions and proteins with great difficulty, through plasma membrane. Permeability on any biological membrane is itself variable within wide limits. The very numerous membranes of animals and plants, *e.g.*, plasma membranes, produce many osmotic effects and are of great importance in determining local differences in composition of the organism. According to Virgin (1953), the permeability is the quality of a living membrane through which different ions and molecules may pass, and during this process the energy obtained from metabolic activities is not utilized. This is the permeability of the protoplasm which is dependable upon the physiochemical properties of the protoplasmic membrane of the cell. Virgin has also propounded that the permeability of the protoplasm is the control of active and passive forces on the particles passing through the living protoplasmic membrane. The cellulose cell wall is permeable for water and other solutes, whereas the protoplasmic membrane is permeable only to water and not to other solutes.

Properties of Protoplasm

The protoplasm is a living matter and makes the physical basis of life. On the basis of the properties given below it may be differentiated from non-living matter. The properties are as follows:

Absorption and excretion. The protoplasm takes essential substances for its growth by absorption and it gets rid of from non-required substances by excretion. The protoplasm of green plants absorbs water and minerals from the soil and carbon dioxide from the atmosphere. Thus, the substances quite different from the protoplasm are being absorbed by it.

Metabolism. In general the chemical processes occurring within an organism, or within part of one. They involve breaking down of organic compounds from complex to simple (catabolism) with liberation of energy available for the organism's many activities; and building up of organic compounds from simple to complex (anabolism) using energy liberated by catabolism and in the case of autotropic organisms, energy from external non-organic sources (particularly from sun-light). Catabolism is by no means confined to the breaking down of the 'food material' necessary for the organism's energy requirements. It involves, continuously, very many constituents of the organism, though they are broken down at various rates, and on the other hand anabolism involves, continuously, synthesis of many constituents. These processes go on even in an apparently static tissue. This metabolic whirlpool is a system of reactions predominantly controlled by enzymes. In most of the aspects of metabolism which have been sufficiently investigated, such as catabolism of carbohydrates, there is a fundamental similarity throughout a wide variety of organisms including plants, animals and bacteria.

Growth and reproduction. Growth means increase in size. It includes differentiation of cells, increase in plant size, even though such differentiation contributes nothing to size change. The growth of protoplasm is the result of the separation and growth of such a small part which has been derived from one or parental living beings. In other words, the reproduction is another form of growth.

Movement. The protoplasm has the power of movement and usually it remains in dynamic condition. The dynamic state of the protoplasm of the cell may be seen under the microscope. This phenomenon is known as Brownian movement. The protoplasm does not only possess the property of movement, but it also helps the living being or its organs to remain in dynamic state. Such movements are more clearly seen in animals than in plants, but in certain plants such as *Mimosa pudica*, it is quite obvious. Besides, the young parts of several plants bend towards the light; several unicellular and other types of water plants move like the animals from one place to another such as *Chlamydomonas, Volvox,* etc.

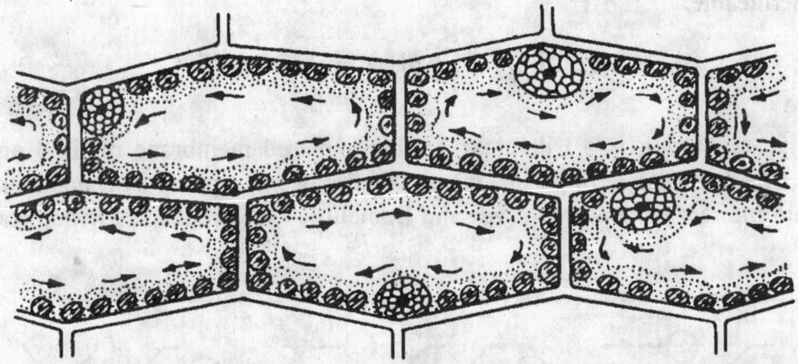

Fig. 39.2. Movement of protoplasm. Rotation in the leaf of *Vallisneria*.

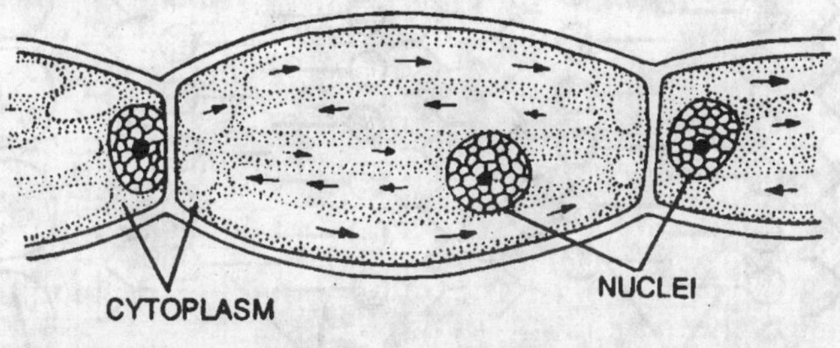

Fig. 39.3. Movement of protoplasm. Circulation in the staminal hair of *Commelina*.

Irritability. This is a universal property of living things (protoplasm). The responsiveness of protoplasm to outer stimulus is known as irritability. Temperature and several chemicals have definite effect upon the movement of the protoplasm. At ordinary temperature the rate of movement increases whereas at low temperature it decreases. The effect of certain chemicals increases the rate of movement while the effect of certain other chemicals decreases it. With the result of the stimulus upon the protoplasm, a complete organ of the plant may be affected, *e.g., Mimosa pudica.*

THE PLASMA MEMBRANE
(Cell Membrane)

All cells remain covered by a **plasma membrane.** The plasma membrane is quite separate and should not be confused with the cell wall which lies outside the cytoplasm. Generally a cell wall is regarded as protoplasmic product and is not believed to be truly living. However, in certain cases the cell wall remains capable of growth.

The plasma membrane is generally considered to be the outer living limit of the cell, but not necessarily its outer boundary. Such outer boundaries are most commonly found in plant cells, many of which possess heavy walls of cellulose, but animal cells and unicellular organisms also exhibit a number of somewhat comparable external substances.

The cell membrane is double in nature and about 10 Å (Å = *Angstrom* unit) thick. This membrane remains connected with the nuclear membrane through the endoplasmic reticulum.

The double nature and molecular make-up of the plasma membrane are depicted in figure. The membrane has a lipoprotein (fat + protein) composition. The protein constituent of the membrane gives the cell wettability and flexibility. Since protein molecules, which are long and complex, can fold or unfold, the membrane can expand or contract, thus providing through molecular spacing a possible means of control over which molecules can enter the cell from the outside environment, or pass to the environment from inside the cell. Such a membrane is known as selectively permeable.

MODELS OF PLASMA MEMBRANE

Ultrastructure

The plasma membrane is a trilaminar or three-layered membrane of lipid and protein molecules. The trilaminar nature of plasma membrane has been proposed by Danielli and Davson (1935) by certain indirect evidences. Harvey and Danielli (1938) produced a hypothetical model

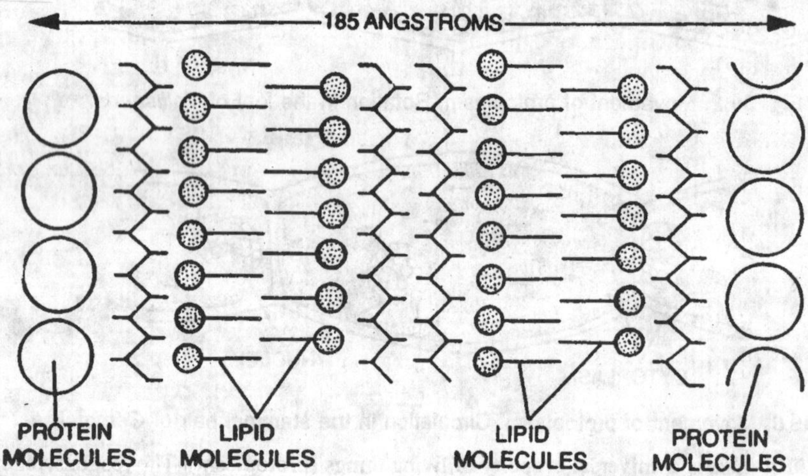

Fig. 39.4. The plasma membrane in molecular terms showing protein and lipid molecules.

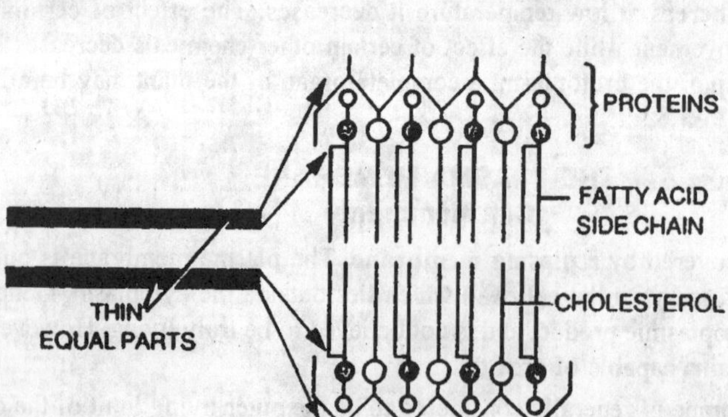

Fg. 39. 5. Symmetrical pattern of plasma membrane.

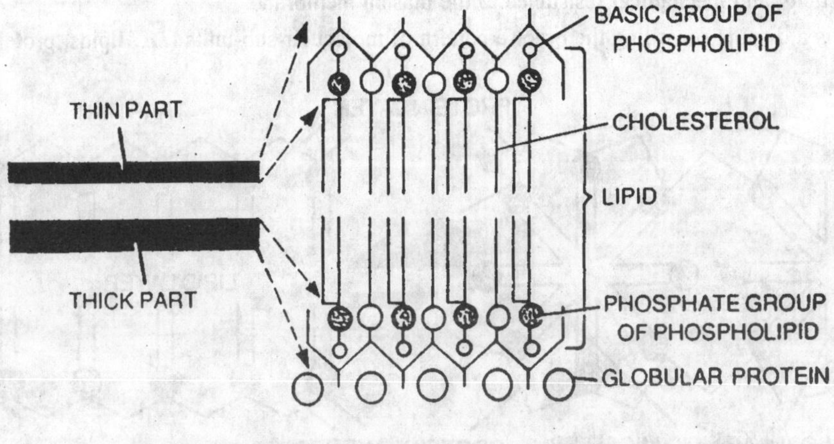

Fig. 39.6. Asymmetrical pattern of plasma membrane.

of the plasma membrane which has shown a bimolecular lipid structure in between two outer and inner layers of protein molecules. The studies by electron microscope have revealed the protein-lipid-protein arrangement in the plasma membrane. Robertson (1959) found wide occurrence of such trilaminar composition in most of the membranes of cellular organelles, and with the result the propounded the concept of the **unit membrane.** A unit membrane possesses the protein-lipid-protein arrangement. The unit membrane has been found in plasma membrane, endoplasmic reticulum, Golgi complex, lysosomes and plastids. It has been found, that both the outer and inner membranes of the mitochondria and the nucleus are the unit membranes.

The plasma membrane of most cells varies from 100 to 215 Å in thickness. The plasma membrane is not a continuous layer but contains certain minute pores of 8 to 15 Å diameter. The opening and closing of these pores depends on the metabolic phase of the cell.

Molecular Structure

The plasma membrane consists of two layers of protein molecules and two layers of lipid molecules. The lipid molecules occur in chains. The two molecular chains of lipids remain parallel to each other and form a bimolecular or double-layered structure. Both lipid layers remain linked with each other by the inner ends of lipid molecules which are non-polar and hydrophobic (Gr. *hydra* = water; *phobe* = hate) in nature. Both the layers of lipids are held together due to Vander waal's forces at these non-polar ends.

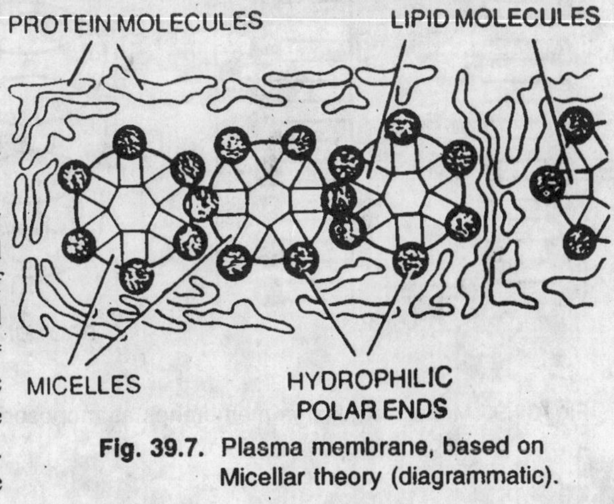

Fig. 39.7. Plasma membrane, based on Micellar theory (diagrammatic).

The lipid layers remain enclosed by outer and inner layers of proteins. The lipid molecules are linked with the molecules of protein layers by their outer, polar and hydrophilic (Gr. *hydra* = water; *phil* = loving) ends. In the hydrogen bonds, ionic linkages, or electrostatic forces bind the molecules of lipids and proteins together. The carbohydrate molecules are found in the association of protein molecules and provide stability to lipo-protein complex. The protein layers provide elasticity and mechanical resistance to the plasma membrane.

There is a dispute regarding the precise pattern of molecular sub-units (*i.e.*, lipids, proteins

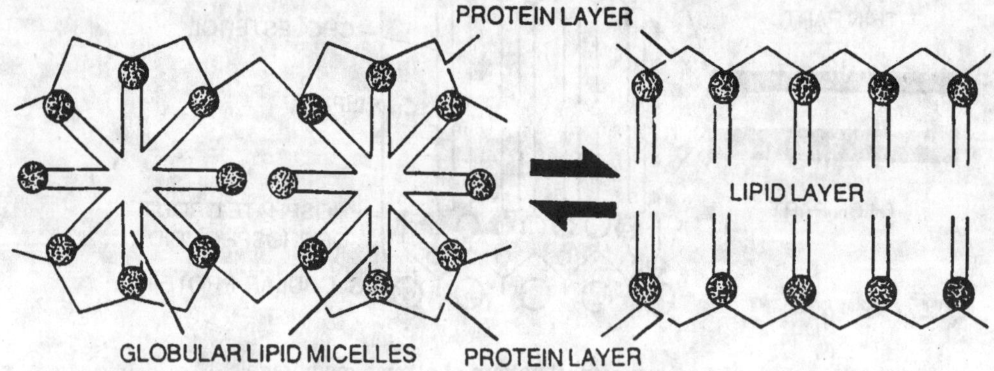

Fig. 39.8. Plasma membrane. Transformation between micellar and lamellar states (globular bi-layertransformation).

and carbohydrates) in the plasma membrane. Following three kinds of theories and models, *viz.*, **lamellar theory, micellar theory** and **fluid mosaic theory**, have been suggested for the possible molecular structure of plasma membrane.

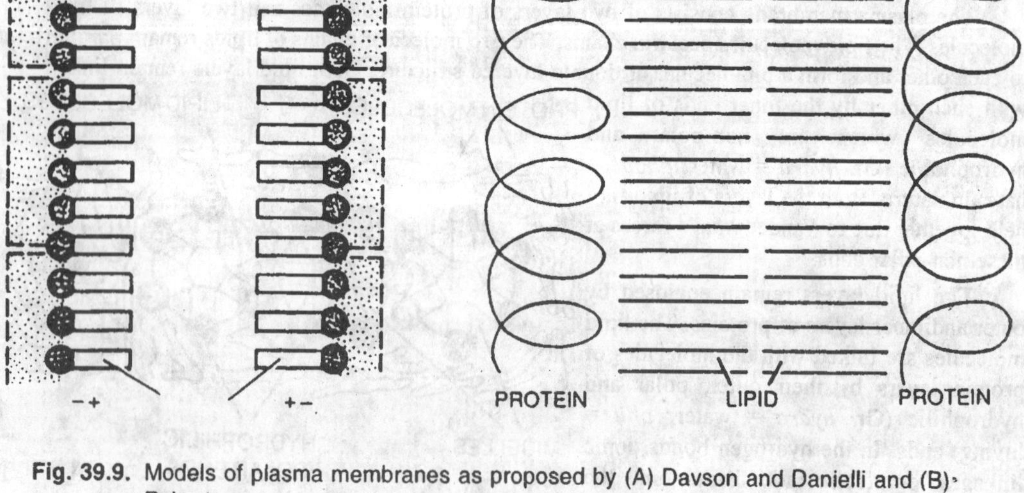

Fig. 39.9. Models of plasma membranes as proposed by (A) Davson and Danielli and (B) Robertson.

MEMBRANE MODELS

To explain the physical and biological features of plasma membranes two main categories have been proposed, *i.e.*, the **bilayer models** and the **micellar** or **sub-unit models**. In the bilayer models the protein and lipid that constitute the membrane are believed to occur in layers, while in the micellar model the membrane is thought to consist of a number of similar units.

Danielli-Davson Model

By studying the surface tension of cells the existence of protein was indicated (Harvey and Cole, 1931; Danielli and Harvey, 1935). This led Davson and Danielli (1935) to propose a lipoprotein model of the cell membrane. According to this model the bimolecular liquid layer consists of two layers of molecules with their polar regions on the outer side. Globular proteins are thought to be associated with the polar groups of the lipid.

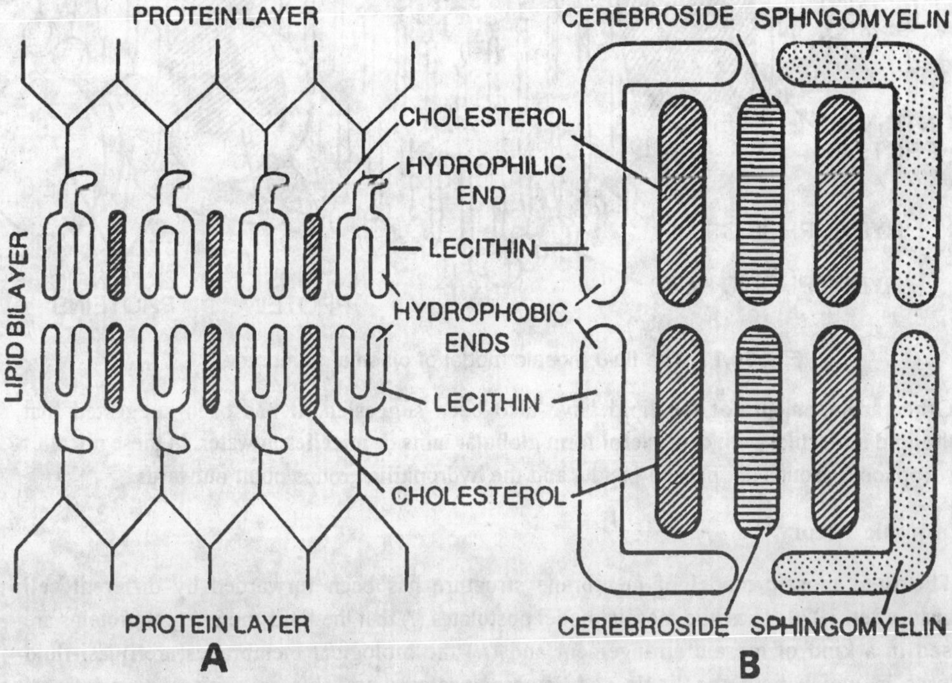

Fig. 39.10. A phospholipid-cholesterol complex of cell membrane.

The lipids in the membrane consist mainly of phospholipids, with their non-polar groups near each other and their polar groups directed outwards. The lipid layer in many cases consists of a phospholipid **lecithin**, alternating with a steroid molecule **cholesterol.** The lecithin molecule consists of two lipid chains of glycerol and a polar head containing **phosphate** and **choline.** According to Finean (1953) the head is bent around like a walking stick, and forms a bond with **cholesterol.**

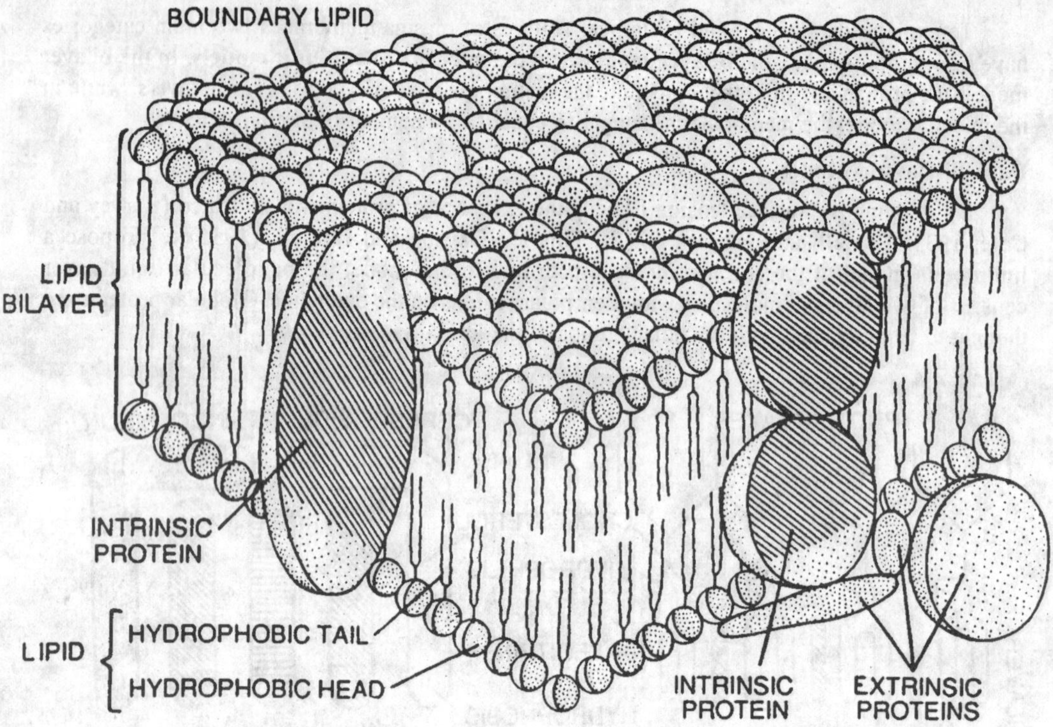

Fig. 39.11. The fluid mosaic model of plasma membrane

Other arrangements of the lipid have also been suggested. It has been suggested that phospholipid molecules with cholesterol form globular units or **micelles** in water. In these micelles the hydrophobic groups are packed inside, and the hydrophilic groups point outwards.

Fluid Mosaic Theory

The fluid mosaic model of membrane structure has been forwarded by different cell biologists, after, 1970. The fluid mosaic model postulates (*i*) that the lipid and integral proteins are disposed in a kind of mosaic arrangement and (*ii*) the biological membranes are quasi-fluid structures in which both the lipids and integral proteins are able to perform translational movements within the overall bilayer. The concept of fluidity implies that the main components of the membrane, *i.e.*, lipids and oligosaccharides, are held in place by means of non-covalent interactions.

The fluid mosaic model was propounded by Singer and Nicolson (1972), is now widely accepted as best explaining the properties of the plasma membrane. This model assumes that there is a continuous bilayer of **phospholipid** molecules in which are embedded **globular proteins**. Here the proteins have been compared to icebergs floating in the sea of the phospholipid bilayer. Thus plasma membranes are considered to be **quasifluid** structures in which lipids and integral proteins are arranged in a **mosaic** manner.

Chemical Nature of Plasma Membrane

The plasma membrane consists of a protein called **stromatin,** which is fibrous in nature and possesses a high molecular weight. These are also glycoproteins and mucoproteins. It also contains large amount of arginine and lysine. In addition to it, histidine, tyrosine, tryptophan, methionine and many other amino acids are also present. The protein is acidic in nature and forms greater percentage of plasma membrane as compared to lipid components. The lipids are mainly phospholipids and cholesterol. The phospholipids mainly consist of lecithin and cephalin. On an average the membrane possesses 75 to 90 molecules of lipid for every molecule of protein. Five phospholipids have been identified from the cell membrane. One is **phosphatidic acid** and the remaining four are more complex being comprising either cholein, inositol ethanolamine or serine attached to the phosphate groups in addition. The one phospholipid containing choline is called **lecithin.** The phospholipid molecules that are made up of glycerol and phosphate are water soluble, whereas the fatty acid molecules that constitute the tail of the whole structure are water insoluble. According to Parpart and Ballantine (1952) the structure of the plasma membrane is different in different cells. Salts are also present in the cell membrane. Lowell and Hokin (1965) demonstrated that the phospholipids are secretory in function and they increase the formation of the membrane phospholipids.

Functions

The main functions of plasma membrane are as follows:

Osmosis. The plasma membrane is semipermeable for differentially permeable membrane because water moves through it more easily than the large molecules. Osmosis accounts for the movement of water through the membrane with the implication that solute moves at slower rate. This means that the solute would remain isolated on one side of the cell membrane—this does not occur in living cell. Undoubtedly the smaller molecules like that of water move with greater facility through the membrane than the large molecules. Thus this membrane is **selective permeable.**

Active transport. Normally, the molecules of dissolved materials diffuse through the membrane towards a region of low concentration. But sometimes they move towards a region of higher concentration. For this the energy is needed to move the molecules in a direction opposite to that in which they would move by diffusion. This type of movement is called **active transport.** In brief, here the substance does not move by itself but is transported through the cell membrane. It can be defined as, **"the movement of molecule of a substance against a concentration gradient and (or) against an electrochemical."**

CELL STRUCTURE

The protoplast of each cell contains the protoplasmic and non-protoplasmic components. The protoplasmic or living components are—nucleus, mitochondria, plastids, endoplasmic reticulum, ribosomes, lysosomes, sphaerosomes, microtubules and Golgi bodies.

The chief non-protoplasmic or non-living components are—vacuoles, food products, secretory products and waste products. The protoplasmic and non-protoplasmic components of the cell are summarised on next page.

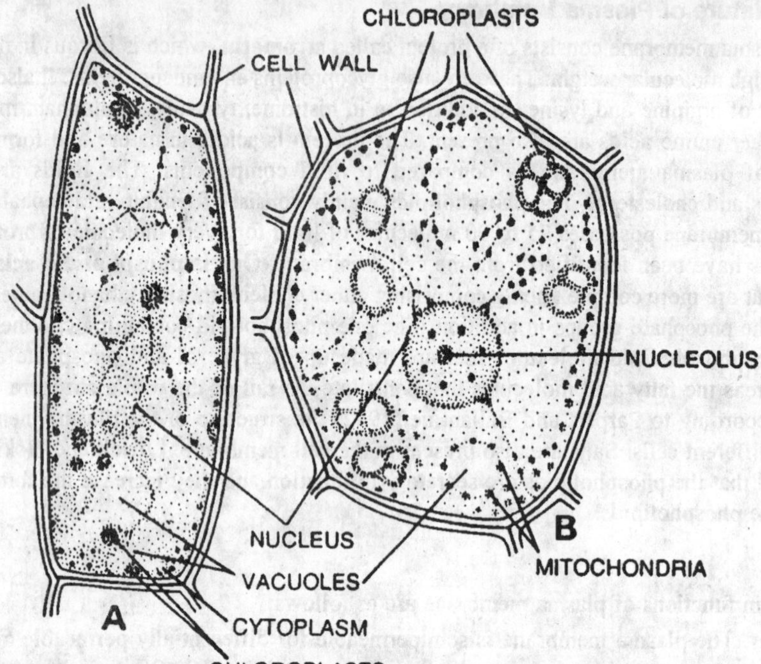

Fig. 39.12. Plant cells. A, cell from sugar-beet leaf with vacuolated cytoplasm, a nucleus and granular chloroplasts; B, a cell from starch-sheath of tobacco stem.

CELL

- **Protoplasmic Components**
  1. Nucleus
  2. Mitochondria
  3. Plastids
     - (*i*) Leucoplasts
     - (*ii*) Elaioplasts
     - (*iii*) Chromoplasts
     - (*iv*) Chloroplasts
  4. Endoplasmic reticulum
  5. Ribosomes
  6. Lysosomes
  7. Sphaerosomes
  8. Microtubules
  9. Golgi bodies
- **Non-Protoplasmic Components**
  - Vacuoles
  - Ergastic Substances
    - Food products
      - Non-nitrogenous (Carbohydrates)
        - (*i*) Starch
        - (*ii*) Inulin
        - (*iii*) Hemicellulose
        - (*iv*) Cellulose
        - (*v*) Sugars
      - Nitrogenous
        - (*i*) Proteins
        - (*ii*) Amino compounds
      - Fats and fatty oils
    - Secretory products
      - (*i*) Enzymes
      - (*ii*) Pigments
      - (*iii*) Nectar
    - Waste products
      - (*i*) Tannins
      - (*ii*) Mineral crystals
      - (*iii*) Latex
      - (*iv*) Essential oils

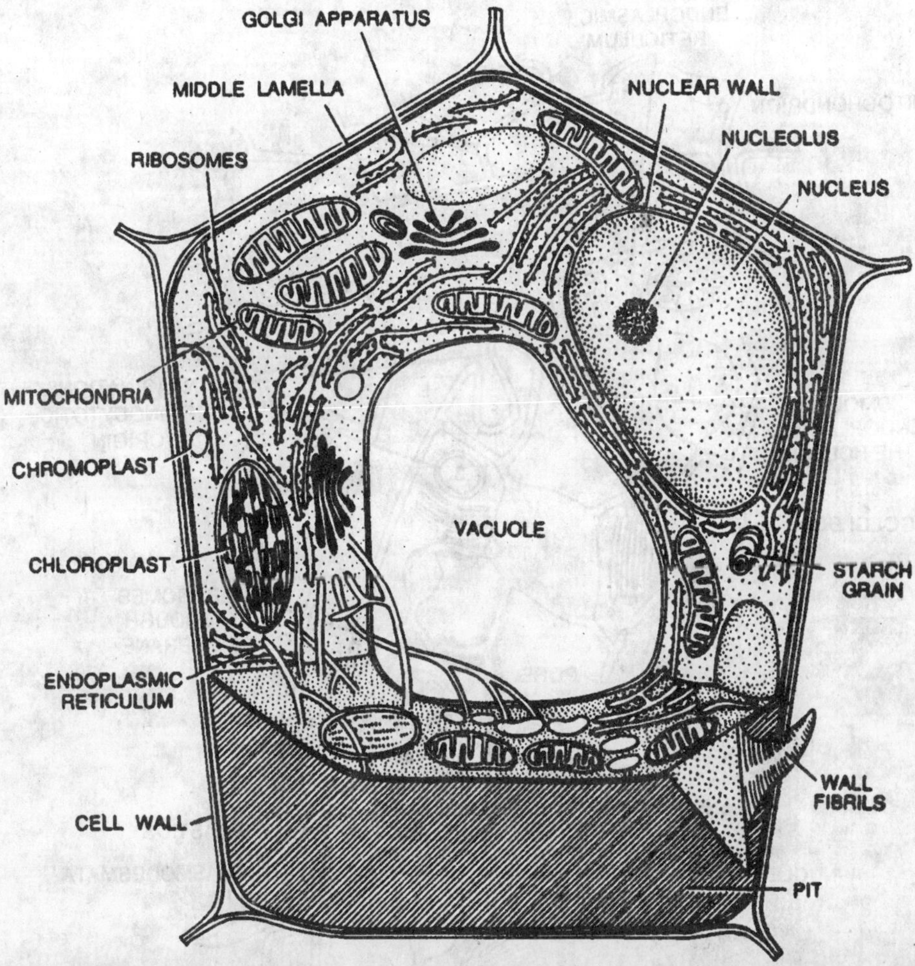

Fig. 39.13. The cell structure. Diagram of an electron micrograph of a cell from a leaf of *Phaseolus vulgaris*.

Cytoplasm. Kolliker (1862) gave the name '*cytoplasm*, to the substance found around the nucleus. According to Guilliermond (1941) and Sharp (1934) the word cytoplasm has been used to designate all the matter in the cell exclusive of the nucleus. The cytoplasm and various protoplasmic bodies (*e.g.*, nucleus, plastids, mitochondria, etc.,) have the same fundamental characteristics.

The cytoplasm is a transparent semifluid substance denser than water with granules, vacuoles and vesicles of various sizes embedded in it. It is highly complex, both physically and chemically. Usually it consists of water which may be 85–90% in it. Many organic and inorganic substances also occur in the cytoplasm either in true solution or in colloidal state. Salts, carbohydrates and other water soluble substances are found in dissolved state. Proteins and fats are also found in the form of very minute particles which are invisible in the microscopes of ordinary light. They are found in colloidal state. The studies of many workers such as Fry–Wyssling (1948); Seifriz (1935, 1936, 1945); Sharp (1943) and many others suggest the presence of a continuous framework of

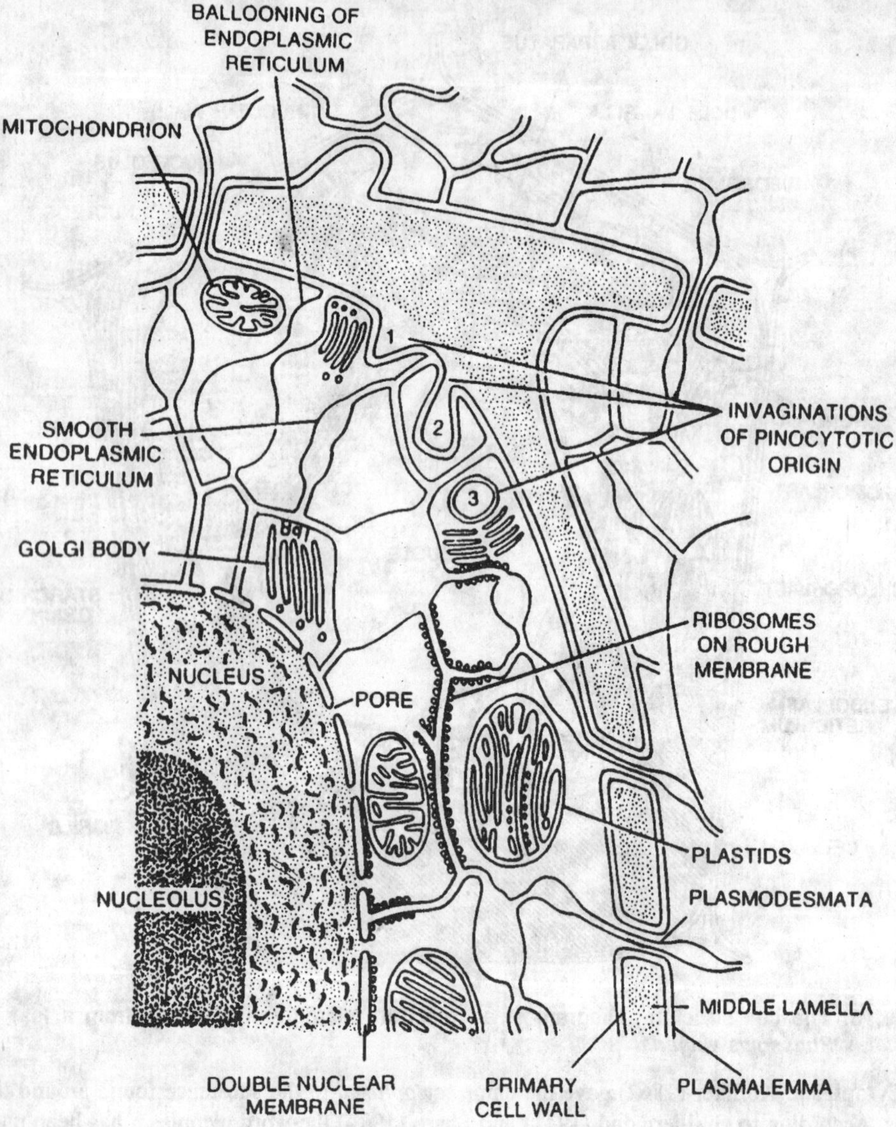

Fig. 39.14. Portion of a plant cell as seen under electron microscope. The invaginations of plasma membrane and ballooning of endoplasmic membrane are clearly seen.

proteins. It remains always in a dynamic state due to constant phase inversions. It is bounded by a monomolecular layer or a multimolecular layer on the outside called **ectoplast** (plasma membrane). Similar second layer on inside called **tonoplast** (vacuolar membrane). The protoplasmic layers are semipermeable in nature which involve in differential absorption. In the cytoplasm, fatty substances such as lipids and certain proteins take part in the formation of ectoplast (plasma membrane). The tonoplast (vacuolar membrane) also develops from the same substance and possesses similar structure to that of plasma membrane.

The electron microscope reveals membranous differentiations in the interior of the cytoplasm notably, the **endoplasmic reticulum** and the **dictyosomes**. The cytoplasm also includes granules of various sizes. Granules of 0.25 to 1 micron in diameter, containing lipids and proteins, constitute the **spherosomes**. These granules are highly mobile in living cells. At the submicroscopic level, a granule about 150 Å in diameter, the **ribosome** a globular macromolecule of ribonucleoprotein that takes part in protein synthesis. Ribosomes occur free in the cytoplasm or they remain associated with the endoplasmic reticulum.

Some of the resolvable entities in the protoplast, such as the **nucleus, plastids** and **mitochondria**, are referred to as **organelles**, whereas the endoplasmic reticulum and the dictyosomes are called sometimes membrane systems and sometimes organelles.

Cytoplasmic membranes. Among the cytoplasmic membranes, ectoplast and tonoplast, have long been associated with the important physiological characteristics of the protoplast. These membranes are difficult to recognize with the light microscope, but the electron microscopy has confirmed their morphologic identity (Mercer, 1960). The tonoplast is thinner than the ectoplast.

The endoplasmic reticulum is a system of membrane-bound cavities or **cisternae**. The cisternae are commonly much flattened and therefore, their sections appear as double lines. The endoplasmic reticulum is responsible for providing the cell with a large internal membrane surface along which enzymes are orderly distributed.

Dictyosomes are stacks of flattened sacks or cisternae, circular in outline, each surrounded by vesicles. The vesicles originate from the margins of the cisternae and pass into the cytoplasm. Dictyosomes are concerned with secretory activities and wall formation.

THE NUCLEUS
(The Controlling Centre)

The controlling centre of a cell is the ***nucleus***. The ***chromosomes*** and ***genes*** are found within it which determine the character, activities and destiny of each individual cell.

Each nucleus is surrounded on the outside by a ***nuclear membrane***. This membrane quite resembles the cell membrane. It is double-layered and consists of proteins and lipids. The main part of the nucleus consists of chromatin, which during cell division becomes more distinctly visible as a definite number of individual chromosomes. Certain coarser granules are also visible in the chromatin. They are known as **chromocentres** which stain darker than the rest of the network of the chromatin. Each nucleus consists of **nuclear membrane, nuclear sap (nucleoplasm), nucleolus or nucleoli and chromatin.**

Structure of the nucleus. Each nucleus remains surrounded by a limiting membrane as the

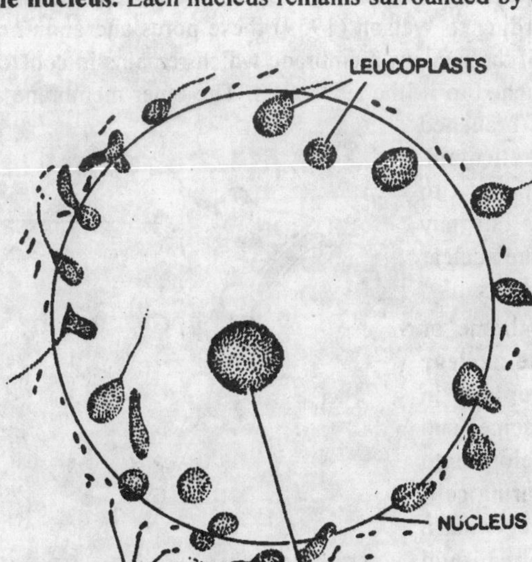

Fig. 39.15. The nucleus. Nucleus, amoeboid leucoplasts, and mitochondria from the cell of sugar-beet hypocotyl.

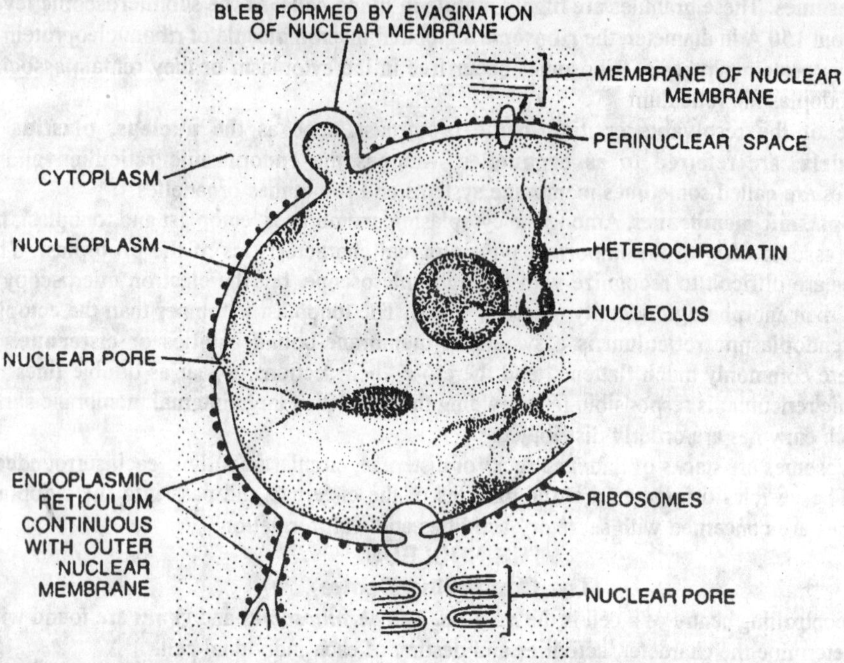

Fig. 39.16. The structure of the interphase nucleus (diagrammatic).

nuclear membrane. As electron microscopy reveals the nuclear membrane consists of two membranes each being 90Å thick and the space in between the two, the **perinuclear space** being 100-115Å wide. The nuclear membrane possesses pores here and there varying in diameter from 400-600Å. Through these pores the nucleoplasm communicates with cytoplasm. At the margins of the pores the two membranes are continuous. The number of pores varies from species to species and even from cell to cell. According to some workers, each pore remains encircled by a circular structure, the **annulus.** According to Watson (1959) these pores and annuli constitute the **pore complex.** The outer surface of the nucleus membrane which remains in contact of cytoplasm has RNA containing granules attached to it, the ribosomes. The outer membrane at places gives out tubular structures which get branched and form the endoplasmic reticulum. The inner membrane exposed to nucleoplasm lacks ribosomes but may have aggregated chromatin. The nuclear membrane consists of lipoproteins.

Inside the nuclear membrane or nuclear envelope their lies the **nuclear sap** or **karyolymph** or **nucleoplasm** in which are found nuclear ribosomes and chromatin network that develops into well defined chromosomes during cell-division. Nucleoplasm is some-what a granular and homogeneous semifluid which contains nucleic acids, nucleoprotein, etc.

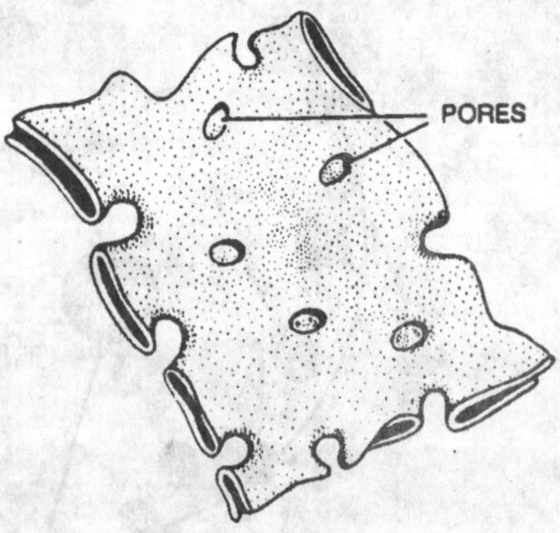

Fig. 39.17. Nucleus. Structure of a part of nuclear membrane. The membrane is two layered and the pores are clearly visible.

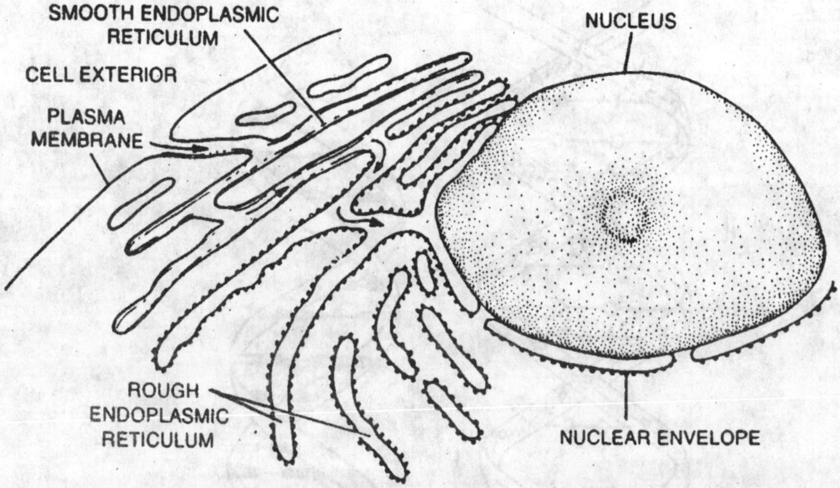

Fig. 39.18. The diagram depicts a eukaryotic cell that shows how the endoplasmic reticulum (ER) connects with both the plasma membrane and the double layered nuclear envelope. Connections of this type may form channels through which materials may pass to and from the cell's surroundings without penetrating the plasma membrane. However, such channels are formed only in cells with a highly developed system of endoplasmic reticulum (ER).

Certain distinct one or more rounded bodies known as **nucleoli** (singular-**nucleolus**) are also found within the nucleus. The number of nucleoli per nucleus of a particular species is definite. For example, nucleus of onion cell possesses four nucleoli, which sometimes fuse together.

The **nucleus** is a relatively large, generally spherical ball-like body found inside the nucleus. The nucleoli are made up of small granules containing proteins and RNA which has got some part to play in the activity of the nucleus. It is thought that nucleoli help in the synthesis of

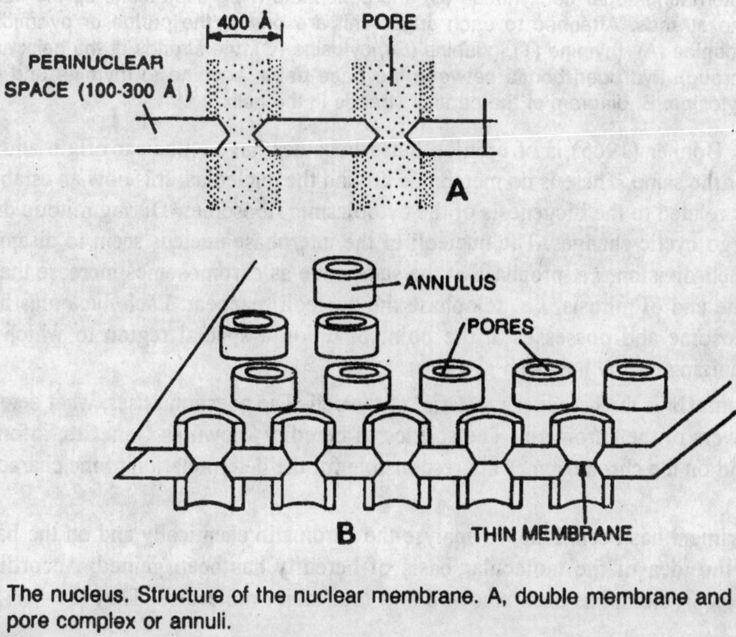

Fig. 39.19. The nucleus. Structure of the nuclear membrane. A, double membrane and pores; B, pore complex or annuli.

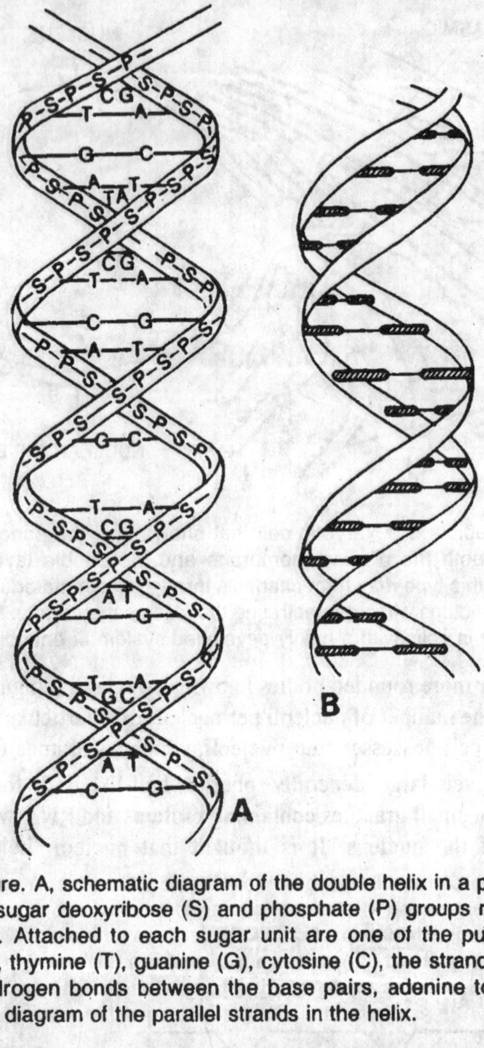

Fig. 39.20. DNA structure. A, schematic diagram of the double helix in a portion of a DNA molecule. Alternating sugar deoxyribose (S) and phosphate (P) groups make up the backbones of the strands. Attached to each sugar unit are one of the purine or pyrimidine bases, adenine (A), thymine (T), guanine (G), cytosine (C), the strands of the helix are together through hydrogen bonds between the base pairs, adenine to thymine and guanine to cytosine; B, diagram of the parallel strands in the helix.

nucleoprotein. Bonner (1965) is of opinion that ribosomes have a nuclear origin and nucleolus plays a role for the same. There is no membrane around the nucleolus. It is now an established fact that nucleus is related to the biogenesis of the cytoplasmic ribosomes. During mitotic division the nucleoli undergo cyclic changes. The nucleoli of the interphase nucleus seem to disappear at the beginning of cell division, *i.e.* prophase at the same time as chromosomes increase their staining property. At the end of mitosis, *i.e.*, telophase the nucleoli reappear. Each nucleolus has contact with a chromosome and possesses at the point of union a special region to which the name nucleolar organizing region has been given.

The **chromatin** is the hereditary material of the cell. The question arises, what determines the hereditary powers of the chromatin. The science of heredity known as **Genetics,** informs us that the genes found on the chromosomes are responsible for the determination of the characters of the species.

An experiment has been done, to analyse the chromatin chemically and on the basis of this experiment : the idea of the molecular basis of heredity has been gained. According to this experiment the chromatin has been resolved into four major molecules. They are—(*i*) **histone,** a low molecular weight protein (2000), (*ii*) a more complex protein than histone; (*iii*) deoxyribonucleic acid (DNA) and (*iv*) ribonucleic acid (RNA). These four molecules constitute the chromatin. But now, with the result of extensive studies this has been demonstrated that DNA is the molecule whose structure determines hereditary uniquences on the cell and the individual. In other words, this can be said that DNA is the hereditary material of the cell. The proteins and RNA are necessary for the functioning of the nucleus but not so important from the point of view of the heredity. In certain plant viruses only RNA is found in their structure and no DNA, in such cases the RNA acts as hereditary molecule.

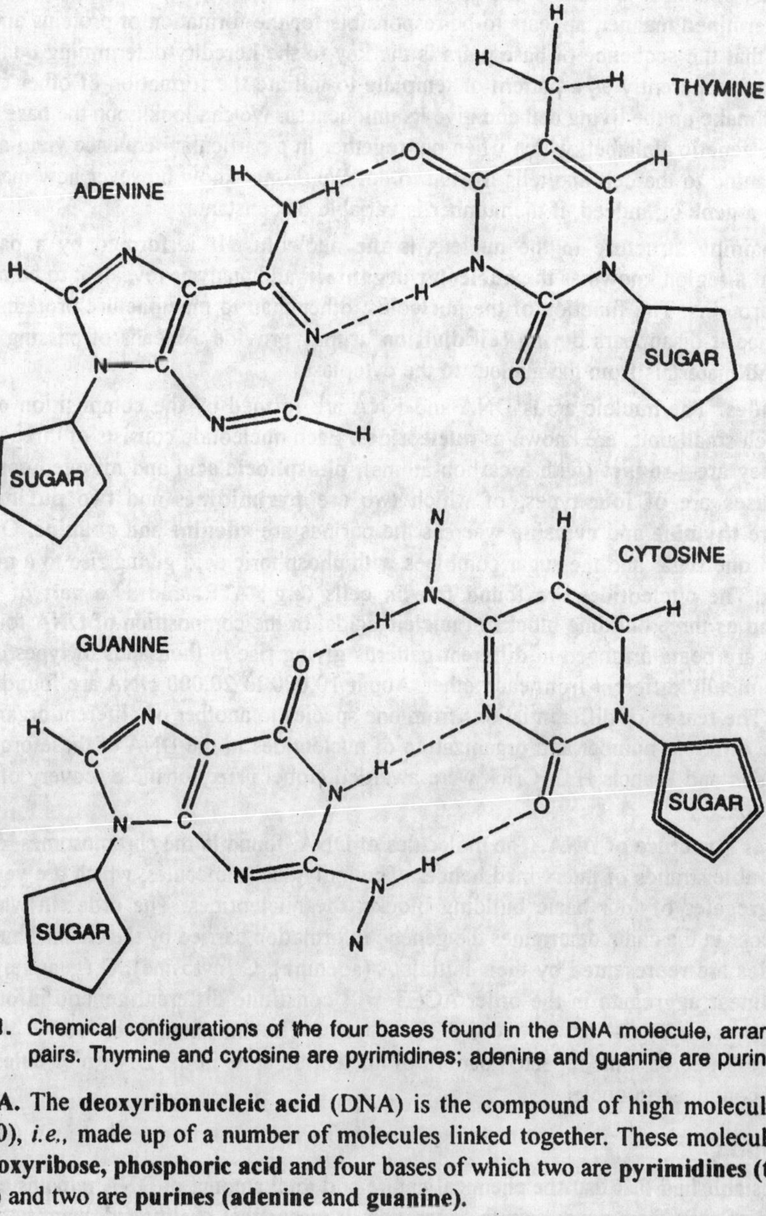

Fig. 39.21. Chemical configurations of the four bases found in the DNA molecule, arranged as base pairs. Thymine and cytosine are pyrimidines; adenine and guanine are purines.

DNA. The **deoxyribonucleic acid** (DNA) is the compound of high molecular wt. (over 1,000,000), *i.e.,* made up of a number of molecules linked together. These molecules include a sugar, **deoxyribose, phosphoric acid** and four bases of which two are **pyrimidines (thymine and cytosine)** and two are **purines (adenine and guanine)**.

Chemical structure of DNA. The alternating sugar and phosphate arrangement forms the outside boundaries of DNA while base pairs link the two sides together. The base pairs, however, are not at random, for adenine and thymine are always paired, as are guanine and cytosine. Hydrogen bonds tie the bases to each other. X-ray analysis of the molecular arrangements reveals that DNA is not a flat structure, as one might suspect, but a double helix, *i.e.*, a sort of spiral' stair case with alternating sugar-phosphate 'bannisters' and 'steps' of base pairs. This is the Watson-Crick model of DNA, so named after its discoverers. The DNA molecule may have thousand of turns in its spiral configuration and the steps, can be arranged in any order. The possible variations therefore are astronomical in number and give an infinite variety to the molecule. Since the DNA, in some undetermined manner, appears to be responsible for the formation of proteins and RNA, it is believed that the sequence of base pairs is the key to the heredity-determining qualities of DNA. These act apparently as a pattern or template to initiate the formation of other complex molecules that make up the living cell and give its uniqueness. We can look upon the base pairs as the letters in a genetic alphabet, which when put together in a particular sequence yield a 'word' which has meaning to the cell and tells it what to do. We do not know however how many base pairs make up a gene or, indeed, if the number is variable or constant.

The remaining structure in the nucleus is the nucleolus. It is formed by a particular chromosome at a region known as the **nucleolar organizer,** and analysis reveals it to be made up of RNA and proteins. The function of the nucleolus, other than to manufacture proteins, is not known but since it disappears during cell division, it may provide a means of passing genetic information and materials from the nucleus to the cytoplasm.

Nucleotides. The nucleic acids DNA and RNA are formed by the composition of small molecules. Such small units are known as **nucleotides.** Each nucleotide consists of three types of molecules. They are—**sugars** (with 5 carbon atoms), **phosphoric** acid and nitrogen containing bases. The bases are of four types, of which two are **pyrimidines** and two **purines.** The pyrimidines are **thymine** and **cytosine** whereas the purines are **adenine** and **guanine.** One base combines with one sugar and the sugar combines with phosphoric acid giving rise to a molecule of nucleotide. The nucleotides are found free in cells (*e.g.*, ATP) and as a part of various coenzymes, and as three building blocks of nucleic acids. In the composition of DNA four types of nucleotides are being arranged in different patterns giving rise to thousands of types of DNA which are chemically different from each other. About 10,000 to 20,000 DNA are found on one chromosome. The reason of differentiations from one species to another of different organisms is because of the different number and organization of nucleotides in the DNA of these organisms. James D. Watson and Francis H.C. Crick were awarded Nobel prize for the discovery of helical structure of DNA.

Molecular structure of DNA. The molecules of DNA, found in the chromosomes, occur in the form of double strands of interwined helices. The individual molecules, which are very long, are linear aggregates of four basic building blocks, the nucleotides. The order in which the nucleotides occur in the chain determines the genetic information carried by the chain. Thus, if the four nucleotides are represented by their initials A (adenine), C (cytosine), G (guanine) and T (thymine), a linear aggregate in the order ACGT will constitute different genetic information from—AGCT—or—ATCG—or ACCA-GTGT—chains. The inheritance or every organism consists in its essence of some repeated pattern of nucleotide units in the DNA molecules of the chromosomes contained in nuclei.

DNA replication

It is an established fact that the chemical nature and total amount of DNA remains constant in similar kind of cells from generation to generation. It means that quality and quantity of DNA remain same in similar cells, derived from the same parent cell. While explaining the DNA replication one has to keep in the view these both requirements. The weak hydrogen bond that holds together the two strands of the double helix works some-what like a zipper. If one starts at one end of the molecule, one can 'unzip' each purine from it pyrimidine partner one by one. This will leave unpaired purine and pyrimidine ends on both strands. It is well known that the cell is a

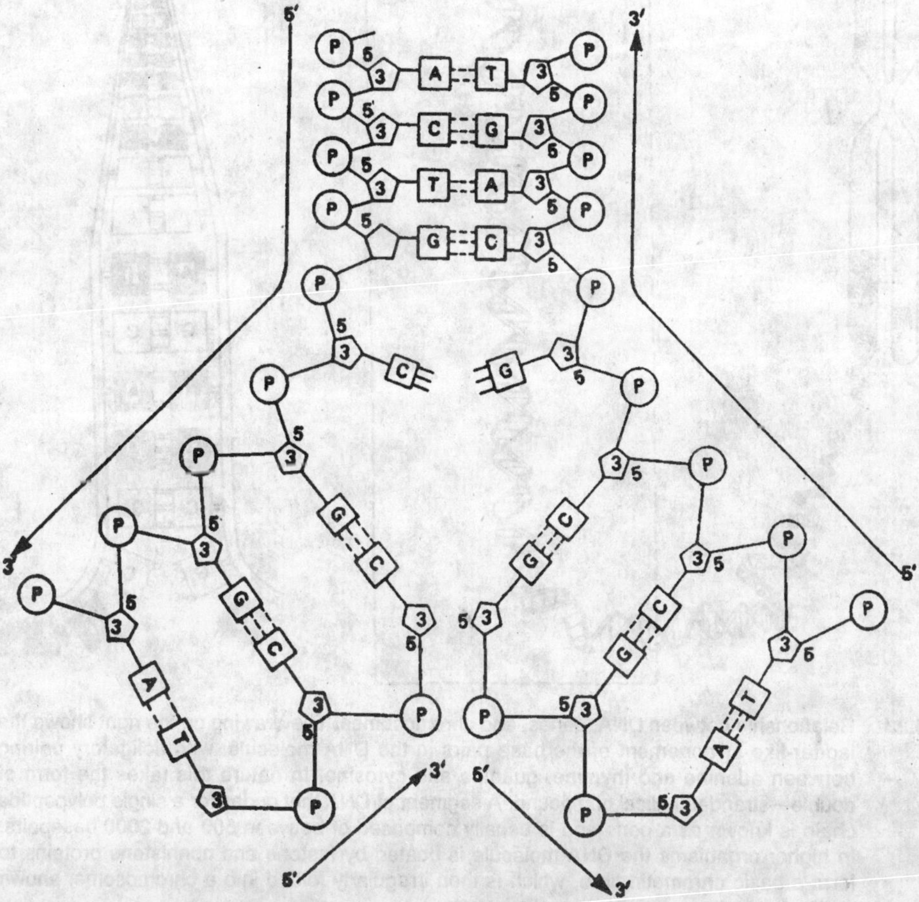

Fig. 39.22. DNA structure. The three components of DNA are the bases adenine, guanine, thymine and cytosine; a sugar molecule, deoxyribose; and phosphate groups. The phosphate groups are attached to the 3' and 5' carbons of the deoxyribose and serve to connect successive pairs of nucleotides. The replication process must one DNA strand by adding bases in the 5' → 3' direction and the other DNA strand, apparently by adding bases in the opposite direction.

storehouse of precursors of the four sorts of building blocks needed to make a new chain. These precursors are nucleotides. As such when the DNA helix 'unzips' new nucleotides from the cell of the proper kind fall into place, the improper ones are rejected as they will not fit. An adenine group will become bounded only with a new thymine group whereas the thymine group of the other strand will become bounded to a new adenine nucleotide thus completing the double chain in the two original strands. In the words of Crick the two strands of DNA 'unzip' as follows—'it is the growth of the two new chain that unwinds the original pair. This is likely in the terms of energy because, for every hydrogen bond that has to be broken, two new ones will be forming".

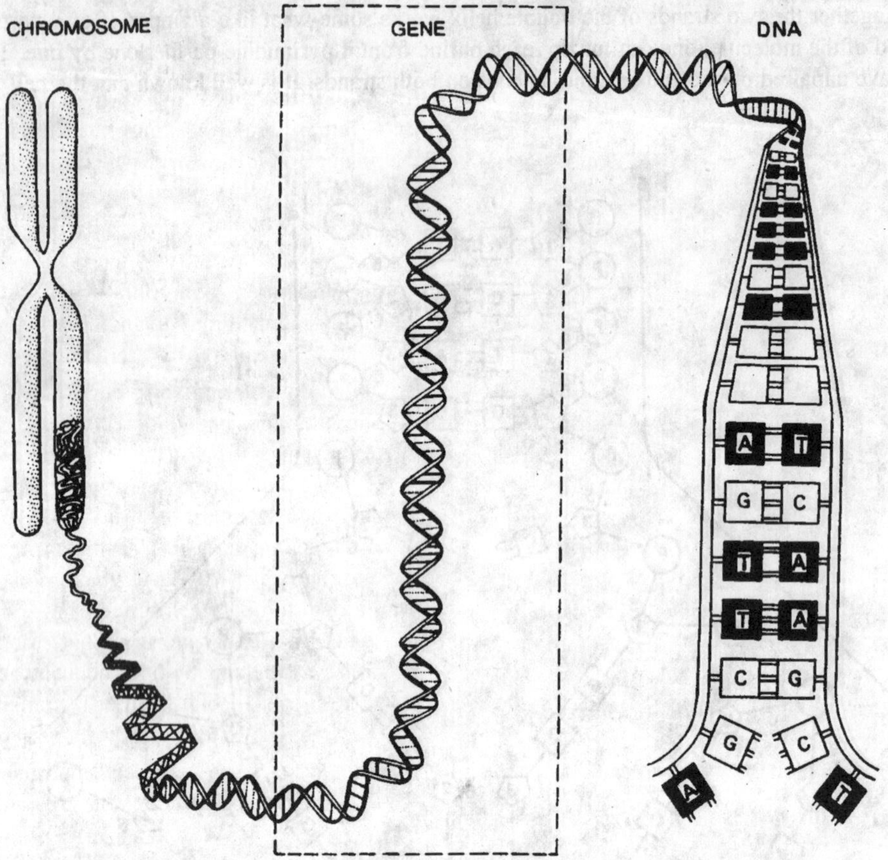

Fig. 39.23. Relationship between DNA, genes, and chromosomes. The drawing on the right shows the ladder-like arrangement of the base pairs in the DNA molecule, with deligatory pairing between adenine and thymine, guanine and cytosine. In nature this takes the form of double—stranded helical compound. A segment of DNA that codes for a single polypeptide chain is known as a gene and is usually composed of between 500 and 2000 basepairs. In higher organisms the DNA molecule is coated by histone and nonhistone proteins to form a basic chromatin fibre, which is then irregularly folded into a chromosome, shown on the left in the metaphase configuration.

The unzipping of DNA molecule at the weak forces (H-bonds) leaves the two strands apart, each strand with a purine or pyrimidine base attached to the sugar molecule. Each strand has not the capacity to replicate and exactly identical strand like the partner from which it has separated.

Classification of DNA

The DNA in the eucaryotic cells may be classified as follows:

(*i*) Nuclear DNA (*n*DNA)—It is found in the chromosomes of nucleus.

(*ii*) Mitochondrial DNA (*m*DNA)—It is found in the mitochondria.

(*iii*) Chloroplast DNA (*c*DNA)—It is found in the chloroplasts.

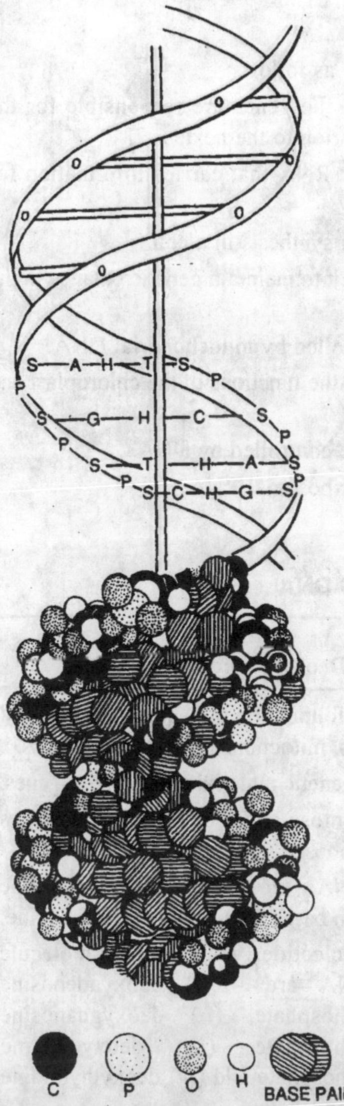

Fig. 39.24. The helix of DNA, with three different ways of representing the molecular arrangement. Top, general diagram of the double helix, with the phosphate sugar combinations making up the outside spirals and the base pairs the cross bars. Middle, a somewhat more detailed representation—phosphate (P), sugar deoxyribose (S), adenine (A), thymine (T), guanine (G), cytosine (C) and hydrogen (H). Bottom, detailed structure showing how the space is filled with atoms—carbon (C), oxygen (O), hydrogen (H), phosphorus (P) and base pairs.

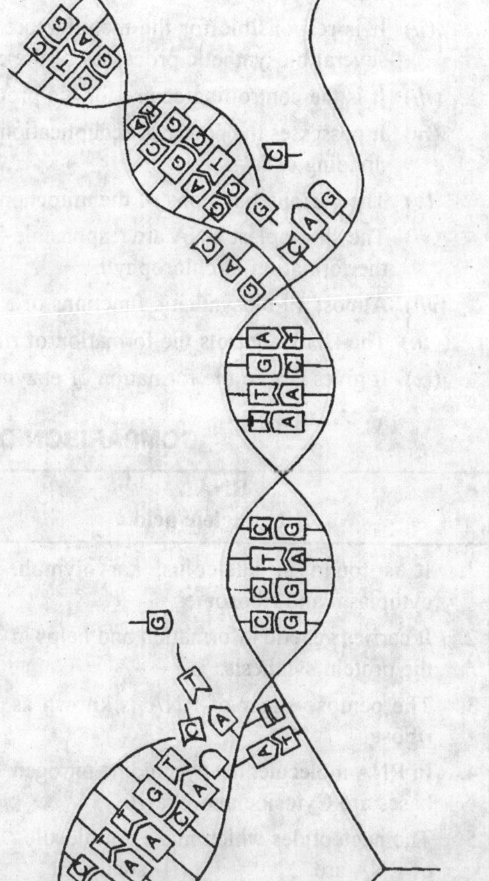

Fig. 39.25. Replication of DNA molecule. Diagrammatic representation.

Functions of DNA

The main functions of deoxyribonucleic acid (DNA) are as follows:

(*i*) It carries genes from one generation to the other; the genes are responsible for the transference of genetic information from one generation to the next.

(*ii*) It is responsible for the manufacture of messenger RNA that carries information for several biosynthetic processes of the cell.

(*iii*) It is the controlling centre for the process of protein synthesis in a cell.

(*iv*) It possesses the power of reduplication which makes it to maintain genetic balance in the dividing cells.

(*v*) The various functions of the mitochondria are controlled by mitochondrial DNA.

(*vi*) The chloroplast DNA are responsible for controlling the functions of the chloroplast and the formation of chlorophyll.

(*vii*) Almost all biosynthetic functions of a living cell are controlled by DNA.

(*viii*) The DNA controls the formation of ribosomes and ribosomal RNA.

(*ix*) It gives rise to the formation of enzymes.

COMPARISON OF RNA AND DNA

RNA **Ribonucleic acid**	**DNA** **Deoxyribonucleic acid**
1. It is found in nucleolus, karyolymph, cytoplasm and ribosomes.	1. It is found in the chromosomes of nucleus, mitochondria and chloroplasts.
2. It carries genetic information and helps in the protein synthesis.	2. It is a genetic material and contains genes.
3. The pentose sugar of RNA is known as ribose.	3. The pentose sugar of DNA is known as deoxyribose.
4. In RNA molecule, the pyrimidine nitrogen bases are Cytosine and Urasil.	4. In DNA molecule, the pyrimidine nitrogen bases are Cytosine and Thymine.
5. The nucleotides which make a molecule of RNA are - (*i*) adenosine monophosphate, (*ii*) guanosine monophosphate, (*iii*) cytidine monophosphate and (*iv*) Uridine monophosphate.	5. The nucleotides which make a molecule of DNA are – (*i*) deoxyadenosine monophosphate, (*ii*) deoxyguanosine monophosphate, (*iii*) deoxycytidine monophosphate and (*iv*) deoxythymidine monophosphate.
6. The nucleotides of a RNA molecule are arranged in a single chain.	6. The paired nucleotides of a DNA molecule are arranged in a double stranded helix.
7. Three main types of RNA are messenger (*m*RNA), transfer (*t*RNA) and ribosomal (*r*RNA).	7. Three main types of DNA are — nuclear (*n*DNA), mitochondrial (*m*DNA) and chloroplast (*c*DNA).

RNA

The molecule of RNA (ribonucleic acid) consists of a single strand, but it may be wound back upon itself in several places, producing helices in these places as found in DNA. In the region of helix formation, the bases are hydrogen bonded. The RNA differs chemically from the DNA in that it contains a ribose sugar instead of deoxyribose sugar. The ribose sugar possesses an additional oxygen molecule which is not found in deoxyribose sugar. The base pairs in RNA are same, *i.e.*, three of the four bases—adenine, guanine and cytosine are the same as found in DNA however, the fourth base, thymine is replaced in RNA by **uracil** which possesses one methyl group less. There are three kinds of RNA—ribosomal RNA (rRNA), soluble or transfer RNA (tRNA) and messenger RNA (mRNA). The RNA contained in the ribosomes are known as rRNA. Electron microscopy reveals that ribosomes are composed of two sub-units—the larger and the smaller. The small subunits are attached to mRNA and the appropriate tRNA are specially bound to the large subunits.

Classification of RNA

The RNA in the eucaryotic cells may be classified as follows:

(*i*) The messenger RNA (mRNA)— This carries message from the DNA to the actual site of protein synthesis.

(*ii*) The transfer RNA (tRNA)— This carries a specific amino acid to the site of protein synthesis.

(*iii*) The ribosomal RNA (rRNA)— It is found in the ribosomes. The function of this is not very clear.

THE MITOCHONDRIA
(Power house of cell)

They are microscopic bodies occurring in cytoplasm of every cell in varying numbers (upto 2500 per cell in rat liver) except in bacteria, blue-green algae and human r.b.c. Most are granular, rod or thread shaped. They are generally known as 'powerhouses of cell'. They are the site of the chemical events that supply the energy to the cell. They are also held responsible for fat synthesis. They range in their size from 0.2μ to 3.0μ. They also vary in their shape from spheres to rods. They are always found in dynamic state.

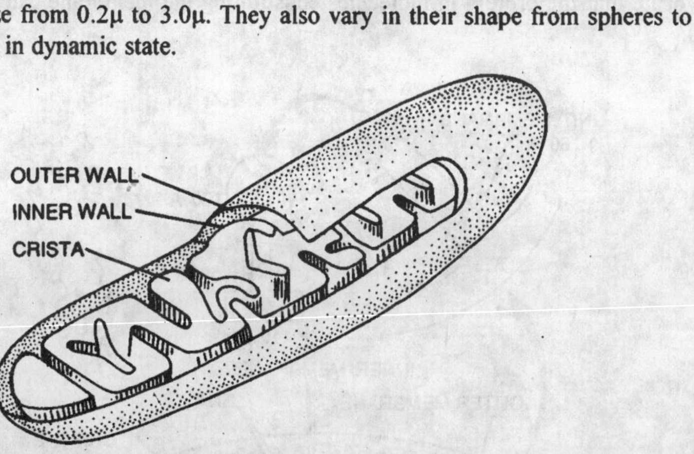

Fig. 39.26. Mitochondrion. Schematic diagram of a typical mitochondrion.

Each mitochondrion has a double-layered envelope with an outer and inner membranes. Each membrane is a typical unit membrane, being about 50–70 Å thick. The two membranes are generally 60–100 Å apart from each other. In between them remain filled the fluid rich in coenzymes. Extending from the inner membrane into the interior of the cavity, there are present a series of folds, called the **cristae.** The cristae are shorter in mitochondria of plant origin that in those of animal cells.In all the cases the purpose of the presence of cristae is to increase the surface area of the interior of the mitochondrion. The number of folds per unit of volume of a mitochondrion is variable. The cristae may be branched, tubular rather than lamellate, and may be

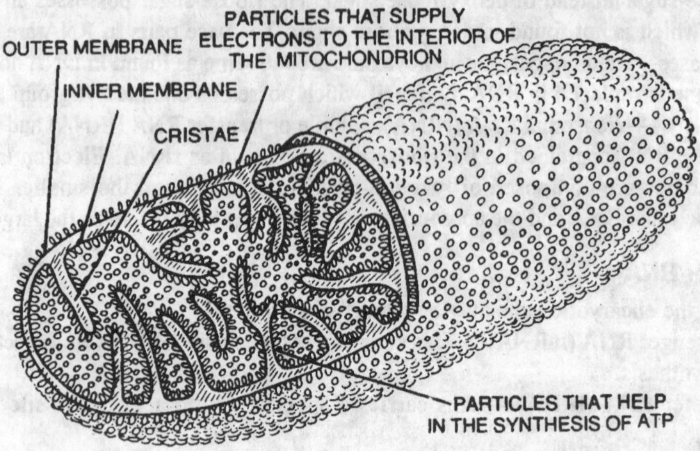

Fig. 39.27. Mitochondrion. Structure as viewed in electron microscope. The particles that supply electrons to the interior of the mitochondrion are clearly seen.

arranged parallel with long axis of mitochondrion, not, as is usual, at right angles. Thus each mitochondrion contains two cavities. The outer cavity found in between the two membranes is called **'outer compartment'** while the cavity limited by the folds of inner membrane is known as **'inner compartment** or **mitochondrial matrix'**. The matrix is normally homogeneous but it contains granules of 300–500 Å diameter. The outer covering membrane of the mitochondrion is quite elastic and may be stretched by swelling sometimes 200 times its normal dimensions. These facts advocate that the protein in molecules constituting the membrane can be greatly folded or stretched.

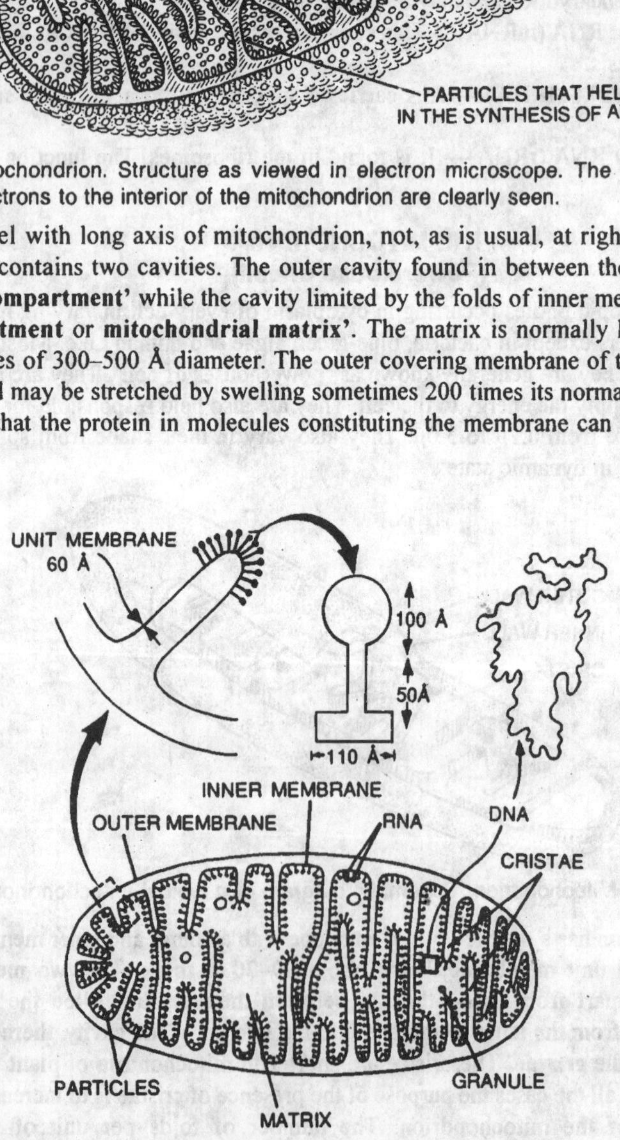

Fig. 39.28. Structure of mitochondrion as seen in electron microscope. Above, the various parts of mitochondrion magnified.

Electron microscopy has also revealed the presence of very small particles adhered to the outside of the outer membrane and the inside of the inner membrane. These particles were first described by Humberto Fernandez-Moran (1962). The particles of the two membranes differ considerably. Depending upon the size and type of the mitochondrion there are from 10,000 to 100,000 particles per mitochondrion. Each particle consists of a base, a stalk and a head. The base which remains attached to the inner membrane has about 80 Å diameter. The stalk is 50 Å long and 33 Å wide while the head has the same diameter as does the base. The length of the complete particle is about 160 Å.

The mitochondria contain DNA and many oxidative enzyme systems.

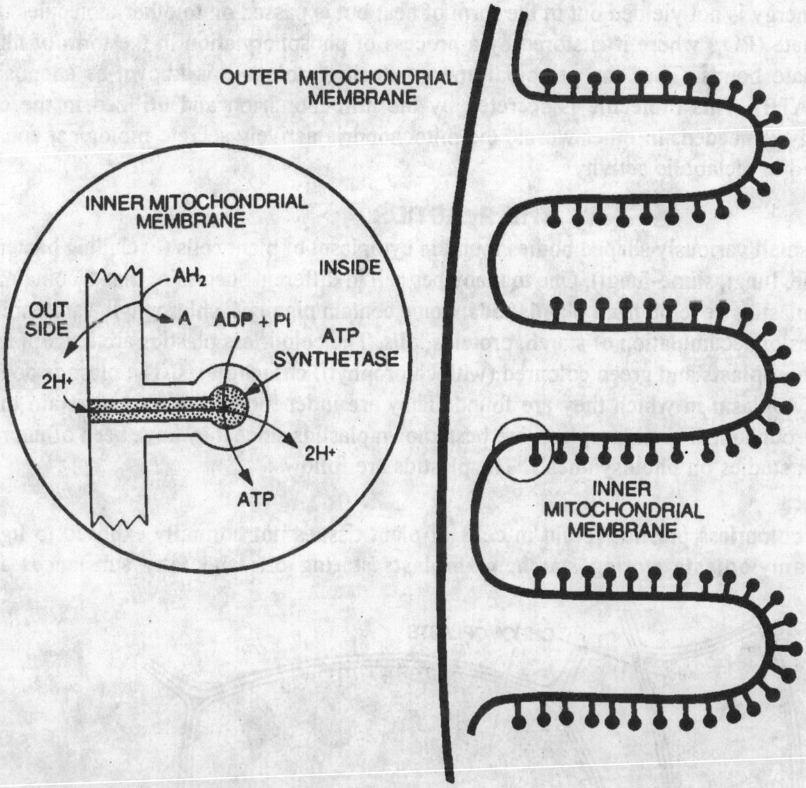

Fig. 39.29. The mitochondria. The figure shows the principle of the chemiosmotic hypothesis of energy conservation. The insert represents a magnified view of the encircled portion of the inner mitochondrial membrane.

Development. The mitochondria are essential structures where combustion of organic substances by oxygen takes place. Since this form of energy supply is essential for the life of most higher organisms the presence of functional mitochondria is essential for life. There are certain organisms, such as yeast, which can grow in the absence of oxygen. When such anaerobic cells are examined critically it is found that they contain small organelles having double membranes but the inner membrane does not have any of the invaginations (*i.e.*, cristae) typical of normal mitochondria. The characteristic enzymes and coenzymes which take part in aerobic respiration are also absent. Upon exposure to oxygen these structures soon develop to become normal respiring organelles. This observation shows that mitochondria can exist in an **embryonic** form, called a **promitochondrion,** and that upon stimulation by environmental factor (*i.e.*, oxygen) they undergo a process of development to become functional structures.

Functions

As regards the functions of the mitochondria they perform two important tasks. They are as follows.

(*i*) The carbohydrates, proteins and fats are broken down gradually into smaller and smaller molecules. During this process there is transference of energy. This process takes place through a series of steps, and each step is controlled by an enzyme. All these energy giving reactions are known as **oxidations.**

(*ii*) The energy is not yielded out in the form of heat but is passed on to other molecules that contain phosphate (PO_4) where it is stored by a process of phosphorylation in the form of high-energy phosphate bonds. Thus the principal energy storing molecule is known as adenosine triphosphate (ATP). This molecule is secreted by the mitochondrion and utilized in the cell wherever energy is needed. In other words, the mitochondria actively secrete biological energy which is utilized in metabolic activity.

THE PLASTIDS

They are small variously shaped bodies found in cytoplasm of plant cells (excluding bacteria, blue-green algae, fungi, slime-fungi), One to many per cell in different species of plants containing pigments. The plastids develop from **proplastids.** Some contain pigments chlorophyll, carotenoids, some are centres of accumulation of starch, proteins, oils. The colourless plastids are **leucoplasts,** pigmented **chromoplasts** and green coloured (with chlorophyll) **chloroplasts.** The plastids do not mix with the cytoplasm in which they are found. They are independent bodies and retain their individuality throughout. The chloroplasts are best known plastids since they have been of interest in the extensive studies on photosynthesis. The plastids are follows:

Leucoplasts

They are colourless plastids found in cells of plant tissues not normally exposed to light. They include **amyloplasts** storing starch, **elaioplasts** storing oils and fatty substances and

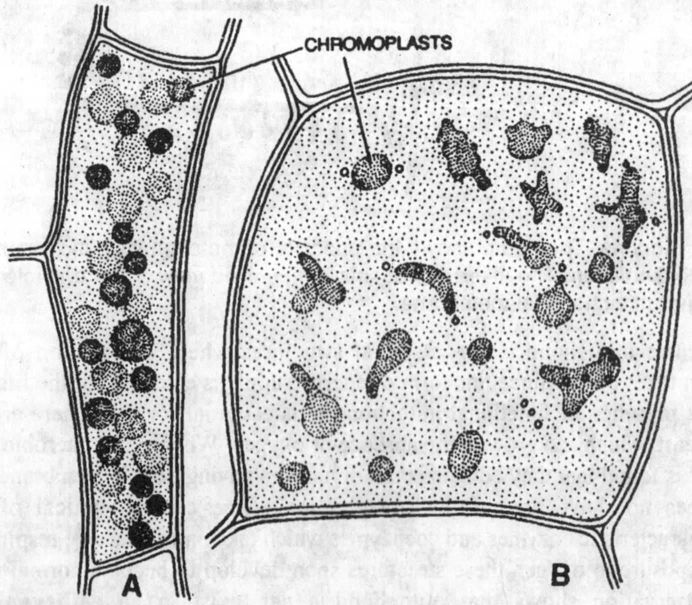

Fig. 39.30. Chromoplasts. A, from *Calendula* petal; B from *Pyracantha* fruit.

aleuroplasts, storing protein. The amyloplasts are found in cotyledons, endosperm and in storage organs such as potato tubers. The elaioplasts are commonly found in the tissues of liverworts and monocotyledons. They are refractive granules and also referred to as fatty or lipoid granules. The leucoplasts are found in many seeds. The leucoplasts often appear as small masses of protoplasm, variable and unstable in form. They commonly aggregate near the nucleus. The plastids of the epidermis frequently appear nonpigmented and are then classified as leucoplasts.

Chromoplasts

They are pigmented plastids of plant cells. They may be red, orange or yellow, *e.g.*, tomato fruits, carrot roots containing carotenoid pigments. They may appear rather granular with the pigments enclosed in it in a dispersed condition.

They show great variety in shape but are chiefly irregular; granular, angular, acicular and forked types occur. The irregular and sharp-pointed shapes are believed to be caused in part by the presence of the coloured substances, especially carotene and carotenoids, in crystalline form, as in the root of *Daucus*. They are associated with colour in flowers, fruits and roots. Usually they represent transformed chloroplasts, but may form directly from small leucoplasts. The development of chromoplasts with globular and fibrous inclusions from chloroplasts involves the destruction of the original grana system.

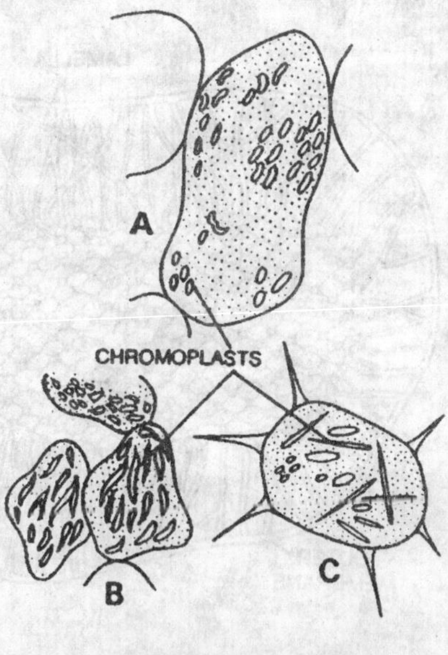

Fig. 39.31. Plastids. The chromoplasts. A, chromoplasts in pulp cells of tomato; B, chromoplasts in pulp cells of fruit of

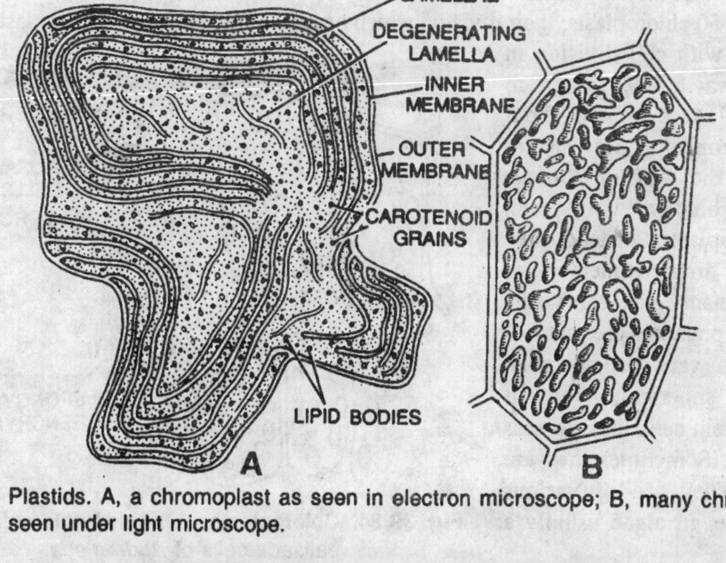

Fig. 39.32. Plastids. A, a chromoplast as seen in electron microscope; B, many chromoplasts as seen under light microscope.

Chloroplasts

The sequence of the trapping of light energy, its conversion into chemical energy, and its storage in molecules derived from CO_2 and water, is known as **photosynthesis.** The photosynthesis is initiated by the capture of light energy through absorption in the green pigment **chlorophyll.** The **chloroplast** is the cytoplasmic particle in which this takes place.

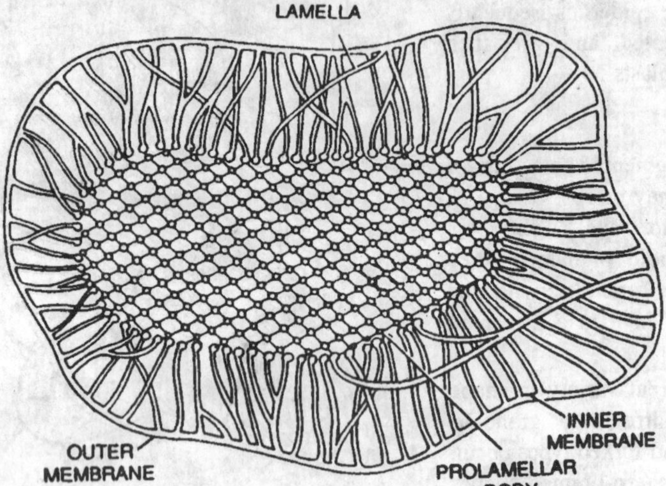

Fig. 39.33. Plastids. A, proplastid which gives rise to a plastid.

Morphology. The chloroplast is one of the largest cytoplasmic structures which can very well be seen under the low power of compound microscope. The size, shape and distribution of chloroplasts vary in different cells and species, but they remain relatively constant within the same tissue. The average size varies from 4 to 6 μ in diameter and 1 to 3 μ in thickness. The chloroplasts may assume many forms, and vary widely in number per cell in different plants. In some algae, such as the filamentous *Spirogyra*, only a single chloroplast is present in each cell; when the cell divides, it divides at the same time. On the other hand, a cell in the spongy tissue of a grass leaf may have 30 to 50 chloroplasts; their division which occurs in the immature, or proplastid state, is not correlated with cell division in any exact way. According to Haberlandt (1914) there are about 400,000 chloroplasts per square millimeter in the leaf of *Ricinus communis*. The blue-green algae lack definite chloroplasts; instead they possess loosely arranged membranes in the cytoplasm on which the photosynthetic pigments are layered. The shape too vary considerably. They may be spherical, ovoid or discoid. In certain cells they possess special shapes. Sometimes they are club-shaped. They are of various shapes in algae. In algae usually a

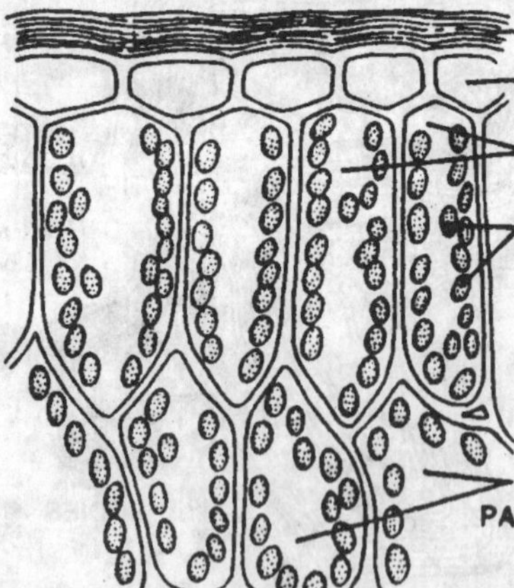

Fig. 39.34. Chloroplasts. Discoid chloroplasts in palisade cells of *Andromeda*.

single large size chloroplast is present which may be reticulate, spiral, band like or stellate. The chloroplass are sometimes homogeneously distributed within the cytoplasm, but are seldom packed near the nucleus or close to the cell wall. Their distribution depends largely on external conditions such as light intensity.

Structure. Electron microscopy reveals that the chloroplast is a structure of considerable complexity. A mature chloroplast remains surrounded by a semipermeable membrane. The membrane comprises of two separate layers, each being 40 to 60 Å thick and the space between

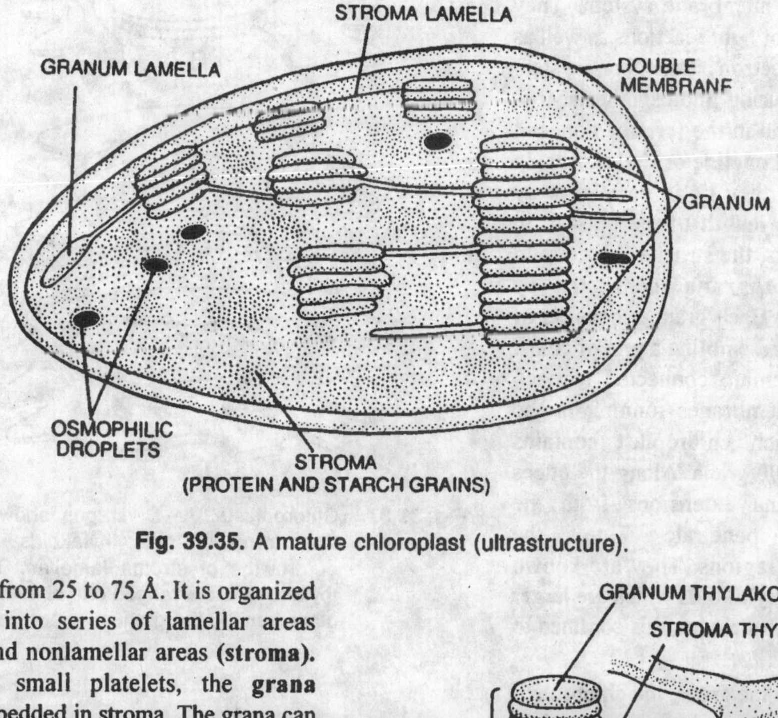

Fig. 39.35. A mature chloroplast (ultrastructure).

them vary from 25 to 75 Å. It is organized internally into series of lamellar areas **(grana)** and nonlamellar areas **(stroma).** Numerous small platelets, the **grana** remain embedded in stroma. The grana can be visualized as pieces of many-layered plywood lying in a less well-organized stroma. The number of grana is variable in different chloroplasts. The mesophyll cell of spinach has 40 to 60 grana per chloroplast whereas one granum per chloroplast is found in *Euglena*. Each granum consists of double membrane **discs** or **lamellae** which vary in thickness and are of two types, *i.e.,* **granum lamellae** and **stroma lamellae.**

Various particles and molecules may be found in the stroma; 175 Å diameter chloroplast **ribosomes;** the proteinaceous **stroma center,** starch grains **pyrenoids** in lower plants; osmophilic globule; and in some cases **phytoferritin** as well as fine

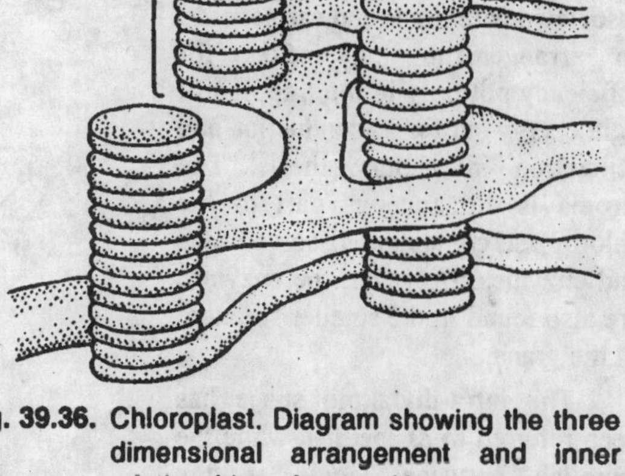

Fig. 39.36. Chloroplast. Diagram showing the three dimensional arrangement and inner relationships of grana (the scheme given in this diagram does not necessarily

fibrils of DNA—different from the nuclear DNA. The osmophilic globuli are generally referred to as **plastoglobuli.** They contain various lipid materials but no chlorophyll or carotenoid pigments.

In the stroma is also found suspended a chlorophyll containing lipoprotein membrane system. They are the site of light reactions as well as of the electron transport system operating during photosynthesis. It is usually found in the form of flattened sacs called **lamellae or thylakoids.** In many algae they lie in parallel array and run the length of the plastid. In higher plants, the structure varies and comprise of **grana,** connected by membranes. Each granum consists of **thylakoids** resembling a pile of coins, and they remain connected to each other by membranes running in the stroma. Each chloroplast contains about 20–100 grana. Along the edges of the grana extensions from the thylakoid penetrate into the intergranal regions. They are known as **stroma thylakoids** which are larger than the **grana thylakoids** confined to grana.

Within the grana, the chlorophyll molecules are precisely oriented in a monolayer sandwiched in between layers of proteins and intimately associated with lipids and carotenoids, an arrangement that makes for efficiency not only in the trapping of light energy but for its conduction and utilization in photosynthesis. The stroma is the aqueous part of the chloroplast, containing dissolved salts and enzymes. However, the enzymes are also found in the smaller structure of the grana.

The intra-thylakoid space has been referred to as **loculus,** while the lamellae between loculi as the **partition.** The connections between grana are termed as **frets** (Weier,

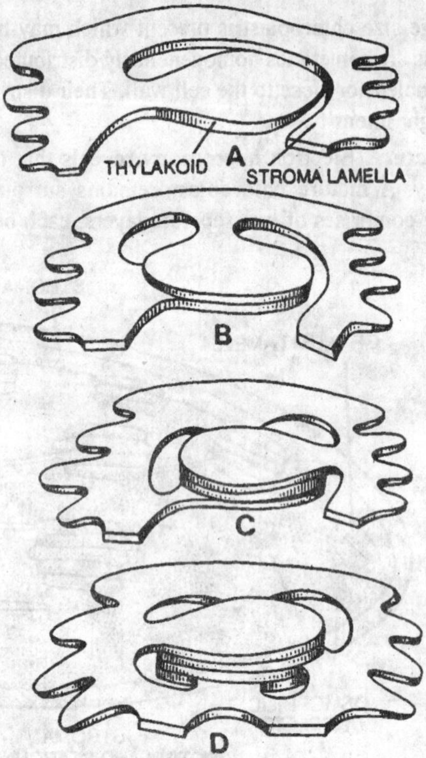

Fig. 39.37. Chloroplasts. A—D, stages showing the formation of thylakoids as outgrowths of stroma lamellae. The thylakoids are arranged one above the other forming the granum.

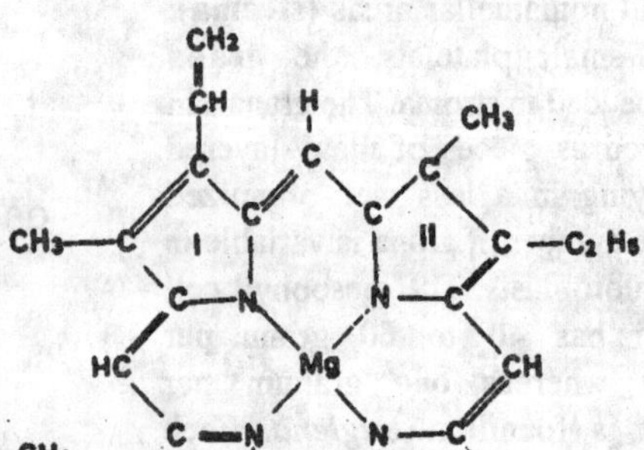

Fig. 39.38. Chlorophyll. Chemical structure of the chlorophyll— a molecule. The four pyrrole rings (1—4) attached to it.

1966). Park and Pon (1961) reported the presence of **quantosome particles,** 100—200 Å in diameter arranged in rows in the chloroplast thylakoid membrane. They are the fundamental units responsible for the conversion of **quantum** of light energy into chemical energy.

Development. When a plant is germinated in the dark, its cells contain small double membraned structures. These structures appear colourless but they can be shown to contain a very low concentration of substances which are precursors of chlorophyll. Upon exposure to light these precursor substances are immediately converted to chlorophylls. At the same time a process of growth and development starts which results in the transformation of the small **prochloroplast** into a typical photosynthetic chloroplast. The entire process takes place in less than twenty four hours.

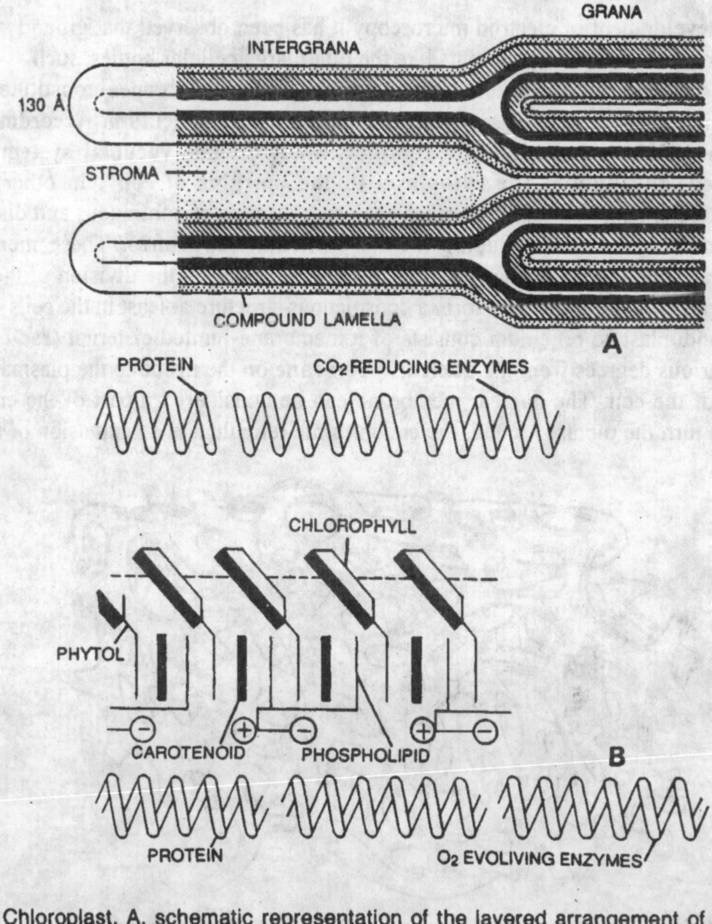

Fig. 39.39. Chloroplast. A, schematic representation of the layered arrangement of lamella, in the grana; B, possible arrangement of molecules in lamellae. The enzymes involved in photosynthesis are part of the protein layers, and the carotenoid and phospholipid molecules assist in the transfer of energy captured by the chlorophyll. (After A.J. Hodge and M. Calvin).

It seems quite obvious that light induces the activation of synthetic processes within the cell that result in the construction of the complex photosynthetic apparatus (*i.e.*, chloroplast). During the induced development process many new enzymes which were not present in the prochloroplasts are synthesized and organized. This phenomenon shows that control systems operate within the cells.

Functions

The main function of chloroplast is to take active part in photosynthesis. The photosynthesis is initiated by the capture of light energy through absorption in the green pigment chlorophyll inside the chloroplast.

The light energy trapped by chlorophyll can also be funneled through a series of enzymatically controlled reactions, into an energy compound called **adenosine triphosphate** (ATP). The chloroplast is, therefore, a dual energy converter, since the energy of sugars and ATP can be utilized by the cell in a variety of ways.

ENDOPLASMIC RETICULUM (ER)

With the development of electron microscopy it has been observed that ground substance of a cell is divided into several compartments like the other large cellular bodies, such as the nucleus and mitochondria. This highly ordered arrangement of the membranes constitute a cellular background which is called the **ergastoplasm** or **endoplasmic reticulum.** According to Porter (1961), **"the endoplasmic reticulum is a complex, finely divided vacuolar system extending from the nucleus throughout the cytoplasm to the margins of cell".** In other words the endoplasmic reticulum consists of membranes enclosing a series of continuous and discontinuous vacuoles, found in cytoplasm excluding all the particulate structures. These membranes of ergastoplasm may found to be arranged variously sometimes during the division of the cells they appear and disappear rapidly. But they form a conspicuous structure at least in the cells of liver and pancreas. The endoplasmic reticulum consists of a membrane-limited cisternal (sac-like) system extending, in various degrees from the **nuclear membrane** on the inside to the plasma membrane on the outside of the cell. The nuclear membrane can be considered a part of the endoplasmic recticulum or to turn the picture around, the endoplasmic reticulum is an extension of the nucleus in the cytoplasm.

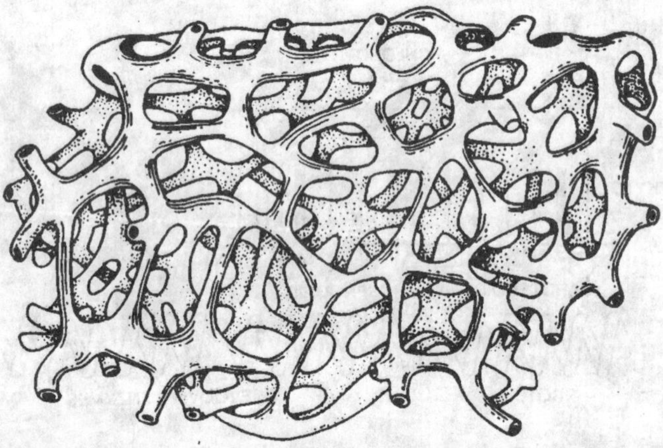

Fig.33.40. Endoplasmic reticulum (ergastoplasm). Three dimensional view.

Morphology. The endoplasmic reticulum is of a variable morphology, and each kind of cell has a characteristic ER. The ER can be loosely organized or its membranes can be tightly packed in the cytoplasm. Furthermore, the membranes can be either **rough** or **smooth.**

The rough, or **granular,** ER is found in great abundance in those cells engaged in protein synthesis. This chemical capacity resides in electron-dense particles (microsomes) that are rich in ribose nucleic acid (RNA). Since ribosomes live free in the cytoplasm, their association with ER is not necessary. On the other hand, the association of ribosomes with membranes, does not provide the intact cell with a means of compartmentalizing specific chemical reactions. **Further** the membranes of ER also provide a tremendous increase in surface area within the cell. If this is accepted that enzymes are part of membrane systems, then the cell can possess local patterns of synthesis.

The smooth, or **agranular,** ER, lacks the ribosomes. There is probably no sharp morphological discontinuity between smooth and rough kinds of ER, but the former is particularly prevalent in those cells engaged in the synthesis of fatty substances, *i.e.*, lipids in the cells of sebaceous glands, or steroid hormones in certain endocrine glands. The enzymes necessary for these syntheses appear to be a part of the membrane itself since they cannot be separated physically from the membrane fragments.

Function

Thus ER is a kind of cytoskeleton providing surfaces for chemical reactions, pathways for the transport of materials, and collection depots for synthesized materials. We also find the smooth ER in particular, in these cells that must maintain a particular shape; in these the ER is a structural component as well. The RNA-rich particles, called **microsomes,** are particularly active in the synthesis of proteins, while the membrane itself appears to be involved in the synthesis of **steroids,** a group of compounds which include certain of the hormones. We therefore look upon the endoplasmic reticulum as the principal manufacturing portion of our factory (cell), although we are far from a complete comprehension of its operation as whole.

RIBOSOMES

For the first time in 1955 Palade discovered the ribosomes in the cytoplasm. They are the intracellular sites of protein synthesis and are present in all the cells. They are very small granules (smaller than 1μ) and are visible only under the electron microscope. They are found frequently associated with membranes of endoplasmic reticulum. They are found attached to the outer surface of the double fold endoplasmic reticulum membrane. Sometimes this association is very tight. Their association with the endoplasmic reticulum has given rise to a number of different names, such as **'rough endoplasmic reticulum'** or **'granular endoplasmic reticulum'** as opposed to the **'smooth endoplasmic reticulum'** or **'agranular endoplasmic reticulum.'** In the smooth or agranular endoplasmic reticulum the membranes remain devoid of ribosomes. In tangential view the ribosomes seem to be arranged in definite patterns such as rosettes, spirals and circles. Though these two components (ER and ribosomes) are closely associated yet they are quite different in their functions and properties. They contain RNA (ribonucleic acid), nucleoproteins and enzymes needed in many synthetic reactions. The RNA is of very high molecular weight. The ribosome globules may be extracted out by centrifuging the cells. It is believed that they are mainly concerned with the synthesis of cellular proteins. These proteins control the chemical reactions going on within the cells. They are enzymic in nature and act as catalysts. The proteins of ribosomes appear to be basic in nature.

As electron microscopy reveals they appear as spherical to ellipsoidal bodies. The size varies from 150 Å in bacteria and chloroplast to 200 Å in the cytoplasm of plant and animal cells. Each ribosome consists of two distinctive sub-units, which differ in sizes. The two subunits are held together by bonds which appear to need magnesium ions for their continued stability.

Sub-units of ribosomes. The ribosome sizes are known in terms of speed with which they sediment in the centrifugal field. **Svedberg unit** (S) is the unit in measuring this speed. In this context, each plant cytoplasmic ribosome is typically a 80 S which possesses typically 60 S and 36 S particles or sub-units which in the natural conditions are probably held together by bonds which appear to need magnesium ions for their continued stability. The 60 S sub-unit (larger one) contains an RNA molecule whose molecular weight is about 1.5 million, *i.e.*, twice than those of

36 S sub-unit (smaller one) RNA. Further, the larger sub-unit contains about 30 proteins—all different from each other while the smaller sub-unit contains only 20.

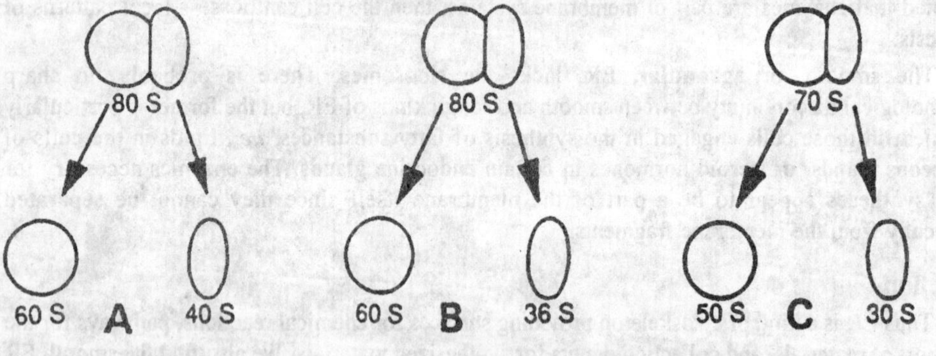

Fig. 39.41. Ribosomes. On the basis of sedimentation constant three classes of ribosomes can be distinguished—A, animal cytoplasmic ribosomes; B, plant cytoplasmic ribosomes; C, organelle bacterial ribosomes. The differences can be noted in the above-mentioned diagrams. (S—Svedberg unit).

The smaller particles are not active in protein synthesis. It is only the larger particles that are active. As regards protein synthesis, mRNA is specifically held by the smaller sub-units while tRNA seems to be specifically held by the larger sub-units. As a matter of fact, a portion of tRNA molecule is bound to the larger sub-unit and portion of it is bound to mRNA on the smaller sub-unit.

LYSOSOMES

They represent a new discovery among the cytoplasmic particles. They are found in most of the animal cells and in some meristematic cells of the plants. C. De Duve (1955) for the first time observed a fluffy layer of particles in the cytoplasm in which number of hydrolytic enzymes were present. The electron microscopy revealed that fluffy layer consists of membrane bounded structures whose appearance is markedly affected by the osmotic conditions present during preparation. De Duve called these structures, the lysosomes because of their contents of hydrolytic enzymes. As regards their origin it has been thought that they have been originated from the Golgi complex and the ribosomes. The lysosomes vary in size from 0.4μ to 0.8μ in diameter, but sometimes they are as large as 5μ in diameter, *e.g.*, in a mammalian kidney. They may be spherical, rod like or irregular in shape, being covered by a single layered membrane composed of lipoprotein. They may be uniformly solid or some of them possess a very dense outer zone and airless dense core. The vacuoles or cavities are found within the granular material. They are distinguished from the mitochondria by their lack of internal cristae and by their characteristic enzyme content. The breakdown products diffuse out of the lysosomes and into the mitochondria, where they are further broken down in the process of respiration. They are also concerned with the digestion of proteins.

SPHAEROSOMES

The sphaerosomes are usually spherical bodies. They remain surrounded by membranes and range in diameter from 0.5 to 1.0μ. They are associated with the synthesis of fats and other such substances. They contain lipids and various types of lysosome-like enzymes. Sorokin (1966) reported the presence of a limiting membrane around each sphaerosome, however, James and Hilton (1972) do not agree with this view; they are in agreement with Yatsu that partial bounding membrane surrounds the sphaerosomes. Besides lipid storage and their transport, they are also thought to be intermediaries in the biosynthesis of waxes, cutin and other allied compounds, which result in cuticularization and suberization of cell walls.

LOMASOMES

They are generally small bodies found in algae, fungi and higher plants. Usually they are found in the periphery of cytoplasm. As regards their function they are supposed to be concerned with cell wall synthesis.

GLYOXYSOMES

They are small bodies and occur only in plant cells. They are supposed to contain enzymes which convert fatty acids into sugars

PEROXISOMES

These are microbodies and measure 0.2 to 2.0 mμ. They are found in all photosynthetic cells of higher plants in etiolated leaf tissue, in coleoptiles and hypocotyls, in tobacco stem and callus, in ripening pear fruits, and also in Euglenophyta, protozoa, brown algae, fungi, liverworts, mosses and ferns.

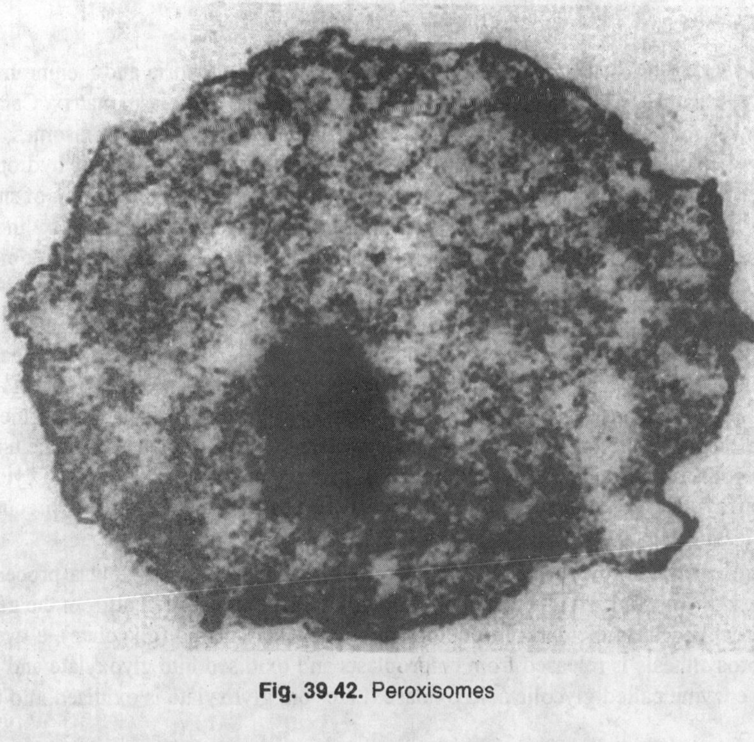

Fig. 39.42. Peroxisomes

Structure

Peroxisomes are variable in size and shape, but usually appear circular in cross section, having diameter between 0.2 and 2.0 mμ. They have a single limiting unit membrane of lipid and protein molecules, which encloses their granular matrix. In some cases (*e.g.*, *Festuca* grass) the matrix contains numerous threads or fibrils, while in others they are observed to contain either an amorphous nucleoid or a dense inner core which in many species shows a regular crystalloid structure (*e.g.*, tobacco leaf cell).

Functions

Peroxisomes are found to perform following two types of biochemical activities:

A. Hydrogen peroxide metabolism: Peroxisomes are so-called, because they usually contain one or more enzymes (*i.e.*), D-amino acid oxidase and urate oxidase) that molecular oxygen to remove hydrogen atoms from specific organic substances (R) in an oxidative reaction that produces hydrogen peroxide.

$$RH_2 + O_2 \longrightarrow R + H_2O_2$$

Catalase (which forms 40 percent of total peroxisome protein) utilises the H_2O_2 generated by other enzymes including alcohols, phenols, formic acid and formaldehyde by the peroxidative reaction.

$$H_2O_2 + R'H_2 \longrightarrow R' + 2H_2O$$

This type of oxidative reaction is particularly important in lirer and kidney cells, whose peroxisomes detoxify various toxic molecules that enter the blood stream. Almost half of alcohol one drinks is oxidised to acetaldehyde in this way. However, when excess H_2O_2 accumulates in the cell, catalase converts H_2O_2 to H_2O

$$2H_2O_2 \longrightarrow 2H_2O + O_2$$

H_2O_2 and aging. Most cytosolic H_2O_2 is produced by mitochondria and membranes of ER, alhough there are also H_2O_2– producing enzymes localised in the cytoplasm matrix. Catalase acts as a "safety valve" for dealing with the large amounts of H_2O_2 generated by peroxisomes; however, other enzymes such as glutathione peroxidase, are capable of metabolizing organic hydroperoxides and also H_2O_2, in the cytosol (cytoplasmic matrix) and mitochondria. The production of superoxide anion (O_2^-) in mitochondria and cytosol (cytoplasmic matrix) is regulated mainly by the enzyme superoxide dismutase. All of these protective enzymes are present in high levels in aerobic tissues.

B. Glycolate cycle. Peroxisomes of plant leaves contain catalase together with the enzymes of **glycolate pathway,** as glycolate oxidase, glutamate glyoxylate, serine-glyoxylate and asparate α-ketoglutarate aminotransferases, hydroxy pyruvate reductase and malic dehydrogenase. They also contain FAD, NAD and NADP coenzymes. The glycolate cycle is thought to bring about the formation of the amino acids - glycine and serene- from the non-phosphorylated intermediates of photosynthetic carbon reduction cycle, *i.e.*, glycerate to serene, or glycolate to glycine and serene in a sequence of reactions which involve chloroplasts, peroxisomes, mitochondria and cytosol. The **glycolate** pathway also generates C_1 compounds and serves as the generator of precursors for nucleic acid biosynthesis.

Photorespiration. In green leaves, these are peroxisomes that carry out a process called photorespiration which is a light stimulated production of CO_2 that is different from the generation of CO_2 by mitochondria in the dark. In photorespiration, glycolic acid (glycolate), a two-carbon product of photosynthesis is released from chloroplasts and oxidised into glyoxylate and H_2O_2 by a peroxisomal enzyme called glycolic acid oxidase. Later on, glyoxylate is oxidised into CO_2 and formate.

$$CH_2OH.COOH + O_2 \longrightarrow CHO\text{—}COOH + H_2O_2$$

$$CHO\text{—}COOH + H_2O_2 \longrightarrow HCOOH + CO_2 + H_2O$$

Photorespiration is so-called because light induces the synthesis of glycolic acid in chloroplasts. The entire process involves intervention of two basic organelles : chloroplasts and peroxisomes.

Lastly, photorespiration is driven by atmospheric conditions in which the O_2 tension is high and the CO_2 tension low. Apparently O_2 competes with CO_2 for the enzyme **ribulose diphosphate carboxylase** which normally is the key enzyme in CO_2 fixation during photosynthesis. When O_2

is used by the enzyme, an unstable intermediate is formed which breaks down into 3-phosphoglycerate and phosphoglycolate. The latter tends to increase the glycolate concentration by removal of its phosphate group, and therefore, more glycolate is available for additional oxidation and CO_2 release.

C.–β– Oxidation. Peroxisomes of rat liver cells contain enzymes of β-oxidation for the metabolism of fatty acids. They are capable of oxidising palmitoyl-CoA (or fatty acyl-CoA) to acetyl–CoA, using molecular oxygen and NAD as electron acceptors. The acetyl-CoA formed by this process is, eventually, transported to the mitochondria where it enters into the citric acid cycle. If alternatively, acetyl-CoA remains in the cytosol, it is reconverted into fatty acids and ultimately to neutral fats. β-oxidation pathway of the peroxisomes is very similar to the one that occurs in mitochondria, with one very important exception. In mitochondria the flavin dehydrogenase donates its electrons to the respiratory chain. It doe not react with molecular oxygen. In peroxisomes, the dehydrogenase reacts directly with O_2 and in so doing generates H_2O_2. Mitochondria contain no catalase and therefore, cannot deal with the formation of toxic hydrogen peroxide. For peroxisomes, this is not a problem.

D. Other functions. Mammalian cells do not contain D-amino acids, but the peroxisomes of mammalian liver and kidney contain **D-amino acid oxidase.** It is suggested that this enzyme is meant for D-amino acids that are found in the cell wall of the bacteria. Thus, the presumed role of this enzyme is to initiate the degradation of D-amino acid that may arise from breakdown and absorption of peptidoglycan material of intestinal bacteria.

Uric acid oxidase (uricase) is important in the catabolic pathway that degrades purines. Thus, peroxisomes are unusually diverse organelles and even in different cells of a single organism may contain very different sets of enzymes. They can also adapt remarkably to changing conditions. For example, yeast cells grown on sugar have tiny peroxisomes. But when in some yeasts are grown on methanol, they develop large-sized peroxisomes that oxidize methanol; when grown on fatty acids, they develop large peroxisomes that break down fatty acids to acetyl-CoA.

Biogenesis of Peroxisomes

At one time it was thought that the membrane 'shell' of the peroxisomes is formed by budding of the endoplasmic reticulum (ER), while the 'content' or matrix is imported from the cytosol (cytoplasmic matrix) However, there is now evidence suggesting that now peroxisomes always arise from pre-existing ones being formed by growth and fission of old organelles similar to mitochondria and chloroplasts.

Thus peroxisomes are a collection of organelles with a constant membrane and a variable enzymatic content. All of their proteins are encoded by nuclear genes and are synthesised in the cytosol.

The proteins present in either lumen or membrane of the peroxisome are taken up post-translationally from the cytosol. For example, catalase enzyme is a tetrameric haeme-containing protein that is made in the cytosol (cytoplasmic matrix) as the haeme-free monomers; the monomers are imported into the lumen of peroxisomes, where they assemble into tetramers in the presence of haeme. Catalase and many peroxisomal proteins are found to have a **signal sequence** (comprising of three amino acids) which is located near their carboxyl ends and directs them to peroxisome. Peroxisomes contain **receptors** exposed on their cytosolic surface to recognise the signal on the imported proteins. All of the **membrane proteins** of the peroxisomes, including signal receptor proteins, are imported directly from the cytosol. The lipids required to make new peroxisomal membrane are also imported from the cytosol, possibly being carried by **phospholipid transfer proteins** from sites of this synthesis in the ER membrane.

MICROTUBULES

For the first time Ledbetter and Porter (1963) demonstrated the presence of fine elongated tubular structures in the peripheral cytoplasm of some plant cells. These tubules are usually found to be attached to the cell wall. They are thought to be responsible for the orientation of cellulose synthesis. These structures are very clearly visible during the process of mitosis as cytoplasmic fibrils. They are several microns in length and their diameter ranges from 150 to 250 Å with a wall of about 60 Å in thickness. According to some workers they are thought to be fibres of spindle apparatus.

GOLGI COMPLEX

Camillio Golgi (1898), an Italian neurologist, first discovered these organelles in animal cells. The **Golgi complex,** so named after its discoverer is characteristic system of cytoplasmic membranes. The term, **dictyosome,** is also used to describe this structure. It is comparable to the smooth endoplasmic reticulum, but discontinuous, smaller and more compact in nature. It is still debatable that there is a direct morphological relation between the endoplasmic reticulum and the Golgi complex. However, it was early recognized by its affinity for osmium of silver-containing stains. In modern days its existence has been clearly demonstrated with the electron microscope. They are found in living cells of both animals and plants, immersed in their cytoplasm.

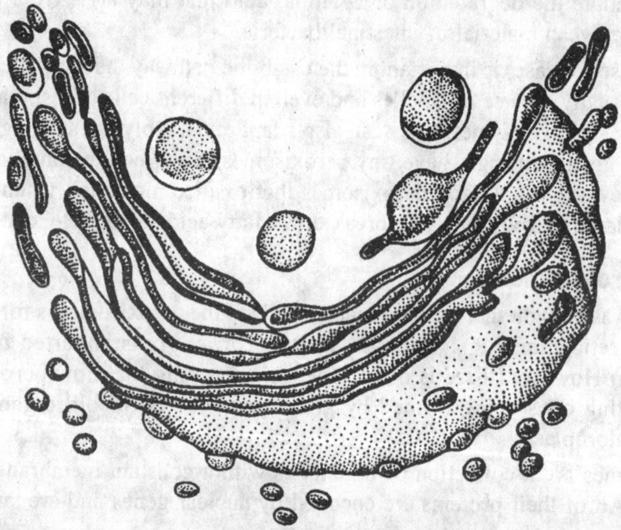

Fig. 39.43. The diagram indicates the organisation of the Golgi complex. At the convex "forming face" small vesicles containing the products of the synthetic activity of the cell are shown coalescing with the outermost saccule or cisterna. At the concave or "maturing face" of the complex, saccules containing-concentrated secretory product are rounding up to form secretory droplets or granules.

Various workers have given various names to this complex, such as **dictyosome,** idiosome, lipochondria, Golgi body, Golgi substance, Golgi apparatus and Golgi complex. Generally the name Golgi complex is used for the material invertebrates and dictyosome in invertebrates and plants. However, the Golgi complex is not found in bacteria and blue green algae.

Structure

The shape of Golgi complex is quite variable in somatic cells of plants and animals. Even in the same cell there are variations with functional stage. However, the shape is characteristic for each cell type. Their appearance depends partly on the position of cells within the plant or animal body and partly on the way in which cells are prepared for microscopic study. These bodies look like the complexes of the droplets and therefore, termed as Golgi complex. They appear thin plate like layers of irregular arrangement. Each complex consists of stacks of parallel lamellae. In some cases, it occurs as a dense reticulum of anastamosing trabeculae while in others as an irregular plaque, a ring, hollow spheres united together. In nerve cells it occurs as a reticulum of wide meshes around the nucleus. The size of Golgi complex is also variable. It is small in muscle cells but quite large in the nerve and gland cells. Generally the complex is well developed in an active cell while in old cells the complex diminishes in size and ultimately disappears.

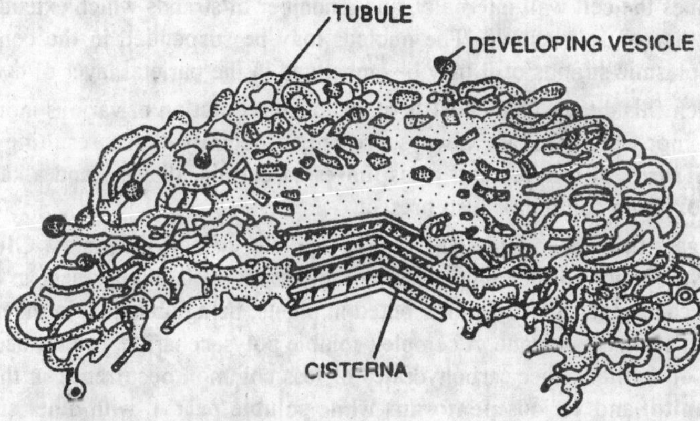

Fig. 39.44. Golgi complex. Diagrammatic representation of the morphology of Golgi body (dictyosome),

The electron microscopic observations reveal as follows. The Golgi complex comprises of 1. flattened sacs or cisternae, 2. large clear vacuoles and 3. clusters of dense vesicles.

1. Flattened sacs. These are also known as **cisternae.** These structures are similar to the smooth surface endoplasmic reticulum and appear in sectional view as dense parallel membranes. The packed cisternae are often arrayed concentrically, enclosing regions of the cytoplasm filled with numerous large vesicles.

2. Large vacuoles. These vacuoles are clear and commonly found at the edge of Complex. These structures represent the modified and expanded flattened sacs. In the cells of liver and pancreas these vacuoles of complex contain dense masses or granules.

3. Vesicles. These are the clusters of dense vesicles. They remain usually associated with cisternae and show continuity with them. The flattened sacs give rise to them by means of budding or pinching off. These structures remain dispersed in the surrounding hyaloplasm.

Functions

The Golgi bodies are believed to function in the manufacture of cellular secretion products. Since its membranes have little RNA it is not connected with protein synthesis. The general consensus of modern days is that it is somehow involved in the storage and possible modification of lipid substances, a point of view supported by observations that the appearance of the Golgi complex in animal cells can be modified greatly by changes in fat diet.

During the maturation of sperm, the Golgi complex plays a role in the formation of acrosome (Burgos and Fawcett, 1955).

The complex also activates mitochondria to produce the ATP which is utilized in respiratory cycle, nervous transmission, and nucleic acid and protein synthesis; the latter occurs in the vicinity of endoplasmic reticulum.

NON PROTOPLASMIC COMPONENTS: VACUOLES

The vacuoles (latin, *vacuus* = empty) are non-living inclusions of cytoplasm. Some of these are found in the form of minute droplets in the cytoplasm of meristematic cells. Each droplet is a small vacuole filled up with cell-sap. These small vacuoles enlarge and finally coalesce to give rise to a large vacuole. The enlargement of the vacuoles is accompanied by the entry of water into the cell. It becomes quite evident that with the entry of water into the cell, the size of the cell will increase, and, in fact, the cell attains a volume many times greater than the volume of the original meristematic cell. During this process of cell enlargement by vacuolation the nucleus and cytoplasm do not greatly increase in size, and in the fully vucuolated cell the cytoplasm forms a parietal layer which lines the cell wall internally, and a number of strands which extend from this parietal layer across the central vacuole. The nucleus may be suspended in the centre of the vacuole by these cytoplasmic strands or it may be embedded in the parietal layer of cytoplasm.

The cell-sap which fills the vacuole consists of an aqueous solution of various inorganic and organic compounds. Inorganic ions are always present, especially those resulting from the dissociation of the **nitrates, sulphates** and **phosphates** of certain alkaline and alkaline-earth metals, and **carbondioxide** in solution is also present.

A number of sugars have been isolated from the cell-sap of various plants. **Glucose** and **fructose,** are specially common in the cell-sap. Sometimes **maltose** is also present in the sap of leaf cells. **Sucrose,** or cane sugar is widely distributed in plants, being abundant in the root of the sugar-beet and the stem of the sugar-cane. A complex soluble polysaccharide, **inulin,** occurs in the cell-sap of the tubers of dahlia. Other carbohydrates of less common occurrence in the cell-sap include **dextrin, mannitol** and various **pentosans** while soluble **pectin**, with other substances, sometimes occurs in appreciable amount. **Glycosides** are also of common occurrence in the cell-sap. **Mucilaginous compounds** also occur in cell-sap and they give the slimy character to the cytoplasm. **Mucilages** are found abundantly in the cell-sap of many bulbs, *e.g.*, onion, and in the leaves of many succulent plants. They are polysaccharides in nature. **Tannins** may also be present in cell-sap. They are complex substances and soluble in water and alcohol. **Anthocyanin pigments** are frequently present in cell-sap. These pigments give blue or red colours to the cell-sap. Malic, citric and tartaric acids are all of common occurrence, and the acidity of many fruits is due to the presence of these acids in the cell-sap. Oxalic acid is also found in the cell-sap, in the form of its insoluble calcium-salt, and as such is usually regarded as a waste product of cell metabolism. Calcium oxalate occurs in a crystalline form and the crystals may be of various types. **Calcium carbonate** occurs only infrequently in plants in the form of **cystoliths.** Soluble **nitrogenous compounds** may also be present in the cell-sap. **Ammonium compounds** may be present too.

Besides the proteins which form a part of living protoplasm, **non-living proteins** may occur either dissolved in the cell-sap or in the form of crystal-like bodies, **crystalloids.** In many seeds, especially those containing oil, the vacuoles contain large amounts of **dissolved proteins,** and as the seed dries out and ripens these proteins may be transformed into **aleurone grains.** Fats and oils are frequently present in plant cells, especially in certain seeds. They occur as droplets or globules, and may be present either in the cell-sap or protoplasm or both. Other substances sometimes present include basic substances such as the **purine bases** and the **alkaloids. Resins** as found also, but are of limited distribution, being confined to special cells or ducts in certain plants and essential oils are produced by some plants. These essential oils are usually mixtures of complex organic compounds such as **alcohols, esters, ketones, aldehydes** and **hydrocarbons. Resin** also is not itself a simple chemical substance, but a mixture of substances insoluble in water and containing **resin acids,** resin esters and **rosenes,** all of which are complex substances of high molecular weight.

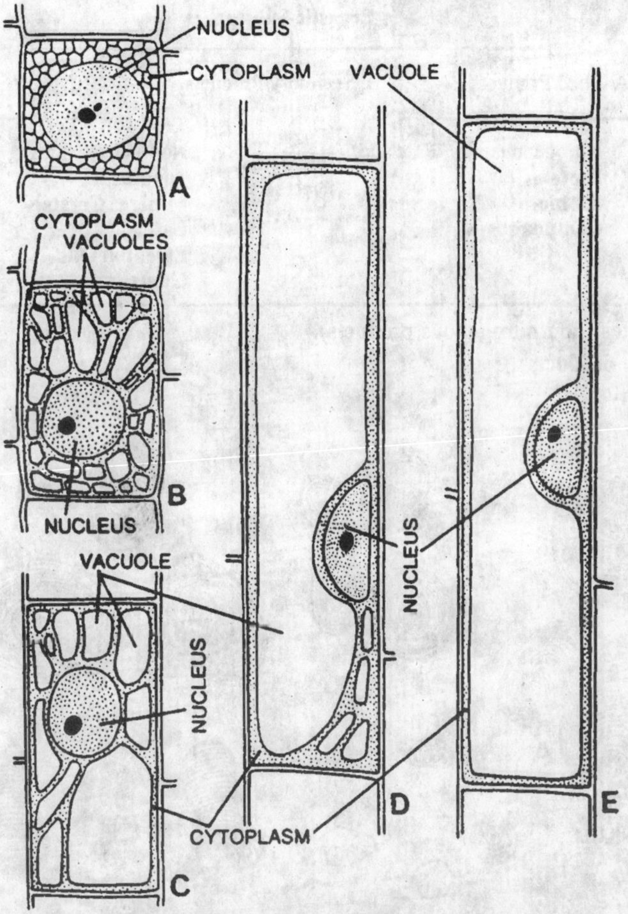

Fig. 39.45. The cell. A, the young cell without vacuoles; B—E. various stages in the formation and enlargement of the vacuole.

Functions

The vacuoles have many functions to their credit. They maintain the rigidity of the plant cell. They are responsible for rapid exchange of material by pushing the cytoplasm towards the periphery of the cell. They contain various substances in their cell sap such as enzymes, acids, salts, etc., which act in several ways. They store waste products. The vacuoles contain ions and molecules, and therefore, they maintain osmotic relationships of the cell. They help in the enlargement of the cell. Several metabolic activities take place in the cell sap of vacuoles.

ERGASTIC SUBSTANCES

Several chemical compounds occur as non-living inclusions in the cytoplasm. These inclusions remain dispersed either in cell-sap or in cytoplasm. Principally they are classified as follows:

A. FOOD PRODUCTS

These are the substances manufactured by the protoplasm of the cells from the simple inorganic substances like carbon dioxide and water and stored in the cells as food materials. The food thus manufactured is partly used up to make new protoplasm and partly it is broken down to provide necessary energy, and remainder of it is stored as reserve food material in protoplasm of cells. The reserve food materials may be classified as follows:

Ergastic Substances

- A. Food Products
  - Non-Nitrogenous: **Starch**, **Inulin**, **Hemicellulose**, **Cellulose**, **Sugars**
  - Nitrogenous: **Proteins**, **Amino-Compounds**
  - **Fats and Fatty acids**
- B. Secretory Products
  - Enzymes, **Pigments**, **Nectar**
- C. Waste Products
  - Non-Nitrogenous: **Tannins**, **Mineral Crystals**, **Latex**, **Essential Oils**, **Gums**
  - Nitrogenous: **Alkaloids**

1. Carbohydrates (non-nitrogenous products).
2. Nitrogenous products
3. Fats and fatty oils.

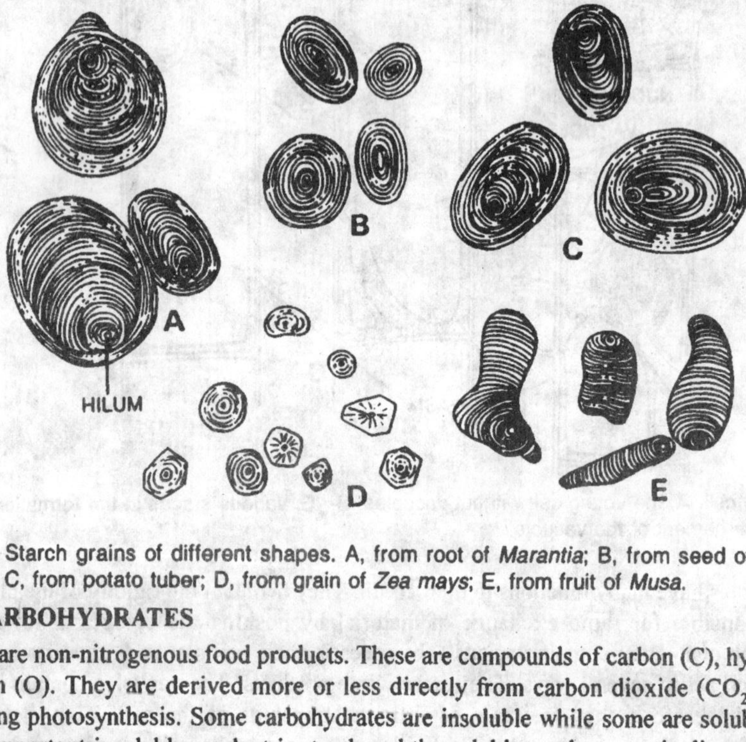

Fig. 39.46. Starch grains of different shapes. A, from root of *Marantia*; B, from seed of *Phaseolus*; C, from potato tuber; D, from grain of *Zea mays*; E, from fruit of *Musa*.

1. CARBOHYDRATES

They are non-nitrogenous food products. These are compounds of carbon (C), hydrogen (H), and oxygen (O). They are derived more or less directly from carbon dioxide (CO_2) and water (H_2O) during photosynthesis. Some carbohydrates are insoluble while some are soluble in water. The most important insoluble product is starch and the soluble products are inulin, sugar, etc.

***(i)* Starch.** It is an insoluble carbohydrate of polysaccharide type formed by the condensation of simple sugars like glucose. The starch is usually found in the form of starch grains of various shapes. The starch grains are abundantly found in the storage organs of plants, *e.g.*, tuberous roots, underground stems, cortex of stems, endodermis, grains of cereals, banana fruits, etc. The starch grains vary in their shape and may be used for the identification of plants. The starch grains are not found in fungi and certain algal groups. The starch grains have different shapes that are characteristic of the plant types, *e.g.*, they are oval-shaped in potato; flat in wheat; polygonal in maize; spherical in pulses and dumbell or rod-shaped in the latex cells of some *Euphorbias*. The starch grains of rice are smallest and those of *Canna* largest. The starch grains vary from 5–100μ in size. The starch is always derived either from chloroplasts of green cells or from leucoplasts (amyloplasts) of storage tissue.

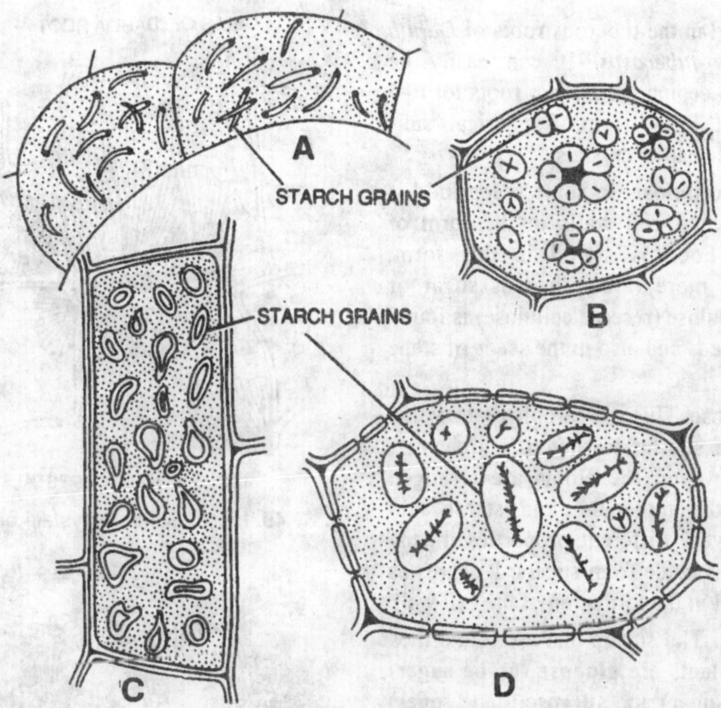

Fig. 39.47. Starch grains. A, starch grains in outer pericarp of *Musa*, B, starch grains in cotyledon of *Pisum*; C, starch grains in ray cell of phloem of *Ailanthus*; D, starch grains in cotyledon of *Phaseolus*.

The structure of the starch grain usually exhibits conspicuous concentric layers formed around a dark roundish spot, the **hilum.**

The layering may be conspicuous in some grains whereas inconspicuous in others. Most of the starch grains show this layering and are known as stratified starch grains. If the concentric layers of the starch are formed on one side of the hilum of starch grain, the grain is said to be **eccentric** (*e.g.*, potato) and when the layers are deposited concentrically around the hilum (*e.g.*, wheat) the grain is known as **concentric.** Concentric types of starch grains are quite common in most of the plants. If the starch grain possesses a single hilum, it is known as **simple.** Sometimes two, three or many grains, arranged in a group with as many hila as the starch grains, they are known as **compound** grains. Compound grains are commonly found in potato, sweet potato, rice and oats. The starch is turned blue or black in aqueous solution of iodine.

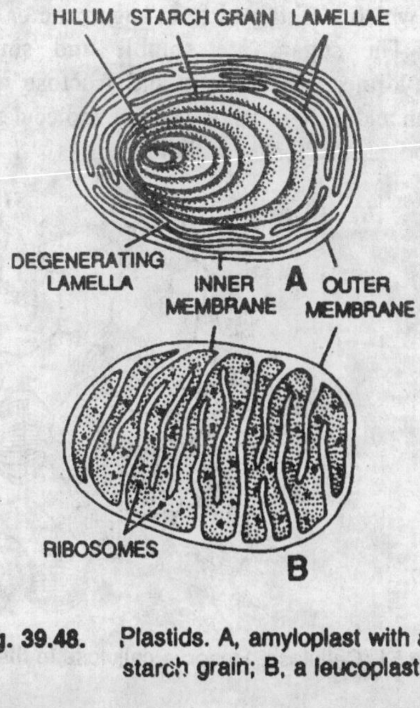

Fig. 39.48. Plastids. A, amyloplast with a starch grain; B, a leucoplast.

(*ii*) **Inulin.** This is also a carbohydrate of polysaccharide type. It is soluble carbohydrate usually found in the cell-sap. Inulin has been reported from the roots of many Compositae. It is commonly found in the tuberous roots of *Dahlia* and *Helianthus tuberosus*. It can easily be precipitated by keeping the *Dahlia* roots for 6–7 days, in alcohol, in the form of spherical, star-shaped or wheel-shaped crystals.

***(iii)* Hemicellulose.** In some seeds food is stored in thickened cell walls in the form of hemicellulose. Food is stored in this form, however, much more rarely than as sugar or starch. Hemicellulose (reserve cellulose) is found in some palm seeds and also in the seeds of some other plants.

***(iv)* Cellulose.** This is a carbohydrate with a general formula similar to that of starch, *i.e.*, $(C_6H_{10}O_5)_n$. However, the atoms are arranged differently in the molecule, and starch and cellulose have very different properties. In the plant, cellulose is made from sugars. It serves as building material in the formation of the cell wall.

***(v)* Sugars.** The sugars that are found most abundantly in plants are **glucose** (grape sugar), **fructose** (fruit sugar) and **sucrose** (cane sugar). Glucose and fructose have the formula $C_6H_{12}O_6$. They are thus composed of the same kinds of atoms in the same proportion, but the arrangement in the molecule is different. The simplest natural sugars are monosaccharides. Sucrose $(C_{12}H_{22}O_{11})$ has twice as many carbon atoms and is a disaccharide. Sucrose is known as the ordinary sugar, which is obtained from sugarcane or sugar beets. The sugars are soluble and simplest carbohydrates. As glucose and fructose are in solution and have relatively simple molecules, they are good material for the building up

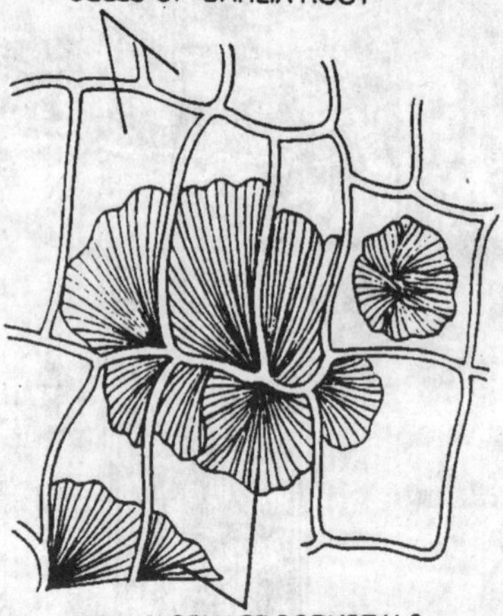

Fig. 39.49. Inulin. Sphaerocrystals of inulin in cells of dahlia root.

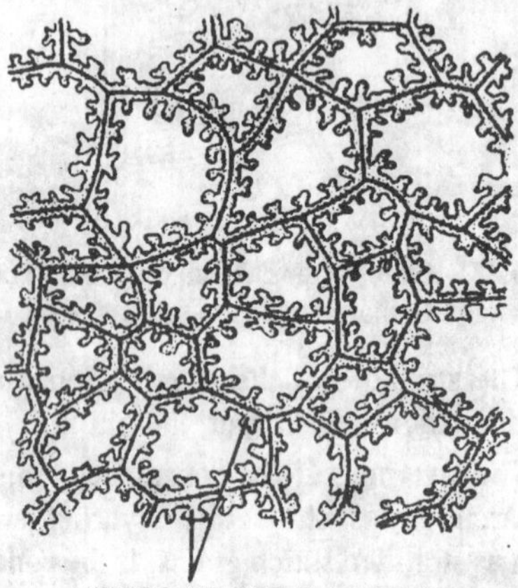

Fig. 39.50. Hemicellulose. Thickened walls of hemicellulose from *Areca* seed.

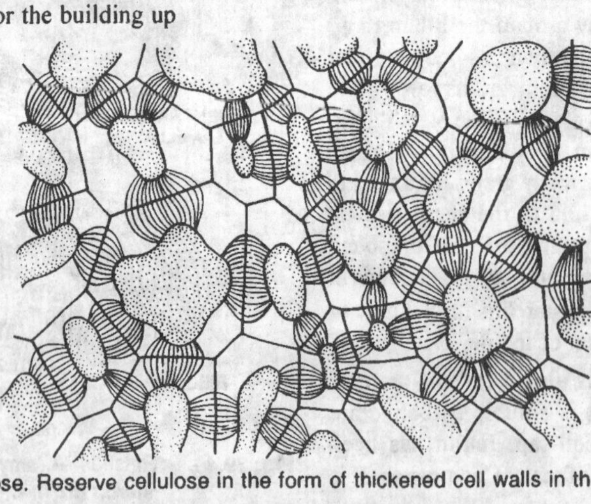

Fig. 39.51. Cellulose. Reserve cellulose in the form of thickened cell walls in the seeds of *Diospyros*.

of other substances or for the furnishing of energy. In sugarcane and sugarbeet sucrose is found as reserve food.

2. NITROGENOUS PRODUCTS

The important nitrogenous food materials are proteins and amino compounds.

***(i)* Proteins.** The proteins are the most important group of compounds found in plants, as they constitute the active matter of protoplasm, and the chemical phenomena of life processes are associated with them. The proteins are exceedingly complex organic nitrogenous substances constituting of carbon (C), hydrogen (H), oxygen (O) and nitrogen (N). In certain more complex proteins sulphur (S) and phosphorus (P) are also present. For example, representative proteins as zein $C_{736}H_{1161}N_{184}O_{208}S_3$ from Indian corn and gliadin $C_{685}H_{1068}N_{196}O_{211}S_5$ from wheat. Proteins are not only the main constituents of protoplasm but, in the form of solid granules, are frequently found in plants as reserve food material. Proteins are formed by a rearrangement of the atoms of carbohydrates with the addition of nitrogen, commonly sulphur and sometimes phosphorus. A protein molecule is made up of hundreds or thousands of amino acid molecules joined together by peptide links into one or more chains, which are variously folded. There are twenty different kinds of amino-acids commonly found in proteins, and most of these usually occur in any one protein molecule; they are arranged in the chain in a sequence which is exactly the same in all molecules of a given kind of protein. The possible different arrangements of the amino acids are evidently practically infinite, and the diversity is fully exploited by living things every species having kinds of protein molecule peculiar to itself.

Amino-acids are peculiar in that they have both basic and acid properties. The proportion of different amino-acids in different proteins varies; and some proteins lack amino-acid found in other proteins. Animal proteins are better for human food than plant protein because the amino-acid content of animal proteins is more like that of human proteins than is the amino acid content of plant proteins. Some plant proteins lack entirely some of the amino acids which are essential for the building of human proteins.

A common form of protein found in the endosperm of castor seed is known as **aleurone grains.** Each aleurone grain is a solid, ovate or rounded body which usually encloses a crystal like body in it,

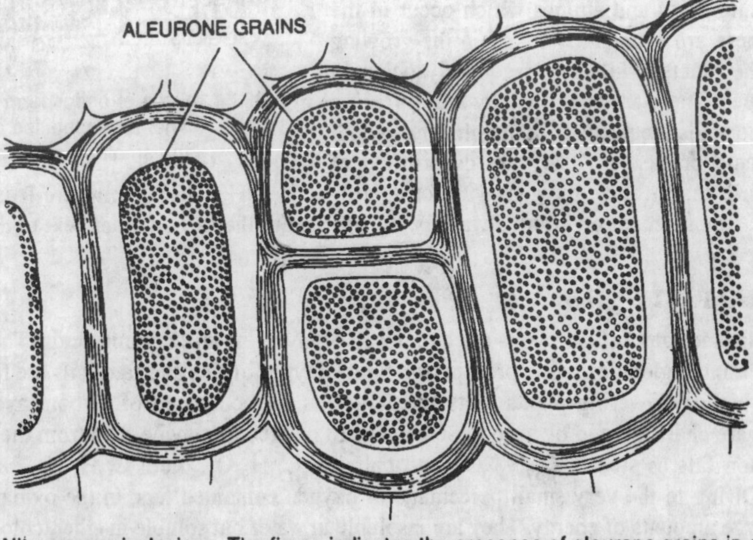

Fig. 39.52. Nitrogenous inclusions. The figure indicates the presence of aleurone grains in endosperm of *Zea mays.*

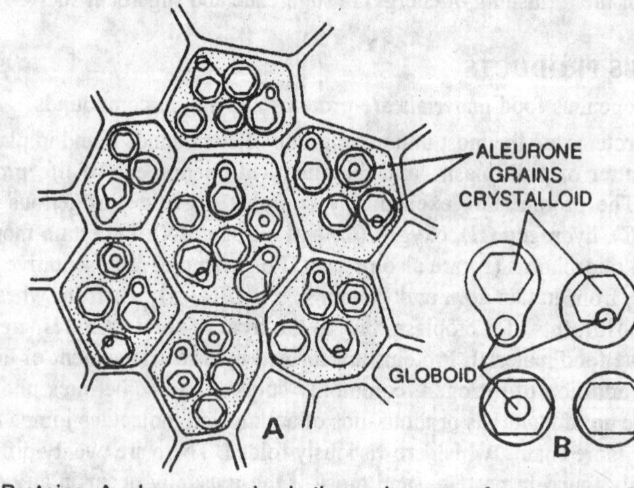

Fig. 39.53. Proteins. A, aleurone grains in the endosperm of castor seed; B, few grains magnified containing crystalloids and globoids in them.

known as **crystalloid** and a globule like body known as *globoid*. The crystalloid is proteinaceous in nature and occupies the major portion of aleurone grain, whereas the globoid is double phosphate of calcium (Ca) and magnesium (Mg) and occupies the narrower part of the grain. The aleurone grains vary in their shape and size in different plants. When they are found in oily seed of castor they are larger in size, while when found with starch they are very minute in size.

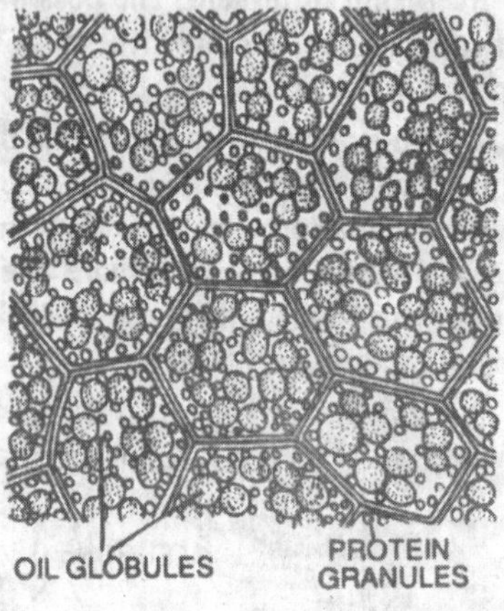

Fig. 39.54. Cells of endosperm of coconut. Thel arge globules are oil and the small granules are protein.

***(ii)* Amino compounds.** They are simple nitrogenous food materials. They are found in the form of amino-acids and amines which occur in the cell sap. These are abundantly found in the growing apices of the plants, while less frequently occur in storage tissues. There are about twenty known amino acids. Amino acids are peculiar in that they have both basic and acid properties. They are constituted of carbon, hydrogen, nitrogen, oxygen, with formula R—CH (NH_2)—COOH, where R is a variable grouping of atoms, an amino group always being attached to the carbon atom next to the carboxyl group.

3. FATS AND FATTY OILS

The fats and fatty oils in plants are composed of glycerine and organic acids. They occur in the form of minute globules in the protoplasm. Special types of fats and fatty oils are found in the seed and fruits of flowering plants. Fats and fatty oils are composed of carbon, hydrogen and oxygen and are characterized by a small percentage of oxygen as may be seen from the formula of such common fats as stearin $C_{57}H_{110}O_6$, and palmitin $C_{51}H_{98}O_6$, olein $C_{57}H_{104}O_6$, and linolein $C_{57}H_{98}O_6$. Owing to the very small percentage of oxygen contained fats, in the oxidation of fats produces large amounts of energy. They are insoluble in water but soluble in ether, chloroform and petroleum. Fats, may be solid or liquid (fatty oils), according to the temperature.

B. SECRETORY PRODUCTS

Besides food material several other products are also secreted by protoplasm which are not useful as nutritional products but they may help or accelerate the various reactions in the cells. These are as follows:

(i) **Enzymes.** They are soluble nitrogenous substances secreted by the protoplasm. They are digestive in function and convert the insoluble substances into soluble and complex compounds into simple ones, *e.g.* **diastase** converts starch into sugar, so that because of the action of this enzyme an insoluble substance converts into soluble one. The **lipase** breaks up fats into their components, glycerine and fatty acids. **Papain** converts proteins into amino acids.

(ii) **Colour in cell.** The substances that give colour to cells are usually found in the plastids. Chlorophyll is a green colouring matter secreted by the chloroplasts and performs the phenomenon of photosynthesis. Chlorophyll is not a single compound but it is mixture of two pigments known as chlorophyll *a* and chlorophyll *b*. The yellow pigments, carotenoids are also found in cell sap and give colours to the petals of the flowers. The anthocyanins are also secretary products of the protoplasm and are stored in the cell sap; they also impart colour to the petals of the flowers.

(iii) **Nectar.** The nectar is another useful secretion of protoplasm. It is secreted by special glands or organs of the flower, called nectaries.

Nectaries. The nectaries occur on flowers (floral nectaries) and on vegetative parts (extrafloral nectaries). The floral nectaries are found in various positions on the flower, whereas the extrafloral nectaries occur on stems, leaves, stipules and pedicels of flowers.

The secretory tissue of the nectary is generally found in the epidermal layer. Usually the secretory epidermal cells have dense cytoplasm and may be papillate or elongated like palisade cells. In many nectaries, the cells found beneath the epidermis are also secretory. They have dense cytoplasm and thin walls. The nectary is covered by a cuticle.

The sugar of the nectaries (both floral and extrafloral), is derived from the phloem. Vascular tissue is found just near the nectary. In some nectaries the vascular tissue is merely that of the organ bearing the nectary, in others it is part of the nectary.

The nectar is excreted either through the cell wall and the ruptured cuticle or sometimes through stomata.

(iv) **Osmophors.** The fragrance of flowers, is generally produced by volatile substances distributed throughout the epidermal region of perianth parts. However, in some plants the fragrance originates in special glands known as **osmophors** (Vogel, 1962). Examples of such special glands are commonly found in Asclepiadaceae, Aristolochiaceae, Araceae, Burmanniaceae and Orchidaceae. Various floral parts are differentiated as osmophors and they assume the form of flaps, cilia or brushes. The prolongation of the spadix of Araceae and the insect-

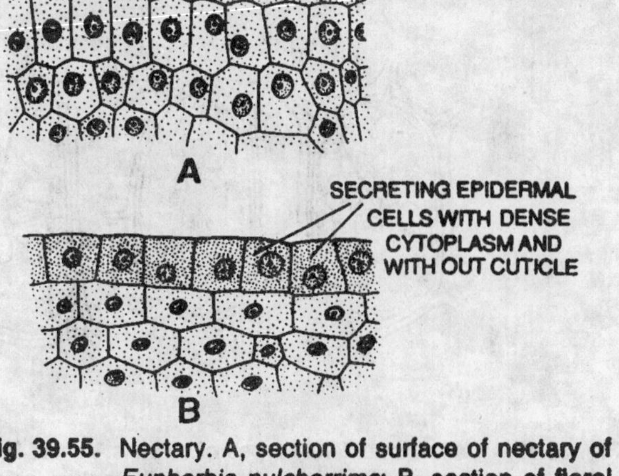

Fig. 39.55. Nectary. A, section of surface of nectary of *Euphorbia pulcherrima*; B, section of floral nectary of *Malus pumila*.

attracting tissue in the flowers of Orchidaceae are osmophors. The osmophors have a secretory tissue usually several layers in depth.

C. WASTE PRODUCTS

They are excretions of the plant cells. Usually these products are stored in the dead cells. These products are formed as a result of metabolic activities of protoplasm, and therefore, they are known as metabolic wastes of the plants. Usually there are two types of metabolic wastes. They are 1. Non-nitrogenous waste products and 2. Nitrogenous waste products.

1. Non-nitrogenous waste products.

They are tannins, mineral crystals, latex, essential oils, gums, resins, and organic acids. They are either found in the cytoplasm or in the cell-sap.

***(a)* Tannins.** They are non-nitrogenous complex compounds, commonly found dissolved in the cell-sap. They are the derivatives of phenol and usually related to glucosides. They are found in the cell walls, in the dead cells, in the heart wood and in the bark. They are also found in abundance in leaves and unripe fruits. On the ripening of the fruits the tannins are being converted into glucose and other substances. The tannins possess a bitter taste and their presence in tea leaves make the tea decoction bitter. They are used

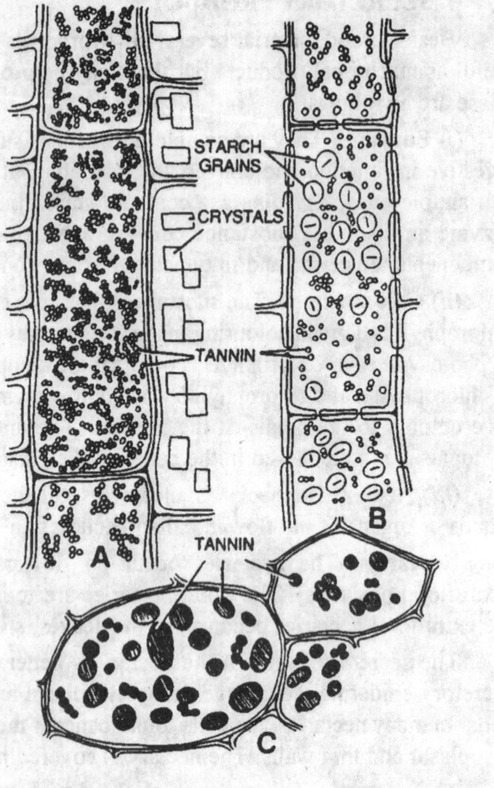

Fig. 39.56. Tannin, starch grains and crystals, A, Tannin and crystals in phloem parenchyma of *Pinus*; B, tannin and starch grains in ray cells of wood of *Malus pumila*; C, tannin in pith cells of *Fragaria*.

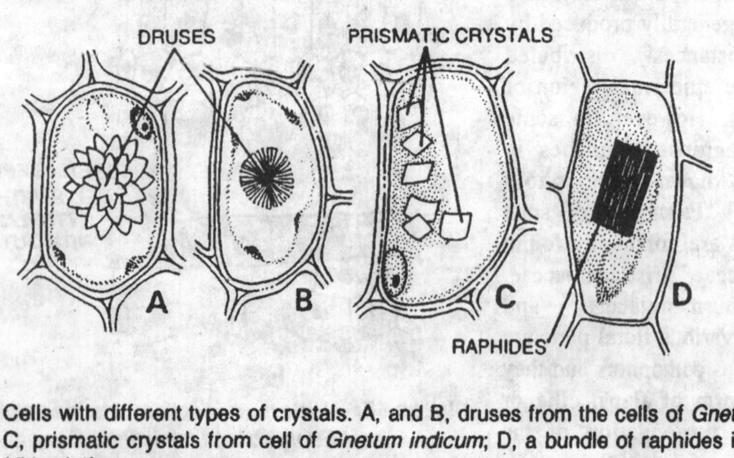

Fig. 39.57. Cells with different types of crystals. A, and B, druses from the cells of *Gnetum gnemon*; C, prismatic crystals from cell of *Gnetum indicum*; D, a bundle of raphides in leaf cell of *Vitis vinifera*.

in tanning industry. The commercial **katha** is prepared from the tannins of the heart wood of *Acacia catechu*. The tannins are poorly developed in monocotyledonous plants. They are either found in individual cells or in special organs, called the **tannin sacs.** The tannin-containing cells often form connected systems. In the individual cells the tannins occur in the protoplast and may also impregnate the walls, in cork tissue. Within the protoplast, tannins are a common ingredient of the vacuoles. As regards their function they act as protectants of protoplasm against injury, decay, termites and pests; as reserve substances related in some manner to the starch and metabolism; as substances associated with the formation and transport of sugars; as antioxidants; and as protective colloids maintaining the homogeneity of the cytoplasm.

(*b*) Mineral crystals. Various types of mineral crystals occur in the plant cells. They may occur either in the cell cavity or in the cell walls. The crystals usually lie loose in the cells but sometimes they are found to be suspended into the cell cavity from the cell wall.

The crystals vary in shape and size. Usually the crystals consist of calcium carbonate, calcium oxalate or silica.

(*i*) Calcium carbonate crystals. These crystals are commonly known as **cystoliths.** Usually they occur in the epidermal cells of leaves of many flowering plants. They are generally found in under mentioned angiospermic families—Moraceae, Urticaceae, Acanthaceae, Cucurbitaceae, etc. The main body of cystolith is a cellulose extension of the cell wall in which the calcium carbonate is deposited in the form of fine granules. In certain plants double cytoliths are also found.

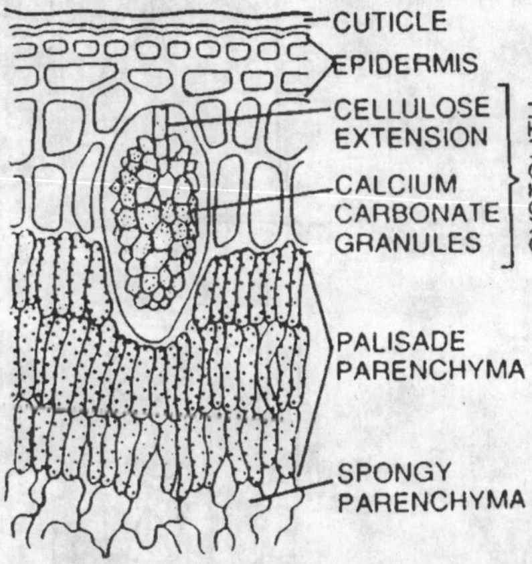

Fig. 39.58. Cystolith (calcium carbonate) in leaf of *Ficus elastica* (India rubber).

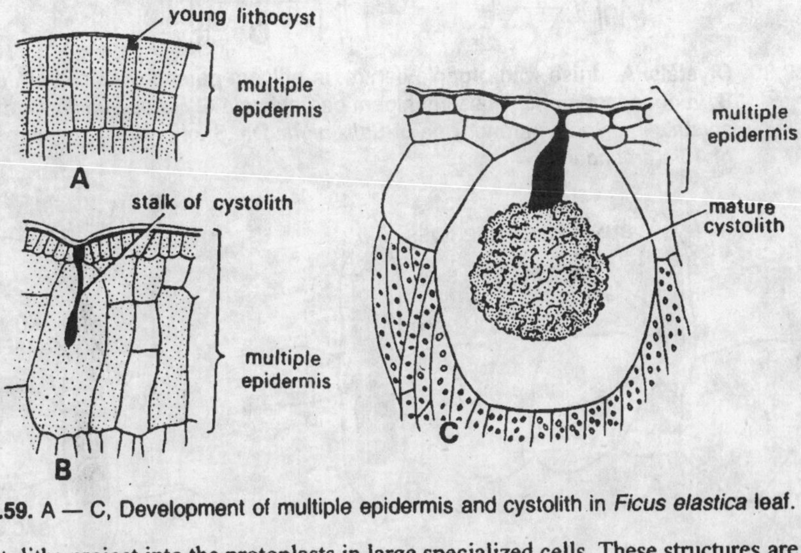

Fig. 39.59. A — C, Development of multiple epidermis and cystolith in *Ficus elastica* leaf.

The cystoliths project into the protoplasts in large specialized cells. These structures are lime-encrusted or lime-infiltrated, stalked projections of the wall. The foundation of the cystolith is a stalked stratified, cellulosic body which arises early in cell development as a local wall thickening. With the addition of large amounts of calcium carbonate this becomes an irregular body which may nearly fill the cell. In shape, cystoliths vary greatly in different genera and families.

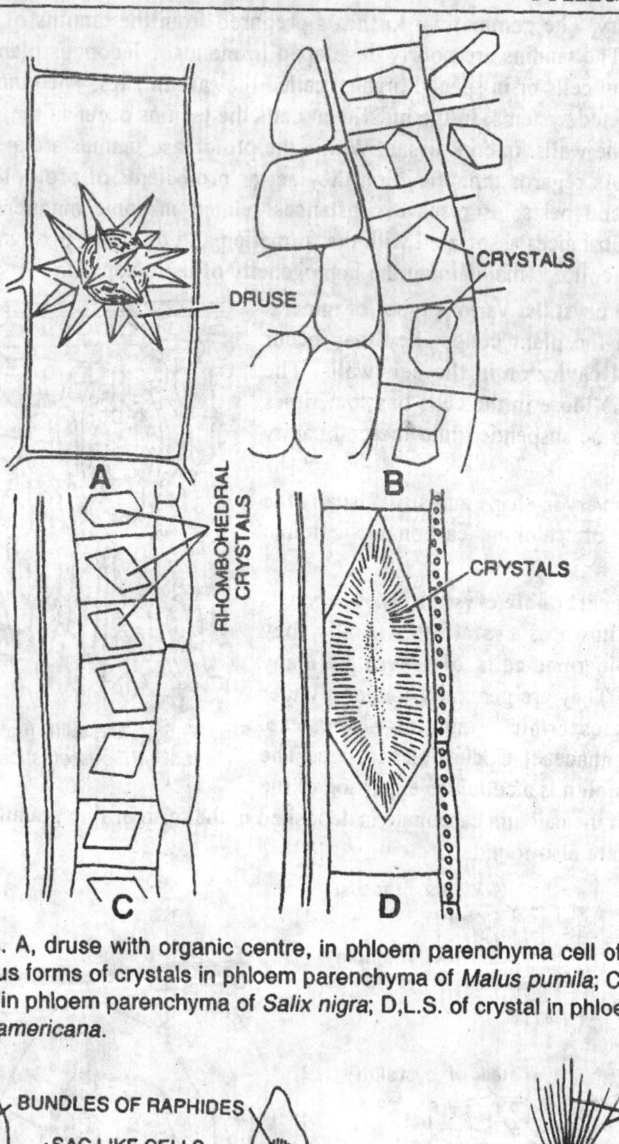

Fig. 39.60. Crystals. A, druse with organic centre, in phloem parenchyma cell of *Juglans nigra*; B, various forms of crystals in phloem parenchyma of *Malus pumila*; C, rhombohedral crystals in phloem parenchyma of *Salix nigra*; D,L.S. of crystal in phloem parenchyma of *Tilia americana*.

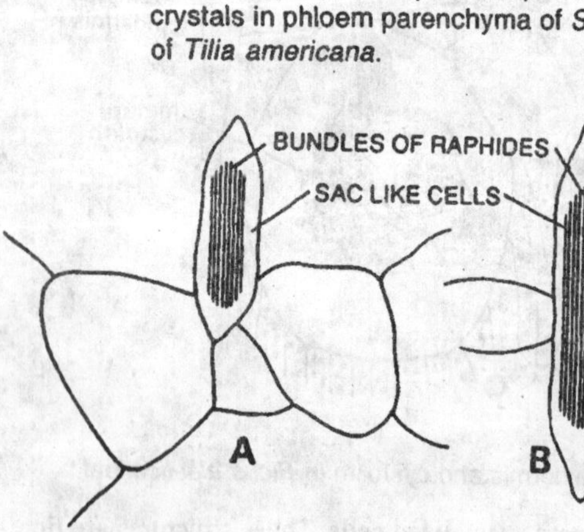

Fig. 39.61. Raphides (calcium oxalate needle like crystals). A, from leaf of *Colocasia*; B, from leaf of *Pistia*.

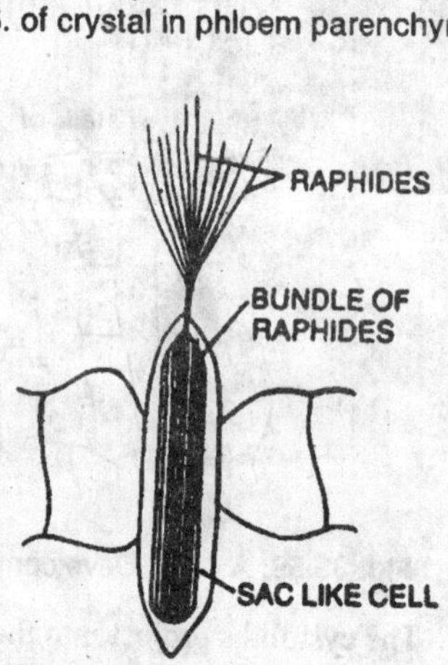

Fig. 39.62. Raphides. Ejection of raphides from sac like cell of leaf of *Colocasia*.

***(ii)* Calcium oxalate crystals.** The leaves and other organs of many plants contain conspicuous crystals of calcium oxalate. The forms of the crystals are very diverse. They are as follows:

Raphides. They are needle-like, long slender crystals usually lying parallel to each other in a bundle, which is sometimes found in a special sac like cell. When the sacs are injured mechanically, the raphides are released out with a jerk through a small hole. The raphides are commonly found in *Alocasia, Colocasia, Pistia,* etc. Certain raphides are very irritating and afford some protection to the plants from animals. Raphides are destroyed by boiling, and so food plants containing them are not irritating when cooked.

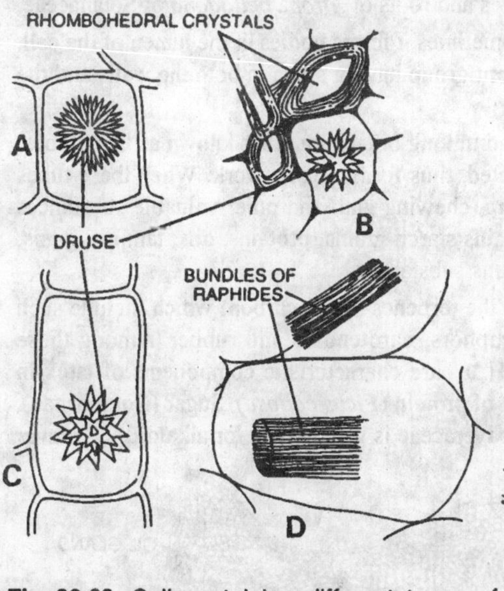

Fig. 39.63. Cell containing different types of crystals, A, druse in cortex cell of stem of Viburnum lentago; B, druse and rhombohedral crystals in stone cell of Carya glabra; C, druse in cortical cell of Carica papaya D, bundles or raphides in cells of fruits of Smilacina racemosa.

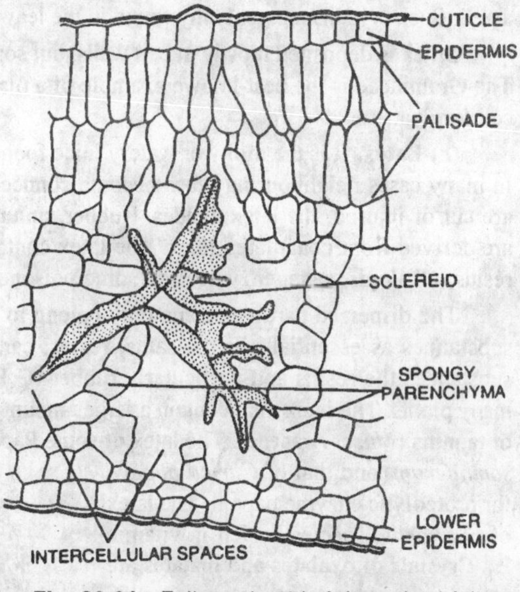

Fig. 39.64. Foliar sclereid. A branched foliar sclereid from the leaf blade of *Trochodendron.*

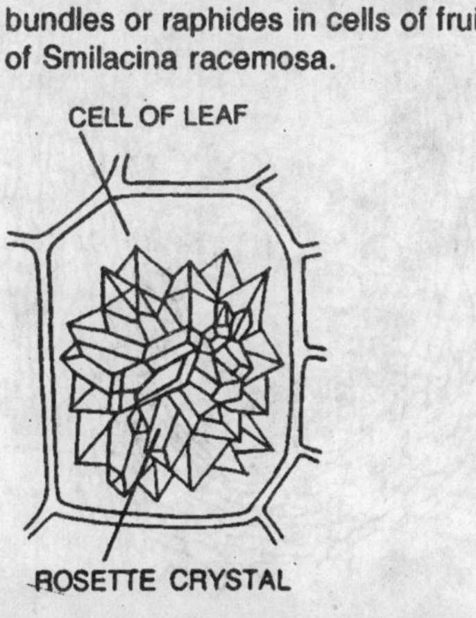

Fig. 39.65. Rosette crystal (calcium oxalate) from cell in a leaf.

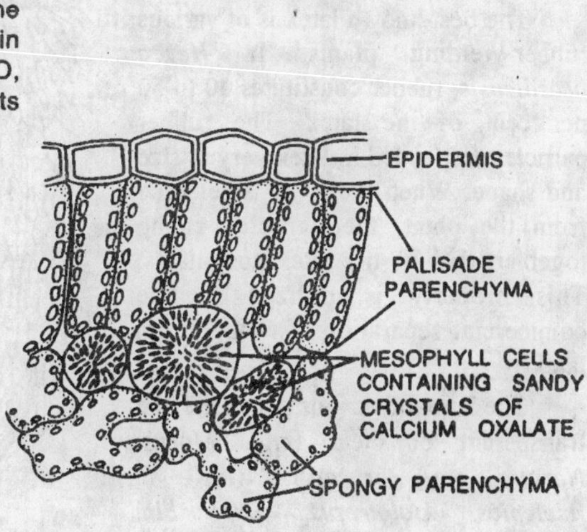

Fig. 39.66. Calcium oxalate crystals. Sandy crystals in leaf of *Atropa belladona.*

Idioblasts. They are stellate calcium oxalate crystals usually found in the aerenchyma of aquatic plants to give support to the tissue. They are quite common in *Limnanthemum*, *Nymphaea, Trapa,* etc.

Druses, rosette, crystals or cluster crystals. This is one of the commonest compound crystal having the appearance of a rosette and known as a **rosette crystal.** Such crystals are quite common in *Eucalyptus, Nerium, Ixora*, etc.

Prismatic crystals. They are single calcium oxalate crystals found in various plants. They may be square, prismatic, rhomboidal or pyramid-like in shape.

Sand crystals. They are commonly found in masses of micro sphenoidal crystals packed into a cell. Such crystals are generally found in the leaves and roots of *Atropa belladona* of Solanaceae.

Silica is deposited mostly in cell walls, but sometimes it forms bodies in the lumen of the cell. The Gramineae is the best-known example of a plant group having silica in both the walls and the cell lumina.

(*c*) Latex. It is the milky or watery juice found in long branching tubes known as latex tubes. In many cases neighbouring tubes become connected, thus forming a network. When these tubes are cut or injured, the latex exudes. Rubber, opium, chewing gum and other valuable substances are derived from coagulated latex. The latex contains starch grains, proteins, oils, tannins, gums, resins, alkaloids, salts, enzymes and some poisonous substances.

The dispersed particles commonly belong to the terpenes (hydrocarbon) which include such substances as essential oils, balsams, resins, camphors, carotenoids and rubber. Among these substances the resins and particularly rubber $(C_5H_8)n$ are characteristic components of latex in many plants. The latex may contain a large amount of protein (*Ficus callosa*), Sugar (Compositae), or tannins (*Musa,* Araceae). The latex of some Papaveraceae is well known for alkaloids (*Papaver somniferum*) and that of *Carica papaya* for proteolytic enzyme papain. The latex of *Euphorbia* species is rich in vitamin B_1. Crystals of oxalates and malates are abundantly found in latex. Certain plants contain starch grains in their latex.

The best-known latex is of various rubber-yielding plants. In *Hevea brasiliensis*, rubber constitutes 40 to 50 per cent of the latex. The rubber particles suspended in latex vary in size and shape. When the latex is released from the plant, the particles clump together; that is, the latex coagulates. This property is utilized in the commercial separation of rubber from latex.

The latex of various plants may be transparent or clear (*e.g., Morus, Nerium,* etc.) or milky (*e.g.*, in *Asclepias, Calotropis, Euphorbia, Ficus,* etc.). It is yellow-brown in

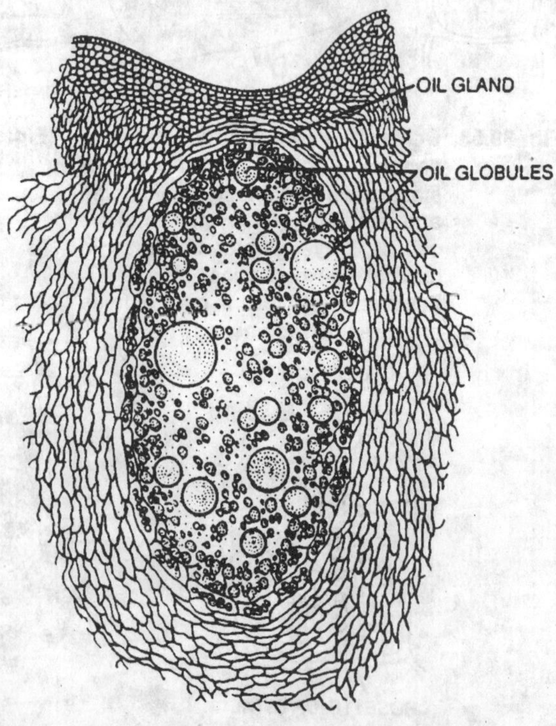

Fig. 39.67. L.S. of oil gland in orange peel.

Cannabis and yellow or orange in several members of Papaveraceae.

(*d*) Essential or volatile oils. The essential or volatile oils frequently occur in oil glands. These oils are volatile and are usually very odoriferous. Well-known examples are eucalyptus oil and the oil from orange peel. The orange peel contains large oval glands. These glands originate in the splitting apart of certain cells, but are formed largely by the breaking down of the cells containing the oil. The disintegration of the cells brings the oil into the large cavity of the gland. The oil glands are also found in the petals of rose, jasmines and many other flowers.

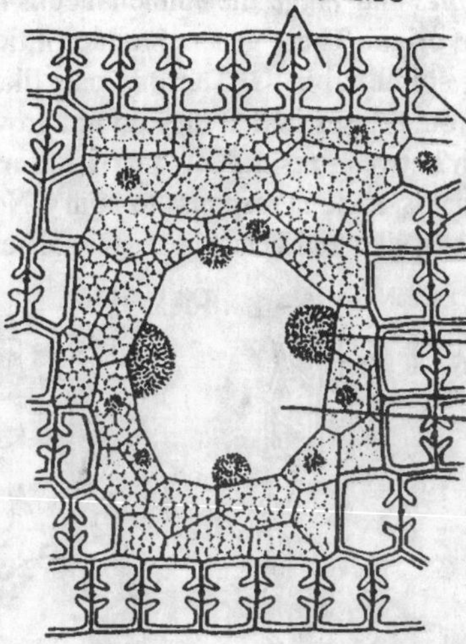

Fig. 39.68. Schizogenous cavities. Resin-duct of pine stem with resin.

(*e*) Gums. The gums are exuded out from the stems of many plants. The species of *Acacia* produce best gum. These spacies are *Acacia senegel, A modesta* and *A. arabica.* The gums are soluble in water and insoluble in alcohol. They swell up in water to produce a viscous mass.

(*f*) Resins. The resins are frequently found in the resin ducts of various conifers. The resin ducts are formed either by the separation of the neighbouring cells or by disintegration of cells. Turpentine obtained by cutting through the resin ducts of pine trees, after which the turpentine exudes and is collected. Various kinds of varnish and other resins are obtained by the same method from other conifers. The resins are insoluble in water but soluble in alcohol and turpentine. The well known mounting fluid, canada balsam is a resinous product of *Abies balsamea.*

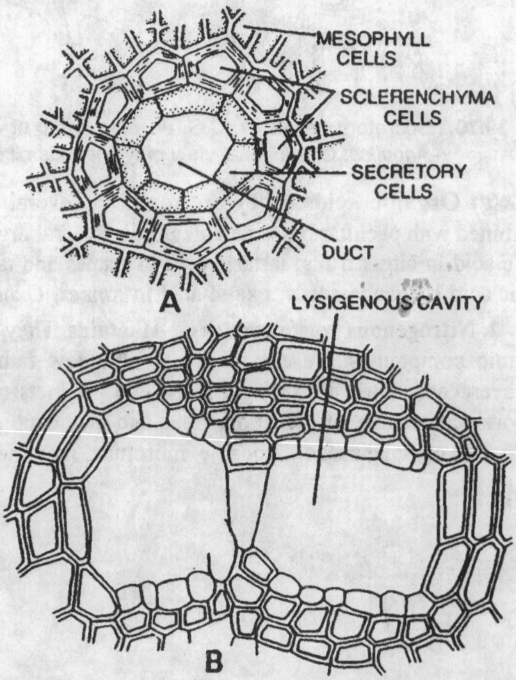

Fig. 39.69. Glands. A, internal schizogenous gland (resin duct of *Pinus*); B, lysigenous gland (secondary xylem of *Copaifera*).

Resin ducts. Resin ducts are long passages surrounded by glandular cells. They occur not only in stems but also in other parts of plants.

In *Pinus* and allied genera the resin ducts develop in the axial system or in both the axial and ray systems. Typically, resin ducts develop as schizogenous intercellular spaces by separation of parenchyma cells from each other. After some divisions these cells form the lining, or the **epithelium,** of the resin ducts and excrete resin. In *Pinus* the epithelial cells are thin-walled, remain active for several years, and produce abundant resin. In *Abies* and *Tsuga* the epithelial cells have thick lignified walls and most of them die during the year of origin. These genera produce little resin. Eventually a resin duct may become closed by enlarging epithelial cells. These tylosis like intrusions are called **tylosoids** (Record, 1934). They differ from tyloses in that they do not grow through pits. According to some workers there is a distinction between resin ducts that are **normal** and those that are **traumatic** (Greek *trauma*; a wound), that is, arise in response to injury. Normal ducts are elongated and occur singly; traumatic ducts are cyst-like and occur in tangential series.

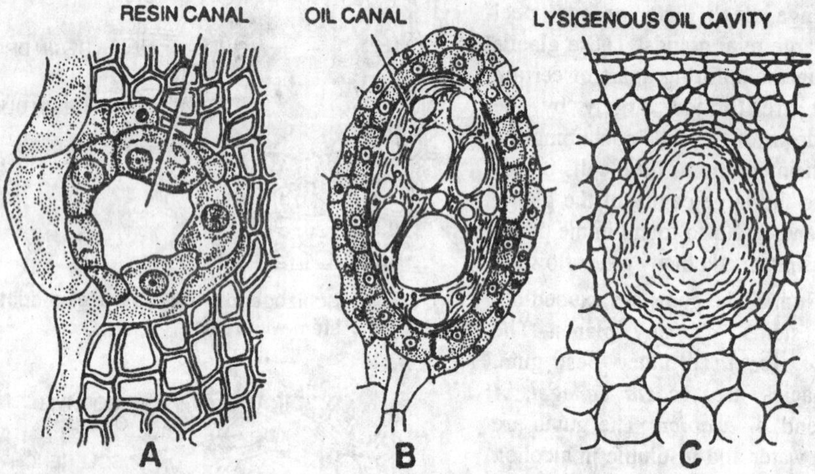

Fig. 39.70. Secretory tissue. A, C.S. of resin canal of *Pinus*; B, C.S. of oil canal of young fruit of *Angelica*; C, sectional view of lysigenous oil cavity of rind of *Citrus*.

***(g)* Organic acids.** They are found in several vegetable and fruit juices and are often combined with peculiar bases and alkaloids. Several organic acids are found in various plants, *e.g.*, citric acid in citrus fruits; tartaric acid in grapes and tamarinds; malic acid in the fruits of apple; gallic acid in mango seeds; oxalic acid in *Rumex, Oxalis* and *Nepenthes*.

2. Nitrogenous waste products. Alkaloids. They make a group of nitrogen-containing, basic organic compounds present in plants of a few families of Dicotyledons, *e.g.*, Solanaceae, Papaveraceae. They are thought to be end products of nitrogen metabolism. They are of great importance because of their poisonous and medicinal properties, *e.g.*, atropine (found in *Atropa belladona* of Solanaceae.), cocaine, morphine, nicotine, quinine, strychnine, etc.

40

CHAPTER

The Cell Wall

The cells of the plant tissue possess protective cell wall in near about all flowering plants. The presence of non-protoplasmic walls is considered the outstanding characteristic differentiating the cell of plants from those of animals. Few plant cells lack cell walls. Examples of cells without walls in plants are the motile spores in algae and fungi and the sexual cells in lower and higher plants. As we know the cells are composed of very soft and delicate substance, called protoplasm and thus they ~~need~~ protection against other injurious agencies. The cell walls protect the protoplasts. The cell wall was discovered before the protoplast, and in the early history of botany has received more attention than the cell contents. Later the protoplast became the main object of study. In modern days the origin and the structure of cell wall have received critical attention and are now much better understood.

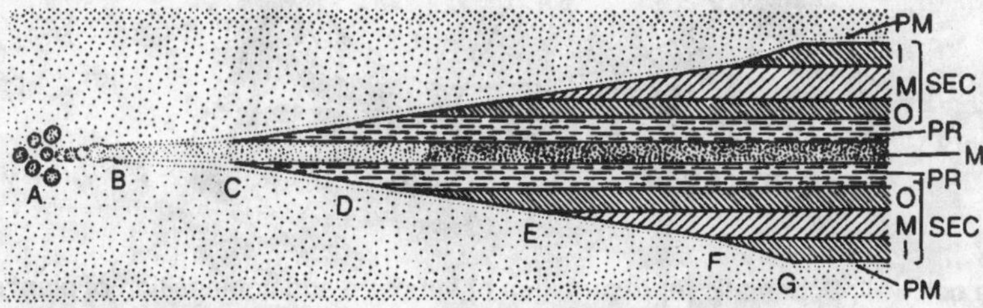

Fig. 40.1. The cell wall. Diagrammatic representation of successive stages (from left to right) in formation of cell wall with secondary layers. Walls of both daughter cells are shown in the figure. A, origin of cell plate; B, beginning of transformation of cell plate into middle lamella; C, beginning of deposition of primary wall D, E and F, beginning of deposition of outer, middle and inner layers (O, M.I.); G, completion of wall thickening.

THE WALL LAYERS

Each cell within a tissue has its own cell wall. The cell walls of plants vary much in thickness in relation to age and type of cells. Generally, young cells have thinner cell walls than the fully developed ones, but sometimes the wall does not thicken much after the cell ceases to grow. In mature thick-walled cells, a concentric layering is usually distinct in the cell wall. The layers differ from one another in physical and chemical nature. The cell wall is complex in its structure and usually consists of three layers, the **primary wall, the intercellular substance** or **middle lamella,** and the **secondary wall.** The intercellular substance cements together the primary walls of two contiguous cells, and the secondary wall is laid over the primary, that is, next to the lumen of the cell. The primary wall usually consists of a single layer, whereas the secondary wall is made up of one to many layers, most frequently of three.

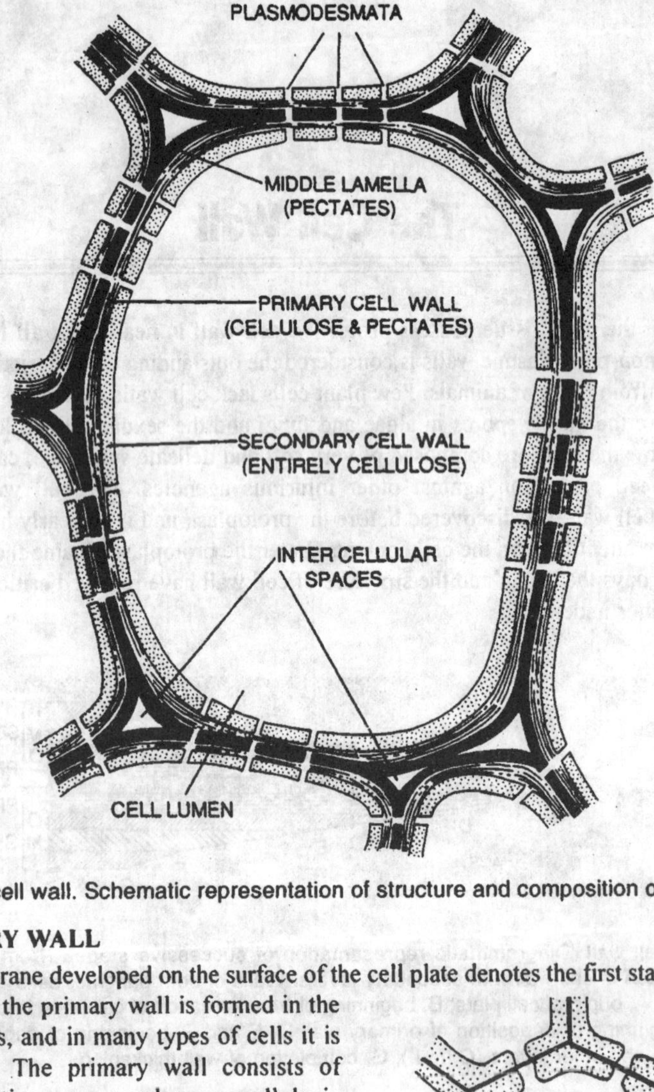

Fig. 40.2. The cell wall. Schematic representation of structure and composition of plant cell walls.

THE PRIMARY WALL

The membrane developed on the surface of the cell plate denotes the first stage of the primary wall. Generally the primary wall is formed in the developing cells, and in many types of cells it is the only wall. The primary wall consists of cellulose, pectic compounds, noncellulosic polysaccharides and hemicelluloses (Bonner, 1950). Sometimes it becomes lignified. The primary walls are usually associated with living protoplasm. The walls of dividing and growing meristematic cells are primary. The primary wall may change its shape and volume according to the growth of young protoplast. This wall is not uniformly thickened and may maintain its thickness and unevenness, or be alternately thickened and thinned.

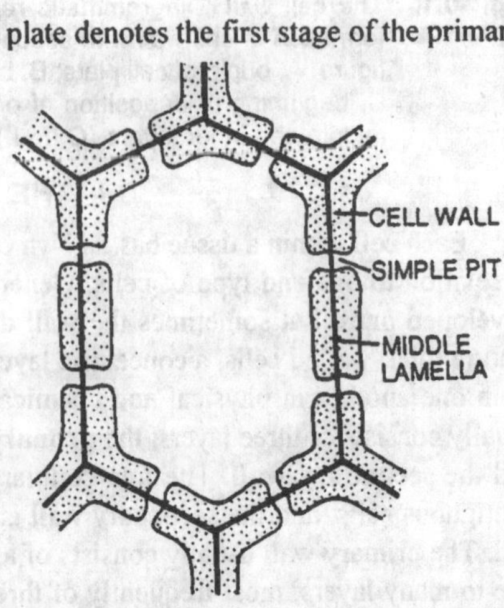

Fig. 40.3. The cell wall. Simple pits. A cell in sectional view showing simple pits in its wall.

As already mentioned, the walls of dividing and growing meristematic cells are primary, and so are those of most of the cells which retain

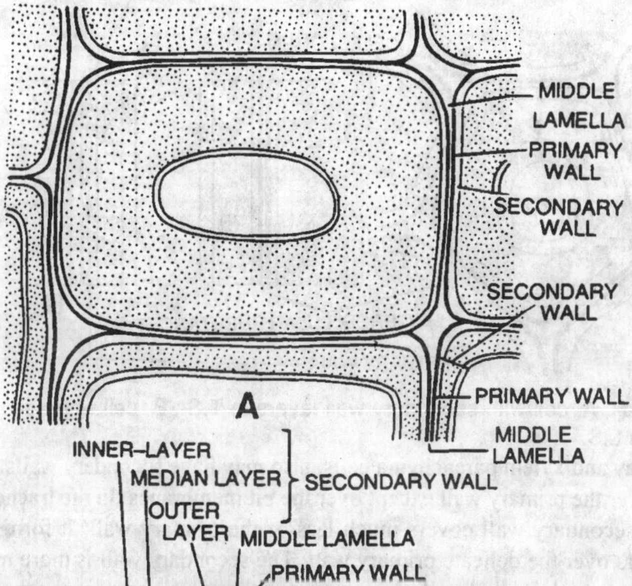

Fig. 40.4. The cell wall. The figure shows wall structure and middle lamella in wood fibres. A, T.S. of one wood fibre and parts of seven adjacent fibres; B, cross section of adjacent walls and middle lamella (highly magnified).

living protoplast. The changes that occur in primary walls are therefore reversible. The wall may lose a thickening previously acquired and chemical substances may be removed or replaced by others. For example, cambial walls show seasonal changes in thickness and in colloidal properties (Kerr and Bailey, 1934). In other cases the thick primary walls of the endosperm in many seeds are digested during germination.

THE MIDDLE LAMELLA

The intercellular substance which cements together the primary walls of two contiguous cells very firmly is called **middle lamella.** This is a complex layer in its structure and morphology. It is amorphous, colloidal, and optically inactive. It is composed mainly of a pectic compound which appears to be a mixture of calcium and magnesium pectate. In woody tissues the middle lamella is commonly lignified. The distinction between intercellular lamella and the primary wall is frequently obscured during the extension growth of the cell. In such cells as tracheids and fibres, which typically develop prominent secondary walls, the intercellular layer becomes extremely tenuous. As a result, the two primary walls of contiguous cells and the intervening middle lamella appear as a unit, particularly when all three become strongly impregnated with lignin. This triple structure is often known as middle lamella.

THE SECONDARY WALL

Usually in many fully developed cells further thickening of cell wall occurs. The wall then formed is the **secondary wall.** The secondary wall maybe considered a supplementary wall whose principal function is mechanical. Generally the cells with secondary walls are devoid of protoplasts at maturity. These walls are most characteristic of cells that are highly specialized and undergo irreversible changes in their development. However, cells with active, living protoplasts,

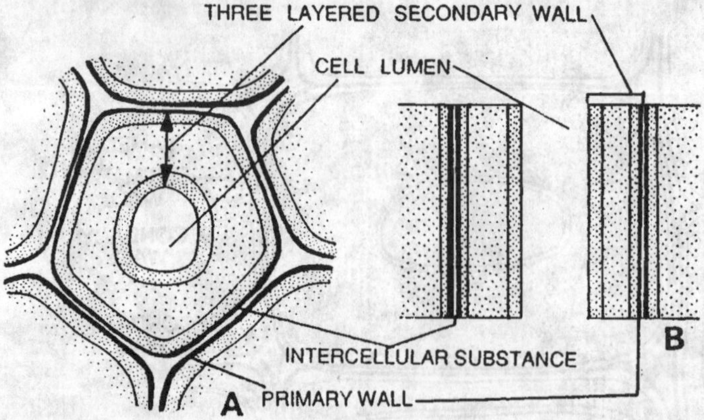

Fig. 40.5. A cell wall. A, cell with secondary wall layers in T.S.; B, cell with secondary wall layers in L.S.

such as the xylem ray and xylem parenchyma cells, also may have secondary walls. The secondary wall is laid down over the primary wall except over the pit membranes. In the tracheids and vessels of protoxylem the secondary wall covers much less of the primary wall; it forms only as rings, spiral bands and bars over the delicate primary wall. The secondary wall is more massive than the primary, and in most thick-walled cells it constitutes the major part of the wall. Usually the secondary wall constitutes of three layers—**inner, middle** and **outer.** This wall may consist of cellulose or mixtures of cellulose, non-cellulosic polysaccharides and hemicelluloses. Sometimes the number of layers of secondary wall may exceed three, and the innermost sometimes only of a helical band and such bands are called **tertiary spirals or spiral thickenings** (Eames and Mac Daniels, 1947).

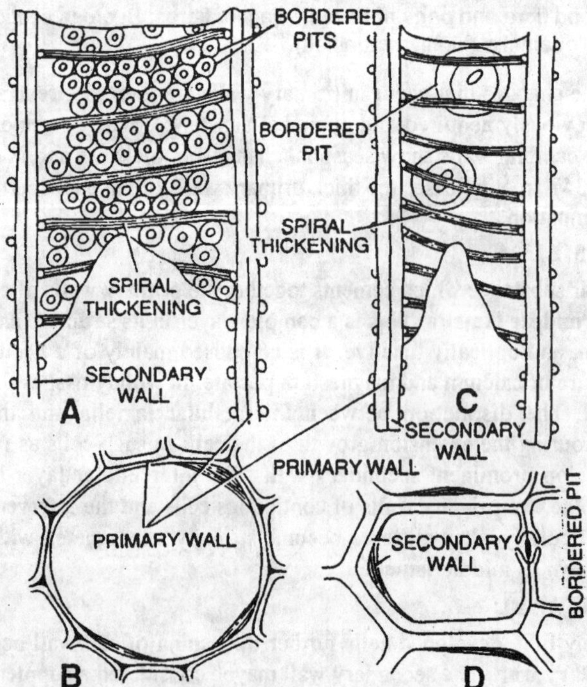

Fig. 40.6 The cell wall. This figure shows the primary wall and secondary wall with tertiary spirals. A and B, L.S. and T.S. of vessel of *Tilia;* C and D, L.S. and T.S. of tracheid of *Taxus* (a gymnosperm).

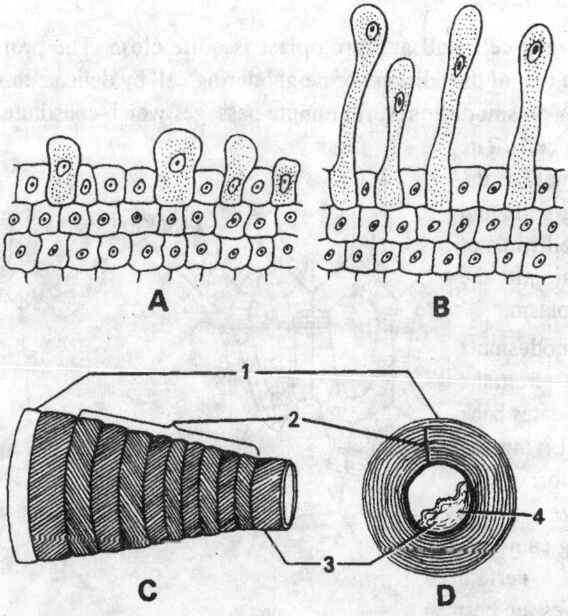

Fig. 40.7. Structure and growth of cotton fibre. A, outer layer of cells of young cotton seed showing the beginning enlargement of the fibre on the day of flowering; B, same after 24 hours, C, diagram of the various layers of the cellulose laid down in a mature cotton fibre (1) outer primary wall (2) concentric inner layers revealing the different orientation of the cellulose in the secondary thickenings, (3) last inner layer of the secondary wall, (4) remains of cell contents.

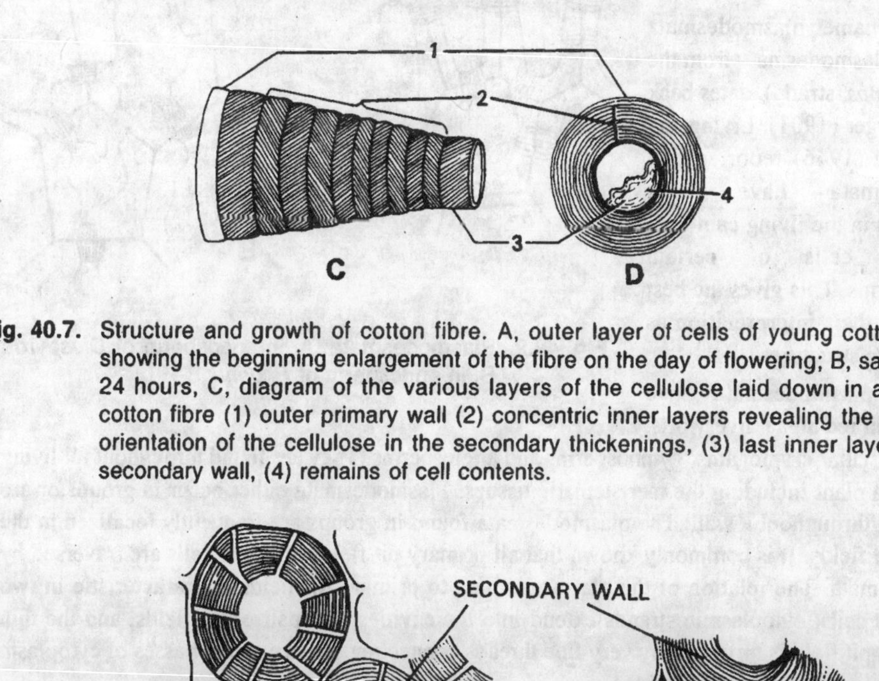

Fig. 40.8. The cell wall. Secondary cell wall sclereids from a T.S. of *Cydonia* fruit; B, phloem fibres from a transection of *Nicotiana* stem.

Plasmodesmata

The relation between cell wall and protoplast is quite close. The protoplast of one cell remains connected with that of the adjacent or neighbouring cell by delicate threads of cytoplasm. These threads known as **plasmodesmata,** fill minute passages which constitute the only breaks in the primary wall of two cells. The presence of plasmodesmata is the characteristic of living cells and they are found in the cell walls of all living cells to maintain the continuity of the protoplasm.

The name plasmodesmata (singular plasmodesma—from the Greek *desmos*, strand), dates back to Strasburger (1901). Livingston and Bailey (1946) reported that plasmodesmata have been recognized in the living cambium and ray cells of certain gymnosperms. This gives the best support to their interpretation as cytoplasmic structures.

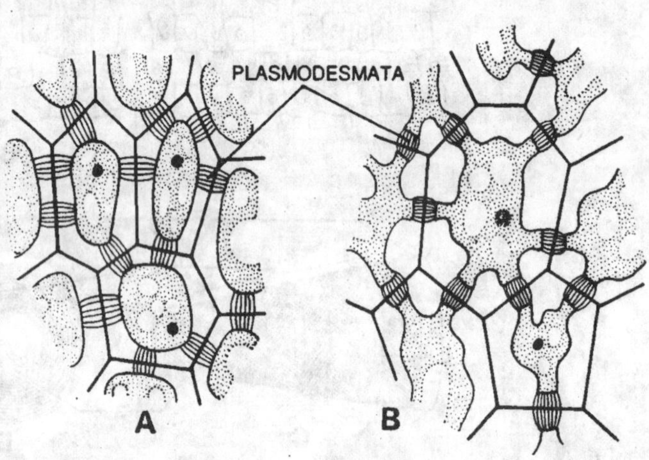

Fig. 40.9. Plasmodesmata. A, in endosperm of *Diospyros;* B, in endosperm of *Phoenix*.

The plasmodesmata have been seen in red algae, liverworts, mosses, vascular cryptogams, gymnosperms and angiosperms. They are found throughout all living tissues of a plant including the meristematic tissues. Plasmodesmata either occur in groups or are distributed throughout a wall. The plasmodesmata found in groups are frequently localized in the primary pit fields. It is commonly known that all primary pit fields of living cells are traversed by plasmodesmata. The relation of the plasmodesmata to primary pit fields is characteristic in two contiguous cells, cytoplasmic strands extend into the cavities of a pair of pit fields, and the thin wall of the pit field is traversed by very fine threads connecting the two small masses of cytoplasm filling the depression of the pit field.

As regards their origin, it has been suggested that young, growing walls are permeated with cytoplasm, which later withdraws except in localized areas where it then makes the plasmodesmata. It is also thought that plasmodesmata are formed *de novo* in older walls.

As regards their function, they are thought to be concerned with material transport and conduction of stimuli. The plasmodesmata are also regarded as channels permitting the movement of viruses from cell to cell. In the case of the angiospermic parasites such as *Cuscuta*, *Viscum* and *Orobanche*, the presence of plasmodesmata between the haustoria-like structures and the cells of their host plants is thought to be related to food and virus movement (Esau, 1948).

Plasmodesmata are most readily seen in the endosperm of some seeds (*e.g., Phoenix, Aesculus, Diospyros*) where food storage has greatly increased wall thickness.

Thickening of the Cell Wall

The cells cease to increase in size and become mature. At this stage, the cells become modified according to the function they have to perform. During the process of their maturation, the cells undergo additional or secondary thickening deposition of new materials such as cellulose, lignin, suberin, cutin, etc. Some of the cells (*e.g.*, parenchymatous cells) remain unthickened. The cells of certain parts (*e.g.*, pericycle, phloem, xylem, etc.) of the plants undergo heavy thickening of their walls. The thickening materials of the cells are secreted by the protoplasm. These materials are deposited in the cell walls in such manner that cell wall becomes stratified in appearance. The cells which ultimately develop into vessels, tracheids and fibres show the thickening of the cell wall in various ways. This thickening takes place due to the deposition of a hard substance, called **lignin,** on the inner surface of the cell wall. Usually the thickening material (*e.g.*, lignin) of the secondary wall is not laid down in uniform thickness but it may form the special patterns such as **annular, spiral, scalariform, reticulate** and **pitted.** In such patterns the whole of the wall is not thickened. Only those portions of the cell walls are thickened where the thickening material is laid down in the form of above mentioned patterns and the remaining portion of the wall remains thin. The details of these thickenings are as follows:

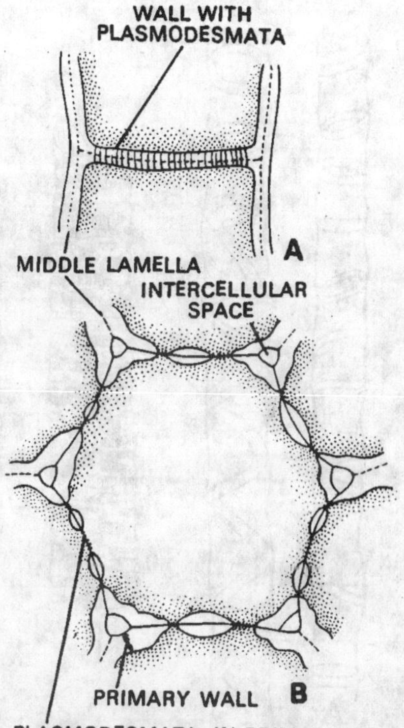

Fig. 40.10. Plasmodesmata. A and B, parenchyma cells without secondary walls from *Nicotiana* stem. Plasmodesmata dispersed throughout

Annular or ring-like thickenings: The deposition of lignin takes place in the form of rings on the inner surface of the cell wall. These lignified rings are placed one above the other like coins leaving sufficient space in between each other. The gaps of the walls remain unthickened. Such thickenings are commonly found in the vessels and tracheids.

Spiral thickenings. In such cases the deposition of thickening material (lignin) takes place in the form of complete spiral bands. The number of such bands may be one or more than one. This type of thickening is commonly found in the vessels or tracheae of angiosperms.

Scalariform or ladder-like thickenings. In such thickenings of the cell wall the lignin is being deposited in the form of the transverse rods of the ladder, and thus known as scalariform or ladder-like. The unthickened areas between the successive thickening layers appear as elongated transverse pits. This type of thickenings are common in xylem vessels and tracheids of protoxylem.

Reticulate or net-like thickenings. In such thickenings of the cell wall the thickening matter or lignin is being deposited in the form of a net or reticulum and thus known as reticulate or net like thickening of the cell wall. In such cases the unthickened areas of the cell wall are irregular in shape. These thickenings are commonly found in the vessels of the stems, roots and leaves of angiosperms and in the tracheids of protoxylem.

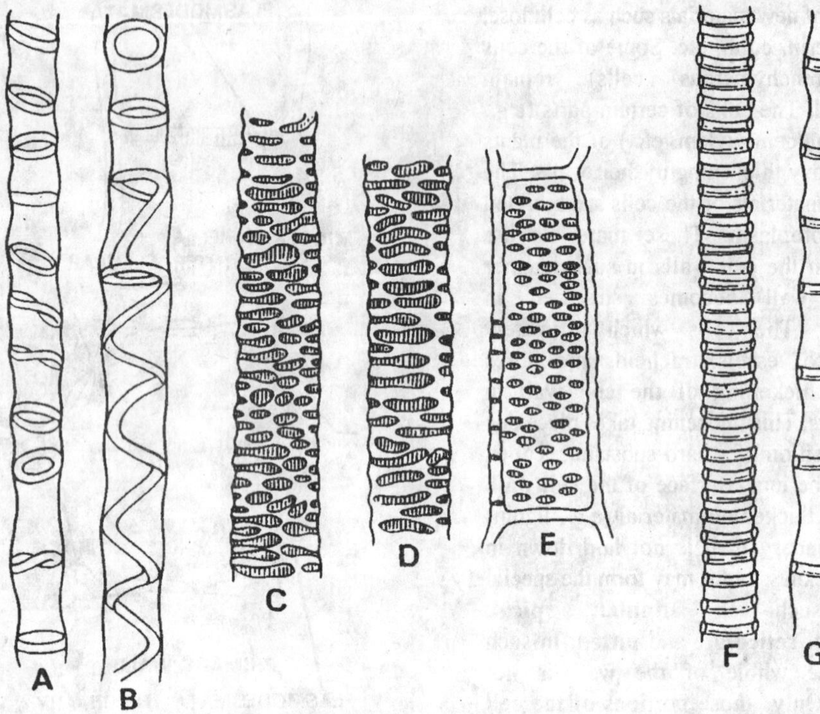

Fig. 40.11. Xylem-vessels. Secondary wall structure in primary tracheary (vessel) elements, the thickenings are visible. A, annular; B, partly annular, partly helical; C, reticulate; D, scalariform reticulate; E, pitted; F, annular in an unstretched vessel element; G, annular in a stretched vessel element.

Pitted thickenings. In such thickenings of the cell wall, the whole inner wall is more or less uniformly thickened, leaving here and there some small unthickened areas, the **pits.**

Pits

The pits are formed in pairs lying against each other on the opposite sides of the wall, and morphologically more correct they are called **'pit pairs'.** A pit pair is structural and directional unit constituted by two pits lying opposite to each other of contiguous cells.

Structure. The space found inside the pit is called the **pit cavity** or **pit chamber.** The separating membrane which separates the two chambers or cavities of a pit pair, is called the **pit membrane,** or **pit aperture.** The pit cavity opens internally in the lumen of the cell and is closed by the closing or pit membrane along the line of junction of two contiguous cells. A pit has two pit cavities, two pit apertures, and one pit or closing membrane. The pit membrane is common to both pits of a pit pair and consists of two primary walls and a middle lamella or intercellular substance. Usually two types of pits are met within the cells of various plants, *viz.*, **simple pits** and **bordered pits.** Two bordered pits make up a bordered pit pair, two simple pits form a simple pit pair. A bordered pit and a simple pit lying opposite to each other in contiguous cells, constitute a **half bordered pit pair.** A pit occurs opposite an intercellular space has no complementary pit and is known as **blind pit.** Fundamentally the bordered pit differentiates from a simple pit in having a secondary wall arching over the pit cavity, which constitutes the actual border and becomes narrow

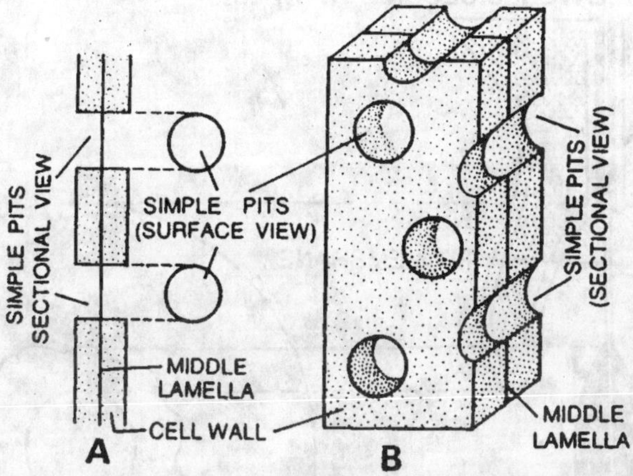

Fig. 40.12. Simple pits. A, cell-wall having two simple pits showing sectional and surface views; B, portion of a cell wall showing some simple pits—sectional view (right top) surface view (front).

like a funnel towards the lumen of the cell. In the simple pit, no such arching of the secondary wall and narrowing of the pit towards the lumen of the cell occurs.

Simple pits. Simple pit pairs occur in parenchyma cells, in medullary rays, in phloem fibres, companion cells, and in tracheids of several flowering plants. In the simple pits, the pit cavity remains of the same diameter and the pit or closing membrane also remains simple and uniform in its structure. The simple pit may be circular, oval, polygonal, elongated or somewhat irregular in its facial view. The simple pits occurring in the thin walls are shallow, whereas in thick wall the pit cavity may have the form of a canal passing from the lumen of the cell towards the closing or common pit membrane. The diffusion of protoplasm takes place through these pits.

Bordered pits. They are abundantly found in the vessels of many angiosperms and in the tracheids of many conifers. They are more complex and variable in their structure than simple pits. The overarching secondary wall which encloses a part of the pit cavity is called, the **pit border,** which opens outside by a small rounded mouth known as **pit aperture.** The overarching rim forms a border around the aperture and thus named 'bordered pits'. The pit aperture may be of various shapes in the facial view. It may be circular, lenticular, linear or oval. In the case of relatively thick secondary walls, the border divides the cavity into two parts. The space between the closing membrane and the pit aperture may be called the pit chamber and the canal leading from pit chamber to the lumen of the cell may be termed as **pit canal.** The pit canal opens in the pit chamber by an outer aperture and at the same time it opens in the lumen of the cell by an inner aperture. The closing membrane of a bordered pit pair which consists of the parts of two primary walls and the intercellular substance or middle lamella, is somewhat thickened in its central part. This thickening is called **torus** which remains surrounded by a delicate margin. In many bordered pits, the closing membrane may change its position within pit cavities. The torus may remain in central position or it may shift to the lateral position. As the torus is shifted to the lateral position the pit aperture closes, and the passage of the protoplasm may take place only by diffusion through torus.

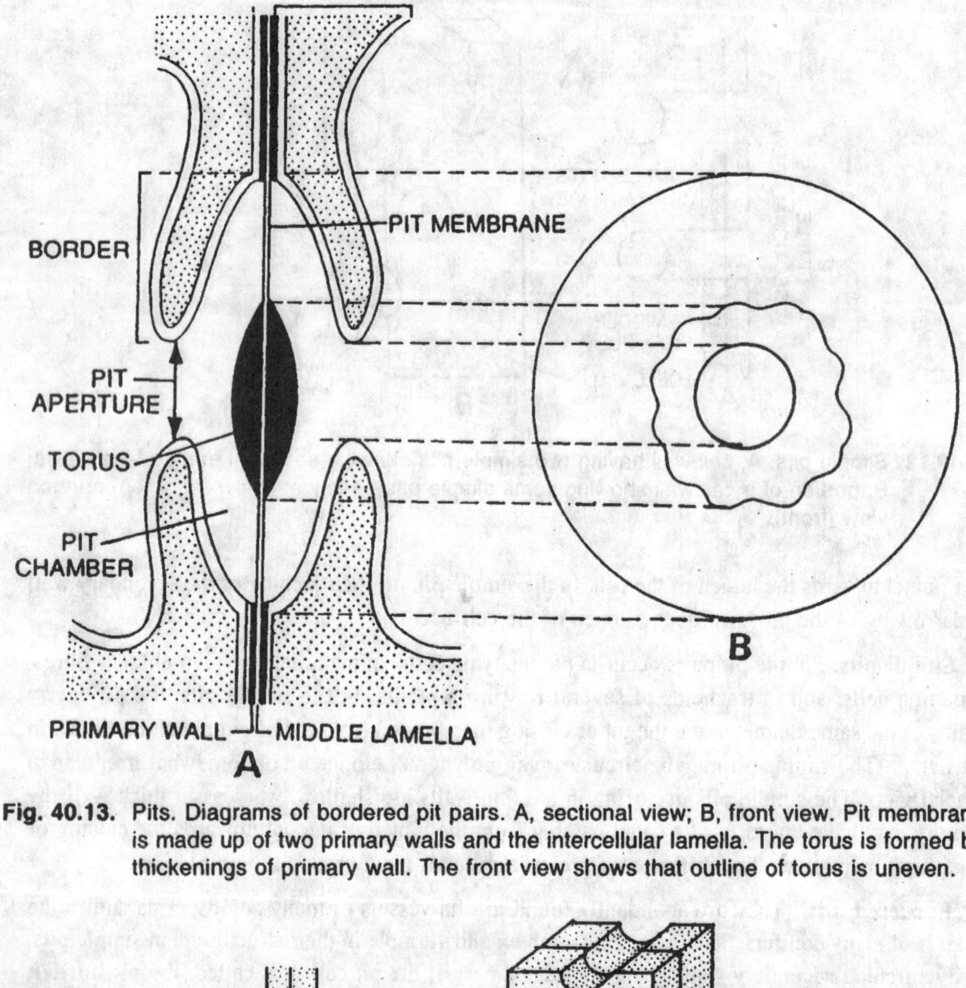

Fig. 40.13. Pits. Diagrams of bordered pit pairs. A, sectional view; B, front view. Pit membrane is made up of two primary walls and the intercellular lamella. The torus is formed by thickenings of primary wall. The front view shows that outline of torus is uneven.

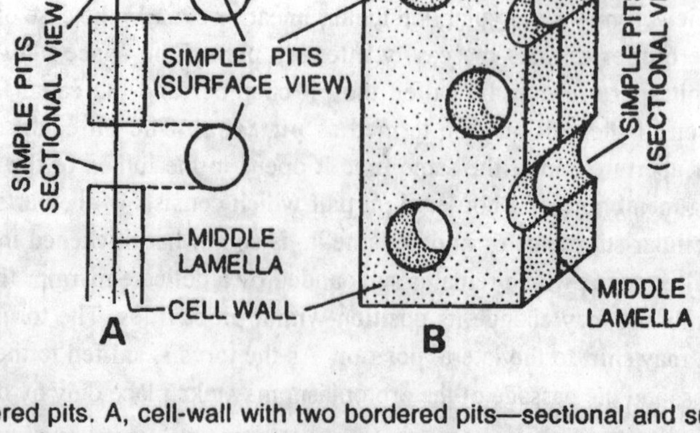

Fig. 40.14. Bordered pits. A, cell-wall with two bordered pits—sectional and surface views; B, a portion of the cell-wall with two bordered pits—sectional view (bottom) and surface view (top).

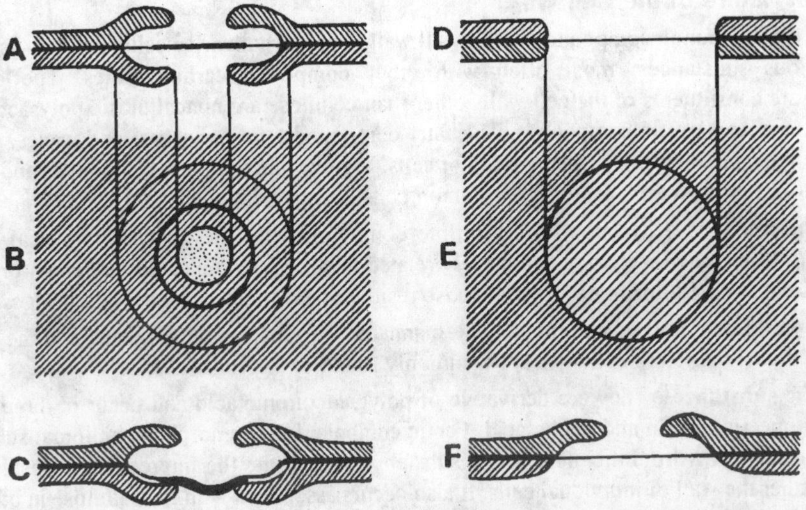

Fig. 40.15. The pits—diagrams of three kinds of pit-pairs. A, B, section and face view of bordered pit-pair showing overarching borders, pit cavities, closing membrane and torus; C, section of same showing closing mombrane in lateral position, the torus closely appressed to the pit aperture; D, E, section and face view of a simple pit-pair, the closing membrane has no torus; F, section of a half bordered pit-pair, arches only on one pit cavity, no torus.

Patterns of bordered pits. The bordered pits in vessel walls of angiosperms show *three* main types of arrangement : (*i*) scalariform, (*ii*) opposite and (*iii*) alternate. If the pits are elongated or linear and make ladder-like arrangement, it is called **scalariform pitting** (Fig. 40.16 A). When the pits are arranged in horizontal pairs, it is called **opposite pitting** (Fig. 40.16 B). If such pits are crowded, their borders assume rectangular outlines in face view. When the pits occur in diagonal rows, the arrangement is called **alternate pitting** (Fig. 40.16C). Generally small simple pits are arranged in clusters, and such arrangement is called **sieve pitting.**

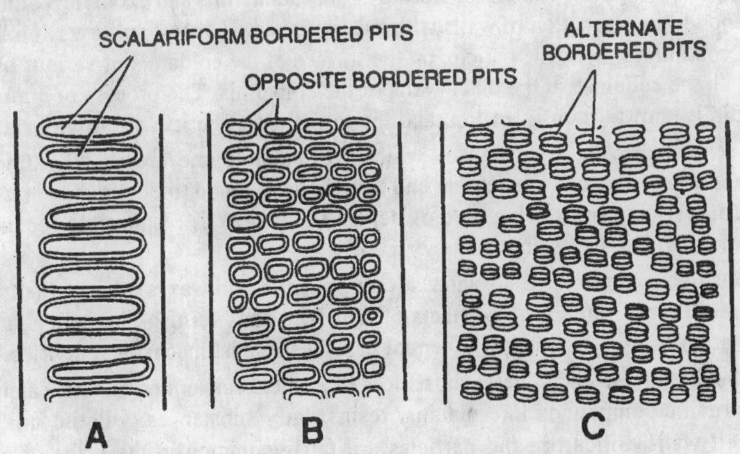

Fig. 40.16. Pits. Arrangement of bordered pits in vessel walls of angiosperms as seen in face view. A, scalariform in *Magnolia*; B, opposite in *Liriodendron*; C, alternate in *Salix*.

Chemical Nature of the Cell Wall

The most-common compound in plant cell wall is the carbohydrate cellulose. It is associated with various substances, most often with other compound carbohydrates. The common carbohydrate constituents of the cell walls other than cellulose are noncellulosic polysaccharides, hemicellulose, and pectic compounds. The fatty compounds, cutin, suberin and waxes, occur in varying amounts in the walls of many types of cells. Various other organic compounds and mineral substances are also present. Water is a common constituent of cell walls.

Cellulose. It is a hydrophilic crystalline compound with the general empirical formula $(C_6H_{10}O_5)_n$. It is a polysaccharide and closely related to starch. Its molecules are chain-or ribbon-like structures with 100 or more of the glucose residues held together by oxygen bridges.

Non-cellulosic polysaccharides. The mannans, the galactans, the xylans and the arabans which are closely allied to cellulose are commonly found in the cell walls.

Pectic substances. They are derivative of polygalacturonic acid and occur in three general types, protopectin, pectin and pectic acid. Pectic compounds are amorphous colloidal substances plastic and highly hydrophilic. The pectic substances constitute the intercellular substance that binds together the wall of individual cells. It also occurs associated with the cellulose in other wall layers, mainly the primary.

Gums and mucilages. They are also the compound carbohydrates of the cell walls. They are related to the pectic compounds, and both possess the property of swelling in water (Bonner, 1950). Gums exude as a result of physiological or pathological disturbances that induce a break down of walls and cell contents, whereas the mucilages occur in some gelatinous or mucilaginous type of cell walls.

Lignin. It is an organic compound of high carbon content, distinct from the carbohydrates. Lignin is found in all three wall layers—the primary wall, the middle lamella, and the secondary wall. The impregnation with lignin usually starts in the intercellular lamella and then spreads centripetally through the primary and secondary walls. The process of conversion of cellulose into lignin is called **lignification.**

Cutin, suberin and waxes. The cutin and suberin are fatty substances which are not meltable and exhibit considerable insolubility in fat solvents. Cutin and suberin are closely related, highly polymerized compounds consisting of fatty acids. Suberin occurs in association with the cellulose in cork cells of the periderm. Suberin also occurs in the endodermis and exodermis of many plants. The phenomenon of impregnation of walls with suberin is referred to as **suberization.** Usually the cutin forms a continuous layer, the cuticle, on the surface of the epidermis of various plants. Cutin also occurs with the cellulose in the outer walls of the epidermis. The process of impregnation of walls with cutin is known as **cutinization,** and the formation of cuticle as **cuticularization.**

The waxes are also fatty substances which are meltable and are easily extracted by fat solvents. Waxes are associated with suberin and cutin and are found to be deposited on the surface of the cuticle in various forms. This type of deposition of wax is responsible for the glaucous condition of many fruits, leaves and stems.

The deposition of these fatty substances (cutin, suberin and waxes) checks the transpiration and protects the leaves from leaching effects of rain. The hard varnish-like cuticle, may protect against penetration of living tissues by potential parasites against mechanical injuries.

Mineral substances. The mineral substances like silica, calcium carbonate, calcium oxalate and several organic compounds like tannins, resins, fatty substances, volatile oils, etc., may impregnate cell walls. Silica or sand particles are fairly common in the walls of grasses and horsetails (*Equisetum* sp.). Calcium carbonate is being deposited in the form of cystoliths in many species of *Ficus* and other plants. Organic compounds are frequently deposited in the xylem walls when this tissue changes from sapwood into heartwood.

INTERCELLULAR SPACES

Usually the meristematic or young cells do not possess any intercellular spaces among them but as they become older their walls split at certain places giving rise to small spaces called intercellular spaces, usually these are filled up with air or water. Generally there are two types of intercellular spaces—1. Schizogenous intercellular spaces and 2. Lysigenous intercellular spaces.

Schizogenous intercellular spaces. The most common intercellular spaces result from separation of cell walls from each other along more or less extended areas of their contact. In such cases, the intercellular substance dissolves partly and an intercellular space develops. Ultimately this becomes quite big in size and is known as **schizogenous cavity.** The ordinary intercellular spaces and schizogenous cavities form an intercommunicating system of long intercellular canals which facilitate diffusion of gases and liquids from one part of the plant body to the other. The resin ducts in the Coniferales, and the secretory ducts in the Compositae and Umbelliferae are the typical examples. The cells lining the cavity are secretory in nature and release their product in the intercellular canal.

Lysigenous intercellular spaces. This type of intercellular space arises through dissolution of entire cells, which are therefore called lysigenous intercellular spaces (*lysis*, loosening, Greek). These cavities of intercellular spaces store up water, gases and essential oils in them. The examples are commonly found in water plants and many monocotyledonous plants. The secretory cavities in *Eucalyptus*, *Citrus* and *Gossypium* are good examples.

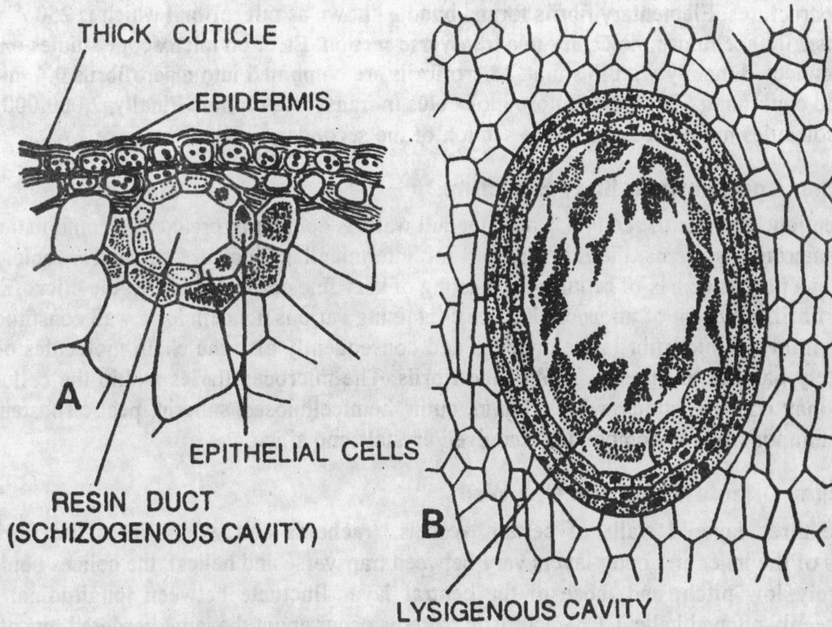

Fig. 40.17. Intercellular spaces. A, a schizogenous intercellular space in *Bryophyllum* stem; B, a schizogenous intercellular space in leaf of *Sequoia sempervirens*.

MICROSCOPIC AND SUBMICROSCOPIC STRUCTURE OF CELL WALLS

The chemical substances of cell walls remain combined physically and chemically with each other. Several physical and chemical methods have been employed for such investigations. At first the secondary wall was the main object of study, but with the refinement of methods the primary wall has been also investigated successfully. The significance of the study of primary walls is that it yields information on the methods of growth of cell walls in surface area. Investigators combine observations on differential staining; differential solubilities; coarse and fine structure variations; reaction to polarized and fluorescent light, to X-rays, and to dark-field illumination; refractive indices; and composition of ash. In modern days, the electron microscope is the main tool for the study of cell walls.

Micellar and Intermicellar Systems

The organization of the structure of the cell walls is based on cellulose. The fundamental units of the system are the chain-like cellulose molecules of different lengths. These chains are not dispersed at random but occur in aggregates and generally known as **micelles.** The chain molecules possess a parallel arrangement in a micelle and the glucose residues within a chain are spaced at uniform distances from each other. Thus, a bundle of cellulose molecules, the micelle, may be compared to a crystal in that its units are arranged symmetrically. This way, the bundles of cellulose molecules are interconnected by means of the lower chain molecules and from a porous coherent system, the **micellar system,** interpenetrated by an equally coherent **intermicellar system** in which various wall substances other than the cellulose are present.

Frey Wyssling (1959) graphically described these structural elements and their interrelations on the basis of the secondary wall of the fibre of *Boehmeria.* Here one cellulose molecule is 8 Å wide. Cellulose molecules are combined into an **elementary microfibril** which has a widest diameter of 100 Å and is discernible with the electron microscope. It contains 100 cellulose molecules in a transverse section. Both the cellulose molecules and the elementary fibrils are ribbon like structures. Elementary fibrils form a bundle known as **microfibril** which is 250 Å wide and contains 2,000 cellulose molecules in a transverse section. Electron microscope studies on cell walls are connected mainly with this unit. Microfibrils are combined into macrofibrils 0.4 micron (μ) wide and containing 500,000 cellulose molecules in transverse section. Finally, 2,000,000,000 cellulose molecules make up a transverse section of the secondary wall of the fibre.

Microfibrillar and Microcapillary Structure

As mentioned earlier the cellulose of plant cell walls is being interpreted as a combination of two interpenetrating systems, the micellar and the intermicellar. They are submicroscopic. The walls contain a porous matrix of cellulose consisting of very fine coalesced fibrils, the **microfibrils** and an interfibrillar system of **microcapillaries** containing various noncellulosic wall constituents. However, within the microfibrils the micelles and consequently also the chain molecules occur approximately parallel to the long axis of the fibrils. The microcapillaries within the cellulose framework may contain liquids, waxes, lignin, cutin, hemicelluloses, suberin, pectic substances, other less common organic compounds, and even crystals and silica.

Microfibrillar Orientation in the Cell Wall

In the three layered walls of certain vessels, tracheids and wood fibres the fibrillar orientations of the inner and outer layers vary between transverse and helical, the helices being of comparatively low pitch, and those of the central layer fluctuate between longitudinal and relatively steeply pitched helical. Characteristic patterns occur about the large bordered pits of the early wood tracheids.

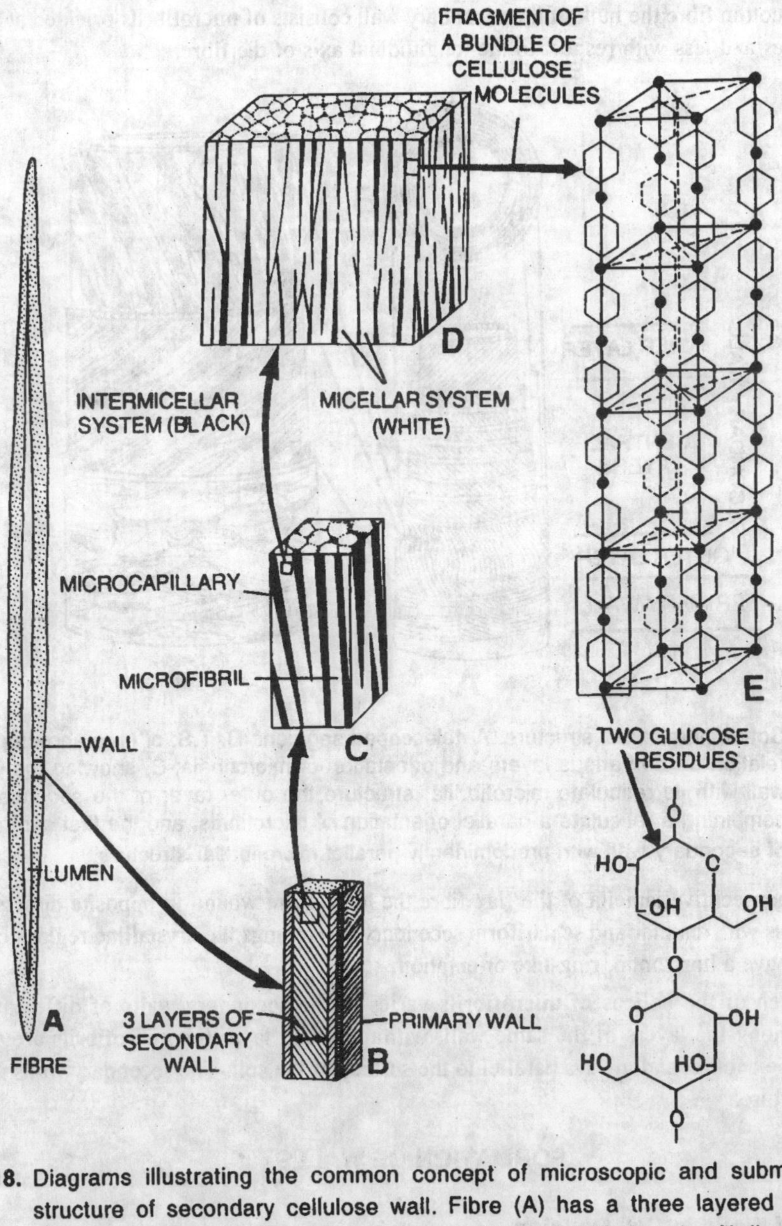

Fig. 40.18. Diagrams illustrating the common concept of microscopic and submicroscopic structure of secondary cellulose wall. Fibre (A) has a three layered secondary wall (B), In a fragment of the central layer of this wall (C), the microfibrils of cellulose (white), the other of micro capillaries (black) containing various noncellulosic wall materials. Microfibrils consist of inter micellar (black) and micellar (white) systems (D). The intermicellar system contains noncellulosic wall constituents, whereas the micellar system is composed of bundles of chain like cellulose molecules (E). The bundles of cellulose chains, the micelles, show an orderly arrangement of the glucose residues (F) that make the basic units of the cellulose molecules.

In the cotton fibre the bulk of the secondary wall consists of microfibrils oriented at an angle of 45 degrees and less with respect to the longitudinal axis of the fibre.

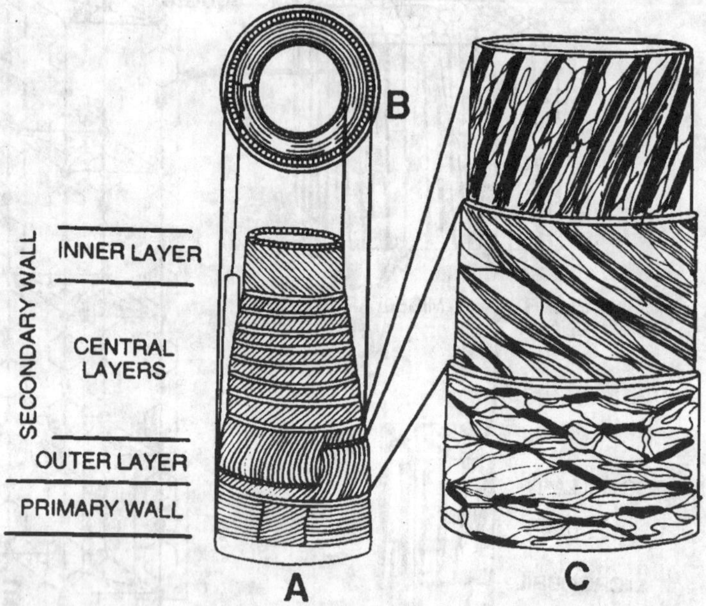

Fig. 40.19. Cotton fibre's wall structure. A, telescoped segment; B, T.S. of fibre showing spatial relation of the various layers and orientation of microfibrils; C, showing the primary wall with its reticulate microfibrillar structure the outer layer of the secondary wall combining a reticulate a parallel orientation of microfibrils, and the first central layer of secondary wall with predominantly parallel microfibrillar structure.

In the consecutive lamella of the flax fibre the helices are wound in opposite directions. In tracheary cells with annular and scalariform secondary thickenings the crystalline regions of these thickenings have a horizontal, ring-like orientation.

The pitch of the helices of microfibrils varies in the secondary walls of different cells. However, among the layers of the same wall, within a given layer the microfibrils are usually parallel to one another and always parallel to the surface of the cell. The secondary walls possess a parallel texture.

FORMATION OF WALLS

Initiation of Walls in Cell Division

The process of somatic division of a protoplast may be separated into two parts—(*i*) The division of the nucleus (*i.e.,* **mitosis** or **karyokinesis**) and (*ii*) The division of the part of the protoplast other than nucleus (*i.e.*, **cytokinesis**). In the cells which have cell walls the new wall develops during cytokinesis. The partition between the newly formed protoplasts, when first appears, is referred to as the **cell plate.** If cytokinesis takes place immediately after the nuclear division, the cell plate develops in the equatorial plane of a fibrous spindle, the **phragmoplast,** extending between the two groups of chromosomes that move apart during the anaphase of mitosis. As these two groups develop into the telophase nuclei, the phragmoplast becomes wider

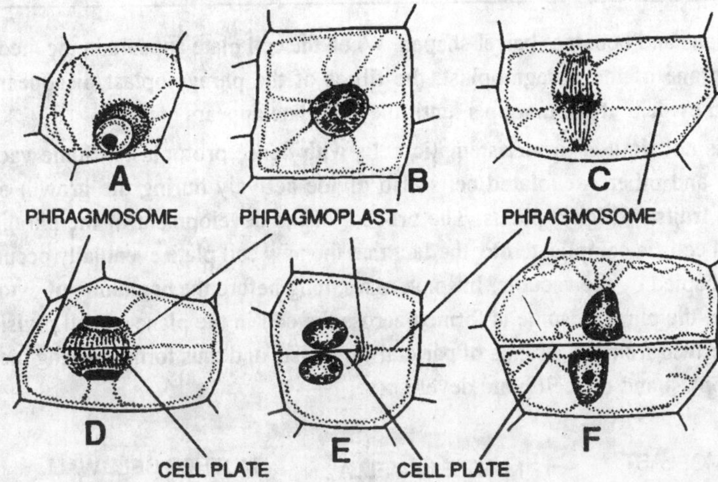

Fig. 40.20. Division of highly vacuolated cells. A, cell in a non-dividing state; B, nucleus in prophase and located in the middle of the cell; C, nucleus in early anaphase; laterally mitotic spindle is connected to parietal cytoplasm by a cytoplasmic layer the, phragmosome; D, daughter nuclei in telophase, the barrel-shaped spindle between the nuclei is the phragmoplast; cell plate appears in its equatorial plane; E, cell plate intersects one of the walls of mother cell; F, cell division is completed and the cell plate occupies the former position of phragmosome.

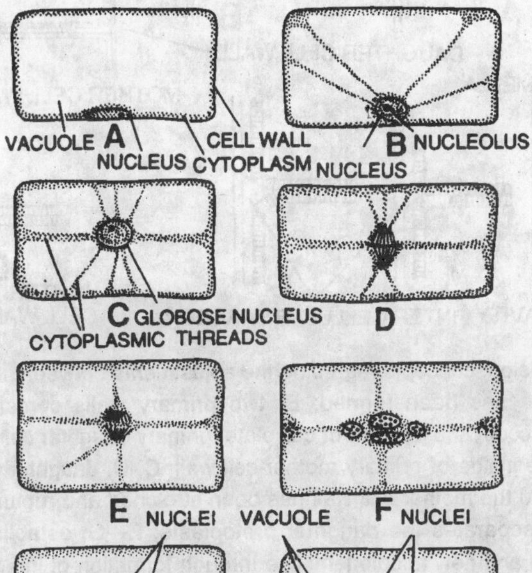

Fig. 40.21. Origin of the cell wall. Division in cell with large central vacuole. The cytoplasm increases in amount forming layer in position of new wall; nucleus becomes rounded and shifts to central position; normal nuclear division takes place with extending phragmoplast.

in the equatorial plane and becomes barrel-shaped. When the cell plate appears in the median part of the equatorial plane of the phragmoplast, the fibres of the phragmoplast disappear in this position but remain evident at the margin's, until the cell plate appears here too.

Cytokinesis is not limited to meristematic cells with dense protoplasts. Some vacuolated meristematic cells and other vacuolated cells also divide actively during the growth of roots, shoots, leaves and fruits of higher plants. The process of the development of the phragmoplast through vacuolated cells is complicated by the fact that the new cell plate eventually occurs in the region formerly occupied by the vacuole. In some cases, long before the beginning of cytokinesis, a cytoplasmic plate, the phragmosome is formed across the cell in the plane of cell division. The phragmosome is derived from the strands of parietal cytoplasm and thus forms a living medium in which the phragmoplast and the cell plate develop.

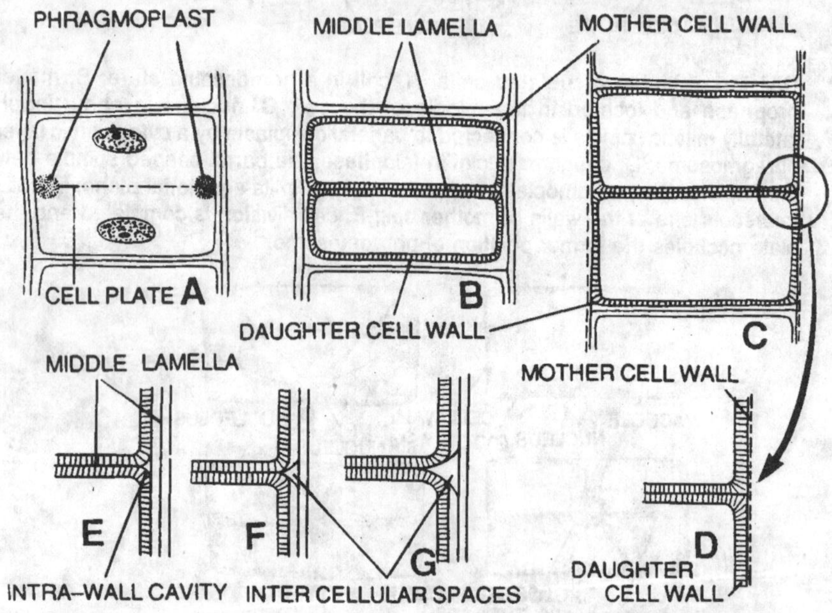

Fig. 40.22. After cell division, concepts regarding the adjustments between new and old cell walls. A, cell plate has been formed; B, two primary walls cemented by intercellular substance occupy the position of cell plate; primary daughter cell walls have been laid down on the inside of primary mother-cell wall; C, D, daughter cells have expanded vertically and the mother cell wall has been stretched and ruptured opposite the new wall which separates the daughter protoplasts; E—G, establishment of continuity between old and new middle lamellae through formation of intercellular space.

Division in cells with a large central vacuole involves predivision changes in form and position of nucleus and in structure of the vacuole. The cytoplasm increases in amount extending in strands through the vacuole; the nucleus becomes more rounded and moves away from the wall along one of the cytoplasmic strands; the strands gradually become concentrated in the **'phragmosome'** in the plane where the new wall is to be formed. Nuclear division and wall formation then take place as in other meristematic cells or cells with enough cytoplasm.

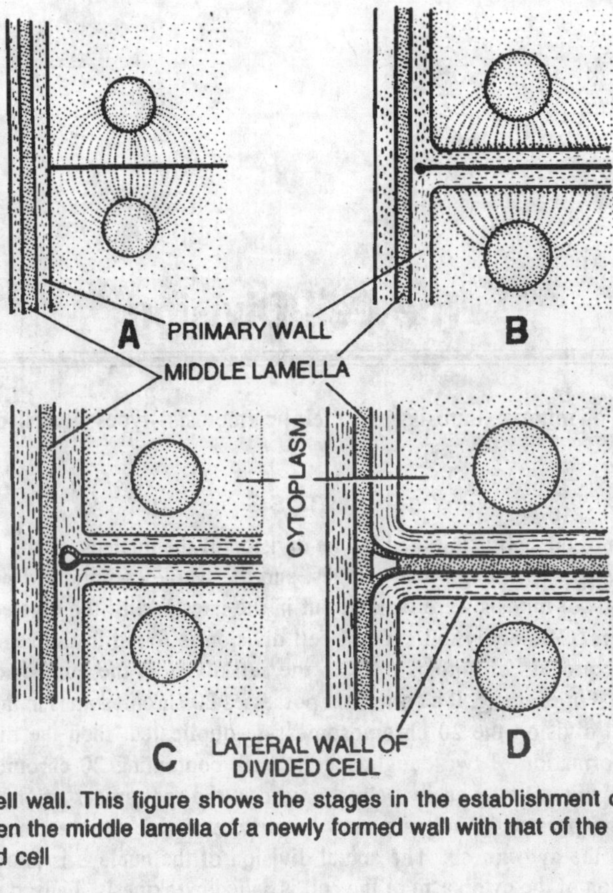

Fig. 40.23. The cell wall. This figure shows the stages in the establishment of the connection between the middle lamella of a newly formed wall with that of the lateral wall of the divided cell

Growth of Walls

Growth in thickness of walls is evident in secondary walls as well as in primary walls. It occurs by a successive deposition of wall material, layer upon layer that is, by a process known as **apposition.** Growth of walls by apposition is usually centripetal, that is, it occurs from outside and toward the lumen of the cell. Centripetal growth is characteristic of cells forming tissues. Another important aspect of wall growth establishment of continuity between the new intercellular lamella and that located outside the primary wall of the mother cell. There is an extension and break down of the parent wall opposite the new middle lamella. The formation of intercellular spaces is thought to be associated with this phase of wall growth.

41

CHAPTER

The Cell Division

The details of mitotic (mitosis) and meiotic (meiosis) types of cell division have been discussed here.

MITOSIS

The division of the cell is initiated by the division of the nucleus. In the ordinary method of division a nucleus passes through many stages, and the whole complicated process is known as **mitosis.** The details of mitosis were worked out in the later part of the nineteenth century by W. Flaming and others. Commonly this type of cell division is found in the vegetative parts of the plant body. In the process of mitosis prior to the cell division, the number of chromosomes is always duplicated. For example, if a corn plant possesses 20 chromosomes in the somatic cell, then prior to each cell division the 20 chromosomes are duplicated, then the division takes place resulting in the formation of two daughter cells each containing 20 chromosomes again. The different stages of mitosis may easily be recognised in the root apices of onion. From the study point of view, the process of mitosis may be differentiated into two main phases — The **karyokinesis** and the **cytokinesis.** The actual division of the nucleus is known as karyokinesis whereas the division of the cytoplasm of the cell is called cytokinesis. Thus, during the process of mitosis the nucleus undergoes several changes which may easily be studied in the onion root apex by special cytological techniques. The chief function of mitosis seems to be to divide all parts of the chromatin equally between the two daughter nuclei. The important phases of mitosis are — **prophase, metaphase, anaphase** and **telophase.**

Prophase. In the resting nucleus the chromatin is spread out as a reticulum. It is actually composed of a number of separate units, the **chromosomes.** The number of chromosomes in the nuclei is definite in different species. Gradually the chromosomes become thick and condensed and each of them splits lengthwise forming two **chromatids.** The chromatids remain coiled around each other throughout their length. Gradually, they become much more thick and smooth. The chromatids coil around each other spirally and each chromosome itself remains surrounded by a membrane. In well fixed chromosomes some unstained gaps or constrictions are seen; they are the attachment regions, called **centromeres.** The nucleoli lose their staining power and disappear completely. The nucleus then rapidly passes into the next stage, the metaphase, through a complicated series of changes.

Metaphase. The nuclear membrane disappears and simultaneously a new structure, the **spindle,** appears in the cytoplasm, which chemically, consists of long chain protein molecules oriented longitudinally between two poles. The **fibres** of the spindle, however, are really fine tubules, not just protein threads. Chemical analysis of the cells has indicated that approximately 15 per cent of the cytoplasmic proteins go into its make-up. Once the spindle is formed, the chromosomes move through the cytoplasm to it, and become fastened by their **centromeres** to a region midway between the poles called the **equator** of the spindle, a position of apparent

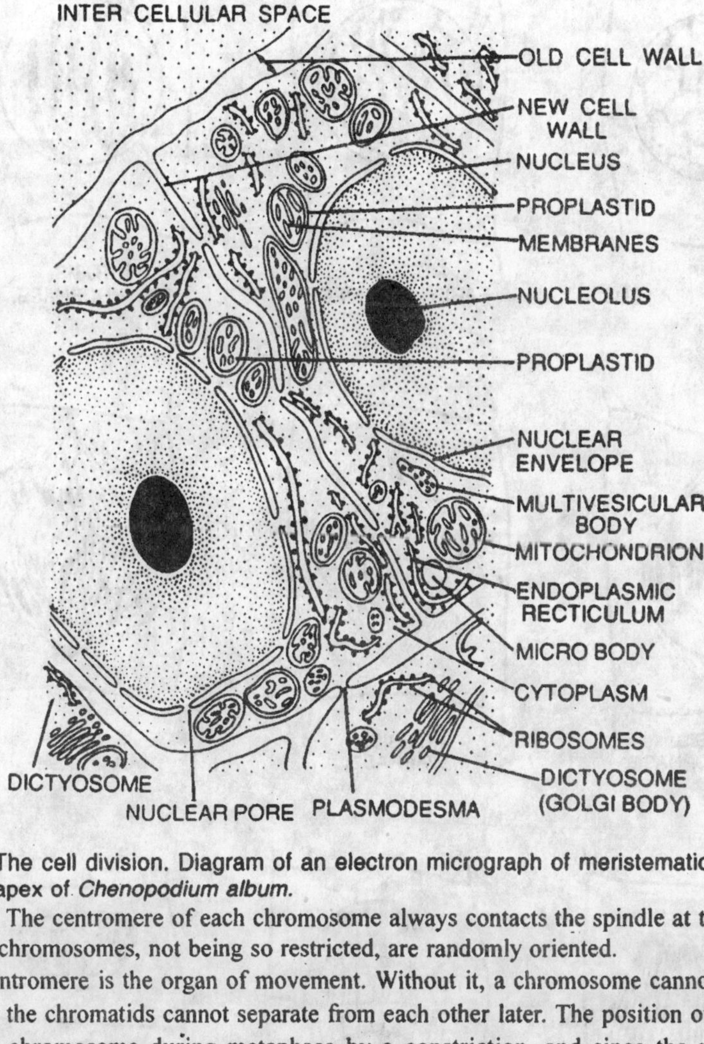

Fig. 41.1. The cell division. Diagram of an electron micrograph of meristematic cells in shoot apex of *Chenopodium album.*

equilibrium. The centromere of each chromosome always contacts the spindle at the equator; the arms of the chromosomes, not being so restricted, are randomly oriented.

The centromere is the organ of movement. Without it, a chromosome cannot orient on the spindle, and the chromatids cannot separate from each other later. The position of centromere is visible in a chromosome during metaphase by a constriction, and since the position of the constriction is characteristic for each chromosome, the centromere divides the chromosome into two arms of varying lengths. Very few chromosomes have strictly terminal centromeres.

Anaphase. Anaphase follows metaphase. At the end of the metaphase the centromeres of each pair of chromatids appear to repel each other. The centromeres now divide so that each chromatid has its own centromere; they then move apart from each other to initiate a slow movement that will take sister chromatids to opposite poles. Termination of anaphase movement occurs when the chromosomes form a densely packed group at the two poles.

Telophase. As soon as the chromosomes reach the poles, they collect into a more or less solid-appearing mass. This marks the beginning of telophase. The mass of chromosomes gradually converts into a nucleus. A new nuclear membrane forms. Spindle gradually disappears. The formation and enlargement of the spaces containing nucleoplasm continue until the

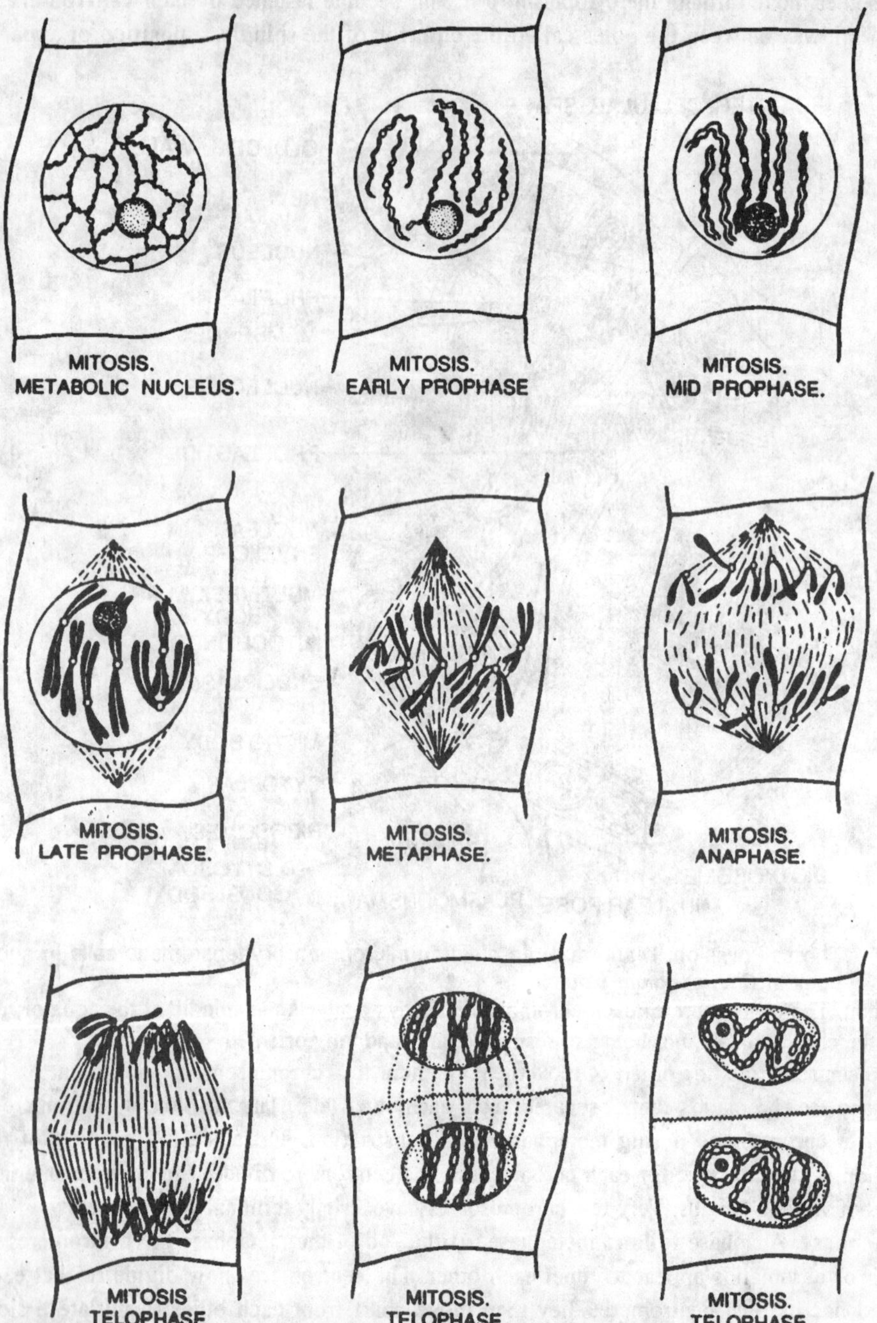

Fig. 41.2. Cell division. Mitosis.

chromosomes again become scattered in the form of a network typical of the resting stage. As the mass of chromosomes becomes more and more spread on by the formation of nucleoplasm a new nucleolus makes its appearance. The newly formed nucleus contains the same number of chromosomes, as this was in parent nucleus.

Cytokinesis. Just after the nuclear division, the division of cytoplasm takes place which is known as **cytokinesis.** The cytokinesis takes place in two ways. According to one method, much of the cellulose is being deposited in the centre of the cell, and the cell is resulted. This method is known as **cell plate method.** According to other method after the formation of young nuclei, a furrow develops in the cytoplasm and the cytoplasm is being divided into two equal parts, thus completing the cytokinesis.

Duplication of DNA and its transfer to daughter cells. With the result of mitotic cell division one parental cell gives rise to two daughter cells, and this process continues indefinitely. The newly formed daughter cells behave in the similar way as their parent cells. This shows that the daughter cells bearing the DNA molecule of one type, and they are also similar in quantity. As we know, the DNA molecules consist of two spirally coiled threads. This model of DNA is known as double helix DNA. During cell division, because of the presence of weak hydrogen bonds the threads of DNA helix separate from each other. In prophase stage of mitosis each chromosome splits into two chromatids. One of the DNA threads goes to one chromatid and the other to another chromatid. All the chemical substances, that give rise to the new thread of DNA are found in the protoplasm of the daughter cell. The newly formed thread coils around the old DNA thread and forms the double helix of DNA. The newly developed DNA is similar to that of original DNA of parental nucleus. By this process, the DNA molecules reach in the same quantity to each of the daughter cells.

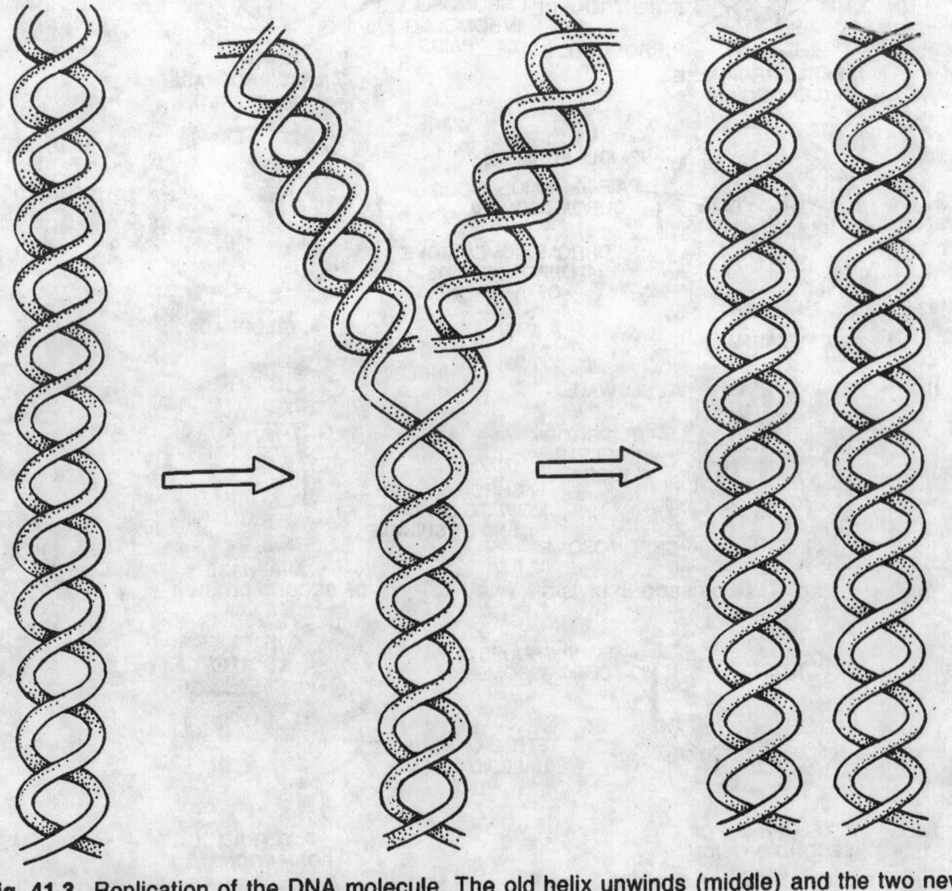

Fig. 41.3. Replication of the DNA molecule. The old helix unwinds (middle) and the two new helices are being formed.

Significance of mitosis

With the result of mitosis, the chromosomes split lengthwise into two chromatids. Each chromatid bears all those characteristics which were present in mother chromosome. In other words, with the result of mitosis, two identical cells have the same genetic constitution, qualitatively and quantitatively, as the parental cell from which they arose. Thus, the maintenance of the genetic integrity of the cell population and ultimately of the organism and its descendent depends upon the mechanism of mitosis. This process has been proved to be beneficial to vegetative reproduction. In the similar way, the characters of the plants grown by vegetative reproduction may be preserved for long time.

MEIOSIS

The division during which the number of chromosomes are reduced are known as the reducing or meiotic divisions, and the process of reduction division as **meiosis.** For the first time

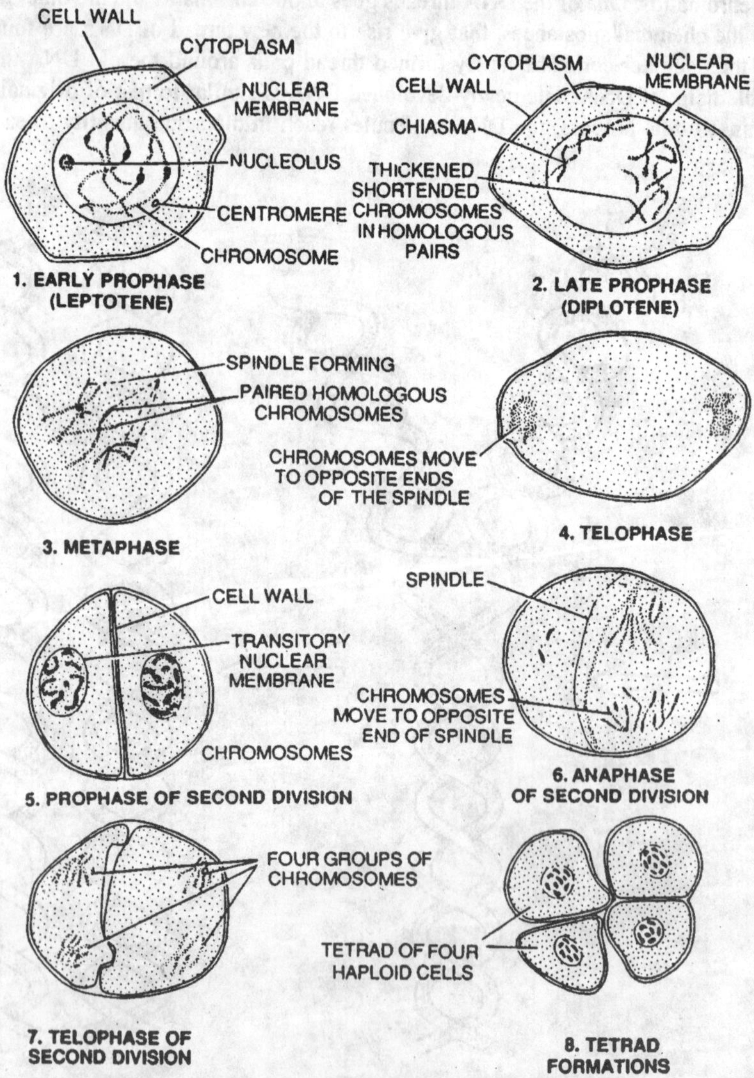

Fig. 41.4. The Cell Division. Stages in Meiosis.

in 1888, Strasburger discovered this phenomenon. There are two phases in the life-cycle of lower and higher plants — **sporophyte** and **gametophyte.** The sporophyte contains the 2n number of chromosomes, whereas the gametophyte possesses n number of chromosomes. If the nucleus of sporophyte contains 6 chromosomes, then its nucleus of gametophyte contains only 3 chromosomes, *i.e.*, half the number of the chromosomes of the nucleus of the sporophyte. With the result of meiotic division (meiosis), from one nucleus of the sporophyte four nuclei of the gametophyte are formed, and the number of chromosomes for each nucleus becomes half of the number of chromosomes of the nucleus of the sporophyte. In all the plants which are sexually reproduced, the meiosis takes place. In the sporophyte, the spore mother cells represent the last phase of the sporophytic status. Thus, each spore mother cell bears 2n number of chromosomes. Each spore mother cell eventually divides reductionally producing four haploid (n) spores. In such division, the first division is known as **heterotypic division.** The number of chromosomes is reduced to half during this division. The division is immediately followed by another ordinary division, which is known as **homotypic division.** The spore denotes the beginning of the gametophytic stage. The spore, when germinates gives rise to the gametophyte, that bears male and female gametes. The number of chromosomes in the gametes is always n. With the result of fertilization or conjugation the nuclei of male and female gametes fuse together forming **zygote** or **oospore.** The oospore (2n) is the beginning of the sporophytic stage. It bears 2n number of chromosomes. The oospore develops into the embryo and thereafter the young plant is formed. The mitotic division goes on continuously, and the plant remains diploid (2n). During the spore formation the meiosis takes place, thus the sporophytic and gametophytic stages of the plant bear 2n and n number of chromosomes in their nuclei respectively. This is only because of meiosis, the species of the plants bear definite number of chromosomes in their nuclei.

Mechanism of meiosis

It is already mentioned that during meiosis the mother nucleus divides twice, *i.e.*, heterotypic division is followed by homotypic division. The number of chromosomes is reduced to half in the heterotypic division whereas the homotypic division is mitotic one and here number of chromosomes remains same. The mechanism consists of four important phases — **prophase, metaphase, anaphase** and **telophase.**

Prophase. The prophase of meiosis is longer in duration, and consists of five separate states — **leptotene, zygotene, pachytene, diplotene** and **diakinesis**. When chromosomes first appear they are separate fine threads; this is the **leptotene** stage. The homologous members of each pair of chromosomes then associate closely side by side, corresponding loci (chromosomes) adhering together, a process called **pairing** or **synapsis;** each associated pair is a **bivalent;** this is the **zygotene** stage. The bivalents shorten and thicken. Each individual chromosome is now manifestly double; hence each bivalent consists of four **chromatids;** this is the **pachytene** stage. The two chromatids derived from one chromosome remain paired but they separate from the other two chromatids derived from the homologous chromosome; this is **diplotene** stage, followed by **diakinesis.** At certain places, however, they are held together by interchanges **(chiasmata)** occurring between chromatids derived from homologous chromosomes. Chiasmata are the visible expression of crossing-over of genes. There are usually one or more chiasmata per chromosome pair per meiosis. In a chiasma two chromatids, one from each of the original chromosomes, have apparently broken at corresponding places; and the broken ends of one chromatid have fused with the broken ends of the other. Where there is more than one chiasma in a single bivalent they may involve different pairs of chromatids, but always one from each of the original chromosomes.

As each of the two chromosomes which compose the bivalent chromosome is split into two chromatids, the bivalent chromosome is really a quadruple structure and is called a tetrad chromosome. After the formation of tetrad chromosomes, the nucleus has only half the number of

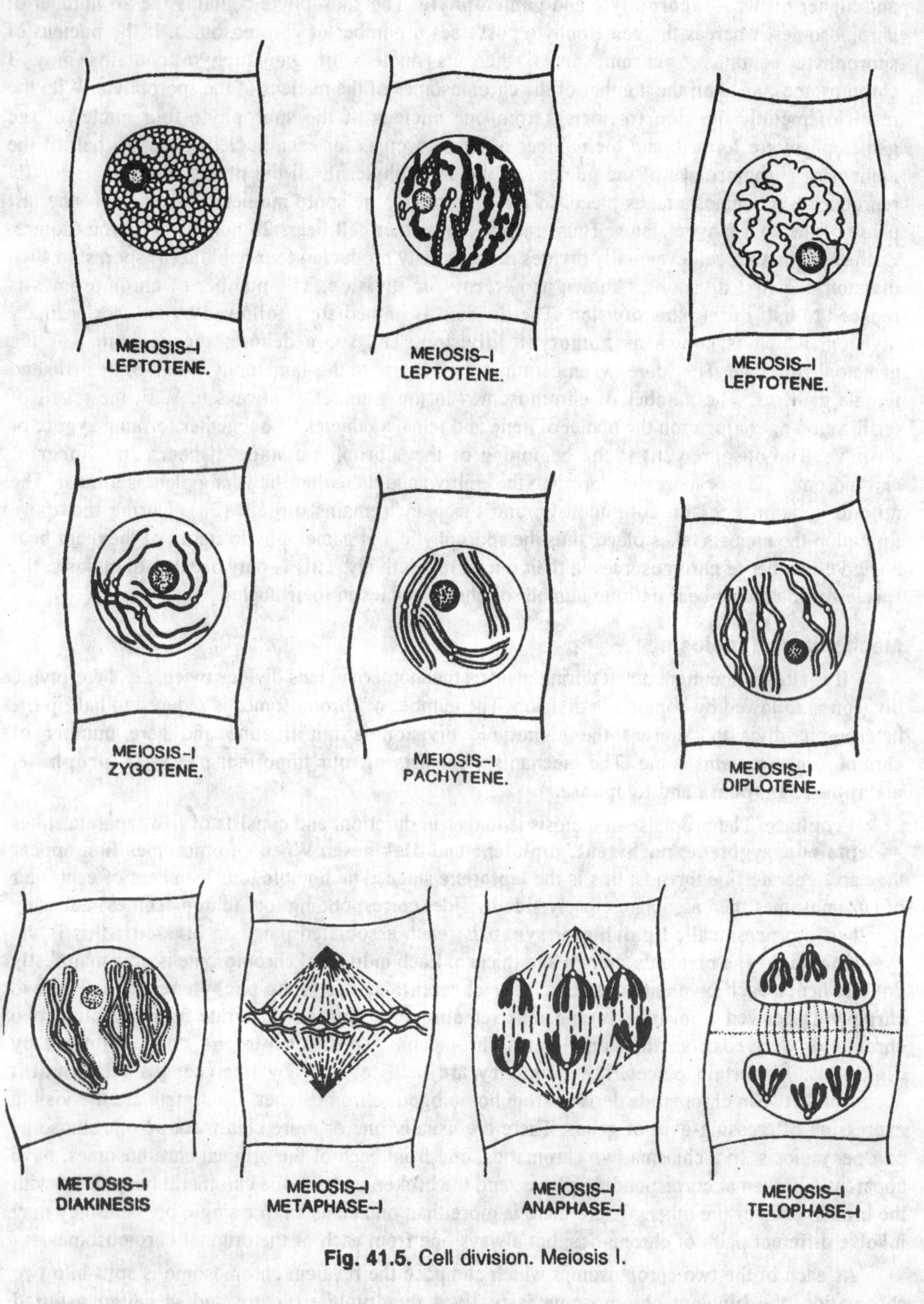

Fig. 41.5. Cell division. Meiosis I.

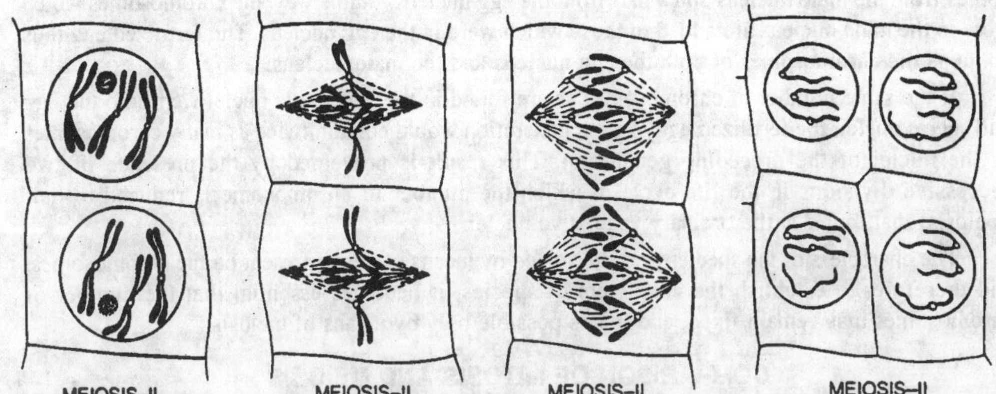

Fig. 41.6. Cell division. Meiosis II.

chromosomes that are found in ordinary vegetative cells. The subsequent events in this and the next division distribute one of the chromatids of the tetrad to each of the four cells.

Metaphase. At metaphase each of tetrad chromosomes is separated longitudinally into two daughter chromosomes which pass to opposite poles. Each of these chromosomes is, however, already split into two chromatids. At metaphase of the second of the reduction divisions these chromatids are separated from each other. We can now see why there are two reduction divisions. This is connected with the fact that the chromosomes which are formed in the prophase of the first meiotic division are quadruple and that it takes two divisions to divide them up into their constituent chromatids. At the end of the second reduction division not only has each chromosome been reduced to a single chromatid but the total number of chromosomes is also haploid (n).

Anaphase. At anaphase two of the four chromatids from each bivalent go to one pole of the spindle, and the other two to the other pole. The chromatids go in pairs because the spindle attachment of each original chromosome has not yet duplicated, so that two chromatids are united at that point. Owing to the effects of chiasmata, however, the united chromatids are not usually derived throughout their length from the same chromosome but are mixtures of one or more pieces from each of the original chromosomes. It is a matter of chance, and quite uninfluenced by behaviour of other bivalents, which spindle attachment with its chromatids, goes to which pole of the spindle.

Telophase. After anaphase there may be a short telophase and resting stage, or the second meiotic division may follow immediately, usually in both the daughter-cells formed by the first division. It is like a mitosis, except that it starts prophase with only half the normal number of chromosomes, each already divided into two chromatids before the previous prophase. The two chromatids separate at anaphase, one going to each daughter cell. Again, the distribution of the chromatids is a matter of chance, except that the two from each chromosome must go to opposite poles. On this chance distribution of the chromatids at both anaphase depends the law of independent assortment. Each daughter-cell, therefore, eventually receives only the haploid number of chromosomes. The reduction from the diploid number of the original cell to the haploid number of the four products is one of the bases of genetic segregation.

Significance of Meiosis

During the process of fertilization the male nucleus and the egg nucleus come together and the contents of the two nuclei come to be enclosed by a single nuclear membrane, a part of which comes from the male nucleus and a part from the egg nucleus. In this way, the chromosomes which were in the male nucleus are added to those which were in the egg nucleus. The fertilized egg thus contains the chromosomes of both the egg nucleus and the male nucleus.

If the same number of chromosomes as are found in the vegetative nuclei went into the egg and sperm nuclei, the fertilized egg of each generation would contain twice as many chromosomes as the nuclei of the preceding generation. This result is prevented by the presence of two successive divisions in the life cycle in which the number of chromosome is reduced to half (meiosis) that found in the ordinary vegetative nuclei.

The characters of the species are determined by means of genes present on the chromosomes, and therefore, to establish the characters of species, it becomes essential that the number of chromosomes may remain fixed, and this is possible only by means of meiosis.

COMPARISON OF MITOSIS AND MEIOSIS

Mitosis	Meiosis
1. It takes place in all the somatic cells, except those of spore mother cells, or germinal cells.	1. It always takes place either in the spore mother cells or in germinal cells.
2. The whole process is being completed in one sequence; two daughter cells or nuclei are produced from the mother cell.	2. The whole process is being completed in two sequences; with the result four daughter cells or nuclei are produced from one spore mother cell or germinal cell.
3. The daughter cells are identical to the parent cell as each cell possesses the similar number of chromosomes, *i.e.*, diploid (2n).	3. The daughter cells are dissimilar to that of parent cells as crossing over takes place and the number of chromosomes is reduced to half in each of daughter cells or nuclei, *i.e.*, haploid (n).
4. The prophase stage is of short duration and it does not bear any sub-stages. From the very beginning the chromosomes are double structures each formed of two chromatids. The split homologous chromosomes are not attracted towards each other. There is no chiasma formation and the crossing over does not take place. Synapsis does not occur.	4. The prophase is of long duration and it consists of several sub-stages. The chromosomes are granular and single structures in the beginning. In zygotene and later sub-stages, the homologous chromosomes attract towards each other forming bivalents. Each chromosome splits into two but the chromatids are not separated. The chromatids of one chromosome exchange with the chromatids of the second chromosome during the process of diplotene. The process of chiasma formation and crossing over takes place during diplotene. Synapsis takes place in the homologous chromosomes.
5. During metaphase the centromere of each chromosome divides, and the chromatids travel towards the opposite poles. No	5. During metaphase the centromeres of chromosome do not divide, and the homologous chromosomes travel towards

	change takes place in the number of chromosomes and the resultant daughter cells remain similar to parent cells. In the last stage of metaphase, the chromatids are separated from each other in the divided parts of centromeres. This separation takes place because of repulsion.		the opposite poles themselves. The number of chromosomes travelling towards one of the poles remain half to the normal number. The resultant daughter cells are dissimilar to parent cell. The maternal and paternal chromosomes are separated because of repulsion of homologous chromosomes.
6.	In anaphase the chromosomes travel upto poles.	6.	As in mitosis.
7.	As the result of telophase the two nuclei bear diploid (2n) number of chromosomes.	7.	Two haploid (n) nuclei are formed during first telophase stages.
8.	There is no second division in mitosis.	8.	The second division occurs in meiosis. The reduction division takes place during the first telophase, whereas during second telophase ordinary mitotic division takes place.
9.	As the result of mitosis, the number of chromosomes, their characters and constitution do not change.	9.	As the result of meiosis, four daughter cells are formed. Each daughter cell or nucleus is haploid (n), *i.e.*, it contains half number of the chromosomes, thus the characters and the constitution of the chromosomes also change.
10.	Cytokinesis always takes place after each division.	10.	Cytokinesis does not necessarily occur in telophase one, normally it occurs in second telophase.

Unit 9: Genetics–
Continuity of Life

42
chapter

Genetic Basis of Inheritance

All the living organisms fundamentally have the capacity of reproduction. The offspring of all the organisms (plants and animals) resemble their parents in the several respects. Why is it so? The answer lies in the phenomenon of heredity. Heredity literally means "**tendency of like to beget like**", *i.e.*, all living organisms tend to produce young ones like themselves. It involves the transfer of biological information of parental generation to the new organism via the egg and sperm. For example, cow can produce cow and never cats or elephants. This tendency of individuals to resemble their progenitors is called heredity. Though the offspring of a species may resemble very closely to their parents, but they never resemble a particular set of parents differ from each other and from their parents in many respects and to different degrees. In other words we can say that each species has its **individuality**, *i.e.*, each species is recognisable by its certain specific morphological, physiological and behavioural characteristics. For example, each person has certain peculiar characteristics by which he is easily recognised by other persons. Similarly the dogs of same breed are distinguishable from each other by certain structural differences.

Thus the offspring are similar to their parents but not exactly. They differ not only one another but from their parents also in many characters. These differences are called **variations.** The variations may be of two types. 1. The variations which are inherited from one generation to other are called **hereditary variations**, and 2. The variations which are not inherited but are because of temperature, moisture, food, light or other environmental factors affecting the development of organism are called **environmental variations.** For example, the differences between a well-nourished and malnourished person are environmental because they are due to food factor.

The branch of biological science that deals with heredity and variations is termed **genetics.** Both heredity and variations play significant role in the organic evolution as well as in speciation, *i.e.*, formation of new species. The word **genetics** (Greek, *gen* to grow into or to generate) was proposed by William Bateson (1906). This branch of science seeks to understand the laws governing the transmission of hereditary potentialities from parents to offspring. The aim of the science of genetics was defined by **Bateson** in 1905 as "the elucidation of the phenomena of heredity and variation." The geneticist studies the causes both of the similarities and of the dissimilarities between the developmental patterns of different organisms.

Modern biologists know that the units of heredity are **genes** which are transmitted from generation to generation. The parallel behaviour of genes and chromosomes during inheritance demonstrates the location of genes on chromosomes. The genetic material which carries the information and the programme of biological potential of an organism is **deoxyribonucleic acid** (DNA), whereas in somes viruses this function is carried on by **ribonucleic acid** (RNA).

Several experiments have been performed which reveal the mechanisms how genes function in prokaryotic and eukaryotic cells. However, differential gene expression forms the molecular basis of normal processes of growth and differentiation as well as cancer. Advances in molecular biology have developed techniques to isolate individual genes and to transfer them from one kind of organism to another. Such researches have revolutionised the field of agriculture and medicine.

As scientists map **genome,** the total genetic content of organisms including of humans, the prospects of curing diseases, solving mysteries of forensics and biological evolution have become easy and within reach. The birth of the first human **clone** a baby girl called Eve by scientists, was announced by Brigite Boisselier, head of a company named **Clonaid.** This was announced in December, 2002.

There is an old proverb that "like begets like." Human babies always cast in the human mould and usually resemble in particular ways their parents. On the other hand puppies always grow to be dogs and usually have the body shape, size, colour and other characteristics of their breed. It involves the transfer of biological information of parental generation to the new organism *via* the egg and sperm. Thus, the offspring of the dogs always resemble with their parents and never with cats or tigers. This tendency of individuals to resemble their progenitors is called **heredity.** A scientific understanding of heredity could arise only out of knowledge of the basic facts of biology, that is, reproduction and the means by which living matter perpetuates, in particular.

It is obvious that a living individual always arises from another living individual of the same species and never from another species or from lifeless matter. It is a well known fact that individual living things grow old and die, and therefore, the continuity of life must be maintained by the transmission of heredity to new offspring. This process of reproduction occurs in different organisms in different ways. For example, in **asexual** or **vegetative** reproduction, the body of the parent is divided into two or more parts and each part grows into a new individual. In such cases only one "parent" inherits all its traits. It is really a carbon copy of parent and is called its **clone**, rather than offspring. In some plants a small portion of the body, when removed and placed under favourable conditions, may establish itself as a new individual. For example, potatoes are cultivated more easily from pieces of tubers than from seeds, and many plants of horticultural importance are propagated by the union of two sex cells, or **gametes** (*i.e.*, egg and sperm), which form a **zygote** from which the new individual develops. In both sexual and asexual reproduction there exists a physical, living link between the parents and the offspring/clone. A part, however small, of the parent grows and develops to become the body of the offspring/clone. Whatever is inherited must be contained in this part.

However, every living organism has a set of characters by which it is identified as a member of a particular species. Now question arises, what is that which makes a species having certain set of characters and how are they maintained generation after generation. The science which deals with the answers of these questions is **genetics.** Though genetics is a relatively young discipline, yet this has gained enormous importance.

Inheritance-Heredity and Variation

No two persons or individuals, even of the same sex, are never exactly alike. The characters that provide individuality to a species are said to cause **variation** among the species. The primary reason for this is that the environment of the organisms is never the same in different places and at different times. So long as an organism is alive, its heredity interacts with its environment; this interaction determines what an individual organism is like at a given moment and what it can develop into in the future. To facilitate this the Danish geneticist Johannsen (1911) proposed to distinguish the **genotype** of the organism from its **phenotype.** The genotype is the sum total of heredity, the genetic constitution that an organism receives from its parents. The observable characteristics, of an organism such as colour, form, size, behaviour, chemical composition, and structure, both external and internal gross and microscopic, constitute the **phenotype.** Two individuals with the same genotype may become different in phenotype when they come into contact witn different conditions of food, temperature, light, humidity and other external factors. Such differences among organisms of similar heredity are known as **environmental variations.**

Among the sexually reproducing organisms no two individuals possess the same heredity, except for identical twins, which are likely to have identical genotypes. This is **hereditary** or genotypic variation. It arises from variations in the elements responsible for heredity, the genes, which may undergo changes called **mutations.**

However, hereditary component explains the variations which exist within a species. Another component of heredity and variation is associated with the mode of reproduction of a species.

Pre-Mendelian Ideas about Inheritance

In early nineteenth century, Schleiden and Schwann proposed their famous Cell Theory, and formerly proposed notion of spontaneous generation was rejected. Charles Darwin proposed the hypothesis of pangenesis. This hypothesis suggested that every part of the body produces a 'gemmule' which by the blood circulation, gets collected in the semen and thereafter these 'gemmules' transmit the characteristics to the offspring. Later on in 1892, this hypothesis was discarded by August Weismann. He proposed that living organisms consist of two kinds of materials, *i.e.*, (*i*) somatoplasm and (*ii*) germplasm. According to him the somatoplasm makes the whole body that undergoes growth, development and ultimately death. He believed that germplasm is responsible for continuity of subsequent generations.

Mendel provided the first proof for a theory that explained heredity by the transmission of units in the reproductive cell and thus put an end to vague notions such as those concerning 'bloods'.

Gregor Mendel and his Theory of Inheritance

Mendel was born in 1822 in a small village of Czech Republic. He made singular contributions in the field of genetics. He joined the Augustinian Monastery at Brno in 1843 and now he became Gregor Johann Mendel. He continued research throughout his life. In 1856, Mendel performed his first set of hybridization experiments with the garden pea. His interest in genetics was immense even when he did not get any recognition for his work in his life time. He died in 1884.

Mendel and his methods. Gregor Mendel (1822-1884) was a monk in the Augustinian Monastery at Brunn, Austria (now Brno, Czechoslovakia). He conducted his researches over a period of eight years on the common garden pea plant *Pisum sativum.* Thereafter he presented the results of his experiments, together with the generalization known as "Mendel's laws". The principle of segregation was formulated by Gregor Mendel in 1866 under peculiar circumstances that the scientific world failed to recognize or to appreciate it until after a lapse of 34 years. In 1900 A.D. when the law of segregation was rediscovered almost simultaneously by three different investigators, who had obtained results like Mendel's. These three scientists were — De Vries in Holland, Correns in Germany and Tschermark in Austria. They found Mendel's forgotten paper and proclaimed its importance. Immediately after his conclusions began to be confirmed and extended by experiments carried on in various parts of the world on many kinds of animals and plants. Mendel died in 1884, long before his scientific work came into its own.

About a century back Mendel did his experiments with garden peas which led to the discovery of the basic principles of inheritance. Subsequent work of several plant breeders showed three basic characteristics of inheritance. 1. Traits could be hidden or masked for one or more generations to reappear unchanged. 2. Traits may remain together in one generation and separate out in a later generation. 3. One form of a particular trait may be seen more often than its alternate form.

All sexually arising organisms owe their birth to the union of the male and female gametes and are the outcome of a single cell, the zygote. From this it follows that all resemblances between the offsprings and the parents must have come through the gametes. Thus the gametes are the carriers of all inheritance.

Why Mendel used garden pea for his experiments? Mendel's experimental use of the garden pea, *Pisum sativum* was evidently not an accident but the result of long careful thought. First, pollination could easily be controlled in this plant. Normally, the pea plant was self-fertilizing and, therefore, the use of Mendel's main techniques, 'selfing', presented no difficulties. When cross-fertilization between two pea plants was necessary, Mendel had merely to remove the stamens from one plant and transfer them to another plant without stamens. Second, the pea plant was easy to cultivate, and from one generation to the next took only a single growing season. Third, peas had many sharply defined inherited differences that had been long collected by seedsmen in the form of individual varieties. For his experiments. Mendel chose among these varieties seven different "**unit characters**" to follow in inheritance, ranging from stem size to shape of seed. Each character that he followed had two alternative appearances or "**traits**", *i.e.*, tall or short stems, round or wrinkled seeds, etc.

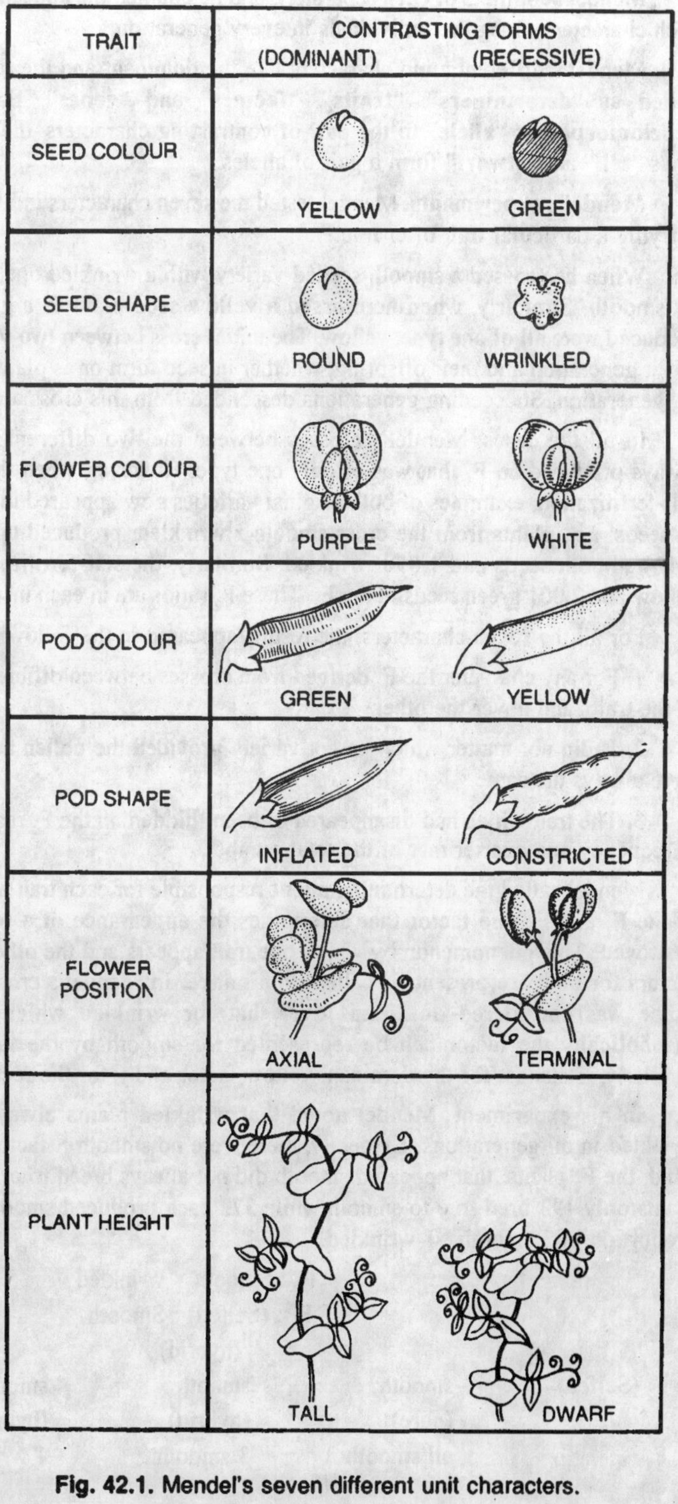

Fig. 42.1. Mendel's seven different unit characters.

Mendel kept traits of each separately, and he counted the appearance of the different traits for each character among the individuals in every generation.

Mendel's differentiating characters like the dominant and the recessive have been variously called as "**determiners**", "**traits**", "**factors**" and "**genes**". Bateson proposed the name "**allelomorph**" or "**allele**" to the pair of contrasting characters–the dominant and its recessive. Thus "**tall**" and "**dwarf**" form a pair of alleles.

Mendel's experiments. Mendel tested the seven characters individually by crossing a variety carrying a particular trait of character.

When he crossed a smooth-seeded variety with a wrinkled one, he obtained seeds that were all smooth. Similarly, when he crossed a yellow seed plant to a green seed variety, the seeds produced were all of one type, yellow. The initial cross between two varieties is called the parental, or P_1, generation and their offspring, whether in seed form or as plants are called the first filial, or F_1, generation. Succeeding generations descended from this cross are labelled F_2 and so on.

In all the cases, Mendel's crosses between the two different varieties for each character always produced an F_1 that was of only one type. However, when these F_1 plants reproduced by self-fertilization, examples of both original varieties now appeared in F_2. For example, the smooth F_1 seeds, *i.e.*, plants from the cross smooth *x* wrinkled, produced upon self-fertilization of F_2 of 5,474 smooth seeds and 1,850 wrinkled. Similarly, the self-fertilized yellow F_1 produced 6,022 yellow and 2,001 green seeds in the F_2. These F_2 ratios are in each instance very close to 3 : 1 ratio.

For all the seven characters, the results appeared in the following pattern:

1. For any character the F_1 derived from crosses between different varieties showed only one of the traits and never the other.

2. It did not matter which parent variety provided the pollen and which the ova; the results were always the same.

3. The trait which had disappeared or been 'hidden' in the F_1 reappeared in the F_2 but only in a frequency one quarter that of the total number.

Mendel called the determining **agent** responsible for each trait a "**factor**". From the evidence of the F_1 and F_2, the factor that determines the appearance of a trait could be hidden but not destroyed. This phenomenon by which one trait appears and the other does not, even through the factors for both are present, is called **dominance.** In Mendel's cross the factor for smooth seed shape was considered **dominant** over that for wrinkled which was considered **recessive.** Symbolically the factor can be represented for smooth by the **letter** S, and s for wrinkled. Similarly, Y stands, for the dominant yellow factor and *y* for the recessive green.

In his experiment, Mendel noted that wrinkled plants always gave rise ('bred true') to wrinkled in all generations. Evidently, there were no smooth S factors within them. On the other hand, the F_2 plants, that appeared smooth did not always breed true; of 565 self-fertilized smooth plants only 193 bred true to smooth while 372 each produced smooth and wrinkled plants in the proportion of 3 smooth : 1 wrinkled.

P_1 : Smooth × wrinkled
F_1 : (Selfed) : Smooth
(hybrid)

F_2 (Selfed)	:	smooth (pure)	:	smooth (hybrid)	:	smooth (hybrid)	:	wrinkled (pure)
F_3		all smooth		3 smooth		1 wrinkled		all wrinkled

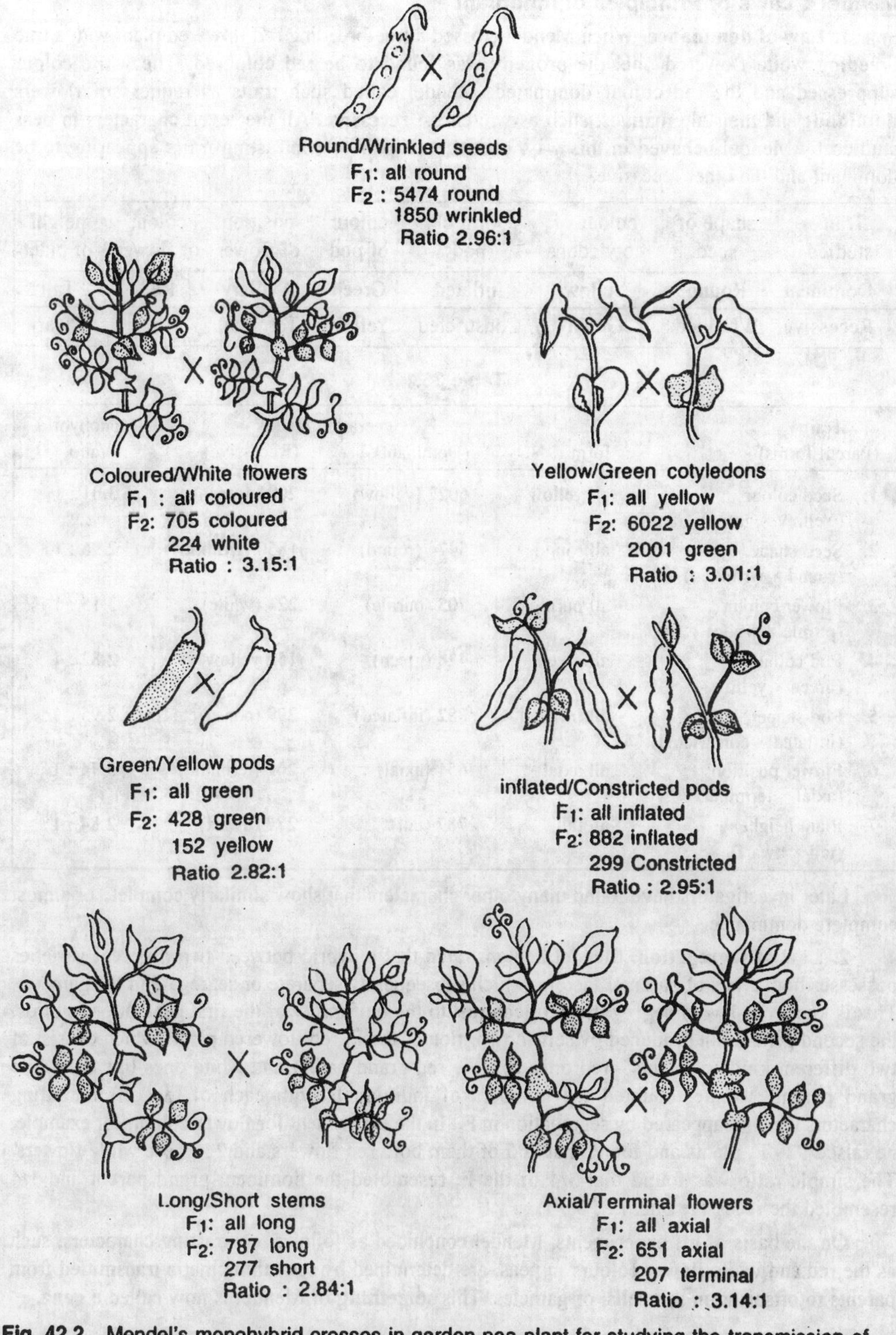

Fig. 42.2. Mendel's monohybrid crosses in garden pea plant for studying the transmission of seven different phenotypic traits of pea plants.

Mendel's Laws or Principles of Inheritance

1. Law of dominance. When Mendel crossed a true-breeding red flowered plant with a true breeding white flowered one, the progeny was found to be red coloured. The white colour suppressed and the red colour dominated. Mendel called such traits as redness of flowers **dominant** and their alternatives, such as whiteness, **recessive.** All the seven characters in peas studied by Mendel behaved in this way, one of each pair of contrasting traits appearing to be dominant and the other recessive.

Trait studied	shape of seed	colour of cotyledons	form of pod	colour of pod	position of flower	colour of flower	height of plant
Dominant	Round	Yellow	Inflated	Green	Axillary	Red	Tall
Recessive	Wrinkled	Green	Constricted	Yellow	Terminal	White	Dwarf

Table 36.1

Trait (Parent forms)	F_1 form	F_2 Generation results (Dominant)	(Recessive)	Monohybrid ratio
1. Seed colour (Yellow × green)	all yellow	6022 (yellow)	2001 (green)	3.01 : 1
2. Seed shape (round × wrinkled)	all round	5474 (round)	1850 (wrinkled)	2.96 : 1
3. Flower colour (purple × white)	all purple	705 (purple)	224 (white)	3.15 : 1
4. Pod colour (green × yellow)	all green	428 (green)	152 yellow	2.82 : 1
5. Pod shape (inflated × constricted)	all inflated	882 (inflated)	299 (constricted)	2.95 : 1
6. Flower position (axial × terminal)	all axial	651 (axial)	207 (terminal)	3.14 : 1
7. Plant height (tall × dwarf)	all tall	787 (tall)	277 (dwarf)	2.84 : 1

Later investigators have found many other characters that show similarly complete or almost complete dominance.

2. Law of segregation. Mendel demonstrated that a hybrid between two different varieties possesses both types of parental factors, which subsequently separate or segregate in the gametes. This is known as law of **segregation.** In contrast to the uniformity of the first generation hybrids, the second generation produced by self-fertilization of the F_1 red flowered plants which consist of two different kinds of plants—red ones like the red grand parent and white ones like the white grand parent. Mendel counted the numbers of individuals with each of the differentiating characters which reappeared by segregation in F_2. In the experiment for flower colour, for example, he raised 929 F_2 plants and found that 705 of them bore red flowers and 224 bore white flowers. The simple ratio was found that 3/4 of the F_2 resembled the dominant grand parent and 1/4 resembled the recessive one, *i.e.*, 3 : 1.

On the basis of his experiments, Mendel concluded as follows. contrasting characters, such as the red and white flower colours in peas, are determined by something that a transmitted from parents to offspring in sex cells, or gametes. This **something** of Mendel is now called a **gene.**

The different genes, for different flower colours or for round wrinkled seeds, do not blend, contaminate or affect each other while they are together in the hybrid. These different genes segregate, separate pure and uncontaminated, pass into different gametes formed by a hybrid and then go to different individuals in the offspring of the hybrid.

To understand how the genes are transmitted and distributed they are symbolized by letters. The dominant genes are provided with capital letters and their recessive alternatives by corresponding small letters. For example, in the cross of red and white peas *R* stand for the gene for red flowers and *r* for the alternative, or allelic, form of this gene, which gives white flowers *R* and *r* are allelic genes or **alleles.**

Since an individual develops from the union of two gametes, it receives a gene for flower colour from both parents. The true breeding red flowered parent is, therefore, represented by *RR* and its gametes are *R*; the true breeding white parent is *rr* and its gametes, *r*, or *vice versa*; and the resulting hybrid zygote will have both *R* and *r*; its genetic formula will be *Rr*.

When a gene pair in an organism contains two identical alleles, *e.g.*, *R* and *R*, the organism is considered **homozygous** for that gene pair and is called a **homozygote**. When two different alleles are present in a single gene pair, *e.g.*, *R* and *r*, the organism is **heterozygous** for that gene pair and is called a **heterozygote.** The red-flowered plants obtained by Mendel in the F_1 generation (*Rr*) were heterozygotes. They were red because the allele *R* is dominant over *r*.

3. Law of independent assortment. 'When two pairs of independent alleles enter into combination in the F_2, they exhibit independent dominant effects. In the formation of gametes the law of segregation operates but the factors assort themselves independently at random and freely.

Dihybrid and monohybrid crosses. Mendel studied seven pairs of characters in peas. These were—seed colour, seed surface, flower colour, plant height, colour of unripe pods, pod shape and position of flowers. One of his crosses was between a pea plant with round and yellow seed and one with wrinkled and green ones. This type of cross, which involves two character differences separable in inheritance is called a **dihybrid** cross and a cross which involves a single pair of alleles is **monohybrid.** The hybrids of F_1 possessed yellow and round seeds, since the yellow colour is dominant over the green and the round shape is dominant over the wrinkled. When F_1 hybrids were selfed, an F_2 generation was obtained consisting of 556 seeds of the following types:

315 round yellow

108 round green

101 round yellow

032 round green

In terms of proportion, these numbers are very close to a 9 : 3 : 3 : 1 ratio

P_1 : round × wrinkled	Yellow × green
F_1 : round	Yellow
F_2 : 423 round : 133 wrinkled	416 yellow : 140 green
or about	or about
3/4 round : 1/4 wrinkled	3/4 yellow : 1/4 green

The F_2 ratios therefore fit close to the ratios expected from crosses involving single gene pairs in which dominance occurs. When these two sets of results are combined in a single dihybrid cross, one finds that each gene pair acts independently of the other. This means that the chances for a plant to be round or wrinkled do not interfere with, or are independent of, its chances to be yellow or green. Therefore, if a seed has a 3/4 chance of being round and a 3/4 chance of being yellow, its chances to be round and yellow at the same time would be 3/4 × 3/4 = 9/16. The ratio

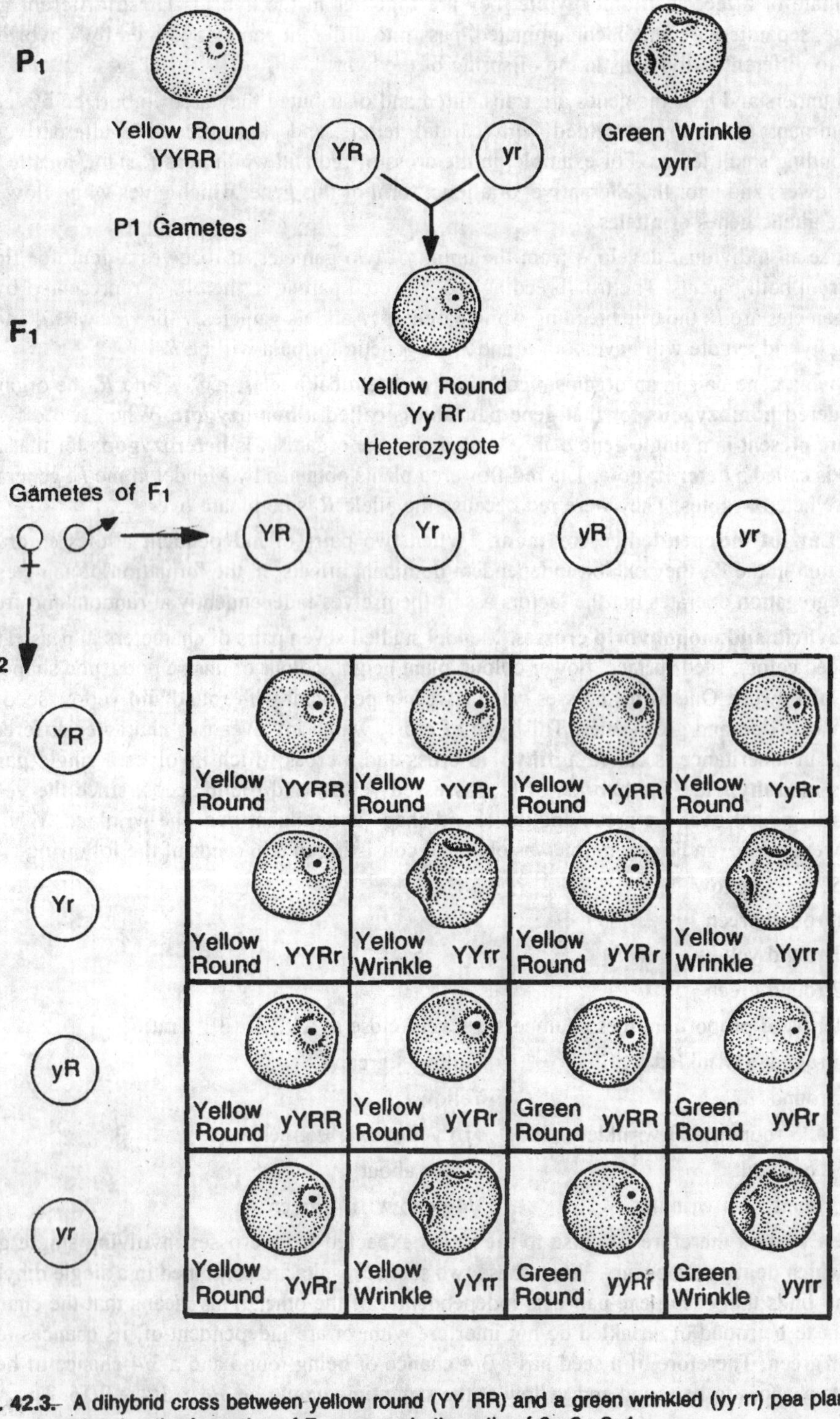

Fig. 42.3. A dihybrid cross between yellow round (YY RR) and a green wrinkled (yy rr) pea plant showing the formation of F_2 progeny in the ratio of 9 : 3 : 3: 1.

of each phenotypic combination may be obtained by multiplying the probabilities of the individual phenotypes:

3/4 round × 3/4 yellow	=	9/16 round yellow
3/4 round × 1/4 green	=	3/16 round green
1/4 wrinkled × 3/4 yellow	=	3/16 wrinkled yellow
1/4 wrinkled × 1/4 green	=	1/16 wrinkled green
		16/16 and a ratio of 9 : 3 : 3 : 1

Independent assortment. The gene for the round seeds is represented by *R* and its allele for wrinkled seeds by *r*, while the gene for yellow seeds by *Y* and for green seeds by *y*. Mendel's original yellow round seeded parent thus had the genes *RRYY*, and the green wrinkled parent *rryy*. The gametes produced by these parents were represented by *RY* and *ry*, and consequently the F_1 hybrid zygote formed by their union had the genotype *Rr Yy*. When the seed surface alone is considered, it is found that the F_1 *Rr* individuals produce gametes half of which carry *R* and half *r*. Every gamete must contain within itself not only a gene for seed surface but one for seed colour as well and indeed genes affecting every other character of the plant. Half these same gametes must, therefore, contain the allele *Y* and half the allele *y*; but in any given gamete it is a matter of chance as to whether the gene for round seeds is associated with that for yellow seeds or with that for green seeds. The assortment of the genes is independent. The F_1 hybrid produces four kinds of gametes in equal numbers *RY*, *Ry*, *rY* and *ry*. Now if two such F_1 plants are crossed, there will be 16 possible combinations among their gametes, because there are four kinds of pollen grains (♂) and four kinds of egg cells (♀). The 16 possible combinations that appear among the F_2 offspring will, therefore, equal in number. The parents, the F_1 and the F_2 of the cross, are represented diagrammatically in figure as to both their genotypes and their appearance, the 16 squares in F_2 represent the 16 possible combinations of gametes. Nine out of the 16 individuals are phenotypically round and yellow, 3 are wrinkled and yellow, 3 are round and green and only 1 is wrinkled and green. The ratio is 9 : 3 : 3 : 1.

Mendel's Postulates

The consistent pattern of results obtained from different monohybrid crosses led Mendel to propose four postulates which are also called **principles of inheritance.**

Postulate 1. Mendel proposed that each genetic character is controlled by a **pair of unit factors**, now known as **alleles** or **allelomorphic pair**

On the analysis of a monohybrid cross as per this postulate in the true bred parents, there are two unit factors for tallness and in the similar way two unit factors for dwarfness.

Thus, three combinations are possible: (*i*) either these are two factors for tall, or (*ii*) two factors for dwarf stems, or (*iii*) one of each factor in an individual.

Postulate 2. This postulate is based on the results obtained in F_1 generation. Mendel proposed that when two dissimilar unit factors are present in a single individual, only one is able to express and not the other.

The one which expresses itself is the **dominant unit factor** and the other which does not express is the **recessive unit factor**, and thus, tall stem is said to be dominant over the recessive dwarf stem. The dominant and recessive terms are used to denote a trait, *e.g.*, tall trait or recessive trait.

Now the unit factors of Mendel are called **genes.**

Postulate 3. This postulate is popularly known as the **principle of segregation** or **purity of gametes.** During gamete formation, the unit factors of a pair segregates randomly, so that, each gamete receives one or the other unit factor with equal probability. This ensures the purity of gametes.

During the formation of gametes in P generation (tall × dwarf) each gamete from the parent will receive one but the same unit factor either for tallness or for dwarfness.

After fertilization, F_1 plants will receive one unit factor for tallness and one for dwarfness.

With the former (*i.e.*, factor for tallness) being dominant, all F_1 plants will be tall.

When F_1 tall plants will form gametes, the principle of segregation will demand that each gamete randomly received either the tall or the dwarf unit factor.

With subsequent fertilisation, which is a chance event, four combinations of these unit factors will result in equal frequency in F_2 generation:

(*i*) tall/tall (*ii*) tall/dwarf (*iii*) dwarf/tall (*iv*) dwar/dwarf.

When any individual produces gametes, the **alleles segregate**; so each gamete receives only one member of the pair of alleles and the paired condition is restored by random fusion of gametes during fertilisation.

Application of postulate 2. When postulate 2 is applied the combinations (*i*), (*ii*) and (*iii*) will result into tall plants, and only combination (*iv*) will result into dwarf plants. This means that the F_2 generation consists of three-fourths tall and one-fourth dwarf or a phenotypic ratio of 3 : 1. This is exactly what Mendel observed, and is found in all the monohybrid crosses.

Application of postulate 3. When postulate 3 is applied, the combinations (*i*) and (*iv*) will result into homozygous tall and homozygous dwarf respectively and combinations (*ii*) and (*iii*) will result in heterozygous tall and homozygous dwarf, respectively in F_2 generation.

Postulate 4. This postulate is popularly known as the **Principle of Independent Assessment of Factors.** As already described, Mendel extended his work by conducting dihybrid or two factor crosses, in which the parent plants differed in two pairs of contrasting traits.

For example, a cross in which plants producing round and yellow seeds were crossed with plants producing wrinkled and green seeds.

The F_1s were all yellow and round seeded, which suggests that yellow is dominant over green and round seed is dominant over wrinkled seed.

When F_1s were selfed, Mendel postulated that the segregation of one pair of unit factors will occur independently of the other pair or they will assort independently.

As per rule, the gametes must carry all possible combinations of the unit factors in equal frequency.

In such example, gametes with random distribution of unit factors will give following combinations: (*i*) yellow, round (*ii*) green, wrinkled (*iii*) green, round and (*iv*) green, wrinkled.

During fertilisation, each zygote will have equal probability of receiving two of these combinations, one from each parent. This will result into progeny as follows: 9/16 yellow round; 3/16 yellow, wrinkled; 3/16 green, round; 1/16 green, wrinkled, *i.e.*, 9 : 3 : 3 : 1. Mendel's dihybrid results.

On the other hand, if the two pairs of contrasting traits are inherited independently, the principle of independent assortment can also be stated as when two independent events occur simultaneously the combined probability of two outcomes is equal to the product of their individual probabilities of occurrence.

For example, the segregation of yellow × green and also of round seed × wrinkled seed is 3/4 yellow : 1/4 green, and 3/4 round seed : 1/4 wrinkled seed

If these two events are combined:

(3/4) yellow × (3/4) round seed	=	9/16 yellow, round;
(3/4) yellow × (1/4) wrinkled seeds	=	3/16 yellow, wrinkled
(1/4) green × (3/4) round	=	3/16 green, round seeds; and
(1/4) green × (1/4) wrinkled	=	1/16 green, wrinkled seeds

This ratio is obtained in dihybrid cross.

Genetic Terms and Symbols

The pioneering study of Mendel led to a scientific study of heredity, which is known as **Genetics.** Central to this study is the **gene**, a unit of heredity and equivalent to the **factor** of Mendel. It is essentially a unit of information. The various forms of gene are called **alleles,** and therefore, the dominant and recessive factors of Mendel are alleles of a gene. A pair of alleles exists for each trait in the zygote of an organism, and in every cell of its body thereafter. However, the gametes it produces contain only one allele of a pair. Individual organisms in which the members of a pair of alleles are different, as in an Aa hybrid, are said to be **heterozygous.** Those in which they are alike are **homozygous** as in AA and aa forms. When selfed or inbred, homozygous organism will be truebreeding for the particular trait determined by the particular allele. However, the gene is chemically a stretch of DNA (or RNA in certain viruses).

The **genotype** is the genetic constitution of an organism. AA, Aa and aa are the genotypes of organisms with reference to these particular pair of alleles. The 1 : 2 : 1 ratio is a **genotypic ratio.** The observable characteristics of an organism constitutes its **phenotype.** The same dominant phenotype can be, as a result of two genotypes, homozygous dominant (AA) or heterozygous (Aa). The 3 : 1 monohybrid ratio is a **phenotypic ratio.** The phenotype is a result of how its genotype is expressed.

Symbols are assigned to the alleles of the genes determining a genetic trait. By the earlier convention of Mendel, genetic traits are usually assigned a letter symbol referring to their dominant state. Thus where yellow seed colour is dominant over green seed colour in peas, the dominant allele is symbolized by capital Y and the recessive allele with small y. Thus homozygous dominant will be genotype YY (phenotype yellow) and homozygous recessive genotype yy (phenotype green) and the heterozygous or hybrid form Yy (phenotype yellow).

Methods of Analysis

Punnett square. A monohybrid cross between yellow and green seeded forms is symbolized as follows. The visual diagram is called the **Punnett square.** The genotypes and phenotypes which result from various combinations of gametes can easily be determined by **Punnett squares.** Such squares were devised by Reginald C. Punnett (1875-1967). Here, each of the possible gamete is placed in an individual column or a row. The gametes are then arranged all possible combinations and the resulting genotypes are entered in the boxes along with phenotypes.

Testcross. A dominant phenotype (*e.g.,* yellow seed colour) may be exhibited by homozygous (*e.g.,* YY) or a heterozygous (*e.g.,* Yy) genotype, that is a '**pure**' or an '**impure**' form. For determining the genotype of such an offspring. Mendel devised a simple test, called '**testcross**'. The offspring with the unknown dominant phenotype is crossed with an individual homozygous recessive for the trait (green seed) and the phenotype of F_1 progeny is examined. This is illustrated as follows:

F_2 phenotypic ratio : 3 yellow (1 YY and 2Yy) : 1 green (yy)
genotypic ratio : 1 : 2 : 1 (1 YY : 2 Yy : 1 yy).

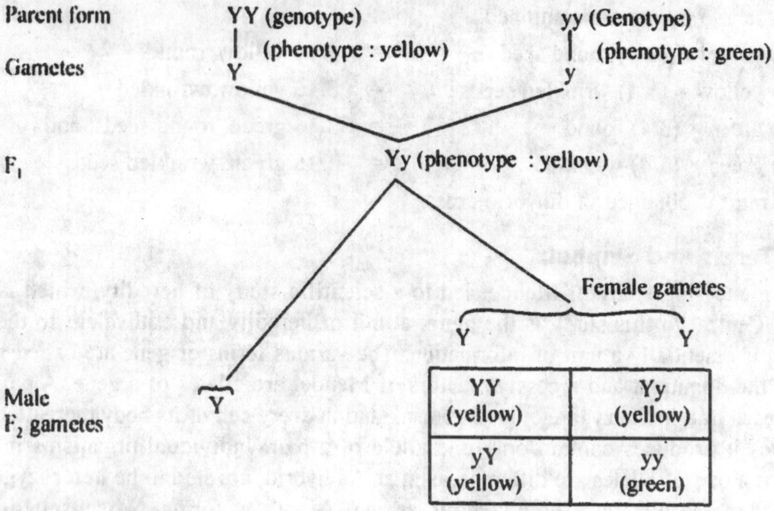

F_2 phenotypic ratio : 3 yellow (1 YY and 2 Yy) : 1 green (yy)
genotypic ratio : 1 : 2 : 1 (1 YY : 2 Yy : 1 yy).

Possibility 1. If the unknown homozygous (YY), then crossing with green recessive (yy) gives all yellow offspring, *i.e.,* all Yy. YY × yy: all offspring Yy, *i.e,* 100 per cent yellow.

Possibility 2. If the unknown is heterozygous (Yy), then crossing with green recessive (yy) result in 50 per cent yellow (Yy) and 50 percent green (yy) progeny as undermentioned:

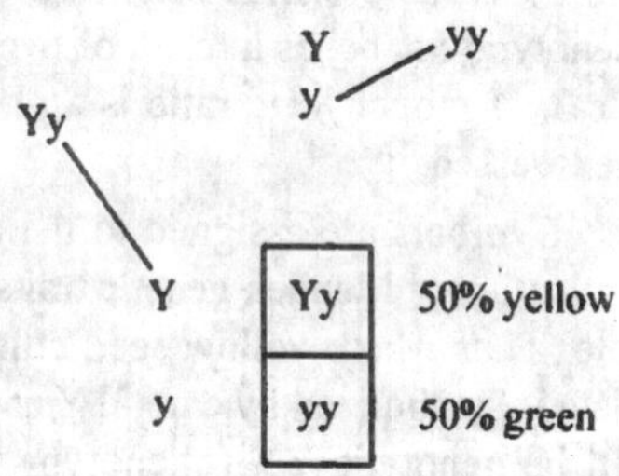

Backcross. This is another cross devised by Mendel where the F_1 is crossed with an individual with the same genotype as one or the other parent. Such crosses are used by animal and plant breeders to rapidly improve a breed or variety by making a useful trait (gene) homozygous, that is 'pure'.

Rediscovery of Mendel's Work

Mendel started his work on pea in 1856 but presented it for the first time in 1865. Mendel's work was unfortunately paid no attention from the biologists of his time. This is perhaps due to the controversies arose from the publication of Darwin's book 'Origin of Species'. Before the rediscovery of Mendel's paper in 1900, several investigators had almost deduced Mendelian principles, from their own experiments. But three biologists, who took pain and considered the conclusions of Mendel, were Hugo de Vries of Holland, Karl Correns of Germany and Erich Tschermark-Seysenegg of Austria. De vries had made many of the same observations in the course of his studies. In 1900, he reported that Mendelian principles apply to different groups of seed plants. De Vries also made an important contribution to genetics as a result of his investigations with the Evening Primrose. Such experiments of these three biologists led to the rediscovery of Mendelian work and birth of the science of Genetics.

Post-Mendelian Era-Other Patterns of Inheritance

After the re-establishment of Mendel's laws of inheritance in 1900, geneticists were used to repeat Mendel's experiments using other organisms and different phenotypes. Mendel explained inheritance in terms of separate hereditary determinants or factors now called **genes.** What Mendel discovered in peas for the first time that was later shown to be generally true for a variety of traits in many plants and animals. However, not all patterns of inheritance could be explained exclusively on the basis of Mendel's original principles alone and complexities were observed by later workers. However, many such complex situations could be resolved within the framework of his principles with suitable modifications and extensions.

1. Incomplete dominance. In many cases, however, dominance is absent, and the hybrid individuals resemble neither parent exactly but are more or less intermediate between the two. For example, in the snapdragon or four'o clock (*Mirabilis jalapa*) a red flowered plant crossed with a white one gives first generation hybrids that possess flowers of pink colour. In certain other cases the hybrid offspring resembles one parent much more closely than the other but does not resemble it exactly, so that dominance is incomplete. This is termed as **incomplete dominance.**

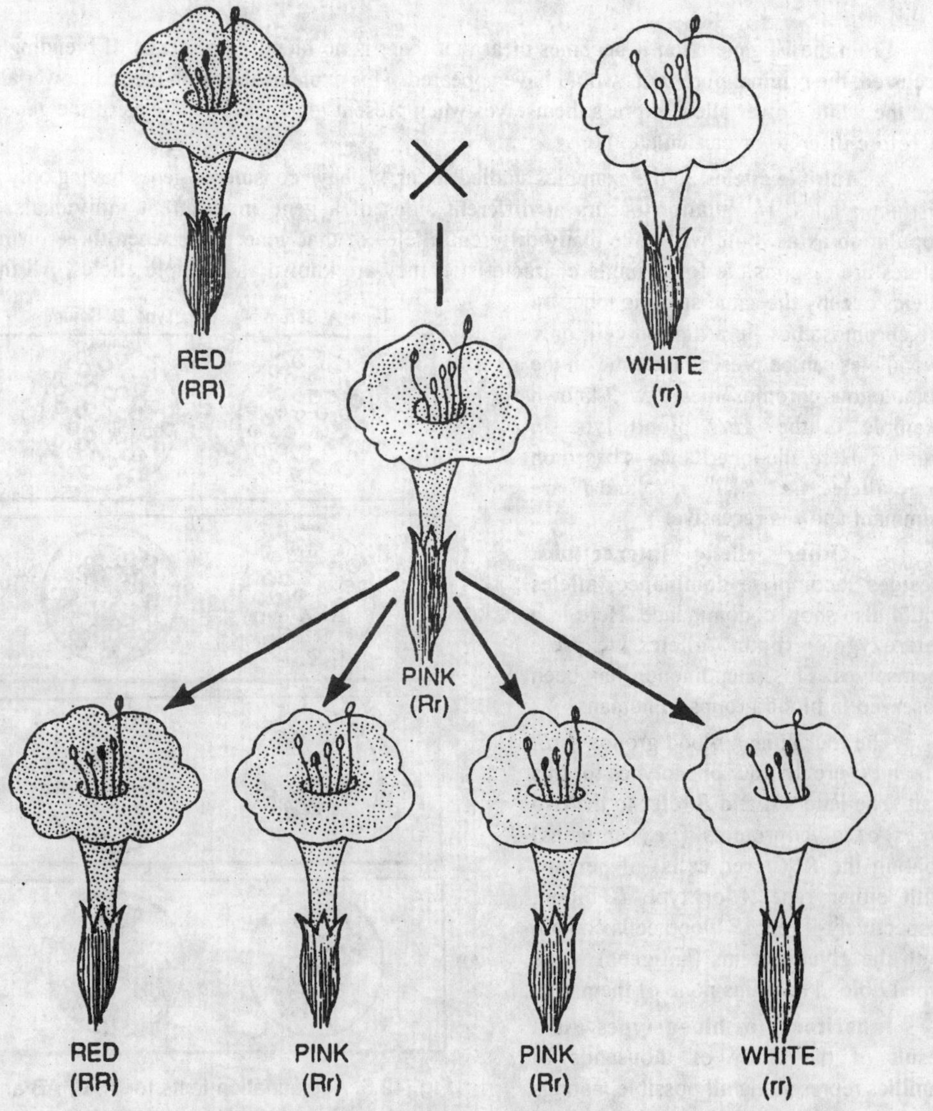

Fig. 42.4. Mendel's laws. Incomplete dominance in *Mirabilis jalapa*.

The F_1 when selfed gives F_2 progenies which are red, pink and white in the ratio of 1 : 2 : 1. Pink is therefore the heterozygous phenotype. The phenotypic and the genotypic ratio are the same in the case of incomplete dominance.

	Dominance		Incomplete dominance	
P_1	RR (Red)	rr (white)	RR (Red)	rr (white)
P_1 Gametes	R	r	R	r
F_1	Rr (Red)		Rr (Pink)	

From the F_2 generation it becomes clear that there is no blending of genes. If blending had occurred, the original pure traits would have appeared. This explains that both the red flower allele and the white flower allele express themselves when present together. The alleles of the gene are therefore discrete or particulate.

2. Multiple alleles. In the examples studied so far, we have considered genes having only two distinct alleles. If mutation occurs at different sides of a gene in different individuals, the population as a whole will have many different alleles of that gene. Thus when three or more alleles are responsible for a single characteristic, they are known as multiple alleles. All these alleles occupy the same specific locus on the chromosomes. In a diploid cell, only two alleles can be present at a time on the homologous chromosomes. A well-known example is the *ABO* blood type in humans. Here, the inheritance is based on three alleles, *i.e.*, I^A, I^B, i, I^A and I^B are dominant and i is recessive.

3. Other allelic interactions. Besides incomplete dominance, alleles could also show codominance. Here in a heterozygote both alleles express themselves. This phenomenon has been observed in blood groups in humans.

The four human blood groups *A*, *B*, *AB* and *O* are the four phenotypes for this trait. The letters *A* and *B* refer to the two types of glycoproteins (*i.e.*, antigens) coating the *RBC* (red cells) of persons with either type *A* or type *B* blood, respectively. Type *AB* blood cells contain both the glycoproteins (antigens) while type *O* blood contains none of them.

Inheritance of blood types. As a result of the study of thousands of families representing all possible matings between and within the various blood

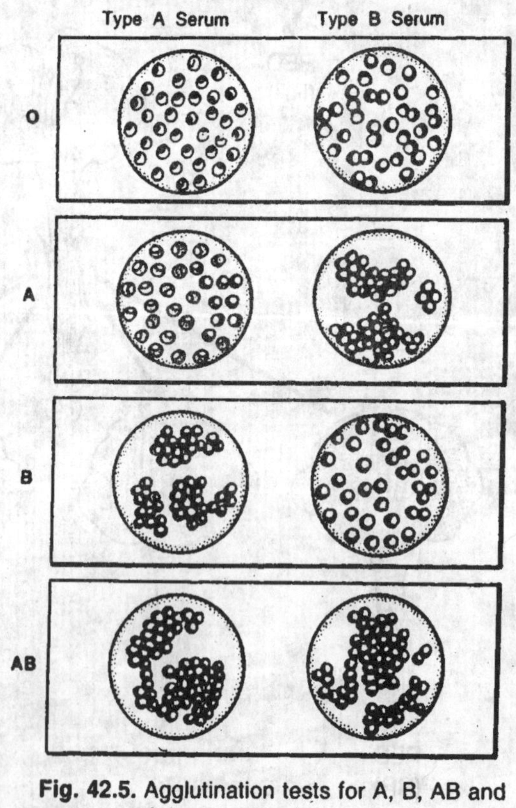

Fig. 42.5. Agglutination tests for A, B, AB and O human blood groups.

groups, the inheritance of the *A*, *B* and *O* alleles has been determined. The accumulated data support the hypothesis that there are three alleles concerned with the determination of the blood group of any given person. Each individual can have any two of these alleles, which are located in one of the 22 autosomes.

The method of inheritance of blood type is quite definite and well understood. We know that *A* antigen is produced by an autosomal gene. No person can carry this gene without having the *A* antigen, and, except for the very rare event of mutation, no child can have the *A* antigen unless at least one of his parents had it. In this respect the gene appears to act as a dominant, but it is not dominant in the same sense that the gene for normal pigmentation is dominant over the gene for albinism. When a person carries a gene for *A* antigen and the gene for *B* antigen, his blood will contain both antigens. Hence neither gene dominant over the other, a condition similar to intermediate inheritance, but which is more accurately described as a case of lack of dominance. Each of the blood group alleles seems to act independently and is not suppressed by the presence of any of the others.

Table 42. 2. The genotypes which produce the four blood types

Genotype	*Blood type*
I^oI^o	O
I^AI^A & I^AI^o	A
I^BI^B & I^BI^o	B
I^AI^B	AB

Table 42.3. Blood groups of parents and the possible blood groups of their children.

Blood groups of parent	*Possible genotypes of parents*	*Possible genotypes of children*	*Possible blood groups of children*
A × O	I^AI^A × ii I_Ai × ii	I^Ai I_A i and ii	A A O
B × O	$I_B I_B$ × ii I_B i × ii	I_B i I_B i and ii	B B O
A × B	$I_A I_A$ × $I_B I_B$ I_A i × $I_B I_B$ I_B i $I_A I_A$ × I_B i I_A i I_A i × I_B i	$I_A I_B$ $I_A I_B$ and I_b i $I_A I_B$ and I_A i I_B i and ii	AB AB B AB A A B or O
AB × O	$I_A I_B$ × ii	I_A i and I_B i	A B

Because of this rather unusual method of inheritance, it has become customary to use the letter I (Isohemagglutinogen) as a basic symbol for the genes at this locus, with a second letter as an exponent to indicate which variation of the allele is represented. For instance, I^A represents the gene which produces the A antigen, and I^B represents the gene which produces the B antigen

Persons heterozygous for these two genes will have both antigens in their blood, and it will therefore be classed as type *AB*. The third gene in the series is I^o. This gene is usually considered recessive to the other two. since a person heterozygous for the A and O genes to type A and a person heterozygous for B and O genes to type B. The type O individuals must therefore be homozygous, I^oI^o.

Table 42.4. Differences between co-dominance and incomplete dominance.

Co-dominance	Incomplete dominance
1. The heterozygotes show traits of both the alleles, *e.g.*, blood group *AB* has both the antigens *A* and *B*.	1. The heterozygote is of the intermediate type and shows none of the original parental forms, *e.g.*, pink flower colour in F_1 generation in Four 'O clock plant (*Mirabilis jalapa*).
2. Both the alleles are equally dominant, and therefore, both express themselves fully.	2. There is partial dominance of one allele, and therefore, the intermediate type is formed in F_1.
3. For example *ABO* blood group system in man.	For example colour of flowers in snapdragon and four 'o clock plants.

Two Gene Interactions

There are examples where a phenotype is not controlled by one gene but is an outcome of the contribution of more than one non-allelic genes. Such genes show an interaction at the phenotypic level depending upon the type of the alleles carried by an individual. Some cases of two gene interactions are as follows:

(*i*) In each case a distinct phenotype is produced.

(*ii*) Genes under consideration show normal dominance and assort independently.

(*iii*) On phenotypic level, homozygotes and heterozygotes, such as AA or Aa and BB or Bb, will show their respective phenotype governed by the dominant allele, such as A- or B- Here dash indicates the presence of either allele.

(*iv*) The F_1 generation must be heterozygous for the two gene pairs (Aa Bb) which will be selfed or intercrossed.

(*v*) In a normal dihybrid cross, the F_2 genotypes fall into four phenotypic classes, (*i*) 9/16 A-B-, (*ii*) 3/16 A-bb, (*iii*) 3/16 aa B-, and (*iv*) 1/16 aa bb.

Epistasis. This is a phenomenon that takes place when the presence of one gene suppresses the action of another gene at a different locus. In other words epistasis represents the marking of the effect of one gene locus by the effect of another gene locus. The epistatic genes are also called inhibiting genes. The gene that suppresses the effect is called **epistatic gene**, while the gene whose effect gets suppressed is called **hypostatic gene.**

In none of the combination of traits studied by Mendel did one gene affect the phenotypic expression of the other. The result was the typical phenotypic dihybrid ratio of 9 : 3 : 3 : 1. However, several types of mutual influences are now known, and termed as **epistasis.** This means *standing on.* Thus epistatic interactions between genes cause departures from the Mendelian phenotypic dihybrid ratio.

The suitable examples of epistasis is the expression of flower colour in sweet pea (*Lathyrus odoratus*):

Here the dominant allele *P* determines the formation of purple flower colour. However, neither *PP* nor *Pp* will show colour unless another gene *C* is also present in the dominant form (*CC* or *Cc*). Recessive (cc) will interfere with colour formation by *PP* or *Pp* thereby resulting in white flowers. A cross of purple *PPCC* and white ppcc gives all purple *PpCc* F_1 hybrid. Selfing the hybrid gives purple and white flowers progeny in the phenotypic ratio of 9 : 7 instead of normal 9 : 3 : 3 : 1.

All the genotypes recessive for *P* or *C*, or *P* and *C*, *i.e.*, *ppcc*, *PPcc*, *PpCC* or *ppCc* express white phenotype.

Epistasis may be differentiated from dominance. The epistasis is due to the interaction of two separate genes, while the dominance is the interaction of the two alleles of the same gene.

Complementary Genes

A colour expression is observed in dramatic way when the two white genotypes ppCC and PPcc are crossed. All the progeny, *i.e.* PpCc are coloured. Here as one gene complements the expression of the other, they are called complementary genes.

Polygenic Traits

All the traits studied by Mendel has an either/or quality, and no intermediate forms. The seeds were either round or wrinkled, the plants tall or dwarf, the flowers purple or white. There were no intermediate or graded forms. However, several

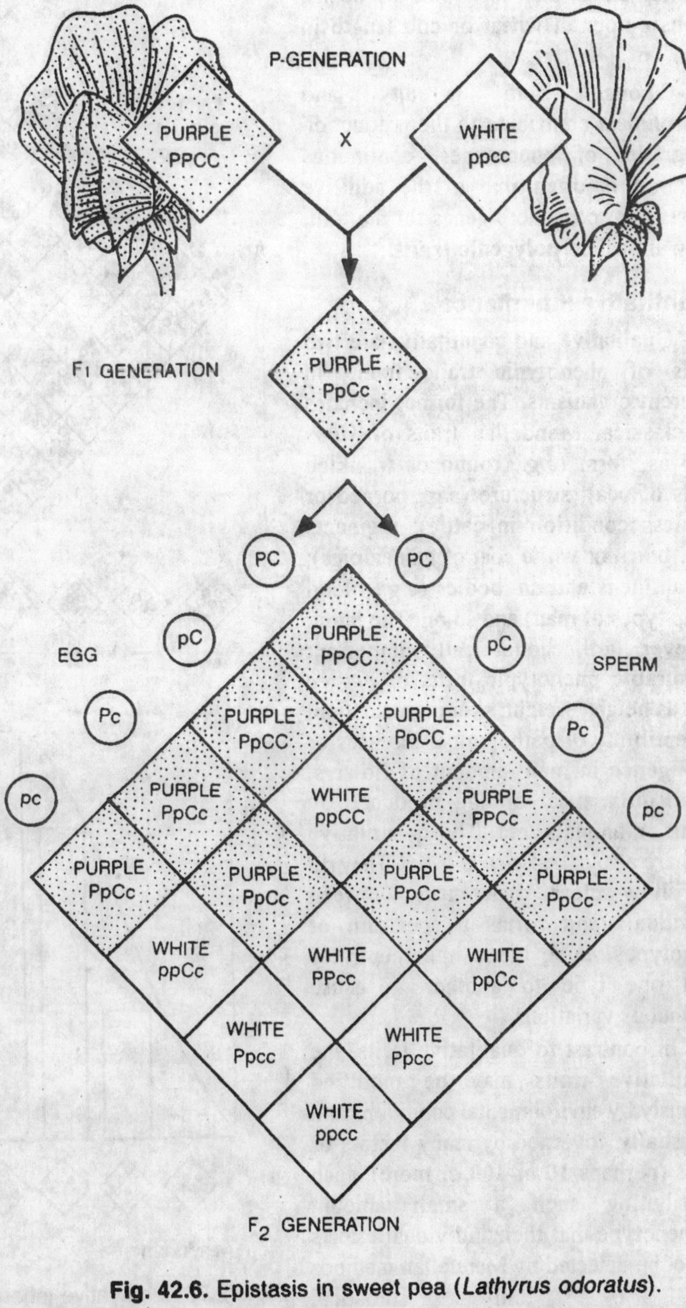

Fig. 42.6. Epistasis in sweet pea (*Lathyrus odoratus*).

traits show gradation. For example, humans skin colour can grade from black to white with all intermediate shades, and so the human height also exhibits a gradation from short to tall forms. Gradations may also be seen in many less familiar traits like seed size of beans, grains colour in wheat or cob length in corn.

Though both heredity and environment contribute to the production of grades of phenotypes, continuous variation is often due to the additive effects of two or more genes for the trait. They are called **polygenic traits.**

Quantitative Inheritance

Qualitative and quantitative are two kinds of phenotypic traits found in different organisms. The former includes the classical Mendelian traits of *kinds* such as, form (*e.g.*, round or wrinkled seeds of pea); structure (*e.g.*, horned or hornless condition in cattle); pigments (*e.g.*, black or white coat of guinea pigs); and antigens and antibodies (*e.g.*, blood group types of man) and so on. The latter, however, are economically important measurable phenotypic traits of *degree* such as height, weight, skin pigmentation, susceptibility of pathological diseases or intelligence in man; amount of flowers, seeds, milk, meat or egg produced by plants or animals, etc. The quantitative traits are also called *metric traits*. They do not show clear differences between individuals and forms a spectrum of phenotypes which blend imperceptively from one type to another to cause continuous variations..

In contrast to qualitative traits, the quantitative traits may be modified variously by environmental conditions and are usually governed by many factors or genes (perhaps 10 or 100 or more), each contributing such a small amount of phenotype that their individual effects cannot be detected by Mendelian methods but by only statistical methods. Such genes which are non-allelic

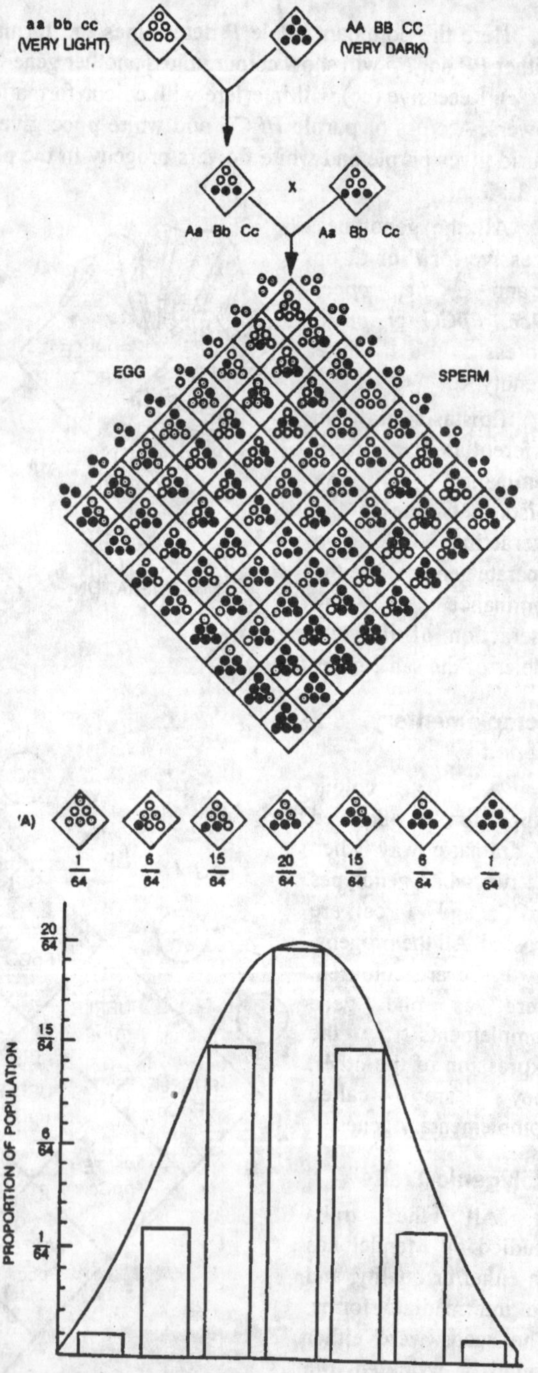

Fig. 42.7. Quantitative inheritance of human skin colour, A and B.

and affect the phenotype of a single quantitative trait, are called *polygenes* or *cumulative genes.* The inheritance of polygenes or quantitative traits is called *quantitative inheritance.*

Human skin colour. Human skin colour is generally controlled by three separate genes. Each gene contributes to a unit of darkness due to incomplete dominance.

Here these three genes can be designated as A, B and C, and thus the skin shade has to vary from a very dark in a AABBCC individual to very light in aabbcc individual.

A person with AaBbCc, *i.e,* heterozygous for all three genes, will possess an intermediate colour.

The number of possible allele combinations in the gametes is eight for such a person, and therefore, a total of 64 phenotypic combinations are possible when two persons of similar genic constitution marry.

As shown in the figures (36.7 A-B), the phenotypic frequency for skin colour will gradually increase from 1/64 for the very dark coloured, *i.e.,* AABBCC to a maximum of 20/64 for the intermediate coloured AaBbCc, and again reduces to 1/64 for the very light coloured aabbcc.

The frequency distribution for skin colour can be shown by a bell-shaped normal distribution curve (Fig. 42.7.B).

Such inheritance is called **quantitative inheritance.**

Kernel colour in wheat. Nilsson-Ehle made a very interesting study of the colour of grain in wheat. He found that, when he crossed a variety of wheat bearing dark red kernels with a variety having white kernels, he obtained an intermediate shade of red in the first generation. This might suggest incomplete dominance, but when the offspring of this F_1 generation were crossed among themselves the zygotes in F_2 generation showed five different phenotypic classes in a ratio of 1 : 4 : 6 : 4 : 1. Noting that 1/16 of F_2 was an extreme in colour as either of the parental plants (red or white), they theorized that two pairs of genes controlling production of red pigment were operating in this cross. Each gene was supposed to contain two alleles. One allele produces a given quantity of the red pigment, while its counterpart did not produce any pigment. All alleles were equally potent in the production or lack or production of pigment.

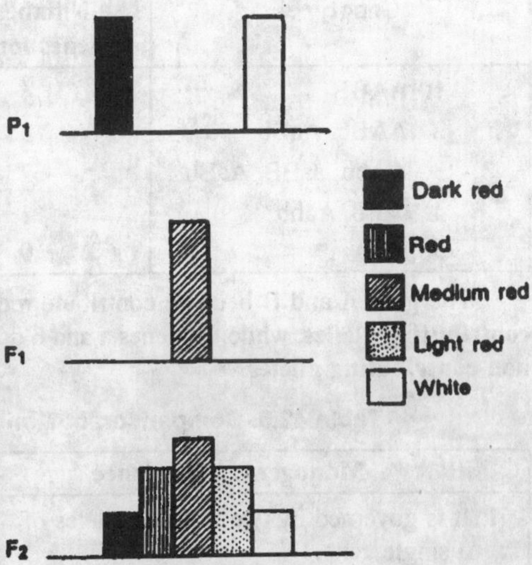

Fig. 42.8. Wheat colour as an example of quantitative trait.

If we symbolize the genes for red with the capital letters A and B and their alleles resulting in lack of pigment production by a and b. We can illustrate the results of this cross as follows:

P:	Red		White
	AABB	×	aabb
Gametes:	(AB) (AB)		(ab) (ab)
F_1: Medium			Medium
Aa Bb		×	Aa Bb

F_1 gametes: Male ♂

Female ♀

	AB	Ab	aB	ab
AB	AABB Red AABb	AABb Dark AAbb	AaBB Dark AaBb	AaBb Medium Aabb
Ab	Dark AaBB	Medium AaBb	Medium aaBB	Light aaBb
aB	Dark AaBb	Medium Aabb	Medium aaBb	Light aabb
ab	Medium	Light	Light	White

or 1/16 Red: 4/16 Dark: 6/16 Medium: 4/16 Light: 1/16 White.

If we suppose that each dose of a gene for pigment production increases the depth of colour, we can arrange the F_2 phenotypes according to the number of genes for red in the following table:

Table 42.5. Contributing and non-contributing alleles

Genotype	Number of genes for red	Phenotype	Fraction of F2
1. AABB	4	Dark red	1/16
2. AABb, AaBb	3	Medium red	4/16
3. AAbb, aaBB, AaBb	2	Intermediate	6/16
4. aaBb, Aabb	1	Light red	4/16
5. aabb	0	White	1/16

The gene A and B because contribute red colour in this case, therefore, are referred to as **contributing alleles**, while the genes a and b do not contribute red colour to kernel and are called **non-contributing alleles.**

Table 42.6. Comparison of Monogenic and Polygenic Inheritance.

Monogenic inheritance	Polygenic inheritance
1. It is governed by two or more alleles of a single gene.	**1.** It is governed by many non-allelic genes.
2. It gives a discontinuous variation.	**2.** It gives a continuous variation.
3. This is called qualitative inheritance.	**3.** This is called quantitative inheritance.
4. There are no intermediates.	**4.** Numerous intermediates may occur giving a complete gradation from one extreme to another.
5. Phenotype is not influenced by environment.	**5.** Phenotype is influenced by the environment.
6. Analysis of progeny is done by counting.	**6.** It is done by statistical method.
7. Example: All seven Mendelian traits.	**7.** Examples: Human skin colour, wheat kernel colour.

Pleiotropy

A single gene often influences more than one phenotypic traits. However, it may be that one gene may cause evidently well marked expression of some phenotypic trait (*i.e.*, **major effect**) than the others with less evident phenotype (*i.e.* **secondary effect**). Most genes have their multiple effects and are called pleiotropic genes. The ability of a gene to have many effects is known as **pleiotropy.** An important example of a pleiotropy is a hereditary disease called **sickle-cell anemia** or **cooley's anemia** found among certain African tribes. A recessive gene causes the disease. A codominant gene Hb^s in homozygous condition produces the disease sickle-cell anaemia which leads to death, generally at least by later adolescence. The gene causes the production of an abnormal hemoglobin. As a result the shape of the red blood cell containing it becomes sickle-shaped and distorted. However, heterozygous individuals which possess both normal and abnormal hemoglobin and have mild anaemia, are naturally protected against malaria as the malarial parasite cannot live in these distorted cells. The heterozygous individuals inherit the genes from generation to generation as shown here. $Hb^{\wedge}$ and Hb^s are the genes for the normal and abnormal hemoglobin.

SUMMARY

1. Heredity is the transmission of traits from one generation to following generations.
2. Variation in heredity is found in sexually produced offspring but not in asexually produced clones unless and until mutation occurs.
3. Traits combined in one generation may separate in later generations suggesting a particular nature for heredity.
4. Mendel selected seven distinct traits in garden pea (*Pisum sativum*) for his experiments.
5. Mendel hybridized alternate forms of single traits in the garden pea and studied their inheritance in subsequent generations following self-pollination.
6. Mendel selected garden pea as it normal self-pollinated but can readily be cross-pollinated.
7. Besides true breeding alternate forms for several traits such as yellow or green seeded forms were available.
8. For each of the seven traits hybridized. Mendel found that:

   (*i*) The F_1 hybrids always exhibited only one of the parental forms; (*ii*) both parental forms were present in F_2 and (*iii*) The form of the trait in F_1 called **dominant** form was present three times as frequently as its alternate **recessive** form, *e.g.*, a 3 : 1 ratio of dominant to recessive forms is termed Mendelian monohybrid ratio.
9. When F_3 generation was raised by selfing F_2 plants, all recessive F_2 plants produced only recessives. They were pure or true breeding.
10. On the other hand, only one-third of dominant F_2 were pure, the rest were impure and produced both dominant and recessive offspring like the F_1.
11. The phenotypic ratio of 3 : 1 was in reality a hidden 1 : 2 : 1 ratio, *i.e.*, of pure dominant: impure dominant or hybrid: pure recessive forms.
12. Mendel interpreted the 1 : 2 : 1 ratio as follows: pea plants possess two factors for each trait whereas each of its male or female gametes has only one factor (Mendel's law of segregation). If dominant factor is represented by symbol A and recessive factor by symbol a, the pure or homozygous dominant parent is AA and the pure recessive parent is aa. The gametes of dominant parent have only factor A and those of recessive parent have only a. These gametes unite to form F_1 hybrid offspring with factors Aa. The F_1 hybrid offspring form two types of male and female gametes having factors A and a. During random fertilisation the male and female gametes can unite in four possible ways, *i.e.*, AA, Aa, aA

and aa giving a 1AA (pure dominant): 2 Aa (impure or hybrid dominant): 1 aa (pure recessive) offspring.

13. Mendel's factor is now called a gene, and its alternative forms are termed alleles. The alleles lie in homologous chromosomes. The ratio 1 : 2 : 1 is known as Mendel's monohybrid genotypic ratio.
14. The separation of two alleles during gamete formation and the restoration of paired condition during random fertilization is called principle of segregation.
15. A cross between F_1 individual and a recessive parent is called test cross. A test cross can distinguish the pure dominant from the hybrid dominant.
16. When alternate forms of two traits controlled by two genes, *e.g.*, dominant round, yellow and recessive wrinkled green are hybridized, the F_1 generation shows the dominant trait of both genes, say round, yellow F_1 plants, on selfing, produce F_2 progeny, with two parental and two new recombinant phenotypes, *i.e.*, round yellow: round green: wrinkled yellow: wrinkled green in the dihybrid ratio of 9 : 3 : 3 : 1.
17. During the inheritance of two or more genes at a time, their distribution in the gametes and in the progeny is independent of each other. This is called Mendel's principle of independent assortment.
18. The results of genetic crosses can be predicted by Punnett squares, which use the principles of mathematical probability to follow the union of gametes.
19. Heterozygotes of incomplete dominance have phenotypes intermediate between the phenotypes of the two homozygotes. This is the law of incomplete dominance, or blended dominance.
20. Some genes have more than two alleles in a population and are called multiple alleles. For example the three I^A, I^B and i alleles of *ABO* blood groups. Here alleles I^A and I^B are codominant, both express themselves when in combination.
21. Epistasis is the influence of one gene on the expression of another gene.
22. Two independent pairs of genes, which interact to produce a trait together, but each dominant allele does not show its effect are called complementary genes. In the sweet pea complementary genes show the unusual 9 : 7 phenotypic ratio.
23. Polygenic traits are controlled by more than one gene such as human skin colour expression. They are called quantitative traits and show a gradation in their expression.
24. A gene affecting more than one trait is called a pleiotropic gene. For example, sickle cell gene.
25. Pedigree analysis is a method to analyse the distribution and movement of traits in human families.

TERMS TO REMEMBER

Allele. The various forms of a gene are called alleles. For example, blue colour and black colour of eye are two alleles of the eye colour gene.

Asexual reproduction. Any reproduction process that does not involve meiosis and fertilization.

Back cross. A cross between an individual offspring and one of its parents.

Clone. A carbon copy of the parent. A group of cells that are derived by mitotic divisions from a single ancestral cell.

Co-dominance. The condition in heterozygotes where both members of an allelic pair contribute to phenotype.

Complementary genes. As one gene complements the expression of the other, they are called complementary genes. The phenotypic ratio is 9 : 7.

Dominant allele. The allele that expresses itself in the homozygous and heterozygous condition. It masks the effect of recessive allele.

Dihybrid cross. A cross in which inheritance of two pairs of contrasting characters is studied simultaneously. The phenotypic ratio is 9 : 3 : 3 : 1.

Epistasis. The phenomenon where one gene suppresses the action of another gene at a different focus. The masked gene is called hypostatic.

Factor. The term used by Mendel. Now this is called gene. Each trait is controlled by a pair of factors.

F_1 generation. The first filial generation. The first generation resulting from a cross.

F_2 generation. The second filial generation. The generation that results from interbreeding members of F_1.

Gene. A basic unit of heredity located on a chromosome. It is equivalent to the 'factor' of Mendel. These words are units of information from one generation to another.

Genetics. The study of genes and how they produce characteristics and their inheritance.

Genotype. Genetic expression of an organism.

Heredity. The transmission of characteristics from one generation to successive generations of living things.

Heterozygous. A condition where a diploid organism has different allelic forms of a gene.

Homozygous. A condition where a diploid organism has same allelic forms of a gene.

Hybrid. An offspring resulting from a cross between two genotypically different parents.

Locus. The position on a chromosome occupied by a particular gene or one of its alleles.

Monohybrid. Individuals produced as a result of monohybrid cross. It contains genes of both the parents.

Monohybrid cross. A cross between two parents in which inheritance of only one pair of contrasting characters is studied.

Multiple alleles. More than two allelic forms exist for certain genes. A well known example is the *ABO* blood types in humans.

Offspring. Organisms produced as a result of sexual reproduction.

P. Parental generation in a cross.

Pedigree analysis. A system for following the movement and distribution of certain genetic traits.

Phenotype. The visible expression of the hereditary constitution possessed by an organism.

Pleiotropy. The ability of a gene to have many effects. Example: sickle-cell anaemia.

Polygenic traits. Very often the continuous variation is due to the additive effects of two or more genes for the traits. They are polygenic traits.

Polygenic inheritance. A particular trait is determined by interaction of more than one pair of non allelic genes. It is also known as quantitative inheritance.

Progeny. Offspring individuals.

Pure line. Pure breeding. A strain of individuals homozygous for all genes being considered.

Punnett square. A checker board that helps to study all possible results of crosses in genetics.

Quantitative inheritance. A particular trait is determined by interaction of more than one pair of non-allelic genes. Also known as polygenic inheritance.

Recessive allele. An allele that does not express itself when present along with the dominant cell.

Reciprocal cross. A second cross of the same genotype where gametes from the parental generation are reversed.

Supplementary genes. Where the obtained ratio is 9 : 3 : 4.

Siblings. Brother and sister relationship; where the individuals having the same material and paternal parents.

Test cross. A cross between an individual (F_1) with one having recessive phenotype.

Trait. It is any recognisable feature of an individual.

Zygote. A fertilized egg; the protoplast resulting from the fusion of two gametes (♂ and ♀).

QUESTION BANK

N.B. Undermentioned questions are asked repeatedly in various Indian Universities and competitive examinations.

Very Short Answer Questions

1. What is heredity?
2. Define variation.
3. What is 'genetics'?
4. Give name of father of genetics.
5. Name the plant on which Mendel worked.
6. How many different contrasting traits did Mendel notice in garden pea?
7. What term is used for a class of individuals which are morphologically similar?
8. What is a monohybrid cross?
9. What is a dihybrid cross?
10. What is the character that does not allow the expression of a contrasting character in a hybrid?
11. What are Mendel's hypothetical factors in modern terminology?
12. What is Mendel's monohybrid ratio?
13. What is dominant factor–round seeds or wrinkled seeds?
14. What is mendel's dihybrid ratio for phenotypes?
15. What do the letters P, F_1 and F_2 represent in heredity?
16. What is a recessive trait?
17. What is allele?
18. What does the phenomenon means where one gene suppresses the action of another gene at different loci?
19. What is the generic expression of an organism known as?
20. What is a locus?
21. What is hybrid?
22. What is a back cross?
23. When a hybrid of F_1 is crossed with the homozygous recessive parent, what is it called?
24. What is a gene pool?
25. What is principle of dominance?

26. Name three principles put forth by Mendel.
27. Blood groups in man is an example of.
28. What is a pleiotropic gene?
29. Which of the genes studied by Mendel in pea is now known as pleiotropic?
30. What is a clone?
31. Name the plant that shows incomplete dominance in respect to the colour of the flower?
32. Which type of inheritance deals with quantitative traits?
33. What is a Punnett square?
34. What are the phenotypes of TT and tt plants?
35. What is the allele of T?
36. What was the total number of true-breeding varieties of garden pea which Mendel had taken to start his experiments?

Answers

1. Study of transmission of characteristics from one generation to the next. **2.** When there is dissimilarities of characteristics in the individuals of a species or by the offspring of the same parents. **3.** The study of various traits and genes and how they are inherited from one generation to next. **4.** Gregor Johann Mendel. **5.** Garden pea (*Pisum sativum*). **6.** Seven. **7.** Phenotype. **8.** A cross between parents differing in a pair of contrasting characters. **9.** A cross of a dihybrid with a homozygous recessive individual. **10.** Dominant. **11.** Genes. **12.** 3 : 1 **13.** Round seeds. **14.** 9 : 3 : 3 : 1. **15.** Parental generation, first filial generation, second filial generation. **16.** It is a form of trait that has inability to express itself in the presence of the allele for other form of same trait. **17.** Alternative forms of a gene, *e.g.*, blue and black colour of eye are two alleles of the eye colour gene. **18.** Epistasis. **19.** Genotype. **20.** The point where an allele is located on chromosome. **21.** An individual resulting from a cross between two genetically unlike persons. **22.** The cross of a progeny individual with one of the parents. **23.** Test cross **24.** All genotypes of all the individuals in a population. **25.** Out of two contrasting alleles only one expresses itself in one individual. The factor which expresses itself if dominant and the other which has not shown its effect is recessive. **26.** (*i*) Principle of independent assortment, (*ii*) principle of segregation and (*iii*) principle of dominance. **27.** Co-dominance. **28.** A gene affecting more than one trait is called pleiotropic gene. **29.** Flower and seed coat colour. **30.** A group of cells derived by mitotic divisions from a single ancestral cell. **31.** *Mirabilis jalapa* (four 'o clock plant). **32.** Polygenic. **33.** The representation of a monohybrid or dihybrid cross by making squares. **34.** Tall and dwarf plants. **35.** t. **36.** Seven.

Short Answer Questions

1. What is Mendel's law of dominance?
2. Give a comprehensive account of law of segregation.
3. Describe Mendel's law of independent assortment.
4. What is epistasis? How does it differ from dominance?
5. What do you mean by a polygenic trait? Cite an example.
6. What heredity principle can be derived from a cross showing 3 : 1 ratio in the F_2 generation?
7. What heredity principle can be derived from a cross showing 9 : 3 : 3 : 1 ratio in the F_2 generation?
8. What do you mean by continuous variation?
9. Define clone. How does variation arise in a clone?
10. Make a list of the 7 pairs of contrasting traits selected by Mendel for breeding experiments.
11. A man with blue eyes and black hair (homozygous for both characters) marries a woman with black eyes and red hair. Black eyes (E) are dominant over black eyes (e) and black hair (H) is dominant over red hair (h). Work out the probabilities of phenotypes of the children of this couple using Punnett square method. Use only symbols for characters as given above.
12. How is skin colour inherited in man?
13. What kind of plants will be produced in F_1 and F_2 generations in the following crosses?
(*a*) Pure Tall × Pure Tall (*b*) Pure Tall × Pure Dwarf (*c*) Hybrid Tall × Pure Tall.

14. A pea plant with purple flowers was crossed with a plant with white flowers producing 40 plants with only purple flowers. On selfing, these plants produced 470 plants with purple flowers and 162 with white flowers. What genetic mechanisms account for these results?
15. The F_2 plants obtained in the Q. 4 were selfed. The white-flowered plants produced only white-flowered F_3 plants. Some of the purple flowered F_2 produced only purple-flowered F_3, while other produced both white and purple-flowered F_3 plants. Provide the genetic basis for this observation.
16. In dogs the barking trait is dominant over the silent one and crest ears are dominant over drooping ears. What is the expected phenotypic ratio of the offspring when dogs, heterozygous for both the traits are crossed? What would be the phenotypic ratio, if dogs, heterozygous for both traits are crossed with dogs homozygous recessive for both traits?
17. A man with type A blood has a wife with type B. They have a child with type O blood. Give the genotypes of all the three. What other blood groups can be expected in the future offspring of this couple?
18. What are the problems faced by a sickle cell anaemia carrier? Why is this defective gene still not eliminated by nature?
19. Taking the example of *ABO* blood types of humans, explain the phenomenon of multiple alleles and co-dominance.
20. What is a test cross? How does it differ from reciprocal cross.

Long Answer Questions

1. Give the scientific name of the plant selected by Mendel for his experiments. State three laws given by him. Briefly explain the law of independent assortment with the help of an example.
2. What are multiple allelic genes? Explain the blood groups in man as an example of multiple allelic genes.
3. Describe the phenomenon of epistasis as found in the flower colour of sweet pea and mention how epistasis is different from dominance.
4. What are complementary genes? Cite one example. Explain their interaction with the help of a cross.
5. What is pedigree analysis? What are the symbols used in such an analysis?
6. Why did Mendel choose garden pea for his experiments? How did he make sure that the plants were true-breeding?
7. Describe the mechanism of inheritance of the *ABO* system of blood groups, highlighting the principle of genetics involved in it.
8. State and explain Mendel's law of segregation.
9. State and explain Mendel's law of independent assortment.

Multiple Choice Questions (Objective type questions)

1. Father of genetics is
   (*a*) Morgan (*b*) Darwin
   (*c*) Mendel (*d*) Hutchinson.
2. Mendel worked on
   (*a*) *Lathyrus* (*b*) *Pisum*
   (*c*) *Dolichos* (*d*) *Vigna*
3. An organism with two unlike genes of a trait is called
   (*a*) heterozygous (*b*) homozygous
   (*c*) hermaphrodite (*d*) monozygous
4. When F_1 plants heterozygous for tallness are selfed, F_2 generation has both tall and dwarf plants. This depicts the principle of
   (*a*) dominance (*b*) law of segregation
   (*c*) law of independent assortment (*d*) blended inheritance

5. The principle of segregation was formulated by Mendel in
(*a*) 1766 (*b*) 1866
(*c*) 1900 (*d*) none of the above.

6. Mendel experimented on
(*a*) wild pea (*b*) sweet pea
(*c*) garden pea (*d*) lablab.

7. The law of segregation was rediscovered by
(*a*) De Vries (*b*) Correns
(*c*) Tschermark (*d*) all of the above.

8. Polygenic traits show
(*a*) discontinuous variation (*b*) continuous variation
(*c*) both (*d*) none of the above.

9. Inheritance of skin colour in man
(*a*) monogenic (*b*) bigenic
(*c*) trigenic (*d*) polygenic

10. A gamete contains
(*a*) only one allele of a gene (*b*) two alleles of a gene
(*c*) all alleles of a gene (*d*) none of the above

11. A breeding experiment dealing with a single trait is called
(*a*) monohybrid (*b*) monozygous
(*c*) dihybrid (*d*) heterozygous.

12. Mendel noted as many pairs of contrasting traits in pea plants
(*a*) 2 (*b*) 5
(*c*) 7 (*d*) 9

13. A cross that shows the principle of independent assortment is
(*a*) monohybrid (*b*) dihybrid
(*c*) both (*d*) none of the above

14. Human blood groups are determined by
(*a*) single gene (*b*) two genes
(*c*) alleles (*d*) multiple genes

15. An important example of pleiotropy is
(*a*) bleeder's disease (*b*) smallpox
(*c*) sickle-cell anaemia (*d*) none of the above

Answers

1. (*c*) **2.** (*b*) **3.** (*a*) **4.** (*b*) **5.** (*b*) **6.** (*c*) **7.** (*d*) **8.** (*b*) **9.** (*c*) **10.** (*a*)
11. (*a*) **12.** (*c*) **13.** (*b*) **14.** (*d*) **15.** (*c*)

43

chapter

Chromosomal Basis of Inheritance

As shown by Mendel the units of heredity, the factors or genes are stable and particulate. However, the location of these factors (now genes) in the cell was unknown to him. In those days neither the role of the nucleus in reproduction nor the existence of chromosomes in the nucleus was known. Mendel published his results in 1866 without the knowledge of genetic material. The processes of mitosis and meiosis were worked out only after Mendel had published his work in 1866. Mendel's observations remained unattended until 1900, less when De Vries, Corens and Tschermak realised the significance of his work.

(*i*) Mendel published his results in 1866 without the knowledge of genetic material.

(*ii*) Mendel's observations remained unattended until 1900, when De Vries, Corens and Tschermak realised the significance of his work.

(*iii*) By the time Mendel was finalising his work on pea, chromosomes were seen in the nuclei of Salamander cells by William Flemming in 1879. Flemming suggested the role of nucleus in the process of inheritance.

(*iv*) In 1902, Walter Sutton and Theodor Boveri came to the conclusion that the behaviour of chromosomes at meiosis can serve as the cellular basis of both segregation and independent assortment. They suggested that chromosomes can be equated with the Mendel's unit factors. Their work led to the chromosome theory of heredity.

(*v*) Work of W. Sutton and T. Boveri was further expanded by Thomas H. Morgan, Alfred H. Sturtevant and Calvin Bridges on fruit fly, *Drosophila.*

(*vi*) The term **factor** as the basic unit of inheritance was replaced by Johannsen, in 1909 with the term **gene.**

Now this is an established fact that in order to maintain the genetic continuity from cell to cell and from one generation to the next, in sexually reproducing organisms an orderly and coordinated process in required. During this process the haploid gametes are formed and there after by means of fertilisation diploid cells are produced. The structure which acts as the vehicle of transmission of genes in subsequent generations is **chromosome.** The manner in which the chromosomes and thus the genetic material is transmitted from one generation to another is accomplished by two cell divisional processes known as **mitosis** and **meiosis.** During mitosis the genetic material is duplicated and distributed equally to the two daughter cells, whereas in meiosis, the number of chromosomes is reduced to half and thus known as **reduction division.**

The principles of inheritance and the modifications in the phenotypic ratio by various types of interactions both at the allelic and non-allelic levels have already been discussed in previous chapter. The principles of inheritance are applicable to all living organisms including humans. In this chapter, the inheritance on the basis of chromosomes shall be dealt with. Though inheritance takes place by means of **genes,** yet it will be greatly influenced by their location on the chromosomes. However, several experiments have revealed that on many occasions genes do not follow the principle of independent assortment and they segregate en block. This type of segregation of genes was referred to as **linkage.** Later on this was also revealed that this characteristic could be assigned to genes located on the same chromosome. This was also demonstrated that linkage between two genes, located on the same chromosome can be broken by the process of **crossing over.** Crossing over takes place during prophase I of meiosis and results in the formation of new combination of alleles. This is called **recombination.**

Recombination is an important source of variation. This brings about allelic variation, which is called **mutation**. Alterations in chromosome number and structure may also bring about phenotypic changes.

Parallelism between Genes and Chromosomes

How genes control phenotypes, and how they are transmitted to the following generations have already been discussed. Now we shall have to learn how a parallelism can be drawn between genes and chromosome. The points in support are as follows :

(1) Each species has a specific and characteristic number of chromosomes in its somatic cells.

(2) In a diploid cell, these chromosomes are found in pairs called homologous pairs which resemble in their morphology and genetic content.

(3) One member of a homologous pair comes from maternal parent and the other comes from the paternal parent.

(4) In the similar way, each gene also exists in allelomorphic pair which are contributed equally by the maternal and paternal parents.

(5) Each chromosome has a double structure which consists of sister chromatids.

(6) During the process of mitosis, the two chromatids get separated into two daughter nuclei and then cells.

(7) Each member of an allele pair also goes in every daughter cell during mitosis, and thus a genetic composition is maintained in the cells of a multicellular organism.

(8) During meiosis the members of a chromosome pair are separated from each other and go to daughter nuclei.

(9) In the similar way, members of an allele pair also separate during meiosis, and therefore, each haploid cell or gamete contains only one allele.

(10) During process of fertilisation two haploid gametes unite and the chromosome number becomes diploid and also every allele pair is restored.

The Chromosome Theory of Inheritance

After the discovery of Mendel's laws of inheritance, biologists soon noticed the undermentioned similarities between the behaviour of genes (Mendel's factors) during inheritance and of chromosomes and genes during cell division.

1. Both (chromosomes and genes) were formed in pairs in diploid cell.
2. Homologous chromosomes separated and gene pairs (alleles) segregated during meiosis.
3. The paired condition of both chromosomes and genes was restored during fertilization.

Sutton and Boveri (1902) propounded **the chromosome theory of inheritance** on the basis of these similarities. According to this theory Mendelian genes are located on chromosomes, and the chromosomes are segregated and assorted independently. This takes place during meiotic cell division. Since Mendel's factors or genes, the units of heredity are present on the chromosomes, Mendel's principles of segregation and independent assortment can be explained better by the chromosome theory.

As the genes are located on the homologous pairs of chromosomes, both the principles of segregation and independent assortment can be explained in better form.

When the members of a homologous pair separate, alleles carried on them will also segregate and go to different gametes. This explains the segregation of alleles controlling the contrasting traits.

Contrary to it when two homologous pairs are considered, each carrying an allele pair, one chromosome pair will segregate independently of the other, and will give rise to four combinations which form the basis of independent assortment.

The number of genes are always much more than the number of chromosomes. This means that each chromosome must carry a large number of genes.

Whenever a gene is assigned a position on the chromosome, it is called a **locus.**

Each allele pair though specifies the same character, it must carry slightly different information so as to depict contrasting forms.

Table 43.1. Comparison of Behaviour of Chromosomes with Mendel's Factors/Genes.

Behaviour of factors at the time of Mendelian inheritance	Behaviour of chromosomes at the time of meiosis
1. The factors behave as independent units. In monohybrid cross in F_1, the factor that expresses is dominant, however, in F_2, recessive factor exhibits its unaltered expression.	1. The chromosomes behave as individual units during inheritance, and this can be studied directly under microscope during meiosis.
2. Mendel's factors maintain stability in the expression of characters.	2. The chromosomes also maintain their stability such as number, structure and functions.
3. The Mendel's factors are found in pairs, and each allelic pair segregates at the time of the formation of gametes.	3. Homologous chromosomes also segregate during meiosis at the time of formation of gametes.
4. Only one factor is present in a gamete.	4. Only one chromosome of a homologous pair passes into a gamete.
5. During fertilization the gametes unite to form a zygote. Each organism contains two factors, one from each parent.	5. During fertilization gametes unite to restore the chromosome number. Each homologous pair contains one paternal and one maternal chromosome.
6. Mendelian factors remain unchanged from generation to generation. Each factor segregates independently of every other pair.	6. Chromosomes also maintain their individuality during segregation. Each pair of homologous chromosomes segregates independently of every other pair.

Chromosomal Theory – Principle of Independent Assortment

As shown in the fig 37.1 it depicts the movement of the alleles of two genes (*i.e.*, seed shape and seed colour) located on two different chromosomes during a dihybrid cross of round-yellow (R–Y) and wrinkled-green (r-y) pea seed varieties which were studied earlier. There are two pairs of chromosomes, one pair carries the alleles for seed shape (R and r) and the other carries the alleles for seed colour (Y and y).

In the F_1 generation the genotype of the offsprings is YyRr. It can be depicted on the chromosomes as shown in Fig. 43.2. The two duplicated and paired homologous chromosomes assembled at the metaphase stage of meiosis I can separate in two possible ways, and this leads to independent assortment of the chromosomes and the genes they carry in four possible ways. Four types of gametes are formed after meiosis II (Fig. 43.2), each with half the number of

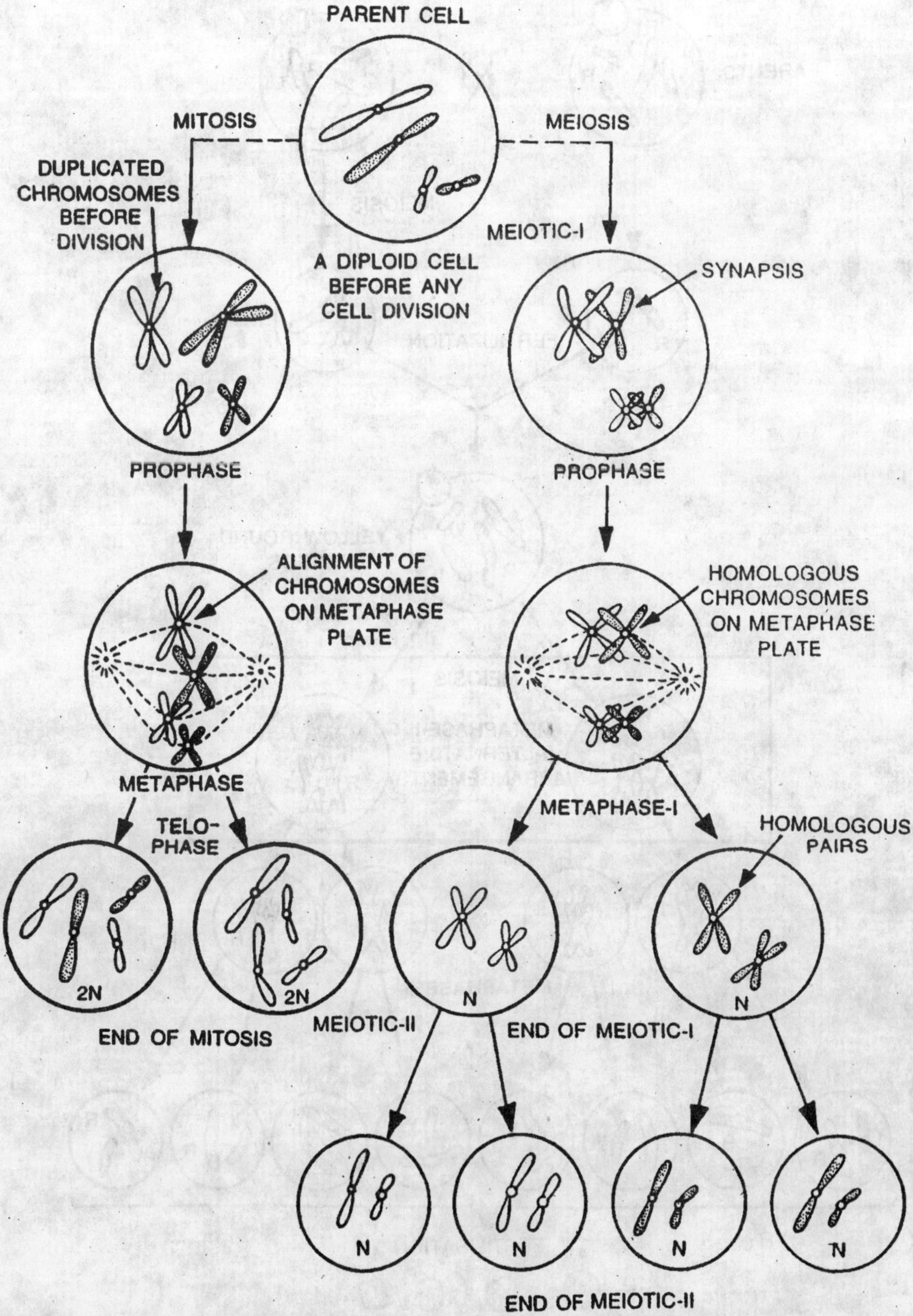

Fig. 43.1. Meiosis reduces chromosome number from diploid (2*n*) to haploid (*n*). Mitosis conserves chromosome number.

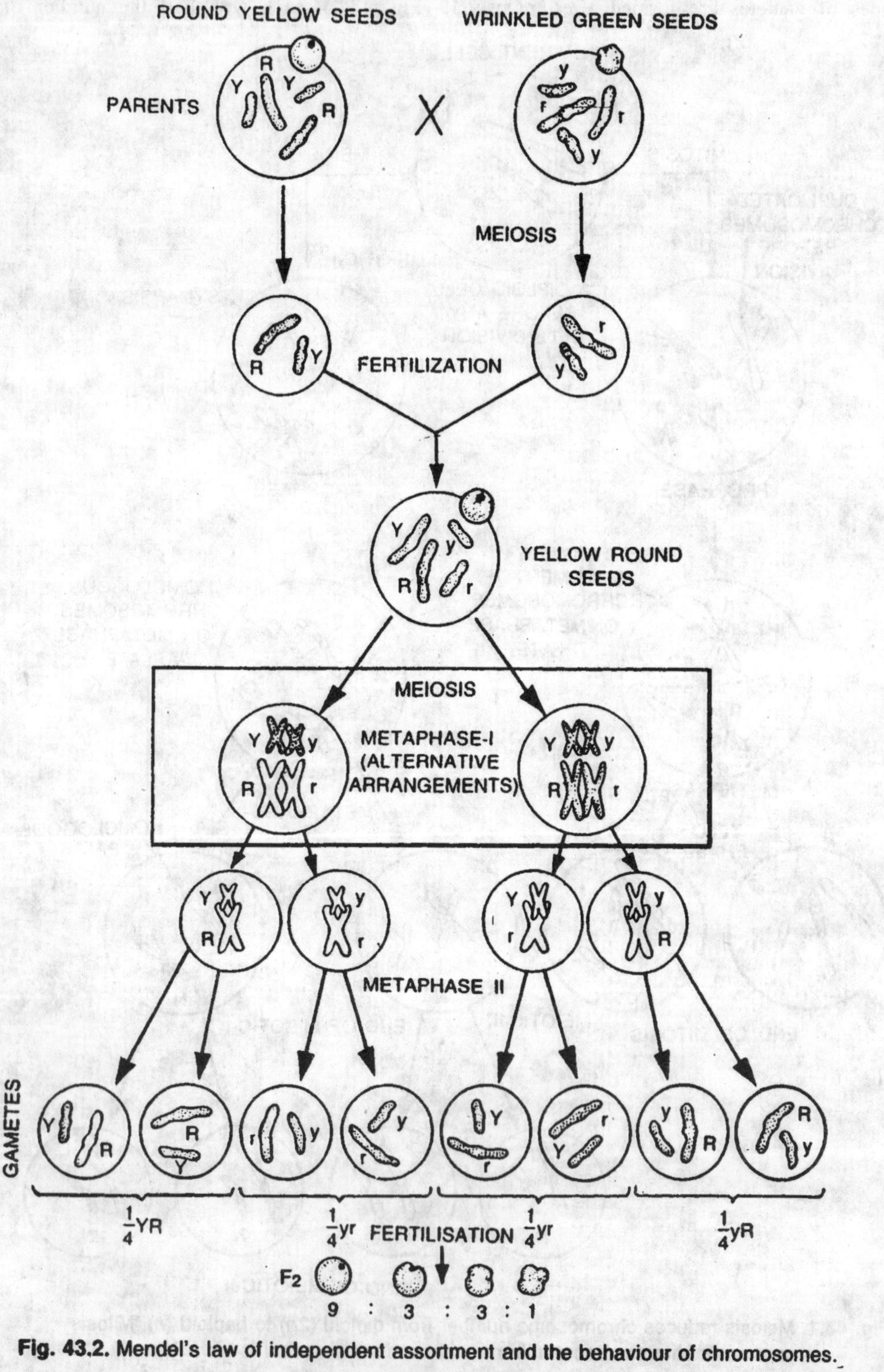

Fig. 43.2. Mendel's law of independent assortment and the behaviour of chromosomes.

chromosomes and genes. The two parental types and the two new recombinants are formed in equal proportions, *i.e.*, 25 per cent each. Two genes located on separate chromosomes produce 50 per cent recombinants during meiosis. This results in the F_2 progeny showing a phenotypic dihybrid ratio of 9 : 3 : 3 : 1. There are millions of cells where meiosis occurs during gamete formation, and four types of possible gametes in equal numbers are produced from genotype RrYy when meiosis occurs in thousands of cells.

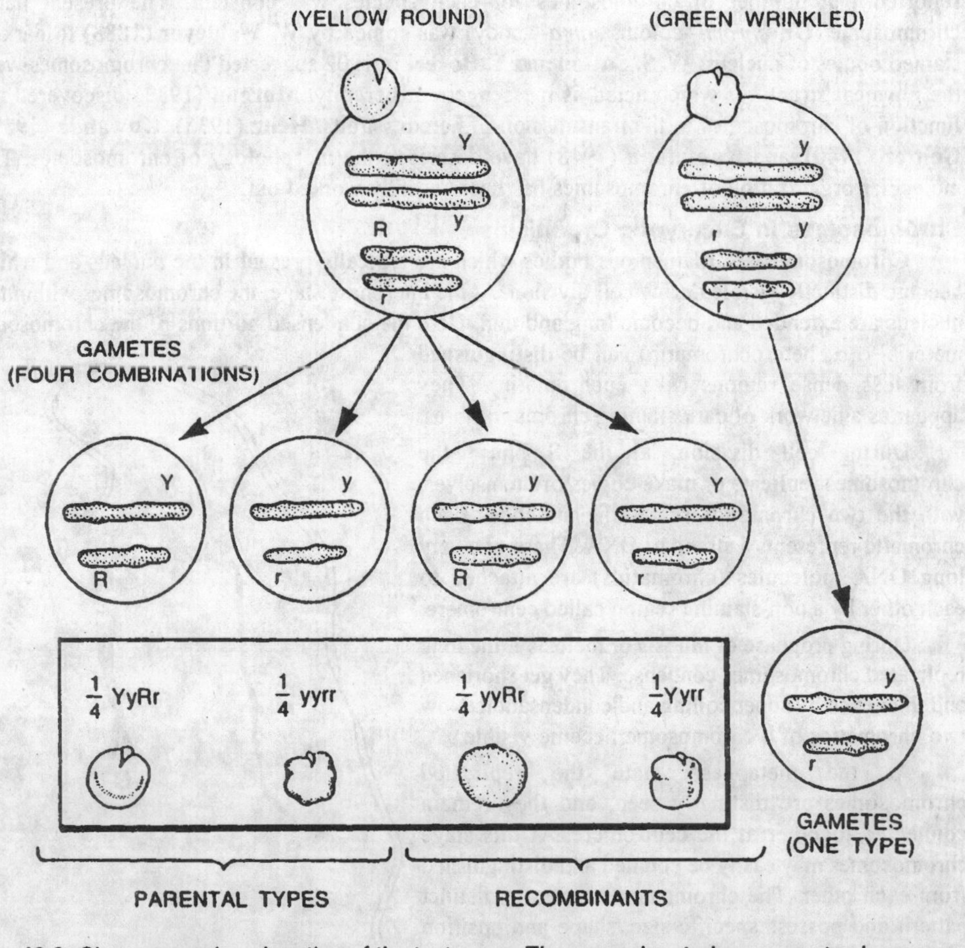

Fig. 43.3. Chromosomal explanation of the test cross. The genes located on separate chromosomes. Four types of progeny are obtained in equal proportions 50% parental and 50% recombinants.

Chromosomal Theory – Explanation of Test Cross

The progeny of a test cross between a dihybrid (heterozygous) round-yellow offspring and the double recessive wrinkled-green parent depicts as follows. With the genes located on separate chromosomes, four types of progeny are obtained in equal proportions. Two of these are of parental types and two are recombinants. Parental and recombinant frequencies are 50 per cent each. The two parental types (*i.e.*, round-yellow and wrinkled-green) and the two recombinants (*i.e.*, round-green and wrinkled-yellow) are formed in equal proportion, *i.e.*, 25 per cent each (Fig. 43.3). This shows the confirmation of the proportion of each type of gamete formed by the dihybrid following independent assortment of chromosomes, that carry the alleles of two genes.

CHROMOSOMES

The chromosomes are the nuclear compounds of special organization and function. They are capable of self-reproduction and play a vital role in heredity, mutation, variation and evolutionary development of the species. **W. Fleming** (1879) first of all described the splitting of chromosomes and coined the term **chromatin** for stainable material of the nucleus. **W. Roux** (1883) suspected the involvement of the chromosomes in the mechanism of inheritance. **Benden and Bovery** (1887) reported that number of chromosomes for each species was constant. The present name chromosome (**Gr.** *chrom*—colour, *soma*—body) was coined by **W. Waldeyer** (1888) to darkly-stained bodies of nucleus. **W. S. Sutton** and **T. Boveri** in 1902 suggested that chromosomes were the physical structures which acted as messengers of heredity. **Morgan** (1933) discovered the function of chromosomes in the transmission of heredity traits. **Heitz** (1935), **Kuwanda** (1939), **Geitter** (1940), and **Kaufmann** (1948) have described the morphology of chromosomes. The molecular organization of chromosomes has been recently worked out.

Chromosomes in Eucaryotic Organisms

Chromosomes are filamentous bodies which are typically present in the nucleus and which become distinctly visible during cell division. At the interphase stage, the chromosomes within the nucleus are extended and become long and thin. Here the condensed portions of the chromosome material (*i.e.*, heterochromatin) can be distinguished from less dense regions (*i.e.*, euchromatin). They appear as a network of dark staining chromatin fibres.

During cell division, at the S phase the chromosomes replicate or make copies of themselves, with the two chromatids remaining attached. Each chromatid represents a strand of DNA. These two very long DNA molecules (chromatids) are attached to each other by a non-staining region called centromere.

During prophase of mitosis or meiosis I, the long replicated chromosomes condense. They get shortened and thickened by super coiling and condensation. Now two chromatids of a chromosome become visible.

At the metaphase state the replicated chromosomes are distinctly seen, and they remain connected together at the centromere. At this stage chromosomes may easily be counted and distinguished from each other. The chromosomes reveal a distinct pattern and possess specific size, shape and position of the centromere. At this stage the karyotyping may be done. A karyotype is systematic arrangement of chromosomes as per their size and shape.

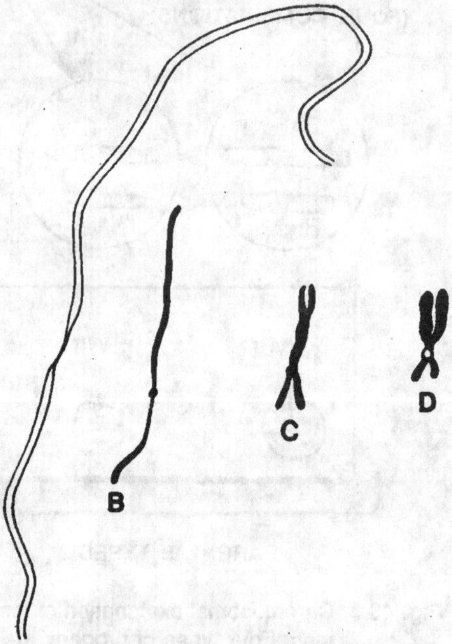

Fig. 43.4. Relative shape and size of a replicated chromosome at different stages of the cell cycle.

Chromosome Number in Eucaryotes

The number of chromosomes is constant for a particular species. Therefore, these are of great importance in the determination of the phylogeny and taxonomy of the species. The organism with the lowest number of the chromosome is the nematode, *Ascaris megalocephalus univalens* which has only two chromosomes in the somatic cells. Human body cells contain 46 chromosomes. This is the diploid (2n) number. Of these one set of 23 chromosomes (haploid, n) is derived from mother's egg cell and a set of 23 chromosomes from the father's sperm cell. The chromosome numbers vary a lot in different organisms.

The males of certain species of insects and round worms have one chromosome less than the females. Male honey bees are haploid, whereas females are diploid. Male honey bees are derived parthenogenetically from unfertilized egg cells. The chromosome numbers are not of much significance as the organisms such as *Amoeba*, adder's tongue fern, etc., are polyploids.

Chromosome numbers of some eucaryotes are tabulated here :

Table 43.2. Chromosome Number of Some Organisms.

Group	Common name	Scientific name	Chromosome number
Animals :			
Protozoa (Protist)	Paramecium	*Paramecium aurelia*	30-40
Cnidaria	Hydra	*Hydra vulgaris*	32
Nematoda	Round worm	*Ascaris lumbricoides*	24
Arthropoda	House fly	*Musca domestica*	12
	Mosquito	*Culex pipiens*	6
	Fruit fly	*Drosophila*	8
	Honey bee (male)	–	16 (n)
	Honey bee (female)	–	32 (2n)
	Cockroach (male)	*Blatta* sp.	23
	Cockroach (female)	*Blatta* sp.	24
Chordata	Frog	*Rana esculenta*	26
	Pigeon	*Columba livia*	80
	Rabbit	*Oryctolagus cuniculus*	44
	Gorilla	*Gorilla gorilla*	48
	Man	*Homo sapiens*	46
	Rat	–	42
	Chimpanzee	–	48
	Cow	–	60
	Horse	–	64
Plants :			
Algae	Chlamydomonas	*Chlamydomonas reinhardii*	10? 12? 16? (Haploid sets)
Fungi	Bread mold	*Mucor hiemalis*	2
		Neurospora	7
		Saccharomyces	17
Pteridophyte		*Ophioglossum*	1262 (largest number)
Gymnosperm	Yellow pine	*Pinus ponderosa*	24
Angiosperms	Cabbage	*Brassica oleracea*	18
	Coffee	*Coffea arabica*	44
	Potato	*Solanum tuberosum*	48
	Sugar cane	*Saccharum officinarum*	80
	Onion	*Allium cepa*	16
Protists (normally haploid)			
	Slime mold	*Dictyostelium*	7
		Amoeba proteus	250

Chromosomes in Procaryotic Organisms (Bacteria)

(1) It has been established now that a bacterial chromosome is always present in the centre of bacterial cell which is not capable of mitotic and meiotic divisions and is not enclosed within a definite nuclear membrane.

(2) The genetic material is found in a compact structure called **nucleoid.** The nucleoid consists of generally a large circular chromosome approximately 1.2 mm in length in the bacterium, *Escherichia coli.*

(3) An average bacterial cell contains one thousandth the DNA content of a typical eucaryotic cell.

(4) The bacterial chromosome is a thin elongated flexible and circular filament of DNA molecule associated with few proteins.

(5) These proteins have close similarities with histones found in eucaryotic cells. Also a large proportion of positively charged ions help them to counter balance the negative charge of phosphate groups in DNA.

(6) A chromosome of a bacterial cell (*Escherichia coli*) is a covalently closed circular structure consisting of several loops of supercoiled DNA.

Most fungi and protists are normally haploid (n) having one basic set of chromosomes. Wild plants may be diploid ($2n$) or polyploid having more than two basic sets of chromosomes. Bread wheat containing 42 chromosomes is a hexaploid, and many edible banana are triploid. Commonly the animals are diploid ($2n$), and some are polyploid. However, the organisms with large number of chromosomes as *Amoeba* and *Ophioglossum* (adder's tounge fern) are likely to be polyploids.

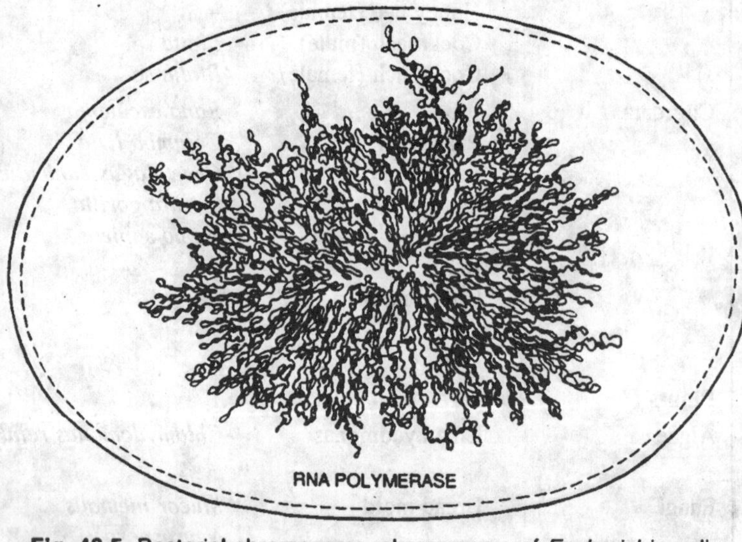

Fig. 43.5. Bacterial chromosome, chromosome of *Escherichia coli.*

Haploid and diploid. The number or set of the chromosomes of the gametic cells such as sperms and ova is known as the gametic, reduced or **haploid** sets of chromosomes. The haploid set of chromosomes is also known as the **genome.** The somatic or body cells of most organisms contain two haploid sets or genomes and are known as the **diploid cells.** The diploid cells achieve the diploid set of the chromosomes by the union of the haploid male and female gametes in the sexual reproduction.

Structure of Chromosome

Size. The size of the chromosomes varies from species to species and relatively remains constant for a particular species. The length of the chromosomes may vary from 0.2 to 50 µ. The diameter of the chromosome may become 0.2 to 20 µ. For instance, the human chromosomes are 6 µ in length. Moreover, the organisms with less number of chromosomes contain comparatively large sized chromosomes than the chromosomes of the organisms having many chromosomes. The monocotyledon plants contain large-sized chromosomes than the dicotyledon plants. The plants in general have large sized chromosomes in comparison to the animals. Further, the chromosome in a cell are never alike in size, some may be exceptionally large and others may be too small. The largest chromosomes are lampbrush chromosomes of certain vertebrate oocytes and polytene chromosomes of certain dipteran insects.

Shape. The shape of the chromosome is changeable from phase to phase in the continuous process of the cell growth and cell division. In the resting phase or interphase stage of the cell, the chromosomes occur in the form of thin, coiled elastic and contractile, thread-like stainable structures, the chromatin threads. In the metaphase and the anaphase, the chromosomes become thick and filamentous. Each chromosome contains a clear zone, known as **centromere** or **kinetocore**, along their length. The centromere divides the chromosomes into two parts, each part is called **chromosome arm.**

Chromonema. In less compact chromosomes, under the optical microscope, a coiled filament is seen in the chromosome. The coiled filament was called **chromonema** by **Vejdovsky** in 1912. The chromonema may be composed of two, four or more fibres according to the species. Further, the number of threads in the chromonema may depend on the different phases because at one phase the chromonema may contain one thread and at other phase it may contain three or four threads. The threads or fibrils of the chromonema remain coiled with each other.

Chromomeres. The chromonema of thin chromosomes of mitotic and meiotic prophases have been found to contain alternating thick and thin regions and thus giving the appearance of a necklace in which several beads occur on a string. The thick or bead-structures of the chromonema are known as the **chromomeres** and the thin region in between the chromomeres is termed as the **inter-chromomeres.** The position of the chromomeres in the chromonema is found to be constant for a given chromosome.

Centromere. The centromere consists of small granules or spherules. The centromere of the chromosome of the *Tilium* has the diameter of 3μ and the spherules have the diameter of 0.2μ. The chromonema remains connected with the spherules of the centromere. The chromosomes of most organisms contain only one centromere and are known as **monocentric** chromosomes. Certain chromosomes may have two or more centromeres and can be termed as **diçentric** and **polycentric** chromosomes respectively.

Material of the Chromosome

The composing material of the chromosomes is the chromatin substance which may be of the following two types :

1. Euchromatin. The euchromatin is the extended form chromatin and it forms the major portion of the chromosomes. It shows affinity to the basic nuclear stains. The euchromatin is rich in DNA. The euchromatin is considered as genetically active substance.

2. Heterochromatin. The highly stained region of the chromosome is said to contain heterochromatin. In the inter-phase the heterochromatin forms condensed chromosomal regions which are known as the **chromocenters** or false **nucleoli.** The heterochromatin remains closely associated with the nucleolus. The heterochromatin is considered as genetically inert substance but it controls the metabolism of the chromosome, biosynthesis of the nucleic acids and the energy metabolism. The sex chromosomes of the animals have been found rich in the heterochromatin.

Molecular compounds of chromosomes. The major molecular constituents of the eukaryotic chromosomes are DNA, RNA, histone and non-histone proteins and metallic ions. Recent studies have established that the chromosomes consist of a single, double stranded DNA molecule. The DNA is the most stable chemical molecule of biological world and carries genetic informations of one generation to next (Ris, 1969). The RNA is transcribed by the DNA. Most of the RNA is transported to the cytoplasm but some RNA remains associated with DNA along with proteins. The histone proteins are basic proteins and contain basic amino acids such as arginine and lysine in their molecules. They remain associated with DNA and serve as repressors of gene activity. The non-histone proteins are mostly acidic and most of them act as enzymes. The important non-histone proteins of chromosomes are phosphoproteins, DNA polymerase, RNA polymerase, DPN pyrophosphorylase and nucleoside triphosphatase. The chromosomes contain many metallic ions, *e.g.*, Mg^{++}, Ca^{++}, etc., which make the organization of chromosomes intact.

Functions of the Chromosomes

The chromosomes are the most significant components of the cell. They control most of the cell biological and genetical activities of a species. They contain the genetical material, the DNA which ultimately influences all the biological phenomena at molecular, physiological and gross morphological levels.

The chromosomes are considered as the organs of heredity because of the following reasons :

(*i*) They form the only link between two generations.

(*ii*) A diploid chromosome's set consists of two morphologically similar (except the X and Y sex chromosomes) sets, one is derived from the mother and another from the father at fertilization.

(*iii*) The genetic material, DNA or RNA is localized in the chromosome and its contents are relatively constant from one generation to the next.

(*iv*) The chromosomes maintain and replicate the genetic informations contained in their DNA molecule and this information is transcribed at the right time in proper sequence into the specific type of RNA molecules which directs the synthesis of different types of proteins to form a body form like the parents.

LINKAGE AND CROSSING OVER

Mendel's principle of independent assortment applies both to genes and chromosomes. It is very obvious that larger the number of chromosomes, the greater will be the number of combinations of the genes and trait resulting from independent assortment. For example, in *Drosophila,* hundreds of genes have been studied, yet there are only four pairs of chromosomes. Each chromosome contains many genes. Thus genes in the same chromosome will not be assorted independently. Mendel's principle of independent assortment is not universal but is limited to genes in different chromosomes.

An exception of law of independent assortment was discovered by Bateson and Punnett in 1906 in which they found two pairs of alleles in sweet peas which did not assort independently. They noted, when two alleles such as A and B, came from the same parent (AA BB × aa bb) they tended to enter the same gamete and to be transmitted together. This was called **coupling**. On the other hand, when the same alleles came from different parents (AA bb × aa BB), they tended to enter different gametes and to remain apart this phenomenon was called **repulsion**. No satisfactory reply of coupling and repulsion was developed until Morgan (1910) found similar situation in *Drosophila* and noted that coupling and repulsion are two aspects of a single phenomenon known as linkage.

Linkage

General definition. "The phenomenon in which linked genes tend to go together in the same gamete as a result of which the parental combinations are obtained in greater frequency than expected in the progeny, is known as **linkage** or the co-existence of two or more genes or factors in the same chromosome as a result of which they are transmitted from one generation to another in group is known as **linkage**".

In other words genes on same chromosome are called **linked genes,** and the phenomenon is termed as **linkage.**

According to Morgan the tendency of two genes to remain together in the same chromosome during hereditary transmission is called linkage. Morgan supposed that this tendency of linked genes to remain in their original combinations was due to their location in the same chromosome. Further, he advanced the basic idea that the degree or strength of linkage depends upon the distance between the linked genes in the chromosome.

Linkage groups. All the genes that are linked together form the linkage group. If a certain gene A is linked with B and B with C and C with D and so on then all the genes AB, CD, etc., are linked together and all the genes that exhibit linkage with one another form a linkage group. Extensive work on *Drosophila melanogaster* has shown that the known genes fall into four linkage groups. The haploid number or the number of pairs of chromosomes which this species possesses is also four. The number of genes which form into linkage groups are also somewhat relative to the lengths of the chromosomes. The smallest linkage group corresponds to the shortest chromosome pair. In maize there are ten linkage groups and ten pairs of chromosomes; in *Pisum sativum* seven linkage groups and seven pairs of chromosomes and in tomato 10 linkage groups for 12 chromosomes have been identified. Thus it can be said that the number of linkage groups is restricted to the haploid number of chromosomes. This principle is known as the **limitation of linkage groups.**

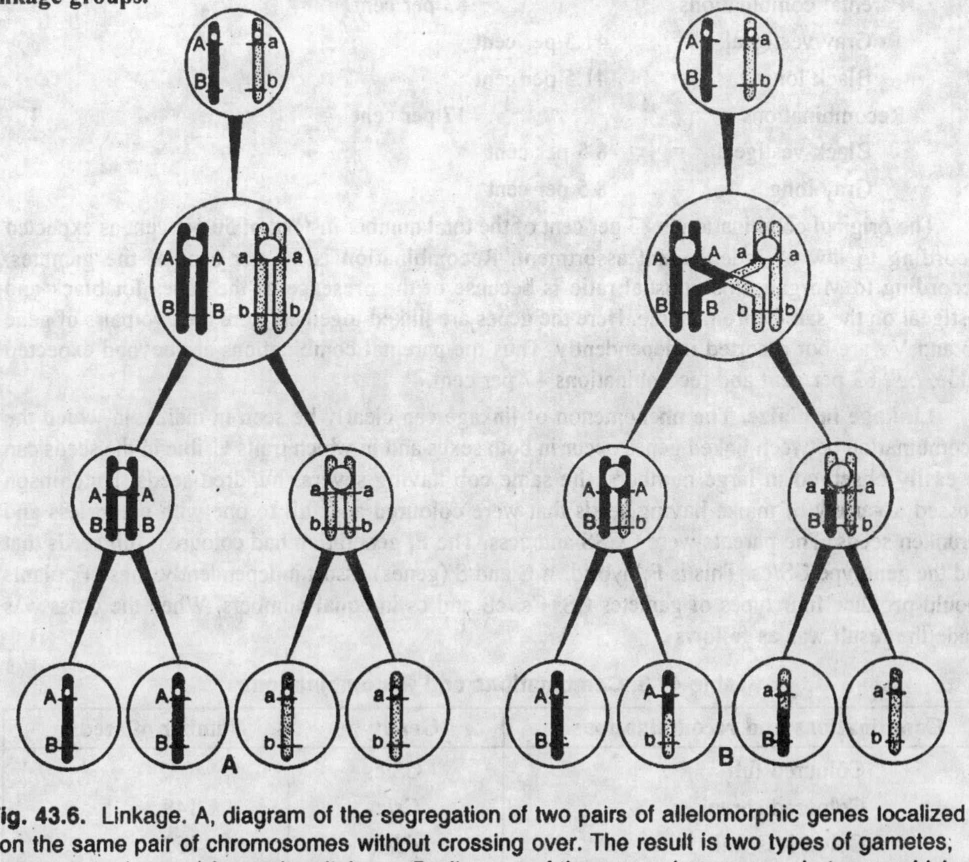

Fig. 43.6. Linkage. A, diagram of the segregation of two pairs of allelomorphic genes localized on the same pair of chromosomes without crossing over. The result is two types of gametes, AB and ab. A case of complete linkage. B, diagram of the same chromosome between which crossing over takes place during meiosis. Four types of gametes result AB, ab, aB and ab. A case of incomplete linkage.

Types of linkage. There are two main types of linkage : (1) complete and (2) incomplete. In complete linkage two or more characters are inherited together and these characters appear in two or more generations. This type of linkage is rarely found in nature. This takes place due to non-break in the gene combinations, situated on any chromosome. It is found in *Drosophila* and certain other insects.

The incomplete type of linkage has been found in many plants and animals. Here, the chromosomes break accidentally either in one or several places. Such type of linkage is found in maize.

Linkage in Drosophila. Morgan (1920) discovered two recessive mutants in *Drosophila* one gray-bodied vestigeal-winged and the other black-bodied long-winged. If a gray-bodied vestigeal-winged fly is crossed to a black-bodied long-winged one, the F_1 generation consists of gray long-winged (normal) flies. Thus the gene for gray body colour, B, is dominant over its allele, which is responsible for black body colour, b, : and the gene for long wings, V, is dominant over its vestigeal allele, v. When the F_1 male hybrids are crossed to double recessive females (*i.e.*, black-bodied vestigeal-winged females), only two kinds of offspring are produced, *i.e.*, gray vestigeal and black long. The expected types, *i.e.*, gray long and black vestigeal do not appear at all. If F_1 female fly is crossed with a black vestigeal male the four expected types are produced as follows :

Parental combinations			83 per cent
Gray vestigeal	=	41.5 per cent	
Black long	=	41.5 per cent	
Recombinations			17 per cent
Black vestigeal	=	8.5 per cent	
Gray long	=	8.5 per cent	

The original combination is 83 per cent of the total number instead of 50 per cent as expected according to law of independent assortment. Recombination is 17 per cent of the gametes. According to Morgan, this unusual ratio is because of the presence of the genes for black and vestigeal on the same chromosome. Here the genes are linked together. Here the two pairs of gene Bb and Vv are not assorted independently. Thus the parental combinations are beyond expected value, *i.e.*, 83 per cent and recombinations 17 per cent.

Linkage in maize. The phenomenon of linkage can clearly be seen in maize, in which the recombination between linked genes occur in both sexes and in which traits visible in the seeds can be easily observed in large numbers, the same cob having several hundred seeds. Hutchinson crossed a variety of maize having seeds that were coloured and full to one with colourless and shrunken seeds. The parents were CCSS and ccss. The F_1 generation had coloured, full seeds that had the genotype CS/cs. This is F_1 hybrid. If C and S (genes) assort independently, these F_1 plants should produce four types of gametes CS, Cs, cS and cs in equal numbers. When the cross was made the result was as follows :

Table 43.3. Combinations and Recombinations

Combinations and recombinations	Genotype	Number of seeds
Coloured full	CS/cs	4032
Coloured shrunken	Cs/cs	149
Colourless full	cS/cs	152
Colourless shrunken	cs/cs	4035

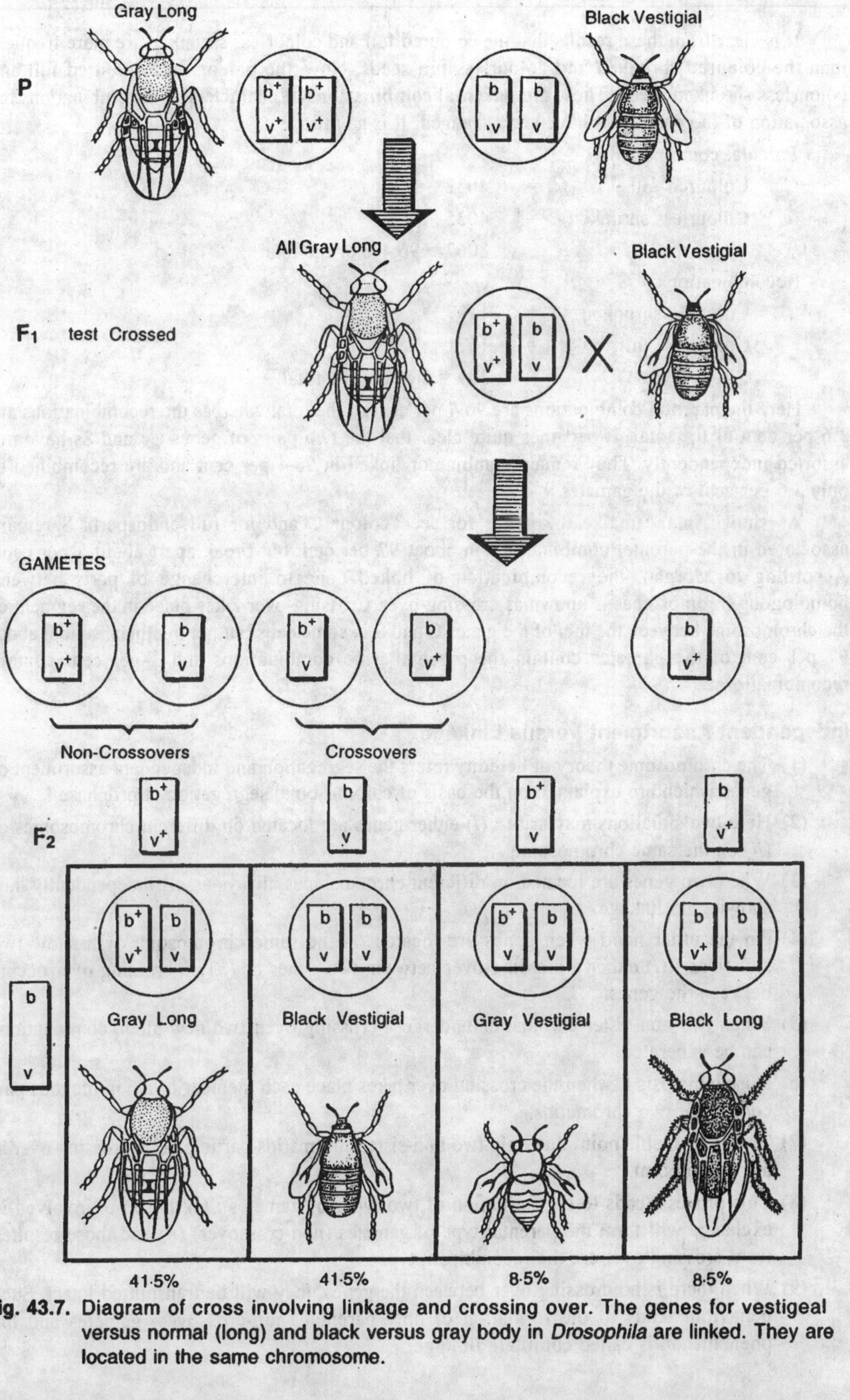

Fig. 43.7. Diagram of cross involving linkage and crossing over. The genes for vestigeal versus normal (long) and black versus gray body in *Drosophila* are linked. They are located in the same chromosome.

It is clear from these results that the coloured full and colourless shrunken are more frequent than the coloured shrunken and colourless full seeds. Now, the parents had coloured full and colourless shrunken seeds. These are **parental combinations** of characters. In recombinations the association of the characters have been changed. It is as follows :

Parental combinations

Coloured full	=	4032
Colourless shrunken	=	4035
		8067 = 96.4% of the total

Recombinations

Coloured shrunken	=	149
Colourless full	=	152
		301 = 3.6% of the total

Here the parental combinations are 96.4 per cent of the total whereas the recombinations are 3.6 per cent of the total. It becomes quite clear that the two pairs of genes Cc and Ss have not assorted independently. They remain combine or linked in 96.4 per cent and are recombined in only 3.6 per cent of the gametes.

As shown in the maize the genes for seed colour C and for full endosperm S remain associated in the parental combinations in about 97 per cent but break apart about 3 per cent. According to Morgan, the recombination of linked gene to interchange of parts between homologous chromosomes is known as crossing-over. Crossing-over takes place in the segment of the chromosome between the loci of the genes C and S in some cells but not in others, so that about 97 per cent of the gametes contain the parental gene combinations and 3 per cent contain recombinations.

Independent Assortment Versus Linkage

(1) The chromosome theory of heredity refers the segregation and independent assortment of genes which are explained on the basis of chromosomal segregation at prophase I.

(2) Here two situations may arise : (*i*) either genes are located on different chromosomes or (*ii*) on the same chromosome.

(3) When two genes are located on different chromosomes always assort independently thus showing no linkage.

(4) On the other hand when genes are located on the same chromosome will show two situations : (*i*) either a crossing over between two genes or (*ii*) no crossing over occurs between the genes.

(5) When two non-sister chromatids undergo a crossing over, two new allele combinations can be generated.

(6) During meiosis I, when the crossing over takes place each member of a homologous pair consists of two chromatids.

(7) This is a notable point that only two non-sister chromatids participate in crossing over at any given point.

(8) This process leads to the formation of two types of gametes : (*i*) those not involved in exchange will form the parental type of gametes (non-crossover) (*ii*) and those resulted from crossing over are the recombinant types.

(9) When there is no crossing over between the genes, they will be transmitted intact. Such behaviour leads to the formation of only parental (non-crossover) gametes and the phenomenon is called **complete linkage.**

(10) The frequency of crossing over between any two genes is generally proportional to the distance between them on the chromosome.

Complete and Incomplete linkage

When two genes located on the same chromosome are considered, the situations may be explained as follows :

If the two genes are very far from each other, crossing over is possible in all the meiotic cells. In such a case 50 per cent of parental and 50 per cent of recombinants will be produced and the gametes will appear in a genotypic ratio of 1 : 1 : 1 : 1. In such a case, transmission of two genes can not be distinguished from that of two genes located on different chromosomes and thus assorting independently.

Contrary to above situation, when the two genes are close to each other there can be two situations. In situation (*i*) because of it, no crossing over will result into only parental or non-cross over types of gametes (*i.e.*, complete linkage). Actually, such a situation does not exist and crossing over takes place even between closely situated genes. This situation is referred to as incomplete linkage. Here, there is a clear predominance of parentals or non-cross over types of gametes. This relationship was demonstrated for the first time in 1911 in *Drosophila* (fruit fly) by Morgan and Sturtevant.

This shows that all the genes located on the same chromosome will show some linkage between them.

The strength of linkage shall be determined by the distances between them.

When the genes are farther, linkage can be easily broken by crossing over.

Thus, genes located on the same chromosome constitute a linkage group.

The number of linkage groups in any organism is proportional to its haploid chromosome number.

Crossing Over

According to Morgan the linkage is caused due to linked genes being carried out by the same chromosome. He also pointed out that the phenomenon of complete linkage occurs rarely because sometimes the linked genes show the tendency to separate during meiosis. This way, the crossing over may be defined as "a mechanism of the recombination of the genes due to interchange of chromosomal segments at the time of pairing."

The cross-over between linked genes allows their recombination during meiosis. The mechanism of cross-over is as follows :

Mechanism of crossing over. The figure shows that crossing over, leading to recombination of linked genes, is due to interchange of sections of homologous chromosomes. At meiosis, the homologous (maternal and paternal) chromosomes come together and pair, or synapse, during prophase. The pairing is remarkably precise and is evidently brought about by mutual attraction of the parts of the chromosomes that are similar or homologous because they contain allellic genes. Further, during the transition between the pachytene and the diplotene of the prophase of meiosis, the paired chromosomes divide each into two chromatids, so that the bivalent is now composed of four chromatids. At about the time when the chromosomes are first seen to be divided, the chromatids establish one or more exchange, or chiasmata, per bivalent. At each chiasma, two of the chromatids have become broken and then rejoined, so that the new chromatids are now formed of sections of the original ones. Owing to chiasma formation, maternal and paternal chromosomes are not transmitted as indivisible units; they exchange sections, and the new chromosomes that arise as a result of meiosis carry genes that before meiosis were located in different members of the pair of homologous chromosomes. Janssens (1909) for the first time discovered the process of chiasma formation. This is a highly precise process since the two chromatids at a chiasma exchange exactly equivalent segments, so that, with very rare exception, neither chromatid gains or loses any genes.

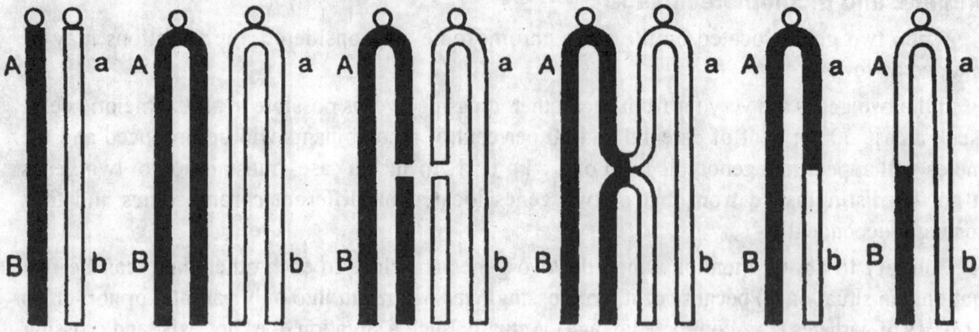

Fig 43.8. Diagram showing the mechanism of crossing over.

Absence of crossing over in Drosophila males. In most of the organisms, recombination of linked genes takes place both in females and males. Similarly, in most organisms, chiasmata formation takes place in both female and male meiosis. But in *Drosophila* the situation is very different. In *Drosophila* crossing over rarely or never takes place in the male. However in the silkworm moth it seems to be absent in the females.

Recombination and crossing over. The cytological observations have established one important fact about crossing over that the exchanges of chromosome segments which cause recombination of linked genes occur at the four-strand, or tetrad stage, in the prophase of meiotic division. Here the homologous chromosomes have paired, each homologue has split into two chromatids held together by undivided centromere, and chiasmata are observed in the tetrad. It is revealed by careful observation that at each chiasma only two of the four chromatids cross over whereas the two other chromatids preserve their original continuities. Genetically it means that of the four chromosomes which emerge from meiosis, only two can show crossing over at any one level.

Recombination is a process which can occur in a variety of situations but the most popular one is in relation to meiosis. Thus, this is a meiotic process that generates haploid product whose genotype is different from the two haploid genotypes constituting the diploid. The product of recombination is a **recombinant.**

Chiasma – type hypothesis. Morgan suggested that the formation of recombinants can be explained by the occurrence of crossing over (*i.e.,* chiasma formation) during meiosis I. This led to chiasma-type hypothesis. The points in support of this hypothesis are as follows :

1. During prophase I (*i.e.*, zygotene), homologous chromosomes pair (*i.e.*, synapsis), with each chromosome consisting of two chromatids.
2. During pachytene of prophase I two non-sister chromatids break at homologous sites and then rejoin.
3. Such rejoining takes place between non-sister chromatid and leads to physical exchange.
4. This physical exchange leads to reshuffling of genes and thus recombination takes place.

Synaptonemal complex and the process of crossing over. Since it is an established fact that DNA is the material of the gene it becomes clear that crossing over involves break and rejoining of DNA. During synapsis, a molecular scaffold known as **synaptonemal complex** aligns the DNA molecules of the two homologous chromosomes side by side. With the result the DNA strand of one chromosome, *i.e.*, a chromatid becomes able to pair with the corresponding DNA strand of the other where their base sequence match. Break and new synthesis of one DNA strand using a strand of other chromatid DNA as the template results in crossing-over.

Crossing-over involves the breaking and rejoining of chromosomes in the synaptonemal complex, which can be observed by cytological methods. However, no crossing-over has been observed in male *Drosophila* during sperm formation. Likewise no recombination of genes occur during meiosis.

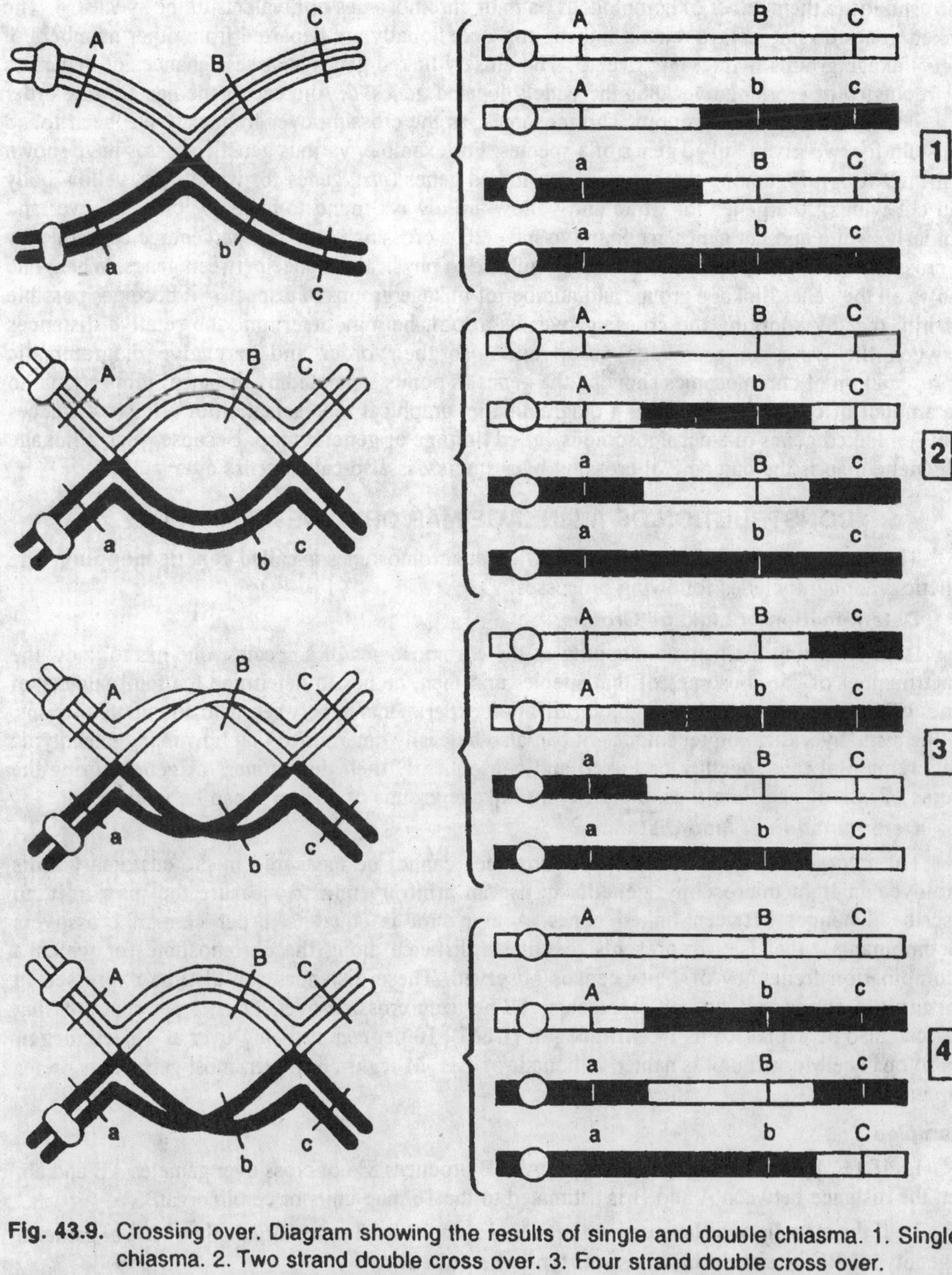

Fig. 43.9. Crossing over. Diagram showing the results of single and double chiasma. 1. Single chiasma. 2. Two strand double cross over. 3. Four strand double cross over. 4. Three strand double cross over.

MAPPING OF CHROMOSOMES

Study of linkage and crossing over has made clear so far, that 1. Because the number of genes usually exceeds the number of chromosomes in different species, therefore, many genes have to be located on same chromosomes. 2. The genes remain arranged linearly on the chromosomes and they have no option before them, except to behave according to the chromosomes during gametogenesis and inheritance, therefore, all the genes on a chromosome inherit together and are said to be linked with each other to form linkage groups. 3. The number of linkage groups corresponds to the number of homologous pairs of chromosomes or bivalents of the species. 4. The linked genes do not always remain linked, but, occasionally are departed from other members of their linkage groups by crossing over. 5. The closely linked genes have less chances of departure or frequency of crossing over than the widely located genes. 6. And each gene has definite order and location in a linkage group or chromosomes, as the crossing over frequency has been found constant for two given linked genes of a species. For example, various genetic crosses have shown that in *Drosophila*, among three mutant sex-linked genes (*viz*., genes for white eyes, yellow body and cut wings), the genes for white and yellow are always found to have 1% crossing over and similarly, white and cut genes are found to have 20% crossing over. The percentage or frequency of crossing over, thus, appears to be closely related to physical distance between genes, When, one knows all the genes, linkage groups and number of linkage groups of a species, it becomes possible for him that by adopting the crossing over as a tool, he may determine the relative distances between the genes in a linkage group and also their order and may give diagrammatic representation of chromosomes showing the genes as points separated by distances proportional to the amount of crossing over. Such a diagrammatic, graphical representation of relative distances between linked genes of a chromosome is called **linkage** or **genetic map.** Because, such a linkage or genetic map is the outcome of crossing over studies, is also called **cross over map.**

CONSTRUCTION OF A LINKAGE MAP OR GENETIC MAPPING

The method of construction maps of different chromosomes is called **genetic mapping**. The genetic mapping includes following processes:

1. Determination of Linkage Groups

Before starting the genetic mapping of the chromosomes of a species, one has to know the exact number of chromosomes of that species and then, he has to determine the total number of genes of that species by undergoing hybridization experiments in between wild and mutant strains. By the same hybridization techniques, it can also be easily determined that how many phenotypic traits remain always together or linked and consequently their determiners or genes during the course of inheritance. And thus, the different linkage groups of a species can be worked out.

2. Determination of Map Distance

The intergene distance on the chromosomes cannot be measured in the customary units employed in light microscopy, geneticists use an arbitrary unit to measure the **map unit**, to describe distances between linked genes. A map unit is equal to 1 per cent of crossovers (recombinants); that is, it represents the linear distance along the chromosome for which a recombination frequency of 1 per cent is observed. These distances can also be expressed in **morgan units;** one morgan unit represents 100 per cent crossing over. Thus, 1 per cent crossing over can also be expressed as **1 centimorgan (1 cM),** 10 per cent crossing-over as **1 decimorgan** and so on. The Morgan unit is named in honour of **T.H. Morgan**; however, most geneticists prefer map units.

Examples

1. If a F_1 hybrid having the genotypes Ab/aB produces 8% of cross over gametes AB and ab, then the distance between A and B is estimated to the 16 map units or centimorgan.

2. If the map distance between the gene loci B and C is 12 centimorgan, then 12% of gametes of genotypes BC/bc should be crossover types, *i.e.,* 6% bC.

Because, each chiasma produces 50% crossover products, 50 per cent crossing over is equivalent to 50 map units or centimorgans. If the mean number of chiasmata is known for a chromosome pair, the total length of the map for that linkage group may be predicted :

Total length = mean number of chiasmata × 50

Two Point Test Cross

The percentage of crossing over between two linked genes is calculated by test crosses in which a F_1 dihybrid is crossed with a double recessive parent. Such crosses because involved crossing over at two points, so called **two point test crosses.** For example, a dihybrid having the genotype Ac/ac is test crossed with a double recessive parent (ac/ac), then among F_2 test cross hybrids we may get 37% dominant genes at both gene loci (AC/ac), 37% recessive genes at both gene loci (ac/ac), 13% dominant gene at first gene locus and recessive gene at the second gene locus (Ac/ac). The last two groups (*i. e.,* 13% Ac/ac) and 13% aC/ac) were produced by crossover gametes (13 + 13) from the dihybrid parent. Thus 26% of all gametes (13 + 13) were of cross over types and the distance between the loci A and C is estimated to be 26 centimorgans. Because, double crossovers usually do not occur between genes less than 5 centimorgans apart, so for genes further apart, the **three point test crosses** are used.

Three Point Test Cross

A three point test cross or trihybrid test cross (involving three genes) gives us information regarding relative distances between these genes, and also shows us the linear order in which these genes should be present on chromosome. Such a three point test cross may be carried out if three points or gene loci on a chromosome pair can be identified by marker genes. If, in addition to genes A and C indicated above, a third marker gene B is located in fairly close proximity in the same linkage group, all three markers may be used together in conducting a more precise analysis of the map distance and the relative position of the three points.

Suppose that we testcross trihybrid individuals of genotype ABC/abc and find in the progeny the following:

36% ABC/abc	9% Abc/abc	4% ABc/abc	1% AbC/abc
36% abc/abc	9% aBC/abc	4% abC/abc	1% aBc/abc
72% Parental type	18% Single crossovers between A and B (region I)	8% Single crossovers between B and C (region II)	2% Double crossovers

To find the distance A–B we must count all crossovers (both singles and doubles) that occurred in region I = 18% + 2% or = 20% or 20 map units between the loci A and B. To find the distance B–C we must again count all crossovers (both singles and doubles) that occurred in region II = 8%+2% = 10% or 10 map units between the loci B and C. The A–C distance is, therefore, 30 map units when double crossovers are detected in a three point linkage experiment and 26 map units when double crossovers are undetected in the two-point linkage experiment above.

Without the middle marker (B), double crossovers would appear as parental types and hence we underestimate the true map distance (crossover percentage). In this case the 2% double crossovers would appear with the 72% parental types, making a total 74% parental types and 26% recombinant types. Therefore, for any three linked genes whose distances are known, the amount of detectable crossovers between the two outer markers A and C when the middle marker B is missing is; (A–B crossover percentage) plus (B–C crossovers percentage) minus (2 × double crossover percentage).

3. Determination of Gene Order

After determining the relative distances between the genes of a linkage group, it becomes easy to place genes in there proper linear order. For example, if the linear order of three genes

ABC is to be determined, then these three genes may be in any one of three different orders depending upon that which gene is in the middle. For the time being we may ignore left and right end alternatives. If double crossovers do not occur, map distances may be treated as completely additive units. Now, if we suppose that the distance between the genes A–B = 12, B–C = 7, A–C = 5, we can determine the order of genes correctly in the following manner :

Case I. Let us assume that gene A is in the middle (*e. g.*, B–A–C) :

[B 12 A] [A 5 C]

[B 7 C]

In this case because, the distances between B–C are not equitable, genes A cannot be in the middle.

Case II. Let us assume that gene B is in the middle (*e. g.*, A–B–C) :

[A 12 B] [B 7 C]

[A 5 C]

In this case, because the distance between A–C are not equitable, therefore, gene B cannot be in the middle.

Case III. Let us assume that gene C is in the middle (*e. g.*, A–C–B).

[A 5 C] [C 7 B]

[A 12 B]

In this case, because the distances between A–B are equitable, therefore, gene C must be in the middle.

Thus, the relative distances and ordering of genes in a linkage group are determined in separate segments by two point test crosses or three point crosses, as the case may be.

4. Combining Map Segments

Finally, the different segments of maps of a complete chromosome are combined to form a complete genetic map of 100 centimorgans long for a chromosome.

Example: For example, suppose we have to combine following three map segments.

(I) [a 8 b 10 c]

(Ii) [c 10 b 22 d]

(III) [c 30 e 2 d]

We can superimpose each of these segments by aligning the genes shared in common.

(I) [a 8 b 10 c]

(II) [d 22 b 10 c]

(Iii) [d 2 e 30 c]

Then finally we may combine the three segments into one map:

The a to d distance = (d to b) – (a to b) = 22 – 8 = 14

The a to e distance = (a to d) – (d to e) = 14 – 2 = 12

[d 2 e 12 a 8 b 10 c]

Interference and Coincidence

In most higher organisms it has been found that one chiasma formation reduces the probability of another chiasma formation in an immediately adjacent region of the chromosome, probably because of physical inability of the chromatids to bend back upon themselves within certain minimum distances. The tendency of one crossover to interfere with the other crossover is called **interference.** Thus, the proximity of one crossover to another decreases the probability of another very close by. The centromere has a similar interference effect; frequency of crossing over is also reduced near the ends of the chromosome arms. The net result of this interference in the observation of fewer double crossover types than would be expected according to map distances. The strength of interference varies in different segments of the chromosome and is usually expressed in terms of a **coefficient of coincidence,** or the ratio between the observed and the expected double crossovers.

$$\text{Coefficient of coincidence} = \frac{\%\ \text{observed double crossovers}}{\%\ \text{expected double crossovers}}$$

The coincidence is the complement of interference, so:

Coincidence + Interference = 1.0

When interference is complete (1.0), no double crossovers will be observed and coincidence becomes zero. When, interference decreases, coincidence increases. Coincidence values ordinarily vary between 0 and 1. Coincidence is generally quite small for short map distance. There is no interference across centromere.

Example:

For explaining interference and coincidence, we can consider the results of one of the experiment of **Hutchison** (1922). He reported the map distance for three genes, c(colourless aleurone), Sh (shrunken grains), and wx (waxy endosperm) of corn and observed following crossing over frequencies between these genes:

Table 43.4. Crossing over frequencies between genes c, Sh and wx of corn.

Regions	Genes	Percentage crossovers	Map-distances (in map units)
I	c-Sh	3.4	3.4 + 0.1 = 3.5
II	Sh-wx	18.3	18.3 + 0.1 = 18.4
Double corssover	c-Sh-wx	0.1	

If crossing over in region I and II were independent, we should predict 0.035 ×0.184 = 0.6 per cent double crossovers, where as only 0.1 per cent was observed.

$$\text{So, coincidence} = \frac{0.1}{0.6} = 0.167$$

Linkage Maps of different Organisms

By adopting the above mentioned techniques, geneticists have constructed the linkage or genetic maps of various organisms, such as, viruses, bacteria, fungi, tomato, barley, wheat, rice, sorghum, morning glory, garden pea, maize, *Drosophila,* chickens, mice man, etc. The first linkage map has been constructed for two chromosomes of *Drosophila* by **Strutevant** in 1911. The linkage or genetic mapping in maize has been done by **McClintock** under the leadership of **R. A. Emerson.**

Syntenic Genes

If two or more specific human gene products and a given human chromosome are both present in the same hybrid cells, then those genes are located in the same chromosome ; that is, they are **syntenic.** The term **synteny** refers to genes that are located on the same chromosome, whether or not they show recombination; **linkage** refers only to genetic loci that have been shown by recombination studies to be in the same chromosome. Syntenic genes may be so far apart in their chromosome that they seem to segregate independently; that is, they may show as much as 50 per cent recombination as would be exhibited by non-syntenic genes.

Linkage Map of Drosophila melanogaster

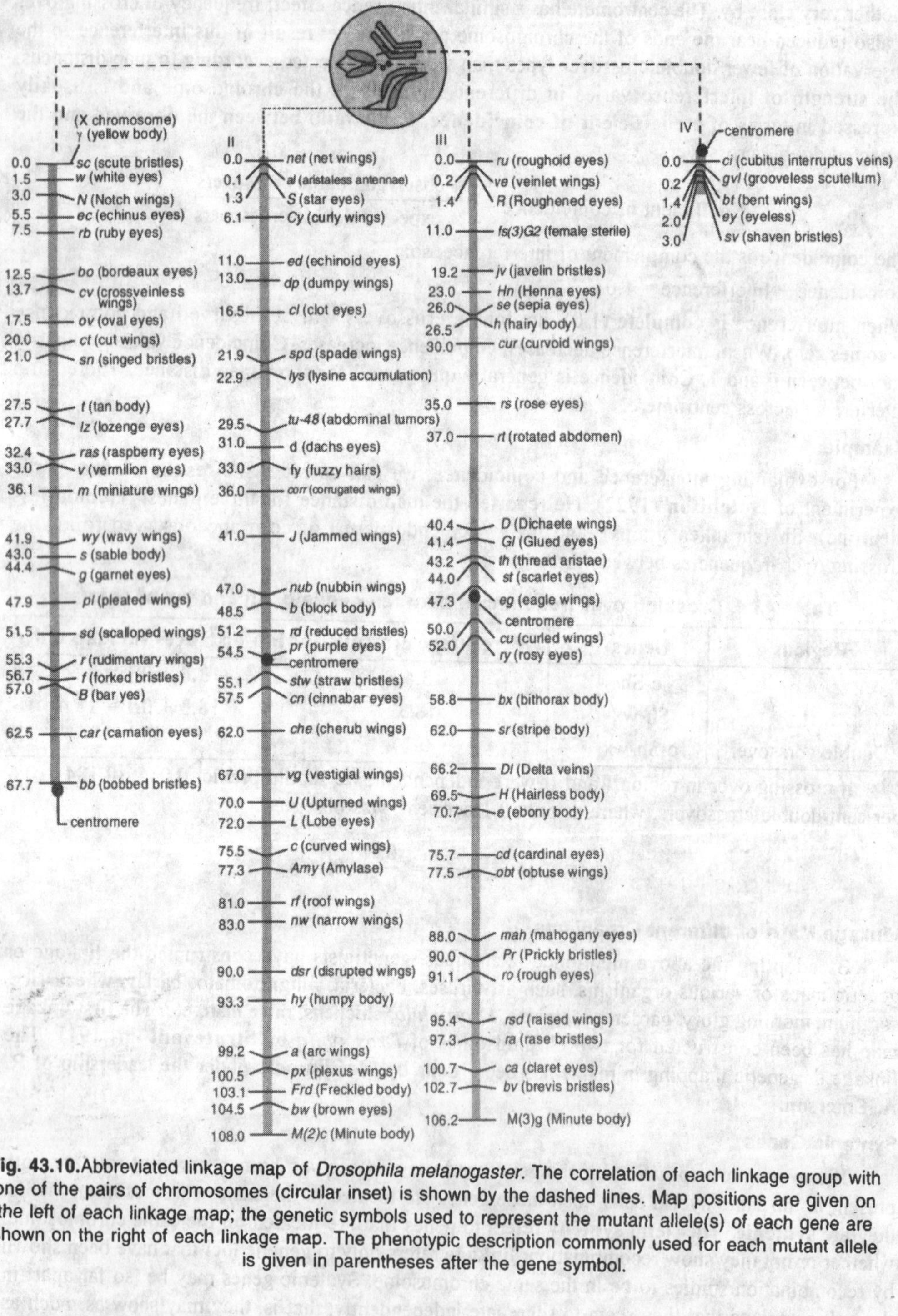

Fig. 43.10. Abbreviated linkage map of *Drosophila melanogaster.* The correlation of each linkage group with one of the pairs of chromosomes (circular inset) is shown by the dashed lines. Map positions are given on the left of each linkage map; the genetic symbols used to represent the mutant allele(s) of each gene are shown on the right of each linkage map. The phenotypic description commonly used for each mutant allele is given in parentheses after the gene symbol.

Linkage Map of Maize *(Zea Mays)*

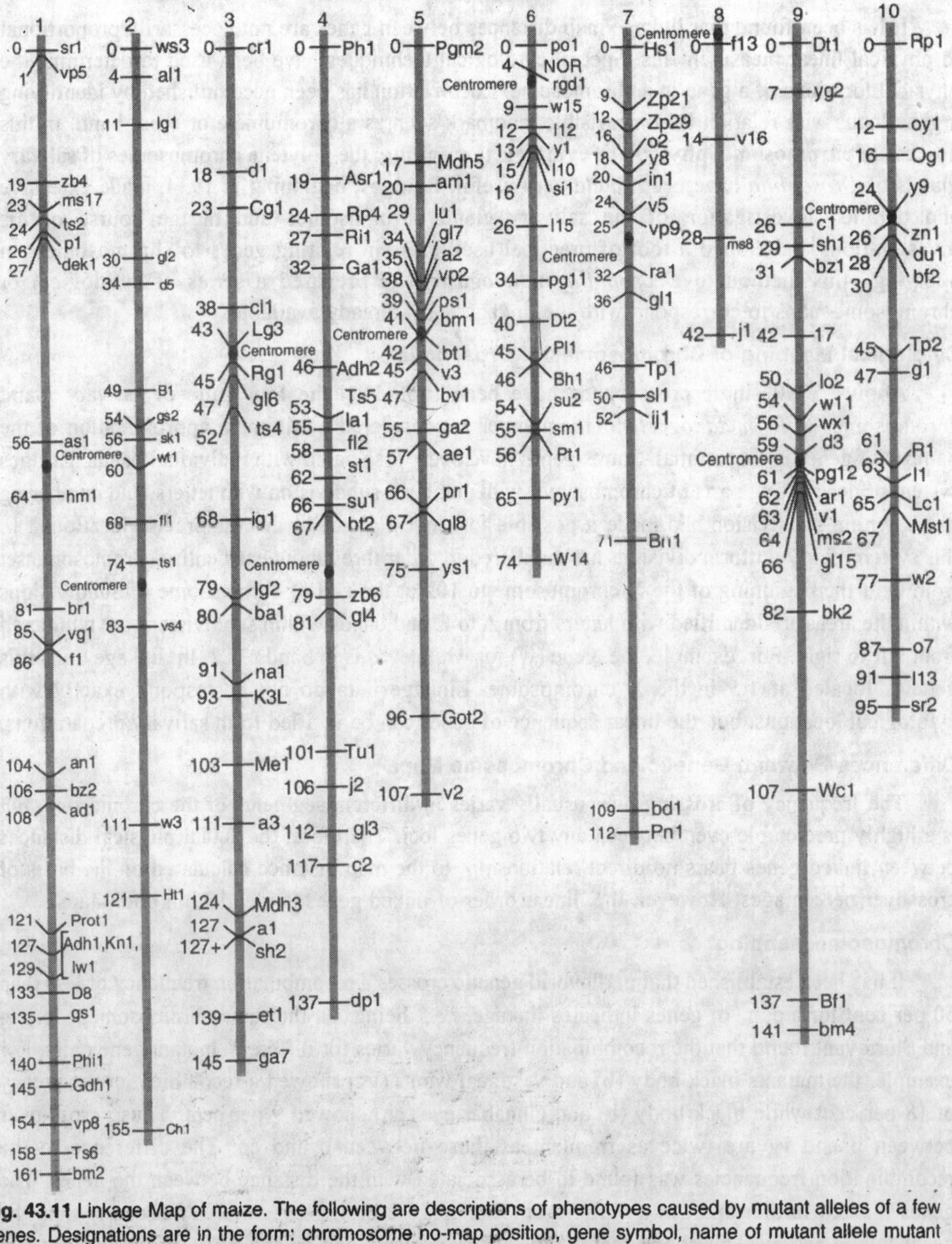

Fig. 43.11 Linkage Map of maize. The following are descriptions of phenotypes caused by mutant alleles of a few genes. Designations are in the form: chromosome no-map position, gene symbol, name of mutant allele mutant phenotype. 1-0 sr1, striate-1, white striations on leaves;; 1-56, as1, asynaptic-1 failure of the meiotic prophase chromosomes to synapse; *2-30, g12,* glossy-2, cuticle wax altered such that leaf surface appears glossy; 2-121, *Ht1, Helminthosporium turcicum* resistance, resistance to the northern leaf blight caused by this fungus; *3-0, cr1,* crinkly-1, leaves broad and crinkled; *3-139, et1,* etched-1, pitted or scarred endosperm; *4-24, Rp4, rust resistance-4, resistance to the fungus Puccinia sorghi*; 4-101, *Tu1,* tunicate-1, kernels enclosed in long glumes; *5 -20, am1, ameiotic-1, meiosis fails; 6*-3 NOR, *nucleolus* organizer tandem repeats of genes coding for rRNA; 6-74, *w14,* white-14, white seedling; 7-16, *o2,* opaque-2, endosperm starch soft and opaque, has high lysine content; 8-28, *ms8,* male sterile-8, anthers not exserted; 9-26, c1, *colorless-1,* nonpigmented aleurone; 9-56, *wx1,* waxy-1, no amylose in endosperm or pollen; 10-16, *Og1, old gold1,* old gold-1, variable bright yellow stripes on leaf blades.

B. CHROMOSOME, PHYSICAL OR CYTOLOGICAL MAPPING

It has been found that linkage map distances between genes are not necessarily proportional to physical linear measurements. Special cytological techniques have been used to determine the physical locations of a gene in a chromosome. Localization has been accomplished by identifying a gene locus with relation to some visible landmark such as a chromomere or cross band. In this process of **chromosome, physical** or **cytological mapping,** the polytene chromosomes of salivary glands of *Drosophila* have been found very useful. **Bridges,** beginning in 1934, made extensive and detailed investigation of the salivary gland chromosomes and in the course of his investigations, developed a tool of practical usefulness in relating genes to chromosomes. In applying this method to *Drosophila melanogaster,* he prepared a series of cytological or chromosome maps to correspond with the linkage maps already available.

Cytological Mapping of Chromosomes of *Drosophila*

About 5000 single cross bands have been noted on the four pairs of salivary gland chromosomes in *D. melanogaster.* This number is considered a minimum approximation of the number of genes in that animal. Some genes have been associated with individual bands. Bridges system of designating parts of chromosomes with numbers, subdivision with letters, and numbering bands within subdivision had made it possible for investigators to discuss precise locations . In this system, fairly uniform divisions are numbered in order throughout each entire chromosome set from O at the beginning of the X chromosome to 102 at the end of chromosome 4. Subdivisions within the areas are identified with letters from A to F, and bands within subdivisions are numbered from left to right. For example, the gene (w) for white eyes is in bands 3C2. In linkage units this gene is located at 1.5 in the X chromosome. Linkage data do not correspond exactly with cytological locations, but the linear sequence of genes can be verified from salivary preparations.

Differences Between Genetic and Chromosome Maps

The frequency of crossing over usually varies in different segments of the chromosome but is a highly predictable even between any two genes loci. Therefore, the actual physical distances between linked genes bears no direct relationship to the map distance calculated on the basis of crossover percentages. However, the linear order of linked genes is identical in both maps.

Chromosome Mapping

It has been established that in dihybrid genetic crosses a recombination frequency of less than 50 per cent for a pair of genes indicates linkage, *i.e.,* being on the same chromosome, Morgan and Sturtevant found that the recombination frequency varies for different mutant gene pairs. For example, the mutants black body (b) and vestigeal wings (vg) showed a recombination frequency of 18 per cent while black body (b) and cinnabar eye (cn) showed 9 per cent. Thus, cross-over between b and vg are twice as frequent as those between b and cn. The difference in the recombination frequencies was found to be associated with the distance between the genes. The genes located farther apart in a chromosome undergo crossing-over more frequently than the genes laying nearby. This shows that the distance between b and vg should be about twice as that between b and cn. Hence, the recombination frequencies can help in the determination of the positions called **loci,** of the genes in the chromosomes and in preparing chromosome maps.

Thus, a **chromosome map** is a graphic representation of a linkage group in the form of a line which shows by points the sequence of the genes and the relative distances between the genes it contains. A chromosome map is also called a **linkage map** or **genetic map.** The method of preparing chromosome map of a species is known as **chromosome mapping.**

Chromosome mapping is based on two undermentioned genetic principles. They are –

1. That the genes are arranged in a linear order in the chromosome.

2. That the frequency of crossing over between two genes is directly proportional to the distance between them in the chromosome. Since the frequency of crossing over is used in preparing chromosome maps, the latter are also called **cross over maps.**

Chromosome map unit. A frequency of one per cent crossing over between two genes is known as one unit of map distance between these genes and it is termed a **morgan** after the name of T. H. Morgan.

How to prepare chromosome maps. Certain examples are quoted here to explain the technique of preparing a chromosome map. Suppose the five genes A, B, C, D and E are located in a single chromosome. If the crossing over percentage between A and B is 10 morgans, these genes are plotted 10 arbitrary units apart in a linear scale (Fig. 43.12 A).

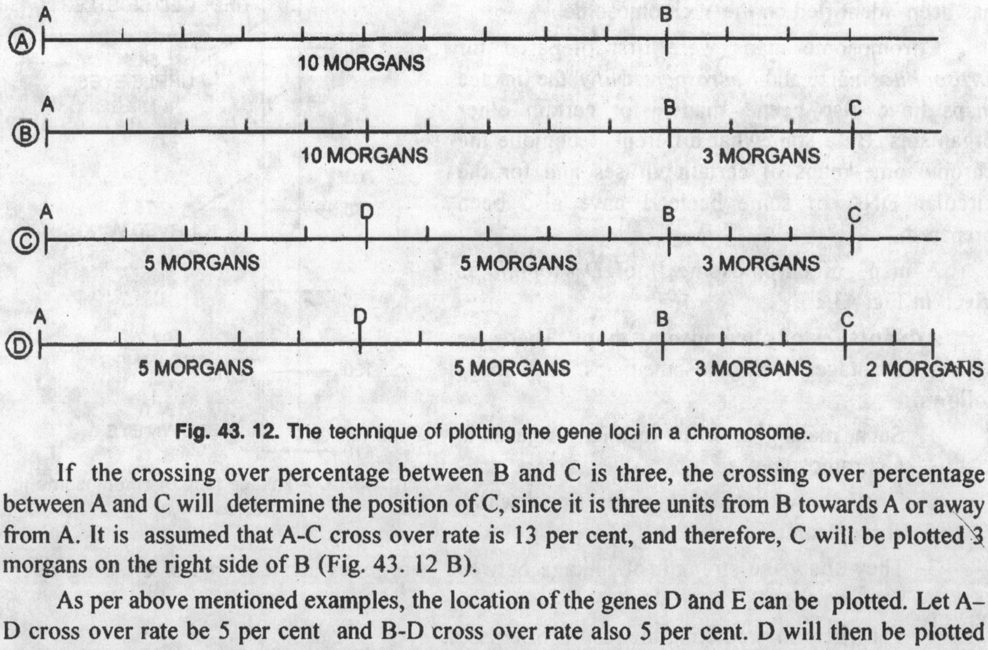

Fig. 43. 12. The technique of plotting the gene loci in a chromosome.

If the crossing over percentage between B and C is three, the crossing over percentage between A and C will determine the position of C, since it is three units from B towards A or away from A. It is assumed that A-C cross over rate is 13 per cent, and therefore, C will be plotted 3 morgans on the right side of B (Fig. 43. 12 B).

As per above mentioned examples, the location of the genes D and E can be plotted. Let A-D cross over rate be 5 per cent and B-D cross over rate also 5 per cent. D will then be plotted between A and B, *i.e.*, 5 morgans from each (Fig. 43. 12 C). If cross over rate between C and E happens to be two per cent and between B and E 5 per cent. E will be plotted two morgans on the right side of C (Fig. 43. 12D).

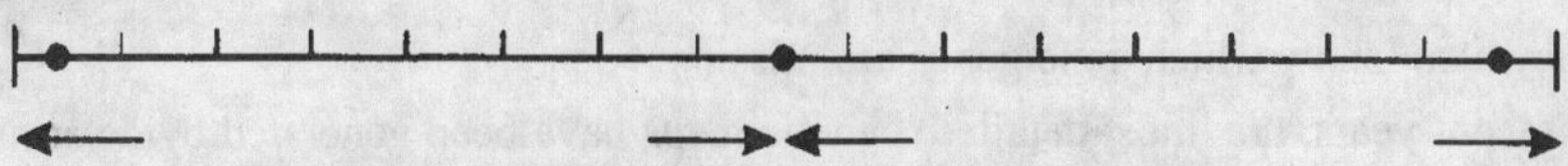

Fig. 43.13 (*a*). Morgan and Sturtevant. Mapping genes.

Morgan and Sturtevant got recombination frequencies of (*i*) 18 between the genes B for black body and for vestigial wings, (*ii*) 9 between the genes b for black body and cn cinnabar eye and (*iii*) 9.5 between the genes cn for cinnabar eye and vg for vestigial wings. If the gene b is plotted at one end of the chromosome, the gene vg will be 18 morgans away from it (Fig. 43. 13 (a). The gene *cn* being 9 morgans from *b* and 9.5 morgans from *vg* will be plotted approximately in the middle between the genes *b* and *vg*. Thus, the sequence of genes on the chromosome is *b, cn* and *vg*.

The recombination frequency of 9.5 was obtained between *cn* and *vg*. This revealed the sequence to be *b* – *cn* – *vg* with a total distance of 9 + 9.5 = 18.5 map units which is close to the observed 18 map units for *b* – *vg*. If it were *cn* – *b* – *vg*, *c* – *vg*, distance should be 9 + 18 = 27 map units apart. Using this method the relative distances and position of hundreds of mutant genes of *Drosophila* have been mapped.

All these mutants cluster together to form four groups of linked genes called **linkage groups.** *Drosophila* possesses four types of chromosomes, *i.e.*, I, II, III and IV. Each linkage group remains associated with a particular chromosome. No gene has been identified on the Y chromosome.

Chromosome maps were first prepared for *Drosophila*, maize and *Neurospora*. Now the linkage maps have also been made for certain other organisms. By a somewhat different technique the chromosome maps of certain viruses and for the circular DNA of some bacteria have also been prepared.

A map of chromosome II of *Drosophila* is given in Fig. 43.13.

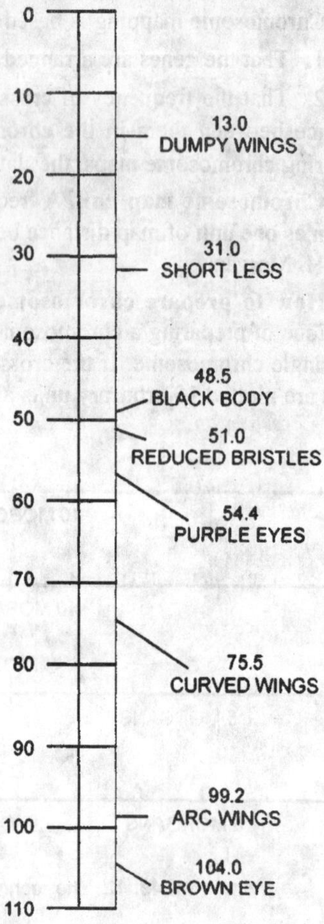

Fig. 43.13. A linkage map of chromosome II of *Drosophila*.

Advantages of chromosome maps. There are several advantages of chromosome maps. They are as follows:

1. Such maps give exact location of genes in a chromosome.
2. They show that which genes lie in which chromosome.
3. They show the strength of linkage between two genes and chances of crossing over between them.
4. They help in predicting the results of crosses.
5. According to these, the genes have linear arrangement in chromosomes; they have definite positions, the **loci,** in the chromosomes, they indicate specific genes in specific chromosomes.
6. They also show which gene/genes are missing.
7. In recent years, the most detailed genetic maps have been generated by determining the nuculeotide sequence of the DNA that makes up each chromosome.
8. Such mapping is not only important in genetic engineering, but is also of fundamental importance in understanding the overall architecture of the chromosome and in fact of the entire genome.

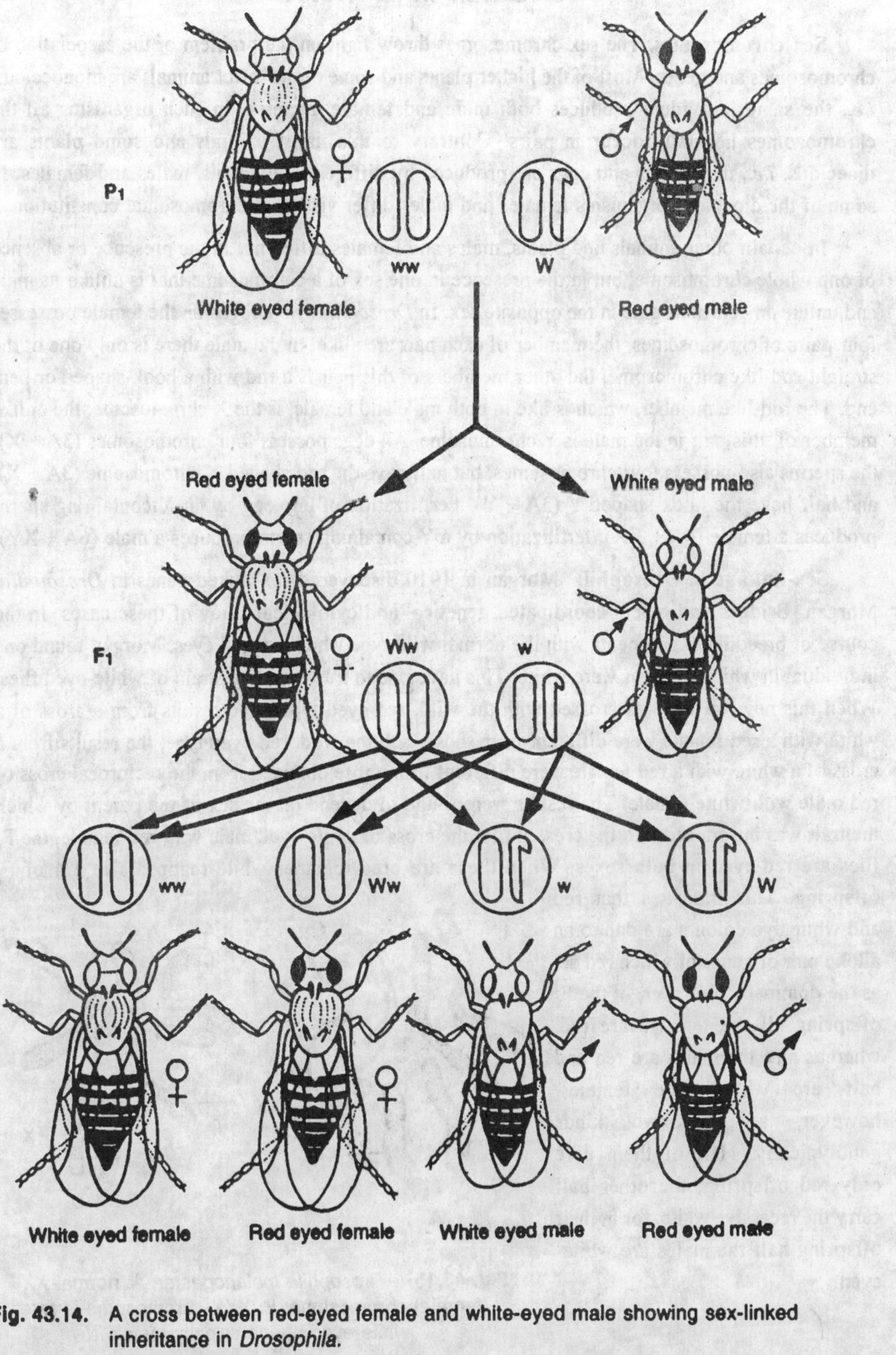

Fig. 43.14. A cross between red-eyed female and white-eyed male showing sex-linked inheritance in *Drosophila*.

SEX LINKED INHERITANCE

Sex chromosomes. The sex chromosomes throw light on the problem of the association of chromosomes and genes. Most of the higher plants and some of the lower animals are monoecious, *i.e.*, the same individual produces both male and female gametes. In such organisms all the chromosomes normally occur in pairs. Contrary to this, most animals and some plants are dioecious, *i.e.*, the sperms and eggs are produced by different individuals, males and females. In some of the dioecious organisms females and males differ visibly in chromosomal constitution.

In certain other animals and plants, males and females differ, not in the presence or absence of one whole chromosome, but in the presence in one sex of a chromosome that is unlike its male and unlike any chromosome in the opposite sex. In *Drosophila melanogaster,* the female possesses four pairs of chromosomes, the member of each pair are alike. In the male there is only one of the straight rod-like chromosome, the other members of this pair is a rod with a hook-shaped or bent end. The rod-like member, which is like in both male and female, is the X chromosome; the unlike member of this pair in the male is Y chromosome. All eggs possess four chromosomes (3A + X); the sperms also possess four chromosomes, but half have the rod-shaped X chromosome (3A + X), and half have the hook-shaped Y (3A + Y). Fertilization of any egg by an X-containing sperm produces a female (6A + XX); fertilization by a Y-containing sperm produces a male (6A + XY).

Sex-linkage in Drosophila. Morgan in 1910 discovered sex-linked genes in *Drosophila.* Morgan, Bridges and others coordinated genetical and cytological study of these cases. In the course of breeding experiments with the normal wild type which has red eyes, Morgan found one individual in which the eyes were white. This gave rise to true breeding strain of white-eyed flies. When this new variety was crossed with the wild, red-eyed typed, the results from a cross of a white with a red female were different from those with the wild, red-eyed type, the results from a cross of a white with a red female were different from those obtained from the reciprocal cross of red male with white female. The results were found to depend on the sex of the parent by which the trait was introduced into the cross. From the cross of white-eyed male with red female, the F_1 flies are red-eyed in both sexes. When these are bred together white reappears in 1/4 of F_2 offspring. This indicates that red and white eye colours are due to an allelic pair of genes of which red act as the dominant. However, of the F_2 offspring all the females are red, whereas half the males are red and half are white. The females, however, are of two kinds genotypically. Half of them give only red offspring; the other half carry the recessive white, for in their offspring half the males are white-eyed.

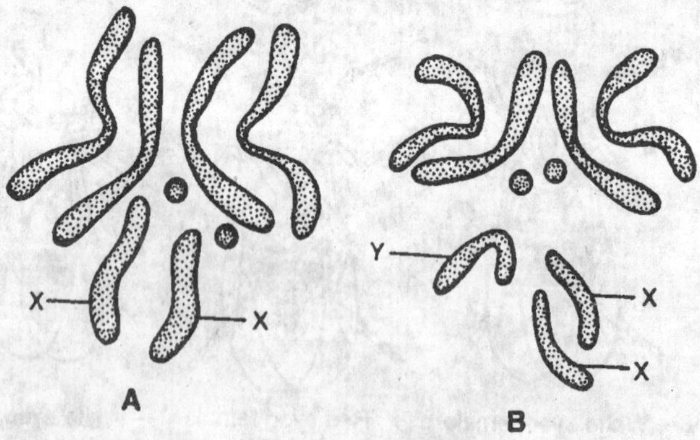

Fig. 43.15. *Drosophila melanogaster.* A, normal *XX* (female) chromosome; B, XXY chromosome in rare white-eyed phenotypically female.

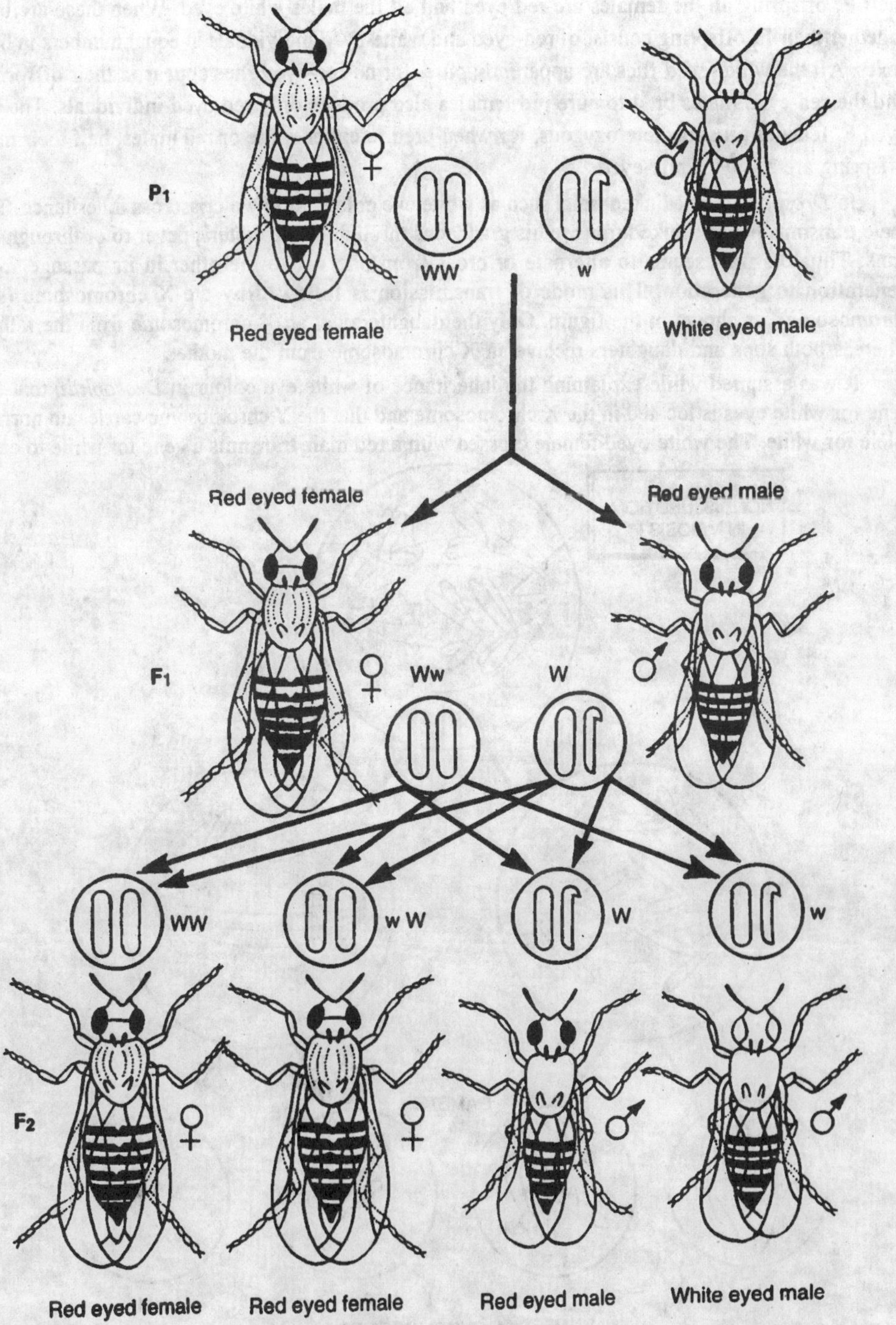

Fig. 43.16. A cross between white eyed-female and white-eyed male showing sex-linked inheritance in *Drosophila*.

When a red male bred to a white female, however, quite a different result is obtained. Among their F_1 offspring all the females are red-eyed and all the males white eyed. When these are bred together their F_2 offspring consist of red-eyed and white-eyed individuals in equal numbers in both sexes. All the white-eyed flies are apparently pure, for no red-eyed flies appear in their offspring; and the red-eyed males bred to pure red females also produce only red-eyed individuals. The red eyed F_1 females must be heterozygous, for when bred to either white or red males, half their male offspring are always white-eyed.

In *Drosophila,* sex-linked traits such as white eye colour follow a crisscross inheritance. The male transmits his sex-linked traits to his grandsons through his daughters, never to or through his sons. Thus the trait seems to alternate or cross from one sex to the other in its passage from generation to generation. This mode of transmission is followed by the X chromosome (sex chromosome), as shown in the figure. Only the daughters get an X chromosome from the father, whereas both sons and daughters receive an X chromosome from the mother.

It was assumed while explaining the inheritance of white eye colour in *Drosophila* that the gene for white eyes is located in the X chromosome and that the Y chromosome carries no normal allele for white. The white-eyed female crossed with a red male transmits a gene for white to each

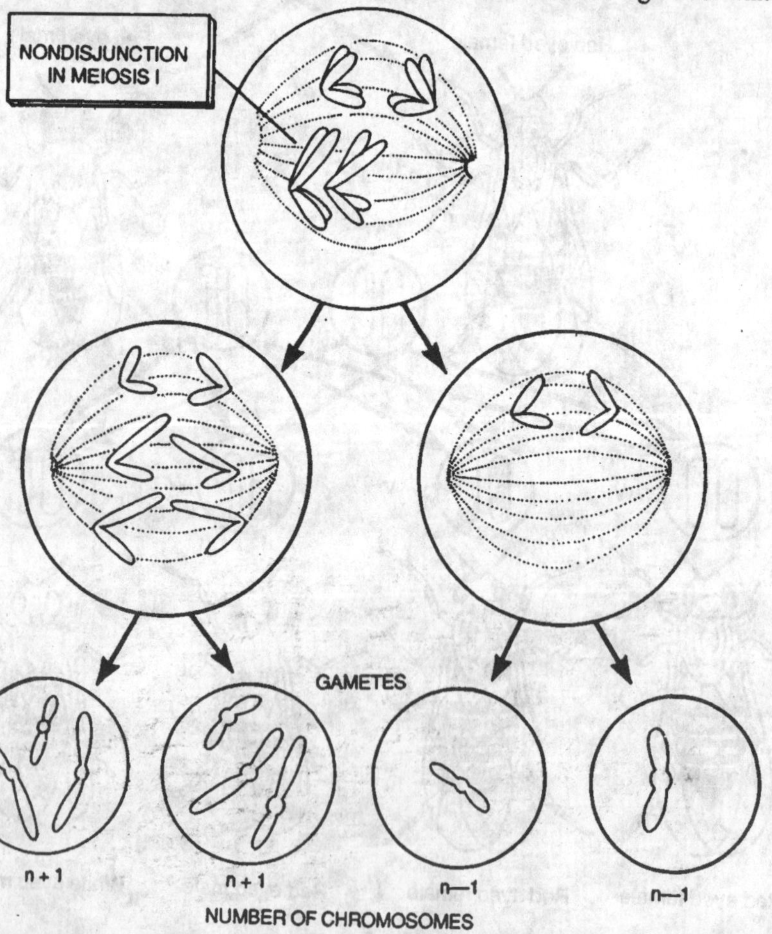

Fig. 43.17. Non-disjunction of a pair of homologous chromosomes during meiosis I produces abnormal gametes with (n + 1) and (n – 1) chromosomes in the gametes.

offspring and an X chromosome to each offspring. The daughters receive also an X chromosome from the father carrying the dominant allele of white and therefore, are red-eyed. The sons, however, receive a Y chromosome from the father and hence no allele of white and they are thus white eyed. The gene for white follows exactly the transmission of the X chromosome. According to Morgan this is actually carried in the X chromosome.

The evidence that the white-eye gene allele is indeed located on the X chromosome was obtained by Bridges, an associate of Morgan. In crosses of white-eyed female and red-eyed male, an exceptional white-eyed female was sometimes found among the otherwise all red-eyed female offspring. Bridges proved by genetic and cytological experiments that such white-eyed females had an unusual XXY rather than the normal XX sex-chromosome complement in its cells (Fig. 43.16)

The XXY condition arises as follows : Sometimes homologous chromosomes do not separate during meiosis. This phenomenon is termed **non-disjunction**, as shown in figure (Fig. 43.17). Non-disjunction of X chromosomes in the white-eyed female parent results in an egg with two XX chromosomes having only the white eye alleles. When such an XX egg is fertilized, by a Y chromosome containing sperm which has no allele for eye colour, the resulting offspring is a white-eyed XXY individual that shows in *Drosophila* a female phenotype.

A mutant trait located on the X chromosome exhibits the same pattern of inheritance as the white-eye allele in *Drosophila.* Fathers pass the X-linked allele trait to their daughters but not to their sons. Mothers pass the allele of the trait to both sons and daughters. If the trait is recessive, a female has to be homozygous to express it, and she should receive the mutant allele from both her parents. On the other hand, any male receiving the mutant allele from his mother will express the trait as he has only one X chromosome.

BASIS OF SEX DETERMINATION

Sex Chromosomes and Autosomes

In diploid ($2n$) organisms, where the sexes are separate, a particular chromosome or a pair of chromosomes are concerned with sex determination. They are designated as **sex chromosomes.** The other chromosome pairs are called **autosomes.** For example, *Drosophila* (fruit fly) has four pairs of chromosomes. Three pairs are identical in both the sexes while the fourth pair differs. The pair that differs is known as sex chromosome pair, while the rest are called autosomes. Also in humans and other mammals the similar situation is found. Here females have two X chromosomes (*i.e.*, XX) whereas males have one X and a morphologically distinct Y chromosome (*i.e.*, XY). Y chromosome, though different in size and shape, pairs with X during meiosis. Thus females are XX and the males are XY.

Since males produce two types of gamètes either X or O in XO type, and X or Y in XY type.

They are known as **heterogametic** whereas females are **homogametic**, and produce only one type of gamete with an X chromosome.

Table. 43.4. Sex Chromosomes in Different Organisms.

Genotype of female		Genotype of male
Insects (*Drosophila*)	XX	XO
Round worms	XX	XO
Humans and other mammals	XX	XY

The females having XX genotype are termed as **homogametic**, and they produce only one type of gametes. All gametes contain X chromosome.

The males having XY genotype are termed as **heterogametic**, and they produce two kinds of gametes. 50 per cent of gametes contain X chromosomes and 50 per cent Y chromosomes.

The chromosomal determination of sex in XY organisms is as follows. Here the sex is determined at the time of fertilization. Since the two sexes are produced in equal numbers, there is equal probability for an egg to be fertilized by a sperm having an X or a Y chromosome.

Parent :	Female ×	Male
	XX	XY
Gametes :	Egg	Sperm
	X	X or Y
Offspring :	Female	Male
	XX	XY
Probability	50 per cent	50 per cent.

In birds and some reptiles, females are heterogametic while males are homogametic. To avoid confusion with the male heterogametic X-Y system, this is referred to as W-Z system. Here males are WW and females WZ respectively.

Sex determination in XX-XY organism. The sex determination in the offspring is being done by the chance union of an egg and a sperm. All eggs have a single X chromosome, whereas half of the sperms contain the X chromosome, and half the Y chromosome. The results are as follows :

(*i*) If the sperm containing X chromosome fertilises with the egg, the offspring is female.

(*ii*) If the sperm containing Y chromosome fertilises with the egg, the offspring is male.

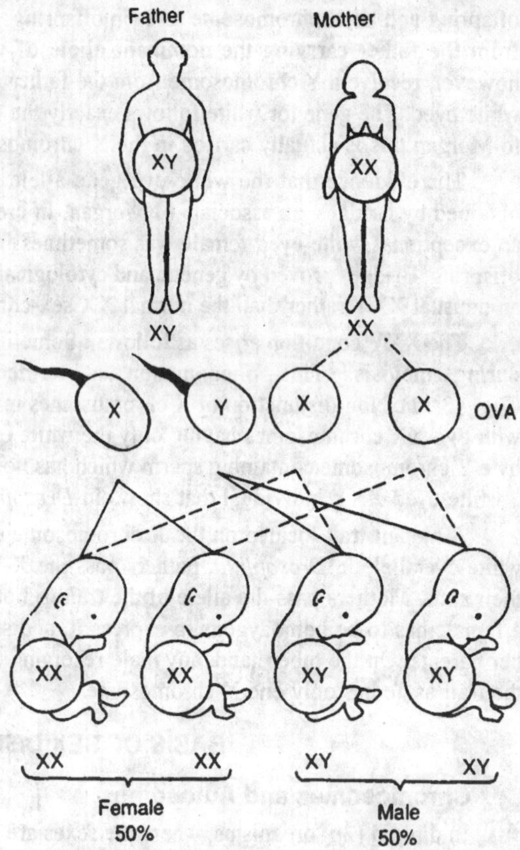

Fig. 43.18. Sex determination in man. Here all the ova carry X chromosome, but one-half of the sperm carry an X chromosome, and one-half carry a Y chromosome.

Morgan and *Drosophila*

Morgan (1910) began his genetical work with the fruit fly, *Drosophila melanogaster.* Thomas H. Morgan was an American Zoologist, and he was awarded with Nobel Prize in 1933 (in medicine or physiology) for his research in genetics. T. H. Morgan's study to work on *Drosophila* proved most rewarding for investigations in genetics. The fruit fly, *Drosophila melanogaster*, a small fly about 2 mm. in size seen hovering around over ripe fruits such as banana, papaya, mango, etc. The fly is attracted due to yeast cells that grow on the fruit surface.

Drosophila is a suitable material for the genetical research experiments due to the undermentioned reasons :

(*i*) The fruit flies breed quickly and prolifically.

(*ii*) A large number of flies are produced to each progeny. A pair of flies in a small milk bottle can produce in a single mating hundreds of progeny.

(*iii*) A new generation can be bred every two weeks.

(*iv*) Fly breeding could be done throughout the year inside laboratory with inexpensive material.

(*v*) Each cell of *Drosophila melanogaster* has four pairs of chromosomes, *i.e.*, I, II, III and IV. All different in size and easily distinguishable. Three pairs, *i.e.*, II, III and IV are autosomes and the fourth pair, *i.e.*, I, sex chromosomes; XX in females and XY in males. The Y chromosome is hook shaped.

Morgan and his associates with their breeding experiments on *Drosophila* concluded that genes are located on chromosomes in a linear fashion. Some of them lie close to each other and tendency to have linked together. They concluded that the genes are physically associated with chromosomes. Morgan's discovery of sex linked traits in *Drosophila* led to the identification of genes carried by each chromosome and the approximate location of each gene on a chromosome (chromosome maps).

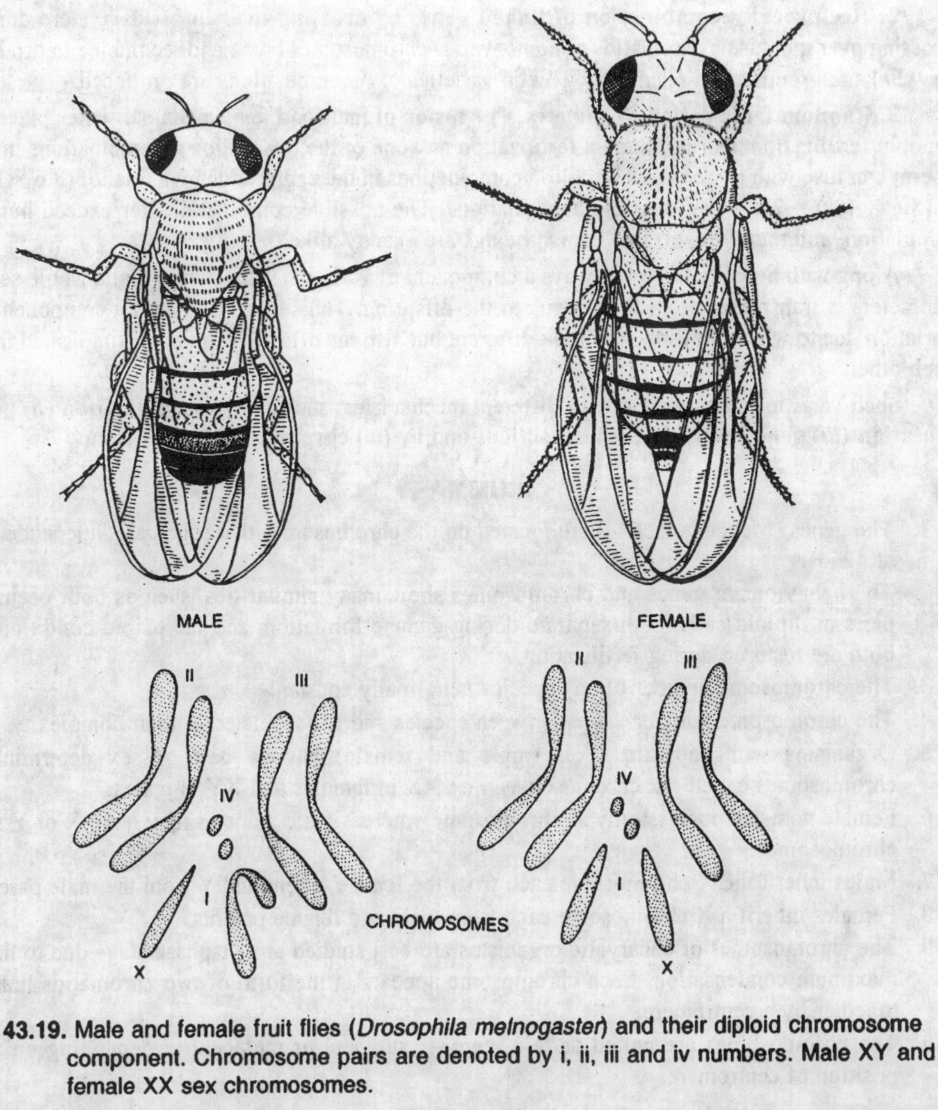

Fig. 43.19. Male and female fruit flies (*Drosophila melnogaster*) and their diploid chromosome component. Chromosome pairs are denoted by i, ii, iii and iv numbers. Male XY and female XX sex chromosomes.

GENETIC VARIATION

This is not always that offspring only resemble partners but they also vary from them. Of course, the resemblances are due to the units of information, the **genes,** they inherit. However, not all the inherited genes express themselves, *i.e.*, exhibit their phenotype. Some may be hidden or be recessive in the presence of dominant counter-parts, during expression. Genetic variation in sexually reproducing species develops primarily because parental genes are shuffled into new combinations, *i.e.*, new genotypes, in the offspring. The recombinations are produced by the routine reshuffling of genes as follows :

1. Independent assortment of chromosomes during meiosis. During the formation of gametes in the metaphase I of meiosis homologous chromosomes come together in pairs and then segregate into daughter cells independent of each other.

For example the maternal and paternal chromosomes of an organism with two pairs of chromosomes can recombine in $2^2 = 4$ possibilities in the gametes. With 3 pairs of chromosomes $2^3 = 8$ possible types of gametes are formed. The humans have 23 pairs of chromosomes which can give rise to 2^{23} or about 8.6 million combinations.

2. Reciprocal recombination of linked genes by crossing-over in meiosis. Here during crossing over in meiosis chromatids of homozygous chromosomes break and recombine to produce new linkage groups. As a result new genetic varieties or recombinations are produced.

3. Random fertilization of gametes. The fusion of male and female gametes takes place by random fertilization. During random fertilization any one of the 8.6 million recombinations in the sperm can fuse with any of the 8.6 million combinations in the egg producing a total of $(8.6 \times 10^6) \times (8.6 \times 10^6) = 70 \times 10^{12}$ possible combinations. The possible combinations far exceed human population, and therefore, no two human beings are exactly alike.

Along with heredity there is always a component of variation. This means that a whole set of characters is transmitted from the parents to the offspring. Thus, there is always a component of variation due to which they not only look different but also the offspring can be distinguished from each other.

Such variations may arise due to different mechanisms, such as (*i*) **recombination** (*ii*) **gene mutation** (*iii*) **gene environment interactions** and by (*iv*) **chromosomal aberrations.**

SUMMARY

1. The genes (Mendel's factors) are located on the chromosomes that segregate independently at meiosis.
2. The behaviour of genes and chromosomes show many similarities, such as both occur in pairs in diploid cells, both separate during gamete formation, and the paired condition of both are restored during fertilization.
3. The chromosome number of any species is normally constant.
4. The chromosome number varies between species and is not related to their complexity.
5. Organisms with separate sexes (male and female) have a pair of sex determining chromosomes called sex chromosomes, *i.e.*, XX in females and XY in males.
6. Female gametes possess only X chromosome whereas male gametes may have X or Y sex chromosomes.
7. Males inherit the X chromosome each from the female parent and Y from the male parent.
8. Females inherit a X chromosome each from male and female parents.
9. The chromosomes of eucaryotic organisms are best studied at metaphase stage due to their maximum condensation. Each chromosome appears in the form of two chromatids linked together by a centromere.
10. The chromosomes are called as telo, acro—, submeta or metacentric depending on the position of centromere.

11. Morgan carried out his experiments on the fruit fly (*Drosophila melanogaster*) and brought out the conclusions that eye colour is present on the X-chromosome, and follows a different pattern called sex-linked inheritance.
12. In all sex-linked or X-linked traits, males express them more often as they have only X chromosome.
    (*i*) The heterozygous female is normal but a carrier of the trait and can pass it on to both male and female offspring.
    (*ii*) For a female to have a disease, it has to be homozygous for the trait.
13. Non-disjunction at meiosis may give rise to abnormal individuals with monosomic (XO) or trisomic (XXY) condition giving rise to various disorders.
14. The genes located on the same chromosome are called linked genes and the phenomenon is known as 'linkage'. The linked genes move together and do not independently assort completely.
15. The linked genes show a recombination frequency of less than 50 per cent.
16. The linked genes can show recombination by crossing-over, *i.e.*, the physical change of parts of non-sister chromatids of homologous chromosomes just after synapsis at meiosis.
17. Even linked genes do not remain together due to crossing over. Cytologically crossing-over, is observed as a chiasma.
18. The crossing-over occurs at the equivalent locus of the non-sister chromatids.
19. When the genes are closer, there are less changes of crossing-over that occurs between them. The crossing-over between two genes near each other is directly proportional to the distance between them.
20. Genes on chromosome can be mapped by determining the recombination frequency between pairs of genes and arranging them in the order of their relative distance.
21. A linkage map shows a linear arrangement of linked genes on a chromosome. Distances between genes can be expressed in map unit, where one map unit is defined as one per cent recombination.
22. All genes on a chromosome form a linkage group. The number of linkage groups is equivalent to the haploid number of chromosomes in an organism. For example, in *Drosophila* there are four linkage groups.
23. Genetic variations occur due to recombinations and mutations. Recombinations take place due to independent assortment of chromosomes, crossing-over of genes during meiosis and by random fertilization of gametes.
24. Gametic variation also takes place by mutation. Mutation is a heritable change in the structure of a gene or chromosome, or change in chromosome number.
25. Gene mutations alter the information conveyed by a gene. Chromosomal mutations may be deletions, duplications, inversion or tanslocation. Mutations are random spontaneous changes but can also be induced by mutagens like X-ray, UV-rays and several chemicals.
26. Sex-linked or X-linked genes are transmitted with a definite regular pattern. Fathers pass the X-linked trait to daughters but not to sons, while the mothers pass the trait to both sons and daughters.
27. Certain extranuclear genes are present in mitochondria and plastids, found in the cytoplasm and are inherited by the offspring through egg cytoplasm only. This type of cytoplasmic inheritance is also known as maternal inheritance and does not exhibit Mendelian inheritance pattern.

28. Haploid organisms have only allele of a gene, and so their genotype directly expresses the phenotype. Phenotypic ratio of haploid offspring after meiosis give a ratio of 1 : 1 instead of the 3: 1 ratio in diploid organisms.

TERMS TO REMEMBER

Acentric chromosome. A chromosome having no centromere.

Allopolyploid. A polyploid having chromosome sets from different sources.

Amphidiploid. Having two different diploid ($2n$) chromosome sets.

Aneuploid. Having non-balanced number of chromosomes, and not an exact multiple of haploid set.

Aneuploidy. A condition where the cells have either one less or one more chromosome than the usual normal number.

Ascus. A sac that contains meiotic ascospores.

Autopolyploid. A polyploid where all chromosomes come from the same species.

Autosomes. Chromosomes other than the sex chromosomes. They are similar in both males and females.

Centromere. The region of a chromosome to which spindle fibre attaches.

Chiasma. The X-shaped structure found in diplotene following a cross-over.

Chromosomal mutation. The mutation that involves a change in the number or structure of a chromosome.

Colchicine. A chemical that inhibits the mitotic division.

Cytoplasmic inheritance. Inheritance that takes place the genes present in cell organelles or the particles present in the cytoplasm.

Deletion. The absence of chromosome segment.

Dicentric. Having two centromeres.

Disjunction. Regular separation and movement of chromosomes to opposite poles during cell division.

Euploid. Having a balanced number of chromosomes, *i.e.*, an exact multiple of the haploid chromosome set.

Extranuclear genes. The genes that present outside the nucleus, *e.g.*, in mitochondria and plastids.

Gene mutation. Mutation that involves a minor change in a DNA sequence, such as deletion, substitution or insertion of a base.

Heterogametic. Organisms with XY genotype that produce two different kinds of gametes, half containing X and half containing Y chromosomes.

Homogametic. Organisms with XX genotype producing only one kind of gametes, *i.e.*, containing only X chromosome.

Isogenic. Having identical genotypes.

Linked gene. Genes present in the same chromosome.

Linkage group. Genes that are present on the same chromosome make one linkage group. They inherit together.

Monosomy. The occurrence of a single chromosome instead of a pair of homologous chromosomes in a diploid cell.

Mutagens. A chemical or some other agent that causes mutations.

Mutations. A permanent heritable change in the DNA molecule of an organism.

Non-disjunction. The chromosomes that fail to go to opposite poles during cell division and lead to unequal number of chromosomes in the daughter cells.

Polyploidy. The occurrence of more than two haploid sets of chromosomes in a cell.

Sex chromosomes. The X or Y chromosome, or the chromosomes that determine sex in a species.

Sex-linked genes. Genes occurring on the X chromosomes. They are inherited in sex-linked patterns, and also known as X-linked genes.

Transition. Mutation of a purine to another purine, or pyrimidine to another pyrimidine.

Transversion. Mutation of a purine to a pyrimidine or pyrimidine to a purine.

Trisomy. Having three representatives of chromosome instead of two homologous of a chromosome in the cells of a normal diploid organism.

QUESTION BANK

N.B. Undermentioned questions are asked repeatedly in various Indian Universities and competitive examinations.

Very Short Answer Questions

1. Who discovered the chromosomes ?
2. Who had proposed the chromosomes theory of inheritance ?
3. Name the scientist, who had proposed the mutation theory.
4. What is the least number of chromosomes a eukaryotic organism can have?
5. Who was the scientist to associate a specific gene with a specific chromosome ?
6. What is the number of chromosomes found in human cells ?
7. You know that the number of chromosomes is specific to a species. Give the number of chromosomes in *Drosophila melanogaster*?
8. Define autosomes.
9. What are sex chromosomes ?
10. How many sets of chromosomes does a diploid cell have ?
11. What do you understand by the term aneuploidy ?
12. When a cell has more than two cells of chromosomes what is it called ?
13. What is the characteristic shape of Y chromosomes of *Drosophila* ?
14. Which genes are known as linked ?
15. What is the tendency of genes located in the same chromosome to stay together in heredity called ?
16. What are the two types of linkages ?
17. Which scientists had shown that genes lie in chromosomes ?
18. How many homologous chromosomes are present in male *Drosophila* ?
19. The gametes of which parent in human determine the sex of the offspring during fertilization ?
20. What is a locus ?
21. What is known as pea of animal kingdom?
22. What is a karyotype ?
23. Who for the first time suggested a close relation between genes and chromosomes?
24. What is a linkage map ?
25. Name the process which is antagonistic to linkage.
26. What is crossing over ?

27. What is variation ?
28. What organisms are called recombinations?
29. What term Hugo de Vries used to describe phenotypic changes that are heritable ?
30. On which plant Hugo de Vries did his work ?
31. Why is gene mutation called point mutation?
32. What are mutagens ?
33. What is an exchange of segments between two non homologous chromosomes called?
34. Name two sex-linked diseases.
35. What are homologous chromosomes ?
36. What is the primary constriction of a chromosome ?
37. How many chromatids are involved in crossing over at one chiasma ?
38. How many linkage groups are found in man ?
39. Name the two main types of mutations.
40. Name three kinds of mutagens.
41. When was the foundation of human genetics laid ?

ANSWERS

1. Hofmeister; **2.** Sutton and Boveri; **3.** Hugo de Vries; **4.** Two; **5.** T. H. Morgan; **6.** 46; **7.** Four; **8.** The chromosomes other than the sex chromosomes; **9.** The pair of chromosomes associated with sex determination; **10.** Two; **11.** Not having an exact number of chromosomes in a multiple of haploid set, either one less or one more chromosome than the usual number; **12.** Polyploid; **13.** J-shaped; **14.** The genes present on the same chromosome; **15.** Linkage; **16.** Complete and incomplete; **17.** Morgan and Bridges; **18.** Three pairs; **19.** Male parent; **20.** Site of a gene in a chromosome; **21.** *Drosophila*; **22.** When chromosomes are systematically arranged and grouped according to length and position of the centromere, it is called karyotype; **23.** Beadle and Tatum.; **24.** Diagrammatic representation of relative distance between the genes in the chromosomes in linear fashion; **25.** Crossing over; **26.** Mutual exchange of blocks of homologous genes between a pair of homologous chromosomes; **27.** The process by which closely related organisms come to differ amongst themselves; **28.** The organisms which express characters of both the parents; **29.** Mutation; **30.** *Oenothera lamarckiana* (Evening primrose); **31.** Since a gene is located at a fixed point on the chromosome; **32.** The agents which may be physical, chemical or biological that bring about attraction in the chemical structure of genes; **33.** Translocation; **34.** Haemophilia and colour blindness; **35.** Chromosomes similar in form, size and traits; **36.** Where a kinetochore lies to which spindle fibres join in cell division; **37.** Two; **38.** 23; **39.** Chromosomal and genic; **40.** Radiation, temperature and chemicals; **41.** 1901.

Short Answer Questions

1. Why *Drosophila* considered suitable for genetic experiments ?
2. How is sex determined in *Drosophila* or human beings ?
3. What are the types of chromosomes present in *Drosophila* ?
4. Why is man unable to pass a sex linked gene to his son ?
5. Why is *Neurospora* selected as a material for genetic studies ?
6. What is aneuploidy and polyploidy ? Give an example of each.
7. What are lampbrush chromosomes ?
8. Briefly explain the structure of a metaphase chromosome ?
9. Explain the terms (*a*) crossing-over (*b*) linkage group ?
10. How does recombination occur in linked-genes ?
11. Why is karyotype done at metaphase stage ? How has karyotype analysis helped in solving some of the human genetic disorders ?
12. How does banding pattern help in studying human chromosomes ?
13. The diploid chromosome number of garden pea is 14. How many linkage groups does this represent ?

14. The map distance between genes A and B is three units, between B and C 10 units, and between C and A 7 units. What is the order of genes on a linkage map ?
15. How is sex determined in human beings?
16. A normal man marries a woman who is a carrier for colour blindness. What will be the phenotypes of the children born to them.
17. If marriage has taken place between a colour blind female and a normal male what will the offspring be ?
18. In humans the sex of the child is determined by the father and not by the mother. How ?

Long Answer Questions

1. What is linkage ? What is its relationship with independent assortment and crossing-over ?
2. Give a comprehensive account of the types of crossing-over.
3. Discuss the salient features of the mechanism of crossing-over.
4. Enumerate the modern approaches to human genetics.
5. Give an account of the types of mutation.
6. What are mutagens ? Give the nature of chemical and physical mutagens.
7. Give a comprehensive account of the role of mutations in evolution.
8. What are continuous and discontinuous variations ? Give details.
9. Give a brief and complete account of sex-linked inheritance.
10. Give a comprehensive account of sex-linkage of *Drosophila*.
11. Give a comprehensive account of cytoplasmic inheritance.
12. Describe the structure of eucaryotic chromosome.
13. Discuss the functions of the chromosome.
14. What is the significance of chromosome number ? Write down the chromosome number of four animals and four plants.
15. Point out the factors affecting the crossing-over.
16. What are linkage groups ?
17. Give the structure of chromosomes of man.
18. Write short notes on : (*a*) polyploidy in man, (*b*) Down syndrome, (*c*) Turner's syndrome, (*d*) chimera, (*e*) gynandromorphism in man.
19. What is mutation ? How this phenomenon was discovered ?
20. What is the role of mutation in agriculture and animal husbandry ?
21. How cytoplasm is held responsible for inheritance of characters ?
22. With the help of diagram only, give the morphological types of the chromosomes according to the position of centromere.
23. Give the diagram of a cross involving linkage and crossing-over in *Drosophila*.
24. With the help of diagram only, show the human chromosomes.
25. Give a cross between red-eyed female and white-eyed male showing sex-linked inheritance in *Drosophila*.
26. Give a cross between white-eyed female and red-eyed male showing sex-linked inheritance in *Drosophila*.
27. What is a chromosome map ? What is its basis ? How can it be prepared ?
28. Describe various kinds of gene mutations.
29. Discuss the modes of inducing mutations.
30. A heterozygous red-eyed *Drosophila melanogaster* female fly is crossed with a white-eyed male.
    (*a*) What type of cross is this ?
    (*b*) Represent the cross schematically.
    (*c*) Give the genotypes and phenotypes of the progeny.
    (*d*) What special type of inheritance does this trait show in this fly.

Multiple Choice Questions (Objective Type Questions)

1. The number of chromosomes in *Drosophila melanogaster* is
   (*a*) six (*b*) eight
   (*c*) ten (*d*) twelve.
2. *Homo sapiens* has
   (*a*) 23 pairs of chromosomes (*b*) 24 pairs of chromosomes
   (*c*) 25 pairs of chromosomes (*d*) 26 pairs of chromosomes
3. Sex chromosomes in human male are known as
   (*a*) XX (*b*) XY
   (*c*) XO (*d*) XZ
4. The prokaryotic chromosomes are found in
   (*a*) *Bacillus* (*b*) *Nostoc*
   (*c*) *Escherichia* (*d*) all of above.
5. Extrachromosomal hereditary determinants are known as
   (*a*) plastids (*b*) ribosomes
   (*c*) plasmids (*d*) none of above.
6. Eucaryotic chromosomes are found in
   (*a*) cyanobacteria (*b*) blue-green algae
   (*c*) fungi (*d*) none of above.
7. Chromosomes are best seen in
   (*a*) interphase (*b*) prophase
   (*c*) metaphase (*d*) telophase.
8. The components of the chromosome that controls heredity is
   (*a*) proteins (*b*) DNA
   (*c*) RNA (*d*) none of above.
9. A chromatid has
   (*a*) one chromosome (*b*) two chromonemata
   (*c*) four chromonemata (*d*) many chromonemata
10. Homologous chromosomes similar in both sexes are called
    (*a*) androsomes (*b*) autosomes
    (*c*) heterosomes (*d*) none of above
11. The term mutation was introduced by
    (*a*) Mendel (*b*) Hugo de Vries
    (*c*) Darwin (*d*) Lamarck.
12. Point mutations are caused by
    (*a*) substitution (*b*) deletion
    (*c*) insertion (*d*) all of above.
13. Mutation can be induced by
    (*a*) radiation (*b*) temperature
    (*c*) chemicals (*d*) all of above.
14. Crossing over during meiosis occurs in
    (*a*) leptotene (*b*) zygotene
    (*c*) pachytene (*d*) diplotene.

Answers

1. (*b*) **2.** (*a*) **3.** (*b*) **4.** (*d*) **5.** (*c*) **6.** (*c*) **7.** (*c*) **8.** (*b*) **9.** (*a*) **10.** (*b*)
11. (*b*) **12.** (*d*) **13.** (*d*) **14.** (*d*)

44
CHAPTER

Nature of Gene: Its Expression and Regulation

As we know, the children acquire the characteristic physical features of their parents or grand-parents. The inheritance of these hereditary characters can be explained on the basis of ancestral genes that are found to be arranged on chromosomes, and they make the total genomic make-up of the organism. The specific questions may be asked about these genes such as what are their functions and what is their chemical nature, and how the characters are transmitted from the parent to the progeny ?

Now this is an established fact that parents transmit the heritable characters to the offspring.

Such transmission forms the basis of maintaining continuity among the numbers of a species.

Factors or genes responsible for this purpose are located on the chromosomes and through the gametes enter a diploid zygote cell.

This process is found in all sexually reproducing organisms.

Thus each offspring receives 50 per cent component of chromosomes and the genes from male parent and 50 per cent from female parent.

On the basis of modern genetic knowledge a gene is expected to have following important characteristics :

1. A gene should be able to store and express information of the heritable characters of living organisms.

2. A gene should be capable to make its own replica so that a copy of it may be transmitted to the offspring.

3. A gene should have a mechanism so that it can undergo mutations which will generate the biological variation essential for evolution.

DNA (deoxyribonucleic acid) and RNA (ribonucleic acid) are the principal genetic materials of living organisms. They are chemically called **nucleic acids** and are complex molecules larger than most proteins and contain carbon, oxygen, hydrogen, nitrogen and phosphorus. The nucleic acids were first isolated by **F. Miescher** in 1868 from the nuclei of pus cells and gained their name from the fact that they are acidic and were first identified in nuclei.

Genetic Material and its Nature

Highly purified DNA extracted from a wide variety of plants, animals, bacteria and viruses has been found to be complex macromolecular or polymeric chemical compound which contains, four kinds of similar building blocks (monomers) called **deoxyribotids** or **deoxyribonucleotides**. Each deoxyribonucleotide is made up of three molecules : **a phosphoric acid molecule** (biologically called phosphate and discovered by **Levene** in 1910's); a pentose sugar called 2 **deoxyribose** (discovered by **Levene** in 1910's); and **pyrimidine** and **purine** nitrogenous bases (discovered by **Fischer** in 1880's). Four major kinds of nitrogenous bases have been found in four kinds of deoxyribonucleotides of DNA : two are heterocyclic and two-ringed purines, **adenine** (A) and **guanine** (G), and two one-ringed pyrimidines, **cytosine** (C) and **thymine** (T).

It is now known that the material in the genes responsible for heredity is capable of performing *three* main functions. They are as follows :

1. The genes should be able to replicate and be inherited by the progeny.

2. The genes should be susceptible to an occasional change by mutation and such a change should be inheritable.

3. The genes should be able to carry all the information necessary for the functions of a cell.

Formerly this was thought that proteins could make an ideal genetic material. As we know, proteins are made up of twenty amino acids and thus the diversity that could be generated on the basis of the number of residues of each amino acid in a given protein and the sequence of amino acids would be enormous. However, this has been proved on the basis of experimental evidence that deoxyribonucleic acid (DNA) is the genetic material.

Bacterial Transformation : Griffith's Experiment

The lines of inquiry that led to an understanding of the chemical nature of genetic material arose from a study of the pestilent organism *Diplococcus pneumoniae.* This bacterium causes pneumonia in mammals. In 1928, Frederick Griffith, found that there are two strains of *D. pneumoniae*, one that forms smooth colonies protected by a capsule, and the other one that formed irregular or rough colonies without a capsule when grown on a suitable medium in petri dishes. When injected into mice (A) only capsulated smooth cells (virulent) produced the disease, but not the non-virulent rough cells (B). On the other hand when the heat killed capsulated (virulent) smooth cells were mixed with non-virulent rough cells (D) and then were injected in the mice the disease was produced. This shows that some factor from the dead capsulated smooth cells, converted the living non-virulent rough cells into living smooth capsulated (virulent) cells.

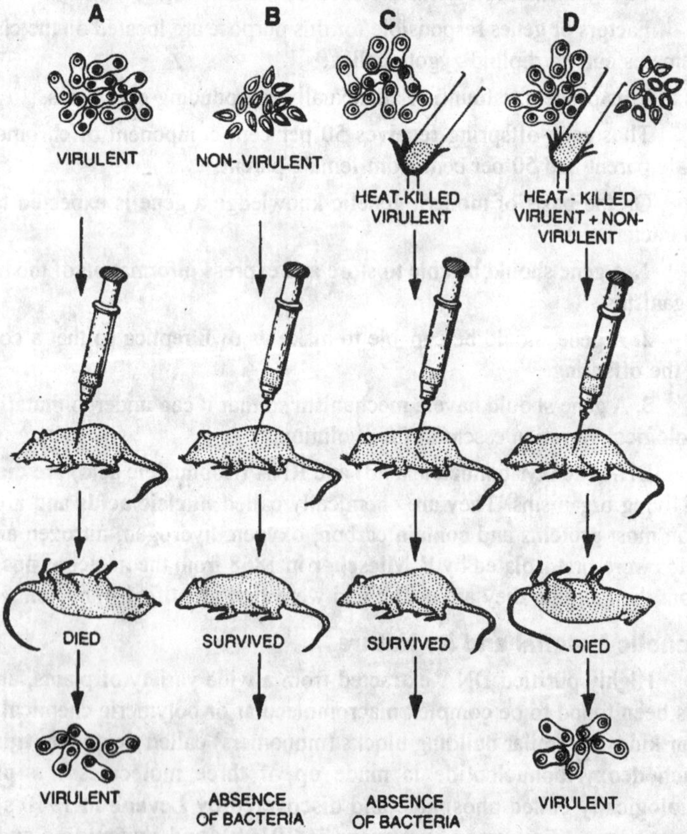

Fig. 44.1. Griffith's experiments with *Diplococcus pneumoniae* and mice.

In 1944, Avery, McCarty and Macleod supported the Griffith's experiment by molecular explanations. They found that the DNA isolated from the heat killed smooth (S) cells, when added to rough (R) cells changed their surface character from rough (R) to smooth (S), and also made them virulent. By this experiment, this was shown that DNA was the genetic material responsible for inducing the smooth (S) character of the cells and their property of virulence in mice. Their experiment proved that bacterial transformation involves transfer of a part of DNA from the dead bacterium (*i.e.*, donor) to the living bacterium (*i.e.*, recipient), that expresses the character of dead cell, and so is known as a **recombinant.**

The phenomenon by which the DNA isolated from one type of cell, when introduced into another type, is able to bestow some of the properties of former to the latter. This phenomenon is known as **transformation.**

Live S + mice ⟶ mice died

Live R + mice ⟶ mice survived

Heat killed S + mice ⟶ mice survived

Heat killed S + live R + mice ⟶ mice died.

Blood of the dead mice showed the presence of live S bacteria.

Another definitive evidence came from experiment on T_2 bacteriophage (virus). This is as follows :

Viral-infecting Agent is DNA : Hershey and Chase Experiment

A bacteriophage (T_2 virus) infects the bacterium *Escherichia coli.* After infection, the virus multiplies and the T_2 phages are released with the lysis of the bacterial cells. As we know, the T_2 phage contains both DNA and proteins. Now the question arises, which of the two components has the information to programme for the multiplication of more viral particles.

To solve this problem, Hershey and Chase (1952) devised an experiment with two different preparations of T_2 phage. In one preparation they made protein part radioactive and in the other preparation the DNA was made radioactive. Thereafter a culture of *E. coli* was made infected by these two phage preparations. Immediately after infection, and before lysis of bacteria the *E. coli* cells were gently agitated in a mixer so that the adhering phage particles were loosened and then the culture was centrifuged. With the result the heavier pellets of infected bacterial cells were settled down in the bottom of the tube. The lighter viral particles and those particles which did not enter the bacterial cells were found in the supernatant. It was found that when T_2 phage with radioactive DNA was used to infect *E. coli* in the experiment, the heavier bacterial pellet was also radioactive. On the other hand when T_2 phage with radioactive protein was used, the bacterial pellet had very little radioactivity and most of the radioactivity was found in supernatant. This experiment has proved, that during infection with T_2 phage, it is DNA that actually entered the bacteria when such infected bacterial cells were developed further they lysed and new phage particles were formed. This famous experiment conducted by Hershey and Chase (1952) has proved that it is the viral DNA and not protein that contains information for the production of more T_2 phage particles hence DNA is genetic material. However, in some viruses (*e.g.*, TMV, influenza virus and polio virus) RNA serves as genetic material.

Hershey and Chase conducted two experiments. In one experiment *E. coli* was grown in a medium containing the radio-isotope S^{35} and in the other experiments *E. coli* was grown in a medium containing the radio-isotope P^{32}. In these experiments *E. coli* cells were made infected with T_2 phage released from *E. coli* cells grown in S^{35} medium have S^{35} in their protein capsid, and those from P^{32} medium had P^{32} in their DNA. When these phages were used to infect new *E.coli* cells in normal medium, the bacterial cells which had infection by S^{35} labelled phages showed the radioactivity in their cell wall and not in cytoplasm. Whereas the bacteria infected with P^{32} labelled phages had shown the reverse condition. Thus it can be said that when T_2 phage infects the bacterial cell, its protein capsid remains outside of the bacterial cell but its DNA enters the cytoplasm of the bacterium. When the infected cells of bacteria gets lysed, new complete viral particles (T_2 phages) are formed. This proves, that viral DNA carries the information for synthesis of more copies of DNA and protein capsids. This shows that DNA is genetic material.

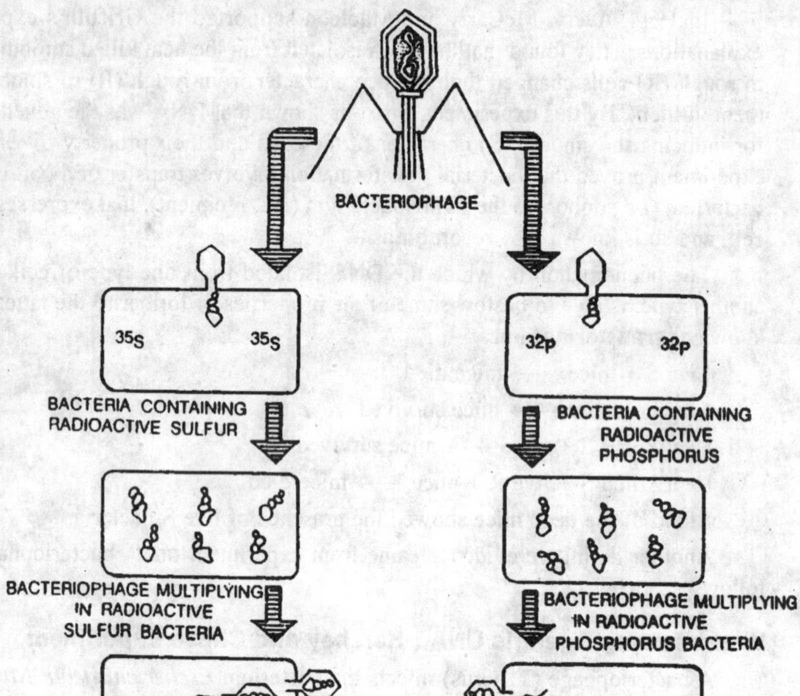

Fig. 44.2. Hershey and Chase's experiments show that DNA is hereditary material in bacteriophages.

That part of each nucleotide which contains a nitrogenous base and deoxyribose is called **deoxyribonucleoside**.

The four deoxyribonucleotides besides occurring in DNA molecule, occur also in nucleoplasm and cytoplasm, but in their triphosphate forms such as deoxyadenosine triphosphate (dATP), deoxyguanosine triphosphate (dGTP), deoxycytidine triphosphate (dCTP) and thymidine triphosphate (TTP). The significance of occurrence of deoxyribonucleotides in triphosphate forms lies in fact that during DNA polymerase enzyme can act only on triphosphates of deoxyribonucleotides.

This experiment shows that only the phage DNA enters the bacterial cell and not the protein coat. It depicts clearly that DNA alone is responsible for the synthesis of new viruses inside the bacterial cells. This shows that DNA is genetic material and not protein. In tobacco mosaic virus

(TMV) the inner core is made up of RNA instead of DNA, hence in this case RNA is genetic material.

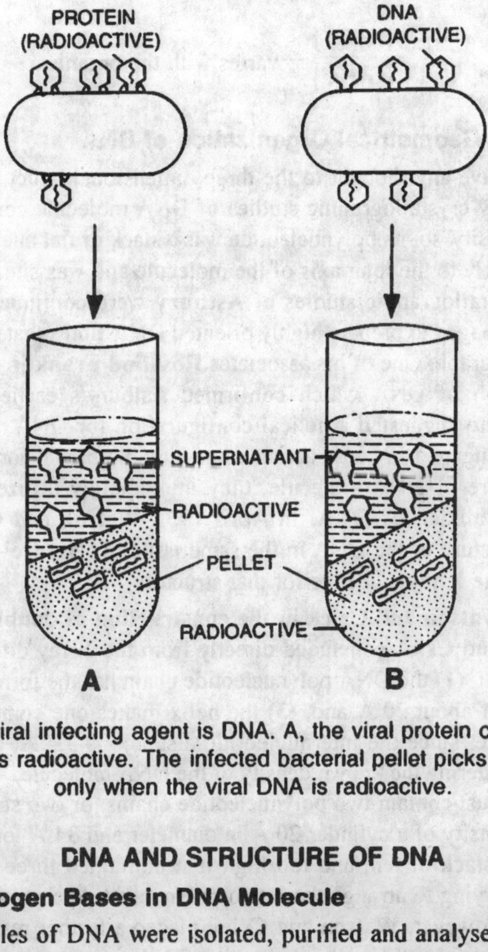

Fig. 44.3. The viral infecting agent is DNA. A, the viral protein coat is radioactive; B, viral DNA is radioactive. The infected bacterial pellet picks up radioactivity only when the viral DNA is radioactive.

DNA AND STRUCTURE OF DNA

Molar Ratios of Nitrogen Bases in DNA Molecule

When many samples of DNA were isolated, purified and analysed by various techniques, such as paper chromatography, etc., it was found by **Hotchkiss** and **Chargaff** in 1948 that contrary to **Levene's** (1920's) tetranucleotide theory which considered DNA as a monotonous polymer having four DNA bases in approximately equal molar proportions, the four nucleotide bases are not necessarily present in DNA in exactly equal proportions. Thus **Chargaff** reported that the DNA extracted from calf-thymus nuclei contains the four bases in following molar proportion : 28% adenine, 24% guanine, 20% cytosine and 28% thymine. When he analyzed the DNA samples of varied animals, he found that the exact base composition of DNA differs according to its biological source.

These different values of A, G, C, and T in different samples of DNA are suggesting that DNA rather than being a monotonous polymer, carries genetic information in the form of specific nucleotide base sequences.

Erwin Chargaff in 1949 proposed Chargaff's rules regarding the composition of bases in DNA are as follows :

(*i*) Total amount of purine nucleotides always equals the total amount of pyrimidine nucleotides, *i.e.*, [A] + [G] = [T] + [C] (*ii*) The proportion of A is equal to T and so also of G is equal to C, but amount of [A] + [T] is not necessarily equal to [G] + [C].

Therefore [A] = [T] : [G] = [C]

But $$\frac{[A]+[T]}{[G]+[C]} = \text{varies with the organism}$$

Physical, Molecular or Geometrical Organization of DNA

The first person to give any thought to the three dimensional structure of DNA was **W. T. Astbury** who by his X-ray crystallographic studies of DNA molecule concluded in 1940's that because DNA has high density, so, its polynucleotide was a stack of flat nucleotides, each of which was oriented perpendicularly to the long axis of the molecule and was situated every 3.4 Å along the stack. The X-ray crystallographic studies of **Astbury** were continued by **Wilkins** and his associates (1953), who managed to prepare highly oriented DNA fibres that allowed them to obtain an X-ray diffraction photograph. One of his associates **Rosalind Franklin** obtained a superior X-ray diffraction photograph of DNA which confirmed Astbury's earlier inference of 3.4 Å internucleotide distance and suggested a helical configuration for DNA molecule. **Watson** and **Crick** who were already engaged in constructing some suitable model for DNA structure, when observed Franklin's picture of DNA molecule, they immediately utilized that information in constructing a molecular model for DNA. In April 1953 **Watson** and **Crick** published their conclusions about the structure of the DNA in the same issue of **'Nature'** in which **Wilkins** and his colleagues presented the X-ray evidence for that structure.

Considerations of Watson and Crick in the construction of double helical structure of DNA molecule. Watson and **Crick** concluded directly from the X-ray diffraction photograph of DNA taken by Franklin that **(1)** the DNA polynucleotide chain has the form of a regular helix, **(2)** the helix has a diameter of about 20 Å and, **(3)** the helix makes one complete turn every 3.4 Å along its length, and hence, since the internucleotide distance is 3.4 Å, consists a stack of ten nucleotides per turn. Considering the known density of the DNA molecule, **Watson** and **Crick** next concluded that the helix must contain two polynucleotide chains, or two stacks of ten nucleotides each per turn, since the density of a cylinder 20 Å in diameter and 34 Å long would be too low if it contained but a single stack of ten, and too high if it contained three or more stacks of ten nucleotides each. Before trying to arrange these two polynucleotide chains into a regular helix of the required dimensions, however, **Watson** and **Crick** placed a further restriction on their model — a restriction that derived from their knowledge that DNA, is after all, the genetic material. If DNA is to contain heredity information so they reasoned, and if that information is inscribed as a specific sequence of the four bases along the polynucleotide chain, then the molecular structure of DNA must be able to accommodate any arbitrary sequence of bases along its polynucleotide chains. Otherwise, the capacity of DNA as an information carrier would be too severely limited. Hence, they felt the need of construction of such a regular helix that though composed of two polynucleotide chains containing an arbitrary sequence of nucleotide bases every 3.4 Å along their length, would nevertheless has a constant diameter of 20 Å. Since the dimension of the purine ring is greater than that of the pyrimidine ring **Watson** and **Crick** hit upon the idea that the two chain helix could have a constant diameter if there existed a complementary relation between the two nucleotide stacks, so that at every level one stack harbours a purine base and the other a pyrimidine base. Finally, to endow the helix with thermodynamic stability, the structure would have ample opportunities for the formation of hydrogen bonds between amino-or-hydroxyl hydrogen and keto-oxygens or immuno-nitrogens of the purines and pyrimidine bases. These considerations led them to construct a double helix model for the molecular structure of DNA molecule.

Watson and Crick's Structural Model of DNA

In DNA molecule the adjacent deoxyribonucleotides are joined in a chain by phosphodiester bridges or bonds which link the 5 carbon of the deoxyribose of one mononucleotide unit with the 3 carbon of the deoxyribose of the next mononucleotide unit. According to **Watson** and **Crick** DNA molecule consists of two such polynucleotide chains wrapped helically around each other, with the sugar-phosphate chain on the outside (forming ribbon like back bone of double helix) and purines and pyrimidines on the inside of the helix (projecting between two sugar-phosphate backbones as transverse bars). The two polynucleotide strands are held together by hydrogen bonds between specific pairs of purines and pyrimidines.

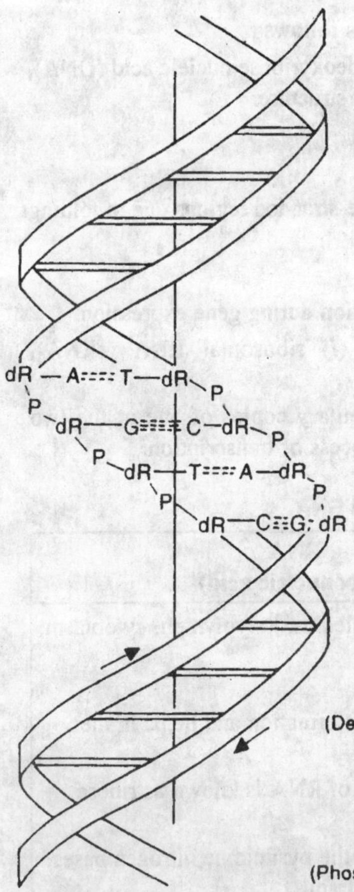

Fig. 44.4. Watson and Crick's double helical DNA molecule.

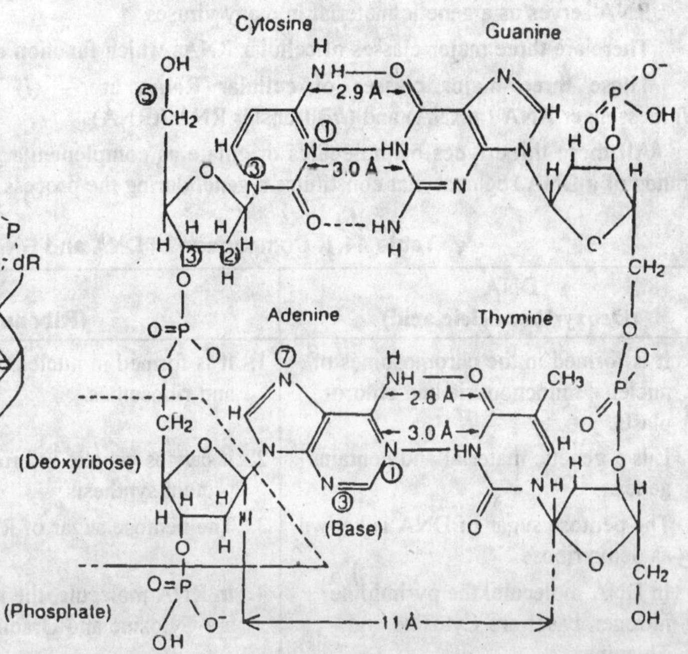

Fig. 44.5. Segment of a DNA molecule.

The hydrogen bonds between purines and pyrimidines are such that adenine can bond only to thymine by two hydrogen bonds, and guanine can bond only to cytosine by three hydrogen bonds and no other alternative is possible between them. The specificity of the kind of hydrogen bonds that can be formed assures that for every adenine in one chain there will be thymine in the other. For every guanine in first chain there will be a cytosine in the other and so on. Thus, the two chains are complementary to each other; that is sequence of necleotides in one chain dictates the sequence of nucleotides in the other. The two strands run antiparallely – that is, have opposite directions. One strand has phosphodiester linkage in $3' - 5'$ direction, while other strand has phosphodiester linkage in just reverse or $5' - 3'$ direction. Further, both polynucleotides strands remain separated by 20 Å distance. The coiling of double helix is right handed and a complete turn occurs every 34 Å. Since each nucleotide occupies 3.4 Å distance along the length of a polynucleotide strand, ten mononucleotides occur per complete turn.

The most crucial outcome of Watson and Crick's double helix model of DNA was the implicit suggestion for a mechanism by which the genetic material (DNA) can be copied and transmitted to progeny. This is known as **DNA replication**.

RNA AND STRUCTURE OF RNA

The characteristic features of ribonucleic acid (RNA) are as follows :

Ribonucleic acid (RNA) is another nucleic acid type. Like deoxyribose nucleic acid (DNA), this is a polynucleotide but several differences are found in their structure.

In RNA, the pentose sugar is ribose and not deoxyribose

RNA contains uracil in place of thymine.

Most RNAs are generally single stranded with partial double-stranded regions due to folding back of its single chain.

RNA serves as a genetic material in many viruses.

There are three major classes of cellular RNAs which function during gene expression.

These three major classes of cellular RNAs are – (*i*) ribosomal RNA (rRNA), (*ii*) messenger RNA (mRNA) and (*iii*) transfer RNA (tRNA).

All these three types of molecules originate as complementary copies of one of the two strands of a DNA segment that constitutes a gene, during the process of transcription.

Table 44.1. Comparison of DNA and RNA

DNA (Deoxyribonucleic acid)	**RNA (Ribonucleic acid)**
1. It is formed in the chromosomes of nucleus, mitochondria and chloroplasts.	1. It is formed in nucleolus, karyolymph, cytoplasm and ribosomes.
2. It is a genetic material and contains genes.	2. It carries genetic information and helps in the protein synthesis.
3. The pentose sugar of DNA is known as deoxyribose.	3. The pentose sugar of RNA is known as ribose.
4. In DNA molecule, the pyrimidine nitrogen bases are Cytosine and Thymine.	4. In RNA molecule, the pyrimidine nitrogen bases are Cytosine and Uracil.
5. The nucleotides which make a molecule of DNA are (*i*) deoxyadenosine monophosphate (*ii*) deoxyguanosine monophosphate, (*iii*) deoxycytidine monophosphate and (*iv*) deoxythymidine monophosphate.	5. The nucleotides which make a molecule of RNA are (*i*) adenosine monophosphate, (*ii*) guanosine monophosphate, (*iii*) cytidine monophosphate and (*iv*) Uridine monophosphate.
6. The paired nucleotides of a DNA molecule are arranged in a double stranded helix.	6. The nucleotides of a RNA molecule are arranged in a single chain.
7. Three main types of DNA are – nuclear (n DNA), mitochondrial (m DNA). and chloroplast (c DNA).	7. Three main types of RNA are – messenger (m RNA), transfer (t RNA) and ribosomal (r RNA).

This shows that RNA will have the same sequence as the other strand of DNA, except that uracil will replace thymine against adenine.

The abovementioned RNA types can be differentiated on the basis of their size, sedimentation behaviour and genetic functions.

Ribosomal RNA (rRNA) is generally the largest and most prevalent of the cellular RNA species. This is an important structural component of ribosomes, the sites where translation occurs during protein synthesis.

Messenger RNA (mRNA) is responsible to carry the genetic message from DNA to the ribosome. Their length and sequence vary depending upon the gene which is being transcribed into m RNA.

Transfer RNA (tRNA) is the smallest of the three types. It carries amino acids to the ribosomes during translation. This species of RNA contains number of modified bases.

REPLICATION OF DNA

As a carrier of genetic informations DNA has following two important functions :

1. Heterocatalytic function. When DNA directs the synthesis of chemical molecules other than itself (*e.g.*, synthesis of RNA, proteins, etc.), then such functions of DNA are called heterocatalytic functions. **2. Autocatalytic function.** The functions of DNA which direct the synthesis of DNA itself, are called autocatalytic functions. Here, we are concerned only with autocatalytic function of DNA.

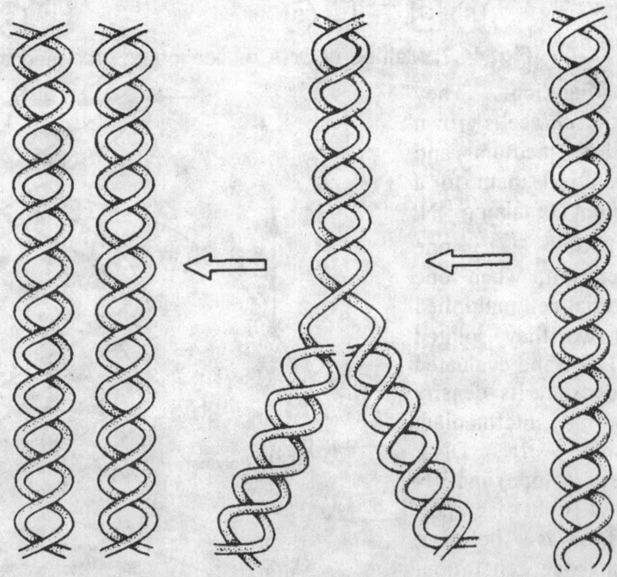

Fig. 44.6. Replication of the DNA molecule. The old helix unwinds (middle) and the new helices are being formed.

The copying mechanism proposed by Watson and Crick is quite simple. When the two strands of DNA separate and each strand serves as a template to form a new strand, one can easily predict how the new strand would look. Since the bases in the old strand would automatically decide the complementary bases that would appear in the new strand on the basis that A will pair with T and G will pair with C. Thus, one DNA molecule gives rise to two DNA molecules identical to that of the parent. However, in the newly formed daughter DNA molecule, one strand will be old (that comes from the parent) and another will be new. This is known as **a semi-conservative model of replication.**

Meselson and Stahl (1958) Experiment. This experiment showed that DNA replication is **semi-conservative.** In their experiment these scientists grew the bacterium *Escherichia coli* in a medium containing nitrogen salts labelled with the heavy isotope, *i.e.*, ^{15}N. ^{15}N was incorporated into both strands of DNA and this DNA was heavier than the DNA obtained from *E. coli* cells grown in ^{14}N medium (*i.e.*, common isotope of N). The heavier DNA was separated by

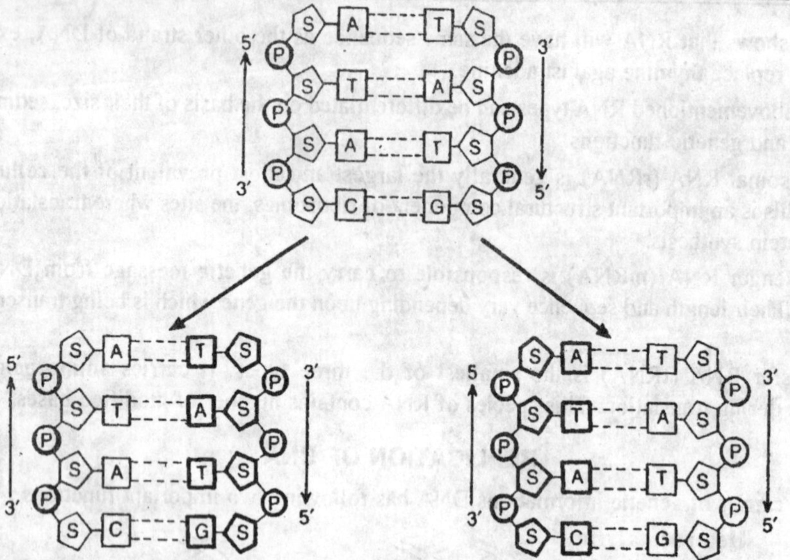

Fig. 44.7. Method of DNA replication as proposed by Watson and Crick.

centrifugation. They took *E. coli* cells grown in ^{15}N medium and transferred them to a medium containing ^{14}N.

After one generation, when one bacterial cell multiplied into two, they isolated the DNA and evaluated its density. Its density was intermediate between ^{15}N DNA (heavy isotope) and ^{14}N DNA (light isotope). This was because, during one generation, new DNA molecules with one ^{15}N old strand and a complementary ^{14}N new strand were formed and this had an intermediate density between the ^{15}N DNA in both the strands and ^{14}N DNA in both the strands. This experiment showed the semi-conservative nature of DNA replication.

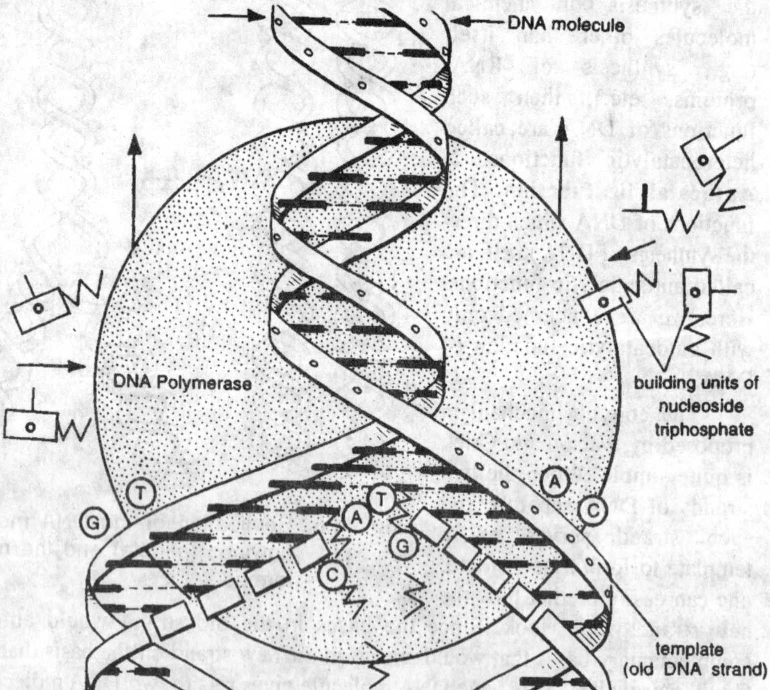

Fig. 44.8. Semi-conservative method of replication of DNA molecule.

Details of DNA Replication in Procaryotes and Eucaryotes

DNA replication in procaryotes and viruses. The procaryotes, such as bacteria possess a single circular molecule of DNA. This type of DNA molecule is much smaller in comparison to a single chromosome of a eucaryote. In this circular DNA molecule there is only one origin of replication. From this point of origin, two replication forks move in opposite direction and ultimately meet at half way round the circle at the termination points. Since each replication fork makes a replica of the original chromosome and therefore in the end the identical daughter DNA circles are formed. In viruses also DNA is in the form of single strand and there is only one origin of replication.

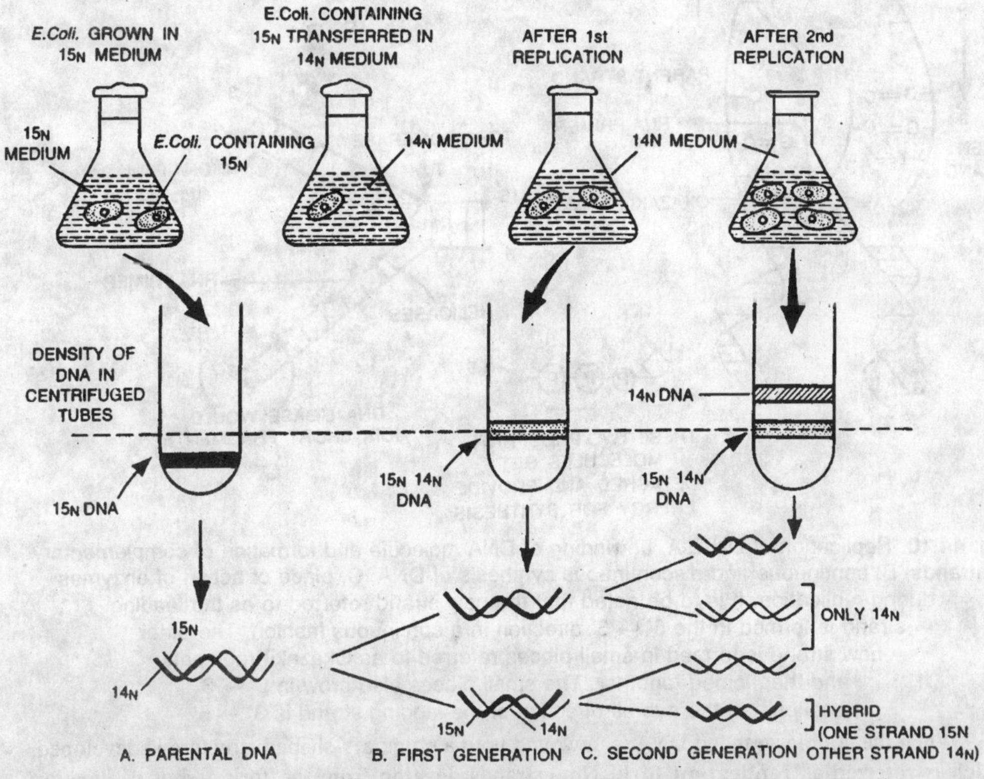

Fig. 44.9. Meselson and Stahl's experiment to demonstrate the semi-conservative replication of DNA.

DNA replication in eucaryotes. In eucaryotes with giant DNA molecules, there are several origins of replication and they can merge with each other while replication is under progress.

The second point is that the two strands of DNA should separate, before each acts as a template for the synthesis of a new strand. For this purpose of unwinding there are enzymes called **helicases** that unwind the helix. There are other enzymes known as **topoisomerases** which are responsible for breaking and resealing of one strand of DNA.

A **primer** is also needed for replication of DNA, that is also formed on the template. This primer is actually a short stretch of RNA formed on the DNA template and the enzyme that polymerases the RNA building blocks, *i.e.*, A, U, G, C into the primer is known as **primase.** The primers are later removed, and the gaps so left are filled up with deoxyribonucleotides make DNA strand continuous.

Synthesis of new strand. The synthesis of new strand of DNA takes place as follows : Here the enzyme DNA polymerase plays an important role in adding the building blocks to the primer in a sequence as influenced by the template. Formation of the complementary DNA strand cannot begin without the formation of an RNA primer.

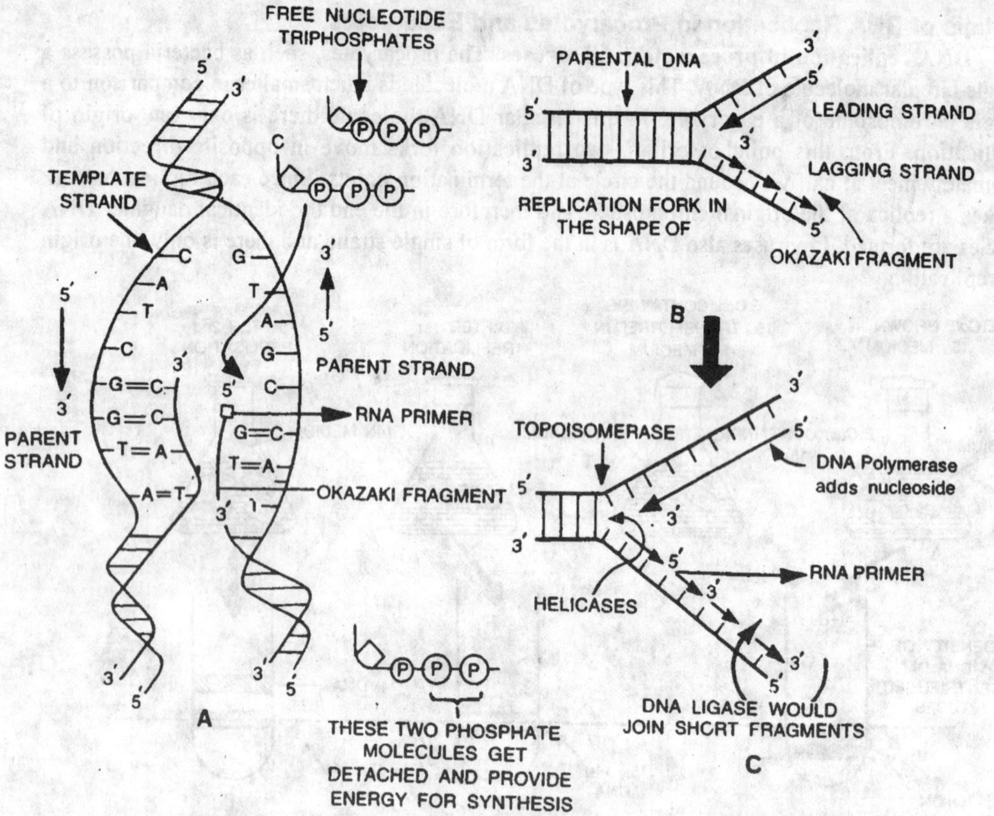

Fig. 44.10. Replication of DNA. A, unwinding of DNA molecule and formation of complementary strands; B, continuous and discontinuous synthesis of DNA; C, place of action of enzymes during replication. It is to be noted that the new strand referred to as the leading strand is formed in the $5' \rightarrow 3'$ direction in a continuous fashion. The other new strand is formed in small pieces referred to as Okazaki fragments and then joined together. The small pieces also grow in $5' \rightarrow 3'$ direction, but the overall direction of the lagging strand is $3' \rightarrow 5'$.

When the double stranded DNA is unwound upto a point, a Y-shaped structure is developed, which is referred as **replication fork.** New strands develop from the fork and as replication progresses this appears as if the point of divergence at fork is moving. The enzyme DNA polymerase can polymerise the nucleotides only in the $5' \rightarrow 3'$ direction. Since the two strands of the DNA are formed in antiparallel orientation, the two new strands will form by the growth taking place in opposite directions. Here the enzyme forms one new strand in a continuous stretch in the $5' \rightarrow 3'$ direction and this is referred to as the **leading strand.**

On the other parent strand, the enzyme forms short stretches of DNA once again in the $5' \rightarrow 3'$ direction starting from an RNA primer. The primer is synthesized by the enzyme primase. These DNA short fragments are known as **Okazaki fragments**, and the strand is called as **lagging strand**, because it is synthesized in small pieces and then joined to each other. These short fragments of DNA are joined together by the enzyme DNA ligase after replacing the RNA primer with DNA.

Proof reading and DNA repair. During DNA replication the specificity of base-pairing introduces a high degree of accuracy. Any error that may be one in 10,000, is corrected by removing the wrong base and replacing the correct one by repair enzymes.

However, bacterial DNA polymerase can do proof reading where it goes back and removing the wrong before it proceeds to add new bases in the $5' \rightarrow 3'$ direction. This type of proof reading ensures formation of identical DNA strands during DNA replication.

Sometimes abnormal base pairs are formed in the DNA due to mutation, that escape the proof reading mechanism of DNA polymerase can still be rectified by repair enzymes, which excise the damaged region and replace it with normal segment.

Enzymes involved in DNA replication. Several enzymes are involved in DNA replication. They are as follows :

(*i*) **Helicases.** They are unwinding enzymes, and help in breaking the weak hydrogen bonds that hold the two strands of DNA together.

(*ii*) **Topoisomerases.** These enzymes are responsible for breaking and resealing of one strand of DNA.

(*iii*) **Primase.** This helps in the formation of primer. Primer is a short RNA segment that is formed on the DNA template. It is absolutely essential.

(*iv*) **DNA polymerase.** This enzyme can link free DNA nucleotides to form the complementary strand of DNA. It polymerases nucleotides in $5' \rightarrow 3'$ direction only.

(*v*) **DNA ligase.** This enzyme can join together the short fragments after replacing RNA primer with DNA.

(*vi*) **Repair enzymes.** There may be some errors during DNA replication. Repair enzymes can excise the wrong bases and replace them with correct ones.

Functions of DNA

The DNA has a key role in all biosynthetic and hereditary functions of the living organisms. Its few important functions are as follows :

1. The most important function of the DNA is that it acts as a carrier of genetic informations from generation to generation. It is most stable compound of the biological world which can be considered immortal.

2. The DNA controls all the life activities of the cell directly or indirectly.

3. The DNA synthesizes the RNA.

4. The DNA guides the process of protein synthesis.

Mechanism of DNA Replication

The process of DNA replication is much complicated. The major steps of the process are as follows : (Fig. 44.10.)

During this process a whole range of enzymes is required to take care of various steps.

The DNA replication in procaryotic cells (bacteria) starts at a single point known as **origin of replication**, and moves bidirectionally.

On the other hand, in eucaryotic cells there are several points of origin on the length of DNA per chromosome.

The first requirement before any type of synthesis is to unwind the double helix of DNA, so that the two strands become free to act as templates.

This function of unwinding of double helix is carried out by the enzyme **helicase**, which unzips the two strands beginning at the origin site.

As soon as unwinding takes place, other proteins called single-stranded binding proteins, associate with single strands and make this condition stable.

Unwinding also creates a coiling tension ahead of the moving **replication fork**, a structure that will be formed when DNA replication begins.

The coiling tension created by unwinding of double helix is reduced by the enzymes known as **topoisomerases**.

One of the most important DNA synthesizing enzyme is DNA polymerase III. This enzyme along with other DNA polymerases (*i.e.*, I and II) can elongate an existing DNA strand but cannot initiate the synthesis of DNA.

All the above mentioned three DNA polymerases (*i.e.*, I, II, and III) function in $5'$ to $3'$ direction only for DNA polymerisation and have $5'$ to $3'$ direction for exonuclease activity.

Now, to initiate DNA synthesis, a small segment of RNA, known as RNA primer complementary to the template DNA is synthesized by an unique RNA polymerase known as **primase**.

It is to this RNA primer, that DNA polymerase III adds $5'$ deoxyribonucleotides and extends the DNA.

A problem arises, when two strands of DNA run antiparallel to each other and DNA polymerase III can act only in $5' \rightarrow 3'$ direction. This problem is solved as follows :

While on the one strand, the DNA synthesis goes on continuously in $5' \rightarrow 3'$ direction, on the other strand, DNA is synthesised in small stretches resulting in discontinuous DNA synthesis.

This process takes place in the opposite direction to the first strand but maintains the over all $5' \rightarrow 3'$ direction as required and such a process is sometimes called semi-discontinuous replication.

The short stretches of DNA, each primed by RNA are called **Okazaki fragments**, named after Japanese scientist who discovered them.

Thereafter RNA primers are removed, and the gap is filled by DNA synthesis. Both these steps are performed by DNA polymerase I.

Now the Okazaki fragments are sealed by the enzyme **ligase**.

The strand which supports the continuous DNA synthesis is the **leading strand** and one which is replicated in short stretches is called the **lagging strand.**

The process of DNA replication ensures the accuracy to maintain the nucleotide sequence of the original DNA.

DNA synthesis is slower in eucaryotes, as larger DNA's need to be replicated.

The general steps of DNA replication are similar both in eucaryotes and procaryotes.

GENE EXPRESSION

The another important characteristic of the gene is to store and express the genetic information which will contribute towards the phenotype and will be passed on to successive generations.

In 1902, an English physician Archibald Garrod, advocated that the diseases which inherit from the parent by the progeny are **inborn errors of metabolism** and they are due to a defect in an enzyme that catalyses the conversion of one metabolic substance to another. Hence this inherited genetic defect is due to the deficiency of an enzyme. This was believed that genes directly influenced the biochemical metabolism by determining the pressure or absence of a specific enzyme and that the genes have the information to produce enzymes.

For example, in one disorder alkaptonuria, afflicted individuals cannot metabolise homogentisic acid, as a result it gets accumulated and is excreted in the urine.

Garrod found that this disorder is inherited as a recessive trait and reasoned that normal individuals must be metabolising homogentisic acid. On the other hand, in affected individuals, the metabolic pathway is blocked resulting into disorder alkaptonuria.

Later on, several other human diseases were identified and described which fell into the category of inherited metabolic defects. This led to idea that many disorders may be inherited as any other gene and that genes function by controlling the metabolism.

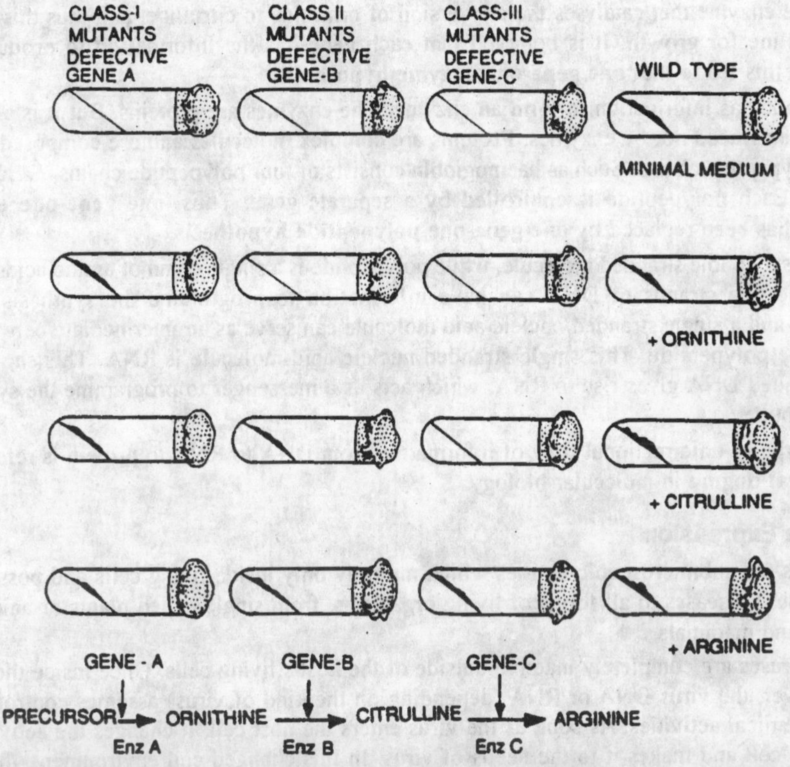

Fig. 44.11. One gene-one enzyme hypothesis—Experiments with *Neurospora crassa.* Wild type of *N. crassa* will grow in minimal condition and it does not require any supplement for growth. Class I mutants are defective in gene A (enzyme A) and thus cannot grow on minimal medium unless supplemented with ornithine or citrulline or arginine. Class II mutants are defective in gene B (enzyme B) and will grow in medium supplemented with citrulline or arginine. Class III mutants are defective in gene C (enzyme C) and will grow in medium supplemented with arginine.

The concept that genes have to information to produce enzymes which are proteinaceous in nature was put on a firm footing by the geneticist George W. Beadle and the biochemist Edward L. Tatum, for which they were awarded the Nobel Prize in medicine in 1959. It is known that UV rays, X-rays and environmental chemicals can bring about a change in the nucleotide sequence of DNA and thus cause mutations.

In 1941, Beadle and Tatum proved the **one gene one enzyme hypothesis**, for which they used X-rays to cause mutations in the mould *Neurospora crassa.* This mould can normally grow in a simple minimal medium containing salts and sugar, making all other chemicals, *i.e.*, amino acids, purines, pyrimidines, etc., through enzyme-catalysed reactions.

However, the mutants cannot grow on a minimal medium. Each type of mutant needs some extra nutrients, and such nutritional mutants are called **auxotrophs.** In their experiments, Beadle and Tatum obtained different mutants that require the amino acids ornithine or citrulline or arginine for growth. It is established that in the cell ornithine converts into citrulline which in turn converts into arginine, here each step is being catalysed by a specific enzyme. Beadle and Tatum proved that the mutant requiring ornithine for growth is defective in the enzyme producing ornithine as a result of gene mutation. In the similar way, a defect in another gene may lead to a defect in the enzyme that catalyses the conversion of ornithine to citrulline, and thus this mutant needs citrulline for growth. It is believed that each gene has the information to produce one enzyme and this led to the **'one gene-one enzyme hypothesis.**

The gene has information to form an enzyme. The enzymes are proteins. But it is also true that all proteins need not be enzymes. Proteins are complex molecules and are composed of one or more polypeptide chains. Such as haemoglobin consists of four polypeptide chains, *i.e.*, 2α and 2β chains. Each polypeptide is controlled by a separate gene. Thus, **one gene-one enzyme hypothesis** has been replaced by **one gene-one polypeptide hypothesis.**

DNA is a double stranded molecule, while polypeptide is a single chain of amino acids. Thus, either of the two strands of DNA can have information to programme the synthesis of the polypeptide and a single stranded nucleic acid molecule can serve as an intermediate between the gene and the polypeptide. This single stranded nucleic acid molecule is RNA. This shows that double stranded DNA gives rise to RNA, which acts as a messenger to programme the synthesis of a polypeptide.

This type of unidirectional flow of information from DNA to RNA to protein is referred to as the **central dogma** in molecular biology.

Viral Gene Expression

Viruses are submicroscopic entities which multiply only inside living cells and possess the ability to cause diseases to all forms of living organisms, from single-celled plants or animals to large trees and mammals.

The viruses are completely inactive outside of the host's living cells. Once inside the host's cells, however, the virus DNA or RNA (depending on the kind of virus) assumes control of the cell's biochemical activities. As soon as the virus enters the host cell, it changes the activities of the infected cell and makes it to the needs of virus. In this changed cell environment, the virus replicates. Hundreds of virus particles may be produced, all exactly like the one that infected the host cell.

Tobacco mosaic virus (TMV) contains RNA as the genetic material. Other viruses may contain DNA as the genetic material. There are also viruses that contain single stranded DNA as the genetic material. Viruses are diverse in size and shape but basically contain the genetic material wrapped around by a protein coat, generally known as the **capsid.**

Viral genomes are small and possess the information to code for a few proteins only. Thus, viruses use the host machinery such as enzymes, ribosomes and other components to replicate, to form the coat and to form more virus particles. The viruses infecting bacteria are known as **bacteriophages.** The expression of viral genes is regulated in such a way that the lysis of the host cells is caused. Thereafter many virus particles **(lytic)** are liberated which can infect new host cells to repeat the **lytic-cycle.** In some viruses after infection of the host cells viral particles get integrated with the host chromosome (DNA) and replicate along with it **(lysogeny).**

Lytic-cycle

Bacteriophages are the best understood viruses in terms of their gene structure and expression. For example T_2-bacteriophage infects *Escherichia coli* and causes lytic cycle. This phage has a double stranded circular DNA enclosed in a hexagonal proteinaceous head, cylindrical hollow tail and six tentacles for attachment to the host. The phage gets attached to bacterial wall by its tentacles. The lysozyme found at the tip of the tail dissolves the host cell wall to form a pore. The tail now contracts and injects the viral DNA into the host cell. Thereafter the viral DNA synthesises an enzyme known as nuclease which degrades the host DNA. Only after few minutes the host DNA is destroyed by nuclease. On the other hand, the viral DNA is resistant to nuclease because its cytosine residues are methylated. Now the viral genes make use of host ribosomes for multiplication. First of all the replication of viral DNA takes place. Thereafter, the proteins of head, tail and tentacles are synthesized. An independent synthesis of viral components occur within the cell followed by an assembly of those components into complete virus particles. After a well defined period the bacterial cell bursts and releases the newly formed virus particles. The liberated virus particles again infect the bacterial cells and the lytic cycle is repeated.

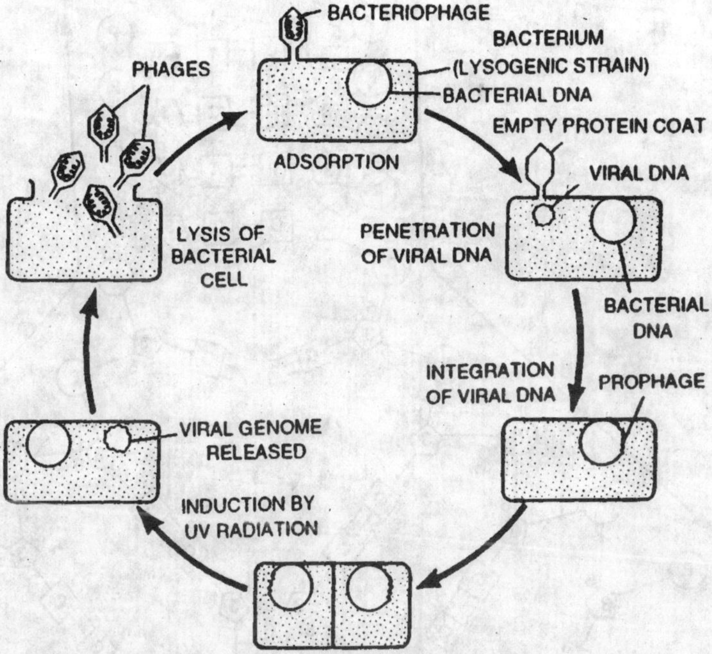

Fig. 44.12. Bacteriophages-life cycle.

Gene Expression in Prokaryotes

Bacterial chromosomes. It has been established now that a bacterial chromosome is always present in the centre of bacterial cell which is not capable of mitotic and meiotic divisions and is not enclosed within a definite nuclear membrane. An average bacterial cell contains one thousandth the DNA content of a typical eucaryotic cell. The bacterial chromosome is a thin elongated flexible and circular filament of DNA molecule associated with few proteins. The bacterial cells can divide very rapidly. The cell division is completed by the doubling of all the cell constituents followed by partition of the cell into two daughter cells. The first step in cell division is DNA duplication. The duplication of bacterial chromosome is semiconservative. Two chains of parental double helix of DNA unwind by breaking of hydrogen bonds between the bases in the presence of the **unwinding enzyme.** The separation of the parental chains results in the formation of Y-shaped growing points called replication forks. The free single chain is used as template and DNA synthesized is started. The chain with $3'$ end has continuous strand called **leading strand** is synthesised by DNA **polymerase** in $5' \rightarrow 3'$ direction only. The second complementary free parental chain with $5'$ end cannot be copied by DNA polymerase in the same direction, and so is copied in the opposite direction but in discontinuous fashion strand with the initial action of an enzyme called DNA

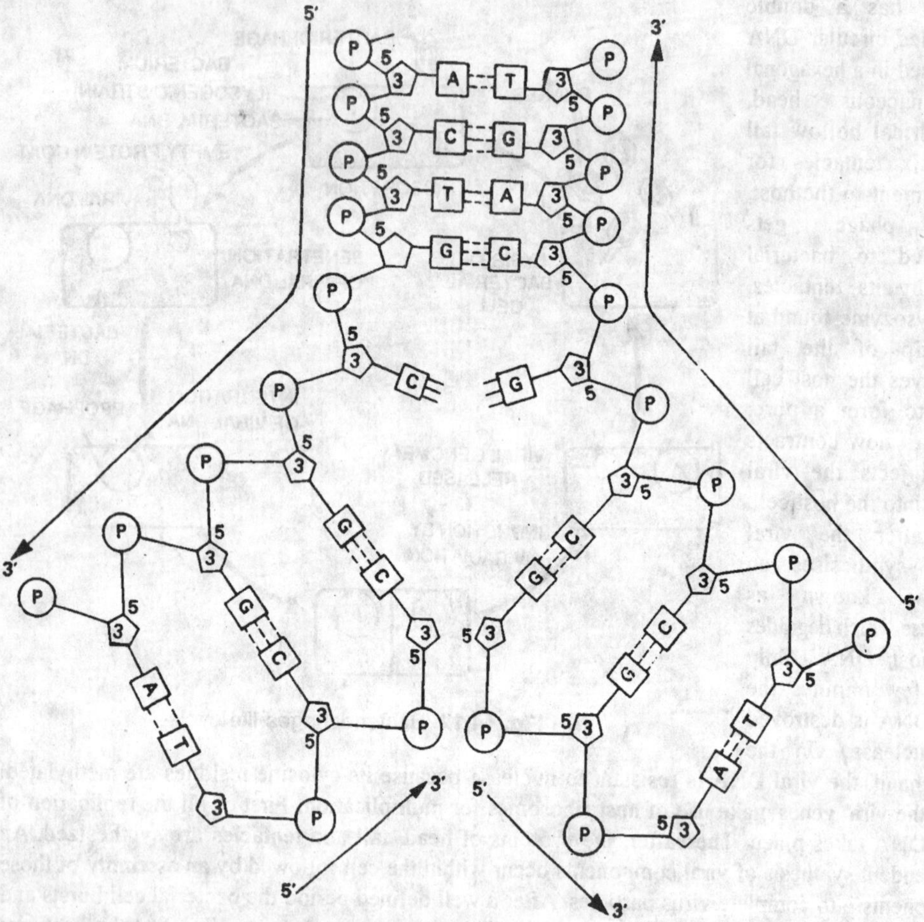

Fig. 44.13. DNA structure. The three components of DNA are the bases adenine, guanine, thymine and cytosine; a sugar molecule, deoxyribose; and phosphate groups. The phosphate groups are attached to the 3′ and 5′ carbons of the deoxyribose and serve to connect, successive pairs of nucleotides. The replication process must be of one DNA strand by adding bases in the 5′ → 3′ direction and the other DNA strand, apparently by adding bases in the opposite direction.

dependent RNA **polymerase**, which lays down a short stretch of RNA. This RNA acts as a primer at its 3—OH end for the enzyme DNA polymerase which then results the synthesis of lagging strand. Finally the enzyme DNA **ligase**, bonds the strands together and closes DNA 'nicks' with the result a continuous strand is formed like the leading strand. After the synthesis of new strands two new double helical DNA molecules are formed each with an old strand from the mother molecule. Now, each of the DNA strands still attached to the cell membrane, are distributed in two daughter cells by a simple pinching off process.

Genetic Recombination in Bacteria

This is a process where genetic materials, contained in two separate genomes, are brought together within one unit. In bacteria the recombination takes place by **(1) transformation, (2) transduction** and **(3) conjugation.**

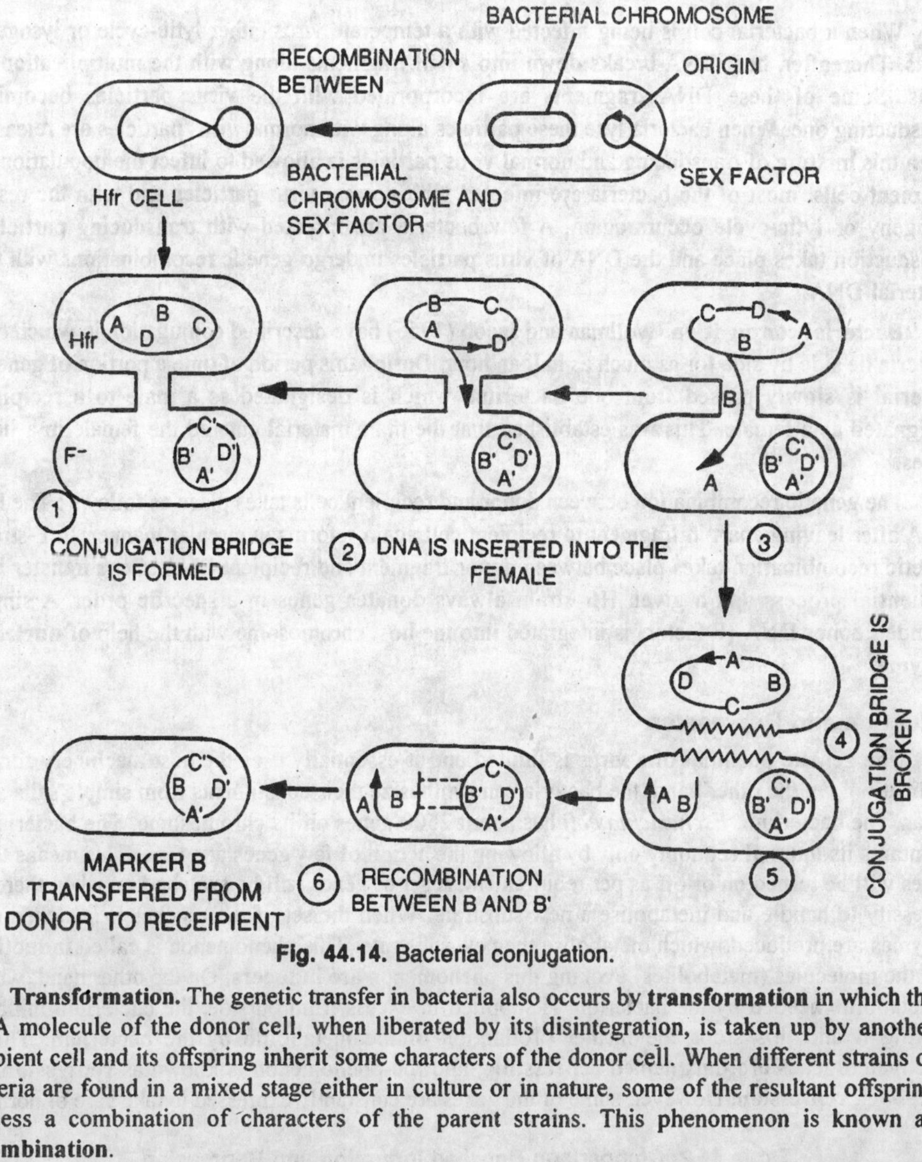

Fig. 44.14. Bacterial conjugation.

Transformation. The genetic transfer in bacteria also occurs by **transformation** in which the DNA molecule of the donor cell, when liberated by its disintegration, is taken up by another recipient cell and its offspring inherit some characters of the donor cell. When different strains of bacteria are found in a mixed stage either in culture or in nature, some of the resultant offspring possess a combination of characters of the parent strains. This phenomenon is known as **recombination**.

The phenomenon of transformation was first recorded by Griffith (1928). Avery, Macleod and McCarty (1944) demonstrated that the transforming principle being DNA in the sequence of events in bacterial transformation.

Transduction. The genetic transfer in bacteria is achieved by a process known as **transduction.** Laderberg and Zinder's (1952) experiment in U-tube *Salmonella typhimurium* indicated that bacterial viruses or phages are responsible for the transfer of genetic material from one to the other lysogenic and lytic phages. Thus the host acquires a new genotype. Transduction has been demonstrated in many bacteria.

In this process, the DNA molecule that carries the hereditary characters of the donor bacterium, is being transferred to the recipient cell through the agency of the phage particle. In this process very few closely linked characters can be transferred by each particle. Thus the bacteriophage bring about genetic changes in those bacteria which survive the phage attack.

When a bacterial cell is being infected with a temperate virus either lytic-cycle or lysogeny starts. Thereafter, host DNA breaks down into small fragments along with the multiplication of virus. Some of these DNA fragments are incorporated with the virus particles becoming transducting one. When bacteria lyse these particles along with normal virus particles are released when this mixture of transducing and normal virus particles is allowed to infect the population of recipient cells, most of the bacteria are infected with normal virus particles and with the result lysogeny or lytic-cycle occurs again. A few bacteria are infected with transducing particles, transduction takes place and the DNA of virus particles undergo genetic recombinations with the bacterial DNA.

Bacterial conjugation. Wollman and Jacob (1956) have described conjugation in which two bacteria lie side by side for as much as half an hour. During this period of time a portion of genetic material is slowly passed from one bacterium which is designated as a male to a recipient designated as a female. This was established that the male material entered the female in a liner series.

The genetic recombination between donor and recipient cells takes place as follows : The Hfr DNA after leaving apart in fragment to recipient cell again reforms in circular manner. In F-strain genetic recombination takes place between donor fragment and recipient DNA. Gene transfer is a sequential process and a given Hfr strain always donates genes in a specific order. A single stranded donor DNA (F factor) is integrated into the host chromosome with the help of **nuclease enzyme.**

Induction and Repression

The genetic potential of a virus is limited and it essentially uses the host machinery for its replication. On the other hand, the bacteria can synthesize their constituents from simple salts and sugar. The bacterium, *Escherichia coli* has about 2500 genes on its chromosome. The bacterium, maintains its internal economy only by allowing the action of few genes at a time. This means that genes will be turned on or off as per requirement. A set of genes will be switched on when there is necessity to handle and metabolise a new substrate. When the set of these genes is switched on, enzymes are produced, which metabolise the new substrate. This phenomenon is called **induction** and the molecules (metabolites) evoking this phenomenon are **inducers**. On the other hand, when a metabolite needed by the bacterium is supplied in excess from outside, the bacterium inhibits making it and this stops the further production of the metabolite by the bacterium. These inactivated genes are thus named **repressible**, and the phenomenon is known as **repression** or **feed-back repression**. However, some of the genes are constantly expressed to take care of normal

Table 44.2. Comparison Between Induction and Repression.

Induction	Repression
1. It is responsible for starting transcription and translation.	1. It stops transcription and translation.
2. It turns the operon on.	2. It turns the operon off.
3. It acts in a catabolic pathway.	3. It acts in an anabolic path way.
4. It is caused by new metabolite that requires enzymes to get metabolised.	4. It is due to excess of existing metabolite.
5. Repressor is checked by the inducer from combining with operator gene.	5. Repressor is helped by a co-repressor to combine with operator gene.

cellular activity such as glycolysis. These genes are known as **constitutive**, and the enzymes produced by them are known as **constitutive enzymes**, such as dehydrogenases.

Gene Expression in Eucaryotes

Higher eucaryotes have thousands of genes, in comparison to procaryotes. They are multicellular organisms which can also undergo differentiation. Thus, the cells in the undifferentiated stage not only grow and divide, but they also become part of specialised tissues such as the liver, spleen, heart, etc., in an animal and the leaf, root, stem, flower, etc., in a flowering plant (angiosperm). Hence, regulation gene expression in the eucaryotic cell is very complex.

The structure of the eucaryotic gene is also complex (Fig. 44.15).

For example, in bacteria, if the base sequence of the DNA is known, the amino acid sequence of the protein can be predicted. Here the gene and the protein are collinear indicating that the linear arrangement of nucleotides (bases) in the gene correlates with the linear arrangement of amino acids in proteins. In most eucaryotic genes the match between the bases in the gene and the amino acids in the protein will only hold in parts. Here the gene will have stretches of bases, which will code for amino acids, that are interspersed with stretches of bases, which do not code for any amino acid. Thus, the information on the eucaryotic gene for assembling a protein is not continuous, but split.

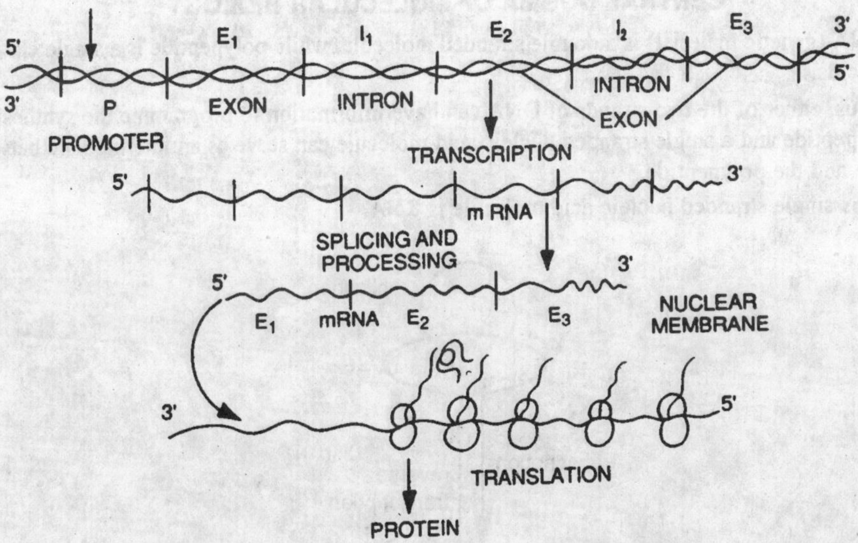

Fig. 44.15. Eucaryotic gene structure. Details in the text.

However, when mRNA is formed from such eucaryotic genes, the unwanted RNA regions are removed and the regions coding for amino acids are joined together, and this process is called **splicing.**

Thus, bases in mRNA and amino acids in proteins are collinear in eucaryotic cells also, though the genes are split. The regions of a gene that become part of mRNA and code for different regions of the protein are known as **exons.** The regions which do not form part of mRNA and are removed during RNA processing before mRNA formation are known as **introns.**

In eucaryotes, genes involved in coding for the enzymes of a definite metabolic pathway need not be linked. Sometimes they are found even on different chromosomes. However, such genes are regulated together as in bacterial operons.

The basic processes of induction and repression operate in eucaryotic cells, but through a complex network of regulatory genes. The gene expression is constantly regulated by the changing environment in the cell. Thus during growth and development, small molecules such as hormones, vitamins, metal ions, chemicals and invading pathogens can induce or repress certain genes, and this will result in the production or absence of certain proteins. This ultimately leads to the operation or non-operation of metabolic pathways leading to altered cell function. This is how the environment influences the molecular basis of the gene action.

Gene and Protein

Now this has been established that DNA is the genetic material, and the genes function by exerting their control over proteins or enzymes.

Now, we shall study, how is the genetic information stored in DNA and then how this information coded in DNA is transmitted in the process of protein synthesis.

The work done in the late 1950s and early 1960s proved that a specific sequence of four bases in the DNA serves as the store house of all genetic information and makes the basis of all life on earth.

The unique way in which these bases are arranged serve as genetic code, which determines the basic structure and function of the whole variety of proteins.

CENTRAL DOGMA OF MOLECULAR BIOLOGY

DNA (genetic material) is a double stranded molecule, while polypeptide is a single chain of amino acids.

Thus, either of the two strands of DNA can have information to programme the synthesis of the polypeptide and a single stranded nucleic acid molecule can serve as an intermediate between the gene and the polypeptide.

This single stranded nucleic acid molecule is RNA.

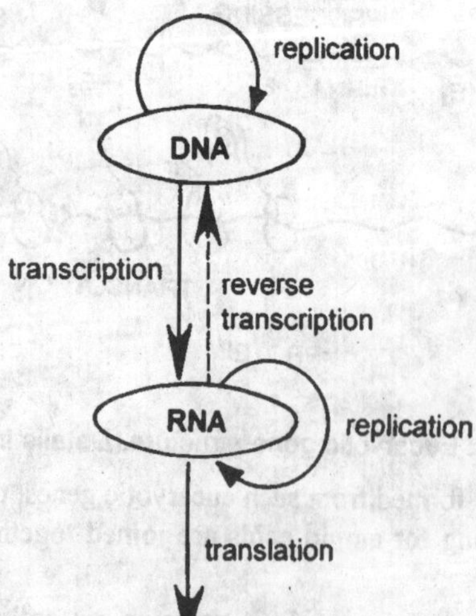

Fig. 44.16. The flow of genetic information.

This shows that double stranded DNA gives rise to RNA, which acts as a messenger to programme the synthesis of a polypeptide.

This type of unidirectional flow of information from DNA to RNA to protein is referred to as the **central dogma of molecular biology.**

The expression of the genetic material (DNA) which occurs generally through the production of protein involves two consecutive steps.

These two steps are known as (*i*) transcription and (*ii*) translation.

In transcription, the genetic information, stored in DNA, is transferred to an RNA intermediate, which in turn uses this information to direct the synthesis of proteins during translation.

This unidirectional flow of information was described by F.H.C. Crick in 1958 as the **central dogma of molecular biology.**

However, in 1970, an important modification of this information was brought to light by H. M. Temin and D. Baltimore.

According to them many tumor viruses contain RNA as genetic material and replicate by first synthesising a complementary DNA. This process is called **reverse transcription.**

Such process is carried out by an RNA- dependent DNA polymerase called reverse transcriptase.

These viruses are known as retroviruses and include **Human Immunodeficiency Virus** (HIV) which is responsible for causing AIDS.

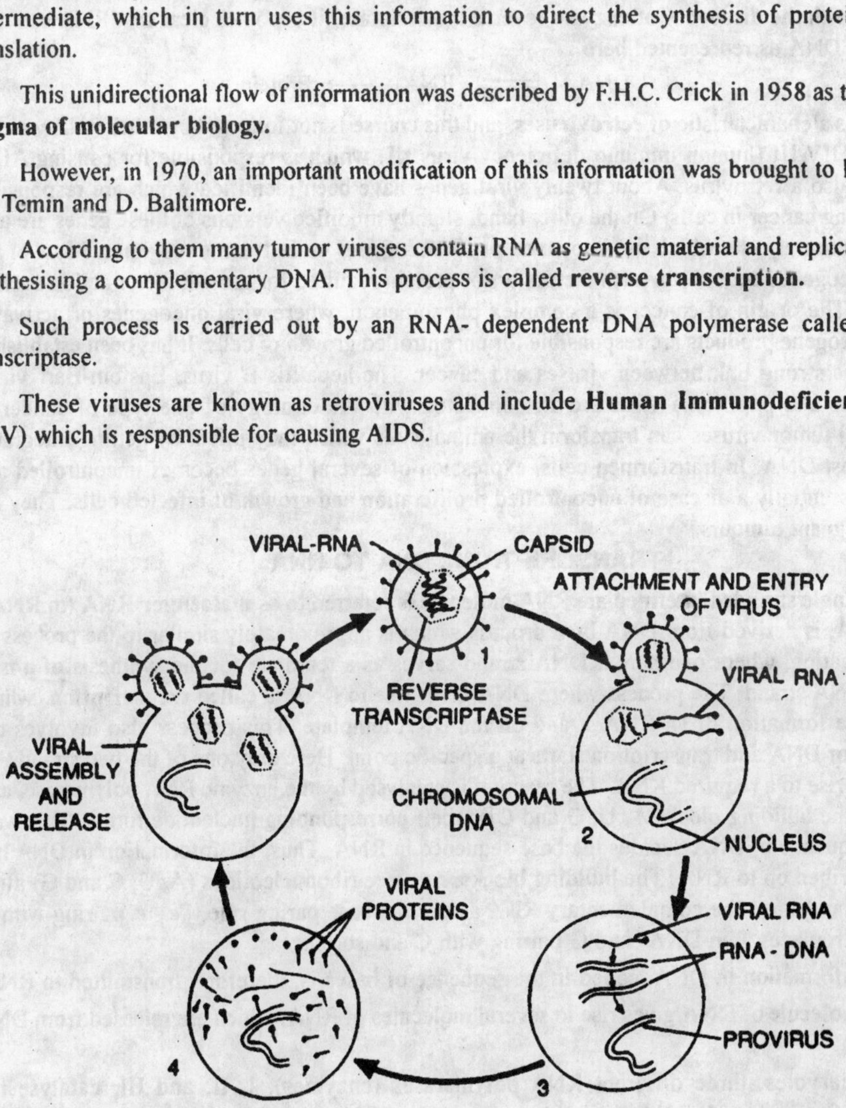

Fig. 44.17. Life-cycle of retrovirus. Details in the text.

Reverse Transcription

This phenomenon was studied by Temin and Baltimore (1972), and thus known as **Teminism.** While studying the activity of double stranded RNA containing Rous sarcoma virus (RSV) in the cancerous tissue, they found that viral RNA synthesized DNA complementary to its strands. As soon as the RNA of RSV comes in contact of the cytoplasm of host cell, it synthesizes the enzyme **reverse transcriptase** that catalyses the conversion of RNA to DNA copy and exhibits a reverse phenomenon of the normal process. Such phenomenon is known as **reverse transcription** or **Teminism.** Once the DNA complementary to viral RNA is synthesized it follows the normal rule and synthesizes viral RNA and viral proteins as depicted in the figure (Fig. 44.16). The central dogma says that the flow of information is unidirectional, *i.e.*, DNA $\rightarrow$ RNA $\rightarrow$ Protein. However, with the discovery of enzyme reverse transcriptase, it becomes clear that RNA can also go back to DNA as represented here :

$$\text{DNA} \rightleftharpoons \text{RNA} \longrightarrow \text{Protein}$$

This is a characteristic of **retroviruses**, and this course is not followed by other RNA viruses. The virus HIV-III (human immuno deficiency virus III) which is responsible for causing AIDS disease is also a retrovirus. About twenty viral genes have been identified which are responsible for triggering cancer in cells. On the other hand, slightly modified versions of these genes are also present in normal cells which are known as **protooncogenes** or **cellular oncogenes**. Most of the cellular oncogenes code for growth factors or for protein required for growth factor action such as receptors. The origin of cancer is a complex phenomenon, where viral oncogenes or activated cellular oncogene products are responsible for uncontrolled growth of cells. It has been established that there is strong link between viruses and cancer. The hepatitis B virus, Epstein-Barr virus, herpes virus and papilloma virus are all connected with the etiology of one type of cancer or another. All tumor viruses can transform the animal cells which they infect by getting integrated with the host DNA. In transformed cells, expression of several genes becomes uncontrolled and cancer is essentially a disease of uncontrolled proliferation and growth of infected cells. They are called malignant tumours.

TRANSCRIPTION : DNA TO RNA

The single stranded intermediate RNA molecule is referred to as **messenger RNA** (m RNA). The m RNA, is derived from DNA by a process which is approximately similar to the process of DNA replication, where one parent DNA strand serves as a template for the synthesis of a new daughter DNA strand. The process where DNA gives rise to RNA is called **transcription**, which involves the formation of an RNA strand on the DNA template. This process also involves the unwinding of DNA and transcription starts at a specific point. Here only one of the two strands, of DNA gives rise to a required RNA. The reaction is catalysed by the enzyme RNA polymerase, and it requires the building blocks A, U, G and C as their corresponding nucleotide forms. This way, the base sequence in DNA decides the base sequence in RNA. Thus, the information in DNA has been transcribed on to RNA. The building blocks, *i.e.*, free ribonucleotides (A, U, C and G) align themselves and form the complementary RNA as per the base paring rule, *i.e.*, A pairing with U (U in RNA replaces T in DNA) and G pairing with C and so on.

The information in DNA, coded in the sequence of bases is, therefore, transmitted to RNA.

One molecule of DNA gives rise to several molecules of RNA, which are released from DNA template.

In eucaryotes, three different RNA polymerases (enzymes), I, II, and III, catalyse the synthesis of **ribosomal RNA** (r RNA), **messenger RNA** (m RNA), and **transfer RNA** (t RNA) respectively.

However, in procaryotes, a single RNA polymerase (enzyme) that has different subunits performs this function.

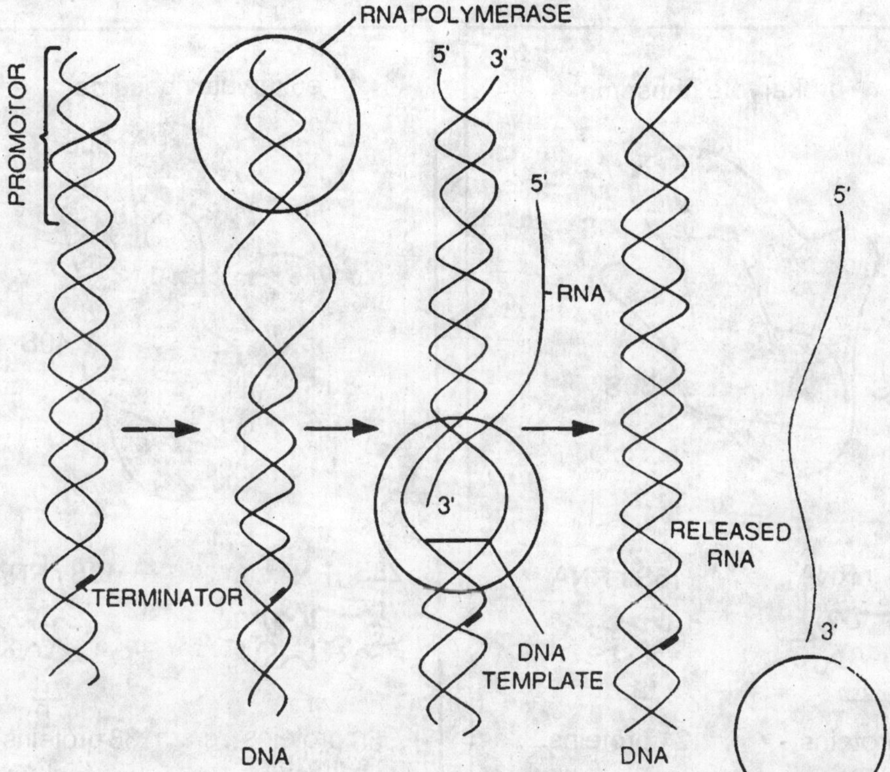

Fig. 44.18. Process of transcription. RNA polymerase binds to the promoter region of the DNA and starts the transcription process. The DNA unwinds and one of the two strands serves as a template for RNA synthesis, and a complementary copy of RNA is formed on the template strand.

TRANSLATION : BIOSYNTHESIS OF PROTEINS

Translation is the process in which genetic message carried by messenger RNA (m RNA) from the DNA is converted in the form of a polypeptide chain having a specific sequence of amino acids, *i.e.*, RNA to protein.

Besides m RNA there are three other key components which take part in this process. They are ***(i)*** ribosomes, ***(ii)*** transfer RNA (t RNA) and ***(iii)*** amino acids.

(i) **Ribosomes.** They are ribonucleoprotein particles which provide the sites for protein synthesis. On the basis of their sedimentation coefficients, procaryotic and eucaryotic ribosomes are characterised, *i.e.*, 70 S and 80 S respectively. Both of them consist of a small and a large subunit.

In procaryotes, the large or 50 S subunit consists of 23 S r RNA and 5 S r RNA + 32 different proteins and the 30 S small subunit consists of 16 S r RNA + 21 different proteins. (see Fig. 44.19).

In eucaryotes, the large or 60 S subunit consists of 28 S r RNA and a 5 S r RNA + 50 different proteins and the 40 S small subunit consists of 18 S r RNA and a 5.8 S r RNA + 33 different proteins.

(ii) **Transfer RNA (t RNA).** The t RNA is the smallest of the known RNA species. This displays somewhat identical structure in procaryotes and eucaryotes.

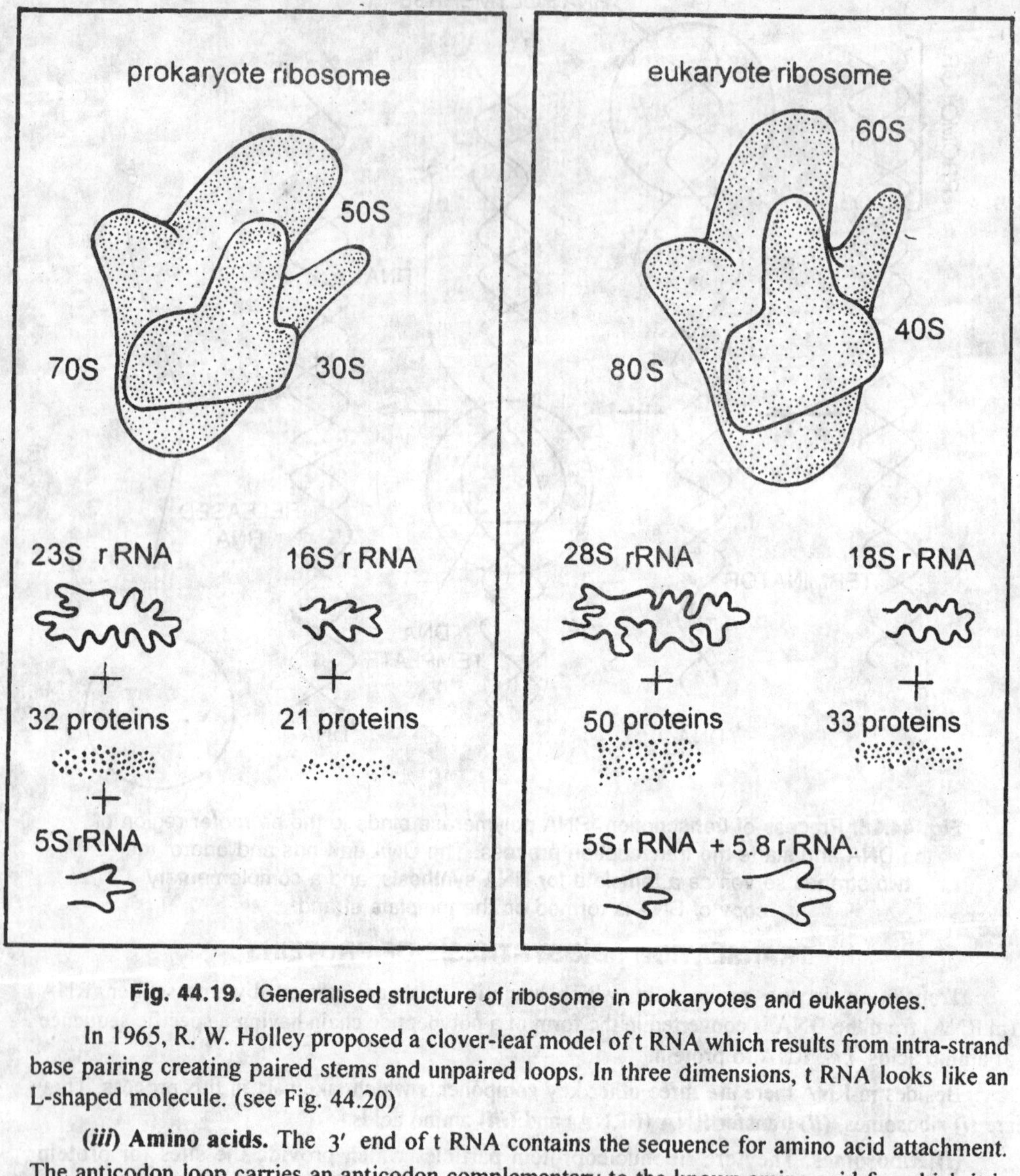

Fig. 44.19. Generalised structure of ribosome in prokaryotes and eukaryotes.

In 1965, R. W. Holley proposed a clover-leaf model of t RNA which results from intra-strand base pairing creating paired stems and unpaired loops. In three dimensions, t RNA looks like an L-shaped molecule. (see Fig. 44.20)

***(iii)* Amino acids.** The 3′ end of t RNA contains the sequence for amino acid attachment. The anticodon loop carries an anticodon complementary to the known amino acid for which it is specific.

Steps in Translation

Twenty naturally occurring amino acids take part in protein synthesis.

Translation exhibits that a t RNA is specifically linked to an amino acid and this process is known as charging. This process is brought about under the direction of an enzyme called aminoacyl t RNA synthetase which is highly specific, *i.e.*, each recognizes only one amino acid.

Charging takes place in two steps. They are as follows :

$$\text{1. Amino acid + ATP} \xrightarrow[\text{t RNA synthetase}]{\text{Aminoacyl}} \text{Aminoacyl adenylic acid + P} \sim \text{P}$$

2. Aminoacyl adenylic acid + t RNA $\rightarrow$ Charged t RNA (t RNA-amino acid)
= P – A + aminoacyl t RNA synthetase

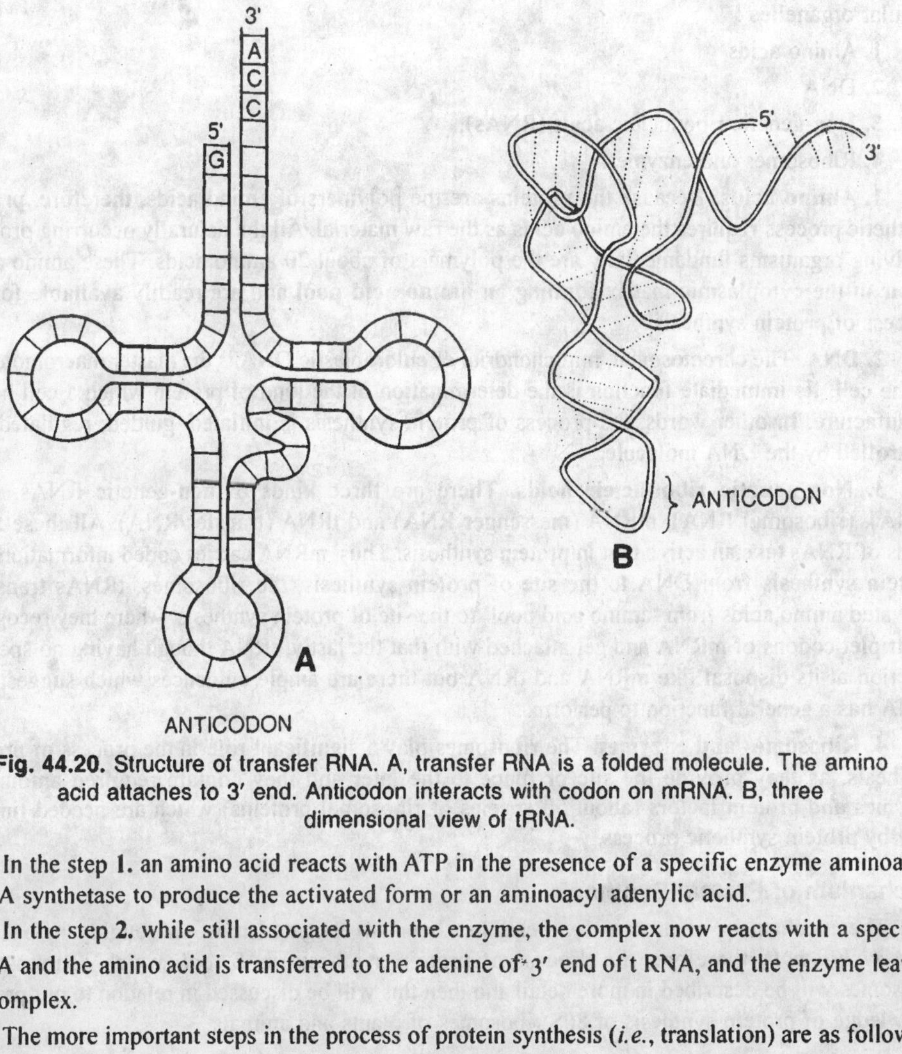

Fig. 44.20. Structure of transfer RNA. A, transfer RNA is a folded molecule. The amino acid attaches to 3′ end. Anticodon interacts with codon on mRNA. B, three dimensional view of tRNA.

In the step **1.** an amino acid reacts with ATP in the presence of a specific enzyme aminoacyl t RNA synthetase to produce the activated form or an aminoacyl adenylic acid.

In the step **2.** while still associated with the enzyme, the complex now reacts with a specific t RNA and the amino acid is transferred to the adenine of 3′ end of t RNA, and the enzyme leaves the complex.

The more important steps in the process of protein synthesis (*i.e.*, translation) are as follows :

PROTEIN SYNTHESIS

The proteins have significant role in the structural and functional organisation of the cell. The structural proteins constitute various cellular components and some extracellular parts such as cuticle and fibres, etc. The functional (*e.g.*, enzymatic and hormonal) proteins control almost all metabolic, biosynthetic, bioenergetic, growth regulating sensory and reproductive activities of the cell. All the proteins which are required by the cell for its different purposes are synthesized by the cell itself intracellularly.

A cell, however, cannot synthesize all the required proteins of multicellular individual, therefore, different kinds of proteins are synthesized by different types of cells. Thus, the liver cells are specialized for the synthesis of liver and plasma proteins, the β-cells of pancreatic islets are specialized for synthesis of proteins of insulin hormone and cells of pituitary are specialized of synthesis of protein component of pituitary hormone and so on.

Components of Protein Synthetic Machinery

The process of protein synthesis is complicated and it employs following molecules and cellular organelles :

1. Amino acids
2. DNA
3. Non-genetic ribonucleic acids (RNAs),
4. Ribosomes and enzymes.

1. Amino acids. Because the proteins are the polymers of amino acids, therefore, protein synthetic process requires the amino acids as the raw material. All the naturally occurring proteins of living organisms fundamentally are the polymers of about 20 amino acids. These amino acids occur in the cytoplasmic matrix forming an **amino acid pool** and are readily available for the process of protein synthesis.

2. DNA. The chromosomal, mitochondrial or chloroplastic DNA is the master macromolecule of the cell. Its immediate function is the determination of the kind of protein which a cell has to manufacture. In other words, the process of protein synthesis is initiated, guided, regulated and controlled by the DNA molecule.

3. Non-genetic ribonucleic acids. There are three kinds of non-genetic RNAs, (*i.e.*, rRNA), (ribosomal RNA), mRNA (messenger RNA) and tRNA (transfer RNA). All these three kinds of RNAs take an active part in protein synthesis. Thus, mRNA carries coded informations for protein synthesis from DNA to the site of protein synthesis, the ribosomes; tRNAs transport activated amino acids from 'amino acid pool' to the site of protein synthesis, where they recognise the triplet codons of mRNA and get attached with that the lastly, rRNA though having no specific function at its disposal like mRNA and tRNA but there are ample evidences which suggest that rRNA has a general function to perform.

4. Ribosomes and enzymes. The ribosomes play a significant role in the process of protein synthesis, as they provide the site or place to the later and they contain required amount of enzymes and prøtein factors (about 50 species of ribosomal proteins) which are needed time to time by protein synthetic process.

Mechanism of Protein Synthesis

The mechanism of protein synthesis has been investigated most thoroughly in bacteria *Escherichia coli*, therefore, the process of protein synthesis in *E. coli* which contains 70S ribosomes will be described in more detail and then this will be discussed in relation to our present knowledge of protein synthesis of 80S ribosomes of plants and animals.

A. Protein Synthesis on 70S Ribosomes

The mechanism of protein synthesis on 70S ribosomes includes the following stages :

1. The transcription. The process of protein synthesis is started by the uncoiling of strands of DNA molecule. One strand of DNA molecule acts as a template for the formation of mRNA. The mRNA is formed according to the triplet codes of DNA by the copying or transcription process. As soon as the mRNA is formed it leaves the nucleus and reaches in the cytoplasm where it attaches with the 30S subunit of the ribosomes. The mRNA carries the triplet codons for the synthesis of the proteins.

2. The attachment of mRNA with 30S ribosome and formation of polyribosome. In prokaryotic cells it has been observed that before the process of protein synthesis the ribosomes occur in dissociated and inactive state. The mRNA binds with the 30S ribosomal subunit in the presence of F_2 protein factor. Soon the N-formylmethionyl-tRNA (F-met-tRNAf) comes from the cytoplasm and binds with the first triplet codon (AUG or AUA) of the mRNA to initiate the process of protein synthesis and to form the **initiation complex.** The formation of initiation complex is aided by the GTP (Guanosine triphosphate) and 3 protein factors (F_1, F_2 and F_3). After the formation of initiation complex the 30S ribosomal subunit unites with 50S ribosomal subunit to form the 70S ribosome. The union of ribosomal subunits occurs in the presence of Mg^{++} ions and F_1 and F_2 factors. The codes of mRNA are not read only by one ribosome but many ribosomes move and read the codes of the mRNA. When many ribosomes bind with the mRNA the formation of polysome or polyribosome occurs.

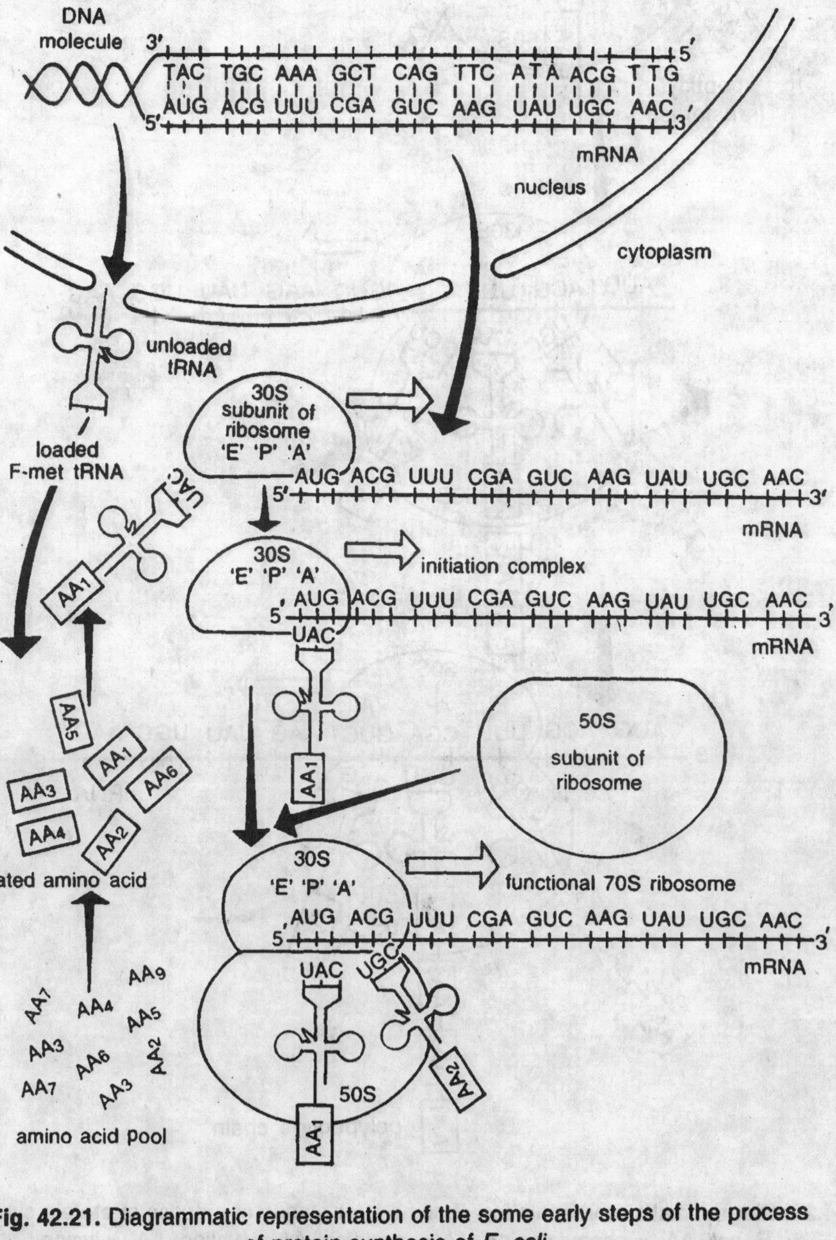

Fig. 42.21. Diagrammatic representation of the some early steps of the process of protein synthesis of *E. coli.*

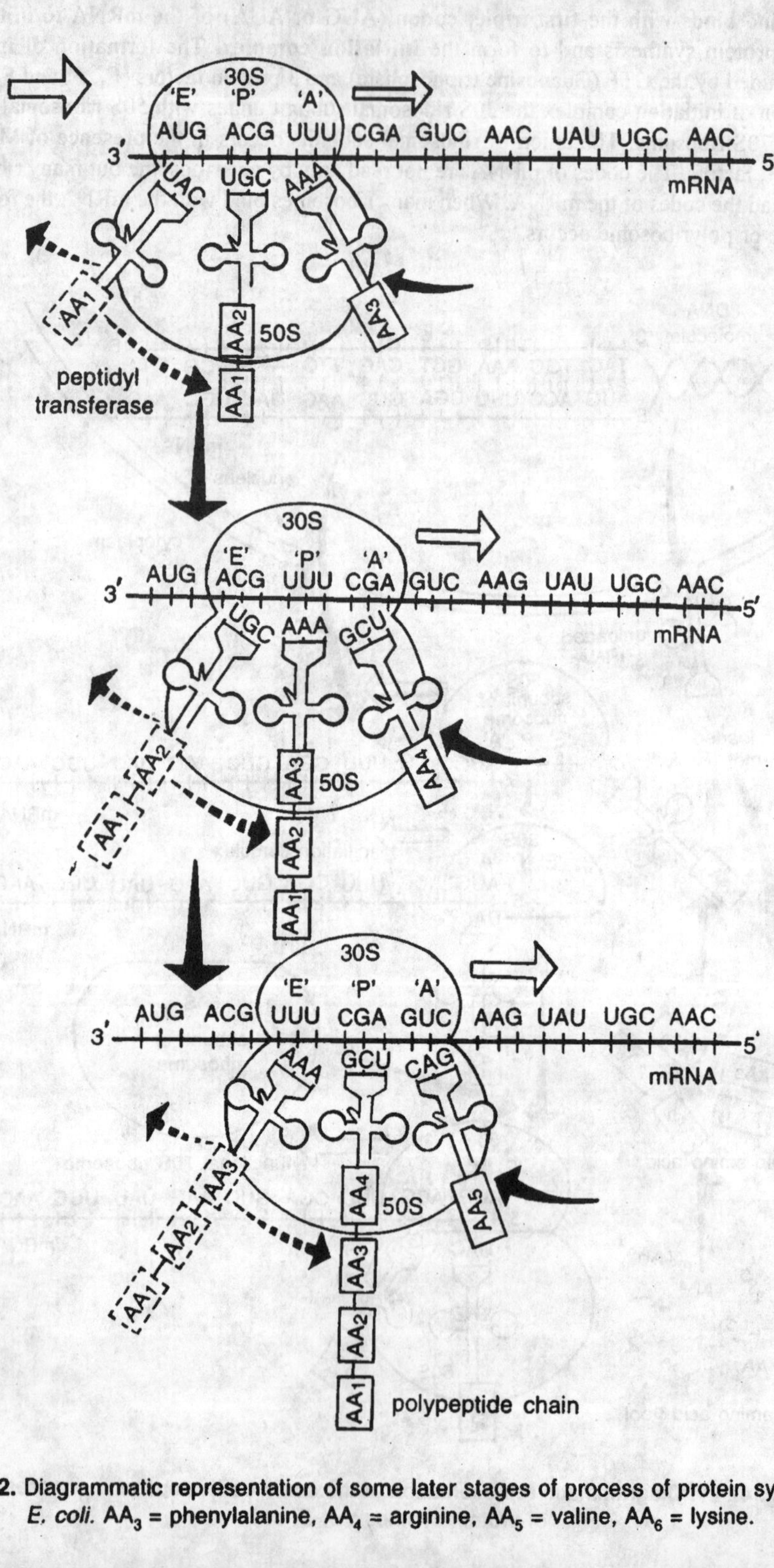

Fig. 44.22. Diagrammatic representation of some later stages of process of protein synthesis of *E. coli.* AA_3 = phenylalanine, AA_4 = arginine, AA_5 = valine, AA_6 = lysine.

3. The transfer of amino acids to the site of protein synthesis. The amino acids are transferred from the intra-cellular amino acid pool to the ribosomes by the tRNA. The transfer processes occur in various stages which are as follows.

***(a)* Activation of amino acids.** Each of the 20 amino acids occurs in the cytoplasm in an inactive state. Each amino acid before its attachment with its specific tRNA is activated by a specific activating enzyme known as the **aminoacyl synthetase** and ATP. The free amino acids react with ATP, resulting the production of aminoacyl adenylate and pyrophosphate :

$$\underset{\text{Amino acid}}{AA} + ATP + \underset{\text{Aminoacyl synthetase}}{\text{enzyme}} \longrightarrow \underset{\text{Aminoacyl adenylate synthetase complex}}{AA \sim AMP - \text{enzyme}} + \underset{\text{Pyrophosphate}}{PP}$$

The reaction product aminoacyl adenylate is bound to the enzyme in the form of a monocovalent complex. This aminoacyl adenylate enzyme complex then esterifies to specific tRNA molecule. The cell has at least 20 aminoacyl synthetase enzymes for the 20 amino acids. Each enzyme is specific and it attaches with the specific amino acid without any error.

***(b)* Attachment of activated amino acid to tRNA.** The aminoacyl adenylate remains bounded with enzyme until it collides with the specific tRNA molecule. Then, the carboxyl group of acid of amino acid residuc of aminoacyl adenylate is transferred to the 3 OH group of the ribose of the terminal adenosine at CCA end of tRNA. As a result AMP and enzyme are released and a final product **aminoacyl tRNA** is formed by the following method :

'A' = aminoacyl site or decoding site, 'P' = peptidyl site or condensing site, 'E' = exist site,

AA_1 = N-formyl methionine.

AA_2 = threonine.

$$\underset{\text{Aminoacyl adenylate and enzyme}}{AA—AMP—\text{Enzyme}} + tRNA \longrightarrow \underset{\text{Aminoacyl—tRNA}}{AA — tRNA} + AMP + \text{Enzyme}$$

The aminoacyl-tRNA moves towards the site of protein synthesis, *i.e.*, ribosomes with mRNA.

4. Initiation of protein synthesis. As we have already mentioned that the initiation of protein synthesis in the bacterium *Escherichia coli* (*E. coli*) involves the formation of 70S complex. In it the mRNA always has first triplet codon as AUG at its beginning (*i.e.*, 5′ end). The AUG codons are the codes for the amino acid methionine. The methionine remains formulated and it has a very important role in initiating the process of protein synthesis. In every type of protein the formyl methionine occupies the first place in the molecule and when the protein molecule is completely synthesized then the formyl methionine often detaches from the newly synthesized protein molecule by the activity of a hydrolytic enzyme.

Since in protein synthesis the peptide chain always grows in the sequence from the free terminal amino ($—NH_2$) group towards the carboxyl (—COOH) end, the function of formyl methionine —tRNA (AA_1—tRNA in figs. 38.22 and 38.23) is to ensure that proteins are synthesized in that direction. In the formyl methionine—tRNA, the amino ($—NH_2$) group is blocked by the formyl group leaving only the —COOH group available to react with the$—NH_2$ group of the second amino acid (AA_2). In this way the synthesis of protein chain follows in the correct sequence.

5. Elongation of polypeptide chain. With the formation of functional 70S ribosome (*i.e.*, 70S—mRNA—F met tRNA), the elongation of polypeptide chain is brought about by the regular addition of amino acids and relative movements of ribosome and mRNA in the presence of GTP molecules, so that a new triplet codon remains available for new aminoacyl tRNA at the decoding or 'A' site of ribosome in each step. Thus, F-met tRNA, must move from decoding site ('A' site) to peptidyl site or 'P' site before the second aminoacyl—tRNA (*i.e.*, AA_2 tRNA) can bind to the next triplet codon occurring at decoding or 'A' site of ribosome. The aminoacyl-tRNA (AA_2 tRNA) binds with the codon of 'A' site in the presence of GTP and two proteins, called **transfer factors** (designated Tn and Ts) which remain associated with ribosomes. During this binding process, a complex is formed between GTP, the transfer factors and the aminoacyl tRNA (*viz.*, AA_2 -tRNA), which ultimately deposits aminoacyl tRNA at the 'A' site of ribosome with the release of transfer factors-GDP complex and inorganic phosphate.

In the next step, due to relative movement of ribosome and mRNA in the presence of single GTP molecule, the next triplet codon (*i.e.*, UUU codon in figs. 38.21 and 38.22) becomes available for next aminoacyl tRNA (*viz.* AA_3-tRNA) at the 'A' site of ribosome. At this stage, f met-tRNA occurs at exit of 'E' site, while, AA_2-tRNA occurs at peptidyl 'P' site. Now, an enzyme known as **transferase** I kicks off tRNA from formyl-methionine (f-met or AA_1) and flips the formyl-methionine to the aminoacyl-tRNA (AA_2-tRNA) bound at the peptidyl or 'P' site. The **'G' factor** is supposed to release the discharged or deacylated tRNA from the 'E' site of the ribosome.

It follows the next stage of elongation process which involves the synthesis of a peptide bond by a reaction between the free amino group of the incoming amino acid (*i.e.*, AA_2) and the carboxyl group of the first amino acid (AA_1) which is esterified to tRNA. The enzyme which catalyses this reaction is called **peptidyl transferase** (or peptide synthetase) and is an integral part of the 50S subunit. The energy for peptide bond synthesis is derived from cleavage of the ester link between an amino acid and its tRNA.

Thus, during the elongation of polypeptide chain each charged or loaded tRNA (Aminoacyl tRNA) enters the decoding or 'A' site, moves to the condensing or 'P' site, transfers its amino acid to the carboxyl end of the polypeptide, moves to the exit site, where the polypeptide chain is transferred to the adjacent tRNA on the condensing site, and tRNA is then released from the ribosome. This process is known as **translocation.** This results in the third codon coming into the A site and an appropriate tRNA charged with a third amino acid would bind at the A site. The process of peptide bond formation and translocation would be repeated. Thus, as the mRNA moves with respect to the ribosome, all the codons would be exposed at A site and the peptide chain grows. This sequence of events involved in elongation must take place very rapidly since it has been calculated that, *E. coli* growing under optimal conditions, a polypeptide chain of about 40 amino acids can be produced in 20 seconds.

6. Termination and release of polypeptide chain. When the synthesis of polypeptide chain is completed according to the codons of mRNA, then process of termination and release of polypeptide chain takes place. The termination of the polypeptide chain and the release of the completed chain from the ribosome is controlled by two factors. The termination of the chain is indicated by three special termination triplets in the mRNA which, in bacteria, are UAG, UAA and UGA. These are the so called **non-sense codons** which do not encode for any amino acid. The polypeptide chain, however, still bound to the tRNA which in turn is attached to the mRNA. The chain is released from the ribosome under the direction of three distinct proteins which are called **release factors** and are designated R_1 R_2 and S. These are bound to the ribosome and control the hydrolysis of the ester link between tRNA and the polypeptide chain. Once the chain has been terminated and released, the ribosome separates from mRNA and dissociates into its two subunits due to the action of F_3 factor. It is ready to enter a new cycle of polypeptide synthesis.

7. Modification of released polypeptide. The released polypeptide chain contains the formulated methionine at its one end. An enzyme **deformylase** removes the formyl group of methionine. The **exopeptidase** enzyme may remove some amino acids from N-terminal end or the C-terminal end of polypeptide chain. At this stage the polypeptide (protein) possesses its primary structure; at least some portion of many proteins have a secondary structure in the form of an alpha-helix. The protein chain may then fold back up itself, forming internal bonds (including storing disulphide bonds) which stabilize its tertiary structure into a precisely and often intricately folded pattern. Two or more tertiary structures may unite into a functional quarternary structure. For example, haemoglobin consists of four polypeptide chains, two identical α-chains and two identical β-chains. A protein does not become an active enzyme until it has assumed its tertiary or quaternary pattern.

The process of initiation, elongation and termination involve the mediation of several protein factors and hydrolysis of GTP (guanosine triphosphate) to provide energy. The detailed steps discussed are applicable to procaryotes and with some modifications also to eucaryotes.

B. Protein Synthesis of 80S Ribosomes

The process of protein synthesis in eukaryotes is found to be similar to the mechanism of protein synthesis of 70S ribosomes of prokaryotes. However, the process of initiation of polypeptide of 80S ribosomes of eukaryotes, differs with that of prokaryotes, in following two aspects :

1. In eukaryotes, formulation of methionine does not take place.

2. In eukaryotes, the smaller subunit associates with met $t\text{RNA}_f^{met}$ without the help of *m*RNA.

The initiation process of eukaryotes (*e.g.*, mammals, wheat and bean) is found to include following stages :

(*i*) $40S + met - t\text{RNA}_f^{met} \longrightarrow 40S - met - t\text{RNA}_f^{met}$

(*ii*) $40S— met - t\text{RNA}_f^{met} + m\text{RNA} \longrightarrow 40S\text{-}m\text{RNA-met-}t\text{RNA}_f^{met}$

(*iii*) $40S—m\text{RNA-met-}t\text{RNA}_f^{met} + 60S \longrightarrow 80S\text{-}m\text{RNA-met—}t\text{RNA}_f^{met}$

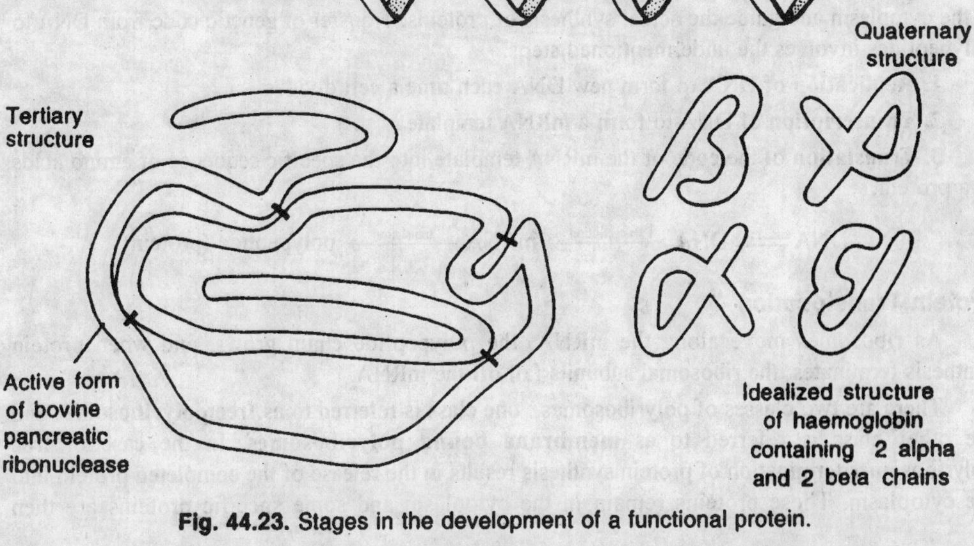

Fig. 44.23. Stages in the development of a functional protein.

Role of Polyribosomes

Since each ribosome moves along the mRNA that synthesises a polypeptide chain by translating the base sequence into the amino acid sequence, more ribosomes get attached one after another. Each ribosome takes the course from the initiation codon the termination codon. The

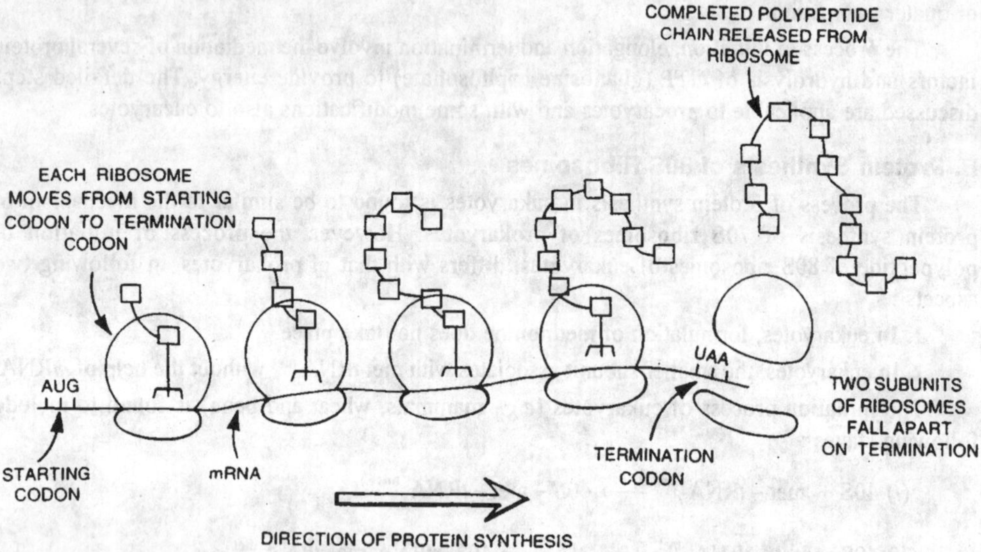

Fig. 44.24. A polyribosome (polysome).

whole complex with several ribosomes attached to a single mRNA looks like beads on a string and is known as **polyribosome** or **polysome.** This ensures the synthesis of several polypeptides simultaneously.

DNA, the Master Copy

DNA does not directly control the formation of a polypeptide. However, it forms an intermediate template mRNA molecule, which directs the synthesis of polypeptide. The DNA can be compared to a **master copy** that is carefully preserved in the nucleus and used for preparing **working copies** in the form of mRNA molecules. The mRNA molecules pass out to the ribosomes in the cytoplasm and guide the actual synthesis of proteins. Transfer of genetic code from DNA to polypeptides involves the undermentioned steps.

1. Replication of DNA to form new DNA each time a cell divides.

2. Transcription of DNA to form a mRNA template

3. Translation of the code of the mRNA template into the specific sequence of amino acids in a protein.

$$\text{DNA} \rightleftharpoons \text{DNA} \xrightarrow{\text{transcription}} \text{mRNA} \xrightarrow{\text{translation}} \text{polypeptide (protein)}$$

Protein Translocation

As ribosomes move along the mRNA, the polypeptide chain grows, and when protein synthesis terminates, the ribosomal subunits fall off the mRNA.

There are two classes of polyribosomes : one class is referred to as **free polyribosomes** and the other class is referred to as **membrane bound polyribosomes**. In the case of free polyribosomes termination of protein synthesis results in the release of the completed protein into the cytoplasm. These proteins remain in the cytoplasm and some specific proteins are then

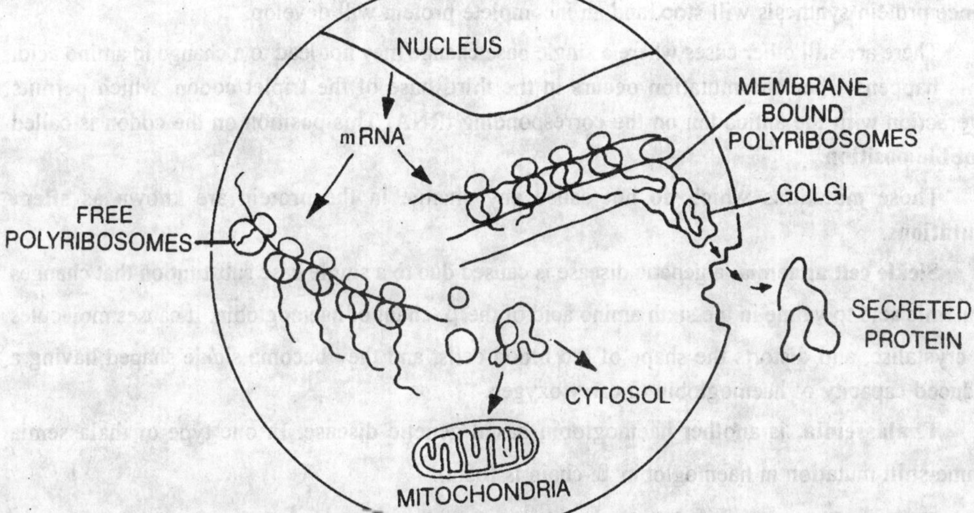

Fig. 44.25. Synthesis of proteins on free and membrane bound polyribosomes.

translocated into mitochondria and nucleus through special mechanisms. While in the case of membrane-bound polyribosomes, the polypeptide chain as it grows on the mRNA is inserted into the lumen of the ER (endoplasmic reticulum) membrane. Some of the proteins are integrated into the membrane and become integral membrane proteins. Some others are released into the lumen and are incorporated in Golgi vesicles. Now by the addition of certain sugar residues, these proteins undergo **glycosylation.** The Golgi vesicles fuse with the plasma membrane and the proteins are secreted out.

Effect of Mutations on Protein Structure and Function

As already stated that during DNA replication, the positioning of the correct base is maintained; and if any error persists, that is being corrected by proof reading and repair mechanisms. However, base changes are possible in DNA due to environmental mutagens such as UV rays, X-rays and certain chemicals. Hence, an A-T base pair may be changed into a G-C pair and this point mutation may be inherited by the progeny. In the similar way, insertion of an additional base may also cause mutation.

Under certain special condition cross-over and recombination between DNA strands can also lead to chunks of DNA being deleted or added. Thus mutations in genes lead to changes in mRNA and hence changes in the protein structure and function.

As already stated during cross-over and recombination between DNA strands may lead to chunks of DNA being deleted or added. Here shuffling of genes from one location to another is possible based on similarity of DNA sequences on the flanks of these genes. Such genes are popularly known as '**jumping genes**'.

The effect of such mutations will be reflected in the proteins. This is because the mRNA derived from the gene will lack a base, or will have an altered base. If the mutation involves loss or addition of a single base or a segment of DNA, then the enter reading frame will change from the site of mutation and one may end up in a protein with a new set of amino acids, and this is known as **frameshift mutation**.

In certain other instances, mutation can convert a normal codon to a non-sense codon and hence protein synthesis will stop, and an incomplete protein will develop.

There are still other cases where a single base change may not lead to a change in amino acid. This happens when the mutation occurs in the third base of the triplet codon, which permits interaction with the anticodon on the corresponding tRNA. This position on the codon is called **wobble position.**

Those mutations which do not cause any change in the protein are known as **silent mutations.**

Sickle cell anaemia, a genetic disease is caused due to a single base substitution that changes glutamic acid to valine in the sixth amino acid of the β-chain of haemoglobin. It causes molecules to crystalise, and distorts the shape of red blood cells, and they become sickle shaped having a reduced capacity of haemoglobin to carry oxygen.

Thalassemia, is another haemoglobin based genetic disease. In one type of thalassemia frame-shift mutation in haemoglobin β-chain is found.

Cancer. Chromosomal deletions and translocations have been reported in a variety of experimentally induced cancers.

Molecular Mechanism of Mutation

With the identification of biochemical nature of gene as a defined segment of DNA (deoxyribose nucleic acid), mutation mechanisms were worked out at molecular level.

This is now known that in DNA specific sequence of bases forms the reading frame in the form of genetic code for a gene.

Mutations are brought about by two main mechanisms which, alter the reading frame. (*i*) substitution and (*ii*) frame-shift mutations.

(*i*) **Substitution**. Here, one base is replaced by another base. For example, substitution of purine to purine or pyrimidine to pyrimidine is called **transition**, and purine to pyrimidine and *vice-versa* is known as **transversion**.

(*ii*) **Frame-shift mutation**. When the mutation involves loss or addition of a single base or a segment of DNA, then the entire reading frame will change from the site of mutation and one may end up in a protein with a new set of amino acids.

A specific base sequence within gene is crucial for it to express a particular phenotype.

Any change in the base sequence may change the codon and leads to mutation.

Each living cell has repair mechanisms to rectify such alterations. Only when these mechanisms are defective, the mutations can be induced.

GENETIC CODE

As DNA is a genetic material, it carries genetic informations from cell to cell and from generation to generation. At this stage, an attempt will be made to determine that in what manner the genetic informations are existed in DNA molecule? Are they written in articulated or coded language on DNA molecule? If in the language of codes what is the nature of genetic code?

A DNA molecule is composed of three kinds of moieties: (i) phosphoric acid,(ii) deoxyribose sugar, and (iii) nitrogen bases. The genetic informations may be written in any one of the three moieties of DNA. But the poly-sugar-phosphate backbone is always the same, and it is, therefore, unlikely that these moieties of DNA molecule carry the genetic informations. The nitrogen bases, however, vary from one segment of DNA to another, so the informations might well depend on their sequences. The sequences of nitrogen bases of a given segment of DNA molecules, actually, has been found to be identical to linear sequence of amino acids in a protein molecule. The proof of such a **colinearity** between DNA nitrogen base sequence and amino acid sequence in protein molecules has first obtained from an analysis of mutants of head protein of bacteriophage T_4 and the A protein of tryptophan synthetase of *Escherichia coli.* The colinearity of protein molecules and DNA polynucleotides has given the clue that the specific arrangement of four nitrogen bases (*e.g.*, A, T, C and G) in DNA polynucleotide chains, somehow, determines the sequence of amino acids in protein molecules. Therefore, these four DNA bases can be considered as four alphabets of DNA molecule. All the genetic informations, therefore, should be written by these four alphabets of DNA. Now the question arises that whether the genetic informations are written in articulated language or coded language? If genetic informations might have occurred in an articulated language, the DNA molecule might require various alphabets, a complex system of grammar and ample amount of space on it. All of which might be practically impossible and troublesome too for the DNA. Therefore, it was safe to conclude for molecular biologists that genetic informations were existed in DNA molecule in the form of certain special language of code words which might utilize the four nitrogen bases of DNA for its symbols. Any coded message is commonly called **cryptogram.**

BASIS OF CRYPTOANALYSIS

The basic problem of such a genetic code is to indicate how information written in a four letter language (four nucleotides or nitrogen bases of DNA) can be translated into a twenty letter language (twenty amino acids of proteins). The group of nucleotides that specifies one amino acid is a **code word** or **codon**. By the **genetic code** one means the collection of base sequences (codons) that correspond to each amino acid and to translation signals. The simplest possible code is a **singlet code** (a code of single letter) in which one nucleotide amino acid could be specified. A **doublet code** (a code of two letters)is also inadequate, because it could be specify only sixteen (4 × 4) amino acids, whereas a **triplet code** (a code of three letters) could specify sixty four (4 × 4 × 4) amino acids. Therefore, it is likely that there may be 64 triplet codes for 20 amino acids. The possible singlet, doublet and triplet codes, which are customarily represented in terms of "**mRNA language**" [mRNA is a complementary molecule which copies the genetic informations (crytogram of DNA) during its transcription], have been illustrated in Table 38.3

The first experimental evidence in support to the concept of triplet code is provided by **Crick** and coworkers in 1961. During their experiment, when they added or deleted single, or double base pairs in a particular region of DNA of T_4 bacteriophages of *E. coli,* they found that such bacteriophages ceased to perform their normal functions. However, bacteriophages with addition or deletion of three base pairs in DNA molecule, had performed normal functions. From this experiment, they concluded that a genetic code is in triplet form, because the addition of one or two nucleotides has put the reading of the code out of order, while the addition of third nucleotide resulted in a return to the proper reading of the message.

Table 44.3. Possible singlet, doublet and triplet codes of mRNA.

Single code (4 words)	Doublet code (16 words)				Triplet code (64 words)			
					AAA	AAG	AAC	AAU
					AGA	AGG	AGC	AGU
					ACA	ACG	ACC	ACU
					AUA	AUG	AUC	AUU
					GAA	GAG	GAC	GAU
					GGA	GGG	GGC	GGU
A	AA	AG	AC	AU	GCA	GCG	GCC	GCU
G	GA	GG	GC	GU	GUA	GUG	GUC	GUU
C	CA	CG	CC	CU	CAA	CAG	CAC	CAU
U	UA	UG	UC	UU	CGA	CGG	CGC	CGU
					CCA	CCG	CCC	CCU
					CUA	CUG	CUC	CUU
					UAA	UAG	UAC	UAU
					UGA	UGG	UGC	UGU
					UCA	UCG	UCC	UCU
					UUA	UUG	UUC	UUU

CODON ASSIGNMENT

(Cracking the Code or Deciphering the Code)

The genetic code has been cracked or deciphered by the following kinds of approaches :

A. Theoretical Approach

George Gamow proposed the **diamond code** (1954) and the **triangle code** (1955) and suggested the following properties of the genetic code :

(*i*) **A triplet codon** corresponding to one amino acid of the polypeptide chain.

(*ii*) **Direct template translation** by codon-amino acid pairing.

(*iii*) Translation of the code in an **overlapping** manner.

(*iv*) **Degeneracy** of the code, *i.e.*, an amino acid being coded by more than one codon.

(*v*) **Colinearity** of nucleic acid and the primary protein synthesized.

(*vi*) **Universality** of the code, *i.e.*, the code being essentially the same for different organisms.

B. The *in vitro* codon Assignment

1. Discovery and use of polynucleotide phosphorylase enzyme. Manago and **Ochoa** isolated an enzyme from the bacteria (*e. g., Azobacter vinelandii*) that catalyzes the breakdown of RNA in bacterial cells. This enzyme is called **polynucleotide phosphorylase.** They found that outside of the cell (*in vitro*), with high concentrations of ribonucleotides, the reaction could be driven in reverse and an RNA molecule could be made. Incorporation of bases into the molecule is random and does not require a DNA template. Thus, in 1955 **Manago** and **Ochoa** made possible the artificial synthesis of polynucleotides (=mRNA) containing only a single type of nucleotides (U, A, C, or G respectively) repeated many times.

Polynucleotide	Configuration
1. Polyuridylic acid or poly (U)	UUUUUU
2. Polyadenylic acid or poly (A)	AAAAAA
3. Polycytilic acid or poly (C)	CCCCCC
4. Polyguanidylic acid or poly (G)	GGGGGG

Thus, the action of polynucleotide phosphorylase can be represented in the following way:

$$(RNA)_n + \text{ribonucleoside diphosphate} \xrightleftharpoons[\text{phosphorylase}]{\text{polynucleotide}} (RNA)_{n+1} + Pi$$

The polynucleotide phosphorylase enzyme differs from RNA polymerase used to transcribe mRNA from DNA polymerase used to transcribe mRNA from DNA in that : (i) it does not require a template or primer; (ii) the activated substrates are ribonucleoside diphosphates (*e. g.*, UDP, ADP, CDP and GDP) and not triphosphates; and (iii) orthophosphate (Pi) is produced instead of pyrophosphates (PPi).

The deciphering of the genetic code was made possible by the use of synthetic (or artificial) polynucleotides and trinucleotides. The different types of techniques used include the use of polymers containing a single type of nucleotide (called **homopolymers**), the use of mixed polymers (**copolymers**) containing more than one type of nucleotides (**heteropolymers**) in random or defined sequences and the use trinucleotides (or **"minimessengers"**) in ribosome-binding or filter-binding.

2. Codon assignment with unknown sequence. (i) Codon assignment by homopolymer. The first clue to codon assignment was provided by **Nirenberg and Matthaei** (1961) when they used in *vitro* system for the synthesis of a polypeptide using an artificially synthesized mRNA molecule containing only one type of nucleotide (*i.e.*, homopolymer). Prior to performing the actual experiments, they tested the ability of a cell-free protein synthesizing system to incorporate radioactive amino acids into newly synthesized proteins. Their cell-free extracts of *E.coli* contained ribosomes, tRNAs, aminoacyl-tRNA synthetase enzymes, DNA and mRNA. The DNA of this extract was eradicated by the help of **deoxyribonuclease** enzyme, thus, the template which might synthesize new mRNA was destroyed. When twenty amino acids were added to this mixture along with ATP, GTP, K^+ and MG^{2+}, they were incorporated into proteins. This incorporation continued so long as mRNA was present in such a cell-free suspension. It also continued in the presence of synthetic polynucleotides (mRNAs) which could be made with the help of polynucleotide phosphorylase enzyme.

The first successful use of this technique was made by **Nirenberg and Matthaei** who synthesized a chain of uracil molecules (poly U) as their synthetic mRNA (homopolymer). Poly (U) seemed a good choice, because there could be no ambiguity in a message consisting of only one base. Poly (U) was good choice for other reasons: it binds well to ribosomes and, as it turned out, the product protein was insoluble and easy to isolate. When poly(U) was presented as the message to the cell-free system containing all the amino acids, one amino acid was exclusively selected from the mixture for incorporation into the polypeptide, called **polyphenylalanine.** This amino acid was phenylalanine and it could be concluded that some sequence of UUU coded for phenylalanine. Other homogeneous chains of nucleotides (Poly A, Poly C and Poly G) were inactive for phenylalanine incorporation. The mRNA code word of phenylalanine was, therefore, shown to be UUU. The corresponding DNA code word for phenylalanine can be deduced to be AAA. Thus, the first code word to be deciphered was UUU.

This discovery was extended in the laboratories of **Nirenberg and Ochoa.** The experiment was repeated using synthetic **poly (A)** and **poly (C)** chains, which gave **polylysine** and **polyproline** respectively. Thus, AAA was identified as the code for lysine and CCC as code of proline. A poly

(G) message was found non-functional in *vitro,* since it attains secondary structure and, thus, could not attach to the ribosomes. In this way three of 64 codons were easily accounted for.

(ii) Codon assignment by heteropolymers (Copolymers with random sequences). Further exposition of the genetic code took place by using synthetic messenger RNAs containing two kinds of bases. This technique was used in the laboratories of **Ochoa** and **Nirenberg** and led the deduction of the composition of codons for the 20 amino acids. The synthetic messengers contained the bases at random (called **random copolymers).** For example, in a random copolymer using U and A nucleotides eight triplets are possible, such as UUU, UUA, UAA,UAU, AAA, AAU, AUU and AUA. Theoretically, eight amino acids could be coded by these eight codons. Actual experiments, however, yielded only six phenylalanine, leucine, tryosine, lysine asparagine and isoleucine. By varying the relative compositions of U and A in the random copolymer and determining the percentage of the different amino acids in the proteins formed, it was possible to deduce the composition of the code for different amino acids.

3. Assignment of codons with known sequences. (i) Use of trinucleotides or minimessengers in filter binding (Ribosome-binding technique). Ribosome binding technique of **Nirenberg** and **Leder** (1964) made use of the finding that aminoacyl-tRNA molecules specifically bind to ribosome-mRNA complex. This binding does not require the presence of a long mRNA molecule; in fact, the association of a **trinucleotide** or **minimessenger** with the ribosome is sufficient to cause aminoacyl-tRNA binding. When a mixture of such small mRNA molecules-ribosomes and amino acid-tRNA complexes are incubated for a short time and then filtered through a **nitrocellulose membrane,** then the mRNA-ribosome-tRNA-amino acid complex is retained back and rest of the mixture passes through the filter. By using a series of 20 different amino acid mixtures, each containing one radioactive amino acid at a time, it is possible to find out the amino acid corresponding to each triplet by analysing the radioactivity absorbed by the membrane, *e.g.*, the triplet GCC and GUU retain only alanyl-tRNA and valyl-tRNA respectively. All 64 possible triplets have been synthesized and tested in this way. Forty five of them have given clear-cut results. Later on, with the help of longer synthetic messages it has been possible to decipher 61 out of the possible 64 codons.

C. The *in vivo* Codon Assignment

The cell free protein synthetic systems, though have proved of great significance in decipherment of the genetic code, but they could not tell us whether the genetic code so deciphered is used in the living systems of all organisms also. Three kinds of techniques are used by different molecular biologists to determine whether the same code is also used in *vivo* (a) amino acid replacement studies (*e.g.*, tryptophan synthetase synthesis in *E. coli* (**Yanofsky** *et al.* 1963) and haemoglobin synthesis in man), (b) frameshift mutations (*e.g.*, investigations of **Terzaghi** *et. al.* 1966, on lysozyme enzyme of T_4 bacteriophages, and (c) comparison of a DNA or mRNA polynucleotide cryptogram with its corresponding polypeptide clear text (*e.g.*, comparison of amino acid sequence of the R_{17} bacteriophage coat protein with the nucleotide sequence of the R_{17} mRNA in the region of the molecule that dictates coat-protein synthesis by **S. Cory** *et. al.*, 1970).

Thus, *in vitro* and *in vivo* studies, so far described, gave the way to formulate a code table for twenty amino acids (see Table 38.4 and Table 38.5).

CHARACTERISTICS OF GENETIC CODE

The genetic code has the following general properties:

1. The code is a triplet codon. The nucleotides of mRNA are arranged as a linear sequence of codons, each codon consisting of three successive nitrogenous bases, *i.e.*, the code is a triplet codon. The concept of triplet codon has been supported by two types of point mutations: frameshift mutations and base substitutions.

Table 44.4. The genetic dictionary. The trinucleotide codons are written in the 5'→3' direction.

First base	Second base: U		Second base: C		Second base: A		Second base: G		Third base
	U		C		A		G		
U	UUA	Phe	UCU	Ser	UAU	Tyr	UGU	Cys	U
	UUC	Phe	UCC	Ser	UAC	Tyr	UGC	Cys	C
	UUA	Leu	UCA	Ser	UAA	Non-sense codon	UGA	Non-sense codon	A
	UUG	Leu	UCG	Ser	UAG	Non-sense codon	UGG	Trp	G
C	CUU	Leu	CCU	Pro	CAU	His	CGU	Arg	U
	CUC	Leu	CCC	Pro	CAC	His	CGC	Arg	C
	CUA	Leu	CCA	Pro	CAA	Gln	CGA	Arg	A
	CUG	Leu	CCG	Pro	CAG	Gln	CGG	Arg	G
A	AUU	Ileu	ACU	Thr	AAU	Asn	AGU	Ser	U
	AUC	Ileu	ACC	Thr	AAC	Asn	AGC	Ser	C
	AUA	Ileu	ACA	Thr	AAA	Lys	AGA	Arg	A
	AUG*	Met	ACG	Thr	AAG	Lys	AGG	Arg	G
G	GUU	Val	GUC	Ala	GAU	Asp	GGU	Gly	U
	GUC	Val	GCC	Ala	GAC	Asp	GGC	Gly	C
	GUA	Val	GCA	Ala	GAA	Glu	GGA	Gly	A
	GUG	Val	GCG	Ala	GAG	Glu	GGG	Gly	G

***AUG** – Met or chain initiation codon.

Table 44.5. Amino acids and their messenger RNA codons.

Alanine – (Ala)	GCA GCG GCC GCU	Glycine – (Gly)	GGA GGC GGC GGU	Leucine – (Leu)	CUA CUG CUC CUU UUA UUG	Threonine – (Thr)	ACA ACG ACC ACU
Arginine – (Arg)	AGA AGG CGA CGG CGC CGU	Glutamine – (Gln; Glun)	CAA CAG	Methionine – (Met) (Starting codon)	AUG	Tryptophan – (Trp)	UGG
Aspartic acid – (Asp)	GAC GAU	Glutamic acid – (Glu)	GAA GAG	Phenylalanine – (Phe)	UUC UUU	Tyrosine – (Tyr)	UAC UAU
Asparagine– (Asn; Aspn)	AAC AAU	Histidine – (His)	CAC CAU	Proline – (Pro)	CCA CCG CCC CCU	Valine – (Val)	GUA GUG* GUC GUU
Cysteine – (Cys)	UGC UGU	(Isoleucine – (Ile)	AUC AUU AUA	Serine – (Ser)	AGC AGU UCA UCG UCC ICU	Terminator – (Nonsense codons)	UAA (ocher) UAG (amber) UGA (opal)
		Lysine – (Lys)	AAA AAG				

*GUC is also used as a start codon for some proteins.

(i) Frameshift mutations. Evidently, the genetic message once initiated at a fixed point is read in a definite frame in a series of three letter words. The framework would be disturbed as soon as there is a deletion or addition of one or more bases. When such frameshift mutations were intercrossed, then in certain combinations they produce wild type normal gene. It was concluded that one of them was deletion and the other an addition, so that the disturbed order of the frame due to mutation will be restored by the other (Fig. 44.26).

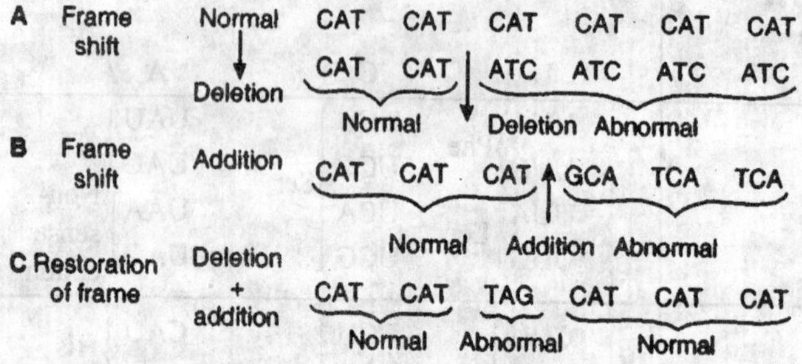

Fig. 44.26. Frame-shift mutations: A — Delection; B— Addition; C—Restoration of frame.

Fig. 38.27. Basses in mRNA are read sequentially in the 5′ to 3′ direction, in group of three bases.

(ii) Base substitution. If in a mRNA molecule at a particular point, one base pair is replaced by another without any deletion or addition, the meaning of one codon containing such an altered base will be changed. In consequence, in place of a particular amino acid at a particular position in a polypeptide, another amino acid will be incorporated. For example, due to substitution mutation, in the gene for tryptophan synthetase enzyme in *E.coli*, the GGA codon for glycine becomes a missence codon AGA which codes for arginine. **Missence codon** is a codon which undergoes an alteration to specify another amino acid.

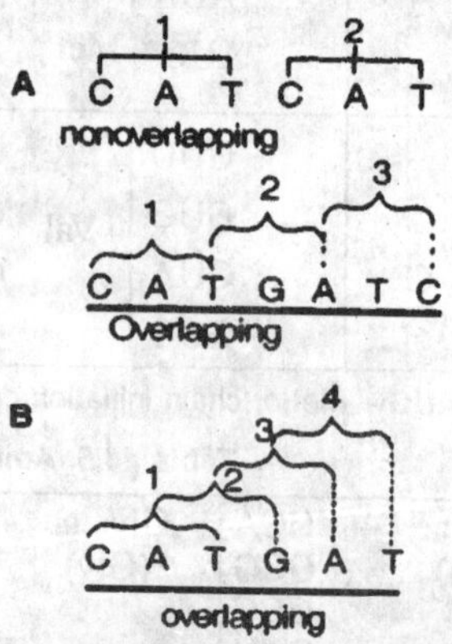

Fig. 44. 28. A — Non-overlapping codons; B— Overlapping of codon due to one base; C—Overlapping of codon due to two bases.

A more direct evidence for a triplet code came from the finding that a piece of mRNA containing 90 nucleotides, corresponded to a polypeptide chain of 30 amino acids of a growing haemoglobin molecule. Similarly, 1200 nucleotides of "satellite" tobacco necrosis virus direct the synthesis of coat protein molecules which have 372 amino acids.

2. The code is non-overlapping. In translating mRNA molecules the codons do not *overlap* but are "read" sequentially (Fig. 44.27). Thus, a **non-overlapping code** means that a base in a mRNA is not used for different codons. In Figure 38.28, it has been shown that an overlapping code can mean coding for four amino acids from six bases. However, in actual practice six bases code for not more than two amino acids. For example, in case of an overlapping code, a single change (of substitution type) in the base sequence will be reflected in substitutions of more than one amino acid in corresponding protein. Many examples have accumulated since 1956 in which a single base substitution results into a single amino acid change in insulin, tryptophan synthelase, TMV coat protein, alkaline phosphatase, haemoglobin, etc.

However, it has been shown that in the bacteriophage $\phi \times 174$ there is a possibility of overlapping the genes and codons (**Barrel** and coworkers, 1976; **Sanger**, et al., 1977).

3. The code is commaless. The genetic code is commaless, which means that no codon is reserved for punctuations. It means that after one amino acid is coded, the second amino acid will be automatically, coded by the next three letters and that no letters are wasted as the punctuation marks (Fig. 44.29).

4. The code is non-ambiguous. Non-ambiguous code means that a particular codon will always code for the same amino acid. In case of ambiguous code, the same codon could have different meanings or in other words, the same codon could code two or more than two different amino acids. Generally, as a rule, the same codon shall never code for two different amino acids. However, there are some reported exceptions to this rule: the codons AUG and GUG both may code for *methionine* as initiating or starting codon, although GUG is meant for *valine*. Likewise, GGA codon codes for two amino acids *glycine* and *glutamic acid.*

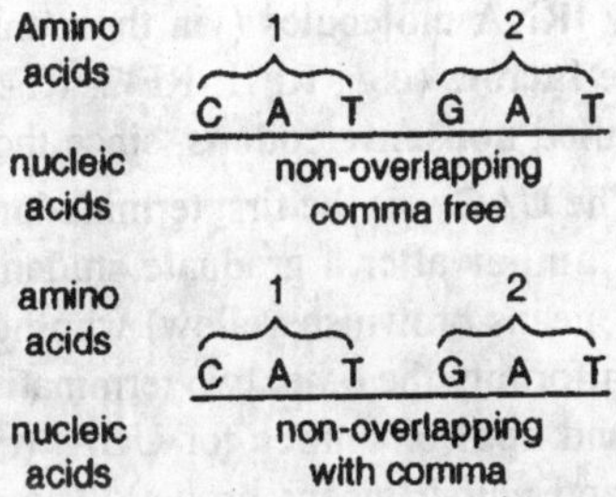

Fig. 44.29. Two forms of genetic code. A—Genetic code without comma; B—Genetic code with comma.

5. The code has polarity. The code is always read in a fixed direction, *i.e.*, in the 5′→3′ direction. In other words, the codon has a **polarity**. It is apparent that if the code is read in opposite directions, it would specify two different proteins, since the codon would have reversed base sequence :

Codon :	UUG	AUC	GUC	UCG	CCA	ACA	AGG
Polypeptide:→	Leu	Ile	Val	Ser	Prof	Thr	Arg
	Val	Leu	Leu	Ala	Thr	Thr	Gly←

6. The code is degenerate. More than one codon may specify the same amino acid; this is called **degeneracy** of the code. For example, except for *tryptophan* and *methionine*, which have a single codon each, all other 18 amino acids have more than one codon. Thus, nine amino acids, namely *phenylalanine, tyrosine, histidine, glutamine, asparagine, lysine, aspartic acid, glutamic acid* and *cysteine*, have two codons each. Isoleucine has three codons. Five amino acids, namely *valine, proline, threonine, alanine* and *glycine*, have four codons each. Three amino acids, namely *leucine, arginine* and *serine,* have six codons each (see Table 38.5).

The code degeneracy is basically of two types : partial and complete. **Partial degeneracy** occurs when first two nucleotides are identical but the third (*i.e.*, 3′ base) nucleotide of the degenerate codons differs, *e.g.*, CUU and CUC code for leucine, **Complete degeneracy** occurs when any of the four bases can take third position and still code for the same amino acid (e.g., UCU, UCC, UCA and UCG code for serine).

Degeneracy of genetic code has certain biological advantages. For example, it permits essentially the same complement of enzymes and other proteins to be specified by microorganisms varying widely in their DNA base composition. Degeneracy also provides a mechanism of minimising mutational lethality.

7. Some codes act as start codons. In most organisms, AUG codon is the **start or initiation codon**, *i.e.*, the polypeptide chain starts either with **methionine** (eukaryotes) or **N-formylmethionine** (prokaryotes). Methionyl or N-formylmethionyl-tRNA specifically binds to the **initiation site** of mRNA containing the AUG initiation codon. In rare cases, GUG also serves as the initiation codon, *e.g.*, bacterial protein synthesis. Normally, GUG codes for valine, but when normal AUG codon is lost by deletion, only then GUG is used as initiation codon.

8. Some codes act as stop codons. Three codons UAG, UAA and UGA are the chain **stop or termination** codons. They do not code for any of the amino acids. These codons are not read by any tRNA molecules (via their anticodons), but are read by some specific proteins, called **release factors** (e.g., RF-1, RF-2, RF-3 in prokaryotes and RF in eukaryotes). These codons are also called **nonsense codons**, since they do not specify any amino acid.

The UAG was the first termination codon to be discovered by **Sidney Brenner** (1965). It was named **amber** after a graduate student named **Bernstein** (= the German word for 'amber' and amber means brownish yellow) who help in the discovery of a class of mutations. Apparently, to give uniformity the other two termination codons were also named after colours such as **ochre** for UAA and **opal** or **umber** for UGA. (*ochre* means yellow red or pale yellow; *opal* means milky white and *umber* means brown). The existence of more than one stop codon might be a safety measure, in case the first codon fails to function.

9. The code is universal. Same genetic code is found valid for all organisms ranging from bacteria to man. Such universality of the code was demonstrated by **Marshall, Caskey** and **Nirenberg** (1967) who found that *E.coli* (Bacterium), *Xenopus laevis* (Amphibian) and guinea pig (mammal) amino acyl-tRNA use almost the same code. **Nirenberg** has also stated that the genetic code may have developed 3 billion years ago with the first bacteria, and it has changed very little throughout the evolution of living organisms.

Recently, some differences have been discovered between the universal genetic code and mitochondrial genetic code (Table 38.6).

Table 44.6. Differences between the 'universal genetic code' and two mitochondrial genetic codes.

Codon	Mammalian mitocondrial code	Yeast mitochondrial code"	"Universal Code
1. UGA	*Trp* *	*Trp*	Stop
2. AUA	*Met*	*Met*	Ile
3. CUA	Leu	*Thr*	Leu
4. AGA	*Stop*	Arg	Arg
5. AGG			

* Italic type indicates that the code differs from the 'universal' code.

Codon and Anticodon

The codon words of DNA would be complementary to the mRNA code words (*i.e.*, DNA codes run in 3′→5′ direction and mRNA code words run in 5′→3′ direction) and so thereby the three bases forming the **anticodon** of tRNA (*i.e.*, bases of anticodon run in 3′→5′ direction). Three bases of anticodon pair with the mRNA on the ribosomes at the time of aligning the amino acids during protein synthesis (*i.e.*, translation of mRNA into proteins which proceeds in mRNA → COOH direction). For example, one of two mRNA and DNA code words for the amino acid phenylalanine is UUC and AAG respectively, and the corresponding anticodon of tRNA is CAA. This indicates that codon and anticodon pairing is antiparallel. In this case, C pairs with G and U pairs with A.

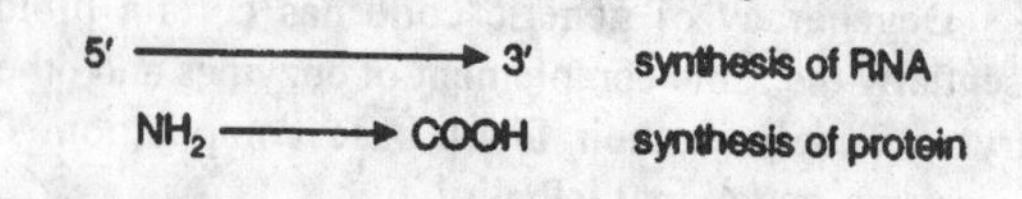

Fig. 44.30. Directions of synthesis of RNA and protein with respect to the coding strand of DNA.

WOBBLE HYPOTHESIS

To explain the possible cause of degeneracy of codons, **Crick** (1966) proposed the **wobble hypothesis** (wobble means to sway or move unsteadily). Since there are 61 codons specifying amino acids, the cell should contain 61 tRNA molecules, each with a different anticodon. Actually, however, the number of tRNA molecule types discovered is much less than 61. This implies that the anticodons of tRNAs read more than one codon on mRNA. For example, yeast $tRNA^{ala}$ with anticodon bases 5′ IGC 3′ (where I stands for inosine, a derivative of adenine or A) could bind to three codons in mRNA such as 5′ GCU 3′, 5′GCC3′ and 5′GCA3′. Inosine is frequently found as the 5′ base of the anticodon; at the time of pairing with the base of the codons it wobbles and can pair either with U, C or A of three codons (see Table 38.7). Thus, Crick's wobble hypothesis states that the *base at 5′ end of the anticodon is not spatially confined as the other two bases allowing it to form hydrogen bonds with any of several bases located at the 3′ end of a codon* (Fig. 44.31).

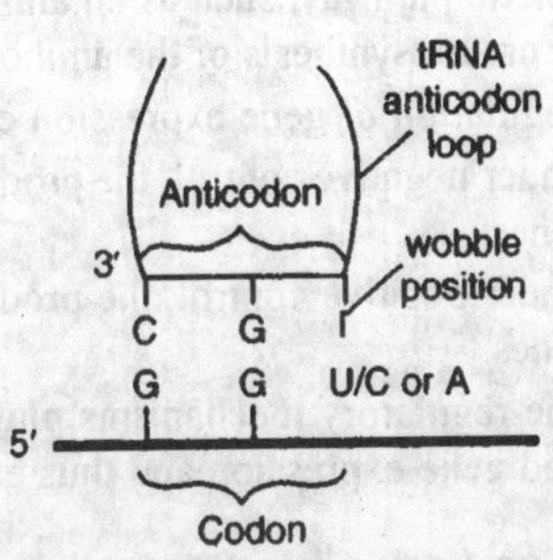

Fig. 44.31. Wobble hypothesis. In the third site (5′ end)) of the anticodon I can take either of three wobble positions, thus, being able to pair with either U, C or A. This means that a single tRNA species carrying an amino acid can recognize three codons in mRNA: GCU, GCC and GCA.

Table 44.7. Allowed base-pairing combinations according to the wobble hypothesis.

5′ base of codon	3′ base of anticodon
C	G
A	U
U	A or G
G	U, C or A
I	U, C or A

REGULATION OF GENE EXPRESSION

Now this is known to us that how the genetic information stored in DNA or gene is expressed through the process of protein synthesis.

The analysis reveals, there are vast differences in the concentration of different proteins, even in a simple bacterium *Escherichia coli*, where some proteins may be synthesised in low concentration as 5 to 10 molecules, while in others may be produced as 100,000 molecules per cell.

This phenomenon shows the regulation of gene expression.

Since 1900, this was known that lactose-metabolising enzymes are synthesised by yeast only when it is grown in the presence of lactose sugar.

Thereafter, bacteria were shown to adapt to their chemical environment by synthesising certain enzymes depending upon the substrate present.

Such adaptive enzymes are called **inducible enzymes.**

Contrary to it, some enzyme types were synthesised all the times irrespective of the chemical constitution of the environment, and are called **constitutive enzymes.**

Another type of regulation of gene expression was revealed when the end product of a biosynthetic pathway, such as an amino acid is provided in the medium. Under such a condition, the internal biosynthesis of the amino acid stops. Such regulation is called **repressible** regulation.

Regulation of gene expression can also be described as **negative** or **positive** control.

Under negative control, the product of the regulatory gene shuts off the expression of the said gene/genes.

Under positive control, the product of the regulatory gene activates transcription of the said gene/genes.

The regulatory mechanisms play an important role in the life of a cell as they prevent any unwanted gene expression and thus efficient energy management is ensured.

Induction (Inducible Control) and Repression (Repressible Control)

Induction. As we know, the genetic potential of a virus is limited, as it uses the host machinery for its replication.

On the other hand, the bacterial cell can synthesise its constituents from simple salts and sugar.

The bacterium *Escherichia coli* has about 2500 genes. The expression of these genes is usually controlled to achieve maximum cellular economy. This shows that genes will be turned on or off as per requirement.

A set of genes will be switched on when there is necessity to metabolise a new substrate.

This phenomenon is called **induction** and the small molecules responsible for this are known as **inducers.**

Repression. Similarly, when a metabolite needed by the bacterium (*E. coli*) is provided in excess from out side, the bacterium stops making it and thus conserves its reserves.

This condition is achieved by the added metabolite turning off a set of genes involved in producing that metabolite in the bacterial cell. This phenomenon is called **feed-back repression.**

The phenomena of induction and repression can be described on the basis of **operon concept.** This is as follows :

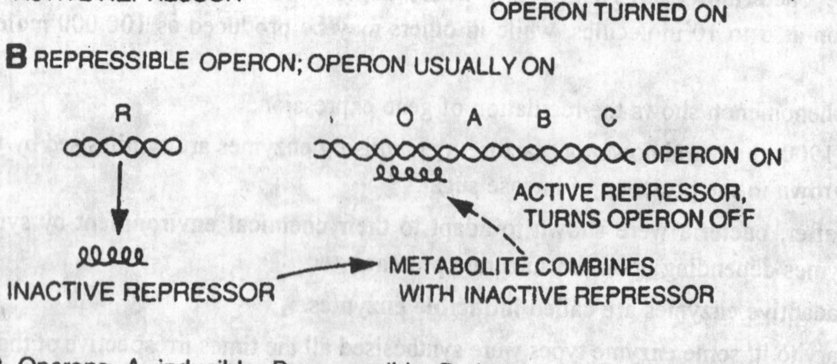

Fig. 44.32. Operons. A, inducible; B, repressible. Both the operons become off when operator site is bound by the repressor formed by regulator gene R.

Operon Concept

Francois Jacob and Jacques Monod (1961), while working at the Pasteur Institute, Paris, proposed that metabolic pathways are regulated as a unit. They studied the change in the nature of enzymes of *E. coli* when provided with different kinds of sugars. They found, when the sugar lactose is added to the cultures of *E. coli*, it induces three enzymes necessary to break down the lactose into galactose. These newly synthesized enzymes are – ***(i)*** β -galactosidase, ***(ii)*** permease and (*iii*) transacetylase. According to them, the synthesis of these three enzymes is controlled by a long DNA segment known as **operon** which is divisible into an operator site O and three structural genes Z, Y and A. The action of structural genes is regulated by operator site with the help of a **repressor** protein produced by the action of gene 'i' known as the **regulator gene.** The genes are expressed or not expressed that depends on whether the operator switch is on or off. When the switch is on, the three genes are transcribed by RNA polymerase into a single stretch of messenger RNA covering all the three genes. Each structural gene is generally known as **cistron** and the transcribed long m RNA covering all the cistrons is known as **polycistronic.**

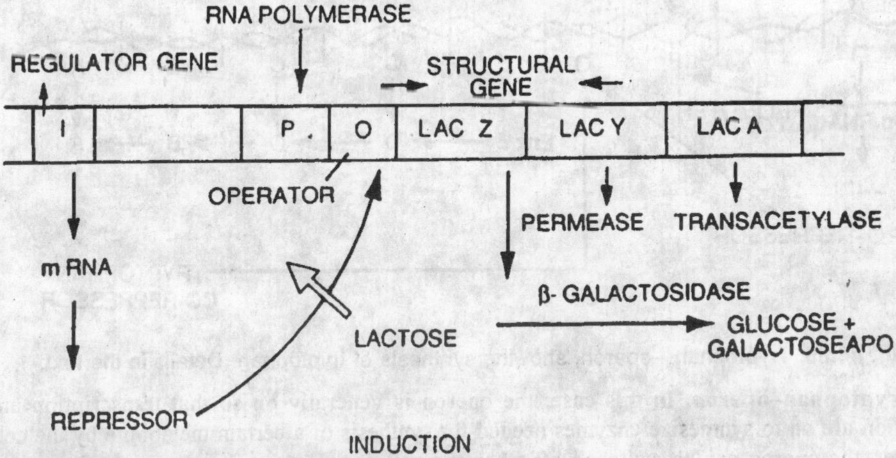

Fig. 44.33. Lac operon. Details in the text.

The switching on or off of the operator switch is achieved by a protein known as **repressor.** When this protein ties together to the operator (O) and blocks it, the switch is turned off and the three genes (Z, Y, A) are not expressed.

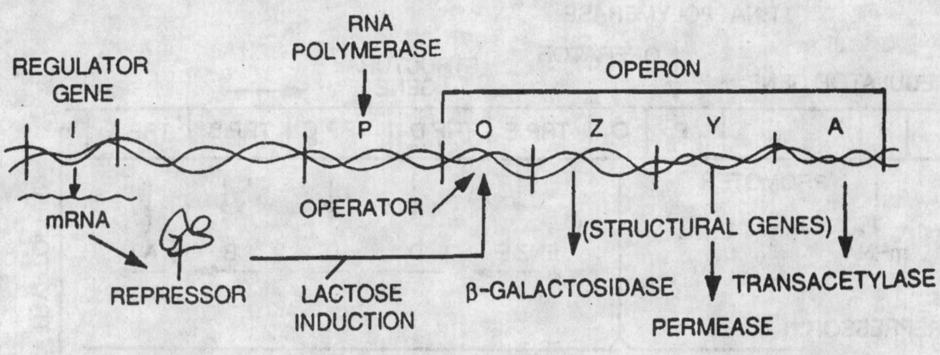

Fig. 44.34. Lac-operon. Lactose acts as inducer and activates repressor, removes it from operator site with the result operon is activated that transcribes mRNA and within the cell metabolism of lactose begins.

Lac-operon. This is an example of **inducible operon.** A few molecules of lactose are added into the cell by the action of the enzyme permease, a small quantity of which is found even under repressed conditions. These few molecules are then converted into an active form of lactose which binds to the repressor (i gene product) and thus, the repressor cannot bind to the operator switch any more. When the operator is free of repressor RNA polymerase starts the transcription of the operon by binding the promotor site P. Messenger RNA corresponding to all the three enzymes is synthesized which gets translated to produce the three enzymes— β -galactosidase, permease and transacetylase. With the production of these three enzymes metabolism of lactose begins. The synthesis of enzymes is continued unless and until all lactose molecules are consumed by the cell. When the last molecules of lactose bound to repressor are also consumed, the inactive repressor becomes active and binds to operator site (O) to switch off the operon as normal.

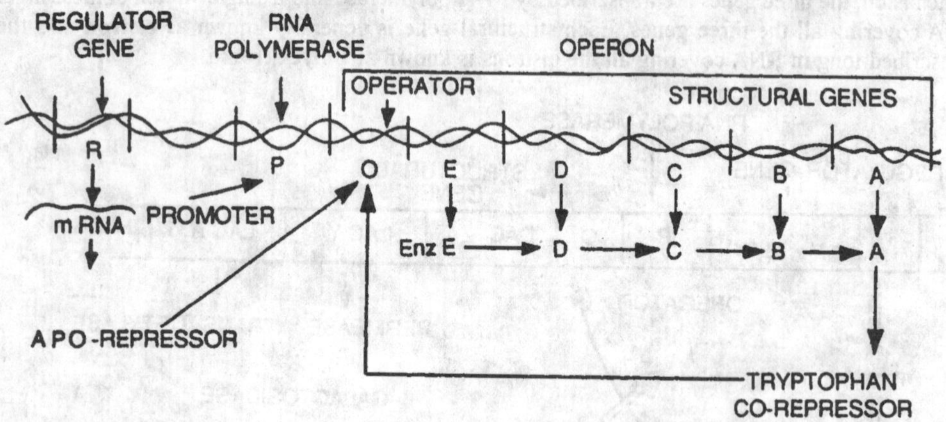

Fig. 44.35. Tryptophan—operon, showing synthesis of tryptophan. Details in the text.

Tryptophan–operon. In this case, the operon is generally on so that transcription and translation are on to synthesize enzymes needed for synthesis of a certain metabolite by the cell. However, the operon can be switched off when the cell does not require the metabolite or the metabolite has been produced in excess. The tryptophan operon consists of five genes (trp E, D, C, B and A) coding for five enzymes (Enz E, D, C, B and A) catalysing the synthesis of tryptophan (an amino acid) and thus constituting an anabolic pathway. The presence of tryptophan serves to repress the synthesis of the enzymes responsible for its manufacture.

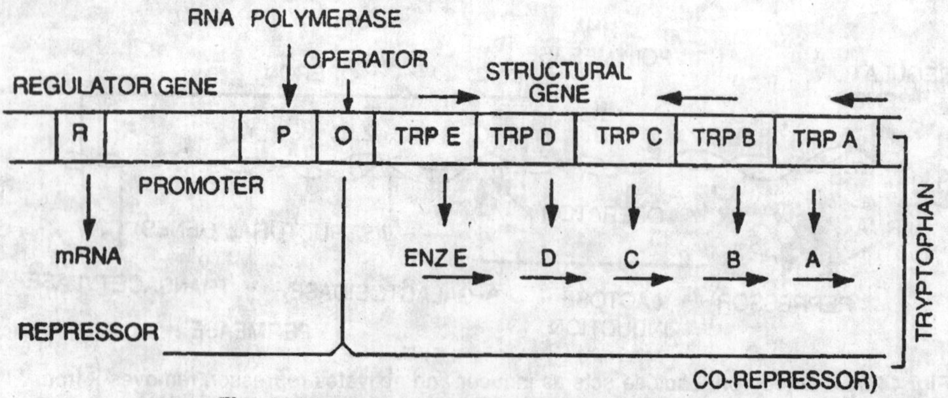

Fig. 44.36. Tryptophan operon. Details in the text.

The five structural genes coding for these five enzymes are regulated by a single operator switch. Here, the repressor protein produced by the regulatory genes does not bind to the operator by itself. However, when tryptophan is added, it binds to the repressor and is known as the **co-repressor.** The repressor-corepressor complex binds to the operator and blocks the expression of this operon.

The structure of the tryptophan operon is more or less similar to that of the lac operon, but has a functional variation. In this case the R gene product is equivalent to the i gene of lac operon. The R gene product produces protein which by itself is unable to bind to operator. This is referred to as **apo-repressor.** In the presence of tryptophan a co-repressor, the functional repressor is formed which now binds to the operator and prevents the transcription of the operon and production of tryptophan. Here the operon model explains both the induction and repression phenomenon in procaryotes.

House-keeping Genes

However, all the information present in the gene is not always used. Many genes remain silent, and expressed only when the gene product is needed. There are certain genes whose products are constantly needed during various metabolic activities of a cell, and therefore, they are known as **house-keeping genes,** and their function is referred to as house-keeping or constitutive activity.

DIFFERENTIATION AND DEVELOPMENT

The most complex of all the physiological processes is **growth**. The process of growth results from an increase in protoplasm, leading to an irreversible increase in size and weight. The growth involves three stages-stage of **cell division**, stage of **cell elongation** and stage of **cell differentiation.** Growth is associated with differentiation of cells which is a change in form and physiological activity. Development refers to the sequence of processes in the overall life history of a cell or an organism including growth, differentiation, maturation and senescence. In unicellular organisms growth involves increase in their volume and numbers. Cell division serves as a means of reproduction in these organisms, and leads to increase in population. In the multicellular organisms, however, growth is much more complex.

The life of flowering plant begins with the fertilized egg. Through a series of divisions an embryo is formed which is enclosed in a seed. Germination then takes place leading to the formation of a seedling. After passing through the juvenile phases a mature plant is finally formed.

When we observe the changes in the zygote as if gradually develops into an embryo and later into an adult organism (plant or animal), we find that physiological behaviour of cells changes with time. Generally the embryonic cells remain totipotent, or in other words each embryonic cell is capable of giving rise to an embryo and give rise to all tissues of the adult organism. However, as cell division proceeds, the cells, of the adult organism lose the property of totipotency. Now the group of cells give rise to specialized tissues such as leaf and stem in a plant and brain and liver in an animal. This process, where the totipotent embryonic cells are being converted into specialized cells forming specific tissues is known as **differentiation**. As embryonic cells divide, and the function of these specialized cells becomes restricted, to an organ of an adult organism, it is known as **determination.** This way, development contains both growth and differentiation. It has been revealed that these developmental changes are preceded by many molecular changes. Some of the developing cells start producing a new set of proteins and at the same time, they stop producing those proteins which were synthesized earlier. For example, muscle cells synthesize myosin; erythroid cells synthesize globin; brain cells synthesize myelin and leaf cells synthesize Ru BP carboxylase. The synthesis of these proteins is due to differentiation.

Robert Briggs and Thomas King have brought out some experiments on nuclear transplantation to prove that how these primary events trigger differentiation along a particular pathway. They isolated some mature cells from the body of frog and toad. They destroyed the nuclei of these cells and transplanted fresh nuclei from embryonic and tadpole cells into the enucleated eggs. Many of the embryos having transplanted nuclei developed into normal tadpoles, on the other hand, if the cells were transplanted with nuclei from differentiated organs such as intestine, tadpoles were not developed. Thus it becomes clear that the nuclei undergo some change during differentiation. Further investigations revealed that totipotency in animal systems was retained by embryonic cells upto a specific stage, and beyond that the cells acquired the function of the developed organ. However, in plants even a mature differential cell of leaf or stem can be dedifferentiated to form a **callus** which can give rise to a whole plant.

The main process of differentiation involves altered gene activity. Thus, different genes act at different times to suit the requirement of the organism. It is believed that the change in gene activity is brought about by its interaction with the cytoplasm. The components of the cytoplasm are further determined by a wide variety of environmental factors such as nutrition, light, temperature, cell to cell interaction and the pH. In other words the modulation of the gene and its cytoplasm is interdependent.

A lot of information has been collected by using *Drosophila melanogaster* (fruit fly), as a working model and the developmental mutants that have been isolated.

It is quite clear that during development, a single fertilized egg gives rise to cells that have different developmental fates.

This asymmetry may be a part of the egg itself in terms of distribution of its cytoplasmic components as in *Drosophila* or in the initial division cycles of mammals.

It is supposed that each cell type is characterised by its pattern of gene expression or by particular gene products which it produces.

In fruit fly, many types of genes have been identified by mutation and analysing their functions.

These genes not only regulate on another but perhaps also code for structural proteins.

Many of these genes have conserved motifs, the most common of which is known as **homebox**. Such homeboxes are distributed in other eukaryotes also, such as worms, frogs and mammals. It is thought that they may be characteristics of all animals.

Cancer and Oncogenes

Cancer can be cited as a problem associated with differentiation and development. The process of growth and differentiation are regulated by various growth controlling mechanisms, which operate to maintain the structure and coordinated function of the various parts of the organism. In malignant disease (cancer) there is a breakdown in this process-a cell/cells escapes from the usual growth control restrictions and is able to grow and divide, and to move more freely than normal cells. This results frequently in the ability to invade and damage normal tissues, and to spread by way of blood or lymphatic systems to other regions of the organism. Malignant cells may arise in any tissue in which cell proliferation takes place.

Thus, cancer may be defined as unorganized growth in which the controlling and regulating mechanisms have disappeared or have been ineffective.

The cancer cells continue to divide unchecked, resulting in an ever-increasing number of cancerous cells and, therefore, the size of the tumour keeps growing. Two hypotheses have been proposed to explain how a normal cell changes into a cancerous cell — (*i*) According to one hypothesis cancer may be essentially due to alterations in one or more chromosomes or gene mutations in the nuclei of the somatic cells. (*ii*) According to the other hypothesis, a genetic change may not be an essential factor. Instead, some change occurs in the cytoplasm, resulting in the loss of control on the nuclear and cytoplasmic divisions.

There are three main differences between the cancer cells and the normal cells. They are as follows.

(*i*) Unlike the normal cells, cancer cells show indefinite growth.

(*ii*) As the cancer cells are derived from normal cells they seem to arise from **transformation** where normal constraints of growth are bypassed.

(*iii*) At some stage cancer cells acquire the ability to **metastasize**, that is, they become capable of invading normal tissue and start a new chain of transformation away from the original site.

Oncogenesis. Multiple genetic changes also occur during the transformation of a normal cell to cancer cell. This process is called **oncogenesis**. Such a transformation may be caused spontaneously or by the agents known as **carcinogens.** They include agents such as radiations, chemical compounds and viruses.

Viruses and cancer. Rous (1910) observed that a particular type of virus causes tumours to develop in chickens. The virus is an RNA virus now known as the Rous sarcoma virus. Recently, viruses have been associated with several kinds of tumours in mammals, especially in mice. The virus transforms the cells from their normal state to a cancerous state; the transformation is accompanied by changes in the DNA of the infected cell and profound functional disturbances, including changes in cell surface, properties and behaviour. Although viruses have been isolated from human tumour material, in no case has any human cancer yet been conclusively shown to have been caused by a virus.

Now, two types of genes, *i.e.*, (*i*) **oncogenes** and (*ii*) **tumour suppressor genes** have been identified, whose mutations result in cancerous transformations.

Oncogenes. Oncogenes stimulate cell division. However, these genes have normal cellular counterparts known as proto-oncogenes (c- onc) which are involved in normal cell functions. Mutations of proto-oncogenes lead to the formation of oncogenes.

Many tumour causing viruses may carry similar c-onc gene (v-onc) which induce carcinogenesis.

Tumour suppressor genes. Such genes normally suppress the tumours and the disease appears only when the appropriate active gene is lacking or both the alleles are lost. They impose some constraints on cell cycle. Their absence leads to the release of these constraints and the tumours are initiated.

Regeneration

As already mentioned that development does not end with the completion of embryogenesis. Development potentialities persist into the post-embryonic life more or less in all organisms. These enable them to replace or repair the lost or damaged structures during their larval and adult life. For example, when you cut off part of the tail of a frog tadpole or a house wall-lizard, the missing part is developed again from the remaining portion of the tail. This restoration of the removed part of the tail is called **regeneration.** Thus, regeneration may be defined as replacement, repair or restoration of the lost or damaged structures or reconstitution of a whole body from a small fragment of it during the post-embryonic life of an organism.

The mammals have great capacity to regenerate the liver. When a part of the liver is removed the remaining portion grows by repeated division of its cells until the original volume of the liver tissue is attained.

In many respects, the process of regeneration is similar to the process of the development of embryo. As in the embryonic development, regeneration involves cell division, cell movements, cell and tissue differentiation and morphogenesis. However, for the process of regeneration cells arise through a process of de-differentiation from the already differentiated and specialized cells of well-developed tissues.

Aging

Failing disease or injury, a multicellular organism dies from the process of **aging**, which takes different forms in different types of cell. The average lifespan differs very widely for different organisms. While some live for only short periods, other may have a life of several decades or even centuries. For example, in plants there are giant sequoia and redwood trees at one end of the longevity scale, living to thousands, of years and always continûing to grow, whereas annual plants largely cease to grow soon after the flowering period when the fruit begins to form, after which they soon age and die. On the other hand among animals, the process of aging appears to be accompanied by obvious external changes in warm blooded animals, whereas in some long-living animals such as the sturgeon (with a lifespan of more than 100 years) and the tortoise (a life-span of more than 150 years), in which continuous growth during life occurs, the process of aging is so slow as to almost undetectable. However, none lives for ever. Even if an individual meets no total accident, is not eaten up by a predator or does not suffer a killing disease, death still comes as the natural final result of old age.

Thus *aging is defined as the process of progressive deterioration in the structure and function of the cells, tissues and organs of the organism as it grows older.* The area of developmental biology that is concerned with the study of the process of aging is known as **gerontology.**

Hormonal changes affecting adversely the functioning of various organs, the accumulation of waste material from various metabolic processes inside certain cells, loss of elasticity in elastic fibres and an increase in the amount of collagen in connective tissue—all play a part in aging, resulting in such well known changes as stiffening of the joints and hardening of the arteries. No new nerve cells are formed, but there is a replacement of intracellular material at the molecular level, and this process also becomes slower with advancing age. In the absence of death from injury or disease, the changes brought about by aging eventually results in death due to the breakdown of some vital structure such as the rupture of a blood vessel.

The reason why the various processes of aging take place are not yet clear. However, some biologists suggest that adverse changes in the environment are the causes of aging in the organism. Others believe that aging is an intrinsic genetic property of the cells of an organism. According to another theory aging is due to an interaction between hereditary factors (*i.e.*, genes) and the environment. Another theory proposes that the cells and the organisms with a high rate of metabolism are more rapidly and die sooner than those with a relatively lower rate of metabolic activity. The theory of immunity suggests that the decline and disappearance of the thymus gland by late middle age in man is the primary cause of aging. However, the cell death is programmed by the cell itself. As the cell ages the gene activity of it is altered to the extent that it gradually shows impaired metabolic reaction. It may involve the stop of synthesis of an essential enzyme (*e.g.*, dehydrogenase) or production of a toxin which stops electron transport system in the cell leading to its death.

Thus, it becomes clear that every development change in a biological cell takes place at the gene level that is DNA, which is directly exposed to cytoplasm in procaryotes and located in the nucleus of eucaryotes. The constant interaction of the genes (*i.e.*, DNA) with the cytoplasm and environment leads to the end result.

The problems of cell death, cell growth, malignancy and aging are all different aspects of cell development.

SUMMARY

1. Deoxyribonucleic acid (DNA) is the genetic material.
2. The identification of DNA is based on bacterial transformation and viral infection experiments.
3. In the bacterial transformation experiments it has been shown that DNA is responsible for inducing a smooth surface character and the property of virulence, when introduced into cells do not have these properties.
4. In the case of viral infection experiments it has been shown by radioactive labelling that the ability to infect and to give rise to more viral particles rests with the DNA and not with the proteins.
5. In certain viruses RNA also serves as genetic material.
6. The semi-conservative mode of replication is easily explained by the double stranded structure of DNA.
7. In this semi-conservative mode, the daughter cells derive from the parent one old strand of DNA and new strand is formed using the former as template.
8. The DNA replication involves unwinding of DNA and formation of new strands on the separated old strands. Third process is catalysed by the enzyme DNA polymerase.
9. During DNA replication, accuracy of replication and insertion of correct bases are preserved by proof-reading mechanisms.
10. In molecular biology the central dogma involves-DNA $\longrightarrow$ RNA $\longrightarrow$ Proteins.
11. The process by which DNA gives rise to RNA is called transcription.
12. The transcription is involved by unwinding of DNA, where one DNA strand gives rise to complementary RNA. This reaction is catalysed by the enzyme RNA polymerase.
13. The process by which proteins are derived from RNA is known as translation.
14. The sequence of bases in mRNA decides the sequence of amino-acids in proteins. Each amino acid is formed by a triplet code, which consists, of a sequence of three bases in the DNA and the complementary bases in mRNA.
15. Protein synthesis involves the step of —(*i*) initiation, (*ii*) elongation and (*iii*) termination. After termination the proteins are translocated to different parts of the cell or transported out of the cell.
16. The mutations cause changes in the genes, and thus the mutations in the genetic material are reflected in the proteins. Hence, a single base change in the DNA can affect the sequence of amino acids in the protein and its function too.
17. All processes of life are controlled by genes.
18. The genes have the information to code for proteins.
19. The gene expression that leads to the protein synthesis is regulated. Some genes are expressed only when their products are required.
20. The regulation of the expression of genes operates in all forms of life ranging from viruses to eucaryotic organisms.

21. In viruses, regulation of gene expression decides whether it follows the lytic or lysogenic cycles.
22. In retroviruses, RNA is the genetic material. /Here, DNA is formed from RNA by the catalysis of enzyme reverse transcriptase. With the invention of this enzyme, the central dogma has been modified to read as —

    DNA $\rightleftharpoons$ RNA → Proteins. Hence this type of conversion is bidirectional.
23. The expression of retroviral genes, referred to as oncogenes, is responsible for the onset of cancer in various living cells.
24. The regulation of gene expression in bacteria is generally effected through operons. Each operon is made up of a group of genes to code for enzymes involved in a specific metabolic pathway.
25. The operon concept can explain the phenomenon of both induction and repression.
26. During induction some enzymes are induced by an inducer, so that, it (inducer) could be metabolized.
27. Repression is the phenomenon by which the synthesis of a set of enzymes takes place that leads to a product is shut down when the product is provided from outside.
28. The regulation of gene expression in eucaryotic cells is more complex than in procaryotic cells.
29. The eucaryotic gene is splitted into exons and introns whereas procaryotic gene does not.
30. When the DNA is transcribed, the exonic portions of DNA are spliced together to give rise to functional mRNA, whereas the intronic portions are removed and degraded.
31. Cancer and ageing are basically due to differential gene expression.

TERMS TO REMEMBER

Aging. A progressive deterioration in structure and function of cells as the age advances. It is found that each type of animal cells starts dying after a certain number of mitotic divisions.

A-site. (Amino acyl site). A functional site in larger subunit of ribosome where the second and next amino acyl tRNA gets attached.

Anticodon. A triplet of bases present on tRNA complementary to the triplet code of mRNA.

Auxotrophs. The term refers to nutritional mutants of *Neurospora* that need one extra nutrient to grow on minimal medium.

Bacteriophages. The viruses that infect the bacterium, also termed bacterial viruses.

Cancer. The cells continue to divide and give rise to a malignant tumour. These cells can also invade other tissues and tumours can arise in new locations.

Capsid. In viruses, the genetic material is wrapped around by a protein coat called capsid.

Cistron. A unit of function, *i.e.,* segment of DNA that determines a single polypeptide chain.

Costitutive genes. The genes that are constantly expressed.

Co-repressor. A molecule that binds with the repressor protein to form a functional repressor complex.

Conjugation. The genetic transfer from one bacterial cell to another.

Central dogma. The unidirectional flow of information from DNA ⟶ RNA ⟶ proteins.

Core enzyme. The enzyme without the subunit, and capable of transcribing bacterial DNA into RNA.

Codon. Triplet (group of three) of bases on mRNA that specify a particular amino acid in protein synthesis.

DNA. Deoxyribonucleic acid.

DNA ligase. An enzyme that joins newly synthesized short fragments of DNA.

DNA polymerase. An enzyme responsible for linking free DNA nucleotides to form the complementary strand. It can polymerise the nucleotides only in 5′ – 3′ direction.

Exons. The regions of a gene which contain the information necessary to form a protein.

Feed-back repression. When a metabolite needed by the bacterium is provided in excess from outside, the bacterium stops making it and thus conserves its resources.

F factor. Fertility factor on sex faction present in the bacterium. F^+ is male bacterium while F^- is female bacterium.

Frameshift mutation. Mutation caused due to shifting of entire reading frame by loss or addition of single base or a segment of DNA.

Genetic code. The complex process by which the information in RNA is decoded into a polypeptide chain.

Glycosylation. The addition of sugar residues by modification of some proteins, that are released in the lumen and are incorporated in Golgi vesicles.

Helicases. The enzymes which help in unwinding of two strands of DNA.

Hemizygous. The genotype of a male with regard to an X-trait, since males have only one set of X-linked genes.

Hydrogen bond. The bond found in between nitrogen bases of DNA forming two nucleotide chains.

Hfr strain. High frequency strain of bacteria. This donates all or large portion of their DNA into another bacterial cell.

Inducer. The small molecules eliciting the phenomenon of induction are referred to as inducers.

Induction. When the genes are turned on enzymes are produced, which metabolize the new substrata, this is called induction.

Inducible enzymes. The enzymes whose production is induced by a compound called inducer, such as β-galactosidase.

Intron. Those regions of a gene which do not have the information for a protein.

Jumping genes. The genes which are reshuffled from one place to another.

Lysogenic cell. It refers to the bacterial cell that carries the provirus or prophage.

Lysogeny. The phenomenon by which the phage DNA integrate with the host chromosome and replicate along with it.

Oncogene. It involves the origin of cancer.

Operator. Gene that regulates the activity of structural genes.

Operon. The structural genes and an operator made an operon.

Okazaki fragments. Newly synthesized short fragments of DNA that are formed on the lagging strand of DNA during DNA replication.

P-site or peptidyl site. A functional site in ribosomes, where tRNA from A-site are translocated to P-site.

Phenocopy. When a normal gene under different environmental conditions copies down the phenotypic characters of a mutant.

Phosphodiester bond. The bond between two adjacent nucleotides of two adjacent sugar molecules at 3′ and 5′ positions with phosphoric acid.

Polyribosome or polysome. The series of ribosomes translating the same single strand of mRNA.

Primer. This is a short RNA segment formed on DNA template prior to the beginning of replication.

Primase. It polymerises ribonucleotide bases in the formation of a primer.

Plasmids. They are extrachromosomal DNA elements found mostly in bacteria.

Polycistronic mRNA. The long mRNA covering all the cistrons is known as polycistronic mRNA.

Promoter gene. Gene that forms the binding site of RNA polymerase.

Protooncogenes. Oncogenes present in the normal cell before triggering cancer in cells.

Prophage or provirus. A stage, when the DNA of virus gets incorporated in the host DNA.

Regulatory gene. A gene that regulates the function of the operator gene.

Repressor. The functioning of the operator by a protein is referred to as repressor.

Repression. A phenomenon by which the synthesis of a set of enzymes leading to a product is switched off when the product is provided from outside.

Repressible enzymes. Enzymes whose production is stopped or repressed by the presence of certain metabolite.

Repressor protein. Protein formed by regulatory gene.

Restriction enzyme. An enzyme that recognises specific nucleotide sequences in DNA and then makes a double strand cleavage of DNA molecule.

Retroviruses. A group of viruses possessing RNA as a genetic material. These viruses carry the gene for reverse transcription, *i.e.*, RNA $\rightarrow$ DNA.

Reverse transcriptase. The enzyme responsible for catalysing the conversion of RNA to DNA.

Replication. A phenomenon that refers to DNA synthesis or duplication.

RNA. Ribonucleic acid.

RNA polymerase. An enzyme that acts as a catalyst in the formation of RNA from one strand of DNA.

Silent mutation. Mutation that does not cause any change in the protein.

Semi-conservative. That conserves half of the original self as in the replication of DNA.

Structural genes. The genes that contain the information to determine the sequence of amino acids present in the proteins. They have the information to code for the amino acid sequence and decide the structure and function of the individual proteins.

Template. That refers to a DNA strand from which complementary or RNA strand is formed.

Transcription. Where a single strand of RNA is transcribed from one of the strands of DNA.

Transformation. The process by which DNA isolated from one type of cells is introduced into another type and that inherits some of the properties from former to the latter.

Translation. A phenomenon that changes the coded message of mRNA into the sequence of amino acids.

Translocation. In protein synthesis, where a tRNA molecule moves from A site to P site because of relative movement of ribosomes on mRNA.

Viral oncogenes. The origin of cancer is a complex phenomenon where viral oncogenes lead to uncontrolled growth of cells.

Wobble position. The position on the codons of the third base of the same amino acid.

QUESTION BANK

N.B. Undermentioned questions are asked repeatedly in various Indian Universities and competitive examinations.

Very Short Answer Questions

1. Who had first proposed the double helix structure of DNA ?
2. Which British medical officer had put forth the phenomenon of bacterial transformation ?
3. Who had coined the term gene ?
4. Who proposed the theory of continuity of germplasm ?
5. Which bonds hold the two polynucleotides chains of DNA molecule ?
6. Who had deciphered the genetic code?
7. Who had used X-rays to cause mutations in *Neurospora* ?
8. Who proved experimentally that DNA replication is semi-conservative ?
9. What does a nucleotide comprise of ?
10. Name the enzyme which can break and reseal the strand of DNA ?
11. In which direction $5'-3'$ or $3'-5'$ are the new strands of DNA formed during replication ?
12. Name the enzymes that catalyse (*a*) replication of DNA, (*b*) formation of RNA.
13. What is the linkage between two adjacent nucleotides called ?
14. What is a codon ?
15. Who performed the experiment that showed that DNA is the genetic material in bacteriophages ?
16. What is considered to be the central dogma in molecular biology ?
17. What is the sugar in DNA and RNA called?
18. Name the two types of nitrogenous bases.
19. Name the purines and pyrimidines.
20. Name the enzymes that unwind DNA helices.
21. What is transformation ?
22. What is an anti-codon?
23. What is transcription ?
24. Name the process that blocks the amino group of the first amino acid and thereby preventing the formation of dipeptide bond.
25. What are non-sense codons ?
26. Give two examples of amino acids that have one codon ?
27. Which triplet is known as terminating codon ?
28. What is wobble position ?
29. What is a genetic code ?
30. How many bases code for one amino acid?
31. Give two significant functions of DNA.
32. Which base triple are to code for the amino acid, phenylalanine ?
33. What does RNA control ?
34. What are the initiation codons for protein synthesis ?
35. Which is the first amino acid in any polypeptide chain ?

36. Who had proposed the one gene, one enzyme hypothesis ?
37. What is a polyribosome ?
38. What are Okazaki fragments ?
39. What are auxotrophs ?
40. Who had discovered jumping genes ?
41. Of the 64 possible code triplets how many code for amino acids and how many for stop signals ?
42. The amino acid arginine has 6 mRNA codons : CGU, CGC, CGA, CGG, AGA and AGG. Give the DNA codon for it.
43. What are virus infecting bacteria called?
44. Name the virus which is composed entirely of protein and RNA ?
45. What is the protein coat of virus cells ?
46. Name the group of virus to which the human immuno deficiency virus belong?
47. What is the phenomenon of destruction of a cell following infection by virus ?
48. Which is the enzyme that catalyses synthesis of DNA from RNA ?
49. Name the scientists who proposed the operon model ?
50. What are oncogenes ?
51. Which are the three modes of genetic transfer between bacterial cells ?
52. What is transduction ?
53. What are plasmids ?
54. What are inducers ?
55. Which is the strain of bacterial cells that have the chromosomal F-factor ?
56. Name the gene that controls the functioning of structural genes ?
57. Which gene is responsible for the switching on and off a structural gene?
58. What is the entire unit of regulator gene, operator gene and structural gene called?
59. What is splicing ?
60. Give the name of the science of ageing.
61. What is recombinant DNA ?
62. What is the enzyme that cuts DNA at specific sites ?
63. What is the process that synthesises protein on mRNA ?
64. Name the virus that is responsible for causing AIDS in humans.
65. What is the phenomenon that controls the expression of genes to achieve maximum cellular economy?
66. What is genetic engineering ?
67. Name a method for producing new combination of genetic material in bacterial cells.
68. Expand HIV.
69. Who synthesised the first artificial gene without a primer ?
70. Name the enzymes which cut the DNA molecule into fragments with sticky ends.

ANSWERS

1. Watson and Crick; **2.** Griffith; **3.** Johannsen; **4.** Weismann; 5. Hydrogen bond between the base pairs; **6.** Nirenberg, Ochoa, Hargobind Khorana and Francis Crick; **7.** Beadle and Tatum; **8.** Messelson and Stahl; **9.** It consists of a sugar, phosphate and nitrogen base; **10.** Topoisomerase; **11.** $5' - 3'$ direction; **12.** (*a*) DNA polymerase, (*b*) RNA polymerase; **13.** Phosphodiester bonds; **14.** Triplet of bases on mRNA coding for one amino acid; **15.** Hershey and Chase; **16.** The unidirectional flow of genetic information for DNA ⟶ RNA ⟶ Protein ; **17.** Deoxyribose and Ribose; **18.** Purines and Pyrimidines; **19.** Purines are — adenine (A) and guanine (G); Pyrimidines are-cytosine (C), thymine and uracil (U); **20.** Helicases;

21. The phenomenon where DNA is isolated from one type of cell, and is able to bestow some of its properties to another type of cell where the former is introduced; **22.** A triplet of bases present on tRNA, complementing the mRNA codon; **23.** The process of formation of a RNA strand on the DNA template; **24.** Formylation; **25.** The codon that do not code for any amino acid; **26.** Methionine and Tryptophan; **27.** The triplets UUA, and UAG, UGA are terminating codons; **28.** The third position in the codon; **29.** Sequence of base triplets in DNA molecule; **30.** Three; **31.** Replication and expression of genetic information; **32.** UUU, UUC; **33.** The synthesis of enzymes; **34.** AUG, GUC; **35.** Formylated methionine; **36.** Beadle and Tatum; **37.** During protein synthesis a group of ribosomes line up on the mRNA chain are called polyribosomes; **38.** Short segments of DNA formed in $5'-3'$ direction starting from a RNA primer are called Okazaki fragments; **39.** The nutritional mutants; **40.** Barbara McClintock; **41.** 61,3; **42.** GCA, GCG, GCC, TCT and TCC. **43.** Bacteriophage; **44.** Tobacco Mosaic Virus (TMV); **45.** Capsid; **46.** Retrovirus; **47.** Lysis; **48.** Reverse transcriptase; **49.** Francis Jacob and Jacques Monod; **50.** They are genes that trigger the normal cells to become cancerous; **51.** Transformation, transduction and conjugation; **52.** It is the transfer of DNA from one bacterial cell to another with the help of bacteriophage; **53.** In addition to chromosome there are circular DNA molecules in bacteria called plasmids; **54.** Metabolites that activate the inactive genes in the cells; **55.** H fr (High frequency recombination); **56.** Operator gene; **57.** Operator gene; **58.** Operon; **59.** The process of removing unwanted regions of mRNA and joining the wanted regions again; **60.** Gerontology; **61.** DNA formed as a result of combination of DNA's from two organisms; **62.** Restriction endonuclease; **63.** Translation; **64.** HIV-III; **65.** The phenomenon of induction and repression; **66.** The science that deals with the synthesis of artificial genes, repair of genes, combining of genes from two organisms and manipulation of artificial genes for improvement of organisms; **67.** Gene cloning; **68.** Human immuno-deficiency virus; **69.** Hargobind Khorana; **70.** Restriction endonucleases.

Short Answer Questions

1. What are the essential requirements of the genetic material ?
2. Draw a neat, labelled diagram of the DNA molecules as suggested by Watson and Crick.
3. Do the two complementary strands of DNA carry the same or different biological message ?
4. What do you mean by proof-reading in DNA synthesis ?
5. What is DNA repair ?
6. What is genetic code ?
7. What is the role of non-sense codons in protein synthesis ?
8. DNA polymerase and RNA polymerase differ in their requirements while functioning. Explain.
9. What do you mean by frameshift mutation ? Give an example.
10. Write the transcribed m-RNA from DNA strand with the base sequence TAG TAC ACT. What is the specific term used for the last codon of the transcribed m-RNA in this case ?
11. Why are DNA and ribosomes are located at different sites ?
12. How is protein synthesis initiated in a cell?
13. Draw a neat and labelled diagram of T_4 bacteriophage.
14. What are oncogenes ?
15. Define ageing. What are the genetic causes of ageing ?
16. Differentiate between :
    (*a*) Lysis and lysogeny; (*b*) Induction and repression.
17. Explain the concept of colinearity of gene and protein structure.
18. What is contact inhibition ? What is its significance in cell division ?
19. What is an operon ? Name the three types of genes which make up an operon.
20. Viruses are intracellular obligately parasitic organisms. Discuss.
21. How does a bacterial chromosome differ from an eukaryotic chromosome.
22. How does an excess of tryptophan cause a switch off of the tryptophan-operon ?
23. How would you differentiate the following :
    (*a*) DNA and RNA; (*b*) initiation codon and termination codon.

24. What was Avery, Macleod and McCarty's contribution to confirm the transformation principles in *Diplococcus* ?
25. What did Hershey and Chase prove by their blender experiment ? Explain how they did the experiment to prove it.
26. Why is genetic code a triplet one ?
27. Explain the following :
    Replication, Transcription, Translation, Codon, Anticodon.
28. Which molecule bears codons and which molecules anticodons ?
29. How is the DNA content in our diet digested in the body?
30. What are the functions of m-RNA and t-RNA ? What anticodons will be required to recognize the following codons :
    (*i*) AAU (*ii*) CGA (*iii*) UAU (*iv*) GCA.
31. Give the structure of a t-RNA molecule.
32. Write a note on central dogma of molecular biology.
33. A tRNA is charged with the amino acid phenylalanine.
    (*i*) At what end of tRNA is this amino acid attached.
    (*ii*) What is the mRNA codon that coded for phenylalanine.
    (*iii*) What is its anticodon ?
    (*iv*) Name the enzyme responsible for this attachment.
34. How did Hershey and Chase prove that DNA is the genetic material ?
35. What are genomic and cDNA libraries ? How can they be prepared ? What are its advantages ?
36. What are plasmids ? How does transfer of genetic material take place by employing plasmids ?
37. All cells in a multicellular organism have same genetic constitution, yet they function differently. How would you account for it ?
38. What are introns and exons ? What process ensures a linear arrangement of amino acids although the genes are discontinuous.
39. How is functioning of lac operon different from that of tryptophan operon ?

Long Answer Questions

1. Provide experimental evidence for the semi-conservative mode of replication of DNA.
2. Genetic material is DNA and not protein. How did Griffith prove this experiment ?
3. How did Hershey and Chase prove that DNA is the genetic material in bacteriophage ?
4. Discuss the mechanism of DNA replication.
5. Explain briefly the steps of protein synthesis.
6. Explain one gene-one enzyme concept with experiments on *Neurospora* by Beadle and Tatum.
7. Describe the transcription of RNA from DNA.
8. Discuss the characteristics of genetic code.
9. Discuss the effect of mutations on the structure and function of proteins.
10. Why is the DNA molecule compared to spiralling stair-case ? Which three components made up the nucleotide ?
11. Give the structure of DNA molecule.
12. Define bacterial transformation. Who demonstrated it experimentally and how?
13. Describe bacterial conjugation as a means of genetic transfer. What is the significance of this process?
14. Explain the steps involved in a polypeptide synthesis. How are the amino acids activated during polypeptide synthesis ?
15. What is reverse transcription ? Explain how single-stranded RNA of viruses give rise to double stranded RNA.
16. What is conjugation in bacteria ? With the help of labelled diagrams explain the process.

17. Explain the operon concept by Jacob and Monod with the help of a suitable example.
18. Describe the modes of genetic transfer between the bacterial cells.
19. What is the inducer in a lac operon ? How does it ensure the switching off of genes ?
20. How is gene expressed in eukaryotes ?
21. What is genetic engineering ? Briefly describe the benefits of genetic engineering to human welfare.
22. What does lac operon consist of ? How is the operon switch turned on and off in the expression of genes in this operon? Explain.

Multiple Choice Questions (Objective Type Questions)

1. The principal genetic material of living beings are
(*a*) DNA (*b*) RNA
(*c*) both a and b (*d*) none of above.
2. Synthesis of DNA is known as
(*a*) replication (*b*) transcription
(*c*) translation (*d*) migration.
3. Transcription means the synthesis of
(*a*) RNA (*b*) DNA
(*c*) Proteins (*d*) Lipids.
4. Transfer of information from m RNA to a polypeptide chain is called
(*a*) amination (*b*) deamination
(*c*) translation (*d*) transamination.
5. Genetic code is
(*a*) singlet (*b*) doublet
(*c*) triplet (*d*) none of above.
6. The initiation codons are
(*a*) AUG (*b*) GUG
(*c*) both (*a*) and (*b*) (*d*) none of above.
7. Autocatalytic function is depicted by
(*a*) hormones (*b*) enzymes
(*c*) RNA (*d*) DNA.
8. Transfer of information from DNA to mRNA is called
(*a*) transcription (*b*) translation
(*c*) transduction (*d*) migration.
9. RNA is genetic material in
(*a*) bacteria (*b*) mycoplasma
(*c*) plant viruses (*d*) fungi.
10. DNA molecule has a uniform diameter of
(*a*) 20 Å (*b*) 60 Å
(*c*) 80 Å (*d*) 27 Å.
11. Griffith's experiment was with
(*a*) *Escherichia coli*
(*b*) *Diplococcus pneumoniae*
(*c*) *Rhizobium* (*d*) *Mycorrhiza.*
12. New strands of DNA are formed in the direction
(*a*) 5′ to 3′ (*b*) 4′ to 3′
(*c*) 3′ to 3′ (*d*) 2′ to 3′.
13. The segments of DNA strand on which a new strand is produced is known as
(*a*) codon (*b*) template
(*c*) nucleotide (*d*) none of above.

14. The genes that shuffle from one location to another are called
(*a*) walking genes (*b*) running genes
(*c*) jumping genes (*d*) none of above.

15. The abnormal ratio 2 : 1 brought about due
(*a*) normal genes (*b*) lethal genes
(*c*) jumping genes (*d*) none of above.

16. One gene-one enzyme hypothesis was proposed by
(*a*) Mendel (*b*) Morgan
(*c*) Punnett (*d*) Beadle and Tatum.

17. Synthesis of a gene in a test tube and its transfer to a cell is known as
(*a*) conjugation (*b*) hybridization
(*c*) genetic engineering (*d*) transduction.

18. The more correct statement is
(*a*) one gene-one enzyme (*b*) one gene-one protein
(*c*) one gene-one polypeptide (*d*) one gene-one nucleotide.

19. The transfer of genetic material from one cell to another by a phage is
(*a*) transduction (*b*) transcription
(*c*) transformation (*d*) conjugation.

20. The enzyme that cleaves DNA at specific sites producing sticky ends is known as
(*a*) cleaving enzyme (*b*) lysing enzyme
(*c*) endonuclease (*d*) restriction endonuclease.

21. HIV is responsible for
(*a*) cancer (*b*) AIDS
(*c*) pneumonia (*d*) tuberculosis.

22. Phages infect the
(*a*) algal cells (*b*) bacterial cells
(*c*) fungal cells (*d*) none of above.

23. TMV contains a genetic material
(*a*) chromosome (*b*) DNA
(*c*) RNA (*d*) none of above.

24. Reverse transcription was studied by
(*a*) Temin and Baltimore (*b*) Smith
(*c*) Jacob (*d*) Watson and Crick.

25. *Escherichia coli* hydrolyses lactose to glucose by
(*a*) β-galactosidase (*b*) permease
(*c*) transacetylase (*d*) all of the above.

ANSWERS

1. (*c*) **2.** (*a*) **3.** (*a*) **4.** (*c*) **5.** (*c*) **6.** (*c*) **7.** (*b*) **8.** (*a*) **9.** (*c*) **10.** (*a*)
11. (*b*) **12.** (*a*) **13.** (*b*) **14.** (*c*) **15.** (*b*) **16.** (*d*) **17.** (*c*) **18.** (*a*) **19.** (*a*) **20.** (*d*)
21. (*b*) **22.** (*b*) **23.** (*c*) **24.** (*a*) **25.** (*d*)

45

CHAPTER

Allelic and Non - allelic Interactions

We know that for determination of single phenotypic trait of an organism, two alleles or allelomorphs of a single gene interact in various ways. Out of the two alleles one may show dominance over the other (recessive) or both have partial or incomplete dominant relationship or both may be codominant.

Different kinds of genic or genetic interactions occur between the two allelomorphs of a single gene. These interactions are called **intraallelic or allelic or interallelic genetic or genic interactions** also. In such case the independent or non homologous genes located on the same or on different chromosomes interact with one another for expression of single phenotype.

According to **Bateson** and **Punnett,** the genes were not merely separate elements producing distinct individual effects, but they could interact with each other to give completely novel phenotypes.

For example, If 'A' allele is characterised by 'A' phenotype and 'B' allele is characterised by 'B' phenotype. But an organism with 'AB' both, is characterised by 'C' phenotype. It suggests that phenotype is not present in a gene but arises from a complicated developmental process. They are no genes which individually create specific organ structure or organisms. This concept is called **epigenetic concept,** where development occurs through a complex network of reactions and interactions influenced by genes.

When two gene pairs, each having two alleles, *i.e.,* A, a and B, b segregate independently in a diploid organism, the genetic consequences are easily predictable. A cross between heterozygotes for both pairs Aa Bb × Aa Bb will give offspring with following genotypes.

1/16	AABB
2/16	AABb
2/16	AaBB
4/16	AaBb
1/16	AAbb
2/16	Aabb
1/16	aaBB
2/16	aaBb
1/16	aabb

As long it is independently associated the above genotype exists. Phenotypic ratio is directly affected in changes as in the phenotype which can be observed and not in the genotype.

Time of genetic Interaction

Gene is a chemical determiner. Phenotypic trait results from the combined action of many genes and their products. Environment and ecological factors, *e. g.,* temperature, quality of light and internal factors, *e. g.,* hormones and enzymes also play an important role. Enzymes are proteins and organization of proteins is determined by genes. Each biosynthetic pathway includes various steps catalysed by specific enzyme which in turn depends on a specific gene. The reaction starts with a **precursor** and ends at the **product.** In between, it includes many metabolities which are produced by various genes. Mutant genes may cause **metabolic blocks** in the pathway.

INTRA ALLELIC GENIC INTERACTION

The expression of gene in the form of phenotype is dependent on product. The genotype can hide or mask the phenotype expression of alleles at one locus. The gene which suppresses or masks the other gene is called **epistatic gene** and the gene which is suppressed is called **hypostatic gene.**

Difference between epistasis and dominance

The phenomenon of dominance involves intraallelic gene suppression on the same locus while the epistasis involves intraallelic gene suppression or masking of other gene locus.

Kinds of epistasis

The epistasis is in between two genes, that is atleast a dihybrid and the phenotypes are less than 4.

(a) Dominant epistasis (12 : 3 : 1)

When dominant allele 'A' masks the expression of 'B' 'A' is epistatic gene of 'B'. A can express itself only in the presence of 'B' or b allele. Therefore it is called **dominant epistasis. B** expresses only when **'aa'** is present. Therefore, in 9 : 3 : 3 : 1 ratio both **9 and 3** are expressing the **'A'** gene the ratio is now 12 : 3 : 1.

Example :Complete dominance at both gene pairs, but one gene, when dominant, epistatic to the other.

Fruit colour in summer squash

Gene pair **A** : White dominant to colour 12/16 white

Gene pair **'B'** – Yellow dominant to green 3/16 yellow

Green – 1/16 both recessive aabb

Dominant white hides the effect of yellow or green.

AaBb × AaBb
white | white

	AB	Ab	aB	ab
AB	AA BB White	AA Bb White	Aa BB White	Aa Bb White
Ab	AA Bb White	AA bb White	AA Bb White	Aa bb White
aB	Aa BB White	Aa Bb White	aa BB Yellow	aa Bb Yellow
ab	Aa Bb White	Aa bb White	aa Bb Yellow	aa bb Green

AB – 9 White
Ab – 3 White
aB – 3 Yellow
ab – 1 Green

(b) Recessive epistasis (9 : 3 : 4)

Recessive alleles at one locus (aa) mask the phenotypic expression of other gene locus (BB, Bb or bb) such epistasis is called **recessive epistasis.** The alleles of 'B' locus express themselves only when epistatic locus 'A' has dominant allele like AA or Aa. The phenotypic ratio is 9 : 3 : 4.

Example : Complete dominance at both gene pairs, but one gene, when homozygous recessive, is epistatic to the other.

In Mouse coat colour.

Gene pair **A** : colour dominant over albino.

Gene pair **'B'** agouti colour dominant over black.

Interaction : homozygous albino is epistatic to aguoti and black.

Agouti 9/16

black 3/16

albino 4/16

Agouti (gray) × white albino

AABB ↓ aabb

Aa Bb × Aa Bb

Agouti Agouti

AB = 9 Agouti

Ab = 3 Albino

Ba = 3 Black

ab = 1 Albino

	AB	Ab	aB	ab
AB	AABB Agouti	AABb Agouti	AaBB Agouti	Aa Bb Agouti
Ab	AABb Agouti	AAbb Albino	AaBb Agouti	Aabb Albino
aB	AaBB Agouti	AaBb Agouti	aaBB Black	aaBb Black
ab	AaBb Agouti	Aabb Albino	aa Bb Black	aabb Albino

9/16 : 3/16 : 4/16

Agouti : Black : Albino

(c) Duplicate recessive gene (9 : 7)

If both gene loci have homozygous recessive alleles and both of them produce identical phenotype the F_2 ratio 9:3:3:1 would be 9:7. The genotype aaBB, aaBb, AAbb, Aabb and aabb produce same phenotype. Both dominant alleles when are present together only then they can complement each other. This is known as **complementary gene.**

Examples : Complete dominance at both gene pairs, but either recessive homozygote is epistatic to the effect of the other gene.

In sweet pea flower colour.

Gene pair **'A'** - Purple dominant over white.

Gene pair **'B'** - Colour dominant over colourless (white).

Interaction: Homozygous recessive of either gene A or B produce white

9/16 Purple

7/16 White

White flowers White flower

CCpp × PPcc

CcPp × CcPp

Purple Purple

CP = 9 Purple

Cp = 3 White

cP = 3 White

cp = 1 White

9 : 7

Purple White

	CP	Cp	cP	cp
CP	CCPP Purple	CCPp Purple	CcPP Purple	CcPp Purple
Cp	CCPp Purple	CCpp White	CcPp Purple	Ccpp White
cP	CcPP Purple	CcPp Purple	ccPP White	ccPp White
cp	CcPp Purple	Ccpp White	ccPp White	ccpp White

(d) Duplicate genes with cumulative effect (9 : 6 :1)

Certain phenotypic traits depend on the dominant alleles of two gene loci. When dominant is present it will show its phenotype. The ratio will be 9 : 6 : 1.

Example: Complete dominance at both gene pairs, interaction between both dominance to give new phenotypes.

Fruit shape in summer squash

Gene pair **'A'** sphere shape dominant over long.

Gene pair **'B'** sphere shape dominant overlong.

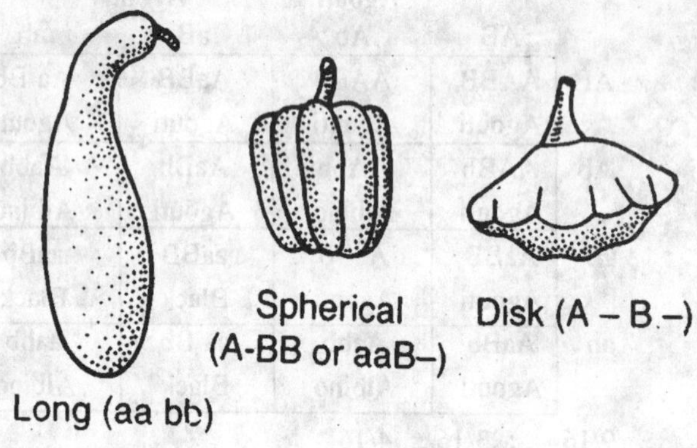

Fig. 45.1. Shape of summer squash.

Interaction at 'AB' when present together, form disc-shaped fruit (Fig .39.1)

Disc shaped fruits 9/16

Sphere shaped fruits 6/16

Long shaped fruit 1/16

Sphere shape × Sphere shape

AAbb aaBB

AaBb × AaBb

Disc shape ↓ disc shape

AB = 9 Disc shape

Ab = 3 = Sphere shape

aB = 3 = Sphere shape

ab = 1 = Long shape

= 9 : 6 : 1

Disc Sphere Long

	AB	Ab	aB	ab
AB	AABB Disc	AABb Disc	AaBB Disc	AaBb Disc
Ab	AABb Disc	AAbb Sphere	AaBb Disc	Aabb Sphere
AB	AaBB Disc	AaBb Disc	aaBB Sphere	aaBb Sphere
ab	AaBb Disc	Aabb Sphere	aaBb Sphere	aabb Long

(e) Duplicate dominant genes (15 :1)

If a dominant allele of both gene loci produces the same phenotype without cumulative effect, *i.e.*, independently the ratio will be 15 :1.

Example : Complete dominance at both gene pairs, but either gene when dominant, epistatic to the other.

Seed capsule of **shepherd's purse** (*Capsella bursa-pestoris)*

Gene pair **'A'** : Triangular shape dominant over ovoid

Gene pair **'B'** : Triangular shape dominant over ovoid (double recessive)

15/16 = Triangular

1/16 = ovoid (topshaped)

AABB × aabb

Triangular Ovoid

AaBb × AaBb

Triangular ↓

	AB	Ab	aB	ab
AB	AABB Triangular	AABb Triangular	AaBB Triangular	AaBb Triangular
Ab	AABb Triangular	AAbb Triangular	AaBb Triangular	Aabb Triangular
aB	AaBb Triangular	AaBb Triangular	aaBB Triangular	aaBb Triangular
ab	AaBb Triangular	Aabb Triangular	aaBb Triangular	aabb ovoid

AB = 9 = Triangular

Ab = 3 Triangular

aB = 3 Triangular

ab = 1 Ovoid (top shaped)

15 : 1

Triangular : Ovoid

(f) Dominant and recessive interaction (13 : 3)

Sometimes the dominant alleles of one gene locus (A) in homozygous and heterogygous (AA, Aa) condition and homozygous recessive alleles bb of another gene locus (B) produce the same phenotype. The F_2 ratio will become **13 : 3.** The genotype AABB, AaBB, AAbb, Aabb and aabb produce one type of phenotype and genotype aaBb, aaBB will produce another type of phenotype.

Example: Complete dominance at both gene pairs, but one gene when dominant epistatic to the other, and the second gene when homozygous recessive, epistatic to the first.

Feather Colour of Fowl

Gene pair **'A'** : colour inhibition is dominant to colour appearance.

Gene pair **'B'** : colour is dominant to white.

Interaction. Dominant colour inhibition prevents colour even when colour is present, colour gene, when homozygous recessive prevents colour even when dominant inhibitor is absent.

13/16 = White

3/16 = coloured

White leg horn × White plymouth Rock

AABB ↓ aabb

AaBb × AaBb

White White

	AB	Ab	aB	ab
AB	AABB White	AABb White	AaBB White	AaBb White
Ab	AABb White	AAbb* Coloured	AaBb White	Aabb* Coloured
aB	AaBB White	AaBb White	aaBB White	aaBb White
ab	AaBb White	Aabb* Coloured	aaBb White	aabb White

AB = 9 white

Ab = 3 coloured

aB = 3 white

ab = 1 white

13 : 3

White : Coloured

Non epistatic Inter allelic genetic interaction

In some cases two pairs of genes determine same phenotype but assorted independently, produce new phenotypes by mutual epistatic interaction. The F_2 ratio remains the same as 9 : 3 : 3 : 1.

Example : Each gene pair affecting the same character complete dominance at both gene pairs, new phenotypes resulting from interaction between dominants, and also from interaction between both homozygous recessives.

Comb Shape in Poultry (Fig. 45.2)

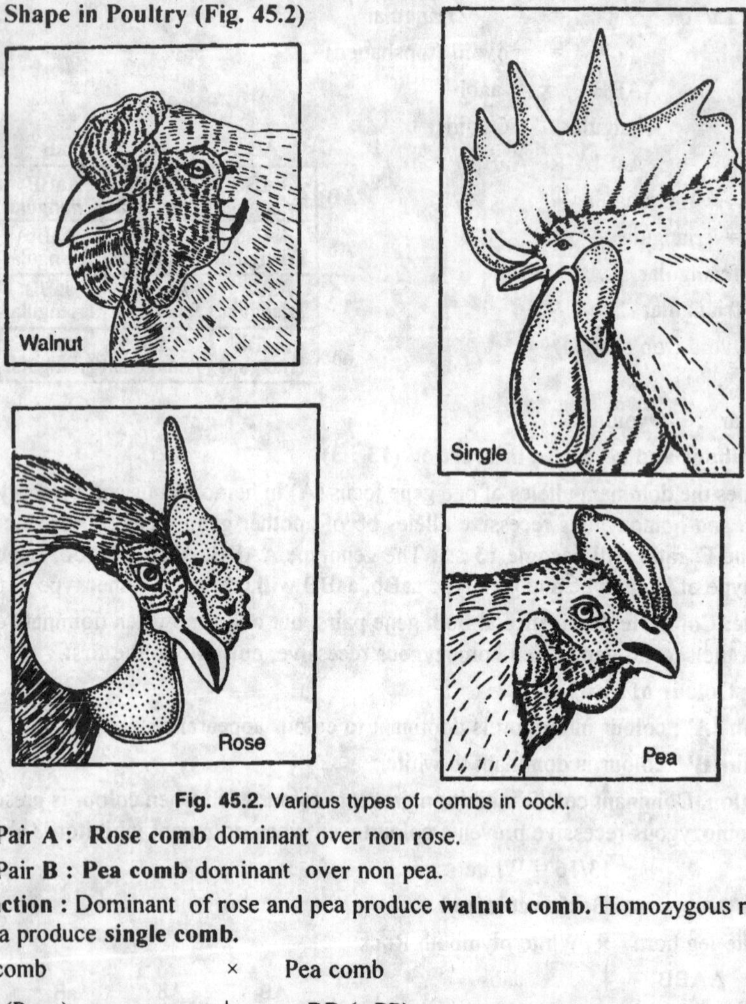

Fig. 45.2. Various types of combs in cock.

Gene Pair **A** : **Rose comb** dominant over non rose.

Gene Pair **B** : **Pea comb** dominant over non pea.

Interaction : Dominant of rose and pea produce **walnut comb.** Homozygous recessive for rose and pea produce **single comb.**

Rose comb × Pea comb

AAbb (Rrpp) ↓ aaBB (rrPP)

× AaBb (RrPp AaBb(RrPp)

Walnut Walnut

9/16 = Walnut

3/16 = rose

3/16 = Pea

1/16 = single

AB = 9 = Walnut

Ab = 3 = Rose

aB = 3 = Pea

ab = 1 = Single

	AB	Ab	aB	ab
AB	AABB Walnut	AABb Walnut	AaBB Walnut	AaBb Walnut
Ab	AABb Walnut	AAbb* Rose	AaBb Walnut	Aabb* Rose
aB	AaBB Walnut	AaBb Walnut	aaBb+ Pea	aaBb+ Pea
ab	AaBb Walnut	Aabb* Rose	aaBb+ Pea	aabb* Single

9 : 3 : 3 : 1

Walnut Rose Pea Single

According to **Bateson** and **Punnett** such result is obtained because by combination of homozygous recessive genes (bb) and a homozygous or heterozygous dominant AA or Aa the Rose comb is produced ; and by combination of homozygous recessive (aa) and homozygous or heterozygous dominant condition **BB** or Bb produce pea comb while the single type comb is produced by double recessive **aabb** genes. **'A'** gene determines the shape of rose comb and 'B' gene determines the shape of Pea comb, but when both genes combine a new shape Walnut appears. In the cross between two types of Walnut chickens 4 phenotypes appear. The genes here do not determine themselves in the development of character but modify the character determined by a basic gene. These genes are called **supplementary** or **modifying** genes.

LETHALITY

In 1905 a French geneticist **Cuenot** reported that on the inheritance of a mouse body colour gene, **yellow**, that did not appear to fit the **Mendelian** segregation pattern. **Yellow** has a dominant phenotypic effect on coat colour of mouse whenever yellow x yellow the progeny is yellow and agouti but when yellow is test crossed it is always found **heterozygotic. Castle and Little** explained it as some effect where homozygotes for yellow die. It has a lethal effect. **Robertson, Eaton, Green,** *et al* also have shown that approximately 25% inviable embryos can be obtained. **Xeroderma pigmentosum** of human is also a heterozygotic lethal form. The gene is called **recessive** lethal as long as it is lethal in homozygous condition.

Dominant lethal genes are having the effect on heterozygote individuals, *e.g.*, *Epiloia* gene causes abnormal skin growth, severe mental defect and multiple tumors in human. Heterozygotes die in young age. In *Drosophila* X-ray treatment of male spermatozoa may cause the death of fertilized offspring through the entire range of developmental stages, *i.e.*, from egg of adult. In *Drosophila* curly wings (Cy), plum eyes (Pm) and stubble bristles (Sb) influence the viability of flies in homozygous conditions.

Penetrance of lethals, recessive or dominant, may also vary, so that not all genotypically affected individuals are phenotypically lethal. Some genes have high degree of penetrance and expression so that no survival beyond embronic or infant stage is found. Some are called **Semilethal** or **subvitals** which permit larger proposition of genotype to survive. Lethal genes in general are regarded as those whose effects cause death to the organism, usually in the early growth stage.

Balanced lethal system

Muller in 1918 reported an unusual stock of *Drosophila* heterozygous for a particular lethal gene **beaded**. The beaded gene has dominant effect on the shape of the wings but has been shown to be lethal in homozygous conditions. A cross between **beaded x beaded** always shows 2:1 ratio (Fig 39.3).

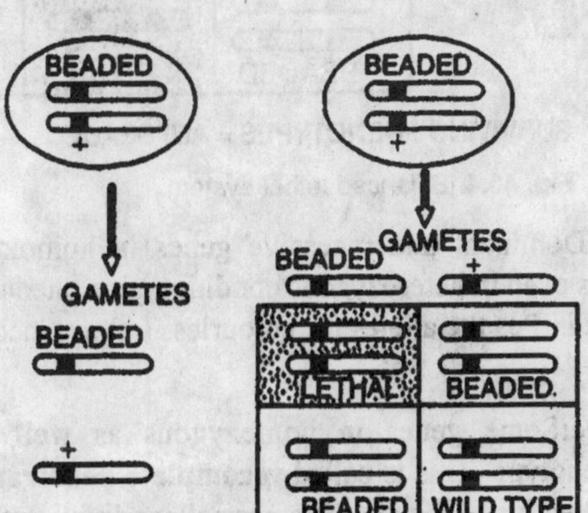

Fig. 45.3. Lethal system.

Muller analysed that the homologous chromosomes carry a normal allele for **beaded** gene also carry a gene which was lethal in homozygous condition, *i.e.*, **le.** But this was not an allele of beaded gene. In addition to beaded heterozygotes **the beaded x beaded** produce two types of homozgyous lethal **Beaded/Beaded, le** (Fig. 45.4). Since **Beaded** and **le** are recessive lethals and are not allelic, it is only the Beaded +/+ le individuals that survive because each of these homologous chromosomes carries the wild-type allele for the recessive lethal factor. Balancing effect between two different lethals in a self perpetuating stock was called **balanced lethal system** by **Muller.**

Changes in lethality

Lethality is also influenced by the environment many times. **Dobzhansky** in 1946 in certain genotypes of *Drosophila pseudoscura* showed that the temperature upto 16.5°C is optimum for growth but is lethal at 25.5°C. Such lethals are called **conditional lethals.**

Suzuki, *et al,* suggested that the conditions of lethality may be restricted to certain phase of life *e.g.*, ***D. melanogaster*** at high temperature, during post larval stage is lethal.

Some strains of yeast are unable to ferment the sugar galactose which may be lethal to them on galactose medium but no effect in glucose medium.

PENETRANCE

The ability of a given gene or gene combination to be expressed phenotypically to any degree is called **penetrance**. It may be of 2 types.

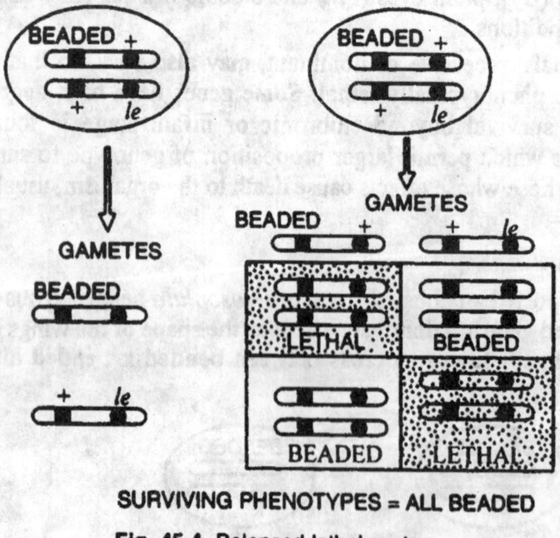

Fig. 45.4. Balanced lethal system.

(a) Complete penetrance: Dominant and recessive genes in homozygous condition and many completely dominant genes even in heterozygous condition give phenotypic expression. It is called complete penetrance, *e.g.*, in Pea the alleles for colourless (rr) are incomplete penetrance in homozygous condition.

(b) Incomplete penetrance: Some genes in homozygous as well as in heterozygous condition fail to express the phenotype. This is called **incomplete penetrance,** *e.g.*, polydactyly in man was thought to be controlled by a gene *'P'*. The normal condition with 5 digits is produced by recessive (pp). Some heterozygous individuals (Pp) are not polydactylus. The penetrance is less than 7%.

EXPRESSIVITY

The expression of different traits is different. The degree of effect produced by a penetrant genotype is called **expressivity,** *e.g.*, if the penetrance of gene is in left side, the man will have 6 digits in left hand and 5 in right.

PLEIOTROPISM

If a single gene influences more than one phenotypic trait, it is called **pleiotropic gene**. If it has more expressive effect on the phenotype, called as a **major effect** and if less effective it is **secondary effect**. The phenomenon of multiple effect of a single gene is known as **pleiotropism,** *e.g.*, in *Drosophila* the recessive gene for vestigial wings cause vestigial wings in homozygous condition. It also affects tiny wing like balancer behind the wings, bristles, structure of reproductive organs, egg production and longevity, etc.

In human the gene for **Phenylketonuria** has pleiotropic effect as it produces many effects called **syndrome**. The diseased individual secretes excessive quantity of amino acid phenylalanine in urine, cerebrospinal fluid and blood. The major characteristics are short stature, mentally retarded, pigmented patches on skin, non pigment hair and eyes, excessive sweating and wide spaced incisors, etc.

MULTIPLE ALLELES

An allele is specific form of a given gene. An allele may be a mutant allele, resulting, in an altered phenotype, or a wild type allele producing an active gene product and a 'normal' phenotype. Different wild type alleles are found in populations producing phenotypes within the 'wild type' range. When more than two different forms of a given gene exist in a species, they are called **multiple alleles.**

In *Drosophila melanogaster,* wild type *Drosophila* have red eyes, but a vast array of eye colour mutants are present. The colour ranges from pure white to intermediate types to red colour. They are named as w^a (white apricot). w^e (white eosin), w^{ch} (white cherry). w^{co} (white coral), w^{col} (white coloured), w^w (white wine), w^{bl} (white blood), w^{cre} (white carrot), w^{cf} (white coffee), etc. Different colours are the result of relative concentration of total pigment.

The number of different genotypes possible among diploid organisms is, a function of the number of alleles that exist for any given gene. If n is the number of alleles of a given gene, the number of different genotypes possible is $n(n + 1)/2$. Thus with 2, 3, 4 or 5 alleles there are 3, 6, 10 and 15 possible genotypes respectively.

Since each diploid organism has only two copies of the gene, an individual must be either

(a) homozygous for allele a_1.

(b) homozygous for allele a_2.

(c) heterozygous for alleles a_1 and a_2.

This individual organism can not have a_3 and a_4 alleles. These may be present in some other organism in the population.

In case of crosses involving multiple alleles standard monohybrid ratio will be observed as $1/4\ a_1 a_1 : 2/4\ a_1 a_2 : 1/4\ a_2 a_2$, etc.

A, B, O Blood groups in Human

Important multiple allele in human involves genetic locus controlling blood types A, B, AB and O. The locus has three common alleles I^A I^B, I^O, I^A and I^B are codominant as I^A I^B (in heterozygotes with both A and B antigens in their red blood cells). I^O is recessive ($I^O I^O$ homozygous has no A, B, O, antigen)while $I^A I^O$ has A antigen and $I^B I^O$ has B antigen in RBC. ABO locus controls the types of glycolipids found on the surface of RBC by specifying the type of glycosyl transferase (enzyme catalysing systems of polysaccharide) synthesized in the RBC. It determines the antigenic reaction with specific antibodies present in the blood serum. When 'A' blood is given to 'B' type, A antibodies will react with 'B' antibodies in the serum or vice versa; producing agglutination or dumping of cells (Fig. 45.5). And therefore before transfusion of blood, the blood groups are matched. Type O is **universal donor** and type 'AB' is **universal recipient** of blood (Table 39.1).

Table 45.1. Blood transfusion capabilities for AB blood group.

Blood Group	Terminal sugars of antigens present	Antibodies present	Red cell types agglutinated	Transfusion accepted from
A	A (galactosamine)	Anti – B	B, AB	A or O
B	B (galactose)	Anti A	A, AB	B or O
AB	A (galactosamine) and B (galactose)	None	None	A, B, AB or O.
O	None	Anti A and Anti B	A, B and AB	O

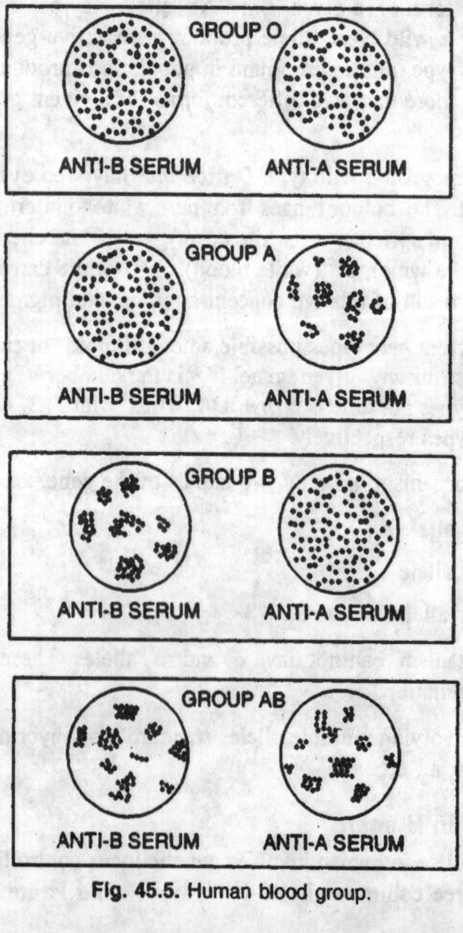

Fig. 45.5. Human blood group.

Rh factor allele in human

The **Rh** factor was discovered in 1940 by **K. Landsteiner** and **A. S. Wiener** from rabbits immunized with the blood of *Macaca rhesus* monkey. The resulting antibodies were found to agluttinate not only the RBC of monkey but those of a high percentage of **Caucasian** people of New York. Individuals whose RBC react with **Rh** antibody are called **Rh positive**, those who do not react are **Rh negative.** If a drop of blood from the individual is mixed with anti **Rh serum** agglutination of erythrocytes takes place, it indicates incompatibility. Rh negative mothers are often immunised by blood from Rh-positive foetus. (When father is Rh positive) to which they give birth (Rh positive is dominant over Rh negative). If the mother is not treated properly for anti Rh serum the subsequent child may show haemolytic jaundice, anemia, etc., called **erythroblastosis fatalis** which may result even in death of the foetus or newborn infant.

SUMMARY

1. Influence of alleles and nonalleles on the normal phenotype expression of genes is callled **gene interaction.**
2. The interaction of gene may be **intergenic** (non allelic) or **intragenic** (allelic).
3. When the interference of genes cause death of individual such genes are called **lethal genes.**
4. Alleles expressing themselves within the same phenotypic range are called **isoalleles.**
5. When one gene hides the effect of the other, it is called **epistasis.**
6. If the epistasis is due to recessive allele ('a' hides the effect of 'B') the result will be 9 : 3 : 4.
7. If the epistasis is due to dominant allele ('A' hides the effect of 'B' or vice versa) the result will be 13 : 3.
8. The result of double recessive epistasis is 9 : 7.
9. When a character is controlled by two different genes, it is called complementary gene.
10. **Shull** studied in shepherd's purse (*Capsella bursa-pestoris)* the fruit shape is either triangluar or top shaped. The triangular shape is controlled by two dominant genes. It is called **duplicating** genes, the result will be 15 : 1.
11. The genes modifying the effect of other genes is called **modifier gene.**
12. The genes with more than one effect are called **pleiotropic genes.**
13. The effect of pleiotropic gene may be more for one trait (major effect) and less evident for other trait (secondary effect).
14. The characters which were expressed as intermediate in F_1 generation, *i.e.*, **blending inheritance** and incomplete dominance are controlled by many genes called **multiple factors** and polygenes.
15. **Penetrance** is the percentage of individuals with a given genotype exhibiting the phenotype associated genotype.
16. The degree or extent to which a given genotype is expressed phenotypically in a particular individual is called **expressivity.**
17. Mendelian genetics is also known as **forward genetics** where the study is **phenotype** to **DNA sequence in gene.**
18. Mapping and isolation of genes with unknown protein products is **reverse genetics.**
19. **Paul Berg** (1991) suggested the use of term **reverse genetics** to the studies starting with **DNA sequences with unknown phenotypic effect.**
20. Reverse genetics is used in production of transgenic plants and animals.

QUESTION BANK

Very Short Answer Questions

1. Give one example of pleiotropism.
2. Define penetrance.
3. Define expressivity.

4. In which type of interaction the result is 9 : 3 : 4.
5. In which type of interaction the result is 13 : 3.
6. What is dominant epistasis.
7. Give one example of complementary genes.
8. Give one example of intraallelic non epistatic interaction of genes.
9. Give one example of lethality.
10. Give one example of interallelic interaction of gene.
11. What will be the results of dominant recessive epistasis.
12. Who studied the effect of duplicating genes in shepherd's purse.
13. What are isoalleles.
14. In chiken when rose and pea comb types were crossed what will be the result of F_1.
15. What is major effect.

Short Answer Questions

1. Explain recessive epistasis.
2. Explain duplicating genes with the help of one example.
3. Describe complementary genes.
4. What is dominant and recessive interaction.
5. Explain non epistatic interallelic genetic interaction.
6. Write short notes on lethality.
7. Explain balanced lethal system.
8. Write short note on penetrance.
9. Write short note on expressivity.
10. Write short note on pleiotropism.

Long Answer Questions

1. Describe allelic and non allelic interaction with the help of suitable examples.
2. Explain different types of epistasis with the help of examples.

Multiple Choice Questions (Objective Type Questions)

1. Inherited traits tend to remain discrete was shown by a german botanist:
   (a) Ubish (b) Nageli
   (c) Kolreuter (d) Von Mohl
2. The trait which does not blend at all is:
   (a) Colour (b) Shape
   (c) Size (d) Sex
3. If pure form black and white andulasian fowls were crossed together the F_1 generation will show
   (a) Black fowls (b) White fowls
   (c) Blue fowls (d) Grey fowls
4. Influence of alleles and non alleles on the normal phenotype expression of genes is called:
   (a) Gene expression (b) Gene interaction
   (c) Gene mixing (d) Gene overlapping
5. If the interference of a particular gene is fatal, it is called:
   (a) Epistatsis (b) Lethal
   (c) Mixed (d) Duplicating
6. When more than two alternate forms of a gene are present on the same locus; they are called:
   (a) Intergenic alleles, (b) Intragenic alleles
   (c) Multiple alleles (d) Lethal genes

7. Human blood groups were established by:
(a) Wakesman (b) Landsteiner
(c) Kolreuter (d) Weisman
8. Universal recipient of Blood is :
(a) A (b) B
(c) AB (d) O
9. Universal donor of Blood is :
(a) A (b) B
(c) AB (d) O
10. Antigens are also called as :
(a) Agglutinogen (b) Agglutinin
(c) Thrombin (d) None of the above
11. Antigens are present in :
(a) Serum (b) RBC
(c) WBC (d) Cytoplasm
12. Antibodies are present in :
(a) Serum (b) RBC
(c) WBC (d) Cytoplasm
13. When two gene pairs affect the same character it is called :
(a) Supplementary gene (b) Duplicating genes
(c) Complementary gene (d) Lethal gene
14. Agglutinins are also called as :
(a) Antigens (b) Antibodies
(c) Agglutinogen (d) All the above
15. When a gene hides the effect of other, it is called:
(a) Epistasis (b) Complementary gene
(c) Incomplete dominance (d) Codominance
16. The result of F_2 generation in recessive epistasis is :
(a) 9 : 3 : 3 : 1 (b) 9 : 3 : 4
(c) 15 : 1 (d) 12 : 3 : 1
17. When one character is controlled by two different genes, it is called :
(a) Duplicating gene (b) Complementary gene
(c) Lethal gene (d) Supplementary gene
18. The F_2 ratio of complementary gene :
(a) 9 : 3 : 4 (b) 9 : 3 : 3 : 1
(c) 9 : 7 (d) 15 : 1
19. 15 : 1 is the result of F_2 generation is :
(a) Duplicating gene (b) Complementary gene
(c) Lethal gene (d) Supplementary gene
20. When a character is controlled by two different genes independently or together the effect is called :
(a) Duplicating genes (b) Supplementary gene
(c) Epistasis (d) Complementary gene
21. The result of F_2 generation in dominant epistasis is :
(a) 9 : 7 (b) 12 : 3 : 1
(c) 3 : 1 (d) 9 : 3 : 4

22. Genes modified the effect of other gene is called :
(a) Modifier (b) Suporter
(c) Suppressor (d) Multiplier

23. The genes with more than one effect are known as :
(a) Pleiotropic genes (b) Polygene
(c) Complementary gene (d) Multiple allele

24. The degree or extent to which a genotype is expressed phenotypically in an individual is called :
(a) Polygene (b) Pentrance
(c) Expressivity (d) Aclamatization

25. The percentage of individuals with a given genotype exhibiting the phenotype associated of genotype is known as :
(a) Expressivity (b) Penetrance
(c) Both 'a' and 'b' (d) None of the above

26. In *Lathyrus odoratus*, cross between two purple flowered plants give a pink/white progeny, it is due to :
(a) Incomplete dominance (b) Codominane
(c) Epistasis (d) Segregation

27. Gene on one locus influence the gene on other locus, it is called :
(a) Epistatic (b) Complementary
(c) Duplicating (d) None

ANSWERS

1. (c)	2. (d)	3. (c)	4. (b)	5. (b)	6. (c)
7. (b)	8. (c)	9. (d)	10. (a)	11. (b)	12. (a)
13. (a)	14. (b)	15. (a)	16. (b)	17. (b)	18. (a)
19. (a)	20. (a)	21. (b)	22. (a)	23. (a)	24. (c)
25. (b)	26. (d)	27. (b).			

46

CHAPTER

Genetic Variations: Mutations

Genetic variations are brought about by crossing over in meiosis and mutations. **Mutations** are inheritable changes. **Hugo de Vries** was first to use the term **mutation.**

GENETIC VARIATION

This is not always that offspring only resemble partners but they also vary from them. Of course, the resemblances are due to the units of information, the **genes,** they inherit. However, not all the inherited genes express themselves, *i.e.,* exhibit their phenotype. Some may be hidden or be recessive in the presence of dominant counter-parts, during expression. Genetic variation in sexually reproducing species develops primarily because parental genes are shuffled into new combinations, *i.e.,* new genotypes, in the offspring. The recombinations are produced by the routine reshuffling of genes as follows :

1. Independent assortment of chromosomes during meiosis. During the formation of gametes in the metaphase I of meiosis homologous chromosomes come together in pairs and then segregate into daughter cells independent of each other.

For example, the maternal and paternal chromosomes of an organism with two pairs of chromosomes can recombine in $2^2 = 4$ possibilities in the gametes. With 3 pairs of chromosomes $2^3 = 8$ possible types of gametes are formed. The humans have 23 pairs of chromosomes which can give rise to 2^{23} or about 8.6 million combinations.

2. Reciprocal recombination of linked genes by crossing-over in meiosis. Here during crossing over in meiosis chromatids of homozygous chromosomes break and recombine to produce new linkage groups. As a result new genetic varieties or recombinations are produced.

3. Random fertilization of gametes. The fusion of male and female gametes takes place by random fertilization. During random fertilization any one of the 8.6 million recombinations in the sperm can fuse with any of the 8.6 million combination in the egg producing a total of $(8.6 \times 10^6) \times (8.6 \times 10^6) = 70 \times 10^{12}$ possible combinations. The possible combinations far exceed human population, and therefore, no two human beings are exactly alike.

Along with heredity there is always a component of variation. This means that a whole set of characters is transmitted from the parents to the offspring. Thus, there is always a component of variation due to which they not only look differnt but also the offspring can be distinguished from each other.

Such variations may arise due to different mechanisms, such as *(i)* **recombination** *(ii)* **gene mutation** *(iii)* **gene environment interactions** and by *(iv)* **chromosomal aberrations.**

MUTATIONS

It is sudden and heritable change independent of the environment and liable to provide a permanent step of which evolutionary changes may be built. Very precisely, mutation is a sudden change in chromosomal DNA, *i.e.,* in a strict sense it covers ony those changes which alter the chemical structure of the gene at the molecular level. These are commonly called **gene mutations** or **point mutations.**

From where the new genetic traits come from ? For example, how can a white-eyed fruit fly suddenly appears in a pure culture of red-eyed flies ? Or how can a short-legged sheep appears in a population of sheep with legs of normal length ? In the early 1900s, Hugo de Vries attempted to answer this question. At the time, he was working on the genetics of the primrose plant (*Oenothera lamarckiana)*. He noticed that several new traits appeared in the offpsring of the plants. He guessed the cause of the new traits to be permanent changes in the genetic material. Such changes are now called **mutations.** Thus, (*i*) a mutation is a permanent change in the DNA molecule of an organism (*ii*) Mutations are heritable changes, that is, if they appear in somatic cells they are inherited to daughter cells by mitosis, and if they appear in gametes, they are inherited to the offspring. The former are known as **somatic mutations** and latter as **germ mutations,** (*iii*) Mutations bring about a change in the genetic message. (*iv*) Mutations occur randomly and spontaneously.

Types of Mutations

There are two types of mutations : (*i*) **Gene mutations** or **point mutations,** and (*ii*) **Chromosomal mutations.**

1. Gene mutations. A chemical change that occurs in the DNA of a cell is called a **gene mutations** or **point mutations.** Such a mutation may alter the sequence of the nucleotides within a part of the DNA molecule. This alternation changes the information on the DNA chain and results in differences in the proteins being produced. For example, in sickle cell anemia, the mutation of a single gene causes a slight change in the structue of the protein molecule of hemoglobin, and because of that slight change, the blood cell that carries the hemoglobin takes a sickle shape.

According to many scientists, the mutations may be caused naturally by the radiation that constantly enters the earth's atmosphere from the cosmos. For example, gene mutations are probably caused when the sex cells (gametes) of an organism are exposed to X-rays, gamma rays, cosmic rays and ultraviolet rays. In addition to this radiation, certain chemicals called **mutagens** can change nucleotides within DNA molecules. The details of mutagens are as follows :

Physical mutagens. Energetic, penetrating radiations such as X-rays and ultraviolet light are powerful physical mutagens. Very high energy radiations can penetrate all organisms and produce large number of a great variety of mutations. For example,X-radiation is a powerful physical mutagen which can break chromosomes, oxidise deoxyribose, deaminate and dehydroxylate bases and form peroxides. Although less energetic than X-rays, ultraviolet light is also a powerful mutagen, largely because the base of nucleic acids absorb energy of its wavelengths. While UV's energy can also break chromosomes, its chemical effect on bases is particularly significant mutagenesis.

Chemical mutagens. Chemical mutagens such as nitrous acid, formaldehyde, ethylethane, sulphonate, etc., produce mutations by the addition or subtraction of whole nucleotides. C. Auerbach was the first to find mutations can also be induced due to certain chemicals . She made this important discovery during World War II.

The chance for a particular human gene to mutate in one generation is between 1 in 10,000 to 1 in 1,000,000. Since humans have atleast 30,000 genes, it is likely that each person carries atleast one mutation.

2. Chromosomal Abberrations (Chromosome mutations). Another way for the genetic traits of an organism to be altered is through changes involving whole chromosomes or parts of chromosomes. Structural changes in chromosomes are also caused by radiation, chemicals, and even by some virus infections.

Changes occur in the structure of chromosomes, during cell division. When homologous chromosomes pair up, linked genes on the chromosomes may break apart. The genes may join another chromosome, or they may be lost.

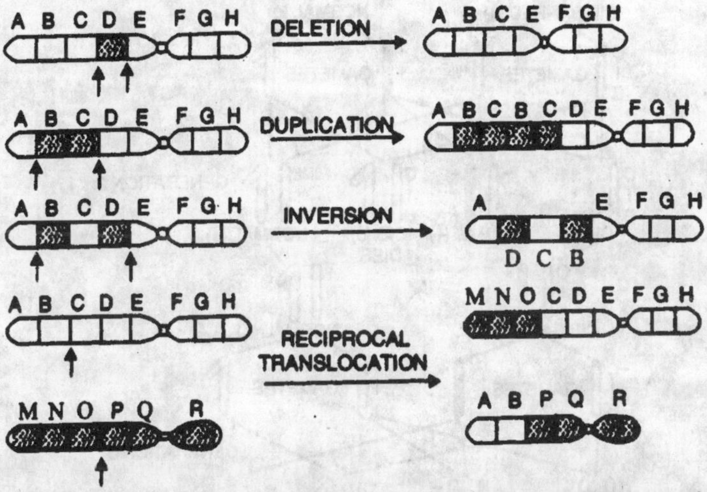

Fig. 46.1. Forms of chromosomal mutations showing deletion, duplication, inversion and reciprocal translocation. Apart of chromosome may be deleted, duplicated or inverted. It brings about the loss of genes, duplication of genes or inversion of gene order in a chromosome. A segment of one chromosome may be reciprocally exchanged with a pair of another chromosome.

Thus, a **deletion** involves the loss of a piece of chromosome. If a chromosome breaks and the parts do not reattach, the pieces may be lost. This is the most serious kind of chromosome mutation. Here, bits of genetic information are not available to the offspring.

A **duplication** occurs when one extra, but identical piece of chromosome is added to the normal chromosome.

When an **inversion** occurs, the pieces of chromosome break apart and pieces rejoin the same chromosome in a different order. Usually inversions have no harmful effects on the offspring.

Due to the mutagens two types of mutation **visible** and **lethal** are found. Mutations are located on either sex chromosomes or autosomes.

Detection of Sex linked lethals

CIB Method : The method involves use of CIB stock carried inversion of heterozygous state to work as **crossover supressor (C), a recessive lethal (i) X chromosome in heterozygote state and a dominant marker for barred eye (B)** or narrow eye.

Female heterozygote fly carries all the three features on one X chromosome (Fig. 46.2) and termed as **CIB X** flies. Male with CIB X chromosome will die. When male normal is irradiated for induction of mutation and crossed to CIB barred female in F_1 progeny male receiving **CIB X** chromosome will die. The **CIB** female will be barred type while the other female though normal but has one irradiated X chromosomes. When barred CIB female is crossed with normal male again the CIB male will die but 50% male will survive with irradiation X chromosome.

Muller-5-method : *Muller-5-Drosophila* with 2 marker genes, dominnant **Bar** (barred eye) and recessive **apricot.** It does not carry a lethal gene (Fig. 46.3) When **Muller-5** ♀ barred apricot is crossed with irradiated normal male the progeny will have heterozygote barred ♀ (female) with one X chromosome irradiated and **Muller 5 barred aprict** ♂ (male) type. If a lethal mutation is induced in X chromosome of irradiated male, no wild type male would apper in F_2 generation. The absence of wild type male in F_2 indicates induction of lethal mutation.

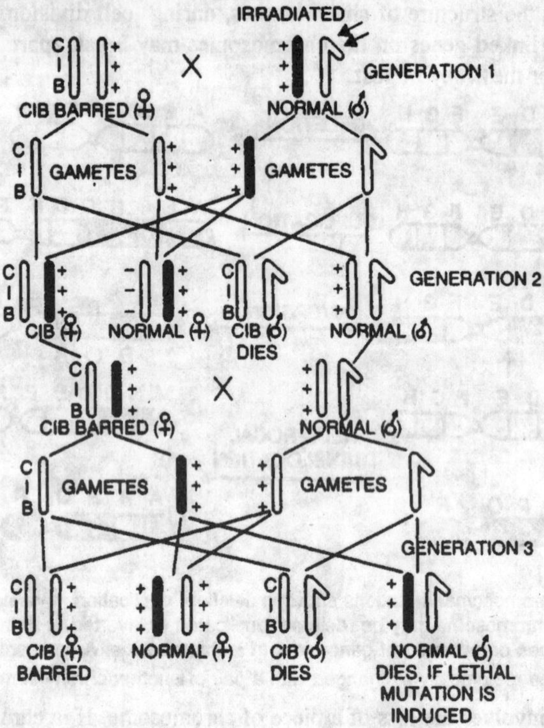

Fig. 46. 2. CIB method for detection of sex linked lethilnulat in *Drosophila*.

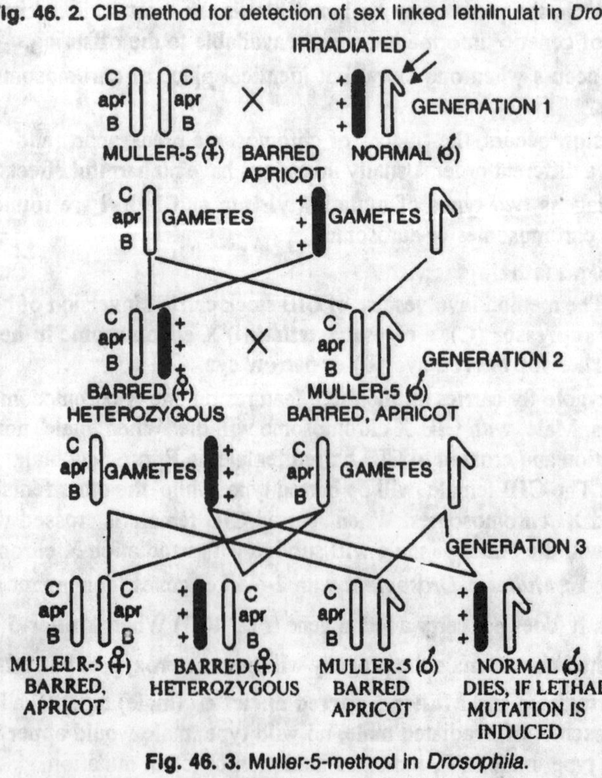

Fig. 46. 3. Muller-5-method in *Drosophila*.

Detection of sex linked visible mutation attached 'X' method : Muller-5 and attached **X** chromosomes were used to detect visible mutation. The attached X female (XXY) is crossed with irradiated male. Irradiated 'X' chromosome of male will form a superfemale (XXX) with visible induced mutation (Fig. 46.4).

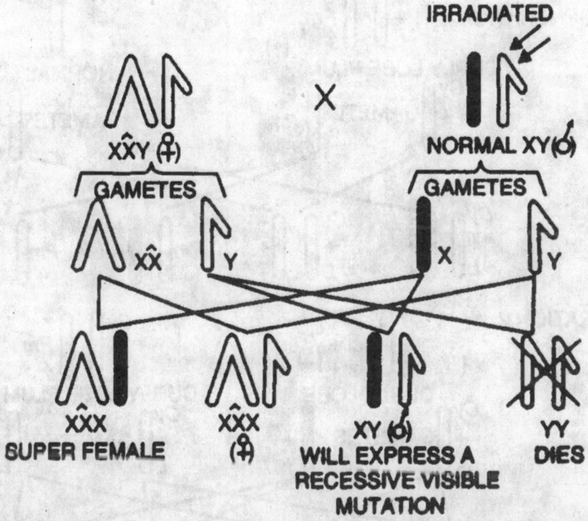

Fig. 46.4. Detection of sex linked visible mutator attached X method.

Balanced lethal system and detection of autosomal mutation

In *Drosophila* the female carrying dominant **Cy** gene (curly wing) and **L** (lobed eye) and the other homologous chromosome carrying gene of plum eye **(pm)** is crossed with same type of male, *i.e.,* curly, lobe, plum type (cyL/pm). the progeny is always heterozygous. Because homozygous with same genes on both the homologous chromosomes Cy L/Cy L or pm/pm will die. (Fig. 46.5).

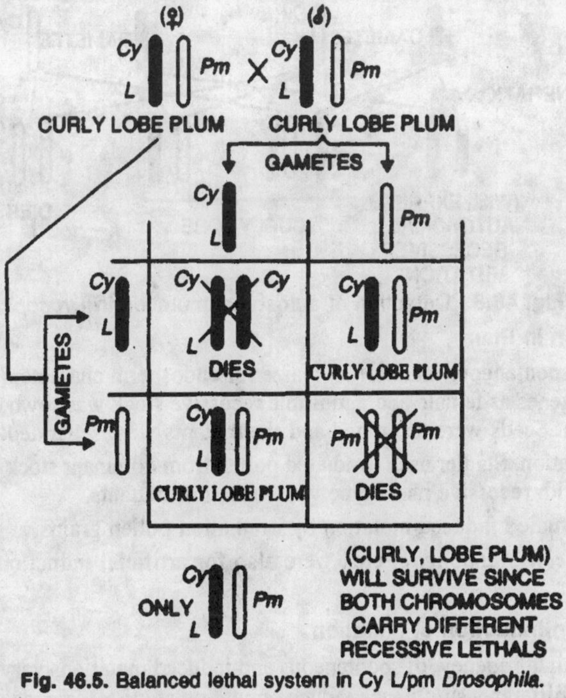

Fig. 46.5. Balanced lethal system in Cy L/pm *Drosophila*.

If Cy L/pm female is crossed with normal irradiated male, recessive mutated forms in females will survive but homozygous Cy L/cy L type will die (Fig. 46.6).

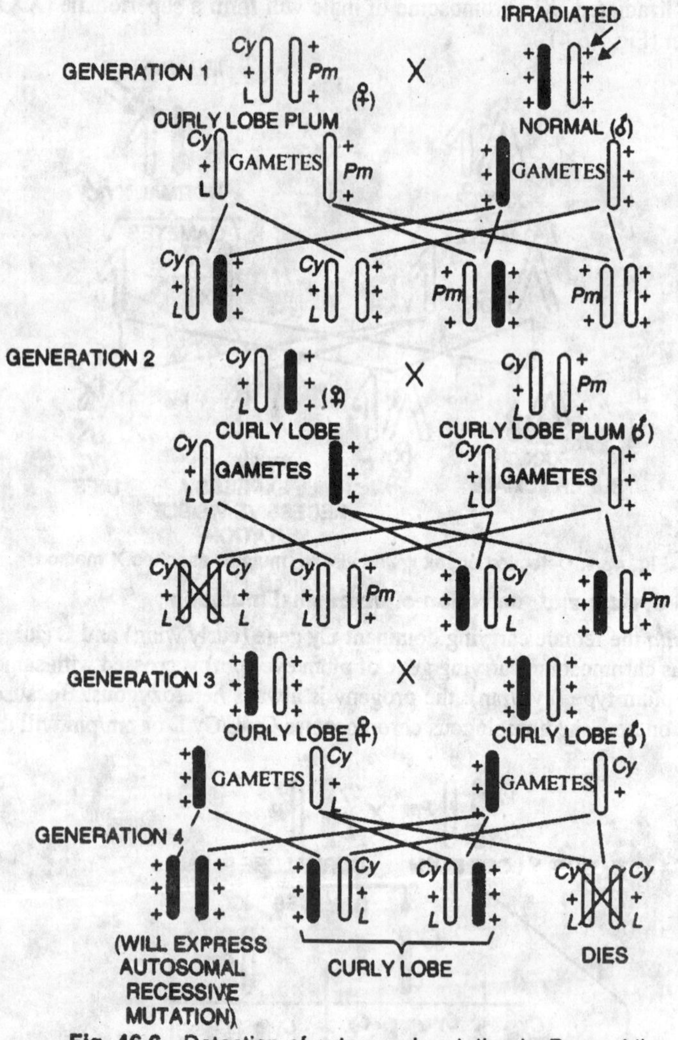

Fig. 46.6. Detection of autosomal mutation in *Drosophila.*

Detection of mutation in Plant

Stadler studied spontaneous mutation in maize for endosperm characters by growing a stock dominant for several genes as female and a multiple recessive stock was sown on every 5th row as male for pollens grain. Seeds were examined and the mutants were separated.

For induced mutation, Stadler used irradiated pollen from dominant stock and a recessive was pollinated. Progeny with recessive phenotype were called as mutants.

Singleton also studied induced mutation by irradiation pollen grains.

Neurospora, E. coli, Salmonella, etc., were also for artificial induction of mutation using various mutagens.

Effect of genotype on induction of Mutation

Stadler showed that freqency of spontaneous and induced mutations vary from locus to locus in maize. The genetic differences influence induced mutation at **mutator** gene and **paramutation.**

Mutator gene : In maize a gene 'a' is located on chromosome 3 causing absence of anthocyanin leading to loss of purple colour in kernel endosperm and other parts. If chromosome 9 has a dominant gene **'Dt'**, 'a' gets mutated to 'A' and allows anthocyanin product in heterozygote (Aa). The kernel will have spots in aleurone layer (Fig. 46.7) or stipes in leaves. Such gene is called mutator gene.

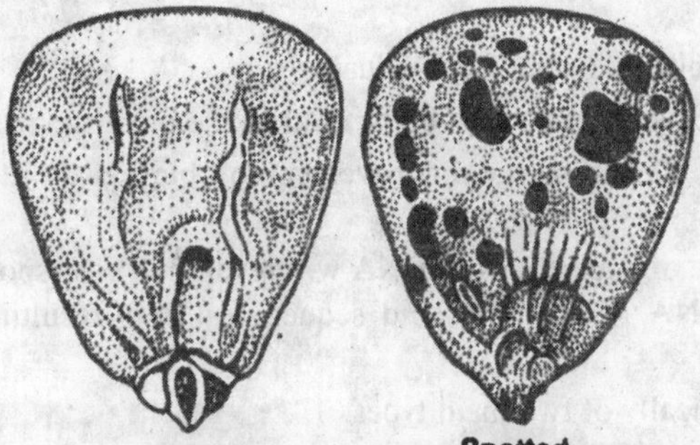

Colourless (aa) Spotted (aa, with mutator gene Dt)

Fig. 46. 7. Effect of mutator gene (Dt) in corn.

Ds-Ac system in cron was studied by **Barbara Mc Clintock. Ds is dissociation gene on** chromosome causing breakage but it is only active in the presence of **Ac (activator) gene located** on other chromosome.

Paramutation:

Brink (1956) discovered the phenomenon of paramutation in corn. He showed that the gene 'R' is for pigment with various phenotype effect R^r (full colour), R^{st} (stippened) and R^{mb} (marble) alleles is called paramutation. It is a rare phenomenon. The examples are found in *Oenothera*, tomato and fern, etc.

Practical applications of Mutation

According to **Gustafsson** less than one in 1,000 mutations produced may be useful in plant breeding.

Mutant varieties in wheat are produced for branched ears, high protein lysine control, amber seed colour, resistance and awned spikelets, etc. **M.S. Swaminathan** in IARI (Indian Agricultural Research Institute) New Delhi has produced a very important mutant variety of wheat, *i.e.*, **Sarbati sonara.**

Reimei is mutant variety of Rice produced by gamma radiation. Mutant varities of rice for increased protein, lysine content, etc., are produced. Mutations in *japonica* variety are created for *indica* type grains.

Erectoides and *Eceriferum* are the mutants of Barley for high yield. **Todd's Mitchem variety** of peppermint which is disease resistant and with improved quality of oil. **Aruna variety of castor** plant is an early maturing variety (110 days instead of 270). It can be harvested before the spread of disease and insects.

Penicillium is irradiated for increased yield of **penicillin.**

GENE MUTATION

Genes are segments of DNA molecules. Mutation is an abrupt qualitative or quantitative change in the genetic material of an organism. Mutations are **intragenic or intergenic. Intragenic mutations are called point mutations.** It includes change or alteration in DNA molecule in a gene. Change in base sequence of DNA molecule may bring about point mutation. The unit of gene bringing about mutation is called **'muton'. Intergenic mutations** involve changes in many genes (long chain of DNA). It includes changes in chromosomes.

Mutations occur in random manner. The frequency of spontaneous mutations is usually low, ranging from 10^{-7} to 10^{-12} per organism. The rate of detectable mutations in average gene is 1 in 10^6. the regions of gene where mutations occur much frequently is called **hot spots.** Mutations are classified as :

Lethal mutation : Results in death of individual.

Subvital mutation : Reduce the chances of survival of the organism in which they occur.

Supervital mutation: Result in the improvement of biological fitness under certain conditions.

Any change in sequence of nucleotides of DNA will result in a corresponding change in the nucleotide sequence of *m*RNA. The amino acid sequence differs resulting in structure and properties of enzyme formed.

Gene mutations are basically of two main types.

(a) Base pair mutation and (b) Frame shift mutations

(a) Base Pair Substitutions

This is the commonest type of mutation. The base pair switches are A-T, G-C, C-G or T-A. One base of a triplet codon is substituted by another, resulting is a changed codon.

(1) Original message reading frame CAT GAT CAT GAT CAT

(2) **Substitution or replacement A** is replaced by **'G'** CAT GAT **CGT** GAT CAT, message out of frame.

The mutated codon specifies another amino acid it will result in amino acid substitution in the polypeptide chain during translation (Fig. 46.8). Such changes are called *missense mutations*. If a single base substitution modifies a codon to a termination codon (CAG → UAG) the chain terminates at the place of mutation. This mutation is called **nonsense mutation**. Base pair substitution is of two types (Fig. 46.9).

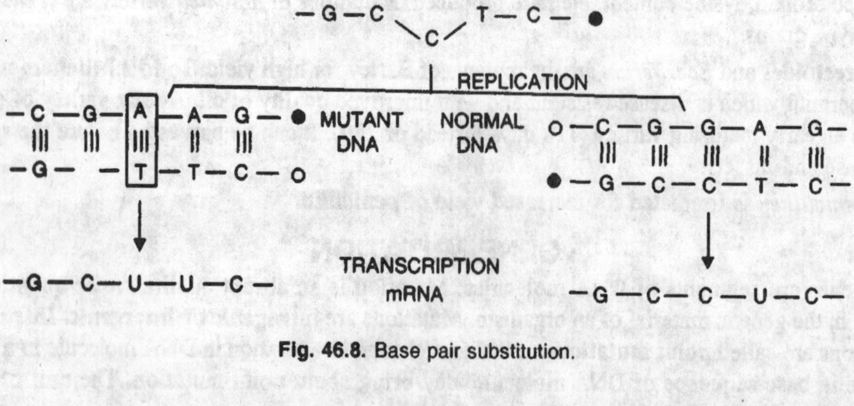

Fig. 46.8. Base pair substitution.

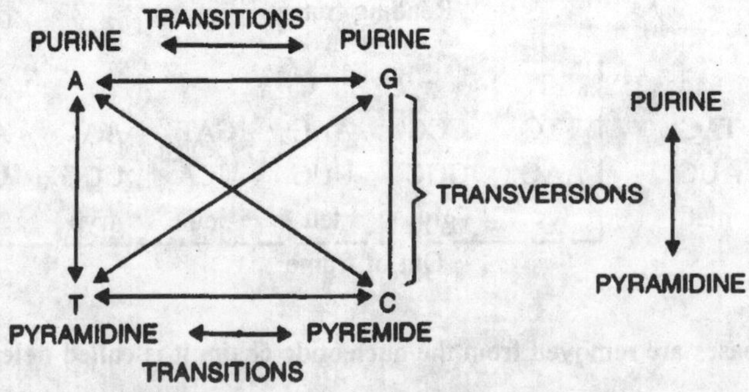

Fig. 46.9. Transition and Transversion.

(i) **Transititon :** Purine base is replaced by another purine, *i.e.*, 'A' by 'G' or 'G' by 'A', and pyramidine base is replaced by another pyramidine, *i.e.*, 'T' by 'C' or 'C' by 'T'.

(ii) **Transversion:** Purine base is substituted by pyramidine base is called transversion, *e.g.*, 'A' or 'C' is replaced by 'T' or 'G'.

Transition mutation generally code for chemically similar amino acids. Transversion shows change in amino acid (Fig. 46.10).

(b) Frame Shift mutation

A mutation in which there is deletion or insertion of one or a few nucleotides is called a **frameshift mutation.** Addition or deletion of one or two bases results in a new sequence of codons coding for entirely different amino acids. The protein synthesized will be entirely different.

Insertion

If one or more bases added to the message, it is called **insertion,** *e.g.*,

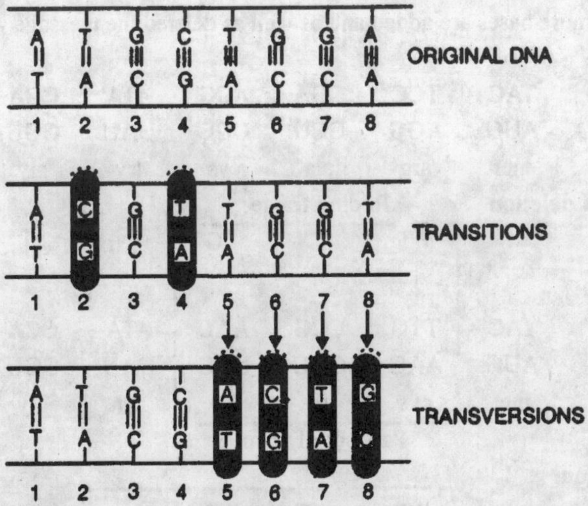

Fig. 46.10. Example of specific base pair change in transition and transversion.

Wild type

DNA	TAC	TCC	CGA	ACG	ATA	CCA	GAG
mRNA	AUG	AGG	GCU	UGC	UAU	GGU	CUC
Protein	met	arg	ala	cys	tyr	gly	leu

Reading frame

After Insertion

+T

DNA	TAC	TTC	CCG	AAC	GAT	AAC	AGA
mRNA	AUG	AAG	GGC	UUG	UCA	UGG	UCU
Protein	met	lys	gly	leu	leu	tryp	Ser

Out of frame

Deletion

If one or few bases are removed from the nucleotide chain, it is called **deletion,** *e.g.*,

Wild type

DNA	TAC	TCC	CGA	ACG	ATA
mRNA	AUG	AGG	GCU	UGC	UAU
Protein	met	arg	ala	cys	tyr

Reading frame

After deletion

–G

↑

DNA	TAC	TCC	CGA	ACA	TAC
mRNA	AUG	ACG	GCU	UGU	AUG
Protein	met	arg	ala	cys	met

Frame out

Insertion and deletion

When one or more bases are added and as well as deleted the message will be changed, *e.g.*,

Wild type

DNA	TAC	TCC	CGA	ACG	ATA	CCA
mRNA	AUG	AGG	GCU	UGC	UAU	GGU
Protein	met	arg	ala	cys	try	gly

Insertion and deletion Reding frame

+T – G

↓ ↓

DNA	TAC	TTC	CCG	AAC	ATA	CCA
mRNA	AUG	AAG	GGC	UUG	UAU	GGU
Protein	met	cys	gly	leu	tyr	gly

Part out of frame

Triple insertion

+ T + T + G

↓ ↓ ↓

DNA	TAC	TTC	CCT	GAA	GCG	ATA	CCA
mRNA	AUG	AAG	GGA	CUU	CGC	UAU	GGU
Protein	met	lys	gly	leu	arg	tyr	gly

Part out of phase

Triple deletion

		−T	−A	−T		
		↑	↑	↑		
DNA	TAC	CCC	GAC	GAA	CCA	GAG
mRNA	AUG	GGG	CUG	CUU	GGU	CUC
Protein	met	gly	leu	leu	gly	leu

part out of frame

Example of **sickle cell anaemia** is of point mutation. The haemoglobin protein in RBC molecule consists of 4 polypeptide chains among which 2 are α chains and 2 are β chains, changes in haemoglobin structure results in certain types of anaemia. In sickle cell anaemia RBC become sickle shaped. Normal haemoglobin has amino acid **glutamic acid** in 6th position. In sickle cell gutamic acid substituted by **valine** and in haemoglobin C it is substituted by **lysine**.

	1	2	3	4	5	6	7	8
A.	Val	his	leu	thr	Pro	**glu acid**	glu acid	lys
B.	Val	his	leu	thr	pro	**val**	gly acid	lys
C.	Val	his	leu	thr	pro	**lys**	glu acid	lys

Where 'A' is normal haemoglobin 'B' is sickle cell haemoglobin and 'C' is haemoglobin 'C'.

Missense mutation

Due to change in one base the amino acid in a polypeptide chain is replaced by other amino acid, the protein has only one different amino acid, *e.g.*, **UUU** codes for phenyl alanine and the base **'U'** is substituted by **'G'** the code will be **UGU** coding for **cysteine** (Fig. 46.11)

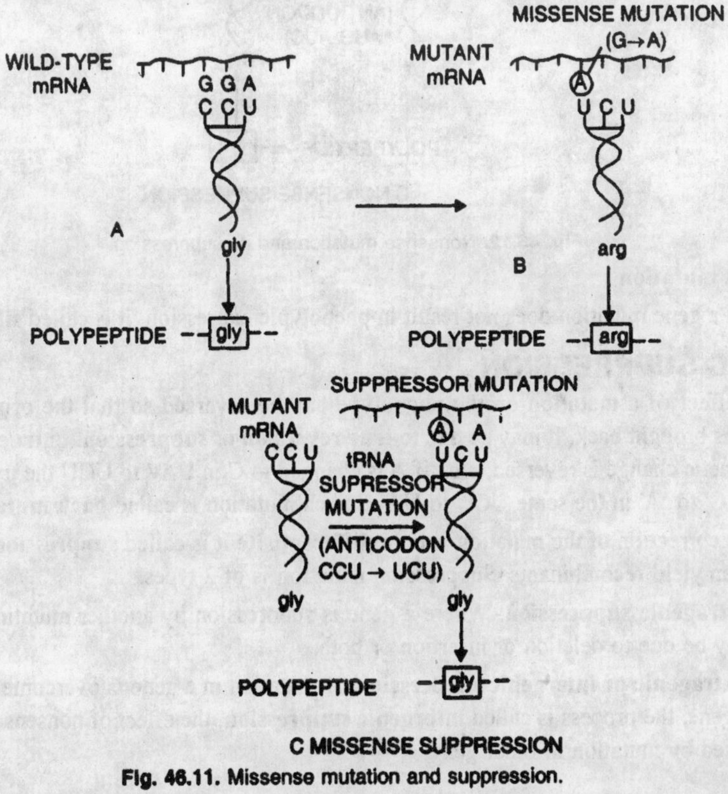

Fig. 46.11. Missense mutation and suppression.

Nonsense mutation

If the change in base sequence codes for termination codon UAA, UAG and UGA the mutation is called nonsequence mutation, *e.g.*, in UAC if C is substituted to G it will become UAG which is a termination codon (Fig. 46.12).

In the same way a termination codon may also be converted into nonsense codon, *e.g.*, in UAA, U is substituted by 'C' then it will become CAA coding glutamine.

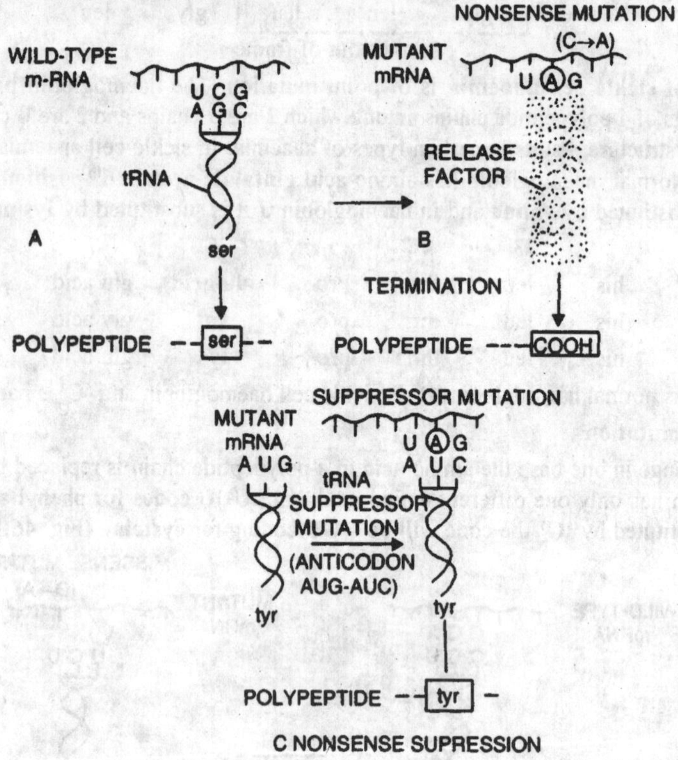

Fig. 46.12. Nonsense mutation and its suppression.

Silent mutation

When a gene mutation does not result in phenotypic expression, it is called **silent mutation**.

GENETIC SUPPRESSION

The effect of a mutation on the phenotype can be reversed so that the original wildtype phenotype is brought back. It may be due to **true reversion** or **suppression**. In **true reversion** the original genetic change is reversed, *e.g.*, if **A** is changed to C in UAV to UCU the true reversion is change to 'C' to 'A' in the same UCU to UAU. Such mutation is called **back mutation**.

When correction of the mutation is on a **different site** it is called **suppression.** Suppression mutation can yield recombinants. Suppression mutation is of 2 types.

(a) **Intragenic suppression**: Where a gene is suppression by another mutation in the same gene. It may be due to deletion or insertion or both.

(b) **Extragenic or intergenic suppression**: If mutation in a gene is overcome by a mutation in another gene, the process is called **intergenic suppression**, the effect of nonsense mutation can be suppressed by mutation in other gene.

Suppressor genes: Genes whose activity results in suppression of mutation in other genes are called **suppressor genes.** Suppressor genes are present for each termination codon. The **amber** (UAG) mutants of T_4 bacteriophage are able to grow on only **permissive** strains (mutant strain containing suppressor genes) of *E. coli*. The suppressor genes restore the function of mutant genes in T_4 DNA enabling them to grow on host cells. 3 **amber** suppressor genes **Su¹, Su²** and **Su³** or **sup D, sup E,** and **sup F** are known for amber termination codon. These genes produce changes in the anticodons of *t*RNA so that they can read the termination codon UAG. Among the three suppressor genes are, inserts **serine,** other **glutamine** and the third **tyrosine** in the termination position.

Ochre (UAA) mutant suppresses the mutation of **ochre** termination codon and **opal** (UGA) mutant suppresses opal termination codon.

Frameshift suppression

Certain suppressor genes can mask the frameshift mutations resulting from the insertion of nucleotides, *e.g.*, anticodon for phenyl alanine *t*RNA reads quadruplet UUUC instead of UUU as codon for phenylalanine. The extra nucleotide permits the reading of form nucleotides in *m*RNA at a time and thus restores the reading frame to the original position. In *Salmonella typhimerinum* glycine *t*RNA contains the nucleotide quadruplet CCCC instead of triplet (CCC) in the anticodon position. The extra nucleotide permits the reading of 4 nucleotides in *m*RNA. (Fig. 46.13)

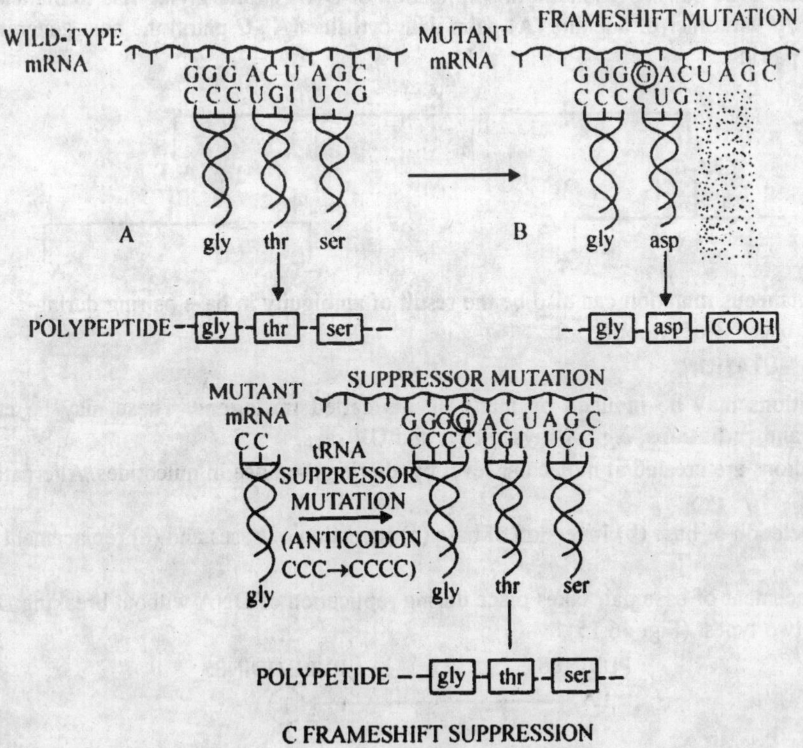

Fig. 46.13. Frameshift mutation and suppression.

SPONTANEOUS MUTATION

Mutation occurring under natural conditions are called **spontaneous mutations.** Such mutations arise by action of mutagens, *e.g.*, cosmic radiation, radioactive compounds, heat, etc.

Tautomerism

The ability of a molecule to exist in more than one form is called **tautomerism.** Normal base pairing in DNA is A-T and G-C. The tautomerism forms are, however capable of unusual base pairing like G-T,T-G,C-A and A-C (Fig. 46.14).

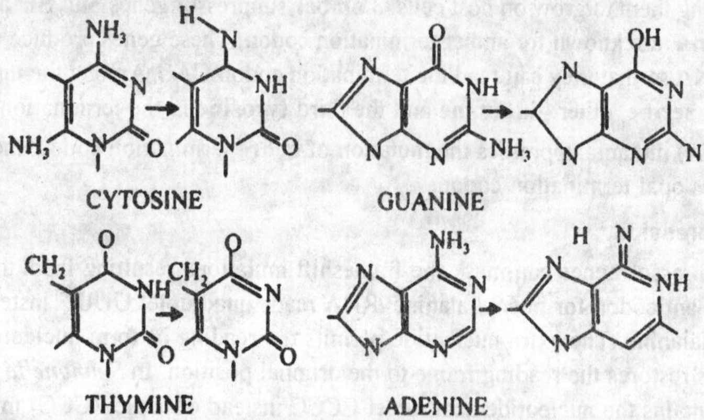

Fig. 46.14. Tautomeric forms.

Unusual base pairing results in misreplication of DNA strand giving rise to mutants in the progeny if A* tautomer of adenine (A) pairs with cytosine (A*-C pairs) the next generation will show G-C pairing.

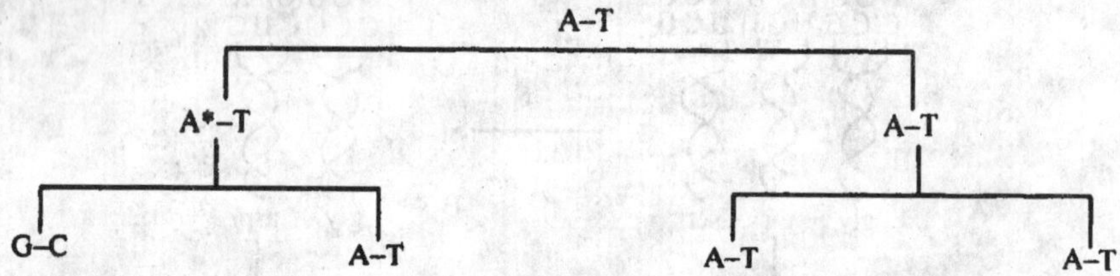

Spontaneous mutation can also be the result of ambiguity in base pairing during replication because of 'wobble'.

INDUCED MUTATION

Mutations may be induced by many agents called **mutagens.** These may be chemical **mutagens and radiations,** *e.g.*, X-rays, γ-rays and UV rays.

Mutations are created at molecular level by altering the **base** in nuleotides. Alternations are created by :

(a) Deletion of base (b) Inversion of base (c) Inversion of bases and (d) replacement of base pairs.

Replacement of base pair takes place during replication of DNA without breaking DNA. It may be of two types. (Fig. 46.15)

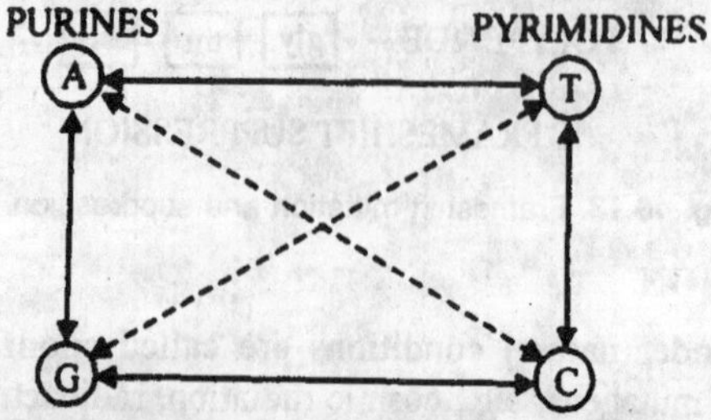

Fig. 46.15. Induced transition and transversion.

(a) **Transition** :Purine is replaced by another purine or pyrimidine is replaced by another pyrimidine.

(b) **Transversion** : Purine is replaced by pyrimidine.

The discovery of mutagenic effects produced by various types of radiations was shown for the first time as an experimental probe for changine gene structure and function. It was very difficult to distinguish between direct or indirect effects of irradiation and to analyse the exact nature of biochemical compounds produced. Chemical mutagens are more effective and their results are characterized.

Thomas and **Steinberg** found nitrous acid effective causing mutation in *Aspergillus.* **Auerbach** and **Robson** found that mutations can be induced by nitrogen and sulphur gas in *Drosophila.* Mutagenic activity in formaldehyde, diethylsulfate, diazomethane, etc., are discovered by **Rapoport.** Chemical mutagens cause severe skin irritations in mammals and also can produce cancer. There are some chemicals which affect some organisms but not other. **Watson** and **Crick** were first to suggest that mutation could occur as a result of occasional changes in the hydrogen bonding of nucleotodie bases, *e.g.*, **adenine** normally bears an NH_2 (amino) group providing hydrogen atom for bonding with the complementary **keto** (C = O) group of thymine. In a **Tautomeric shift** the amino group is changed to amino group (NH). This base now bonds with **cytosine** (instead of thymine). In **thymine** the tautomeric shift from keto to **enol** (COH) form allows it to bond with **guanine** (instead of adenine) (Fig. 46.16).

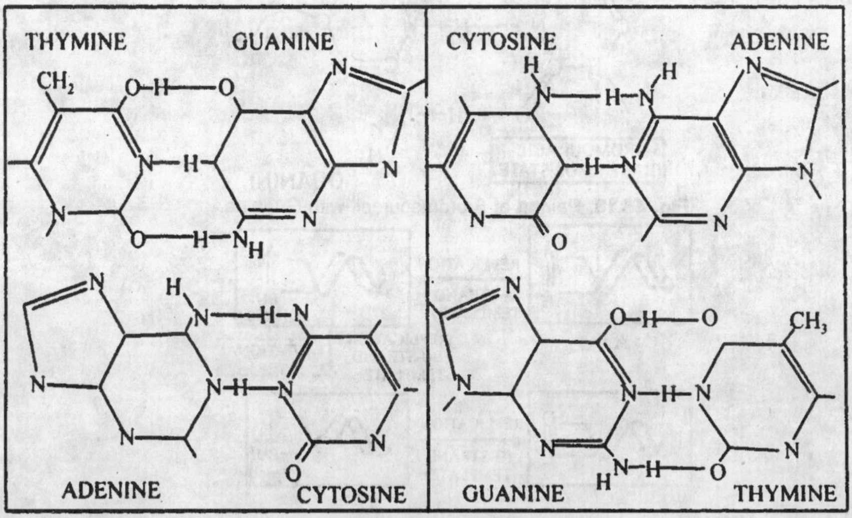

Fig. 46.16. Tautomeric shift : T with G instead of 'A', 'C with 'A' instead of 'G', A with 'C' instead of 'T', G with 'T' instead of 'C'.

If the tautomeric shift produces the error, it is necessary that DNA replication should take place.

Base analogues

A chemical substance resembling a base is called **base analogue.** It may be incorporated into newly synthesized DNA instead of a normal base. Pyrimidine analogue 5-bromouracil (5-BU) is structurally similar to thymine. 5-chlorouracil (5 CU) and 5 iodouracil (5 IU)can also replace thymine in DNA. 2-amino purine (2 AP) is incorporated in very small amount that it could not be possible to find out which base it replaces. 2,6 diamino purine is highly mutagenic. **5-bromouracil** can pair with adenine just like **thymine** (Fig. 46.17).

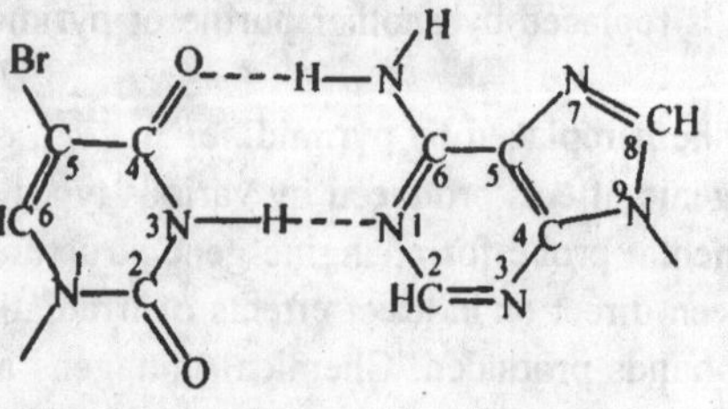

Fig. 46.17. Pairing of "5" bromouracil (keto form) with adenine.

5-bromouracil (5-BU)and bromodeoxyuridine (BUdR) are analogues of thymine which are **keto** forms but can undergo tautomeric shifts, they are **enol** form and pairs with Guanine (G) instead of Adenine (A) (Fig. 46.18). 5-BU produces G-C substitution for the original A-T,or it may occasionally be incorporated in the **enol** form as a pairing mate with guanine and then revert to its keto form to produce A-T substituion for the original G-C. **Lawley** and **Brookes** suggested that mispairing may be caused by ionization of bases rather than by tautomeric shifts. In this mechanism a base, *e.g.*, 5-BU loses the hydrogen normally associated with its 3 nitrogen atom (Fig. 46.19 A,B).and may now pair with guanine (G).

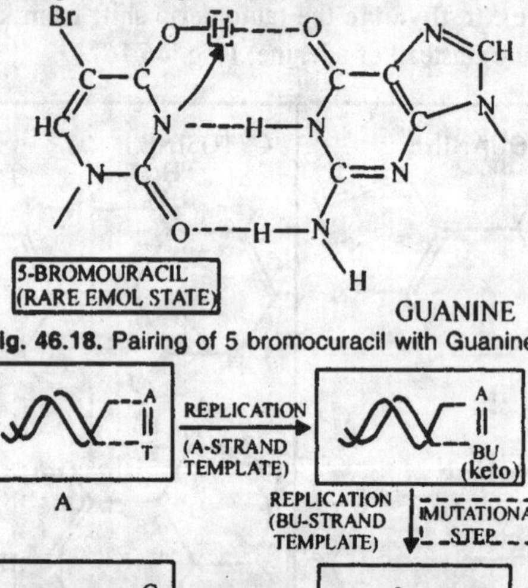

Fig. 46.18. Pairing of 5 bromocuracil with Guanine.

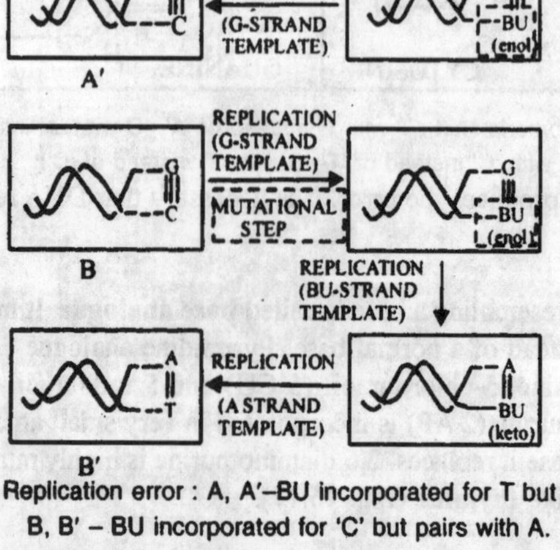

Fig. 46.19. Replication error : A, A′–BU incorporated for T but pairs with G, B, B′ – BU incorporated for 'C' but pairs with A.

The base analogue 2 amino purine (2 AP) shows mutational properties enabling it to be incorporated as a substitute of adenine but to pair subsequently with cytosine, or to pair initially with cytosine and subsequently with thymine. Incorporation a of AP at place of guanine (G) to give AP–C base pair will cause mutation in subsequent generation.

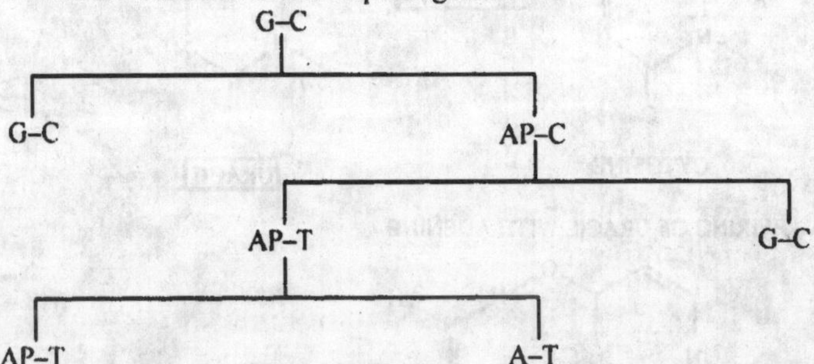

A mistake in replication after incorporation of 2–AP leads to the formation of AP–T base pair inducing transition.

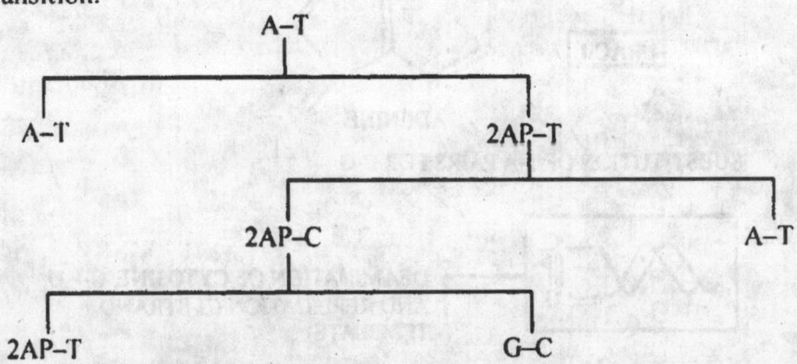

Agents modifying purines and pyrmidines

The agents which modify purines and pyrimidines or agents which stabilize the bases include **nitrous oxide** (HNO_2), hydroxylamine and alkylating agents.

Nitrous oxide (HNO_2): It reacts with bases containing amino groups. It changes the structure by deamination (removal of the amino group). The **amino group** (NH_2) is replaced by **hydroxyl group** (OH^-). Nitrous acid deaminates, the bases, G, C and A with decreasing frequency. Deamination of **adenine** results in the formation of **hypoxanthine** (Fig. 46.20). Hypoxanthine pairs with **cytosine** instead of thymine. Thus **A–T** pairing is replaced by G–C pairs. Deamination of **cytosine** at 6 position results in the formation of uracil (U) (Fig. 46.21) and the pairing of C–G instead of U–A is formed. **Guanine** deaminates to **xanthine. Xanthine** behaves like Guanine and pairs with cytosine, the pairing is **X–C** instead of G–C. Deamination of Guanine has no mutagenic affect (Fig. 46.22). The change in base pairing result in change in DNA in the 50% progeny. Deamination of gaunine, does not show any heritable mutation.

Table: 46.1. The structural and pairing behaviour change of DNA due to deamination by nitrous oxide.

Normal Base	Normal pairing	Deaminated Base	New pair
Adenine	A–T	Hypoxanthine	G–C
Cytosine	C–G	Uracil	U–A
Guanine	G–C	Xanthine	X–C

Hydroxylamine (NH_2OH): It reacts with **cytosine** and **guanine**, the hydroxylation of cytosine at amino group forms **hydroxylcytosine** which pairs with **adenine** because the hydroxyl amino group should be more electronegative than amino group. The hydroxylated molecule is in tautomeric form having a hydrogen atom in place of nitrogen at position 3. The effect of hydroxylamine on 'C' produces a transition in base pairing (Fig. 46.23)

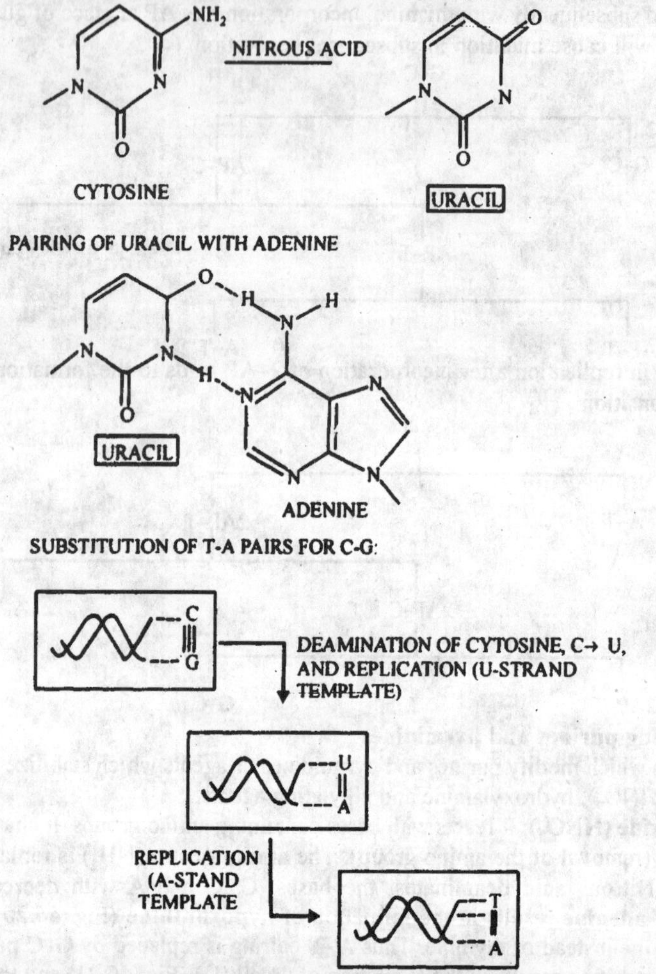

Fig. 46.20. Action of nitrous acid on cytosine.

Hydrazine (NH_2NH_2) breaks the rings of **uracil** and **cytosine** forms **pyrazolone** and **3-aminopyrasole.** When DNA is treated with hydrazine it produces **"apyrimidinic acid".** While when RNA is treated with hydrazine it produces **"ribo-apyrimidinic acid".**

Alkylating agents : Many mutagenic agents carry one or more **alkyl** groups. These are called **mono- , bi-** or **poly** functional alkylating agents, *e.g.*, **dimethyl sulphate** (DES), **dimethyl sulphate** (MMS), ethyl ethane sulphonate (DMS), **methyl methane sulphonate** (EES) and **ehtyl methane sulphonate (EMS),** etc. All of them act as mono-functional groups.

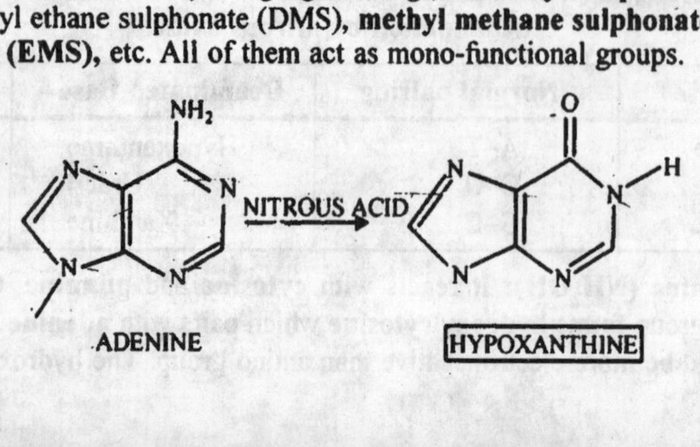

PAIRING OF HYPOXANTHYINE WITH CYTOSINE:

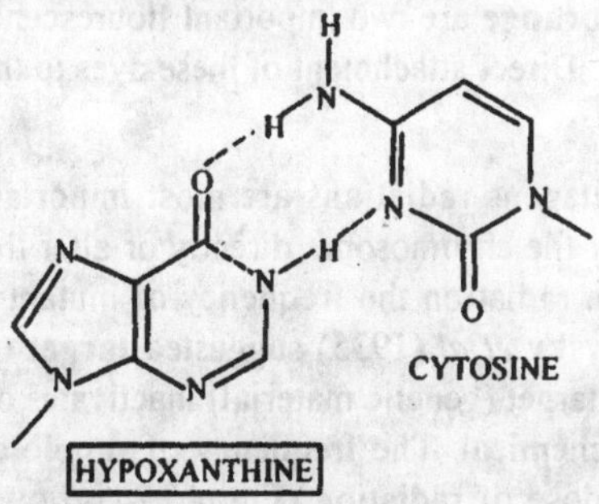

SUBTITUTION OF G-C PAIRS FOR A-T:

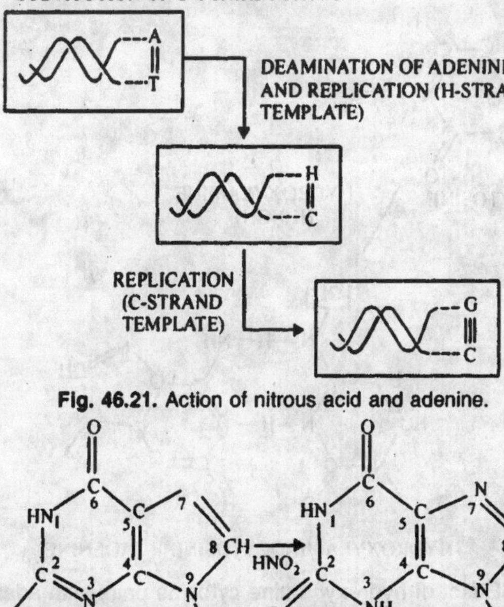

Fig. 46.21. Action of nitrous acid and adenine.

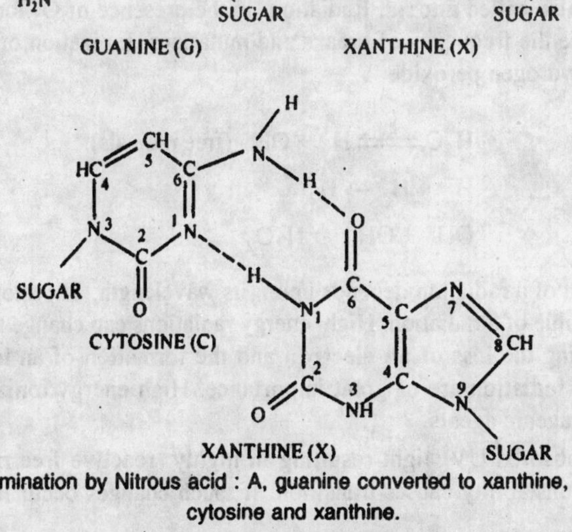

Fig. 46.22. Deamination by Nitrous acid : A, guanine converted to xanthine, B.Base pairing in cytosine and xanthine.

Agents producing distortion in DNA

Proflavin and **acridine orange** are two important flourescent dyes which cause mutation by **insertion** or **deletion** of bases. Direct attachment of these dyes to the nucleic acid causes mutation.

RADIATIONS

Among the physical mutagens radiations are most important. They have direct effect on chromosome. They may break the chromosome directly or alter the DNA bases. If chromosomes at meiotic prophase are given radiation the frequency of mutant per viable organism increases linearly with the dose. **Ressovsky** *et al* (1935) suggested **target theory** stating that single hit of the particle (radiation) on the target (genetic material) inactivates or mutates it. The radiation may act through production of a chemical. The frequency of simple chromosomal aberrations, *e.g.*, deletion, is proposed to the dose of radiation (Fig. 46.24). Low O_2 concentration reduces the frequency of chromosome breaks induced by radiations.

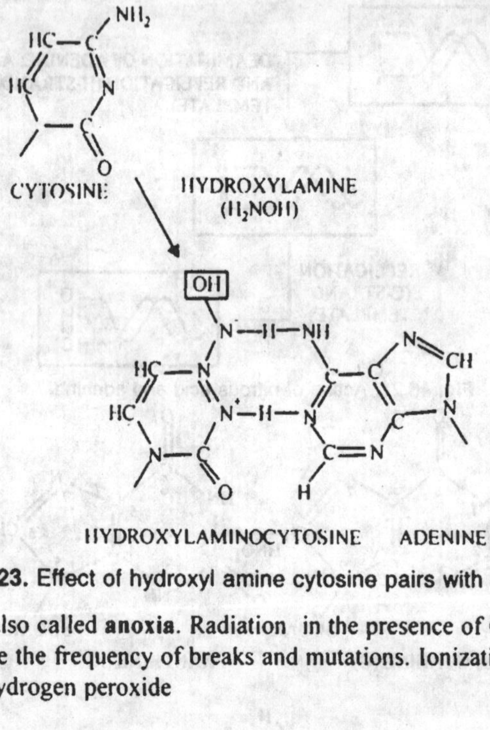

Fig. 46.23. Effect of hydroxyl amine cytosine pairs with adenine.

Oxygen effect is also called **anoxia**. Radiation in the presence of O_2 forms some **peroxide radicals** which influence the frequency of breaks and mutations. Ionization of water in cells may give free radicals and hydrogen peroxide

$$H_2O \rightleftharpoons H^+ + OH^- \text{ (free radicals)}$$

$$H^+ + H^+ \rightarrow H_2$$

$$OH^- + OH^- \rightarrow H_2O_2$$

The energy content of a radiation depends upon its wavelength. The shorter the wavelength the greater the energy value of a radiation. High energy radiations can change the atomic structure of a substance by causing the **loss of an electron** and the formation of an **ion.** Alternations in nucleic acid caused by radiation are of great importance. High energy ionizing radiations and ultraviolet light are mutagenic agents.

DNA and RNA absorbs UV light resulting in highly reactive free radicals in nitrogen containing bases. The unstability causes transition. If such changes occur in *m*-RNA only few inactive proteins are formed in substitution in DNA have lasting effect producing defective protein. UV light produces **thymine dimers** (Fig. 46.25). 5, 6 unsaturated bonds of adjacent pyrimidines become covalently linked and form **cyclobutance** ring. Three possible types of pyrimidine dimers in DNA are found in irradiated bacterial culture.

Thymine–thymine–50%

Thymine–cytosine–40%

Cytosine–cytosine–10%

In RNA pyrimidine dimers are formed between adjacent **uracil** and cytosine ring. These dimers cannot fit into the DNA double helix causing distortion of DNA molecules. If this damage is not repaired the replication is blocked and it is lethal. **Exonuclease** recognizes the distorted region and corrects it. **DNA polymerase** inserts correct bases in the gap and **DNA ligases** joins the inserted base.

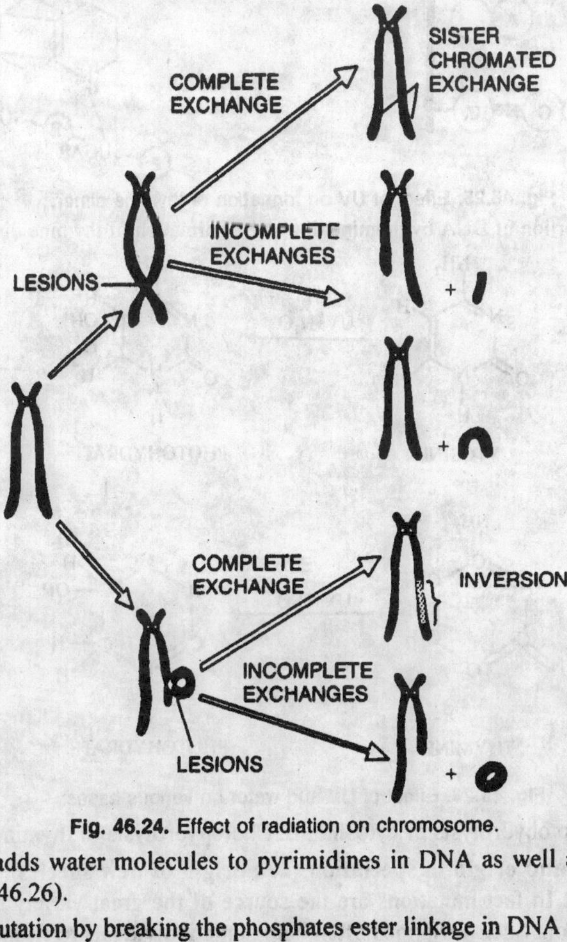

Fig. 46.24. Effect of radiation on chromosome.

UV radiation adds water molecules to pyrimidines in DNA as well as RNA resulting in photohydrates (Fig. 46.26).

X-ray causes mutation by breaking the phosphates ester linkage in DNA at one or more points causing a large number of deletion of bases or rearrangement. In double stranded DNA breaks may occur in one or both the strands. If it is found in both the strands it is lethal. Sometimes two double stranded breaks may occur in the same molecule and the two broken ends may rejoin. The part of DNA between the two breaks is eliminated resulting in deletion.

Photoreactivation: UV induced mutation discovered by **Kelner** *et al* shows that UV effect can be reversed by exposing cells to visible light containing wave length in the blue region of spectrum. It is called **photoreactivation.** It was observed in bacteria and bacteriophages. It is caused by enzyme which splits thymine dimers and repair the DNA molecule. When DNA repair system is absent in humans **xeroderma pigmentosum** appears in the patients susceptible to sunlight.

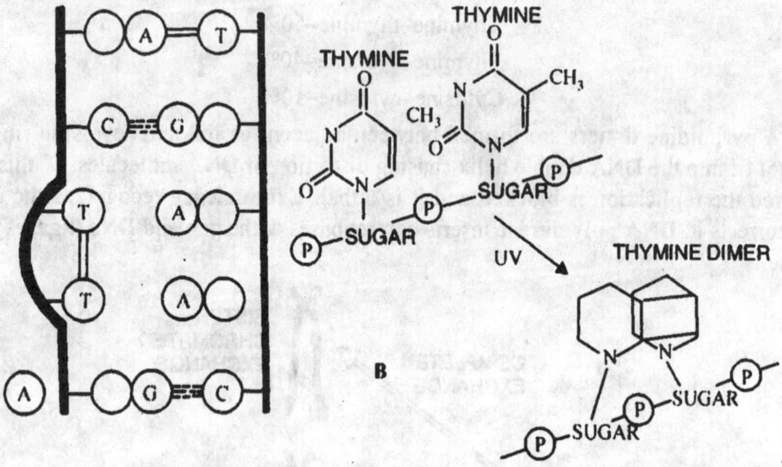

Fig. 46.25. Effect of UV on formation of thymine dimer:
A. Distortion of DNA by thymine dimer; B. Formation of thymine dimer.

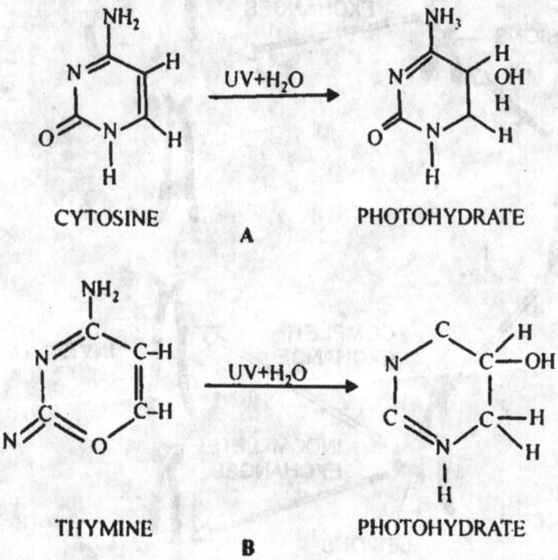

Fig. 46.26. Effect of UV and water on various bases:
A Photohydrolysis of cytosine; B. Photohydrolysis of thymine.

Mutation's role and origin in speciation (*i.e.*, origin of new species). It is learnt that all mutations are not bad. In fact mutations are the source of the great variety that we see among members of a population. Such variations often help some individuals to fit into the environment better than other individuals. However, in general, random mutations are of no help. In fact, most cause the death of the organism. Mutations that survive are usually recessive and remain hidden for many generations.

A species is one or more populations of similar organisms. They are similar because they share a common **gene pool.** A gene pool of a population is the total number of different kinds of genes (alleles) pooled by all its members. Thus, a gene pool is available to a population for adapting itself to the environment. Populations of a species that live in different geographical areas and in different environment conditions, pass through the elemental forces of mutation and natural selection. Thus, the population get adapted to their environment.

Selection of mutations. When a beneficial mutation occurs, this will probably appear with increasing frequency in subsequent generations. The rate at which the new gene replaces the original one in the population will be determined by many factors, such as (i) whether the new mutation is dominant or recessive, (ii) the intensity of the selection, (iii) the rate at which the mutation occurs in the population, and (iv) the size of the population. For this process, many generations are needed for the incorporation of an ordinary mutation into the majority of the individuals of a large population.

Mutations and their origin in organisms. All organisms living in the world are the products of hundreds of thousands of years of this process of selecting favourable mutations, and they are well adapted for the particular environment in which they live. During this process of evolving, when the environmental conditions have remained relatively constant for a long period of time, most of the mutations that could give survival value have occurred and have been selected. Thus, the beneficial mutations occurred with great frequency. George Simpson, in his study of horse evolution, has established that something over five million years was required for the formation of each of the genera in the evolution of the horse.

Under changed environmental conditions, populations either become adapted or die out. As a result of the adaptive changes, originally identical populations become more and more dissimilar. Over a period of time, a population may become so different, from the ancestral population that they are no longer able to interbreed with one another. They then become different species.

Mutations in haploid organisms. In all haploid organisms every mutation behaves as if it were a dominant. Because of this valuable characteristic, many important genetic discoveries have been made on such organisms during recent years. An example of how *Neurospora* can be used will illustrate how mutations with a biochemical effect can be detected. We start with a wild-type mold growing on a minimal medium. Asexual spores from this culture are transferred to a complete medium containing vitamins and amino acids. These spores may be treated with X-rays or in other way to increase the mutation rate. From this tube single spores of sexual fruiting bodies are transferred to tubes containing complete media. Then from these tubes transfers are made to tubes which are deficient vitamins and amino acids. Whenever a tube is found with no growth, that is a sign that a mutation has occurred in some gene which is necessary to synthesize the specific vitamin or amino acid which is lacking in this particular tube.

Among animals there are certain insects, such as male honey bees, which have only one of each type chromosome in their bodies. Unfortunately for genetics, the breeding habits of the bees and the problems of studying them do not make them favourable subjects for investigation. However, other members of the order Hymenoptera make very satisfactory forms for genetic breeding and study. One is the small parasitic wasp, *Habrobracon juglandis,* which has been investigated extensively by P. W. Whiting who has found that females carrying recessive genes yield male offspring which show these genes regardless of what type of male the female is mated to. This is due to the fact that the males develop from the unfertilized eggs. These tiny wasps are parasitic on the meal worm, *Tenebrio,* and may be raised very conveniently in the laboratory with a little corn meal and the *Tenebrio* worms.

Thus, haploids are better for mutation work becaue in them all the mutations, whether recessive or dominant, are expressed, as there is only one allele of each gene present in each cell.

Role of mutations in evolution. On the basis of the sudden changes in organisms. Hugo de Vries (1840-1935) proposed **mutation theory** for evolution. According to it mutation was the whole truth of evolution. Since mutations were known to be random, evolution was also considered to proceed at random. Many geneticists supported such a theory and they did not attach any importance, whatsoever, to the natural selection. They also thought that there are no adaptations, but only chance preadaptions.

Mutation theory of de Vries could explain some of the objections raised against Darwin's natural selection theory. As opposed to Darwin's hypothesis, de Vries attached importance to sudden changes or discontinuous variations, called "sports" by the former and "mutations" by the latter. On the basis of this, cases of overspecialization can be easily explained. One can also explain how the hereditary variations could originate and distinguish them from other environmental variations.

Considerable amount of work on frequency, nature, spectrum and size of mutations has been done in the modern times. It should be realized that hereditary changes can be brought about due to structural changes in chromosomes or due to changes at the genic level. These are called chromosomal mutations and gene mutations, respectively. Both kinds of changes play their roles in evolution. There are a large number of cases like *Drosophila, Crepis,* etc., where speciation has proceeded due to structural changes in chromosomes.

Hugo de Vries thought that mutations would always involve bigger and sudden changes. We now definitely know that the changes due to single mutation may vary from a major change, used for distinguishing species, genera or families to the changes which cannot be easily detected. The former are called **systematic macromutations,** while the latter are **micromutations.** Here, the cases are known where bigger mutations could be important, but in majority of the cases the smaller changes are more important. It is because if a genotype which is well adjusted into an environment, is too drastically altered, it will not be able to adjust. Minute changes, on the other hand, can be useful and help the organism to adjust in the new environmental conditions. Thus, mutation theory in its original form, as proposed by de Vries, does not hold good. However, evolution is a complex process and involves a complex set of factors. Mutation does play a very important role in evolution, but by no means is the only force working for organic evolution.

SUMMARY

1. Mutations can be artificially induced by **X-rays, gamma rays, mustard** gas, etc.
2. Mutation from the wild type to a new type is called **forward mutation.**
3. When mutant type is changed to the wild type is called **reverse mutation.**
4. Mutation involves deletion and insertion of base (s), the condition is known as **frame shift** mutations.
5. Mutation takes place at a definite locus in **point mutation.**
6. In **transition** purine base is replaced by other purine base or a pyrimidine is replaced by another pyrimidine base.
7. In **transversion** purine is replaced by pyrimidine base or vice-versa.
8. *Neurospora* or red bread mold is haploid in its vegetative phase and has a very short life cycle.
9. **Beadle and Tatum** (1941) used *Neuropora* to show biochemical mutations.
10. The whole process in *Neurospora* is controlled by a specific enzyme under control of specific gene.
11. One gene-one enzyme hypothesis in *Neurospora* was suggested by **Beadle** and **Tatum.**
12. Haemoglobin consists of 4 polypeptide chains (2α and 2β). Hence, one gene one enzyme hypothesis has become one gene-one polypeptide hypothesis.
13. **C. Auerback** first of all explained that certain chemicals can induce mutations. These are called as **chemical mutagens, *e.g.*, phenol, mustard gas, formaldehyde, maleic hydrazide,** etc.

14. A **gene pool** is the total number of genes in reproductive gametes of a population.
15. **Gene frequency** is the proportion of different alleles of a gene in a population.
16. Changes in genetic frequencies are due to mutations, selection, genetic drift and migration.
17. Ionizing radiations X-rays, γ-rays, β-rays, neutrons and UV light can produce point mutations or chromosomal aberrations. The number of mutations increases proportionally with the dose of the effect of radiations cumulative.
18. Somatic mutations are not transmitted from one generation to another. But germ cell mutations may be passed to offsprings.
19. Mendelian recombinants are due to crossing over.
20. Mutant strains are called **auxotrophs.**
21. Wild strain capable of growing in minimal media is called **prototroph.**
22. All mutations are easily and immediately expressed because alleld of each gene is present.
23. Mutation theory was proposed by **Hugo de Vries.**
24. Lethal mutations are mostly **recessive.**
25. **Hereditary variations** in plant can be produced by **X-rays.**
26. No two individuals exhibit exactly similar characters (except identical twins). This is known as **variation.**
27. Variations are not necessarily heritable.
28. **Variations** are more prominent in sexually reproducing organisms.
29. Sexual reproduction results in the formation of monoparental offspring, a carbon copy of parent called **clone.**
30. The progeny formed after sexual reproduction is called as **offspring.**
31. Huntigatons disease is due to insertion of copier of a repeat of CAG triplet in the working gene itself.
32. Cancers are due to mutation contains genes, *e.g.*, oncogenes and Tumor suppressor gene.
33. In colorectal cancers there is genetic instability in cancer cells with the expansion of trinucleotide repeats.
34. Certain carcinogens are also bacterial mutagens.
35. Superoxide dismutase (enzyme) destroys mutagen.
36. Sickle cell anaemia is due to change in single gene (point mutation).

QUESTION BANK

Very Short Answer Questions

1. Name various types of mutations.
2. What is mutation?
3. Name 3 chemical mutagens.
4. Name 2 physical mutagens.
5. Who noticed the **ancon** sheeps for the first tisue?
6. Who was the discover of mutations?
7. Who worked on ***Oenothera lmarckiana*?.**
8. Who worked on mutagenic effect on *Drosophila*?
9. What is micromutations?
10. What is Muller-5-method?
11. Who worked on detection of mutation in plant?
12. Who worked in induced irradaition effects on *Neurospora*?.
13. What is 5 bromouracil?
14. What is the effect of HNO_2?

15. What happens when DNA is exposed to low pH?

Short Answer Questions

1. What are the practical applications of mutation?
2. What are the agents producing distortion in DNA?
3. Write short notes on:
   (a) Alkylation agents (b) Base analogue
4. Write notes on effect of radiation on mutation.
5. Write short note on photoreactivation.
6. Write short note on spontaneous mutations.
7. Write short note on silent mutations.
8. Write short note on base pair substitution.
9. Write short note on frame shift mutation.
10. Write short note on mutator gene.
11. Write note on detection of sex linked lethals by CIB method.

Long Answer Questions

1. Describe genetic induced variation.
2. Describe gene mutation.
3. Describe induced gene mutation.
4. Describe missense and nonsense mutations.
5. Write an essay on mutations.

Multiple Choice Questions (Objective Type Questions)

1. Replacement of a purine nucleotide with a pyrimidine nucleotides:
   (a) Transversion (b) Transition
   (c) Frame shift (d) Inversion
2. De Vries attributed evolution to:
   (a) Slow differentiation (b) Polygenes
   (c) Continuous variations (d) Discontinuous variation
3. The major source of variations are:
   (a) Mutations (b) Polyploidy
   (c) Segregation (d) Chromosome abberation
4. Superoxide dismutase enzyme helps in destroying:
   (a) Mutagen (b) Carcinogen
   (c) Enzyme receptor (d) None of the above
5. Mutations used in agriculture are commonly:
   (a) Recessive and lethal (b) Lethal
   (c) Spontaneous (d) Induced
6. Gene mutation is due to:
   (a) Linkage and crossing over (b) Change in base sequence
   (c) Change is sequence of cistrons in DNA (d) Randomsegregation
7. Point mutation results in:
   (a) Free martin (b) Intersex
   (c) Sickle cell anemia (d) Down's syndrome
8. When mutation is from wild type to new type it is called as:
   (a) Forward mutation (b) Backward mutation
   (c) Reverse mutation (d) Point mutation

9. Lethal mutations are:
(a) Recessive (b) Dominant
(c) Homozygous (d) Fragile

10. Lethal gene of *Drosophila* is:
(a) Curly wings (Cy) (b) Plum eyes (Pm)
(c) Stubbles (Sub) (d) All the above

11. Gene mutation is produced in:
(a) Nucleus (b) Chromosome
(c) DNA (d) RNA

12. 5' bromouracil is a :
(a) Nucleotide (b) Base analogue
(c) Purine (d) All the above

13. Which of the following is the genetical induced (irradiated) variety:
(a) Sharbati sonara (b) Pusa Parwati
(c) Co 997 (d) All the above

14. Prof. M.S. Swaminathan has produced a mutant variety (irradiation) of wheat called:
(a) Pusa larma (b) Pusa 96
(c) Sharbati sonara (d) Pusa Parwati

15. Sudden change in structure and activity of gene is called:
(a) Variation (b) Evolution
(c) Mutation (d) Hybridization

16. Lethal mutants were first time observed by:
(a) Mischer (b) Muller
(c) Morgan (d) Mc Clincook

17. The rays absorbed by chromosome is:
(a) X rays (b) Gamma rays
(c) UV rays (d) β rays

18. Superoxide dismutase destroy:
(a) Mutagens (b) Transposon
(c) Virus (d) Fungus

19. Acridine mutagens, *e.g.*, acridine orange and proflavin, etc., are discovered by:
(a) Watson (b) Crick
(c) Wobble (d) Nirenberg

20. Ethyl ethane sulphonate, ethyl methane sulphonate, mustard gas, etc., are:
(a) Base analogues (b) Chemical mutagens
(c) Radiation (d) Physical Mutagens

ANSWERS

1. (a)	2. (d)	3. (a)	4. (a)	5. (d)	6. (b)
7. (c)	8. (a)	9. (c)	10. (d)	11. (c)	12. (b)
13. (d)	14. (c)	15. (c)	16. (b)	17. (a)	18. (a)
19. (b)	20. (b).				

47

CHAPTER

Transposable Genetic Elements

In fact, most genes occupy fixed sites on the chromosomes, and the overall structure of the genetic map is practically invariant. However, in early 1940's researchers have found that some DNA sequences (*viz.*, genes) can actually change their position.

These mobile elements have been variously called **'jumping genes'**, **'mobile elements'**, **'cassettes'**, **'insertion sequences'** and **'transposons'**. The formal name for this family of mobile genes is **transposable elements**, and their movement is called **transposition**. The term transposon was coined by **Hedges** and **Jacob** in 1974 for a DNA segment which could move from one DNA molecule (or chromosome) to other and carried resistance for antibiotic ampicilin. Transposable elements can be defined as small, mobile DNA sequences that move around chromosomes with no regard for homology and insertion of these elements may produce deletions, inversions, chromosomal fusions and even more complicated rearrangements.

MODE OF DISCOVERY OF TRANSPOSABLE ELEMENTS

Transposable elements were discovered by **Barbara McClintock** (1965) through an analysis of genetic instability in maize (corn). The instability involved chromosome breakage and was found to occur at sites where transposable elements were located. In McClintock's analysis, the events of breakage were detected by following the loss of certain genetic markers. In some experiments, McClintock used a marker (gene) that controlled the deposition of pigmentation in the aleurone which is the outer most layer of endosperm of maize kernels. Recall that the endosperm is **triploid**, being produced by the union of two maternal nuclei and one paternal nucleus. McClintock's marker was an allele of the *C* locus on the short arm of chromosome 9. Since this allele, called C^I, is a dominant inhibitor of aleurone colouration, any kernel possessing it should be colourless. McClintock fertilized *CC* ears with pollen from C^IC^I tassels, producing kernels in which the endosperm was C^ICC. Although many of these kernels were colourless, as expected, some showed patches of brownish-purple pigment. **McClintock** (1951) guessed that in such mosaics, the inhibitory C^I allele had been lost sometime during endosperm development, leading to a clone of tissue that was capable of producing pigment. Thc genotype in such a clone would be *–CC*, where the dash indicates loss of the C^I allele. Further study demonstrated that C^I allele had been lost through chromosome breakage.

As shown in Fig. 47.1 a break at the site labelled by the arrow would detach a segment of the chromosome from its centromere, creating an **accentric fragment**. Such a chromosomal fragment tends to be lost during cell division, so all the descendants of this cell would lack part of the paternal chromosome. Since the lost fragment carried the C^I allele, none of the cells in this clone would be inhibited from forming pigment, and if any of them produced a part of the aleurone, a patch of colour would appear.

McClintock established that such kernel mosaics frequently resulted from breaks at a particular site on chromosome 9. She named the factor that produced these breaks, ***Ds***, for **"dissociation"**. In her experiments, the chromosome that carried the C^I allele also carried the *Ds* factor. However, by itself, the *Ds* factor was not capable of inducing chromosome breakage. She found that *Ds* had to be activated by another factor, called *Ac*, for "**activator**". The *Ac* factor was present in some maize stocks, but absent in others. By crossing different stocks, *Ac* could be combined with *Ds*, creating the condition that led to chromosome breakage.

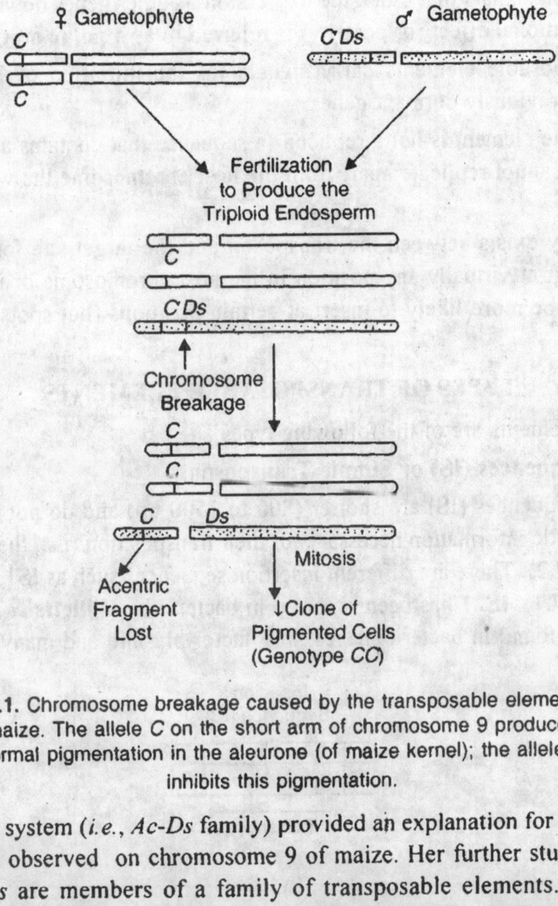

Fig. 47.1. Chromosome breakage caused by the transposable element *Ds* in maize. The allele *C* on the short arm of chromosome 9 produces normal pigmentation in the aleurone (of maize kernel); the allele *C* inhibits this pigmentation.

This two-factor system (*i.e.*, *Ac-Ds* family) provided an explanation for the genetic instability that McClintock had observed on chromosome 9 of maize. Her further studies have established that both *Ac* and *Ds* are members of a family of transposable elements. These elements are structurally related to each other and can insert at many different sites on the chromosomes. In fact, there often are multiple copies of the *Ac* and *Ds* elements present in the maize genome. Through genetic analysis, McClintock demonstrated that both *Ac* and *Ds* elements could move. When one of these elemants was inserted in or near a gene, McClintock sometimes found that the gene's function was altered. In extreme cases, the function was completely suppressed. Because of this effect on gene expression; **McClintock** (1956) referred to *Ac* and *Ds* as **controlling elements**.

CHARACTERISTICS OF TRANSPOSABLE ELEMENTS

Some salient features of the transposable elements are the following :

1. They were found to be DNA sequences that code for enzymes which bring about the insertion of an identical copy of themselves into a new DNA site.

2. Transposition events involve both recombination and replication processes which frequently generate two daughter copies of the original transposable elements. One copy remains at the **parent site** while the other appears at the **target site** (on the host chromosome).

3. The insertion of transposable elements invariably disrupts the integrity of their target genes. For example, if an IS (= insertion sequence) becomes inserted into an operon, it interrupts the coding sequence and inactivates the expression of the target gene into which it inserts as well as any gene downstream in that same operon. This is because an IS contains transcription and/or translation termination signals that block the expression of other genes downstream in an operon. This "one-way" mutational effect (or polarity) is referred to as a **polar mutation**.

4. Since transposable elements carry signals for the initiation of RNA synthesis, they sometimes activate previously dormant genes.

5. A transposable element is not a replicon (a sequence that contains a site for the origin of replication), thus, it cannot replicate apart from the host chromosome the way that plasmids and phage can.

6. No homology exists between the transposon and the target site for its insertion. Many transposons can insert at virtually any position in the host chromosome or into a plasmid. Some transposons seem to be more likely to insert at certain positions (hot spots), but rarely at base-specific target sites.

TYPES OF TRANSPOSABLE ELEMENTS

Transposable elements are of the following types :

1. Insertion Sequences (IS) or Simple Transposons

The insertion sequences (IS) are shorter (800 to 1500 bp) and do not code for proteins. In fact, IS carry the genetic information necessary for their transposition (*i.e.*, the gene for the enzyme **transposase**) (Fig. 47.2). There are different insertion sequences such as IS1, IS2, IS3, IS4 and so on in *E.coli* (Table 47.1). **IS21** has been reported in bacteria by **Willetts** *et al.,* (1981). Insertion sequences have been found in bacteriophages, in F factor plasmid and many bacteria.

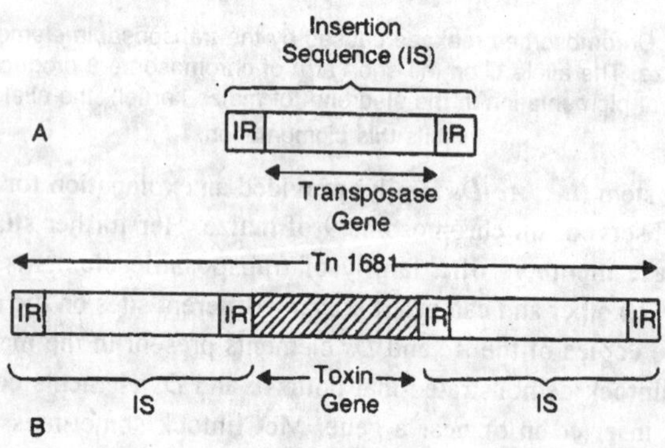

Fig. 47.2. A–A simple transposon (IS) carries only the genetic information necessary for transposition which is often enclosed by short regions of inverted repeat (IR) sequences; B– The complex transposon (Tn) is composed of two insertion sequences (IS) and contains genetic information in addition to that needed for Transposition. In Tn 1681 transposon carries the gene for a heat-labile toxin.

2. Transposons (Tn) or Complex Transposons

Transposons (Tn) are several thousand base pair long, and have genes coding for one or more proteins (including resistance factors in bacteria which act against antibiotics). The hallmark of a transposon is the presence of identical, **inverted terminal repeat (IR) sequences** of 8 to 38 base pairs (b.p.) (Fig. 47.2B). Each type of transposon has its own unique inverted repeat. On either side of a transposon is a short (less than, 10 b.p,) **direct repeat**. If a transposon exists in multiple copies, these direct repeats are of different base composition at each site where the transposon exists in the chromosome; the inverted terminal repeats, however, remain the same for a given transposon. The sequence into which a transposable element inserts is called the target sequence. During insertion of a transposon, the singular target sequence becomes duplicated and, thus, appears as direct repeats flanking the inserted transposable element. The direct repeats are not considered part of the transposon. These repeat sequences themselves act like IS or IS-like segments.

Table 47.1. Some examples of insertion sequences (IS) and complex transposons of *E.coli* (bacterium).

Type of transposable element	Size base pairs (bp)	Target DNA repeat (bp)	Known functions or proteins encoded (besides transposase)
A. Insertion sequences (IS)			
IS 1	768	9	–
IS 2	1327	5	–
IS10-R	1329	9	–
B. Complex Transposons (Tn)			
Tn 3	4957	5	Ampicillin resistance
Tn 5	5700	9 (IS 50 at end)	Kanamycin resistance
Tn 10	9300	9 (IS 10 at end)	Tetracycline resistance
Tn 1681	2100	9 (IS 1 at end)	Heat stable enterotoxin
Tn 2571	23000	9 (IS 1 at end)	Resistance to chloramphenicol, fusidic acid, streptomycin, sulphoamides and mercury.

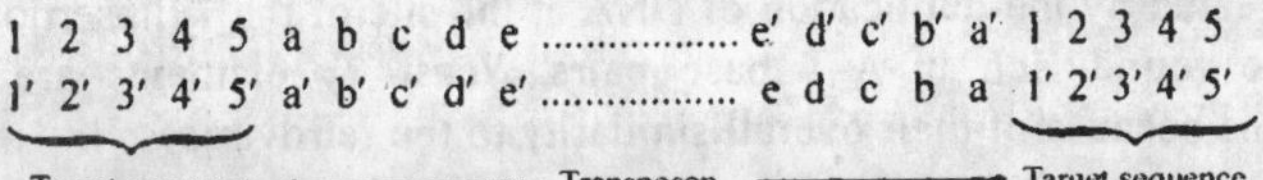

Fig. 47.3. Diagram of a simple transposon. In the diagram, letters and numbers have been used instead of nucleotides to make repeats easier to read. Primed and unprimed symbols of the same kind (*e.g.*, 3 and 3¢, d and d¢) represent complementary base pairs. The ends of a transposon consist of inverted repeats (represented by letters). Direct repeats of the target gene (represented by numbers) flank the transposon. The dotted central region of simple transposons contains only genes necessary for translocation, but in complex transposons it may contain one or more additional genes (consult Fig. 47.2).

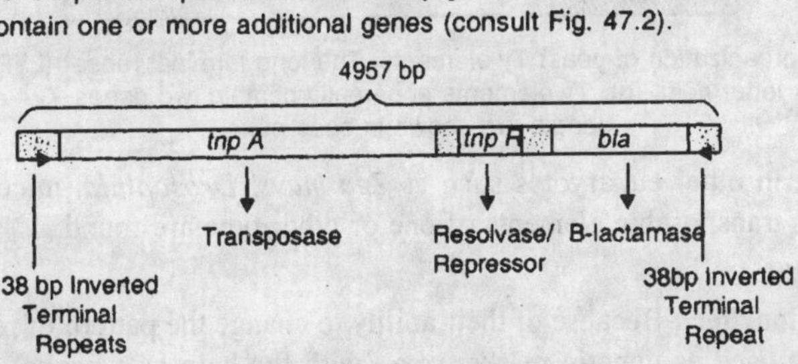

Fig. 47.4. Genetic organisation of Tn 3 transposon of *E.coli*. This complex transposon contains three genes that produce the protein indicated. Lengths of DNA squences are given in base pairs (bp).

Examples of Transposons

1. Tn 3 transposon of *E.coli*. The molecular structure of transposon Tn 3 of *E.coli* has been worked out (Fig. 47.4). Tn 3 has 4957 bp and contains three genes such as *tnp A*, *tnp R* and *bla*, coding respectively for the following proteins : 1. **transposase** having 1015 amino acids and required for transposition; 2. a **repressor** (also called **resolvase**) containing 185 amino acids which regulates the transposase; and 3. β-**lactamase** enzyme which confers resistance to the antibiotic ampicillin. On both sides of the Tn 3 is an inverted repeat of about 38 bp.

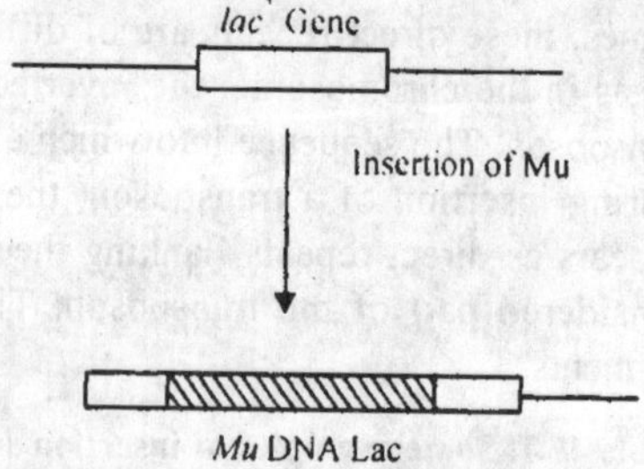

Fig. 47.5. Insertion of phase *Mu* into a *loc* gene renders the gene inactive (lac).

2. Bacteriophage Mu. The bacteriophage *Mu* (*Mu* = mutator) is a temperate bacteriophage having typical phage properties and could be regarded as a giant transposon. Phage *Mu* was thought to behave in a unique manner since it does not multiply in a lytic way. It always starts its life-cycle by inserting itself into the *E.coli* chromosome at random locations. The resulting *prophage* often mutates the genes into which they become inserted (Fig. 47.5). Thus, phage *Mu* was originally known for its mutagenic properties.

During later part of phage life cycle, upon receipt of an appropriate signal, the *Mu* prophage somehow generates its transposition, but also activates the genes encoding for structural proteins which package its DNA. *Mu* phage is unique also in transposing much often than other transposons, providing nearly a hundred new copies of *Mu* during its hour-long life-cycle.

Like other transposons, *Mu* phage has inverted repeats (IR) at or near the ends of its DNA and it makes a short duplication with 5 base pairs of the bacterial DNA into which it is inserted.

3. Yeast *Ty* elements. The yeast *Saccharomyces cerevisiae* carries about 35 copies of a transposable element called *Ty* in its haploid genome. These transposons are about 5900 base pairs long and are bounded at each end by a DNA segment called the **delta (δ) sequence**, which is approximately 340 base-pairs long. Each δ sequence is oriented in the same direction, forming what are known as direct **long terminal repeats** or **LTRs**. *Ty* elements are flanked by five base-pair direct repeats created by the duplication of DNA at the site of the *Ty* insertion. These target site duplications are found rich in A-T base pairs. Yeast ***Ty*** elements are sometimes called **retrotransposons** because of their overall similarity to the retroviruses.

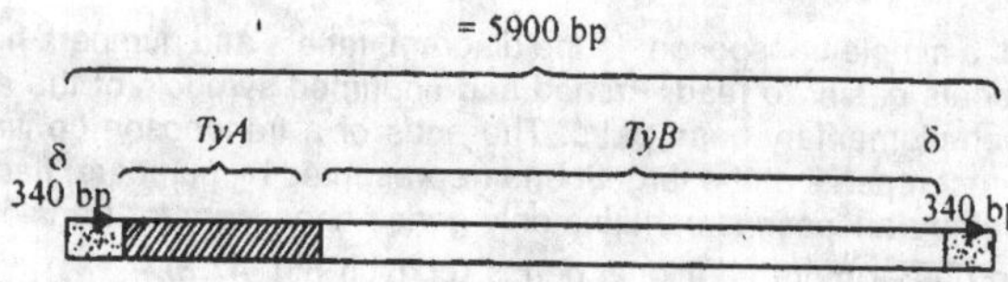

Fig. 47.6. Genetic organization of yeast *Ty* elements. The long terminal repeat (LTR) sequences are denoted by the Greek letter delta (d). *Ty* elements apparently contain two genes *TyA* and *TyB*. Sequence length are shown in base pairs.

Like the yeast, in other eukaryotes such as *Zea mays*, *Drosophila*, mice and snapdragons (*Antirrhinum majus*) transposable elements of one or other type are found.

Uses of Transposons

(1) As genetic marker : Because of their ability to change the pattern of restriction fragment analysis they can be used as genetic marker, *e.g.*, with the help of a probe, it was possible to characterise different strains of *Plasmodium falciparum*. The strains may be identified as they differ in the distribution of transposons.

Transposons are used as genetic markers to construct linkage maps.

Transposons are used in human for distinguishing carriers or non-carriers of sickle cell trait.

(2) As mutagens : Spontaneous mutation can be created by inserting transposons. Transposons cause mutation due to insertion in structural and regulatory region.

(3) For isolation of genes : Transposons are used to search the restriction fragments containing mutant genes. It is used for isolation of genes through **transposon tagging.**

(4) As transformation Vector : Transposons are used in gene transfer artificially if carried in a plasmid.

SUMMARY

1. Mutator genes are supposed to hop around the genome appearing at one place sometimes or on the other place and are known as **transposable elements.**
2. Some genes present in a genome which increase the mutation rate at several loci simultaneously are called **mutator genes.**
3. Transposable element is very typical about 4,500 base pairs long and code for an enzyme called **transposons** that copies the DNA element to another part of chromosome.
4. The effect of transposable elements were found to be due to mobilization of a **'P'-element** which is a piece of transposable DNA.
5. Unstable or hoping DNA is responsible for human mutations also. Parts of human genes are more fluid and open to change the classical geneticist opinion.
6. Inherited mental illness is due to **fragile 'X' syndrome.** The children usually have a distortion of X-chromosome, two small pieces break away from the end of long arm of X-chromosome.
7. **Fragile X-mutation** is unpredictable because of mobile DNA present next to actual locus with repeat triplet of **CCG**.
8. Normally there are 6-60 repeais of sequence but those with fragile X-syndrome have several thousand copies of CCG repeat.

QUESTION BANK

Very Short Answer Questions

1. The first transposable element were observed in which plant ?
2. What is IS element ?
3. T_3 transposon consists of how many base pairs ?
4. What is target sequence ?
5. What is replicon fusion ?
6. Who observed transposable element in Maize ?
7. How many types of transposons are found in eukaryote ?
8. How many copies of Ty elements are found in Yeast ?
9. *Tam* I element in *Snapdragon* has how many base pairs.
10. Name one disease in human due to transposable elements.

Short Answer Questions

1. Write the short note on structure of transposable element.
2. Write short note on IS element.
3. Write short note on T_3 transposon family.
4. Write short note on transposition.
5. Write short note on transposable elements in Eukaryotes.
6. Write short note on transposable elements in Human.
7. Write short note on transposable elements of *Drosophila*.
8. What is Ty element in Yeast ?
9. Write short note on Ac-Ds system.

10. Write short note on suppressor mutation system.
11. Write short note on uses of transposon.

Long Answer Questions

1. What is transposable element. Describe its structure or function.
2. Comment on Ms. Barbara McClintock's investigations regarding the controlling elements of maize.
3. Define the transposable elements. Describe different types of complex transposons of the eukaryotes.
4. Describe the transposable elements of *E.coli* and bacteriophage *Mu*.

Multiple Choice Questions (Objective Type Questions)

1. Mutator gene which hop from one place to the other, 4,500 base pairs long coding for an enzyme that copies that DNA element to another part of the chromosome is called :
(a) Transposable element (b) Transferable element
(c) Transmittable element (d) Transpogene
2. Part of DNA which switch their position are called as :
(a) Exon (b) Transposon
(c) Intron (d) Cistron
3. Transposable element is made up of :
(a) 2,000 bp (b) 4,500 bp
(c) 5,000 bp (d) 1,500 bp
4. Transposable elements were first detected in :
(a) *Drosophila* (b) *Acetabularia*
(c) *E. coli* (d) Human
5. Inverted repeat sequences in the terminus are present in :
(a) Alleles (b) Plasmagens
(c) IS element (d) Tn 3 element
6. R-plasmids are for types containing gene for :
(a) Revolution (b) Resistence
(c) Retranscription (d) All the above
7. The first record of transposable elements from Maize were given by :
(a) Morgon (b) Sutton
(c) Muller (d) Mc Clintock
8. Dotted elements were discovered by Marcus Rhoades in :
(a) 1938 (b) 1928
(c) 1908 (d) 1918
9. Transposable element involving RNA phase is called :
(a) RNA transpose (b) RNA some
(c) Retroelement (d) Retrovirus
10. Transposon caused mutation in human is :
(a) Dowan's syndrome (b) Fragile 'X'-syndrome
(c) Turner's syndrome (d) Edward's syndrome
11. The effect of Transposon is due to mobilization of :
(a) DNA fragment (b) IS element
(c) P-element (d) Rotroelement
12. The fragile X syndrome has several thousands copies of CCG repeats :
(a) At the centromere (b) At the locus
(c) Next to the actual locus (d) At the end of chromosome

ANSWERS

1. (a)	2. (b)	3. (b)	4. (a)	5. (c)	6. (b)
7. (d)	8. (a)	9. (c)	10. (b)	11. (c)	12. (c).

48

CHAPTER

Plasmids

Plasmids are extrachromosomal circular DNA molecules found in most bacterial species and in some species of eukaryotes. Under normal conditions, a particular plasmid is dispensable to its host cell. Many plasmids contain plasmid genes that may be essential in certain environments, *e.g.*, **'R'** plasmid carry genes providing resistance to numerous antibiotics so that the cell containing this plasmid can resist antibiotic action.

With only one exception (killer plasmid of Yeast, a RNA molecule) all known plasmids are supercoiled circular DNA. The molecular weight ranges from $10^6 - 10^8$. The number of copies of a plasmid/cell ranges from 1–2 to 10—60.

Plasmid DNA can be isolated from bacteria by culturing plasmid containing bacteria. Detergent is added to it to get lysed bacteria. The lysate is centrifuged. The smaller plasmid DNA remains in the supernatant. **CsCI and ethidium bromide** is added to the supernatant CsCI forms a density gradient. The supercoiled DNA with high density can be identified by ethidium bromide and easily removed.

Transfer of Plasmid DNA

The bacterium *E. coli* possesses 2 mating types, *i.e.*, **donors** or male and **recipients** or female. The determinant of maleness is the 'F' or **sex plasmid** or donor, a male cell is designated as $\mathbf{F^+}$. Female lacks 'F' plasmid and designated as $\mathbf{F^-}$. When the culture of male and female is mixed, **conjugation** takes place between male-female pairs. Conjugation bridge is formed (Fig. 48.1). Pairing induces looped rolling circle replication of 'F'. One copy of 'F' is transferred to the female in a minute. The female is

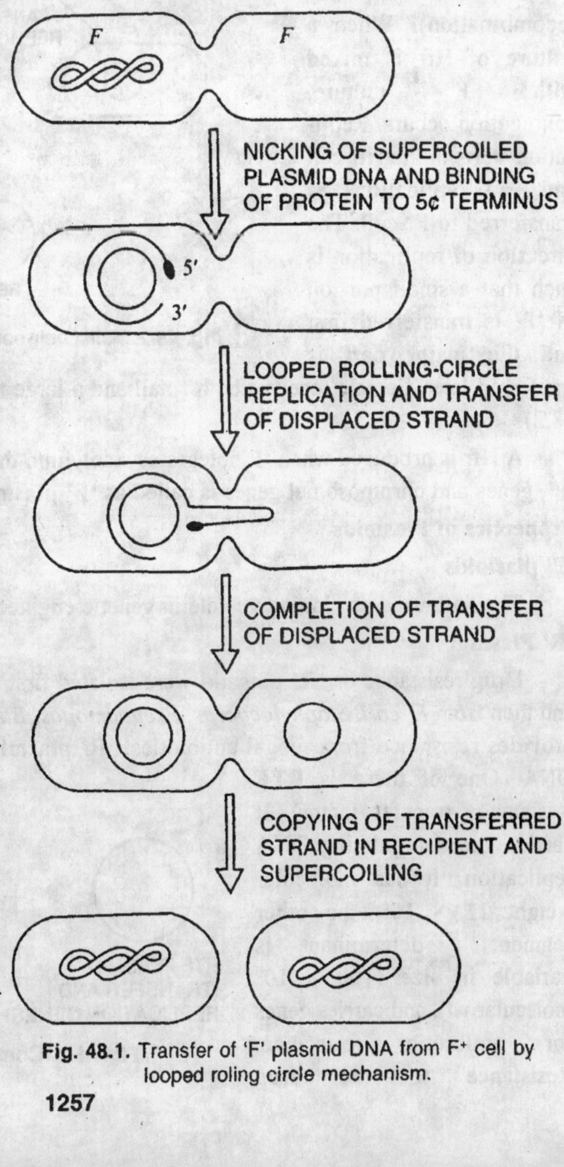

Fig. 48.1. Transfer of 'F' plasmid DNA from F^+ cell by looped roling circle mechanism.

converted to a male often mating, the recipient cell contain the 'F' plasmid. During transfer both Donor and recipient cells show DNA synthesis. In donor, the synthesis replaces single strand to be transferred, synthesis in the recipient converts the transferred single strand to double stranded DNA.

'F' plasmid has an ability to integrate into the bacterial chromosome. 'F' fuses with chromosome increasing its size. The cell is now called **Hfr** cell (high frequency recombination). When a culture of Hfr is mixed with F^- culture, conjugation occurs. Replication starts in the Hfr cell and a replication is transferred to F^- cell. The direction of replication is such that a small portion of 'F' is transferred first and the major part is tranferred later. Female receives both small and a large fragement of the male chromosome (Fig. 48.2).

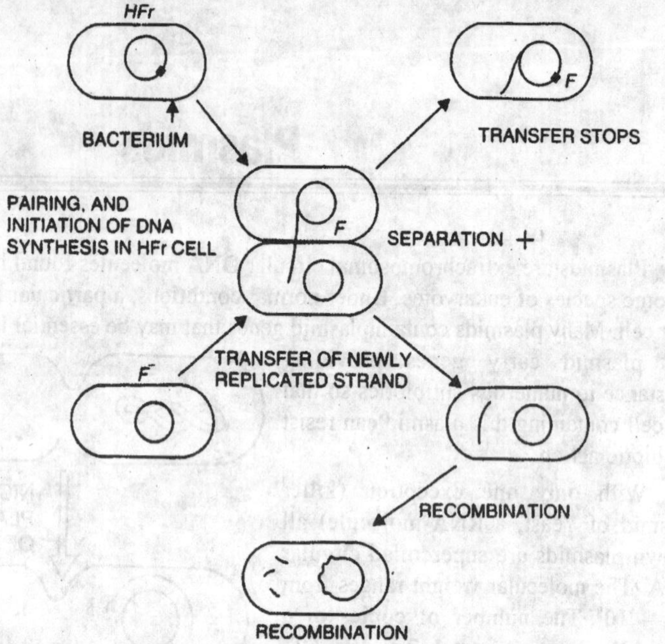

Fig. 48.2. Matrix between and Hfr male and an F^- female bacterium.

A Hfr is produced when 'F' integrates stably into the chromsome A plasmid containing both 'F', genes and chromosomal genes is called as **'F' plasm.**

Properties of Plasmids

'F' plasmids

They are used as cloning vehicle in genetic engineering.

'R' Plasmid

Drug resistance or **'R' plasmid** were isolated first from the bacterium *Shigella dysenteriae* and then from *E. coli*, *Staphylococcus*, *Pseudomonas*, *Bacillus*, *Vibrio*, *Salmonella*, etc. 'R' factor provides resistance from fungal antibiotics. **'R' plasmid** consists of 2 contiguous segments of DNA. One of these is **RTF** (resistance transfer factor). It carries genes regulating DNA replication. It has molecular weight **11 × 10⁶**, the other segment **r** determinant is variable in size (100 × 10^6 molecular wt), and carries genes for antibiotic resistance. Resistance to the drug

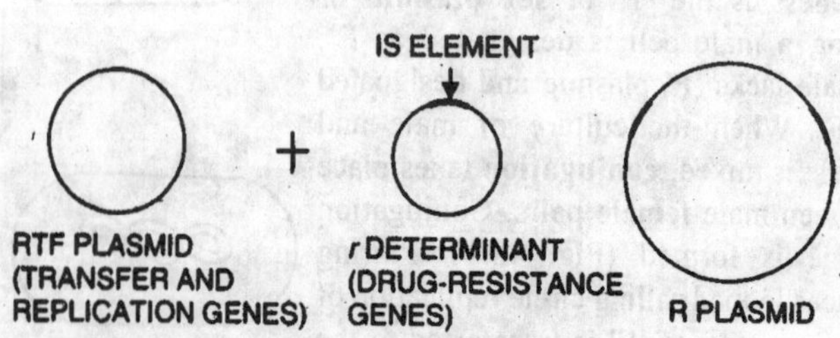

Fig. 48.3. Components of an infectious 'R' plasmid.

penicillin (pen), **ampicillin** (amp), **chloramphanicol** (cam), **streptomycin** (str), kanamycin (kan), and sulphonamide (sul), in combination is common (Fig 42.3).

Col Plasmid

Col plasmid is *E. coli* plasmid encoding colcins, proteins capable of preventing growth of a bacterial strain that does not contain **col** plasmid. Col plasmids are a class of general type of plasmid called **bacteriocinogenic** plasmid, which produce bacteriocins in many bacterial species. Bacteriocins, of which colicins are one example which are proteins binding to the cell wall of sensitive bacterium and inhibit essential processes, *e.g.*, replication, transcription, translation or energy metabolism, etc. The best studied **col** plasmid is col E_1, with a mol wt. 4.2×10^6. It is used in recombination DNA research and in an *in vitro* DNA. replication system.

Ti plasmid

Crown gall tumor is caused by *Agrobacterium tumefaciens.* Ti plasmid is the most important tool in the genetic engineering of plants. The wounds are infected by *A. tumefaciens*

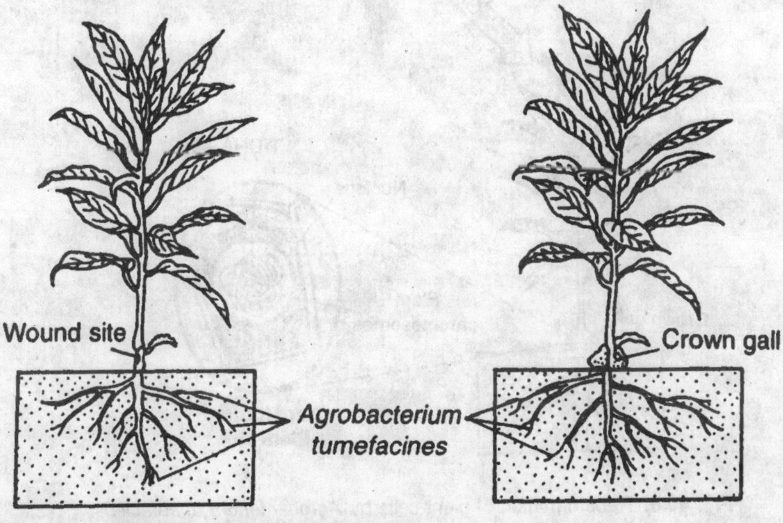

Fig. 48.4. Crown gall formation.

and induce tumour at the site (Fig. 48.4). At the onset of infection they begin to synthesize an arginine derivative called **opine,** *e.g.*, **nopaline** or **octopine** and the cells proliferate to form tumor. The induction of tumor is controlled by genetic information carried on **plasmid** called **Ti** plasmid. **T-DNA** and **vir** region of the Ti plasmid is essential for transformation of plant cells. The plasmid causing tumour is **Ti** plasmid. In an infected plant some of the bacteria enter and grow within the plant cell and lyse there releasing their DNA in the cell. The small fragment of **Ti** plasmid containing genes for replication, becomes integrated into the plant cell chromosomes. The integrated fragment breaks down the hormonally regulated system and control cell divison. The cell turns to tumour cell. **Ti** plasmid of *Agrobacterium tumefaciens* provides an excellent gene-transfer system for use in dicot plants. The host range is limited to dicots only. Fig. 48.5 **Ti** plasmids are very important as specific genes can be inserted into the **Ti** plasmid by recombinant DNA techniques. These genes can be inserted in plant chromosome changing the genotype or phenotype of plant. New varieties of value are produced.

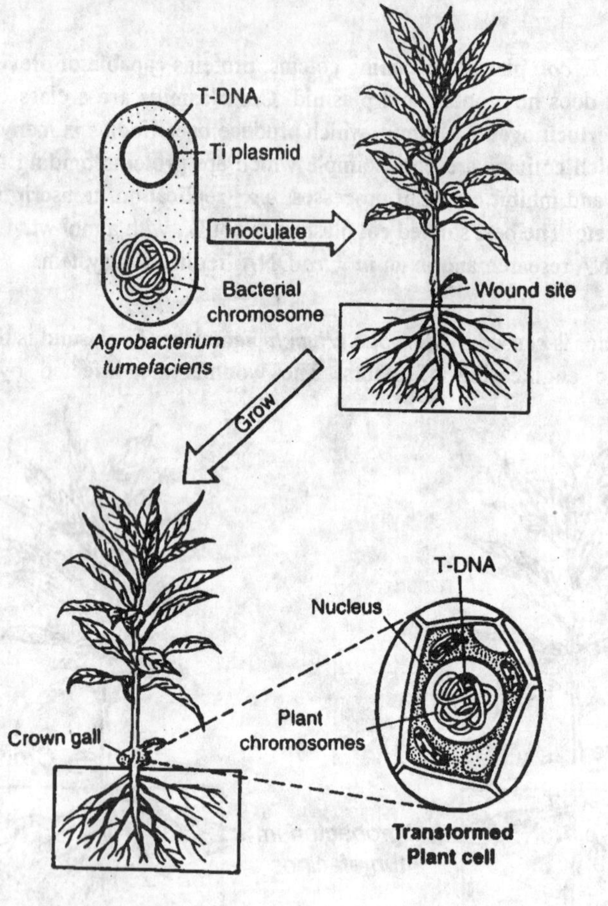

Fig. 48.5. Transformation of plant cells by *Agrobacterium tumefaciens*.

Yeast Plasmid

Yeast have **killer particle** which is double stranded RNA molecule. It is the only plasmid without DNA. It contains 10 genes for replication and several others for synthesis of killer particles (colicin like substance).

Yeast plasmid is 3 μm plasmid and mol. wt. 4×10^6. 60 copies of this plasmid/cell are found in yeast nucleus. Plasmid uses the same enzymes needed for replication of the yeast chromosomes. The plasmid apparently does not integrate into the host DNA. This plasmid is useful system for studying DNA replication in yeast. It acts as a vector for cloning foreign genes in yeast by the recombination DNA techniques.

PLASMID REPLICATION

Plasmid can only replicate within a host cell. The difference of plasmid and phage is :

(i) Reliance on host enzyme : Some plasmids use host enzymes exclusively, other encode some of their own enzymes.

(ii) Identity of polymerase : Most *E. coli* plasmids use Pol III for chain growth and Pol I for synthesis of precussor fragments, as in replication of *E. coli* chromosomes. Where as col E_1 uses Pol I for chain growth.

(iii) Direction : Both purely unidirectional and bidirectional replication is found. Plasmid RK_6 replicates first in one direction and then later in the opposite direction.

(iv) Termination : In unidirectionally replicating plasmids termination necessarily occur at the origin after one cycle of replication.

(v) Replicating form : Plasmids show replication by so called **butterfly** mode (Fig. 48.6). In a partially replicated molecules the replicated portions are untrusted as in 'θ' replication, but the unreplicated part is supercoiled. When the replication completes, one of the circles must be cleaned by DNA gyrase enzymes.

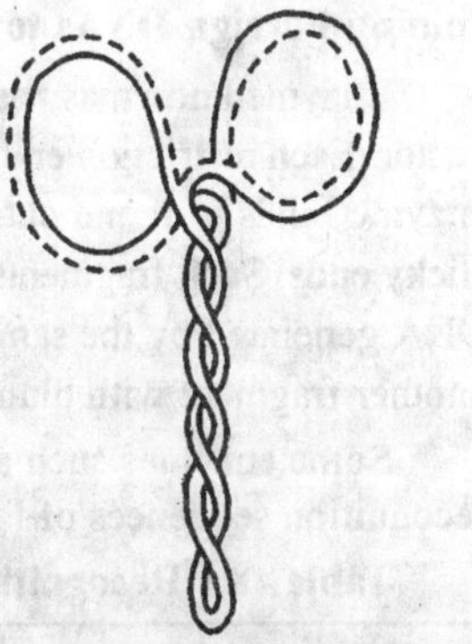

Fig. 48.6. Col E1 DNA replication butterfly molecule.

As plasmids are small circular DNA molecules found in bacteria, containing an origin of replication thus can replicate independently of bacterial chromosome and can produce many copies of itself. Plasmids often carry genes that confer antibiotic resistance on the host bacterium. So it is very easy to select the plasmid containing bacteria from a population of bacteria by applying the antibiotic. Only those bacteria with antibiotic resistance gene will survive (Fig. 48.7). Bacteriophages are viruses that infect bacteria and utilize the host cell's component for their own replication.

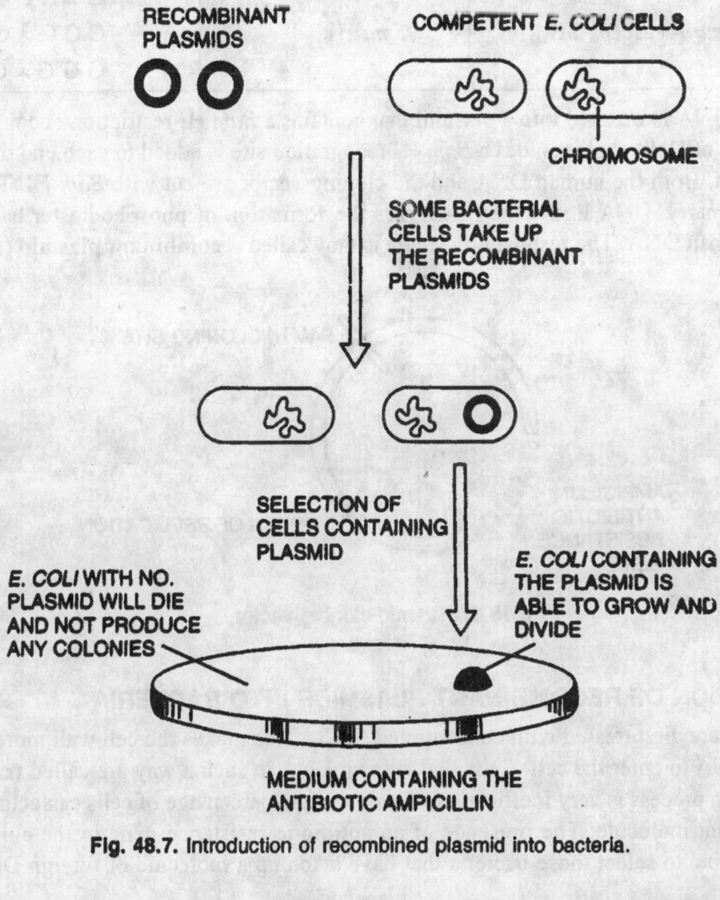

Fig. 48.7. Introduction of recombined plasmid into bacteria.

Joining Foreign DNAs to a Cloning Vector

Enzyme known as **restriction endonucleases** are used to insert foreign DNA into a cloning vector. Each restriction endonuclease recognizes a particular DNA sequence of 4–6 base pairs. The enzyme binds to it and cuts both strands of the double helix. The resultant DNA molecules have sticky ends. Such fragments can associate by complementary base pairing to any other fragment of DNA generated by the same enzyme. DNA fragments produced in this way can only be joined to another fragment with blunt ends.

Some enzymes such as *Bam* HI, *Eco* RI and *Pst* I make cuts one each strand. The names of recognition sequences of few of the common enzymes are shown in Table 48.1.

Table 48.1 Recognition sites of some common restriction enzymes.

Bacterial strain	Enzyme name	Recognition sequences and cleavage sites
1. *Bacillus amyloliquefaciens* **H**	*Bam* H1	G↓G A T C C C C T A G↑G
2. *Escherichia coli* Ry 13	*Eco* R1	G↓A A T T C C T T A A↑G
3. *Provedencia stuartii* 164	*Pst* 1	C T G C A↓G G↑A C G T C
4. *Serratia ma recescens* SB	*Sma* H1	C C C↓G G G G G G↑C C C

Human DNA is inserted into a plasmid that contains a *Bam* HI restriction endonuclease site. A short length of DNA that includes a *Bam* HI recognition site is added to each end of the human DNA fragment. Both the human DNA and the cloning vector are cut with *Bam* HI. The cut ends are complementary. DNA ligase then catalyzes the formation of phosphodiester band between vector and human DNA. The resultant molecule is now called **recombinant plasmid** (Fig. 48.8, 9)

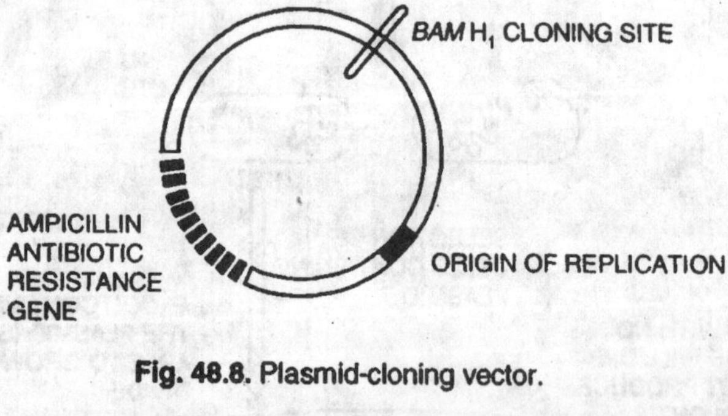

Fig. 48.8. Plasmid-cloning vector.

INTRODUCTION OF RECOMBINANT PLASMIDS INTO BACTERIA

Bacteria are first treated with concentrated $CaCl_2$. This makes the cell wall more permeable and allows DNA to enter the cell. Cells that take up DNA in such a way are called **transformed.** Transformation process is very inefficient and only a small percentage of cells can actually take up the recombinant molecule. The presence of an antibiotic resistance gene in the cloning vector makes it possible to select those bacteria that have taken up a molecule of foreign DNA with its resistance gene. Only transformed cells can survive in the presence of antibiotic. The collection of bacterial colonies produced after this selection process is a **clone library**. Each cell in a colony contain an identical recombinant molecule. Other colonies may contain plasmids carrying different DNA segments. Isolation of these colonies produce different clones of foreign DNA. The collection of such clones is called **c-DNA** library.

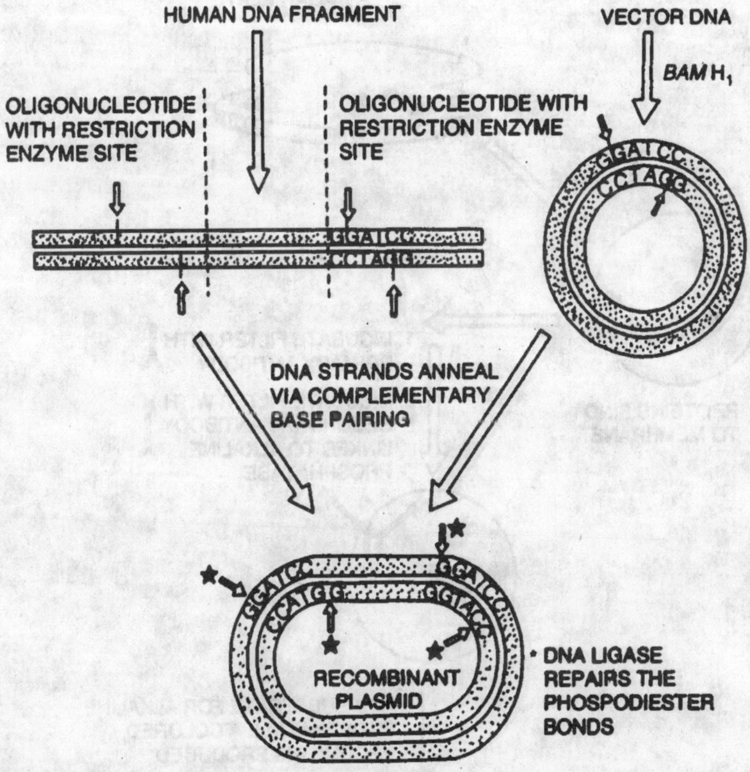

Fig. 48.9. DNA molecule cut at various sites.

SELECTION OF cDNA CLONES

In a library many thousands of different clones are available. The bacteria containing cDNA of particular type is identified. It may be done by various ways, *e.g.*, making use of specific antibodies to detect the bacteria expressing the corresponding antigen. The foreign DNA should be expressed is bacterial cell, its information should be copied first into *m*-RNA and then into protein. To ensure efficient expression the vector with bacterial promoter sequence is used to control transcription of foreign DNA. Such cloning vectors are called **expression vectors.**

To see that bacteria without plasmid will die in antibiotic, a membrane is placed over the bacterial colonies and then lifted off. Bacterial protein stick to the membrane, which is then incubated with appropriate antibody. Bacteria which synthesized corresponding antigen are identified by carrying out a simple colour test for enzyme action (Fig. 48.10).

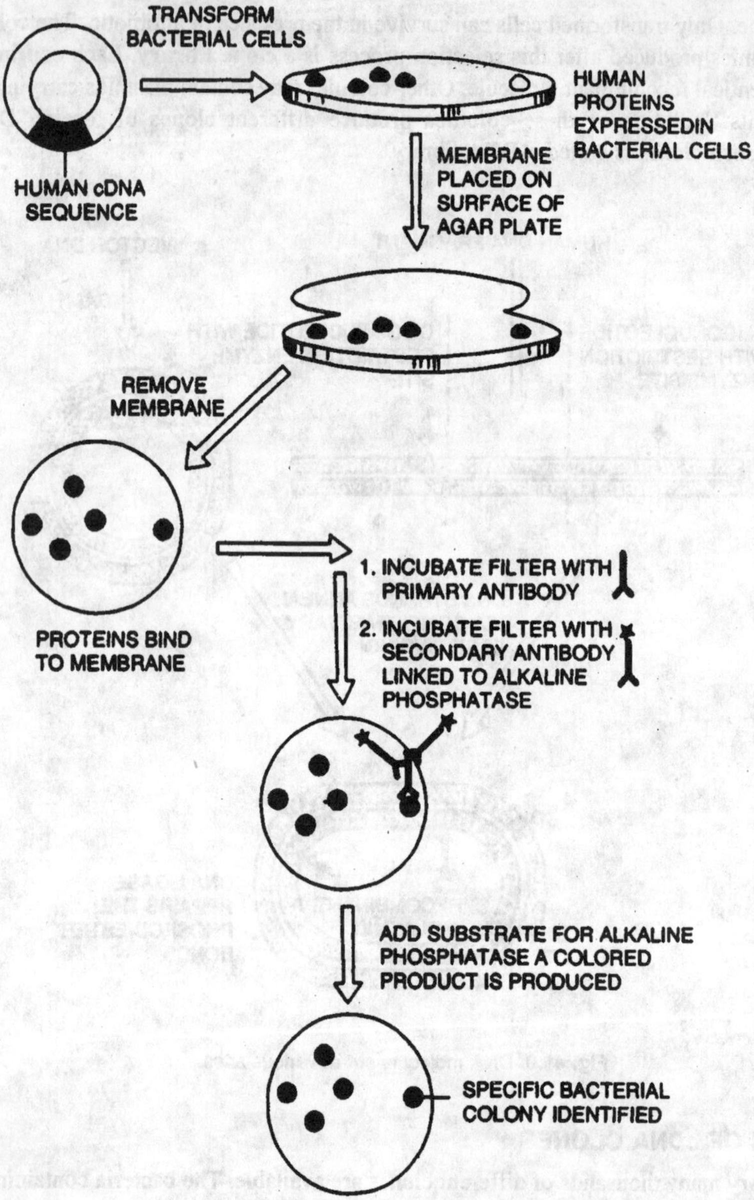

Fig. 48.10. Selection of cDNA clone.

GENOMIC DNA CLONES

The genomic DNA clones containing fragments of chromosomal DNA with promoter gene are developed to study the regulation of transcription of gene. Genomic DNA clones are much larger than cDNA clones as they contain both exon and intron sequences. The cloning vectors for isolation of genomic sequences can accomodate large piece of DNA. Generally vectors based on the bacteriophage lambda (λ) are used as they accept large DNA fragments of about 20,000 base pairs. Large DNA fragments are developed by digesting genomic DNA with a restriction enzyme for a short time. The large fragments are produced by partial digestion. The genomic DNA fragments are joined to bacteriophage vectors in the normal way. Bacteria are infected by bacteriophage with low efficiency of infection so that each bacterium is infected by one phage particle. The collection of bacteria produced in this way is called a **genomic DNA library** (Fig. 48.11).

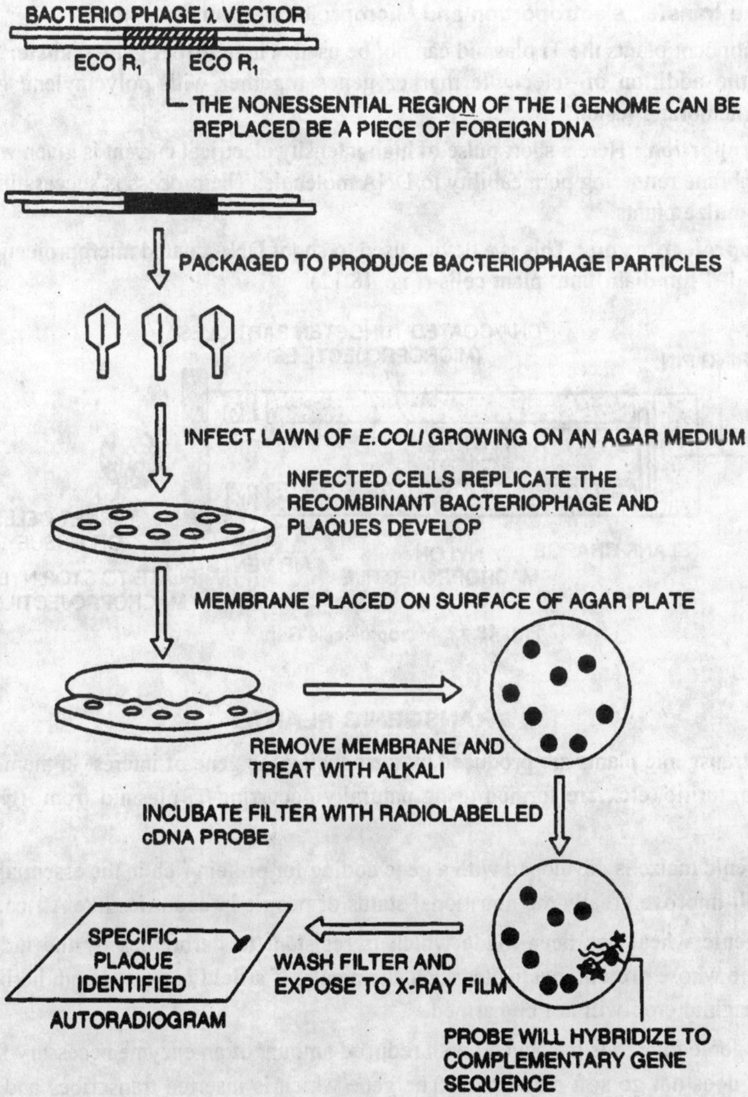

Fig. 48.11. Selection of genomic DNA clone.

To select the genomic DNA sequence of interest, the library is plated onto a layer of cultured bacteria so that many copies of recombinant phages are produced. The recombinant phage multiply inside host bacterial cell. The cell lyses and bacteriophages are spread to surrounded layer of bacteria and infect them. The dead cells give rise to a clear area on the culture plate called **plaque.** Each plaque contains many copies of a recombinant bacteriophage that can be transferred to a membrane. Specific DNA clones are selected by incubating the membrane with a **radiolabelled** *c*DNA probe complementary to the genomic sequence. This produces a radioactive area on the membrane which is identified by autoradiographic technique. If a protein product of a particular gene is unknown, it is impossible to isolate an appropriate *c*DNA clone using conventional techniques. Reverse genetics is applied with a genome and a protein product is identified. It is very time consuming and difficult process.

Direct gene transfer, electroportion and Microprojectile gun

For monocot plants the Ti plasmid can not be used. There **direct gene transfer** is attempted; involving the addition of selectable marker genes together with polyethylene glocyl which stimulates membrane fusion.

Electroportion : Here a short pulse of high intensity electrical current is given which disrupts the all membrane rendering permeability to DNA molecule. The process is successfully employed in 1990 in **maize** plants.

Microprojectile gun : This is a device used to shoot DNA coated microprojectiles (tungsten particles of 1-4 μm diam) into plant cells (Fig. 48.12).

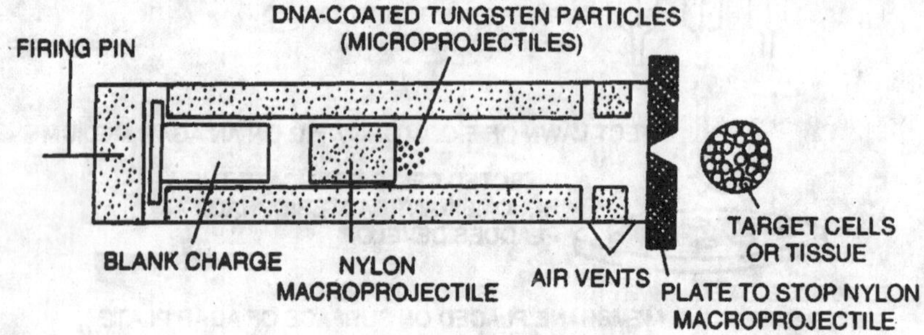

Fig. 48.12. Microprojectile Gun.

TRANSGENIC PLANTS

Many transgenic plants are produced by introducing the gene of interest in them. Transgenic trees, potato, turnip, etc., are formed using naturally occurring Ti plasmid from *Agrobacterium tumifaciens.*

Transgenic maize is developed with a gene coding for protein rich in the essential amino acid **lysine.** It will improve greatly the nutritional status of people in countries like Africa.

Transgenic wheat has been made which is resistant to herbicides by the induction of a bacterial gene whose protein inactivates such chemicals. If a field is treated with herbicide to kill weeds the original crop will not be harmed.

A transgenie tomato is introduced with reduced amount of an enzyme necessary for ripening. This tomato does not go soft on storage. The gene which is inserted transcribes and produces a RNA complementary in sequence to the *m*RNA for the ripening protein. The two RNAs bond by complementary base-pairing, and so the translation of the normal *m*-RNA is inhibited. Genetically engineered **"Flavr Savr"** tomatoes are produced in 1995 in USA. These have increased yield and full development of flavour.

Virus resistant plants of potato, tomato and alfa-alfa are also produced.

Genetically engineered herbicide resistance could double or even quadruple yields. Parasitic weeds such as *Orobanche* and *Striga*, etc., affect the crops a lot.

Herbicide resistent corn, sugarbeet and oil seeds are produced.

Gene for nitrogen fixation into crop plants in introduced. It involves 15 genes called *'Nif'* genes.

Genetic engineering produces transgenic plants for new colour, pattern, shapes of flower. Such plants in **blue roses** are produced.

Medical drug crops are produced which are cheaper, *e.g.*, human **enkephalin** gene has been expressed in plants.

TECHNIQUE OF INTRODUCING TI PLASMID FOR PRODUCING TRANSGENIC PLANTS

The foreign genes are incorporated in 'Ti' plasmid of *Agrobacterium tumefaciens* (Fig. 48.13). It causes a tumorous lump or crown gall. During infection the Ti plasmid is passed from bacterium into the plant cell. It becomes incorporated with plant cell chromosome and induces the cell to proliferate and provide nutrients for the bacterium. The discs cut from leaves or cultured in a culture dish. The transfected cells from leaf cells (discs) are allowed to grow into whole plants. These plants carry transgenes.

Microinjection

Microinjection is the device used for producing transgenic animals. The plasmid is microinjected into the male nucleus (sperm haploid nucleus) of the fertilized egg through a very fine tipped glass needle (Fig. 48.14). The injected DNA can be linear or circular.

TRANSGENIC ANIMAL

The transgenic animal is produced by injecting a foreign gene into the nucleus of a fertilized egg. The egg is then implanted into a foster mother, and the offspring are tested to determine whether they carry the foreign gene. Transgenic mouse are commonly used to investigate the regulation of gene expression in mammals. The production of the protein metallothionein is known to be increased by exposure to heavy metal ions.

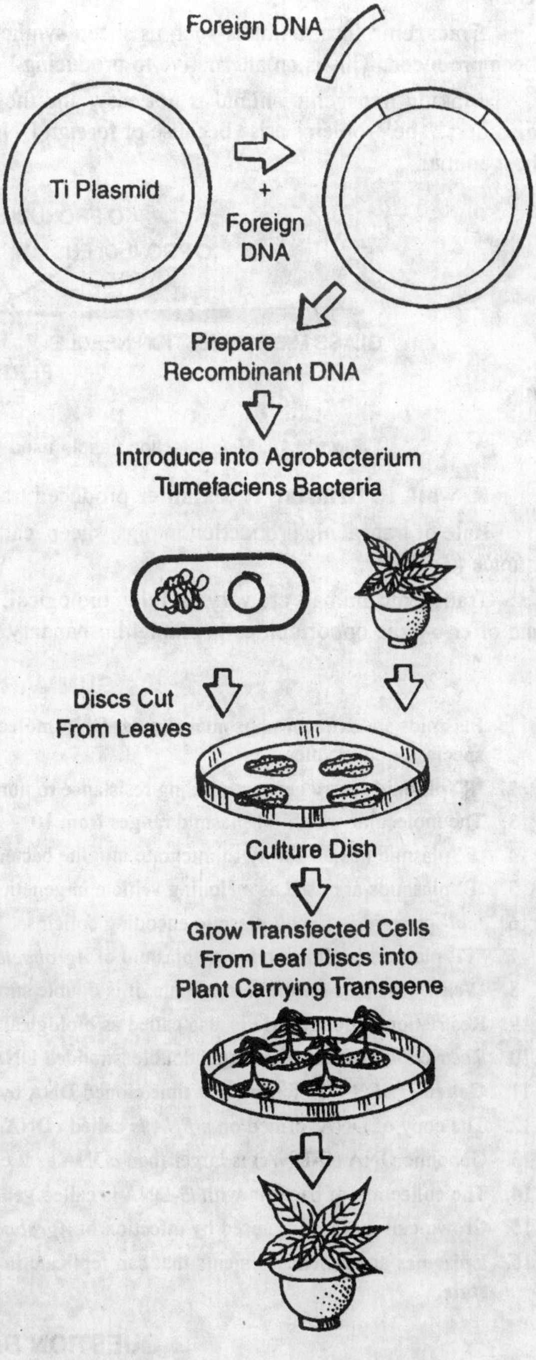

Fig. 48.13. Formation of transgenic plant with the help of Ti plasmid.

Knock out mouse was developed in the late 1980's by **Mario Capecchi** at University of Utah.

Transgenic form animals-such as sheep synthesizing human factor VIII in their milk-have been produced. This is an alternative to producing human proteins in bacteria.

Making transgenic animal is not easy, and they are sometimes sterile or suffer from other disorders. The problems arise because of foreign DNA is integrated at random into the genome of host animal.

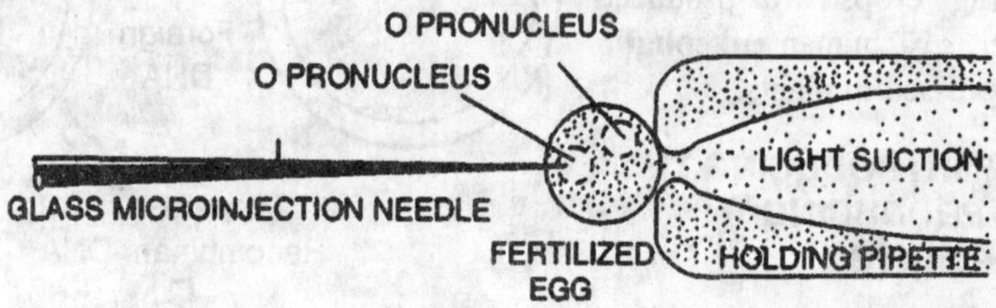

Fig. 48.14. Microinjection needle used for making transgenic animal.

R. wall, R. Brinstar, R. Palmiter produced transgenic pigs.

Rate of transgenic production in pigs, sheep, cattle and goats is much lower (< 1%) than that is mice (3–6%).

Transgenic animals are very useful in biological, biomedical, and biotechnological researches and offer unique opportunities in animal husbandary.

SUMMARY

1. Plasmids are extrachromosomal circular DNA molecules found in most bacterial species and in some species of eukaryotes.
2. 'R' plasmids carry genes providing resistance to numerous antibiotics.
3. The molecular weight of plasmid ranges from $10^6 - 10^8$.
4. 'F' plasmid has an ability to integrate into the bacterial chromosome.
5. 'F' plasmids are used as a cloning vehicle in genetic engineering.
6. '*col*' plasmid is *E. coli* plasmid encoding colicins.
7. **'Ti'** plasmid is tumor inducing plasmid of *Agrobacterium tumefaciens.*
8. 'Yeast' plasmids have killer particle, it is double stranded RNA molecule.
9. Restriction endonuclease is also called as biological scissors.
10. Restriction endonucleases cuts double stranded DNA at a particular place.
11. **Cohen** *et al* (1973) for,the first time cloned DNA by using plasmid as vector.
12. The copy of DNA formed on *mRNA is* called **cDNA.**
13. Genomic DNA (G-DNA) is larger than *c*DNA as it contains both exon and intron sequences.
14. The collection of bacteria with G-DNA is called **genomic DNA library.**
15. Crown gall disease is caused by infection of *Agrobacterium tumefaciens.*
16. **Episomes** are genetic elements that can replicate in an **integrated state,** or in **extra chromosomal state.**

QUESTION BANK

Very Short Answer Questions

1. Ti plasmid is found in natural form in which plant ?
2. Name two transgenic plants.

3. What is 'R' plasmid ?
4. What is 'col' plasmid ?
5. What is the molecular weight of RTF ?
6. Yeast plasmid is made up of which genetic material.
7. Name 2 restriction endonucleases.
8. What is microprojectile gun ?
9. Name one transgenic animal.
10. What is "Flavr savr" Tomato ?

Short Answer Questions

1. Write note on Ti plasmid.
2. What do you understand by Genomic DNA clones ?
3. Write short notes on Transgenic plants.
4. Make only diagrammatic presentation of making transgenic plant by Ti plasmid introduction.
5. Make a diagram of microprojectile gun.
6. Make a diagram of microinjection.
7. Write short note on restriction endnoucleases.

Long Answer Questions

1. What do you mean by plasmids? Describe different types of plasmids.
2. Describe properties of different plasmids.

Multiple Choice Questions (Objective Type Questions)

1. DNA cloning is a part of :
   (a) DNA sequence (b) Recombinant DNA technology
   (c) DNA structure (d) All the above
2. The biological scissors used to cut DNA segment is :
   (a) Protein (b) Restriction endonucleases
   (c) Restriction exonucleases (d) Restriction DNA
3. A number of bacteria with recombinant DNA of same type form :
   (a) Clone library (b) Gene library
   (c) Gene pool (d) Gene frequency
4. *Bam* HI, *Eco* RI, are the types of :
   (a) Restriction endooxidases (b) Restriction endonucleases
   (c) Restriction exonucleases (d) Restriction polymerases
5. Transgenic animals are produced by injecting foreign gene into the :
   (a) Egg (b) Nucleus of unfertilized egg
   (c) Nucleus of fertilized egg (d) Nucleus of sperm
6. Transgenic plants are produced by using Ti plasmid from the :
   (a) *Agrobacterium tumefaciens* (b) *E. coli*
   (c) Bacteriophage (d) *A. varians*
7. The plasmid which carries a foreign DNA molecule of known sequence is called :
   (a) Bacteria (b) Vector
   (c) Viron (d) Virus
8. Plasmid is :
   (a) Linear DNA with several genes (b) A double stranded circular DNA
   (c) A single stranded linear DNA (d) Double stranded RNA

9. Plasmids that can integrate into the bacterial DNA is called :
   (a) Episome (b) Endosome
   (c) Exozyme (d) Hypnosome
10. Transfer of *nif* genes is carried out by :
   (a) Recombinant DNA technology (b) Genetic engineering
   (c) Interferon (d) Both 'a' and 'b'
11. Endonucleases act upon genetic material and :
   (a) Cleave the single strand of DNA
   (b) Cleave the specific point of single stranded DNA
   (c) Cleave the double stranded DNA at any point except the ends
   (d) Cleave the double stranded DNA at the ends only
12. Extrachromosomal self replicating double stranded circular DNA in bacterial cell is called:
   (a) Plasmid (b) Cosmid
   (c) Phasmid (d) All the above
13. Who cloned DNA by, using plasmid as a vector for the first time :
   (a) Robertis (b) Dahl
   (c) Cohen (d) Kornberg
14. Plasmids are :
   (a) Host specific (b) Resistant to antibiotic and heavy metals
   (c) Bacteriocin and toxic materials (d) All the above
15. The disease resistant gene of plasmid is called
   (a) D gene (b) DR gene
   (c) R gene (d) dr gene

ANSWERS

1. (b)	2. (b)	3. (b)	4. (b)	5. (d)	6. (a)
7. (b)	8. (b)	9. (a)	10. (d)	11. (c)	12. (a)
13. (c)	14. (c)	15. (c).			

49
CHAPTER

Chromosomal Aberrations : Structural Changes

The arrangement and presence of many genes on a single chromosome provides a change in genetic information not only through change in chromosome number but also by a change in chromosome structure. The change in chromosome is due to alteration in genetic material through loss, gain or rearrangement of a particular segment. Such changes are called **chromosomal aberrations.** The modification brings about chromosomal mutations. **Chromosomal mutations** are very rare in nature but can be created artificially by 'X' rays, atomic radiation and chemicals, etc.

The structural changes in chromosomes are due to breaks in chromosome, or in its cell division subunit, *i.e.*, chromatid. Each break produces 2 ends which may then follow three different paths. (Fig.43.1).

(a) They may **reunite**, leading to eventual loss of that chromosomal segment which does not contain the centromere.

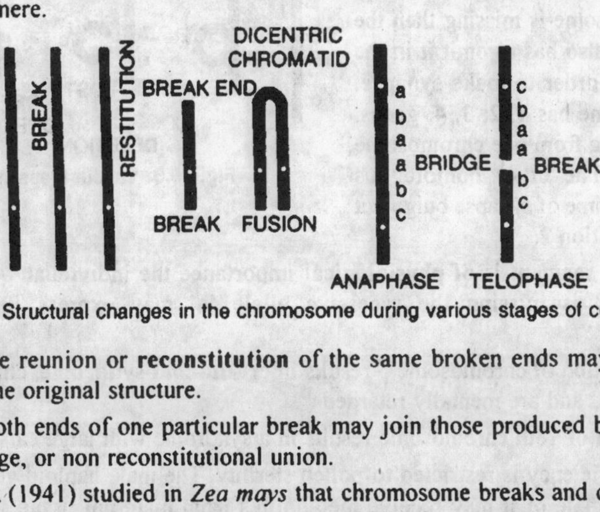

Fig. 49.1. Structural changes in the chromosome during various stages of cell division.

(b) Immediate reunion or **reconstitution** of the same broken ends may occur, leading to reconstitution of the original structure.

(c) One or both ends of one particular break may join those produced by a different break causing an exchange, or non reconstitutional union.

Mc Clintock (1941) studied in *Zea mays* that chromosome breaks and duplication follows. A dicentric chromatid is found. During anaphase spindle fibres are attached to the two centromeres resulting in the formation of bridge from one pole to other. The bridge breaks causing **deficiency** or **duplication.**

Chromosomal aberrations are of 4 major types :

(a) deletion (b) duplication (c) inversion and (d) translocation. (Fig. 49.2).

(A) DELETION OR DEFICIENCY

Deletion or deficiency as the name suggests there is a loss of segment of chromosome. After break the part without centromere is lost. On the other hand the part attached to the centromere acts as deficient chromosome. **Bridges** (1917) for the first time observed deficiency in the *Bar* locus of *Drosophila.*

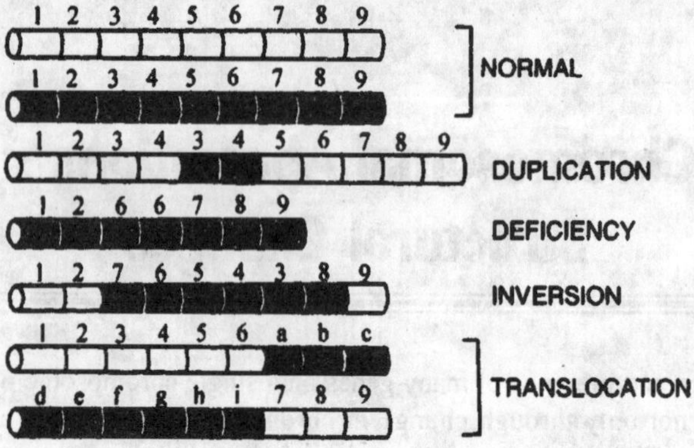

Fig. 49.2. Types of Chromosomal aberrations.

Two types of deletions are found :

Terminal deletion : A single break near the end of the chromosome. Described in maize but otherwise not common.

Interstitial deletion : Chromosome breaks and reunites but the part is lost from in between. (Fig. 49.3). Deletions are detected at the time of homologous pairing. If a part of chromosome is missing then the other chromosome also has to omit it in the form of bulging in order to make synapse. *e.g.*, if a chromosome has 1, 2, 3, 4, genes. The part 2 is missing from one chromosome leaving, 1, 3, 4. The other homologous chromosome at the time of synapse bulge out or form loop at position 2.

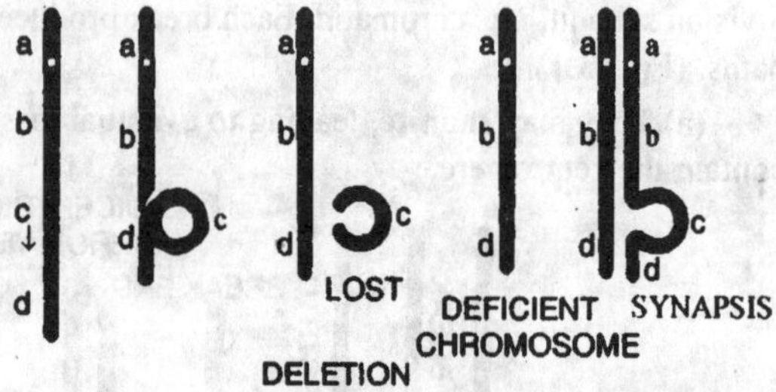

Fig. 49.3. Various steps involved in Deletion

If the missing segment is of physiological importance the individual will not survive. If dominant gene 'A' is missing the recessive allele 'a' may express itself. It is called **pseudodominance.**

In human, deletion of chromosome 5 results in **cri-du-chat syndrome**, children cry like cat, they have small head and are mentally retarded.

Partial deletion of 18th chromosome results in a syndrome with large ears and long fingers.

In corn the deficiency is restricted to pollen sterility. The male haploid gemetophyte shows deficiency while female of it may receive metabolites from maternal tissue supplementing the deficiency. The omitted segment forms buckles. (Fig. 49.4)

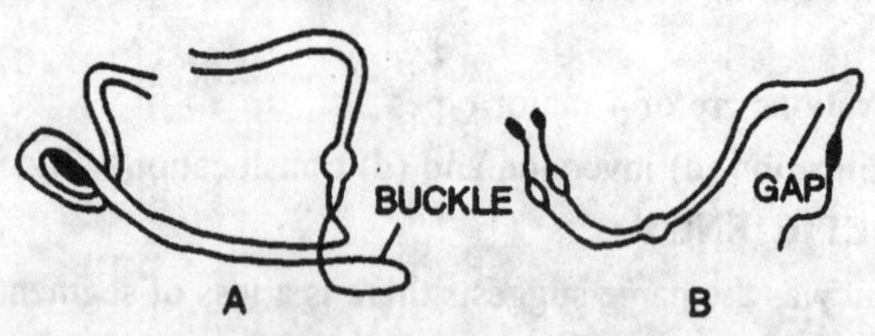

Fig. 49.4. Buckle formation during deletion.

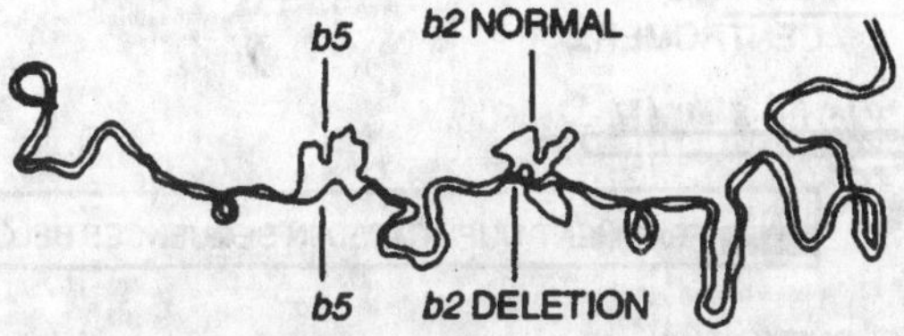

Fig. 49.5. Collapsed loop or brush in single strand DNA due deletion.

Deficiency in *E. coli* is also noted. The deletion points that the DNA is single stranded and looks like collapsed loop or brush. (Fig. 49.5).

(B) DUPLICATION

Here a segment of chromosome is repeated twice, *i.e.*, duplicated. Duplication was discovered in *Drosophila* 'X' chromosome for the first time carrying wild type allele for **vermilion** (v^+) and has been transposed to an 'X' chromosome carrying the mutant **vermilion** allele (v), **Bridges** found that due to the fact that 'X' chromosome was carrying allele v and v^+ both it was wild type instead of vermilion. Equal properties of v and v^+ produced wild type effect. Such 'duplication females' when crossed with nonduplicated vermilion males all female progeny was **vermilion** and all male progeny, *i.e.*, y was **wild type.** (Fig.43.6.)

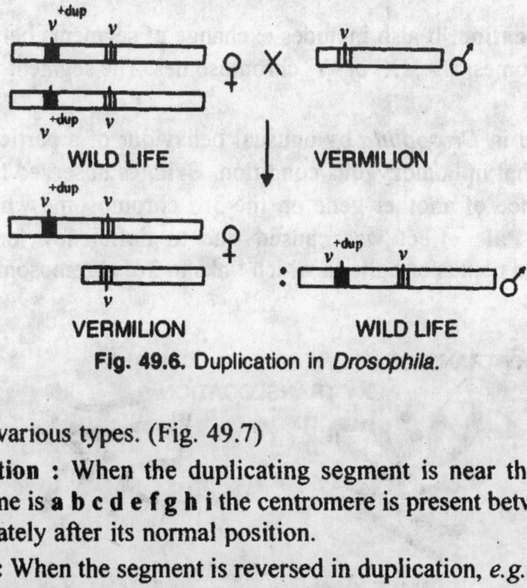

Fig. 49.6. Duplication in *Drosophila.*

Types of duplication

Duplication is of various types. (Fig. 49.7)

Tandem duplication : When the duplicating segment is near the centromeres *e.g.*, the sequence on chromosome is **a b c d e f g h i** the centromere is present between **e** and **f** the segment **d e** is repeated immediately after its normal position.

Reverse tandem : When the segment is reversed in duplication, *e.g.*, it is **d e** segment that is duplicated it will be duplicated as **d e e d** instead of **d e d e.**

Displaced tandem : The segment is repeated some where away from its original location but on the same arm (homobrachial displacement) or on the other arm (heterobrachial displacement).

Transposition : When the segment is duplicated on the non homologous chromosome it is called **transposition.**

Extrachromosomal : Duplication involves centromere it is called extra chromosomal. In salivary gland chromosome duplications are common either as buckling in the duplication heterozygote or as cross pairing between section of different chromosomes.

(C) TRANSLOCATION

Transfer of a section of one chromosome to non homologous chromosome is known as **translocation.** When there is exchange of segments on two **non homologous** chromosomes it is

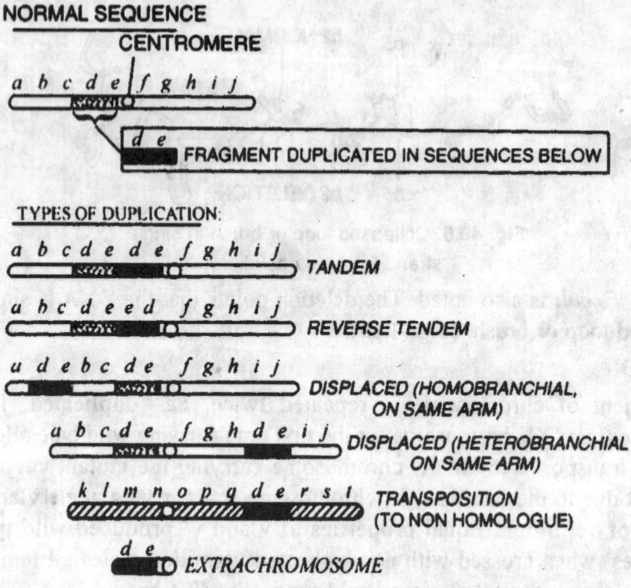

Fig. 49.7. Various types of duplication.

called **reciprocal translocation.** It also includes exchange of segments between non homologous parts of a pair of chromosomes, *e.g.*, 'X' or 'Y' chromosomes. The segment is neither lost or added it is just exchanged.

It was first observed in *Drosophila* by unusual behaviour of a particular 2nd chromosome gene called **Pale.** It is lethal in homozygous condition. **Bridges** observed that its lethality can be suppressed by the presence of another gene on the 3rd chromosome which was also lethal in homozygous condition. **Pale** effect was caused due to deficiency for a small tip of 2nd chromosome including and plexus or balloon which links to 3rd chromosome gene between ebony or rough.

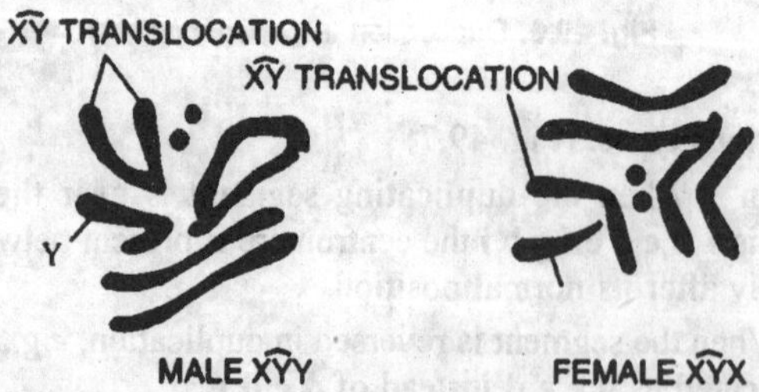

Fig. 49.8. Translocation in *Drosophilla* sex chromosome.

Stern in 1926 observed translocation of some allele (bobbed) on the 'Y' chromosome to the 'X' chromosome. (Fig.43.8)

Types of translocation

(a) Simple translocation : A single break in the chromosome and it is transferred onto the end of the other. (Fig. 49.9)

(b) Shift or intercalary translocation : Common type of translocation involving 3 breaks so that a two break section of one chromosome (*e.g.*, *Pale)* is inserted within the break produced in a non homologous chromosome. (Fig. 49.9B)

(c) Reciprocal translocation or Interchange : Frequently observed translocation where single break in two homologous chromosomes produces an exchange of chromosome segment between them. (Fig. 49.9c)

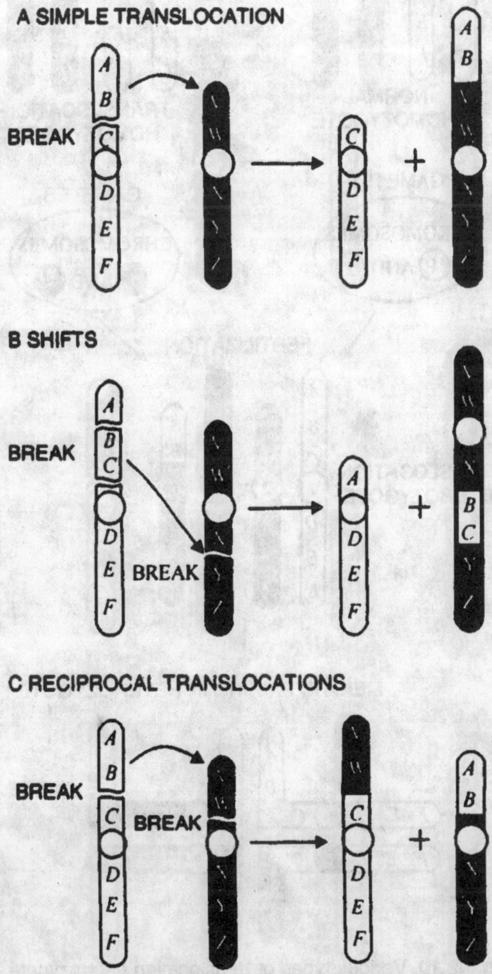

Fig. 49.9. Various types of translocations.

Translocation homozygote forms the same number of homologous pairs as the normal homozygote as long as centromere is not lost.

The result of pairing and meiosis are different in translocation heterozygote bearing two translocated segments and their normal counterpart. (Fig. 49.10). A reciprocal translocation forms a 4 chromosome complex at the pachytene stage. The chiasmata between such chromosomes may form a quadrivalent which can then disjoin in 3 different segregation patterns in the first meiotic division. (Fig. 49.11).

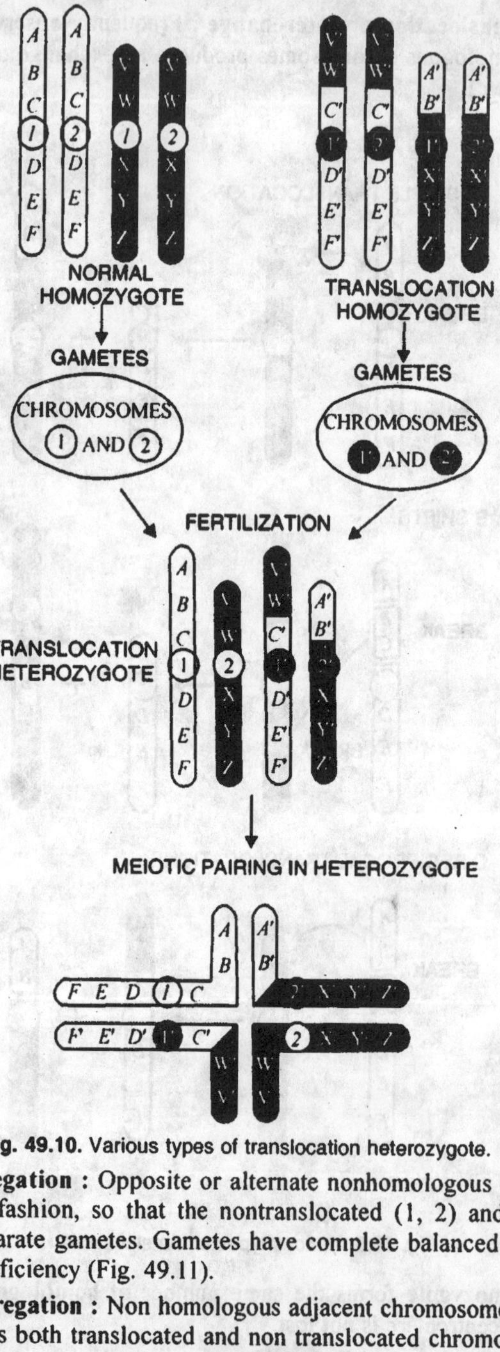

Fig. 49.10. Various types of translocation heterozygote.

(i) Alternate segregation : Opposite or alternate nonhomologous centromeres go to the same pole in a zigzag fashion, so that the nontranslocated (1, 2) and translocated (1′, 2′) chromosomes are in separate gametes. Gametes have complete balanced complement of genes without duplication or deficiency (Fig. 49.11).

(ii) Adjacent-1 segregation : Non homologous adjacent chromosomes go to the same pole but each gamete contains both translocated and non translocated chromosome (1 2′, 1′2) both duplication deficiencies in each gametes are present (Fig. 49.11).

(iii) Adjacent-2 segregation : Adjacent centromeres again go to the same pole but these are now homologous as well as containing both translocated and non translocated chromosomes (1, 1′; 2, 2′). Duplication and deficiencies produce unbalanced components of gene (Fig. 49.11C).

Adjacent-1 and adjacent-2 segregation produce unbalanced gametes. Fertile gametes of translocation heterozygotes will be mostly restricted to alternate segregation.

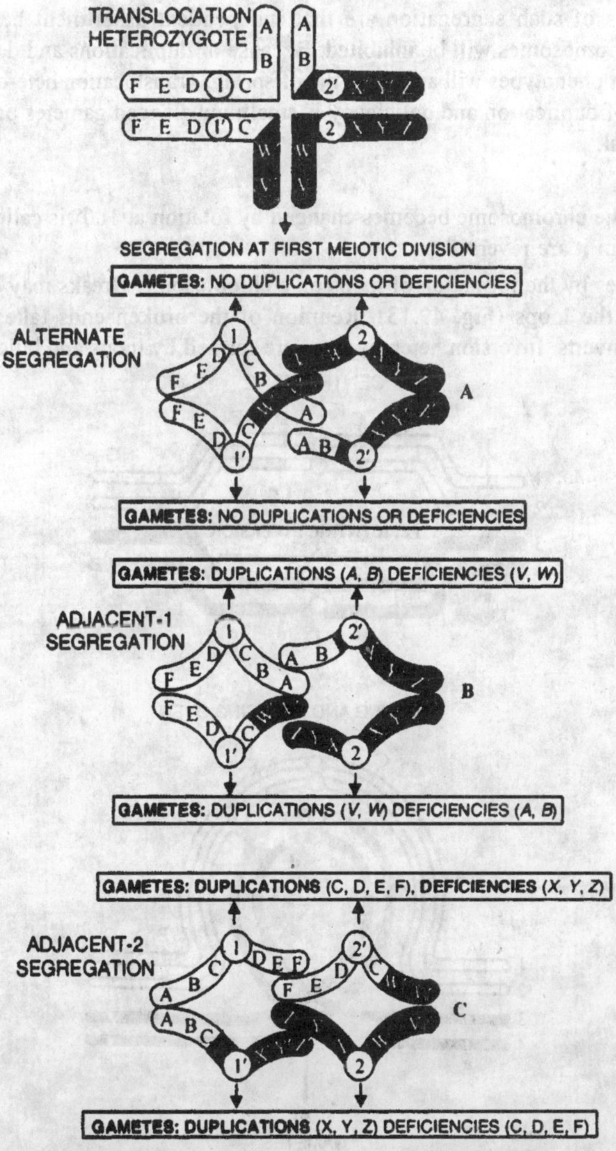

Fig. 49.11. Different segregation pattern in translocation heterozygote.

Synapsis of heterozygous translocation chromosomes showing cross like configuration later on opens out into a ring or a figure of eight (Fig. 49.12).

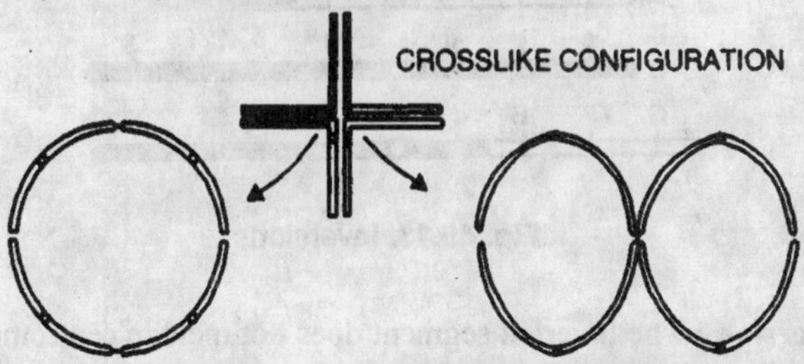

Fig. 49.12. Synapsis of heterozygous translocation.

Consequences of such segregation are that independent assortment between genes and nonhomologous chromosomes will be inhibited. Because of duplications and deficiencies neither of the single mutant phenotypes will appear in the offspring. Translocation heterozygotes have low fertility. If extent of duplication and deficiency is small, unbalanced gametes or zygotes may not necessarily be lethal.

(D) INVERSIONS

A section of the chromosome becomes changed by rotation at 180° is called **inversion.** The order of the genes in it are reversed.

Inversion arises by the formation of loops on a chromosome. Breaks may occur at the point of intersection of the loops (Fig. 49.13). Reunion of the broken ends takes place in a new combination, and inverts. Inversion heterozygotes are formed by loops and bulges in pairs.

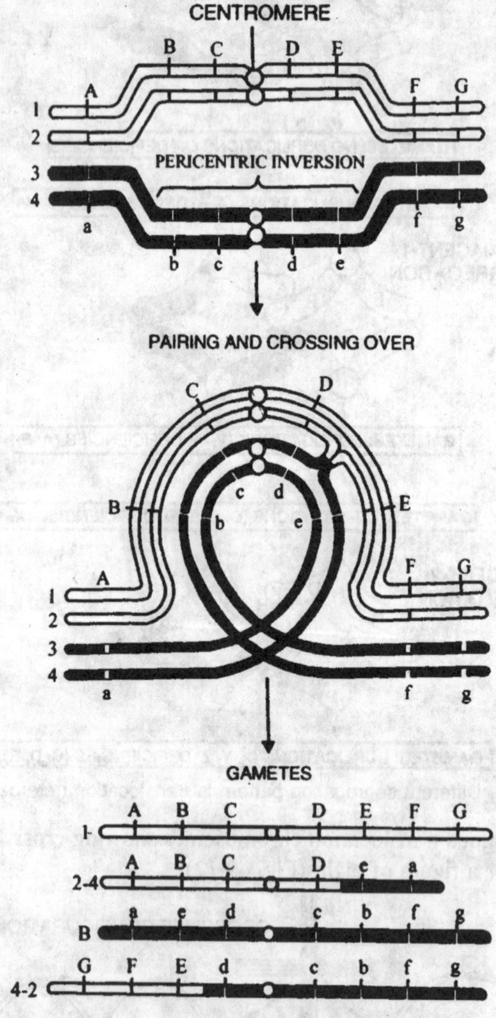

Fig. 49.13. Inversions.

Types of Inversion

Paracentric inversion : The inverted segment does not include centromere.

Pericentric inversion : Inverted segments include centromere.

Paracentric inversion

A single crossing over inverted region will result into formation of a **dicentric** chromosome (with 2 centromeres) and an **acentric** chromosome (with no centromere). Of the remaining 2 chromatids one will be normal and the other will carry inversion. The **dicentric chromatid** and **acentric chromatid** will be observed at anaphase I in the form of a bridge and a fragment (Fig. 49.14). Double crossover shows deficiencies and duplication (Fig. 49.15) giving rise to variations in anaphase I configurations.

Pericentric inversion

In pericentric inversion centromere is in the inverted segments. In pachytene stage 2 of the 4 chromatids resulting after meiosis will have deficiencies and duplications. No dicentric bridge or acentric fragment will be observed (Fig.43.16). In pericentric inversion, if two breaks are not

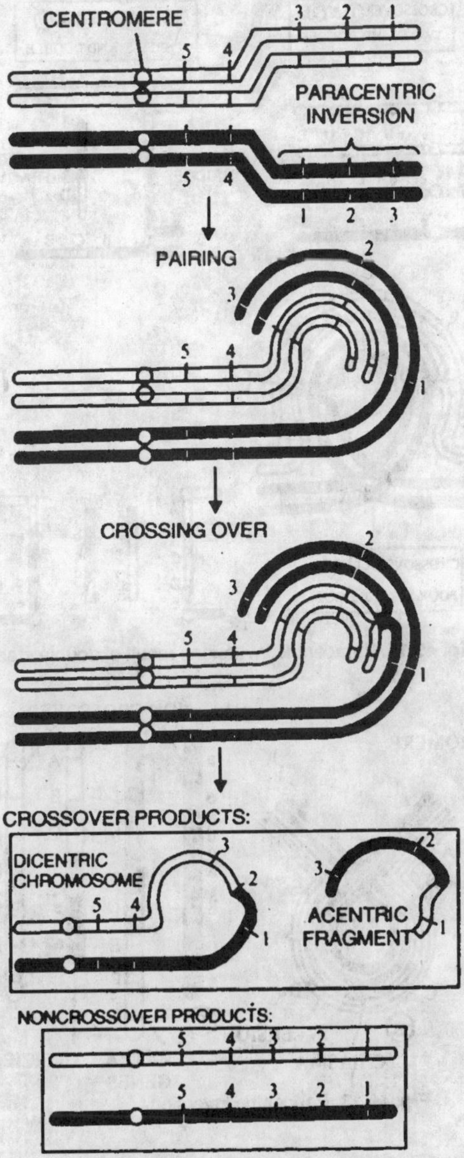

Fig. 49.14. Paracentric inversions.

situated equidistant from the centromere, a change in shape of chromosome results. A metacentric chromosome may become submetacentric and vice versa (Fig. 49.17).

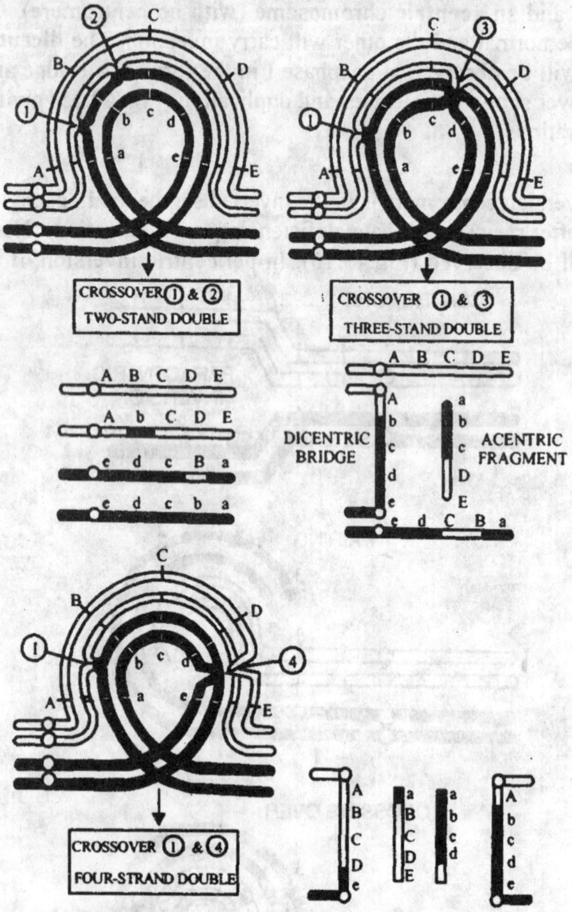

Fig. 49.15. Paracentric inversions result of double cross.

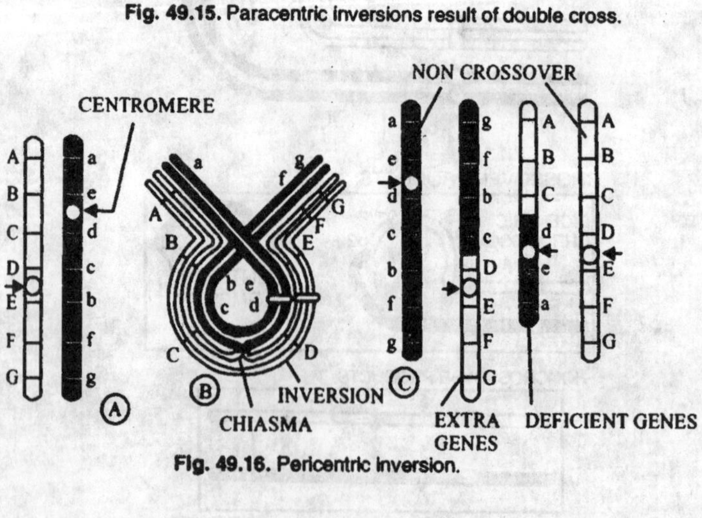

Fig. 49.16. Pericentric inversion.

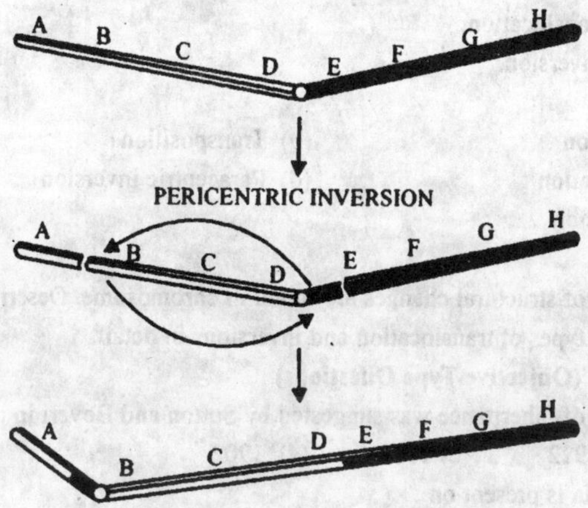

Fig. 49.17. Pericentric inversion and metaphase.

SUMMARY

1. Chromosomal mutations are due to
   (a) **Deletion :** Fragment of chromosome is lost.
   (b) **Duplication :** When the segment is duplicated by joining a homogolous chromosome.
   (c) **Inversion :** Reverse orientation of a segment.
   (d) **Translocation :** Joining of segment of non homologous chromosome.
2. **Cri-du-chat** syndrome is due to deletion of a segment of 5th chromosome.
3. **Myeloid Leukemia** is due to exchange of part of 22nd chromosome with the long arm of 9th chromosome. Such 22nd chromosome is called **philadelphia** chromosome (pH chromosome).
4. Ear and Finger are enlarged when a segment of 18th chromosome is lost.
5. *Drosophila* mutant bar (shape of eye) is the result of doubling up of short piece X chromosome.
6. Loss of a segment of 22nd chromosome (containing gene for **Schizophrenia**) or translocation of the segment cause **Schizophrenia.**

QUESTION BANK

Very Short Answer Questions

1. Define deletion.
2. Give one example of translocation in human.
3. Give one example of deletion in human.
4. In which type of alteration loops are formed.
5. What is reciprocal translocation?
6. What is chromosomal aberration?
7. What is pseudodominance?
8. What is cri du chat syndrome?
9. What is buckle?
10. Give one example of deficiency in *Drosophila.*
11. What is adjacent-1 segregation?
12. What is paracentric inversion?

Short Answer Questions

1. Write short note on deletion.
2. Write short note on insertion or duplication.

3. Write short note on translocation.
4. Write short note on Inversion.
5. Write short note on
   (a) Tandem duplication   (b) Transposition
   (c) Types of translocation   (d) Paracentric inversion
   (e) Pericentric inversion

Long Answer Questions

1. How many types of structural changes are found in chromosome. Describe with diagram.
2. Describe various types of translocation and inversions in detail.

Multiple Choice Questions (Objective Type Questions)

1. Chromosomal theory of inheritance was suggested by Sutton and Boveri in :
   (a) 1932   (b) 1922   (c) 1912   (d) 1902
2. Gene of Schizophrenia is present on :
   (a) 18th chromosome   (b) 22nd chromosome
   (c) 25th chromosome   (d) 17th chromosome
3. The change in the chromosome due to deletion, duplication, etc., is called :
   (a) chromosomal aberration   (b) chromosomal deterioration
   (c) chromosomal arrangement   (d) None of the above
4. Loss of a segment of chromosome is :
   (a) Deletion   (b) Duplication
   (c) Translocation   (d) Inversion
5. When the duplication segment is near the centromere it is called :
   (a) Translocation   (b) Tandem duplication
   (c) Reverse duplication   (d) Reverse tandem
6. When the chromosomal segment is repeated away from the original location the duplication is called :
   (a) Tandem duplication   (b) Reverse tandem
   (c) Displaced tandem   (d) Displaced duplication
7. In transposition the segment duplicates on :
   (a) Same chromosome   (b) Homologous chromosome
   (c) Non-homologous chromosomes   (d) It does not duplicate
8. The second chromosomal gene in *Drosophila* is called :
   (a) Amber   (b) Pale
   (c) Ochre   (d) All the above
9. When the inverted segment do not include centromere the inversion is known as :
   (a) Paracentric inversion   (b) Pericentric inversion
   (c) Reciprocal inversion   (d) Accentric inversion
10. Which statement is correct for pericentric inversion :
    (a) The inversion involves, include centromere
    (b) No dicentric bridge is formed
    (c) No accentric fragement is formed
    (d) All the above.

ANSWERS

1. (d)	2. (b)	3. (a)	4. (a)	5. (b)	6. (c)
7. (c)	8. (b)	9. (a)	10. (d).		

50

CHAPTER

Variation in Chromosome Number

Generally a cell possesses complete set of chromosomes. The condition is called **euploidy.** When the number of chromosomes differs from entire or complete set, *i.e.*, incomplete set of chromosomes it is called **aneuploidy.**

EUPLOIDY

When a cell bears one complete set of chromosomes, it is called **haploid.** Normally individuals bear two similar sets of chromosomes in a cell, the condition is called **diploid.** If an organism bears more than 2 sets of chromosomes in a cell, it is called **polyploid.**

HAPLOID (MONOPLOID)

Haploid organisms possess one complete set of chromosomes. In lower plants, the main plant is a gametophyte and bears haploid set of chromosomes. It is also called **hemizygous.** Among higher organisms, haploidy is found in gametes (sperms, egg). Some insects are also haploids (honey bee). Such haploids reproduce parthenogenetically.

Monoploids may be the result of defective meiosis, *e.g.*, *Datura.* Monoploids are usually sterile. Monoploids are usually smaller in size than the corresponding diploids with less vigour. They show sterility and have small leaves. Monoploids are very important in plants. Doubling of chromosomes in monoploids results in diploids (homozygous).

The chromosome behaviour in haploid differs from normal condition. Haploids of pepper are of same size as diploids.

Haploid generally is half the number of chromosomes. If diploid has 2n then haploid will be having n, *e.g.*, wheat is hexaploid, *i.e.*, 2n=6 X then the haploid will be n = 3 X.

Monoploid means only one set of chromosomes, *e.g.*, n = X *e.g.*, in pea, n = X = 7 or in maize, it is n = X = 10, etc.

POLYPLOIDY

When an organism has more than 2 sets of genomes, *i.e.*, if 3 sets then **triploid,** if 4 sets **tetraploids,** it five sets = **pentaploids,** if 6 sets then **hexaploids,** etc. When the polyploids are even number they are called **primary polyploid.** *e.g.*, 2, 4, 6n, etc.

Secondary polyploids usually arises by crossing between organisms of different ploidy levels, *e.g.*, $4n \times 2n \rightarrow 3n$.

Autopolyploids

The chromosome sets are homologous (ABC, ABC, ABC), etc. Since it is a 'self' (auto) increase in ploidy level. Among the ways in which polyploidy can occur in sexual organisms are (Fig. 50.1) :

(a) The fertilization of egg by more than one sperm then zygote nucleus will have 3 or more sets of chromosomes (Fig. 50.1A).

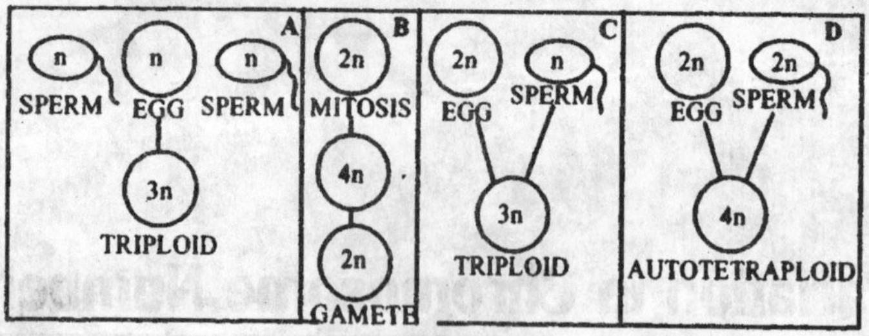

Fig. 50.1. Autopolyploids

(b) Failure of mitosis, multiplying the number of chromosomes there by increasing the number of gametic chromosomes (Fig. 50.1B).

(c) Failure of meiosis producing a diploid gamete instead of a haploid (Fig. 50.1 C, D).

The failure of normal mitotic division in asexual organisms may also produce nuclei with double set of chromosomes. Natural autopolyploids are rare because of the resulting anomalies in cell division.

Triploids may arise by many ways. If normal meiosis fails, a diploid (2n) gamete will be formed. If such gamete (2n) is fertilized by normal haploid gamete (n) an **autotriploid** (3n) is formed (Fig. 50.2A). Autotriploids are generally sterile; because of defective gamete formation. Because of 3 chromosome 2 form a pair **(bivalent)** but one remains **univalent.** If the third also pairs, it forms a **trivalent** (Fig. 50.2C). The gametes will have one and two chromosomes. In the third condition if there are 3 univalents formed, they are randomly distributed in gametes (Fig. 50.2C), *e.g.*, ***Hyacinth*** having triploid constitution 3 n = 8 + 8 + 8 = 24. The gametes may have 8 or 16 chromosomes which is unbalanced.

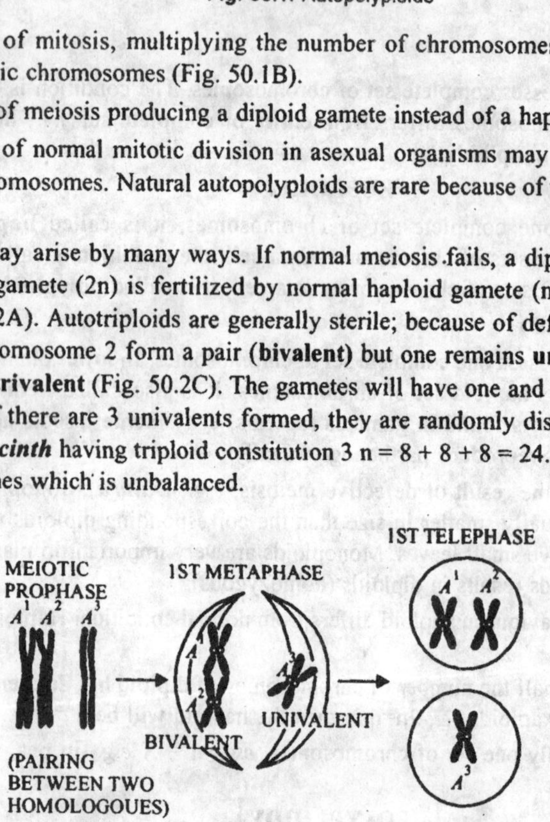

Fig. 50.2. A. Normal Triploid.

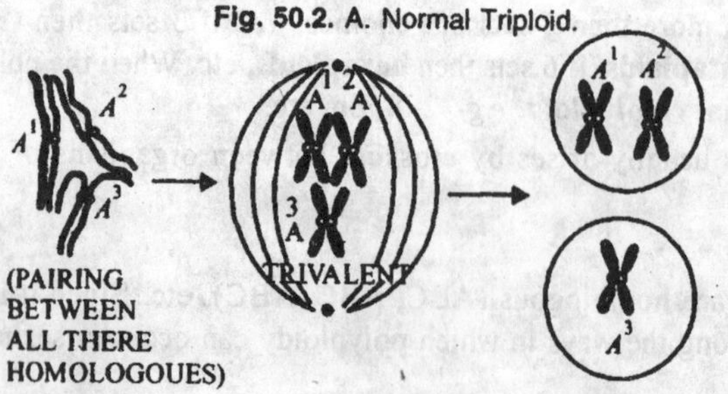

Fig. 50.2 B. In triploid 2 chromosomes forming bivalent and one remains univalent.

Similarly all odd numbered polyploids pentaploids (5n), heptaploids (7n) etc., produce sterile individuals.

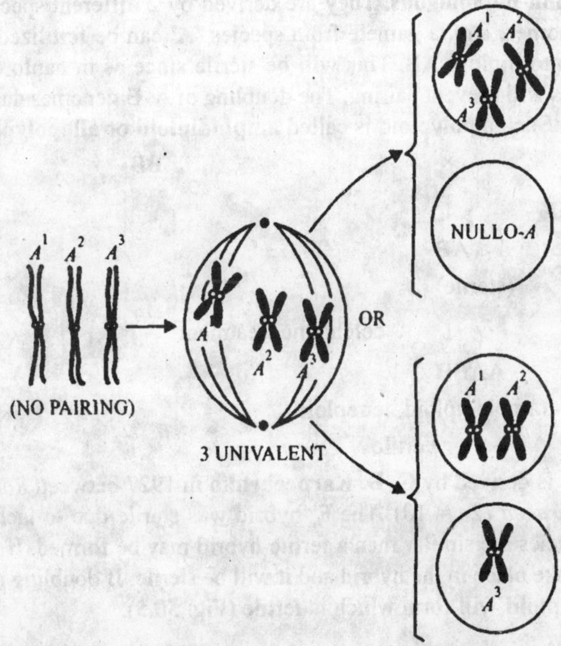

Fig. 50.2 C. Univalents in triploid.

In **autotetraploids** (4n) of *Datura,* there is an equal separation of chromosomes during meiosis. Autopolyploidy was observed by **de Vries** in *Oenothera lamarkiana* (autotetraploid). Autopolyploids are found in plum, moss, tomato, corn, rye, *Datura*, etc.

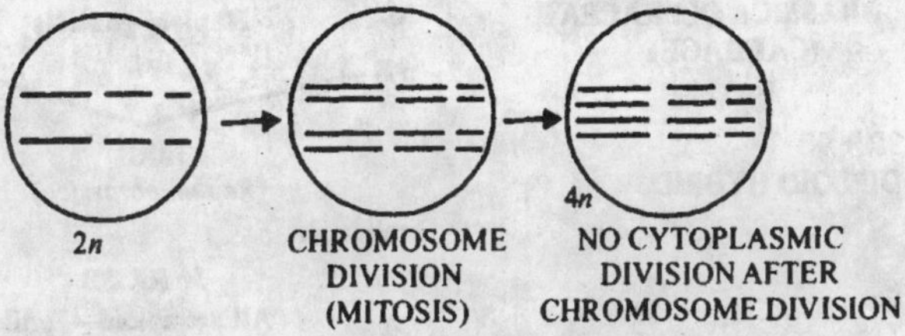

Fig. 50.3. Tetraploids.

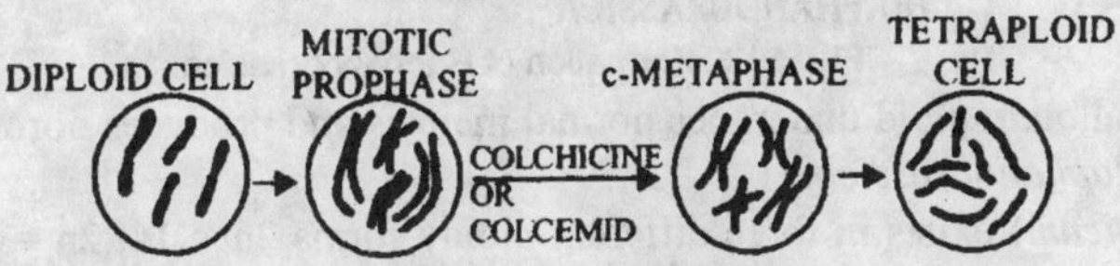

Fig. 50.4. Induced polyploidy.

Normal seedless banana is triploid. Alfa alfa, potato coffee, peanuts, etc., are tetraploids (Fig. 50.3). Polyploidy is induced by inhibiting normal mitosis in some plants. (Fig. 50.4).

The segregation pattern of polyploids is different from normal diploidy. The ratio is based on chromosome segregation or distance of gene form centromere (chromatid segregation). The main effect of autopolyploidy on segregation reveals different kind of inheritance. Tetrasomic inheritance and trisomic inheritance are useful to differentiate between auto and allopolyploids.

Allopolyploidy :

Allopolyploids arise from a heterozygous stock type (ABC, ABC A′B′C′, A′B′C′). The chromosome sets are **non-homologous.** They are derived by 2 different species. Allopolyploids contain 2 different genomes, *e.g.*, a gamete from species **'A'** can be fertilized by a gamete from species **'B'** resulting into diploid **AB.** This will be sterile since as in haploids the homologous between 'A' and 'B' sets will prevent pairing. The doubling of A, B genomes due to (AB) F_1 hybrid gives rise to tetraploid. Such a polyploid is called **amphidiploid** or **allopolyploid.**

AA × **BB**

↓

AB Fi

(sterile)

↓ colchicine treatment

AABB

(amphidiploid, tetraploid)

Fertile

Classical example is derived by **G. D. Karpechenko** in 1927 between *Raphanus sativus* (2n = 18) and *Brassica oleracea* (2n = 18). The F_1 hybrid was sterile due to lack of pairing. If the genomes of the two species are similar then a fertile hybrid may be formed. If they are dissimilar then synapsis will not take place in the hybrid and it will be sterile. If doubling of the chromosome is carried out, **allotetraploid** will form which is fertile (Fig. 50.5).

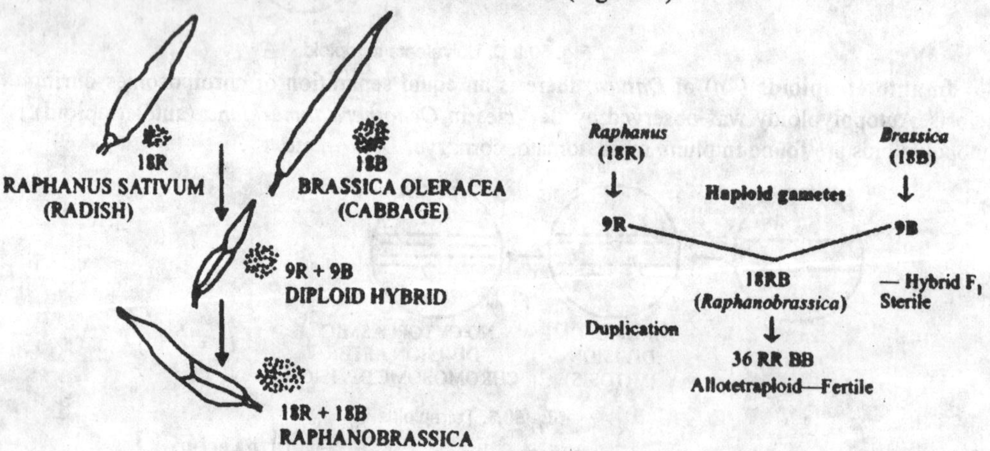

Fig. 50.5. Formation of Raphanobrassica.

The fertile allotetraploid undergoes normal meiosis and produces normal gametes. The new genus is called *Raphanobrassica*.

Wheat (*Triticum*) exists in three different ploidy forms 2n = 14, 2n = 18 and 2n = 42. The common wheat *T. aestivum* is hexaploid, *i.e.*, 2n = 42 and derived from 3 diploid species.

(a) AA = *T. aegilopoides* (2n = 14)

(b) BB = *Aegilops speltoides* (2n = 14)

(c) DD = *Aegilops squarrosa* (2n = 14)

The hexaploid wheat is AABBDD where tetraploid is 2n = 28 and designated as AABB, and diploid is 2n = 14 and designated as AA.

The common hexaploid wheat is **segmental allopolyploid** as the three ancestors are not much different.

Triticum spelta is a hexaploid which was artificially synthesized in 1946 by **E. S. Mc Fadden, E. R. Sears** and **H. Kihara.** It was obtained by crossing *Aegilops squarrosa* (diploid 2n = 14) and *T. dicoccoides* (tetraploid 2n = 28, commonly known as emmer wheat).

T. dicoccoides   *Aegilops squarrosa*

AA BB   DD

2n = 28   ×   2n = 14

ABD

2n = 21

(Triploid hybrid, sterile)

↓ Colchicine treatment

T. spelta

AA BB DD

2n = 42

(*hexaploid wheat*)

Fertile

There are several other natural and synthesized polyploids, *e.g.*, *Gossypium hirsutum* (upland cotton with 2n = 52 is new world cotton raised by crossing *G. herbaceum* (old world cotton 2n = 26) and *G. raimondii* (American cotton 2n = 26).

Triticale is a new man made cereal. It is obtained by crossing *Triticum durum* (2n = 28) and *Secale cereale* (2n = 14). The F_1 hybrids which were sterile (2n = 21) were doubled to get a **hexaploid** *Triticale* (2n = 6X = 42) and **octaploid** *Triticale* (2n = 8X = 56). It was first reviewed by **Muntzing** (1979), **Gupta** and **Priyadarshan** (1982) and **Gupta** and **Reddy** (1991).

(*i*) *Triticum durum*   ×   *Secale cereale*

↓

2n = 28   2n = 14

F_1 hybrid (sterile)

2n = 21

↓ colchicine treatment

2n = 42

Hexaploid *Triticale*

(*ii*) *Triticum aestivum*   ×   *Secale cereale*

2n = 42   ↓   2n = 14

F_1 hybrid (sterile)

2n = 28

↓ colchicine treatment

2n = 56

Octaploid *Triticale*

Clausen and **Goodsped** synthesized a new species of *Tobacco*. They crossed *Nicotiana tabacum* (48 chromosomes, gamete n = 24) with *N. glutinosa* (24 chromosomes, gamete n = 12) and obtained F_1 plants where most of them are sterile but some are viable. Fertile plant was having 72 chromosomes. The new species is called *N. digluta.*

Allopolyploids were also obtained by fusing the protoplast of somatic cells.

Relationship of different kinds of polyploids

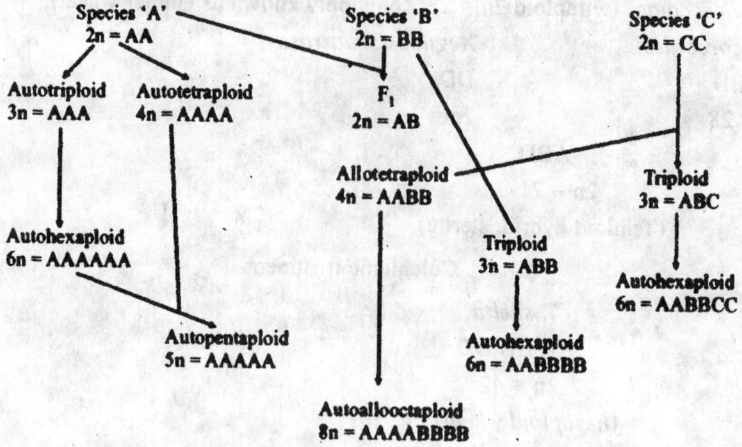

In animal polyploidy is greatly restricted, since the XY mechanism of sex determination is disturbed with duplication of sex chromosome numbers, *e.g.*, male tetraploid with XXYY would produce 'XY' gamete and female tetraploid XXXX will produce XX gamete. The union between XX and XY will form XXXY which is neither male nor female.

Segmental allopolyploids

In some allopolyploids the different genomes which are present are not quite different from one another. In the polyploids chromosomes from different genomes pair together to some extent and multivalents are found. The segments of chromosomes and not the whole chromosomes are homologous. Therefore, such allopolyploids are known as **segmental allopolyploids.** It was suggested by **Stebbins** in 1950. These segmental allopolyploids are intermediate between autopolyploids and allopolyploids. Generally the naturally occurring polyploids are segmental allopolyploids.

APPLICATIONS OF POLYPLOIDY

Tetraploids are more vigourous than diploids bearing larger fruits and seeds. Polyploids are artificially raised for disease resistance, large fruits and high nutritive contents. Disease resistant varieties of tobacco, large fruits of apples and watermelon, large grains in oats and wheat, and disease resistance in wheat, etc., are successfully obtained as polyploids (Fig. 50.6), tetraploid tomato has high vitamin content, tetraploid maize contains 2% more vitamins, etc.

New varieties of wheat, cotton, tobacco, etc., are the examples of polyploids.

INDUCTION OF POLYPLOIDY

Polyploidy may be induced by temperature treatment, decapitation and chemical treatment.

(a) High temperature : High temperatures are helpful in getting polyploids.

(b) Decapitation : The method is used by removing, buds, etc., in tomatoes.

(c) Chemical treatment : Polyploids may be obtained by using colchicine solution. Colchicine inhibits spindle formation. Other chemicals are **acenapthene and indole acetic acid** (IAA).

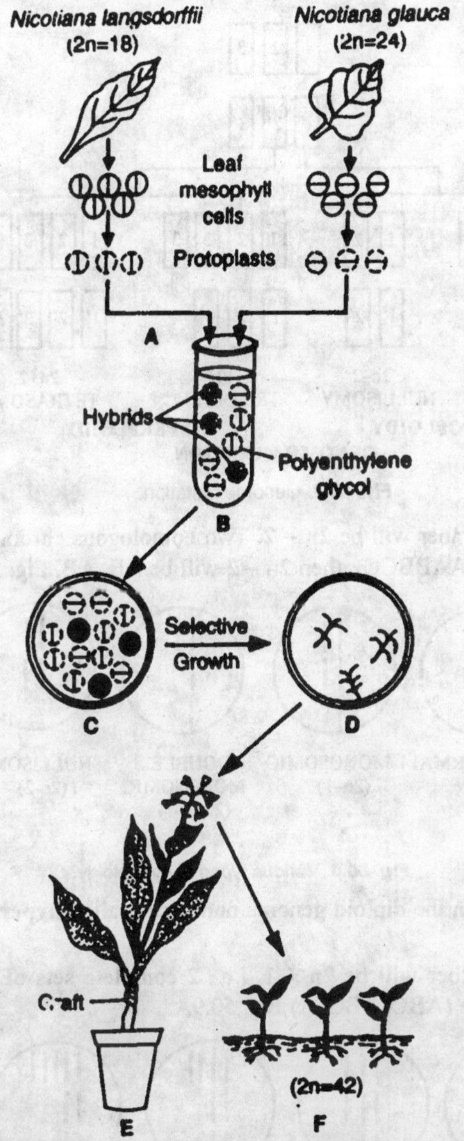

Fig. 50.6. Formation of polyploid in *Nicotiana.*

ANEUPLOIDY

Variation in chromosome number involving individual chromosome is called **aneuploid.** The genome in this is incomplete. It is either less or more than the diploid number. Aneuploidy is also called as **genome mutation** (Fig. 50.7).

Hypoploidy : Less than the diploid genome number (2n) is hypoploidy, *e.g.,*

(a) Monosomic : The number is **2n – 1**. One chromosome less than the diploid complement of 2n = 6 CAABBCC, 2n – 1 will be ABC, AB Fig. 44 .8A.

(b) Double monosomics : The number is **2n – 1 –1**, *i.e.*, two chromosomes less than the whole diploid genome, *e.g.*, 2n = 6. (AABBCC), then 2n – 1 – 1 will be ABC, AB Fig. 50.8B.

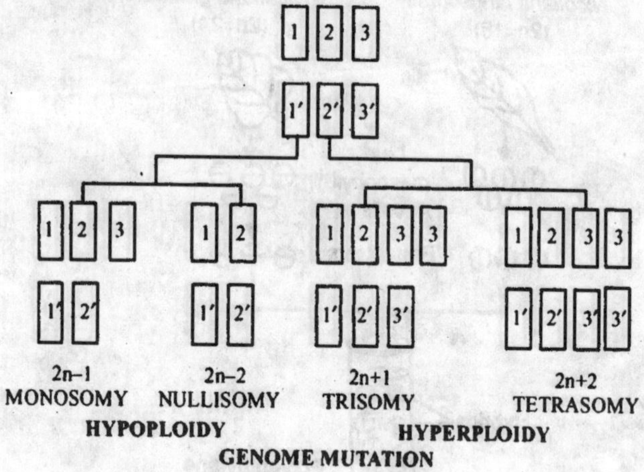

Fig. 50.7. Genome mutation.

(c) Nullisomic : The number will be **2n – 2.** Two homologous chromosomes less than the diploid genome, *e.g.*, 2n = 6 (AABBCC), then 2n – 2 will be AB, AB. Fig. 50.8C.

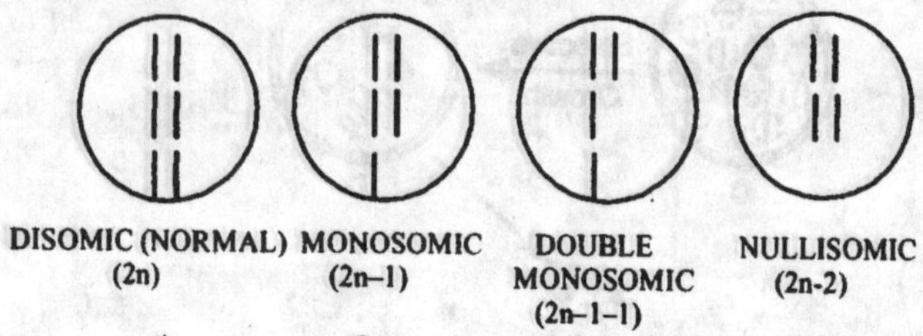

Fig. 50.8. Various types of hypoploidy.

Hyperploidy : More than the diploid genome number is called **hyperploidy** or **polysomy,** *e.g.*,

(a) Trisomic : The number will be 2n + 1, *i.e.*, 2 complete sets of chromosomes but 1 chromosome extra as triplicate (ABC, ABC, A) Fig. 50.9A.

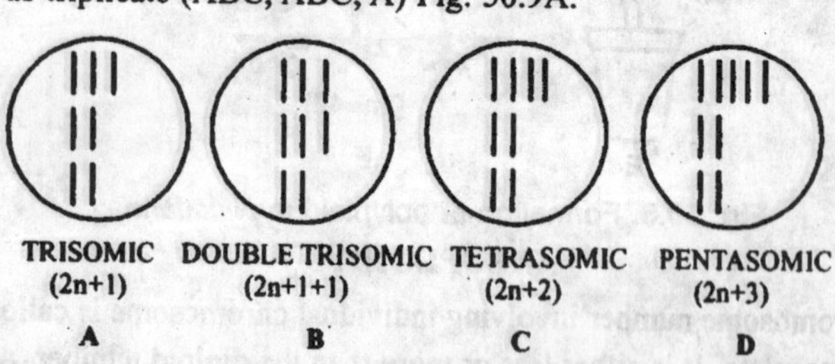

Fig. 50.9. Various types of hyperploidy.

(b) Double trisomics : The number of chromosome will be 2n + 1 + I, *i.e.*, two extra chromosomes than the diploid genome (ABC, ABC, AB) Fig. 50.9B.

(c) Tetrasomics : The number of chromosomes is **2n + 2,** *i.e.*, one chromosome in **quadriplicate** while others are in duplicate number (ABC, ABC, AA) Fig. 50.9C.

(d) Pentasomics : The number is **2n + 3.** One chromosome is **pentaplicate** while others in duplicate (ABC, ABC, AAA) Fig. 50.9D.

Aneuploids are the result of

(a) Union of gametes which contains an unbalanced number of chromosome.

(b) Perpetuation of a cell in which through a failure of mitosis, one or more chromosomes may be added or lost.

Aneuploids generally do not survive. Aneuploids in polyploids are more viable than diploids. Aneuploids in animals are much less viable than in plants.

True aneuploids have one complete set of genome + one fraction of genome. **False aneuploids** contain supernumerary chromosomes or may contain 2 or more complements derived from parents with different chromosome number.

Monosomic and Trisomic in *Drosophila*

Drosophila melanogaster having 2 pairs of chromosomes, among which 3 pairs are of autosomes and one of heterosome or sex chromosomes. In females it is XX and in male it is XY. **First aneuploid** was described by **Bridges** in 1916. Where **non-disjunction** in meiosis produced ***XO*** and XXX or XXY. After meiosis 2 types of eggs are produced one **XX** and one with no sex chromosome. If these eggs mate normal X and Y sperms four types of zygotes XXX, XXY, X and Y are produced. XXX and XXY are **trisomics** while X and Y are **monosomic.**

XX female → gamete X X → normal egg (n)

XX female → gamete X X → n + 1 egg, n - 1 egg → Aneuploids

'XX' x 'X' or 'Y' = XXX – super female (die)

XXY = normal female

'O' x 'X' and 'Y' = XO and normal male

YO = super male (die)

'XXX' will be super female and will die, 'XXY' will act as normal female while 'XO' is normal male and 'YO' is super male and will die without 'X' chromosome.

E.R. Sears produced 2 1 monosomics in wheat variety **chinese spring. J. E. Endrizzi,** etc. have produced monosomics in **cotton** (2n = 52) and **E. R. Clausen** and **D. R. Cameron** produced. In tobacco (2n = 48). Double monosomics or triple monosomics in wheat (2n – 1 – 1 and 2n – 1 – 1 – 1) are also produced. A progeny of monosomic produces a mixture of disomic (2n), monosomic (2n – 1) and nullisomic (2n – 2) but a progeny of nullisomy can not possess a gene on specific chromosome.

Sears isolated all 21 **nullisomic** in wheat.

Trisomic in *Datura* :

Belling and **Blakeslee** obtained trisomics in *Datura stramonium* (Jinsson weed). The haploid chromosome number of it is n = 12. 12 primary trisomics, 24 secondary trisomics are identified by size, shape and other morphological features of fruit (Fig. 50.10).

The trisomics has 25 chromosomes instead of 24 Table 50.1 shows different types of trisomy in *Datura* as 2n + A, 2n + B, etc., and their phenotypes.

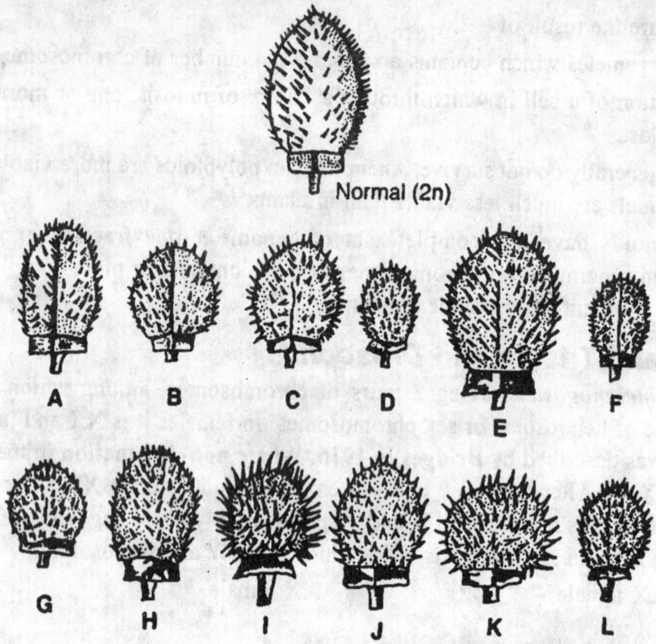

Fig. 50.10. Various shapes of fruits in *Datura* (trisomica).

Table 50.1. Trisomy in *Datura*.

Chromosome no.	Type of Trisomy	Trisomic name	Phenotype
A	2n + A	Rolled	Inrolled leaves
B	2n + B	Glossy	Glossy leaves
C	2n + C	Buckling	Leaves with distorted surface
D	2n + D	Elongate	Elongated leaves
E	2n + E	Echinus	Large capsules very long spines
F	2n + F	Cocklebur	Small, narrow capsule
G	2n + G	Microcarpic	Small, flat capsule
H	2n + H	Reduced	Short, blunt spines
I	2n + I	Poinsettia	Leaves long, clustered
J	2n + J	Spinach	Dark, leaves
K	2n + K	Globe	Globose capsule
L	2n + L	Ilex	Small capsule, sharply toothed leaves

One of the most extensively studied trisomic series is that produced and studied by **T. Tsuchiya** in Barley.

Aneuploidy in Sex chromosome

In *Homosapiens* (man) both monosomics and trisomics of sex chromosomes are found. In monosomic (Fig. 50.11) only one 'X' chromosome is found, *i.e.*, 45 chromosomes. The individuals show **Turner syndrome** (one in 5000). The syndromic individuals are phenotypically female, short statured, webbed neck, under developed breasts, small uterus and reduced overies. Such a condition arises when abnormal eggs without X chromosome fertilizes with 'X' sperm or a normal egg with 'X' chromosome fertilized with sperm without sex chromosome (Fig. 50.12).

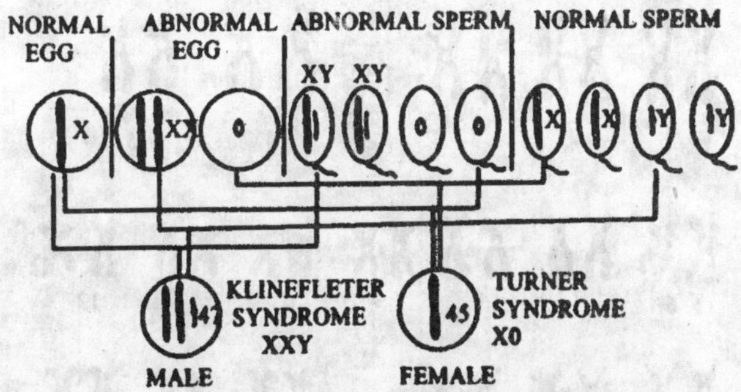

Fig. 44.11. Aneuploidy in sex chromosome of human.

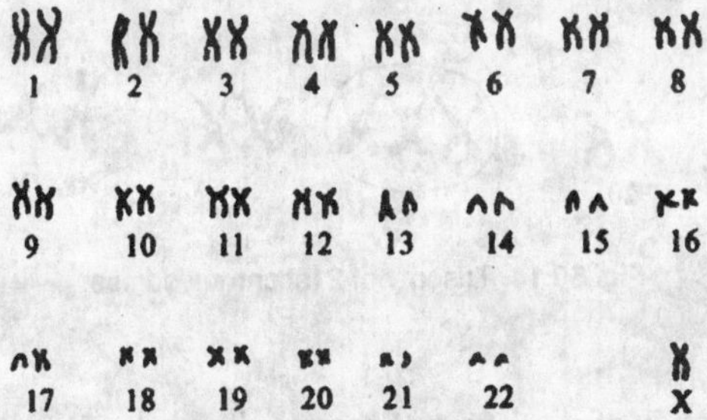

Fig. 44.12. Turner syndrome in human.

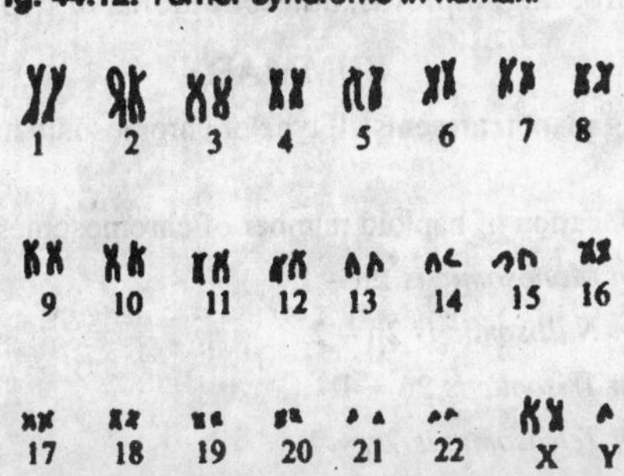

Fig. 50.13. Klinfelter syndrome in human.

Females with XXX (trisomics) XXXX (tetrasomics) and XXXXX (pentasomics) are superfemales with mental abnormality.

Trisomic in human sex chromosome with **XXY** are **Klinefelter syndrome.They** have 47 chromosomes. Such individuals develop small testes, external genitalia of male, female like breasts, sparse body hairs. They develop from abnormal egg (XX) fertilized with normal sperm (Y) or normal egg (X) fertilized with abnormal sperm (XY). XYY males are also found with high criminal tendency (Fig. 50.13).

Aneuploidy in autosome

In human being trisomic of autosome 21st is found. It is called **Down's syndrome** or **Mongolism.** It is characterised by mental retardation, short body, swollen tongue, folded eyelids, etc. (Fig. 50.14). Monosomy of 21st chromosome is fatal. Trisomy of 13, 14, 15, 17, 18 chromosomes results in mental retardation. Trisomy of 18th chromosome results in death within few months after birth. The individuals have laterally flat head, smaller short hands, etc.

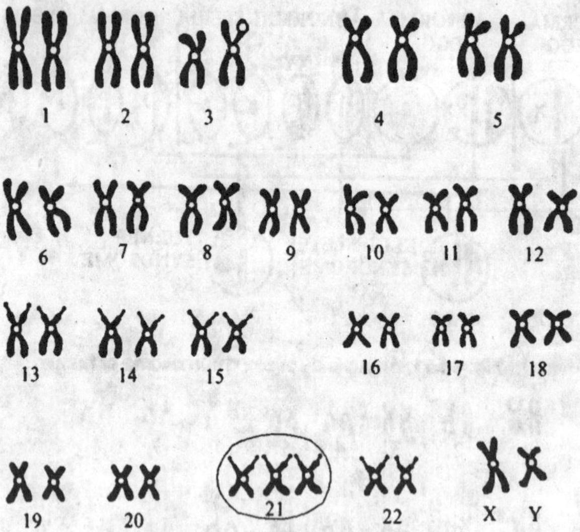

Fig. 50.14. Trisomy of 21st chromosomes.

Production of trisomics

It may be due to production of n + 1 type of gametes because of non disjunction of bivalents. They may be produced by crossing, diploids, autotetraploids or triploid females with diploid male.

SUMMARY

1. Life cycle of a flowering plant represents all type of chromosome numbers, *e.g.*, **haploid**, **diploid** and **polyploid.**
2. Euploidy means multiplication of haploid number of chromosomes.
3. *Chromosome number in Monosomic is* 2n – 1.
4. *Chromosome number in Nullisomic is* 2n – 2.
5. *Chromosome number in Trisomic is* 2n + 1.
6. *Chromosome number in Tetrasomic is* 2n + 2.
7. Chromosome number in a cell can be increased by the treatment with **colchicine.**
8. If a nucleus contains 3 sets of genome the organism is known as triploid and if more it is polyploid.
9. In **aneuploid** the number of chromosome is less than the genome, *i.e.*, 2n – 1. **(hypoploidy)**
10. If the chromosome number is more than the genome, *i.e.*, 2n + 1 **(hyperploidy)**.
11. Aneuploids in mammals are lost in foetus generally.
12. Trisomy of 21st chromosome in human is called **Down's** syndrome.
13. Trisomy of 13th chromosome is called **Patau's** syndrome.
14. Edward's syndrome is due to extra copy of 18th chromosome.
15. **'Klienfelter'** syndrome is due to extra copy of '*X*', *i.e.*, XXY (superfemale) if it is extra copy of 'Y' it will be super male.
16. **Blackslee** discovered induction of polyploidy by colchicine in 1937.
17. **Stebbins** (1950) distinguished 3 types of polyploids : autopolyploids, allopolyploids and autoallopolyploids.
18. **Winklar** (1916) discovered heteroploidy or aneuploidy.
19. **Turners syndrome** is monosomy of sex chromosome with 44A + X.

QUESTION BANK

Very Short Answer Questions

1. What is Edward's syndrome?
2. What is Patau's syndrome?
3. What is Kleinefelters syndrome?
4. Give an example of trisomy in plants.
5. Give an example of trisomy in human.
6. Give an example of monosomy in human.
7. Give an example of allopolyploid.
8. Give the name of one allopolyploid in plants raised by man.
9. Give two examples of sterile hybrids.
10. What is polyploidy ? Define.
11. What is aneuploidy? Define.
12. Name one example of polyploid in plants which is used daily.
13. Name one example of aneuploidy in sex chromosome.
14. Name one example of aneuploidy in autosome.
15. Give two examples of induced polyploidy.

Short Answer Questions

1. Write short notes on autopolyploidy.
2. Write short notes an allopolyploidy.
3. Write short notes on hypoploidy.
4. Write short notes on hyperploidy.
5. Write short notes on.
   (*a*) Monosomy (*b*) *Triticale*
   (*c*) Nullisomy (*d*) Segmental polyploids
6. Write shorts notes on:
   (*a*) *Raphanobrassica* (*b*) Trisomy
   (*c*) Tetrasomy
7. Write short notes on hyperploidy giving suitable examples from human being.
8. Write notes on application of polyploidy.
9. Write short notes on induced polyploidy.
10. Make a line diagram showing relationship between various types of polyploids.

Long Answer Questions

1. What do you mean by polyploidy. Explain polyploidy and give suitable examples.
2. What is aneuploidy? How many types of aneuploidy are found. Explain.

Multiple Choice Questions (Objective Type Questions)

1. If an organism is tetraploid, its haploid will be :
   (a) n (b) 2n
   (c) 3n (d) 4n
2. Banana is generally :
   (a) Triploid (b) Diploid
   (c) Hexaploid (d) Tetraploid
3. Haploid set of chromosome is called :
   (a) Individual (b) Genome
   (c) Nucleus (d) Gene

4. Man made allopolyploid is :
   (a) Water melon (b) *Gossypium*
   (c) *Triticale* (d) *Triticum*
5. Colchicin brings about :
   (a) Polyploidy (b) Cell division
   (c) Cell elongation (d) Cell differentiation
6. Monosomic are :
   (a) n (b) 2n + 1
   (c) 2n – 1 (d) 2n + 2
7. Wheat plant is 6n = 42, what will be the number of chromosomes in its monosomics, haploid and monoploid :
   (a) 43, 21, 7 (b) 15, 7, 7
   (c) 41, 21. 7 (d) 14, 7, 7
8. Chromosome aberration occurs due to :
   (a) Aneuploidy (b) Polyploidy
   (c) Physical effect (d) All the above
9. A material which arrests cell division is obtained from :
   (a) *Chrysanthemum* (b) *Crocus*
   (c) *Cycas* (d) *Colchicum*
10. In Mongolism, the patient has :
   (a) Barr body (b) Trisomy
   (b) Nullisomy (d) Monosomy
11. Extra 18th chromosome in human results in :
   (a) Edwards' syndrome (b) Patau's syndrome
   (c) Down's syndrome (d) None of the above
12. Hexaploid wheat is :
   (a) *Triticum durum* (b) *T. monococcum*
   (c) *T. aestivum* (d) *T turgidum*
13. If haploid number is 10 then what will be the tetrasomic number :
   (a) 19 (b) 40
   (c) 20 (d) 22
14. A polyploid with genome derived from same original species is :
   (a) Autopolyploid (b) Allopolyploid
   (c) Autoallopolyploid (d) Amphiploid
15. A polyploid derived from F_1 hybrid between two species :
   (a) Autopolyploid (b) Autodiploid
   (c) Amphidipioid (d) Hexaploid
16. *Datura* is a classical example of :
   (a) Monoploidy (b) Triploidy
   (c) Trisomy (d) Monosomy
17. A trisomic individual possesses extra chromosomes :
   (a) Three (b) One
   (c) Two (d) Four
18. *Triticale* has been developed from intergeneric hybridization between :
   (a) Wheat and *Aegilops* (b) Rice and Maize
   (c) Wheat and Rice (d) Wheat and Rye

19. Exact multiple of haploid number is :
(a) Heteroploid (b) Euploid
(c) Aneuploid (d) Hypoploid
20. The mule is :
(a) Hybrid (b) Sterile hybrid
(c) Interspecific hybrid (d) All the above
21. Polyploidy means occurrence of :
(a) Diploid set of chromosomes (b) Haploid set of chromosomes
(c) More than diploid set of chromosomes (d) Both 'a' and 'b'
22. The hybrid between *Dianthus* and *Centauria is* called :
(a) Fairchild's mule (b) Hybrid flower
(c) Fairchild's centromic (d) All the above
23. Induction of polyploidy by colchicine treatment was suggested by Blakslee in :
(a) 1930 (b) 1937
(c) 1913 (d) 1952
24. Stebbins in 1950 distinguished :
(a) Aneuploids (b) Barrbodies
(c) Y spot (d) Polyploids
25. Hexaploid wheat is developed through :
(a) Hybridization and chromosome doubling (b) Hybridization
(c) Chromosome doubling (d) Hybridoma
26. Monosomy in sex chromosome in human results in
(a) Klinefelter's syndrome (b) Turner's syndrome
(c) Edward's syndrome (d) Patau's syndrome
27. In Klinefelters syndrome is extra copy of .... is found :
(a) Autosome (b) Sex chromosome
(c) Nucleotide (d) DNA
28. If aneuploid number is less than 2n it is called :
(a) Hyperploid (b) Hypoploid
(c) Polyploid (d) Euploid
29. In trisomic the chromosome number will be :
(a) 2n + 1 + 1 (b) 2n – 1 – 1
(c) 2n + 1 (d) 2n – 1
30. Non disjunction of a chromosome results in :
(a) Polyploidy (b) Aneuploidy
(c) Transversion (d) Inversion.

ANSWERS

1. (b)	2. (a)	3. (b)	4. (c)	5. (a)	6. (c)
7. (a)	8. (d)	9. (d)	10. (b)	11. (a)	12. (c)
13. (d)	14. (a)	15. (c)	16. (c)	17. (b)	18. (d)
19. (b)	20. (b)	21. (c)	22. (a)	23. (b)	24. (d)
25. (a)	26. (b)	27. (b)	28. (b)	29. (c)	30. (b)

51

CHAPTER

Chromosome Organization

Chromosomes are filamentous bodies present in nucleus. They are the carriers of genes (unit of heredity). These are the structure of special organisation and function; playing a vital role in heredity, variation, mutation and evolution. Chromosomes have an ability of self-replication or reproduction.

The chromatin condenses at the time of cell division and becomes clearly visible in the form of **chromosome.** Chromosomes are not visible in the active nucleus due to their high water content. The chromosomes in a cell are of two types (a) **autosomes** and (b) **sex chromosomes** or **heterosomes.**

HISTORY

Chromosomes were first described by **W. Fleming** (1879). He also coined the term **chromatin** to the material that takes stain in nucleus. **W. Roux** (1883) reported the involvement of chromosomes in inheritance. **Bovery** (1887) suggested that the number of chromosomes remain constant in each species. **Waldeyer** in **(1888)** for the first time named **chromosome** for dark stained bodies of nucleus. **Sutton** and **Boveri** 1902 explained chromosomes as **physical basis** of **heredity. Morgan** (1933) discovered that chromosomes are involved in transmission of hereditary traits. The structure of chromosome was described by **Heitz** (1935), **Kuwanda** (1939), and **Geitter** (1940), etc.

NUMBER OF CHROMOSOME

The number of chromosome of a species is constant. Closely related species may also have same number of chromosome. The chromosome number plays an important role in determination of phylogeny and taxonomy of species.

The lowest haploid number recorded in eukaryotes is **'2'** *(Mesotoma,* flat worm and *Ophryotrocha puerilis,* polychaete). In *Ascaris megalocephala*, however, the chromosome number is '1' but it a compound chromosome which divides into about 190 chromosomes in somatic cells. In other animals, the number ranges upto 50 (Table 51.1). The highest chromosome number in animals is upto 127 found in *Eupagurus schotensis* (hermit crab). In plants, the chromosome number ranges from '2' (*Mucor*) to approximately 630 (*Ophioglossum*) (Table 51.1).

Ploidy

Presence of whole set of chromosome is called **euploidy,** *e.g.*, haploid, diploid, triploid, tetraploid, etc. One set of chromosome is called **haploid,** *e.g.*, gamete (n). Somatic cells usually contain 2 sets of chromosomes, *i.e.*, **diploid** (2n). If 3 sets are present it is called **triploid** and so on. Many sets of chromosome in a cell it is called **polyploid.** A change in chromosome number in a set is called **aneuploidy.** If less then it is known as **hypoploidy,** *e.g.*, 2n – 1 is **monosomic,** 2n – n – 1 is nullisomic and if more it is called **hyperploidy,** *e.g.*, 2n + 1 is **trisomic,** 2n + 1 + 1 is **tetrasomic,** etc. Haploid set of chromosome is also called **genome.**

Table 51.1 : Haploid chromosome number of some animals and plants.

S. No.	Name	Scientific name	Chromosome number (haploid)
1.	Flat worm	*Mesotoma*	2
2.	Polychaete	*Ophryotrocha puerilis*	2
3.	Mosquito	*Culex piplesis*	3
4.	Fruit fly	*Drosophila melanogaster*	4
5.	Housefly	*Musca domestica*	6
6.	Frog	*Rana tigrina*	13
7.	Rat	*Rattus rattus*	21
8.	Rabbit	*Oryctogalus cuniculus*	22
9.	Man	*Homosapiens*	23
10.	Gorilla	*Gorilla gorilla*	24
11.	Pigeon	*Columba livia*	40
12.	Hermit crab	*Eupagurus schotensis*	127
13.	Bread mold	*Mucor*	2
14.	Haplopappus	*Haplopappus gracilis*	2
15.	Penicillium	*Penicillium*	2
16.	Neurospora	*Neurospora crassa*	7
17.	Pea	*Pisum sativum*	7
18.	Barley	*Hordeum vulgare*	7
19.	Onion	*Allium cepa*	8
20.	Cabbage	*Brassica oleracea*	9
21.	Mays	*Zea mays*	10
22.	Rice	*Oryza sativa*	12
23.	Yellow Pine	*Pinus* sp	12
24.	Yeast	*Saccharomyces*	17
25.	Wheat	*Triticum aestivium*	21
26.	Oat	*Avena sativa*	21
27.	Coffee	*Coffea arabica*	22
28.	Potato	*Solanum tuberosum*	24
29.	Sugar cane	*Saccharum officinarum*	40
30.	Ophioglossum	*Ophioglossum*	631

SIZE OF CHROMOSOME

The size of chromosome varies from species to species but remains constant in one species. The length varies from 1 μ to 30 μ. The diameter may vary from 0.2 – 20μ. If all the chromosomes of a species are of similar size they are termed **symmetrical karyotype** and if they are of different size they are called as **asymmetrical karyotype.** In man and *Yucca*, etc., there are distinct groups of different sizes. The chromosomes of *Trillium* are hundred times more in length as compared to the related genera *Medeola.* The chromosomes of *Allium porrum* are half the size of chromosomes in *Allium sativum*. Size variations may also take place in different regions or in different stages of the same organism. In *Medeola*, the root tip chromosomes are 50% longer than shoot tip chromosome. The chromosomes of a cell may be very differnt in size, some may be exceptionally large and some are small (human).

SHAPE OF CHROMOSOME

The shape of the chromosome depends on the position of centromere on the chromosome. It may be 'I' shape, 'J' shape, 'V' shape 'L' shape, etc.

STRUCTURE OF CHROMOSOME

Earlier the light microscopic structure of chromosome revealed that it consists of coiled thread called *charomonema* lying in a matrix and covered by membranous **pellicle.** But the electron microscopic studies revealed that there is no definite membranous pellicle present on the chromosome. Chromosome includes centromere, secondary constriction, nucleolar organiser, telomeres and satellite, etc. (Fig. 51.1)

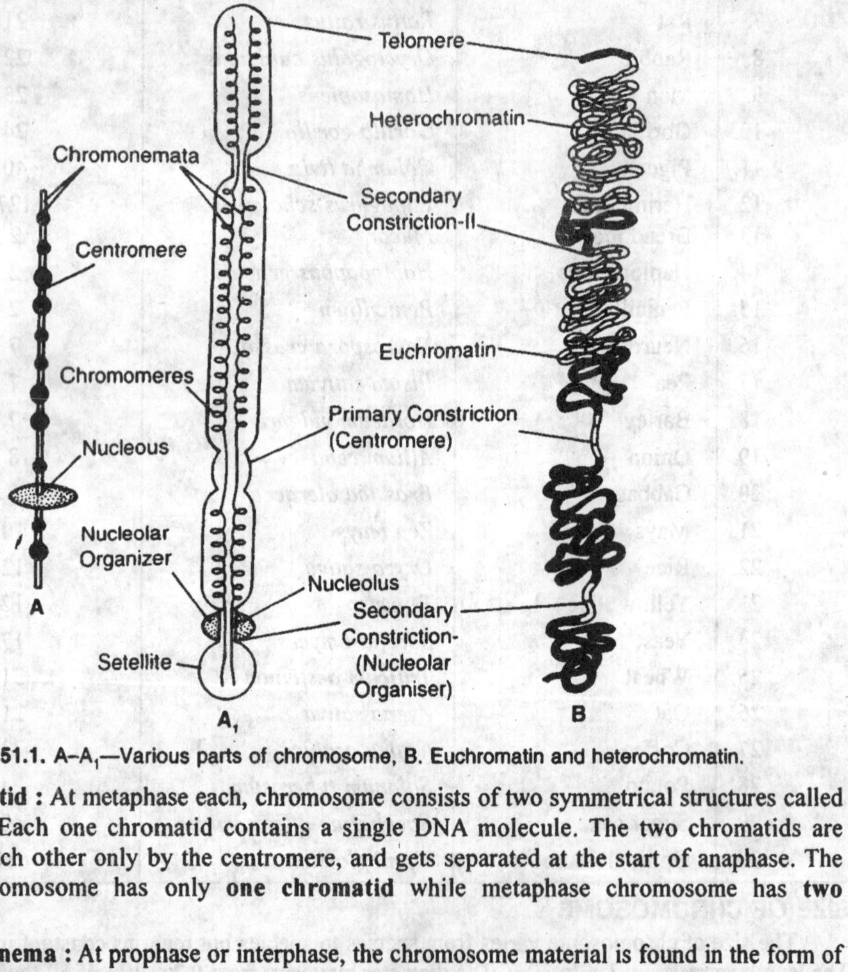

Fig. 51.1. A–A_1—Various parts of chromosome, B. Euchromatin and heterochromatin.

Chromatid : At metaphase each, chromosome consists of two symmetrical structures called **chromatids.** Each one chromatid contains a single DNA molecule. The two chromatids are attached to each other only by the centromere, and gets separated at the start of anaphase. The anaphase chromosome has only **one chromatid** while metaphase chromosome has **two chromatids.**

Chromonema : At prophase or interphase, the chromosome material is found in the form of thread called chromonemata, representing the chromatids in early stages of condensation. Therefore chromanemata is the chromatid as later stage, *i.e.*, a single linear DNA molecule with associated proteins.

(B) Chromomere : The beaded structures present on the chromatid are called **chromomeres.** Chromomeres are visible on the interphase chromosomes also. On polytene chromosomes they are aligned side by side, constituting the chromosome bands. These are the tightly folded regions of DNA. They correspond to the units of genetic function of chromosome. At metaphase, the chromosome is tightly coiled and the chromomeres are not visible.

(C) Centromere or kinetochore : The centromere lies within a linear segment of the chromosome, the **primary constriction.** It is the region of the chromosome that becomes attached to the mitotic spindle. The region adjacent to the centromere frequently contains highly repetitive DNA; and may stain more intensely with basic dyes (heterochromatin). It contains specific DNA sequences with special proteins, forming a disc shape structure. This disc is called **kinetochore.** Electron microscopic picture reveals that the kinetochore disc is **trilaminar structure** with a dense outer proteinaceous, middle low density and inner dense layer tightly bound to centromeric DNA 4–40 microtubules are attached to the kinetochore providing force for chromosomal movement during mitosis.

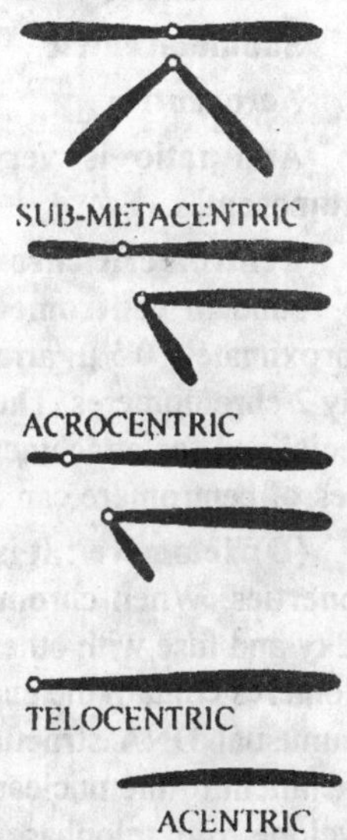

Fig. 51.2. Chromosome : various types of chromosomes based on centromere position.

Depending upon the kinetochores the chromosomes are:

(a) Monocentric chromosomes : Chromosomes have only one kinetochore.

(b) Holocentric chromosomes : The kinetochores are diffuse with microtubules attached along the length of chromosome. In some animals like hemipteran and homopteran insects, *Ascaris*, etc., in some plants also such chromosomes are found. These are also called polycentric chromosomes of diffuse centromere by some cytologits.

(c) Acentric chromosomes : The chromosomes are without any kinetochore. Such type of abnormality is produced by X rays.

(d) Dicentric chromosomes : The chromosome may have two kinetochores. This condition is also an abnormality where a part of other chromosome with centromere gets attached to the chromosome. The condition may not be stable.

According to the position of centromere (kinetochore), the chromosomes are of many types, *e.g.*, (Fig. 51.2).

(a) Metacentric : The centromere is present nearly at the middle of the chromosome (median). The two arms of the chromosome are approxiamtely equal. The chromosome appears 'V' shaped at anaphase. The chromosome is called **metacentric chromosome.**

(b) Submetacentric : The centromere is present away from the middle point on the chromosome. One arm of the chromosome is long and the other is small. The chromosome appears 'J' or `L' shaped. The chromosome is called **submetacentric chromosome.**

(c) Acrocentric : The centromere is present near the end or **subterminus.** It is rod shaped, the one arm is very long and the other arm is very small.

(d) Telocentric : The centromere is **terminal,** present at the tip of the chromosome. The chromosome lies only one arm. Such chromosomes are very rare. The IV chromsome of *Drosophila* was thought to be **telocentric** but now a very small arm has been identified so it is called **acrocentric.** Truely telocentric chromosomes are found in plants, mammals, etc.

In **grasshopper**, all chromosomes are acrocentric and in *Trillium* and *Tradescantia* all the chromosomes are metacentric. In human, the chromosomes are metacentric, submetacentric and acrocentric type.

Arm ratio : The length of the two arms of the chromosome are found in different ratio. It is called arm ratio. The arm ratio is characteristic for each single chromosome. It is important and useful in distinguishing chromosomes with similar total length. In human beings Vogel in 1961 suggested the arm ratio as

Metacentric — from 1·07 - 1.95

Submetacentric — from 2·05 - 3.75

Acrocentric — from 5·00- 11·94.

Arm ratio is very high in acrocentric chromosomes and very low in metacentric chromosomes.

Centromeric chromomeres : In metaphasic chromosomes with two chromatids, 4 granules are found in **centromere** which are called **centromeric chromomeres.** The size of them is approximately 0·5 μ; arrange in square. In anaphase due to separation of each chromatid, it shows only 2 chromomeres. The centromere is also considered to be an extended region of chromonema; specialized for attachment and formation of spindle fibres. Spindle fibres extending from either sides of centromere can be seen during cell division.

(D) Telomere : It is the tip of the chromosome which is called **telomere.** It has very special properties. When chromosomes are broken by **X-rays** the free ends without telomere become **sticky** and fuse with other broken chromosome. They however do not fuse with a normal telomere. Telomeres contain the ends of the long linear DNA molecule contained in each chromatid, so have an unusual DNA structure. Telomeres are specially modified regions of the chromosome for attachment to the nuclear envelope. The ends of the chromosome are associated with the nuclear envelope from telophase to prophase through interphase. Two telomeres never unite. They do not unite with the broken end also.

(E) Secondary constriction : The chromosome has another thin area called **secondary constriction.** The secondary constriction II is different from secondary constriction I which is also called as nucleolar organizer. The location of secondary constriction is constant for a particular chromosome, and is useful for identification of chromosomes. It represents the site of breakage and subsequent fusion. In human beings, the secondary constriction is found on the long arms of chromosome number 1, 10, 13, 16 and Y'chromosome. Secondary constrictions are distinguished from the primary constriction by the absence of marked angular deviations of the chromosomal segment during anaphase.

(F) Nucleolar organizer : This area on the chromosome is also called **secondary constriction I.** It contains the genes coding for **18 S** and **28 S** ribosomal RNA and genes for inducing formation of **nucleolus.** The constriction may arise because the *r*RNA genes are transcribed very actively, interfering with chromosomal condensation. In man, the nucleolar organisers are located in the secondary constrictions of 13, 14, 15, 21, 22 chromosomes (acrocentric with satellites) and 'Y' chromosomes.

Nucleolar organisers have been reported in several animals and plants, and are probably of universal occurrence. Each nucleolar organiser may be associated with the nucleolus or both nucleolar organiser (diploid) may be associated with nucleolus. In polyploids and some diploids, the number of nucleoli and nucleolar organisers may be more than two.

(G) Satellites : In some chromosomes, **satellite** is found. It is a round body separated from the rest of the chromosome by a secondary constriction. It is consant in shape and size for each particular chromosome.

KARYOTYPE AND IDIOGRAM

The whole group of characteristics allowing to identify a particular chromosomal set, *i.e.*, number, relative size, position of cetromere, length of arms, secondary constructions and satellites, etc., are called karyotype. The **karyotype** is characteristic of an individual, species, genus or group. It may be represented by a diagram in which pairs of homologous chromosomes are ordered in a series of decreasing size is called **idiogram.**

Some species may have characteristic features, *e.g.*, plants frequently have heterochromatic regions at the telomeres. Broad beans *(Vicia faba)* or onion (*Allium cepa)* have large chromosomes producing nice pattern in mitotic cells. In mouse, the chromosomes are acrocentric. In amphibians, they are metacentric, etc.

A set of chromosome of an individual or species is called **karyotype.** In man, 23 pairs of chromosomes are found in a somatic cell, forming its karyotype. The chromosomes are identified on the basis of total length, arm ratio, position of secondary constriction and nucleolar organiser and euchromatic and heterochromatic regions. They are grouped in 7 groups (Fig.45.3).

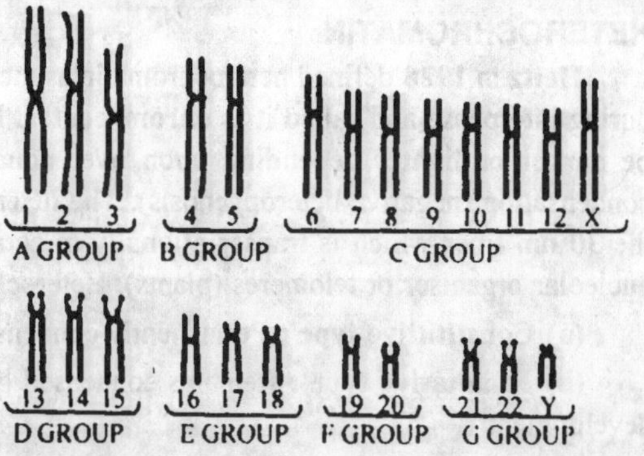

Fig. 51.3. Idiogram of normal human male karyotype

Group I = chromosome no. 1, 2, 3.

Group II = chromosome no. 4, 5

Group III = chromosome no. 6–12 and 'X' chromosome.

Group IV = chromosome no. 13–15

Group V = chromosome no. 16–18

Group VI = chromosome no. 19, 20

Group VII = chromosome no. 21, 22, and 'Y' chromosome

Normally a single chromatid has single DNA molecule to whole of its length which replicates by semiconservative method. The fact is established by using H-thymidine as labelled DNA. The metaphase, chromosomes are symmetrical. The two sister chromatids are mirror images of each other. The morphological characters of each chromatid are same. The sister chromatids contain identical DNA molecules.

COILING OF CHROMOSOME

The coiled filaments are for the first time called **chromosome** by **Velovsky** in 1912.

The chromosome may have one to four threads or fibrils coiled with each other. The coiling may be of following types (Fig. 51.4).

(a) Paranemic coiling : When the fibrils are easily separable from the coils, the coiling is called paranemic.

(b) Plectonemic coiling : When the fibrils are intertwined in such a way that they cannot be separated at all, the coiling is called plectonemic coiling.

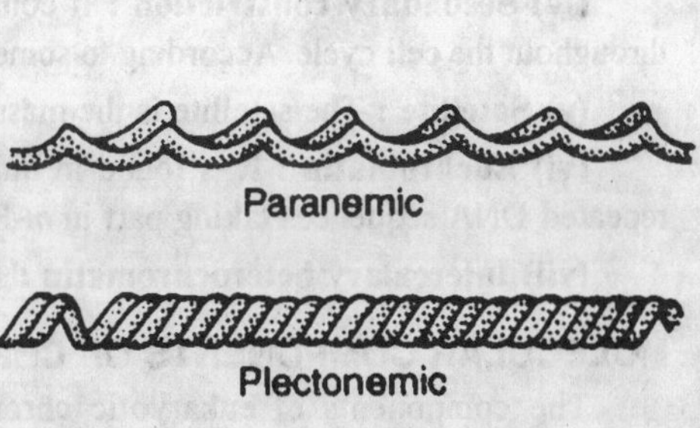

Fig. 51.4. Various type of coiling.

The degree of coiling of fibrils may be different depending upon the length of chromosome. It may be major, minor or standard type.

EUCHROMATIN

It is the segment of chromosome that takes light stain and takes part in cell cycle. This part is non-condensed and extend during interphase, also called as euchromosome. Euchromatin never shows heteropycnosis.

HETEROCHROMATIN

Heitz in 1928 defined heterochromatin as the region of chromosome that remains condensed during interphase and called it as **chromocentre.** It takes dark stain upon staining. The stain may be darker or lighter depending upon over condensation (positive heteropycnosis) or under condensation (negative heteropycnosis). The heterochromatin of DNA remains tightly packed in the 30 nm fiber which is transcriptionally in active chromatin. It is generally present near the nucleolar organiser or telomeres (plants). Heterochromatin is of two types:

(a) Constitutive type : Permanently condensed in all types of cells.

(b) Facultative type : Remains condensed only in certain cell types or at special stages of development.

In facultative heterochromatin, one chromosome of the pair becomes either totally or partially heterochromatic, *e.g.*, 'X' chromosome of mammalian female where one is active and remains euchromatic and the other is inactive and forms sex chromatin or **barr body** at interphase.

The most common heterochromatin is constitutive type. It contains highly repeated DNA sequences called **satellite DNA.** This heterochromatin shows late replication.

The heterochromatin is inactive in RNA synthesis. Genes present on heterochromatic segments are never expressed.

Types of Chromatin in different regions of the chromosome

(i) Telomere : It contains heterochromatin of repetitive DNA sequences.

(ii) Centromere : The chromatin of it is continuous on either sides with the heterochromatin (Rae, 1970). The heterochromatin present is of two types (Heitz, 1934), *i.e.*, α-present around the centromere (compact and resistant to destaining); and β-present in rest of the centromeric region (diffused and less resistant to destaining).

(iii) Nucleolar organiser : Euchromatin is predominantly present. The genes for 18 S and 28 S *r*-RNA are found. RNA synthesis takes place throughout the cell cycle except at mid-mitosis.

(iv) Secondary constriction : It consists of euchromatin taking part in *m*-RNA synthesis throughout the cell cycle. According to some cytologists, it is also the place of 5S *r*-RNA synthesis.

(v) Satellite : The satellite is the mass of heterochromatin.

(vi) Euchromatin : It is found in bulk of the chromosome. It is partly composed of non-repeated DNA sequences taking part in *m*-RNA synthesis during interphase.

(vii) Intercalary heterochromatin : It is found within the euchromatin here and there.

MOLECULAR COMPONENTS OF CHROMOSOME

The components of eukaryotic chromosome are DNA, RNA, histone, and non-histone protein, metallic ions, etc. The DNA is the most stable molecule carrying out transfer of genetic information from one generation to the other. RNA is transcribed over it. Most of *m*-RNA is transported to the cytoplasm where it is translated in terms of proteins. Some *m*RNA remains in the coil associated with the protein.

Proteins : Two types of proteins, *i.e.*, acidic and basic proteins are found associated with DNA in chromosome.

Protamines : These are simple proteins of molecular weight less than 4000 daltons. Rich in basic amino acid **arginine,** found in spermatozoa of some fish (salmon), snail, fowl, etc. They are helically rapped around DNA. Polypeptides of protamine consists of 28 amino acid residue (19 arginines, 8-9 non-basic amino acids).

Histones : Small basic proteins associated with DNA of eukaryotic cells. They are structural proteins of chromatin and act as **gene repressors** also. In a wide variety of plants and animals, the ratio of DNA : Histone = 1 : 1 . There are 5 types of histones *i.e.*, Hl (H5), H2A, H2B, H3 and H4. Histones are rich in **arginine** and **lysine** (basic amino acids). They lack **tryptophan.** Histones are highly modified as well as conserved proteins; with very little difference in amino acid sequences. On the basis of arginine and lysine contents, they are divided into 3 groups.

(i) High lysine rich — Hl

(ii) Lysine rich — H_2A, H_2B

(iii) Arginine rich - H_3, H_4

Histones tend to **depress genetic acitivity.** They make DNA. They are structurally important in packaging DNA molecules.

Non-Histone proteins (NHP) : They have structural, enzymatic and regulatory function in chromatin. They are generally acidic proteins. The acidic to basic residues ratio in these proteins is 1.2 — 1.6.

The molecular weight ranges from 11000-21,500 daltons. They may show structural variation in different species and even tissues. These proteins are synthesised throughout the cell cycle. These proteins stimulate genetic activity.

Enzymes of chromosomal metabolism like nucleic acid polymerase, nucleases, DNA pyrophosphorylases and nucleoside triphosphatases, etc., are non-histone proteins. Such proteins play important role in the interaction of **steroid hormones** with target cell nuclei.

The chromosomes also contain metallic ions like Mg^{++} and Ca^{++}, etc.

ULTRASTRUCTURE OF CHROMOSOME

Electron microscopic studies revealed that chromosomes have very fine fibrils with a thickness of 2nm—4 nm. Since DNA is 2 nm in width a single fibril may correspond to a single DNA molecule. **Dupraw** (1965, 66) suggested that interphase chromatin fibres consist of fibrils of 230 Å and metaphase chromosomal fibrils have 300 Å diam. There are different views about chromosomal strands.

(A) Multistranded view : According to this view, the smallest unit of chromosome is 100 Å thick fibril. Each fibril is made up of 2 DNA molecules at 25 Å distances. A chromosome has 2 chromatids, each chromatid consists of 4 fibrils. According to this view a chromosome has a thickness of 1600 Å suggesting that 16 chromonemal fibrils and 32 DNA molecules. This does not hold the electron microscope observation, so was not supported by cytologists.

(B) Unistrand view : The model was proposed by **Dupraw** (1965) as **folded fibre model** of chromatid. According to this view, the DNA molecule is wrapped in a nucleoprotein and this DNA-protein fibre is coiled tightly to form 250–300 Å fibre (Fig. 51.5). The DNA-protein molecule of both the chromatids remain held at the centromere by a unreplicated fibre segment of DNA until anaphase.

This model was accepted by many workers. But this was discovered after the discovery of **nucleosome.**

STRUCTURE OF CHROMOSOME AT MOLECULAR LEVEL

(A) Nucleosome subunit of chromatin : In 1974, **R. D. Kornberg** and **J. O. Thomas** proposed an active model of DNA and histones. They suggested that DNA interacts with a **tetramer** ($H3_2$ – $H4_2$) and two molecules of an oligomer (H2A-H2B). Tetramer involves 2 molecules each of H3 and H4 histogen is associated with 200 base pairs of DNA. Each repeat unit has one molecule of Hl histone. **P Oudet** *et al* 1975 proposed the term **nucleosome** (Fig. 51.6). Nucleosome contains a **nucleosome core particle** consisting of 146 base pairs of supercoiled

DNA wrapped almost twist around a disc-shaped complex of 8 histone molecules consisting of 2 copies each of histone H2A, H2B, H3B and H4 assembled into an octamer. These nucleosomes are connected by **linker** DNA of about 60 base pairs. Together a nucleosome (12.5 nm in diam) = 200 base pairs + 2 mole each of H2A, H2B, H3 and H4.

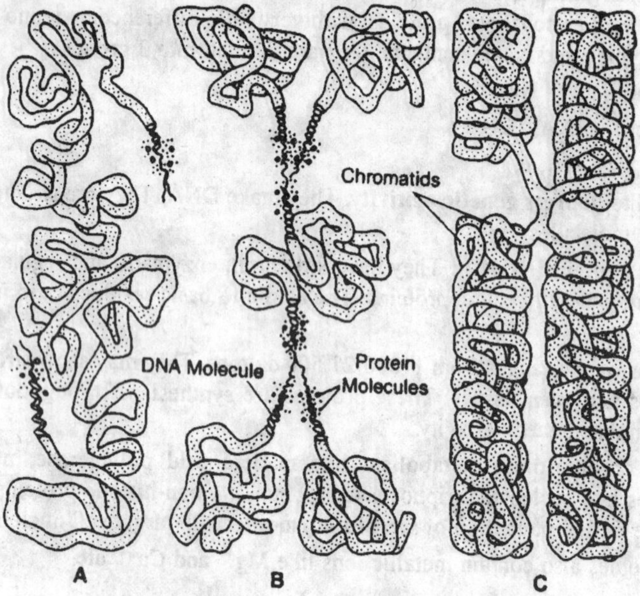

Fig. 51.5. Dupraw's folded fibre model

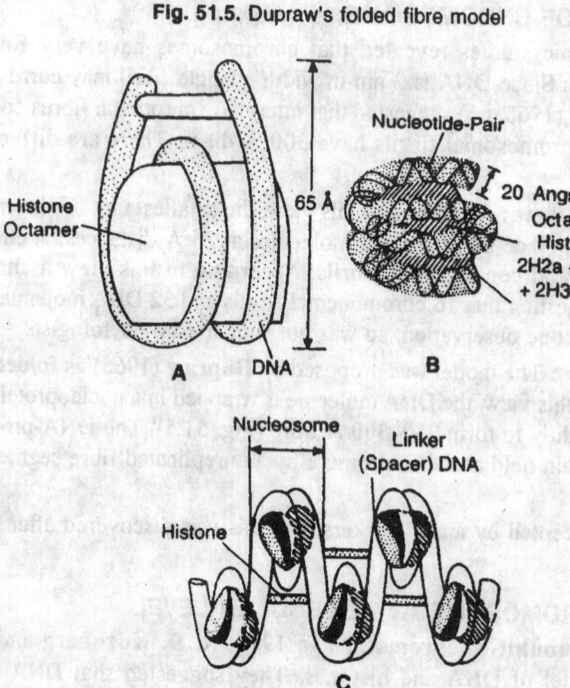

Fig. 51.6. A. Single nucleosome, B. Details of nucleosome, C. Nucleosome with linker DNA.

The model was proposed on the basis of X-ray diffraction, electron microscopy, nuclease digestion and chemical cross-linking (Fig. 51.7).

H1 histone is located just outside the nucleosome core particle and is associated with both ends of the DNA as it enters and exits from the core particle. The nucleosome core particle is a flat structure having dimensions of about 57 × 110 × 110 Å.

The unit fibre according to **Zeuthen** (1978) shows three levels of coiling.

(i) First level of coiling of DNA is in the string of nucleosome.

(ii) The string of nucleosome coils with 300 Å diameter **solenoid** (6–8 nucleosomes).

(iii)Solenoid further coils into **supersolenoid** structure (**Finch and Clug, 1976**) with a diameter of 4000 Å and a wall 300 Å thick. The supersolenoid structure is a **unit fibre.**

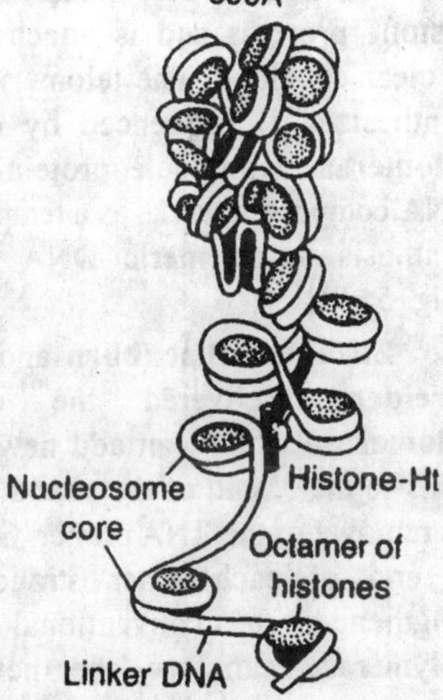

Fig. 51.7. Solenoid structure

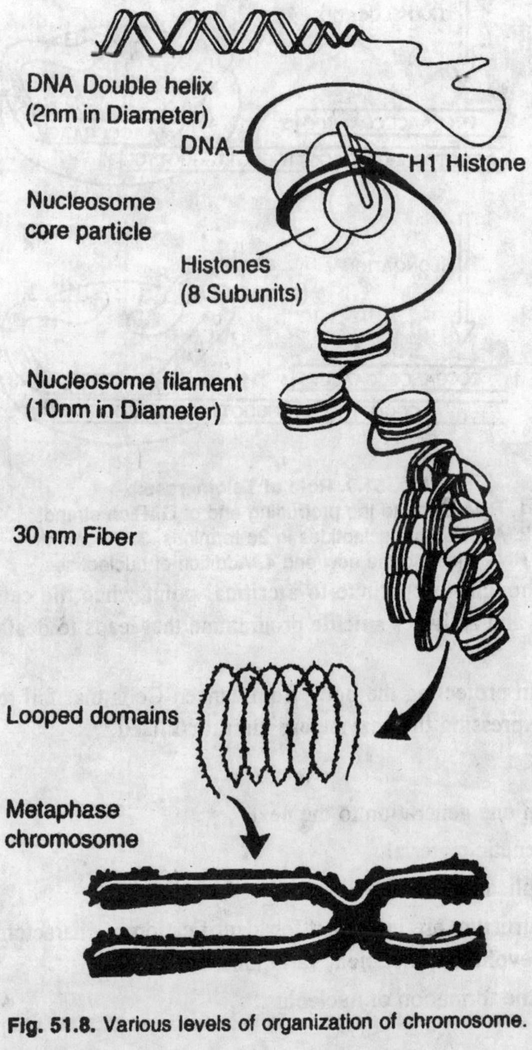

Fig. 51.8. Various levels of organization of chromosome.

The coiling ratio at each level is 7 (nucleosome), 6 (solenoid) and 30–40 (supersolenoid). Overall contraction of DNA within the unit fibre would be 1,300 to 1,500 folds (Fig. 51.8). Unit fibre corresponding **chromonema** which further coils in chromosome.

(B) Telomeres : Telomeres are most conservative elements both in structure and function. Telomeric DNA consists of randomly, repeated sequence of clusters of 'C' on one strand and 'G', on the other. There are 12 + 6 nucleotides in length of G rich strand, *e.g.*, the telomeric repeat sequence in *Tetrahymena* is **GGGGTT,** in *Homosapiens, Neurospora,* slime molds, *Trypanosomas,* etc., it is **AGGGTT,** In *Plasmodium,* it is **AGGG (T/C) TT.** In *Chlamydomonas* it is **AGGGTTTT,** etc.

The same repeated sequence is found at the end of all chromosomes in a species. The same telomeric sequence may occur in widely divergent species. At every telomere at least 10 kilobases of this repeat sequences may occur. The telomeric DNA is associated with non-histone proteins and is attached with nuclear envelope. The telomeric DNA synthesized is influenced by enzyme **telomerase** (ribonucleoprotein whose RNA component works as a template for synthesis of telomeric DNA repeats (Fig. 51.9).

Elizabeth Blackburn and **Carol Greider** discovered the enzyme **telomerase** which can add new repeat units to the 3′ end of the strand created by removal of the RNA primer. Once the 3′ end of each other strand been lengthened, a conventional RNA polymerase can use the newly 3′ segment as a template to return the 5′ ends of the complementary strands to their previous length. Telomerase is a reverse transcriptase that synthesizes DNA using an RNA temptale. The enzyme itself contains the RNA that serves as its template.

Telomere is very important part of a chromosome. It is required for the complete replication of the chromosome. It forms caps that protect the chromosome from nuclease. It prevents the ends of chromosomes from fusing with one another. It facilitates interaction between the ends of the chromosome and the nuclear envelope in some types of cells.

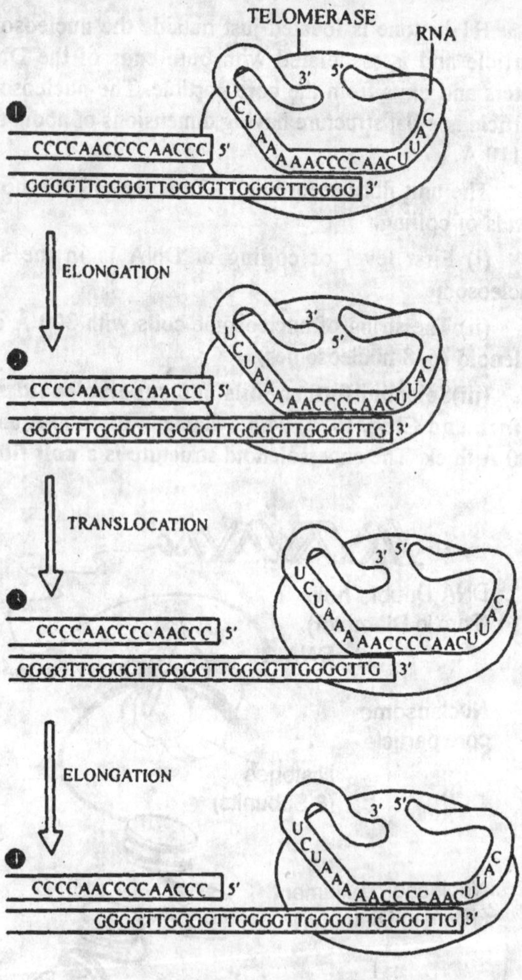

Fig. 51.9. Role of Telomerase: 1. RNA binds to the protruding end of G. Rich strand, 2. Addition of nucleotides in 3¢ terminus, 3. Telomeric RNA slides to the new end 4. Addition of nucleotides.

Telomere shrinking or shortening is thought to continue to a critical point when the cell recognizes the impending loss of a telomere and activates **suicide** programme that leads to death of a cell.

Telomere shortening plays a key role in protecting the body from cancer. Cells that fail to express telomerase die out, where as cells expressing the enzyme are **"immortalized."**

FUNCTIONS OF CHROMOSOME

(i) It carries genetic information from one generation to the next.

(ii) DNA of the chromosome is the genetic material.

(iii) Chromosome replication is the replication of DNA.

(iv) The number of chromosome and structure are important for identification of characters of an organism as they can cause evolution, mutation, variations, etc.

(v) Nucleolar organiser takes part in the formation of nucleolus.

SPECIAL TYPES OF CHROMOSOMES

In certain organisms special types of chromosomes are found, *e.g.*, **lampbrush chromosomes** of vertebrate and **giant chromosmes** of salivary glands of certain insects.

Lampbrush Chromosome

Such type of chromosomes are found in primary oocyte nuclei in amphibians and in some vertebrates. These are found during the prolonged diplotene stage of first meiotic division in primary oocytes of amphibians, and in spermatocyte nuclei of *Drosophila.* The chromosome is very lengthy. Upto 1 mm long chromosomes are observed in urodeles, amphibians.

Lampbrush chromosomes are so named because of their appearance like glass chimneys of kerosene lamps. The first description of lampbrush chromosomes was given by **Flemming** in 1882. The details were provided by **J. Ruckert** in 1982 in oocytes of Shark. Lampbrush chromosomes are also observed in *Sagitta, Sepia, Echinaster,* Shark, reptiles and birds beside amphibians and insects.

Lampbrush chromosomes of vcrtebrates are larger than invertebrates. **Grun** (1958) reported them in plant cells.

The size of lampbrush chromosomes may be more than 1,000 μ in length and 20 μ in width. At dikinesis, the chromosomes contract and reduce in size. The lampbrush chromosome of salamander oocytes is of 5900 μ in length.

Structure of Lampbrush Chromosome

During early prophase, they are in the form of homologous chromosomes with some **chiasmata.** It has an **axis** along which a row of dense granules or **chromomeres** are found. From each chromomere a pair of lateral loop arises (Fig.45.10).

Chromosomal axis : The two chromatids of the chromosome are made up of **axial filaments.** The pair of homologous chromosomes has **four** filametns in all. The axial filaments and chromomeres consist of DNA. The loops are extensions of axial filaments. The ends of axial filaments without loops is the **telomere.** Centromere is also present which is loop free.

Chromomere : The axial filaments at some points are tightly coiled. These points are the **chromomeres.** According to **Ris,** (1957) they are found in pairs, *i.e.*, one chroromomere on each filament; corresponding to heterochromatin.

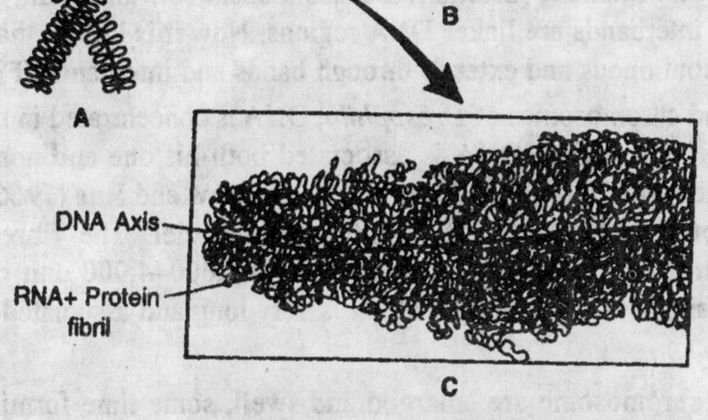

Fig. 51.10. Structure of Lampbrush chromosome.

Loops : Loops are **typical** and **special** type. **Typical loops** consist of a central axis from where RNA fibrils of progressively increasing length come out, making the loop thick. **Special loops** show asymmetry and have granules at the fibrils. Length of each loop may vary between 5-100 μm.

Each loop consists of an **axial fibre** covered with matrix (Fig. 51.11). The loop is made up of DNA and the matrix is made up of RNA. Because when the loop is treated with **deoxyribonuclease** enzyme the loop breaks down and when treated with **ribonuclease** the matrix breaksdown. The loop is believed to represent one long operon consisting of a series of identical copies of structural genes or cistron. Each gene codes for 45 S *r*-RNA and produces a very long RNA molecule interacting with protein to form ribonuceloprotein. If the activity of genes is stopped by **actinomycin** D, the loops will collapse. The matrix free regions between genes loci is the region of 'spacer' DNA which do not produce RNA. At one end of spacer DNA region, dense granules of RNA-polymerase are attached to the **promoter region** the other end is the termination region. Many of the loops correspond to a single transcriptional unit and show a continuous thin thick matrix. Other loops contain several units of transcription. Some transcriptional units in lampbrush chromosomes are extremely long even upto 100 μm in length (1 μm of DNA = 3000 base pairs). The long transcriptional units of lampbrush chromosomes may be due to a failure of transcription termination.

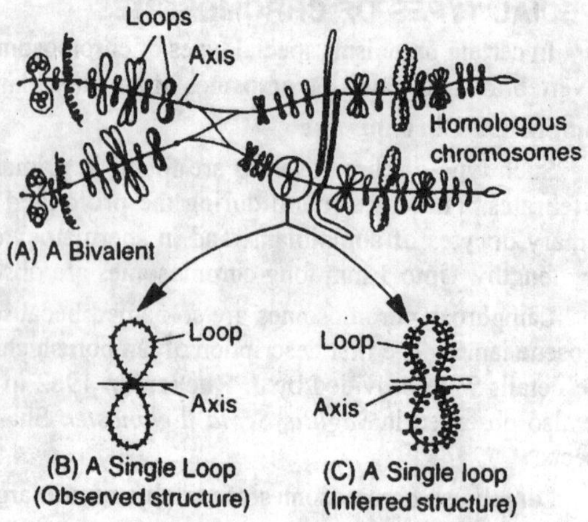

Fig. 51.11. Detailed structure of lampbrush chromosome.

Some *m*RNA produced by lampbrush chromosome is also stored as **informosome,** *i.e.*, *m*-RNA coated by protein for producing biochemicals during the early development of embryo.

Polytene chromosome

These are also called as **salivary gland chromosomes;** normally visible during interphase. Polytene chromosomes are observed first **by Balbiani** (1881) in the salivary gland of *Chironomous*. The first description of these chromosomes was given by **Kollar** (1882). All the chromosomes of a particular type in the individual have an equal number of bands with similar distribution. Topographical maps of bands and interbands are parallel to genetic maps.

Painter (1933) and **Bridges** (1936) showed that the bands of polytene chromosomes have close relationship to genes. Mutations (deletion) are also associated with certain bands. The bands are the sites of genes or interbands are linker DNA regions. Now it is known that interbands also contain genes. DNA is continuous and extends through bands and interbands (Fig. 51.12).

In the salivary gland chromosomes of *Drosophila*, DNA is concentrated in the bands while it is very little in the interband region. DNA is associated both histone and non-histone protein forming nucleoprotein fibres of 100-500 Å. According to **Dupraw** and **Rae** (1966) these fibres are comparable to nucleoprotein fibres found in interphasic nuclei. The fibres correspond to chromatids. The polytene chromosome is formed by about 1,000–4,000 unit chromatids. Each chromatid consists of a single DNA molecule which is very long and associated with protein.

Chromosome puffs

The bands of this chromosome are enlarged and swell, some time forming **chromosome puffs** or **Balbiani** rings. According to **Beerman and Bahr** (1954) the puff represent the regions of tightly coiled chromosomal fibres to form many loops. Puffing is due to unfolding or uncoiling of individual chromomere in a band. Puffs are active genes and sites of RNA synthesis. This can be proved as :

(a) The puffs contain large amount of RNA while puffless area contain DNA and histones. This can be seen by staining the area with toludine blue; RNA takes violet strain and DNA blue.

(b) Radioactive **uridine** when injected, the chromosome shows black spots indicating RNA.

(c) Actinomycin D inhibits RNA formation.

(d) Radioactive leucine is injected to see that protein is labelled but the protein in puff is not labelled. It shows that the proteins in the puff are not made in chromosome. **Chloramphenicol** and **puromycin** (protein synthesis inhibitor) has no effect on puffs.

***m*-RNA synthesis**

Puffs actively synthesise ***m*-RNA** but no protein synthesises the *m*-RNA of one puff varies from the *m*-RNA of other. The *m*RNA formed in puffs moves out in the cytoplasm where it synthesises special type of protein.

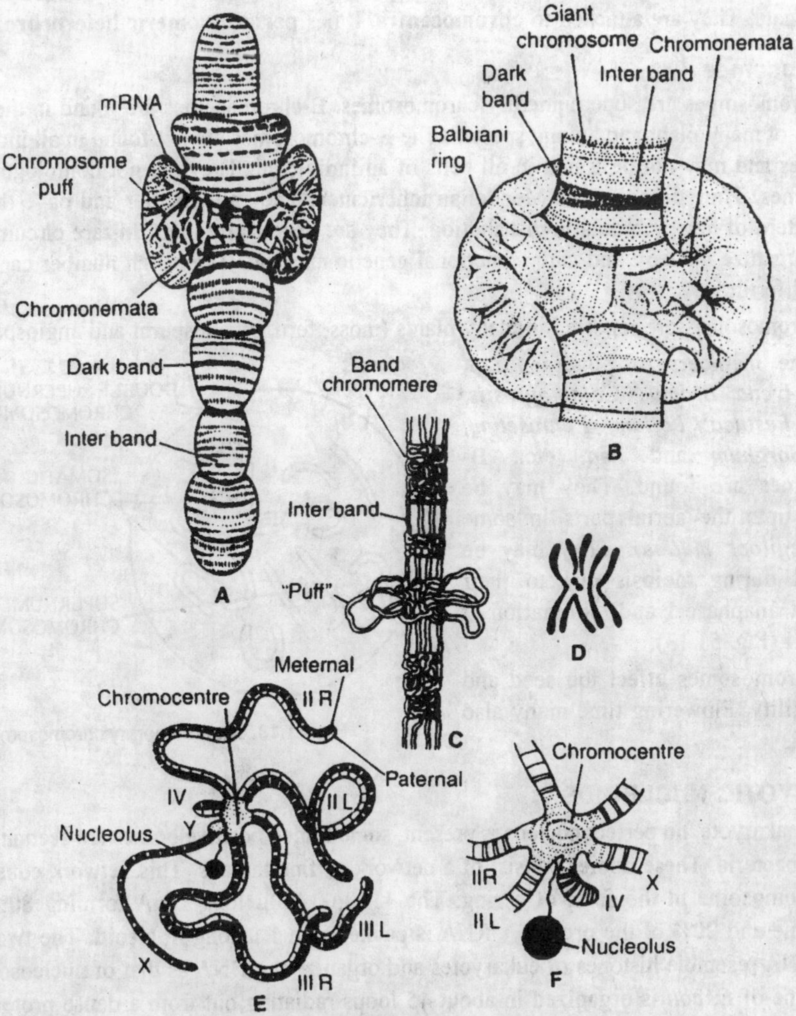

Fig. 51.12. Details of polytene chromosome.

The giant chromosomes represent a bundle of fibrils which arise by repeated cycles of endoreduplication of single chromatids. The chromatin replicates without cell division resulting into a number of chromonemata. Due to many chromosomes, it is also called as **polytene chromosome** and the process as **polyteny.** The number of chromonemata/chromosome may reach upto 2000 to 16000.

In *Drosophila melanogaster,* the giant chromosome is in the form of 5 long and 1 short strand radiating from a single chromocentre (Fig. 51.12 E, F). Qne long strand represents the 'X' chromosome and the other four long strands are the arms of II and III chromosomes. The centromeres of these chromosomes fuse to form **chromocentre.** In male flies, Y chromosome also fuses with chromocentre.

Polytene chromosomes are found in malpighian tubules, fat bodies, ovarian nurse cells, gut epithelium, etc., apart of salivary gland.

Polytene chromosomes are reported in endosperm cells of embryosac by **Malik** and **Singh** (1979). Length of this chromosome may be upto 2000 μm. The chromosome is formed by somatic pairs between homologous chromosomes and repeated replication or endomitosis of chromonemata. They are attached to **chromocentre.** It has **pericentromeric heterochromatin.**

B-Chromosomes

B-chromosomes are supernumerary chromosomes. B-chromosomes are found in the natural population of many plant and animal species. The B-chromosomes are not found in all individuals of a species and may not be found in all cells of an individual. They are not homologous to A-chromosomes. They do not show Mendelian inheritance. They are smaller and have their own unique pattern of heterochromatin distribution. They are genetically inert. In rare circumstances, they can organize nucleoli and carry functional genetic material. Their high number can supress vigour and fertility.

B-chromosomes are reported in many plants (moss, fern, gymnosperm and angiosperm).

In the members of poaceae, *e.g., Agrostis, Avena, Bromus, Calamogrostis, Dactylis, Festuca, Lolium, Pennisetum, Secale, Sorghum* and *Zea*, etc., B-chromosomes are found. They may be restricted upto the aerial parts in some plants *(Aegilops mutica).* They may be eliminated during meiosis due to their division at anaphase I and elimination at anaphase II (Fig. 51.13).

B chromosomes effect the seed and pollen fertility. Flowering time many also be delayed.

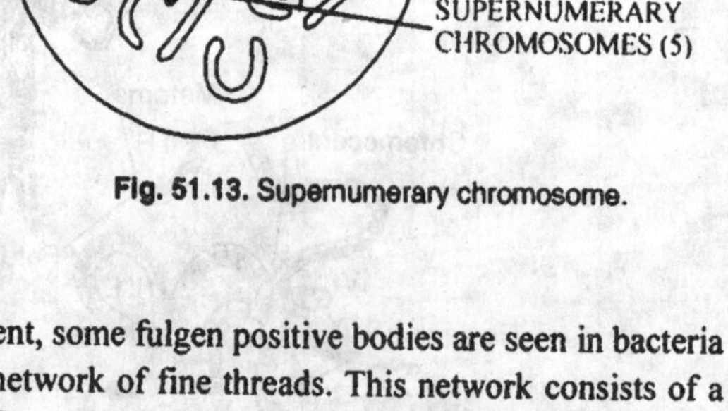

Fig. 51.13. Supernumerary chromosome.

PROKARYOTIC NUCLEOIDS

In proakaryote, no perfect nucleus is present, some fulgen positive bodies are seen in bacteria and cyanobacteria. These bodies consist of a network of fine threads. This network consists of a single chromosome in the form of a ring. The 1100μ-1400μ long DNA forming 80% of the chromosome and 20% of the protein + RNA is packed in a 1 μ long **nucleoid.** The two protein binding DNA resemble histones of eukaryotes and organize the DNA as that of nucleosome. The chromosome of *E. coli* is organized in about 45 loops radiating out from a dense proteinaceous scaffold. In each of the 45 loops, DNA is supercoiled and complexed with protein (Fig. 51.14).

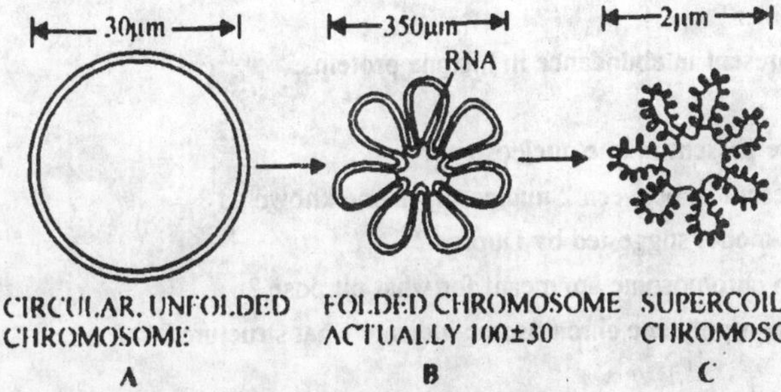

Fig. 51.14. Structure of nucleoid.

SUMMARY

1. Chromosomes were first observed by **Strasburger** (1875) who gave the law of constant number of chromosomes.
2. **Waldeyer** (1888) coined the term chromosome.
3. **Sutton** and **Boveri** (1902) proved that chromosome is physical basis of heredity.
4. Chromosome is so called because it is stained by basic stains.
5. **Morgan** (1933) showed the importance of chromosome in heredity.
6. Chromosome number for a species remain always the same. It is diploid in somatic cell and haploid in gametes.
7. Haploid number is shown in 'n' and diploid by '2n'.
8. Length of chromosome is 0.1μ – 30μ and diameter 0.2μ–2μ.
9. Shape of chromosome is clear in anaphase of cell division. On the basis of centromere position, they are I, J, L and V shaped.
10. The secondary constriction possessing chromosomes are called SAT chromosome.
11. Beaded structures present on chromosome are called chromomeres.
12. Thread-like structures at the metaphase stage of cell division in each chromosome are called **chromatid.** Each chromatid is made up of one molecule of DNA.
13. Barenetzky (1888) first observed chromatid in *Tradescantia* pollen grains.
14. The term **chromonema** is coined by **Vegdovsky** (1912).
15. **Balbiani** (1876) discovered chromomeres.
16. **Belling** (1928) shown 1500-2500 chromomere on a haploid chromosome in *Aloe* and *Lilium.*
17. **Johanssen** (1909) coined the term gene.
18. **Callened Lloyd** (1960) suggested that one loop of lampbrush chromosome is equal to a gene.
19. **Berman** (1967) suggested that one black band of polytene chromosome is equal to a gene.
20. **Woodcock** (1973) termed the beaded structure on chromosome as **nucleosome.**
21. Nucleosome is an octomer of 4 histone proteins complexed with DNA (Oudet *et al*).
22. Every 3/4 turns of DNA have 166 base pairs. When H_1 histone is added the nucleotide number becomes 200.
23. 6 nucleosomes coil to form a solenoid.
24. Many solenoids coil to form a chromatid.
25. **Klug** (1982) discovered **solenoid.**

QUESTION BANK

Very Short Answer Questions

1. Write the names of chromosomes according to the position of centromere.
2. What is primary construction known as?

3. What is nucleolar organizer?
4. Name the amino acids present in abundance in histone proteins.
5. What is solenoid?
6. How many base pairs are present in one nucleosome?
7. What is the structure present in between 2 nucleosomes one known as ?
8. What is the name of the model suggested by Dupraw?
9. The loops of Lampbrush chromosome are meant for what purpose ?
10. The interbands or bands on polytene chromosome indicate what structure ?

Short Answer Questions

1. What is nucleosome; describe and make well labelled diagram.
2. Draw the diagram of chromosome structure.
3. Write short note on giant chromosome.
4. Write in brief the strucutre of polytene chromosome.
5. Write about the structure of chromosome at molecular level.
6. Write briefly about folded fibre model of Dupraw.
7. Write short notes on (a) Telomere (b) Centromere.
8. Write notes on :
   (*a*) Histone protein (b) Non-histone protein
9. Write briefly about the different types of chromatin present at different parts of chromosome.
10. Write short note on kinetochore.

Long Answer Questions

1. Write in detail the structure of chromosome. Describe its various functions with suitable diagrams.
2. Describe the structure and functions of Lampbrush chromosome.
3. Describe the structure and functions of Polytene chromosome.

Multiple Choice Questions (Objective Type Questions)

1. One genome is equal to :
   (a) A set of chromosome (b) A name of animal
   (c) A name of plant (d) A set of gene
2. Centromere is found in :
   (a) ER (b) Ribosome
   (c) Golgi body (d) Chromosome
3. Kinetochore is related to :
   (a) Centrosome (b) Centriole
   (c) Centromere (d) Chromomere
4. The basic unit of eukaryotic chromosome is :
   (a) DNA (b) Chromonema
   (c) Nucleosome (d) Nucleoid
5. Salivary gland chromosomes or polytene chromosomes are found in salivary glands of :
   (a) Rabbit (b) Mouse
   (c) Dog (d) Insect
6. One chromatid has :
   (a) One DNA molecule (b) Two DNA molecules
   (c) Three DNA molecules (d) One DNA and one RNA molecule
7. Nucleolar organizer is :
   (a) Primary constriction (b) Secondary constriction
   (c) Centromere (d) Chromatid

8. Chromosomes are chemically made up of :
   (a) DNA only (b) DNA + RNA
   (c) RNA only (d) DNA + protein
9. The term gene was given by :
   (a) Johanssen (b) Waldeyer
   (c) de Duve (d) Virchow
10. Centromere is related with :
   (a) DNA replication (b) Breaking of chromosomes
   (c) Polar movement of chromosome (d) Spindle formation
11. Balbiani rings contain high amount of :
   (a) DNA and *m*-RNA (b) Only DNA
   (c) Only *m*-RNA (d) Heterochromatin
12. Chromosome number of hexaploid is 48, then its basic chromosome number would be :
   (a) 8 (b) 16
   (c) 32 (d) 24
13. Prokaryotic organism lack :
   (a) True nucleus (b) Nuclear membrane
   (c) Histone protein (d) All the above
14. Histone proteins have large amount of :
   (a) Glycine and glutamic acid (b) Prolein and phenylalanine
   (c) Lysine and argenine (d) Methionine and argenine
15. Chromosomes with equal arms are called:
   (a) Telocentric (b) Acentric
   (c) Metacentric (d) Acrocentric
16. Allosomes are:
   (a) Sex chromosomes (b) Autosomes
   (c) Somatic chromosome (d) Supernumerary chromosome
17. Histone rich in arginine is :
   (a) H_3 (b) H_1
   (c) H_2A and H_2B (d) H_3 and H_4
18. Nucleosome contains :
   (a) 8 carbohydrate molecules (b) 8 histone molecules
   (c) 8 lipid molecules (d) 8 nucleotide molecules
19. Part of chromosome staining dark is :
   (a) Euchromatin (b) Heterochromatin
   (c) Histone protein (d) All the above
20. Non-histone chromosomal protein help in :
   (a) Transcription (b) Translation
   (c) Both 'a' and 'b' (d) Transduction
21. Physical basis of heredity is :
   (a) Protoplasm (b) Nucleus
   (c) Chromosome (d) DNA
22. Paranemic coiling is found in .... stage of cell division.
   (a) Interphase (b) Prophase
   (c) Metaphase (d) G_o phase

23. Nucleosomes are also called as :
(a) Histone core (b) nu particles
(c) Gamma particles (d) All the above

24. Nucleosomes do not contain :
(a) H_1 histone (b) H_2A histone
(c) H_2B histone (d) H_4 histone

25. 'L' shaped chromosomes are :
(a) Acrocentric (b) Submetacentric
(c) Telocentric (d) Subcentric

26. A genophore or nucleoid consists of :
(a) A single stranded DNA (b) Histones only
(c) Double stranded DNA (d) Protein and non-histones

27. Spring *et al* in 1975 reported lampbrush chromosomes in :
(a) *Drosophila* (b) *Lychnis*
(c) *Acetabularia* (d) *Coccinia*

28. B-chromosomes are also called as :
(a) Autosome (b) Allosome
(c) Holandric chromosome (d) Supernumerary chromosome

29. Malik and Singh in 1979 reported presence of Polytene chromosomes in :
(a) *Drosophila* (b) Salivary glands
(c) Endosperm cells of embryosac (d) Oocytes

30. **Lampbrush** chromosomes are also called diplotene chromosomes because they :
(a) Resemble-diplotene chromosomes (b) Show chiasmata
(c) Are in permanent diplotene stage (d) All the above

ANSWERS

1. (a)	2. (d)	3. (c)	4. (c)	5. (d)	6. (a)
7. (b)	8. (d)	9. (a)	10. (c)	11. (b)	12. (a)
13. (d)	14. (c)	15. (c)	16. (a)	17. (d)	18. (b)
19. (b)	20. (a)	21. (c)	22. (b)	23. (b)	24. (a)
25. (b)	26. (c)	27. (c)	28. (d)	29. (c)	30. (c)

52

CHAPTER

Sex Chromosomes

Every cell of the organism bears two types of chromosomes.

(a) Autosomones

(b) Allosomes

Allosomes are the **sex chromosomes** which are very much necessary. One set of sex chromosomes is necessary to determine the sex of the organism. **Sex linkage** occurs when the genes controlling various traits are present on the **sex chrumosome.** The sex chromosomes are not necessarily present in morphologically identical pairs in both sexes. The traits present on them exhibit unique **sex-linked patterns of Inheritance.**

The sexually reproducing organisms are classified into 3 types:

(a) Hermaphrodite : In plants, generally both male and female reproductive parts are present in the single individual.

(b) Monoecious : When the flowers are unisexual (male or female) but present on the same plant.

(c) Dioecious : When both male or female individiuals are different.

Sexus means section or separation. The male has **male gonad** and the female has ovaries or **female gonad.** Such kind of separation is called **gonochorism.** The difference in sex cells and reproductive organs is called **primary sexual characters.** The somatic or morphological differences between male and female is called **secondary sexual character.**

The phenomenon of molecular, morphological, physiological or behavioural differentiation between male and female sexes is known as **sexual dimorphism.**

Genetically controlled sex determining mechanism is classified into following categories:

(a) Sex chromosome mechanism or heterogamesis

(b) Genic balance mechanism

(c) Male haploidy or haplo-diploidy mechanism

(d) Single gene effect

(a) Sex chromosome mechanism (Heterogamesis)

Besides sexual dimorphism, the chromosomes also differ in the male and female organisms. **Henking** (1891) a German biologist studied the spermatogenesis of **squash bug,** *Pyrrhocoris*, and observed that half of the spermatozoa contained an extra chromosome and called them as **'X'** body. In 1902 **McClung** observed gametogenesis in grasshoppers and suggested the importance of 'X' body in determination of sex. He reported that the somatic cells of the female grasshopper (*Xiphidium fasciatum*) contained 24 chromosomes where as the male grasshopper has only 23 chromosomes. After intensive studies by **Stevens** and **Wilson** it was confirmed that 'X' body is nothing but the **'X' chromosome.**

The 'X' chromosome is also called sex chromosome because it is important in determining the sex. In *Lygaeus turicicus* (milkweed bug) both male and female carry 14 chromosomes. In female, all chromosomes are paired and the homologues are of equal size, while in male all chromosomes are paired but the homologue of 'X' chromosome is not identical it is called 'Y' chromosome.

STRUCTURE OF SEX CHROMOSOME

There is definite difference between 'X' and 'Y' chromosome. 'X' chromosomes are straight rod like and larger than 'Y' chromosome. However, the 'Y' chromosome is smaller and **curved** in *Drosophila* (Fig 46.1). In man and *Melandrium* the 'Y' chromosome is also straight (Fig. AB). The 'X' chromosomes have large amount of euchromatin. The 'Y' chromosomes have little amount of euchromatin. The 'X' chromosome contains many genes and 'Y' a few genes. 'Y' chromosome is also called genetically **inert** chromosome.

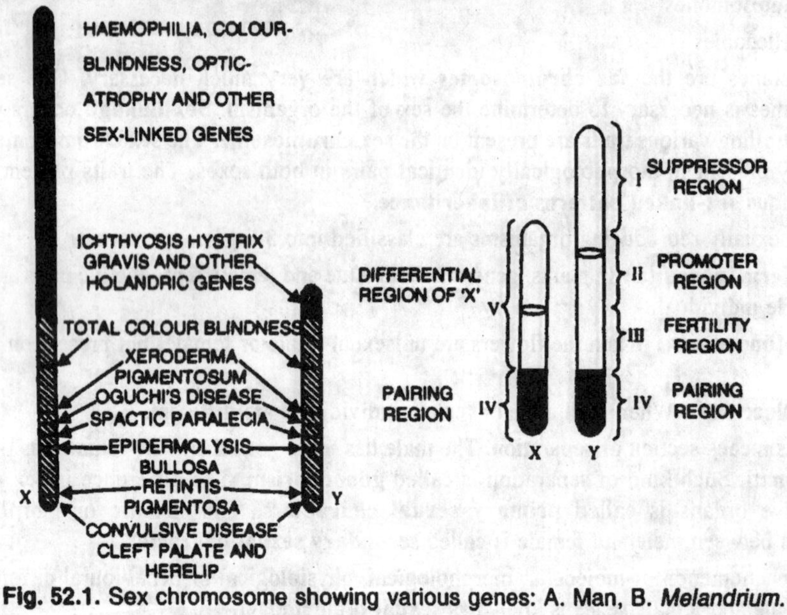

Fig. 52.1. Sex chromosome showing various genes: A. Man, B. *Melandrium.*

COMPOUND SEX CHROMOSOME

'X' chromosome is most commonly found as a single chromosome on single homologous pair of chromosomes. In some species, it is compound or more than one kind of 'X' chromosome that act together as a **sex-determining** group. In such species, there is a large difference in the number of chromosomes between male and females, *e.g.*, in the nematode *Ascaris incurva* the number of autosome pair is **13** but the number of compound **X** chromosome is **8.** A male therefore forms two types of gametes 8 X + A (21 chromosome) and Y +A (14 chromosomes). While the female forms only 8X+A (21 chromosome type), upon fertilization, the diploid number of chromosomes is therefore **35** in males and **42** in females

$$\underset{\text{sperm}}{(8X + A)} + \underset{\text{egg}}{(8X + A)} = 16X + 2A = \text{female}$$

$$\underset{\text{sperm}}{(Y + A)} + \underset{\text{egg}}{(8X + A)} = 8X + Y + 2A = \text{male}$$

The 'Y' chromosome may also exist as a compound group, and in some cases both compound Xs and compound Ys may be found together in the same species. *Blaps polychresta* (beetle) also has compound sex chromosome. The male has 12 Xs and 6 Ys in addition to 18 autosomes.

SEX DETERMINATION

Types of sex chromosomal mechanism in sex determination

In dioecious organism two system of sex chromosomal determination of sex is observed.

(A) Heterogametic male

The female sex has 2 'X' chromosomes (XX) while male has only one 'X' chromosome and at the time of gametogenesis produces 2 types of gametes. 50% with 'X' chromosome while other 50% without 'X' chromosome. Because of 2 types of gametes produced by males it is called **heterogametic sex** (male). While the females are **homogametic.**

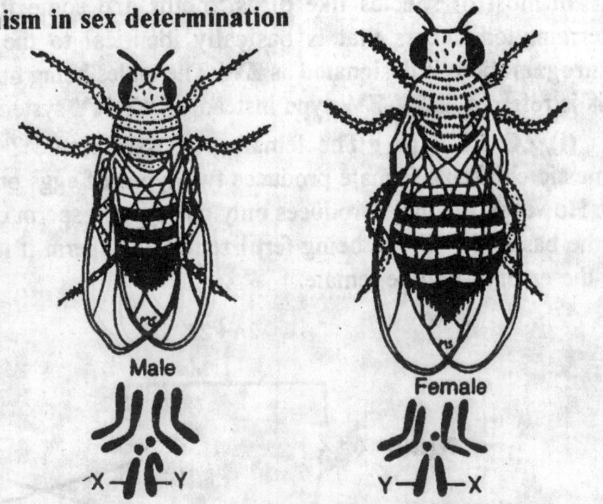

Fig. 52.2. Sex chromosomes in *Drosophila:* A. Male and female. B. Shape of chromosomes in male and female

Heterogametic males are of two types :

(i) XX-XY type : In man, other mammals, plants and many insects like *Drosophila,* etc., the female has homogametic XX type while male has X and Y chromosomes. The female produces only one type of gametes while male produces two types of gametes 'X' and 'Y'. The sex of the embryo depends on the type of sperm or male gamete (X or Y type). If the female gamete is fertilized by 'X' sperm the embryo will be carrying female sex while if it is fertilized by 'Y' sperm the embryo will be male (Fig. 52.2).

(ii) XX-XO type : In some insects like grasshopper, bugs, etc., females are homogametic XX type but the male has only one sex chromosome, *i.e.*, 'X' only, there is no 'Y' chromosome, hence the chromosome number of the male and female will be different. The male has chromosome number one less than that of female. The female will produce only one type of eggs ('X') but male produces 50% sperm with 'X' and other 50% without 'X'. The sex of offspring depends upon the sperm that fertilizes the egg (Fig. 52.3).

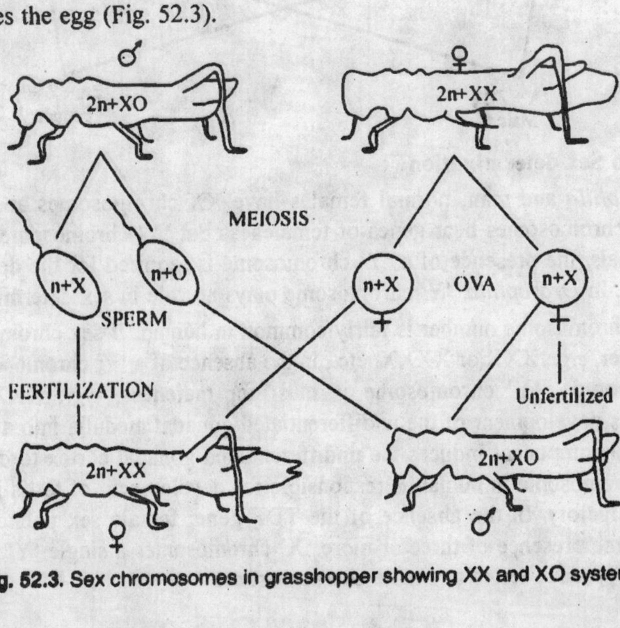

Fig. 52.3. Sex chromosomes in grasshopper showing XX and XO system.

(B) Heterogametic females

In most of species like birds, moths and some fish a chromosomal mechanism of sex determination occurs that is basically identical to the **XX-XY** mechanism. As females are **heterogametic** it is designated as **ZW.** The males being **homogametic,** they are designated as **ZZ.** This is referred as **ZZ-ZW** type instead of **XX-XY** system.

(i) ZO-ZZ type : The female possesses single Z chromosome in moth, butterflies and domestic chickens. Female produces two types of eggs one with 'Z' chromosomes other without 'Z'. However, the male produces only one type of sperm carrying 'Z' only. The sex is determined on the basis of egg type being fertilized by the sperm if it contains Z the embryo will be male if not the embryo will be female.

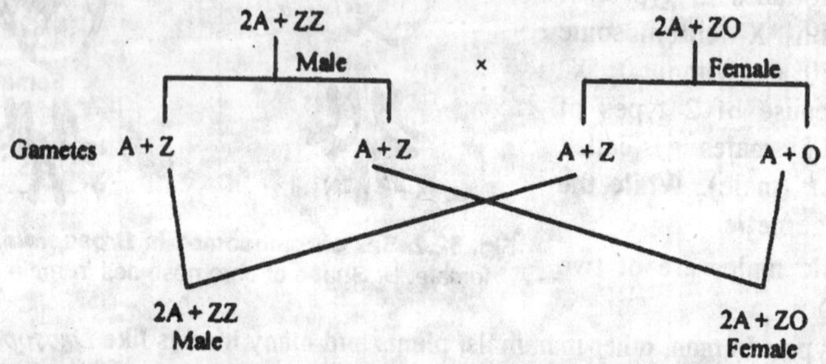

(ii) ZW-ZZ type : It is common in insects, vertebrates like fish reptiles, birds, etc. Females are heterogametic with ZW and males are homogametic with ZZ. Female produces two types of eggs, *i.e.*, 50% with 'Z' or 50% with 'W' while male produces only one type of sperms, *i.e.*, with 'Z'. The sex of the offspring depends on the type of egg it was fertilized.

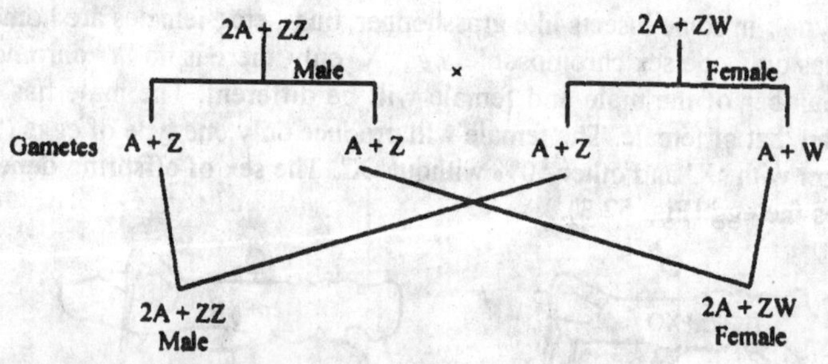

'Y' Chromosome in Sex determination

In both *Drosophila* and man, normal females have XX chromosomes and male has XY chromosomes. 'X' chromosomes bear genes of femaleness but 'Y' chromosome bears genes of maleness. In mammals, the presence of a 'Y' chromosome is required for the development of a male sex phenotype. In *Drosophila,* 'Y' chromosome plays no role in sex determination.

Irregular sex chromosome number is fairly common in human. If sex chromosomes 'X' are present in any number, *e.g.*, XXX or XXXX, etc., in the absence of a 'Y' chromosome give rise to a female sex phenotype. 'Y' chromosome is must for maleness, *e.g.*, XXXXY. The 'Y' chromosome induces development of the undifferentiated gonadal medulla into a **testis,** whereas an XX chromosomal component induces the undifferentiated gonadal cortex to develop ovaries. The gene on 'Y' chromosome in human is responsible for development of testis is called **'TDF'** (testis determining factor). In the absence of the TDF gene, female sex phenotype would be expressed. Even in the presence of three or more 'X' chromosomes a single 'Y' chromosome is usually sufficient to produce testes and male characteristics.

In *Melandrium album* (XY type) **Warmke and Westergaard** and others have shown that sex is determined by a balance between male-determining genes on the 'Y' chromosome and female determining genes on the 'X' and autosomes. In this plant, which is dioecious 'XY' individuals are staminate and 'XX' plants are pistillate. The 'Y' chromosome is the largest and most conspicuous (Fig. 52.1B). Three distinct regions of this chromosome influence in sex determination and male fertility.

Region I suppresses femaleness, in the absence of it plants are bisexual, *i.e.*, they express both male and femaleness.

Region II promotes male development when this region is missing with or without I region a female plant is produced.

Region III carries male fertility genes loss of this region results in male sterility. Only a part of 'Y' chromosome (Region IV) is homologous to 'X' but the major part of 'X' is differentiated with no structural counterpart on the 'Y'. **Westergaard** found that autosomes were also involved in female determination.

Genic Balance Concept of Sex determination In *Drosophila*

C. B. Bridges showed that female determiners were located on the 'X' chromosomes and male determiners were on autosomes. No specific loci were identified at that time. But recent evidences demonstrate that many chromosome segments are involved specifically, female determining genes were shown to be carried on the 'X' chromosomes and male determiner genes were shown to be located on the three autosomal chromosomes of *Drosophila.* The **genic balance theory** of sex determination was devised to explain the mechanics of sex determination in *D. melanogaster.* (Fig. 52.4)

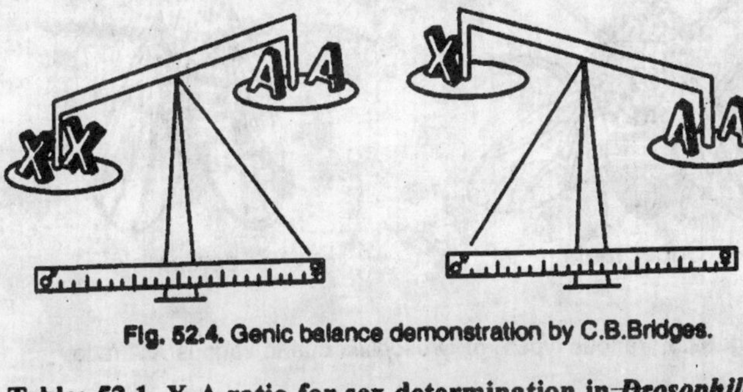

Fig. 52.4. Genic balance demonstration by C.B.Bridges.

Table: 52.1. X-A ratio for sex determination in *Drosophila*.

'X' chromosome	'A' chromosome	Ratio X/A	Sex
1X	2A	0.5	Male
2X	2A	1.0	Female
3X	2A	1.5	Metafemale
4X	3A	1.33	Metafemale
4X	4A	1.0	Tetraploid female
3X	3A	1.0	Triploid female
3X	4A	0.75	Intersex
2X	3A	0.67	Intersex
2X	4A	0.5	Tetraploid male
1X	3A	0.33	Meta male

Bridges experimentally produced various combinations of X chromosomes and autosomes (A) in *Drosophila* and deduced from comparisons that one 'X' chromosome and two sets of autosomes (A) produce a normal male. Normal males had a ratio of 'X' chromosomes to sets of autosomes of 0.5 (Table 52.1) (Fig. 52.5).

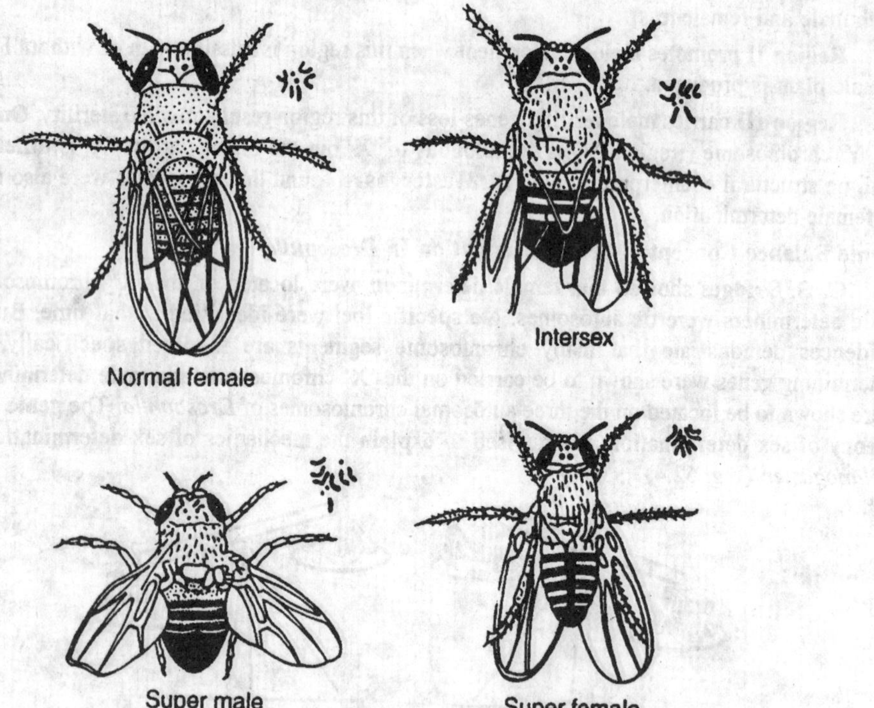

Fig. 52.5. Various types of *Drosophila* due to various *X/A* ratio.

The first irregular chromosome arrangement from **Bridges** experiment resulted from **non-disjunction**, the failure of paired chromosomes to separate in anaphase. X chromosomes, which ordinarily come together in pairs during the meiotic prophase of oogenesis and separate to opposite poles during anaphase, remain together and migrate to the same pole. As a result some female gametes receive 2X chromosomes and the other no X chromosome (Fig. 52.6). After fertilization by sperm from wild type males (2A + XY), all zygotes had 2 sets of autosomes (2A) but some received 2X (XX) from mother and one X from father and became 3X (XXX). The ratio of A/X chromosome was 3 : 2 and the flies were metafemales. The XO males were sterile and those with aY chromosomes and no X chromosome did not survive (Fig. 52.7).

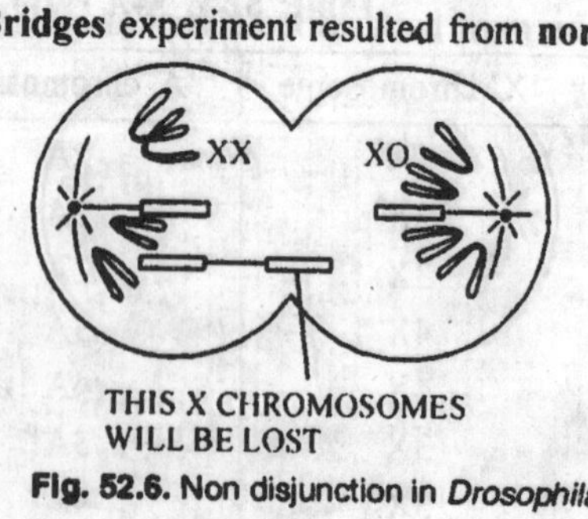

Fig. 52.6. Non disjunction in *Drosophila*.

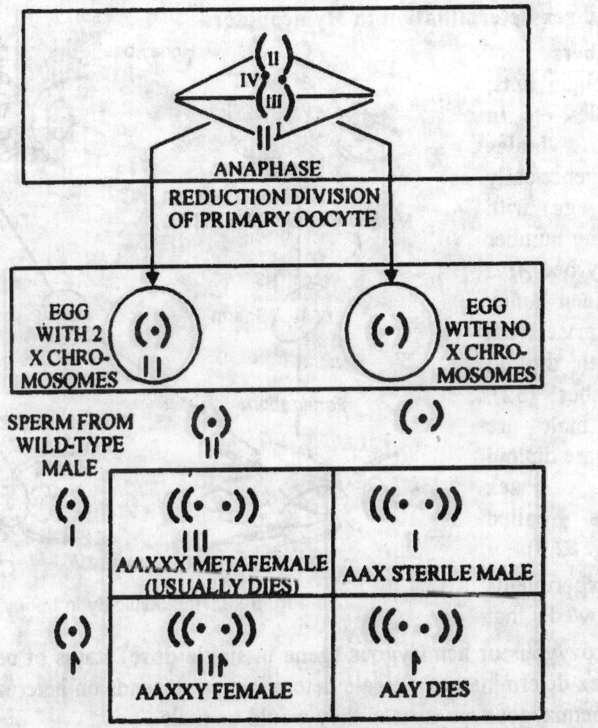

Fig. 52.7. Results of anaphase non-disjunction in *Drosophila*.

2A+XX♀ × 2A+XY♂

	A+X	A+Y
A+XX	2A+XXX Super female (dies)	2A+XXY Female
A + O	2A+XO male	2A+Y (die)

The presence of triploid intersexes in the experiment conducted by Bridges (Fig. 52.8) is a definite proof of autosome carrying factors of sex determination. According to it (genic balance theory) ratio of number of 'X' chromosome and number of complete sets of autosomes determine the sex. The female determiners were located on X chromosome and male determiners on **autosomes.** Recent evidence has demonstrated that many chromosome segments are involved in this process. Female determining genes are carried on 'X' and male determiner genes were located on the three autosomes of *Drosophila.*

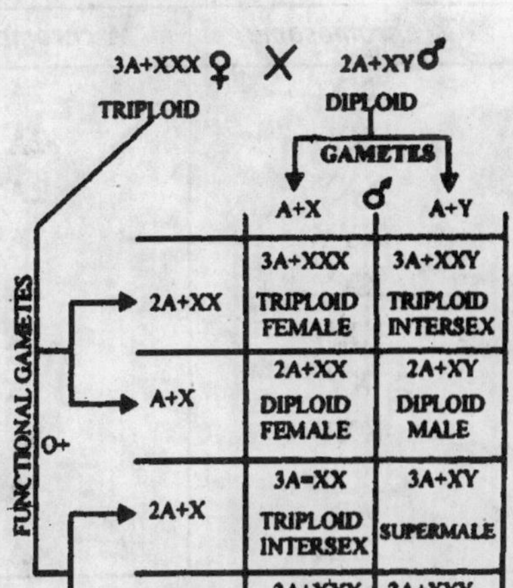

Fig. 52.8. Triploid intersex formation.

Haploidiploidy and sex determination in Hymenoptera

The members of **Hymenoptera** include ants, bees, wasps, sawflies, etc. In several species, **males develop** parthenogenetically (from unfertilized egg) with haploid chromosome number (16 in drone honey bee *Apis mellifera).* The **queen** honey bee and **workers** arise from **fertilized** egg with diploid chromosome number (32). Because normal male are haploid and female are diploid the mechanism of sex determination is called **haplodiploidy** (Fig. 52.9).

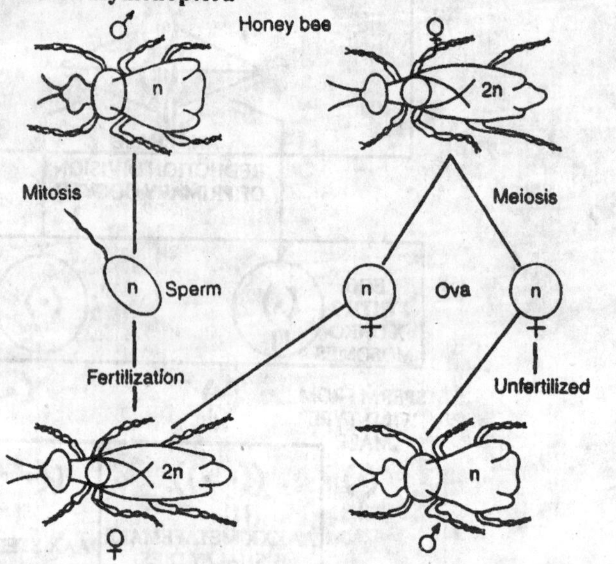

Fig. 52.9. Haplodiploidy in honey bee.

Results of experiments by **Whiting** showed that homozygous, heterozygous or hemizygous (gene in single dose) status of certain chromosome segments control sex determination. Female determination depends on heterozygosity for part of a chromosome. If hemizygous are formed they would be male.

Genic Balance Theory of Sex Determination in Plants

M. Westergaard was first who demonstrated sex determination in plants considering X/A ratio. **R. P. Roy** also studied in detail the sex determination in *Coccinia* and *Melandrium* (unisexual plant). In these plants, 'Y' chromosome is very important. Only 'Y' chromosome's presence makes it male. X/A ratio has nothing to do in it, if even one 'Y' chromosome is present in diploid or polyploid condition the plant will show male characters.

Table 52.2. Sex determination in *Coccinia* and *Melandrium*

X chromosome	*A chromosome*	*X/A ratio*	*Sex*
XX	2A	1.00	Female
XY	2A	0.50	Male
XXY	2A	1.00	Male
XYY	2A	0.50	Male
XXY	3A	0.67	Male
XXX	3A	1.00	Female
XY	4A	0.25	Male
XXY	4A	0.50	Male
XXXY	4A	0.75	Male
XXXXY	4A	1.00	Hermaphrodite

Sex chromosomal mechanism of sex determination has also been observed in monoploid **bryophytes,** *e.g., Spaerocarpos.* **Allen** (1919) found that the sporophyte of *Spaerocarpos* contains **two sex chromosomes (XY)** and it produces two kinds of meiospores (X and Y type) 'X' meiospores germinate into female gametophyte and 'Y' meiospores germinate into male gametophyte.

Mosaic and Gynandromorphs

Abnormal chromosomal behaviour in insect can result in the formation of **'gynandromorph'** or **sexual mosaic,** in which half part of the animal is male and the other half is female. Gynandromorphs in ***Drosophila*** (Fig.46.10) are bilateral intersexes, with male colour pattern, body shape and sexcomb on one half of the body and female charactersitics on the other half. Both male and female gonads and genitalia are present.

Such gynandromorphs are the result of irregularity in mitosis at the first cleavage of zygote. A chromosome lags in division and does not arrive at the pole in time to be included in the reconstructed nucleus. When one of the 'X' chromosomes of an XX (female) zygote lags in the spindle, one daughter nucleus receives only one 'X' chromosome. A mosaic body pattern is established one nucleus in the two nuclei stage would be **XX** (female) and the other would be **XO** (male). It develops into one-half as female and the other as male. In *Bracon bebetor,* gynandromorphs may occur in the anterior posterior plane giving rise to wasp with such peculiar arrangement as **male head** with **female abdomen** or **female head** with **male abdomen.**

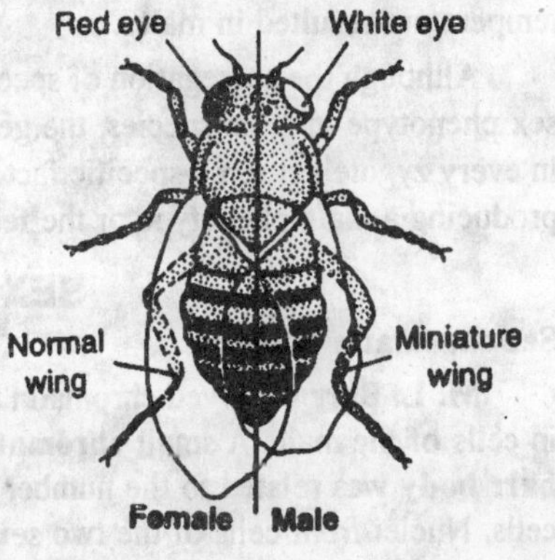

Fig. 52.10. Gynandromorph in *Drosophila.*

Environment factor and sex determination

In some lower animals, the sex determination is non-genetic and depends on factors in the external environment. The genotype of male and female is the same. Stimuli from environment help initiate development toward one sex or the other, *e.g.*, male of marine worm *Bonellia* are small and degenerate and live within the reproductive tract of the larger female (Fig. 52.11). All

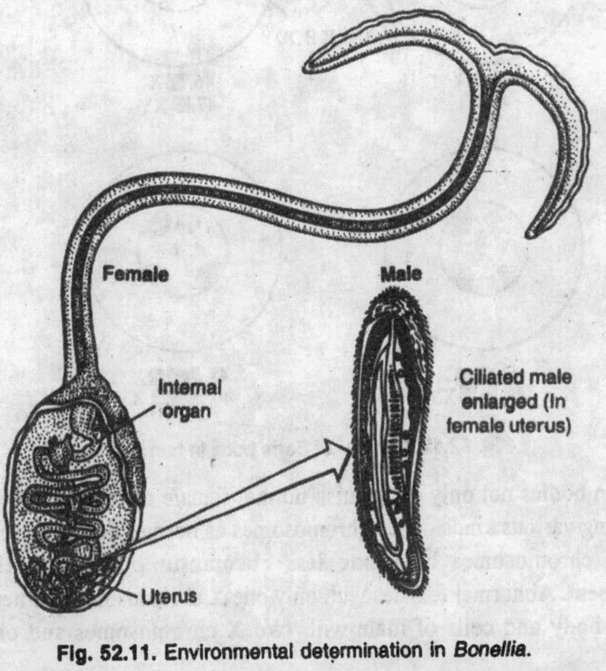

Fig. 52.11. Environmental determination in *Bonellia.*

organs of its body degenerate except the reproductive system. **F Baltzer** found that young worm reared from a single isolated egg became a female. Newly hatched worms in water containing mature females attach to the female proboscis transform into males, and eventually migrate into the female reproductive tracts as parasite. It shows that extract of female proboscis influence the young worm to become male.

In some reptiles, the temperature at the time of incubation prior to hatching plays a major role in determinting sex of offspring. The eggs hatched at 26-27°C developed into female and at 29°C they became male. In turtles (*Chrysema picta*) incubation high temperature (more than 30°C) produced female and at low temperature as male. In lizard (*Agama agama*) high incubation temperature resulted in males.

Although the segregation of specific sex determiner gene and chromosome is responsible for sex phenotype in most species, the genetic potential for both maleness and femaleness is present in every zygote yet some specific factor in the environment triggers the expression of either genes producing a male phenotype or the female phenotype.

SEX DIFFERENTIATION

Sex chromatin bodies

M. L. Barr observed chromatin bodies in the nerve cells of female cats that were not present in cells of the male. A small **chromatin** body was identified in the nucleus of female cells. This **barr body** was related to the number of 'X' chromosomes and was not observed in normal male cells. Nuclei from cells of the two sexes are shown in (Fig.46.12).

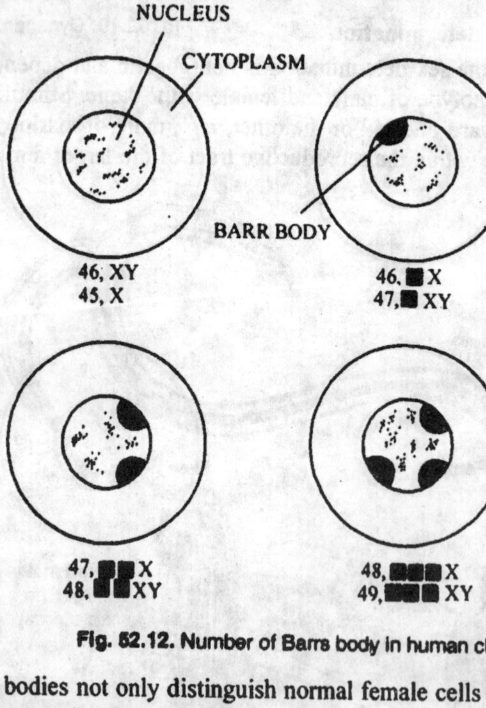

Fig. 52.12. Number of Barrs body in human chromatin.

Sex chromatin bodies not only distinguish normal female cells from male cells, but are also useful for diagnosing various kinds of sex chromosomes as normalities in human. Those who have two or more 'X' chromosomes have **one less chromatin body than the number of X chromosomes present.** Abnormal females with only one X chromosome (Turner's syndrome) have **no sex chromatin body** and cells of male with **two X** chromosomes and one **Y** chromosome

(Klinefelter's syndrome) have one sex chromatin body. Abnormal females with three **X** chromosomes have two sex chromatin bodies in their nuclei.

The sex chromatin appears in the interphase nucleus as a small chromocentre heavily stained with basic dyes (feulgen). It can be found in four positions

(a) Attached to the nucleus of nerve cells,

(b) Attached to the nuclear membrane (epidermis or oral mucosa),

(c) Free in the nucleoplasm (neurons)

(d) As nuclear expansion (neutrophil leucocyte of female where the barr body appears as a small rod called **drum stick**)

The relationship between sex chromatin and sex chromosome is elucidated by **Ohno, Kapan** and **Kinosita** in 1959. The sex chromatin is derived only from one of the 2 **'X'** chromosomes. The other X behaves like autosome and is not **heteropycnotic** at interphase.

Fragile 'X' chromosome

The inactivation of one of the two chromosomes in female mammals must be reversible since female transmit both 'X' chromosomes to their progeny, in functional state 'X' chromosome contains many genes that are vital to growth and development or to survival. The reactivation of the inactive or heterochromatic `X' chromosomes of mammalian females occur in germ cell prior to oogenesis. The abnormal reactivation of heterochromatic X chromosome is partly responsible for inherited mental retardation disease called **'fragile X'syndrome.**

This **'fragile X' chromosome** of humans contains a **fragile site** near the end of long arm (Fig. 52.13). It is the specific region that exhibits constriction. gap or break in cells growing in culture. This particular 'X' chromosome contains a fragile site at position X_q 27 (Fig. 52.13B). The fragile site is inherited as a codominant with both normal and gapped X chromosomes in cells from heterozygotes. The affected individuals show a wide range in severity of mental retardation and other phenotypic manifestation of the syndrome, *i.e.*, hyperactive behaviour, prominant jaws and foreheads, longer than normal ears.

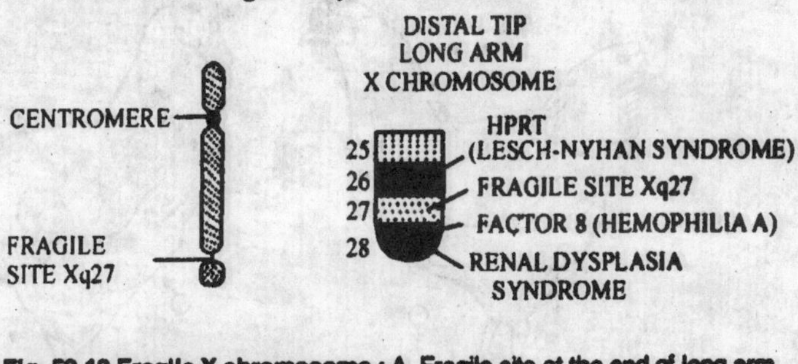

Fig. 52.13 Fragile X chromosome : A. Fragile site at the end of long arm B. Fragile site at position Xq27

The daughter of male who carried the "fragile X" chromosome, did not exhibit phenotypic characteristics of the syndrome, and did not show any manifestation of the syndrome. Fathers always transmit the "fragile X" to their daughters in the same state as they received it from their mothers.

Hormone and Sex differentiation

The hromonal system that regulates the internal or physiological environment of the organism does not directly influence the fundamental process of sex determination. Hormones are necessary to develop the **secondary sex characters.** Sex hormones of higher animals are secreted by ovaries, testes and adrenal glands with stimulation from pituitary gland hormones. Ovaries and testes have dual functions, *i.e.*, production of gamete (sperms or egg) and sex hormones. Hormones influence the development of sexual characters, *e.g.*, physiological difference, bone structure, voice, breast development and hairs, etc. Adrenal gland produces steroids.

Sex Influenced Dominance

The dominance of alleles may differ in heterozygote of the two sexes. This phenomenon is called "sex influenced dominance", *e.g.*, autosomal genes responsible for horns in some breeds of sheep may behave differently in the presence of the **male and female** sex **hormones.**

Some human traits like enlargement of the terminal joints of the fingers, premature patterns of baldness, etc., are types of **sex influenced inheritance. The traits that show the pattern of inheritance characteristic of sex influenced dominance are controlled by genes located on autosomal chromosomes, not on sex chromosomes.** Traits that are governed by genes located on the sex chromosomes exhibit a very distinctive pattern of transmission called sex-linked inheritance.

Sex Limited Gene Expression

One sex may be uniform in expression of a particular trait and yet transfer genes that produce a different phenotype in offspring of the other sex. It is called **sex limited gene expression. Sex hormones** are apparently the **limiting factors** in the expression of some genes, *e.g.*, milk production in mammals is limited to females, but certain bulls are in great demand among dairy breeders and artificial insemination association because their mothers and daughters have increased milk production records. In chickens, redostem generally have long, pointed tail feathers, whereas hens have rather short, blunt tail feather. Same type of feathers are found in many domestic birds (Fig 46.14).

Fig. 52.14. Feathers in hen.

Single gene control of sex

In some organisms like *Chlamydomonas, Neurospora,* yeast, *Asparagus*, maize, *Drosophila*, etc., individual single gene is responsible for the determination or expression of sex.

(a) Sex determination in *Asparagus* : It is a dioecious plant. The female flowers may bear rudimentary anthers and male flowers can bear rudimentary pistils. Rarely a male flower can

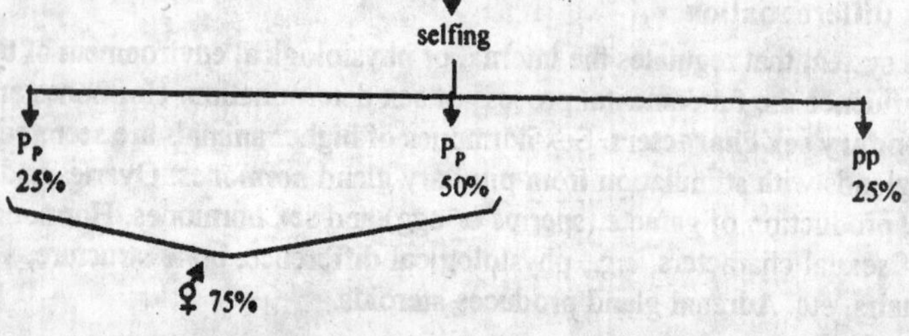

develop pistil and may set seeds. Plants raised from such seeds show male and female plants in 3 : 1 ratio. When male plants are used to pollinate female flowers of female plant only two-third of them segregate. It shows that the sex is controlled by single gene.

(b) Monogenic sex determination in maize : It is a monoecious plant with male inflorescence called **tassel** and female inflorescence as **silk.**

A gene **tassel seed** converts the tassel into seed bearing inflorscence. While gene **silkness** (Sk) is responsible for the absence of silks. A plant with genotype Sk/Sk will be a male plant. Plant with ts/ts will be female. But individual with Sk ts can impose bisexuality in maize.

Metabolically controlled sex determination

Crew suggested that sex is a physiological equitable division between catabolic and anabolic types. **Shull** and **Whitney** showed that by increasing metabolic rate in rotifers the occurrence of male individuals increases than females. **Riddle** suggested that metabolism in pigeon and doves plays an important role as increased rate of metabolism develop maleness.

Hormonally controlled sex determination

Sexual differentiation is controlled by hormones controlling sex of an individual.

Sex reversal in hen : In birds only one gonad of a normal female develops into a functional ovary. If this is destroyed the rudimentary other gonad develops into testes (**Crew** 1925). The female sex is reversed to male. It is called **sex reversal.** Birds have heterogametic (ZW) female. The ovary cells produce female hormones in such an amount that it supresses the male hormone producing cells. If ovary is removed the adrenal gland produces steroid which develops the rudimentary gonad into testis.

Witschi reported sex reversal by hormones in **salamender** also.

Hormones and free martin : In cattle when twin calves of different sexes occur, the female member is usually a sterile intersex called a **free martin.** The freemartin has external female genitalia but internal sex organs are more or less like those of male. The male twin is usually normal. Freemartin is due to a fusion of the foetal membranes of the twin calves, while they are in uterus of the mother. The fusion of the foetal membranes permits blood of each twin to circulate in the blood vessel of the other. The male hormones produced by the male twin are presumed to suppress the differentiation of the female internal sex organs of the co-twin.

XX males and XY females

Sex reversal in mice

Some mice are identified as XX male and XY females. It is due to the transfer of a sex reversing factor (sxr) from Y chromosome (translocation of genes). The Y chromosome is called Y^{sxr}. The duplicated segment of $\mathbf{Y^{sxr}}$ is transferred to X-chromosomes due to crossing over during male meiosis; and gets attached to long arm of 'X' chromosome, which pairs with a segment of 'Y' chromosome (Fig. 52.15). When X derived from male parent sxrXX was inactivated. The sxrXX develops into hermaphrodites or female instead of male.

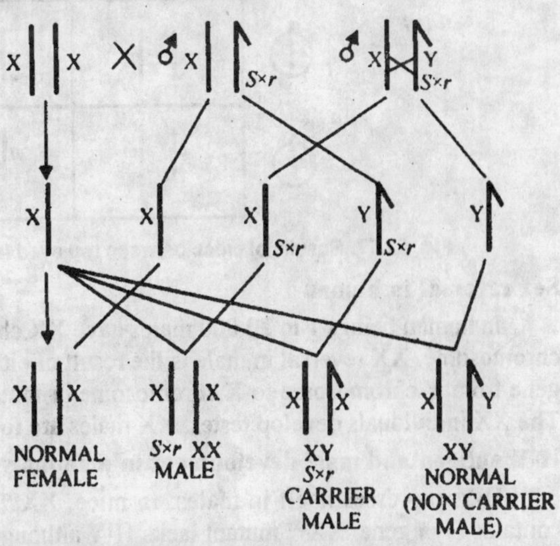

Fig. 52.15. Sex reversal in mice.

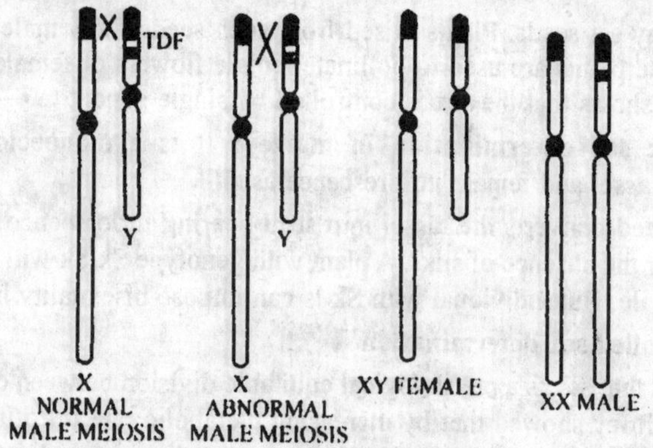

Fig. 52.16. Sex reversal in man.

When a chromosome specific DNA sequence like **Bkm** (present on Y chromosome) was used for *in situ* hybridization could be located on X chromosome of **sxrXX** males.

If a normal female is crossed with an XY^{sxr} carrier male, the normal female, sxrXX males, XYsxr carrier males and non-carrier XY males are obtained (Fig. 52.17).

XY females or hermaphrodite are due to the involvement of **Tdy** (testis determining Y) gene lying close to **Bkm** gene in centromeric region of 'Y" and **Tda-1** (Testis determining autosomal) gene which is autosomal.

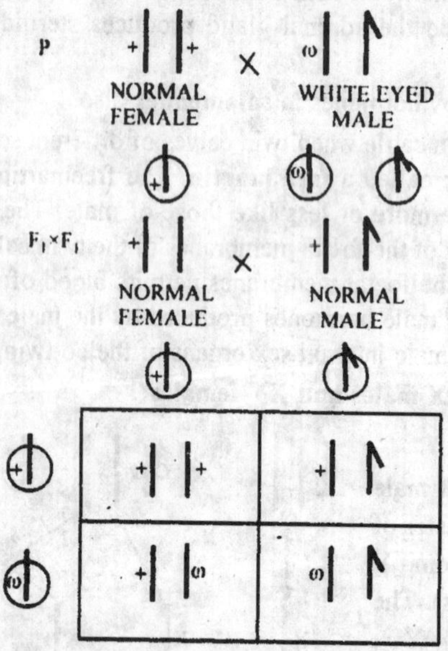

Fig. 52.17. Results of cross between red eyed female and white eyed male in *Drosophila*.

Sex reversal in human

In human beings 1 in 20,000 males have **XX** chromosome and 1 is 1,00,000 females have **XY** chromosome. **XX** reversal in male is the result of either transfer of **TDF** (testes determining factor) gene from **Y** chromosome to **X** chromosome or mutation in a locus which represses development. The XX individuals develop testes. XX males are found to possess 'Y' derived genes (Fig. 52.18).

H-Y antigen and male development in mammals

H-Y expresses itself in males. In mice, XX^{sxr} males also express H-Y because **sxr** region contains **Hya** gene. XX^{sxr} mutant lacks H-Y although it was male. **Hya** is closely linked with **Tdy** but is not necessary for testis development. In human, **Hya** is present on short arm of Y chromosome and TDF is present on long arm. XX males are H-Y negative suggesting that HY antigen does not play any role in male sex development.

SEX-LINKED INHERITANCE

Genes other than sex determiners are also located on the 'X' chromosomes. Many mutant genes in human have been shown to be located on **X** chromosome. The inheritance of such genes are called **sex-linked inheritance.**

The first evidence for sex linkage in a particular species was given by T.H. Morgan in 1910 in white-eyed mutant in *Drosophila.* When white-eyed male was mated with a red-eyed female the F_1 flies were all red-eyed. F_2 generation of it included 3 : 1 ratio of red and white-eyed flies. But all white eyed flies of F_2 generation were males only. When normal female of F1 is crossed with normal male 50% of males were white-eyed and 50% were red-eyed (Fig. 52.17). It shows that the recessive allele is expressed in male only. **Morgan** explained it as the association of the gene on 'X' chromosome. Because male has only one X chromosome all characters present on it will be expressed. The mutant allele (white eye) of the male is transferred to the female (heterozygous). The hemizygous males obtain their X chromosome from their heterozygous mother only then they will be 50% red-eyed (w^+) and 50% white eyed (w).

The female can be white-eyed (ww) only when both 'X' carry gene for it. When heterozygous female (w^+) is crossed with white-eyed male (w) then white-eyed females can be obtained (Fig. 52.18).

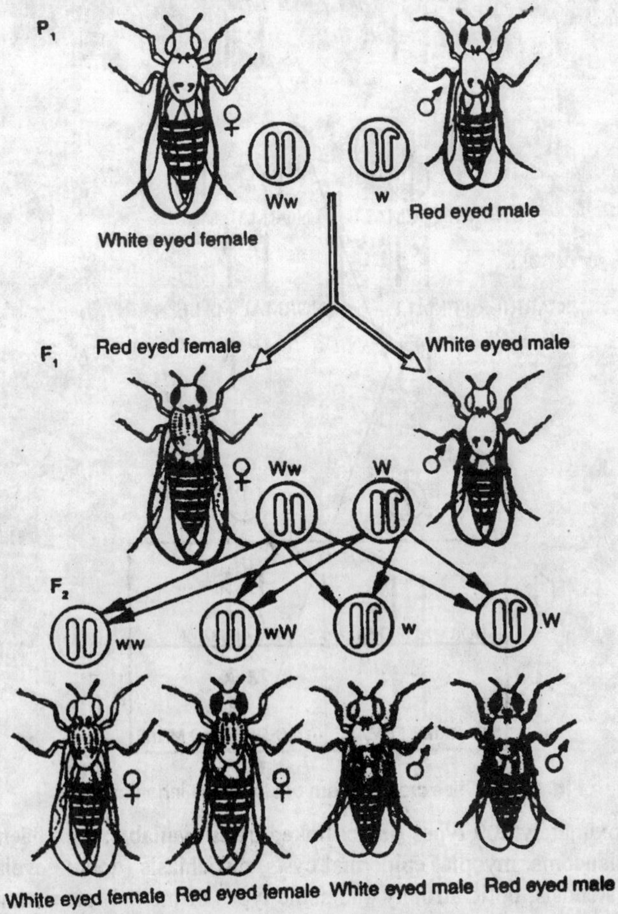

Fig. 52.18. Results of cross between white, eyed female and red, eyed male in *Drosophila.*

'Y' linked inheritance

Most sex-linked genes in male (heterogametic) are on 'X' chromosome. But a few genes are present on 'Y' chromosome also. These are called **'Y' linked** or **holandric** genes. They are transmitted from father to son directly.

'Y' chromosome in *Drosophila* is mostly heterochromatic. The X chromosomes with many genes and 'Y' with virtually none establish the characteristic pattern of inheritance for sex-linked traits. The mother with two 'X' chromosomes transmit one X to each gamete. Zygotes that receive a Y chromosome from father, develops into male. The hemizygous male progeny expresses the sex-linked genes received from the mother. The expression of sex-linked traits in females follow the same pattern as autosomal traits with the recessive phenotype appearing only in homozygous condition.

'X' linked traits in human

The inheritance pattern associated with sex linkage was recorded by Greek philosopher for the first time. An inherited character was observed in a father but not in any of his children (either male or female) and then it reappears in the males of next generation. It is the **criss cross** pattern, from father to daughter to grandson. It is the 'X' linked inheritance. (Fig. 52.19).

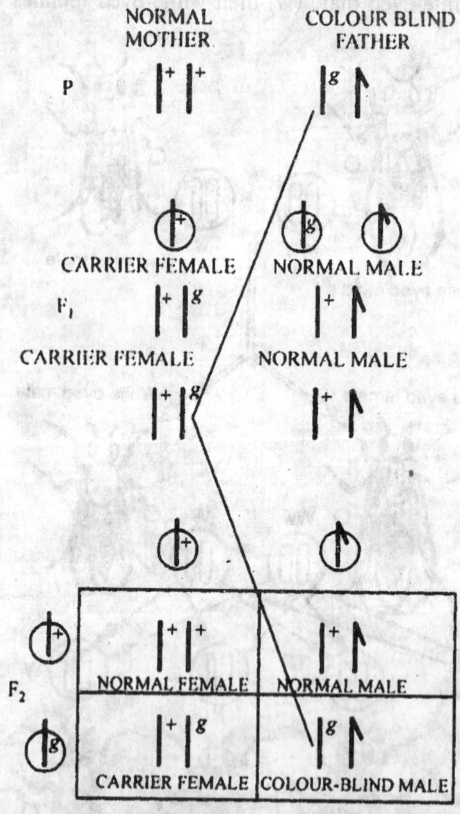

Fig. 52.19. Criss cross pattern of sex linked inheritance.

There are approximately 200 types of sex-linked traits available, *e.g.*, haemophilia, colour blindness, juvenile glaucoma, myopia, epidermal cysts, distichiasis (double eyelashes), occipital lock of hair, miteral stenosis, optic atrophy and some types of mental retardation, etc. Defect in distinguishing green or red colour is sex linked but that of **blue is autosomal.**

Sex-linked (X-linked) recessive traits are transmitted as:

(a) The traits occur much more frequently in males than in females.

(b) Traits are transmitted from an affected man through his daughter to half of his grandsons.

(c) An X-linked allele is never transmitted directly from father to son.

(d) All affected females have an affected father and a carrier or affected mother.

Dominant X-linked traits : Males expressing the trait would be expected to transmit it to all of their daughters but none of their sons. Heterozygous females would transmit the trait to half of their children of either sex. If a female expressing the trait is homozygous, all her children will inherit the trait. Sex linked dominant inheritance cannot be distinguished from autosomal inheritance in the progeny of females expressing the trait, but only in the progeny of affected males.

Sex-linked disease **hemophilia** and pedigree analysis in European royalty which generally showed transmission through females who were unaffected to some of their male offspring who were hemophilic. The disease starts with **Queen Victoria of England.** Who passed the hemophilic gene to 3 of 9 children half of her son were hemophilic. Queen was heterozygous for X chromosome. The females in the pedigree have no phenotypic effect. They may be the carriers and their mating partners are normal and the male who are free of the disease do not pass it on. Male shows hemophilia. The homozygotic diseased female will not survive.

Three general types of hemophilia are known, each affecting the production of a **prothrombin proteinase** (factor X), an enzyme necessary for blood clotting.

(a) The 'classic' sex linked type, or hemophilia 'A' which can be detected by a reduction in the amount of a substance called **antihemophilic factor** (AHF or factor VIII) accounts for approximately 80 per cent of hemophilia.

(b) **Hemophilia 'B'** or **christmas disease** is caused by reduction in the amount of **plasma thromboplastin component** (PTC or Factor IX) while accounts for 20 per cent of **hemophiliacs.** The gene for hemophilia 'B' is not allelic to that of hemophilia 'A'.

(c) **Hemophilia** 'C' is due to the interaction of rare autosomal gene with the production of **plasma thromboplastin antecedent** (PTA or factor XI) is responsible for less than 1 per cent hemophiliacs.

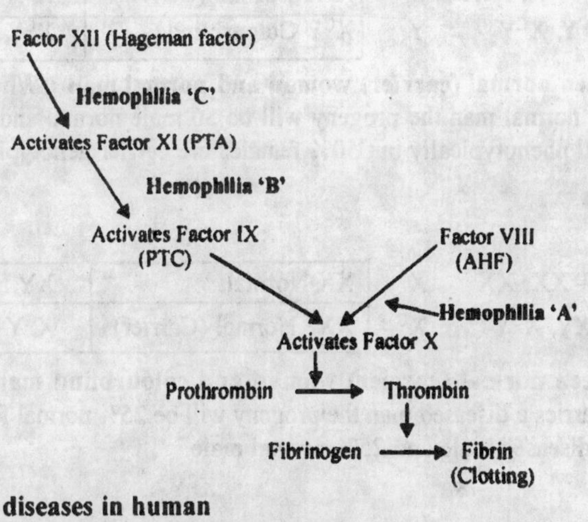

Some X-linked diseases in human

1. Glucose-6-phosphate dehydrogenase deficiency.
2. α-galactosidase deficiency.
3. Hemophilia A (factor VIII deficiency)
4. Hemophilia B (factor IX deficiency)
5. Phosphoglycerate kinase (Glycolysis)
6. Hypoxanthin-guanine-phosphoriboryl transferase (HGPRT or Lesch Nyhan syndrome).

7. Duchenne-Becker muscular dystrophy.
8. Vitamin D resistant ricketts (hypophosphatemia).
9. Ornithine transcarbamylase deficiency.
10. Anhydrotic ectodermal dysplasia.
11. Xg blood cell antigen.
12. Copper transport deficiency (Menkes Kinky-hair syndrome).
13. Bruton type agammaglobulinemia.
14. Testicular feminization syndrome (Tfm).

Various results of crosses in sex-linked inheritance (*e.g.*, colourblindness (X^c) or hemophilia (X^h).

(i) Cross between colourblind man X^CY and normal woman (XX) : When colourblind man marries normal woman the progeny will be, female normal visioned and male 50% colourblind and 50% normal. Though female will be carrier genotypically but normal phenotypically (carrier).

XX × X^CY

↓

		X^C	Y
Female = XX^C, XX^C	X	XX^C Normal carrier	X^CY Colourblind
Male = X^CY, XY	X	XX^C Normal (Carrier)	XY Normal

(ii) Cross between colourblind woman and normal man : When colourblind woman marries a normal man the progeny will be all male colourblind and all female normal but carriers.

XY × X^CX^C

↓

		X^C	X^C
Female —X^CX, X^CX	X	X^CX Normal (Carrier)	X^CX Normal (Carrier)
Male—X^CY, X^CY	Y	X^CY Colourblind	X^CY Colourblind

(iii) Cross between normal (carrier) woman and normal man : When woman is normal (carrier) and marries a normal man the progeny will be 50 male normal and 50% male diseased while all female normal phenotypically but 50% females are carrier genotypically

XX^C × XY

↓

		X	Y
Female — XX, XX^C	X	XX Normal	XY Normal
Male — XY, X^CY	X^C	XX^C Normal (Carrier)	X^CY Colourblind

(iv) Cross between normal (carrier) woman and colourblind man : When woman is normal (carrier) and marries a diseased man the progeny will be 25% normal female (carrier), 25% diseased female, 25% diseased male and 25% normal male.

XX^C × X^CY

↓

		X^C	Y
Female — X^CX^C, XX^C	X	XX^C Normal (Carrier)	XY Normal
Male — XY, X^CY	X^C	X^CX^C Colourblind	X^CY Colourblind

Sex-linkage In *Drosophila*

Example in *Drosophila* where the red eye is dominant over white eye. The genes are present on 'X' chromosome.

(i) **White eyed female crossed with red eyed male** the progeny will be all red eyed female and all white eyed male.

X^WX^W × X^+Y

↓

	X^+	Y
Female = X^WX^+, X^WX^+ X^W	X^WX^+ Red eye	X^WY White eye
Male = X^WY, X^WY X^W	X^WX^+ Red eye	X^WY White eye

(ii) **When red eyed-female is crossed with white eyed male** the progeny will be all female and male red eyed.

X^+X^+ × X^WY

↓

	X^W	Y
Female =X^+X^W, X^+X^W X^+	X^+X^WRed eye	X^+Y Red eye
Male =X^+Y, X^+Y X^+	X^+X^W Red eye	X^+Y Red eye

(iii) **When red eyed female (carrier) is crossed with red eyed male** the progeny will be all female red eyed (50% female are red eyed carrier) and 50% male red eyed and 50% male white eyed.

X^+X^W × X^+Y

↓

	X^+	Y
Female = X^+X^+, X^+X^W X^+	X^+X^+ Red eye	X^+Y Red eyed
Male = X^+Y, X^WY X^W	X^+X^W White eyed	X^WY White eyed

The reciprocal cross in sex linked inheritance are always different.

Inheritance of X-Y linked genes

The genes present in the homologous part of X-Y chromosome show inheritance same as autosomal genes. The X-Y linked genes are partially sex linked because some times crossing over may occur in the homologous part of X and Y chromosomes (Fig. 52.20). In human beings several

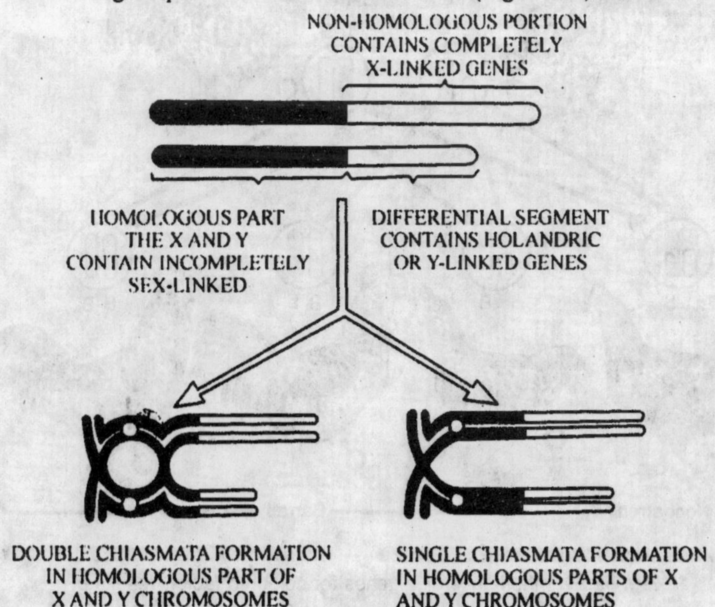

Fig. 52.20. Inheritance of XY linked genes.

diseases are XY linked, *e.g.*, **xeroderma pigmentosum and epidermolysis bulloso**, (skin disease), **retinitis pigmentosa** and **spastic paraplegia**, etc.

Inheritance of Z-linked gene for coloured feathers in chicken.

In birds, the males are homogametic (ZZ) and females are heterogametic (ZW). The sex linked genes follow Criss cross pattern.

In plymoth rock chicken, the gene for barred feather is dominant (B) and for red or black unbarred feathers is recessive (b). Both the genes are Z linked. When barred male chicken is crossed with non barred female, F_1 produces only barred males and females. F_1 barred males when crossed with hemizygous barred female the F_2 shows 50% non-barred and 50% barred females but 100% barred males (Fig. 52.21).

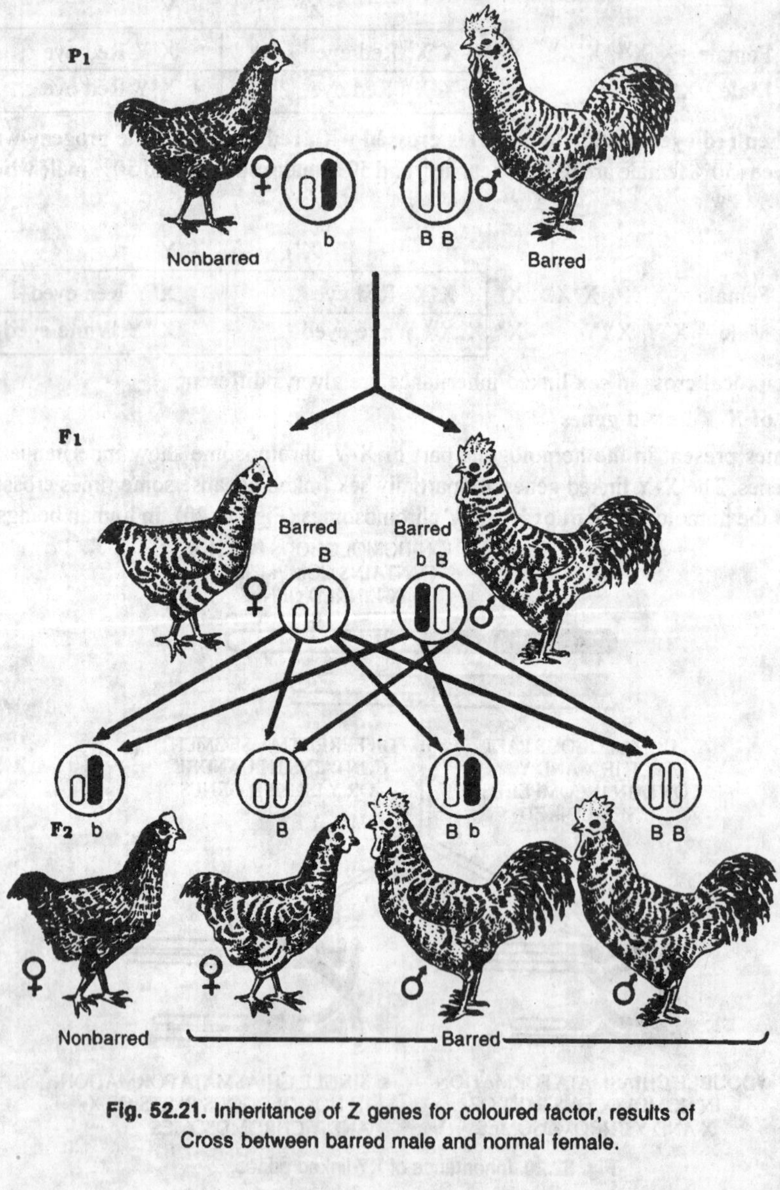

Fig. 52.21. Inheritance of Z genes for coloured factor, results of Cross between barred male and normal female.

When barred female is crossed with non-barred male the F_1 produces 50% non-barred female and 50% barred male when F_1 is self crossed in F_2 generation among the females (hen) 50% are barred and 50% non-barred while among the males (cock) 50% are barred and 50% are non-barred (Fig.46.22)

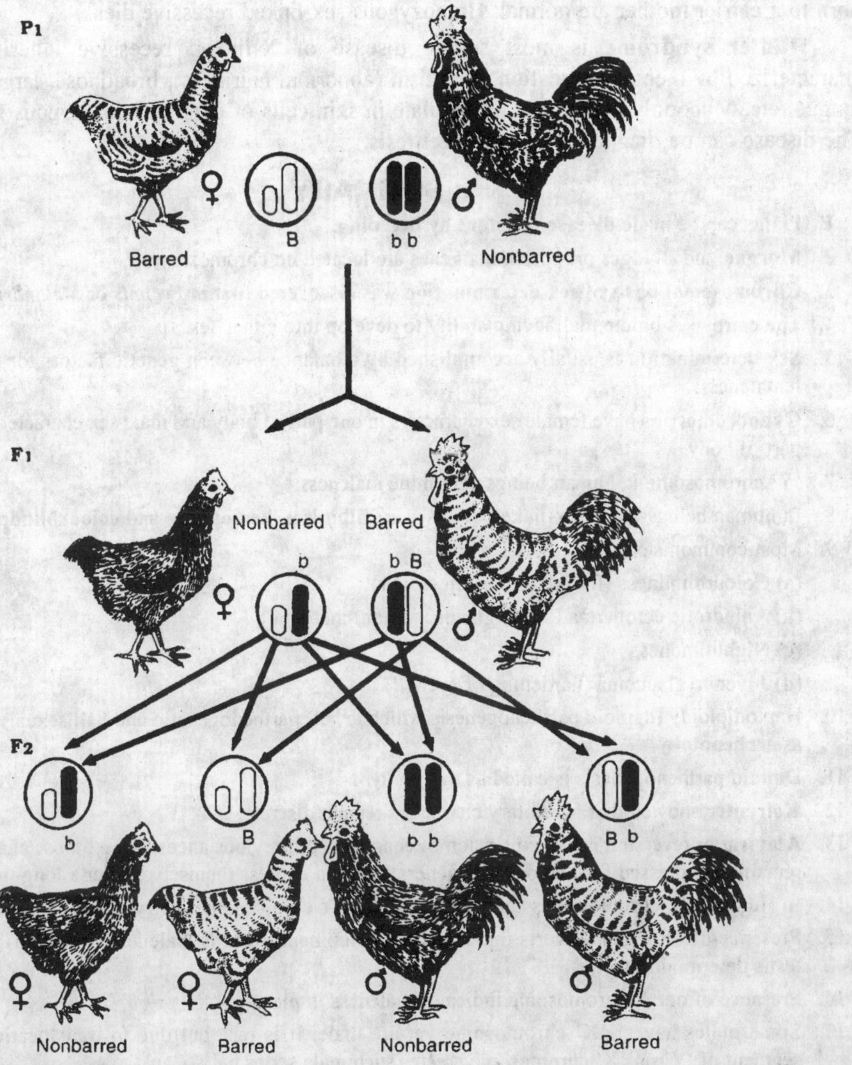

Fig. 52.22. A cross between a barred hen and a non-barred cock showing sex linked (z-linked) inheritance.

Deleterious Recessive sex-linked genes is human

Congenital hyperuricemia (Lesch-Nyhan syndrome), is characterized by excess production of uric acid, inherited through a **sex-linked recessive** gene. The gene for this is transferred from mother's 'X' chromosome to the zygote. The individual is deficient for enzyme **hypoxanthine guanine phosphoribosyltransferase** (HGPRT) which is involved in nucleotide synthesis. The symptoms start at the age of 10 months with orange uric acid crystal in urine; weak flabby muscles the child is unable to sit, walk, speak normally. Death is due to severe renal and neurological damage at the age of twenties.

Duchene type muscular distrophy

It is another sex-linked recessive gene disease. If mother is carrier of this gene half of her male children are expected to be affected. The disease affects males usually before they reach their teens with muscular deterioration. The individual dies before the age of 21. All female children born to a carrier mother are normal. Homozygous sex-linked recessive dies.

Hunter syndrome is most severe disease of X-linked recessive inheritance. It is characterized by mental retardation, hirsutism (abnormal hairiness), broadnose, large protruding tongue, etc. Mucopolysaccharides accumulate in skin cells of persons homozygous for the gene. The disease can be diagnosed by **amniocentesis.**

SUMMARY

1. Plants can be made **disease resistant** by **breeding.**
2. **Morgan** and **Bridges** proposed that genes are located on chromosomes.
3. **Chromosomal basis** of **sex determination** was discovered first in *Lychnis* or *Melandrium.*
4. The emrbyo is bipotential having ability to develop into either sex.
5. Sex determination is usually accomplished by a balance between genetic factors for maleness and femaleness.
6. **Gynadromorphs** have female sex characters in one part of body and male sex characters on the other part of body.
7. 'Y' chromosome in human beings determine maleness.
8. In human beings-some sex-linked diseases are **albinism, hemophilia** and **colourblindness,** etc.
9. Most common sex-linked diseases
   (a) Colourblindness (for red and green colour)
   (b) Anhidrotic ectoderma (sweat glands are nonfunctional)
   (c) Nightblindness
   (d) Juvenile glaucoma (hardening of eyeball).
10. Haplodiploidy (haploid parthenogenesis which is half parthenogenetic and half sexual) is also called as **arrhenotoky**.
11. Diploid parthenogenesis is called as **thelytoky.**
12. **Kolreuter** showed that hereditary characters remain discrete.
13. **Atavism** or reversion is the expression of characters of previous ancestor, *i.e.*, those characters which remain unexpressed for two or more generations can express themselves after a long time also.
14. In Human, 'X' chromosomes carry 102 genes and Y chromosomes carry only 10 genes.
15. Presence of SRY gene diverts the embryo development towards maleness. It is also called TDF or testis determining factor.
16. Presnece of one Y chromosome indicates maleness in plants.
17. Some males have 'XX' chromosome yet are male. It is rare but due to translocation of a small segment of 'Y' on 'X' chromosome creates such male series.
18. In alligators, sex is determined by temperature at which the egg is incubated.
19. Pseudogenes have poly 'A' tail.
20. Male worm *Ophryotrocha* produces sperm when young (male) but when it grows older it elongates upto 20 segments and become female and start producing eggs. If the size of it is reduced by cutting it again becomes male.
21. The discovery of sex-linked inheritance showed that genes were on sex chromosomes.
22. Sex-linked diseases inherited from X chromosomes in human beings are: colourblindness, hemophilia, opticatrophy, hairlessness, myopia, juvenile glaucoma, juvenile muscular dstrophy. distichiasis (double eye lashes), mitrasterosis (abnormal oscillation of eyeball).
23. XY-linked inheritance is due to genes located on homologous parts of X and Y chromosomes.

24. In X-linked inheritance, the characters are controlled by genes located on X chromosomes.
25. In Y linked inheritance, the characters are controlled by genes located on non-homologous points of 'Y' chromosome. These genes are called **holandric** genes.
26. In poultry, the sex iinkage is **abraxis** type (ZZ, ZW).
27. **R. P. Roy** from Patna University studied the sex in diploid, triploid and tetraploid plants with and without 'Y' chromosome.
28. **C. B. Bridges** (1922) studied **genic balance** mechanism of sex determination in *Drosophila*.
29. **Allen** for the first time studied sex determination in liverworts (male gametophyte has 7A + Y, female gametophyte contains 7 A + X and the sporophyte has 14A + XY).
30. In human beings, 'Y' chromosome plays a definie role in sex determination (XO=Turner syndrome with sterile female; XXY = Klinefelter's syndrome with superfemales).
31. XY females are due to deletion of IA segment of short arm of 'Y' chromosome.
32. XY linked diseases are **epidermolysis bullosa** and **xeroderma pigmentosum.**
33. The genes on 'Y' chromosome are SRY (sex determing) or TDF (testis determins factor); ZFY (sperm formation), P ϕ 2V, hypertrichosis, keratoderma dissiapalum, etc.
34. *Asparagus* and maize show single gene cotnrol of sex.
35. Hormonal control of sex is shown by *Bonellia viridis*, some female owl, and cattles, etc.

QUESTION BANK

Very Short Answer Questions

1. Give an example of sex reversal.
2. Give an example of environment factor affecting sex determination.
3. Give an example of harmonal factor controlling sex determination.
4. What are holandric genes?
5. What is criss cross inheritance?
6. The character present on which chromosome will be transferred from father to son.
7. Give an example of sex linked inheritance.
8. Give an example of sex influenced expression.
9. In which plant single gene control of sex detrmination is studied.
10. What is X-Y linked gene.
11. Give two name of sex-linked diseases present on 'X'-chromosome.
12. Give two traits present on 'Y' chromosomes.
13. Is 'Y' chromosome important in *Drosophila* for sex determination.
14. Is 'Y' chromosome important is *Melandrium* for sex determination.
15. Name two sex-linked syndromes in man.

Short Answer Questions

1. Write notes on types of sex determining mechanism.
2. Write various types of combinations in sex linked inheritance.
3. Write short notes on 'Y' chromosome and sex determination in human.
4. Describe various regions on X and Y chromosomes of *Melandrium*.
5. Write notes on genic balance concept of sex determination in *Drosophila*.
6. Write short notes on hapdiploidy in insect.
7. Write short notes on gynandromorph.
8. Write short notes on genetic balance theory of sex determination in plants.
9. Write notes on environmental factors of sex determination.

10. Write short notes on : (a) Fragile X chrorrosome (b) Sex differentiation.
11. Write short notes on :
    (a) Sex linked traits (b) Sex influenced traits
12. Write short notes on single gene control of sex.
13. Write short notes on sex reversal.
14. Write short notes on compound sex chromosome.
15. Write in brief sex linked inheritance.

Long Answer Questions

1. What is sex chromosome ? What is its role in sex determination ?
2. How does a sex chromosome take part in sex-linked inheritance.
3. Describe the structure of sex chromosome in *Drosophila*, man and *Lychnis* or *Melandrium*.
4. Describc by giving various example environment factors and hormonal factors or sex determination.

Multiple Choice Questions (Objective Type Questions)

1. Chromosomes responsible for sex differentiation is called :
   (a) Sex chromosome (b) Somatic chromosome
   (c) Genome (d) Autosome
2. Males are generally :
   (a) Heterogametic (b) Homogametic
   (c) Homozygotic (d) Heterozygotic
3. Heterogametic females are found in :
   (a) Birds (b) Human
   (c) Both 'a' and 'b' (d) Insects
4. 'Y' chromosome is also known as :
   (a) Autosome (b) Androsome
   (c) Sex chromosome (d) Allosome
5. Morgan in *Drosophila* suggested that 'X' chromosome is rod-like and 'Y' chromosome is:
   (a) Rod-like (b) Hook-like
   (c) Cross-like (d) Dot-like
6. 'XO' method was proposed in 1902 while studying grasshopper by :
   (a) Mcclung (b) Thury
   (c) Morgan (d) Corrus
7. Haplodiploidy is also called as :
   (a) Arthotoky (b) Arrhenotoky
   (c) Thalytoky (d) Epigamic
8. Sex determination in dioecious plants was studied by:
   (a) Morgan (b) Wastergared and Warne
   (c) Mcclung (d) Avery and Mclead
9. Gynandromorphs are the result of first division in zygote as :
   (a) 2A + XX, 2A + X (b) 2A + XXX, 2A + Y
   (c) 2A + 2X, 2A + 2Y (d) 2X + 2Y, 2A + XX
10. Gynandromorph suggests that in sex determination in *Drosophila* there is no role of :
    (a) A-chromosome (b) B-chromosome
    (c) X-chromosome (d) Y-chromosome
11. In human sex determination major role is played by:
    (a) X-chromosome (b) Y-chromosome
    (c) A-chromosome (d) B-chromosome

12. Sterile female with abnormalities in XO condition is found in :
(a) Turner's syndrome (b) Down's syndrome
(c) Klinefelter's syndrome (d) Patau's syndrome

13. Despite the presence of **2X** chromosome and additional **Y** chromosome giving maleness to the individual in :
(a) Down's syndrome (b) Klinefelter's syndrome
(c) Turner's syndrome (d) Super male

14. In human being, rare XY females and XX males are found respectively due to:
(a) Deletion and translocation (b) Translocation and deletion
(c) Additon and addition (d) Translocation and transversion

15. IA region on segment of Y chromosome is responsible for
(a) Maleness (b) Femaleness
(c) Intersex (d) Sexual dimorphism

16. Single gene control of sex is founa in :
(a) Maize (b) *Asparagus*
(c) Mango (d) Both 'a' and 'b'

17. In human female XX can be converted into XY male by the presence of :
(a) Sex linked genes (b) Sex reversal gene sxr
(c) Sex determination gene (SRY) (d) All the above

18. In *Bonellia viridis* (a marine worm), if the larva settles near the proboscis of adult female it will develop into :
(a) Male (b) Female
(c) Superfemale (d) Intersex

19. The studies of hormonal control of sex in fowl where fertile fowl changes to fertile male due to damage of ovary in female were done by :
(a) Puri and Garg (b) Hutington
(c) Crew (d) Grahm

20. 22 AA + XO and 22 AA + XXY show no bars body or one barr body respectively in :
(a) Turner's syndrome, Klinefelter's syndrome (b) Klinefelter's syndrome, Turner's syndrome
(c) Down's syndrome, Turner's syndrome (d) Turner's syndrome, Down's syndrome

21. Holandric inheritance is form :
(a) Female to son (b) Male to son
(c) Male to daughter (d) Female to daughter

22. Sex limited traits are those for which the genes are present but expressed due to some hormones :
(a) In males only (b) In females only
(c) Both male and female (d) Either male or female only

23. Sex influenced traits are those :
(a) Influenced by sex of bearer (b) Not influenced by sex of bearer
(c) Both 'a' and 'b' (d) Either 'a' or 'b'

24. Gene transfer froms parent to grand children by opposite sex children is called as :
(a) Sex linked inheritance (b) Autosomal inheritance
(c) Cris cross inheritance (d) Mitotic inheritance

25. Heteropyenotic X chromosome occurs as a round pedunculated body remains attached with nucleus is called as :
(a) Drumstick (b) Red spot
(c) Round body (d) Heteropycnotic body

26. A colourblind girl will only be born when her :
(a) Parents are normal but grand parents are colourblind
(b) Father and maternal grand father colourblind
(c) Mother and maternal grand father are colourblind
(d) Mother and paternal grand father are colourblind

27. If a physically female develops secondary male character the syndrome is called as :
(a) Down's syndrome
(b) Turner's syndrome
(c) Klinefelter's syndrome
(d) Patau's syndrome

28. Gynandromesph in *Drosophila* represent :
(a) Head of female and abdomen of male
(b) Half side (lateral) female and half male
(c) Young male and old female
(d) Old male and young female

29. Homogenetic member with ZZ sex chromosome was found in :
(a) Hen
(b) Cock (fowl)
(c) *Drosophila*
(d) All the above

30. What is the name of Indian scientist from Patna University who studied sex is diploid, triploid and tetraploid plants with and without 'Y' chromosomes :
(a) C. B. Gupta
(b) R. P. Singh
(c) R. P. Roy
(d) S. P. Roychaudhry

ANSWERS

1. (a)	2. (a)	3. (a)	4. (b)	5. (b)	6. (a)
7. (b)	8. (b)	9. (a)	10. (d)	11. (b)	12. (a)
13. (b)	14. (a)	15. (a)	16. (d)	17. (b)	18. (a)
19. (c)	20. (a)	21. (b)	22. (d)	23. (a)	24. (c)
25. (a)	26. (b)	27. (c)	28. (b)	29. (b)	30. (c)

53

CHAPTER

Extra-Nuclear or Cytoplasmic Inheritance

Although, the genes of nuclear chromosomes have a significant and key role in the inheritance of almost all traits from generations to generations, yet they altogether cannot be considered as the sole vehicles of inheritance, because certain experimental evidences suggest the occurrence of certain extranuclear genes or DNA molecules in the cytoplasm of many prokaryotic and eukaryotic cells. For example, bacterial cells such as *Escherichia coli* possesses a single main chromosome in the nucloid and often extra DNA elements called **plasmids** in the cytoplasm; the eukaryotic cells possess a main complement or chromosomes in the nucleus and extra-DNA molecules or chromosomes in their mitochondria and chloroplasts. Qualifying also as extra hereditary elements are certain viruses, bacteria, and algae (which live as endosymbionts inside the eukaryotic cells). These cytoplasmic extra-nuclear genes or DNA molecules of plasmids, mitochondria, chloroplasts, endosymbionts and cellular surfaces have a characteristic pattern of inheritance which does not resemble with that of genes of nuclear chromosomes and is known by different terms such as **non-Mendelian, non-chromosomal, uniparental, maternal, extra-chromosomal, cytoplasmic** and **extra-nuclear** inheritance.

EVIDENCES FOR CYTOPLASMIC FACTORS

Traits with extranuclear basis are identified by the accumulated evidence from a number of diagnostic criteria such as follows :

1. Because the female gamete contributes almost all of the cytoplasm to the zygote and male gamete (sperm or pollen) contributes only a nucleus, an inheritance pattern that differs between reciprocal crosses suggests a cytoplasmic involvement. This is clearly the basis for **uniparental** or **maternal inheritance** where the progeny always resemble one parent, most commonly the female parent (*e.g.*, shell coiling in *Limnaea peregra*).

2. Differences in reciprocal crosses which cannot be attributed to sex-linkage or some other chromosomal basis tend to implicate extranuclear factors (*e.g.*, chloroplast inheritance in *Mirabilis jalapa*).

3. The uniparental inheritance of a trait which cannot be attributed to unequal cytoplasmic contributions from parental gametes may, however, involve cytoplasmic factors (*e.g.*, streptomycin resistance in *Chlamydomonas*).

4. Whenever trait fails to demonstrate the classical segregation patterns and deviates from standard ratios, the conclusion is again a cytoplasm based type of inheritance (*e.g.*, mitochondrial inheritance in yeast).

5. When the trait fails to show linkage to any known nuclear linkage groups and assort independently from nuclear genes, a cytoplasmic mode of inheritance is suggested.

6. Many types of mutants that fit the above criteria will show segregation during mitotic division. This is very common in variegated plants that carry more than one type of plastid (chloroplast) per cell.

The cytoplasmic inheritance, therefore, will be, understood to be based on cytoplasmically located, independent, self-replicating nucleic acids, which differ from chromosomal genes by their location within the cell, and have their own nucleotide sequences. The smallest heritable extra chromosomal unit is called a **plasmagene.** All of the plasmagenes of a cell constitute the **plasmon.**

A. EXTRA-NUCLEAR INHERITANCE IN EUKARYOTES

Many geneticists have studied various cases of extra-nuclear inheritance in different eukaryotes. Certain most important examples of extra-nuclear inheritance in eukaryotes are the following:

1. Maternal Inheritance

In certain cases, it has been observed that certain characteristic phenotypic traits of F_1, F_2 or F_3 progeny are not the expression of their own genes, but rather those of the maternal parents. Such phenotypic expressions of maternal genes (genotype) may be short-lived or may persist throughout the life-span of the individual. The substances which produce the maternal effects in the progeny are found to be transcriptional products (*i.e.*, mRNA, rRNA and tRNA) of maternal genes which have been manufactured during oogenesis and which exist in the ooplasm of unfertilized eggs in the form of inactive protein coated and late translating mRNA molecules **(informosomes)** or inactivated rRNA and tRNA. These transcriptional products of maternal genes produce their phenotypic effects during early cleavage and blastulation when there occur little or no transcription since, maternal and paternal genes of zygote remain engaged in mitotic replication or duplication of DNA. There may be other reasons of maternal affect which are still little understood. The maternal inheritance has been studied in ***Limnaea*** (a snail).

Shell coiling in *Limnaea.* In the snails (gastropods), the shell is spirally coiled. In most cases the direction of coiling of the shell is clockwise, if viewed from apex of the shell. This type of coiling is called **dextral.** However, in some snails the coiling of shell may be counter clockwise or **sinistral.** Both types of coilings are produced by two different types of genetically controlled cleavages, one being **dextral cleavage,** another being **sinistral cleavage** (Fig. 53.1).

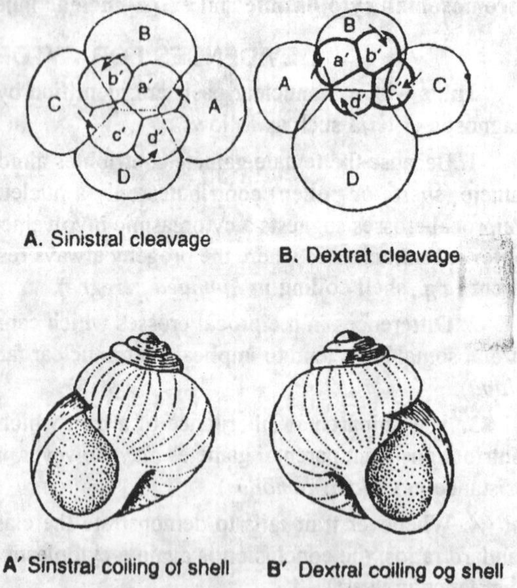

Fig. 53.1. Correlation of sinistral (A) and dextral (B) cleavage with sinistral (A′) and dextral (B′) coiling of the shell in gastropods.

There are some species of gastropods in which all the individuals are sinistral but the main interest attaches to a species in which sinistral individuals occur as a mutation among a population of normal dextral animals. Such a mutant was discovered in the freshwater snail *Limnaea peregra* (**A. Sturtevant,**1923). Breeding and cross breeding of dextral and sinistral snails showed that the difference between the two forms is dependent on a pair of allelomorphic genes, the gene for sinistrality being recessive (S), and the gene for the normal dextral coiling being dominant (S^+). The two genes are inherited according to Mendelian laws, but the action of any genic combination is visible only in the next generation after the one in which a given genotype is found.

The eggs of a homozygous sinistral individual (SS) are fertilized by the sperm of a dextral individual (S^+S^+), the eggs cleave sinistrally and all the snails of this F_1 generation show a sinistral coiling of the shell. Thus, the gene of sperm (S^+) do not manifest themselve, although the genotype of the F_1 generation is S^+S. If a second generation (F_2) is bred from such F_1 sinistral individuals, it is all dextral, instead of showing segregation as would be expected in normal Mendelian inheritance. In fact, segregation does take place in the F_2 generation so far as the genes are concerned, but the new genic combinations fails to manifest themselves, since the coiling is determined by the genotype of the mother.

The genotype of F_1 mother being S^+S, the gene for dextrality dominates and is responsible for the exclusively dextral coiling of the second generation. Only in the F_3 generation does segregation in the ratio of 3 : 1 becomes apparent, since the individuals of the F_2 generation had the genotypes —1S^+S^+; 2 S^+S, 1 SS, 1/4 of them, on the average, produce eggs developing into sinistral individuals (Fig. 53.2).

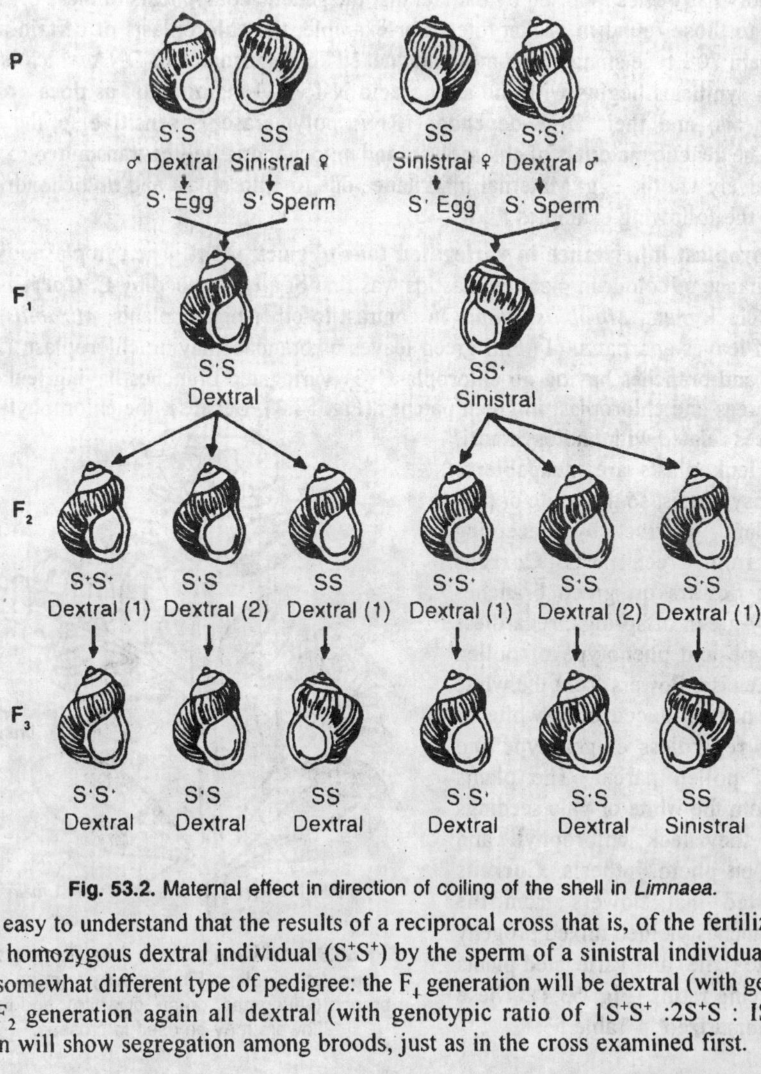

Fig. 53.2. Maternal effect in direction of coiling of the shell in *Limnaea*.

It is easy to understand that the results of a reciprocal cross that is, of the fertilization of the eggs of a homozygous dextral individual (S^+S^+) by the sperm of a sinistral individual (SS)—will lead to a somewhat different type of pedigree: the F_1 generation will be dextral (with genotype S^+S) and the F_2 generation again all dextral (with genotypic ratio of 1S^+S^+ :2S^+S : 1SS). The F_3 generation will show segregation among broods, just as in the cross examined first.

The whole case becomes clear if it is realized that the type of cleavage (sinistral or dextral) depends on the organization of the egg which is established before the maturation division of the oocyte nucleus. The type of cleavage is, therefore, under the influence of the genotype of the maternal parent. The sperm enters the egg after this organization is already established. Lastly, the direction of coiling of shell depends upon the orientation of the mitotic spindle of first cleavage of the zygote. If the spindle is tipped toward the left of the median line of the egg cell, the sinistral pattern will develop; conversely if the mitotic spindle is tipped toward the right of the median line of the cell, the dextral pattern will develop. The spindle orientation is, thus, controlled by the organization of ooplasm which becomes established during oogenesis and before fertilization.

2. Extra-nuclear Inheritance by Cellular Organelles

Chloroplasts and mitochondria and organelles that contain their own DNA and protein-synthesizing apparatus. A widely held theory concerning their origin proposes that they were once infectious endosymbiotic prokaryotes that evolved such a dependence on the gene products of the host that they are no longer able to function autonomously.

This theory has been supported by the fact that the genetic components of these organelle are often similar to those found in prokaryotes. For example, the chloroplasts of certain algae and *Euglena* contain 70S type small ribosomes and "naked" chromosomes or DNA which is circular. Their protein synthesis begins with the amino acid N-formyl methionine, as does prokaryotic protein synthesis, and their DNA-dependent RNA polymerase is sensitive to the inhibitor **rifampicin.** The genetic materials of chloroplasts and mitochondria will be transmitted to offspring almost exclusively via the egg. Maternal inheritance due to chloroplast and mitochondria is well illustrated by the following examples :

(a) Chloroplast inheritance in variegated four o' clock plant. The cytoplasmic or extra-nuclear inheritance of colour in plant by plastids was first of all described by **C. Correns** in 1908 in the four o'clock plant, *Mirabilis jalapa.* In contrast to other higher plants, *Mirabilis* contains three types of leaves and parts: (1) Full green leaves or branches having chloroplast, (2) White (pale) leaves and branches having no chloroplast, (3) Variegated branches having leukoplast in white (pale) areas and chloroplast in green patches (Fig. 53.3). Because, the chlorophyll pigment of chloroplast is related with photosynthesis of food and leukoplasts are incapable to perform photosynthesis, so the white or pale parts of plant survive by receiving nourishment from green parts. **Correns** reported that flowers on green branches produced only green offsprings, regardless of the genotype and phenotype of pollen parent and likewise, flowers from the white or pale branches produced only white or pale seedings regardless of genotype and phenotype of pollen parent. The plants developing from the white or pale seedings die because they lack chlorophyll and cannot carry on photosynthesis. **Correns** further reported that flowers from the variegated branches yielded mixed progeny of green, white (pale) and variegated plants in widely varying ratios (Fig. 53.4). These results are summarized in Table 53.1.

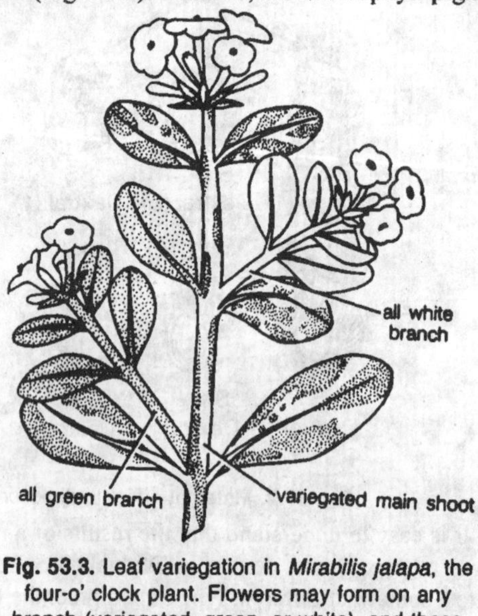

Fig. 53.3. Leaf variegation in *Mirabilis jalapa*, the four-o' clock plant. Flowers may form on any branch (variegated, green, or white), and these flowers may be used in crosses.

The irregularity of transmission from variegated branches could be understood by considering cytoplasmic genes (plasmagenes) of plastids. A study of the egg during oogenesis in *Mirabilis* reveals that the ooplasm contains plastids like cytoplasm of other plant cells. If the egg cell is derived from green plant tissues, its ooplasm will contain coloured plastids; if derived from white plant tissues, its ooplasm will contain white plastids; if derived from variegated tissues, its cytoplasm may contain coloured plastids only, white plastids only or a mixture of coloured and white plastids. A study of the pollenogenesis, however, reveals that pollen contains very little cytoplasm which in most cases is devoid of plastids. Without the plastids, the pollen cannot affect this aspect of the offspring's phenotype.

Mitotic segregation. Variegated branches of *Mirabilis jalapa* produce three kinds of eggs : some contain only white chloroplasts, some contain only green chloroplasts and some contain both types of chloroplasts. In the subsequent mitotic divisions, some form of cytoplasmic segregation occurs that segregate the chloroplast types into pure cell lines, thus, producing the variegated phenotype in the progeny individual. This process of sorting might be described as **"mitotic segregation"** of this is a pure extranuclear phenomenon. In mitotic segregation since both segregation and recombination of organelle genotype takes place, so it is called **cytoplasmic segregation and recombination** (its acronym is **CSAR**).

(b) Maternal inheritance by iojap gene of corn: Another example from higher plants also suggests the existence of plastid genes controlling plastid integrity. A gene in corn plant called **iojap (ij)** has been mapped by **M. Rhoades** (1946) to nuclear chromosomes 7. Plants homozygous for ij are either inviable white seedings or variegated with a characteristic white striping, the phenotype being known as **striped.** When the variegated plants serve as females in a cross, they give rise to green, white, and striped progeny, regardless of the nuclear genotype of the paternal parent. Thus, if the pollen derives from a normal green Ij/Ij plant as in Figure 47.5 b, the resulting progeny will be Ij/ij heterozygotes, but many will exhibit abnormal plastid pigmentation: the presence of the "normal" Ij gene has no curative effect. In the reciprocal Ij/Ij female X ij/ij male cross (Fig. 53.5). On the other hand, the Ij/ij progeny are all normally pigmented.

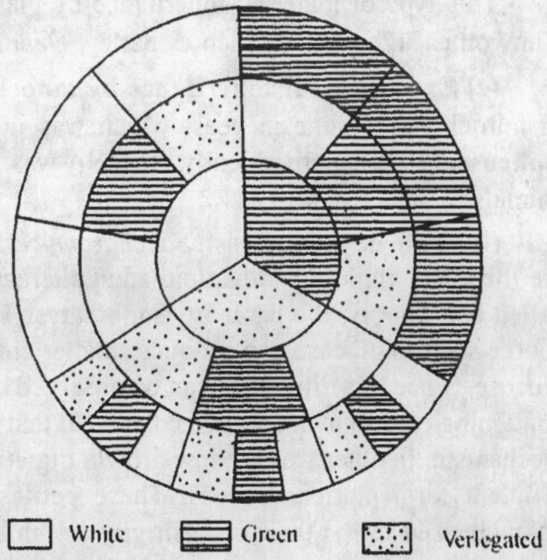

Fig. 53.4. Plastid inheritance of *Mirabilis jalapa*. The central circle represents the type of branch that produces flowers which are pollinated. Intermediate circle represents branch from which pollen is used and outer circle shows the progeny.

The iojap trait, thus, exhibits classical maternal inheritance once it has become established in an ij/ij plant. Moreover, once established, it becomes independent of the ij gene, as can be demonstrated by crossing F_1 Ij/ij variegated females to Ij/Ij normal males. As shown in Figure (47.5c), a mixture of green, striped and white progeny again results, even though some of the striped and white plants now have an Ij/Ij genotype. Thus, the iojap trait, once established, is permanent.

Table 53.1. Chloroplast inheritance in variegated four o'clock plants.

Branch of origin of the male parent	Branch of origin of the female parent	Progeny
Green	Green	Green
	Pale or white	Pale or white
	Variegated	Green, pale or white, variegated
Pale or white	Green	Green
	Pale or white	Pale or white
	Variegated	Green, pale or white, variegated
Variegated	Green	Green
	Pale or white	Pale or white
	Variegated	Green, pale or white, variegated

The iojap phenomenon has been explained by two hypotheses. One hypothesis holds that the ij/ij genetic constitution could bring about or permit, frequent mutations in the chloroplast genome that result the production of lines of abnormal plastids. Another hypothesis suggests that certain cytoplasmic elements other than chloroplast mutations come into being or residence in ij/ij cells, are later inherited in the absence of this "susceptible" or "permissive" genotype, and bring about the bleaching of chloroplasts.

This type of maternal inheritance by plasmagenes of chloroplasts has been also studied in many other higher plants such as barley, *Oenothera* sp., rice, etc.

(c) Extra-nuclear inheritance by mitochondria. The most important work on the genetics of mitochondria done in yeast which was initiated by the discovery of petite mutants by **B. Ephrussi** (1953). Subsequently mt DNA was studied in several organisms including plants and animals.

(i) Petite in yeast. Yeast, *Saccharomyces cerevisiae,* are single-celled ascomycetes fungi. In the life cycle, diploid and haploid adult alternates, the former reproducing by asexual meiospores called **ascospores**, the latter by **isogametes.** The **petite** mutants in yeast fail to grow on carbon source such as glucose and produce smaller colonies (the "littles") when grown on sugars such as glucose. Since this difference can be observed only when such yeast cultures are kept in a oxygen-containing environment; so it is concluded that petite mutants have a defective aerobic respiratory mechanism. In other words, slow growth of petite can be attributed to yeast cells utilization of less efficient fermentation process. These petites differ from wild type, called **grande** and are characterized by (i) their insensitivity to inhibitors of aerobic pathways (such as cyanide), (ii) absence of cytochromes a, a_3, b and a number of other changes in mitochondrial respiratory enzymes; (iii) incomplete development of mitochondria; and (iv) lack of stainability of petite mitochondria.

The petite mutants can be **segregational**, *i.e.*, they follow mendelian segregation and, therefore, presumably controlled by chromosomal genes. They may also be **vegetative,** *i.e.*, non-segregational or extra-chromosomal. The genetic basis of petite character is a cytoplasmic factor ρ^+ (rho) which may be absent or defective in petites. Thus, a vegetative petite can be **neutral** (ρ^0) which completely lack $\rho^+_/$ or it may be **suppressive** (ρ^-) having a defective ρ^+. The neutral petites are not transmitted while suppressive petites are transmitted to a fraction of vegetative diploid progeny. In various strains of yeast, the suppressiveness varies from 1–99 per cent petites. The

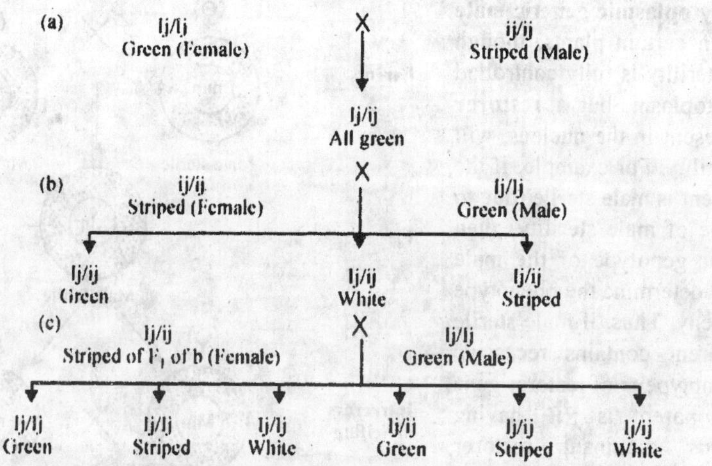

Fig. 53.5. (a) Cross between green (normal) and striped (iojap) plants. (b) Reciprocal of cross (a) (c) Cross of F_1 striped females (of cross b) to normal (green) males.

following two lines of evidences have suggested the association of ρ^+ with mitochondrial DNA (mt DNA); (1) **Ethidium bromide,** which induces petite mutations with 100 per cent efficiency, causes degradation of mt DNA after prolonged exposure of cells. In fact, neutral petites have been found lacking in mt DNA. (2) Supressive petites contain mt DNA which is greatly altered in base composition with respect to wild mt DNA.

(ii) Poky strain of *Neurospora*. In fungi, *Neurospora crassa* a number of mutations of mitochondria are inherited via the female parent. The best studied of these is the **poky strain** of *N. crassa,* first isolated by **Mitchell** and **Mitchell** (1952). A poky mutant differs from wild type strain of *Neurospora* in the following aspects: (1) it is slow growing; (2) it shows maternal inheritance, and (3) it has abnormal cytochromes. Of the three cytochromes—cyt a, b and c found in wild type, cyt a and cyt b are absent, and cyt c is in excess in poky mutant. In reciprocal crosses, poky character shows maternal inheritance:

poky (female) × wild type (male) → all poky

wild type (female) × poky (male) → all wild type

However, there are other marker nuclear genes (ad^+/ad^-) which show 1:1 mendelian segregation. The following evidences suggested that poky trait may be located in mitochondrial DNA: (i) slow growth may be due to lack of ATP energy and source of this energy is mitochondria; (ii) cytochromes in poky strain differ from those in wild type in quality and quantity and these cytochromes are found in mitochondria.

(iii) Male sterility in plants. In plants, the phenotype of male sterility is found to be controlled either by nuclear genes or plasmagenes (cytoplasm) or by both. Therefore, the trait of male sterility of plants is controlled by the following three methods :

(a) Genetiç male sterility. In this type of male sterility the sterility is controlled by a single nuclear gene which is recessive to fertility, so that the F_1 progeny would be fertile and in F_2 generation, the fertile and sterile individuals will be segregated in the typical 3:1 ratio (Fig 47.6).

(b) Cytoplasmic male sterility (CMS). In maize and many other plants, cytoplasmic control of male sterility is known. In such cases, if the female parent is male sterile (having plasmagene for male sterility), the F_1 progeny would always be male sterile, because the cytoplasm is mainly derived from the egg which is obtained from the male sterile female parent (Fig 47.7).

(c) Cytoplasmic genetic male sterility. In certain plants, though the male sterility is fully controlled by the cytoplasm, but a **restorer gene** if present in the nucleus, will restore fertility. For example, if the female parent is male sterile (due to plasmagene of male sterility) then the nuclear genotype of the male parent will determine the phenotype of F_1 progeny. Thus, if male sterile female parent contains recessive nuclear genotype rr of restorer gene and male parent is RR, having homozygous dominant restorer genes. Their F_1 progeny would be male fertile Rr. However, if the male parent is male fertile rr, the F_1 progeny would be male sterile rr. If the F_1 male fertile heterozygote (Rr) is test crossed with male fertile rr male, a progeny with 50 per cent male fertile and 50 per cent male sterile will be obtained (Fig. 53.8).

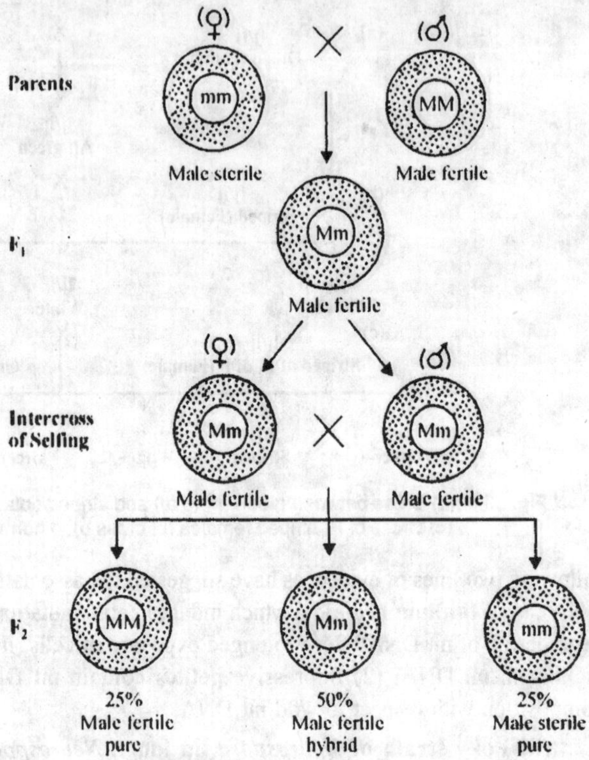

Fig. 53.6. Inheritance pattern of genetic male sterility.

Since, in maize expression of male sterility depends on an interaction between nuclear and extrachromosomal genes. Male sterile lines can bear seeds only after cross-pollination. For this reason they are useful in raising hybrid seeds, especially on large scale.

Later on, in maize the following four types of cytoplasms have been recognized : the normal (N) cytoplasm and three types of male sterile cytoplasms (T, C and S). The recent studies of mitochondria in these cytoplasm revealed that the factors responsible for cytoplasmic male sterility are located in mitochondrial DNA (mt DNA) and mt DNA of N, T, C and S cytoplasms are found to be different. The cytoplasmic male sterility (CMS) of C and S type can be reversed by nuclear storer genes, however, the CMS-T cannot.

3. Extra-Nuclear Inheritance by Endosymbionts

Certain intra-cellular parasites such as bacteria and virus particles maintain symbiotic relationship with host cells. They are self-reproducing and look like the cytoplasmic inclusions. Sometimes they exhibit an infection like transmission with a hereditary continuity of their own. Generally such symbionts are coined by letters of the Greek alphabets (sigma, kappa, mμ, etc.). The various types of infective symbionts are as follows :

(i) Sigma virus in *Drosophila* **L. Heritier** and **Teissier** found that a certain strain of *Drosophila melanogaster* shows a high degree of sensitivity to carbon dioxide, where as the wild type strain can be exposed for long periods to pure CO_2 without permanent damage, the sensitive strain quickly becomes uncoordinated in even brief exposure to low concentrations. This trait (extra-sensitivity) is transmitted primarily, but not exclusively, through the maternal parent. Tests have disclosed that CO_2 sensitivity is dependent upon an infectious DNA virus called **sigma**, found in the cytoplasm of **CO_2 sensitives** *Drosophila*. These infective particles are transmitted normally via the egg's larger amount of cytoplasm but occasionally through the sperms as well. Carbon dioxide sensitivity may even be induced in normal flies by injections of cell free extracts of sigma particles from CO_2 sensitive flies.

(ii) Spirochaetes and maternal sex ratio in *Drosophila*. Females of many *Drosophila* species can harbour a population of **spirochaete bacteria** known generally as **SR.** When **SR** spirochaetes infect the eggs of the host and when these eggs are fertilized, virtually all XY zygotes are killed early in embroyonic development and XX zygotes survive. Thus, the spirochaete can be considered as an endosymbiont of female but not of male *Drosophila*, and its presence in the female gives rise to the condition called **maternal sex ratio**, in which the progeny are exclusively or almost entirely female.

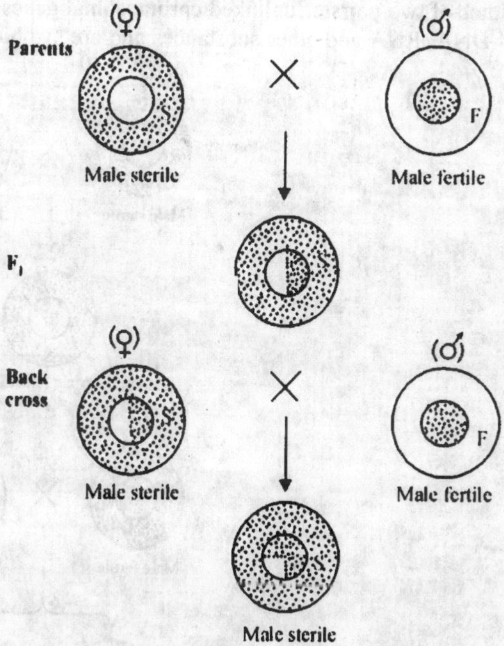

Fig. 53.7. Maternal inheritance of cytoplasmic male sterility.

The SR spirochaete is infectious, for when isolated from the haemolymph of female carriers and introduced into normal females the latter become carriers. Why the female genotype permits their retention and conversely, why XY cells are sensitive to their presence is not yet known. **K. Oishi** and **D. Poulson** (1970) have reported DNA-containing viruses in these endosymbiont spirochaetes of female *Drosophila*.

(iii) Kappa particles. In 1938, **T.M. Sonneborn** reported that some races (known as **"killers"** or **killer strain**) of the common ciliate protozoan, *Paramecium aurelia* produce a poisonous substance, called **paramecin** which is lethal to other individuals called **"sensitives"**. The paramecin is water soluble, diffusible and depends for its production upon cytoplasmically located particles called **kappa.** Electron microscopic observations have shown that kappa particles are about 0.4μ long symbiotic bacteria, *Caedobacter taeniospiralis*; 20 per cent of kappa bacteria of the killer strain contain a refractile protein containing **"R body"** and are called **"brights"**. They are infected with a virus that controls the synthesis of toxic viral protein, the paramecin. A killer *Paramecium* may contain hundreds (*e.g.*, 400) of kappa particles. The presence of kappa particles in the killer *Paramecium* is dependent for their maintenance and replication on the chromosomal dominant gene K. Paramecia with nuclear genotype kk are unable to harbour kappa particles.

When a *Paramecium* of killer strain having the genotype KK or (K^+) conjugates with the *Paramecium* of non-killer strain having , the genotype **kk**, the exconjugants are all heterozygous for Kk gents (Fig. 53.9). The Kk genotype suggests that both exconjugant should be killers. But this is not the case. If conjugation is normal, *i.e.*, lasts only for a short time, and no exchange of cytoplasm takes place between the two, both killers and non-killers (sensitive) are produced. However, rare or prolonged conjugation (*i.e.*, lasting for long time) permits mixing of cytoplasm of both conjugants and results killers only. The killer trait is stable only in killer strain with KK genotype and is suitable in sensitive strain with kk genotype.

(iv) mμ particle. Another type of killer trait known as **mate killer** has been reported in *Paramecium* by **R.W. Siegel** in 1952. The mate killer trait is imparted by a cytoplasmic mμ particle and a *Paramecium* with a mμ particle is called **mate killer** because when it conjugates with a *Paramecium* without any mμ particle is called **mate sensitive**, then it kills the latter. The mμ particles exist only in those cells whose micronucleus contains at least one dominant gene of either of two pairs of unlinked chromosomal genes (M_1 and M_2). The mμ particles are composed of DNA, RNA and other substances and are symbionts.

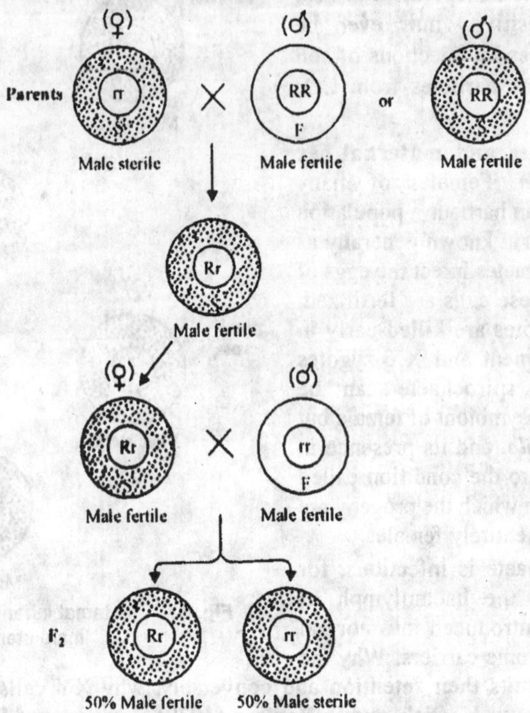

Fig. 53.8. Inheritance of cytoplasmic male sterility and effect of restorer gene in making male steriles into male fertiles.

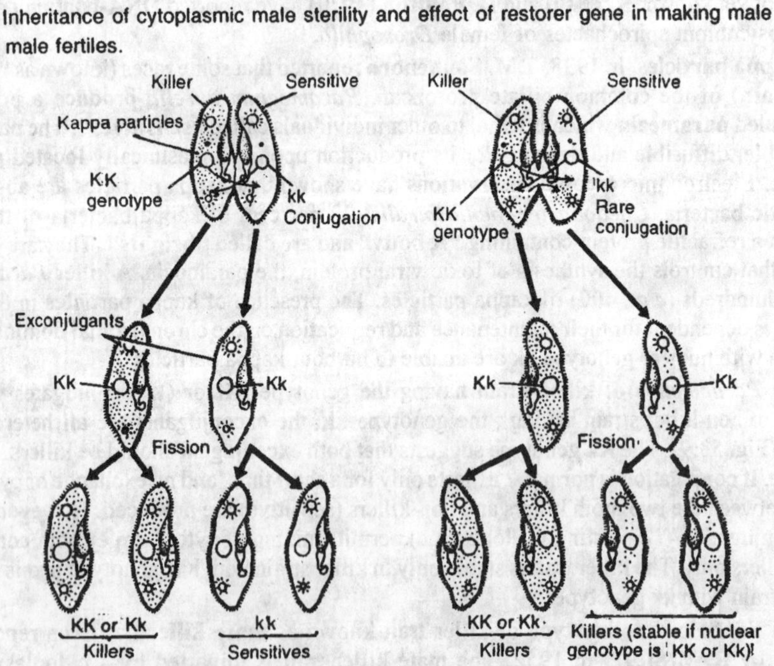

Fig. 53.9. Conjugation in *Paramecium* and the killer trait. Progeny of sensitives are killers only in rare situations where conjugation persists for a longer period so that kappa-containing cytoplasm is introduced into the conjugating sensitive. Kappa particles, however, are maintained only in the presence of K-nuclear genotype.

(v) Milk factor in mice. Bittner found that females of certain lines of mice are hightly susceptible to mammary cancer and this trait was found to be maternally transmitted trait. Result of reciprocal crosses between these and animals of low-cancer-incidence strain depend on the characteristic of the female parent. When the young mice of a low-incidence strain are allowed to be nursed by susceptible foster mothers produces a high rate of cancer in them. Apparently this is a case of infective agent transmitted in the milk. This so called milk factor resembles in many respects with a virus and has been discovered to be transmissible also by saliva and semen. The presence of milk factor also depends on nuclear genes.

4. Uniparental Inheritance *in Chlamydomonas reinhardi*

Like fungi, algae rarely have different sexes, but they do have mating types. In many algal and fungal species, there are two mating types that are determined by alleles at one locus. A cross can occur only if the parents are of different mating types. The mating types are physically identical but physiologically different. Such species are called **heterothallic** (literally "different bodied"). In *Chlamydomonas,* the mating type alleles are called mt^+ and mt^- (in *Neurospora* they are A and a; in yeast a and α).

In 1954, **Ms. Ruth Sagar** isolated a **streptomycin-sensitive (sm-s)** mutant of *Chlamydomonas* with a peculiar inheritance pattern. In the following crosses, sm-r and sm-s indicate streptomycin resistance and streptomycin sensitivity, respectively, and mt is the mating-type gene :

$$mt^+ \text{ sm-r} \times mt^- \text{ sm-s} \rightarrow \text{progeny all sm-r}$$
$$mt^+ \text{ sm-s} \times mt^- \text{ sm-r} \rightarrow \text{progeny all sm-s}$$

Here, occurs a difference in reciprocal crosses; all progeny cell show the streptomycin phenotype of the mt^+ parent. Like the maternal inheritance this is a case of **uniparental inheritance.** In fact, **Sagar** now refers to the mt^+ mating type as the female, using this analogy.

Uses of Extra-nuclear Genome

1. It prevents total loss of organelles due to a single mutation in nuclear gene.
2. It provides a reservoir of cytoplasmic mutations.
3. It is useful under adverse environmental condition.

SUMMARY

1. Cytoplasmic inheritance due to chloroplastic genome is called **plastidome.**
2. Cytoplasmic inheritance includes the transfer of characters from mother (egg) only.
3. Cytoplasmic inheritance never shows mendalian ratio.
4. Cytoplasmic inheritance is carried out by **plasmagenes.**
5. Plastid transmission in plants is reported by **Correns** in *Mirabilis jalapa.*
6. **T. M. Sonneborn** studied the transmission of certain cytoplasmic particles in *Paramecium aurelia.* These particles are called **kappa** paticles.
7. **L. Heritier** and **Teissier** studied *Drosophila melanogaster* sensitive to CO_2 due to transmission of **sigma factor** to the zygote cells through ova.
8. **J. J. Bittner** studied a strain of mice developing breast cancer which are transmitted to offspring through milk of mother. This is called **'milk factor'.**
9. **B. Ephrussi** investigated that yeast red strain is due to the presence of some cytoplasmic particles.
10. **M. B, Mitchell** and **H. K. Mitchell** reported some poky (p^0) strains in *Neurospora.*
11. **Episomes in bacteria** are the best examples of cytoplasmically located genetic determiner called bacterial episome 'F'.
12. **Shell coiling of *Limnaea*** (snail) is determined by a pair of genes.The coiling may be sinistral (left) or dextral (right). The coiling is determined by maternal snail. It was studied by **Conklin** et al.
13. Cytoplasmic inheritance is significant because :
    (a) It prevents the total loss of organelles due to a single mutation in nuclear genes.
    (b) It enhances the chances of cytoplasmic mutation useful under favourable conditions.
14. **Cytoplasmic** inheritance is usually **uniparental.**
15. When maternal genes have effect on the offspring through cytoplasm of egg but not involving plasmagenes, it is called **predetermination effect.**

QUESTION BANK

Very Short Answer Questions

1. Cytoplasmic inheritance in maize is studied by whom ?
2. Name one example of plastidal inheritance.
3. Who explained the streptomycin resistance gene in *Chlamydomonas* ?
4. Name two examples studied by you for haploid cytoplasmic inheritance.
5. Who discovered cytoplasmic male sterility in maize.
6. Name the types of plasmon.
7. In which plant **poky** mutants are found.
8. Write 2 uses of extra nuclear genome.

Short Answer Questions

1. Write the characters of extrachromosomal inheritance.
2. Explain the type of inheritance giving example of snail coiling.
3. Describe streptomycin resistance in *Chlamydomonas*.
4. Describe in short one example of plastogene inheritance.
5. Give one example of chondriogene inheritance.
6. Write short notes on :
   (a) Petite mutants (b) Sigma factor (c) rho factor
7. What are the resemblances between chloroplast and prokaryotes.

Long Answer Questions

1. What is cytoplasmic inheritance. Explain it with two suitable examples.
2. Explain the inheritance of kappa particles in *Paramecium*.
3. Give an illustrated account of the extra chromosomal inheritance in maize.
4. Describe in brief the cytoplasmic inheritance in yeast cells.

Multiple Choice Questions (Objective Type Questions)

1. Extranuclear chromosome is :
   (a) Circular and without protein coat (b) Circular and with protein coat
   (c) Linear and without protein coat (d) Linear and with protein coat
2. Cytoplasmic inheritance is also known as :
   (a) Paternal inheritance (b) Cris cross inheritance
   (c) Maternal inheritance (d) Sexlinked inheritance
3. Cytoplasmic inheritance in *Mirabilis jalapa* was reported by :
   (a) Morgan (b) Correns (c) Mc clincook (d) De Veries
4. Cytoplasmic inheritance of kappa particles was reported by T.M. Sonneborn in :
   (a) *Paramecium aureus* (b) *Paramecium aurelia*
   (c) *Entamoeba histolytica* (d) *Ascaris lumbricoides*
5. Studies on *Drosophila melanogaster* that is sensitive to CO_2 due to **sigma** particles transmission from ova to zygote was reported by :
   (a) Korper and Kappa (b) Bittner (c) Morgan (d) Heritier and Teisier
6. Bacterial episome 'F' is cytoplasmically located :
   (a) Genetic factor (b) Milk factor (c) Genetic determiner (d) Environmental factor
7. If dextral female snail is crossed with sinistral male, the resultant will be :
   (a) All female snails dextral (b) All male snails dextral
   (c) All snails dextral (d) 3 snails dextral and one sinistral
8. *Drosophila is* CO_2 sensitive due to the presence of :
   (a) *rho* factor (b) *sigma* factor (c) *milk* factor (d) none of the above
9. Iojap inheritance in corn is due to the presence of gene :
   (a) IJ (b) Ij (c) iJ (d) ij
10. Non chromosomal genes in *Chlamydomonas* is studied by :
    (a) Sagar (b) Strutvent (c) Correns (d) Morgan
11. Petite mutants of yeast are due to :
    (a) Genome (b) Chondriogenes (c) Plastogenes (d) Kinetogenes

ANSWERS

1. (a)	2. (c)	3. (b)	4. (b)	5. (d)	6. (c)
7. (c)	8. (b)	9. (d)	10. (a)	11. (b).	

54

CHAPTER

Protein Structure

Proteins are most important component of cell. Proteins are the work horses of the cell. **Berzelius** (Swedish chemist) coined the term **protein** (*Protios* = holding the first place; Greek word). **Mulder** (Dutch chemist) extracted very similar nitrogen rich substances from animal and plant sources and depending upon the properties called them proteins. More than half dry weight of a cell is of protein.

Proteins are polymer of Amino acids

The unit constituent of protein in **amino acid.** So they are called as **polymers of amino acids.** Protein amino acids have a central **carbon atom** called **α-carbon;** to which a carboxyl group (—COOII) and amino group (—NH_2) are attached. The general formula may be represented as **ball and stick formula** and **Fischer projection formula** (Fig. 54.1). As the amino group is attached to the α-carbon, the amino acids are called α-amino acids. If R-group is not equivalent to 'H' the α-carbon atom is known as asymmetric; α-amino acids are **chiral** or optically active compounds..

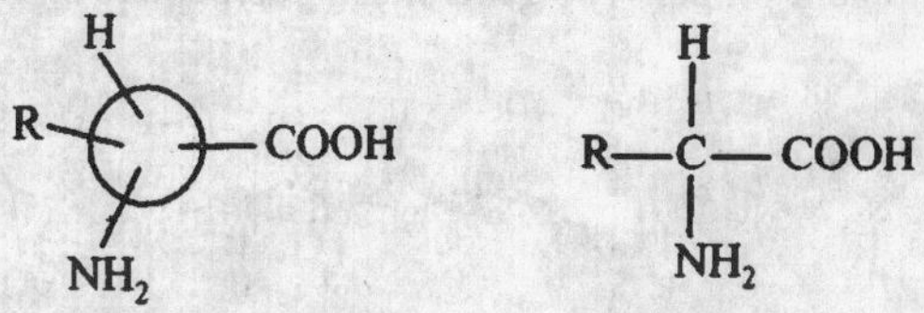

BALL AND STICK MODEL FISCHER PROJECTION FORMULA

Fig. 54.1 Structure of Amino acid.

Amino acids are also known as other, **zwitter ions,** since amino acids have both **carboxyl** – and **amino** + group balancing each. They can react with acids and alkalies. Such compounds are called **amphoteric substances,** *e.g.*, if solid **alanine** (R = CH_3) is dissolved in water, the pH of this solution will be approximately neutral.

Bjerrum in 1923 proposed the term zwitter ion, derived from German word **'zwitter'** meaning hybrid :

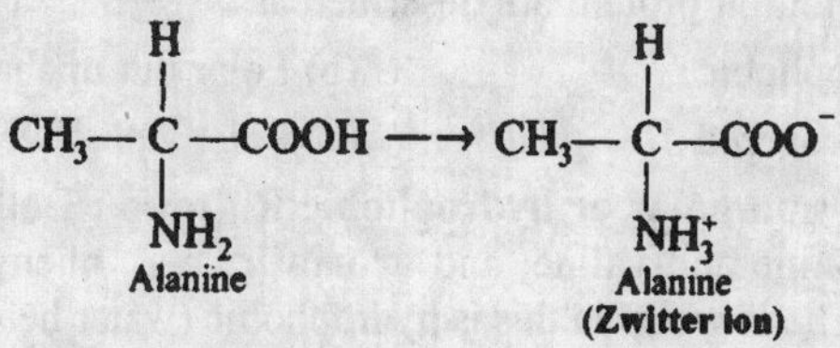

The fundamental structural unit of protein is α-amino acid. The proteins are high molecular weight compounds. The atomic structure of protein molecule generally has 30-33% 'C', 50% H, 9-11% 'O' and 7 to 9% N with small amount of 'S'. The atomic structure of hemoglobin is

$$C_{2796}H_{4592}O_{832}N_{812}S_8$$

PRIMARY STRUCTURE OF PROTEIN

The covalent structure of protein is essentially linear. Amino acids are connected together in the form of a chain with **peptide** bonds to form a **polypeptide.** The peptide bond is simply an amide bond between carboxyl carbon of one amino acid and the amino nitrogen of another

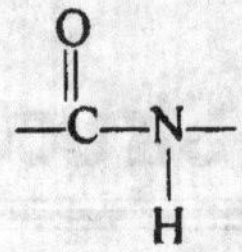

Oxygen is removed from carboxyl group of amino acid I and two protons from the alkyl ammonium group of amino acid II in the formation of peptide bond.

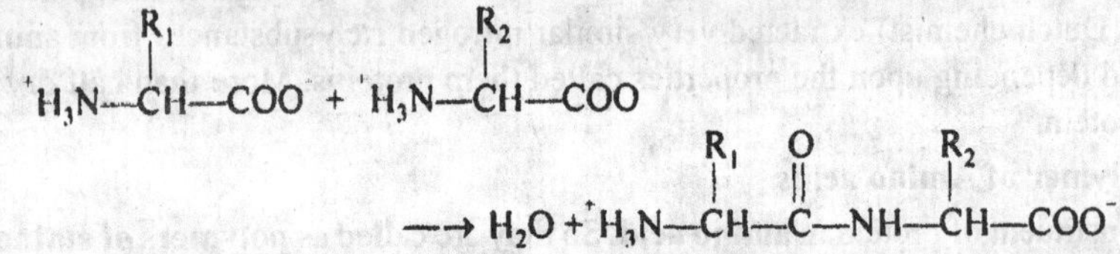

When an amino acid is incorporated into a polypeptide chain it is called **amino acid residue,** because water is 'split out' in the formation of peptide bond; and the remaining part cannot be called as amino acid proper. The generalised polypeptide structure is shown in (Fig. 54.2).

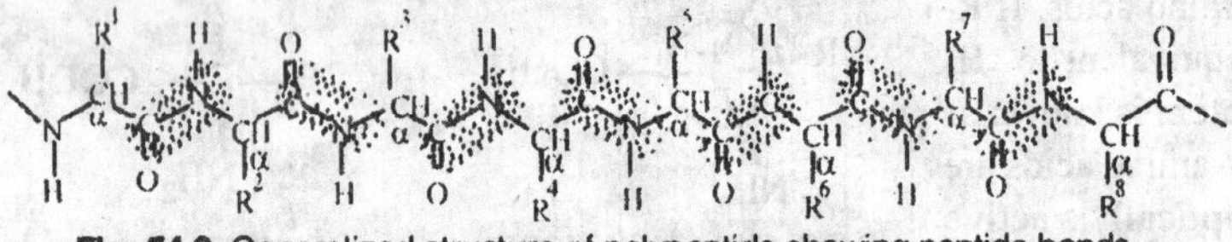

Fig. 54.2. Generalized structure of polypeptide showing peptide bonds.

Twenty different amino acid residues account for the vast majority of protein structures. Except **proline** (imino group) all amino acids are **α-amino acids.** They differ only in the type of 'R' group. The average weight of protein amino acid is approximately **110 kD.**

The primary structure of a protein is simply the order of amino acid residues in polypeptide chain. 20 types of amino acids are found in live forms. According to their chemical nature they are classified as **aliphatic, aromatic** and **heterocyclic** types depending upon 'R' group. On the bases of polarity of 'R' group, functional roles and contribution to the folding of the peptide chain the 20 amino acids found in protein are described as

(a) Non-polar or hydrophobic (b) Polar but uncharged

(c) Polar - negatively charged (d) Polar - positively charged

(a) **Amino acids with non-polar or hydrophobic R group :** Both **aliphatic,** *e.g.*, alanine; leucine, isoleucine, methionine and valine; and **aromatic,** *e.g.*, phenylalanine and tryptophan residues are included in it. The R group in this is hydrophobic (water healing). **Proline** amino acid is unusual in that its nitrogen atom present is a **secondary** rather than a primary amine. It is called **imino acid rather than an amino acid.**

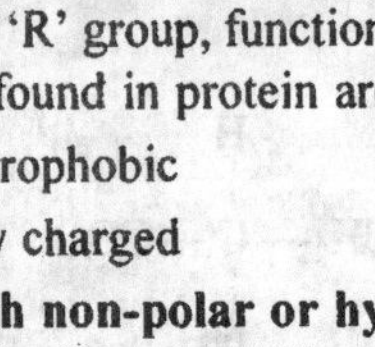

L_α-Alanine

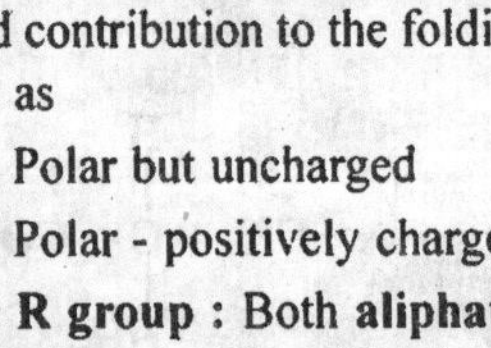

L_α-Valine

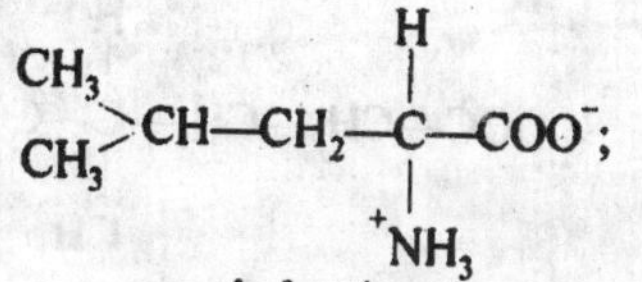

L_δ-Leucine

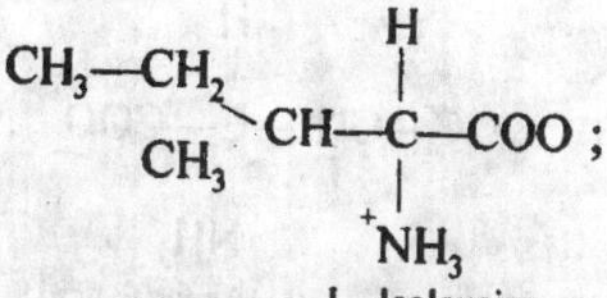

L_δ-Isoleucine

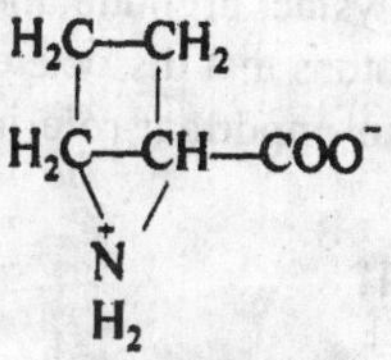

L_δ-Proline

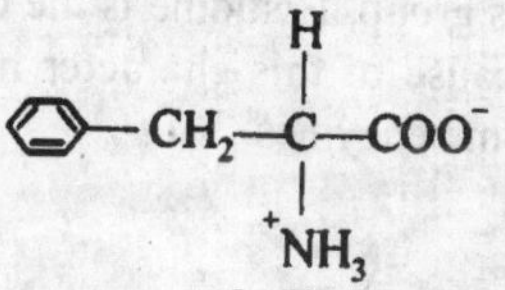

L_δ-Phenylalanine

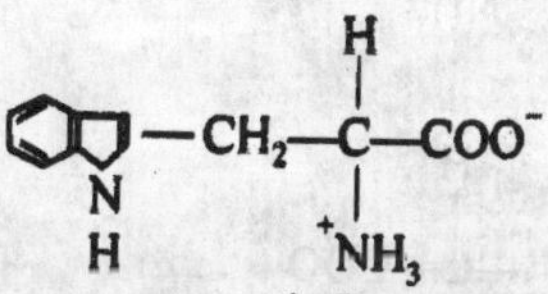

L_δ-Tryptophan

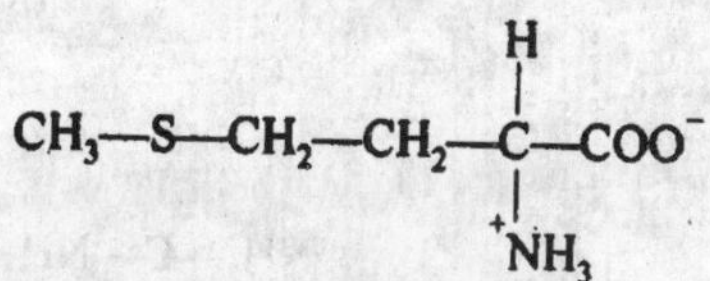

L_δ-Methionine

(b) **Amino acids with polar but uncharged 'R' group :** These amino acids contain polar **'R'** residues participating in hydrogen bond formation. Several of the amino acids in this group possess a **hydroxyl group,** *i.e.*, serine, threonine and tyrosine, or **sulfhydryl group,** *e.g.*, cysteine and **amide group,** *e.g.*, asparagine and glutamine etc. **Glycine** lacks 'R' group. Both aliphatic and aromatic compounds are included in this group.

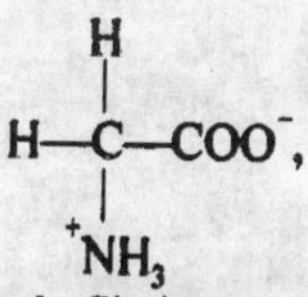

L_δ-Glycine

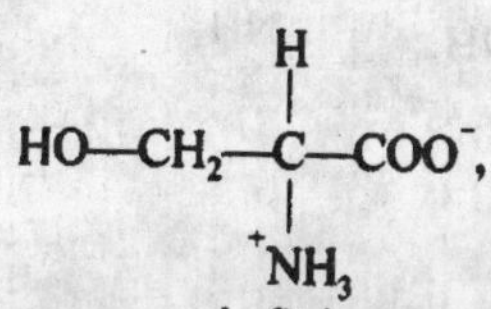

L_δ-Serine

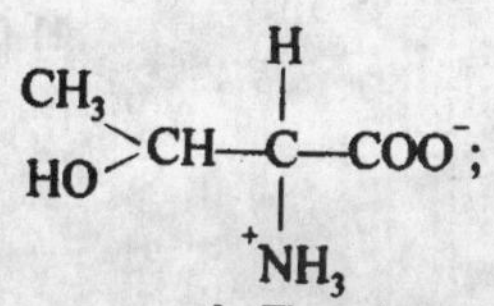

L_δ-Threonine

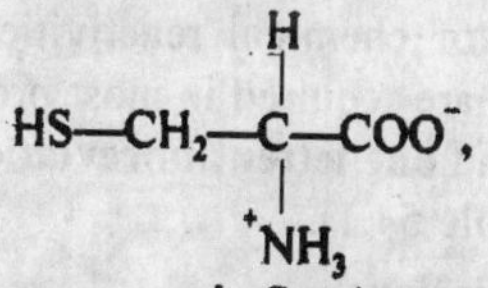

L_δ-Cysteine

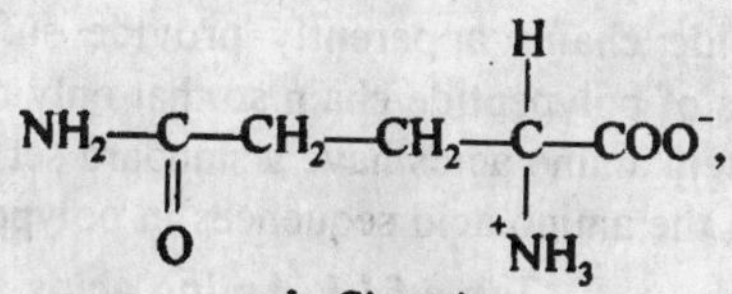

L_δ-Glutamine

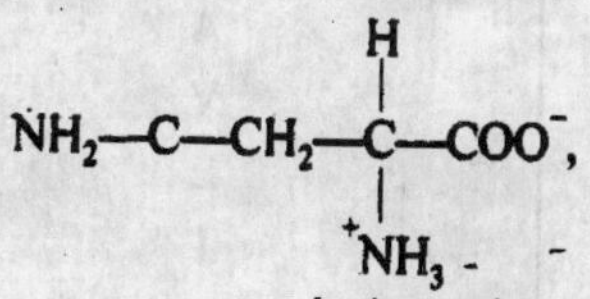

L_δ-Asparagine

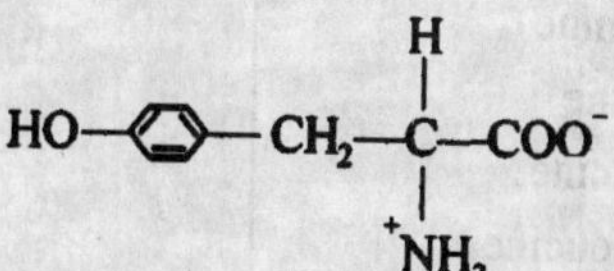

L_δ-Tyrosine

(c) **Amino acids with negatively charged 'R' groups :** It includes the two dicarboxylic amino acids aspartic and glutamic acid.

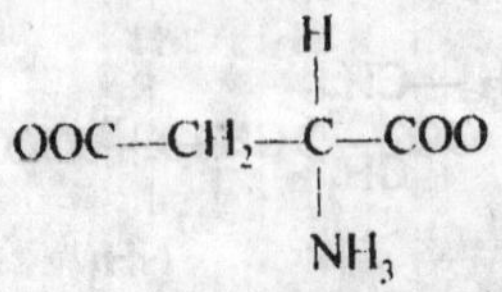

L_α-Aspartic acid

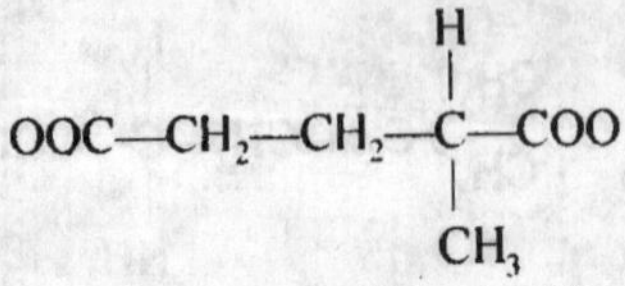

L_α-Glutamic acid

(d) **Amino acids with positively charged 'R' group** : Lysine, arginine and histidine are included in this group. Histidine is the only amino acid with protons that dissociate in the neutral pH range. Because of this character histidine residue plays an important role in the catalytic activities of some enzymes.

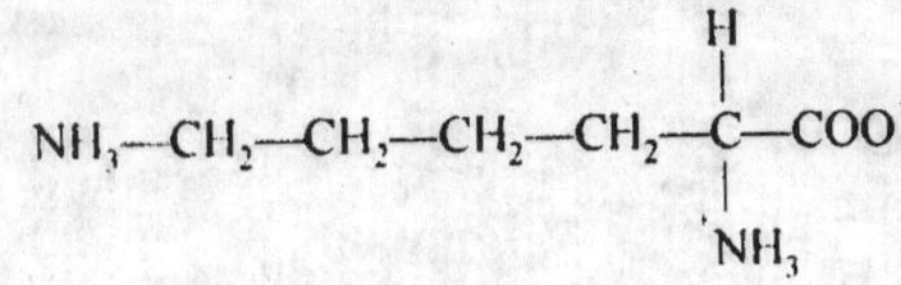

L_α-Lysine

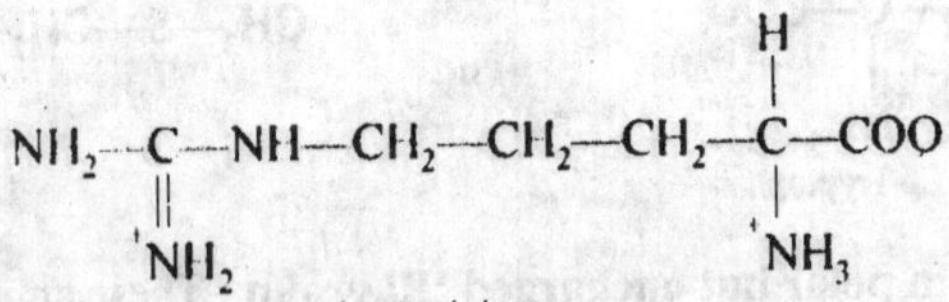

L_α-Arginine

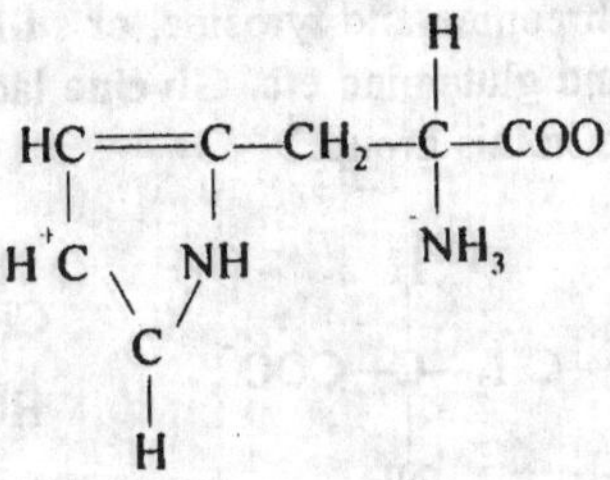

L_α-Histidine

These 20 amino acids constitute the bulk of protein in bacteria, plants and animals in living system. 20 side chains apparently provide sufficient diversity of chemical reactivities and conformations of polypeptide chain so that only these amino acids are required in most proteins. Common protein amino acids have a standard set of **three letter** and **one letter abbreviation** for use in writing the amino acid sequences in polypeptide chains (Table 54.1).

Table 54.1. Amino acids and their abbreviations.

Amino acid	3 letter symbol	One letter symbol
Alanine	Ala	A
Valine	Val	V
Leucine	Leu	L
Isoleucine	Ile	I
Proline	Pro	P
Phenylalanine	Phe	F
Tryptophan	Trp	W

Methionine	Met	M
Glycine	Gly	G
Serine	Ser	S
Threonine	Thr	T
Cysteine	Cys	C
Glutamine	Gln	Q
Asparagine	Asn	N
Tyrosine	Tyr	Y
Lysine	Lys	K
Arginine	Arg	R
Histidine	His	H
Aspartic acid	Asp	D
Glutamic acid	Glu	E

Biologically Active Oligopeptides

An oligopeptide is simply a short polypeptide. It is composed of a smaller number of amino acids (10 or less amino acids.) A peptide has an α-amino and an α-carboxyl group. Peptides have roles in horomones, antibiotics, toxins and metabolic intermediates. Metabolically important peptide is **glutathione.**

It is a tripeptide (3 aminoacids). It is required in mammals to prevent oxidative damage to RBC. Glutathione is also called as V glutaminyl cysteinyl glycine.

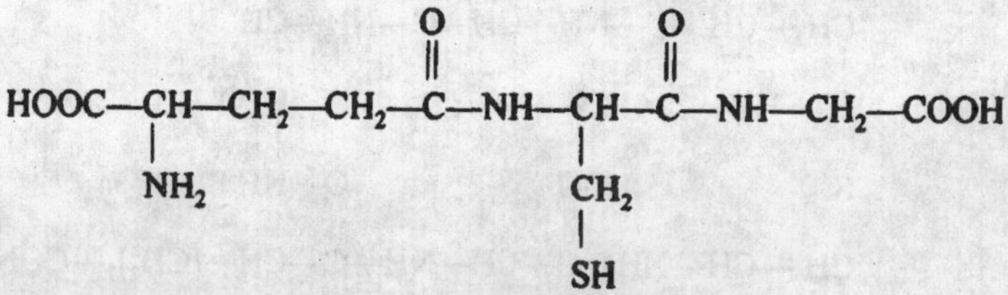

V Glutaminyl cysteinyl glycine
(Glutathione)

Peptide hormones responsible for intercellular and interorgan communication are important group of naturally occurring peptides. Vasopressin and oxytocin (nonapeptides) are formed in pituitary gland. 7 of the 9 peptides are similar in both but the physiological activities are very different. Oxytocin causes contraction of smooth muscles and vasopressin causes a rise in high blood pressure constricting peripheral blood vessels. (Fig. 54.3).

Several antibiotics are peptides of comparatively simple structure. Penicillin contains the valine and cysteine residues but are not linked by peptide bonds.

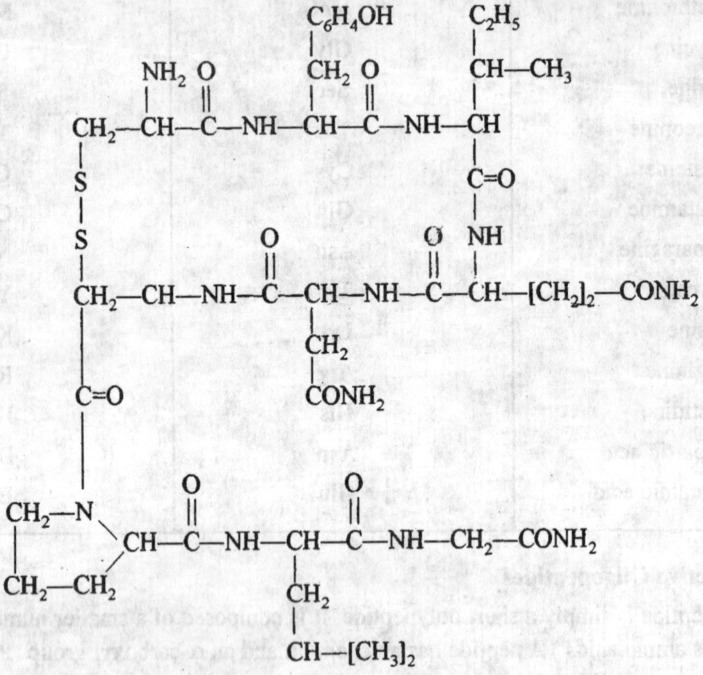

OXYTOCIN

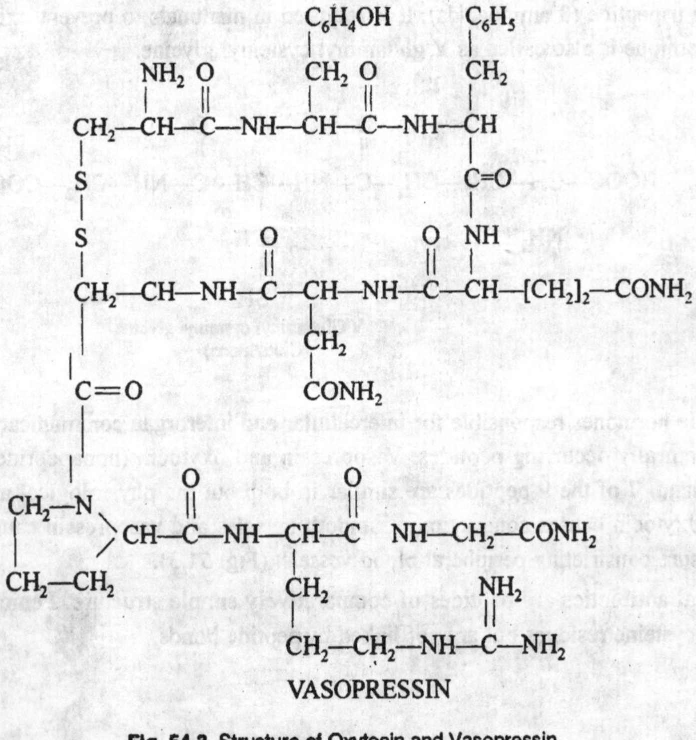

VASOPRESSIN

Fig. 54.3. Structure of Oxytocin and Vasopressin.

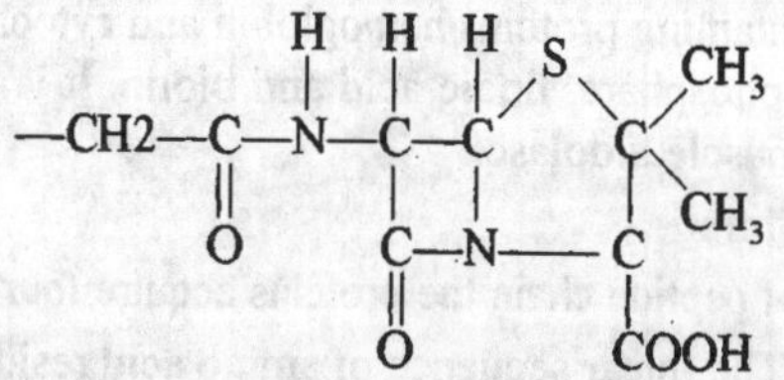

Penicillin G (Benzyl penicillin)

Artificial sweetner **aspartame** is L-aspartyl-L-phenyl alanyl-methyl ester. It is 200 times as sweet as sucrose and is considered to lack some of the unpleasant after taste associate with other synthetic sweetner.

FORMS OF PROTEIN

Proteins have not only a definite covalent structure but also a definite **3-dimensional** structure.

3D structure is controlled primarily by the order of amino acid residues. The stability of 3D structure is due to the non-covalent bonds. The position of reactive functional groups relative to one another in an environment of controlled polarity allows proteins to bind with other molecules.

Globular Protein

General form of the protein is **globular.** They are roughly spherical. X-ray crystallography studies show that globular protein is packed as tightly with amino acid residues as amino acids are packed in amino acid crystals.

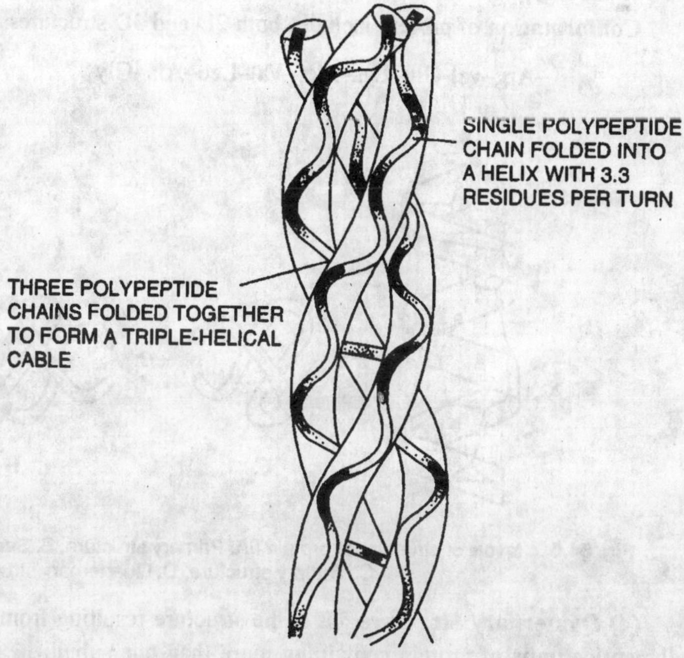

Fig. 54.4. Triple helix structure of protein.

Most of the side chains of amino acids are non-polar, the interior of the protein molecule is predominantly a polar. Polar amino acids are confined mainly to the exterior side of the protein.

Fibrous protein

The major fibrous proteins are **keratins,** the main constituents of hair, beaks, nail and claws, scales, horn, hoove and wool, etc. Collagen of skin, cartilage and bone also are fibrous proteins. Collagen are the glycoproteins composed of glycine, proline hydroxyproline and alanine. Collagen forms a **triple** helix (Fig. 54.4), cross-linked to give a rigid and inextensible material. Silk and the contractile proteins **tropomyosin** and paramyosin are also fibrous protein.

Some proteins are neither globular nor fibrous. **Myosin,** a muscle protein which non-contractile system as well, is one of the largest protein known with more than 1700 amino acid residues in its polypeptide chain. It is neither fibrous nor globular structure. Histidine with its lone electron pair in the ring nitrogen often acts as an efficient acid-base catalyst. Histidine also serves as a metal ligand in the iron containing proteins hemoglobin and cytochrome-c. Lysine is intimately involved in binding pyridoxal phosphate, lipoic acid and biotin. It is the component of the active site of certain enzymes, *e.g.*, muscle aldolase.

The folding of polypeptide chain

According to the folding of peptide chain the proteins acquire four structural levels (Fig. 54.5).

(1) Primary Structure : The linear sequence of amino acid residues in the polypeptide chain is called **primary** structure or 1-D structure.

(2) Secondary Structure : Regular folding pattern of contiguous parts of the polypeptide chain give a protein the secondary structure or 2D structures, *e.g.*, α-helix, β-pleated sheet form.

(3) Tertiary Structure : It is the 3D structure formed by the bonds between amino acid residues which are distant from each other in the polypeptide chain and the arrangement of secondary structure elements relative to one another. The term is applied generally to globular protein and rarely to fibrous proteins.

Conformation of protein includes both 2D and 3D structures.

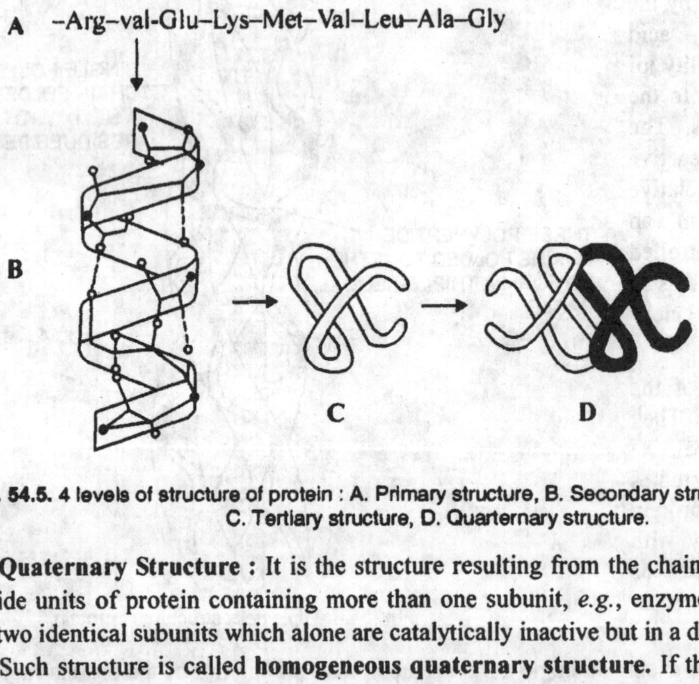

Fig. 54.5. 4 levels of structure of protein : A. Primary structure, B. Secondary structure (a helix). C. Tertiary structure, D. Quarternary structure.

(4) Quaternary Structure : It is the structure resulting from the chains between separate polypeptide units of protein containing more than one subunit, *e.g.*, enzyme **phosphorylase** a contains two identical subunits which alone are catalytically inactive but in a dimer form an active enzyme. Such structure is called **homogeneous quaternary structure.** If the two subunits are dissimilar it is **heterogeneous quaternary structure.** The subunits are also called as **protomers.** Protein made up of more than one protomer is called **oligomeric** protein, *e.g.*, **hemoglobin** is an oligomeric protein with heterogeneous quaternary structure consisting of 2 identical α-chain protomers and two identical β-chain protomers (*i.e.*, α_2 β_2).

Secondary Structure of Protein (2D)

The secondary structure of protein molecule generally is accomplished by consideration of polypeptide back bone alone, without analysis of amino acid side chain. The secondary structures are stabilized by **hydrogen bonds** between peptide imide and carboxyl groups of polypeptide back bone and not by bonds between -side chains. 3 classes of secondary structure are recognised.

(a) Helices, (b) Sheets and (c) Bonds.

The peptide bond, which is an imide (substituted amide) bond, has a planner structure. The electrons are delocalized in amide linkage, giving the C—N bond show considerable double bond characters.

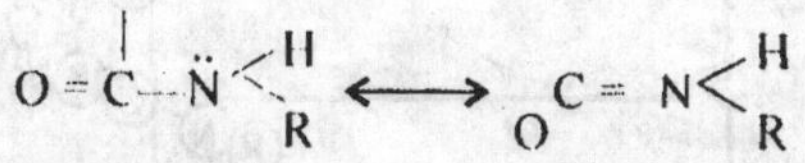

Planner peptide bonds can be shown as

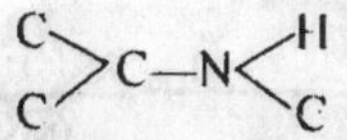

3 bonds make peptide chain, *i.e.*, α-carbon to carboxyl carbon bond, imide nitrogen to α-carbon bond and C—N bond. Double bond of C—N bond limits rotation about it (Fig. 54.6). Due to rotations of groups around α-carbon (ψ and ϕ value) the chain assumes a helical configurations or a circle or a zig-zag structure (Fig. 54.6B).

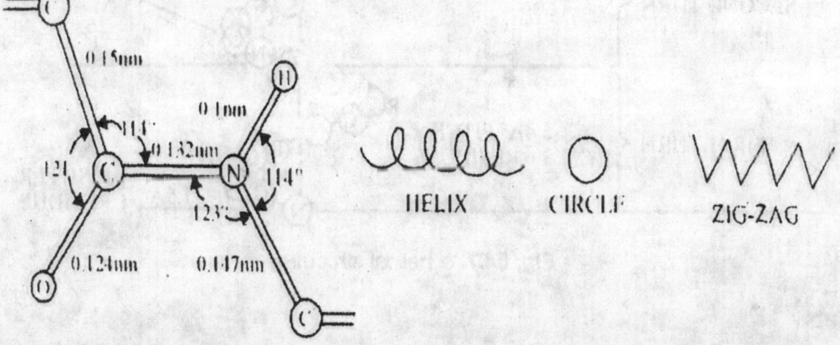

Fig. 54.6. A. Various angles between elements of amino acid, B. Various shapes of secondary structure of protein

All combinations of ϕ a ψ angles are not possible, as many lead to clashes between atoms in adjacent residues. **Ramachandran** worked on possible combinations of ϕ of ψ angles that do not clash and plotted on a conformation map. It is called **Ramachandran plot.**

α-Helix

The protein α-helix is a right handed helix. It was demonstrated by **L. Pauling** and **R.B. Torey** in 1955. The chain rotates clockwise as one views down the helix axis at the polypeptide chain proceeding into the distance. The α-helix has 3.6 amino acid residues per turn and is stabilized by nearly straight hydrogen bonding between an imide group (—NH—) in the polypeptide chain and a carboxyl group (—CO—) at a position four residue away in the same chain (Fig. 54.7). Every —NH— and —CO— group can form a straight hydrogen bond, in this manner the α-helix is especially well stabilized.

The α-helix is characterized by the location of the atoms of the polypeptide chain, the amino acid side chains do influence the probability that a given sequence of amino acid residues will be four in an α-helix. Glycine residues do not foster α-helix as in the side chain only an 'H' atom is present. The polypeptide chain is too flexible at a glycine residue. Protein can also assume value necessary for the α-helix. Both glycine and protein residue are considered to be **helix breakers.** Glutamic acid, leucine, methionine, phenylalanine, etc., occur very frequently in α-helices and are considered to be α-helix promoting residues. Other features of α-helix are :

(a) Overlapping of repeating units after 18 amino acid residues, *i.e.*, after, 5 turns.

(b) Pitch (centre to centre) per turn = 5.4 Å.

(c) Pitch (rim to rim) of each turn = 5.1 Å.

(d) Rise per residue = 1.5 Å.

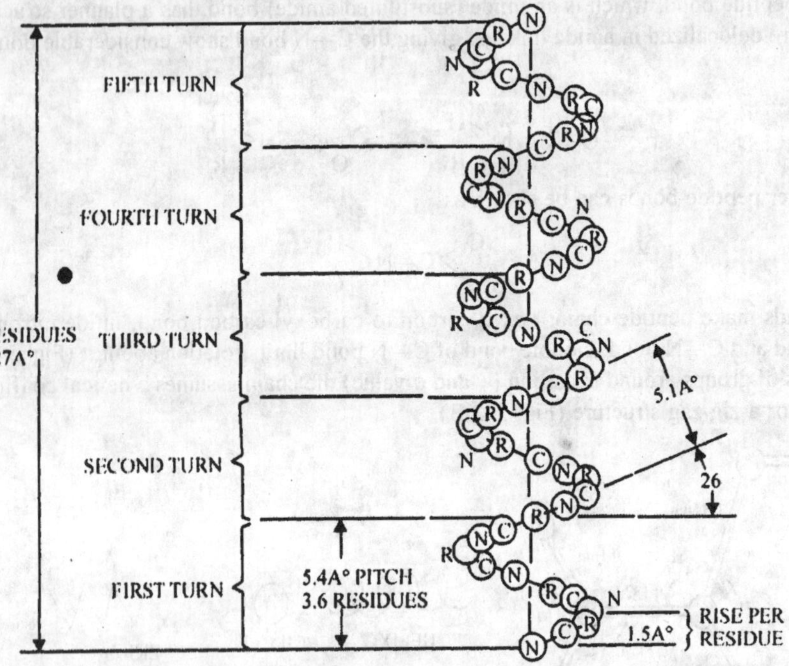

Fig. 54.7. α helical strucutre.

β-pleated Sheets

The β-pleated sheet structure in protein is not exactly in the same plane. The sheets are pleated (Fig. 54.8). The atoms lie in folded plane, and the side chains of succeeding residues along the polypeptide chain protrude alternately above and below the general plane of the structure.

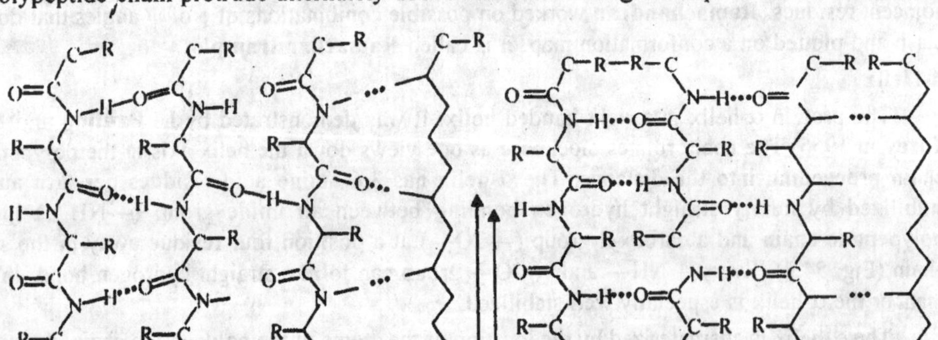

Fig. 54.8. β-Pleated structure.

The β-pleated sheet structures, like the α-helix, allow the maximum amount of hydrogen bonding between polypeptide back bone inside and carboxyl groups, and the H-bonds formed are straight enough to be stable. The β-pleated sheets seen in protein structures are not only pleated but also slightly twisted.

α-helix and β-pleated sheet structures are found in both globular and fibrous proteins. The wide and frequent occurrence of the α-helix and β-pleated sheet structures appears to be due to the combination of sterically favoured disposition of the polypeptide chain and favourable hydrogen bonding.

α-keratin and paramyosin are examples of fibrous proteins that have α-helix structures. Parallel β-pleated sheets and antiparallel β-pleated sheets form the structures of the fibrous proteins stretches of polypeptide chain entirely folded into the secondary structures. In globular proteins the α-helical and β-pleated structures are smaller than those of fibrous proteins.

Reverse Bending

Reverse turn or reverse bending occurs at the surface of protein in globular protein.

Super secondary structure is presented by some fibrous proteins like collagen. The amino acid composition of callagen is unusual being composed of 25% glycine and 25% proline and hydroxyproline. Because of high **glycine and proline** contain no α-helic occurs.

Tertiary Structures of Protein (3D Structure)

The next level after secondary structure is tertiary structure, which describes the conformation of the entire protein. The secondary structure is stabilized primarily by hydrogen bonds between atoms that form the peptide bonds of the backbone. The tertiary structure is stabilized by an array of non-covalent bonds between the diverse side chains of the protein. The secondary structure is limited to the small number of conformations but tertiary structure is virtually unlimited.

The detailed tertiary structure of a protein is usually determined using X-ray crystallography technique. Most proteins can be categorized on the basis of their overall conformations being either **fibrous** (elongated shape) or **globular** (compact shape).

Myoglobin : The first globular protein whose tertiary structure was determined. The polypeptide chains of globular proteins are folded and twisted into complex shapes. Distant points on the linear sequence of amino acids are brought next to each other and linked by various types of bonds. **John Kendrew** *et al* in 1957 produced the 3D structure of myoglobin. Myoglobin is present in muscle tissue as a storage site for oxygen. The oxygen molecule is bound to an iron atom in the centre of a heme group. Heme is the prosthetic group, *i.e.*, a part of protein not composed of amino acids. The heme of myoglobin gives most muscle tissue a red colour. Myoglobin is a globular protein the polypeptide chain was folded back on itself in a complex arrangement. Myoglobin is composed of δ-rodlike stretches of a α-helix ranging from

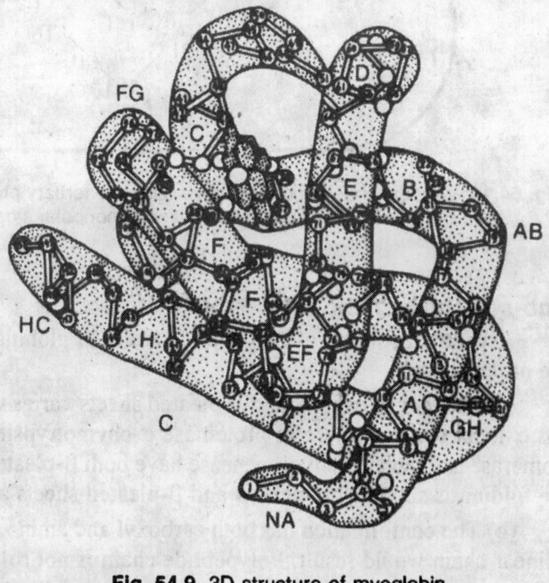

Fig. 54.9. 3D structure of myoglobin.

7-24 amino acids. 75% of the 153 amino acids in the polypeptide chain are in the α-helical conformation. No, β-pleated sheet is present. (Fig. 54.9). The 3D structure reveals that heme is present within a pocket of hydrophobic side chains that promotes the binding of oxygen without the oxidation of iron atom. No disulphide bond is present in myoglobin. Tertiary structure is held together purely by non-covalent bonds between side chains within proteins, *i.e.*, hydrogen bonds, ionic bonds and hydrophobic interactions (Fig. 54.10).

Triosephosphate isomerase (enzyme) consists of β-pleated sheets largely and some α-helices.

There are various types of non-covalent bonds stabilizing tertiary protein structure, *e.g.*, ionic bonds due to electrostatic interaction, hydrogen bonds between heteroatoms of side chains and between side chain and polypeptide backbone, hydrophobic interaction between non-polar side chains and disulphide bonds (Fig. 54.10).

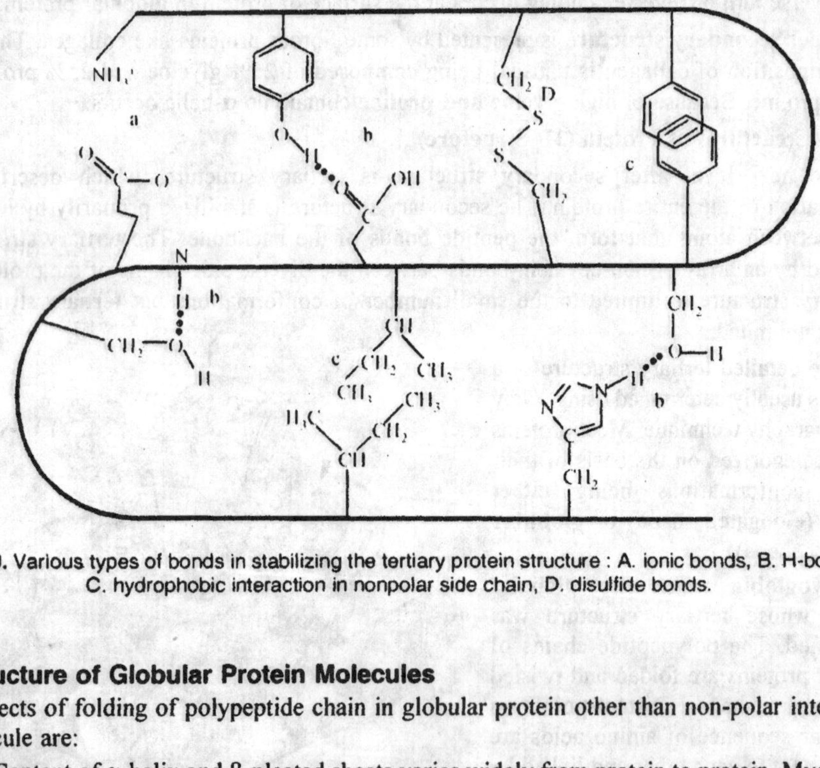

Fig. 54.10. Various types of bonds in stabilizing the tertiary protein structure : A. ionic bonds, B. H-bonds, C. hydrophobic interaction in nonpolar side chain, D. disulfide bonds.

Sub-structure of Globular Protein Molecules

Aspects of folding of polypeptide chain in globular protein other than non-polar interior of the molecule are:

(a) Content of α-helix and β-pleated sheets varies widely from protein to protein. Myoglobin has α-helix content where as proteinase α-chymotrypsin has β-sheet structures. Triose phosphate isomerase and lactate dehydrogenease have both β-pleated sheets and α-helices. In these molecules the folding is such that α-helices and β-pleated sheets alternate along the chain.

(b) The conformation has both carboxyl and amino terminus free, *i.e.*, if they are stretched out a linear chain would result. Polypeptide chain is not rolled up like a ball or string; but the course is from one surface of the molecule to another where it reverses its course.

(c) Useful general concept of globular protein structure is that of **domain.** Statistical tests that analyse the density of atom population around each amino residue in the 3D structure sometimes detect domains not apparent by viewing the protein structure model. Often, the course of the, polypeptide chain leaves one domain for a second and, after forming the second domain, returns to the first, making two polypeptide connections between the two domains. Most recognized domains have 100-200 amino acid residues, though both larger and smaller domains have been identified.

Domains have structural and evolutionary significance. An active site of an enzyme is the localized region of the molecule at which the enzyme bonds and acts on its substrate. Active sites are formed on the junction of 2 or more domains of the enzyme protein.

Domains have been postulated to facilitate the evolution of protein by providing **preformed** sequences of amino acids that will assume a stable conformation and provide a specific function.

The enzyme phosphofructokinase is an example of gene duplication. The phosphofructokinase of some bacteria and mammals are homogeneous tetramers, but mammalian enzyme is twice the size of bacterial enzyme. The two halves of the mammalian enzyme appear to be related **super domains.**

Bacterial and mammalian enzymes have the same number of active sites, *i.e.*, four per tetramer.

STRUCTURE OF SOME PROTEINS

(1) Wool α-Keratin

(i) It is a fibrous protein made up of α-helix, β-pleated sheet and form collagen triple helix structure.

(ii) Secondary structure of wool α-keratin is the right handed α-helix.

(iii) Three such α-helices form a left handed coil called a protofibril which is stabilized by cross linking disulphide bonds.

(iv) Protofibrils coil into cablelike **microfibrils** of 8 nm diameter.

(v) Several hundred **microfibrils embedded** in are amorphous protein matrix form a **macrofibril.**

(vi) Many macrofibrils together form a fiber of wool.

(vii) When α-keratin is exposed to moist heat and stretched, it converts to β-keratin.

The hydrogen bonds stabilizing the α-helical structure are broken and an extended parallel β-pleated sheet results.

(2) Cytochrome c

(i) Cytochrome c is small, stable and coloured globular protein.

(ii) Single iron atom in cytochrome c molecule alternates between the Fe II and Fe III oxidation states.

(iii) Cyt c has 104-111 amino acid residues, 35 of which are found to be invariant from species to species.

(3) Hemoglobin (Fig. 48.11)

(i) It is the transport protein of RBC.

(ii) Heme iron is bonded to a histidine residue on one side of the heme plane.

(iii) On oxygenation, the iron is liganded to oxygen on the opposite side of the heme in a pocket on the surface of the hemoglobin molecule.

(iv) Heme iron remains in the Fe II state during oxygenation and deoxygenation.

(v) The tetramer $\alpha_2\beta_2$ bind with 4-oxygen molecules.

(vi) Association of α_1-β_1 pair with α_2-β_2 is weaker than within them.

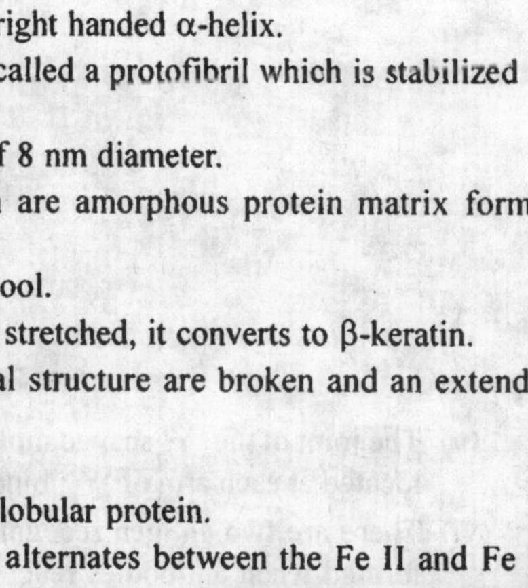

Fig. 54.11. Hemoglobin structure.

(4) Immunoglobin G

(i) It is the most important globular protein related with antibody molecule of immune system.

(ii) It is the serum protein that combines with antigen.

(iii) The quaternary structure of I_gG is made up of 4 polypeptide chains two are **'light'** chains of about 215 amino acid residues and two are **'heavy chains'** of 500 amino acid residues.

(iv) 4 chains are linked by disulfide bridges as form 12 domains. (Fig. 54.12).

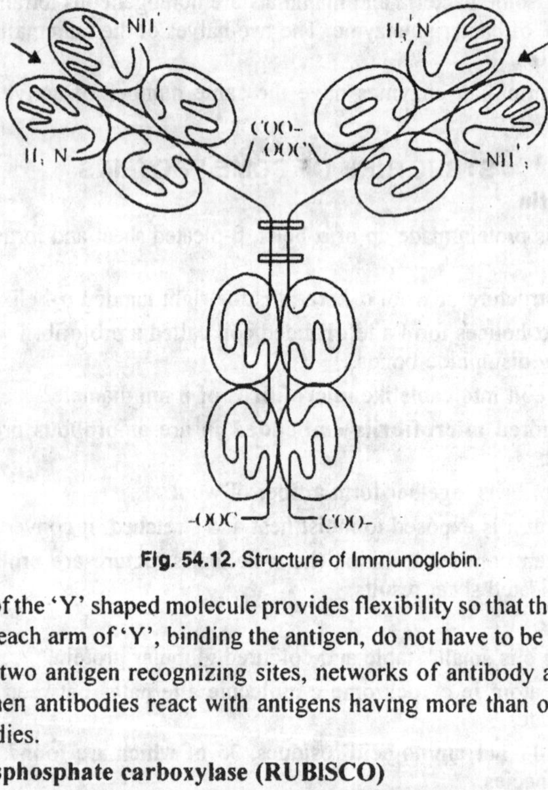

Fig. 54.12. Structure of Immunoglobin.

(v) The joint of the 'Y' shaped molecule provides flexibility so that the two combining sites, located at each arm of 'Y', binding the antigen, do not have to be a fixed distance apart.

(vi) There are two antigen recognizing sites, networks of antibody antigen chains will be formed when antibodies react with antigens having more than one site recognized by the antibodies.

(5) Ribulose bisphosphate carboxylase (RUBISCO)

(i) It is the most important protein in plants catalyzing reaction of ribulose 1, 5, bisphosphate with CO_2 to produce two molecules of 3 phosphoglycerate in CO_2 fixing reaction. RUBISCO has a quaternary structure with 8 small, 100 amino acid residue proteins and 8 large 500 amino acid residue protomers.

The polypeptide within our bodies are folded into complex 3D structures. The 3D structure of **lysozyme** was deciphered in 1965. It is made up of 129 amino acids in linear order and joined by disulphide bridges to form the 3D conformation.

The primary structure of it reads as (NH_2) K V F G R C E L A A A M K R H G L D N Y R G Y S L G N W V C A A K F E S N F N T Q A T N R N T D G S T D Y G I L Q I N S R W W C D N G R T P G S R N L C N I P C S A L L S S D I T A S V N C A K K I V S D G D G M N A W V A W R N R C K G T D V Q A W I R G C R L (COOH).

The linear model of molecule (Fig. 54.13) is some what irregular. If the side chains are stripped away and path of the peptide bond backbone is drawn some regions of protein are ordered in a repeating pattern. It shows both α-helix and β-sheet pattern (Fig. 54.14). In the α-helix region the chain twists around in a spiral while in β-sheet region the polypeptide run alongside each other. In tertiary conformation there can be grooves, clefts and protrusions on the surface of protein where particular amino acid side chains are positioned to form site that bind ligands and catalyse reactions.

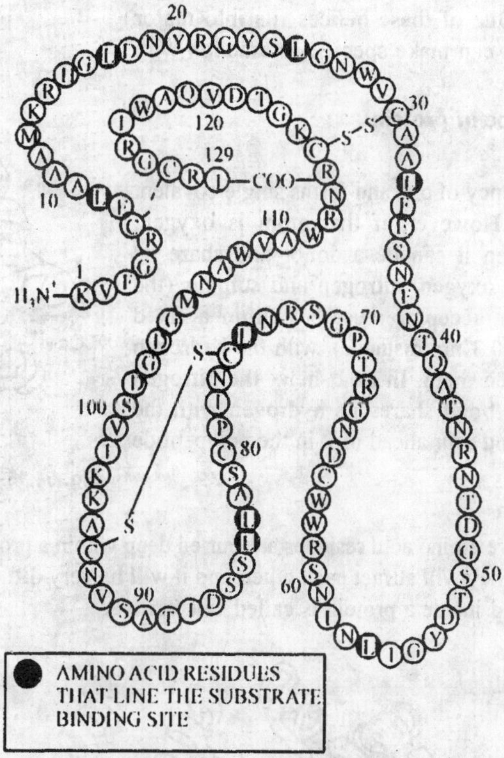

Fig. 54.13. Structure of Lysozyme. (Primary structure).

In calmodulins (calcium binding proteins) the single chain is organized into two domains, joined by only one strand of polypeptide chain. The two domains are very similar and might be originated by duplication of gene (Fig. 54.15).

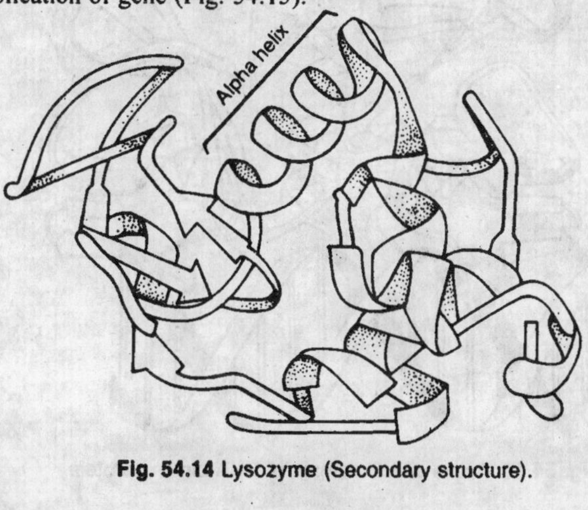

Fig. 54.14 Lysozyme (Secondary structure).

The catabolite activating protein (CAP) of *E. coli* binds to specific sequences of bases on DNA assisting RNA polymerase to bind to its promoters and initiate transcription of *lac* operon. One of the domains of CAP has the job of binding cAMP and another recognizes DNA sequences using a helix turn helix motif. One of these helices fits into major groove of DNA where it can make specific interaction with exposed edges of the bases.

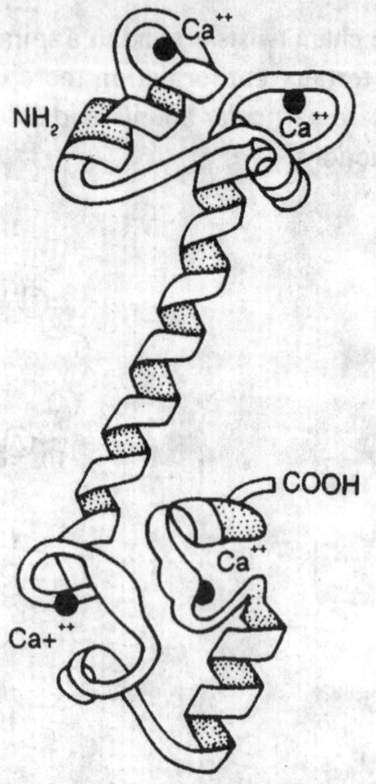

Fig. 54.15. Calmodulin Structure.

Forces molding the shape of protein

Hydrogen bonds

Hydrogen has a valency of one and forms single covalent bond with other atom. However, if that atom is oxygen, nitrogen and sulphur then it can be a donor and share its hydrogen with a second oxygen, nitrogen and sulphur (the acceptor): The donor or acceptor must be within a fixed distance of one another (0.3 nm distance), with the hydrogen on a straight line between them. In an α-helix the nitrogen atom within the peptide bond shares its hydrogen with the oxygen of the peptide bond four ahead of it in the polypeptide chain.

Electrostatic Interaction

If positive or negative amino acid residues are buried deep within a protein, where neither can interact with water, then they will attract each other, and it will be very difficult to tear them apart Such an electrostatic bond inside a protein is called **salt bridge.**

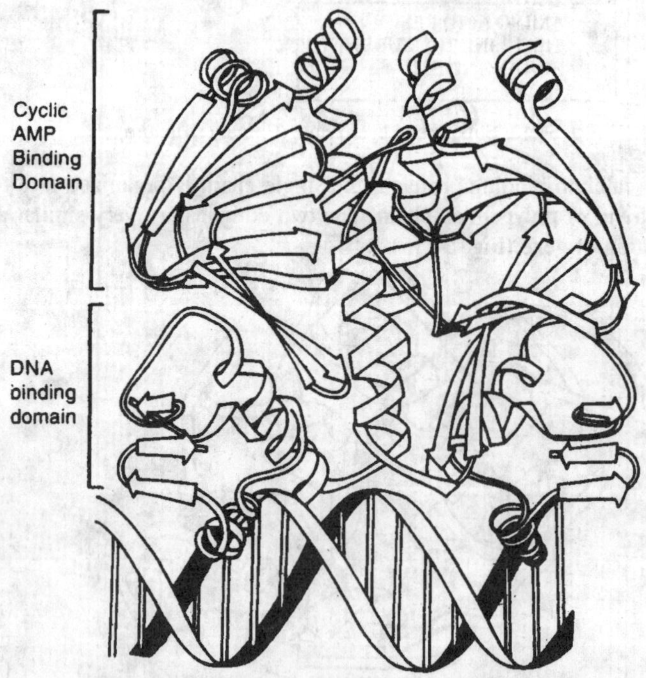

Fig. 54.16. Active cAMP domain of DNA binding protein

Polar groups such as hydroxyl and amide groups are dipoles: they have an excess of electrons on one atom and a compensating deficiency at the other. The partial cnarges of dipoles will be attracted to other dipoles and to fully charged ions.

van der Wall's Forces

These are relatively weak close range interactions between atoms. These forms are important in the interiors of proteins and membranes and in the specific binding of a ligand to its binding site.

Hydrophobic interactions

A polypeptide with hydrophilic and hydrophobic residues will spontaneously adopt a configuration in which the hydrophobic residues are not exposed to water, either by sitting in a lipid bilayer or by adopting and globular shape in which the hydrophobic residues hide in the centre of the protein.

Disulphide bonds

Extra cellular proteins often have disulphide bonds between specific cysteine residues. These tend to lock the molecules into its conformation. Few proteins contain disulphide bonds. But these are more stable.

SUMMARY

1. Polypeptides are linear polymer of α-amino acids linked by peptide bonds.
2. There are 20 amino acids coded for by the genetic code.
3. Amino acids differ in the properties of their side chains which range from hydrophobic groups to charged and uncharged hydrophilic groups.
4. Proteins are polypeptides that have a complex 3D shape.
5. Proteins have four levels of structures, *i.e.*, primary secondary tertiary and quaternary.
6. Primary structure is the linear sequence of the amino acid monomers.
7. Secondary structures possess regular, repeated folding of the peptide chains.
8. Secondary structures are held together by hydrogen bonds between the carboxyl oxygen and the hydrogen of the amino group of the peptide bonds.
9. Common types of secondary structures are
   (a) α-helix where the chain coils upon itself making a spring like spiral with hydrogen bonds running parallel to the length of the spiral.
   (b) In β-sheets the hydrogen bonds are between extended strands of polypeptide that runs along side of one another.
10. Tertiary structure includes complex foldings.
11. Tertiary structures are stabilized by interactions between side chains.
12. Proteins also have quaternary structures that is an association of subunits, each of which has a tertiary structure.

QUESTION BANK

Very Short Answer Questions

1. Name one imino acid.
2. What is the one letter symbol of leucine and phenyl alanine?
3. Name one example of globular protein.
4. Name one example of triple helix fibrous protein.
5. Who discovered α-helix model of secondary structure of protein.
6. What is RUBISCO?
7. What is immunoglobin G?
8. Draw the structure of immunoglobin G.
9. Draw the structure of α-helix model.
10. Draw the structure of hemoglobin.

Short Answer Questions

1. Explain that proteins are polymers of amino acid.
2. Write notes on primary structure of protein.

3. Write short notes on : (a) amino acids with positively chaged 'R' group. (b) amino acids with polar but unchanged 'R' group.
4. Make structures of Histidine, Lysine,- Aspartic acid and Glutamine.
5. Write three letter and one letter symbols of atleast 10 amino acids.
6. Write short note on forms of protein.
7. Write note on tertiary structure of proteins.
8. Write notes on secondary structures of proteins.
9. Write short notes on : (a) α-helix (b) β-pleated sheets.
10. Write short notes on : (a) Cytochrome c (b) Hemoglobin
11. Write short notes on RUBISCO.

Long Answer Questions

1. Describe the structures of protein.
2. Describe various forces that mold the shape of protein.

Multiple Choice Questions (Objective Type Questions)

1. Which amino acid has no asymmetric carbon atom
   (a) Proline (b) Glycine
   (c) Aspartic acid (d) Cystine
2. Basic unit of protein is
   (a) Polypeptide (b) Peptide
   (c) Amide (d) Amino acid
3. Proteins were named by
   (a) Flemming (b) Sanger
   (c) Berzelius (d) Kunhe
4. α-helix and β-pleated sheats are folding pattern of
   (a) Primary structure of protein (b) Secondary structure of protein
   (c) Tertiary structure of protein (d) Quaternary structure of protein
5. Three dimensional structure of protein is stabilized by
   (a) Ionic bonds (b) Covalent disulphide bonds
   (c) Hydrogen bond (d) All the above
6. Primary structure of protein is maintained by
   (a) Hydrogen bonds (b) Peptide bonds
   (c) Glycosidic linkage (d) Phenolic linkage
7. Hemoglobin and collagen are examples of ...... respectively.
   (a) Fibrous protein and chromoprotein (b) Chromoprotein and fibrous protein
   (c) Nucleoprotein and cell sap protein (d) Chromosomal protein and cytoplasmic protein
8. Which of the two amino acids are essential for growth.
   (a) Arginine and Histidine (b) Cystine and Valine
   (c) Leucine and Isoleucine (d) Arginine and Methionine
9. Histone proteins have large amount of
   (a) Glycine and glutamic acid (b) Protein and phenyl alanine
   (c) Lysine and Arginine (d) Methionine and Arginine
10. Which of the following is imino acid
    (a) Proline (b) Hydroxyproline
    (c)Phenylalanine (d) Both 'a' and 'b'
11. Amino acids are
    (a) Negatively charged (b) Positively charged
    (c) Zwitter ions (d) Cations

ANSWERS

1. (b)	2. (d)	3. (c)	4. (b)	5. (d)	6. (b)
7. (b)	8. (a)	9. (c)	10. (d)	11. (c).	

55

CHAPTER

DNA Damage and Repair

The first demonstration about the damage repair was given by **Kelner** *et al* where they have shown that UV induced effects could be reversed by exposing the cells to visible light in blue spectrum region. The process is called **photoreactivation**. It can only be done before the genetic material is permanently affected.

Setlow and **Setlow** demonstrated that photoreactivation effect primarily depends upon a specific enzyme **photolyase** which can split the pyrimidine dimer produced by UV radiation.

There are also several ways of DNA repair other than that of photoreactivation. The changes in DNA are mainly of 2 types.

(i) Single base change: Which are corrected through DNA replication leading to change in DNA sequence.

(ii) Structural distortions : Resulting from a single stranded nick, removal of a base or covalent link between bases of same or different strands.

In dark repair system, enzyme recognition of the distorted section of a DNA strand, is carried out by excision of defective sequence and replacement of section by new sequence of nucleotides formed as a complement to the undamaged DNA strand. In *E. coli.*, ultraviolet repair (*uvr*) mutation may affect different steps in these processes.

Polymerase I enzyme was used by **Kornberg** *et al* for *in vitro* replication of DNA. This method is used in the dark repair process by **polymerase I mutants** (Pol A) which are extremely sensitive to UV radiation.

In *Micrococus luteus* a different method for elimination of thymine dimer involves a **glycosylase** enzyme which C leaves the glycosylic bond between are of the dimerized thymine bases and its deoxyribose sugar. It leaves a vacant baseless 'AP' (apyrimidinic or apurinic) site on the DNA chain which is then nicked by special AP endonucleases. Glycosylase enzyme is highly specific in helping to remove damaged bases, *e.g.*, hypoxanthine, 7-methyl guanine, deaminated cytosine (uracil), etc., methylnitronitrosoguanidine (MNNG) involves enzymes acting specifically on damaged bases by directly removing methyl or ethyl group from the O^6 position of guanine.

Those DNA aberrations which are not directly repaired by excision and replacement may be more indirectly impaired by enzymes involved in recombination process. The procedure of multiplicity reactivation depends upon recombination events between the various intact parts of damaged phages leading to the formation of recombinant viable phages.

According to **Howard Flanders** the recombination repair process acts mostly on DNA strand carrying gaps caused by intra or interstrand cross links (Fig. 49.1). When such strands replicate gaps remain enabling 'free' end of a single strand section to initiate and exchange with a similarly oriented strand on a homologous DNA molecule. The exchange forms a new unbroken single strand which can serve as template for an enzyme complex to remove and replace the defective DNA part.

Excision repair involves different lengths of DNA as **very short patch repair (VSP); short patch repair** and **long patch repair.** VSP repairs single base damage. VSP also deals with mismatch repair, *e.g.*, **GC—GT** type which gives rise to mutant type.

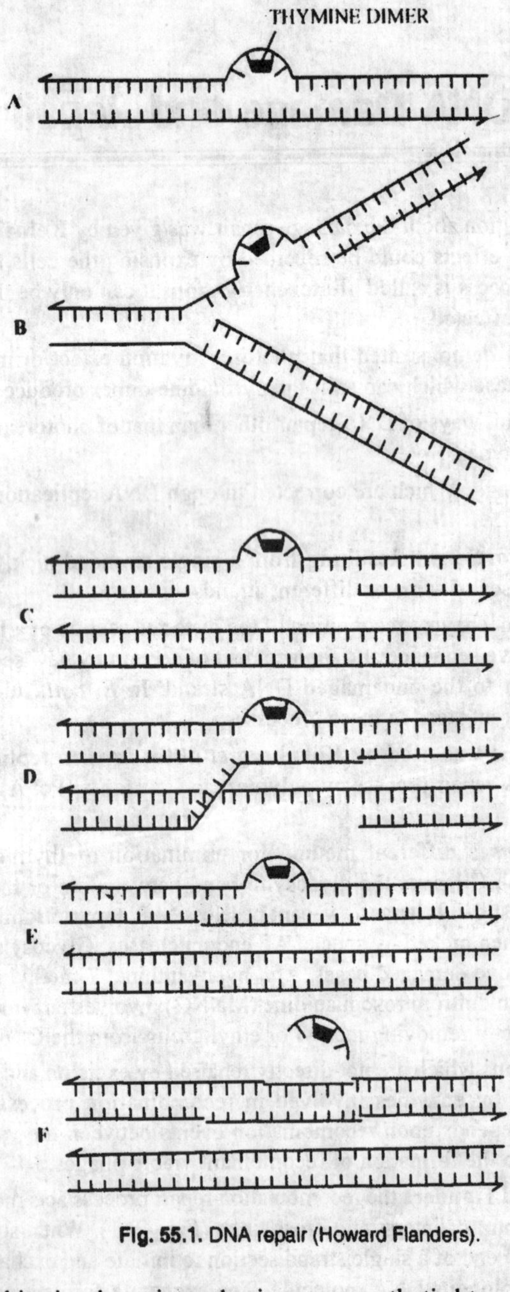

Fig. 55.1. DNA repair (Howard Flanders).

In *E. coli* recombinational repair mechanisms are mostly tied to *rec* A protein which has a dual function catalyzing both **recombination** and **protein cleavage.** The ability of *rec* A to cleave particular proteins regulates its own abundance. The protein repressor (a product of the *lex* A gene) restricts *rec* A gene activity is susceptible to cleavage by *rec* A protein. Due to mutational defects at replication forks an increase in single stranded DNA sections activiting *rec* A proteins to cleave its *lex* A repressor amplifing *rec* A protein production. This type of cellular response was called **"SOS"**.

In *E. coli* many treatments carry DNA damage or inhibition of DNA replication, induce a complex series of phenotypic changes are called **SOS response.** It initiates the interaction of *Rec* A protein with **lex** A repressor. It involves damaging treatment activating *Rec* A protein (protease), *Rec* A protease interacts with *Lex* A pressor (**Lex** A gene) all operons to which **Lex** A is bound are induced including many operons or genes, *e.g.*, *din* genes (*uvr* A, *uvr* B, *uvr* C and *hin* A). Each such gene has a **SOS** box. After DNA damaging signal is removed *Rec* A is not induced and *Lex* A accumulates repressing all other genes belonging to SOS system (Fig. 49.2)

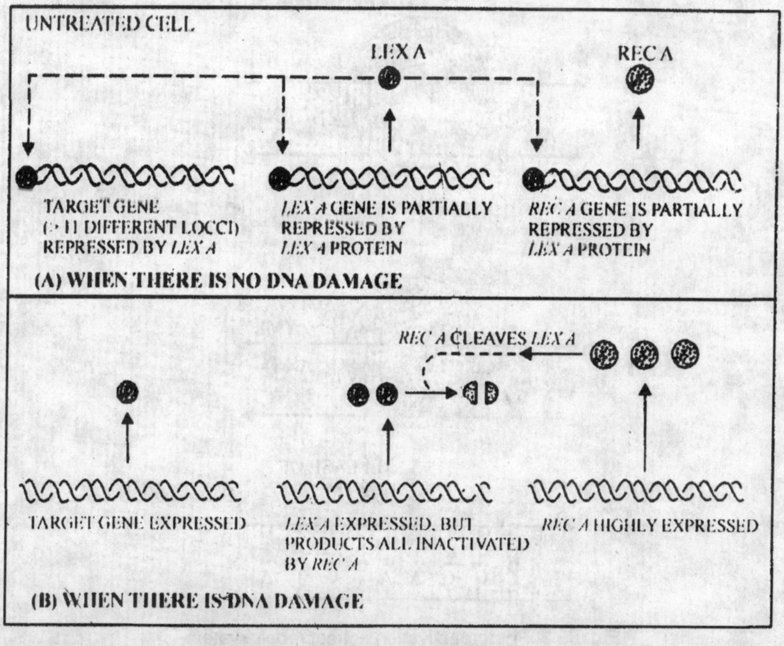

Fig. 55.2. SOS DNA repair system in *E.coli.*

The mechanism of DNA modification is carried out by methylating DNA bases (addition of CH_3). The enzyme taking part in this activity is **methylase.** In *E. coli* 3 types of mechanisms of DNA repair are found

(a) Photoreactivation

(b) Excision repair

(c) Post replication recombination repair

Photoreactivation : It involves an enzyme which splits thymine dimer directly without the removal of nucleotides (Fig. 49.3). Enzyme binds with thymine dimer in DNA in the dark but can not catalyze cleavage of the bonds joining the thymine molecules without energy derived from visible light; light of blue region of spectrum. Enzyme also activates cytosine dimers and cytosine thymine dimers. When ultraviolet light is used as an experimental mutagen, the treatment is usually carried out in the dark to maximize the mutation frequency, photoreactivation is also called **direct repair system** (Fig. 49.3).

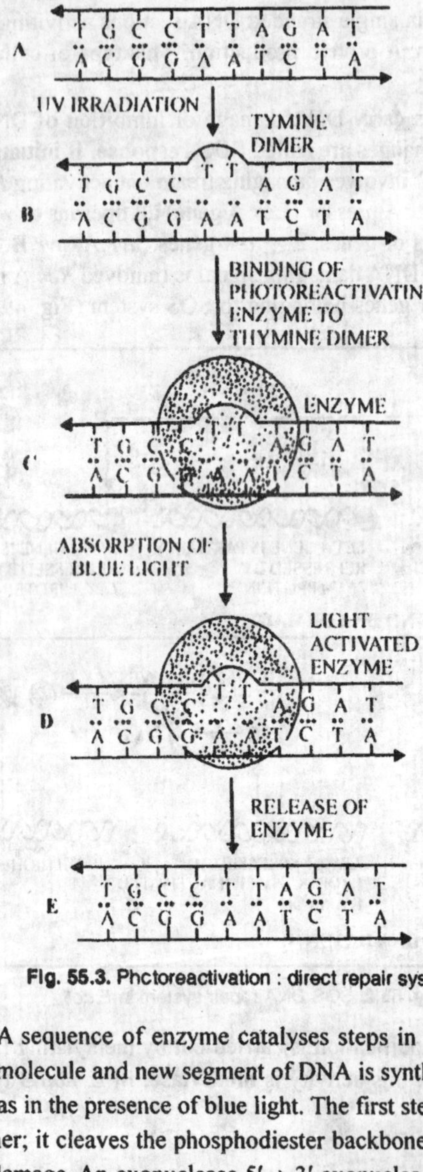

Fig. 55.3. Photoreactivation : direct repair system.

Excision repair : A sequence of enzyme catalyses steps in which the thymine dimers are removed from the DNA molecule and new segment of DNA is synthesized. Excision repair occurs as efficiently in the dark as in the presence of blue light. The first step is catalyzed by endonuclease recognizing thymine dimer; it cleaves the phosphodiester backbone of DNA strand containing the dimer at a site near the damage. An exonuclease 5′→ 3′ exonuclease activity of DNA polymerase I removes the dimer *in vitro.* (Fig. 49.4).

The segment adjacent to the endonuclease is then removed including dimer. DNA polymerase I fills the gap using complementary strand as template. DNA ligase catalyzes covalent closure or phosphodiester linkage between the adjacent nucleotides. Mutant lacking in enzyme DNA polymerase I are defective in excision repair. In addition uvr A, uvr B and uvr C genes are also required.

Post replication recombination: When DNA molecules containing thymine dimers are replicated gaps are formed in the nascent complementary strand opposite the dimers because DNA

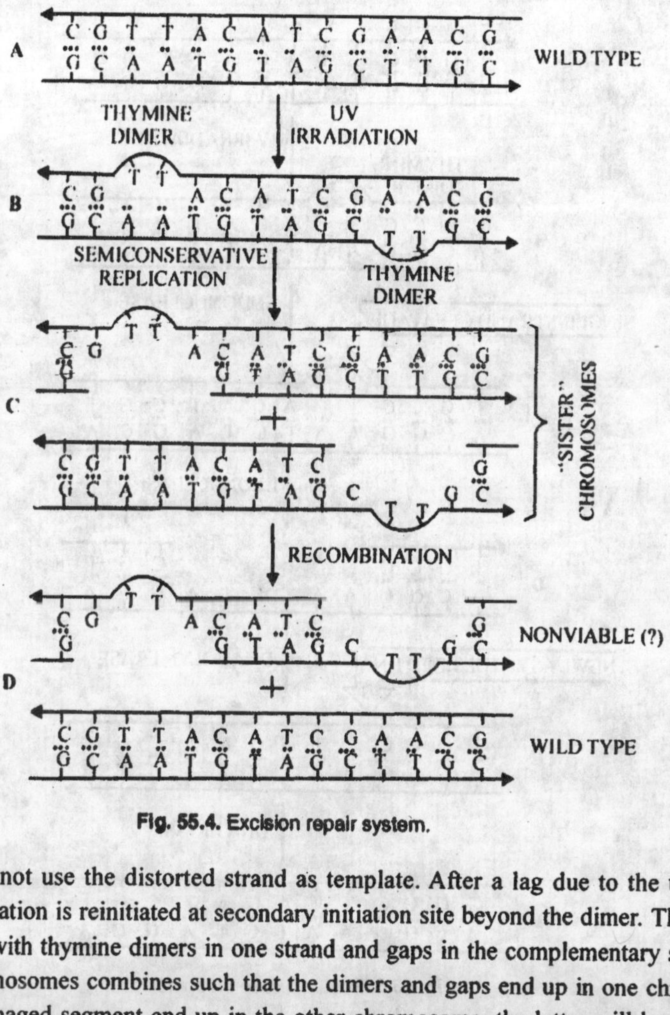

Fig. 55.4. Excision repair system.

polymerase cannot use the distorted strand as template. After a lag due to the thymine dimer blockage, replication is reinitiated at secondary initiation site beyond the dimer. The progeny has double helices with thymine dimers in one strand and gaps in the complementary strand. If these two sister chromosomes combines such that the dimers and gaps end up in one chromosome and the intact undamaged segment end up in the other chromosome, the latter will be functional and produce a viable cell (Fig. 49.5).

Another DNA repair enzyme, **uracil DNA glycosylase** has been characterized in *E. coli.* It efficiently removes **uracil** from DNA. It is called glycosylase because it removes uracil by cleaving the glycosidic bond between base and sugar. It produces a pyrimidinic site in DNA. Such apyrimidinic site undergoes an excision repair mechanism. Uracil is produced in DNA by deamination of cytosine. *E. coli* mutants deficient in uracil DNA glycosylase exhibit increased sensitivity to deaminating agents such as nitrous acid, indicating that enzyme is important in the repair of this type of damage to DNA (Fig. 49.6).

The larger the number of **essential genes** the more sites at which a lethal mutations occur and given equivalent repair process, the greater the probabilities that a given dose of mutagen will cause a lethal mutation

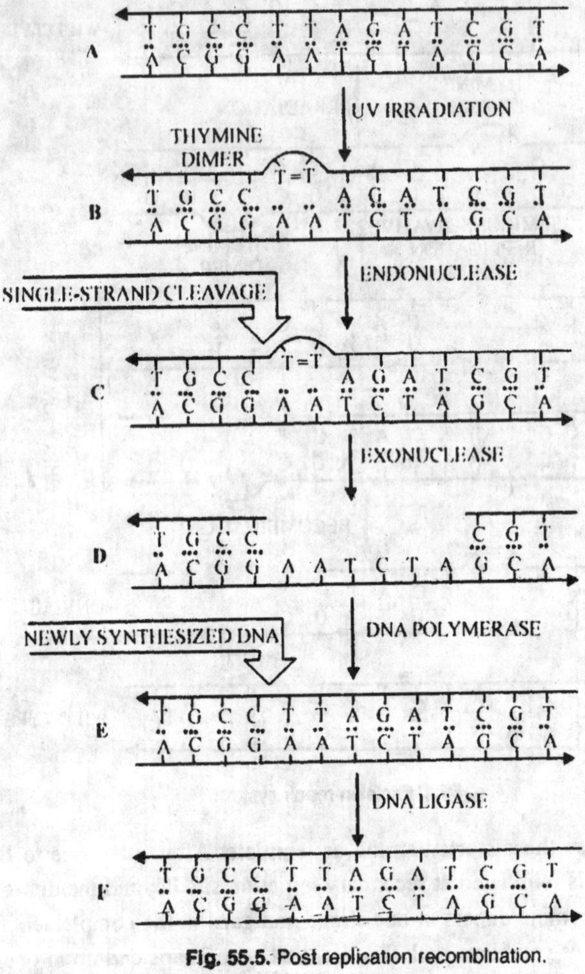

Fig. 55.5. Post replication recombination.

DNA repair and genetic disease in human

In human many diseases are caused by DNA damage. These are recessively inherited, *e.g.*, **Xeroderma pigmentosum** (XP), **Ataxia telangiectasia; Fanconi anaemia,** and **Bloom's syndrome,** etc. The damages are caused by UV rays, ionizing radiation, etc. **Cleaver** has shown that the cells of such affected individuals are unable to repair DNA damage induced by UV.

The best known example of an inherited deficiency in the repairs of radiation damage in human is the autosomal recessive disease **Xeroderma pigmentosum**. The skin of individuals with **Xeroderma pigmentosum** exhibit extreme sensitivity to sunlight resulting in a high frequency of tumors in the epidermal cells of exposed areas such as face. The cells are deficient in the repair of UV induced damage to DNA, such as thymine dimer. Therefore high incidence of skin cancer results directly from the inability of individuals with xeroderma pigmentosum to repair damage in DNA induced by UV in sunlight. The defective enzyme may be endonuclease which recognize as the thymine dimer and excise them. Mutation in about 6 genes can cause the disease.

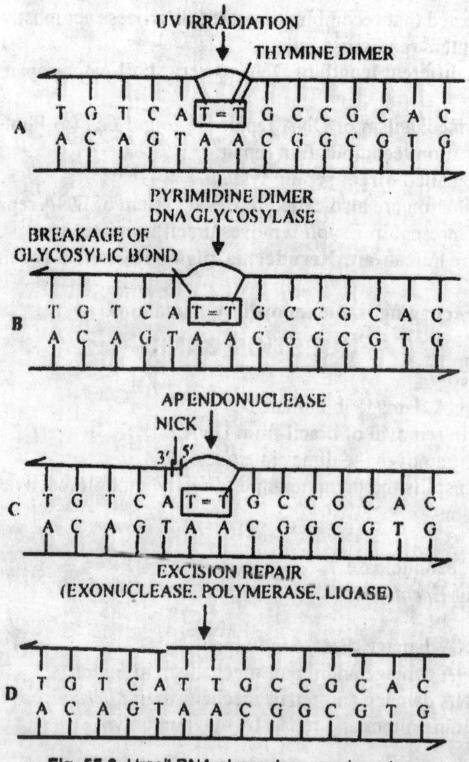

Fig. 55.6. Uracil DNA glycosylase repair system.

Some individuals suffering from this disease may develop neurological abnormalities resulting from premature death of cells. Mutation also contribute in the process of aging. According to **F. M. Burnet**, aging is the consequence of low level mutations **Fanconis anemia, ataxia telangiectasia** and **Bloom's syndrome** are the other three inherited (autosomal recessive) diseases in humans in which the primary defect may be in a DNA repair pathway. Leukemia is found in Fanconis anemia, cells are abnormally sensitive to ionizing radiations in **ataxia telongiectasia.** Individuals with Bloom's syndrome exhibit a high frequency of chromosome breakage resulting in aberration. All the three diseases are due to defect in DNA metabolism, *i.e.*, repair process.

The DNA damage repair system are grouped under

(a) Direct repair of DNA system (or) Photoreactivation

(b) Excision repair system : The damaged section is first excised and then repaired, it involves.

(i) Very short patch repair

(ii) Short patch region

(iii) Long patch repair

(iv) Involves excision of about 1500 bases long segment to 9000 bases long segments.

(c) Mis match repair system : Single base alters due to methylation or deamination.

(d) Retrieval system : Post replication repairs.

(e) Tolerance repair system : Damages blocking normal replication at the damaged site.

SUMMARY

1. The first demonstration about the damage repair was given by **Kelner** *et al* where they have shown that UV induced effect can be reverse by visible light.
2. **Setlow and Setlow** demonstrated that photoreactivity depends upon the enzyme which can split the pyrimidine dimer produced by UV radiation.

3. **Howard Flanders** suggested that recombinational repair process act mostly on DNA strands carrying gaps caused by intra or interstrand cross links.
4 Excision repair involves different length of DNA as very short patch repair (VSP), short patch repair and long patch repairs.
5. In *E.* coli three types of mechanism of DNA repair are found *i.e.*, (a) Photoreactivation (b) Excision repair and (c) Post replication recombination repair.
6. Photoreactivation is also called **direct repalr system.**
7. Post replication recombination are also called retrieval system of DNA repair.
8. Uracil DNA glycosylase present in *E. coli* removes uracil from DNA.
9. DNA damage disease in human are **Xeroderma pigmentosum, Fancom's anemia** and **Bloom's syndrome,** etc.
10. According to **F. M. Burnet** aging is due to low level mutations.

QUESTION BANK

Very Short Answer Questions

1. Name two diseases of DNA damage in human.
2. Name the enzyme used in removal of uracil from DNA.
3. Name the enzyme which removes the dimer in *istio.*
4. Name the enzyme which splits the thymine dimer directly in photoreactivation.
5. What is 'SOS' type response?
6. What is endonuclease?
7. What is the function of 'exonuclease'?
8. What is SOS ıesponse in *E. coli*?

Short Answer Questions

1. Write short notes on DNA damage disease in human.
2. Write short notes on DNA damage and repair mechanism in *E. coli.*
3. Write short notes on DNA damage and repair mechanism in *Micrococcus luteus.*
4. Explain removal of thymine dimer and repair by diagram only.

Long Answer Questions

1. Write an essay on DNA damage and repair.

Multiple Choice Questions (Objective Type Questions)

1. The mechanism of DNA modification is carried out by :
(a) Acetylation (b) Methylation (c) Both 'a' and 'b' (d) None
2. The enzyme which splits thymine dimer directly during photoreactivation is :
(a) Photolyase (b) Polymerase (c) Lignase (d) Invertase
3. In *E. coli* the treatments causing DNA damage induce a complex series of phenotypic changes are called :
(a) Excise repairs (b) 'SOS' response (c) Photoreactivation (d) All the above
4. Who used polymerase I enzyme for *invued* replication of DNA :
(a) Kornberg (b) Flanders (c) Setlow (d) Kelner
5. Glycosylase enzyme is specific in helping the removal of damaged bases:
(a) Hypoxanthine (b) 7-methyl guanine (c) Uracil (d) All the above
6. The disease due to DNA damage in human are :
(a) Xeroderma pigmentosum (b) Bloom's syndrome (c) Albinism (d) Both 'a' and 'b'
7. Who for the first time observed DNA damaged repair :
(a) Kelner (b) Stelon (c) Kornberg (d) None of the above
8. Who suggested that aging is due to low level of mutation :
(a) Kelner (b) Burnet (c) Setlow (d) Flanders
9. Removal of Uracil from DNA is called :
(a) Mismatch repair system (b) Excision repair system
(c) Retrieval repair system (d) Tolerance repair system
10. Photoreactivation was demonstrated by :
(a) Setlow ans Setlow (b) Setlow and Kelner (c) Kelner and Burnet (d) Setlow and Burnet.

ANSWERS

1. (b)	2. (a)	3. (b)	4. (a)	5. (d)	6. (d)
7. (a)	8. (b)	9. (a)	10. (a)		